Using parallelism   3
Using a synthesis chart   2, 21, 22, 2

Drafting
Writing rough drafts   3, 13, 14
Writing paragraphs   12
Writing introductions and conclusions   3, 15
Using paraphrase and quotation   3, 16
Writing clear and focused sentences   34

Revising
Practicing peer review   4, 17
Interpreting and applying comments   17
Revising to make your audience and purpose clear   4, 6
Revising to focus your topic or strengthen your thesis   4, 10, 11
Revising to reorganize your essay   4, 7, 13
Revising for paragraph development   4, 12
Revising to integrate quotations and paraphrases   4, 16
Revising to avoid plagiarism   16, 18, 20

Editing
Reading your essay out loud   4
Reading backwards   4
Editing for fragments   28
Fixing errors in verb use   27
Fixing pronoun errors   30
Editing for comma errors   31
Finding and fixing fused sentences and comma splices   29
Finding and fixing common sentence-structure problems   33
Finding and fixing parallelism errors   32
Editing for clarity and focus   34
Recognizing active and passive voice   34
Varying sentence structure   25, 26, 33
Creating a title for your essay   6

Proofreading
Proofreading for errors and format   4
Finding and correcting your errors   24
Finding and fixing apostrophe errors   35
Correcting spelling and capitalization   36
Correcting citation and documentation   20

Reflection
Interpreting and applying instructor's comments   17
Creating a personalized grammar log   24
Reflecting on your writing   Portfolios e
Using portfolios   Portfolios e
Becoming a more successful student   1, 17, 18, 19, Essay Exams, Managing Your Time and Avoiding Procrastination e

W9-BYU-847

Icons indicate additional Integrated Media resources available at bedfordstmartins.com /readwriteconnect.

Read
Write
Connect

Read
Write
Connect

A Guide to College Reading and Writing

Kathleen Green
Pasadena City College

Amy Lawlor
City College of San Francisco

Bedford/St. Martin's
Boston ◆ New York

For Bedford/St. Martin's

Executive Editor Developmental Studies: Alexis Walker
Senior Developmental Editor: Ellen Darion
Senior Production Editor: Deborah Baker
Senior Production Supervisor: Lisa McDowell
Senior Marketing Manager: Christina Shea
Market Development Manager: Vivian Garcia
Editorial Assistant: Rachel Greenhaus
Copyeditor: Jennifer Greenstein
Indexer: Mary White
Photo Researcher: Sherri Blaney
Senior Art Director: Anna Palchik
Text Design: Jerilyn Bockorick
Cover Design: Marine Miller
Cover Photo: (composite) Spanish Sparrow perching in tree
  © J-P Lahall/Getty Images. Grass-covered hill and blue cloudy sky
  © Heidi Orcino Photography/Getty Images.
Composition: Cenveo Publisher Services
Printing and Binding: RR Donnelley and Sons

President, Bedford/St. Martin's: Denise B. Wydra
Editor in Chief: Karen S. Henry
Director of Marketing: Karen R. Soeltz
Production Director: Susan W. Brown
Director of Rights and Permissions: Hilary Newman

Manufactured in the United States of America.

9 8 7 6 5 4
f e d c b a

For information, write: Bedford/St. Martin's, 75 Arlington Street, Boston, MA 02116
  (617-399-4000)

ISBN 978-1-4576-2074-4 (Student Edition)
ISBN 978-1-4576-6697-1 (Loose-leaf Edition)

Acknowledgments

Preface

Born out of our collective years of experience in the classroom, as well as countless hours of one-on-one tutoring sessions with inquisitive students in office hours and tutoring centers, *Read, Write, Connect* helps students understand that being a good writer requires being a good reader, both of published texts and one's own writing. With lots of guidance and practice in both reading and writing, *Read, Write, Connect* is designed to help students meet the challenges of college courses that require them to integrate reading and writing skills and make connections among a wide variety of texts.

Our students are like most college students: diverse in their backgrounds and experiences, varied in their educational and career interests, and eager for challenging work that will inspire them. We wrote *Read, Write, Connect* for them. Our guiding principles in deciding what to include in this book have been the questions: "Do students need help with that?" "Is that the way you explain it in class?" and "Does it work?" As a result, the explanations in the book are student-centered and eminently practical.

Organization

In order to meaningfully integrate the recursive processes of reading and writing, *Read, Write, Connect*'s design and organization take a steep departure from traditional rhetorics.

CHAPTERS 1–4: THE WALK-THROUGH

Designed as a walk-through of the entire reading and writing process, Chapters 1–4 guide students step-by-step from pre-reading college-level reading selections to proofreading their first essay. The walk-through provides the core components of the reading and writing processes, beginning with how to read actively and ending with revising and proofreading their first out-of-class essay. The walk-through forms the basis of a strong reading and writing practice that students will follow not only in subsequent essays, but ideally in all of their college courses requiring reading and writing.

READING AND WRITING WORKSHOPS

The workshop chapters (Chapters 5–20) offer a deeper understanding of the reading and writing processes by focusing on and expanding coverage of specific topics that many students need to practice more deeply to master—such as note taking, essay organization and outlining, and vocabulary building. The workshops offer tremendous flexibility to instructors, who can assign them at any point in the semester to emphasize a particular topic in more depth for the class as a whole or for an individual student struggling with a particular concept. The instruction, examples, and practice exercises make the workshop chapters fairly self-contained; as such, they can serve as the focus of classroom instruction or for independent practice. Many of the reading and writing workshops highlight the recursive nature of both reading and writing processes by deepening the discussion and practice of elements first introduced in the walk-through. By making connections between the initial lessons of the semester and the more advanced lessons and activities of the reading and writing workshops, students can reflect on the increasing sophistication of their writing and reading skills.

THEMATIC READING CHAPTERS

The thematic reading chapters (Chapters 21–23) combine readings from a variety of sources into a conversation around a popular theme that most college students will find relevant and thought provoking. The themes—Fame and Celebrity, Siblings, and Public Art—cover many disciplines and interests, ranging from business and finance to the arts to psychology and science, so they will appeal to students with a variety of career interests and majors. Each of the thematic reading chapters includes texts of varying lengths as well as pre- and post-reading activities, comprehension and discussion questions, and vocabulary activities. The thematic reading chapters are designed to be flexible so that an instructor can assign all or a few of the readings. One additional reading and one multimedia text are available online in the e-Pages for each themed unit for instructors looking to supplement the print book's selections. Each thematic reading chapter closes with a synthesis chart to help students organize their thoughts, a variety of writing prompts in different modes, and a list of additional resources.

GRAMMAR, STYLE, AND MECHANICS WORKSHOPS

The grammar section of *Read, Write, Connect* (Chapters 24–36) begins with a workshop that encourages students to take stock of their strengths and weaknesses as writers. Chapter 24 leads students through the process of identifying the errors that they commonly make, studying the rules about their errors, recording those errors and notes about how to fix them in a personalized Grammar Log, and undertaking systematic practice in editing for those particular errors. The remainder of the grammar workshops offer focused instruction and practice in the areas of grammar and mechanics. While many instructors may spend some class time with those chapters that cover the major errors, such as fragments, the chapters can also be studied individually, on an as-needed basis. Like the rest of the book, this section explains how to find and fix errors in a student-friendly, straightforward manner. All the grammar workshops have detailed explanations as well as realistic examples, practice exercises, helpful tips, and chapter reviews.

e ONLINE READINGS AND WORKSHOP CHAPTERS

Available online in the e-Pages are an additional thematic reading chapter on the topic of education, and three additional workshops: Taking Essay Exams, Portfolios, and Time Management and Avoiding Procrastination. These additional workshops highlight important student skills and include the same kind of instruction, examples, and practice exercises that are in the print book workshop chapters. In addition, the e-Pages offer one additional reading for each of the themed reading chapters in the print text (Money and Wealth; Fame and Celebrity; Public Art; and Siblings) as well as interactive multimodal activities.

Features

"PRACTICE IT" ACTIVITIES

Students need to practice the techniques of successful readers and writers, so we created the "Practice It" activities to provide lower-stakes assignments that prepare them for their larger assignments and offer them an immediate opportunity to apply what they learn to a concrete, real-life practice of reading or writing. These activities are deeply embedded in the instruction—often asking students to refer to the readings in the themed chapters for models, or requiring them to apply what they learn to their own assignments. Such activities are designed to offer authentic and useful practice to students, and can be assigned individually or to the class as a whole, as homework or as in-class activities.

✔ INTERACTIVE READING AND WRITING PRACTICE VIA LEARNINGCURVE

LearningCurve's innovative adaptive online quizzing lets students learn at their own pace, and features a game-like interface that encourages them to keep at it. Quizzes are keyed to instruction in the book, so what is taught in class gets reinforced at home. Instructors can also check in on each student's activity in a grade book.

A student access code is printed in every new student copy of *Read, Write, Connect*. Students who do not buy a new print book or e-Book can purchase access by going to **bedfordstmartins.com/readwriteconnect**. Instructors can also get access at this site.

TIPS BOXES

These boxes appear in the margins of the book to offer students helpful hints. Practical in nature, these tips guide students so that they can avoid repeating some common mistakes that our students have made over the years. They also provide students with an easier way to perform a task in the writing or reading process.

LOOK OUT BOXES

Similar to Tips, these boxes appear in the grammar chapters, and alert students to typical patterns of errors.

VOCABULARY PRACTICE

Read, Write, Connect addresses vocabulary in several ways. Students are instructed to mark, look up, and write definitions for unfamiliar words they encounter as part of annotating. Additionally, in all the readings in the print book and e-Pages, potentially unfamiliar words are italicized to prompt students to practice their annotation skills, and each reading has a specific vocabulary activity following it. Finally, Chapter 8 is devoted entirely to vocabulary building.

Acknowledgments

The following reviewers were very helpful through several drafts of this book: Emory Reginald Abbott, Georgia Perimeter College; Christie L. Anderson, Spokane Falls Community College; Angelina Arellanes-Nunez, El Paso Community College; Brenda Ashcraft, Virginia Western Community College; Marta Brown, Community College of Denver; Wendy Crader, Alamo Colleges–Northeast Lakeview; Bethany Davila, University of New Mexico; Deborah De La Rosa, Evergreen Valley College; Cynthia DeLauder, Spokane Falls Community College; Melissa Dickman, Community College of Denver; Mary Downing-Gardner, John Tyler Community College; Maryann Errico, Georgia Perimeter College; Kevin Ferns, Woodland Community College; Christopher Gibson, Skyline College; Larry Giddings, Pikes Peak Community College; Sarah Gilliam, Mountain Empire Community College; Anissa Graham, University of North Alabama; Rose Grotjan, Lincoln University; Ashley Horak, Kankakee Community College; Lauri Humberson, St. Philip's College; Tom Hyder, Piedmont Virginia Community College; Judith I. Johnson, John Tyler Community College; Brent Kendrick, Lord Fairfax Community College; Amber Kinonen, Bay College; Linda Koffman, College of Marin; Mary S. Leonard, Wytheville Community College; Glenda Lowery, Rappahannock Community College; Jill Maggs, University of Rio Grande; Jane Maguire, Valencia College; Elizabeth Marsh, Bergen Community College; Jennifer McCann, Bay College; Josie Mills, Arapahoe Community College; Miriam Moore, Lord Fairfax Community College; Robbi Muckenfuss, Durham Technical Community College; Mary Ellen Muesing, University of North Carolina at Charlotte; Alexis Nelson, Spokane Falls Community College; Sheila Nicholson, Texas State University–San Marcos;

Julie Odell, Community College of Philadelphia; Liana J. Odrcic, University of Wisconsin–Milwaukee; Sandra Padilla, El Paso Community College; Jacqueline Pena, Miami Dade College; Calisa A. Pierce, Kanawha Valley Community & Technical College; Robert Pontious, Brunswick Community College; Betty Raper, Pulaski Technical College; Nancy M. Risch, Caldwell Community College and Technical Institute; Carolee Ritter, Southeast Community College; Becky Rudd, Citrus College; Kara M. Ryan-Johnson, Tulsa Community College; Patricia Sansbury, Florida State College at Jacksonville; James Shackle, Owens Community College; Eric Paul Shaffer, Honolulu Community College; Benjamin Sloan, Piedmont Virginia Community College; Lori Smalley, Greenville Technical College; Sallie Stone, Pitt Community College; Claudia Swicegood, Rowan-Cabarrus Community College; Judi Salsburg Taylor, Monroe Community College; Patrick Tompkins, John Tyler Community College; Kathryn Y. Tyndall, Wake Technical Community College; Barbara Urban, Central Piedmont Community College; Lana Velez, Central Virginia Community College; Maria C. Villar-Smith, Miami Dade College; and Michelle Zollars, Patrick Henry Community College.

Working with a publishing company that values collaboration as much as Bedford/St. Martin's, necessarily we have many people to thank. Among them, we owe a deep debt of gratitude to Nick Carbone and Kimberly Hampton, our first contacts at Bedford/St. Martin's, who encouraged us and helped us gain the confidence to develop our ideas in this form. We are also indebted to the Bedford team, who met with us en masse in Boston, showed us the power of collaborative work, asked hard questions, listened, and encouraged us, especially Joan Feinberg, who first had the vision of putting our ideas into a textbook. We want to thank Denise Wydra, who trekked all the way to Paso Robles for the most intense weekend work session imaginable, in which the book found its bones. We thank the following people for their guidance and efforts to make us look polished: Deborah Baker, Senior Production Editor; Anna Palchik, Senior Art Director; Jennifer Greenstein, copyeditor; Sheri Blaney and Natalie Turner for art and text permissions research, respectively; and Rachel Greenhaus, for all manner of tasks large and small. For their marketing efforts, we thank Christina Shea and Vivian Garcia.

We would also like to especially thank our editors: Ellen Darion, who is infallibly cheerful and good-natured and has provided the nuts-and-bolts guidance for the completion of this book, and Alexis Walker, who has given us incomparable guidance and encouragement and has been our friend and constant touchstone throughout this long journey.

And finally, to all of our students, who have been guinea pigs and sources of inspiration, we owe the deepest thanks. Every time we tried to explain something and didn't get through, and a student had the strength of mind and purpose to say "Wait, that doesn't make sense" made us better teachers, teachers who had to reach down a little deeper to find a way to explain it all better.

xii   Preface

Amy would like to thank her many students over the years who have given her as many opportunities to learn as to teach. She would also like to thank her many colleagues who have offered inspiration, courage, guidance, humor and, on countless occasions, copies of excellent hand-outs! She is grateful especially to her parents, Marty and Bill, who were her first and continue to be her most important teachers. She would also like to thank her brothers and sister and friends who have supported her and keep asking "When can we see the book?" And finally, she would like to thank Brian for his tireless support, love, and understanding while she was buried in the writing of this book.

Kathy would like to thank the students of Pasadena City College who taught her how to teach developing students, and her teacher friends over many years and institutions—especially Liana Odrcic, Teri Keeler, Bev Tate, Amy Ulmer, and Paige Wilson—whose passion for developing writers is a constant source of inspiration. She would also like to thank the village who helped her muddle through domestic life during the long weeks of finishing the rough draft—ye who watch over children and offer respite to weary writers. Finally, the biggest thanks go to Jo, Hana, and Ben, for enduring a mother and wife who was MIA for countless weekend activities, who had to take conference calls on vacation, and who "always had too much to do" while writing this book.

Kathleen Green
Amy Lawlor

You Get More with *Read, Write, Connect*

Read, Write, Connect does not stop with a book. Online, you will find resources to help students get even more out of the book and your course. You will also find free, convenient instructor resources, such as a downloadable instructor's manual. For more information, visit **bedfordstmartins .com/readwriteconnect/catalog**.

STUDENT RESOURCES

Premium Resources

- **WritingClass** provides students with a dynamic, interactive online course space preloaded with exercises, diagnostics, video tutorials, writing and commenting tools, and more. WritingClass helps students stay focused and lets instructors see how they are progressing. It is available at a significant discount when packaged with your print text. To learn more about WritingClass, visit **yourwritingclass.com**.

- **SkillsClass** offers all that WritingClass offers, plus guidance and practice in reading and study skills. This interactive online course space comes preloaded with exercises, diagnostics, video tutorials, writing and commenting tools, and more. It is available at a significant discount when packaged with the print text. To learn more about SkillsClass, visit **yourskillsclass.com**.

- *Re:Writing Plus*, **now with VideoCentral**, gathers all of our premium digital content for the writing class into one online collection. This impressive resource includes innovative and interactive help with writing a paragraph; tutorials and practices that show how writing works in students' real-world experience; VideoCentral, with more than 140 brief videos for the writing classroom; the first ever peer-review game, *Peer Factor*; *i-cite: visualizing sources*; plus hundreds of models of writing and hundreds of readings. *Re:Writing Plus* can be purchased separately or packaged with *Read, Write, Connect* at a significant discount.

Free* with the Print Text

- **The *Bedford/St. Martin's ESL Workbook*** includes a broad range of exercises covering grammatical issues for multilingual students of varying language skills and backgrounds. Answers are at the back. ISBN: 978-0-312-54034-0

*NOTE: There is a limit of one free supplement per order. Additional supplements can be packaged at a significant discount.

- The *Make-a-Paragraph Kit* is a fun, interactive CD-ROM that teaches students about paragraph development. It also contains exercises to help students build their own paragraphs, audiovisual tutorials on four of the most common errors for basic writers, and the content from *Exercise Central to Go: Writing and Grammar Practices for Basic Writers*. ISBN: 978-0-312-45332-9

- The *Bedford/St. Martin's Planner* includes everything that students need to plan and use their time effectively, with advice on preparing schedules and to-do lists plus blank schedules and calendars (monthly and weekly). The planner fits easily into a backpack or purse, so students can take it anywhere. ISBN: 978-0-312-57447-5

- *Journal Writing: A Beginning* is designed to give students an opportunity to use writing as a way to explore their thoughts and feelings. This writing journal includes a generous supply of inspirational quotations placed throughout the pages, tips for journaling, and suggested journal topics. ISBN: 978-0-312-59027-7

e-Book Options

- *Read, Write, Connect* e-Book. Available as a value-priced e-Book, either as a CourseSmart e-Book or in formats for use with computers, tablets, and e-Readers—visit **bedfordstmartins.com/readwriteconnect /catalog** for more information.

INSTRUCTOR RESOURCES

- *Instructor's Guide for Read, Write, Connect* includes sample syllabi, answers to practice exercises, and chapter-by-chapter pointers for using *Read, Write, Connect* in the classroom. To download, see **bedfordstmartins.com/readwriteconnect/catalog**.

- *Testing Tool Kit: Writing and Grammar Test Bank* **CD-ROM** allows instructors to create secure, customized tests and quizzes from a pool of nearly two thousand questions covering 47 topics. It also includes ten prebuilt diagnostic tests. ISBN: 978-0-312-43032-0

- *TeachingCentral* at **bedfordstmartins.com/teachingcentral** offers the entire list of Bedford/St. Martin's print and online professional resources in one place. You will find landmark reference works, sourcebooks on pedagogical issues, award-winning collections, and practical advice for the classroom.

Brief Contents

Preface   vii

PART 1   Getting into a College Mind-Set   2

1   Reading and Responding to College Texts ✓   2

PART 2   From Pre-Reading to Proofreading: The Reading
and Writing Processes   36

2   Active and Critical Reading   36

3   Putting Ideas into Writing ✓   92

4   Revising, Editing, and Proofreading   118

PART 3   How Do I Do That? Reading and Writing Workshops   138

5   Additional Reading Strategies   138

6   Audience, Purpose, and Topic   169

7   Rhetorical Patterns in Reading and Writing ✓   187

8   Vocabulary Building ✓   198

9   Pre-Writing   214

10   Thesis and Main Idea ✓   223

11   Argument ✓   238

12   Topic Sentences and Paragraphs ✓   253

13   Essay Organization and Outlining   267

14   Drafting   286

15   Introductions and Conclusions   291

16   Quotation and Paraphrase   307

17   Giving and Receiving Feedback   323

18   Note Taking   339

19   Research   351

20   MLA Documentation   362

e   Essay Exams

e   Portfolios

e   Managing Your Time and Avoiding Procrastination

e ✓ **Icons indicate additional Integrated Media resources
available at bedfordstmartins.com/readwriteconnect**

PART 4   Food for Thought: Thematic Readings and Sources   379

21   Siblings 🄴   379

22   Public Art 🄴   441

23   Fame and Celebrity 🄴   508

🄴   Education

PART 5   How Do I Make My Sentences Say What I Mean? Grammar, Style, and Mechanics   576

24   How to Learn the Rules and Apply Them to Your Own Writing   576

25   Parts of Speech ✓   586

26   Basic Sentence Components ✓   600

27   Verbs ✓   617

28   Fragments ✓   635

29   Run-Ons: Fused Sentences and Comma Splices ✓   649

30   Pronouns ✓   654

31   Commas ✓   664

32   Parallelism ✓   674

33   Common Sentence-Structure Problems ✓   682

34   Writing Clear and Focused Sentences ✓   692

35   Apostrophes ✓   701

36   Spelling and Capitalization ✓   708

Index   I-1

🄴 ✓ **Icons indicate additional Integrated Media resources available at bedfordstmartins.com/readwriteconnect**

Contents

Preface   vii

PART 1   Getting into a College Mind-Set   2

1   Reading and Responding to College Texts ☑   2

How to Approach a Text: Pre-Reading Strategies   3
   Taking Stock of What You Already Know about a Topic   3
   Previewing the Text   4
   Carol S. Dweck, *The Perils and Promises of Praise*   6

Annotating While You Read   14
   Active Readers Annotate   14
   Recording Your Thoughts about the Text   15
   Asking Questions about the Text   16
   Identifying New Words   16

Finding Main Ideas and Supporting Evidence   25
   What Is the Main Idea?   25
   What Is Support?   25
   How Do You Find the Thesis, Major Points, and Support in an Essay or Article?   26
   Chart 1: Main Idea and Support ⒠

Writing a Summary   29
   How Do You Write a Summary?   30

Reading Textbooks Effectively   32

Chapter Review   34

PART 2   From Pre-Reading to Proofreading: The Reading and Writing Processes   36

2   Active and Critical Reading   36
Reading Critically   38
Reading With and Against the Grain   38

Read With the Grain   38

Read Against the Grain   39

Compare Your Notes   39

Readings on Money, Wealth, and Financial Literacy   41

SHERIE HOLDER AND KENNETH MEEKS, *Teach Your Children the Building Blocks of Finance*   43

OLIVIA MELLAN, *Men, Women, and Money*   50

Chart 2: Finding Meaningful Quotations 1 e

BUREAU OF LABOR STATISTICS, *Education Pays* (Chart)   59

MARK C. SCHUG AND ERIC A. HAGEDORN, *Milwaukee's Youth Enterprise Academy: An Eight-year Study of a Model Program for Urban Youth*   62

Chart 3: Pros and Cons e

RAKESH KOCHHAR, RICHARD FRY, AND PAUL TAYLOR, *Wealth Gaps Rise to Record Highs between Whites, Blacks, Hispanics: Twenty-to-One*   72

Chart 4: Finding Evidence e

PAM FESSLER, *Making It in the U.S.: More Than Just Hard Work*   81

Chart 5: Comparing Evidence e

SHIRA BOSS, *Money Envy* e

PBS, *Digging out of Debt* e

Chart 6: Synthesis Chart for Chapter 2 e

Working with Multiple Sources   88

Additional Online and Media Sources   90

Chapter Review   91

3   Putting Ideas into Writing ✓   92

What Is an Essay and How Do You Write One?   93

The Essay   93

The Writing Process   94

How to Read an Essay Assignment   94

Essay Writing Time Management   96

Chart 7: Essay Writing Time Management 1 e

Pre-Writing for Your Essay   98
  Freewriting   99
  Listing   100

Thesis Statements   102

Outlining Your Ideas   105

Generating Evidence to Support Your Thesis   107

Topic Sentences   108
  Finding Topic Sentences   108
  Writing Topic Sentences   110

Drafting a Rough Essay   111

Introductions and Conclusions   112

Finishing the Rough Draft   115

Essay Assignments for Money, Wealth, and Financial Literacy
  Unit   115

Chapter Review   117

4 Revising, Editing, and Proofreading   118

Revising as Re-Seeing Your Work   119
  Chart 8: Essay Writing Time Management 2

Practicing Peer Review   125

Revision Strategies   126
  Revising to Make Your Audience and Purpose Clear   127
  Revising to Focus Your Topic or Strengthen Your
  Thesis   127
  Revising to Reorganize an Essay   128
  Revising to Reorganize a Paragraph   129
  Revising for Paragraph Development   130
  Revising to Integrate Quotations and Paraphrases   131

Editing Strategies   134
  Reading Your Essay Out Loud   135
  Reading Backwards   135

Proofreading   136

Chapter Review   137

Icons indicate additional Integrated Media resources
available at bedfordstmartins.com/readwriteconnect

PART 3   How Do I Do That? Reading and Writing Workshops   138

5   Additional Reading Strategies   138

Reading Comprehension Strategies   138
   SQ3R   139
   KWL+   140
   Chart 9: KWL+ 🄴
   David J. Flaspohler *In Hakalau, a Modern Success Story*   142
   Mapping   145

Reading Textbooks   149
   SQ3R   150
   Annotating Textbooks   150
   Outlining or Mapping Textbooks   150
   Muscle Reading   164

Reading Fiction   164
   Elements of Fiction   165
   Annotating Fiction   165
   Taking Notes on Fiction   166
   Story Star Maps   166

Chapter Review   168

6   Audience, Purpose, and Topic   169

Audience and Purpose   169
   Determining the Audience and Purpose in a Reading   170
   Reading for Audience and Purpose   171

Topics   176
   Finding Something to Say and Caring about It   176
   Making a Broad Topic More Specific   178

Crafting Your Paper's Audience, Purpose, and Tone   180
   Writing for a Particular Audience   180
   Writing with a Purpose   182
   Chart 10: Audience and Purpose 🄴
   Writing in a Particular Tone   183

🄴 ✓ **Icons indicate additional Integrated Media resources available at bedfordstmartins.com/readwriteconnect**

      Sharpening Your Topic with a Title   184
      Titles of Academic Articles   185
   Chapter Review   186

7 Rhetorical Patterns in Reading and Writing ✓   187

What Is a Rhetorical Pattern?   187

A Detailed Look at the Patterns   188
   Example/Illustration   189
   Definition   190
   Classification/Categorization   190
   Narration   191
   Description   192
   Process Analysis   192
   Comparison and Contrast   193
   Cause and Effect   193

Using Rhetorical Patterns   195

Chapter Review   197

8 Vocabulary Building ✓   198

Strategies for Discovering the Meanings of Words   199
   Using Context Clues   199
   Using a Dictionary   201

Understanding Word Parts   203
   Prefixes   203
   Roots   204
   Suffixes   206

Committing New Words to Memory   207
   Using Mnemonics   207
   Making Graphic Flash Cards   207

Using a Thesaurus   210
   Using New Vocabulary   210

Chapter Review   213

9 Pre-Writing   214

Freewriting   214

Clustering   216

Listing   219

Questioning   220

Chapter Review   222

10   Thesis and Main Idea ☑   223

The Purpose of a Thesis   223

  The Explicit Thesis or Main Idea   224

  The Implied Thesis or Main Idea   224

  Sample Thesis Statements from Different Types of Readings   224

Finding the Main Point in a Reading   225

Shaping Your Thesis   226

  Characteristics of a Thesis   227

  How Do You Know What Claim You Want to Make?   228

Drafting Your Thesis, Step by Step   229

  Sharpening Your Thesis   230

  Improving Weak Thesis Statements   231

Chapter Review   236

11   Argument ☑   238

What Is an Argument?   238

Taking a Position   238

Evidence and Reasons   240

  Evidence versus Opinion   241

  Kinds of Evidence   242

  Making Inferences from Evidence   244

Counterarguments and Rebuttals   246

  Concession Words   248

Chapter Review   252

12   Topic Sentences and Paragraphs ☑   253

Topic Sentences   253

  Identifying Topic Sentences   253

    CATHERINE MAYER AND KATIE HARRIS *Hold the Relish*   254

The Topic Sentence and the Thesis 256

Writing Topic Sentences 257

Paragraphs 258

Understand Paragraph Structure 258

Evaluate Your Paragraphs 261

Develop Your Point (P) 262

Strengthen the Information (I) 262

Strengthen the Explanation or Elaboration (E) 263

Double-Check for Paragraph Unity and Coherence 264

Turn Your Topic Sentence into a Question 264

Chapter Review 266

13 Essay Organization and Outlining 267

Outlining as a Reader 267

Outlining as a Writer 272

Formal Outlines 273

Informal Outlines 274

Two Commonly Assigned Essay Structures 276

Compare and Contrast Essays 276

Cause and Effect Essays 278

Outlining Your Own Rough Draft 280

Transitions 281

Transitional Words and Expressions 281

Transitions from Paragraph to Paragraph 282

Sequencing Transitions 284

Chapter Review 285

14 Drafting 286

Writing the Very Rough Draft 286

Exploratory Drafts 287

Evidence Drafts 287

Conversation Drafts 288

Writing the Public First Draft 289

Chapter Review 290

Icons indicate additional Integrated Media resources available at bedfordstmartins.com/readwriteconnect

15 Introductions and Conclusions 291

Introductions 291
>   The Hook 293
>   The Topic 295
>   Background Information 296
>   The Thesis 298

Conclusions 299
>   Summing Up Your Essay 300
>   Providing Context and Adding Final Thoughts 302
>   Strategies for Writing Strong Conclusions 304

Chapter Review 306

16 Quotation and Paraphrase 307

Evaluating Sources for Credibility 308
>   Making Sure Quotations and Paraphrases Are Relevant 309

The Importance of Citation 309

When and How to Use Quotations 309
>   How to Quote Correctly 310
>   How to Enclose Quotations in Quotation Marks Correctly 311
>   How to Alter Quotations 312

When and How to Use Paraphrase 314

Introducing a Quotation or Paraphrase 316
>   Basic Signal Phrases 316
>   Use Signal Phrases to Add Meaning 317
>   Use More Sophisticated Signal Phrases 318

Explaining a Quotation or Paraphrase 320

Chapter Review 322

17 Giving and Receiving Feedback 323

Feedback Is Essential 323

Guidelines for Peer Review 324

Interpreting and Applying Instructors' Comments 325
>   Corrections 327
>   Comments 329

How to Use a Rubric   331

Meeting with an Instructor or Tutor   336

Chapter Review   338

18   Note Taking   339

The Cornell Method of Note Taking   340

Note Taking in Other Situations   342

    Class Discussions   342

    Small-Group Activities   343

    Film and Video Screenings   343

    Interviews   344

Avoiding Plagiarism When Taking Notes   346

    The Note Card System   346

    The Notebook System   347

    Electronic Note-Taking Systems   347

Chapter Review   350

19   Research   351

What to Look for in Source Materials   351

    Credibility   352

    Relevance   352

    Currency   352

Your College Library   353

The Role of the Internet in Academic Research   355

Evaluating Web Sources   355

Working with Sources   360

Chapter Review   361

20   MLA Documentation   362

Citation and Credibility   363

    A Note about Plagiarism   363

The Three Components of MLA Format   364

    Document Format   367

    The Works Cited Page   368

    In-Text (Parenthetical) Citation   375

Chapter Review   377

 Icons indicate additional Integrated Media resources available at bedfordstmartins.com/readwriteconnect

e Essay Exams

Preparing Mentally and Physically for an Essay Exam

Understanding the Expectations for the Essay Exam
   Essay Exams in General
   The Specific Exam

Studying for an Essay Exam
   Starting with an Overview
   Brainstorming Sample Questions
   Charting
   Chart 11: Comparing Readings e

Dissecting the Question

Making and Sticking to a Plan of Attack
   Interpreting the Question and Brainstorming Stage
   Outlining Stage
   Drafting Stage
   Revising, Editing, and Proofreading Stage

Chapter Review

e Portfolios

Why Create a Writing Portfolio?

Selecting Work for Your Portfolio

Reflecting on Your Writing
   Thinking about Your Reflective Letter or Statement
   Writing Your Reflective Letter or Statement

Chapter Review

e Managing Your Time and Avoiding Procrastination

Time Management

Setting Goals

Making and Using Schedules
   Your Typical Weekly Schedule
   Chart 12: Your Typical Weekly Schedule e
   A Schedule for Each Specific Week

Organizing for College

 Icons indicate additional Integrated Media resources available at bedfordstmartins.com/readwriteconnect

Your Study Space and Your Study Routine
Your Virtual Life

Avoiding Procrastination
Why We Procrastinate
Cutting Back on Procrastination

Chapter Review

PART 4 Food for Thought: Thematic Readings and Sources   379

21 Siblings   379

SHARON OLDS, *Killing My Sister's Fish*   380

Theme Overview   380

Readings on Siblings   382

JANE MERSKY LEDER, *Close Encounters of a Special Kind*   382

JEFFREY KLUGER, *The New Science of Siblings*   395

JEFFREY KLUGER, *The Power of Birth Order*   403

LAUREN SANDLER, *The Only Child: Debunking the Myths*   412

PO BRONSON AND ASHLEY MERRYMAN, *The Sibling Effect*   423

MIKAL GILMORE, *Secrets and Bones* e

ABC TV, *Sibling Secrets* (video) e

Chart 13: Synthesis Chart for Chapter 21 e

Synthesizing the Readings   434

Writing Your Essay   436

Writing Assignments   437

Additional Online and Media Sources   439

22 Public Art   441

Theme Overview   442

Readings on Public Art   443

PATRICK FRANK, *Public Art: Street Art*   443

JACK BECKER, *Public Art: An Essential Component of Creating Communities*   450

Icons indicate additional Integrated Media resources available at bedfordstmartins.com/readwriteconnect

TERESA PALOMO ACOSTA, *Chicano Mural Movement*   465

WILL SHANK, *Whose Art Is This Anyway?*   469

KOON-HWEE KAN, *Adolescents and Graffiti*   474

LOS ANGELES POLICE DEPARTMENT, *What Graffiti Means to a Community*   484

JAMES GADDY, *Nowhere Man*   487

ROSANNA XIA, *Lighthearted Street Art Delights (and Confuses) Downtown L.A. Visitors*   493

BUFFALO LAW JOURNAL, *Battles over Yard Art Sometimes Turn Ugly*   497

AMY KUPERINSKY, *Yarn Bombing: The Worldwide Web of Knit Graffiti, from N.J. to Dubai* **e**

Chart 14: Synthesis Chart for Chapter 22 **e**

Synthesizing the Readings   500

Writing Your Essay   502

Writing Assignments   503

Additional Online and Media Sources   505

23 Fame and Celebrity   508

Theme Overview   509

Readings on Fame and Celebrity   510

ANDREA CHANG, *The Kardashians: Cashing in with a Capital K*   510

CARLIN FLORA, *Seeing by Starlight: Celebrity Obsession*   516

MARY LOFTUS, *The Other Side of Fame*   523

Chart 15: Finding Meaningful Quotations 2 **e**

JAKE HALPERN, *The Desire to Belong: Why Everyone Wants to Have Dinner with Paris Hilton and 50 Cent*   538

DREW PINSKY, *Broadcasting Yourself*   550

MARK HARRIS, *How to Train Your Celebrity: Five Hollywood Charity Myths* **e**

LOOKTOTHESTARS.ORG, *LooktotheStars.org* **e**

Chart 16: Synthesis Chart for Chapter 23 **e**

Synthesizing the Readings   570

Writing Your Essay   571

Writing Assignments   572

Additional Online and Media Sources   574

[e] Education

Theme Overview

Readings on Education

> **GALE OPPOSING VIEWPOINTS IN CONTEXT,** *Education*

> **LUCINDA ROSENFELD,** *How Charter Schools Can Hurt*

> **DIANE RAVITCH,** *Stop the Madness*

> **GERARD ROBINSON AND EDWIN CHANG,** *The Color of Success: Black Student Achievement in Public Charter Schools*

> **ROBERT MARANTO AND JAMES V. SHULS,** *Lessons from KIPP Delta*

> Chart 17: Synthesis Chart for Chapter 24 [e]

Synthesizing the Readings

Writing Your Essay

Writing Assignments

Additional Online and Media Sources

PART 5   How Do I Make My Sentences Say What I Mean? Grammar, Style, and Mechanics   576

24   How to Learn the Rules and Apply Them to Your Own Writing   576

Understanding Editing and Proofreading   576

Pinpointing Your Errors   577

> Errors That Make Your Writing Unreadable   578
> Errors That Make Your Writing Unclear   578
> Errors That Make Your Writing Distracting   579
> Creating a Grammar Log   579
> Chart 18: Grammar Log [e]
> Identifying and Prioritizing Errors: One Student's Paragraph   580

Learning the Rules   582

Applying What You've Learned to Your Own Writing   582

Chapter Review   584

25 Parts of Speech ✓ 586

Nouns and Pronouns   589

   What Are Nouns and Pronouns?   589

   Identifying Nouns and Pronouns   589

Adjectives   590

   What Are Adjectives?   590

   Identifying Adjectives   591

   Definite and Indefinite Articles   591

Verbs   592

   What Are Verbs?   592

   Identifying Verbs   592

Adverbs   594

   What Are Adverbs?   594

   Identifying Adverbs   594

Conjunctions   595

Prepositions   597

Interjections   598

Chapter Review   599

26 Basic Sentence Components ✓ 600

What Is a Sentence?   600

Verbs   600

   Time-Testing to Find the Verb   601

   Compound Verbs   602

Subjects   603

   Sentences That Begin with *There Is* or *There Are*   604

   Verbals: The Verbs That Aren't Verbs   604

   Compound Subjects   605

Phrases   605

Clauses   606

Subordination   607

e ✓ Icons indicate additional Integrated Media resources available at bedfordstmartins.com/readwriteconnect

Comma Placement with Subordinating Words or Phrases 608

Finding and Correcting Subordination Errors 609

Coordination 611

Finding and Correcting Choppy Sentences 612

Sentence Variety 614

Chapter Review 615

27 Verbs ☑ 617

What Exactly Is a Verb? 617

Agreement, Tense, and Irregular Verbs 618

Subject-Verb Agreement 619

Verb Tense 619

Irregular Verbs 620

Fixing the Three Main Errors in Verb Use 621

Errors in Subject-Verb Agreement 622

Errors in Verb Tense 627

Errors in Irregular Verb Usage 631

Chapter Review 633

28 Fragments ☑ 635

What Exactly Is a Fragment? 635

Fragments That Are Missing a Subject 636

Fragments That Are Missing a Verb or Part of a Verb 638

Fragments That Are Incomplete Thoughts 640

Fragments That Begin with Prepositions 640

Fragments That Begin with Subordinators (Dependent Words) 642

Fragments That Add Additional Information: *Who, Like, When*, and *Which* Fragments 643

Recognizing Fragments in Your Own Writing 645

Chapter Review 647

29 Run-Ons: Fused Sentences and Comma Splices ☑ 649

What Are Fused Sentences and Comma Splices? 649

Icons indicate additional Integrated Media resources available at bedfordstmartins.com/readwriteconnect

Finding and Fixing Fused Sentences and Comma Splices   651

Chapter Review   653

30 Pronouns ✓ 654

What Exactly Is a Pronoun?   654
   Subject Pronouns   654
   Possessive Pronouns   654
   Indefinite Pronouns   655
   Demonstrative Pronouns: *This/These/That/Those*   655
   Antecedents   656

Common Pronoun Errors   656
   Pronoun-Reference Errors   656
   Pronoun-Agreement Errors   658
   Pronoun-Shift Errors   660

Fixing Pronoun Errors   662

Chapter Review   662

31 Commas ✓ 664

What Is a Comma?   664

Rules for Using Commas   665
   Use a Comma to Separate Items in a List   665
   Use a Comma to Separate Place Names, Dates, and People's Titles   665
   Use a Comma When You Introduce a Quotation, *Unless* You Use the Word *That*   666
   Use a Comma When You Have Two or More Adjectives in a Row   666
   Use a Comma with Introductory Elements   667
   Use a Comma When Joining Two Sentences with a Coordinating Conjunction   668
   Use Commas with Sentence Interrupters   670

Building Sentences Using These Comma Rules   672

Editing Your Work for Comma Errors   673

Chapter Review   673

32 Parallelism ✓ 674

What Is Parallelism?   674

Icons indicate additional Integrated Media resources available at bedfordstmartins.com/readwriteconnect

Common Parallelism Errors   675
   Lists with Colons   675
   List Interrupters   676
   That Tricky Word *That*   677
   Maintaining Parallelism When Quoting   677
Finding and Fixing Parallelism Errors   678
Chapter Review   681

33 Common Sentence-Structure Problems ☑ 682

What Is a Mixed Construction?   682
   What Are Predication Errors?   684
Finding Mixed Constructions   685
Fixing Mixed Constructions   685
What Is a Modifier?   687
   Misplaced Modifiers   688
   Dangling Modifiers   688
Finding and Fixing Misplaced and Dangling Modifiers   689
Chapter Review   691

34 Writing Clear and Focused Sentences ☑ 692

What Are Clear and Focused Sentences?   692
Wordiness   693
   What Is Wordiness?   693
   Fixing Wordiness   693
Avoid Vague or Unclear Pronouns   695
Use Active Voice Whenever Possible   696
Avoid Clichés, Empty Phrases, and Slang   697
Chapter Review   700

35 Apostrophes ☑ 701

What Is an Apostrophe?   701
   Using Apostrophes to Make Contractions   701
   A Few Exceptions   702
   Using Apostrophes to Show Ownership   703

Icons indicate additional Integrated Media resources available at bedfordstmartins.com/readwriteconnect

Finding and Fixing Apostrophe Errors with Possessives   705

Chapter Review   706

36 Spelling and Capitalization ✅   708

Spelling   708

Commonly Confused Words   708

Tricky Spelling Rules   710
  Plural Endings   711
  Silent *E*   711
  To Double or Not to Double the Final Consonant   712
  Foreign Words   712

Capitalization   713
  Proper Nouns   713
  Titles   714

Chapter Review   715

Index   I-1

Read
Write
Connect

1

Reading and Responding to College Texts

in this chapter

- What Is Pre-Reading?
- What Is Annotation?
- How Do You Read Actively?
- How Do You Find Main Ideas and Supporting Evidence?
- What Is a Summary?
- How Do You Read Textbooks Effectively?

You already know how to read and write. But do you know how to read and write well? How many times have you read something, only to forget a few days or even minutes later what you just read? Have you ever studied for a test but blanked out when it came time to write your answers? Do you know how to write with your own voice about what you read? *Read, Write, Connect* is designed to help you think critically and become a more effective and efficient reader and writer and to prepare you for college work.

This book's central premise is that reading and writing are both processes. No one is born a good writer or a good reader. There are many steps to reading and writing well, and all students can learn those steps, practice them, and improve their reading, critical thinking, and writing. Unfortunately, there is no "quick fix" to learning how to read and write well, but we believe that when you see reading and writing as processes and practice the steps outlined in this book, you'll make serious progress as a reader, writer, and thinker.

This chapter gives a quick overview of active reading and summary writing to jump-start your college semester and to get you into the college "mind-set." The rest of the book goes into far more detail about these important skills. The book begins with a short article that provides valuable information on the learning process and can give you a quick introduction to the skills of pre-reading, annotating, and summarizing, which are the foundation of college-level work.

LearningCurve
For extra practice in the skills covered in this chapter, visit **bedfordstmartins.com /readwriteconnect.**

How to Approach a Text: Pre-Reading Strategies

Strong readers don't just begin reading at the first sentence. They follow a process. Very experienced readers follow the process almost automatically, so they may not even be aware of what they are doing. It makes them look naturally "smart," but actually they just have had a lot of practice at something everyone can learn. The first step in the process is called pre-reading because you do it before you actually start to read. Here, we'll begin with two basic techniques:

1. Taking stock of what you already know about a topic
2. Previewing the text

For more on pre-reading and becoming a strong reader, see Chapter 5, Additional Reading Strategies, page 138.

TAKING STOCK OF WHAT YOU ALREADY KNOW ABOUT A TOPIC

To get you thinking about the selections you'll read later on, complete the following Your Project activity. Don't worry; this is not a formal writing assignment to be graded. You don't need to worry about organization or writing the perfect sentence. This sort of writing is called "freewriting," and its purpose is to help you generate as many ideas as possible.

For more on freewriting, see Chapter 9, Pre-Writing, page 214.

Taking Stock of What You Already Know

Spend ten minutes writing nonstop about one or more of the questions below:

- Recall a time when someone's praise really mattered to you. Describe what happened. What did the person say? How did it make you feel?
- What does it mean to be smart?
- What does it mean to be a good student?
- How do you feel when you struggle with something you are learning?
- Think of a time you overcame a difficult problem in life or at school. How did you handle the problem? What helped you to bounce back afterward?

Read over what you have written and reflect on it. Highlight or underline any particularly good points or ideas that you generated. Add any additional thoughts that come to you. What three or four words come to your mind when you think about learning, overcoming obstacles, and praise? List them on your freewrite.

You've just practiced one of the most effective techniques for becoming a strong college reader. Why is taking stock of what you know so helpful? Consider for a moment all the knowledge and information you hold in your mind. Readers understand and remember what they read much better when they can connect the reading to what they already know. So by thinking about what you already know of the topic you are going to read about, you are drawing from all the knowledge and information you already have and getting ready to understand the reading and make connections.

PREVIEWING THE TEXT

Previewing means flipping through the reading to get a sense of what it might be about, how it is organized (into sections or paragraphs), how long it is, and what tools the writer has provided to help you read it. (You probably already check the length of assigned readings, just to see what you're in for!) Previewing the text in this way will help you to get a sense of the scope of the topic and the organization of the text. Previewing a reading takes very little time, and it really helps you understand the material.

Why is previewing so effective? Imagine you have to go someplace in an unfamiliar part of town. You may have a rough idea of how to get there, but looking up the route on a map will give you a clear picture of how to get from where you are to where you want to end up, and it will let you know what landmarks to look for along the way so you will know you are on the right path. Similarly, previewing a text before reading it will give you a sense of the map of the text. What points will it cover to get you from the introduction to the conclusion? Previewing will give you a sense of what main points (landmarks) you should be noticing along the way.

To use another analogy, think back to your first day of college or of a new job. Probably much of that first day is one big blank in your mind because you were so overwhelmed by all the new information. Something similar happens with reading. Plunging into a reading without previewing it is like dropping in on an event without prior preparation: It's easy to overlook the main points and get lost in the details. Getting a sense of the big picture before you read will prepare you to absorb the information right away.

practice it   Previewing the Text

Previewing the text is quick. Practice right now with Carol S. Dweck's article "The Perils and Promises of Praise," published in the journal *Educational Leadership* in October 2007 (pp. 6–13). You can do this by yourself or with some classmates, or even as a whole class. Keep these questions in front of you as you work. Here's how to do it:

Step 1: Look at the title of the text. Based on the title, what might you predict the article will be about? Look for words that suggest an opinion or point of view (words like "best" or "against"), a topic range (words like "from _____ to _____"), or titles that ask questions.

Step 2: Find out who the author is and where the text was published. What does this tell you about the audience and purpose? Is this a reading intended for students, parents, or teachers? How will the intended audience shape the information presented?

Step 3: Flip through the pages of the article. How long is it? How is it laid out? What kinds of pictures does it have? Is the reading broken up by sections or paragraphs? Are there any section headers? If so, what do they tell you about the subtopic of each section? What kind of information is at the end of the article? What can you learn about the author, topic, audience, and/or purpose of the text?

Step 4: Quickly skim the first paragraph. What did you learn? What do you expect the article will discuss?

Step 5: Quickly skim the last paragraph. What did you learn? What point(s) do you think Dweck is going to make?

continued ❂

Step 6: Check whether there are any comprehension or discussion questions at the end of the reading. If so, read those before you read the article or chapter. The questions will clue you in on what important points or ideas you should be looking for in the text.

Step 7: Take a few minutes to write what you learned in the margins of the text. (That's right: Write your thoughts directly on the pages of your book.) Writing down what you learned will help you make sense of the text, even if you are just guessing or making predictions.

Important words and phrases have been italicized in this reading. Look up those words you don't know, and write the definitions in your personal vocabulary list.

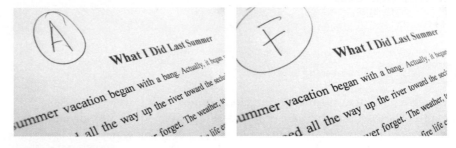

CAROL S. DWECK

The Perils and Promises of Praise

The wrong kind of praise creates self-defeating behavior.
The right kind motivates students to learn.

We often hear these days that we've produced a generation of young people who can't get through the day without an award. They expect success because they're special, not because they've worked hard.

Is this true? Have we *inadvertently* done something to hold back our students?

I think educators commonly hold two beliefs that do just that. Many believe that (1) praising students' intelligence builds their confidence and motivation to learn, and (2) students' *inherent* intelligence is the major cause of their achievement in school. Our research has shown that the first belief is false and that the second can be harmful—even for the most competent students.

As a psychologist, I have studied student motivation for more than thirty-five years. My graduate students and I have looked at thousands of children, asking why some enjoy learning, even when it's hard, and why they are *resilient* in the face of obstacles. We have learned a great deal. Research shows us how to praise students in ways that yield motivation and resilience. In addition, specific interventions can reverse a student's slide into failure during the *vulnerable* period of adolescence.

Fixed or Malleable?

Praise is *intricately* connected to how students view their intelligence.   5
Some students believe that their intellectual ability is a fixed trait. They have a certain amount of intelligence, and that's that. Students with this fixed mind-set become excessively concerned with how smart they are, seeking tasks that will prove their intelligence and avoiding ones that might not (Dweck, 1999, 2006). The desire to learn takes a backseat.

Other students believe that their intellectual ability is something they can develop through effort and education. They don't necessarily believe that anyone can become an Einstein or a Mozart, but they do understand that even Einstein and Mozart had to put in years of effort to become who they were. When students believe that they can develop their intelligence, they focus on doing just that. Not worrying about how smart they will appear, they take on challenges and stick to them (Dweck, 1999, 2006).

More and more research in psychology and *neuroscience* supports the growth mind-set. We are discovering that the brain has more *plasticity* over time than we ever imagined (Doidge, 2007); that fundamental aspects of intelligence can be enhanced through learning (Sternberg, 2005); and that dedication and persistence in the face of obstacles are key ingredients in outstanding achievement (Ericsson, Charness, Feltovich, & Hoffman, 2006).

Alfred Binet (1909/1973), the inventor of the IQ test, had a strong growth mind-set. He believed that education could transform the basic capacity to learn. Far from intending to measure fixed intelligence, he meant his test to be a tool for identifying students who were not profiting from the public school curriculum so that other courses of study could be devised to foster their intellectual growth.

The Two Faces of Effort

The fixed and growth mind-sets create two different psychological worlds. In the fixed mind-set, students care first and foremost about how they'll be judged: smart or not smart. Repeatedly, students with this mind-set reject opportunities to learn if they might make mistakes (Hong, Chiu, Dweck, Lin, & Wan, 1999; Mueller & Dweck, 1998). When they do make mistakes or reveal deficiencies, rather than correct them, they try to hide them (Nussbaum & Dweck, 2007).

They are also afraid of effort because effort makes them feel dumb. They believe that if you have the ability, you shouldn't need effort (Blackwell, Trzesniewski, & Dweck, 2007), that ability should bring success all by itself. This is one of the worst beliefs that students can hold. It can cause many bright students to stop working in school when the curriculum becomes challenging.

Finally, students in the fixed mind-set don't recover well from setbacks. When they hit a setback in school, they *decrease* their efforts and consider cheating (Blackwell et al., 2007). The idea of fixed intelligence does not offer them *viable* ways to improve.

Let's get inside the head of a student with a fixed mind-set as he sits in his classroom, confronted with algebra for the first time. Up until then, he has breezed through math. Even when he barely paid attention in class and skimped on his homework, he always got As. But this is different. It's hard. The student feels anxious and thinks, "What if I'm not as good at math as I thought? What if other kids understand it and I don't?" At some level, he realizes that he has two choices: try hard, or turn off. His interest in math begins to *wane*, and his attention wanders. He tells himself, "Who cares about this stuff? It's for nerds. I could do it if I wanted to, but it's so boring. You don't see CEOs and sports stars solving for x and y."

By contrast, in the growth mind-set, students care about learning. When they make a mistake or exhibit a deficiency, they correct it (Blackwell et al., 2007; Nussbaum & Dweck, 2007). For them, effort is a *positive* thing: It ignites their intelligence and causes it to grow. In the face of failure, these students *escalate* their efforts and look for new learning strategies.

Let's look at another student—one who has a growth mind-set—having her first encounter with algebra. She finds it new, hard, and confusing, unlike anything else she has ever learned. But she's determined to understand it. She listens to everything the teacher says, asks the teacher questions after class, and takes her textbook home and reads the chapter over twice. As she begins to get it, she feels *exhilarated*. A new world of math opens up for her.

It is not surprising, then, that when we have followed students over challenging school transitions or courses, we find that those with growth mind-sets outperform their classmates with fixed mind-sets— even when they entered with equal skills and knowledge. A growth mind-set fosters the growth of ability over time (Blackwell et al.,

10

15

2007; Mangels, Butterfield, Lamb, Good, & Dweck, 2006; see also Grant & Dweck, 2003).

The Effects of Praise

Many educators have hoped to maximize students' confidence in their abilities, their enjoyment of learning, and their ability to thrive in school by praising their intelligence. We've studied the effects of this kind of praise in children as young as four years old and as old as adolescence, in students in inner-city and rural settings, and in students of different ethnicities—and we've consistently found the same thing (Cimpian, Arce, Markman, & Dweck, 2007; Kamins & Dweck, 1999; Mueller & Dweck, 1998): Praising students' intelligence gives them a short burst of pride, followed by a long string of negative consequences.

In many of our studies (see Mueller & Dweck, 1998), fifth-grade students worked on a task, and after the first set of problems, the teacher praised some of them for their intelligence ("You must be smart at these problems") and others for their effort ("You must have worked hard at these problems"). We then assessed the students' mind-sets. In one study, we asked students to agree or disagree with mind-set statements, such as, "Your intelligence is something basic about you that you can't really change." Students praised for intelligence agreed with statements like these more than students praised for effort did. In another study, we asked students to define intelligence. Students praised for intelligence made significantly more references to *innate*, fixed capacity, whereas the students praised for effort made more references to skills, knowledge, and areas they could change through effort and learning. Thus, we found that praise for intelligence tended to put students in a fixed mind-set (intelligence is fixed, and you have it), whereas praise for effort tended to put them in a growth mind-set (you're developing these skills because you're working hard).

We then offered students a chance to work on either a challenging task that they could learn from or an easy one that ensured error-free performance. Most of those praised for intelligence wanted the easy task, whereas most of those praised for effort wanted the challenging task and the opportunity to learn.

Next, the students worked on some challenging problems. As a group, students who had been praised for their intelligence *lost* their confidence in their ability and their enjoyment of the task as soon as they began to struggle with the problem. If success meant they were smart, then struggling meant they were not. The whole point of intelligence praise is to boost confidence and motivation, but both were gone in a flash. Only the effort-praised kids remained, on the whole, confident and eager.

When the problems were made somewhat easier again, students   20
praised for intelligence did poorly, having lost their confidence and
motivation. As a group, they did worse than they had done initially on
these same types of problems. The students praised for effort showed
excellent performance and continued to improve.

Finally, when asked to report their scores (anonymously), almost 40
percent of the intelligence-praised students lied. Apparently, their egos
were so wrapped up in their performance that they couldn't admit
mistakes. Only about 10 percent of the effort-praised students saw fit to
falsify their results.

Praising students for their intelligence, then, hands them not
motivation and resilience but a fixed mind-set with all its vulnerability. In contrast, effort or "process" praise (praise for engagement,
perseverance, strategies, improvement, and the like) fosters *hardy*
motivation. It tells students what they've done to be successful and
what they need to do to be successful again in the future. Process
praise sounds like this:

- You really studied for your
  English test, and your improvement shows it. You read the
  material over several times,
  outlined it, and tested yourself on
  it. That really worked!
- I like the way you tried all kinds
  of strategies on that math problem until you finally got it.
- It was a long, hard assignment,
  but you stuck to it and got it done. You stayed at your desk, kept up
  your concentration, and kept working. That's great!
- I like that you took on that challenging project for your science class.
  It will take a lot of work—doing the research, designing the machine,
  buying the parts, and building it. You're going to learn a lot of great
  things.

What about a student who gets an A without trying? I would say, "All
right, that was too easy for you. Let's do something more challenging that
you can learn from." We don't want to make something done quickly and
easily the basis for our admiration.

What about a student who works hard and *doesn't* do well? I would
say, "I liked the effort you put in. Let's work together some more and
figure out what you don't understand." Process praise keeps students
focused, not on something called ability that they may or may not have
and that magically creates success or failure, but on processes they can
all engage in to learn.

Motivated to Learn

Finding that a growth mind-set creates motivation and resilience—and   25
leads to higher achievement—we sought to develop an intervention that
would teach this mind-set to students. We decided to aim our intervention at students who were making the transition to seventh grade because
this is a time of great vulnerability. School often gets more difficult in
seventh grade, grading becomes more *stringent*, and the environment
becomes more impersonal. Many students take stock of themselves and
their intellectual abilities at this time and decide whether they want to
be involved with school. Not surprisingly, it is often a time of disengagement and plunging achievement.

We performed our intervention in a New York City junior high
school in which many students were struggling with the transition and
were showing plummeting grades. If students learned a growth mind-
set, we reasoned, they might be able to meet this challenge with
increased, rather than decreased, effort. We therefore developed an
eight-session workshop in which both the control group and the growth-
mind-set group learned study skills, time management techniques, and
memory strategies (Blackwell et al., 2007). However, in the growth-
mind-set intervention, students also learned about their brains and
what they could do to make their intelligence grow.

They learned that the brain is like a muscle—the more they exercise
it, the stronger it becomes. They learned that every time they try hard
and learn something new, their brain forms new connections that, over
time, make them smarter. They learned that intellectual development is
not the natural unfolding of intelligence, but rather the formation of new
connections brought about through effort and learning.

Students were *riveted* by this information. The idea that their intellectual growth was largely in their hands fascinated them. In fact, even
the most disruptive students suddenly sat still and took notice, with the
most unruly boy of the lot looking up at us and saying, "You mean I don't
have to be dumb?"

Indeed, the growth-mind-set message appeared to unleash students'
motivation. Although both groups had experienced a steep decline in their
math grades during their first months of junior high, those receiving the
growth-mind-set intervention showed a significant rebound. Their math
grades improved. Those in the control group, despite their excellent study
skills intervention, continued their decline.

What's more, the teachers—who were unaware that the intervention   30
workshops differed—singled out three times as many students in the
growth-mind-set intervention as showing marked changes in motivation.
These students had a heightened desire to work hard and learn. One
striking example was the boy who thought he was dumb. Before this

experience, he had never put in any extra effort and often didn't turn his homework in on time. As a result of the training, he worked for hours one evening to finish an assignment early so that his teacher could review it and give him a chance to revise it. He earned a B+ on the assignment (he had been getting Cs and lower previously).

Other researchers have obtained similar findings with a growth-mind-set intervention. Working with junior high school students, Good, Aronson, and Inzlicht (2003) found an increase in math and English achievement test scores; working with college students, Aronson, Fried, and Good (2002) found an increase in students' valuing of academics, their enjoyment of schoolwork, and their grade point averages.

To *facilitate* delivery of the growth-mind-set workshop to students, we developed an interactive computer-based version of the intervention called *Brainology*. Students work through six modules, learning about the brain, visiting virtual brain labs, doing virtual brain experiments, seeing how the brain changes with learning, and learning how they can make their brains work better and grow smarter.

We tested our initial version in twenty New York City schools, with encouraging results. Almost all students (anonymously polled) reported changes in their study habits and motivation to learn resulting directly from their learning of the growth mind-set. One student noted that as a result of the animation she had seen about the brain, she could actually "picture the *neurons* growing bigger as they make more connections." One student referred to the value of effort: "If you do not give up and you keep studying, you can find your way through."

Adolescents often see school as a place where they perform for teachers who then judge them. The growth mind-set changes that perspective and makes school a place where students vigorously engage in learning for their own benefit.

Going Forward

Our research shows that educators cannot hand students confidence on a silver platter by praising their intelligence. Instead, we can help them gain the tools they need to maintain their confidence in learning by keeping them focused on the *process* of achievement.   35

Maybe we have produced a generation of students who are more dependent, fragile, and entitled than previous generations. If so, it's time for us to adopt a growth mind-set and learn from our mistakes. It's time to deliver interventions that will truly boost students' motivation, resilience, and learning.

References

Aronson, J., Fried, C., & Good, C. (2002). Reducing the effects of stereotype threat on African American college students by shaping theories of intelligence. *Journal of Experimental Social Psychology, 38*, 113–125.

Binet, A. (1909/1973). *Les idées modernes sur les enfants* [Modern ideas on children]. Paris, France: Flammarion. (Original work published 1909).

Blackwell, L., Trzesniewski, K., & Dweck, C. S. (2007). Implicit theories of intelligence predict achievement across an adolescent transition: A longitudinal study and an intervention. *Child Development, 78*, 246–263.

Cimpian, A., Arce, H., Markman, E. M., & Dweck, C. S. (2007). Subtle linguistic cues impact children's motivation. *Psychological Science, 18*, 314–316.

Doidge, N. (2007). *The brain that changes itself: Stories of personal triumph from the frontiers of brain science.* New York, NY: Viking.

Dweck, C. S. (1999). *Self-theories: Their role in motivation, personality, and development.* Philadelphia, PA: Taylor and Francis/Psychology Press.

Dweck, C. S. (2006). *Mindset: The new psychology of success.* New York, NY: Random House.

Ericsson, K. A., Charness, N., Feltovich, P. J., & Hoffman, R. R. (Eds.). (2006). *The Cambridge handbook of expertise and expert performance.* New York, NY: Cambridge University Press.

Good, C., Aronson, J., & Inzlicht, M. (2003). Improving adolescents' standardized test performance: An intervention to reduce the effects of stereotype threat. *Journal of Applied Developmental Psychology, 24*, 645–662.

Grant, H., & Dweck, C. S. (2003). Clarifying achievement goals and their impact. *Journal of Personality and Social Psychology, 85*, 541–553.

Hong, Y. Y., Chiu, C., Dweck, C. S., Lin, D., & Wan, W. (1999). Implicit theories, attributions, and coping: A meaning system approach. *Journal of Personality and Social Psychology, 77*, 588–599.

Kamins, M., & Dweck, C. S. (1999). Person vs. process praise and criticism: Implications for contingent self-worth and coping. *Developmental Psychology, 35*, 835–847.

Mangels, J. A., Butterfield, B., Lamb, J., Good, C. D., & Dweck, C. S. (2006). Why do beliefs about intelligence influence learning success? A social-cognitive-neuroscience model. *Social, Cognitive, and Affective Neuroscience, 1*, 75–86.

Mueller, C. M., & Dweck, C. S. (1998). Intelligence praise can undermine motivation and performance. *Journal of Personality and Social Psychology, 75*, 33–52.

Nussbaum, A. D., & Dweck, C. S. (2007). Defensiveness vs. remediation: Self-theories and modes of self-esteem maintenance. *Personality and Social Psychology Bulletin.*

Sternberg, R. (2005). Intelligence, competence, and expertise. In A. Elliot & C. S. Dweck (Eds.), *The handbook of competence and motivation* (pp. 15–30). New York, NY: Guilford Press.

Carol S. Dweck is the Lewis and Virginia Eaton Professor of Psychology at Stanford University and the author of *Mindset: The New Psychology of Success* (Random House, 2006).

COMPREHENSION QUESTIONS

1. What sort of research study did Dweck and her colleagues conduct? How did they design the study? Who participated? What were they trying to discover?

2. How does a fixed mind-set differ from a growth mind-set?

3. What kinds of praise encourage a growth mind-set?

4. What does "resilience" mean, and why is it so important to learning?

5. What does Dweck suggest about people who like to be challenged versus those who prefer to take on easy tasks?

6. Why did Dweck and her colleagues decide to focus on seventh graders in the study described in the "Motivated to Learn" section?

DISCUSSION QUESTIONS

1. How does a person develop a fixed mind-set or a growth mind-set?

2. Do you believe that praising students' intelligence does more harm than good? Why or why not?

3. Do you think the study would have had different results if it had been conducted in a different area, such as a rural or suburban location?

4. Can a person change from a fixed mind-set into a growth mind-set? How?

5. What can a parent do to create a growth mind-set? What can a teacher or coach do? What can a student do?

6. Is it possible to have a dual mind-set?

7. Is the IQ test relevant today?

Annotating While You Read

Strong readers read actively rather than passively. Passive readers scan the words on the page, but after reading a sentence or two, can't remember what they've just read. (Sound familiar?) Active readers, on the other hand, do a number of things to keep them engaged and focused, and to help them understand and remember what they have read. When you listen to a story your friend is telling you, do you find yourself nodding your head and maybe adding comments like "Really? He said that?" or "I know what you mean" or "That's too bad"? If you hear something you don't understand, you probably ask for clarification: "What do you mean you couldn't find your car? Was it gone or had you just forgotten where you parked it?" These are all signs of active listening.

Active readers do the same kinds of things when they read. Although the author isn't present to answer our questions or notice if we are nodding our heads in agreement, by responding in this way—especially in writing, through annotations—we are participating in a conversation. The most common active reading strategy is annotating your text.

ACTIVE READERS ANNOTATE

Annotating—writing in your book in a specific and productive way—may be difficult for you to wrap your mind around, especially if you are a new college student. From elementary school through high school, students are told over and over again not to write in their books. Get ready for a change: The best readers write in their books constantly, and in college your professors will expect you to write in your books. Once you can shift your mind-set into finding this acceptable, you'll see that annotating helps you process and remember information, study for tests, and write papers. There are many ways to annotate, and you will find your own style of annotation with practice.

RECORDING YOUR THOUGHTS ABOUT THE TEXT

Another reason to annotate is to record your ideas as they come to you, particularly the first time you read something. Briefly write your thoughts in the margins near the sentences that inspired your reaction. Do you agree or disagree with what the author has to say? Why? How does the reading make you feel? What does it make you think? Chances are the reading is making you feel something, so start with that.

Sample Reactions

Huh?	Yes! I agree!	No! I disagree!
How can that be?	Exciting!	Losing interest . . .
Really?!	Interesting!	Frustrating!
Lacking support	This sounds like me	I don't think so
Don't get it . . .	Good point	Funny
Confusing	Sad :(	

Recording your honest personal reactions to the text can help you later when you analyze the reading. You often start with an emotional response, but then you think through the reasons for your response.

Another type of annotation helps you draw connections between your previous experiences and the reading. Readers frequently compare and contrast what the reading says to what they already know. While reading, you may compare people you know to those described in the text. You might also relate information you've learned in other classes or through personal experience to what you are reading.

Sample Connections

Sounds like my brother
Like the theory of motivation from psychology class
Like the Golden Rule—do unto others
Happened to me once—but turned out differently

Connecting the ideas in a reading to other things you have read or studied becomes increasingly helpful as you move on in college. You will get more out of your studies when you see the connections between, for instance, your psychology and English class readings, or your math and business class.

ASKING QUESTIONS ABOUT THE TEXT

Strong readers also make note of any questions they have about the text while annotating. You may think you already know a lot about the topic of the reading, but finding some questions to ask about the text is good:

1. Asking questions helps you identify what you don't understand.
2. Asking questions sparks your critical thinking about a topic.

Thinking over your questions, talking about them in class, and asking for clarification about them will all increase your comprehension of the text.

So, as you read, write down any questions you have. You might ask clarifying questions like "What does 'peril' mean?" or bigger picture questions like "Can someone have both a fixed and growth mind-set?" or "How does she come to that conclusion?" or "How does this apply to me?" Your instructor will likely ask the class what questions you have about the reading; here's your chance to keep track of those questions.

IDENTIFYING NEW WORDS

As part of annotating, make sure to also underline or circle any words you don't know. Sometimes you can figure out the meaning of a word by examining the words or phrases near it in the sentence or paragraph; we call this looking at context clues. If you can't figure out a word's meaning this way, look it up in a dictionary and write the meaning in the margin in your own words. Keep a glossary of new vocabulary and key terms in your notebook or make flash cards of important vocabulary words as you read. Every time you see a new vocabulary word, in addition to writing the definition in your own words in the margin, add it to your list or make a flash card for it, and note the page number of your reading or textbook so that you can find it again later if necessary. This is a great way to build your vocabulary. An example of one student's annotations of Carol Dweck's article "The Perils and Promises of Praise" follows.

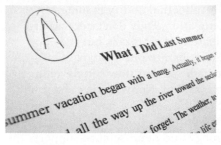

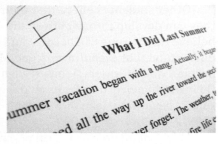

CAROL S. DWECK

The Perils and Promises of Praise

(dangers)

) isn't praise/feedback from teachers also important?

) I didn't know there was a <u>wrong</u> kind of praise...?

The wrong kind of praise creates self-defeating behavior. The right kind motivates students to learn.

We often hear these days that we've produced a generation of young people who can't get through the day without an award. They expect success because they're special, not because they've worked hard.

Is this true? Have we inadvertently done something to hold back our students?

I think educators commonly hold two beliefs that do just that. Many believe that (1) praising students' intelligence builds their confidence and motivation to learn, and (2) students' inherent intelligence is the major cause of their achievement in school. Our research has shown that the first belief is false and that the second can be harmful—even for the most competent students.

doesn't it?

) really?

export

As a psychologist, I have studied student motivation for more than thirty-five years. My graduate students and I have looked at thousands of children, asking why some enjoy learning, even when it's hard, and why they are resilient in the face of obstacles. We have learned a great deal. Research shows us how to praise students in ways that yield motivation and resilience. In addition, specific interventions can reverse a student's slide into failure during the vulnerable period of adolescence.

able to bounce back

Fixed or Malleable? *able to be molded*

Praise is intricately connected to how students view their intelligence. Some   5
students believe that their intellectual ability is a fixed trait. They have a certain amount of intelligence, and that's that. Students with this fixed mind-set become excessively concerned with how smart they are, seeking tasks that will prove their intelligence and avoiding ones that might not (Dweck, 1999, 2006). The desire to learn takes a backseat.

Other students believe that their intellectual ability is something they can develop through effort and education. They don't necessarily believe that anyone can become an Einstein or a Mozart, but they do understand that even Einstein and Mozart had to put in years of effort to become who they were. When students believe that they can develop their intelligence, they focus on doing just that. Not worrying about how smart they will appear, they take on challenges and stick to them (Dweck, 1999, 2006).

true!

More and more research in psychology and neuroscience supports the growth mind-set. We are discovering that the brain has more plasticity over time than we ever imagined (Doidge, 2007); that fundamental aspects of intelligence can be enhanced through learning (Sternberg, 2005); and that dedication and persistence in the face of obstacles are key ingredients in outstanding achievement (Ericsson, Charness, Feltovich, & Hoffman, 2006).

what does that mean?

Alfred Binet (1909/1973), the inventor of the IQ test, had a strong growth mind-set. He believed that education could transform the basic capacity to learn. Far from intending to measure fixed intelligence, he meant his test to be a tool for identifying students who were not profiting from the public school curriculum so that other courses of study could be devised to foster their intellectual growth.

interesting!

The Two Faces of Effort

The fixed and growth mind-sets create two different psychological worlds. In the fixed mind-set, students care first and foremost about how they'll be judged: smart or not smart. Repeatedly, students with this mind-set reject opportunities to learn if they might make mistakes (Hong, Chiu, Dweck, Lin, & Wan, 1999; Mueller & Dweck, 1998). When they do make mistakes or reveal deficiencies, rather than correct them, they try to hide them (Nussbaum & Dweck, 2007).

isn't praise/feedback from teachers also important?

They are also afraid of effort because effort makes them feel dumb. 10
They believe that if you have the ability, you shouldn't need effort (Blackwell, Trzesniewski, & Dweck, 2007), that ability should bring success all by itself. This is one of the worst beliefs that students can hold. It can cause many bright students to stop working in school when the curriculum becomes challenging.

I never thought about that—but true!

Finally, students in the fixed mind-set don't recover well from setbacks. When they hit a setback in school, they decrease their efforts and consider cheating (Blackwell et al., 2007). The idea of fixed intelligence does not offer them viable ways to improve.

Let's get inside the head of a student with a fixed mind-set as he sits in his classroom, confronted with algebra for the first time. Up until then, he has breezed through math. Even when he barely paid attention in class and skimped on his homework, he always got As. But this is different. It's hard. The student feels anxious and thinks, "What if I'm not as good at math as I thought? What if other kids understand it and I don't?" At some level, he realizes that he has two choices: try hard, or turn off. His interest in math begins to wane, and his attention wanders. He tells himself, "Who cares about this stuff? It's for nerds. I could do it if I wanted to, but it's so boring. You don't see CEOs and sports stars solving for *x* and *y*." *[I can relate]*

By contrast, in the growth mind-set, students care about learning. When they make a mistake or exhibit a deficiency, they correct it (Blackwell et al., 2007; Nussbaum & Dweck, 2007). For them, effort is a positive thing: It ignites their intelligence and causes it to grow. In the face of failure, these students escalate their efforts and look for new learning strategies. *[increases desire to learn]* *[increase]*

Let's look at another student—one who has a growth mind-set—having her first encounter with algebra. She finds it new, hard, and confusing, unlike anything else she has ever learned. But she's determined to understand it. She listens to everything the teacher says, asks the teacher questions after class, and takes her textbook home and reads the chapter over twice. As she begins to get it, she feels exhilarated. A new world of math opens up for her.

It is not surprising, then, that when we have followed students over challenging school transitions or courses, we find that those with growth mind-sets outperform their classmates with fixed mind-sets— even when they entered with equal skills and knowledge. A growth mind-set fosters the growth of ability over time (Blackwell et al., 2007; Mangels, Butterfield, Lamb, Good, & Dweck, 2006; see also Grant & Dweck, 2003). *[15]*

The Effects of Praise

Many educators have hoped to maximize students' confidence in their abilities, their enjoyment of learning, and their ability to thrive in school by praising their intelligence. We've studied the effects of this kind of praise in children as young as four years old and as old as adolescence, in students in inner-city and rural settings, and in students of different ethnicities—and we've consistently found the same thing (Cimpian, Arce, Markman, & Dweck, 2007; Kamins & Dweck, 1999; Mueller & Dweck, 1998): Praising students' intelligence gives them a short burst of pride, followed by a long string of negative consequences. *[wow!]*

In many of our studies (see Mueller & Dweck, 1998), fifth-grade students worked on a task, and after the first set of problems, the teacher praised some of them for their intelligence ("You must be smart at these problems") and others for their effort ("You must have worked hard at these problems"). We then assessed the students' mind-sets. In one study, we asked students to agree or disagree with mind-set statements, such as, "Your intelligence is something basic about you that you can't really change." Students praised for intelligence agreed with statements like these more than students praised for effort did. In another study, we asked students to define intelligence. Students praised for intelligence made significantly more references to innate, fixed capacity, whereas the students praised for effort made more references to skills, knowledge, and areas they could change through effort and learning. Thus, we found that praise for intelligence tended to put students in a fixed mind-set (intelligence is fixed, and you have it), whereas praise for effort tended to put them in a growth mind-set (you're developing these skills because you're working hard).

good evidence to support author's claim

We then offered students a chance to work on either a challenging task that they could learn from or an easy one that ensured error-free performance. Most of those praised for intelligence wanted the easy task, whereas most of those praised for effort wanted the challenging task and the opportunity to learn.

Next, the students worked on some challenging problems. As a group, students who had been praised for their intelligence *lost* their confidence in their ability and their enjoyment of the task as soon as they began to struggle with the problem. If success meant they were smart, then struggling meant they were not. The whole point of intelligence praise is to boost confidence and motivation, but both were gone in a flash. Only the effort-praised kids remained, on the whole, confident and eager.

wow ... really?

When the problems were made somewhat easier again, students praised for intelligence did poorly, having lost their confidence and motivation. As a group, they did worse than they had done initially on these same types of problems. The students praised for effort showed excellent performance and continued to improve.

20

Finally, when asked to report their scores (anonymously), almost 40 percent of the intelligence-praised students lied. Apparently, their egos were so wrapped up in their performance that they couldn't admit mistakes. Only about 10 percent of the effort-praised students saw fit to falsify their results.

Praising students for their intelligence, then, hands them not motivation and resilience but a fixed mind-set with all its vulnerability. In contrast, effort or "process" praise (praise for engagement, perseverance, strategies, improvement, and the like) fosters (hardy) motivation. It tells

sturdy, strong

students what they've done to be successful and what they need to do to be successful again in the future. Process praise sounds like this:

- You really studied for your English test, and your improvement shows it. You read the material over several times, outlined it, and tested yourself on it. That really worked!
- I like the way you tried all kinds of strategies on that math problem until you finally got it.
- It was a long, hard assignment, but you stuck to it and got it done. You stayed at your desk, kept up your concentration, and kept working. That's great!
- I like that you took on that challenging project for your science class. It will take a lot of work—doing the research, designing the machine, buying the parts, and building it. You're going to learn a lot of great things.

What about a student who gets an A without trying? I would say, "All right, that was too easy for you. Let's do something more challenging that you can learn from." We don't want to make something done quickly and easily the basis for our admiration.

What about a student who works hard and *doesn't* do well? I would say, "I liked the effort you put in. Let's work together some more and figure out what you don't understand." Process praise keeps students focused, not on something called ability that they may or may not have and that magically creates success or failure, but on processes they can all engage in to learn.

focus on the process of learning=success!

Motivated to Learn

Finding that a growth mind-set creates motivation and resilience— and leads to higher achievement—we sought to develop an intervention that would teach this mind-set to students. We decided to aim our intervention at students who were making the transition to seventh grade because this is a time of great vulnerability. School often gets more difficult in seventh grade, grading becomes more stringent, and the environment becomes more impersonal. Many students take stock of themselves and their intellectual abilities at this time and decide whether they want to be involved with school. Not surprisingly, it is often a time of disengagement and plunging achievement.

25

? what does she mean by intervention?

We performed our intervention in a New York City junior high school in which many students were struggling with the transition and were showing plummeting grades. If students learned a growth mind-set, we reasoned, they might be able to meet this challenge with increased, rather than decreased, effort. We therefore developed an eight-session workshop in which both the control group and the growth-mind-set group learned study skills, time management techniques, and memory strate-gies (Blackwell et al., 2007). However, in the growth-mind-set interven-tion, students also learned about their brains and what they could do to make their intelligence grow.

yes!   They learned that the brain is like a muscle—the more they exer-cise it, the stronger it becomes. They learned that every time they try hard and learn something new, their brain forms new connections that, over time, make them smarter. They learned that intellectual develop-ment is not the natural unfolding of intelligence, but rather the formation of new connections brought about through effort and learning.

Students were riveted by this information. The idea that their intellectual growth was largely in their hands fascinated them. In fact, even the most disruptive students suddenly sat still and took notice, with the most unruly boy of the lot looking up at us and saying, "You mean I don't have to be dumb?"

exciting idea!   Indeed, the growth-mind-set message appeared to unleash students' motivation. Although both groups had experienced a steep decline in their math grades during their first months of junior high, those receiv-ing the growth-mind-set intervention showed a significant rebound. Their math grades improved. Those in the control group, despite their excellent study skills intervention, continued their decline.

that's good evidence!

did they do better on assignments though?

    What's more, the teachers—who were unaware that the intervention   30
workshops differed—singled out three times as many students in the growth-mind-set intervention as showing marked changes in motivation. These students had a heightened desire to work hard and learn. One striking example was the boy who thought he was dumb. Before this experience, he had never put in any extra effort and often didn't turn his homework in on time. As a result of the training, he worked for hours one evening to finish an assignment early so that his teacher could review it and give him a chance to revise it. He earned a B+ on the assignment (he had been getting Cs and lower previously).

does this work for college students too?!?

    Other researchers have obtained similar findings with a growth-mind-set intervention. Working with junior high school students, Good, Aronson, and Inzlicht (2003) found an increase in math and English achievement test scores; working with college students, Aronson, Fried, and Good (2002) found an increase in students' valuing of academics, their enjoyment of schoolwork, and their grade point averages.

yes!
☺

To facilitate delivery of the growth-mind-set workshop to students, we developed an interactive computer-based version of the intervention called *Brainology*. Students work through six modules, learning about the brain, visiting virtual brain labs, doing virtual brain experiments, seeing how the brain changes with learning, and learning how they can make their brains work better and grow smarter.

We tested our initial version in twenty New York City schools, with encouraging results. Almost all students (anonymously polled) reported changes in their study habits and motivation to learn resulting directly from their learning of the growth mind-set. One student noted that as a result of the animation she had seen about the brain, she could actually "picture the neurons growing bigger as they make more connections." One student referred to the value of effort: "If you do not give up and you keep studying, you can find your way through."

Adolescents often see school as a place where they perform for teachers who then judge them. The growth mind-set changes that perspective and makes school a place where students vigorously engage in learning for their own benefit.

yes

cool!

Going Forward

Our research shows that educators cannot hand students confidence on a silver platter by praising their intelligence. Instead, we can help them gain the tools they need to maintain their confidence in learning by keeping them focused on the *process* of achievement.   35

Maybe we have produced a generation of students who are more dependent, fragile, and entitled than previous generations. If so, it's time for us to adopt a growth mind-set and learn from our mistakes. It's time to deliver interventions that will truly boost students' motivation, resilience, and learning.

References

lots of research went into this study/article— well supported!

Aronson, J., Fried, C., & Good, C. (2002). Reducing the effects of stereotype threat on African American college students by shaping theories of intelligence. *Journal of Experimental Social Psychology, 38*, 113–125.

Binet, A. (1909/1973). *Les idées modernes sur les enfants* [Modern ideas on children]. Paris, France: Flammarion. (Original work published 1909).

Blackwell, L., Trzesniewski, K., & Dweck, C. S. (2007). Implicit theories of intelligence predict achievement across an adolescent transition: A longitudinal study and an intervention. *Child Development, 78*, 246–263.

Cimpian, A., Arce, H., Markman, E. M., & Dweck, C. S. (2007). Subtle linguistic cues impact children's motivation. *Psychological Science, 18*, 314–316.

Doidge, N. (2007). *The brain that changes itself: Stories of personal triumph from the frontiers of brain science.* New York, NY: Viking.

Dweck, C. S. (1999). *Self-theories: Their role in motivation, personality and development.* Philadelphia, PA: Taylor and Francis/Psychology Press.

Dweck, C. S. (2006). *Mindset: The new psychology of success*. New York, NY: Random House.

Ericsson, K. A., Charness, N., Feltovich, P. J., & Hoffman, R. R. (Eds.). (2006). *The Cambridge handbook of expertise and expert performance*. New York, NY: Cambridge University Press.

Good, C., Aronson, J., & Inzlicht, M. (2003). Improving adolescents' standardized test performance: An intervention to reduce the effects of stereotype threat. *Journal of Applied Developmental Psychology, 24*, 645–662.

Grant, H., & Dweck, C. S. (2003). Clarifying achievement goals and their impact. *Journal of Personality and Social Psychology, 85*, 541–553.

Hong, Y. Y., Chiu, C., Dweck, C. S., Lin, D., & Wan, W. (1999). Implicit theories, attributions, and coping: A meaning system approach. *Journal of Personality and Social Psychology, 77*, 588–599.

Kamins, M., & Dweck, C. S. (1999). Person vs. process praise and criticism: Implications for contingent self-worth and coping. *Developmental Psychology, 35*, 835–847.

Mangels, J. A., Butterfield, B., Lamb, J., Good, C. D., & Dweck, C. S. (2006). Why do beliefs about intelligence influence learning success? A social-cognitive-neuroscience model. *Social, Cognitive, and Affective Neuroscience, 1*, 75–86.

Mueller, C. M., & Dweck, C. S. (1998). Intelligence praise can undermine motivation and performance. *Journal of Personality and Social Psychology, 75*, 33–52.

Nussbaum, A. D., & Dweck, C. S. (2007). Defensiveness vs. remediation: Self-theories and modes of self-esteem maintenance. *Personality and Social Psychology Bulletin*.

Sternberg, R. (2005). Intelligence, competence, and expertise. In A. Elliot & C. S. Dweck (Eds.), *The handbook of competence and motivation* (pp. 15–30). New York, NY: Guilford Press.

clearly an expert in her field!

Carol S. Dweck is the Lewis and Virginia Eaton Professor of Psychology at Stanford University and the author of *Mindset: The New Psychology of Success* (Random House, 2006).

practice it   Annotating the Text

Ready to try your hand at annotating? Let's review first:

- You've done freewriting on what you think about intelligence, praise, and motivation, key topics Dweck covers in her article.
- You've scanned the text to see how long it is, how it's structured, and what the introduction and conclusion might cover.
- You've learned how to annotate to keep track of your reactions to the text.
- You've learned how to annotate to ask questions of the text and make note of unfamiliar words.
- You've read another student's annotations, to give you an idea of how to get started.

Now, carefully read Carol S. Dweck's article "The Perils and Promises of Praise," on page 6 (the version without annotations). Annotate the text by writing your questions and reactions in the margins as you read.

your project   Reflecting on Your Reactions and Questions

Now that you have practiced recording your reactions and asking questions of the text in your annotations, share and compare your reactions with other students. Then, on your own, write a one-paragraph reader response that describes your initial thought of Dweck's points.

Finding Main Ideas and Supporting Evidence

After you have read and annotated to record your reactions and questions, it's time to identify the main ideas and support in the reading. Well-constructed readings generally have one main idea and support for that idea. Marking these elements in the text as you read will help you understand the text better and recall it more effectively later. An experienced college reader can probably record reactions, ask questions, and read for main ideas—all at the same time. However, for now, we have separated those steps.

WHAT IS THE MAIN IDEA?

Nonfiction essays in a newspaper, magazine, or textbook are generally persuasive or informative, so the main idea will usually be the overall point that the author is trying to get across. We often call this the thesis. Sometimes the thesis is stated directly (this is called an explicit thesis) and can be found right away. In many types of writing, though, the thesis is not clearly indicated. It is not stated directly, but is instead implied, or suggested. It can take some practice to determine the thesis in those cases.

WHAT IS SUPPORT?

Support is the evidence that the author uses to prove and develop the main idea. A reading's main idea is usually broken down into a series of major points, which in turn will be supported by evidence. When you write an essay, you support your main idea or thesis with a variety of information, which is generally made up of facts, details, examples, explanations, statistics, quotations, paraphrases, and anecdotes. To find the support in a reading, look for this kind of information. Often, readers can pick out the examples and evidence and then work backward from there to figure out what main idea the examples illustrate. If that works better for you, especially with those difficult readings where the thesis or main idea is implied rather than stated directly, then begin with the support and work your way backward to the main idea.

TIP

Use highlighters sparingly. When most of a page is highlighted, essentially nothing is: All you end up with is a brightly colored page. Highlighters also discourage more in-depth annotation. If you have a pen or pencil in your hand instead, you are likely to make notes in the margins.

You'll learn more about implied main ideas in Chapter 10, Thesis and Main Idea, page 223.

For more on paraphrases and anecdotes, see Chapter 4, Revising, Editing, and Proofreading, page 118.

HOW DO YOU FIND THE THESIS, MAJOR POINTS, AND SUPPORT IN AN ESSAY OR ARTICLE?

STEP 1: Find the Thesis.   Begin by rereading the introduction and conclusion, looking for the main idea. Ask yourself what overall point the author makes or proves. Try to find an explicit thesis in the introduction of the reading. Sometimes it's there; other times, the main idea is nicely summed up in the conclusion.

If you have trouble locating the main idea, perhaps it is not stated explicitly and is only implied. If that's the case, you need to read the text again carefully, asking yourself what the purpose of the reading is. If you can answer that question, you've probably found the main idea. Try to write it in your own words in a sentence or two. Run your ideas by your instructor or classmates to see if they agree and to help you make your ideas more clear.

Another trick for finding the main idea is to look at the title of the article or chapter. If the title is a question, the thesis might be the answer to the question. If the title is not in the form of a question, turn it into a question and see if the answer is the main idea of the reading. For example, Dweck's title "The Perils and Promises of Praise" can be phrased as "What are the perils and promises of praise?"

If you are still having trouble locating the main idea, take your reading to a tutor or visit your instructor during his or her office hours to get help.

STEP 2: Find the Major Points by Looking at the Structure of the Reading. The reading is probably broken down into chunks of some sort. Are there subheadings dividing sections or just paragraphs? If it is not divided into clear sections, can you determine where the reading shifts from one major point to the next? Can you group the paragraphs together in some way to identify when the author covers one major point and then moves on to a new point? Looking at the structure in this way helps you break the main idea down into smaller parts. You will see how one major point leads to another and to another. All the section or paragraph points together support the overall thesis. Some authors indicate the major points or topics by dividing the paragraphs into sections with subheadings. These subheadings can give you a clue about the major points or topics covered.

For more about structure, see Chapter 13, Essay Organization and Outlining, page 267.

For example, Dweck's article is divided into the following sections:

Introductory paragraphs
Fixed or Malleable?
The Two Faces of Effort
The Effects of Praise
Motivated to Learn
Going Forward

What major points or topics does Dweck emphasize through these subheadings?

STEP 3: Find the Main Ideas by Figuring out the Main Point of Each Paragraph.
You can usually figure out the main point of each paragraph by finding
the topic sentence. Often, the topic sentence is the first sentence of a
paragraph, but sometimes it is elsewhere. The topic sentence is the
"umbrella" sentence that all the other sentences relate to or support.

If you can't find a topic sentence, the topic sentence may be in a previous paragraph or maybe the author hasn't written one. In newspaper or
magazine writing, frequently two or three paragraphs support one major
point from a previous paragraph. In these cases, finding the topic sentence might mean looking in a preceding paragraph. Some paragraphs,
however, have what is called an implied topic sentence, meaning the
author did not include it in the paragraph, but kept one in mind as the
paragraph was written. In these cases, ask yourself what overall point is
being made by that paragraph and write a "nutshell summary" in the margin of each paragraph. To do this, ask yourself what the point of the paragraph is, and see if you can jot it down in a phrase or sentence. Making
nutshell summaries for all the paragraphs gives you a rough outline of the
whole essay. If you still can't find the main point of the paragraph, move
on to the next step, and then work your way backwards to this step again.

When you come to a part of a reading that is hard to understand, it's
easier to figure it out if you slow down, figure out the topic sentence or
main point of each paragraph, and then put all the topic sentences into
your own words. This helps you find and keep track of the major points
as you go through the reading. It's like you're building a wooden foot-
bridge, one plank of wood at a time. If you understand this point, and
then the next one, and the next one, eventually you will put them all
together and understand the whole reading.

Here's a sample student nutshell summary of a short passage from
Dweck's article.

**For more on topic
sentences, see Chapter 12,
Topic Sentences and
Paragraphs, page 253.**

Fixed or Malleable?

Praise is intricately connected to how students view their intelligence. Some students believe that their intellectual ability is a fixed
trait. They have a certain amount of intelligence and that's that.
Students with this fixed mind-set become excessively concerned with
how smart they are, seeking tasks that will prove their intelligence
and avoiding ones that might not (Dweck, 1999, 2006). The desire to
learn takes a backseat.

Other students believe that their intellectual ability is something
they can develop through effort and education. They don't necessarily believe that anyone can become an Einstein or a Mozart, but they
do understand that even Einstein and Mozart had to put in years of
effort to become who they were. When students believe that they
can develop their intelligence, they focus on doing just that.
Not worrying about how smart they will appear, they take on challenges and stick to them (Dweck, 1999, 2006).

Nutshell Summaries

praise can cause
students to think of
their intelligence as
set in stone

some students don't
care how they look—
they know they can
learn through trying

research shows
brains keep growing
if we keep trying

More and more research in psychology and neuroscience supports the growth mind-set. We are discovering that the brain has more plasticity over time than we ever imagined (Doidge, 2007); that fundamental aspects of intelligence can be enhanced through learning (Steinberg, 2005); and that dedication and persistence in the face of obstacles are key ingredients in outstanding achievement (Ericsson, Charness, Feltovich, & Hoffman, 2006).

Binet originally
thought of IQ as a
way to figure out who
needed help, not label
people as smart or
stupid!

Alfred Binet (1909/1973), the inventor of the IQ test, had a strong growth mind-set. He believed that education could transform the basic capacity to learn. Far from intending to measure fixed intelligence, he meant his test to be a tool for identifying students who were not profiting from the public school curriculum so that other courses of study could be devised to foster their intellectual growth.

STEP 4: Find the Support.   Make a vertical line in the margin next to any facts, statistics, examples, and quotes. These pieces of evidence probably support a point the author is making. Ask yourself what the author is trying to say about that fact (or statistic or quote). The support can be easier to identify than the main idea, so if you have trouble locating the main idea, you might have better luck by looking for the support first. A good trick is to ask yourself: What does this fact/example/statistic show? The answer will likely be the thesis or a major point.

In the following paragraphs from Dweck's essay, we have underlined the evidence and examples.

Students were riveted by this information. The idea that their intellectual growth was largely in their hands fascinated them. In fact, even the most disruptive students suddenly sat still and took notice, with the most unruly boy of the lot looking up at us and saying, "You mean I don't have to be dumb?"

Indeed, the growth-mind-set message appeared to unleash students' motivation. Although both groups had experienced a steep decline in their math grades during their first months of junior high, those receiving the growth-mind-set intervention showed a significant rebound. Their math grades improved. Those in the control group, despite their excellent study skills intervention, continued to decline.

STEP 5: Check Your Accuracy.   Look back at your answers to the comprehension and discussion questions that followed the reading. If you skipped any, see if you can answer them now that you have read the article more critically. Compare your ideas about the reading's thesis and main point to the ideas that were raised in the comprehension and discussion questions. Can the questions help you fill in any gaps in your understanding of the article now?

When reading to find the main idea and support, follow the steps and keep working with the text until you get it. Some readings are structured in such a way that the main idea is obvious. With others, you have to work a little harder to figure it out. Let's practice now with Dweck's article "The Perils and Promises of Praise," which you have already read carefully once.

your project   Finding the Main Idea and Support

Follow the steps listed above to find the thesis and main points of "The Perils and Promises of Praise." You can copy the chart below into your notebook, or download a version of the chart from the e-Pages. (Go to **bedfordstmartins.com/readwriteconnect** and click on **Charts**.) Your entries should look like this:

CHARTING MAIN IDEA AND SUPPORT

Thesis: _____

Main point of "Fixed or Malleable?" section: _____

> **Example:** Some students believe intelligence is fixed, but others believe that intelligence can grow and be developed.

Main point of "The Two Faces of Effort" section: _____
Main point of "The Effects of Praise" section: _____
Main point of "Motivated to Learn" section:
Main point of "Going Forward" section: _____

Compare your ideas with your classmates' responses. If you had very different ideas about the thesis or main points, reread the article with the various responses in mind. Which ideas are a better fit? Why?

Writing a Summary

Being able to summarize a text you have read—or a presentation you have seen, or anything else for that matter—is one of the most fundamental skills of college life and a very important post-reading strategy. Once you become comfortable writing summaries, you will begin to feel more at ease with college readings. Writing a summary helps you clarify and remember what you read. Summary skills will help you in just about every career, too, because summarizing is something you will do pretty much on a daily basis: You might summarize a complex problem for your boss, summarize a patient's symptoms for another doctor or nurse, or summarize your own work for your coworkers or clients.

So what makes a good summary? Good summaries restate in your own words the major points contained in a text. They do not include your opinion or reaction to the text (no "I" statements). They present a lot of complex information in a clear, coherent, brief way. A summary is much shorter than the original and includes only the most important points, not specific details. For example, a one-sentence summary of the story of *Romeo and Juliet* might read:

> William Shakespeare's tragic play *Romeo and Juliet* tells the story of two teenagers in love who end up dying because their families forbid their relationship.

Although the length of your summary will depend on the length of the text you are summarizing, summaries are often a single paragraph. Here is a one-paragraph summary of *Romeo and Juliet*:

> *Romeo and Juliet* is William Shakespeare's tragic play about two teenagers in love against the wishes of their families. The problem is their families were feuding and wouldn't let them get married, but against their parents' wishes, they got married in secret. After a fight breaks out, Romeo kills Tybalt, Juliet's cousin, and is banned from the city, and Juliet's family wants her to marry another boy, Paris. To avoid having to marry Paris, Juliet fakes her death by drinking a sleeping potion, thinking that she will be able to run away with Romeo after her family mourns her. However, Romeo finds her and, thinking she is really dead, he kills himself. Juliet wakes up from her fake death and sees that Romeo is, in fact, really dead, and so she kills herself for real. The families are distraught and realize that their feud caused these deaths and agree to fight no more.

While this summary isn't perfect, this student did a good job of putting the main points of the play in his own words and staying concise.

HOW DO YOU WRITE A SUMMARY?

STEP 1: Look at Your Annotations.   Skim over any marginal notes that identify the main point of a paragraph or section. Make a list of the main points. (If you skipped annotating for any reason, you will quickly discover how difficult it is to write a summary without a thorough understanding of the reading. You'll have to go back and reread, annotating carefully. Get help from an instructor or a friend if you don't understand the material after several attempts to master it.)

STEP 2: Make a List of All the Key Terms.   This will jog your memory about important points, and give you some terminology to use in your summary. For instance, for Dweck's article, you might include words like "fixed mind-set," "growth mind-set," "resilience," "motivation," and "praise." This list is not complete, so go ahead now and add other key concept words that you believe are important.

STEP 3: Draft a Summary of the Central Idea and Main Points.   Cover up the text so that you can't see it. Then, in your own words, write down a sentence or two that states the main idea (thesis) of the text. Once you have something written down, look back at the text and see how well you got the author's main idea across and if you have forgotten anything. Skim through your annotations or use your list of main points, and restate the main points in your own words. Look at your list of key terms for ideas of what else to include.

Read your summary over several times to make sure you have included all the main points, have not included details or examples, and have put the author's ideas into your own words. Check to be sure you haven't included your thoughts or opinions. Add and delete as needed until you feel confident about your summary paragraph.

STEP 4: Write an Introductory Sentence.   In your introductory sentence, mention the author's full name and the full title of the original text with a very general statement about the purpose of the text. It might sound something like this:

> In her article "The Perils and Promises of Praise," Carol S. Dweck presents research on how to praise students appropriately to help them become motivated learners.

STEP 5: Reread and Revise.   Read over and revise your summary a few more times so that it reads smoothly and makes sense and that it is entirely in your own words. Try reading it out loud, too, to catch any errors you might have made. Realize that everyone will summarize a reading slightly differently, though all summaries should include the same major points.

---

your project   Writing a Summary

Follow the preceding steps to write a summary of "The Perils and Promises of Praise."

summary checklist

☐ Does the summary include the full name of the article and the full name of the author?

☐ Is the summary an objective statement of Dweck's ideas, rather than a subjective response (your opinions, thoughts, or feelings)? Remember, you shouldn't use "I" in a summary.

☐ Does it have an introductory sentence that states the main idea of the text in your own words?

☐ Does it use the vocabulary words and key concepts from the text, such as "fixed mind-set" and other words?

☐ Does it include all the major points of the reading? Is it missing any important points? What more should be included?

☐ Does the summary go into too much detail anywhere? What could be cut?

☐ Does the paragraph feel coherent and finished? How might you make it better?

Reading Textbooks Effectively

Carol S. Dweck's article "The Perils and Promises of Praise" gives you a sense of the challenges that college-level reading can bring. The reality is, though, that much of what you read in college will be in the form of college textbooks. The reading strategies we have gone through so far in this chapter apply to college textbooks too. When reading your textbooks, use all the strategies that you have learned so far:

• Pre-reading to get a sense of what you know about the topic and to get a sense of structure, audience, purpose, and other features
• Annotating for reactions and questions you have about the reading and to find main points and support
• Summarizing the text

If you follow these steps with all your college reading, we can guarantee that you will do better on your college exams than if you do not.

In addition to the steps above, college textbooks present some unique features, many of which, if used well, make your reading and writing even more efficient, productive, and interesting. From taking previous classes, you are probably familiar with the typical features of a textbook, like the table of contents, index, glossary, and chapter reviews. However, if you are like many students, you might not be using those features to your best advantage. Here are a few tips and techniques for smart textbook reading:

- **Read the book title and the table of contents.** Book titles often suggest the scope and purpose of the content. Can you guess the book's purpose from reading the title? The table of contents is a map of the entire book and gives you a clue about what the authors plan to address. Additionally, the table of contents shows you the organizational structure of the book. What comes first? Why? What does the order of chapters suggest about the purpose of the book? By looking at the number of pages devoted to each chapter, you can get a preview of how much attention is paid to the various topics. What predictions can you make about the book's audience and purpose based on the table of contents?
- **Spend time skimming the chapter openers and closers.** Chapters often start with chapter outlines or activities and end with chapter reviews, activities, or questions. These features give you clues about the important points covered in the chapter. Read these thoroughly before you read the textbook chapter, so that you can know in advance what to look for. In your notes, jot down what you expect the scope of the chapter will be. What overall lesson do you predict the chapter will teach?
- **Pay particular attention to the section headings, charts, boxes, and glossary.** Turn the headings into questions to predict what each section will be about.
- **Keep a personalized glossary or make flash cards of important vocabulary words.**

---

practice it   Pre-Reading a Textbook Chapter

Use *Read, Write, Connect* to practice these strategies. Be sure to:

- Read the book title and the table of contents. What does the title suggest about the book's purpose and content? Based on the table of contents, what topics does this book cover? How is the material organized? What kinds of topics are addressed in each part of the book? What can you learn about the audience and purpose from reading the table of contents? Does the table of contents reflect the title of the book? In what ways? How does this book compare to other English textbooks you have used?
- Preview the text by reading the title and skimming over the section headings for each chapter. Pay particular attention to any charts, boxes, and tables that call out key aspects of the chapter's topic. What kind of material is covered in the chapters?

continued ❍

- Look for chapter-opening and chapter-ending reviews, outlines, questions, and activities to anticipate what important points might be covered.
- Think about the intended purpose and audience (in this case, students). What do the authors think students should learn? What can you expect to learn by the time you are finished using this textbook? What is the relationship between reading and writing?

your project   Bringing a College Mind-Set to Writing

In this chapter, you have been introduced to some fundamental reading and writing skills, and you have read Dweck's research on student motivation. Now you can put those skills and ideas into practice by writing a short essay for one of the following assignments.

1. Examine your experiences as a student. Do you think you have a fixed or growth mind-set? In explaining why, be sure to discuss what messages you have received from others (teachers, parents, peers) about your potential, as well as how you have responded when faced with challenges in school.
2. Write about a time you have been resilient and adopted a growth mind-set in the face of adversity. Describe what happened, and then explain how you might apply that life lesson to your future academic success.

chapter review

Chapter 1 introduces strategies for pre-reading, annotating while you read, and summarizing after you read. By understanding these concepts and practicing them regularly, you will become a stronger student. Taking the initiative to use the critical reading strategies outlined in this chapter—even if an instructor does not require you to—means you are definitely in the college mind-set.

To review this chapter, choose one or more of the following strategies:

1. Read through any notes you took and your responses to the activities. Make a list of the ideas you generated while doing the activities.
2. Review the words you are unfamiliar with from the readings. Keep a glossary—a list of new words and their definitions—in your notebook or a word-processing document to help you review new words and boost your

vocabulary. Skim through the reading in this chapter and add words to your glossary. Remember to write definitions in your own words.

3. Try to explain what you have learned to someone you know. Discuss the key concepts and give your own examples to illustrate those concepts. It might be especially interesting to talk to your family members about Dweck's research on growth mind-set and motivation.

4. If you skipped any activities, do them now as a way to deepen your understanding of the material.

2
Active and Critical Reading

in this chapter

- What Is Critical Reading?
- How Do You Read With the Grain?
- How Do You Read Against the Grain?
- What Is Financial Literacy?
- How Can a Chart Help You Understand Readings?

Chapter 1 introduced a few key strategies for college-level reading and writing: pre-reading, annotating, and summarizing. Chapter 2 gives you more practice with those skills and adds new techniques, as you move from comprehending and summarizing your readings to reading them critically. To practice all of these skills, you'll work with a number of reading selections on the topics of financial literacy (an understanding of personal money topics, like saving, budgeting, and planning), money, and wealth.

For more readings that go with this chapter, go to **bedfordstmartins.com/readwriteconnect** and click on **e-Readings**.

---

practice it   Previewing the Chapter

Take a few minutes to preview this chapter. Note its content, structure, and features. What can you learn from the titles of the readings? How do the opening pages of this chapter help you predict the topic, audience, and purpose? Does the "Education Pays" chart below confirm or challenge your preconceived notions about money and wealth? What do you already know about financial literacy? Overall, what do you expect to learn about critical reading or the other topics covered in this chapter? Make a list of your predictions.

EDUCATION PAYS

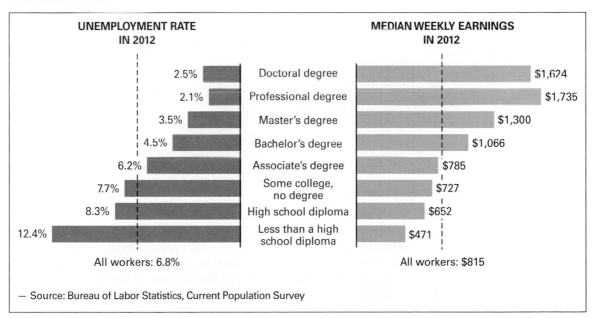

UNEMPLOYMENT RATE IN 2012		MEDIAN WEEKLY EARNINGS IN 2012
2.5%	Doctoral degree	$1,624
2.1%	Professional degree	$1,735
3.5%	Master's degree	$1,300
4.5%	Bachelor's degree	$1,066
6.2%	Associate's degree	$785
7.7%	Some college, no degree	$727
8.3%	High school diploma	$652
12.4%	Less than a high school diploma	$471
All workers: 6.8%		All workers: $815

— Source: Bureau of Labor Statistics, Current Population Survey

Reading Critically

Reading critically means reading closely, asking questions, and thinking about what you're reading. Critical reading helps you move beyond merely understanding (or comprehending) what authors are saying; it helps you analyze how they say it and evaluate whether or not they do a good job. When you read and think critically, you analyze by looking at how the author established the text's purpose, argument, evidence, and audience. You also evaluate the text when you establish your own opinion about how well the author achieved his or her purpose in writing. Analyzing and evaluating prepare you to write essays about what you have read, and they are skills that strong readers practice regularly.

For most essays that you write in college, you read about or research a topic extensively before writing about it. These readings will give you substantial information and background knowledge on a topic, but in most cases the writing you do in response has to go beyond merely reporting this information. Instead, you will be expected to contribute your own ideas on the topic, joining the conversation that the articles and books have already begun.

The good news is that in Chapter 1 you already learned and practiced several key steps necessary for getting into conversation with other texts:

- Considering what you already know and previewing the text
- Annotating to respond, ask questions, identify and define new words, and find main ideas and support
- Summarizing the text you have read

The next step to learn and practice is how to read critically by analyzing or evaluating the strengths and weaknesses of a piece of writing. Using the strategies described below will help you do so.

Reading With and Against the Grain

READ WITH THE GRAIN

You bring some relevant ideas and opinions to most of the reading that you do. Critical college readers are open-minded and consider the strengths and weaknesses of a piece of writing, whether they agree or disagree with some (or all) of its ideas. To read with the grain, try to share the author's point of view (or that of people likely to agree with him or her) as much as possible. Whether you personally agree, disagree, or are neutral on the topic at hand, reading with the grain helps you understand the topic as your author sees it, and possibly enrich or even alter your perspective on it.

To read with the grain, assume the author is a reasonable person, and ask yourself why he or she takes a particular position. Why is the position compelling and the support convincing? Even if you remain unconvinced of the author's main point, trying to read with the grain makes it more likely that you will honestly acknowledge any solid supporting points, examples, or evidence the author includes. If you're still unconvinced of the main idea but you do find some interesting evidence, ask yourself whether this evidence would support a slightly different point from the one the author is making. In other words, is there common ground to be found between your perspective and the author's perspective? Take notes on what you discover.

If you already agree with an author's main point, it won't be very difficult for him or her to win you over. Most likely, you will find the evidence and examples very convincing because you already see things from the same perspective; however, that doesn't necessarily mean the author has done a great job of making his or her case in writing.

READ AGAINST THE GRAIN

To read against the grain, read the text skeptically—that is, read it as if you don't agree with the author's point. This will give you a better perspective when evaluating how well the author has supported his or her points and whether the author offers credible support or evidence. Try to see things from a viewpoint different from or opposite to that of the author. Ask critical questions of the text. Is the support provided convincing? Has the author left out important points or perspectives? Does the author have any hidden bias or preexisting beliefs about the subject matter that influence the way he or she presents it? As always, take notes on your responses to the text.

COMPARE YOUR NOTES

After making serious efforts to read both with and against the grain, compare your notes on each approach. These notes will help you do a thorough job of thinking critically about the strengths and weaknesses of the article as a whole. Form a careful response to each of the following questions:

- Does the main idea represent a reasonable perspective on the topic?
- Is the evidence used to support the main idea persuasive and credible? Is there enough evidence to support the point?
- Does the author have any biases that you can detect, or is the material fairly and objectively presented?

As usual, save these notes and ideas; they come in handy when you start to write your own essay.

practice it   Reading with and against the Grain

Here is a short passage from the magazine article "Teach Your Children the Building Blocks of Finance," by Sherie Holder and Kenneth Meeks (the complete article appears on p. 43). Read this passage from the middle of the article, and then follow the steps listed.

> **Show children how to pay bills.** With so many people paying bills online, this is an opportunity to get children involved. Show them how money is deposited into an account, and how you're subtracting from those dollars to pay your obligations for gas, the lights, and food.
>
> [Single-mother Yvette] Saul discusses her finances with her daughter because it gives her a better sense of household expenses. When Saul receives her paycheck, she sits down with [her daughter] Savannah on a monthly basis and explains her income and the expenses she has to meet. "I would sit down with Savannah every month when I pay my bills and she would pull out her calculator and start adding things up. It becomes like a game to her but her thought process is moving."
>
> According to [certified financial planner Gwendolyn] Kirkland, this is good for children to see. "This makes it real to the children—the specific dollars you have left in your account," says Kirkland. "This instills an appreciation for what it takes to run a household." Savannah sees exactly where her mother's money is going.

STEP 1: Read the Paragraphs "With the Grain."   Look for the strengths in what Holder and Meeks write. What examples do they use that you find particularly persuasive? On the left side of the page, make some annotations commenting on the points, examples, or evidence. An example of a "with the grain" comment might be: "This is a good real-life example of managing money."

STEP 2: Reread the Paragraphs "Against the Grain."   Now, look again at the same paragraphs, but this time try to poke holes in the ideas. Are there places where the authors have not provided enough explanation or examples? Are their points well supported? If not, what other information might you need to be convinced to see things from their point of view? Can you detect any bias in the writing? Make some annotations in the right-hand margin pointing out what might be flaws or weaknesses in the presentation of the material. An example of an "against the grain" comment might be: "Young children shouldn't be stressed out by their family's finances. Let them be kids."

STEP 3: Compare Your Notes. Now, compare your notes from reading with and against the grain (the left and right margins), and make a list of the strengths and weaknesses of this particular passage.

Readings on Money, Wealth, and Financial Literacy

Money drives many of our decisions and behaviors, from what we eat for breakfast to what we choose to do with our lives. Even those people who choose their life paths without considering how much money they'll make, like monks and artists, do so partly because they understand how money influences us. For those millions of people who live at or near the poverty level and want to do better, money is certainly one of the major concerns of daily life. Even middle-class people often struggle to live happily within their means—to spend less than they make and put some aside for emergencies. Financial well-being isn't important only for individuals, either. A healthy economy is important for all of us, and when our national and global economies are in trouble, our local communities suffer too.

Despite the importance of money in our personal lives and our society at large, many of us have major misconceptions about money and wealth. Few students are offered financial management courses in grade school or high school. Many Americans—even highly educated ones—are financially illiterate. We might confuse the cost of an item with its value. We might struggle to figure out the relationship between money and happiness. We might have no meaningful information about how to save and spend. These problems affect many Americans, no matter how much money they actually have in the bank—or at home in a sock drawer.

The readings in this unit invite you to think about what money and wealth mean to you personally and to Americans as a group. These resources provide some factual information about the basics of the economy and personal finance, ask you to think about your own priorities and values, and challenge you to consider the philosophical issues surrounding money and our world.

To get the most out of the collection of texts that follow, annotate them using the steps outlined in Chapter 1 (pp. 14–16). Your annotations will help you answer the questions and complete the activities that follow each reading. Remember to read with and against the grain as you annotate.

your project   Considering What You Already Know

Below is a list of pre-reading questions for you to answer, either in your notebook or in group discussion, to determine your knowledge of, and biases about, money.

- What are your own experiences with money? What do you wish for yourself in terms of money? What sacrifices might you be willing to make to attain your goals?
- Do you know people who have money troubles? What are some obvious causes of those troubles? What are some of the underlying causes?
- How is money represented in the media? What television shows or movies have you seen that focus on money and wealth? What sorts of messages do those examples send to their audiences?
- What do you know about how our economy works? List the economic terms that you can define or that you want to know more about.
- How have you learned about money? How have you learned about the economy?
- What does it mean to be wealthy or poor? What characteristics do you use to determine someone's economic status?

MAGAZINE

This article is from the magazine *Black Enterprise*, which offers news and advice about business and personal finance for African American entrepreneurs. This particular article (published on February 6, 2006) uses real-life people as examples to illustrate its points. The authors, Sherie Holder and Kenneth Meeks, are freelance writers who have written other articles as well as several books on topics ranging from NASCAR to racial profiling. *Important words and phrases have been italicized in this reading. Look up those you do not know, and write the definitions in your personal vocabulary list.*

practice it   Pre-Reading

Before you begin reading, do the following:

- Look at the layout of the article, the use of pictures, the headings, bolded lines, and other graphic features. What do they tell you about the topic, audience, and purpose of the article?
- Note your first impression: Do you want to read this article? Why or why not? Write down your feelings in the margins near the top of the article.

- Think about your own knowledge, experience, and biases. Do you believe in giving children allowances or not? Did your parent(s) tell you much about the family finances when you were growing up? Why or why not? How well did older family members teach you about managing money? What could they have done differently? Freewrite for five minutes on these questions in your notebook.
- Turn the title into a question, such as "How can you teach your children the building blocks of finance?" or "Why should you teach your children the building blocks of finance?" As you read, look to see how and where the authors attempt to answer your question.

SHERIE HOLDER AND KENNETH MEEKS

Teach Your Children the Building Blocks of Finance

As a thirty-seven-year-old single mother, Yvette Saul knows that the key to her financial empowerment starts with her ability to create and maintain a savings initiative and to adequately manage her family's finances. And while she didn't learn this as a child, she is determined to make sure that her eleven-year-old daughter, Savannah Gay, learns the concept of proper money management. By educating her daughter at an early age, Saul is ensuring that little Savannah is more inclined to practice sound budgeting as she gets older. In doing so, Saul is adopting Declaration of Financial *Empowerment* principle No. 7: to provide access to programs that will educate my children about business and finance.

"It's extremely important for me to teach her about money and financial planning," says Saul. "Although money is not the root of happiness, it certainly is the pathway to happiness by being fiscally responsible as an adult."

In a *turbulent* economic environment, and with the uncertain future of Social Security, it's even more important that parents pass

Saul and her daughter, Savannah, meet regularly to discuss financial matters.

on the basics of personal finance. The learning process should start when you're a child. Parents have to teach children the value of money and guide them in their spending, encourage them to save, explore *entrepreneurship* opportunities, and expose them to solid financial planning. By using a few of the principles found in our Black Wealth Initiative, we offer you a step-by-step guide to help start your children down the right path.

Open a savings account and show children how to save.   Since the age of five, when Savannah opened her first savings account with $100, she has been on a path toward saving and money management. And while she is *tucking* away 40% of her $20 weekly allowance into a savings account, Savannah is following DOFE principle No. 2: to save and invest 10% to 15% of my after-tax income. Savannah has spent some of the money while on family vacations and on other personal items. She currently has about $700 in her account. According to New York City–based financial consultant Ivanhoe Ffriend, of Ffriend Enterprises, parents cannot *underscore* enough the importance of exposing their children to the sacrifices that go into planning the family budget. The value of money can be taught early on by teaching children how to bargain shop or collect coupons.

Teach children to respect the value of money.   A child's attitude toward money will determine how he or she uses it in life, according to Laura Levine, executive director of Jumpstart Coalition, a Washington, D.C.–based national organization that develops standards to teach kids about finance in grades K–12. "A lot of times it's a value decision, but we encourage parents to include a lesson at home that teaches their children about the value of money."

Inspire children to budget.   Getting children to track their own spending is a great way to start and follow DOFE principle No. 4: to engage in sound *budget*, *credit*, and tax management practices. Parents might have to give children an incentive to keep track of their expenses, such as a financial reward or a day off from chores. Showing them the importance of budgeting for items they need versus spending extravagantly is critical.

"Children must realize that there is an inflow and an outflow of money and you don't want the outflow to be greater than the inflow or else we become financially *overextended*," says Gwendolyn Kirkland, a certified financial planner at Kirkland, Turnbo & Associates, in Chicago. "A budget establishes financial boundaries. So when they're asking for different things, parents can say they either budgeted or they didn't budget for it."

Encourage children under the age of eight to divide money into different categories.   Perhaps they should have one piggy bank for saving and another piggy bank for spending. By the time your child turns nine, talk to him or her about creating a small budget to keep track of income and expenses. Teenagers should already understand the basics of personal finance and budgeting and be allowed to make their own financial decisions, with your guidance. By then, budgets should be a *cornerstone* of their money management.

Plant the seeds of entrepreneur-ship.   Not all children receive weekly allowances. When Angelina and Marvin Lipford, of Hampton, Virginia, were married twenty years ago, they entered into their marriage carting around $15,000 to $20,000 worth of credit card and student loan debt. They spent the first five years of their marriage paying off the debt along with the accompanying high interest rates. The couple was determined to keep their three children from falling into the same trap.

The Lipfords encourage their children to earn money rather than receive an allowance.

Knowing the financial sacrifices they had to make early in their mar-   10
riage, the Lipfords are making sure their three children keep a tight *rein* on their finances and avoid the same pitfalls. They have an eighteen-year-old daughter, Jasmine, who is attending Howard University on a basketball scholarship; a fifteen-year-old son, Marvin Jr., who is a sophomore in high school; and a nine-year-old, Nehemiah. A natural progression in teaching their children the building blocks of finances was to encourage their children to either work, as Jasmine had done before going to college, or to start their own business. Instead of giving their children allowances, the Lipfords encourage them to earn their own money by doing chores around the house. It was on a pay-per-work arrangement. And if the children asked their parents for additional money, they were required to pay their parents back with interest.

This arrangement encouraged Marvin Jr. to earn money on his own. In 2002, he took the financial and entrepreneurial lessons he learned from attending a weeklong financial camp to cut grass during the summer months using his father's lawn mower. This past summer, he charged $20 a yard and earned $1,000, which he put into his savings account.

Show children how to pay bills.   With so many people paying bills online, this is an opportunity to get children involved. Show them how money is deposited into an account, and how you're subtracting from those dollars to pay your obligations for gas, the lights, and food.

Saul discusses her finances with her daughter because it gives her a better sense of household expenses. When Saul receives her paycheck, she sits down with Savannah on a monthly basis and explains her income and the expenses she has to meet. "I would sit down with Savannah every month when I pay my bills and she would pull out her calculator and start adding things up. It becomes like a game to her but her thought process is moving."

According to Kirkland, this is good for children to see. "This makes it real to the children—the specific dollars you have left in your account," says Kirkland. "This *instills* an appreciation for what it takes to run a household." Savannah sees exactly where her mother's money is going.

Expose your children to investing.   Many people can go online to monitor their 401(k) account, change the contribution they make, and change their asset allocation. This is an excellent time to introduce children to this concept.   15

Kirkland suggests getting children to invest early and to invest in what they know or what they use. As an example of practicing DOFE principle No. 6: to be *proactive* and knowledgeable about investing, money management, and consumer issues, Kirkland suggests giving stock as a gift to children when they turn twelve. "If it's something that they wear, they want, they eat, something that they can relate to, buying stock in that company introduces them to the concept of ownership. You own a part of this company."

While parents will have to open a *custodial account* for children under eighteen, the process of doing it together exposes young people to investing.

Kirkland suggests introducing children to other *tax-deferred* investment vehicles, such as a 529 Plan. "While control of the 529 Plan rests with the parents, the benefit is that it is tax-deferred," he explains. "One of the things a child will learn early on is that wherever it is legitimate, they should *defer* taxes as much as possible, so they can have more income in the future."

Hold family financial meetings.   On a regular basis, parents should hold meetings where family finances are discussed. Go over spending habits with your children. Examine how they track their spending and what they spend money on. Let the kids explain why they are making certain purchases, and make the total family finances a discussion with input from everyone. Use the same principles, standards, and *parliamentary* procedures that a board of directors in any multimillion-dollar corporation might use. This is the meeting where you, as a family, map out long-term and short-term financial goals and develop strategies to accomplish those goals. This is also a good time to invite a professional financial planner to attend and let him or her offer individual professional help.

These are but a few of the tips to teach your children about money management. There are other everyday practices you can do, from reading the business or money section of the local newspaper with your children, to watching television programs that follow the market and our national economy. Have discussions about what's in the financial news. It's important to do something that puts your children on the correct path to good money management. And as always, follow the coverage of our Black Wealth Initiative. For a Wealth Building Kit or to open a ShareBuilder Custodial Account for your child (an online brokerage account), visit blackenterprise.com.   20

A resource guide to help you teach your children about money management

Here at *Black Enterprise*, we encourage our readers to introduce the children in their lives (including nieces, nephews, and grandchildren) to the fundamental principles of money management. We know that building wealth and teaching solid money-management skills to our children is a continuous process. Therefore, the following resources are designed to help parents teach today's children the basics of financial empowerment.

Web sites

- *blackenterprise.com. Black Enterprise* magazine seeks out, analyzes, and *disseminates* information that is helpful to, and provides a forum for, the ideas, ambitions, and expression of African American businesspeople.
- *www.myownbizkit.com.* This Web site offers business opportunities to parents and their children who are highly motivated and interested in learning about entrepreneurship.
- *www.youthventure.org.* This Web site helps young people across the country start new youth-led organizations that achieve a lasting benefit for their schools and communities.
- *www.youthinvestor.com.* This Web site offers insightful information that introduces young people to the concept of investing.
- *www.fleetkids.com.* This Web site contains a wealth of knowledge to help parents teach their children about money and investing.
- *www.bankingonourfuture.org.* Helping children take control of their financial future, this Web site offers the basics in banking and credit unions, checking and savings accounts, insurance, credit, and investments.
- *www.jumpstart.org.* This site's direct objective is to encourage curriculum enrichment to ensure that basic personal financial management skills are attained during grades K–12.
- *www.ncee.net/ea/program.php.* This organization provides materials and programs to help schools across the country meet state academic standards in economics, personal finance, and social studies.
- *www.teachingkidsbusiness.com.* This is a free online resource that helps kids in grades K–12 discover, explore, and gain experience in the world of business.
- *www.ja.org.* Junior Achievement uses hands-on experiences to help young people understand the economics of life.

Organizations

- NAACP Reginald F. Lewis Youth Entrepreneurial Institute; 410-580-5745; *www.naacp.org*
- National Association of Investment Corp. (trade group for investment clubs); 877-275-6242; *www.better-investing.org/subjects/youth*

- The Institute for Entrepreneurship; 414-302-9922; *www.theeplace.org*
- The National Foundation for Teaching Entrepreneurship; 800-367-6383; *www.nfte.com*

Books and Publications

- *Banking on Our Future: A Program for Teaching You and Your Kids about Money* by John Bryant and Michael Levin (Beacon Press; $14.00)
- *Raising Financially Fit Kids* by Joline Godfrey (Ten Speed Press; $19.95)
- *Money Doesn't Grow on Trees: A Parent's Guide to Raising Financially Responsible Children* by Neale S. Godfrey and Carolina Edwards (Simon & Schuster; $12.00)
- *Make More Than Your Parents: Your Guide to Financial Freedom* by Micke Bundlie, Kevin O'Donnell, and Bart DiLiddo (HCI; $12.95)

Camps and Programs

- Black Enterprise Kidpreneurs Conference; 800-543-6786; *blackenterprise.com*
- The Bull and Bear Investment Camp (conducted by Moody Reid Financial Advisors Inc.); 800-761-0274
- Camp $tart-Up, Summer$tock, and Who's Behind the Noise; 805-965-0457; *www.independentmeans.com*
- Securities Industry Foundation for Economic Education Stock Market Game; 212-618-0519; *www.smg2000.org*
- YoungBiz Better Investing and YoungBiz 'Trep Camps; 888-543-7929; *www.youngbiz.com*

---

practice it   **Post-Reading**

Review the article again and underline any particular sentences that indicate that the audience for this article is parents. Without the images and the title, how clear is the intended audience? What types of words and examples reveal the intended audience?

For more on audience and purpose, see Chapter 6, Audience, Purpose, and Topic, page 169.

For more on audience and purpose, see Chapter 6, Audience, Purpose, and Topic, page 169.

COMPREHENSION QUESTIONS

1. What is Social Security?

2. What is a 401(k)?

3. What does "financial empowerment" mean?

4. What does "entrepreneurship" mean?

5. According to the article, what are the best ways to teach children about money?

SUMMARY ACTIVITY

Write a brief summary of "Teach Your Children the Building Blocks of Finance" in your notes. Refer back to the steps for summary writing in Chapter 1 (pp. 30–31) if necessary.

VOCABULARY ACTIVITY

Look back over your annotations for this article and begin to compile a glossary of words that pertain to the topic of financial literacy. Do your best to write your own definition of the word, using context clues or word parts. For any words you cannot figure out, look up the definition in a dictionary, and then restate it in your own words on your glossary.

DISCUSSION QUESTIONS

1. Why do many parents prefer not to discuss their finances with their children?

2. Do you think children should be given a set allowance for doing regular chores, or should they earn money for each individual chore? Why?

3. Who else outside of the intended audience for this article might find the information helpful or interesting?

4. Why do you think the article begins with the story of Yvette Saul?

5. Besides the personal examples, what other types of evidence does the article include? What pieces of evidence do you find most convincing?

6. The article refers to the "Declaration of Financial Empowerment" but never explains it. From the context of the article, what can you guess about what this is?

MAGAZINE

Magazine articles are enjoyable because they blend real-life examples with facts and statistics and appeal to emotion as well as logic. This helps them appeal to a large, general audience. Olivia Mellan does this in her article "Men, Women and Money," from the January 1999 issue of *Psychology Today*, a magazine covering psychology for a general audience. Mellan gets her expertise from her own practice as a psychotherapist and money coach, and draws on that experience to describe common problems that people have communicating about money. The most recent of her five books—*Money Harmony: A Road Map for Individuals and Couples*, second edition, by Olivia Mellan and Sherry Christie—expands on concepts expressed in this article. For more about Mellan's work, see her Web site www.moneyharmony.com. *Important words and phrases have been italicized in this reading. Look up those you do not know, and write the definitions in your personal vocabulary list.*

practice it   Pre-Reading

Take stock of what you already know about the topic by recalling real-life examples of couples' money disagreements you have had or witnessed.
  Preview the article:

- What do you predict the article will be about?
- Review how the article is structured. Does the structure help you understand the material?
- Look at the length of the article. How much time do you think you will need to read it?
- What do you want to know about the topic based on your preview of the article?

OLIVIA MELLAN

Men, Women, and Money

For most people, money is never just money, a tool to accomplish some of life's goals. It is love, power, happiness, security, control, dependency, independence, freedom, and more. Money is so *loaded* a symbol that to unload it—and I believe it must be unloaded to live in a fully *rational* and balanced relationship to money—reaches deep into the human *psyche*. Usually, when the button of money is pressed, deeper issues emerge that have long been neglected. As a result, money matters are a perfect *vehicle* for awareness and growth.

Most people relate to money much as they relate to a person—in an ongoing and complex way that taps deep-seated emotions. When two individuals form an *enduring* relationship with each other, money is always a partner, too. In these *liberated* times, couples discuss many things before marriage, but the meaning of money is not one of them. Money is still a *taboo* topic. Often, the silence is a shield for the shame, guilt, and anxiety people feel about their own ways with money. I, for one, would not want to tell a date that I'm an overspender.

Many individuals have a troubled relationship with money. Then, when they get into a couple relationship, money matters get explosive. Other people may have no problem with money individually; the trouble starts after they're in the relationship.

In two decades as a *psychotherapist* specializing in resolving money conflicts, I have observed that couples usually *polarize* around money. Partners tend to assume defense styles, or personalities, in relation to money that are direct opposites to each other. I call it Mellan's Law: If opposites don't attract right off the bat, then they will create each other eventually.

Commonly, a *hoarder* marries a spender. The United States is in fact a   5
nation of overspenders. We live in a *market economy* and we are led to believe that we are good citizens to the degree that we go out and spend. Because of our community breakdown and spiritual *alienation*, many people feel a core emptiness that they try to fill up with things. If we're not overspending, we're typically worrying about money or compulsively hoarding it.

We grow up in families where nobody talks about money. Most people will immediately protest: "Not true. My family talked about money all the time." When I ask, "How did you talk?" they reply, "My father worried about not having enough, and he yelled at my mother for spending too much."

The fact remains that people do not grow up with educational or philosophic conversations about what money is and isn't, what it can and can't do. We don't examine the societal messages telling us that *gratification* lies in spending or that keeping up with the Joneses is important. Information-based money discussions are so taboo that we usually reach adulthood without a realistic sense of our family's finances.

I once met a man who had no idea that he grew up in a wealthy family. He said, "We had a family restaurant and my mother was always worrying about how we were at the edge of doom. As a child I developed a *stammer* from all that money anxiety. As an adolescent, I worked day and night to keep the restaurant afloat. Years later, my mother was talking about the good old days when we were making so much money in the restaurant business. I started screaming at her about all the money anxiety I carried. I was outraged that it wasn't even based on a real threat. When I stopped screaming, I noticed that my stammer was gone."

And it never returned. That's a therapist's dream story: one *catharsis*, no symptom. But it does show how money carries a huge emotional load.

Doing What Doesn't Come Naturally

Growth, creativity, intimacy, and flexibility come from doing what is not automatic. For a hoarder, spending money on one's self or a loved one for immediate pleasure changes the pattern. For a spender, it's saving or investing money, or going on a slow, choreographed binge. Breaking habits doesn't happen all at once; it's a slow process. For example, I can't say, "Don't worry!" to a worrier. But I can say, "Pick one hour to worry, write down your worries for that time, and give up worrying for the rest of the day."

Partners can begin to change their ingrained habits by taking the following steps:

- Do what doesn't come naturally once a week. Eventually you and your partner will have moved enough toward some middle ground that you are not locked into your roles.
- While practicing a new behavior, write down how it feels in order to monitor your progress.
- Reward yourself for that new behavior.

As a result of the money taboo, I grew up as most kids do: imitating my   10
parents' way of handling money without being aware of it. My father, affected by the Depression, worried out loud about money. My mother was a shopaholic, expressing love by buying me and herself clothes. She'd hide the purchases behind a living room chair until my father was in a good mood. As an adult, whenever I felt either depressed or particularly happy, I too would go out and shop. And even if I bought everything at a thrift store, I'd hide all the items behind a chair until my husband was in a good mood. Actually, I alternated between shopping and worrying about money.

Some people do the opposite. They typically say, "My father was a hoarder and a worrier. I hated the way he made me account for every penny of my allowance. I made a vow to myself that I'd never be like that." Such people, however, are anything but free of the parental attitude; their behavior is still defined by it.

In addition to *irrational* attitudes and beliefs about money that we *internalize* from our *families of origin*, we carry our own emotionally charged memories of money from childhood. I remember being in a barbershop with my father when I was six, and some kid asked his father for a quarter. The father said no. The kid started to sob uncontrollably. I remember being so *gripped by* the child's sense of deprivation, I made a vow right then that I was never going to feel deprived like that. If you tell yourself at six that you're never going to feel deprived, you have the makings of a chronic overspender.

Couples polarized over money engage in a balancing dance of opposites. Two spenders who come together will fight each other for the superspender role; the other, as a defense, will learn to hoard because someone has to set limits. When it comes to defense styles, there's always a pursuer (or clinger) and a withdrawer. With two withdrawers, one will become the superwithdrawer. The other will become a pursuer, because if they both withdrew there would be no connection at all.

An equally common polarity is the worrier and avoider. Avoiders don't focus on the details of their money life, such as whether they have enough money or how much interest they're paying on their credit cards; they just spend. A worrier will turn a mate into an avoider just as a way of escaping the avalanche of worry. And an avoider will turn a mate into a worrier. Two partners couldn't both avoid forever; somebody will eventually get concerned and take on the worrier role. Doubling the trouble, hoarders are usually worriers and spenders are usually avoiders.

As with all polar personality styles, hoarders and spenders live in different   15 universes marked by opposing beliefs. What feels good to one feels horrible to the other. When not spending, a hoarder feels *virtuous*, in control. A spender when not spending feels anxious and deprived. Indeed, spenders can't tolerate the word "budget"; financial planners have to draw up a "spending plan."

Other money personalities include planners, who are detail-oriented, and dreamers, who are global *visionaries*. In addition, there are money *monks*, often ex-hippies, political activists, or spiritual souls, who feel that money corrupts and it's better to not have too much. Sometimes they marry money *amassers*, who believe that the guy with the most money wins. Amassers are not hoarders; they don't simply save, they invest to make their money grow. They save, spend, and invest.

What makes each of the personality types is the operation of internal belief systems, what I call money myths—all the money messages, vows, and emotional memories acquired from the family of origin, the peer group, the culture at large and filtered through a person's *intrinsic* temperament. Many spenders, for example, don't give away just money; they are *effusive* with feelings, words, everything. Hoarders are typically *taciturn* and withholding. Even in therapy, they have to be encouraged to open up.

Here is the ironic part. The longer couples are married, the more they lock into polarized roles. Then they attack each other for their differences, projecting onto the other attitudes about every other spender or hoarder they have encountered in their life. They fail to acknowledge the positive aspects of their partner's personality type and of the balancing dance itself.

The failure of people to explore their money personalities leads to deep misunderstanding and hurt. Take the case of a man who views money as security. He does not believe in spending a great deal on gifts; he believes in saving. He's married to a woman who believes that money is both love and happiness; she's a spender. They are about to celebrate a major anniversary. He spends days in record stores searching for the song they danced to when they were dating in the '60s, "their song." When she gets his gift, she thinks he's *chintzy* and is insulted. He's *inconsolably* hurt. She, meanwhile, has bought him an expensive gift.

Conversing with Cash

How do you turn your consciousness to an area that's usually in the dark? When a couple comes in fighting about money, I first have them clarify their own personal history and private relationship with money before turning to the dynamic between them.

I want people to see what money symbolizes to them. Then they can "unload" the symbol.

As an exercise at home, I ask each to engage in a dialogue with their money, and not share the conversation until they come back. The goal is to see what money symbolizes for each person, and to recognize that money is just a tool to accomplish certain of life's goals.

In the dialogue, imagine your money is being interviewed on *Oprah*. Ask how it thinks the relationship between you two is going, how it feels about the way you treat it.

Perhaps Money will reply, "You know, you're squeezing me so tight, I can't breathe. You need to let go a little." Or, "You throw me around, but you don't treat me with respect. You need to pay more attention to me." Either speak into a tape recorder or write the conversation down on paper.

After this dialogue, draw on at least three voices in your head—mother, father, and any other figure and have them comment on what has transpired. Finally, consider what God, a Higher Power, or inner wisdom might say.

Either Money or God, or both, will help you see the direction you need to move in to achieve money harmony.

Occasionally, a couple is unable to have a dialogue with Money. I then ask them to write down all their childhood memories and associations relating to money and start there.

Money issues rarely *manifest* themselves openly in relationships. Instead,   20
couples fight over what money represents. And while money issues can *rear* their head anytime; there are specific transition periods in relationships that force them to the surface: tax time, starting a family, and buying a house. Couples may complain, "We can't agree on where we want to live." Or, "He wants to go on vacation and I want to save our money for retirement." Or, "She keeps indulging the children, getting them everything they want, and I don't think that's good for the kids."

In addition to money personalities, there are male-female differences in approaches to money that haunt many relationships. It could be said that some differences reflect men as hunters and women as gatherers. In his theater piece *Defending the Caveman*, Rob Becker describes men: They go out and buy a shirt, wear it until it dies, then go out and kill another shirt. Women, in contrast, gather. They shop for this for next Christmas for their niece and for that for their son-in-law.

Other pervasive money differences exist between the genders. First, men and women have differences of personal boundaries because they are both raised largely by women. Men have to psychologically separate more rigidly from women because of the sex difference; women do not have to separate so rigidly, and therefore can afford less distinct boundaries.

Second, men are raised to see the world as *hierarchical* and competitive. There's always a one-up and one-down position, a winner and a loser. Women see the world as cooperative and democratic; they share. In addition, they are allowed—even encouraged—to be needy and *vulnerable*, while men are discouraged from such display.

The boundary and hierarchical differences between men and women lead to clashes around money decision making. Men think nothing of going out alone and buying a big-screen TV, or even the family car or computer, then coming home and saying, "Hi honey I have a new car." She says, "Why didn't you consult me? I thought we were a team." And he says, "Are you my mother? Do I have to ask your permission?"

Because of their more rigid boundaries, men think of themselves as islands   25
and withdraw when facing difficulties of *intimacy*. They don't see themselves as part of a team. And, of course, men and women are raised to believe different things about the way they should actually handle money. Despite many social changes, men are still bred to believe they will be good at dealing with money—although nobody tells them how to do it. In that way, money is like sex; they're just supposed to know. Women are raised to believe they won't be good at it and, if they're lucky, some man will take care of the details of money and investing.

One of the major financial houses recently *canvassed* high school students and asked how good they were about math and money. The boys said, "We're pretty good." The girls said, "We're not very good." In fact, they both knew the same amount about money; but their confidence levels were vastly different.

Moreover, when men make money in the stock market, they credit their own cleverness. When they lose money, they blame the incompetence of their advisers or bad luck. When women make money in the market, they credit the cleverness of their advisers, good luck, or even the stars. When they lose money, they blame themselves.

This explanatory style is *literally* and *figuratively* depressing. In addition, women are still paid three-quarters of what men are paid for the same job. These events *conspire* to reduce women's confidence and inspire "bag-lady" nightmares. Because of the forced dependency on men to make decisions about money, women fear being out on the street with nothing.

When men make more money than their spouse, they believe their superior earnings entitle them to greater power in decision making. By contrast, women who make more than their mates almost always desire democratic decision making.

As a woman and a therapist, I have a definite bias towards shared   30
decision making and shared power. It is the only arrangement that works. I prefer to think of men's sense of money not as an *entitlement* but as a defense against the terrible provider burden they carry.

Men are trained to believe that money equals power and that power is the path to respect. However, power and control are not compatible with intimacy. Relationships succeed only when both partners are willing to display their vulnerabilities to each other. It's important for men to know that failing to share power cheats them of the intimacy and love they want.

Another important difference between men and women concerns their interests in merging their money. Typically, men want to *merge* all the couple's money—while maintaining primary decision-making power. Women want to keep at least some money separate.

The fight goes like this:

HE: "Why do you want separate money? You must not trust me. Are you planning to file for a divorce?"

SHE: "Why do you want to merge all of our money? It must be that you   35
want to control me."

There may be truth in both positions. Still, experience has led me to see a very positive, and probably unconscious, longing in both views, and it has to do with the challenge of intimacy. Merging, getting connected and staying connected, is more difficult for men. At the first sign of conflict, it's easy for them to withdraw.

I believe that men's desire to merge the family money is a loving expression of the desire for intimacy and connection. Perhaps it is even a safeguard against their withdrawing. I have come to see that women want separate money as a loving expression of their need for healthy autonomy. Their biggest challenge in relationships is not losing themselves; it's holding on to their own sense of self.

Neither his demand for merged money nor her desire for separate funds is a position taken up against the spouse—although that is how partners tend to see it. When couples understand this, their new perspective has the power to transform their entire relationship.

American culture, I believe, makes a big mistake in pressuring married couples to merge all their money. It is in fact unwise for couples to merge money right away. Since couples don't talk about money before they marry, you don't know if you're tying yourself to an overspender in debt or a worrier who could drive you crazy.

Couples can merge some of their common assets for joint expenses,   40
savings, and investing and keep the rest separate. That definitely *averts* some kinds of conflicts. Your partner doesn't get to comment on how you spend your money. I've always kept a portion of money apart because I knew I was an overspender and I didn't want to mess up the family finances or credit rating.

8 Tips to Talking about Money

Never try to negotiate about money before airing your feelings; otherwise, negotiations will always break down.

1. Find a nonstressful time when money is not a loaded issue (not tax season, please) and when the kids are not around. Agree on some ground rules: no interrupting each other; no long tirades; after one person shares a difficult piece of information, the partner will try to mirror it back before responding.
2. Take turns sharing your childhood messages about money. How did your parents save it, spend it, talk about it? How did they deal with allowances? What specific money messages did you get and how might they be affecting you today?
3. Share your old hurts, resentments and fears about money.
4. Mention your concerns and fears about your partner's money style. Then acknowledge what you admire about their methods and what you secretly envy. Hoarders secretly admire spenders' capacity to enjoy life in the present, while spenders secretly envy hoarders' ability to set limits, to budget and delay gratification. But typically they won't tell each other because they're afraid it confers license to continue in that style. In reality, positive statements help to make partners feel safe enough to give up the negative aspects of their behavior.
5. Talk about your goals for the future, short and long term.
6. Share your hopes and dreams.
7. Consider making a shared budget or a spending plan together by merging the hopes and the goals that have come up on your list more than once.
8. Set a time to have the next money talk. Aim for weekly conversations in the beginning, then monthly ones.

Alternatively, couples could merge some money and only the woman could have separate funds. Solutions do not have to be *symmetrical* to work well. They just have to appeal to the deeper needs of both partners. The difficulty is in making clear to the other what your own needs are.

Money issues are different from other problems in relationships. They're harder to talk about and harder to resolve because of our extensive cultural conditioning. The most important thing in couples communication is *empathy*, or putting yourself in your partner's place. It is almost always more important to be heard and understood than to have a partner agree with what you say.

Spouses who start talking genuinely about what they like about each other's money style create an atmosphere of safety and nondefensiveness. Once such a way of talking about money is established and once couples understand the positive intent of the partner, they can then work out a solution to almost any problem, a solution that best fits their own unique needs.

| practice it | Post-Reading |

To spark your thinking and deepen your participation in class discussion, pick a few quotes that you really liked and copy them out in a chart like this. You can copy the chart into your notebook or download a version of the chart from the e-Pages. Add rows to the chart as needed. (Go to **bedfordstmartins.com/readwriteconnect** and click on **Charts**.)

FINDING MEANINGFUL QUOTATIONS

Quotation You Find Meaningful (page no.)	Why Quotation Is Meaningful
"...couples usually polarize around money. Partners tend to assume defense styles, or personalities, in relation to money that are direct opposites to each other." (51)	I see this in my own parents, and I have seen how feeling like they are on different teams with money makes them argue

It will be helpful to return to these quotes later when you begin to do essay writing. For now, reflect on them in writing or share them in class discussion.

COMPREHENSION QUESTIONS

1. Who is the audience and what is the purpose of this article? How do you know?

2. What is "Mellan's Law"? Give one or two examples from the article and/or your experience to illustrate Mellan's Law.

3. What is "keeping up with the Joneses"? How does this idea relate to the article?

4. What are the characteristics of hoarders and spenders? Planners and dreamers? Money monks and amassers?

5. How do traditional male and female gender roles contribute to our money personalities, according to the author?

SUMMARY ACTIVITY

Write a brief summary in your notes of "Men, Women, and Money." Refer back to the steps for summary writing in Chapter 1 (pp. 30–31) if necessary.

VOCABULARY ACTIVITY

Add words from this article to your ongoing glossary of financial terms. Remember to write definitions in your own words.

DISCUSSION QUESTIONS

1. Do you agree that money is a "taboo" subject for most dating couples (para. 2)?

2. Do you think that same-sex couples have the same issues with money as opposite-sex couples?

3. What do you think of Mellan's advice for couples on how to talk about money? How do her professional background and experience influence her perspective on this topic?

4. What do you think is the most important thing couples can do to prevent (or at least reduce) arguments about money?

5. How might a couple's money problems affect their children's financial attitudes?

6. Are Mellan's examples and evidence fair and useful? Why or why not?

CHART

You will read many different types of texts in college, including textbooks, scholarly articles, Web sites, and magazine articles, as well as documents like the following chart that are primarily visual. Charts, such as this one from the U.S. Bureau of Labor Statistics, convey much helpful information if you know how to interpret them. Published every three years, it shows the relationship between how much education a person has and his or her average salary and likelihood of unemployment.

practice it   **Pre-Reading**

In order to "read" the chart, spend some time looking at its title, the numbers it presents, its structure, and the degree categories it lists. Try looking at it from top to bottom as well as from left to right.

BUREAU OF LABOR STATISTICS

Education Pays (Chart)

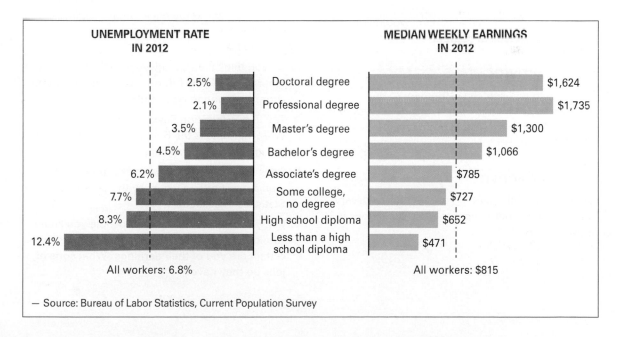

Source: Bureau of Labor Statistics, Current Population Survey

Post-Reading

Many of us have a love-hate relationship with statistics: We find them compelling, but we know they can be taken out of context, misquoted, and abused by advertisers and others, so we don't always trust them.

- Find the "Education Pays" chart on the Bureau of Labor Statistics Web site (www.bls.gov).
- Look at the Web page where the chart is located, and then click around a little to other parts of the site, taking notes as you go. What did you learn about the Bureau of Labor Statistics? Does what you learned make you more or less likely to think of the evidence as reliable and credible? Why? Would you use this site as a source in college papers? Why or why not? What parts of it would be most useful?

COMPREHENSION QUESTIONS

1. Where do these statistics come from? Who collected them? How can you find out more about the Bureau of Labor Statistics?

2. What does *median* mean? How does "median" differ from "average"? What is the significance of an "average" when considering information like that presented in the chart?

3. What is the main point of the chart?

4. What is the difference between a doctoral and professional degree? What careers would you have with each type of degree?

SUMMARY ACTIVITY

Write a one- to two-sentence summary of the "Education Pays" chart in your notes. Refer back to the steps for summary writing in Chapter 1 (pp. 30–31) if necessary.

VOCABULARY ACTIVITY

Add words from this chart to your ongoing glossary of financial terms. Remember to write definitions in your own words.

DISCUSSION QUESTIONS

1. How much would you make per month with a high school degree, assuming you earned the median amount indicated by the chart? How much would you make per month with some college and no degree? An associate's degree? A bachelor's degree? Do the math. Would you be able to live on those salaries where you live now?

2. The economy "crashed" in 2008; this chart reflects 2012 data. How does the recession of 2008 seem to have affected the unemployment rates and earnings of more educated and less educated workers?

3. Do you think the chart gives reliable evidence? In other words, is the information trustworthy and current enough to be useful?

4. The title "Education Pays" is short and sweet. What message is the Bureau of Labor Statistics trying to send? Do you agree with this message?

5. Does the chart's design (as a bar graph, rather than a pie chart) help convey the Bureau of Labor Statistics' message?

6. Can you think of examples of people you know who don't fit the trend shown in the chart? How certain are you of their earnings? What sorts of jobs do they have?

SCHOLARLY ARTICLE

Now that you have more experience with reading magazine articles, and a bit more basic knowledge of financial management, you're better prepared to tackle another major type of college reading, the scholarly journal article. A scholarly journal article differs from a magazine article in three key ways. First, it is written by experts for other experts in the same profession. The article "Milwaukee's Youth Enterprise Academy" was written by sociologists Mark Schug and Eric Hagedorn, and it describes an experimental program they developed. It was originally published in the journal the *Social Studies* in 2006. The audience for the article is most likely other sociologists or education professionals. Second, you'll notice that it doesn't have pictures, inset quotes, or any decorative features—scholarly articles tend to include only text and data (like charts and graphs), though most of them have features such as subheadings that help you navigate through them. A third feature of scholarly journal articles is that they are peer-reviewed. This simply means that experts in the field (in this case, other sociologists) read the article and agreed that it was good research before the journal agreed to publish it. *Important words and phrases have been italicized in this reading. Look up those you do not know, and write the definitions in your personal vocabulary list.*

practice it **Pre-Reading**

Preview the text by scanning the article, noticing the subheadings. Does the format look familiar? How does it compare to a lab report you may have written for a science class? Look at the charts and other special features. How do you think you will begin to read a scholarly journal article?

MARK C. SCHUG AND ERIC A. HAGEDORN

Milwaukee's Youth Enterprise Academy: An Eight-year Study of a Model Program for Urban Youth

Twenty-five years ago, adults worked for companies that provided defined benefit pensions. Banks offered routine services like savings accounts and checking accounts. People bought homes and saved what money they could. Today, the situation has changed. Most companies no longer offer defined benefit pension plans and, instead, allow employees to enroll in 401(k) programs, which are defined contribution programs. Banks and other financial institutions offer a complex range of financial instruments and services, with many services available on the Internet. Accompanying this changing financial environment is an increase in the population's financial misbehaviors, including a greater number of bankruptcies, accumulations of large amounts of credit debt, and low rates of personal saving.

The problem is more serious for minority populations in urban households. Nonwhites are more likely to file for bankruptcy and have lower credit scores than whites. Table l is an illustration of the large gap between whites and nonwhites in net wealth, which is the net value of all assets, including homes, cars, stocks, and savings accounts. Differences in asset ownership between whites and nonwhites appear to be one of the important contributors to the gap. The Federal Reserve (Aizcorbe, Kennickell, and Moore 2003) reports that nonwhites or Hispanics own homes at a lower rate than do white non-Hispanics and hold less business equity. Nonwhites or Hispanics are less likely to invest in bonds, mutual funds, retirement, stocks, or certificates of deposits. Although an economic and financial education is certainly important for all young people, one can make the case for it being of particular importance to minorities. Alas, economic education is less frequently offered in large urban high schools than it is in suburbs or medium-sized cities (Walstad 2001).

Many studies and reports indicate the need to improve programs for financial and economic education. Former Federal Reserve Chairman Alan Greenspan, a leading voice advocating for increased economic education, has stated.

The importance of basic financial skills underscores the need to begin the learning process as early as possible. Indeed improving basic financial education at the elementary and secondary school level will provide a foundation of financial literacy that can help prevent younger people from making poor decisions that can take years to overcome. (Greenspan 2005, 65)

TABLE 1. MEDIAN FAMILY NET WORTH

Family Characteristic	1992	1995	1998	2001
White, non-Hispanic	$86,200	$88,500	$103,800	$120,000
Nonwhite or Hispanic	$14,800	$18,300	$17,900	$17,100

Source. Adapted from *Federal Reserve Bulletin.* January 2003.

In several studies, researchers suggest that young people can learn economics at young ages (see Schug and Hagedorn 2005). New evidence suggests that financial knowledge is the key ingredient for success. Writing in the *Federal Reserve Bulletin*, Hilgert, Hogarth, and Beverly (2003) found that improved financial knowledge is linked to improved financial behavior in such areas as money management, credit management, saving, and investment. That study is typical of a growing set of studies that suggest that carefully designed programs with clearly stated expectations can help individuals to achieve better financial outcomes. The especially good news is that improving knowledge is something that we know how to do in schools.

University of Wisconsin–Milwaukee's Youth Enterprise Academy

The Youth Enterprise Academy (YEA) is a program developed at the University of Wisconsin–Milwaukee Center for Economic Education through the partnership of a private foundation, the state government, a private not-for-profit organization, and the local public schools. The program was started with funding from the Helen Bader Foundation and now enjoys support from several organizations. The Lynde and Harry Bradley Foundation and the Wisconsin Department of Public Instruction are the largest supporters, but other local foundations and individuals also provide financial support.

The YEA is designed to improve the financial and economic understanding of urban youth. An analysis of the pre- and posttest scores combined over a seven-year period reveals large and significant effect sizes in terms of student gains on tests of economic and financial knowledge. Based on the statistical analysis, we are confident that the curriculum used in Milwaukee's YEA is effective in influencing students' knowledge. We believe that the program is a model for others to consider.

Youth Enterprise Academy Summer "Boot Camp"

The YEA is a ten-day summer program for high school students (see the appendix for the syllabus) and is conducted on the campus of the

University of Wisconsin–Milwaukee. Each year, approximately twenty-five Milwaukee public school students from the ninth and tenth grades participate.

The goal of the YEA is to increase the economic and financial education of urban youth and their participation in the economy. Three areas are emphasized. First, students study personal finance and participate in several activities that stress saving, investing, credit, and the importance of getting a good education (investing in their own human capital). Students act as stock analysts, researching various companies for their clients and eventually recommending whether a company's stock should be bought, held, or sold. The students use materials developed by the National Council on Economic Education (NCEE) and materials published by the National Association of Investors Corporation. Students are required to read and complete most of the exercises in *Financial Fitness for Life: Going for the Gold*, a curriculum for grades 9–12. They also receive a copy of *Your Credit Counts Challenge* and are assigned specific activities. Both texts are published by the National Council on Economic Education.

Second, the YEA emphasizes basic economics. Students participate in several activities to learn such basics as scarcity, choice, opportunity cost, incentives, profit, laws of supply and demand, market price, price ceilings, and price floors. The students participate in two simulations—auction market and private property rights—and hear presentations from successful minority business people. A highlight of this part of the program is an all-day field trip to visit the Chicago Board of Trade and the Federal Reserve Bank of Chicago.

Finally, YEA focuses on developing leadership skills. We assume   10
that becoming a leader in today's economy requires being successful academically in high school and college. Students in the YEA examine career options, decide what courses to take in high school to get ready for college, and discuss how to finance a college education. Using the Internet, students visit the Web pages of numerous colleges and examine various academic majors and tuition costs.

Real-World Investment Experiences

Students who successfully complete the YEA receive $500 U.S. Savings Bonds. Ten students in two teams of five from each Youth Enterprise Academy take the next step when they are invited to join a Youth Enterprise Investment Club. Here, the students manage a Youth Enterprise College Fund—a fund with an initial value of $2,000 per student or $10,000 for each team. The goal of a Youth Enterprise College Fund is to increase the value of the fund to pay as much as possible of the first year of tuition at a typical college or university. When a member of the Youth Enterprise Investment Club graduates from high school, that student can designate that his or her share of the whole fund be paid into the individual account at the postsecondary education institution in which he or she is enrolled.

Methods of Reaching Our Conclusion

Data were collected to evaluate the YEA over an eight-year period. A total of 198 ninth- and tenth-grade students participated in the Youth Enterprise Academy—an average of twenty-five students per year. Two measures were administered at the beginning and end of each YEA session. First, twenty multiple-choice items were selected from the Basic Economics Test (BET) published by the NCEE. The BET is designed to measure the economic understanding of intermediate elementary students. Second, a Personal Finance Test (PFT) was developed, based on test items published in *Learning from the Market*, which is another publication of NCEE. The PFT is a twenty-two-item, multiple-choice test designed to assess middle grade students' knowledge in personal finance.

Analysis of Student Performance on the Basic Economics Test

The average pretest score on the BET, over the eight-year period, was 70.9 percent correct (SD = 16.7 percent). This very high pretest score is almost certainly because the test was designed for upper-elementary grade students. The average posttest score was 83.4 percent correct (SD = 15.7 percent). The average gain was 12.5 percent (SD =12.1 percent). To evaluate whether this 12.5 percent increase during the eight-year period was statistically significant, we used a paired-samples t test, as we did in each of the individual program years. Table 2 contains those results. A paired-samples t test for this gain indicated a statistically significant change in score from pre- to posttest (t = −14.60, df = 197, p < .001). In addition to reporting the statistically significant changes each year (and for the eight years) from the pre- to posttests, we also included Cohen effect sizes for the significant gains. Measuring effect size is a way of denoting whether a statistically significant effect has any practical meaning. The Cohen effect size for the 12.5 percent gain over the eight-year period was 1.04. That is considered a "large" effect (with effects of .2 being considered "small," those of .5 "medium," and those more than .8 "large").

Analysis of Student Performance on the Test of Personal Finance

The average pretest score on the PFT was 55.4 percent correct (SD = 15.1). The average posttest score was 71.8 percent correct (SD = 15.2 percent). The average gain was 16.4 percent (SD = 12.69 percent). A paired-samples t test for this gain indicated a statistically significant change in score from pre- to posttest ($t = -18.26$, $df = 197$, $p < .001$). The Cohen effect size for this gain was 1.30, which Cohen describes as a large effect. Table 3 contains the results for the individual years and the eight-year period.

Do Members of the Youth Enterprise Investment Clubs Attend College?

The second feature of the YEA is the Youth Enterprise Investment   15
Clubs. The students in the club spend two years managing a college scholarship fund to be used eventually to pay a portion of their college tuition. Since 1999, all but two of the students who partici-pated in the investment clubs graduated from high school and have gone to college. Those students enrolled in the following colleges:

- Carroll College, Wisconsin
- Chicago College of Performing Arts
- Drake University
- Embry-Riddle Aeronautical University
- Florida Agricultural and Mechanical University
- Johns Hopkins University
- Marquette University
- Milwaukee Area Technical College
- Milwaukee School of Engineering
- University of Minnesota–Twin Cities
- Tennessee State University
- University of Arkansas–Pine Bluffs
- University of Minnesota–Morris Campus
- University of Wisconsin–Eau Claire
- University of Wisconsin–Madison
- University of Wisconsin–Whitewater
- Virginia Polytechnic Institute and State University

Discussion and Conclusion

During the eight years of the program, students who participated in the Youth Enterprise Academy significantly improved their knowledge of economics and personal finance. The large effect sizes suggest robust gains in learning. Those results lead us to three conclusions. First, urban youth can learn key concepts and principles of economic and financial education. What is necessary is that instruction be provided through the use of age-appropriate materials. Second, the materials and overall approach used in the program are easily available to school districts or other colleges and universities, and most activities used in the YEA are drawn from materials published by the NCEE and not extraordinary or exotic teaching approaches. Finally, the Youth Enterprise Academy

TABLE 2. BASIC ECONOMICS TEST

Year	N	Pretest mean (*SD*)	Posttest mean (*SD*)	Gain score	*t* value (*df, p*)	Effect size
1998	23	72.8 (14.2)	87.2 (9.1)	14.4	6.57 (22, .000)	1.4
1999	23	75.9 (14.5)	88.7 (10.7)	12.8	5.19 (22, .000)	1.1
2000	25	70.2 (18.3)	84.6 (17.7)	14.4	6.90 (24, .000)	1.1
2001	30	72.3 (15.1)	84.8 (10.9)	12.5	6.98 (29, .000)	1.3
2002	23	69.6 (13.0)	86.7 (10.3)	17.1	6.84 (22, .000)	1.4
2003	25	74.2 (13.4)	79.2 (18.0)	5.0	1.47 (24, .153*)	
2004	26	61.0 (22.7)	75.4 (23.2)	14.4	6.25 (25, .000)	1.0
2005	23	71.7 (17.7)	81.5 (17.0)	9.8	5.02 (22, .000)	1.0
Total	198	70.9 (16.7)	83.4 (15.7)	12.5	14.60 (197, .001)	1.0

Not a significant change.

TABLE 3. TEST OF PERSONAL FINANCE

Year	N	Pretest mean (*SD*)	Posttest mean (*SD*)	Gain score	*t* value (*df, p*)	Effect size
1998	23	49.0 (13.9)	66.0 (12.5)	17.0	7.66 (22, .000)	1.6
1999	23	46.8 (11.1)	69.6 (11.4)	22.8	11.36 (22, .000)	2.4
2000	25	48.7 (16.3)	74.4 (13.3)	25.7	11.60 (24, .000)	2.3
2001	30	57.3 (11.6)	70.0 (14.9)	12.7	5.11 (29, .000)	.9
2002	23	59.5 (11.5)	75.7 (9.8)	16.2	6.56 (22, .000)	1.4
2003	25	61.3 (16.8)	76.2 (16.1)	14.9	4.97 (24, .000)	1.0
2004	26	58.2 (14.7)	68.2 (20.7)	10.0	4.05 (25, .000)	.8
2005	23	61.3 (16.9)	75.1 (18.0)	13.8	7.52 (22, .000)	1.6
Total	198	55.4 (15.1)	71.8 (15.2)	16.4	18.26 (197, .001)	1.3

Investment Clubs provide evidence that students who participate in such real-life investment programs are likely to go on to college.

The results we report in this article should come as good news to educational leaders in urban school districts who believe that they can do little to improve the economic and financial prospects of their students. Educators in schools and universities who consider the current state of economic and financial knowledge to be unacceptably low may wish to consider the Youth Enterprise Academy and the Youth Enterprise Academy Investment Clubs, well-tested programs that have been successful for several years. We hope that they will agree that such programs are worthy of emulation.

APPENDIX

Syllabus for the Youth Enterprise Academy University of
   Wisconsin–Milwaukee Center for Economic Education

Day 1
- Registration and Welcome
- Overview and Introductions
- Complete Pretests
- Introduction to the Stock Analyst Project
- Why Investing Is Important
- What Is a Corporation?
- Check Your Stock Market IQ
- Review

Day 2
- Review and Overview
- Reading Stock Tables in the Newspaper
- Assign Pairs to Work on Stock Analyst Reports
     Select companies to research
     Begin to chart and graph companies' performance
- Wise Investment Practices: Risk and Reward
- NAIC Stock Checklist and How to Use Value Line Reports
- Review

Day 3
- Review and Overview
- Three Strategies for Wealth Building over the Long Term
- Why Go to College?
- How You Can Pay for College
- Review

Day 4
- Review and Overview
- Selecting the Career That's Right for You
- Time Is Everything: The Magic of Compound Interest
- There Is No Such Thing as a Free Lunch in Investing
- Spending and Credit Are Serious Business
- Review

Day 5
- Review and Overview
- Dynamics of Professional Speaking
- The Economic Way of Thinking
- Greed Video
- Review and Overview

Day 6
- Review and Overview
- The Basics of a Market Economy: Scarcity, Opportunity Cost, Market Systems, Productivity
- Introducing the Laws of Demand and Supply: Highs and Lows of Washing Cars
- Market Price: Market Simulation
- Shortages and Surpluses: Price Ceilings and Price Floors
- Review

Day 7
- Review and Overview
- What Is Money? Barter? Banks?
- The Federal Reserve System
- The Chicago Board of Trade
- Banks and Financial Institutions: Is Your Family "Unbanked?"
- Review

Day 8
- Field Trip to the Federal Reserve Bank of Chicago and the Chicago Board of Trade

Day 9
- Review and Overview
- Income and Choices: Living Below Your Means
- Panel Discussion: What You Need to Know to Be a Success in Business
- Presentation and Judging of Stock Analyst Reports
- Review

Day 10
- Review and Overview
- Global Economy: Grab Bag
- Mystery Nations
- The YEA College Bowl (Cash Awards for Best Performance!)
- Posttests
- Luncheon and Awards Ceremony
- Group Photographs

REFERENCES

Aizcorbe, A. M., A. B. Kennickell, and K. B. Moore. 2003. Recent changes in U.S. family finances: Evidence from the 1998 and 2001 survey of consumer finances. In *Federal Reserve Bulletin*, 1–32. Washington, DC: Federal Reserve Division of Research and Statistics.

Greenspan, A. 2005. The importance of financial education today. *Social Education* 69 (2): 65–66.

Hilgert, M. A., J. M. Hogarth, and S. G. Beverly. 2003. Household financial management: The connection between knowledge and behavior. In *Federal Reserve Bulletin*, 309–22. Washington, DC: Federal Reserve Division of Research and Statistics.

Schug, M. C., and E. A. Hagedorn. 2005. The money savvy pig™ goes to the big city: Testing the effectiveness of an economics curriculum for young children. *The Social Studies* 96 (5): 68–71.

Walslad, W. B. 200I. Economic education in U.S. high schools. *Journal of Economic Perspectives* 15 (3): 195–210.

practice it   Post-Reading

Make a chart of the pros and cons of the Youth Enterprise Academy program. You can copy the chart into your notebook or download a version of the chart from the e-Pages. Add rows to the chart as needed. (Go to **bedfordstmartins.com/readwriteconnect** and click on **Charts**.) Did you list more pros or cons? What does this lead you to conclude about the program? Did others in your class come up with the same conclusions?

CHARTING PROS AND CONS

Pros of YEA	Cons of YEA

COMPREHENSION QUESTIONS

1. What is "financial literacy"?

2. According to the authors, why has financial literacy become more important today than ever before?

3. What is "net worth"?

4. What problem is Milwaukee's Youth Enterprise Academy trying to solve?

5. How does the MYEA try to solve the problem, and does its solution work?

6. What would the authors like to see happen next?

SUMMARY ACTIVITY

Write a brief summary of "Milwaukee's Youth Enterprise Academy" in your notes. Refer back to the steps for summary writing in Chapter 1 (pp. 30–31) if necessary.

VOCABULARY ACTIVITY

Add words from this article to your ongoing glossary of financial terms. Remember to write definitions in your own words.

DISCUSSION QUESTIONS

1. Do you think the Youth Enterprise Academy would work in your community? Why or why not?

2. The authors cite a study that shows "economic education is less frequently offered in large urban high schools than it is in suburbs or medium-sized cities" (para. 2). Do a quick reading with and against the grain of the paragraph that includes this quote. Why do you think suburban kids get more economic education than urban kids? What about rural kids?

3. Should financial education be left solely to parents and families? Why or why not?

4. This article was written in 2006. Do you think its conclusions are still relevant? Why or why not?

5. How does the presentation of information in this scholarly article compare and contrast to a reading intended for general audiences, such as Mellan's "Men, Women, and Money"?

RESEARCH REPORT

The Pew Research Center report that follows offers numerous hard facts about the realities of wealth in America. Many believe that the wealth gap described in this report is the biggest economic problem in our country today, though they might differ on how to solve the problem. The Pew Research Center describes itself on its Web site as a "fact tank," which means it employs researchers to conduct polls of public opinion, collect statistics and information, and analyze the data. As you will see later in Pam Fessler's article (pp. 81–86), many magazine, newspaper, and radio journalists use Pew's information as the basis for their stories about American life and its economy. Pew is considered a highly credible source of information. The report that you will read was published in July 2010. (We present the Executive Summary of the report, but you can find the full report online.) *Important words and phrases have been italicized in this reading. Look up those you do not know, and write the definitions in your personal vocabulary list.*

practice it   Pre-Reading

Before you begin reading, do some background research about the Pew Research Center:

- Spend some time on the Pew site (www.pewresearch.org) to become familiar with its goals and mission. Note that this is a ".org" site, which means it is a nonprofit organization. (Pew uses U.S. Census information, but it is not, strictly speaking, a government organization.)
- Click through a few topics listed on the site, and skim through a few of the articles to see if you can identify any biases in the sources.
- Think about the similarities and differences between this site and others that deal with the same topic. You might, for example, compare it to the Bureau of Labor Statistics Web site. You might even click over to a commercial news Web site, like CNN or ABC News, to compare the presentation of facts.

Pew Research Center Site

Wealth Gaps Rise to Record Highs between Whites, Blacks, Hispanics: Twenty-to-One

Rakesh Kochhar, Richard Fry, and Paul Taylor

Executive Summary

The *median* wealth of white households is twenty times that of black households and eighteen times that of Hispanic households, according to a Pew Research Center analysis of newly available government data from 2009.

These *lopsided* wealth *ratios* are the largest since the government began publishing such data a quarter century ago and roughly twice the size of the ratios that had prevailed between these three groups for the two decades prior to the Great Recession that ended in 2009.

The Pew Research analysis finds that, in percentage terms, the bursting of the housing market bubble in 2006 and the recession that followed from late 2007 to mid-2009 took a far greater toll on the wealth of minorities than whites. From 2005 to 2009, inflation-adjusted median wealth fell by 66 percent among Hispanic households and 53 percent among black households, compared with just 16 percent among white households.

As a result of these declines, the typical black household had just $5,677 in wealth (assets minus debts) in 2009; the typical Hispanic household had $6,325 in wealth; and the typical white household had $113,149.

MEDIAN NET WORTH OF HOUSEHOLDS, 2005 AND 2009
in 2009 dollars

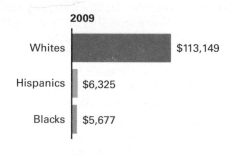

2009

Whites — $113,149
Hispanics — $6,325
Blacks — $5,677

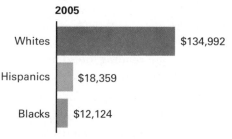

2005

Whites — $134,992
Hispanics — $18,359
Blacks — $12,124

— Source: Pew Research Center tabulations of Survey of Income and Program Participation data

Pew Research Center

Moreover, about a third of black (35 percent) and Hispanic (31 percent) households had zero or negative net worth in 2009, compared with 15 percent of white house-holds. In 2005, the comparable shares had been 29 percent for blacks, 23 percent for Hispanics and 11 percent for whites.

Hispanics and blacks are the nation's two largest minority groups, making up 16 percent and 12 percent of the U.S. population *respectively*.

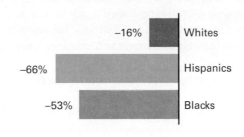

PERCENTAGE CHANGE IN MEDIAN NET WORTH OF HOUSEHOLDS, 2005 TO 2009

-16% Whites
-66% Hispanics
-53% Blacks

— Source: Pew Research Center tabulations of Survey of Income and Program Participation data

Pew Research Center

These findings are based on the Pew Research Center's analysis of data from the Survey of Income and Program Participation (SIPP), an economic questionnaire distributed *periodically* to tens of thousands of households by the U.S. Census Bureau. It is considered the most *comprehensive* source of data about household wealth in the United States by race and ethnicity. The two most recent administrations of SIPP that focused on household wealth were in 2005 and 2009. Data from the 2009 survey were only recently made available to researchers.[1]

Plummeting house values were the principal cause of the recent *erosion* in household wealth among all groups, with Hispanics hit hardest by the meltdown in the housing market.

From 2005 to 2009, the median level of home equity held by Hispanic homeowners declined by half—from $99,983 to $49,145—while the homeownership rate among Hispanics was also falling, from 51 percent to 47 percent. A geographic analysis suggests the reason: A disproportionate share of Hispanics live in California, Florida, Nevada and Arizona, which were in the *vanguard* of the housing real estate market bubble of the 1990s and early 2000s but that have since been among the states experiencing the steepest declines in housing values.

1. Data on the wealth of households are also collected in the Survey of Consumer Finances (SCF) and the Panel Survey of Income Dynamics (PSID), neither with as large a sample size as SIPP. The SCF was last conducted in 2010 and the PSID last collected wealth data in 2009. However, the final sets of data from those surveys were not available as of the writing of this report.

The following chart shows the Pew Research Center's estimates of   10
the wealth ratios for 2009 and those published by the Census Bureau for
1984 to 2004. As the chart demonstrates, the white-to-black and white-to-
Hispanic wealth ratios were much higher in 2009 than they had been at
any time since 1984, the first year for which the Census Bureau published
wealth estimates by race and ethnicity based on SIPP data.

MEDIAN NET WORTH OF HOUSEHOLDS, 2005 AND 2009

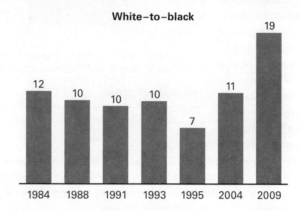

White-to-black

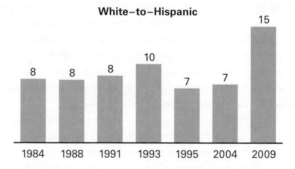

White-to-Hispanic

Note: Blacks and whites include Hispanics. The Survey of
Income and Program Participation was redesigned for the 1996
panel. The redesign may have affected the comparability of the
data from 1998 and later years with the data from earlier panels.

— Sources: For 2009: Pew Research Center tabulations of Survey
of Income and Program Participation data from the 2008 panel; for
1984 to 2004: various U.S. Census Bureau P–70 *Current Population
Reports*

Pew Research Center

Note that the ratios shown in the chart for 2009 differ slightly from the 2009 estimates used in the rest of this report: 19-to-1 for the white-to-black ratio, compared with 20-to-1 elsewhere in the report, and 15-to-1 for the white-to-Hispanic ratio, compared with 18-to-1 elsewhere in the report. That is because, in order to make the estimates in the chart consistent over time, the 2009 figures were adjusted to allow the racial groups "white" and "black" to include Hispanic members of these groups, consistent with methods used by the Census Bureau from 1984 to 2004. In the rest of this report, the white and black (and Asian) racial groups include only the non-Hispanic components of these populations. (Changes in racial identification methods and a redesign of SIPP in 1996 may also have had an impact on the comparability of the wealth ratios over time.)

White and black homeowners also saw the median value of their *home equity* decline during this period, but not by as much as Hispanics. Among white homeowners, the decline was from $115,364 in 2005 to $95,000 in 2009. Among black homeowners, it was from $76,910 in 2005 to $59,000 in 2009. There was little or no change during this period in the homeownership rate for whites and blacks; it fell from 47 percent to 46 percent among blacks and was unchanged at 74 percent among whites.[2]

An Alternative Approach to Measuring the Wealth Gap Trend

This report measures the changing wealth gaps between whites, Hispanics and blacks using ratios. An alternative approach would be to measure the changes in absolute levels rather than ratios. By that yardstick, the median wealth gaps between these groups decreased from 2005 to 2009. For example, in 2005, the median wealth of white households was $116,632 more than the median wealth of Hispanic households. By 2009, the difference had shrunk to $106,824. The same is true for white-black difference in median wealth. This means that white households experienced a greater absolute drop in their wealth. However, because the wealth base for white households is so much larger than it is for Hispanics and blacks, the proportional decrease in wealth was much less for whites. That is reflected in the sharp rise of the white-to-Hispanic and white-to-black wealth ratios reported in this study.

Household wealth is the accumulated sum of assets (houses, cars, savings and checking accounts, stocks and mutual funds, retirement accounts, etc.) minus the sum of debt (mortgages, auto loans, credit card debt, etc.). It is

---

2. The homeownership rates cited in this report are derived from SIPP data. They differ from homeownership rates published by the Census Bureau from other data sources.

different from household income, which measures the annual inflow of wages, interest, profits and other sources of earning. Wealth gaps between whites, blacks and Hispanics have always been much greater than income gaps.

The 2005 to 2009 time frame allows for a before-and-after look at the impact of the Great Recession. However, those dates do not *align* perfectly with the downturn, which ran from December 2007 to June 2009, according to the National Bureau of Economic Research.

In 2005, both the stock and housing markets were still rising. Thus, had the base year for these measurements of wealth been closer to the top of these markets in 2006 or 2007, the recorded declines are likely to have been even steeper.   15

Moreover, since the official end of the *recession* in mid-2009, the housing market in the United States has remained in a slump while the stock market has *recaptured* much of the value it lost from 2007 to 2009. Given that a much higher share of whites than blacks or Hispanics own stocks—as well as mutual funds and 401(k) or individual retirement accounts (IRAs)—the stock market rebound since 2009 is likely to have benefited white households more than minority households.

Other key findings from the report:

Hispanics: The net worth of Hispanic households decreased from $18,359 in 2005 to $6,325 in 2009. The percentage drop—66 percent—was the largest among all groups. Hispanics *derived* nearly two-thirds of their net worth in 2005 from home equity and are more likely to reside in areas where the housing meltdown was concentrated. Thus, the housing downturn had a deep impact on them. Their net worth also diminished because of a 42 percent rise in median levels of debt they carried in the form of unsecured liabilities (credit card debt, education loans, etc.).

Blacks: The net worth of black households fell from $12,124 in 2005 to $5,677 in 2009, a decline of 53 percent. Like Hispanics, black households drew a large share (59 percent) of their net worth from home equity in 2005. Thus, the housing downturn had a strong impact on their net worth. Blacks also took on more *unsecured debt* during the economic downturn, with the median level rising by 27 percent.

Whites: The drop in the wealth of white households was *modest* in comparison, falling 16 percent from $134,992 in 2005 to $113,149 in 2009. White households were also affected by the housing crisis. But home equity accounts for relatively less of their total net worth (44 percent in 2005), and that served to lessen the impact of the housing bust. Median levels of unsecured debt among whites rose by 32 percent.

Asians: In 2005 median Asian household wealth had been greater than the median for white households, but by 2009 Asians lost their place at the top of the wealth hierarchy. Their net worth fell from $168,103 in 2005 to $78,066 in 2009, a drop of 54 percent. Like Hispanics, they are geographically concentrated in places such as California that were hit hard by the housing market meltdown. The arrival of new Asian immigrants since 2004 also contributed significantly to the estimated decline in the overall wealth of this racial group. Absent the immigrants who arrived during this period, the median wealth of Asian households is estimated to have dropped 31 percent from 2005 to 2009. Asians account for about 5 percent of the U.S. population.

No Assets: About a quarter of all Hispanic (24 percent) and black (24 percent) households in 2009 had no assets other than a vehicle, compared with just 6 percent of white households. These percentages are little changed from 2005.

Medians and Means: Just as the gap in median household wealth among racial and ethnic groups rose from 2005 to 2009, so too did the gap in *mean* household wealth. However, the mean differences are not as dramatic as the median differences. (A median is the midpoint that separates the upper half from the lower half of a given group; a mean is an average, and, in this case, the average is driven upward by households with high net worth.) In 2005, mean white household wealth was 2.3 times that of Hispanics and 3 times that of blacks. By 2009, it was 3.7 times that of both Hispanics and blacks.

Wealth Disparities within Racial and Ethnic Groups: During the period under study, wealth disparities not only increased between racial and ethnic groups, but also rose within each group. Even though the wealthiest 10 percent of households within each group suffered a loss in wealth from 2005 to 2009, their share of their group's overall wealth rose during this period. The increase was the greatest among Hispanics, with the top 10 percent boosting their share of all Hispanic household wealth from 56 percent in 2005 to 72 percent in 2009. Among whites, the share of wealth owned by the top 10 percent rose from 46 percent in 2005 to 51 percent in 2009. These trends indicate that those in the top 10 percent of the wealth ladder were relatively less impacted by the economic downturn than those in the remaining 90 percent.

SIPP Net Worth

SIPP data include the following assets and liabilities:

Assets

- Financial institution accounts
  - Savings accounts
  - Money market deposit accounts
  - Certificates of deposit (CD)
  - Interest-earning checking accounts
  - Regular checking accounts
- Other interest-earning assets
  - U.S. government securities

- Municipal or corporate bonds
- U.S. savings bonds
- Stocks and mutual fund shares
- Business or profession
- Motor vehicles
- Owned home
- Rental property
- Vacation homes and other real estate
- IRA and Keogh accounts
- 401(k) and Thrift Savings Plans
- Mortgages held for sale of real estate
- Amount due from sale of business or property
- Other financial assets

Liabilities

- Secured liabilities
  - Margin and broker accounts
  - Debt on business or profession
  - Vehicle loans
  - Mortgages on own home
  - Mortgages on rental property
  - Mortgages on other homes or real estate

- Unsecured liabilities
  - Credit card and store bills
  - Student loans
  - Doctor, dentist, hospital, and nursing home bills
  - Loans from individuals
  - Loans from financial institutions
  - Other unsecured liabilities

Major assets not captured by SIPP are equities in defined-benefit pension plans, the cash value of life insurance policies, the value of household furnishings and jewelry, and future claims on Social Security. Thus, wealth estimates from SIPP are typically less than the estimates from the Survey of Consumer Finances.

Terminology

References to whites, blacks and Asians are to the non-Hispanic components of those populations. The only exception to this rule is when historical comparisons are drawn with data published by the Census Bureau.

"Asian" refers to (non-Hispanic) persons reporting their racial origin as Asian alone and does not include native Hawaiians or other Pacific Islanders. "Black" refers to black alone, and "white" refers to white alone.

The racial and ethnic identity of a household is determined on the   20
basis of the racial and ethnic identity of the head of the household.

Household "net worth" is the sum of the market value of assets owned by every member of the household minus their liabilities (debt).

Unless otherwise stated, all estimates in this report are expressed in 2009 dollars.

About the Report

This report presents net worth and asset ownership figures from wave 6 of the 2004 panel of the Survey of Income Program and Participation (SIPP) and wave 4 of the 2008 SIPP panel. These waves were conducted at the end of 2005 and 2009, respectively. SIPP is a *longitudinal* survey of households conducted by the U.S. Census Bureau. By design, SIPP oversamples low-income households and thus surveys large numbers of minority households. SIPP has periodically collected detailed wealth data since 1984 and is considered an authoritative source on the wealth of American households. As with any survey, estimates from SIPP are subject to *sampling* and *nonsampling* errors. See the *appendix* for more details.

This report was edited and the overview written by Paul Taylor, executive vice president of the Pew Research Center and director of its Social and Demographic Trends project. Senior researcher Rakesh Kochhar and senior economist Richard Fry researched and wrote the report. Research assistant Seth Motel helped with the preparation of charts. The report was number-checked by Motel and Pew Research Center staff member Gabriel Velasco. The report was copy-edited by Marcia Kramer. The Center is grateful for the expeditious assistance of Nasrin Dalirazar of the Housing and Household Economic Statistics Division of the U.S. Census Bureau on the definition of SIPP net worth components, weighting issues, and the replication of wealth tabulations published by the Census Bureau.

---

practice it   Post-Reading

This article has many facts, figures and new concepts, so make sure you understand the material before you analyze it. Copy this chart into your notebook, or download a version of the chart from the e-Pages. (Go to **bedfordstmartins.com/readwriteconnect** and click on **Charts**.) Then list the main points and supporting evidence. One student's first entries are below.

FINDING EVIDENCE

Point the Article Makes	Examples, Statistics, and Evidence Given as Support
The housing crash hurt minorities far more than whites.	Median wealth for Hispanics dropped 66 percent, for blacks 53 percent, and only 16 percent for whites.

COMPREHENSION QUESTIONS

1. What is net worth, and why do we examine that instead of salary or income?
2. What is the "wealth gap"?
3. What is the "housing market bubble," and when and why did it burst? What was its impact?
4. Why do experts categorize the statistics by ethnic group?
5. What reasons does the article give for why Hispanics were influenced more than other groups by the decline in housing prices?
6. What does it mean to have diversified assets?

SUMMARY ACTIVITY

Write a brief summary of this excerpt of the Pew Study in your notes. Refer back to the steps for summary writing in Chapter 1 (pp. 30–31) if necessary.

VOCABULARY ACTIVITY

Add words from this article to your ongoing glossary of financial terms. Remember to write definitions in your own words.

DISCUSSION QUESTIONS

1. Why do you think blacks and Hispanics keep most of their assets in real estate? Are there cultural, historical, or other reasons for this?
2. Are you surprised by the statistics? Why or why not?
3. What impact does the wealth gap have on the United States as a whole? How big a deal is it for you?
4. What can or should the United States as a nation do to decrease the wealth gap?
5. This article is mostly a presentation of evidence—lots of facts. What arguments about the wealth gap could you make using this evidence?

AUDIO REPORT

Pam Fessler is one of the many journalists inspired by the Pew report on pages 72–79. She studied that research and then wrote the article you are about to read. Fessler has over thirty years of experience as a journalist covering economic issues. A version of this two-part news analysis originally aired in Fall 2011 on National Public Radio; they then published the following version online. Notice that the paragraphs here are far shorter than in the other readings in this chapter. Pay attention to how the article sounds, and try reading it out loud yourself. *Important words and phrases have been italicized in this reading. Look up those you do not know, and write the definitions in your personal vocabulary list.*

practice it   **Pre-Reading**

What factors lead a person to financial success? Certainly, education is one important factor, as we have seen in the "Education Pays" chart. What other factors do you think are important for a person in finding and keeping a solid financial footing? Make a list, and compare lists with one or more classmates.

Making It in the U.S.: More Than Just Hard Work

Pam Fessler

PART 1

Here's a *startling* figure: The typical white family has twenty times the wealth of the median black family. That's the largest gap in twenty-five years. The recession widened the racial wealth gap, but experts say it's also due to deeply ingrained differences in things such as inheritance, home ownership, taxes, and even expectations.

WEALTH GAP GROWS, MEDIAN WEALTH, 1984–2007

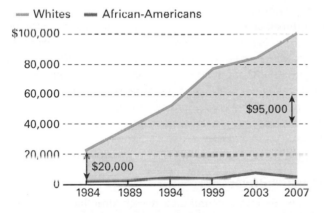

Notes: Figures do not include home equity. The data is based on more than 2,600 families tracked by the study's researchers, Thomas M. Shapiro, Tatjana Meschede and Laura Sullivan. The researchers published their findings in a brief, "The Racial Wealth Gap Increases Fourfold."

— Source: Institute on Assets and Social Policy, Brandeis University
Credit: Stephanie d'Otreppe

Take the example of two California women, Dametra Williams and Stephanie Upp, who aren't that different in many ways. Both were raised by single mothers who struggled financially. Both worked hard to get where they are today.

But how they describe basically the same thing about how they got to where they are today differs.

Williams is forty, black, and a single mother of one. She just started her own business.

"It's funny, the American dream is sort of *steeped* in this myth of 5 work hard, be self-sufficient and push yourself forward, pull yourself up by your *bootstraps*, that kind of thing. But much of the wealth in this country was not built on that, in no way, fashion or form," Williams says.

Upp, forty-three, is white, a mother of two and a part-time *consultant*.

"I think about the little things, like when I went to college. When I graduated, my mom had enough *resources* to give me her car so that I had a car to get to work so that I could earn money that I could then save to help put me into the next position," Upp says. "I could then save more money and have opportunities. So it wasn't like we had a lot, but there was enough. I didn't do it all by myself."

And that's the difference. Study after study shows that white families are more likely than blacks and Hispanics to enjoy certain economic advantages—even when their incomes are similar. Often it's the subtle things: help from Mom and Dad with a down payment on a home or college tuition, or a tax break on money passed from one generation to the next.

Tom Shapiro of Brandeis University has tracked hundreds of families for almost thirty years and says the gap *perpetuates* itself.

"The larger the amount of financial wealth a family starts with, the 10 more financial wealth it accumulated over that period of time," he says.

In other words, it's easier to get richer if you already are. Since blacks and Hispanics are less likely to have much wealth to begin with, they're less likely to have money to invest in the stepping-stones to success—a small business, college, or home.

Stephanie Upp: "A Richer Life"

Upp, her husband Ben Corson and their two children live in a small *bungalow* in Oakland. This family is well on its way to achieving the American dream. Corson works in software. Upp consults for *nonprofits*.

Upp credits her success, in part, to something that happened a long time ago. When her parents divorced, her mother insisted on keeping their home in suburban Kansas. They didn't have much money, but they had stability and good schools, where college was a given and expectations were high.

"In my mind, there wasn't a question that I would have a richer life than I grew up with both financially and then also in terms of experience," Upp says.

College led to graduate school, then a career, then Corson. They 15 started a family, and when they wanted to buy their first house, they got an unexpected boost.

"We were able to have a down payment for this house, thanks to my great-aunt," says Corson. "So that definitely helped us."

His great-aunt left the couple $60,000 in her will.

Shapiro says inheritance is a big factor when it comes to the racial wealth gap. White families are four times more likely than blacks to inherit. When they do, the median inheritance is ten times greater.

Now, Upp and Corson plan to *leverage* their house into a new and bigger one, which will mean better public schools.

Stephanie says they aren't rich by any means, but they have options.   20

Their six-year-old daughter, Clare, reads a poem from the Dr. Seuss book *Oh, the Places You'll Go* that is painted on the wall above her bed: "You have brains in your head, you have feet in your shoes, you can steer yourself any direction you choose."

Experts say choices and expectations can make all the difference.

Dametra Williams: Making Things Work

"When you don't have enough money to make any mistakes, the bottom line is you just don't, there's no room," Williams says.

Today, Williams thinks she finally has choices. Her home health-care business in Berkeley is getting off the ground. She beams when her eighteen-year-old daughter, Yvonne, talks about getting into Mount Holyoke for college.

"I applied to so many [schools]," Yvonne says.   25

Williams says Yvonne applied to about twenty-three or twenty-four schools. "And she was offered admission and scholarships to about eighteen of them, so I'm very, very proud," she says.

But it's been a tough journey. Only twelve years ago, Williams and her daughter were poor and homeless. She says that in her family, growing up in Texas, education wasn't a priority and college wasn't in the cards.

"My plan was to work and start my family," she says.

Unlike Upp's mother, Williams' didn't own a home. That's not uncommon among black and Hispanic families. In fact, about a third have no assets at all or are in debt, according to a recent study by the Pew Research Center. That's double the rate for white families. This means no *home equity* to draw upon and no *mortgage interest deduction* to ease the cost of housing. Williams knew when she left home at seventeen, she was on her own.

"There was no cushion for me to go back to, so the reality for me was   30 either make things work [or] be homeless," she says. "I remember my grandmother telling us we could do anything we wanted to do." But, she adds, she doesn't remember getting advice on how to do it.

Like inheritance, financial know-how is key to closing the racial wealth gap, says Stuart Butler of the Heritage Foundation. He says families that don't expect to climb the economic ladder often don't acquire the skills to do so. After decades of discrimination, he adds, blacks especially can be discouraged about their prospects.

"If somebody thinks they will not succeed, there's a high probability that they won't succeed. Because if they don't expect to go to college, if they don't expect to be *affluent*, they start doing things with that in mind," he says.

"A Formula for It"

At the urging of a school counselor, Williams attended the University of California at Berkeley, but she says she dropped out when she realized she didn't have the right skills. Instead, she started a family. When she and Yvonne's father split, though, her one income as a youth counselor wasn't enough. Williams and her daughter wound up homeless, then in public housing.

"It was really hard," Williams says.

But here's where her story takes a turn. Williams was poor but smart.   35 With the help of a housing authority savings program she eventually returned to college and got her degree.

She also got Yvonne into private schools through a special program for inner-city youth. A San Francisco nonprofit called EARN helped her save money for tutors and a business. Today, she thinks she might be breaking the cycle that has kept so many others in poverty.

"Families of color in particular are becoming much more knowledge-able and much more aware of how to create wealth here in America," she says. "I think there is a formula for it, and it's not work hard and do well. Most poor people work really hard."

Williams says she's still trying to figure out the formula and working hard to catch up. But she thinks that Yvonne at least is going into the world with the head start she never had.

PART 2

The gap in the wealth of white families and what's owned by blacks and Hispanics has widened in recent years. Researchers say it will widen even more unless steps are taken to break what's become a vicious cycle—the rich getting richer and the poor struggling to keep from falling further behind.

The city of San Francisco is taking one step to help even the playing   40 field. Children entering the city's kindergartens are getting their own college savings accounts.

"It's all about building *aspirations* in that child's mind," says City Treasurer Jose Cisneros.

The city will deposit $50 in each account—$100 for those students who get free and reduced-price lunches. Local nonprofits will match parents' contributions up to another $200.

The amounts are *modest*, Cisneros admits. But he says, in a city where many public school children are poor, it's more about the message than the money.

"When a child grows up and sees—'Oh, look at this, concrete evidence, a college savings account, my name on it. That must mean I'm going,'" he says. "And we wanted to bring that kind of success to San Francisco."

Right now, half the kindergarten classes are participating. Soon, it will be all of them.   45

Kindergarten to College: The Fine Print

Here, details about San Francisco's Kindergarten to College accounts:

Who Can Contribute?   The city will deposit $50 in each account, $100 for those students who get free and reduced-price lunches. After the initial deposit from the city, students and their parents and guardians may make contributions to the account for as long as the student is enrolled in a city public school. In some cases, nonprofits will also match contributions.

How Much?   Contributions to an account may not exceed $2,500 a year.

For What?   Withdrawals may only be made for tuition, fees, books, supplies, and equipment at private and public universities, community colleges and graduate and trade schools. Contributions not used after the student turns 25 will be returned to the student— except for that initial deposit. That goes back to the program.

—Source: The Kindergarten to College program

This program is part of an effort nationwide by government and nonprofit groups to narrow the racial wealth gap. The Pew Research Center recently found that the *median* white household has net *assets* worth 20 times that of the median black household and 18 times that of a Hispanic family—assets such as housing, savings, and investments, minus any debt.

Ben Mangan runs a nonprofit group in San Francisco called EARN, which helps low-income families save money for long-term investments, such as college, a home, or business. He says the racial wealth gap itself is *propelling* the economic divide.

"The fact is, communities of color have less of the dollars across the generations and so they're at a disadvantage in their ability to invest in the things that would allow them to get ahead," he says.

His group has helped people such as thirty-four-year-old Helena Edwards, who today lives in a three-bedroom condominium in the Bayview section of San Francisco. She bought the place about a year ago, after she, her partner, their daughter, a niece, and a nephew came home one day to find an *eviction* notice on their door.

"The apartment we was living at, the landlord went into *foreclosure*   50
and he didn't tell us," Edwards says.

First, she got the eviction delayed. Then, with the help of EARN, she started a matched savings account for a down payment on a home. The group also gave her financial advice. Edwards grew up in foster care, and no one really showed her how to handle money, let alone how to buy a house.

"Lot of stuff that I never knew about. Never. I don't even know anybody who owned a house but one person," she says.

Edwards learned how to have money automatically withheld from her paycheck to put into a savings account. And she got her favorite tip of all—something she calls a "credit card condom"—to help control debt.

"It's a little envelope you put over your credit card and you write your goal," she explains. "Every time you use that credit card, you had to pull it out of that sleeve. So you got to read, 'Do I need this, or do I need to save for a house?'"

Now that she has her house, Edwards says she can focus on other   55
things, such as finishing her college education.

Tom Shapiro of Brandeis University, who has studied the racial wealth gap extensively, says families that participate in these individual development accounts, as they're called, have shown promising results.

"Their foreclosure rates have been much lower. Their savings are much higher. Indicators around their children's education are much better," he says. "But we're talking about maybe thousands of families, not even tens of thousands in a state."

And there are millions who need help. These programs are also expensive, which makes them difficult to fund at a time when government at all levels is stretched for resources. San Francisco's Kindergarten to College accounts will cost the city about $500,000 a year.

Shapiro says it will take a lot more than that to narrow a gap that's so firmly *entrenched*. He thinks one solution might be tax breaks to encourage low-income families to save more. Shapiro says that might *offset* the many tax breaks today—on things such as estates and investments—that tend to favor those who already have wealth and help to widen the economic divide.

Stuart Butler of the Heritage Foundation says another way to encour-   60
age more savings by low-income families might be for employers to automatically enroll people in savings plans—for things such as 401(k) plans—instead of waiting for them to sign up, which they often don't do. Once enrolled, he says, people are more likely to keep saving.

practice it   Post-Reading

What tools, resources, or factors helped or limited Dametra Williams's and Stephanie Upp's ability to make their way in life? Add other specific ideas about each woman to a chart like the one shown here. Copy this chart into your notebook, or download a version of the chart from the e-Pages. Add rows to the chart as needed. (Go to **bedfordstmartins.com/readwriteconnect** and click on **Charts**.) One student's first entries are listed to help you get started.

COMPARING EVIDENCE

Dametra Williams's Resources	Stephanie Upp's Resources
Williams's mother rented, which meant that there was little safety net for Williams.	Upp's mother had a home in the suburbs and managed to hang onto it even through a divorce.

What conclusions, if any, can you draw from this comparison? These notes will be useful if you write an essay using this article as evidence.

COMPREHENSION QUESTIONS

1. What are the similarities and differences between Stephanie Upp, Dametra Williams, and Helena Edwards? What plans does each woman have? What resources, information, or tools has each used to reach her goals?

2. What role does inheritance play in the wealth gap?

3. What can help close the wealth gap?

4. What is EARN?

SUMMARY ACTIVITY

Write a brief summary in your notes of "Making It in the U.S.: More Than Just Hard Work." Be objective, even if you have strong feelings about the topic. Refer back to the steps for summary writing in Chapter 1 (pp. 30–31) if necessary.

VOCABULARY ACTIVITY

Add words from this article to your ongoing glossary of financial terms. Remember to write definitions in your own words.

DISCUSSION QUESTIONS

1. This article focuses on the stories of three women to help illustrate the information about the wealth gap. Is this strategy effective? Why or why not?

2. Aside from the stories about Upp, Williams, and Edwards, the article does not address other racial or ethnic groups in the discussion of the wealth gap. Is it important to include every racial or ethnic group in the examples? Why or why not?

3. How can financial literacy programs, such as EARN, influence the wealth gap?

4. How important is owning a home? What are the pros and cons of home ownership?

5. This text is based on the Pew study presented earlier in this chapter, but it puts personal faces on the data. Which type of article do you prefer? Which type do you find more persuasive? Why?

Working with Multiple Sources

When you grapple with many authors' ideas and try to figure out your own position, take a few minutes to collect and organize your thoughts. It's time well spent. Often, when you step back and record your thoughts in an organized fashion, you clarify your ideas, or new ideas emerge. You can begin by answering questions that bring out some of the central themes of the unit as a whole.

DISCUSSION QUESTIONS

1. What is financial literacy and why is it important? What might happen if more Americans were financially literate?
2. Now that you have read these texts, what do you believe is the relationship between money and personal happiness?
3. How do you determine where the line is between "enough" and "too much" money? Does drawing that line become easier or harder as you have more money?
4. How is it that we talk openly about the economy but are very private about our personal finances in America? What are the effects of the taboo on discussing money with family and friends?
5. Given the large and complicated nature of the global economy, what can or should an individual do about money and the economy? What responsibility does an individual have for his or her own financial health?
6. Read through the glossary you created for the articles in this unit. What key terms did you identify about financial literacy? What important themes do these key terms suggest? Compare your list to your classmates' lists, if possible.

CHARTING TO ORGANIZE IDEAS

One effective and efficient tool used by many successful students is a chart like the one on page 89. Transferring some of your best and most important observations about the texts from your annotations and class notes onto one well-organized chart will help you draw some conclusions about the articles and how they relate to one another. Copy this blank chart into your notebook or download the chart from the e-Pages, and then fill in your own ideas.
    Here's how it works:

1. Look at the chart to see how it is structured.
2. For each topic listed across the top, write down key points, quotes, and/or paraphrases from each article (refer to Chapter 1 for more on these topics). Think of the chart as a tool, not a test: You won't write the same amount in every box, and you might end up leaving some of them blank. That's fine.

3. Reread what you have written and think about what the authors might say to one another about each topic. Then, in the bottom row, record your thoughts and ideas on each topic. What do you think about the readings? With whom do you most agree? Why?

SYNTHESIS CHART

	Financial literacy	Factors that add to financial stability and/or wealth	Money in personal relationships	Wealth gap	Other
Holder and Meeks, "Teach Your Children the Building Blocks of Finance"					
Mellan, "Men, Women, and Money"					
Bureau of Labor Statistics, "Education Pays" (Chart)					
Schug and Hagedorn, "Milwaukee's Youth Enterprise Academy"					
Kochhar, Fry, and Taylor, "Wealth Gaps Rise to Record Highs between Whites, Blacks, and Hispanics"					
Fessler, "Making It in the U.S.: More Than Just Hard Work"					
My Thoughts					

Charts like this one serve many purposes, and as you move through your college classes, you will likely adapt chart making to various writing and studying situations. Sometimes, when you make such a chart, you begin to realize what the focus of your paper will be. Other times, making a chart helps you predict essay exam questions or otherwise study for a test. Essentially, charts prepare you to synthesize texts, which is a very high-level type of thinking. In later chapters, you'll get more practice with synthesis charts. For now, keep adding to your chart as you get ready to begin the essay-writing process.

Additional Online and Media Sources

The readings in this chapter may spark your thinking and leave you wanting more information, and possibly even a little personal financial help. In the e-Pages, you can read Shira Boss's article "Money Envy" and watch the PBS video "Digging Out of Debt." Go to **bedfordstmartins .com/readwriteconnect** and click on **e-Readings**. You might also want to consult the following online and media sources.

WEB RESOURCES

- **Bureau of Labor Statistics, www.bls.gov** This site provides current data on the U.S. labor market. The Occupational Outlook Handbook portion of the site presents data on employment and salaries in various professions.
- **CNN Money.com's Money 101 Lessons, http://money.cnn.com/ magazines/moneymag/money101/** This series of lessons gives a brief but comprehensive view of the major areas of financial planning.
- **Council for Economic Education, www.councilforeconed.org/** This comprehensive site about economic education includes reports, video presentations, games, and other materials. These resources will definitely be interesting to students who are also parents.
- **EconEdLink, www.econedlink.org/** This site is a subsidiary of the Council for Economic Education. It offers lesson plans on financial literacy for various K–12 grade levels. Although this site is directed at teachers, it provides an insight into how financial education is taught in the schools.
- **Federal Student Aid, http://studentaid.ed.gov/** This U.S. Department of Education Web site provides information on student aid.
- **FinAid! The Smart Student Guide to Financial Aid, www.finaid.org/** This site gives substantial information about resources to help pay for college and counsels students to beware of financial aid scams.
- **Jump$tart Coalition, www.jumpstart.org/** This site offers information about financial literacy for children and has a thorough handout on the K–12 standards for a financial literary program.
- *Planet Money*, **blogs and podcasts, www.npr.org/blogs/money/** Economics explained.
- **TED Talk: "Paradox of Choice," http://blog.ted.com/2006/09/26/ paradox_of_choi/** Sociologist Barry Schwartz talks about how too much choice makes us miserable.

- **U.S. Census, www.census.gov** The U.S. Census provides well-respected data on people's lives. Begin with the more reader-accessible reports on common questions and the "Highlights" sections, not the more difficult-to-interpret raw data.

RADIO & TELEVISION

- *Frontline*, **www.pbs.org/wgbh/pages/frontline/** *Frontline* episodes dealing with economics include *The Card Game, Inside the Meltdown, The Secret History of the Credit Card*, and *Is Wal-Mart Good for America?*
- *This American Life*, **episode 355, "Giant Pool of Money" (May 9, 2008)** This radio program on the Great Recession explains how the mortgage industry crisis developed, focusing on real people, including a man who went from being a bartender to being a mortgage broker of shoddy loans.

chapter review

Chapter 2 explains how to actively and critically read a text, annotating it to record your thoughts and reactions and to connect the material with your prior knowledge and experiences. These skills give you the foundation for analyzing and getting into conversation with a reading. This chapter also introduced you to a variety of texts on money, wealth, and financial literacy, which probably included much new vocabulary. In working through the texts, you are building a knowledge base.

To review this chapter, choose one or more of the following strategies:

1. Reread your writing and notes from the Practice It activities. Make a list of the ideas you generated while doing them.
2. The idea of reading "with the grain" or "against the grain" uses the metaphor of wood. Research working with wood grain and why it is important to paint or sand wood with the grain, and what happens when you go against the grain. How is this a good metaphor for reading with or against an author's ideas? Is it a useful metaphor? Why or why not? Write for five minutes about what it means to read with the grain and what it means to read against the grain.
3. If you skipped any activities, do them now as a way to deepen your understanding of the material.
4. Try to explain what you have learned to someone you know. Discuss the key concepts and give your own examples to illustrate those concepts.

3
Putting Ideas into Writing

in this chapter

- What Is an Essay?
- What Is the Writing Process?
- How Do You Pre-Write?
- What Is a Thesis?
- How Do You Support Your Ideas?
- How Do You Write a Rough Draft?

What Is an Essay, and How Do You Write One?

There are many names and labels for the different types of writing a student does in college. Depending on the classes you take, you might be asked to write paragraphs, essays, journals, summaries, research papers, or lab reports. These types of writing have one thing in common: Each is an attempt to connect to the reader, to share ideas. Good writing communicates ideas, makes a connection with the reader, and has a clear purpose. By carefully reading your assignment (also known as a "prompt") and listening and participating in class, you should have a good idea about the type of essay you have been assigned to write.

Your assignment should also get you thinking about two key issues you need to consider for any piece of writing: your audience and your purpose. In most college writing assignments, the assumed audience is "college-level readers," people who can read and understand a sophisticated essay but may not be experts in the particular topic and may not have read the books or articles referred to in the paper. The purpose of most college writing is to argue a point, to persuade the reader into adopting the writer's viewpoint.

LearningCurve
For extra practice in the skills covered in this chapter, visit **bedfordstmartins.com /readwriteconnect**.

To learn more about audience and purpose, see Chapter 6, Audience, Purpose, and Topic, on page 169.

THE ESSAY

The most common assignment you will be asked to write and read in college is the essay. The word *essay* itself can mean lots of different things. Generally, people use the term to mean a piece of nonfiction writing that focuses on a specific topic. Essays can be short or long. They can be personal and fun to read, or factual and dry. They may include a list of sources or not, be serious or not, be formal or not. For each college writing assignment you get, determine which type of essay is required and figure out the instructor's expectations. Instructors also give writing assignments that help you figure out your essay thesis, like lists, ideas, and short answers to questions. Just as pre-reading helps you comprehend readings, pre-writing activities prepare you for writing by generating ideas and getting you into the mind-set to write the assigned essay. So don't forget about all those smaller in-class and homework assignments your instructors may ask you to do. Look for the ways they are connected to the larger essay.

What does a college essay look like? This varies from course to course; for instance, sociology, biology, and English instructors have different expectations about what a paper should be. Your instructor will tell you about specific rules and expectations for writing in a specific discipline. In general, though, most college essays follow these guidelines:

- They have an introduction, body, and conclusion. This means they usually have at least three paragraphs, but often they are longer, especially when they involve research.
- They have a thesis statement or main idea, which is often an argument.

- They have one or more body paragraphs that focus on and develop a single idea or point.
- They require thought, planning, and revision.
- They require you to give credit when you use someone else's ideas.

THE WRITING PROCESS

So how do you write an essay? Although there is no magic formula, the process is fairly simple. It requires time and effort, but works like a charm: It's called "the writing process," and real writers do it every day when faced with a writing task. What is this thing called the writing process? First, let's talk about what it's not. It's not the stay-up-late-and-write-the-whole-paper-the-night-before-and-then-run-into-the-computer-lab-to-print-it-out-five-minutes-before-class method. Sorry. While that method may have worked for you sometimes in the past, it certainly never helped you produce your best work, and it definitely won't work in college, where the paper assignments get far more challenging. Think of it this way: Even if you are able to pull off the "write it the night before" approach with a short, three-page paper, that won't work when you have to write ten- and twenty-page papers later in your college career or papers that require more complex use of outside sources. Our advice? Learn and practice good reading and writing process skills now so that you will know how to do it when your paper assignments get longer.

The writing process is actually quite simple. It looks like this:

pre-writing ⟶ outlining/ ⟶ drafting/ ⟶ editing ⟶ proofreading
organizing   revising

You'll have plenty of practice in these stages throughout your course and college.

How to Read an Essay Assignment

Writing the college essay begins with understanding the assignment. Generally, essay prompts have three types of information:

1. Background information about the topic, including specifics on what you have read or studied
2. The question stem, which is the main part of the assignment prompt that tells exactly what you should write
3. Hints, guidelines, and expectations about length, number of sources, and other things your instructor wants you to include

These three elements won't always appear exactly in this order, so take your time and read the assignment carefully to sort them out. Sometimes the instructor gives a written assignment with just the question stem and then explains the background information and hints, guidelines, and expectations during class. Write down oral instructions so that you can refer to them later.

Since argument writing is the core of most college subjects, let's look at a typical argument essay assignment. While some writing prompts will not require you to respond to outside readings, as this one does, all assignments require you to understand a question stem, background information, and guidelines or expectations.

In the following example, the background information is yellow; the question stem is green and underlined; and hints, guidelines, and expectations are blue.

> Wealth Gap Essay: The Pew Research Report "Wealth Gaps Rise to Record Highs between Whites, Blacks, and Hispanics" offers data about the wealth gap in America that many people find disappointing. It shows that the economic downturn that began in 2008 "took a far greater toll on the wealth of minorities than whites." Pam Fessler's article "Making It in the U.S.: More Than Just Hard Work" puts a personal face on this data. What are some of the factors that create financial stability and/or wealth for Americans? Write an essay in which you identify what you think are the most important factors that create wealth and financial stability and explain how and why they are important in helping Americans achieve financial stability. Refer to at least three texts from the unit, and use at least one quotation from each article. Final drafts must be three to four pages, typed and double-spaced.

How do you know the yellow-highlighted text is background information? It states facts about the articles that no one could really argue against. How do you know the underlined green part is the question stem? (It doesn't have a question mark, unfortunately, and sometimes sentences that do aren't even the question stem, so watch out for that!) You'll know it's the question stem because it outlines the specific task that the essay requires you to do. In this case, there are two tasks:

1. Identify the most important factors that create wealth and financial stability.
2. Explain why they are important.

The blue-shaded section, which offers hints, guidelines, and expectations, reminds the student to use quotations as evidence. The second sentence shaded in blue explains length expectations.

Take a look at those two main tasks again. Words like *identify* and *explain* each require a specific type of response, so you need to do both. The chart on page 96 provides a list of words commonly used in writing assignments.

WORDS TO LOOK FOR IN WRITING ASSIGNMENTS

Word	Means in plain English . . .
analyze; interpret	explain what you think is going on and why
anecdote	a little story used to support or explain a point
argue; make an argument	take a stance and defend it, giving evidence to support your opinion; also note counterarguments
compare	describe the similarities
contrast	describe the differences
compare and contrast	describe the similarities and differences
counterargument	the opposite or other side of an argument
describe in detail	use vivid language and lots of specific examples so the reader can picture what you are saying
evidence	quotes and paraphrases, usually from course readings, that help your reader understand why you believe what you do
explain	give the meaning of something, usually answering some "why" question
narrative	a story
paraphrase	ideas or facts from a source that you put in your own words and also cite properly
quotation	exact words taken directly from a source and properly cited
summarize	give an overview of an event or text but do not comment on it
support your ideas	provide quotes, paraphrases, and/or other evidence to explain why you believe what you believe
thesis	the main point or claim of your essay

e For more on interpreting essay assignments see the Managing Your Time chapter in your e-Pages. Go to **bedfordstmartins.com /readwriteconnect** and click on **e-Chapters**.

Essay Writing Time Management

Once you understand writing as a process, you will realize that creating a good workflow and schedule is part of a writer's job. Organizing a big project—whether it's an essay or term paper for a college course or a project at work—requires you to get a sense of all the steps involved, how long each step will take, and the most logical order for the steps. Not budgeting enough time to do your best at each step in the writing process can lead to extra stress, "writer's block," difficulty coming up with enough to say, and poor proofreading. However, when you plan your time wisely so that you have the right amount of time to complete each step, you will find the writing process much more enjoyable.

A time-management chart like the one in the following Practice It activity will help you plan and manage the essay-writing process. Keep track of the amount of time you spend on each part of the writing process. Consult your calendar to schedule when you will do each part of the process and estimate how much time you think each step will take.

practice it   Make a Schedule

Copy the following chart into your notebook, or download a version from the e-Pages. (Go to **bedfordstmartins.com/readwriteconnect** and click on **Charts**.) Right now, fill in the first two columns of this chart. If your assignment does not require you to respond to readings, start with the fourth row down, pre-writing. After you finish your essay, return to this chart and complete the last column. Recording how much time you spent on each task and a few reflections on your process helps you accurately estimate the time needed for the next essay.

ESSAY WRITING TIME MANAGEMENT CHART 1

Task	Planned day to complete	Estimated time to complete	Actual time to complete
Reading and annotating the articles in Chapter 2	Wednesday by noon	4 hours	6 hours
Organizing thoughts about the articles in Chapter 2			
Reading and understanding the essay prompt			
Pre-writing			
Thesis development			
Outlining			
Generating support and evidence			

continued ❯

Task	Planned day to complete	Estimated time to complete	Actual time to complete
Writing topic sentences			
Writing rough, rough draft			
Adding an introduction and conclusion			

your project   Analyze Your Essay Assignment

Step 1: Take a few minutes to analyze the assignment you have selected or your instructor has assigned. Label or use different colored highlighters to mark the background information, the question stem, and any hints, guidelines, or expectations. Make a note of anything you don't understand so you can ask for clarification.

Step 2: What exactly are you being asked to do? Rewrite the question stem in your own words, breaking it down into parts if necessary as in the list following the highlighted example (p. 95). Note the specific "question words" included in the prompt.

Step 3: Make a quick list of the requirements of the essay. For example, how long should it be? Should it include support from readings? If so, how many readings? Is there a rough draft due first? Add all essay-related due dates to your calendar.

Pre-Writing for Your Essay

Pre-writing is a broad term that applies to all the thinking, doodling, sketching, writing, and discussing that you do before you actually sit down to write the first rough draft. Some people prefer the term "brainstorming" for this kind of work. Many writers enjoy the pre-writing stage because it allows them to explore various creative ideas without having to worry about being perfect. Pre-writing may be fun, but it's also a serious and helpful stage of the writing process. Students in a hurry who think they can skip pre-writing usually end up wasting lots of time later on, because they didn't prepare well enough to start writing. If you spend too much time staring at a blank piece of paper or blank screen, or believe you suffer from "writer's block," or feel you can never meet the length requirement for assignments, then the problem is most likely that you didn't do enough pre-writing.

Often, you have read about your topic already, before you start your writing assignment. Remember that the reading and writing activities you did while reading in Chapters 1 and 2 are also a sort of pre-writing. They prepared you to formulate your own ideas about the topic. It is important to make those thoughts conscious, to put them on paper through pre-writing.

Literally hundreds of pre-writing techniques and warm-up exercises exist. Some writers pre-write by talking into a recorder as they kick around ideas. Others draw extensive diagrams and charts. Some writers talk about their topic with friends and experts, and then sit down and their ideas just flow. For now, we'll focus on two strategies: freewriting and listing.

For demonstrations of many pre-writing techniques, see Chapter 9, Pre-Writing, on page 214.

FREEWRITING

Freewriting is exactly what it sounds like: writing freely. It's easy to do as long as you don't think of it as having to be perfect. Just take out a piece of paper and write anything that comes to mind about your topic. Start writing, and write for at least five minutes without stopping. Do not tell yourself that an idea isn't interesting enough or clear enough to write down. Just write it anyway. Freewriting can include examples, bits of evidence, points you want to make, or even questions you have.

Here's a sample of a piece of freewriting by a college student named Thalia, who is responding to the prompt on page 95.

> The major factors that create wealth and stability, I think they are to own a home. A lot of people want to own home, because that offers stability instead of an apartment, because an apratment offers leases for depending how many months or years the owner wants you to live there. So that creates instability, because you're always moving around. Especially if you have kids, because then they would grow up with that instability, and that creates more instability. Another factor is owning a car, because with a car you can go anywhere you want. You will have more freedom to do whatever you want and go to wherever place you want, without asking for permission or money to anyone. Another factor could be education. Having an education can give you wealth and stability, because you're studying to get a living. To have a carreer that would give you and your family stability in the future.

As you can see, this piece of freewriting reflects Thalia's personal reactions to the material. Also, she didn't worry about spelling, punctuation, or grammar. She just wrote her ideas down as quickly as they came to her. It can take a while to get started, but once you relax and let yourself just write, the ideas usually flow. Give it at least five minutes, and if you can't think of anything to say, write anything you know about the topic, even if it seems really obvious. Getting the "obvious" ideas down on paper often leads you to your more original ideas. (Plus, what's "obvious" to you is often quite interesting and not at all obvious to others—you just don't realize it.)

Once you finish freewriting, reread your work, and locate one or two gems. A gem does not have to be a completed thought. Usually, it's a theme or the start of an idea that you recognize as worth developing. In the above freewrite, the student has a couple of good examples, but the point about education that she ends with seems most relevant. Now she can take that idea and do another, more focused five-minute freewrite on it and see where it leads. Often, repeating these freewriting steps two or three times puts into words the focus of your essay. That's pretty good for fifteen to twenty minutes of work!

LISTING

Listing is just that: making a list of all the ideas, thoughts, and examples that come to mind about your topic. It's different from freewriting because rather than writing sentences or a paragraph, you just jot down a few words or phrases for your ideas. Listing after you have already done some freewriting helps you focus the ideas you are generating and begin to shape, in a rough form, your essay structure.

After doing her freewriting, Thalia determined that the Bureau of Labor Statistics' "Education Pays" chart, Fessler's "Making It in the U.S.: More Than Just Hard Work," and Holder and Meeks's "Teach Your Children the Building Blocks of Finance" were most relevant to how she wanted to approach the essay assignment. She made a list that looked like this:

community that has good schools and homes

inheritance

whether or not you have money—how much money you start with

debt

money habits

financial literacy

education

college degree

Then she paged through her annotations of the articles, her pre-reading and post-reading writing about the articles, and her class notes from the days the articles were discussed. As she did that, she listed the points that seemed most relevant to her essay topic, like this:

"Education Pays" chart

You're likely to be successful if you have a bachelor's degree—you'll be average at least

Doctoral degree you're the most successful

No high school diploma you're likely to be unemployed

I better work toward my doctoral degree

So far I don't even have enough education to be average

"Making It in the U.S.: More Than Just Hard Work"

It's good to have nonprofit groups that help you save and at the same time teach you about money

The typical white family has 20 times the median wealth of a black family

Inheritance is a big factor when it comes to the wealth gap

Experts say that choices and expectations can make all the difference

Like inheritance, financial know-how is key to closing the racial wealth gap

Kindergarteners are getting their own college savings accounts

EARN is a nonprofit group that helps families save money for long-term investments

"Teach Your Children the Building Blocks of Finance"

It is important to teach children about money

Open savings accounts for children

Show them how to pay bills

Expose them to investing

Have financial meetings

Once you've created a list like Thalia's, take a short break and then examine your list. You might want to share it with a friend for some brief comments. If you're satisfied you have enough ideas, move on to the next step in the writing process: developing a thesis.

your project   Pre-Writing

If you did the activities in Chapter 2, have your notes handy. Feel free to look through them at any point in the process.

Step 1: Do a five-minute freewrite on your essay assignment. Then stop and read what you have written. Is there one gem or good idea? Underline it or summarize it in a new sentence. If your essay prompt has more than one part, try doing a separate freewrite for each part.

Step 2: Reread your essay prompt and then reread that good idea from your first freewrite. Write that idea at the top of another blank page. Now freewrite for five more minutes, this time making more of an effort to stay focused on the prompt and your gem or good idea.

Step 3: Next, try listing. Make a quick list of ideas you think you want to include in your essay. Then skim through the articles and your annotations on them, making lists of important terms,

continued ⊚

ideas, or quotes to include in your paper. If you include a quote, write down the page number so you don't have to waste time tracking it down again later.

Step 4: Now, return to your essay prompt. Reread it, with your free-write and list on your desk. Are you developing some good ideas to begin the assignment? If so, great! Move on to the next section on thesis statements. If not, spend more time pre-writing, either by yourself or in consultation with classmates or your instructor.

Thesis Statements

Developing your own point of view, argument, or thesis for the essay grows out of your pre-writing activities. Most writers significantly revise their thesis statement several times throughout the writing process, so don't get stuck in your writing if you can't get your thesis statement perfect early in the process. Write a good "working" thesis, and know that you will revise it as you go.

What, exactly, is a thesis statement? The thesis is the central claim of your essay. It's the overall point you want to make. The thesis statement is the *answer* to the *question* posed by the assignment. This is why properly reading the prompt and identifying the question stem helps so much in writing a good thesis. For instance, suppose this is the question stem:

> How would you describe a financially stable middle-class standard of living where you live? What kind of lifestyle and assets does a person who is considered "financially stable" usually have?

The answer, in its most rough form, might be something like this:

> A financially stable middle-class standard of living in [name of your city] includes _____ and _____, and middle-class people usually are able to _____.

Of course, the details are missing at this point, but formulating such a statement helps you get a handle on what you're trying to say. Then you'll refine and improve your statement as you write the essay drafts. The thesis is usually one sentence long in early college papers, though as you take on longer and more complicated writing projects, your thesis statements may grow too.

In general, good thesis statements:

- Respond directly to the assignment.
- Make claims about the topic, and are not merely restatements of the topic.

- Develop a complete idea about what the writer believes about the topic as well as why he or she believes it.
- Are written as statements, not questions.
- Are clearly worded.
- Are not too broad or too narrow.
- Do not include words like "I," "we," or "this essay will. . . ."

Let's look again at our sample student's assignment to see how she begins to write her thesis. Here's the prompt. (To see the different parts of the assignment identified, return to p. 95.)

> Wealth Gap Essay: The Pew Research Report "Wealth Gaps Rise to Record Highs between Whites, Blacks, and Hispanics" offers data about the wealth gap in America that many people find disappointing. It shows that the economic downturn that began in 2008 "took a far greater toll on the wealth of minorities than whites." Pam Fessler's article "Making It in the U.S.: More Than Just Hard Work" puts a personal face on this data. What are some of the factors that create financial stability and/or wealth for Americans? Write an essay in which you identify what you think are the most important factors that create wealth and financial stability and explain how and why they are important in helping Americans achieve financial stability. Refer to at least three texts from the unit, and use at least one quotation from each article. Final drafts must be three to four pages, typed and double-spaced.

Thalia's first attempt at a thesis, based on her previous brainstorming, began by breaking down the question stem:

What are all the possible factors that help create wealth and financial stability?

money habits

education

inheritance

family discussions

financial literacy

Which two are most important?

education

financial literacy

Based on this thought process, the first draft of Thalia's thesis might look something like this:

The key to create financial stability in America is to have a good education and good financial literacy.

This is a good start. However, the thesis should include the specific reasons why these are the most important factors, so this needs to be added to the thesis.

What are Thalia's reasons?
Our bad economy hurts people without an education more.
People who start off life with less money still want to provide their children with
    good financial security.

Now, Thalia revises the thesis, adding those new ideas. The revised working thesis looks like this:

The key to create financial stability in America is to have a good education and good
financial literacy, because in today's bad economy, people without good money
habits can't compete with people who start off life with more money.

Again, Thalia will probably continue to revise the thesis throughout the writing process, but this working thesis provides a solid enough foundation to begin outlining the body of the essay.

your project   Brainstorm to Create Your Thesis

An effective way to begin putting a thesis together is to simply answer the questions of the assignment. Try these steps in your notebook:

Step 1: Write down the question stem, either in your own words or as it appears in your prompt.
Step 2: Break the stem down into its specific parts and transform them into questions.
Step 3: Answer each question in one sentence.
Step 4: Look over your answers and think in which direction you would most like to go with the essay. Write the idea up in one or two complete sentences. That's your working thesis.

For more help developing a thesis, see Chapter 10, Thesis and Main Idea, page 223.

practice it   Evaluate Working Thesis Statements

Evaluate the following three working thesis statements for the essay assignment on page 95.

• This essay will explain how not having financial know-how about money can cause problems.
• I think that learning how to save money at a young age can lead to financial stability.
• Is education really the answer to financial instability?

For each sample thesis, answer the following questions:

1. What works?
2. What is missing or unclear?
3. How can the thesis be revised?

Finally, rewrite each thesis statements as necessary until you feel like it gives a clear idea of where the essay will go.

Here are one student's answers for a different thesis statement.

Thesis: Living in a community that has programs can lead to building wealth.

1. What works?
The thesis is on the topic of wealth and financial stability, and it's a claim.

2. What is missing or unclear?
It isn't clear which kinds of programs help build wealth. The thesis also doesn't mention financial stability. Is it only going to talk about wealth? What about people who don't want to be "wealthy" but at least want financial stability?

3. How can the thesis be revised?
Living in a community that has financial literacy programs and job-training programs can lead to developing financial stability and even to building wealth.

Outlining Your Ideas

Once you have a working thesis, you can make a rough or sketch outline to help you sort out your ideas. Writers organize their ideas in many different ways.

Sketch out a rough outline to clarify and develop your ideas as you organize them. The method seems simple at first, but it requires pretty intense thinking, so be prepared to spend some time on it. Here are the steps:

STEP 1: Jot down ideas.   Looking over your pre-writing, jot down a list of all the ideas you think you will cover in your essay. Do not worry about the order of ideas now. Just make a list of phrases about the ideas you believe you want to include. It might look like this:

Education

- inheritance that helps you start your life with a good set of money
- family discussions that give you background information about money and good money habits

TIP
In the early stages of writing, formal outlines with Roman numerals and capital letters are difficult to create because you won't know all the points and examples of your essay until you do more prep work. So start with a rough outline: At this stage of the writing process, messy is best.

STEP 2: Now, examine that list.   What does each item really mean? Have you explained your meaning clearly and specifically enough? Which points are related? Clarify each point, adding details, combining ideas if necessary, or breaking one idea into two or more if necessary. This is the part that takes significant time and thought, so don't rush. By the time you finish, your rough list might look like this:

> money habits
> family discussion
> high level of education
> inheritance

STEP 3: Order Your Points.   Now, put the ideas in order. The order of your ideas depends on your overall thesis. Sometimes, it makes sense to begin with background or context and then move on to ideas that explain and prove your thesis. Other times, you might begin with the simpler points and then move on to more complex ones. In other cases, the assignment itself suggests a logical order: Your prompt may ask for a cause-and-effect essay, or one that moves from problem to solution, or from past to present. The main rule of thumb is that your points should be in whatever order makes the most sense to support your thesis.

For more on outlining, see Chapter 13, Essay Organization and Outlining, page 267.

your project   Group Activity to Organize Ideas

Sometimes two, or three, or four heads are better than one. In the case of organizing ideas, additional minds (and eyes) can help you see possible patterns of organization. For this activity, you need several index cards or small pieces of paper.

Step 1: Have each group member write his or her thesis on one card and label it "thesis."

Step 2: Then each group member writes each point of his or her rough outline on a separate card. Spread one person's cards out on the desk. Discuss different ways to put the cards in order, moving them around as you do. If you decide that a new idea needs to be added, or that two ideas should be combined, make new cards that show this. (If some cards have evidence instead of ideas, note that and put them aside. The author of the cards should keep those ideas handy for a later stage of the writing process: generating support for the thesis.)

Step 3: When the group arrives at an order of points that works well, the author of the cards writes the points down in that order on his or her paper.

Step 4: Repeat with the other group members.

Generating Evidence to Support Your Thesis

Now that you have a working thesis and some idea of the points you intend to include in your paper, you need examples and evidence to support your thesis and points. Review your earlier pre-writing, gather quotes and paraphrases from the readings, and consider new ideas that no doubt emerged while you were writing your working thesis and sketching out a rough order for your points. As you search for evidence, bear in mind your audience. For instance, if you write to a college-level audience, your readers may be more convinced by facts and figures, whereas if you write to a general audience or a younger audience, your readers might find personal anecdotes more compelling. A mixture of types of evidence often appeals most to readers. Your instructors will likely be impressed if you handle a variety of types of sources in an essay, as long as you do enough analysis of the evidence you present.

practice it   Finding Evidence and Connecting It to Claims

Look back at the "Education Pays" chart (p. 59). This chart offers many pieces of evidence, but you have to interpret the chart to find the evidence. Pull three statistics out of the chart and paraphrase them so that they can be included in an essay. Then write down the point that each of these paraphrases might support.

your project   Gather Quotations and Paraphrases

Complete this activity on a computer if you can, so you won't have to recopy quotations and paraphrases. To begin, type up the outline you created in the previous stage of the writing process. Gather your notes and books, and give yourself plenty of time and space for this task. Slowly work your way through the articles you have read, your pre-writing, and any other notes. Each time you find a piece of evidence that interests you—a quotation, paraphrase, fact, example, observation, or anecdote— ask yourself why it is interesting, to whom it might be convincing, and where you could put it in your paper. If you think you might use it in your essay, type up the information under the relevant point, being sure to include the source and page number so that you don't have to find it again later. For now, just insert the author's last name and the page number in parentheses, like this: (Mellan 00). When you are finished, print the document out and review all the material you have so far.

Topic Sentences

Each paragraph should develop one idea or make one clear point in support of the thesis. This idea or clear point is stated by the paragraph's topic sentence. You can think of a topic sentence like a mini-thesis; it is usually a claim and tells the reader what to expect of the paragraph. Topic sentences are important because they help guide the reader through your essay.

A topic sentence states two things:

1. The topic of the paragraph
2. The point the paragraph will make about the topic in support of the thesis

In academic writing, topic sentences are generally the first sentence of each paragraph so they indicate to the reader what point the paragraph will make. In professional writing (articles, stories, essays), topic sentences may be located in the beginning, middle, or even the end of the paragraph. In professional writing, the topic sentence sometimes isn't even in the paragraph at all—it's implied. For college writing, however, the topic sentence should usually start the paragraph.

For more on topic sentences, see Chapter 12, Topic Sentences and Paragraphs, on page 253.

FINDING TOPIC SENTENCES

Because the topic sentences in a piece of writing are usually clear statements of the major claims of that writing, they help you understand the reading. By practicing finding and evaluating topic sentences you also improve your writing skills: By seeing examples of various ways to write topic sentences you learn through experience what makes a good, clear topic sentence.

---

practice it   Finding Topic Sentences

Take a look at the following excerpt from Pam Fessler's article "Making It in the U.S.: More Than Just Hard Work" (pp. 81–86). This is the middle portion of the text. When you first saw the article in Chapter 2, it was broken down into many short paragraphs. It was published that way to mimic the way it was read out loud on the radio. Here all the paragraph breaks are removed. Your task is to find the topic sentences and re-paragraph this portion of the text. Hint: You are likely to find about three topic sentences. Remember that topic sentences are often, but not always, the first sentence in the paragraph.

Step 1: Read the excerpted text, underlining main points / topic sentences.

Step 2: Insert the paragraph symbol (¶) where you would add a paragraph break.

Step 3: Evaluate the topic sentences you have identified:

   a. Do they cover the material from the entire paragraph?
   b. Are they clearly written?

Feel free to change your underlining if you find a sentence that works better as the topic sentence.

Step 4: Reread just the topic sentences you have identified, skipping the rest of the sentences in the paragraph. Do they make sense? Do the topic sentences present a coherent map of the ideas in the excerpt?

The Excerpt

Upp, her husband Ben Corson, and their two children live in a small bungalow in Oakland. This family is well on its way to achieving the American dream. Corson works in software. Upp consults for nonprofits. Upp credits her success, in part, to something that happened a long time ago. When her parents divorced, her mother insisted on keeping their home in suburban Kansas. They didn't have much money, but they had stability and good schools, where college was a given and expectations were high. "In my mind, there wasn't a question that I would have a richer life than I grew up with both financially and then also in terms of experience," Upp says. College led to graduate school, then a career, then Corson. They started a family, and when they wanted to buy their first house, they got an unexpected boost. "We were able to have a down payment for this house, thanks to my great-aunt," says Corson. "So that definitely helped us." His great-aunt left the couple $60,000 in her will. Shapiro says inheritance is a big factor when it comes to the racial wealth gap. White families are four times more likely than blacks to inherit. When they do, the median inheritance is 10 times greater. Now, Upp and Corson plan to leverage their house into a new and bigger one, which will mean better public schools. Stephanie says they aren't rich by any means, but they have options. Their six-year-old daughter, Clare, reads a poem from the Dr. Seuss book *Oh, the Places You'll Go* that is painted on the wall above her bed: "You have brains in your head, you have feet in your shoes, you can steer yourself any direction you choose." Experts say choices and expectations can make all the difference. "When you don't have enough money to make any mistakes, the bottom line is you just don't, there's no room," Williams says. Today, Williams thinks she finally has choices. Her home health-care business in Berkeley is getting off the ground. She beams when her eighteen-year-old daughter, Yvonne, talks about getting into Mount Holyoke for college. "I applied to so many [schools]," Yvonne says. Williams says Yvonne applied to about twenty-three or twenty-four schools. "And she was offered admission and scholarships to about eighteen of them, so I'm very, very proud," she says.

WRITING TOPIC SENTENCES

Now it's time to write your own topic sentences for your essay. Take your outline, which lists the topic of each paragraph and some evidence under each bullet point. Make each topic into a complete thought by asking yourself: What point do I want to make about that topic? Answer in just one sentence. Check that the point you made supports the thesis and matches the evidence you have collected so far. Each sentence will then serve as the topic sentence of one paragraph of your essay.

Sounds simple, right? To be honest, it's easier said than done. Sometimes, when you try to write up your sentences, they come out easily and you feel confident about your work. Other times, you struggle and have to go back to the brainstorming stages to figure out exactly what you are trying to say. That's fine. It happens to all writers. Don't forget to adopt the growth mind-set. If you expect struggles to be part of the learning process, you are less likely to give up when you encounter difficulties.

A few hints will help you get through this tricky stage of the writing process. First, think about the key terms of your essay, which may even be words from the assignment. Try to use those key terms in your topic sentences. For instance, if the prompt asks what factors lead to wealth and financial stability, the terms *factors*, *wealth*, and *financial stability* will likely show up in one or more of your topic sentences.

Here's Thalia's thinking process in getting from a list to topic sentences. She started with this list of topics for the body paragraphs:

money habits

family discussion

high level of education

inheritance

Then she wrote up a rough topic sentence for each point:

In order for people in America to be financially stable, people need to learn to have good money habits.

Another key for people to be financially stable is to have family discussions about how money works.

Having a high level of education is a must when it comes to having good financial stability.

Another key that can help America achieve a high level of education in order to have financial stability is inheritance.

These topic sentences are not set in stone, but they are a good start. Thalia can continue to revise them as she moves through the writing process.

Drafting a Rough Essay

You spent a serious chunk of time pre-writing; you have a focused topic, a working thesis, and some decent topic sentences; and you feel good enough about your outline to start writing. How do you write that first draft? One. Word. At. A. Time. Seriously, the drafting stage is the most overrated stage of the writing process. Most people think of that first draft as the most important part of writing, when really it's probably the least important part. So don't sweat it; just get writing. You'll be impressed with what you have, once you start putting it all together.

TIP

Write out or print out your thesis and tape it to the top of your computer screen so you have it clearly in view as you write. This little reminder will help you stay focused as you draft the body paragraphs.

your project   The Quick Draft

Gather your working thesis, topic sentences, and notes about what support you plan to use. Also, print out all your notes and put them on the desk beside you so you can easily look at them while you write.

Start writing the beginning of the essay. Don't worry about an introduction; just start with your first point. Keep writing, sticking to your outline as much as possible. Don't worry about making every sentence perfect yet. Don't worry about spelling or other things that might make you stop writing. Just keep putting sentences down. If you get stuck, feel free to put in a placeholder note to yourself like:

Say more here about how hard it is to teach financial literacy to teenagers

or:

Need a good example for this idea

Jot down a note to yourself about what you still need in this part of your essay and keep writing. You can come back to it later.

When you think you are finished, give yourself a pat on the back! Then save your document (in more than one place and with a sensible name, like "Money Essay 1") and print it out. If you are writing by hand, now is a good time to type up your draft; then save and print the document.

Read what you have written. Does it really feel like a complete rough draft? Have you answered all parts of the prompt (even in a rough form)? Add any information that needs to be added. Don't cut too much yet. You can always cut later. If you do delete large amounts, put the deleted material into a "junk" file that has the same document name (for example, "Money Essay 1 Junk"), just in case you need it later.

For additional drafting strategies, see Chapter 14, Drafting, page 286.

Introductions and Conclusions

Introductions set the tone for your essay right away, and conclusions leave a lasting impression. Strong writers spend considerable time thinking about an essay's introduction and conclusion. Possibly you wrote a decent introduction and conclusion when you did the quick rough draft, but if you're like most college students, you didn't know quite what to include in the introduction, and so you left it rather short, and perhaps you didn't write a conclusion at all yet.

For now, think of the introduction as the place to draw in the reader, explain the topic, give readers background information they need, and state the thesis. For instance, if you are writing about two articles, the introduction should provide the full titles of the articles, the authors' full names, a one- to two-sentence summary of each article, and perhaps some information about where and when they were published. In short, the introduction should include the following things:

- One or two sentences that "hook" your reader and get him or her interested in your topic. The hook could be a fact or quote that really stands out or gets to the heart of the issue.
- A statement about the focused topic of the essay
- Background information on your topic so your reader knows a bit about the context of your essay
- Your thesis statement

Here's a sample introduction for the paper our student writer, Thalia, is drafting. Key components of the paragraph are coded as follows: The hook is green; background information is yellow; the topic is blue; the thesis is orange.

> Money is something that is really important to everyone, especially in today's economy, where everyone needs to save to have future financial stability. For many people, money is never just money, it is a tool that accomplishes many of life's goals, like going to college, open up a business, go on a trip, buy a car, buy a house, and so on. Today to have a good financial stability is very important, because parents want to leave their children with good financial security, but for some parents it's hard to achieve this goal, because they don't have the same privileges that some other parents have. The key to create financial stability in America is to have a good education and good financial literacy, because in today's bad economy, people without good money habits can't compete with people who start off life with more money.

Thalia's introduction provides adequate background information and states the topic, but she will probably decide later to revise the hook and thesis.

The conclusion, usually one-paragraph long, should sum up the paper and leave the reader with some last thoughts. In summing up the paper, think of the main points you covered in your body paragraphs. Sum up each one along with your thesis. When offering your final thoughts on the essay, think about whether you learned something, want to make a recommendation, or have a prediction or suggestion for your reader. Conclusions can refer back to an idea sparked in the introduction, particularly if the introduction was especially creative in getting the reader's attention. Here is Thalia's sample, with parts that sum up the main points noted in blue and those that offer final thoughts highlighted in green:

> In order to create financial stability in America is to have a good education and good financial literacy, because otherwise we won't make it in today's economy and future economy, which by today it is still a disaster that will take us years to overcome. Money is a big discussion in all countries, not only in America so that's why learning to have good money habits, to have family discussions about money, having a good education and having an inheritance can help you achieve financial stability for the future since we still don't know what the future holds for us It's better to be well-informed and have money saved than to have nothing and regret it later on.

Like many first draft conclusions, Thalia's is very rough. She will certainly revise it later.

Evaluating a text's introductory and concluding paragraphs serves as a useful strategy for reading comprehension because those paragraphs usually state and restate the thesis, or main point, of the reading. Looking at how an author introduces and concludes a reading also provides an example of how to write an introduction and conclusion. These examples can serve as models for you in creating your own introductions and conclusions.

practice it   Evaluating the Introduction and Conclusion

Reread the introductory paragraph and the two concluding paragraphs to Olivia Mellan's article "Men, Women, and Money," which are reprinted here. Follow the steps below to evaluate the paragraphs in a group or individually.

Step 1: Read over the introduction and conclusion two or three times.
Step 2: Find and label each of the major parts of the introduction:

- The hook / attention grabber
- The statement of the article's topic

continued ❯

- The background information a reader might need to know to read the article
- The thesis or main point

Step 3: Find and label in the conclusion the sentences that do each of the following:

- Sum up the main ideas of the article
- Give the reader some final thoughts to consider or something they can do with the information that has been presented

Step 4: Evaluate the effectiveness of the introduction. Does it make you want to read the article? Why or why not? Discuss.

Step 5: Evaluate the effectiveness of the conclusion. Does it make the article feel finished, complete, and meaningful? Why or why not? Discuss.

Mellan's Introductory Paragraph

For most people, money is never just money, a tool to accomplish some of life's goals. It is love, power, happiness, security, control, dependency, independence, freedom, and more. Money is so loaded a symbol that to unload it—and I believe it must be unloaded to live in a fully rational and balanced relationship to money—reaches deep into the human psyche. Usually, when the button of money is pressed, deeper issues emerge that have long been neglected. As a result, money matters are a perfect vehicle for awareness and growth.

Mellan's Concluding Paragraphs

Money issues are different from other problems in relationships. They're harder to talk about and harder to resolve because of our extensive cultural conditioning. The most important thing in couples communication is empathy, or putting yourself in your partner's place. It is almost always more important to be heard and understood than to have a partner agree with what you say.

Spouses who start talking genuinely about what they like about each other's money style create an atmosphere of safety and nondefensiveness. Once such a way of talking about money is established and once couples understand the positive intent of the partner, they can then work out a solution to almost any problem, a solution that best fits their own unique needs.

Note: Mellan's article was originally published in a magazine, where paragraphs are typically short so readers' eyes can follow along with the long, thin text columns. What might have been one longer concluding paragraph in a book or essay is therefore broken into two shorter paragraphs for the magazine. Both paragraphs are shown here, since together they serve as the conclusion.

Finishing the Rough Draft

You have come a long way from the beginning of this chapter, and you probably have a solid rough draft of your essay. Read it over a few more times, make any changes you need to, and print it out. As you move into the revision stages, you will make significant changes to it, but hopefully you budgeted your time well so that you can take a short break. A few days or even hours away from the essay can give you some perspective.

At this point, if you haven't already done so, go back to the Essay Writing Time-Management chart you made for the Practice It activity on page 97 and fill in the last column. What might you do to tweak your time management next time around? Make a note of that before you move on to Chapter 4, Revising, Editing, and Proofreading.

Essay Assignments for Money, Wealth, and Financial Literacy Unit

To give you an idea of the kinds of assignments you might see in college, the following prompts show some possible essay questions that might be asked in response to the readings on financial literacy in Chapter 2.

Financial Literacy Essay:

"Teach Your Children the Building Blocks of Finance" by Sherie Holder and Kenneth Meeks and "Milwaukee's Youth Enterprise Academy" by Mark Schug and Eric Hagedorn each describe ways to teach young people financial literacy. The authors of both articles would agree on what young people need to learn about money, but they offer different proposals for how to teach that information. Write a clear, well-organized essay in which you summarize both plans, explain the fundamental differences between them, and then take a position on which of the two approaches to teaching financial literacy would be most effective for young people in America today. Give specific reasons for why you think a particular proposal would be more effective in teaching young people to become financially literate.

Definition Assignment

Write an essay that defines one of the following terms: *wealth, poverty, money taboo, needs, wants,* or *financial literacy.*

Narration Assignment

Write an essay that explains your money history and your level of financial literacy. To answer this prompt, think about the following questions: Did you grow up with an allowance? Do you remember having money worries? Was money discussed openly in your family or was it a taboo topic? Did you witness arguments about money in your family? What were your family's values about money, and how were they passed on to you or not passed on to you? Refer to at least two of the texts from the unit on Money, Wealth, and Financial Literacy as you write your essay.

Process Analysis Assignment

What can individuals or families do to become more financially stable in America today? Write an essay that explains what you believe are the most important steps to take in the process of becoming financially stable. You may use yourself or your family as an example or create a hypothetical family, but make sure you give some details about who is in the family, what their educational levels are, and what their goals are.

Compare/Contrast Assignment

Choose two people you know who are in an important relationship (your parents, you and your significant other, two friends) and compare and contrast their money personalities, using the psychological types outlined in Olivia Mellan's article "Men, Women, and Money." Make sure you give details from real life that show why they fit the personality type that you believe they fit. In the concluding paragraph, show how their different money personalities affect their relationship.

Review Assignment

Find out what course offerings in economics or personal finance are available in your public school district. Learn what the courses are about, who takes them, and if they are required or elective. Write a review of your school system's curriculum. You may choose to structure your review as a letter to the editor of your local newspaper or as an academic essay or paragraph.

Research Assignment

What are your life goals? Where do you hope to see yourself in fifteen years? Freewrite on your future life, brainstorming specifics about where you wish to live, what kind of career and family you hope to have, how you plan to give to children or others, and how you plan to retire. Next, research that dream life, using your school's career center, the online resources listed in Chapter 2, and Web sites that will give you information about salaries and housing costs. Would the salary of your dream career support the lifestyle you hope to have? What do you need to do to achieve success in your chosen career? Write an essay that explains the path you will need to take to achieve your dream life. If you discover that your dream life needs to be revised, write an essay about what you need to change and how you will decide to rearrange your priorities.

chapter review

Chapter 3 walked you through the planning, organizing, and drafting stages of writing an academic essay. By now, you have learned that college-level reading and writing require you to follow a process. In your own project, you have moved from pre-reading the texts you will write about to drafting. Take time now, though, to reflect on all that you have learned about reading and writing academic texts.

To review this chapter, choose one or more of the following strategies:

1. Read through all your writing and notes from the Practice It activities. Make a list of the ideas you generated while doing them.

2. In your notebook, draw a flowchart or time line of the processes you have learned so far. What are the steps in the reading and writing process? What techniques have you learned for each of these steps? List them under each relevant point on your flowchart or time line. Which techniques are you using successfully? Which techniques might require more practice for you? Mark those as well.

3. If you skipped any activities, do them now as a way to deepen your understanding of the material.

4. Try to explain what you have learned to someone you know. Discuss the key concepts and give your own examples to illustrate those concepts.

4

Revising, Editing, and Proofreading

in this chapter

- What Is Revision?
- What Is Peer Review?
- How Do You Revise?
- What Is Editing?
- How Do You Proofread?

Once you have a complete rough draft, the most serious work of writing begins. Writing the first draft of an essay is a major accomplishment, but good writing comes from rewriting, which includes revising for major changes, editing to make your sentences clear, and proofreading to polish your final product. In the real world, writers go through this process every day. It takes work, but the good news is that you do not have to do it alone. In fact, revising is most productive when done in consultation with others; we call this peer review.

In Chapter 3, you filled out an essay-writing time-management chart to give yourself an idea of how long each step in the drafting process takes. (If you skipped this activity, take a moment to fill in the top part of the Essay Writing Time Management chart on page 120 now to help you with time management in essay writing.) The bottom half of the following chart includes the steps in the revising process. You can copy this chart into your notebook or download a version of the chart from the e-Pages. (Go to **bedfordstmartins.com/readwriteconnect** and click on **Charts**.) Estimate how long the revising, editing, and proofreading steps will take you. By the time you complete this chapter, you will have an accurate idea of how long it takes you to write a complete essay, from reading and brainstorming to editing and proofreading.

Revising as Re-Seeing Your Work

The revising stage of the writing process requires that you switch hats: You have been working on your essay as a writer; now it's time to review your essay as a critical reader. It's important to be able to identify which parts of your essay are strong and which parts need more attention and work. In fact, revising is perhaps the most important step in the writing process. Revising can make a garbled mess of ideas into a decent paper, and it makes a decent rough draft into a very good second draft. Successful writers always revise their work many times before considering it "done." The American writer Ernest Hemingway had an intense revision process; he told one interviewer that he often rewrote the first chapter of a book forty or fifty times! We don't expect you to rewrite or revise that many times, but a successful college writer must be open to making major changes to a draft.

What exactly is revising? Revising is the process of working out the thesis and structural support of your essay. Revising requires you to think about big-picture concerns and analyze your focus, points, support, and/or organization. Frequently, your first rough draft will have an unfocused thesis, insufficient support, or major organizational problems. You may need to cut out paragraphs, rearrange your essay entirely, or add substantial amounts of new information. Occasionally, writers figure out their thesis only at the end of the first draft, and they have to

ESSAY WRITING TIME MANAGEMENT CHART 2

Task	Planned day to complete	Estimated time to complete	Actual time to complete
Reading and annotating the articles in Chapter 2			
Organizing thoughts about the articles in Chapter 2			
Reading and understanding the essay prompt			
Pre-writing			
Thesis development			
Outlining			
Generating support and evidence			
Writing topic sentences			
Writing rough, rough draft			
Adding an introduction and conclusion			
Peer review			
Making a plan of action for big-picture and sentence-level concerns			
Revising thesis			
Organizing from one paragraph to the next			
Organizing inside paragraphs			
Revising for clear transitions			
Developing paragraphs			
Integrating quotations and paraphrases			
Editing for sentence errors			
Proofreading for minor errors and format			

shift the paper around completely to make the thesis clear and focused. As you can see, being open to revision means being open-minded about your writing.

Many students confuse revision with editing and proofreading, which are separate stages of the writing process. Editing, the stage that follows major revision, focuses on making your sentences clear. During the proofreading stage, the last stage in the writing process, you correct spelling and other minor errors. Make sure you complete your revisions before you attempt to edit or proofread. After all, there is really no point in struggling to find the perfect word if you may end up cutting the entire paragraph.

When working with a rough draft, work on big-picture issues first so you can make clear what it is you are trying to say. Once your thesis, ideas, logic, and organization are solid, you can work on concerns at the sentence level, fine-tuning your words and proofreading for errors. Think of it like building a house: Once the structure is complete (a solid foundation, framing, walls, and roof), you can add details, paint, and decorate. Similarly, when writing, you need a solid foundation for your essay (the thesis, audience, purpose, organization, topic sentences, and support) before you can polish it by finding the just-right word or perfecting your punctuation.

Big-picture issues include:

Audience and purpose
Topic and thesis
Organization
Paragraph development and coherence
Introduction and conclusion

Sentence-level issues include:

Sentence clarity / Grammar
Word choice
Punctuation
Spelling

---

practice it   Finding Big-Picture and Sentence-Level Concerns

Look over the following student essay and read the comments and editing marks. What **big-picture** issues should this student focus on in revision? What are the **sentence-level** concerns? What would you suggest this student focus on while revising? How would you prioritize the instructor's comments? Discuss how this student should proceed with a revision.

continued ❯

Siebrecht 1

Thalia Siebrecht

Ms. Lawlor

English 95

March 21, 2013

Perhaps use an example of the importance of money as your hook?

Financial Stability

Money is really important to everyone, especially in today's economy, where *Yes!*

everyone needs to save to have future financial stability. For many people, money is

never just money, it is a tool that accomplishes life's goals, like going to college, open up   *parallel structure error*

a business, go on a trip, buy a car, buy a house, and so on. Today to have a good financial   *v. form*

stability is very important, because parents want to leave their children with good

financial security, but for some parents it's hard to achieve this goal, because they don't

have the same privileges that some other parents have. The key to create financial

stability in America is to have a good education and good financial literacy, because in   *good*

today's bad economy, people without good money habits can't compete with people who

start off life with more money.

v. form

In order for people in America to be financially stabled, people need to learn to

have good money habits. To create this good money habits, people should stop buying | *agree!*

things they don't need and limit their money spending. They should start saving and

investing their money in better ways, because what they do right now will affect not only   *review comma rules*

them, but their children in the future. To have a good understanding about good money

habits, there are nonprofits groups that help you understand about how the economy   *What are the non-profit groups? Examples?*

works and what can you do to save your money. In the article "Making It in the U.S.:

More Than Just Hard Work" by Pam Fessler, she mentions one woman named Dametra

Siebrecht 2

WW

Williams, whom got help from one of this nonprofit groups and explains how they helped

CS

her achieve her American Dream, she said, "A San Francisco nonprofit called EARN   *CS = comma splice*

helped her save money for tutors and a business" (5). This nonprofit group helps anyone   *Is this true? Are there No income requirements?*

that needs help on how to save money, like how they helped Dametra, that way creating

good money habits. Now families of all races are becoming more knowledgeable about

how to invest their money on the right things, and that helps them be more financially   *good connection back to thesis*

stabled for the future.

Another key for people to be financially stabled is to have family discussions

about how money works. As kids we don't know anything about money, but parents now   *Good point*

should opt for the idea of teaching their kids about money at a very young age, because

is

the economy of today it's really bad, and it's going to keep getting worse before it gets   *why?*

better. The more kids know now how to handle money, the better it would be for them for

WW

when they grow up, because that way they would be more knowledgeable in how to

spend it right. In the article, "Teach Your Children the Building Blocks of Finance" by

the authors   *is | missing subject*

Sherie Holder and Kenneth Meeks explains, "Parents should examine their children

spending and what they spend money on. Let kids explain why they are making certain   *check accuracy of quote*

purchases, and make the total family finances a discussion with input from everyone"   *comma error*

(46). Letting kids explain what they spend their money on, will help them understand if it   *How will explaining what they spend $ on lead to this understanding?*

CS

was a necessary purchase or not, they will learn what it's worth buying and what it's not.

This also is a great way for them to get well-informed at how a family budget is built and

help them understand how a house is bought and kept by investing on the right things,

that way they can be financially stabled for when they grow up.

continued ❯

Siebrecht 3

Having a high level of education is a must for when it comes to have a good

financial stability. As kids we were always told that education is everything, but we   *good point!*

didn't necessarily know how important it was. We thought that once we got our

associate's degree, which is two years of college, we were off to a good start, but the

reality is different because of the economy we face right now. Before it would have been

fine to have studied until you got your associate's degree, but now most of the time jobs   *who is doing the hiring? Jobs or employers?*

don't hire you unless you have a higher education than that. In the Bureau of Labor

Statistics' "Education Pays" chart, the U.S. government uses a chart with various

examples of education and how much ~~worth~~ of a salary you might likely make. One   *awkward*

example that the chart shows is that having only a high school education will most likely   *good. Say more about the level of salary*

make you unemployed, but a bachelor's degree at least would make you have an average

salary. The chart pretty much explains itself and it's scary to know that you can be   *No! please explain*

unemployed in the future if you don't a higher education, especially with how the

economy is right now, that's why to achieve good financial stability in America, you   *CS*

need to start saving to have a higher education so that in the future you would earn a lot

of money and won't have to struggle financially.

Another key that can help America achieve high education in order to have

financial stability is inheritance. Inheritance plays a big factor for when you want to start   *explain what you mean here*

your life, it helps you achieve more things than you can imagine for instead of having to

find a job and work really hard to achieve an education, which why inheritance is mostly

saved for. Some parents start saving money as early as possible for their kids to have a   *check + watch for comma errors in this ¶*

high education so that they will be able to survive in the future, so kids should take   *succeed?*

advantage of this great opportunity and not waste that money on things that would do no

Siebrecht 4

good for them since some families don't have that privilege. In the article "Making It in

the U.S.: More Than Just Hard Work" by Pam Fessler, she mentions a married woman

which

named Stephanie Upp who got an inheritance from her aunt ~~and~~ helped her have better

options not only to live in a better place, but for the education of her daughter, Fessler

said that Upp and her family "plan to leverage their house into a new and bigger one,

which will mean better public schools" (83). Inheritance alone helped her achieve one of

the most desired dreams of many Americans which is to have your own home in a very   *good*

nice community and to be able to give your kids a better education. In order for

inheritance to work more in the future, families of color should start saving money for

their kids, telling their children the importance of having an inheritance, because that way

they will know how important money is for their education in order to achieve financial

stability.

| predication error

In conclusion, in order to create financial stability in America is to have a good   *?*

education and good financial literacy, because otherwise we won't make it in today's

economy and future economy, which by today it is still a disaster that will take us years

to overcome (Money is a big discussion in all countries, not only in America) so that's   *| logic error*

why learning to have good money habits, to have family discussions about money,   *Learning # habits is important because*

having a good education and having an inheritance can help you achieve financial   *# is a big topic around the world?*

stability for the future since we still don't know what the future holds for us. It's better to

true!

be well-informed and have money saved than to have nothing and regret it later on.

Practicing Peer Review

Peer review, which is also sometimes called "workshopping," is when a group of writers read and offer constructive criticism about one another's work. Peer review has two distinct purposes: It provides you with feedback on your draft during the revision process, and it helps you become a better reader and evaluator of good writing. As you get feedback on

For more detailed information about peer review, see Chapter 17, Giving and Receiving Feedback, page 323.

your essay, you evaluate other essays and hone your critical reading skills by practicing evaluating the strength of a thesis, organizational logic, and the thoroughness of evidence and support. It's certainly valuable to get feedback from your peers, but by giving others feedback, you strengthen your ability to recognize what needs work, and this helps you when writing and evaluating your own essays.

Your peers can offer you feedback on your ideas and organization. They can also point out parts of the essay that just don't seem quite right, which can be immensely helpful. For students, peer review works best when comments focus on big-picture issues.

Guidelines for Peer Review

- The more complete your rough draft is, the more thorough the peer feedback can be. So, although it's typically fine to have a rough version of your essay, if half the essay is missing, your peer reviewer obviously can't give you feedback on what isn't there.
- If you have been struggling with a particular aspect of your essay while writing the rough draft (for example, your topic sentences or your introduction), let your peer reviewers know so they can pay particular attention to that part of your essay.
- When you respond to a peer's work, always begin by saying something positive, but make sure you include constructive criticisms as well, since the purpose of peer review is to suggest ways to improve a piece of writing.

your project   Asking for Specific Feedback on Your Draft

Whether you have a formal peer review in your class or not, seek out a classmate, friend, or tutor to give you feedback on some specific areas of the rough draft that you'd like the most help on. Ask your reviewer for feedback on how well you address both the big-picture and the sentence-level issues. This activity will help you figure out what parts need the most work, so you can prioritize these problem areas of your essay. You should end up with a list of the big-picture and sentence-level concerns that need the most attention.

Revision Strategies

To begin revising, reread the assignment prompt. Keep it on your desk as you reread your essay a few times. Read critically, and determine the strengths and weaknesses of your work. Make a list of what things you do well and what needs improvement. Once you have identified your areas of weakness, review them in more depth by working your way through the steps in the following sections.

REVISING TO MAKE YOUR AUDIENCE AND PURPOSE CLEAR

Reread the prompt. Are you being asked to write to a particular audience? If you are not being asked to write to a particular audience, do you have an audience in mind? Your classmates? Your campus community? Residents of your city? Young people? People with children? Once you determine your audience, look over your introductory paragraph. The introduction sets the tone for the essay and introduces your topic and thesis as well as any background information. All of these parts of your introduction should be written with your audience in mind. How much background information you include about your topic depends on how well-informed your audience is about it. If your audience is young people, for example, you need to consider whether your topic is something young people are likely to know much about. If necessary, revise to add enough background information for your audience. This focuses the start of your essay by establishing a clear audience right from the beginning.

Your writing assignment probably makes your purpose clear: For instance, you may be asked to explain the difference between two plans for educating young people about the complicated issues of money, wealth, and financial literacy. If your writing prompt allows for a range of possible purposes, use your thesis to state the goal or purpose of your essay. Sometimes instructors provide broad prompts so that you can narrow the focus and purpose to something specific that interests you.

For more help with audience and purpose, see Chapter 6, Audience, Purpose, and Topic, page 169.

REVISING TO FOCUS YOUR TOPIC OR STRENGTHEN YOUR THESIS

When you preview a text as part of pre-reading, you try to anticipate the scope of what an article will cover. In a well-structured essay, you should also get the gist of the whole essay just by reading the thesis statement and the topic sentences. Because these key parts of the essay direct the focus of the information, you want to make sure there is coherence from one topic sentence to the next.

In Chapter 3, you wrote a "working thesis" that gave you a focus for the draft as you wrote it. Now that you have a completed rough draft, it's time to revise the thesis and your overall essay to make a stronger point.

---

practice it   Preview to Revise the Thesis

Copy your thesis out and then list your topic sentences. Taken together, the thesis and topic sentences should read like an overview of your entire paper. Ask someone who has not read your essay to read the thesis and topic sentences, and determine if the points made in the topic sentences logically flow from and support the thesis. The reader should answer these questions:

continued ○

1. Based on the thesis, what do you anticipate the essay will be about?
2. After reading the topic sentences, can you understand the flow of the ideas? Do they progress naturally and logically from one idea to the next?
3. Is the essay focused? Do the topic sentences relate back to and support the thesis? Are there any topic sentences that seem out of place? (If so, the next section will help you get them back in place.)
4. Are these topic sentences enough to support the thesis? Are there other points the writer needs to add?

Look over the feedback. What did your reviewer expect the essay to say based on your thesis? Is this how you see your essay? If not, then reconsider what your thesis promises. It could be that your thesis is exactly what you want to say, but the body paragraphs veer off topic or are missing supporting topics. If this is the case, you have two options: Revise the thesis to fit the body paragraphs, or revise the body paragraphs to fit the thesis.

REVISING TO REORGANIZE AN ESSAY

A disorganized draft is a common problem among writers. Sometimes this happens because you didn't plan enough in the first place—if this is the case, for your next paper, try starting with the pre-writing activities in Chapter 3, especially the Group Activity to Organize Ideas (p. 106). Other times, though, you end up with a disorganized draft because new ideas came up as you wrote, and you just stuck them in anywhere. Now you have to figure out how to fix this. When revising for organization, be very open-minded and ready to work. Essays need to be organized on two levels: overall and within each paragraph. Sometimes you only need to move a paragraph or add a transition. However, if you find that your ideas have no clear order, or that ideas from various topics are sprinkled throughout your body paragraphs, a more fundamental reorganization may be needed.

Writers who don't make some kind of outline often have extremely disorganized first drafts. Other writers outline but don't use their outlines, ignoring important work they have already done. Either way, if your entire essay needs an organization overhaul, start by determining what you have already written and where exactly your organization went off course. Follow these steps:

STEP 1: **Make a list of your paragraph topics or points.**

STEP 2: **Gather a handful of colored pens, pencils, crayons, or highlighters.**   You need as many colors as you have paragraph topics. Assign each topic a color.

STEP 3: Print out your essay.   Go through the essay with one colored pen or pencil at a time, and underline sentences that directly support or relate to that color's assigned topic. Read carefully through all the body paragraphs. If a sentence fits more than one topic, underline it in both colors; later you can decide where it ultimately should go.

STEP 4: After you color-code all the sentences, look over your paper.   Does it resemble rainbow sprinkles on an ice cream cone, with a little of each color everywhere? Or maybe you have mostly one color per paragraph with only a few odd colors stuck in here and there? The idea is to put all the sentences underlined in the same color together in a paragraph. You should end up with all the pink sentences in one paragraph and all the blue sentences in another, for example.

STEP 5: Evaluate the "leftovers."   Are there some sentences that you didn't underline in any color? Evaluate them one at a time. Possibly they don't fit at all, and should just be deleted. However, if you think they are important, maybe you need to add a new point to your paper and put those sentences in a new paragraph.

STEP 6: Return to the document on your computer.   Save it as a new document. Using your word-processing program, cut and paste the sentences into the correct paragraphs, based on the color-coding steps. Print it and read it out loud, paying particular attention to transitions that may need to be changed in the new organizational structure.

REVISING TO REORGANIZE A PARAGRAPH

Sometimes your essay is generally well organized, but you need to revise one particular paragraph's structure. When you add new information as you write, you may end up with paragraphs that include more than one topic. Revising for this problem can get messy, but it's also a very valuable strategy to practice and the result will be a much clearer essay. Determine the main point of the paragraph, and whether or not you have a clear topic sentence for this main point. Then evaluate the support. Quite frequently, student writers have good topic sentences and decent supporting evidence, but the evidence doesn't truly fit the point it is supposed to support. Next, check to see if the paragraph includes enough analysis of the evidence it presents. Is it clear how and why the evidence supports the point? Finally, review the transitions: Are there adequate transitions from idea to idea, or does the paragraph jump around? Reading your work against the grain and thinking critically about whether or not the paragraph coheres helps you to improve the paragraph.

For more information on paragraph structure, see Chapter 12, Topic Sentences and Paragraphs, page 253.

For more on transitions, see pages 281–85 of Chapter 13, Essay Organization and Outlining.

practice it   Organization within a Paragraph

Look over the following paragraph. Based on the point made in the topic sentence, what single topic/point will the paragraph cover? Does the paragraph stray off topic by addressing or introducing additional ideas not suggested by the topic sentence? Underline sentences that make this paragraph disorganized by addressing other topics. How can this paragraph be fixed? Suggest possible strategies for removing off-topic material or relating off-topic material to the topic sentence.

Learning financial literacy at a young age gives someone the best chance to gain financial stability. A big problem with many people is that they never learned financial literacy. This prevents them from knowing how to budget their money and can lead to overspending or debt. Not everyone can rely on an inheritance for their future stability. In fact, not everyone has family resources or support to help them if they get in a financial jam or want to try to buy a house and need help with the down payment. If you don't get an inheritance and you haven't gone to college, you might consider going back to school to get your A.A. degree or your B.A. According to the "Education Pays" chart, people with only a high school education are twice as likely to be unemployed as people with a bachelor's degree. Also, having a bachelor's degree will likely give you a higher paycheck than just having a high school diploma or an associate's degree. Teaching kids to save early in life will ensure that they are able to save money for unexpected problems that may come up later, or will help them to buy a home one day.

REVISING FOR PARAGRAPH DEVELOPMENT

For help with paragraph development, see Chapter 12, Topic Sentences and Paragraphs, page 253.

The body paragraphs have a very specific job: They explain and support the claim of the thesis. Each body paragraph should cover one point and should begin with a topic sentence that states that point or idea and provides information and explanations. After the topic sentence, paragraphs should be made up of information, examples, details, and explanations to help prove the paragraph's main point. Generally, college essays use some information from one or more readings or from research, so all those great annotations you did when reading and those notes you took during class discussion will be very useful when building up your paragraphs. Problems with paragraph development usually emerge from an unclear topic sentence, a lack of supporting details, or not enough explanation or elaboration. Take note of the following common indicators of a lack of development in body paragraphs:

- Paragraphs that begin with evidence (such as a quotation) instead of a topic sentence / point in your own words
- Paragraphs that contain very little supporting evidence
- Paragraphs that end with evidence (such as a quotation) instead of some explanation of how that evidence supports your point

REVISING TO INTEGRATE QUOTATIONS AND PARAPHRASES

Develop your paragraphs by adding more evidence—in the form of well-chosen quotations or paraphrases—to prove your point. A quotation is the *exact words* of a writer, surrounded with quotation marks. A paraphrase is a restatement of an author's words or ideas in your own words.

For more information about quotation and paraphrase, see Chapter 16, Quotation and Paraphrase, page 307.

Use either quotations or paraphrases to support your point, but be careful not to just drop a quotation or paraphrase into your essay. You need to provide a framework so that the reader understands where it comes from and how it helps you make your point. Integrating quotations and paraphrases well make for a more coherent paragraph. Whenever you use a quotation or paraphrase, it should be part of a "sandwich." Here's how to make a quotation sandwich:

- Introduce the quotation.
- Copy the exact words of the author, and surround them with a pair of quotation marks.
- Explain *what* the quotation means.
- Explain *how* the quotation supports your point.

Introducing and explaining the quotation are ways to smoothly integrate the quotation into your essay. Be aware that when you quote (or paraphrase), you must always let the reader know where you got the information.

For detailed information on citing sources, see Chapter 20, MLA Documentation, page 362.

Introduce a Quotation.   Someone once suggested that a quotation is like a dinner guest; you would never think of inviting a guest over and then not introducing him or her to everyone else. In the same way, you should never just drop a quotation into your paper without a proper introduction. Dropping a quotation into an essay without introducing it is generally abrupt and doesn't provide enough transition between your ideas and those of the author you are citing. The same is especially true of a paraphrase because the reader won't know that you are citing information from someone else.

Introduce a quotation or paraphrase using a signal phrase, or introductory word(s), to let the reader know its source. Most of the time, the best way to do this is to use the full name of the author and the title of his or her work the first time you mention them. You can just refer to the author by his or her last name after that, but don't ever refer to an author by first name.

Common Signal-Phrase Words

argues	illustrates	says
claims	makes the point that	suggests
explains	reveals	writes

Here's the formula for a full-introduction signal phrase (for the first mention of an author in your essay):

> **Full title of work (book or article) + full name of author + signal-phrase word + quote**

Here's an example of a quotation introduced with a signal phrase:

> **In her article "Men, Women, and Money," Olivia Mellan claims,** "The failure of people to explore their money personalities leads to deep misunderstanding and hurt" (53).

Here's an example of a paraphrase introduced with a signal phrase:

> **In the article "Teach Your Children the Building Blocks of Finance," Sherie Holder and Kenneth Meeks reinforce** the importance of saving at least 10 to 15 percent of after-tax income (44).

If you already introduced the author fully earlier in the essay, you can use a shortened signal phrase:

> **Last name of author or speaker + signal-phrase word + quote**

Here's a second or later quotation, once you've already fully introduced an author in an earlier quotation:

> **Mellan reveals** that "silence is a shield for the shame, guilt, and anxiety people feel about their own ways with money" (51).

Here's a second or later paraphrase:

> **Holder and Meeks claim** that how children feel about money will affect their money habits later in life (43).

Explain What the Quotation Means.   Often, students assume that the reader understands what the quotation means or that it explains itself. This is rarely the case. Different readers can interpret a quotation differently. Remember, you have carefully read and annotated the text, probably several times, and possibly even discussed it in class or elsewhere. Assume your reader is seeing it for the first time, so be sure you explain what you think the author means in your own words.

Explain How the Quotation Supports Your Point.   Again, a quotation does not speak for itself. You introduced it into the essay—now explain why. Let's look back at Thalia's essay, which appeared earlier in this chapter. In the following paragraph from a later, revised draft, we can see an example of how a quote sandwich might look in a paragraph. The signal phrase is in bold, the quote is underlined, and the explanation is in italics.

Another key for people to be financially stable is to have family discussions about how money works. As kids we don't know anything about money, but parents now should opt for the idea of teaching their kids about money at a very young age, because the economy of today is really bad, and it's going to keep getting worse before it gets better. The more kids know now how to handle money, the better it would be for them for when they grow up, because that way they would be more knowledgeable about how to spend it right. **In the article "Teach Your Children the Building Blocks of Finance," Sherie Holder and Kenneth Meeks explain that parents should** "examine how they track their [children's] spending and what they spend money on. Let kids explain why they are making certain purchases, and make the total family finances a discussion with input from everyone" (00). *Letting kids explain what they spend their money on will help them understand if it was a necessary purchase or not.* They will learn what is worth buying and what is not. This also is a great way for them to get well-informed about how a family budget is built and help them understand how a house is bought and kept by investing in the right things. That way they can be financially stable when they grow up.

---

your project   Revising to Make Major Changes

Read your essay once or twice, bearing in mind the list of questions below. As you read, annotate the parts of your paper that need more time and attention.

Audience and purpose
- Who is the audience for your paper?
- How are you communicating to this particular audience?
- Why are you writing? To persuade? To inform? To argue? To describe? To compare? Is your purpose clear in your paper?

Topic and thesis
- Does your essay respond to the prompt? Does it fit the topic?
- Do you have a clear, strong thesis that states a claim?
- Does the thesis address all parts of the question stem?

continued ❯

Organization
- Are the major sections in a logical order?
- Are the transitions from one paragraph to the next logical and clear? Are the transitions from sentence to sentence within the paragraphs clear?

Paragraph development and coherence
- Does each body paragraph have a clear topic sentence that states the point that the paragraph will make?
- Do all the sentences in a paragraph focus on the same topic?
- Do the evidence and examples appropriately support the main point of the paragraphs?
- Are quotations and paraphrases integrated well?
- Does each body paragraph feel complete and finished?

Introduction and conclusion
- Does the introduction hook the reader and provide some good, general background about the topic?
- Does the conclusion sum up the ideas and offer final thoughts?

Finally, review what you marked on your essay and make a plan for your revision. What big-picture and sentence-level issues do you need to focus your revision on? List your specific "next steps" for your essay in detail and consult the relevant sections below for help.

Editing Strategies

As you can see, revising takes time, effort, and focus. It is difficult, if not impossible, to edit sentences at the same time you make major changes to content and organization. If you find yourself hitting the delete key far more than you are typing words, you probably need to loosen up, stop censoring everything you write, and remember that there will be a time for editing after all your ideas are in place.

Now that you are at that editing stage, there are specific techniques that you can use to make sure your writing is clear and correct. Give each a try and see which ones you like best. Ideally, you will have more than one strategy that works well for you.

Guidelines for Editing
- Always edit from a printed copy; never edit from the computer screen.
- Make corrections by hand on your paper and enter them into your computer. Then go back and compare your handwritten marks to the new printout to make sure you didn't miss anything. Then read the paper over again.

- Editing requires that you read the paper several times. Reading it over once is not enough.
- Give yourself adequate time to edit. You might spend fifteen minutes or more on each page of text that you have to edit.
- Try not to edit immediately after you finish writing something. Give yourself a break between revising and editing; editing requires a fresh mind and clear focus.
- Take a three-minute break every twenty minutes if you are working on a long document.
- Never skip editing.

READING YOUR ESSAY OUT LOUD

Reading your work out loud is one of the most effective ways to edit. Sure, it may be embarrassing to read your writing out loud, especially in your local coffee shop or, even worse, in class. You'll get over the embarrassment pretty quickly, though, once you have tried it a few times. Most student writers find five or more errors per page when they use this technique. Here's how it works:

STEP 1: Print a copy of your paper and grab a pencil or pen.

STEP 2: Read your paper out loud.   Read slowly, clearly, and carefully, as if you are a newscaster reading the evening news. As you read, underline the places that sound wrong or bad. Do *not* stop to fix them as you are reading. This will break the rhythm. Just read and underline the mistakes.

STEP 3: When you finish reading the whole document, go back and focus on those underlined parts.   Make corrections.

STEP 4: Edit your document on the computer.   Print it.

STEP 5: Repeat steps 1–4 until your paper sounds great.

If you can't bear to read your own writing, or if English is not your first language, enlist a friend, classmate, or relative to help. In that case, print two copies of your paper. Give your friend a copy and keep a copy for yourself. Have your friend read it while you listen, watch, and underline the bad parts. (Seriously, keep your eyes open: Your friend's face will show it when he or she gets confused by something that isn't clear.) Then make the changes yourself.

READING BACKWARDS

Reading your essay backwards may sound funny, but it is a highly effective editing technique. If you can get the answers right when you take multiple-choice tests and do grammar exercises, but still can't figure out how to find and fix your own errors, this may be the best editing technique for you. When editing, you look for lots of different kinds of things: grammar errors, punctuation, and word choice. You need several read-throughs to adequately search for each kind of issue. This takes some time, especially at the beginning, but it is worth it. Here's how you edit by reading backwards:

STEP 1: Choose your most serious error.   Review your instructor's comments from past assignments.

STEP 2: Print your essay and also find a blank piece of paper.

STEP 3: Turn to the last page of your essay.   Use the blank piece of paper to cover up everything except the last sentence.

STEP 4: Read that last sentence.   Does it include the error you're looking for? If it doesn't, move on to the second-to-last sentence in the essay. If it does, try to fix the error. Check the relevant chapter of this book and if you can't fix it on your own, see your instructor or a tutor for advice and for help learning the grammar rule.

STEP 5: Continue on throughout the essay, one sentence at a time, back to front.   Remember to look for only one error at a time.

STEP 6: Take a break between passes so you are always looking at your essay fresh.   For example, if you know that you have trouble with sentence fragments and commas, read your essay backwards first for sentence fragments, and then start over and read it backwards again for comma errors. You are much more likely to find errors when you focus your search.

STEP 7: Repeat the steps with your next-most-serious error and then the next.   Do this until you have covered all the errors you commonly make.

If you're not sure what kinds of errors you tend to make, look over older writing assignments to see what errors your instructors marked, or go to Chapter 24, How to Learn the Rules and Apply Them to Your Own Writing, to begin keeping a Personalized Grammar Error Log of your frequent errors. Knowing what kinds of errors you are most likely to make is valuable information!

Proofreading

You are nearly finished! You have brainstormed, organized, drafted, revised, and edited your essay. It's time to put the final polish on it by carefully proofreading and correcting any minor errors you may have missed. After you have the major ideas in place and have made changes to your sentences by using one or more editing techniques, double-check your work by proofreading. Careful proofreading of your document will catch errors that you make, such as when you make a change in one paragraph but forget to follow through with the change in the next. The proofreading stage is also a good time to catch your own commonly made spelling or word-choice errors, such as if you always mix up *there/their/they're*. Finally, if you haven't already done so, now is the time to double-check that your typed document includes your name, the course number, and other necessary information and is properly formatted with the correct margin size, line spacing, and font. If your instructor hasn't stated a preference for font size, 12-point Times New Roman is a good bet.

---

your project Proofreading for Errors and Format

Print a copy of your essay and proofread for typographical errors. Then compare it to the sample MLA formatted essay on pages 365–67. Make sure you include the correct information in your header and that your margins and font size are correct. Remember to delete extra spaces between paragraphs—they just look like "filler."

---

chapter review

Chapter 4 walked you through the revision, editing, and proofreading stages of the writing process. Academic reading and writing are challenging, but you have learned many new ways to improve your reading and writing skills. By now, you have finished an impressive college essay.

To review this chapter, choose one or more of the following strategies:

1. Reflect on your reading and writing processes in the entire Money, Wealth, and Financial Literacy unit. Specifically, freewrite or make a list of ideas in response to the following questions:

    What strategies helped you the most when reading?
    Which strategies helped you the most during the writing process?
    Which strategies will you use in the next unit of this course?
    If you could improve anything about the way you did your reading and writing for this unit, what would it be?

2. If you skipped any activities, do them now as a way to deepen your understanding of the material.

3. Try to explain what you have learned to someone you know. Discuss key concepts and give your own examples to illustrate those concepts.

5
Additional Reading Strategies

in this chapter

- What Are Reading Comprehension Strategies?
- What Strategies Should You Use for Reading Textbooks?
- What Is the Difference between Reading Textbooks and Fiction?
- What Are Strategies for Reading Fiction?

Because we learn to read as children, we often take this skill for granted. You might ask why you need to learn reading strategies. You already know how to read! While this is true, there is always room to improve your reading skills. Reading is not like riding a bike, where there is only one set of basic skills (balancing, steering, pedaling) to master. Reading involves a more complex set of skills that continue to grow and improve the more you practice and develop them. As you progress in your academic career, reading tasks become more challenging and require stronger comprehension and analysis skills.

Strong readers do more than just understand and recall what they read; they also have a growth mind-set about the challenges of reading. All college students face difficult readings at times, but one main difference between strong readers and struggling readers is that strong readers can evaluate the challenges in a reading and can draw from an arsenal of reading strategies in order to meet a reading challenge.

For more on "growth mind-set," see Carol S. Dweck's article "The Perils and Promises of Praise," in Chapter 1 (pp. 6–13).

Reading Comprehension Strategies

There are many reading strategies; some are very similar to one another, but each has a slightly different purpose. The more reading strategies you know, the easier it will be to pick the right one to help you tackle a challenging reading task. Think of it this way: If you are a chef but you only know how to sauté, what happens when you are faced with ingredients that don't sauté well? Lots of foods are delicious sautéed, but that cooking strategy won't work for everything. Knowing several reading strategies makes you a more flexible reader.

Following are three important strategies to help you prepare to read and understand what you read. Note that some strategies can be used throughout the reading process, while others apply only to certain stages.

READING STRATEGIES

Strategy	Reading Stage
SQ3R	pre-reading and during reading
KWL+	pre-reading, during reading, and post-reading
Mapping	post-reading

SQ3R

SQ3R stands for Scan, Question, Read, Recite, Review. This reading strategy will help you get ready to read a short work like an article, essay, or book chapter.

For more on previewing, see Chapter 1, Reading and Responding to College Texts, page 2.

Scan.   This step is about previewing the text by scanning it.

- Look at the title of the reading, the headings or subheadings, the length, and any pictures or graphs. What do you already know about the topic? What does the title tell you about the topic?
- Read the introductory paragraphs. How does this information relate to the title? What connections can you make?
- Read the last paragraph and any questions at the end of the essay or chapter. How do these parts relate to the introduction and the title? What connections can you make between them?
- Read the topic sentences or the first sentence of each paragraph of the essay or article. What can you figure out about the different points the essay will cover? Even if you can't identify all the main points, this step will help you with the next step.
- Notice any words that are highlighted, italicized, or in bold type. These are probably key words or new vocabulary words to learn.

Question.   Turn the headings, subheadings, and topic sentences into questions, to anticipate questions that the article, essay, or chapter might answer. Write all the questions down in your notebook or a computer file, leaving space between each section or paragraph so you can fill in the answers later. What information or points do you think you will learn? Write questions for all the pictures, graphs, and charts as well. What do you anticipate they will help you learn? Start with the journalist's six questions: who, what, where, when, why, how?

Read.   Read the whole work, but not all at once. If the reading is divided into sections, read one section at a time while actively looking for answers to your questions. As you find answers, write them down under each question. Don't forget to "read" the pictures, graphs, and charts. If the reading is not divided into sections, read each paragraph separately while looking for answers. If the paragraphs are very short, group related paragraphs together and treat these like a section. Also write main points or significant examples in the margins and in your notes.

Recite.   This step is the fun one. After reading a section, look away or cover the reading and recite out loud or in your head the answers to the questions you wrote. Summarize the points you learned in this section. Reciting is important because it builds a mental link to the information. Write down your answers, including any helpful or important examples. After you do this, move on to the next section and repeat the QRR.

Review.   After reading the whole text by questioning, reading, and reciting, you are ready to review. You will be amazed at how much you learned. Go back to the start of the reading and, looking at the title, try to remember what the first section was about. Summarize it out loud or at least in your head. If you can remember the points from the first section, move on to the next section and repeat the review. If you have trouble with any section, go back and do the QRR for that section again. The notes you create while doing SQ3R are a perfect study guide for a reading. Review them occasionally, especially before a quiz or exam.

KWL+

A second reading strategy is called KWL+. KWL+ is an acronym—a phrase created from the first letter of a series of words. The acronym KWL+ stands for:

K = What do I **Know** about the topic?
W = What do I **Want**/expect to learn?
L = What have I **Learned**?
+ = What questions do I still have about the topic?

KWL+ is a strategy that helps you prepare to read and engage actively with the text to improve comprehension.

STEP 1: Create a chart with four columns.   Label the first column "K," the second column "W," and so on.

STEP 2: In the first column, under "K," write down what you already know about the topic.   Now, you haven't done the reading yet, so you may not think you know very much about the topic, but fortunately we don't learn

KWL+ CHART

K What do I Know about the topic?	W What do I Want/expect to learn about the topic?	L What did I Learn about the topic?	+ What questions do I still have about the topic?

everything new, from scratch, every day. We have *some* prior knowledge about almost everything. What words or phrases are associated with the topic? It's fine if you don't know a lot about a topic, but what do you know? Write it down in this column.

STEP 3: Preview the reading, taking note of the title, any headers or topic sentences, images, graphs, and questions. Based on your preview, write what you want to learn or expect you will learn from this reading in the second, "W," column. When filling in the "W" column, make a list of things that you think might be important to know about your textbook or your chapter.

STEP 4: Read, annotating as you go, and making note of the places in the text where your questions are answered or your knowledge on the topic is expanded.

STEP 5: After reading, fill the "L" column up with information about what you learned in the reading. This is a good time to look back at the "K" column to see if there is anything you thought about the topic that needs correcting or clarifying. In the "L" column, correct any misinformation that you might have had before reading. For example, if there is an idea you had about the reading that now seems incomplete or perhaps inaccurate, you might write something like, "So X is not what I thought it was before I read the article," in order to clarify what you now know. Be sure to include main points and concepts from the reading in the "L" column as well as anything you found interesting.

STEP 6: Look over the "W" column to see if you learned everything you expected to learn about this topic. If there is anything that the reading did not address, write down any remaining questions you still have about the topic in the "+" column. This is also a place to write down any questions you have about the reading itself.

practice it   Using KWL+ 1

Try your hand at KWL+ with the following article, using the preceding steps. Copy the chart into your notebook or download a version of the chart from the e-Pages. (go to **bedfordstmartins.com/readwriteconnect** and click on **Charts**.) Fill out the "K" and "W" columns before reading the article. Once you complete the reading, fill out the last two columns.

KWL+ CHART FOR "IN HAKALAU, A MODERN SUCCESS STORY"

K What do I Know about the topic?	W What do I Want/expect to learn about the topic?	L What did I Learn about the topic?	+ What questions do I still have about the topic?
• Hakalau sounds Hawaiian. I haven't been there, but I have been to Hawaii and there are lots of unique plants and birds there. • I think a lot of birds started becoming endangered because of tourism. • "Avian" means bird, I think. • There are lots of endangered animals in the world like the polar bear, panda bear, and Bengal tiger. • I think the bald eagle was endangered too.	• Are some birds endangered? Why? • Where do the birds live? • How many are left? • Is there still hope for this species of bird? • What can be done to help save the bird? • What other birds might be endangered in Hawaii? • What/where is Hakalau?		

DAVID J. FLASPOHLER

In Hakalau, a Modern Success Story

David J. Flaspohler, an avian ecologist and conservation biologist at Michigan Technological University, writes from Hawaii, where he is studying the influence of human activities on birds and the natural ecosystems that support them. This article originally appeared in the *New York Times' Scientists at Work* blog.

Tuesday, May 29

Pelican Island, Fla., is a long way from the Big Island of Hawaii, but human vanity, high fashion, and bird feathers feature prominently in the history of both. Teddy Roosevelt created the first national wildlife refuge at Pelican Island in 1903, after years of unrestricted plume hunting of egrets to ornament ladies' hats nearly led to their extinction. The Polynesians who colonized Hawaii centuries ago shared a similar love of feathers as adornment, and the ruling class, or ali'i, wore cloaks made from tens of thousands of honeycreeper feathers.

It is difficult to know what role this practice had in the decline and extinction of birds before European contact with Hawaii. What we do know is that for those bird species that have survived into the 21st century, Hakalau Forest National Wildlife Refuge is both their final redoubt and a laboratory for the audacious possibility of recovery.

So this morning, Eben Paxton, biologist with the United States Geological Survey Pacific Island Ecosystem Research Center; Jessie Knowlton, a postdoctoral researcher; and I rumble among saffron-colored cinder cones up the steep slopes of Mauna Kea volcano. We have the good fortune to be visiting a small corner of this modern success story in Hawaiian bird conservation.

Hakalau was created in 1985 after surveys revealed an extraordinary diversity of native and endangered birds in this remnant forest. Somehow Hakalau survived as many lowland Hawaiian forests were converted to agriculture by ancient Hawaiians, a process that accelerated after modern Euro-Americans arrived.

We drive through Hawaiian Home Lands to reach the high elevation in Hakalau. For 30 minutes, we pass through zones overrun with the aggressive and invasive European shrub gorse (*Ulex europaea*). Turkeys, francolins, California quail, pigs, and even feral cows wander across our path as we near the refuge.

Entering the refuge on foot, we pass widely scattered native ohia and koa trees. Some are 15 feet tall, the products of an ambitious forest restoration campaign; others are 70-foot-tall giants left over from the vast forest that once covered this area.

Immediately, we hear the songs of native apapane, amakihi and i'iwi. Then, not five minutes after we reach the entrance, Eben points out a bird foraging at eye level just 12 feet away: an 'akepa! This small, endangered orange honeycreeper has appeared before we could even begin searching for it. It is a "life bird" for me, meaning it is the first one I have ever seen. Still absorbing this thrill, Eben points out a Hawaii creeper, another endangered species that gleans insects from the bark of trees like a nuthatch.

Over the next four hours, we see five more 'akepas and all of the more common native birds. The 'akiapola'au is also relatively common in Hakalau, although we don't see one on this morning. Woodpeckers never reached Hawaii, and the aki, as it is known, evolved to fill the wood-boring niche. It uses its stout lower mandible to dig into tree bark and its long, curved upper bill to extract insects.

Birds are not the only endangered species in Hawaii. We sit down for lunch near a rare endemic plant, a six-foot-tall lobelia that is in bloom. Over evolutionary time, particular Hawaiian bird species became more efficient plant pollinators, reaching their bills into the curved flowers to drink the sweet nectar. Birds with slightly longer bills could reach the nectar more efficiently and thus had a selective advantage over others. Similarly, flowers whose shape more closely matched the curve of their more efficient pollinating birds produced more offspring. This co-evolutionary dance between the honeycreepers and lobelias is partly what produced the remarkable biodiversity of Hawaii.

Finishing our sandwiches, we notice that pigs have chewed off some of the lobelia's lower branches. Then, suddenly, a Hawaii amakihi flies down and, inserting his curved bill into the curved corolla of the flower, recapitulates his argument for co-evolution between plant and pollinator.

Two simple features explain the remarkable diversity and density of endemic birds at Hakalau: Most of the refuge is above the mosquito-borne malaria zone, and the forest is composed of native trees of many ages. Indeed, large-scale plantings of koa in the 1990s have already been colonized by native birds, suggesting that such an approach could greatly expand available habitat— and thus population size—of many rare and endangered Hawaiian birds. This could accomplish more than simply slowing population declines. Forest restoration of the kind at Hakalau on a large enough scale could be a game changer for Hawaiian forest birds.

Endangered species conservation at times resembles a protracted chronic disease, like a malarial fever that haunts the infected patient with cyclic bouts of acute symptoms that can never be fully cured. Hawaiian forest bird conservation sometimes feels this way. Although the koa planting experiments at Hakalau are continuing, they and other restoration work on the Big Island offer a vision for the future of Hawaii's remarkable birds that is both practical and inspiring. If, 500 years from now, this remote archipelago is still graced by the songs and brilliant colors of its native birds and the ecosystems that support them, it will be this kind of bold action that our descendants will thank us for.

| practice it | Using KWL+ 2 |

All reading strategies require practice in order to be able to use them well. Try KWL+ on an assigned reading for a class. Be sure to take the time to fill out every column. When you finish, assess how well the strategy worked for you. When would you use this strategy?

MAPPING

The third reading strategy, mapping, involves using visual cues to help you navigate long or difficult texts. There are many ways to map a reading selection. You can use words and graphics, such as circles, arrows, and underlining, or draw images that suggest the literal content of the reading. You can also outline a reading, an approach described in Chapter 13, Essay Organization and Outlining (p. 267).

Mapping is often used as a post-reading strategy. In this case the first task is to read, always making sure to carefully annotate and to determine the main points. Once you determine the main points in the reading, here's how to get started mapping a reading.

For more help finding the main points, see Chapter 10, Thesis and Main Idea, page 223.

- Write or draw major points, and underline them or draw a box or circle around them with a heavy marker so they stand out.
- Draw arrows to show sequence from one point to the next.
- Leave enough space between main points or images to write the supporting examples clearly.
- Use different shapes or different colors to show the difference between main and supporting points or examples.

Here's one example, based on the article you just read, "In Hakalau, a Modern Success Story" (pp. 142–44).

STEP 1: After you complete the reading, in the center of a large, blank piece of paper, draw a circle or box and write the topic in it.   Be as specific about the topic as you can. In this case, the reading is about birds. What, specifically, does the reading say about birds?

Is it about birds in general? No
Is it about bird-watching as a hobby? No
Is it about the environmental effects of
  pollution on a specific bird population? No
Is it about an endangered bird species in
  Hawaii? Yes

Endangered bird species
in Hawaii

STEP 2: Draw lines out from the central topic and write the main points the reading makes about the topic on these lines. You can leave these as words on a line or make a box around the words.

STEP 3: Beneath each main point, draw lines on which to write the main point's supporting details. Be careful not to overdo it with too many examples or details; identify the significant supporting detail and examples only.

Here's one example of what your map might look like after following the preceding steps.

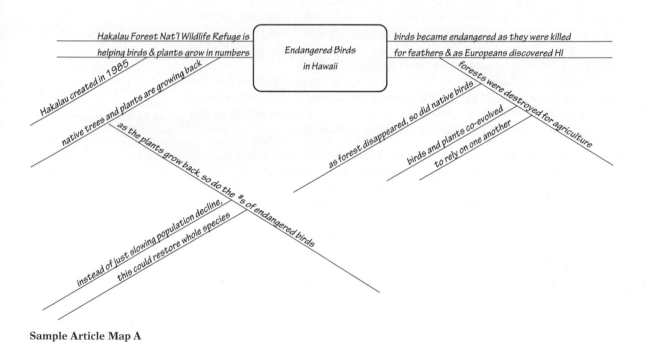

Sample Article Map A

There are many ways to organize information, so no two maps will look exactly the same. Mapping a reading helps you understand the concepts in the reading and how these concepts connect; there's no one "right" way to map. Following is another map of the same article, one that relies more heavily on images than on words.

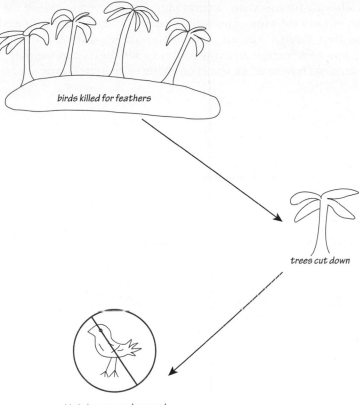

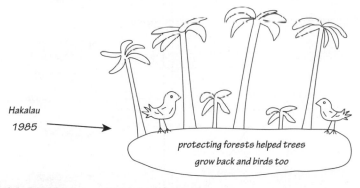

Sample Article Map B

practice it   **Mapping a Reading**

Create a map of any article you have been assigned to read for this course. Preview the text before you read and annotate. Use any headers or topic sentences to help guide you to the main and supporting points.

The following figures show several map formats you may find useful, depending on both the kind of material you are mapping and your assignment. The first three maps all offer different ways of visualizing, or picturing, how to structure an essay around your thesis and support. The last map suggests how to think about one kind of comparison or argument paper.

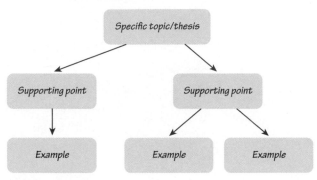

Map 1

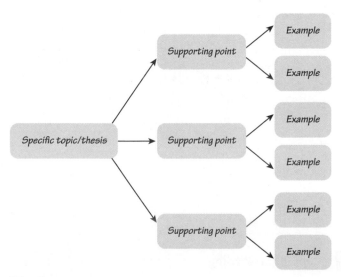

Map 2

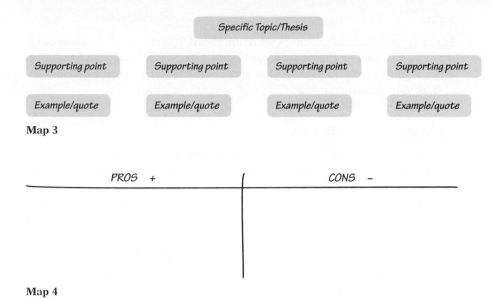

Map 3

<table>
<tr><td>PROS +</td><td>CONS –</td></tr>
</table>

Map 4

Reading Textbooks

Perhaps the most common textbook-reading strategy students use is underlining. Underlining sounds easy, but you have to recognize the main points and important concepts in order to underline them. That's the tricky part. Without this information, underlining is random (not helpful) or so extensive that too much of the page is underlined (also not helpful). Not only that, but underlining doesn't assist you in understanding or remembering new information. Because of this, underlining by itself is not the most helpful textbook-reading strategy. Of course, any of the comprehension strategies you have learned so far can be applied to textbook reading, but because textbooks tend to be loaded with facts and information that you need to recall, there are several specific strategies that work very well with this reading task.

STRATEGIES FOR READING TEXTBOOKS

Strategy	Reading Stage
SQ3R	pre-reading and during reading
Annotating	during reading
Outlining/mapping	during reading and post-reading
Muscle Reading	during reading

SQ3R

Again, SQ3R stands for Scan, Question, Read, Recite, Review. Look back at the discussion of this strategy on page 139. SQ3R is equally effective when reading textbooks; it helps you increase your comprehension as well as your reading speed.

ANNOTATING TEXTBOOKS

As with an article or book chapter, when you annotate a textbook, you add explanations and brief notes in the margins for what you have learned. These annotations are an excellent study tool for preparing for tests and quizzes. Annotating is a highly valuable reading strategy because it requires you to process the information as you read it, so you understand it and remember it. Many textbooks have key terms highlighted on the page, often with the definition in the margin. However, paraphrase the meaning by putting it in your own words in the margin. This way you learn and remember the meaning much better than by simply reading it.

For a review of annotating techniques, see Chapter 1, Reading and Responding to College Texts, page 2.

OUTLINING OR MAPPING TEXTBOOKS

Creating an outline or map of a textbook chapter is a fantastic reading strategy that doubles as a study guide. Both outlining and mapping help you understand and identify the organization of the chapter material as well as identify how that information is categorized. Because textbook chapters hold a ton of information, outlining or mapping breaks it down to a clear structure, from broader concepts to specific examples and terms.

STEP 1: First, preview the chapter. Textbooks often have features that show you how the information is organized.   Read the chapter title, a list of chapter contents, and headings that break up the information into manageable sections. Then look at the end of the chapter for a chapter review or for chapter questions. These can also give you a clue as to the main ideas and concepts the author wants you to understand. Often textbooks list these at the beginning of the chapter; they're sometimes called "objectives."

If you create an outline, list the section headings on a piece of paper with space between them to fill in later with specifics from each section. If you create a map, write the chapter title in a circle in the middle of the page. Draw circles or boxes in each corner for each heading (or spaced around the edge of the paper depending on how many headings there are).

STEP 2: Read one section at a time and try to identify the major point of each section.   You might get extra clues from bold or highlighted words or section subheadings. Write the main idea or point under the section heading. If a specific example or person is connected with that idea, write down that information as well. Don't forget to read graphs, charts, and images too. These can provide clues to the important concepts or terms that the author wants to reinforce.

STEP 3: Continue to read each section, adding major points and significant examples to your outline or map.

STEP 4: When you complete the outline or map, congratulate yourself.   Then read through the whole chapter from start to finish with your outline or map in hand, referring back to it as you read. If you find anything additional that you left out the first time through, add it now.

STEP 5: Periodically review your outline or map, particularly before a quiz or exam.   You have now created a perfect chapter study guide. Here's one example: a map of the first ten pages of Chapter 10 of the textbook *Psychology* by David G. Myers. The chapter follows the map.

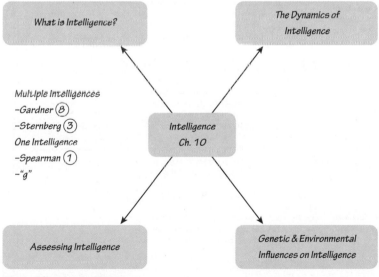

Map of Textbook Chapter

CHAPTER 10

Intelligence

Three huge controversies have sparked recent debate in and beyond psychology. First is the "memory war," over whether traumatic experiences are repressed and can later be recovered, with therapeutic benefit. The second great controversy is the "gender war," over the extent to which nature and nurture shape our behaviors as men and women. In this chapter, we meet the "intelligence war": Does each of us have an inborn general mental capacity (intelligence), and can we quantify this capacity as a meaningful number?

School boards, courts, and scientists debate the use and fairness of tests that attempt to assess people's mental abilities and assign them a score. Is intelligence testing a constructive way to guide people toward suitable opportunities? Or is it a potent, discriminatory weapon camouflaged as science? First, some basic questions:

- What is intelligence?
- How can we best assess it?
- To what extent does it result from heredity rather than environment?
- What do test score differences among individuals and groups really mean? Should we use such differences to rank people, to admit them to colleges or universities, to hire them?

This chapter offers answers. It will also remind you that there are a variety of mental gifts and that the recipe for high achievement in any field blends talent and grit.

What Is Intelligence?

PSYCHOLOGISTS DEBATE: Should we consider intelligence as one aptitude or many? As linked to cognitive speed? As neurologically measurable? Yet, intelligence experts do agree on this: Although people have differing abilities, intelligence is a concept and not a "thing." When we refer to someone's "IQ" (short for *intelligence quotient*) as if it were a fixed and objectively real trait like height, we commit a reasoning error called *reification*—viewing an abstract, immaterial concept as if it were a concrete thing. To reify is to invent a concept, give it a name, and then convince ourselves that such a thing objectively exists in the world. When someone says, "She has an IQ of 120," they are reifying IQ; they are imagining IQ to be a thing this person *has*, rather than a score she once obtained on a particular **intelligence test.** Better to say, "She scored 120 on the intelligence test."

Intelligence is a socially constructed concept: Cultures deem "intelligent" whatever attributes enable success in those cultures (Sternberg & Kaufman, 1998). In the Amazon rain forest, intelligence may be understanding the medicinal qualities of local plants; in an Ontario high school, it may be superior performance on cognitive tasks. In each context, **intelligence** is the ability to learn from experience, solve problems, and use knowledge to adapt to new situations. In research studies, *intelligence* is what intelligence tests measure. Historically, as we will see, that has been the sort of problem solving displayed as "school smarts."

WHAT IS INTELLIGENCE?

Is Intelligence One General Ability or Several Specific Abilities?

Intelligence and Creativity

Emotional Intelligence

Is Intelligence Neurologically Measurable?

ASSESSING INTELLIGENCE

The Origins of Intelligence Testing

Modern Tests of Mental Abilities

Principles of Test Construction

THE DYNAMICS OF INTELLIGENCE

Stability or Change?

Extremes of Intelligence

GENETIC AND ENVIRONMENTAL INFLUENCES ON INTELLIGENCE

Twin and Adoption Studies

Heritability

Environmental Influences

Group Differences in Intelligence Test Scores

The Question of Bias

Is Intelligence One General Ability or Several Specific Abilities?

1: What argues for and against considering intelligence as one general mental ability?

You probably know some people with talents in science, others who excel at the humanities, and still others gifted in athletics, art, music, or dance. You may also know a talented artist who is dumbfounded by the simplest mathematical problems, or a brilliant math student with little aptitude for literary discussion. Are all of these people intelligent? Could you rate their intelligence on a single scale? Or would you need several different scales?

Charles Spearman (1863–1945) believed we have one **general intelligence** (often shortened to **g**). He granted that people often have special abilities that stand out. Spearman had helped develop **factor analysis,** a statistical procedure that identifies clusters of related items. He had noted that those who score high in one area, such as verbal intelligence, typically score higher than average in other areas, such as spatial or reasoning ability. Spearman believed a common skill set, the g factor, underlies all of our intelligent behavior, from navigating the sea to excelling in school.

This idea of a general mental capacity expressed by a single intelligence score was controversial in Spearman's day, and it remains so in our own. One of Spearman's early opponents was L. L. Thurstone (1887–1955). Thurstone gave 56 different tests to people and mathematically identified seven clusters of primary mental abilities (word fluency, verbal comprehension, spatial ability, perceptual speed, numerical ability, inductive reasoning, and memory). Thurstone did not rank people on a single scale of general aptitude. But when other investigators studied the profiles of the people Thurstone had tested, they detected a persistent tendency: Those who excelled in one of the seven clusters generally scored well on the others. So, the investigators concluded, there was still some evidence of a g factor.

We might, then, liken mental abilities to physical abilities. Athleticism is not one thing but many. The ability to run fast is distinct from the strength needed for power lifting, which is distinct from the eye-hand coordination required to throw a ball on target. A champion weightlifter rarely has the potential to be a skilled ice skater. Yet there remains some tendency for good things to come packaged together—for running speed and throwing accuracy to correlate, thanks to general athletic ability. So, too, with intelligence. Several distinct abilities tend to cluster together and to correlate enough to define a small general intelligence factor.

Satoshi Kanazawa (2004) argues that general intelligence evolved as a form of intelligence that helps people solve *novel* problems—how to stop a fire from spreading, how to find food during a drought, how to reunite with one's band on the other side of a flooded river. More common problems—such as how to mate or how to read a stranger's face or how to find your way back to camp—require a different sort of intelligence. Kanazawa asserts that general intelligence scores *do* correlate with the ability to solve various novel problems (like those found in academic and many vocational situations) but do not much correlate with individuals' skills in *evolutionarily familiar* situations—such as marrying and parenting, forming close friendships, displaying social competence, and navigating without maps.

Theories of Multiple Intelligences

2: How do Gardner's and Sternberg's theories of multiple intelligences differ?

Since the mid-1980s some psychologists have sought to extend the definition of *intelligence* beyond Spearman's and Thurstone's academic smarts. They acknowledge that

:: **intelligence test** a method for assessing an individual's mental aptitudes and comparing them with those of others, using numerical scores.

:: **intelligence** mental quality consisting of the ability to learn from experience, solve problems, and use knowledge to adapt to new situations.

:: **general intelligence** *(g)* a general intelligence factor that, according to Spearman and others, underlies specific mental abilities and is therefore measured by every task on an intelligence test.

:: **factor analysis** a statistical procedure that identifies clusters of related items (called *factors*) on a test; used to identify different dimensions of performance that underlie a person's total score.

people who score well on one sort of cognitive test have some tendency to score well on another. But maybe this occurs not because they express an underlying general intelligence but rather because, over time, different abilities interact and feed one another, rather as a speedy runner's throwing ability improves after being engaged in sports that develop both running and throwing abilities (van der Maas et al., 2006).

Gardner's Eight Intelligences   Howard Gardner (1983, 2006) views intelligence as multiple abilities that come in packages. Gardner finds evidence for this view in studies of people with diminished or exceptional abilities. Brain damage, for example, may destroy one ability but leave others intact. And consider people with **savant syndrome,** who often score low on intelligence tests but have an island of brilliance (Treffert & Wallace, 2002). Some have virtually no language ability, yet are able to compute numbers as quickly and accurately as an electronic calculator, or identify almost instantly the day of the week that corresponds to any given date in history, or render incredible works of art or musical performances (Miller, 1999). About 4 in 5 people with savant syndrome are males, and many also have autism, a developmental disorder (see Chapter 5).

Memory whiz Kim Peek, a savant who does not have autism, was the inspiration for the movie *Rain Man.* In 8 to 10 seconds, he can read and remember a page, and he has learned 9,000 books, including Shakespeare and the Bible, by heart. He learns maps from the front of phone books, and he can provide Mapquest-like travel directions within any major U.S. city. Yet he cannot button his clothes. And he has little capacity for abstract concepts. Asked by his father at a restaurant to "lower your voice," he slid lower in his chair to lower his voice box. Asked for Lincoln's Gettysburg Address, he responded, "227 North West Front Street. But he only stayed there one night—he gave the speech the next day" (Treffert & Christensen, 2005).

:: savant syndrome a condition in which a person otherwise limited in mental ability has an exceptional specific skill, such as in computation or drawing.

TABLE 10.1	
GARDNER'S EIGHT INTELLIGENCES	
Aptitude	**Exemplar**
1. Linguistic	T. S. Eliot, poet
2. Logical-mathematical	Albert Einstein, scientist
3. Musical	Igor Stravinsky, composer
4. Spatial	Pablo Picasso, artist
5. Bodily-kinesthetic	Martha Graham, dancer
6. Intrapersonal (self)	Sigmund Freud, psychiatrist
7. Interpersonal (other people)	Mahatma Gandhi, leader
8. Naturalist	Charles Darwin, naturalist

Using such evidence, Gardner argues that we do not have *an* intelligence, but rather *multiple intelligences.* He identifies a total of eight (**TABLE 10.1**), including the verbal and mathematical aptitudes assessed by standard tests. Thus, the computer programmer, the poet, the street-smart adolescent who becomes a crafty executive, and the basketball team's point guard exhibit different kinds of intelligence (Gardner, 1998). He notes,

> If a person is strong (or weak) in telling stories, solving mathematical proofs, navigating around unfamiliar terrain, learning an unfamiliar song, mastering a new game that entails dexterity, understanding others, or understanding himself, one simply does not know whether comparable strengths (or weaknesses) will be found in other areas.

A general intelligence score is therefore like the overall rating of a city—which tells you something but doesn't give you much specific information about its schools, streets, or nightlife.

Wouldn't it be wonderful if the world were so just, responds intelligence researcher Sandra Scarr (1989). Wouldn't it be nice if being weak in one area would be compensated by genius in some other area? Alas, the world is not just. General intelligence scores predict performance on various complex tasks, in various jobs, and in varied countries; *g* matters (Bertua et al., 2005; Gottfredson, 2002a,b, 2003a,b; Rindermann, 2007). In two digests of more than 100 data sets, academic intelligence scores that predicted graduate school success also predicted later job success (Kuncel et al., 2004; Strenze, 2007; see also **FIGURE 10.1**).

Even so, "success" is not a one-ingredient recipe. High intelligence may help you get into a profession (via the schools and training programs that take you there), but it won't make you successful once there. The recipe for success combines talent with *grit:* Those who become highly successful are also conscientious, well-connected, and doggedly energetic. Anders Ericsson (2002, 2007; Ericsson et al., 2007) reports a *10-year rule:* A common ingredient of expert performance in chess, dancing, sports, computer programming, music, and medicine is "about 10 years of intense, daily practice."

• For more on how self-disciplined grit feeds achievement, see Chapter 11. •

Sternberg's Three Intelligences Robert Sternberg (1985, 1999, 2003) agrees that there is more to success than traditional intelligence. And he agrees with Gardner's idea of multiple intelligences. But he proposes a *triarchic theory* of three, not eight, intelligences:

- *Analytical (academic problem-solving) intelligence* is assessed by intelligence tests, which present well-defined problems having a single right answer. Such tests predict school grades reasonably well and vocational success more modestly.
- *Creative intelligence* is demonstrated in reacting adaptively to novel situations and generating novel ideas.
- *Practical intelligence* is required for everyday tasks, which may be ill-defined, with multiple solutions. Managerial success, for example, depends less on academic problem-solving skills than on a shrewd ability to manage oneself, one's tasks, and other people. Sternberg and Richard Wagner's (1993, 1995) test of practical managerial intelligence measures skill at writing effective memos, motivating people, delegating tasks and responsibilities, reading people, and promoting one's own career. Business executives who score relatively high on this test tend to earn high salaries and receive high performance ratings.

"You have to be careful, if you're good at something, to make sure you don't think you're good at other things that you aren't necessarily so good at. . . . Because I've been very successful at [software development] people come in and expect that I have wisdom about topics that I don't."
Bill Gates (1998)

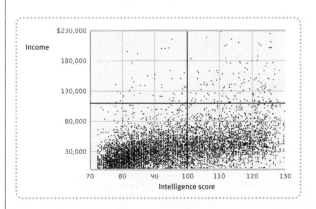

➤ **FIGURE 10.1**
Smart and rich? Jay Zagorsky (2007) tracked 7403 participants in the U.S. National Longitudinal Survey of Youth across 25 years. As shown in this scatterplot, their intelligence scores correlated +.30 with their later income.

Street smarts This child selling candy on the streets of Manaus, Brazil, is developing practical intelligence at a very young age. ▲

With support from the U.S. College Board (which administers the widely used SAT Reasoning Test to U.S. college and university applicants), Sternberg (2006, 2007) and a team of collaborators have developed new measures of creativity (such as thinking up a caption for an untitled cartoon) and practical thinking (such as figuring out how to move a large bed up a winding staircase). Their initial data indicate that these more comprehensive assessments improve prediction of American students' first year college grades, and they do so with reduced ethnic-group differences.

Although Sternberg and Gardner differ on specific points, they agree that multiple abilities can contribute to life success. (Neither candidate in the 2000 U.S. presidential election had scored exceptionally high on college entrance aptitude tests, Sternberg [2000] noted, yet both became influential.) The two theorists also agree that the differing varieties of giftedness add spice to life and challenges for education. Under their influence, many teachers have been trained to appreciate the varieties of ability and to apply multiple intelligence theory in their classrooms. However we define *intelligence* (**TABLE 10.2**), one thing is clear: There's more to creativity than intelligence test scores.

Intelligence and Creativity

3: What is creativity, and what fosters it?

Pierre de Fermat, a seventeenth-century mischievous genius, challenged mathematicians of his day to match his solutions to various number theory problems. His most famous challenge—*Fermat's last theorem*—baffled the greatest mathematical minds, even after a $2 million prize (in today's dollars) was offered in 1908 to whoever first created a proof.

Princeton mathematician Andrew Wiles had pondered the problem for more than 30 years and had come to the brink of a solution. Then, one morning, out of the blue, the final "incredible revelation" struck him. "It was so indescribably beautiful; it was so simple and so elegant. I couldn't understand how I'd missed it and I just stared at

410 CHAPTER 10 :: INTELLIGENCE

TABLE 10.2

COMPARING THEORIES OF INTELLIGENCE

Theory	Summary	Strengths	Other Considerations
Spearman's general intelligence (*g*)	A basic intelligence predicts our abilities in varied academic areas.	Different abilities, such as verbal and spatial, do have some tendency to correlate.	Human abilities are too diverse to be encapsulated by a single general intelligence factor.
Thurstone's primary mental abilities	Our intelligence may be broken down into seven factors: word fluency, verbal comprehension, spatial ability, perceptual speed, numerical ability, inductive reasoning, and memory.	A single *g* score is not as informative as scores for seven primary mental abilities.	Even Thurstone's seven mental abilities show a tendency to cluster, suggesting an underlying *g* factor.
Gardner's multiple intelligences	Our abilities are best classified into eight independent intelligences, which include a broad range of skills beyond traditional school smarts.	Intelligence is more than just verbal and mathematical skills. Other abilities are equally important to our human adaptability.	Should all of our abilities be considered *intelligences*? Shouldn't some be called less vital *talents*?
Sternberg's triarchic	Our intelligence is best classified into three areas that predict real-world success: analytical, creative, and practical.	These three facets can be reliably measured.	1. These three facets may be less independent than Sternberg thought and may actually share an underlying *g* factor. 2. Additional testing is needed to determine whether these facets can reliably predict success.

it in disbelief for 20 minutes. Then during the day I walked around the department, and I'd keep coming back to my desk looking to see if it was still there. It was still there. I couldn't contain myself, I was so excited. It was the most important moment of my working life" (Singh, 1997, p. 25).

Wiles' incredible moment illustrates **creativity**—the ability to produce ideas that are both novel and valuable. Studies suggest that a certain level of aptitude—a score of about 120 on a standard intelligence test—is necessary but not sufficient for creativity. Exceptionally creative architects, mathematicians, scientists, and engineers usually score no higher on intelligence tests than do their less creative peers (MacKinnon & Hall, 1972; Simonton, 2000). So, clearly there is more to creativity than what intelligence tests reveal. Indeed, the two kinds of thinking engage different brain areas. Intelligence tests, which demand a single correct answer, require *convergent thinking*. Creativity tests (*How many uses can you think of for a brick?*) require *divergent thinking*. Injury to the left parietal lobe damages the convergent thinking required by intelligence test scores and for school success. Injury to certain areas of the frontal lobes can leave reading, writing, and arithmetic skills intact but destroy imagination (Kolb & Whishaw, 2006).

Sternberg and his colleagues have identified five components of creativity (Sternberg, 1988, 2003; Sternberg & Lubart, 1991, 1992):

1. **Expertise,** a well-developed base of knowledge, furnishes the ideas, images, and phrases we use as mental building blocks. "Chance favors only the prepared mind," observed Louis Pasteur. The more blocks we have, the more chances we have to combine them in novel ways. Wiles' well-developed base of knowledge put the needed theorems and methods at his disposal.

2. **Imaginative thinking skills** provide the ability to see things in novel ways, to recognize patterns, and to make connections. Having mastered a problem's basic elements, we redefine or explore it in a new way. Copernicus first developed expertise regarding the solar system and its planets, and then creatively defined

:: **creativity** the ability to produce novel and valuable ideas.

the system as revolving around the Sun, not the Earth. Wiles' imaginative solution combined two partial solutions.

3. *A venturesome personality* seeks new experiences, tolerates ambiguity and risk, and perseveres in overcoming obstacles. Inventor Thomas Edison tried countless substances before finding the right one for his lightbulb filament. Wiles said he labored in near-isolation from the mathematics community partly to stay focused and avoid distraction. Venturing encounters with different cultures also fosters creativity (Leung et al., 2008).

4. *Intrinsic motivation* is being driven more by interest, satisfaction, and challenge than by external pressures (Amabile & Hennessey, 1992). Creative people focus less on extrinsic motivators—meeting deadlines, impressing people, or making money—than on the pleasure and stimulation of the work itself. Asked how he solved such difficult scientific problems, Isaac Newton reportedly answered, "By thinking about them all the time." Wiles concurred: "I was so obsessed by this problem that for eight years I was thinking about it all the time—when I woke up in the morning to when I went to sleep at night" (Singh & Riber, 1997).

5. *A creative environment* sparks, supports, and refines creative ideas. After studying the careers of 2026 prominent scientists and inventors, Dean Keith Simonton (1992) noted that the most eminent among them were mentored, challenged, and supported by their relationships with colleagues. Many have the *emotional intelligence* needed to network effectively with peers. Even Wiles stood on the shoulders of others and wrestled his problem with the collaboration of a former student. Creativity-fostering environments often support contemplation. After Jonas Salk solved a problem that led to the polio vaccine while in a monastery, he designed the Salk Institute to provide contemplative spaces where scientists could work without interruption (Sternberg, 2006).

Emotional Intelligence

4: What makes up emotional intelligence?

Also distinct from academic intelligence is *social intelligence*—the know-how involved in comprehending social situations and managing oneself successfully. The concept was first proposed in 1920 by psychologist Edward Thorndike, who noted, "The best mechanic in a factory may fail as a foreman for lack of social intelligence" (Goleman, 2006, p. 83). Like Thorndike, later psychologists have marveled that high-aptitude people are "not, by a wide margin, more effective . . . in achieving better marriages, in successfully raising their children, and in achieving better mental and physical well-being" (Epstein & Meier, 1989). Others have explored the difficulty that some

"You're wise, but you lack tree smarts."

rationally smart people have in processing and managing social information (Cantor & Kihlstrom, 1987; Weis & Süß, 2007). This idea is especially significant for an aspect of social intelligence that John Mayer, Peter Salovey, and David Caruso (2002, 2008) have called **emotional intelligence.** They have developed a test that assesses four emotional intelligence components, which are the abilities to

- *perceive* emotions (to recognize them in faces, music, and stories).
- *understand* emotions (to predict them and how they change and blend).
- *manage* emotions (to know how to express them in varied situations).
- *use* emotions to enable adaptive or creative thinking.

Mindful of popular misuses of their concept, Mayer, Salovey, and Caruso caution against stretching "emotional intelligence" to include varied traits such as self-esteem and optimism, although emotionally intelligent people are self-aware. In both the United States and Germany, those scoring high on managing emotions enjoy higher-quality interactions with friends (Lopes et al., 2004). They avoid being hijacked by overwhelming depression, anxiety, or anger. They can read others' emotions and know what to say to soothe a grieving friend, encourage a colleague, and manage a conflict. Such findings may help explain why, across 69 studies in many countries, those scoring high in emotional intelligence also exhibit modestly better job performance (Van Rooy & Viswesvaran, 2004; Zeidner et al., 2008). They can delay gratification in pursuit of long-range rewards, rather than being overtaken by immediate impulses. Simply said, they are emotionally in tune with others, and thus they often succeed in career, marriage, and parenting situations where academically smarter (but emotionally less intelligent) people fail (Ciarrochi et al., 2006).

Brain damage reports have provided extreme examples of the results of diminished emotional intelligence in people with high general intelligence. Neuroscientist Antonio Damasio (1994) tells of Elliot, who had a brain tumor removed: "I never saw a tinge of emotion in my many hours of conversation with him, no sadness, no impatience, no frustration." Shown disturbing pictures of injured people, destroyed communities, and natural disasters, Elliot showed—and realized he felt—no emotion. He knew but he could not feel. Unable to intuitively adjust his behavior in response to others' feelings, Elliot lost his job. He went bankrupt. His marriage collapsed. He remarried and divorced again. At last report, he was dependent on custodial care from a sibling and a disability check.

Some scholars, however, are concerned that emotional intelligence stretches the concept of intelligence too far. Multiple-intelligence man Howard Gardner (1999) welcomes our stretching the concept into the realms of space, music, and information about ourselves and others. But let us also, he says, respect emotional sensitivity, creativity, and motivation as important but different. Stretch "intelligence" to include everything we prize and it will lose its meaning.

Is Intelligence Neurologically Measurable?

5: To what extent is intelligence related to brain anatomy and neural processing speed?

Using today's neuroscience tools, might we link differences in people's intelligence test performance to dissimilarities in the heart of smarts—the brain? Might we anticipate a future brain test of intelligence?

Brain Size and Complexity

After the brilliant English poet Lord Byron died in 1824, doctors discovered that his brain was a massive 5 pounds, not the normal 3 pounds. Three years later, Beethoven died and his brain was found to have exceptionally numerous and deep convolutions.

::**emotional intelligence** the ability to perceive, understand, manage, and use emotions.

Such observations set brain scientists off studying the brains of other geniuses at their wits' end (Burrell, 2005). Do people with big brains have big smarts?

Alas, some geniuses had small brains, and some dim-witted criminals had brains like Byron's. More recent studies that directly measure brain volume using MRI scans do reveal correlations of about +.33 between brain size (adjusted for body size) and intelligence score (Carey, 2007; McDaniel, 2005). Moreover, as adults age, brain size and nonverbal intelligence test scores fall in concert (Bigler et al., 1995).

One review of 37 brain-imaging studies revealed associations between intelligence and brain size and activity in specific areas, especially within the frontal and parietal lobes (Jung & Haier, 2007). Sandra Witelson would not have been surprised. With the brains of 91 Canadians as a comparison base, Witelson and her colleagues (1999) seized an opportunity to study Einstein's brain. Although not notably heavier or larger in total size than the typical Canadian's brain, Einstein's brain was 15 percent larger in the parietal lobe's lower region—which just happens to be a center for processing mathematical and spatial information. Certain other areas were a tad smaller than average. With different mental functions competing for the brain's real estate, these observations may offer a clue to why Einstein, like some other great physicists such as Richard Feynman and Edward Teller, was slow in learning to talk (Pinker, 1999).

If intelligence does modestly correlate with brain size, the cause could be differing genes, nutrition, environmental stimulation, some combination of these, or perhaps something else. Recall from earlier chapters that experience alters the brain. Rats raised in a stimulating rather than deprived environment develop thicker, heavier cortexes. And learning leaves detectable traces in the brain's neural connections. "Intelligence is due to the development of neural connections in response to the environment," notes University of Sydney psychologist Dennis Garlick (2003).

Postmortem brain analyses reveal that highly educated people die with more synapses—17 percent more in one study—than their less-educated counterparts (Orlovskaya et al., 1999). This does not tell us whether people grow synapses with education, or people with more synapses seek more education, or both. But other evidence suggests that highly intelligent people differ in their *neural plasticity*—their ability during childhood and adolescence to adapt and grow neural connections in response to their environment (Garlick, 2002, 2003).

One study repeatedly scanned the brains of 307 children and teens ages 5 to 19. The surprising result: Kids with average intelligence scores showed modest cortex thickening and thinning—with a peak thickness at age 8, suggesting a short developmental window (Shaw et al., 2006). The most intelligent 7-year-olds had a *thinner* brain cortex, which progressively thickened to age 11 to 13, before thinning with the natural pruning of unused connections. Agile minds came with agile brains.

Efforts to link brain structure with cognition continue. One research team, led by psychologist Richard Haier (2004; Colom et al., 2006), correlated intelligence scores from 47 adult volunteers with scans that measured their volume of *gray matter* (neural cell bodies) and *white matter* (axons and dendrites) in various brain regions. Higher intelligence scores were linked with more gray matter in areas known to be involved in memory, attention, and language.

Brain Function

Even if the modest correlations between brain anatomy and intelligence prove reliable, they only begin to explain intelligence differences. Searching for other explanations, neuroscientists are studying the brain's functioning.

As people contemplate a variety of questions like those found on intelligence tests, a frontal lobe area just above the outer edge of the eyebrows becomes especially active—in the left brain for verbal questions, and on both sides for spatial questions (Duncan et al., 2000). Information from various brain areas seems to converge in this spot,

• Recall from Chapter 1 that the lowest correlation, -1.0, represents perfect disagreement between two sets of scores—as one score goes up, the other goes down. A correlation of zero represents no association. The highest correlation, +1.0, represents perfect agreement—as the first score goes up, so does the second. •

"I am, somehow, less interested in the weight and convolutions of Einstein's brain than in the near certainty that people of equal talent have lived and died in cotton fields and sweatshops."

Stephen Jay Gould,
The Panda's Thumb, 1992

suggesting to researcher John Duncan (2000) that it may be a "global workspace for organizing and coordinating information" and that some people may be "blessed with a workspace that functions very, very well."

Are more intelligent people literally more quick-witted, much as today's speedier computer chips enable more powerful computing than did their predecessors? On some tasks they seem to be. Earl Hunt (1983) found that verbal intelligence scores are predictable from the speed with which people retrieve information from memory. Those who recognize quickly that *sink* and *wink* are different words, or that *A* and *a* share the same name, tend to score high in verbal ability. Extremely precocious 12- to 14-year-old college students are especially quick in responding to such tasks (Jensen, 1989). To try to define *quick-wittedness*, researchers are taking a close look at speed of perception and speed of neural processing of information.

Perceptual Speed   Across many studies, the correlation between intelligence score and the speed of taking in perceptual information tends to be about +.3 to +.5 (Deary & Der, 2005; Sheppard & Vernon, 2008). A typical experiment flashes an incomplete stimulus, as in **FIGURE 10.2**, then a *masking image*—another image that overrides the lingering afterimage of the incomplete stimulus. The researcher then asks participants whether the long side appeared on the right or left. How much stimulus inspection time do you think you would need to answer correctly 80 percent of the time? Perhaps .01 second? Or .02 second? Those who perceive very quickly tend to score somewhat higher on intelligence tests, particularly on tests based on perceptual rather than verbal problem solving.

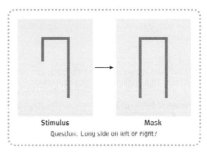

Stimulus   Mask

Question: Long side on left or right?

➤ **FIGURE 10.2**

An inspection time task A stimulus is flashed before being overridden by a masking image. How long would you need to glimpse the stimulus at the left to answer the question? People who can perceive the stimulus very quickly tend to score somewhat higher on intelligence tests. (Adapted from Deary & Stough, 1996.)

Neurological Speed   Do the quicker processing and perceptions of highly intelligent people reflect greater neural processing speed? Repeated studies have found that their brain waves do register a simple stimulus (such as a flash of light or a beeped tone) more quickly and with greater complexity (Caryl, 1994; Deary & Caryl, 1993; Reed & Jensen, 1992). The evoked brain response also tends to be slightly faster when people with high rather than low intelligence scores perform a simple task, such as pushing a button when an *X* appears on a screen (McGarry-Roberts et al., 1992).

Neural processing speed on a simple task seems far removed from the untimed responses to complex intelligence test items, such as, "In what way are *wool* and *cotton* alike?" As yet, notes intelligence expert Nathan Brody (1992, 2001), we have no firm understanding of *why* fast reactions on simple tasks should predict intelligence test performance, though he suspects they reflect one's "core information processing ability." Philip Vernon (1983) has speculated that "faster cognitive processing may allow more information to be acquired." Perhaps people who more quickly process information accumulate more information—about wool, cotton, and millions of other things. Or perhaps, as one Australian-Dutch research team has found, processing speed and intelligence may correlate not because one causes the other but because they share an underlying genetic influence (Luciano et al., 2005).

The neurological approach to understanding intelligence (and so many other things in psychology) is currently in its heyday. Will this new research reduce what we now call the *g* factor to simple measures of underlying brain activity? Or are these efforts totally wrongheaded because what we call intelligence is not a single general trait but several culturally adaptive skills? The controversies surrounding the nature of intelligence are a long way from resolution. . . .

BEFORE YOU MOVE ON . . .

> ### ASK YOURSELF
The modern concept of multiple intelligences (as proposed by Gardner and Sternberg) assumes that the analytical school smarts measured by traditional intelligence tests are important abilities but that other abilities are also important. Different people have different gifts. What are yours?

> ### TEST YOURSELF 1
Joseph, a Harvard Law School student, has a straight-A average, writes for the *Harvard Law Review*, and will clerk for a Supreme Court justice next year. His grandmother, Judith, is very proud of him, saying he is way more intelligent than she ever was. But Joseph is also very proud of Judith: As a young woman, she was imprisoned by the Nazis. When the war ended, she walked out of Germany, contacted an agency helping refugees, and began a new life in the United States as an assistant chef in her cousin's restaurant. According to the definition of *intelligence* in this chapter, is Joseph the only intelligent person in this story? Why or why not?

Answers to the Test Yourself Questions can be found in Appendix B at the end of the book.

twins raised together are more similar than those of other siblings, and the scores of identical twins raised apart are slightly less similar (though still very highly correlated) than the scores of identical twins raised together. Other studies, of children reared in extremely impoverished, enriched, or culturally different environments, indicate that life experiences can significantly influence intelligence test performance.

11: How and why do gender and racial groups differ in mental ability scores?

Males and females average the same in overall intelligence. There are, however, some small but intriguing gender differences in specific abilities. Girls are better spellers, more verbally fluent, better at locating objects, better at detecting emotions, and more sensitive to touch, taste, and color. Boys outperform girls at spatial ability and related mathematics, though girls outperform boys in math computation. Boys also outnumber girls at the low and high extremes of mental abilities. Psychologists debate evolutionary, brain-based, and

cultural explanations of such gender differences. As a group, Whites score higher than their Hispanic and Black counterparts, though the gap is not as great as it was half a century and more ago. The evidence suggests that environmental differences are largely, perhaps entirely responsible for these group differences.

12: Are intelligence tests inappropriately biased?

Aptitude tests aim to predict how well a test-taker will perform in a given situation. So they are necessarily "biased" in the sense that they are sensitive to performance differences caused by cultural experience. But bias can also mean what psychologists commonly mean by the term—that a test predicts less accurately for one group than for another. In this sense of the term, most experts consider the major aptitude tests unbiased. *Stereotype threat,* a self-confirming concern that one will be evaluated based on a negative stereotype, affects performance on all kinds of tests.

Terms and Concepts to Remember

intelligence test, p. 406
intelligence, p. 406
general intelligence (*g*), p. 406
factor analysis, p. 406
savant syndrome, p. 407
creativity, p. 410
emotional intelligence, p. 412
mental age, p. 416

Stanford-Binet, p. 417
intelligence quotient (IQ), p. 417
achievement tests, p. 418
aptitude tests, p. 418
Wechsler Adult Intelligence Scale (WAIS), p. 418
standardization, p. 419
normal curve, p. 419

reliability, p. 421
validity, p. 421
content validity, p. 421
predictive validity, p. 421
mental retardation, p. 425
Down syndrome, p. 425
stereotype threat, p. 438

 WEB

Multiple-choice self-tests and more may be found at www.worthpublishers.com/myers

MUSCLE READING

Muscle reading is a great strategy for both textbook reading and any dense reading packed with information.

STEP 1: Preview the chapter or reading.

STEP 2: If the chapter has sections, follow those.   If it doesn't, use a pencil to mark off sections based on paragraph topics. This doesn't have to be exact; you want to end up with manageable sections to work with.

STEP 3: Read the first section quickly.   Don't stop to look up words you don't know, but do underline or circle them for later.

STEP 4: Go back and reread the section, this time more carefully, trying to really understand the material.   Annotate as you go. This read-through should be slower. Take the time to figure out words you don't know using context clues. Don't forget to note their meanings in the margin when you can figure them out. If you can't figure out the meaning of a word from context clues, look it up in a good dictionary. Remember to write the definition in your own words so that you know you understand the meaning fully.

STEP 5: Take a break.   Stretch, stand up, or close your eyes for a minute.

STEP 6: Review the previous section's annotations.

STEP 7: Move on to the next section.

Reading Fiction

Reading fiction requires slightly different strategies, since fictional texts are not organized in the same ways as most nonfiction texts you will read in college. There are many genres of fiction: literary fiction, science fiction, fantasy, historical fiction, mysteries and thrillers, graphic novels, romance, and young adult, to name a few. Some nonfiction—such as histories, biographies, memoirs, autobiographies, and true crime—feels a lot like fiction, and you can use most of the techniques for fiction

STRATEGIES FOR READING FICTION

Strategy	Reading Stage
Annotating	during reading
Note taking	during reading
Story star map	post-reading

reading on those types of nonfiction. For instance, biographies often have compelling characters and settings and plots like fiction does.

ELEMENTS OF FICTION

When reading fiction, look for and analyze the following basic elements of a short story or novel.

Characters. These people populate the story. Most short stories have at least one or two main characters; a novel might have more. Often, there are also minor characters who appear less frequently in the story.

Setting. The setting is both the location where the story takes place and the time period (era) in which it is set. The same location one hundred years apart is not the same setting: For example, one story that takes place in New York City in the 1960s and another that takes place in New York City in 2060 do not have the same setting.

Plot. The plot is, essentially, what happens during the story. It's what makes us want to turn the page to see what happens next. Some people refer to the plot as the story arc.

Conflict. The conflict is the main problem that the characters are trying to deal with. A short story generally has one central conflict; a longer work might have one central and several other smaller conflicts.

Symbol. A symbol is something that stands for something else. We use symbols all the time in our daily lives. We give the "thumbs up" symbol to mean that everything is good, or okay, and we use hearts to symbolize love.

Theme. The theme is a central topic or subject of the story.

ANNOTATING FICTION

Should you really write in the margins of your novel or short story? Absolutely! Annotating fiction is one of the best reading and study activities you can practice. Because works of fiction are not thesis driven or evidence based, it might not seem clear what you should annotate while you read. Really, though, you are annotating many of the same kinds of things that you would for an essay or article: interesting or significant passages, unfamiliar words, and questions or confusing sections. In addition, make notes in the margins when a new character is introduced or when a character behaves atypically—both might become something to discuss in class or in an essay. Underline important passages. Also annotate any symbols that seem important, themes that you recognize, and places where the plot "thickens."

TAKING NOTES ON FICTION

Taking notes requires discipline, but it does not have to take the fun out of reading. It should help you better appreciate the way the author writes. And it will definitely help you write a better paper. Take several different types of notes as you read.

Plot notes.   In your notes, write down what happens in the novel as you finish reading each chapter or section. It's great if you can also write down page numbers so you can find things more easily. We always think we'll remember what happened where, but we often don't. This is especially true in a novel that does not follow a chronological time line. Does it begin at the beginning and then end at the end? Does the story begin at the end and then go backwards in time through memory or flashbacks? Nutshell summaries of each chapter's plot help you keep track of a novel's structure.

For more on nutshell summaries, see Chapter 1, Reading and Responding to College Texts, page 2.

Thematic notes.   As you read, you start to notice themes that keep emerging. A theme is a central topic or subject of a story or book. These themes vary from story to story or novel to novel. For instance, in Shakespeare's *Romeo and Juliet*, themes include love, family, coming of age, sexuality, and rebelliousness. Usually a novel or short story has a few major themes and several minor ones. Once you identify a theme, keep a running list of page numbers where it is mentioned. By the time you finish the book, you will have a chart with various themes and lists of page numbers under them. The inside of the book's back cover or a blank page at the end is a great place to keep your list. This list makes essay writing much easier; you just have to look back at those passages, figure out how they all relate, and develop your thesis from the material.

Character notes.   Keep a chart, family tree, or list of all the characters. Write down the page number where they are first introduced. This is usually where they are described in most detail. Depending on the novel, you might find it useful to make a list of the major scenes with each major character.

STORY STAR MAPS

A third strategy for reading fiction is the story star map. After reading a short story or novel, answer the following five questions on the star graph:

1. When does the story take place?
2. Where does the story take place?
3. Who are the major characters in the story?
4. What happens in the story?
5. How does the story end?

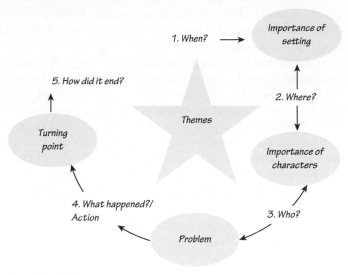

Story Star Map

These basic elements of the story assist you in understanding the larger meaning of the story and the themes. Once you have these five elements filled out on the star, the next task is to think about how they relate. Add bubbles for the following questions:

6. Setting: Taking both the location and the time into consideration, what is the importance of the setting? Is the story set in Germany during World War II? The American South during the civil rights movement? A rural location in the present day? What does setting add to the story? Write this in a bubble connected to both "Where?" and "When?"

7. Characters: Taking both setting and the characters into consideration, what is the importance of the characters? For example, if the setting is Germany during World War II and the character is a German Jewish girl, the significance is that she is in danger. If the character is a German Christian girl, the significance might be that she has to make difficult moral decisions about what she sees and participates in. Write the importance of the characters in a bubble connected to the "Where?" and "Who?" points of the star.

8. Problem: Taking into consideration the importance of the character(s) and the action, what problem does the character face? Write the problem in a bubble connected to the "Who?" and "What happened?/Action" points of the star.

9. Turning point and resolution: The turning point is the point in the story where the character takes an action or makes a decision that determines the outcome. The resolution is the outcome. In a bubble between the "What happened?/Action" and "How did it end?" bubbles, write down the turning point in the story and the resolution.

10. Theme(s): The theme(s) might be clear to you as you read, but often, we won't have enough understanding of the central subject or message until after thinking about how all the other elements of the story relate to one another. Now that the story star is filled out almost completely, think about what subject or idea relates to all the points of the star. There are often big themes and smaller themes, especially in a longer work or novel. Write down the major theme(s) inside the star.

chapter review

Chapter 5 introduces additional reading strategies that help you tackle the more challenging readings of college. After reading through this chapter, you should have a variety of strategies to choose from during all stages of the reading process: pre-reading, during reading, and post-reading. Although you won't use all the strategies all the time, the goal of this chapter is to give you a range of strategies that you can draw from whenever you need one.

To review this chapter, choose one or more of the following strategies:

1. Skim back over the chapter and make a list of the reading strategies you learned. Then make a list of all your reading this semester in all your classes (textbooks, Web sites, articles, and so on). Next to each reading assignment, make notes about which strategies you might use to help you tackle these readings.

2. Make a map of this chapter as a way to practice mapping.

3. If you skipped any activities, do them now as a way to deepen your understanding of the material.

4. Try to explain what you have learned to someone you know. Discuss the key concepts and give some of your own examples to illustrate those concepts.

6
Audience, Purpose, and Topic

in this chapter

- Why Do Audience and Purpose Matter?
- How Do You Find a Topic You Care About?
- What Is Tone?
- How Does Your Title Help You Focus Your Topic?

Imagine that you just started a new job and your boss invites you to attend a party. You know you have to go, but you don't know whether the party will be big or small, formal or casual, really about making friends or about impressing the higher-ups. You might be very nervous, right? When you arrive, you might need a few minutes to get your bearings and relax. Unfortunately, during those first few minutes, you are likely to be introduced to a lot of people, whose names you probably will promptly forget. Horrible, right?

Now imagine that you are invited to the same party, but some nice coworker calls you beforehand to give you the lowdown: It's a suit and tie event, don't bring a date, and you're not there to have fun but to make connections and meet the upper-level executives, who are the people who decide how big your bonus will be that year. Now you might still be nervous—who wouldn't be?—but you would walk in there with a clear sense of what to expect, and be prepared to remember the names of all the people you met.

What's the major difference between these two scenarios? Knowing the audience and purpose of the event. Once you know who will be in the room and why they are there, you can get a lot more out of the event, right from the start.

> **LearningCurve**
> For extra practice in the skills covered in this chapter, visit **bedfordstmartins.com /readwriteconnect**.

Audience and Purpose

Knowing the audience and purpose is equally important while reading. When you start reading something, if you don't know the audience and purpose, you spend the first few minutes with your mind racing, trying to figure out what type of text you have in your hands. It's not that you aren't paying attention. In fact, your brain is very active. It's just that you are still trying to figure out *why* the author is writing the text, and *for whom*, and that makes you unable to focus on *what* the author is actually saying—just like at the party.

Figuring out the audience and purpose of a text *before* you start actually reading will help you understand the text much better. Once you know the audience and purpose, you will be better equipped to understand the vocabulary, point of view, voice, and tone of the reading. When you have a clear idea of the audience and purpose, you can also respond to the text more critically: You will find yourself asking and answering questions as you read like "Is the author doing a good job choosing examples?" or "Why didn't the author talk about X?" Such questioning deepens your reading experience.

DETERMINING THE AUDIENCE AND PURPOSE IN A READING

For more on pre-reading, see Chapter 1, Reading and Responding to College Texts, pages 3–6.

So how do you figure out an author's audience and purpose? Remember the pre-reading strategies from Chapter 1? Before you begin to read something, quickly skim over it to evaluate the following fundamentals:

- The title, subtitle, headings, and format of the article
- Any pictures or graphics
- Any "apparatus" surrounding the reading—the author's biography, glossed words, or questions/activities intended to guide the reader's response to the reading
- The context of the reading—when and where it was published

As you scan these features of the reading, look for clues about audience and purpose. For instance, if there are pictures, what types of pictures are they? Who might be their target audience? What might their purpose be?

Another way to learn about audience and purpose is to look at the type of publication in which the material was originally published. For instance, the purpose of the front page of a newspaper is to give news as objectively as possible. If you are looking at the editorial page, then the purpose is to give an opinion or news analysis. The audience is the same—newspaper readers, who are a diverse group—but the purpose is different.

Most successful college readers pre-read an article for the features listed here. They then read the opening lines and pause to ask themselves a few questions:

- What kinds of words are being used in this reading? Is this formal or informal writing? Is it full of jargon and technical terms or does it mostly use common words?
- What's the point of view of this reading? Objective or subjective? Third person or first person? How does the point of view relate to the author's purpose?
- What does the language sound like? What words best describe the tone, voice, and style of the writing? (For example, is it engaging? Dry? Sarcastic?)

READING FOR AUDIENCE AND PURPOSE

Imagine three different types of readings about the topic of drug addiction: a chapter from a college-level introductory psychology textbook; a scholarly journal article; and a personal memoir. Let's see how the features of the text provide clues to audience and purpose.

Textbook chapter.   Take a look at the excerpt on page 172 on drug addiction from the introductory college psychology textbook *Psychology*, Ninth Edition, by David G. Myers.

The fact that the excerpt is from an introductory college textbook tells us that it is intended for an audience of college students, most of whom are fairly new to the material. The features highlighted in the excerpt reinforce this conclusion and suggest that the book's purpose is primarily informative, and the author's goal is to convey a lot of information as efficiently as possible. Textbooks often have a side column that might include points of importance and interest to the student reader: vocabulary, interesting facts, and even humor. The chart in the middle creates an easy visual aid, and the use of bolded and colored subheadings helps the reader quickly determine the overall structure of the information.

Scholarly article.   Now take a look at the excerpt on page 173 from a scholarly journal article.

Again, knowing where the reading was published gives us information about the audience. The fact that this article was published in a scholarly journal suggests that the audience is scholars and experts—academics, researchers, and perhaps very advanced students. As the title, headings, and abstract indicate, its purpose is more narrow than that of the college textbook; the authors' goal is to tell this group of readers about a new scientific study on teenage use of ecstasy. The writing is full of specialists' jargon or terminology, and the highly detailed and technical charts in the middle of the article would likely be difficult for a nonexpert reader to interpret.

Personal memoir.   Now take a look at one final example: an excerpt from a blog-based memoir focused on drug addiction on page 174.

hormone-delivering "libido patches" for middle-aged women, and Adderall for students hoping to focus their concentration. Before drifting off into REM-depressed sleep, our hypothetical drug user is dismayed by news reports of pill-sharing, pill-popping college students and of celebrity deaths (Anna Nicole Smith, Heath Ledger) attributed to accidental overdoses of lethal drug combinations.

Dependence and Addiction

12: What are tolerance, dependence, and addiction, and what are some common misconceptions about addiction?

Why might a person who rarely drinks alcohol get tipsy on one can of beer, but an experienced drinker show few effects until the second six-pack? Continued use of alcohol and other psychoactive drugs produces **tolerance.** As the user's brain adapts its chemistry to offset the drug effect (a process called *neuroadaptation*), the user requires larger and larger doses to experience the same effect (**FIGURE 3.17**). Despite the connotations of alcohol "tolerance," an alcoholic's brain, heart, and liver suffer damage from the excessive alcohol being "tolerated."

Users who stop taking psychoactive drugs may experience the undesirable side effects of **withdrawal.** As the body responds to the drug's absence, the user may feel physical pain and intense cravings, indicating **physical dependence.** People can also develop **psychological dependence,** particularly for stress-relieving drugs. Such drugs, although not physically addictive, can become an important part of the user's life, often as a way of relieving negative emotions. With either physical or psychological dependence, the user's primary focus may be obtaining and using the drug.

::**psychoactive drug** a chemical substance that alters perceptions and moods.

::**tolerance** the diminishing effect with regular use of the same dose of a drug, requiring the user to take larger and larger doses before experiencing the drug's effect.

::**withdrawal** the discomfort and distress that follow discontinuing the use of an addictive drug.

::**physical dependence** a physiological need for a drug, marked by unpleasant withdrawal symptoms when the drug is discontinued.

::**psychological dependence** a psychological need to use a drug, such as to relieve negative emotions.

::**addiction** compulsive drug craving and use, despite adverse consequences.

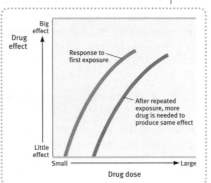

▶ **FIGURE 3.17**
Drug tolerance With repeated exposure to a psychoactive drug, the drug's effect lessens. Thus, it takes bigger doses to get the desired effect.

Misconceptions About Addiction

An **addiction** is a compulsive craving for a substance despite adverse consequences and often with physical symptoms such as aches, nausea, and distress following sudden withdrawal. Worldwide, reports the World Health Organization (2008), 90 million people suffer from such problems related to alcohol and other drugs.

In recent pop psychology, the supposedly irresistible seduction of addiction has been extended to cover many behaviors formerly considered bad habits or even sins. Has the concept been stretched too far? Are addictions as irresistible as commonly believed? Many drug researchers believe the following three myths about addiction are *false:*

Myth 1. Addictive drugs quickly corrupt; for example, morphine taken to control pain is powerfully addictive and often leads to heroin abuse. People given morphine to control pain rarely develop the cravings of the addict who uses morphine as a mood-altering drug (Melzack, 1990). But some people—perhaps 10 percent—do indeed have a hard time using a psychoactive drug in moderation or stopping altogether. Even so, controlled, occasional users of drugs such as alcohol and marijuana far outnumber those addicted to these substances (Gazzaniga, 1988; Siegel, 1990). "Even for a very addictive drug like cocaine, only 15 to 16 percent of

Sample Textbook Page

Drugs: education, prevention and policy,
October 2010; 17(5): 507–527

informa
healthcare

*Article comes from a
specialized academic
journal*

ORIGINAL ARTICLE

Factors associated with teenage ecstasy use

*Title is plain and
informative*

PATRICK MCCRYSTAL & ANDREW PERCY

*Institute of Child Care Research, School of Sociology Social Policy and Social Work,
Queens University Belfast, 6 College Park, Belfast BT7 1LP, UK*

*Authors are academic
researchers who are open
to communication from
other experts*

Abstract
Aims: The aim of this article was to investigate the factors associated with ecstasy use in
school-aged teenagers.
Methods: This was a longitudinal study of adolescent drug use, which was undertaken
in three towns in Northern Ireland. A questionnaire was administered annually to
participants. In this article ecstasy use patterns amongst a cohort of young people aged
14–16 years participating in the Belfast Youth Development Study (BYDS) was explored.
Findings: The percentage of those who had used ecstasy at least once increased from 7%
when aged 14 years to 9% at 15 and 13% at 16 years. Female gender, delinquency,
problem behaviours at school and the number of evenings spent out with friends each
week were found to be significant variables predicting 'ever use' of ecstasy in all 3 years by
logistic regression.
Conclusions: The findings suggest that ecstasy use patterns may be changing from their
historical perception as a 'party' drug, as the demographic profile ecstasy of users in this
study reflected the traditional profile of illicit drug use during adolescence, which raises
challenges for addressing the problems associated with this drug.

*Article begins with an
abstract*

*Article is structured
according to the scientific
method (like high school
lab reports)*

Introduction

Despite being a relatively new drug (van Ours, 2005) ecstasy (3,4-methylene-
dioxymethamphetamine, MDMA) has become widely used as a recreational drug
by young people around the world (Christophersen, 2000), and for over a decade
has been an established part of youth culture in some countries (WHO, 1996)
and part of the acid house, rave and dance scene in the UK for 20 years now. It is
labelled one of the 'party' or 'club' drugs with use highest amongst teenagers and
young adults in social settings including bars, concerts and dance parties
(Koesters, Greenberg, Pollack, & Dolezal, 2002). Early studies of ecstasy users

Correspondence: Patrick McCrystal, Institute of Child Care Research, School of Sociology, Social
policy and Social Work, Queens University Belfast, 6 College Park, Belfast BT7 1LP.
Tel: 00442890975991. Fax: 00442890975900. E-mail: P.McCrystal@qub.ac.uk

ISSN 0968–7637 print/ISSN 1465–3370 online © 2010 Informa UK Ltd.
DOI: 10.3109/09687630902810691

Blog title shows it's about her life

First person, confessional article title

Opens with strong, emotional personal anecdote

Mamapundit.com

A Parenting Secret I Am No Longer Willing to Keep
Mamapundit / Katie Allison Granju

I worried and fretted, when my eldest child was brought to the intensive care unit three days ago, that the nurses and doctors might treat him differently, maybe even give him substandard care once they knew why he was there. That's because he was admitted not after a car accident in which he was blameless. Not due to some mysterious, unknown fever. No, he was rushed to the hospital, nearly lifeless, after a massive drug overdose and a brutal physical assault related to his involvement with drugs. But I was wrong to worry about this; in the time since we began our bedside hospital vigil—could it really only have been three or four days ago?—every single medical professional on the staff here at the hospital has been wonderful—skilled, compassionate, and just plain amazing.

This wasn't the first time I've been concerned about what people would think if they found out. In fact, I've been worried about what would happen if our family's terrible secret "got out"—that my son suffers from a life threatening drug addiction—for several years now. I mean, some people DID know—the people closest to us. And as someone who has been writing essays and blogging about her family life for many years, I had alluded to the issue obliquely here and there since about 2008—so I am sure some readers had their suspicions. However, until this week, until H overdosed and ended up on life support in the ICU, I had never said it clearly, proactively, without obfuscation or minimizing.

But I am saying it now, out loud, in public, for the first time: I am the mother of a drug addict.

My beloved, firstborn child suffers from a terrible disease, addiction, and he has been struggling with it for several years. It started with early juvenile experimentation with marijuana at about age 14 and has progressed to where he is now, addicted to hard street drugs and as a result, lying in a critical care hospital bed, dealing with a horrific brain trauma along with various other physical injuries that are the direct result of that disease.

He has been to drug treatment (almost a year, inpatient), 12 step meetings, jail and on the streets. I have cried, begged, threatened, prayed, and beat myself up every way a mother can possibly beat herself up. I know I made mistakes in raising him. My first and biggest mistake—and one that I implore other parents reading this not to make themselves—was to minimize and rationalize my child's earliest drug use as the kind of "experimentation" that "lots of kids" try when they are adolescents. In fact, however, this "experimentation" was an early warning signal, a huge, blaring, shrieking, flashing early warning sign, and I chose not to see or hear it for what it really was. It was akin to early stage pediatric cancer and instead, I treated it like he had made a "D" on his report card or something similarly inconsequential.

When he was admitted to the hospital earlier this week, they warned us he might not make it. He has pulled through the critical first few days, and we are now looking at weeks and months of neurological and physical rehabilitation to bring our son back. I will fight like hell to get him where he needs to be, but then what? Then are we right back where we were at the beginning of this week, before the overdose? Back to a place where a beautiful, brilliant, sensitive, amazing, loved-beyond-all-reason teenage boy can't see past his next fix? Can't or won't stop careening down a one way path straight to hell?

I don't know. I don't know what our next steps will be. But I know this: I am no longer willing—or ABLE—to keep this secret. Maybe people will judge me. Maybe they will label me the bad mother I fear that I am to have ended up in this place. Maybe they will shun me, my son, my family. I don't know. But I do know that the disease has now declared itself to such a degree that it's no longer possible to keep it a secret, even if I wanted to.

By the end, the tone shifts—she seems to be taking a stand

The author, Katie Allison Granju, is a regular blogger on parenting issues with a large following, but before this entry, she had never before admitted to having a drug-addicted son. Since this blog is published online, you can assume the audience is a general one, made up of people who are curious to know what it's like to suffer from or recover from an addiction. In this case, as in many such memoirs, the author's purpose is to express her experience and to convey how painful and awful addiction is. How do the tone, voice, and use of examples in this blog differ from those in the other two sources? How does the use of first person influence your reading of the piece?

> **practice it**   Pre-Reading for Audience and Purpose
>
> Look over the readings from Chapter 21, 22, or 23. Although each of the readings is about the same basic topic or theme, they vary in audience and purpose. Choose three readings, and evaluate their audience and purpose:
>
> 1. How can you make an educated guess about audience and purpose before you even start reading?
> 2. What specific features of each text did you use to determine the audience and purpose?

Topics

FINDING SOMETHING TO SAY AND CARING ABOUT IT

When deciding on a topic for a college writing assignment, student writers often face two common problems:

1. They were assigned a topic that just doesn't inspire them.
2. They choose a topic only because they think they will be able to write enough about it to meet the page requirement.

Good writing rarely results from either situation. Why? Because the best writing comes from actually having something to say—from having a purpose and wanting to communicate to an audience.

As the old saying goes, "Write what you know." Whenever possible, choose a topic that truly interests you, and worry about the page limit later. If your instructor gives you three or four essay assignment options, don't rush to pick the first one or the one that seems easiest. Give it some thought. Which topic really interests you most? Which readings for the class did you like best, and how might you incorporate them into the assignment? Take the time to decide on your essay topic and to focus the topic in the way that is most interesting to you.

If you have an assigned topic that doesn't immediately thrill you, create a sense of excitement by connecting it to other things that *do* interest you, and by molding the purpose and audience to suit the ideas you want to express. The big difference between a successful student and one who is just getting by is how the student approaches an assignment that doesn't immediately create a spark of interest.

So how do you motivate yourself to get interested in an assigned topic? There are as many approaches to the topic as there are students in the room. Really. So make your essay interesting—maybe even fun—to write. Choose a particular focus that speaks to you. (Don't worry about limiting the topic too much—by focusing a topic more closely, you often actually make it easier to fill up the required pages.)

Convinced? Ready to get started? You probably already have the brainstorming skills you need. Start by taking out the essay assignment and reading it over a couple of times. Highlight words or phrases that refer to the topic of the assignment. Then list these words at the top of a freewriting page, or put these words into cluster bubbles. Elsewhere on the page, make a list or cluster about something that you're currently very passionate about, even if it seems to have nothing in common with the assignment topic.

For example, let's say you just finished reading the unit on siblings. Your essay assignment looks like this:

> Write a thesis-driven argument essay about some aspect of sibling relationships. You might consider the following topics: sibling rivalry, only children, and adult siblings.

Imagine that you couldn't care less about siblings, don't really get along with your older brother, who lives across the country, and don't feel inspired by this topic. However, you are really interested in running track. There seems to be no possible connection between running and siblings at first glance. When you think further about it, though, and brainstorm a little on both topics, you see that the competitive spirit that you feel when running has some similarities with the rivalries siblings sometimes feel. Use this connection, and your natural curiosity about things related to running, as springboards to a topic that matters to you.

For instance, in terms of running, you might be curious about the following questions:

- What types of competition or rivalry are helpful?
- When can competition or rivalry become too extreme or in some way bad for you?
- How does the coach influence rivalry within a team? Between teams? Should a coach create rivalries or downplay them?

Now, think about how these questions might relate to siblings. You could substitute the word *parent* for coach and *family* for team, and ask essentially the same questions about siblings that you asked about athletes.

After trying brainstorming exercises like these, you may discover that the topic now intrigues you, or that you still don't care about siblings. At the very least, though, this exercise gives you a better sense of how to focus your writing assignment and help you get started.

practice it Brainstorming to Find a Topic That Matters to You

Look at your essay assignment (or, if you aren't working on one currently, choose one of the sample prompts from Chapter 21, 22, or 23). What interests you about this essay prompt? What doesn't interest you? How can you spark some curiosity in yourself about this assignment? What can you connect it to that *does* really matter to you?

MAKING A BROAD TOPIC MORE SPECIFIC

Once you have arrived at a topic you like, if you are like most students, you still need to tweak it to make it specific enough. For example:

Unclear Topic   This paper will be about video games.

This topic is far too broad. What *about* video games? Ask yourself: Why did I think of the topic in the first place?

Clear Topic   Many people are concerned about children who sit at home and play video games alone every day after school. Should they be?

The second topic clearly states the *who* (children who play video games alone), *where* (at home), and *when* (every day after school). It also suggests a *what* (people's concern—is it warranted?). Now the topic is much more clear and specific.

Peer review.   To figure out how specific you need to be, start by listening to your peers and friends. State your topic to them, and then sit quietly and take notes while they brainstorm a list of all the things they think you might be talking about. This method will give you a good idea of how clear and specific your topic is, because it will reveal their preconceived notions about the topic. Next, look at the list and use it to help focus your topic. Make your idea as specific as possible and write it up clearly in a complete sentence. Don't begin with "this paper is about" or "my topic is" or any other phrases that refer to yourself or the paper.

For example, tell your friends that your topic for your English class essay is money and how we manage it. Ask them what they think of when they hear the phrase "money management" and then sit back and see what they say. They are likely to brainstorm a list that looks something like this:

- debt
- credit cards
- never having enough money to buy stuff
- paying for college
- student loans—good idea or not?
- shopping and spending too much
- running out of money
- parents' money problems and fights about money
- buying presents for boyfriend/girlfriend
- college expenses—books, food, going out
- paying bills
- saving for vacations, cars, etc.

Take a close look at the list. It gives you a good idea about potential readers' expectations. The fact that this list is so wide-ranging demonstrates that you need to focus your topic. Maybe you are just talking about money management for college students, not everyone. Maybe you're just talking about avoiding credit card debt. In order to ensure that you are being clear and specific, carefully describe your topic so your reader knows exactly what you will discuss in your essay (and what you won't be covering).

Once you have a list like this, highlight the items on it that directly pertain to your topic and cross out those that don't. Then write a sentence that explains your topic, sticking to the words on the list. Here's an example:

> College students often struggle to pay their school expenses and have a hard time deciding whether student loans are a wise choice.

Ask questions.   Another way to become specific is to write a very basic topic idea and then revise it by asking questions. Often, you can take a vague or broad topic and make it more clear and specific by asking questions to get important details and then adding a few words.

STEP 1: In your notebook, write your topic as best you can.

STEP 2: Now circle each word that could be made more specific.   Brainstorm more detail about each word.

STEP 3: Finally, take your best words and phrases and rewrite a more focused, specific topic.

Let's look at an example:

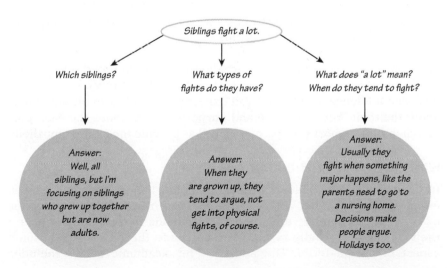

Now, take that information that you've added and rewrite the topic with more specifics:

> Adult siblings often argue during holidays or whenever major family decisions need to be made.

Much better! Incorporating the words and specific details from the question and answer process really helps focus the topic. Now your readers won't waste time wondering what exactly you mean, and won't question why you're not discussing children's squabbles over toys.

---

practice it   Identifying the Topic

Reread the article "Men, Women, and Money" (see pp. 50–57). Underline or highlight the topic in the first few paragraphs of Mellan's essay. Can you clearly identify the topic? Do you understand it? How would you explain the topic to a friend who hadn't read the article? Write down your thoughts in the margins of the essay.

Crafting Your Paper's Audience, Purpose, and Tone

Once your curiosity is sparked and you have a clear, specific topic, you might be tempted to jump right in and start brainstorming all that you can on the topic. As part of your brainstorming, though, you must consider the audience and purpose of your writing. Remember, audience and purpose often shape the tone, word choice, style, content, and even the structure of a piece of writing, as we have seen in the three types of writing about drug use earlier in this chapter.

Audience and purpose also often determine what you put into a text and what you leave out. For instance, how much background information you include in an introductory paragraph depends entirely on whom your intended audience is and what you expect your readers to already know about the topic. Your audience and purpose will influence the examples you choose to support your points, as well as provide the context for them.

WRITING FOR A PARTICULAR AUDIENCE

In the majority of college writing assignments, the assumed audience is a "college-level reader." What exactly does this mean? Essays written for a "college-level reader" are generally academic in tone and style, and their purpose is usually to argue or persuade the reader about some aspect of the material. The audience for academic essays includes college students and college-educated general readers—people who read and understand sophisticated essays but who may not be experts in the particular topic under discussion, and who may not have read the books or articles referred to in the paper. (This is why you should briefly identify books and articles you discuss somewhere early in your paper, and also identify experts to whom you refer, even if you know that your instructor knows who the expert is because he or she assigned the text.)

In most written and oral communication outside the college class-room, the audience you write to changes constantly, and your ability to adapt to these changes largely determines how successful your written and oral communication will be. For instance, an e-mail about your bro-ken computer to your good friend who works in the IT department might be phrased very differently from a formal request to your boss justifying your need for an expensive replacement. A phone message left for a best friend differs significantly from one left for a potential employer.

If you are allowed to choose your audience for a college assignment, then use these basic demographic categories to determine your ideal reader:

- Age
- Gender
- Ethnicity
- Educational level
- Ability level
- Career/profession
- Role in society
- Other important and relevant factors (for example, if your topic is drug use, then it would be important to know if your audience had used drugs, had thought about using drugs, or had never used drugs)

Audiences are, after all, made up of people, and knowing something about the people you hope to reach with your writing will help you write better. Age, for instance, can be divided in many ways: babies, toddlers, preschool-ers, grade schoolers, tweens, teens, young adults, thirty-somethings, middle-aged adults, and the elderly. You might group some of these together, depending on their shared experiences. An essay might speak to tweens and teens, or teens and young adults. Be aware, though, that as with topics, narrowing the focus of the audience sometimes makes it easier to generate ideas. In other words, the more you focus, the more you have to say.

For instance, if your instructor assigned a paper about the topic of fame and celebrity, but allowed you to choose your audience and purpose, you might decide to focus on teen readers or parent readers, women or men, pro-ducers of media or consumers of media. How would an essay intended for teenagers who watch reality television differ from an essay intended for par-ents who want their young children to become stars? The purpose in both cases might be similar: to caution readers to be careful about valuing fame too much. However, the approach you would take—from the language used to the examples given—would probably be quite different because of the audience.

WRITING WITH A PURPOSE

Most writers determine the audience and purpose together, developing one alongside the other. For instance, if you want to write to teens who watch too much reality television, then you probably already know your purpose in choosing that specific audience: to convince them to turn off the television and do something else. Sometimes, though, you cannot quite articulate your purpose to the audience you have in mind or which has been assigned to you. If that's the case, ask yourself the following questions:

- What do I want to say to this audience?
- Why do I want to say this? What do I hope to accomplish?
- What can I say to this audience that might be original or unique, that they don't already know?
- Am I part of the group to whom I am speaking or not? In other words, am I speaking as an insider or an outsider? What advantages can I offer either way?

practice it   Brainstorming Audience and Purpose 1

Imagine that your instructor assigned a paper on the topic of public art, but gave you complete freedom to choose the audience and purpose. Brainstorm a list of as many possible types of audiences as you can. Then, for each possible audience, brainstorm one or two possible purposes you might have in writing to that audience about that topic. (The process has been started on the chart below. Fill in the rest of the chart with your own ideas. You can copy the chart into your notebook or download a version of the chart from the e-Pages. Go to **bedfordstmartins.com/readwriteconnect** and click on **Charts**.)

Possible Audiences	Possible Purposes
experienced professional artists	1. to showcase important new works of public art 2. to share art techniques 3. to inform them of opportunities to promote their work
untrained artists and art students	
homeowners	
commercial property owners	
taxpayers/citizens	

educators		
others?		

Brainstorming Audience and Purpose 2

Once you select a specific audience and purpose in part 1, ask yourself these questions:

- What types of evidence will resonate most with this audience? Statistics? Facts? Expert testimony? Stories? Case studies? Personal experiences? Some combination?
- If I make an argument, what kinds of appeals will be most persuasive to this type of reader?
- How formal of a tone should I take when writing to this audience? What kind of language should I use, or avoid using?
- Is humor appropriate for this audience? Why or why not?
- Should I use vivid sensory descriptions or stick to the facts?
- What comparisons or analogies are these readers most likely to find convincing and engaging?

Use these questions to spark your brainstorming about information to include in a paper with this topic and audience.

WRITING IN A PARTICULAR TONE

Tone is hard to define but easy to recognize—especially when someone uses an inappropriate tone. (Think of what provokes an irritated-looking mother to say to her teenage daughter, "Are you getting sassy with me, young lady?") "Tone of voice" refers to the way a person says something, which influences the meaning of the words. For instance, imagine people sitting down to a formal holiday dinner. One person says to another, "Please pass me the knife." The tone of that statement might be described as polite, ordinary, or untroubled. Imagine, however, that a hostage is trying to convince one of his captors to set him free while the other one is distracted. If the hostage says the same words—"Please, pass me the knife!"—the tone would be totally different.

Actors do a great job capturing the tone of voice of their characters. Writers, however, don't have the benefit of an actor, setting, costumes, props, or an action-packed scenario. All writers have to control tone are words, punctuation, and document format, so we have to use them extremely well.

Most academic writing has a fairly neutral tone, as you can see from the essays you have been reading. A neutral tone means that the writing doesn't use too much humor, doesn't reveal too much about the author, and doesn't sound like it's looking for a fight. Academic writers usually try to appear neutral and objective—or at least fair to opposing viewpoints. A neutral tone doesn't mean the writer doesn't have strong feelings; it just means that the writer is capable of putting his or her feelings aside in order to present the information clearly and logically and to examine an issue from all sides. (Since a neutral tone can be difficult to learn, some instructors discourage students from using "I" in all academic writing to ensure a neutral tone; others suggest using it sparingly.)

In addition, academic writers usually avoid slang because they do not wish to alienate or offend their readers. Slang words or phrases such as *crappy, for real, LOL,* and *u* when you mean "you" are very informal and are not considered Standard English. We often use informal language when talking with friends or when e-mailing or texting. But for the same reason that we talk differently with our friends than we do during a job interview, we use more formal language when writing for academic or job-related purposes than we do when e-mailing or texting friends.

SHARPENING YOUR TOPIC WITH A TITLE

Good titles are like doors cracked open: They make you want to open them wider and take a look around. One of Ernest Hemingway's novels is titled *The Sun Also Rises*. What if it had been called *The Sun Rises* instead? We might read it and shrug: "Of course the sun rises. So what?" When Hemingway puts the word "also" in the title, he implies its opposite: The sun sets. "Yes," we might think, "The sun sets, but it *also* rises. So there's light as well as darkness. Hmm . . . which way is this book going to go?" We might be intrigued enough to open the book to find out. The titles of the essays you write in college can also spark the reader's curiosity, and hint at some of the subtle or metaphorical ideas in your piece of writing.

Few student writers think too much about their titles. In fact, here's a list of some of the phrases—hardly even titles—that appeared at the top of student papers for a class writing about the theme of money and wealth:

"Essay 1"
"Money and Wealth Paper"
"Money Essay"
"Wealth Essay"
"Does Money Buy Happiness?"

You get the picture. None of these titles inspire you to read the paper. The last one in the list is the best of the bunch, but when you realize that three students from the same class used the exact same title, it hardly seems original.

How do you create a focused title that reflects the ideas in your paper and piques the reader's curiosity? Group brainstorming for title ideas can be extremely helpful. In addition, try these strategies:

- Reread your introduction and conclusion. Are there any words or phrases that jump out at you that could be developed into an interesting title?
- Reread your thesis statement. What keywords do you use there? Can they be made into a title?
- Look at an important quotation or example that you used in your essay. Can a word or phrase from it be the basis for a title?
- Is there an image, analogy, metaphor, or symbol that you use in your paper, or that you might be able to weave into your writing? Perhaps you can use that as your title.

practice it   **Brainstorming Titles**

Brainstorm three or four possible titles for an essay you are writing now. Run them by your peers, and ask them to put them in order from most to least interesting.

TITLES OF ACADEMIC ARTICLES

You may have noticed that many of the titles of the articles you read in college are rather dry, such as "Factors Associated with Teenage Ecstasy Use." Articles of this kind are meant to inform, not entertain, and their titles are as precise as possible in order to save their readers time. Many academic articles of this kind have a title and a subtitle, such as "Milwaukee's Youth Enterprise Academy: An Eight-year Study of a Model Program for Urban Youth." Partly, the reason for this is practical. Authors want you to be able to find their articles in searchable online databases, such as EBSCO and JSTOR, so they use the subtitle to include other words that may be search terms. The other reason authors use a subtitle as well as a title is that it allows them to be creative *and* informative; the subtitle conveys the main purpose of the article in a traditional, informative way, freeing up the main title for creative license.

Titles do vary by discipline. The humanities allow authors more freedom than the sciences or social sciences in terms of writing titles that are metaphoric or otherwise creative. In college writing courses, unless your instructor tells you otherwise, determine whether a more creative or a more informative title best fits your essay's tone. In other courses, follow the expectations of the discipline; look at the titles of the course readings for clues to title tone, length, and style. (Ask your instructor for guidelines if you're unsure.)

> **practice it**   Evaluating Titles
>
> Turn to the table of contents for this book, and look over the titles of the essays in Chapter 21, 22, or 23. Make a list of the titles that inspire you to read, and make another list of those that don't spark your curiosity. Compare your lists with those of your classmates.

chapter review

In Chapter 6 you learned how to figure out who is at the party, so to speak, when you are reading and how to decide what kind of party you want to throw when you set out to write. Understanding how topic, audience, purpose, tone, and title all work together definitely pushes you to a more sophisticated level as both a reader and writer.

To review this chapter, choose one or more of the following strategies:

1. Skim through the chapter again, making an outline of the major points in your notes as you do.

2. Create a personal glossary of the words you learned in this chapter (or add to the one you are already keeping) with your own examples to explain the meaning of the words.

3. If you skipped any activities, do them now as a way to deepen your understanding of the material.

4. Try to explain what you learned to someone you know. Discuss the key concepts and give some of your own examples to illustrate those concepts.

7

Rhetorical Patterns in Reading and Writing

in this chapter

- What Is a Rhetorical Pattern?
- How Can You Recognize a Particular Rhetorical Pattern?
- When and Why Do You Use the Rhetorical Patterns?

What Is a Rhetorical Pattern?

Rhetorical patterns are ways of thinking, strategies that everyone uses on a daily basis, often unconsciously. Writers use these patterns consciously and thoughtfully to make their ideas strong. Take comparison and contrast as an example. On a daily basis, you often think in comparisons and contrasts. When you question whether you should eat at a fast-food restaurant for lunch or bring your own lunch, you weigh the similarities and differences, such as taste, convenience, cost, and healthiness, between the two options. Most people who live in a consumer society like America have highly developed comparison and contrast skills, since there are so many choices to be made each minute of the day.

It may seem odd to take a step back and think about how we think (we call this metacognition), but categorizing our ways of thinking can be very helpful. In doing so, you will become more aware of the rhetorical choices readers and writers make, and better able to evaluate and control these choices.

First, rhetorical patterns often form the basis of essay structures, so being aware of these rhetorical strategies helps you understand readings. Imagine, for example, that you are reading an article that describes the current economic situation by comparing and contrasting it to the Great Depression. Why might that be effective, or ineffective, as a strategy? Which readers would find such an approach to the material useful? If you know nothing about the history of the Great Depression, how much can comparing and contrasting our present situation to it tell you? A lot? A little? If the author extensively compares and contrasts the present with the past, how can a bit of quick research about that historical period improve your understanding of the article? If you as a reader take the time to think about why the author refers to the Great Depression, your reading comprehension will improve.

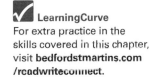

LearningCurve
For extra practice in the skills covered in this chapter, visit **bedfordstmartins.com /readwriteconnect**.

Second, we also become more critical readers when we question whether the author has chosen the most effective and appropriate rhetorical pattern. Perhaps within an essay the author overuses contrast and doesn't focus enough on comparisons between subjects. Perhaps the body paragraphs use only personal narrative as evidence, which might be interesting and emotionally compelling, but not logically persuasive. As a reader, once you begin to recognize the rhetorical patterns the author uses, you will analyze the text in a more sophisticated way.

Third, when we write, we can do our best to choose the rhetorical strategy that fits our topic, audience, and purpose. For the student writer, this often means understanding the assignment (for more on reading essay assignments, see Chapter 3, Putting Ideas into Writing, p. 92). If your instructor asks you to compare and contrast two topics, but instead you describe them both but never get around to comparing and contrasting, then you won't earn a very strong grade.

Being aware of rhetorical patterns also helps deepen your thinking and your writing. Maybe you overuse narration and illustration to prove your points. You might be missing opportunities to expand your ideas by bringing some cause and effect thinking to the topic. Even taking the time to ask yourself, "Is what I'm writing about a cause or an effect?" can be helpful in generating your ideas.

e For more on reading essay assignments, log into your Integrated Media at **bedfordstmartins.com /readwriteconnect**, click on **e-Chapters**, and select **Essay Exams**.

A Detailed Look at the Patterns

There are many rhetorical patterns. In fact, even the idea of categorizing thought is itself a pattern: categorization or classification. Scientists classify every living thing into kingdom, phylum, class, order, family, genus, and species, so it's no wonder philosophers and writers want to classify the way we think, write, and speak into the various rhetorical patterns. Such metacognition is what distinguishes us from other mammals. Some of the more commonly used rhetorical patterns in college writing are:

- Example/illustration
- Definition
- Classification/categorization
- Narration
- Description
- Process
- Compare-contrast
- Cause-effect
- Argument

Argument is such a rich and varied strategy that it merits an entire chapter in this book; see Chapter 11, Argument, page 238. Here's a detailed look at all the other patterns.

EXAMPLE/ILLUSTRATION

We routinely use examples in writing and speech, and our choice of examples often says a lot about us. Does your best friend use a sports example to illustrate every new topic? Does your sister use examples from her workplace every time she's trying to give you advice? In college essay writing, you can sometimes draw examples from your own personal observation and experience, but usually you need to do reading and research to find additional examples. Nearly every piece of academic writing offers examples of one type or another, and your job as a critical reader is to evaluate these illustrations, reading them both with and against the grain to see if they serve well to support the author's points.

Take a look at how one writer in a Milwaukee college student newspaper, the *UWM Post*, begins an article about charter schools with an example from the director of UW–Milwaukee's Office of Charter Schools ("Laboratories of Education," April 2, 2012):

> For Dr. Robert Kattman, it's the little things that best demonstrate his success.
>
> On a routine visit to the Seeds of Health Elementary campus on 32nd and Greenfield Ave., Kattman ran into a fifth grader that was bawling inconsolably.
>
> "I stopped and asked him what's wrong," Kattman recalled. The boy responded, "My RIT score went down!"
>
> Retelling the story, Kattman chuckled with pride, telling me how he calmed the boy down and discussed how he might improve his RIT score, a routine test that tracks a student's achievement over a school year.
>
> "He was devastated that his score had gone down," Kattman said. "[I]n many schools kids blow their tests off and they don't care—but in these schools they do."

The student journalist made some good decisions in interviewing Kattman and choosing this particular illustration. The example of the child crying is a personal, real-life appeal to our emotions; we can imagine this little kid and even, possibly, identify with him. We also have an educational expert who offers an intelligent, logical interpretation of the story that differs from what we might expect. Dr. Kattman is pleased to see the boy crying, because he knows the boy will get over this momentary setback. The bigger picture illustrated here—a child who cares desperately about his education—is the more important point for Kattman. Even that expert, however, is humanized: he "chuckled with pride" at the little boy's tears. The example, then, works on several levels, and it is personal and human while also citing a credible authority.

DEFINITION

When we think of definition, usually we think of simple meanings of specific words. Indeed, much of the work you do in college involves learning definitions of new terminology. The rhetorical mode, however, moves beyond simple dictionary definitions to include historical definitions, cultural definitions, and extended definitions.

Notice how this paragraph from Koon-Hwee Kan's article "Adolescents and Graffiti" (pp. 474–83) begins with a simple definition (highlighted in purple) but then moves on to include a historical and cultural definition for *latrinalia* (highlighted in yellow):

> Another type of private graffiti is "latrinalia," the kind of graffiti found near toilets (Abel & Buckeley, 1970). In most civilizations throughout history, its creators were usually suppressed individuals in society, for example, slaves working in monumental construction or prisoners inside jail cells. In contemporary times, such creation is not the sole responsibility of adolescence; people of all ages are equally likely to perform such acts (Kan 477).

The addition of the history of latrinalia deepens our understanding of it, for we see its social context. By showing that it's not just done by teenagers, the author challenges some of our assumptions about how latrinalia ought to be defined.

CLASSIFICATION/CATEGORIZATION

To classify means to put something into categories so that you can understand it better. Carol S. Dweck's (pp. 6–12) classification of students into two groups—growth mind-set and fixed mind-set—is one good example. As we already noted, much of scientific learning is about classifying and categorizing: the different systems of the body; the states of matter (solid, liquid, gas); the elements; the types of animals; and so on. Here Jeffrey Kluger (see "The Power of Birth Order," pp. 403–10) categorizes siblings. We've highlighted the key categories.

> If eldest sibs are the dogged achievers and youngest sibs are the gamblers and visionaries, where does this leave those in between? That it's so hard to define what middle-borns become is largely due to the fact that it's so hard to define who they are growing up. The youngest in the family, but only until someone else comes along, they are both teacher and student, babysitter and babysat, too young for the privileges of the firstborn but too old for the latitude given the last. Middle children are expected to step up to the plate when the eldest child goes off to school or in some other way drops out of the picture—and generally serve when called. The Norwegian intelligence study showed that when firstborns die, the IQ of second-borns actually rises a bit, a sign that they're performing the hard mentoring work that goes along with the new job.

What do you think of this way of classifying children within a family? Does it hold up for blended families, with stepchildren entering the picture at various stages? How long does one's classification last—until one is out of the house or for a lifetime? Whenever authors define categories, or accept established ones, we should think about whether the categories they use are effective or not.

NARRATION

Narration tells a story, often but not always in a chronological way. While a full story has a beginning, middle, and end, often in writing an author will tell part of a story. This fragment is intended to spark the reader's interest, illustrate a concept, or give some background information about a topic. Readers gravitate toward narration, partly because it feels human and conveys "real life" topics, and partly because narrative writing usually uses strong description. Narration creates a tension, or suspense, that makes the reader want to keep reading to find out what happens next.

Certainly, narration is the primary rhetorical mode used in fiction, biography, autobiography, and memoir. Narrative can also be used effectively within expository (factual) or argument writing of all sorts. Writers often tell a brief story, sometimes called an anecdote, to illustrate a point. They then reflect on that story, exploring what it means and why it matters. For instance, Carlin Flora opens her article "Seeing by Starlight" (pp. 516–21) with the following anecdote. Narration is highlighted in yellow; reflection in blue.

> A couple of years ago, Britney Spears and her entourage swept through my boss's office. As she sashayed past, I blushed and stammered and leaned over my desk to shake her hand. She looked right into my eyes and smiled her pageant smile, and I confess, I felt dizzy. I immediately rang up friends to report my celebrity encounter, saying: "She had on a gorgeous, floor-length white fur coat! Her skin was blotchy!" I've never been much of a Britney fan, so why the contact high? Why should I care? For that matter, why should any of us?

The narration, while short, has a clear beginning, middle, and end: Britney arrived, Flora shook her hand, and then Flora called her friends. It leads up well to the questions and reflections, which express the central question the article tries to answer: Why are we so affected by fame? Narration works particularly well here to hook the reader, because the author is so honest. She's not telling a story that makes her look great; rather, she's revealing something about herself that surprised her, something that she wants to invite her readers to explore. We are drawn in, both by the invitation and by the juicy tidbits that might follow.

DESCRIPTION

Good description is the key to telling a great story, and it is also useful in any writing where you want to offer a concrete, detailed example. Furthermore, descriptive writing serves as the basis for much nonfiction process analysis, definition, and illustration. Take this example from the article "Whose Art Is This Anyway?" by Will Shank (pp. 469–72). Strong descriptive words are highlighted.

> Consider this contentious mural. An innocent-looking, almost-white wall sits quietly on a sun-blasted, south-facing building in a warehouse neighborhood where San Francisco's largely Latino Mission District creeps toward the foot of Potrero Hill. There is nothing remarkable about the southern wall of the windowless building except for its massive sixty-by-sixty stance at the intersection of several narrow industrial streets that gets lots of cars but little foot traffic.

The paragraph describes a building that once had a mural on it but now does not. Notice how the author makes the building seem almost human through the descriptive language that personifies it.

How do you write descriptively? Think about the who, what, where, when, and how questions. What details can you add to your description to make it more vivid for a reader? What details does the reader most need to know to grasp the larger point you are trying to make? Can you show these details, instead of telling them? In the example above, the author aims to help readers visualize the building, but he also hints that it reflects the soul of the neighborhood.

Good descriptive writing often happens during the editing process, when the writer polishes the words until they shine. For starters, though, begin by choosing words that capture the senses. In Shank's short passage, he uses words that capture the human qualities of the building, such as "innocent-looking" and "stance." Strong descriptive writing means that you must also choose good verbs, such as "creeps" in the passage. If you find your paragraphs filled with words like *is, are, was, were, have, had,* and *seems,* then you have opportunities to rewrite and restructure the sentence around stronger verbs.

For more on how to use strong verbs, see Chapter 34, Writing Clear and Focused Sentences, page 694.

PROCESS ANALYSIS

Process analysis writing describes the steps of an activity, such as how a plant grows or how a volcano erupts. Read the following paragraph from the article "Milwaukee's Youth Enterprise Academy" by Mark Schug and Eric Hagedorn (pp. 62–70). Transitional expressions are highlighted.

> Students who successfully complete the YEA receive $500 U.S. Savings Bonds. Ten students in two teams of five from each Youth Enterprise Academy take the next steps when they are invited to join a Youth

Enterprise Investment Club. Here, the students manage a Youth Enterprise College Fund—a fund with an initial value of $2,000 per student or $10,000 for each team. The goal of the Youth Enterprise College Fund is to increase the value of the fund to pay as much as possible of the first year of tuition at a typical college or university. When a member of the Youth Enterprise Investment Club graduates from high school, that student can designate that his or her share of the whole fund be paid into the individual account at the postsecondary education institution in which he or she is enrolled.

Essentially the entire paragraph explains the process of a student progressing from the YEA to the investment clubs and then on to college. The passage is factual, clear, and easy to follow, largely because of the transitional expressions that indicate when and how the student moves forward.

COMPARISON AND CONTRAST

Comparison and contrast are two of the most common rhetorical patterns in school assignments. Perhaps on a history test you have been asked to compare and contrast World War II with the American Revolutionary War, or in a biology class you have been asked to compare the human brain to that of the dolphin. To compare means to describe the similarities; to contrast means to point out the differences.

Carol S. Dweck's article "The Perils and Promises of Praise" (pp. 6–13) relies extensively on comparison and contrast: She compares and contrasts the fixed-mind-set and the growth-mind-set students, the different types of praise, and the resulting educational outcomes. In this short passage, you can see how she encapsulates her argument. Comparison is highlighted in blue, while contrast is highlighted in yellow.

> It is not surprising, then, that when we have followed students over challenging school transitions or courses, we find that those with growth mind-sets outperform their classmates with fixed mind-sets—even when they entered with equal skills and knowledge.

Here the comparison goes last, and the contrast is listed first. Does this strategy emphasize the contrast or the comparison, or weigh them both equally?

CAUSE AND EFFECT

Cause and effect is one of the more common rhetorical patterns, and your ability to analyze and understand causes and effects is crucial to your success in college courses. While cause and effect seems simple enough on the surface, cause and effect is one of the most challenging rhetorical strategies. Often, writers assume that just because two things happened at the same time, one caused the other. Sometimes, they jump to the conclusion that the simplest or most obvious "cause" of something is the actual or only cause, without investigating carefully hidden or underlying causes which may be more important. You will improve at this sort of thinking with time and practice, and as you gather more knowledge and research skills, your ability to think critically about the causes and effects of complex issues will develop quickly.

Let's look at an example of an author who outlines multiple possible causes. In her article "The Only Child: Debunking the Myths" (pp. 412–21), Lauren Sandler writes about reasons for having more than one child:

> There are certain time-honored reasons for having that [second] baby: in many countries and communities, the mandate to be fruitful and multiply is a powerful religious directive. And family size can be dictated by biology as much as by psychology. But the entrenched aversion to stopping at one mainly amounts to a century-old public-relations issue. Single children are perceived as spoiled, selfish, solitary misfits. No parents want that for their kid (413).

Here she lists powerful forces that cause parents to have multiple children: religion, psychology, and biology. Ultimately, though, she jokingly calls it a "public-relations issue." The ugly and unfair stereotypes about only children are the main cause, according to Sandler, who spends much of the rest of the article describing how these stereotypes began. Here Sandler's writing engages because she takes time to list the ideas likely to pop into her reader's mind before she lays out what she thinks is the underlying cause.

practice it   Recognizing Rhetorical Patterns

Here are some paragraphs that use a particular rhetorical style to make a point. Read the paragraphs below to determine the rhetorical strategy the author is using and compare your answers in groups or pairs. (These paragraphs are all from Olivia Mellan's article "Men, Women, and Money," which you can find in full on pp. 50–57.)

1. As a result of the money taboo, I grew up as most kids do: imitating my parents' way of handling money without being aware of it. My father, affected by the Depression, worried out loud about money. My mother was a shopaholic, expressing love by buying me and herself clothes. She'd hide the purchases behind a living room chair until my father was in a good mood. As an adult, whenever I felt either depressed or particularly happy, I too would go out and shop. And even if I bought everything at a thrift store, I'd hide all the items behind a chair until my husband was in a good mood. Actually, I alternated between shopping and worrying about money.

2. Other money personalities include planners, who are detail-oriented, and dreamers, who are global visionaries. In addition, there are money monks, often ex-hippies, political activists, or spiritual souls, who feel that money corrupts and it's better to not have too much. Sometimes they marry money amassers, who believe that the guy with the most money wins. Amassers are not hoarders; they don't simply save, they invest to make their money grow. They save, spend and invest.

3. Moreover, when men make money in the stock market, they credit their own cleverness. When they lose money, they blame the incompetence of their advisers or bad luck. When women make money in the market, they credit the cleverness of their advisers, good luck, or even the stars. When they lose money, they blame themselves.

Using Rhetorical Patterns

How do we actually use the rhetorical patterns in writing? How do they work together? Using the patterns to make your point is most likely not new to you, although you may not have been aware of using them before. If you ever used an example to illustrate your point or described the steps to follow to accomplish something, you used a rhetorical pattern.

Let's look at the opening paragraphs of Jeffrey Kluger's essay "The Power of Birth Order" from Chapter 21, Siblings (pp. 403–10). Kluger uses a nice mix of rhetorical strategies to draw us into the article and explain his topic, how birth order in a family often determines one's life experiences.

Parents insist that how kids turn out depends on when they were born. More and more, science agrees.

It could not have been easy being Elliott Roosevelt. If the alcohol wasn't getting him, the morphine was. If it wasn't the morphine, it was the struggle with depression. Then, of course, there were the constant comparisons with big brother Teddy.

Example/illustration: Elliott Roosevelt serves as an example of a younger sibling. Even though his family was not typical, his experience is said to be typical of the experiences of younger siblings of famous people.

In 1883, the year Elliott began battling melancholy, Teddy had already published his first book and been elected to the New York State assembly. By 1891—about the time Elliott, still unable to establish a career, had to be institutionalized to deal with his addictions—Teddy was U.S. Civil Service Commissioner and the author of eight books. Three years later, Elliott, 34, died of alcoholism. Seven years after that, Teddy, 42, became President.

Narration: A slice of the life story of Elliott Roosevelt makes him more compelling and believable. The power of the first story carries us through the rest of the examples, so the author doesn't have to spend much time on stories of the other presidents' siblings.

Elliott Roosevelt was not the only younger sibling of an eventual President to cause his family heartaches—or at least headaches. There was Donald Nixon and the loans he wangled from billionaire

Howard Hughes. There was Billy Carter and his advocacy on behalf of the pariah state Libya. There was Roger Clinton and his year in jail on a cocaine conviction. And there is Neil Bush, younger sib of both a President and a Governor, implicated in the savings-and-loan scandals of the 1980s and recently gossiped about after the release of a 2002 letter in which he lamented to his estranged wife, "I've lost patience for being compared to my brothers."

Welcome to a very big club, Bro. It can't be easy being a runt in a litter that includes a President. But it couldn't have been easy being Billy Ripken either, an unexceptional major league infielder craning his neck for notice while the press swarmed around Hall of Famer and elder brother Cal. It can't be easy being Eli Manning, struggling to prove himself as an NFL quarterback while big brother Peyton polishes a Super Bowl trophy and his superman stats. And you may have never heard of Tisa Farrow, an actress of no particular note beyond her work in the 1979 horror film *Zombie*, but odds are you've heard of her sister Mia.

Of all the things that shape who we are, few seem more arbitrary than the sequence in which we and our siblings pop out of the womb. Maybe it's your genes that make you a gifted athlete, your training that makes you an accomplished actress, an accident of brain chemistry that makes you a drunk instead of a President. But in family after family, case study after case study, the simple roll of the birth-date dice has an odd and arbitrary power all its own.

Comparison: Kluger calls the younger sibling the "runt in a litter." By comparing siblings to animals, and by doing so in a very familiar, perhaps even clichéd way, he makes the concept clearer to his readers.

Kluger's writing style, with its mix of rhetorical patterns, is actually quite persuasive to most people. While many of us may say that we are persuaded most by cold, hard facts, we respond to writing that mixes the patterns, offering us a smorgasbord of illustrations, examples, stories, and analogies along with the analysis and other, more scientific evidence.

practice it   Critical Reading for Rhetorical Patterns

Turn to pages 403–10 and read the rest of Kluger's article. As you read, annotate the article to make notes about the types of rhetorical strategies the author uses. Hint: He moves from narration and example to more factual arguments, but returns again and again to analogies and personal examples to illustrate the scientific facts he presents more objectively.

practice it   Changing Rhetorical Patterns

Look at an essay you are writing or one that you recently finished. Find a passage in the essay that doesn't quite work well, that could be more powerful. Analyze what you have already written in the passage. What rhetorical pattern did you use? How might you make the same point or convey the same information by using a different—perhaps more interesting or persuasive—rhetorical pattern? Rewrite the passage one or more times, using different approaches. Which do you like best? Why? Gather opinions from peers, if possible, too.

chapter review

Chapter 7 introduces the rhetorical patterns and helps you think about how you might employ these patterns in your college-level reading and writing. Understanding how a text functions rhetorically is a key part of critical thinking.

To review this chapter, choose one or more of the following strategies:

1. Think about a topic about which you recently wrote or are currently writing. Brainstorm a list of possible approaches to the topic based on the various rhetorical patterns. How would you write a definition essay about the topic? A compare-contrast essay? How might you mix the rhetorical patterns?

2. Create a personal glossary of the words you learned in this chapter (or add to the one you are already keeping) with your own explanations and examples to explain the meaning of the words.

3. If you skipped any activities, do them now to deepen your understanding of the material.

4. Try to explain what you have learned, or at least part of it, to someone you know. Explain the key concepts and give some of your own examples to illustrate those concepts.

8

Vocabulary Building

in this chapter

- How Do You Build Your Vocabulary?
- What Are Context Clues?
- How Do You Use a Dictionary?
- How Do You Remember New Words?
- What Is a Thesaurus and How Do You Use One?

✔️ **LearningCurve**
For extra practice in the skills covered in this chapter, visit **bedfordstmartins.com /readwriteconnect**.

Building a bigger vocabulary makes you a more flexible writer because you will have more words to choose from to express your point. It also allows you to tackle more difficult readings because you won't be hampered by unfamiliar words as often. Finally, having a broader vocabulary gives you confidence in speaking—which is critical, because the majority of our communication is still oral.

According to *The Oxford English Dictionary*, there are 171,476 words currently in use in the English language. We don't recommend that you try to learn all 171,476 of them (at least not in one semester!), but learning new words that you encounter in your readings is a good place to start. In many cases, to understand a reading fully, you must know how certain words are being used and what they mean. You definitely need to look up these words as part of your annotating process while reading.

Of course, learning new vocabulary is not confined to the books and articles you read for class. In addition to learning words from your readings, be on the lookout for words used frequently in class lectures and discussions. If you hear your instructor using a new term or if it appears on a list of words to learn for a test, then you should figure out the meaning and practice using the term.

Even outside of particular classes, your college experience is full of new terms and words that are important to know but may be unfamiliar, like *syllabus*, *prerequisite*, or *matriculation*. You also encounter unfamiliar words in everyday contexts—in conversations, in watching television or browsing Web sites, or in reading for pleasure. The dictionary is not the only way to find out the meanings of these words. You learn the meanings of some words in specialized sources like textbook glossaries; others you learn by asking people or by using context clues. It's extremely useful to keep a list of all these new words and their definitions in a dedicated notebook.

| practice it | Learning College Vocabulary |

Make a list of unfamiliar academic words you have heard or read as a student. You might draw from your syllabi and assignment sheets, registration material, student handbook, or other campus documents. Then join a few classmates and combine your lists.

Step 1: As a group, try to define as many words as possible on the list. In cases where you have differing opinions about the meaning of a word, write down more than one definition or explanation.

Step 2: Divide the words among the group members.

Step 3: Research your list of words. What can you deduce about what a word means from the context or from the information you gathered?

Step 4: At the next class meeting, update other group members with the results of your new word investigation. Add the meanings to your word list.

Step 5: Discuss how knowing these words will help you be more prepared as a student.

Strategies for Discovering the Meanings of Words

USING CONTEXT CLUES

Reading is the best way to build up your vocabulary. The more you read, the more words you encounter, and the more you practice learning vocabulary through context (the surrounding words or sentences). You won't always be able to figure out the meaning of a word from its context, but by using context clues, you have a good chance of understanding it.

Context clues are pieces of information in a sentence or sentences that help you decipher the meaning of a word you don't know. These might include a definition of the word, an example of the word, or an antonym that shows a contrasting meaning.

Did you notice the context clue for the word *antonym* in that last sentence? The phrase "that shows a contrasting meaning" is a context clue that gives a definition.

Deriving the meaning of a word in its "natural habitat"—that is, in a sentence or paragraph—is an effective way to learn its meaning. Often, when we look up a new word in the dictionary, the definition is not enough to show how the word is really used. Dictionaries that include example sentences do a better job of showing you the word in context, so keep an eye out for these. Using context clues also helps you keep a steadier reading pace because you don't stop to look up words as often.

When you come across context clues in a reading, mark both the new word and the context clue that helps you understand the word. Jotting down your understanding of the word in the margin is also a good practice that helps cement the meaning in your brain. In the following examples, the word being defined is underlined twice, and the context clues are underlined once.

Common Types of Context Clues

Context Showing an Example

"In most civilizations throughout history, [latrinalia's] creators were usually <u>suppressed</u> individuals in the society, <u>for example, slaves working in monumental construction or prisoners inside jail cells</u>" (Kan 477).

"His early images showcased drawing and stencil-cutting prowess with an added edge: his seemingly effortless wit. Using an engaging tromp l'oeil technique, he created a range of <u>visual puns</u>—<u>rats taking photos of pedestrians, policemen kissing, the *Mona Lisa* with a rocket launcher</u>" (Gaddy 489).

"Public art can assume many forms. It is <u>malleable</u>, <u>able to meet the needs of different communities and contribute to many types of projects, from city planning or a river cleanup to a memorial for a lost hero</u>" (Becker 455).

Context Showing a Definition

"[M]en are raised to see the world as <u>hierarchical</u> and competitive. <u>There's always a one-up and one-down position, a winner and a loser</u>" (Mellan 55).

"Another type of private graffiti is '<u>latrinalia</u>,' <u>the kind of graffiti found near toilets</u>" (Kan 477).

Context Showing a Synonym

"Couples <u>polarized</u> over money engage in a balancing dance of <u>opposites</u>" (Mellan 53).

Context Using Contrast

"Typically, men want to <u>merge</u> all the couple's money—while maintaining primary decision-making power. Women want to keep at least some money <u>separate</u>" (Mellan 56).

Because using context clues is not an infallible, airtight strategy for understanding a word's meaning, it's important to look up the new word in the dictionary to make sure you accurately understand the word. If the definition is different from the one you derived from context clues, write the dictionary definition in your own words in the margin.

| practice it | Finding Context Clues |

In your reading for class, find one or two instances of each kind of context clue that help you figure out the meaning of an unfamiliar word in your reading. Circle or underline the unfamiliar word and underline the context clue. Write down your understanding of the definition in the margin, and then look up the word in the dictionary. If necessary, modify or correct the definition you wrote in the margin. Assess how well you were able to figure out the meaning using the context clues.

TIP

Fold a blank piece of paper in half and use it as a bookmark. While reading, when you come across a word you can't figure out from context clues, circle or underline it as part of your annotations, and then write it on the bookmark to look up later.

USING A DICTIONARY

Sometimes there won't be enough clues in the context to allow you to figure out the meaning of a word; in that case, you need to consult a dictionary. Your first impulse might be to look up unfamiliar words online. While this can work, you won't always have Internet access while reading, so we strongly recommend purchasing a paperback collegiate dictionary as a backup. Online searches yield highly variable results, so when you do look up a word online, be aware of the following guidelines.

First, don't just search for the word on Google or Yahoo or another Web browser. Go to an actual dictionary site like Dictionary.com or Merriam-Webster.com. Once you type in the word, what comes up should look similar to the entry in a print dictionary. Words are generally broken into syllables followed by the part(s) of speech of the word. Most words can appear as more than one part of speech, so look for the part of speech that matches the way it is being used in the reading. Because words often have more than one direct meaning, there will probably be numbered definitions listed. A good dictionary will have one or more examples of the word used in a sentence. Some online dictionaries allow you to hear a recording of the pronunciation.

Second, read through all the definitions of the word; don't assume the first one is the right meaning for your reading. If it's not immediately clear to you which definition the author intends, look again at the sentence in your reading. Use the various meanings of the word from the dictionary and the context of the sentence to think through which definition fits best.

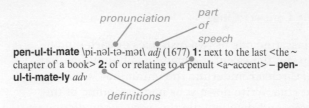

pronunciation   part of speech

pen·ul·ti·mate \pi-nəl-tə-mət\ *adj* (1677) **1:** next to the last <the ~ chapter of a book> **2:** of or relating to a penult <a~accent> – **pen·ul·ti·mate·ly** *adv*

definitions

Online Dictionary Entry

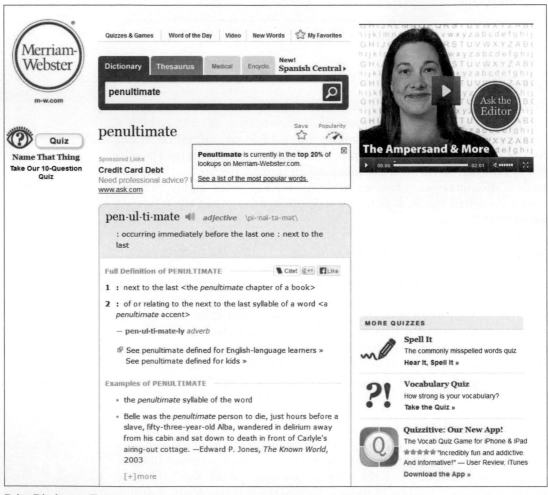

Print Dictionary Entry

practice it	Evaluating Online Dictionaries

There are many online dictionaries, but not all are created equal. To evaluate an online dictionary, pick a word and look it up in three or four different dictionaries. (Use your Web browser to find several; search for "online dictionary.") Compare the results. Do the dictionaries provide all the basic information (word broken into syllables, part(s) of speech, pronunciation, examples of the word used in a sentence)? How do the actual definitions compare? Most online dictionaries include ads and other distractions; which one has the fewest? Identify the online dictionary that provides the best information presented in the clearest way and bookmark the site. Having a go-to dictionary helps you get the information you need more quickly.

Understanding Word Parts

Many words are made up of parts: prefixes, roots, and suffixes. Understanding the meaning of the most common word parts can help you determine the meaning of many words. Combined with using context clues, knowing word parts improves both your vocabulary and your reading comprehension.

PREFIXES

Prefixes are the word parts added to the beginning of a word. Many of these will look familiar, and you might be reminded of other words that use the same prefix and have a similar meaning. For example, the prefix *ex-* means "out" or "away from," which we can readily see from words like *expel* (to force out), *exoskeleton* (an external supportive covering of an animal), *exile* (one who is cast out), and *exit* (a way out of an enclosed space). What other words can you think of that begin with the prefix *ex-* that share the meaning of "out" or "away from"?

COMMON PREFIXES AND THEIR MEANINGS

Prefix	Meaning	Prefix	Meaning
a-, an-	not, without	hetero-	mixed, unlike
ab-	away from	homo-	same
ad-	toward, addition	ideo-	idea
ante-	before	il-, im-, in-, ir-	not

(continued)

COMMON PREFIXES AND THEIR MEANINGS (*CONTINUED*)

Prefix	Meaning	Prefix	Meaning
anti-	opposite	mal-, mis-, ne-	bad
aud-, aur-	hear	pan-	all, every
ben-, bon-	good	poly-	many
co-,col-,con-,cor-	with	post-	after
de-, ex-	out, away from	pre-	before
di-	two, double	pro-	big, much
dis-	not, apart	re-	back, again
dys-	bad, abnormal		

practice it   Understanding Prefixes

Using the preceding chart, think of at least three words that begin with each prefix, and write down the meaning of each word.

Examples: *il-, im-, in-,* and *ir-*

illegitimate = not legitimate
improper = not proper
inconsistent = not consistent
irreplaceable = not replaceable

ROOTS

The root is the base of the word. Words can be customized based on the various combinations of prefixes (added to the beginning of the root) and suffixes (added to the end of the root). For example, the root *enn* means "year." Add the prefix *bi-*, meaning "two," and the suffix *-ial*, denoting a descriptive word, and you have the word *biennial*, which is an adjective describing something that happens every two years. However, change the prefix to *per-* (meaning "through") and you have *perennial*, an adjective describing something lasting through an indefinite number of years.

Not all words have prefixes *and* suffixes. Sometimes, words have only a root and a suffix, in which case the root might look like a prefix, but it's not. Consider the words *audio, biological, captivate,* and *equal.* These words begin with a root and have a suffix attached at the end.

Look over the following roots and see how many you recognize. When you come across a word you don't know, check the following root list to figure out the meaning by understanding the word parts.

COMMON ROOTS AND THEIR MEANINGS

Root	Meaning	Root	Meaning
ann, enni	year	mym, onym	word, name
arch	chief, leader	ortho	straight, correct
aud	sound	pac	peace
biblio	book	pater	father
bio	life	path	feeling, suffering
cap	take, seize	ped, pod	foot
ced	yield, go	phon, phono	sound
chron	time	psych	soul, mind
corp	body	sci	know
crac, crat	rule, ruler	sec, sect	cut
cred	believe	sed, sess	sit
demo	people	sens, sent	to be aware, feel
dox	belief	sol	sun
duc, duct	lead	son	sound
equ	equal	soph	wisdom
fac	make, go	spec, spic	look, see
frater	brother	stat	stay, position
geo	earth	tact, tang	touch
grad, gress	step	temp	time
graph	writing, printing	ten, tent	hold
gyn	woman	terr	earth
hem, hema, hemo	blood	theo	god, deity
hydro	water	therm	heat
man	hand	vac	empty
mater	mother	ven, vent	come, go
met, meta	behind, between	ver	truth
mor, mort	death	vert	turn
morph	structure, form	voc	call
mut	change		

> **practice it**   Understanding Roots
>
> For this activity, pick a root from the preceding list and, without looking
> at the meaning, think of other words with the same root to see if you can
> figure out the meaning. These roots often come from Greek or Latin, so
> if you know a Romance language—like Spanish, French, or Italian—you
> might be able to recognize the Latin root from a non-English word.
>
> **Example:** The root *temp* is recognizable from the words *temporary* and
> *contemporary*. It is probably related to time.

SUFFIXES

Suffixes are word parts attached to the ends of roots or words to add or
change the meaning. For example, the suffixes *-ist* and *-er* both indicate
a person, like in *zoologist* or *treasurer*. Suffixes often clue you in on the
part of speech of a word. For example, you may remember that adverbs
often end in *-ly*. Words that end in *-ism* are generally nouns, while words
that end in *-ical* are typically adjectives. (Keep in mind, however, that
these are clues, not hard-and-fast rules.)

COMMON SUFFIXES AND THEIR MEANINGS

Suffix	Meaning	Suffix	Meaning
-able, -ible	capable of	-ette, -illo	little
-ac, -ic, -ical, -tic	having to do with	-ia, -y	act, state
-ate, -efy, -ify, -ise, -ize,	make	-ism	belief in
-cede, -cess	yield, go	-ist	a person
-cide	kill	-ite	connected with
-cis	cut	-logy, -ology	study
-er, -orone	who takes part in	-ous	full of

> **practice it**   Using Word Parts
>
> Armed with the charts of word parts on the preceding pages, look
> over one of the readings you've been assigned from this text and
> find the italicized words. Can you use the word parts and context
> clues to figure out their meanings? Once you have a good idea of the

meaning of a word, check a dictionary to see how accurate you are. Remember to write the definition in the margin of your reading in your own words.

The more practice you have using this strategy, the more accurate you will become.

Committing New Words to Memory

It's easy to identify unfamiliar words in a reading. Looking them up takes a bit of effort, but committing them to memory so that you really learn them is more difficult. Most people have to use new words many times before really mastering them.

USING MNEMONICS

Mnemonics, or memory aids, are a good way to commit new words to memory. Did you ever learn "Please Excuse My Dear Aunt Sally" in a math class? It's a mnemonic device to help you remember *PEMDAS*, the order of operations (Parentheses, Exponents, Multiplication, Division, Addition, Subtraction). Mnemonics like this work because they are shorter and simpler than what they stand for, and also give us the first letter of the words we're trying to remember. Forming a sentence from the letters also helps us remember the order of terms, because a sentence has a built-in order that most of us recognize and use without difficulty.

You should use all the mnemonics you can to learn new words and commit them to memory, including making rhymes with words and their definitions ("*syllabus*—what you expect of us"), using word associations ("*penultimate*—I use a pen second to last, before the eraser"), or creating graphic images that represent a word's meaning (a runner jumping a hurdle, something they are required to get through, for *prerequisite*). Try a few of these methods to see which work best for your memory.

MAKING GRAPHIC FLASH CARDS

Flash cards are another good way to remember important words. Adding an image to the flash cards helps you visualize the meaning of a word, which is a great memory device. Here's how to do it.

STEP 1: You will need a set of 3 × 5 inch note cards.

STEP 2: Identify vocabulary words and terms you are trying to learn from your annotations or elsewhere.

STEP 3: Write each word on one side of a note card.

STEP 4: On the other side of the note card, write:

a. A definition of the term in your own words.
b. A sentence (at least six words) using the word. If you are struggling with the sentence, go back to the reading. Seeing the word in context might help.
c. The part of speech. If you aren't sure what part of speech the word is, you can find this information in the dictionary entry just after the word. Dictionaries use the following abbreviations for the parts of speech:

Noun = **n**
Verb = **v, vt** (transitive verb—a verb like *love* that takes an object), **vi**
    (intransitive verb—a verb like *appear* that does not take an object)
Adjective = **adj**
Adverb = **adv**

STEP 5: On the front of the card, below the word, draw a picture to help you remember the meaning.   You don't need to be an artist or spend more than a few moments on the image for it to be effective. The image helps anchor the definition in your memory.

STEP 6: Practice with your flash cards.   Making them is the first step, but to use them to help you improve your vocabulary, you have to practice with them.

Sample Graphic Flash Cards

putrid

Front

Having a horrible smell from decomposing

The rotting garbage was putrid.

adj

Back

reminisce

Front

To think about past experiences

On his 15th wedding anniversary, he reminisces about his wedding day.

v

Back

Using a Thesaurus

All words have shades of meaning (or *connotations*), so even though two words might be *synonyms* (words sharing the same meaning), they may not both work in the same context. For example, when describing a sky darkened with storm clouds, you might refer to the sky as *frightening*. But perhaps you want to use a more sophisticated word, so you decide to try a thesaurus. You look up *frightening* in a thesaurus, and you see that *macabre* is listed as a synonym. Great, right? Not so fast. Although *macabre* is related to *frightening*, it doesn't mean quite the same thing: *macabre* more precisely means *horrifying* or *gruesome*. A Halloween haunted house might be macabre with its monsters and ghostly images, but storm clouds are not likely to be macabre, so describing a sky as *macabre* is likely to be more confusing than impressive.

What's the point here? A thesaurus is a good tool, but needs to be used correctly. Once you find a synonym for the word you want to replace, you need to look up the new word in the dictionary. So use a thesaurus by all means, but you also need to look up the word in the dictionary to be sure that you use it correctly.

---

practice it   **Using the Right Word in Context**

Choose the best word to complete this sentence from the choices below.

> If a person is not knowledgeable about finances, we might say that they are financially _____.

a. ignorant
b. unacquainted
c. unfamiliar
d. insensible
e. oblivious

Each of these words means "not having knowledge," but they wouldn't all work in this context. Look up each word in the dictionary to determine which word is the best fit for this context and explain why.

USING NEW VOCABULARY

TIP
Challenge yourself to use a new word in conversation and/or in writing five times each day for a week.

Practice the strategies in this chapter when you identify new words, and you will build a robust vocabulary for yourself. Don't forget, however, that learning what the new word means is only the beginning of developing an *active* vocabulary; in order to really benefit from knowing the word, you have to use it, whether in writing or in speech.

Most people understand more words than they use regularly when they write. Have you noticed that you tend to use the same verbs repeatedly? Or that you often describe people as "nice" or "mean," places as "beautiful" or "boring"? You may know many words that could replace each of these words, but out of habit, you use the same ones repeatedly. Try to shake this habit and instead create a style and tone to fit your audience. Do you want to sound academic? Sophisticated? Familiar with current events? Replace *nice* or *mean* with words that reflect how you would like to sound.

As you experiment, try out new words from your readings. It's particularly useful to use new words from the readings when you write essays based on the readings or their topics, but keep an eye out for other opportunities: Post new words on social media, use them when writing e-mails, or weave them into conversations. Also, listen for instances when other people use any of the new words you are learning. You might hear them in lectures or conversations or on the news.

One useful strategy for fully understanding newly acquired vocabulary is finding and making connections between new words—even if they seem unrelated.

practice it   Making Connections between Words

Make a list of new words from a reading and divide them into two columns. Pick any two words (one from each column) and find a way to compare or connect the two words in a sentence that shows the meaning of both words. Continue making sentences with words from both columns until you use up all the words in both lists. Try different match-ups to practice using words in different contexts. It might be helpful to write down the definition in your own words to help you come up with a good sentence.

Example 1

Words	gratuitous	anecdote
Definitions	unnecessary	a short story
Sentence	A gratuitous anecdote in an essay is unnecessary and can make the essay too wordy.	

Example 2

Words	indict	plaintiff
Definitions	make a formal accusation	person who begins a lawsuit
Sentence	A plaintiff indicts someone when they sue them.	

Another way to improve your vocabulary and style in your writing is to look over your writing during the editing stage to identify words you use repeatedly and words that sound vague or bland, and replace them. Check your signal phrases for quotations. Do you use the same verb to introduce your quotations every time? Vary the signal verbs. Also, look out for the passive voice ("The ball was thrown" rather than "The girl threw the ball") and replace passive verbs with active ones. If you find that you use the verb *to be* frequently, replace it in at least some instances with strong, active verbs.

practice it   Improving Style through Word Choice

In the following paragraph, vague, repetitive, or slang words are underlined, as are passive verbs. Find better replacements for these words to improve this paragraph's style.

Being famous is not all it's cracked up to be. Most people think they want fame, but they don't think of all the problems with fame. Being famous is isolating; it is thought that a famous person will always have lots of friends around, but it must be even harder to know who your real friends are and who is just a groupie. Being famous is also hard because you have no privacy. Imagine being photographed all the time, even when you go grocery shopping or wash your car. You can't ever have a bad hair day without it showing up in a magazine. Once you are famous, there are expectations that you will stay famous; it would be difficult to ever have a "normal" job after being famous. This shows that being famous is not all that.

practice it   Stretching Your Vocabulary

Reread a few pages of essays you have written. Circle words that you use repeatedly. Do you notice patterns? Are there particular words that you seem to overuse? Words that seem vague or bland? Circle those too. Then, without using a dictionary or thesaurus, replace the circled words with different words that you know. Think hard. Spend some time and really rack your brain, and come up with some alternatives.

Building your vocabulary doesn't end when class is over. Using the strategies in this chapter will help you not only increase your vocabulary, but use your new words well. Be diligent about looking up unfamiliar words or using context clues to determine their meaning, and then apply these new words to your own writing and experiences. As always, the best way to keep your vocabulary growing is to read, read, read!

chapter review

Vocabulary building is a lifelong endeavor, and Chapter 8 gives you a good start in that direction. Getting the most out of learning new vocabulary goes well beyond just looking up new words, so this chapter has shown you strategies for figuring out the meanings of unfamiliar words and remembering and using new terms.

To review this chapter, choose one or more of the following strategies:

1. Make flash cards of word parts—prefixes, roots, and suffixes—and review them regularly. See how well they can help you figure out word meanings while reading.

2. If you skipped any activities, do them now as a way to deepen your understanding of the material.

3. Try to explain what you have learned to someone you know. Discuss the key concepts and give some of your own examples to illustrate those concepts.

9
Pre-Writing

in this chapter

- Why Pre-Write?
- What Is Freewriting?
- How Will Clustering Help You Find Your Topic?
- Why Write a List?
- How Do You Ask Good Questions?

For more on pre-writing, see Chapter 3, Putting Ideas into Writing, pages 98–102.

Pre-writing is a key phase of the writing process; in pre-writing you move from reading and thinking about a topic to writing about it. If you are like many writers, you may find this phase the most fun because it captures the first thoughts or ideas about your topic, and unlike the rest of drafting, you don't need to worry about perfect grammar or organization or spelling. Instead, you focus on thinking creatively to generate ideas and make connections. You've probably already done some pre-writing, earlier in this class, or in other classes.

In pre-writing you essentially get all your thoughts and ideas onto paper so you can see what you have and evaluate it. This chapter covers four popular pre-writing activities: freewriting, clustering, listing, and questioning. Practice them all so you have more than one strategy at your fingertips the next time you start a writing assignment. It's always good to have several techniques to choose from.

Freewriting

Freewriting is what it sounds like: writing freely. When you freewrite, you begin with a topic or question and write freely, without stopping, for five or ten minutes. You generally freewrite in sentence or paragraph form.

Freewriting sounds easy because it's informal writing that isn't graded, but students often find this technique a bit challenging at first. Since you're usually asked to produce writing for a grade or to be evaluated, it can be hard to get used to the idea that freewriting can be rough. Really rough. In fact, freewriting is supposed to be messy and disorganized and full of grammar or spelling errors, so you focus on your ideas and not on editing. As long as you can read it and understand it, it's good enough.

Freewriting is like free association. Don't stop to consider whether what you're writing is good enough: This should be nonstop writing. This instruction often produces a blank stare from students who wonder, "Nonstop? What if I can't think of what to write?" Well, exactly. The idea of freewriting is to stop censoring your ideas. Stopping to think of what you should write or whether your ideas are any good actually gets in the way of the activity. If you can't think of what to write, just keep rewriting what you previously wrote, or write over and over: "I can't think of what to write. I can't think of what to write." Pretty soon, your brain will come up with something related to the topic, which will lead to another thought about the topic, and another, and so on. If you have ever meditated, the concept is similar. By trying not to direct your thinking, your mind will focus on what you need to.

Here's a student freewrite on the question "What is art?":

> What is art? Hmmmm. What is art? Well, art is pictures on the wall. It's also photographs and sculptures. Not all photos though--like, school photos from when you were a kid, those aren't art. unless an artist did something with those pictures like put them in a collage or something. that would be artistic. but by themselves, they are just embarrassing! I always seemed to have the worst haircuts in grade school. Blech. Ummmm, I don't really know what else art is. i guess computer graphics are art. but i don't consider video games playable art. I guess art is made with the idea that is going to be art. or it is things collected and put together like art. I used to love art day in school when I was little. My mom still has my ceramic hand print hanging on her wall. parents think almost anything their kids do is art. That makes me wonder if art has to be any good for it to be considered art. I guess not because I don't even like or get a lot of the art in museums. Everyone has different tastes when it comes to art.

Notice that this writer didn't correct grammar or worry about going off topic. In this case, going "off topic" about parents always loving kids' art was a good thing, because it led the writer to an important question about art: Does it have to be "good" to be considered art?

After freewriting, the next step is to reread the freewrite, underlining ideas you want to think about more or examples that seem useful. Here's an example of what this writer might have underlined:

> What is art? Hmmmm. What is art? Well, art is pictures on the wall. It's also photographs and sculptures. Not all photos though—like, school photos from when you were a kid, those aren't art. unless an artist did something with those pictures like put them in a collage or something. that would be artistic. but by themselves, they are just embarrassing! I always seemed to have the worst haircuts in grade school. Blech. Ummmm, I don't really know what else art is. i guess computer graphics are art. but i don't consider video games playable art. <u>I guess art is made with the idea that is going to be art. or it is things collected and put together like art.</u> I used to love art day in school when I was little. My mom still has my ceramic hand print hanging on her wall. parents think almost anything their kids do is art. <u>That makes me wonder if art has to be any good for it to be considered art.</u> I guess not because I don't

even like or get a lot of the art in museums. Everyone has different tastes when it comes to art.

Either of the underlined phrases could be the starter question for another freewrite to develop each idea more fully. In this way, freewriting has unlimited potential as an idea-generating activity.

| practice it | **Freewriting** |

Pick one of the following topics, or use a topic for an essay you are working on, and write freely for five minutes. Remember, don't try to direct your thinking or edit your writing. Write continuously for the full five minutes, and if you can't think of what to write, recopy what you just wrote or copy down "I can't think of what to write" until you can.

Hint: Set a timer for five minutes so you don't have to focus on the time.

Do you wish you were famous?
What makes a school good?
What does it mean to be educated?
Why is financial literacy important?
What is art?
What are the advantages of having siblings or being an only child?

Clustering

Clustering is sometimes called mapping, webbing, or bubbling. A cluster is essentially a graphic organizer that you can make to help you generate ideas. Because it's a series of bubbles or boxes that you connect with lines, you can roughly organize your ideas while you create it.

STEP 1: **Begin a cluster by putting your idea, topic, or thesis, if you have one, in a central circle in the middle of a blank piece of paper.** Write down anything you think relates to that central idea or claim, and circle that. Draw lines from your circle in the center to the other circles, connecting them. At this point, don't worry about whether your ideas are organized or even whether they are any good; the main point of this activity is to get as many related ideas down on paper. Here's what a cluster on the question "What is art?" might look like:

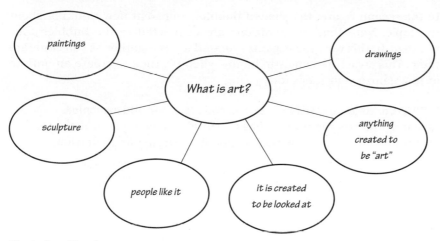

Clustering, Step 1

STEP 2: **After you spend a few minutes mapping out your ideas, review your cluster.** See if there are more ideas you'd like to add or clarify or ask questions about. This additional step is just as important as Step 1.

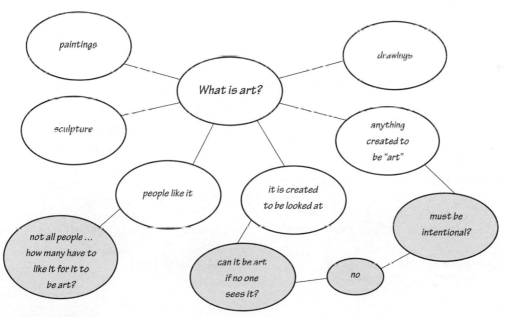

Clustering, Step 2

In the second figure, the shaded bubbles represent new thinking about the topic. Note that the additions are connected to the bubbles they relate to. In this way, you organize related ideas together as you generate them. This structure comes in handy when it's time to create an outline or to organize your ideas for writing.

STEP 3: **Continue to clarify questions and ideas and add examples, repeating the process several times.**   Here's an example of a cluster that went through four or five stages of clarifying and addition:

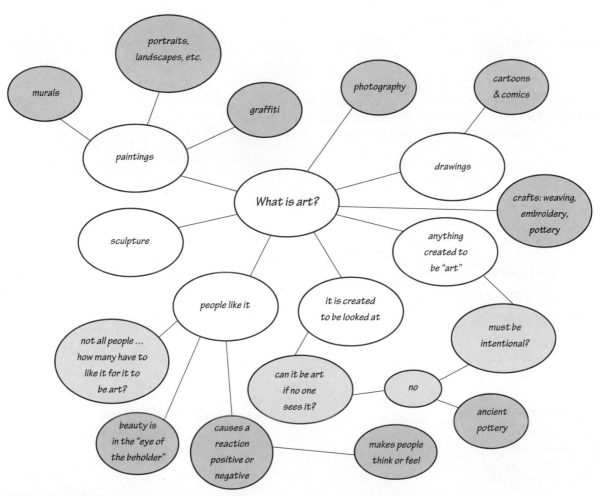

Clustering, Step 3

Listing   219

practice it   Clustering

After looking over the "What is art?" cluster, make your own cluster in response to a topic you are writing about. Add to and clarify ideas through several stages of clustering before you consider it done.

TIP
There are several good clustering computer programs that make it very easy to create pre-writing clusters. Ask if any are installed at your campus computer lab, or do a search online. Clustering software programs are sometimes referred to as "mind mapping" programs.

Listing

Listing is just that, making a list of everything you can think of that's related to your topic. Begin by writing your topic, thesis, or idea at the top of a piece of paper, and then beneath that, list as many related ideas as you can.

> What is art?
> paintings
> sculpture
> drawing
> people like it
> it's created to be looked at
> anything created to be "art"

Note that in this list, the first things that come to mind are written down. Like in clustering or freewriting, you should look over your list once you generate it and then take another pass at adding and clarifying.

> What is art?
> paintings
> sculpture
> drawing
> people like it—not all people . . . how many have to like it for it to be "art"?
> it's created to be looked at—can it be art if no one sees it?
> anything created to be "art"—must it be intentional?
> portraits
> murals, graffiti
> photography
> cartoons, comics
> can it be art if no one sees it? no . . .
> crafts like weaving, embroidery, pottery
> art has to cause a reaction—positive or negative
> makes people think or feel
> doesn't need to be intentional—think of ancient pottery—we consider it art
>   today but it prob. wasn't when it was made

Remember that a list is not the same as an outline. Your list is generated quickly and spontaneously, to help you get your ideas into writing, but it is not structured. Just because you brainstorm an idea first doesn't mean it should be the first point in your paper.

For more on outlining, see Chapter 13, Essay Organization and Outlining, page 267.

> **practice it**   Listing
>
> Make your own list in response to a topic you are writing about. Add to and clarify ideas through several stages of listing before you consider it done.

Questioning

When it comes to generating ideas for an essay, asking increasingly complex questions will help you develop a much richer selection of ideas on which to base your essay.

Not all questions are equal, however. Some questions result in straightforward, factual answers, which are good for starters, but don't engage more complex thinking. To use the right kinds of questions for this pre-writing strategy, it's important to first understand what the different kinds of questions are. The following chart shows six different levels of questions, moving from the easiest to the most difficult. (This chart is based on the research of Benjamin Bloom, an educator who created this system of questions, known as Bloom's Taxonomy.)

Level	Kind of Question and Purpose	Examples
1	Knowledge: to get facts	What is the issue? Who is involved? Where does it take place? How long has it been going on?
2	Comprehension: to understand	How do you summarize the article, topic, or event? How can you explain the issue or topic? What is the main idea/purpose? Whom does this issue affect? How? Who might benefit from change? How?
3	Application: to show you can use information	How can you apply this information to a new situation? How is this used? How would changing this change the outcome? What are examples of this?
4	Analysis: to explain the whole by understanding parts	What do you think about [a certain part]? How are [one part] and [another part] related? What evidence is there for this? How does this compare with other things? Why is this effective/not effective? What can you infer from this? What does this mean? What are the most important parts/reasons/issues, and why?

Level	Kind of Question and Purpose	Examples
5	Synthesis: to make new meaning	How do the various sources relate? What is a different solution? What would you change or modify? How could this situation/issue be improved? What needs to change, and why?
6	Evaluation: to assess and judge information	What is your opinion on the issue? What works well? What doesn't work? What would you suggest or recommend? How valid are the various points of view? How would change benefit some people? How would change put some people at a disadvantage?

Start with questions from level 1, and then move down the list to the more complex questions, to deepen your critical thinking.

In the following example, a student uses questioning to develop ideas for the essay "Is Graffiti Art?"

1. What is the issue? Is graffiti art or vandalism?
   Who is involved? Graffiti artists, art critics, anyone who likes art
   Where does it take place? Graffiti is all over the place—urban centers and suburban as well.
   How long has it been going on? Graffiti as a "scene" really started in the 1970s and 1980s, but it goes back much further

2. How do you summarize the article, topic, or event?
   A lot of people think of graffiti as vandalism and gang markings. But some think graffiti is art, especially the colorful and very complex "pieces" that are seen in cities mostly. Even museums have recognized graffiti as art. Some owners of buildings hire graffiti artists to paint elaborate "pieces" on their walls.

3. Whom does this issue affect? Building owners and members of a community are affected by seeing graffiti in their neighborhood, perhaps even on their buildings. They might have to pay to have graffiti removed. Also, though, members of a community might be positively affected by the color and brightness that lots of graffiti adds to a community, especially a run-down neighborhood.

4. How is graffiti/art/vandalism used? Graffiti is used to express the personality of the "writers" as well as their design skills and use of color. It's also used to promote their names and to get attention or "street cred," particularly for pieces in hard-to-reach locations. Art is used to express personality and skill as well. Art is often sold, so it's used to make money for the artist as well as recognition. Vandalism is used to express anger or frustration or mark territory.

5. How would changing art and graffiti change the outcome?
   Changing the definition of art to include graffiti would make graffiti officially art. It would also make this paper a lot easier ☺ If graffiti was done only on approved surfaces (on art gallery walls, on buildings that allow it, etc.), it would probably change most people's view of it being art. But probably graffiti artists would be less interested in it and probably move on to do something else. They like being outside the art world.

You can see that by moving from easier to increasingly complex question levels, you are writing down much more specific and interesting ideas. After answering as many questions as you can, you have a lot of great material to then organize into an outline and topic sentences.

practice it   Asking Questions

With a small group of classmates, put your heads together to brainstorm or do the questioning activity to generate ideas. Either work independently for the first five to ten minutes and then compare and share your ideas, or work together from the beginning. Just remember, all group members should take their own notes during the group pre-writing so they have ideas to take home.

Now that you have learned several good pre-writing strategies, practice them whenever you begin a writing project or whenever you have trouble coming up with something to say as you are writing. Many writers continue to brainstorm throughout the writing process, so feel free to revisit this chapter at any point.

chapter review

Chapter 9 covers the basics of pre-writing to help you get started on any kind of writing assignment. You may have been familiar with some of the strategies, but you also probably learned some new steps or techniques. It's always a good idea to have a variety of strategies to draw from so you are ready to tackle any kind of college writing.

To review this chapter, choose one or more of the following strategies:

1. Pick a pre-writing strategy that is new to you and practice it with an old or a new writing assignment from your class.

2. Reflect on your favorite method of pre-writing. What does it reveal about the kind of thinker and learner you are?

3. If you skipped any activities, do them now as a way to deepen your understanding of the material.

4. Try to explain what you have learned, or at least part of it, to someone you know. Discuss the key concepts and give some of your own examples to illustrate those concepts.

10
Thesis and Main Idea

in this chapter

- What Does a Thesis Do?
- How Do You Find the Main Point in a Reading?
- How Do You Shape and Draft Your Thesis?
- How Do You Make Your Thesis Stronger?

The Purpose of a Thesis

The thesis statement is the central, controlling idea in a piece of writing; it states the writer's main point or purpose. As the central purpose or idea, the thesis is almost always a claim, meaning that it is the perspective or position of the author. Another way to think about the thesis is to distinguish it from the topic. The topic is what the author is writing about, and the thesis is what the author is saying about that topic.

Most articles or essays have many points, so the thesis is the central point, the umbrella point that all the other points help prove. All the paragraphs, examples, explanations, and evidence in an essay support the thesis. Without a thesis, an essay would be much harder for the writer to organize and much harder for the reader to follow.

Not all kinds of writing have a thesis statement, but all academic essays do, and much of what you read in college will have a central, controlling idea. For example, letters or e-mails may have a purpose, but they usually won't have a thesis. Short stories have messages and themes that drive them, but they won't have a thesis. Academic writing is driven by a thesis that aims to inform, analyze, or argue.

You may have been taught at some point to write a five-paragraph essay with a three-part (or tripartite) thesis that has three major supporting points. If you learned this kind of thesis, practice stretching your thinking beyond it, and think of the tripartite thesis as you would riding a bike with training wheels: Training wheels help you get comfortable with the general feeling of riding a bike, but eventually you take them off and ride that two-wheeler on your own. Similarly, the three-part thesis has limitations. It assumes you have three points to make, and only three. So when you use this format, you don't develop your thinking beyond three points, even if there are many more points to be made. Your writing assignments become longer and more complex as you move through college, and you need to know how to organize an essay around your arguments or ideas, which rarely come in threes.

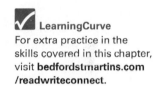

LearningCurve
For extra practice in the skills covered in this chapter, visit **bedfordstmartins.com /readwriteconnect**.

THE EXPLICIT THESIS OR MAIN IDEA

In Chapter 3, Putting Ideas into Writing, you learned that a thesis statement should express a complete idea about what the writer believes about the topic as well as why he or she believes it. In your own writing, your thesis should appear toward the beginning of your essay and should be an arguable claim. For academic essays, assume your instructor wants to see an explicit (that is, directly and clearly stated) thesis statement.

THE IMPLIED THESIS OR MAIN IDEA

In essays and articles that you read, you won't always find the thesis at the beginning. Professional writers sometimes put a thesis in the conclusion. Other readings may not have an obvious thesis statement at all, but instead require you to figure it out. We call this kind of thesis implied. An implied thesis does not mean there is no thesis. This type of thesis is thought out as much as a directly stated thesis. In these cases, the author has the central claim in mind when developing the essay; he or she has just decided to let the reader figure out the thesis rather than stating it. This kind of writing is a bit trickier—both reading it and writing it takes much practice.

SAMPLE THESIS STATEMENTS FROM DIFFERENT TYPES OF READINGS

Different kinds of writing require different kinds of thesis statements, but they all have some common features. Here are some examples of different kinds of thesis statements. Some may be familiar to you from readings you encountered in Chapter 2, Active and Critical Reading. Looking over this selection, you can see some of the breadth and variety of kinds of thesis statements.

Thesis from a Magazine Article, "Teach Your Children the Building Blocks of Finance" by Sherie Holder and Kenneth Meeks

Parents have to teach children the value of money and guide them in their spending, encourage them to save, explore entrepreneurship opportunities, and expose them to solid financial planning.

Thesis from a Student Literature Paper on Kate Chopin's Short Story

In "The Story of an Hour," the main character Louise Mallard was unhappy until she had a moment of self-discovery; unfortunately, she died shortly thereafter.

Thesis from a Student Psychology Paper on Freud's Theory of Defense Mechanisms

Defense mechanisms operate in every person all throughout their lives, and to help better understand ourselves, it is important to look at how defense mechanisms work for and against us.

Thesis from a Book Chapter, "Broadcasting Yourself" by Drew Pinsky
Whatever the reaction, these two media (TV and the Internet) are changing our relationship to celebrity in dramatic and potentially dangerous ways.

The next thesis example is from the "Education Pays" chart in Chapter 2. The chart has no explicit thesis; in fact, it has very little text at all, but it does make a clear point to its readers. In this case, it has an *implied thesis*, meaning that you can figure out the central argument from reading the whole chart.

Implied Thesis from the "Education Pays" Chart by the Bureau of Labor Statistics
The higher your level of education, the less likely you are to be unemployed and the more likely you are to earn a higher salary.

Note that in all these examples, the thesis does more than just state the topic of the work. The topic is *what* the reading is about, and the thesis is the central claim and overall point the author makes about the topic.

Finding the Main Point in a Reading

Finding the thesis is an important part of reading comprehension and analysis. In order to find the thesis, begin by following these steps.

STEP 1: Preview the text. Previewing the text gives you an idea of what the overall purpose or point of the reading is, which is the first step in identifying the thesis. What is the topic of the reading? Write it down in the margin as part of your annotations or in your notebook. Then write down in one sentence the point you expect the author might make about that topic.

STEP 2: Read the introductory and the concluding paragraphs. Is there a broad claim that the author is making? If so, that might be the thesis. Make a note of it and move on to Step 3. If there is more than one claim, check to see if one of them is a broader, more general claim that the other claims might serve. If you can't tell, make a note of the various claims and move on to Step 3.

STEP 3: Read the entire article or essay. As you read, keep in mind the claim or claims you have found to see if they are developed and supported in the essay. If you haven't already found a claim, keep a lookout for the point the author seems to be making about the overall topic. If you have already read the article or essay, read through it again. Annotate any places where the author makes claims, particularly at the beginning of paragraphs (topic sentences).

For more on pre-reading strategies, see Chapter 1, Reading and Responding to College Texts, page 2, and Chapter 5, Additional Reading Strategies, page 138.

STEP 4: At the end of the reading, go back to any claims you wrote down in Step 2 and evaluate whether any of them are the thesis.   Consider the following:

- Do any of the claims seem too narrow? Do they only fit one paragraph or one section of the overall reading? If so, those claims are probably not the thesis.
- Does the essay support one claim throughout by proving it, developing examples of it, or discussing it in detail? If yes, then you probably have found the thesis. If you can answer yes about more than one claim, see if one of those claims can support the other (for instance, two different claims about specific threats of animal extinction might support a thesis about climate change). If so, the claim supported by the other is probably the broader claim. If the claims are equal, go to the next step.

STEP 5: If there is no stated claim, or if there are a few that seem equally important to the essay, the thesis may be implied rather than written into the essay.   Cover the essay with a blank piece of paper and ask yourself, what was the main point of this essay? Write down the answer without thinking too much about it. If you have trouble answering this question, pretend that a classmate just asked you what the reading was about. What would you tell him or her? Be as specific as you can. Write the answer down, and then uncover the essay and look it over with this statement in mind. Does it fit the essay? Is it the main point the author is trying to make?

practice it   Finding the Thesis

Choose an article or essay that your instructor has assigned and follow the preceding five steps to find the thesis. Check with a few class-mates or with your instructor to see if you have correctly identified the thesis. Remember, finding the thesis takes practice, so if you don't get it at first, keep reading and practicing. Soon, it will become second nature to you.

Shaping Your Thesis

Shaping your own thesis is one of the most important steps in the writing process. It takes practice and usually several drafts to write a good the-sis, but that's because you have to figure out what you're really trying to say before you can write one. Remember, the thesis is the controlling, central idea or claim in the essay. It is the claim that all the body paragraphs and evidence will support, so your thesis should clearly reflect the point you want to make.

CHARACTERISTICS OF A THESIS

Your thesis should:

- **Be an arguable claim.** A claim is what you think about the topic. Not everyone would agree with your claim, which makes it arguable. Claims differ from opinion in that opinions aren't arguable. You are entitled to any opinion you happen to have, but a claim must be supported by evidence to be considered valid.

Opinion	I like soup.
Claim	Soup is often thought of as healthy, but cream-based soups are among the unhealthiest dishes you can eat.

- **Be a statement, *not* a question.** A question is a thought-provoking way to get someone to think about your topic and be interested in it. In fact, questions make great "hooks" for the introduction, but because a thesis is a claim, it can never be a question.

Question	What is the meaning of life?
Statement	Developing close relationships with family and friends is the meaning of life.

- **Address the question/task of the assignment.** Your thesis must respond directly to the essay prompt and fulfill all parts of the assignment.

Sample Assignment	Evaluate your city's public transit options and argue which is the best method of getting around town.

  In this case you are being asked to do two things: Evaluate all the public transit options and pick one to argue is the best method of public transportation. If your thesis doesn't answer both parts of the prompt, your essay won't either.
- **Not announce the topic of your essay.** You want your reader to know your specific topic, but don't use announcements like "this essay will discuss" or "in this essay, I will prove." Such statements may be appropriate in some disciplines, like the sciences, but they are not appropriate for general academic essay writing and are definitely not suitable for English papers.
- **Be significant.** Ask yourself "So what?" about your claim. Why does the point you're making matter? Why is your claim relevant? What difference should it make to your reader? If you can't answer these questions, your claim isn't strong enough to support an essay. See the section on sharpening your thesis (p. 231) for more about this.

HOW DO YOU KNOW WHAT CLAIM YOU WANT TO MAKE?

It's true that it takes practice and usually several drafts to write a good thesis, but that's because you have to figure out what you're trying to say before you can write a great thesis. Many writers—even professional writers—need to do an entire rough draft before they determine what they really want to say. Some people write a draft without a thesis and then go back and figure out what the thesis should be. Other writers won't start until they have what they believe is a perfectly crafted thesis. Beginning writers should probably take the middle road: Draft a thesis you think is good, but be open to changing it as your ideas evolve. Here's a definition of a thesis statement that might make the process easier:

A thesis statement is what you will argue is true about your topic.

For more on essay assignments, see the section How to Read an Essay Assignment in Chapter 3, Putting Ideas into Writing, pages 94–96.

In academic writing, the thesis usually begins with the essay assignment. What is your assignment? What are you being asked to do? Usually the thesis is an answer to the essay question or the prompt.

Let's say the essay assignment is to take a position on whether schools should stop selling soft drinks and other sugar-filled drinks like juices at school. (In fact, many school districts already have such a ban in place and many others are debating whether to make this change.) Your topic is this:

Banning sugary drinks at school

Your assignment is to take a position on this topic. To create a thesis from the topic, in this case, you would state your position on the issue. Suppose you think the topic is a good idea. Your position would be:

Schools should ban the selling of sugary drinks.

That's a good start because it's a clear position on the issue, but it's not yet a strong thesis. To make this a stronger thesis, include the reason for your position, which will help focus your essay. By asking why schools should ban the selling of sugar-laden drinks, you will come up with a reason or two. (If you have trouble coming up with reasons, you haven't done enough brainstorming and probably aren't ready to write a thesis yet.) Here are the reasons you might generate:

For more on developing your ideas, see Chapter 9, Pre-Writing, page 214.

- Sugary drinks are unhealthy (lots of calories, bad for teeth, no nutritional value).
- Kids don't make the best choices about what to eat or drink.
- Sugary drinks are partly to blame for high rates of childhood obesity.

In this case, you can combine the first two reasons into one:

Not having sugary drinks at school will help students make healthier choices.

Great! Now you can add the reasons to the thesis:

> Schools should ban the selling of sugary drinks <u>in order to help kids</u>
> <u>maintain a healthier diet and reduce childhood obesity.</u>

Much stronger! Next, let's look at an example taking the opposite position:

> **Schools should not ban soft drinks and juices.**

This thesis has the same weakness as our first draft of the previous thesis: There are no reasons given. Why should schools not ban selling soft drinks and juices?

> It's not the school's job to tell kids what they can or can't drink. That's the parents' responsibility. Parents are responsible for teaching kids healthy habits.

Great! Now let's put that all together:

> Parents, not schools, are responsible for teaching kids to have a
> healthy diet.

Here's the much-improved thesis with the reasons added:

> Schools should not ban selling soft drinks and juices because parents, not schools, are responsible for teaching kids to have a healthy diet.

Notice that each thesis in this case is a direct answer to the prompt. But what if your position isn't clearly for (pro) or against (con)? Remember that all thesis statements are claims, so even if your position is not clearly pro or con, you are still taking some sort of position. For example, if you write a paper on siblings and your topic is birth order, you wouldn't take a pro or con position on birth order—it's not the kind of topic one would be for or against. However, you can still make a *claim*, based on evidence, about the effect of birth order: For instance, do you think evidence indicates that birth order determines personality? Whether you answer yes or no, this position can be developed into your claim.

Drafting Your Thesis, Step by Step

STEP 1: Brainstorm the assignment. Have your essay prompt in front of you and underline the question stem. Spend at least five minutes writing down your initial response to the prompt.

STEP 2: Read through the results of your brainstorming. Underline places where you state your opinion about the topic that fits the assignment.

STEP 3: Draft the thesis.   A good way to begin putting a thesis together is to simply answer the questions of the prompt. You may have some of these answers already jotted down in your brainstorming material. If not, write out each part of the question stem and answer each part separately.

Here is an example for an essay on Education.

Assignment   What are the problems with public education today? Are charter schools the answer?

In one sentence each, answer the following questions:

1. What are the problems with education?
2. What is good about charter schools?
3. What is not good about charter schools?
4. Can charter schools alleviate the problems of public education? Why or why not?

STEP 4: Look over your answers and think about which one you have the strongest claim for, or which one you are most interested in writing about.   Your answers to questions 2 and 3 should help you come up with a good answer for question 4. Your answers for questions 1 and 4 should be your working thesis. Remember, it's a *working thesis* because you might revise it a few more times before the essay is finished, but it's a good start for building the rest of your paper.

SHARPENING YOUR THESIS

Thesis statements are generally written and then revised many times. The first draft of your thesis is really a working thesis, which means it is good enough to work from, but will probably still need development. Let's look at an example of a working thesis about siblings:

Adult siblings often argue whenever major family decisions need to be made.

This is a good start, but it needs to be more of an argument. To make your thesis better, try to make it more arguable and more specific. Your thesis might answer one or more of the following questions:

- Why is this true?
- What impact will this have on other people or things?
- Who should care about this?

Here are some possible thesis statements that "answer" those questions:

Why?
Adult siblings often argue when major family decisions need to be made, because stress makes them go back to the ways they acted as children.

What impact?
When adult siblings argue during a family crisis, it can make it hard for the next generation of cousins to become close friends.

Who cares?
Elderly parents continue to get upset by their children's arguments, especially when those fights are about the parents' care.

Each of these thesis statements is deeper than the earlier draft of the thesis, though each takes the paper in different directions. Extensive pre-writing helps you generate a variety of options for how to focus your essay's thesis, so you can choose the direction you wish to go, instead of feeling as though there is only one possible way to write the paper.

IMPROVING WEAK THESIS STATEMENTS

Part of the reason why thesis statements seem difficult to write is that there are so many possible variations of thesis statements. Although much college writing assigns you to take some kind of position, you may also be asked to write other kinds of essays. Following are examples of working thesis statements for specific kinds of assignments. Each one starts out weak, but ends up strong. With practice, you'll accomplish the same thing.

Definition Thesis Statement

Poor Thesis   The definition of *voting*, according to *Merriam-Webster's Dictionary*, is to "exercise political franchise."

In a definition paper, your instructor is not looking for the dictionary's meaning of a concept; he or she is looking for what the word means to you, to a specific group, or to people generally. The thesis of a definition essay should state your interpretation of the word, in a way that shows your point of view. The thesis above misses the mark completely. With these things in mind, the student revises the thesis:

Better Thesis   Voting means having a voice.

Ah, better! This revision is much closer to stating what voting means to the author. The thesis still needs work, though. What is meant by "having a voice"? How does that relate to voting, and why is it important?

Best Thesis   Voting is much more than a quiet democratic exercise; it is about having a voice in important issues.

Now the thesis states what kind of voice (a voice in important issues), and it puts the definition in context by stating how voting may be thought of (a quiet democratic exercise). These big improvements make the thesis a much stronger claim.

Narration Thesis Statement

Poor Thesis   I remember the first time I voted.

There is no claim here; this is just a fact. What point does the author want to make about the first voting experience? What was significant about that experience? These considerations go into writing the revised thesis:

Better Thesis   When I stood at the voting booth for the first time, I realized what an amazing right it is to vote.

This is a big improvement on the first thesis draft because the author has added the significance of the experience by including the claim that the right to vote is amazing. The thesis is still a bit generic, though—what is amazing about this new right? What caused the realization? These questions help the student revise the thesis again:

Best Thesis   Having the right to vote was not exactly the highlight of turning eighteen, but when I stood at the voting booth for the first time, I was struck by what an amazing privilege it is to vote, since women have only had the right to vote for less than one hundred years.

This thesis does a much better job of showing how the experience of voting didn't hit the author until she actually voted and why the experience of voting was so meaningful (because women have only had the right to vote for less than one hundred years). The addition of "Having the right to vote was not exactly the highlight of turning eighteen" emphasizes how much her thinking about voting shifted.

Process Analysis Thesis Statement

Poor Thesis   There are several steps to achieving democracy.

This thesis draft doesn't make a strong point other than saying there are steps involved in achieving democracy. What are these steps? Why are these steps important or significant?

Better Thesis   The steps to achieving real democracy begin with the critical thinking of voters.

This revision is an improvement: The addition of the word *real* tells us more about what the author thinks of the current state of democracy— that it's not a "true" or "real" democracy. It also includes some of the process required to achieve that—"the critical thinking of voters." The author could improve the thesis a bit here by clarifying what role "the critical thinking of voters" has in the process of achieving real democracy.

Best Thesis   The steps to achieving real democracy begin with critical thinking, which will lead voters to make informed choices at the voting booth.

This is now a really terrific thesis. It is much stronger because it is now clear how critical thinking can lead to "real democracy"—by helping voters make informed choices at the voting booth.

Compare-Contrast Thesis Statement

Poor Thesis Which are ultimately more important, local or national elections?

This thesis breaks one of the important standards of thesis writing: It is in the form of a question, not a statement. As a question, it's not taking a position about which kind of election is more important, so it is not a claim.

Better Thesis National elections seem more important than local elections.

This is a definite improvement because the thesis is a claim and no longer a question. It's far from perfect, though, because it doesn't make a strong point. It says that one kind of election seems more important, but doesn't say why or whether it actually is or not. This thesis still needs a stronger position and a reason for that position.

Best Thesis National elections seem more important, but local elections have a bigger impact on your day-to-day life.

Much improved! The thesis now includes a specific, strong claim: Local elections have a bigger impact than national elections. By starting with a general assumption that national elections seem more important, this thesis immediately interests the reader by claiming the opposite.

Cause-Effect Thesis Statement

Poor Thesis If more people voted, things would be really different.

This thesis doesn't make a specific claim. Because the wording is left vague ("things" and "different"), it's not clear what the focus of this essay will be. What things would be different? How would they be different?

Better Thesis If more people voted, it would show that they have a stake in current issues.

This thesis is an improvement because now we know what would be different, but the significance is not specifically stated. Which people is the author referring to? Why is it important for them to show that they are interested and care about current issues?

Best Thesis If more young adults voted, they could dispel the myth that they're apathetic and show that they have a stake in current issues.

Excellent revisions! Now it's very clear what this essay is going to discuss. We now know whom the essay will be about (young adults) and some important context (young adults are often thought of as apathetic).

It is also clear what effect an increase in voting would have (it would show that they are not apathetic, but concerned about current issues).

Problem-Solution Thesis Statement

Poor Thesis   If you are unhappy, the solution is to vote.

There are a couple of problems with this thesis. First, although the solution is clear (voting is the solution), the problem is so generic as to be meaningless. There are many reasons people might be unhappy that have nothing to do with politics or elections, so voting is not logically a solution to general unhappiness. It was probably clear in the writer's mind that he meant unhappy with elections or politics, but if it's not clear on the paper, the reader won't know what the connection is. Second, the writer directly addresses the reader in the second person by writing "you," In academic writing, you should avoid using "you." The standard is to write in third person ("people are unhappy"), or sometimes in first person, but generally not in second person.

Better Thesis   If people are unhappy with society, the solution is to vote.

Here the writer has made a good change by replacing "you" with the third-person perspective ("people"). It's a little clearer now what people are unhappy about, but the writer still needs to make this even clearer. How would voting make people happy with society? What about society are people unhappy with? *Society* is one of those really broad words that get seriously overused in essays. Be careful when using it. Unless you really are referring to all of society, it's a generic word that is hard to live up to.

Best Thesis   If young adults are generally unhappy with the decisions of elected officials, the solution is to vote and campaign.

Wow, a big improvement here. This thesis has gone from very unclear to very clear and specific. Can you see how much stronger the writer made the thesis by taking out the vague word "society" and replacing it with more concrete, specific words/ideas? The problem is that young people are unhappy with decisions of elected officials, and the solution is for them to vote and campaign. This writer decided to add more clarity to the solution as well.

Argument Thesis Statement

Poor Thesis   This essay will explain why the voting age should not be lowered to sixteen.

Although there is a clear position (voting age should not be lowered to sixteen), this thesis doesn't provide the reasons why the author takes this position. Another problem with this thesis is that it announces that the reasons will be provided in the essay. Don't include a discussion of what you are going to discuss. In an academic argument essay, a thesis should state a clear position and one or more reasons for that position.

Better Thesis   The voting age should not be lowered to sixteen because teenagers are not ready for that.

The writer has greatly improved this thesis by getting rid of the announcement "this essay will explain." And the writer has started to indicate the reason behind this position, which is good. It could still be improved by clarifying the reason. Why are teens not ready? What does it mean to be ready to be a voter? Are there any other significant reasons why age sixteen is too young for voting?

Best Thesis   At age sixteen, teenagers are still learning how to be responsible, which is often trial and error, but because voting is a big responsibility, the voting age should remain eighteen.

This thesis is now a winner. It states the author's position clearly (voting age should not change), and it gives a solid reason: Voting is a big responsibility and sixteen-year-olds are still learning responsibility.

practice it   Improving Weak Thesis Statements

Evaluate the four working thesis statements below about fame and celebrity. Then write your own working thesis statement. What works and what needs more work for each thesis statement? Revise each one based on the following criteria. A thesis statement should:

- Be an arguable claim (not everyone would agree with it; it can be supported by evidence)
- Be clearly and specifically phrased
- Address the question/task of the assignment
- Be a statement (*not* a question)

Thesis statements:

1. The question is, what is fame?

   What works?
   What is missing or unclear?
   Revise to improve the thesis.

2. This essay will explore the downsides of celebrity and why we still want it despite the negatives.

   What works?
   What is missing or unclear?
   Revise to improve the thesis.

3. Casually following celebrities' lives can be inspirational for many who relate to the struggles some celebrities have overcome, but celebrity obsession can cause a person to lose their identity and live in a fantasy world far from reality.

What works?
What is missing or unclear?
Revise to improve the thesis.

4. Michael Jordan is not just the world's most famous athlete; he is a role model.

What works?
What is missing or unclear?
Revise to improve the thesis.

After practicing with these sample student thesis statements, evaluate and revise your own working thesis, using the same criteria:

Write down your working thesis.
Evaluate and revise your working thesis as needed.
What works?
What is missing or unclear?
Revise to improve the thesis.

Writing a strong thesis is a skill that takes time and practice to acquire. Sufficient brainstorming will create the foundation for a strong working thesis. This strategy will save you time. Remember, it can be very helpful to consult with your instructor, a tutor, or a classmate or two to get feedback on your thesis.

chapter review

Chapter 10 strives to deepen your understanding of the role of the thesis in an essay and to broaden your view of the range of thesis statements you can write. Understanding how a thesis functions is an essential part of both finding thesis statements in reading and shaping your own thesis statements in writing.

To review this chapter, choose one or more of the following strategies:

1. Look over the readings you have been assigned for class to find one that has an implied thesis. Read through the text carefully to identify the implied thesis, and then write it out in your own words in the margin of the text.

2. Make flash cards that define, in your own words, the following terms: *thesis, topic, claim, evidence, argument*, and *opinion*. Be sure to differentiate between the terms to show how they are distinct from one another.

3. If you skipped any activities, do them now as a way to deepen your understanding of the material.

4. Try to explain what you have learned to someone you know. Discuss the key concepts and give some of your own examples to illustrate those concepts.

11

Argument

in this chapter

- What Is an Argument?
- What Are the Main Parts of an Argument?
- What Is the Difference between Evidence and Opinion?
- Why Should You Make a Counterargument?
- How Do You Make Inferences?

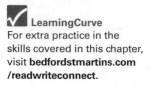

LearningCurve
For extra practice in the skills covered in this chapter, visit **bedfordstmartins.com /readwriteconnect**.

What Is an Argument?

When you hear the word *argument*, what comes to mind? Two people in a heated disagreement? This may be the most obvious kind of argument, but in most kinds of academic writing you are asked to make a claim about something. That claim is, in fact, a statement of opinion that then must be *argued*. In argument essays, your thesis states a clear position or claim, and the body of the essay provides ample support to convince your reader of your position.

Taking a stand and making an argument are skills we have honed since childhood, such as when we made a case for staying up past our bedtime or negotiated for an extra dessert after dinner. In fact, if you spend any time around kids, you will recognize in their behavior the early development of some of the strategies that college writers use: making a claim, sizing up the audience, offering reasons and evidence for support, and sometimes concluding with a tantrum (college writers should avoid this last strategy).

Let's begin by looking at the parts of an argument. A solid argument has four major components:

- Position
- Evidence and reasons
- Counterargument
- Rebuttal

Taking a Position

Your position is your claim about an issue or stand on an issue, and it will be stated in your thesis. Your position is more than a simple opinion;

238

it must be an arguable claim. For example, suppose you make the following assertion:

Graffiti is my favorite form of art.

This statement is an opinion. It is not arguable because it is a matter of personal taste, and therefore it couldn't be your position in an argument paper.

However, suppose you make this assertion:

Graffiti is one of the most controversial art forms.

This statement is both your opinion and an arguable position to take. It is arguable because another person could argue that graffiti is not art at all. A different person might take the position that graffiti isn't all that controversial. Your position would need to be supported by reasons and evidence. If your assignment asks you to argue for or against something, your position will be one or the other. If you argue for a compromise or third option, then that will be your position. The position must be stated clearly in the thesis at the beginning of the essay, and the body of the essay must prove and support it.

Before you decide on the position you wish to take on an issue, prewrite to figure out and evaluate all the possibilities. Begin by working out what you think about an issue and evaluating the reasons and support for the various positions you can take. For example, if you are asked to write an essay arguing whether graffiti is art or vandalism, you might begin by sketching out the following brainstorm:

Graffiti is art.	Graffiti is vandalism.
• Most graffiti is made up of big "pieces" that are colorful and very stylistic.	• Graffiti created without the authorization of the building owner is vandalism and often costs small business owners a lot of money to cover up, not to mention time.
• "Tagging" is usually considered different from graffiti and that's more vandalism.	• Graffiti pops up on public property like schools, parks, subways, freeway walls, buses, overpasses, and signs. It's vandalism b/c it messes up the space and requires public funds to clean up or cover.
• Graffiti "pieces" or murals are often requested from building owners to add to their building walls.	
• Many graffiti images are very artistic and can even be murals.	• When graffiti covers freeway or street signs, it's a hazard for the public who can't read the information on the signs. This could cause people to miss a freeway exit or even get lost.
• Although some graffiti is done without permission, it's often done on abandoned building walls or public walls like overpasses, and walls of freeways or subways.	

- Even graffiti that is unauthorized can really beautify a neighborhood, esp. when neighborhood is falling apart.
- Graffiti can be artistic with lots of colors and images.
- Not all "art" through the ages was necessarily popular or accepted as art when it was made.
- Not all art is authorized—just because it is illegal or might vandalize a building doesn't make it not artistic, and therefore it is art.

- Just because some might find graffiti to be cool or even beautiful doesn't mean it's everyone's taste. It's still vandalism.

Based on the brainstorm, which position would you take? Explain why.

> **practice it**   Choosing a Position
>
> If your assignment is to write an argument paper based on what you have read, pick a side or a position by first going over your reading notes and annotations, and then listing or brainstorming all the reasons why you chose that position. If you are still unsure which position to take, do this for both sides or more than one position to see which one you have more support for or interest in.

Evidence and Reasons

The evidence in your argument is like the soldiers in an army. It provides the ground support for your reasons and claim. Evidence is made up of facts, statistics, observations, quotations, and paraphrases. Your reasons are what led you to your position. Strong and logical reasons provide the rationale for your position. The reasons answer the question "why" about your position. For example, suppose you take the following position:

Graffiti is one of the most controversial art forms.

You can then ask yourself a few questions: Why is graffiti considered art? What makes graffiti controversial? Your answers would be your reasons. You should have several reasons to support any position, and your reasons usually become your topic sentences.

Position   Graffiti is one of the most controversial art forms.

Reasons

- Much of the graffiti in urban areas is painted illegally and is expensive to clean up.
- Major museums, such as the Los Angeles County Museum of Art, have had street art exhibits including graffiti.
- Some people find that the artistic quality of graffiti beautifies a community.

EVIDENCE VERSUS OPINION

Most people choose a position on an issue because they have an opinion about it. Opinions are often based on several things: values, beliefs, reasons, evidence, experience, and others' beliefs. We all have opinions on just about everything, and this is good because opinions, in part, shape who we are and what we like and don't like. When crafting support for an argument, opinions are essential, but it's important to clearly understand the difference between opinions and evidence.

Evidence is made up of facts and information as well as expert opinion, which is supported by knowledge of the facts, and not by simple belief. We often need to rely on the expert opinion of others because it's impossible to research every fact personally. For instance, in choosing a new computer to buy, we might call on the expert opinion of a friend who works in the technology industry and follows computer trends. Or we might rely on the expert opinion of a publication like *Consumer Reports* that reviews products and their reliability. Either of these choices is reasonable since the source in both cases is someone more informed than us, and his or her opinion is based on research and knowledge of the product. Opinions not based on evidence cannot support an academic argument. How can you tell if an opinion is based on evidence? If an opinion is supported by clear facts or information, it might be a good basis for an argument.

However, if an opinion is based less on evidence and mostly on belief, you should not use it as support for an argument. For example, imagine that a strong swimmer refuses to swim in the ocean because he or she fears sharks. Now, admittedly, sharks are the kinds of creatures you want to avoid when swimming, but this person is a terrific swimmer, loves to swim, and otherwise would be happy swimming in the ocean if not for fear of a shark attack. Where does the belief that swimming in the ocean is dangerous because of sharks come from? Is it based on recent reports of shark attacks or sightings? Is it based on movies like *Jaws* or *Deep Blue Sea* or *Mega Shark versus Giant Octopus*? All oceans have sharks and, unfortunately, people have been attacked by them, but it's also true, according to the department of ichthyology at the Florida Museum of

Natural History, that the chances of being the victim of a fatal shark attack are smaller than the chances of being killed by falling into a sand hole on the beach. Does the frightened swimmer see only the negatives and ignore the rest? Now, there might be many valid reasons why someone would not want to swim in the ocean (for instance, not being a strong swimmer), but without more evidence about the danger of potential shark attacks, this opinion that the ocean is too dangerous for swimming is not well supported.

KINDS OF EVIDENCE

In addition to expert opinion, evidence also includes facts, statistics, anecdotes, observations, quotations, and paraphrases that come from your readings, experience, and observations. Not all evidence is equally useful or convincing. When crafting an argument, you must consider your audience. This determines how much and what kind of evidence you need to support your position. If you write to a well-informed group, you need less background information or detail. If you write to an audience that already agrees with some of your points, you can choose evidence suited to what they already know or believe. If you write to an audience that disagrees with your point of view, then you need to carefully select the most convincing evidence and be sure to address counterarguments thoroughly.

For more information and practice understanding audience, see Chapter 6, Audience, Purpose, and Topic, page 169.

Just as you learned to critically evaluate the credibility of an author or source, you should apply the same scrutiny to your own evidence to test its strength. If you gathered facts, statistics, anecdotes, and observations from several readings and the information is well documented and/or comes from a reputable source, you should consider your information to be strong. Here are some examples of evidence to support the argument that graffiti is vandalism:

Reason	It is costly to remove graffiti.
Fact as Evidence	The four main methods of removing graffiti all cost money for supplies and labor: paint-overs, chemicals, replacing or removing structure that has graffiti on it, and cleaning with sandblasting or other methods. (This fact comes from a U.S. Department of Justice guide for police; government documents are widely considered to be credible sources.)
Statistic as Evidence	The city of Seattle, Washington, spent over $1 million on graffiti cleanup and prevention in 2009. (This fact comes from a well-known national newspaper; newspapers are expected to research what they publish to verify that it is true.)

Reason	*Graffiti can be hazardous when it covers freeway or street signs.*
Anecdote as Evidence	*I was almost hit by a car that didn't stop because a stop sign was covered up by graffiti.*
Observation as Evidence	*Freeway signs on overpasses are sometimes covered up by graffiti tags, which make it difficult or impossible to read names of exits.*

practice it   Reasons and Evidence

Underline the reasons and evidence in the following sample paragraph supporting the position that graffiti is art:

> Graffiti may not be everyone's cup of tea, but graffiti can definitely be considered art because of its use of color, its stylistic design, and the pride graffiti artists take in their work. Most urban graffiti is made up of big "pieces," short for masterpieces, that use lots of color. In many poor urban neighborhoods, these bright bursts of color that pop up on walls of abandoned buildings or freeway underpasses are usually the only colorful spots. Most graffiti artists take pride in their creations and are very thoughtful and creative in their designs. According to Deborah Lamm Weisel in her publication *Graffiti*, "Some tagger graffiti may involve creative expression, providing a source of great pride in the creation of complex works of art" (8). The complexity of the designs and the pride that the "tagger" takes in his or her work make the graffiti artistic rather than pure vandalism. Although many graffiti pieces are considered vandalism because they are not painted with permission, vandalism includes the intent to deface property. These creative, stylistic, freestyle masterpieces may be painted without permission, but they are not painted with the intention to deface. On the contrary, they are painted with the purpose of beautifying.

After you identify the reasons and evidence in the paragraph, evaluate how convincing they are. Is this paragraph well supported? Why or why not? Would you add anything? If so, discuss what you would add and why.

practice it **Taking a Side**

Working with a classmate or friend, select one of the following issues, and have each person take a different position. (Put aside your own personal beliefs for the moment if you need to argue a side opposite to your own views.) Sketch out a quick brainstorm to gather evidence and reasons to support the position you have selected, and then compare the reasons and evidence with your partner.

Children should get an allowance.
Schools should have metal detectors.
Dogs should always be on leashes.
Colleges should be tuition-free.
Fame is overrated.
You should always maintain contact with your siblings.

practice it **Building an Argument**

Now that you have learned how to craft a good argument, take time to work on your own argument. First, list reasons that support your position, and then list the evidence. If you take evidence from a reading, be sure to include the author, title, and page number, whether you paraphrase or quote directly.

MAKING INFERENCES FROM EVIDENCE

An inference is an educated guess based on available evidence and information. We make inferences all the time in everyday life, in what we read, and in making arguments. For example, let's say Brian is waiting for a bus. It's later than he usually leaves work, and no one else is waiting at the bus stop. He knows that during rush hour, the bus stops here every fifteen minutes, but he's been waiting over thirty minutes. He can infer two things from the available information:

1. The bus runs less frequently after rush hour. Instead of every fifteen minutes, perhaps the bus only runs once an hour at this point in the day.
2. The bus no longer services this stop after rush hour.

Brian has no way of knowing which of these, if either, is the case, but based on the available information, either of these scenarios is a reasonable inference.

Reading critically requires making inferences, as does building a well-reasoned argument. In order to fully support your argument, make sure you draw a logical and reasonable conclusion based on your evidence. In order to do that, support your argument with the right evidence, so your readers believe your conclusion.

When reading, making inferences is like "reading between the lines." We tend to automatically make inferences as we read, but to really understand and to build your own argument, add these inferences to your annotations as you read, so that you can easily refer back to them later.

practice it   Making Inferences

Practice reading between the lines of the following blog post from the *New York Times*. Read the post and then answer the questions that follow it.

NewYorkTimes.com

Disney Limits Junk-Food Ads
KJ Dell'Antonia, *MotherLode: Adventures in Parenting blog*

Finally, an entity powerful enough to challenge food manufacturing   1
conglomerates takes affirmative action against advertising food to
children that we don't, as a society, actually want them to eat. The Food
and Drug Administration? No, not them. The Federal Communications
Commission? Not them, either.

What we need, it turns out, in order to find someone willing to stand   2
up and put some limit on exactly what kinds of products we will put
millions of dollars into encouraging children to eat, is someone that's able
to be largely independent of those millions of dollars. Maybe it takes a
powerful corporation to take on powerful corporations.

Disney announced today that all products advertised on its child-   3
focused television channels, radio stations and Web sites must comply
with a strict new set of nutritional standards. Many products that already
advertise on Disney, like Capri-Sun and Kraft Lunchables meals, won't
make the cut as they currently stand. Disney will also "reduce the amount
of sodium by 25 percent in the 12 million children's meals served annually
at its theme parks, and create what it calls fun public service announcements promoting child exercise and healthy eating."

Will it help? It can't hurt. It could be argued by the cynical that most   4
large businesses involved in selling food to consumers, including
children, have an incentive (if not an active duty) to encourage consumers
to eat as much as possible. If they don't create products that are unique to
them and encourage us to eat them, their business won't prosper—and if
we as a society don't recognize the power (and the origin) of that incentive, all of our efforts at change will go nowhere.

continued ❯

Disney is the rare company with a huge marketing and media reach   5
to children whose revenues aren't dependent on food products or closely
tied to their advertising, and its initiative fits in well with the national
conversation. Like Walmart, it's powerful enough (and profitable enough)
to take a stand. Does Disney think that stand will ultimately benefit its
bottom line? Of course. Disney, as a company, needs consumers' love
more than it needs their tastebuds. But just because Disney sees encouraging good health as an area in which it can profit doesn't mean it can't
help promote positive change. On the contrary—that financial incentive
may be the only thing that will work.

Answer these questions about the reading:

1. What is the specific topic of the article?
2. What position does this author take? Underline the evidence and reasons that lead you to that conclusion.
3. In paragraph 2, the author states, "What we need, it turns out, in order to find someone willing to stand up and put some limit on exactly what kinds of products we will put millions of dollars into encouraging children to eat, is someone that's able to be largely independent of those millions of dollars"? What can you infer is the reason for this claim?
4. In paragraph 3, what inference can you draw from Disney's announce-ment that "all products advertised on its child-focused television channels, radio stations and Web sites must comply with a strict new set of nutritional standards"?
5. In paragraph 4, what can be inferred about the role of large food corporations in our national diet?
6. In paragraph 5, what can you infer the "national conversation" means here?

Counterarguments and Rebuttals

Imagine that a skeptical reader is reading an essay; the *counterargu-ments* are the ideas that he or she would use to counter, or argue against, the text. You can think of the counterarguments as the "reading against the grain" ideas. A counterargument is an opposing position to the one you take in your paper. A *rebuttal* is your response to the counterargu-ment that you introduced.

Why would you include an argument opposing your central claim in your paper? A good writer knows there is more than one side to every story, and it's important to acknowledge the other positions and evidence. Including counterarguments intelligently in your writing accomplishes two things. First, acknowledging counterarguments shows that you are well-informed about the issue. Second, rebutting or accommodating counterarguments addresses concerns that readers might have. Consider the following situation: Francesca wants to get a group of friends together to take a vacation in Hawaii, but Anthony has another vacation destination in mind. See how Anthony uses counterargument and rebuttal to address concerns about Francesca's proposition.

> **Francesca:** Hawaii has great beaches, sun, and tropical sunsets. Pack your bags, and let's go!

What's wrong with this position? It only acknowledges one side of the issue. Are there any reasons *not* to go to Hawaii that ought to be considered?

> **Anthony:** While Hawaii is a beautiful tropical destination with great beaches and warm water for snorkeling, which makes it a popular vacation spot, these "benefits" also make it a very crowded place to visit, and it's a long plane flight away and can be very expensive. Camping at a nearby lake can provide warm days and plenty of swimming on less crowded beaches, at one-fifth of the cost of a trip to Hawaii.

In the preceding example, the counterargument is highlighted in blue, and the rebuttal to the counterargument is in yellow.

Anthony's counterargument and rebuttal may not convince Francesca to give up her dream of a Hawaiian vacation, but the counterargument that such a vacation is expensive, is crowded, and requires a lot of travel time identifies the weaknesses in the argument. Addressing counterarguments is important so you don't look like you are ignoring the obvious or, worse, are ignorant of it.

When reading, look for places in the text where the author considers the evidence for other sides of the argument and rebuts that evidence or offers alternatives or a solution. This indicates that the author is aware of the complexity of the issue and shows respect for his or her readers by acknowledging the potential questions or weaknesses represented by counterarguments.

practice it   Find the Parts of the Argument

The following paragraph is taken from Lucinda Rosenfeld's opinion piece "How Charter Schools Can Hurt." Just by pre-reading the title alone, how do you know what position Rosenfeld is taking on the issue of charter schools? Armed with that information, find the counterargument and her rebuttal. Underline the counterargument and put brackets around the rebuttal.

You'll find the full text of this article in the e-pages for *Read, Write, Connect.* Go to **bedfordstmartins .com/readwriteconnect** and click on **e-Chapters /Education.**

continued ❯

> The apparent reason for opening a charter school in a gentrified neighbor-hood like Cobble Hill (or the Upper West Side, where a Success Academy opened last year) is to bring more middle-class and upper-middle-class families into the publicly funded charter system. But if the Success Academy succeeds in its mission, it could well end up destroying schools like P.S. 261 that already succeed in attracting these families. My daughter's new friends include the children of both marketing executives and maintenance workers. At drop-off recently, I watched as she and a friend who lives in a nearby housing project walked hand in hand down the hall. In its promise of a more just world, the sight made me almost teary-eyed. I wonder how much longer those kinds of scenes will prevail.

CONCESSION WORDS

Concession words are words that show you acknowledge or accept a point or position. Because the most important part of a counterargument is to accept or concede a point for another position, concession words are an important tool to help you do that. Concession words are especially useful for counterarguments because they allow you to acknowledge the merits of an opposing point of view while still giving more emphasis to your position. Consider the following example:

Arguing to Prevent New Freeway Construction
Although *traffic levels have reached a tipping point*, adding another freeway will be costly and won't provide immediate relief.

Arguing to Construct a New Freeway
Although *adding another freeway will be costly and won't provide immediate relief,* traffic levels have reached a tipping point.

Notice how each sentence uses essentially the same words, but the con-cession word *although* gives less emphasis to the part of the sentence that the word is attached to (in italics), which can shift the meaning of the sentence.

Here are two more examples:

Although the restaurant only got two out of five stars in an online review, my neighbor recommends it highly.

Although my neighbor recommends it highly, the restaurant only got two out of five stars in an online review.

Which sentence suggests the speaker wants to try the new restaurant? Which sentence implies the speaker doesn't think the new restaurant is worth trying?

Common Concession Words
although
even though
though
whereas
while

The key to using these words is to remember that the part of the sentence the concession word is attached to gets less emphasis. When using a concession word to join two sentences, the sentence the concession word is attached to becomes a dependent clause and can no longer stand on its own. Join the dependent clause to the second sentence with a comma. See the example below:

Vanilla is often thought of as a boring ice cream flavor. It's the best ice cream to pair with a really good hot fudge or caramel sauce.

Use a concession word to emphasize that vanilla is a boring flavor.
Even though + it's the best ice cream to pair with a really good hot fudge or caramel sauce, vanilla is often thought of as a boring ice cream flavor.

Use a concession word to emphasize that vanilla is the best flavor for toppings.
Even though + vanilla is often thought of as a boring ice cream flavor, it's the best ice cream to pair with a really good hot fudge or caramel sauce.

practice it　Concession Words

Use concession words to combine the following sentences:

Dogs are not allowed off leashes. The park is empty.

Combine to emphasize that dogs are not allowed off leashes.
Combine to emphasize that the park is empty.

Fame is something many people secretly yearn for. It comes with many problems such as lack of privacy and unrealistic expectations.

Combine to emphasize that people want fame.
Combine to emphasize that fame is problematic.

Using concession words to add emphasis to your point while acknowledging other positions or information is an excellent way to show more sophistication in your writing and is especially useful in argumentative writing. Practice using these words when you can and keep an eye out as you read for writers using them in articles and books.

---

practice it   Understanding an Argument

Read the following opinion piece, from the *New York Times*, June 2012. Mark Bittman is the author of the book *Food Matters: A Guide to Conscious Eating* as well as the cookbook *How to Cook Everything* and is a regular contributor to the *New York Times* Opinion Pages. As you read, remember to:

For more on reading with and against the grain, see pages 38–41 in Chapter 2, Active and Critical Reading.

- Identify the author's claim.
- Read with and against the grain.
- Identify types of reasons and evidence.
- Evaluate the quality of the evidence.
- Identify any counterarguments.
- Make inferences—what conclusions can you draw from this article?

MARK BITTMAN

Limit Soda for Kids' Sake

For some people, the central knock on Mayor Bloomberg is his eagerness to institute a "nanny state," the most recent example of which is his administration's attempt (opposed by nearly two-thirds of Americans) to ban large servings of sugar-sweetened beverages (SSBs). In this scenario a nanny is unquestionably a bad thing: an excessive and patronizing intrusion, something to be feared and reviled.

A nanny—at her worst—is someone who treats people like children. At her best and most basic, however, she takes care of and protects our children while we're not around. And off the top of my head I can think of one group of people who deserve to be treated and protected like children: children.

What might Mayor Bloomberg's proposal accomplish? Will it get grown-ups who are dead set on drinking two liters of soda a day to drink less? Probably not. Will it create an environment for the next generation of kids in which it is no longer normal to be served a 32-ounce cup of soda? Yes.

And if that's nannying, I'm all for it. Here's the question: Who do you want taking care of your kids while you're not looking—governments interested in improving public health, or corporations interested in improving the bottom line at the expense of same?

There is a maddeningly false "choice" being put forth by the staunchest crit- 5 ics of this plan: either the government tells us what we can and cannot eat and drink, or we exercise our unbridled freedom in making those decisions for ourselves. If we were truly free to make our own uncorrupted choices about what to eat and drink, then corporations wouldn't be allowed to spend hundreds of millions of dollars marketing junk food to kids (including on school buses), and the federal government would subsidize fruits and vegetables (otherwise known as "specialty crops") at the same rate as the commodity crops that are often used to produce junk. Whether we acknowledge it or not, we're already being told what to eat, and more often than not it's the wrong thing.

For sure, the government doesn't always act in our best interest when it comes to nutrition—an understatement, really—but Big Food *never* does, nor should we expect it to. If somebody with some real political clout is willing to stick his neck out for the public health of his city, then good for him and lucky for us. It's easy to forget sometimes, but that's what government is supposed to do: identify the activities that are bad for us or for others and make it harder for us to do them; activities like smoking cigarettes, wearing seat belts or drinking 32 ounces of soda at a stretch.

Some critics are more worried that the plan just won't work. As the mayor himself admitted, there is nothing besides mild inconvenience preventing people from drinking just as much soda as ever; maybe that inconvenience will work and maybe it won't. Either consumers will find it too burdensome to carry two cups at once or to go back for more, or they'll exercise their right to free refills with a renewed sense of purpose (perhaps burning off some extra calories in the process of walking back and forth from the soda fountain).

Strangely enough, I don't think it actually matters much if, in the short-term, consumption of SSBs drops off a bit or stays level. The battle to reverse the calamitous turn that the American diet has taken is long and uphill. The average portion sizes of our dietary staples (burgers, fries and soda) have increased at an alarming rate since the 1950s. A four-ounce burger, 2.5-ounce fries and seven-ounce soda used to be called a meal. Now it's called *tapas*. We've created a new normal in which eating the average amount of the average American foods all too often leads to the average case of obesity or Type 2 diabetes. The real promise of the Bloomberg plan is not in immediately changing the habits of our adults, but in slowly beginning to change the environment for our kids.

Drinking 64 ounces of soda in one sitting was likely as hard to imagine in the 1950s as drinking just four ounces is now. But somewhere down the road,

continued ❯

when we've fully acknowledged the disastrous health implications of added sugars and elected enough people willing to do something about it, we'll look back at the Double Gulp and say, "What the hell were we thinking?" The shift back to a sane diet (and make no mistake, drinking ourselves sick with sugar is insane) has to start somewhere. Is a ban on giant cups the most effective deterrent? No. But could it begin to pave the road (or the slippery slope, as some would call it) towards more aggressive and successful forms of legislation like taxation? Yes. And I hope it does.

Largely because of obesity, we are now raising the very first American 10 generation with a shorter life expectancy than their parents. If this is where we've gotten without a nanny, I think it's about time we get one. Several, in fact.

chapter review

Crafting a strong argument and being able to identify the strengths and weaknesses of arguments you read are essential critical thinking skills for college and beyond. You will often practice the reading and writing strategies in Chapter 11 simultaneously. When taking a stand on an issue, you must assess sources (articles, essays, book chapters) for evidence and information before taking a stand and making a claim. Then you should reevaluate the information carefully, selecting the most fitting evidence to support your position, being sure to address counterarguments along the way.

To review this chapter, choose one or more of the following strategies:

1. In Chapter 2, Active and Critical Reading, you learned about an important reading strategy called reading with and against the grain, which helps you evaluate the support for an argument. This strategy is useful not only when evaluating arguments as a reader, but also when evaluating your own arguments as a writer. You can use this method to assess how well your evidence will support your claim, and what, if any, counterarguments you might need to include. Practice reading with and against the grain on an argument essay of your own. Identify the strengths and weaknesses in your argument.
2. If you skipped any activities, do them now as a way to deepen your understanding of the material.
3. Go to the Opinion Pages of the *New York Times* Web site (or any newspaper or news Web site you read) and pick an opinion piece to read. Look for and identify any reasons, evidence, and opinions. Evaluate how well the author makes his or her case and addresses counterarguments.
4. Try to explain what you have learned to someone you know. Discuss the key concepts and give your own examples to illustrate those concepts.

12

Topic Sentences and Paragraphs

in this chapter

- What Makes a Good Topic Sentence?
- What Is PIE Paragraph Structure?
- How Do You Improve Your Paragraphs?

Writing coherent, clear, well-organized, and well-developed paragraphs will help you throughout your life, as we are often asked to write a one-paragraph response to a question posed by a teacher or co-worker. In addition, strong body paragraphs are the core of a well-written essay, so the more you understand how paragraphs work, the better a college reader and writer you will be.

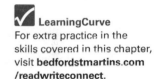

LearningCurve
For extra practice in the skills covered in this chapter, visit **bedfordstmartins.com /readwriteconnect**.

Topic Sentences

A topic sentence is the sentence that states the main point of a paragraph. You've already read about topic sentences in Chapters 1–4; this chapter will help you both recognize and write topic sentences.

Good topic sentences:

- Make one point that the paragraph will cover
- Are the most general sentence of the paragraph
- Are appropriately focused—not too broad or too narrow
- Have a direct relationship to the thesis

IDENTIFYING TOPIC SENTENCES

In some types of writing, especially college textbooks, the topic sentence is often the first sentence of the paragraph. Topic sentences that are the first sentence in a paragraph are easy to find, but what if the first sentence is clearly not the topic sentence? What if it is buried further within the paragraph, or is a question or a statement of fact? Read the whole paragraph, paying careful attention to the point being made. If this doesn't lead you to the topic sentence, look for the most general sentence of the paragraph: Because the topic sentence is the broadest point made in the paragraph, it should be the most general sentence. Or look for examples or quotes in the paragraph and ask yourself: What point does that evidence support? Then try to find a sentence that answers that question. In most cases, you will find the topic sentence using one of these critical reading strategies.

---

practice it   Identifying Topic Sentences

Find and underline the thesis and topic sentences in the following short article on engineered meat, published in *Time* magazine in 2013. If you cannot find an *explicit thesis* (written out in the article) see if you can come up with the author's *implied thesis* and write it out. After identifying the thesis and topic sentences, read just the thesis and the topic sentences together to get a sense of the overall structure of the article. Does each topic sentence make a point? Is each the most general sentence in the paragraph? How does each topic sentence connect back to the thesis?

CATHERINE MAYER AND KATIE HARRIS

Hold the Relish

True beef or not true beef? That is the question two volunteers masticating a burger in front of an invited audience in a London theater attempted to answer Aug. 5. Developing this version of the global fast-food staple in a laboratory had taken three months and eaten up €250,000 ($331,400). "It's close to meat," mused the first taster, Hanni Rützler, a nutritional scientist, swallowing with some difficulty. "This is kind of an unnatural experience," confessed the second taster, Josh Schonwald, a writer, as he chewed on history. He meant the lack of ketchup.

Schmeat—or "cultured beef," as the patty's progenitor, Mark Post, a professor of physiology and biomedical technology at Maastricht University in the Netherlands, calls it—is the culinary product of stem cells harvested from a cow's shoulder and lab-nurtured into strips of muscle. It's hailed by proponents as a potential solution to several juicy existential problems. The demand for cheap meat has been met at a high price to the environment—contributing greenhouse gases and diminishing biodiversity as ever more land is given over to feed crops—as well as risking human health and animal welfare. In Britain, beef eaters have experienced some of the downsides of industrialized farming and food production: an epidemic of bovine spongiform encephalopathy that spiked in the early 1990s, a foot-and-mouth epidemic a decade later and, this year, the revelation that the "beef" in certain prepared foods was actually horse meat. Schmeat production, if scaled up enough to bring prices down, could help feed the world and reduce some of the pressures on the planet.

The quest to develop in vitro meat is riven with apparent contradictions. Can this most processed of processed foods be healthy? Is it possible to solve problems created by our greed for meat by making more meat more cheaply? Post macerates the muscle cells in a broth that includes fetal-calf serum, obtained by slaughtering pregnant cows, yet his work is lauded by some vegetarians. "Our goal is to promote foods that don't use animals at all," says Ingrid Newkirk, president of People for the Ethical Treatment of Animals (PETA), an animal-rights organization. "But enormous swaths of the population can't bring themselves to become vegan, so it's logical to support in vitro meat if its goal is to reduce suffering."

PETA has funded research into in vitro meat for seventeen years, says Newkirk. And the deep-pocketed mystery backer of Post's project was unveiled in London along with the burger: Google cofounder Sergey Brin. In a short film screened before the burger tasting, Brin acknowledged that some critics dismiss the prospects for mass-produced schmeat as science fiction. He added, "I actually think that's a good thing. If what you're doing is not seen by some people as science fiction, it's probably not transformative enough."

But if this really is the food of the future—and the most optimistic esti-   5
mates suggest schmeat won't make it into supermarkets for ten to twenty years—it will have to overcome what Kenneth A. Cook, president of the U.S. environmental-health research and advocacy organization Environmental Working Group, calls "the ick factor." In Post's earlier career as a physician specializing in pulmonary and vascular conditions, he learned to grow tissue to repair the damage that can be caused by fatty diets. Now he is trying to figure out how to put tasty fat into his burgers by culturing the right kinds of fat cells.

"If consumers don't accept it, it won't work. It will end up having been a science experiment," says Cook, who flew to London for the event and believes the technology is "worth a look."

And that is what cultured beef's theatrical debut was all about: drawing attention—and funding. With time and additional resources, Post is confident he can improve on the too solid flesh of the prototype patty. A little ketchup wouldn't go amiss either.

THE TOPIC SENTENCE AND THE THESIS

Once you identify the topic sentences, you can see how they work together to support the thesis of an essay (in other words, how the topic sentence links the thesis and the paragraph information). The topic sentence states the point the paragraph will make and must clearly relate back to the thesis. The body paragraph explains, develops, or supports the topic sentence, and in so doing, supports the thesis. One helpful metaphor is that of a wooden plank bridge. Each topic sentence is like one plank of wood in the bridge. If you put them all together, they add up to the thesis, the bridge itself, across which you may lead your readers.

A visual example of the relationship between the topic sentences and the thesis will help. Look at the following first page of a student essay on murals. The annotations and highlighting show how the topic sentences in blue relate back to the thesis (in yellow).

Murals are not only a way to decorate neighborhoods and public buildings; they also are a way to honor people who have contributed to society and to help pass on lessons about a culture. One such mural is painted on the side of a drugstore and it's called *Mission Celebration*. This mural takes up about half of the wall of the building. It is painted with vibrant, bright colors and includes scenes of Latino culture, and it has a very large image of Cesar Chavez. This mural is hard to miss. The mural *Mission Celebration* is a piece of art created with the purpose of motivating the general public to celebrate and learn about Cesar Chavez and Mexican folklore.

The thesis claims the purpose of the mural is to get the public to know about Cesar Chavez and Mexican folklore

By prominently portraying Cesar Chavez, the mural encourages the community to know about this Mexican American leader. Many people are already aware of who Cesar Chavez was, but if someone didn't know, this mural would make him or her want to know. The image of Cesar Chavez in this mural is positioned in such a way as to suggest he is someone important. His portrait is just of his head, and it's by far the largest image in the mural. Anyone driving or walking by would wonder who this man is and what he might mean to the community. The muralist used size to show him as an important figure.

Topic sentence 1 relates back to the thesis and helps develop it by discussing one aspect of the thesis: encouraging community to learn about CC

Mission Celebration, by depicting Cesar Chavez's legacy, is an inspiration for other political and social leaders. The community is shown celebrating Cesar Chavez in the mural by depicting him surrounded by other things that are important to the community. This is inspiring to others who want to make a difference in their community, because they can see how honored someone like Cesar Chavez is and aim to be like him. In this way, the mural serves as a positive inspiration to all.

Topic sentence 2 relates back to thesis and helps develop it further by showing how learning about CC is inspiring

One common problem in student writing is that while the topic sentences might be interesting, they don't always relate back to the thesis. Take a look at two examples from student essays. How well does each topic sentence connect to the thesis? Ask yourself the following questions to help you evaluate the examples.

1. Looking at the topic sentences, what point will the paragraph make? Underline that point.
2. Does the topic sentence relate back to the thesis?
3. If the topic sentence does not relate back to the thesis, what is missing?
4. Which topic sentence is a better fit with the stated thesis? Why?

Example 1

Thesis	**The mural *Revive* conveys the message that the wildlife of Golden Gate Park could be restored with the help of the San Francisco community.**
Topic Sentence A	The red-tailed hawk symbolizes creation on the top of the mural because it is part of nature and one of the original inhabitants of the San Francisco Bay Area.
Topic Sentence B	The possibility of the park being restored can be seen in the images of the volunteers and the growth of new plants in the mural.

Example 2

Thesis	**The mural *A Past That Still Lives* shows the struggle the people from El Salvador have had healing from their civil war.**
Topic Sentence A	The colors of the mural—bright yellows, oranges, reds, and greens—make the mural vibrant.
Topic Sentence B	The shadow images of past events painted throughout the mural show that what happened during the civil war still haunts people.

WRITING TOPIC SENTENCES

To draft good topic sentences, begin by reviewing your pre-writing. Generally speaking, topic sentences are written after the thesis to ensure that your topic sentences fully support and develop your thesis's central claim.

One way to generate topic sentences is to list all the points you want to make in support of your thesis. You might already have a list like this from your pre-writing; if so, use that. Write down your points with plenty of room between each one, so you have room to work on topic sentences. For each point, create a sentence that can be developed into a paragraph. Check the topic sentence criteria at the start of the chapter (p. 253) to see if these sentences work as topic sentences. If they don't, revise until they fit.

If you aren't sure what points to make in support of your thesis, begin with the broader topics or evidence you have selected during the pre-writing stage. If you have done the Post-Reading activities in this book, you probably already have an idea of what quotations or examples from the class readings you think will support your thesis. Make a list of either the topics or the evidence you have gathered, and then one by one, ask yourself what you want to say about each topic or piece of evidence and write it out in a sentence.

practice it   **From Topics to Topic Sentences**

Make a rough list of your topics that support your thesis. The next step is to turn each of these phrases into a complete, grammatically correct sentence stating the point the paragraph will make about that topic. This way, you will know *what* you plan to say about each of these ideas. For example, if the topic is financial literacy, you can ask yourself what point you want to make *about* financial literacy. Put the answer into a complete sentence, such as "Financial literacy leads to a better understanding of one's financial situation and good decision making about money." This sentence certainly gives you a clearer sense of where you're going with the paragraph. Write a topic sentence for each topic that you have.

PARAGRAPHS

The function of the body paragraphs is to develop the information that supports the topic sentence and the thesis. Body paragraphs are the muscle behind the thesis: They do all the heavy lifting to prove the claim that your thesis makes. That's a lot of work. To convince the reader the thesis is valid, body paragraphs begin with their own point, the topic sentence. Each body paragraph must have sufficient evidence to fully support its topic sentence.

A well-built paragraph has several important features:

- Purpose—a clear point is stated in the topic sentence.
- Unity—all the sentences relate to and address the point of the paragraph.
- Development—the paragraph provides enough information and explanation to make the point that the topic sentences promise and also to help support the thesis.

UNDERSTAND PARAGRAPH STRUCTURE

An easy way to understand how a paragraph works is to remember the acronym PIE. *PIE* stands for Point, Information, and Explanation/Elaboration, the three main parts of a body paragraph in academic writing.

PIE PARAGRAPH STRUCTURE

Point = your topic sentence	Topic Sentence
Information = observations, facts, statistics, examples, anecdotes, quotes, and other types of evidence	Evidence
Explanation/elaboration = your reasons why the information supports and explains the point of the paragraph or thesis; your discussion of what the information means, and how the information is relevant	Analysis

The PIE paragraph structure serves two main purposes: (1) to help you analyze your paragraph to see if your information and explanation are well balanced, and (2) to help you develop your paragraph if your topic sentence is not well supported.

Each body paragraph (not the introduction or conclusion) should have P, I, and E. Although you will only have one P per paragraph, you should have several I and E sentences, and they don't necessarily have to be in that order. Let's look at a student's sample body paragraph where the P, I, and E are highlighted in different colors. The P (point) is highlighted in yellow, the I (information) is highlighted in blue, and the E (explanation/elaboration) is highlighted in green.

Ruben's Paragraph

Financial know-how is necessary for an individual to become debt-free and **P**
learn to grow their wealth. Financial knowledge includes learning how to **I**
save and keep a budget. In the article "Teach Your Children the Building **I**
Blocks of Finance," Sherie Holder and Kenneth Meeks reinforce the importance of the practice of saving at least 10 to 15 percent of after-tax income
(44). Getting into the practice of automatically saving a certain amount **E**
every month will help you grow your wealth. Another part of financial **E**
know-how is learning how to manage money, which includes knowing how
to avoid getting into debt in the first place. By knowing how to budget your **I**
money, you can learn how much money you actually have, which can help **E**
you spend within your means. When you spend within your means, you are **E**
able to avoid having to use credit cards, which, in turn, will prevent you
from having to pay costly interest fees and prevent you from getting further
into debt.

You can see that the pattern for this paragraph is P/I/I/E/E/I/E/E. It has a good balance of both information and explanation/elaboration.

practice it   Identifying Information and Explanation

Look over the two student sample paragraphs and label each sentence with P, I, or E. Does each paragraph have a good balance of information and explanation/elaboration? Does either paragraph need development in one or both of these areas?

Lisa's Paragraph

Many parents who have their children enrolled in some sort of financial education are happy with the results. The students are more confident in their approach to spending, and more inclined to save or wait instead of having an immediate gratification. Parents then feel more at ease when they are getting ready to send their children to school or on an outing instead of worrying that their children will spend frivolously. More importantly, the pupils will be ready to go on to a job or higher education with the skills and knowledge to succeed financially. Their financial literacy will ensure that they are capable of managing bills and student loans instead of going into severe debt. They will be able to understand the importance of saving and of postponing gratification for a later time when they might be more stable in their finances.

Holly's Paragraph

Parents who are unintentionally sending their children down the path of financial illiteracy may not even fully understand the results of their actions. Parents who send mixed messages about money by telling their children to do one thing while they demonstrate another are making one of the most common mistakes that can be made. Unless they are personally setting the right example themselves, their children will not be willing to follow their advice. If their parents are not doing it, then why should they? It must not be that important, right? Parents who show their children that it is possible to borrow money when you cannot afford to, hinder their children's decision-making process, in turn teaching them to take shortcuts to get what they want, instead of working hard. Using credit cards as a means to supplement the difference between one's income and one's spending is also a nasty shortcut that children have been known to pick up on. This will lead them to believe that living beyond their means is a normal and acceptable way of life. Children will then use this mentality to easily talk themselves into getting or buying whatever they desire, whether they can afford it or not. Also, parents who refuse to ever say no to their children's every wish will set them up for failure. In the end, these tactics can make children unable to say no to things that they do not need, ultimately teaching them that spending is fun! This will lead children to believe that money equals happiness.

---

practice it   Balancing Body Paragraphs

In the essay you are writing, review your body paragraphs one at a time and label each sentence with P, I, or E. Determine if your paragraphs have a good balance of information and explanation or if they need development in one or both of these areas.

Evaluate Your Paragraphs

A paragraph without a clear topic sentence and sufficient evidence won't convince your reader of your point. Labeling the sentences in your body paragraphs with P, I, or E identifies your paragraph's strengths and weaknesses. If you find you are missing the P (topic sentence), think about what point that paragraph is trying to make. Sometimes you can figure that out by looking at the I in the paragraph and asking yourself, "Okay, why did I include that information/example/quotation? What does it support?" Often this will help you focus on the point of the paragraph. Labeling all the sentences with P, I, or E shows whether or not your paragraph is balanced with both information and explanation, and what you need more of. If your paragraph is low on I, remedy the situation by adding more examples, facts, observations, or other forms of information. Just make sure the new information you add to the paragraph fits the point you are making. The most common piece of PIE missing from body paragraphs is usually E. If your paragraph lacks enough explanation or elaboration, now is the time to add it: You need to explain how all the information in your paragraph supports your overall point.

Each paragraph is a unit of writing that focuses on supporting one point, the topic sentence. Strengthening the I and E of your PIE paragraph structure adds texture and sophistication to your writing.

For more help on developing support, see the Quote Sandwich activity in Chapter 16, Quotation and Paraphrase, pages 321–22.

DEVELOP YOUR POINT (P)

If you can't find the sentence that states the point your paragraph will make, you may be missing a topic sentence in that paragraph. Take a step back and read over the whole paragraph, and then ask yourself what single point the paragraph makes. Write that point in the form of a sentence and then check the topic sentence criteria on page 253 of this chapter. If you find the paragraph makes more than one point, you will probably want to develop each point into its own paragraph. Review the section in this chapter on writing topic sentences (see p. 257) for more help.

STRENGTHEN THE INFORMATION (I)

Sometimes strengthening the information in a paragraph is simply a matter of adding more. If you are missing the I in the paragraph, go back to your annotated articles and pre-writing to see what evidence, examples, quotes, or anecdotes you found interesting but have not yet included. Would anything there help provide support for your point in this paragraph? List all the possible pieces of information you might use to support your topic sentence, and then choose the best ones. Peer or instructor feedback can be useful at this point in the writing process.

You may have lots of sentences of information, but they aren't varied enough. Some beginning writers mistakenly use only one kind of support in a paragraph, which weakens the paragraph. If you begin creating a paragraph by choosing a quote or example, you might have a harder time seeing how other sources or kinds of information relate to your main point. But if you begin building your paragraph with an idea, you can often find many pieces of evidence to help you make your point.

When building and developing paragraphs, use a variety of examples, facts, anecdotes, quotations, personal experiences, reasons, and statistics. For example, look at Martha's paragraph from an essay about celebrity and fame. The paragraph is adequate, but the writer could have made it much stronger by using more than one kind of support to prove the point of the topic sentence. The entire paragraph is focused only on support from "Seeing by Starlight" by Carlin Flora. Read the paragraph and then brainstorm additional support that this author could have used to make a stronger paragraph.

Martha's Paragraph

We are drawn to celebrities not only because they are beautiful people, but because they seem to be living the lives most of us can only dream of. Carlin Flora writes about our fascination with celebrities in her article "Seeing by Starlight." The huge salaries and lavish homes of stars keep us interested because "our lives seem woefully dull by comparison" (Flora 518). They are elegant walking the red carpet in couture fashion and dripping with real jewels, perfect hair, and makeup. Flora also argues, however, that some of the beauty we attach to stars is based more on how often we see images of them than their actual beauty. "The more we see a certain face, the more our brain likes it, whether or not it's actually beautiful," writes Flora (520). It helps, too, that they have access to the best skin and hair professionals in the business. Whether it is because of their looks or their lavish lives, we can't stop looking at stars.

This writer misses an opportunity to use quotations from additional sources about celebrity attraction, as well as anecdotes from personal experience. Also, most of us have daydreamed about fame and celebrity for the very reason that we are, at least occasionally, drawn to the glitz and glamour of celebrity lifestyles. This kind of personal perspective could really add variety and broader support to the paragraph.

STRENGTHEN THE EXPLANATION OR ELABORATION (E)

Once you have sufficient and varied information to support your topic sentence, make sure you elaborate on or explain it. In journalistic writing, you see many paragraphs simply end with a quotation, but in college writing, you are expected to say something about the information in your paragraphs. Start by reviewing every piece of information in the paragraph and ask yourself, how does this support my point? Ask yourself why you picked that information to include in your paragraph. The answer is your E. Often we think it's obvious how the information in our paragraphs proves the point, but what's obvious to you is not always obvious to your reader.

Here is a body paragraph from a student essay on branding, the marketing practice of creating an easily identifiable brand identity. The author, William, is making the claim in this essay that Apple's brand identity is sophisticated and modern. Read through the paragraph and see where, if at all, he could develop the paragraph further by adding more, and more varied, kinds of evidence as well as explanation.

William's Paragraph

Apple is selling more than computers and iPhones; it is selling an image of being sophisticated and cutting edge. All of Apple's products have a sleek, modern design. We often think of computers as highly complex machines, but Apple's products look simple and modern because of their signature white and silver computers and iPhone cases. iPhones only have one button; everything is controlled through a touch screen, which is also very modern. Apple was the first to introduce a touch screen on a phone. Apple is always on the cutting edge of both design and features, so when people buy Apple products, they are showing that they, too, are cutting edge and modern. Apple's brand identity of sophistication and the cutting edge is obviously what consumers want. Luckily for Apple, the company is setting the trends of tomorrow, which means it will always have followers.

Now, look at William's revised paragraph. The highlighted sentences are evidence that he added to develop the paragraph. How do his additions improve the paragraph?

William's Revised Paragraph

Apple is selling more than computers and iPhones; it is selling an image of being sophisticated and cutting edge. All of Apple's products have a sleek, modern design. We often think of computers as highly complex machines, but Apple's products look simple and modern because of their signature white and silver computers and iPhone cases. White is a very futuristic color and iPhones were the first cell phone to have the signature white design, which gave them an edge in marketing. iPhones only have one button; everything is controlled through a touch screen, which is also very modern. Apple was the first to introduce a touch screen on a phone. Apple is always on the cutting edge of both design and features, so when people buy Apple products, they are showing that they, too, are cutting edge and modern. In his book *Buying In*, media critic Rob Walker says in the chapter "Very Real," "Nobody wants to drive their parents' car of choice," and this can apply to computers and smartphones too (136). Since technology changes so fast, no one wants to be associated with yesterday's smartphone or laptop. Apple's brand identity of sophistication and the cutting edge is obviously what consumers want, because between January 1 and March 31 of 2012, Apple sold approximately 35 million iPhones (Elmer-Dewitt). I admit, I jumped on the bandwagon and am now on my fourth iPhone. Luckily for Apple, the company is setting the trends of tomorrow, which means it will always have followers.

Margin labels:
I (fact)
E
I (quotation)
I (observation)
E
I (fact)
I (personal experience)

DOUBLE-CHECK FOR PARAGRAPH UNITY AND COHERENCE

In revising your paragraphs for Point, Information, and Explanation/Elaboration, you have improved their development, focus, and clarity. Great! At this point, you should take a step back and reread them again to make sure they are unified and coherent. In other words, read your own paragraphs against the grain. Does each paragraph still cover one point? Does it do so well?

See Chapter 2, Active and Critical Reading, page 36, for more on reading with and against the grain.

TURN YOUR TOPIC SENTENCE INTO A QUESTION

Another way to check whether your body paragraphs are well developed, unified, and coherent is to turn the topic sentences into questions. By turning the topic sentence into a question, you essentially take on the role of a reader. Based on the question, what do you expect the paragraph to cover? Try a few different questions to see which one best fits the purpose of the paragraph; then scan the paragraph to see if it adequately answers the question. If it doesn't, there's a good chance you need more evidence. What part(s) of the question does it not answer? What additional evidence and explanation would help the paragraph answer the question?

Let's practice with a body paragraph from a student essay on the importance of financial literacy. Here is Jabal's paragraph:

Jabal's Paragraph

Having financial literacy also helps you become stable in your personal finances. Having financial literacy will help you be stable financially. A big reason people in the United States are having trouble with money is that they don't know how to use it wisely. But the thing is that nobody teaches you how to manage your personal finances. From my experience, there is no class in school that teaches you how to budget. So people go on to graduate high school and go into the real world without having any financial literacy. When those people get jobs, they end up using their paychecks on all the wrong things and might end up losing all their hard-earned money.

If we turn the topic sentence into questions, they might look like this:

1. When does having financial literacy help you become stable in your personal finances?
2. Why does having financial literacy help you become stable in your personal finances?
3. How does having financial literacy help you become stable in your personal finances?

The topic sentence seems to be trying to answer the third question, *How does having financial literacy help you become stable in your personal finances?* because the paragraph does not give examples about when or why financial literacy leads to stability. Instead, it focuses on the result of not budgeting or not knowing how to spend money.

Now, write down the question the topic sentence is trying to answer, and then read the paragraph looking for answers to the question. When you find an answer to the question, jot it down. Here's how that might look for Jabal's paragraph:

How does having financial literacy help you become stable in your personal finances?

- Not knowing how to use money leads to trouble with money.
- Not budgeting can cause you to lose your money or spend it on unnecessary things.

Hmm. Jabal's paragraph doesn't really have much evidence to show how financial literacy makes you stable in your personal finances. Instead, it spends more time discussing how *not* having financial literacy makes you *not* stable. This tells us that the paragraph needs to be fixed.

Fortunately, there is a lot of room for development in Jabal's paragraph because there are several claims that can each be developed into a full paragraph:

- Having financial literacy also helps you become stable in your personal finances.
- A big reason people in the United States are having trouble with money is that they don't know how to use it wisely.
- But the thing is that nobody teaches you how to manage your personal finances.

To improve his essay, Jabal needs to develop each of these claims into a full paragraph, providing support (information and explanation) for each point. Not only will this method help him develop the paragraph, but it will help him develop a couple of pages for his essay.

practice it | Asking Questions to Improve Paragraph Unity and Coherence

Practice the preceding strategy on your own essay, turning your topic sentences into questions. Then take on the role of a critical reader to see if your paragraphs have appropriate evidence and elaboration. If they don't, add information and explanation to fill up the gaps in support. If you find that you have more than one claim, develop each claim into a new paragraph.

chapter review

You have seen in Chapter 12 that the job of a topic sentence is seemingly never done. The topic sentence is a key component in helping readers follow your flow of ideas. It also sets up the point the body paragraphs will develop.

To review this chapter, choose one or more of the following strategies:

1. Reread a couple of readings for this class and analyze the kinds of support that the authors use in their paragraphs. Which kinds of support do you find most effective, and why?
2. Make a bookmark or graphic flash card of the PIE structure with the definitions of the three parts and examples.
3. If you skipped any activities, do them now as a way to deepen your understanding of the material.
4. Try to explain what you have learned to someone you know. Describe the role of a topic sentence or paragraph support and give your own examples to illustrate those concepts.

13
Essay Organization and Outlining

in this chapter

- How Do You Outline as a Reader?
- How Do You Outline as a Writer?
- What Are Transitions, and Why Do They Matter?

Sometimes we talk about being organized as a person—knowing where we put our keys, paying bills on time, meeting deadlines, that sort of thing. But in writing, the word organization can mean a few different things. With texts, we talk about organization within each paragraph as well as among the paragraphs of an essay, and organization refers to the order of information, from sentence to sentence and then paragraph to paragraph, as well as the transitions from one idea to the next. Paying attention to the organization, or structure, as we read helps us work through difficult readings and see deeper meanings in the text. Paying attention to organization as we write saves us time and frustration by decreasing the likelihood that we will have to do major structural revisions.

There is no one right way to organize a piece of writing. The order of information and the types of transitions used will vary depending on the author's purpose, audience, and style. Some types of texts have an expected order of information, such as a lab report or a scholarly journal article. Other texts are organized more organically, with authors making choices based on what they wish to express and how they wish to express it. If a piece of writing is organized well, the content and ideas of the writing shine. In contrast, poor organization results in a text that is confusing and hard to follow.

e For help with organizing in general, read the Managing Your Time and Avoiding Procrastination chapter in the e-Pages for *Read, Write, Connect*. Go to **bedfordstmartins.com /readwriteconnect** and click on **e-Chapters**.

Outlining as a Reader

One effective critical reading strategy is to make an outline as you read or as you reread. Essentially, this involves locating the topic sentence and highlighting it or inferring the main point or idea. (You did this in Chapter 1 when you wrote "nutshell summaries" of main points as you annotated your readings.) Recognizing the topic sentences as you read and writing down a list of main points helps you see the underlying structure of a text, leading to a deeper understanding of the reading. When you complete the process, you have created an informal outline of the reading, one the author might have used while writing it. Informal outlines help us think through the structure of a piece of writing; they are also known as "working outlines" as opposed to formal outlines, which are generally much more detailed and can serve as a study guide for a chapter or article.

Making informal outlines as you read also helps you identify places where you don't understand the main point the author is trying to convey. If you can't sum it up in a few words, then you probably didn't catch it, and you may need to reread a few times or backtrack to figure out from the context what the author is saying. Outlining is an especially helpful technique when you work with a particularly long or difficult text. Additionally, outlining a reading serves as an excellent study tool to review material before a test or as part of pre-writing for an assignment.

Let's try the technique first on a short article to see how it works. Here's an annotated version of the article "Income Inequality within Families Is Emerging as a Major Issue" by Janna Malamud Smith, published in 2013 in the online periodical, *The Daily Beast*. The annotations identify the thesis and topic sentences to help you figure out how the text is structured.

---

thedailybeast.com

Income Inequality within Families Is Emerging as a Major Issue
Janna Malamud Smith

Income inequality isn't just bad for our economic health. It's bad for our   1
mental health. Working for decades as a psychotherapist has accustomed
me to listening closely. And—in and outside the office—I've lately been
hearing painful stories told about how families, friendship circles, and
neighborhoods are being strained by ever greater wealth differences
among their members. Yes, some folks have always earned more than
others, and people have always had greater or lesser luck and success.
The small town in Vermont where I grew up for a while had its local
millionaire, and his children owned a trampoline and we didn't. But the
thesis   situation now is different. As the rich have gotten massively richer, the
emotional climate has deteriorated for all of us. People now routinely tell
me about the impact on them of wealth gaps so yawning they threaten
the bonds of affection and blood.

Some examples? A woman who could easily afford to pay the college tuition for much less well off nieces and nephews, doesn't. She feels she's worked harder than the others, and resents being put in the position of seeming selfish. Meanwhile, the rest of the family resents her turning her back . . . A man sells the beloved family property because he's tired of maintaining it alone—though it breaks the hearts of his kin who cannot pay what would be their fair share, and who consequently have no say in the decision. A brother, guilty that he had better educational opportunities than his siblings, repeatedly pays off his sister's credit card debt—even as he dislikes the way she implies that he owes her. A businessman jets half a dozen neighbors to his home in a warm climate to give them a vacation they cannot afford; he feels beneficent. While grateful, they feel small and weird. Kind of like they've just received charity from a feudal lord.

2 no topic sentence

examples of problem defined in thesis

The evidence of stress is not just anecdotal. Research suggests that people indeed feel worse as disparity increases. An abstract in the *British Journal of Psychiatry* succinctly sums up a global overview: "Greater income inequality is associated with higher prevalence of mental illness and drug misuse in rich societies. There are threefold differences in the proportion of the population suffering from mental illness between more and less equal countries. This relationship is most likely mediated by the impact of inequality on the quality of social relationships and the scale of status differentiation in different societies."

3   topic sentence

In other words, people feel generally worse about themselves the more they feel they earn less and have lower social rank than those around them. The term "relative deprivation," used in other disparity studies, applies. We are acutely sensitive to slight differences of status, and the wider the income gap grows, the more people experience relative deprivation, even if by objective measures they have more than enough. Dissonance emerges between what people know (I have plenty) and what they feel (I don't have as much as he does). That breeds first envy or resentment, and then shame. And when many people feel relatively deprived, and a few feel on top of the heap, not only do real interests diverge, but interpersonal tensions increase. The sibling with children in private school, and the one who can't afford it, no longer have the same stake in passing the budget override to fund local public schools. And, at Thanksgiving dinner, that conversation about taxes can quickly go south.

4   topic sentence

Conversely, when people feel more equal, they feel happier and closer. For the past few years, I've been interviewing fishermen and their families on a Maine island, and over and over I've heard islanders utter more or less the same words. (I'm offering a composite here.) "We had little when we were growing up. But, you know, it didn't matter. We had a good

5   topic sentence

time." Why? I ask. Well, . . . really—I get told repeatedly—I think it was because everybody was in the same boat.

examples to support topic sentence of previous paragraph

Gradually I caught on. My interviewees knew that they could deal with backbreaking work and the tough times because they felt they were in it together with everyone else. Or, as one woman observed, "We didn't know we were poor until I grew up and then I was like, 'Wow we were poor!'" No one earned much. Everyone pitched in to help when someone was slammed.   6

Meanwhile, in suburban and city worlds many people have siblings or friends who go into finance, or start a business, or join a lucrative law firm. And even if other siblings do well and become firemen, plumbers, teachers or architects, or even pediatricians and public defenders, the income differences, decade by decade, just keep growing. And the ones who don't make it into the top 1 percent, or 10 percent, just keep finding it harder not to feel one down, their labors subtly—or not so subtly—devalued.   7

topic sentence

examples to support topic sentence of previous paragraph

A brother, guilty that he had better educational opportunities than his siblings, repeatedly pays off his sister's credit card debt—even as he dislikes the way she implies that he owes her.

topic sentence

We're unsure just how to traverse this new terrain. Years ago, visiting Ghana, I heard stories about how, when families became more affluent, they added rooms to their houses for their relatives. But that seems not to be our way. Here owners of McMansions tend to favor empty rooms over poor kin. So, too, with friendship. True or not, our national myths suggest that the ambitious, like Jay Gatsby, know to leave old ties behind as they jump aboard the passing yacht and begin their journeys toward "crazy" rich.   8

examples to support topic sentence of previous paragraph

Meanwhile, I hear stories of friends who stop traveling together because the luxury one pair takes for granted is out of reach of the others. Or of dinners where the wealthiest friend picks up the check while everyone else looks at his/her sneakers. Or of extended families whose Christmas celebrations seem modest to some and like a nightmare of materialist extravagance to others. Or of kids' birthday parties when the mom who bakes cupcakes and makes a piñata feels like a chump beside her children's friends' parents who hire caterers and entertainers. Meanwhile, she implies that "homemade" is morally superior.   9

counterargument

summary of main point / restatement of thesis

In part, I'm just describing the normal discomfort that constitutes adulthood. But the wealth gap has stretched us so far apart that the disparities heighten negative feelings among people who would otherwise feel closer and more at ease. On the one side, there is envy, shame, inadequacy, longing, deprivation, and a sense of being left out.   10

On the other, superiority, disdain, guilt, and a fear of being befriended or loved for all the wrong reasons. I don't know what will happen next. Some people may simply find ways to sever their awkward ties that chafe. But the experiences of the Maine fishermen suggest that *reducing* extremes of rich and poor would be the better way for us to go; even, perhaps, worth its weight in gold.

As you can see from the annotations, the reader has underlined some of the topic sentences and, in places where exact topic sentences were unclear, has made marginal notes about the main topic. Brackets link some of the paragraphs that share the same point. Look back at just the underlined topic sentences and the annotations. Next, you can translate those annotations into a list.

Paragraph 1: Thesis: "As the rich have gotten massively richer, the emotional climate has deteriorated for all of us. People now routinely tell me about the impact on them of wealth gaps so yawning they threaten the bonds of affection and blood."

Paragraph 2: No clear topic sentence; this paragraph gives examples of the thesis.

Paragraph 3: "Research suggests that people indeed feel worse as disparity increases."

Paragraph 4: "In other words, people feel generally worse about themselves the more they feel they earn less and have lower social rank than those around them."

Paragraph 5: "Conversely, when people feel more equal, they feel happier and closer."

Paragraph 6: No clear topic sentence; more examples to support the point in paragraph 5.

Paragraph 7: "[T]he income differences, decade by decade, just keep growing. And the ones who don't make it into the top 1 percent, or 10 percent, just keep finding it harder not to feel one down, their labors subtly—or not so subtly—devalued."

Paragraph 8: "We're unsure just how to traverse this new terrain."

Paragraph 9: No clear topic sentence; the implied point is that relationships break down because we don't talk openly about our differences in wealth.

Paragraph 10: Counterargument and conclusion: It's hard when your siblings or friends make very different amounts of money.

As you move from the annotations to the list, the structure starts to emerge. The author describes a problem in paragraphs 1–6, and then in the last half of the article, she tries to understand the deeper implications of this problem. In fact, the article follows a fairly common essay structure, where an author explains the cause(s) of a complex problem. Here, understanding the reasons for the problem—the breakdown in social relationships—is the author's primary goal. She reports on what her patients and others have told her recently, and tries to work out the root cause of the problem. Note that Smith is not writing a problem-solution paper; she doesn't outline a complete solution, but her final line, which includes the words "reducing extremes of rich and poor would be ... worth its weight in gold," hints at her preference. Still, she does not explain how we might go about that difficult task, since that is not her focus.

Once we see Smith's overall structure, we can evaluate the choices she makes as a writer. Are the Maine fishing communities a good example? Do you think she should have suggested more solutions to this problem? How does the expertise and experience she brings to the subject affect the focus she chooses for this article? Does she offer enough evidence and examples to prove her points? Why does she only bring up the counter-argument in the end, and then only briefly? How would you approach this topic if you were writing about it? Questions like these emerge when we take a step back and look at a reading's organizational structure. These sorts of critical-thinking questions will deepen your understanding of the material. The more you outline as a reader, the better you get at seeing the possibilities for organizing your own thoughts in writing.

practice it   Outlining as a Reader

Choose an article you have been assigned to read and, working independently or in groups, make an informal outline of it.

Step 1: Find the topic sentence of each paragraph, or figure out the main point and summarize it briefly in the margin.

Step 2: In your notes, translate your annotations into a list of the main points in the order they appear in the reading.

Step 3: Review the list to see how the author builds his or her discussion. What do you notice about the overall structure of the essay or article? Are there some main points that can be grouped together? In other words, are some paragraphs subtopics of other paragraphs? Does the author repeat the same point with a new example? Group together any similar points and subdivide any points, as necessary.

Step 4: Make your list into a bullet-point outline to reveal the text's organizational structure.

Outlining as a Writer

For you as a writer, outlining is one of the best ways to organize your thoughts before you start writing a draft of an essay. Generally, outlining comes after you do a fair amount of pre-writing and already have a good idea about what you want to say in your essay. Most writers start with informal outlines and then, if necessary, make the informal outline into a formal one. Since you are probably familiar with formal outlines, we will begin with a review of those.

FORMAL OUTLINES

Take a look at this formal outline for a researched argument essay on siblings:

I. Introduction
II. Overview of Research on Advantages and Disadvantages of Siblings
    A. Advantages
        1. Sharing Resources
        2. Learning Collaboration and Competition
        3. Sharing Burden of Parents' Care When Older
    B. Disadvantages
        1. Fewer Resources per Child
            a. Parents' Time and Attention
            b. Money
        2. Sibling Rivalry
III. Overview of Research on Advantages and Disadvantages of Only Children
    A. Advantages
        1. Only Children Often Successful
        2. Only Children More Individualistic
    B. Disadvantages
        1. Possible Lack of Peer Interaction
        2. Child Behaves More Like Adult
IV. Arguments in Favor of Raising an Only Child
    A. More Attention and Financial Support
    B. Can Find Other Ways to Socialize and Collaborate
    C. Myths of Only Children Not Proven Scientifically
V. Conclusion

Another example of a formal outline would be the table of contents for this book. Flip to the front and take a look at both the brief and the full tables of contents now. Though the table of contents evolved as we wrote this book, as an outline, it was a constant guide to help us stay organized and on track. We kept a printed version of the full table of contents on our desks as we worked. As you compare the student outline on siblings and the tables of contents, what features do you see in common?

- They include a clear plan of what will be covered in what order.
- They are very neat and precise in terms of format.
- They are generally parallel—care was taken so that each point and subpoint is the same form.

Formal outlines are especially useful for longer writing projects and collaborative writing projects, where you need to communicate clearly the structure of what you are writing as you write it. Many writers find comfort in outlines like this that guide them and give them confidence that they have enough material to flesh out their ideas.

INFORMAL OUTLINES

Despite the advantages of a nice, clear formal outline, the reality is that few writers can successfully create a formal outline while they are in the early planning stages of writing. Early in the writing process, an informal outline is much more useful. You can polish it later into a formal outline, if your audience requires one—for instance, if your instructor wants to see the fully developed structure of your intended essay or if you need to turn a research paper into a slide presentation. Indeed, the outlines that many writers use in thinking through the structure of a piece of writing are very messy. (You should see all the notes that were scribbled on our table of contents at various points!) We call these working outlines rough or informal outlines.

For more on rough or informal outlines, see Chapter 3, Putting Ideas into Writing, page 92.

Outlines often start out as a bullet-point list and then are fleshed out in more detail. When you're not worrying about making points parallel, you feel more free to move them around, juggle things, and experiment with different options. This informal outlining is one of the most creative—and difficult—parts of the writing process. If you're having trouble with organization, you may want to sit down with a tutor or instructor to talk through ideas. It helps to have someone ask questions like "What would happen if you moved this here?" or "Don't you need to explain X before you make an argument about Y?" As you become a more experienced writer, you can ask these questions of yourself more and more, but even professional writers work with a fellow writer or editor during this process.

So how do you do this type of informal outlining?

STEP 1: Figure out what you need or want to include in your essay.   Write down a quick bullet-point list of these ideas, referring to the essay prompt to make sure you fulfill the purpose of the assignment.

STEP 2: Think about each point on the list.   Should any points be combined or divided? Are they clear? How many paragraphs will it take to cover each point? If you think it will take more than one paragraph, can you rewrite the list so that each point corresponds to one paragraph? You will probably need to rewrite one or more of the points during this step.

STEP 3: Decide the order of your rewritten list of points.   Too often, writers tend to use the idea they brainstormed first as the first point in their paper, and that is not always the best choice. What principles, then, should guide you as you decide upon an order for your points? While there is never only one "correct" way to write, generally, the order of paragraphs in an essay is based in part on your essay's audience and purpose. Usually, we put ideas in order in one of these ways:

- From the simplest to the most complex
- From the ones your readers will agree with most easily to the ones they will need to be persuaded to accept
- From the most obvious/least interesting to the most original/most interesting
- From the ones you talk about the least to the ones you talk about the most
- From the ones that are closely related to the ones that are less related
- In chronological order (the order in which they happen or happened), if applicable

Depending on your audience and purpose, you may want to begin with simple information then build toward complex evidence and ideas. This works well with an audience unfamiliar with your topic. If your purpose is to persuade, you might begin with paragraphs that readers are most likely to agree with before hitting them with controversial points.

Now, let's create a sample informal outline. Imagine you are planning to write an essay about how financial literacy can lead to financial stability and your audience is young adults. You have brainstormed the points in the following list, and you plan to write one full paragraph on each idea:

- How to become financially literate
- The costs of not being financially literate
- The importance of financial literacy and how it can lead to financial stability
- What does financial literacy mean?

In what order would you put these ideas for this audience and purpose? It would make the most sense to define *financial literacy* first, wouldn't it? In order to understand the *importance* of financial literacy or the costs of *not* being financially literate, your reader needs to first understand *what* financial literacy is. Since your overall point is to show how financial literacy can lead to financial stability and your audience is young adults who may not have much experience with either financial literacy or its potential benefits, you might organize like this:

1. What does *financial literacy* mean?
2. The importance of financial literacy and how it can lead to financial stability
3. The costs of not being financially literate
4. How to become financially literate

What other ways are there to reorganize these topics? Would you reorganize them differently if you were arguing why schools should teach financial literacy? Why or why not? Considering the organization of your ideas is an important way to strengthen their logic and make your point really hit home.

---

practice it   **Outlining as a Writer**

Go through the preceding steps to make an informal outline for your next essay assignment. As you try to decide upon the order of the information, outline it in two different ways. Show both options to a peer or your instructor and talk them through the pros and cons of each possible organizational structure.

Two Commonly Assigned Essay Structures

Sometimes, especially on timed essays and final exams, the assignment is to write an entire essay in one rhetorical mode or with a set structure. When instructors give these sorts of assignments, they expect you to use certain organizational structures. For instance, in a problem-solution paper, you are usually expected to outline various solutions and argue why yours is the best solution, requiring you to explain what's wrong with other people's solutions. Although some assignments might be flexible, there is wisdom in the idea that you need to know the "rules" before you break them. So let's take a look at some common essay structures that can help you organize your writing.

For more on structuring an argument paper, see Chapter 11, Argument, page 238.

COMPARE AND CONTRAST ESSAYS

The compare and contrast essay is a classic college assignment, and there are a few different ways you can structure such a paper, based on the type of information you plan to include. Each structure begins with an introduction and ends with a conclusion, but the content in the body paragraphs differs.

Point-by-Point Structure.   If you are comparing and contrasting two very similar things, use a point-by-point structure because you can then do the comparing and contrasting right there in each body paragraph. For instance, if you compare and contrast regular college classes with online college classes in order, ultimately, to argue which one is better, you might structure your paper according to key features of education, which you would evaluate. The sample outline below is for a student essay that focuses on the classroom activities, the student-class fit, the data on student performance, and the potential for collaboration in each type of class:

1. Introduction
2. What types of activities can be offered in each type of class?
   A. Details about regular class
   B. Details about online class
   C. Discuss the similarities and differences
3. Which types of students do well in each type of class?
   A. Details about regular class
   B. Details about online class
   C. Discuss the similarities and differences
4. How well does each type of class increase individual student performance?
   A. Details about regular class
   B. Details about online class
   C. Discuss the similarities and differences
5. How well does each type of class foster collaborative learning?
   A. Details about regular class
   B. Details about online class
   C. Discuss the similarities and differences
6. Conclusion

This outline clearly follows a formula, and we encourage you to use it only as a starting point in your writing. The format works well for this topic because, generally, you have the same kinds of things to say, and the same kinds of questions to ask, about online classes as you do about regular classes. The benefit of this structure is that you do the comparing and contrasting right in each body paragraph, so you are certain to do it.

Similarities and Differences Structure.   If you are writing about more of an "apples and oranges" topic, comparing and contrasting two very different things, the point-by-point structure outlined previously just won't work. For instance, imagine you are writing an essay comparing and contrasting taking a class in the summer and getting a summer job. These two options have different features, advantages, and disadvantages, and trying to force them into the preceding structure might not work. Your first step is, of course, to brainstorm your ideas about each option. Then you have a couple of different ways to structure the essay.

The first possible structure is the similarities and differences approach. Your essay will look something like this if you want to emphasize the differences between the two options:

1. Introduction
2. Similarities between the two options
3. Differences between the two options
4. Conclusion, often where you take a position on which option is best

The same type of essay will look like this if you want to emphasize the similarities:

1. Introduction
2. Differences between the two options
3. Similarities between the two options
4. Conclusion, often where you take a position on which option is best

As you might expect, the information that comes later in the essay carries more weight, so if you want to emphasize similarities, put those last; if you want to emphasize differences, put those last. Either structure could work well for an essay four paragraphs or longer. It's fine to have one paragraph on similarities and two or three on differences: Allow the number of genuine ideas you have to dictate the length. It's comforting, though, to be familiar with some of the more basic structures when you write under pressure, as in a timed essay situation or a final exam.

Subject-by-Subject Structure.   Another type of compare-contrast structure, one that is the most difficult to do well, is the subject-by-subject method. Let's take the same essay topic from the example above, writing an essay comparing and contrasting taking a class in the summer and getting a summer job. You might structure your essay like this:

1. Introduction
2. Working during the summer
3. Taking classes during the summer
4. Conclusion

This may seem like the easiest way to structure a compare and contrast essay, but what often happens is that you describe one topic, then describe another topic, and you never really compare and contrast them. In this essay structure, you must do significant writing in the conclusion to thoroughly discuss the similarities and differences. Such a conclusion will often become longer than the body paragraphs themselves. Whenever possible, choose one of the other options, even though this structure appears to be easier. Remember, looks can be deceiving!

For more on compare and contrast essays, see Chapter 7, Rhetorical Patterns in Reading and Writing, page 187.

CAUSE AND EFFECT ESSAYS

If you're the type of person who always wonders why things happen the way they do, you will enjoy writing cause and effect essays in college. Such assignments ask you to dig deep and figure out why things have happened, or evaluate the effects of various possible scenarios. Cause and effect thinking is the core of problem solving, so, like the problem-solution paper, this type of essay helps you develop key critical-thinking skills that you will need on the job and in the world.

While brainstorming for causes and effects tends to go hand in hand, often the essays you produce based on that brainstorming emphasize cause more than effect—or vice versa. A history professor, for example, might ask you to write an essay in which you identify and describe the effect of the Boston Tea Party of 1773, in which case you would talk about the Tea Party's role in the American Revolution. However, the professor might ask you to write an essay about the cause of the Boston Tea Party; here, you would talk about the fact that the British government passed the Tea Act, which unfairly taxed the American colonists. In either essay, you would need to be sure that you did not merely cover the most obvious causes or effects, but also did your research and discovered any hidden causes or effects.

In structuring an essay about the effects of something, you might use this format as a starting place:

1. Introduction
2. Describe the event or topic in detail
3. Explain effect 1, including what the effect was, why it happened, and its significance
4. Explain effect 2, including what the effect was, why it happened, and its significance (Repeat as necessary for as many effects as you have)
5. Conclusion

Generally, in listing the effects, you would put them in some logical order. You might list them chronologically, or in order of most obvious effect to least obvious effect. You might also list them in order of least significant to most significant. Think of it this way: Save your best ideas for last, so your reader isn't disappointed. If you reveal your most interesting or original effect first, then the other paragraphs will be a disappointment for your reader.

In structuring an essay about the causes of something, you might use a similar format to begin:

1. Introduction
2. Describe the event or topic in detail
3. Explain reason 1 (cause 1), for why the event happened the way it did
4. Explain reason 2 (cause 2), for why the event happened the way it did (Repeat as necessary for as many reasons as you have)
5. Conclusion

Again, especially with causes, you should give significant thought to the deeper or hidden causes and order your points well. Do not assume that just because two things happen at the same time, one caused the other. Nor can you assume that the most obvious reason for something is the most important.

For instance, if you try to work out why your best friend is always broke, you might jump to the obvious conclusion that he's always broke because he doesn't have a job. Sure, that's an important reason, but push your thinking further: Why doesn't he have a job? Maybe it's because the economy is bad and he couldn't find one despite lots of work on his resume and interview skills. Or maybe it's because he doesn't want a job and hasn't tried to find one because he believes his parents should still provide for him. While the obvious cause—not having a job—is the immediate reason he's broke, if you want to help him change the situation, address the deeper, hidden cause: that his values and beliefs don't line up with getting a job.

For more on cause-and-effect essays, see Chapter 7, Rhetorical Patterns in Reading and Writing, page 187.

| practice it | Sample Structures for Problem-Solution Papers |

One common type of paper you may be asked to write in college is the problem-solution paper. These are fun papers to write because you choose how you focus and organize your ideas. You might focus more on the problem, more on the solution(s), or equally on both problem and solution. Using the sample structures for the compare and contrast and cause and effect papers as examples, make sample outlines for problem-solution papers. Try to come up with as many possible sample structures as you can, and then evaluate them.

Outlining Your Own Rough Draft

Despite our best intentions, sometimes our rough drafts suffer from serious organizational problems. Fortunately, the strategy for outlining a reading that you learned at the beginning of this chapter can also be applied to your own rough draft! If your draft is disorganized, stepping back from it and doing your own "reverse outline" reveals ways to make substantial revisions to the essay's structure. Go through the essay, paragraph by paragraph, asking yourself, what does this paragraph accomplish? Don't ask yourself, what did I intend for this paragraph to accomplish? Stick to the facts. What did you actually accomplish? Write nutshell summaries in the margins as you go, and then type up the points in a list. Play around with the list, reordering the information in a way that makes sense. Then return to your draft, and copy and paste the old material into a new document in the new order. You may be surprised that a complete restructuring of the essay isn't as time-consuming as it sounds and can produce huge rewards in terms of the overall quality of your work.

practice it	Reverse Outlines

Make a reverse outline of a rough draft of a paper you are working on or have recently finished. You can do this on a computer by inserting comment boxes, but most people prefer to work by hand. Remember, as you create the reverse outline, that your paragraphs might not be unified—which could be one of your problems. So don't just assume every paragraph only covers one topic. Perhaps one paragraph includes topics A and B; another paragraph includes topics B, C, and D; and a third paragraph includes material related to topics A and C. In such a case—not uncommon in student writing—a major reorganization greatly improves the paper without much significant new material being added.

Transitions

Good writing flows. This means that the reader can easily follow the organization of the piece as the author transitions from one idea or point to the next. Well-placed transitions not only give your essay a good flow, but also help you make your point by indicating how one idea relates to another. You should pay attention to transitions while you draft, of course. However, most writers also make extensive improvements to their transitions during the revision and editing stages. In other words, don't feel you have to make your transitions perfect the first time. Writing, after all, is all about revision.

TRANSITIONAL WORDS AND EXPRESSIONS

Within your paragraph, use transition words or phrases to show how your information is connected. You can also begin a paragraph with a transition word to reveal how that paragraph's ideas or points grew out of the previous paragraph. Transition words can show contrast between ideas, cause and effect, or compare and contrast. Within a paragraph, they are useful to introduce examples, to indicate meaning, or to outline a sequence of events or a time line. Here's an example of a paragraph you just read with the transitional expressions highlighted:

> Good writing flows. This means that the reader can easily follow the organization of the piece as the author transitions from one idea or point to the next. Well-placed transitions not only give your essay a good flow, but also help you make your point by indicating how one idea relates to another. You should pay attention to transitions while you draft, of course. However, most writers also make extensive improvements to their transitions during the revision and editing stages. In other words, don't feel you have to make your transitions perfect the first time. Writing, after all, is all about revision.

COMMON TRANSITION WORDS

To Show Contrast	To Show Cause/Effect	To Give Examples
but	as a result	for example
however	because	to illustrate
on the contrary		
still		
yet		

To Compare	To Show Meaning	To Concede a Point
despite	of course	although
like	in other words	even though
nevertheless	therefore	that is
on the contrary		though
on the other hand		whereas
similarly		while
still		
unlike		

To Show Additional Meaning	To Show Sequence or Time
in addition	after
this too	before
	finally
	now
	then

practice it   Transition Words

In "Making It in the U.S.: More Than Just Hard Work," Pam Fessler begins her paragraphs with transitions, showing the reader how one paragraph or idea relates to another. Scan Fessler's article on pages 81–86 and circle the transition words. Which types of transition words does she use? How do they help the reader follow her points and interpret her information?

TRANSITIONS FROM PARAGRAPH TO PARAGRAPH

Sometimes transitional words and phrases don't provide enough information to show how you are getting from one idea to the next. Be careful not to overuse transitions instead of thinking through the connections between ideas more thoroughly. If a word or phrase like *in addition*, *for example*, or *on the one hand* appears at the start of every single sentence in a paragraph, you are probably overusing transitional words and phrases, expecting them to do more than they are capable of doing to guide the reader through your ideas.

Instead of just throwing in a transitional word here and there, use more substantive transitions, up to a sentence or two long. Such transitional sentences—or even, in a very long work, a short transitional paragraph—use repeated words or synonyms to connect for the reader one idea to the next. In this way, they show the reader the connections between two ideas. Take a look at this excerpt from "Teach Your Children the Building Blocks of Finance" by Sherie Holder and Kenneth Meeks:

> **Plant the seeds of entrepreneurship.** Not all children receive weekly allowances. When Angelina and Marvin Lipford, of Hampton, Virginia, were married 20 years ago, they entered into their marriage carting around $15,000 to $20,000 worth of credit card and student loan debt. They spent the first five years of their marriage paying off the debt along with the accompanying high interest rates. The couple was determined to keep their three children from falling into the same trap.
>
> Knowing the financial sacrifices they had to make early in their marriage, the Lipfords are making sure their three children keep a tight *rein* on their finances and avoid the same pitfalls. They have an 18-year-old daughter, Jasmine, who is attending Howard University on a basketball scholarship; a 15-year-old son, Marvin Jr., who is a sophomore in high school; and a 9-year-old, Nehemiah. A natural progression in teaching their children the building blocks of finances was to encourage their children to either work, as Jasmine had done before going to college, or to start their own business. Instead of giving their children allowances, the Lipfords encourage them to earn their own money by doing chores around the house. It was on a pay-per-work arrangement. And if the children asked their parents for additional money, they were required to pay their parents back with interest.
>
> This arrangement encouraged Marvin Jr. to earn money on his own. In 2002, he took the financial and entrepreneurial lessons he learned from attending a weeklong financial camp to cut grass during the summer months using his father's lawn mower. This past summer, he charged $20 a yard and earned $1,000, which he put into his savings account.

Transition from poor financial management to teaching their children successful financial management

Refers back to the arrangement described in paragraph 2

As you can see, the repetition of ideas forms a bridge from one paragraph to another, so we see that the decision Angelina and Marvin made in how to raise Jasmine, Marvin Jr., and Nehemiah grew out of the experience of the couple early in their marriage, and then came full circle when Marvin Jr. made different financial choices from his parents. The repetition encourages us to see the cause-effect connections, in this case, without even using words like *cause* and *effect*. Such repetition of key ideas, concepts, and even words and phrases makes logical connections for your readers: problem to solution, comparison to contrast, or cause to effect, to name a few.

SEQUENCING TRANSITIONS

When you describe events that take place over a period of time, transitions need to be especially clear so that the reader can follow the ideas. For instance, process writing, such as step-by-step instructions, uses sequencing transitions because the reader needs to keep track of where he or she is in the process. Words like *first, next*, and *finally* serve well, but most readers will need additional transitions. Authors of process writing, in fact, use a significant number of transitional expressions, as you can see in this excerpt from the article "Influence of Licensed Characters on Children's Taste and Snack Preferences," published in 2010 in *Pediatrics*, a journal for pediatricians. This passage describes an experiment in which the investigators, Christina Roberto et al., tried to determine if children would choose snack foods in packages with licensed cartoon characters (such as Scooby-Doo, Dora the Explorer, and Shrek) over other foods. Transitional words and phrases are highlighted.

Each participant sat at a table across from the investigator, who began by saying "I am going to give you 2 foods to taste." The child was then presented with 2 samples of 1 of 3 food products. The 3 different food items were presented to each child in a randomized order, and the 3 licensed characters and 3 foods were paired randomly for each child. Therefore, participants were exposed to all 3 food conditions and all 3 characters but not in the same order or combination. Throughout the procedure, children could view only the food item they were currently evaluating.

The investigator placed the 2 food items on paper plates in front of the child and said, "I'd like you to take a bit of this food," pointing to one side of the table. The side of the table that was pointed to first was alternated, as was the side for the licensed-character sample. Next, the investigator pointed to the other sample on the table and said, "Now take a bite of this food." After the child finished tasting the 2 samples, the investigator asked the child, "Tell me if they taste the same to you, or point to the food that tastes the best to you." After recording the child's response, the investigator placed a smiley-face Likert scale, as a secondary measure or taste preference, in front of the child and asked, while pointing to one side of the tray, "How much do you like the way this food tastes? Do you love it, like it, it's OK, you don't like it, or you hate it?" After the child gave an answer, the investigator asked him or her to rate the taste of the other food sample by using the Likert scale. Next, the investigator asked, "If you had to pick one of these 2 foods for a snack, which one would you pick?" After the child's responses were recorded, the investigator repeated the procedure for the remaining food pairs. At the end of the study, the investigator presented the child with images of Scooby-Doo, Dora, and Shrek and asked the child to identify the characters and to rate how much he or she liked each character, by using the smiley-face Likert scale.

You can see that the writers use some transitional expressions—like *next* and *then*—but more often, the transitions are longer and convey some real information. One action happened after another action. This helps the reader visualize what happened during the experiment, as if he or she were there. Remember, transitions don't just flow magically from your pen as you write the first draft. Transitions need a lot of attention during revising and editing, as they are usually some of the roughest spots in a draft.

practice it   Identifying Transitions

Take out an essay you are currently drafting or a finished piece. Highlight all the transitional words and phrases you find. What did you discover? Did you use adequate transitions? Did you repeat the same words? What could you do to improve? If you are currently revising the essay, work on all the transitions to make them clearer.

chapter review

As you have seen in Chapter 13, most of the time you spend working on organization and outlining will be before you draft and after you draft—not during the drafting stage. If you take the time to plan out your essay in advance, you will be happy you did, but remember that you will also need to double-check your organization—especially your transitions—as you revise.

To review this chapter, try one or more of the following strategies:

1. Make a "reverse outline" of this chapter in your notes.
2. Look back over the common essay structures for compare and contrast and cause and effect papers. Then make your own essay structure template for an essay you are working on now. Remember, there are probably multiple ways you could structure your essay, but deciding on one structure before you begin drafting can be helpful.
3. Review your annotations for this chapter and summarize in your notes your biggest strength and your biggest weakness in terms of essay structure. What can you do to improve the structure of your essays?
4. If you skipped any activities, do them now as a way to deepen your understanding of the material.
5. Try to explain what you have learned to someone you know. Discuss the key concepts and give your own examples to illustrate those concepts.

14
Drafting

in this chapter

- What Is a Rough Draft?
- How Do You Write a Rough Draft?
- What Is the Public First Draft?

Sitting in front of a blank computer screen or a blank piece of paper trying to write a perfect first draft would make anyone unhappy. That's why writers don't do it much, if at all. Successful writers—and college students in a writer's mind-set—do loads of reading and pre-writing to get the ideas flowing. By the time a writer gets to the drafting stage, he or she has already written pages of notes, ideas, freewrites, outlines, and perhaps even a thesis and topic sentences. The rough draft is just an extension of all that thinking.

You'll get the best results if you think of the rough draft as taking at least two stages: First, you write a very rough draft, just to get something on the page. Then, you revise that first draft, asking yourself important questions such as whether your draft responds to the assignment given and whether your thesis is clear. That revised first draft will be your public first draft, the one you show your first readers.

There are going to be times when you're having difficulty, and some concrete strategies for getting started writing can be very helpful. This chapter gives you strategies for getting those first sentences on paper and then shaping them into something you might be willing to share as a rough draft.

For more on pre-writing, see Chapter 6, Audience, Purpose, and Topic, page 169, and Chapter 9, Pre-Writing, page 214. You can't start writing without some ideas to write about.

Writing the Very Rough Draft

Writer Anne Lamott has a quote that writers love: "For me and most of the other writers I know, writing is not rapturous. In fact, the only way I can get anything written at all is to write really, really shitty first drafts." We should all listen to Anne Lamott. Getting rid of the idea that the rough draft should be perfect is crucial to writing. While you write that first rough, rough draft, don't erase or delete anything. Don't censor yourself. Too often, student writers judge themselves too harshly, think every word they write is wrong, and spend more time erasing than thinking about what they want to say. If you are stuck on the rough draft, sitting in front of a blank piece of paper with a mind that feels even more blank, try one of the following strategies so you can just get started.

EXPLORATORY DRAFTS

Some people work best when they take away all the pressure of having to write a perfect first draft. If that's you, then give yourself permission to write an exploratory or idea draft and be willing to throw much of it away. Here's how.

STEP 1: **Open a new document or get a blank piece of paper.**

STEP 2: **Read over your outline, your notes, and your working thesis.** If you have a thesis already, put that at the top of the page. If not, put your best idea at the top, or choose one quote or idea from the readings that really speaks to you.

STEP 3: **Put your notes away and write a "quick, throwaway draft."** Don't make corrections or stop to make anything perfect. Think of this draft as almost freewriting, but try your best to stay focused on your topic and thesis. Get all your ideas down on paper as quickly as you can. Don't spend more than a half hour on this draft. (If you spend more time, you won't be willing to throw it away.)

STEP 4: **Take a short break.**

STEP 5: **Go back and read what you have written.** Compare it to your outline. What's usable? Can you cut and paste some paragraphs into the points on your outline? Save what's good and use it to build your confidence to start the first public rough draft in a more careful way. Chances are good that you will find you do have something to say.

EVIDENCE DRAFTS

Other people work best when they start with the source material, support, and examples. If this strategy sounds like it might work for you, begin by writing up your sources or examples and write your way around them. Here's how to start.

STEP 1: **Type up your outline.**

STEP 2: **Find all the quotes or examples that you want to use in the paper and type them up under the relevant point in the outline.** Don't forget to include the source information and page number (if there is one).

STEP 3: **Now, write a sentence or two after each quote or example to explain how it supports that particular point.**

STEP 4: **Save, print, and read what you've written.** (If you write by hand, type up what you have written so far. Double-check that you are accurately typing all quotations.) Reread all you have accomplished so far. You have probably written half the draft just by typing up your examples and supporting points.

STEP 5: Go back to the beginning of the document and fill in the gaps until you have fleshed-out body paragraphs.   Review the strategies in Chapter 12, Topic Sentences and Paragraphs, page 253, for help here.

STEP 6: Finally, add an introduction and conclusion.   Write down what interested you in the topic, and begin with that as your hook. Then think about the final thoughts you want to leave your reader with, and include these in your conclusion.

CONVERSATION DRAFTS

Some writers know what they want to say and just need to get their ideas down on paper without worrying about how their ideas fit with sources. If that's you, then think of the rough draft as a conversation you are having and write down all the things you want to say in the draft. Here's how.

STEP 1: Imagine you are explaining your ideas to a friend.   Imagine your friend is asking you questions about your topic and you are answering them. (If you have a friend who is willing to help you, ask him or her to take notes on what you say as you speak your way through the following steps.)

STEP 2: Write down all the questions your friend would ask.   Don't worry about the exact wording, since you're going to be changing it later anyway.

STEP 3: Under each question, fill in your answers.   Write just like you would talk. Don't worry about making it sound like a college paper right now.

STEP 4: Type up this conversation.   As you type, you might discover that you are rewriting as you go, making it sound more like an essay and less like people talking. Or you might just type it up as is; that's fine too.

STEP 5: Read what you have written.   Think about the strengths and weaknesses of the ideas and the organization; don't worry yet about sentence-level concerns.

STEP 6: Make an outline based on what you have on the paper, leaving room to add or subtract major points, if necessary.

STEP 7: Read over all the other notes that you made for the paper earlier in the writing process, and reread the essay assignment to make sure you're on track.

TIP
Some writers actually start off by recording themselves talking out their ideas. Then they play back the recording and type it up. Check your smartphone or computer to see if it has a voice recorder you can use for this purpose.

STEP 8: **Write your very rough draft based on the conversation notes, your outline, and your other notes.** Make it as complete and clear as possible, but do not worry about how it sounds, since you will revise it later.

> **practice it**   **Writing a Rough Draft**
>
> Choose one of the three strategies outlined above and write a very rough draft of your current essay project. Then let it sit for a day or two—or at least a couple of hours. Then reread it, and identify three or four things you did well. Forget about the weaknesses for the moment. Concentrate on your strengths. Hopefully, you'll be ready to work on making that very rough draft into something you might, possibly, be eager to show your peer group or your instructor.

Writing the Public First Draft

What do you need to do to your rough draft to make it suitable for that first round of peer review? Most writers ask themselves the following questions to make a solid public first draft:

- Have I finished the draft? Are all the points and examples that you can think of right now actually in the draft somewhere? Check your outline to see if you included all your points. If not, make a list directly on the paper where you wish to include more ideas.
- Does the draft change its topic, focus, or thesis? If the draft shifts topic, focus, or thesis, think about in what direction you want to take the draft, and adjust the draft so that it is coherent—in other words, change the thesis, points, or evidence as necessary so that the paper sticks to the same topic, focus, and thesis. (This happens more often than you might expect; we think we want to write about one topic, but as we write without censoring ourselves, another, more interesting topic or thesis emerges. Go with it!)
- Does the essay as it is fit the assignment and address all parts of the prompt? Are there some expectations in the assignment (about source material, type of writing, or anything else) that you need to meet? Reread the essay prompt and adjust the paper to fit it if necessary.
- Have I included a complete introduction and conclusion? Many writers write their introduction after the body, which is fine so long as you remember to do it. Write a conclusion, too, even though it may be difficult at this early stage in your essay. No one will hold you to it.
- Is the essay divided into paragraphs in a sensible way? If you forgot to break it up into paragraphs, do so as you make the rough, rough draft into a public first draft.

After answering these questions and scribbling notes on your rough, rough draft, rewrite it into the first public draft. Read it over a few times, make the changes you need to, and get ready for peer review. At this point in the writing process, you will probably have some specific questions about your paper, such as "Does my thesis make sense?" or "Is it okay to use that example in paragraph four?" Go ahead and jot down the questions you have so that you can remember to ask your peer reviewers or your instructor.

chapter review

Chapter 14 outlines some concrete strategies to help you conquer writer's block, that horrible feeling of having no idea how to start. These methods will help you build up the confidence to start putting words on paper.

To review this chapter, choose one or more of the following strategies:

1. Spend some time reflecting on your own process as a writer. What parts of the writing process do you enjoy most and least? Are you good at finding examples, but have difficulty figuring out what to do with them? Do you see yourself as an "idea person" who has trouble following through with your thoughts? Determine which of the three quick drafting strategies suits your strengths and weaknesses best.

2. Drafting is like . . . what? Write a simile or metaphor to describe how you experience the drafting process.

3. If you skipped any activities, do them now as a way to deepen your understanding of the material.

4. Try to explain what you have learned to someone you know. Discuss the key concepts and give your own examples to illustrate those concepts.

15

Introductions and Conclusions

in this chapter

- What Is the Purpose of an Introduction?
- What Are the Parts of the Hook?
- What Is the Role of a Conclusion?
- How Do You Write a Strong Conclusion?

Introductions and conclusions are like the bookends around your essay. They give the first and last impressions, and get and keep your reader interested in what you have to say. In the simplest terms, the purpose of the introduction is to set the scene for your main points, and the purpose of the conclusion is to reinforce why your ideas are relevant or important. It's usually easiest to write the introduction and conclusion if you think about what motivated you to choose the topic or focus of the paper. Even if your instructor assigned a particular topic, your paper differs from everyone else's, right? Think about what most interests you, whether it is a particular anecdote, a burning question you have, or simply a statistic that amazes you. Then share that interesting idea to introduce your ideas to your reader, and build on that idea to conclude the paper.

You may know people who like to write their introductions last. These are usually experienced writers or people who write many, many drafts of a paper and are very open to revising their ideas. This can lead to wonderful essays, but it usually takes more time. Beginning writers or writers with a deadline usually do better with a bit more structure to the writing process. Try writing an introduction paragraph as you write the rough draft. You can always change it later.

Introductions

Introductions are as important in writing as they are in life. Readers pick up an article or book, read the first couple of lines or paragraphs, and then decide whether or not they want to continue. To make your readers care about your writing, you have to grab their attention and keep it. In an essay, the introduction is the place to get their attention. The good news is that you probably already have what you need to write

If you have a thesis but aren't confident about it, see Chapter 10, Thesis and Main Idea, page 223.

a good introduction. You know what you're talking about—your topic and thesis. If you don't have a good sense of your topic and some idea about a thesis, you're not ready to write your introduction and conclusion. Thesis development is a major part of the pre-writing process, so look back at Chapter 3, Putting Ideas into Writing, page 92.

There are four elements to an introduction:

1. The hook grabs the reader's attention.
2. The topic is what the paper is about.
3. Background information gives the reader context for the topic.
4. The thesis states your position or main idea about the topic.

Let's look at an example of an introduction for a student paper about young people and voting:

> As many studies have proven, only about one-third of American youth aged eighteen to twenty-two usually vote in presidential elections. Voter apathy among young Americans is a problem in America today. Issues such as college funding, abortion laws, military recruitment, and even taxes and global warming affect young people. Voting rates among young people have not always been so low. Young people give a variety of reasons for why they don't care about politics, ranging from lack of education about the issues to not knowing how to register to vote. Martin P. Wattenberg discusses some of these reasons in his book *Is Voting for Young People? With a Postscript on Citizen Engagement* (2007). He explains why young people don't vote and how it is undermining our democracy. Young people need to take the responsibility to educate themselves about the issues and to vote, or else they will have to live with the laws that older people make for them.

This introduction is a good-sized paragraph that gives real information: It's not just a couple of sentences stuck on at the beginning of an essay to please the instructor. It sets up the paper so the writer can say something meaningful. This paragraph has a clear hook, a clear topic, background information, and a strong thesis. They are color-coded below so you can identify them and see how they fit together.

Hook

Statement of topic

Background information

As many studies have proven, only about one-third of American youth aged eighteen to twenty-two usually vote in presidential elections. Voter apathy among young Americans is a problem in America today. Issues such as college funding, abortion laws, military recruitment, and even taxes and global warming affect young people. Voting rates among young people have not always been so low. Young people give a variety of reasons for why they don't care about politics, ranging from lack of education about the issues to not knowing how to register to vote. Martin P. Wattenberg discusses some of these reasons in his book *Is Voting for Young People? With a Postscript on Citizen Engagement* (2007). He explains why young people don't vote and how it is undermining our democracy. Young people need to take the responsibility to educate themselves about the issues and to vote, or else they will have to live with the laws that older people make for them.

If you have trouble seeing the difference between the parts, ask your instructor for help. You will get better at identifying the parts—and therefore making sure your own introductions are complete—as you practice more.

---

practice it   Evaluating Introductions

Look at the essays by professional writers that you have read so far, and determine where their introduction begins and ends. (In a short college paper, the introduction is usually one paragraph, but in longer pieces, the introduction is often more than one paragraph.) What sorts of strategies do they use to gain your interest? Choose the introduction you like best and make a list of the reasons you like it. Next, choose the one you like least and make a list of the reasons you don't like it. What can you learn from these examples to improve your own introductions?

THE HOOK

The hook is what interests the reader in your writing, whether your reader is your instructor, with a stack of thirty papers in front of her; a scholarship or job application committee; or someone just curious about what you have to say. Hooks are one of the most fun things to write because you get to be a little creative. You can think like an advertising executive or a storyteller, even in the most formal research paper.

The hook can take many forms, and can be called many different things, like attention grabber or dramatic opening. It can be a short sentence or several sentences. The hook can be emotional (provoking laughs, tears, or shock in the reader), or it can appeal to readers' logic and reason, or their sense of ethics, their sense of right and wrong. To get started, think about what made you interested in the topic in the first place. If you were assigned the topic, why did you choose this particular approach to it? What about the topic sparks your curiosity? Most likely, you can develop a well-written hook based on whatever drew you into the topic. What quote from the course readings really jumped out at you? What question did you find yourself asking? What story from your personal experience illustrates the topic well? Trust your own instincts. Good writing comes from having something to say.

TIP

Sometimes you are assigned to write on a topic that doesn't interest you. Instead of focusing on the fact that you don't like the subject, find a way to get curious about it. Ask good questions. Get your brain going. Successful writers can make any topic interesting and can see the significance of topics where it might not be obvious.

To write an effective hook, you can:

- Give a statistic or fact to capture the reader's interest.
- Ask a question.
- Tell an anecdote, a brief interesting story.
- Give a quote.
- Dramatize a key idea.
- Do some combination of the above.

Whichever approach you take, the hook should grab your readers, fire their interest, and make them want to continue reading.

Let's look at some examples. Here's a hook that uses an interesting statistic to draw the reader into a paper on wealth:

> According to a Pew Research Report in 2009, the average white family had $113,149 in net worth, compared to $6,325 for Hispanics and $5,677 for blacks mostly because of the decline in house prices. When your home is your main asset, your life goes up and down with the price of real estate.

What's good about this hook is that it's not just a shocking fact about the wealth gap today. It also shows the reason behind the statistic and makes the reader start to ask questions, such as: "Why do Hispanics and blacks put more of their money into real estate? That hurt them recently, but has it ever helped them? I wonder why the gap is so huge?" This hook gives the source for the statistic through the signal phrase. This is important because you want your reader to know where you got your information and that your information is valid.

Here's another example. This time, the writer uses an anecdote (or brief story) to hook the reader into reading a paper about college student success:

> When Paula Mason wanted to go to college, her parents told her to go to the mall and get a job. When her brother wanted to go to college, they paid his way to a four-year university. He dropped out and got a job as a truck driver. She worked her way through community college at night and is now a branch manager for a bank.

This hook tells a brief story related to the topic of college student success. It also prompts the reader to reflect on some "big life questions" and to wonder what happened in the rest of the story. A reader might think, "Wow! That's amazing—not what I would expect. I wonder what made Paula so successful. Maybe making your own way in life is more meaningful? Still, it must have been hard. What makes some people successful in upper-level careers and others unsuccessful? Why didn't Paula's parents expect her to go to college?" The hook did its job. It made the reader curious. The rest of the introductory paragraph will provide the paper's topic, some background information, and the thesis.

practice it   Finding the Hook

Turn to one of the readings in Chapter 21, 22, or 23. Find two great hooks that you like. Underline or highlight these hooks. Jot down notes in the margins or in your notebook, answering the following questions. The annotations will be handy later when you do more work with the article.

- What kind of hook is it?
- Why do you like the hook? Why is it effective?
- When could you use this sort of hook in your own writing?

practice it   Revising the Hook

What "hooked" you about your current writing project? List as many ideas for hooks as you can. Remember to note the source if you're taking information (like a statistic) from someone else. If you have already drafted an introduction to your paper, take a look at its hook. Are any of your new ideas better than what you already have? Rewrite your hook to make it more interesting and meaningful. You may want to get a second or third opinion from a classmate or friend too.

After you have drawn readers into reading your paper, you need to let them know what hooked you about your topic so that they keep reading. You can do this with the next three parts of the introduction: the topic, background information, and the thesis. We'll look at each of these in more detail.

THE TOPIC

The introduction is your chance to establish what your topic is so that your reader doesn't assume you're trying to cover everything related to that subject. Take the topic of video games, for example. If you just write "Video games are a big part of American culture" as your topic, that's too broad. Your reader might assume you're going to discuss all types of video games—the games for children or for adults, online gaming, console gaming, handheld gaming, playing games on company time, maybe even arcade games. You know you won't include all these, but your reader doesn't. In your introduction, be specific and clear about exactly what your topic is. Remember, the topic (subject) is not the same as the thesis (your position on the topic). Your reader needs to know exactly what your topic is before he or she will be ready to read your thesis.

For help generating topics, see Chapter 6, Audience, Purpose, and Topic, page 169.

BACKGROUND INFORMATION

Once you've hooked the reader and stated a clear topic, you then need to provide necessary background information. Ask yourself: What does my reader need to know about my topic? For college papers that focus on a particular book, article, or film, your background information should always include:

- The full author's name
- The full title
- The year published, if available
- A short summary of the text

Here is an example:

> Beth Kobliner's 2009 book *Get a Financial Life: Personal Finance in Your Twenties and Thirties* provides basic financial planning advice on budgeting, paying off debt, and making good long-term financial decisions.

Sometimes, the necessary background information comes from a text you are reading in class, as in the preceding example. Other times, it's more generally about the concept or historical period you have been studying. In papers about a concept or historical period that is not well-known or is often misunderstood, explain it as clearly and succinctly as you can in your own words. For example, if you're writing about graffiti, you might say:

> Many people think that the word *graffiti* just refers to illegal tagging done by gangs in cities, but graffiti is created by all different types of people and is found in the suburbs and on farms as well as in cities. Actually, modern graffiti in America started in the railroad cars during the Depression and later was used by American soldiers and airmen.

This background information helps the reader who might have some sense of what *graffiti* means but might need some clarification. Since you will be going into more detail in the body of the paper, this is enough for now.

Let's look at what happens when a student doesn't provide sufficient background information in the introduction, as in the following example:

Twenty Dollars?!

Micah Yu

After many attempts to perfect an NBA game, Visual Concepts may have finally created an avid basketball fan's fantasy. The ESPN NBA series has been among the best of its kind since it entered the basketball gaming scene in 1999. Now, after battling its rival NBA Live for six consecutive years, ESPN is offering the new 2K5 at a bargain price of twenty dollars. Does this game have the features of a twenty-dollar game, or is it a gem at an amazingly low price?

Read Micah Yu's paragraph again. This time, circle all the words or phrases that you don't understand. Make a list of questions in the margins. Here's a list of some of the questions the typical reader (that is, a reader who does not play video games) might have:

> What is Visual Concepts?
> I know what ESPN is, but I don't get how it's a rival for NBA Live. Is that a show or a network?
> What is the 2K5?

Imagine how confused the reader would be if he or she didn't know the answer to these questions. Here's how Micah could rewrite the paragraph, sprinkling background information in here and there, so that his reader would understand the context of his topic. Added information is highlighted in yellow.

> ### Twenty Dollars?! [Revised Introduction]
>
> After many attempts to perfect an NBA video game based on the National Basketball Association (NBA), video game developer Visual Concepts may have finally created an avid basketball fan's fantasy. Their ESPN NBA game series has been among the best of its kind since it entered the basketball gaming scene in 1999. Now, after battling its rival Electronic Arts (EA) Sports' NBA Live for six consecutive years, ESPN Visual Concepts is offering the new ESPN NBA 2K5 game at a bargain price of twenty dollars. Does this game have the features of a twenty-dollar game, or is it a gem at an amazingly low price?

You may have figured out by now that background information is related to audience. A reader who knows the sports video game industry wouldn't need this information, but a general reader would.

practice it   What Background Does Your Reader Need?

What background information is needed to understand your paper? Remember to think about the audience you are trying to reach. Do you need to give them information about a reading, explain what you mean by a certain term or concept, or provide any historical, cultural, or other information? Jot down ideas in your notebook. Then take these notes and draft a sentence or two of background information that you want to add to your introduction.

practice it   Evaluating Background Information

Look at the introduction below written by a student. Does it confuse you because it does not offer sufficient background information? Does it

continued ❯

provide too much background information? Annotate it to indicate where you think the author needs to add or cut background information. Make sure you say what the writer needs to add or why the writer needs to cut. Write down your thoughts in your notebook or in the margins.

> In our world today, having a proper education can be a make-or-break factor when considering our financial futures. It's very common to see a college graduate's salary substantially higher than that of those who have discontinued their education after high school. However, being properly educated is not the only asset that will pave your way to a more comfortable, financially stable life. Having resources and financial assistance from family or close friends can make a world of difference. Sadly, not all of us have these options and the racial wealth gap is blatant evidence. Along with helpful financial resources, financial know-how is a key necessity for being financially stable and avoiding the stress of poverty.

THE THESIS

As the central idea or claim of your essay, the thesis lets the reader know what point your essay will make. For this reason, the thesis belongs in the introduction for academic essay writing. You want readers to know exactly what you intend to discuss before you begin discussing it. If you don't have a thesis yet or you don't feel confident enough in your ideas to write one at this point, remember that thesis development is a major part of the pre-writing process, so look back at Chapter 3, Putting Ideas into Writing, page 92, or Chapter 10, Thesis and Main Idea, page 223.

The thesis differs from the topic in that the topic is the subject and the thesis is what you believe about your topic (specifically). It's important to first introduce your reader to the general topic before stating your claim about it.

Here are some thesis examples:

Elderly parents continue to get upset by their children's arguments, especially when these fights are about the parents' care.

When adult siblings argue during a family crisis, it can make it hard for the next generation of cousins to become close friends.

Adult siblings often argue when major family decisions need to be made, because stress makes them go back to the ways they acted as children.

Let's take a thesis and see how it looks at the end of a complete introduction paragraph:

The image of the huge happy family is all over television, especially during all those holiday specials. As everyone knows, most real-life families do not look like the ones on television, though. In reality, adult siblings often argue during holidays or whenever important family decisions need to be made. They fight about stupid things like who is going to make the Thanksgiving turkey, or they fight about major things like whether or not to put Grandma in a nursing home. This happens in most families, especially in families where there is not a set of cultural "rules" about who does what. But what the adults do not realize is that it's not all about them. When adult siblings argue at family get-togethers or during a family crisis, this can make it hard for the next generation of cousins to become close friends.

practice it   Finding the Parts of the Introduction

Identify the four parts of the introduction in the preceding sample introduction paragraph. Label them in the margins of your book.

practice it   Moving from Topic to Thesis

If you don't have a thesis but think you are ready to write one now, practice moving from topic to thesis. Select an essay topic that you are writing about in your English class. Rewrite your topic in your notebook. Then draft a list of questions you could ask about the topic. Next, decide which direction you most wish to go with your paper. Finally, take some time to draft (or revise) your thesis.

If you have followed along with all the Practice It activities, you practically have an introduction already. Look at your work and put your sentences together. Feel free to tweak things, and revise as you rewrite so that transitions are smooth. You'll probably want to do this in your notebook or on your computer.

Conclusions

Once you feel confident about the ways in which you revised your introduction, review your draft conclusion. Reading and revising the introduction and conclusion at the same time makes your essay more coherent as a whole. Conclusions are often completed in a hurry: You have a deadline looming, so you slap a quick summary paragraph onto the end of the paper and call it finished. For the reader, this feels like having a burnt cookie for dessert after a fantastic meal—it's a letdown. Taking the time to brainstorm, draft, and revise the conclusion makes your whole essay more interesting and powerful. Your reader will feel that the essay finished well and will engage with your ideas. A strong conclusion can even motivate the reader to change his or her way of thinking about a topic.

Essentially, an essay's conclusion should accomplish two things:

- Sum up the essay's major points
- Make the reader care about the information you presented in the paper by offering final thoughts

Sometimes you have to bring in new information and ideas in the conclusion in order to make the reader care, but your job as a writer is to do that without adding so much new information that it reads like a body paragraph or the beginning of another essay. You will learn to strike the right balance with practice and a little help from your peers.

SUMMING UP YOUR ESSAY

Let's start with summarizing your essay's main points, which is one of the two major purposes of the conclusion. Don't just copy your thesis or main points word for word into your conclusion. Rephrase them in a way that shows how and why they are important. In other words, restate the thesis, by including all the fantastic main ideas you have just presented.

Let's look at a few examples from one of our readings. Take a look at Carol S. Dweck's article "The Perils and Promises of Praise" (pp. 6–13). We've placed her thesis and her summary statement side by side below:

Thesis (from the Introduction)	Summary Statement (from the Conclusion)
"Research shows us how to praise students in ways that yield motivation and resilience. In addition, specific interventions can reverse a student's slide into failure during the vulnerable period of adolescence" (7).	"Our research shows that educators cannot hand students confidence on a silver platter by praising their intelligence. Instead, we can help them gain the tools they need to maintain their confidence in learning by keeping them focused on the process of achievement" (12).

What similarities do you notice? What differences? By closely comparing and contrasting the language in these two statements, it becomes clear how to shape a strong summary statement for the conclusions. Here we have highlighted some of the similarities in the two passages:

Thesis (from the Introduction)	Summary Statement (from the Conclusion)
"Research shows us how to praise students in ways that yield motivation and resilience. In addition, specific interventions can reverse a student's slide into failure during the vulnerable period of adolescence" (p. 7).	"Our research shows that educators cannot hand students confidence on a silver platter by praising their intelligence. Instead, we can help them gain the tools they need to maintain their confidence in learning by keeping them focused on the process of achievement" (p. 12).

In the yellow-highlighted areas, the language is almost identical, but these are the only words that match in these passages. Clearly, Dweck wants to emphasize that her ideas are research based, not just hunches or anecdotes. In the blue-highlighted areas, Dweck is conveying one of the main points: She wants to help students become more motivated, resilient, and confident. These qualities all relate to one another, but in the conclusion, she develops the point by including the word "tools." One major point of her article is that being good at learning is itself a learned behavior. Students can learn to use the tools of learning.

Now, let's look at some of the differences between the passages. Differences are highlighted in purple:

Thesis (from the Introduction)	Summary Statement (from the Conclusion)
"Research shows us how to praise students in ways that yield motivation and resilience. In addition, specific interventions can reverse a student's slide into failure during the vulnerable period of adolescence" (7).	"Our research shows that educators cannot hand students confidence on a silver platter by praising their intelligence. Instead, we can help them gain the tools they need to maintain their confidence in learning by keeping them focused on the process of achievement" (12).

In the thesis, Dweck mentions "specific interventions." Then, in the conclusion, she explains what kind of interventions these are: ones that help students "[focus] on the process of achievement." These are the types of interventions that she has spent the article describing, and this phrasing sums that up nicely.

As you can see, when Dweck summarizes the main point of her essay in her conclusion, she does more than just restate the thesis. She sums up the major ideas she has covered in the body of the essay as well. She does not list each intervention, but she does mention the factor they all have in common: All the interventions emphasize "the process of achievement."

So how do you summarize the main points for your own essay? First, don't be intimidated by Dweck. She's had years of experience with this. You might start by listing all the key words you used in your essay, so you know what to include in your summary statement. You should also reread your introduction, but don't copy the thesis exactly. Instead, imagine that you have to restate your whole essay in one or two clear sentences. One way to do this is to imagine that you are explaining your essay to a person who doesn't know anything about it. What would you say? Say that out loud to a friend and ask him or her to write down what you say. Then read it over and edit it until you like the way it sounds.

PROVIDING CONTEXT AND ADDING FINAL THOUGHTS

The second important job of a conclusion is to leave your readers with the feeling that the information they just read matters. The job of the conclusion is to wrap up all the great points you made in your body paragraphs and conclude something about them; show readers why your ideas matter and what it all means. Readers need to know why they should care about what they've read. At the back of their minds, questions often lurk: "So what?" "Why should I care?" "Why does this matter to me?" (We're pretty sure you've asked these questions yourself once or twice, even while reading this book.) You don't want readers to finish your paper, put it down, say "So what?" to themselves, and forget everything they just read.

You need to answer the lingering "So what?" question in their minds. Sometimes this answer can be direct: They should care about the information in your paper because it will directly influence their lives. More often, it's indirect: They should care about the information because in some way—sometimes in an abstract way—it will influence the society they live in, the world around them, or the future. Writers often use the conclusion to offer recommendations or make predictions about the issue. They have some idea about how their topic could change society or how it might affect people in the future. This shows the context of your essay: how the topic relates to people and why they should care.

For example, let's say you are writing a paper about financial literacy. This topic has a direct and clear influence on most of us, as we have to manage our money, keep a budget, and set financial goals. It's easy for readers to see how the information matters, and your job in the conclusion may be to inspire them to act, rather than to just convince them that the topic matters. Maybe you want to push your readers to communicate better about money with their own family members by making that recommendation in your conclusion.

Imagine, though, that your essay is about something more narrowly focused, like the budget of your college. Clearly, people who attend or work at your college would care about that topic, but others might not see themselves as stakeholders. So, if you want to reach a wide audience, show in the conclusion why the issue matters. You might, for instance, show that your college is typical of a general trend going on across the country, and then explain the implications of that trend for taxpayers in general or for education as a whole. You could even go a step further and make a prediction by discussing the long-term consequences of the issue as you describe it in your paper. Maybe you could talk about what will happen to the workforce in your state if the trend you describe continues. In other words, you need to demonstrate the significance of the ideas you express in your essay, answering any lingering "So what?" questions that your readers might have.

Let's look at an example. Here again is the beginning of a paper about young people and voting.

> As many studies have proven, only about one-third of American youth aged eighteen to twenty-two usually vote in presidential elections. Voter apathy among young Americans is a problem in America today. Issues such as college funding, abortion laws, military recruitment, and even taxes and global warming affect young people. Voting rates among young people have not always been so low. Young people give a variety of reasons for why they don't care about politics, ranging from lack of education about the issues to not knowing how to register to vote. Martin P. Wattenberg discusses some of these reasons in his book *Is Voting for Young People? With a Postscript on Citizen Engagement* (2007). He explains why young people don't vote and how it is undermining our democracy. Young people need to take the responsibility to educate themselves about the issues and to vote, or else they will have to live with the laws that older people make for them.

Now, let's imagine that we wrote out the paper's conclusion:

> Clearly, young people have shown at certain times that they can be educated and involved voters. Not everyone ignores his or her responsibility or thinks that someone else will take care of it. However, the percentage of young people who make it out to the polls is still shockingly low. What if young people had a habit of voting all the time? How might our country make decisions differently? Would America be better off or worse? Whether young Americans would vote intelligently or not is not clear, but politicians would definitely have to pay more attention to issues that affect young people. One thing is clear, though: The more they take the time to vote, the more likely they are to become more educated about voting, and the more involved they will be in our democracy later in life. So getting people involved in voting when they are young does not merely influence a current election. It makes the entire country move in a positive direction over the long term. That's definitely something we can all support.

Does this conclusion work? Does it leave you feeling satisfied and full of ideas? What might you change? Why?

> **practice it**   Evaluating Conclusions
>
> Look at the essays you have read so far for this course. Reread their conclusions. Remember that for a long essay, the conclusion could be more than one paragraph. For scholarly journal articles, the conclusion is often even labeled for you as "Conclusion" or "Discussion." As you skim through a few conclusions, choose the one you like best and make a list of the reasons you like it. Choose the one that you like least and list the reasons you don't like it. What can you learn about conclusions that you can apply to your own writing?

STRATEGIES FOR WRITING STRONG CONCLUSIONS

Remember how we said that the introduction and conclusion can function as bookends around your essay? If you are stuck on how to conclude your paper, you might return to the ideas expressed in the introduction, particularly the hook. (Remember, the hook makes the reader want to read your paper, and it's usually the first thing in the introductory paragraph.) This strategy works especially well if you wrote a hook based on what "hooked" you on the paper topic. If you did, then building on that for the conclusion will likely get right to what you consider the heart of the issue. Here are a few types of hooks with their corresponding conclusion strategy:

BOOKENDING YOUR CONCLUSION AND HOOK

Type of Hook	Example	Corresponding Strategy for Conclusion	Example
statistic or fact	As many studies have proven, only about one-third of American youth aged eighteen to twenty-two usually vote in presidential elections.	Refer back to the statistic and add another, more inspiring fact.	Although only about one-third of American youth now vote, the potential for big change is there. There are many young nonvoters in America. If even half of them started to vote, we could see more turnout in local and state elections, and then make an even bigger difference in the presidential election.

(Continued)

Type of Hook	Example	Corresponding Strategy for Conclusion	Example
anecdote (real-life or hypothetical story)	My friend Paul turned eighteen six weeks before the last election. He never registered to vote. Six months later, budget cuts forced his college to raise tuition 12 percent. He's not sure he can pay for school this year.	Finish the story in a thought-provoking or inspiring way.	Paul is managing to get more loans for this semester, but he wonders if he can continue next year. Now that his education is on the line, he makes sure to vote in all local and state elections. He realizes now how important voting is to his future.
quotation	I once saw a bumper sticker that said: "The Vote: Use It or Lose It!"	Restate the quotation in your own words, and then add a new thought.	Maybe "Use it or lose it" is a little simplistic, but it's a good start. We need to remember that we didn't always have the rights we [have] now, and to keep them we need to participate in politics.
question	You would never let someone tell you what to wear every day, so why would you let someone else make even bigger life decisions for you?	Answer the question.	Obviously, young people want freedom. We want freedom to dress the way we want, listen to the music we want, and be who we want. We don't vote because we don't always see the connection between voting and freedom, but once we understand it, we begin to take part.

For more on peer review, see Chapter 17, Giving and Receiving Feedback, page 323.

The technique of revisiting the hook works well so long as it doesn't become too predictable or boring. Good writing offers surprises. Good writing makes the reader want to read more. Have fun with the introduction and conclusion, and use these tips and techniques as a starting point for your own creativity. When in doubt, do what all writers do: Ask your peers, instructors, friends, and family to read your work and give you ideas.

chapter review

Now that you have read Chapter 15, you should be able to recite the four parts of an introduction and the two functions of a conclusion. A well-written introduction and conclusion not only provide important information for your reader, but also set up and wrap up the tone of your essay, respectively. Now that you have learned the important functions and steps for these significant paragraphs, you are ready to nicely frame your essay.

To review this chapter, choose one or more of the following strategies:

1. Skim through the chapter again, writing notes on a page in your notebook for the entire chapter.

2. If you skipped any activities, do them now as a way to deepen your understanding of the material.

3. Try to explain the four parts of an introduction and the two major functions of the conclusion to someone you know. Discuss the key concepts and give your own examples to illustrate those concepts.

16

Quotation and Paraphrase

in this chapter

- How Do You Know If the Source You Are Using Is a Good One?
- Why Is Citation Important?
- When and How Do You Use Quotations?
- When and How Do You Paraphrase?
- What Is a Signal Phrase?
- How Do You Explain a Quotation or Paraphrase?

When you make a claim in writing, it's not enough that you believe in your position; you need to provide the evidence to support it. Quotations and paraphrases provide evidence for your points. In academic writing, quotations and paraphrases usually make up the bulk of your support in a paragraph. This chapter will help you decide when to quote and when to paraphrase and will help you integrate source material well into your own writing.

- A *quotation* is a direct copy of words from another source. Because you want to make it clear to your reader that these words are not your own, you use quotation marks (" ") at the start and end of the quotation.
- A *paraphrase* is your own rewording of the ideas from another source. Because the words are your own, quotation marks are not necessary, but citation (formal acknowledgment of the original source) is necessary.
- A *summary* is a shorter version of someone else's writing; when you summarize, you take a whole paragraph, essay, or longer work and reduce it to its most important points, entirely in your own words. Note that paraphrase should not be confused with *summary*, which is used for a different purpose. The key distinction between summary and *paraphrase* is that in a summary, you restate the overall point, whereas in a paraphrase, you rephrase more directly the meaning of a single sentence or short passage. Usually you summarize a text to provide background information about it, often in your introductory paragraph, or when you introduce a source if you plan to refer to it extensively in your paper.

   Whether you decide to quote a piece of text or paraphrase it, you absolutely must do the following:

For more on finding and
evaluating sources, see
Chapter 19, Research,
page 351.

- evaluate the source for credibility
- make sure the quotation or paraphrase you choose is relevant
- cite the source material properly
- integrate the source material well using signal phrases and explanation

In addition, there are a few specific rules for quotations and for paraphrases that you need to master.

Evaluating Sources for Credibility

Quotations and paraphrases are only as good as the sources they come from, so be sure the sources you use are *credible*—that is, trustworthy or reliable. Credible source material tends to be written by experts or professional journalists, with some form of review provided by editors or fellow experts. As a result, the information these sources provide is accurate and unbiased.

Virtually all nationally distributed newspapers, magazines, journals, and books have the advantage of professional or expert authors and editors who help make sure the author has his or her facts straight, so the information in them tends to be credible.

Other sources need to be evaluated carefully for credibility: Web sites in particular are like the Wild West when it comes to standards of credibility and accuracy. You have probably encountered this issue when you are surfing the Internet. Perhaps you are researching information about a soccer player and come across a Web site that says this player has been traded to another team, only to find out later that the trade was rumored to happen, but never did. The truth is, you can post almost anything on the Internet—there is no Internet editorial board keeping information accurate and current.

So how can you tell if your source is reliable? For starters, consider the reputation and editorial procedures of the publication. Next, read any biographical information you can find about the author. Is this person an expert in his or her field? Let's say Michael Jones is a professor of biology at an accredited college and he's writing about biodiversity; you can assume he is an expert on this topic. As a professional, too, he has a reputation to maintain, which makes him less likely to publish inaccuracies.

If you cite from a newspaper, there are two general categories of writer: journalists and op-ed ("opposite the editorial page") writers. Journalists follow a code of ethics that requires them to maintain a standard of accuracy and objectivity. (Of course, even journalists make mistakes, and they don't always intend to show all sides of an issue, so don't assume what they write is absolutely true and unbiased.) Op-eds are written not by a newspaper's staff writers, but by outside contributors who are generally well-informed on the topic, but who are not necessarily bound by a code of journalistic ethics. You can often learn more about the author of an op-ed piece by reading the biographical information that the newspaper offers, which should help you judge whether the piece is likely to be credible.

Web sites are the trickiest sources to evaluate because often the information about the Web site and its author(s) is not available. Since just about anybody can publish a Web site, you don't always know who wrote the content. While a quick search on the Internet might seem like a researching shortcut, determining the reliability of Web sources often requires a lot more work. You may need to search for information about the author, or even track down the original version of the article.

MAKING SURE QUOTATIONS AND PARAPHRASES ARE RELEVANT

Once you have determined that a source is credible, check to be sure it is relevant to your point. Does the particular quotation or paraphrase that you have selected really fit the point you want to make, or is there a more appropriate piece of evidence that you could quote or paraphrase? Sometimes, we are drawn to a quotation because it is very well written, or we find a statistic that we wish to paraphrase because it is so interesting. While it's great to be enthusiastic about your source material, make sure that you have considered several possible pieces of evidence before you select the best one to use.

The Importance of Citation

It's crucial that you properly cite any quotations, paraphrases, and summaries you include in your writing. In college, original thoughts and ideas are highly valued, so when you use someone else's ideas, you must give them credit. In fact, when you acknowledge your sources, your credibility increases because your reader will see you have done your research. Not properly giving credit—by acknowledging the source and including a proper citation—is considered plagiarism, and plagiarism is a very serious offense in academic writing. Most colleges and universities have codes of student conduct that spell out the penalties for students caught plagiarizing, which can range from a zero on the assignment to expulsion.

For a complete discussion of when and how to cite your sources, see Chapter 20, MLA Documentation, page 362.

When and How to Use Quotations

In general, you use a quotation for one of two reasons:

1. First, the source says it better than you could rephrase it. Here's an example:

   According to Koon-Hwee Kan in "Adolescents and Graffiti," "The 1980s were the Golden Age of graffiti art with the emergence of 'wild style,' an intertwined and decorative lettering that mixes icons and images from popular culture to form a complex composition" (477).

In this case, the best way to say something was the Golden Age is to say it was the Golden Age. The language Kan uses to make her point is vivid, precise, and skillfully constructed, so it both conveys her message well and adds to her credibility as an academic expert.

Here's another example:

According to art education specialist Koon-Hwee Kan, for adolescents "[school] becomes a boring, frustrating, stressful, or anxious experience" (475).

Finding synonyms for "boring, frustrating, stressful, or anxious" so that you could paraphrase would be awkward and difficult.

2. The second reason to use a direct quotation is to draw specific attention to the language or the author's use of words. This situation often occurs when you are quoting literature. In this case, the purpose of the quotation is to highlight the author's particular use of language. For this reason, a quotation is preferred over a paraphrase. Here's an example:

In Shakespeare's *Hamlet*, Hamlet begins his famous soliloquy by questioning whether life is worth living by saying, "To be, or not to be: that is the question" (3.1.55).

Putting the quotation in your own words in this case simply wouldn't capture the spirit of Shakespeare.

HOW TO QUOTE CORRECTLY

When you have evaluated your source and have decided to quote from the source material, take care to quote correctly to avoid confusing the reader. Make sure that:

- **Quotations are enclosed correctly in quotation marks.**
- **Quotations work with the grammar of your sentence.** It is your responsibility to complete the sentence if the quotation is not already complete or to otherwise change the quotation, using very specific rules, to make it grammatically correct.

As with all material taken from an outside source, you must also remember the following:

- **Cite your sources.** At all times. No exceptions. None. Ever.
- **Introduce and explain your source material.** In other words, don't just drop a quotation into your writing and move on. It's your responsibility to let your reader know why it's there and what it means. (We'll cover this in more detail on pp. 316–20.)

HOW TO ENCLOSE QUOTATIONS IN QUOTATION MARKS CORRECTLY

Use double quotation marks (" ") when quoting. The following example incorporates a quote from the article "Adolescents and Graffiti" by Koon-Hwee Kan:

> Artist and teacher Koon-Hwee Kan describes interviewing people who "felt personally connected to the graffiti-art style and deliberately copied and learned its forms" (478). Kan shows how influential graffiti is in the overall artistic production of adolescents, even those who are not out there writing in the streets.

The words from the source are in quotation marks, and the quotation is introduced and cited.

However, if the text you are quoting already has quotation marks in it, you can see that just putting quotes around the source material makes it hard to distinguish where Kan's quote begins and ends:

Incorrect   As artist and teacher Koon-Hwee Kan writes, "My interviews with some adolescents interested in graffiti and former "writers" have given me insights" (478). Kan draws on her interviews to understand what role graffiti serves for adolescents, rather than trying to guess.

To fix this problem, when you quote something that already contains quotation marks, replace the double quotation marks in the original with single quotation marks (the apostrophe key on a keyboard: ' '). Here's how it should look (see the highlighted word below):

Correct   As artist and teacher Koon-Hwee Kan writes, "My interviews with some adolescents interested in graffiti and former 'writers' have given me insights." (478). Kan draws on her interviews to understand what role graffiti serves for adolescents, rather than trying to guess.

Note, too, that the quotation is properly introduced, commented on, and cited, and it's placed as part of a complete, grammatically correct sentence.

practice it   Basic Quotations

Choose a basic quotation to incorporate into an essay you are writing. Copy the quotation out, inserting the quotation marks and citation correctly. Ask your instructor or a tutor to review your work to make sure you understand the basics of quotation marks.

HOW TO ALTER QUOTATIONS

Sometimes the quotation that you want to use doesn't quite fit, because the verb tense or a pronoun doesn't work with the grammar of your sentence. In such cases, it's acceptable to make slight changes to the quotation. However, you need to indicate to your reader that you are making a change to the quotation; there are specific rules about how to do so. Common reasons to make a change within a quotation include:

- To clarify a pronoun reference (for example, *he* becomes the name of the actual person)
- To change the part of speech (for example, *schooling* becomes *school*)
- To change the verb tense (for example, from past to present)
- To add necessary explanatory information (such as to spell out the name of an acronym or provide other information from nearby in the text)

If these reasons do not apply, you should always copy a quotation exactly as it is written in the original, punctuation and all. If you do change a quotation, you need to follow certain rules.

Modifying a Quotation.   If you need to add or change a word in a quotation, you must use square brackets [ ], not parentheses ( ), and you must change the text as little as possible to make the quotation work with the rest of your sentence.

Imagine, for example, that you want to quote the following passage from page 1 of Jane Mersky Leder's essay "Close Encounters of a Special Kind" (see p. 382 for the entire selection):

> Thanksgiving one year taught me a lot about strange things that can happen when adult brothers and sisters get together in the house where they grew up. The house was for sale, and that made the holiday scene even crazier. My brother, my sister, and I were charged not only with readjusting to one another but also with helping my parents divide up the spoils of their nearly fifty years together—an unsettling task.

Say you want to introduce part of this quotation from a third-person perspective. To adjust the pronoun, you might write:

> Any discussion of adult sibling relationships has to address holiday get-togethers. Writer Jane Mersky Leder describes how "Thanksgiving one year taught [her] a lot about strange things that can happen when adult brothers and sisters get together in the house where they grew up" (382).

Here, *me* is changed to *her* because that makes more sense in the sentence. Similarly, you may need to change the capitalization of a word so that it fits the rules of capitalization for your sentence. For instance, you might write:

> In describing one particularly strained holiday with her adult siblings, Jane
> Mersky Leder concedes that "[t]he house was up for sale, and that made the
> holiday scene even crazier" (382).

The letter "T" was capitalized in the original, but it shouldn't be capitalized here, so it has been changed to lowercase, as the square brackets indicate.

A more substantial change may be needed to make your sentence grammatically correct. For example, to change the verb tense, you might write:

> In the opening passage of her book, Jane Mersky Leder describes her
> experience of the "strange things that [happened] when adult brothers and
> sisters [got] together in the house where they grew up" (382).

Here *can happen* is changed to *happened* because that fits the sentence's verb tense better. To add explanatory information, you might write:

> Leder writes, "Thanksgiving one year taught me a lot about strange things [like
> arguments about dividing parents' belongings] that can happen when adult
> brothers and sisters get together in the house where they grew up" (382).

Here the additional information—dividing parents' belongings—refers directly to something that Leder discusses in the next couple of paragraphs. This is not information that you made up; it is an actual paraphrase of some of Leder's ideas that need to be clarified for your reader.

Omitting Words from a Quotation.   Sometimes you find a really great quotation, but it's rather long or part of it is unrelated to your point. In these cases, you can leave part of the quotation out, but you must not change the meaning of the original material. In other words, you can leave out part of the quotation as long as this doesn't change the author's intended meaning. Use an ellipsis, three little dots (. . .), to replace any part of the quotation you have removed. Here's an example with Leder's passage on page 382.

> Jane Mersky Leder describes one of the common problems of adult
> siblings: being "charged . . . with helping [their] parents divide up the spoils
> of their nearly fifty years together—an unsettling task" (382).

The ellipsis (. . .) replaces the few words that were omitted, yet Leder's meaning is maintained even with the omission. Notice how a pronoun had to be changed using square brackets to match the grammar of the sentence as well.

Note: You will sometimes see writing using four dots at the end of a quotation, which is really an ellipsis plus a period. MLA bibliographic style no longer requires the use of ellipses at the end of a sentence, so just go ahead and end the quotation where you want to end it, as long as it accurately represents the meaning of the quotation and makes sense in your sentence.

Square brackets and ellipses are extremely useful to help you manipulate a quotation so it fits smoothly into your writing. However, if you need to make major changes to a quotation to make it fit your sentence, that's a good indication that you would be better off paraphrasing instead of quoting.

---

practice it   Altering Quotations

Choose a quotation from a source that you would like to incorporate into an essay you are writing. Alter the quotation to shorten it, modify its grammar, or otherwise make it fit into your sentence. Show your work to your instructor or a tutor to make sure you understand how to alter quotations.

Once you master the nuts and bolts of how to use quotations, you can also become a more critical reader, examining how the authors you read use quotation, and if they really choose their quotations well.

---

practice it   Examining Quotations in a Published Work

Almost all the reading you do in college will be the work and ideas of others. Reread a few previously assigned articles and find examples of quotations. What kinds of quotations did the author include? How did he or she introduce these quotations? How did the quotations help support his or her point? How did he or she cite sources? Does the text look like MLA style or another style? Does the source omit citation? How does that influence your assessment of the source's credibility?

When and How to Use Paraphrase

Why paraphrase? Essentially, you paraphrase for the same reasons you use a quotation: to add support to your point, to provide an example to discuss, or to show what others think about a topic. You paraphrase rather than quote when you don't need the exact sentence or paragraph from a source, just a few of its points. Paraphrasing is also a good choice when the sentence or phrase you would quote is written in an awkward way or in a style or tone that doesn't fit your paper. There is one additional benefit of paraphrasing for students: Paraphrasing shows your instructor that you have a good grasp of the material, because you are putting it into your own words.

How do you paraphrase? When you paraphrase, whether it's a sentence or a paragraph, you put the author's words into your own. This does not mean just changing a few key words here or there. It means rewriting the sentence, using your own words to convey the author's information. However, it is essential that you maintain the *meaning* of the original sentence or paragraph. Here is an example from Koon-Hwee Kan's article "Adolescents and Graffiti" (the full selection can be found on p. 474).

Quotation	"The undesirable fact is graffiti has become an expensive social problem in many cities in the world."
Paraphrase	The problem of graffiti exists in urban centers worldwide, and it costs a lot of money to deal with.

The highlighted words hold the key meaning in this sentence and need to be stated in a different way, while keeping their same point. If you match the colored highlighting in the quotation and the paraphrase, you can see how each key part of the original sentence was reworded in the second sentence. (A word like *graffiti* is okay to keep; since that's the topic of the sentence and not easily replaced, it can remain in the paraphrase.)

Here's another example, from the article "Teach Your Children the Building Blocks of Finance" by Sherie Holder and Kenneth Meeks (the full selection can be found on p. 43).

Quotation	"By the time your child turns nine, talk to him or her about creating a small budget to keep track of income and expenses."
Paraphrase	Parents should encourage kids before they're nine to track both their savings and their spending.

Finally, here's one more example from Chapter 10 of David G. Myers's textbook *Psychology* (the excerpt can be found on p. 153).

Quotation	"This idea of a general mental capacity expressed by a single intelligence score was controversial in Spearman's day, and it remains so in our own."
Paraphrase	Using an IQ score to represent a person's intellectual ability has been debated ever since Spearman introduced the concept.

Note that each of these paraphrases closely maintains the meaning of the original.

practice it | Paraphrasing Sentences

First, underline the key words in the sentence that convey the meaning of the sentence. Then rewrite the sentence in your own words, making sure to keep the meaning of the underlined words.

1. From Carol S. Dweck's "The Perils and Promises of Praise":

   "Praise is intricately connected to how students view their intelligence" (7).

2. From Pam Fessler's "Making It in the U.S.: More Than Just Hard Work":

   "Like inheritance, financial know-how is key to closing the racial wealth gap, says Stuart Butler of the Heritage Foundation" (83).

3. From Olivia Mellan's "Men, Women, and Money":

   "Typically, men want to merge all the couple's money—while maintaining primary decision-making power. Women want to keep at least some money separate" (56).

4. From Carol S. Dweck's "The Perils and Promises of Praise":

   "Many educators have hoped to maximize students' confidence in their abilities, their enjoyment of learning, and their ability to thrive in school by praising their intelligence" (9).

Introducing a Quotation or Paraphrase

As you learned in Chapter 4, a signal phrase is the group of words that introduces a quotation or a paraphrase so that the reader knows where you got your information. The signal phrase also hints at the reasons you chose to include this particular information in your writing. For instance, you might give the author's credentials in your signal phrase, or you might provide some other contextualizing information. At the most basic level, the signal phrase should work together with the citation to give your reader enough information to find the source if she or he so desires. Successful writers also skillfully use the signal phrase to help the reader take in the information presented in the quotation or paraphrase.

BASIC SIGNAL PHRASES

The simplest way to introduce a quotation or paraphrase is to use the full name of the author and the title of his or her work the first time you mention them. This information can go before or after the quotation or paraphrase. After you mention an author by his or her full name the first time, refer to him or her by last name only. (Never refer to an author by first name only.) Here's a general pattern, followed by some examples:

Full-Introduction Signal Phrase (for the First Mention of an Author in Your Essay)
Full name of author or speaker + full title of work (book or article) + signal-phrase word + quotation or paraphrase

Example of a Quotation | **In her article "Men, Women, and Money," Olivia Mellan claims,** "The failure of people to explore their money personalities leads to deep misunderstanding and hurt" (53).

Example of a Paraphrase | **Sherie Holder and Kenneth Meeks, in their article "Teach Your Children the Building Blocks of Finance,"** reinforce the importance of the practice of saving at least 10–15% of after-tax income (44).

If you already introduced the author fully earlier in the essay, use a shortened signal phrase:

Shortened Signal Phrase (for Additional References to a Previously Introduced Author)
Last name of author or speaker + signal-phrase word + quotation or paraphrase

Example of a Quotation | **Mellan reveals that** "[o]ften, the silence is a shield for the shame, guilt, and anxiety people feel about their own ways with money" (51).

Example of a Paraphrase | **Holder and Meeks claim** that how children feel about money will affect their money habits later in life (53).

practice it Locating and Evaluating Signal Phrases in Published Works

Flip through any of the readings in this book and find places where the author uses signal phrases to introduce a quotation and where the author doesn't use signal phrases. Compare the articles that include signal phrases with those that don't. Which are clearer? Smoother? Easier to follow?

USE SIGNAL PHRASES TO ADD MEANING

Signal phrases can do more than simply identify the source: They can also make your point clearer by emphasizing the meaning of the author. For example, look at the differences between the following signal phrases:

Carol S. Dweck writes that "students in the fixed mind-set don't recover well from setbacks" (19).

Carol S. Dweck argues that "students in the fixed mind-set don't recover well from setbacks" (19).

Carol S. Dweck proposes that "students in the fixed mind-set don't recover well from setbacks" (19).

Each of these signal phrase verbs makes a different statement. When you use *writes*, you merely state that this is what the author says. There is no hint of what the author thinks about the information you cite. However, when you use *argues* or *proposes*, you give the reader more information about the point the author makes. Sometimes it makes the most sense to use *says* or *writes*, but if the author is clearly making a claim or disputing an argument, use a signal phrase to show that. The right signal phrase adds meaning not only to your reader's understanding of the quotation, but to the overall point you are making.

Common Signal Words and Phrases

according to	illustrates	refutes
admits	implies	reveals
argues	informs	says
as stated by (or in)	maintains	states
claims	makes the point	suggests
demonstrates	that	thinks
discusses	proposes	writes
explains	recalls	

practice it   Using Different Signal Phrases

Find a place in one of your readings where the author uses a quotation. Rewrite the quotation with different signal phrase verbs to introduce the quotation. Which signal phrases best fit the meaning of the quotation?

USE MORE SOPHISTICATED SIGNAL PHRASES

You can use other types of signal phrases to eliminate repetition of information, or to de-emphasize the source author and title. If you have already established the author and title, and it's clear you are referring to them, repeating the same information over and over will get boring. Or perhaps the author and title are not the most important factor that you wish to emphasize in your signal phrase; this is often the case with news articles, scholarly studies, and even some video materials. In these cases, you might use a different type of signal phrase, taking care to include a complete citation in the parenthetical reference.

To generate more sophisticated signal phrases, ask yourself again the questions: What will best set up this quotation or paraphrase for my reader? What context is most important for the reader to see the quoted or paraphrased information the way I want them to see it? Again, once you clearly establish the source, you can highlight other important information about the reading.

For example, you might decide to use the date of the information, as with this example that quotes the Pew study on the wealth gap that you read in Chapter 2:

> A 2011 analysis of some key data from the recession found that "since the official end of the recession in mid-2009, the housing market in the United States has remained in a slump while the stock market has recaptured much of the value it lost from 2007 to 2009" (Taylor et al. 76).

You might want the signal phrase to emphasize some other important context for the information, such as how it fits into the history of the topic you are discussing, as in this example that quotes Po Bronson and Ashley Merryman's chapter from *NurtureShock* entitled "The Sibling Effect":

> Since the Biblical story of Cain and Abel, our lifelong relationships with siblings has been determined early: "For the most part, the tone established when [siblings] were very young, be it controlling and bossy or sweet and considerate, tended to stay that way" (Bronson and Merryman 425).

The signal phrase can also indicate how the quoted or paraphrased information fits into the argument you are outlining, as with this example that paraphrases Koon-Hwee Kan's article, "Adolescents and Graffiti":

> One counterargument to the common belief that graffiti is purely vandalism is the argument that graffiti is a way for teenagers to rebel against the consumer culture of their lives (Kan 479).

With works of fiction or memoir, once you've established the title and author, you may want to use the signal phrase to let readers know when in the story the action you are describing occurs, as in this example that quotes the opening soundtrack of Banksy's film *Exit through the Gift Shop*, a documentary about street art:

> The film opens with a montage of graffiti artists while a song plays with the refrain "tonight, the streets are ours" (*Exit through the Gift Shop*).

As you gain more experience with signal phrases, you will see how much heavy lifting they can do for you in your writing.

Explaining a Quotation or Paraphrase

After you learn to write good signal phrases and quote or paraphrase properly, you need to explain the quotation or paraphrase in order for it to be fully integrated into your paragraph. You can think of it as a "sandwich": Your words are the pieces of bread that come before and after the filling (the quoted or paraphrased information).

Quotation/Paraphrase Sandwich
1. Introduce the quotation or paraphrase with a signal phrase.
2. Copy the exact words of the author and surround them with a pair of quotation marks (" "), *or* paraphrase the author's ideas using your own words.
3. Explain what the quotation or paraphrase means.
4. Explain how the quotation or paraphrase supports your point.

The introduction is the signal phrase, and the quotation or paraphrase itself comes next. What follows determines how useful the quotation is in your writing: Quotations and paraphrases are evidence, and you need to explain exactly how that evidence supports the point you want to make.

Explain what the quotation or paraphrase means as objectively as you can so that you are true to the original meaning of the information. In some cases, the meaning will be easy for most people to understand, but think carefully about the material before assuming that is the case. Depending on both your audience and the context of the quotation or paraphrase in the original source, its meaning might need some explaining.

Once you're sure you've made the meaning of the quotation or paraphrase clear, show the reader how it supports your point. Again, don't assume the reader sees the connection between your information and your overall point. You picked the source material for a reason, so explain to the reader how it provides insight or support for the point that you are making.

The following paragraph by student writer Ariel is a great example of the use of the quotation sandwich. In the paragraph, the signal phrases and citations are highlighted in yellow, the quotations are highlighted in blue, and the explanations of the significance of the quotations are highlighted in purple. Ariel is writing about Carlin Flora's "Seeing by Starlight," which she has summarized in prior paragraphs of the essay.

We constantly see celebrities flaunt their lifestyles, and we become jealous of them. We read and constantly watch celebrities put their lives on display for the world to see, and we become envious of what they have. In the article, "Seeing by Starlight," Carlin Flora quotes Francisco Gil-White when he explains that we start to follow the celebrities' clothes and fashion by stating, "Humans naturally copy techniques from high-status individuals" (519). Gil-White means that with the constant reminder of what celebrities have, we become so attracted to the material things these celebrities have that we go out and copy their style. When we go out and buy these clothes, shoes, cars, and so on, we feel as though we are one step closer to becoming like these celebrities and having this lifestyle we look up to. When we are jealous, we often feel as though we can pass judgment on celebrities as well. Flora states, "We're quick to judge when stars behave too outrageously or live too extravagantly" (519). As observers, we constantly pass judgment on celebrities whether it's wearing an ugly outfit on the red carpet or how much weight they have gained or lost. By judging celebrities, we make ourselves feel good because we constantly compare ourselves to them and when they do something wrong we feel like it's our need to pass judgment on them so we can feel confident about ourselves.

Note that the signal phrase for the first quotation explains that Flora is quoting someone else in her article. It's important to let your reader know whose words are being quoted. The words of Gil-White quoted in Flora's article are followed by an explanation of the quoted material, highlighted in purple, where Ariel explains what it means to "copy techniques from high-status individuals." The meaning of the quoted material "we're quick to judge when stars behave too outrageously or live too extravagantly" becomes clear when Ariel writes, "As observers, we constantly pass judgment on celebrities whether it's wearing an ugly outfit on the red carpet or how much weight they have gained or lost. By judging celebrities, we make ourselves feel good because we constantly compare ourselves to them and when they do something wrong we feel like it's our need to pass judgment on them so we can feel confident about ourselves."

practice it   Identifying the Parts of the Quotation Sandwich

For the following two paragraphs from student essays, identify the parts of the quotation sandwich. Underline the signal phrase, highlight the quotation, and put brackets around the explanation of the quotation. How well did each author use the elements of the quotation sandwich? How effective is the quotation sandwich in helping the reader understand the use of the quotations? What advice would you give these authors for revision?

1. From Julie's essay "Marketing to Children":

> The effects of marketing vary with age. As stated in *Pediatrics*, "Among U.S. preschool-aged children (2–5 years of age), obesity rates have more than doubled since the 1970s; among 6- to 11-year-old children, rates have more

continued ❯

than tripled" (Roberto et al. 89). Young children are easily persuaded and manipulated with popular cartoon characters and fancy labeling on junk food. As a mother of a two-year-old, I realize my son can easily identify popular cartoon characters and prefers junk food that is packaged with their images. This must come to a stop; if it doesn't, our children can develop any of the many disorders that come from eating unhealthy food.

2. From Karla:

"Overspending has been a huge problem throughout America, especially among young teens. Parents are not aware of ways to inform teens about smart purchasing habits. "Advertising is a pervasive influence on children and adolescents" (Committee on Communications 2563). "This targeting occurs because advertising is a $250 billion/year industry with 900,000 brands to sell" (Committee on Communication 2563). Young teens are spending $155 billion a year and those younger are spending $25 billion. The teens living on the West Coast prefer to purchase clothes from brands like American Eagle, Forever 21, and Hollister. Specifically among brands ranked by young women, Hollister took the "most preferred" position (Committee on Communication 2563), while West Coast brands continued to be a favorite among young men. Men and women today are choosing these top brands because they're the brands that are being worn here in California and among teens.

chapter review

Chapter 16 covers important information about how to properly use source material in your writing. Using quotations and paraphrases correctly gives your writing texture and adds to your credibility as a writer. Feel free to revisit this chapter any time you work on a writing assignment that calls for quotations or paraphrase.

To review the material in this chapter, choose one or more of the following strategies:

1. Look through some of the essays you have written for this class or others and highlight the signal phrases you have used. Did you include all the parts of the signal phrase? Did you have a good variety of signal phrase words? How might you improve your signal phrases? Make a list in your notebook of effective signal phrases you have found, and add any additional ways to introduce a quotation to the list.

2. If you skipped any activities, do them now as a way to deepen your understanding of the material.

3. Try to explain the concepts of this chapter to someone you know. Explain the difference between a quotation and a paraphrase; the parts of a quotation sandwich; the meanings of various signal phrases. Give your own examples to illustrate those concepts.

17

Giving and Receiving Feedback

in this chapter

- Why Is Feedback Essential?
- What Is Peer Review?
- How Do You Understand and Apply Instructors' Comments?
- What Is a Rubric, and How Do You Use One?
- When Should You Meet with an Instructor or Tutor?

Before you were able to purchase this book, approximately sixty people read drafts of it, made suggestions, and offered their advice and opinions about everything from the title to the content to the size of the margins. Surprised? Many people who see writing as a solitary process— a tortured artist sitting in a cold, damp room—are shocked to find out how collaborative it really is. Even writers who do work alone typically have a small group of writer friends, as well as editors and other people, they go to for advice. Your English class will help you begin to see yourself as a writer by offering opportunities for your classmates to provide feedback on your writing.

Feedback Is Essential

So why do writers so often ask for feedback from others? What do they do with that feedback? Writers seek feedback for many reasons, including these:

- To check whether something they are trying to do "works"
- To answer that nagging "I know what I mean to say, but am I really saying it?" question
- To get ideas for how to expand and develop a piece of writing
- To identify strengths and weaknesses in a piece of writing

Do writers always follow the advice they get? Definitely not. Sometimes readers have a difference of opinion about a piece of writing, but if three out of four peer reviewers all agree that your introduction isn't clear, you should probably listen to them. You might not change it the way they would like you to, but you should consider revising it.

The other important key to peer review may also surprise you: You learn just as much—if not more—by giving feedback as you do by receiving it. Why is that? Think for a moment about a time when you had to teach someone something. Maybe you had to teach your little sister how to make a foul shot, or your cousin how to balance his checkbook. Sure, you know how to do it, but explaining it is another matter. You have to understand something far more deeply to teach it than you do to just do it. This is true of everything—writing included. So, if you are in a peer-review writing group with classmates and one of the writers doesn't have a strong enough thesis, being able to recognize the problem and then explain why the thesis is not strong will help you develop a deeper knowledge of thesis statements, the assignment prompt, and the content of your own paper.

Peer review can be a scary thing. Even though you ask for honest, constructive criticism, hearing negative comments can be tough, especially when you worked hard on something. Still, the rewards far, far outweigh these difficulties. While peer review may never be a totally comfortable process, as you practice it, you will probably find that you enjoy working on your writing with your classmates and friends. By the end of the course, you will probably discover that your peer-review skills have improved significantly and that you revise and edit your essay more confidently because of the experience.

Guidelines for Peer Review

Many models for peer review exist, and your instructor will choose one that best suits your class. Most frequently, peer review in college English classrooms happens in a writing workshop, where students working in small groups exchange drafts, read and comment on them, and then discuss ways the authors can improve them. Another model is a written peer response, usually accompanied by a set of specific written questions. One student reads another student's draft and fills out a questionnaire about the paper, often as homework. Then the students collect one or more responses to their work and interpret these responses on their own. Sometimes, your instructor will ask for a volunteer to have his or her paper "workshopped" by the entire class. This is a fantastic opportunity to get feedback on your writing from the instructor as well as your classmates; try to volunteer if asked, even if you are nervous.

Whatever method of peer review your instructor chooses, adhering to some basic principles of peer review will make the entire experience more worthwhile and pleasant.

- **Always say something positive first.** This is the cardinal rule of peer review among writers. People learn from what they did right, not just from having what they did wrong pointed out to them repeatedly.

- **Refer to the assignment.** Have the essay assignment and any notes about the assignment that your instructor gave you out on your desk and refer to them as you do peer review.
- **Consult the sources.** As much as possible, return to the books and articles referred to in your classmate's paper as you work with it.
- **Make your criticism constructive.** If you find a weak point, offer a couple of possible suggestions for improvement.
- **Be specific and detailed in your feedback.** Just saying "It's good" doesn't help anyone. Instead, say something specific, such as "Your hook really makes me want to read the paper." If you find a weakness, be specific in that too. Saying "This paragraph doesn't work" might be somewhat helpful, but it would be more helpful if you said, "This paragraph doesn't work because the example you give doesn't really fit with the point you're trying to make."
- **Follow the directions that your instructor gave.** Perhaps in this round of review, your instructor only wants you to focus on the thesis statement because you're going to work on the rest of the essay next week. If he or she gave handouts or wrote lists of items to discuss on the board, use them.
- **Have an open mind, have fun, and stay focused.** Peer review is the place where you can admit mistakes, figure out better ways to do things, and have a little fun. Peer review works best, though, when you stay on track, so be disciplined about it.
- **Make a real effort.** There's nothing worse than being in a peer group with a bunch of writers who don't really try to give feedback. For the process to work, everyone needs to participate. For shy students, that means speaking up. For talkative students, that means giving others the chance to speak, sometimes by asking for their opinions. Make sure no one person dominates the conversation.
- **Establish a time frame and appoint a timekeeper.** Often, peer groups run out of time, which isn't fair to the last person. Divide the amount of time you have equally among the participants and set an alarm or appoint a timekeeper to make sure you stay more or less on schedule.

Interpreting and Applying Instructors' Comments

Wouldn't it be wonderful to get a paper back from your instructor with just the words "You're Brilliant!" written at the top and a big fat A grade? Of course we all want that, but even if it did happen, it wouldn't be great for you. Instructor comments, like the comments you receive from peers in writing groups, are a way to teach and learn, and a paper with no comments means a lost opportunity for you to learn. Usually instructors provide you with positive as well as negative feedback, but even if the comments you get are mostly about ways to improve, you can use that information positively for your next paper if you follow these guidelines:

- **Understand the difference between a correction and a comment.** Instructors often make corrections by circling errors or actually correcting errors on your papers. Typically, these are errors in document format or sentence-level issues, and usually when an instructor circles or fixes a problem, there is one right way to fix it—for instance, you spelled a word wrong, had the wrong margins, made a mistake in subject-verb agreement, or left off a citation.

  Comments, on the other hand, are like annotations. Comments address larger issues (often called higher-order concerns), like your ideas, support, or writing style. For example, an instructor might comment that your evidence doesn't fit your point, or that you misunderstood the tone of the text you are discussing. Being able to distinguish between a correction and a comment helps you prioritize your revisions. When in doubt about what your most pressing writing problems are, ask your instructor.

- **Do your best to fix your errors.** Instructors often wish that students would look at their corrections, figure out how to fix the errors, and never make those errors again. This is a big wish, and they know it doesn't really happen like that, but they do expect you to try your best. Start in the right direction by keeping track of your common mistakes, and recognizing the ones you make most often. The Grammar Log described in Chapter 24 (p. 579) is a useful tool for learning to edit your writing. You need to track your errors and edit specifically for those errors you tend to make so that you will eventually, with lots of practice, stop making these same mistakes.

- **Really *think* about the comments.** Instructors expect you to read their comments, especially the comments they write at the end of the paper, and really think about them. Instructors who write substantial comments see them as the beginning of a conversation about your work. They expect you to think carefully about their comments, and hope to see some of that thought process reflected in your revisions or in your next papers.

  For instance, if your instructor writes on your paper that you often seem to have trouble with conclusions, but you do not have another chance to revise that paper, you should make a special effort on your conclusion in the next paper. If you need help figuring out how to apply the comment to your next paper, ask your instructor or see a tutor if one is available.

- **Study the course or assignment rubric (if there is one).** A *rubric* is a document that divides up the writing task into different skills so they

To download the Grammar Log, go to **bedfordstmartins.com /readwriteconnect** and click on **Charts**.

can be evaluated one by one. For example, a rubric might have sections for content, organization, use of evidence, and editing. (See p. 331 for more on rubrics.) If your instructor grades with a rubric, he or she may show it to you before the assignment is due so that you understand the grading standards better and, hopefully, produce better work.

As you look over the rubric, take time to distinguish between big-picture concerns and sentence-level concerns. Sometimes the sentence-level concerns are listed in greater detail on the rubric because this format allows the instructor to check off boxes and save time, but that does not mean he or she sees those items as more important than big-picture concerns—in fact, the opposite is almost always true.

- **Spend time reviewing your efforts.** If you really worked hard on an assignment and got a lower grade than expected, reread the assignment, your work, and the instructor's comments. Then, if you are still confused, set up an appointment to speak privately with the instructor. Make sure you ask the instructor what you can do better next time.

Comparing your grade to another student's grade can be tempting, but try to avoid it. Two papers both earning C grades might have different problems and strengths, and instructors often have to weigh the quality of the ideas against the actual writing of the paper to arrive at a fair grade.

CORRECTIONS

The following chart explains some common marks or correction symbols instructors write on papers. Many instructors hand out their own personalized editing chart at the beginning of the semester. When in doubt about what a correction means—or when you can't read the handwriting—make sure you ask for clarification.

Correction	What It Might Mean	Related Chapters in This Book; Other Places to Go for Help
frag: fragment incomplete sentence	You do not have a complete sentence. You are making a sentence fragment.	Chapter 28, Fragments
run-on: RO fused sentence; cs: comma splice	You have two (or more) complete sentences joined together improperly, either with or without a comma.	Chapter 29, Run-Ons/Fused Sentences and Comma Splices

continued

(Continued)

Correction	What It Might Mean	Related Chapters in This Book; Other Places to Go for Help
verb s/v agr tense tense shift verb form	You have a problem with your verbs in this sentence.	Chapter 27, Verbs
(,)	Either you have a comma that shouldn't be there or you need a comma.	Chapter 31, Commas
pro agr / pro ag pro ref / pronoun ref pronoun circled pronoun with "?" next to it	Either you used the wrong pronoun or the reader cannot tell what noun your pronoun is replacing.	Chapter 30, Pronouns
awk awkward unclear mixed sentence predication error	Your sentence is hard to follow. It needs a total rewrite. (Don't worry; we've all been there.)	Chapter 33, How to Fix Common Sentence-Structure Problems
// parallel faulty parallel	You have a sentence with a series of items, but the items in the series do not match up grammatically.	Chapter 32, Parallelism
wordy	You used too many words to say something. You need to be more clear and succinct.	Chapter 34, Writing Clear and Focused Sentences
word choice wc ww	You used a word that doesn't quite mean what you intended. This error is often caused by an over-reliance on a thesaurus.	Try looking the word up in a dictionary; then figure out a better word for what you meant to say by looking at synonyms. See also Chapter 8, Vocabulary Building.
sp	You spelled a word incorrectly.	Use a dictionary. See also Chapter 36, Spelling, Commonly Confused Words, and Capitalization.

(Continued)

Correction	What It Might Mean	Related Chapters in This Book; Other Places to Go for Help
cap C (or three lines drawn under a letter)	You have a capitalization error.	Chapter 36, Spelling, Commonly Confused Words, and Capitalization
proof! proofreading edit!	You have many mistakes. If your instructor uses exclamation points, chances are good he or she thinks you are being sloppy and knows you can do better.	Chapter 4, Revising, Editing, and Proofreading; Chapter 24, How to Learn the Rules and Apply What You've Learned to Your Own Writing

COMMENTS

The chart below lists some shorthand terms for the comments instructors make on papers. Remember, a correction addresses a problem—usually small or sentence level—that has a right or wrong answer. In contrast, a comment targets ideas, organization, purpose, audience, and other big-picture areas of writing, where there is no one "right" way to revise.

Comment	What It Might Mean	Related Chapters in This Book; Other Places to Go for Help
plus sign (+) check mark (✓)	A plus sign usually means you made a strong point. A check mark probably means you made a good point or did something the instructor wanted you to accomplish. It could also mean you made a mistake.	Do yourself and your classmates a favor by politely asking what a check mark on your paper means, if your instructor forgets to explain it when handing back the first stack of papers.
underlining	Underlining probably means you wrote something particularly good, but it could mean something else.	Ask your instructor what underlining means.

continued

(Continued)

Comment	What It Might Mean	Related Chapters in This Book; Other Places to Go for Help
good! great!	Congratulate yourself—you did well! Now take the time to figure out what was so good. We learn from what we do right, not just from what we do wrong.	If your instructor neglected to put any positive feedback on your paper, set up a private time to go over the paper and ask what strengths he or she sees in your writing.
TS?	You may not have a topic sentence, or your topic sentence may not fit your paragraph.	Chapter 12, Topic Sentences and Paragraphs
organization? structure? org prob	Perhaps you have a paragraph where all the information does not fit under the topic sentence, or a paragraph that does not fit with the rest of the essay. Check to see if the instructor drew arrows or brackets to suggest how you might change the order of information or the paragraph breaks.	Chapter 13, Essay Organization and Outlining
¶	You may need to break up your paragraph into two paragraphs, which will probably require some revising to smooth over the transition and make sure both paragraphs are complete.	Chapter 12, Topic Sentences and Paragraphs
thesis?	Clarify or strengthen your thesis, or another revision.	Chapter 10, Thesis and Main Idea
confusing clarity ?	You expressed your idea unclearly. This may require editing, but you probably need to think more about your content.	Reread what you wrote, and try to identify what is unclear. Then choose the chapter that applies. When in doubt, ask your instructor.

(Continued)

Correction	What It Might Mean	Related Chapters in This Book; Other Places to Go for Help
more support expand say more	You began to make a good point, but you need more evidence or examples to support your idea well.	Chapter 9, Pre-Writing; Chapter 11, Argument
focus off-topic	You drifted away from the main point you were making or the assigned paper topic generally.	Chapter 10, Thesis and Main Idea; Chapter 13, Essay Organization and Outlining
relate to thesis connection? How does this relate?	You may offer a good example or other piece of evidence, but you don't explain how it supports your point or thesis.	Chapter 12, Topic Sentences and Paragraphs

Eventually, you will learn to interpret your instructor's corrections and comments. To speed this process along, ask questions if you do not understand what your instructor has written.

practice it   Reviewing Comments and Corrections

Find an essay your instructor has graded and marked, even one from a previous class. Examine the different corrections and comments that were made. Which corrections or comments did you find most helpful to you? Why? Which corrections or comments do you still not fully understand? How might those corrections or comments still apply to your writing? Make notes, if applicable, on your Grammar Log of any sentence-level issues.

How to Use a Rubric

As we mentioned earlier, some instructors grade with a rubric—an assessment tool that lists the categories on which you are graded, such as content, organization, mechanics, and citations. Rubrics can be simple or very detailed. Sometimes all the instructors who teach a specific course use the same rubric, whereas other times an instructor will personalize rubrics, perhaps for every assignment. A couple of examples follow.

This rubric is point-based, which means it lists specific values for each area:

POINT-BASED RUBRIC

Area	Possible Points	Your Points
Thesis and supporting points	5	
Evidence: amount and quality of quotes, paraphrases, and examples	5	
Organization: paragraphing, order of ideas, transitions	5	
Grammar and mechanics	3	
Proper use of bibliographic (MLA) style	2	
TOTAL	20	

The next rubric is holistic, which means it records strengths and weaknesses in an overall way:

HOLISTIC RUBRIC

	Excellent	Good	Average	Poor	Failing
Content/ quality of argument/ development and support of thesis	Clear thesis; detailed examples; excellent analysis	Same qualities as for excellent, but some examples need more detail or analysis	Insufficient examples to support thesis; examples lack detail; insufficient analysis	Lacks a thesis and/or supporting examples; provides partial argument	Lacks thesis and supporting examples; examples are off-topic; thesis inappropriate for assignment
Use of source material	Appropriate source material supports argument; introduces all quotes and paraphrases; summarizes well; uses citation correctly	Appropriate source material supports argument; generally introduces quotes and paraphrases; 1–2 minor errors in citation	Uses source material but does not clearly tie it to argument; 3 or more errors in citation	Lacks appropriate source material; multiple errors in citation	Plagiarism (intentional or inadvertent); lacks appropriate source material; multiple errors in citation

(Continued)

	Excellent	Good	Average	Poor	Failing
Organization/ structure	Clear and logical structure for introduction, body, and conclusion; uses effective transition sentences; has a coherent paragraph structure	Same qualities as for excellent, but may have 1–2 problems with organization, such as missing transition, misplaced paragraph break, or ineffective order of information	Organization is solid and predictable; may have 3–4 problems with some aspect of organization, but these problems do not substantially undermine the argument	Essay has enough problems with organization, structure, and coherence that they get in the way of understanding the argument	Essay is disorganized and hard to follow; introduction does not include basic background information; paper lacks a conclusion
Grammar, mechanics, and style	The prose is readable, clear, and free of major errors	The prose is generally readable; 1–2 recurring errors, but they do not impede meaning	The prose is generally readable; 3–4 recurring errors, but they do not impede meaning	The prose has more than 4 recurring errors or errors that are significant enough to impede meaning	The prose has sufficient major errors that it is frequently unreadable
MLA style	The essay follows all aspects of MLA style	The essay has minor errors in MLA style	The essay has several or more serious errors in MLA style	The essay has fundamental problems with MLA citation	The essay has fundamental problems with MLA; may include inadvertent plagiarism

practice it   Using a Rubric

Score one of your previous essays or several essays from your classmates according to the preceding holistic rubric. Identify specific examples from the essay(s) to justify your scoring. Give the essay an overall grade. Compare your scoring with that of your peers.

Here is an example of a rubric that might be used to assess the first essay assignment in an introductory English course:

Rubric for the First Essay in a Course

4 = Excellent   3 = Adequate   2 = Below Average   1 = Far Below Average

Content

Paper offers an appropriate and focused argument	4 3 2 1
Paper uses sufficient evidence to support points	4 3 2 1
Paper analyzes the evidence well	4 3 2 1

Organization

Essay uses an effective structure	4 3 2 1
Topic sentences are well written and match content	4 3 2 1
There is a clear and complete introduction	4 3 2 1
There is a meaningful conclusion	4 3 2 1

Grammar and Mechanics   (if checked, you have a problem in this area)

____ Run-ons and comma splices	____ Comma rules
____ Fragments	____ Semicolons
____ Subject-verb agreement	____ Colons
____ Pronoun agreement	____ Apostrophes
____ Pronoun reference	____ Quotation marks
____ Pronoun shifts	____ End punctuation
____ Verb tense	____ Capitalization
____ Wordiness	

Editing and Proofreading Skills   4 3 2 1

Initial grade: _____

Minus points for lateness or missing workshops: _____

What do you notice about the rubric? What does the point scale of 1–4 mean? What writing tasks or skills is the instructor trying to evaluate at this point in the term? Remember, the extensive checklist for Grammar and Mechanics does not mean this area is more important than the others. It's just a time-saving device that allows your instructor to communicate quickly and efficiently.

Now, here is an example of a rubric that might be used later in the term:

Rubric for the Third Essay in a Course

4 = Excellent   3 = Adequate   2 = Below Average   1 = Far Below Average

Content

Paper uses sufficient evidence to support points	4 3 2 1
Paper analyzes the evidence well	4 3 2 1
Paper introduces quotes and paraphrases well	4 3 2 1
Author moves beyond obvious arguments	4 3 2 1

Organization

Essay uses an effective structure	4 3 2 1
Topic sentences are well written and match content	4 3 2 1
There is a clear and complete introduction	4 3 2 1
There is a meaningful conclusion	4 3 2 1
There are good transitions between points and paragraphs	4 3 2 1

Grammar and Mechanics   (if checked, you have a problem in this area)

____ Run-ons and comma splices	____ Comma rules
____ Fragments	____ Semicolons
____ Subject-verb agreement	____ Colons
____ Pronoun agreement	____ Apostrophes
____ Pronoun reference	____ Quotation marks
____ Pronoun shifts	____ End punctuation
____ Verb tense, mood, and voice	____ Capitalization
____ Wordiness	

Editing and Proofreading Skills   4 3 2 1

MLA

____ one-inch margins all around

____ double-spaced throughout, including Works Cited list and block quotes

____ proper format for name, instructor, course title, and date in upper left corner

____ proper format for page numbers

____ Works Cited list alphabetized

____ proper format for block quotes

____ proper format (period in the right place, correct spacing) for parenthetical references

____ parenthetical citations used correctly and appropriately, citing when necessary

____ proper format for entries in the Works Cited list

MLA Skills   4 3 2 1

Initial grade: _____

Minus points for lateness or missing workshops: _____

What new skills are being evaluated with this rubric? What has stayed the same?

Whatever type of rubric your instructor uses, refer to the rubric to understand the grade you earned and prepare to do better on the next essay. The best way to use a rubric, though, is to keep it on hand during the rough draft and revision stages, and refer to it as a checklist to guide your revisions. The clearer the instructor's expectations, the better you will be at following them.

The rubric can be a helpful tool as a checklist during peer review too. In fact, if you pay careful attention, you may notice that some instructors hand out a form to use for peer review that is strikingly similar to the grading rubric. Making this connection—seeing how the peer-review and grading processes fit together—will lead you to succeed more quickly.

---

practice it   Making Your Own Rubric

Make a rubric of your own. Imagine that you are the instructor and you are creating a grading rubric for a major assignment in one of your college classes. Looking at the assignment instructions, design a rubric for the assignment. Show it to your instructor for that class and ask his or her opinion. Did you correctly predict the evaluation criteria?

Meeting with an Instructor or Tutor

When you were in high school, being asked to stay after class to meet with your teacher usually meant trouble. College, however, is the complete opposite. In college, students often meet with the instructor outside of class to discuss their work, even when their work is pretty good already. In fact, most full-time instructors are required to have a certain number of regularly scheduled office hours so that students can see them privately to discuss the course material. (Part-time or adjunct faculty members often do not have office hours, but they should have other ways to touch base with you, so ask.)

Meeting with your instructor should be a part of your college mindset. When you need help, knock on his or her door, send an e-mail, or stay after class to ask a question. (If it's a basic question—like the date for a test—then ask a classmate or consult the course schedule, of course.) Generally, your instructors are happy to help you with anything related to the course, and they can even help guide you to appropriate resources on campus if you have other problems—such as difficulty adjusting to college life—affecting your work. Getting to know at least one instructor, especially one in a field of study that you are considering pursuing, will benefit you because he or she can offer advice about your educational and career path and often write you letters of recommendation later.

Sometimes you may be advised by your instructor to visit a tutor on campus. Again, this may require a mental shift for you. Seeing a tutor does not mean you are "dumb" or "don't get it." In fact, once you get to the tutoring center, you discover that the one thing the students there have in common is their motivation to improve, a hallmark of successful students. Sometimes students who need to review basic skills seek tutoring, but just as often, the most advanced students pull up a chair with a tutor to improve their work. How do you think they got so good at writing? Tutors are sort of halfway between your instructor and your peer group, and they usually offer a unique perspective. The more feedback the better, right?

Whatever you do, don't wait until it's too late to seek help. Coming to your instructor for help fifteen minutes before an essay is due won't accomplish much—except maybe irritate your instructor. However, students who show a solid track record of seeking help and try their best are generally treated with fairness and respect by instructors, especially when an emergency arises.

So, once you decide to see your instructor or a tutor, how can you make the most of the visit? Come prepared by bringing:

- A copy of your paper, outline, or notes for wherever you are in the writing process
- The sources (books, articles, and printouts of Web pages) you are planning to use in the essay
- A specific list of questions you have or a specific problem to work on

When you sit down with a tutor, he or she will probably start by asking what kind of help you need. The more specific you are, the better. If you just show a tutor your draft, he or she may focus on grammar errors, when you really need more help with the thesis of a very rough draft. Remember, tutors are not taking the class with you and aren't familiar with the readings or assignment, but they can still tell whether a piece of writing makes sense or not. In fact, they serve as good outside readers exactly for this reason. Be clear about the type of help you want at this stage of the process, and both you and the tutor will find the meeting more useful and enjoyable.

chapter review

As you have seen in Chapter 17, giving and receiving feedback requires some of the most sophisticated reading skills you will employ in college. Not only are you reading for tone, style, structure, and content; you are also conveying your constructive criticism back to the writer in a way that requires close attention to your own word choice. Indeed, the collaborative nature of feedback provides a great training ground for your future work life, too, since so much of what we do in the world requires us to engage in back-and-forth thinking and revising ideas with others. The benefits of peer review and expert consultation to your personal growth and development are worthwhile in their own right, quite apart from the actual improvement that you are able to make to your draft.

To review this chapter, choose one or more of the following strategies:

1. Freewrite about your prior experiences working in groups on school assignments. What worked? What didn't? Then review the material from the chapter and find one or two practical suggestions to address any previous problems you had working in groups. For example, if you found in the past that in your groups you ended up doing all the work, what specific action could you take to change that next time? Review the chapter for ideas.
2. Make a list of all your questions for your instructor about a piece of writing you are working on now or recently completed. Determine which questions would require a correction from the instructor and which would require a comment. Then use the corrections chart on pages 327–29 to find the chapter in the book that addresses your corrections. Discuss the areas that need a comment with your instructor, tutors, or peer group.
3. If you skipped any activities, do them now as a way to deepen your understanding of the material.
4. Try to explain what you have learned to someone you know. Discuss the key concepts and give your own examples to illustrate those concepts.

18
Note Taking

in this chapter

- Why Is Note Taking Important?
- What Is the Cornell Method?
- How Do You Avoid Plagiarism When Taking Notes?
- How Do You Create Good Note-Taking Systems?

Taking good notes requires discipline, but it pays off immensely. When you translate what you see and hear in class through your own hand into your own words and pictures, you understand it more fully and are able to recall it more easily. Studying your notes later makes the learning even deeper, but the very action of taking the notes increases learning more than you probably realize.

Taking notes is similar to the reading and writing processes in many ways. To take useful notes:

- Prepare your mind to receive the information *before* you take notes
- Process the information *during* note taking
- Synthesize the information *after* receiving it

Just before class, for instance, you might jot down in your notes a few thoughts about the topic, answering questions such as these:

- What do you already know about the topic?
- What have you learned so far in this class? In other classes?
- What key terms or vocabulary apply to the topic for the day?
- Why is the instructor spending time on this topic now? How does it fit into the course as a whole?

Once the presentation begins—whether it is a formal lecture or a class discussion—take notes on the main points, taking time to write down your responses to that information as much as possible. Finally, at the end of the lecture or class, or later that day if necessary, add some comments about what you learned, write down questions about things you still do not understand, and generally organize your thoughts on the topic.

Notes are rarely complete sentences; capture the ideas you've heard accurately but quickly, since instruction continues while you're taking notes. Abbreviations will help you do this. Efficient note takers also develop their own shorthand, leaving out letters. You may already have developed your own system, but here are some common abbreviations and symbols you can use if you haven't:

Common Abbreviations and Symbols

@ = at	govt = government
b/c = because	w/ = with
btwn = between	← → = relates to
dif = different or difference	+ = positive, pro, or good point
esp = especially	– = negative, con, or bad point
ex = example	~ = approximately or about

The Cornell Method of Note Taking

You will eventually develop your own style for taking notes, but a good place to begin is with the Cornell method, developed at Cornell University. This method gives you space to write down what the instructor says and to record your thoughts, reactions, questions, and connections to the material. In essence, the Cornell note method allows you to record notes on the material and then annotate your notes, just as if you were reading a text. This level of thought means you process the material more deeply than if you just listen.

Here's how it works:

STEP 1: Note Taking.   Divide your page into two columns; the right column should be wider than the left. On the right side of your page, take notes as you read or listen to a lecture or class discussion, summarizing the main ideas and points and jotting down examples.

STEP 2: Annotating with Your Ideas and Questions.   On the left side of the page, you take notes on your notes. While you take notes—or, if you feel pressured for time, shortly afterwards—write down your responses, key terms, and any questions you have. For example, if the lecture you're taking notes on is about the wealth gap, you might write, "What is the wealth gap?" in the left column. Then, when you study the notes, fold the paper to cover the right side (the "answer") and quiz yourself using the questions you wrote about the material. Try to write *how* and *why* questions as well as *who*, *what*, *where*, and *when* questions. Having a range of questions allows you to think more fully about the material.

You can also use the left column for your reflections about the material, especially ideas that come up as you are reviewing the material after class. In classes that are more about critical thinking than memorization of information, the left column becomes a space for you to generate your ideas about the course material, while in class or after.

STEP 3: Summarizing.   After class, spend a short time briefly summarizing the information. Your summary can go at the bottom of the page of notes. You can also use this space to reflect more deeply on the material—for example, by connecting the ideas to a previous day's information or even another course you have taken.

STEP 4: Reviewing and Reciting.   On a daily or weekly basis, reread, recite, and rethink your notes, questions, and summaries. Actually reciting the information—saying it out loud—can be more effective for people who learn best by listening and speaking. Waiting until the day before the test to read your notes is not as effective as reviewing them more frequently.

Here's a sample of what your notebook page would look like in the Cornell notes system:

LIST THE COURSE NAME, TOPIC, AND DATE HERE:

Your Annotations on Your Notes	Your Notes on the Lecture or Discussion
List key terms, specific questions that will help you recall the material, and anything you don't understand. In a content-heavy class, like biology, use this section to write down questions to use while quizzing yourself later.	List, in your own words, the main points from the presentation, lecture, or class discussion. Don't try to copy down everything. Focus on the main points. Make drawings or diagrams to help you remember the key points. If you think you missed something, draw a line and remember to ask a classmate or your instructor after class about what you missed.

Your Summary of the Lecture or Discussion
Review all your notes from both columns. Write a summary of the entire lecture or discussion, and make comments about how this information fits in with the other information from the course.

practice it   The Cornell Method

Make a Cornell notes page in your notebook. Then take notes on your next class lecture, discussion, or reading using the Cornell notes method. Afterward, reflect on how well the method worked for you. Were you able to study the information more or less effectively than with your current note-taking method? Why? Did you stay more engaged with the material when you forced yourself to take notes on it? Remember, you will need practice if the method is new to you.

Note Taking in Other Situations

The Cornell notes method described in the preceding section was designed for students to use during lectures, where the instructor presents large amounts of information and expects students to record it accurately in their notes. You can adapt the Cornell method in your own ways to many situations, but sometimes you need additional techniques, such as for classroom discussions, small-group activities, film viewings, and interviews.

CLASS DISCUSSIONS

It's easy to neglect to take notes on classroom discussions, either because you get so wrapped up in the conversation that you forget or because you—erroneously—believe that you should only take notes on material the instructor presents. Remember, any classroom discussions or small-group activities your instructor has you do are part of the planned coursework. Class discussion provides additional perspectives on a reading or topic. The instructor expects you to take new knowledge or skills away from the experience, and recording notes about what you heard, observed, or said is the best way to ensure that you will recall the information later.

When you take notes on a classroom discussion, it is not necessary to write down each student's name with his or her comments (though if you can, that's great). Rather, you might put people's comments into categories or groups based on the content of what they say. For instance, if you have a class debate, you might create two columns in your notes, one for "comments from people who are for X" and another for "comments from people who are against X." You might even add a third column for miscellaneous comments and your own ideas.

Here's an example from a student's notes on a class discussion about whether financial literacy should be taught in the school system or at home:

taught at school	taught at home	other ideas
parents don't know enough to teach kids—just look at the mess the older gen. has already created—we need schools to do it	different cultural values—money is personal—I don't want someone else teaching my kid those kinds of values	why can't you do both? first @ home then @ school?
it's a basic life skill—we teach home ec, why not how to balance a checkbook or pick the best credit card?	kids need to focus on reading, writing, and math, not "extras" like finance	
	if it's supposed to start early, then it has to start in the home b/c kids don't go to school until age 5	

Taking notes in this way helps you see the different sides of the debate—and the holes in each side's thinking. Remember, you don't have to end up in the same place you started. Maybe after listing all the ideas that come out of class discussion, you will decide to change your own position a little or a lot.

SMALL-GROUP ACTIVITIES

Small-group activities are another situation in which students often don't take good notes. Too often, when an instructor assigns students to a small group to complete a specific task, the students agree to let one person—usually the one with the neatest handwriting—take all the notes. This causes trouble for a few reasons. First, what happens if that person misses the next class period? The notes are usually gone. Second, note taking has really nothing to do with handwriting, so there's no reason why the person with the best handwriting would be the best note taker. Third, and most importantly, the very process of taking notes is a learning experience. By writing down your thoughts and other people's ideas, you are processing and learning the information. Sure, it's work, but it's very worthwhile work—hardly the busywork that many people believe it to be. So make sure you take your own notes, even if a group note taker has been appointed, so you have the information to study and for future assignments.

TIP
Sharing notes electronically is a good way to keep everyone involved; this way if someone is out sick, the group does not fall behind.

FILM AND VIDEO SCREENINGS

Taking notes during a film is an art developed by film reviewers decades ago, before videos and DVDs allowed multiple viewings. While you may have the opportunity to watch a film a second time, this won't always be the case. Taking good notes the first time around saves time and helps you remember the film's contents. Here are a few tips:

- Before the film starts, predict what it will be about from its title. Consider all the ways you might want to refer to the film in your upcoming writing assignments. Determine why the instructor chose to show this film at this time. What do you expect to get out of it?
- Jot down the title, director, date (if known), and company that made the film at the top of your notes. This information is usually in the credit sequence. If you miss it, consult an online database, like the Internet Movie Database, to fill in details.
- For fiction films, make note of characters' names, music, repeated lines, frequently used colors, repeated shots, significance of clothing, symbolism in props, and anything else that seems important, even if you don't know why it is important yet. If you have a particular reaction to the film—like you laugh or get scared—note when in the film this happened.
- For documentary films, make notes on the arguments presented through the information, just as you would annotate an article that tries to inform and/or persuade. Note down the types of experts used—and their names, if you can catch them—and if any "ordinary" people's opinions are included. Write down facts that you might want to look up in more detail later. If the documentary presents an argument, you might divide your notes into two columns marked "argument" and "counterargument."
- After the film, take ten to fifteen minutes to summarize it and to record your thoughts while they are fresh in your mind.
- Remember to take notes on anything your instructor mentions about the film, as well as on any class discussion of it afterward.

While you are not expected, usually, to catch entire quotes from films, make your best attempt to include accurate information in your essays. Good notes help you earn credibility.

INTERVIEWS

One of the most difficult note-taking situations that you are likely to encounter in college is when you have to interview someone. Interviewing requires several sophisticated tasks: asking good questions, listening, interpreting someone's tone, being open and pleasant even if you're nervous or confused, and thinking on the spot. Add to that the need to take absolutely accurate notes on what your interview subject says, and you understand why most reporters actually study formal shorthand, a very rapid system for writing. Ask your subject in advance for permission to record the interview: If he or she agrees, this will be very helpful. Either way, however, preparation is key to successful interviews. These steps will help you prepare for an interview:

STEP 1: **Brainstorm a list of questions you hope to ask.** Open-ended questions (those without a yes-or-no answer) work best. For instance, "What was it like to major in engineering?" is an open-ended question. If you ask "Did you like majoring in engineering?" you will likely get a simple "yes" or "no" answer.

STEP 2: **Review your list of questions.** Group items into categories, starting at basic information and moving to deeper and/or more personal questions. Always end on one or two positive questions. Don't try to cover more than ten deeper questions during an interview. Usually, you only have time to ask five or six intensive questions during a short interview with a talkative person.

STEP 3: **Type up a note-taking page, with spaces for all the basic information you need to gather, followed by your questions with spaces below to jot down notes.**

STEP 4: **Highlight the questions that are your top priorities so that you can skip ahead to them if you are running out of time.**

Here's a sample of what a note-taking page might look like for a student interviewing another student on his or her attitudes about money.

My interview with: _____

Date: _____

Interview conducted at _____

Sex: M/F Age: _____ Live with parents? Yes/No

Major: _____

Career goals? _____

Paying for school yourself? Yes/No

Credit cards? Yes/No How many? _____

What kinds of early experiences do you remember having with money as a kid?

How does money influence your career goals?

What, in your view, is the relationship between money and happiness?

How much control do you feel you have over your finances?

What is your biggest strength in terms of money?

Thank you for your time.

Coming to the interview prepared with a sheet like this saves you from having to write down the basics, giving you more time to make eye contact and create a rapport with the interview subject.

Avoiding Plagiarism When Taking Notes

You have probably heard of plagiarism and know it is bad, but if you are like most college students, you may not fully understand it or know how to avoid it. Plagiarism means that you improperly take credit for someone else's work, whether intentionally or unintentionally. Intentional or not, it's wrong, and it will get you into all sorts of trouble—not to mention that you'll never learn much if you let other people do your thinking for you. Unintentional plagiarism often comes about as a result of improper note taking, so avoiding plagiarism is one more important reason to develop strong note-taking skills.

For more on citing sources properly, see Chapter 20, MLA Documentation, page 362.

Develop good note-taking and study habits now so that you do not get into crisis mode or even inadvertently plagiarize. It is best to develop these good habits now, when paper assignments are relatively short, instead of waiting until you have a massive paper with multiple sources to juggle. To develop good organizational habits while doing research, begin with consistently using an organized system for note taking, such as one of the following:

THE NOTE CARD SYSTEM

In a note card system, you write all the bibliographical information for each source on a separate note card and assign each card a number: 1, 2, 3, and so on. These are called the bibliography cards. Then you take notes from your sources, writing one piece of information (one quotation or paraphrase) on each card. These are called the note cards. Write the source number and page number (if there is one) on the note card as well. Be extremely careful to add the quotation marks around the exact words you take from a source, so that you do not get confused later on, think those are your words, and unintentionally plagiarize. Making the quotation marks extremely large can help. Some students write quotes in one color pen and their own words in another color to make clear which words are theirs.

When you are planning your essay, you can move the note cards around to help you visualize how the essay might be organized. Then, when typing up the draft, add in the appropriate citations for each note, which you find by looking at the corresponding bibliography card. Make sure you include the parenthetical documentation when you write the sentence, or else you will waste time later looking it up again.

THE NOTEBOOK SYSTEM

To use a handwritten notebook system, make sure you use a clean page of your notebook for each source so that you are clear about which piece of information came from which source. At the top of the page, write the full bibliographic citation in MLA style. (Writing it up in proper style now helps you avoid the problem of leaving out information you didn't know you needed, information that might take you precious time to track down again.) Then take notes from that source—and that source only—on that page. List the page numbers directly next to each note, and copy quotations carefully. If you run onto a second page, recopy the MLA citation at the top of the page so that you don't lose the source if the pages get separated later.

ELECTRONIC NOTE-TAKING SYSTEMS

Note cards and notebooks work perfectly well, but many students become frustrated quickly with the time it takes to copy out citations and quotations, and then type them up. Since the majority of your information is accessed in an online form, you may decide to take all your notes for a project on a computer. If you have established a good system for online document management, with folders for each college course, use it to stay organized and avoid accidental plagiarism.

Here's what one student's online folders for her English course look like:

Many commercial note-taking software products are available, and they may be useful as you continue your college career. Essentially, these programs allow you to create a personal database of all the notes you have from your classes. For example, suppose you are writing an essay on twins for your English class. You would add notes on all your sources directly into the database. Then, two semesters later, when you are in a psychology class and are asked to write a research paper on twins, you can easily access those potentially useful English class notes. For students who plan to major in medical fields, this can be especially helpful, as you can track all the studies you have read and can access your notes on them later, when you start your career. If you plan to purchase note-taking software, sign up for a free trial first to make sure you like it. Also, check for educational software discounts online or at your school bookstore if you decide to purchase.

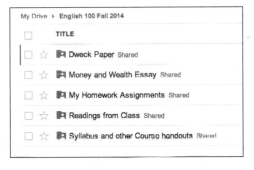

My Drive ▸ English 100 Fall 2014

TITLE

☆ 🏴 Dweck Paper Shared

☆ 🏴 Money and Wealth Essay Shared

☆ 🏴 My Homework Assignments Shared

☆ 🏴 Readings from Class Shared

☆ 🏴 Syllabus and other Course handouts Shared

Alternatively, here's an easy system for taking research notes within your word-processing program. While it may not provide a comprehensive searchable database of notes, if you organize all your course notes into folders, you will be able to access the information years later.

STEP 1: Create a folder on your computer, flash drive, or online documents storage for each class.   Label folders and subfolders clearly and consistently. For example, you might have a folder called "English 100 Fall 2014" and within that folder, subfolders for each major essay you are writing. You might have separate folders for homework, readings, and course handouts.

STEP 2: As you research additional outside sources, save PDFs or other electronic versions of articles you find, if possible, with clear document titles, like "Speaker article on Dweck Mind-Set book"   (see below).

STEP 3: For each source that you consult, create a new note-taking document and save it in the appropriate folder.   Name the document with the author's last name and a shortened version of the title of the article or book so that you will recognize it easily. For example, for the article by Carol S. Dweck called "The Perils and Promises of Praise" in Chapter 1, you might label the document "Dweck Perils and Promises of Praise NOTES" (as below) or "Dweck NOTES."

STEP 4: At the top of the note-taking document, type out the full citation in whatever bibliographic style your instructor requires (probably MLA style in an English class).   Do this now, at the beginning. Then, when it comes time to write your paper, you can copy and paste the citation into your paper and you will not be rushed. You will also know what to put into the parenthetical citations because you will have already completed your citation. The References tab in MS Word will help you create your Works Cited citation.

STEP 5: After you write up the full citation, type up your notes from that source.   If you copy and paste material from an online source, be especially careful to add quotation marks around it so you do not later think those are your own words and unintentionally plagiarize. Record page and paragraph numbers for all information from your sources, whether a

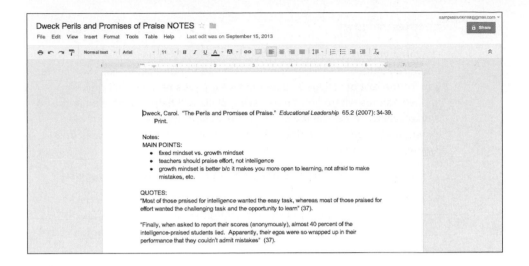

quote or something you put in your own words. If you take notes from a Web site, include the date you looked at the material (called the "access date"). As you take notes, write up all the relevant information, using questioning: Who? What? Where? When? Why? How? If you mention a person, make sure you note that person's credentials and/or area of expertise. Also be sure to spell first and last names correctly.

STEP 6: When you finish gathering notes and are ready to begin planning your paper, print out all your notes, looking for patterns and ideas. As you read and arrange the notes, use different-colored highlighters to mark different subtopics. Once you complete your outline, keep your highlighted notes on the table as you write. That way, you can copy and paste quotes and paraphrases into your paper, making sure to include the correct parenthetical citation as you do. Having the hard copy on your desk can really help you keep your thoughts organized, and you can check off information as you put it into your draft so that you do not reuse the same example or forget a point. This will save you time and ensure that you do not accidentally leave out a source, mistype a quote, or get confused about which source you are using.

practice it   Taking Notes

Check your syllabus to see the next reading assignment you have for this course. Create a note-taking document for the source and begin to take notes on it. Remember to give the document a title you'll be able to find in your computer files.

chapter review

Now that you have read Chapter 18, you are ready to become a more organized student and a better note taker. Good note taking skills will serve you for the rest of college and beyond. Many jobs require staff meetings and workshops where good note-taking skills will help you do well in the workplace. Of course, many students take good notes already, but even experienced students can find ways to improve, and college classes often require some new skills.

To review this chapter, choose one or more of the following strategies:

1. Think about the courses you are taking this term. What are the best note-taking methods for each of the different courses you are taking? How does the academic discipline of the course affect the type of notes you need to take?
2. Review your current notes for a class you are taking. What are their strengths and weaknesses? How useful will your notes be when you need to prepare for course assignments and tests? What could you do to improve your notes? Choose at least one specific suggestion from this chapter and try to apply it in the next week.
3. If you skipped any activities, do them now as a way to deepen your understanding of the material.
4. Try to explain what you have learned to someone you know. Discuss the key concepts and give your own examples to illustrate those concepts.

19
Research

in this chapter

- What Should You Look for in Source Materials?
- What Resources Can a College Library Provide?
- What Is the Role of the Internet in Academic Research?
- How Do You Work with Sources?

With the digital culture in which we now live, information is easily accessible and in many cases free. However, more access to information doesn't necessarily make researching easier. In fact, sifting through vast amounts of information—online or in a library database—can prove challenging and require more finely tuned skills. Information literacy—the ability to find, evaluate, and organize information from a wide variety of types of sources—will play a growing role in your education and professional lives. Acquiring excellent research skills begins with understanding the fundamentals of good sources, the different avenues you can use to find them, and the best way to present them in your own work.

What to Look for in Source Materials

If you are reading this chapter, either you have been assigned to write an essay that requires research or you have decided on your own to seek out extra information to flesh out the ideas in your paper. Remember that your instructor has already selected your course materials, so be sure to rely on your instructor-provided course content first, before you tackle research. Then, if there are gaps in your knowledge, or you are curious to find out more about an issue covered in your course materials, use research to supplement your evidence. As you do research, bear in mind certain key factors about the information you find: its source, credibility, relevance, and currency.

The *source* of information means simply that: Where does it come from and who wrote it or said it? With the expansion of the Internet, it can be difficult to figure out where a piece of information originated. Some sites simply plagiarize from other sources, often badly misrepresenting the information in the process. Many sites pick up information from other places and present it with an acknowledgment of where it originally appeared. In other cases, an article that is published in a scholarly journal, like *Pediatrics*, might get rewritten for a more general audience in a magazine like *Psychology Today*. Your best bet when researching information is to find the place where that information comes from, its original publication. It's sort of like that old game of telephone; when information is repeated several times, the facts become distorted.

CREDIBILITY

Credibility is the cornerstone of good research: As you look for sources, you always need to judge whether the author and publication should be trusted. Ask yourself, "What qualifications does this author have to write about this topic?" and "What kind of reputation does the publication have? Why did it publish this work?" Ideally, you will find sources where the author's background is clearly indicated, either at the start or the end of the article. If you cannot find the author's credentials, search for that person on a biographical database or the Internet. Figuring out the quality of a particular publication can be trickier. How does the *New York Times* compare to the *Toledo Blade*? An Internet search can also help here, to some extent. Research librarians and your instructor can help, too. You will also learn through experience, which you will accumulate much more quickly if you ask for help from instructors and librarians.

RELEVANCE

In research, *relevance* refers to how appropriate the information is for your project. With so much information available at our fingertips, sometimes we get fascinated by a statistic or example and want to include it, even when it might not be directly relevant to the point we are trying to support. One common problem with doing open-ended Google searches is that the search results are based on popularity, or companies pay to have their results listed first, and the top-listed search results don't always fit your topic. You have to sort through pages and pages of links to find something relevant. Learning to focus your search strategies can help solve that problem, and library databases are a great place to start.

CURRENCY

Finally, note the currency of a piece of researched information. *Currency* refers to how current, or recent, a source is. Your writing topic is important in determining currency. For instance, if you are writing about computer technology, a source that is three years old will probably be so outdated as to be completely useless, but a well-written ten-year-old book about the Civil War might be just fine.

Essentially, in the digital age, you need fairly sophisticated skills in reading and interpreting a wide variety of sources, from books to Web sites, and everything in between. As you research, annotate sources to determine their usefulness and quality, just as you would with a book or article. Use the same critical-reading strategies in choosing sources that you use in reading the texts that your instructor has selected for you.

For more on reading critically, see Chapter 2, Active and Critical Reading, page 36.

Your College Library

Your research should begin with your college library's resources, whether these are in the physical library or online. College and university libraries—also known as academic libraries—operate somewhat differently from public libraries. In your college life, you will mostly use your school's library, but you may need to supplement your research with books and articles from your public library or other academic libraries.

---

practice it   **Web Resources**

Visit the following important Web sites and bookmark them for quick reference.

Your college library
Your public library or libraries
Nearby academic libraries, especially those that have an exchange with your campus
WorldCat: www.worldcat.org (WorldCat allows you to search worldwide library catalogs simultaneously.)

Take a library tour, if one is available, whether your instructor requires it or not. It's best to take your tour early in the semester, before you are in a big rush to finish a major project. Take the time to get familiar with the layout of the place and you will feel far more comfortable doing research there. Many libraries offer research orientations online or in person, so ask about this while you visit the library. Also, freshen up your knowledge of your library from time to time. Information databases are always changing, and as you progress in your education, you will be required to consult more and more specialized resources. So in the beginning of your college career, you will use some of the more general materials, such as the ProQuest or EBSCO periodical databases, but as you move into your field of study, you need to learn more about the specialized resources the library offers.

The college library offers many resources for research:

- **Books** are usually available on open library shelves, but special or rare books might be held in special collections, which you can access by permission. Some colleges have e-books that you can electronically check out to download or read on e-readers. Most colleges offer

Interlibrary Loan to get books you need from other libraries, though there may be a fee for this service. If you need a book that your college does not have, it is usually best to also check your local public library or other area academic libraries for it first. You can use WorldCat to do that.

- **Media,** including movies, television shows, taped lectures, music, and sometimes even art works or other artifacts, are often available for check out. Find out whether there are separate catalogs that you have to check to find these materials.

- **Periodicals** include newspapers, magazines, and scholarly journals. Increasingly, we access most of these materials in an online format through a periodical database. ProQuest, EBSCOhost, SIRS, JSTOR, and Project MUSE are examples of databases to which your school might subscribe. What this means is that the college pays a fee so that students can quickly and easily locate information on and, often, gain online access to articles that were published in many different newspapers, magazines, or journals. Specialized databases in specific disciplines— like ProQuest Nursing & Allied Health Source, PsycARTICLES, or Literature Resource Center—will be important as you do more advanced research in your field of study. Take time to visit your library or go online to see which databases your school provides and how to access them. You will probably need to log in with a student ID or library card to gain access. Your school may offer an orientation to the databases or an online tutorial.

- In addition to being a place to find information, your school's library is a great place to study, work on group projects with other students, use a computer on campus, or get reserve materials, which are books, articles, or other course materials, such as videos, sample tests, and class notes, that your instructor has provided. Usually you can check these out for a specified period, from an hour to a day or two. This system allows many students to share the materials fairly. Ask your instructors if they have put any materials on reserve for your classes.

practice it   Tour Your College Library

Many people are nervous about going to new places. Your college library might seem huge, and you might worry that you'll have trouble finding what you need in it. Find a map of your library, either at the library or on its Web site. Scan the map to get a general sense of what the different sections of your college library are and where they are located. Once you have an idea of where things are, visit the library for a half hour or so. Make sure that during your visit you learn how to check out a book, find course reserves, and get access to articles.

The Role of the Internet in Academic Research

The best thing about the Internet is that it offers so much free information. The worst thing about the Internet is that it offers so much free information. Anyone can create a Web site, but relatively few sites are worthwhile. Often, a Google search of the open Web (that is, the nonsubscription, freely accessible portions of the Internet) returns too many sites to sort through efficiently, so inexperienced researchers end up just following the top few results, which do not necessarily provide credible or relevant information.

When you have a question that requires research, it's tempting to turn on your computer or smartphone or tablet, type a phrase into Google, and consider your research done. The truth is, all of us—and certainly the authors of this book—use this research strategy for some purposes every day, and that's okay. An expert researcher, though, knows when a quick search is adequate—like when you can't remember particular dates from the U.S. Civil War—and when it isn't. For any academic project that requires research, you'll need to hunt for and evaluate a variety of relevant sources before considering your research complete.

Your best tools as a college researcher are the online periodical databases, like ProQuest, JSTOR, and Opposing Viewpoints, to which your college library subscribes. Learning to use these databases well saves you time and gives you access to a wider array of credible resources than you can find through a Google search. Online periodical databases comb through millions of articles—many of which are not freely accessible through an Internet search—and organize them in a clear, easily searchable way. They also eliminate most of the questionable sources that pop up in a random online search. Think of it this way: If a group of experts were willing to search all the source material on the Internet and present you with the best sources, wouldn't you be happy to let them?

Evaluating Web Sources

When you do go to the open Web for information, take particular care in examining the information's quality and credibility. First, look at the site's title, sponsor, and URL. For many Web sites, the extension (the last three letters of the URL) gives clues about the type of organization or person that created the site. Here are a few common examples:

.com = commercial, for-profit organization, which refers to a profit-making business (such as adweek.com or amazon.com)
.edu = educational organization (such as your college)
.gov = government organization (such as census.gov, the Web site for the U.S. Census)

TIP

Be particularly careful if you're thinking of citing a blog. Blogs can look professional, and might be hosted by a newspaper or magazine site, but they are not always checked by editors or other experts to verify facts or review claims. If you want to cite a blog, do some research on the blog's author first. It's also a good idea to search for a source that confirms the information in a database like EBSCOhost.

.org = charitable or nonprofit organization (such as www.lls.org, for the
  Leukemia and Lymphoma Society)
.net = network (such as an Internet service provider)
.mil = military organization (such as the U.S. Army)

Web sites with any of these extensions might be good sources in the right context, but be aware of any political or profit motive behind a Web site. Information from a government or nonprofit organization might be more objective than that from a commercial Web site, particularly about topics such as product safety. Information on Web sites ending in .edu may be credible information from academic professionals, but students can sometimes have Web sites with .edu URLs, and teachers sometimes post student projects and assignments on their class Web pages. Elementary and high schools also generally have an .edu extension, so it doesn't necessarily indicate a college or university. So follow the usual process of evaluating the information, even with an .edu URL.

In addition to a site's URL, look for other clues about credibility. Ask the same questions about Web sources as you would about any sources: Is the author some sort of expert? Does he or she provide a list of sources and references (a bibliography)? Is the information on the site confirmed by other sources? Are there any obvious errors on the site? What sorts of biases might the Web site or author have? College instructors usually prefer to see sources from reputable nonprofit organizations, like the American Academy of Pediatrics or the U.S. Department of Energy, rather than commercial sites, like BabyCenter or Solar Power USA.

Another part of evaluating sources is evaluating their currency. Find out how recently the Web site has been updated. Page or site updates are often listed at the bottom of a Web site; article dates tend to be under the article title. If no dates are given on the Web site or the article within the Web site, the absence of a date should make you suspicious.

Sometimes you find online information that appears useful, but you can't find enough background knowledge to determine whether it's credible. There are a few strategies, though, to help you figure this out:

- Ask whether the site was recommended to you by an expert. Did your instructor or textbook refer to it? Was it listed as a resource in another reputable source? (Chapters 21–23 list several of the best Web sites on the topics covered in those chapters; those sites would be good places to start.)
- Look carefully at the area of the Web site that lists information about the sponsoring organization—usually in a tab labeled "About Us" or a link through the name of the organization. Is the organization endorsed by other reputable groups? Is it for profit or not? What is its purpose in providing this information?
- Ask the reference librarian in your college library to look at the Web site if you are really stuck. Some libraries even have an online chat feature,

TIP
The fact is, usually you can find similar information on more than one Web site if you look. Frequently, the same article is reposted on many different sites. Because the information is more likely to be accurate, your credibility increases if you quote or paraphrase from the *original* place of publication, rather than, say, a reposting on someone's blog or another Web site.

or a twenty-four-hour "ask a librarian" service, so you can send a librarian the link, explain your topic, and ask if the site is a good one. If it isn't a good source, he or she may even have time to point you to better ones.

Let's look at a sample from the Web site of the American Academy of Pediatrics:

For most credible Web sites, at the bottom of their home page is a link to the site map, and information about the sponsoring organization.

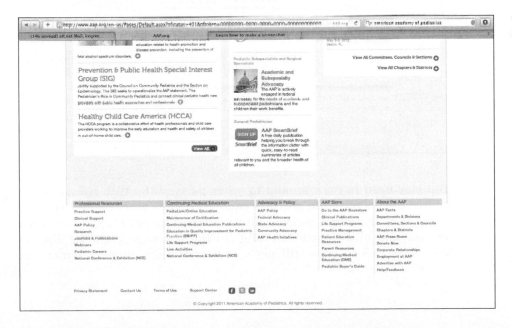

Now look at the home page for the American Montessori Society, an educational organization. Think about the perspective that is represented here. What sorts of biases are probably reflected in articles from this Web site? Does the possibility of bias rule it out as a source in your research? How might you read articles from this Web site with and against the grain in order to determine their usefulness for your research?

For a review of reading with and against the grain, see Chapter 2, Active and Critical Reading, page 36.

You may need to click around to other parts of the Web site to determine if the organization provides enough credible and current research. If you do click around, you will find a thorough bibliography of research sources and other documentation, so the research might be fine to use. Nevertheless, you still need to acknowledge in your paper the perspective, or bias, of the source. Obviously, this organization will emphasize the strengths, not the problems, with the Montessori method of education.

Here's a closer look at one article titled the "Benefits of Montessori" from the Web site:

For details on the various
methods of note-taking,
consult Chapter 18, Note
Taking, page 339.

practice it   Evaluating Web Sites for Bias

Look at the following Web sites:

> www.adweek.com
> www.pbs.org/wgbh/pages/frontline/view
> www.councilforeconed.org
> www.monacaron.com
> www.nea.org

What kinds of biases, or perspectives, might each of these sites have?
How might you acknowledge the perspective of the source if you were
to use a quotation or paraphrase from it in an essay? Where might you
go to find other articles that would balance the perspective?

Working with Sources

Once you locate sources that are credible, relevant, and current, you need
to be organized when taking notes so that you do not accidentally plagiarize, and so that you do not waste precious minutes of your life tracking
down a source that you had in your hand or on your computer screen a
week ago. Whether you use a note card system, a notebook, or an electronic
style of organization, be consistent. Good research-organization habits
save you hours of time in the long run and prepare you well for any future
profession.

For more on PIE paragraph
structure, see Chapter 12,
Topic Sentences and
Paragraphs, page 253.

Remember that research should yield evidence that supports the
points you make in your writing. Research supplies the I in the PIE body
paragraph structure.

Good writers adapt their views based on the research they find, but
do not lose their own sense of style, perspective, or voice. Make sure your
sources do not "take over" your paper. Avoid long blocks of quotations
unless they are absolutely necessary, and be sure to integrate source
material effectively and to quote document source material correctly.
Research, when done well, can be one of the most fun parts of writing.
Enjoy all the resources at your fingertips!

For more on using
quotations, see Chapter 16,
Quotation and Paraphrase,
page 307.

For more on documenting
sources, see Chapter 20,
MLA Documentation,
page 362.

chapter review

Becoming a skilled researcher serves you well in all aspects of your life, particularly as the digital age provides us with more and more information to navigate. The difference between adequate and excellent research often translates directly into your paper grades as you take more advanced courses, so it's crucial that you use the strategies provided in Chapter 19 to begin to build these information literacy skills now.

To review this chapter, choose one or more of the following strategies:

1. Review your college library's home page to determine where you might go for research in each of the classes you are taking this term.
2. Evaluate a Web site that you used recently for a college assignment. How credible is it? How do you know?
3. If you skipped any activities, do them now as a way to deepen your understanding of the material.
4. Explain what you learned, or at least part of it, to someone you know. Explain the key concepts and give some of your own examples to illustrate those concepts.

20
MLA Documentation

in this chapter

- How Does Citing Sources Increase Your Credibility?
- What Are the Three Components of MLA Format?
- How Do You Create a Template for Your MLA Research Paper?
- When Should You Make Your Works Cited Page?
- How Do You Cite Sources in the Body of Your Paper?

MLA stands for the Modern Language Association, an organization made up of professors, writers, and graduate students working in English, foreign languages, and the humanities. Usually, students in English classes learn MLA style for documenting sources because it is one of the simplest and most common systems. You may use other documentation methods, such as APA (American Psychological Association) style, in a health sciences or social science class down the road. Always check with your instructor to make sure you use the documentation style required.

Why, you might wonder, do you need to use a standard style of documentation? For the same reasons that we use standards in anything. When a recipe calls for a cup of sugar, we all know how much sugar that means. If ten different recipes each meant something different by "one cup," then coming up with edible results would be much harder. Similarly, standard rules for formatting a document and including references to sources help the writer and the reader communicate effectively and efficiently. This is especially necessary because so many sources are online, and merely listing the author and title of an article won't give the reader enough information to find the correct version of it.

Your main goal in using any system of documentation (MLA, APA, or any other) is to show your readers exactly where you got any information from outside sources that you include in your paper. Proper documentation provides readers with all they need to find the articles, books, Web sites, or other materials you refer to in your paper. Not providing such information makes it look like you are plagiarizing, or trying to pass off other people's ideas as your own.

This chapter explains the basics of MLA style as simply as possible. As you move on in college, you might need other, more detailed guides to MLA style, but this chapter will get you on the right track.

Citation and Credibility

Once you master the nuts and bolts of MLA style—or any style you are assigned to use—you will come to appreciate how it helps increase your credibility as a writer. Credibility means believability—essentially, if you are a credible writer, your reader believes that you are fairly and accurately representing the ideas of others. Using sources well demonstrates that you have done your homework on the topic, and it builds your reader's trust. Shoddy or sloppy use of MLA style can leave readers wondering, "What else did this person get wrong? If this author can't even remember to put down the source's page number, should I trust that this person got the information right?"

At worst, making an error or leaving something out of a citation leaves you open to the charge of plagiarism, which means that you have unfairly copied someone else's ideas and presented them as your own. Plagiarism is a serious offense, and you can earn a zero or "failing grade" on an assignment or, in severe cases, be expelled from college for plagiarizing. Mastering the rules of MLA style allows you to integrate material from outside sources correctly and confidently into your writing.

A NOTE ABOUT PLAGIARISM

Clearly, intentionally copying and taking credit for someone else's work or buying a paper off the Internet is plagiarism, and it's wrong. Why, then, do good students sometimes do bad things? Sometimes, students experience anxiety about their ability to do well in a course, and think someone else's work will be better than their own. Other times, students—not you, of course!—procrastinate on an assignment and then search the Web for "ideas" and end up taking information from a Web site without properly documenting it or worse, without documenting at all. Other students may have seen cheating in high schools—or in the "real" world around them—and figure that "everyone else is doing it."

Here's a news flash, though: Most colleges and universities have much stricter policies about plagiarism than high schools. Consequences for plagiarizing might be earning a failing grade or receiving no credit on an assignment or failing an entire course. So be ethical, do the right thing, and realize that plagiarism in college has serious repercussions. You can do well in college based on your own work if you give yourself a chance. Good study skills and time-management techniques should reduce your anxiety about doing well and give you a buffer against any crisis that life throws your way, and learning proper MLA documentation will enable you to use additional material credibly. Still, there might be a time that you feel like the only option is to cheat. It's not. Go to your instructor, explain your situation without trying to make excuses for yourself, and ask for a reasonable extension with a reasonable penalty. If your instructor won't make accommodations—and he or she does not have to do so—then chalk it up to a life lesson learned. Plagiarizing will haunt you far more than one bad grade on an assignment, and it could cost you your college career.

The Three Components of MLA Format

MLA style has three major components: document format, the Works Cited page, and in-text (parenthetical) citation. Let's take a quick look at each part:

1. **Document format** refers to the design and layout of your document. This includes margins, spacing, page numbers, and headings.
2. The **Works Cited page** lists all the sources you referred to in the paper, with all the information readers would need to find your sources. Note that this list does not include all the sources you might have casually looked at while writing the paper; it includes just the ones you actually quoted, paraphrased, or summarized in the paper.
3. **In-text (parenthetical) citation** refers to the source information you add, in parentheses, following material that you've found in an outside source. This information leads your reader to one of your Works Cited entries, and to the particular page/section (if available) where you found the material.

Let's look at a sample paper to see the various parts:

Your last name and the page number go in the upper right. Use the "insert page number" and "header" functions in your word-processing program.

The entire text is double-spaced. Use an easy-to-read font such as Times New Roman.

Smith 1

Sally Smith

Professor Green

English 100

20 April 2014

When Siblings Grow Up

Hollywood loves siblings who fight. In *Brothers*, Captain Sam Cahill (Tobey Maguire) and his brother, Tommy (Jake Gyllenhaal), both are in love with Sam's wife. In *Rachel Getting Married*,

Smith 2

recovering drug addict Kym (Anne Hathaway) seems to want to wreck the wedding of her sister, Rachel (Rosemarie DeWitt). Movies about siblings almost always have the obligatory scene of the two brothers duking it out or the two sisters hurling insults and ending up in tears. Watching such dramatic scenes, one wonders if all adult siblings are doomed to bad relationships, and if all pairs of siblings end up as opposites. While stormy sibling relationships make for great movie drama, many siblings have successful relationships as adults. How do they do it? Siblings can have strong adult relationships if they start off well in childhood and continue to nurture their relationship as they grow older.

Most people envision that the path to family harmony is to minimize arguments when children are little. Good intentions might actually undermine the sibling relationship, though. Ironically, young siblings who barely fight may not be on the path to a happy adult relationship. Researchers who study sibling interaction have observed that playing and fighting makes siblings friends as adults, and that young "siblings who simply ignored each other had less fighting, but their relationship stayed cold and distant long term" (Bronson and Merryman 426). So while all the arguments about whose turn it is or who got more might drive parents crazy at times, siblings who take the time to argue it out as children often end up with more positive communication as adults.

As siblings grow into adults, one of the major hurdles they face has to do with the roles they had as children and their ability to relate outside those roles. As Jane Mersky Leder writes, "Our siblings push buttons that cast us in roles we felt sure we had let go of long ago—the baby, the peacekeeper, the caretaker, the avoider" (383). Even if we as adults have outgrown those roles, when we step into the house we grew up in, we are seen and even sometimes act in ways that we did as children. Our siblings, who

Smith 3

usually outlive our parents, have a huge impact on our sense of self: "Our brothers and sisters bring us face to face with our former selves and remind us how intricately bound up we are in each other's lives" (Leder 383). Sometimes that former self is not someone we want to know anymore—as was the case of Kym, the recovering drug addict in *Rachel Getting Married*, who wanted so badly to move beyond her addiction but would always be seen with a certain amount of suspicion by her family.

Family harmony is possible, once you realize that "harmony" doesn't mean the absence of all arguments. Getting conflicts out in the open and working them through is important. We learn how to do that as children, if our parents don't step in to solve our problems for us. However, we need to keep practicing it as adults, and we need to allow our siblings to change and grow. Good sibling relationships might not make their way into a movie script, but most of us would probably prefer them to the storminess of the popular images.

This sentence summarizes a movie, but movies do not have page numbers, so there is no parenthetical citation. The source is included in the Works Cited list, though.

Smith 4

Works Cited

Bronson, Po, and Ashley Merryman. "The Sibling Effect." *Read, Write, Connect: A Guide to College Reading and Writing.* Eds. Kathleen Green and Amy Lawlor. Boston: Bedford, 2014. 423–33. Print.

Brothers. Dir. Jim Sheridan. Perf. Jake Gyllenhaal, Natalie Portman, and Tobey Maguire. Lionsgate, 2009. Film.

Leder, Jane Mersky. "Close Encounters of a Special Kind." *Read, Write, Connect: A Guide to College Reading and Writing.* Eds. Kathleen Green and Amy Lawlor. Boston: Bedford, 2014. 382–93. Print.

Rachel Getting Married. Dir. Jonathan Demme. Perf. Anne Hathaway, Rosemarie DeWitt, and Debra Winger. Sony, 2008. Film.

The Works Cited page starts on a new page, with the title "Works Cited" centered.

The Works Cited page lists all sources you quote or paraphrase in the paper. The citations give the reader enough information to find the sources mentioned in the paper. The Works Cited page is not very different from a bibliography.

DOCUMENT FORMAT

Computers are wonderful things, and, if you use yours wisely, you only have to set up your MLA document format once in your entire college life. If you are unfamiliar with word-processing basics, like how to set the margins on a document and insert a page number, you should go to the computer lab with this book and have a lab assistant—or even just the student sitting next to you—help you set up an MLA template.

Your first task in mastering MLA style is to create a document in your computer files that you title "MLA Template." Set this up as a blank sample paper, and then every time you need to write an essay for your English class, you will open up the document, use it to type your essay, and re-save it under a different name. That way, your template will always be there, and you never have to worry about setting the margins or font again. If you do not have a preinstalled MLA template in your word-processing program, follow these steps, in this order:

1. Open a new document.
2. Change the document line spacing to 2 to double-space the entire document. You will never change this because MLA uses only double spacing.
3. Set the margins at 1 inch on top, bottom, left, and right.
4. Change the font to 12-point Times New Roman. You should not use different or fancy fonts to try to make your work unique. Times New Roman translates universally among computer programs with no problems. Stick to it.
5. Create a header for the document that has your last name, a space, and then the page number. If you don't know how to do automatic page numbering in your word-processing program, ask someone or use the Help function. Do not type the number "1" on the first page; if you do, "1" will appear as the number on all the pages.
6. On the top left of the first page only, type the following:

   Your name
   Instructor's name
   Course title
   Date

7. Type the words "Title Goes Here" centered, and then hit "enter" or "return" once. Do not use bold, underlining, or quotation marks for your title.
8. Set up a tab to indent paragraphs ½ inch.
9. Hit "enter" or "return" a few times.
10. Insert a page break.
11. Type the words "Works Cited" centered at the top of the page. Do not use bold, underlining, or quotation marks for these words.

12. Set up your ruler or tabs for the Works Cited page so that the first line of each new paragraph starts at the left margin and all following lines indent five spaces. (This is the exact reverse of a normal paragraph.) To set the ruler, you need to see it. Generally, find the "View" drop-down menu and select "Print Layout."
13. Save the document as "MLA Template."
14. Whenever you write a paper, open this document, type in your current instructor's name and your current class number, add your new title, and begin to write your paper. Make sure you "save as" a different title so that you do not save over your MLA template.

The final product should look like the sample on pages 364–66, so check yours against that example to see if you did everything correctly.

Done correctly and used regularly, the template should prevent mistakes in MLA document format. Your work will look professional instead of sloppy. Once the document format is out of the way, you can focus on the more important task of citing your outside sources properly.

practice it   Creating a Template for an MLA Paper

Set up an online template for a sample MLA paper, and save it in an appropriate folder on your computer or online file management system.

THE WORKS CITED PAGE

Most people think that the Works Cited page should be completed last because it always appears as the last page of the paper. Wrong! Creating your Works Cited page as you gather information, and before you even start to write your rough draft, saves you lots of time in the end. How do we know this? We have seen literally thousands of students over the years waste precious minutes, hours, and sometimes even days of their lives trying to track down the correct information for a source that they had in their hands previously. We have also seen students struggle to figure out in-text parenthetical documentation, when it's relatively simple if you do your Works Cited page first. Countless students turn in sloppy work, which destroys their credibility, because they rush to do the Works Cited page at the last minute.

Understanding the Elements of the Works Cited Page.   What do you put on the Works Cited page, and what does it look like? Let's take a closer look at the Works Cited page of our short example paper from page 366:

Smith 3

Works Cited

Bronson, Po, and Ashley Merryman. "The Sibling Effect." *Read,*
    Write, Connect: A Guide to College Reading and Writing. Eds.
    Kathleen Green and Amy Lawlor. Boston: Bedford, 2014.
    423–33. Print.

Brothers. Dir. Jim Sheridan. Perf. Jake Gyllenhaal, Natalie Portman,
    and Tobey Maguire. Lionsgate, 2009. Film.

Leder, Jane Mersky. "Close Encounters of a Special Kind." *Read,*
    Write, Connect: A Guide to College Reading and Writing.
    Eds. Kathleen Green and Amy Lawlor. Boston: Bedford, 2014.
    382–93. Print.

Rachel Getting Married. Dir. Jonathan Demme. Perf. Anne Hathaway,
    Rosemarie DeWitt, and Debra Winger. Sony, 2008. Film.

Use the ruler toolbar to adjust the indentation.

List each source only once, even if you use it more than once.

Citations differ but they all have the same type of information, like titles and publication dates.

Bronson, Po, and Ashley Merryman. "The Sibling Effect." *Read,*
    Write, Connect: A Guide to College Reading and Writing. Eds.
    Kathleen Green and Amy Lawlor. Boston: Bedford, 2014.
    423–33. Print.

Start with the authors' names and article title.

List the full title and subtitle of the book the article is taken from.

Give the names of the book editors if they differ from the author.

Creating Your Own Works Cited Page.

Ready to give it a try with your sources? Follow the steps below.

STEP 1: Gather the sources you think you will use in your paper. (If you create a citation for a source and end up not using it, that's good practice. Just delete it from your final version of your paper.)

STEP 2: Open up your MLA template document and save it under the name of your new essay, such as "Fame Essay 1" or "Siblings Essay" or whatever your title or topic might be.

STEP 3: Go to the Works Cited page you created. The margins, spacing, and ruler should already be set up properly.

STEP 4: Type up the citation for each of your sources, following the sample formats on pages 370–74.

List the city and year of publication, and the name of the publisher. You'll find this information on the first pages of the book.

Note whether the source is print, Web, film, or some other medium.

STEP 5: Drag and drop to put your citations in alphabetical order after you are sure you have the format for each citation correct.

Sample Formats for Works Cited Citations. Works Cited citations are basically broken down into several categories:

- Books
- Newspaper, journal, and magazine articles
- Web and electronic sources
- Articles and other materials that you get from a database, like ProQuest, EBSCOhost, ERIC, or SIRS from your college library
- Media sources
- Other (for example, interviews, drawings, and performances)

Examples of some of the most common types of citations appear on the following pages.

Print Books and Articles. Sometimes you will have a book or article in a physical form. These Works Cited citations are the simplest.

TIP

Most newer word-processing programs will format citations for you, once you enter basic source information, but the result is often incorrect. Make sure the program is based on the most recent version of the *MLA Handbook for Writers of Research Papers*. Software commonly makes errors such as not properly capitalizing titles, giving too much information, and including the URL for Web sources. Remember, you are responsible for the accuracy of your citations; you can't blame the computer for getting it wrong.

BOOK

Author, Last Name First	Book Title, Italicized	City of Publication

Shell, Ellen Ruppel. *Cheap: The High Cost of Discount Culture*. New York:

Publisher	Date	Medium

Penguin, 2009. Print.

ARTICLE IN AN ANTHOLOGY OR TEXTBOOK

Author of Selection, Last Name First	Title of Selection, in Quotation Marks	Title of Anthology, Italicized

Bohjalian, Chris. "My Brother's a Keeper." *Brothers: 26 Stories of Love and*

	Editor(s) of Anthology, Name(s) in Normal Order	City of Publication	Publisher	Date	Pages of Selection

Rivalry. Ed. Andrew Blauner. San Francisco: Jossey-Bass, 2009. 91–96.

Medium

Print.

NEWSPAPER ARTICLE

Author, Last Name First	Second Author, in Normal Order	Article Title, in Quotation Marks

Braudy, Leo, and Michael Cieply. "Hollywood's High-Powered Image

	Newspaper Title, Italicized	Date: Day + Month + Year	Page	Medium

Machine." *Los Angeles Times* 10 July 1988: 10A. Print.

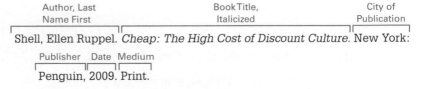

MAGAZINE ARTICLE

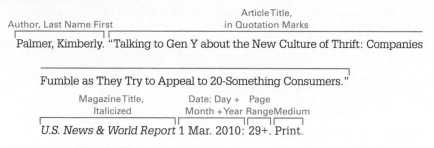

Author, Last Name First   Article Title, in Quotation Marks

Palmer, Kimberly. "Talking to Gen Y about the New Culture of Thrift: Companies

Fumble as They Try to Appeal to 20-Something Consumers."

Magazine Title, Italicized   Date: Day + Month + Year   Page Range   Medium

U.S. News & World Report 1 Mar. 2010: 29+. Print.

SCHOLARLY JOURNAL ARTICLE

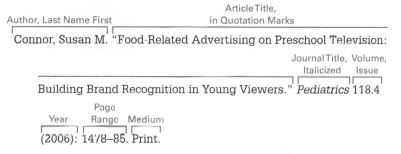

Author, Last Name First   Article Title, in Quotation Marks

Connor, Susan M. "Food-Related Advertising on Preschool Television:

Journal Title, Italicized   Volume, Issue

Building Brand Recognition in Young Viewers." *Pediatrics* 118.4

Year   Page Range   Medium

(2006): 1478–85. Print.

Online Books and Articles. More often than not, though, you will access articles and other sources online. You need to show that in your citations, generally by replacing the word "Print" with "Web." Notice, however, that it also makes a difference where online you got the article. Specifically, did you get it just by searching through a Web browser, or did you find it by going through a paid subscription database, like ProQuest or SIRS? Take a look at these examples:

ONLINE BOOK

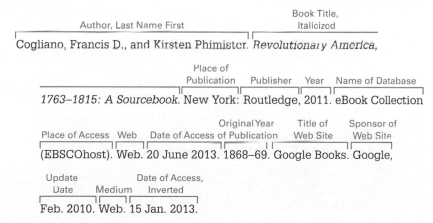

Author, Last Name First   Book Title, Italicized

Cogliano, Francis D., and Kirsten Phimister. *Revolutionary America,*

Place of Publication   Publisher   Year   Name of Database

1763–1815: A Sourcebook. New York: Routledge, 2011. eBook Collection

Place of Access   Web   Date of Access   Original Year of Publication   Title of Web Site   Sponsor of Web Site

(EBSCOhost). Web. 20 June 2013. 1868–69. Google Books. Google,

Update Date   Medium   Date of Access, Inverted

Feb. 2010. Web. 15 Jan. 2013.

ONLINE NEWSPAPER ARTICLE ON THE NEWSPAPER'S WEB SITE

Author, Last Name First	Article Title, in Quotation Marks	Title of Online Newspaper, Italicized	Sponsor or Publisher

Banks, Sandy. "Where Poor Students Soar." *LATimes.com. Los Angeles Times*,

Date of Publication, Inverted	Medium	Date of Access, Inverted

5 Nov. 2011. Web. 15 Jan. 2013.

ONLINE NEWSPAPER ARTICLE FROM A DATABASE

Note that in the following example, Newspaper Source Plus is a part of EBSCOhost.

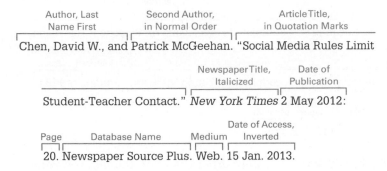

Author, Last Name First	Second Author, in Normal Order	Article Title, in Quotation Marks

Chen, David W., and Patrick McGeehan. "Social Media Rules Limit

	Newspaper Title, Italicized	Date of Publication

Student-Teacher Contact." *New York Times* 2 May 2012:

Page	Database Name	Medium	Date of Access, Inverted

20. Newspaper Source Plus. Web. 15 Jan. 2013.

Web Sites.   Another frequently used type of source is a Web site. The content and format of your citation will vary, depending on whether you are using just one page or article from the Web site or clicking around to various places in the site. Note the abbreviation "n.d." in one of the entries below: This stands for "no date." If you can't find any information about a source or sponsor, use the abbreviation "n.p." for "no publisher."

SINGLE PAGE FROM A WEB SITE

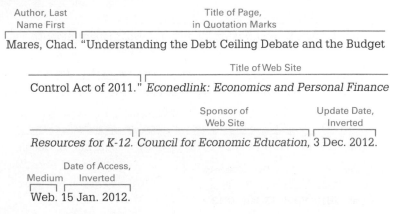

Author, Last Name First	Title of Page, in Quotation Marks

Mares, Chad. "Understanding the Debt Ceiling Debate and the Budget

	Title of Web Site

Control Act of 2011." *Econedlink: Economics and Personal Finance*

	Sponsor of Web Site	Update Date, Inverted

Resources for K-12. Council for Economic Education, 3 Dec. 2012.

Medium	Date of Access, Inverted

Web. 15 Jan. 2012.

ENTIRE WEB SITE

Organization Name | Title of Web Site | Update Date, Inverted

U.S. Department of Commerce. *United States Census Bureau*. n.d.

Medium | Date of Access, Inverted

Web. 15 Jan. 2013.

Other Sources

FILM

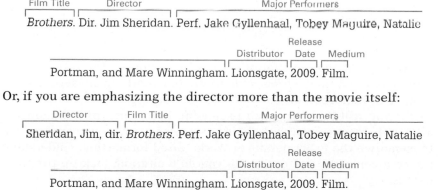

Film Title | Director | Major Performers

Brothers. Dir. Jim Sheridan. Perf. Jake Gyllenhaal, Tobey Maguire, Natalie

Distributor | Release Date | Medium

Portman, and Mare Winningham. Lionsgate, 2009. Film.

Or, if you are emphasizing the director more than the movie itself:

Director | Film Title | Major Performers

Sheridan, Jim, dir. *Brothers*. Perf. Jake Gyllenhaal, Tobey Maguire, Natalie

Distributor | Release Date | Medium

Portman, and Mare Winningham. Lionsgate, 2009. Film.

RADIO SHOW

For radio and television shows, the narrator, writer, director, producer, or star is often significant. Include this key additional information as shown in the examples below.

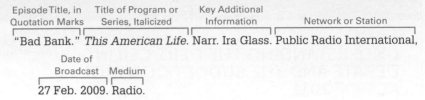

EpisodeTitle, in   Title of Program or   Key Additional
Quotation Marks   Series, Italicized   Information   Network or Station

"Bad Bank." *This American Life*. Narr. Ira Glass. Public Radio International,

Date of
Broadcast   Medium

27 Feb. 2009. Radio.

RADIO SHOW ACCESSED ONLINE

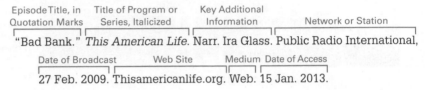

EpisodeTitle, in   Title of Program or   Key Additional
Quotation Marks   Series, Italicized   Information   Network or Station

"Bad Bank." *This American Life*. Narr. Ira Glass. Public Radio International,

Date of Broadcast   Web Site   Medium Date of Access

27 Feb. 2009. Thisamericanlife.org. Web. 15 Jan. 2013.

TELEVISION SHOW ACCESSED ONLINE

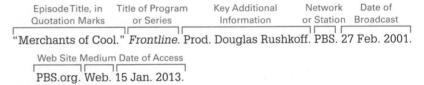

EpisodeTitle, in   Title of Program   Key Additional   Network   Date of
Quotation Marks   or Series   Information   or Station Broadcast

"Merchants of Cool." *Frontline*. Prod. Douglas Rushkoff. PBS. 27 Feb. 2001.

Web Site Medium Date of Access

PBS.org. Web. 15 Jan. 2013.

INTERVIEW YOU CONDUCTED PERSONALLY

Subject of Interview,
Last Name First   Date of Interview

Shepherd, Trixie. Personal interview. 15 Sept. 2013.

This list of sample citations is hardly complete. The official *MLA Handbook for Writers of Research Papers* (currently in its seventh edition) lists hundreds of samples, and at some point in your college career you will probably need to refer to it or some other handbook. MLA style may seem overwhelming, but remember, no one expects you to memorize the exact details of Works Cited formatting. Understand the core concepts, and each time you do a citation, look up the finer details.

Formatting Titles

When you are learning to cite sources in MLA style, formatting titles correctly can sometimes be challenging. Here are some tips:

- Big things are italicized. Little things go in quotation marks. So a book title is italicized, and the title of a chapter from a book—which is smaller than a book—goes in quotation marks. A CD title is italicized; a song title goes in quotation marks.
- If you italicize a title in your Works Cited list, then you should italicize it everywhere in the paper, any time you mention it, even in parenthetical documentation. The same goes for titles that are in quotation marks.
- Whether the document or book in front of you capitalizes all the letters in a title, capitalizes none of them, or makes the letters out of elbow macaroni, you should use what are called "title caps" for all titles all the time. This means that you capitalize the first word and all the big words in a title, and you capitalize the first word and all the big words in a subtitle.
- Just type the title of your own paper in regular 12-point Times New Roman with title caps. Don't use a fancy font, a bigger font, bold, underlining, or italics.
- Errors with titles drive most instructors batty for some reason. Take time to do titles correctly, and your instructors will look kindly on you.

---

practice it   Creating a Sample Works Cited Page

Practice doing a sample Works Cited citation for two or three of the sources you think you might use in your essay. Handwrite or type them clearly, with proper margins and spacing. Ask your instructor or a tutor to check them for accuracy.

IN-TEXT (PARENTHETICAL) CITATION

The third component of MLA style, in-text (parenthetical) citation, is truly the most important from a writing perspective because the information you put into the parentheses at the end of your sentences communicates the most to the reader. The basic concept of MLA style is that when a reader reaches a passage in an essay that includes information (a quotation, paraphrase, or summary) that the writer found in another source, the writer will at this point let the reader know where the information comes from. To do this, the writer puts the information in parentheses.

For example, here's an original passage taken from the article "The Perils and Promises of Praise" by Carol S. Dweck:

> We often hear these days that we've produced a generation of young people who can't get through the day without an award. They expect success because they're special, not because they've worked hard.
>
> Is this true? Have we inadvertently done something to hold back our students?
>
> I think educators commonly hold two beliefs that do just that. Many believe that (1) praising students' intelligence builds their confidence and motivation to learn, and (2) students' inherent intelligence is the major cause of their achievement in school. Our research has shown that the first belief is false and that the second can be harmful—even for the most competent students.

This article is one of many in an anthology, in this case your textbook, which has page numbers. This article has an author and a title. The citation in the Works Cited page would look like this:

> Dweck, Carol S. "The Perils and Promises of Praise." *Read, Write, Connect: A Guide to College Reading and Writing*. Eds. Kathleen Green and Amy Lawlor. Boston: Bedford, 2014. 6–13. Print.

Now, let's say we want to include a quotation from the article in an essay. The sentence might look like this if we want to emphasize the idea that Dweck is the author of the article being quoted:

> Educational psychologist Carol S. Dweck's research shows that many teachers are wrong when they think that "praising students' intelligence builds their confidence and motivation to learn" (6).

Or the sentence could look like this if we don't want to emphasize Dweck herself, but care more about the date that the study was originally done:

> A groundbreaking study published in 2007 suggests that teachers do more harm than good by "praising students' intelligence" (Dweck 6).

What do you notice? In both examples, we use Dweck's name and the page number. The only difference is that in the first example, we include Dweck's name in the sentence, so we don't need to repeat it in the parentheses. In the second example, we don't include Dweck's name in the sentence, but we include it in the parentheses, so that the reader can locate the source on the Works Cited page. We don't include any other publication information, nor do we use "page" or "p." or "pg." Simple, right?

Remember, the key to MLA style is that when the reader notices the source name, he or she can flip back to the Works Cited page (which is conveniently alphabetized and designed to make finding the names easy) for more information about the source. Either in your sentence or in your parentheses—or some combination—you need to provide your reader with the first word in the Works Cited list. If the source has a page number, that has to go into parentheses. Never introduce a quote by saying "On page 3 of her article, . . ." The fact that the quote is on page 3 does not add useful information to the meaning of your sentence, so you always keep the page number in the parentheses.

To review again, in the second example, why did we choose to put "Dweck" in the parentheses? Why not the title of the article? Or the title of the book in which it was published? The answer is simple, and it is the basic rule of MLA style:

> **In your sentence and/or parenthetical reference, you need to include the first word(s) in the Works Cited citation.**

Usually, the first word is an author's last name, but sometimes it's the first word(s) in the title, if the article has no author. That's why you should create the Works Cited page first: so you know what you need to put in the parentheses as you write, and you can do it correctly the first time.

Students who skip listing their citations as they research and say to themselves "I'll put all the sources in later" are wasting their time and almost always make mistakes. Not only do they often forget to do the citations, but when they do remember, they spend more time on this task, because they have to find the quotes and paraphrased text all over again. Why not just create the citations first and spare yourself the effort? The quicker you develop this mind-set, the less time you'll spend on the details of MLA style, and the more time you'll have to think about what you want to say in your writing.

chapter review

Documenting your sources may seem like one of the tedious parts of writing. While this task may seem like nitpicking, citing your sources correctly increases your credibility as a writer, so it is a good idea to develop an organized and efficient process for documenting sources that you can use throughout your college life. Chapter 20 gives you the tools to do this.

To review this chapter, choose one or more of the following strategies:

1. Try to list for yourself—without looking back at the chapter—the three major components of MLA format. If you can't, review the chapter, make sure you understand the three components, and test yourself again.

2. If you skipped any activities, do them now as a way to deepen your understanding of the material.

3. Compare and contrast academic writing—which requires careful documentation of sources—with your local television news—which often "borrows" from other news sources and does not always adequately show where it is getting its information. Make a list of the differences between the two in terms of audience and purpose.

4. Try to explain what you have learned to someone you know. Discuss the key concepts and give your own examples to illustrate those concepts.

21
Siblings

in this chapter

- **Sharon Olds**
  Killing My Sister's Fish
- **Jane Mersky Leder**
  Close Encounters of a Special Kind
- **Jeffrey Kluger**
  The New Science of Siblings
- **Jeffrey Kluger**
  The Power of Birth Order
- **Lauren Sandler**
  The Only Child: Debunking the Myths
- **Po Bronson and Ashley Merryman**
  The Sibling Effect

Serena and Venus Williams, tennis superstars.

Killing My Sister's Fish
Sharon Olds

I picked up the bottle with its gladiator shoulders—
inside its shirred, greyish plastic
ammonia, more muscular than water, pungent—
I poured one dollop, gleaming genie,
into the bowl with my sister's goldfish
just because they were alive, and she liked them.
It was in the basement, near the zinc-lined sinks
and the ironing-board, next to the boiler,
beside the door to the cellar from which
I could get into the crawl space
under the corner of the house, and lie
on the dirt on my back, as if passed out.
I may have been on my way there
when I saw the bowl, and the ammonia curled
for a moment in the air like a spirit. Then I crawled up
under the floor-joists, into the tangent
where the soil curved up, and I lay there
at the ends of the earth, as if without
regret, as if something set in motion
long before I had been conceived
had been accomplished.

Theme Overview

The longest relationships you will have in your life will most likely be with your brothers and sisters, your siblings. For many people, the sibling bond lasts from the earliest childhood memories until old age. Your siblings have an immense impact on your life, your personality, and your identity—even if you aren't friendly with them. For most people, the sibling relationship is deep and messy and changes a great deal over the years. Despite the importance of siblings, we don't pay much attention to them in American culture. In psychology and sociology classes, a great deal of time is spent studying parent-child relationships and romantic relationships, but very little time is devoted to sibling relationships. The psychology section of your local bookstore has shelf after shelf about how to be a better parent, a more successful person, and a better lover and spouse, but very few books about how to be a better sibling. Why is that? What gets left out when we ignore a discussion of the impact our siblings have on us? How can understanding the role of siblings in our lives help us understand human behavior better and possibly even live better lives? This chapter will begin to help you understand some of the current science and psychology about siblings and will spark a debate about how siblings influence one another. You will read scientific studies as well as personal accounts.

No doubt some of this material will strike a nerve, whether you grew up in a house full of brothers and sisters, are an only child, or are part of a blended family with step-siblings, half-siblings, or cousins. Note whether or not you overgeneralize based on your own experiences when you discuss and write about the material. The following questions will help you take stock of your own initial responses and ideas. By using these questions you will get your thoughts on paper in a coherent way, making it easier for you to read more critically, speak more in class discussion, and generate ideas for papers on this topic. So take time to write down answers to the following questions in your journal or notebook. Keep this writing and refer back to it as you read the articles and begin your assignments.

practice it Taking Stock of What You Already Know

If you have siblings, half-siblings, or step-siblings, think about what your relationships with them are like. If you don't have any siblings of your own, think about sibling relationships that you know (your parents' or friends' siblings or even siblings from a television show).

- How have those relationships changed over the years?
- Are you a twin or do you know any twins? Do you think being a twin intensifies the sibling relationship? Why or why not?
- Do you know any elderly siblings? What is their relationship like? Have they grown closer as they have become older? Why or why not?
- If you are an only child, did you ever wish to have a sibling? Why or why not? Do you have a parent or another relative who has siblings? How do sibling relationships influence your parent or relative?
- What is a good metaphor to describe older siblings? Are they guides on a hike toward adulthood? Teammates in a battle against parents? Enemies locked in eternal combat for their parents' attention? What other metaphors can you think of that would describe older siblings? What metaphors can you create about younger siblings and middle siblings?
- Do brother-brother relationships differ from sister-sister relationships? If so, in what ways do they differ?
- How does favoritism have an impact on a child? What are the pros and cons of being the parents' "favorite"?
- Think about the images of siblings that you see on television and in the media. List all the examples that come to mind. What are some of the stereotypes about siblings that these images encourage us to believe?
- Do you have experience of another culture outside of America? If so, what are the similarities and differences between that culture's ideas about siblings and American culture's ideas about siblings?

Jane Mersky Leder regularly publishes magazine articles and educational materials and has written three nonfiction books. Though she is not trained as a psychologist, her books have focused on psychological themes, which she researches thoroughly. She has published books on topics as diverse as teen suicide and siblings. Her most recent book, *Thanks for the Memories: Love, Sex, and World War II* (2009), chronicles the romantic experiences of young people during World War II. This reading selection comes from the first chapter of her book *Brothers and Sisters: How They Shape Our Lives* (1991), where she makes a case for the importance of siblings in shaping our identities. *Important words and phrases have been italicized in this reading. Look up those you do not know, and write the definitions in your personal vocabulary list.*

practice it Pre-Reading

Think back on any psychology or sociology courses you have had in high school or college, or on any other research or reading you have done about siblings. What do you know about the study of siblings? What theories are there about sibling behavior? What do you know about these theories? Write down in your notes your own prior knowledge on the topic.

Jane Mersky Leder

CLOSE ENCOUNTERS OF A SPECIAL KIND

Thanksgiving one year taught me a lot about the strange things that can happen when adult brothers and sisters get together in the house where they grew up. The house was up for sale, and that made the holiday scene even crazier. My brother, my sister, and I were charged not only with *readjusting* to one another but also with helping my parents divide up the spoils of their nearly fifty years together—an unsettling task. "You don't know when you'll be back here," my mother said. "And I want to get this out of the way."

When my mother is on a mission, there is no stopping her. And there was no stopping Liz, John, and me from sliding back into our childhood roles as easily as successful dieters fit back into their old clothes.

The time had come to divide up my grandmother's china and the silverware with the pearl handles.

"I'm in the process of simplifying my life," my sister said. "I don't need any of this. Besides, when would I ever use it?"

My mother glared at her.   5

I'd have to do something fast. Anything to keep the peace. "I'll take this set," I said, sliding spoons, knives, and forks over in front of me.

"Well, wait a minute," Liz said. "I might want those."

I wanted to punch her. "Just make up your mind. It really doesn't matter to me."

Where the hell was John? "Isn't John a part of this?" I asked.

"He's resting," my mother said.   10

"How convenient," I mumbled. Nothing had changed. John had bailed out like he always did, leaving us to juggle a *ticklish* situation.

Liz picked up two spoons. She was acting like a *petulant* little girl. Why couldn't she just choose the damn silverware and make things easier for all of us?

I stared out the floor-to-ceiling windows at the bare trees. They looked *vulnerable*, caught unprotected in the blustery November wind.

"I guess I'll take these," Liz said, picking a simple pattern.

"It's about time," I said, relieved.   15

The quickness with which all the "stuff" from childhood can reduce adult siblings to kids again *underscores* the strong and complex connections between brothers and sisters. We can enter a family gathering as confident adults and exit feeling as unsettled as we did during childhood. Our siblings push buttons that cast us in roles we felt sure we had let go of long ago—the baby, the peacekeeper, the caretaker, the avoider . . . It doesn't seem to matter how much time has *elapsed* or how far we've traveled. Our brothers and sisters bring us face to face with our former selves and remind us how intricately bound up we are in each other's lives.

Given the importance of the relationship between brothers and sisters—particularly adult siblings—why has it not been thoroughly studied? Has Freud's *myopic* version of the family drama, which minimized the significance of siblings, so blinded those in the mental health field that they could not consider the diversity of roles siblings play? Has personality development theory handcuffed us to the belief that our personalities are set in stone by the age of eighteen or twenty? Has the fact that until recently males have dominated the field of sibling research had an impact on *methodology* and theory? Bent on finding some answers, I questioned researchers, educators, and clinicians about why they felt the powerful connections between siblings have been underemphasized in a culture that presumably places great importance on family.

Some felt the answer lies in the overemphasis our society has placed on the parent/child relationship. Parents and children have different power sources, different areas of authority, different kinds of responses within the family. The relationship between siblings, on the other hand, is much more *egalitarian*; it is considered a relationship between peers. As such, scientists haven't seen as much *differentiation* between siblings as between parent and child and have consequently assumed the sibling relationship needn't be studied as fully or taken as seriously. "We've underemphasized peer relationships," said Stephen Bank, coauthor of *The Sibling Bond*, "and sibling relationships are part of that. Siblings are viewed as minor actors on the stage of human development. If there were an opera, they would be there in the chorus, not as key players."[1]

Bank sees this lack of interest in brothers and sisters as a bias of both researchers (most of whom are firstborns or only children[2]) and of our culture, a culture that is very hard on parents. "We attribute a great deal to parental influence," he said in a phone interview. "There is a certain level of blame that occurs, since parents are seen as the originators of all good things in this culture and all bad things."

For Bank and others, such as Douglas Breunlin, Director of Training at the Institute for Juvenile Research in Chicago, most family therapy theory is based on the belief that things go wrong either because one generation has passed "crazy things" down to another generation or because parents aren't doing what they should to raise their children properly.

"The family," said Breunlin, "is usually centered on the *pathology* of the parents, the style of the parents, or the way the child is being caught up in marital conflict. Therapists often don't know how to involve siblings because they don't have a theory that says siblings are essential."[3]

We are not a society that pays much attention to siblings. There are no rituals to *cement* or *sever* the sibling bond. Although writers and artists have used the drama of sibling relations in their works from the Bible on, the typical American family raises its children to be individuals, who often compete for the spoils their parents have to offer. "We call that sibling rivalry," said Breunlin, "but I'm not sure that sibling rivalry would be nearly as bad if we didn't have the social structure that reduces the importance of siblings."

20

Other societies place a much higher value on brothers and sisters and the attachment between them. A study of child care in 186 societies has shown that forty percent of the infants were looked after by people other than their mothers, often by their siblings.[4] There are African societies in which the brother *kinship* is more important than parental kinship and where it is the brothers who make decisions about the family. "There exists a sense of loyalty between siblings in other societies," said Breunlin, "and a determination to resolve differences . . . elements often missing among brothers and sisters in the United States."

Contemporary American society emphasizes individual achievement, not *collaborative* accomplishments. Children have their own bedrooms, their own television sets, their own telephones. When Breunlin suggested that, for the most part, parents are raising families that consist of a group of only children, I was intrigued. I hadn't considered how this emphasis on individualism gave brothers and sisters very few good reasons to interact. Yet as I thought about all the families I've observed, I realized how little time is spent by parents *orchestrating* activities in which their children work together. What ever happened to all those lemonade stands with siblings at the helm? Much more common is Johnny going off to soccer or karate practice and his sister being shuttled off to ballet or gymnastic lessons. There is, of course, the annual family vacation in which everyone piles into the station wagon or boards a plane. Despite good intentions, these once-a-year affairs too often deteriorate into Excedrin Plus headaches, with the kids at each other's throats and the parents at their wits' end. It's no wonder that this most sacred of American family traditions turns nightmarish. Kids aren't encouraged to spend long hours together in a spirit of cooperation and purpose during the rest of the year, so why should they be expected to do so this time?

If the *interconnectedness* between family members, siblings in particular, needs redefining, it can be argued that the women's rights movement has begun to help us to do just that. When I spoke with Karen Lewis, a counseling psychologist and coeditor of *Siblings in Therapy*, she pointed out that up until the publication of *Siblings: Love, Envy, and Understanding* by Judy Dunn and Carol Kendrick in 1982, males had dominated the field of sibling research.[5] And when most of these men studied brothers and sisters, they observed them in school or at a playground, not in the context of the home. "What information they got," said Lewis, "was often limited and lopsided."[6] I agreed, adding that this male perspective, colored by the more distant, competitive dynamics that mark the relationships between many brothers, distorted some of the "scientific" theories concerning siblings.

Sigmund Freud's theory of sibling rivalry is a case in point. A first-born male, Freud produced a concept of brothers and sisters *vying* for parental attention that minimized the significance of the sibling experience and completely ignored the relationship between sisters. Subsequent theories were developed based on Freud, and very few people expanded the framework he established. The professional training and personal therapy of those in the mental health field were based on the same idea. "We started out with a half-open eye," said Lewis, "ignoring the role brothers and sisters play, and this limited view has been passed down over the generations. It's easier to ignore what we don't understand."

No doubt the complexity of the sibling relationship makes it difficult for both researchers and siblings to understand. A child may take many roles in interactions with siblings: friend, model, teacher, pest, caretaker, rival, and more. And it is likely that through the years a child will play a number of these roles, some of them simultaneously.

Not only are the dynamics of sibling interaction complex; so are the demands of sibling research design. A researcher must use adequate *controls* to determine which differences between siblings are due to their interaction and which are due to such variables as gender, birth order, age spacing, access, and a family's ethnic background.

Deborah Gold, assistant professor of medical sociology and Senior Fellow in the Center for Aging and Human Development at Duke University, knows only too well the complexity of such research. As she began her work with siblings in their old age, she talked with several researchers who had written one paper about siblings and quit. "They all said, 'You'll see why when you get into it.' I quickly learned that by the time you take into account the number of sibs, the gender of those sibs, the birth order of those sibs, the relationships of those sibs with their parents, you're controlling for so much that it makes it very difficult to analyze data. There is never going to be a Dr. Spock book for the sibling relationship."[7]

For Gold and other researchers interested in the sibling relationship across the life span the *dominant literature* on personality development has been of little help. "The studies," said psychologist Joel Milgram, "all theorized that major influences on development, changes, or *modifications* in one's personality occur between birth and late adolescence. Once you are an adult, you are an adult. The idea that something can happen to dramatically change a person later in life was almost unheard of until the 1960s, when a whole group of studies on men and women as adults appeared."[8]

30

Gail Sheehy's landmark best-seller *Passages* (first published in 1976) did for adults what Gesell and Spock had done for children. It detailed inner changes we all experienced on the way to full adulthood. While not a book about siblings per se, *Passages* validated the now more readily accepted theory that things do happen to dramatically change a person's life after the age of eighteen or twenty. If we buy this concept of human development, we acknowledge the roles brothers and sisters continue to play throughout life, and we can more readily predict certain stages at which their influence may be stronger than at others.

The decade between ages thirty-five and forty-five, for example, provides us with the chance to rework the identities we defined for ourselves in the first half of life. This, says Sheehy, can create a "full-out *authenticity* crisis." But somewhere in the mid-forties, if we have confronted ourselves in the mid-life passage, a new level of stability is reached. This may result in forgiving our parents for their "sins," and reconnecting with brothers and sisters whose influence may have diminished or been downplayed over the years.

Still another understanding that can grow out of the "*mid-life crisis*" is that marriage cannot carry the burden of all our needs and wants. We start to understand the real benefits to be gained by developing rich relationships with other adults, including our siblings. Siblings share a common history yet a unique experience within the family. To find out what each sibling remembers and to put all the pieces together helps each of us know ourselves better and expands our understanding and appreciation for the brothers and sisters with whom we shared our childhood.

Divorce, shrinking family size, longer life spans, geographic *mobility*, employment of mothers, and various forms of parental insufficiency are placing brothers and sisters in a position of greater *accessibility* to one another and may be giving the sibling relationship even greater relevance.[9] "With increases in abandonment by parents, child abuse, divorce, and families being fragmented," said Michael Kahn in a phone interview, "kids are less likely to be able to know *intrinsically* and implicitly that they can always count on their parents. They can't. But human beings, needing to count on somebody or something, turn to whatever is close at hand. Very often, the sibling group is what's available. I think that is primarily why the sibling relationship is coming into focus now."[10]

Getting the sibling relationship into focus is no easy task. Professionals are being asked to dive into new territory, to put aside *operative* theories that have dominated their training and work and to consider different ways of looking at the family and the roles each member plays. Sisters and brothers are being asked to consider influences of relationships that have been traditionally underplayed or just plain ignored. We're more *adept* at talking about peers outside the family than about our peers within. Yet our quest for *intimacy* in an unsure world pulls us back to the family; the call of *kin* offers the promise of support and continuity. What we do along the way to keep those connections alive and meaningful or distant and painful will surely help us to understand and have an effect on who we are as individuals, partners, parents, and peers.

Intimate Bonds

Janis G. was born the third of six children and the first girl. The arrangement of two boys, then two girls, then two boys established three distinct sibling subgroups within her family: the "big boys," the "girls," and the "little boys." While each group had its own rules, history, and *hierarchy*, the close contact Janis and her siblings had every day as they waited for a turn in the bathroom, tried to get to the dinner table on time, and *vied* for parental attention shaped not only Janis as a young girl but Janis as the woman she's become.

"I really feel that I come from a very blessed situation," Janis told me as we sat in her museum office. "My mother and father tried to create a very strong sense of unity with their children that has marked each of us in different ways. Certainly where you come in the family means that you have a different experience and a different view of the family unit. But all of us share a very strong sense of family that is central to our worldview."

As the first girl, Janis's views and experiences were unique and sometimes frustrating. "Being the first girl is tough. The standard is different. My father had very strict ideas about what girls could or could not do." Janis's brothers—the "big" boys—were allowed more freedom. They could stay out later and didn't have to battle to wear stockings and makeup or the rest of the "girl kinds of things." Such hard-won rights came later for Janis than they did for many of her friends.

Did the double standard create *animosity* between Janis and her brothers? "I came to understand and accept that it was my father and his old-fashioned attitudes, not my brothers, who set the different rules. My brothers were empowered because of my father, and I eventually understood that."

Besides, the advantages of having two older brothers outweighed the disadvantages. The "big boys" provided Janis with a "wonderful 40 feeling of being protected" and a group of male friends who were "really very interesting." "I loved to make these guys sandwiches. Whatever they wanted, I would do." And when she was old enough to travel in the same social set, Janis was always surprised to see her brothers taking on a protective air toward her. She'll never forget the times when fights broke out at parties and a brother "hightailed it in there to yank her out."

That "protective air" shaped Janis's expectations of the opposite gender. While she described herself as "very *liberal* in her thinking and independent in her approach," she admitted to falling back in a minute on looking for that kind of champion in her relationships with other men. "I still like for men to open doors and do things for me, and I know that comes from the values my father instilled in my brothers that was passed on to me."

Not surprisingly, the ideal of taking care of one's kin, a pattern passed down on both sides of Janis's family, prepared Janis to assume a caretaking role with her sister Samantha, not quite two years younger. Though they were known *collectively* as the "girls," the two sisters were very different from one another: Janis was the public one, much more social; Samantha was the private one, *conservative*, *naive*, and accident prone. "She was called '*Calamity* Sam' at one point because she was always falling down or messing up something. I felt that I needed to take care of her. I was definitely the big sister. Even when she was in high school, I looked after her, checking out the guys who were checking her out, helping her put her outfits together." Janis tossed her head and chuckled. "God knows her color *schemes* were always different."

Sam didn't always take a backseat. Her musical talent blossomed early on. Janis described a wonderful two-month period when there were two baby grand pianos in the house. She and Sam played duets, each sister with her own baby grand. But then Sam passed Janis in skill, and Janis lost interest. "Her artistic talent was one of the things that I envied. And her intelligence. She was a much better student than I was. I know it was hard for her to be 'Janis's sister,' that she resented being compared to me, but fortunately she excelled in many areas of her own. Her *resentment* at being known as the sister of somebody else never drove a wedge between us. There were times when we each went our own way. But that was important. Sam could carve out her own space."

As an adult, each sister has carved a space that *complements* the other. The director of education at a large, metropolitan museum, Janis, who has not married, remains in the public eye; Sam is married and has four children. Janis recalled a four-hour phone conversation she and Sam had recently in which each sister *yearned* for the other's life.

Here she was wishing that she had my life because I have privacy and do things on my own without the responsibility of kids. And there I was miserable because she has four children and a husband and a nice little house. And at that moment, we wanted to change lives. I *coveted* those wonderful faces that wake you up and say "I love you, Mom," and she wanted my life because she could work and sleep and do whatever she wanted. I listened to her frustrations at trying to be an artist and a mother. And she listened to my disappointment at not having a family. Ours is a very *equitable*, supportive relationship . . . a real source of comfort.

The adult relationships between Janis and her two older brothers, 45 though not as close as Samantha and her, provided her with models of successful marriages and examples of how to cope with whatever life has to offer. Her oldest brother, though somewhat of a "loner" and "very private," has been happily married for many years. "His wife was very good for him, and that's all we can ask for, that he is happy in that relationship." Janis's number-two brother, a very "opinionated lawyer who tells everyone what to do," is married to a woman who can harness his energy and "help us know how he's feeling or why he's feeling a certain way and how to deal with it. None of us likes *discord* in the family. If there is discord between any two of us, it affects us all. It's important to find a way to connect."

The connection between Janis and the "little boys"— six and eight years younger—is, in many ways, an extension of their childhood relationships. Growing up, Janis was a caretaker for the boys, getting them dressed, taking them to school, and babysitting for them when she was older. "I felt a sense of responsibility, but I also thought they were real cute." Jasper, the older of the two, is an architect who has "done a lot of searching." "I play a supportive role, an encouraging role, a 'bring-him-up-on-the-stuff-he-should-have-done-better' role. But as adults, we share the same taste in music, art, and intellectual *endeavors*, which puts us at an equal place at the table." Like his older two brothers, Jasper is married, but his wife is, according to Janis, "the problem of the family." "His marriage hasn't *diminished* our relationship," said Janis, "but there's a frustration, a need for him to resolve that marriage because of the tension in the family. It makes me upset with him, but it hasn't changed the dynamics of our connection."

The very special connection Janis has with her "baby" brother Stephen developed during childhood and has been strengthened as adults. "He was always special to me, even as a child. He was the one whose hair I really liked to brush, the one I really liked to get dressed. I watched for him as he grew up. It's not more love than I feel for my other brothers; it's just special." As the two "unmarrieds" in the

family, Janis feels even more *camaraderie* with Stephen, who looks out 25
for her in a certain way because he understands life as a single person.
"As the youngest of four boys," said Janis, "he had a lot of inherited
expectations. That was hard for him. But I think he came through it
very well. He's been finding his own place and feeling very comfortable about that. He has become the anchor for my parents, taking care
of their home and other properties. That position has given him a new
respectability as the youngest son. He's a special person."

Janis's sibling experiences serve as good examples of how gender
and closeness in age can affect the connections between brothers and
sisters. As the first girl, she faced a different standard that caused its
share of problems and forced her to work harder at getting what she
wanted. Janis is convinced that the struggle as a child shaped the *perseverance* that has served her so well in the outside world. Her father's
old-fashioned expectations of what a girl should or shouldn't do were
fortunately balanced by love and a set of values that, in the long run,
created unity, not *dissension,* among Janis and her siblings.

Growing up with two older brothers shaped Janis's expectations *vis á
vis* men. Their protective and gentlemanly manner provided a sense of
security and comfort that she has come to expect. Janis let all of her boyfriends know that she had two older brothers and claims that she was
never mistreated because her brothers would have "killed any guy who
tried to get away with something." Janis's brothers taught her what to
expect from the opposite sex and their feelings about females. And while
these expectations don't necessarily *jibe* with her self-described *feminist*
views, she admits to easily falling back into the being-taken-care-of mode.

As reflected in myths and fairy tales like "Snow White and Rose 50
Red" (the tale of two sisters who are devoted to one another) and supported by scientific research, the gender of siblings may also affect
the emotional bond between them. Relationships between sisters
seem to be more intense and emotionally intimate than those between
brothers or between brothers and sisters. Janis's close connection with
her sister, deeper and more intense than the relationships with her
brothers, reflects the influence of gender as well as the high number
of life experiences they have shared.

Only twenty months apart, Janis and Samantha shared the same
bedroom, attended the same schools at the same time, and had many
friends in common. Such closeness between the two sisters increased
the influence each had on the other. But as Janis recognized, this close
contact had its disadvantages. Samantha often felt as if she were standing in her older sister's shadow, while Janis couldn't help comparing
herself to her sister and feeling that she came up on the short end of

the stick artistically and academically. Over the long haul, though, the differences between the two sisters gave them a sense of wholeness and helped them recognize the infinite possibilities in their own lives.

As Janis clearly pointed out, the role her parents played in "fostering a strong sense of unity" between her and her siblings helped mold the positive emotional bonds that have carried into adulthood. Not surprisingly, a majority of the siblings I interviewed, whether in their twenties or in their eighties, talked about their parents' role in either *fostering* cooperation and a sense of specialness among their children or in *perpetuating* hurtful comparisons and *ineptitude* when it came to solving problems and settling arguments. While Janis acknowledged the tough task her parents faced raising six children and keeping a balance between them, she gave them high marks for "making us all feel that we were loved and that there were no favorites." Working to change some of the dynamics within their own sibling groups and between them and their parents, Janis's mother and father "consciously tried to correct the problems of their childhoods." Janis's mother, who came from a family of thirteen children, remembered a lot of tension between her and her siblings, tension that she wanted her own six children to avoid. "My mother and my father helped each of us look at what were our good qualities," said Janis. "It was never a comparison, never a 'You should be more like so and so.'"

The significance of parents treating their children differently and the effects such treatment has on the siblings themselves are issues that are discussed again and again in the current literature on siblings. The value of equal treatment of siblings within the family, of *nonintervention* in sibling conflict, and of parents "distancing" themselves from the siblings' relationships have been shown to enhance the growth of positive sibling bonds and feelings of healthy cooperation within the family as a whole. When Janis said she'd been blessed, coming from such parents, she gave thanks for their unqualified love and astute parenting.

Adult siblings who were not blessed with such thoughtful parents will have to work harder at understanding that their childhood rivalries are left over from a struggle that was most likely not their fault. If they can see that, it will help them stop feeling guilty or blaming each other the way they did when they were children. Of course, talking to one another about such revelations is crucial. It is often wondrous how a few kind words ("I'm beginning to see that Mom's favoritism wasn't your fault," or "it must have been horrible to have the rest of us picking on you all the time") can go a long way in restoring positive feelings. If we adult siblings want to improve our relationships, parental *blunders* need to be discussed, forgiven, and put to rest.

Notes

1. Stephen P. Bank, telephone interview with the author, 19 October 1989.
2. B. N. Adams, "Birth Order: A Critical Review," *Sociometry* 35 (3): 411–39.
3. Douglas Breunlin, interview, 18 December 1989, Chicago, Illinois.
4. Judy Dunn, *Sisters and Brothers: The Developing Child* (Cambridge, Mass.: Harvard University Press, 1985), p. 13.
5. This is not to overlook the important contributions of other women, including Deborah Gold, Frances Fuchs Schachter, Victoria Bedford, Elinor Rosenberg, Helen Koch, Helgola Ross, Toni Falbo, and others.
6. Karen Lewis, telephone interview with the author, 18 October 1989.
7. Deborah Gold, telephone interview with the author, 2 October 1989.
8. Joel Milgram, telephone interview with the author, 10 November 1989.
9. Stephen P. Bank and Michael D. Kahn, *The Sibling Bond* (New York: Basic Books, 1982), p. 12.
10. Michael D. Kahn, telephone interview with the author, 5 November 1989.

---

practice it   Post-Reading Activity

This reading selection shifts from very interesting and readable anecdotes and case studies to more difficult sections about the history of psychological theories. Find a passage two to three paragraphs long that you find very difficult to understand. Reread the passage, perhaps multiple times, using all your annotation skills. Look up words you don't know, ask questions of the text, and take notes in a notebook to sketch out the ideas. How well did your critical reading skills help you dig in and get through this difficult passage? What further help might you need to understand it? Make a list of questions you still have about the passage and ask them in class discussion, talk to a friend about them, or visit your instructor in office hours for help.

To review annotating techniques, see Chapter 1, Reading and Responding to College Texts, page 2.

COMPREHENSION QUESTIONS

1. According to Leder, why haven't siblings been discussed much by psychologists and other experts who study human behavior?

2. Why is doing reliable research on siblings so difficult?

3. What does Freud say about sibling rivalry?

4. What is family therapy theory? What does family therapy theory say about family problems?

5. How does American culture compare and contrast to other cultures in terms of the importance placed on siblings? How does American individualism influence siblings?

6. According to Leder, what do adult siblings need to do if they are to have healthy relationships as adults?

VOCABULARY ACTIVITIES

1. Refer back to your annotations to begin a glossary of words related to the study of siblings. Try to use context clues or roots, prefixes, and suffixes to determine the meaning of the words, and if you have to use a dictionary, try to restate the definition in your own words.

2. Create graphic flash cards for the difficult terminology you found in the readings.

3. Generate a list of synonyms for the words *sibling*, *brother*, and *sister*. Identify how formal or informal each synonym is. Are any of your choices slang? In what context(s) would it be appropriate to use each of the various terms?

SUMMARY ACTIVITY

Underline Leder's thesis statement and the topic sentence of each paragraph. Then go back and reread just the thesis and topic sentences. How well does this help you summarize the main points of the article? Based on this activity, write a one- to three-sentence summary of the reading.

DISCUSSION QUESTIONS

1. How do the issues surrounding adult siblings differ from those of child siblings?

2. In the opening anecdote about Thanksgiving, Leder writes, "I'd have to do something fast" (para. 6). What does this mean? What does she have to do, and why does she have to do it? What does this conversation convey about adult sibling relationships?

3. Leder writes, "Relationships between sisters seem to be more intense and emotionally intimate than those between brothers or between brothers and sisters" (para. 50). She uses the case study of Janis to back up this claim but offers no other research. What do you think of her claim? Do you agree or disagree? What counter-arguments could you offer? What evidence would you use to support those counterarguments?

4. Do you agree or disagree that it is important to have good bonds with adult siblings? Why might it be important? How can sibling relationships help you as an adult?

MAGAZINE

Jeffrey Kluger, author of "The New Science of Siblings" as well as the next reading, "The Power of Birth Order," is a senior editor for *Time* magazine's science and technology areas. In addition, he regularly writes about psychology and science for a wide variety of magazines and has written more than seven books. His book *The Sibling Effect: What the Bonds among Brothers and Sisters Reveal about Us* (2011) expands on his scientific articles about siblings—such as the two included here—and includes his personal memories of growing up in a family with four children. For Kluger, the sibling bond plays a fundamental role in his identity. This article originally appeared in *Time* magazine in 2006. *Important words and phrases have been italicized in this reading. Look up those you do not know, and write the definitions in your personal vocabulary list.*

For a review of previewing, see Chapter 1, Reading and Responding to College Texts, page 2.

practice it   Pre-Reading

Preview the text. What can you predict about the article's topic, audience, and purpose from previewing? Annotate your preview notes directly on the text.

JEFFREY KLUGER

The New Science of Siblings

There are a lot of ways to study a painting, and one of the best is to get to know the painter. The splash or splatter of color makes a lot more sense when you understand the rage or *whimsy* or heart behind it. The songwriter, similarly, can lay bare the song, the poet the poem, the builder the building.

So what explains the complex bit of artistry that is the human personality? We may not be born as *tabulae rasae*. Any parent can tell you that each child comes from the womb with an individual *temperament* that seems preloaded at the factory. But from the moment of birth, a lot of things set to work on that temperament—*moderating* it, challenging it, *annealing* it, wounding it. What we're left with after 10 or 20 or 50 years is quite different from what we started out with.

For a long time, researchers have tried to nail down just what shapes us—or what, at least, shapes us most. And over the years, they've had a lot of *eureka* moments. First it was our parents, particularly our mothers. Then it was our genes. Next it was our peers, who show up last but hold great *sway*. And all those ideas were good ones—but only as far as they went.

The fact is once investigators had strip-mined all the data from those theories, they still came away with as many questions as answers. Somewhere, there was a sort of temperamental *dark* matter *exerting* an invisible *gravitational* pull of its own. More and more, scientists are concluding that this unexplained force is our siblings.

From the time they are born, our brothers and sisters are our *collaborators*   5
and co-conspirators, our role models and *cautionary tales*. They are our *scolds*, protectors, *goads*, tormentors, playmates, counselors, sources of envy, objects of pride. They teach us how to resolve conflicts and how not to; how to conduct friendships and when to walk away from them. Sisters teach brothers about the mysteries of girls; brothers teach sisters about the puzzle of boys. Our spouses arrive *comparatively* late in our lives; our parents eventually leave us. Our siblings may be the only people we'll ever know who truly qualify as partners for life. "Siblings," says family sociologist Katherine Conger of the University of California, Davis, "are with us for the whole journey."

Within the scientific community, siblings have not been wholly ignored, but research has been limited mostly to discussions of birth order. Older sibs were said to be strivers; younger ones rebels; middle kids the lost souls. The stereotypes were broad, if not entirely untrue, and there the discussion mostly ended.

But all that's changing. At research centers in the U.S., Canada, Europe and elsewhere, investigators are launching a wealth of new studies into the sibling *dynamic*, looking at ways brothers and sisters steer one another into—or away from—risky behavior; how they form a protective *buffer* against family upheaval; how they educate one another about the opposite sex; how all siblings compete for family recognition and come to terms—or blows—over such impossibly charged issues as parental *favoritism*.

From that research, scientists are gaining intriguing insights into the people we become as adults. Does the manager who runs a *congenial* office call on the peacemaking skills learned in the family playroom? Does the student struggling with a professor who plays favorites summon up the coping skills acquired from dealing with a sister who was Daddy's girl? Do husbands and wives benefit from the *intergender* negotiations they waged when their most important partners were their sisters and brothers? All that is under investigation. "Siblings have just been off the radar screen until now," says Conger. But today serious work is revealing exactly how our brothers and sisters influence us.

Why Childhood Fights between Siblings Can Be Good

The first thing that strikes contemporary researchers when they study siblings is the sheer quantity of time the kids spend in one another's presence and the power this has to teach them social skills. By the time children are 11, they *devote* about 33% of their free time to their siblings—more time than they spend with friends, parents, teachers or even by themselves—according to a well-regarded Penn State University study published in 1996. Later research, published last year, found that even adolescents, who have usually begun going their own way, devote at least 10 hours a week to activities with their siblings—a lot when you consider that with school, sports, dates and sleep, there aren't a whole lot of free hours left. In Mexican-American homes, where broods are generally bigger, the figure tops 17 hours.

"In general," says psychologist Daniel Shaw of the University of Pittsburgh, "parents serve the same big-picture role as doctors on grand rounds. Siblings are like the nurses on the ward. They're there every day." All that *proximity* breeds an awful lot of *intimacy*—and an awful lot of friction.   10

Laurie Kramer, professor of applied family studies at the University of Illinois at Urbana-Champaign, has found that, on average, sibs between 3 and 7 years old engage in some kind of conflict 3.5 times an hour. Kids in the 2-to-4 age group top out at 6.3—or more than one *clash* every 10 minutes, according to a Canadian study. "Getting along with a sister or brother," Kramer says dryly, "can be a frustrating experience."

But as much as all the fighting can set parents' hair on end, there's a lot of learning going on too, specifically about how conflicts, once begun, can be settled. Shaw and his colleagues conducted a years-long study in which they visited the homes of 90 2-year-old children who had at least one sibling, observing the target kids' *innate* temperaments and their parents' discipline styles. The researchers returned when the children were 5 and observed them again, this time in a structured play session with one close-in-age sib. The pairs were shown three toys but given only one to play with. They were told they could move onto the next one only when both agreed it was time to switch and further agreed which toy they wanted next.

That, as any parent knows, is a *scenario* trip-wired for fights—and that's what happened. The experimenters ranked the conflicts on a five-point scale, with one being a single cross word and five being a full-blown brawl. The next year, they went to the same children's schools to observe them at play and interview their teachers. Almost universally, the kids who practiced the best conflict-resolution skills at home carried those abilities into the classroom.

Certainly, there are other things that could account for what makes some kids battlers in school and others not. But the most powerful *variables*—parents and personality—were identified and their influence isolated during the course of the two-year-long observations. Socioeconomic status, an X factor that *bedevils* studies like this one, was controlled by selecting all the families from the same economic *stratum*. *Distill* those influences away and what is left is the interaction of the sibs. "Siblings have a socializing effect on one another," Shaw says. "When you *tease out* all the other variables, it's the play styles that make the difference. Unlike a relationship with friends, you're stuck with your sibs. You learn to negotiate things day to day."

It's that permanence, researchers believe, that makes siblings so valuable a 15 rehearsal tool for later life. Adulthood, after all, is practically defined by peer relationships—the workplace, a marriage, the church building committee. As siblings, we may *sulk* and *fume* but by nighttime we still return to the same twin beds in the same shared room. Peace is made when one sib offers a toy or shares a thought or throws a pillow in a mock *provocation* that releases the lingering tension in a burst of roughhousing. Somewhere in there is the early training for the e-mail joke that breaks an office silence or the husband who signals that a fight is over by asking his wife what she thinks they should do about that fast-approaching vacation anyway. "Sibling relationships are where you learn all this," says developmental psychologist Susan McHale of Penn State University. "They are relationships between equals."

How Not Being Mom's Favorite Can Have Its Advantages

Multichild households can be nothing short of palace courts, with *alliances*, feuds, grudges and loyalties, all changing day to day. Perhaps the touchiest problem in most such families is favoritism.

Parents feel a lot of guilt over the often evident if rarely admitted preference they harbor for one child over another—the sensitive mom who goes gooey over her son the poet, the hard-knocks dad who adores his tough-as-nails daughter. If favorites exist, however, it may be not the parents' fault, but evolution's.

The family began as—and remains—a survival unit, with parents agreeing to care for the kids, the kids agreeing to carry on the genes and all of them doing what they can to make sure no one gets eaten by wolves. But the resources that make this possible are limited. "Economic means, types of jobs, even love and affection are in *finite* supply," says psychologist Mark Feinberg of Penn State. Parents, despite themselves, are programmed to notice the child who seems most worthy of the investment. While *millenniums* of socialization have helped us resist and even reverse this impulse, and we often pour much of a family's wealth and energy into the care of the disabled or difficult child, our *primal* programming still draws us to the pretty, gifted ones.

Conger devised a study to test how widespread favoritism is. She assembled a group of 384 adolescent sibling pairs and their parents, visiting them three times over three years and questioning them all about their relationships, their sense of well-being and more. To see how they interacted as a group, she videotaped them as they worked through sample conflicts. Overall, she concluded that 65% of mothers and 70% of fathers exhibited a preference for one child—in most cases, the older one. What's more, the kids know what's going on. "They all say, 'Well, it makes sense that they would treat us differently, because he's older or we're a boy and a girl,'" Conger reports.

At first, kids appear to adapt well to the *disparity* and often learn to game   20
the system, flipping *blatant* favoritism back to their shared advantage. "They'll say to one another, 'Why don't you ask Mom if we can go to the mall because she never says no to you,'" says Conger. But at a deeper level, second-tier children may pay a price. "They tend to be sadder and have more self-esteem questions," Conger says. "They feel like they're not as worthy, and they're trying to figure out why."

Think you're not still living the same reality show? Think again. It's no accident that employees in the workplace instinctively know which person to send into the lion's den of the corner office with a risky proposal or a bit of bad news. And it's no coincidence that the sense of hurt feelings and adolescent envy you get when that same colleague emerges with the proposal approved and the boss's applause seems so familiar. But what you summon up with the feelings you first had long ago is the knowledge you gained then too—that the smartest strategy is not to compete for approval but to strike a partnership with the favorite and spin the situation to benefit yourself as well. This idea did not occur to you *de novo*. You may know it now, but you learned it then.

Why Your Sibling Is—or Isn't—Your Best Role Model

It's no secret that brothers and sisters *emulate* one another or that the learning flows both up and down the age ladder. Younger siblings mimic the skills and strengths of older ones. Older sibs are prodded to attempt something new because they don't want to be shown up by a younger one who has already tried it. More complex—and in many ways more important—are those situations in which siblings don't mirror one another but *differentiate* themselves—a phenomenon psychologists call *de-identification*.

Alejandra and Sofia Romero, 5-year-old *fraternal twins* growing up in New York City, entered the world at almost the same instant but have gone their own ways ever since—at least in terms of temperament. Alejandra has more of a tolerance—even a taste—for rules and regimens. Sofia observed this (and her parents observed her observing it) and then distinguished herself as the looser, less disciplined of the two. Sofia is also the more *garrulous*, and Alejandra eventually became the more *taciturn*. "Sofie served as their mouthpiece," says Lisa Dreyer, 39, the girls' mother, "and Alejandra was perfectly happy to let her do it."

De-identification helps kids stake out personality turf inside the home, but it has another, far more important function: pushing some sibs away from risky behavior. On the whole, siblings pass on dangerous habits to one another in a depressingly predictable way. A girl with an older, pregnant teenage sister is four to six times as likely to become a teen mom herself, says Patricia East, a developmental psychologist at the University of California, San Diego. The same pattern holds for substance abuse. According to a paper published in the *Journal of Drug Issues* earlier this year, younger siblings whose older sibs drink are twice as likely to pick up the habit too. When it comes to smoking, the risk increases fourfold.

But some kids break the mold—and for surprising reasons. East con- 25
ducted a five-year study of 227 families and found that those girls who don't follow their older sisters into pregnancy may be drawn not so much to the wisdom of the choice as to the mere fact that it's a different one. One teen mom in a family is a drama; two teen moms has a been-there-done-that quality to it. "She purposely goes the other way," says East. "She decides her sister's role is teen mom and hers will be high achiever."

Younger sibs may avoid tobacco for much the same reason. Three years ago, Joseph Rodgers, a psychologist at the University of Oklahoma, published a study of more than 9,500 young smokers. He found that while older brothers and sisters often do introduce younger ones to the habit, the closer they are in age, the more likely the younger one is to resist. Apparently, their *proximity* in years has already made them too similar. One *conspicuous* way for a baby brother to set himself apart is to look at the older sibling's smoking habits and then do the opposite.

How a Sibling of the Opposite Sex Can Affect Whom You Marry

Far subtler—and often far sweeter—than the risk-taking modeling that occurs among all sibs is the gender modeling that plays out between opposite-sex ones. Brothers and sisters can be fierce de-identifiers. In a study of adolescent boys and girls in central Pennsylvania, the boys unsurprisingly scored higher in such traits as independence and competitiveness while girls did better in empathic characteristics like sensitivity and helpfulness. What was less expected is that when kids grow up with an opposite-sex sibling, such exposure *doesn't* temper gender-linked traits but *accentuates* them. Both boys and girls *hew* closer still to gender stereotype and even seek friends who conform to those norms. "It's known as *niche* picking," says Kimberly Updegraff, a professor of family and human development at Arizona State University and the person who conducted the study. "By having a sibling who is one way, you strive to be different."

But as kids get older, that distance from the other gender must, of necessity, close. Here kids with opposite-sex siblings have a marked advantage. Last year William Ickes, a psychologist at the University of Texas at Arlington, published a study in which he paired up male and female students—all of whom had grown up with an opposite-sex sibling—and set them to chatting with one another. Then he questioned the subjects about how the conversation went. In general, boys with older sisters or girls with older brothers were less fumbling at getting things going and kept the exchange flowing much more naturally.

"The guys who had older sisters had more involving interactions and were liked significantly more by their new female acquaintances," says Ickes. "Women with older brothers were more likely to strike up a conversation with the male stranger and to smile at him more than he smiled at her."

If siblings can indeed be as powerful an influence on one another as all the   30
research suggests, are all siblings created at least potentially equal? What about half-sibs and stepsibs? Do they *reap*—and *confer*—the same benefits? Research findings are a bit scattered on this, if only because shared or reconstituted families can be so complicated. A dysfunctional home in which parents and siblings *hunker* behind barricades alongside the ones they're biologically closest to does not lend itself to good sibling ties. Well-blended families, on the other hand, may produce step- or half-siblings who are extraordinarily close. One of the best studies on this topic is being conducted in Britain with a large group of many different kinds of nontraditional families. In general, the researchers have found that the intensity of the relationships closely follows the degree of physical relatedness. No hard rules have emerged, but the more genes you share, the more deeply invested you tend to grow. "Biological siblings just get into it more," says Thomas O'Connor, an associate professor of

psychiatry at the University of Rochester Medical Center. "They are warmer and also more conflicted."

How Those Early Bonds Can Grow Stronger with Age

One of the greatest gifts of the sibling tie is that while warmth grows over time, the conflicts often fade. After the shooting stops, even the fiercest sibling wars leave little lasting damage. Indeed, siblings who battled a lot as kids may become closer as adults—and more emotionally skilled too, often clearly recalling what their long-ago fights were about and the lessons they took from them. "I'm very sensitized to the fact that it's important to listen to others," a respondent wrote in a recent study conducted in Britain. "People get over their anger, and people who disagree are not terrible," wrote another. Even those with troubled or self-destructive siblings came away with something valuable: they learned patience, acceptance and cautionary lessons. "[You] cannot change others," wrote one. "[But] I wasn't going to be like that."

Full-blown childhood crises may *forge* even stronger lifelong links. The death of a parent blows some families to bits. But when older sibs step in to help raise younger ones, the dual role of contemporary and caretaker can lay the foundation for an indestructible closeness later on. Wayne Duvall, 48, a television and film actor in New York City and the youngest of three brothers, was just 13 when his father died. His older brothers, who had let him get away with all manner of mischief when both parents were in residence, intuitively knew that the family no longer had that luxury. "I vividly remember them leaning down to me and saying, 'The party's over,'" Duvall recalls. "My brothers are my best friends now, though they still consider me the little brother in every imaginable way."

Such powerful connections become even more important as the inevitable illnesses or widowhood of late life lead us to lean on the people we've known the longest. Even siblings who drift apart in their middle years tend to drift back together as they age. "The relationship is especially strong between sisters," who are more likely to be *predeceased* by their spouses than brothers are, says Judy Dunn, a developmental psychologist at London's Kings College. "When asked what contributes to the importance of the relationship now, they say it's the shared early childhood experiences, which cast a long shadow for all of us."

Of course, that shadow—like all shadows—is a thing created by light. Siblings, by any measure, are one of nature's better brainstorms, and all the new studies on how they make us who we are is one of science's. But the rest of us, outside the lab, see it in a more primal way. In a world that's too big, too scary and too often too lonely, we come to realize that there's nothing like having a band of brothers—and sisters—to venture out with you.

practice it   Post-Reading Activity

Reread the first few paragraphs of "The New Science of Siblings" in order to evaluate the introduction. Where does the introduction end? How do you know? Can you find a thesis for this article? Underline the thesis and write a brief summary of it in your own words. Then think about what else Kluger includes in his introductory paragraphs. What tone and style does he use? What does his language use suggest about his audience and purpose?

COMPREHENSION QUESTIONS

1. In what ways are siblings "a rehearsal tool for later life" (para. 15)?

2. Kluger goes into detail to explain how the scientists isolated the variable of sibling relationship in their experiments. How did they do this? Why is this so important to do?

3. How common is it for parents to have a favorite child? What are the possible positive and negative outcomes of favoritism, according to Kluger?

4. What is de-identification? What examples of sibling de-identification does Kluger explain?

5. What conclusions have researchers made about siblings in blended families?

VOCABULARY ACTIVITIES

1. Add any words from this article to your ongoing sibling glossary. Remember to write definitions in your own words.

2. One of Kluger's strengths as a writer is his use of strong verbs. Choose one paragraph, underline the verbs in it, and then analyze how interesting and active his verbs are. How does this contribute to his writing style? What happens if you substitute various synonyms for the verbs he is currently using?

SUMMARY ACTIVITY

Make an outline of the reading, using the technique described in Chapter 13, Essay Organization and Outlining, page 267.

DISCUSSION QUESTIONS

1. Reflect on the concept of de-identification as it applies to siblings. Think about sibling pairs you know, paying attention to how close the pairs are in age. Do your personal observations fit with the research conclusions? What specific anecdotal evidence could you use to support the claims of the researchers? To refute those claims?

2. Has your own behavior at school or work been shaped by your sibling experience? If so, how? If you don't think it has, why hasn't it?

3. This article essentially emphasizes the importance of siblings as "partners for life" (para. 5). What arguments can you make for and against this claim?

MAGAZINE

Our second selection by Jeffrey Kluger originally appeared in *Time* magazine in 2007. *Important words and phrases have been italicized in this reading. Look up those you do not know, and write the definitions in your personal vocabulary list.*

practice it   **Pre-Reading**

What are the stereotypes about the oldest, middle, and youngest children in a family? Freewrite for five minutes about this question, recalling images from the media (such as *Modern Family* or *The Middle*) as well as comments you have heard from regular people over the years. After you freewrite, make a list (by yourself or with classmates) of the qualities that are stereotypically associated with these categories of siblings.

JEFFREY KLUGER

The Power of Birth Order

It could not have been easy being Elliott Roosevelt. If the alcohol wasn't getting him, the *morphine* was. If it wasn't the morphine, it was the struggle with depression. Then, of course, there were the constant comparisons with big brother Teddy.

In 1883, the year Elliott began battling *melancholy*, Teddy had already published his first book and been elected to the New York State assembly. By 1891—about the time Elliott, still unable to establish a career, had to be *institutionalized* to deal with his addictions—Teddy was U.S. Civil Service Commissioner and the author of eight books. Three years later, Elliott, 34, died of alcoholism. Seven years after that, Teddy, 42, became President.

Elliott Roosevelt was not the only younger sibling of an eventual President to cause his family heartaches—or at least headaches. There was Donald Nixon and the loans he *wangled* from billionaire Howard Hughes. There was Billy Carter and his advocacy on behalf of the *pariah* state Libya. There was Roger Clinton and his year in jail on a cocaine conviction. And there is Neil Bush, younger sib of both a President and a Governor, implicated in the savings-and-loan scandals of the 1980s and recently gossiped about after the release of a 2002 letter in which he lamented to his *estranged* wife, "I've lost patience for being compared to my brothers."

Welcome to a very big club, Bro. It can't be easy being a runt in a litter that includes a President. But it couldn't have been easy being Billy Ripken either, an unexceptional major league infielder *craning* his neck for notice while the press swarmed around Hall of Famer and elder brother Cal. It can't be easy being Eli Manning, struggling to prove himself as an NFL quarterback while big brother Peyton polishes a Super Bowl trophy and his superman stats. And you may have never heard of Tisa Farrow, an actress of no particular note beyond her work in the 1979 horror film *Zombie*, but odds are you've heard of her sister Mia.

Of all the things that shape who we are, few seem more arbitrary than the sequence in which we and our siblings pop out of the *womb*. Maybe it's your genes that make you a gifted athlete, your training that makes you an accomplished actress, an accident of brain chemistry that makes you a drunk instead of a President. But in family after family, case study after case study, the simple roll of the birth-date dice has an odd and arbitrary power all its own.   5

The importance of birth order has been known—or at least suspected—for years. But increasingly, there's hard evidence of its impact. In June, for example, a group of Norwegian researchers released a study showing that firstborns are generally smarter than any siblings who come along later, enjoying on average a three-point IQ advantage over the next eldest—probably a result of the intellectual boost that comes from mentoring younger siblings and helping them in day-to-day tasks. The second child, in turn, is a point ahead of the third. While three points might not seem like much, the effect can be enormous. Just 2.3 IQ points can correlate to a 15-point difference in SAT scores, which makes an even bigger difference when you're an *Ivy League* applicant with a 690 verbal score going head to head against someone with a 705. "In many families," says psychologist Frank Sulloway, a visiting scholar at the University of California, Berkeley, and the man who has for decades been seen as the U.S.'s leading authority on birth order, "the firstborn is going to get into Harvard and the second-born isn't."

The differences don't stop there. Studies in the Philippines show that later-born siblings tend to be shorter and weigh less than earlier-borns. (Think the slight advantage the 6-ft. 5-in. Peyton Manning has over the 6-ft. 4-in. Eli doesn't help when he's trying to throw over the outstretched arms of a leaping lineman?) Younger siblings are less likely to be vaccinated than older ones, with last-borns getting immunized sometimes at only half the rate of first-borns. Eldest siblings are also *disproportionately* represented in high-paying professions. Younger siblings, by contrast, are looser cannons, less educated and less *strapping*, perhaps, but statistically likelier to live the exhilarating life of an artist or a comedian, an adventurer, entrepreneur, GI or firefighter. And middle children? Well, they can be a puzzle—even to researchers.

For families, none of this comes as a surprise. There are few extended clans that can't point to the firstborn, with the *heir-apparent bearing*, who makes the best grades, keeps the other kids in line and, when Mom and Dad grow old, winds up as caretaker and *executor* too. There are few that can't point to the lost-in-the-*thickets* middle-born or the wild-child last-born.

Indeed, to hear families tell it, the birth-order effect may only be getting stronger. In the past, girls were usually knocked out of the running for the job and college *perks* their place in the family should have accorded them. In most other ways, however, there was little to distinguish a first-, second- or third-born sister from a first-, second- or third-born brother. Now, with college and careers more equally available, the remaining differences have largely melted away.

"There are stereotypes out there about birth order, and very often those   10
stereotypes are spot-on," says Delroy Paulhus, a professor of psychology at the University of British Columbia in Vancouver. "I think this is one of those cases in which people just figured things out on their own."

But have they? Stack up enough *anecdotal* maybes, and they start to look like a scientific definitely. Things that appear definite, however, have a funny way of surprising you, and birth order may conceal all manner of hidden dimensions—within individuals, within families, within the scientific studies. "People read birth-order books the way they read horoscopes," warns Toni Falbo, professor of educational psychology at the University of Texas. "'I'm a middle-born, so that explains everything in my life'—it's just not like that." Still, such *skepticism* does not prevent more and more researchers from being drawn to the field, and as they are, their findings, and the debate over them, continue to grow.

Humans Aren't Alone

If you think it's hard to manage the birth-order issues in your family, be thankful you're not an *egret* or an orange blossom. Egrets are not the intellectual heavyweights of the animal kingdom—or even the bird world—but nature makes them remarkably *cunning* when it comes to planning their families. Like most other birds, egrets lay multiple eggs, but rather than brooding them all the same way so that the chicks emerge on more or less the same day, the mother begins incubating her first and second eggs before laying the remaining ones in her *clutch*. That causes the babies to appear on *successive* days, which gives the first-arriving chick the earliest crack at the food and a 24-hour head start on growth. The second-hatched may not have too difficult a time catching up, but the third may struggle. The fourth and beyond will have the hardest go, getting pushed aside or even pecked to death if food, water and shelter become scarce.

All that makes for a nasty nursery, but that's precisely the way the mother wants it. "The parents overproduce a bit," says Douglas Mock, professor of zoology at the University of Oklahoma, "maybe making one more baby than they can normally afford to raise and then letting it take the fall if the resource budget is limited."

Orange trees are even tougher on their young. A typical orange tree carries about 100,000 pollinated blossoms, each of which is a potential orange, complete with the seeds that are potential trees. But in the course of a season, only about 500 oranges are actually produced. The tree determines which ones make the cut, shedding the blossoms that are not receiving enough light or that otherwise don't seem *viable*. It is, for a tree, a sort of selective *termination* on a *vast* scale. "You've got 99% of the babies being thrown out by the parent," says Mock. "The tree just drops all the losers."

Even mammals, warm-blooded in *metabolism* and—we like to think—*temperament*, can play a similarly *pitiless* game. Runts of litters are routinely ignored, pushed out or *consigned* to the worst nursing spots somewhere near Mom's *aft* end, where the milk flow is the poorest and the outlook for survival the bleakest. The rest of the *brood* is left to fight it out for the best, most milk-rich positions.

Humans, more sentimental than birds, trees or litter bearers, don't like to   15
see themselves as coming from the same child-rearing traditions, but we face many of the same pressures. As recently as 100 years ago, children in the U.S. had only about a 50% chance of surviving into adulthood, and in less developed parts of the world, the odds remain *daunting*. It can be a sensible strategy to have multiple offspring to continue your line in case some are claimed by disease or injury.

While the eldest in an overpopulated brood has it relatively easy—getting 100% of the food the parents have available—things get stretched thinner when a second-born comes along. Later-borns put even more pressure on resources. Over time, everyone might be getting the same *rations*, but the firstborn still enjoys a *caloric* head start that might never be overcome.

Food is not the only resource. There's time and attention too and the emotional nourishment they provide. It's not for nothing that family scrapbooks are usually stuffed with pictures and report cards of the firstborn and *successively* fewer of the later-borns—and the later-borns notice it. Educational opportunities can be unevenly shared too, particularly in families that can afford the tuition bills of only one child. Catherine Salmon, an assistant professor of psychology at the University of Redlands in Redlands, Calif., *laments* that even today she finds it hard to collect enough subjects for birth-order studies from the student body alone, since the campus population is typically overweighted with eldest sibs. "Families invest a lot in the firstborn," she says.

All of this favoritism can become self-reinforcing. As parental *pampering* produces a fitter, smarter, more confident firstborn, Mom and Dad are likely to invest even more in that child, placing their bets on an offspring who—in survival terms at least—is looking increasingly like a sure thing. "From a parental perspective," says Salmon, "you want offspring who are going to survive and reproduce."

Firstborns do more than survive; they thrive. In a recent survey of corporate heads conducted by Vistage, an international organization of *CEOs*, poll takers reported that 43% of the people who occupy the big chair in boardrooms are firstborns, 33% are middle-borns and 23% are last-borns. Eldest siblings are *disproportionately* represented among surgeons and M.B.A.s too, according to Stanford University psychologist Robert Zajonc. And a recent study found a *statistically significant* overload of firstborns in what is—or at least ought to be—the country's most *august* club: the U.S. Congress. "We know that birth order determines occupational prestige to a large extent," says Zajonc. "There is some expectation that firstborns are somehow better qualified for certain occupations."

Little Sibs, Big Role

For eldest siblings, this is a pretty sweet deal. There is not much incentive for 20
them to change a family system that provides them so many goodies, and typically they don't try to. Younger siblings see things differently and struggle early on to shake up the existing order. They clearly don't have size on their side, as their physically larger siblings keep them in line with what researchers call a high-power strategy. "If you're bigger than your siblings, you punch 'em," Sulloway says.

But there are low-power strategies too, and one of the most effective ones is humor. It's awfully hard to resist the charms of someone who can make you laugh, and families *abound* with stories of last-borns who are the clowns of the *brood*, able to get their way simply by being funny or outrageous. Birth-order scholars often observe that some of history's great *satirists*—Voltaire, Jonathan Swift, Mark Twain—were among the youngest members of large families, a pattern that continues today. *Faux bloviator* Stephen Colbert—who yields to no one in his ability to get a laugh—often points out that he's the last of 11 children.

Such examples might be little more than *anecdotal*, but personality tests show that while firstborns score especially well on the dimension of temperament known as *conscientiousness*—a sense of general responsibility and follow-through—later-borns score higher on what's known as agreeableness, or the simple ability to get along in the world. "Kids recognize a good low-power strategy," says Sulloway. "It's the way any sensible organism sizes up the *niches* that are available."

Even more impressive is how early younger siblings develop what's known as the theory of mind. Very small children have a hard time distinguishing the things they know from the things they assume other people know. A toddler who watches an adult hide a toy will expect that anyone who walks into the room afterward will also know where to find it, *reckoning* that all knowledge is *universal* knowledge. It usually takes a child until age 3 to learn that that's not so. For children who have at least one elder sibling, however, the realization typically comes earlier. "When you're less powerful, it's advantageous to be able to anticipate what's going on in someone else's mind," says Sulloway.

Later-borns, however, don't try merely to please other people; they also try to provoke them. Richard Zweigenhaft, a professor of psychology at Guilford College in Greensboro, N.C., who revealed the *overrepresentation* of firstborns in Congress, conducted a similar study of *picketers* at labor demonstrations. On the occasions that the events grew unruly enough to lead to arrests, he would interview the people the police rounded up. Again and again, he found, the majority were later- or last-borns. "It was a statistically significant pattern," says Zweigenhaft. "A *disproportionate* number of them were choosing to be arrested."

Courting Danger

Later-borns are similarly willing to take risks with their physical safety. All sibs   25
are equally likely to be involved in sports, but younger ones are likelier to choose the kinds that could cause injury. "They don't go out for tennis," Sulloway says. "They go out for rugby, ice hockey." Even when siblings play the same sport, they play it differently. Sulloway is currently collaborating on a study of 300 brothers who were major league ballplayers. Though the work is not complete, he is so far finding that the *elder* brothers excel at skills that involve less physical danger. Younger siblings are the ones who put themselves in harm's way—crouching down in catcher's gear to block an incoming runner, say. "It doesn't just hold up in this study but a dozen studies," Sulloway says.

It's not clear whether such behavior extends to career choice, but Sandra Black, an associate professor of economics at UCLA, is intrigued by findings that firstborns tend to earn more than later-borns, with income dropping about 1% for every step down the birth-order ladder. Most researchers assume this is due to the educational advantages eldest siblings get, but Black thinks there may be more to it. "I'd be interested in whether it's because the second child is taking the riskier jobs," she says.

Black's *forthcoming* studies will be designed to answer that question, but research by Ben Dattner, a business consultant and professor of industrial and organizational psychology at New York University, is showing that even when later-borns take *conservative* jobs in the corporate world, they approach their work in a high-wire way. Firstborn CEOs, for example, do best when they're making *incremental* improvements in their companies: shedding underperforming products, maximizing profits from existing lines and generally making sure the trains run on time. Later-born CEOs are more inclined to blow up the trains and lay new track. "Later-borns are better at *transformational* change," says Dattner. "They pursue riskier, more innovative, more creative approaches."

If eldest sibs are the dogged achievers and youngest sibs are the gamblers and visionaries, where does this leave those in between? That it's so hard to define what middle-borns become is largely due to the fact that it's so hard to define who they are growing up. The youngest in the family, but only until someone else comes along, they are both teacher and student, babysitter and babysat, too young for the privileges of the firstborn but too old for the *latitude* given the last. Middle children are expected to step up to the plate when the eldest child goes off to school or in some other way drops out of the picture— and generally serve when called. The Norwegian intelligence study showed that when firstborns die, the IQ of second-borns actually rises a bit, a sign that they're performing the hard *mentoring* work that goes along with the new job.

Stuck for life in a center seat, middle children get shortchanged even on family resources. Unlike the firstborn, who spends at least some time as the only-child eldest, and the last-born, who hangs around long enough to become the only-child youngest, middlings are never alone and thus never get 100% of the parents' investment of time and money. "There is a U-shaped distribution in which the oldest and youngest get the most," says Sulloway. That may take an emotional *toll.* Sulloway cites other studies in which the self-esteem of first-, middle- and last-borns is plotted on a graph and follows the same *curvilinear trajectory.*

The phenomenon known as *de-identification* may also work against a   30
middle-born. Siblings who hope to stand out in a family often do so by observing what the elder child does and then doing the opposite. If the firstborn gets good grades and takes a job after school, the second-born may go the slacker route. The third-born may then de-de-identify, opting for *industriousness*, even if in the more unconventional ways of the last born. A Chinese study in the 1990s showed just this kind of zigzag pattern, with the first child generally scoring high as a "good son or daughter," the second scoring low, the third scoring high again and so on. In a three-child family, the very act of trying to be unique may instead leave the middling lost, a pattern that may continue into adulthood.

The Holes in the Theories

The birth-order effect, for all its seeming *robustness*, is not indestructible. There's a lot that can throw it out of balance—particularly family *dysfunction*. In a 2005 study, investigators at the University of Birmingham in Britain examined the case histories of 400 abused children and the 795 siblings of those so-called *index* kids. In general, they found that when only one child in the family was abused, the *scapegoat* was usually the eldest. When a younger child was abused, some or all of the other kids usually were as well. Mistreatment of any of the children usually breaks the bond the parents have with the firstborn, turning that child from parental *ally* to protector of the *brood*. At the same time, the eldest may pick up some of the younger kids' agreeableness skills—the better to deal with irrational parents—while the youngest learn some of the firstborn's self-sufficiency. Abusiveness is going to "totally disrupt the birth-order effects we would expect," says Sulloway.

The sheer number of siblings in a family can also *trump* birth order. The 1% income difference that Black detected from child to child tends to flatten out as you move down the age line, with a smaller earnings gap between a third and fourth child than between a second and third. The IQ-boosting power of tutoring, meanwhile, may actually have less influence in small families, with parents of just two or three kids doing most of the teaching, than in the six- or eight-child family, in which the eldest sibs have to pitch in more. Since the Norwegian IQ study rests on the tutoring effect, those findings may be open to question. "The good birth-order studies will control for family size," says Bo Cleveland, associate professor of human development and family studies at Penn State University. "Sometimes that makes the birth-order effect go away; sometimes it doesn't."

The most *vocal* detractors of birth-order research question less the findings of the science than the methods. To achieve any kind of statistical significance, investigators must assemble large samples of families and look for patterns among them. But families are very different things—distinguished by size, income, hometown, education, religion, ethnicity and more. Throw enough random factors like those into the mix, and the results you get may be nothing more than interesting junk.

The alternative is what investigators call the in-family studies, a much more *pointillist* process, requiring an exhaustive look at a single family, comparing every child with every other child and then repeating the process again and again with hundreds of other families. Eventually, you may find threads that link them all. "I would throw out all the between-family studies," says Cleveland. "The proof is in the in-family design."

Ultimately, of course, the birth-order debate will never be entirely settled.   35
Family studies and the statistics they yield are cold and *precise* things, *parsing* human behavior down to decimal points and margins of error. But families are a good deal sloppier than that, a *mishmash* of competing needs and moods and clashing emotions, better understood by the people in the thick of them than by anyone standing outside. Yet *millenniums* of families would swear by the power of birth order to shape the adults we eventually become. Science may yet overturn the whole theory, but for now, the smart money says otherwise.

Post-Reading Activity

Look back at the list you generated from the pre-reading freewrite. How does the research compare with your list? Choose one idea from your list—such as the view that the eldest sibling is the smartest or that the youngest is wild—and carefully list all the evidence you can find in Kluger's article to support or refute that claim. Include specific quotes from the article and be as detailed as possible in recording your personal observations and examples.

COMPREHENSION QUESTIONS

1. What does the scientific evidence generally suggest about the power of birth order?

2. What resources do children need to thrive?

3. What is the difference between a high-power strategy and a low-power strategy?

4. In the last section of the article, Kluger explains the counterarguments against the importance of birth order. What are they? How does he handle those counterarguments?

VOCABULARY ACTIVITIES

1. Add any words from this article to your ongoing sibling glossary. Remember to write definitions in your own words.

2. Kluger uses some jargon in this article. Make a list of all the terms that you would identify as "jargon" or technical language, and then identify the discipline(s)—such as psychology, sociology, or biology—that would be most likely to use that terminology. Use roots, prefixes, and suffixes that you know from those disciplines to help you figure out the meanings if necessary. For more on roots, prefixes, and suffixes, see Chapter 8, Vocabulary Building, page 198.

SUMMARY ACTIVITY

Make a list of all the qualities that Kluger attributes to oldest, middle, and youngest siblings. Then write a one-sentence summary for each of the three categories. Add an introductory sentence and a concluding sentence, so you have a complete, coherent paragraph. For help writing a summary, see Chapter 1, Reading and Responding to College Texts, page 2.

DISCUSSION QUESTIONS

1. Why does Kluger refer to famous siblings? How well does this serve his purposes as a writer?

2. What is the point of bringing in the example of egrets, orange trees, and mammal "runts of litters" (para. 14)? Do you find this information useful? Why or why not? What does it suggest about Kluger's audience that he includes this information?

3. Overall, are you convinced by the research Kluger offers? Why or why not? Which claims are well supported with a variety of types of evidence? Which claims seem to need more support to convince you?

4. After you have carefully considered the evidence and reflected on your personal observations, what is your opinion about the influence of birth order in shaping personality? Can you sum up your views in one clear statement?

MAGAZINE

Journalist and essayist Lauren Sandler has covered a range of issues, including the American family, the Christian youth movement, and cultural politics. She is the author of *Righteous: Dispatches from the Evangelical Youth Movement* (2006) and *One and Only: The Freedom of Having an Only Child, and the Joy of Being One* (2013), and she also writes the blog *One and Only: A Journalist—and Only Child—Investigates the Choice to Have Just One Kid*. Herself an only child, Sandler is also the parent of an only child, so her perspective on the research seems inclined to challenge stereotypes about only children. This article was a *Time* cover story in July 2010. *Important words and phrases have been italicized in this reading. Look up those you do not know, and write the definitions in your personal vocabulary list.*

practice it Pre-Reading

As the title suggests, this article is about debunking—or challenging—the "myths" of the only child. What are your preconceived ideas about only children? What are the stereotypes of only children that you have seen in popular culture? Make a list or cluster diagram of all the only children that you can remember from television or movies or books and describe their overall characteristics in these depictions. How do your own feelings about only children compare and contrast to the media images?

To review strategies such as listing and clustering, see Chapter 9, Pre-Writing, page 214.

LAUREN SANDLER

The Only Child: Debunking the Myths

It's a conversation I have most weeks—if not most days. This time, it happens when my 2-year-old daughter and I are buying milk at the supermarket. The cashiers *fawn over* her pink cheeks and applaud when she twirls for them, and then I endure the usual dialogue.

"Your first?"

"Yup."

"Another one coming soon?"

"Nope—it might be just this one."

"You'll have more. You'll see."

"At the moment, I'm not planning on it."

"You wouldn't do that to your child. You'll see."

5

I offer no *retort*, but if I did, I'd start by asking these young minimum-wage earners to consider the following: the U.S. Department of Agriculture reports that the average child in the U.S. costs his or her parents about $286,050—before college. Those costs have actually risen during the recession. The milk I'm buying adds up to $50 a month, and we're pushing toilet training just to drop the cost of diapers—about $100 a month—from our monthly budget. It's a marvel to me these days that anyone can manage a second kid—forget about a third.

And since I celebrated my 35th birthday, I have to ask myself not when   10 but if. My parents asked themselves that question when I was my daughter's age and decided the answer was no. They wanted the experience of parenting but also their careers, the freedom to travel and the lower cost and *urbane* excitement of making a home in an apartment rather than a suburban house. Back then, their choice was rare, but if we too choose to stop at one child, my daughter will likely feel far less alone in her only status than I did.

"The *recession* has dramatically reshaped women's childbearing desires," says Larry Finer, the director of *domestic* policy at the Guttmacher Institute, a leading reproductive-health research organization. The institute found that 64% of women polled said that with the economy the way it is, they couldn't afford to have a baby now. Forty-four percent said they plan to reduce or delay their childbearing—again, because of the economy. This happens during financial meltdowns: the Great Depression saw single-child families spike at 23% of all families, and that was back when onlies were still an *anomaly*. Since the early '60s, according to the National Center for Health Statistics, single-child families have almost doubled in number, to about 1 in 5—and that's from before the markets crashed. Birth control has quickly become one of the recession's few growth industries.

Meanwhile, friends and relatives—not to mention supermarket cashiers, pastors and, I've found, strangers on the subway—continue to urge parents of only children to have another baby. There are certain time-honored reasons for having that baby: in many countries and communities, the *mandate* to be fruitful and multiply is a powerful religious *directive*. And family size can be dictated by biology as much as by psychology. But the entrenched *aversion* to stopping at one mainly amounts to a century-old public-relations issue. Single children are perceived as spoiled, selfish, solitary misfits. No parents want that for their kid. Since the 1970s, however, studies devoted to understanding the personality characteristics of only children have *debunked* that idea. I, for one, was happy without siblings. A few ex-boyfriends aside, people seem to think I turned out just fine. So why, at a time when so many parents worry about being able to support more than one, do we still worry that there's something wrong with just one? And what will it mean for future generations if more parents than ever before decide that one is enough?

A Stereotype Is Born

The image of the lonely only—or at least the *legitimizing* of that idea—was the work of one man, Granville Stanley Hall. About 120 years ago, Hall established one of the first American psychology-research labs and was a leader of the child-study movement. A national network of study groups called Hall Clubs existed to spread his teachings. But what he is most known for today is supervising the 1896 study "Of Peculiar and Exceptional Children," which described a series of only-child oddballs as permanent misfits. Hall—and every other *fledgling* psychologist—knew close to nothing about *credible* research practices. Yet for decades, academics and advice columnists alike *disseminated* his conclusion that an only child could not be expected to go through life with the same capacity for adjustment that children with siblings possessed. "Being an only child is a disease in itself," he claimed.

Later generations of scholars tried to correct the record, but their findings never filtered into popular parenting *discourse*. Meanwhile, the "peculiar" only children—"overprivileged, asocial, royally autonomous . . . self-centered, aloof and overly intellectual," as sociologist Judith Blake describes them in her 1989 book *Family Size and Achievement permeated* pop culture, from the demon children in horror films (*The Omen, The Bad Seed*) to the oddball sidekicks in '80s sitcoms (*Growing Pains, Family Ties*). Even on the new show *Modern Family*, the *tween singleton* is a *cringingly precocious* loner with a *coddling* mother. Such vehicles have evangelized Hall's teachings more than his clubs did. Of course we ask when someone is going to have "kids," not "a kid." Of course we think that one is the loneliest number.

No one has done more to disprove Hall's stereotype than Toni Falbo, a   15
professor of educational psychology and sociology at the University of Texas at Austin. An only child herself and the mother of one, Falbo began investigating the only-child experience in the 1970s, both in the U.S. and in China (where the government's one-child policy, the world's biggest experiment in population control, went into effect in 1979), drawing on the experience of tens of thousands of subjects. Twenty-five years ago, she and *colleague* Denise Polit conducted a *meta-analysis* of 115 studies of only children from 1925 onward that considered developmental outcomes of adjustment, character, sociability, achievement and intelligence. The studies, mainly from the U.S., cut across class and race.

Generally, those studies showed that singletons aren't measurably different from other kids—except that they, along with firstborns and people who have only one sibling, score higher in measures of intelligence and achievement. No one, Falbo says, has published research that can demonstrate any truth behind the stereotype of the only child as lonely, selfish and *maladjusted*. (She has spoken those three words so many times in the past 35 years that they run together as one: lonelyselfishmaladjusted.) Falbo and Polit later completed a second *quantitative* review of more than 200 personality studies.

By and large, they found that the personalities of only children were indistinguishable from their peers with siblings.

"For most people, this still hasn't sunk in," she tells me after a meeting of her graduate seminar in social psychology. She's just spent a couple of hours pacing a *linoleum* classroom floor in platform heels, presenting data to her students—all of whom have siblings, except for an exchange student from China (who is a product of the one-child policy)—but they still don't seem to have *internalized* the lesson. After class, a student from West Texas chats with a student from India. He had *astute* things to say during class regarding how cultures adapt over time, offering sharp observations about the psychology of *collectivism*. But now he refers to how there's "no only-child problem" in his big family. "I'm not saying only children are socially retarded or anything, but, you know . . ." he laughs.

Undiluted Resources

At California State University at Dominguez Hills, Adriean Mancillas—an only child and the mother of triplets—has studied the *prevalence* of only-child stereotypes. They can be found cross-culturally from Estonia to Brazil, she says, dating to "when people needed bigger families to farm the land." And they stick. "You can tell people all the research in the world that contradicts it," she says, but the same *cognitive psychology* that maintains any sort of prejudice, large or small, applies.

Of course, part of the reason we assume only children are spoiled is that whatever parents have to give, the only child gets it all. The argument Blake makes in *Family Size and Achievement* as to why onlies are higher achievers across *socioeconomic* lines can be stated simply: there's no *"dilution* of resources," as she terms it, between siblings. No matter their income or occupation, parents of only children have more time, energy and money to invest in their kid, who gets all the dance classes, piano lessons and prep courses, as well as all their parents' attention when it comes to helping work out an algebra problem. That attention, researchers have noticed, leads to not just higher SAT scores but also higher self-esteem.

And as Falbo tells her students, the cocktail of *aptitude* and confidence 20 yields results: only children tend to do better in school and get more education—college, medical or law degrees—than other kids. Not that having siblings will necessarily *thwart* you; Einstein had a sister and did just fine. But for every Venus and Serena Williams you can find a *luminary* singleton: Cary Grant, Elvis Presley, John Updike, Lance Armstrong or Frank Sinatra.

But if only children do get it all, doesn't that mean there's truth to the stereotype that they're *overindulged*? In Austin, I seek out the counseling practice of psychologist Carl Pickhardt, who meets with patients in his office on the ground floor of a Victorian house. The low lamplight—and Kleenex box on his coffee table—*renders* an *inversion* of Falbo's fluorescent-lit classroom. Pickhardt, author of *The Future of Your Only Child*, is neither cheerleading nor *hectoring*, as participants in the *stratified* conversation about only children tend to be. His soft-voiced presence is a reminder that clinical sampling can take us only so far, that human behavior cannot be entirely reduced to numbers on a questionnaire.

"There's no question that only children are highly indulged and highly protected," he tells me. But that doesn't mean the stereotype is true, he says, at least not based on his four decades of seeing singletons—both kids and adults—unburden themselves in his office. "You've been given more attention and nurturing to develop yourself. But that's not the same thing as being selfish. On balance, that level of parental involvement is a good thing. All that attention is the energy for your self-esteem and achievement." But, he adds, "everything is double-edged. And everything is *formative*."

In a suburb outside Austin, Zoe and Don Mullican live with their 9-year-old daughter Sophia in a rented house with a red pickup parked outside. The beige sectional couch in the family room was a free Craigslist find; folding mesh chairs make up the outdoor furniture in the yard. On the tailgate of their truck is a purple sticker that bears the name of the private Austin Waldorf School, which Sophia attends. Zoe recently lost her job as an executive assistant in a law firm, and the new *gig* she found is only part time, resulting in a significant cut in their family income. (Don works as a civil engineer.) They've scaled back on "everything from gas to groceries to clothing," Zoe says, but Sophia's attendance at her school is nonnegotiable. As is her status as an only child. "We have such limited resources financially, and we want to give one person the best we could give," Zoe tells me over Don's home-brewed beer at a backyard barbecue.

Researchers have crunched the numbers from years of standardized tests like the National Merit Scholarship exam to measure verbal and mathematical abilities. In each category, only children performed better than children from larger families. Furthermore, they're expected to. Falbo tells her class that parents have significantly higher expectations of academic achievement and attainment when they have just one kid. But Pickhardt notes that parental expectations are merely part of the pressure only children can feel. Much of it is self-imposed, he says, because of their notions of themselves as performing at a peer level with their parents. It's the other edge of all that adult-icizing: pressure and responsibility usually accompany success, and neither feels much like childhood.

But Zoe doesn't sound that worried about it as we talk over the sound of   25
Sophia belting out *High School Musical* karaoke upstairs in her room with two other singleton friends. Zoe was an only child herself until she was a teenager; so was her oldest friend, whose only child's voice joins the chorus of Vanessa Hudgens impersonators. When Sophia and her friends come downstairs for grilled turkey burgers, Sophia expresses dismay that I haven't heard of the band Ghostland Observatory, which she saw perform at Austin City Limits with her parents last year. "Mom, you gotta play it for her!" she says. "They're one of our favorite bands," the 9-year-old tells me. Zoe puts on the album, sits

down next to Sophia and gives her a hug. "Isn't this great?" they say together. To my only-child eyes, their *dynamic* looks ideal, but I can hear the nay-saying voices in my head wondering if this is the fullest form of childhood.

Will It Make Us Happier?

As parents, we tend to ask ourselves two questions when we talk with our partners about having more children. First, will it make our kid happier? And then, will it make us happier?

When University of Pennsylvania *demography* professor Samuel Preston was conducting research to help him predict the future of fertility, he told me the discovery that surprised him most was that parents felt so madly in love with their first child, they wanted a second. That's an unusual finding. Talk to parents and you'll often hear that they opt to have another because they think it will be better for the child they already have. Not many say they do it for themselves, no matter how much they may love the experience of parenting.

But I bring it up because of how deeply I feel all that love for my kid. I am not someone who spent my first three decades imagining a glowing pregnancy followed by maternal *bliss*. In fact, I used to suspect that mothers who talked about their children with such unbridled wonder didn't have much else going on in their lives. Then I had my daughter—and now I *gush* like the rest of them. When I was interviewing the parents of only children, several *paraphrased* the words of one mother I spoke with: "If I knew I could have him all over again, I'd do it in a heartbeat. But being a mother, and loving being a mother, means being his mother—at least that's how I experience it." I can relate, which is why it amazes me when people seem to think that parents who choose to have one kid don't love their child as much as parents who have more—that somehow they are doing their kid harm.

Parents who intend to have only one say they can manage the *drudgery* with an eye on the light at the end of the tunnel. Beth Nixon, a Pennsylvania artist and mother of a 1-year-old, says she finds reassurance every day in the fact that "it's not going to be an endless chain of need which is going to be fulfilled for years and years." When her daughter Ida wakes up every hour and a half, screaming with the pain of teething, Nixon feels like it's no big deal. "I can be fully present for this and do my best at trying to appreciate it, because it's like, this is the only time I am going to do this."

Rochelle Rosen works full time running her own educational-consulting   30
firm in Massachusetts while a nanny stays with her young daughter. "People judge me for working full time and for saying I don't want another kid, like these things mean I don't love my daughter. They tell me I'd be happier if I didn't work as much, if I had another kid," she says. "If I have another child, in five years or 10 years will I be happy that I did it? Maybe. But I try to imagine the first couple of years and try to imagine the impact on my daughter. I am so torn in different directions already."

A 2007 survey found that at a rate of 3 to 1, people believe the main purpose of marriage is the "mutual happiness and fulfillment" of adults rather than the "bearing and raising of children." There must be some balance between the joy our kids give us and the sacrifices we make to care for them. Social scientists have *surmised* since the 1970s that singletons offer the rich experience of parenting without the consuming efforts that multiple children add: all the wonder and giggles and shampoo mohawks but with leftover energy for sex, conversation, reading and so on. The research of Hans-Peter Kohler, a population sociologist at the University of Pennsylvania, gives weight to that idea. In his analysis of a survey of 35,000 Danish twins, women with one child said they were more satisfied with their lives than women with none or more than one. As Kohler told me, "At face value, you should say that you'll stop at one child to *maximize* your subjective well being."

"Most people are saying, I can't divide myself anymore," says social psychologist Susan Newman. Before technology made the office a 24-hour presence, we actually spent less time actively parenting, she explains. "We no longer send a child out to play for three hours and have those three hours to ourselves," she says. "Now you take them to the next practice, the next class. We've been consumed by our children. But we're moving back slowly to parents wanting to have a life too. And people are realizing that's simply easier with one."

The New Traditional Family

While singleton households may become "the new traditional family," as Newman puts it, in Leslie and Jarrod Moore's church community in Amarillo, Texas, tradition means something quite different. The couple decided to become parents when Leslie was 25, but pregnancy didn't come easily. It was years before Leslie finally conceived, and by the time Bryar—now 9—arrived healthy, the Moores decided their hard-won baby boy was "the one God meant for us to have and the only one we want." Jarrod, who has his own home-design company, is one of six and says he knows how hard it is to share resources with siblings. Bryar plays four sports, and "it's already expensive," says Leslie. "Forget college, insurance and a car. Imagine if we were running around to twice as many sporting events, buying twice as many uniforms and tennis shoes," she says. "People around here think we're crazy. But to tell you the truth, if by some weird twist I got pregnant accidentally, we would be devastated."

If you comb the World Values Survey, you'll find *religiosity* and fertility go hand in hand, whether in more *secular* Europe or in more *pious* America. As much as family size is a deeply personal issue, for many people it is also a spiritual one. And as Samuel Preston writes in his 2008 paper "The Future of American Fertility," high fertility can *beget* high fertility: children who inherit their parents' religious beliefs inherit at least one of the reasons to have many children themselves. No wonder churches nationwide *vied* to book Jon and Kate Gosselin (predivorce) for guest spots in their pulpits. Evangelicals—the biggest share of their viewership—saw the Gosselins' brood as proof of pure piety.

Back when the *mandate* to be fruitful and multiply was first *chiseled* in   35
stone, there was a true *impetus* behind the idea. It was pretty elementary evolutionary psychology: the more you bred, the more likely your line was to survive. Large families were social networks and insurance policies. More kids meant more helping hands, more productivity, more comfort. In much of the world, that is still the case.

Most American families aren't of *biblical* proportions any longer, but a *plurality* of adults (46%) say two children is the ideal number, according to a 2010 Pew survey on American motherhood. Only 3% said one child was ideal—the same number that said zero. But Kohler says his happiness study contributes to a *consensus* that a *metamorphosis* is afoot. "If people feel they have to give in to these social expectations to have more children, then they might have another child for reasons other than their own happiness," he told me. "But as the acceptability of one-child families increases over time, there's an absence of these pressures to have more children—and so people don't."

Falbo has observed that in some urban areas in China where the one-child policy has been relaxed and permission has been given to have more than one child, families still choose to have only one—largely because of economic uncertainty. And that's not just an Asian phenomenon. A paper by Joshua Goldstein, a director of the Max Planck Institute for Demographic Research in Germany, made a stir at population conferences: he presented research on how the next generation of German and Austrian parents will be the first in Europe to see only children as more common.

Ascent of the Onlies?

Goldstein's paper is just one of many *exacerbating angst* about the current low-fertility "crisis" that has European economists and *policy wonks* in a panic. In the early 1960s, Europe represented 20% of the world's population. About a century later, those numbers are projected to drop to about 7.5%, despite the rise in minority and immigrant birthrates. Between now and 2030, demographers forecast the E.U. will have lost 13 million—or almost 4%—of people ages 15 to 64. Meanwhile, the number of people over 65 will increase by more than 40%. On a continent where the fertility rate is well below 2, these questions arise: Who will make up the workforce? Who will care for the disproportionate number of elderly citizens?

The latter is a question felt even more *acutely* on a personal level—particularly in the *microcosm* of the single-child family. A 2001 study found that one of the most consistent self-perceived challenges for only children was concern about being the sole caretaker for aging parents (including feelings of anxiety about being the sole survivor in the family once their parents died). My parents address my unspoken anxiety with monthly payments into a long-term health care insurance plan. But there are limits to what can be managed by *logistics*, even for families with the resources to plan ahead. Like many only children, I've lined up emotional and practical support—in my case, my spouse. My husband is like a son to my parents. He will be the first to spoon *pureed* food into my mother's mouth, like he did for my grandmother, or help my father in the bathroom, like he did for my grandfather. And yet I know my parents are not his. I know it's not the same.

Of course, having siblings is no guarantee that the burden of elder care will be shared equally or even shared at all. But imagining this emotionally fraught inevitability *impels* many people I know to have more kids, especially if they can afford them. (As one Park Avenue obstetrician told me, in her practice "three is the new black.")   40

It may be tough to trace the overall impact of single-child families in the U.S., if, as some experts predict, they trend upward alongside an increase in larger families—not of the *9 by Design ilk* but three- and four-child families. While demographers expect to see a slip in population because of the recession, the champion breeders among us will likely offset the continuing ascent of onlies. Preston, the University of Pennsylvania demographer, projects that in the U.S. both the number of larger families and the number of only children will keep growing. But our national picture will probably look a little different: the recent Pew study on American motherhood shows a major uptick in the share of births to Hispanic women, who now give birth to 1 in 4 babies, while white motherhood has declined by 12 percentage points since 1990. (The share of births to Asian mothers has also increased, though not nearly as dramatically, while African-American families have stayed stable.)

Even with those population segments in mind, Andrew Oswald, a professor at the University of Warwick who studies the relationship between economics and happiness, predicts many families will continue to shrink, assuming the nation doesn't slide far deeper into economic crisis. *Ironically*, it seems that if economic pressures can bring about lower fertility, so can economic prosperity. "I love my own daughters to bits. But skiing and sports cars without baby seats can be fun too," he says. "That's why only children are the *secular* trend of a rich society we've been moving toward for the past 100 years."

That trend is what is known as the second *demographic transition*, a concept Ron Lesthaeghe at the University of Michigan advanced 25 years ago. It refers to the fertility shift that occurred when the *industrial* world moved from high birth and death rates to low ones. Now postponement of parenthood—or refusal of it—in favor of greater focus on education and career, longer periods of searching for the ideal mate and a more flexible and pleasure-seeking life has given us the second demographic transition. Because of these "rich society" tendencies, Oswald guesses that 50-odd years from now, the U.S. will be worrying about declining population, just like Europe and Japan are today.

What shape might that worry take? Nicholas Eberstadt of the American Enterprise Institute has furrowed his brow a great deal over what he calls "the depopulation bomb" in Russia and China, but he says even if it were to go off in the U.S., we wouldn't face the same kinds of *collective* problems. "It's not like we don't have the *social capital*, the rule of law, the sorts of *institutional infrastructure* that we in the West take for granted," he told me. He says he's not even that worried about Europe. "That's a whole lot less consequential than in China, where there is no national public pension system, where people have relied on relatives for economic backup since *time immemorial*." He's not just talking about siblings: in China, as generations of only children follow each other, the cousin disappears from the family tree.

On the other hand, no one in the U.S. is taking Social Security for granted   45
these days. If they needed it, I wouldn't be able to financially support my parents in their decline without their long-term-care plan—especially with another year or two of day care still to go. If it were easier to be a parent in this country and if the current economic situation weren't so *dire*, I might feel more inclined to have a second child myself.

As I enter what my obstetrician calls advanced maternal age, it's a choice my husband and I need to make soon. In doing so, we talk about the idea that to be good parents, we have to be happy people. How we determine our happiness and our daughter's will be based on the love we feel for her and the realities—both joyful and trying—of what a larger family would mean. What we won't consider is whether being an only child will screw her up; we'll do that fine in other ways.

If we end up having no other children, we'll have to be mindful to raise her to be part of something bigger than just us three. But must we share DNA to do that? Stepparents and stepsiblings have become firmly *normative* in American culture. Single, unmarried and gay parents have headed in that direction too. As Susan Newman tells me, "What really changes, the fewer siblings we have, is how we define family." I've been part of this redefinition all my life. Like most only children, I've cast cousins and friends as *ersatz* siblings since I was a child, knowing it's not the same as having a brother or a sister but not necessarily missing what I don't have. For now, my kid is happy enough to dance down supermarket aisles by herself or with her friends and cousins. And with her, sometimes, I do too.

---

practice it   **Post-Reading Activity**

Look up Granville Stanley Hall in your library databases and online. What can you learn about him? What books did he publish? What was his contribution to the fields of child development and psychology? Based on your brief research, do you think Sandler treats him fairly? If you wanted to investigate further, what steps would you take?

For research tips, see Chapter 19, Research, page 351.

COMPREHENSION QUESTIONS

1. The opening conversation Sandler describes ends with the line "'You wouldn't do that to your child. You'll see'" (para. 8). What is "that"? What is it that many people believe parents are doing to their only children?

2. Why do people try to suggest that parents should have (and sometimes even pressure parents into having) more than one child?

3. In the past, what were the economic reasons to have a large family?

4. What are the economic reasons not to have a second child in twenty-first-century America?

5. Who is Granville Stanley Hall? What role did he play in the development of stereotypes about only children?

6. What does the research prove? Are only children worse off or better off or no different from children with siblings?

7. What is the "new traditional family," according to Sandler?

8. What is the "second demographic transition" (para. 43)? Why is it significant with regard to Sandler's points?

VOCABULARY ACTIVITIES

1. Choose the paragraph in the article that has the most challenging vocabulary for you. Using roots/prefixes/suffixes and context clues but not the dictionary, define as many of the words as you can. Then look up the words in the dictionary to check your accuracy. For more on roots, prefixes, and suffixes, see Chapter 8, Vocabulary Building, page 198.

2. Add any words from this article (including those from Vocabulary Activity 1) to your ongoing sibling glossary. Remember to write definitions in your own words.

3. Create graphic flash cards for the difficult terminology you found in the readings. For help creating flash cards, see Chapter 8, Vocabulary Building, page 198.

SUMMARY ACTIVITY

Sandler refers to various historical periods, events, and people, but her essay is not structured chronologically. Make a time line of the phases, periods, events, people, and publications that she mentions. Does making a time line give you a better overview of the history she traces? Do you have a better sense of how attitudes toward only children have evolved? In what ways can a time line be an effective tool in summarizing a text? For help writing a summary, see Chapter 1, Reading and Responding to College Texts, page 2.

DISCUSSION QUESTIONS

1. How well does Sandler blend personal anecdotes and short narratives with statistics to make her case? Which type of evidence do you remember most? Which type do you find most convincing?

2. Have you thought about who will support your parent(s) in old age? If you are an only child, have you worried about the burden of taking care of your parent(s)? If you have siblings, do you think you and your siblings will work together to provide the emotional, physical, and financial support your parent(s) might need?

3. Do you believe we are in a period that might be known as the "ascent of the onlies," as Sandler calls it? What evidence convinces you that we are or are not? If we are, how big of an impact do you predict this change will have on American culture and society?

BOOK

Po Bronson and Ashley Merryman's collaborative writing about parenting has garnered them many awards, including one for science journalism from the American Association for the Advancement of Science. Bronson has written several nonfiction books about self-development and relationships and one novel. Merryman is an attorney as well as a writer; she has written for the *National Catholic Reporter*, *Time*, and many other publications. Their book *NurtureShock* (2009) is a well-researched study that challenges some of the currently accepted assumptions about parenting. This chapter on siblings from that book provides for a general audience an overview of some of the most recent academic research on siblings. Both authors have lectured on the topic and maintain a robust Web site (www.nurtureshock.com) devoted to the book, where readers and parents voice their views. Merryman and Bronson have used a bibliographic style rather than MLA or APA for their list of references; students should always use the format specified by their instructors. *Important words and phrases have been italicized in this reading. Look up those you do not know, and write the definitions in your personal vocabulary list.*

practice it   Pre-Reading

What are your thoughts about sibling rivalry? Do you think siblings are destined to fight? How much bickering do you consider normal? What would you consider too much fighting in a sibling relationship? Do you expect siblings to "grow out" of arguing? Do you expect siblings who are closer in age to fight more or less than those with a wider age gap? Free-write for five minutes about your thoughts and feelings about sibling rivalry, touching on at least one of these questions.

Po Bronson and Ashley Merryman

THE SIBLING EFFECT

Dr. Laurie Kramer, Associate Dean at the University of Illinois at Urbana-Champaign, is attempting to do the impossible: get brothers and sisters to be nicer to each other.

It was clear what she's up against, after just a few minutes with parents who have enrolled their children in Kramer's six-week program, "More Fun with Sisters and Brothers." We were sitting on a circle of couches in a small room, watching their children on a closed-circuit television. On the other side of the wall, in a living room wired with seven hidden cameras, the children were working with Kramer's undergraduate students.

"When they get going, it's like a freight train. It's paralyzing," remarked one mother about the fighting between her five-year-old daughter and six-year-old son. In her professional life, she's a *clinical* psychiatrist working with wounded veterans. But it's seeing her kids battling that she described as "painful to watch."

Another mother sighed in frustration as we watched her seven-year-old son constantly *taunt* his four-year-old sister. "He knows what to say, but he just can't be nice about it." She stared into space for a moment, fighting a tear.

A mother of five-year-old twin girls felt that her kids are usually 5 great together—but for some *inexplicable* reason, they can't get through cooking dinner without a nightly argument.

The families in Kramer's program are well-educated and well-off. Many of the parents are Illinois faculty, and their children attend one of the best private elementary schools in Urbana. These parents have done everything to provide their children with a positive environment. But there's one wild card in the environment that they can't control, undermining everything—how well the siblings get along.

Mary Lynn Fletcher is the program coordinator for Dr. Kramer; she's on the receiving end of the phone calls from parents who want to get their kids in the program. "Many are shaking when they call. My heart goes out to them," Fletcher said. "They are so stressed. Others, the stress isn't so bad, but they are feeling so helpless. Every day, there's a moment they have to deal with. One parent was driving her kids home from school, and she said, 'Listen to this,' then held the cell phone up to the back seat so I could hear the yelling."

It might sound like these children were the problem cases, but Ashley and I had reviewed videotapes of the children made a month earlier, in their homes. Each tape recorded a half-hour stretch of the sibling pairs playing beside each other with their toys, without any parents in the room to *mediate*. On these videotapes, there was definitely some tension, but what we saw looked better than normal.

Observational studies have determined that siblings between the ages of three and seven clash 3.5 times per hour, on average. Some of those are brief clashes, others longer, but it adds up to ten minutes of every hour spent arguing. According to Dr. Hildy Ross, at the University of Waterloo, only about one out of every eight conflicts ends in compromise or *reconciliation*—the other seven times, the siblings merely withdraw, usually after the older child has bullied or *intimidated* the younger.

Dr. Ganie DeHart, at State University of New York College at Geneseo, compared how four-year-old children treat their younger siblings versus their best friends. In her sample, the kids made seven times as many negative and controlling statements to their siblings as they did to friends.

Scottish researcher Dr. Samantha Punch found similar results in her interviews of ninety children. She determined that kids don't have an incentive to act nicely to their siblings, compared to friends, because the siblings will be there tomorrow, no matter what. She concluded, "Sibship is a relationship in which the boundaries of social interaction can be pushed to the limit. Rage and irritation need not be *suppressed*, whilst politeness and toleration can be neglected."

So do they grow out of it, by having thousands of interactions of practice? Not really, according to Kramer. Back in 1990, she and her mentor, Dr. John Gottman, recruited thirty families who were on the verge of having a second child; their first child was three or four years old. Twice a week, for months, Kramer went into their homes to observe these siblings at play until the youngest were six months old. She was back again at fourteen months, then four years. Each time, Kramer scored the sibling relationship quality, by *coding* how often the kids were nice or mean to each other. Nine years later, Kramer tracked these families down again. By then, the older siblings were on the verge of college. Again, she videotaped them together. To make sure they didn't ignore each other, she gave the sibling pairs some tasks—solve some puzzles together, and plan an imaginary $10,000 weekend for their family.

Kramer learned that sibling relationship quality is remarkably stable over the long term. Unless there had been some major life event in the family—an illness, a death, a divorce—the character of the relationship didn't change until the eldest moved out of the house. For the most part, the tone established when they were very young, be it controlling and bossy or sweet and considerate, tended to stay that way.

"About half of these families are still in the Urbana-Champaign area," said Kramer. "They're now into their twenties. I see their graduation and wedding announcements in the paper. I bump into their parents at the grocery store. I ask how they're getting along. It's really more of the same."

• • •

Kramer often hears, "But I fought with my brothers and sisters all the time, and we turned out great." She doesn't disagree. Instead, she points out that in many sibling relationships, the rate of conflict can be high, but the fun times in the backyard and in the basement more than balance it out. This *net-positive* is what predicts a good relationship later in life. In contrast, siblings who simply ignored each other had less fighting, but their relationship stayed cold and distant long term.

Before she began "More Fun with Sisters and Brothers," Kramer had parents fill out questionnaires about their expectations for their children's sibling interactions. The parents actually accepted conflict as a way of life for siblings; instead, what really troubled them was that their children so often just didn't seem to *care* about each other. Their feeling toward their brother or sister was somewhere between *blasé ambivalence* and annoyance.

So Kramer's program is unique in the field—she doesn't attempt to teach children some kinder version of conflict *mediation*. Grown-ups have a hard enough time mastering those techniques—*attentive* listening, *de-escalation*, avoiding negative generalizations, offering compliments. Instead, the thrust of Kramer's program is made in its title— getting siblings to *enjoy* playing together. The six hour-long sessions are meant to be a fun camp for siblings to attend. Most activities that kids have scheduled into their lives are age-*segregated*—siblings go off with children their own size. Here, they stick together.

In the first session, four papier-mâché hand puppets appear on a puppet stage. They announce they're alien children from the planet Xandia. The clouds on Xandia produce rain whenever brothers and sisters argue, and the planet is at risk of flooding. The aliens have come to Earth to attend the camp with the human children, in order to learn how to have more fun together. All the children—alien and earthling—spend the next six sessions playing board games, creating art projects, role playing, and dancing to a custom-made rap song. They take home bedtime books and a board game set on Xandia.

Along the way, the children adopt a *terminology* for how to initiate play with their siblings, how to find activities they both like to do together, and how to gently decline when they're not interested. They consciously role play these steps. What these steps are called (Stop, Think, and Talk) probably isn't important; what's crucial is the kids are given a way to bridge the age-divide, so the older child doesn't always end up in a bossy role. During one of the sessions, the children are visited by an annoying woman in a trench coat named Miss Busy Bossy—she's a clownlike caricature of a boss, too busy to even put down her cell phone. The children teach her to be less bossy.

Many of the games and art projects teach the kids to recognize the feelings being broadcast in the faces of their siblings. The catchphrase 20 they're taught is, "See it your way, see it my way." They draw these facial expressions on paper plate masks, then listen to stories and hold up the masks that correspond to how each child in the story would be feeling.

Kramer has fine-tuned her scripts for the sessions over the years, but probably the most *innovative* aspect of her program isn't in those details—it's that she focuses on the children at all. Other scholars assumed that four-year-olds were too young, so they directed their training at parents, trying to coach them how to respond to sibling fights. In Kramer's program, fewer fights are the *consequence* of teaching the children the *proactive* skills of initiating play on terms they can both enjoy. It's conflict *prevention*, not conflict *resolution*. Parents are mere facilitators; when back at home, their job is to reinforce the rule that the kids should use their steps together to work it out, *without* the parents' help.

Kramer's program is effective, by every measure. The before-and-after videotapes of the kids playing at home reveal more positive, *mutual* involvement, and the parent questionnaires indicate the parents spend less time breaking up arguments between the kids. The children seem to enjoy the camp, but an hour never goes by without at least one classic display of sibling tension, as the older child turns controlling, or the younger plays the *provocateur*. In fact, the entire premise of the camp—the idea that brothers and sisters should *enjoy* one another—is an objective not all kids are ready to accept.

● ● ●

"I have two special talents," seven-year-old Ethan announced to the instructors and the children in the program. "The first is soccer with my dad. The second is I'm really good at beating people up. When I beat my sister up, it makes me feel good."

His four-year-old sister, Sofia, sat not more than two feet away from him as he said this. But she didn't react to his shocking claim.

The truth was that Ethan had never actually hit his sister, who was 25 half his size. Instead, he often *fretted* that she was so tiny that he might accidentally hurt her. But that session, Ethan seemed to delight in being verbally cruel to Sofia. He mocked her—loudly protesting when an instructor helped her read aloud. He said he didn't want a younger sister: "She wants to play princess, and she always wants me to be the prince, but I want to play ninja. Right now, she's really annoying, and not a worthy opponent."

At the end of the session, Ethan's mother confronted him in the hallway, demanding an explanation. Ethan made a particularly insightful point: "But Mom, it's not *cool* to like a little sister."

Ethan was convinced he had to *act* mean toward Sofia. He couldn't let the other older siblings in the program know that he liked his sister—thus the false brag about beating her up.

Curious about how Ethan and Sofia really got along, we sat down with Kramer to watch the videotape of them at home. Over the half-hour, Ethan led Sofia in the construction of a fort made of couch cushions. The tension was excruciating; it felt like a scene out of film noir—a banal little event that could explode into tragedy at any moment.

Designating himself construction manager, Ethan bossed the four-year-old around constantly. He yelled and chided her when she couldn't hold a cushion perfectly straight. When she wanted to leave for a snack, Ethan threatened, "If you do one more thing—you'll lose your job and you can't come back." When Sofia misunderstood something, the seven-year-old snapped, "No excuses! There are no excuses! You can only keep your job if you promise never, ever to make up an excuse ever again. And don't talk with your mouth full!"

However, Kramer actually saw a lot of hope in the tape. Without 30 question, Ethan *berated* his sister—but the two kids had chosen, on their own, to play together, and they remained engaged in joint play the entire time. They didn't hit each other. They kept talking. Ethan threatened his sister, but he changed the rules so she could keep playing. He made an effort to help Sofia understand she had an important role in the game. When he stopped ordering her around, Sofia would ask him for guidance—which he delighted in. When Sofia tried to drag a big cushion to the fort, Ethan said, "Good job," then came over to help her.

"The kids are still connected," Kramer ultimately concluded. "There's an attempt to manage conflict. The kids like each other—they are looking out for each other. I think there's a lot to work with." She had not yet scored this tape, but at a glance she estimated it would rate a 50 out of 100—an equal balance of negative and positive moments. "I would imagine, in their tape after the program, they'll be around a 70."

So if Ethan actually liked his sister, where was he getting the message that it was uncool and he had to hide it? Ethan's mother, Rebecca, pointed out that Ethan's best friends all were nice to their little brothers and sisters. It wasn't coming from them. She believed Ethan was picking up the message from the books he was reading. He was an exceedingly gifted reader and *consumed* books constantly.

Rebecca was *reticent* to mention her theory, afraid it might come off that she was looking for a scapegoat. However, Kramer's research suggests that Rebecca may be right on target. In one of her studies,

Kramer had a control group of kids come in for six weeks of reading books aloud and discussing cartoons that depicted sibling story lines. These were typical products any parent might share with his kids, hoping they would help the kids get along better—the Berenstain Bears series, *Sesame Street* books, and the like. Kramer figured these kids' relationships with their siblings would improve, but she crossed her fingers that they wouldn't improve *more* than the kids in *her* program.

But Kramer started getting complaints from parents after just a couple weeks. While the books and videos always ended on a happy note, with siblings learning to value and appreciate each other, the first half of the stories portrayed in vivid detail ways that children can fight, insult, and *devalue* their siblings. "From these books, the kids were learning novel ways to be mean to their younger siblings they'd never considered," Kramer recalled. Sure enough, after six weeks, the sibling relationship quality had *plummeted*.

Kramer went on to analyze 261 common children's books that portray sibling relationships. These ranged from picture books for preschoolers to chapter books for third graders. Kramer scored the books as she might score a videotape of kids playing together. She noted the number of times a sibling argued, threatened, excluded, and teased, as well as the positive moments of sharing, affection, problem-solving, and inclusion. The average book demonstrated virtually as many negative behaviors as positive ones. Despite all but one being overtly crafted to have a happy ending, along the way kids were constantly taunting each other, *belittling* a sib, and blaming others for their wrongdoing.   35

• • •

It turns out that Shakespeare was right, and Freud was wrong. For almost a century, Freud's argument—that from birth, siblings were locked in an eternal struggle for their parents' affection—held huge influence over scholars and parents alike. But Freud's theory turns out to be incomplete. Sibling rivalry may be less an *Oedipal* tale of parental love, and more King Lear.

A team of leading British and American scholars asked 108 sibling pairs in Colorado exactly what they fought about. Parental affection was ranked dead last. Just 9% of the kids said it was to blame for the arguments or competition.

The most common reason the kids were fighting was the same one that was the ruin of Regan and Goneril: sharing the castle's toys. Almost 80% of the older children, and 75% of the younger kids, all said sharing physical possessions—or claiming them as their own—caused the most fights.

Nothing else came close. Although 39% of the younger kids did complain that their fights were about . . . fights. They claimed, basically, that they started fights to stop their older siblings from hitting them.

Mindful of the Freudian *paradigm*, the scholars *tempered* their 40 findings, wondering if the children were too young to understand the depths of the family *psychodrama* they were starring in. But these brothers and sisters weren't toddlers. The younger kids were in elementary school, and some of the older kids were already teenagers. The scholars felt that the psychological community needed to recognize that "siblings have their own *repertoire*, of conflict issues separate from their parents." The struggle to win a greater share of parental love may be a factor, they wrote, but kids in mid-childhood don't think about it, recognize it, or *articulate* it.

Laurie Kramer also came to this same conclusion. She reviewed 47 popular parenting manuals, analyzing how much of their advice regarding sibling relationships was rooted in *empirical* research, versus how much was just unproven theory. Kramer found that every single parenting manual recited the *psychodynamic* paradigm, that sibling resentment stems from a loss of parental attention when the younger child is born. Kramer noted that there's certainly research making this point. For instance, one recent study showed that an older sibling's jealousy when the younger is 16 months old predicts what kind of relationship they'll have a couple years later. But Kramer feels this *fixation* on competition for parental love masks and distracts from a more important truth: even in families where children are given plenty of affection by both parents, "young children may fail to develop prosocial relationships with their siblings if nobody teaches them how." Less emphasis needs to be placed on the psychology, and more needs to be on skill-building.

What else is overrated? Parents imagine that the difference in age between siblings is an important factor. Some think it's preferable to have kids less than two years apart, so they are close enough in age to play together; others feel they should wait three or four years, to help each child develop independence. But the research is entirely mixed—for every study that concludes age differences matter, there's another study proving it doesn't. "*Relative* to other factors," said Kramer, "age spacing is not as strong a predictor. Nor is gender. There's many other things to be concerned about."

As for what does matter, Kramer's work offers one big surprise. One of the best predictors of how well two siblings get along is determined *before* the birth of the younger child. At first glance, this is astounding—how can it be possible to predict a clash of personalities, if one of the personalities at issue doesn't even exist yet? How can their future relationship be knowable? But the explanation is quite reasonable. It has nothing to do with the parents. Instead, the predictive factor is the quality of the older child's relationship *with his best friend.*

Kramer studied young kids from families who were expecting another child. She observed these kids playing one-on-one with their best friends. The kids who could play in a *reciprocal, mutual* style with their best friend were the ones who had good rapport with their younger sibling, years later.

It's long been assumed that siblings learn on one another, and 45 then apply the social skills they acquire to their relationships with peers outside the family. Kramer says it's the other way around: older siblings train on their friends, and then apply what they know to their little brothers and sisters.

After monitoring these relationships with best friends, Kramer saw that one factor stood out as especially telling: shared fantasy play. As Kramer and John Gottman explained, "Fantasy play represents one of the highest levels of social involvement for young children." In order for joint fantasy play to work, children must emotionally commit to one another, and pay attention to what the other is doing. They have to articulate what's in their mind's eye—and *negotiate* some scenario that allows both their visions to come alive. When one kid just announced the beginning of a ninja battle, but the other wants to be a cowboy, they have to figure out how to still ride off into the sunset together.

If, however, the child hasn't developed these good habits on friends, and the younger sibling comes along, now there's very little *incentive* to learn the skills of shared play (choosing an activity both can enjoy, inviting the other and/or asking to be included, recognizing when someone is busy or wants to play alone). The incentive's not there because, as Samantha Punch pointed out, the sibling will be there tomorrow no matter what. Siblings are prisoners, genetically sentenced to live together, with no time off for good behavior. There is simply no motivation to change.

Kramer also considered children's behavior in day care and preschools. The fact that kids could cooperate in class or remain engaged in a group setting didn't predict improved sibling relationships. It was that real connection between friends—that made a child care how his behavior impacted someone he liked—that was the *catalyst* for the difference.

"A parent is going to work hard to meet his child's needs. They are highly motivated by love," Kramer explained. "Other kids don't care if you're hungry or have a bruise on your knee—they have one, too."

In other words, getting what you need from a parent is easy. It's 50 getting what you want from friends that forces a child to develop skills.

"It's not that parents are unimportant," Kramer has concluded. "But they are important in very different ways."

Which is why, in a sense, what Kramer is really trying to do is transform children's relationships from sibship to something more *akin* to a real friendship. If kids enjoy one another's presence, then quarreling comes at a new cost. The penalty for fighting is no longer just a time-out, but the loss of a worthy opponent.

Selected Sources and References

DeHart, Ganie B., Bobette Buchanan, Carjah Dawkins, and Jill Rabinowitz, "Preschoolers' Use of Assertive and Affiliative Language with Siblings and Friends," Poster presented at the Biennial Meeting of the Society for Research in Child Development, Boston (2007).

Kennedy, Denise, and Laurie Kramer, "Building Emotion Regulation in Sibling Relationships," Poster presented at the Biennial Meeting of the Society for Research in Child Development, Boston (2007).

Kramer, Laurie, e-mails with authors (2007–2008).

Kramer, Laurie, "The Essential Ingredients of Successful Sibling Relationships: An Emerging Framework for Advancing Theory and Practice," Manuscript under review (2009).

Kramer, Laurie, and Lisa A. Baron, "Intergenerational Linkages: How Experiences With Siblings Relate to the Parenting of Siblings," *Journal of Social and Personal Relationships*, vol. 12, no. 1, pp. 67–87 (1995).

Kramer, Laurie, and John Gottman, "Becoming a Sibling: With a Little Help from My Friends," *Developmental Psychology*, vol. 28, no. 4, pp. 685–699 (1992).

Kramer, Laurie, and Amanda K. Kowal, "Sibling Relationship Quality from Birth to Adolescence: The Enduring Contribution of Friends," *Journal of Family Psychology*, vol. 19, no. 4, pp, 503–511 (2005).

Kramer, Laurie, Sonia Noorman, and Renee Brockman, "Representations of Sibling Relationships in Young Children's Literature," *Early Childhood Research Quarterly*, vol. 14, no. 4, pp. 555–574 (1999).

Kramer, Laurie, Lisa A. Perozynski, and Tsai-Yen Chung, "Parental Responses to Sibling Conflict: The Effects of Development and Parent Gender," *Child Development*, vol. 70, no. 6, pp. 1401–1414 (1999).

Kramer, Laurie, and Chad Radey, "Improving Sibling Relationships among Young Children: A Social Skills Training Model," *Family Relations*, vol. 46, no. 3, pp. 237–246 (1997).

Kramer, Laurie, and Dawn Ramsburg, "Advice Given to Parents on Welcoming a Second Child: A Critical Review," *Family Relations*, vol. 51, no. l, pp. 2–14 (2002).

Punch, Samantha, "'You Can Do Nasty Things to Your Brothers and Sisters Without a Reason: Siblings' Backstage Behaviors," *Children & Society*, vol. 22, no. 5, pp. 333–344 (2007).

Ram, Avigail, and Hildy S. Ross, "Problem Solving, Contention, and Struggle: How Siblings Resolve a Conflict of Interests," *Child Development*, vol. 72, no. 6, pp. 1710–1722 (2001).

Ross, Hildy S., "Negotiating Principles of Entitlement in Sibling Property Disputes," *Developmental Psychology*, vol. 32, no. 1, pp. 90–101 (1996).

Ross, Hildy, Michael Ross, Nancy Stein, and Tom Trabasso, "How Siblings Resolve Their Conflicts," *Child Development*, vol. 77, no. 6, pp. 1730–1745 (2006).

Smith, Julie, and Hildy Ross, "Training Parents to Mediate Sibling Disputes Affects Children's Negotiation and Conflict Understanding," *Child Development*, vol. 78, no. 3, pp. 790–805 (2007).

practice it | Post-Reading Activity

Look back at the section of the article on pages 423–27 that describes Kramer's program. Reread this passage, using the technique of reading with and against the grain, as outlined in Chapter 2 (pages 38–41). Make sure you distinguish between your annotations for reading with the grain and those for reading against the grain. (You can use two different-colored pens, if you like.) Afterward, review your annotations and decide whether the passage is well written, and how the authors could improve it.

COMPREHENSION QUESTIONS

1. What is the goal of the "More Fun with Sisters and Brothers" program? How does the program aim to accomplish its goals?

2. What is the "net-positive" balance between conflict and fun (para. 15)? Why is this concept so essential to understanding sibling relationships?

3. What is the value in fantasy play for children?

4. How does an older sibling's best-friend relationship influence the relationship he or she will have with a younger sibling?

5. What messages about sibling relationships are presented in children's books?

6. What conclusions can be drawn from Dr. Laurie Kramer's research?

VOCABULARY ACTIVITIES

1. Add any words from this book excerpt to your ongoing sibling glossary. Remember to write a definition in your own words.

2. Paragraph 41 uses terminology from psychology. Underline or circle words you do not know, and then try to figure out from context clues what each one means. Why do the authors use this language? Can you think of synonyms for any words on your list?

SUMMARY ACTIVITY

The authors use only small design graphics to break up the chapter, yet these mark important shifts in topic. Map the text, and then write subheadings for each section as a way of summarizing it. For help mapping a text, see Chapter 5 (p. 138).

DISCUSSION QUESTIONS

1. Bronson and Merryman present research that shows "that siblings between the ages of three and seven clash 3.5 times per hour, on average. Some of those are brief clashes, others longer, but it adds up to ten minutes of every hour spent arguing" (para. 9). Does this surprise you? Does it seem like a long time or not? As an adult, particularly as a parent, how might you feel if you were observing such clashes this frequently?

2. In the last section of the chapter, Bronson and Merryman write, "It turns out that Shakespeare was right, and Freud was wrong. . . . Sibling rivalry may be less an Oedipal tale of parental love, and more King Lear" (para. 36). Do you understand these references to Shakespeare and Freud? Look up these references and try to figure out how they apply to the authors' thesis.

3. The "More Fun with Sisters and Brothers" program primarily serves highly educated, upper-middle-class families (para. 6). Do the educational levels or the incomes of the parents matter? Would children from lower-income families have any different experiences? Why or why not?

4. How does this view of sibling conflict compare and contrast to some of the other readings you have done in the chapter, such as "Close Encounters of a Special Kind" or "The New Science of Siblings"?

Synthesizing the Readings

Now that you have read a wide variety of texts on the topic of siblings, you have enough schema, or background information, to begin to synthesize the material and build arguments of your own. It's helpful, though, to pause and discuss how the various readings "converse" with one another before you jump right into a writing assignment. Here are some post-reading discussion questions to help direct your thinking:

DISCUSSION QUESTIONS

1. After reading several pieces about siblings, what do you think of sibling rivalry? How would you define it? Do you think siblings are inherently in competition? If so, for what do they compete?

2. What images of siblings and only children do you see in the media? What values are those images presenting?

3. Given the choice, would you prefer to have siblings or be an only child? If you are a parent or plan to become one, would you prefer to have an only child or multiple children? What economic and psychological factors would you consider? Justify your answer with evidence and examples from your readings.

4. Most U.S. families are not made up of two parents with children. There are a variety of formations of families. How do those differences influence the debate on birth order and siblings?

5. Several of the readings in this chapter were written by journalists who specialize in scientific topics but are not scientists. What are the strengths and

weaknesses of this type of writing? How does it compare to science text-books? To fiction?

6. If you were an instructor and had to write an essay-exam question about the topic of siblings based on these readings, what would you ask? Why?

CHARTING TO ORGANIZE YOUR IDEAS

After your discussion, take some time to organize your thoughts on the topic of siblings before you proceed to your specific assignment. You can begin by gathering ideas and quotations about the various issues that emerged in more than one of the readings. Use the following chart to record your thoughts and any interesting information or quotations that you pull from the readings. You can copy the chart into your notebook or, to download a version, log onto **bedfordstmartins.com/readwriteconnect** and click on **Charts**.

SYNTHESIS CHART: SIBLINGS

	Sibling Rivalry	Birth Order	Adult Sibling Relationships	Pros and Cons of Having Siblings	Other
Olds, "Killing My Sister's Fish"					
Leder, "Close Encounters of a Special Kind"					
Kluger, "The New Science of Siblings"					
Kluger, "The Power of Birth Order"					
Sandler, "The Only Child: Debunking the Myths"					
Bronson and Merryman, "The Sibling Effect"					
My thoughts					

Writing Your Essay

The following steps review how to get into the mind-set to write your essay on siblings. These steps are outlined in greater detail in Chapters 2, 3, and 4.

STEP 1: What type of essay are you assigned to write about siblings? Look over the question or your instructor's prompt, and write it in your own words.

STEP 2: Which readings from this chapter do you think you will include? List them in your notes, including any quotations that you think you might use. (Don't forget to include the author and page number when you write down the quotation or paraphrase so that you don't have to find it again later.)

STEP 3: What ideas from class discussion or your own experience and observations would you like to include? Look over your notes, and add those thoughts to your brainstorming for this assignment.

STEP 4: Take a few more minutes to brainstorm in your favorite method: listing, freewriting, clustering, questioning, or group discussion.

STEP 5: Look back at the assignment prompt, and write up a tentative thesis or main idea based on your work so far. Remember, one way to think of the thesis is as the answer to the question posed in the assignment prompt. Don't worry that your thesis has to be perfect or set in stone right now. It's a working thesis that you will probably revise as you make decisions about what you want to say.

STEP 6: Make a bullet-point outline for your essay. Remember to first put the ideas down and then reorganize them into a logical order.

STEP 7: Copy or type up the relevant quotations and examples under each appropriate bullet point.

STEP 8: Pat yourself on the back! You have a lot of material so far, don't you?

STEP 9: Write the rough, rough draft, remembering that you'll be revising it.

STEP 10: Reread the assignment sheet one more time, and then make big-picture revisions to your focus, content, and organization. Peer review may help.

STEP 11: Once you are generally satisfied that your work is focused, complete, and organized, edit for sentence-level issues. Remember to use the editing techniques of reading your work out loud, reading "backward," and isolating your common errors. Refer to your Grammar Log frequently during this process. Edit and print your paper again and again until you are satisfied with the way each sentence sounds.

STEP 12: Take a break.

STEP 13: Proofread your essay one or two more times to correct any minor errors and to make sure your document format is correct for this assignment.

To learn how to use the Grammar Log, see Chapter 24, page 579. To download a copy of this log, go to **bedfordstmartins .com/readwriteconnect** and click on **Charts**.

Writing Assignments

DEFINITION ASSIGNMENT

How would you define *brotherhood* or *sisterhood*? Write an essay that explains how one qualifies for the label of *brother* or *sister*, what qualities we associate with those terms, and how we stretch the label to include a variety of people.

NARRATION ASSIGNMENT

Write a narrative essay that tells the detailed story of one key incident in the life of a pair or group of siblings whom you know well—the most likely choices are people in your family or close friends whom you have observed for several years. Remember, a narrative has a beginning, middle, and end, so make sure your story does too. Try to describe in detail what happened. Include some commentary—probably as a concluding paragraph—about the significance of this event for their relationship. You might answer one or more of the following questions: How is this event typical of their relationship? How did it change their relationship? What does this event suggest about how one or both of the siblings feel about themselves and/or their sibling(s)?

DESCRIPTION ASSIGNMENT

Spend an hour or two observing a set of siblings as they interact. Take notes on their activities, conversations, and body language. If they feel comfortable with you recording them, do that too. (Make sure you get their permission or their parents' permission if they are under eighteen.) Write an essay in which you profile the siblings. Describe their interactions in detail to illustrate the characteristics of their sibling relationship. Before you begin, you should reread some of the writing that describes people in the articles that you read for class. Underline parts that you think are strong, and make note of what types of details really work.

PROCESS ANALYSIS ASSIGNMENT

Write an essay addressed to parents who are about to create a new blended family with step-siblings. Describe in a step-by-step way how they should go about setting up a successful household. Guide them through the process as they undertake this major life change.

COMPARE AND CONTRAST ASSIGNMENT

Drawing on the examples given in the readings, write an essay in which you compare and contrast only children and children with siblings.

RESEARCH ASSIGNMENT

Do some research on the advice given to parents about how to handle sibling rivalry. (This part of the assignment can be done individually, in small groups, or as an entire class.) Collect articles and books, including older materials so you have examples of how things have changed. For instance, each student in a group could take one decade and look at a women's magazine, a parenting manual, and a movie or television show from that period. Make a chart to compile your results, with categories for the type of source, its audience, the way it defines sibling rivalry, how it suggests parents should handle sibling rivalry, and other points from your research. Then, working individually, write a paper in which you analyze the data you collected. The focus might be on how the definition of sibling rivalry has changed, how the advice about how to handle it has changed, or anything else that emerges from your research.

ARGUMENT ASSIGNMENTS

1. Does birth order really matter, as Kluger suggests in his article "The Power of Birth Order"? Write an essay in which you take a position strongly in support of the importance of birth order or strongly against it. Use specific examples from Kluger's essay and at least one other reading from the chapter to support your points. Be sure to address counterarguments fairly.
2. For years, psychologists and parenting experts have suggested that sibling rivalry is at its root a fight for the parents' attention, but Bronson and Merryman, the authors of "The Sibling Effect," argue that siblings fight mostly over stuff, like the remote control and the best toys. Are fights about stuff really a hidden way to fight for the parents' attention? Or are they simply arguments to get the best material goods? What do you think is the primary motivation behind sibling arguments? Look back over the sibling articles that you have read for the class and find quotations about sibling fights to help you think about your answer to this question.

Additional Online and Media Sources

The readings in this chapter may spark your thinking and leave you wanting more information for further study or personal reflection. In the e-Pages you can read Mikal Gilmore's essay "Secrets and Bones," and watch the *20/20* video "Sibling Secrets." Go to **bedfordstmartins.com/readwriteconnect** and click on **e-Readings**. You might also want to consult the following online and media sources.

WEB RESOURCES

The Compassionate Friends (www.compassionatefriends.org): An organization that provides support and resources to grieving families, including siblings.

The Donor Sibling Registry (www.donorsiblingregistry.com): An organization that helps people who were conceived through sperm, egg, or embryo donation locate their biological siblings.

National Organization of Mothers of Twins Clubs, Inc. (www.nomotc .org): A nonprofit organization that functions as a national clearinghouse and support for twins organizations.

Parents (www.parents.com): A Web site sponsored by one of the best-selling parenting magazines, which offers information about parenting siblings, only children, and blended families.

The Sibling Support Project (www.siblingsupport.org): A nonprofit organization that supports siblings of people with developmental or mental health disabilities.

FILMS

Adaptation. Dir. Spike Jonze. Perf. Nicolas Cage, Meryl Streep, and Chris Cooper. Beverly Detroit, 2002.

Brothers. Dir. Jim Sheridan. Perf. Jake Gyllenhaal, Natalie Portman, and Tobey Maguire. Lionsgate, 2009.

Cinderella. Disney. RKO Pictures, 1950.

Legends of the Fall. Dir. Edward Zwick. Perf. Brad Pitt, Anthony Hopkins, and Aidan Quinn. TriStar, 1994.

Margot at the Wedding. Dir. Noah Baumbach. Perf. Nicole Kidman, Jennifer Jason Leigh, and Jack Black. Paramount, 2007.

My Sister's Keeper. Dir. Nick Cassevetes. Perf. Cameron Diaz and Abigail Breslin. Curmudgeon Films, 2009.

Rachel Getting Married. Dir. Jonathan Demme. Perf. Anne Hathaway, Rosemarie DeWitt, and Debra Winger. Sony, 2008.

Rain Man. Dir. Barry Levinson. Perf. Dustin Hoffman and Tom Cruise. United Artists, 1988.

Step Brothers. Dir. Adam McKay. Perf. Will Ferrell and John C. Reilly. Columbia, 2008.

Sweetie. Dir. Jane Campion. Perf. Genevieve Lemon and Karen Colston. New South Wales Film Corp., 1989.

The Virgin Suicides. Dir. Sofia Coppola. Perf. James Woods, Kathleen Turner, and Kirsten Dunst. American Zoetrope, 1999.

TELEVISION AND RADIO

Band of Brothers (HBO/DreamWorks miniseries), 2001.

Brothers & Sisters

Keeping Up with the Kardashians

"Sibling Rivalry." *This American Life.* Narr. Ira Glass. Chicago Public Media. 9 Jan. 1998. thisamericanlife.org. Web.

22
Public Art

- **James Gaddy**
  Nowhere Man
- **Rosanna Xia**
  Lighthearted Street Art Delights (and Confuses) Downtown L.A. Visitors
- *Buffalo Law Journal*
  Battles over Yard Art Sometimes Turn Ugly

in this chapter

- **Patrick Frank**
  Public Art and Street Art
- **Jack Becker**
  Public Art: An Essential Component of Creating Communities
- **Teresa Palomo Acosta**
  Chicano Mural Movement
- **Will Shank**
  Whose Art Is This Anyway?
- **Koon-Hwee Kan**
  Adolescents and Graffiti
- **Los Angeles Police Department**
  What Graffiti Means to a Community

Mural by Francisco Aquino and Banksy, San Francisco.

Theme Overview

We as a species have always wanted to represent ourselves—our emotions, hopes, dreams, and fears—in a visual way. Art began as a public expression of personal or social ideas. As our cultures developed, the field of art became more professional, and as it did so, experts arose and were given the power to define and evaluate art. Art museums became the place where we "put" art. And for some, art museums became a way of defining what is art and what is not art. (If it's not museum quality, it's not art, some people think.) Public art, however, has never been held to the same standards as private art. As art intended for public view, public art is often more durable and more massive in scale than works that collectors or museums can accommodate. Public art includes both sanctioned and unsanctioned works, such as sculpture, installation art, fountains, murals, graffiti, tile art, and art built into the structure of public walkways, railings, or walls.

The readings in this chapter invite you to study a variety of examples of human expression in order to investigate this human motivation to make a mark on the world in a very public way. The readings address a range of different types of public art, from the commissioned public mural by the famous artist, to the yard art of artistic property owners, to the unsanctioned street art and graffiti of youth. Along the way, you will investigate some related questions: What is art? Who decides what art is good? What separates the private world from the public world? And, finally, what rights does owning a piece of property give you?

practice it   Taking Stock of What You Already Know

What do you know about the following types of creative expression? How would you compare and contrast the types listed? Answer the questions, taking stock of your beliefs about how we define and value art.

Art: What is art? What are the differences between public and private art? What kinds of public art exist in your community? Is art an individual interest or a community experience?

Graffiti: What do you think of graffiti? Who is affected by it? Is it in your community? Have you ever made graffiti? If so, why?

Murals: Does your community have any mural art? If so, where are the murals located? How are murals and graffiti similar? How are they different? Have you ever helped make a mural?

Yard art: What do you think of decorated yards? Have you seen any yards with yard art or farms with barn paintings? Have you ever decorated any of the space around where you live? If so, when, how, and why? Do you think about how those in the community will respond to your creative expressions?

Prebles' Artforms is a well-regarded visual arts textbook that covers, among many other topics, public art and street art. As a textbook selection, this reading provides a peek into the design and coverage common in many college-level textbooks. The excerpt here explains public art and street art. Author Patrick Frank is an art historian who writes general art history texts as well as specialized books on Latin American art history. *Important words and phrases have been italicized in this reading. Look up those you do not know, and write the definitions in your personal vocabulary list.*

practice it   **Pre-Reading**

Preview the text by looking carefully at the images and headings. What can you predict the reading will be about? What do you expect to learn from this text? Write your pre-reading notes directly on the text.

Patrick Frank

PUBLIC ART

Public art is art that you might encounter without intending to; it exists in a public place, accessible to everyone. The idea of public art originated in ancient times, as government and religious leaders commissioned artists to create works for public spaces. In our time, artists still make public art that responds to the needs and hopes of broad masses of people.

The *Vietnam Veterans Memorial,* located on the Mall in Washington, D.C., is probably America's best-known public art piece. The 250-foot-long, V-shaped black granite wall bears the names of the nearly sixty thousand American servicemen and women who died or are missing in Southeast Asia. The nonprofit Vietnam Veterans Memorial Fund, Inc., was formed in 1979 by a group of Vietnam veterans who believed that a public monument to the war would help speed the process of national reconciliation and healing after the conflict.

Maya Lin. *Vietnam Veterans Memorial*. The Mall, Washington, D.C. 1980–1982. Black granite. Each wall 10'1" × 246'9".

After examining 1,421 *entries*, the jury selected the design of twenty-one-year-old Maya Lin of Athens, Ohio, then a student at Yale University. Lin had visited the site and created a design that would work with the land rather than dominate it. "I had an impulse to cut open the earth . . . an initial violence that in time would heal. The grass would grow back, but the cut would remain, a pure, flat surface, like a geode when you cut it open and polish the edge. . . . I chose black granite to make the surface reflective and peaceful."

Lin's bold, eloquently simple design creates a memorial park within a larger park. It shows the influence of *Minimalism* and site works of the 1960s and 1970s. The polished black surface reflects the surrounding trees and lawn, and the tapering segments point to the Washington Monument in one direction and the Lincoln Memorial in the other. Names are *inscribed* in chronological order by date of death, each name given a place in history. As visitors walk toward the center, the wall becomes higher and the names pile up *inexorably*. The monument's thousands of visitors seem to testify to the monument's power to *console* and heal.

When the Museum of Modern Art in New York expanded in 2004, 5 the neighbors in high-rise buildings complained about having to look down onto new ugly roof structures. The museum responded by turning to landscape architect Ken Smith, who said, "Let's camouflage

Ken Smith. *MOMA Roof Garden* (*Museum of Modern Art Roof Garden*). 2005. Outdoor garden at the Museum of Modern Art, New York.

it!" He made the humorous *MOMA Roof Garden* out of colored gravel, asphalt, and plastic bushes. The composition is a *camouflage* pattern, the better to "hide" the building. This piece of public art is not visible from inside the museum and, more important, requires no maintenance. When the neighbors complained yet again that the garden was completely fake, Smith responded that it was about as fake as nearby Central Park, which had been carefully planted on a stripped and leveled field. The *tongue-in-cheek* humor of this piece and its witty quotation of camouflage patterns make this work a rare example of *postmodern* landscape architecture.

A great deal of public art in the United States is created under a *mandate* that one-half of one percent of the cost of public buildings be spent on art to *embellish* them. Sometimes the results can turn out unsatisfactorily, as the case of Richard Serra's *Tilted Arc* shows. But when a community-minded artist works with the local people, the results can be much more successful, as in the following case.

Seattle-based Buster Simpson specializes in public art, and one of his recent commissions *embodies* the environmental concerns of an eastern Washington agricultural community. *Instrument Implement: Walla Walla Campanile* begins with a core of metal farmers' disks arranged in a repeating bell-shape pattern. Sensors track environmental conditions in nearby Mill Creek: water temperature, flow level, and amount of dissolved gases. All three of these measures are critical for the annual salmon migration, which has been diminishing in recent years. The data are processed by a computer that *encodes* them into musical notes. Hammers on the piece then strike the proper disks to ring a chime, which becomes an hourly auditory update on the condition of the river. The health of the salmon is a

Buster Simpson. *Instrument Implement: Walla Walla Campanile.* 2008. William A. Grant Water & Environmental Center, Walla Walla Community College, Walla Walla, WA. Height 25'6".

"canary in the coal mine," an early warning of other environmental problems. Simpson included a yellow *effigy* of a salmon as an indicator of this. The entire piece is powered by an attached solar collector. *Instrument Implement* is located at Walla Walla Community College, within sight and earshot of hundreds of people each day.

STREET ART

In the late 1990s, many galleries in various cities began to exhibit work by artists who had previously made illegal graffiti. Many of these "street artists" were based in the culture of skateboards and punk music, and they used materials bought at the hardware store rather than the art supply house. Their creations were only rarely related to gang-oriented graffiti, which usually mark out territories of influence. Nor were they mere tags with names or initials. Rather, the street artists made much broader statements about themselves and the world in a language that was widely understandable. The ancestors of the movement in the 1980s were Keith Haring and Jean-Michel Basquiat, both of whom worked illegally for years before exhibiting in galleries. By the turn of the twenty-first century, street art was a recognized movement, and most of its main practitioners work both indoors and out. All of our artists here create under pseudonyms. While sometimes illegal, the boldness and personal risk-taking that street artists engage in inspires many in a society with strong corporate and government power.

Faile. *A Continuing Story*. 2009. Acrylic, spraypaint, and screenprint on canvas. 62" square.

Faile is a collaborative of two Brooklyn-based artists. They create imagery that seems as though it were lifted from magazines and advertisements, but it is their own work in silkscreen, stencil, and paint. They layer these images and then rip through them to leave a worn surface like a decaying urban wall. Some of their work at first seems self-promotional, such as *A Continuing Story,* but a better way to describe Faile is that they *mock* the style of billboards. The *brazenness* and *flair* of their works has attracted viewers since 1999 when the team began.

Some of today's most skill- 10 ful street art is created by Swoon. She carves large linoleum blocks and makes *relief prints* from them, usually life-size portraits of everyday people. She prints them on large sheets of cheap (usually recycled) newsprint and pastes them on urban walls, beginning on the Lower East Side of Manhattan, but now in cities on every continent. Her *Untitled* installation at Deitch Projects was a recent indoor work. Against objections that her work is mostly illegal, she replies that her creations are far easier to look at than advertising, that they lack any persuasive agenda, and that they *glorify* common people. Moreover, the newsprint that she uses decays over time so that her work is impermanent. Although she works mostly outdoors, she sometimes shows in galleries because, she admits, "I have to make a living," but she charges far less for her work than most other artists of wide *repute*.

Probably the most famous street creator today is the English artist Banksy. His street art is generally witty, as we see in *Stone Age Waiter*. This piece adorns an outdoor location in a Los Angeles neighborhood with many restaurants; a cave man has apparently joined the ranks of the pleasure-seekers. Well-heeled Angelenos who walk the (always short) distance from their cars to their favorite restaurants will pass this stencil-and-spray-paint creation. Banksy is currently one of the most popular artists in his homeland, and many of his outdoor works

Banksy. *Stone Age Waiter*. 2006. Spray paint and stencils. Height 5'6". Outdoor location, Los Angeles.

have been preserved. When a *prominent* street work of his was recently *defaced* by another graffiti artist, protests *ensued* and the *defacer* was arrested for vandalism! Thus, street artists often blur the line between legal and illegal.

---

practice it   Post-Reading Activity

This art textbook includes images to help clarify the ideas presented. Go back through the reading and annotate the images, connecting them to the text that they support. How do the images help you understand the concepts introduced in the reading?

COMPREHENSION QUESTIONS

1. What is public art?

2. What is the role of public art like the *Vietnam Veterans Memorial*?

3. What other ways does public art function, according to the reading?

4. How is public art subsidized?

5. How does street art differ from more traditional art forms?

VOCABULARY ACTIVITIES

1. Add any words from this textbook excerpt to your ongoing public art glossary. Remember to write definitions in your own words.

2. The selection titled "Street Art" questions how different people might define "legal" and "illegal" artistic activities. Searching carefully through this reading, create one cluster diagram of the group of italicized vocabulary words that you associate with "legal," and another cluster

diagram of the group of italicized vocabulary words that you associate with "illegal." What associations and ideas emerge? How might these associations and ideas help you define the legality of different types of street art? For more on cluster diagrams, see Chapter 9, Pre-Writing, page 214.

SUMMARY ACTIVITY

Write a one-sentence summary of each paragraph in this textbook excerpt. Add an introductory sentence and a concluding sentence, so you have a complete, coherent paragraph. For help writing a summary, see Chapter 1, Reading and Responding to College Texts, page 2.

DISCUSSION QUESTIONS

1. Is public art important? Why or why not?
2. According to Frank, "Many . . . 'street artists' were based in the culture of skateboards and punk music" (para. 8). Is the origin of street art significant? Why or why not?
3. Some street artists like Banksy have achieved widespread fame and recognition, to the point that people protect and even sell their street art. Who owns street art?
4. Should street art be protected or removed as illegal graffiti? Explain.

As the founder and artistic director of FORECAST Public Artworks in Minnesota, Jack Becker has been heavily involved in public art and recognized as a leader in the field of public art. In his role as director of FORECAST Public Artworks, he created a statewide grant program for emerging artists and the national journal *Public Art Review*. He holds a Ph.D. in American art and is currently the executive director of the Joslyn Art Museum in Omaha, Nebraska. His writing has been published in both books and periodicals, including the *Utne Reader* and the *Boston Globe*. The following article, published in 2004, is excerpted from the *Americans for the Arts Monograph* series, which is intended mostly for people working in the art world or interested art patrons. *Important words and phrases have been italicized in this reading. Look up those you do not know, and write the definitions in your personal vocabulary list.*

practice it   Pre-Reading

Preview the article, looking carefully at the section headings as well as the images and the boxes to try to determine the audience and purpose. What clues provide information about this? What do you expect this reading to be about?

AmericansfortheArts.org

Public Art: An Essential Component of Creating Communities
Jack Becker

Defining Public Art

A definition of public art is essential to establish *ordinances*, develop permits, and educate broad audiences. However, as the field grows and evolves at a rapid pace, developing a fixed definition is very difficult. The intention and the desired outcomes of each program vary. For most public agencies, public art may be defined as "work created by artists for places accessible to and used by the public," but the variety of public art encompasses a much broader spectrum of activities and approaches.

It is important to distinguish between public art, which takes into account its site and other *contextual* issues, and art in public places.

Simply placing a sculpture on a street corner is not the same as designing a sculpture specifically for that site by considering its audience, environmental conditions, the history of the site, etc. Regardless, art placed in public can still be quality art and offer the general public an art experience outside a museum or gallery setting.

As more artists have entered the public arena, their art has taken many forms. The field today encompasses place-making, environmental activism, cause-related art, sound installations, interdisciplinary performance events, community-based initiatives, and much more. Indeed, public art is a *multifaceted* field, open to artists of all stripes, without *predetermined* rules or a mutually agreed upon critical language. This open-endedness can be a *liability* for public agencies seeking to serve a diverse community. Artists may view it as an asset, however, *liberating* them from the constraints imposed by the commercial marketplace.

Survey Highlights: Public Art Ordinances

A public art ordinance is the legislation establishing a public art program within a unit of government. Generally, a public art ordinance establishes the financial mechanism that funds the public art program, identifies the unit of government or private contractor that will manage the public art program, and establishes a basis for the development of public art policies and/or guidelines.

Three quarters of the programs that responded to the survey report that they operate with an active public art ordinance. A few ordinances serve only to establish the public art program (13.7 percent), while most also allocate funding (86.3 percent).

Among those that allocate funding:

- 91 percent mandate the allocations (the rest are voluntary funds);
- 41 percent allocate funds for conservation;
- 29 percent allocate funds for program staff; and
- 21 percent allocate funds for educational programming.

Interestingly, public art programs that operate with a public art ordinance tend to have significantly larger and faster-growing budgets than those without an ordinance. This is not surprising since by definition, most ordinances create a consistent and reliable funding stream for public art.

Tribute in Light initiative: John Bennett, Gustavo Bonevardi, Richard Nash Gould, Julian Laverdiere, Paul Marantz, Paul Myoda. Produced by the Municipal Art Society and Creative Time, with support from the Battery Park City Authority.

The process of creating public art necessarily involves interaction among many interests; it is a cooperative, somewhat theaterlike production with many individuals playing a part in creating a common goal. As people of different perspectives and positions seek to make decisions cooperatively, the result can be *dynamic*, *inviting*, engaging, and sometimes contentious.

Likewise, the experience of viewing public art is *dynamic*. The relationship between the work and its site, its audience, and other contextual factors all contribute to its impact. Successful public art *evokes* meaning in the public realm while retaining a high artistic quality. Perhaps most exciting is the fact that the field is evolving to include different art forms, traditions, and perspectives.

5

Why Is Public Art Important?

Imagine, if you can, a world devoid of public art: no *Statue of Liberty*, no *Eiffel Tower*, no *Vietnam Veterans Memorial*, no *Tribute in Light*. No murals, memorials, or monuments. What would life be like without fireworks displays, puppet parades, sculpture parks, and visionary roadside folk art? These landmarks and special events enhance our experience of a place and our quality of life. They *engender* a sense of pride and community identity. They reach audiences outside museums, galleries, and theaters, and they add to the beauty of everyday life. They declare the worth of a place and a time in our shared culture.

How important is the design of our shared public *realm*? What is the value of a park or plaza, or of a free exchange in a welcoming environment? Public art projects offer us a way to participate in the planning, design, and creation of *communal* space. For this reason, many refer to public art as a democratic art form. And while democracy can be a messy process, public art is an integral part of the fabric of American culture.

Public art does many things, most of which can be divided into four areas. It can:

- engage civic dialogue and community;
- attract attention and economic benefit;
- connect artists with communities; and
- enhance public appreciation of art.

Engage Civic Dialogue and Community

During the mid-1990s, in a run-down row of shotgun houses in Houston, artist Rick Lowe saw an opportunity to return life and vitality to an endangered part of that city's African American history. *Project Row Houses*, a public art effort involving numerous public and private *entities*, demonstrated successful community building. In addition to artists in residence, the area around the restored homes featured events and festivals, renewing residents' faith in the power of *civic dialogue*.

In addition to grand monuments like the *Gateway Arch* or *Mount Rushmore*, which *foster* pride and contribute to our cultural *heritage*, strategically executed public art can raise awareness of issues such as racism, gang violence, and environmental *degradation*. The *AIDS Memorial Quilt*, featuring over 70,000 individual quilts, has been displayed on the National Mall in Washington, D.C. Beyond the *spectacle* of a colorful, monumental folk art installation, the quilt raises awareness of the AIDS *epidemic*, generates significant media attention, and *leverages* increased support for research and education.

10

> "[Public art] adds vitality, and it adds liveliness. It's important because it's an amenity you can add to a building. It's a way of showing tenants that you care about the public space and that you want to give back to the building."
>
> —Developer Michael Staenberg, THF Realty, Overland, MO

> "Public artworks can be more than objects in space—they can be ideas, places, and actions. They can reveal the dynamics of

ecological and social processes, tap into imaginations, and create a sense of place. I think of my artworks as theaters that regenerate the environment while triggering internal emotions and narratives."

—Lorna Jordan, environmental artist

"The incorporation of art in our public space helps give expression to our community values. When we encourage art, we also encourage creativity and thoughtfulness."

—Mayor Kevin Foy, Chapel Hill, NC

Attract Attention and Economic Benefit

Providence, Rhode Island, experienced a *revitalization* of its downtown due in part to *WaterFire Providence*, a public art event conceived in 1995 by artist Barnaby Evans. While the concept is simple—burning fires in the middle of a restored river channel through downtown, accompanied by original musical compositions from artists around the world—it draws thousands of people several times each year, stimulating the economy and creating pride.

Thanks to Kathleen Farrell and a handful of other artists, Joliet, Illinois, became a mural capital, attracting positive media attention, tour groups, and increased community support for the arts. Many of the murals relate to Joliet's colorful history and connect with the city's Heritage Walk.

Significant funds and attention have been generated by such projects as *Cows on Parade* in Chicago and *Art on the Street* in Cedar Rapids, Iowa, supporting a wide variety of causes. Public art can help visitors *navigate* a city and can generate *cultural tourism*. The economic benefits of public art also include the many businesses contributing to the field, such as design, fabrication, engineering, lighting, insurance, and installation. Indeed, public art services are a growth industry in communities such as Los Angeles, Minneapolis, Phoenix, and San Francisco.

Connect Artists with Communities

Public art can assume many forms. It is *malleable*, able to meet the needs of different communities and contribute to many types of projects, from city planning or a river cleanup to a memorial for a lost hero. Artists bring creative perspectives to the strategies and management of such projects, and their efforts often improve the end result.

The artist riding the Charlotte Robinson figure from Red Grooms's *Tennessee Foxtrot Carousel*.

As an audience development tool, public art provides *unparalleled* access to the arts. Street-painting festivals, such as the Italian Street Painting Festival held annually in San Rafael, California, encourage audiences to watch as artists create temporary masterpieces in chalk on the street. The May Day Parade in Minneapolis, hosted by Heart of the Beast Puppet and Mask Theatre, features community art-making workshops that invite hundreds of neighborhood residents to create their own contribution to a celebratory festival that draws an audience of 50,000 annually. 15

Enhance Public Appreciation of Art

Public art can inspire *awe*, draw out deep emotions, make us smile, engage young people, and refresh our perspective. Sometimes, appreciation of public art is found in the details, the fine craftsmanship, and the sheer artistry. Red Grooms's *Tennessee Foxtrot Carousel* in Nashville, Tennessee, features a rideable Davy Crockett, Kitty Wells, Chet Atkins, a big catfish, and many more colorful characters from the region's musical *legacy*. It's fun, it's educational, and it *oozes* creativity.

Artists can deliver messages—*unfiltered* by galleries, agents, or the media—to targeted audiences. In fact, every site comes with an audience. Creative expressions can be directed to businesspeople downtown; children at a playground; seniors at a community center; or farmers at a grain elevator, such as Tacoumba Aiken's giant mural in Good Thunder, Minnesota. Public art can teach us about the diverse cultures inhabiting our community, and invite us to consider the role of art and artists in our society.

Great public art reveals its meaning over time, rewarding repeated visits. Beyond all that, public art has the distinct ability to add beauty to our shared environment; to *commemorate*, memorialize, and celebrate;

and to transport us, if only momentarily, out of our daily routine. Public art is for everyone and it is free. Many people don't visit museums or attend the theater; anybody can experience public art.

Critical Issues

Given the complexities of developing and managing public art programs, working as a professional in the field, and connecting public art with a broad and diverse audience, critical issues abound. Discussing complex topics such as selection processes, funding, conservation, contracts, copyright, and insurance could fill a book; many of these issues will be dealt with in subsequent Public Art Network publications and on its Web site. What follows is intended to *illuminate* a select number of critical issues facing contemporary public art production and administration, and offer possible solutions or methods for addressing them.

Survey Highlights: Working with Artists

- The 102 public art programs that provided information on the number of artists they have commissioned report that they have commissioned an average of 79.5 artists since the inception of their program.
- According to responding programs, the most common method used by artists to apply for a public art commission is an open call (86 percent). Of the open calls that are circulated, 72 percent of the programs issue requests for qualifications and 68 percent issue requests for proposals. Nearly one half (46 percent) report that artists apply for commissions by invitation or nomination. Fewer public art programs report that artists typically apply by joining a slide registry (30 percent). Fifteen percent of programs use all three methods to commission artists. The least common method used by artists to apply for commissions is proposing projects directly to the program (15 percent).
- The vast majority (83 percent) of public art programs report that they pay artists for their proposals when they are finalists for a project.
- According to both government and private nonprofit programs, artist selection panels tend to include the representation of architects, artists, arts professionals, business leaders, and community members, as well as representatives from the commissioning agency and the public art program. In general, artist selection panels consist of an average of 8.6 people.

Education and Incubation

How do artists gain experience in the field of public art? If you have never   20
had a commission, how are you going to get one? The Public Art Network's field survey found that less than one half of the responding public
art programs provide educational and/or training opportunities for artists.
Programs that do offer training are likely to offer open meetings and
lecturers. Far fewer programs offer mentoring or provide resources for
public art educators. Only nine of the responding programs report that
they have a *mentorship* program for artists.

American educational institutions are just beginning to recognize the
importance of public art and design. These are challenging yet teachable
subjects, but few schools have developed *curricula*. A handful, like the
University of Southern California and the University of Washington, offer
public art courses or degree programs for artists or administrators
seeking to enter the field.

From preschool through college and beyond, we can learn something
from public art, and we can also learn about public art: how to get started;
find support; negotiate with site owners; deal with *bureaucracies*; and,
most importantly, make a living at it. More educational tools are needed.
Books, journals, and slide shows are helpful, but first-hand experience is
essential. To gain this, visit an artist's studio, attend a community meeting,
and listen to the stories that each project has to tell and the lessons
learned.

For artists new to public art, only a few *grant* programs exist that
fund artist-initiated projects. Often, artists need to have experience in
public art in order to gain commissions. The lack of opportunities for
artists to receive funding for their own public art initiatives makes it
challenging for them to receive that breakthrough project from a commissioning organization.

FORECAST Public Artworks, a 25-year-old nonprofit in St. Paul, MN,
established a statewide funding program in 1989 for independent artists
of all disciplines, offering support for research and development and for
small-scale "demonstration" projects. FORECAST's national journal,
Public Art Review, has served as a valuable educational tool since 1989,
with many instructors, students, schools, and libraries as subscribers.
Apprenticeships and internships are also effective ways to gain hands-on
experience with artists and program administrators.

Diversity

Public art reflects the changing *demographics* of our society, but it could   25
do even more. Creating opportunities for diverse and immigrant populations to participate in public art will strengthen the overall fabric of our

I have a story to tell you . . . (2003). Pepón Osorio, artist. Photo by Gregory Benson.

culture and inform audiences about the creative impulse found in all cultures.

Unlike the traditional world of art museums, diverse artists now figure prominently in the public art field, including such visionaries as Maya Lin, Suzanne Lacy, Mel Chin, Pepón Osorio, and Rick Lowe. These and countless other artists have *championed* public art as a *humanizing* force; strengthened our connections to the natural world and to each other; and created a means of communicating ideas and sharing experiences in a changing, culturally diverse world.

Philadelphia's Latino community, for example, recently celebrated the installation of internationally renowned artist Pepón Osorio's *I have a story to tell you . . .*, a set of large-scale photographic images in the newly renovated headquarters of Congreso de Latinos Unidos. The installation was commissioned by the Fairmount Park Art Association as part of their groundbreaking New-Land-Marks program. The windows of the main building and the *adjacent*, more intimate *casita* (little house) are fabricated with photographic images on glass. To create this community photograph album, Osorio collected photographs from community members, seeking images that reflect shared experience and *depict* local events that have impacted community life. Beyond its empowering *attributes* for the Latino community, Osorio's project offers the community at large a glimpse at a growing population and with it a sense of their culture and their values.

Critical Language

Shared vocabulary in the public art field urgently needs development. Not everybody is on the same page. Each of us brings a different perspective and a distinct set of *criteria* when deciding what makes good public art. Can the field develop critical language through shared sets of evaluation criteria?

Few public art programs currently conduct evaluations. Only 27 percent of the programs responding to the field survey stated that they had conducted an evaluation or assessment of an individual public art project; 22 percent had conducted an evaluation or assessment of their entire program. It is interesting to note that the survey found that programs that have completed an evaluation of their entire program have much larger and more aggressively growing budgets than those that have not.

Public art programs can develop their evaluation methods by   30 gathering information from local and national grantmaking organizations about evaluation processes, working with an evaluation consultant, and learning about the evaluations conducted by other public art programs. Reporting back to the field about the evaluation mechanism and results via the Public Art Network, websites, conferences, *listservs*, and articles is an essential step toward advancing awareness of the need and benefits of evaluation.

Critical writing and analysis on public art is scarce, but it is a skill that needs to be fostered among the many talented writers in the United States. Beyond art critics, who tend to be more interested in *aesthetics* or art historical concerns, investigative journalists, social critics, anthropologists, social workers, and the articulate *layperson* should all be encouraged to write and talk publicly about public art more often.

Public artists and program administrators, both of whom have the greatest involvement and familiarity with the field, need to gain more objective critical writing skills to effectively share their experiences with public art's larger audience. Public art programs and their parent agencies should consider partnering with foundations and the media to support fellowships for writers and commentators. Newspapers undoubtedly could do a better job covering what's important about public art; many regard it merely as a photo opportunity or a human interest story.

Every project has a story to tell, making film and video and the Internet effective tools for talking about public art. The complex process, the many talented artists, and the wide range of projects can be edited and organized for a broad audience. We can walk around a sculpture, observe it during different seasons, hear the comments of those passing by, and go behind the scenes.

Television programs such as PBS's *Art 21* and segments occasionally aired on *CBS Sunday Morning* are good examples of ways to explore contemporary art and artists, as they are accessible to a broad audience and they don't "talk down" to viewers. Noteworthy films include *Running Fence*, documenting Christo and Jeanne-Claude's struggle to install a 22 mile fabric sculpture in California. More recent documentaries include the Academy Award–winning *A Strong Clear Vision* about Maya Lin's experience creating the Vietnam Veterans Memorial and other projects, and the 2003 documentary *Rivers and Tides* about artist Andy Goldsworthy and his persistent struggle to create *meticulous*, fragile, and *ephemeral*—and stunningly beautiful—outdoor works of art. These and other records are tremendous resources that begin to break down the language barriers between public art and its many audiences.

Controversy

Public art can become a *lightning rod*, especially in complex capital projects, because it is often the only area where public participation is invited. Public art can also attract controversy because it uses public funds and occupies a prominent place in public spaces. The meaning of great public art is often not grasped immediately upon installation; consider the *Eiffel Tower*, the *Gateway Arch*, the *Statue of Liberty*, and the *Vietnam Veterans Memorial*—all controversial. It wasn't until years—or even decades—later that these projects became valued icons, able to withstand the test of time. It isn't hard to offend someone with nudity, political incorrectness, social commentary, the perceived unnecessary use of public funds, etc. And sometimes public art simply doesn't work.

35

Let's face it, there's plenty of *mediocre* art out there, making it difficult to build a case for future support.

Controversy is a magnet for the media, and there are plenty of examples. Dennis Oppenheim's *Blue Shirt* project for Milwaukee's General Mitchell International Airport faced overwhelming opposition after the design was approved by the county's art committee in 2000. The monumentally scaled wall-mounted sculpture of a blue work shirt was the subject of a legal dispute, based on the fact that the artist did not complete installation on time. Oppenheim said the problems with the piece were not about timing or money, but about politics. The city government and local press mounted a campaign against the sculpture, characterizing it as a *pejorative* comment on Milwaukee's reputation as a blue-collar town. The dispute kept the project on hold for months, until a revised installation was approved for completion.

Survey Highlights: Visual Artists Rights Act

The Visual Artists Rights Act of 1990 (VARA) is Section 106A of the copyright law. It applies to any work created after 1990. VARA establishes a definition of visual art, which includes sculpture. VARA provides protection beyond the economic rights of the copyright law, and is distinct from ownership of a copy of an artwork or of a copyright or any exclusive right under copyright to that artwork.

VARA is personal to the artist, its protection is for the life of the artist, and an artist's VARA rights cannot be transferred. VARA provides for the artist's right of attribution to claim authorship of his or her work; to prevent the use of his or her name on any work he or she did not create; and to have his or her name removed from any work that is distorted, mutilated, or modified that would reflect with prejudice on the artist's reputation.

VARA provides for the artist's right of integrity to prevent any intentional distortion, alteration, or destruction of a work of recognized stature, and any intentional or grossly negligent destruction of a work in violation of that right. The artist can waive his or her VARA rights, but a waiver has to be in writing and must specifically identify the artwork and the uses of that artwork. The waiver applies only to the artwork and uses so identified.

Eighty-eight percent of responding public art programs report that their artist contract complies with VARA. Similarly, 90 percent of public art programs say that the artists that they commission retain the copyright of their work. When the copyright is not maintained by the artists, most often it becomes the property of the public art program. A few programs report that they share a joint copyright with the artists.

Definition by William Gignilliat, Esq., PAN Council committee member.

Everyone's a critic. If you want to find fault with a public art project at any point in the process, you can. And, depending on the situation, there may be a need for "damage control." Obtaining written support from key community leaders and project *stakeholders* early on can help.

Strategic planning and obtaining early feedback helps avoid unwanted controversy. Play your own devil's advocate and determine the risks carefully, then move forward with assurance and conviction. If you consider the examples listed here—all considered great works of public art—controversy can be viewed as a good sign. Controversy and an abundance of attention indicate that people are interested, concerned, or even outraged. This begs the question: why? The root of this question is at the heart of what makes public art so compelling.

Conclusion

Communities that desire meaningful public art need to work at it by reaching out and participating in the effort. After all, the public is the final beneficiary of public art. As the *demographics* and the economics in our   40 communities change, public art must constantly prove its value to the public.

Based on the significant number of programs, the size of their budgets, and the millions of people affected every day, public art appears to be gaining recognition. As public art *infiltrates* almost every *facet* of our culture, in *myriad* forms, it can help all the arts to regain a position of value and priority in our society. We must continue to support public artists; help them to give shape to our shared identity; and bring their visions, their energy, their spirit, and their creative solutions to the world. Shaping places—with landmarks and landscapes, events and ideologies— sets the stage for a critical part of our existence: our connection with our environment; with our past, present, and future; and with other human beings.

About Public Art Network

PAN is a program of Americans for the Arts designed to provide services to the diverse field of public art and to develop strategies and tools to improve communities through public art. PAN's key constituents are public art professionals, visual artists, design professionals, arts organizations, and communities planning public art projects and programs. For more information about PAN, e-mail pan@artsusa.org or visit the Web site at www.AmericansForTheArts.org/PAN.

Resources

For more information on the artists, projects, and organizations in this Monograph, please see the following Web sites.

Artists and Projects

Art on the Street
http://artonthestreet.info/index.html

Blue Shirt Project, Dennis Oppenheim, artist
www.home.earthlink.net/~dennisoppenheim

Mel Chin, artist
www.pbs.org/art21/artists/chin

Christo and Jeanne-Claude, artists
www.christojeanneclaude.net

Suzanne Lacy, artist
www.suzannelacy.com

Maya Lin, artist and architect
www.pbs.org/art21/artists/lin

May Day Parade
www.heartofthebeasttheatre.org/mayday

PBS's *Art 21*
www.pbs.org/art21

Project Row Houses, Rick Lowe, artist
www.projectrowhouses.org

A Strong Clear Vision (documentary)
www.pbs.org/pov/pov1996/mayalin/

WaterFire Providence, Barnaby Evans, artist
www.waterfire.com

Programs and Organizations

Creative Time
www.creativetime.org

FORECAST Public Artworks
www.forecastart.org

Public Art Fund
www.publicartfund.org

Regional Arts and Culture Council
www.racc.org

Seattle Office of Arts and Culture
www.cityofseattle.net/arts

Tucson Pima Arts Council
www.tucsonpimaartscouncil.org

University of Southern California's Public Art Studies Program
http://finearts.usc.edu/pas

---

practice it   **Post-Reading Activity**

Look up two or three of the various artists, programs, and organizations referenced in "Public Art: An Essential Component of Creating Communities." After doing some brief research, add additional information to your annotations.

COMPREHENSION QUESTIONS

1. What is the role of a public art ordinance?

2. What does Becker mean when he says that "the experience of viewing public art is dynamic?" (para. 5).

3. How can public art become a "lightning rod" (para. 35)?

4. Why does the author introduce examples of famous public art projects like the *Eiffel Tower*, the *Gateway Arch*, and the *Statue of Liberty*? How is he using these examples to make a point? Does he succeed?

5. What is the Visual Artists Rights Act? How does it relate to artists who display their work in public?

6. Becker says that "controversy can be viewed as a good sign" (para. 39). Why does he say this? Do you agree? Why or why not?

VOCABULARY ACTIVITIES

1. Refer back to your annotations to begin a glossary of words related to the study of public art. Try to use context clues or roots, prefixes, and suffixes to determine the meaning of the words, and if you have to use a dictionary, try to restate the definition in your own words. For more on roots, prefixes, and suffixes, see Chapter 8, Vocabulary Building, page 198.

2. Make graphic flash cards for the top ten challenging vocabulary words from this article. For help creating flash cards, see Chapter 8, Vocabulary Building, page 198.

SUMMARY ACTIVITY

Create a nutshell summary of each section of this article. Use these nutshell summaries to write a one-paragraph summary overview of the whole reading beginning with Becker's main point or purpose. For help writing a summary, see Chapter 1, Reading and Responding to College Texts, page 2.

DISCUSSION QUESTIONS

1. Becker writes that "art placed in public can still be quality art and offer the general public an art experience outside a museum or gallery setting" (para. 2). What does this mean and is this important? What does public art do for a community? Explain.

2. Why does Becker suggest that public art is a "democratic art form" (para. 7)? What does he mean? Do you agree?

3. The creation of public art requires the cooperation of many: city officials, artists, and the public, among others. How does graffiti art skirt this process? What are the pros and cons of both commissioned public art and graffiti art?

4. What suggestions does the author make about ways that public art can be fostered?

RESEARCH REPORT

Teresa Palomo Acosta researches and writes about the history of Texas. She is the author of three books of poetry, and the coauthor *of Las Tejanas: 300 Years of History* (2003). Her article on the Chicano Mural Movement was published in the *Handbook of Texas Online*, a publication featured on the Web site of the Texas State Historical Association (TSHA). The TSHA was founded in 1897 to preserve and promote Texas history by publishing books and articles, maintaining an online database of state historical records, and offering educational workshops and online resources for students and historians. *Important words and phrases have been italicized in this reading. Look up those you do not know, and write the definitions in your personal vocabulary list.*

practice it   Pre-Reading

What is significant about the geographic locations of El Paso, San Antonio, and Houston? Look the cities up on a map if you aren't familiar with them. What do you know about these cities or the state of Texas? Spend a few minutes freewriting on these places before you begin the reading.

---

tshaonline.org

Chicano Mural Movement
Teresa Palomo Acosta

The Chicano mural movement began in the 1960s in Mexican-American barrios throughout the Southwest. Artists began using the walls of city buildings, housing projects, schools, and churches to depict Mexican-American culture. Chicano muralism has been linked to pre-Columbian peoples of the Americas, who recorded their rituals and history on the walls of their pyramids, and Mexican revolutionary-era painters José Clemente Orozco, Diego Rivera, and David Alfaros Siquieros, collectively known as *los tres grandes*, who painted murals in the United States. Two other Latino predecessors were Antonio García and Xavier González, who painted murals in the 1930s under the auspices of the Work Projects Administration art projects. In 1933 at San Diego (Texas) High School, García produced *March on Washington*, which has since been moved to the Duval County Museum. It embodies the idea that President Herbert Hoover failed to rebuild the nation's finances after the stock-market crash of 1929 and that President Franklin Delano Roosevelt triumphed in putting Americans back to work. García also painted murals for Corpus Christi Cathedral and an academy in Corpus Christi. González, who went on to international acclaim as a sculptor, painted a mural for the San Antonio Municipal Auditorium in 1933. It was later removed because of public outcry over the "upraised fist and a palm with a bleeding wound" depicted in it.

During the Mexican-American artistic and literary renaissance that occurred throughout the Southwest in the 1960s and 1970s mural production became part of the effort of Hispanics to reinvigorate their cultural heritage, which was manifested in the rise of the Raza Unida party, the United Farm Workers Union, and the Mexican American Youth Organization, all of which tried to affirm cultural identity and challenge racism. The mural movement depicted such cultural motifs and heroes as Quetzalcoatl from the pre-Columbian era, Francisco (Pancho) Villa from the revolutionary period, and Cleto L. Rodríguez from Tejano history. Nuestra Señora de Guadalupe (Our Lady of Guadalupe) is the only representation of a woman. Around the state, most of the artists, some formally trained and others self-taught, worked in collaboration with community volunteers, often teenagers who were recruited for specific projects, to fashion the murals.

In El Paso more than 100 murals have been painted since the mid-1960s. Manuel Acosta painted *Iwo Jima*, perhaps the earliest of the city's known Chicano murals, at the Veterans of Foreign Wars office in 1966. Carlos Rosas, Felipe Adame, and Gaspar Enríquez usually worked in conjunction with student painters. Mago Orona Gándara, one of the few known female muralists working in El Paso, has painted at least two as a solo artist, *Señor Sol* and *Time and Sand*. Two other women, Irene Martínez and Monika Acevedo, participated in the team that completed *Myths of Maturity* at the University of Texas at El Paso library in 1991. The murals, located throughout the city's various corridors, often depict themes common to Chicano muralism, such as mestizo heritage or social problems, but they also tell unique stories about the "merging of ideas, cultures, and dreams" along the United States-Mexico border. An attempt to preserve the murals, as well as to restore older ones or paint new ones, was sponsored in the early 1990s by the city's artists and the Junior League, which also published a brochure entitled *Los Murales, Guide and Maps to the Murals of El Paso*.

San Antonio also has a strong Chicano mural tradition, with the majority of murals concentrated on the city's predominantly Mexican-American West Side. The Cassiano public-housing project, for instance, has been the site of numerous murals, many of them painted under the direction of the Community Cultural Arts Organization, which was organized in 1979. CCAO chief artist Anastacio "Tacho" Torres has recruited teams of student artists to complete works that depict an array of subjects: labor leader César Chávez, lowriders, the San Antonio missions, Tejano military and political heroes, and others. More than 130 murals had been completed in the city by the early 1990s. Some have been privately commissioned for a variety of locales such as the convention center, Mario's Mexican Restaurant, and Our Lady of the Lake University. As in El Paso, efforts to record the existence of these works have occurred. In the early 1980s, for example, historian Ricardo Romo developed a slide show on them called "Painted Walls of the Barrio" for the University of Texas Institute of Texan Cultures.

In Houston, Leo Tanguma painted *Rebirth of our Nationality* on the 5 wall of the Continental Can Company. Because of the politically charged content of Tanguma's mural art, several of his works have been erased. In Austin muralist Raúl Valdez has led volunteer teams in painting murals at several public sites on the city's predominantly Mexican-American east side, including the Pan American Recreation Center. Some of his work, like Tanguma's, has been lost in recent years. *Los Elementos*, for instance, which was painted on the exterior of the Juárez-Lincoln University building in 1977, was destroyed in 1983; city officials could not save it when the building was sold to a new owner. Sylvia Orozco, codirector of Mexic-Arte, has also painted murals, among them one for the Chicano Culture Room in the student union building of the University of Texas at Austin. Murals have also been reported in Crystal City, Dallas, Lubbock, Levelland, Lockhart, and other cities. Whether in small or large towns, artists in the Chicano mural movement have offered an opportunity to the barrios' "untrained" painters. Art historians Shifra Goldman and Tomás Ybarra-Frausto call the murals a significant contribution to public art.

Bibliography

Arriba, November 15–December 15, 1989.

Shifra Goldman and Tomás Ybarra-Frausto, *Arte Chicano. A Comprehensive Annotated Bibliography of Chicano Art, 1965–1981* (Chicano Studies Library Publications Unit, University of California, Berkeley, 1985).

---

practice it **Post-Reading Activity**

Look back at the freewrite you wrote as your pre-reading activity. Has reading the Web article provided you with more information, not only about the topic of mural art, but also about these three cities and the people who live there? Add new information and thoughts to your freewrite based on what you learned from the reading.

COMPREHENSION QUESTIONS

1. What is the historical basis of the 1960s Chicano mural movement?

2. What kinds of topics or scenes did early murals depict?

3. What were the goals of the Mexican American mural movement in the 1960s and 1970s?

4. What kind of mural activity has there been in El Paso, San Antonio, and Houston since the 1960s?

DISCUSSION QUESTIONS

1. What is the significance of mural artists being self-taught versus formally trained?

2. How might a mural "affirm cultural identity and challenge racism"? How might a mural not be successful in challenging racism? Can you think of any examples of murals you have seen that work to challenge racist attitudes? If so, explain how. If not, explain why they don't.

3. Why are Chicano murals "concentrated on the city's predominantly Mexican-American West Side"? What does that suggest about the intended audience and purpose of the murals? How might the murals function differently in other neighborhoods?

4. What rights should a community have to remove art that the majority of residents find politically objectionable? How should decisions be made about which murals to remove and which to preserve?

VOCABULARY ACTIVITIES

1. Add any words from this article to your ongoing public art glossary. Remember to write definitions in your own words.

2. "Chicano Mural Movement" makes references to a number of artists and organizations or agencies throughout the text. Look up some of these and make annotations in the margin of your text indicating their significance to the mural movement.

SUMMARY ACTIVITY

Write a nutshell summary for each paragraph of the text. How well does this help you summarize the main points of the article? Based on this activity, write a short, one-paragraph summary of the reading. (For help writing a summary, see Chapter 1, Reading and Responding to College Texts, p. 29.)

Will Shank is an art historian and conservator who was educated and trained in art conservation at Villa Schifanoia, Florence; the Institute of Fine Arts of New York University; and the Harvard University Art Museums. In addition to writing numerous articles and a book, *Celluloid San Francisco: The Film Lover's Guide to Bay Area Movie Locations*, he was the head of conservation at the San Francisco Museum of Modern Art for many years. He is also an adviser and cocreator of the Rescue Public Murals project, which is part of the national nonprofit organization Heritage Preservation in Washington, D.C. The following article was originally published in the book *Street Art San Francisco: Mission Muralismo* (2009). *Important words and phrases have been italicized in this reading. Look up those you do not know, and write the definitions in your personal vocabulary list.*

practice it   Pre-Reading

Freewrite about the differences and similarities between museum art and public art. Who decides what art is museum-worthy? Why would people prefer to display their art in a public place?

Will Shank

WHOSE ART IS THIS ANYWAY?

As a *conservator* of modern art, my job is to understand and preserve precious museum objects. But I am also a former Mission resident who has biked and jogged up and down every street and alley in order to seek out the neighborhood's mural treasury. The layers of art in *the Mission* are an invitation for exploration to a *conservator*. As the cofounder, with mural historian Tim Drescher, of an initiative called Rescue Public Murals, I am hoping to accomplish something that contemporary public art frequently does not do well. Thanks to the *Getty Foundation* and other supporters, we are able to examine what is *enduring* in a *temporal* medium. While stone sculptures and ceiling frescoes were designed to address eternity, outdoor murals are subject to the *tyranny* of time, street life, politics, and fashion.

  Consider this contentious mural. An innocent-looking, almost-white wall sits quietly on a sun-blasted, south-facing building in a warehouse neighborhood where San Francisco's largely Latino Mission

District creeps toward the foot of Potrero Hill. There is nothing remarkable about the southern wall of the windowless building except for its massive sixty-by-sixty stance at the intersection of several narrow industrial streets that get lots of cars but little foot traffic. But, if you look closely, you will notice a rectangle of faded color here, and some splotches of dripped colors there, apparently made by someone hurling a paint-filled balloon at the white wall. The Lilli Ann building, built as a garment factory and currently housing offices, holds a secret.

Until 1998, a brightly hued, abstract, geometric mural by Chicano artist Chuy Campusano filled this wall. Then suddenly it was gone. The building had changed hands, and the owners took steps to seal out moisture that was creeping into the interior through the painted wall. They used an opaque layer of sealant, which turned the once-colorful wall white.

Hysteria ensued. Death threats were made against the building's owners. The family of the deceased artist sued the owners of the building but encouraged local supporters to cease the vandalism, which had begun when the mural was covered over. The option was explored of transferring the aged paint film, in a variation of the traditional Italian fresco technique known as *strappo*, from a wall that consisted of hundreds of cinderblocks, mortar, and cement patches. The family eventually settled for monetary compensation, and the wall remains blank.

Jesus "Chuy" Campusano, *Lilli Ann*, 1986.

Lilli Ann Building after mural was whitewashed, 1998.

The principles of conservation treatments for contemporary murals 5
are among the few areas whose ethics are not specifically addressed by
my profession. When called upon to address the condition problems of
a deteriorating outdoor mural, the average conservator will apply the
standard principles of conservation to his or her task: documentation,
reversibility, and design compensation restricted to areas of loss. But is
this approach always, or even usually, appropriate?

I have questioned several managers of public art collections about
the special case of outdoor murals. From their point of view, painted
walls should by-and-large be considered temporary artworks. Some city
collections have *quantified* the number of years that a mural should be
expected to last: ten years, say, or fifteen. In spite of this hard line
about the limited life span of outdoor murals, there is almost universal
hesitation when the time comes to state that all murals should fall into
this somewhat disposable category.

The tricky *sociological* matter is that a highly visible work of art on
constant public display develops a life, and sometimes a *cult*, of its
own—even if an authoritative body, or the community that created it,
decides that it is time to do away with a mural. Even if *adequate* notice
is posted, as is required by law, the destruction of any sort of art in the
public eye can have violent *repercussions* when the artist, or the

community, objects. The Visual Artists Rights Act grants to artists certain "moral" or "aesthetic" rights in the *integrity* of their work.

As the matter was resolved, the Lilli Ann mural itself was the loser. This sort of highly publicized conflict certainly discourages other building owners from welcoming such public works of art on their walls or *arbitrarily* destroying the ones that already exist. Happily, in test cases elsewhere, those who would eliminate a mural without the approval of the artist(s) who created it have paid a high price.

Rescue Public Murals has begun to bring together the communities that create murals, the owners of buildings whose walls they grace, the caretakers of these powerful visual statements, and the professionals whose job it is to save works of art in order to come to some *consensus* about how best to proceed. The Mission was the breeding ground of this initiative.

Damaged mural in Cullmann, Alabama, 2011.

practice it   Post-Reading Activity

Review the Visual Artists Rights Act (VARA) that you read about in Jack Becker's "Public Art: An Essential Component of Creating Communities" earlier in this chapter. What are the "moral" and "aesthetic" rights an artist has over his work? Do you think VARA gives more rights to the artist or to the owner of the artwork? In what ways? Based on your research, who should be responsible for the life of a mural? Why?

COMPREHENSION QUESTIONS

1. We often hear about "conservation" in relation to the environment. What does it mean to conserve art?

2. He refers to murals as "enduring in a temporal medium" (para. 1). What does this mean? And how does it apply to the way people view murals?

3. What factors affect the longevity and condition of both indoor and outdoor murals?

4. Shank writes that "a highly visible work of art on constant public display develops a life, and sometimes a cult, of its own" (para. 7). What does he mean by that? How does this happen?

VOCABULARY ACTIVITIES

1. Add any words from this article—especially those related to art techniques—to your ongoing public art glossary. Remember to write definitions in your own words.

2. What does the root of the word *conservator* mean? List as many other words that you can find that use this same root. How does this help you understand the full meaning of the term *conservator*? Why might Shank call himself a "conservator" rather than something else? What other possible synonyms are there? For more on roots, see Chapter 8, Vocabulary Building, page 198.

SUMMARY ACTIVITY

If a picture is truly worth a thousand words, this reading has a lot to say just through its images. Write a paragraph explaining how the images summarize the ideas of mural ownership presented in this reading. For help writing a summary, see Chapter 1, Reading and Responding to College Texts, page 2.

DISCUSSION QUESTIONS

1. The title of the article raises an interesting question about ownership of public art. Does the article provide an answer to this question?

2. The author is both a conservator of art in the art industry and a former resident of a mural-rich neighborhood. How does this experience equip him to write on the topic of public art? What other affiliations or expertise does he have in relation to this topic?

3. How do the images in this reading selection help you understand murals as one form of "temporary" public art?

4. In the case of the Campusano mural, should the building owners have acted differently in your opinion? Should the family of Chuy Campusano have acted differently?

JOURNAL

Koon-Hwee Kan is a practicing artist as well as an associate professor in the art education department at Kent State University's School of Art. She is also the coordinator for the Saturday Art Program, a ten-week outreach program for children in the community. Kan has received several awards for her research and presents nationally and internationally on art education. In addition to publishing this article in the journal *Art Education in 2001*, she has also published numerous articles in other art and art education journals, including a number of studies on art and youth in Singapore. She is working on a book, *Playful Mindfulness: How Artists and Artisans Embody Meanings with Life. Important words and phrases have been italicized in this reading. Look up those you do not know, and write the definitions in your personal vocabulary list.*

practice it   Pre-Reading

What kinds of graffiti do you notice in your environment? What locations are most likely to have graffiti? Is the graffiti you see on bathroom walls on campus different from the other graffiti you see on campus? How?

KOON-HWEE KAN

Adolescents and Graffiti

What is graffiti, and why are many adolescents attracted by it? Art teachers recognize that there are great variations of visual art forms nowadays. As conceptions of art change, so will the ideas about art education. Wilson (1997) has proposed an expanded concept of "child art" to include activities that are common to the youth of today. This view could encourage teachers to broaden their *curriculums* and incorporate new art forms that are more engaging to young people.

This article uses teenage psychology to interpret adolescents' involvement in both private and public graffiti. Graffiti art will be examined in different contexts with its educational implications considered for the secondary school art curriculum and instruction.

Private Graffiti

Doodling

Doodling is a form of private graffiti. These scrawls and scribbles are created when attention is supposed to be focused elsewhere, so their completeness and aesthetic quality are seldom recognized. Adolescents' doodling may seem totally formless and meaningless, but it fits perfectly into certain aspects of adolescents' psychology.

Living in multiple realities, including the "daydream reality," is common among adolescents. My personal experience of interviewing and observing adolescents has alerted me that even when they seem to be very engaged in an activity or a conversation, their thoughts can change dimension and direction at any time without warning. This scattered attention continues to puzzle and worry many parents and teachers. However, adolescents' accomplished "divided attention" and "selective attention" can easily allow them to concentrate on different things simultaneously, switching focus instantly to activities that interest them while allowing others to fade into the background (Higgins & Turnure, 1984).

Thus, the elongated concentration span of adolescence that guides   5
curriculum planning has certain limitations. As academic achievement is not valued by many teenagers today (Meyer, 1994), schooling becomes a boring, frustrating, stressful, or anxious experience for them. In such cases, their natural tendency to drift in and out of multiple realities increases. From this perspective, adolescent doodling is a form of escape. It can be interpreted as an unconscious rejection of the kind of learning that is not helping them to construct personal meanings and effectively integrate their inner needs to promote growth.

"Latrinalia"

Another type of private graffiti is "latrinalia," the kind of graffiti found near toilets (Abel & Buckley, 1970). In most civilizations throughout history, its creators were usually suppressed individuals in the society, for example, slaves working in monumental construction or prisoners inside jail cells. In contemporary times, such creation is not the sole responsibility of adolescence; people of all ages are equally likely to perform such acts. Yet, latrinalia is common in school toilets and poses a major vandalism problem.

Creation of latrinalia satisfies the emotional needs of adolescents in an unusual manner. Adolescence is a stage of life in which the individuals seek autonomy. When trying to secure a sense of personal space and time, the presence of others, especially adults, is often deemed threatening. At home, parents may regularly notice the strange behaviors of their adolescents, either behind frequently locked bedroom doors or during unusually extended times inside the bathrooms. Yet, many such episodes end almost immediately with the flushing of the toilet and a speedy reappearance of their teenagers without clues to what had happened just before. For many adolescents, parents' caring questionings are regarded as tight supervision. Nor is the school community perceived as supportive and accommodating of their unique growing-up experience. Thus, latrinalia in schools may be a form of silence and mindless protest for them against the large educational system that alienates their primary needs. There is evidence that school vandalism decreases or is absent in schools that manage a successful community of learning (Flaherty, 1987).

Public Graffiti

In contrast to private graffiti, public graffiti always makes its debut known. The main distinction between the two types of graffiti is that the latter is often created with an intended audience and special motives, while the former is created more unconsciously. Different forms of public graffiti, like gang graffiti, "tags," and "pieces," provide different means to satisfy the psychology and emotional needs of their creators, who are not exclusively adolescents.

Gang Graffiti

Gang graffiti appeared in the United States in the 1950s. It is the most unacceptable form of public graffiti because of the notorious reputation of gangs. "These are primitive scrawls focusing on the gang names or symbols adopted to mark territory and war zones" (Gomez, 1993, p. 644). They are often simple alphabets written backwards, numbers marked in sets, or letters intentionally crossed out to send coded messages among gang members or warn away intruders. Usually, these activities are carried out by junior members within the gang hierarchy or by newly recruited young members to prove their worth and courage by entering the territory of another gang and leaving an insulting mark.

Tags

"Tags are simple, stark lettering like signatures . . . that Taggers 10 have adopted for different personal reasons" (Gomez, 1993, p. 645). The invention of magic markers and improvement of spray paint in the late 1960s made tagging possible and popular in the United States, as these two mediums can easily and quickly mark on any surface.

Pieces

Deriving from the word "masterpiece," these are large, elaborate works with refined details often found on the exterior of subway trains and buildings. "Style" of pieces is important since they distinguish how different creators, known as "artists" or "writers" (Gomez, 1993), express their imaginations. Pieces can be a form of political protest or social statement as in the example of works found on the former Berlin Wall (Walderburg, 1990). Many creators of "pieces" consider their work as public art, an improvement to their surrounding environment and community (Geer & Rowe, 1995). Some families of victims of crime and violence in New York have commissioned graffiti artists to paint murals in memory of the deceased (Cooper & Sciorra, 1994). In the 1970s, a Union of Graffiti Artists (UGA) was formed that organized exhibitions and sales.

How Did Graffiti Become Art?

The 1980s were the Golden Age of graffiti art with the emergence of "wild style," an intertwined and decorative lettering that mixes icons and images from popular culture to form a complex composition (Fineberg, 1995). A big avant garde art show at Times Square in 1980 featured many graffiti artists, including Jean-Michel Basquiat, Futura 2000, Lee Quinones, and Keith Haring. Most of them seemed to become famous overnight. At that time, high art was being criticized as too *institutionalized* and intellectual. A huge discrepancy existed between art in museums and the experience of common people. Witnessing the gradual decline of *Minimalism* in the previous decade, art critic Rene Richard highlighted graffiti art in *Art Forum*, a distinguished high art magazine. Art dealers sought "new blood" to stimulate the art market. Graffiti thus became an art commodity worth investing in.

Graffiti art was also indebted to the Hip-Hop culture popular at that time, which included rap music, disc jockeys and break dancing (Hager,

1985). This subculture gained attention in the *New Yorker* magazine, films, and movies. American popular culture made heroes of graffiti artists like Jean-Michel Basquiat, portraying in the movie *Break-in* the young talent who died prematurely at age 29. Another young rising star was Keith Haring, who soon became the most widely renowned graffiti artist.

By the 1990s, Hip-Hop culture had lost its initial vibrancy, but had become known worldwide and accepted as part of mainstream U.S. culture. Graffiti art became commercialized at about this time, appearing in the advertisements of Nike and Sprite, while other marketing strategies targeted at youth culture continued to reinforce the notion of graffiti as an artistic form of expression to the younger generations.

Most graffiti creators in the United States today are estimated to be 15 between the ages of 12 to 30, with the majority younger than 18 years old. Half are from white middle- and upper-middle-class families (Walsh, 1996). My research findings, generated from 50 survey forms given to anonymous adolescents in a small midwestern community have convinced me of the validity of these figures. Most respondents regarded graffiti as a means of expression and honestly admitted their involvement in some form of graffiti, especially when they felt bored or stressed out in school. Only one student used graffiti seriously as a coping mechanism: "Yes, only once, I drew a figure balled up holding the word 'why' in her hands on a school desk. My neighbor had just committed suicide, I was torn apart . . . neurotic almost, I created it absentmindedly and during French class."

Should a child-centered art curriculum that emphasizes personalized learning of students by actively engaging their environment and community, exclude lessons on graffiti?

My interviews with some adolescents interested in graffiti and former "writers" have given me insights. A white female interviewee felt personally connected to the graffiti-art style and deliberately copied and learned its forms for her own artistic creation. Another interviewee demonstrated a convincing expertise in "graffiti appreciation" when we looked through pictures of graffiti together. The scribbling found around a complete "piece" can "teach you insight into the attitude of the artist too. If he writes something funny, then you know that the guy has a light mood or something. Or if he like writes something really political, then it is like he really feels like an artist. . . . [It is] information, . . . like what year it is made and who they are affiliated with."

A third interviewee recalled how his own "angular" an "typographic" graffiti-art style had evolved from his initial involvement in gang graffiti when he was young. As the only minority person growing up in that underprivileged environment, he was eager to gain acceptance into another ethnic group and wanted desperately to join their gang. His "graffiti-artistic development" began when "it was like sort of copying all those things that I have seen, do stuff like big S.C. [representing Spanish Cobra, his gang's name]. Like in black and white, very style like, like some of the older kids would do . . . so, that's all I had. No magazine, no anything at that time, very little to go on, as far as like learning style or something. Just copying." Despite his humble beginning, with self-improvised equipment, "using empty paper towel tubes or toilet paper tubes . . . [that] we use to control the flow of the spray paint." Gradually, his graffiti *connoisseurship* improved.

Graffiti art provides novelty in both language and visual representation with a unique and holistic aesthetic naturally favored by youth. It directly borrows popular icons from the saturated mass media to which teenagers are continually exposed and also incorporates common slang as text (Chalfant & Prigoff, 1987). For many adolescents who despise following social norms and cultural conventions, graffiti represents the means to rebel against the established taste of society (Ferrell, 1995). Museum exhibitions that they visit on school field trips may represent traditional adult tastes but not "their cup of Coke [tea]." Seeking an alternative form of expression is equivalent to the *non-normative* way of communication, like using *coded* language amongst their own peer group. Moreover, for many living in certain parts of the city, the naturalistic settings where graffiti appears is right in their surrounding. Thus, graffiti is the most familiar form of their "visual culture" of everyday living and a must in their art curriculum.

What if a disciplined-based art curriculum introduced the aesthetic and history of graffiti or the artist Keith Haring without inquiry into the social and cultural context of its creation?

"You're standing there in the station, everything is gray and gloomy and all of a sudden one of those graffiti trains slides in and brightens the place like a big bouquet from Latin America," famous artist Claes Oldenburg *lauds* the beauty of graffiti (Horworth, 1989). Many young graffiti artists have captured the attention of the mass media with their "unique artistic courage." For example, young TAKI 183 was featured in the *New York Times*, on July 21, 1971, after tagging on almost every line of the New York subway.[1] Keith Haring's graffiti art is widely recognized too. His work appears in all forms of commercial arts and museum souvenirs, in many contemporary art history textbooks, in exhibits all over the United States, and even in a number of children's art books.

It is indeed easy to compare the characteristics of graffiti to other art forms and highlight its *aesthetics* or to simply introduce the graffiti artists' work and learn their graffiti-like art styles. However, will this 20 represent graffiti art adequately in an art curriculum? What about the vulgarity and often explicit hostility in some of the contents that may include biased, racist, and sexist statements and images?

The undesirable fact is graffiti has become an expensive social problem in many cities in the world. U.S. cities spent an estimated four billion dollars cleaning graffiti in 1994 (Walsh, 1996). Cleaning graffiti in schools is also a struggle for many teachers, principals, and school staff. School vandalism is an increasing problem in many western countries; it depletes educational reform budgets and delays upgrading plans (Zwier & Vaughan, 1984). As a result, there has been strong advocacy in recent years for stricter state legislation against such juvenile delinquency on school property. There are 12 states with legislation addressing vandalism and damage to school property (Menacker & Mertz, 1994, p. 6). These include Alabama, Arkansas, California, Colorado, Hawaii, Indiana, Kentucky, Mississippi, North Carolina, New Mexico, Pennsylvania, and Tennessee.

My survey indicates that most young adolescents (12–13 years old) cannot differentiate between graffiti art and vandalism. For them, it is confusing when the art world and society send them contradictory messages; while one highly honors the achievement of individual graffiti artists, the other prohibits the work of unknown artists and even severely prosecutes those who are arrested.

Can school art curriculum relate to social critical theory's call of reconsidering sub-cultural phenomena like graffiti, but without resolving the issue of vandalism, a social problem and a crime with punishment?

For some adolescents who find the desire to engage in activities unacceptable to adults, public graffiti becomes enormously attractive when society pronounces it illegal. This rebellious attitude against the whole society is one that many adolescents exhibit, often manifested in their defiance against parental authority and revolt against codes and order. Adolescents may seek autonomy primarily in this way, establishing their own identity by breaking away from their earlier dependent and compliant role. However, the undesirable truth is that anti-social behavior is often contagious within youth peer groups. Indeed, adolescents seeking group belonging and acceptance may be subjected to great peer pressure for conformity, even though individual relationships in the groups may not actually be satisfactory (Pabon, Rodriguez & Gurin, 1992).

In addition, when the culture and mass media send out messages that value youth heroism, graffiti can easily spark the risk-taking tendency amongst some male adolescents. They would "bravely" cross the fatal third rail that carries high voltages of electricity while tagging and creating their "masterpieces" in the dark tunnels. A great sense of achievement is derived reaching areas that are deemed impossible for normal accessibility. Climbing high on bridges and hanging in dangerous positions to leave their marks proves courage more than words (Anonymous, 1998). Adolescents' high risk-taking tendency contradicts their improved cognitive abilities. The ability to think about possibilities, to employ abstract concepts, and to engage in meta-cognition, or thinking about their own thinking (Keating, 1990), is supposed to make adolescents better decision-makers since they can reflect critically, hypothesize before making judgments, rationalize their choices and preferences, and consider their options. Yet, even a tragic accident[2] in 1973 that nearly killed a young writer could not deter the die-hard youngsters.

The dilemma of adolescents' psychological and emotional needs 25 versus the creation of graffiti did not reach the consciousness of the U.S. public until 1994. Michael Fay, an American teenager, was caned in the Republic of Singapore after his conviction on criminal mischief charges for spray-painting graffiti on 18 cars.

The *polarized* conflicts of interest surrounding the definition of graffiti and its place within the art world present challenges for art teachers. How should they approach it?

Tips for art teachers to minimize the "red tape" in order to incorporate graffiti as part of their curriculum in school:

1. There must always be a serious consideration of age appropriateness in pedagogy. Do not try to introduce controversial art forms and content to a whole student body. For example, most art teachers recognize that sharp linoleum-cutting tools or acid are inappropriate printmaking materials for younger students. Concepts and ideas may sometimes be more dangerous than sharp tools and toxic materials.
2. Seek the approval of all the authorities in the school and district, including the principals and other colleagues. Take it as an opportunity to educate them about the multiple dimensions of art in the present time, so that they may become aware of art as a social-ethical activity instead of a beautiful and fun act to kill time. Perhaps in this way, the marginal role of the arts in school can be revised.
3. Fully consider the community and its interests. If it is necessary, speak to the community leaders and parents instead of sending letters home. Sincerity matters. Use this as an opportunity to advocate the importance of arts to learning.
4. Try to involve a decent graffiti writer or artist who may be already known in the neighborhood. The kids can sometimes help to locate one easily. However, always double-check his or her philosophy of life, thoughts on education, and the meaning of his or her "art" (Gomez, 1993).

Acknowledgments

Special thanks to Christine Thompson, Julia Kellman, and Reed Larson for insightful comments on this manuscript. I am indebted to Irena Kola, Aida Orgocka, and Silvana Dushku for reading numerous revisions of this article.

References

Abel, E. L., & Buckley, B. E. (1977). *The handwriting on the wall: Towards a sociology and psychology of graffiti.* Westport, CT: Greenwood Press.

Anonymous (1998). Racking, bombing, tagging . . . my career as a writer. In P. Kay, A. Estepa, & A. Desetta (Eds.), *Things get hectic: Teens write about the violence that surrounds them* (pp. 141–145). New York, NY: Simon & Schuster.

Chalfant, H., & Prigoff, J. C. (1987). *Spraycan art.* London: Thames & Hudson.

Cooper, M., & Sciorra, J. (1994). *R.I.P. New York spraycan memorials.* London, United Kingdom: Thames & Hudson.

Ferrell, J. (1995). Urban graffiti: Crime, control, and resistance. *Youth & Society, 27*(1), 73–92.

Fineberg, J. (1995). *Art since 1940: Strategies of being.* Englewood Cliffs, NJ: Prentice Hall.

Flaherty, G. (1987). Reducing vandalism by changing the school community. *Trust for Educational Leadership, 16*(5), 28–30.

Geer, S., & Rowe, S. (1995, spring/summer). Thoughts on graffiti as public art. *Public Art Review,* 24–26.

Gomez, M. (1993). The writing on our walls: Finding solutions through distinguishing graffiti art from graffiti vandalism. *University of Michigan Journal of Law Reform, 26,* 633–707.

Hager, S. (1985). *Hip Hop: The illustrated history of break dancing, rap music, and graffiti.* New York, NY: St. Martin's.

Higgins, A., & Turnure, J. (1984). Distractibility and concentration of attention in children's development. *Child Development, 44,* 1799–1810.

Horworth, L. N. (1989). Graffiti. In M. Thomas Inge (Ed.), *Handbook of American popular culture* (pp. 556–557). New York, NY: Greenwood Press.

Keating, D. (1990). Adolescent thinking. In S. Feldman & G. Elliott (Eds.), *At the threshold: The developing adolescent* (pp. 54–89). Cambridge, MA: Harvard University Press.

Menacker, J., & Mertz, R. (1994). State legislative responses to school crime. *West's Education Law Reporter, 85,* 1–9.

Meyer, L. (1994). *Teenspeak: A bewildered parent's guide to teenagers.* Princeton, NJ: Peterson's.

Pabon, E., Rodriguez, O., & Gurin. G., (1992). Clarifying peer relationships change during puberty? *Psychological Bulletin, 10,* 47–66.

Walderburg, H. (1990). *The Berlin Wall book.* New York, NY: Thames & Hudson.

Walsh, M. (1996). *Graffito.* Berkeley, CA: North Atlantic Books.

Wilson, B. (1997). Child art, multiple interpretations, and conflicts of interest. In A. Kindler (Ed.), *Child development in art* (pp. 81–94). Reston, VA: National Art Education Association.

Zwier, G., & Vaughan, G. M. (1984, summer). Three ideological orientations in school vandalism research. *Review of Educational Research*, 54(2), 263–292.

Endnotes

1. The same article also reported the annual expenditure that the Mass Rapid Transportation of New York was spending to clean graffiti, an alarming figure that was revealed to the public for the first time.
2. That particular teenager was hiding under a stationed subway train while avoiding another passing train; his faulty spray paint caught fire and nearly burned him to death.

practice it   Post-Reading Activity

Make a map of this article, outlining the various kinds of graffiti Kan discusses. Use the headings as a guide. Include illustrative examples to help fill out the map.

For more on mapping, see Chapter 5, Additional Reading Strategies, page 138.

COMPREHENSION QUESTIONS

1. What is art education?
2. What connection does Kan make between adolescence and graffiti?
3. What are the differences between "private" and "public" graffiti?
4. According to the article, what are the differences between "gang graffiti," "tags," and "pieces"?
5. What does it mean that graffiti art has become "commercialized"?

VOCABULARY ACTIVITIES

1. Add any words from this article to your ongoing public art glossary. Remember to write definitions in your own words.
2. Many people use the word *writer* to refer to those who make graffiti. What are the connotations of this term in this context? To help you answer this question, look up the word *graffiti* in a good dictionary so that you can learn the history and root of that word. For more on connotations and roots, see Chapter 8, Vocabulary Building, page 198.

SUMMARY ACTIVITY

Write a one-sentence summary of each section of Kan's article. Add an introductory sentence and a concluding sentence, so you have a complete, coherent paragraph. For help writing a summary, see Chapter 1, Reading and Responding to College Texts, page 2.

DISCUSSION QUESTIONS

1. How does Kan relate doodling to other forms of graffiti? Do you agree with the comparison? Why or why not?
2. According to Kan, historically writers of latrinalia were usually "suppressed" people, and today "people of all ages are equally likely to perform such acts" (para. 6). Why do people write on bathroom walls? What kind of outlet does it provide?
3. Kan references the former Berlin Wall as a location of works of political graffiti art. Do an online search to learn more about the Berlin Wall, including a search for images. Why might graffiti artists have been drawn to this location?
4. Kan raises the question of whether lessons on graffiti should be included in art curricula for adolescents. What do you think, and why?

The Los Angeles Police Department's Web site provides a robust assortment of information for the community. In addition to the 2013 Web article "What Graffiti Means to a Community," the organization offers a "newsroom" with current issues, a blog, and a newsletter published on a quarterly basis called *The Beat. Important words and phrases have been italicized in this reading. Look up those you do not know, and write the definitions in your personal vocabulary list.*

practice it   Pre-Reading

Preview the whole article before reading. What can you infer about the topic, audience, and purpose of this Web article? Would you say this article is a credible source? Why or why not?

www.lapdonline.org

What Graffiti Means to a Community
Los Angeles Police Department

The more social disorder and graffiti in a neighborhood, the louder the message is sent that "nobody cares." This sets off a vicious cycle that encourages further crime in affected neighborhoods.

Most vandals are young people, from grade school age to young adults, who damage property for reasons of boredom, anger or revenge. Others vandalize to show defiance toward rules, laws and authority or to draw attention to a "cause." Graffiti is often the first sign that gangs are taking over a neighborhood. Gangs use graffiti as their street *"telegraph,"* sending messages about turf and advertising their exploits. Graffiti identifies territorial boundaries, lists members, and communicates threats to rival gangs.

Each year millions of dollars are spent to clean up graffiti. Communities can adopt a *zero tolerance* policy for vandalism. The first step is to identify locations or objects *prone* to graffiti and to teach property owners effective removal methods. Participants should include property owners victimized by graffiti, schools, government, businesses, recreation facilities, public transportation, utilities, public works, and shopping malls among others.

Beautification projects such as trash cleanups, landscape *enhancements*, and gardens also serve as a focus for community organizing.

Community groups working with law enforcement, public works, or parks and recreation staff clean up public areas and abandoned lots. The project may reclaim a public space for neighborhood use, establish new green space, or mark neighborhood boundaries. The Los Angeles Police Department has a number of such projects. For more information, contact your local Los Angeles Police Department Community Relations Office.

A community's first step in taking back its streets is getting rid of   5
graffiti immediately. This power struggle cannot be won overnight, but *persistent* communities working in partnership with law enforcement almost always *emerge* as victors. Once the graffiti is gone, use landscape designs (such as prickly shrubs or closely planted hedges), building materials (such as hard-to-mark surfaces), lighting, or fences to discourage vandalism. This philosophy, known as Crime Prevention Through Environmental Design, can help diminish the possibility of graffiti by changing landscaping, lighting, fencing, etc.

Since 1990, the Los Angeles Police Department (LAPD) in an effort to combat graffiti, implemented the Police Assisted Community Enhancement Program (PACE) which coordinates other City agencies to *alleviate adverse* conditions affecting the quality of life in neighborhoods citywide. Conditions such as graffiti, abandoned cars, *vagrants*, *accumulative* trash, street vendors and abandoned buildings are examples of conditions that cause fear among residents and are a sign that residents have lost control of their neighborhood. If minor problems such as broken windows are left unattended, it could foster serious crimes such as robbery, assault, etc. The PACE program is the method by which these problems are addressed and the core of the Department's community based policing efforts.

The PACE program is heavily dependent on the hard work of the Senior Lead Officers (SLOs) who maintain an active *liaison* with area residents and other City entities. Once a problem has been identified, officers will complete the Community Enhancement Request (CER) form. This form is reviewed by a supervisor who then forwards it to the proper City department that will handle the specified problem.

Public works agencies, such as the City of Los Angeles' Board of Public Works, can supply equipment and staff for larger projects, while landscaping firms or other businesses can donate supplies and plants. Publicity and coordination with other police-advised beautification projects help *enhance* the success of such efforts. Volunteer patrols help support maintenance, and publicity helps protect areas from future *deterioration.*

practice it   Post-Reading Activity

Compare and contrast the perspective of this article with the perspective of one other reading in this chapter. How are the perspectives similar? Where do they differ? What might account for their differences? Go back to your annotations for each article and add notes about the similarities and differences between the two articles.

COMPREHENSION QUESTIONS

1. How does this Web article portray graffiti and the people who make graffiti? Where in the text do you find evidence of these portrayals?

2. According to the article, how do gangs use graffiti?

3. What are some of the suggestions the article makes for preventing graffiti?

4. What is the PACE program? Why was it created and whom does it serve?

VOCABULARY ACTIVITIES

1. Add any words from this article to your ongoing public art glossary. Remember to write definitions in your own words.

2. Graffiti is a controversial issue, with some people seeing it as art and others seeing it as vandalism. Make two columns in your notes, one headed "graffiti as art" and the other headed "graffiti as vandalism." Then generate as many terms associated with each position as you can. For example, in the "graffiti as vandalism" column, you might list words like *trashy*, *dirty*, and *gangs*. In the "graffiti as art" column, you might list words like *expression* or *community*.

SUMMARY ACTIVITY

In a few sentences, sum up the policies and efforts of the LAPD to educate and address graffiti in the community. For help writing a summary, see Chapter 1, Reading and Responding to College Texts, page 2.

DISCUSSION QUESTIONS

1. What is the thesis of this Web article?

2. In order to adopt a "zero tolerance policy" toward graffiti, the LAPD suggests uniting "property owners victimized by graffiti, schools, government, businesses, recreation facilities, public transportation, utilities, public works, and shopping malls among others" (para. 3) in the cause. How are each of these groups related to or affected by graffiti?

3. The article cites graffiti as one of the "adverse conditions" (para. 6), along with vagrancy, trash, and abandoned vehicles, that make people fearful. What is graffiti's role in this list of conditions that create fear? Do you agree that it can make people fearful? Why or why not?

4. What is the role of a police department in a community? What position should a police department take on graffiti?

MAGAZINE

James Gaddy is a senior editor at *Print* magazine, and he writes about design and visual art. Founded in 1940, *Print* magazine covers a wide variety of visual arts and design, from advertising and packaging to street art and animation. In this article, published in 2007, Gaddy writes about traveling to Los Angeles to attend street artist Banksy's show "Barely Legal," which was held in a downtown warehouse. He ruminates about whether Banksy, an artist known for keeping tight control of his image, has lost control of his fame. *Important words and phrases have been italicized in this reading. Look up those you do not know, and write the definitions in your personal vocabulary list.*

practice it   Pre-Reading

Whether you have already heard of him or not, do a quick Internet search for Banksy. In ten or fifteen minutes, what can you learn about him and his art? Follow this up with a five-minute freewrite in which you summarize what you found out in your quick search and comment on it.

JAMES GADDY

Nowhere Man

Banksy, the most famous street artist alive, is *waffling*. I don't realize this until I'm flying back to JFK from LAX, suspended in the air somewhere over the Ozarks. I had gone out to L.A. to see "Barely Legal," his first major U.S. show, where I was hoping to find him, talk, and try to understand his appealing *mystique*. (And hey, maybe cut some *stencils* together.) I was curious to see what Banksy, an artist who is himself suspended in midair between cult figure and *bona fide* star, would have to offer this time. What would he do next?

But let's start with the headlines, because for many, that's where he begins and ends. "Animals Sprayed by Graffiti Artist," *BBC News* declared in July 2003. The report claimed that a young man, whose real name was Robin Banks, had tagged a *cadre* of pigs, cows, and sheep, enraging the local animal-rights activists (and farmers). He had already sneaked into the London Zoo and sprayed "We're bored of fish" in the penguin cages. In October 2003, "Graffiti Star Sneaks Work into Tate," sang the BBC headlines. Having stenciled "Mind the Crap" on the steps of the Tate Modern in time for the 2002 Turner Prize ceremony, Banksy had gotten inside this time. "I thought my work belonged in

Image painted on the Israeli Palestinian wall near the Ramallah checkpoint, 2005.

there and I got tired of waiting," he had said. In July 2004, the *London Evening Standard* published his photo and identified him as Robert Banks, from East Bristol. But the photos were never fully *verified*.

"Need Talent to Exhibit in Museums?" *The New York Times* asked in March 2005, the day after Banksy, dressed in fake beard, hat, and trench coat, *punked* four major New York art institutions—the Met, MoMA, the Museum of Natural History, and the Brooklyn Museum—by hanging (and most important, filming himself hanging) his own adapted paintings inside the museums. "Spray Can Prankster Tackles Israel's Security Barrier," said *The Guardian* in August 2005, after Banksy painted the Palestinian side of the wall with optical illusions.

Lost in the *hoopla* and media coverage was serious consideration of the graphic power of Banksy's work. His early images showcased drawing and stencil-cutting prowess with an added edge: his seemingly effortless wit. Using an engaging *trompe l'oeil* technique, he created a range of visual puns—rats taking photos of pedestrians, policemen kissing, the *Mona Lisa* with a rocket launcher—and expanded on the stencil-graffiti *syntax* established by Blek le Rat, softening the hard edge of the stencil with clever takes on *clichéd* images of war, government, religion, and art.

His vandalism also interacted with the city's urban furniture on a *visceral*   5
level: Rats spilled toxic fluid off the wall and into the street, policemen spray-painted their own graffiti on the walls, a diver appeared from a public

What Are You Looking At?, which appeared on the Marble Arch, London 2004.

fountain holding a drain plug. The style reflects its environment, says Tristan Manco, the Bristol-based author of the book *Stencil Graffiti*, by blending elements of official signage with those of punk bands like Crass, who used stencils to make their logo. The pranks were a natural outgrowth of his sense of humor as well: A mixture of *meta-graffiti* and *wry* social commentary, they were a pie in the face of stuffy *elitism*.

Marc Schiller, who runs the Wooster Collective graffiti Web site with his wife, Sara, has promoted Banksy—and street art in general—tirelessly in the U.S. He started an outcry when the publisher IDW appropriated Banksy's imagery without notification, and he provided pictures of the museum pranks to *The New York Times*. "Every once in a while, you meet someone who can do things other people can't do, and I put Banksy in that category," he says. "Graffiti is something very *inaccessible*; it's not something everyone likes or understands. But Banksy's work appeals to everyone; it crosses cultural borders and age. He's become a truly mythic hero."

A mythic hero with a PR handler, however, who informed me that a sit-down interview with Banksy would be impossible. Yet last June, she called to give a few details about his L.A. gallery show in September, so I made plans to attend. In the *intervening* months, Banksy put up two stencil pieces in my neighborhood in Brooklyn, replaced 500 copies of Paris Hilton's album with his own artwork, and planted an inflatable doll dressed as a Guantánamo Bay prisoner behind the fence of the Thunder Mountain Railroad ride at Disneyland. All of a sudden, Banksy was everywhere—and nowhere.

An elephant painted red with gold fleurs-de-lis in "Barely Legal."

The show began on a Thursday night in a warehouse at the end of a deserted industrial alley east of downtown L.A. The address was announced on Banksy's Web site the day of the show, and when I arrived on Friday at noon, word had it that Angelina Jolie, Brad Pitt, and Jude Law had been there the night before. The show itself was what you'd expect: half greatest hits—video footage of the Met prank, several altered paintings, reproductions of some of his famous *icons*—and half new work, including a sculpture of Michelangelo's *David* wearing a bulletproof vest and a painting of a white family eating a picnic among starving Africans. The ideas driving the newer work, however, *teetered* on the *hackneyed*. In one, a group of punks lines up to buy a shirt that says "Destroy Capitalism"; in another, an auctioneer sells a painting that reads, "I can't believe you morons actually buy this shit."

And then there was the elephant. Painted red with gold *fleurs-de-lis*, it wandered *dourly* within a fenced-off area where a man and woman sat on a couch and read magazines. The elephant was *emblematic* of the show: It was a *motif* Banksy had used before, but this time it was bigger, much as the attention paid him has grown massive, and the subsequent *validation* even greater. By the time Saturday rolled around, the alley played host to an ad hoc block party of gawkers and news vans.

I thought maybe fellow street artist Shepard Fairey could help me find Banksy, so I went to his show on Saturday night, where the line outside stretched down the street. "He might stop by here tonight," Fairey said cryptically. When we spoke by phone a few weeks later, he said he thinks Banksy has kept his identity secret for two reasons: "Number one, he can do this and not get arrested, but number two, the rebel pose is the most market-able pose ever." Angelina Jolie bought three of Banksy's pieces from the show,

10

some upward of $30,000. He's working on Africa-related campaigns for Bono. Nike has contacted him several times (he declined), as has Puma (he accepted). Although he's done commercial jobs in the past, he has recently made it clear that, with his success in the art world, he's done with work for hire. "It's not black and white," admits Schiller.

Whether or not he's *eschewing* commercial clients these days, Banksy had his detractors before the "Barely Legal" show; they *harped* on his self-promotion, his endless media baiting, his *pithy* one-liners that disintegrate on close examination. His apparent *ambivalence* might explain why I felt a little let down on the flight home, trying to *reconcile* how an artist who had spent his career criticizing celebrity culture was now actively *courting* that market. And I wasn't the only one. "Banksy—slowly becoming what he is against," read a recent thread on his fan site. The general *consensus* on the boards is that Banksy is at a crossroads, trying to "keep it real" for those who want to see more street art, but charging hundreds of thousands of dollars for those who can afford pricey canvases. The hope is that he'll take the money he made from "Barely Legal" and invest in more street work.

The more crucial question, however, is what he does next. His style remains *iconic*, but it doesn't reproduce well in the gallery; there, it has little of the power the street produces in him. But as prices rise, and as his fame grows, street work becomes more difficult to pull off. And how do you top a painted elephant, anyway? A painted whale? How do you top the Met? The White House? Now that Banksy has been properly introduced to this side of the Atlantic, we're again suspended, wondering. For now, I don't mind the anticipation.

---

practice it   **Post-Reading Activity**

Choose one Banksy image you found online that you find particularly intriguing, appealing, or offensive. Analyze the following elements of the image: its message, its use of color, the interplay between text and image (if there is any text), its similarity to other images you have seen, and, if you know it, its original location. Write a paragraph that explains your interpretation of the image, using these elements to support your points.

COMPREHENSION QUESTIONS

1. What does "iconic" mean (para. 12), and in what ways is Banksy's work iconic?

2. Gaddy starts his article with a review of news headlines about Banksy. Gaddy gives his rationale by saying "because for many, that's where he [Banksy] begins and ends" (para. 2). What does he mean by this?

3. What are the "clichéd images of war, government, religion, and art" that Gaddy refers to in paragraph 4?

4. Street artist Shepard Fairey believes Banksy keeps his identity secret for two reasons. What are they?

5. According to the author, what is the crossroads that Banksy is facing?

VOCABULARY ACTIVITIES

1. Add any words from this article to your ongoing public art glossary. Remember to write definitions in your own words.

2. Since this article uses a fairly elevated vocabulary, you may need to study some of the words you added to your list. Choose your top ten challenging words and make graphic flash cards of them to help you remember them. For help creating flash cards, see Chapter 8, Vocabulary Building, page 198.

SUMMARY ACTIVITY

Beneath each image in the reading, write an informational sentence that explains how each image relates to Banksy's overall approach to art.

DISCUSSION QUESTIONS

1. Like some other readings in this chapter, Gaddy's article includes images to provide a visual story to accompany the text. How do the images enrich the discussion of Banksy's work? How necessary are they to the effectiveness of the article?

2. What does the title of the article, "Nowhere Man," suggest about Banksy? How does his anonymity add to his appeal?

3. Marc Schiller says, "Graffiti is something very inaccessible; it's not something everyone likes or understands. But Banksy's work appeals to everyone; it crosses cultural borders and age" (para. 6). Do you agree with Schiller's sentiments about graffiti and Banksy? Why or why not?

4. Does fame diminish Banksy's "street credibility"? Why or why not?

NEWSPAPER

As a copy editor for the Minority Editorial Training Program at the *Los Angeles Times*, Xia has written and contributed to articles on diverse topics, the appearance of papier-mâché street art being one of them. Living among some of the best art museums and most prolific graffiti artists on the West Coast, Los Angelenos are no strangers to art. However, this news article, published in 2012, shows that public art can still surprise. *Important words and phrases have been italicized in this reading. Look up those you do not know, and write the definitions in your personal vocabulary list.*

practice it   **Pre-Reading**

Where do you generally expect to see works of art? What kinds of art do you expect to see in public places? Have you ever seen a spontaneous display of art? Have you ever seen a flash mob? If so, what was your reaction? If not, how do you think people in general (other than in musicals) react to spontaneous displays of art or theater or dance?

ROSANNA XIA

Lighthearted Street Art Delights (and Confuses) Downtown L.A. Visitors

The artists intended to be anonymous, but their papier-mâché creations generated so much buzz that soon friends and strangers were showering them with praise.

With the chilling pulse of the *Drive* movie soundtrack flooding their van, Calder Greenwood and his *cohort* sped into the shadows of the bridges overlooking the L.A. River east of downtown Los Angeles. They were on a mission to humanize the harsh industrial landscape of concrete, rusting metal, graffiti and whitewash.

Their installation: A life-size papier-mâché surfer.

Deftly using wires and a concrete block, Greenwood placed the surfer smack in the middle of the waterway. The next morning, it was there to delight—and, in some cases, confuse—motorists driving across the river during the morning commute.

Downtown L.A. has no shortage of street art, from the historic murals that   5
grace freeway walls and aging brick buildings to the flowering graffiti and the
more graphical works from the likes of Shepard Fairey. Some of it is political.
Some of it is social commentary. Much of it is serious.

But over the last several weeks, downtown has been the site of a *decidedly*
lighter form of *guerrilla* street art that has generated much buzz and debate
over its deeper meaning.

It started in May when Greenwood and his partner, known only as Wild
Life, placed a family of life-size sunbathers in an empty downtown lot, the site
of a *stalled* federal courthouse. Later, papier-mâché deer popped up in the
untrimmed weeds by 4th and Hill streets. Then a *wooden* tree sprouted from a
stump near Spring and 2nd streets.

The pieces created a sensation as bloggers and passers-by *pondered* the back
story: Was this some statement on *blight* or *urban renewal*? Or was it a work of
subtle advertising?

Neither, said Greenwood, a transplanted New Yorker who moved to downtown L.A. last fall. His only goal was to get people to notice things they pass
every day but never see.

"I'm inspired by downtown," Greenwood said. "What some see as an eye-   10
sore, I think is beautiful. It's just getting people to look up and see what's otherwise invisible."

Street art veterans said the simplicity and *fanciful* nature of the pair's work
set it apart.

"I find that *purity* refreshing," said Daniel Lahoda, founder of LA Free-
walls, an unofficial art initiative that invites international muralists to paint,
technically illegally, on the walls of downtown buildings.

"The sunbathers weren't done along with a brand, or a marketing stunt for
the artist's career. It was done just for art's *sake*. . . . I think there's a lot of
power behind this type of *uncommissioned* art."

Lahoda said other artists have also found ways to *enliven* downtown, including one graphic designer who creates 3D *quartz* formations with shiny paper,
filling in *defunct* telephone booths and holes in brick walls.

Greenwood, 32, who creates short films and visual effects, said he was taking   15
his parents to the Walt Disney Concert Hall when they walked by a dirt pit, half-
filled with rainwater, and "this image of sunbathers just popped in my head."

By chance, he met Wild Life, a longtime L.A. artist who once created street
signs that said "DRUGS" and "HEROIN" and placed them around skid row.
Within minutes of their first conversation, the two had committed to the same
artistic vision.

During their downtime, in a packed windowless workroom in the back of
Greenwood's apartment, the two spend a few days each week creating realistic
sculptures out of recycled cardboard and papier-mâché.

Their installations have been *subtle* enough to stand unnoticed by many, but bring a brief moment of amusement to those who pause long enough to see them. In the parking lot by an unattended grassy *slope*, one valet said the deer's arrival made him want to clean up the weeds and trash that he had barely noticed before.

"I both live and work in downtown, and it still doesn't have a lot of green space and you can't really get away from the concrete landscape," said Estela Lopez, executive director of the Central City East Assn. "So to be able to walk around that area and have something to laugh at is fabulous."

She likened it to a pop-up store that comes and goes without advance notice. 20

Another longtime downtown resident, Brady Westwater, said everyone he knows is talking about it.

"It's all over Facebook," he said. "It's hard to find something that stands apart from the regular type of street art we've seen around here. . . . They're not damaging property. They have a very light touch, but a very strong presence."

Roger Gastman, *co-curator* of last year's "Art in the Streets" show at L.A.'s Museum of Contemporary Art, said this kind of art is popular because it's accessible.

"It's much more *digestible* to the public than traditional graffiti," he said, noting that it's also an increasingly popular way for artists to quickly "build a buzz."

Although Greenwood said he intended to remain anonymous, he posted 25 photos of the work-in-progress on his Facebook page and didn't realize the installations would go viral.

But after the sunbathers drew media attention, friends showered Greenwood with praise. Even his parents in New York heard about it when family friends called and asked: Is this *your* Calder Greenwood?

And when Wild Life walked into a Santa Monica cafe popular among the art crowd, the owner laughed and said: "Well, Mr. Ano-ny-mous. What an honor."

Before they *carted* out the sunbathers, the duo had their eyes on other holes and "loosely abandoned" *parcels* around town. Cardboard is cheap and flexible to work with, Greenwood said, and with practice, each project has gotten more creative and durable.

Even without the buzz, Greenwood said, it's worth it. "Building it is fun," he said. "Installing it is a rush."

For their most recent installation, Greenwood and Wild Life *donned* dark 30 clothes and hit the streets after midnight to relocate the deer. They awkwardly cradled the life-size *herbivores* under their arms, sidestepping bar-lined Main Street in favor of skid row.

At the spot, they fell silent, glancing over their shoulders as they raced into the brush. In less than 10 minutes, Greenwood and Wild Life hammered the deer into their latest home: a trash-speckled slope of grass overshadowed by the Walt Disney Concert Hall and the Stanley Mosk Courthouse.

From the pair's *vantage* point, Wild Life could see a *scaffold* that's been hanging off a building for years. He's already envisioning what's next.

practice it   Post-Reading Activity

Draw a map of the ideas presented in this article. Use images that come to mind or from the article to help you recall and note key concepts or ideas from the reading. See Chapter 5, Additional Reading Strategies (p. 138), for more information about and an example of a map that uses images.

COMPREHENSION QUESTIONS

1. What does Daniel Lahoda mean when he says, "It [the papier-mâché artwork] was done just for art's sake" (para.13)? Does he consider that a good or bad thing?

2. What has the public's reaction been to Greenwood and Wild Life's art?

3. What is a "pop-up store"? Does the comparison of this art to a pop-up store make sense? Why or why not?

4. Brady Westwater, a resident of downtown L.A., said, "They [Greenwood and Wild Life] have a very light touch, but a very strong presence" (para. 22). What does this mean? Do you agree?

5. What do you think Roger Gastman, co-curator of the Museum of Contemporary Art's show "Art in the Streets," meant when he called this art "accessible" (para. 23)?

6. What does it mean that the artwork went "viral"?

VOCABULARY ACTIVITIES

1. Add any words from this article to your ongoing public art glossary. Remember to write definitions in your own words.

2. Look up a street art group (such as Global Street Art or Street Art) on Facebook. As you skim over the comments, make a list of adjectives that are used to describe the art put online. How many ways do people find to say they like or don't like something, besides merely hitting the "like" button? Look back over your list, marking any nonslang examples that you found. If you found fewer than ten nonslang examples, generate a list of at least ten nonslang words that you might use in the college environment to express the same ideas.

SUMMARY ACTIVITY

Make a list of the quotations from the reading that you think summarize the ideas and the point of the article. Add some context or additional information to help make the quotations make sense.

DISCUSSION QUESTIONS

1. Xia contrasts the "serious" street art of downtown L.A. with the "lighthearted" street art of Greenwood and his partner known as Wild Life. What does this comparison suggest about their art? Is this a good comparison? Why or why not?

2. Papier-mâché is a fragile construction of paper and glue, easily destroyed by the elements. What does this choice of medium suggest about the artists' attitude about temporary art?

3. What role did Facebook play in the popularity of the artwork?

4. Why do you suppose Greenwood and Wild Life chose the locations that they did for their artwork? How does the combination of the papier-mâché figures and the location suggest a contrast or irony?

NEWSPAPER

Most news articles focus on facts and straightforward information, but the human interest story is a newspaper staple that has a greater focus on personal experience. This kind of writing looks at news and events from a more personal perspective. As a human interest story, the following 2007 article, "Battles over Yard Art Sometimes Turn Ugly," uses interviews to show the personal impact of conflicts over a particular kind of public art: yard art. Although it has the word "journal" in its title, the *Buffalo Law Journal* is a newspaper with a specific focus on legal, real estate, and financial news. Its readership is most likely to be those who follow legal news, like this article's topic of the rights of homeowners to decorate their home and yard with art. *Important words and phrases have been italicized in this reading. Look up those you do not know, and write the definitions in your personal vocabulary list.*

practice it   **Pre-Reading**

Recalling your prior knowledge of a subject can be very helpful for pre-reading. Think about a time you looked at art (in a museum, gallery, book, or online) that you didn't like. What didn't you like about it? Did it change your opinion of the museum or gallery that hosted the art? Have you ever found someone's yard decoration to be really tacky or really beautiful? Do you think people should have total control over the way they paint their houses or decorate their yards? Why or why not?

BUFFALO LAW JOURNAL

Battles over Yard Art Sometimes Turn Ugly

Chesterfield, Mo. (AP) — For Dwight DeGolia's neighbors, the last straw was the fake palm trees.

The 62-year-old retiree had spent years fixing up the sliver of sloping land outside his home, adding two putting greens that were almost 30 feet long, a small creek and a *gazebo*.

Then he added 50 tons of beach sand to complete the illusion of a tropical golf vacation, as well as a portable golf hitting cage and a bar with a *pergola* roof.

"We had that place really shining," DeGolia said.

But the 8- to 12-foot palm trees made it impossible for neighbors   5
to ignore DeGolia's project anymore, a passion that they said was making the neighborhood look tacky and led them to take DeGolia to court.

"We gave it a nickname," said Dennis Taylor, a former subdivision trustee. "Wally World."

Cities and neighborhood associations have struggled for years with how to handle situations in which *eccentric* people with a *penchant* for lawn decoration get into fights with nearby homeowners.

The battles often feature issues that are far from straightforward, such as whose property rights are more important—the woman who *fancies* dozens of cupid statues on her front lawn, or the next door neighbor who has to look at it?

"It's a hard balancing act," said Carlos Trejos, planning and *zoning* administrator for the City of Olivette, Mo. "We are not there to determine taste."

Two months ago, members of a Ballwin, Mo., neighborhood   10
demanded action from their Board of *Aldermen* after retired art teacher Lewis Greenberg built clusters of colorful, twisted metal and wooden spikes on his front lawn and hung silver bowls from the trees. Greenberg said it was to commemorate the Holocaust.

City officials cited Greenberg for littering, but that's not the end of it, said his attorney, David Howard.

"It's going to be extremely expensive, the route they've chosen," Howard said.

He has argued that Greenberg's art is no different from the neighbor who hangs Christmas lights or installs a bird bath or rose trellis. He said the issue isn't that Greenberg put up art but that people don't like the art he put up.

"Once you go down that slippery slope, where do you stop?" Howard asked.

But not all self-expressive yards lead to confrontation.   15

Ronald Kuper has stone lions guarding the sidewalks to his Webster Groves house, which also features seven collectible automobiles displayed in a couple of driveways and a backyard rimmed with a waist-high iron fence and several stone columns. In the backyard are a dozen seminude female statues surrounding a couple of *ornate* birdbaths.

"Some people collect women," said Kupet, 66. "Some people collect beer cans. I collect female statues and Rolls-Royces. They don't talk back."

Julie Jacobs said she wasn't *deterred* when she moved into the neighborhood a few years ago.

"I guess I said to myself, 'That has to be an interesting person,'" she said. "People ask where we live and we say we live next to the statue house."

When Rebecca Pickens moved into her Olivette house a few years 20 ago, she said she *despaired* that her small backyard looked like everyone else's.

"It just wasn't my style," she said. "It just wasn't me."

So she built a human-sized bird's nest, complete with ceramic eggs. A post next to the nest reads "2014," the year Pickens' son will leave for college.

"This is my empty nest," she said.

Trejos, the city's zoning administrator, said his office inspected Pickens' property after a neighbor filed a complaint, worried about rodent infestation. While the inspector found branches and foliage scattered around the yard, Pickens later e-mailed him a picture of the yard and nest cleaned up.

DeGolia's fight for his golf paradise didn't end as easily. 25

In December, after incurring about $12,000 in legal fees, DeGolia agreed to remove the palm trees and the golf cage, while the Greenleaf Valley *subdivision*, which forked over $20,000 in fees, allowed the gazebo, putting greens and some bridges to remain.

DeGolia said he should have communicated better with the subdivision, and vice versa.

In any event, he and his wife have moved to Oklahoma, partly because of the fight over his landscaping.

"We didn't feel very welcome where we were at," he said, adding that he took the palm trees with him.

practice it   Post-Reading Activity

Reread this short article, using the technique of reading with and against the grain, as outlined in Chapter 2 (pages 38–41). Make sure you distinguish between your annotations for reading with the grain and those for reading against the grain. (You can use two different-colored pens, if you like.) Afterward, look back over your annotations and decide for yourself which side of the position is more convincing.

COMPREHENSION QUESTIONS

1. A former subdivision trustee, Dennis Taylor, referred to DeGolia's yard art as "Wally World." What is Wally World, and what did he mean by the comment?

2. In paragraph 8, the author writes, "The battles [over yard art] often feature issues that are far from straightforward." What complicates these conflicts?

3. What is the job of a planning and zoning administrator for a city?

4. What is an alderman?

VOCABULARY ACTIVITIES

1. Add any words from this article to your ongoing public art glossary. Remember to write definitions in your own words.

2. Find words in the article that describe the yard art positively, and then find words that describe it negatively. Which words are more convincing? How can totally different descriptions refer to the same piece of yard art?

SUMMARY ACTIVITY

Make a list of arguments on both sides of the yard art debate, as it is described in this article, and then briefly summarize the two sides in a paragraph. For help writing a summary, see Chapter 1, Reading and Responding to College Texts, page 2.

DISCUSSION QUESTIONS

1. Why do people adorn their yards with art?

2. The article cites several neighbors of various yard art aficionados. How do their attitudes toward yard art differ? What might cause the differences in their attitudes?

3. How does yard art relate to other kinds of public art?

4. David Howard, attorney for Lewis Greenberg, says, "[T]he issue isn't that Greenberg put up art but that people don't like the art he put up" (para. 13). Do you agree? Do you think Greenberg's neighbors would behave differently if they had the same taste in art? Why or why not?

5. Would the audience of the *Buffalo Law Journal* likely be interested in this article? Why or why not?

Synthesizing the Readings

Now that you have read a wide variety of texts on the topics of public art, you have enough schema, or background information, to begin to synthesize the material and build arguments of your own. It's helpful, though, to pause and discuss how the various readings "converse" with one another before you jump right into a writing assignment. Here are some post-reading discussion questions to help direct your thinking:

DISCUSSION QUESTIONS

1. Some graffiti art is not only accepted, but highly valued and even protected, while other graffiti is removed and the artists are prosecuted. What differentiates the two kinds? How is this message contradictory? What effect might this message have on graffiti artists?

2. What is the meaning of public art? How is public art different from museum art or art sold in galleries?

3. How does the more temporary nature of some public art affect the way people view it?

4. How are graffiti, murals, and yard art related? What connects these three forms of public art? What differentiates them from one another?

5. Consider the locations of public art. Some public art is located in plazas, libraries, parks, and yards, or on the walls of buildings and other structures. Does the location determine people's attitude toward the art? Why or why not?

6. How do the readings in this chapter challenge your notions of what qualifies as private and what qualifies as public? Can private property function as public space? Can public property function as private space?

7. Who decides what makes something "art"? Who decides whether artwork is "good" or "great"?

8. What connections can you make between the readings in this chapter and those in Chapter 23, Fame and Celebrity (p. 509), if you have completed that chapter? Is Banksy a celebrity? Are graffiti artists? If a street artist or a graffiti artist gains some level of fame or notoriety, does this change your estimation of his or her art? Why or why not?

9. What is the meaning of "self-expression"? Do we value self-expression? How does it compare with other needs, rights, or responsibilities?

10. The discussion of graffiti art tends to focus on male artists, but there are female graffiti artists as well. Some of them use spray paint and markers, but others use different materials, like yarn. (See Amy Kuperinsky's article on yarn bombing in your e-Pages; go to **bedfordstmartins .com/readwriteconnect** and click on **e-Readings**.) Does graffiti in general appeal more to males than females? Why or why not?

CHARTING TO ORGANIZE YOUR IDEAS

After your discussion, take some time to organize your thoughts on the topic of public art before you proceed to your specific assignment. You can begin by gathering ideas and quotations about the various issues that emerged in more than one of the readings. Use the following chart below to record your thoughts and any interesting information or quotations that you pull from the readings. You can copy the chart into your notebook or, to download a version, go to **bedfordstmartins .com/readwriteconnect** and click on **Charts**.

SYNTHESIS CHART: PUBLIC ART

	What Is Art?	Ownership of Art	Art and Community	Legal versus Illegal Art	Other:
Becker, "Public Art: An Essential Component of Creating Communities"					
Frank, "Public Art" and "Street Art"					
Acosta, "Chicano Mural Movement"					
Shank, "Whose Art Is This Anyway?"					

(Continued)

Kan, "Adolescents and Graffiti"					
Los Angeles Police Department, "What Graffiti Means to a Community"					
Gaddy, "Nowhere Man"					
Xia, "Lighthearted Street Art Delights (and Confuses) Downtown L.A. Visitors"					
Buffalo Law Journal, "Battle over Yard Art Sometimes Turns Ugly"					
My thoughts					

Writing Your Essay

The following steps review how to get into the mind-set to write your essay on public art. These steps are outlined in greater detail in Chapters 2, 3, and 4.

STEP 1: What type of essay are you assigned to write about public art? Look over the question or your instructor's prompt, and write it in your own words.

STEP 2: Which readings from this chapter do you think you will include? List them in your notes, including any quotations that you think you might use. (Don't forget to include the author and page number when you write down the quotation so that you don't have to find it again later.)

STEP 3: What ideas from class discussion or your own experience and observation would you like to include? Look over your notes, and add those thoughts to your brainstorming for this assignment.

STEP 4: Take a few more minutes to brainstorm in your favorite method: listing, freewriting, clustering, questioning, or group discussion.

STEP 5: Look back at the assignment prompt, and write up a tentative thesis or main idea based on your work so far. Remember, one way to think of the thesis is as the answer to the question posed in the assignment prompt. Don't worry that your thesis has to be perfect or set in stone right now. It's a working thesis that you will probably revise as you make decisions about what you want to say.

STEP 6: Make a bullet-point outline for your essay. Remember to first put the ideas down and then reorganize them into a logical order.

STEP 7: Copy or type up the relevant quotations and examples under each appropriate bullet point.

STEP 8: Pat yourself on the back! You have a lot of material so far, don't you?

STEP 9: Write the rough, rough draft, remembering that you'll be revising it.

STEP 10: Reread the assignment sheet one more time, and then make big-picture revisions to your focus, content, and organization. Peer review may help.

STEP 11: Once you are generally satisfied that your work is focused, complete, and organized, edit for sentence-level issues. Remember to use the editing techniques of reading your work out loud, reading "backward," and isolating your common errors. Refer to your Grammar Log frequently during this process. Edit and print your paper again and again until you are satisfied with the way each sentence sounds.

STEP 12: Take a break.

STEP 13: Proofread your essay one or two more times to correct any minor errors and to make sure your document format is correct for this assignment.

> **e** To learn how to use the Grammar Log, see Chapter 24, page 579. To download a copy of this log, go to **bedfordstmartins .com/readwriteconnect** and click on **Charts**.

Writing Assignments

DEFINITION ASSIGNMENT

How would you define *public art* or *street art*? Write an essay that explains what constitutes public or street art. What are the differences between public and private art? What characteristics do they share? What qualities do we associate with those terms, and how do we stretch the labels to include a variety of artworks?

NARRATION ASSIGNMENT

Whether you like them or not, you can probably agree that murals, yard art, street art, and graffiti are all the attempt of an individual or community to make a mark on the world. This is a common human desire. For this essay, recall a time—either when you were a child or an adult—when you tried to make some mark on your world. (Make sure you choose a specific event or a focused time period, not a general phase of your life.) Tell the story of that experience, recalling as many vivid details as you can. What happened? Did you feel successful in making your mark? Did others recognize it? How? What were the ramifications or outcomes of the experience? Refer in your introduction or conclusion to at least one of the readings as a touchstone for your own story.

DESCRIPTION ASSIGNMENT

Imagine that you are asked to create a mural for your community or school. What message would you want to present to or about your community or school? What images would you include in the mural to get that message across? What colors would you use? Would you use traditional paint or spray paint? Would you create a mosaic? Where would you locate your mural, and what would be significant about that location? Before you begin, visit some murals in your community or do an online image search for mural art. Consider how the artists use both color and imagery. As a pre-writing activity, sketch out a concept of your mural.

PROCESS ANALYSIS ASSIGNMENT

Considering the complicated nature of street art, how would you design a lesson on street art for a high school class? What would you highlight? What visuals would you include, and why? Is there anything specific about this topic that you would emphasize to this age group? Why or why not? Write a process analysis essay that outlines the steps of the lesson, with explanations and justifications for each step.

COMPARISON AND CONTRAST ASSIGNMENT

Drawing extensively on the examples given in the readings, compare and contrast two of the following: murals, yard art, street art, graffiti. What is similar about the art forms and about the artists? What differences do you find?

PROBLEM-SOLUTION ASSIGNMENT

Choose one form of public art (yard art, graffiti, or murals) and, noting the causes, identify the potential problems in the community with that art form and evaluate a possible solution. For example, if graffiti is considered a blight in your community, discuss the reasons graffiti exists and what problems it causes. Come up with a potential solution for the problem of graffiti. Or consider the same situation with either yard art and unhappy neighbors or mural art and its potential problems.

ANALYSIS ASSIGNMENT

Murals are a very public kind of artwork. The artwork on a mural is not intended to hang in someone's home or sit in a museum; rather, murals, in a sense, belong to everyone. Some murals are political in nature; others tell a story about the dreams, achievements, and cultural identity of the artist or community. Choose a mural that tells a story or responds politically or socially to the community, and analyze the message of that mural. Explain the importance of that mural's message to the community. How does the mural reflect the identity of the community?

RESEARCH ASSIGNMENT

Walk one square mile near your home and document all the public expressions of creativity you see. Or research the public art in your community, considering civic spaces like city hall, libraries, and schools, and the sculptures or fountains that often adorn business buildings. What kinds of art do you find? What themes emerge from the public art in your neighborhood or city? What is your neighborhood or community's attitude toward public art? Are there any places where installing public art would improve your surroundings? In what ways?

ARGUMENT ASSIGNMENTS

1. Street art, which can include murals as well as graffiti "pieces," "tags," or stenciled art, is often a temporary and publicly shared art form. Using a variety of examples of graffiti art, write an essay about the role of graffiti art in a community. Is it art? Is it vandalism?
2. Is public art important in a community? Write an essay in which you take a position about the role of public art. Use specific examples from the readings to support your position.

Additional Online and Media Sources

The readings in this chapter may spark your thinking and leave you wanting some more information for further study or personal reflection. In your e-Pages, you can read Amy Kuperinsky's article on yarn bombing. Go to **bedfordstmartins.com/readwriteconnect** and click on **e-Readings**. You may also want to consult the following online and media sources.

WEB RESOURCES

Banksy (www.banksy.co.uk): The official Web site of street artist Banksy, which includes a gallery of a sampling of images of his street art.

Blek le Rat (http://bleklerat.free.fr/stencil%20graffiti.html): The robust official site of Blek le Rat, a pioneer of street art stencil graffiti; the site includes several galleries of images, press, and a personal manifesto.

Mona Caron (www.monacaron.com): The official site of muralist Mona Caron, with images of a range of her public art murals.

City of Philadelphia Mural Arts Program (http://muralarts.org): As the largest public art program in the United States, the City of Philadelphia Mural Arts Program offers program information on its Web site, as well as a well-documented history of its mural projects.

Federal Art Programs (www.gsa.gov/portal/content/101818): The U.S. Federal Art Programs site provides a short history of public art programs in America; the site includes links to the oldest fine arts public art collection as well as the controversial Ariel Rios Federal Building murals.

"Female Writers," @149st The Cyber Bench: Documenting New York Graffiti (www.at149st.com/women.html): A brief history of female graffiti artists in New York City, along with images of their work.

NoLa Rising (http://nolarising.org): The Web site for the nonprofit art initiative to revitalize a post-Katrina New Orleans through public art works.

***Project Row Houses*, Public Art** (http://projectrowhouses.org/public-art): The Web site for the public art community of Houston's Third Ward neighborhood.

San Francisco Arts Commission, Public Art (www.sfartscommission .org/pubartcollection): The Web site for the city agency in San Francisco that oversees the installation and care of public art, as well as education about it.

Street Art Utopia (www.streetartutopia.com): An online gallery of street art from around the world.

FILMS

Basquiat. Dir. Julian Schnabel. Perf. Jeffrey Wright, Dennis Hopper, and Gary Oldman. Miramax, 1996.

Bomb It. Dir. Jon Reiss. Perf. Cope 2, Kid Acne, Antonio. Gravitas Ventures, 2008.

Cave of Forgotten Dreams. Dir. Werner Herzog. Perf. Werner Herzog, Jean Clottes, Julien Monney. Creative Differences, 2010.

Exit through the Gift Shop. Dir. Banksy. Perf. Banksy, Mr. Brainwash, and Debora Guetta. Paranoid Pictures, 2010.

Jean-Michel Basquiat: The Radiant Child. Dir. Tamra Davis. Perf. Jean-Michel Basquiat, Julian Schnabel, Larry Gagosian. Arthouse, 2010.

Style Wars. Dir. Tony Silver. Perf. Cey Adams, Cap, Daze. Public Art Films, 2005.

Vigilante Vigilante: The Battle for Expression. Dir. Max Good. Perf. Stefano E. Bloch, Joe Connolly, Michael Dingler. Open Ranch, 2011.

Wild Style. Dir. Charlie Ahearn. Perf. Easy A.D., A.J., Almighty K.G., and Lee Quinones. Rhino, 1983.

23
Fame and Celebrity

in this chapter

- **Andrea Chang**
  The Kardashians: Cashing in with a Capital K
- **Carlin Flora**
  Seeing by Starlight: Celebrity Obsession
- **Mary Loftus**
  The Other Side of Fame
- **Jake Halpern**
  The Desire to Belong: Why Everyone Wants to Have Dinner with Paris Hilton and 50 Cent
- **Drew Pinsky**
  Broadcasting Yourself

"In the future, everybody will be world famous for fifteen minutes."

—Andy Warhol

"I'm not a businessman; I'm a business, man."

—Jay-Z

Theme Overview

Everyone wants to be famous, right? Who wouldn't? Fame often brings money and attention, sometimes even adoration. However, as we often see in celebrity gossip news, fame can also bring pain, addiction, and a complete loss of privacy. Many people who gain public fame have private lives that do not match their image. When we look beneath the surface, we begin to ask whether the gains of fame outweigh the losses. Is celebrity worth the price in our media-saturated world? Why do some people want to be famous? Why do others shun attention? How has fame changed as new media outlets have evolved? Most of us don't get even fifteen minutes of fame, but we may yearn for celebrity status or be drawn to those who have achieved it for reasons we don't fully understand.

Drawing on research in psychology, medicine, history, and business, the writers in this chapter will get you thinking about the value of fame and celebrity, the values that underlie America's apparent celebrity obsession, and the way new forms of brand marketing help create what might be called a "celebrity culture." This chapter may also help you begin to define what success might mean for you personally.

While you read, it is tempting to get caught up in celebrity gossip. Try not to do so; instead, focus on the overall point of the articles rather than the specific stars under discussion. Also, since celebrity is a short-lived type of fame, the articles in this chapter may seem outdated. Celebrities' marriages dissolve at an alarming pace, and no textbook could possibly keep current with the latest gossip or fads. Remember, it's not the minute details of a star's clothes, hair, or persona that are so important. Focus instead on the broader arguments that the writers are making about the role of fame and celebrity in American culture.

> **practice it**   Taking Stock of What You Already Know
>
> Think about your own knowledge and feelings about fame and celebrity. Then try to answer the following questions:
>
> - Have you ever met anyone famous? If so, what was your experience? If you could meet that person again, would you do anything differently? Why or why not?
> - What famous people would you like to meet, and why? What do you hope would happen if you met them?
> - What are the benefits of fame and celebrity? What are the downsides?
> - Do you want to be famous? Why or why not? If so, what would you want to be famous for doing?

NEWSPAPER

Andrea Chang is a staff writer for the *Los Angeles Times* newspaper; she covers retail, business, and technology. This article about the Kardashian family shows in precise detail how the family functions as a celebrity brand. The specific details of the Kardashian family should not be the main reason you read the article, as they will quickly become dated. Rather, the article is useful because of the detailed way it describes the process of celebrity self-branding. This year it might be the Kardashians, and next year someone else, but the process of idolizing celebrities and making them into commodities remains similar. Indeed, celebrity self-branding has been going on in Hollywood for as long as films have been around, though one might argue that the Kardashian family has taken the business of self-promotion to a more intense level. *Important words and phrases have been italicized in this reading. Look up those you do not know, and write the definitions in your personal vocabulary list.*

practice it **Pre-Reading**

This article about the Kardashian family of reality TV fame was originally published in the Business section of the *Los Angeles Times*, not in one of the sections usually devoted to celebrities and popular culture. Preview the article, thinking about its title, its place in the newspaper, and its lead paragraph, "There are Kardashian boutiques, fragrances, jewelry, apparel, bikinis, skin-care products and candles. And the reality-TV family says it's just getting started. But with a less-than-wholesome image, will the brand have staying power?" What perspective can you predict this article will take on the Kardashians? What types of information do you think you will learn as you read? Write your predictions directly on the article.

ANDREA CHANG

The Kardashians: Cashing in with a Capital K

There are Kardashian boutiques, fragrances, jewelry, apparel, bikinis, skin-care products and candles. And the reality-TV family says it's just getting started. But with a less-than-wholesome image, will the brand have staying power?

Having conquered reality television, the Kardashians are fashioning a celebrity retail powerhouse.

Beyond the glittery red carpets and steamy tabloid *fodder*, the famous family has transformed itself into a branding machine, quickly *leveraging* the hype into a retail empire worth tens of millions of dollars.

Unlike other reality-stars-turned-*entrepreneurs* such as Snooki of *Jersey Shore* fame or Lauren Conrad of *The Hills*, the Kardashians are in a class by themselves and *unfazed* by skeptics who doubt they can keep it up for the long haul.

There are Kardashian boutiques, fragrances, jewelry, apparel, bikinis, self-tanner, skin-care products, candles—even bottled water, if you're willing to shell out $10 for it.

Whether it's business *savvy* or shameless self-promotion, it's paid off: 5 Kardashian Inc. raked in an estimated $65 million last year, according to the *Hollywood Reporter*, a trade publication. And with the family signing on to a *slew* of new projects, it's poised to make even more in 2011.

This year alone, sisters Kourtney, Kim and Khloe released their own "glam pack" of Silly Bandz, the wildly popular rubber-band shapes that kids trade and wear as bracelets. They're also opening Kardashian Khaos, a celebrity retail store at the Mirage in Las Vegas. Kim has been promoting her jewelry line Belle Noel and touting Midori liqueur as a company spokeswoman; she and mother Kris are also the new faces of Skechers Shape-Ups sneakers. Khloe and Laker husband Lamar Odom, who are starring in their own spin-off series on E!, recently released a *unisex* fragrance called Unbreakable.

The sisters' biggest project this year is the launch of the Kardashian Kollection, an ambitious "shop-within-a-shop" concept that will launch at Sears stores in late August and in international markets.

The global lifestyle brand is Sears' biggest celebrity deal ever. The line will span categories including dresses, outerwear, T-shirts, denim, footwear, jewelry, handbags and lingerie, and will reflect the sisters' individual styles: classic red-carpet glamour for Kim, bohemian chic for Kourtney and edgy rocker for Khloe.

"It's new and exciting and different, and they're going to be a big part of that change," said John Goodman, executive vice president of apparel and home for parent company Sears Holdings Corp. "In order to evolve and move forward, you're going to have to step out of the comfort zone."

Not everything the Kardashians have lent their name to has been a success.   10 In November, the sisters were forced to pull their prepaid debit card, called the Kardashian Kard, amid slow sales and an outcry about high fees. After releasing "JAM (Turn It Up)," a dance-pop-infused single last month, Kim was criticized as having an uneven voice and talking her way through the song.

But for the most part, strong sales have followed their many pursuits. Kim's *eponymous* perfume was Sephora's No. 1-selling fragrance last year and the sisters' exclusive Bebe collection was a huge success, a company spokeswoman said. Their memoir and style guide, *Kardashian Konfidential,* debuted at No. 4

on the *New York Times* bestseller list in December. Unbreakable, available exclusively at Perfumania, has sold out twice since its February launch.

In recent interviews with *The Times*, the Kardashians said they're just getting started.

"There's some days we definitely go crazy," Khloe said during a recent appearance at the Beverly Center, where hundreds of hysterical fans lined up for photos and autographs. Added Kourtney: "There's no way I could do this alone. . . . We all kind of pick up the pieces for each other."

The Kardashians became household names in 2007 with the debut of *Keeping Up with the Kardashians* on the E! channel, which was conceived of by Kris as a modern-day Brady Bunch–esque reality show.

At the time, Kim Kardashian, still the most well-known of the brood, had   15 already made a name for herself as Paris Hilton's sidekick and fellow socialite. And like Hilton, Kim was also facing *notoriety* over the release of a sex tape made with her then-boyfriend.

The family's less-than-wholesome reputation has earned the Kardashians a fair amount of criticism that retail experts say could hinder the family's long-term viability as a brand.

"The Kardashians are a great example of, in my mind, talentless celebrities or celebrity for celebrity's sake who took advantage of their looks, a sex tape, a lot of pretty raw and low-level stuff that *titillated* and fascinated the American public," said Eli Portnoy, a marketing and branding expert in Los Angeles.

Led by Kris, who describes herself as the family's "momager," the Kardashian *brood* includes Kourtney, 32, Kim, 30, Khloe, 26, and Rob, 24, her children with her first husband, former O. J. Simpson lawyer Robert Kardashian, who died of esophageal cancer in 2003.

After divorcing Robert in 1989, Kris married Olympic gold medalist Bruce Jenner, who also had four kids. Kris and Bruce have two daughters together, Kendall, 15, and Kylie, 13.

Also part of the family are Odom, the Lakers basketball player who married   20 Khloe in 2009 after a month of dating, and Scott Disick, Kourtney's on-again, off-again boyfriend and father of her 1-year-old son, Mason.

As a group, the Kardashian-Jenner-Odom-Disick clan is capitalizing on its multi-generational, multiethnic appeal, actively pursuing and inking deals for everyone in the family.

But celebrity branding is a *fickle* beast. Too many missteps or a slump in popularity could see the Kardashian franchise headed the way of Lindsay Lohan's infamous leggings line or Sarah Jessica Parker's clothing collection at now-*defunct* Steve and Barry's.

If successful, they could join the elite ranks of celebs-turned-lucrative-designers such as Victoria Beckham, Mary-Kate and Ashley Olsen and Jessica Simpson, whose retail empire is expected to bring in $1 billion in sales this year.

Whether the nonstop rollout of new products will damage the brand or lead to a *bona fide* franchise with lasting appeal will depend on the family's ability to maintain product quality and exclusivity, said Howard Davidowitz, chairman of national retail consulting and investment banking firm Davidowitz & Associates Inc.

"If you're everywhere and you become a mass brand, that means you better 25 really be good," he said. "The Kardashians are hot as a pistol, but they're no Oprah. This stuff can *dissipate* very quickly."

The Sears deal in particular is a curious choice, marketing and branding experts say, given the sisters' sought-after, fashion-forward styles—a *stark* contrast to Sears' image as a place to buy power tools or a new washing machine.

"The Sears thing—I have a question mark," Portnoy said. "In my mind, Sears and the Kardashians are not consistent at all. It hurts both properties. That one strictly comes off as about more greed, more money."

Not so, said Bruno Schiavi, president of Jupi Corp., which will produce the Kardashian Kollection.

"It's not a one-off collection—this is a long-term goal for us," he said, noting that other celebrity *mavens* have partnered with Sears. Most *notably*, Martha Stewart offered an exclusive line for years at Kmart, a Sears Holdings company.

Another challenge is the fact that the public's fascination still mostly centers 30 on the family's real-life dramas and not the products. For Kim especially, being seen as a serious businesswoman has been a struggle.

At recent Los Angeles events promoting the sisters' various products, the women were mobbed by hordes of paparazzi and tabloid reporters who lobbed a few throwaway questions about whatever the Kardashians were hawking— clothes, shoes, jewelry—before spending most of the time grilling them on what new words Kourtney's baby was saying, Khloe's latest diet tricks and Kim's new boyfriend (she's currently dating Kris Humphries of the New Jersey Nets; previous boyfriends include NFL players Reggie Bush and Miles Austin).

The sisters admit that fame sometimes gets in the way of getting the job done.

In Calabasas, where they opened their first Dash boutique before becoming tabloid fixtures, Khloe said it was no longer possible to swing by and work the cash register or greet customers—"it almost causes a scene where people can't shop."

For the Kardashian sisters, who don't have business backgrounds, running a burgeoning empire has been about being heavily involved and carefully vetting projects. Only Kourtney, who attended the University of Arizona, graduated from college.

"We all approve everything together," Kim said at a recent event at Kitson in 35 Los Angeles, where she and her sisters were promoting their Silly Bandz rubber-band shapes. "I could love something but they hate it, so two out-rule the one."

"We're in every design meeting, we pick everything from the buttons to the fabric to the fit, we pick the fit models," Khloe said. "We're very hands-on."

The companies that are signing the Kardashians say they're not concerned that their own brands might be hurt by the family's sexually charged, drama-driven image.

"This is just nonsense," said Silly Bandz creator Robert Croak. "They're having fun. There's always going to be the *naysayers* who say someone's famous for nothing, and I really don't see that with the girls."

Not surprisingly, the family is open for even more business ventures. Among the categories they'd like to tackle next include home decor and children's products, Kourtney said; they are also in talks with nail polish maker OPI for a not-yet-announced project.

"We have to, No. 1, make sure that it's something that we really want to spend our time doing," Kim said. "Time is really precious now." 40

So far, the overexposure isn't turning off their fans.

"Get it while you can get it," said Amanda Lopez, 29, after buying a $140 dress at Dash Calabasas recently. "I think it's great that they're branching out. They're hot right now; why wouldn't they?"

practice it   Post-Reading Activity

You may be familiar with the idea of brands, since you see brands in the products you use all day long, from your morning coffee to your toothpaste at night. What does it mean, though, to suggest that a person—or an entire family, as the Kardashians have shown—can function as a brand? Think of another major celebrity who has his or her own product line. What products are sold with that person's name? Does the person have a well-known logo or look that has been used for selling products unrelated to his or her initial fame? What are that person's admirable qualities? What are his or her flaws? Write a well-developed paragraph that answers these questions.

COMPREHENSION QUESTIONS

1. How does the entrepreneurship of the Kardashians go beyond the marketing of other reality stars?

2. Kris Kardashian refers to herself as the "momager" of her client-daughters. What does this mean?

3. What does Chang mean by "celebrity branding is a fickle beast" (para. 22)? How is it fickle?

VOCABULARY ACTIVITIES

1. Refer back to your annotations to begin a glossary of words related to the study of fame and celebrity. Try to use context clues or roots, prefixes, and suffixes to determine the meaning of the words, and if you have to use a dictionary, try to restate the definition in your own words. For more on context clues, see Chapter 8, Vocabulary Building, page 198.

2. Look at the word "eponymous" (para. 11). How can you figure out from context clues what this word means? Once you figure out the meaning, can you determine the root of the word? What other words share this same root? How can knowing the root help you remember the meaning of *eponymous*?

SUMMARY ACTIVITY

Write a one- to two-sentence summary of "The Kardashians: Cashing in with a Capital K." Try to stay focused and not stray into your opinion of the Kardashians, even if you have strong feelings about them. For more help with summary writing, see Chapter 1, Reading and Responding to College Texts, page 2.

DISCUSSION QUESTIONS

1. How has the Kardashian family transformed themselves into a brand? What is the Kardashian brand?

2. How does the partnership between the Kardashians and Sears benefit each party? Which partner has more to gain or more to lose? Explain.

3. After reading the article, do you think of the Kardashians more as entrepreneurs or celebrities? Why?

4. Is the celebrity entrepreneur a new role for stars? Can you think of any other celebrity entrepreneurs? How successful have they been at promoting their fame?

5. Have you ever purchased a celebrity-branded product? If so, were you drawn to the celebrity name? Why or why not?

MAGAZINE

Carlin Flora is trained as a journalist, and she worked as a writer and editor for *Psychology Today*, a well-respected magazine for general readers, when she wrote this article, published in 2004. Her journalistic specialty is science, particularly psychological issues such as narcissism, self-representation, and friendship. She has published articles in a variety of health and beauty magazines, and her most recent book is *Friendfluence: The Surprising Ways Friends Make Us Who We Are. Important words and phrases have been italicized in this reading. Look up those you do not know, and write the definitions in your personal vocabulary list.*

practice it   **Pre-Reading**

For more on identifying audience, purpose, and topic, see Chapter 6, Audience, Purpose, and Topic, page 169.

Identify the audience, topic, and purpose of this article by using the pre-reading techniques that you have learned so far. Answer these questions:

- What do you think the focused topic is? How do you know?
- Who do you think the audience of *Psychology Today* is? Who do you think the audience for this particular article might be?
- What is the author's purpose, and what clues did you use to figure that out?

Write down your answers in your notes.

CARLIN FLORA

Seeing by Starlight: Celebrity Obsession

From Princess Diana to The Donald, A-listers teach us how to grab life's goodies—or so we're wired to think. What we actually learn from celebrities may surprise you.

A few years ago, Britney Spears and her entourage swept through my boss's office. As she *sashayed* past, I blushed and stammered and leaned over my desk to shake her hand. She looked right into my eyes and smiled her pageant smile, and I confess, I felt dizzy. I immediately rang up friends to report my celebrity encounter, saying: "She had on a gorgeous, floor-length white fur coat!

Her skin was blotchy!" I've never been much of a Britney fan, so why the contact high? Why should I care? For that matter, why should any of us? Celebrities are fascinating because they live in a parallel universe—one that looks and feels just like ours yet is light-years beyond our reach. Stars cry to Diane Sawyer about their problems—failed marriages, hardscrabble upbringings, bad career decisions—and we can relate. The paparazzi catch them in wet hair and a stained T-shirt, and we're thrilled. They're ordinary folks, just like us. And yet . . .

Stars live in another world entirely, one that makes our lives seem woefully dull by comparison. The teary chat with Diane quickly turns to the subject of a recent $10 million film fee and honorary United Nations ambassadorship. The magazines that specialize in gotcha snapshots of *schleppy*-looking celebs also feature Cameron Diaz wrapped in a $15,000 couture gown and glowing with youth, money and star power. We're left hanging—and we want more.

It's easy to blame the media for this *cognitive* whiplash. But the real celebrity *spinmeister* is our own mind, which tricks us into believing the stars are our lovers and our social intimates. Celebrity culture plays to all of our *innate* tendencies: We're built to view anyone we recognize as an acquaintance ripe for gossip or for romance, hence our powerful interest in Anna Kournikova's sex life. Since catching sight of a beautiful face bathes the brain in pleasing chemicals, George Clooney's killer smile is impossible to ignore. But when celebrities are both our intimate daily companions and as distant as the heavens above, it's hard to know just how to think of them. Reality TV further confuses the picture by transforming ordinary folk into bold-faced names without warning. Even celebrities themselves are not immune to celebrity watching. Magazines print pictures of Demi Moore and "Bachelorette" Trista Rehn reading the very same gossip magazines that stalk them. "Most pushers are users, don't you think?" says top Hollywood publicist Michael Levine. "And, by the way, it's not the worst thing in the world to do."

Celebrities tap into powerful motivational systems designed to foster   5
romantic love and to urge us to find a mate. Stars summon our most human yearnings: to love, admire, copy and, of course, to gossip and to *jeer*. It's only natural that we get pulled into their gravitational field.

Exclusive: Fan's Brain Transformed by Celebrity Power!

John Lennon infuriated the faithful when he said the Beatles were more popular than Jesus, but he wasn't the first to suggest that celebrity culture was taking the place of religion. With its myths, its rituals (the red carpet walk, the Super Bowl ring, the handprints outside Grauman's Chinese Theater) and its ability to *immortalize*, it fills a similar cultural *niche*. In a *secular* society our need for *ritualized idol* worship can be displaced onto stars, speculates psychologist James Houran, formerly of the Southern Illinois University School of Medicine and now director of psychological studies for True Beginnings dating service. Nonreligious people tend to be more interested in celebrity culture, he's found, and Houran speculates that for them, celebrity fills some of the same roles the church fills for believers, like the desire to admire the powerful and the drive to fit into a community of people with shared values. Leo Braudy, author of *The Frenzy of Renown: Fame and Its History*, suggests that celebrities are more like Christian calendar saints than like spiritual authorities (Tiger Woods, patron saint of *arriviste* golfers; or Jimmy Carter, protector of down-home liberal farmers?). "Celebrities have their *aura*—a debased version of charisma that stems from their all-powerful captivating presence," Braudy says.

Much like spiritual guidance, celebrity-watching can be inspiring, or at least help us *muster* the will to tackle our own problems. "Celebrities motivate us to make it," says Helen Fisher, an anthropologist at Rutgers University in New Jersey. Oprah Winfrey suffered through poverty, sexual abuse and racial discrimination to become the wealthiest woman in media. Lance Armstrong survived advanced testicular cancer and went on to win the Tour de France five times. Star-watching can also simply point the way to a grander, more dramatic way of living, publicist Levine says. "We live lives more dedicated to safety or quiet desperation, and we transcend this by connecting with bigger lives—those of the stars," he says. "We're afraid to eat that fatty muffin, but Ozzy Osbourne isn't."

Don't I know you?!

Celebrities are also common currency in our socially fractured world. Depressed college coeds and laid-off factory workers both spend hours watching Anna Nicole Smith on late night television; Mexican villagers trade theories with hometown friends about who killed rapper Tupac Shakur; and Liberian and German businessmen critique David Beckham's plays before hammering out deals. My friend Britney Spears was, in fact, the top international Internet search of 2003.

In our global village, the best targets for gossip are the faces we all know. We are born to dish dirt, evolutionary psychologists agree; it's the most efficient way to navigate society and to determine who is trustworthy. They also point out that when our brains evolved, anybody with a familiar face was an "in-group" member, a person whose alliances and *enmities* were important to keep track of.

Things have changed somewhat since life in the Pleistocene era, but our *neural*   10 hardwiring hasn't, so on some deeper level, we may think NBC's *Friends* really are our friends. Many of us have had the celebrity-sighting *mishap* of mistaking a minor star—a local weatherman, say, or a bit-part soap opera actor—for an acquaintance or former schoolmate. Braudy's favorite example of this mistake: In one episode of the cartoon show *King of the Hill*, a character meets former Texas Governor Ann Richards. "You probably know me," he says. "I've seen you on TV." That's also why we don't get bored by star gossip, says Bonnie Fuller, editorial director of American Media, which publishes *Star* and *The Enquirer*: "That would be like getting bored with information about family and friends!"

The brain simply doesn't realize that it's being fooled by TV and movies, says sociologist Satoshi Kanazawa, lecturer at the London School of Economics. "Hundreds of thousands of years ago, it was impossible for someone not to know you if you knew them. And if they didn't kill you, they were probably your friend." Kanazawa's research has shown that this feeling of friendship has other repercussions: People who watch more TV are more satisfied with their friendships, just as if they had more friends and socialized more frequently. Another study found that teens who keep up to date on celebrity gossip are popular, with strong social networks—the interest in pop culture indicates a healthy drive for independence from parents.

The *penchant* for gossiping about the stars also plays into our species' obsession with status. Humans naturally copy techniques from high-status individuals, says Francisco Gil-White, professor of psychology at University of Pennsylvania. It's an attempt to get the same rewards, whether that's "attention, favors, gifts, [or] *laudatory* exclamations." Stars get all kinds of perks and pampering: Sarah Jessica Parker was allowed to keep each of her *Sex and the City* character's extravagant getups; Halle Berry borrowed a $3 million diamond ring to wear to the Oscars. Understandably, we look to get in on the game.

The impulse to copy is behind the popularity of celebrity magazines, says Fuller. Regular women can see what the stars are wearing, often with tips on how to buy cheap knockoffs of their outfits. Taken to extremes—which television is only too happy to do—the urge to copy produces spectacles like the MTV reality show *I Want a Famous Face*. By dint of extensive plastic surgery, ordinary people are made to look more like their famous heroes. In one episode, two *gangly* 20-year-old twin brothers are molded into Brad Pitt look-alikes. The brothers want to be stars, and they've decided that looking more like Pitt is the fastest road to fame. No wonder makeover shows are so popular, points out Joshua Gamson, an associate professor of sociology at the University of San Francisco. These shows offer *drab* nobodies a double whammy: simultaneous beauty and celebrity. The most fascinating measure of status is, of course, sex. "We want to know who is mating with whom," says Douglas Kenrick, professor of psychology at Arizona State University. He *speculates* that we look to stars to evaluate our own sexual behavior and ethics, and mistake them unconsciously for members of our prospective mating pool. Given this me-too drive to imitate and adore, why are celebrity flame-outs and meltdowns so fascinating? Even though we love to hear about the *lavish* rewards of fame—remember *Lifestyles of the Rich and Famous*?—we're quick to judge when stars behave too outrageously or live too extravagantly. We suspect some stars are enjoying society's highest rewards without really deserving them, says University of Liverpool anthropologist Robin Dunbar, so we monitor their behavior. "We need to keep an eye on the great-and-the-good because they create a sense of community for us, but also because we need to make sure that they are holding to their side of the bargain."

Diva Alert: Beauty Isn't Everything (Being Nice Helps!)

The beauty bias is well-known. We all pay more attention to good-looking people. Kenrick's eye-tracking research has shown that both men and women spend more time looking at beautiful women than at less attractive women. Babies as young as 8 months old will stare at an attractive female face of any race longer than they will at an average-looking or unattractive female face. Certain human traits are universally recognized as beautiful: symmetry, regularity in the shape and size of the features, smooth skin, big eyes and thick lips, and an hourglass figure that indicates fertility. Men interpret these features as evidence of health and reproductive fitness. Women's responses are more complex, says psychologist and Harvard Medical School instructor Nancy Etcoff, author of *Survival of the Prettiest*. Women stare at beautiful female faces out of *aesthetic* appreciation, to look for potential tips—and because a beautiful woman could be a rival worth monitoring.

It's not surprising that gorgeous people wind up famous. What's less obvious is that famous people often wind up gorgeous: The more we see a certain face, the more our brain likes it, whether or not it's actually beautiful. Thanks to what is known as "the exposure effect," says James Bailey, a psychologist at George Washington University, the pleasurable biological cascade that is set off when we see a certain celebrity "begins to wear a neurochemical groove," making her image easier for our brains to process. It begins to explain why Jennifer Aniston—not exactly a classic cover girl—was again named one of *People* magazine's 50 "most beautiful" in the world this year. 15

On the flip side, celebrity overload—let's call it the J.Lo effect—can leave us all thoroughly sick of even the most beautiful celeb. With the constant *deluge* of celebrity coverage, says Etcoff, "they at first become more appealing because they are familiar, but then the *ubiquity* becomes *tedious*. That is why the stars who reign the longest—Madonna is the best example—are always changing their appearance." Every time Madonna *reconfigures* her look, she resets our responses back to when her face was recognizable but still surprising.

Just as in pageants, personality plays a part in the beauty contest, too. State University of New York at Binghamton psychology professors Kevin Kniffin and David Sloan Wilson have found that people's perceptions of physical appeal are strongly influenced by familiarity and likability. "Almost all of the beauty research is based on subjects looking at strangers in photos or computer-generated images—but we don't live in a world of strangers!" Kniffin points out.

In one of Kniffin's experiments, students worked on an archeological dig together toward a shared goal. Those who were deemed cooperative and likable were rated as more attractive after the project was finished than they were at the outset. *Conversely*, students who were not as hardworking were rated as less attractive after the chore was done.

Kniffin believes this same mechanism is at work in our feelings toward celebrities, who rank somewhere between strangers and intimates. Athletes are an obvious example: Team spirit gives even ugly guys a boost. NBA great Wilt Chamberlain might have been a bit goofy-looking, but his astonishing abilities to *propel* his team to victory meant that he was a hero, surrounded with adoring—and *amorous*—fans. Kniffin points to William Hung, the talent-free and *homely* also-ran on the contest show *American Idol*, as evidence of his theory at work. In part because of his enthusiasm and his good-natured willingness to put up with ridicule, Hung became a bigger star after he was kicked off the show: His album, *Inspiration*, sold more than 37,000 copies in its first week. "William doesn't display the traits of universal attractiveness, but people who have seen the show would probably rate him as more attractive because of nonphysical traits of likability and courage. He's even received some marriage proposals." Kniffin's theory also explains why models are less compelling objects of fascination than actresses or pop stars. They're beautiful, but they're *enigmatic*: We rarely get any sense of their personalities.

Saved from Oblivion!

What's the result of our simultaneous yearning to be more like celebrities and our desire to be wowed by their unattainable perfection? We've been watching it for the past decade. Reality television is an express train to fame, unpredictably turning nobodies into somebodies. Reality TV now gives us the ability to get inside the star factory and watch the transition to fame in real time.   20

"The appeal of reality stars is that they were possibly once just like you, sitting on the couch watching a reality TV program, until they leaped to celebrity," says Andy Denhart, blogger and reality TV junkie. "With the number of reality shows out there, it's inexcusable to not be famous if you want to be!" In the past, ambitious young men who idolized a famous actor might take acting lessons or learn to dance. Now, they get plastic surgery and learn to tell their life stories for the camera. In fact, says editor Fuller, the newly minted stars of reality TV are better at the celebrity game than many of the movie and television stars: "They are more accessible, more cooperative. They enjoy publicity. They will open up and offer insight, often more than a 'traditional' celeb, because they want the attention, whereas an actress might have *ambivalent* feelings about fame and how it is tied in with her 'craft.'" At the same time, shows like *The Simple Life* and *The Newlyweds* (and amateur videotapes like Paris Hilton's) let us gawk at the silly things that stars do in the privacy of their own home. As a result, the distance between celebrity *stratosphere* and living room couch dwindles even further.

Yet there's still something about that magic dust. A celebrity sighting is not just about seeing a star, author Braudy points out, but is about being seen by a star: "There is a sense that celebrities are more real than we are; people feel more real in the presence of a celebrity." It wasn't just that I saw Britney, it was that Britney saw me.

practice it   Post-Reading Activity

Look back at your predictions about audience, topic, and purpose that you made before you started reading the article. How accurately did you predict them? What, if anything, about the article's audience, topic, or purpose was surprising to you? What did you learn about celebrity watching? What questions do you still have about the topic?

COMPREHENSION QUESTIONS

1. In paragraph 4, what does Flora mean by "cognitive whiplash"?

2. What is the "cultural niche" (para. 6) that celebrity watching fulfills in our society, according to Flora?

3. Flora writes that celebrities provide a "common currency in our socially fractured world" (para. 8). What does she mean by this? Do you agree with her? Can you think of any instances where celebrities provide us with a way to connect?

4. What is the "exposure effect" (para. 15)?

5. Why, according to Flora, are we so drawn to stars?

6. How might a reality TV star and an actor deal with fame differently?

VOCABULARY ACTIVITIES

1. Add any words from this article to your ongoing fame and celebrity glossary. Remember to write definitions in your own words.

2. Reread the first two paragraphs of this article, underlining all the words you consider really strong or interesting. Did you already know these words, or are they new to you? How does the author's vocabulary make her writing style engaging but still understandable?

SUMMARY ACTIVITY

Write a brief summary of "Seeing by Starlight: Celebrity Obsession" by turning Flora's section subheadings into main points. Try to stay objective, even if you have strong feelings about the topic. For more help with summary writing, see Chapter 1, Reading and Responding to College Texts, page 2.

DISCUSSION QUESTIONS

1. In what ways can star watching be inspiring? What inspirational celebrities can you think of who fulfill this role? What needs can celebrity watching fulfill?

2. How does celebrity watching affect your friendships?

3. Using the reading-against-the-grain strategy, can you find any flaws in Flora's argument?

4. Think of a current big celebrity; do Flora's points about our fascination with celebrities apply to this celebrity? Why or why not?

MAGAZINE

Mary Loftus is the associate editor of *Emory Magazine*, a publication of Emory University. As a journalist and freelance writer, she has worked for the *New York Times*, *Psychology Today*, and a variety of other publications, writing about a wide range of topics. This article, which considers the negative effects of fame and celebrity, appeared in *Psychology Today* magazine in 1995. *Important words and phrases have been italicized in this reading. Look up those you do not know, and write the definitions in your personal vocabulary list.*

practice it   Pre-Reading

Imagine for a moment that you could be famous. What would you want to be famous for? What would it be like to be famous? Would your life be drastically changed? What would be better and what would be worse? Freewrite for five minutes on these questions to help you identify your preconceived notions about what it would be like to be famous.

MARY LOFTUS

The Other Side of Fame

Behind the glitz and glamour—sex, drugs, and rock 'n' roll. Celebrities suffer from drug abuse and addiction.

For some reason, perhaps because it's far removed from the L.A.-N.Y. continuum, celebrities' siblings are drawn to Central Florida. Not only that, but they feel compelled to become journalists here.

I've sat two desks over from Jennifer Deals's brother, Greg. Been at newspaper parties with Susan Sarandon's brother, Terry Tomalin, and shared journalistic turf with Gretchen Letterman, Dave's sis.

These relationships occasionally bring the mild-mannered reporters some fall-out fame. Terry, while on a backpacking trip with his sister and her pal Julia Roberts, noticed that Roberts was listening to Lyle Lovett cassettes on her Walkman, and set the two up for their first date. Gretchen made the newspapers when her brother dropped by for a visit in St. Petersburg and had a car accident.

But mostly, they're close-mouthed about their celebrity sibs.

"It's not just that you get tired of people asking about them," says Arthur McCune, a reporter whose stepbrother, Daniel Waters, wrote *Heathers* and   5

Batman Returns. "It's also that, in comparison, you feel kind of like a failure. I mean, he comes home for Christmas and has been at some exotic locale for his new movie, or just had lunch with Winona Ryder, and then it's, 'So what's new with you?'"

Celebrity and success have become *synonymous* in a culture that judges by how rich, seductive, and *riveting* the image; where the name recognition of teenage waif models rivals that of Nobel Peace Prize recipients.

"Celebrity [is] the reward of those who project a vivid or pleasing exterior or have otherwise attracted attention to themselves," Christopher Lasch wrote in *The Culture of Narcissism.* "It is *evanescent.* . . . In our time, when success is so largely a function of youth, glamour, and novelty, glory is more *fleeting* than ever, and those who win the attention of the public worry incessantly about losing it."

Stars, then, have their own problems, not the least of which is contemplating their own *half-lives.* Some worries intrude from outside: rabid fans, gold diggers, paparazzi, critics, competition. Others gnaw from within: self-doubt, addiction, wanderlust.

Entertainers—whether actors, artists, evangelists, writers, musicians, politicians, or athletes—survive by peddling themselves and their talents to the masses. They're put on display, consumed, evaluated and achieve either dismissal or acclaim. Feedback is received through Gallop polls, Nielsen ratings, and box-office draw.

Like the tree-in-the-forest *conundrum*, this presents a philosophical puzzle: 10 If a celebrity doesn't rivet the public's attention, does he exist?

Fame has always had a bad reputation among thinkers. Poets sung of its seductiveness, and its tendency to breed vanity and superficiality. But the worst you could say of the old kind of fame, the kind based on accomplishment, was that it clouded your vision. The new, less *durable* fame, the kind refracted through images, proves especially *corrosive* to the self.

"To be a celebrity means to have more than the usual assaults on one's ego," says Charles Figley, Ph.D., director of the Psychosocial Stress Research Program at Florida State University. "You're very vulnerable to the personal evaluations of other people. The public is ultimately in control of whether your career continues."

Figley, who is writing a book on the stresses peculiar to celebrities, conducted a survey in which 200 questionnaires were mailed out to names randomly selected from a list of the public's top-ranked celebrities. From 51 replies, he compiled a list of the primary sources of stress for celebrities and their families, as well as their reactions and solutions. Most of the questionnaires were completed by the celebrities, the rest by a spouse, friend, or adult child of the celebrity. The top 10 stressors, in order, were:

- the celebrity press
- critics
- threatening letters/calls

- the lack of privacy
- the constant monitoring of their lives
- worry about career plunges
- stalkers
- lack of security
- curious fans
- worries about their children's lives being disrupted

The celebrities' reactions to this stress were: depression, loss of sleep, crying over nothing, bad moods, acting out and misbehavior on the part of their children, lack of concentration, stomach problems, paranoia, over-spending, lack of trust, and self-hatred.

"There's a certain amount of insecurity," Figley says. "One of the respon-   15
dents said that, at any time, he expected someone to come up and tap him on the shoulder and say, 'Go back to being a waiter. What do you think you're doing here, anyway?' There's a constant need for reassurance that they deserve what they've received."

Stress-busting solutions celebrities mentioned included: talking to friends or therapists, beefing up security, having friends outside the business, protecting their kids, laughing as much as possible, finding faith and religion, getting out of L.A.

"A sense of humor was one thing that kept coming up when they were asked about coping," Figley says. "One family had fun with it, and made a game out of trying various disguises to not be recognized." But another respondent, a well-known celeb, said he vividly remembers a painful moment when his family was going out for pizza, and his youngest child asked his mother, "Does Dad have to come?"

"There tends to be a wide variation among the children," Figley says. "Some don't mind the attention, or even look forward to it. Others hate it."

Kate Capshaw, wife of Steven Spielberg, recently said their three young children were the reason she wants to move her family out of Los Angeles. "L.A. is kind of a one-horse town—because of the entertainment industry— and their daddy's riding on a pretty damn big horse."

Although Figley asked respondents to focus on the negatives, he said   20
most acknowledged that celebrity comes with "tremendous highs, an extraordinary sense of pleasure and reward. They enjoy the sense of influence."

Show Biz

Let's state up front, nobody's feeling sorry for people who get $4.5 million a picture, own three mansions on various hills, have tired of being invited to so many glamorous parties, and fly to Paris on a whim. As Jerry Seinfeld, star and creator of the *eponymous* un-sitcom, told *TV Guide*, "I think people want to see you enjoy what you've done. If I were depressed and complaining, people would say, 'Oh, for crying out loud, what the hell does it take?' "

But even this expectation—that celebs should be modest and grateful, zenfully happy, and content in their accomplishments—is just another larger-than-life role that we expect them to play.

Brad Pitt, he of the undead, who, ironically, was also named "Sexiest Man Alive" by *People* magazine, says, "Being in the movies doesn't make you laugh any harder, or any less sad." Pitt collects live chameleons that hang in cages behind his California home, which he fills with old-wood furniture and antiques. Changelings in confinement, surrounded by things that are solid and lasting; the symbolism is not subtle. "The house is very, very important as this [fame] thing builds and builds and gets completely out of hand. Proportion, materials, light, perspective," he told *Rolling Stone*, just after the release of *Interview with a Vampire*.

And Jodie Foster, on the set of the movie *Nell*, tells reporters that she's suffering from bad dreams and sleeplessness because she doesn't live any-where anymore. She bought a house in a remote location years ago, when she was in an "L.A. is a scuzzy Hollywood town" frame of mind, and now, she says, it's too far away from everything. A home, a place of comfort and security, is vitally important to her. Foster endured a madman's obsession after John Hinckley claimed that he made his assassination attempt on President Reagan to impress her. "The problem is, I can't really go out all the time and feel okay about what might happen to me. I don't get to go out like other people do. I can't go to McDonald's, or a coffee shop," Foster says. And, in a later interview, "I've gotten more fragile as I've gotten older."

Celebrities by Association

Celebrityhood—being well known and recognized either by face or name to large groups of people—isn't confined to a few towns or professions. Dr. Jack Kevorkian has it. Joey Buttafuoco has it. JFK Jr. has it. Ivana Trump married and divorced it.   25

People who acquire fame quickly or due to reasons outside their control deal with it less well than those who have struggled for years before making it or who were born into high-achieving families, observes psychotherapist Marcia Lasswell, M.A., a professor at California State University and private practitioner in L.A.

Lasswell has surveyed almost 40 other therapists who counsel celebrities, asking them about their clients' most frequent problems. "I believe the most difficult areas in which to be a celebrity are religion and politics," said Lasswell. "You've got the same types of stress as other celebrities, but you're held to a higher standard." Drugs or affairs are verboten. And while it might be trendy in Los Angeles to have a therapist, for politicians it can be seen as a sign of weakness and, for religious leaders, a crisis of faith. Take, for example, the debate over whether Florida governor Lawton Chiles was fit for office after it was disclosed that he was on Prozac for depression.

"Politicians can't lead reclusive lives," Lasswell says.

Indeed, the media frenzy that surrounded Henry Foster, M.D., when he was nominated for Surgeon General in February took him from respected obstetrician to controversial candidate overnight. "Now, when I wake up in the morning and look out my window, the press is out there waiting and watching," Foster said. "I have even picked up a new lexicon: Sound bites. Boom mikes. Stakeouts. Live shots. Talking heads. On-air analysis. All dissecting me over and over again. And all before I uttered one word at my Senate confirmation hearings."

Face recognition is the most stressful part of being a celebrity, the thera-   30
pists reported. People who are famous but not easily recognized, such as authors, have an easier time of it.

Self vs. Image

In his book *The Image*, Daniel J. Boorstin writes, "The celebrity is a person who is known for his well-knownness. . . . The hero was distinguished by his achievement, the celebrity by his image or trademark." Even the most enduring, respected actors question which of these categories they fall into.

Paul Newman, in a recent interview, says he continually wonders if his entire career was based on his arctic-blue eyes. "You're constantly reminded. There are places you go and they say, 'Take off your dark glasses so we can see your beautiful blue eyes.' And you just want to, I dunno, um . . . thump them," Newman says. "They could say, 'Hey, it's very nice to meet you'— that's great. Or, 'Thanks for a bunch of great performances,' and you can feed off that for a half. But the other thing, which is always there, is a never-ending reminder.

"The bloodshot blue eyes," he says, laughing.

Newman, 70, says despite his years of philanthropy and dozens of classic movie roles, this issue perplexes him. "I am thoroughly and predictably concerned about what was my accomplishment, and what was the accomplishment of my appearance, which I have no control over," he says. "What was attributable to me?"

Celebrities live in a world of myth and fantasy, where limits have been   35
peeled back by money and fame. Boundless opportunities, however, can feel like a prison with silken walls, luxurious in its isolation. However much the world opens up to celebrities, a part of it also closes down. There is a massive loss of privacy. It is a challenge to maintain human contact.

The seclusion and grandeur imparted by fame can trigger paths of thinking that resemble schizophrenic or paranoid delusions. "I don't know who to relate to," says musician Eddie Vedder. "I don't know how people relate to me. I don't feel like people relate to me as a normal human."

Therapists say their celebrity clients often develop an adaptive form of personality disorder: a split between their private and public selves. "There are constant accolades from outside based on how they look, who their characters are," says Annie Coe, a Los Angeles therapist who has done research on celebrity couples. "It's easy to lose track of who they are. Holding on to a sense of self is difficult."

Celebrities struggle every day with their private persona, notes Lasswell: "Who am I to the world, who am I to myself, who am I to my family?"

There are two types of celebrities, says Coe, who estimates that about 60 percent of her clients are celebrities, or on their way up. The first type is self-confident and secure, and retains their ego strength. The second is driven by inferiority to gain approval and masks this with narcissism, constantly demanding special attention.

But there are commonalities in people who are drawn to the genre and   40
succeed. "They tend to be iconoclasts, people who need to live the gypsy life. They love challenges, stimulation, verbal expression. They're usually social and gregarious, and have great charm and wit," Coe says.

Chutes and Ladders

"Things are going very well for me," says actor Tom Sizemore, who played the love-besotted detective in *Natural Born Killers*. "Unless, of course, people don't like me."

Celebrities ply their wares in a business that the Screen Actors Guild says has an 85 percent unemployment rate at any given moment, which is bound to create a bit of tension, even for the 15 percent lucky enough to be at work that day.

"The main stressor I've seen in our clients is the cyclical nature of the entertainment business," says psychologist Michele Harway, Ph.D., director of the California Family Study Center in North Hollywood. "And, when working, the incredible hours. There's no time or energy left over for family. Then, during the hiatus, there's anxiety about if they'll ever work again. Commitments are not made from year to year. Fame is elusive—you're the darling today, and can't get a job tomorrow."

Celebrities, then, can scarcely enjoy their fame for fear of it slipping away. And while you are on top, the people who sign your paycheck, fickle lot though they may be, insist on following you everywhere. Stardom, Harway says, means that "you can't even go pee without being followed by hordes of fans demanding autographs."

Harway sat behind Don Johnson and Barbra Streisand, back when they were   45
a couple, at a Dodgers game, and when Johnson got up to go to the bathroom, a whole crowd of people followed him, waving slips of paper in his face.

Don, and even Barbra, may not have to worry about this for long. "There are more famous people than ever before, but most of their lives are parables of perishability," says author Neal Gabler in *Winchell: Gossip, Power and the Culture of Celebrity*, a biography of gossip columnist Walter Winchell. "For decades, an ever-expanding pool of celebrities has been competing for a finite public attention. . . . Viewed in more ruthless economic terms, these movie stars, athletes, artists, journalists, and socialites were human commodities."

In a speech she wrote for acceptance of the Lifetime Achievement Award from the Screen Actors Guild, the late Audrey Hepburn thanked those who "guided an unknown, insecure, inexperienced, skinny broad into a marketable commodity."

But most celebrities don't like to think of themselves as passing fads, or even plan for that possibility, for fear of jinxing their careers. They tend, instead, to make huge amounts of money in short amounts of time, then spend it very quickly. In a business that is feast or famine, celebs may reward themselves when the big checks come in, assuming that they will be able to sustain their new lifestyle.

Body Image

In a business where what you sell is, ultimately, yourself, appearance takes on a special significance. In acting and modeling, it has become almost chic to step away from your own image. "I don't really look as good as I do in pictures," Christie Brinkley once said during a television interview, straight to the camera.

Stars, like most of us, often fixate on their flaws, not on their best attributes.   50 Women in the business seem especially anxious about fulfilling expectations of willowy beauty and ever-sustainable youth. It may be an understandable response, given the built-in insecurities of fame: There's always another talent arriving on the celebrity shuttle.

Demi Moore, as surely as Hester Prynne, knows the power of her dark eyes and throaty voice. And yet, in a recent interview with *Rolling Stone*, the highest-paid actress in Hollywood history details why she believes she's a plain Jane. "You know . . . eyes too small, I don't have a good smile, I'm square, I have no waist, and I'm never thin enough."

The late Gilda Radner spoke about dealing with fame in her autobiography, *It's Always Something*. "With fame, and the constant display of my image on television, came anorexia. I became almost afraid to eat," she said. But New York streets are filled with tempting kiosks. "During the second year of *Saturday Night Live*, I taught myself to throw up. I became bulimic before medical science had given it that name."

After her hair fell out from chemotherapy, Radner could go out in public and not be recognized. But with that freedom came the loss of her sense of self. "I started introducing myself by saying, 'I used to be Gilda Radner.' That was how I felt. I used to be her, but now I was someone else." Radner finally broke through the desolation and joined a cancer support group, where she established friendships and made people laugh. "Finding that part of myself again," she said, "was wonderful."

Drugs and Destruction

English actor Gary Oldman seems to take pride in finding the oddest roles imaginable; he's played Count Dracula, Beethoven, Sid Vicious, and Lee

Harvey Oswald. "Acting comes too easy for Gary. He's a genius at the craft. It bores him," says Douglas Urbanski, Oldman's agent.

The *nemesis* Oldman is struggling to conquer is more challenging than a   55
difficult screen persona. "He's 61 days sober as of today," Urbanski says. "Isabella (Rossellini), Gary, and I have been on the most incredible journey together. The work he has done on himself is awesome."

Oldman is the son of an alcoholic welder who abandoned his family when Gary was seven. While Oldman was gliding to the top of the film industry, his personal life was in shambles, with two broken marriages. "Sometimes acting gets in the way of living life," Oldman has said. "It's very consuming,"

After five weeks of rehab, Oldman now plays his Steinway to relieve stress, attends AA meetings, and stays grounded by establishing a routine in his life. "He's got children, dogs, nannies, housekeepers, a whole menagerie up there [at his home]," Urbanski said. "But this is the first time he's experienced it all from a point of sobriety."

"People are naive about chemical dependence," Oldman now tells reporters, "about how destructive, powerful, and overwhelming it is."

David Wellisch, Ph.D., a professor of psychiatry at UCLA's medical school, says Oldman may well have two of the factors associated with alcohol abuse—a genetic *predisposition* and an environmental influence from childhood, with at least one parent modeling addictive behaviors.

But because of his talent, Oldman, like many celebs, had a third risk   60
factor—one that Wellisch calls a "crisis of mobility," in which his fame transported him from one world to another. "He knew how to act when he was the son of a welder, but then he became a stranger in a strange land. His life had, at some level, lost its bearings. Drugs can be a stabilizer, at least temporarily, providing anxiety reduction, feelings of *omnipotence* and power, or a soothing, deep peace otherwise unattainable," Wellisch says.

For celebrities, especially in the entertainment field, the pressure is always on to turn in a perfect performance, to be better than before, to constantly hit the mark. At the same time, artists tend to be sensitive souls, in touch with naked emotions they mine for our *perusal*.

"Artists are the lenses through which life is transmitted. They show us what we think and feel in a way that is profound, intense, and highly emotional," Wellisch says. "They experience life more dearly than the rest of us." Drugs are a way to mute these feelings, which threaten to overwhelm.

And with the riches that accompany their fame, drugs are an escape route celebrities can afford at least for a while. The list of celebrity deaths from drugs is long, and continually updated—Elvis Presley, Judy Garland, Marilyn Monroe, Jim Morrison, Janis Joplin, Scott Newman, David Kennedy, John Belushi, River Phoenix.

"I think it has to be remembered that he was 23 and he made the choice," said Judy Davis, who was set to star opposite Phoenix in his next movie.

"There's something about stardom and the way it empowers people—he thought he was immune." Fame, therapists agree, can draw stars into a kind of magical thinking, wherein the laws of humankind are suspended.

Or, perhaps, River Phoenix felt he was unworthy. "There's embarrassment 65 and guilt among those who become superstars quickly," Figley says. "They may have a self-destructive streak."

Jib Fowles, professor of media studies at the University of Houston–Clear Lake and author of *Starstruck: Celebrity Performers and the American Public* (Smithsonian Institute Press), found in a study of 100 stars from all fields— Hollywood entertainers, sports stars, musicians—that celebrities are almost four times more likely to kill themselves than the average American.

"It's an enormously stressful profession," Fowles says. "There is unrelenting pressure coupled with diminishing private lives. They have to be on every time they step out their front door."

In fact, Fowles found that the average age of death for celebrities, overall, was 58, compared to an average of 72 years old for other Americans.

Celebrities, he believes, are the sacrificial victims of our adoration.

"Never in a society has the individual been anywhere near as important 70 as in contemporary America," Fowles says. And, as old heroic figures—military, political, and religious leaders—have fallen by the wayside, entertainers have taken their place. "They are delivered to us as perfect human beings. We look to them as ideals, and that gives us orientation. But the burden falls heavily on them. There's an argument to be made that stars aren't paid nearly enough for the cultural service they provide."

"You have to wonder if anyone set limits for these people, if anyone said, 'You're nuts, you're going to the hospital,'" Wellisch says. "Take it from me, I've seen celebrities who are household names, and it's tough to tell them things. Everyone else is telling them what magnificent, otherworldly creatures they are, and you have to tell them they have all these problems they need to deal with . . ."

Show business, like police work and medicine, is a high-risk profession, says Wellisch. "You experience too much, you see too much."

Some of the celebrities who have kicked drugs and come through to the other side attribute the change to settling down and having children. Actor Dennis Quaid battled drugs and alcohol for years, finally checking into rehab to kick a cocaine addiction before marrying Meg Ryan and having their son, Jack.

Children can pull their parents, famous or not, outside themselves. There is no longer the luxury of complete self-indulgence, if one takes parenting seriously. And, perhaps for the first time, there is someone more important, someone more deserving. For celebrities, who are at the center of so many orbits, it's especially important to have a little Copernicus around.

"As soon as Sam was born," said proud papa Michael J. Fox, "I knew that 75 I would throw myself in front of a truck for him."

Privacy Protected

Sharon Stone, who's had a reputation for being outspoken and forthright in interviews, recently switched tacks. "My new policy is this: I have a life of my own. Just a little, tiny one, but it's mine," she told the *Entertainment Tonight* crew when they asked about her latest love interest.

Celebrities understandably become more protective when they achieve the level of fame where fans begin to swarm, track, or target them obsessively, says therapist Coe, whose office is across from the entrance to Warner Bros. Studios. "They'll buy burglar alarms, cars with tinted windows, guard dogs, bodyguards. Some of them even border on paranoia, like the stars who have four bodyguards with them at all times, even on a movie set, and change clothes five times a day. It's a fine line.

"You've got the upside, where celebrities have the freedom and opportunities to go places and do things that bring them wonderment and joy. But their boundaries are constantly being pushed back, physically and mentally. Also, their trust level is down. They don't trust a lot of people."

Through their prominence and visibility, celebrities become living *Rorschach tests*, valued by their adoring public not for who they are, but for who their fans want them to be. With the casual fan, this could mean confusing actors with the roles they play, or feeling a sense of false intimacy with someone they've never actually met. For the lunatic, it could mean that the celebrity becomes the fantasy half of a dangerous delusion. Take the woman who, after breaking into David Letterman's home, took to driving his cars and referring to herself as "Mrs. Letterman."

Michelle Pfeiffer has said that she acts for free—but charges for the   80
inconvenience of being a celebrity. She tells about one day on the set of *The Age of Innocence*, when people were gathered around her trailer. "I kept trying to find a place where they couldn't see in. So I find myself in the back of the trailer and they can't see me, but I can hear them. Now, these are people who are usually like, 'Michelle, Michelle, we love you.' And I hear somebody say, 'Hey, man, I saw her and she looks old,'" Pfeiffer recounted, laughing. "I'm not worried about age. But I'm very aware that this is my window of time."

Moving away from fans to "get away from it all" might work too effectively, however. Garrison Keillor, radio host from the banks of Lake Wobegon, left St. Paul for Denmark, homeland of his Scandinavian wife. He claimed he wanted anonymity, the freedom to "live the life of a shy person." Eventually, he moved back to Minneapolis and resumed broadcasting live. Nothing's worse than *adulation*, till it's gone.

Family Ties

Celebrity parents may produce celebrity *progeny*: Janet Leigh begat Jamie Lee Curtis, Debbie Reynolds begat Carrie Fisher, Kirk Douglas begat Michael, Lloyd

Bridges begat Beau and Jeff, Martin Sheen begat Charlie and Emilio, Henry Fonda begat Jane and Peter, who begat Bridget.

But for the most part, celebrities have ordinary moms, dads, dogs, and siblings back in the great American heartland who serve as touchstones in their lives. Families and old friends, say the stars, counteract the dizzying seduction of a world in which you can endlessly reinvent yourself, losing track of who you are and where you came from.

Sarah Jessica Parker says she takes "self-appointed *sabbaticals*" from the demands of filming to "see my family, go to the market, and cook every day." Heather Locklear told Barbara Walters that her parents live nearby, visit often, and keep her sane.

When your parents are the ones who are famous, though, it can be a tough 85 act to follow. It is the children who often pay the price of parental celebrity. The insecurity in the household, the tension, the career and mood ups and downs, the *errant*, hectic schedules, and the long absences all *coalesce* to shift a great deal of the emotional burden to the kids.

"I feel so for the kids," says Coe. "You're always dealing with having that name, or that face." No surprise, then, that the children of celebrities, like the *prodigal* minister's daughter, often act out in effective and embarrassing ways.

Alison Eastwood, now a model, grew up in Carmel as not only the daughter of actor Clint, but also as the rebellious child of the town's mayor. "I was feeling my oats," she says. "I dyed my hair orange and drove around fast with my stereo blaring. I was one of the big noise-makers in town. I bet people were happy to see me go to college."

The trappings of fame—frequent travel, drug use, affairs—can estrange celebrity parents from their children, preventing a normal relationship during their formative years. Actress Liv Tyler is the daughter of model Bebe Buell and Aerosmith's Steven Tyler. Raised in Maine, Liv was nine before she learned that Tyler was her father. Her mother blocked Tyler from his daughter's life due to his drug and alcohol abuse. "He was a screwed-up mess, and I chose not to have him in her life until he chose sobriety," Buell says.

Tyler's daughters now accept and acknowledge their rock-legend dad, although his daughter Mia says he does embarrass her sometimes while on stage. "I mean, he stands there and he's groping himself . . . and he should not be doing that," she told *A Current Affair* in an interview. "It disgusts me."

Celebrities' children, like the children of the very wealthy, also run the risk 90 of wasted lives due to dysgradia, a syndrome where there is a complete lack of connection between doing and getting. "This is extremely amotivational," says Wellisch. "You know that no matter what you do, everything's still going to be there."

In addition to blood relations, celebs often have extended "families" nearby, made up of friends, employees, and other stars. Celebrities often work out of their homes, scheduling appointments, reading scripts, conducting meetings, and having networking parties. "The household is filled with people always coming and going. There's quite a bit of entertainment. It's rather chaotic. Managers and agents who have been with them for a long time become close friends, and like aunts and uncles to their children," Figley says.

With a support staff comes a payroll, employees and associates who depend on the celebrity for their own livelihood. "That puts a celebrity under constant pressure to be famous," Figley says. "So if an actor is in a movie that gets bad reviews or does poorly, he is inclined to self-blame, which leads to depression."

And, as always when there's a lot of money involved, there's the potential for corruption, for a trust violated. Indeed, celebrities are usually inundated by people who want to work for them. It can be difficult to scrutinize who to hire, never knowing what anyone really wants of you.

The Home Front

Hardest of all, perhaps, is the stress that fame can place on a celebrity's marriage.

Temptations are abundant. *Legends of the Fall* star Aidan Quinn, who has a   95
wife, Elizabeth Bracco, and a young daughter, has women slipping notes to him even while he's getting his teeth cleaned at the dentist. "One time," he recounts, "I was out with my wife at dinner, and this woman walks up to the table and puts down a card with her name and number. She just laid it down and she walked away. I had to almost physically restrain my wife. Pretty fucking ballsy."

Without a separate, strong commitment to a career or other interests, it is particularly difficult for a celebrity's partner to maintain a clear sense of identity in a relationship. The attainment of celebrity almost automatically shifts the power balance. The spouse of a celebrity may live in constant fear of abandonment. What's more, the frequent absences of the celebrity mean the partner winds up with the extra burden of domestic responsibility. And the unpredictability of employment puts constant tension on the relationship.

But the biggest stress on relationships may come from the celebrity's own psyche. Does a star give up the role at home? The shift is almost always difficult for celebrities, therapists say. After a day in front of the camera, being catered to by teams of workers, not to mention sought out by hordes of fans, a request to take out the garbage can feel extremely claustrophobic.

Jennifer Sils, a Santa Monica therapist wed to comedy magician Mac King, says being in a relationship with an entertainer provides as many benefits as drawbacks to the spouse. Sils interviewed in depth eight women married to or living with men in the performing arts. Erratic schedules, long hours, unpredictable income, and periods of unemployment can make living with performers difficult, they admitted.

The financial ups and downs add a profound level of unpredictability in scheduling important life events, such as when to have children. There are difficulties in establishing a personal identity when married to a performer, who is often a strong personality. Parties and other social events supply more stress, because they tend to make the spouse feel unimportant. The frequent long absences of their mates require adjustments on leaving and reentry.

But, Sils found, most of the women said their relationships gave them opportunities they might not have otherwise experienced, like travel and rubbing shoulders with other stars. For the most part, said the women, their lives were exciting, filled with creativity, and seldom boring. 100

For celebrity spouses anchored by children, homes, and careers, however, home can be a long way from the latest movie set.

And then there are those celebrities who feel destined to stay single due to their star status. Joan Lunden, co-host of *Good Morning America*, bemoaned her lack of romantic companionship three years after her divorce. "Since then, I've only had a few dates—and believe me, that hasn't been my choice. I can't understand why men are so intimidated. There must be someone wonderful out there. But I'm certainly finding him hard to find."

Media

Ah, the press. The Fourth Estate, defender of the First Amendment, the No. 1 source of celebrity stress.

The tabloids, both print and TV, lead the pack, certainly. But even the mainstream press has incredible *leeway* when it comes to reporting on public figures. Where a private person must prove only negligence to claim libel, public figures (such as celebrities, politicians, and others who have sought the spotlight) must claim actual malice or knowledge that the statement is false.

The creative-expression defense goes a long way with courts intent on upholding the freedom of the press. When *Hustler* magazine discussed Jerry Falwell having sex with his mother in an outhouse, the Supreme Court ruled it satire. 105

But those on the receiving end say the press can be relentless in trying to capture, then condemn, their celebrity prey.

"I was walking down the street to go and get a newspaper and I was followed by this van, and this man with a video camera was filming me," Julia Roberts said in an interview. "This popped up on TV a few days later. I mean, I'm going to get the paper, and it's early in the morning and I have my hair pulled back and I have on some little dress or whatever. This woman on the television had the nerve to be completely obsessed by how I looked."

"Now, I don't have a clue what she looks like when she's going to get the paper," Roberts continued, "but I doubt it is the same as she does on television. She was saying, 'Julia, I have the name of a great hairdresser.' I thought, well, why should I do my hair to go and get a paper on the off-chance that somebody is going to videotape it and put it on TV?"

Being constantly judged and evaluated by their appearance, whether attending the Academy Awards or stepping out to get a newspaper, denies celebrities any part of their life that is truly and exclusively their own. Therein lies madness . . . or, at least, resentment. Does buying a movie ticket, owning a television, or subscribing to a magazine give us automatic rights to 24-hour surveillance?

We build 'em up, just to knock 'em down. 110

Accomplishments

The late Tony Perkins, said his wife, Berry, never gloried in his cinematic successes. "He was very strong, and very intelligent, but I don't think he thought he really contributed a hell of a lot to this world, which is really sad."

"I've always felt . . . that it was a very exposable myth that I was somebody," Perkins told the *Saturday Evening Post* in 1960. "I've felt this was an absurd dishonesty and that if I were close to people, it would be instantly evident and that they would say, 'Well, gee, he's nothing at all. What do we want to see him for?'"

Many celebrities suffer from this "impostor *phenomenon*," says Harway, and attribute their successes to good luck rather than hard work.

Just as we have created celebrities, we have created the hall of mirrors in which they so *precariously* exist. For the famous today, said Lasch, self-approval depends on public recognition and acclaim.

"The good opinion of friends and neighbors, which formerly informed a man 115 that he had lived a useful life, rested on appreciation of his accomplishments.

"Today, men seek the kind of approval that applauds not their actions, but their personal attributes," Lasch continued. "They wish to be not so much esteemed as admired. They crave not fame, but the glamour and excitement of celebrity. They want to be envied rather than respected. Pride and acquisitiveness . . . have given way to vanity."

The Last Word

Sure. But some celebrities refuse to give in to the *sanctimonious* seriousness of it all. Wisdom can be found in the most unlikely places. MTV VJ Karen Duffy says that her newfound recognition is really no big deal.

"I still live in the same neighborhood. I still spend a lot of time with my family in New Jersey. I still volunteer at a nursing home when I can," Duffy says. "I'd rather have a good life than a good career. So I treat my career like a rental car. I take changes, and have a lot of fun with it."

---

practice it | **Post-Reading Activity**

To spark your thinking and deepen your participation in class discussion, pick out five to ten quotations that you really like and copy them out into the following chart. You can copy the chart into your notebook or to download a version, go to **bedfordstmartins.com/readwriteconnect** and click on **Charts.**

continued ❯

Quotation You Find Meaningful (p. no.)	Why Quotation Is Meaningful

It will be helpful to return to these quotes later when you begin to do essay writing. For now, reflect on them in writing or share them in class discussion.

COMPREHENSION QUESTIONS

1. What are the major stressors of being a celebrity, according to the article?

2. What is the difference between the "old kind of fame" and the "new, less durable fame" (para. 11)?

3. Why do so many celebrities seem to have what one of the celebrity survey respondents called "a constant need for reassurance" (para. 15)?

4. Why do religious people and politicians who become famous have a harder time than performers?

5. Although this article was not published recently, it references books about fame and celebrity that have served as a foundation for current studies. List all the books Loftus references, and determine their topic and purpose from the information that she provides.

VOCABULARY ACTIVITIES

1. Add any words from this article to your ongoing fame and celebrity glossary. Remember to write definitions in your own words.

2. How does Lasch define celebrity (para. 7)? What does his definition demonstrate about his attitude about the topic? How might someone else define celebrity differently? Write down a definition of celebrity from a different perspective.

SUMMARY ACTIVITY

Write a clear, one-sentence summary of each section of "The Other Side of Fame." Use the subheadings to get hints about the overall point of each part of the article. For more help with summary writing, see Chapter 1, Reading and Responding to College Texts, page 2.

DISCUSSION QUESTIONS

1. Most Americans are somewhat aware of the bad sides of being famous, but that doesn't seem to stop them from aspiring to be famous. Like River Phoenix, many young people think they are "immune" to the problems of fame (para. 64). Why do so many of us feel this way? Should the adult world try to discourage young people from seeking celebrity? Why or why not?

2. Brad Pitt has been quoted as saying that "being in the movies doesn't make you laugh any harder, or any less sad" (para. 23). Why is it so easy to forget that celebrities have typical human emotions like we do?

3. Do you agree that stars and celebrities have replaced older types of heroes, like military, political, and religious leaders? If so, why do you think that is? If you disagree, what examples and evidence can you give to counter Loftus's claim?

4. Do the benefits of fame and celebrity outweigh the downsides? Why or why not?

BOOK

Jake Halpern is a prolific writer whose works spans several genres: magazine journalism, radio, fiction, and book-length nonfiction. Educated at Yale University, Halpern dropped the suit-and-tie cubicle life as a young man to pursue writing. This selection is excerpted from his book *Fame Junkies: The Hidden Truths behind America's Favorite Addiction* (2007), which served to launch an original radio series on National Public Radio. This chapter posits a difference between "old fame," which was based on accomplishments and talents, and "new fame," which is based on self-promotion and self-branding and not necessarily on accomplishments, outside of sports and acting or modeling. *Important words and phrases have been italicized in this reading. Look up those you do not know, and write the definitions in your personal vocabulary list.*

practice it   Pre-Reading

Make a list of ten to fifteen famous people and then group them into two categories: those born before 1950 and those born after 1950. If you don't have any born before 1950, brainstorm a few more people. What do you notice about the two groups? What types of things are the pre-1950 people famous for doing? What types of things are the post-1950 people famous for? Reflect on the list you have generated. What does your list tell us about contemporary fame?

Jake Halpern

THE DESIRE TO BELONG: WHY EVERYONE WANTS TO HAVE DINNER WITH PARIS HILTON AND 50 CENT

I got a chance to talk on the phone with one of my longtime heroes, "the Edge," who is the lead guitarist for the band U2. His ambivalence about celebrity struck me immediately. "After our *Joshua Tree* album, we were as famous as you could be in music," he said, "and frankly, it was kind of overpowering for a while, but it really wasn't that interesting. If anything, it was something we tried to downplay. I don't think we ever *really* wanted celebrity, in and of itself, because we came out of the whole punk-rock thing, which was all about tearing that system down."

More than anything else, he said, fame was a kind of psychological torment for the band, especially in the beginning. "Early on, we were kind of overwhelmed by it," he explained. "At the big U2 concerts we were really just hanging on to make it through. There was an element of desperation in which we were just trying to focus on our music. And if we got seduced by fame, I think our version of that was being too self-conscious, taking ourselves a little too seriously, and wondering, *Did we measure up? Were we a good enough band? Were we really able to do this?*" According to the Edge, fame's effect on the band was the opposite of a high—it induced a kind of low in which they constantly questioned themselves. Apparently, it had taken them years to outgrow this.

"I think now we are a little older, and we don't beat ourselves up quite so much," he said. "We feel extremely fortunate to have such great fans and to have written some great songs. Now, without being *complacent*, we're really enjoying what we're doing in a way that we probably wouldn't have earlier on, when there was an element of struggle, and nothing was ever good enough. We were always trying to reach beyond our abilities. We still do that now, but we also accept that we have certain limitations. It just gets to a point where you go, 'This is me. I am not everything I would like to be as an artist, but that doesn't mean I don't have anything worth saying.'"

We chatted about celebrity and the emptiness of fame for almost an hour. The *irony* of this whole episode was that as soon as our conversation was over, I felt compelled to call a number of my friends and tell them I had just talked with the Edge. I was especially excited because he had offered me two tickets and backstage passes for U2's concert in Boston the following evening. For the next thirty-six hours I actually walked around under the blissful *delusion* that he and I were on the verge of becoming pals. On some level I realized that I was falling into the very trap I was meant to be objectively observing, but it made no difference. In my heart I admit that I felt thrilled, privileged, and special.

The following evening, before the concert started, I made my way backstage. It was a mob scene. The small concrete room was crawling with people—doctors, business executives, schoolteachers, fashion models, and more than a few squealing children, all of whom had a connection to someone in the band. Needless to say, I never got even close to the Edge. I felt completely deflated. I also worried about what I would say to the friends I'd told about my budding *rapport* with him. Eventually I shook off my *malaise*, and enjoyed one of the best concerts I've ever attended. Still, somewhere deep down, well beyond the reach of rational thought, lurked a hunger that left me feeling supremely uncomfortable.

5

Why was I so desperate to talk to the Edge that night? For that matter, why did people in general *pine* to bond with and befriend celebrities? The answer may be found in something called Belongingness Theory. Some research psychologists have come to believe that the need to belong is every bit as urgent as the need for food and shelter. Supporters of this theory contend that the desire to belong is actually humankind's driving psychological force. As they see it, Freudian theories about sexuality are compelling, but not nearly as important as the *primal* yearning for social acceptance.

Belongingness Theory is rooted in evolution. It holds that humans who formed groups in ancient times increased their chances of survival and reproduction. When it came to hunting large animals or defending the campfire against *marauders*, groups fared better. Anthropologists point out that groups were *resilient* in a way that individuals weren't, because their members could spread out and offer a number of services, such as hunting, firewood gathering, and even healing. Groups are especially important for children. Those who stayed close to the group probably received more food, care, and protection. Perhaps most important, at least in terms of evolution, adults in groups were more likely to find mates, reproduce, and form long-term parental relationships, increasing the chances that their children would reach maturity and reproduce themselves.

Belongingness Theory posits that over time, evolution has created a sort of internal mechanism that makes us crave social acceptance. This mechanism prompts us to feel stressed when we are isolated and pleased when we interact with others. Some psychologists, including Jaak Panksepp, of the Medical College of Ohio at Toledo, claim that the formation of social relationships actually stimulates the production of opioids—chemicals in the brain that make us feel pleasure. Panksepp goes so far as to say that "social affect and social bonding are in some fundamental neurochemical sense opioid addictions." In other words, what started as a basic survival mechanism has evolved into an addiction to natural chemicals that our bodies release whenever we socialize.

This has direct implications for how we react to famous actors and even to the fictional characters they portray on television and in the movies. I've always been a fan of the TV show *Cheers*. In fact, not far from where I live in Boston, there is a sign for the bar Cheers, and I'm frequently tempted to stop in and have a beer at the place where Norm, Cliff, Carla, and Sam hung out—only it's not the place where they hung out, because *that place* never really even existed except on some Hollywood back lot.

Evidently, I've formed what research psychologists call a "para- 10
social" relationship with the characters on the show. The notion of
such a relationship was first discussed by two psychologists, Donald
Horton and R. Richard Wohl, in a 1956 article for the journal *Psychiatry*.
They argued that television gives viewers "the illusion of a face-to-face
relationship with the performer." Over the course of many episodes,
viewers come to feel that they know a given performer or a fictional
persona. Horton and Wohl write:

> The persona offers, above all, a continuing relationship. His appear-
> ance is a regular and dependable event, to be counted on, planned
> for, and integrated into the routines of daily life. His devotees "live
> with him" and share the small episodes of his public life—and to
> some extent even of his private life away from the show. Indeed,
> their continued association with him acquires a history. . . . In time,
> the devotee—the "fan"—comes to believe that he "knows" the per-
> sona more intimately and profoundly than others do.

There are numerous examples of this phenomenon. Soap-opera
viewers send flowers and condolence cards to TV studios when a favorite
character is injured or killed in a tragic episode. Hordes of "Trekkies"
obsess over Captain Kirk, Mr. Spock, and the other fictional personae
on *Star Trek*. Perhaps the most extreme example involves Robert Young,
the actor who starred in the series *Marcus Welby, MD*. In the early 1970s,
during his first five years on the show, he received some 250,000 letters
from viewers, most of them asking for medical advice.

One important thing that has changed since the 1950s, when Horton and Wohl introduced their theory, is that we (the public) can now
know as much about the personal lives of our favorite stars as we do
about the fictional lives they portray on TV and in the movies. In the
early 2000s, for example, fans could follow the romantic entangle-
ments of Rachel Green on the TV show *Friends*, and they could also
then watch *Access Hollywood*, or pick up a copy of *Us Weekly*, to catch
up on the love life of Jennifer Aniston, who played Rachel. According
to Robert Thompson, of Syracuse University, the upshot of this is it is
now easier than ever to form para-social relationships—not just with
fictional personae but with actual celebrities as well. It all comes down
to access, Thompson says, and the venues that offer glimpses into the
lives of celebrities—magazines, books, Web sites, online chat rooms,
radio and TV talk shows—seem endless.

"Just look at the rise in TV talk shows," Thompson says. "In the six-
ties you had just a few TV talk-show hosts, like Johnny Carson and Dick
Cavett, who interviewed celebrities, whereas nowadays—especially

with cable and satellite channels—you've got dozens of these hosts interviewing every last celebrity. You've got Oprah Winfrey, David Letterman, Jay Leno, Carson Daly, Conan O'Brien, Ellen DeGeneres, Jon Stewart, Martha Stewart, Jenny Jones, Jimmy Kimmel, Montel Williams, Maury Povich, Jerry Springer, Ricki Lake, Rosie O'Donnell, Sally Jessy Raphael, Tony Danza, Tyra Banks—and the list goes on." All these hosts offer us a chance to meet celebrities "being themselves," he says.

Another major change since the 1950s is that Americans now appear to be lonelier than ever. In his book *The Loss of Happiness in Market Democracies*, the Yale political scientist Robert Lane notes that the number of people who described themselves as lonely more than quadrupled in the past few decades. We have increasingly become a nation of loners—traveling salesmen, Web designers, phone-bank operators, and online day traders who live and work in isolation. According to the U.S. Census Bureau, we also marry later in life. In 1956 the median age for marriage was 22.5 for men and 20.1 for women; by 2004 it was 27.4 for men and 25.8 for women. This helps to explain something else the Census Bureau has noted: Americans are increasingly living alone. The share of American households including seven or more people dropped from 35.9 percent in 1790, 5.8 percent in 1950, and 1.2 percent in 2004. Meanwhile, the number of households consisting of just one person rose from 3.7 percent in 1790 to 9.3 percent in 1950 and 26.4 percent in 2004. Nowadays, one out of four American households consists of a single person. In recent years this trend has been especially discernible among young people. Since 1970 the number of youths (ages fifteen to twenty-five) living alone has almost tripled, and the number of young adults (ages twenty-five to thirty-four) living alone has more than quadrupled.

The combination of loneliness and our innate desire to belong 15 may be fueling our interest in celebrities and our tendency to form para-social relationships with them. Only a few research psychologists have seriously explored this possibility, among them Lynn McCutcheon and Dianne Ashe. McCutcheon and Ashe compared results from 150 subjects who had taken three personality tests—one measuring shyness, one measuring loneliness, and one measuring celebrity obsession, on something called the Celebrity Attitudes Scale, or CAS. The CAS asks subjects to rate the veracity of statements such as "I am obsessed by details of my favorite celebrity's life" and "If I were lucky enough to meet my favorite celebrity, and he/she asked me to do something illegal as a favor, I would probably do it." McCutcheon and Ashe found a *correlation* among scores on loneliness, shyness, and the CAS. Their results led McCutcheon to observe in a subsequent paper, "Perhaps one of the ways [we] cope with shyness and loneliness is to cultivate a 'safe,' non-threatening relationship with a celebrity."

Another investigation, led by Jacki Fitzpatrick, of Texas Tech University, looked at the correlation between para-social relationships and actual romantic relationships. Fitzpatrick asked forty-five college students to complete a questionnaire containing several psychological measures, including one that gauged para-social relationships (the Para-social Interaction Scale) and another that gauged romantic relationships (the Multiple Determinants of Relationship Commitment Inventory). She and her colleague, Andrea McCourt, discovered that subjects who were less invested in their romantic relationships were more involved in para-social relationships. They concluded, "It makes sense that individuals may use para-social relationships as one way to fulfill desires or address needs (e.g., for attention, companionship) that are unmet in their romances."

The Rochester survey, too, provides evidence that lonely teenagers are especially susceptible to forming para-social relationships with celebrities. Boys who described themselves as lonely were almost twice as likely as others to endorse the statement "My favorite celebrity just helps me feel good and forget about all of my troubles." Girls who described themselves as lonely were almost three times as likely as others to endorse that statement.

Another survey question asked teens whom they would most like to meet for dinner: Jesus Christ, Albert Einstein, Shaquille O'Neal, Jennifer Lopez, 50 Cent, Paris Hilton, or President Bush. Among boys who said they were not lonely, the clear winner was Jesus Christ; but among those who described themselves as lonely, Jesus finished last and 50 Cent was the clear winner. Similarly, girls who felt appreciated by their parents, friends, and teachers tended to choose dinner with Jesus, whereas those who felt underappreciated were likely to choose Paris Hilton. One possible interpretation of these results is that lonely and underappreciated teens particularly want to befriend the ultimate popular guy or girl.

For the older generation, that guy was Steve McQueen; nowadays he appears to be 50 Cent. Regardless of who exactly this figure is at a given time, it's clear that many of us—lonely people in particular—yearn to belong to the popular crowd.

I also got to know a Hollywood publicist named Michael Levine. I'd 20 first seen Levine on television as Michael Jackson's publicist during Jackson's first child-molestation scandal, in the early 1990s. He'd been in the business more than twenty years, representing quite a few stars, and had written a number of books on public relations, including *Charming Your Way to the Top: Hollywood's Premier PR Executive Shows You How to Get Ahead*, and *Raise Your Social I.Q: How to Do the Right Thing in Any Situation*.

Levine and I met for tea one afternoon at the Century Plaza Hotel in Los Angeles. We found each other in the hotel's soaring, sun-drenched lobby, where a pianist in a tuxedo played soft jazz while a *svelte* waitress whose nametag read "Queenie" served drinks to tourists *laden* with Gucci and Versace shopping bags. Levine was a tall, handsome man in his midfifties with watery blue eyes, an aquiline nose, and a shock of gray hair slicked back with gel.

When we shook hands, he greeted me loudly, as if he were greeting everyone in our section of the lobby. I quickly discovered that Levine had two modes of speaking. The first was his broadcast mode, in which he spoke with the volume and authority of a courtroom lawyer. The second was his intimate mode, in which he drew close, made unwavering eye contact, and spoke in a hushed manner as if letting me in on a secret that was far too sensitive for public consumption. His intimate voice was rare, and when he used it, I had the impression I might be speaking with Michael Levine the person.

"Are you familiar with my Tiffany's theory?" he asked as we sat down.

I told him I wasn't.

Levine cleared his throat and explained. "If I visit you today and 25 give you a present, and I give it to you in a Tiffany's box, in your mind the gift that I gave you has a higher perceived value than if I gave it to you in *no* box or a box of lesser prestige. The reason that's true is not because you are a psychological jackass"—he smiled briefly, presumably to convey that no offense was intended—"but because you and I and your wife and this waitress live in a culture in which we gift-wrap everything. We gift-wrap our politicians, our corporate heads, our TV and movie stars, and even our toilet paper."

"So you see yourself as gift-wrapping celebrities?"

"Yes," he replied. "That is the analogy."

When I asked him to clarify one aspect of his theory, he responded by asking which of the ninety-nine words I wanted him to repeat. I said I'd like to hear the entire theory again. Levine nodded, gathered himself for a minute, and then repeated his words *verbatim*, with the same seemingly *nonchalant* facial expressions and hand gestures he'd used before. Clearly, this was a man who had perfected the art of speaking in sound bites; I began to worry that he wasn't going to tell me anything he hadn't already composed, edited, and delivered dozens of times before.

Nonetheless, I pressed on, and asked Levine how he had become, as his books claimed, "Hollywood's premier PR executive."

"The arc of anyone's career . . . ," he began, and then paused to 30 reconsider his approach. "Scratch that," he said. "Yours is a multidimensional question. Is it luck? Is it timing? Is it skill? I'm not sure, but I have represented some of the most successful people in the world." He paused again and then rattled off the following names in rapid-fire succession: "Michael Jackson, Charlton Heston, Nancy Kerrigan, Demi Moore, Michael J. Fox, Sandra Bullock, David Bowie, Prince, Kareem Abdul-Jabbar, Jon Stewart, Dave Chappelle, Cameron Diaz, Bill O'Reilly, Ozzy Osbourne, Bob Evans, and Barbra Streisand. I learned something very important when I was working for Barbra Streisand on New Year's Eve. It was an event at the MGM in Las Vegas, and she hadn't performed in many years—two decades, actually—and right at midnight, or perhaps twelve-thirty, she asked me whether I could find her some plum sauce. Plum sauce—like you get in a Chinese restaurant. And I figured something out real quick. When Barbra Streisand asks you for plum sauce on New Year's Eve in Las Vegas, 'No' is a really bad answer. And 'I don't know' is a really bad answer. 'Yes,' however, is a really good answer. You've got to figure that out! And the higher you get, the harder it gets. The demands get more intensified."

I asked him how he, as a professional at the top of his field, coped with such demands.

"This is a question that goes through your head at the beginning of your career," he admitted in a quiet voice. "But I want you to understand: Getting someone plum sauce in Las Vegas at midnight on New Year's Eve is challenging, but it's not murder. It's not so ludicrous. And professionals who work at the top of their field in the fame game realize that this is simply part of the game."

In the end, Levine said, any misgivings he had about occasionally being asked to fetch plum sauce were far outweighed by the status he gained in performing such duties. "Look," he said, "I've seen strangers look at Mike Tyson and say, 'What a scumbag, what a vermin, what a douche bag.' Then, as he gets closer, they start getting excited. And then, three minutes later, they want their picture taken with him. Fame is a validator. The conflict is that I want it. You want it. We all want it—or want to be close to it. But what is the price? It's the *Faustian* bargain. You see what I mean? Celebrities offer you the drug of validation, but you can't talk straight to the pusher, or you won't get your drag. That's the deal."

Hollywood, like Washington, D.C., is known for being an insular company town where everybody competes for recognition, status, and, above all, proximity. In Washington it is commonly said that your status can be measured by how many degrees of separation exist between you and the president; in Hollywood the same is often said of Jack Nicholson or Steven Spielberg.

One could argue that this fight for *proximity*, in which we strive to   35 *ingratiate* ourselves with famous and prestigious people, goes well beyond those power vortexes and plays itself out in many corners of America. Perhaps the best example of this can be found in studies on the social dynamics of cheerleaders. According to the sociologists Pamela Bettis and Natalie Adams, 3.3 million people participate in cheerleading each year. They observe, "Numerous scholars have documented that cheerleading is often perceived as the highest-status activity for girls in middle school, and girls who cheer often occupy positions of power, prestige, and privilege in their schools."

In a landmark study Donna Eder examined the social dynamics of cheerleaders at an unspecified middle school in the Midwest. Eder and several research assistants spent more than a year interviewing students during lunch, between classes, and at special after-school events such as dances and picnics. In the process Eder identified an elite group—composed primarily of cheerleaders—that most of the other girls wanted to join. The members of this elite group were typically referred to as the "popular girls" by the rest of the students. According to Eder, these girls commanded the school's attention. Eder observed that girls throughout the school discussed the activities of the popular girls, but the popular girls paid almost no attention to anyone but themselves. She also noted that non-cheerleaders often went to great lengths to *ingratiate* themselves with the cheerleaders:

> Many of the girls wanted to sit with the cheerleaders at lunch and made special attempts to be friendly toward them. For example, when it looked as though cheerleading might be eliminated from the school budget, Sylvia made a point of telling Carrie, one of the new cheerleaders, that she had written a letter to President Reagan telling him how important cheerleading was for school spirit and how hard some of her friends had worked to become cheerleaders. Also, if one of the new cheerleaders was upset about something, there were usually many girls around to comfort her.

Eder concluded that there were "two main avenues for mobility into the elite group—becoming a cheerleader or becoming a friend of a cheerleader." But few cheerleading positions were ever available, so all the other girls engaged in a desperate race to befriend the school's pompom-toting elite. The upshot of all this, observed Eder, is that teenage girls often become more self-conscious and preoccupied with being liked.

The social lives of cheerleaders and celebrities are strikingly similar. Both groups consist of and are defined by two types of people: the "stars," who appear talented, glamorous, and popular; and the "*acolytes*," who strive to endear themselves to the stars. The question is: What exactly motivates the acolytes? To a certain extent, Belongingness Theory explains why so many of us yearn to belong to groups in general, but not why we prefer these highly prestigious groups above all others, or why we toil to ingratiate ourselves with the leaders of these groups.

Francisco Gil-White, an evolutionary anthropologist at the University of Pennsylvania, offers one explanation. In 2001 he and a colleague, Joseph Henrich, of Emory University, proposed the idea of Prestige Theory. The core of the theory is based on the notion that humans—unlike chimps, orangutans, and other primates—have the unique ability to learn and perfect highly *nuanced* skills. Perhaps the best example of this involves an experiment conducted by two Emory *primatologists*, Josep Call and Michael Tomasello, who tested and compared the learning abilities of adult orangutans and four-year-old humans. According to Call and Tomasello, orangutans have a reputation among primatologists for being skillful problem solvers. To test just how clever they were, the researchers built a small contraption that dispensed M&M chocolate candies. It had a long steel handle that could be pushed, pulled, or rotated. During the experiment a researcher would manipulate the handle in a combination of ways, and if the orangutan successfully mimicked this motion, it received an M&M. Call and Tomasello discovered that the adult orangutans were not nearly as successful as the four-year-old humans at doing this. They concluded that orangutans "did not use imitative learning to help them solve the problem presented," whereas children "did use their observations of the demonstrations to help them solve the task."

Gil-White and Henrich relied on experiments like this one to argue that only humans have the ability to observe and then mimic complex behaviors. They claim that this uniquely human ability eventually created "prestige hierarchies" in which those with the most valuable skills sat at the top. So when a truly talented hunter emerged in prehistoric times, he was revered both because he brought home food and because his skill could be learned. *Disciples* soon gravitated toward this hunter. They "paid" for access by doing favors for him, excusing him from certain obligations, and siding with him politically. Posses of studious disciples eventually formed. According to Gil-White and Henrich, these posses served as *beacons*, allowing hungry tribe members to identify a mentor, learn a skill, and begin feeding themselves as quickly as possible.

The premise of Prestige Theory is that it has been evolutionary advantageous for human beings to identify prestigious people and befriend them in order to gain skills. In ancient times the disciple of a successful hunter stood a better chance of surviving, having children, and then feeding them. By this rationale, over the *millennia astute* disciples have flourished. But perhaps even more interesting is the notion that human beings have developed a conditioned response to entourages. In theory, at least, we are genetically predisposed to identifying posses of admirers and gravitating toward the leaders (or people with the skills) because historically this is how our ancestors survived and reproduced. So when Michael Levine fetches plum sauce for Barbra Streisand, or Sylvia tries to ingratiate herself with a "skilled" cheerleader, the invisible hand of evolution is simply pushing them along.

These instincts still help us in modern-day scenarios. In many work settings, for example, it pays to identify and endear oneself to the man or woman at the center of a posse of admirers. This allows one to learn valuable skills—today's equivalent of hunting school. But according to Gil-White, whom I interviewed, this goes all wrong when it comes to celebrities. When we see them on TV, we sense that they are at the center of a truly enormous entourage, so our conditioned "posse response" is activated, and we gravitate toward them. A few savvy operators, like Michael Levine, can actually find their way into the posse and become disciples or insiders. The overwhelming majority of us, however, can't. And we are the real losers in this scenario because we subconsciously attempt to ingratiate ourselves with our idols—buying Paris Hilton's jewelry and Nicole Kidman's perfume—without really gaining anything. In essence we are still chasing the great hunters; but, of course, most of these hunters have no interest in teaching us, and worse yet, many of them have little of real value to teach.

Whatever motivated Michael Levine to run errands for his famous clients, he at least had the satisfaction of knowing that he had been invited to the party.

practice it   Post-Reading Activity

This reading begins with Halpern's anecdote about his own brush with a celebrity. What other types of evidence does he give to support his points? Which types of evidence do you find most effective, and why?

COMPREHENSION QUESTIONS

1. What is Belongingness Theory? Find the definition in the chapter, and then rephrase it in your own words, using your own example.

2. What is a "para-social" relationship (para. 10), and how do we form para-social relationships with television characters or other celebrities?

3. According to Halpern, how does our loneliness contribute to our love of celebrities?

4. What is Prestige Theory? How does it apply, according to Halpern, to understanding the power of celebrity?

5. Why are we the "real losers" in our attempt to "ingratiate ourselves with our idols" (para. 42)? What do we lose, according to Halpern?

VOCABULARY ACTIVITIES

1. Add any words from this book excerpt to your ongoing fame and celebrity glossary. Remember to write definitions in your own words.

2. Halpern calls fame a "Faustian bargain" (para. 33). This is called an allusion, which means that the author alludes to a well-known outside text to make a point. However, if the reader does not understand the allusion, the point will be lost. Who was Faust? If you don't know, how would you find out? Figure out what this allusion means, and then analyze Halpern's use of it. Does the comparison seem appropriate? Why or why not?

SUMMARY ACTIVITY

Briefly summarize Halpern's argument about why we are addicted to stars, taking care to include the theories he relies on to make his argument. Keep your summary concise and objective. For more help with summary writing, see Chapter 1, Reading and Responding to College Texts, page 2.

DISCUSSION QUESTIONS

1. Reflect on Halpern's book title, *Fame Junkies: The Hidden Truths behind America's Favorite Addiction.* What do you think of the metaphor of addiction? How does celebrity addiction compare and contrast to more physical addictions?

2. Does the evidence Halpern gives convince you that, as he says, "Americans now appear to be lonelier than ever" (para. 14)? What types of evidence does he provide? How do you value that evidence, as compared to your own personal experiences and observations?

3. Think back to your own experience of high school. How effective is Halpern's comparison between celebrities and cheerleaders?

4. Presuming you agree with Halpern's argument that celebrity worship is caused by our desire to belong, what could be done to change our culture of celebrity worship? What else besides celebrity worship might help us feel like we "belong"?

BOOK

Drew Pinsky—or "Dr. Drew" as he is known in the world of television and radio—has hosted radio talk shows like *Loveline* and reality television shows such as *Celebrity Rehab*. He is also a psychiatrist and works as a professor of psychiatry at the University of Southern California, where he specializes in treating dependency issues. This selection is a chapter from his book *The Mirror Effect: How Celebrity Narcissism Is Seducing America* (2009), which offers his critique of the very world that he participates in on television. *Important words and phrases have been italicized in this reading. Look up those you do not know, and write the definitions in your personal vocabulary list.*

practice it   Pre-Reading

Think about Drew Pinsky's credibility as an author. What do you know about him that might influence your reading of this book chapter? Does his performance on reality television shows influence your views on his ethics or his expertise? What might his reasons be for writing a book that criticizes reality television, given that he has clearly profited from it financially and professionally?

Drew Pinsky

BROADCASTING YOURSELF

This is the true story . . . of seven strangers . . . picked to live in a house . . . work together and have their lives taped . . . to find out what happens when people stop being polite . . . and start getting real.

—The introduction to the MTV series *The Real World*

As a reality show producer, there are many times when things will happen and you will look at an edit and think, "Oh my gosh, this person is going to be devastated when they see this scene play out." I think it's damaging to their reputation or who they think they are. And what happens is, they see the scene, and they call you and say, "Oh my god! I loved that scene; it was amazing." . . . They're not worried about their reputation because it's catapulting them into fame. Any attention is good attention.

—L., reality TV producer

Both reality television and the Internet have been around for more than a decade. However, in the past five years the explosion of reality TV programming, combined with the widespread accessibility of the Internet, have reshaped the landscape of fame and dramatically influenced the public's relationship with celebrity. Celebrity has become *uncoupled* from talent or performance; today, being famous seems like a game anyone can play. And the price of admission, apparently, is to indulge in the same unregulated, often troubling, behavior that dominates reality TV and the Internet. The behavior modeled in those two *venues* can have different effects on different audiences. Some viewers take a celebrity's bad behavior as inspiration or license to act out in similar ways. Others may use it as an occasion to sit in self-righteous judgment, thereby *shoring* up their own weak self-esteem. Whatever the reaction, these two media are changing our relationship to celebrity in dramatic and potentially dangerous ways.

An important *precursor*, of today's explosion of reality TV shows was *The Real Word*, which *debuted* in 1992. The first season installed seven young people between the ages of seventeen and twenty-five in a Soho loft in Manhattan and rolled the cameras 24/7. One of the show's creators, Jon Murray, told Mark that the show was initially conceived to showcase the modern-day melting pot of youth culture, showing strangers from diverse backgrounds sorting out their differences and living together.

When *The Real World* premiered, no one knew if it was going to be a success. But from my radio experience I knew that the young audience at that time was craving a "really real," that is, authentic, mirror of their personal experiences. They wanted to be able to see their generation portrayed as they saw themselves. Teenagers were far more media *savvy* than they'd been in previous generations, and they'd become restless with traditional radio and TV programming, which they recognized as the product of an older generation trying to *pander* to their tastes. *The Real World resonated* with this audience, and over time it has provided an accurate, though amplified, reflection of the culture of young adults.

Early in the show's run, the cast members discussed, or hinted at, their housemates' more questionable behaviors in *titillating* confessionals, sharing their feelings with the camera (and us). Later, this behavior became more explicit: Cast members were shown acting out sexually, drinking heavily, even referring to their drug use. The unacknowledged fallout of such open discussions was that adolescent viewers, who strongly identified with the show's characters, were at risk of relating to this behavior without analyzing it. Whether it was Ruthie passing out from drinking, prompting the roommates to call paramedics (season eight); Steven, Trishelle, and Brynn's hot-tub threesome (season twelve); Davis and Tyrie's rage-filled blowout (season eighteen); or Joey's alcoholic rampage, his denial that he had a problem, his angrily blaming his housemates for his drinking, and his ultimately leaving the house to go to rehab (season twenty), these behaviors were portrayed without *framing* commentary. Beyond the fleeting reactions of the housemates themselves, no one ever clarified that such behavior was part of a *pathology*, or even hinted that it was troubling. And how did the culture at large respond? With a *resounding* shrug. *After all*, we seemed to say, *kids will be kids*.

As someone who came of age in the era of sex, drugs, and rock 'n' roll rebellion that followed the sexual revolution, I can understand why so many parents today are so reluctant to second-guess such imagery. They don't understand that while youthful experimentation can be normal, it can quickly spill into pathology. And parents are not given the information they need to know the difference. When I am evaluating an adolescent, I know that signs of mental illness can be expressed through obsession with one's body, sexual acting out, *volatile* anger, or excessive drinking or drug use. Unfortunately, it is precisely those behaviors that were highly valued in the parents' youthful rebellions of the 1960s and '70s, and that are glamorized in magazines and on TV today.

The same sorts of behavior, from obsession with one's body to sexual acting out to anger to excess drinking and drug use, are staples of reality show story lines today.

When callers on my radio shows bring up these types of behavior, I can explain why they are harmful and offer appropriate advice, often as a counterpoint to messages the caller has heard elsewhere in the culture. But when reality TV exploded, and viewers started watching such behaviors as entertainment, I became deeply worried. Reality was flooding a vulnerable audience with potentially damaging messages without offering any balancing commentary.

The success of *The Real World* marked a television *watershed*, but it was around the year 2000 that reality programming really exploded. The cable channels, and even the mainstream networks, jumped on the *bandwagon*, creating shows like *Who Wants to Marry a Multi-Millionaire*, *Big Brother*, *Survivor*, *The Amazing Race*, *The Simple Life*, and *America's Next Top Model*. There were many different types of reality show, and some generated spinoff after spinoff, but they all shared one hallmark: They exploited *narcissistic* behaviors for dramatic effect.

Competition shows like *Survivor*, *American Idol*, *America's Next Top Model*, *I'm a Celebrity . . . Get Me Out of Here!*, *The Apprentice*, *Project Runway*, *Dancing with the Stars*, *Hell's Kitchen*, and *Celebrity Circus* pit contestants in no-holds-barred battles for supremacy and financial reward. It's debatable whether talent has much to do with winning on these shows, but one thing is certain: They reward their contestants for being ruthless, *exploitative*, *authoritarian*, self-sufficient, and *vain*. It's hard to imagine anyone without a heavy reserve of narcissism carrying on after a dressing-down from one of their *acerbic* judges. Many of the shows, especially *Top Model* and *Celebrity Fit Club*, focus on body image, following their contestants as they obsess over their weight and appearance, and then subject themselves to potentially *withering* critique. Nearly all of them highlight bad behavior, giving extra camera time to cast members who blow up, break down, or, alternatively, scheme and conspire to grasp every advantage. As Omarosa Manigault-Stallworth, the villain of *The Apprentice*, told *Time*, "When I was a good girl, there were no cameras on. The minute I started arguing, there was a camera shooting me from every angle." Even the judges, from Donald Trump to Janice Dickinson to Paula Abdul, join in the divalike behavior. These shows invite the audience to indulge its own narcissistic feelings of superiority, whether by *jeering* at the TV screen in their living rooms or by posting *snide* commentary on the shows' Web sites.

Dating competition shows like *The Bachelor*, *The Bachelorette*, *Joe Millionaire*, and *Mr. Personality* combine all of the traits above, with more emphasis on sex and *treachery*. The figure at the center of the competition—the prize, as it were—is always extremely attractive and *charismatic*, carefully coached to appear sincere and vulnerable. On television, such figures become *idealized* romantic *idols*, even if in real life they're vain, arrogant, and *entitled*. One talent agent I know was repeatedly called by one of his clients, a former star of *The Bachelor*, who wanted to know why he wasn't being offered leading man roles in films. Though he'd never acted, he saw himself as the star of a romantic blockbuster. While people were paying him thousands of dollars to show up at a restaurant or a shopping mall, he couldn't understand why his agent couldn't get him a movie role.

There were plenty of dating shows in the early years, offering endless variations on the basic cat-and-mouse game. Dating voyeur shows like *Blind Date*, *Room Raiders*, and *Next* featured noncelebrities angling to hook up with sexy contestants—no promise of deeper relationships here—in a hot-tub stew of competition, outrageous behavior, and sexploitation. A series of *surreal* celebrity-bachelor shows, including *Flavor of Love*, *I Love New York*, *Rock of Love*, and *A Shot at Love with Tila Tequila* blended the house-of-misfit-toys *absurdism* of *The Surreal Life* with the spectacle of unconventional romance featuring such *eccentric* characters as rapper Flavor Flav, Poison lead singer Bret Michaels, and the so-called reality star known as New York. And parental boundaries were thrown out the window in the surprisingly *robust subgenre* of shows like *Meet My Folks*, *Date My Mom*, *Who Wants to Marry My Dad?*, and *Parental Control*, in which parents and children judged each other's dates for entertainment value.

Shows like *The Simple Life*, *The Surreal Life*, *Newlyweds: Nick and Jessica*, *Tommy Lee Goes to College*, *Hogan Knows Best*, and *Tori & Dean: Inn Love* invite audiences to laugh at celebrities in fish-out-of-water situations. Whether it's watching Paris and Nicole work on a dairy farm or Tommy Lee at marching band practice, the last laugh is usually on the audience: In most cases, the celebrities *flaunt* their narcissistic superiority, determined to prove that they're different from, that is, better than, the average folks who surround them. The audience might have enjoyed the spectacle of Paris and Nicole *bungling* the normal tasks they were assigned, but after an episode's worth of juvenile *sabotage*, stubbornness, and whining, Paris and Nicole just returned to their glamorous lives. Jessica and Nick weren't fish out of water, exactly, but Jessica's dumb-girl *antics* were a riff on the Paris-and-Nicole act, and the show somehow managed to make Jessica seem idiotic while preserving her glamorous *aura*. The point of these programs was to showcase celebrities being themselves, in other words, to document how narcissistic personalities cope with everyday life. They gave viewers an opportunity to indulge their own feelings of envy or superiority toward the celebrities, while flattering viewers by letting them in on the celebrities' little joke on the rest of the world.

A whole host of narcissistic traits—extreme self-importance, inflated sense of specialness, vanity, envy, and entitlement—come into play in diva shows like *Gastineau Girls*, *My Super Sweet 16*, *Real Housewives of Orange County*, *Kimora: Life in the Fab Lane*, and *Keeping Up with the Kardashians*. These shows offer hope to all narcissistic viewers who ever dreamed that fame, or even just *ostentatious* wealth, could be theirs simply by demanding it. The people who succeed on these shows appear to have little use for education, hard work, or the discipline of climbing a career ladder. Instead, they pout, throw tantrums, stomp their feet, manipulate friends, family, and coworkers, and otherwise act out, all while *wallowing* in the lap of luxury.

A similar narcissistic drive is the *subtext* of body-image shows such as *Dr. 90210*, *The Biggest Loser*, *The Swan*, *Look-a-Like*, *I Want a Famous Face*, and *Celebrity Fit Club*. These programs glorify the improvement of the body—by any means necessary. Unfortunately for most of the contestants, though, such extreme makeovers couldn't possibly solve the problems that may have driven them to the show in the first place. These shows may motivate some viewers to make positive changes in their lives, but for more vulnerable individuals their preoccupation with appearance, and the fantastic promise that internal struggles can be solved by external changes, risk triggering other harmful behavior, including eating disorders or other damaging habits.

The most *malicious* reality shows, however, are the train-wreck 15 series: *The Anna Nicole Show*, *The Osbournes*, *Britney and Kevin: Chaotic*, *Breaking Bonaduce*, and *Hey Paula*, in which unstable individuals' lives and *interpersonal* chaos are served up as entertainment. Several of these shows, especially *Anna Nicole* and *The Osbournes*, got huge attention when they debuted. Yet there was little public outcry about what their stars' behavior suggested about their own mental health. In many cases, the stars of these shows were deeply in trouble. It's appalling that their behavior was broadcast without acknowledging all the circumstances underlying their *dysfunction*. When *Celebrity Rehab* was created, I told VH1 producers that my goal was to do exactly the opposite of these shows: to *humanize* the celebrities we would feature, and to use the show to explain what really was behind the participants' outrageous and *inconceivable* behavior.

I was fortunate that VH1 was on board with my goals for the show. Perhaps my insistence on the importance of providing context to the sometimes unrestrained and incomprehensible behavior of addicts hit home with them, as VH1 had only recently completed the *grueling* experience of filming Danny Bonaduce's reality show, *Breaking Bonaduce*.

The producers certainly had some *inkling* of what they were getting into when they built a show around the former child actor: Bonaduce's long struggle with drugs, his police record, and his history of violence were no secret, and they were all red flags for an unstable personality. The producers were forced to walk a fine line as they decided how much "reality" they could present in the absence of full context of the behavior. The footage was often raw, and sometimes frightening. As viewers watched, Bonaduce hit bottom in real time— abusing drugs including steroids, harming himself, and unleashing violent and uncensored emotion on those around him.

In a *New York Daily News* interview, Bonaduce talks about what was really going on during filming—the downward spiral of his life brought about by a return to abusing alcohol before the cameras even started rolling. "If I had known that I was going to *implode*," Bonaduce told the reporter, "I would never in a million years have done [the show]."

But by the time VH1 producers tried to pull the plug on filming, Bonaduce admitted that his regular cocktail of prescription drugs and alcohol had left him powerless to *temper* his behavior. "When VH1 said, 'We think you're probably going to die and we don't want to film you dying,'" said Bonaduce, "I said, 'What kind of TV show quits when the lead is going to die?' I thought the death of a B-lister on tape would be pretty cool. . . . Plus I wouldn't have to muscle through this crap anymore, and I'd be James Dean. Anyone can die in a car crash. It takes a special guy to actually be the car crash."

In the end, Bonaduce didn't die and the producers ran with the 20 raw, and in this case, unscripted reality. What emerged was a painful and eye-opening look at a troubled soul in the grip of personal demons. In the end, Bonaduce's decision to seek therapy for his addictions, psychological problems, and in the hopes of saving his marriage, revelations about his abusive childhood may have encouraged at-risk viewers who identified with certain of his behaviors to seek professional help. This type of audience response has been typical of the reaction to *Celebrity Rehab*, with new patients showing up for treatment and saying they had been motivated by seeing a celebrity they admired going through the process of rehab.

Most recently, the exploitative qualities of reality TV have been heightened in a host of next-generation shows, including *The Ashlee Simpson Show*, *Living Lohan*, and *Rock the Cradle*, in which the children or younger siblings of celebrities *vie* for their chance at the spotlight, often at the manipulative direction of parents, who are clearly acting out their own narcissistic tendencies through their *grandiose* promotion of their families.

Even noncelebrity reality shows tend to exploit dysfunctional behavior. Family counseling shows like *Wife Swap*, *Nanny 911*, *Shalom in the Home*, and *The Baby Borrowers* all promise to shed light on common family struggles, and offer advice to those at home struggling with similar issues. Yet even these shows thrive on exploiting dysfunctional behavior—without ever exploring the complexities of the situations—and in so doing they allow viewers to sit in self-righteous judgment of these unfortunate families.

Whatever the genre, the formula for a successful reality show has long been clear: The more *outlandish* the behavior, the more successful the show. As Ellis Cashmore points out in his book *Celebrity/Culture*, "Reality television tended to turn its characters' *vices* into *virtues*, so that people who displayed ignorance, dishonesty or some other kind of *depravity* became praiseworthy."

Reality shows have influenced more than their viewers' notions that anyone could become a celebrity. They have promoted a new *ethos* of morality, in which superficial hooking up and intoxicated *improprieties* become *rites of passage*. The subtext of constant interpersonal drama speaks directly to the young viewers who personally relate to the conflicts being played out in each episode: *I am important. My problems are more important than yours. So watch me.*

Reality TV requires *complicity* from its audience. Viewers must 25 willingly suspend disbelief to indulge in a fantasy that's portrayed as reality. How else can we explain the guilty pleasure of watching *pseudo-reality* shows like the MTV series *The Hills*? When Mark asked his students at USC why they watched the show, they said they knew it was scripted, and admitted that the dialogue often seemed forced, but they insisted that parts of the show still resonated with their actual lives. And it's these small pieces of truth that make the show feel real and *compel* them to keep watching, even as they feel guilty about it. This goes a long way toward explaining the popularity of reality shows: Viewers can easily project themselves and their lives onto characters and situations that, however extreme, have a kernel of realness that triggers an emotional, and often narcissistic, response.

Anyone watching reality TV should keep in mind that it's not just the circumstances on these shows that make the cast members behave as they do. Nor, for that matter, is it a matter of personality, dysfunctional or not. One hidden element in every reality show is the influence of the producers, who manipulate the environment constantly to keep the contestants feeling unsettled and challenged, to encourage conflict and thus create drama. The result should really be called *hyper-reality* TV, since what it offers is a parade of reactions *coaxed* out of fragile people in extreme circumstances.

When we're watching a reality show, even one of the many that involve extreme circumstances—strangers locked in a house together, or stranded far from civilization, or engaged in ruthless competition under the *guise* of pursuing a relationship—it's easy to overlook the fact that we're also watching sick people struggle with very real problems. Having served as a consultant to several reality shows, I know what the producers are looking for in contestants. The standards regarding mental health are extremely *fluid*. In some cases, as long as the psychological evaluations indicate that contestants are unlikely to seriously harm themselves or others, they're good to go. If they're psychologically disturbed enough to create some real drama, so much the better. As far as reality shows are concerned, emotionally healthy, stable people just don't make "good TV."

The purpose of drama has always been to examine the human emotional condition through *allegory*, and today reality TV *purports* to fill this role, but there are *subtler*, and more dangerous, forces at work here as well. After all, one of the *hallmarks* of narcissism is a lack of *empathy*, so it's highly unlikely that either participants in the shows or viewers with narcissistic tendencies could ever learn any real lessons about the human condition from these chaotic reality story lines. Certainly the cast members themselves tend to react to conflict in a typically narcissistic fashion, often with an immediate, intense, even violent response and the certainty that their point of view is the only perspective worth considering. While this may make for high-tension television, presenting such behavior as reality allows the audience to validate their own preexisting narcissistic responses and encourages them to mirror the behavior in their own lives.

The *phenomenon* of reality TV has certainly *democratized* fame, but by normalizing narcissistic behaviors on a public stage, it has also fueled narcissism among everyday people. Reality television has a great capacity for taking challenging, even tragic dysfunctions and making them seem glamorous and even beneficial. When night after night we watch the "real" people on these shows become famous for acting out, drinking, using drugs, engaging in hypersexual behavior, indulging in *exhibitionism*, *flaunting* their vanity and *entitlement*, or drawing attention through self-harming actions, it's easy to conclude that the road to fame is paved with bad behavior. And when we realize that few of these individuals ever suffer consequences for these actions, it only seems to prove that celebrity offers special protections to the famous. That's a powerfully seductive message, particularly to vulnerable audience members *predisposed* to narcissistic thinking.

One of the earliest reality-show blockbusters, *Big Brother*, also became   30 the first to exploit the power of the Internet to *lure* audiences by promising to make them part of the show. At first, the appeal was that the online content was only subject to a twelve-second delay before it was transmitted. The nightly ninety-minute shows were lightly edited to meet broadcast standards, but watching online gave the viewer the voyeuristic chance to witness behavior, like nudity or sex, that would be edited from the TV broadcast. Another aspect of the online episodes proved even more attractive.

What the *Big Brother* producers hit upon was a way to allow viewers to participate actively in a reality-show community via the Internet. Before long, the interactions of the people who visited the Web site were as interesting as the program itself. *Big Brother* also used the Internet to give the audience power over the outcome of the show by allowing them to vote off cast members. The audience now had two ways of participating in reality shows: Those who weren't lucky enough to become contestants could nevertheless indulge their judgmental side to knock down those who were. For the first time, narcissistic individuals had a direct way to act out their feelings toward the characters on one of their favorite shows.

This came at a time when other cultural trends had already begun weakening the boundaries between public and private, redefining the meaning of exhibitionism and creating new kinds of celebrity. President Bill Clinton exposed his private life to scrutiny: first willingly, as he took personal questions from MTV viewers (boxers or briefs?), then less so when his behavior in office led to a blistering inquiry into his extramarital affairs. A flood of personal tell-all memoirs, dubbed *reality literature* by some critics, became a growing trend. The talk shows of the 1980s and '90s, hosted by Geraldo Rivera, Sally Jessy Raphael, Maury Povich, Montel Williams, Ricki Lake, Jenny Jones, and Jerry Springer, specialized in *probing* the deeply dysfunctional lives of their guests. For an audience eager to experience a supposedly real moment of *illicit* behavior, reality TV transformed voyeurism into a mainstream hobby, and created modern-day celebrities out of ordinary individuals whose high levels of exhibitionism were perfect *fodder* for constant *scrutiny* and commentary.

Then the world went online. In its short life as a public phenomenon, the Internet has proven its enormous potential to transform our culture in ways we're only beginning to understand. It has already changed journalism, *commerce*, communication, research, and entertainment. It has been welcomed by some quarters of society for its ability to spread information quickly and democratically, and *scorned* by others for the platform it offered to more *insidious* forces, from Internet scams to pornography.

In particular, when broadband Internet access became widespread, it gave young people the opportunity to project their own images, in words, music, photographs, and video, to unknown viewers the world over. In less than a decade, this has had enormous, and troubling, implications for young people who were vulnerable to exploitation.

By the early 2000s, a handful of entrepreneurs recognized the potential to use this technology to create an entirely new form of communication and began creating what became known as social networking sites. First Friendster, then MySpace and Facebook, allowed their members, at that time predominantly young women and men looking for connection, to create Web pages on which they could share personal information, photos, and running commentary about their lives. These unmonitored sites invited users to create new *personae* whose connection with their real lives were often *tenuous* at best, a high-tech version of what psychiatric professionals call a *pseudo-self*, a classic social coping mechanism among narcissists. And the perceived goal of these sites was to connect with others by "friending" them, thus establishing an *ambiguous*, but *alluring*, connection with strangers who might be hiding behind false fronts of their own.

Beyond the social networks, other platforms offered more specialized ways for vulnerable users to share their private worlds with strangers, often without any adult supervision. YouTube and Flickr allowed users to post video and still images (respectively) of whatever they wanted, making them accessible to anyone in the world. Twitter offered users the chance to share their experiences in brief instant messages up to

140 characters long, perfect for a generation already accustomed to IM'ing and text-messaging on their computers and phones. Some used webcams to broadcast their every move in real time on their own Web pages. By the mid-2000s it seemed like everyone had a blog, a kind of personal online journal for posting everything from photos to political commentary to a running chronicle of the bloggers' most intimate thoughts and feelings.

All these services have their legitimate purposes, but they can also feed the narcissism of adolescents and adults alike by allowing people to document their experiences in words, pictures, and videos solely for the purpose of broadcasting them to (often anonymous) others. The very act of creating an artfully crafted image of oneself, in words, photos, or video, and posting it for universal consumption can make the poster feel suddenly important, *gratified*, glamorous, even powerful. Ultimately, these sites act as *incubators* for those who harbor narcissistic traits.

With its open invitation to broadcast to the world from the privacy of your bedroom, the Internet paved the way for voyeurs to evolve into exhibitionists. Blogs, webcams, and social networking sites present themselves as miraculous new avenues of self-expression, but they also encourage users to give *free rein* to their narcissistic side. They turn personal information into a *commodity* and give those on the Internet a rare opportunity to manipulate the opinions of others. Any average person can now become a cyber-celebrity: the star of his or her own documentary, broadcast through the ether to an anonymous audience who then *validates* his or her existence by offering encouraging or critical feedback. It's hard to imagine a more perfect *venue* for the narcissist.

In a June 2008 article in *Wired* magazine, Jason Tanz profiled Julia Allison, one of the most visible Internet celebrities who have blogged their way to *notoriety* in recent years. Of Allison, Tanz wrote: "She can't act. She can't sing. She's not rich. But thanks to a genius for self-promotion—plus Flickr, Twitter, and her blogs—she's become an Internet celebrity. . . . Allison has done it on her own and on the cheap, armed only with an *insatiable* need for attention and a healthy helping of Web savvy."

Julia Allison is young, attractive, and ambitious. She's a graduate 40 of Georgetown University. No doubt she could have been successful in any number of ventures, but when she moved to New York City in 2004, she decided that her goal would be to brand herself, to "become a cult figure." Her strategy began with writing a dating column for *AM New York*, a free commuter newsletter. She then used the tip line on Gawker, a media-gossip site with millions of readers each month, to link to her articles. Allison upped her visibility on the site by becoming a frequent commenter on stories, until the site's editors banned her for a level of "*gratuitous* self-promotion that makes even the most gratuitous self-promoters at Gawker blush."

Allison remained determined to become a Gawker regular, but once she could no longer spread her name around on their comments boards, she knew she had to take more drastic measures; she translated her online personality into real life, showing up at Gawker owner Nick Denton's Halloween party in a skimpy, low-cut costume accessorized with condom wrappers. Denton noticed the condom fairy and told his managing editor to run an item about her. The 800-word item was *scathing*, and a thinner-skinned individual might have given up on the idea of taking Manhattan by storm. Not Allison. Her next move was to befriend the Gawker writers, sending them personal *anecdotes* from her blog. As the writers started picking up her stories and readers began to comment, Allison continued revealing intimate information about herself, particularly the made-for-the-Internet drama of her love life, and then begged Gawker *not* to link to it. It was a brilliant stroke of reverse psychology, and it worked: After a few months, everyone who read Gawker knew who Julia Allison was.

Having achieved name recognition, and a following, though much of her audience loved to hate her for her spotlight-hungry *antics*, Allison continued her media *onslaught* with a job as a talking head for *Star* magazine, appearing on various news and talk shows to *parse* the latest celebrity dramas. She used Flickr and Twitter to amplify her cyberpresence, updating followers on her activities every few hours throughout the day.

Allison's online life eventually *netted* her—you guessed it!—a deal to develop her very own reality show. In June 2008, the Bravo network signed a series called *IT Girls*, which will follow Allison and her partners as they launch an Internet start-up *venture*. As with most reality TV, whether the business succeeds or fails hardly seems to matter. Narcissists are largely *undeterred* by failure. Their protective mechanisms are always on hand to reassure them that the blame lies with others; before long, other helpful traits, like vanity, exploitativeness, superiority, and entitlement, will kick into gear and they're on to their next adventure.

Not every Internet celebrity has it quite as easy as Julia Allison. Another blogger's *notorious* oversharing cost her relationships and eventually drove her from her job (though it did land her a *New York Times Magazine* cover story). Emily Gould, a book editor turned Gawker writer and editor, says she left the media blog in despair after being deluged with criticism about her *glib* commentary on the site, and after her personal life overlapped once too often with her blogging personality. Gould told the *Times* just how all-consuming blogging about oneself can become: "The will to blog is a complicated thing, somewhere between inspiration and *compulsion*. It can feel almost like a biological impulse. You see something, or an idea occurs to you, and you have to share it with the Internet as soon as possible." That's the kind of language that often crops up when narcissists talk about their feelings: Because they're so detached from their emotions, they often seem bewildered by otherwise normal behaviors, and can truly feel driven by a mysterious force.

It's not just bloggers who use the Internet to achieve widespread 45 notoriety. For anyone with a digital camera and an Internet connection, a rise from obscurity to celebrity can be just one short video away. Twenty-year-old Chris Crocker was an openly gay adolescent living in a small town, posting frustrated *rants* and performance art videos about his life on his MySpace page, when one of his video posts went viral, making him an Internet icon and opening the door to a whole new level of celebrity.

Crocker's moment came in September 2007, after Britney Spears opened the MTV Video Music Awards with a disoriented and *sluggish* performance. The event had been billed as her comeback, and when she fell short the critics savaged her, amping up the media frenzy that had been swirling around her for months. Crocker posted a *plaintive* video on YouTube and MySpace begging viewers to "leave Britney alone," a phrase that eventually gave the video its name. A tearful identification with his fellow Southerner, and a hysterical *indictment* of Britney's critics, the video immediately went viral, with two million views in the first twenty-four hours. Although Crocker's persona and MySpace page already had a dedicated following, the Britney video set him on the path of the modern version of celebrity: national press, a consulting gig with MTV, a development deal for a reality show (fittingly called *Chris Crocker's 15 Minutes More*), and a recording deal.

Crocker *leveraged* his newfound fame into a move to LA and a very public amplification of his feminine appearance and gay lifestyle. While he has abandoned his MySpace channel and his reality show development deal, citing "censorship," in September 2008 he announced on his newest blog that he had acquired another badge of modern celebrity: an unauthorized Internet sex tape.

When I first saw the "Britney" video, my immediate reaction was that Crocker's behavior indicated a simple but extreme narcissism. He does not use his real name, presenting instead a deeply *entrenched*, false persona, a pseudo-self. After becoming more familiar with his story, I began to see a young man who is obviously suffering. His demeanor and blog lead me to suspect a background of sexual trauma and abuse. Like any severe narcissist, he is so helpless and shattered that he appears to seek control by projecting his pain out into the world. He may even *derive* some satisfaction from being an object of ridicule, but this type of emotional arousal comes at serious expense. And while his level of self-absorption and preoccupation is profound, I suspect that he suffers quiet moments of *self-loathing*.

The interesting thing about those who achieve fame through the Internet is that society elevates them to celebrity status not because they *exude* glamour or have any proven talent as artists or performers, but because they present a model of hypersexualized, damaged behavior, and because they project a certain vulnerability. Whether the audience attacks or supports them doesn't seem to matter. When narcissistic individuals are singled out, from millions of others on the same Internet platforms, it feeds their narcissism and propels them to increasingly exhibitionistic revelations. This kind of random reinforcement is the same mechanism that drives gamblers to continue to bet even when they're deep in the hole: Convinced that lightning can strike twice, they keep on broadcasting the persona that first got them attention. A vicious cycle can develop: Some of these individuals become famous when a sudden *flurry* of Internet attention *piques* the interest of the commercial media. That kind of *implicit* endorsement by the mainstream only amplifies their behavior before reflecting it back to us under the affirming banner of celebrity. Before you know it, other narcissistic individuals start seeing similar behavior as normal, even desirable, and mirroring the behavior back themselves, copycat style.

When eighteen-year-old Disney star Vanessa Hudgens poses nude 50 for "private photos" for her boyfriend that are then leaked over the Internet, or when fifteen-year-old Miley Cyrus's provocative cell phone pictures are uploaded for all the world to see, the message being sent to thousands of tween and teen girls is: "This kind of behavior is okay. It's how really popular girls have fun." Furthermore, despite a flare of negative publicity surrounding each episode, neither girl appears to have suffered any long-term consequences from such public overexposure. For a teenage girl with a digital camera or cell phone, imitating a celebrity couldn't be easier.

Without appropriate monitoring, these social networking platforms are subject to abuse by those who are most vulnerable to the endless feedback loop they create. This is known as an *urge/compulsion/reinforcement cycle*, and it's very similar to what happens to those who crave drugs or other addictive substances. The Mirror Effect has the potential to turn a vulnerable young person with some narcissistic traits into a Narcissus on *OxyContin*.

Don't misunderstand me: The mass media aren't responsible for introducing narcissism into society, but narcissistic celebrity behavior can have a powerful magnifying effect on the *latent* narcissism in all of us. When some new celebrity incident strikes a narcissistic chord in a wide audience, the result is like an effective *opioid*. It gives relief, a sense of *euphoria*, focuses aggression, and gives users a chance to get outside the body and escape. It may not be physically addictive, but can have a deep and lasting effect on a person's psychological cravings.

The Internet's broadcasting power offers anyone a chance to manufacture a new self-image (that is, a pseudo-self), to project it into the world, and to *bask* in the global audience's reaction. It gives people with dominant narcissistic traits a chance to indulge their most dangerous impulses before literally millions of viewers. If they're lucky, their fantasies might even become reality, making them *bona fide* celebrities with the opportunity to interact with an audience of fans, and accept a real-time stream of admiration and validation in return.

One of the most successful Internet celebrities I've met is Tila Tequila, who *parlayed* a drive for fame and an attention-getting MySpace page into a self-described career as a singer, actor, stripper, model, and businesswoman. When Tila appeared on *Loveline*, Mark and I watched as she spent the two hours in the studio simultaneously answering questions and comments from listeners, replying to online and text messages, and updating her MySpace page. Tila says she set out to become popular just to prove everyone wrong who ever said she couldn't be famous. But in an interview with Time.com she may have come closer to the core reasons for her fame: "There's a million hot naked chicks on the Internet," she says, but "there's a difference between those girls and me. Those chicks don't talk back to you."

Despite her constant communication with them, Tila Tequila   55
doubtless has a more arm's-length relationship with her millions of MySpace friends than she does with her flesh-and-blood acquaintances. Yet the irony is that her MySpace audience may be more meaningful to her career, at least in the short term. Years ago, in his essay "The Strength of Weak Ties," sociologist Mark Granovetter argued that weaker relationships, such as those formed with colleagues at work or minor acquaintances, are more useful in spreading certain kinds of information than our networks of close friends and family. In a recent issue of *The New Atlantis*, author Christine Rosen applies this argument to today's social networks. "The activities social networking sites promote are precisely the ones weak ties foster, like *rumor-mongering*, gossip, finding people, and tracking the ever-shifting movements of popular culture and fad. If this is our small world, it is one that gives its greatest attention to small things."

One of the best examples of the "weak ties" theory, and a powerful online manifestation of the Mirror Effect, is the popularity of the gossip blog. Over the past few years, celebrity gossip sites have become destination reading for those with a constant thirst for celebrity news updates. There are hundreds of gossip blogs, but some of the most heavily trafficked are those owned by media *conglomerates*, including TMZ.com (Time Warner), People.com (Time Warner), E!Online.com (Comcast), and Scandalist.com (VH1/Viacom). Gawker Media, a company devoted to blogs covering everything from celebrity (Gawker.com, Defamer.com) and sports (Deadspin.com) to pornography (Fleshbot .com) and the automotive industry (Jalopnik.com), has at least a dozen active sites.

Though most users may never give it a second thought, the corporations maintain these gossip sites because they help to promote their other entertainment interests—the latest movies, TV shows, or CDs by the stars whose personal lives are hung out like laundry on the sites. However, there are other, independent gossip sites, and in some cases, these have *catapulted* individual bloggers to celebrity beyond the Internet. The best known among these is the blogger Mario Lavandeira, who calls himself Perez Hilton. Since launching his blog, perezhilton.com, in 2005, Perez has gone on to establish a radio and TV presence, sign a book deal, make innumerable personal appearances, and create a clothing line.

Perez is known for the often-cruel commentary that's a regular feature of his blog, and for the *scatological* "doodles" he inks over certain celebrities' pictures. Perez himself protests that it's all in good fun. He once told me that, growing up in a strongly matriarchal family, he internalized his mother's and grandmother's attraction for gossip as a means of exchanging important information. But of course one person's gossipy run can lead to another's hurtful consequences, and it's hard to defend his *knee-jerk* habit of referring to women as "sluts" (he has repeatedly referred to fifteen-year-old Miley Cyrus as a "Disney slut"), especially when you're playing to an audience of millions.

All these innovations in technology and media programming have fueled today's narcissistic notion that everyone is entitled to be famous. They've paved a slick road between the celebrity media machine and the consumer, speeding the vicious cycle of supply and demand that drives the Mirror Effect. Tabloid reporting and reality TV were the first venues that allowed us to indulge our obsession with turning ordinary people into celebrities (and celebrities into ordinary people), but the Internet has served as a powerful *accelerant*.

And this new relationship to the media has created a *hybrid* breed 60 of celebrity that exists only as long as we keep watching: celebrities like Tila Tequila, Perez Hilton, Kim Kardashian, even Paris and Nicole. In the past few years, professional and amateur online commenters have created a whole new celeb *lexicon* for these figures: They've been *dubbed celebutantes* (debutante-age girls famous only because of their wealth, lifestyle, and perceived glamour); *celebuspawn* (offspring of a celebrity or celebrity couple); and, most cruelly, *celebutards* (stars known for ignorant behavior or opinions).

These quasicelebrities fuel the Mirror Effect, *insinuating* themselves into the public consciousness by inspiring equal measures of attraction, judgment, and envy. They are famous only as long as they can keep themselves in front of the media and in the eye of the public. It takes work to maintain this kind of celebrity, striving to always stay in the limelight. But it's not the kind of work ethic that results in a lasting career. These people aren't spending their time studying for their next audition, or writing songs for their new CD. They're too busy being *famous*.

The individuals who manage to attain this most *ephemeral* level of celebrity are also the ones who are most intent on preventing it from fading. Having clawed their way to fame by surviving the trials of reality television, or by parading themselves in frankly sexual fashion on the Internet and the red carpet, they're *petrified* of what will happen if they lose their fame. And they're supported by the entertainment media that thrives on their *antics*, as well as a corporate culture that's invested in their continued celebrity. Actress Julia Stiles is one young star who believes that extensive press coverage only encourages Hollywood's party-loving elite to misbehave. "We reward bad behavior. They get a lot of attention for misbehaving, and it reinforces the idea [that] this is who they're supposed to be. . . . And they're surrounded by people who won't stop them, because they're making so much money for everybody."

Here's how to recognize these new celebrities, those whose behavior is most clearly *underpinned* by narcissistic traits, and whose example most clearly sparks the phenomenon we call the Mirror Effect.

They identify themselves as celebrities first and foremost. Their résumés may present them as actors or actresses, singers, or models or, often, as all of the above. However, their simple celebrity is more important than any of their *fleeting* career achievements.

They are immature and unregulated. Jamie Lynn Spears, Britney's 65 little sister, got pregnant at the age of sixteen. Seventeen-year-old Nick Hogan was arrested on felony reckless-driving charges after a car accident that critically injured his passenger. At fifteen, *Gossip Girl* star Taylor Momsen already has a reputation as a party girl on the New York scene. The first *whiff* of scandal came when pictures allegedly leaked from her MySpace showed her kissing a scantily clad girl. Now gossip sites track her every move and rumors on everything from her health to her behavior surface regularly.

They spend much of their time courting media attention—good, bad, or inappropriate. As Vanessa Hudgens told *GQ*: "If you have paparazzi, you know you've gotten somewhere."

And finally, they have an almost all-encompassing sense of entitlement. The roar of the modern celebrity is "Don't you know who I am?" Consider just a few examples:

> *Don't you know who I am? I almost won*
> American Idol*!*

—Singer Chris Daughtry, trying to claim stage space next to Scott Weiland and Billy Corgin at an Alice in Chains concert.

> *Don't you know who I am?*

—Actor Jeremy Piven to a hostess at a Hollywood restaurant after he was unable to get a table there. In the tirade that followed, he screamed at the hostess, belittling her for working in a restaurant.

> *Do you know who I am?*

—Singer John Mayer, throwing a "diva fit" on being asked for ID in a Circuit City store in Santa Monica, California.

> *Do you know who I am?*

—Actress Tatum O'Neal, a former child star, as police arrested her for buying crack from a street dealer in New York City. O'Neal claimed she was doing research for a role.

> *Do you know who I am? I'm a big star, and I can look you*
> *up, find where you live and blow you up.*

—Talk show host Montel Williams, intimidating a teenage newspaper intern who asked him a question at a press event.

> *Do you know who I am? I'm Tara f***ing Reid!*

—Actress Tara Reid on the rope line at a Hollywood nightclub.

From the severe dysfunctions of the patients I treat, to celebrity meltdowns glamorized by the media, to the reaction and participation of the increasingly self-dramatizing audience, I see evidence every day that narcissism is the common thread weaving through much of our pop-culture universe. The influence of drugs and alcohol may fuel some celebrities' extreme behavior, but substance abuse can't explain the escalating media coverage of this dysfunctional *exhibitionism*, or our responses. And I feel strongly that it's time for us to stop accepting these narcissistic behaviors as natural by-products of fame, and start recognizing them for what they are: a sign of danger for our culture.

For decades now, I've treated thousands of patients who acted out in these same extreme ways, with *flagrant* displays of exhibitionism, entitlement, self-abuse, and more. And it's clear to me that the underlying psychological condition driving both that behavior and our reaction to it is an unhealthy level of narcissism. The fact is, some celebrities *have* gotten sicker over the past ten years, and their *indiscretions* are more public than ever before, thanks largely to today's media delivery system, which relays such stories almost instantaneously. While it's troubling that certain dysfunctional behaviors have become the celebrity media's daily bread, what's even more distressing is the way we, the audience, respond to this phenomenon. Why is it that we're so eager to read more and more about our favorite stars' troubles, instead of responding with concern and sympathy? In part, it's because the media glamorizes such behavior. It's also because of deep-rooted psychological *constructs* that *predispose* us to accept *salacious* gossip and disturbing behavior as entertainment.

This exchange of narcissistic behaviors between celebrities and 70 the vulnerable audience who *dotes* on them is at the heart of the Mirror Effect. The increasingly amplified and dysfunctional behavior of celebrities, the size and speed of the distribution system, and the response of the consumers add up to a perfect storm of conditions, with troubling implications for our value systems and society at large. And our children, who are more fully immersed in media culture than any previous generation, are at risk of internalizing such behaviors at a developmental stage when it could permanently affect their emotional well-being.

Before we can truly understand the dangers of the Mirror Effect, however, it's important to look more closely at what narcissism actually is, to appreciate which personality traits are amplified by unhealthy levels of narcissism, to consider why we as human beings are biologically predisposed to mimic the narcissistic strategies of others we consider successful, and to examine how prolonged exposure to narcissistic celebrity behavior can affect anyone who follows celebrity gossip, especially children. Finally, it's crucial to explore steps we can take in our daily lives to connect consciously and empathetically with people we actually know, as well as the celebrities we think we know, if we're going to bring a healthy perspective to the celebrity and entertainment news we consume every day.

For more on organizational patterns such as cause-and-effect, see Chapter 7, Rhetorical Patterns, page 187.

practice it   Post-Reading Activity

Look over the organizational pattern of "Broadcasting Yourself." Where does Pinsky use cause and effect to discuss reality TV? What are the various causes and effects he outlines in the chapter?

COMPREHENSION QUESTIONS

1. According to Pinsky, what are some of the dangers of watching reality TV shows?

2. Which type of reality show is, in Pinsky's opinion, the worst?

3. What influence do the producers have on reality shows? How do they manipulate the cast members?

4. Pinsky writes that "the road to fame is paved with bad behavior" (para. 29). What does he mean by this? Can you think of examples from current reality TV shows?

5. What is narcissism, and why is it so damaging? What does the myth of Narcissus have to do with narcissism?

6. What are "weak ties" (para. 56), and why are they important to Pinsky's argument?

7. This reading is a chapter from Pinsky's book titled *The Mirror Effect*. Based on this chapter, what do you think the "Mirror Effect" is?

VOCABULARY ACTIVITIES

1. Add any words from this book excerpt to your ongoing fame and celebrity glossary. Remember to write definitions in your own words.

2. Pinsky describes a "whole new celeb lexicon" and gives a few examples (para. 60). What is a lexicon? How does the "celeb lexicon" play with roots, prefixes, and suffixes? For more on roots, prefixes, and suffixes, see Chapter 8, Vocabulary Building, page 198.

3. Can you think of more examples to add to Pinsky's list? Why would such a slang lexicon evolve, in your opinion?

SUMMARY ACTIVITY

Summarize the chapter in two or three sentences. You'll have to be very concise and focus on the main point(s). For more help with summary writing, see Chapter 1, Reading and Responding to College Texts, page 2.

DISCUSSION QUESTIONS

1. Would you be willing to be a contestant on a reality television show? Why or why not? If you had or have children, would you want your children to be on such a show? Why or why not?

2. Andy Warhol's famous quote "In the future, everybody will be world famous for fifteen minutes" refers to short-lived, meaningless fame; how is Chris Crocker an example of this? Can you think of other examples of flash-in-the-pan celebrities? What qualities do they share?

3. In addition to asserting that reality TV makes stardom seem within anyone's grasp, Pinsky claims that reality TV has created "a new ethos of morality" (para. 24). What does he mean by that? Do you agree or disagree?

4. Do you agree that narcissism is a serious problem in American society? Why or why not?

5. Does social networking encourage narcissistic behavior among people? Why or why not?

Synthesizing the Readings

Now that you have read a wide variety of texts on the topic of fame and celebrity, you have enough schema, or background information, to begin to synthesize the material and build arguments of your own. It's helpful, though, to pause and discuss how the various readings "converse" with one another before you jump right into a writing assignment. Here are some post-reading discussion questions to help direct your thinking:

DISCUSSION QUESTIONS

1. What are the key themes of the readings in this chapter? How do these themes intersect with one another?

2. Compare and contrast the effects of fame and celebrity on people of different ages (young children, teens, young adults, and older adults). What are the similarities and differences in the impacts fame and celebrity have on their lives?

3. How deep of a problem is the celebrity culture in America? If you think it is a large problem, how might we address it in our families or communities? Should this become a nationwide issue?

4. Do local heroes or other "old fame" figures still exist in our communities? How do they compare and contrast to "new fame" celebrities?

5. Compare Loftus's and Halpern's ideas about fame. On what points do they agree? On what points do they differ?

6. Thinking back to the quotations from Andy Warhol and Jay-Z that opened this chapter, which authors best support each man's quote?

CHARTING TO ORGANIZE YOUR IDEAS

After your discussion, take some time to organize your thoughts on the topic of fame and celebrity before you proceed to your specific assignment. You can begin by gathering ideas and quotations about the various issues that emerged in more than one of the readings. Use the following chart to record your thoughts and any interesting information or quotations that you pull from the readings. You can copy the chart into your notebook or to download a version, go to **bedfordstmartins.com /readwriteconnect** and click on **Charts**.

SYNTHESIS CHART: FAME AND CELEBRITY

	Main Idea in Your Own Words	Key Terms	My Thoughts, Ideas, and Questions	Relates to . . . (Which Other Author's Ideas?)
Chang, "The Kardashians: Cashing in with a Capital K"				
Flora, "Seeing by Starlight: Celebrity Obsession"				
Loftus, "The Other Side of Fame"				
Halpern, "The Desire to Belong: Why Everyone Wants to Have Dinner with Paris Hilton and 50 Cent"				
Pinsky, "Broadcasting Yourself"				
My thoughts				

Writing Your Essay

The following steps review how to get into the mind-set to write your essay on fame and celebrity. These steps are outlined in greater detail in Chapters 2, 3, and 4.

STEP 1: What type of essay are you assigned to write about fame and celebrity? Look over the question or your instructor's prompt, and write it in your own words.

STEP 2: Which readings from this chapter do you think you will include? List them in your notes, including any quotations that you think you might use. (Don't forget to include the author and page number when you write down the quotation so that you don't have to find it again later.)

STEP 3: What ideas from class discussion or your own experience and observation would you like to include? Look over your notes, and add those thoughts to your brainstorming for this assignment.

STEP 4: Take a few more minutes to brainstorm in your favorite method: listing, freewriting, clustering, questioning, or group discussion.

STEP 5: Look back at the assignment prompt, and write up a tentative thesis or main idea based on your work so far. Remember, one way to think of the thesis is as the answer to the question posed in the assignment prompt. Don't worry that your thesis has to be perfect or set in stone right now. It's a working thesis that you will probably revise as you make decisions about what you want to say.

STEP 6: Make a bullet-point outline for your essay. Remember to first put the ideas down and then reorganize them into a logical order.

STEP 7: Copy or type up the relevant quotations and examples under each appropriate bullet point.

STEP 8: Pat yourself on the back! You have a lot of material so far, don't you?

STEP 9: Write the rough, rough draft, remembering that you'll be revising it.

STEP 10: Reread the assignment sheet one more time, and then make big-picture revisions to your focus, content, and organization. Peer review may help.

e-Pages
To learn how to use the Grammar Log, see Chapter 24, page 579. To download a copy of this log, go to **bedfordstmartins.com /readwriteconnect** and click on **Charts**.

STEP 11: Once you are generally satisfied that your work is focused, complete, and organized, edit for sentence-level issues. Remember to use the editing techniques of reading your work out loud, reading "backward," and isolating your common errors. Refer to your Grammar Log frequently during this process. Edit and print your paper again and again until you are satisfied with the way each sentence sounds.

STEP 12: Take a break.

STEP 13: Proofread your essay one or two more times to correct any minor errors and to make sure your document format is correct for this assignment.

Writing Assignments

DEFINITION ASSIGNMENT

What do *fame* and *celebrity* really mean? Write an essay in which you offer your own extended definition of *fame* and/or *celebrity*. You may want to distinguish between fame and celebrity as a way to help make your points. Be sure to use specific examples to illustrate your points.

DESCRIPTION ASSIGNMENT

Think of a celebrity who, like the Kardashians, functions as a brand. What is the celebrity's brand identity? Describe in specific detail the image, products, and values associated with this celebrity.

COMPARE-CONTRAST ASSIGNMENT

Drawing on Jake Halpern's book chapter "The Desire to Belong: Why Everyone Wants to Have Dinner with Paris Hilton and 50 Cent" from *Fame Junkies*, write an essay that compares and contrasts one person who has "new fame" with one person who had "old fame." You may need to use outside library sources to research your people. Use these examples to make a larger point about new and old fame.

ANALYSIS ASSIGNMENT

Choose a popular magazine from the past or from today. (Older magazines are available in libraries and many are now archived online.) Look at all the facets of the magazine, including the cover, articles, regular columns, photo spreads, and advertisements. Analyze how the magazine presents fame and/or celebrity. In developing your thesis, realize that magazines might not offer one coherent "message" but instead might offer contradictory messages about fame and celebrity.

RESEARCH ASSIGNMENT

Choose someone famous and research the path he or she took to achieve fame and the contributions this person made to his or her field or the world at large. What did this person actually do to achieve fame? What were the critical moments in the development of his or her career? What is/was the value of fame to this person and to those around him or her?

ARGUMENT ASSIGNMENT

As the authors in this chapter have shown, celebrities have a hold on us. We obsessively watch them on TV, follow their lives in gossip magazines and on Twitter, and buy the trendy clothes and gadgets they promote. Why are we so obsessed with celebrity watching? Is there any value in it, or does it have a solely negative impact? Drawing on the readings by Halpern and Pinsky, write an essay in which you take a position on the psychological and/or social impact of celebrity culture on America as a whole or on some segment of the population.

Additional Online and Media Sources

The readings in this chapter may spark your thinking and leave you wanting some more information for further study or personal reflection. In the e-Pages, you can read Mark Harris's article "How to Train Your Celebrity" and explore the Web site for the organization Look to the Stars. Go to **bedfordstmartins.com/readwriteconnect** and click on **e-Readings**. You might also want to consult the following online and media sources.

WEB RESOURCES

Check your college library's online databases to see if you have access to the Biography Resource Center or other databases that provide information about famous people. You might also familiarize yourself with the various fan and gossip sites, if you haven't seen them previously. In addition, you can consult the following:

Andy Warhol Museum (www.warhol.org): The robust Web site of the Andy Warhol Museum, which offers information about Warhol along with images of his art.

Bio. True Story (www.biography.com): Biographies of a wide variety of famous people and celebrities.

CelebYouth (www.celebyouth.org): An online research project from the United Kingdom that explores the impact of celebrities on youth.

Federal Resources for Educational Excellence, U.S. History Topics: Famous People (http://free.ed.gov/subjects.cfm?subject_id=172): Research resources for famous people in American history.

Museum of Modern Art, Learning: Pop Art (www.moma.org/learn/moma_learning/themes/pop-art/celebrity): Art, discussion questions, and activities about celebrity culture and art that reflects on celebrity.

FILMS

Almost Famous. Dir. Cameron Crowe. Perf. Billy Crudup, Frances McDormand, and Kate Hudson. Columbia, 2000.

Bamboozled. Dir. Spike Lee. Perf. Damon Wayans, Savion Glover, and Jada Pinkett Smith. New Line Cinema, 2000.

The Bling Ring. Dir. Sofia Coppola. Perf. Katie Chang, Israel Broussard, and Emma Watson. American Zoetrope, 2013.

Consuming Kids: The Commercialization of Childhood. Dir. Adriana Barbaro and Jeremy Earp. Perf. Daniel Acuff, Enola Aird, and Michael Brody. Media Education Foundation, 2008.

Exit through the Gift Shop. Dir. Banksy. Perf. Banksy, Mr. Brainwash, and Debora Guetta. Paranoid Pictures, 2010.

The Hunger Games. Dir. Gary Ross. Perf. Stanley Tucci, Jennifer Lawrence, and Liam Hemsworth. Lionsgate, 2012.

I Love Your Work. Dir. Adam Goldberg. Perf. Marisa Coughlan, Judy Greer, and Shalom Harlow. Cyan Pictures, 2003.

The Joneses. Dir. Derrick Borte. Perf. David Duchovny, Demi Moore, and Amber Heard. Echo Lake Productions, 2009.

Notting Hill. Dir. Roger Michell. Perf. Julia Roberts, Hugh Grant, and Richard McCabe. Polygram, 1999.

Somewhere. Dir. Sofia Coppola. Perf. Stephen Dorff and Elle Fanning. Focus, 2010.

"Tennessee Williams: Wounded Genius." *Biography.* Prod. Paul Budline. Perf. Tennessee Williams, Helena Carroll, and Candy Darling. A&E, 9 June 1998. Television.

The Truman Show. Dir. Peter Weir. Perf. Jim Carrey, Laura Linney, and Noah Emmerich. Paramount, 1998.

24

How to Learn the Rules and Apply Them to Your Own Writing

in this chapter

- What Is Editing and Proofreading?
- How Do You Pinpoint Your Errors?
- How Do You Learn the Rules?
- How Do You Apply What You've Learned?

Understanding Editing and Proofreading

Writing involves more than just stringing words together correctly. Writing involves generating ideas, forming logical arguments, and organizing thoughts, among other things. Correcting your sentence-level errors—sometimes referred to generally as errors in "grammar"—is a key part of writing, but often problems with sentences occur because your ideas are not yet clear and focused. For this reason, it's important to work on idea development and larger concerns before you attend to sentence-level issues. Also, make sure you understand the difference between editing and proofreading:

- *Edit:* When you edit your work, you find and fix grammar errors and make changes to improve sentence clarity.
- *Proofread:* When you proofread your work, you find and fix typos, minor punctuation errors, and misspellings, and correct document format.

That said, when you spend time on your sentence-level errors, you want that time to be productive. Too often, students spend hours doing multiple-choice exercises that don't really help them improve. So how do you learn to find and fix your own errors in your own writing?

Correcting grammar is a process much like working out to get into shape: You have to work on it repeatedly in order to get the results you want. It also helps to be organized about noting what kinds of errors you make. One of the best ways to track these errors so you can find them and fix them is to keep a Grammar Log of the kinds of errors you are prone to making. This chapter will show you how to do that. If you take the time to learn the rules and correct your errors, eventually you will write fluently and correctly.

As you work to improve your grammar, you will most likely make progress yet have some setbacks. That's completely normal. (In dieting or working out, it's called a plateau.) In writing, you might plateau for a while because you still need to master some basic rules and apply them in a disciplined, consistent way. You might also plateau in the area of grammar because you are focusing on and progressing in other areas of the reading and writing processes. As you move through your college English course, you will be asked to read increasingly difficult texts and write and think in more and more sophisticated ways. Often, when you are reaching a new level intellectually, you will make a few more errors for a while. Try not to see this as a negative thing. Instead, realize that your grammar is suffering because you are hitting new highs intellectually. This is the growth mentality that Carol S. Dweck describes in her work (see Chapter 1, pages 6–13). You will have to spend more time than usual, perhaps, in the editing stage of writing on a particular assignment, but the end result will be well worth the effort.

So what is the process of correcting grammar errors?

STEP 1: First, you need to figure out exactly what your problems are. Do you repeatedly write fragments? Comma splices? Do you use commas incorrectly? The more you can pinpoint and identify the exact errors you make, the easier it will be to fix them.

STEP 2: Next, you need to learn the rules for the specific errors you make. After you feel confident with the rules, you can test yourself.

STEP 3: Finally, you need to apply your knowledge to your own writing by finding and fixing those errors in your own papers.

Note that this process does not involve trying to memorize every aspect of American English grammar. We don't think that is an effective or efficient way to learn to read and write well. So we won't ask you to diagram random sentences, but you will need to turn a microscope on your own work.

Pinpointing Your Errors

Let's look in depth at the first step, identifying your particular errors. How do you do that? Your English instructor is your best resource here. She or he will review your writing and comment in the margins about the

For more help finding your own errors, see Chapter 17, Giving and Receiving Feedback, pages 327–29.

errors you make, sometimes correcting those errors to show you how it should be done. Take the time to make a list of all the errors your instructor marks. You might also think back to past classes to remember what other instructors have told you about your writing.

| practice it | **Compile a List of Your Errors** |

Start to compile a list of your common errors in your notebook. Include examples from your writing of each error you make frequently.

Once you have a list of the errors you tend to make, you will likely need to prioritize them, especially if you make many errors. Now, this may come as a surprise, but the spelling and apostrophe errors that your high school teachers might have constantly corrected—while common—are not the worst errors you can make. Let's take a look at the most common types of errors, in order of importance.

ERRORS THAT MAKE YOUR WRITING UNREADABLE

First, we have the major errors, those that make your writing unreadable:

- Verb problems
- Fragments
- Run-ons and comma splices
- Mixed constructions

Tackle these problems first because they hide the meaning of your sentences. If you make these mistakes frequently, your reader won't understand what you are trying to say.

ERRORS THAT MAKE YOUR WRITING UNCLEAR

Next up, we have the errors that make your writing unclear or difficult to follow.

- Pronoun problems
- Some comma errors
- Parallelism errors
- Misplaced and dangling modifiers
- Overuse of passive voice
- Wordiness and other style problems

In some cases, these errors occur because you are trying to do something more sophisticated with your work, but aren't quite getting it right.

In other cases, these are errors of style. If you focus on being clear and concise, your work will have more impact.

ERRORS THAT MAKE YOUR WRITING DISTRACTING

Last, but not least, we have the errors that make your writing distracting:

- Apostrophe errors
- Some comma errors
- Most punctuation errors
- Spelling and capitalization errors

These errors concern minor issues, but they make your writing unpolished and unprofessional and can easily distract your reader from your ideas. Errors like these may seem minor, but they add up and undermine your credibility.

If your list of errors includes one or two from each of these categories, begin with the errors that make your writing unreadable, and work your way down to the other categories.

CREATING A GRAMMAR LOG

Copy the following chart into your notebook or download a version of this chart from the e-pages. Add rows to the chart as needed. Instructions in each column explain how the Grammar Log works.

e To download the Grammar Log, log into your Integrated Media at **bedfordstmartins.com /readwriteconnect** and click on **Charts**.

GRAMMAR LOG

My Error	The Rules in My Own Words	Example of Corrected Error	My Notes
Here, list your most common errors, in order of priority.	Here, write the rules for finding and fixing the error. Putting the rule in your own words will help you understand the rule.	Here, write an example of a sentence with the error corrected.	Add any notes that will help you understand or remember how to fix the error.

> **practice it**   **Prioritize Your Errors**
>
> Look back over the list of your common errors in your notebook. Prioritize your errors based on the categories above. Then write the name of your two or three most important errors in your Grammar Log. These are the errors you will begin to address first this semester.

IDENTIFYING AND PRIORITIZING ERRORS: ONE STUDENT'S PARAGRAPH

Let's take a look at a sample student's writing. This student, Andrea, wrote a paragraph about budgeting and financial literacy.

> Financial literacy is important for everyone. Like college students, young couples, and retired people. Most people think that having a budget is enough but they do not realize that budgeting is just the first step. Making long-term plans, setting goals, and building an emergency fund as well. Their are so many resources available to help. Such as Web sites, books, government publications and even online lessons for children. The U.S. council on economic education has one of the best Web sites i have seen for children. (My little Sister even liked it!) Starting young makes all the difference in the world. If people start thinking about finances when they are little they will do it regularly when they actually have a job later in Life. From that point on the road to success is certain.

Clearly, this student made many errors. This is just a quick rough draft, however, so she probably knows how to correct some of these errors but just hasn't fixed them yet. Based on the preceding paragraph, though, we can list the following errors (they are color-coded to correspond to the paragraph):

- Fragments (-*ing* and example fragments)
- Commas (after introductory element and when joining two main clauses with a coordinating conjunction)
- Capitalization ("i")
- Commonly confused words (*there/their/they're*)

Now, when we look at the list, the most important errors are the fragment errors, followed by the comma errors. The capitalization problems and the commonly confused–word problem are distracting and make the writing look unprofessional, but the fragment and comma errors make it hard to follow. Most likely, too, the student made the capitalization and commonly confused–word errors out of haste or laziness, and that means she needs to edit more carefully. She probably already knows the rules for these.

This student's instructor would advise her to work on the fragments first, but some comma rules might help her fix the fragments, so she should probably address the commas at the same time or shortly afterward. Most likely, when the student lists her errors, she will realize that she knows to spell *I* with a capital letter, so she can omit this error from her Grammar Log. Her personalized Grammar Log, then, will look something like this:

GRAMMAR LOG

My Error	The Rules in My Own Words	Example of Corrected Error	My Notes
fragments, especially with -ing			
fragments with examples			
comma rules			
there/their/they're			

Remember, you probably won't be able to pinpoint all your own errors yourself. Look over comments and corrections made on your past work, and ask your instructor for help.

Learning the Rules

Once you figure out what you need to work on, how do you learn the rules? A few students do well with self-study—they can read the chapters in a grammar handbook and figure it out pretty well. Most students, though, learn best in an interactive way, either with classmates outside of class or through in-class instruction. Though your instructor may devote class time to the major errors that appear frequently in student work, you will probably need some one-on-one help also. Make sure to read and study the relevant material in Chapters 25–36 of this book, and try your hand at the Practice It activities. One good way to check your understanding of a particular rule is to test how well you can explain it in your own words. Try teaching the rule to another student, or at least repeat it back in your words to your tutor or instructor. Then, when you are sure you have the right idea, write it down in your Grammar Log.

Don't be surprised if you have some trouble figuring out the rules by yourself. You may need to see a tutor or your instructor for personalized help. If so, come prepared with samples of your own writing where the error appears.

practice it   Define the Rules

Read the appropriate chapters (see Chapters 25–36) and fill in the column labeled "The Rules in My Own Words" in your Grammar Log for the errors you have identified. Seek help from a tutor or instructor if you don't fully understand the rules.

Applying What You've Learned to Your Own Writing

Once you are confident that you know the rules pertaining to the errors you make, it's time for the final step: finding and fixing the errors in your own work. Follow these steps.

STEP 1: Take out one or two current pieces of your own writing, preferably writing that has *not* been corrected by an instructor.

STEP 2: Read your writing out loud, looking for one specific error at a time. For instance, if you make fragments and comma errors, read through it once looking just for fragments. Then read through it a second time looking just for comma errors. As you read, underline any problem sentences, but don't stop to fix them now.

STEP 3: When you have finished reading the whole paper, go back and fix your errors. You might find it helpful to have your book open to the relevant chapter.

STEP 4: Have a tutor or your instructor check your corrections to be sure you are editing correctly. Make sure you show them the original and the corrected versions.

STEP 5: Repeat this process until you find that you are no longer making these errors. Then move on down your list to the other errors that you need to correct.

Remember, learning to write without errors is a process. You get better in time if you study, test yourself, and apply what you know. Regularly taking the time to check your work for errors will reduce the number of errors you make.

Study ——▶ Test yourself ——▶ Apply what you've learned ——▶ Repeat

practice it   Find and Correct Your Errors

Find in your own writing one common example of each error you make. Copy it out exactly in your Grammar Log. Then, with a different-colored pen, correct the sentence. Do not erase the mistake. You need to see the original error and the way it was fixed when you study in the future.

Here's what Andrea's Grammar Log looked like after she had reviewed all the rules, found examples from her own writing, and corrected them:

My Error	The Rules in My Own Words	Example of Corrected Error	My Notes
fragments, especially with -ing	You can't have an -ing verb all by itself as a sentence.	Financial literacy includes making Making long-term plans, setting goals, and building an emergency fund as well.	Look out for any -ing words starting a sentence.
fragments with examples	Examples should be attached to the thing they are giving an example of.	Financial literacy is important for everyone. Like college students, young couples, and retired people.	Double-check sentences that start with like or such as.
comma rule before conjunction	Two sentences joined by and or but need a comma before the and or but.	Most people think that having a budget is enough, but they do not realize that budgeting is just the first step.	Use the cover-it-with-your-hand technique to check.
comma rule after introductory material	Use a comma after any introductory word or phrase that is separate from the main part of the sentence.	From that point on, the road to success is certain.	You can hear this one when you read it out loud.
there/their/they're	They're over there in their underwear.	There Their are so many resources available to help.	Use the Find feature to check while proofreading.

chapter review

Understand that editing and proofreading are two distinct tasks that help you work more efficiently as you finalize a piece of writing. We often overlook errors when we do too much at one time. Chapter 24 shows you how to identify the kinds of errors you tend to make and then prioritize them. If you address your errors in an organized way, your writing will become clearer.

To review this chapter, choose one or more of the following strategies:

1. Try to explain what you have learned, or at least part of it, to someone you know. Discuss the key concepts and give some of your own examples to illustrate those concepts.

2. Having identified your most common errors, make flash cards of the grammar rules for each error and practice learning how to identify and fix these errors.

3. If you skipped any of the Practice It activities in the chapter, go back and do them now as a way to deepen your understanding of the material.

4. If you skipped making your own Grammar Log, do it now.

25

Parts of Speech

in this chapter

- What Are Parts of Speech?
- What Are Nouns and Pronouns?
- What Are Adjectives?
- What Are Verbs?
- What Are Adverbs?
- What Are Conjunctions?
- What Are Prepositions?
- What Are Interjections?

e To download the Grammar Log, log into your Integrated Media at **bedfordstmartins.com /readwriteconnect** and click on **Charts**.

✔ **LearningCurve**
For extra practice in the skills covered in this chapter, visit **bedfordstmartins.com /readwriteconnect**.

Any word used in a sentence fits into one of eight *parts of speech*. The parts of speech are defined by how they function *grammatically*—in other words, by what their job is in a sentence. Because many words can play the role of more than one part of speech, you won't be able to identify what part of speech a word is until you see how it is used.

Why is it important to know the parts of speech? For starters, to build strong, clear sentences, you need to understand how words function in sentences. You also need a basic understanding of the major parts of speech in order to communicate *about* writing. You can't understand the explanations for how to fix your grammar errors if you don't know this basic vocabulary. It would be like trying to learn how to hit a baseball without knowing what *swing* means.

You have probably heard of the parts of speech before, but you may have forgotten what they are or why it's useful to know them.

Part of Speech	Purpose	Example
Noun	person, place, thing, or idea	Professor Peacock, library, candlestick, honesty
Pronoun	stands for a person or thing	he, she, it, they, my, that, which
Adjective	modifies nouns	purple, cold, awesome
Verb	action or state of being	sat, thinks, is
Adverb	modifies verbs, adjectives, or other adverbs	quietly, very
Preposition	links nouns and phrases to the rest of a sentence; often indicates location	to, in, by, through, after
Conjunction	joins complete sentences or ideas	and, but, or
Interjection	expresses emotion	No! Wow! Huh?

Dictionaries are a great resource for determining a word's part of speech. After every word in a dictionary entry, you will find its part(s) of speech listed. Here, for example, is the beginning of the definition of *check* found at Merriam-Webster.com:

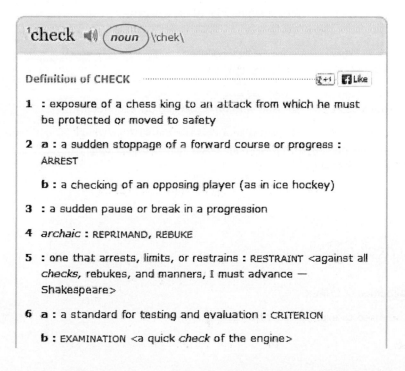

¹**check** 🔊 (*noun*) \chek\

Definition of CHECK ···································· 👍+1 👍 Like

1 : exposure of a chess king to an attack from which he must be protected or moved to safety

2 a : a sudden stoppage of a forward course or progress : ARREST

   b : a checking of an opposing player (as in ice hockey)

3 : a sudden pause or break in a progression

4 *archaic* : REPRIMAND, REBUKE

5 : one that arrests, limits, or restrains : RESTRAINT <against all *checks*, rebukes, and manners, I must advance — Shakespeare>

6 a : a standard for testing and evaluation : CRITERION

   b : EXAMINATION <a quick *check* of the engine>

In English, many words are used—sometimes with a slight change—for more than one purpose, so they serve as different parts of speech. For example, as you can see in the following excerpt of the rest of the definition, the word *check* can also be used as a verb and as an interjection.

---

²**check** (*verb*)

Definition of CHECK

transitive verb

1 : to put (a chess king) in check

2 *chiefly dialect* : REBUKE, REPRIMAND

3 a : to slow or bring to a stop : BRAKE <hastily *checked* the impulse>

   b : to block the progress of (as a hockey player)

4 a : to restrain or diminish the action or force of : CONTROL

   b : to slack or ease off and then belay again (as a rope)

5 a : to compare with a source, original, or authority : VERIFY <needs to *check* her facts>

   b : to inspect, examine, or look at appraisingly —usually used with *out* or *over* <*checking* out new cars>

   c : to mark with a check as examined, verified, or satisfactory —often used with *off* <*checked* off each item>

6 a : to consign (as luggage) to a common carrier from which one has purchased a passenger ticket <*checked* our bags before boarding>

---

³**check** (*inter*)

Definition of CHECK

   —used to express assent or agreement

If someone asked you what part of speech the word *check* was, you couldn't answer until you saw how it was used in a sentence. In the following sentences, it's used as a noun, a verb, and an interjection.

Verb   Noun   Interjection
I check my check every payday to see if there's an error. Check! No error.

Nouns and Pronouns

WHAT ARE NOUNS AND PRONOUNS?

A *noun* is a person, place, thing, or idea. Nouns are the most basic building blocks of writing. Examples of nouns include *athlete*, *beach*, *dream*, *car*, and *loyalty*. In the following sentence, all the underlined words are nouns:

It was the Olympic athlete's dream to own a house at the beach.

A *pronoun* is a word that stands in for a noun. (Hint: Imagine that its job is to "play" a noun.) Examples include *I*, *you*, *he*, *she*, *it*, *we*, *they*, *everybody*, and *one*.

Pronouns are helpful because they allow us to avoid repeating the same noun over and over, which can get tedious.

The bus was so crowded, the bus looked like a can of sardines; I still had to get on the bus though.

The bus was so crowded, it looked like a can of sardines; I still had to get on it, though.

Notice how much smoother the sentence is with pronouns in the place of the noun *bus*?

To avoid a common pitfall in using pronouns, be aware that pronouns must clearly refer back to a particular noun in order for a sentence to make sense.

Mike and Paul ran to the store, but he didn't go in.

Which *he* didn't go in? In this case, repeating the noun (either *Mike* or *Paul*) is essential.

Mike and Paul ran to the store, but Mike didn't go in.

IDENTIFYING NOUNS AND PRONOUNS

Both nouns and pronouns can be used as the *subject* of a sentence—generally speaking, the person, place, thing, or idea that performs the action of the sentence.

Clarence feels bad.

TIP

If you can put *a*, *an*, or *the* in front of a word, it is most likely a noun. Some examples:

an athlete, a beach, the dream, a car, the loyalty.

To identify the subject, ask yourself: Who or what feels bad? In this case, *Clarence* is the one who feels bad, so *Clarence* is the subject. You could also write this:

> He feels bad.

Again, who or what feels bad? *He* feels bad, so *he* would be the subject. Here's another example:

> Freedom is a founding principle of America.

Ask yourself: Who or what is a founding principle? *Freedom* is, so *freedom* is the subject. Let's look at one final example:

> It is also the subject of a song Janis Joplin made famous.

Ask yourself: Who or what is also the subject? *It* is also the subject. Don't get fooled by the fact that this sentence has a person's name in it. The subject isn't necessarily a person.

Nouns and pronouns can also serve as the *object* of the action in the sentence, as the object of a *preposition*, or as part of a *subordinate clause*.

> Janis Joplin sang the song. [What did she sing? The *song*, the object of the action.]

> Janis Joplin sang it. [What did she sing? *It*, the object of the action.]

> Janis Joplin sang about freedom. [What did she sing about? About *freedom*, the object of the preposition *about*.]

For more on subordinate clauses, see Chapter 26, Basic Sentence Components, page 600.

> Janis Joplin died young because she abused drugs. [*She* and *drugs* are part of a subordinate clause, *because she abused drugs*, which is subordinate because it can't stand on its own as a sentence.]

What else do you need to know about nouns and pronouns? Nouns and pronouns are *modified* (a fancy word for described) by adjectives, which we'll discuss in the next section.

Adjectives

WHAT ARE ADJECTIVES?

An **adjective** is a word that modifies or describes a noun. Adjectives answer three questions about nouns or pronouns:

1. What kind/kinds?
2. How many/much?
3. Which one/ones?

Adjectives are an interesting part of speech because they add description. Adjectives are also immensely helpful to us because they provide clarifying information about the nouns in a sentence. You may be familiar with the lyrics to the old tune "How Much Is That Doggie in the Window?" Of course, if you worked in a pet store and someone asked you this question, you wouldn't know which dog the customer was referring to. But the second line of the song goes: "The one with the waggly tail." Okay, now it's clear which dog the customer is interested in: the pup wagging its tail. It wouldn't be enough to just say "the one with the tail"; since the majority of dogs have tails, this wouldn't be enough information. In this case, *waggly* gives us more information about the noun *tail* by answering the question, what kind of tail?

IDENTIFYING ADJECTIVES

Adjectives answer one or more of the three questions listed previously about nouns and pronouns. Here are some examples:

I ended up buying an old car.

This answers the question, what kind of car? An *old* car.

My feet are tired.

I have tired feet.

Both of these sentences answer the question, what kind of feet? *Tired* feet.

Raisin Bran has two scoops of raisins.

This answers the question, how many scoops? *Two* scoops.

I have little homework to do this weekend.

This answers the question, how much homework? *Little* homework.

Use the sharp scissors.

This answers the question, which ones? The *sharp* scissors.

Now, let's see how nouns, pronouns, and adjectives might appear in a sentence together:

adj.   adj. noun   pron. noun   adj. noun
The quick, brown fox jumped carefully over his friend, the lazy dog.

What kind of fox? A *quick* and *brown* fox. Which dog? The *lazy* dog.

DEFINITE AND INDEFINITE ARTICLES

A, an, and *the* are adjectives that have a special function. They are called **articles** and are sometimes considered a separate part of speech. They are typically used before nouns and are used to show whether you are referring to a specific or a general noun. Articles are divided into two categories: definite (*the*) and indefinite (*a/an*).

A *definite article* is used when you are referring to specific nouns or pronouns.

Can you pass the bread?

Here, you are not referring to any bread, but some specific bread you have your eye on, probably sitting at the other end of the table just out of reach.

The pipes in the sink are leaking again; I need to call the plumber.

This sentence refers to specific pipes (not just any pipes in the house), a specific sink (not all the sinks, thankfully), and a specific plumber (your regular plumber).

An *indefinite article* is used when you aren't referring to a specific noun or pronoun.

I would love a piece of fruit.

In this example, it's not clear what kind of fruit the speaker wants. No specific fruit has been specified.

A pipe is leaking somewhere; I need to call a plumber.

In this sentence, it's not clear which pipe is leaking, and there is no specific plumber needed—any plumber will do.

TIP
Generally, native speakers of English don't misuse definite and indefinite articles. Using the correct one comes automatically from years and years of speaking English. However, if English is not your first language, it's important to understand the difference between them so you know when to use *a*, *an*, or *the*.

Verbs

WHAT ARE VERBS?

For more help with verbs, see Chapter 27, Verbs, page 617.

A *verb* indicates an action or state of being. Examples include *laugh, laughing, is laughing, laughed, is, was, were, has been*, and *seems*.

IDENTIFYING VERBS

To find the verb, look for what is happening in a sentence.

Lydia goes to the movies.

What is the action? What is Lydia doing? She *goes* to the movies. Is *going* an action? Yes.

Lydia loves silent films.

What is happening in this sentence? The action is *loves*. That's what Lydia is doing; she *loves*. Although *love* may not seem like an action because you can't see her doing it, it is. Think of *love* this way: Is it something you can do or not do? Can she not love? Yes, she can. Therefore, *loving* is an action.

In the next example there is more than one action. What are the actions?

> Lydia buys popcorn and sits in the front row.

What is Lydia doing? She *buys* and *sits*, so these are the verbs in the sentence.

Often action verbs get a little help from their friends, the *helping verbs.*

Helping Verbs

is, am, are, was, were, be, being, been	may, might, must	shall, should
do, does, did	can, could	will, would
have, has, had		

Memorize these or keep a list of them, and when you see them, know they are part of the main verb.

> A noisy couple <u>was sitting</u> behind her.

In this case, the verb includes the helping verb *was* and the action *sitting.*

In some sentences, the verb is not an action but a state of being. This means that something simply exists—something is or was—as in the following sentence:

> The movie <u>was</u> in black and white.

When looking for the verb in this sentence, you might have difficulty at first because there is no action. The movie didn't do anything. It just existed; the movie *was.* Here are some more examples of verbs that show state of being:

> The sky <u>is</u> a cloudless, perfect blue.

> The traffic on the freeway <u>was</u> at a standstill.

> There <u>are</u> two sides to every story.

> I <u>am</u> optimistic about the new semester.

What else do you need to know about verbs? Verbs are modified by (described by) adverbs, which we'll discuss in the following section.

Adverbs

WHAT ARE ADVERBS?

An *adverb* is a word that describes a verb, an adjective, or another adverb. Adverbs answer the following five questions:

1. Where?
2. How?
3. Why?
4. When?
5. To what extent?

Adverbs are similar to adjectives in that they both describe or provide more information about another word, but remember, adjectives modify nouns and pronouns, and adverbs modify verbs, adjectives, and other adverbs. In the following examples, the adverbs are underlined twice and the word being modified is underlined once.

Verbs   Melanie ran tirelessly. [How did she run? She ran *tirelessly*.]

Adjectives   The sky at sunset was extremely pretty.

To find the adjective, ask: What kind of sky was it at sunset? It was *pretty*. Then ask the adverb question about the adjective. How pretty was it? It was *extremely* pretty.

Other adverbs   If you make errors, you should proofread more cautiously.

How should you proofread? *Cautiously.* How cautiously should you proofread? *More* cautiously.

IDENTIFYING ADVERBS

Adverbs answer the five questions listed previously. Many adverbs end in -*ly*, but not all do. In the following examples, the word being modified is underlined.

Lydia laughed loudly during the movie.

Ask yourself: How did Lydia laugh? Lydia laughed *loudly*.

The movie was over too soon.

Ask yourself: When was the movie over? *Soon.* How soon? *Too* soon. In this case, as you can see, there are *two* adverbs. The first modifies the verb *was*; the second modifies the adverb *soon*.

The movie was very good.

How good was the movie? *Very* good.

Sometimes Lydia will s̄ēe a double feature.

When will she see a double feature? She'll see a double feature *sometimes*.

Now let's see how nouns, pronouns, adjectives, verbs, and adverbs might appear in a sentence.

     adj.   adj. noun verb   adverb   pron. noun   adj. noun

The quick, brown fox jumped carefully over his friend, the lazy dog.

Wow—we've learned the function of almost all the words in the sentence. What about those other words, though? We'll cover them in the next section.

Conjunctions

A **conjunction** is a word that joins other words and phrases and sentences together and shows the relationship between them. There are four kinds of conjunctions: coordinating conjunctions, correlative conjunctions, subordinating conjunctions, and conjunctive adverbs. Let's take a look at each of these.

Coordinating Conjunctions. Coordinating conjunctions join words, phrases, or clauses that are parallel in structure. In the following example, *but* joins two complete sentences, each with a subject (underlined once) and a verb (underlined twice).

The desserts here are delicious, *but* the coffee is on the weak side.

There are only seven coordinating conjunctions and you can remember them easily by the catchword "FANBOYS":

For
And
Nor
But
Or
Yet
So

Correlative Conjunctions. Correlative conjunctions come in pairs and, like coordinating conjunctions, join parallel grammatical structures. In the first sentence, the conjunctions join nouns that function as subjects.

In the second sentence, the conjunctions join two verb phrases. In the following sentences, the conjunctions are underlined.

Both the apple pie and the pecan pie are outstanding.

We should either share a piece or skip dessert.

Here's the full list of correlative conjunctions:

as/as
both/and
either/or
neither/nor
not only/but also
whether/or

Subordinating Conjunctions.   Subordinating conjunctions, also referred to as subordinators, introduce a clause. They are great words to help relate the ideas of the clause to the rest of the sentence, but these words make a powerful change to the clause they are attached to: They make it a *dependent clause*, which means it can no longer stand on its own. In the following example, the dependent clause is underlined:

Because I am trying to cut down on sugar, I think I'll skip dessert after all.

For more on subordinators, see Chapter 26, Basic Sentence Components, page 600.

Common Subordinating Conjunctions

after	if	unless
although	now	until
as	once	when
as if	provided that	where
because	since	whereas
before	so that	which
even	than	while
even if	that	who
even though	though	whoever

Conjunctive Adverbs.   These are mostly used as transition words leading from one sentence to the next, as in the following example:

I'll skip dessert. However, coffee might be nice.

LOOK OUT
Writers often create comma splices when trying to write sentences with this sentence pattern.

When joining two complete sentences together, use a semicolon before the conjunctive adverb and a comma after it:

I really enjoyed the whole dining experience; nevertheless, I now regret that I didn't order dessert.

Common Conjunctive Adverbs

also	consequently	however	on the other hand
altogether	finally	meanwhile	similarly
as a result	further	moreover	then
besides	furthermore	nevertheless	therefore

Prepositions

A *preposition* is a word that shows location in time or space. Prepositions are always part of a *prepositional phrase*, which begins with a preposition and ends with a noun or pronoun.

> The troll lived <u>under the bridge</u>.

Under is the preposition; *bridge* is its object; and the underlined portion is the prepositional phrase.

Common Prepositions

about	besides	in regard to	over
above	between	in spite of	since
according to	beyond	inside	through
across	by	instead of	throughout
after	by way of	into	till
against	down	like	to
around	during	near	toward
at	except	of	under
because of	for	off	until
before	from	on	up
behind	in	on account of	upon
below	in addition to	out	with
beneath	in front of	out of	without
beside	in place of	outside	

Prepositional phrases add interesting material to a sentence, but they are never the main subject or main verb of the sentence. In the examples below, the prepositional phrase is underlined.

> Ellie surfs the Internet <u>in her spare time</u>.

The prepositional phrase *in her spare time* adds information, but it's not the subject. Who surfs? Ellie does, so *Ellie* is the main subject. What does Ellie do? She *surfs*, so surfs is the main verb. *In her spare time* tells us when Ellie surfs.

Once you get the hang of prepositional phrases, you can see that you can use them to add all kinds of information to the sentence:

> <u>In the morning</u>, Ellie surfs the Internet.

TIP

Any word you can put in the blank of the following sentence is probably a preposition.

The ant ran _____ the picnic basket.

There are prepositions that won't work in this sentence, but many will.

Ellie surfs the Internet <u>after school</u> <u>at the school's computer lab.</u>

<u>Instead of writing her paper,</u> Ellie surfs the Internet.

Still, the subject is *Ellie,* and she's still surfing.

Interjections

An *interjection* is a word like *Aha!, Oh!, Wow!,* or *Whoops!* used to indicate emotion. Here are a few examples:

<u>Darn!</u> There is no more milk left!

<u>Hey!</u> Hold the elevator!

Now let's see how nouns, pronouns, adjectives, verbs, adverbs, conjunctions, prepositions, articles, and interjections might all appear in a single sentence.

interj.   art.   adj.   adj.   noun   verb   adverb   prep. pron. noun   art.   adj.   noun

Wow! The quick, brown fox jumped carefully over his friend, the lazy dog.

That's almost all eight parts of speech. (Did you notice that there were no conjunctions?) Well done!

| practice it | Identify the Parts of Speech |

In the following paragraph, identify the parts of speech for the words in bold. Either write the part of speech above the word or use the number of the part of speech to identify them.

1. noun
2. pronoun
3. verb
4. adjective
5. adverb
6. preposition
7. conjunction
8. interjection

Not all **penguins** live **among** ice and snow. **Although** the penguins of

Antarctica are the most famous, only five species of penguin **live** on

that icy continent. There are twelve other **species** of penguin that live

elsewhere **in** the Southern Hemisphere from the Galapagos Islands to the

very southern tip of the African continent. Many of these African penguins

live **on** islands off the coast of mainland Africa, although several colonies of the African penguins live **contentedly** on the actual continent. **They were** the first penguins that **European** explorers encountered, **and** by the middle of the twentieth century much of the African penguin population had died out. **Wow! Both** the birds **and** their eggs **were used** for food **or** their habitats were destroyed. Since then, the African penguin population has been dwindling; **consequently**, unless there is more effort to save these lovable birds, **their** future **is** in peril.

chapter review

As Chapter 25 points out, learning the parts of speech is important so that you can communicate about sentences and how to improve them. This chapter may have been review for you, or perhaps you learned these concepts for the first time here; either way, the parts of speech are the fundamental building blocks of writing, so they are important to understand.

To review this chapter, choose one or more of the following strategies:

1. Try to explain what you have learned, or at least part of it, to someone you know. Discuss the key concepts and give some of your own examples to illustrate those concepts.

2. Take a single paragraph of your writing and try to identify all the parts of speech in your sentences. If you get stuck, visit a tutor or your instructor for help. You can also consult a dictionary to help figure out the part of speech, but remember that many words can be used as different parts of speech depending on the context.

3. Make flash cards of the eight parts of speech. For each part of speech, include the definition and several sample sentences with the part of speech highlighted.

4. If you skipped the Practice It activity in the chapter, go back and do it now as a way to deepen your understanding of the material.

5. Update your Grammar Log to include your most frequent errors with parts of speech. Don't forget to refer to the Grammar Log every time you edit a piece of writing, and don't forget to take the time to edit everything you write for all your college classes.

26

Basic Sentence Components

in this chapter

- What Is a Sentence?
- What Are Verbs?
- What Are Subjects?
- What Are Phrases?
- What Are Clauses?
- What Is Subordination?
- What Is Coordination?
- How Do You Build Better Sentences?

e To download the Grammar Log, log into your Integrated Media at **bedfordstmartins.com /readwriteconnect** and click on **Charts**.

✔️ **LearningCurve**
For extra practice in the skills covered in this chapter, visit **bedfordstmartins.com /readwriteconnect**.

What Is a Sentence?

At the minimum, a sentence is made up of a subject, a verb, and a complete thought or idea. It must include all these elements. However, most sentences you write are more complex. While it's not necessary to understand how every word is working in a sentence to write well, knowing the basic components of sentences will help you understand how to fix problems when they occur and will also help you avoid them.

Verbs

A *verb* (sometimes called a *predicate*) is a word that is an action or a state of being or existence. In sentences that express actions, the verb tells us what the subject of the sentence is doing. Because actions are usually easier to spot in a sentence than some of the other sentence components, for many students it is easier to find the verb first and then work backwards to find the subject. Strictly speaking, *verb* refers to the part of speech (the word) and *predicate* refers to the way a verb functions in the sentence, though very often both the word and its use in the sentence are simply referred to as a *verb*.

Not all verbs describe actions, however. Some verbs describe states of being. Some verbs, *helping verbs* (sometimes called *auxiliary verbs*), accompany main verbs to show tense. Still others, *linking verbs*, connect subjects to the words that describe them. These verbs may not always be immediately recognizable as verbs, but it is important to know how to find them in a sentence.

For more information on active, helping, and linking verbs, see Chapter 27, Verbs, page 617.

Helping Verbs

is, am, are, was, were, be, being, been	may, might, must	shall, should
do, does, did	can, could	will, would
have, has, had		

TIME-TESTING TO FIND THE VERB

Since looking for the action will only help you part of the time, you need a more surefire way of finding the main verb in a sentence. Luckily there is a fairly easy way to do this, which we call "time-testing."

Let's use this sentence as an example:

The Grand Canyon seems to go on forever.

STEP 1: Put the words *last week* at the beginning of the sentence, and see what word you have to change as you read it out loud.

Last week, the Grand Canyon seemed to go on forever.

STEP 2: Put the words *next week* at the beginning of the sentence, and see what word you have to change as you read it out loud.

Next week, the Grand Canyon will seem to go on forever.

STEP 3: Put the word *today* at the beginning of the sentence, and see what word you have to change as you read it out loud.

Today, the Grand Canyon seems to go on forever.

Aha! In our three time tests, the only word we had to change from the original sentence was *seems*. (Not in every case, but in two of three.) That tells us that *seems* is the verb of the sentence. *Seems* is not an action; it's a linking verb connecting *Grand Canyon* with *to go on forever.*

Let's try another example. In this case, there are two sentences. Each sentence needs to have its own verb. You do the time test to see if you can find them.

It doesn't look real. It looks like a painting.

The first sentence has a slightly more complicated verb situation. Did you notice that the contraction *doesn't* had to change to either *didn't* or *won't*? The part of each of those words that did not change is the *n't* part of the contraction. This is because *n't* is not actually part of the verb. *Doesn't* is a contraction for *does not*, and the word *not* is an adverb modifying *does*, so *not* is not actually part of the verb. The verb here is really *does look*. *Look* is an action verb and *does* is the helping verb that goes with it. Together, they make up the main verb.

The second sentence is a bit easier. Did you find *looks* as the verb? If so, good job! *Looks* is a linking verb, and linking verbs aren't always easily recognizable as verbs.

Try the time test with these next two sentences to locate the verbs.

> The Grand Canyon is about a mile deep and eighteen miles wide.

> It boasts some of the most beautiful sunsets in the world.

In the first sentence, did you identify *is* as the verb? If you did, great job. *Is* is one of those verbs you'll learn to identify right away as a verb. It's probably the most commonly used verb in the English language, and it is always used as a verb. For the second sentence, you should have picked *boasts* as the verb.

Here's another one to try:

> Running along the floor of the canyon, the Colorado River stretches over 1,400 miles.

This sentence is a bit trickier because there are two words that right away seem like actions: *running* and *stretches*. If you do the time test, you discover that the only word that has to change is *stretches*. There's the verb.

COMPOUND VERBS

In some sentences, more than one action is expressed and therefore there is more than one main verb. We write sentences like this all the time. A sentence with more than one main verb has a *compound verb*.

> The hikers climbed the steep trail, admired the view, and guzzled plenty of water before heading back down the mountain.

What is the action of this sentence? *Climbed, admired,* and *guzzled*. There are three verbs in this sentence.

Locate the verb(s) in the following sentence; don't forget to use the time test to find the verb(s).

> Instructors work hard planning and grading and care deeply about their students.

Did you find two verbs? You should have found *work* and *care* as the compound verb. (*Planning* and *grading* don't have helping verbs, and don't change when you time-test.)

TIP

When you see a word that looks like a verb and ends in *-ing*, check whether it's accompanied by a helping verb; if it isn't, it's *not* functioning as a verb in the sentence.

Grammar and sentence syntax (the way words are strung together to make meaning) are endlessly fascinating for English instructors, but many of those details don't really affect day-to-day writers. If you are interested in the workings of parts of speech or sentence components, consider taking a grammar class. It's fascinating to poke around under the hood of sentences. For now, though, know that finding the main verb is extremely important, because the main subject(s) and main verb(s) are the fundamental components of the sentence. You can add other information to sentences in the form of prepositional phrases, modifiers, or clauses, but as long as you can find the main subject and verb, you can tackle (and avoid) a lot of the major sentence errors.

---

practice it   **Time-Testing to Find Verbs**

Time-test to find the verb in the following sentences.

1. Up close to a mural, you might notice some interesting details that you hadn't seen from farther away.
2. Grace wanted to spend her eightieth birthday on a boat in the bay because she has always loved sailing.
3. Martha and Bill spent their honeymoon camping rather than staying at a fancy hotel.
4. Even with all the hills, Norm loves walking around the city watching all the people hustling and bustling about.
5. Luckily Jean's favorite Italian restaurant also happens to be right down the block from where we live.

Subjects

The subject of a sentence is the person or thing doing the action of the verb. Think of the subject as the star of the sentence, so to speak. The subject is essentially what the sentence is about. The easiest way to find the subject of the sentence is to first find the verb and then ask: Who or what is doing the action?

Take a look at this sentence:

The Grand Canyon became a national park in 1919.

Okay, let's find the verb. What is the action in this sentence? *Became* is the only action here, so that must be the verb. So who or what *became*? The *Grand Canyon* became, so, *Grand Canyon* is the subject and *became* is the verb.

Let's try another:

Rafting is fun on this river.

First, locate the verb *is*, and then ask: Who or what is? *Rafting* is, so *rafting* is the subject, even though it might not look like a noun.

SENTENCES THAT BEGIN WITH *THERE IS* OR *THERE ARE*

Consider the following sentence. The verb is underlined once and the subject is underlined twice.

There are many outdoor activities at the Grand Canyon.

In sentences starting with *there is* or *there are*, the subject follows the verb. In the preceding sentence, we've underlined the verb once, and the subject twice.

A good way to check that you have the correct subject is to turn the sentence around, beginning with the word you think is the subject and ending with *there is* or *there are*.

Many outdoor activities at the Grand Canyon are there.

It might sound awkward, but does the sentence make sense? Ask yourself the subject-finding question now: Who or what are there? *Activities* are there, so *activities* is the subject. Here's another example:

There are some trails you can hike from the top to the bottom of the canyon.

Some trails you can hike from the top to the bottom of the canyon are there.

Who or what are there? *Trails* are there, so *trails* is the subject.

VERBALS: THE VERBS THAT AREN'T VERBS

Verbals are verbs that function as nouns, adjectives, or adverbs, in terms of parts of speech. In a sentence, verbals that function as nouns may be used as a subject. Verbals used as adjectives might modify a subject or other noun in the sentence.

Verbals as Nouns/Subjects
Swimming is Jean's favorite exercise.
The *waiting* was the hardest part.
To eavesdrop is rude.

Verbals Used as Adjectives or Adverbs
Every *waking* hour should be spent studying. [adj.]
The *swimming* pool is a perfect 80 degrees. [adj.]
To impress his boss, Bob worked over the weekend. [adv.]

TIP
If the verb is *are*, look for a plural subject; if the verb is *is*, look for a singular subject.

COMPOUND SUBJECTS

Sentences can have more than one subject, just like they can have more than one verb. This is called a *compound subject*. In these sentences, ask yourself: Who or what is doing the action of the verb? If there are two answers, there is a compound subject.

> The icy roads and strong winds keep me off the roads during winter storms.

After locating the verb *keep*, ask: Who or what keep? *Icy roads* and *strong winds* keep, so both are the subjects of the sentence, and make up a compound subject. Here's one more example:

> Both my history class and my English class challenge me in a good way this semester.

Who or what challenge? *History class* and *English class* challenge, so they are the compound subject of the sentence.

---

practice it Find the Subjects and Verbs

Find all the subjects and verbs in the following paragraph. Circle the subjects and underline the verbs.

The Grand Canyon is a great place for people who love the outdoors and crowds. About five million people visit the park every year. Visitors come from all over the world. They camp, hike, raft, backpack, and visit archaeological ruins. Spring and summer are the most crowded seasons. In the summer, it seems less like nature and more like a busy city.

Phrases

A phrase is a group of words that can't stand on its own as a complete thought; therefore, a phrase is not a sentence although it may be part of a sentence. There are prepositional phrases, verb phrases, adverb phrases, adjective phrases, and noun phrases. Most of the time, native English speakers use all the different phrases correctly, so for the purposes of writing, keep doing what you are doing. However, the one phrase that gives writers trouble is the prepositional phrase. This is the most important kind of phrase for you to know because it can muddle up your writing.

We use *prepositional phrases* all the time to add more information to a sentence. Prepositional phrases always begin with a preposition, and

For a definition of prepositions, see Chapter 25, Parts of Speech, page 586.

always end with a noun or pronoun. In the following examples, prepositions are underlined and prepositional phrases are bold.

> I am going **to the gym** **in the morning**.

> **During the power outage**, I had to study **by candlelight**.

> **On Saturday**, I am going to be moving, **with help from friends**.

Notice that in each of these examples, the prepositional phrases stick together as a kind of word unit.

- to the gym
- in the morning
- during the power outage
- by candlelight
- on Saturday
- with help
- from friends

Prepositional phrases are essential sentence components when writing essays. Without them, we couldn't say things like this:

> **In her article**, Olivia Mellan writes **about couples and their attitudes toward money**.

The three bold phrases are prepositional phrases (the prepositions are underlined). See how much they add to academic writing? Without them, all this sentence could say is "Olivia Mellan writes." That is a complete sentence, but it says nothing valuable about her article or her ideas.

Sometimes, however, prepositional phrases get in the way. If you use them incorrectly, you will have trouble writing clear, well-constructed sentences. If this is the case, see Chapter 33, Common Sentence-Structure Problems, page 682.

practice it   Find Prepositional Phrases

Take a look at a paragraph you have written and underline all the prepositional phrases you used. How are they being used in your sentences? What kinds of information do the prepositional phrases add?

Clauses

A **clause** is a group of words that has a subject and verb. (This is the main difference between a phrase and a clause: Phrases don't have subjects and verbs.) There are two kinds of clauses, *independent clauses* and *dependent clauses*. An independent clause is a complete sentence. A dependent clause can't stand on its own. Left by itself, a dependent clause makes a *fragment*, which is a major grammar error.

To learn more about fragments and how to avoid them, see Chapter 28, Fragments, page 635.

Here are some examples of independent clauses; the subjects are underlined once and the verbs are underlined twice.

Our bodies are 75 percent water.

Water is the healthiest drink for you.

Here's an example of a dependent clause; again, the subject is underlined once and the verb is underlined twice.

Although a person can go weeks without food

This may look like a sentence, but it's not. It's a dependent clause because although it has a subject and verb, it does not complete a thought. In order to do so, it needs to be attached to an independent clause.

Although a person can go weeks without food, he can survive only a few days without water.

Because all organs require water to function, it is recommended that you drink sixty-four ounces a day.

The bold parts of the sentence are dependent clauses. Read them by themselves to hear how dependent they are on the rest of the sentence: They can't stand alone even though they have a subject and verb.

Subordination

Understanding subordination is crucial to understanding how we build sentences in English. Once you get this concept and can recognize the common subordinating words, it will be much easier to notice and fix your errors with fragments, commas, and sentence structure.

If something is subordinate, that means it's on a lower level. In writing, *subordination* shows the relationship between ideas or sentences and that one idea is "lower" or deserves less emphasis. If you take a regular sentence and attach a subordinating word or phrase to it, it can no longer stand alone as a sentence. Instructors use words like *dependent clause* or *subordinate clause* to refer to this. For example, take a perfectly good sentence like this:

Mel got a car.

Now add the subordinating word *after*:

After Mel got a car

This is no longer a perfectly good, complete sentence. It's a *subordinate clause*. (It's a clause because it has a subject and verb, and it's subordinate because it can no longer stand alone.) When we read this, we are left wondering what happened after Mel got a car. The thought is not complete. We could attach this clause to some new information, which might look like this:

After <u>Mel</u> <u>got</u> a car, <u>he</u> <u>stopped</u> taking the bus.

Now this is a complete sentence again. Notice that the emphasis in this sentence is placed on the second half: *he stopped taking the bus.* The subordinate part of the sentence, *After Mel got a car*, tells us when he stopped taking the bus.

COMMA PLACEMENT WITH SUBORDINATING WORDS OR PHRASES

Some of the most common comma mistakes have to do with subordination. While there are always exceptions, you can generally follow these rules:

RULE 1: When you begin a sentence with a subordinate clause, put a comma after it.

Subordinate Clause | Main Clause
When I graduate, I will throw a huge party.

Notice that the comma comes after the entire subordinate clause, not right after the word *when.* You might notice a natural pause between the subordinate clause and the main sentence when you read it out loud.

After she studied for several hours, Mara went to a movie.
Whenever it is a holiday weekend, the traffic is out of control.
Since I am trying to sell my car, I need to wash it and get it tuned up.

RULE 2: When the subordinate clause comes after the main sentence, do *not* use a comma to separate them.

I will throw a huge party **when I graduate**.
Mara went to a movie **after she studied for several hours**.
The traffic is out of control **whenever it is a holiday weekend**.
I need to wash it and get it tuned up **since I am trying to sell my car**.

In these sentences, the subordinate clause can come either before the main sentence or after it. The sentences work either way and have the same meaning.

FINDING AND CORRECTING SUBORDINATION ERRORS

Understanding subordination can help you avoid some major grammar errors. Also, a writer can use subordination to make more sophisticated and interesting sentences. (Don't we all want to be more sophisticated and interesting?)

The most common errors associated with subordination are comma errors, sentence fragments, and mixed-construction errors. Follow these steps to find and correct these errors.

STEP 1: Learn to recognize subordinating conjunctions (sometimes called subordinators). Memorize this list if necessary, or at least memorize the subordinators that tend to show up in your mistakes. Add those to your Grammar Log. Whenever any of the subordinators begin a sentence, you should check carefully to make sure you have a complete sentence.

For more on keeping a Grammar Log, see page 579.

Common Subordinators		
after	since	whereas
although	so that	wherever
as	than	whether
as if	that	which
because	though	whichever
before	unless	while
even if	until	who
even though	whatever	whom
ever since	when	whose
however	whenever	why
if	where	

STEP 2: Learn how to tell the difference between a sentence and a fragment. Here's an example:

> **Fragment**   As long as each person takes one step toward reducing greenhouse gases.

How do we know this is a fragment? Ask yourself: Do we know what will happen as long as each person takes one step toward reducing greenhouse gases? Nope. The sentence doesn't tell us that, so the subordinator *as long as* makes this a fragment. Because it adds an independent clause to the dependent clause, the following sentence is complete:

> **Correct**   As long as each person takes one step toward reducing greenhouse gases, we can greatly reduce the threat of climate change.

Notice that we added the comma *before* we added the independent clause.

practice it   Proofread for Subordinators

In the following paragraph, look for subordinate-clause fragments and comma errors. When you find an error, fix it. There are five errors.

When you think of freshly baked cookies or cakes. What person comes to mind? If it is Mrs. Fields or your mother or grandmother you are not alone. Many people associate baking with women and the home kitchen. Although there are plenty of male chefs who, along with female chefs, excel in the pastry arts. Baking is a perfect blend of science and art, and contemporary bakers have taken baking to new heights. Because it relies on chemical changes in the oven you have to be very exact with your measurements and ingredients. Having a background in food chemistry is almost a necessity with baking these days. While there used to be only shows focused on cooking savory appetizers and entrées. There are now several competition cooking shows dedicated strictly to desserts. These shows highlight some of the most intriguing and artistic sweet creations I have ever seen. No longer focused on traditional desserts like cookies, cakes, and pies, these chefs have truly broken the mold when it comes to reinventing dessert. Some of the creations look like modern art pieces— too incredible to eat. Even though they certainly look like they would taste amazing. The proof in this case is not in the pudding, for we never get a chance to try them. We have to instead rely on the culinary wisdom of the celebrity chef judges. Lucky ducks.

practice it   Applying What You've Learned

It's not enough to learn the grammar rules. You have to apply them. Take a look at some of your writing for this class, and see if you are making the errors we've discussed in the preceding sections. Find and correct the errors; then take your work to your instructor or a tutor to have your corrections checked.

Coordination

Coordination is another way of connecting words and ideas in a sentence or between sentences. The most common way to coordinate in sentences is by using the coordinating conjunction, sometimes better known as **FANBOYS** words. FANBOYS is a great acronym to help you remember the seven coordinating conjunctions: *For, And, Nor, But, Or, Yet, So.* These seven little words help you not only connect words and ideas, but also relate them to each other. Look at these two sentences:

I am tired. I got plenty of sleep.

The two sentences are grammatically fine just as they are, but the sentences are choppy, and the relationship between them is unclear. We can guess at what the writer means, but we shouldn't have to do that work (and we might guess wrong). Take a look at this version:

I am tired, but I got plenty of sleep.

Now, with the word *but* combining these sentences, we see that the writer is ruling out lack of sleep as the cause of his or her tiredness. The word *but* is a coordinating conjunction connecting two complete sentences and showing the opposing or negative relationship between them. Each of the FANBOYS coordinating conjunctions expresses a particular kind of relationship between the components it connects:

F	*For* indicates cause/effect
A	*And* indicates addition of two things
N	*Nor* indicates addition of two negatives
B	*But* indicates opposition or negation
O	*Or* indicates alternatives
Y	*Yet* indicates opposition
S	*So* indicates cause/effect

You can use these coordinating conjunctions to join words, phrases, or independent clauses. Note that when you use a FANBOYS word to combine two independent clauses, you need to add a comma before the coordinating conjunction. Here's an example:

Each hour-long episode is like watching a short movie. You don't have to stand in line.

Each hour-long episode is like watching a short movie, but you don't have to stand in line.

FINDING AND CORRECTING CHOPPY SENTENCES

Placing multiple short sentences one after the other in a paragraph produces a choppy effect. Read the following two paragraphs to see which one sounds better.

Paragraph 1

Television shows seem to be getting better and better. I used to love TV dramas like *Dallas* and *Charlie's Angels*, which were fun. They were not very realistic. After a number of years, okay, decades, TV shows have become more true to life. Now there are more great dramas on TV, especially HBO and Showtime. There are police dramas like *CSI*, *Law & Order*, *The Closer*, and *Criminal Minds*. The TV dramas like *Breaking Bad* and *True Blood* keep viewers on the edges of their seats. The production quality of the shows is terrific. Each hour-long episode is like watching a short movie. You don't have to stand in line. You don't have to pay the high prices of the movie theaters. Shows like *CSI*, *The Wire*, *The Sopranos*, and *Law & Order* all deal with emergencies or crime in the same way a blockbuster film might. All the shows have excellent writing, action-packed scenes, and good actors.

Paragraph 2

Television shows seem to be getting better and better. I used to love TV dramas like *Dallas* and *Charlie's Angels*, which were fun, but they were not very realistic. After a number of years, okay, decades, TV shows have become more true to life, and now there are more great dramas on TV, especially HBO and Showtime. There are police dramas like *CSI*, *Law & Order*, *The Closer*, and *Criminal Minds*. The TV dramas like *Breaking Bad* and *True Blood* keep viewers on the edges of their seats. The production quality of the shows is terrific, so each hour-long episode is like watching a short movie, but you don't have to stand in line, nor do you have to pay the high prices of the movie theaters. Shows like *CSI*, *The Wire*, *The Sopranos*, and *Law & Order* all deal with emergencies or crime in the same way a blockbuster film might. All the shows have excellent writing, action-packed scenes, and good actors.

Which paragraph sounds smoother and flows better from one idea to the next? If you aren't sure, read them each again before continuing on.

If you chose the second paragraph, we agree. Why? What makes the first paragraph harder to read? If you look back, you'll see that the first paragraph has lots of short, choppy sentences. Reading it is like driving along a series of short streets, each ending with a stop sign. You can get to the end of the paragraph eventually, but the journey is not an easy one. The second paragraph has the same information, in the same order, but it combines the shorter sentences together, not only to provide better flow, but also to show the relationship between the ideas of the sentences.

In order to combine short, choppy sentences into smoother-sounding sentences, you need to understand the rules for avoiding run-on sentences and fragments. You also need to be able to recognize what you want your sentences to say. Let's look at two of the ways you can combine short sentences.

For more on fragments, see Chapter 28, Fragments, page 635. For more on run-on sentences, see Chapter 29, Run-Ons: Fused Sentences and Comma Splices, page 649.

OPTION 1: Use a FANBOYS word to combine short sentences.   (For examples, see p. 611.)

OPTION 2: Use a semicolon (;).   Semicolons have a unique function in English grammar. The semicolon's main job is to join independent clauses (sentences) together without needing a FANBOYS conjunction or a capital letter.

Choppy   Some TV shows have remained popular even after decades. *The Simpsons* is one example.

Better   Some TV shows have remained popular even after decades; *the Simpsons* is one example.

practice it   Coordination

Rewrite the following choppy paragraph to express the logical relationships between *sentences* and *ideas* and to create a smoother paragraph.

Traveling is not only a luxury. It is an education as well. When visiting the eastern United States, you can learn about the Pilgrims. You can learn about early American life by visiting Plymouth Rock in Massachusetts. If you want to travel back in time, you can also visit the Jamestown Settlement in Virginia and Colonial Williamsburg in Virginia. They both have re-created outdoor living-history areas you can walk through. The states of the Midwest boast picturesque, small-town American life in towns throughout Ohio, Illinois, Michigan, Nebraska, Missouri, and Minnesota. You can really get a feel for the importance of farming by driving through these bountiful states. You have your choice when visiting the Pacific

continued ⊙

Northwest to get a peek into America's logging. Another choice is you can get a peek into the local fishing industry. It would be a shame to leave without learning about the culture of the indigenous people of this region. Don't miss it. The western and southwestern states offer more than just sunshine. They offer interesting historical lessons about the Gold Rush. You won't find any gold there, unless you buy it. The southern states of America provide a rich opportunity to learn more about and understand the history of the civil rights movement. You can visit some very important locales such as the Civil Rights Memorial and Center in Montgomery, Alabama. The Lorraine Hotel in Memphis, Tennessee, where Martin Luther King Jr. was assassinated, is not to be missed. Of course, traveling to our nation's capital, Washington, D.C., is a must for anyone interested in educational travel. This city is home to dozens of museums where you can learn about history, art, and culture all in one place.

Sentence Variety

Now that you have learned the basic components of a sentence, how can you use this information to build better sentences?

Just as you would get bored listening to music that all had the same beat or tempo, your reader would find your essay monotonous if your sentences were all the same length and constructed the same way. You can improve your overall writing quality by getting comfortable with more complex sentence constructions. Following are the three basic sentence constructions. In the examples below, the subject is underlined once and the verb is underlined twice.

Simple sentence: a basic independent clause. It is made up of a subject and a verb and expresses a complete thought. Here are some examples:

I always order popcorn at the movies.

Murals often display culturally or historically significant themes.

A good education is important.

Compound sentence: two independent clauses joined by a coordinating conjunction (FANBOYS: *for, and, nor, but, or, yet, so*). In the following examples, the conjunction and the second independent clause are in bold.

Some students are already good at keeping a budget, **but others need a class on financial literacy.**

Learning good money habits is a start toward financial stability, **and practicing them regularly helps maintain it.**

Public schools are overcrowded, **so students get too little time from their teachers.**

Complex sentence: an independent clause joined with a dependent clause. In the following examples, the *dependent clause* is in bold.

Because most jobs require strong writing skills, learning to improve writing in college is a smart career move.

Although you can't choose your siblings, they can be a source of great comfort and support.

| practice it | Vary Your Sentence Structure |

You have learned all the basic parts of a sentence, so you should now be able to construct all three kinds of sentences: simple, compound, and complex. Try your hand at sentence variety by writing a short paragraph on one of the following topics. Be sure to practice writing at least two of each kind of sentence.

Suggested Paragraph Topics
Your favorite TV show
The last meal you cooked
Your study plan for the week or month
A summary of the last article you read

chapter review

Chapter 26 covers the basic unit of communication—the sentence. Although you have been writing sentences for many years, this chapter provides important information for understanding how the parts of a sentence work together, which will help you untangle problem sentences. Varying your sentence structure will also keep your writing from sounding monotonous and predictable.

To review this chapter, choose one or more of the following strategies:

1. Try to explain what you have learned, or at least part of it, to someone you know. Discuss the key concepts and give some of your own examples to illustrate those concepts.

2. Make a list of the FANBOYS words and their functions to keep handy until you have them memorized.

3. Make a flash card with the three kinds of sentence structure and example sentences. Tape this card to your desk or keep it in your notebook, so you can refer to it the next time you write an essay.

4. Look over any previous writing assignment you have to see if you can identify the basic sentence components in your own writing. Underline clauses, put parentheses around phrases, and circle or highlight any coordinators and subordinators that you use. Keep this chapter open as you do this so you can refer back to it for help identifying the components.

5. If you skipped any of the Practice It activities throughout the chapter, go back and do them now as a way to deepen your understanding of the material.

6. Update your Grammar Log to include your most frequent errors and corrections. Don't forget to refer to the Grammar Log every time you edit a piece of writing, and don't forget to take the time to edit everything you write for all your college classes.

27
Verbs

in this chapter

- What Do Verbs Do?
- What Is Agreement?
- What Is Tense?
- What Are Irregular Verbs?
- How Do You Find and Fix Errors in Verb Use?

What Exactly Is a Verb?

A *verb* is a word that shows an action or a state of being.

- *Action verbs* are the things that someone or something can do—for example, *laugh, jump,* or *run.*
- *State of being verbs* show that something exists or how it exists—for example, *is, are, was,* or *were.*
- *Linking verbs*—like *feel, look, seem, become,* and *appear*—link the subject with a word that describes the subject.
- *Helping verbs,* also called *auxiliary verbs,* are used with other verbs—for example, *is* running or *had* been. Often, when we talk about the main verb in a sentence, we actually mean two or more verbs together, also called the *verb phrase.* The helping verbs don't necessarily look like verbs, but there are only twenty-three of them, so they are easy to learn and recognize.

To download the Grammar Log, log into your Integrated Media at **bedfordstmartins.com /readwriteconnect** and click on **Charts.**

LearningCurve
For extra practice in the skills covered in this chapter, visit **bedfordstmartins.com /readwriteconnect.**

Helping Verbs		
is, am, are, was, were, be, being, been	may, might, must	shall, should
do, does, did	can, could	will, would
have, has, had		

How can you locate the verb in a sentence? Let's look at an example:

Regina is going to the art studio after lunch.

What is Regina doing? She *is going.* Both of the italicized words are verbs, and together they make up the main verb of the sentence.

617

Let's look at another example, one without a clear action:

Wayne was a little ill from the roller coaster.

What was Wayne doing? Well, nothing—he just *was*. In this case, the verb is the state of being *was*. The state-of-being verbs are not very action packed as verbs go, but they are still verbs.

Let's try another:

Marjorie seems upset again.

Seems isn't an action, but in a way it is what Marjorie is doing: She is seeming. In this sentence, *seems* links Marjorie with the word *upset*.

Let's try one more:

Gabriel appears angry.

What is the verb? Ask yourself: Can you appear? Yes. Can you angry? No. So *appears* is the verb. This method won't always work, but it will often help you locate the verb.

Though a sentence can include multiple clauses, there might be more than one verb in a sentence, there will only be one *main* verb. Remember, a clause is a group of words that has a subject and a verb. (For a refresher about what a clause is, see Chapter 26, Basic Sentence Components, p. 600.) Here's an example, with the subjects underlined once, the verbs underlined twice, and the subjects and verbs that go together linked by arrows:

The books that I need for this class are in the campus bookstore.

Both *need* and *are* are verbs in this sentence. The word *are* is the main verb. The verb *need* is part of the clause *that I need*, which modifies *books* but can't stand on its own.

To review, a verb can be an action or a state of being. A sentence can have more than one verb, and to correct some verb errors, you need to figure out which verb is serving as the main verb of the sentence.

Agreement, Tense, and Irregular Verbs

You need to understand three main things about verbs to avoid making errors in using them:

1. Subject-verb agreement
2. Verb tense
3. Irregular verbs

It's no wonder that verbs are some of the hardest things for people to get right when they are learning English—and that even those who grew up

TIP
Think of a linking verb as an equal (=) sign. Marjorie = upset. The equal sign is a good way to check if a verb is linking or not. If you can use the equal sign instead of the verb, it's a linking verb.

For more practice finding the main verb, see Chapter 26, Basic Sentence Components, page 600.

speaking only English still make mistakes. Verbs are downright tricky sometimes.

SUBJECT-VERB AGREEMENT

Let's start with subject-verb agreement. Your instructor might write "s/v agr" on your paper, and what he or she means is that you have a verb that doesn't match the subject you used. Let's look at an example:

Jennifer laugh at the comedian.

What's wrong here? The verb *laugh* doesn't agree with the subject *Jennifer*. We can't really change the subject because only Jennifer is performing the action, so we have to change the verb to match the subject.

Jennifer laughs at the comedian.

Can you hear the difference between *Jennifer laugh* and *Jennifer laughs*? If you can't, then you probably grew up—as many of us did—hearing this error frequently, and you are likely to make it when you write. You will need to pay special attention while editing your writing, using the specific strategies described in the section on how to fix errors in subject-verb agreement (see p. 622).

VERB TENSE

The second thing to pay attention to is verb tense. Tense indicates time. So when we speak of verb tense, we mean the time period in which the action happened—past, present, or future. It happens; it happened; it will happen—all of these are different verb tenses. If your instructor writes "tense" or "tense shift" while correcting your paper, then you have problems with verb tense.

Let's start with the present tenses. The following types of verbs refer to the various ways you can do something in the **present**:

Present	Jane smiles when she serves ice cream.
Present Progressive	Jane is smiling because she likes serving ice cream.
Present Perfect Progressive	Jane has been smiling while serving ice cream for three hours.

Now, let's look at a few of the ways you can indicate something happened in the **past**, or at least started in the **past**:

Past	Jane smiled at me at the ice cream shop yesterday.

Past Progressive	Jane <u>was smiling</u> when I walked in the door.
Past Perfect	Jane <u>had smiled</u> when I ordered a chocolate malt, but then she frowned when she realized I had no money.
Past Perfect Progressive	Jane <u>had been smiling</u> at me for three minutes when I finally admitted I'm lactose intolerant.

Finally, there are a number of ways you can talk about **future** actions:

Future	Jane <u>will smile</u> at Bob if he comes for ice cream tonight.
Future Progressive	Jane <u>will be smiling</u> when Bob drops his ice cream cone.
Future Perfect	Jane <u>will have smiled</u> at 287 customers by the end of the day.
Future Perfect Progressive	Jane <u>will have been smiling</u> for eight hours by the time her shift is over tonight.

Each verb tense has a name, and if you are learning English as a second language, you may need additional instruction in these tenses. Mostly, though, the goal is to understand the implied time difference enough so that you can figure out from context when something happened or when it happened in relation to another event. For instance, the complicated verb tense *had been smiling* implies that Jane was smiling in the past and had been doing it for some time until something else happened. Both actions are over now. Verb tense becomes a problem when you use the wrong tense or—more commonly—when you shift from one tense to another inappropriately.

IRREGULAR VERBS

The third tricky thing about verbs is that even if you master the rules for verb use, many common verbs in English don't follow the rules. Linguists debate why this is true, but it happens in many languages. For example, the verb "to give" doesn't follow the pattern of a regular verb; in the past tense, we say *she gave me an extra slice of cake* not *she gived me an extra slice of cake.* Of course, anyone who has ever been around small children will remember laughing at their occasional errors, such as this:

"Billy <u>gived</u> me his truck and I <u>hitted</u> him with it!"

This sentence actually uses the logical past tense of *give* and *hit*, but doesn't follow accepted usage. A parent would probably repeat back the corrected sentence to the child:

> "Billy <u>gave</u> you his truck and you <u>hit</u> him with it? That's not very nice!"

The child then hears the verb tense in its irregular form—*gave* instead of *gived* and *hit* instead of *hitted*—and eventually, after hearing this a few times, learns the irregular form. (Though who knows how long it might take to work out the problem with Billy and the truck!)

As adults, many of us—even those whose first language is English—still make errors with certain irregular verbs, though not ones so obvious as those in the previous example. More likely, our errors emerge in more complicated verb forms, especially when a form of the verb *to be* is involved. In fact, the verb *to be* is the most frequently used verb in the English language, so it's a good idea to just memorize the various forms of the verb so you can recognize them when you see them. Here are some of them:

	Singular	Plural
First person	I am	We are
Second person	You are	You are
Third person	He/She/It is	They are

There are many other irregular verbs. Most of the time, it's the past tense that is irregular—*gave* instead of *gived*, *bought* instead of *buyed*. Sometimes, like with *to be* or *to have*, all the forms of the verb are oddballs. Instead of trying to memorize a long list, take care to keep track of the verbs you tend to use incorrectly, and pay attention to the ways that irregular verb forms contribute to your problems with subject-verb agreement or verb tense.

Fixing the Three Main Errors in Verb Use

So, if you are making mistakes with verbs, your first job is to figure out what sort of mistakes you are making. Are your errors mostly with subject-verb agreement? Verb tense? Incorrect usage of irregular verbs? It's possible that you are making all three errors, but most likely you make one error more than the others. Try to pinpoint your problem areas, if possible, by looking over your past work or asking a tutor or instructor to help you identify them.

ERRORS IN SUBJECT-VERB AGREEMENT

Subject-verb agreement means that the verb agrees with—or matches—its subject. We say *José laughs*, not *José laugh*. Errors in subject-verb agreement are serious because they can make a sentence confusing. So how do you get a handle on subject-verb agreement, once you have pinpointed it as one of your trouble areas? If you have studied French or Spanish, the following conjugation chart will look familiar:

	Singular	Plural
First person	I _____	we _____
Second person	you _____	you _____
Third person	he _____	they _____
	she _____	
	it _____	

This chart provides a basic format for conjugating a verb. When you fill in the chart with a nice, normal, regular verb, it looks like this:

	Singular	Plural
First person	I dance	we dance
Second person	you dance	you dance
Third person	he dances	they dance
	she dances	
	it dances	

What do you notice? Most of the forms of *to dance* are the same, except the *he/she/it* form, which we call the third-person singular. That verb form has the letter *s* on the end: *dances*. That box in the chart is always the one that changes.

If the verb ends in a vowel (*a, e, i, o, u*), then add *-es* instead of just *-s* to that third-person singular form. Here's an example with the verb *to do*:

	Singular	Plural
First person	I do	we do
Second person	you do	you do
Third person	he does	they do
	she does	
	it does	

Nice and regular, right? Remember, though, there are three things you have to know about verbs: subject-verb agreement, tense, and irregulars. What happens when we try to figure out the subject-verb agreement for a really irregular verb? Take a look at the verb *to be*:

	Singular	Plural
First person	I am	we are
Second person	you are	you are
Third person	he is	they are
	she is	
	it is	

This is a truly funky irregular verb. It's also one that we use all the time. What do you notice? Take a minute to look at the boxes again. Which one is the most different? The lower left. Granted, they are all pretty bizarre. None of them even start with the letter *b*. The *he/she/it* verb form is the oddest, though. To have subject-verb agreement with the verb *to be*, you have to make sure the verb you are using matches with the subject. You say, "I am," not "I be" or "I are."

Most of the time, if you make subject-verb agreement errors, it's not with simple sentences. Most adults wouldn't say, "I are ready for a nap." Rather, most adults mess up subject-verb agreement in two scenarios:

1. The subject is very complicated.
2. There are words between the subject and the verb.

Let's look at these two scenarios in greater depth.

Complicated Subjects.   *Bob dances. He dances.* That's pretty straightforward, and the subject-verb agreement is easy to hear and see. What happens, though, when the subject is a lot more complicated?

My older sister Sally's ancient VW still gets twenty miles to the gallon.

Trickier, isn't it? You might start to second-guess yourself. What's the subject? *Sister*? *Sally*? *VW*? All of the above? The full subject, really, is the entire phrase *My older sister Sally's ancient VW*; the main subject is *VW*. The verb is *gets*. Do subject and verb agree? Yes, but you may not be as sure as you were with the simpler *Bob dances*.

So how do you know for sure if your subjects and verbs agree? One way to double-check or fix your subject-verb agreement is to replace the subject with its corresponding pronoun. Figure out what you're really talking about in the sentence. In this case,

My older sister Sally's ancient VW = a car

Then figure out which pronoun from the conjugation chart for *to be* fits best. Would you replace *car* with *I*, *we*, *you*, *he*, *she*, *it*, or *they*? In this case,

a car = it

So, if we were to rewrite the sentence using the pronoun, it would read:

It still <u>gets</u> twenty miles to the gallon.

Once you see the sentence this way, it's easier to hear and see that the subject and verb agree.

Some tricky subjects might seem like a *they* or a *we* when they really aren't, so be on the lookout for these. The following indefinite pronouns should be treated as singular:

another	either	no one
anybody	everybody	one
anyone	everyone	somebody
anything	everything	someone
each	neither	something

For example, even though *everybody* sounds like many people, it is treated like a third-person singular (*he/she/it*) form.

Everybody [every individual he/she] <u>hopes</u> for love and success.

There are also some strange nouns that look plural because they end in the letter *s*, but which actually function as the third-person singular (*it*) form. These include words like:

athletics	economics
civics	genetics

mathematics	physics
measles	series
mumps	United States
news	

For example, *United States* would be replaced by the pronoun *it*, not *we*—even if the writer is American.

The **United States** [it] plays a major role in the global economy.

And, of course, some words seem singular but take a plural verb:

both	pliers
few	scissors
jeans	several
many	shears
pants	trousers

For example, *jeans* would be replaced by the pronoun *they*.

My **jeans** [they] fit like a glove.

Did you notice how many words in this list are things that come with two legs or points? It's probably not a coincidence. Perhaps these words came to be treated as plural because they have two parts.

Finally, there are some *indefinite pronouns* that can take a singular or plural verb, depending on the context:

all
any
most
none
some

These words take a singular verb unless they refer to something that has countable components. In general, they are used as singular subjects.

All of my chores are done. [*all* refers to *chores* = plural]

All of the ice cream is gone. [*all* refers to *ice cream* = singular]

Most of my homework is done. [*most* refers to *homework* = singular]

Most of my video games are interesting. [*most* refers to *video games* = plural]

The following words are usually treated as singular, but may be treated as plural depending on context. These are known as *collective nouns*:

audience	group	posse
class	jury	team
crowd	media	
family	orchestra	

Let's look at an example:

> The crowd was cheering wildly when the band came back out for an encore.

Here, *the crowd* refers to one group acting together, so it's treated as singular. Here's another example:

> My family have always argued about politics.

Here, *family* refers to a group made up of individuals, so it's treated as plural.

Words between the Subject and Verb.   The other common reason people make errors in subject-verb agreement is that other words come between the subject and verb, which causes confusion. Consider the following example:

> My physics professor, who has been here since the college first opened and serves on the boards of several internationally ranked academic journals, loves to salsa dance in his spare time.

This sentence conveys a lot of information, but to check the subject-verb agreement, you have to temporarily get rid of some of the information. Look at all the words that come between the subject and verb:

> My physics professor, ~~who has been here since the college first opened and serves on the boards of several internationally ranked academic journals,~~ loves to salsa dance in his spare time.

Once we cut those words out of the sentence, we then see that the subject and verb match:

> My physics professor . . . loves to salsa dance in his spare time.

If you are still confused, you can always change *My physics professor* into the corresponding pronoun:

> He . . . loves to salsa dance in his spare time.

Often, one or more prepositional phrases are between the subject and the verb. Prepositional phrases seem to throw students off because they end with a noun or pronoun, and this sometimes causes confusion about which noun is the subject. For example, take a look at this sentence:

> The bank with the free checking accounts is my favorite.

Accounts is doesn't sound right if you read just those two words together, but in this case you shouldn't read those two words together. *Accounts* is part of the prepositional phrase *with the free checking accounts*. What happens if you eliminate that prepositional phrase temporarily?

> The bank ~~with the free checking accounts~~ is my favorite.

Now it's easier to see that the subject is *bank* and the verb is *is. The bank is* sounds right. The subject and verb do agree.

Simple, right? In fact, simplicity is your best tool for correcting errors in subject-verb agreement. Once you change the subject into a simple pronoun and temporarily eliminate any extra words or phrases, you can simplify the sentence and check its subject-verb agreement.

practice it   Editing for Subject-Verb Agreement Errors

The following paragraph has only subject-verb agreement errors. You should find and fix six errors.

> According to Carol S. Dweck, we have the fixed-mind-set students, who approaches their learning by just doing the bare minimum. On the other hand, there is students who have a growth mind-set. Having a growth mind-set mean you are more eager to learn. A student who has a growth mind-set always try to achieve a lot more. In my opinion, having a growth mind-set is the best way to progress in life. This way of thinking about life show that you believe in yourself and have hope for the future. My sister, who is successful in her career and makes my family proud, have a growth mind-set all the way. I am working hard to be like her.

ERRORS IN VERB TENSE

Remember, verb tense refers to when the action took place. Instead of memorizing grammatical terms for each tense, concentrate on asking yourself the following key questions:

- Did the action happen in the past, present, or future?
- Is the action ongoing, or is it finished or will it finish?
- If there is more than one action happening, which one happened first?

Since the proper use of verb tense is always context specific—meaning it depends on what exactly you are saying—you have to check verb tense on a case-by-case basis. Generally, reading out loud is a good strategy to edit for verb tense, if you are a native speaker of English.

Using the Wrong Verb Tense.   Remember, verb tense means verb *time*. Let's say, for instance, you are describing what happened at a birthday party yesterday. Since the party is in the past, and it is not still going on, you use *simple past*:

> We had a great time at Samantha's birthday party. She had twenty-five different kinds of cupcakes.

How would that sound in the *simple present* tense?

> We have a great time at Samantha's birthday party. She has twenty-five different kinds of cupcakes.

Not quite right, huh? If we were actually still at the party, and, let's say, we called a friend to brag about it while we were still there, we would put it this way, using the simple present:

> We are having a great time at Samantha's birthday party. She has twenty-five different kinds of cupcakes.

A bit conceited, but grammatically correct. Now, what about the future tense? How would that sound?

> We will have a great time at Samantha's birthday party. She will have twenty-five different kinds of cupcakes.

That sounds okay. The question is, did the party already happen or not? Only you, the author/guest, know what you are trying to say. Choose the right verb tense so that your reader knows when the party took place. The verb tense is the only indication of this information in the sentence.

The Literary Present.   One unusual thing about academic writing is the use of the "literary present tense." What this means is that we are expected to write in the present tense when writing about what happens in literature, films, and other creative works. Why? It's a convention, or a rule. It does have some logic to it as well: Every time you open a book, the characters are always doing the same actions—Huck's always going down the river; Harry Potter's always battling Voldemort. They always exist in the present; frozen in the literary present, they never change. This same logic applies when referring to the author writing the text. Here's what it looks like:

> As Mark Twain writes in *Huckleberry Finn*, "We went to a clump of bushes, and Tom made everybody swear to keep the secret, and then showed them a hole in the hill, right in the thickest part of the bushes" (9).

Sure, Mark Twain has been dead for over a century, but in academic writing we still say "Mark Twain writes . . ."

Shifting Incorrectly between Tenses.   Most verb-tense errors are actually verb-tense-shift errors. The rules for these can be complex because the correct verb tense always depends on the context. Let's look at a couple of common student verb-tense errors, starting with this example:

| Incorrect | She **was** in a bad mood because she **is** in an awkward position between her bickering friends. |

Here the writer shifts from *was* to *is*—from past to present—a shift for which there is no reason in the sentence.

| Correct | She **was** in a bad mood because she **was** in an awkward position between her bickering friends. |

OR

| Correct | She **is** in a bad mood because she **is** in an awkward position between her bickering friends. |

Only the writer knows whether past or present is preferable; the important thing is to stay consistent, since there is no logical reason to shift tenses. Here's another example:

| Incorrect | Yesterday, he <u>was</u> being weird because he <u>gets</u> too little sleep. |

Here, we clearly have a time marker, the word *yesterday*. So we know this action took place in the past.

| Correct | Yesterday, he **was** being weird because he **got** too little sleep. |

When you write a paragraph, you often need to shift from one verb tense to another because of what you are trying to say. The problem comes when you do so incorrectly. Look at the following short paragraph:

> Financial literacy <u>used</u> to be taught in most high schools, but it <u>has</u> not <u>been taught</u> since school boards <u>cut</u> home economics classes in order to focus more on English, math, and science. They <u>might have moved</u> the financial literacy component of the curriculum into the math classes, but for some reason they <u>didn't</u>. Unfortunately, most students <u>are</u> no longer <u>taught</u> how to read a contract, balance a checkbook, or make a home budget.

As you can see, the basic verb tense is past (*used, cut, didn't*). The verb tense shifts when appropriate, though, to more complicated tenses like *has not been taught*. In fact, there are many appropriate verb tense shifts in the paragraph.

So, then, how do you shift verb tense appropriately while writing? Try following these steps.

STEP 1: Figure out what time frame you want to use throughout the piece of writing: past, present, or future.   For example:

It **was** August 29, 2012, the first day of my college career. I nervously <u>took</u> a seat in the front row of my English class. [time frame: past]

OR

It **is** August 29, 2012, the first day of my college career. I nervously <u>take</u> a seat in the front row of my English class. [time frame: present]

STEP 2: When something happens outside of your basic time frame, change the verb tense.   Be sure to return to your basic time frame immediately afterwards. In the following example, the basic time frame is the simple past, and most of the verbs are in the simple past (they are in bold italic so you can see them). However, some of the verbs (the ones that are underlined) indicate actions that happened prior to August 29, 2012 so the verb tense shifts appropriately.

My College Career by Joe Mangaro, February 2013

It ***was*** August 29, 2012, the first day of my college career. Just a few days earlier, I <u>had decided</u> to quit my job and register for classes at City College. I nervously ***took*** a seat in my first class, English 100. For the past ten years, I <u>had been working</u> in a small factory, bored out of my skull. Now, all of a sudden, I ***found*** myself ***crammed*** into a chair too small for me, ***surrounded*** by a bunch of teenagers. I ***felt*** too old to be in college, and they ***looked*** too young to ever be my friends. I ***found*** out that I ***had*** more in common with them than I <u>had thought</u>.

If the tense shifts in this paragraph are confusing, it might help to make a time line of the events. It would look like this:

2000–2011	approx. August 23, 2012	August 29, 2012	February 2013
working in a factory, bored	decided to quit job and register for college	first day of college	writing this essay

Having a clear sense of the time line makes it much easier to get your verbs right, so take the time to draw one if you find that you are not sure about what happened when.

ERRORS IN IRREGULAR VERB USAGE

To fix errors with irregular verbs, begin by writing up a list of the verbs that you use incorrectly. Then make flash cards with their proper usage and spend time memorizing them. For instance, if you have trouble with forms of the verb *to be*, write out the conjugation chart a few times. We rarely suggest that you use rote memorization to solve your grammar problems, but this is one of those times when it might be necessary to drill the right information into your head through constant repetition. Most likely, if you struggle with irregular verbs, it is because English is your second (or third) language, or because you grew up hearing the "wrong" verb over and over. Constant repetitive practice, such as making and practicing with flash cards, may be necessary to break the habit.

For example, in many regions of the country, people might say, "He *snuck* into the movie theater." This is a regionalism that probably sounds just perfect to you if you live in the American South. It is, however, not proper grammar. The correct way to say it is, "He *sneaked* into the movie theater." But if you grew up hearing *snuck*, then it's going to be a hard habit to break. Constant repetition will be necessary to break yourself of the habit.

If you regularly make one or two errors like this, people will consider it a cute regionalism. If you make many such errors, they will start to question your grasp of the English language. Certain errors also attract more unwelcome attention than others. Simply using *snuck* instead of *sneaked*, for example, will fly below most people's radar, but using *gived* instead of *gave* will not. So target your most serious errors and practice correcting them. Start by looking at the errors your instructor has marked on your papers. Be sure to add those errors to your Grammar Log with some of your own sample sentences.

For more on keeping a Grammar Log, see page 579.

practice it   Editing for Verb-Tense Errors

Verb-tense errors are context specific, so there will be more than one way to fix the following paragraph. Maintain consistent simple past tense unless specific time markers require you to shift to another tense. You should find and fix fifteen verb errors.

On April 23, 1967, Bobby McGregor, who was then seventeen, stolen fifteen dollars from the home of his aunt and uncle, Mr. and Mrs. Neal McGregor. Since Bobby was a family member, the McGregors do not press charges. Now, looking back on it after all these years, the

continued ◉

McGregors wishing they had. Perhaps, they might stop Bobby from developing into one of the worst petty thieves in town history. For on April 24, 1967, thrilling at how easy it would be to take the fifteen dollars, Bobby breaked into the local general store and stolen some perfume for his little sister, Kate, and a baseball glove for his brother, Sammy. Two days later, he was slipping into the school cafeteria after the lunch period and walked off with fourteen chocolate chip cookies. From there, things are going downhill quickly: A lawn mower was pilfer from the local hardware shop, a historical brass bell was remove from the town museum, and fourteen glass rabbit figurines vanish from the mayor's wife's personal collection. No one could quite identify the thief, but everyone in town had their suspicions. The McGregor name was tarnish forever. Little Kate had no friends at school, and Sammy's dream of becoming president is crushed. Ashamed but silent, Bobby left town when he turned eighteen, never to be seen or hearing from again.

practice it   Editing for Multiple Errors in Verb Use

Correct the following paragraph, which has a mixture of types of verb problems. Remember, there is more than one correct way to rewrite the paragraph. Check with your instructor or tutor if you get stuck.

Portable music are not a recent invention. It used to be common to see teens with transistor radios, which are small and easy to carry around, but you couldn't play your own music on them. With radios you can only listen to what the station played. Then came boom boxes blasting the latest new music. The problem is that boom boxes were bulky and everyone could have to hear your music. In the eighties, Sony invented the Walkman, which is a small, portable tape player. This was a good change because you could have played any music you wanted. They even made a waterproof version that you could take to the beach or pool. The main problem with a Walkman is that the sound quality of tapes were pretty bad. Sony eventually made a Discman that was the same idea, but it played CDs instead of tapes. The Discman were an improvement from the Walkman, but songs skipped a lot when the Discman gets bumped. With more recent technology came the MiniDisc player, which was a huge improvement, but it didn't last long because even better technology are just around the corner: the MP3 player. The MP3 player is the latest in portable music technology, and its strongest feature is that you can store tons of songs in a compact player. It seems like everyone have an iPod these days. My iPod can hold up to six thousand songs, and it's tiny! It has a long battery life, and I can even watch movies or TV shows on it. Portable music did really evolved over the years, and I can't imagine what's next: probably a microchip that you would drop into your ear.

chapter review

Verb errors are like ingrained bad habits. You can replace them with new, better habits by following the guidelines in Chapter 27, but it takes work. The truth is that verb errors are some of the hardest errors to eliminate from your writing, partly because you most likely have been hearing the verbs incorrectly and writing them incorrectly for a long time. You have to pay special attention to verbs for a while, and then you'll be able to find and fix your errors.

To review this chapter, choose one or more of the following strategies:

1. Try to explain what you have learned, or at least part of it, to someone you know. Discuss the key concepts and give some of your own examples to illustrate those concepts.

2. Reread every single thing you write to try to eliminate verb errors. This goes for everything, even e-mails to friends. By looking only at the verbs, you will isolate those errors, which will make you more likely to see problems.

3. Make a flash card with the kinds of verb errors you tend to make. Look over essays you have gotten back in your current English class or previous ones, and see if your instructor has noted any verb errors. On the flash

card, include one of your own sentences with the verb error and a corrected version of the sentence. Keep this flash card handy when you edit your papers.

4. If you skipped any of the Practice It activities throughout the chapter, go back and do them now as a way to deepen your understanding of the material.

5. Update your Grammar Log to include your most frequent verb errors. Don't forget to edit the Grammar Log every time you edit a piece of writing, and don't forget to take the time to edit everything you write for all your college classes.

28

Fragments

in this chapter

- What Is a Fragment?
- How Do You Recognize Fragments in Your Own Writing?
- How Do You Fix Fragments?

What Exactly Is a Fragment?

Fragments are a very common sentence error, and they can seriously affect the meaning of your writing. A fragment is also sometimes called an incomplete sentence, and that's a good way to think about it. Fragments occur when you have a partial sentence that is missing something. You can also think of it as a thought that isn't completely finished. The three main causes of fragments are

- A missing subject
- A missing verb or part of a verb
- An incomplete thought—a "cliffhanger," so to speak

Your readers care about sentence fragments because without the verb or subject they don't know what the action of the sentence is, or who performs the action. That's why instructors consider sentence fragments major errors. Instructors will usually take points off your grade for them, so you definitely want to learn how to edit to fix fragments. Luckily, learning a few rules and practicing them can help you tackle this problem.

Take a look at the following example:

Fragment   Going to the bookstore to get my textbooks.

This is a fragment because we don't know who is going to the bookstore. In other words, we don't know the subject of the sentence. Now, you may think, "Well, anybody could figure it out—I am the one going to the bookstore," and that fragment would be fine if you were just talking, but in written English, it's important to say what you mean completely.

Correct   <u>I am</u> going to the bookstore to get my textbooks.

For a sentence to be complete, it needs to have all these things: a subject, a complete verb, and a complete thought. An incomplete-thought

LearningCurve
For extra practice in the skills covered in this chapter, visit **bedfordstmartins.com /readwriteconnect.**

fragment might occur when you begin to write what seems like a sentence but don't quite finish it. Basically, this fragment occurs when your sentence does not complete your thought. The sentence leaves the reader hanging on to hear the rest of the thought; this type of fragment is sometimes referred to as a "cliffhanger." Sometimes authors write fragments on purpose because they are acceptable in certain kinds of writing like newspaper headlines, magazine articles, literature, or children's picture books. Fragments in these cases are produced intentionally for stylistic purposes, but in academic writing, fragments are always considered errors.

FRAGMENTS THAT ARE MISSING A SUBJECT

TIP
To find the subject of a sentence, ask yourself: Who or what is doing the action of the verb?

Typically, if there's a problem with a fragment's subject, it's simply that you left it out. This error usually happens when the subject is in the previous sentence or when the subject seems obvious. Most of the time, you can't get away with this type of fragment. Without a subject, you don't have a complete sentence. Take a look at the following example of a fragment:

Fragment   Gave up playing pro basketball to coach.

Ask yourself: Who or what gave up playing basketball? Let's say Samantha did.

Correct   <u>Samantha</u> gave up playing pro basketball to coach.

Let's examine another fragment:

Fragment   Interesting to compare the two readings.

What is interesting to compare? Think about what your sentence is about. What are you trying to say? In this case, you are basically saying *it* is interesting or *comparing* is interesting. Either of these could be the subject.

Correct   <u>It</u> is interesting to compare the two readings.

OR

Correct   <u>Comparing</u> the two readings <u>is</u> interesting.

When you find fragments that are missing subjects, the fix is to add a subject. Sometimes the subject is actually in the sentence before or after the fragment, and the best fix is to combine the fragment with that sentence. Remember that when you use a semicolon, the parts that come before and after it must be able to stand as complete sentences.

Fragment   Jeremy loved the beach and ocean; also wanted to learn to scuba dive.

Who wanted to learn to scuba dive? *Jeremy.* You can join the fragment to the independent clause to avoid repeating the same subject, or add a subject to the fragment after the semicolon.

For more on independent clauses, see Chapter 26, Basic Sentence Components, page 600.

Correct   Jeremy loved the beach and ocean <u>and</u> also wanted to learn to scuba dive.

OR

Correct   Jeremy loved the beach and ocean; <u>he</u> also wanted to learn to scuba dive.

Now, let's take a look at a special kind of sentence:

***Not* a Fragment**   Finish your coffee before entering the computer lab.

Although this sentence begins with a verb and there is no subject visible in the sentence, it is not a fragment. This sentence is a command, and most command sentences have an implied *you* as the subject even though it won't appear in the sentence.

(Hey, you:) Finish your coffee before entering the computer lab.

practice it   Finding a Fragment

Find an example from your own writing of a fragment that is missing a subject. Jot it down in your Grammar Log and correct it. If you can't find any, try to make one up, and then correct it.

For more on keeping a Grammar Log, see page 579.

practice it   Editing for Fragments Missing Subjects

1. Read the paragraph and underline all the fragments you find. You should find five problem sentences.
2. Decide how to fix the parts you've underlined. Remember, you can combine sentences, add words, or totally rewrite. Make your corrections by hand in the space above the sentence you are fixing.

Fast Food Nation by Eric Schlosser is an eye-opening book about the fast-food industry in America. Not just about fast-food restaurants, but is revealing about the entire industry from cattle ranching to marketing. The book taught me a lot. Didn't know what went on behind the scenes at a slaughterhouse. The way employees are treated at many fast-food restaurants was disappointing to read

continued ❯

about. McDonald's doesn't want any of their employees to belong to a union. Preferring to close down a restaurant sometimes instead of allowing the employees to create a union to protect workers' rights and wages. What was most surprising, though, was learning about how bad for you the food is. Of course, never thought cheeseburgers and fries were healthy, but I had no idea that they caused so much obesity in people. Not only is the fat bad for you, but there's lots of sugar in the food too. Causing childhood obesity. I will never look at another McBurger the same way again after reading this book.

FRAGMENTS THAT ARE MISSING A VERB OR PART OF A VERB

For more help finding verbs, see "Time-Testing to Find the Verb," page 601, in Chapter 26, Basic Sentence Components.

Sometimes sentences have words that look like verbs, but the verb is not complete or isn't actually a verb at all. The two most common problems with verbs are using an *-ing* verb all by itself or using the *to* _____ form of the verb. Watch out for words ending in *-ing* that look like verbs but are not complete on their own. If they do not have a helping verb, then the sentence won't be complete. Also look out for *to* verbs, which are in their infinitive form and can't work as the main verb of the sentence.

Take a look at the following fragment:

Fragment   The waiter carefully balancing several plates on the way back to the kitchen.

For a list of helping verbs, see Chapter 25, Parts of Speech, page 586.

Can the waiter *balancing*? No, he *was balancing* or maybe he *balanced*. Either add a helping verb to make the verb complete, or turn *balancing* into a verb on its own. In this case, either works.

Correct   The waiter <u>was</u> carefully balancing several plates on the way back to the kitchen.

OR

Correct   The waiter carefully <u>balanced</u> several plates on the way back to the kitchen.

Let's look at another sample fragment:

Fragment   Maya for mayor.

Is there a verb here? Can you *for*? Nope. You can be for something or run for mayor, but you can't *for*. This is a popular campaign slogan, and it fits easily on election posters, but in writing this phrase is considered a fragment. Add a verb.

Correct   Maya <u>ran</u> for mayor.

Here's another example:

> **Fragment**   My history professor to return our exams today.

Is there a verb here? In this sentence, *to return* seems like a verb (action), but the *to* form can never be the verb. Either add a verb to the sentence, or change the *to* form into a verb.

> **Correct**   My history professor <u>promised</u> to return our exams today.
>
> OR
>
> **Correct**   My history professor <u>returned</u> our exams today.

---

practice it   **Finding a Fragment**

Find an example from your own writing of a fragment that is missing a verb or part of a verb. Jot it down in your Grammar Log, and then correct it. If you can't find any, try to make one up, and then correct it.

---

practice it   **Editing for Fragments Missing Verbs**

1. Read the paragraph and underline all the fragments you find. You should find five problem sentences.
2. Decide how to fix the parts you've underlined. Remember, you can combine sentences, add words, or totally rewrite. Make your corrections by hand in the space above the sentence you are fixing.

Everybody knows the three Rs of waste disposal: reduce, reuse, and recycle, right? Recycling is easy to do. So why don't more people recycle? People are busy and stressed in their daily lives. People feeling inconvenienced. Recycling takes effort, and so people don't do it. An increase in recycling bins around town. However, the problem is also created by our impatient lifestyle. People buy lots of disposable products. For example, plastic razors, disposable cleaning products, plastic diapers, which account for a large amount of the landfill waste. Instead, we could shop smarter to reduce the amount of disposables and packaging that gets thrown away. Also, so much food and yard waste that ends up in landfills that could be composted instead. You probably never thought of recycling your old coffee grounds or banana peels, but you can. The end result makes soil. Composting, an easy solution.

FRAGMENTS THAT ARE INCOMPLETE THOUGHTS

Another kind of fragment is an incomplete thought fragment, also known as a "cliffhanger." This type of fragment occurs when the idea or thought is not complete. These fragments may look a lot like sentences, but they do not complete a thought—they are cliffhangers, because they leave us needing more information. This kind of fragment has several variations. Cliffhangers might be a phrase adding information to another sentence or beginning with a preposition or a subordinator.

For more on subordinators, see Chapter 25, Parts of Speech, page 586, and Chapter 26, Basic Sentence Components, page 600.

With these kinds of fragments, it's often easiest to look at the sentence before or after the fragment to figure out what is missing. In some cases, cliffhanger fragments need both subjects and verbs, like in the following example:

> **Fragment**   Wishing he had more time to study.

Wishing seems like a verb, but it's not complete without a helping verb, and in this case, it needs a subject as well. An *-ing* verb alone can't be the main verb of the sentence; you need a helping verb as well:

> **Fragment**   Was wishing he had more time to study.

Okay, that fixes the verb problem, but the sentence is still a fragment. *Who* was wishing? Let's say *Carlo*.

> **Correct**   <u>Carlo was wishing</u> he had more time to study.

Now that we have added enough information to make the thought complete, this is no longer a cliffhanger; it's now a complete sentence.

FRAGMENTS THAT BEGIN WITH PREPOSITIONS

For more on prepositions, see Chapter 25, Parts of Speech, page 586, and Chapter 26, Basic Sentence Components, page 600.

Beware of sentences that begin with prepositional phrases. They often add a bunch of words to a sentence and give you the illusion that it's a complete thought. Don't fall for it! Learn to recognize a prepositional phrase so it doesn't trick you.

Common Prepositions		
after	by	into
among	for	like
as	from	since
before	in	with

Let's look at an example. Here, the second sentence, which is actually a fragment, begins with a prepositional phrase.

> **Fragment**   The author starts off making an argument. *For increasing the number of healthy snacks available to school kids who are currently at the mercy of fast-food manufacturers.*

The prepositional phrase "For increasing the number of healthy snacks available to school kids who are currently at the mercy of fast-food manufacturers" cannot stand alone; it is not a complete thought. It should be a part of the previous sentence because it tells us what kind of argument the author is making. Fix this fragment by removing the period after *argument* and making the F in *For* lowercase.

Correct	The author starts off making the <u>argument for</u> increasing the number of healthy snacks available to school kids, who are currently at the mercy of fast-food manufacturers.

Here's another example:

Fragment	In an attempt to impress the other guests.

What happened in an attempt to impress the other guests? You need to explain what happened.

Correct	<u>Cynthia wore a fancy hat</u> in an attempt to impress the other guests.

Fragments can often occur when you use a preposition to introduce an author or quote. Be especially on the lookout for fragments like this one:

Fragment	In the beginning of his essay "The Fifteen Appeals of Advertising," states that the appeal for affiliation—friends, family, and romantic relationships—is actually more common than most people would think.

Who is doing the stating? The author, Jib Fowles.

Correct	In the beginning of his essay "The Fifteen Appeals of Advertising," <u>Jib Fowles</u> states that the appeal for affiliation—friends, family, and romantic relationships—is actually more common than most people would think.

Often, fragments are created when a preposition is used to add examples or explanation to a sentence. Watch out for fragments like the one in this example:

Fragment	To do well this semester, I have mapped out all my major assignments. *Like my art history term paper, my English semester project and paper, and all my final exams.*

Like suggests that you are going to provide examples of something. What are the art history term paper, the English semester project and paper, and the final exams examples of? They are examples of *major assignments.* A list of examples cannot stand on its own as a sentence, because there is no subject. In this case, it should be joined with the sentence before it.

> **Correct**   To do well this semester, I have mapped out all my major <u>assignments, like</u> my art history term paper, my English semester project and paper, and all my final exams.

---

practice it   **Editing for Fragments That Begin with Prepositions**

Make a list of prepositions that you often use and want to keep an eye on in your own writing. Find an example from your own writing of a fragment that begins with a preposition. Jot it down in your Grammar Log, and then correct it. If you can't find any, try to make one up, and then correct it.

FRAGMENTS THAT BEGIN WITH SUBORDINATORS (DEPENDENT WORDS)

For more on subordinates, see Chapter 25, Parts of Speech, page 586, and Chapter 26, Basic Sentence Components, page 600.

Even if you've never heard of a subordinator or think it sounds like an engine part, don't let this grammar word confuse you. As we discuss in Chapter 25, a subordinate is someone who is lower than someone else; for instance, an employee is the subordinate of the boss.

A subordinating word is a word that makes one part of the sentence "lower" in rank, or dependent on the main sentence. In this position, this part of the sentence can't stand alone; it becomes a fragment. You make a fragment if you put a subordinator on a sentence and don't add anything else to the sentence. This would be a bad idea, as we can see in the following example.

> **Fragment**   *Unless there is a great demand for change.* The school district won't improve the snacks or lunches it provides for students.

What won't happen unless there is great demand for it? *The school district won't change the snacks or lunches.* In this case, it makes the most sense to simply combine the fragment with the sentence following it, since they are really two parts of the same thought.

> **Correct**   Unless there is a great demand for <u>change, the</u> school district won't improve the snacks or lunches it provides for students.

Some Common Subordinators

after	even	when
although	if	whenever
anywhere	since	whereas
as	so that	wherever
because	though	while
before	unless	

Let's take a look at another example:

| Fragment | *Although TV news programs can provide video footage and up-to-the-minute information on developing news stories. News on the Internet is updated even more frequently throughout the day and night.* |

Can the first sentence here stand on its own? Does it complete a thought? No. Words like *although* set up a two-part sentence kind of like *if . . . then . . .* You need both parts for the sentence to make sense and to complete the thought. Here, the second part of the two-part thought is in the next sentence. In this case, combine the two thoughts by replacing the period with a comma. Any time you begin a sentence with a dependent word, you need a comma to separate the first part of the sentence from the rest of the sentence.

| Correct | Although TV news programs can provide video footage and up-to-the-minute information on developing news <u>stories,</u> <u>news</u> on the Internet is updated even more frequently throughout the day and night. |

Which of the following sentences is a fragment?

| Fragment | To me, this party is boring. Since my best friend just met a cute guy. Maybe we'd better stay a while longer. |

The fragment is *Since my best friend just met a cute guy. Since* is a subordinator, and it creates a cliffhanger because we are left wanting to know what will happen since the best friend just met a cute guy. Once again, you can use a comma to combine the two thoughts.

| Correct | To me, this party is boring. Since my best friend just met a cute guy, maybe we'd better stay a while longer. |

> **practice it**   **Finding a Fragment**
>
> Make a list of subordinators that you often use and want to keep an eye on in your writing. Find an example from your own writing of a fragment that begins with a subordinator and jot it down in your Grammar Log. If you can't find any, try to make one up, and then correct it.

FRAGMENTS THAT ADD ADDITIONAL INFORMATION: *WHO, LIKE, WHEN,* AND *WHICH* FRAGMENTS

Some fragments are created when you write a phrase that might be adding more information or explanation to a previous sentence, but the phrase can't stand alone. Often, these phrases begin with words like *who*, *like*, *when*, and *which*. These fragments are usually best fixed by combining the additional information to another existing sentence. Here's an example:

Fragment   Cosmetic ads especially appeal to teens. *Who might feel insecure about their appearance.*

To whom does *Who might feel insecure about their appearance* refer? *Who* refers to *teens* in the previous sentence and should be a part of that sentence.

Correct   Cosmetic ads especially appeal to <u>teens who might feel insecure</u> about their appearance.

Here's another instance where added information can't stand alone:

Fragment   Of course we are going to have high standards for beauty. *When advertisers only use young, beautiful models to sell their products.*

What is going to happen *When advertisers only use young, beautiful models to sell their products*? *We are going to have high standards for beauty* when that happens, so this fragment is really finishing the thought of the previous sentence and should be joined with it.

Correct   Of course we are going to have high standards for <u>beauty when</u> advertisers only use young, beautiful models to sell their products.

Take a look at one more example:

Fragment   Barney is a great guy and a really fantastic dancer. *Which is why he always gets invited to parties.*

Why does he always get invited to parties? He always gets invited to parties because he is a great guy and a really fantastic dancer. Connect the *which* clause to the previous sentence to make it complete the thought.

Correct   Barney is a great guy and a really fantastic <u>dancer, which</u> is why he always gets invited to parties.

practice it   Words That Lead You to Write Fragments

Look at papers you have gotten back from your instructors. In your Grammar Log, make a note about what kinds of words might trigger fragments for you. It's likely that there is a pattern to the types of fragments you write. Once you see your fragment pattern, it's easier to find and fix the errors. (If there is a pattern, your instructor can help you find it too.)

Recognizing Fragments in Your Own Writing

The trick to identifying fragments in your own writing is to know what a complete sentence needs and then make sure each sentence has all the necessary parts. When in doubt, ask yourself the following three questions:

For more on keeping a Grammar Log, see Chapter 24, How to Learn the Rules and Apply Them to Your Own Writing, page 576.

1. Does it have a subject?
2. Does it have a verb?
3. Does it complete a thought?

If the answer to any of these questions is "no," you've found a fragment.

Most often, we end up with fragments when the sentence seems long enough to be complete, but isn't. Just because a sentence is long does not mean it is complete; even a long sentence can be a fragment. Look at the following example:

> Cleaner-burning fuels, hybrid cars, and better public transportation have led to improved air quality, which continues to improve. Because older cars are removed from the roads and no longer pollute the air with harmful carbon dioxide.

This seems like two sentences when we read them together, but one is actually a fragment. See what happens when we read them separately:

> Cleaner-burning fuels, hybrid cars, and better public transportation have led to improved air quality, which continues to improve.

Ask yourself: Does it have all the necessary parts?

1. Does it have a subject? Yes: *fuels, cars, and transportation*
2. Does it have a verb? Yes: *have led*
3. Does it complete a thought? Yes: *They've led to improved air quality.*

So that one checks out. How about the next one?

> Because older cars are removed from the roads and no longer pollute the air with harmful carbon dioxide.

1. Does it have a subject? Yes: *cars*
2. Does it have a verb? Yes: *are removed*
3. Does it complete a thought? No: *What happens when older cars are removed from the roads?*

So the second "sentence" is not a sentence at all, but a fragment. Generally, you have two choices when fixing a fragment:

1. Add the missing necessary part.
2. Combine the fragment with the previous or following sentence to complete the thought or to add the necessary part.

In this case, the missing part (what happens when older cars are removed from the roads) is in the previous sentence (air quality will continue to improve).

Correct	Cleaner burning fuels, hybrid cars, and better public transportation have led to improved air quality, which continues to improve <u>because older cars are removed</u> from the roads and no longer pollute the air with harmful carbon dioxide.

You can learn to fix fragments, but it will take practice. The best way to catch sentence errors like fragments is to read your essay out loud, slowly. Often you can "hear" when a sentence is not complete. Not all fragments are easy to spot, so here are some good tips for finding them:

- **Keep a list of words to look out for** and check your paragraph or essay for sentences that begin with them. When you find them, pay careful attention to whether or not you have created a fragment.
- **Look for sentences that begin with verbs** in your writing and check to make sure you haven't created a fragment.
- **When you edit, get into the habit of reading your writing from back to front.** This helps because you often blend sentences together in your mind when reading. In the case of "cliffhanger" fragments, you won't always be able to tell when a sentence is really missing information without isolating it. To do this, begin at the last sentence of the paragraph or essay and read it through. Check to see if it has a subject, verb, and complete thought. If it does, great, move to the next-to-last sentence and repeat this process all the way through your writing. This trick is a bit time-consuming, but it really helps you find cliffhangers.
- **Don't think that a long sentence is always a complete sentence, or a short sentence is necessarily incomplete.** Fragments can be long or short, and so can sentences. Length is not a good way to determine if something is a fragment or not.

practice it   Editing for Fragments

1. Read the paragraph and underline all the fragments you find. You should find eight problem sentences.
2. Decide how to fix the parts you've underlined. Remember, you can combine sentences, add words, or totally rewrite. Make your corrections by hand in the space above the sentence you are fixing.

Most of the time, Americans spend more money than they earn. Which leads them into debt. However, every so often, you end up with extra money in your pockets from a sudden windfall, like a birthday. Or if you're lucky, a tax refund. Wondering what the best use for that money is? A quick trip to Vegas. Sounds like fun, but most of us know there are better ways to spend it. So what should you do with that extra cash? The first thing to do is to pay off your debt or any money you borrowed from someone else. If you have more than one type of debt, you should pay down the one with the highest interest rate first. Usually your credit card. After that, you should try to save a good chunk of change for emergencies. It's smart to imagine what types of emergencies you might have. For instance, a flat tire or a broken cell phone. Maybe even living expenses for three to six months if you live on your own. Then you can decide how much you need to save for emergencies. Once your emergency fund is as full as necessary, then you can start to save for those little luxuries you want, like that trip to Vegas. Knowing what to do with extra cash is the first step toward not having to worry about money.

practice it   Applying What You've Learned

Take out a draft of your writing and use one or more of the techniques you have learned to search for fragments. If you don't have a current piece of writing, try looking through an older essay or paragraph that you have written. If your instructor has told you that you tend to make fragment errors in your writing, then be especially careful in your search for them.

chapter review

Chapter 28 explains a common writing error—fragments—and shows you how to recognize and correct them in your own writing. This chapter introduces you to various types of fragments and gives you hints for identifying them and strategies for fixing them.

To review this chapter, choose one or more of the following strategies:

1. Define a fragment in your own words, and explain why fragments are considered such a serious grammar error by writers and instructors.

2. If you were confused by any of the explanations or kinds of fragments in this chapter, reread those sections to see if the material makes more sense now that you have made it through the whole chapter. Be sure to ask for clarification from your instructor or a tutor if you are still unsure.

3. Update your Grammar Log to include your personal examples of fragments and the corrected versions. If you tend to make more than one type of fragment, include a sample of each type of fragment you make. Don't forget to refer to the Grammar Log every time you edit a piece of writing, and don't forget to make the time to edit everything you write for all your college classes.

29

Run-Ons: Fused Sentences and Comma Splices

in this chapter

- What Is a Fused Sentence?
- What Is a Comma Splice?
- How Do You Find Fused Sentences and Comma Splices?
- How Do You Fix Fused Sentences and Comma Splices?

What Are Fused Sentences and Comma Splices?

The terms *fused sentence* and *comma splice* refer to sentence errors where two or more sentences are joined incorrectly, creating a *run-on* sentence. (Be aware, however, that some instructors use the term *run-on* to refer to fused sentences only.) Fused sentences and comma splices are errors that can get in the way of your meaning. For instance, take a look at the following fused sentence:

> My car broke down yesterday I took the bus to school.

Which does it mean?

> My car broke down yesterday, so I took the bus to school.

> OR

> My car broke down. Yesterday, I took the bus to school.

It gets even more confusing when you have a longer, more involved thought that you are trying to express. Some writers even pile more than two sentences together without any clear indication of where one stops and the next starts:

> **Run-On**   It might be necessary to take the bus drivers usually can help you find the route you need to give him or her the correct change.

Should we take the bus or the drivers? Do I need to give him or her the correct change or does he or she help me find the route I need? This sentence is confusing, isn't it?

e To download the Grammar Log, log into your Integrated Media at **bedfordstmartins.com /readwriteconnect** and click on **Charts**.

✓ LearningCurve For extra practice in the skills covered in this chapter, visit **bedfordstmartins.com /readwriteconnect**.

649

In the case of a *fused sentence*, the error is that the writer has run one sentence into another without any punctuation between them. Take a look at the following example:

Fused   I will have to make my mom's birthday present the mall is closed.

There are two complete sentences smushed together here. Can you find them?

[I will have to make my mom's birthday present] [the mall is closed.]

Each of these could stand on its own as a complete sentence because each one contains

- A subject (underlined once)
- A verb (underlined twice)
- A complete thought or idea

Let's look at another example:

Fused   I saw *The Hunger Games* I also read the book.

Because the subject of each sentence, *I*, stands out, this fused sentence is probably easier to spot.

[I saw *The Hunger Games*] [I also read the book.]

Here's one final example:

Fused   Some think charter schools may solve the problems of public education they have their own problems.

This fused sentence may be trickier to spot because the sentence is longer.

[Some think charter schools may solve the problems of public education] [they have their own problems.]

To learn how to join two independent clauses with a comma and coordinating conjunction, see Chapter 31, page 664.

Some people think they can fix any fused sentence by inserting a comma into it. But just throwing in a comma usually results in another type of error, a *comma splice*. Commas are great, but on their own they are not strong enough to join complete sentences. Take a look at the following example:

Comma Splice   I will have to make my mom's birthday present, the mall is closed.

This comma splice is essentially the same as the first fused-sentence example; the only difference is the comma between the two sentences.

[I will have to make my mom's birthday present], [the mall is closed.]

The following sentences are also comma splices:

[Baseball is the de facto national sport of America], [football and soccer are gaining in popularity.]

[Regular exercise is great for weight loss], [it is even better for heart health.]

Finding and Fixing Fused Sentences and Comma Splices

In order to find and fix fused sentences and comma splices, you have to find the subject and verb in a sentence. These are the basic sentence components, and knowing them makes it possible for you to determine if a sentence is complete or not.

To review how to find the subject or verb in a sentence, see Chapter 26, Basic Sentence Components, page 600.

Also, you need to understand what an *independent clause* (complete sentence) is and be able to recognize it. Knowing how to find the subject and verb of a sentence allows you to identify independent clauses, which helps you see if there is more than one sentence joined together in a fused sentence or comma splice.

---

practice it   Find and Fix Run-Ons in Your Own Writing

Find an example of a fused sentence or comma splice from your own writing and jot it down. If you can't find any, try to make one up, and then correct it.

Here are some steps to follow for fixing fused sentences and comma splices.

STEP 1: **Locate the subject-verb pairs.**

> I remember the first teacher I had she was the same teacher my older sister had.

STEP 2: **Identify the complete independent clauses.** Double-check that both actually express a complete thought coherently (as they do in this example). The double slashes separate the two complete independent clauses.

> I remember the first teacher I had // she was the same teacher my older sister had.

STEP 3: **Pick a method from the following list to fix the problem.**

- **Add a period and begin each sentence with a capital letter.** This is a good method, but it can lead to two short, choppy sentences, so you need to learn the other methods as well.

> I remember the first teacher I had. She was the same teacher my older sister had.

- **Add a semicolon (;).** This is a good method to use when the sentences are both short and related in meaning.

> I remember the first teacher I had; she was the same teacher my older sister had.

LOOK OUT
Just using a FANBOYS
word alone to join two
sentences is not enough.
All FANBOYS words must
also have a comma before
them to correctly join
complete sentences.

**For more on subordinating
words, see Chapter
26, Basic Sentence
Components, page 600.**

- **Add a comma after the first sentence and a FANBOYS word** *(for, and, nor, but, or, yet, so)*. This solution clarifies the relationship between the two ideas.

  I remember the first teacher I had, **and** she was the same teacher my older sister had.

- **Start one of the independent clauses with a subordinating word** *(because, since, although, when,* **and so on)**. This solution makes your sentence more sophisticated.

  I remember the first teacher I had **because** she was the same teacher my older sister had.

With practice, you'll be able to avoid fused sentences and comma splices. Often, these errors happen during the flurry of drafting, when your ideas are coming fast and furious and you don't pay as much attention to sentence structure as you do to your ideas, and that's okay. There are so many things to keep track of during the writing process that sentence problems are common; however, this means that taking enough time to edit and proofread your sentences carefully is essential.

practice it   Editing for Fused Sentences and Comma Splices

1. Read the paragraph and underline all the fused sentences and comma splices that you find. You should find five problem sentences.
2. Decide how to fix the parts you've underlined. Remember, to fix the fused sentences and comma splices, you can use a
   - Period
   - Semicolon
   - Comma plus a FANBOYS word
   - Subordinating word

   Make your corrections by hand in the space above the sentence you are fixing. To do your best, read slowly and look at every word. If you don't find five errors when you go through the paragraph the first time, try reading the last sentence first. Then read the second-to-last sentence and so on. You will probably find more errors when you read it "backwards" like this because you will be focusing on the sentence itself instead of on the meaning of the paragraph.

   The word *style* is hard to define it means so many different things to different people. Most people think about fashion when they think about style, but it means so much more than that. Style can be the way you walk, style can be the way you talk. Most of all, style is the way you carry yourself. Sometimes your personal style reflects your values when you wear a T-shirt with a political slogan, people assume you believe in that idea. This isn't always true, though, lots of people who aren't hippies wear tie-dyed shirts nowadays, whereas in the old days wearing tie-dye really meant that you were antiwar and into peace, love, and happiness. We shouldn't judge people by their style, sometimes we do, though, especially when someone has no style.

chapter review

Run-ons are very common errors in student writing. They are so common, in fact, that you may have been well acquainted with them before reading Chapter 29. The good news is that they are fairly easy to fix if you use the guidelines you learned here, which means clearer writing is in your future.

To review this chapter, choose one or more of the following strategies:

1. Try to explain what you have learned, or at least part of it, to someone you know. Discuss the key concepts and give some of your own examples to illustrate those concepts.

2. Take a look at some of your writing for your English class, and see if you are making errors involving fused sentences and comma splices. Find and correct these errors; then ask your instructor or a tutor to check your corrections.

3. Make a flash card for each of the ways to fix run-ons that you learned in this chapter; keep this with you when you are editing your writing.

4. If you skipped any of the Practice It activities in the chapter, go back and do them now as a way to deepen your understanding of the material.

5. Try to identify the types of run-ons you make—if you make any at all. Update your Grammar Log to include your most frequent run-on errors and their corrections. Don't forget to refer to the Grammar Log every time you edit a piece of writing, and don't forget to take the time to edit everything you write for all your college classes.

For more on keeping a Grammar Log, see page 579.

30
Pronouns

- What Exactly Is a Pronoun?
- What Are Common Pronoun Errors?
- How Do You Fix Pronoun Errors?

What Exactly Is a Pronoun?

Pronouns are words that can be used in place of nouns. Their job is to fill in for nouns, sort of a like a stunt double fills in for the movie star in certain scenes. We use pronouns all the time without thinking about them. Understanding how they work will help you avoid making certain sentence errors, though, so they're worth paying attention to. We'll start by discussing the different types of pronouns and their purposes.

SUBJECT PRONOUNS

Some pronouns can be used as a subject.

Subject Pronouns	
I	we
you	you
he/she/it	they

We use these pronouns to replace nouns to avoid repeating the noun over and over again. Consider the following example:

> Professor Pippilini talks too quickly when lecturing. Professor Pippilini always lectures for hours and hours too.

Using *she* rather than *Professor Pippilini* a second time would make the sentences much easier to read or say.

> Professor Pippilini talks too quickly when lecturing. She always lectures for hours and hours too.

POSSESSIVE PRONOUNS

Some pronouns are used to show ownership. These are known as the *possessive pronouns*, but we don't use an apostrophe with them.

Possessive Pronouns	
my/mine	his
our/ours	its
your/yours	their/theirs
her/hers	whose

Here's an example:

That shirt is <u>mine</u>, not <u>yours</u>!

INDEFINITE PRONOUNS

Some pronouns don't look very much like pronouns, but they function that way by standing in for nouns. The following is a list of pronouns used when you are stating a general principle or idea and not referring to a specific person or thing:

Indefinite Pronouns		
anybody	everybody	no one
anyone	everyone	nothing
anything	everything	somebody
each	neither	someone
either	nobody	something

Here's an example:

Anybody who wants to board a plane must bring his or her proper identification.

DEMONSTRATIVE PRONOUNS: *THIS/THESE/THAT/THOSE*

Although they do not look or act much like the other pronouns, the words *this*, *that*, *these*, and *those* are, technically speaking, pronouns. When you use one of these words, known as demonstrative pronouns, you are usually using it to replace a group of words. For example, if you and your friend were walking through a neighborhood looking at murals, you might point to one and say, "That is artfully painted." The word *that* replaces the word *mural*, and as long as your friend knows what you're talking about, everything's fine. In writing, we want to be as specific as possible, so we try to avoid overusing *that* in this manner. In other words, we prefer to make *that* or *this* function more as an adjective than a pronoun. So, instead of writing, "That is artfully painted," you should say, "That mural is artfully painted." Since unclear pronoun usage is more a clarity issue than a pronoun issue, you will find more examples of how to address this problem in Chapter 34, Writing Clear and Focused Sentences, page 692.

ANTECEDENTS

Another important term to know if you want to understand pronouns is *antecedent*. Think of the antecedent as the "ancestor" of the pronoun: The antecedent is the thing that a pronoun replaces, usually a noun or a phrase that acts like a noun. Take a look at the following sentence:

> Stefanie changes the oil in <u>her</u> car every six months because she wants to keep <u>it</u> running.

What does *her* refer to? What does *it* refer to? In this sentence, *Stefanie* is the antecedent for *her*, and *car* is the antecedent for *it*. Take a look at another example:

> Going to the mechanic takes a lot of time, but <u>it</u> is worthwhile.

What does *it* refer to? In this case, the entire phrase *Going to the mechanic* is the antecedent for *it*.

Common Pronoun Errors

LOOK OUT

Did you notice how the pronoun agreement and shift errors sound a lot like the two major verb errors? People who tend to make subject-verb-agreement errors sometimes also make pronoun-agreement errors, and people who make verb-tense-shift errors sometimes make pronoun-shift errors, so watch out for these patterns as you try to pinpoint your own personal grammar errors. You might even try studying the errors together. Do whatever works for you.

Pronoun errors are fairly common, and they tend to fall into the following three major categories:

1. *Pronoun reference*: It's not clear what your pronoun refers to.
2. *Pronoun agreement*: You picked the wrong pronoun to go with the noun it is replacing.
3. *Pronoun shift*: You shift from one pronoun to another when you shouldn't.

PRONOUN-REFERENCE ERRORS

If your reader can't tell which word your pronoun replaces, this problem is called unclear pronoun referent, and you need to fix it. Take a look at this example:

> **Unclear**   Gabriel took his dog for a walk because <u>he</u> was restless.

Who was restless, the dog or Gabriel? It's not clear who the *he* in this sentence is supposed to replace.

> **Correct**   His dog was getting restless, so Gabriel took him for a walk.
>
>   OR
>
> **Correct**   Gabriel was getting restless, so he took his dog for a walk.

Here's another example:

> **Unclear**   The San Francisco Giants and the Detroit Tigers played against one another in the 2012 World Series, and <u>they</u> ultimately won.

The reader can't tell from this sentence who won. Does *they* refer to the Giants or the Tigers? Did they tie? In this case, you can't replace the noun with a pronoun because the reader can't tell from the context which team name the pronoun replaces. Here's a possible revision:

Correct   The San Francisco Giants ultimately won when they played against the Detroit Tigers in the 2012 World Series.

In this revised sentence, *they* clearly refers to the Giants, so there is no confusion.

practice it   Editing for Pronoun-Reference Errors

1. Read the paragraph and underline all the pronoun-reference errors you find. You should find five problem sentences.
2. Decide how to fix the parts you've underlined. Make your corrections by hand in the space above the sentence you are fixing.

The Monterey Road Citizens Committee (MRCC) has been given the tasks of evaluating possible street designs, gathering input from the residents and other stakeholders, and making a recommendation about what, if anything, to change about the street. The MRCC has fifteen members, including the architect Mrs. O'Malley, who lives on Monterey Road, and Mr. Watson, who uses his wheelchair to get to the Metro line a block away from Monterey Road. The redesign was prompted by the street's noncompliance with the Americans with Disabilities Act. They are obstructed by light poles and utility boxes. People riding in wheelchairs or pushing baby strollers have great difficulty going down the sidewalk. The street is uneven and badly in need of a new asphalt surface. Mr. Ono, the city planner, recommends the MRCC consider whether bike lanes would be a good addition to the street. Since it has to go to the expense to pave and redesign the sidewalks, other changes should be considered at this time. At the first meeting, they agreed that wheelchair access, bike lanes, and an overall slower traffic pattern are the top priorities. Much to Mr. Ono's surprise, parking is not a high priority on the street. They would prefer to have a bike lane and a quieter street instead of the current number of on-street parking spots. It quickly arrived at a consensus on their goals. The next step is to bring in an engineering consultant to determine the viability of it.

PRONOUN-AGREEMENT ERRORS

The other common pronoun error involves agreement. If you use the wrong pronoun, one that does not agree with the noun it is replacing, you create an error. Usually, the error is that you used a singular pronoun when you should have used a plural one, or vice versa. For instance, if you replace the word *Americans* with a pronoun, you should choose the pronoun *they*—or perhaps *we* if you include yourself in the group. If you replace the phrase *American way of life*, you should choose the pronoun *it*. A way of life is one thing, singular. Look at the following example:

Unclear   Leila liked the songs Eric wrote about her. It made her feel loved.

Here, the pronoun *her* matches with *Leila*, but the pronoun *it* doesn't agree with *songs*. To fix this error, you need to change either the word *songs* or the pronoun.

Correct   Leila liked the song Eric wrote about her. It made her feel loved.

OR

Correct   Leila liked the songs Eric wrote about her. They made her feel loved.

Agreement with Indefinite Pronouns and Collective Nouns.   Two categories of words are particularly tricky when it comes to antecedent agreement: *indefinite pronouns* and collective nouns. (Both groups should be familiar friends if you have worked on subject-verb agreement at all, since they are some of the biggest hurdles with subject-verb agreement too.) If you recall, the indefinite pronouns are the words beginning with *any-/every-/no-/some-* and ending in *-body/-one/-things*, plus their friends *each*, *either*, and *neither* (p. 655). These pronouns should all take a third-person singular pronoun: *he*, *she*, or *it*. Here are some examples:

Everything in my studio is ready for its shipping container.

Something under the bushes is growling and showing its fangs.

For more on subject-verb agreement, see Chapter 27, Verbs, page 617.

Neither car is available with its original 1964 engine.

Collective nouns should also look familiar if you have studied subject-verb agreement. These are words like *couple* and *jury*. The pronoun you use to replace one of these nouns depends upon the context of the sentence. Do you want to stress the "group-ness" of the word, or do you want to emphasize the individual members of the group?

The couple celebrating its first anniversary is so cute.

The couple dividing up their assets are nearly finished with their divorce proceedings.

The first example stresses the togetherness of the couple; the couple functions as one item, an *it*. The second example stresses the separateness of the two people in the couple; the couple functions as a *they*, so we use the possessive pronoun *their*.

Gender Agreement.   One of the most difficult issues with pronouns is gender agreement. Historically, *he* was used to refer to any person; this was called the "generic *he*." The generic *he* led to sentences like "When an American wants to vote, he must register." (Huh? Didn't women earn the right to vote nearly a hundred years ago?) Most people avoid this usage today because it's sexist and just plain inaccurate. Instead, we say "he or she," "his or her," and so on, as in the following example:

> A student should bring his or her books to class every day.

Eliminating sexist language is great. Figuring out which pronoun to use so that you are not being sexist is sometimes a challenge. The truth is that we aren't used to the sound of gender-neutral pronouns quite yet, so our tongues tend to trip over the "his or her" or the "he or she." While the preceding short sentence about a student's books sounds okay, sentences can become unwieldy pretty quickly.

> **Awkward**   A dog trainer must have patience, for his or her client may need to have his or her basic assumptions about dogs challenged.

Frequently, writers just give up and rewrite such sentences, which usually works.

> **Revised**   A dog trainer must have patience, for the client may need to have basic assumptions about dogs challenged.

Rewriting may work beautifully, as in the preceding example. Because it doesn't always work so well, it's a good idea to learn a few strategies for avoiding sexist language:

- **Switch singular nouns to plural.** This allows your pronouns to shift to the gender-neutral *they*.

  > Dog trainers must have patience, for their clients may need to have their basic assumptions about dogs challenged.

- **Use the generic *one* pronoun.** This can work when the situation is formal; be aware, though, that *one* needs to be used consistently in the sentence. For instance:

  > One must have patience to train dogs, for one is often training one's clients as well.

Sentences with *one* can sound stiff, so use this strategy judiciously.

In everyday speech, the desire to be gender-neutral has triumphed over correctness with the indefinite pronouns. For example, it is grammatically correct to say:

> Everyone in the tour group to France must be responsible for his or her own luggage.

However, in speech, most people use the incorrect version:

> **Everyone** in the tour group to France must be responsible for **their** own luggage.

By the time your grandchildren are in college, the language will have probably evolved out of this conundrum, but for now at least, in writing, you should err on the side of correctness and use "his or her" to replace the indefinite pronouns.

---

practice it   Editing for Pronoun-Agreement Errors

1. Read the paragraph and underline all the pronoun-agreement errors you find. You should find seven problem sentences.
2. Decide how to fix the parts you've underlined. Make your corrections by hand in the space above the sentence you are fixing.

> Julia Alvarez's epic novel *In the Time of the Butterflies* tells the story of the
> four Mirabal sisters, Patria, Dedé, Minerva, and María Teresa. Tracing her
> lives from girlhood until her tragic end, and even beyond, the story follows
> the events of her attempts to overthrow the dictator Trujillo. Readers fall in
> love with the girls, taking sides in our arguments and rooting for them in
> their romantic and religious quests. No more realistic portrait of sisters has
> existed in fiction since the March girls sprang from Louisa May Alcott's pen.
> Alvarez drew on their own family's connection to her parents' homeland in
> writing this novel, and readers can't help but wonder if he is meant to be the
> journalist who bothers Dedé, asking all those questions about the girls. *In
> the Time of the Butterflies* makes readers laugh and cry—and call her sisters.

PRONOUN-SHIFT ERRORS

A pronoun-shift error occurs if you move from one pronoun to a different pronoun (and sometimes back again) when you should not. Take a look at the following example:

Incorrect   When <u>one</u> intends to purchase a house, <u>you</u> should always get an inspection.

This sentence leaves the reader confused: Are *one* and *you* the same person? In addition to being unclear, shifting the pronouns like this is odd for a couple of reasons. First, *one* is very formal and *you* is informal. Second, *one* is a third-person pronoun, and *you* is a second-person pronoun. (Did you notice that the verb *intends* ends in *-s*? That is the third-person form, which you use with *he*, *she*, or *it*.) Correct this pronoun shift by replacing one or the other of the pronouns to stay consistent:

Correct   When <u>one</u> intends to purchase a house, **one** should always get an inspection.

OR

Correct   When <u>you</u> intend to purchase a house, <u>you</u> should always get an inspection.

TIP
When you switch a pronoun to second person (*you*), you also need to double-check the verb. Pronoun and verb problems often go hand in hand, which is why you need to take the time to carefully reread any sentence after you make a change.

practice it   Editing for Pronoun-Shift Errors

1. Read the paragraph and underline all the pronoun-shift errors you find. You should find three problem sentences.
2. Decide how to fix the parts you've underlined. Make your corrections by hand in the space above the sentence you are fixing.

One might think that children's literature is a simplistic form intended only for kids, but the reality is that children's literature is just as sophisticated and rich as literature for adults. Sure, there are plenty of poorly written fairy-tale books out there, but there are probably more badly written romance novels. You cannot judge the genre by its worst examples; we must judge based on the best the field has to offer. Children's classics like *The Wind in the Willows* have endured over time and have probably touched as many minds and hearts as the classics of adult literature. *The Hunger Games* is written so well that you must read it all in a day—or be haunted by nightmares about Katniss in the arena.

Fixing Pronoun Errors

You are likely to make pronoun errors when you rewrite a sentence and don't go back to double-check your writing. Sometimes we change our minds about what we are going to say while we are writing the sentence, and pronouns are usually the biggest casualty. If we change one sentence, this change can have an impact on pronouns later in the paragraph. Therefore, if you don't go back and edit the entire paper at least a couple of times, you are likely to miss pronoun errors.

Often, pronoun errors require some rewriting of the entire sentence structure, and there's usually more than one way you can fix the error. Experiment a little to find the best way to edit the sentence. Editing specifically for pronoun errors is worth the time, especially if your instructor has noted that you make pronoun errors on your papers. Follow these steps, which will help you eliminate most of your mistakes.

STEP 1: **Print out the paper so that you are not working from a computer screen.**   This allows you to write on the draft and to see it all at once.

STEP 2: **Starting at the beginning, read over the draft with a highlighter in hand.**   Highlight every pronoun you find.

STEP 3: **When you have finished highlighting all the pronouns, look at each one individually.**   Ask yourself: What does this pronoun replace? If you can't find the exact word(s) it replaces, that's a red flag that you may have a pronoun-reference problem. If you can find the word(s) it replaces, ask yourself: Does my pronoun match its antecedent? (Remember, the antecedent is what the pronoun replaces.) For example, if your pronoun is *it*, does that fit well with the noun *it* refers back to?

STEP 4: **Check for pronoun shifts by looking at all the highlighted words.**   Did you change from *it* to *he* when you shouldn't have? Did you change from *you* to *one* and back again? Look for these shifts and correct them so you are consistent.

chapter review

Chapter 30 covers pronouns, which are the source of many sentence-level errors. Since we tend to be rather sloppy about our use of pronouns while speaking, pronoun errors frequently appear in our writing, especially if we have rewritten a paragraph and did not go back to reread it for clarity. This chapter shows you how to identify and correct these pronoun errors.

To review this chapter, choose one or more of the following strategies:

1. Try to explain what you have learned, or at least part of it, to someone you know. Discuss the key concepts and give some of your own examples to illustrate those concepts.

2. Turn to one of the articles in this book that you have read recently. Choose two or three paragraphs from somewhere in the middle of the article. Read the paragraphs, underlining all the pronouns you find. Check to see if the author made any errors.

3. If you skipped any of the Practice It activities throughout the chapter, go back and do them now as a way to deepen your understanding of the material.

4. Update your Grammar Log to include your most frequent pronoun errors with corrections. Don't forget to refer to the Grammar Log every time you edit a piece of writing, and don't forget to take the time to edit everything you write for all your college classes.

For more on keeping a Grammar Log, see page 579.

31
Commas

in this chapter

- What Is a Comma?
- What Are the Rules for Using Commas?
- How Do You Build Sentences Using These Comma Rules?
- How Do You Fix Comma Errors in Your Writing?

To download the Grammar Log, log into your Integrated Media at **bedfordstmartins.com /readwriteconnect** and click on **Charts**.

LearningCurve
For extra practice in the skills covered in this chapter, visit **bedfordstmartins.com /readwriteconnect**.

What Is a Comma?

The comma (,) is the punctuation mark that makes a speaker or reader pause when reading. It helps the reader figure out what groups of words go together, and it helps establish the rhythm of the sentence. For instance, read the following sentences out loud:

Too fat to jump the cat Mr. Boots just sat and stared.

Difficult, isn't it? Now try it again, pausing where there is a comma:

Too fat to jump, the cat, Mr. Boots, just sat and stared.

In this example, a reader can barely make out what the sentence is saying without the commas. These are very necessary commas. Other times, the commas may not be so absolutely necessary, but they force the reader to pause where you want him or her to pause. For example:

Hey, Marco, where did you put your hat?

has a slightly different rhythm than

Hey Marco, where did you put your hat?

Can you hear the difference when you read these sentences? If not, try reading them again out loud, emphasizing the pauses where there are commas. Controlling the rhythm of the language means you can control the reader's pacing and emphasis, which in turn influences the tone of the language. That little comma has a lot more power than at first glance.

So, how do you use commas correctly? Read on!

Rules for Using Commas

USE A COMMA TO SEPARATE ITEMS IN A LIST

Use a comma after each item in a list. Most American writers use a comma after the second-to-last item (before *and* or *or*), as in the following examples:

> Siblings may be best friends, enemies, caretakers, or strangers.

> I like punk music, ferocious dogs, and romantic sunsets.

This rule applies whether the list is made up of single words or phrases. For instance, in the following example the items in the list are phrases:

> I spent much of my summer camping among the redwoods, reading great works of literature, hiking until my feet hurt, and waking up with the sunrise.

If you struggle with this rule, one simple trick is to imagine a number on each item in the list:

>   1   2
>
> Trixie likes playing tug-of-war with her favorite rope taking long walks in
>
>   3
>
> the forest and seeing her family at the end of the day.

Once you figure out where the numbers go, simply add a comma after each numbered item:

> Trixie likes playing tug-of-war with her favorite rope, taking long walks in the forest, and seeing her family at the end of the day.

When you have *only two* items in a list joined by *and* or *or*, don't use a comma, no matter how long the items in the list might be. Here's a list with two short items (underlined):

> I like <u>chocolate</u> and <u>vanilla</u>.

Here's an example where each item in the list is very long:

> I like <u>traveling on my summer vacations to exotic locales like the Galàpagos</u> and <u>spending my rather short winter breaks at my brother's house in Maine.</u>

You'll notice that the list is still made up of only two items joined by the word *and*. No comma is used, even though there are many words in the sentence.

USE A COMMA TO SEPARATE PLACE NAMES, DATES, AND PEOPLE'S TITLES

Your teachers no doubt tried to drill this comma rule into your head in elementary school. (You may have been more interested in recess at the time, so here it is again, for old time's sake.) Use a comma in the following situations:

- Between city and state and between city and country
- Between day and year
- Between a person's last name and any official letters (such as Ph.D., M.D., or Esq.)

Here are two examples:

> Brian May, Ph.D., lives in Surrey, England.

> I visited Washington, D.C., on Tuesday, July 15, 2014, and Richmond, Virginia, on Wednesday, July 16, 2014.

USE A COMMA WHEN YOU INTRODUCE A QUOTATION, *UNLESS* YOU USE THE WORD *THAT*

Commas are required most of the time when you use quotation marks, whether you are writing dialogue or quoting from a source.

For more on using source material in your own writing, see Chapter 16, Quotation and Paraphrase, page 307, and Chapter 20, MLA Documentation, page 362.

Dialogue	The waiter asked, "Would you like cheese with that?"
Quotation from Source (with Comma)	The syllabus for my math course reads, "Students who arrive late will not be allowed to take the final exam."

Remember, when using source material, you must cite it to give credit to the original source.

Sometimes when you use quotation marks, the material you are quoting is integrated fully into the grammar of your sentence. Usually such sentences include the word *that* shortly before the quotation. In these cases, do *not* use a comma.

Quotation from Source (No Comma)	The banker said that "a 529 plan is the best college savings vehicle for most middle-class families."

As you read this sentence out loud, notice that you don't naturally pause after the word *that*.

USE A COMMA WHEN YOU HAVE TWO OR MORE ADJECTIVES IN A ROW

When describing a person, place, thing, or idea, sometimes you want to stack up the adjectives to add more detail to the description. In almost all cases, you should use commas to separate the words, even if there are only two adjectives in the list.

> Chad is the cheapest, nastiest boyfriend I have ever had.

> Children should learn to develop positive, respectful relationships with their siblings.

As you might notice, this rule is different from the earlier rule about a list of items using the word *and* or *or*. The lists in that rule usually consist of nouns or of phrases that stand in for nouns. The lists here consist of adjectives.

The exception to this rule is when one adjective modifies an adjective/noun combination, rather than the noun alone. For example:

> The <u>ratty old</u> toy should have been thrown out.

In this case, the *old toy* is ratty, not the *toy*. Try using an exaggerated pause where the comma would go to judge the difference between sentences that follow the rule about using a comma to separate adjectives and those that represent an exception.

USE A COMMA WITH INTRODUCTORY ELEMENTS

Using the comma appropriately with introductory elements clarifies the meaning of your sentence. In many cases, a missing or misplaced comma makes it hard to understand what you're trying to say. For instance, if you leave out the comma in the following sentence, your reader won't be sure exactly what you mean.

> After playing mahjong for several hours I felt sick.

The sentence could mean:

> After playing mahjong, for several hours I felt sick.

Or it could mean:

> After playing mahjong for several hours, I felt sick.

Without the comma, the reader cannot be sure what you mean. Avoid such errors by using a comma after words or groups of words (phrases or clauses) that introduce the main sentence.

> However, Aaron is the better goalie.

> On Valentine's Day, I hope to get some flowers.

Read these sentences out loud, and you can hear the pause. Here are some additional examples:

> Without more funding for education, schools will continue to struggle with limited resources.

> After trying for several hours, Maria finally mastered her math homework.

Finding and Fixing This Comma Error.   Most of the time, you can read the sentence out loud, slowly and clearly, to determine where to place the comma after introductory material. In addition, as you revise, be on the lookout for typical "introductory" words.

Common Introductory Words		
after	even if	in conclusion
although	first/second/third	once
as	furthermore	since
because	however	when
before	if	while
despite	in	

When you see one of these words or others like it, stop and reread the sentence to see if you can remove any words from the start of the sentence and still have a complete sentence. If you can, then you probably need a comma. Consider this example:

> When I miss the bus I am late for work.

If we remove the introductory material, what we are left with could still stand alone as a sentence:

> ~~When I miss the bus~~ I am late for work.

So we definitely need the comma:

> When I miss the bus, I am late for work.

Beware of the Word *Although*. The word *although* is the source of one common error, because *although* does not function in the same way as the word *however. However* can be used in more ways than *although*. For instance, both of the following sentences are correct:

Correct	However, I like macaroni and cheese.
Correct	However much I like macaroni and cheese, I get sick of eating it every day.

With *however*, the introductory material can be just the one word or a whole phrase. Either way, the sentences are complete as written. But you can't do the same thing with *although. Although* is never a one-word introductory phrase. When you see the word *although* at the start of a sentence, the whole phrase it's attached to is the introductory phrase:

Incorrect	Although, I like macaroni and cheese.
Correct	Although I like macaroni and cheese, I get sick of eating it every day.

USE A COMMA WHEN JOINING TWO SENTENCES WITH A COORDINATING CONJUNCTION

If you have trouble with fragments, run-ons, or comma splices, this is the comma rule for you. Understanding this comma rule is fundamental to making clear, correct, compound sentences. Imagine that you have two short, choppy sentences:

> The tree is beautiful. The flowers are dead.

Now, imagine you don't like the sound of these short, choppy sentences. You want to combine them:

> The tree is beautiful. + The flowers are dead.

You need to do more than just throw in the word *and*. You have to include a comma as well:

> The tree is beautiful, and the flowers are dead.

Here's another example:

> I like physics, but my educational plan requires chemistry.

I like physics could be a sentence by itself. *My educational plan requires chemistry* could be a sentence by itself. When you join them with the word *but*, you have to put a comma before *but*.

Notice that you don't use a comma *every* time you use a FANBOYS word. Only use a comma if both halves of the sentence can stand on their own. In the following example, you should *not* use a comma:

> My choice was clearly between physics and my educational plan.

The words *my educational plan* can't stand alone as a sentence, so you don't put a comma before the word *and* in this case.

Finding and Fixing This Comma Error. While editing your paper, stop every time you see one of the FANBOYS words in the middle of a sentence. Take your hand and cover up the FANBOYS word and all the words that come after it. The underlined words in the following example indicate the portion of the sentence you would cover.

> I love pizza <u>so I'm going to eat it every day this week.</u>

Is that first half a complete, correct sentence? The answer is yes, so cover up the first half of the sentence and check the second half.

> <u>I love pizza so</u> I'm going to eat it every day this week.

Is that a complete sentence? The answer is yes, so you need a comma before the FANBOYS word *so*.

> **Correct**   I love pizza, so I'm going to eat it every day this week.

Simple? Yes—but you have to take the time to read each sentence carefully, and you have to be able to tell if a sentence is complete and correct or not.

TIP

Coordinating conjunctions are also known as the FANBOYS words: *for, and, nor, but, or, yet, so.* If you haven't memorized these words yet, do it now. You'll need them for lots of grammar rules.

> **practice it**   Editing for Missing Commas
>
> Add the missing commas to the following paragraph.
>
> I was born in Baldwin Park California on January 1 1986. The attending physician was Nidia Rivera M.D. My mother screamed "Get this baby out!" One nurse says that I "spit up in her face smiled and fell asleep." Everyone says I was the cleverest most beautiful baby in the maternity ward. However my musical talent was not recognized until I was four. On my fourth birthday I received my first drum set. I loved my drums but my mom began getting intense headaches. My choice was clearly between the drums and my mom's sanity. My love for my mom, who is the best mom ever made me switch to the guitar which is why I am now the rock goddess that I am.

USE COMMAS WITH SENTENCE INTERRUPTERS

The last major comma rule has to do with words that interrupt the flow of a sentence or that are tacked on to the end of a sentence. You can think of such words as nonessential information—material you could take out and still be left with a complete sentence. The rule is that you need to use commas to set off words or groups of words that interrupt the flow of the sentence. Take a look at the following example:

My brother Jeff, who graduated with a chemistry degree last June, has a high-paying job with great benefits, which is why he's paying for dinner.

In this example, the main sentence is "My brother Jeff has a high-paying job with great benefits." The words *who graduated with a chemistry degree last June* and *which is why he's paying for dinner* are extra information that interrupt or are added onto the main sentence. Try reading this sentence out loud, and listen for the pauses before and after you read those parts. You could take out either piece of information and the sentence would still make sense:

My brother Jeff, who graduated with a chemistry degree last June, has a high-paying job with great benefits.

OR

My brother Jeff has a high-paying job with great benefits, which is why he's paying for dinner.

You could even take out both parts:

> My brother Jeff has a high-paying job with great benefits.

Another type of extra information is a short description of a noun, usually a person, which comes directly after the noun. Take a look at the following example:

> My cardiologist, <u>Dr. Nathan Flowers</u>, appeared on the news yesterday.

Here, the cardiologist is Dr. Nathan Flowers. The information between the commas is called an *appositive*. It gives details about the subject, in this case his name.

Sometimes it might be a little difficult to tell whether some information is truly essential or not to the sentence. To test whether or not this information is essential, ask yourself if you need it to understand who or what you are talking about. Take a look at these two examples:

> Mr. Ross, who has spent more than a few years in jail, is not exactly my mother's idea of a role model.

> The banker who has spent more than a few years in jail is not exactly my mother's idea of a role model.

In the first example, the phrase *who has spent more than a few years in jail* is interesting, but the reader doesn't need it to know who we are discussing because the person's name is given. There can be no confusion that we are talking about Mr. Ross. Therefore, we use commas around the nonessential information to set it off from the main sentence.

In the second example, however, we don't know which banker is being described without the phrase *who has spent more than a few years in jail*. The additional information is necessary in order to distinguish one banker from all the other possible bankers. Here we do not use commas since that information is part of the main sentence.

Finding and Fixing This Comma Error. When looking for this particular error in your writing, look for phrases (word groups) that come before or after the subject and verb of the sentence. These phrases often—but not always—begin with:

that	who
when	whom
where	whose
which	

Look out for these words to see if the information that follows them is essential to the meaning of the sentence or not. If it isn't, add commas to set the nonessential information apart from the sentence.

---

practice it   Editing for Comma Errors

Add all necessary commas to the following paragraph. You should add ten commas altogether.

Baseball is considered America's favorite pastime but you may not know its athletes are among the most superstitious. These superstitions ranges from pregame rituals to in-game practices and one of the most well-known pregame rituals was Hall of Famer Wade Boggs's habit of eating chicken before every game. In-game rituals include jumping over the foul lines between innings and taking the exact same number of practice swings when up at bat. When a pitcher is pitching a no-hitter the superstitions intensify. His team-mates who are watching with excitement will not sit next to him or even talk to him in order to avoid jinxing such a rare feat. It is also taboo to even mention the fact that a no-hitter is in progress. When a player is doing really well such as having a prolonged hitting streak he may continue to wear the same socks or undershirt while the streak lasts and when a team is doing really well the players may go without shaving to keep the winning streak going. As long as baseball is played one thing is certain: Superstitions will be a part of the game.

Building Sentences Using These Comma Rules

Once you have mastered the comma rules, you can see how they help you build more sophisticated sentences. Take a basic sentence:

The orange cat is purring.

Now add information and set it off with commas:

The orange cat, who is the oldest of my pets, is purring.

Now add even more information:

The orange cat, who is the oldest of my pets, is purring, thinking he's going to be fed soon.

We can even add information to the start of the sentence, as in the introductory-material comma rule:

At the moment, the orange cat, who is the oldest of my pets, is purring, thinking he's going to be fed soon.

This sentence is now quite long, but it is not a run-on sentence. In fact, its grammar is perfect. As you can see, once you gain control of commas, you can express more complicated ideas in a single sentence.

Editing Your Work for Comma Errors

Like most punctuation errors, comma errors are best fixed during the editing and proofreading stages of the writing process. Figure out which comma errors you tend to make, and read through the paper looking for just those comma errors. As you practice fixing your own errors, correct comma usage will become part of how you write, and you will break the rules less and less frequently. Pretty soon you'll put the commas in the right place without even thinking about it.

In the meantime, since many students seem to believe myths about commas, it might be useful to dispel a few of the common ones. The truth is:

- There is no set number of commas that a sentence is allowed to have or not allowed to have.
- A run-on cannot be fixed simply by throwing in a comma. In fact, that's just making a comma splice, another type of error.
- Whether you use a comma before the final *and* in a list or not is up to you, but be consistent. Most American writers use the comma in this case.

chapter review

Chapter 31 focuses on everyone's favorite punctuation mark, the comma. The best editing strategies for commas involve reading your work out loud—either by yourself or with a friend. Determine which comma rules you tend to break and then concentrate on mastering these. Chances are good that you are already doing quite a lot right with commas, so take care to identify errors properly.

To review this chapter, choose one or more of the following strategies:

1. Try to explain what you have learned, or at least part of it, to someone you know. Discuss the key concepts and give some of your own examples to illustrate those concepts.
2. Make flash cards for each of the rules outlined in this chapter.
3. If you skipped any of the Practice It activities in the chapter, go back and do them now as a way to deepen your understanding of the material.
4. Update your Grammar Log to include your most frequent comma errors with corrections. Don't forget to refer to the Grammar Log every time you edit a piece of writing, and don't forget to take the time to edit everything you write for all your college classes.

For more on keeping a Grammar Log, see page 579.

32
Parallelism

in this chapter

- What Is Parallelism?
- What Are the Most Common Parallelism Errors?
- How Do You Find and Fix Parallelism Errors?

To download the Grammar Log, log into your Integrated Media at **bedfordstmartins.com /readwriteconnect** and click on **Charts**.

LearningCurve
For extra practice in the skills covered in this chapter, visit **bedfordstmartins.com /readwriteconnect**.

What Is Parallelism?

Perhaps you have identified a problem you have with parallelism. More likely, your instructor made a note to you about a parallelism problem, and you—being the successful college student that you are—looked it up. Maybe you thought parallelism had something to do with geometry. It sure sounds like it: parallel lines, parallelograms, that sort of thing. Actually, if you're thinking along those lines, you aren't far off. Parallel lines are lines that go in the same direction and never cross. They match, in a way.

In grammar, an error in parallelism means that you have a list of things, but they don't all follow the same path. One or more of the items in the list just doesn't match the others in form. It's not parallel. Here's an example:

> **Incorrect** At the gym, I rotate between cycling, weightlifting, kickboxing, and to go swimming.

Notice how awkward that last part of the sentence is? One of the things that you do at the gym is not in the same grammatical format as the others. The first three items—cycling, weightlifting, and kickboxing—are simply *-ing* words, but *to go swimming* is an oddball. It has *to go* before the *-ing* word. It just doesn't fit. So how do you fix it? Make that oddball parallel with the other words in the sentence by changing its form:

> **Correct** At the gym, I rotate between cycling, weightlifting, kickboxing, and swimming.

Another solution is to change the first three items in the list to fit the last item, but this involves some rewriting:

> At the gym, I like to do cycling, to practice weightlifting, to engage in a bit of kickboxing, and to go swimming.

674

The first possible correction is much cleaner. You can always try revising the sentence a couple of different ways; read each version out loud to see which you prefer.

Correcting errors in parallelism looks pretty easy when you see it like this, right? As with most things grammatical, though, you usually won't make only simple errors. Sure, writers might make the preceding error, but they would probably catch it pretty quickly if they edited the sentence. It's the trickier, more complicated errors in parallelism that may stump you.

Let's try another, trickier example:

Incorrect   College has improved my study habits by helping me to <u>organize my time</u>, <u>taking better notes</u>, and <u>get help from my instructor when I don't understand something</u>.

It can be difficult to figure out where the list of items that need to be parallel starts. In this case, not all items in the list start with the word *to*, so this is not a list of phrases that begin with *to*. You might notice that each item starts with a verb: *organize*, *taking*, and *get*. However, the verbs aren't all parallel. *Taking* is in the *-ing* form, and that doesn't fit with the others. The fix, in this case, is simple:

Correct   College has improved my study habits by helping me to organize my time, <u>take better notes</u>, and get help from my instructor when I don't understand something.

Often, only a slight change in wording will correct an error in parallelism. It's one of those errors that are harder to notice than to fix.

Common Parallelism Errors

Most real-life parallelism errors occur when it's not quite so obvious that you are using a list of things in your writing, such as when the items in the list are each quite long or when the ideas are complicated. The trick is to notice that the items are in a list, figure out what each item is, and make sure that each item uses the same grammatical structure.

LISTS WITH COLONS

Sometimes writers use a colon to indicate a long pause before a list. This is great, so long as you do it correctly and maintain parallel structure. Take a look at this example:

Incorrect   Puppies need several important things to be healthy and happy: proper veterinary care, nutritious puppy food, to be loved and petted by their new owners, and when you get a new puppy, you have to exercise it frequently.

In this example, the items in the list are seriously mismatched, and the sentence seems to go on past the end of the list, which further confuses the reader. The writer needs to decide on the best way to rewrite, and whether or not to move that last part—*and when you get a new puppy, you have to exercise it frequently*—into the list or toward the front of the sentence. Take a look at some possible solutions:

Minor Revision	Puppies need several important things to be healthy and happy: proper veterinary care, nutritious puppy food, loving affection, and frequent vigorous exercise.
Major Revision	When you get a puppy, you must realize that it needs several important things to be healthy and happy: proper veterinary care, nutritious puppy food, and a loving new home.

Both of these options sound good and are grammatically correct; they use the colon, end the sentence with the list, and have parallel forms. The option you choose will depend on what you try to emphasize. The minor revision changes very little, while the major rewrite shifts the focus of the sentence from the puppy to the owner.

LIST INTERRUPTERS

Another tricky but fairly common parallelism problem happens when a writer puts a thought into the middle of the list that shouldn't be there at all. Here's one example:

Incorrect	My girlfriend plays video games all day, I even complain about it, and never takes me out to dinner.

Here we have three things that look like they are in a list, but it's not a parallel list.

My girlfriend plays video games all day, I even complain about it, and never takes me out to dinner.

Actually, the girlfriend does two things:

1. plays video games all day
2. never takes me out to dinner

Who is complaining? Not the girlfriend. She seems pretty happy. That bit in the middle about complaining shouldn't even be in the list. We can move it to the front of the sentence and rewrite it like this:

Correct	Even though I complain about it, my girlfriend plays video games all day and never takes me out to dinner.

Much better! *Plays video games all day* and *never takes me out to dinner* are parallel, and the misfit phrase has been moved out of the list. (Now all that's needed is a new girlfriend.)

THAT TRICKY WORD *THAT*

Often, when your sentences include phrases with the word *that*, you can lose track of your ideas and create a problem with parallelism. Here's an example:

Incorrect	My instructor promised that she would grade our essays within two weeks, that we would be happy with the results, and she was really nice about it.

Where does the list begin?

Incorrect	My instructor promised that she would grade our essays within two weeks, that we would be happy with the results, and she was really nice about it.

Notice how the first two items in the list begin with the word *that* followed by a complete thought. The last item doesn't fit, though, does it? It's not parallel. In fact, it's a comment on the other two things in the list. We might decide to take it out and put it elsewhere, like this:

Correct	My instructor was really nice when she promised that she would grade our essays within two weeks and that we would be happy with the results.

If we want to keep the item in the list, some rewriting would be necessary:

Correct	My instructor promised that she would grade our essays within two weeks, that we would be happy with the results, and that she would be kind to us.

This doesn't work as well, for a couple of reasons. First, it sounds repetitive. Saying "we would be happy" and "she would be kind" is practically the same thing. More important, it's probably not what the writer originally intended.

MAINTAINING PARALLELISM WHEN QUOTING

Probably the trickiest parallelism problem is how to correctly integrate a quotation into your sentence and keep your writing parallel. Read the following passage from *Little Women* by Louisa May Alcott:

> Fifteen-year-old Jo was very tall, thin, and brown, and reminded one of a colt, for she never seemed to know what to do with her long limbs, which were very much in her way. She had a decided mouth, a comical nose, and sharp, gray eyes, which appeared to see everything, and were by turns fierce, funny, or thoughtful. Her long, thick hair was her one beauty, but it was usually bundled into a net, to be out of her way. Round shoulders had Jo, big hands and feet, a flyaway look to her clothes, and the uncomfortable appearance of a girl who was rapidly shooting up into a woman and didn't like it. (10)

Most likely, you would not want to include the entire description of Jo in your essay. Instead, you would pick and choose the details you want to

For help integrating quotations into your own writing, see Chapter 16, Quotation and Paraphrase, page 307.

stress. However, when you do that, you have to be careful to maintain good parallel structure.

First Attempt	Jo, the heroine of Louisa May Alcott's famous sister story, *Little Women*, is a girl who "never seemed to know what to do with her long limbs, . . . sharp, gray eyes, which appeared to see everything, . . . and the uncomfortable appearance of a girl who was rapidly shooting up into a woman and didn't like it" (10).

What's wrong with the way that sounds? Read it out loud, and you'll probably hear the problems with parallelism. Let's take a closer look, this time by underlining the elements of the list:

Jo, the heroine of Louisa May Alcott's famous sister story, *Little Women*, is a girl who "<u>never seemed to know what to do with her long limbs</u>, . . . <u>sharp, grey eyes, which appeared to see everything</u>, . . . and <u>the uncomfortable appearance of a girl who was rapidly shooting up into a woman and didn't like it</u>" (10).

Even though these phrases were fine in Alcott's original passage, the way they have been selected from different sentences makes the grammar a mismatch. The first phrase begins with an adverb/verb combination (*never seemed*), and the other two phrases begin with adjective/noun combinations (*sharp, gray eyes* and *uncomfortable appearance*). It's probably best to go with the majority in this case, so you can fix the passage by eliminating part or all of the first phrase. If you like, you can add new material from elsewhere in the passage to convey similar information.

Revised	Jo, the heroine of Louisa May Alcott's famous sister story, *Little Women*, is a girl ~~who~~ "~~never seemed to know what to do~~ with ~~her~~ <u>long limbs</u>, . . . <u>sharp, grey eyes, which appeared to see everything</u>, . . . and <u>the uncomfortable appearance of a girl who was rapidly shooting up into a woman and didn't like it</u>" (10).

Here's the final result:

Correct	Jo, the heroine of Louisa May Alcott's famous sister story, *Little Women*, is a girl "with . . . long limbs, . . . sharp, gray eyes, which appeared to see everything, . . . and the uncomfortable appearance of a girl who was rapidly shooting up into a woman and didn't like it" (10).

Now, go back and read that sentence out loud to double-check its parallelism.

Finding and Fixing Parallelism Errors

Most likely, you make parallelism errors when you are struggling to say something that you haven't fully articulated yet. That's okay. Take some time to think through what you really mean to say, and then be willing to rewrite the sentence. Quite often, sentences that have parallelism problems are clunky sentences that would benefit from serious editing.

Keep an eye out for any sentences that introduce or explain two or more examples, reasons, actions, or ideas. Sometimes, when we start writing a list like that, we can only think up two good ideas, but we feel compelled for some reason to have three, so the third one that we make up is the clunker that is not parallel. Check over your sentence a few times to see if you can cut something.

Reading your writing out loud is very effective for finding errors in parallelism because parallelism is related to the rhythm of language, so be sure to use this editing strategy as you look over your papers.

Remember, errors in parallelism often do not have only one right solution. Play around with the sentence a little to discover a few different options, and then choose the one that sounds best to you.

LOOK OUT

If you are prone to making errors in parallelism, double-check for parallelism each time you use the words *and* and *or*. This could help you locate your own parallelism errors.

| practice it | Editing for Parallelism 1

1. Read the paragraph and underline all the errors in parallelism. You should find six problem sentences.
2. Go back to the errors that you underlined and decide how to fix them. Remember, you can either make minor changes or rewrite entirely. Make your corrections by hand in the space above the sentence you are fixing.

Richard Louv's *Last Child in the Woods: Saving Our Children from Nature-Deficit Disorder* makes a convincing argument that American culture has made childhood too safe and kids are too clean. In his book, Louv shows that children are no longer allowed to have a free and open relationship to nature because their parents won't let them climb trees or play in the woods, their teachers won't let them take any real risks on the playground, and many children live in high-crime neighborhoods. Even those who don't are often kept inside because the parents fear kidnappers and child predators. These fears, Louv demonstrates through statistical evidence, are not logical; rather, they are created by the media and enhanced by new styles of hands-on parenting that may not be for the best. Louv is right. We need to allow children to climb trees, getting dirty, and run around their neighborhoods a little bit more often. The environmentalist groups also need to lighten up in

continued ❯

their anti-fishing, anti-hunting, and "leave no trace" attitudes. Sure, we want kids to respect nature, but many children who grow up fishing and hunt do have more respect for nature than those who grow up playing video games. Hunters are, ironically, some of the best caretakers of natural lands. "Leave no trace," while good in theory, can go a little overboard. If a child picks up a stick or plucking a flower, maybe he or she will remember that day and enjoying the beauty of nature forever. If all the child hears is "don't touch that," do you think that child will grow up to care about the natural world? Definitely not.

practice it   Editing for Parallelism 2

1. Read the paragraph and underline all the errors in parallelism. You should find four problem sentences.
2. Go back to the errors that you underlined and decide how to fix them. Remember, you can either make minor changes or rewrite entirely. Make your corrections by hand in the space above the sentence you are fixing.

Richard Louv's book *Last Child in the Woods: Saving Our Children from Nature-Deficit Disorder* argues that the current generation of American children has literally lost touch with nature and knowing a lot about environmental issues. While he has tons of great facts to support his argument, his personal anecdotes, especially when he compares his childhood to his son's life, are the most convincing. For example, Louv opens the book with a description of a conversation he had with his son, who asked him why life was more fun when his dad was growing up (1). Louv reflects on this and concluding that "[a] kid today likely will tell you about the Amazon rain forest—but not about the last time he or she explored the woods in solitude, or lay in a field listening to the wind and watching the clouds move" (1–2). In this scene, Louv does not seem like a scientist or philosophical; he seems like a dad who is trying to do his best to raise his son. He is really listening to his son and thoughts are about what his son has to say. You have to admire him for that.

chapter review

Chapter 32 covers one of the more common sentence-structure problems, parallelism. Once you begin to learn about parallelism errors, they tend to jump out at you. That's why, if you make this error, using the "isolate your errors" editing technique is best. Simply review the rule, and then read through your paper looking just for parallelism problems. Then rewrite as needed.

To review this chapter, choose one or more of the following strategies:

1. Try to explain what you have learned, or at least part of it, to someone you know. Discuss the key concepts and give some of your own examples to illustrate those concepts.

2. Write a paragraph with at least four parallel structures. Try to vary the structures (parallel phrases, verbs, nouns, and so on).

3. Look at the subheadings of Carol S. Dweck's article "The Perils and Promises of Praise," in Chapter 1 (pp. 6–13). Are they parallel?

4. If you skipped any of the Practice It activities in the chapter, go back and do them now as a way to deepen your understanding of the material.

5. Update your Grammar Log to include your parallelism problems with corrections. Don't forget to refer to the Grammar Log every time you edit a piece of writing, and don't forget to take the time to edit everything you write for all your college classes.

For more on keeping a Grammar Log, see page 579.

33

Common Sentence-Structure Problems

in this chapter

- What Is a Mixed Construction?
- What Are Predication Errors?
- How Do You Find and Fix Mixed Constructions?
- What Is a Modifier?
- What Are Misplaced Modifiers?
- What Are Dangling Modifiers?
- How Do You Find and Fix Misplaced and Dangling Modifiers?

To download the Grammar Log, log into your Integrated Media at **bedfordstmartins.com /readwriteconnect** and click on **Charts**.

LearningCurve
For extra practice in the skills covered in this chapter, visit **bedfordstmartins.com /readwriteconnect**.

Ever had the experience of finding sentences in your writing that just didn't seem to make sense or work well, but you weren't sure exactly what was wrong or how to fix them? You are not alone. The English language is complex, and when you express your sophisticated ideas in writing, you are bound to create some messy sentences along the way. This chapter covers two major problems students make in their writing: mixed constructions and misplaced or dangling modifiers. In order to get the most out of this chapter, you should have a good understanding of the basic sentence components and how to find the subject and verb in a sentence.

What Is a Mixed Construction?

Mixed constructions occur when you begin a sentence with one kind of structure and then switch to a different structure partway through. This happens sometimes when you edit sentences as you write. It can also happen in long sentences, in sentences including quotations, or in sentences with certain verbs or phrases. Terms like *sentence structure* or *sentence pattern* refer to the basic building blocks of a sentence. Although there is plenty of room for creativity in writing, once you begin a sentence, you are limited in the number of ways you can finish it. For example, suppose a sentence begins:

In her essay . . .

There are limited ways to go from here; logically, you need to tell the reader what the author says or does in her essay.

In her essay, <u>the author claims</u> . . .

At this point, this sentence is on a clear trajectory. Now that you have said *the author claims*, you have to say *what* she claims. This can come in the form of a summary, quotation, or paraphrase.

Prepositional Phrase Showing *Where* the Author Makes Her Claim	Subject and Verb Showing *What* the Author Is Doing	Phrase Stating *What* the Author Is Claiming

In her essay, the author claims **that balloon animals are art**.

Prepositional Phrase Showing *Where* the Author Makes Her Claim	Subject and Verb Showing *What* the Author Is Doing	Clause Stating *What* the Author Is Claiming

In her essay, the author claims, **"Balloon animals are a craft that few people recognize as art, but they are."**

Notice that we have many choices in terms of which author we put in this sentence and which quote or paraphrase we add, but once we begin with a prepositional phrase, we're limited as to how we structure the rest of the sentence. We could, of course, start the sentence by taking the prepositional phrase out, but we'd end up right back where we started.

Subject and Verb Showing *What* the Author Is Doing	Phrase Stating *What* the Author Is *Claiming*

Correct   The author claims **that balloon animals are art**.

Subject and Verb Showing *What* the Author Is Doing	Clause Stating *What* the Author Is *Claiming*

Correct   The author claims, **"Balloon animals are a craft that few people recognize as art, but they are."**

In a mixed-construction sentence, the structure of the sentence doesn't make sense logically—the parts don't match.

Incorrect   In her essay, balloon animals are art.

With this sentence construction, you end up with parts that don't match up. Read each sentence part carefully:

Incorrect   In her essay, balloon animals are art.

The balloon animals are not art *in her essay*, but that's what this sentence suggests.

The following sentence is a mixed construction because the sentence parts don't make sense together.

Incorrect   Even though unauthorized graffiti is technically vandalism, it can also be expensive to remove.

This sentence begins one way and then shifts gears in the middle. The two parts don't match. The words *Even though* are setting up the sentence to suggest something about graffiti despite the fact that it is vandalism, but the second part of the sentence doesn't continue in that direction. To fix this mixed construction, change the conjunctions:

Correct   Unauthorized graffiti is technically vandalism, and it can be expensive to remove.

WHAT ARE PREDICATION ERRORS?

A predication error is a common mixed-construction error that happens when the subject and the predicate (verb part of the sentence) don't match. This often occurs when you use a form of the verb *to be*, which functions like an equals sign between sentence parts. If the two parts connected by the verb *to be* are not equal, you have created a predication error.

Incorrect   Summer vacation is where I get to travel.

What this sentence is saying: Summer vacation = where.

Summer vacation is not a place, so you can't use *where* to refer to it. Summer vacation is a time period, however, so you can fix it by changing the word "where" to "when."

Correct   Summer vacation is when I get to travel.

Here is an example of another common predication error in student writing:

Incorrect   The reason to have charter schools is because they have more autonomy over their budgets and their teachers' salaries.

Using *reason . . . is because* this way is common but incorrect. The word *because* is not a reason. In this instance, the word *because* is actually getting in the way of your reason.

Correct   The reason to have charter schools is they have more autonomy over their budgets and their teachers' salaries.

Let's look at another example of a common error:

Incorrect   Another way that education is in trouble today are not enough supplies for their classes.

In this example, the first part of the sentence (the subject part) does not match the second part (the predicate part). The first part sets up a *way* that education is in trouble, but *not enough supplies* is not a *way* education is in trouble; it is an example of the result of not having enough funding. How could you fix this sentence?

Finding Mixed Constructions

The best way to find mixed-construction sentences is for you or someone else to read your essay aloud while you listen for parts that sound awkward or don't make sense. It's important to hear these kinds of errors because when you read something silently, your brain will "fix" mistakes as you read in order to make broader sense of the sentence or paragraph. Of course, this does not actually fix the mistake in your paper. Another strategy for finding mixed-construction sentences is to look for sentences that

- Include quotations
- Begin with a prepositional phrase
- Are long
- Use *reason* and *because* together
- Use *is when* or *is where*

These may not be the only places mixed-construction errors pop up, but they are the most common. Of course, if your instructor or a tutor has commented on this error in your writing before, be especially on the lookout. Ask for examples of places in your essays where you have made this error if they aren't already marked; this will give you a good idea of where you run into trouble.

Don't be discouraged if you create mixed constructions. Often they emerge in a piece of writing when the writer is trying to express something slightly beyond his or her skill level. This sort of stretching is great. You just have to challenge yourself to make the grammar of the sentence appropriate to the level of your ideas. The worst thing is to simply delete the problematic sentence. Take the time to fix it. The idea in the sentence might be one of your best!

Fixing Mixed Constructions

So, then, how do you fix those awkward sentences? Let's face it, if you knew how to avoid them, you would. What it boils down to is understanding the basic sentence parts and making sure the compatible sentence parts match. Start with the subject and verb. Being able to identify the subject and verb of the sentence will help you unravel the mixed construction. Slowly read through your sentences one at a time. Circle or underline the subject of each sentence, and then underline the main verb of each sentence twice. After you do this for every sentence in your paragraph, look more closely at each sentence. Do the subject and the verb make sense together?

Incorrect   Increases in bus fare make it harder to ride the bus.

The subject and verb are identified in this sentence. Read just the subject and verb together. Do they make sense? Do increases make it harder to ride the bus? No. Maybe they make it more expensive to ride the bus, or they make it harder to afford riding the bus, but increases don't make it harder to ride the bus. One way to rewrite the sentence might be:

Correct   Increases in bus fare make it harder to afford riding the bus.

Another way to check for mixed construction is to underline the phrases or word groups that go together in the sentence.

Incorrect   In the article "Chicano Mural Movement," says that Chicano murals are depictions of Mexican American culture.

Check to see if the underlined parts work together. Do they make sense? In this example, who *says that Chicano murals are depictions of Mexican American culture*? Does *In the article* say? No, *the author* says this. But the author is not in the sentence. Now you know what to add to make this sentence make sense.

Correct   In the article "Chicano Mural Movement," Teresa Palomo Acosta says that Chicano murals are depictions of Mexican American culture.

Much better! Let's look at another example:

Incorrect   My favorite memory was when I walked across the stage at graduation.

By looking at the underlined parts, we can see that the first part of the sentence starts off fine, but the second part goes in a different direction by saying *was when*. When you use *when*, you refer to a time, but a memory is not a time, so you can't refer to it using *when*. How can we fix this sentence?

Correct   My favorite memory was walking across the stage at graduation.

OR

Correct   I remember when I walked across the stage at graduation.

Notice that the second sentence changes the meaning. The sentence is no longer about a "favorite" memory; now it is just about remembering. When you fix your sentences, think about what point you want to get across.

Another way to fix sentences with structure problems is to learn the three basic kinds of sentences and practice using them when you write. There are three basic sentence constructions:

1. *Simple sentence:* an independent clause that makes up the basic sentence unit. It is made up of a subject and a verb and expresses a complete thought. Here are some examples:

   I always <u>order</u> popcorn at the movies.

   <u>Murals</u> often <u>display</u> culturally or historically significant themes.

   A good <u>education</u> <u>is</u> important.

2. *Compound sentence:* two independent clauses joined by a coordinating conjunction (FANBOYS: *for, and, nor, but, or, yet, so*). In the following examples, the conjunction and the second independent clause are bold.

   Some <u>students</u> <u>are</u> already good at keeping a budget with their money, **but others <u>need</u> a class on financial literacy**.

   Learning good money habits <u>is</u> a start toward financial stability, **and practicing them regularly <u>helps</u> maintain it**.

   Public <u>schools</u> <u>are</u> overcrowded, **so <u>students</u> <u>get</u> too little time from their teachers**.

3. *Complex sentence:* an independent clause joined with a dependent clause. In the following examples, the dependent clause is in bold.

   Because most <u>jobs</u> <u>require</u> strong writing skills, <u>learning</u> to improve writing in college <u>is</u> a smart career move.

   Although <u>you</u> can't <u>choose</u> your siblings, <u>they</u> <u>can be</u> a source of great comfort and support.

---

practice it   Finding Mixed Constructions

Look over a few paragraphs from an essay you wrote, and see if you can find any mixed constructions. If you find any, underline the sentence parts and try to fix the sentences.

What Is a Modifier?

A **modifier** is a word or group of words that adds to or changes the meaning of another word. Adjectives and adverbs are modifiers; they describe or add to the meaning of nouns, verbs, adjectives, and other adverbs.

Essentially, you have two parts to the modifying equation: the word or group of words being modified and the modifier.

Zeus, the black cat, is fat and likes to eat broccoli.

In this sentence, all the underlined words or phrases are modifying the word *cat*.

What kind of cat? black, fat, likes to eat broccoli

Modifiers can either be single words (*black*) or phrases (*likes to eat broccoli*). Either way, modifiers should appear next to the word they are modifying in the sentence (or at least very close).

MISPLACED MODIFIERS

A misplaced modifier happens when the word being modified is not close enough to the modifier, so it ends up modifying the wrong word in the sentence.

Misplaced   Jake saw a roach taking out the trash.

Wait, what? He saw a roach carrying garbage? Of course not. This is just a case of a misplaced modifier. In this sentence, *taking out the trash* is the modifier, meaning it gives more information about what Jake was doing. Modifiers end up modifying the words closest to them, and in this case the modifier is seriously misplaced! This phrase is about Jake, not the roach, so it needs to be placed next to the word *Jake* in the sentence. Let's try that again:

Correct   Taking out the trash, Jake saw a roach.

Now that makes a lot more sense. Here's another example of a misplaced modifier:

Misplaced   Raquel served birthday cake to the guests on paper plates.

This sentence reads as though the guests were on paper plates. What part of the sentence is the modifier? And what word is it modifying?

The underlined part of the sentence is the modifier, giving us more information about the birthday cake. To fix this, move this part of the sentence closer to the word it modifies.

Correct   Raquel served birthday cake on paper plates to the guests.

DANGLING MODIFIERS

A dangling modifier occurs when only half of the modifying equation is in the sentence. In the case of a misplaced modifier, the word being modified is in the sentence but is separated from the modifier. In the case of a dangling modifier, the word being modified is missing from the sentence entirely.

| Dangling Modifier | Raised in a very large family, the house was too small for us. |

The house was not raised in a very large family. What or who was? It's not clear from this sentence. *Raised in a very large family* is modifying something, but that something is not in the sentence and needs to be added.

| Correct | I was raised in a very large family, and the house was too small for us. |

OR

| Correct | Raised in a very large family, I always thought our house was too small for us. |

There is no single correct way to fix a dangling or misplaced modifier; the key is to identify what is misplaced or dangling and rewrite the sentence so that the modifier modifies the right word.

---

practice it   Finding Misplaced and Dangling Modifiers 1

Underline the misplaced or dangling modifiers in the following sentences. Then draw an arrow pointing from the modifier to the word it should be modifying.

1. I gave a bite of my steak to my boyfriend skewered with onions and peppers.
2. The mailman left a package outside our house dripping wet from the rain.
3. The sweater once belonged to my grandmother full of moth holes.
4. Cynthia ran out to the scene of the car accident wearing pajamas and a robe.
5. Preparing for the long car ride, the cat paced as I packed.

Finding and Fixing Misplaced and Dangling Modifiers

To find misplaced and dangling modifiers, follow the same careful proofreading techniques outlined earlier in this chapter: Slowly read your essay out loud with a pencil in hand so you can mark sentences that don't sound quite right. Keep a lookout for prepositional phrases or *-ing* words that begin sentences, as these are likely places for misplaced modifiers. If you find a sentence that doesn't sound right, underline the sentence parts to see if they work together. If not, see if there is a part of the sentence that provides more information. Read it carefully a few times to decide whether the word or phrase is modifying the right part of the sentence.

Modifiers aren't picky; they modify anything you put next to them. For this reason, you should keep your modifiers close to the word they modify—right next to them is the best place. When you separate the modifier from the word or group of words that it modifies, confusion and sometimes hilarity ensue, and unfortunately the meaning of your sentence is compromised. In the case of a dangling modifier, the word being modified is actually missing from the sentence.

| Misplaced Modifier | While jogging along the trail, a mountain lion frightened the couple. |

Although a jogging mountain lion would frighten most people, this is not what the writer intended to say here. The modifier *while jogging along the trail* should be modifying the couple, not the mountain lion. The fix is to move this phrase next to *the couple*.

| Correct | A mountain lion frightened the couple, who were jogging along the trail. |

Here's another example:

| Dangling Modifier | The cake was ruined, having forgotten to add baking powder. |

The cake did not forget to add baking powder, but the person who did is not in the sentence. To fix this, add the person in the sentence where he or she belongs.

| Correct | Having forgotten to add baking powder, Don ruined the cake. |

practice it   Finding Misplaced and Dangling Modifiers 2

Underline the misplaced or dangling modifiers in the following sentences. Then draw an arrow pointing from the modifier to the word it should be modifying.

1. Pouring millions of gallons over the waterfall, Bill marveled at Niagara Falls.
2. While walking down the street, a football smashed into my head.
3. Slithering smoothly down the trail, Martha and Jean came across a rattlesnake.
4. Reading the directions while driving, the map looked confusing.
5. Nathaniel saw the Rocky Mountains looking out the airplane window.

6. We ordered a sundae from the waiter with extra whipped cream.
7. Hanging on a lamppost Allegra saw the parade banners.
8. Walking through the door, the dog jumped up and licked Brian's face in welcome.
9. Zola saw a family of ducks on the way to the hospital.
10. Hungry after a day of yard work, the steaks looked mouthwatering.

chapter review

Chapter 33 discusses some of the more complex sentence-structure problems, the types of errors that can make your writing difficult to understand. It is challenging to identify the pattern of your common errors, so you should start by reviewing your instructor's corrections and comments on your previously graded papers. Did your instructor note any mixed constructions or misplaced or dangling modifiers? Often, instructors simply label these sentences "awk" for awkward or note that your sentences are confusing. You definitely need to take some time to rewrite such sentences as practice.

To review this chapter, choose one or more of the following strategies:

1. Try to explain what you have learned, or at least part of it, to someone you know. Discuss the key concepts and give some of your own examples to illustrate those concepts.

2. Make flash cards for each of the rules outlined in this chapter.

3. If you skipped any of the Practice It activities in the chapter, go back and do them now as a way to deepen your understanding of the material.

4. Update your Grammar Log to include your most frequent sentence-structure problems with corrections. Don't forget to refer to the Grammar Log every time you edit a piece of writing, and don't forget to take the time to edit everything you write for all your college classes.

For more on keeping a Grammar Log, see page 579.

34

Writing Clear and Focused Sentences

in this chapter

- What Are Clear and Focused Sentences?
- What Is Wordiness?
- What Are Vague or Unclear Pronouns?
- What Is Active Voice and Passive Voice?
- How Do You Avoid Clichés, Empty Phrases, and Slang?

What Are Clear and Focused Sentences?

Your instructor may have written comments on your paper saying you need to work on sentence clarity or sentence focus, but perhaps you aren't entirely sure what this means. If your sentences lack clarity, your reader can't understand what you are trying to say about the topic. Similarly, lack of sentence focus means the topic of the sentence itself is not clear. The most fundamental purpose of writing is to communicate, and if your sentences lack clarity or focus, you aren't communicating. For instance, can you get a clear sense of what the following sentence is saying?

> Whether it is from the latest trends in fashion or the way people behave, you will come across numerous celebrity obsession stories that all too often hook us in.

How about this one?

> Children with older siblings can affect the behavior of children in many ways.

Neither of these sentences is very clear or focused. After reading them several times, you might get a sense of what the author means, but you don't want your reader to have to work that hard to understand you. Writing clear, focused sentences from the beginning makes you and your ideas stand out in a good way.

Lack of sentence clarity and focus may have any number of causes, but the most common ones in student writing are wordiness, vague or unclear pronouns, passive voice, and poor vocabulary choices (clichés, empty phrases, and slang).

:e To download the Grammar Log, log into your Integrated Media at **bedfordstmartins.com /readwriteconnect** and click on **Charts**.

✔ LearningCurve For extra practice in the skills covered in this chapter, visit **bedfordstmartins.com /readwriteconnect**.

Wordiness

WHAT IS WORDINESS?

Instructors write "wordy" on your paper when you use too many words to say something that could be said in fewer words. Often, wordy sentences also have an overly complicated sentence structure that can be simplified for clarity and focus. Let's look at an example:

Wordy   It is the best way to see a car at the auto show because the auto show is where you can really see what is going to be coming out in the new line of cars.

Sounds wordy, doesn't it? What is the point of this sentence? From reading the sentence a few times, we can see that the real point made here is that car makers reveal their new cars at auto shows. Here's one possible revision:

Revised   The auto show introduces the new line of cars to the public.

This gets to the point more quickly with fewer words and less confusion.

FIXING WORDINESS

Fortunately, you already have the tools you need to correct wordiness. Mostly, you need to be willing to cut out unnecessary words or replace those words with better ones.

Strategy 1: Try to eliminate *there is, there are,* and *it is* from the beginning of your sentences. Once you delete these phrases, you'll need to rewrite the sentence a little, which usually makes the verbs stronger.

Wordy   There are several cures for a hangover, but no cures for hangover have been scientifically proven.

Better   Several cures for a hangover exist, but no cures for hangover have been scientifically proven.

Strategy 2: Look for words used twice in the sentence, or synonyms (words that mean the same thing). Rewrite the sentence to delete these repetitions.

Repetitive   Several cures for a hangover exist, but no cures for hangovers have been scientifically proven.

Better   Several cures for a hangover exist, but none have been scientifically proven.

Strategy 3: Make the verbs in the sentence as strong as possible. Don't turn perfectly good verbs (such as *avoid*) into nouns (like *avoidance*). Try to avoid -*ing* verbs if you can too.

> **Wordy**   One sure way for hangover avoidance is spending more time on the dance floor instead of drinking so much when you go to a club.
>
> **Better**   To avoid a hangover, when you go to a club, dance more and drink less.

Strategy 4: Figure out who or what is really doing the action of the sentence and put that at the beginning of the sentence. This often forces you to make your verbs stronger, as suggested in the previous strategy.

> **Wordy**   The winner of the contest will be the person who has the best dance moves.
>
> **Better**   The person with the best moves will win the dance contest.

Strategy 5: Eliminate inflated or empty language. Sometimes students use big words and fancy phrases when a simple word will do. Of course, having a good vocabulary is great, but an inflated vocabulary just makes you seem like you're trying to impress, which is, well, not impressive.

> **Wordy**   In the event that the executive in charge of production deems it necessary to call for a work stoppage for the day, we will resume our duties in a timely fashion tomorrow.
>
> **Better**   If the production manager thinks we need to stop work today, we will start again early tomorrow.

While the first sentence might seem better to some because it sounds official, experienced readers will find it wordy. The following is a short list of phrases you should avoid whenever possible, as well as some suggested substitutions.

Avoid	Substitute
due to the fact that	because
in the event that	if
in society today, or nowadays	in Texas since the mid-1990s (or other specific time and place)

Wordiness makes your writing hard to understand, and sometimes makes it look like you're trying to sound important, which usually ends up just sounding silly. Avoiding wordiness is the key to having a clear, concise, college writing style.

Avoid Vague or Unclear Pronouns

Vague or unclear pronouns create unclear or unfocused sentences. Although this can happen with almost any pronoun, the following pronouns are most likely to cause trouble:

Pronouns That Refer to People

he	she
hers	their
his	they
one	

Pronouns That Refer to Things

it
that
this

Here's an example:

> **Unclear**   The instructor gave the student his essay.

Whose essay did the instructor give the student? Was it the student's essay or the instructor's essay? It's not clear who *his* refers to in this sentence.

> **Revised**   The student received his essay back from the instructor.

Now we know whose essay it was: the student's. Let's look at another sentence:

> **Unclear**   Taking the bus or walking is a great way to get around the city; this also helps reduce traffic on the streets.

What does *this* refer to? Taking the bus, walking, or both?

> **Revised**   Taking the bus and walking are great ways to get around the city and to reduce traffic on the streets.

Good, now it's clear that *both* methods of transportation reduce traffic on the street. Here's another example:

> **Unclear**   In the trilogy *The Lord of the Rings*, it creates a fantasy world that is very complex.

What does *it* refer to? What creates a fantasy world that is very complex? *The Lord of the Rings* trilogy creates the fantasy world, but in this case it would be too wordy to repeat the title and too vague to use the pronoun *it* to replace it.

In some cases, the best solution is to rewrite the sentence to focus on what you are trying to say. In this instance, the point is that the books create a complex fantasy world. So let's rewrite it with that point as the focus:

> **Revised**   The trilogy *The Lord of the Rings* creates a very complex fantasy world.

Much clearer!

Using the pronoun *one* is sometimes necessary to avoid a lengthy explanation of who *one* refers to, but overuse of this pronoun leads to a vague sentence or paragraph, as in the following example:

> **Unclear**   If one recycled all of one's plastics and cans, one could get by with a smaller garbage can.

This sentence sounds really awkward because of the use of the vague pronoun *one*. It's not clear whom the writer is referring to. The general population? A specific audience? Us? If you know whom you are referring to in the sentence, use a concrete subject instead of the vague pronoun *one*. The following sentence is much clearer:

> **Revised**   If the tenants of the apartment building recycled all of their plastics and cans, they could get by with smaller garbage cans.

Can you see how this sentence becomes clearer and more focused when we replace the vague pronoun with a concrete subject? The use of the pronoun *they* in the second half of the sentence works fine because now that we have clarified the subject (tenants of the apartment building), we know exactly whom that pronoun is referring to. Essentially, if you can't tell what the noun is, then you have an unclear pronoun referent.

For more on pronouns, see Chapter 30, page 654.

Use Active Voice Whenever Possible

An active-voice sentence occurs when the subject of the sentence is doing the action. For example:

> **Active**   Financial literacy programs make sense.

In this sentence, the subject *programs* is doing something; it is making.

In contrast, the action of a passive-voice sentence is done by someone not named in the sentence. For example:

> **Passive**   Financial literacy *programs* should be taught.

Who should teach financial literacy programs? It's not clear because the person or thing doing the action (teaching) is not in the sentence. Passive-voice sentences can really affect the clarity of your writing. Here's another example:

> **Passive**   The problem of having different financial styles is solved through talking.

Who is doing the solving through talking? Couples, maybe? Now look at the following sentence, written in the active voice:

Active   Couples can solve the problem of having different financial styles through talking.

Much better! Let's look at another sentence:

Passive   Yosemite has been visited by many tourists over the years.

This sounds awkward. If it's tourists who are doing the visiting, have tourists be the subject.

Active   Many tourists have visited Yosemite over the years.

Sometimes the passive voice is necessary, specifically in cases where you don't know who is doing the action or where the doers of the action are too large and varied a group to name. However, if you know who is doing the action of the sentence, it is generally better to avoid the passive voice and keep the verb active.

General   The Nike "swoosh" symbol is recognized around the
Group Doing   world.
the Action

In this case, the group recognizing the "swoosh" symbol is so general that it is not necessary to name it.

Unclear   Diamonds can now be manufactured in labs.
Who Is Doing
the Action

It's not clear who is doing the manufacturing; the point is that this technology exists.

To Avoid Naming   During the group obstacle course, mistakes were made.
Who Is Doing
the Action

In this case, the passive voice is used intentionally to protect the identity of the person or people who made mistakes.

Avoid Clichés, Empty Phrases, and Slang

Clichés are literary shortcuts that would be great if they weren't so overused. For example, instead of using the cliché *up in arms*, use *angry* or *frustrated* since that's what the cliché means. Avoid clichés in your writing; instead, come up with a fresh way of describing things or at least attempt to use newer analogies to make your point. Think for a moment about what you are actually trying to say. Often, just saying exactly what you mean is the best choice. Take a look at this example:

| Cliché | Here's some food for thought: Almost 25 percent of students who begin high school never make it to graduation. |

What is this writer really trying to say here? The point is that this statistic might be information you didn't already know. Okay, so how about writing that?

| Revised | Surprisingly, almost 25 percent of students who begin high school never make it to graduation. |

Now the reader can focus on the information, not the worn-out cliché.

Common Clichés
as luck would have it
bored to tears
few and far between
food for thought
larger than life
up in arms

Like clichés, empty phrases don't really say anything. Using them is like adding packing peanuts to your essay; they take up space but provide no valuable content. Most of the time, you can simply cut out the empty phrases or replace them with a simpler expression. For instance:

| Empty Phrase | In today's society, women and men both attend college. |

| Empty Phrase Deleted | Women and men both attend college. |

| Replaced and Revised | Since the late 1970s, women and men have both attended college in equal numbers. |

Common Empty Phrases
the fact of the matter is
I, myself
I, personally
in my opinion
in today's society
since the dawn of time
throughout time

Slang words or phrases are very informal or not considered part of Standard English. Avoiding slang language in an academic paper is important because you want instructors to take you seriously, and using slang makes writing at best informal and at worst sloppy. We often use more informal, slang language when talking with friends or even when e-mailing or texting. But for the same reason that you talk differently with your friends than you do during a job interview, you use more formal language when writing for academic or job-related purposes than you do when writing e-mails or text messages to friends.

Common Slang Expressions
24/7
back in the day
for sure, for real
LOL, OMG (any text abbreviations)
stuff
u (for "you")

practice it   Editing for Clarity and Focus 1

Use the information and skills you learned in this chapter to revise the following paragraph.

In society today, one problem with public schools is the lack of funding. The lack of funding, especially in low-income areas, makes it harder for students to achieve success. It is harder for students to achieve success because the schools don't have a lot of things. They don't have enough books or computers for each student to use. The test scores are very low because when students can't study, they score very low on the test. They can't study because they don't have enough books or materials. The children are suffering. They are not to blame.

practice it   Editing for Clarity and Focus 2

Use the information and skills you learned in this chapter to revise the following paragraph.

Clashes between celebrities and paparazzi are frequent occurrences in the news. A lack of privacy is the result of photographers following celebrities everywhere they go. After one incident between a celebrity photographer

continued ❯

and a bodyguard, it was claimed that the bodyguard took his camera. The allegation was denied by the bodyguard. It was also stated that the reputation of the celebrity was on the line when photos of him being arrested for drunk driving emerged. There are those who blame them for invasion of privacy, and there are others who say that it is a right that celebrities forfeit in exchange for their fame. Shows like *TMZ* (OMG, so funny) always follow celebrities around asking stuff until the celebrities finally get mad, and then the celebrities usually get in a car and drive away. Sometimes they show other paparazzi getting into arguments with celebs. Although I envy their fancy clothes, cars, and vacations, I am glad I don't have anyone following me around with a camera.

chapter review

Chapter 34 explains how to write clear and focused sentences. A lack of sentence focus and clarity, as you now know, can have many different sources: wordiness, vague or unclear pronouns, passive voice, and cliché or slang language. The solution is usually to isolate the sentence and think about what you are trying to say. Rewrite the sentence on a separate piece of paper a few times until you feel you have it clearly focused.

For more on keeping a Grammar Log, see page 579.

To review this chapter, choose one or more of the following strategies:

1. Try to explain what you have learned, or at least part of it, to someone you know. Discuss the key concepts and give some of your own examples to illustrate those concepts.

2. Read through a paper you recently wrote for a college class, highlighting any unclear or unfocused words, phrases, or sentences. Then go back and try to rewrite them, consulting the chapter as needed.

3. If you skipped any of the Practice It activities in the chapter, go back and do them now as a way to deepen your understanding of the material.

4. Update your Grammar Log to include a list of the empty phrases, clichés, or slang that you tend to overuse. Don't forget to refer to the Grammar Log every time you edit a piece of writing, and don't forget to take the time to edit everything you write for all your college classes.

35
Apostrophes

in this chapter

- What Is an Apostrophe?
- What Is a Contraction?
- How Do You Use Apostrophes to Show Ownership?
- How Do You Find and Fix Apostrophe Errors?

What Is an Apostrophe?

The apostrophe—that little thing that looks like a comma but hangs above the word—is one of the most incorrectly used punctuation marks in the English language. People who make signs and banners seem particularly confused by this tiny demon. You, however, can master the apostrophe. The first step is to recognize that it has two totally different purposes: to show a contraction and to show ownership. Next, you need to figure out how to use it correctly. This is pretty easy with contractions, but more difficult with ownership. Luckily, a few simple possession tests can tame this punctuation mark.

USING APOSTROPHES TO MAKE CONTRACTIONS

When something contracts, it shrinks. It pulls together. Your muscles can contract while you run and give you a cramp or a muscle spasm, which is why you should stretch before you jog.

In language, a contraction is the pulling together of two words. You smush them together and leave out a few letters. We do this constantly in spoken English, often in a sloppy, informal way: "Bobby, gimme the shovel." What we really mean is "Bobby, give me the shovel," but we run *give* and *me* together and say it quickly: *gimme*. This is not good English. You can get away with it with Bobby, but definitely not on a job application or a college paper.

Some contractions are acceptable in written English, if you make them properly and spell them correctly. Here are a few of the acceptable ones:

Common Contractions

do not	becomes	*don't*
is not	becomes	*isn't*
she will	becomes	*she'll*
we are	becomes	*we're*
it is	becomes	*it's*

To download the Grammar Log, log into your Integrated Media at **bedfordstmartins.com /readwriteconnect** and click on **Charts**.

LearningCurve
For extra practice in the skills covered in this chapter, visit **bedfordstmartins.com /readwriteconnect**.

LOOK OUT
Some instructors request that you never use contractions in formal papers. Look at the course syllabus and assignment sheets, and listen to your instructor's verbal instructions, to find out his or her preference. When in doubt, leave them out.

TIP
Contractions with the word *is* are the ones that give people the most trouble. To figure out if a word is a contraction with *is*, try reformulating it as a question by reversing the two words that you are contracting. Here's an example: "She's going to call me." Is she? Yes, she is. Here's another example: "It's raining outside." Is it? Yes, it is.

To make a contraction properly, you have to know which words you are trying to contract (or pull together), and you have to know how to spell them. Then, when you pull them together, simply insert the apostrophe where you leave out the letters. Let's look at some examples in closer detail:

1. Begin with the words: do not
2. Run them together: → donot ←
3. Take out the second *o*:   don't

Sometimes you leave out more than one letter. That's okay too.

1. Begin with the words: she will
2. Run them together: → shewill ←
3. Take out *wi*:   she'll

A FEW EXCEPTIONS

Of course, it wouldn't (would not) be the English language if there weren't (were not) some exceptions, which you'll (you will) just have to memorize if they don't (do not) come naturally to you. Here are some exceptions:

will not	→	won't
shall not	→	shan't

Some contractions have more than one meaning, which can make things a bit tricky. For these, the reader has to use context to figure out which one the writer means. Here are a few examples:

Contractions That End in -'s

he's	can mean	he is	OR	he has
that's	can mean	that is	OR	that has
there's	can mean	there is	OR	there has

Contractions That End in -'d

he'd	can mean	he had	OR	he would
you'd	can mean	you had	OR	you would

practice it   Contractions

Look at the last essay you wrote for this class. Circle all the contractions on one page. How many contractions did you use? How formal is this piece of writing expected to be? Does the number of contractions seem appropriate? Correct any errors that you see in any of the contractions you found.

USING APOSTROPHES TO SHOW OWNERSHIP

As we have seen, the first reason to use an apostrophe is to make a contraction. The second reason is to show ownership—also known as possession. In other words, you use an apostrophe to show that one person, place, or thing (one noun) belongs to another person, place, or thing (another noun). For instance:

> my iguana's cage = the cage that belongs to my iguana

Of course, my iguana didn't buy the cage. He got it as a gift. Still, it's his, and he lives there, all by himself, so I use an apostrophe to show ownership.

The tricky part of using apostrophes to show ownership always seems to involve the letter *s*. Let's look at a few more examples. As you read, pay special attention to the word endings. Reading each example twice might help.

> my iguana's cage = one iguana, one cage

Now, say my iguana had two babies, and I'm keeping them all in the same cage. I need to make *iguana* plural (because there are more than one now), but I can keep *cage* singular, since I still have only one cage. So I add an -*s* to *iguana* to make it plural, and then I hang the apostrophe on the outside, like this:

> my iguanas' cage = more than one iguana, one cage

Now, say the babies got too big to share a cage, and I bought each of them its own cage. I now have three iguanas and three cages. I need to make both words—*iguana* and *cage*—plural. Then I need to hang the apostrophe after the *s* on *iguanas*. Here's what it looks like now:

> my iguanas' cages = more than one iguana, more than one cage

Tricky, right? It gets even tougher when the first word ends in an -*s*. Let's start with the word *witness* and imagine our witness has a story about what happened in an accident.

> the witness's story = one witness, one story

For singular nouns that end in -*s*, add an apostrophe and an -*s*.

If more than one witness was there, but they all remembered seeing the same thing, I would need to add *es* to *witness* and write it like this:

> the witnesses' story = more than one witness, one story

If, however, the witnesses had different recollections of the accident—different stories—it would look like this:

> the witnesses' stories = more than one witness, more than one story

We agree that this can get confusing. Luckily, there is a very simple rule to follow to avoid making mistakes with the possessive. Here it is, in two easy steps.

STEP 1: Make the noun showing ownership singular or plural *first*.

STEP 2: Hang an apostrophe + *s* or an apostrophe on the word that is demonstrating ownership of something.

Let's look at one more example:

I have three female siblings, and they own a house together.

Plural   Singular

My sisters own a house.

Since *sisters* already ends in the letter *s*, to make it possessive, just hang an apostrophe on the end:

My sisters' house

Now, let's say they go into a real estate business together and start buying up houses. Now we would say:

My sisters' houses

But if two of them moved to France and left all the houses to one of the sisters, we would say:

My sister's houses

But then let's say she decided to sell all the houses and move into a condo. We would say:

My sister's condo

The mighty apostrophe in combination with the letter *s* certainly can convey a lot of information, right? Unfortunately, though, in English, there is no way to determine from the apostrophe *how many more than one* we have. The reader or listener has to figure that out from the context.

Sometimes nouns form irregular plurals. For instance, *radius* becomes *radii* when you have more than one of them. More than one *life* would be *lives*. Here are some other common examples:

deer = one deer AND more than one deer
mouse = one mouse
mice = more than one mouse

Handle irregular plurals with the same rules given earlier: Make the noun that owns something singular or plural first, and then add the apostrophe or the apostrophe + *s* as necessary.

the mouse's cheese = one mouse, one piece of cheese
the mice's cheese = more than one mouse, one piece of cheese

Finding and Fixing Apostrophe Errors with Possessives

Sure, the spell checker on your computer can catch some apostrophe errors, but that doesn't help you when you're taking an essay exam or doing the sort of on-the-spot report writing common in so many professions. Plus, the spell checker is notoriously wrong much of the time when it comes to apostrophes. You need to learn how to eliminate apostrophe errors from your writing to gain a level of polish and sophistication in your work.

Many times, we've seen students who are trying to fix their apostrophe errors take something that was correct and rewrite it the wrong way. There are so many weird words in English, and it's easy to get overwhelmed. That's why the best way to find and fix your own errors is by repeating this simple rule to yourself while you are editing:

Make the noun showing ownership singular or plural first. Then hang an apostrophe + s or an apostrophe on it to make it possessive.

One more time:

Singular or plural first. Then think about the apostrophe.

It's sort of like the order of operations in math problems. As long as you follow that order, you'll be right every time.

To edit carefully for apostrophes, you may want to read your writing "backwards" by starting at the last sentence and ending with the first. You could use a piece of blank paper to cover the words so you are only looking at one sentence at a time. Some writers like to read out loud as they proofread. Proofreading works best from the printed page, not the computer screen.

---

practice it   Using Apostrophes to Show Possession

Practice using the apostrophe correctly by making possessives with the following:

- Your family name
- The first name of everyone in your family
- The names of all your pets
- Objects you see in the room
- Your favorite dessert
- Your favorite animal
- Your favorite sport

practice it   Correcting Apostrophe Errors

The following paragraph contains twelve apostrophe errors. Some are contraction errors and some are possession errors. The words might be missing an apostrophe or might have it in the wrong place. Proofread the paragraph with a pen or pencil in your hand. Circle each apostrophe error as you find it. Then go back and fix the errors, using this chapter to help you.

Yesterday I went to a seminar on time management. Its about time I went to something like this. My sisters boyfriend told me about it, and he's really smart, so I figured Id give it a try. I wasn't exactly thrilled to go at first, but now I'm totally glad I went. I feel like it will completely change my life. If I can apply some of the strategies' the lecturers were talking about, I can save myself so much time and get so much more done. For instance, they showed us how to make a weekly schedule with a to-do list. They said we should do it every Saturday morning so we have a sense of what our whole week's will look like. They also gave a lot of simple suggestions' that seem so easy. I don't know why I did'nt think of them before. They said that we should pack our backpack for school the night before class. Ive never bothered to do that, which is probably why I'm always rushing and forgetting things every morning. It sure would be nice to have time to have a bowl of cereal in the morning instead of rushing around like mad looking for all my books. Im going to start small and try those two strategies', and then once I've become good at those Ill try some of the other stuff they mentioned, like stopping procrastination, getting all the details' of my life organized, and finishing my homework before I go out to have fun.

chapter review

Apostrophe errors are small errors, but they are quite common, and it's good to take care of them as quickly as you can, using the guidelines in Chapter 35. Remember, the more that you practice correcting your own work, the more quickly you will stop making errors. Because apostrophes are such small marks, apostrophe errors are easy to miss. You have to proofread carefully to find them.

To review this chapter, choose one or more of the following strategies:

1. Try to explain what you have learned, or at least part of it, to someone you know. Discuss the key concepts and give some of your own examples to illustrate those concepts.

2. Reading your paper back to front works great for apostrophe proofreading. This isolates each sentence so you can see it out of context and check it for correctness. Use a paper you've already written to try this technique. Identify any apostrophe errors you find and correct them.

3. As you go through your daily life, whenever you see a sign in a restaurant or shop, check its apostrophe use. Playing this little game will train your brain to catch the errors.

4. If you skipped any of the Practice It activities in the chapter, go back and do them now as a way to deepen your understanding of the material.

5. In your Grammar Log, keep a list of words that cause you trouble with apostrophes. Review this list before you proofread your papers so these words are fresh in your mind. As you read through your paper, circle those words and any other words that don't seem correct. Then go back and double-check all the words you circled, referring to the words described earlier in this chapter.

For more on keeping a Grammar Log, see page 579.

36

Spelling and Capitalization

in this chapter

- What Are the Most Commonly Confused Words?
- What Are Some Tricky Spelling Rules?
- When Do You Capitalize?

Spelling

Sure, computers have spell checkers that can fix your typing or spelling errors, sometimes without your even realizing you've made an error. Such technology can help writers reduce errors and make the finished product look much more polished. However, relying on your spell checker alone can be dangerous for a couple of reasons. First, spell checkers won't alert you if you use the wrong word. For instance, most computers can't tell when you should use *their*, *there*, or *they're*. Such errors are actually the most common spelling mistakes. Second, and more important, not all the writing you do is on a computer, so you won't have your spell checker with you everywhere. In fact, in college some of the most important types of writing you do—midterms and finals—are handwritten, so you need to find and fix spelling errors yourself.

Commonly Confused Words

Let's start with the most common errors, the ones that make your writing look sloppy but are, thankfully, easily fixed.

Confusion between *it's* and *its* is reported to be the most common mistake in English.

it's is a contraction that means "it is" (It's raining.)

its is a possessive pronoun (The dog chased its tail.)

One way to tell whether to use *it's* or *its* is to ask yourself the question, "Is it?" and see if you can create an answer. For instance, take the following sentence:

It's raining.
Ask yourself: Is it raining?
Answer: Yes, it is.
Therefore, use *it's* to mean *it is*.

Now, try it with this sentence:

The dog chased its tail.
Ask yourself: Is it?
Answer: There's no answer that makes sense to that question. We could say
"Did it?" but "Is it?" doesn't fit.
Therefore, use *its* in this sentence.

Another way to remember the difference is to memorize the following sentence:

It's time that the apostrophe took its place at the start of the sentence.

Other commonly confused words are *their*, *there*, and *they're*:

their refers to a person
there refers to a place
they're means "they are"

Fortunately, there are some helpful memorization tricks you can use to remember these words. If you create a sentence that uses all three words in alphabetical order, you can figure out which word to use:

Their car is over there, but they're not in it.

Have a little fun creating your own sentence, one that you might remember better, making sure to keep the words in alphabetical order. Here are a few more examples of commonly confused words:

accept is when you receive or agree to something
except means the one that was left out

The cashier accepted all my coupons except for the one that had expired.

advice is a noun that means the words of wisdom someone gives
advise is what someone does while they are delivering advice

Good advice is rare; I advise you to take it.

affect is usually a verb that means to impact or influence
effect is usually a noun that means the result of something

He suffered from seasonal depression and was affected by the lack of sunshine in the winter. The effect was that he slept all the time and rarely ate.

loose is the opposite of tight
lose is what happens when you can't find something

My pants are loose; I hope I don't lose them when I round third base!

prejudice is a noun that refers to the state of being biased
prejudiced is an adjective that describes something that has prejudice

Racial prejudice is a terrible thing; I won't date anyone who is prejudiced.

quiet is the opposite of loud
quite means "very"

Being quiet is quite important in libraries.

than is used when comparing things
then refers to time or place (now and then)

I'd rather make dinner at home than eat out, but then after dinner I'd like to go out for ice cream.

to serves as a preposition (to the store) or as part of an infinitive (to dance)
too means "also" or "in addition" (I want a million dollars too!)
two is the number (No, I want two million dollars!)

To dance too much is impossible for those two.

weather is the snow, rain, sunshine, and so on
whether refers to possibilities, choices, or alternatives

The weather will determine whether the baseball game is called off.

we're is a contraction that means "we are" (We're going to buy books.)
were is the past tense of the verb to be (They were going to buy books.)
where refers to a place (Where are you going to buy books?)

We're lucky because we were just driving on the road where the avalanche hit, but it missed us by a minute.

Tricky Spelling Rules

The commonly confused words discussed in the preceding section cause most spelling errors among adults. Three types of words seem to cause the majority of the rest of the errors: plurals, words ending in silent *e*, and words for which people are not sure whether to double the final consonant when adding suffixes.

PLURAL ENDINGS

Turning a singular word into a plural causes many spelling errors. The three rules are pretty simple:

1. For regular words, most of the time you simply add *s* to the end to make them plural.

Singular		Plural
bird	→	birds
book	→	books
house	→	houses

(Remember, though, there are some irregular plurals, like *woman* → *women* and *mouse* → *mice*.)

2. For regular words ending in *s*, *sh*, *ch*, *x*, or *es*, add *es* to the end to make them plural.

Singular		Plural
dress	→	dresses
dish	→	dishes
lunch	→	lunches
box	→	boxes

3. For most words ending in *f* or *fe*, change the ending to *ves* to make it plural.

Singular		Plural
thief	→	thieves
knife	→	knives

Note that *safe* (meaning a place to store valuables) does not follow this rule. Its plural is *safes*.

SILENT *E*

Silent *e* is the letter at the end of a word that changes the sound of the vowel in the middle but does not have a sound itself.

For example, take the word *tap* and add silent *e* and you get *tape*. When we say *tape*, it sounds like "tayp," not "tay-pee," right? That's silent *e* in action.

If you need to add a suffix like *-ing*, *-ed*, or *-en* to a word that ends in silent *e*, drop the silent *e* before adding the suffix.

chase + ed = chased
chase + ing = chasing
take + en = taken
take + ing = taking

If the word ends in *ce* or *ge*, keep the *e* when adding the suffix *-able* or *-ous*.

    replace + able = replaceable
    advantage + ous = advantageous

TO DOUBLE OR NOT TO DOUBLE THE FINAL CONSONANT

Knowing whether or not to double a final consonant before adding a suffix is another tricky spelling situation. The rule is that you double the consonant if the word is only one syllable and the final consonant comes after a single vowel, like in the following examples:

    stop + ed = stopped
    rap + ing = rapping

The same rule applies if the word has more than one syllable and the final syllable is stressed.

    submit + ed = submitted
    regret + able = regrettable

If a word has more than one vowel, don't double the consonant.

    feel + ing = feeling (not feelling)
    look + ed = looked (not lookked)

FOREIGN WORDS

Like many languages, English has words that don't follow the rules. Often, this happens when a word enters English from another language. This list includes words like *bourgeois*, *entrepreneur*, *caveat*, *faux pas*, *avant-garde*, and *llama*. You need to memorize these words or look them up in a dictionary. Keeping a list in your Grammar Log may help.

For more on keeping a Grammar Log, see page 579.

practice it   Proofreading for Spelling Errors and Commonly Confused Words

The following paragraph contains ten spelling errors. Proofread the paragraph with a pen or pencil in your hand. Correct each spelling error you find. You may find it easier to read "backwards," going sentence by sentence from the end of the paragraph.

Being an enterpeneure sounds great, right? The idea of being you're own boss seems amazing cuz of the freedom and flexibility. However, they're are many factors that you have to consider before taking the plunge into self-employment. First, you will be giving up the security you might have in your current job. Their's no unemployment insurance for the self-employed. Second, you do not have quiet the same vehicles to save for your retirement. In many cases, 401(k)s are free money. Some employers match all or part of your contributions, and at the very least you should concider the tax-free contributions an automatic return on your investment. The types of retirement savings plans for the self-employed are not as generous. Finally, you have to factor in the cost of health insurance, which will be determined by you're age, health, and smoking habits. Its wise to comparison shop for health insurance before you decide to quit your regular job and start your own business. Overall, the life of an entrepreneur does have many advantages, but their are significant drawbacks as well. Make sure you carefully weigh the costs and benefits and have enough cash to carry you over lean times before you except the challenge of starting your new business.

Capitalization

The basic rules of capitalization are pretty straightforward. Capitalize words at the beginning of sentences, proper nouns, and the first and major words in titles. The devil, as they say, is in the details. What counts as a proper noun? Which words in a title are considered major? When in doubt, you can check a good dictionary, of course, but you should also learn a few specific techniques to help you figure out whether to capitalize or not to capitalize.

PROPER NOUNS

Proper nouns are capitalized because they refer to important things: specific names of people, places, and events. Take, for example, Niko the cat. The word *cat* is a common noun. It refers to all four-legged furry felines. The word *Niko* is a proper noun because it is the name of one specific cat. The same is true for most nouns, as you can see in the following sentences, where the proper nouns are capitalized and the corresponding common nouns are not:

I think Saturday is my favorite day of the week.

Most people believe Earth is the best planet.

The writer Jane Austen is the best novelist.

That guy says Nirvana is the most influential band of all time.

Who knew Paris was the most beautiful city?

Is Halloween the most fun holiday?

Sometimes, though, a word can be either a proper or a common noun, so you capitalize it or don't capitalize it depending on whether or not it refers to a specific person, place, or thing. Look at these examples:

A new study reported that the average mom does twenty-seven hours of housework a week.

I sure hope my mom has some help with all that work.

"Hey, Mom, did you wash my soccer jersey?"

In the first example, the word *mom* refers to the general category of mothers. In the second example, someone is referring to his or her mother but not using the word as a name. In the third example, the person is using "Mom" in place of a name, so it is capitalized. In this case, *Mom* essentially functions as a name, so it gets capitalized. Here's another example:

Any college you attend should be accredited.

Pasadena City College is an accredited institution.

TITLES

The rule for titles is that you capitalize the first and last words in any title or subtitle, plus all the major words. What counts as a major word? Anything except articles (*a, an, the*), coordinating conjunctions (*for, and, nor, but, or, yet, so*), and prepositions (*of, on, with*, and so on) needs to be capitalized. Here are some examples:

I'm Dancing as Fast as I Can
Of Human Bondage
Home to Harlem
All the Pretty Horses

These minor capitalization rules do change from one publication style to the next, so MLA may capitalize something where the *New York Times* does not. Remember, too, that book titles are italicized in MLA style, and essay and short story titles are in quotation marks. Check with your instructor in each class to determine which documentation style you should use, but keep in mind that generally MLA is used in the humanities and APA is used in the social and health sciences.

For more on formatting titles, see Chapter 20, MLA Documentation, page 362.

practice it   Proofreading for Capitalization Errors

The following paragraph contains numerous capitalization errors. Proofread the paragraph with a pen or pencil in your hand. Correct each capitalization error you find. You may find it easier to read "backwards," going sentence by sentence from the end of the paragraph.

The local Public Radio Station, Kacg, has a weekly talk show program about personal finance called *Money Matters And me*. This week, the host, Janice million, was joined by a guest expert on financing a college education, Mr. Edward Most. He explained the difference between student loans backed by the Government and private loans, and he argued that parents should always put their retirement savings ahead of their children's college savings goals. When a college student called in and asked Mr. Most what she should do if her Parents hadn't saved enough for college, he gave her a very informative answer about various options, like work study, postgraduation work opportunities that forgive part or all of your student loan debt, and, of course, the Military, which has the gi bill for veterans as well as some excellent training programs for active duty military personnel. The radio program made a compelling case that parents and students need more education about College Financing, and that most americans probably are not aware of the full array of options available.

chapter review

Chapter 36 covers some basic spelling and capitalization rules. Remember, though, that checking for proper spelling and capitalization is best done in the final stage of the writing process, when you proofread your writing.

To review this chapter, choose one or more of the following strategies:

1. Try to explain what you have learned, or at least part of it, to someone you know. Discuss the key concepts and give some of your own examples to illustrate those concepts.

2. Make flash cards for any of the spelling and capitalization rules that you know you tend to break. Include examples drawn from your own writing to illustrate the rules.

3. If you skipped any of the Practice It activities in the chapter, go back and do them now as a way to deepen your understanding of the material.

4. Update your Grammar Log to include your most frequent spelling and capitalization errors with corrections. Don't forget to refer to the Grammar Log every time you edit a piece of writing, and don't forget to take the time to edit everything you write for all your college classes.

For more on keeping a Grammar Log, see page 579.

ACKNOWLEDGMENTS

Teresa Paloma Acosta. "Chicano Mural Movement," *Handbook of Texas Online* (http://www.tshaonline.org/handbook/online/articles/kjc03), accessed September 4, 2013. Published by the Texas State Historical Association.

Catherine Brittain Allison. "A Parenting Secret I Am No Longer Willing to Keep," babble.com. Used by permission.

Jack Becker. "Public Art: An Essential Component of Creating Communities." Reprinted from *Public Art: An Essential Component of Creating Communities*, Americans for the Arts/Monograph, March 2004 with permission by Americans for the Arts, www.AmericansForTheArts.org and author Jack Becker, Forecast Public Art, www.forecastpublicart.org.

Mark Bittman. "Limit Soda for Kids' Sake," *The New York Times*, June 6, 2006. Used by permission of the author.

Po Bronson and Ashley Merryman. From *NurtureShock*. Copyright © 2009 by Po Bronson. By permission of Grand Central Publishing. All rights reserved.

Andrea Chang. "Kashing In," *LA Times*, April 24, 2011. Used by permission.

"Director of UW–Milwaukee's Office of Charter Schools." *The UWM Post*. Used by permission.

Carol S. Dweck. "The Perils and Promises of Praise." From the October 2007 issue of *Educational Leadership, 65(2)*, pp. 34–39. Copyright © 2007 by ASCD. Reprinted with permission. Learn more about ASCD at www.ascd.org.

Pam Fessler. "Making It in the U.S.: More Than Just Hard Work/New Programs Aim to Close the Wealth Gap," NPR, September 15/September 16, 2011. Used by permission.

David J. Flaspohler. "In Hakalau, a Modern Success Story," *The New York Times*, June 6, 2012. Used by permission.

Carlin Flora. "Seeing by Starlight," *Psychology Today*, July/Aug 2004. Used by permission.

Patrick L. Frank and Sarah Preble. *Prebles' Artforms*, 10th Edition, © 2011. Reprinted by permission of Pearson Education, Inc., Upper Saddle River, NJ.

James Gaddy. "Nowhere Man," *Print Magazine*, 2007. Used by permission.

Jake Halpern. "The Desire to Belong: Everyone Wants to Have Dinner with Paris Hilton and 50 Cent" from *Fame Junkies: The Hidden Truths Behind America's Favorite Addiction* by Jake Halpern. Copyright © 2007 by Jake Halpern. Reprinted by permission of Houghton Mifflin Harcourt Publishing Company. All rights reserved.

Sherie Holder and Kenneth Meeks. "Teach Your Children the Building Blocks of Finance," *Black Enterprise*, February 1, 2006. Used by permission.

Koon-Hwee Kan. "Adolescents and Graffiti." © 2001. Used with permission of the National Art Education Association.

Jeffrey Kluger. "The New Science of Siblings," *Time*, July 10, 2006. Used by permission.

Jeffrey Kluger. "The Power of Birth Order," *Time*, October 29, 2007. Used by permission.

Jane M. Leder. "Close Encounters of a Special Kind," from *Brothers and Sisters: How They Shape Our Lives* (St. Martin's, 1991). Used by permission of the author, Jane Mersky Leder.

Mary Loftus. "The Other Side of Fame," *Psychology Today*, May 1995. Reprinted by permission of the author.

Los Angeles Police Department. "What Graffiti Means to a Community." http://www.lapdonline.org/get_informed/content_basic_view/23481.

Catherine Mayer. "Hold the Relish: A lab-grown burger excites hopes but not taste buds." © 2013 Time Inc. All rights reserved. Reprinted from

TIME and published with permission of Time Inc. Reproduction in any manner in any language in whole or in part without written permission is prohibited.

Patrick McCrystal and Andrew Percy. "Factors associated with teenage ecstasy use," *Drugs: Education, Prevention, and Policy*, copyright © 2010, Informa Healthcare. Adapted with permission of Informa Healthcare.

Olivia Mellan. "Men, Women and Money," *Psychology Today*, January 1, 1999. Used by permission of the author.

Dave Myers. *Psychology*, 9e, Worth Publishers. Used by permission.

Dr. Drew Pinsky and Dr. S. Mark Young. Pages 59–86 from *The Mirror Effect*. Copyright © 2009 by Dr. Drew Pinsky and Dr. S. Mark Young. Reprinted by permission of HarperCollins Publishers.

Christina A. Roberto, et al. "Influence of Licensed Characters on Children's Taste and Snack Preferences," *Pediatrics*, June 21, 2010. Used by permission.

Lauren Sandler. "The Only Child: Debunking the Myths," *Time*, July 8, 2010. Used by permission.

Mark Schug and Eric Hagedorn. "Milwaukee's Youth Enterprise Academy," Routledge, Taylor & Francis. Used by permission.

Will Shank. "Whose Art Is This Anyway?" *Street Art San Francisco: Mission Muralismo* edited by Annice Jacoby. Copyright © 2009 by Precita Eyes Muralists Association, Inc., Annice Jacoby, and Susan K. Cervantes. Used by permission of Abrams, an imprint of Harry N. Abrams, Inc., New York. All rights reserved.

Janna Malamud Smith. "Income Inequality Within Families Is Emerging as a Major Issue," *Newsweek*, January 19, 2013. Used by permission.

Paul Taylor, Richard Fry, and Rakesh Kochhar. "Wealth Gaps Rise to Record Highs Between Whites, Blacks, and Hispanics" (Pew Research Report Executive Summary), Pew Research Social and Demographic Trends, July 26, 2011, http://www.pewsocialtrends.org/2011/07/26/wealth-gaps-rise-to-record-highs-between-whites-blacks-hispanics/.

Rosanna Xia. "Lighthearted Street Art Delights (and Confuses) Downtown L.A. Visitors," *LA Times*, June 24, 2012. Used by permission.

YGS Group. *Buffalo Law Journal*, "Battles Over Yard Art Sometimes Turn Ugly." Associated Press. Used by permission.

PHOTO CREDITS

Page 2: ©iStock/huePhotography.

Page 6: (left) ©Aaron Hsiao/Shutterstock.com. (right) ©Aaron Hsiao/Shutterstock.com.

Page 8: ©Cardinal/RF/Corbis.

Page 10: ©Alloy/Corbis.

Page 17: (left) ©Aaron Hsiao/Shutterstock.com. (right) ©Aaron Hsiao/Shutterstock.com.

Page 18: ©Cardinal/RF/Corbis.

Page 21: ©Alloy/Corbis.

Page 36: ©iStock/huePhotography.

Page 37: Bureau of Labor Statistics, Current Population Survey.

Page 43: ©Steve Widoff, Widoff Photo.

Page 45: ©Keith Lanpher Photography.

Page 59: Bureau of Labor Statistics, Current Population Survey.

Page 72: Courtesy of the Pew Research Center.

Page 73: Courtesy of the Pew Research Center.

Page 74: Courtesy of the Pew Research Center.

Page 81: Courtesy of Institute on Assets and Social Policy, Brandeis University. Shapiro, T., Meschede, T., & Osoro, S. (2013, 02 27). The roots

Index

A

a, basics of, 591–92
Abbreviations, for note taking, 339–40
ABC TV, [e]
-able, adding, 712
accept/except, 709
Acosta, Teresa Palomo, 465–67
Action verbs. *See also* Verbs
    definition of, 617
    identifying, 592–93
    in sentence structure, 600
Active reading, 14–15. *See also* Reading critically
Active voice, 696–97
Adjectives
    basics of, 586, 590–92
    commas between, 666–67
    verbals as, 604
"Adolescents and Graffiti" (Kan), 190, 474–83
Adverbs
    basics of, 586, 594–95
    conjunctive, 596–97
    verbals as, 604
advice/advise, 709
affect/effect, 709
Alcott, Louisa May, 677–78
although, 643, 668
American Academy of Pediatrics, 357
American Montessori Society, 358–59
American Psychological Association (APA) style, 363, 714
an, basics of, 591–92
analyze, meaning of, 96
and. See also Coordinating conjunctions
    comma before, in list, 665, 676
    for compound sentences, 614–15
    as coordinating conjunction, 595, 611–13
    for run-on sentences, 652
anecdote, meaning of, 96
Anecdotes
    as evidence, 243
    in introduction and conclusion, 305
    as introductory hook, 294

    strengthening evidence with, 262–63
Annotating
    Cornell method of note taking and, 340–41
    of fiction, 165
    to outline, 268–72
    of textbooks, 150
    while reading, 14–25
    writing summary after, 30
Antecedents of pronouns, 655
Anthology, article in, MLA format for, 371
APA style, 363, 714
Apostrophes, 701–7
Appositives, commas with, 671
argue, meaning of, 96
Argument, 238–52
    counterarguments and rebuttals in, 246–50
    evidence and reason in, 240–46
    example of assignment for, 95
    sample for analyzing, 250–52
    sample thesis statements for, 230, 235
    taking position in, 238–40
    understanding, 238
Art, public, readings on, 440–506
Art Education in 2001, 473
Articles (*a, an, the*), basics of, 591–92
as/us, 596
Assignments
    analyzing, 97
    examples of, 115–17
    reading, 94–96
    thesis and, 227
Audience
    for argument, 242
    considering, for essay, 93
    determining while reading, 169–76
    revising for, 127, 128
    writing for particular, 180–82

B

Background information, in introduction, 292, 296–98
"Battles over Yard Art Sometimes Turn Ugly"
    (*Buffalo Law Journal*), 497–99

because, with *reason*, 684, 685
Becker, Jack, 450–63
Bibliography. *See* Works Cited
Bibliography cards, 346
Big-picture issues
 instructor feedback and, 327
 revising for, 121
Bittman, Mark, 250–52
Black Enterprise, 42
Blogs, credibility of, 308, 356
Bookending conclusion and hook, 304–6
Books, MLA format for, 371, 372
both/and, 596
Brainstorming. *See also* Pre-writing
 to choose topic, 177
 for thesis statement, 230
"Broadcasting Yourself" (Pinsky), 225, 550–68
Bronson, Po, 423–33
Brothers and Sisters: How They Shape Our Lives
 (Leder), 382
Buffalo Law Journal, 497–99
Bureau of Labor Statistics, 59–60, 225
but. See also Coordinating conjunctions
 for compound sentences, 614–15
 as coordinating conjunction, 595, 611–13
 for run-on sentences, 652

C

Capitalization, 375, 713–15
Categorization, as rhetorical pattern, 190–91
Cause and effect
 as rhetorical pattern, 193
 sample thesis statements for, 230, 234
 structure of, 278–80
Celebrities, readings on, 508–75
Chang, Andrea, 510–14
Chang, Edwin,
Chapter openers/closers, of textbooks, 33
Characters
 as element of fiction, 164
 story star mapping and, 167
 taking notes on, 166
Charts
 for organizing ideas, 88–90
 reading, 59–60

"Chicano Mural Movement" (Acosta), 465–67
Citations. *See* In-text citations; Works Cited
Claims
 in argument, 238–40
 determining which to make, 228–29
 finding thesis in, 225–26
 thesis as, 227
Class discussions, taking notes during, 342–43
Classification, as rhetorical pattern, 190–91
Clauses, in sentence structure, 606–7
Clear and focused sentences, writing, 692–700
Clichés, avoiding, 697–99
Cliffhanger fragment, 636, 640
"Close Encounters of a Special Kind" (Leder), 382–93
Close reading. *See* Reading critically
Clustering, techniques for, 216–19
Coherence, within paragraphs, 264
Collective nouns
 pronoun-agreement and, 658–59
 subject-verb agreement and, 625–26
College-level reader, as audience, 180–81
College library, research at, 353–54
Colons, lists with, parallelism errors and, 675–76
Color-coding, for essay organization, 129–30
"Color of Success, The: Black Student Achievement
 in Public Charter Schools" (Robinson and
 Chang),
.com, 355
Commands, versus fragments, 637
Commas, 664–73
 after conjunctive adverbs, 596
 after dependent clauses, 643
 before coordinating conjunctions, 611
 for run-on sentences, 652
 with subordinate clauses, 608
Comma splices, 649–53
Comments from instructors
 versus corrections, 326
 meaning of, 329–31
Commonly confused words, 708–10
compare, meaning of, 96
compare and contrast, meaning of, 96
Comparison and contrast
 example of, 196
 example of assignment for, 116

as rhetorical pattern, 193
sample thesis statements for, 230, 233–34
structure of, 276–78
as way of thinking, 117
Complex sentences, 615, 687
Compound sentences, 614–15, 687
Compound subjects, 605
Compound verbs, 602–3
Comprehension, reading strategies for, 138–49
Concession words, 248–50
Conclusions
drafting, 112–15
finding thesis in, 26, 225
purpose and content of, 291, 299–306
Conflict
as element of fiction, 165
story star mapping and, 167
Confusing words, 708–10
Conjugation charts for verbs, 622
Conjunctions
basics of, 587, 595–97
coordinating. *See* Coordinating conjunctions
correlative, 595–96
subordinating. *See* Subordinating conjunctions
Conjunctive adverbs, basics of, 596–97
Connotations of words, 210
Consonant, final, doubling, 712
Constructive criticism, in peer review, 325
Context, in conclusion, 302–4
Context clues, for meaning of words, 199–201
Contractions, apostrophes for, 701–2
Contrast
and comparison. *See* Comparison and contrast
in context clues, 200
contrast, meaning of, 96
Conversation drafts, 288–89
Coordinating conjunctions
for compound sentences, 614–15
for coordination, 611–14
mixed construction and, 687
for two sentences joined together, 668–69
understanding, 595
Coordination, 611–14
Cornell method of note taking, 340–46

Corrections from instructors
versus comments, 326
meaning of, 327–29
Correlative conjunctions, basics of, 595–96
counterargument, meaning of, 96
Counterarguments, in argument, 246–50
Creative titles, 185
Credibility
of author, citations and, 363–64
of sources, 308–9, 352
of Web sources, 355–59
Critical reading. *See* Reading critically
Currency
of sources, evaluating, 352
of Web sources, 356

D

Daily Beast, The, 268
Dangling modifiers, 688–91
Dates, commas in, 665–66
Definite articles, basics of, 591–92
Definition
in context clues, 200
example of assignment for, 116
as rhetorical pattern, 190
sample thesis statements for, 229, 232
Dell'Antonia, KJ, 245–46
Demonstrative pronouns, 655–56
Dependent clauses
concession words and, 249
in sentence structure, 607
as subordinating conjunction, 596
Dependent words. *See* Subordinating conjunctions
describe in detail, meaning of, 96
Description, as rhetorical pattern, 192
"Desire to Belong, The: Why Everyone Wants to Have Dinner with Paris Hilton and 50 Cent" (Halpern), 538–49
Dictionaries
for parts of speech, 587–88
with sample sentences, 199–200
using, 201–3
Dictionary.com, 201
Discussions in class, taking notes during, 342–43

"Disney Limits Junk-Food Ads" (Dell'Antonia), 245–46
Documentary films, taking notes during, 344
Document format for MLA style, 364, 367–68
Double quotation marks, 310, 311
Draft, public first, writing, 289–90
Draft, rough
 drafting of, 111–12
 methods for writing, 286–89
 outlining, 280–81
Dweck, Carol S., 6–13, 17–24, 26–28, 190, 193, 300–2

E

e, silent, 711–12
-ed, dropping *e* before adding, 711
Editing
 learning rules for, 582–83
 pinpointing errors for, 577–82
 versus revising, 121
 strategies for, 134–36
 understanding, 576–77
.edu, 355
Education, readings on, [e]
Education (Gale Opposing Viewpoints), [e]
"Education Pays" (Bureau of Labor Statistics), 59–60, 224
Effect, cause and. *See* Cause and effect
effect/affect, 709
either/or, 596
Elaboration (in PIE), 258–61, 263–64
Electronic note taking systems, for avoiding plagiarism, 347–49
Ellipsis, in quotations, 313–14
-en, dropping *e* before adding, 711
Equal sign, linking verbs as, 618
-er, 206
Errors, in grammar, editing, 576–85
-es
 adding to make plural, 711
 adding to verbs, 622–23
-'es/-es', 703–4
Essay
 conclusion for, 112–15
 drafting, 111–12

example assignments for, 115–17
finishing draft of, 115
generating evidence for, 107
introduction for, 112–15
organization of. *See* Organization of essay
outlining of, 105–6
pre-writing for, 98–102
reading assignment for, 94–96
taking essay exams and, [e]
thesis statement for, 102–5
time management and, 96–98
topic sentences for, 108–11
understanding, 93–94
Evidence
 in argument, 240–46
 generating, for essay, 107
 identifying while reading, 25–29
 in paragraphs, strengthening, 261, 262–63
evidence, meaning of, 96
Evidence drafts, 287–88
ex-, 203, 204
Example
 in context clues, 200
 example of, 195
 as rhetorical pattern, 189
 strengthening evidence with, 262–63
Exams, essay, taking, [e]
except/accept, 709
Experiences, personal
 annotating text and, 15
 strengthening evidence with, 262–63
Expert opinion, in argument, 241
explain, meaning of, 96
Explanation (in PIE), 258–61, 263–64
Explanatory information, adding to quotations, 312, 313
Explicit thesis, 25, 224
Exploratory drafts, 287

F

"Factors Associated with Teenage Ecstasy Use," 173
Facts
 as evidence, 242
 in introduction and conclusion, 304
 strengthening evidence with, 262–63

Fame, readings on, 508–75

Fame Junkies: The Hidden Truths behind America's Favorite Addiction (Halpern), 537

FANBOYS, 595, 611, 652. *See also* Coordinating conjunctions

Feedback, 323–38
    as essential, 323–24
    from instructors, interpreting and applying, 325–31
    meeting with instructor or tutor for, 336–37
    peer review guidelines and, 324–25
    rubric and, 331–36

Fessler, Pam, 80, 81–87, 109–11

Fiction, reading, 164–68

Films
    MLA format for, 374
    taking notes during, 343–44

Financial literacy, readings on, 41–87

"Financial Stability" (Siebrecht), 122–25

"Fine Art of Yarn Bombing, The" (*Time*), e

First draft. *See* Draft, rough

Flash cards
    for irregular verbs, 631
    for new vocabulary words, 16, 207–9

Flaspohler, David J., 142–44, 145–47

Flora, Carlin, 191, 516–21

Focused and clear sentences, writing, 692–700

for. See also Coordinating conjunctions
    for compound sentences, 614–15
    as coordinating conjunction, 595, 611–13
    for run-on sentences, 652

Foreign words, 712

Formal outlines, understanding, 273–74

Format of paper in MLA style, 364, 367–68

Fragments, 635–48
    beginning with preposition, 640–42
    beginning with subordinator, 642–43
    editing for, 645–47
    finding and fixing, 607–9
    with incomplete thought, 640
    with missing subject, 636–38
    with missing verb, 638–39
    understanding, 635–36
    with *who, when,* or *which,* 643–44

Frank, Patrick, 443–48

Freewriting
    about topic, before reading, 3–4
    for essay, 99–100
    techniques for, 214–16

Fry, Richard, 71, 72–80

Fused sentences, 649–53

Future tenses, 620

G

Gaddy, James, 487–91

Gale Opposing Viewpoints, e

Gender agreement for pronouns, 659–60

Gender-neutral language, 659–60

Gilmore, Mikal, e

.gov, 355

Grammar errors, editing, 576–85

Grammar Log, 577, 579–80, 582, 584

Granju, Katie Allison, 174–75

Graphic flash cards, for new vocabulary, 207–9

H

Hagedorn, Eric A., 61, 62–70, 192–93

Halpern, Jake, 538–49

Handbook of Texas Online, The, 464

Harris, Katie, 254–55

Harris, Mark, e

Headings, in textbooks, 150

Helping verbs
    basics of, 593
    definition of, 617
    in sentence structure, 600–2

Hemingway, Ernest, 119, 184

he or she, 659

Highlighting, avoiding excess of, 25

his or her, 659, 660

Holder, Sherie, 40, 43–49, 224, 283

"Hold the Relish" (Mayer and Harris), 254–55

Holistic rubric, 332–33

Hook
    bookending with conclusion and, 304–6
    in introduction, 292, 293–95

how, story star mapping and, 166–67

"How Charter Schools Can Hurt" (Rosenfeld), **e**
however, 668
"How to Train Your Celebrity: Five Hollywood
    Charity Myths" (Harris), **e**

I

I
    neutral tone and, 184
    in summaries, 30
-ical, 206
Ideas, organization of, by charting, 88–90
Illustration
    example of, 195
    as rhetorical pattern, 189
Implied thesis, 25–26, 224, 225
Implied topic sentences, 27
"Income Inequality within Families Is Emerging as
    a Major Issue" (Smith), 268–71
Incomplete sentences. *See* Fragments
Incomplete thoughts, fragments and, 640
Indefinite articles, basics of, 591–92
Indefinite pronouns
    pronoun-agreement and, 658–59
    subject-verb agreement and, 624–25
    understanding, 655
Independent clauses, 606–7
Inferences, from evidence, 244–45
Inflated language, wordiness and, 694
*Influence of Licensed Characters on Children's Taste
    and Snack Preferences* (Roberto et al.), 284–85
Informal outlines
    creating, 274–76
    versus formal, 268
Information (in PIE), 258–61, 262
Information literacy, 351
-ing, dropping *e* before adding, 711
-ing verbs
    fragments and, 638
    helping verbs and, 602
"In Hakalau, a Modern Success Story"
    (Flaspohler), 142–44, 145–47
Instructors
    feedback from, 325–31
    meeting with, 336–37

Interjections, 587, 598
Internet. *See also* Online sources
    credibility of, 308, 309
    researching on, 355
interpret, meaning of, 96
Interrupters
    commas with, 670–71
    in lists, 676
Interviews
    MLA format for, 374
    taking notes during, 344–46
In-text citations
    definition of, 365
    format for, 376–77
    importance of, 309
    recording while note taking, 346–50
Introductions
    drafting, 112–15
    finding thesis in, 26, 225
    purpose and content of, 291–99
Introductory sentence, for summary, 31
Introductory words
    comma after, 667–68
    for quotations/paraphrases, 132–33
Irregular verbs
    basics of, 620–21
    errors in, 620–21
is, contractions with, 702
-ism, 206
-ist, 206
Italics, for titles, 375
it is, wordiness and, 693
its/it's, 708–9

J

Journal articles
    audience and purpose of, 172–74
    MLA format for, 371
    peer-reviewed, understanding, 61
Journalists, credibility of, 308–9

K

Kan, Koon-Hwee, 190, 474–83

"Kardashians, The: Cashing in with a Capital K" (Chang), 510–14
Key terms, writing summary from, 31
"Killing My Sister's Fish" (Olds), 380
Kluger, Jeffrey, 190, 195–96, 395–401, 403–10
Know, KWL+ reading strategy and, 140–42
Kochhar, Rakesh, 71, 72–80
Kuperinsky, Amy,
KWL+, 140–42

L

Lamott, Anne, 286
Learn, KWL+ reading strategy and, 140–42
Leder, Jane Mersky, 382–93
"Lessons from KIPP Delta" (Maranto and Shuls),
Library, college, research at, 353–54
"Lighthearted Street Art Delights (and Confuses) Downtown L.A. Visitors" (Xia), 493–95
like, fragments beginning with, 641–42, 644
"Limit Soda for Kids' Sake" (Bittman), 250–52
Linking verbs
    definition of, 617
    recognizing, 618
    in sentence structure, 600, 602
Listing
    for essay, 100–1
    techniques for, 219–20
Lists
    items in, using comma to separate, 665
    parallelism errors in, 675–76
Literary present tense, 628
Literature, quoting, 310
Little Women (Alcott), 677–78
Loftus, Mary, 523–36
LooktotheStars.org,
loose/lose, 710
Los Angeles Police Department, 484–85
Los Angeles Times, 492, 509
lose/loose, 710
-ly
    adverbs ending in, 594
    as suffix, 206

M

Magazine articles, MLA format for, 371
Main ideas. *See also* Thesis statement
    identifying while reading, 25–29
    in summaries, 29–31
Main verb, 618
Major points. *See* Main ideas
make an argument, meaning of, 96
"Making It in the U.S.: More Than Just Hard Work" (Fessler), 80, 81–87, 109–11
Mamapundit, 174
Mangaro, Joe (student writer), 630
Mapping
    for comprehension, 145–49
    of textbooks, 150–51
Maranto, Robert,
Mayer, Catherine, 254–55
Meeks, Kenneth, 40, 43–49, 224, 283
Mellan, Olivia, 50–58
Memoirs, 174–76
Memorization, of new vocabulary, 207–9
"Men, Women, and Money" (Mellan), 50–58
Merriam-Webster.com, 201
Merryman, Ashley, 423–33
.mil, 356
"Milwaukee's Youth Enterprise Academy: An Eight-year Study of a Model Program for Urban Youth" (Schug and Hagedorn), 61, 62–70, 192–93
Mirror Effect, The: How Celebrity Narcissism Is Seducing America (Pinsky), 550
Misplaced modifiers, 688, 689–91
Mixed construction of sentences, 682–84
MLA documentation, 362–78
    capitalization and, 714
    citation and credibility and, 363–64
    document format for, 364, 367–68
    in-text citations for, 365, 376–77
    Works Cited page for, 364–65, 369–75
MLA Handbook for Writers of Research Papers, 375
MLA Template, 367–68
Mnemonics, for new vocabulary, 207
Modern Language Association documentation. *See* MLA documentation
Modifiers, 687–91

Money, readings on, 41–87
MotherLode: Adventures in Parenting blog, 245
Muscle reading, 151, 164
"My College Career" (Mangaro), 630
Myers, David G., 151, 152–63, 171, 172

N

Narration
    example of, 195
    example of assignment for, 116
    as rhetorical pattern, 191
    sample thesis statements for, 229–30, 232–33
narrative, meaning of, 96
National Public Radio, 80
n.d. (no date), 373
neither/nor, 596
.net, 356
Neutral tone, 184
"New Science of Siblings, The" (Kluger), 395–401
Newspaper articles, MLA format for, 371, 372
Newspapers, credibility of, 308–9
New York Times, 250
New York Times' Scientists at Work blog, 142
no date (n.d.), 373
nor. See also Coordinating conjunctions
    for compound sentences, 614–15
    as coordinating conjunction, 595, 611–13
    for run-on sentences, 652
not, verbs and, 602
Notebook system, for avoiding plagiarism, 347
Note card system, for avoiding plagiarism, 346
Note taking, 339–50
    avoiding plagiarism while, 346–50
    Cornell method of, 340–46
    for fiction, 166
not only/but also, 596
Nouns
    basics of, 586, 589–90
    making plural, 703–4
    in prepositional phrases, 606
    verbals as, 604
"Nowhere Man" (Gaddy), 487–91
Nutshell summary, 27

O

Object of preposition, nouns and pronouns as, 590
Object of sentence, nouns and pronouns as, 590
Observations, as evidence, 243
Olds, Sharon, 380
one
    avoiding overuse of, 696
    as gender-neutral pronoun, 659
Online sources
    credibility of, 308, 309
    dictionaries and, 201–3
    evaluating, 355–60
    MLA format for, 372–73, 373
"Only Child, The: Debunking the Myths" (Sandler), 194, 412–21
Op-ed writers, credibility of, 309
Opinions
    argument and, 239
    versus claims, 227
    versus evidence, 241–42
or. See also Coordinating conjunctions
    comma before, in list, 665
    for compound sentences, 614–15
    as coordinating conjunction, 595, 611–13
    for run-on sentences, 652
.org, 356
Organization of essay, 267–85
    common structures for, 276–80
    outlining for, 267–76
    outlining rough draft for, 280–81
    revising for, 127, 129
    transitions for, 281–85
Organization of ideas, by charting, 88–90
"Other Side of Fame, The" (Loftus), 523–36
-ous, adding, 712
Outlining
    for essay, 105–6
    as reader, 267–72
    of textbooks, 150
    as writer, 273–76
Ownership, apostrophes to show, 703–5
Oxford English Dictionary, The, 198

P

Paragraphs
    evaluating, 261–66
    finding topic sentences in, 27
    revising, 127, 130–32
    structure of, 258–61
    topic sentence and, 258
    transitions from one to another, 282–83
Parallelism, 674–81
paraphrase, meaning of, 96
Paraphrasing, 307–22
    definition of, 307
    evaluating sources before, 308–9
    explaining, 320–22
    importance of citation for, 309
    introducing, 316–20
    revising to integrate, 132–34
    when and how to, 314–16
Parentheses, for in-text citations, 377
Parenthetical citations. *See* In-text citations
"Parenting Secret I Am No Longer Willing to Keep, A" (Granju), 174–75
Parts of speech, 586–99
    adjectives as, 586, 590–92
    adverbs as, 586, 594–95
    conjunctions as, 587, 595–97
    interjections as, 587, 598
    nouns and pronouns as, 586, 589–90
    prepositions as, 586, 597–98
    verbs as, 586, 592–93
Passive reading, 14
Passive voice, 696–97
Past tenses, 619–20
Peer review
    as essential, 323–24
    guidelines for, 324–25
    practicing, 125–26
    of topic choice, 178–79
Peer-reviewed journal articles. *See* Journal articles
People's titles, commas in, 665–66
Perfect progressive tenses, 619–20
Perfect tenses, 619–20
"Perils and Promises of Praise, The" (Dweck), 6–13
    annotation of, 17–24, 26–28
    comparison and contrast in, 193

finding main ideas in, 27
    thesis and summary statement in, 300–2
Periodical databases, researching with, 354, 355
Personal experiences
    annotating text and, 15
    strengthening evidence with, 262–63
Personal interviews, MLA format for, 374
Personal memoirs, 174–76
Phrases
    empty, list of common, 698
    in sentence structure, 605–6
PIE, 258–61
Pinsky, Drew, 225, 550–68
Place names, commas in, 665–66
Plagiarism
    avoiding while taking notes, 346–50
    citations and, 363–64
    seriousness of, 309
Plot, 165, 166
Plural nouns
    rules for creating, 703–4
    spelling rules for, 711
Point, Information, Explanation/Elaboration (PIE), 258–64
Point-based rubric, 331–32
Point-by-point structure, 276–77
Point (in PIE), 258–64
Point of paragraph. *See* Topic sentences
Portfolios,
Position, taking in argument, 238–40
Positive remarks, in peer review, 324
Possessive pronouns, 654–55
"Power of Birth Order, The" (Kluger), 190, 195–96, 403–10
Prebles' Artforms, 442
Predicates. *See* Verbs
Predication errors, 684–85
Prefixes, 203, 204
prejudice/prejudiced, 710
Prepositional phrases
    in sentence structure, 605–6
    between subjects and verbs, 626–27
    understanding, 597–98
Prepositions
    basics of, 586, 597–98
    fragments beginning with, 640–42

Pre-reading
   to determine audience and purpose, 170
   strategies for, 3–6
Present tenses, 619
   literary, 628
Previewing, to find thesis, 225
Previewing text, 4–6
Pre-writing
   for argument, 239–40
   for essay, 98–102
   techniques for, 214–22
Print, 486
Problem solving
   sample thesis statements for, 230, 234–35
   structure of, 276
Process analysis
   example of assignment for, 116
   as rhetorical pattern, 192–93
   sample thesis statements for, 230, 233
   transitions in, 284
Procrastination, avoiding,
Progressive tenses, 619–20
Prompts. *See* Assignments
Pronoun-agreement errors, 658–60
Pronoun-reference errors, 656–57
Pronouns
   basics of, 586, 589–90
   changing within quotations, 312
   in prepositional phrases, 606
   types and errors of, 654–63
   vague or unclear, avoiding, 695–96
Pronoun-shift errors, 660–61
Proofreading
   learning rules for, 582–83
   pinpointing errors for, 577–82
   versus revising, 121
   strategies for, 136–37
   understanding, 576–77
Proper nouns, capitalization of, 713–14
Psychology (Myers), 151, 152–63, 171, 172
Psychology Today, 50, 515, 522
"Public Art: An Essential Component of Creating
   Communities" (Becker), 450–63
"Public Art" (Frank), 443–46
Public art, readings on, 441–507

Public first draft, writing, 289–90
Purpose for writing
   considering, for essay, 93
   crafting paper for, 182–83
   determining while reading, 169–76
   revising for, 127, 128

Q

Questioning
   to narrow topic, 179–80
   as prewriting strategy, 220–22
   as reading strategy, 139–40
   while annotating, 16
Questions
   for interviews, 345
   in introduction and conclusion, 305
   thesis as, 227
   turning title into, 26
   turning topic sentences into, 264–66
quiet/quite, 710
quotation, meaning of, 96
Quotation marks
   commas with, 666
   for titles, 375
   using correctly, 310, 311
   when note taking, 346
Quotations, 307–22
   commas with, 666
   definition of, 307
   evaluating sources before using, 308–9
   explaining, 320–22
   importance of citation for, 309
   introducing, 316–20
   in introduction and conclusion, 305
   parallelism errors and, 677–78
   revising to integrate, 132–34
   strengthening evidence with, 262–63
   when and how to use, 309–14

R

Radio shows, MLA format for, 374
Ravitch, Diane,
Reading, 2–35. *See also* Reading critically; Reading
   strategies

annotating while, 14–25
finding supporting evidence while, 25–29
identifying main ideas while, 25–29
pre-reading and, 3–6
sample text for, 6–13
of textbooks, 31–32
writing summary after, 29–31
Reading between the lines, 245
Reading critically, 37–91
about money, wealth and financial literacy, 41–87
with and against the grain, 38–41
multiple sources and, 88–90
understanding, 37–38
Reading out loud. *See* Reciting
Reading strategies, 138–68
for comprehension, 138–49
for fiction, 164–68
for textbooks, 149–64
reason, with *because*, 684, 685
Reasons
in argument, 240–46
strengthening evidence with, 262–63
Rebuttals, in argument, 246–50
Reciting
as editing strategy, 134–35
of notes, 341
as reading strategy, 140
Recording, to write rough draft, 289
Relevance of sources, 352–53
Reliability of sources, 308–9
Repetition, wordiness and, 693
Research, 351–61
college library and, 353–54
evaluating Web sources for, 355–60
example of assignment for, 117
role of Internet in, 355
sources for, qualities to look for, 351–53
working with sources for, 360
Resolution, in fiction, story star mapping and, 168
Reverse outlining, 280–81
Review assignment, example of, 116
Reviewing, as reading strategy, 140
Revising
of essay, 119–25

peer review and, 125–26
strategies for, 126–34
of summary, 31
Rhetorical patterns, 187–97
types of, 188–95
understanding, 187–88
using, 195–97
Roberto, Christina, 284
Robinson, Gerard,
Romeo and Juliet (Shakespeare), 30, 166
Roots of words, 203–6
Rosenfeld, Lucinda,
Rough draft. *See* Draft, rough
Rubrics
instructor feedback and, 326–27
using, 331–36
Run-ons, 649–53

S
-s
adding to make plural, 711
adding to verbs, 622
Salon.com, 245, 268
Sandler, Lauren, 194, 412–21
Scan, question, read, recite, review (SQ3R), 139–40, 150
Scanning, as reading strategy, 139
Schedule, for writing essay, 97–98
Scholarly journal articles. *See* Journal articles
Schug, Mark C., 61, 62–70, 192–93
"Secrets and Bones" (Gilmore),
"Seeing by Starlight: Celebrity Obsession" (Flora), 191, 516–21
Semicolon
before conjunctive adverbs, 596
for coordination, 613
for run-on sentences, 651
Sentence-level issues
instructor feedback and, 327
revising for, 121
Sentences, 600–16
clauses in, 606–7
clear and focused, writing, 692–700
common structure problems of, 682–91
coordination and, 611–14

Sentences (*continued*)
  phrases in, 605–6
  subjects of, 603–5
  subordination and, 607–10
  understanding, 600
  variation in, 614–15
  verbs and, 600–3
Setting
  as element of fiction, 165
  story star mapping and, 167
Sexist language, avoiding, pronouns for, 659–60
Shakespeare, William, 30, 166
Shank, Will, 192, 469–72
Shorthand, for note taking, 340
Shuls, James V., [e]
"Sibling Effect, The" (Bronson and Merryman), 423–33
Siblings, readings on, 379–440
"Sibling Secrets" video (ABC TV), [e]
Siebrecht, Thalia (student writer), 122–25
Signal phrases
  for quotations/paraphrases, 132–33
  when and how to use, 316–20
Silent *e*, 711–12
Similarities and differences structure, 277–78
Simple past tense, 628
Simple present tense, 628
Simple sentences, 614, 687
Single quotation marks, within double, 311
Slang, avoiding, 184, 699
Small-group activities, taking notes during, 343
Smith, Janna Malamud, 268–71
Smith, Sally (student writer), 365–67
so. See also Coordinating conjunctions
  for compound sentences, 614–15
  as coordinating conjunction, 595, 611–13
  for run-on sentences, 652
Social Studies in 2006, The, 61
Sources
  evaluating, 308–9
  good qualities of, 351–53
  more than one, reading critically, 88–90
  online. *See* Online sources
  working with, 360
Speech, parts of. *See* Parts of speech

Spell checkers, relying too much on, 708
Spelling, 708–13
SQ3R, 139–40, 150
Square brackets, to modify quotations, 312
-'*s*/-*s*', 703–4
Statement, thesis as, 227
State of being verbs. *See also* Verbs
  definition of, 617
  recognizing, 593, 618
  in sentence structure, 600–2
Statistics
  as evidence, 242
  in introduction and conclusion, 304
  as introductory hook, 294
  strengthening evidence with, 262–63
"Stop the Madness" (Ravitch), [e]
Story star mapping, 166–68
"Street Art" (Frank), 446–48
Street Art San Francisco: Mission Muralismo, 468
Subheadings, finding main idea from, 26
Subject-by-subject structure, 278
Subject of sentence
  in clauses, 606–7
  fragments without, 636–38
  mixed construction and, 685–86
  nouns as, 589–90
  pronouns as, 589–90, 654
  in sentence structure, 603–5
  verbals as, 604
  words between verb and, 626–27
Subject pronouns, 589–90, 654
Subject-verb agreement
  basics of, 619
  errors in, 622–27
Subordinate clauses
  nouns and pronouns in, 590
  in sentence structure, 607–10
Subordinating conjunctions
  basics of, 596
  fragments beginning with, 642–43
  list of common, 609, 642
  for run-on sentences, 652
Subordination, in sentence structure, 607–10
Subordinators. *See* Subordinating conjunctions
Subtitles, 185, 375

Suffixes, 206
summarize, meaning of, 96
Summarizing
      after note taking, 341
      after reading, 29–31
      definition of, 307
Summary statements, in conclusion, 300–2
Sun Also Rises, The (Hemingway), 184
Support. *See* Evidence
support your thesis, meaning of, 96
Symbols
      as element of fiction, 165
      for note taking, 340
Synonyms
      in context clues, 200
      thesaurus for, 210
Synthesis chart, 89–90

T

Table of contents
      as formal outline, 273
      of textbooks, 33
Taylor, Paul, 71, 72–80
"Teach Your Children the Building Blocks of
      Finance" (Holder and Meeks), 40, 43–49, 224,
      283
Television shows, MLA format for, 374
Textbooks
      article in, MLA format for, 371
      audience and purpose of, 172
      reading, strategies for, 149–64
      reading effectively, 32–33
than/then, 710
that
      as demonstrative pronoun, 655–56
      parallelism errors and, 677
      with quotations, 666
the, basics of, 591–92
their/there/they're, 709
Themes of fiction
      as element of fiction, 165
      story star mapping and, 168
      taking notes on, 166
then/than, 710

there is/there are
      sentences beginning with, 604
      wordiness and, 693
there/their/they're, 709
Thesaurus, using, 210–12
these, as demonstrative pronoun, 655–56
Thesis, 223–37. *See also* Thesis statement
      generating evidence for, 107
      identifying while reading, 26–27, 225–26
      in introduction, 292–93, 298–99
      as main idea, 25
      purpose of, 223–25
      revising to strengthen, 127, 128
      shaping, 226–30
      topic sentence and, 256–57
thesis, meaning of, 96
Thesis statement
      in argument, 239
      definition of, 228
      drafting step by step, 230–37
      for essay, 102–5
they, as gender-neutral pronoun, 659
they're/there/their, 709
Thinking, rhetorical patterns and, 117
this, as demonstrative pronoun, 655–56
those, as demonstrative pronoun, 655–56
Thoughts, recording by annotating, 15
Three-part thesis, 223
Time, 394, 403, 412,
Time management
      methods of,
      for writing essay, 96–98, 119, 120
Time-testing, to find verb, 601–2
Titles
      capitalization of, 714
      finding thesis from, 26
      MLA style format for, 375
      sharpening topic with, 184–85
      of textbooks, 33
to be
      as irregular verb, 621, 623
      predication errors and, 684
Tone, writing in particular, 183–84
too/to/two, 710

Topics. *See also* Topic sentences
    choosing, 176–77
    in introduction, 292, 295
    making more specific, 178–80
    revising to focus, 127, 128
    versus thesis, 223
Topic sentences
    for essay, 108–11
    evaluating paragraphs for, 261, 262
    finding main ideas from, 27
    identifying, 253–55
    outlining, 267–72
    paragraphs and, 258–61
    thesis and, 256–57
    turning into questions, 264–66
    writing, 257–58
to/too/two, 710
to verbs, fragments and, 638–39
Transitions, 130, 281–85
Transition words/phrases, 281–82
Tripartite thesis, 223
Turning point in fiction, story star mapping and, 168
Tutors, meeting with, 336–37
TV shows, MLA format for, 374
"Twenty Dollars?!" (Yu), 296–97
two/to/too, 710

U

Unclear pronoun reference, 656–57
Underlining, of textbooks, 149
Unity, within paragraphs, 264
URL extensions, 355–56
UWM Post, 189

V

Verbals, 604
Verbs, 617–34
    basics of, 586, 592–93
    in clauses, 606–7
    fragments without, 638–39
    irregular, 620–21, 631
    mixed construction and, 685–86
    in sentence structure, 600–3

subject-verb agreement and, 619, 622–27
    tense of. *See* Verb tense
    understanding, 617–18
    words between subject and, 626–27
Verb tense
    basics of, 619–20
    changing within quotations, 312, 313
    errors in, 627–30
Very rough draft. *See* Draft, rough
-ves, adding, 711
Videos, taking notes during, 343–44
Vocabulary, unfamiliar, identifying while annotating, 16
Vocabulary building, 198–213
    memorizing words for, 207–9
    understanding word parts for, 203–7
    using context clues for, 199–201
    using dictionary for, 201–3
    using thesaurus for, 210–12

W

Want, KWL+ reading strategy and, 140–42
Wealth, readings on, 41–87
"Wealth Gaps Rise to Record Highs between Whites, Blacks, Hispanics: Twenty-to-One" (Kochhar et al.), 71, 72–80
weather/whether, 710
Web sites
    credibility of, 308, 309
    evaluating, 355–60
    MLA format for, 373
we're/were/where, 710
what, story star mapping and, 166–67
"What Graffiti Means to a Community" (Los Angeles Police Department), 484–85
when
    fragments beginning with, 643–44
    predication errors with, 684, 686
    story star mapping and, 166–67
"When Siblings Grow Up" (Smith), 365–67
where
    predication errors with, 684
    story star mapping and, 166–67
    versus *were* and *we're*, 710
whether/or, 596

whether/weather, 710

which, fragments beginning with, 643–44

who
>fragments beginning with, 643–44
>story star mapping and, 166–67

"Whose Art Is This Anyway?" (Shank), 192, 469–72

Wordiness, 693–94

Word parts, understanding, 203–7

Word-processing programs, for note taking, 348

Words
>commonly confused, 708–10
>unfamiliar, identifying while annotating, 16

Working outlines, 268

Working thesis. *See also* Thesis; Thesis statement
>drafting, 231
>for essay, 102

Works Cited
>definition of, 364–65
>examples of, 367, 369
>format for, 369–75
>in-text citations and, 377

Workshopping. *See* Peer review

Writer's block, pre-writing and, 98

X

Xia, Rosanna, 493–95

Y

"Yarn Bombing: The Worldwide Web of Knit Graffiti, from N.J. to Dubai" (Kuperinsky), e

yet. See also Coordinating conjunctions
>for compound sentences, 614–15
>as coordinating conjunction, 595, 611–13
>for run-on sentences, 652

Yu, Micah (student writer), 296–97

Inside the Bedford Integrated Media for *Read, Write, Connect*

e-READINGS

Money, Wealth, and Financial Literacy (Chapter 2)
 Shira Boss, *Money Envy*
Siblings (Chapter 21)
 Mikal Gilmore, *Secrets and Bones*
 ABC TV, *Sibling Secrets* (video)
Public Art (Chapter 22)
 Amy Kuperinsky, *Yarn Bombing: The Worldwide Web of Knit Graffiti, from N.J. to Dubai*
Fame and Celebrity (Chapter 23)
 Mark Harris, *How to Train Your Celebrity: Five Hollywood Charity Myths*
 LooktotheStars.org, *LooktotheStars.org* (Web site)

e-CHAPTERS

Essay Exams
Portfolios
Managing Your Time and Avoiding Procrastination
Education
 Gale Opposing Viewpoints in Context, *Education*
 Lucinda Rosenfeld, *How Charter Schools Can Hurt*
 Diane Ravitch, *Stop the Madness*
 Gerard Robinson and Edwin Chang, *The Color of Success: Black Student Achievement in Public Charter Schools*
 Robert Maranto and James V. Shuls, *Lessons from KIPP Delta*

CHARTS

1. Main Idea and Support
2. Finding Meaningful Quotations 1
3. Pros and Cons
4. Finding Evidence
5. Comparing Evidence
6. Synthesis Chart for Chapter 2, Money, Wealth, and Financial Literacy
7. Essay Writing Time Management 1
8. Essay Writing Time Management 2
9. KLW+
10. Audience and Purpose
11. Comparing Readings
12. Time Management
13. Synthesis Chart for Chapter 21, Siblings
14. Synthesis Chart for Chapter 22, Public Art
15. Finding Meaningful Quotations 2
16. Synthesis Chart for Chapter 23, Fame and Celebrity
17. Synthesis Chart for Readings on Education
18. Grammar Log

McGraw-Hill's

NATIONAL ELECTRICAL CODE® HANDBOOK

McGraw-Hill's

NATIONAL ELECTRICAL CODE® HANDBOOK

Twentieth Edition

Based on the Current 1990
National Electrical Code®

by
J. F. McPartland
Editorial Director
Electrical Design and Installation
McPartland Publishing
Englewood Cliffs, NJ 07632

and

Brian J. McPartland
Chief Editor
Electrical Design and Installation
McPartland Publishing
Englewood Cliffs, NJ 07632

McGRAW-HILL PUBLISHING COMPANY

New York St. Louis San Francisco Auckland
Bogotá Hamburg Lisbon London Madrid Mexico Milan
Montreal New Delhi Paris San Juan São Paulo
Singapore Sydney Tokyo Toronto

"The Library of Congress has cataloged this
serial publication as follows:"

McGraw-Hill's national electrical code handbook. — 16th ed- —
  New York: McGraw-Hill, c1979-

  v. : ill. ; 22 cm.

  Editor: J. F. McPartland, 1979-
  Based on 1978-   ed. of: National Fire Protection Association.   National electrical
code.
  Continues: NFPA handbook of the National electrical code.
  ISSN 0277-6758 = McGraw-Hill's national electrical code handbook.

ISBN 0-07-045814-6

  1. Electric engineering—Insurance requirements—Collected works.   I.
McPartland, Joseph F.   II. National Fire Protection Association.   National
electrical code.   III. Title: National electrical code handbook.

TK260.N2   621.319′24′0218   81-642618
                       AACR 2   MARC-S

Library of Congress   [8311]

*Although every effort has been made to make the explanation
of the* **Code** *accurate, neither the Publisher nor the Author
assumes any liability for damages that may result
from the use of the Handbook.*

ISBN 0-07-045814-6

*The sponsoring editor for this book was Harold B. Crawford, the editing supervisor was
Margaret Lamb, and the production supervisor was Thomas G. Kowalczyk. It was set in
Melior by University Graphics, Inc.
Printed and bound by R. R. Donnelley & Sons.*

Contents

Preface   ix
Introduction to the National Electrical Code®   xi
Brief History of the National Electrical Code®   xiii
About the 1990 NE Code®   xv
Highlights of the 1990 NE Code® Changes   xvii

Article   Page
00 Introduction   1

Chapter 1 _____

100 Definitions   9
110 Requirements for Electrical Installations   39

Chapter 2 _____

200 Use and Identification of Grounded Conductors   73
210 Branch Circuits   80
215 Feeders   144
220 Branch-Circuit and Feeder Calculations   154
225 Outside Branch Circuits and Feeders   203
230 Services   211
240 Overcurrent Protection   271
250 Grounding   317
280 Surge Arresters   460

v

Article   *Page*

Chapter 3 _____

300 Wiring Methods   465
305 Temporary Wiring   508
310 Conductors for General Wiring   520
318 Cable Trays   564
320 Open Wiring on Insulators   578
321 Messenger Supported Wiring   579
324 Concealed Knob-and-Tube Wiring   581
325 Integrated Gas Spacer Cable Type IGS   582
326 Medium Voltage Cable   582
328 Flat Conductor Cable Type FCC   583
330 Mineral-Insulated, Metal-Sheathed Cable   586
331 Electrical Nonmetallic Tubing   589
333 Armored Cable   592
334 Metal-Clad Cable   599
336 Nonmetallic-Sheathed Cable   604
337 Shielded Nonmetallic-Sheathed Cable   613
338 Service-Entrance Cable   614
339 Underground Feeder and Branch-Circuit Cable   619
340 Power and Control Tray Cable   623
342 Nonmetallic Extensions   624
344 Underplaster Extensions   624
345 Intermediate Metal Conduit   625
346 Rigid Metal Conduit   628
347 Rigid Nonmetallic Conduit   636
348 Electrical Metallic Tubing   645
349 Flexible Metallic Tubing   649
350 Flexible Metal Conduit   651
351 Liquidtight Flexible Conduit   656
352 Surface Raceways   660
353 Multioutlet Assembly   662
354 Underfloor Raceways   663
356 Cellular Metal Floor Raceways   664
358 Cellular Concrete Floor Raceways   666
362 Wireways   668
363 Flat Cable Assemblies   671
364 Busways   672
365 Cablebus   685
370 Outlet, Device, Pull and Junction Boxes, Conduit Bodies, and Fittings   686
373 Cabinets and Cutout Boxes   722
374 Auxiliary Gutters   729
380 Switches   733
384 Switchboards and Panelboards   744

Chapter 4 _____

400 Flexible Cords and Cables   771
402 Fixture Wires   776
410 Lighting Fixtures, Lampholders, Lamps, and Receptacles   777
422 Appliances   812

Article　　　　　　　　　　　　　　　　　　　　　　　　　*Page*

424 Fixed Electric Space Heating Equipment 818
426 Fixed Outdoor Electric De-Icing and Snow-Melting Equipment 836
427 Fixed Electric Heating Equipment for Pipelines and Vessels 839
430 Motors, Motor Circuits, and Controllers 839
440 Air-Conditioning and Refrigerating Equipment 920
445 Generators 942
450 Transformers and Transformer Vaults 944
460 Capacitors 979
470 Resistors and Reactors 990
480 Storage Batteries 990

Chapter 5

500 Hazardous (Classified) Locations 995
501 Class I Locations 1005
502 Class II Locations 1048
503 Class III Locations 1055
504 Intrinsically Safe Systems 1057
511 Commercial Garages, Repair and Storage 1057
513 Aircraft Hangars 1061
514 Gasoline Dispensing and Service Stations 1062
515 Bulk Storage Plants 1068
516 Spray Application, Dipping, and Coating Processes 1070
517 Health Care Facilities 1072
518 Places of Assembly 1090
520 Theaters and Similar Locations 1091
530 Motion Picture and Television Studios and Similar Locations 1096
540 Motion Picture Projectors 1097
547 Agricultural Buildings 1100
550 Mobile Homes and Mobile Home Parks 1102
551 Recreational Vehicles and Recreational Vehicle Parks 1105
553 Floating Buildings 1106
555 Marinas and Boatyards 1107

Chapter 6

600 Electric Signs and Outline Lighting 1113
604 Manufactured Wiring Systems 1116
605 Office Furnishings 1117
610 Cranes and Hoists 1119
620 Elevators, Dumbwaiters, Escalators, Moving Walks, Wheelchair Lifts, and Stairway Chairlifts 1120
630 Electric Welders 1121
640 Sound-Recording and Similar Equipment 1123
645 Electronic Computer/Data Processing Equipment 1124
650 Pipe Organs 1132
660 X-ray Equipment 1133
665 Induction and Dielectric Heating Equipment 1133
668 Electrolytic Cells 1137
670 Industrial Machinery 1138

Article	*Page*
680 Swimming Pools, Fountains, and Similar Installations	1139
690 Solar Photovoltaic Systems	1173

Chapter 7 _____

700 Emergency Systems	1175
701 Legally Required Standby Systems	1191
702 Optional Standby Systems	1191
705 Interconnected Electric Power Production Sources	1193
710 Over 600 Volts, Nominal	1194
720 Circuits and Equipment Operating at Less Than 50 Volts	1222
725 Class 1, Class 2, and Class 3 Remote-Control, Signaling, and Power-Limited Circuits	1222
760 Fire Protective Signaling Systems	1241
770 Optical Fiber Cables	1242
780 Closed-Loop and Programmed Power Distribution	1246

Chapter 8 _____

800 Communications Circuits	1249
810 Radio and Television Equipment	1249

Chapter 9 _____

A Tables	1251
B Examples	1253
Index follows Chapter 9	

Preface

This is a reference book of commentary, discussion, and analysis on the most commonly encountered rules of the 1990 **National Electrical Code.** Designed to be used in conjunction with the 1990 **NE Code** book published by the National Fire Protection Association, this Handbook presents thousands of illustrations—diagrams and photos—to supplement the detailed text in explaining and clarifying **NEC** regulations. Description of the background and rationale of specific **Code** rules is aimed at affording a broader, deeper, and readily developed understanding of the meaning and application of those rules. The style of presentation is conversational and intended to facilitate a quick, practical grasp of the ideas and concepts that are couched in the necessarily terse, stiff, quasilegal language of the **NEC** document itself.

This Handbook follows the order of "articles" as presented in the **NE Code** book, starting with "Article 90" and proceeding through "Article 810" and "Chapter 9—Tables and Examples." The **Code** rules are referenced by "section" numbers (e.g., "250-45. Equipment Connected by Cord and Plug"). This format assures quick and easy correlation between **NEC** sections and the discussions and explanations of the rules involved. This companion reference to the **NEC** book expands on the rules and presents common interpretations that have been put on the many difficult and controversial **Code** requirements. A user of this Handbook should refer to the **NEC** book for the precise wording of a rule and then refer to the corresponding section number in this Handbook for a practical evaluation of the details.

Because many **NEC** rules do not present difficulty in understanding or interpretation, not all sections are referenced. But the vast majority of sections are covered, especially all sections that have proved troublesome or controversial. And particular emphasis is given to changes and additions that have been made in **Code** rules over recent editions of the **NEC**. Although this new edition of the Handbook does not contain the complete wording of the **NE Code** book, it does contain much greater analysis and interpretation than any other version of the Handbook has ever contained, and it is more thoroughly illustrated than any previous edition.

Today, the universal importance of the **NE Code** has been established by the federal government (OSHA and other safety-related departments), by state and local inspection agencies, and by all kinds of private companies and organizations. To meet the great need for information on the **NEC**, the McGraw-Hill Publishing Company has been publishing a handbook on the **National Electrical Code** since 1932. Originally developed by Arthur L. Abbott in that year, the Handbook has been carried on in successive editions for each revision of the **National Electrical Code**.

One final point—words such as "workmanlike" are taken directly from the **Code** and are intended in a purely generic sense. Their use is in no way meant to deny the role women already play in the electrical industries or their importance to the field.

Joseph F. McPartland
Brian J. McPartland

Introduction to the
National Electrical Code®

McGraw-Hill's National Electrical Code® Handbook is based on the 1990 Edition of the **National Electrical Code** as developed by the **National Electrical Code** Committee of the American National Standards Institute (ANSI), sponsored by the National Fire Protection Association (NFPA). The **National Electrical Code** is identified by the designation NFPA No. 70-1990. The NFPA adopted the 1990 **Code** at the NFPA Annual Meeting held in Washington, D.C., on May 18, 1989.

The **National Electrical Code,** as its name implies, is a nationally accepted guide to the safe installation of electrical wiring and equipment. The committee sponsoring its development includes all parties of interest having technical competence in the field, working together with the sole objective of safeguarding the public in its utilization of electricity. The procedures under which the **Code** is prepared provide for the orderly introduction of new developments and improvements in the art, with particular emphasis on safety from the standpoint of its end use. The rules of procedure under which the **National Electrical Code** Committee operates are published in each official edition of the **Code** and in separate pamphlet form so that all concerned may have full information and free access to the operating procedures of the sponsoring committee. The **Code** has been a big factor in the growth and wide acceptance of the use of electrical energy for light and power and for heat, radio, television, signaling, and other purposes from the date of its first appearance (1897) to the present.

The **National Electrical Code** is primarily designed for use by trained electrical people and is necessarily terse in its wording.

The sponsoring **National Electrical Code** Committee is composed of a Correlating Committee and 20 **Code**-Making Panels, each responsible for one or more Articles in the **Code.** Each Panel is composed of experienced individuals representing balanced interests of all segments of the industry and the public concerned with the subject matter. The internal operations of the sponsoring committee are guided by a *Manual of Procedure for Code-Making Panels.* This Manual is published in pamphlet form, and copies are available from the NFPA, Batterymarch Park, Quincy, MA 02269.

The National Fire Protection Association also has organized an Electrical Section to provide the opportunity for NFPA members interested in electrical safety to become better informed and to contribute to the development of NFPA electrical standards. This new Handbook reflects the fact that the **National Electrical Code** was revised for the 1990 edition, requiring an updating of the previous Handbook which was based on the 1987 Edition of the **Code.** The established schedule of the **National Electrical Code** Committee contemplates a new edition of the **National Electrical Code** every three years. Provision is made under the rules of procedure for handling urgent emergency matters through a Tentative Interim Amendment Procedure. The Committee also has established rules for rendering Formal (sometimes called Official) Interpretations. Two general forms of findings for such Interpretations are recognized: (1) those making an interpretation of literal text and (2) those making an interpretation of the intent of the **National Electrical Code** when a particular rule was adopted. All Tentative Interim Amendments and Formal Interpretations are published by the NFPA as they are issued, and notices are sent to all interested trade papers in the electrical industry.

The **National Electrical Code** is purely advisory as far as the National Fire Protection Association is concerned but is very widely used as the basis of law and for legal regulatory purposes. The **Code** is administered by various local inspection agencies, whose decisions govern the actual application of the **National Electrical Code** to individual installations. Local inspectors are largely members of the International Association of Electrical Inspectors, 802 Busse Highway, Park Ridge, Illinois 60068. This organization, the National Electrical Manufacturers Association, the National Electrical Contractors Association, the Edison Electric Institute, the Underwriters' Laboratories, Inc., the International Brotherhood of Electrical Workers, governmental groups, and independent experts all contribute to the development and application of the **National Electrical Code.**

Brief History of the
National Electrical Code®

The **National Electrical Code** was originally drawn in 1897 as a result of the united efforts of various insurance, electrical, architectural, and allied interests. The original **Code** was prepared by the National Conference on Standard Electrical Rules, composed of delegates from various interested national associations. Prior to this, acting on an 1881 resolution of the National Association of Fire Engineers' meeting in Richmond, Virginia, a basis for the first **Code** was suggested to cover such items as identification of the white wire, the use of single disconnect devices, and the use of insulated conduit.

In 1911, the National Conference of Standard Electrical Rules was disbanded, and since that year, the National Fire Protection Association (NFPA) has acted as sponsor of the **National Electrical Code.** Beginning with the 1920 edition, the **National Electrical Code** has been under the further auspices of the American National Standards Institute (and its predecessor organizations, United States of America Standards Institute, and the American Standards Association), with the NFPA continuing in its role as Administrative Sponsor. Since that date, the Committee has been identified as "ANSI Standards Committee C1" (formerly "USAS C1" or "ASA C1").

Major milestones in the continued updating of successive issues of the **National Electrical Code** since 1911 appeared in 1923, when the **Code** was rearranged and rewritten; in 1937, when it was editorially revised so that all the general rules would appear in the first chapters followed by supplementary rules in the following chapters; and in 1959, when it was editorially revised to incorporate a new numbering system under which each Section of each Article is identified by the Article Number preceding the Section Number.

For many years the **National Electrical Code** was published by the National Board of Fire Underwriters (now American Insurance Association), and this public service of the National Board helped immensely in bringing about the wide public acceptance which the **Code** now enjoys. It is recognized as the most widely adopted **Code** of standard practices in the U.S.A. The National Fire Protection Association first printed the document in pamphlet form in 1951 and has, since that year, supplied the **Code** for distribution to the public through its own office and through the American National Standards Institute. The **National Electrical Code** also appears in the National Fire Codes, issued annually by the National Fire Protection Association.

About the 1990 NE Code®

Based on an all-time record volume of proposals and comments from thousands of electrical industry personnel across the nation, the 1990 **National Electrical Code** contains hundreds of major and minor revisions of existing rules and the addition of many new rules. The new edition contains completely new articles on equipment never covered by the **Code** before, along with radically new regulations and changes in old regulations covering the widest range of everyday electrical details. In particular, the impact of high technology on electrical design, methods, and products is very obvious in this new edition, particularly in new Art. 504 on Intrinsically Safe Systems for use in hazardous locations, in extensive reorganization of Art. 517 on Health Care Facilities, and in the expansion of Art. 645 on Electronic Computer/Data Processing Equipment.

All the discussion and analysis of the changes and additions in the 1990 **NEC** has been published in the two familiar documents, known as *The Technical Committee Reports*, referred to as the *TCR*, and *The Technical Committee Documentation*, known as the *TCD*. Both volumes—which are approaching the size of big-city telephone books—are available from the National Fire Protection Association, Batterymarch Park, Quincy, MA 02269. They are highly recommended as valuable references in using the 1990 **NEC** over the next three years and should be available to all electrical design and construction personnel.

Electrical construction people—contractors, electricians, electrical designers, plant electrical personnel, and electrical inspectors—have a vital, immediate, and awesome task before them. The **NE Code** is today more important than it has ever been. OSHA (the Occupational Safety and Health Administration) has developed its own standard, NFPA 70E, around **NE Code** rules and intends it as a mandatory federal standard, binding under force of legal sanctions. OSHA's application of **NE Code** rules to new electrical construction and to modernization and expansion of existing systems has been deeply and widely felt throughout the nation over recent years. This new edition of the **NE Code** will deepen and intensify the government's insistence on maximum safety and effectiveness in electrical work.

At the state and local levels, electrical inspection agencies everywhere are tightening their control over electrical work and are exercising stricter enforcement. "Listing" and "labeling" of products by nationally recognized testing labs is a "must" with inspectors and engineers. And now the **NE Code** has many rules that virtually insist on the use of certified equipment and materials.

The continuing boom in application of electrical energy for light, power, heat, control, signaling, and communications is still another factor that is demanding greater attention to the **Code.** As the electrical percentage of the construction dollar moves ever upward, the visibility and universality of electrical usage demand closer, more penetrating concern for safety in electrical work. In today's sealed buildings, with the entire interior environments totally dependent on effective electrical usage, the critical role of electrical systems demands not only concern for eliminating fire and shock hazards, but also concern for continuity and reliability of electrical usage as essential to safety of people and property. And this new **NE Code** edition reflects the need for safety regulations in prefabricated subsystems of wiring—like modular ceiling wiring and electrification of partitions for segmenting office space.

And, of course, one of the critical factors that emphasize the importance of the **NE Code** is the highly competitive nature of construction work today. With a constricted electrical market and the universal concern for energy conservation, forces in the industry are promoting maximum economy in such a way as to jeopardize full attention to safety. The **NE Code** is an effective, commendable barrier against any compromises with basic electrical safety. It is a democratically developed industry standard that establishes the essential foundation for design and installation of electrical systems; and, as such, it dictates basic economics in equipment and material costs as well as labor costs.

In this Handbook, the discussion delves into the letter and intent of **Code** rules. Read and study the material carefully. Talk it over with your associates; engage in as much discussion as possible. In particular, check out any questions or problems with your local inspection authorities. It is true that only time and discussion provide final answers on how some of the rules are to be interpreted. But now is the time to start. Do not delay. Use this Handbook to begin a regular, continuous, and enthusiastic program of updating yourself on this big new **Code.**

This Handbook's illustrated analysis of the 1990 **NE Code** is most effectively used by having your copy of the new **Code** book at hand and referring to each section as it is discussed. The commentary given here is intended to supplement and clarify the actual wording of the **Code** rules as given in the **Code** book itself.

Highlights of the 1990 NE Code® Changes

The following listed articles and sections indicate the major areas of change to the 1990 **National Electrical Code**. These articles and sections were amended or are completely new to the 1990 **National Electrical Code**. Detailed discussions of these changes appear in the main body of the text.

Note: In the **National Electrical Code** itself, changes and additions of specific **Code** sections can be readily identified by a vertical line in the margin. A dot in the margin indicates deletions.

Chapter 1. General

Article 100. Definitions
Plenum (new)
Premises Wiring (amended)
Bypass Isolation Switch (new)
Transfer Switch (new)

Article 110. Requirements for Electrical Installations
Sec. 110-14. Electrical Connections
Sec. 110-16(c). Access and Entrance to Working Space
Sec. 110-22. Identification of Disconnecting Means

Chapter 2. Wiring Design and Protection

Article 210. Branch Circuits
Sec. 210-3. Classifications, Exception
Sec. 210-4(d). Identification of Ungrounded Conductors
Sec. 210-6(a). Occupancy Limitation, (2)
Sec. 210-6(c). 277 Volts to Ground
Sec. 210-7(d). Replacements, Exception

Sec. 210-8. Ground-Fault Circuit-Interrupter Protection for Personnel (a). Dwelling Units, (3), (4), and (5)
Sec. 210-22(c). Other Loads
Sec. 210-52(a). General Provisions
Sec. 210-52(b). Small Appliances
Sec. 210-52(c). Counter Tops
Sec. 210-52(e). Outdoor Outlets
Sec. 210-52(h). Hallways
Sec. 210-63. Heating, Air-Conditioning, and Refrigeration Equipment Outlet
Sec. 210-70(a). Dwelling Unit(s)
Sec. 210-70(c). Other Locations

Article 215. Feeders

Sec. 215-2(a). For Specified Circuits
Sec. 215-10. Ground-Fault Protection of Equipment

Article 220. Branch-Circuit and Feeder Calculations

Sec. 220-3(c)(5). Other Loads—All Occupancies
Sec. 220-13. Receptacle Loads—Nondwelling Units
Sec. 220-36. Optional Calculation—New Restaurants

Article 225. Outside Branch Circuits and Feeders

Sec. 225-4. Conductor Covering, Exception
Sec. 225-7(b). Common Neutral
Sec. 225-19(a). Above Roofs
Sec. 225-19(b). From Nonbuilding or Nonbridge Structures
Sec. 225-19(c). Horizontal Clearances
Sec. 225-26. Live Vegetation

Article 230. Services

Sec. 230-2. Number of Services, Exception No. 4a
Sec. 230-50(a). Service-Entrance Cables

Article 240. Overcurrent Protection

Sec. 240-6. Standard Ampere Ratings, Exception, and Fine-Print Note
Sec. 240-13. Ground-Fault Protection of Equipment
Sec. 240-21. Location in Circuit, Exception No. 2
Sec. 240-81. Indicating
Sec. 240-83(c). Interrupting Rating
Sec. 240-83(e). Voltage Marking

Article 250. Grounding

Sec. 250-5. Alternating-Current Circuits and Systems to Be Grounded (b). Alternating-Current Systems of 50 Volts to 1000 Volts, (2) and (3)
Sec. 250-21(d). Limitations to Permissible Alterations
Sec. 250-23(b). Grounded Conductor Brought to Service Equipment and Fine-Print Note
Sec. 250-24. Two or More Buildings or Structures Supplied from a Common Service (d). Grounding Conductor
Sec. 250-26. Grounding Separately Derived Alternating-Current Systems (a). Bonding Jumper, (b). Grounding Electrode Conductor
Sec. 250-43(g). Electric Signs
Sec. 250-43(k). Motor-Operated Water Pumps
Sec. 250-61(a). Supply-Side Equipment

Sec. 250-71(b). Bonding to Other Systems
Sec. 250-75. Bonding Other Enclosures, Exception
Sec. 250-79(d). Size—Equipment Bonding Jumper on Supply Side of Service and
   Main Bonding Jumper
Sec. 250-81. Grounding Electrode System, Exception
Sec. 250-81(b). Metal Frame of the Building, Fine-Print Note
Sec. 250-83. Made and Other Electrodes (a). Metal Underground Gas Piping System,
   (e). Aluminum Electrodes
Sec. 250-91(a). Grounding Electrode Conductor, Exception No. 2
Sec. 250-94. Size of Alternating-Current Grounding Electrode Conductor, Note to
   Table
Sec. 250-95. Size of Equipment Grounding Conductors
Sec. 250-112. To Grounding Electrode
Sec. 250-119. Identification of Wiring Device Terminals

Chapter 3. Wiring Methods and Materials

Article 300. Wiring Methods
Sec. 300-4(d). Cables and Raceways Parallel to Framing Members
Sec. 300-5(a). Minimum Cover Requirements
Sec. 300-11. Securing and Supporting
Sec. 300-18. Raceway Installations
Sec 300-22(c). Other Space Used for Environmental Air

Article 310. Conductors for General Wiring
Sec. 310-4. Conductors in Parallel
Sec. 310-13. Conductor Constructions and Applications, Fine-Print Note
Sec. 310-15. Ampacity
Tables 310-16 through 310-19, Note 3. 120/240 Volts, 3-Wire, Single-Phase Dwelling
   Services, Note 8(a). More than Three Conductors in a Raceway or Cable
Sec. 310-16, Note 8(a), Exception No. 4

Article 318. Cable Trays
Sec. 318-3(b). In Industrial Establishments, (1) Single Conductor
Sec. 318-4. Uses Not Permitted

Article 328. Flat Conductor Cable Type FCC
Sec. 328-17. Crossings

Article 331. Electrical Nonmetallic Tubing
Sec. 331-3. Uses Permitted, (1)
Sec. 331-4. Uses Not Permitted, (8)
Sec. 331-10. Bends—Number in One Run

Article 333. Armored Cable
Sec. 333-6(a). Uses Permitted
Sec. 333-11. Exposed Work, Exception No. 3

Article 336. Nonmetallic-Sheathed Cable
Sec. 336-3. Uses Permitted (b). Type NMC
Sec. 336-4. Uses Not Permitted (a). Type NM or NMC

Article 345. Intermediate Metal Conduit
Sec. 345-11. Bends—Number in One Run

Article 348. Electrical Metallic Tubing

Sec. 348-12. Supports, Exception

Article 350. Flexible Metal Conduit

Sec. 350-3. Minimum Size, Exception No. 3
Sec. 350-7. Number of Conductors

Article 351. Liquidtight Flexible Conduit

Sec. 351-23. Use (a). Permitted, (4)

Article 363. Wireways

Sec. 362-6. Deflected Insulated Conductors
Sec. 362-8. Supports

Article 364. Busways

Sec. 364-4(a). Use Permitted, Exception No. 2

Article 370. Outlet, Device, Pull, and Junction Boxes, Conduit Bodies, and Fittings

Sec. 370-3. Nonmetallic Boxes, Exceptions No. 1 and 2
Sec. 370-6. Number of Conductors in Outlet, Device, and Junction Boxes, and
    Conduit Bodies (a). Standard Boxes
Sec. 370-12. Exposed Surface Extensions, Exception
Sec. 370-13(d). Raceway Supported Enclosure(s), Without Devices or Fixtures
Sec. 370-13(e). Raceway Supported Enclosure(s), With Devices or Fixtures
Sec. 370-13(g). Nonthreaded Nonmetallic Enclosures, Metal Conduit Supported
Sec. 370-18(a)(2). Angle or U Pulls
Sec. 370-52(e). Suitable Covers

Article 384. Switchboards and Panelboards

Sec. 384-4. Installation
Sec. 384-13. General
Sec. 384-16(f). Back-Fed Devices
Sec. 384-20. Grounding of Panelboards

Chapter 4. Equipment for General Use

Article 400. Flexible Cords and Cables

Sec. 400-8. Uses Not Permitted, (6) and Exception

Article 410. Lighting Fixtures, Lampholders, Lamps, and Receptacles

Sec. 410-8. Fixtures in Clothes Closets
Sec. 410-15(b). Metal Poles Supporting Lighting Fixtures, Exception
Sec. 410-16. Means of Support (h). Trees
Sec. 410-56(c). Isolated Ground Receptacles
Sec. 410-67(c). Tap Conductors
Sec. 410-73(f). Recessed High-Intensity Discharge Fixtures
Sec. 410-77(c). Wired Fixture Sections
Sec. 410-80(b). Dwelling Occupancies

Article 422. Appliances

Sec. 422-7. Central Heating Equipment

Article 430. Motors, Motor Circuits, and Controllers

Sec. 430-1. Motor Feeder and Branch Circuits
Sec. 430-6(b). Torque Motors

Sec. 430-7(e). Phase Converter Marking
Sec. 430-19. Phase Converter
Sec. 430-22(b). Phase Converter
Sec. 430-36. Fuses—In Which Conductor
Sec. 430-52(a). General Motor Applications
Sec. 430-52(c). Phase Converters
Sec. 430-86. Phase Converter Power Interruption
Sec. 430-91. Motor Controller Enclosure Types

Article 450. Transformers and Transformer Vaults

Sec. 450-3. Overcurrent Protection, Fine-Print Note
Sec. 450-8(c). Exposed Energized Parts
Sec. 450-9. Ventilation
Sec. 450-22. Dry-Type Transformers Installed Outdoors
Sec. 450-23. Less-Flammable Liquid-Insulated Transformer
Sec. 450-24. Nonflammable Fluid-Insulated Transformers
Sec. 450-42. Walls, Roof, and Floor
Sec. 450-43(c). Locks

Article 460. Capacitors

Sec. 460-9. Rating or Setting of Motor Overload Device

Chapter 5. Special Occupancies

Article 500. Hazardous (Classified) Locations

Sec. 500-2. Location and General Requirements

Article 501. Class I Locations

Sec. 501-4(a). Class I, Division 1, Exception
Sec. 501-4(b). Class I, Division 2
Sec. 501-5(a). Conduit Seals, Class I, Division 1, (1)
Sec. 501-5(f)(3). Canned Pumps, Process or Service Connections, Etc.
Sec. 501-6(b)(1). Type Required
Sec. 501-10(b). Class I, Division 2, (1) Heaters (a), Exception No. 2
Sec. 501-16(a). Bonding
Sec. 501-16(b). Types of Equipment Grounding Conductors

Article 502. Class II Locations

Sec. 502-4(a)(2). Flexible Connections
Sec. 502-4(b). Class II, Division 2

Article 504. Intrinsically Safe Systems (new)

Sec. 504-1. Scope

Article 514. Gasoline Dispensing and Service Stations

Sec. 514-2. Class I Locations
Sec. 514-5. Circuit Disconnects

Article 515. Bulk Storage Plants

Sec. 515-2. Class I Locations
Sec. 515-4. Wiring and Equipment Above Class I Locations

Article 516. Spray Application, Dipping, and Coating Processes

Sec. 516-2. Classification of Locations (a). Class I or Class II, Division 1 Locations, (b). Class I or Class II, Division 2 Locations, (2)

Article 517. Health Care Facilities (Completely Restructured Article)

Sec. 517-13(a). Patient Care Areas
Sec. 517-14. Panelboard Bonding
Sec. 517-18(b). Patient Bed Location Receptacles
Sec. 517-20. Wet Locations (1)
Sec. 517-30(c)(3). Mechanical Protection of the Emergency System, Exception No. 3
Sec. 517-34(b). Equipment for Delayed Automatic or Manual Connection, (1) and (3)

Article 518. Places of Assembly

Sec. 518-4. Wiring Methods, Exception No. 1

Article 530. Motion Picture and Television Studios and Similar Locations

Sec. 530-11. Permanent Wiring, Exception

Article 547. Agricultural Buildings

Sec. 547-8(a). Grounding and Bonding, Exception No. 2
Sec. 547-8(d). Water Pumps and Metal Well Casings

Article 550. Mobile Homes and Mobile Home Parks

Sec. 550-23. Mobile Home Service Equipment

Chapter 6. Special Equipment

Article 645. Electronic Computer/Data Processing Equipment (Complete Rewrite)

Sec. 645-2. Special Requirements for Electronic Computer/Data Processing Equipment Room
Sec. 645-5. Supply Circuits and Interconnecting Cables
Sec. 645-11. Uninterruptible Power Supplies
Sec. 645-15. Grounding

Article 680. Swimming Pools, Fountains, and Similar Installations

Sec. 680-4. Definitions
Sec. 680-21(a). Junction Boxes, (4)
Sec. 680-22(a). Bonded Parts, (6)
Sec. 680-25(c). Motors
Sec. 680-25(c). Motors, Exception No. 3
Sec. 680-41(a). Receptacles
Sec. 680-41(b)(1). Lighting Fixtures and Lighting Outlets, Exception No. 2

Chapter 7. Special Conditions

Article 700. Emergency Systems

Sec. 700-9(a). Identification

Article 710. Over 600 Volts, Nominal

Sec. 710-3(b). Underground Conductors, Table 710-3(b), Exceptions No. 2 and 3

Article 725. Remote-Control, Signaling, and Power-Limited Circuits

Sec. 725-17(a). Class 1 Circuit Conductors
Sec. 725-38(a)(4). In Shafts
Sec. 725-49. Fire Resistance of Cables Within Buildings
Sec. 725-50. Listing and Marking of Class 2, Class 3, and PLTC Cables

Sec. 725-51. Additional Listing Requirements
Sec. 725-53. Applications of Listed Class 2, Class 3, and PLTC Cables

Article 760. Fire Protective Signaling Systems (Extensive Revisions and Additions Throughout)

Chapter 8. Communications Systems

Article 800. Communications Circuits

Sec. 800-52. Installation of Conductors

Chapter 9. Tables and Examples

Table 5B (new)
Table 10 (new)

ARTICLE 90. INTRODUCTION

90-1. Purpose. (a). This section clearly and simply describes the function of the NE Code in relation to electrical design and installation work. But it is important to understand that the NE Code is intended only to assure that electrical work is done safely—that is, to provide a system that is "essentially free from hazard."

The NE Code is recognized as a legal criterion of safe electrical design and installation. It is used in court litigation and by insurance companies as a basis for insuring buildings. Because the Code is such an important instrument of safe design, it must be thoroughly understood by all electrical designers. They must be familiar with all sections of the Code and should know the accepted interpretations which have been placed on many specific rulings of the Code. They should keep abreast of formal interpretations which are issued by the NE Code committee. They should know the intent of Code requirements—i.e., the spirit as well as the letter of each provision. They should keep informed on interim amendments to the Code. And, most important, they should keep this Code handbook handy and study it often.

(b). As stated, compliance with the provisions of the National Electrical Code can effectively minimize fire and accident hazards in any electrical design. The Code (throughout this manual, the word "Code" refers to the National Electrical Code) sets forth requirements, recommendations, and suggestions and constitutes a minimum standard for the framework of electrical design. As stated in its own introduction, the Code is concerned with the "practical safeguarding of persons and property from hazards arising from the use of electricity" for light, heat, power, radio, signaling, and other purposes.

Although the Code assures minimum safety provisions, actual design work must constantly consider safety as required by special types or conditions of electrical application. For example, effective provision of automatic protective devices and selection of control equipment for particular applications involve engineering skill of the designer, above routine adherence to **Code** requirements. Then, too, designers must know the physical characteristics—application advantages and limitations—of the many materials they use for enclosing, supporting, insulating, isolating, and, in general, protecting electrical equipment. The task of safe application based on skill and experience is particularly important in hazardous locations. Safety is not automatically made a characteristic of a system by simply observing codes. Safety must be designed into a system.

(c). The **National Electrical Code** contains provisions considered necessary for safety, but does not provide information of a design nature, other than for safety purposes, and should not be used to ensure adequate or efficient forms of installation. These features should be obtained from design manuals or through the services of a competent consulting engineer or electrical contractor.

90-2. Scope. (a). The **Code** applies to all electrical work—indoors and outdoors—other than that work excluded by the rules of part **(b)** in this section.

By the word "installations" in parts **(a)(1)** through **(a)(4)**, it is made clear that the **NE Code** applies to electrical circuits and systems in their manner of installation as well as in the components used.

Part **(a)(1)** makes clear that the **NE Code** also applies to "floating buildings" because the safety of **Code** compliance is required for all places where people are present. Coverage of floating buildings is contained in **NEC** Art. 553.

The scope of the NEC includes the installation of optical fiber cable, part (a)(4) As part of the high-technology revolution in industrial and commercial building operations, the use of light pulses transmitted along optical fiber cables has become an alternative method to electric pulses on metal conductors for control, signals, and communications. The technology of fiber optics has grown dramatically over recent years as a result of great strides in development of the fiber cables and associated equipment that converts electric pulses to light pulses and vice versa. For high rates of data transmission involved in data processing and computer control of machines and processes, optical fiber cables far outperform metallic conductors carrying electrical currents—all at a small fraction of the cost of metallic-conductor circuiting (Fig. 90-1).

NEC Art. 770, "Optical Fiber Cables," covers the use of such cables in association with conventional metallic-conductor circuits. Nonconductive optical fiber cables are permitted to be installed in the same raceway and enclosures as metallic-conductor circuits where the functions of the two different types of cables are associated with the same equipment, operation, or process.

(b). The rules of the **Code** do not apply to the electrical work described in **(1)** through **(5)**. The most common controversy that arises concerns exclusion of electrical work done by electric utilities (power companies).

The fine-print note after part **(b)(5)** clarifies a long-standing point of controversy about how the **NE Code** applies to electrical circuits and systems on premises belonging to electric utilities. Where part **(b)(5)** indicates that the **Code** does not apply to those circuits, systems, and equipment that are involved solely with the power company's supply of electric power to its customers, the note makes

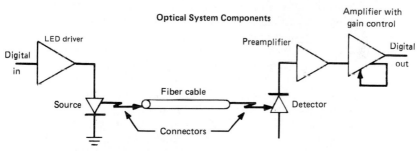

A telephone conversation is first transformed into an electrical signal. This input signal is scanned by a digital encoder, which reduces it to a series of "on's" and "off's." The driver, which activates the laser light source, transmits the digital "on's" as a pulse of light and the "off's" as the absence of a pulse. The light travels through the optical fiber cable to its destination, where it is received, amplified, and fed into a digital decoder. The decoder translates the pulses back into the original electrical signal.

Fig. 90·1. The NEC covers the new technology of fiber optics for communication and data transmission.

clear that other electrical circuits and systems owned and controlled by an electric utility are covered.

This note emphatically explains that not all electrical systems and equipment belonging to utilities are exempted from **Code** compliance. Electrical circuits and equipment in buildings or on premises that are used exclusively for the "generation, control, transformation, transmission, and distribution of electric energy" are considered as being safe because of the competence of the utility engineers and electricians who design and install such work. **Code** rules do not apply to such circuits and equipment—nor to any "communication" or "metering" installations of an electric utility. But, any conventional electrical systems for power, lighting, heating, and other applications within buildings or on structures belonging to utilities must comply with **Code** rules where such places are not "used exclusively by utilities" for the supply of electric power to the utilities' customers.

An example of the kind of utility-owned electrical circuits and equipment covered by **Code** rules would be the electrical installations in, say, an office

Fig. 90-2. CIRCUITS AND EQUIPMENT of any utility company are exempt from the rule of the NEC when the particular installation is part of the utility's system for transmitting and distributing power to the utility's customers—*provided* that such an installation is accessible only to the utility's personnel and access is denied to others. Outdoor, fenced-in utility-controlled substations, transformer mat installations, utility pad-mount enclosures, and equipment isolated by elevation are typical utility areas to which the NEC does not apply. The same is also true of indoor, locked transformer vaults or electric rooms. (Sec. 90-2.) But, electrical equipment, circuits, and systems that are involved in supplying lighting, heating, motors, signals, communications, and other load devices that serve the needs of personnel in buildings or on premises owned (or leased) and operated by a utility are subject to NE Code rules, just like any other commercial or industrial building, provided that the buildings or areas are not integral parts of a generating plant or substation.

building of the utility. But, in the Technical Committee Report for the 1987 **NEC**, the **Code** panel for Art. 90 stated that it is not the intent of this rule to have **NEC** regulations apply to "office buildings, warehouses, etc., that *are* an *integral* part of a utility generating plant, substation, or control center." **NEC** rules would not apply to any wiring or equipment in a utility generating plant, substation, or control center and would not apply to conventional lighting and power circuits in office areas, warehouses, maintenance shops, or any other areas of utility facilities used for the generation, transmission, or distribution of electric energy for the utility's customers. But **NEC** rules would apply to all electrical work in *other* buildings occupied by utilities—office buildings, warehouses, truck garages, repair shops, etc., that are not part of a generating plant or substation. (See Fig. 90-2.)

90-4. Enforcement.   This is one of the most basic and most important of **Code** rules because it establishes the necessary conditions for use of the **Code**.

The **NE Code** stipulates that, when questions arise about the meaning or intent of any **Code** rule as it applies to a particular electrical installation, the electrical inspector having jurisdiction over the installation is the only one authorized by the **NE Code** to make interpretations of the rules. The wording of Sec. 90-4 reserves that power to the local inspection authority along with the authority to approve equipment and materials and to grant the special permission for methods and techniques that might be considered alternatives to those **Code** rules that specifically mention such "special permission" [for instance, Sec. 250-57(c)].

Up until the 1975 **NE Code**, Sec. 90-4 aimed only at giving the inspector the right to "interpret" **Code** rules. But the 1975 **NE Code**, for the first time, specifically gave the inspector the authority to "waive" specific requirements—that is, to disregard the wording and meaning of individual **Code** rules. However, use of this authority by the inspector was allowed (1) only in "industrial establishments and research and testing facilities" and (2) only where the inspector is satisfied that the safety objectives sought by the **Code** rule are achieved by the particular design and/or installation techniques that are used as alternatives to the specifics of the **Code** rule. The 1975 **NE Code** referred to the necessity for "establishing and maintaining effective safety and maintenance procedures" whenever a rule was "waived" or whenever "alternative methods" were accepted.

The present **NE Code** permits the electrical inspector to "waive specific requirements" or "permit alternate methods" in *any* type of electrical installation. The last sentence of Sec. 90-4 no longer limits waiver of **Code** rules to

Fig. 90-3. INSPECTOR'S AUTHORITY may be exercised either by enforcement of that individual's interpretation of a Code rule or by waiver of the Code rule when the inspector is satisfied that a specific non-Code-conforming method or technique satisfies the safety intent of the Code. (Sec. 90-4).

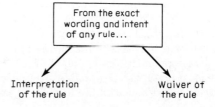

industrial establishments and research and testing facilities. In residential, commercial, and institutional electrical systems—as well as in industrial— inspectors may now accept design and/or installation methods that do not conform to a specific **Code** rule, provided they are satisfied that the safety objectives of the **Code** rule are achieved (Fig. 90-3).

It should be noted that permission for any such variations from normal **NE Code** practice is granted only to the authority having jurisdiction in enforcing the **Code**. This permission is given to the electrical inspectors to permit them to recognize practices at variance with the **Code**, provided such practices are carefully controlled and under rigorously maintained conditions. In addition, such practices must be based on sound engineering principles and techniques which otherwise assure the safety of personnel and freedom from shock and fire hazard that the **NE Code** itself seeks to provide.

This recognition of practices at variance with the **Code** is provided only for special conditions and must not be interpreted as a general permission to engage in non-**Code** methods, techniques, or design procedures. In fact, it is likely that inspectors will exercise this authority only with reluctance and then with great care, because of the great responsibility this places on the inspector.

90·5. Formal Interpretations.   Official interpretations of the **National Electrical Code** are based on specific sections of specific editions of the **Code**. In most cases, such official interpretations apply to the stated conditions on given installations. Accordingly, they would not necessarily apply to other situations that vary slightly from the statement on which the official interpretation was issued.

As official interpretations of each edition of the **Code** are issued, they are published in the NFPA Fire News and press releases are sent to interested trade papers.

All official interpretations issued on a specific **Code** edition are reviewed by the appropriate **Code**-making panel during the period when the specific **Code** edition is being revised. In reviewing an interpretation, a **Code** panel may agree with the interpretation findings and clarify the **Code** text to avoid further misunderstanding of intent, or the panel may reject the findings of the interpretation and alter the **Code** text to clarify the **Code** panel's intent. On the other hand, the **Code** panel may not recommend any change in the **Code** text because of the special conditions described in the official interpretation. For these reasons, the NFPA does not catalog official interpretations issued on previous editions of the **Code**. And in reviewing all previous interpretations, it can be stated that practically none of them would apply to the present edition of the **Code** because of revised **Code** wording that materially changes the intent.

If anyone feels that a past interpretation applies to the present text, they should submit it in the form of a proposed **Code** change when revisions for the next edition of the **Code** are being considered.

With the wide adoption of the **Code** throughout the country, the authority having jurisdiction has the prime responsibility of interpreting **Code** rules in its area and disagreements on the intent of particular **Code** rules in its area; and disagreements on the intent of particular **Code** rules should be resolved at the local level if at all possible. There is no guarantee that the authority having jurisdiction will accept the findings of an official interpretation.

90-6. Examination of Equipment for Safety.   It is not the intent of the National Electrical Code to include the detailed requirements for internal wiring of electrical equipment. Such information is usually contained in individual standards for the equipment concerned.

The last sentence does not intend to take away the authority of the local inspector to examine and approve equipment, but rather to indicate that the requirements of the National Electrical Code do not generally apply to the internal construction of devices which have been listed by a nationally recognized electrical testing laboratory.

Although the specifics of Code rules on examination of equipment for safety are presented in Sec. 110-2 and Sec. 110-3, the general Code statement on this matter is made here in Sec. 90-6. Although the Code does place emphasis on the need for third-party certification of equipment by independent testing laboratories, it does not make a flat rule to that effect. However, the rules of OSHA are very rigid in insisting on product certification.

The clear effect of OSHA regulations is to *require* that "listed," "labeled," "accepted," and/or "certified" equipment be used whenever available. If any electrical system component is "of a kind" that *any* nationally recognized testing lab "accepts, certifies, lists, labels, or determines to be safe," then *that* component *must* be so designated in order to be acceptable for use under OSHA regulations. For instance, because liquidtight flexible metal conduit is a product that is listed and labeled by Underwriters Laboratories Inc. (UL), it is clearly and certainly a violation of the OSHA rule to use any nonlisted, nonlabeled version of liquidtight flexible metal conduit. A nonlisted, nonlabeled, noncertified component may be used *only* if it is "of a kind" that *no* nationally recognized lab covers. And even then, the nonrecognized component must be inspected or tested by another federal agency or by a state, municipal, or other local authority responsible for enforcing occupational safety provisions of the NE Code.

Every electrical designer and installer must exercise great care in evaluating any and all equipment and products used in electrical work to assure compliance with OSHA rules on certification by a nationally recognized testing lab. In many cases, "listed" components are combined to make up an assembled piece of equipment, but the entire assembly is not listed or labeled as an assembly and may constitute an assembly that is not safe for use. For instance, a listed circuit breaker and a listed magnetic starter may be combined in a listed electric cabinet, but that does not of itself constitute a listed "circuit-breaker combination motor starter." A listed "combination motor control unit" is an entire assembly that has been tested as an assembly and is labeled as such. It is critically important to be fully aware of the meaning and extent of the "listing" or "label" for every product. This is particularly true of combination products and custom-made equipment.

Codes and standards must be carefully interrelated and followed with care and precision. Modern work that fulfills these demands should be the objective of all electrical construction people.

Chapter One

ARTICLE 100. DEFINITIONS

Accessible: "(As applied to wiring methods.)"

Accessible: "(As applied to equipment.)"

Accessible, Readily: (Readily Accessible.)

Note that the first definition for "accessible" makes reference to "concealed" and "exposed." Because these words are critically important to applications of wiring methods and equipment, their definitions must be carefully studied and cross-referenced with one another, as well as related to **Code** rules using these words. Since discussions involving the definitions can become complex and murky, it should be noted that Sec. 90-4 gives the local inspector the authority to make the binding interpretation.

Note that there are definitions for words that apply to wiring methods and definitions that apply to equipment. Wiring methods are any of the **NE Code**-recognized techniques for running circuits between equipment. These include conductors in EMT (electric metallic tubing), rigid metal, or nonmetallic conduit; wireway; cable tray; underfloor raceways; all the cable assemblies covered in Arts. 330 to 340; busway; and the other hookup methods covered in Chap. 3. "Equipment" covers all the products that are connected or hooked by any of these recognized wiring methods.

For electrical applications above suspended ceilings with lift-out panels, it is necessary to distinguish between "equipment" and "wiring methods." It also is necessary to distinguish between ceiling spaces used for air handling and those not used as air-handling spaces. Typical applications of **Code** rules to both those categories are as follows for nonair-handling ceilings.

9

1. Wiring methods above lift-out ceiling panels are considered to be "exposed" because the definition of that word includes reference to "behind panels designed to allow access." A typical application of this definition is where wireways are installed in a hung ceiling. Section 362-2 says that wireways are permitted only for exposed work. Therefore, wireway may be installed in the open and visible, or it may be installed above lift-out panels of a suspended ceiling.

    Any wiring methods above a ceiling made up of lift-out ceiling elements are, therefore, accessible, as shown in Fig. 100-1.

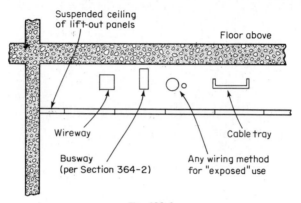

Fig. 100·1

2. The rules on installation of busway used to be worded the same as that quoted above for wireway. But now, Exception No. 1 to Sec. 364-4(a) permits busway above panels, if means of access are provided. It further limits such use to totally enclosed, nonventilated busway, without plug-in switches or CBs on the busway—except for an individual fixture—and only in ceiling space that is not used for air handling. Exception No. 2 to Sec. 364-4(a) permits busway in an air-handling ceiling space when installed in accordance with Sec. 300-22(c)—that is, totally enclosed, nonventilated, insulated busway that "has no provisions" to accommodate any plug-in fuse or CB.

3. Section 318-6(h) requires cable trays to be exposed and accessible. Note that the two words "exposed" and "accessible" must be taken "as applied to wiring methods." Cable tray may be used above a suspended, nonair-handling ceiling; and, if used with a wiring method permitted by Sec. 300-22(c), it may be used also above an air-handling ceiling.

4. In many of the articles on cables it is noted, under "Uses Permitted," that the cable may be used for both "exposed" and "concealed" work. Such cables may, therefore, be used above suspended ceilings.

5. Fuses and circuit breakers that provide overcurrent protection required by the **NE Code** are generally required by Sec. 240-24 to be "readily accessi-

ble"—that is, they must be capable of being reached quickly. Note that the definition for "readily accessible" applies to **equipment** rather than **wiring methods** and is a different concept from that of the word "accessible." Fuses and/or CBs in a distribution panel or switchboard or motor control center are **not** readily accessible, for instance, if a bunch of crates piled on the floor block access and present an obstacle in getting to the fuses or CBs. They also are not readily accessible if it is necessary to get a portable ladder or stand on a chair or table to get at them.

Equipment is not "readily accessible" if conditions shown in Fig. 100-2 obtain.

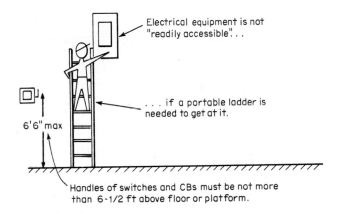

Electrical equipment is not "readily accessible"...

... if a portable ladder is needed to get at it.

6'6" max

Handles of switches and CBs must be not more than 6-1/2 ft above floor or platform.

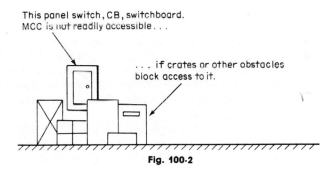

This panel switch, CB, switchboard. MCC is not readily accessible...

... if crates or other obstacles block access to it.

Fig. 100-2

Exception No. 1 in Sec. 240-24 permits overcurrent devices to be used high up on a busway where access to them could require use of a ladder, but not on busway above a suspended ceiling (Sec. 364-4).

Supplementary overcurrent devices—over and above those required by the **NE Code** and which the **Code** defines as supplementary protection [Sec. 424-

22(c) covering fuses or CBs permitted above a suspended ceiling for protection of electric duct heaters]—do not have to be readily accessible (Sec. 240-10 and Exception No. 2 in Sec. 240-24) and may be installed above a suspended ceiling. A CB- or fusible-type panelboard may be used in the ceiling space to satisfy Sec. 424-22(c).

Exception No. 3 of Sec. 240-24 permits service overcurrent protection to be sealed, locked, or otherwise not "readily accessible."

In general, aside from the cases noted above, fuses and CBs must **not** be used above a suspended ceiling because they would be not readily accessible. But equipment that is not required by a **Code** rule to be "accessible" or to be "readily accessible" may be mounted above a suspended ceiling, as indicated in Fig. 100-3.

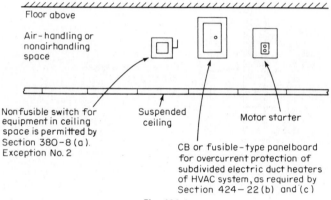

Fig. 100-3

If it is necessary to use a portable (but not a fixed) ladder to get to a switch or CB or transformer or other piece of equipment, then the equipment is not "readily accessible." The term "readily accessible" implies a need for performing promptly an indicated act, for example, to reach quickly a disconnecting switch or circuit breaker without the use of ladders, chairs, etc. The installation of such a switch or circuit breaker at a height above 6½ feet from a standing level is not considered "readily accessible."

An analysis   In judging whether electrical equipment is "readily accessible," it is first necessary to determine if the equipment is "accessible" in the **National Electrical Code** meaning of that word. If it can be determined that the equipment *is* accessible, then the equipment can be judged to be "readily accessible" if, when it is reached, it is not necessary to use a portable ladder or otherwise climb to get at it, and the equipment is not blocked by obstacles that have to be moved.

Any equipment that has to be "readily accessible" must be so only for "those to whom ready access is requisite"—which clearly and intentionally allows for making equipment *not* readily accessible to other than authorized persons, such as by providing a lock on the door, with the key possessed by or available to those who require ready access.

Because the definition of "readily accessible" contains a last phrase that says "See 'Accessible'," logic dictates that it is first necessary to satisfy the definition of the word "accessible." And the wording of that definition clearly establishes that there is no **Code** violation for "readily accessible" equipment to be behind a door under lock and key to make it accessible only to authorized persons.

Note that the definition for "accessible" does not say that a door to an electrical room is prohibited from being locked. In fact, the wording of the definition, by referring to "locked doors," actually presumes the existence and, therefore, the acceptability of "locked doors" in electrical systems. The only requirement implied by the wording is that locked doors, where used, must not "guard" against access—that is, the disposition of the key to the lock must be such that those requiring access to the room are not positively excluded.

To be "accessible," equipment must not be *"guarded"* by locked doors and must not be *"guarded"* by elevation. The critical word is "guarded." The definition is *not* intended to mean that equipment *cannot* be "behind" locked doors or that equipment *cannot* be mounted up high where it *can* be reached with a portable ladder. To make equipment "not accessible," a door lock or high mounting must be such that it positively "guards" against access. For instance, equipment mounted up high where conditions are such that it cannot be reached with a portable ladder is *not* "accessible." Equipment behind a locked door for which a key is not possessed by or available to persons who require access to the equipment is *not* "accessible." A common example of that latter condition occurs in multitenant buildings where a disconnect for the tenant of one occupancy unit is located behind the locked door of another tenant's occupancy unit from which the first tenant is effectively and legally excluded.

The definition of "accessible" has always been intended to recognize that equipment may be fully "accessible" even though installed behind a locked door or at an elevated height. Equipment that is high-mounted but can be reached with a ladder that is fixed in place or a portable ladder *is* "accessible" (although the equipment would not be "readily accessible" if a portable ladder had to be used to reach it). Similarly, it has always been within the meaning of the definition that equipment behind a locked door *is* "accessible" to anyone who possesses a key to the lock or to a person who is authorized to obtain and use the key to open the locked door. In such cases, conditions do *not* "guard" against access.

There is no rule in the **NEC** that prohibits use of a lock on the door of an electrical room. In fact, some **Code** rules *require* equipment to be in rooms with locked doors—while maintaining the condition of the room as "accessible" or "readily accessible."

Section 110-31 says, "Electrical installations in a vault, room, or closet or in an area surrounded by a wall, screen, or fence, access to which is *controlled by lock and key* or other approved means, *shall be considered to be accessible to qualified persons only.*" [Italics supplied.]

In Art. 450 on transformers, where a transformer is used in a vault, two separate **Code** rules must be satisfied simultaneously. Section 450-13 says, "Transformers and transformer vaults *shall be readily accessible* to qualified personnel for inspection and maintenance." [Italics supplied.]

Section 450-43, covering rules on doors for the above-described vaults, which must be "readily accessible," says, "Vault doorways shall be protected as follows: **(c) Locks.** Doors shall be equipped with locks, and doors shall be kept locked, access being allowed only to qualified persons."

Those two rules combine to require that a transformer in a vault *must* be "readily accessible" *and* that the vault must be equipped with a locked door. Obviously, the "locked door" and "readily accessible" are not mutually exclusive and are completely compatible with each other.

Conditions of "accessibility" can be evaluated in accordance with the following:

CASE I—EQUIPMENT IN A LOCKED ROOM, LOCKED SPACE, OR LOCKED, FENCED-IN AREA

Condition A: Accessible, But *Not* Readily Accessible

This condition exists if the key to the locked door or gate is available to anyone requiring access to the equipment within—but, when the room, space, or area is entered, a portable ladder, chair, scaffold, hoist, or lift is needed to reach high-mounted equipment. Such a ladder or climbing or lifting device must be capable of reaching the equipment and be on the premises and available to anyone requiring access to the equipment—that is, the ladders or lifting or climbing devices must be permanently installed. Need for a *portable* ladder or other *portable* climbing or lifting device makes the equipment *not* "readily accessible" although it is "accessible."

Condition B: Accessible and Readily Accessible

This condition exists if the key to the locked door or gate is available to anyone requiring access to the equipment—and, when the room or space is entered, the equipment may be reached by a person standing on the floor or on a readily accessible platform—without need for a portable ladder or other climbing or lifting device and without need to move stored objects, materials, or other obstacles blocking access to the equipment. Any high-mounted equipment—suspended from overhead or located on an elevated platform or balcony—is also "readily accessible" if a permanently installed ladder or stairway provides for reaching the equipment.

Conditon C: Not Accessible

(1) This conditon exists if the key for the locked door or gate is not available to anyone requiring access because that person does not know who has the key and/or does not know how to contact the person with the key who will surrender the key or make its use available. This would typically be encountered in multiple-occupancy buildings like office buildings, apartment houses, shopping centers, etc., where, either as part of original design or as a result of alterations or modernization, a switch or circuit breaker for one tenant is within locked space of another tenant. In such a condition, "close approach" to the equipment by the first tenant is "guarded" by the locked door or gate. OR:

(2) This condition exists if the key for the locked door or gate is available to anyone requiring access—but the equipment is so high-mounted or so otherwise installed that available portable ladders or other climbing or lifting devices cannot reach the equipment. In such a condition, "close approach" to the equipment is "guarded" by "elevation."

CASE II—EQUIPMENT IN AN UNLOCKED ROOM, SPACE, OR FENCED-IN AREA
Condition A: Accessible But *Not* Readily Accessible
This condition exists if a portable ladder, chair, scaffold, hoist, or lift is needed to reach high-mounted equipment and such ladder or climbing or lifting device is capable of reaching the equipment and is on the premises and is available to anyone requiring access to the equipment.
Condition B: Accessible and Readily Accessible
This condition exists if the equipment may be reached by a person standing on the floor or on a readily accessible platform—without need for a portable ladder or other climbing or lifting device and without need to move stored objects, materials or other obstacles blocking access to the equipment. Any high-mounted equipment—suspended from overhead or located on an elevated platform or balcony—is also "readily accessible" if a permanently installed ladder or stairway provides for reaching the equipment.
Condition C: Not Accessible
The equipment is so high-mounted or otherwise so installed that available portable ladders or other climbing or lifting devices cannot reach the equipment. In such a conditon, "close approach" to the equipment is "guarded" by "elevation."

Ampacity:

"Ampacity" is the maximum amount of current in amperes that a conductor may carry under specific conditions of use. This definition provides a clear, logical description of what a conductor's ampacity is: "The current in amperes a conductor can carry continuously *under the conditions of use* without exceeding its temperature rating."

For instance, **NEC** Table 310-16 gives ampacities of various sizes of copper and aluminum conductors, with ampacities being higher for 75°C (THW) conductors and 90°C (THHN, XHHW, RHH) conductors than for 60°C (TW) conductors because the higher-temperature-rated conductors have insulations that are capable of withstanding the higher heat of greater I^2R. And in the table, the ampacities shown are for the "condition" that not more than three conductors are used in raceway or cable and for the "condition" that the ambient temperature of air around the conductors is not over 30°C (86°F). As now covered by the revised wording of Note 8 to Table 310-16 in the 1984 **NEC**, if more than three current-carrying conductors are used in a raceway, *the ampacity of each* *conductor must be reduced as required by the note. And further, where the ambient temperature exceeds 30°C, the ampacity of each conductor must be reduced for elevated ambient temperature in accordance with the table of factors at the bottom of Table 310-16 (or Table 310-18).*

As stated in the **Code**-making panel's substantiation for revision of Note 8 to Table 310-16, "Where *both* conditions (high ambients and four or more conductors in a raceway or cable) exist, *both deratings should be applied, one on the other*."

Note: The above is an important and radical change from the rule of the 1981 **NEC**, which did *not reduce* ampacity but simply required limiting of the load. Now, the "ampacity" value is reduced and conductors must be protected in accordance with the *reduced value* and *not* at the value of current shown in the table. See the full discussion under "Note 8, Tables 310-16 through 310-19."

Approved:

The electrical inspector having jurisdiction on any specific installation is the person who will decide what conductors and/or equipment are "approved." Although inspectors are not required to use "listing" or "labeling" by a national testing lab as the deciding factor in their approval of products, they invariably base their acceptance of products on listings by testing labs. Certainly the **NE Code** almost makes the same insistence as OSHA does that, whenever possible, acceptability must be based on some kind of listing or certification of a national lab. But on this matter, the OSHA law takes precedence— a "listed," "labeled," or otherwise "certified" product must *always* be used in preference to the same "kind" of product that is not recognized by a national testing lab (Fig. 100-4).

Fig. 100-4

Bonding:

This definition covers a general concept that metal parts are conductively connected by a cable, wire, bolt, screw, or some other metallic connection of negligible impedance. The term is used frequently throughout the **Code** to imply that metal parts that are "bonded" together have no potential difference between them. Two common "bonding" techniques are bonding of switchboards and bonding of panelboards. When bonding is done by a short length

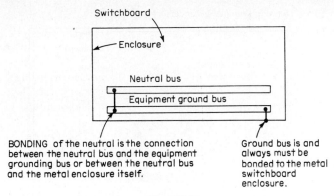

Switchboard

Enclosure

Neutral bus

Equipment ground bus

BONDING of the neutral is the connection
between the neutral bus and the equipment
grounding bus or between the neutral bus
and the metal enclosure itself.

Ground bus is and
always must be
bonded to the metal
switchboard
enclosure.

Fig. 100·5

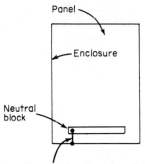

Panel

Enclosure

Neutral
block

BONDING is the insertion of a bonding screw into the panel neutral block to
connect the block to the panel enclosure, or it is use of a bonding jumper from
the neutral block to an equipment grounding block that is connected to the
enclosure.

NOTE: Bonding – the connection of the neutral
terminal to the enclosure or to the ground
terminal that is, itself, connected to the
enclosure – might also be done in an
individual switch or CB enclosure.

Fig. 100·6

of bare or insulated conductor, the conductor is referred to as a "bonding
jumper." Examples of bonding are given in Figs. 100-5 and 100-6.

Bonding Jumper:

This is any bare or insulated conductor used to provide bonding between metal
parts in a system—such as between a metal switchboard enclosure and metal
service conduits that stub-up under a service switchboard. The bonding jumper
or jumpers provide for making an electrically conductive connection between
the metal switchboard enclosure and the metal conduits—as required by **NEC**
Sec. 250-71(a) and (b). An example is shown in Fig. 100-7.

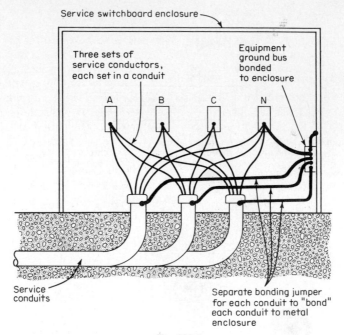

Service switchboard enclosure

Three sets of
service conductors,
each set in a conduit

Equipment
ground bus
bonded
to enclosure

A   B   C   N

Service
conduits

Separate bonding jumper
for each conduit to "bond"
each conduit to metal
enclosure

Fig. 100·7

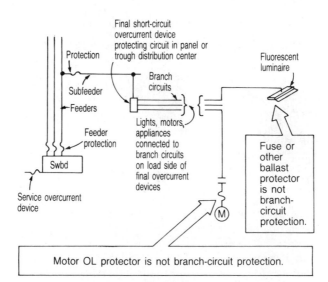

Final short-circuit
overcurrent device
protecting circuit in panel or
trough distribution center

Protection

Branch
circuits

Subfeeder

Feeders

Feeder
protection

Lights, motors,
appliances
connected to
branch circuits
on load side of
final overcurrent
devices

Fluorescent
luminaire

Fuse or
other
ballast
protector
is not
branch-
circuit
protection.

Swbd

Service overcurrent
device

M

Motor OL protector is not branch-circuit protection.

Fig. 100·8

Branch Circuit:

A branch circuit is that part of a wiring system extending beyond the final automatic overload protective device which is approved for use as branch-circuit protection. Thermal cutouts or motor overload devices are not branch-circuit protection. Neither are fuses in luminaires or in plug connections, where used for ballast protection or individual fixture protection. Such supplementary overcurrent protection is not a substitute for branch-circuit protection and does not establish the point of origin of the branch circuit. The extent of a branch circuit is illustrated in Fig. 100-8.

In its simplest form, a branch circuit consists of two wires which carry current at a particular voltage from protective device to utilization device.

The branch circuit represents the last step in the transfer of power from the service or source of energy to utilization devices. First, the loads are circuited. Then the circuits are lumped on the feeders. Finally, the distribution system is connected to one or more sources of power.

Branch Circuit, General Purpose:

Refer to Fig. 100-9.

Fuse or CB:
Rated—15, 20, 30,
40 or 50 amps

A number of
outlets for
lighting and/or
appliances

Circuit voltage shall not exceed 150 volts to ground
for circuits supplying lampholders, fixtures or receptacles
of standard 15-amp rating. For fluorescent, incandescent or
mercury lighting under certain conditions, voltage to
ground may be as high as 300 volts. In certain cases, voltage
for electric discharge lighting may be up to 600 volts ungrounded.

Fig. 100-9

Branch Circuit, Appliance:

Refer to Fig. 100-10.

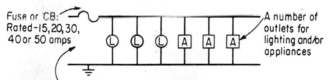

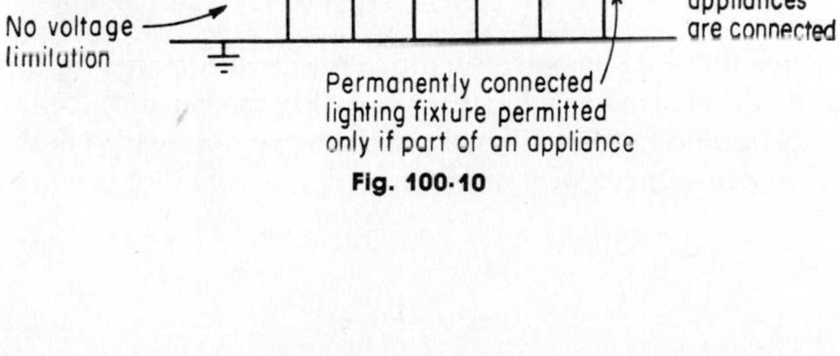

APPLIANCE BRANCH CIRCUIT (RECEPTACLE CIRCUITS)

Fuse or CB:
Rated—15, 20, 30,
40 or 50 amps

No voltage
limitation

Two or more
outlets to
which only
appliances
are connected

Permanently connected
lighting fixture permitted
only if part of an appliance

Fig. 100-10

Branch Circuit, Individual:

Refer to Fig. 100-11.

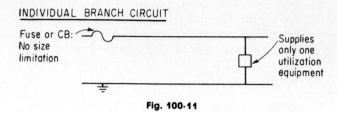

Fig. 100·11

Branch Circuit, Multiwire:

A multiwire branch circuit must be made up of a neutral conductor (grounded) and at least two ungrounded or "hot" conductors. The most common multiwire circuits are shown in Fig. 100-12.

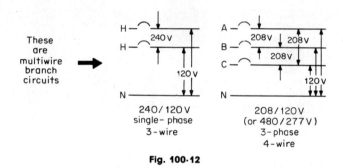

Fig. 100·12

A 3-wire, 3-phase circuit (without a neutral) is not a "multiwire branch circuit," even though it does consist of "multi" wires, as shown in Fig. 100-13.

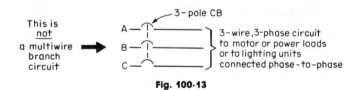

Fig. 100·13

Building:

Most areas have building codes to establish the requirements for buildings, and such codes should be used as a basis for deciding the use of the definition given in the **National Electrical Code.** The use of the term "fire walls" in this definition has resulted in differences of opinion among electrical inspectors and others.

Since the definition of a fire wall may differ in each jurisdiction, the processing of an interpretation of a "fire wall" has been studiously avoided in the **National Electrical Code** because this is a function of building codes and not a responsibility of the **National Electrical Code**.

Cabinet:

The door of a cabinet is hinged to a trim covering wiring space, or gutter. The door of a cutout box is hinged directly to the side of the box. Cabinets usually contain panelboards; cutout boxes contain cutouts, switches, or miscellaneous apparatus.

Concealed:

Any electrical equipment that is closed-in by structural surfaces is considered to be "concealed" as shown in Fig. 100-14.

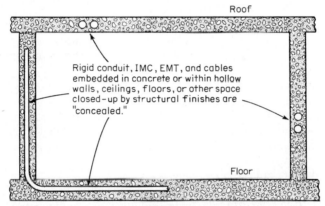

Roof

Rigid conduit, IMC, EMT, and cables embedded in concrete or within hollow walls, ceilings, floors, or other space closed-up by structural finishes are "concealed."

Floor

Fig. 100-14

Circuits run in an unfinished basement or an accessible attic are not "rendered inaccessible by the structure of finish of the building," and are therefore considered as exposed work rather than a concealed type of wiring.

Conduit Body:

An added sentence notes that FS and FD boxes—as well as larger cast or sheet metal boxes—are not considered to be "conduit bodies," as far as the **NE Code** is concerned. Although some manufacturers' literature refers to FS and FD boxes as conduit fittings, care must be used to distinguish between "conduit bodies" and "boxes" in specific **Code** rules. For instance, the last sentence of Sec. 370-6(c) prohibits splicing and use of devices in conduit bodies with less than three conduit hubs (although a provision is made for splicing in conduit bodies under certain conditions). However, FS and FD boxes are not conduit bodies and may contain splices and/or house devices. Table 370-6(a) lists FS and FD boxes as "boxes." See Fig. 100-15.

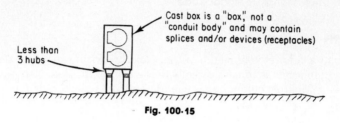

Cast box is a "box," not a "conduit body" and may contain splices and/or devices (receptacles)

Less than 3 hubs

Fig. 100-15

Continuous Load:

Any condition in which the maximum load current in a circuit flows without interruption for a period of not less than 3 hr.

Demand Factor:

Two terms constantly used in electrical design are "demand factor" and "diversity factor." Because there is a very fine difference between the meanings for the words, the terms are often confused.

Demand factor is the ratio of the maximum demand of a system, or part of a system, to the total connected load on the system, or part of the system, under consideration. This factor is always less than unity.

Diversity factor is the ratio of the sum of the individual maximum demands of the various subdivisions of a system, or part of a system, to the maximum demand of the whole system, or part of the system, under consideration. This factor generally varies between 1.00 and 2.00.

Demand factors and diversity factors are used in design. For instance, the sum of the connected loads supplied by a feeder is multiplied by the demand factor to determine the load which the feed must be sized to serve. This load is termed the maximum demand of the feeder. The sum of the maximum demand loads for a number of subfeeders divided by the diversity factor for the subfeeders will give the maximum demand load to be supplied by the feeder from which the subfeeders are derived.

It is common and preferred practice in modern design to take unity as the diversity factor in main feeders to loadcenter substations to provide a measure of spare capacity. Main secondary feeders are also commonly sized on the full value of the sum of the demand loads of the subfeeders supplied.

From power distribution practice, however, basic diversity factors have been developed. These provide general indication of the way in which main feeders can be reduced in capacity below the sum of the demands of the subfeeders they supply. On a radial feeder system, diversity of demands made by a number of transformers reduces the maximum load which the feeder must supply to some value less than the sum of the transformer loads. Typical application of demand and diversity factors for main feeders is shown in Fig. 100-16.

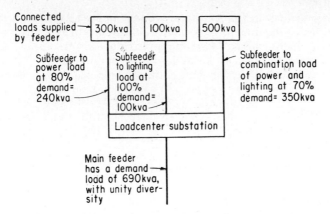

Connected loads supplied → by feeder

| 300kva | 100kva | 500kva |

Subfeeder to power load at 80% demand= 240kva

Subfeeder to lighting load at 100% demand= 100kva

Subfeeder to combination load of power and lighting at 70% demand= 350kva

Loadcenter substation

Main feeder has a demand → load of 690kva, with unity diversity

1. Sum of individual demands = 240 + 100 + 350 = 690 kva.

2. Sizing the substation at unity diversity, the required

$$kva = \frac{690}{1.00} = 690 \ kva.$$

3. To meet this load, use a 750-kva substation.

4. If analysis dictates the use of a diversity factor of 1.4 , the

$$required \ kva = \frac{690}{1.40} = 492 \ kva.$$

5. To meet this load, use a 500-kva substation.

6. Primary feeder to unit substation must have capacity to match the substation load.

Fig. 100-16

Device:

Switches, fuses, circuit breakers, controllers, receptacles, and lampholders are "devices."

Dwelling:

Dwelling unit. Because so many **Code** rules involve the words "dwelling" and "residential," there have been problems applying **Code** rules to the various types of "dwellings"—one-family houses, two-family houses, apartment houses, condominium units, dormitories, hotels, motels, etc. The present **NE Code** includes terminology to eliminate such problems and uses definitions of "dwelling" coordinated with the words used in specific **Code** rules.

A "dwelling unit" is now defined as "one or more rooms" used "as a house-keeping unit" and *must* contain space or areas specifically dedicated to "eating, living, and sleeping" and *must* have "permanent provisions for cooking and sanitation." A one-family house is a "dwelling unit." So is an apartment in an apartment house or a condominium unit. But, a guest room in a hotel or motel or a dormitory room or unit is not a "dwelling unit" if it does not contain "permanent provisions for cooking"—which must mean a built-in range or counter-mounted cooking unit (with or without an oven). However, the rule of Sec. 210-8, which requires GFCI (ground-fault circuit-interrupter) protection of receptacles in bathrooms of "dwelling units," does also require GFCI protection for bathroom receptacles in standard hotel or motel units.

Any "dwelling unit" must include all the required elements shown in Fig. 100-17.

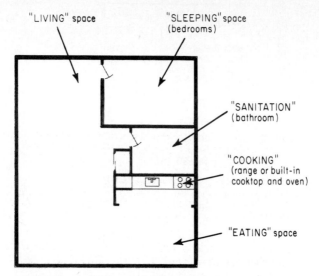

NOTE: Eating, living, and sleeping space could be one individual area, as in an efficiency apartment. But the unit must contain a "bathroom," defined in Section 210-8(a) as "an area including a basin with one or more of the following: a toilet, a tub, or a shower." And the unit must contain permanent cooking equipment.

Fig. 100·17

Exposed: "⟨As applied to wiring methods.⟩"

Wiring methods and equipment that are not permanently closed in by building surfaces or finishes are considered to be "exposed." See Fig. 100-18.

Feeder:

A "feeder" is a set of conductors which carry electric power from the service equipment (or from a transformer secondary, a battery bank, or a generator switchboard where power is generated on the premises) to the overcurrent protective devices for branch circuits supplying the various loads.

A feeder may originate at a main distribution center and feed one or more subdistribution centers, one or more branch-circuit distribution centers, one or

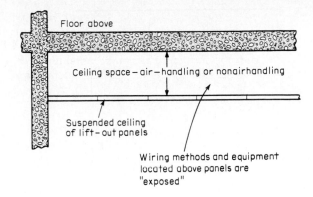

Floor above

Ceiling space – air – handling or nonairhandling

Suspended ceiling
of lift – out panels

Wiring methods and equipment
located above panels are
"exposed"

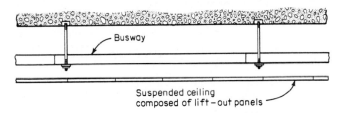

Busway

Suspended ceiling
composed of lift – out panels

BUSWAY above this suspended ceiling is considered
"exposed" as required by Section 364 – 4.

Fig. 100·18

more branch circuits (as in the case of plug-in busway or motor circuit taps to a feeder), or a combination of these. It may be a primary or secondary voltage circuit, but its function is always to deliver a block of power from one point to another point at which the power capacity is apportioned among a number of other circuits. In some systems, feeders may be carried from a main distribution switchboard to subdistribution switchboards or panelboards from which subfeeders originate to feed branch-circuit panels or motor branch circuits. In still other systems, either or both of the two foregoing feeder layouts may be incorporated with transformer substations to step the distribution voltage to utilization levels.

Grounded Conductor:

This is the conductor of an electrical system which is intentionally connected to a grounding electrode at the service of a premises, at a transformer secondary, or at a generator or other source of electric power. See Fig. 100-19. It is most commonly a neutral conductor of a system, but may be one of the phase legs—as in the case of a corner-grounded delta system.

　　Grounding one of the wires of the electrical system is done to limit the voltage upon the circuit which might otherwise occur through exposure to lightning

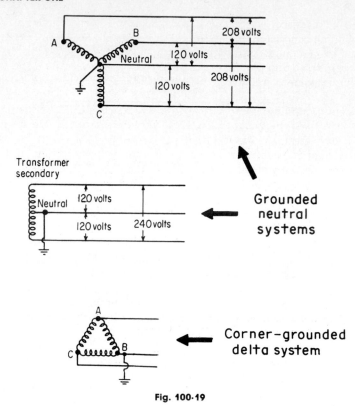

A
B
208 volts
Neutral   120 volts
208 volts
120 volts
C

Transformer
secondary

Neutral   120 volts
120 volts   240 volts

**Grounded
neutral
systems**

A
C   B

**Corner–grounded
delta system**

Fig. 100-19

or other voltages higher than that for which the circuit is designed. Another purpose in grounding one of the wires of the system is to limit the maximum voltage to ground under normal operating conditions. Also, a system which operates with one of its conductors intentionally grounded will provide for automatic opening of the circuit if an accidental or fault ground occurs on one of its ungrounded conductors.

Selection of the wiring system conductor to be grounded depends upon the type of system. In 3-wire, single-phase systems, the midpoint of the transformer winding—the point from which the system neutral is derived—is grounded. For grounded 3-phase wiring systems, the neutral point of the wye-connected transformer(s) or generator is usually the point connected to ground. In delta-connected transformer hookups, grounding of the system can be effected by grounding one of the three phase legs, by grounding a center-tap point on one of the transformer windings (as in the 3-phase, 4-wire "red-leg" delta system), or by using a special grounding transformer which establishes a neutral point of a wye connection which is grounded.

Grounding Conductor, Equipment:

The phrase "equipment grounding conductor" is used to describe any of the electrically conductive paths that tie together the noncurrent-carrying metal enclosures of electrical equipment in an electrical system. The term "equipment grounding conductor" includes bare or insulated conductors, metal raceways (rigid metal conduit, intermediate metal conduit, EMT), and metal cable jackets where the **Code** permits such metal raceways and cable enclosures to be used for equipment grounding—which is a basic **Code**-required concept as follows:

Equipment grounding is the grounding of all metal enclosures that contain electrical wires or equipment when an insulation failure in such enclosures might place a potential on the enclosures and constitute a shock or fire hazard. It is a permanent and continuous bonding together (i.e., connecting together) of all noncurrent-carrying metal enclosures and frames of electrical equipment— conduit, boxes, cabinets, housings of lighting fixtures and machines, frames of motors, etc.—and connection of this interconnected system of enclosures to the system grounding electrode. The interconnection of all metal enclosures must be made to provide a low-impedance path for fault-current flow along the enclosures in the event that one of the energized conductors within a metal enclosure should make contact with the enclosure and thereby energize it. This fault-current flow assures operation of overcurrent devices which will open a circuit in the event of a fault. By opening a faulted circuit, the system prevents dangerous voltages from being present on equipment enclosures which could be touched by personnel, with consequent electric shock to such personnel.

Simply stated, grounding of all metal enclosures of electric wires and equipment prevents any potential-above-ground on the enclosures. Such bonding together and grounding of all metal enclosures are required for both grounded electrical systems (those systems in which one of the circuit conductors is intentionally grounded) and ungrounded electrical systems (systems with none of the circuit wires intentionally grounded).

As shown in the sketch of Fig. 100-20, metal enclosures, metal raceways, and metal cable armors may serve as the "equipment grounding conductor." When nonmetallic raceways or cables are used, a bare or insulated conductor must be used within the raceway or cable to provide the interconnection of all metal enclosures. And the overall equipment grounding system must be connected to a grounding electrode at the service or power source (local transformer or a generator) and must also be connected at the service or source to the system-

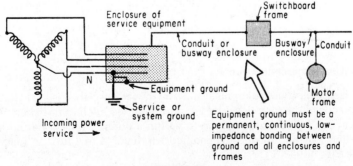

Fig. 100-20

grounded conductor (such as a grounded neutral) if a grounded conductor is used.

Effective equipment grounding depends upon sure connection of all equipment grounding conductors of adequate ampacity. Equipment grounding is extremely important for grounded electrical systems to provide the automatic fault clearing, which is one of the important advantages of grounded electrical systems. A low-impedance path for fault current is necessary to permit enough current to flow to operate the fuses or circuit breakers protecting the circuit.

In a grounded electrical system with a high-impedance equipment ground return path (equipment grounding conductor path), if one of the phase conductors of the system (i.e., one of the ungrounded conductors of the wiring system) should accidentally come in contact with one of the metal enclosures in which the wires are run, not enough fault current would flow to operate the overcurrent devices. In such a case, the faulted circuit would not automatically open, and a dangerous voltage would be present on the conduit and other metal enclosures.

Grounding Electrode Conductor:

The conductor that runs from the bonded neutral block or busbar in service equipment to the system grounding electrode is clearly and specifically identified as the "grounding electrode conductor." See Fig. 100-21. It is also the conductor used to ground the bonded neutral of a transformer secondary or a generator.

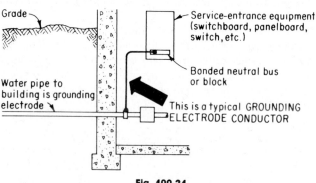

Fig. 100-21

Ground-Fault Circuit-Interrupter:

This revised definition makes clear that the device described is a GFCI (breaker or receptacle) of the type listed by UL and intended to eliminate shock hazards to people. Such devices must operate within a definite time from initiation of ground-fault current above the specified trip level (4 to 6 mA, as specified by UL). See Fig. 100-22.

Fig. 100-22

Ground-Fault Protection of Equipment:

Although any type of ground-fault protection is aimed at protecting personnel using an electrical system, the so-called ground fault protection required by NEC Sec. 230-95 for any 480Y/277-V grounded service disconnect rated 1000 A or more is identified in Sec. 230-95 as "ground-fault protection of equipment." The so-called ground-fault circuit interrupter (GFCI), as described in the previous definition and required by Sec. 210-8 for residential receptacles and by other NEC rules, is essentially a "people protector" and is identified in Sec. 210-8 as "ground-fault protection for personnel." Because there are Code rules addressing these distinct functions—people protection versus equipment protection—this definition distinguishes between the two types of protection.

Identified:

It is the intent of the Code that this single word "identified" be substituted for the phrase "approved for the purpose" *with no change in concept from its definition* as it was given in previous editions of the NE Code. It is intended that this term permit code-making panels to include reference to function, use, environment, or specific purpose in the text of Code rules, for example, "identified for use in wet locations," "identified as suitable for Class I, Div. 1 locations," "identified as weatherproof."

Another purpose of the change from "approved for the purpose" to "identified" was to eliminate the implication that the local inspector (the authority having jurisdiction for Code enforcement) is the sole judge of a product's acceptability as a consequence of the definition for "approved." The term "identified" is intended to make clear that manufacturers and testing laboratories have responsibility to assist the inspector by their own indications of suitability of products for their intended uses.

Although the definition of "identified" does not specifically require that products be marked to designate specific application suitability, there is that suggestion; and such marking on a product, its label, or the box or wrapping in which the product is supplied would best comply with the definition of "identified."

In Sight From:

The phrase "in sight from" or "within sight from" or "within sight" means visible and not more than 50 ft away. These phrases are used in many **Code** rules to establish installation location of one piece of equipment with respect to another. A typical example is the rule requiring that a motor-circuit disconnect means must be *in sight from* the controller for the motor [Sec. 430-102(a)]. This definition in Art. 100 gives a single meaning to the idea expressed by the phrases—not only that any piece of equipment that must be "in sight from" another piece of equipment must be visible, but also that the distance between the two pieces of equipment must not be over 50 ft. If, for example, a motor disconnect is 51 ft away from the motor controller of the same circuit, it is *not* "within sight from" the controller even though it is actually and readily visible from the controller. In the interests of safety, it is arbitrarily defined that separation of more that 50 ft diminishes visibility to an unacceptable level.

Interrupting Rating:

This definition covers both "interrupting ratings" for overcurrent devices (fuses and circuit breakers) and "interrupting ratings" for control devices (switches, relays, contactors, motor starters, etc.).

Labeled:

The label of a nationally recognized testing laboratory on a piece of electrical equipment is a sure and ready way to be assured that the equipment is properly made and will function safely when used in accordance with the application data and limitations established by the testing organization. Each label used on an electrical product gives the exact name of the type of equipment as it appears in the listing book of the testing organization.

Typical labels are shown in Fig. 100-23(a).

Underwriters Laboratories Inc., the largest nationally recognized testing laboratory covering the electrical field, describes its "Identification of Listed Products" as shown in Fig. 100-23(b).

It should be noted that the definitions for "labeled" and "listed" do not require that the testing laboratory be "nationally recognized." The definitions acknowledge that a local inspector may accept the label or listing of a product by a testing organization that is qualified and capable even though it operates in a small area or section of the country and is not "nationally recognized."

Fig. 100-23(a).

The Listing Mark may appear in various forms as authorized by Underwriters Laboratories Inc. Typical forms which may be authorized are shown below:

Listing Marks include one of the forms illustrated above, the word "Listed", and a control number assigned by UL. The product name as indicated in this Directory under each of the product categories is generally included as part of the Listing Mark text, but may be omitted when in UL's opinion, the use of the name is superfluous and the Listing Mark is directly and permanently applied to the product by stamping, molding, ink-stamping, silk screening or similar processes.

Separable Listing Marks (not part of a name plate and in the form of decals, stickers or labels) will always include the four elements: UL's name and/or symbol, the word "Listed", the product or category name, and a control number.

Fig. 100-23(b).

Listed:

As a result of broader, more intensive and vigorous enforcement of third-party certification of electrical system equipment and components, OSHA and the **NE Code** have made it necessary that all electrical construction people be fully aware of and informed about testing laboratories. The following organizations are widely known and recognized by governmental agencies for their independent product testing and certification activities. Each should be contacted directly for full information on available product listings and other data on standards and testing.

Underwriters Laboratories Inc.
333 Pfingsten Rd.
Northbrook, Ill. 60062

Other UL offices and testing stations:

1285 Walt Whitman Rd.
Melville, N.Y. 11746

1655 Scott Blvd.
Santa Clara, Calif. 95050

12 Laboratory Dr.
Research Triangle Park, NC 27709

Factory Mutual Engineering Corp.
1151 Boston-Providence Turnpike
Norwood, Mass. 02062

Electrical Testing Laboratories, Inc.
2 East End Ave.
New York, N.Y. 10021

United States Testing Co., Inc. (UST)
1415 Park Avenue
Hoboken, N.J. 07030

Canadian Standards Association (CSA)
178 Rexdale Blvd.
Rexdale, Ontario, Canada

Note: Although the OSHA law specifically mentions Underwriters Labs and Factory Mutual as "nationally recognized" independent testing laboratories, OSHA recognition is "not limited to" (the actual expression used in the law) the two testing organizations named as typical.

Publications of nationally recognized testing laboratories may be obtained by writing to the various test labs at the above addresses.

Plenum:

This definition is intended to clarify use of this word, which is referred to in Sec. 300-22(b) and other sections. A "plenum" is a compartment or chamber to which one or more air ducts are connected and which forms part of an air distribution system. This definition replaces the fine print note that was in Sec. 300-22(b) of the 1987 **NEC**. As now noted in the text of Sec. 300-22(b), a plenum is an enclosure "specifically fabricated to transport environmental air." The definition further clarifies that an air-handling space above a suspended ceiling or under a raised floor (such as in a computer room) is not a plenum, but is "other spaces" used for environmental air, as covered by Sec. 300-22(c).

Premises Wiring (System):

Published discussions of the **Code** panel's meaning of this phrase make clear the panel's intent that premises wiring includes all electrical wiring and equipment on the load side of the service drop or lateral, including any electrical work fed from a "separately derived system"—such as a transformer, generator, computer power distribution center, an uninterruptible power supply (UPS), or a battery bank. Premises wiring includes all electrical work installed on a premises. Specifically, it includes all circuits and equipment fed by the service or fed by a separately derived electrical source (transformer, generator, etc.). This makes clear that all circuiting on the load side of a so-called computer power center or computer distribution center [enclosed assembly of an isolating transformer and panelboard(s)] must satisfy all **NEC** rules on hookup and *grounding*. When a "computer power center" is supplied with factory-wired branch-circuit "whips" (lengths of flexible metal conduit or liquidtight flex—with installed conductors), the use of equipment grounding conductors and grounding connections at the power center and at receptacles fed by the circuits must satisfy all rules of Art. 250 (especially Sec. 250-26) on grounding, as well as the rules of Art. 645, Electronic Computer/Data Processing Systems.

Raceway:

Whenever this term is used in the **Code**, it must be understood that the meaning includes all the many enclosures used for running conductors between cabinets and housings of electrical distribution components—like panels, switches, motor starters, etc.—and housings of utilization equipment—like lighting fixtures, motors, heaters, etc. Any raceway must be an "enclosed" channel for conductors. Cable tray is a "support system" and not a "raceway." When the **Code** refers to "conduit," it means only those raceways containing the word "conduit" in their title. But "EMT" is not conduit. Table 1 of Chap. 9 in the back of the **Code** book refers to "Conduit and Tubing." The **Code**, thus, distinguishes between the two. "EMT" is tubing.

Receptacle:

Each place where a plug cap may be inserted is a "receptacle," as shown in Fig. 100-24.

Only a single receptacle can be served by an individual branch circuit. See Secs. 210-21(b) and 555-4.

Each box is one receptacle outlet

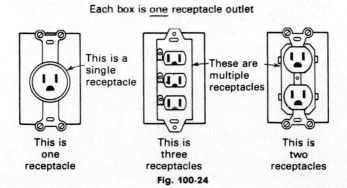

This is a single receptacle

These are multiple receptacles

This is one receptacle

This is three receptacles

This is two receptacles

Fig. 100-24

Receptacle Outlet:

The "outlet" is the outlet box. But this definition must be carefully related to Sec. 220-3(c)(5) for calculating receptacle loads in other than dwelling occupancies. For purposes of calculating load, Sec. 220-3(c)(5) states that "For receptacle outlets, each single or multiple receptacle" must be taken as a load of 180 VA. Because a single, duplex, or triplex receptacle is a device on a single mounting strap, the rule requires that 180 VA must be counted for each strap, whether it supports one, two, or three receptacles.

Remote-Control Circuit:

The circuit that supplies energy to the operating coil of a relay, a magnetic contactor, or a magnetic motor starter is a "remote-control circuit" because that circuit controls the circuit that feeds through the contacts of the relay, contactor, or starter as shown in Fig. 100-25.

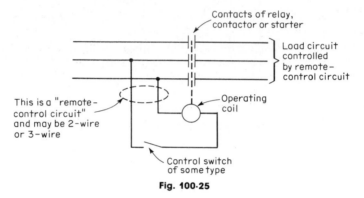

Fig. 100-25

A control circuit as shown is any circuit which has as its load device the operating coil of a magnetic motor starter, a magnetic contactor, or a relay. Strictly speaking, it is a circuit which exercises control over one or more other circuits. And these other circuits controlled by the control circuit may themselves be control circuits, or they may be "load" circuits—carrying utilization current to a lighting, heating, power, or signal device. The sketch clarifies the distinction between control circuits and load circuits.

The elements of a control circuit include all the equipment and devices concerned with the function of the circuit: conductors, raceway, contactor operating coil, source of energy supply to the circuit, overcurrent protective devices, and all switching devices which govern energization of the operating coil.

The NE Code covers application of remote-control circuits in Art. 725 and in Secs. 430-71 through 430-74.

Service:

The word "service" includes *all* the materials and equipment involved with the transfer of electric power from the utility distribution line to the electrical wiring system of the premises being supplied. Although service layouts vary widely, depending upon the voltage and amp rating, the type of premises being served, and the type of equipment selected to do the job, every service generally consists of "service-drop" conductors (for overhead service from a utility pole line) or "service-lateral" conductors (for an underground service from either an overhead or underground utility system)—plus metering equipment, some type of switch or circuit-breaker control, overcurrent protection, and related enclosures and hardware. A typical layout of "service" for a one-family house breaks down as in Fig. 100-26.

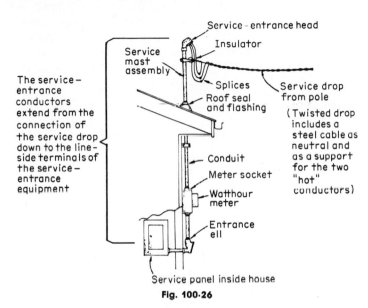

Fig. 100-26

That part of the electrical system which directly connects to the utility-supply line is referred to as the "service entrance." Depending upon the type of utility line serving the house, there are two basic types of service entrances—an overhead and an underground service.

The **overhead service** has been the most commonly used type of service. In a typical example of this type, the utility supply line is run on wood poles along the street property line or back-lot line of the building, and a cable connection is made high overhead from the utility line to a bracket installed somewhere high up on the building. This wood pole line also carries the telephone lines, and the poles are generally called "telephone poles."

The aerial cable that runs from the overhead utility lines to the bracket on the outside wall of the building is called the "service drop." This cable is installed by the utility-line worker. At the bracket which terminates the service drop, conductors are then spliced to the drop cable conductors to carry power down to the electric meter and into the building.

The **underground service** is one in which the conductors that run from the utility line to the building are carried underground. Such an underground run to a building may be tapped from either an overhead utility pole line or an underground utility distribution system. Although underground utility services tapped from a pole line at the property line have been used for many years to eliminate the unsightliness of overhead wires coming to a building, the use of underground service tapped from an underground utility system has only started to gain widespread usage in residential areas over recent years. This latter technique is called "URD"—which stands for Underground Residential Distribution.

As noted above, when a building is supplied by an overhead drop, an installation of conductors must be made on the outside of the building to pick up power from the drop conductors and carry it into the meter enclosure and service-entrance equipment (switch, CB, panelboard, or switchboard) for the building. On underground services, the supply conductors are also brought into the meter enclosure on the building and then are run into the service equipment installed, usually, within the building.

Service Conductors:

This is a general term that covers all the conductors used to connect the utility-supply circuit or transformer to the service equipment of the premises served. This term includes "service-drop" conductors, "service-lateral" (underground service) conductors, and "service-entrance" conductors. In an overhead distribution system, the service conductors begin at the line pole where connection is made. If a primary line is extended to transformers installed outdoors on private property, the service conductors to the building proper begin at the secondary terminals of the transformers. See Sec. 230-200 and Sec. 230-201.

Where the supply is from an underground distribution system, the service conductors begin at the point of connection to the underground street mains.

In every case the service conductors terminate at the service equipment.

Service Drop:

As the name implies, these are the conductors that "drop" from the overhead utility line and connect to the service-entrance conductors at their upper end on the building or structure supplied. See Fig. 100-27.

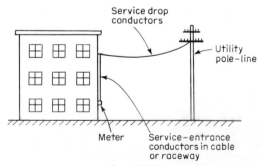

Fig. 100-27

Service Lateral:

This is the name given to a set of underground service conductors. A service lateral serves a function similar to that of a service drop as shown in Fig. 100-28.

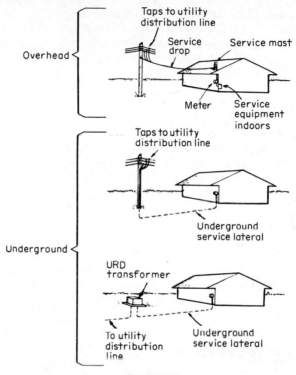

Fig. 100-28

Solar Photovoltaic System:

This refers to the equipment involved in a particular application of the developing technology of solar energy conversion to electric power. This definition correlates to NEC Art. 690 covering design and installation of electrical systems for direct conversion of the sun's light into electric power.

Special Permission:

It *must* be carefully noted that any **Code** reference to "special permission" as a basis for accepting any electrical design or installation technique requires that such "permission" be in *written form*. Whenever the inspection authority gives "special permission" for an electrical condition that is at variance with **Code** rules or not covered fully by the rules, the authorization must be "written" and not simply verbal permission.

Switches:

Bypass isolation switch This is "a manually operated device" for bypassing the load current around a transfer switch to permit isolating the transfer switch for maintenance or repair without shutting down the system. The second paragraph of Sec. 700-6 permits that "means" be provided to bypass and isolate transfer equipment. This definition ties into that rule.

Transfer switch This is a switch for transferring load-conductor connections from one power source to another. And a note indicates that such a switch may be automatic or nonautomatic—but is subject to the applicable rules of Article 230 (Sec. 230-83), 517, 700, 701, and 702.

Voltage to Ground:

For a grounded electrical system, voltage to ground is the voltage that exists from any ungrounded circuit conductor to either the grounded circuit conductor (if one is used) or the grounded metal enclosures (conduit, boxes, panelboard cabinets, etc.) or other grounded metal, such as building steel. Examples are given in Fig. 100-29.

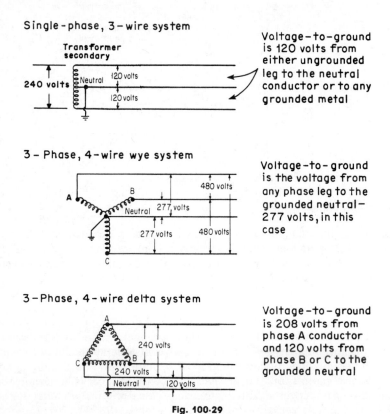

Single-phase, 3-wire system

Transformer secondary

240 volts

Neutral 120 volts

120 volts

Voltage-to-ground is 120 volts from either ungrounded leg to the neutral conductor or to any grounded metal

3 - Phase, 4-wire wye system

A

B

Neutral 277 volts

277 volts

480 volts

480 volts

C

Voltage-to-ground is the voltage from any phase leg to the grounded neutral— 277 volts, in this case

3 - Phase, 4-wire delta system

A

240 volts

C

B

240 volts

Neutral 120 volts

Voltage-to-ground is 208 volts from phase A conductor and 120 volts from phase B or C to the grounded neutral

Fig. 100-29

For an ungrounded electrical system, voltage to ground is *taken to be* equal to the maximum voltage that exists between any two conductors of the system. This is based on the reality that an accidental ground fault on one of the ungrounded conductors of the system places the other system conductors at a voltage aboveground that is equal to the value of the voltage between conductors. Under such a ground-fault condition, the voltage to ground is the phase-to-phase voltage between the accidentally grounded conductor and any other phase leg of the system. On, say, a 480-V, 3-phase, 3-wire ungrounded delta system, voltage to ground is, therefore, 480 V, as shown in Fig. 100-30.

Ungrounded delta system at 480 volts

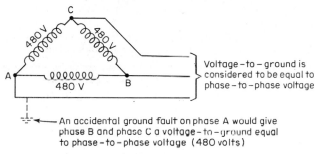

Voltage – to – ground is considered to be equal to phase – to – phase voltage

An accidental ground fault on phase A would give phase B and phase C a voltage – to – ground equal to phase – to – phase voltage (480 volts)

Fig. 100-30

In many **Code** rules, it is critically necessary to distinguish between references to "voltage" and to "voltage to ground." The **Code** also refers to "voltage between conductors," as in Sec. 210-6, to make very clear how rules must be observed.

ARTICLE 110. REQUIREMENTS FOR ELECTRICAL INSTALLATIONS

110-1. Mandatory Rules and Explanatory Material. Although the **NE Code** consists essentially of specific regulations on details of electrical design and installation, there is much explanatory material in the form of notes to rules. Compliance with the **Code** consists in satisfying all requirements and conditions that are stated by use of the word "shall." That word, anywhere in the **Code**, designates a mandatory rule. Failure to comply with any mandatory **Code** rule constitutes a "**Code** violation."

110-2. Approval. This section of the **NE Code** regulates the use of electrical products and equipment. The intent of the **NEC** is to place strong insistence on third-party certification of the essential safety of the equipment and component products used to assemble an electrical installation.

The use of custom-made equipment is also covered in OSHA rules. Every manufacturer of custom equipment must provide documentary safety-test data to the owner on whose work premises the custom equipment is installed. And it seems to be a reasonable conclusion from the whole rule itself that custom-equipment assemblies must make maximum use of "listed," "labeled," or "certified" components.

The word "approved," as used in this rule, must be taken to have the meaning given in the **NE Code** definition for that word. "Approved" is "acceptable to the authority having jurisdiction." The electrical inspector having jurisdiction on any specific installation is the final judge of what conductors and/or equipment are "approved." Although inspectors are not *required* to use "listing" or "labeling" by a national testing lab as the deciding factor in their approval of products, they invariably base their acceptance of products on listings by testing labs. The note in this section almost makes the same insistence as OSHA does that, whenever possible, acceptability must be based on some kind of listing or certification of a national lab.

110-3. Examination, Identification, Installation, and Use of Equipment.   This section presents general rules on "Examination, Identification, Installation, and Use of Equipment." Part **(a)** lists eight factors that must be evaluated in determining acceptability of equipment for **Code**-recognized use.

Section 110-3(a)(1) notes that, in addition to "listing" or "labeling" of a product by UL or another test lab to certify the conditions of its use, acceptability *may* be "identified by a description *marked on* or *provided with* a product to identify the suitability of the product for a specific purpose, environment, or application." This is a follow-through on the definition of the word "identified," as given in Art. 100. The requirement for identification of a product as specifically suited to a given use is repeated at many points throughout the **Code**.

Item **(3)**, an important consideration for electrical inspectors to include in their examination to determine suitability of equipment for safe and effective use, is "wire-bending and connection space." See Fig. 110-1. This factor is included because of increasing concern over inadequate gutter space at conductor terminal locations in enclosures for switches, CBs, and other control and protection equipment. This general mention of the need for sufficient conductor bending space is aimed at avoiding poor terminations and conductor damage that can result from excessively sharp conductor bends required by tight gutter spaces at terminals. Specific rules that cover this consideration are given in Sec. 373-6 on "Deflection of Conductors" at terminals or where entering or leaving cabinets or cutout boxes—covering gutter widths and wire-bending spaces.

Part **(b)** of this section is a critically important **Code** rule because it incorporates, as part of the **NE Code** itself, all the application regulations and limitations published by product-testing organizations, such as UL, Factory-Mutual, ETL, etc. That rule clearly and certainly says, for instance, that any and every product listed in the UL *Electrical Construction Materials Directory* (Green Book) must be used exactly as described in the application data given with the listing in the book. Because the *Electrical Construction Materials Directory* and the other UL books of product listings, such as the *Hazardous Location Equipment Directory* (Red Book) and the *Electrical Appliance and Utilization Equipment Directory* (Orange Book), contain massive amounts of installation and application instruction, all those specific bits of application data become mandatory **NE Code** regulations as a result of the rule in Sec. 110-

Fig. 110-1. Equipment must be evaluated for adequate gutter space to assure safe and effective bending of conductors at terminals. [Sec. 110-3(a)(3).]

3(b). The data given in the UL listing books supplement and expand upon rules given in the **NE Code**. In fact, effective compliance with **NE Code** regulations can be assured only by careful study and observance of the limitations and conditions spelled out in the application instructions given in the UL listings books or similar instructions provided by other national testing labs.

In the preface to its *Electrical Construction Materials Directory* (the Green Book), UL points out certain basic conditions that apply to products listed.

1. In general, equipment listed is intended for use in ordinary locations, which may be dry, damp, or wet locations, as defined in the **NE Code**. All limitations on use specified in the **NE Code** and in the general information preceding the section on listing in the Green Book must be carefully observed. Equipment and products for use in hazardous locations are covered in the UL Red Book, *Hazardous Location Equipment Directory*.

2. Listed equipment has been investigated only for use indoors in dry locations, unless outdoor use is specifically permitted by **NE Code** rules, is indicated in the UL listing information, or is obvious from the designation of the equipment in the listing (such as "Swimming Pool Fixtures").

3. The amperage or wattage marking on power-consuming equipment is valid only when the equipment is supplied at its marked rated voltage. In general, current input to resistive loads increases in direct proportion to input voltage increase. Current input to an induction motor with a fixed load increases in direct proportion to decrease in input voltage.

4. All permanently connected equipment and appliances provided with terminals are intended for use with *copper* supply conductors. Terminals that are suitable for *either* copper or aluminum conductors are marked to indicate that. Such marking must be independent of any marking on terminal connectors and must be on a wiring diagram or other readily visible location. Permanently connected equipment and appliances with pigtail leads are intended for use with copper supply conductors. But aluminum supply wires may be used if they are spliced to the pigtails by splicing devices that are suitable for joining copper to aluminum.

5. A very important qualification is indicated for the temperature ratings of terminations. Although application data on minimum required temperature ratings of conductors connected to equipment terminals are not given in the **NE Code**, it nevertheless becomes part of the mandatory regulations of the **Code** because of Sec. 110-3(b).

A basic general rule in the preface of the listing of "Equipment for Use in Ordinary Locations" in the UL *Electrical Construction Materials Directory* states that, for distribution and control equipment,

Except as noted in the following paragraphs or in the information at the beginning of some product categories, the termination provisions are based on the use of 60°C ampacities for wire sizes No. 14-1 AWG and 75°C ampacities for wire sizes Nos. 1/0 AWG and larger, as specified in Table 310-16 of the **National Electrical Code.**

Some distribution and control equipment is marked to indicate the required temperature rating of each field-installed conductor. If the equipment, normally intended for connection by wire sizes within the range 14-1 AWG, is marked "75°C only" or "60/75°C", it is intended that 75°C insulated wire may be used at full 75°C ampacity. Where the connection is made to a circuit breaker or switch within the equipment, such a circuit breaker or switch must also be marked for the temperature rating of the conductor.

A 75°C conductor temperature marking on a circuit breaker or switch normally intended for wire sizes 14-1 AWG does not in itself indicate that 75°C insulated wire can be used unless (1) the circuit breaker or switch is used by itself, such as in a separate enclosure or (2) the equipment in which the circuit breaker or switch is installed is also so marked.

"A 75 or 90°C conductor temperature marking on a terminal (e.g., AL7, CU7AL, AL7CU, or AL9, CU9AL, AL9CU) does not in itself indicate that 75 or 90°C insulated wire can be used unless the equipment in which the terminals are installed is marked for 75 or 90°C."

Higher temperature rated conductors than specified may be used if the size is based on the above statements.

Application of these data to various types of equipment is repeated in many sections of the *Electrical Construction Materials Directory*. And, as the UL wording says, this temperature limitation on terminals applies to the terminals on all equipment—circuit breakers, switches, motor starters, contactors, etc.—except where some other specific condition is recognized in the general information preceding the product category. This is a vitally important matter, which has been widely disregarded in general practice.

When terminals are tested for suitability at 60 or 75°C, the use of 90°C conductors operating at their higher current ratings poses definite threat of damage to terminals on switches, breakers, etc. Many termination failures experienced in electrical equipment suggest overheating even where the load current did not exceed the current rating of the breaker or switch or other equipment.

When a 60°C-rated terminal is fed by a conductor operating at 90°C, there will be substantial heat conducted from the 90°C conductor metal to the 60°C-rated terminal; and, over a period of time, that can damage the termination—even though the load current does not exceed the equipment current rating and does not exceed the ampacity of the 90°C conductor. Whenever two metallic parts at different operating temperatures are tightly connected, the higher-temperature part (say, the 75 or 90°C wire) will give heat to the lower-temperature part (the 60°C terminal) and thereby raise its temperature over 60°C.

The basic UL limitation on termination temperature rating for all distribution and control equipment is shown in Fig. 110-2.

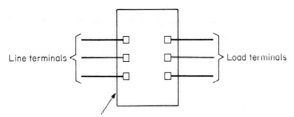

Panelboard, switch, transformer, motor starter, etc.

UNLESS A PIECE OF ELECTRICAL EQUIPMENT IS MARKED OTHERWISE, circuit conductors connected to the terminals must not operate at more than 60°C ampacity for conductor sizes No.14 up to No.1 and must not operate at more than a 75°C ampacity for conductor sizes No.1/O and larger (refer to *NEC* Tables 310-16 through -19).

FOR SWITCHES, CONTACTORS, ETC. WIRED WITH No. 14-1 AWG: Use TW wire (or use THW, THHN, RHH, XHHW, or other higher-temperature wire at the ampacity of the corresponding size of TW wire).

FOR SWITCHES, CONTACTORS, ETC. WIRED WITH No.1/O AWG OR LARGER: Use TW, THW, THWN or XHHW wire at their ampacities permitted up to 75°C (or use RHH, THHN, or other higher-temperature wire at the ampacity of the corresponding size of 75°C wire).

Fig. 110-2. [Sec. 110-3(b), Example.]

The same UL Directory contains the following regulations on circuit-breaker terminals:

Circuit breakers and circuit-breaker enclosures as listed herein are for use with copper conductors unless marked to indicate which terminals are suitable for use with aluminum conductors. Such markings shall be independent of any marking on terminal connectors and shall be on a wiring diagram or other readily visible location.

1. Circuit-breaker enclosures are marked to indicate the temperature rating of all field-installed conductors.

2. Circuit breakers of continuous current rating of 125 A or less are marked as being suitable for 60°C only, 75°C only, or 60/75°C wire.

3. Circuit breakers rated 125A or less and marked suitable for use with 75°C-rated wire are intended for field use with 75°C wire at full 75°C ampacity only when the circuit breaker is installed in a circuit-breaker enclosure or individually mounted in an industrial control panel with no other component next to it, unless the end-use equipment (panelboard, switchboard, service equipment, power outlet, etc.) is also marked suitable for use with 75°C wire.

4. A circuit breaker of continuous current rating of more than 125 A is suitable for use with 75°C wire.

A suitable marking is required in a circuit-breaker enclosure, whether or not terminals are mounted therein, if it is intended that the breaker to be mounted therein is to be used with aluminum wire. All equipment manufactured after October 1, 1986, will be marked to show a tightening torque for all wire connectors intended for use with field wiring.

Note: That last sentence will make it mandatory to use a torque wrench or screwdriver when tightening terminals on circuit breakers. And Sec. 110-3(b) makes such torquing a mandatory **NEC** rule.

For any given size of conductor, the greater ampacity of a higher-temperature conductor is established by the ability of the conductor insulation to withstand the I^2R heat produced by the higher current flowing through the conductor. But it must not be assumed that the equipment to which that conductor is connected is also capable of withstanding the heat that will be thermally conducted from the metal of the conductor into the metal of the terminal to which the conductor is tightly connected.

Although this limitation on the operating temperature of terminals in equipment does reduce the advantage that higher-temperature conductors have over lower-temperature conductors, there are still many advantages to using the higher-temperature conductors because of their reduced cross-section areas that permit more economical raceway fills—either smaller conduit for a given number of conductors or more conductors in a given size of conduit. However, where higher-temperature conductors are used, they must be applied at the ampacities of corresponding sizes of 60 or 75°C conductors—as required.

In conductor sizes No. 14, No. 12, and No. 10, with their 15-, 20-, and 30-A load ratings, as set by the footnote to **NE Code** Table 310-16, there is no difference in load rating between the same size conductors of different temperature rating. A No. 12 TW copper conductor, for instance, has a 20-A basic rating; and a No. 12 THW (75°C), a No. 12 RHH (90°C), a No. 12 XHHW (75°C in wet or dry locations or 90°C in dry locations only), and a No. 12 THHN (90°C) are all rated at a basic loading value of 20 A. Even though the different types of conductors in sizes No. 14, No. 12, and No. 10 have the same load-current ratings, there is still an advantage in using the thin-wall-insulated, higher-temperature wires because they permit greater conduit fill.

In those conductor sizes where there are differences in ampacity between conductors of different temperature ratings (conductors No. 8 and larger), careful consideration must be given to a number of factors involved in selection of the correct and most effective conductor for any specific circuit application. Attention must certainly be paid to the above-described temperature limitation at equipment terminals. Selection of circuit conductors must also be based on load limitation required by **NE Code** Secs. 210-22(c), 220-3(a), and 220-10(b) for "continuous load"—that is, any case "where the maximum current is expected to continue for three hours or more," such as branch circuits and feeders for commercial and industrial lighting or similar loads that are left on all day or for periods over 3 hr. And the greater conduit fill of thin-wall-insulated, high-temperature conductors (offering use of smaller conduits) must also be factored into conductor selection, along with the impact of conductor load-current derating due to conduit fills over three current-carrying conductors. All these considerations are interrelated, and the most effective and most economical circuit makeup for any case can be determined only by thorough study and careful calculation. For typical details of this kind of analysis to relate all the applicable NE Code and UL rules, see Sec. 310-15 on ampacity of conductors.

110-4. Voltages.   In all electrical systems there is a normal, predictable spread of voltage values over the impedances of the system equipment. It has been common practice to assign these basic levels to each nominal system voltage. The highest value of voltage is that at the service entrance or transformer secondary, such as 480Y/277 V. Then considering voltage drop due to impedance in the circuit conductors and equipment, a "nominal" midsystem voltage designation would be 460Y/265, and finally a "load" or "outlet" voltage is given as 440Y/254. Variations in "nominal" voltages have come about because of (1) differences in utility-supply voltages throughout the country, (2) varying transformer secondary voltages produced by different and often uncontrolled voltage drops in primary feeders, and (3) preferences of different engineers and other design authorities.

110-6. Conductor Sizes.   In this country, the American Wire Gage (AWG) is the standard for copper wire and for aluminum wire used for electrical conductors. The American Wire Gage is the same as the Brown & Sharpe (B & S) gage. The largest gage size is No. 0000; above this size the sizes of wires and cables are stated in circular mils.

The circular mil is a unit used for measuring the cross-sectional area of the conductor, or the area of the end of a wire which has been cut square across. One circular mil (commonly abbreviated CM or cmil) is the area of a circle $\frac{1}{1,000}$ in. in diameter. The area of a circle 1 in. in diameter is 1,000,000 CM; also, the area of a circle of this size is 0.7854 sq in.

To convert square inches to circular mils, multiply the square inches by 1,273,200.

To convert circular mils to square inches, divide the circular mils by 1,273,200 or multiply the circular mils by 0.7854 and divide by 1,000,000.

In interior wiring the gage sizes 14, 12, and 10 are usually solid wire; No. 8 and larger conductors in raceways are required to be stranded. (See Sec. 310-3.)

A cable (if not larger than 1,000,000 CM) will have one of the following numbers of strands: 7, 19, 37, or 61. In order to make a cable of any standard size, in nearly every case the individual strands cannot be any regular gage number but must be some special odd size. For example, a No. 00 cable must have a total cross-sectional area of 133,100 CM and is usually made up of 19 strands. No. 12 has an area of 6,530 CM and No. 11, an area of 8,234 CM; therefore each strand must be a special size between Nos. 12 and 11.

110·7. Insulation Integrity. Previous editions of the **Code** contained *recom-mended* values for testing insulation resistance. It was found that those values were incomplete and not sufficiently accurate for use in modern installations, and the recommendation was deleted from the **Code**. However, basic knowl-edge of insulation-resistance testing is important.

Measurements of insulation resistance can best be made with a megohm-meter insulation tester. As measured with such an instrument, insulation resist-ance is the resistance to the flow of direct current (usually at 500 or 1,000 V for systems of 600 V or less) through or over the surface of the insulation in elec-trical equipment. The results are in ohms or megohms, but insulation readings will be in the megohm range.

110·8. Wiring Methods. All **Code**-recognized wiring methods are covered in Chap. 3 of the **NE Code**—Arts. 300 through 384.

110·9. Interrupting Rating. **Interrupting rating** of electrical equipment is divided into two categories: current at fault levels and current at operating levels.

Equipment intended to clear fault currents must have interrupting rating equal to the maximum fault current that the circuit is capable of delivering at the line (not the load) terminals of the equipment. See Fig. 110-3. The internal

All short-circuit protective devices. . .

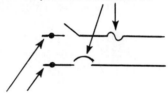

. . . . must have an interrupting rating at least equal to the maximum fault current that the circuit could deliver into a short circuit on the *line side* of the device.

NOTE: That means that the fault current "available" at the line terminals of all fuses and circuit breakers *must be known* in order to assure that the device has a rating sufficient for the level of fault current.

Fig. 110·3. (Sec. 110-9.)

impedance of the equipment itself may not be factored in to use the equipment at a point where the available fault current on its line side is greater than the rated, marked interrupting capacity of the equipment.

If overcurrent devices with a specific IC (interrupting capacity) rating are inserted at a point on a wiring system where the available short-circuit current exceeds the IC rating of the device, a resultant downstream solid short circuit between conductors or between one ungrounded conductor and ground (in grounded systems) could cause serious damage to life and property.

Since each electrical installation is different, the selection of overcurrent devices with proper IC ratings is not always a simple task. To begin with, the amount of available short-circuit current at the service equipment must be known. Such short-circuit current depends upon the capacity rating of the utility primary supply to the building, transformer impedances, and service conductor impedances. Most utilities will provide this information.

Downstream from the service equipment IC ratings of overcurrent devices may be reduced to lower than those at the service, depending on lengths and sizes of feeders, line impedances, and other factors. However, large motors and capacitors, while in operation, will feed additional current into a fault, and this must be considered when calculating short-circuit currents.

Manufacturers of overcurrent devices have excellent literature on figuring short-circuit currents, including graphs, charts, and one-line-diagram layout sheets to simplify the selection of proper overcurrent devices.

Equipment intended only for control of load or operating currents, such as contactors and unfused switches, must be rated for the current to be interrupted, but does not have to be rated for interrupting available fault level, as shown in Fig. 110-4.

All switches, contactors, starters, relays. . .

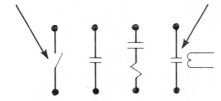

. . . must have an interrupting rating at least equal to "the current that must be interrupted"—which could be full-load current or, in the case of isolating or disconnect switches, some lesser value of operating current (such as transformer magnetizing current).

Fig. 110-4. (Sec. 110-9.)

110-10. Circuit Impedance and Other Characteristics. This section requires that all equipment be rated to withstand the level of fault current that is let through by the circuit protective device in the time it takes to operate—without "extensive damage" to any of the electrical components of the circuit as illustrated in Fig. 110-5.

The phrase "the component short-circuit withstand ratings" has been added to this rule. The intent of this addition is to require all circuit components that are subjected to ground faults or short-circuit faults to be capable of withstanding the thermal and magnetic stresses produced within them from the time a fault occurs until the circuit protective device (fuse or CB) opens to clear the fault, without extensive damage to the components.

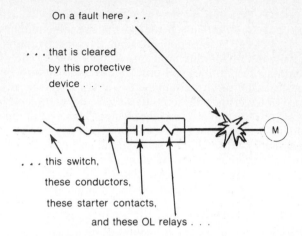

On a fault here ‚ ‚ ‚

‚ ‚ ‚ that is cleared
by this protective
device . . .

. . . this switch,

these conductors,

these starter contacts,

and these OL relays . . .

. ‚ . must all be rated to safely withstand the energy of the fault let-through current

Fig. 110·5. (Sec. 110-10.)

"Identified"—This kind of marking on a product makes it "recognizable as suitable for the specific purpose" as indicated on the labels.

Fig. 110·6. "Identified." This kind of marking on a product makes it "recognizable as suitable for the specific purpose" as indicated on the labels.

110·11. Deteriorating Agents.   Equipment must be "identified" for use in the presence of specific deteriorating agents, as shown on the typical nameplate in Fig. 110-6.

110-12. Mechanical Execution of Work. This statement has been the source of many conflicts because opinions differ as to what is a "neat and workmanlike manner."

The **Code** places the responsibility for determining what is acceptable and how it is applied in the particular jurisdiction on the authority having jurisdiction. This basis in most areas is the result of:

1. Competent knowledge and experience of installation methods
2. What has been the established practice by the qualified journeyman in the particular area
3. What has been taught in the trade schools having certified electrical training courses for apprentices and journeymen

Examples which generally would not be considered as "neat and workmanlike" include nonmetallic cables installed with kinks or twists; unsightly exposed runs; wiring improperly trained in enclosures; slack in cables between supports; flattened conduit bends; or improvised fittings, straps, or supports. See Fig. 110-7.

It has long been required in specific **Code** rules that unused openings in boxes and cabinets be closed by a plug or cap (see Secs. 370-8 and 373-4). The requirement for such plugging of open holes is also a general rule to provide

Fig. 110-7. Stapling of BX to bottoms of joists and ragged drilling of joists add up to an unsightly installation that does not appear "workmanlike." (Sec. 110-12.).

Fig. 110-8. Unused openings in any electrical enclosure must be plugged or capped. Any punched knockout that will not be used must be closed, as at arrow.

fire-resistive integrity of all equipment—boxes, raceways, auxiliary gutters, cabinets, equipment cases or housings (Fig. 110-8).

As required by Sec. 110-12(b), in concrete manholes and pull boxes for underground electrical systems, safe and ready access demands proper training and racking of conductors. This rule requires "racked" conductors in "subsurface" enclosures to provide adequate room for safe and easy movement of persons who have to do installation and maintenance work in such enclosures.

110·14. Electrical Connections.   Proper electrical connections at terminals and splices are absolutely essential to ensure a safe installation. Improper connections are the cause of most failures of wiring devices, equipment burndowns, and electrically oriented fires.

Terminals and splicing connectors must be "identified" for the *material* of the conductor or conductors used with them. Where in previous **NEC** editions this rule called for conductor terminal and splicing devices to be "suitable" for the material of the conductor (i.e., for aluminum or copper) the wording now requires that terminal and splicing devices must be "identified" for use with the material of the conductor. And devices that combine copper and aluminum conductors in direct contact with each other must also be "identified for the purpose and conditions of use."

Although the **NEC** definition of *identified* does not specifically require that products be marked to designate specific application suitability, there is that suggestion; and such marking on the product, its label, or the box or wrapping in which the product is supplied would best comply with the definition "identified," and such marking is widely done by manufacturers to satisfy requirements of UL. Specific rules of UL require terminals and splice devices to be marked to indicate suitability with copper or aluminum conductors. The term "identified" is intended to make clear that the manufacturers and testing laboratories have a responsibility to assist the inspector by their own indications of suitability of products for their intended uses.

In general, approved pressure-type wire splicing lugs or connectors bear no marking if approved for only copper wire. If approved for copper, copper-clad aluminum, and/or aluminum, they are marked "AL-CU"; and if approved for aluminum only, they are marked "AL." Devices listed by Underwriters Laboratories Inc. indicate the range or combination of wire sizes for which such devices have been listed. Terminals of 15- and 20-A receptacles not marked "CO/ALR" are for use with copper and copper-clad aluminum conductors only. Terminals marked "CO/ALR" are for use with aluminum, copper, and copper-clad aluminum conductors.

The vast majority of distribution equipment has always come from the manufacturer with mechanical set-screw-type lugs for connecting circuit conductors to the equipment terminals. Lugs on such equipment are commonly marked "AL-CU" or "CU-AL," indicating that the set-screw terminal is suitable for use with *either* copper or aluminum conductors. But, such marking on the lug itself is not sufficient evidence of suitability for use with aluminum conductors. UL requires that equipment with terminals that are found to be suitable for use with *either* copper or aluminum conductors must be marked to indicate such use on the label or wiring diagram of the equipment—completely independent of a marking like "AL-CU" on the lugs themselves. A typical safety switch, for instance, would have lugs marked "AL-CU," *but also must have* a notation on the label or nameplate of the switch that reads like this: "Lugs suitable for copper or aluminum conductors."

There are two possible ways to go when using aluminum conductors with distribution equipment that comes with mechanical set-screw terminals about which there may be some reservations on their effectiveness:

1. A termination device or copper pigtail may be put on the end of each aluminum conductor to provide an "end" that is suitable, tested, and proved for effective use in a set-screw-type lug. A number of manufacturers make "adapters" which are readily crimped onto the end of an aluminum conductor to "convert" the end to copper or an alloy that will not exhibit the creep and cold-flow disadvantages of aluminum in a set-screw termination. This is shown in Fig. 110-9.

2. Another way to attack the problem is to remove the set-screw lug from the switch or breaker or panel and replace the set-screw lug with a crimp-type lug designed to accept an aluminum conductor which is crimped in the barrel of the lug.

UL-listed equipment must be used in the condition as supplied by the manufacturer—in accordance with **NE Code** rules and any instructions covered in the UL listing in the *Electrical Construction Materials Directory* (the UL Green Book)—as required by **NE Code** Sec. 110-3(b). Unauthorized alteration or modification of equipment in the field voids the UL listing and can lead to very dangerous conditions. For this reason, any arbitrary or unspecified changing of terminal lugs on equipment is *not acceptable unless such field modification is*

Method 1

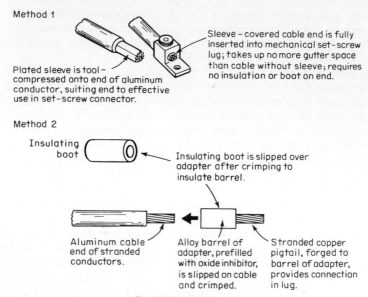

Plated sleeve is tool-
compressed onto end of aluminum
conductor, suiting end to effective
use in set-screw connector.

Sleeve – covered cable end is fully
inserted into mechanical set-screw
lug; takes up no more gutter space
than cable without sleeve; requires
no insulation or boot on end.

Method 2

Insulating boot

Insulating boot is slipped over
adapter after crimping to
insulate barrel.

Aluminum cable
end of stranded
conductors.

Alloy barrel of
adapter, prefilled
with oxide inhibitor,
is slipped on cable
and crimped.

Stranded copper
pigtail, forged to
barrel of adapter,
provides connection
in lug.

Fig. 110-9. (Sec. 110-14.)

recognized by UL and spelled out very carefully in the manufacturers' literature and on the label of the equipment itself.

For instance, UL-listed authorization for field changing of terminals on a
safety switch is described in manufacturers' catalog data and on the switch
label itself. It is obvious that field replacement of set-screw lugs with compression-type lugs can be a risky matter if great care is not taken to assure that the
size, mounting holes, bolts, and other characteristics of the compression lug line
up with and are fully compatible for replacement of the lug that is removed.
Careless or makeshift changing of lugs in the field has produced overheating,
burning, and failures. To prevent junk-box assembly of replacement lugs, UL
requires that any authorized field replacement data *must* indicate the specific
lug to be used and *also must* indicate the tool to be used in making the crimps.
Any crimp connection of a lug should always be done with the tool specified
by the lug manufacturer. Otherwise, there is no assurance that the type of crimp
produces a sound connection of the lug to the conductor.

Section 110-14(a), last sentence, prohibits use of more than one conductor in
a terminal (see Fig. 110-10) *unless the terminal is approved for the purpose*
(meaning approved for use with two or more conductors in the terminal).

WATCH OUT!

Fig. 110-10. [Sec. 110-14(a).]

Use of the word "identified" in the last sentence of Sec. 110-14(a) could be interpreted to require that terminals suited to use with two or more conductors must somehow be marked. For a long time terminals suited to and acceptable for use with aluminum conductors have been marked "AL-CU" or "CU-AL" right on the terminal. Twist-on or crimp-type splicing devices are "identified" both for use with aluminum wires and for the number and sizes of wires permitted in a single terminal—with the identification marked on the box in which the devices are packaged or marked on an enclosed sheet.

For set-screw and compression-type lugs used on equipment or for splicing or tapping-off, suitability for use with two or more conductors in a single barrel of a lug could be marked on the lug in the same way that such lugs are marked with the range of sizes of a single conductor that may be used, e.g., "No. 2 to No. 2/0." But the intent of the **Code** rule is that any single-barrel lug used with two or more conductors must be tested for such use (such as in accordance with UL 486B standard), and some indication must be made by the manufacturer that the lug is properly suited and rated for the number and sizes of conductors to be inserted into a single barrel. Again, the best and most effective way to identify a lug for such use is with marking right on the lug, as is done for "AL-CU." But the second sentence of Sec. 110-3(a)(1) also allows such identification to be "provided with" a product, as on the box or on an instruction sheet. See Fig. 110-11.

Fig. 110-11. A TERMINAL with more than one conductor terminated in a single barrel (hole) of the lug (at arrows) must be "identified" (marked, listed or otherwise tested and certified as suitable for such use).

A fine-print note after the first paragraph of Sec. 110-14 calls attention to the fact that manufacturers are marking equipment, terminations, packing cartons, and/or catalog sheets with specific values of required tightening torques (pound-inches or pound-feet). Although the **National Electrical Code** does not presently contain explicit requirements on torquing, it is certainly true that the **NEC** objective of providing for the "practical safeguarding of persons and property from hazards arising from the use of electricity" cannot be fulfilled without diligent attention to so safety-related a consideration as proper connections. **NEC** Sec. 110-3(b), which requires all listed and labeled products to be used in accordance with any instructions included with the listing and labeling, can and should be construed to require that all electrical connections be torqued to values specified in UL standards. Although that puts the installer to the task of finding out appropriate torque values, many manufacturers are presently publishing "recommended" values in their catalogs and spec sheets. In the case of connector and lug manufacturers, such values are even printed on the boxes in which the devices are sold.

A proposal was submitted for the **NE Code** to make torquing of terminals mandatory. In response to that, the **Code**-making panel commented that "The proposal is adequately covered in Section 110-3(b)." That statement appears to say that torquing is, in fact, already a **Code** requirement, because Sec. 110-3(b) incorporates as **Code** rules all the requirements on torquing contained in UL standards. Torque is the amount of tightness of the screw or bolt in its threaded hole; that is, torque is the measure of the twisting movement that produces rotations around an axis. Such turning tightness is measured in terms of the force applied to the handle of the device that is rotating the screw or bolt and the distance from the axis of rotation to the point where the force is applied to the handle of the wrench or screwdriver:

$$\text{Torque (lb ft)} = \text{force (lb)} \times \text{distance (ft)}$$
$$\text{Torque (lb in.)} = \text{force (lb)} \times \text{distance (in.)}$$

Because there are 12 inches in a foot, a torque of "one pound foot" is equal to "12 pound inches." Any value of "pound feet" is converted to "pound inches" by multiplying the value of "pound feet" by 12. To convert from "pound inches" to "pound feet," the value of "pound inches" is divided by 12.

Note: The expressions "pound feet" and "pound inches" are preferred to "foot pounds" or "inch pounds," although the expressions are used interchangeably.

Torque wrenches and torque screwdrivers are designed, calibrated, and marked to show the torque (or turning force) being exerted at any position of the turning screw or bolt. Figure 110-12 shows typical torque tools and their application.

Section 110-14(b) covers splice connectors and similar devices used to connect fixture wires to branch-circuit conductors and to splice circuit wires in junction boxes and other enclosures. Much valuable application information on such devices is given in the UL *Electrical Construction Materials Directory*, under the heading of "Wire Connectors and Soldering Lugs."

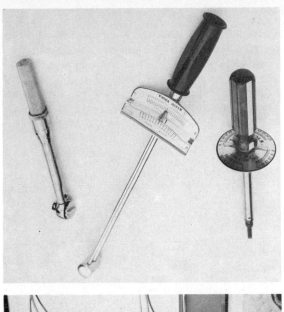

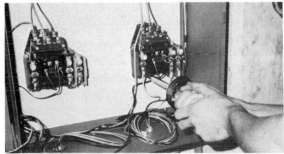

Fig. 110-12. Readily available torque tools are (at top, L–R): torque screw-driver, beam-type torque wrench, and ratchet-type torque wrench. These tools afford ready compliance with the implied requirement of the fine-print note in the **Code** rule. [Sec. 110-14.]

110-16. Working Space About Electric Equipment (600 Volts, Nominal, or Less). The basic rule of Sec. 110-16(a) calls for safe work clearances in accordance with Table 110-16(a). The intent of the second paragraph of Sec. 110-16(a), which calls for a work space at least 30 in. wide in front of electrical equipment, is to provide sufficient "elbow room" in front of such equipment as column-type panelboards and single enclosed switches (e.g., 12 in. wide) to permit the equipment to be operated or maintained under safer conditions (Fig. 110-13).

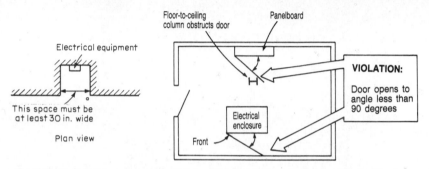

Fig. 110-13. Working space required in front of electrical equipment for side-to-side clearance and door opening. [Sec. 110-16(a).]

And, as required by the second sentence of the second paragraph of Sec. 110-16(a), clear workspace in front of any enclosure for electrical equipment must be deep enough to allow doors, hinged panels, or covers on the enclosure to be opened to an angle of at least 90°. Any door or cover on a panelboard or cabinet that is obstructed from opening to at least a 90° position makes it difficult for any personnel to install, maintain, or inspect the equipment in the enclosure safely. Full opening provides safer access to the enclosure and minimizes potential hazards (Fig. 110-13).

In **Code** Table 110-16(a), the dimensions of working space in the direction of access to live electrical parts operating at 600 V or less must be carefully observed. All minimum clearances are 3 ft. Section 110-16(d) requires a working space at least 3 ft deep in front of switchboards or motor control centers that have live parts normally exposed on their front. The minimum of 3 ft was adopted for **Code** Table 110-16(a) to make all electrical equipment—panelboards, switches, breakers, starters, etc.—subject to the same 3-ft minimum to increase the level of safety and assure consistent, uniform spacing where anyone might be exposed to the hazard of working on any kind of live equipment. Application of **Code** Table 110-16(a) to the three "conditions" described in Sec. 110-16(a) is shown in the sketches making up this handbook's Table 110-1. Figure 110-14 shows a typical example of Condition 3.

Exception No. 2 of Sec. 110-16(a) allows working clearance of less than the distances given in Table 110-16(a) for live parts that are operating at not over 30 V ac or 42 V dc. The last phrase recognizes the safety of low-voltage circuits

Table 110·1. Clearance Needed in Direction of Access to Live Parts in Enclosures for Switchboards, Panelboards, Switches, CBs, or Other Electrical Equipment—Plan Views [Sec. 110·16(a)]

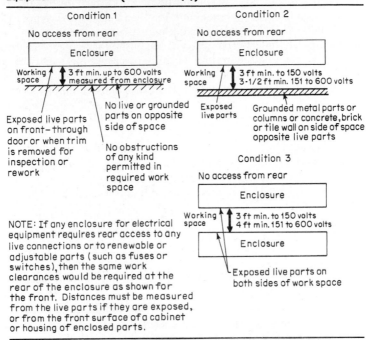

Condition 1

No access from rear

| Enclosure |

Working space ↕ 3 ft min. up to 600 volts measured from enclosure

Exposed live parts on front–through door or when trim is removed for inspection or rework

No live or grounded parts on opposite side of space

No obstructions of any kind permitted in required work space

NOTE: If any enclosure for electrical equipment requires rear access to any live connections or to renewable or adjustable parts (such as fuses or switches), then the same work clearances would be required at the rear of the enclosure as shown for the front. Distances must be measured from the live parts if they are exposed, or from the front surface of a cabinet or housing of enclosed parts.

Condition 2

No access from rear

| Enclosure |

Working space ↕ 3 ft min. to 150 volts 3-1/2 ft min. 151 to 600 volts

Exposed live parts

Grounded metal parts or columns or concrete, brick or tile wall on side of space opposite live parts

Condition 3

No access from rear

| Enclosure |

Working space ↕ 3 ft min. to 150 volts 4 ft min. 151 to 600 volts

| Enclosure |

Exposed live parts on both sides of work space

Fig. 110·14. Condition 3 in Code Table 110-16(a) for the rule covered by Sec. 110-16(a) applies to the case of face-to-face enclosures, as shown here where two switchboards face each other. The distance indicated must be at least 3 or 4 ft depending on the voltage of enclosed parts. [Sec. 110-16(a).]

like the Class 2 control and power-limited circuits covered by Art. 725. It is intended to allow less than the 3-ft minimum spacing of Table 110-16(a) for live parts of low-voltage control or power-limited circuits that *are integral parts of* switchboards or control centers that contain other bus and equipment rated at 208/120 V or 480/277 V, for which the table clearances do apply.

As an added safety measure, to prevent the case where personnel might be trapped in the working space around burning or arcing electrical equipment, the rule of Sec. 110-16(c) requires *two* "entrances" or directions of access to the working space around any equipment enclosure that contains "overcurrent devices, switching devices, or control devices," where such equipment is rated 1,200 A or more and is over 6 ft wide. (Note that this rule is no longer limited just to "switchboards and control panels," as it was in the 1987 and previous **Code** editions.) Sec. 110-16(c) requires *two* "entrances" or directions of access to the working space around switchboards, motor-control centers, distribution centers, panelboard lineups, UPS cubicles, rectifier modules, substations, power conditioners, and any other equipment that is rated 1,200 A or more and is over 6 ft wide.

At each end of the working space at such equipment, an entranceway or access route at least 24 in. wide must be provided. Because personnel have been trapped in work space by fire between them and the only route of exit from the space, rigid enforcement of this rule is likely. Certainly, design engineers should make two paths of exit a standard requirement in their drawings and specs. Although the rule does not *require* two doors into an electrical equipment room, it may be necessary to use two doors in order to obtain the required two entrances to the required work space—especially where the switchboard or control panel is in tight quarters and does not afford a 24-in.-wide path of exit at each end of the work space.

In Fig. 110-15, sketch "A" shows compliance with the **Code** rule—providing two areas for entering or leaving the defined dimensions of the work space. In that sketch, placing the switchboard with its front to the larger area of the room and/or other layouts would also satisfy the intent of the rule. It is only necessary to have an assured means of exit from the defined work space. If the space in front of the equipment is deeper than the required depth of work space, then a person could simply move back out of the work space at any point along the length of the equipment. That is the objective of Exception No. 2 to Sec. 110-16(c), which recognizes that where the space in front of equipment is twice the minimum depth of working space required by Table 110-16(a) for the voltage of the equipment and the conditions described, it is not necessary to have an entrance at each end of the space (Fig. 110-16). In such cases, a worker can move directly back out of the working space to avoid fire. For any case where the depth of space is not twice the depth value given in Table 110-16(a) for working space, an entranceway or access route at least 24 in. wide must be provided at each end of the working space in front of the equipment.

Sketch "B" in Fig. 110-15 shows the layout that must be avoided. With sufficient space available in the room, layout of any equipment rated 1,200 A or more with only one exit route from the required work space would be a clear violation of the rule. As shown in sketch "B," a door at the right end of the working space would eliminate the violation. *But,* if the depth *D* in sketch "B"

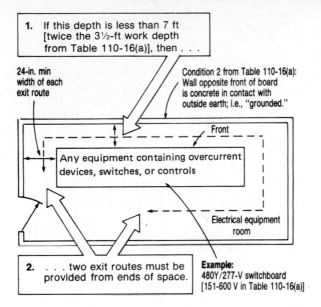

1. If this depth is less than 7 ft [twice the 3½-ft work depth from Table 110-16(a)], then . . .

24-in. min width of each exit route

Condition 2 from Table 110-16(a): Wall opposite front of board is concrete in contact with outside earth; i.e., "grounded."

Front

Any equipment containing overcurrent devices, switches, or controls

Electrical equipment room

2. . . . two exit routes must be provided from ends of space.

Example: 480Y/277-V switchboard [151-600 V in Table 110-16(a)]

(A) Complies

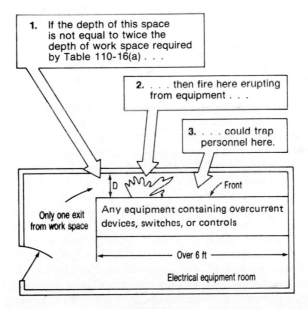

1. If the depth of this space is not equal to twice the depth of work space required by Table 110-16(a) . . .

2. . . . then fire here erupting from equipment . . .

3. . . . could trap personnel here.

Only one exit from work space

D

Front

Any equipment containing overcurrent devices, switches, or controls

Over 6 ft

Electrical equipment room

(B) Violation

Fig. 110-15. There must be *two* paths out of the work space required in front of any equipment containing fuses, circuit breakers, motor starters, switches, and/or any other control or protective devices, where the equipment is rated 1,200 A or more and is over 6 ft wide. [Sec. 110-16(c).]

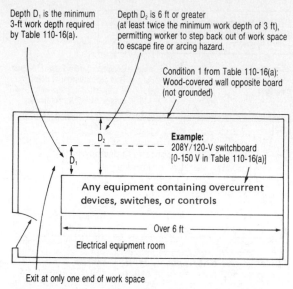

Depth D₁ is the minimum 3-ft work depth required by Table 110-16(a).

Depth D₂ is 6 ft or greater (at least twice the minimum work depth of 3 ft), permitting worker to step back out of work space to escape fire or arcing hazard.

Condition 1 from Table 110-16(a): Wood-covered wall opposite board (not grounded)

D_2

D_1

Example: 208Y/120-V switchboard [0-150 V in Table 110-16(a)]

Any equipment containing overcurrent devices, switches, or controls

Over 6 ft

Electrical equipment room

Exit at only one end of work space

Fig. 110-16. This satisfies Exception No. 2 to Sec. 110-16(c).

is equal to or greater than twice the minimum required depth of working space from Table 110-16(a) for the voltage and "conditions" of installation, then a door at the right is *not* needed and the layout would *not* be a violation.

The paragraph following Exception No. 2 states that when the defined work-space in front of an electrical switchboard or other equipment has an entranceway at only one end of the space, the edge of the entrance nearest the equipment must be at least 3, 3½, or 4 ft away from the equipment—as designated in Table 110-16(a) for the voltage and conditions of installation of the particular equipment. This **Code** requirement requires careful determination in satisfying the precise wording of the rule. Figure 110-17 shows a few of the many possible applications that would be subject to the rule.

Section 110-16(e) requires lighting of workspace at "service equipment, switchboards, panelboards, or motor control centers installed indoors." The basic rule and its exception are shown in Fig. 110-18.

The important Exception to this rule excludes "service equipment or panel-boards, in dwelling units, that do not exceed 200 amperes" from the need to have lighting installed at their locations. But note that the Exception applies only to such equipment in "dwelling units"—which means in a one-family house or in an apartment within an apartment house. The narrow definition of "dwelling unit" does not make this Exception applicable to service equipment or panelboards that are in an apartment building but are located outside any of the "dwelling units"—such as in hallways, electric closets, and basements.

It should be noted that although lighting is required for safety of personnel in work spaces, nothing specific is said about the kind of lighting (incandescent, fluorescent, mercury-vapor), no minimum footcandle level is set, and such details as the position and mounting of lighting equipment are omitted. All that

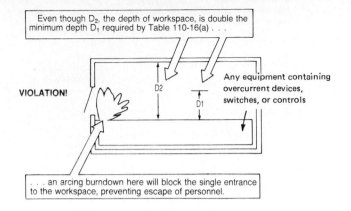

Even though D₂, the depth of workspace, is double the
minimum depth D₁ required by Table 110-16(a) . . .

VIOLATION!

D2

D1

Any equipment containing
overcurrent devices,
switches, or controls

. . . an arcing burndown here will block the single entrance
to the workspace, preventing escape of personnel.

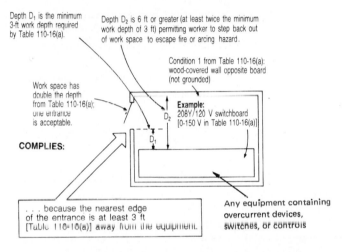

Depth D₁ is the minimum
3-ft work depth required
by Table 110-16(a).

Depth D₂ is 6 ft or greater (at least twice the minimum
work depth of 3 ft) permitting worker to step back out
of work space to escape fire or arcing hazard.

Condition 1 from Table 110-16(a):
wood-covered wall opposite board
(not grounded)

Work space has
double the depth
from Table 110-16(a);
one entrance
is acceptable.

D₂

Example:
208Y/120 V switchboard
[0-150 V in Table 110-16(a)]

COMPLIES:

D₁

. . . because the nearest edge
of the entrance is at least 3 ft
[Table 110-16(a)] away from the equipment.

Any equipment containing
overcurrent devices,
switches, or controls

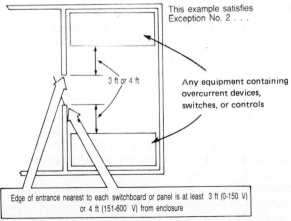

This example satisfies
Exception No. 2 . . .

3 ft or 4 ft

Any equipment containing
overcurrent devices,
switches, or controls

Edge of entrance nearest to each switchboard or panel is at least 3 ft (0-150 V)
or 4 ft (151-600 V) from enclosure

Fig. 110-17. Arcing burndown must not block route of
exit. [Sec. 110-16(c).]

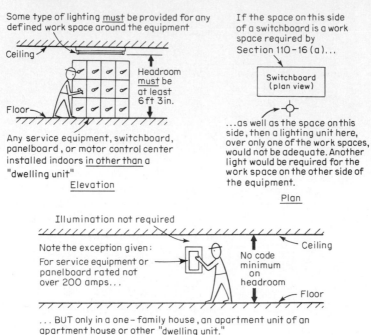

Fig. 110·18. Electrical equipment requires lighting and 6¼-ft headroom at *all* work spaces around equipment. [Secs. 110-16(e) and (f).]

is left to the designer and/or installer, with the inspector the final judge of acceptability.

In Sec. 110-16(f), a minimum headroom of 6¼ ft in working spaces is required around electrical equipment. The rule applies to "service equipment, switchboards, panelboards, or motor control centers." The same Exception as in Sec. 110-16(e) permits "service equipment or panelboards, in dwelling units, that do not exceed 200 amperes" to be installed with less than 6¼ ft of headroom—such as in crawl spaces under single-family houses. But the permission for reduced headroom of the equipment described in the Exception applies only in "dwelling units" that meet the definition of that phrase. In any space other than a dwelling unit, all indoor service equipment, switchboards, panelboards, or control centers must have 6¼-ft headroom in any space around the equipment that is work space required by Sec. 110-16(a).

Details on lighting and headroom are shown in Fig. 110-18. But, in that sketch, it should be noted that the 6-ft 3-in. headroom must be available for the entire length of the work space. It must be clearance from the floor up to the light fixture or to any other overhead obstruction—and not simply to the ceiling or bottom of the joists.

110·17. Guarding of Live Parts (600 Volts, Nominal, or Less). After the 1968 NEC, old Sec. 110-17(a)(3), accepting guard rails as suitable for guarding live parts, was deleted. It was felt that a guard rail is not proper or adequate protection in areas accessible to other than qualified persons.

Live parts of equipment should in general be protected from accidental contact by complete enclosure; i.e., the equipment should be "dead-front." Such construction is not practicable in some large control panels, and in such cases the apparatus should be isolated or guarded as required by these rules.

110-18. Arcing Parts.   The same considerations apply here as in the case covered in Sec. 110-17. Full enclosure is preferable, but where this is not practicable, all combustible material must be kept well away from the equipment.

110-21. Marking.   The marking required in Sec. 110-21 should be done in a manner which will allow inspectors to examine such marking without removing the equipment from a permanently installed position. It should be noted that the last sentence in Sec. 110-21 requires electrical equipment to have a marking durable enough to withstand the environment involved (such as equipment designed for wet or corrosive locations).

110-22. Identification of Disconnecting Means.   As shown in Fig. 110-19, it is a mandatory **Code** rule that all disconnect devices (switches or CBs) for load

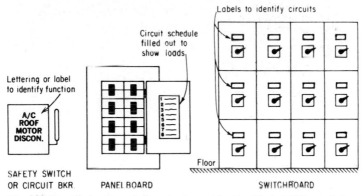

Fig. 110-19. All circuits and disconnects must be identified. OSHA regulations make NE Code Sec. 110-22 mandatory and retroactive for existing installations and for all new, expanded or modernized systems—applying to switches as well as circuit breakers. (Sec. 110-22.)

devices and for circuits be clearly and permanently marked to show the purposes of the disconnects. This is a "must" and, under OSHA, it applies to all existing electrical systems, no matter how old, and also to all new, modernized, expanded, or altered electrical systems. This requirement for marking has been widely neglected in electrical systems in the past. Panelboard circuit directories must be fully and clearly filled out. And all such marking on equipment must be in painted lettering or other substantial identification.

Effective identification of all disconnect devices is a critically important safety matter. When a switch or CB has to be opened to de-energize a circuit quickly—as when a threat of injury to personnel dictates—it is absolutely necessary to identify quickly and positively the disconnect for the circuit or equipment that constitutes the hazard to a person or property. Painted labeling or embossed identification plates affixed to enclosures would comply with the requirement that disconnects be "legibly marked" and that the "marking shall be of sufficient durability." Paste-on paper labels or marking with crayon or chalk could be rejected as not complying with the intent of this rule. Ideally, marking should tell exactly what piece of equipment is controlled by a disconnect (switch or CB) and should tell where the controlled equipment is located and how *it* may be identified. Figure 110-20 shows a case of this kind of iden-

Fig. 110-20. Identification of disconnect switch and pushbutton stations is "legibly marked" in both English and French—and is of "sufficient durability to withstand the environment"—as required by the **Code** rule. (Sec. 110-22).

tification as used in an industrial facility where all equipment is marked in two languages because personnel speak different languages. And that is an old installation, attesting to the long-standing recognition of this safety feature.

The second paragraph of Sec. 110-22 says that where circuit breakers or fused switches are used in a series combination with downstream devices that do not have an interrupting rating equal to the available short-circuit current but are dependent for safe operation on upstream protection that is rated for the short-circuit current, enclosure(s) for such "series rated" protective devices must be marked in the field "Caution—Series Rated System."

Manufacturers make available multimeter distribution equipment for multiple-occupancy buildings with equipment containing a main service protective device that has a short-circuit interrupting rating of some value (e.g., 65,000 A) that is connected in series with feeder and branch-circuit protective devices of considerably lower short-circuit interrupting ratings (say 22,000 or 10,000 A). Because all of the protective devices are physically very close together, the feeder and branch-circuit devices do not have to have a rated interrupting capability equal to the available short-circuit current at their points of installation. Although such application is a literal violation of **NEC** Sec. 110-9, which calls for all protective devices to be rated for the short-circuit current available at their supply terminals, "series rated" equipment takes advantage of the ability of the protective devices to operate in series (or in *cascade* as it is sometimes called) with a fault current interruption on, say, a branch circuit being shared by the three series protective devices—the main, feeder, and branch circuit. Such operation can enable a properly rated main protective device to protect downstream protective devices that are not rated for the available fault. When manufacturers combine such series protective devices in available distribution equipment, they do so on the basis of careful testing to assure that all of the protective devices can operate without damage to themselves. Then UL tests such equipment to verify its safe and effective operation and will list such equipment as a "Series Rated System."

Because UL listing is based on use of specific models of protective devices to assure safe application, it is critically important that all maintenance on such equipment be based on the specific equipment. For that reason, this **Code** rule demands that the enclosure(s) for all such equipment be provided with "readily visible" markings to alert all personnel to the critical condition that must always be maintained to assure safety. Thus, all series rated equipment enclosure(s) must be marked.

Although the **Code** calls for the marking on such enclosure(s) to read "Caution—Series Rated System," addition of the phrase "Identical Component Replacement Required" would provide direction for appropriate action, as has been determined through litigation to be necessary for similar **Code**-required warning signs. For example, Sec. 710-43 requires all enclosures used with mobile and portable high-voltage equipment to be marked "Warning—High Voltage." Such a warning sign has been found in the courts to be inadequate because it gives the reader no instruction as to what action to take. Even though the **Code** still does not require more complete wording, failure to include the command "Keep Out" following the **Code**-required wording would not be defensible in a court of law. Because the prescribed wording for the marking required by the new rule of Sec. 110-22 seems similarly incomplete, addition of instructional wording such as suggested above would be a most prudent approach.

110-30. General.   Figure 110-21 notes that high-voltage switches and circuit breakers must be marked to indicate the circuit or equipment controlled. This requirement arises because Sec. 110-30 says that high-voltage equipment must comply with preceding sections of Art. 110. Therefore, the rule of Sec. 110-22 calling for marking of all disconnecting means must be observed for high-voltage equipment as well as for equipment rated up to 600 V.

110-31. Enclosure for Electrical Installations.   Figure 110-22 illustrates the rules which cover installation of high-voltage equipment indoors in places accessible to unqualified persons. Installation must be in a locked vault or locked area, or equipment must be metal-enclosed.

For any equipment, rooms, or enclosures where the voltage exceeds 600 V, permanent and conspicuous warning signs reading WARNING—HIGH VOLTAGE, KEEP OUT should always be provided. It is a safety measure that alerts unfamiliar

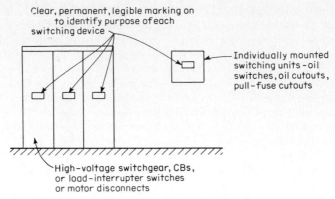

Fig. 110·21. High-voltage switches and breakers must be properly marked to indicate their function. (Sec. 110-30.)

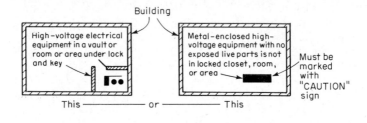

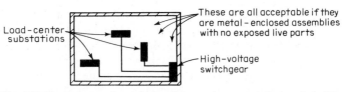

Fig. 110·22. NE Code rules on high-voltage equipment installations in buildings accessible to electrically unqualified persons. [Sec. 110-31(a).]

or unqualified persons who may for some reason gain access to a locked, high-voltage area.

Section 110-31(b) specifies that outdoor installations *with exposed live parts* must *not* provide access to unqualified persons. Elevation may be used to prevent access [Sec. 110-34(e)], or equipment may be enclosed by a wall, screen, or fence under lock and key, as shown in Fig. 110-23. Outdoor installations that are open to unqualified persons must comply with Art. 225, "Outside Branch Circuits and Feeders."

Where high-voltage equipment is installed in places accessible only to qualified persons, the rules of Secs. 110-34, 710-32, and 710-33 apply. In such areas,

Fig. 110-23. High-voltage equipment enclosed by a wall, screen, or fence at least 8 ft high with a lockable door or gate is considered as accessible only to qualified persons. [Sec. 110-31(b).]

circuit conductors may be installed in conduit, in duct systems, in metal-clad cable, as bare wire, cable, and busbars, or as nonmetallic-sheathed cables or conductors as permitted by **NE Code** Secs. 710-3 through 710-6.

The last sentence of Sec. 110-31(c) recognizes a difference in safety concern between high-voltage equipment accessible to "unqualified persons"—who may not be qualified as electrical personnel but are adults who have the ability to recognize warning signs and the good sense to stay out of electrical enclosures and "the general public," which includes children who cannot read and/or are not wary enough to stay out of unlocked enclosures (Fig. 110-24).

The rationale submitted with the proposal that led to this change in the **Code** rule noted:

Where metal-enclosed equipment rated above 600 volts is accessible to the general public and located at an elevation less than 8 feet, the doors should be kept locked to prevent children and others who may be unaware of the contents of such enclosures from opening the doors.

However, in a controlled environment where the equipment is marked with appropriate caution signs as required elsewhere in the **NE Code**, and only knowledgeable people have access to the equipment, the requirement to lock the doors on all metal-enclosed equipment rated above 600 volts and located less than 8 feet above the floor does not contribute to safety and may place a burden on the safe operation of systems by delaying access to the equipment.

Note that Sec. 110-31(a)(1) does not require locking indoor metal-enclosed equipment that is accessible to unqualified persons, but such equipment is required to be marked with "CAUTION" signs.

Fig. 110·24. METAL-ENCLOSED high-voltage equipment accessible to the general public—such as pad-mount trans- formers or switchgear units installed outdoors or in indoors areas where the general public is not excluded—must have doors or hinged covers locked (arrow) if the bottom of the enclo- sure is less than 8 ft above the ground or above the floor.

110·32. Work Space about Equipment. Figure 110-25 points out the basic **Code** rule of Sec. 110-32 relating to working space around electrical equipment.

Figure 110-26 shows the rules on adequate headroom and necessary illumi- nation for safely working on high-voltage electrical equipment.

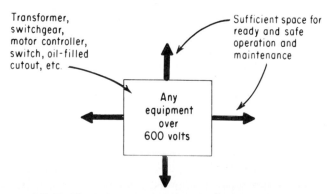

Fig. 110·25. This is the general rule for work space around any high- voltage equipment. (Sec. 110-32.)

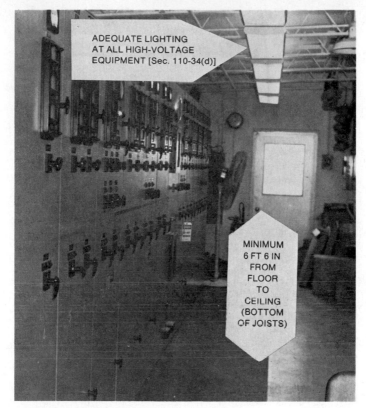

ADEQUATE LIGHTING
AT ALL HIGH-VOLTAGE
EQUIPMENT [Sec. 110-34(d)]

MINIMUM
6 FT 6 IN
FROM
FLOOR
TO
CEILING
(BOTTOM
OF JOISTS)

Fig. 110-26. Sufficient headroom and adequate lighting are essential to safe operation, maintenance, and repair of high-voltage equipment. (Sec. 110-32.)

Figure 110-27 shows required side-to-side working space for adequate elbow room in front of high-voltage equipment.

110-33. Entrance and Access to Work Space.   Entrances and access to working space around high-voltage equipment must comply with the rules shown in Fig. 110-28.

Exception No. 2 says that if the depth of space in front of a switchboard is at least twice the minimum required depth of working space from Table 110-34(a), any person in the working space would be capable of moving back out of the working space to escape any fire, arcing, or other hazardous condition. In such cases, there is no need for a path of exit at either end or at both ends of the working space. But where the depth of space is not equal to twice the minimum required depth of working space, there must be an exit path at each end of the working space in front of switchgear or control equipment enclosures that are wider than 6 ft. And what applies to the front of a switchboard also applies to working space at the rear of the board if rear access is required to work on energized parts.

Fig. 110-27. Working space in front of equipment must be at least 3 ft wide measured parallel to front surface of the enclosure. (Sec. 110-32.)

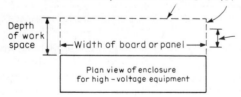

Defined work space from Table 110–34(a)

Depth of work space

Width of board or panel

Plan view of enclosure for high–voltage equipment

One entrance 24 in. wide by 6-1/2 ft high must be provided to the defined work space. But, if the board or panel is over 6 ft wide, there must be one entrance at each end of of the work space, except where the depth of space is at least twice the value in Table 110-34 (a).

Fig. 110-28. Access to required work space around high-voltage equipment must be assured. (Sec. 110-33.)

The paragraph after Exception No. 2 specifies minimum clearance distance between high-voltage equipment and edge of entranceway to the defined workspace in front of the equipment, where only one access route is provided. Based on Table 110-34(a)—which gives minimum depths of clear working space in front of equipment operating at over 600 V—the rule in this section presents the same type of requirement described for Sec. 110-16(c), Exception No. 2. Based on the particular voltage and the conditions of installation of the high-voltage switchgear, control panel, or other equipment enclosure, the nearest edge of an entranceway must be a prescribed distance from the equipment enclosure. Refer to the sketches given for Sec. 110-16(c).

110-34. Work Space and Guarding. Application of **Code** Table 110-34(a) to working space around high-voltage equipment is made in the same way as shown for **Code** Table 110-16(a)—except that the depths are greater to provide more room because of the higher voltages.

As shown in Fig. 110-29, a 30-in.-deep work space is required behind enclosed high-voltage equipment that requires rear access to "de-energized"

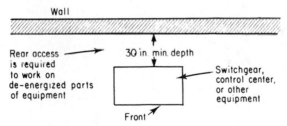

Fig. 110-29. Space for safe work on de-energized parts. [Sec. 110-34(a).]

parts. The Exception to Sec. 110-34(a)(3) notes that working space is not required behind dead-front equipment when there are no fuses, switches, other parts, or connections requiring rear access. But the rule adds that if rear access is necessary to permit work on "de-energized" parts of the enclosed assembly, the work space must be at least 30 in. deep. This is intended to prohibit cases where switchgear requiring rear access is installed too close to a wall behind it, and personnel have to work in cramped quarters to reach taps, splices, and terminations. However, it must be noted that this applies only where "de-energized" parts are accessible from the back of the equipment. If energized parts are accessible, then Condition 2 of Sec. 110-34(a) would exist, and the depth of working space would have to be anywhere from 4 to 10 ft, depending upon the voltage [see Table 110-34(a)].

Section 110-34(c) requires that the entrances to all buildings, rooms, or enclosures containing live parts or exposed conductors operating in excess of 600 V be kept locked, except where such entrances are under the observation of a qualified attendant at all times. The last paragraph in this section requires use of warning signs to deter unauthorized personnel.

The rule of Sec. 110-34(d) on lighting of high-voltage work space is shown in Fig. 110-26. Note that the rule calls for "adequate illumination," but does not specify a footcandle level or any other characteristics.

Figure 110-30 shows how "elevation" may be used to protect high-voltage live parts from unauthorized persons.

Fig. 110-30 Elevation may be used to isolate unguarded live parts from unqualified persons. [Sec. 110-34(e).]

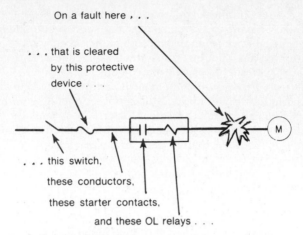

On a fault here , . .

. . . that is cleared
by this protective
device . . .

. . . this switch,

these conductors,

these starter contacts,

and these OL relays . . .

. . . must all be rated to safely withstand the energy of the
fault let-through current

Fig. 110-5. (Sec. 110-10.)

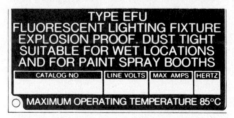

"Identified"—This kind of marking on a product makes it "recognizable as suitable for the specific purpose" as indicated on the labels.

Fig. 110-6. "Identified." This kind of marking on a product makes it "recognizable as suitable for the specific purpose" as indicated on the labels.

110-11. Deteriorating Agents.   Equipment must be "identified" for use in the presence of specific deteriorating agents, as shown on the typical nameplate in Fig. 110-6.

Table 110-1. Clearance Needed in Direction of Access to Live Parts in Enclosures for Switchboards, Panelboards, Switches, CBs, or Other Electrical Equipment—Plan Views (Sec. 110-16(a))

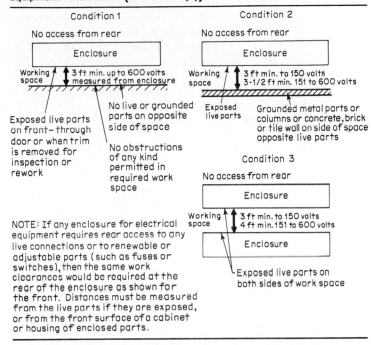

Condition 1

No access from rear

Enclosure

Working space ↑↕ 3 ft min. up to 600 volts measured from enclosure

Exposed live parts on front – through door or when trim is removed for inspection or rework

No live or grounded parts on opposite side of space

No obstructions of any kind permitted in required work space

NOTE: If any enclosure for electrical equipment requires rear access to any live connections or to renewable or adjustable parts (such as fuses or switches), then the same work clearances would be required at the rear of the enclosure as shown for the front. Distances must be measured from the live parts if they are exposed, or from the front surface of a cabinet or housing of enclosed parts.

Condition 2

No access from rear

Enclosure

Working space ↑↕ 3 ft min. to 150 volts 3-1/2 ft min. 151 to 600 volts

Exposed live parts — Grounded metal parts or columns or concrete, brick or tile wall on side of space opposite live parts

Condition 3

No access from rear

Enclosure

Working space ↑↕ 3 ft min. to 150 volts 4 ft min. 151 to 600 volts

Enclosure

Exposed live parts on both sides of work space

Fig. 110-14. Condition 3 in Code Table 110-16(a) for the rule covered by Sec. 110-16(a) applies to the case of face-to-face enclosures, as shown here where two switchboards face each other. The distance indicated must be at least 3 or 4 ft depending on the voltage of enclosed parts. [Sec. 110-16(a).]

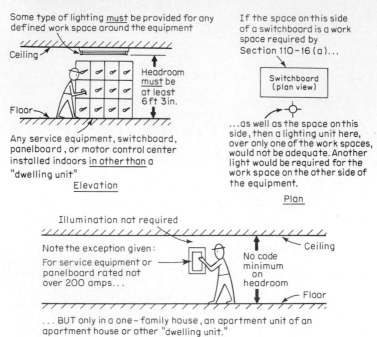

Some type of lighting <u>must</u> be provided for any defined work space around the equipment

Ceiling

Headroom <u>must</u> be at least 6ft 3in.

Floor

Any service equipment, switchboard, panelboard, or motor control center installed indoors <u>in other than a</u> "dwelling unit"

Elevation

If the space on this side of a switchboard is a work space required by Section 110-16(a)...

Switchboard (plan view)

...as well as the space on this side, then a lighting unit here, over only one of the work spaces, would not be adequate. Another light would be required for the work space on the other side of the equipment.

Plan

Illumination not required

Note the exception given:

For service equipment or panelboard rated not over 200 amps...

Ceiling

No code minimum on headroom

Floor

... BUT only in a one-family house, an apartment unit of an apartment house or other "dwelling unit."

Fig. 110-18. Electrical equipment requires lighting and 6¼-ft headroom at *all* work spaces around equipment. [Secs. 110-16(e) and (f).]

is left to the designer and/or installer, with the inspector the final judge of acceptability.

In Sec. 110-16(f), a minimum headroom of 6¼ ft in working spaces is required around electrical equipment. The rule applies to "service equipment, switchboards, panelboards, or motor control centers." The same Exception as in Sec. 110-16(e) permits "service equipment or panelboards, in dwelling units, that do not exceed 200 amperes" to be installed with less than 6¼ ft of headroom—such as in crawl spaces under single-family houses. But the permission for reduced headroom of the equipment described in the Exception applies only in "dwelling units" that meet the definition of that phrase. In any space other than a dwelling unit, all indoor service equipment, switchboards, panelboards, or control centers must have 6¼-ft headroom in any space around the equipment that is work space required by Sec. 110-16(a).

Details on lighting and headroom are shown in Fig. 110-18. But, in that sketch, it should be noted that the 6-ft 3-in. headroom must be available for the entire length of the work space. It must be clearance from the floor up to the light fixture or to any other overhead obstruction—and not simply to the ceiling or bottom of the joists.

110-17. Guarding of Live Parts (600 Volts, Nominal, or Less). After the 1968 **NEC**, old Sec. 110-17(a)(3), accepting guard rails as suitable for guarding live parts, was deleted. It was felt that a guard rail is not proper or adequate protection in areas accessible to other than qualified persons.

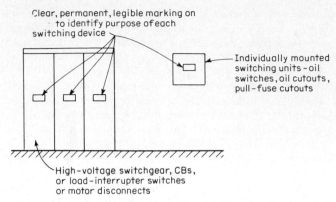

Fig. 110-21. High-voltage switches and breakers must be properly marked to indicate their function. (Sec. 110-30.)

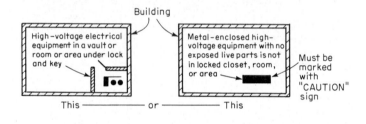

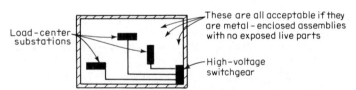

Fig. 110-22. NE Code rules on high-voltage equipment installations in buildings accessible to electrically unqualified persons. [Sec. 110-31(a).]

or unqualified persons who may for some reason gain access to a locked, high-voltage area.

Section 110-31(b) specifies that outdoor installations *with exposed live parts* must *not* provide access to unqualified persons. Elevation may be used to prevent access [Sec. 110-34(e)], or equipment may be enclosed by a wall, screen, or fence under lock and key, as shown in Fig. 110-23. Outdoor installations that are open to unqualified persons must comply with Art. 225, "Outside Branch Circuits and Feeders."

Where high-voltage equipment is installed in places accessible only to qualified persons, the rules of Secs. 110-34, 710-32, and 710-33 apply. In such areas,

Fig. 110-24. METAL-ENCLOSED high-voltage equipment accessible to the general public—such as pad-mount transformers or switchgear units installed outdoors or in indoors areas where the general public is not excluded—must have doors or hinged covers locked (arrow) if the bottom of the enclosure is less than 8 ft above the ground or above the floor.

110-32. Work Space about Equipment.   Figure 110-25 points out the basic **Code** rule of Sec. 110-32 relating to working space around electrical equipment.

Figure 110-26 shows the rules on adequate headroom and necessary illumination for safely working on high-voltage electrical equipment.

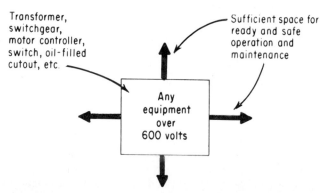

Fig. 110-25. This is the general rule for work space around any high-voltage equipment. (Sec. 110-32.)

Fig. 110·27. Working space in front of equipment must be at least 3 ft wide measured parallel to front surface of the enclosure. (Sec. 110-32.)

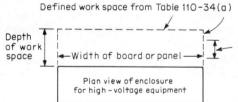

One entrance 24 in. wide by 6-1/2 ft high must be provided to the defined work space. But, if the board or panel is over 6 ft wide, there must be one entrance at each end of of the work space, except where the depth of space is at least twice the value in Table 110-34 (a).

Fig. 110·28. Access to required work space around high-voltage equipment must be assured. (Sec. 110-33.)

Chapter Two

ARTICLE 200. USE AND IDENTIFICATION OF GROUNDED CONDUCTORS

200-2. General. As indicated in the Exception, some circuits and systems may be operated without an intentionally grounded conductor—that is, without a grounded neutral or a grounded phase leg. Sections 250-7, 503-13(a), and 517-63 *require* use of *ungrounded* circuits. Ungrounded circuits are required in anesthetizing locations where flammable anesthetics are used—which include hospital operating rooms, delivery rooms, emergency rooms, and any place where flammable anesthetics are administered. (See Sec. 517-63.)

The rule in the last paragraph of this section requires that an insulated grounded-neutral conductor must have the same insulation voltage rating as the ungrounded conductors in all circuits rated up to 1,000 V—which means in all the commonly used 240/120-, 208/120-, and 480/277-V circuits. To correlate with Sec. 250-152 on minimum voltage rating of insulation on grounded neutrals of high-voltage systems, Secs. 250-152 and 200-2 state that where an insulated, solidly grounded neutral conductor is used with any circuit rated over 1,000 V—such as in 4,160/2,400- or 13,200/7600-V solidly grounded neutral circuits—the neutral conductor does *not* have to have insulation rated for either phase-to-phase or phase-to-neutral voltage, but must have insulation rated for at least 600 V. See Sec. 250-152. [Of course, a bare, solidly grounded neutral conductor may be used in such circuits that constitute service-entrance conductors, are direct-buried portions of feeders, or are installed overhead, outdoors—as specified in Sec. 250-152. But when an insulated neutral is used, the above rule on 600-V rating applies.] Both Sec. 250-152 and Sec. 200-2 represent exceptions to Sec. 310-2 requiring conductors to be insulated.

200-6. Means of Identifying Grounded Conductors. The basic rule in part **(a)** requires that any grounded neutral conductor or other circuit conductor that is

73

operated intentionally grounded must have a white or natural gray outer finish for *the entire length* of the conductor *if* the conductor is No. 6 size or smaller. See Fig. 200-1.

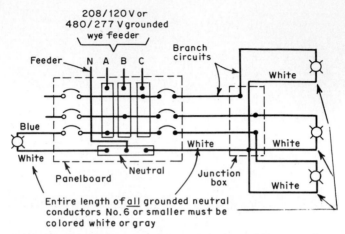

Fig. 200-1. Generally any grounded circuit conductor that is No. 6 size or smaller must have a continuous white or natural gray outer finish. [Sec. 200-6(a).]

Exempted from the basic requirement for a white or gray neutral are multi-conductor varnished-cloth insulated cables, fixture wires as covered by Sec. 402-8, branch-circuit neutrals with color tracer stripes (other than green) to distinguish among multiple neutrals of different systems in the same raceway or other enclosure, and neutrals of aerial cable—which may have a raised ridge on the exterior of the neutral to identify them.

Exception No. 3 to the basic rule that requires use of continuous white or natural gray color along the entire length of any insulated grounded conductor (such as grounded neutral) in sizes No. 6 or smaller permits use of a conductor of other colors (black, purple, yellow, etc.) for a grounded conductor in a *multiconductor cable* under certain conditions (see Fig. 200-2):

1. That such a conductor is used only where qualified persons supervise and do service or maintenance on the cable—such as in industrial and mining applications.
2. That every grounded conductor of color other than white or gray will be effectively and permanently identified at all terminations by distinctive white marking or other effective means applied at the time of installation.

This permission for such use of grounded conductors in multiconductor cable allows the practice in those industrial facilities where multiconductor cables are commonly used—although the rule does not limit the use to industrial occupancies.

An Exception identical to the one described above under Sec. 200-6(a) also follows the rule of Sec. 200-6(b) that requires any grounded conductor larger than No. 6 to be either white or gray color for its whole length or to be marked

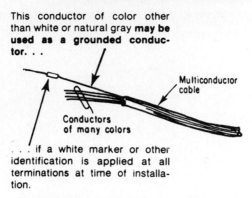

This conductor of color other than white or natural gray **may be used as a grounded conductor. . .**

Multiconductor cable

Conductors of many colors

. . . if a white marker or other identification is applied at all terminations at time of installation.

NOTE: This permission applies to No. 6 and smaller conductors. —as well as to conductors larger than No. 6.

Fig. 200-2. [Sec. 200-6(a), Exception No. 3.]

with white identification (like white tape) at all terminations at time of installation.

For conductors installed in raceways or in general-use cable assemblies like NM cable or BX cable [NEC Type (AC)], continuous white or gray marking along the entire lengths of grounded conductors is not required for conductors larger than No. 6. Such grounded conductors may be of color other than white or gray provided that a "distinctive white marking"—such as white tape or paint—is applied to the conductor surface at all points of splice or termination to readily designate that it *is* a grounded conductor. See Fig. 200-3.

In the rule of part **(d),** color coding must distinguish between grounded circuit conductors where branch circuits and/or feeders of different systems are in the same raceway. This rule assures that differentiation between neutral (grounded circuit) conductors of different wiring systems in the same raceway or other enclosure is provided for feeder circuits *as well as* branch circuits. Section 210-5(a) has long required such differentiation for branch circuits—requiring, for instance, that if a 208/120-V, 3-phase, 4-wire circuit is in the same conduit with a 480/277-V, 3-phase, 4-wire circuit, one neutral must be white or natural gray; but the neutral of the other circuit of a different voltage must be white with a color tracer stripe along the conductor length or must have some other means of distinguishing between the two neutrals of the different systems. The rule here makes the same requirement for differentiating neutrals when a conduit contains more than one feeder (or feeder and branch circuit) of different systems. (See Fig. 210-10.)

200-7. Use of White or Natural Gray Color.   Although the basic rule here limits conductors with white or gray outer covering to use only as grounded conductors [that is, as grounded neutral or grounded phase conductors (see Fig. 200-4)], a number of exceptions to the rule are noted:

Figure 200-5 shows a white-colored conductor used for an ungrounded phase conductor of a feeder to a panelboard. As shown in the left side of the panel bottom gutter, the white conductor has black tape wrapped around its end for

Fig. 200-3. Conductors of colors other than white or gray—in sizes larger than No. 6—may be used as grounded neutrals or grounded phase legs if marked white at all terminations—such as by white tape on the grounded feeder neutrals, at left. [Other color tapes are used on other circuit conductors to identify the three phases as A, B, and C—as required by Sec. 384-3(f).] [Sec. 200-6(b).]

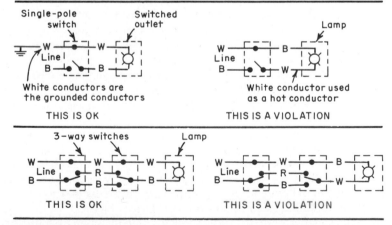

Fig. 200-4. A white or gray-colored conductor must normally be used *only* as a grounded conductor (the grounded circuit neutral or grounded phase leg of a delta system). (Sec. 200-7.)

Fig. 200-5. White conductor in lower left of panel gutter is used as an ungrounded phase conductor of a feeder, with black tape wrapped around the conductor end to "reidentify" the conductor as *not* a grounded conductor. (Sec. 200-7, Exception No. 1.)

a length of a few inches. This almost satisfies Exception No. 1 of Sec. 200-7, which permits a white conductor to be used for an ungrounded (a hot phase leg) conductor if the white is "permanently reidentified"—such as by wrapping with black or other color tape—to indicate clearly and effectively that the conductor is ungrounded. The wording of the Exception, however, might be interpreted to require that the black or other color tape be wrapped over the entire visible length of the conduit bushing.

Exception No. 2 indicates conditions under which a white conductor in a cable (such as BX or nonmetallic-sheathed cable) may be used for an ungrounded (hot-leg) conductor—*without need* for "reidentification" (such as painting or taping). When used as described, the white conductor is acceptable even though it is *not* a grounded conductor. Figure 200-6 shows examples of correct and incorrect hookups of switch loops where hot supply is run first to the switched outlet, then to switches.

Exception No. 3 covers flexible cords for connecting appliances to a receptacle outlet. Exception No. 4 applies to circuits derived from the secondary side of transformers that step down to less than 50 V. Such circuits may use a white conductor.

200-10. Identification of Terminals. Part **(b)** permits a neutral terminal on a receptacle to be identified by the word "white" marked on the receptacle as an alternative to identification of a neutral terminal by use of terminal parts (screw, etc.) that are "substantially white in color."

Marking of the word "white" provides the required identification of the neutral terminal on receptacles that require white-colored plating on *all* terminals of a receptacle for purposes of corrosion resistance or for connection of aluminum conductors. Obviously, if all terminals are white-colored, color no longer serves to identify or distinguish the neutral as it does if the hot-conductor

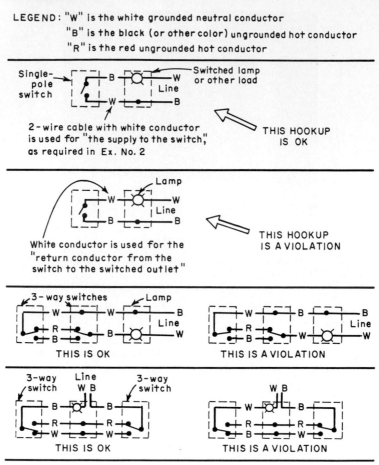

LEGEND: "W" is the white grounded neutral conductor
"B" is the black (or other color) ungrounded hot conductor
"R" is the red ungrounded hot conductor

Single-pole switch

B — Switched lamp or other load
W
Line
B

2-wire cable with white conductor is used for "the supply to the switch" as required in Ex. No. 2

THIS HOOKUP IS OK

Lamp
W — W
Line
B — B

White conductor is used for the "return conductor from the switch to the switched outlet"

THIS HOOKUP IS A VIOLATION

3-way switches   Lamp
W — W — B
Line
R
B — B — W

THIS IS OK

W — B — B
Line
R
B — W — W

THIS IS A VIOLATION

3-way switch   Line W B   3-way switch
B — B
R — R
W — W

THIS IS OK

W B
W — B
R — R
B — W

THIS IS A VIOLATION

Fig. 200·6. For switch loops from load outlets with hot supply to the load outlet, white conductor in cable must be the "supply to the switch." (Sec. 200-7, Exception No. 2.)

terminals are brass-colored. And as the rule is worded, the marking "white" may be used to identify the neutral terminal on receptacles that have all brass-colored terminal screws. See Fig. 200-7.

The third sentence of part **(b)** permits a push-in-type wire terminal to be identified as the neutral (grounded) conductor terminal either by marking the word "white" on the receptacle body adjacent to the conductor entrance hole or by coloring the entrance hole white—as with a white-painted ring around the edge of the hole.

The Exception to part **(b)** makes clear that a 2-wire plug cap must have its neutral terminal identified if the plug is of the polarized type required by Sec. 410-42(a).

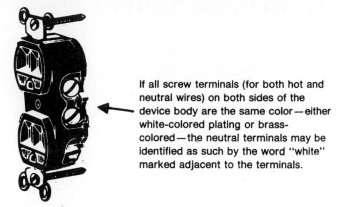

If all screw terminals (for both hot and neutral wires) on both sides of the device body are the same color—either white-colored plating or brass-colored—the neutral terminals may be identified as such by the word "white" marked adjacent to the terminals.

Fig. 200-7.

The rule of part (c) is shown in Fig. 200-8.

Part (e) of Sec. 200-10 requires that the neutral terminal of appliances be identified—to provide proper connection of field-installed wiring (either fixed wiring connection or attachment of a cord set).

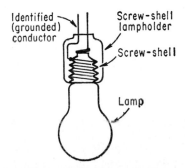

Identified (grounded) conductor — Screw-shell lampholder — Screw-shell — Lamp

SCREW-SHELL LAMPHOLDERS are wired so that ungrounded conductor is connected to center terminal to reduce shock hazard. The identified (grounded) conductor is connected to the screw-shell.

Fig. 200-8. Screw-shell sockets must have the grounded wire (the neutral) connected to the screw-shell part. [Sec. 200-10(c).]

The rule applies to "appliances that have a single-pole switch or a single-pole overcurrent device in the line or any line-connected screw-shell lampholder" and requires simply that some "means" (instead of "marking") be provided to identify the neutral. As a result, use of white color instead of marking is clearly recognized for such neutral terminals of appliances.

ARTICLE 210. BRANCH CIRCUITS

210·1. Scope. Article 210 covers all branch circuits other than those "which supply only motor loads," which are covered in Art. 430. This section makes clear that the article covers branch circuits supplying lighting and/or appliance loads as well as branch circuits supplying any combination of those loads plus motor loads or motor-operated appliances. Where motors or motor-operated appliances are connected to branch circuits supplying lighting and/or appliance loads, the rules of *both* Art. 210 and Art. 430 apply. Article 430 alone applies to branch circuits that supply only motor loads.

210·2. Other Articles for Specific-Purpose Branch Circuits. Exceptions to the requirements for general-purpose branch circuits are indicated for "Closed-Loop and Programmed Power Distribution" as covered in new **NEC** Art. 780. Design and hookup details for that type of branch-circuit distribution system are given in **Code** Art. 780 and represent special conditions which substantially differ from the usual **Code** rules on conventional branch-circuit wiring systems.

210·3. Classifications. A branch circuit is rated according to the rating of the overcurrent device used to protect the circuit. A branch circuit with more than one outlet *must* normally be rated at 15, 20, 30, 40, or 50 A (Fig. 210-1). That is, the protective device must have one of those ratings for multioutlet circuits, and the conductors must meet the other size requirements of Art. 210. Under the definition for "receptacle" in **NE Code** Art. 100, it is indicated that a duplex convenience outlet (a duplex receptacle) is two receptacles and not one—even though there is only one box. Thus, a circuit that supplies only one duplex receptacle has "more than one outlet," that is, more than one point at which current is taken from the circuit to supply utilization equipment.

The Exception to this section gives limited permission to use multioutlet branch circuits rated over 50 A—but *only* to supply nonlighting loads and *only* in industrial places where maintenance and supervision assure that only qualified persons will service the installation. This Exception recognizes a real need in industrial plants where a single machine or piece of electrically operated equipment is going to be provided with its own dedicated branch circuit of adequate capacity—in effect, an individual branch circuit—but where such machine or equipment is required to be moved around and used at more than one location, requiring multiple points of outlet from the individual branch circuit to provide for connection of the machine or equipment at any one of its intended locations. *But at any time, only one machine or equipment will be connected to the branch circuit.*

It is important to note that it is the size of the overcurrent device which determines the rating of any circuit covered by Art. 210, even when the conductors used for the branch circuit have an ampere rating higher than that of the protective device. In a typical case, for example, a 20-A circuit breaker in a panelboard might be used to protect a branch circuit in which No. 10 conductors are used as the circuit wires. Although the load on the circuit does not exceed 20 A and No. 12 conductors would have sufficient current-carrying capacity to be used in the circuit, the No. 10 conductors with their rating of 30 A were selected

BASIC RULE —

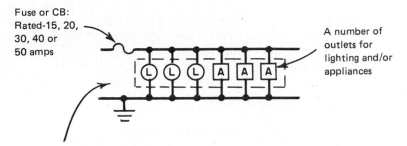

Fuse or CB:
Rated-15, 20,
30, 40 or
50 amps

A number of
outlets for
lighting and/or
appliances

Circuit voltage shall not exceed 150 volts to ground for circuits
supplying lampholders, fixtures or receptacles of standard 15-amp
rating. For incandescent or electric-discharge lighting under certain
conditions, voltage to ground may be as high as 300 volts. In certain
cases, voltage for electric discharge lighting may be up to 500 volts
"between conductors" and may be an ungrounded circuit.

EXCEPTION —

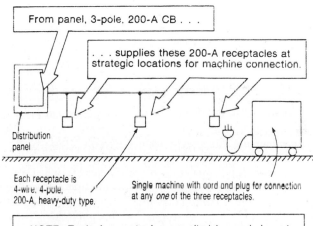

From panel, 3-pole, 200-A CB . . .

. . . supplies these 200-A receptacles at
strategic locations for machine connection.

Distribution
panel

Each receptacle is
4-wire, 4-pole,
200-A, heavy-duty type.

Single machine with cord and plug for connection
at any *one* of the three receptacles.

NOTE: Typical receptacles supplied by such layout
could be rated 60 A, 100 A, 200 A or 400 A — with
their supply circuit of the same rating. Such hookups
are common in jet airplane hangars for supplying
cord-connected equipment used for servicing individual planes in their hangar bays.

Fig. 210-1. A multioutlet branch circuit must usually have a rating (of its overcurrent protective device) at one of the five values set by Sec. 210-3. (Sec. 210-3.)

to reduce the voltage drop in a long homerun. The rating of the circuit is 20 A because that is the size of the overcurrent device. The current rating of the wire does not enter into the ampere classification of the circuit.

Although multioutlet branch circuits are limited in rating to 15, 20, 30, 40, or 50 A, a branch circuit to a single-load outlet (for instance, a branch circuit to one machine or to one receptacle outlet) may have any ampere rating (Fig. 210-2). For instance, there could be a 200-A branch circuit to a special receptacle outlet or a 300-A branch circuit to a single machine.

INDIVIDUAL BRANCH CIRCUIT

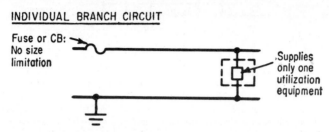

Fig. 210-2. A circuit to a single load device or equipment may have any rating. (Sec. 210-3.)

210-4. Multiwire Branch Circuits. A "branch circuit" as covered by Art. 210 may be a 2-wire circuit or may be a "multiwire" branch circuit. A "multiwire" branch circuit consists of two or more ungrounded conductors having a potential difference between them and an identified grounded conductor having equal potential difference between it and each of the ungrounded conductors and which is connected to the neutral conductor of the system. Thus, a 3-wire circuit consisting of two opposite-polarity ungrounded conductors and a neutral derived from a 3-wire, single-phase system or a 4-wire circuit consisting of three different phase conductors and a neutral of a 3-phase, 4-wire system is a *single* multiwire branch circuit. This is only one circuit, even though it involves two or three single-pole protective devices in the panelboard (Fig. 210-3). This is important, because other sections of the **Code** refer to conditions involving "one branch circuit" or "the single branch circuit." (See Secs. 250-24 and 410-31.)

The wording of part **(a)** of this section makes clear that a multiwire branch circuit may be considered to be either "a single circuit" or "multiple circuits." This coordinates with other **Code** rules that refer to multiwire circuits as well as rules that call for two or more circuits. For instance, Sec. 220-4(b) requires that at least *two* 20-A small appliance branch circuits be provided for receptacle outlets in those areas specified in Sec. 210-52—that is, the kitchen, dining room, pantry, and breakfast room of a dwelling unit. The wording of this rule recognizes that a single 3-wire, single-phase 240/120-V circuit run to the receptacles in those rooms is equivalent to *two* 120-V circuits and satisfies the rule of Sec. 220-4(b).

In addition, a "multiwire" branch circuit is considered to be a single circuit of multiple-wire makeup. That will satisfy the rule in Sec. 410-31, which rec-

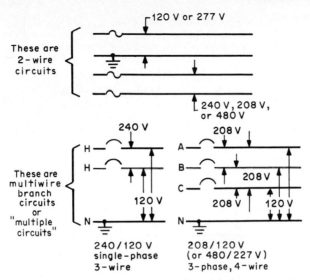

Fig. 210-3. Branch circuits may be 2-wire or multiwire type. (Sec. 210-4.)

ognizes that a multiwire circuit is a single circuit when run through end-to-end connected lighting fixtures that are used as a raceway for the circuit conductors. Only *one circuit*—either a 2-wire circuit or a multiwire (3- or 4-wire) circuit—may be run through fixtures connected in a line.

Part **(b)** is discussed after part **(c)**.

The basic rule of part **(c)** of this section states that multiwire branch circuits (such as 240/120-V, 3-wire, single-phase and 3-phase, 4-wire circuits at 208/120 V or 480/277 V) may be used only with loads connected from a hot or phase leg to the neutral conductor (Fig. 210-4). The two exceptions to that rule are shown in Fig. 210-5.

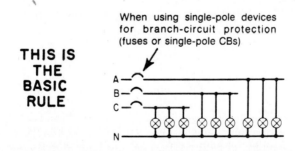

. . . multiwire branch circuits shall supply only line-to-neutral connected loads.

Fig. 210-4. With single-pole protection only line-to-neutral loads may be fed. (Sec. 210-4.)

Ex. No. 1 A multiwire branch circuit may supply a single utilization equipment with line-to-line and line-to-neutral voltage using single-pole switching devices in branch-circuit protection.

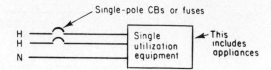

Single-pole CBs or fuses

H ——
H ——
N ——

Single utilization equipment

← This includes appliances

Ex. No. 2 If a multipole CB is used, loads may be connected line-to-line and/or line-to-neutral.

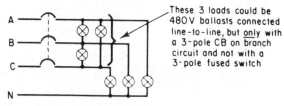

A ——
B ——
C ——
N ——

These 3 loads could be 480V ballasts connected line-to-line, but only with a 3-pole CB on branch circuit and not with a 3-pole fused switch

Fig. 210-5. Line-to-line loads may only be connected on multiwire circuits that conform to the Exceptions given. (Sec. 210-4.)

Exception No. 1 permits use of single-pole protective devices for an individual circuit to "only one utilization equipment"—in which load may be connected line-to-line as well as line-to-neutral. "Utilization equipment," as defined in Art. 100, is "equipment which utilizes electric energy for mechanical, chemical, heating, lighting, or similar purposes." The definition of "appliance," in Art. 100, notes that an appliance is "*utilization equipment, generally other than industrial, normally built in standardized sizes or types* . . . such as clothes washing, air conditioning, food mixing, deep frying, etc." Because of those definitions, the wording of Exception No. 1 opens its application to commercial and industrial equipment as well as residential.

Exception No. 2 permits a multiwire branch-circuit to supply line-to-line connected loads only when it is protected by a multipole CB. The intent of Exception No. 2 is that line-to-line connected loads may be used (other than in Exception No. 1) *only* where the poles of the *circuit protective device* operate together, or simultaneously. A multipole CB satisfies the rule, but a fused multipole switch would not comply because the hot circuit conductors are *not* "opened simultaneously by the branch-circuit overcurrent device." This rule requiring a multipole CB for any circuit that supplies line-to-line connected loads as well as line-to-neutral loads was put in the **Code** to prevent equipment loss under the conditions shown in Fig. 210-6. Use of a 2-pole CB in the sketch would cause opening of both hot legs on any fault and prevent the condition shown.

At the end of part **(c)**, a fine-print note calls attention to Sec. 300-13(b), which requires maintaining the continuity of the grounded neutral wire in a multiwire branch circuit by pigtailing the neutral to the neutral terminal of a receptacle.

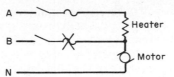

Should fuse B open, the heater and motor would be
in series on 115 volts, and the motor could burn out
if not properly protected.

Fig. 210-6. Single-pole protection can expose equipment to
damage. (Sec. 210-4.)

Exception No. 2 of Sec. 210-4(c) and Sec. 300-13(b) are both aimed at the same
safety objective—to prevent damage to electrical equipment that can result
when two loads of unequal impedances are series-connected from hot leg to
hot leg as a result of opening the neutral of an energized multiwire branch circuit or are series-connected from hot leg to neutral. Section 300-13(b) prohibits
dependency upon device terminals (such as internally connected screw terminals of duplex receptacles) for the splicing of neutral conductors in multiwire
(3- or 4-wire) circuits. *Grounded neutral wires* must not depend on device connection (such as the break-off tab between duplex-receptacle screw terminals)
for continuity. White wires can be spliced together, with a pigtail to the neutral
terminal on the receptacle. If the receptacle is removed, the neutral will not be
opened.

This rule is intended to prevent the establishment of unbalanced voltages
should a neutral conductor be opened *first* when a receptacle or similar device
is replaced on energized circuits. In such cases, the line-to-neutral connections
downstream from this point (farther from the point of supply) could result in a
considerably higher-than-normal voltage on one part of a multiwire circuit and
damage equipment, because of the "open" neutral, if the downstream line-to-
neutral loads are appreciably unbalanced. Refer to the description given in
Sec. 300-13 of this book.

Some electrical inspectors have applied an interpretation to the rule of part
(c) and its Exception No. 2 to require a multipole CB on multiwire circuits with
line-to-line loads to provide safety to maintenance personnel or any persons
working on or replacing lighting fixtures or receptacle outlets connected line-
to-line in existing systems. This has been a widely discussed and very controversial problem in Code interpretation over recent years. Shock hazard may
exist in replacing or maintaining any piece of electrical equipment where *only
one* of *two* hot supply conductors has been opened. If only one of the two single-pole CBs or single-pole switches controlling a 240-V circuit or a 240/120-V,
3-wire circuit is shut off, the load will be de-energized and electrical workers
may presume that they will not contact any hot terminals of equipment supplied and then be surprised by electric shock from the other hot leg.

Part **(b)** of this section requires a 2-pole (simultaneously operating) circuit
breaker or switch to be used at the panelboard (supply) end of a 240/120-V,
single-phase, 3-wire circuit that supplies one or more split-wired duplex receptacles or combination wiring devices *in a dwelling unit* (a one-family house, an

apartment in an apartment house, a condominium unit, or any other occupancy that conforms to the definition of "dwelling unit" given in Art. 100). In addition to covering split-wired receptacles, this rule applies the same concept of safety to cover duplex switches and switch-receptacle combinations, as found in the "combination line" of wiring devices that have either two receptacles, two switches, or a switch and receptacle on a single mounting strap (yoke), with a break-off fin for isolating the devices—as well as night-lights, pilot-light lamps, or other visual or audible indicators which are incorporated into common-yoke assemblies of wiring devices.

Figure 210-7 shows that a 2-pole CB, two single-pole CBs with a handle tie that enables them to be used as a 2-pole disconnect, or a 2-pole switch ahead of branch-circuit fuse protection will satisfy the requirement that both hot legs must be interrupted when the disconnect means is opened to de-energize a multiwire circuit to a split-wired receptacle. This **Code** rule provides the greater safety of disconnecting both hot conductors simultaneously to prevent shock hazard in replacing or maintaining any piece of electrical equipment where *only one* of *two* hot supply conductors has been opened.

Note: Circuits supplying split-wired receptacles in commercial, industrial, and institutional occupancies (places that are not "dwelling units") may use single-pole CBs, plug fuses without switches, or single-pole switches ahead of fuses.

It should also be noted that although a 2-pole switch ahead of fuses may satisfy as the simultaneous disconnect required ahead of split-wired receptacles, such a switch does *not* satisfy as the simultaneous multipole "branch-circuit protective device" that is required by Exception No. 2 of Sec. 210-4 when a multiwire circuit supplies any loads connected phase-to-phase. In such a case, a 2-pole CB *must* be used because fuses are single-pole devices and do not assure simultaneous opening of all hot legs on overcurrent or ground fault.

It should be noted that the threat of motor burnout shown in the diagram of Fig. 210-6 can exist just as readily where the 230-V resistance device and the 115-V motor are fed from a dual-voltage (240-V, 120-V) duplex receptacle as where loads are fixed wired. As shown in Fig. 210-8, the rule of Sec. 210-4 does clearly call for a 2-pole CB (and not single-pole CBs or fuses) for a circuit supplying a dual-voltage receptacle. In such a case, a line-to-line load and a line-to-neutral load could be connected and subjected to the condition shown in Fig. 210-6.

In part **(d)**, an important rule for multiwire branch circuits requires some means of identification of each of the hot (ungrounded) conductors of branch circuits in a building that contains wiring systems operating at two or more different voltage levels.

This **Code** rule restores the need to identify phase legs of circuits where more than one voltage system is used for multiwire branch circuits in a building. For instance, a building that utilizes both 208Y/120-V circuits and 480Y/277-V circuits must have separate and distinct color coding of the hot legs of the two voltage systems—or must have some means other than color coding, such as tagging, marking tape (color or numbers), or some other identification that will

ANY SPLIT-WIRED WIRING DEVICE IN A <u>DWELLING UNIT</u> MUST HAVE MULTIPOLE, SIMULTANEOUS DISCONNECT MEANS AT CIRCUIT ORIGIN. . .

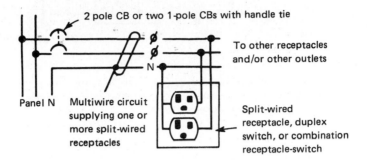

2 pole CB or two 1-pole CBs with handle tie

To other receptacles and/or other outlets

Panel N Multiwire circuit supplying one or more split-wired receptacles

Split-wired receptacle, duplex switch, or combination receptacle-switch

. . . OR THIS MAY BE DONE . . .

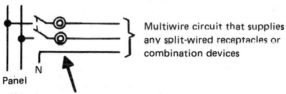

Multiwire circuit that supplies any split-wired receptacles or combination devices

Panel

2-pole switch ahead of plug fuses will satisfy as disconnect on circuit to one or more split-wired receptacles, provided there are no phase-to-phase-connected loads on the circuit.

. . . BUT THIS WOULD BE A VIOLATION!

2-pole switch with plug fuses

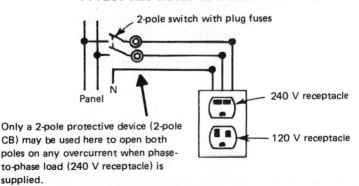

Panel

240 V receptacle

120 V receptacle

Only a 2-pole protective device (2-pole CB) may be used here to open both poles on any overcurrent when phase-to-phase load (240 V receptacle) is supplied.

Fig. 210-7.

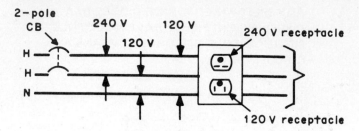

If any load on a multiwire circuit supplying more than one outlet is
connected line-to-line (such as a 240-volt load on the receptacle
above), a multipole CB must be used.

Fig. 210·8. A dual-voltage receptacle requires a 2-pole CB on its circuit. (Sec.
210-4.)

satisfy the inspecting agency. And this new rule further states that the "means
of identification must be permanently posted at each branch-circuit panelboard"—to tell how the individual phases in each of the different voltage systems are identified (Fig. 210-9).

The wording of the new rule requires that the "means of identification" must
distinguish between all conductors "by phase and by system." But, if a building
uses only one voltage system—such as 208Y/120 V or 240/120 V single phase—
then, no identification is required for the circuit phase (the "hot" or
ungrounded) legs. And where a building utilizes two or more voltage systems,
the separate, individual identification of ungrounded conductors must be done
whether the circuits of the different voltages are run in the same or separate
raceways.

210·5. Color Code for Branch Circuits.   Code rules on color coding of conductors (Sec. 210-5) apply only to branch-circuit conductors and do not directly
require color coding of feeder conductors. However, **NE Code** Sec. 384-3(f) does
require identification of phase legs of feeders to panelboards, switchboards,
etc.—and that requires some technique for marking the phase legs. Many
design engineers do insist on color coding of feeder conductors to afford effective balancing of loads on the different phase legs.

Color coding of branch-circuit conductors is divided into three categories:

Grounded conductor: The grounded conductor of a branch circuit (the neutral of a wye system or a grounded phase of a delta) must be identified by a
continuous white or natural gray color, for the entire length of conductors No.
6 or smaller. Where wires of different systems (such as 208/120 and 480/277)
are installed in the same raceway, box, or other enclosure, the neutral or
grounded wire of one system must be white; and the neutral of the other system
must be gray or white with a color stripe. If there are three or more systems in
the same raceway or enclosure, the additional neutrals must be white with colored tracers other than green. The point is that neutrals of different systems
must be distinguished from each other when they are in the same enclosure
[Code Sec. 210-5(a) and Fig. 210-10].

WHEN BUILDING CONTAINS ONLY
ONE SYSTEM VOLTAGE FOR CIRCUITS:

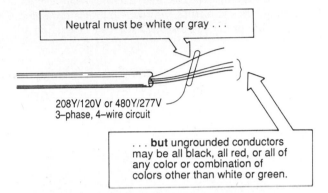

Neutral must be white or gray . . .

208Y/120V or 480Y/277V
3–phase, 4–wire circuit

. . . **but** ungrounded conductors
may be all black, all red, or all of
any color or combination of
colors other than white or green.

IF THERE ARE TWO SYSTEM VOLTAGES:

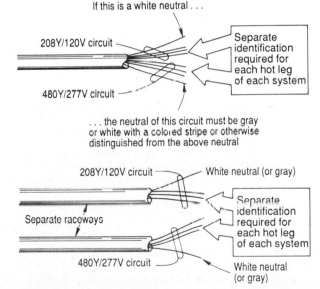

If this is a white neutral . . .

208Y/120V circuit

480Y/277V circuit

Separate
identification
required for
each hot leg
of each system

. . . the neutral of this circuit must be gray
or white with a colored stripe or otherwise
distinguished from the above neutral

208Y/120V circuit   White neutral (or gray)

Separate raceways

Separate
identification
required for
each hot leg
of each system

480Y/277V circuit   White neutral
                                     (or gray)

Fig. 210-9. Separate identification of ungrounded conductors is
required only if a building utilizes more than one nominal voltage
system. Neutrals must be color-distinguished if circuits of two voltage
systems are used in the same raceway (Sec. 210-5), but *not* if different
voltage systems are run in separate raceways. [Sec. 210-4(d).]

As already noted, Exceptions to Sec. 200-6 modify the basic rule that requires use of continuous white or natural gray color along the entire length of any insulated grounded conductor (such as a grounded neutral) in size No. 6 or smaller. Likewise, Exception No. 2 to Sec. 210-5(a) also permits use of a conductor of other colors (black, purple, yellow, etc.) for a grounded conductor in a *multiconductor* cable under the conditions given in Exception No. 3 of Sec. 200-6(a).

WHEN THERE IS ONLY ONE SYSTEM VOLTAGE:

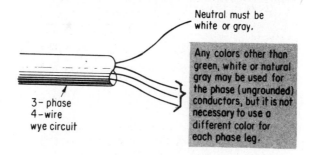

Neutral must be white or gray.

Any colors other than green, white or natural gray may be used for the phase (ungrounded) conductors, but it is not necessary to use a different color for each phase leg.

3-phase
4-wire
wye circuit

BUT, Neutrals of different systems must be distinguished

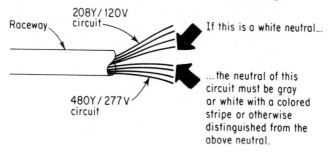

Raceway

208Y/120V circuit

480Y/277V circuit

If this is a white neutral...

...the neutral of this circuit must be gray or white with a colored stripe or otherwise distinguished from the above neutral.

Fig. 210-10. Grounded circuit conductors (neutrals) must have color identification. [Sec. 210-5(a).]

That permission for such use of grounded conductors in multiconductor cable allows the practice in commercial and industrial facilities where multiconductor cables are commonly used.

Hot conductors: The NE Code requires that individual hot conductors of a multiwire circuit be identified where a building has more than one nominal voltage system. [See Sec. 210-4(d).]

Grounding conductor: An equipment grounding conductor of a branch circuit (if one is used) must be color-coded green or green with one or more yellow stripes—or the conductor may be bare [Sec. 210-5(b)].

However, Exception No. 1 refers to Sec. 250-57(b), which says that an equipment grounding conductor larger than No. 6 may be other than a green-insulated conductor or a green-with-yellow-stripe conductor. Section 250-57 permits an equipment grounding conductor with insulation that is black, blue, or any other color—provided that one of the three techniques specified in Sec. 250-57 is used to identify this conductor as an equipment grounding conductor.

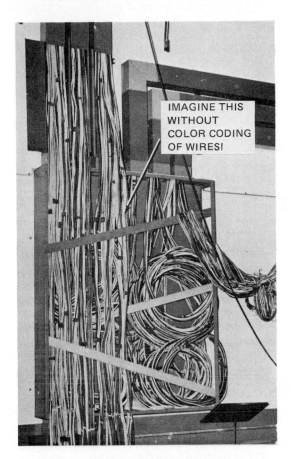

IMAGINE THIS WITHOUT COLOR CODING OF WIRES!

Fig. 210-11. Although not Code required, color identification of branch-circuit phase legs is needed for safe and effective work on grouped circuits. (Sec. 210-5.)

The first technique consists of stripping the insulation from the insulated conductor for the entire length of the conductor appearing within a junction box, panel enclosure, switch enclosure, or any other enclosure. With the insulation stripped from the conductor, the conductor then appears as a bare conductor, which is recognized by the **Code** for grounding purposes. A second technique which is acceptable is to paint the exposed insulation green for its entire length within the enclosure. If, say, a black insulated conductor is used in a conduit coming into a panelboard, the length of the black conductor within the panelboard can be painted green to identify this as an equipment grounding conductor.

The third acceptable method is to mark the exposed insulation with green-colored tape or green-colored adhesive labels. Figure 210-12 summarizes the rules on identification of equipment grounding conductors. Green-colored conductors must not be used for any purpose other than equipment grounding.

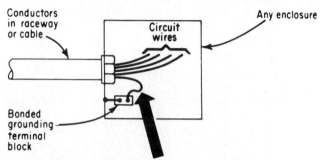

Equipment grounding conductor may be bare, or covered to show a green color or green with one or more yellow stripes.

Exception No. 1

But, for a grounding conductor larger than No. 6, an insulated conductor of other than green color or green with yellow stripes may be used provided *one* of the following steps is taken:

1. Stripping the insulation from an insulated conductor of another color (say, black) for the entire length that is exposed in the box or other enclosure— so that the conductor appears as a bare conductor.

2. Painting the exposed insulation green for its entire length within the enclosure.

3. Wrapping the entire length of exposed insulation with green-colored tape or green-colored adhesive labels.

Fig. 210-12. Equipment grounding conductor for branch circuit. [Sec. 210-5(b).]

Color coding of circuit conductors (or some other method of identifying them), as required by Sec. 210-4(d), is a wiring consideration that deserves the close, careful, complete attention of all electrical people. By providing ready identification of the two or three phase legs and neutrals in wiring systems, color coding is the easiest and surest way of balancing loads among the phase legs, thereby providing full, safe, effective use of total circuit capacities. In circuits where color coding is missing or not effectively applied, loads or phases get unbalanced, many conductors are either badly underloaded or excessively loaded, and breakers or fuses often are increased in size to eliminate tripping due to overload on only one phase leg. Modern electrical usage—for reasons of safety and energy conservation, as well as full, economic application of system equipment and materials—demands the many real benefits that color coding can provide.

For the greater period of its existence, the **NE Code** required a very clear, rigid color coding of branch circuits for good and obvious safety reasons. Color coding of hot legs to provide load balancing is a safety matter. Section 220-4(d) requires balancing of loads from branch-circuit hot legs to neutral. Section 220-22 bases sizing of feeder neutrals on clear knowledge of load balance in order to determine "maximum unbalance." And mandatory differentiation of voltage levels is in the safety interests of electricians and others maintaining or working on electrical circuits, to warn of different levels of hazard.

Because 99 percent of electrical systems involve no more than two voltage configurations for circuits up to 600 V, and because there has been great standardization in circuit voltage levels, there should be industrywide standardization on circuit conductor identifications. A clear, simple set of rules could cover the preponderant majority of installations, with exceptions made for the relatively small number of cases where unusual conditions exist and the local inspector may authorize other techniques. Color coding should follow some basic pattern—such as the following:

- 120-V, 2-wire circuit: grounded neutral—white; ungrounded leg—black.
- 240/120-V, 3-wire, single-phase circuit: grounded neutral—white; one hot leg—black; the other hot leg—red.
- 208Y/120-V, 3-phase, 4-wire: grounded neutral—white; one hot leg—black; one hot leg—red; one hot leg—blue.
- 240-V, delta, 3-phase, 3-wire: one hot leg—black; one hot leg—red; one hot leg—blue.
- 240/120-V, 3-phase, 4-wire, high-leg delta: grounded neutral—white; high leg (208-V to neutral)—orange; one hot leg—black; one hot leg—blue.
- 480Y/277-V, 3-phase, 4-wire: grounded neutral—gray; one hot leg—brown; one hot leg—orange; one hot leg—yellow.
- 480-V, delta, 3-phase, 3-wire: one hot leg—brown; one hot leg—orange; one hot leg—yellow.

By making color coding a set of simple, specific color designations, standardization will assure all the safety and operating advantages of color coding to all electrical systems. Particularly today, with all electrical systems being subjected to an unprecedented amount of alterations and additions because of continuing development and expansion in electrical usage, conductor identification is a regular safety need over the entire life of the system.

A second step in clarification and expansion of color coding would require color coding for all circuits—multiwire branch circuits, branch circuits without a neutral or other grounded conductor, feeders, and even for service conductors. As now indicated in Sec. 384-3(f) of the **NE Code**, correct, effective loading of all circuits—to get full capacity of all phases and to prevent unknown unbalances with the attendant chance of oversizing of protection and overloading of conductors—depends upon ready identification of all conductors at all points in a system.

Of course, there are alternatives to "color" identification throughout the length of conductors. Color differentiation is almost worthless for color-blind electricians. And it can be argued that color identification of conductors poses problems because electrical work is commonly done in darkened areas where color perception is reduced even for those with good eyesight. The **NE Code** already recognizes white tape or paint over the conductor insulation end at terminals to identify neutrals where conductors are larger than No. 6 (Sec. 200-6). Number markings spaced along the length of a conductor on the insulation (1, 2, 3, etc.)—particularly, say, white numerals on black insulation—might prove very effective for identifying and differentiating conductors. Or the letters "A," "B," and "C" could be used to designate specific phases. Or a combination of color and markings could be used. But some kind of conductor identification is essential to safe, effective hookup of the ever-expanding array of conductors used throughout buildings and systems today. And the method used for identifying ungrounded circuit conductors must be posted at each branch-circuit panelboard to comply with requirements of Sec. 210-4(d). Although not required by Sec. 210-5(a), the method used to distinguish the grounded (neutral) conductors for the different systems should also be included with that information required for the ungrounded (phase) conductors.

210·6. Branch Circuit Voltage Limitations.   Voltage limitations for branch circuits are presented in Sec. 210-6. In general, branch circuits serving lampholders, fixtures, or receptacles of the standard 15-A or less rating are limited to operation at a maximum voltage rating of 120 V.

Part **(a)** applies specifically to dwelling units—one-family houses, apartment units in multifamily dwellings, and condominium and co-op units—and to guest rooms in hotels and motels and similar residential occupancies. In such occupancies, any lighting fixture or any receptacle for plug-connected loads rated up to 1,440 VA or for motor loads of less than ¼ hp must be supplied at not over 120 V between conductors.

Note: The 120-V supply to the above-type loads may be derived from (1) a 120-V, 2-wire branch circuit, (2) a 240/120-V, 3-wire branch circuit, or (3) a 208/120-V, 3-phase, 4-wire branch circuit. Appliances rated 1,440 VA or more (ranges, dryers, water heaters, etc.) may be supplied by 240/120-V circuits in accordance with Sec. 210-6(c)(5).

Part **(b)** permits a circuit with not over 120 V between conductors to supply medium-base screw-shell lampholders, ballasts for fluorescent or HID lighting fixtures, and plug-connected or hard-wired appliances—in any type of building or on any premises (Fig. 210-13).

Part **(c)** applies to circuits with over 120 V between conductors (208, 240, 277, or 480 V) but not over 277 V (nominal) to ground. This is shown in Fig. 210-14, where all of the circuits are "circuits exceeding 120 V, nominal, between conductors and not exceeding 277 V, nominal, to ground." Circuits of any of those voltages are permitted to supply incandescent lighting fixtures with mogul-base screw-shell lampholders, ballasts for electric-discharge lighting fixtures or

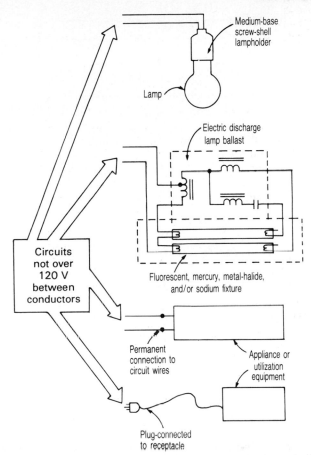

Fig. 210-13. In any occupancy, 120-V circuits may supply these loads. [Sec. 210-6(b)]

plug-connected or hard-wired appliances, or other utilization equipment. It is important to note that this section no longer contains the requirement for a minimum 8-ft mounting height for incandescent or electric-discharge fixtures with mogul-base screw-shell lampholders used on 480/277-V systems.

A UL-listed electric-discharge lighting fixture rated at 277 V nominal may be equipped with a medium-base screw-shell lampholder and does not require a mogul-base screw-shell. The use of the medium-base lampholder, however, is limited to "listed electric-discharge fixtures." for 277-V incandescent fixtures, Sec. 210-6(c)(2) continues the requirement that such fixtures be equipped with "mogul-based screw-shell lampholders."

Fluorescent, mercury-vapor, metal-halide, high-pressure sodium, low-pressure sodium, and/or incandescent fixtures may be supplied by 480/277-V, grounded-wye circuits—with loads connected phase-to-neutral and/or phase-to-phase. Such circuits operate at 277 V to ground even, say, when 480-V bal-

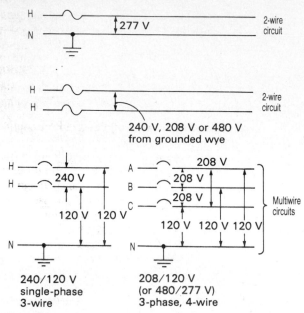

Fig. 210·14. These circuits may supply incandescent lighting with mogul-base screw-shell lampholders for over 120 V between conductors, electric-discharge ballasts, and cord-connected or permanently wired appliances or utilization equipment. [Sec. 210-6(c).]

lasts are connected phase-to-phase on such circuits. Or lighting could be supplied by 240-V delta systems—either ungrounded or with one of the phase legs grounded, because such systems operate at not more than 277 V to ground.

Use of incandescent lighting at over 150 V to ground is accepted by the **NE Code** in commercial, institutional, and industrial buildings and premises.

Although 277-V incandescent lamps are available with medium screw bases, and fixtures for them are available with medium screw-shell lampholders, use of such equipment violates the **NE Code** rule in Sec. 210-6(c) (1). And Sec. 210-6(b) (1) limits medium base, screw-shell lampholders to use only where connected to circuit wires with not more than 120 V between the wires—such as 2-wire 120-V circuits.

Section 210-6(c) permits installations on 480/277-V, 3-phase, 4-wire wye systems—with equipment connected from phase-to-phase (480-V circuits) or connected phase-to-neutral (277-V circuits). In either case, the voltage to ground is only 277 V. In any such application, it is important that the neutral point of the 480/277-V wye be grounded to limit the voltage aboveground to 277 V. If the neutral were not grounded and the system operated ungrounded, the voltage to ground, according to the **Code**, would be 480 V (see definition "voltage to ground," Art. 100), and lighting equipment could be used on such circuits only for outdoor applications as specified under Sec. 210-6(d) (discussed later).

On a neutral-grounded 480/277-V system, incandescent, fluorescent, mercury-vapor, metal-halide, high-pressure sodium, and low-pressure sodium equipment can be connected from phase-to-neutral on the 277-V circuits. If fluorescent or mercury-vapor fixtures are to be connected phase-to-phase, some **Code** authorities contend that autotransformer-type ballasts cannot be used when these ballasts raise the voltage to more than 300 V, because, they contend, the **NE Code** calls for connection to a circuit made up of a grounded wire and a hot wire. (See Sec. 410-78.) On phase-to-phase connection these ballasts would require use of 2-winding, electrically isolating ballast transformers. The wording of Sec. 410-78 does, however, lend itself to interpretation that it is only necessary for the *supply system* to the ballast to *be grounded*—thus permitting the two hot legs of a 480-V circuit to supply an autotransformer because the hot legs are derived from a neutral-grounded "system." But Sec. 210-9 can become a complicating factor. Use of a 2-winding (isolating) ballast is clearly acceptable and avoids all confusion.

    Section 210-6(d) of the **NE Code** permits fluorescent and/or mercury-vapor units to be installed on circuits rated over 277 V (nominal) to ground and up to 600 V between conductors—but only where the lamps are mounted in permanently installed fixtures on poles or similar structures for the illumination of areas such as highways, bridges, athletic fields, parking lots, at a height not less than 22 ft, or on other structures such as tunnels at a height not less than 18 ft. (See Fig. 210-15.) Part **(d)** covers use of lighting fixtures on 480-V ungrounded circuits—such as fed from a 480-V delta-connected or wye-connected ungrounded transformer secondary.

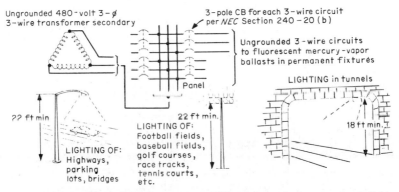

Fig. 210-15. Ungrounded circuits, at up to 600 V between conductors, may supply lighting only as shown. [Sec. 210-6(d).]

    This permission for use of fluorescent and mercury units under the conditions described is based on phase-to-phase voltage rather than on phase-to-ground voltage. This rule has the effect of permitting the use of 240- or 480-V ungrounded circuits for the lighting applications described. But as described above, autotransformer-type ballasts may not be permitted on an ungrounded system if they raise the voltage to more than 300 V [Sec. 410-78]. In such cases, ballasts with 2-winding transformation would have to be used.

    Certain electric railway applications utilize higher circuit voltages. Infrared lamp industrial heating applications may be used on higher circuit voltages as allowed in Sec. 422-15(c) of the **Code**.

Caution: The concept of maximum voltage not over "120 V ... *between* conductors," as stated in Sec. 210-6(a), has caused considerable discussion and controversy in the past when applied to split-wired receptacles and duplex receptacles of two voltage levels. It can be argued that split-wired general-purpose duplex receptacles are not acceptable in dwelling units and in hotel and motel guest rooms because they are supplied by conductors with *more* than 120 V between them—that is, 240 V on the 3-wire, single-phase, 120/240-V circuit so commonly used in residences. The two hot legs connect to the brass-colored terminals on the receptacle, with the shorting tab broken off, and the voltage between those conductors *does* exceed 120 V. The same condition applies when a 120/240-V duplex receptacle is used—the 240-V receptacle is fed by conductors with more than 150 V between them. But, the **Code**-making panel ruled that the use of duplex receptacles connected on 240/120-V, 3-wire, single-phase circuits in dwelling units and guest rooms in hotels, motels, dormitories, etc., is **not** prohibited. See Fig. 210-16.

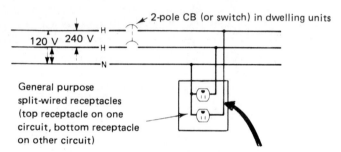

Fig. 210-16. Split-wired receptacles *are* permitted in residential occupancies ("dwelling units") and in all types of occupancies (commercial, institutional, industrial, etc.).

Objection to split-wired receptacles in dwelling units has a sound basis: Two appliances connected by 2-wire cords to a split-wired receptacle in a kitchen do present a real potential hazard. With, say, a coffee maker and a toaster plugged into a split-wired duplex, if the hot wire in each appliance should contact the metal enclosure of the appliance, there would be 240 V between the two appliance enclosures. The user would be exposed to the extremely dangerous chance of touching each appliance with a different hand—putting 240 V across the person, from hand-to-hand, through the heart path (Fig. 210-17). Use of nonsplit-wired receptacles on the usual spacing of up to 4 ft does tend to separate appliances on different hot legs.

Use of split-wired receptacles and other receptacles with more than 120 V between terminals is, of course, completely acceptable in any commercial, institutional, or industrial location. And it is also perfectly acceptable at any time to use a split-wired receptacle for switch control of one plug-in point leaving the other hot all the time (Fig. 210-18).

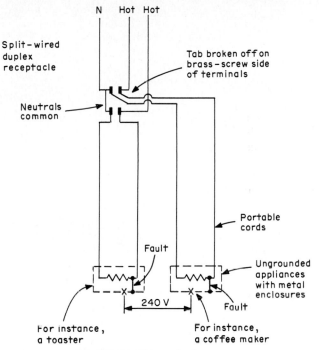

Fig. 210-17. This can be dangerous.

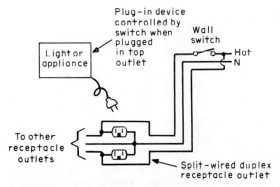

Fig. 210-18. Split-wiring of receptacles to control one of the receptacles may be done from the same hot leg of a 2-wire circuit or with separate hot legs of a 3-wire, 240/120-V circuit. (Sec. 210-6.)

Section 210-6(c) (5) clearly permits "permanently connected utilization equipment" to be supplied by a circuit with voltage between conductors in excess of 120 V, and permission **is** intended for the use of 277-V heaters in dwelling units, as used in high-rise apartment buildings and similar large buildings that may be served at 480/277 V.

210-7. Receptacles and Cord Connectors. Section 210-7 states that "receptacles installed on 15- and 20-A branch circuits shall be of the grounding type." This requires that on all new installations a grounding-type device must be used (Fig. 210-19). This rule came into effect in 1968. Prior to that, ungrounded

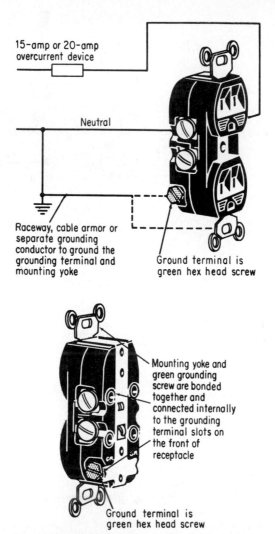

Fig. 210-19. Any receptacle on a 15- or 20-A branch circuit must be a grounding type. (Sec. 210-7.)

devices were permitted on branch circuits. If a residence or office is equipped with these older devices, it is not necessary to replace them as long as they are serviceable.

In all cases where a grounding-type receptacle is installed, it shall be grounded. For nonmetallic-sheathed cable the grounding conductor is run with the branch-circuit conductors. The armor of Type AC metal-clad cable, the sheath of ALS cable, and certain metallic raceways are acceptable as grounding means (Fig. 210-20).

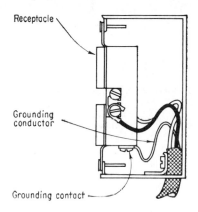

GROUNDING TERMINALS on receptacles may be grounded by the cable armor or sheath, by metallic conduit, or by a grounding conductor.

SELF–GROUNDING RECEPTACLE includes mounting screw equipped with pressure clip to assure tight contact between screws and device yoke, eliminating the need for a grounding jumper from green hex-head screw to metal box.

Fig. 210-20. The grounded terminal must be grounded in an approved manner. [Sec. 210-7(c).]

The purpose here is to make certain that grounding-type receptacles are used and grounded where a ground is available, and nongrounding-type receptacles are used where grounding is impractical so that no one will be deceived as to the availability of a grounding means for appliances.

The rule of Sec. 210-7(b), requiring grounding of the ground terminal of receptacles and cord connectors, has an important Exception. It permits receptacles mounted on portable or vehicle-mounted generators, in accordance with Sec. 250-6, to have their ground terminals left ungrounded, when the generator frame itself is not grounded (Fig. 210-21). But where such receptacles are mounted on portable or vehicle-mounted generators, the grounding terminal of the receptacle *must* be bonded to the generator frame [Sec. 250-6(a) (2)].

For correlation purposes, a note after Sec. 210-7(c) refers to the use of "quiet grounding" for electrical noise reduction for sensitive equipment, as covered in Sec. 250-74, Exception No. 4.

Very important!

On replacement of receptacles that become defective in an already existing installation, the Exception to Sec. 210-7(d) clarifies the rule. Although the

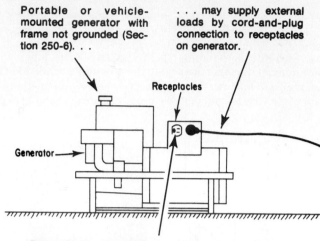

Portable or vehicle-mounted generator with frame not grounded (Section 250-6)...

... may supply external loads by cord-and-plug connection to receptacles on generator.

Receptacles

Generator

Receptacle grounding terminals do not have to be grounded but *must* be bonded to generator frame.

Fig. 210-21. Grounding is not required for generator-mounted receptacles. [Sec. 210-7(b).]

basic rule is that grounding-type receptacles be used as replacements for existing nongrounding types, the Exception covers replacement of *a nongrounding*-type receptacle in any case where the box or other enclosure of the existing receptacle is *not* grounded and *does not* contain an equipment grounding conductor—as with older installations of nonmetallic-sheathed cable without a ground wire or knob-and-tube wiring (Fig. 210-22). In an existing system, a nongrounding-type receptacle in a box that does not include an equipment grounding conductor is permitted to be replaced by either a new nongrounding-type receptacle, by a GFCI-type receptacle, or by a grounding-type receptable (with a U-ground terminal that is not connected to the supply circuit)—*if* the grounding-type receptacle is fed from an upstream GFCI receptacle that provides feed-through protection on its load side (the downstream side). A GFCI receptacle with feed-through protection will provide shock and electrocution protection to any type of receptacle on its load (or protected) side. Replacement of nongrounding-type receptacles by 3-slot grounding-type receptacles offers the advantage of being able to connect 3-prong grounding-type cord plugs to the grounding-type receptacles—eliminating the practice of snapping off the ground prong or using a plug-adapter (or "cheater") on the cap to permit insertion into a nongrounding-type receptacle. Greater safety is the result, even without the ground wire connection to the grounding receptacle. Another advantage is the fact that even 2-wire cord caps are now polarized and cannot be plugged into a nongrounding (2-wire) receptacle, but such cord caps do readily fit the into the two slots of a 3-wire grounding-type receptacle.

The Exception recognizes that a GFCI-type receptacle may be used as replacement for a nongrounding-type receptacle that is installed in a box and

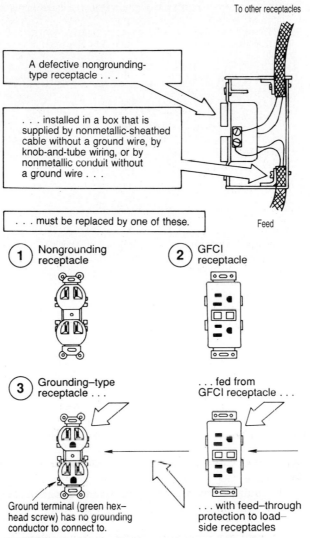

To other receptacles

A defective nongrounding-
type receptacle . . .

. . . installed in a box that is
supplied by nonmetallic-sheathed
cable without a ground wire, by
knob-and-tube wiring, or by
nonmetallic conduit without
a ground wire . . .

. . . must be replaced by one of these.   Feed

(1) Nongrounding
    receptacle

(2) GFCI
    receptacle

(3) Grounding–type
    receptacle . . .

. . . fed from
GFCI receptacle . . .

Ground terminal (green hex–
head screw) has no grounding
conductor to connect to.

. . . with feed–through
protection to load–
side receptacles

Fig. 210-22. A nongrounding-type receptacle, a GFCI-type receptacle, or GFCI protection, must always be used when replacing a nongrounding receptacle in any case where the box does not contain an
equipment grounding conductor. [Sec. 210-7(d).]

fed by a wiring method that does not include an equipment grounding conductor—even if there are other existing receptacles downstream from the GFCI
receptacle. And the wording of the Exception specifies that an equipment
grounding conductor "shall **not** be connected" from the GFCI receptacle to any
downstream receptacles (Fig. 210-23). A GFCI receptacle will still function to
provide protection against shock hazard or electrocution even though it is connected to a 2-wire circuit without an equipment grounding connector. This

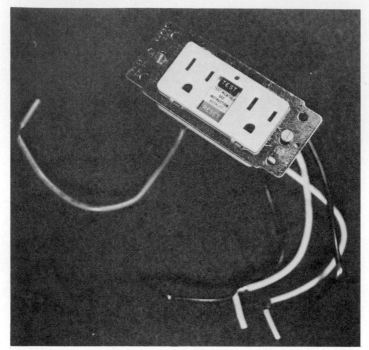

Fig. 210-23. A GFCI receptacle may replace existing nongrounding device in box without an equipment grounding means and may feed downstream receptacles. [Sec. 210-7(d), Exception.]

Code rule has long recognized that it could be misleading and therefore dangerous to replace a nongrounding receptacle with a grounding receptacle without grounding the green hex-head screw (or other ground terminal) of the receptacle or providing line-side GFCI protection.

210-8. Ground-Fault Circuit-Interrupter Protection for Personnel. Part **(a)** of Section 210-8 of the **NE Code** is headed "Dwelling Units." The very clear and detailed definition of those words, as given in Art. 100 of the **NE Code**, indicates that all the ground-fault circuit interruption rules apply to:

- all one-family houses
- each dwelling unit in a two-family house
- each apartment in an apartment house
- each dwelling unit in a condominum

GFCI protection is required by Sec. 210-8 for all 125-V, single-phase, 15- and 20-A receptacles installed in **bathrooms** of dwelling units [part **(a)(1)**] and hotel or motel units [part **(b)**] and in garages of dwelling units only (Fig. 210-24). The requirement for GFCI protection in "garages" is included because home owners do use outdoor appliances (lawn mowers, hedge trimmers, etc.) plugged into garage receptacles. Such receptacles require GFCI protection for the same reason as "outdoor" receptacles. In either place, GFCI protection may be provided by a GFCI circuit breaker that protects the whole circuit and any receptacles connected to it, or the receptacle may be a GFCI type that incorporates the

PROVIDE THIS PROTECTION. . .

Single-phase,125-V, 15A or
20A receptacles

Either GFCI CB
in panel or GFCI
receptacles
at box locations   In bathrooms   In Garages

If a receptacle is in-
stalled to supply a
freezer in a garage, it
does *not* have to be
GFCI protected . . .

. . . BUT AT LEAST ONE OTHER
RECEPTACLE must be installed in the
garage for using hand-held electric
tools or appliances, and it MUST be
GFCI-protected.

CEILING-MOUNTED RECEPTACLE for plugging in the power
cord from an electric garage-door operator is "not readily accessible," and Exception No. 1, therefore, permits it to be non-GFCI
protected.

Fig. 210-24. GFCI protection is required for receptacles in garages
as well as in bathrooms. [Sec. 210-8(a) (2).]

components that give it the necessary tripping capability on low-level ground
faults.

A lot of the controversy that was generated by the question "What is a bathroom?" is eliminated because a definition of the word "bathroom" is given at
the end of Sec. 210-8. A "bathroom" is "an area" (which means it could be a

room or a room plus another area) that contains first a "basin" (sometimes called a "sink") and then at least one more plumbing fixture—a toilet, a tub, and/or a shower. A small room with only a "basin" (a washroom) is not a "bathroom." Neither is a room that contains only a toilet and/or a tub or shower (Fig. 210-26).

As noted above, GFCI protection is required by Sec. 210-8(b) in bathrooms of hotel or motel rooms but not in dormitory rooms or any other residential occupancy that does not conform to the definition of "dwelling unit" (Fig. 210-25).

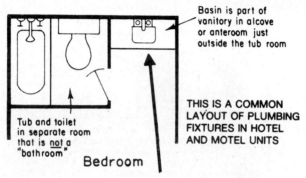

Basin is part of vanitory in alcove or anteroom just outside the tub room

THIS IS A COMMON LAYOUT OF PLUMBING FIXTURES IN HOTEL AND MOTEL UNITS

Tub and toilet in separate room that is _not_ a "bathroom"

Bedroom

Guest rooms in hotels and motels are required by Section 210-60 to have the same receptacle outlets required by Section 210-52 for "dwelling units." The requirement for a wall receptacle outlet at the "basin location" applies to bathrooms; and the anteroom area with only a basin is, by definition and intent, part of the "bathroom." A receptacle at the basin would, therefore, be required. Section 210-8(b) applies to bathrooms, in hotels and motels — and GFCI protection is required for this receptacle.

Fig. 210-25. GFCI is needed in bathrooms of hotel and motel "guest rooms." [Sec. 210-8(b).]

The rule here extends the same protection of GFCI breakers and receptacles to bathrooms in hotel and motel guest rooms as for receptacles in bathrooms of dwelling units. Because Sec. 210-60 has required guest rooms in hotels and motels to have the same availability of receptacle outlets as required in Sec. 210-52 for dwelling units, it is logical that such required receptacles in hotel and motel guest rooms be subject to the rules on GFCI protection for bathrooms in dwelling units.

The rule of Sec. 210-8(a) (2) requiring GFCI protection in garages applies to both attached garages and detached (or separate) garages associated with "dwelling units"—such as one-family houses or multifamily houses where each unit has its own garage. Section 210-52 requires at least one receptacle in an attached garage and in a detached garage if electric power is run out to the garage. Any receptacle in a detached garage must have GFCI protection.

TYPICAL BEDROOM SUITE IN ONE-FAMILY
HOUSE OR APARTMENT UNIT

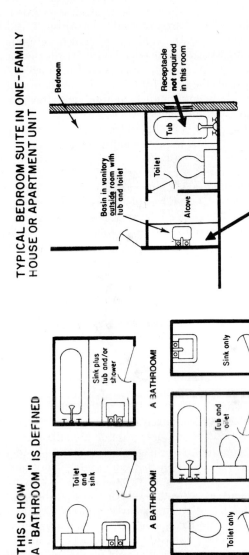

THIS IS HOW
A "BATHROOM" IS DEFINED

Although this **area** with basin is **outside** room with tub and toilet, the intent of Section 210-52 requires a receptacle at basin; and Section 210-8(a) requires that it be GFCI-protected.

NOTE: It is important to understand that the *Code* meaning of "bathroom" refers to the total "area" made up of the basin in the alcove *plus* the "room" that contains the tub and toilet. Although a receptacle is *not* required in the "room" with the tub and toilet, if one is installed in that room, it must be GFCI-protected because such a receptacle is technically "in the bathroom," just as the one at the basin location is "in the bathroom."

NOTE: If a room is not a bathroom according to the definition of Section 210-8(b), then the requirement of Section 210-52 for "at least one wall receptacle outlet . . . adjacent to the basin location" does not apply. If, however, a receptacle is installed in a room that is *not* a "bathroom"—such as the one above containing a basin *only*—GFCI protection is not required for the receptacle because it is not a bathroom receptacle.

Fig. 210-26. For GFCI use, a bathroom may be a "room" or an area that includes one or more "rooms." [Sec. 210-8(b).]

Although the basic rule of part **(a)(2)** requires **all** 125-V, single-phase, 15- or 20-A receptacles installed in garages to have ground-fault circuit-interrupter protection, Exception No. 1 excludes a ceiling-mounted receptacle that is used solely to supply a cord-connected garage-door operator. And, as worded, the Exception excludes *any* receptacles that "are not readily accessible"—that is, any receptacle that requires use of a portable ladder or a chair to get up to it.

From Exception No. 2 to part **(a)(2),** garage receptacles for "dedicated appliances"—those that are put in place and not normally moved because of their weight and size—are excluded from the need for GFCI because they will not normally be used to supply hand-held cord-connected appliances (lawn mowers, hedge trimmers, etc.) that are used outdoors.

Note: Any receptacle in a garage that is excluded from the requirement for GFCI protection, as noted in the two Exceptions of this section, may not be considered as the receptacle that is required by Sec. 210-52(g) to be installed in an attached garage or detached garage with electric power. Thus if a non-GFCI-protected receptacle is installed in a garage at the ceiling for connection of a door operator or if a non-GFCI-protected receptacle is installed in a garage for a freezer, at least one additional receptacle must be installed in the garage to satisfy Sec. 210-52(g) for general use of cord-connected appliances, and such a receptacle *must* be installed not over 5½ ft above the floor and **must** have GFCI protection (either in the panel CB or in the receptacle itself).

Application of the two Exceptions of Sec. 210-8(a)(2) may prove troublesome, because receptacle outlets are most commonly installed in a garage during construction of a house and before it is known what appliances might be used. Under such conditions, GFCI receptacles would be required because "dedicated space" appliances are not in place. Then if, say, a freezer is later installed in the garage, the GFCI receptacle could be replaced with a non-GFCI device. But such replacement would not be acceptable for a receptacle that is the only one in the garage, because such a receptacle is required by Sec. 210-52(g) and is not subject to Exception No. 2 of Sec. 210-8(a).

Part **(a)(3)** of Sec. 210-8, on outdoor receptacles, requires GFCI protection of "all 125-V, single-phase, 15- and 20-A receptacles installed outdoors" at dwelling units. Because hotels, motels, and dormitories are not "dwelling units" in the meaning of the **Code** definition, outdoor receptacles at such buildings do not require GFCI protection. The rule specifies that such protection of outdoor receptacles is required only "where there is direct grade level access to the dwelling unit and to the receptacles . . ." (Fig. 210-27). The phrase "direct grade level access" is defined in part **(a)(3)** and means not over 6½ ft above grade and readily accessible. Because there is no "grade level access" to apartment units constructed above ground level, there would be no need for GFCI protection of receptacles installed outdoors on balconies for such apartments or condominium units. Likewise, GFCI protection would not be required for any outdoor receptacle installed on a porch or other raised part of even a one-family house provided that there was not grade-level access to the receptacle, as in the examples of Fig. 210-27.

The definition of "direct grade level access" in the 1987 **NEC** said that the receptacle requiring GFCI protection had to be "readily accessible without

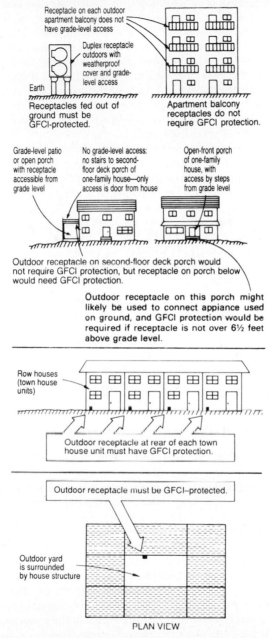

Fig. 210-27. For dwelling units, only outdoor receptacles with "direct grade level access" require GFCI protection. [Sec. 210-8(a) (3).]

entering or passing through a dwelling unit." That phrase was interpreted to exclude from the need for GFCI protection any outdoor receptacles behind "townhouses" (contiguous single-family dwelling units) because such receptacles are readily accessible only by passing through the unit to get to its outdoor back yard. The same is true of "atrium" yards, which are outdoor areas totally surrounded by the structure of a dwelling unit. To make it clear that any outdoor receptacle mounted not over 6½ ft above the ground and readily accessible must be GFCI protected, even though you have to go through the house to reach it, the phrase "without entering or passing through a dwelling unit" was removed from this rule for the 1990 **NEC**.

In any case of an outdoor receptacle at a dwelling unit, GFCI protection is not required if there is no access to the receptacle from the grade level of ground around the building. This important rule on GFCI protection of outdoor outlets reflects the **Code**-making panel's conviction that such protection is not needed where the receptacle cannot readily be used by someone plugging in a tool or appliance and making contact with earth or any masonry walk or other surface or grade.

According to the rule of Sec. 210-8(a)(4), all 125-V, single-phase, 15- and 20-A receptacles installed in crawl spaces at or below grade and/or in unfinished basements must be GFCI-protected. This is intended to apply only to those basements or portions thereof that are unfinished (not habitable). Sec. 210-52(g) requires that at least one receptacle outlet must be installed in the basement of a one-family dwelling, in addition to any installed for laundry equipment. This rule applies to basements of all one-family houses but not to apartment houses, hotels, motels, dormitories, and the like.

Exception No. 1 to Sec. 210-8(a)(4) eliminates the need for GFCI protection of any single receptacle (not duplex or triplex) that is fed by a "dedicated" (an individual) branch circuit that is "located and identified" for use by a plug-in refrigerator or freezer.

Exception No. 2 exempts a laundry circuit from the need for GFCI protection of its receptacle outlets.

Exception No. 3 eliminates the need for GFCI protection of a single receptacle supplying a permanently installed sump pump.

According to part **(a)(5)**, GFCI protection is required for all 125-V, single-phase, 15- or 20-A receptacles installed within 6 ft of any kitchen sink "to serve the counter-top surfaces"—whether such receptacles are above or below the counter top. This will provide GFCI protected receptacles for appliances used on counter tops in kitchens. This would include any receptacles installed in the vertical surfaces of a kitchen "island" that includes counter-top surfaces with or without additional hardware such as a range, grill, or even a sink. Because so many kitchen appliances are equipped with only 2-wire cords (toasters, coffee makers, electric fry pans, etc.), their metal frames are not grounded and are subject to being energized by internal insulation failure, making them shock and electrocution hazards. Use of such appliances close to a sink creates the strong possibility that a person might touch the energized frame of such an appliance and at the same time make contact with a faucet or other grounded part of the sink—thereby exposing the person to shock hazard. Use of GFCI receptacles within arm's reach of the sink (6 ft to either side of the sink) will protect personnel by opening the circuit under conditions of dangerous fault current flow through the person's body (Fig. 210-28).

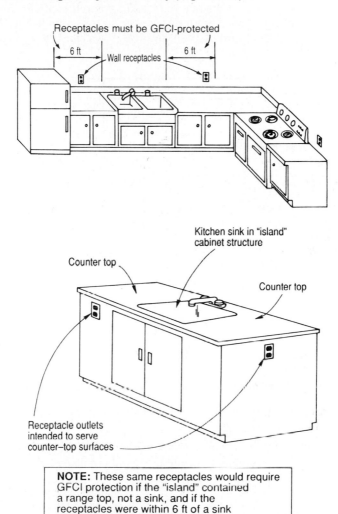

NOTE: These same receptacles would require GFCI protection if the "island" contained a range top, not a sink, and if the receptacles were within 6 ft of a sink installed in cabinets along a wall.

Fig. 210-28. GFCI protection must be provided for receptacles within 6 ft of kitchen sink, whether above or below the counter top. Receptacles in face of island cabinet structure in kitchen must be GFCI-protected if "within 6 ft of kitchen sink." [Sec. 210-8(a)(5).]

Part **(a)(6)** requires that all general-use receptacles in a boathouse of a dwelling unit must have GFCI protection. This rule is in recognition of the potential shock hazard due to damp or wet conditions in a boathouse.

210·9. Circuits Derived from Autotransformers.   The top of Fig. 210-29 shows how a 110-V system for lighting may be derived from a 220-V system by means of an autotransformer. The 220-V system either may be single phase or may be one leg of a 3-phase system. Note that the hookup complies with Exception No. 1. In the case illustrated the "supplied" system has a grounded wire solidly connected to a grounded wire of the "supplying" system: 220-V single-phase system with one conductor grounded.

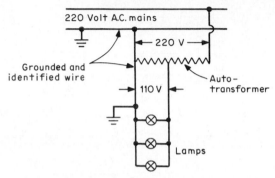

Autotransformer used to derive a 2-wire 110-V system for lighting from a 220-V power system. (Sec. 210-9, Exception No. 1.)

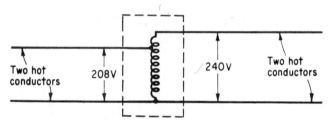

Fig. 210·29. Autotransformers with and without grounded conductors are recognized. (Sec. 210-9, Exceptions No. 1 and No. 2.)

Autotransformers are commonly used to supply reduced voltage for starting induction motors.

Exception No. 2 permits the use of an autotransformer in existing installations for an individual branch circuit without connection to a similar identified grounded conductor where transforming from 208 to 240 V or vice versa (see Fig. 210-29). Typical applications are with cooking equipment, heaters, motors, and air-conditioning equipment. For such applications transformers are commonly used. This has been long-established practice in the field of voltage ranges where a hazard is not considered to exist.

Buck or boost transformers are designed for use on single- or 3-phase circuits to supply $^{12}\!/_{24}$-V or $^{16}\!/_{32}$-V secondaries with a $^{120}\!/_{240}$-V primary. When connected as autotransformers the kVA load they will handle is large in comparison with their physical size and relative cost.

210-10. Ungrounded Conductors Tapped from Grounded Systems. This section permits use of 2-wire branch circuits tapped from the outside conductors of systems, where the neutral is grounded on 3-wire DC or single-phase, 4-wire, 3-phase, and 5-wire 2-phase systems.

Figure 210-30 illustrates the use of unidentified 2-wire branch circuits to supply small motors, the circuits being tapped from the outside conductors of a 3-wire DC or single-phase system and a 4-wire 3-phase wye system.

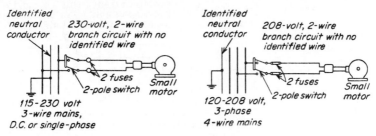

Fig. 210-30. Tapping circuits of ungrounded conductors from the hot legs of grounded systems. (Sec. 210-10.)

All poles of the disconnecting means used for branch circuits supplying permanently connected appliances must be operated at the same time. This requirement applies where the circuit is supplied by either circuit breakers or switches.

In the case of fuses and switches, when a fuse blows in one pole, the other pole may not necessarily open and the requirement to "manually switch together" involves only the manual operation of the switch. Similarly, when a pair of circuit breakers is connected with handle ties, an overload on one of the conductors with the return circuit through the neutral may open only one of the circuit breakers; but the manual operation of the pair when used as a disconnecting means will open both poles. The words "manually switch together" should be considered as "operating at the same time," i.e., during the same operating interval, and apply to the equipment used as a disconnecting means and not as an overcurrent protective device.

Circuit breakers with handle ties are, therefore, considered as providing the disconnection required by this section. The requirement to "manually switch together" can be achieved by a "master handle" or "handle tie" since the operation is intended to be effected by manual operation. The intent was not to require a common trip for the switching device but to require that it have the ability to disconnect ungrounded conductors by one movement of the hand. For service disconnecting means see Sec. 230-71.

210-19. Conductors—Minimum Ampacity and Size. In past NEC editions, the basic rule of this section has said—and *still does* say—that the conductors of a branch circuit must have an ampacity that is not less than the maximum current load that the circuit will supply. Obviously, that is a simple and straightforward rule to assure that the conductors are not operated overloaded. But up to the 1981 NEC, the rule further required that branch-circuit conductors have "an ampacity of not less than the rating of the branch circuit" (Fig. 210-31). Because Sec. 210-3 clearly notes that the amp rating of a multioutlet circuit (typical lighting and appliance branch circuits) is set by the rating of the circuit protective device, the conductors of the circuit were, therefore, always required to have an ampacity of not less than the rating of the fuses or circuit-breaker poles that protect them. And there were no exceptions to that rule.

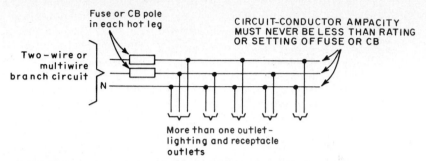

Fig. 210·31. This is the basic rule for any multioutlet branch circuit supplying one or more receptacles. [Sec. 210-19(a).]

The wording of this rule now requires the circuit conductors to have an ampacity not less than "the rating of the branch circuit" **only** for a multioutlet branch circuit that supplies receptacles for cord- and plug-connected loads. The concept here is that plug receptacles provide for random, indeterminate loading of the circuit; and, by matching conductor ampacity to the amp rating of the circuit fuse or CB, overloading of the conductors can be avoided. But for multioutlet branch circuits that supply fixed outlets—such as lighting fixture outlets or hard-wired connections to electric heaters or other appliances—it is acceptable to have a condition where the conductor ampacity is adequate for the load current but, where there is no standard rating of protective device that corresponds to the conductor ampacity, the circuit fuse or CB rating is the next higher standard rating of protective device above the ampacity value of the conductor.

For multioutlet branch circuits (rated at 15, 20, 30, 40, or 50 A), the ampacities of conductors usually correspond to standard ratings of protective devices when there is only one circuit in a cable or conduit. Standard rated protective devices of 15, 20, 30, 40, or 50 A can be readily applied to conductors that have corresponding ampacities from Tables 310-16 through 310-19 and their footnotes—i.e., 15 A for No. 14, 20 A for No. 12, 30 A for No. 10, and 40 A for No. 8, with 55-A rated No. 6 used for a 50-A circuit. But when circuits are combined in a single conduit so that more than three current-carrying conductors are involved, the ampacity derating factors of Note 8 to Table 310-16 often result in reduced ampacity values that do not correspond to standard fuse or CB ratings. It is to such cases that the rule of Sec. 210-19(a) may be applied.

For instance, assume that two 3-phase, 4-wire multioutlet circuits supplying fluorescent lighting are run in a single conduit. Two questions arise: (1) How much load current may be put on the conductors? and (2) What is the maximum rating of overcurrent protection that may be used for each of the six hot legs?

The eight wires in the single conduit (six phases and two neutrals) must be taken as eight conductors when applying Note 8 of Table 310-16 because the neutrals to electric-discharge lighting carry harmonic currents and must be counted as current-carrying conductors [Note 10(c) of Table 310-16]. Note 8 then shows that the No. 14 wires must have their ampacity reduced to 70 percent (for 7 to 9 wires) of the 20-A ampacity given in Table 310-16 for No. 14 TW. With the eight No. 14 wires in the one conduit, then, each has an ampacity of 0.7 × 20, or 14 A. Because Sec. 210-19(a) requires circuit wires to have an ampacity at least equal to the rating of the circuit fuse or CB if the circuit is supplying receptacles, use of a 15-A fuse or 15-A circuit breaker would **not** be acceptable in such a case because the 14-A ampacity of each wire *is* less than "the rating of the branch circuit" (15 A). **But** because the circuits here are supplying fixed lighting outlets, as stated in the original assumption, Sec. 210-19(a) would accept the 15-A protection on wires with 14-A ampacity. In such a case, it is only necessary that the design load current on each phase must not exceed 14 A if the load is noncontinuous. Or if the lighting load **is** continuous (operating steadily for three or more hours), the load on each 15-A CB or fuse must not exceed 0.8 × 15, or 12 A [as required by Sec. 210-22(c) and Sec. 384-16(c)].

Refer to the discussion of Sec. 210-20 and the discussion of ampacity and derating under Sec. 310-15.

In part **(b)**, the rule also calls for the same approach to sizing conductors for branch circuits to household electric ranges, wall-mounted ovens, counter-mounted cooking units, and other household cooking appliances (Fig. 210-32).

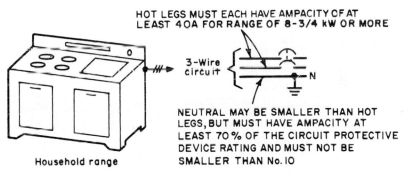

HOT LEGS MUST EACH HAVE AMPACITY OF AT LEAST 40A FOR RANGE OF 8-3/4 kW OR MORE

3-Wire circuit   N

NEUTRAL MAY BE SMALLER THAN HOT LEGS, BUT MUST HAVE AMPACITY AT LEAST 70% OF THE CIRCUIT PROTECTIVE DEVICE RATING AND MUST NOT BE SMALLER THAN No. 10

Household range

Fig. 210·32. Sizing circuit conductors for household electric range. [Sec. 210-19(b).]

The maximum demand for a range of 12-kW rating or less is sized from NEC Table 220-19 as a load of 8 kW. And 8,000 W divided by 230 V is approximately 35 A. Therefore, No. 8 conductors with an ampacity of 40 A may be used for the range branch circuit.

On modern ranges the heating elements of surface units are controlled by five-heat unit switches. The surface-unit heating elements will not draw current from the neutral unless the unit switch is in one of the low-heating positions. This is also true to a greater degree as far as the oven-heating elements are concerned, so that the maximum current in the neutral of the range circuit seldom exceeds 20 A. Because of that condition, Exception No. 2 permits a smaller-size neutral than the ungrounded conductors, but not smaller than No. 10.

A reduced-size neutral for a branch circuit to a range, wall-mounted oven, or cook-top must have ampacity of not less than 70 percent of the circuit rating, which is determined by the current rating or setting of the branch-circuit protective device. This is a change from previous wording that required a reduced neutral to have an ampacity of at least 70 percent of "the ampacity of the ungrounded conductors." Under that wording, a 40-A circuit (rating of protective device) made up of No. 8 TW wires for the hot legs could use a No. 10 TW neutral—because its 30-A ampacity is at least 70 percent of the 40-A ampacity of a No. 8 TW hot leg (0.7 × 40 = 28 A). But if No. 8 THHN (55-A ampacity) is used for the hot legs with the same 40-A protected circuit, the neutral ampacity would have to be at least 70 percent of 55 A (0.7 × 55 = 38.5 A) and a No. 10 TW (30 A) or a No. 10 THW (35 A) could not be used. The new wording bases neutral size at 70 percent of the protective-device rating (0.7 × 40 A = 28 A), thereby permitting any of the No. 10 wires to be used, and does not penalize use of higher-temperature wires (THHN) for the hot legs.

Exception No. 1 permits taps from electric cooking circuits (Fig. 210-33). Because Exception No. 1 says that taps on a 50-A circuit must have an ampacity of at least 20 A, No. 14 conductors—which have an ampacity of 20 A in Table 310-16—may be used.

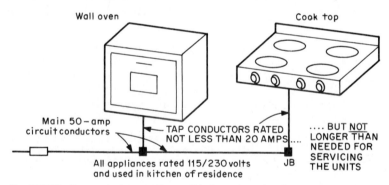

Fig. 210·33. Tap conductors may be smaller than wires of cooking circuit. [Sec. 210-19(b), Ex. No. 1.]

Exception No. 1 applies to a 50-A branch circuit run to a counter-mounted electric cooking unit and wall-mounted electric oven. The tap to each unit must be as short as possible and should be made in a junction box immediately adjacent to each unit. The words "no longer than necessary for servicing the appliance" mean that it should be necessary only to move the unit to one side in order that the splices in the junction box be accessible.

Section 210-19(c) sets No. 14 as the smallest size of general-purpose circuit conductors. But tap conductors of smaller sizes are permitted as explained in Exceptions No. 1 and No. 2 (Fig. 210-34). No. 14 wire, not longer than 18 in., may be used to supply an outlet unless the circuit is a 40- or 50-A branch circuit, in which event the minimum size of the tap conductor must be No. 12.

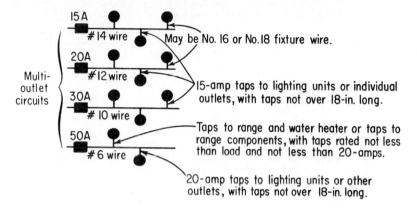

Multi-
outlet
circuits

15A

#14 wire → May be No. 16 or No.18 fixture wire.

20A

#12 wire

30A → 15-amp taps to lighting units or individual outlets, with taps not over 18-in. long.

#10 wire

50A → Taps to range and water heater or taps to range components, with taps rated not less than load and not less than 20-amps.

#6 wire

20-amp taps to lighting units or other outlets, with taps not over 18-in. long.

Branch circuit taps—as covered in 210-19 and 210-20— are considered protected by the branch circuit overcurrent devices.

Fig. 210-34. Tap conductors may be smaller than circuit wires. [Sec. 210-19(c), Exception Nos. 1 and 2.]

210-20. Overcurrent Protection. According to the basic **Code** rule of this section, the rating or setting of an overcurrent device in any branch circuit must not exceed the current-carrying capacity of the circuit conductor or may be the next higher value of overcurrent device where conductor ampacity does not match the rating of a standard fuse or CB. Section 240-3 applies to the rating of overcurrent protection. Figure 210-35 shows the basic rules that apply to use of overcurrent protection for branch circuits. (Section 240-2 designates other **Code** articles that present data and regulations on overcurrent protection for branch circuits to specific types of equipment.)

Branch-circuit taps—as covered in Secs. 210-19 and 210-20—are considered protected by the branch-circuit overcurrent devices, even where the rating or setting of the protective device is greater than the amp rating of the tap conductors, fixture wires, or cords.

When only three No. 12 TW or THW conductors of a branch circuit are in a conduit, each has a load-current rating of 20 A (see the footnote to Table 310-16, Art. 310) and must be protected by a fuse or CB rated not over 20 A. This satisfies Sec. 210-19, which requires branch-circuit conductors to have an ampacity not less than the rating of the branch circuit—and Sec. 210-3 notes

Branch circuit for other than motor load

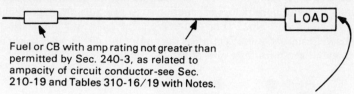

Fuel or CB with amp rating not greater than
permitted by Sec. 240-3, as related to
ampacity of circuit conductor-see Sec.
210-19 and Tables 310-16/19 with Notes.

If load on circuit operates for any period of 3 or
more hours, load current must not exceed 80%
of fuse or CB rating.

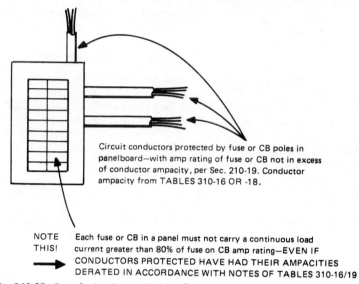

Circuit conductors protected by fuse or CB poles in
panelboard—with amp rating of fuse or CB not in excess
of conductor ampacity, per Sec. 210-19. Conductor
ampacity from TABLES 310-16 OR -18.

NOTE   Each fuse or CB in a panel must not carry a continuous load
THIS!   current greater than 80% of fuse on CB amp rating—EVEN IF
            CONDUCTORS PROTECTED HAVE HAD THEIR AMPACITIES
            DERATED IN ACCORDANCE WITH NOTES OF TABLES 310-16/19

Fig. 210-35. Branch-circuit protection involves a number of rules. (Sec. 210-20.)

that the rating of a branch circuit is established by the rating of the protective
device. It also satisfies Sec. 210-20, which says:

> Branch-circuit conductors ... shall be protected by overcurrent protective devices
> having a rating or setting ... *not exceeding that specified in Section 240-3* for conduc-
> tors. ...

The basic rule of Section 240-3 says:

> Conductors ... shall be protected against overcurrent *in accordance with their ampac-
> ities* as specified in Tables 310-16 through 310-19 and all applicable notes to these
> tables.

That rule says that conductors are required to be protected at a current value
indicated by the table and its accompanying notes, such as Note 8, which
reduces ampacities from the table values.

In Table 310-16, which applies to conductors in raceways and in cables and
covers the majority of conductors used in electrical systems for power and light,

the ampacities for sizes No. 14, No. 12, and No. 10 are particularly significant because copper conductors of those sizes are involved in the vast majority of branch circuits in modern electrical systems. No. 14 has an ampacity of 20, No. 12 has an ampacity of 25, and No. 10 has an ampacity of 30. The typical impact of that on circuit makeup and loading is as follows:

No. 12 TW or THW copper is shown to have an ampacity of 25; and based on the general UL requirement that equipment terminals be limited to use with conductors loaded not in excess of 60°C ampacities for wires up to No. 1 AWG, No. 12 THHN or XHHW copper conductors must also be treated as having a 25-A continuous rating (the ampacity of 60°C No. 12) and **not** 30 A, as shown in Table 310-16. *But,* the footnote to Table 310-16 limits all No. 12 copper to not over 20-A load current by requiring that they be protected at not more than 20 A.

The ampacity of 25 A for No. 12 TW and THW copper wires interacts with Note 8 to Tables 310-16 to 310-19 where there are, say, six No. 12 TW current-carrying wires for the phase legs of two 3-phase, 4-wire branch circuits in one conduit supplying, say, receptacle loads. In such a case, the two neutrals of the branch circuits do not count in applying Note 8, and only the six phase legs are counted to determine how much all conductors must have their ampacities *derated* to the "Percent of Values in Tables"—as stated at the top of the table in Note 8. In the case described here, that literally means that each No. 12 phase leg may be used at an ampacity of 0.8 × 25, or 20 A. And the footnote to Table 310-16 would require use of a fuse or CB rated not over 20 A to protect each No. 12 phase leg. Each No. 12 would be protected at the current value that represents the maximum I^2R heat input that the conductor insulation can withstand. In that example, the derated ampacity of the No. 12 conductors (20 A) is not in excess of "the rating of the branch circuit"—that is, the 20-A rating of the fuse or CB protecting the circuit. Thus, Sec. 210-19(a) is completely and readily satisfied because the ampacity and protective device rating came out to the same value. Thus the circuits described could be used for supplying receptacles and/or fixed-load outlets. The only other possible qualification is that Sec. 384-16(c) would require the load current on each of the phase legs to be further limited to no more than 80 percent of the 20-A rating of the overcurrent device—that is, to 16 A—if the load current is "continuous" (operates steadily for 3 hr or more), a condition not likely for receptacle-fed loads. Refer to further analysis in Sec. 310-15.

210-21. Outlet Devices.   Specific limitations are placed on outlet devices for branch circuits: Lampholders must not have a rating lower than the load to be served; and lampholders connected to circuits rated over 20 A must be heavy-duty type (that is, rated at least 660 W if it is an "admedium" type and at least 750 W for other types). Because fluorescent lampholders are not of the heavy-duty type, this excludes the use of fluorescent luminaires on 30-, 40-, and 50-A circuits. The intent is to limit the rating of lighting branch circuits supplying fluorescent fixtures to 20 A. The ballast is connected to the branch circuit rather than the lamp, but by controlling the lampholder rating, a 20-A limit is established for the ballast circuit. Most lampholders manufactured and intended for use with electric-discharge lighting for illumination purposes are rated less than 750 W and are not classified as heavy-duty lampholders. If the luminaires are individually protected, such as by a fuse in the cord plug of a luminaire cord connected to, say, a 50-A trolley or plug-in busway, some inspectors have permitted use of fluorescent luminaires on 30-, 40-, and 50-A circuits. But such protection in the cord plug or in the luminaire is supplementary (Sec. 240-10), and branch-circuit protection of 30-, 40-, or 50-A rating would still exclude use of fluorescent fixtures according to Sec. 210-21(a).

Section 210-21(b) contains two paragraphs of importance. Part **(b)(1)** reads: "A **single** receptacle installed on an individual branch circuit shall have an ampere rating of not less than that of the branch circuit." Since the branch-circuit overcurrent device determines the branch-circuit rating (or classification), a single receptacle (not a duplex receptacle) supplied by an individual branch circuit cannot have a rating **less than** the branch-circuit overcurrent device, as shown in Fig. 210-36.

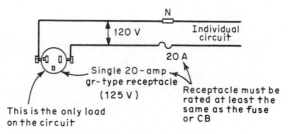

Fig. 210-36. Receptacle amp rating must *not* be less than circuit protection rating for an individual circuit. [Sec. 210-21(b).]

Receptacles must have ratings at least equal to the load. On circuits having two or more outlets, receptacles shall be rated as follows:

- On 15-A circuits—not over 15-A rating
- On 20-A circuits—15- or 20-A rating
- On 30-A circuits—30-A rating
- On 40-A circuits—40- or 50-A rating
- On 50-A circuits—50-A rating

For multioutlet branch circuits rated over 50 A, as permitted under the limited conditions described in the discussion on the Exception to Sec. 210-3, every receptacle must have a rating not less than the branch-circuit rating.

210-22. Maximum Loads.   Part **(c)** of this section says that a branch circuit supplying a continuous current load must have a rating (the rating of the circuit fuse or CB) not less than 125 percent of the continuous-current load. The concept is the same as that described in Sec. 220-3(a). The idea of the rule is that 125 percent of a total continuous-load current gives a circuit rating such that the continuous-load current does "not exceed 80 percent of the rating of the branch circuit." One is the reciprocal of the other.

Sec. 210-22(c) says that (for loads other than motor loads) the rating of a branch circuit must be at least equal to 1.25 times the continuous-load current when the load will constitute a continuous load—such as store lighting and similar loads that are on for periods of 3 or more hr.

Continuous load current must be limited:

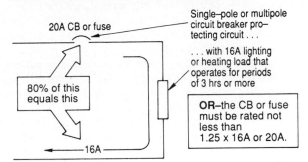

Fig. 210-37. Branch-circuit protective device must be rated not less than 125 percent of the continuous load current. [Sec. 210-22(c).]

Because multioutlet branch circuits, such as lighting circuits, are rated in accordance with the rating or setting of the circuit overcurrent protective device, this rule has the effect of saying that the rating of the protective device must equal at least 1.25 times the continuous-load current (Fig. 210-37). Where a circuit also supplies some noncontinuous load (not "on" for periods of 3 hr or more) in addition to continuous-load current, the branch circuit protective device must have a rating not less than the noncontinuous-load current plus 1.25 times the continuous-load current.

Although the above-mentioned limitation applies only to loads other than motor loads, Sec. 384-16(c) says that "the total load on any overcurrent device located in a panelboard shall not exceed 80 percent of its rating where in normal operation the load will continue for 3 hours or more," which is the same rule stated reciprocally.

NOTE: In both of the above cases, neither the 125 percent of continuous load nor the 80 percent load limitation applies "where the assembly including the overcurrent device is approved for continuous duty at 100 percent of its rating,"

It is very important to understand that the UL and **Code** rules calling for load limitation to 80 percent of the rating of the protective device are based on the inability of the protective device itself to handle continuous load without overheating. And, if a protective device has been designed, tested, and "listed" (such as by UL) for continuous operation at its full-load rating, then there is no requirement that the load current be limited to 80 percent of the breaker or fuse rating (or that the breaker or fuse rating must be at least 125 percent of continuous load). The 80 percent continuous limitation is not at all based on or related to conductor ampacity—which is a separate, independent determination.

Section 384-16(c) requires any CB or fuse in a panelboard to have its load limited to 80 percent; and only one exception is made for such protective devices in a panel: A continuous load of 100 percent is permitted only when the protective device assembly (the CB unit or fuses in a switch) is approved for 100 percent continuous duty. (And there are no such devices rated less than 600 A. UL has a hard and fast rule that any breaker not marked for 100 percent of continuous load must have its continuous load limited to 80 percent of its rating.) Based on Sec. 384-16(c) and the UL rules described, use of conductors that have had their ampacity derated because more than three are in a raceway (Note 8 to Tables 310-16 through 310-19) does not eliminate the requirement for an 80 percent limit on continuous load.

210-23. Permissible Loads. A single branch circuit to one outlet or load may serve any load and is unrestricted as to amp rating. Circuits with more than one outlet are subject to **NE Code** limitations on use as follows: (The word "appliance" stands for any type of utilization equipment.)

1. Branch circuits rated 15 and 20 A may serve lighting units and/or appliances. The rating of any one cord- and plug-connected appliance shall not exceed 80 percent of the branch-circuit rating. Appliances fastened in place may be connected to a circuit serving lighting units and/or plug-connected appliances, provided the total rating of the fixed appliances fastened in place does not exceed 50 percent of the circuit rating (Fig. 210-38). *Example:* 50 percent of a 15-A branch circuit = 7.5 A. A room-air-conditioning unit fastened in place, with a rating not in excess of 7.5 A,

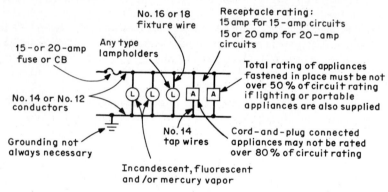

Fig. 210-38. General-purpose branch circuits—15 or 20 A. [Sec. 210-23(a).]

may be installed on a 15-A circuit having two or more outlets. Such units may not be installed on one of the small appliance branch circuits required in Sec. 220-4(b).

However, modern design provides separate circuits for individual fixed appliances. In commercial and industrial buildings, separate circuits should be provided for lighting and separate circuits for receptacles.

2. Branch circuits rated 30 A may serve fixed lighting units (with heavy-duty-type lampholders) in other than dwelling units or appliances in any occupancy. Any individual cord- and plug-connected appliance which draws more than 24 A may not be connected to this type of circuit (Fig. 210-39).

Because an *individual* branch circuit—that is, a branch circuit supplying a single outlet or load—may be rated at any ampere value, it is important to note that the omission of recognition of a 25-A **multioutlet** branch circuit does not affect the full acceptability of a 25-A **individual** branch cir-

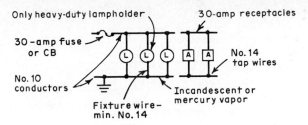

Fig. 210-39. Multioutlet 30-A circuits. [Sec. 210-23(b).]

cuit supplying a single outlet. A typical application of such a circuit would be use of No. 10 TW aluminum conductors (rated at 25 A in Table 310-16), protected by 25-A fuses or circuit breaker, supplying, say, a 4,500-W water heater at 230 V. The water heater is a load of 4,500 ÷ 230, or 19.6 A— which is taken as a 20-A load. Then, because Sec. 422-14(b) designates water heaters as continuous loads (in tank capacities up to 120 gal), the 20-A load current multiplied by 125 percent equals 25 A, and satisfies Sec. 422-4(a), Exception No. 2, on the required minimum branch-circuit rating. The 25-A rating of the circuit overcurrent device also satisfies Sec. 422-27(e), which says that the overcurrent protection must not exceed 150 percent of the ampere rating of the water heater.

No. 10 aluminum, with a 60°C ampacity of 25 A, may be used instead of No. 12 copper (rated 20 A). But the need for and the application possibilities of a 25-A **multioutlet** branch circuit have always been extremely limited. Such a circuit has never been considered suitable to supply lighting loads in dwelling units (where aluminum branch-circuit conductors have been primarily used). But for heavy-current appliances (16 to 20 A) realistic loading dictates use of an **individual** branch circuit, which **may** be rated at 25 A.

3. Branch circuits rated 40 and 50 A may serve fixed lighting units (with heavy-duty lampholders) or infrared heating units in other than dwelling units or cooking appliances in any occupancy (Fig. 210-40). It should be noted that a 40- or 50-A circuit may be used to supply any kind of load equipment—such as a dryer or a water heater—where the circuit is an individual circuit to a single appliance. The conditions shown in that figure apply only where more than one outlet is supplied by the circuit. Figure 210-41 shows the combination of loads.

4. A multioutlet branch circuit rated over 50 A—as permitted by Sec. 210-3— is limited to use only for supplying industrial utilization equipment (machines, welders, etc.) and may *not* supply lighting outlets.

Except as permitted in Sec. 660-4 for portable, mobile, and transportable medical x-ray equipment, branch circuits having two or more outlets may supply only the loads specified in each of the above categories. It should be noted that any other circuit is not permitted to have more than one outlet and would be an individual branch circuit.

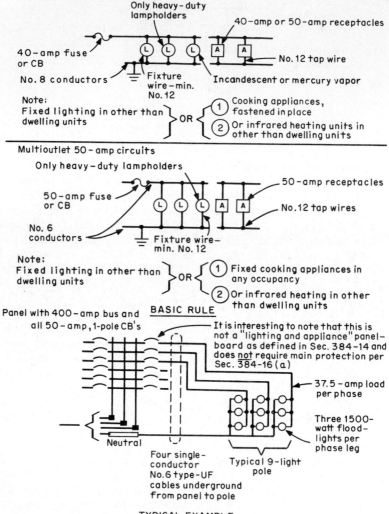

Multioutlet 40-amp circuits

Only heavy-duty lampholders

40-amp or 50-amp receptacles

40-amp fuse or CB

No. 8 conductors

Fixture wire—min. No. 12

No. 12 tap wire

Incandescent or mercury vapor

Note:
Fixed lighting in other than dwelling units } OR {
(1) Cooking appliances, fastened in place
(2) Or infrared heating units in other than dwelling units

Multioutlet 50-amp circuits

Only heavy-duty lampholders

50-amp receptacles

50-amp fuse or CB

No. 6 conductors

Fixture wire— min. No. 12

No.12 tap wires

Note:
Fixed lighting in other than dwelling units } OR {
(1) Fixed cooking appliances in any occupancy
(2) Or infrared heating in other than dwelling units

BASIC RULE

Panel with 400-amp bus and all 50-amp, 1-pole CB's

It is interesting to note that this is not a "lighting and appliance" panelboard as defined in Sec. 384-14 and does **not** require main protection per Sec. 384-16(a)

37.5-amp load per phase

Three 1500-watt flood-lights per phase leg

Neutral

Four single-conductor No.6 type-UF cables underground from panel to pole

Typical 9-light pole

TYPICAL EXAMPLE

50-amp, 3-phase, 4-wire circuits to supply incandescent floodlights on pole for lighting of a baseball field.

Fig. 210-40. Larger circuits. [Sec. 210-23(c).]

Application of those rules—and other **Code** rules that refer to "dwelling unit"—must take into consideration the **NE Code** definition for that phrase. A "dwelling unit" is defined as "one or more rooms" used "as a housekeeping unit" and must contain space or areas specifically dedicated to "eating, living, and sleeping" and must have "permanent provisions for cooking and sanitation." A one-family house is a "dwelling unit." So is an apartment in an apart-

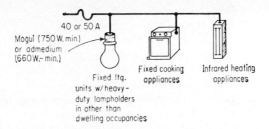

NOTE: Usually, all outlets on the circuit would supply
     the same type of load — i.e., all lamps or all
     cooking units, etc.

Fig. 210-41. Only specified loads may be used for multioutlet circuit.
[Sec. 210-23(c).]

ment house or a condominium unit. But, a guest room in a hotel or motel or a
dormitory room or unit is not a "dwelling unit" if it does not contain "permanent provisions for cooking"—which must mean a built-in range or counter-
mounted cooking unit (with or without an oven).

It should be noted that the requirement calling for heavy-duty type lampholders for lighting units on 30-, 40-, and 50-A multioutlet branch circuits
excludes the use of fluorescent lighting on these circuits because lampholders
are not rated "heavy-duty" in accordance with Sec. 210-21(a) (Fig. 210-42). Mercury-vapor units with mogul lampholders may be used on these circuits provided tap conductor requirements are satisfied.

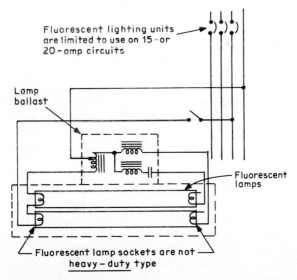

Fig. 210-42. Watch out for this limitation on fluorescent equipment. (Sec. 210-23.)

As indicated, multioutlet branch circuits for lighting are limited to a maximum loading of 50 A. Individual branch circuits may supply any loads. Excepting motors, this means that an individual piece of equipment may be supplied by a branch circuit which has sufficient carrying capacity in its conductors, is protected against current in excess of the capacity of the conductors, and supplies only the single outlet for the load device.

Fixed outdoor electric snow-melting and de-icing installations may be supplied by any of the above-described branch circuits. (See Sec. 426-4 in Art. 426, "Fixed Outdoor Electric De-Icing and Snow-Melting Equipment.")

210-24. Branch-Circuit Requirements—Summary. Table 210-24 summarizes the requirements for the size of conductors where two or more outlets are supplied. The asterisk note also indicates that these ampacities are for copper conductors where derating is not required. Where more than three conductors are contained in a raceway or a cable, Note 8 to Tables 310-16 through 310-19 specifies the load-current derating factors to apply for the number of conductors involved. A 20-A branch circuit is required to have conductors which have an ampacity of 20 A and also must have the overcurrent protection rated 20 A where the branch circuit supplies two or more outlets. Refer to the detailed discussion of conductor ampacity and load-current limiting under Sec. 310-15, where Table 310-16 and its notes are explained.

As noted at the end of the first paragraph of this section, a branch circuit in a dwelling unit must not have outlets in any other dwelling unit. This rule is intended to prevent overloading of a circuit that could result from tenants in different dwelling units attempting to simultaneously connect heavy-current appliances to a single circuit. But, as noted in the Exception, common branch circuit(s) may be used to supply more than one dwelling unit in a two-family or multifamily dwelling (apartment house, condominiums, etc.) for purposes of alarm, signal, communication, or similar safety or security functions. The Exception recognizes that apartment houses and similar multifamily dwelling units under single management do make use of *common* systems for the safety of all of the tenants or occupants of the building (fire alarm, intrusion systems, communications systems, etc.). Such systems run from a common "house" panel or enclosure to and through individual dwelling units. The same permission is also extended to two-family dwellings.

210-50. General. Part **(b)** simply requires that wherever it is known that cord- and plug-connected equipment is going to be used, receptacle outlets must be installed. That is a general rule that applies to any electrical system in any type of occupancy or premises.

210-52. Dwelling Unit Receptacle Outlets. This section sets forth a whole list of rules requiring specific installations of receptacle outlets in all "dwelling units"—i.e., one-family houses, apartments in apartment houses, and other places that conform to the definition of "dwelling unit." As indicated, receptacle outlets on fixed spacing must be installed in every room of a dwelling unit except the bathroom. The **Code** rule lists the specific rooms that are covered by the rule requiring receptacles spaced no greater than 12 ft apart in any continuous length of wall.

In part **(a)**, the required receptacles must be spaced around the designated rooms and any "similar room or area of dwelling units." The wording of this section assures that receptacles are provided—the correct number with the indicated spacing—in those unidentified areas so commonly used today in residential architectural design, such as *greatrooms* and other big areas that combine living, dining, and/or recreation areas.

As shown in Fig. 210-43, general-purpose convenience receptacles, usually of the duplex type, must be laid out around the perimeters of living room, bedrooms, and all the other rooms. Spacing of receptacle outlets should be such

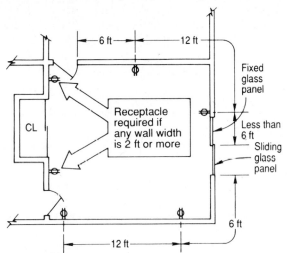

Fig. 210-43. From any point along wall, at floor line, a receptacle must be not more than 6 ft away. Required receptacle spacing considers a fixed glass panel as wall space and a sliding panel as a doorway. [Sec. 210-52(a).]

that no point along the floor line of an unbroken wall is more than 6 ft from a receptacle outlet. Care should be taken to provide receptacle outlets in smaller sections of wall space segregated by doors, fireplaces, bookcases, or windows. Although Sec. 210-52(h) calls for one receptacle outlet for each dwelling-unit hallway that is 10 ft or more in length, this section does not specify location or require more than a single receptacle outlet. However, good design practice would dictate that a convenience receptacle should be provided for each 10 ft of hall length. And they should be located as close as possible to the middle of the hall.

In determining the location of a receptacle outlet, the measurement is to be made along the floor line of the wall and is to continue around corners of the room, but is not to extend across doorways, archways, fireplaces, passageways, or other space unsuitable for having a flexible cord extended across it. The location of outlets for special appliances within 6 ft of the appliance [Sec. 210-50(c)] does not affect the spacing of general-use convenience outlets but merely adds a requirement for special-use outlets.

Figure 210-44 shows two wall sections 9 ft and 3 ft wide extending from the same corner of the room. The receptacle shown located in the wider section of the wall will permit the plugging in of a lamp or appliance located within 6 ft of either side of the receptacle. The same rule would apply to the other wall shown.

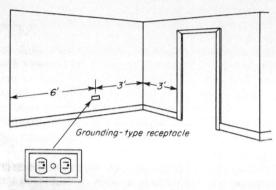

Fig. 210-44. Location of the receptacle as shown will permit the plugging in of a lamp or appliance located 6 ft on either side of the receptacle. [Sec. 210-52(a).]

Receptacle outlets shall be provided for all wall space within the room except individual isolated sections which are less than 2 ft in width. For example, a wall space 23 in. wide and located between two doors would not need a receptacle outlet.

In measuring receptacle spacing for exterior walls of rooms, the fixed section of a sliding glass door assembly is considered to be "wall space" and the sliding glass panel is considered to be a doorway. In previous **NEC** editions the entire width of a sliding glass door assembly—both the fixed and movable panels— was required to be treated as wall space in laying out receptacles "so that no point along the floor line in any wall space is more 6 feet" from a receptacle outlet. The wording takes any fixed glass panel to be a continuation of the wall space adjoining it, but the sliding glass panel is taken to be the same as any other doorway (such as with hinged doors) (Fig. 210-43).

The last sentence of the first paragraph of part **(a)** requires fixed room dividers to be considered in spacing receptacles. This is illustrated by the sketch of Fig. 210-45. In effect, the two side faces of the room divider provide additional

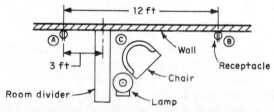

Fig. 210-45. Fixed room dividers must be counted as wall space requiring receptacles. [Sec. 210-52(a).]

wall space, and a table lamp placed as shown would be more than 6 ft from both receptacles A and B. Also, even though no place on the wall is more than 6 ft from either A or B, a lamp or other appliance placed at a point such as C would be more than 6 ft from B and out of reach from A because of the divider. This rule would ensure placement of a receptacle in the wall on both sides of the divider or in the divider itself if its construction so permitted.

As noted in the next-to-last paragraph of Sec. 210-52(a), any receptacle that is an integral part of a lighting fixture or an appliance or a cabinet may not be used to satisfy the specific receptacle requirements of the section. For instance, a receptacle in a medicine cabinet or lighting fixture may not serve as the required bathroom receptacle. And a receptacle in a post light may not serve as the required outdoor receptacle for a one-family dwelling.

In spacing receptacle outlets so that no floor point along the wall space of the rooms designated by Sec. 210-52(a) is more than 6 ft from a receptacle, a receptacle that is part of an appliance must not generally be counted as one of the required spaced receptacles. However, the Exception at the end of part **(a)** states that a receptacle that is "factory installed" in a "permanently installed electric baseboard heater" (not a portable heater) may be counted as one of the required spaced receptacles for the wall space occupied by the heater. Or a receptacle "provided as a separate assembly by the manufacturer" may also be counted as a required spaced receptacle. But, such receptacles must not be connected to the circuit that supplies the electric heater. Such a receptacle must be connected to another circuit.

Because of the increasing popularity of low-density electric baseboard heaters, their lengths are frequently so long (up to 14 ft) that required maximum spacing of receptacles places receptacles above heaters and produces the undesirable and dangerous condition where cord sets to lamps, radios, TVs, etc., will droop over the heater and might droop into the heated-air outlet. And UL rules prohibit use of receptacles above certain electric baseboard heaters for that reason. Receptacles in heaters can afford the required spaced receptacle units without mounting any above heater units. They satisfy the UL concern and also the preceding note near the end of Sec. 210-52(a) that calls for the need "to minimize the use of cords across doorways, fireplaces, and similar openings"— and the heated-air outlet along a baseboard heater is a "similar opening" that must be guarded (Fig. 210-46).

A fine-print note at the end of part **(a)** points out that the UL instructions for baseboard heaters (marked on the heater) may prohibit the use of receptacles above the heater because cords plugged into the receptacle are exposed to heat damage if they drape into the convection channel of the heater and contact the energized heating element.

Part **(b)** requires that the two or more 20-A branch circuits required by Sec. 220-4(b) supply all the receptacle outlets in the kitchen, pantry, dining room, breakfast room, and any similar area of any dwelling unit—one-family houses, apartments, and motel and hotel suites with cooking facilities or serving pantries.

The two or more small appliance circuits serving the kitchen and other specified rooms must not have outlets in any other rooms (Fig. 210-47). Part **(b)(2)**

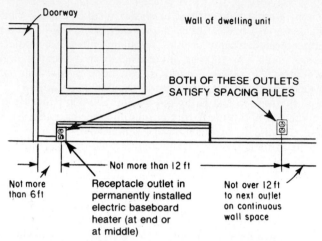

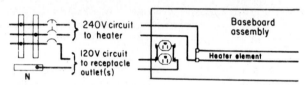

Fig. 210-46. Receptacles in baseboard heaters may serve as "required" receptacles. [Sec. 210-52(a), Exception.]

requires that at least two such circuits must supply countertop receptacle outlets in the kitchen itself. The two circuits feeding outlets in the kitchen may also feed outlets in the other areas above (dining room, pantry, etc.). What the **Code** prohibits is, say, one circuit feeding the kitchen outlets and the other circuit or circuits feeding the outlets in the other prescribed areas. And it would not be acceptable for one 2-wire circuit to supply all of the countertop kitchen receptacles and the other circuit to supply kitchen wall outlets that are not located above countertop area. Of course, use of a 3-wire, 240/120-V, 20-A circuit feeding all of the kitchen receptacles with each receptacle split-wired to the different circuit hot legs would satisfy the rule, because each countertop receptacle would be fed by two circuits (a 3-wire, 240/120-V circuit is equivalent to two 120-V circuits) (Fig. 210-48).

It should be noted that the wording of Part **(b)(1)** requires that the "two or more" small appliance circuits must supply the receptacle outlets for any "refrigeration equipment" in the designated rooms. Therefore, receptacles for refrigerators and freezers in those rooms must be connected on the 20-A small appliance circuits. Because such appliances are often high-amperage appliances, some inspectors require a single (not duplex) receptacle fed by an individual 20-A branch circuit. And in such cases, the inspector usually requires

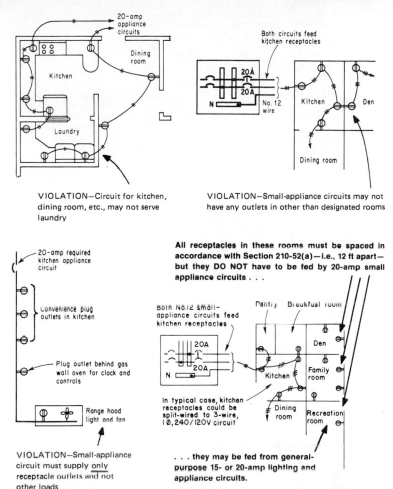

Fig. 210-47. Small appliance circuits for eating areas must not have outlets for other rooms or uses. [Sec. 210-52(b).]

that there must be two 20-A small appliance circuits, in addition to the separate circuit for the refrigerator or freezer, to supply the general purpose receptacle outlets spaced around the kitchen and other designated rooms. Such requirements are defended on the basis that the rule of the NEC calls for two "or more" circuits, that it is not acceptable to allow a refrigerator or freezer to consume the major capacity of one small appliance circuit when only two such circuits are provided, and that it is the intent of the Code to require at least *two* small appliance circuits in addition to any individual appliance circuits.

Note: Part **(b)(1)** requires that the two or more 20-A small appliance circuits must supply "all" receptacle outlets in the kitchen, dining room, etc., *and must also* supply receptacle outlets in any "similar area of a dwelling unit." That

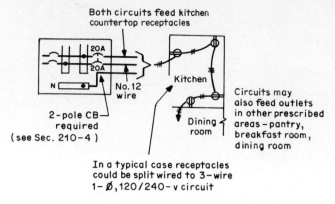

METHOD 1 – A 3-wire circuit to all outlets in prescribed areas.

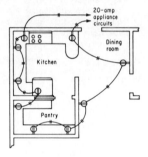

METHOD 2 – Two 2-wire circuits, each with at least one kitchen countertop receptacle outlet.

Fig. 210-48. Two appliance circuits must have outlets in area specified in Sec. 210-52(b). [Sec. 210-52(b).]

phrase *suggests* that all the rules on small appliance circuits and receptacles *might* apply to *family rooms, recreation rooms, greatrooms, dens,* and any other room that would be used for preparing and/or serving food.

As noted in Exceptions to part **(b)(1)**, electric clock-hanger outlets and/or outdoor receptacle outlets may be connected on *either* a small appliance circuit *or* a general-purpose circuit (Fig. 210-49).

The intent of Sec. (b)(1), Exception No. 3, is that a wall switch-controlled receptacle(s) may be used to supply a plug-in lamp for lighting in a dining room, breakfast room, or pantry of a dwelling unit, *but* the switched receptacle(s) must not be connected on the one or more required 20-A small appliance circuit(s) supplying those rooms (Fig. 210-50). This Exception correlates the rule of Sec. 210-52(b)(1) with Exception No. 1 of Sec. 210-70(a), as follows:

- The basic rule of Sec. 210-70(a) requires a wall switch-controlled lighting outlet in each habitable room of a dwelling unit—which includes the kitchen, dining room, breakfast room, and pantry.

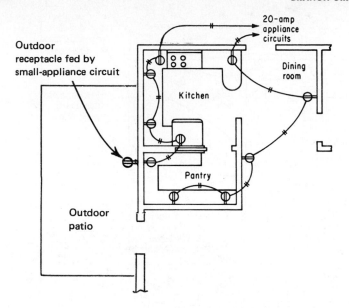

Outdoor receptacle

3-wire grounding. Outlet recessed for plug cup, allows
clock to hang flush with wall. Clock hook furnished
with each device.

**Clock-hanger
receptacle**

Fig. 210-49. Certain outlets may be fed by small appliance circuit or other circuit. [Sec.
210-52(b)(1), Exceptions No. 1, 2, and 3.]

- Exception No. 1 of Sec. 210-70(a) says that a wall switch-controlled receptacle may be used instead of a switch-controlled outlet to a lighting fixture,
  with a floor or table lamp plugged into the switched receptacle to provide
  lighting in a room. But this may be done only in rooms other than the
  kitchen or bathroom, which must always have a switched lighting outlet for
  a ceiling or wall-mounted fixture.
- If a wall switch-controlled receptacle is used to supply a plug-in lamp for
  lighting in a dining room, breakfast room, or pantry—as permitted by
  Exception No. 1 of Sec. 210-70(a)—that poses a conflict with the rule of Sec.
  210-52(b)(1), which says that two or more 20-A small appliance branch cir-

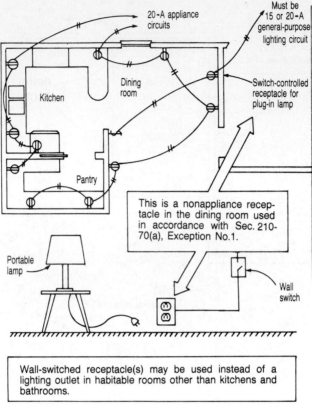

20-A appliance circuits

Must be 15 or 20-A general-purpose lighting circuit

Dining room

Kitchen

Switch-controlled receptacle for plug-in lamp

Pantry

This is a nonappliance receptacle in the dining room used in accordance with Sec. 210-70(a), Exception No.1.

Portable lamp

Wall switch

Wall-switched receptacle(s) may be used instead of a lighting outlet in habitable rooms other than kitchens and bathrooms.

Fig. 210·50. This type of circulating correlates Sec. 210-52(b)(1) with Sec. 210-70(a), Exception No. 1. [Sec. 210-52(b)(1), Exception No. 3.]

cuits must be used to supply *all* receptacle outlets in the kitchen, dining room, breakfast room, pantry and that those circuits must not have outlets other than for plug-in applicances—meaning no outlets supplying lighting.

- Section 210-52(a) requires the small appliance receptacle outlets in the dining room, breakfast room, and/or pantry to be installed so that "no point along the floor line in any wall space is more than 6 ft, measured horizontally, from an outlet in that space."

- Exception No. 3 of Sec. 210-52(b)(1) says that, *in addition* to the number of small appliance receptacle outlets required to satisfy the above rules, it is permissible to install one or more switched receptacle outlets for plug-in lamps *provided* that such receptacles are supplied from a general-purpose 15-A or 20-A branch circuit and *not* from one of the required 20-A small appliance circuits.

Part **(c)** requires a receptacle outlet in kitchens and dining areas at each counter space wider than 12 in., defines counter spaces, and disqualifies as "required outlets" any receptacles rendered inaccessible by the installation of appliances that are either fastened in place or positioned in a space that is "dedicated"—i.e., assigned for permanent positioning of an appliance. Refrigerators and freezers would be typical of appliances "occupying dedicated space" (Fig. 210-51).

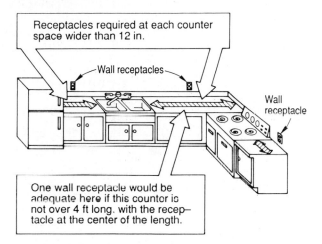

Any point along the wall line of each length of counter top must *not* be over 24 in., measured horizontally, from a receptacle outlet.

Receptacles required at each counter space wider than 12 in.

Wall receptacles

Wall receptacle

One wall receptacle would be adequate here if this counter is not over 4 ft long. with the recep— tacle at the center of the length.

COUNTER SPACES in kitchen and dining rooms such as shown by arrows (above) must be supplied with receptacles if they are over 12 in. wide. Appliances are frequently used even on narrow counter widths; this requirement is designed to remove the dangerous practice of stretching cords across sinks, behind ranges, etc., to feed such appliances.

Inaccessible receptacles.

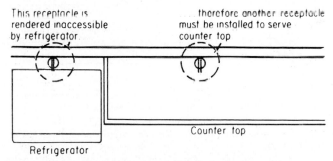

This receptacle is rendered inaccessible by refrigerator.

therefore another receptacle must be installed to serve counter top

Counter top

Refrigerator

RECEPTACLE LOCATED behind an appliance, making the receptacle inaccessible, does not count as one of the required "counter-top" receptacles. (Neither does it count as one of the appliance-circuit receptacles required to be located every **4** ft.)

Fig. 210-51. Counter-top receptacles are needed and must be accessible. [Sec. 210-52(c).]

The rule of part **(c)** further requires that, at any countertop space, "no point along the wall line" of the countertop is permitted to be more than 24 in. from a receptacle outlet, measured horizontally along the wall line. The same section also calls for the installation of at least one receptacle outlet every 4 ft for any "island" or "peninsula" countertop that is 12 in. wide or wider. Such receptacles would have to be installed in the vertical surfaces of those kinds of counter constructions. Although the **Code** here does not specifically prohibit the installation of such receptacles "face-up" in the horizontal surfaces of the countertop, this is expressly prohibited by Sec. 551-41(d) for recreational vehicles, and such an installation would be contrary to good practice.

Part **(d)** requires the installation of at least one wall receptacle outlet adjacent to the wash basin location in bathrooms of dwelling units—and Sec. 210-60 requires the same receptacle in bathrooms of hotel and motel guest rooms (Fig. 210-52).

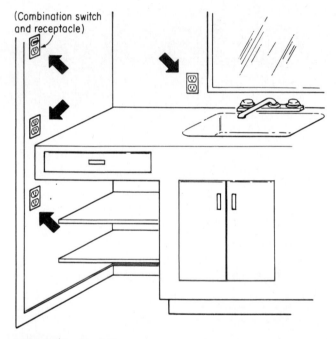

LOCATION of receptacle will vary, depending upon available wall space. Arrows show several possibilities. A receptacle in a medicine cabinet or in the bathroom lighting fixture does not satisfy this rule.

Fig. 210-52. Receptacle required adjacent to wash basin in residence. [Sec. 210-52(d).]

Part **(e)** requires that at least one outdoor receptacle must be installed for every one-family house ("a one-family dwelling"). The definition of "one-family dwelling" (Art. 100) makes clear that an outdoor receptacle is not required for outdoor balconies of apartment units, motels, hotels, or other units in multiple-occupancy buildings.

The second sentence of part **(e)** says that townhouse-type one-family dwellings require one GFCI-protected outdoor receptacle outlet at the front of each dwelling and one at the rear of each dwelling. This rule is aimed at providing adequacy in the availability of outdoor receptacles for one-family dwelling units. Any one-family dwelling that does not have direct grade-level access from the front to the rear of the unit—as is commonly the case with row houses (so-called "townhouses"), which are one-family dwellings attached to each other—must have an outdoor receptacle that is accessible at grade level at the front and the rear of the dwelling. And all such receptacles must be GFCI-protected (Fig. 210-53).

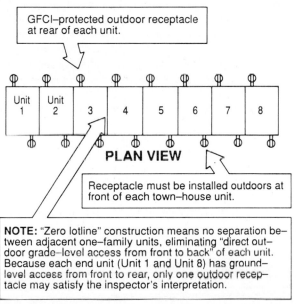

Fig. 210·53. Front and rear receptacle outlets are required outdoors for "zero-lotline" construction. [Sec. 210-52(e).]

The use of outdoor appliances at two-family houses has been judged to be as common as at one-family houses, and the need for outdoor receptacles to eliminate use of extension cords from within the house is recognized by the rule calling for outdoor receptacles for two-family houses.

For a two-family dwelling, the rule requires a separate outdoor receptacle outlet for each dwelling unit in a two-family house where each dwelling unit is an upstairs-and-downstairs unit—that is, each unit has living space (i.e., kitchen and living room) located "at grade level." And, as with a one-family dwelling, the receptacle outlet could contain a single, duplex, or triplex receptacle—installed on the outside wall or fed underground. [Note that a receptacle in a post light does not qualify as the required outdoor receptacle, because a receptacle "that is part of any lighting fixture" is excluded by the last paragraph of Sec. 210-52(a).] The clear intent of the rule, however, is *not* to require an outdoor receptacle for a dwelling unit that is totally on the second floor of a two-family house, with only its entrance door on the first floor, providing access to the stairway.

In a multiple-occupancy building—such as adjacent up-and-down duplex units in "townhouses"—if adjacent units are separated by fire-rated walls, each unit is considered to be a separate building and each is, by **Code** definition, a "one-family dwelling," even though the appearance of a continuous structure might make it seem like a multifamily dwelling or apartment house. Each such unit is, therefore, required to have at least one outdoor receptacle.

Part **(f)** requires that at least one receptacle—single or duplex or triplex— must be installed for the laundry of a dwelling unit. Such a receptacle and any other receptacles for special appliances must be placed within 6 ft of the intended location of the appliance. And part **(g)** requires a receptacle outlet in a basement in addition to any receptacle outlet(s) that may be provided as the required receptacle(s) to serve a laundry area in the basement. One receptacle in the basement at the laundry area located there may *not* serve as *both* the required "laundry" receptacle and the required "basement" receptacle. A separate receptacle has to be provided for each requirement to satisfy the **Code** rules.

Section 210-52(g) requires that at least one receptacle (other than for the laundry) must be installed in the basement of a one-family dwelling, one in an attached garage, and one in a detached garage *if* power is run to the detached garage. This rule calls for at least one receptacle outlet in the basement of a one-family house, in addition to any required for a basement laundry (Fig. 210-54). It calls for at least one receptacle in an attached garage of a one-family

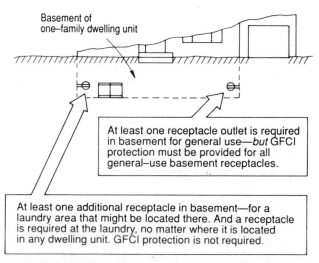

Fig. 210·54. Only one basement receptable is required (in addition to any for the laundry), *but* all general-purpose receptacles in *unfinished* basements must be GFCI protected. [Sec. 210-52(g).]

house. But for a detached garage of a one-family house, the rule simply requires that one receptacle outlet must be installed in the detached garage *if*— for some reason other than the NEC—electric power is run to the garage, such as where the owner might desire it or some local code might require it (Fig. 210-55). The rule itself does *not* require that electric power be run to a detached garage to supply a receptacle there.

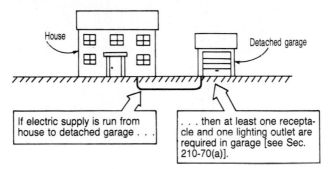

Fig. 210-55. Detached garage may be required to have a receptacle and lighting outlet. [Sec. 210-52(g)]

If the required "basement" receptacle is installed in an "unfinished" basement—that is a basement that has NOT been converted to, or constructed as, a recreation room, bedroom, den, etc.—such a receptacle would be required to be provided with GFCI protection [Sec. 210-8(a)(4)]. And, that same rule requires that any additional receptacles in an unfinished basement be GFCI-protected. In addition, *all* receptacles installed in a dwelling-unit garage (attached or detached) must have GFCI protection, as required by Sec. 210-8(a)(2).

With the wording of the rules of Sec. 210-52(f) and Sec. 210-8(a)(4), it would be acceptable for a one-family dwelling to have one basement receptacle with GFCI protection if the basement is unfinished, but any other receptacles that are optionally installed must also have GFCI protection. The one or more receptacles provided for a laundry area in the basement are *excluded* from need for GFCI protection by Exception No. 2 of Sec. 210-8(a)(4).

In part **(h)**, a receptacle outlet is required in any dwelling-unit hallway that is 10 ft or more in length. This provides for connection of plug-in appliances that are commonly used in halls—lamps, vacuum cleaners, etc. The length of a hall is measured along its centerline.

Figure 210-56 shows required receptacles for a one-family dwelling.

210-60. Guest Rooms.   The number of receptacles in a guest room of a hotel or motel must be determined by the every-12-ft rule of Sec. 210-52(a) but *may* be located where convenient for the furniture layout, exempted from the rule that "no point along the floor line in any wall space is more than 6 ft. . . from an outlet." The intent of the rule is that the *number* of receptacles must satisfy Sec. 210-52(a) but *spacing* of the receptacles is exempted from the every-12-ft

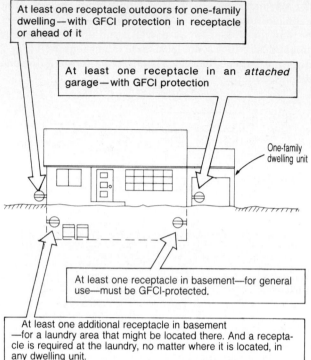

At least one receptacle outdoors for one-family dwelling—with GFCI protection in receptacle or ahead of it

At least one receptacle in an *attached* garage—with GFCI protection

One-family dwelling unit

At least one receptacle in basement—for general use—must be GFCI-protected.

At least one additional receptacle in basement —for a laundry area that might be located there. And a receptacle is required at the laundry, no matter where it is located, in any dwelling unit.

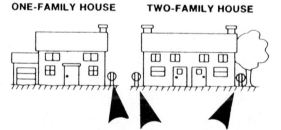

ONE-FAMILY HOUSE   TWO-FAMILY HOUSE

At least one receptacle must be installed out-doors for a one-family dwelling and for each dwelling unit of a two-family dwelling — with GFCI protection in or ahead of each receptacle.

Fig. 210-56. These specific receptacles are required for dwelling occupancies. [Sec. 210-52(e), (f), and (g).]

rule. In such cases, the spacing requirements of not more than 12 ft between receptacles, etc., do not have to be observed.

210-62. Show Windows.   The rule here calls for one receptacle in a show window for each 12 ft of length (measured horizontally) to accommodate portable window signs and other electrified displays (Fig. 210-57).

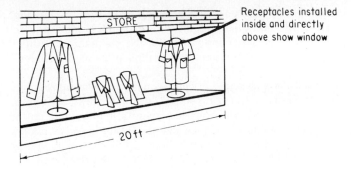

For a 20-ft-long store show window,

a minimum of two receptacles must be installed, one for

each 12 linear ft or major fraction thereof of show window

length.

Fig. 210·57. Receptacles are required for show windows in stores or other buildings. [Sec. 210-62.]

210.63. Heating, Air-Conditioning, and Refrigeration Equipment Outlet. A general-purpose 125-V receptacle outlet must be installed within 75 ft of heating, air-conditioning, refrigeration equipment on rooftops *and* in attics and crawl spaces (Fig. 210-58).

This rule provides a readily accessible outlet for connecting 120-V tools and/or test equipment that might be required for the maintenance or servicing of mechanical equipment in attics and crawl spaces as well as rooftops. Each such

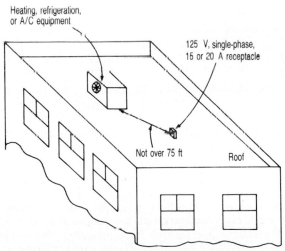

Fig. 210·58. Maintenance receptacle outlet required for rooftop mechanical equipment as well as for such equipment in attics and crawl spaces. [Sec. 210-63.]

receptacle must be on the same level and within 75 ft of the heating, refrigeration, and air-conditioning equipment. This receptacle must not be fed from the load side of the disconnecting means for the mechanical equipment. Only rooftop units on one- and two-family dwelling units are excluded from this requirement.

210·70. Lighting Outlets Required. The basic rule of part **(a)** requires "at least one wall switch-controlled lighting outlet" in rooms, halls, stairways, attached garages, "detached garages with electric power," and at outdoor entrances. This rule requires a wall switch-controlled lighting outlet in *every attached* garage of a dwelling unit (such as a one-family house). But, for a *detached* garage of a dwelling unit, a switch-controlled lighting outlet is required *only* if the garage is provided with electric power—whether the provision of power is done as an optional choice or is required by a local code. Note that the **NEC** rule here does not itself require running power to the detached garage for the lighting outlet, but simply says that the lighting outlet must be provided *if* power is run to the garage.

The word "bathrooms" is in the basic rule because various building codes do not include bathrooms under their definition of "habitable rooms." So the word "bathroom" was needed to assure that the rule covered bathrooms. The rule does not stipulate that the required "lighting outlets" must be ceiling lighting outlets; they also may be wall-mounted lighting outlets (Fig. 210-59).

A note clarifies that "a vehicle door in an attached garage is *not* considered as an outdoor entrance." This makes it clear that the **Code** does not require such a light outlet at any garage door that is provided as a vehicle entrance because the lights of the car provide adequate illumination when such a door is being used during darkness. But the wording of this note does suggest that a rear or side door that is provided for personnel entry to an attached garage would be "considered as an outdoor entrance" because the note excludes only "vehicle" doors. Such personnel entrances from outdoors to the garage would seem to require a wall-switched lighting outlet.

At least one lighting outlet must be installed in every attic, underfloor space, utility room, and basement if it is used for storage or if it contains equipment requiring servicing. In such cases, the lighting outlet must be controlled by a wall switch at the entrance to the space. A lamp socket controlled by a pull chain or a canopy switch cannot be used. And each such required lighting outlet must be installed "at or near the equipment requiring servicing."

The last paragraph of part **(a)**, just before the Exceptions, states that lighting outlets for indoor stairways are required and must be controlled by a wall switch at each floor level connected by a stairway of six or more steps. This rule has the effect of requiring 3-way switching for control of the lighting outlet illuminating such stairways.

Two exceptions are given to the basic requirements. Exception No. 1 notes that in rooms other than kitchens and bathrooms, a wall switch-controlled receptacle outlet may be used instead of a wall switch-controlled lighting outlet. The receptacle outlet can serve to supply a portable lamp, which would give the necessary lighting for the room. Exception No. 2 states that "in hallways, stairways, and at outdoor entrances remote, central, or automatic control of

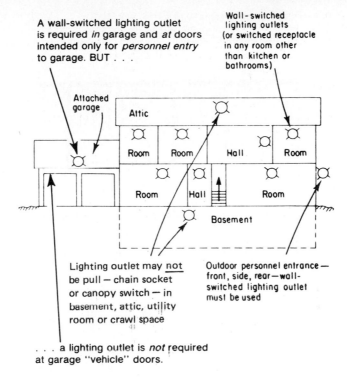

A wall-switched lighting outlet
is required *in* garage and *at* doors
intended only for *personnel entry*
to garage. BUT . . .

Wall-switched
lighting outlets
(or switched receptacle
in any room other
than kitchen or
bathrooms)

Attached
garage

Attic

Room   Room   Hall   Room

Room   Hall   Room

Basement

Lighting outlet may <u>not</u>
be pull — chain socket
or canopy switch — in
basement, attic, utility
room or crawl space

Outdoor personnel entrance —
front, side, rear—wall-
switched lighting outlet
must be used

. . . a lighting outlet is *not* required
at garage "vehicle" doors.

EXCEPTION:

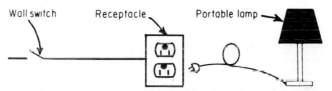

Wall switch   Receptacle   Portable lamp

Wall-switched receptacle(s) may be used instead of a lighting
outlet in habitable rooms other than kitchens and bathrooms.

Fig. 210-59. Lighting outlets required in dwelling units. (Sec. 210-70.)

lighting shall be permitted." This latter recognition appears to accept remote, central, or automatic control as an alternative to the wall switch control mentioned in the basic rules.

But note carefully that every kitchen and every bathroom must have at least one wall switch-controlled lighting outlet (Fig. 210-60).

Section 210-70(b) notes that "at least one wall switch controlled lighting outlet or wall switch controlled receptacle shall be installed in guest rooms in hotels, motels, or similar occupancies."

Part **(c)** requires that a wall switch–controlled lighting outlet must be provided in attics or underfloor spaces housing heating, A/C, and/or refrigeration

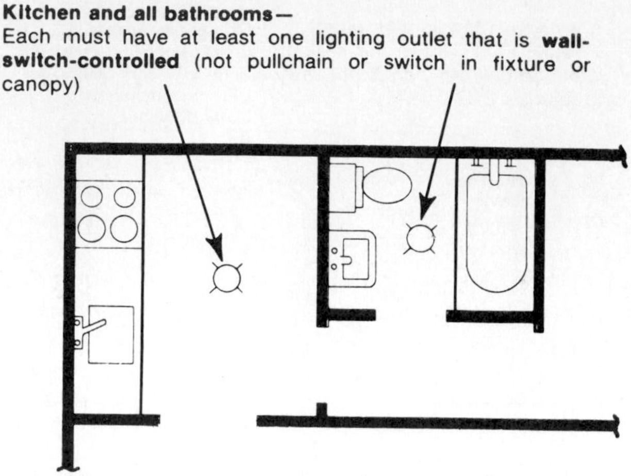

Kitchen and all bathrooms—
Each must have at least one lighting outlet that is **wall-switch-controlled** (not pullchain or switch in fixture or canopy)

Fig. 210-60. Switch-controlled lighting outlet in kitchen and bathroom. [Sec. 210-70(a).]

equipment—*in other than dwelling units.* The lighting outlet must be located at or near the equipment to provide effective illumination. And the control wall switch must be installed at the point of entry to the space.

ARTICLE 215. FEEDERS

215-1. Scope. "Feeders" are the conductors which carry electric power from the service equipment (or generator switchboard, where power is generated on the premises) to the overcurrent protective devices for branch circuits supplying the various loads. "Subfeeders" originate at a distribution center other than the service equipment or generator switchboard and supply one or more other distribution panelboards, branch-circuit panelboards, or branch circuits. **Code** rules on feeders apply also to all subfeeders (Fig. 215-1).

For the given circuit voltage, feeders and subfeeders must be capable of carrying the amount of current required by the load, plus any current which may be required in the future. Selection of the size of a feeder depends upon the size and nature of the known load computed from branch-circuit data, the anticipated future load requirements, and voltage drop.

Article 215 deals with the determination of the minimum sizes of feeder conductors necessary for safety. Overloading of conductors may result in insulation breakdowns due to overheating; overheating of switches, busbars, and terminals; the blowing of fuses and consequent overfusing; excessive voltage drop; and excessive copper losses. Thus the overloading will in many cases create a fire risk and is sure to result in very unsatisfactory service.

The actual maximum load on a feeder depends upon the total load connected to the feeder and the demand factor. If at certain times the entire connected

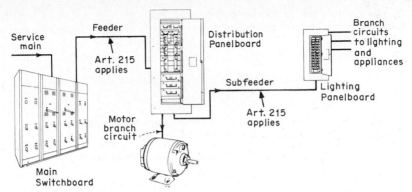

Fig. 215-1. Article 215 applies only to those circuits that conform to the **NEC** definition of "feeder." (Sec. 215-1.)

load is in operation, the demand factor is 100 percent; i.e., the maximum load, or maximum demand, is equal to the total connected load. If the heaviest load ever carried is only one-half the total connected load, the demand factor is 50 percent.

215-2. Minimum Rating and Size. There are two steps in the process of predetermining the maximum load that a feeder will be required to carry: first, a reasonable estimate must be made of the probable connected load; and, second, a reasonable value for the demand factor must be assumed. From a survey of a large number of buildings, the average connected loads and demand factors have been ascertained for lighting and small appliance loads in buildings of the more common classes of occupancy, and these data are presented in Sec. 220-3 and part **B** of Art. 220 as minimum requirements.

The load is specified in terms of voltamperes per square foot for certain occupancies. These loads are here referred to as standard loads, because they are minimum standards established by the **Code** in order to assure that the feeders and branch circuits will have sufficient carrying capacity for safety.

In this section, the last two sentences of the first paragraph note that it is never necessary for feeder conductors to be larger than the service-entrance conductors (assuming use of the same conductor material and the same insulation). In particular, this is aimed at those cases where the size of service-entrance conductors for a dwelling unit is selected in accordance with the higher-than-normal ampacities permitted by Note 3 to **Code** Table 310-16 for services to residential occupancies. If a set of service conductors for an individual dwelling unit are brought in to a single service disconnect (a single fused switch or circuit breaker) and load and the service conductors are sized for the increased ampacity value permitted by Note 3 to Table 310-16, diversity on the load-side feeder conductors gives them the same reduced heat-loading that enables the service conductors to be assigned the higher ampacity. This rule simply extends the permission of Note 3 to those feeders and is applicable for any such feeder for a dwelling unit (a one-family house or an apartment in a two-family or multifamily dwelling, such as an apartment house) or for mobile-home feed (Fig. 215-2). See the discussion on Note 3 of Table 310-16 in Art. 310.

Part **(a)** specifies that the feeder wires must never have an ampacity of less than 30 A when the feeder supplies at least the number of circuits as shown in Fig. 215-3.

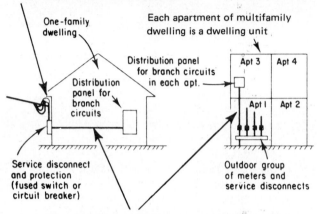

If Note 3 of Table 310-16 is used to assign higher ampacity to the service entrance conductors . . .

One-family dwelling

Each apartment of multifamily dwelling is a dwelling unit

Distribution panel for branch circuits in each apt.

Distribution panel for branch circuits

Apt 3   Apt 4

Apt I   Apt 2

Service disconnect and protection (fused switch or circuit breaker)

Outdoor group of meters and service disconnects

. . .then these feeder conductors may also be assigned the higher ampacities of Note 3 (for instance, No. 2/0 copper THW is rated at 200 amps instead of 175 amps). (They do not have to be larger than the service conductors.)

Or, a multifamily dwelling might be fed like this —

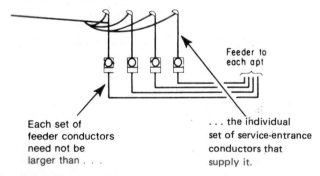

Feeder to each apt

Each set of feeder conductors need not be larger than . . .

. . . the individual set of service-entrance conductors that supply it.

Fig. 215-2. Feeder conductors need not be larger than service-entrance conductors when higher ampacity of Note 3, Table 310-16, is used. (Sec. 215-2.)

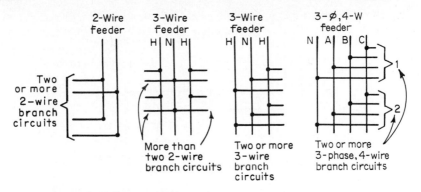

EXAMPLE

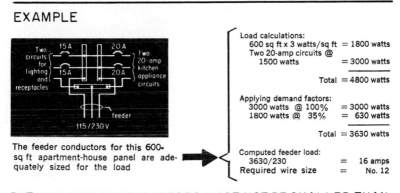

Load calculations:
    600 sq ft x 3 watts/sq ft = 1800 watts
    Two 20-amp circuits @
        1500 watts   = 3000 watts

                    Total = 4800 watts

Applying demand factors:
    3000 watts @ 100%   = 3000 watts
    1800 watts @ 35%   = 630 watts

                    Total = 3630 watts

The feeder conductors for this 600-sq ft apartment-house panel are adequately sized for the load

Computed feeder load:
    3630/230   =   16 amps
    Required wire size   =   No. 12

BUT, THE FEEDER CONDUCTORS MUST <u>NOT</u> BE SMALLER THAN No. 10 FROM SEC. 215-2 (a) (3).

Fig. 215-3. Feeder must have an ampacity of at least 30 A in these cases. Conductors must not be smaller than No. 10 TW copper or No. 8 TW aluminum. [Sec. 215-2(a).]

As shown in Fig. 215-4, the rule of part **(b)** of this section requires that the ampacity of feeder conductors must be at least equal to that of the service conductors where the total service current is carried by the feeder conductors. In the case shown, No. 4 TW aluminum is taken as equivalent to No. 6 TW copper and has the same ampacity (55 A).

A note at the end of Sec. 215-2 comments on voltage drop in feeders. It should be carefully noted that the **NEC** does not establish any mandatory rules on voltage drop for either branch circuits or feeders. The references to 3 and 5 percent voltage drops are purely advisory—i.e., recommended maximum values of voltage drop. The **Code** does not consider excessive voltage drop to be unsafe.

The voltage-drop note suggests not more than 3 percent for feeders supplying power, heating, or lighting loads. It also provides for a maximum drop of 5 percent for the conductors between the service-entrance equipment and the connected load. If the feeders have an actual voltage drop of 3 percent, then only 2 percent is left for the branch circuits. If a lower voltage drop is obtained in

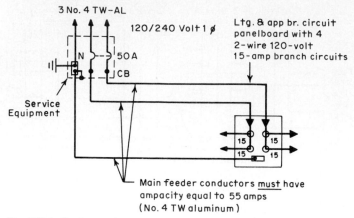

Fig. 215-4. Feeder conductors must not have ampacity less than service conductors. [Sec. 215-2(b).]

the feeder, then the branch circuit has more voltage drop available, provided that the total drop does not exceed 5 percent. For any one load, the total voltage drop is made up of the voltage drop in the one or more feeders plus the voltage drop in the branch circuit supplying that load.

Again, however, values stated in the FPN on voltage drop are recommended values and are not intended to be enforced as a requirement.

Voltage drop must always be carefully considered in sizing feeder conductors, and calculations should be made for peak load conditions. For maximum efficiency, the size of feeder conductors should be such that voltage drop up to the branch-circuit panelboards or point of branch-circuit origin is not more than 1 percent for lighting loads or combined lighting, heating, and power loads and not more than 2 percent for power or heating loads. Local codes may impose lower limits of voltage drop. Voltage-drop limitations are shown in Fig. 215-5 for **NEC** levels and better levels of drop, as follows:

1. For combinations of lighting and power loads on feeders and branch circuits, use the voltage-drop percentages for lighting load (at left in Fig. 215-5).
2. The word *feeder* here refers to the overall run of conductors carrying power from the source to the point of final branch-circuit distribution, including feeders, subfeeders, sub-subfeeders, etc.
3. The voltage-drop percentages are based on nominal circuit voltage at the source of each voltage level. Indicated limitations should be observed for each voltage level in the distribution system.

There are many cases in which the above-mentioned limits of voltage drop (1 percent for lighting feeders, etc.) should be relaxed in the interests of reducing the prohibitive costs of conductors and conduits required by such low drops. In many installations 5 percent drop in feeders is not critical or unsafe—such as in apartment houses.

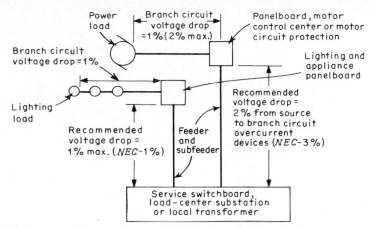

Fig. 215·5. Recommended basic limitations on voltage drop. (Sec. 215-2, FPN.)

Voltage-drop tables and slide calculators are available from a good number of electrical equipment manufacturers. Voltage-drop calculations will vary according to the actual circuit parameters, e.g., AC or DC, single- or multiphase, power factor, circuit impedance, line reactance, types of enclosures (nonmetallic or metallic), length and size of conductors, and conductor material (copper, copper-clad aluminum, or aluminum).

Calculations of voltage drop in any set of feeders can be made in accordance with the formulas given in electrical design literature, such as those shown in Fig. 215-6. From this calculation, it can be determined if the conductor size initially selected to handle the load will be adequate to maintain voltage drop within given limits. If it is not, the size of the conductors must be increased (or other steps taken where conductor reactance is not negligible) until the voltage drop is within prescribed limits. Many such graphs and tabulated data on voltage drop are available in handbooks and from manufacturers. Figure 215-7 shows an example of excessive voltage drop—over 10 percent in the feeder.

215·4. Feeders with Common Neutral.   A frequently discussed Code requirement is that of Sec. 215-4, covering the use of a common neutral with more than one set of feeders. This section says that a common neutral feeder may be used for two or three sets of 3-wire feeders or two sets of 4-wire feeders. It further requires that all conductors of feeder circuits employing a common neutral feeder must be within the same enclosure when the enclosure or raceway containing them is metal.

A common neutral is a single neutral conductor used as the neutral for more than one set of feeder conductors. It must have current-carrying capacity equal to the sum of the neutral conductor capacities if an individual neutral conductor were used with each feeder set. Figure 215-8 shows a typical example of a common neutral, used for three-feeder circuits. A common neutral may be used only with feeders. It may never be used with branch circuits. A single neutral of a multiwire branch circuit is not a "common neutral." It is the neutral of only

Two-wire, single-phase circuits (inductance negligible)

$$V = \frac{2k \times L \times I}{d^2} = 2R \times L \times I$$

$$d^2 = \frac{2k \times L \times I}{V}$$

V = drop in circuit voltage (volts)
R = resistance per ft of conductor (ohms/ft)
I = current in conductor (amperes)

Three-wire, single-phase circuits (inductance negligible)

$$V = \frac{2k \times L \times I}{d^2}$$

V = drop between outside conductors (volts)
I = current in more-heavily loaded outside conductor (amps)

Three-wire, three-phase circuits (inductance negligible)

$$V = \frac{2k \times L \times I}{d^2} \times 0.866$$

V = voltage drop of 3-phase circuit

Four-wire, three-phase balanced circuits (inductance negligible)

Lighting loads
Voltage drop between one outside conductor and neutral equals one-half of drop calculated by formula above for 2-wire circuits.

Motor loads
Voltage drop between any two outside conductors equals 0.866 times the drop determined by formula above for two-wire circuits.

In the above formulas:

L = one-way length of circuit (ft)
d^2 = cross-section area of conductor (circular mils)
k = resistivity of conductor metal (cir mil-ohms/ft)
= 12 for circuits loaded to more than 50% of allowable circuit capacity
= 11 for circuits loaded less than 50%
= 18 for aluminum or copper-clad aluminum conductors

Example: 230-V two-wire heating circuit. Load is 24 A. Circuit size is No. 10 AWG copper, and the one-way circuit length is 200 ft.

An 11-V drop on a 230-V circuit is about a 5 percent drop (11/230 = 0.0478). No. 8 AWG copper conductors would be needed to reduce the voltage drop to 3 percent on the branch circuit and allow 2 percent more on the feeder.

$$VD = \frac{24 \times 200 \times 24}{10,380} = \frac{115,200}{10,380} = 11$$

Fig. 215-6. Calculating voltage drop in feeder circuits. (Sec. 215-2, FPN.)

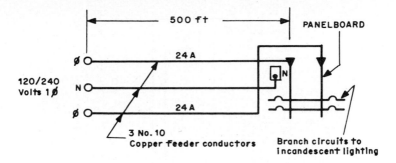

1. No. 10 copper conductor has a resistance of 1.018 ohms per 1000 ft
   (Table 8, Chapter 9).
2. The two 500-ft lengths of circuit conductors total 1000 ft and have a resistance
   of 1.018 ohms.
3. Voltage Drop = load current x conductor resistance
                = 24 amps x 1.018 ohms = 24.43 volts
4. $\frac{24.43}{240}$ = 10.2% VOLTAGE DROP–*NEC* SUGGESTS MAX. 3%

Fig. 215-7. Feeder voltage drop should be checked. [Sec. 215-2, FPN.]

a single circuit even though the circuit may consist of 3 or 4 wires. A feeder common neutral is used with more than one feeder circuit.

215-7. Ungrounded Conductors Tapped from Grounded Systems. Refer to Sec. 210-10 for a discussion that applies as well to feeder circuits as to branch circuits.

215-8. Means of Identifying Conductor with the Higher Voltage to Ground. The wording of this section recognizes orange as the preferred color of the high leg of a 4-wire delta supply without disturbing current practices in various local areas where other colors (such as red, yellow, or blue) or other means of identification are required by electric utility regulations or by local code (Fig. 215-9).

Note that identification of the phase leg with 208 V to ground is required only at those points in the system where the neutral is present—such as in panelboards, motor-control centers, and other enclosures where circuits are connected. The purpose of this is to warn that 208 V, not 120 V, exist from the high leg to the neutral. Such indication minimizes the chance that a 208-V circuit might be accidentally or unwittingly connected to 120-V loads, such as lamps or appliances of 120-V operating coils in motor starters. Such connection would burn out 120-V equipment and presents a hazard to personnel.

215-9. Ground-Fault Protection for Personnel. A ground-fault circuit-interrupter may be located in the feeder and protect all branch circuits connected to that feeder. In such cases, the provisions of Sec. 210-8 and Art. 305 on temporary wiring will be satisfied and additional **downstream** ground-fault protection on the individual branch circuits would not be required. It should be mentioned, however, that downstream ground-fault protection is more desirable than ground-fault protection in the feeder because less equipment will be de-energized when the ground-fault circuit-interrupter opens the supply in response to a line-to-ground fault.

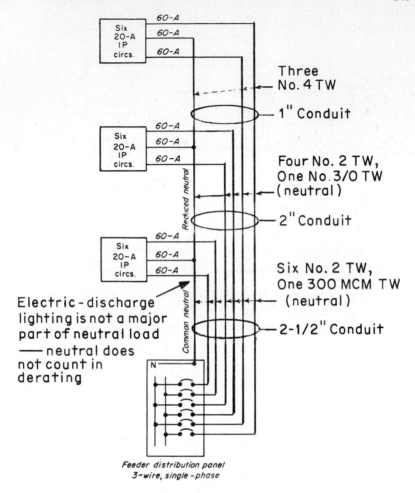

Fig. 215·8. Example of three feeder circuits using a single, "common neutral"—with neutral size reduced as permitted. (Sec. 215-4.)

As shown in Fig. 215-10, if a ground-fault protector is installed in the feeder to a panel for branch circuits to outdoor residential receptacles, this protector will satisfy the NEC as the ground-fault protection required by Sec. 210-8 for such outdoor receptacles.

215·10. Ground-Fault Protection of Equipment. This section mandates equipment ground-fault protection for every feeder disconnect switch or circuit used

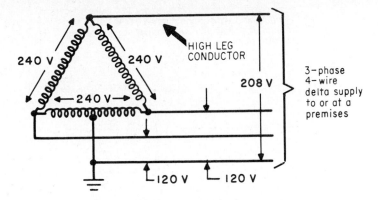

HIGH-LEG CONDUCTOR may be orange in color or may be some other color—such as red or yellow—as long as the color or tagging or other identification clearly distinguishes this as the one with higher voltage to ground at any connection point where the neutral is present.

Fig. 215·9. Identifying the high leg of 4-wire delta circuits. (Sec. 215-8.)

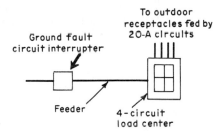

Fig. 215·10. GFCI in feeder does satisfy as protection for branch circuits. (Sec. 215-9.)

on a 480Y/277-V, 3-phase, 4-wire feeder where the disconnect is rated 1,000 A or more, as shown in Fig. 215-11. This is a very significant **Code** requirement for ground-fault protection of the same type that has long been required by Sec. 230-95 for every *service* disconnect rated 1,000 A or more on a 480Y/277-V service.

An exception notes that feeder ground-fault protection is not required on a feeder disconnect if equipment ground-fault protection is provided on the supply (line) side of the feeder disconnect.

The substantiation submitted as the basis for the addition of this new rule stated as follows:

Substantiation: The need for ground-fault equipment protection for 1000 amp or larger 277/480 grounded system is recognized and required when the service equipment is 277/480 volts. This proposal will require the same needed protection when the service equipment is not 277/480 volts. Past proposals attempted to require these feeders be treated as services in order to achieve this protection, but treating a feeder like a service created many other concerns. This proposal only addresses the feeder equipment ground-fault protection needs when it is not provided in the service equipment.

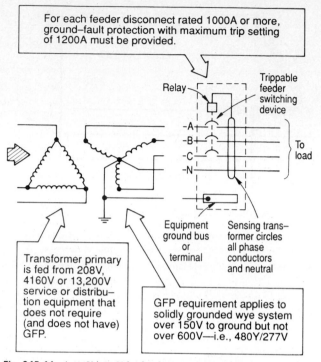

For each feeder disconnect rated 1000A or more, ground–fault protection with maximum trip setting of 1200A must be provided.

Relay

Trippable feeder switching device

-A-
-B-
-C-
-N-

To load

Equipment ground bus or terminal

Sensing transformer circles all phase conductors and neutral

Transformer primary is fed from 208V, 4160V or 13,200V service or distribution equipment that does not require (and does not have) GFP.

GFP requirement applies to solidly grounded wye system over 150V to ground but not over 600V—i.e., 480Y/277V

Fig. 215-11. A 480Y/277-V feeder disconnect rated 1,000 A or more must have ground-fault protection (GFP) if there is not GFP on its supply side. (Sec. 215-10.)

As noted, this rule calls for this type of feeder ground-fault protection when ground-fault protection is not provided on the supply side of the feeder disconnect, such as where a building has a high-voltage service (say, 13,200 V) or has, say, a 208Y/120-V service with a load-side transformer stepping-up the voltage to 480Y/277 V—because a service at either one of these voltages (e.g., 13.2 kV and 208 Y/120 V) is not required by Sec. 230-95 to have GFP.

ARTICLE 220. BRANCH-CIRCUIT AND FEEDER CALCULATIONS

220-1. Scope.   All the calculations and design procedures covered by Art. 220 involve mathematical manipulation of units of voltage, current, resistance, and other measures of electrical conditions or characteristics.

220-2. Voltages.   NE Code references to voltages vary considerably. The Code contains references to 120, 125, 115/230, 120/240, and 120/208 V. Standard voltages to be used for the calculations that have to be made to observe the rules of Art. 220 are 120, 120/240, 208Y/120, 240, 480Y/277, 480, and 600 V. But use of lower voltage values (115, 230, 440, etc.) as denominators in calculations would not be a **Code** violation because the higher current values that result would assure **Code** compliance because of greater capacity in circuit wires and other equipment.

In all electrical systems there is a normal, predictable spread of voltage values over the impedances of the system equipment. It has been common practice to assign these basic levels to each nominal system voltage. The highest value of voltage is that at the service entrance or transformer secondary, such as 480Y/277 V. Then considering voltage drop due to impedance in the circuit conductors and equipment, a "nominal" midsystem voltage designation would be 460Y/265. Variations in "nominal" voltages have come about because of (1) differences in utility-supply voltages throughout the country, (2) varying transformer secondary voltages produced by different and often uncontrolled voltage drops in primary feeders, and (3) preferences of different engineers and other design authorities.

Because the **NE Code** is produced by contributors from all over the nation and of varying technical experiences, it is understandable that diversity of designations would creep in. As with many other things, we just have to live with problems until we solve them.

To standardize calculations, part **B** of Chap. 9 also specifies that nominal voltages of 120, 120/240, 240, and 208/120 V are to be used in computing the ampere load on a conductor. [Dividing these voltages into the watts load will produce lower current values than would 230 and 115 V; thus use of the lower voltage values results in larger (safer) conductor sizes.] *All* branch-circuit, feeder, and service conductor calculations made at those lower voltage levels would obviously satisfy the **NEC** minimum requirements on conductor sizes.

In some places, the **NE Code** adopts 115 V as the basic operating voltage of equipment designed for operation at 110 to 125 V. That is indicated in Tables 430-148 to 430-151. References are made to "rated motor voltages" of 115, 230, 460, 575, and 2,300 V—all values over 115 are integral multiples of 115. The last note in Tables 430-149 and 430-150 indicates that motors of those voltage ratings are applicable on systems rated 110–120, 220–240, 440–480, and 550–600 V. Although the motors can operate satisfactorily within those ranges, it is better to design circuits to deliver rated voltage. These **Code** voltage designations for motors are consistent with the trend over recent years for manufacturers to rate equipment for corresponding values of voltage.

Where calculations result in values involving a fraction of an ampere, the fraction may be dropped if it is less than 0.5. A value such as 20.7 A should be continued to be used as 20.7 or rounded off as the next higher whole number, in this case 21 A. Again, this is on the safe side. There are occasions, however, when current values must be added together. In such cases, it is on the safe side to retain fractions less than 0.5, since several fractions added together can result in the next whole ampere.

220-3. Computation of Branch Circuits. Part **(a)** is essentially the same as the requirement of Sec. 210-22(c). (Refer to that discussion.) As pointed out in a fine-print note, calculation of branch-circuit and feeder loads must comply with the rules of Art. 600 for circuits to signs and outline lighting.

Although Art. 220 gives the basic rules on calculations of loads for branch circuits and feeders, this note warns that Sec. 600-6(c) is another rule on this subject and requires that the 20-A branch circuit that must be supplied for a sign on the outside of every commercial occupancy must be taken as a computed load of 1,200 VA.

The task of calculating a branch-circuit load and then determining the size of circuit conductors required to feed that load is common to all electrical system calculations. Although it may seem to be a simple matter (and it usually is), there are many conditions which make the problem confusing (and sometimes controversial) because of the **NE Code** rules that must be observed.

The requirements for loading and sizing of branch circuits are covered in Art. 210 and in Sec. 220-3. In general, the following basic points must be considered.

- The ampacity of branch-circuit conductors must not be less than the maximum load to be served [Sec. 210-19(a)].
- The ampacity of branch-circuit conductors must generally not be less than the rating of the branch circuit. Section 210-19(a) requires that the conductors of a branch circuit that supplies any receptacle outlets must have an ampacity not less than the rating of the branch circuit, which rating is determined by the rating or setting of the overcurrent device protecting the circuit.
- The rating of a branch circuit is established by the rating or setting of its OC (overcurrent) protective device (Sec. 210-3).
- The normal, maximum, continuous ampacities of conductors in cables or raceways are given in Tables 310-16 to 310-19 for both copper and aluminum.
- These normal ampacities of conductors may have to be derated where there are more than three conductors in a cable or raceway (Note 8 to Tables 310-16 through 310-19).
- The current permitted to be carried by the branch-circuit protective device (fuse or CB) may have to be reduced if the load is continuous [Sec. 210-22(c) and Sec. 220-3(a)].

Section 210-20 says that the rating or setting of the branch-circuit overcurrent protective device is not to exceed that specified in Sec. 240-3 for conductors. Section 240-3 says that conductors shall be protected against overcurrent in accordance with their ampacities; but Exception No. 4 to that rule allows that where the ampacity of the conductor does not correspond with the standard ampere rating of a fuse or a circuit breaker, the next higher standard device rating shall be permitted if this rating does not exceed 800 A and if the wire being protected is not part of a branch circuit supplying receptacles for plug-connected portable tools, appliances, or other plug-in loads. In selecting the size of the branch-circuit overcurrent device, the rule of *both* Secs. 210-19(a) and 210-20 must be satisfied, because **all Code** rules bearing on a particular detail must always be observed.

Section 210-19(a) does not permit *any* case where branch-circuit conductors supplying one or more receptacle outlets would have an ampacity of less than the ampere rating of the circuit protective device. Section 210-19(a) thereby correlates to and repeats the last phrase in Exception No. 4 to Sec. 240-3 to prohibit using a protective device of "the next higher standard rating" on branch circuits to receptacles. However, a branch circuit that supplies only hard-wired outlets—such as lighting outlets or outlets to fixed electric heaters—may have its overcurrent protection selected as the next higher standard rating of protective device above the ampacity of a conductor when the conductor ampacity does not correspond to a standard fuse or CB rating—as permitted by Exception No. 4 of Sec. 240-3.

Section 220-3(a) must be evaluated against all those background data from Art. 210. Although determination of ampacities from Tables 310-16 through 310-19 yields the maximum allowable *continuous* current ratings of conductors, there are **Code** rules that limit the load that may be carried continuously (3 hr or more) to no more than 80 percent of the rating of the circuit protective device. Section 210-22(c) says that the total load on a branch circuit must not be more than the sum of noncontinuous load *plus* 125 percent of the continuous load. Although the rating of the branch circuit is set by the ampere rating or setting of the overcurrent device protecting the circuit, the conductors of a branch circuit supplying any receptacles may not have ampacity (either normal or derated) of less than the rating of the protective device [Section 210-19(a)]. As a repetition of the rule of Sec. 210-22(c), Sec. 220-3(a) requires a branch-circuit protective device to be rated not "less than the noncontinuous load plus 125 percent of the continuous load."

This wording is the reciprocal way of saying what Sec. 384-16(c) says—that the continuous load of a circuit must not exceed 80 percent of the rating of the branch-circuit protective device. (From Sec. 210-3, the "rating" of a branch circuit is determined by the "ampere" rating or setting of the overcurrent device.") The wording of both Sec. 210-22(c) and Sec. 220-3(a) states the need to limit heating effect. As shown in Fig. 220-1, although circuit has a total load current

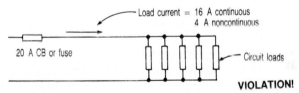

Fig. 220-1. Continuous load does not exceed 80 percent of the circuit rating (20 A); but the 20-A CB rating is *less* than "the noncontinuous load plus 125 percent of the continuous load" and violates Sec. 220-3(a).

of 20 A, the loading satisfies the wording that the continuous load shall not exceed 80 percent of the rating of the branch-circuit overcurrent protective device. (0.8 × 20 = 16 A.) But, according to the rule of Sec. 220-3(a), with 4 A of noncontinuous load, the above circuit could carry only that amount of continuous load which, when multiplied by 1.25, would equal 16 A. Then, 16/1.25 = 12.8 A. Thus the maximum continuous load that would be permitted in addition to the 4 A noncontinuous load is 12.8 A. The branch-circuit rating (20 A) is "not less than the noncontinuous load [4A] plus 125 percent of the continuous load" (1.25 × 12.8 A = 16 A).

[Section 220-10(b) also has the effect of limiting a continuous load to not more than 80 percent of the rating of any feeder CB or fuse protection that is not UL-listed for continuous loading to 100 percent of its rating.]

The continuous-current limitation, as set forth in those **NE Code** sections, is not established because the conductors cannot carry 100 percent of their rated current continuously. The conductors still have the same ampacity—the same maximum allowable continuous current rating. Likewise, a fused switch or circuit breaker can, itself, withstand the heat produced within it by 100 percent of its current rating. The 80 percent limit is set because of the following:

1. Conductors of any circuit must connect to the terminals of the fusible switch or circuit breaker that provides disconnect and protection for a branch circuit or feeder.
2. Current flow through a circuit produces heating in the fusible switch or circuit breaker as well as in the conductors.
3. The heat produced in the switch or CB does not generally harm the switch or CB itself, but that heat is readily conducted into the end lengths of conductors that are attached to the terminals.
4. Although the conductors can take the heat input from 100 percent of their own current rating, the extra heat conducted into the conductor from the switch or CB adds to the heat load on the conductors adjacent to the terminations.
5. For a continuous load, excessive heat will be produced in the conductor insulation if the conductor is already carrying its full rated current; and that can cause damage to the conductor insulation.

The effect of the rule of Sec. 220-3(a) is that any CB or fuse for a branch circuit supplying a total continuous load must have its load current limited to 80 percent, and only one exception is made for such protective devices—a continuous load of 100 percent of the fuse or CB rating is permitted *only* when the protective device assembly (fuse in switch or CB) is approved for 100 percent continuous duty. (And there are no such devices rated less than 225 A, so the exceptions referring to 100 percent rated devices do not apply to any branch circuits of less than 225 A. In addition, UL has a hard and fast rule that **any** breaker *not* marked for 100 percent continuous load must have its load limited to 80 percent of its rating.)

Code Table 220-3(b) lists certain occupancies (types of buildings) for which a minimum general lighting load is specified in voltamperes per square foot. In each type of building, there must be adequate branch-circuit capacity to handle the total load that is represented by the product of voltamperes per square foot times the square-foot area of the building. For instance, if one floor of an office building is 40,000 sq ft in area, that floor must have a total branch-circuit capacity of 40,000 times 3½ VA/sq ft [**Code** Table 220-3(b)] for general lighting. Note that the total load to be used in calculating required circuit capacity must never be taken at less than the indicated voltamperes per square foot times square feet for those occupancies listed. Of course, if branch-circuit load for lighting is determined from a lighting layout of specific fixtures of known voltamp rating, the load value must meet the previous voltamperes-per-square-foot minimum; and if the load from a known lighting layout is greater, then the greater voltamp value must be taken as the required branch-circuit capacity.

Note that the bottom of Table 220-3(b) requires a minimum general lighting load of ½ VA per square foot to cover branch-circuit and feeder capacity for halls, corridors, closets, and all stairways.

As indicated in Sec. 220-3(b), when load is determined on a voltamperes-per-square-foot basis, open porches, garages, unfinished basements, and unused areas are not counted as part of the area. Area calculation is made using the *outside* dimensions of the "building, apartment, or other area involved."

When fluorescent or mercury-vapor lighting is used on branch circuits, the presence of the inductive effect of the ballast or transformer creates a power factor consideration. Determination of the load in such cases must be based on the total of the voltampere rating of the units and not on the wattage of the lamps.

Based on extensive analysis of load densities for general lighting in office buildings, Table 220-3(b) requires a minimum unit load of only 3½ VA/sq ft—rather than the previous unit value of 5—for "office buildings" and for "banks."

A double-asterisk note at the bottom of the table requires the addition of another 1 VA/sq ft to the 3½ value to cover the loading added by general-purpose receptacles in those cases where the actual number of receptacles is not known at the time feeder and branch-circuit capacities are being calculated. In such cases, a unit load of 4½ VA/sq ft must be used, and the calculation based on that figure will yield minimum feeder and branch-circuit capacity for both general lighting and all general-purpose receptacles that may later be installed.

Of course, where the actual number of general-purpose receptacles is known, the general lighting load is taken at 3½ VA/sq ft for branch-circuit and feeder capacity, and each strap or yoke containing a single, duplex, or triplex receptacle is taken as a load of 180 VA to get the total required branch-circuit capacity, with the demand factors of Table 220-13 applied to get the minimum required feeder capacity for receptacle loads.

Part **(c)** covers rules on providing branch-circuit capacity for loads other than general lighting and designates specific amounts of load that must be allowed for each outlet. This rule establishes the minimum loads that must be allowed in computing the minimum required branch-circuit capacity for general-use receptacles and "outlets not used for general illumination." Item **(3)** requires that the actual voltampere rating of a recessed lighting fixture be taken as the amount of load that must be included in branch-circuit capacity. This permits local and/or decorative recessed lighting fixtures to be taken at their actual load value rather than having them be taken as "other outlets," which would require a load allowance of "180 voltamperes per outlet"—even if each such fixture were lamped at, say, 25 W. Or, in the case where a recessed fixture contained a 300-W lamp, allowance of only 180 VA would be inadequate.

Receptacle Outlets

The last sentence of Sec. 220-3(c)(5) calls for "each single or each multiple receptacle *on one strap*" to be taken as a load of "not less than 180 voltamperes"—in commercial, institutional, and industrial occupancies. The rule requires that every general-purpose, single or duplex or triplex convenience receptacle outlet in nonresidential occupancies be taken as a load of 180 VA, and that amount of circuit capacity must be provided for each such outlet (Fig. 220-2). **Code** intent is that each individual device strap—whether it holds one, two, or three receptacles—is a load of 180 VA. This rule makes clear that branch-circuit and feeder capacity must be provided for receptacles in nonresidential occupancies in accordance with loads calculated at 180 VA per receptacle strap.

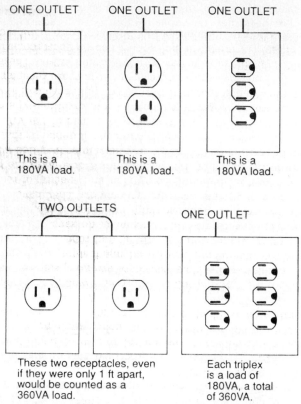

Fig. 220-2. Classification of single, duplex, and triplex receptacles. (Sec. 220-3.)

If a 15-A, 115-V circuit is used to supply *only* receptacle outlets, then the maximum number of general-purpose receptacle outlets that may be fed by that circuit is

$$15 \text{ A} \times 115 \text{ V} \div 180 \text{ VA or 9 receptacle outlets}$$

For a 20-A, 115-V circuit, the maximum number of general-purpose receptacle outlets is

$$20 \text{ A} \times 115 \text{ V} \div 180 \text{ VA or 12 receptacle outlets}$$

See Fig. 220-3.

15A, 115V CIRCUIT—Maximum of 9 receptacle outlets

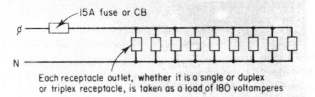

Each receptacle outlet, whether it is a single or duplex
or triplex receptacle, is taken as a load of 180 voltamperes

20A, 115V CIRCUIT—Maximum of 12 receptacle outlets

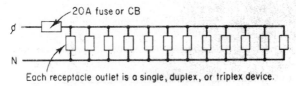

Each receptacle outlet is a single, duplex, or triplex device.

Fig. 220-3. Number of receptacles per circuit, nonresidential occupancy. [Sec. 220-3(c) (4).]

Note: In these calculations, the actual results work out to be 9.58 receptacles on a 15-A circuit and 12.77 on a 20-A circuit. Some inspectors round off these values to the nearest integral numbers and permit 10 receptacle outlets on a 15-A circuit and 13 on a 20-A circuit.

Although the **Code** gives the above-described data on maximum permitted number of receptacle outlets in commercial, industrial, institutional, and other nonresidential installations, there are no such limitations on the number of receptacle outlets on residential branch circuits. There are reasons for this approach.

In Sec. 210-50, the **Code** specifies where and when receptacle outlets are required on branch circuits. Note that there are no specific requirements for receptacle outlets in commercial, industrial, and institutional installations other than for store show windows in Sec. 210-62 and roof A/C equipment in Sec. 210-63. There is the general rule that receptacles do have to be installed where flexible cords are used. In nonresidential buildings, if flexible cords are not used, there is no *requirement* for receptacle outlets. They have to be installed only where they are needed, and the number and spacing of receptacles are completely up to the designer. But because the **Code** takes the position that receptacles in nonresidential buildings only have to be installed where needed for connection of specific flexible cords and caps, it demands that where such receptacles are installed, each must be taken as a load of 180 VA.

A different approach is used for receptacles in dwelling-type occupancies. The **Code** simply assumes that cord-connected appliances will always be used in all residential buildings and requires general-purpose receptacle outlets of the number and spacing indicated in Secs. 210-52 and 210-60. These rules cover one-family houses, apartments in multifamily houses, guest rooms in hotels and motels, living quarters in dormitories, etc. But because so many receptacle outlets are required in such occupancies and because use of plug-connected loads is intermittent and has great diversity of load values and operating cycles, the **Code** notes at the bottom of Table 220-3(b) that the loads connected to such receptacles are adequately served by the branch-circuit capacity required by Sec. 220-4, and no additional load calculations are required for such outlets.

In dwelling occupancies, it is necessary to first calculate the total "general lighting load" from Sec. 220-3(b) and Table 220-3(b) (at 3 VA/sq ft for dwellings or 2 VA/sq ft for hotels and motels, including apartment houses without provisions for cooking by tenants) and then provide the minimum required number and rating of 15-A and/or 20-A general-purpose branch circuits to handle that load as covered in Sec. 220-4(a). As long as that basic circuit capacity is provided, any number of lighting outlets may be connected to any general-purpose branch circuit, up to the rating of the branch circuit if loads are known. The lighting outlets should be evenly distributed among all the circuits. Although residential lamp wattages cannot be anticipated, the **Code** method covers fairly heavy loading.

When the above **Code** rules on circuits and outlets for general lighting in dwelling units, guest rooms of hotels and motels, and similar occupancies are satisfied, general-purpose convenience receptacle outlets may be connected on circuits supplying lighting outlets; or receptacles only may be connected on one or more of the required branch circuits; or additional circuits (over and above those required by **Code**) may be used to supply the receptacles. But no matter how general-purpose receptacle outlets are circuited, *any number* of general-purpose receptacle outlets may be connected on a residential branch circuit—with or without lighting outlets on the same circuit.

And when small appliance branch circuits are provided in accordance with the requirements of Sec. 220-4(b), *any number* of small appliance receptacle outlets may be connected on the 20-A small appliance circuits—*but only* receptacle outlets may be connected to these circuits and only in the specified rooms.

Section 210-52(a) applies to spacing of receptacles connected on the 20-A small appliance circuits, as well as spacing of general-purpose receptacle outlets. That section, therefore, establishes the *minimum* number of receptacles that must be installed for greater convenience of use.

Exception No. 1 to Sec. 220-3(c) requires branch-circuit capacity to be calculated for multioutlet assemblies (prewired surface metal raceway with plug outlets spaced along its length). Exception No. 1 says that each 1-ft length of such strip must be taken as a 180-VA load when the strip is used where a number of appliances are likely to be used simultaneously. For instance, in the case of industrial applications on assembly lines involving frequent, simultaneous use of plugged-in tools, the loading of 180 VA/ft must be used. (A loading of 180 VA for each 5-ft section may be used in commercial or institutional applications of multioutlet assemblies when use of plug-in tools or appliances is not heavy.) Figure 220-4 shows an example of such load calculation.

Exception No. 3 permits branch-circuit capacity for the outlets required by Sec. 210-62 to be calculated as shown in Fig. 220-5—instead of using the load-per-outlet value from part **(c)**.

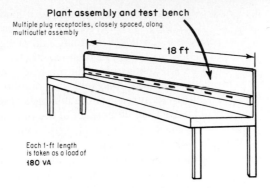

Plant assembly and test bench

Multiple plug receptacles, closely spaced, along multioutlet assembly

18 ft

Each 1-ft length is taken as a load of **180 VA**

Load allowed for this bench = *18 X 180 VA = 3240 VA*

THEREFORE, 3240 VOLTAMPERES OF CIRCUIT CAPACITY MUST BE PROVIDED IN THIS EXAMPLE

Fig. 220-4. Calculating required branch-circuit capacity for multioutlet assembly. (Sec. 220-3(c), Exception No. 1.)

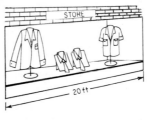

Required branch-circuit capacity for show window } = 200 VA X 20 linear ft = 4000 VA

Fig 220-5. Alternate method for calculating show-window circuit capacity. (Sec. 220-3(c), Exception No. 3.)

As noted in Exception No. 5, in calculating the size of branch-circuit, feeder, or service conductors, a load of 5000 VA may be used for a household electric dryer when the actual dryer rating is not known. This is an Exception to Sec. 220-3(c) (1), which specifies that the "ampere rating of appliance or load served" shall be taken as the branch-circuit load for an outlet for a specific appliance. And where more than one dryer is involved, the demand factors of Table 220-18 may be used.

220-4. Branch Circuits Required.   After following the rules of Sec. 220-3 to assure that adequate branch-circuit capacity is available for the various types of load that might be connected to such circuits, Sec. 220-4(a) requires that the minimum required number of branch circuits be determined from the total computed load, as computed from Sec. 220-3, and from the load rating of the branch circuits used.

For example, a 15-A, 115-V, 2-wire branch circuit has a load rating of 15 A times 115 V, or 1,725 VA. If the load is resistive, like incandescent lighting or electric heaters, that capacity is 1,725 W. If the total load of lighting, say, that was computed from Sec. 220-3 were 3,450 VA, then exactly two 15-A, 115-V, 2-wire branch circuits would be adequate to handle the load, provided that the load on the circuit is not a "continuous" load (one that operates steadily for 3 hr or more). Because Sec. 220-3(a) requires that branch circuits supplying a continuous load be loaded to not more than 80 percent of the branch-circuit rating, if the above load of 3,450 VA was a continuous load, it could not be supplied by *two* 15-A, 115-V circuits loaded to full capacity. A continuous load of 3,450 VA could be fed by *three* 15-A, 115-V circuits—divided among the three circuits in such a way that no circuit has a load of over 15 A times 115 V times 80 percent, or 1,380 VA. If 20-A, 115-V circuits are used, because each such circuit has a continuous load rating of 20 times 115 times 80 percent, or 1,840 VA, the total load of 3,450 VA can be divided between two 20-A, 115-V circuits. (A value of "120 V" could be used instead of "115 V.")

example Given the required unit load of 3 VA/sq ft for dwelling units [Table 220-3(b)], the **Code**-minimum number of 20-A, 120-V branch circuits required to supply general lighting and general-purpose receptacles (not small appliance receptacles in kitchen, dining room, etc.) in a 2,200-sq-ft-one-family house is three circuits. Each such 20-A circuit has a capacity of 2,400 VA. The required total circuit capacity is 2,200 times 3 VA/sq ft, or 6,600 VA. Then dividing 6,600 by 2,400 equals 2.75. Thus, at least three such circuits would be needed.

example In Sec. 220-3(b), the **NE Code** requires a minimum unit load of 3 VA/sq ft for general lighting in a school, as shown in Table 220-3(b). For the school in this example, *minimum capacity for general lighting* would be

1,500 sq ft $\times$ 3 VA/sq ft   or 4,500 VA

By using 115-V circuits, when the total load capacity of branch circuits for general lighting is known, it is a simple matter to determine how many lighting circuits are needed. By dividing the total load by 115 V (using "120 V" would yield a lower current), the total current capacity of circuits is determined:

$$\frac{4,500 \text{ VA}}{115 \text{ V}} = 39.1 \text{ A}$$

But, because the circuits will be supplying continuous lighting loads (over 3 hr), it is necessary to multiply that value by 1.25 in order to keep the load on any circuit to not more than 80 percent of the circuit rating. Then, using either 15- or 20-A, 2-wire, 115-V circuits (and dropping the fraction of an ampere) gives

$$\frac{1.25 \times 39 \text{ A}}{15 \text{ A}} = 3.25$$

which means four 15-A circuits, or

$$\frac{1.25 \times 39 \text{ A}}{20 \text{ A}} = 2.43$$

which means three 20-A circuits. And then each circuit must be loaded without exceeding the 80 percent maximum on any circuit.

Part **(b)** of Sec. 220-4 requires that two or more 20-A branch circuits be provided to supply all the receptacle outlets required by Sec. 210-52(b) in the kitchen, pantry, dining room, breakfast room and any similar area of any dwelling unit—one-family houses, apartments, and motel and hotel suites with cooking facilities or serving pantries. That means that at least one 3-wire, 20-A, 240/120- or 208/120-V circuit shall be provided to serve only receptacles for the small appliance load in the kitchen, pantry, dining room, and breakfast room of any dwelling unit. Of course, two 2-wire, 20-A, 120-V circuits are equivalent to the 3-wire circuit and could be used. If a 3-wire, 240/120-V circuit is used to provide the required two-circuit capacity for small appliances, the 3-wire circuit can be split-wired to receptacle outlets in these areas.

Part **(c)** of Sec. 220-4 requires that at least one 20-A branch circuit be provided for the one or more laundry receptacles installed, as required by Sec. 210-52(f), at the laundry location in a dwelling unit. Further, the last sentence of part **(c)** prohibits use of the laundry circuit for supplying outlets that are not for laundry equipment. And because laundry outlets are required by Sec. 210-50(f) to be within 6 ft of the intended location of the appliance, it would seem that any receptacle outlet more than 6 ft from laundry equipment could not be connected to the required 20-A laundry circuit (Fig. 220-6).

Part **(d)** of Sec. 220-4 makes clear that a feeder to a branch-circuit panelboard and the main busbars in the panelboard must have a minimum ampacity to serve the *calculated* total load of lighting, appliances, motors, and other loads supplied. And the amount of feeder and panel ampacity required for the general lighting load must not be less than the amp value determined from the circuit voltage and the total voltamperes resulting from the minimum unit load from Table 220-3(b) (voltamperes per square foot) times the area of the occupancy supplied by the feeder—even if the actual connected load is less than the calculated load determined on the voltamperes-per-square-foot basis. (Of course, if the connected load is greater than that calculated on the voltamperes-per-square-foot basis, the greater value of load must be used in determining the number of branch circuits, the panelboard capacity, and the feeder capacity).

It should be carefully noted that the first sentence of Sec. 220-4(d) states, "Where the load is computed on a voltamperes-per-square-foot (0.93 sq m) basis, the *wiring system* up to and including the branch-circuit panelboard(s) shall be provided to serve not less than the calculated load." Use of the phrase "wiring system up to and including" requires that a feeder must have capacity for the total minimum branch-circuit load determined from square-foot area times the minimum unit load [voltamperes per square foot from Table 220-3(b)]. And the phrase clearly requires that amount of capacity to be allowed in every part of the distribution system supplying the load. The required capacity would, for instance, be required in a subfeeder to the panel, in the main feeder from which the subfeeder is tapped, and in the service conductors supplying the whole system.

Actually, reference to "wiring system" in the wording of Sec. 220-4(d) presents a requirement that goes beyond the heading, "Branch Circuits Required,"

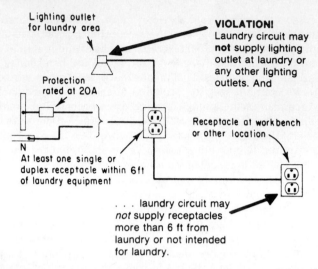

Lighting outlet
for laundry area

Protection
rated at 20A

N

At least one single or
duplex receptacle within 6ft
of laundry equipment

VIOLATION!
Laundry circuit may
not supply lighting
outlet at laundry or
any other lighting
outlets. And

Receptacle at workbench
or other location

. . . laundry circuit may
not supply receptacles
more than 6 ft from
laundry or not intended
for laundry.

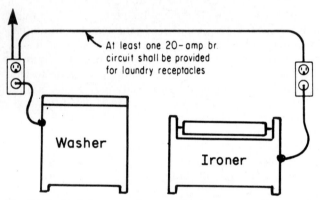

At least one 20-amp br.
circuit shall be provided
for laundry receptacles

Washer

Ironer

Fig. 220-6. No "other outlets" are permitted on 20-A circuit required for laundry receptacle(s). [Sec. 220-4(c).]

of Sec. 220-4 and, in fact, constitutes a requirement on *feeder* capacity that supplements the rule of the second sentence of Sec. 220-10(a). This requires a feeder to be sized to have enough capacity for "the computed load"—as determined by part **A** of this article (which means, as computed in accordance with Sec. 220-3).

A second part of Sec. 220-4(d) affects the required minimum number of branch circuits. Although the feeder and panelboard must have a minimum ampacity for the *calculated* load, it is only necessary to install the number of branch-circuit overcurrent devices and circuits required to handle the actual connected load in those cases where it is less than the calculated load. The last sentence of Sec. 220-4(d) is clearly an exception to the basic rule of the first sentence of Sec. 220-4(a), which says that "The minimum number of branch circuits *shall* be determined from the *total computed* load. . . ." Instead of having to supply *that minimum* number of branch circuits, it is necessary to have only the number of branch circuits required for the actual total "connected load."

example   For an office area of 200 × 200 ft, a 3-phase, 4-wire, 460/265-V feeder and branch-circuit panelboard must be selected to supply 277-V HID lighting that will operate continuously (3 hr or more). The actual continuous connected load of all the lighting fixtures is 92 kVA. What is the minimum size of feeder conductors and panelboard rating that must be used to satisfy Sec. 220-4?

$$200 \text{ ft} \times 200 \text{ ft} = 40{,}000 \text{ sq ft}$$
$$40{,}000 \text{ sq ft @ minimum of 3.5 VA/sq ft} = 140{,}000 \text{ VA}$$

The minimum computed load for the feeder for the lighting is

$$140{,}000 \text{ VA} \div [(480)(1.732)] = 168 \text{ A per phase}$$

The actual connected lighting load for the area, calculated from the lighting design, is

$$92{,}000 \text{ VA} \div [(480)(1.732)] = 111 \text{ A per phase}$$

Sizing of the feeder and panelboard must be based on 168 A, *not* 111 A, to satisfy Sec. 220-4(d).

The next step is to correlate the rules of Sec. 220-4(a) and (d) with those of Sec. 220-10. Section 220-10(a) requires a feeder to be sized for the "computed load" as determined by part **(A)** [Sec. 220-3(b)]. The feeder to the continuous calculated load of 168 A must have an ampacity at least equal to that load, and the feeder protective device must be sized at 125 percent of the continuous load of 168 A, when using a CB or fused switch that is not UL-listed for continuous operation at 100 percent of rating, as required by Sec. 220-10(b).

$$168 \times 1.25 = 210 \text{ A [Sec. 220-10(b)]}$$

1. Assuming use of a non-100 percent rated protective device, the overcurrent device must be rated not less than 1.25 x 168 A, or 210 A—which calls for a standard 225-A circuit breaker or fuses (the standard rating above 210-A).

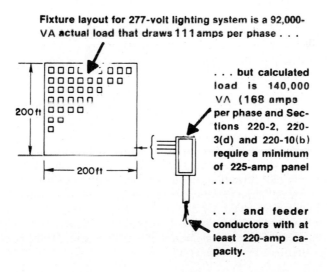

Fixture layout for 277-volt lighting system is a 92,000-VA actual load that draws 111 amps per phase . . .

. . . but calculated load is 140,000 VA (168 amps per phase and Sections 220-2, 220-3(d) and 220-10(b) require a minimum of 225-amp panel . . .

. . . and feeder conductors with at least 220-amp capacity.

200 ft

200 ft

2. Although feeder conductors with an ampacity of 168 A would be adequate for the load, they would not be properly protected (Sec. 240-3) by 225-A protection.
3. Using Table 310-16, the smallest size of feeder conductor that would be protected by 225-A protection is a No. 3/0 THHN or XHHW copper, with an ampacity of 225 A.
4. Because the UL requires that conductors larger than No. 1 AWG must be used at no more than their 75°C ampacities to limit heat rise in equipment terminals, the selected No. 3/0 THHN or XHHW copper conductor must not operate at more than 200 A—which is the table value of ampacity for a 75°C No. 3/0 copper conductor. And the load current of 168 A is well within that 200-A maximum.

Thus, all requirements of Sec. 220-10(b) and UL are satisfied.

Section 384-13 requires the panelboard here to have a rating not less than the minimum required ampacity of the feeder conductors—which, in this case, means the panel must have a busbar rating not less than 168 A. A 225-A panelboard (i.e., the next standard rating of panelboard above the minimum calculated value of load current—168 A) is therefore required, even though it might seem that a 125-A panel would be adequate for the actual load current of 116 A.

The number of branch-circuit protective devices required in the panel (the number of branch circuits) is based on the size of branch circuits used and their capacity related to connected load. If, say, all circuits are to be 20-A, 277-V phase-to-neutral, each pole may be loaded no more than 16 A because Sec. 220-3(a) requires the load to be limited to 80 percent of the 20-A protection rating. With the 111 A of connected load per phase, a single-circuit load of 16 A calls for a minimum of 111 ÷ 16, or 8 poles per phase leg. Thus a 225-A panelboard with 24 breaker poles would satisfy the rule of Sec. 220-4(d).

220·10. General.
Calculating Feeder Load

The key to accurate determination of required feeder conductor capacity in amperes is effective calculation of the total load to be supplied by the feeder. Feeders and subfeeders are sized to provide sufficient power to the circuits they supply. For the given circuit voltage, they must be capable of carrying the amount of current required by the load, plus any current which may be required in the future. The size of a feeder depends upon known load, future load, and voltage drop.

The minimum load capacity which must be provided in any feeder or subfeeder can be determined by considering **NE Code** requirements on feeder load. As presented in Sec. 220-10, these rules establish the minimum load capacity to be provided for all types of loads.

Part **(a)** of Sec. 220-10 requires feeder conductors to have ampacity at least equal to the sum of loads on the feeder, as determined from Sec. 220-3. Then part **(b)** rules on the rating of any feeder protective device.

If an overcurrent protective device for feeder conductors is not UL-listed for continuous operation at 100 percent of its rating, the load on the device must not exceed the noncontinuous load plus 125 percent of the continuous load. The first paragraph of part **(b)** applies to feeder overcurrent devices—circuit breakers and fuses in switch assemblies—and requires that the rating of any such protective device must generally never be less than the amount of noncontinuous load of the circuit (that amount of current that will not be flowing for 3 hr or longer) plus 125 percent of the amount of load current that will be continuous (flowing steadily for 3 hr or longer) (Fig. 220-7).

THE RULE

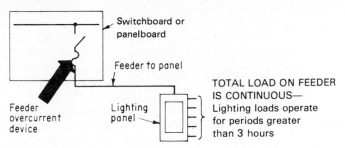

Switchboard or
panelboard

Feeder to panel

Feeder
overcurrent
device

Lighting
panel

TOTAL LOAD ON FEEDER
IS CONTINUOUS—
Lighting loads operate
for periods greater
than 3 hours

FEEDER OVERCURRENT DEVICE must be rated not less
than 125% of the continuous load *and* the feeder
conductors must be sized so they have an ampacity such
that they are properly protected by the rating of the feeder
CB or fuses, as required by Sec. 240-3. Another way of
saying that is "the continuous load must not exceed 80%
of the rating of the protection."

EXAMPLE: For this feeder, with conductors rated at 380 A,
the maximum continuous load permitted for a conventional
fused switch is 80% of the 400-A fuse rating [400X0.8 =
320A].

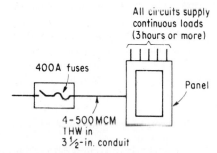

All circuits supply
continuous loads
(3 hours or more)

400A fuses

Panel

4 – 500 MCM
THW in
3½-in. conduit

Rating of fuses must be at least equal to 125% times the
continuous load and the 400-A rating is proper
protection for conductors with an ampacity of 380 A.

Fig. 220-7. Feeders must generally be loaded to no more than 80 percent
for a continuous load. [Sec. 220-10(b).]

For any given load to be supplied by a feeder, after the minimum rating of
the overcurrent device is determined from the above calculation (noncontinuous plus 125 percent of continuous), then a suitable size of feeder conductor
must be selected. For each ungrounded leg of the feeder (the so-called "phase
legs" of the circuit), the conductor ampacity must be at least equal to the amount
of noncontinuous current plus the amount of continuous current, from the **NEC**
tables of ampacity (Tables 310-16 through 310-19 and their accompanying
notes).

But because the amount of load current results in conductor ampacity
requirement lower than the rating of the protective device selected at 125 per-

cent times the continuous current, that condition violates the rule of Sec. 240-3 that calls for conductors to be protected "in accordance with their ampacities" from the tables. To satisfy Sec. 240-3, then, it becomes necessary to increase the size of the current conductors so that the rating of the protective device *either* does not exceed the ampacity of the conductors or, for circuits up to 800 A, the rating of the protective device is the next standard rating of device (from Sec. 240-6) above the conductor ampacity where the conductor ampacity does not correspond to a standard rating of protective device.

Note that the conductor size increase described above applies only to the ungrounded or phase conductors because they are the ones that must be properly protected by the rating of the protective device. A neutral or grounded conductor of a feeder does not have to be increased; its size must simply have ampacity sufficient for the neutral load as determined from Sec. 220-22.

The Exception for Sec. 220-10(b) notes that a circuit breaker or fused switch that is UL-listed for continuous operation at 100 percent of its rating may be loaded right up to a current equal to the device rating. Feeder ungrounded conductors must be selected to have ampacity equal to the noncontinuous load plus the continuous load. The neutral conductor is sized in accordance with Sec. 220-22, which permits reduction of neutral size for feeders loaded over 200 A that do not supply electric-discharge lighting, data processing equipment, or similar loads that generate high levels of harmonic currents in the neutral.

Fuses for feeder protection   The rating of a fuse is taken as 100 percent of rated nameplate current when enclosed by a switch or panel housing. But, because of the heat generated by many fuses, the maximum continuous load permitted on a fused switch is restricted by a number of NEMA, UL, and **NE Code** rules to 80 percent of the rating of the fuses. Limitation of circuit-load current to *no more than* 80 percent of the current rating of fuses in equipment is done to protect the switch or other piece of equipment from the heat produced in the fuse element—and also to protect attached circuit wires from excessive heating close to the terminals. The fuse itself can actually carry 100 percent of its current rating continuously without damage to itself, but its heat is conducted into the adjacent wiring and switch components.

NEMA standards require that a fused, enclosed switch be marked, as part of the electrical rating, "Continuous Load Current Not to Exceed 80 Percent of the Rating of Fuses Employed in Other Than Motor Circuits" (Fig. 220-8). That derating compensates for the extra heat produced by continuous operation. Motor circuits are excluded from that rule, but a motor circuit is required by the **NE Code** to have conductors rated at least 125 percent of the motor full-load current—which, in effect, limits the load current to 80 percent of the conductor ampacity and limits the load on the fuses rated to protect those conductors. But, the UL *Electrical Construction Materials Directory* does recognize fused bolted-pressure switches and high-pressure butt-contact switches for use at 100 percent of their rating on circuits with available fault currents of 100,000, 150,000, or 200,000 rms symmetrical A—as marked (Fig. 220-9). (See "Fused Power Circuit Devices" in that UL publication.)

Manual and electrically operated switches designed to be used with Class L current-limiting fuses rated 601 to 4,000 A, 600 V AC are listed by UL as "Fused

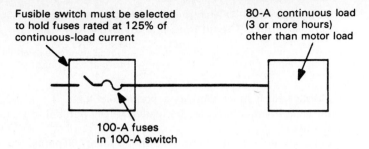

Fusible switch must be selected
to hold fuses rated at 125% of
continuous-load current

80-A continuous load
(3 or more hours)
other than motor load

100-A fuses
in 100-A switch

Circuit conductors must be sized so 100-A protection is equal to
conductor ampacity or is the next higher standard rating of protective
device above ampacity of conductors.

Fig. 220·8. For branch circuit or feeder, fuses in enclosed switch must be limited
for continuous duty. [Sec. 220-10(b).]

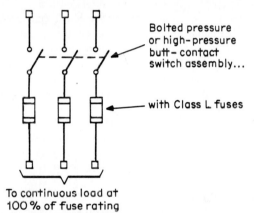

Bolted pressure
or high-pressure
butt-contact
switch assembly...

with Class L fuses

To continuous load at
100% of fuse rating

Fig. 220·9. Some fused switches may be used at 100
percent rating for continuous load. [Sec. 220-10(b).]

Power Circuit Devices." This category covers bolted-pressure-contact switches
and high-pressure, butt-type-contact switches suitable for use as feeder devices
or service switches if marked "Suitable for Use As Service Equipment." Such
devices "have been investigated for use at *100 percent of their rating* on circuits
having available fault currents of 100,000, 150,000 or 200,000 rms symmetrical
amperes" as marked.

CB for feeder protection   The nominal or theoretical continuous-current rating of a CB generally is taken to be the same as its trip setting—the value of
current at which the breaker will open, either instantaneously or after some
intentional time delay. But, as described above for fuses, the real continuous-
current rating of a CB—the value of current that it can safely and properly
carry for periods of 3 hr or more—frequently is reduced to 80 percent of the
nameplate value by codes and standards rules.

The UL *Electrical Construction Materials Directory* contains a clear, simple rule in the instructions under "Circuit Breakers, Molded-Case." It says:

> Unless otherwise marked, circuit breakers should not be loaded to exceed 80 percent of their current rating, where in normal operation the load will continue for three or more hours.

A load that continues for 3 hr or more is a *continuous* load. If a breaker is marked for *continuous* operation, it may be loaded to 100 percent of its rating and operate continuously.

There are some CBs available for continuous operation at 100 percent of their current rating, but they must be used in the mounting and enclosure arrangements established by UL for 100 percent rating. Molded-case CBs of the 100 percent continuous type are made in ratings from 225 A up. Information on use of 100 percent rated breakers is given on their nameplates.

Figure 220-10 shows two examples of CB nameplate data for two types of UL-listed 2,000-A, molded-case CBs that are specifically tested and listed for continuous operation at 100 percent of their 2,000-A rating—*but* only under the conditions described on the nameplate. These two typical nameplates clearly indicate that ventilation may or may not be required. Because most switchboards have fairly large interior volumes, the "minimum enclosure" dimensions shown on these nameplates (45 by 38 by 20 in.) usually are readily achieved. *But,* special UL tests must be performed if these dimensions are *not* met. Where busbar extensions and lugs are connected to the CB within the switchboard, the caution about copper conductors does not apply, and aluminum conductors may be used.

If the ventilation pattern of a switchboard does not meet the ventilation pattern and the required enclosure size specified on the nameplate, the CB must be applied at 80 percent rating. Switchboard manufacturers have UL tests conducted with a CB installed in a specific enclosure, and the enclosure may receive a listing for 100 percent rated operation even though the ventilation pattern or overall enclosure size may not meet the specifications. In cases where the breaker nameplate specifications are not met by the switchboard, the customer would have to request a letter from the manufacturer certifying that a 100 percent rated listing has been received. Otherwise, the breaker must be applied at 80 percent.

To realize savings with devices listed by UL at 100 percent of their continuous-current rating, use must be made of a CB manufacturer's data sheet to determine the types and ampere ratings of breakers available that are 100 percent rated, along with the frame sizes, approved enclosure sizes, and the ventilation patterns required by UL, if any. According to UL Standard 489, paragraph 33.37A, "a circuit breaker having a frame size less than 600 amperes shall not be marked suitable for continuous operation at 100 percent of rating." Of course, trip units with lower ampere ratings may be installed in the 600-A frame.

It is essential to check the instructions given in the UL listing to determine **if** and under what conditions a CB (or a fuse in a switch) is rated for continuous operation at 100 percent of its current rating.

EXAMPLE 1

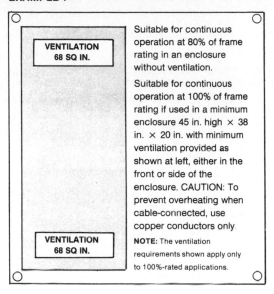

VENTILATION
68 SQ IN.

VENTILATION
68 SQ IN.

Suitable for continuous operation at 80% of frame rating in an enclosure without ventilation.

Suitable for continuous operation at 100% of frame rating if used in a minimum enclosure 45 in. high × 38 in. × 20 in. with minimum ventilation provided as shown at left, either in the front or side of the enclosure. CAUTION: To prevent overheating when cable-connected, use copper conductors only.

NOTE: The ventilation requirements shown apply only to 100%-rated applications.

EXAMPLE 2

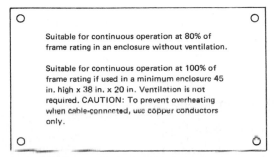

Suitable for continuous operation at 80% of frame rating in an enclosure without ventilation.

Suitable for continuous operation at 100% of frame rating if used in a minimum enclosure 45 in. high x 38 in. x 20 in. Ventilation is not required. CAUTION: To prevent overheating when cable-connected, use copper conductors only.

Fig. 220·10. Nameplates from CBs rated for 100 percent continuous loading. [Sec. 220-10(b).]

220·11. General Lighting.   For general illumination, a feeder must have capacity to carry the total load of lighting branch circuits determined as part of the lighting design and not less than a minimum branch-circuit load determined on a voltamperes-per-square-foot basis from the table in Sec. 220-2(b).

Demand factor permits sizing of a feeder according to the amount of load which operates simultaneously.

Demand factor is the ratio of the maximum amount of load that will be operating at any one time on a feeder to the total connected load on the feeder under consideration. This factor is frequently less than 1. The sum of the connected loads supplied by a feeder is multiplied by the demand factor to determine the load which the feeder must be sized to serve. This load is termed the maximum demand of the feeder:

Maximum demand load = connected load × demand factor

Tables of demand and diversity factors have been developed from experience with various types of load concentrations and various layouts of feeders and subfeeders supplying such loads. Table 220-11 of the **NE Code** presents common demand factors for feeders to general lighting loads in various types of buildings (Fig. 220-11).

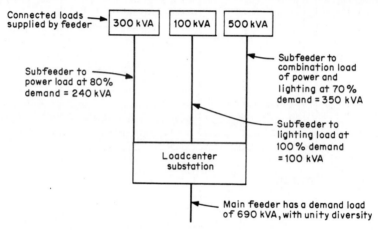

Fig. 220·11. How demand factors are applied to connected loads. (Sec. 220-11.)

The demand factors given in Table 220-11 may be applied to the total branch-circuit load to get required feeder capacity for lighting (but must not be used in calculating branch-circuit capacity). Note that a feeder may have capacity of less than 100 percent of the total branch-circuit load for only the types of buildings designated in Table 220-11, that is, for dwelling units, hospitals, hotels, motels, and storage warehouses. In all other types of occupancies, it is assumed that *all* general lighting will be operating at the same time, and each feeder in those occupancies must have capacity (ampacity) for 100 percent of the voltam-peres of branch-circuit load of general lighting that the feeder supplies.

example If a warehouse feeder fed a total branch-circuit load of 20,000 VA of general lighting, the minimum capacity in that feeder to supply that load must be equal to 12,500 VA plus 50 percent times (20,000 − 12,500) VA. That works out to be 12,500 plus 0.5 × 7,500 or 16,250 VA.

But, the note to Table 220-11 warns against using any value less than 100 percent of branch-circuit load for sizing any feeder that supplies loads that will all be energized at the same time.

220·12. Show·Window Lighting. If show-window lighting is supplied by a feeder, capacity must be included in the feeder to handle 200 VA per linear foot of show-window length. Because that is the same loading as given in Sec.

220-3(c), Exception No. 3, it works out to be a 100 percent demand for the entire branch-circuit load of show-window lighting.

220-13. Receptacle Loads—Nondwelling Units. This rule permits two possible approaches in determining the required feeder ampacity to supply receptacle loads in "other than dwelling units," where a load of 180 VA of feeder capacity must be provided for all general-purpose 15- and 20-A receptacle outlets. (In dwelling units and in guest rooms of hotels and motels, no feeder capacity is required for 15- or 20-A general-purpose receptacle outlets. Such load is considered sufficiently covered by the load capacity provided for general lighting.) But in other than dwelling units, where a load of 180 VA of feeder capacity must be provided for all general-purpose 15- and 20-A receptacle outlets, a *demand factor* may be applied to the total calculated receptacle load as follows. Wording of this rule makes clear that *either* Table 220-11 or Table 220-13 may be used to apply demand factors to the total load of 180-VA receptacle loads when calculating required ampacity of a feeder supplying receptacle loads connected on branch circuits.

In other than dwelling units, the branch-circuit load for receptacle outlets, for which 180 VA was allowed per outlet, may be added to the general lighting load and may be reduced by the demand factors in Table 220-11. That is the basic rule of Sec. 220-13 and, in effect, requires any feeder to have capacity for the total number of receptacles it feeds and requires that capacity to be equal to 180 VA (per single or multiple receptacle) times the total number of receptacles (straps)—with a reduction from 100 percent of that value permitted only for the occupancies listed in Table 220-11.

Because the demand factor of Table 220-11 is shown as 100 percent for "All Other" types of occupancies, the basic rule of Sec. 220-13 as it appeared prior to the 1978 NE Code required a feeder to have ampacity for a load equal to 180 VA times the number of general-purpose receptacle outlets that the feeder supplied. That is no longer required. Recognizing that there is great diversity in use of receptacles in office buildings, stores, schools, and all the other occupancies that come under "All Others" in Table 220-11, Sec. 220-13 contains a table to permit reduction of feeder capacity for receptacle loads on feeders. Those demand factors apply to any "nondwelling" occupancy.

The amount of feeder capacity for a typical case where a feeder, say, supplies panelboards that serve a total of 500 receptacles is shown in Fig. 220-11.

Although the calculation of Fig. 220-12 cannot always be taken as realistically related to usage of receptacles, it is realistic relief from the 100 percent demand factor, which presumed that all receptacles were supplying 180-VA loads simultaneously.

220-14. Motors. Any feeder that supplies a motor load or a combination load (motors plus lighting and/or other electrical loads) must satisfy the indicated NEC sections of Art. 430. Feeder capacity for motor loads is usually taken at 125 percent of the full-load current rating of the largest motor supplied, **plus** the sum of the full-load currents of the other motors supplied.

220-15. Fixed Electric Space Heating. Capacity required in a feeder to supply fixed electrical space heating equipment is determined on the basis of a load equal to the total connected load of heaters on all branch circuits served from

Take the total number of general-purpose receptacle outlets fed by a given feeder. . .

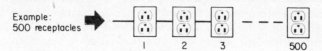

Example:
500 receptacles

. . . multiply the total by 180 voltamperes [required load of Section 220-2(c) (5) for each receptacle]. . .

500 × 180 VA = 90,000 VA

Then apply the demand factors from Table 220-13:

First 10 kVA or less @ 100% demand   = **10,000 VA**
Remainder over 10 kVA @ 50% demand
    = (90,000 − 10,000) × 50%
    = 80,000 × 0.5   = **40,000 VA**

Minimum demand-load total = **50,000 VA**

Therefore, the feeder must have a capacity of 50 kVA for the total receptacle load. Required minimum ampacity for that load is then determined from the voltage and phase-makeup (single- or 3-phase) of the feeder.

Fig. 220-12. Table 220-13 permits demand factor in calculating feeder demand load for general-purpose receptacles. (Sec. 220-13.)

the feeder. Under conditions of intermittent operation or where all units cannot operate at the same time, permission may be granted for use of less than a 100 percent demand factor in sizing the feeder. Sections 220-30, 220-31, and 220-32 permit alternate calculations of electric heat load for feeders or service-entrance conductors (which constitute a service feeder) in dwelling units. But reduction of the feeder capacity to less than 100 percent of connected load must be authorized by the local electrical inspector. Feeder load current for heating must not be less than the rating of the largest heating branch-circuit fed.

220-16. Small Appliance and Laundry Loads—Dwelling Unit. For a feeder or service conductors in a single-family dwelling, in an individual apartment of a multifamily dwelling with provisions for cooking by tenants, or in a hotel or motel suite with cooking facilities or a serving pantry, at least 1,500 VA of load must be provided for each 2-wire, 20-A small appliance circuit (to handle the small appliance load in kitchen, pantry, and dining areas). The total small appliance load determined in this way may be added to the general lighting load, and the resulting total load may be reduced by the demand factors given in Table 220-11.

A feeder load of at least 1,500 VA must be added for each 2-wire, 20-A laundry circuit installed as required by Sec. 220-4(c). And that load may also be added to the general lighting load and subjected to the demand factors in Table 220-11.

220-17. Appliance Load—Dwelling Unit(s). For fixed appliances (fastened in place) other than ranges, clothes dryers, air-conditioning equipment, and space heating equipment, feeder capacity in dwelling occupancies must be provided for the sum of these loads; but, if there are at least four such fixed appliances, the total load of four or more such appliances may be reduced by a demand factor of 75 percent (**NE Code** Sec. 220-17). Wording of this rule makes clear that a "fixed appliance" is one that is "fastened in place."

As an example of application of this **Code** provision, consider the following calculation of feeder capacity for fixed appliances in a single-family house. The calculation is made to determine how much capacity must be provided in the service-entrance conductors (the service feeder):

Water heater.........	2,500 W	230 V =	11.0 A
Kitchen disposal.......	½ hp	115 V = 6.5 A + 25% =	8.1 A
Furnace motor.........	¼ hp	115 V =	4.6 A
Attic fan...........	¼ hp	115 V = 4.6 A	0.0 A
Water pump ...	½ hp	230 V =	3.7 A

Load in amperes on each ungrounded leg of feeder = 27.4 A

To comply with Sec. 430-24, 25 percent is added to the full-load current of the ½ hp, 115-V motor because it is the highest-rated motor in the group. Since it is assumed that the load on the 115/230-V feeder will be balanced and each of the ¼-hp motors will be connected to different ungrounded conductors, only one is counted in the above calculation. Except for the 115-V motors, all the other appliance loads are connected to both ungrounded conductors and are automatically balanced. Since there are four or more fixed appliances in addition to a range, clothes dryer, etc., a demand factor of 75 percent may be applied to the total load of these appliances. Seventy-five percent of 27.4 = 20.5 A, which is the current to be added to that computed for the lighting and other loads to determine the total current to be carried by the ungrounded (outside) service-entrance conductors.

The above demand factor may be applied to similar loads in two-family or multifamily dwellings.

220-18. Electric Clothes Dryers—Dwelling Unit(s). This rule prescribes a **minimum** demand of 5 kVA for 120/240-V electric clothes dryers in determining branch-circuit and feeder sizes. Note that this rule applies only to "household" electric clothes dryers, and not to commercial applications. This rule is helpful because the ratings of electric clothes dryers are not usually known in the planning stages when feeder calculations must be determined (Fig. 220-13).

When sizing a feeder for one or more electric clothes dryers, a load of 5,000 VA or the nameplate rating, whichever is larger, shall be included for each dryer—subject to the demand factors of Table 220-18 when the feeder supplies a number of clothes dryers, as in an apartment house.

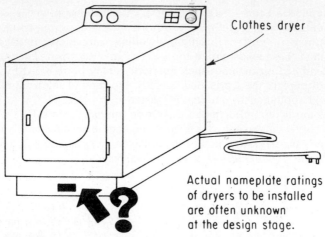

Clothes dryer

Actual nameplate ratings
of dryers to be installed
are often unknown
at the design stage.

Fig. 220·13. Feeder load of 5 kVA per dryer must be provided if actual load is not known. (Sec. 220-18.)

220·19. Electric Ranges and Other Cooking Appliances—Dwelling Unit(s). Feeder capacity must be allowed for household electric cooking appliances rated over 1¾ kW, in accordance with Table 220-19 of the **Code.** Feeder demand loads for a number of cooking appliances on a feeder may be obtained from Table 220-19.

Note 4 to Table 220-19 permits sizing of a branch circuit to supply a single electric range, a wall-mounted oven, or a counter-mounted cooking unit in accordance with that table. That table is also used in sizing a feeder (or service conductors) that supplies one or more electric ranges or cooking units. Note that Sec. 220-19 and Table 220-19 apply only to such cooking appliances in a "dwelling unit" and do not cover commercial or institutional applications.

Figure 220-14 shows a typical **NEC** calculation of the minimum demand load to be used in sizing the branch circuit to the range. The same value of demand load is also used in sizing a feeder (or service conductors) from which the range circuit is fed. Calculation is as follows:

A branch circuit for the 12-kW range is selected in accordance with Note 4

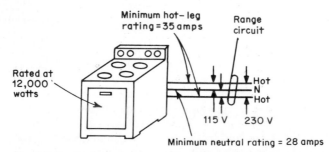

Fig. 220·14. Minimum amp rating of branch-circuit conductors for a 12-kW range. (Sec. 220-19.)

of Table 220-19, which says that the branch-circuit load for a range may be selected from the table itself. Under the heading "Number of Appliances," read across from "1." The maximum demand to be used in sizing the range circuit for a 12-kW range is shown under the heading "Maximum Demand" to be not less than 8 kW. The minimum rating of the range-circuit ungrounded conductors will be

$$\frac{8{,}000 \text{ W}}{230 \text{ V}} = 34.78 \text{ or } 35 \text{ A}$$

NE Code Table 310-16 shows that the minimum size of copper conductors that may be used is No. 8 (TW—40 A, THW—45 A, XHHW or THHN—50 A). No. 8 is also designated in Sec. 210-19(b) as the minimum size of conductor for any range rated 8¾ kW or more.

The overload protection for this circuit of No. 8 TW conductors would be *40-A fuses or a 40-A circuit breaker.* If THW, THHN, or XHHW wires are used for the circuit, they must be taken as having an ampacity of not more than 40 A and protected at that value. That requirement follows from the UL rule that conductors up to No. 1 AWG size must be used at the 60°C ampacity for the size of conductor, regardless of the actual temperature rating of the insulation—which may be 75°C or 90°C. The ampacity used must be that of TW wire of the given size.

Although the two hot legs of the 230/115-V, 3-wire circuit must be not smaller than No. 8, Exception No. 2 to Sec. 210-19(b) permits the neutral conductor to be smaller, but it specifies that it must have an ampacity not less than 70 percent of the rating of the branch-circuit CB or fuse and may never be smaller than No. 10.

For the range circuit in this example, the neutral may be rated

70% × 40 A (rating of branch-circuit protection) = 28 A

This calls for a No. 10 neutral.

Figure 220-15 shows a more involved calculation for a range rated over 12 kW. Figure 220-16 shows two units that total 12 kW and are taken at a demand load of 8 kW, as if they were a single range. Figure 220-17 shows another calculation for separate cooking units on one circuit. And a feeder that would be used to supply any of the cooking installations shown in Figs. 220-14 through 220-17 would have to include capacity equal to the demand load used in sizing the branch circuit.

A feeder supplying more than one range (rated not over 12 kW) must have ampacity sufficient for the maximum demand load given in Table 220-19 for the number of ranges fed. For instance, a feeder to 10 such ranges would have to have ampacity for a load of 25 kW.

Other Calculations on Electric Cooking Appliances

The following "roundup" points out step-by-step methods of wiring the various types of household electric cooking equipment (ranges, counter-mounted cooking units, and wall-mounted ovens) according to the **NEC**.

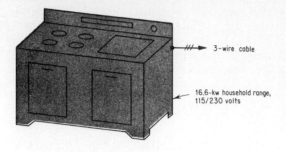

3-wire cable

16.6-kw household range,
115/230 volts

Refer to *NE Code* Table 220-19.
1. Column A applies to ranges rated not over 12 kW, but this range is rated 16.6 kW.
2. Note 1, below the Table, tells how to use the Table for ranges over 12 kW and up to 27 kW. For such ranges, the maximum demand in Column A must be increased by 5% for each additional kW of rating (or major fraction) above 12 kW.
3. This 16.6-kW range exceeds 12 kW by 4.6 kW.
4. 5% of the demand in Column A for a single range is 400 watts (8000 watts x 0.05).
5. The maximum demand for this 16.6-kW range must be increased above 8 kW by 2000 watts:
    400 watts (5% of Column A) X 5 (4 kW + 1 for the remaining 0.6 kW)
6. The required branch circuit must be sized, therefore, for a total demand load of
        8000 watts + 2000 watts = 10,000 watts
7. Required size of branch circuit—

$$\text{amp rating} = \frac{10,000 \text{ w}}{230 \text{ v}} = 43 \text{ amps}$$

USING 60C CONDUCTORS, AS REQUIRED BY UL, THE UNGROUNDED BRANCH CIRCUIT CONDUCTORS WOULD CONSIST OF NO. 6 TW CONDUCTORS.

Fig. 220-15. Sizing a branch circuit for a household range over 12 kW. (Sec. 220-19.)

Tap Conductors

Section 210-19(b), Exception No. 2, gives permission to reduce the size of the neutral conductor of a 3-wire range branch circuit to 70 percent of the rating of the CB or fuses protecting the branch circuit. However, this rule does not apply to smaller taps connected to a 50-A circuit—where the smaller taps (none less than 20-A ratings) must all be the same size. Further, it does not apply when individual branch circuits supply each wall- or counter-mounted cooking unit and all circuit conductors are of the same size and less than No. 10.

Section 210-19(b), Exception No. 1, permits tap conductors, rated not less than 20 A, to be connected to 50-A branch circuits that supply ranges, wall-mounted ovens, and counter-mounted cooking units. These taps cannot be any longer than necessary for servicing. Figure 220-18 illustrates the application of this rule.

In Sec. 210-19(b), Exception No. 1, the wording "no longer than necessary for servicing" encourages the location of circuit junction boxes as close as possible to each cooking and oven unit connected to 50-A circuits. A number of counter-mounted cooking units have integral supply leads about 36 in. long, and some ovens come with supply conduit and wire in lengths of 48 to 54 in. Therefore, a box should be installed close enough to connect these leads.

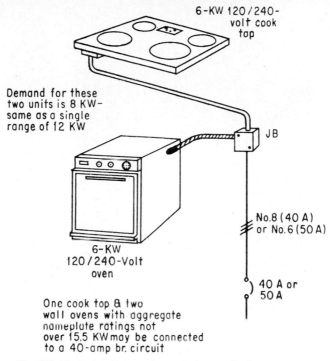

6-KW 120/240-
volt cook
top

Demand for these
two units is 8 KW—
same as a single
range of 12 KW

JB

6-KW
120/240-Volt
oven

No.8 (40 A)
or No.6 (50 A)

40 A or
50 A

One cook top & two
wall ovens with aggregate
nameplate ratings not
over 15.5 KW may be connected
to a 40-amp br. circuit

Fig. 220-16. Two units treated as a single-range load. (Sec. 220-19.)

Feeder and Circuit Calculations

Section 220-19 permits the use of Table 220-19 for calculating the feeder load for ranges and other cooking appliances that are individually rated more than 1¾ kW.

Note 4 of the table reads: "The branch circuit load for one wall-mounted oven or one counter-mounted cooking unit shall be the nameplate rating of the appliance." Figure 220-19 shows a separate branch circuit to each cooking unit, as permitted.

Common sense dictates that there is no difference in demand factor between a single range of 12 kW and a wall-mounted oven and surface-mounted cooking unit totaling 12 kW. This is explained in the last sentence of Note 4 of Table 220-19. The mere division of a complete range into two or more units does not change the demand factor. Therefore, the most direct and accurate method of computing the branch-circuit and feeder calculations for wall-mounted ovens and surface-mounted cooking units within each occupancy is to total the kilowatt ratings of these appliances and treat this total kilowatt rating as a single range of the same rating. For example, a particular dwelling has an 8-kW, 4-burner, surface-mounted cooking unit and a 4-kW wall-mounted oven. This is a total of 12 kW, and the maximum permissible demand given in Column A of Table 220-19 for a single 12-kW range is 8 kW.

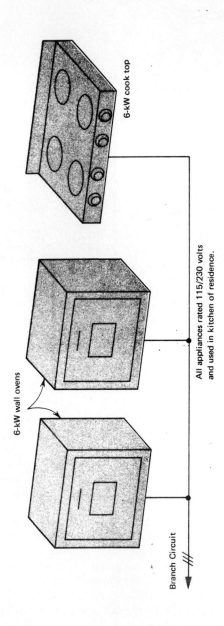

6-kW cook top

6-kW wall ovens

Branch Circuit

All appliances rated 115/230 volts
and used in kitchen of residence.

1. Note 4 of Table 220-19 says that the branch-circuit load for a counter-mounted cooking unit and not more than two wall-mounted ovens, all supplied from a single branch circuit and located in the same room, shall be computed by adding the nameplate ratings of the individual appliances and treating this total as a single range.

2. Therefore, the three appliances shown may be considered to be a single range of 18-kW rating (6 kW + 6 kW + 6 kW).

3. From Note 1 of Table 220-19, such a range exceeds 12 kW by 6 kW and the 8-kW demand of Column A must be increased by 400 watts (5% of 8000 watts) for each of the 6 additional kilowatts above 12 kW.

4. Thus, the branch-circuit demand load is—

$$\boxed{\text{8000 WATTS} + (6\times400 \text{ WATTS}) = 10,400 \text{ WATTS}}$$

A 50-AMP CIRCUIT IS REQUIRED.

Fig. 220-17.   Determining branch-circuit load for separate cooking appliances on a single circuit. (Sec. 220-19.)

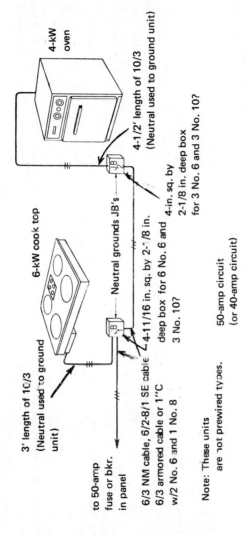

3' length of 10/3
(Neutral used to ground unit)

6-kW cook top

4-kW oven

Neutral grounds JB's

4-1/2' length of 10/3
(Neutral used to ground unit)

4-11/16 in. sq. by 2-1/8 in.
deep box for 6 No. 6 and
3 No. 10?

4-in. sq. by
2-1/8 in. deep box
for 3 No. 6 and 3 No. 10?

to 50-amp
fuse or bkr.
in panel

6/3 NM cable, 6/2-8/1 SE cable
6/3 armored cable or 1"C
w/2 No. 6 and 1 No. 8

50-amp circuit
(or 40-amp circuit)

Note: These units
are not prewired types.

NEC rules permit a 50-amp circuit to supply cook tops and ovens. Typical arrangement shows such a circuit. Junction box sizes are computed from Table 370-6(a) and Table 370-6(b) for No. 6 conductor combinations. Taps to each unit are No. 10 to permit the use of the neutral as an equipment ground. Using the neutral to ground the junction boxes is permitted by Sec. 250-60.

Fig. 220-18. One branch circuit to cooking units. (Sec. 220-19.)

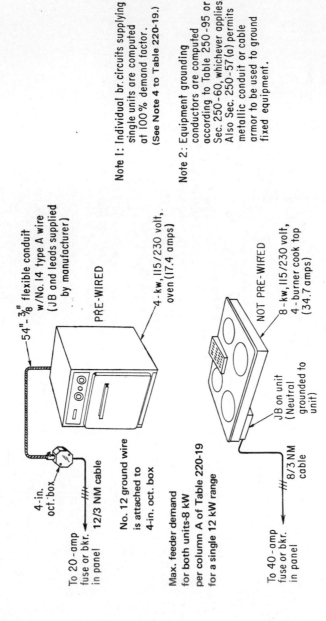

Note 1: Individual br. circuits supplying single units are computed at 100% demand factor. (See Note 4 to Table 220-19.)

Note 2: Equipment grounding conductors are computed according to Table 250-95 or Sec. 250-60, whichever applies. Also Sec. 250-57(a) permits metallic conduit or cable armor to be used to ground fixed equipment.

54" - 3⁄8" flexible conduit w/No. 14 type A wire (JB and leads supplied by manufacturer)

PRE-WIRED

4-kw, 115/230 volt, oven (17.4 amps)

4-in. oct. box

To 20-amp fuse or bkr. in panel   12/3 NM cable

No. 12 ground wire is attached to 4-in. oct. box

Max. feeder demand for both units-8 kW per column A of Table 220-19 for a single 12 kW range

NOT PRE-WIRED

8-kw, 115/230 volt, 4-burner cook top (34.7 amps)

JB on unit (Neutral grounded to unit)

To 40-amp fuse or bkr. in panel   8/3 NM cable

An 8-kW cook top is supplied by an individual No. 8 (40-amp) branch circuit, and a No. 12 (20-amp) branch circuit supplies a 4-kW oven. Such circuits are calculated on the basis of the nameplate rating of the appliance. In most instances individual branch circuits cost less than 50-amp, multi-outlet circuits for cooking and oven units.

Fig. 220-19.   Separate branch circuit to cooking units. (Sec. 220-19.)

Similarly, it follows that if the ratings of a 2-burner, counter-mounted cooking unit and a wall-mounted oven are each 3.5 kW, the total of the two would be 7 kW—the same total as a small 7-kW range. Because the 7-kW load is less than 8¾ kW, Note 3 of Table 220-19 permits Column C of Table 220-19 to be used in lieu of Column A. The demand load is 5.6 kW (7 kW times 0.80). Range or total cooking and oven unit ratings less than 8¾ kW are more likely to be found in small apartment units of multifamily dwellings than in single-family dwellings.

Because the demand loads in Column A of Table 220-19 apply to ranges not exceeding 12 kW, they also apply to wall-mounted ovens and counter-mounted cooking units within each individual occupancy by totaling their aggregate nameplate kilowatt ratings. Then if the total rating exceeds 12 kW, Note 1 to the table should be used as if the units were a single range of equal rating. For example, assume that the total rating of a counter-mounted cooking unit and two wall-mounted ovens is 16 kW in a dwelling unit. The maximum demand for a single 12-kW range is given as 8 kW in Column A. Note 1 requires that the maximum demand in Column A be increased 5 percent for each additional kilowatt or major fraction thereof that exceeds 12 kW. In this case 16 kW exceeds 12 kW by 4 kW. Therefore, 5 percent times 4 equals 20 percent, and 20 percent of 8 kW is 1.6 kW. The maximum feeder and branch-circuit demand is then 9.6 kW (8 kW plus 1.6 kW). A 9,600-W load would draw over 40 A at 230 V, thereby requiring a circuit rated over 40 A.

For the range or cooking unit demand factors in a multifamily dwelling, say a 12-unit apartment building, a specific calculation must be made, as follows:

1. Each apartment has a 6-kW counter-mounted cooking unit and a 4-kW wall-mounted oven. And each apartment is served by a separate feeder from a main switchboard. The maximum cooking demand in each apartment feeder should be computed in the same manner as previously described for single-family dwellings. Since the total rating of cooking and oven units in each apartment is 10 kW (6 kW plus 4 kW), Column A of Table 220-19 for one appliance should apply. Thus, the maximum cooking demand load on each feeder is 8 kW.

2. In figuring the size of the main service feeder, Column A should be used for 12 appliances. Thus, the demand would be 27 kW.

As an alternate calculation, assume that each of the 12 apartments has a 4-kW counter-mounted cooking unit and 4-kW wall-mounted oven. This would total 8 kW per apartment. In this case Column C of Table 220-19 can be used to determine the cooking load in each separate feeder. By applying Column C on the basis of a single 8-kW range, the maximum demand is 6.4 kW (8 kW times 0.80). Therefore, 6.4 kW is the cooking load to be included in the calculation of each feeder. Notice that this is 1.6 kW less than the previous example where cooking and oven units, totaling 10 kW, had a demand load of 8 kW. And this is logical, because smaller units should produce a smaller total kilowatt demand.

On the other hand, it is better to use Column A instead of Column C for computing the main service feeder capacity for twelve 8-kW cooking loads. The reason for this is that Column C is inaccurate where more than five 8-kW ranges (or combinations) and more than twelve 7-kW ranges (or combinations) are to be used. In these instances, calculations made on the basis of Column C result in a demand load greater than that of Column A for the same number of ranges. As an example, twelve 8-kW ranges have a demand load of 30.72 kW (12 times 8 kW times 0.32) in applying Column C, but only a demand load of 27 kW in Column A. And in Column A the 27 kW is based on twelve 12-kW ranges. This discrepancy dictates use of Column C only on the limited basis previously outlined.

Branch-Circuit Wiring

Where individual branch circuits supply each counter-mounted cooking unit and wall-mounted oven, there appears to be no particular problem. Figure 220-19 gives the details for wiring units on individual branch circuits.

Figure 220-18 shows an example of how typical counter-mounted cooking units and wall-mounted ovens are connected to a 50-A branch circuit.

Several manufacturers of cooking units provide an attached flexible metal conduit with supply leads and a floating 4-in. octagon box as a part of each unit. These units are commonly called "prewired types." With this arrangement, an electrician does not have to make any supply connections in the appliance. Where such units are connected to a 50-A circuit, the 4-in. octagon box is removed, and the flexible conduit is connected to a larger circuit junction box, which contains the No. 6 circuit conductors.

On the other hand, some manufacturers do not furnish supply leads with their cooking units. As a result, the electrical contractor must supply the tap conductors to these units from the 50-A circuit junction box. See Fig. 220-18. In this case, connections must be made in the appliance as well as in the junction box.

Figure 220-20 shows a single branch circuit supplying the same units as shown in Fig. 220-18.

40-A Circuits

The NEC does recognize a 40-A circuit for two or more outlets, as noted in Sec. 210-23(c). Because a No. 8 (40-A) circuit can supply a single range rated not over 15.4 kW, it can also supply counter- and wall-mounted units not exceeding the same total of 15.4 kW. The rating of 15.4 kW is determined as the maximum rating of equipment that may be supplied by a 40-A branch circuit, which has a capacity of 9,200 W (40 A $\times$ 230 V). From Note 1 to Table 220-19, a 15.4-kW load would require a demand capacity equal to 8,000 W plus [(15.4 − 12) $\times$ 0.05 $\times$ 8,000] = 8,000 W plus 3 $\times$ 0.05 $\times$ 8,000 = 8,000 plus 1,200 = 9,200 W.

Figure 220-21 shows an arrangement of a No. 8 (40-A) branch circuit supplying one 7.5-kW cooking unit and one 4-kW oven. Or individual branch circuits may be run to the units.

220-20. Kitchen Equipment—Other than Dwelling Unit(s). Commercial electric cooking loads must comply with Sec. 220-20 and its table of feeder demand factors for **commercial** electric cooking equipment—including dishwasher

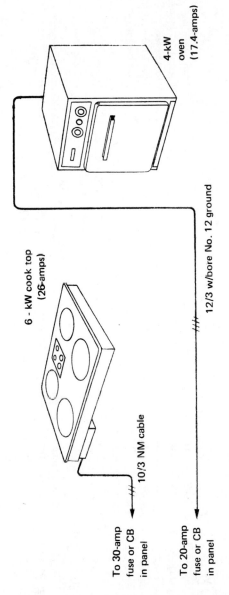

4-kW
oven
(17.4-amps)

6 - kW cook top
(26-amps)

12/3 w/bare No. 12 ground

10/3 NM cable

To 30-amp
fuse or CB
in panel

To 20-amp
fuse or CB
in panel

Same size and type of units as in Fig. 220-18,
but wired on individual circuits

Individual branch circuits supply the same units that appear in Fig. 220-18. With this arrangement, smaller branch circuits supply each unit with no JBs required. Although two additional fuse or CB poles are required in a panelboard, overall labor/material costs are less than the 50-amp circuit shown in Fig. 220-18. However, one disadvantage to individual circuits is that smaller size circuits will not handle larger units, which may be installed at a later date.

Fig. 220-20. Separate circuits have advantages. (Sec. 220-19.)

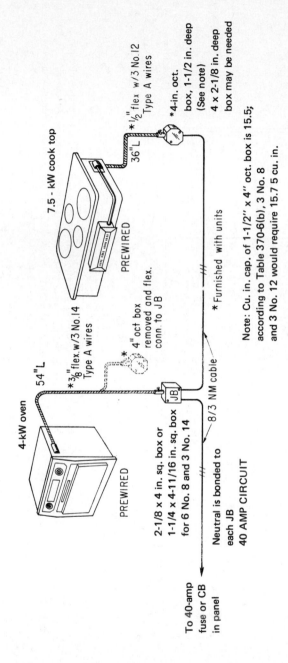

7.5 - kW cook top

*½" flex w/3 No.12 Type A wires

36"L

*4-in. oct. box, 1-1/2 in. deep (See note)

4 x 2-1/8 in. deep box may be needed

PREWIRED

*Furnished with units

Note: Cu. in. cap. of 1-1/2" x 4" oct. box is 15.5; according to Table 370-6(b), 3 No. 8 and 3 No. 12 would require 15.7 5 cu. in.

4-kW oven

54"L

*⅜" flex w/3 No.14 Type A wires

*4" oct box removed and flex. conn. to JB

* Furnished with units

PREWIRED

JB

8/3 NM cable

2-1/8 x 4 in. sq. box or 1-1/4 x 4-11/16 in. sq. box for 6 No. 8 and 3 No. 14

Neutral is bonded to each JB

40 AMP CIRCUIT

To 40-amp fuse or CB in panel

Fig. 220-21. A single 40-A circuit may supply units. (Sec. 220-19.)

The *NEC* permits 40-amp circuits in lieu of 50-amp circuits where the aggregate nameplate rating of cook tops and ovens is less than 15.5 kW. Most ranges are less than 15.5 kW and so are most combinations of cook tops and ovens.

booster heaters, water heaters, and other kitchen equipment. Space-heating, ventilating, and/or air-conditioning equipment are excluded from the phrase "other kitchen equipment."

At one time, the **Code** did not recognize demand factors for such equipment. **Code** Table 220-20 is the result of extensive research on the part of electric utilities. The demand factors given in Table 220-20 may be applied to **all** equipment (except the excluded heating, ventilating, and air-conditioning loads) that is **either** thermostatically controlled **or** is used only on an intermittent basis. Continuously operating loads, such as infrared heat lamps used for food warming, would be taken at 100 percent demand and not counted in the "Number of Units" that are subject to the demand factors of Table 220-20.

The rule says that the minimum load to be used in sizing a feeder to commercial kitchen equipment must not be less than the sum of the largest two kitchen equipment loads. If the feeder load determined by using Table 220-20 on the total number of appliances that are controlled or intermittent and then adding the sum of load ratings of continuous loads like heat lamps is less than the sum of load ratings of the two largest load units—then the minimum feeder load must be taken as the sum of the two largest load units.

example   Find the minimum demand load to be used in sizing a feeder supplying a 20-kW quick-recovery water heater, a 5-kW fryer, and four continuously operating 250-W food-warmer infrared lamps—with a 208Y/120V, 3-phase, 4-wire supply.

Although the water heater, the fryer, and the four lamps are a total of 1 + 1 + 4 or 6 unit loads, the 250-W lamps may not be counted in using Table 220-20 because they are continuous loads. For the water heater and the fryer, Table 220-20 indicates that a 100 percent demand must be used where the "Number of Units of Equipment" is 2. The feeder minimum load must then be taken as

$$\text{Water heater @ 100\% 20 kW}$$
$$\text{Fryer @ 100\% } \underline{\text{5 kW}} = \text{25 kW}$$
$$\text{Four 250-W lamps @ 100\% 1 kW} + \text{25 kW} = \text{26 kW}$$

Then, the feeder must be sized for a minimum current load of

$$\frac{26 \times 1000}{208 \times 1.732} = 72 \text{ A}$$

The two largest equipment loads are the water heater and the dryer:

$$20 \text{ kW} + 5 \text{ kW} = 25 \text{ kW}$$

and they draw

$$\frac{25 \times 1000}{208 \times 1.732} = 69 \text{ A}$$

Therefore, the 72-A demand load calculated from Table 220-20 satisfies the last sentence of the rule because that value is "not less than" the sum of the largest two kitchen equipment loads. The feeder must be sized to have at least 72 A of capacity (a minimum of No. 3 TW, THW, THHN, RHH, etc.).

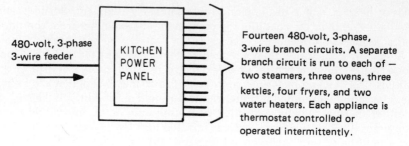

480-volt, 3-phase 3-wire feeder → KITCHEN POWER PANEL

Fourteen 480-volt, 3-phase, 3-wire branch circuits. A separate branch circuit is run to each of — two steamers, three ovens, three kettles, four fryers, and two water heaters. Each appliance is thermostat controlled or operated intermittently.

Kitchen panel supplies fourteen 480-volt, 3-phase, 3-wire branch circuits.

A separate branch circuit is run to each of—
    Two steamers,
    Three ovens,
    Three kettles,
    Four fryers, and
    Two water heaters
The 14 appliances make up a total connected load of 303.3 kVA

QUESTION:
Is a full-capacity feeder (303.3 kVA/480 X 1.73 = 366 amps) required here? Or can a demand factor be applied?

ANSWER:
Although it is possible that all of the appliances might operate simultaneously, it is not expected that they will all be operating at full connected load. Table 220-20 of the *NE Code* does permit use of a demand factor on a feeder for commercial electric cooking equipment (including dishwasher, booster heaters, water heaters and other kitchen equipment). As shown in the Table, for six or more units, a demand factor of 65% can be applied to the feeder sizing:

366 amps × 0.65 = 238 amps

The feeder must have a least that much capacity, and that amp rating must be at least equal to or greater than the sum of the amp ratings of the two largest load appliances served. Capacity must be included in the building service entrance conductors for this load

Fig. 220·22. Demand factor for commercial-kitchen feeder. (Sec. 220-20.)

Figure 220-22 shows another example of reduced sizing for a feeder to kitchen appliances.

220·21. Noncoincident Loads. When dissimilar loads (such as space heating and air cooling in a building) are supplied by the same feeder, the smaller of

the two loads may be omitted from the total capacity required for the feeder if
it is unlikely that the two loads will operate at the same time.

220-22. Feeder Neutral Load. This section covers requirements for sizing the
neutral conductor in a feeder, that is, determining the required amp rating of
the neutral conductor. The basic rule of this section says that the minimum
required ampacity of a neutral conductor must be at least equal to the "feeder
neutral load"—which is the "maximum unbalance" of the feeder load.

"The maximum unbalanced load shall be the maximum net computed load
between the neutral and any one ungrounded conductor. . . ." In a 3-wire, 120/
240-V, single-phase feeder, the neutral must have a current-carrying capacity
at least equal to the current drawn by the total 120-V load connected between
the more heavily loaded hot leg and the neutral. As shown in Fig. 220-23, under
unbalanced conditions, with one hot leg fully loaded to 60 A and the other leg
open, the neutral would carry 60 A and must have the same rating as the loaded
hot leg. Thus No. 6 THW hot legs would require No. 6 THW neutral (copper).

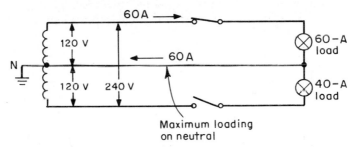

Fig. 220-23. Neutral must be sized the same as hot leg with heavier load. (Sec.
220-22.)

It should be noted that straight 240-V loads, connected between the two hot
legs, do not place any load on the neutral. As a result, the neutral conductor of
such a feeder must be sized to make up a 2-wire, 120-V circuit with the more
heavily loaded hot leg. Actually, the 120-V circuit loads on such a feeder would
be considered as balanced on both sides of the neutral. The neutral, then,
would be the same size as each of the hot legs if only 120-V loads were supplied
by the feeder. If 240-V loads also were supplied, the hot legs would be sized
for the total load; but the neutral would be sized for only the total 120-V load
connected between one hot leg and the neutral, as shown in Fig. 220-24.

But, there are qualifications on the basic rule of Sec. 220-22, as follows:

1. When a feeder supplies household electric ranges, wall-mounted ovens,
   counter-mounted cooking units, and/or electric dryers, the neutral conductor may be smaller than the hot conductors but must have a carrying
   capacity at least equal to 70 percent of the current capacity required in the
   ungrounded conductors to handle the load (i.e., 70 percent of the load on
   the ungrounded conductors). Table 220-19 gives the demand loads to be
   used in sizing feeders which supply electric ranges and other cooking
   appliances. Table 220-18 gives demand factors for sizing the ungrounded
   circuit conductors for feeders to electric dryers. The 70 percent demand

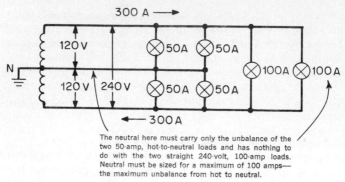

The neutral here must carry only the unbalance of the two 50-amp, hot-to-neutral loads and has nothing to do with the two straight 240-volt, 100-amp loads. Neutral must be sized for a maximum of 100 amps—the maximum unbalance from hot to neutral.

Fig. 220-24. Neutral sizing is not related to phase-to-phase loads. (Sec. 220-22.)

factor may be applied to the minimum required size of a feeder phase (or hot) leg in order to determine the minimum permitted size of neutral, as shown in Fig. 220-25.

From Table 220-19—DEMAND LOAD for 8 10-kW ranges = 23 kW

$$\text{LOAD ON EACH UNGROUNDED LEG} = \frac{23{,}000 \text{ W}}{230 \text{ V}} = 100 \text{ amps}$$
(e. g., No. 1TW)

$$\text{Required minimum Neutral capacity} = 70\% \times 100 \text{ amps} = 70 \text{ amps}$$
(e.g., No. 4TW)

Fig. 220-25. Sizing the neutral of a feeder to electric ranges. (Sec. 220-22.)

2. For feeders of three or more conductors—3-wire, DC; 3-wire, single-phase; and 4-wire, 3-phase—a further demand factor of 70 percent may be applied to that portion of the unbalanced load in excess of 200 A. That is, in a feeder supplying only 120-V loads evenly divided between each ungrounded conductor and the neutral, the neutral conductor must be the same size as each ungrounded conductor up to 200-A capacity, but may be reduced from the size of the ungrounded conductors for loads above 200 A by adding to the 200 A only 70 percent of the amount of load current above 200 A in computing the size of the neutral. It should be noted that this 70 percent demand factor is applicable to the unbalanced load in excess of 200 A and not simply to the total load, which in many cases may

include 240-V loads on 120/240-V, 3-wire, single-phase feeders or 3-phase loads or phase-to-phase connected loads on 3-phase feeders. Figure 220-26 shows an example of neutral reduction as permitted by Sec. 220-22.

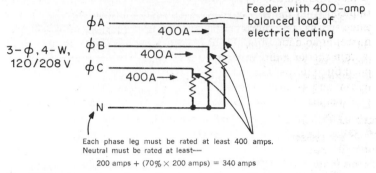

Fig. 220-26. Neutral may be smaller than hot-leg conductors on feeders over 200 A. (Sec. 220-22.)

WATCH OUT!

The size of a feeder neutral conductor may **not** be based on less than the current load on the feeder phase legs when the load consists of electric-discharge lighting, data processing equipment, or similar equipment. The foregoing reduction of the neutral to 200 A plus 70 percent of the current over 200 A does not apply when all or most of the load on the feeder consists of electric-discharge lighting, electronic data processing equipment, and similar electromagnetic or solid-state equipment. In a feeder supplying ballasts for electric-discharge lamps and/or computer equipment, there must not be a reduction of the neutral capacity for that part of the load which consists of discharge light sources, such as fluorescent mercury-vapor or other HID lamps. For feeders supplying only electric-discharge lighting or computers, the neutral conductor must be the same size as the phase conductors no matter how big the total load may be (Fig. 220-27). Full-sizing of the neutral of such feeders is required because, in a balanced circuit supplying ballasts or computer loads, neutral current approximating the phase current is produced by third (and other odd-order) harmonics developed by the ballasts. For large electric-discharge lighting or computer loads, this factor affects sizing of neutrals all the way back to the service. It also affects rating of conductors in conduit because such a feeder circuit consists of *four* current-carrying wires, which requires application of an 80 percent reduction factor. [See Note 8 and Note 10(c) of the "Notes to Tables 310-16 through 310-19" in the **NE Code**.]

In the case of a feeder supplying, say, 200 A of fluorescent lighting and 200 A of incandescent, there can be no reduction of the neutral below the required 400-A capacity of the phase legs, because the 200 A of fluorescent lighting load cannot be used in any way to take advantage of the 70 percent demand factor on that part of the load in excess of 200 A.

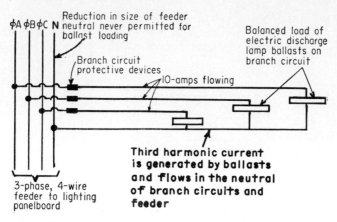

ΦA ΦB ΦC N   Reduction in size of feeder
             neutral never permitted for
             ballast loading
             Branch circuit
             protective devices
             10-amps flowing

Balanced load of
electric discharge
lamp ballasts on
branch circuit

**Third harmonic current
is generated by ballasts
and flows in the neutral
of branch circuits and
feeder**

3-phase, 4-wire
feeder to lighting
panelboard

EXAMPLE:

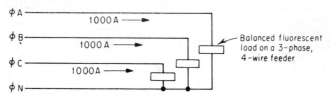

ΦA ———— 1000A ——▶
ΦB ———— 1000A ——▶
ΦC ———— 1000A ——▶
ΦN ————

Balanced fluorescent
load on a 3-phase,
4-wire feeder

There must be no reduction in amp rating of this neutral.
It must have 1000-amp rating like the phase conductors.

Fig. 220-27. Full-size neutral for feeders to ballast loads or computers.
(Sec. 220-22.)

It should be noted that the **Code** wording in Sec. 220-22 prohibits reduction in the size of the neutral when electric-discharge lighting and/or computers are used, even if the feeder supplying the electric-discharge lighting load over 200 A happens to be a 120/240-V, 3-wire, single-phase feeder. In such a feeder, however, the third harmonic currents in the hot legs are 180° out of phase with each other and, therefore, would not be additive in the neutral as they are in a 3-phase, 4-wire circuit. In the 3-phase, 4-wire circuit, the third harmonic components of the phase currents are in phase with each other and add together in the neutral instead of canceling out. Figure 220-28 shows a 120/240-V circuit.

Figure 220-29 shows a number of circuit conditions involving the rules on sizing a feeder neutral.

220-30. Optional Calculation—Dwelling Unit. This section sets forth an optional method of calculating service demand load for a residence. This method may be used instead of the standard method as follows:

1. Only for a one-family residence or an apartment in a multifamily dwelling, or other "dwelling unit"
2. Served by a 120/240-V or 120/208-V 3-wire, 100-A or larger service or feeder

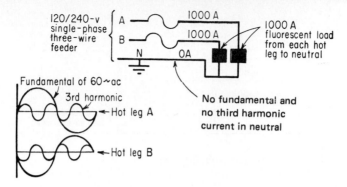

As shown, both the fundamental and harmonic currents are 180° out of phase and both cancel in the neutral. Under balanced conditions, the neutral current is zero. But the literal wording of Sec. 220-22 says there can be no reduction in neutral capacity when fluorescent lighting is supplied. As a result, there should be no use of the 70% factor for current over 200 amps as there would be for incandescent loading. Neutral here must be rated for 1000 amps.

Fig. 220-28. No reduction of neutral capacity even with zero neutral current. (Sec. 220-22.)

3. Where the total load of the dwelling unit is supplied by one set of service-entrance or feeder conductors

This method recognizes the greater diversity attainable in large capacity installations. It therefore permits a smaller size of service-entrance conductors for such installations than would be permitted by using the load calculations of Sec. 220-10 through Sec. 220-22.

In making this calculation, the heating load or the air-conditioning load may be disregarded as a "noncoincident load," where it is unlikely that two dissimilar loads (such as heating and air conditioning) will be operated simultaneously. In previous **NEC** editions, 100 percent of the air-conditioning load was compared with 100 percent of the total connected load of four or more separately controlled electric space heating units, and the smaller of the two loads was not counted in the calculation. In the present **NEC**, 100 percent of the air-conditioning load is compared with only *40 percent* of the total connected load of four or more electric space heaters, and the lower value is omitted from the calculation.

For instance, if a dwelling unit had 3 kW of air-conditioning load and 6 kW of electric heaters, the electric heating load of 6 kW was formerly used in the calculation because it is greater than the 3-kW air-conditioning load—even though the heating load was then subjected to the diversity factor of 40 percent in the calculation itself. *Now,* with these same loads, the 3-kW air-conditioning load is greater than 40 percent of the 6-kW heating load (0.40 × 6 = 2.4 kW) and the calculation will be made using the 3-kW air-conditioning load at 100 percent demand, and the electric heating load will be disregarded.

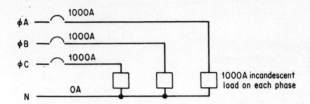

1. Incandescent lighting only

Serving an incandescent load, each phase conductor must be rated for 1000 amps. But neutral only has to be rated for 200 amps plus (70% x 800 amps) or 200 + 560 = 760 amps.

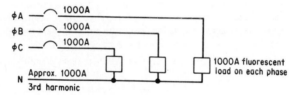

2. Electric discharge lighting only

Because load is electric discharge lighting, there can be no reduction in the size of the neutral. Neutral must be rated for 1000 amps, the same as the phase conductors, because the third harmonic currents of the phase legs add together in the neutral. This applies also when the load is mercury-vapor or other metallic-vapor lighting.

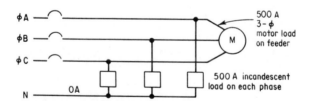

3. Incandescent plus motor load

Although 1000 amps flow on each phase leg, only 500 amps is related to the neutral. Neutral, then, is sized for 200 amps plus (70% x 300 amps) or 200 + 210 = 410 amps. The amount of current taken for 3-phase motors cannot be "unbalanced load" and no capacity has to be provided for this in the neutral.

Fig. 220-29. Sizing the feeder neutral for different conditions of loading. (Sec. 220-22.)

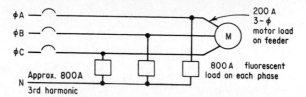

4. Electric discharge lighting plus motor load

Here, again, the only possible load that could flow on the neutral is the 800 amps flowing over each phase to the fluorescent lighting. But because it is fluorescent lighting there can be no reduction of neutral capacity below the 800-amp value on each phase. The 70% factor for that current above 200 amps DOES NOT APPLY in such cases.

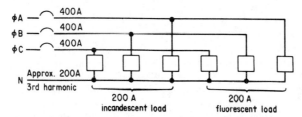

5. Incandescent plus electric discharge lighting

Each phase leg carries a total of 400 amps to supply the incandescent load plus the fluorescent load. But because there can be no reduction of neutral capacity for the fluorescent and because the incandescent load is not over 200 amps, the neutral must be sized for the maximum possible unbalance, which is 400 amps.

Fig. 220-29. (Continued)

example　A typical application of the data and table of Sec. 220-30, in calculating the minimum required size of service conductors, is as follows:

A 1,500-sq ft house (excluding unoccupied basement, unfinished attic, and open porches) contains the following specific electric appliances:

12-kW range
2.5-kW water heater
1.2-kW dishwasher
9 kW of electric heat (in five rooms)
5-kW clothes dryer
6-A, 230-V AC unit

When using the optional method, if a house has air conditioning as well as electric heating, there is recognition in Sec. 220-21 that if "it is unlikely that two dissimilar loads will be in use simultaneously," it is permissible to omit the smaller of the two in calculating required capacity in feeder or in service-entrance conductors. In Sec. 220-30, that concept is spelled out in the table to require adding only the larger of either the total air-conditioning load or 40 percent of the connected load of four or more separately controlled electric space heating units. For the residence considered here, these loads would be as follows:

Air conditioning = 6 A × 230 V = 1.38 kVA
40% of heating (five separate units) = 9 kW × 0.4 = 3.6 kW (3600 VA)

Because 3.6 kW is greater than 1.38 kVA, it is permissible to omit the air-conditioning load and provide a capacity of 3.6 kW in the service or feeder conductors to cover *both* the heating and air-conditioning loads.

The "other loads" must be totaled up in accordance with Sec. 220-30:

	Voltamperes
1. 1,500 VA for each of two small appliance circuits (2-wire, 20-A) required by Sec. 220-4(b) (1)	3,000
Laundry branch circuit (3-wire, 20A)	1,500
2. 3 VA/sq ft of floor area for general lighting and general-use receptacles (3 × 1,500 sq ft)	4,500
3. Nameplate rating of fixed appliances:	
Range	12,000
Water heater	2,500
Dishwasher	1,200
Clothes dryer	5,000
Total	29,700

In reference to Table 220-30, load categories 1, 3, and 4 are not applicable here: "Air conditioning" has already been excluded as a load because 40 percent of the heating load is greater. There is no "central" electric space heating; and there are *not* "less than four" separately controlled electric space heating units.

The total load of 29,700 VA, as summed up above, includes "all other load," as referred to in **Code** Table 220-30. *Then:*

1. Take 40% of the 9000-W heating load	3,600
2. Take 10 kVA of "all other load" at 100% demand	10,000
3. Take the "remainder of other load" at 40% demand factor: (29,700 − 10,000) × 40% = 19,700 × 0.4	7,880
Total demand	21,480

Using 230- and 115-V values of voltage rather than 240- and 120-V values, ampacities may then be calculated. At 230 V, single phase, the *ampacity of each service hot leg would then have to be*

$$\frac{21{,}480 \text{ W}}{230 \text{ V}} = 89.5 \text{ or } 90 \text{ A}$$

But, Sec. 230-42(b) (2) requires a minimum conductor rating when demand load is 10 kW (10 kVA) or more:

$$\text{Minimum service conductor required} = 100 \text{ A}$$

Then the neutral service-entrance conductor is calculated in accordance with Sec. 220-22, based on Sec. 220-10. All 230-V loads have no relation to required neutral capacity. The water heater and electric space heating units operate at 230 V, 2-wire and have no neutrals. By considering only those loads served by a circuit with a neutral conductor and determining their maximum unbalance, the minimum required size of neutral conductor can be determined.

When a 3-wire, 230/115-V circuit serves a total load that is balanced from each hot leg to neutral—that is, half the total load is connected from one hot leg to neutral and the other half of total load from the other hot leg to neutral—the condition of maximum unbalance occurs when all the load fed by one hot leg is operating and all the load fed by the other hot leg is off. Under that condition, the neutral current and hot-leg current are equal to half the total load watts divided by 115 V (half the volts between hot legs). But that current is exactly the same as the current that results from dividing the *total* load (connected hot leg to hot leg) by 230 V (which is twice the voltage from hot leg to neutral). Because of this relationship, it is easy to determine neutral-current load by simply calculating hot-leg current load—total load from hot leg to hot leg divided by 230 V.

In the example here, the neutral-current load is determined from the following steps that sum up the components of the neutral load:

	Voltamperes
1. Take 1,500 sq ft at 3 VA/sq ft [Table 220-3(b)]	4,500
2. Add three small appliance circuits	
(two kitchen, one laundry) at 1,500 VA each (Sec. 220-16)	4,500
Total lighting and small appliance load	9,000
3. Take 3,000 VA of that value	
at 100% demand factor (Secs. 220-11 & 220-16; Table 220-11)	3,000
4. Take the balance of the load	
(9,000 − 3,000) at 35% demand factor:	
6,000 VA × 0.35	2,100
Total of 3 and 4	5,100

Assuming an even balance of this load on the two hot legs, the neutral load under maximum unbalance will be the same as the total load (5,100 VA) divided by 230 V (Fig. 220-30):

$$\frac{5,100 \text{ VA}}{230 \text{ V}} = 22.17 \text{ A}$$

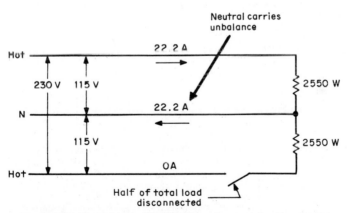

Fig. 220-30. Neutral current for lighting and receptacles. (Sec. 220-30.)

And the neutral unbalanced current for the range load can be taken as equal to the 8,000-W range demand load multiplied by the 70 percent demand factor permitted by Sec. 220-22 and then divided by 230 V (Fig. 220-31):

$$\frac{8,000 \times 0.7}{230} = \frac{5,600}{230} = 24.34 \text{ A}$$

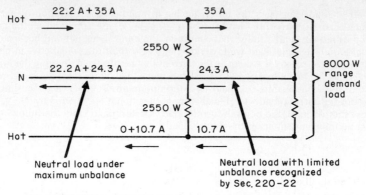

Fig. 220·31. Neutral for lighting, receptacles, and range. (Sec. 220-30.)

Then, the neutral-current load that is added by the 115-V, 1,200-W dishwasher must be added [Fig. 220-32]:

$$\frac{1,200 \text{ W}}{115 \text{ V}} = 10.43 \text{ A}$$

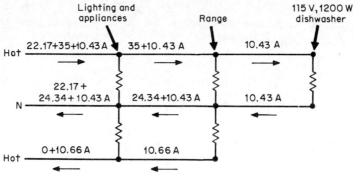

Fig. 220·32. Neutral current for all but dryer. (Sec. 220-30.)

The clothes dryer contributes neutral load due to the 115-V motor, its controls, and a light. As allowed in Sec. 220-22, the neutral load of the dryer may be taken at 70 percent of the load on the ungrounded hot legs. Then (5000 VA × 0.7) ÷ 230 V = 15.2 A.
The minimum required neutral capacity is, therefore,

	22.17 A	
	24.34 A	
	10.43 A	
	15.2 A	
Total:	72 A	(Fig. 220-32)

From **Code** Table 310-16, the neutral minimum for 72 A would be:

No. 3 copper TW, THW, THHN or XHHW
No. 2 aluminum TW, THW, THHN or XHHW

And the 75 or 90°C conductors must be used at the ampacity of 60°C conductors, as required by UL instructions in the UL's *Electrical Construction Materials Directory.*

Note: The above calculation of the minimum required capacity of the neutral conductor differs from the calculation and results shown in Example No. 2(a) in Chap. 9 in the **NE Code** book. In the book, the 1,200-W dishwasher load is added as a 230-V load to the range load and general lighting and receptacle load. To include a 115-V load as a 230-V load (and then divide the total by 230 V, as shown) does not accurately represent the neutral load that the 115-V, 1,200-W dishwasher will produce. In fact, it yields exactly half the neutral load that the dishwasher represents. The optional calculation method of Sec. 220-30 does indicate in part **(3)** that fixed appliances be added at nameplate load and does not differentiate between 115-V devices and 230-V devices. It simply totals all load and then applies the 100 percent and 40 percent demand factors as indicated. That method clearly is based on well-founded data about diversity of loads and is aimed at determining a reasonable size of the service hot legs. But, calculation of the feeder neutral in accordance with Sec. 220-22 is aimed at determining the *maximum unbalanced current* to which the service neutral might be subjected.

Although the difference is small between the **NE Code** book value of 64 A (or 67 A if 15,400 VA is divided by 230 V) and the value of 72 A determined here, precise calculation should be made to assure real adequacy in conductor ampacities. The difference actually changes the required minimum size of neutral conductor from No. 4 up to No. 3 for copper. A load like a dishwasher, which draws current for a considerable period of time and is not just a few-minute device like a toaster, should be factored into the calculation with an eye toward adequate capacity of conductors.

220·31. Optional Calculation for Additional Loads in Existing Dwelling Unit.   This covers an optional calculation for additional loads in an existing dwelling unit that contains a 120/240- or 208/120-V, 3-wire service of any current rating. The method of calculation is similar to that in Table 220-30.

The purpose of this section is to permit the *maximum load* to be applied to an *existing* service without the necessity of increasing the size of the service. The calculations are based on numerous load surveys and tests made by local utilities throughout the country. This optional method would seem to be particularly advantageous when smaller loads such as window air conditioners or bathroom heaters are to be installed in a dwelling with, say, an existing 60-A service, as follows:

If there is an existing electric range, say, 12 kW (and no electric water heater), it would not be possible to add any load of substantial rating. Based on the formula 13,800 VA (230 V × 60 A) = 8,000 + 0.4 (X − 8,000), the total "gross load" that can be connected to an existing 115/230-V, 60-A service would be X = 22,500 VA. Actually, it can be greater if a value of 240 V is used [240 V × 60 A = 14,400 VA].

example   Thus, an existing 1,000-sq ft dwelling with a 12-kW electric range, two 20-A appliance circuits, a 750-W furnace circuit, and a 60-A service would have a gross load of:

	Voltamperes
1,000 sq ft × 3 VA/sq ft	3,000
Two 20-A appliance circuits @ 1,500 VA each	3,000
One electric range @	12,000
Furnace circit @	750
Gross voltamperes	18,750

Since the *maximum* permitted gross load is 22,500 VA, an appliance not exceeding *3,750* VA could be added to this existing 60-A service. However, the tabulation at the end of this section lists air-conditioning equipment, central space heating, and less than four separately controlled space heating units at 100 percent demands; and if the appliance to be added is one of these, then it would be limited to *1,500 VA*:

From the 18,750-VA gross load we have 8,000 VA @ 100 percent demand + [10,750 VA (18,750 − 8,000) × 0.40] or 12,300 VA. Then, 13,800 VA (60 A × 230 V) − 12,300 VA = 1,500 VA for an appliance listed at *100 percent demand*.

220-33. Optional Calculation—Two Dwelling Units. This section provides an optional calculation for sizing a feeder to "two dwelling units." It notes that if calculation of such a feeder according to the basic long method of calculating given in part **B** of Art. 220 exceeds the minimum load ampacity permitted by Sec. 220-32 for three identical dwelling units, then the *lesser* of the two loads may be used. This rule was added to eliminate the obvious illogic of requiring a greater feeder ampacity for two dwelling units than for the three units of the same load makeup. Now optional calculations provide for a feeder to one dwelling unit, two dwelling units, or three or more dwelling units.

220-34. Optional Method—Schools. The optional calculation for feeders and service-entrance conductors for a school makes clear that feeders "within the building or structure" must be calculated in accordance with the standard long calculation procedure established by part **B** of Art. 220. **But** the ampacity of any individual feeder does not have to be greater than the minimum required ampacity for the whole building, regardless of the calculation result from part **B**.

The last sentence in this section excludes portable classroom buildings from the optional calculation method to prevent the possibility that the demand factors of Table 220-34 would result in a feeder or service of lower ampacity than the connected load. Such portable classrooms have air-conditioning loads that are not adequately covered by using a watts-per-square-foot calculation with the small area of such classrooms.

220-35. Optional Calculations for Additional Loads to Existing Installations. Because of the universal practice of adding more loads to feeders and services in all kinds of existing premises, this calculation procedure is given in the **Code**. To determine how much more load may be added to a feeder or set of service-entrance conductors, at least one year's accumulation of measured maximum-demand data must be available. Then, the required spare capacity may be calculated as follows:

$$\text{Additional load capacity} = \text{ampacity of feeder or service conductors} - [(1.25 \times \text{existing demand kVA} \times 1{,}000) \div \text{circuit voltage}]$$

where "circuit voltage" is the phase-to-phase value for single-phase circuits and 1.732 times the phase-to-phase value for 3-phase circuits.

A third required condition is that the feeder or service conductors be protected against overcurrent, in accordance with applicable **Code** rules on such protection.

ARTICLE 225. OUTSIDE BRANCH CIRCUITS AND FEEDERS

225-4. Conductor Covering. The wiring method known as "open wiring" is recognized in Art. 225 as suitable for overhead use outdoors—"run between buildings, other structures or poles" (Fig. 225-1). This is derived from Secs. 225-1, 225-4, 225-14, 225-18, and 225-19. Section 225-4 requires open wiring to be insulated *or* covered if it comes within 10 ft of any building or other structure, which it must do if it attaches to the building or structure. Insulated conductors have a dielectric covering that prevents conductive contact with the conductor when it is energized. Covered conductors—such as braided, weatherproof conductors (sometimes referred to as TBWP)—have a certain mechanical protection for the conductor but are not rated as having insulation, and thus there is no protection against conductive contact with the energized conductor.

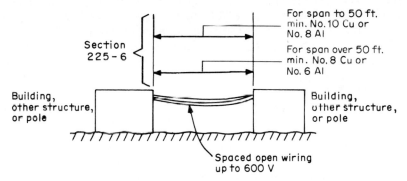

Fig. 225-1. Open wiring is OK for overhead circuits. (Sec. 225-4.)

Because Sec. 225-4 says that conductors in "*cables*" (except Type MI) must be of the rubber or thermoplastic type, a number of questions arise.

1. What kind of "*cable*" does the **Code** recognize for overhead spans between buildings, structures, and/or poles?
2. May an overhead circuit from one building to another or from lighting fixture to lighting fixture on poles use service-entrance cable, UF cable, or Type NM or NMC nonmetallic-sheathed cable?

The **Code** covers specific types of cables in turn (Arts. 330 through 340), but only in Art. 321 does the **Code** refer to use for outdoor overhead applications. And no other mention is made in the **Code** of cable suitable for overhead, outdoor spans.

The **Code** refers to overhead cable assemblies in Art. 342, "Nonmetallic Extensions." This includes a nonmetallic cable assembly with an integral supporting messenger cable (within the assembly) for "aerial" applications. But this aerial cable is suitable only for limited use indoors, in industrial plants that are dry locations. This cable assembly is listed as an "aerial cable" by UL, but it is the *only* aerial cable listed by UL. But again, *it may not be used outdoors.*

Use of service-entrance cable between buildings, structures, and/or poles is not supported by Art. 338. No mention is made of overhead use; and Sec. 338-4 requires that "unarmored" SE cable be supported as required by Sec. 336-15, which says that the cable must be "secured in place at intervals not exceeding 4½ feet." No exceptions are given. It could be argued that such support could be made to a messenger cable to which the SE cable is secured, and such practice is recognized in Sec. 321-3(a)(3).

Where Sec. 338-3(b) refers to SE cable as "a feeder to supply other buildings," it clearly refers only to "type SE" cable with a bare neutral and an overall outer jacket. (Type USE cable is recognized by UL and the **Code** for use as a feeder or branch circuit underground where all conductors are insulated.) The UL listing on type SE cable recognizes it only for aboveground installation. That certainly means on building surfaces or in raceway, but there is no mention of aerial or overhead use.

Use of Type MI, MC, or UF cable for outdoor, overhead circuits is supported by Sec. 321-3. There are no exceptions given to the support requirements in Sec. 336-15 that would let NM or NMC be used aerially, and such cables are not recognized by Sec. 321-3 for use as "messenger supported wiring."

Service-Drop Cable

The **NE Code** has Art. 321, "Messenger Supported Wiring," which covers use of "service-drop" cable, but the UL has no listing for or reference to such cable. The **NE Code** does make reference to it; and its use for aerial circuits between buildings, structures, and/or poles is particularly dictated (Fig. 225-2). Experience with this cable is very extensive and highly satisfactory. It is an engineered product specifically designed and used for outdoor, overhead circuiting.

NE Code Secs. 230-21 through 230-29 cover use of service-drop cable for overhead service conductors. Because the general rules of Art. 225 on outside branch circuits and feeders do make frequent references to other sections of Art. 230, it is logical to equate cables for overhead branch circuits and feeders to cables for overhead services. Although the rules of Art. 321 refer to a variety of messenger-supported cable assemblies, for outdoor circuits, use of service-drop cable is the best choice—because such cable is covered by the application rules of Secs. 230-21 through 230-29. Other types of available aerial cable assemblies, although not listed by UL, might satisfy some inspection agencies. But, in these times of OSHA emphasis on codes and standards, use of service-drop cable has the strongest sanction.

One important consideration in the use of service-drop cable as a branch circuit or feeder is the general **Code** prohibition against use of bare circuit conductors. Section 310-2 requires conductors to be insulated. An exception notes that bare conductors may be used where "specifically permitted." Bare *equipment grounding conductors* are permitted in Sec. 250-91(b). A bare conductor for SE cable is permitted in Sec. 338-1(c). Bare neutrals are permitted for service-entrance conductors in Sec. 230-41, for underground service-entrance (service lateral) conductors in Sec. 230-30, and for *service-drop conductors* in Sec. 230-22, Exception *when used as service conductors*. When service-drop

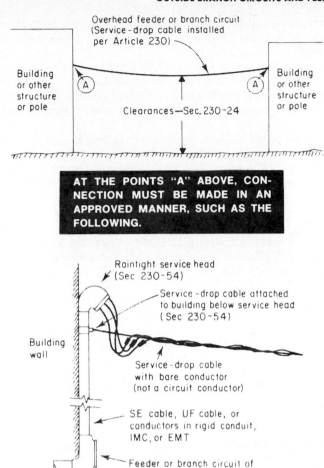

Fig. 225·2. Aerial cable for overhead circuits. (Sec. 225-4.)

cable is used as a feeder or branch circuit, however, there is no permission for use of a bare circuit conductor—although it may be acceptable to use the bare conductor of the service-drop cable as an equipment grounding conductor. And where service-drop cable is used as a feeder from one building to another, it would seem that a bare neutral could be acceptable as a grounded neutral conductor—as permitted in the last sentence of Sec. 338-3(b), first paragraph. (If service-drop cable is used as a feeder to another building and the bare conductor is *not* used as an equipment grounding conductor, then a grounding electrode *must* be installed at the other building in accordance with Sec. 250-24.)

When service-drop cable is used between buildings, the method for leaving one building and entering another *must* satisfy Secs. 230-43, 230-52, and 230-54. This is required in Sec. 225-11.

The Exception to Sec. 225-4 excludes equipment grounding conductors and grounded circuit conductors from the rules on conductor covering. This Exception permits equipment grounding conductor *and* grounded circuit conductors (neutrals) to be bare or simply covered (but not insulated) as permitted by other **Code** rules.

Because the matter of outdoor, overhead circuiting is complex, check with local inspection agencies on required methods. As **NE Code** Sec. 90-4 says, the local inspector has the responsibility for making interpretations of the rules.

225·6. Minimum Size of Conductor.   Open wiring must be of the minimum sizes indicated in Sec. 225-6 for the various lengths of spans indicated.

Section 225-6 gives a definition of *festoon lighting* as "a string of outdoor lights suspended between two points more than 15 feet apart" (Fig. 225-3). Such lighting is used at carnivals, displays, used-car lots, etc. Such application of lighting is limited because it has a generally poor appearance and does not enhance commercial activities.

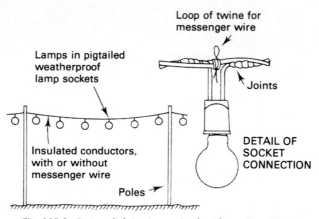

Fig. 225·3. Festoon lighting is permitted outdoors. (Sec. 225-6.)

Overhead conductors for festoon lighting must not be smaller than No. 12; and where any span is over 40 ft (Sec. 225-13), the conductors must be supported by a messenger wire, which itself must be properly secured to strain insulators. But the rules on festoon lighting do not apply to overhead circuits between buildings, structures, and/or poles.

225·7. Lighting Equipment Installed Outdoors.   Part **(b)** permits a common neutral for outdoor branch circuits—something not permitted for indoor branch circuits (a neutral of a 3-phase, 4-wire circuit is *not* a common neutral). For two 208Y/120-V multiwire circuits consisting of six ungrounded conductors (two from each phase) and a single neutral (serving both circuits) feeding a bank of floodlights on a pole, if the maximum calculated load on any one circuit is 12 A and the maximum calculated load on any one phase is 24 A, the ungrounded circuit conductors may be No. 14, but the neutral must be at least No. 10. This rule clearly states the need to size a common neutral for the *maximum* (most heavily loaded) phase leg made up by multiple conductors connected to any one phase and supplying loads connected phase-to-neutral.

Part **(c)** covers use of 480/277-V systems for supplying incandescent and electric-discharge lighting fixtures. A minimum mounting height of 8 ft is no longer required for lighting fixtures installed outdoors on buildings, structures, or poles on industrial or commercial premises and fed by 480/277-V circuits. This section rules that such fixtures must be not less than 3 ft from "windows, platforms, fire escapes, and the like." And the wording of this section is not just limited to fixtures mounted on buildings, structures, or poles but could apply to fixtures mounted at ground level for lighting of signs, building facades, and other decorative or ornamental lighting.

225-10. Wiring on Buildings. Compared with the 1984 and previous NEC editions, additional wiring methods are recognized for installation on the outdoor surfaces of buildings. Rigid, nonmetallic conduit may be used for outside wiring on buildings, as well as the other raceway and cable methods covered in this section. For a long time, rigid PVC was not permitted for such application.

225-14. Open-Conductor Spacings. Open wiring runs must have a minimum spacing between individual conductors (as noted in Sec. 225-14) in accordance with Table 230-51(c), which gives the spacing of the insulator supports on a building surface and the clearance between individual conductors on the building or run in spans (Fig. 225-4).

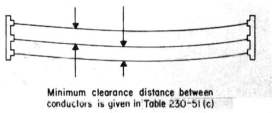

Minimum clearance distance between
conductors is given in Table 230-51(c)

Fig. 225-4. Spacing of open-wiring conductors. (Sec. 225-14.)

It should be noted that Sec. 225-14 and Table 230-51(c) require that the *minimum spacing* between individual conductors in spans run overhead be 3 in. for circuits up to 300 V (such as 120, 120/240, 120/208, and 240 V). For circuits up to 600 V, such as 480 Δ and 480/277 V, the *minimum spacing* between individual conductors must be at least 6 in.

225-18. Clearance from Ground. Open conductors must be protected from contact by persons by keeping them high enough aboveground or above other positions where people might be standing. And they must not present an obstruction to vehicle passage or other activities below the lines (Fig. 225-5).

Section 225-18 applies only to "open conductors" and gives the conditions under which clearances must be 10, 12, 15, or 18 ft—for conductors that make up either a branch circuit or a feeder [not service-drop conductors, which are

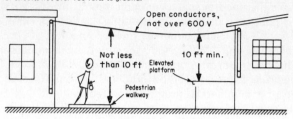

Open conductors are strung from one building to another, for circuits not over 150 volts to ground.

Open conductors, not over 600 V

Not less than 10 ft   Elevated platform

10 ft min.

Pedestrian walkway

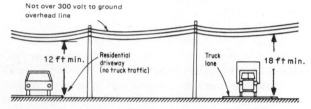

Individual open conductors supported by poles pass over both a residential driveway and a road bearing truck traffic:

Not over 300 volt to ground overhead line

12 ft min.   Residential driveway (no truck traffic)   Truck lane   18 ft min.

Fig. 225·5. Conductor clearance from ground. (Sec. 225-18.)

subject to Sec. 230-24(b)]. Although the wording of the third, fourth, and fifth paragraphs is the same as that of those referring to corresponding clearances in Sec. 230-24(b), application of Sec. 225-18 is limited to "open conductors"— and Art. 225 gives no clue as to minimum clearances for triplex or quadruplex cables commonly used for outdoor overhead branch circuits and feeders. This does pose a serious problem in **Code** application, especially in relation to Art. 321, which recognizes both indoor and outdoor use of a variety of messenger supported assemblies (not "open conductors") for overhead branch circuits or feeders. Article 321 gives no clearances from ground for such circuits, but Sec. 321-2 does make such circuits subject to "applicable provisions of Article 225"—which, as noted, gives clearances only for "open conductors."

As Secs. 225-18 and 230-24(b) stand, "open conductors" for an overhead *branch circuit or feeder* require only a 10-ft clearance from ground for circuits up to 150 V to ground; *but* "open conductors" for a service drop up to 150 V must have a clearance of not less than 12 ft from ground.

The rules of this section agree with the clearances and conditions set forth in the NESC *(National Electrical Safety Code)* for open conductors outdoors. The distances given for clearance from ground must conform to maximum voltage at which certain heights are permitted.

225·19. Clearances from Buildings for Conductors of Not Over 600 Volts, Nominal. The basic minimum required clearance for outdoor conductors running above a roof is 8-ft vertical clearance from the roof surface.

The wording of this section is substantially different from that of the 1987 and previous editions of the **NEC** and completely changes the concept involved. The rule no longer differentiates between "conductors not fully insulated" and "fully insulated conductors"—as was done in the 1987 Sec. 225-19(a). The basic ideas behind the rules are as follows:

1. Any branch-circuit or feeder conductors—whether insulated, simply covered, or bare—must have a clearance of at least 8 ft vertically from a roof surface over which they pass. And that clearance must be maintained not less than 3 ft from the edge of the roof in all directions. (The use of fully insulated conductors with only a 3-ft vertical or diagonal clearance above a roof is *no longer* allowed.)

2. A roof that is subject to "pedestrian or vehicular traffic" must have conductor clearances "in accordance with the clearance requirements of Sec. 225-18." This is an extremely obscure rule that is impossible to apply with comprehension. It might be interpreted to require 10 or 15-ft clearance for a roof subject to pedestrian traffic and 18 ft for a roof subject to vehicular traffic. This rule is made difficult by the reference to Sec. 225-18 because that section applies only to "open conductors" and does not at all cover the several types of insulated (and sometimes jacketed) cable assemblies that are far more commonly used than "open conductors."

In parts **(b)** and **(c)**, overhead conductor clearance from signs, chimneys, antennas, and other nonbuilding or nonbridge structures must be at least 3 ft—vertically, horizontally, or diagonally. The minimum required clearance here was reduced from a 5-ft requirement in the 1987 **NEC**.

As indicated in Fig. 225-6, Exception No. 2 to Sec. 225-19(a) may apply to circuits that are operated at 300 V or less.

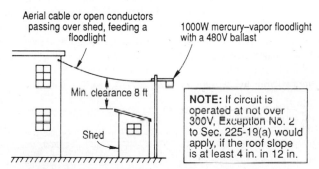

Fig. 225·6. Conductors—whether or not they are fully insulated for the circuit voltage—must have at least 8-ft vertical clearance above a roof over which they pass. (Sec. 225-19.)

225·22. Raceways on Exterior Surfaces of Buildings.   Condensation of moisture is very likely to take place in conduit or tubing located outdoors. The conduit or tubing should be considered suitably drained when it is installed so that any moisture condensing inside the raceway or entering from the outside cannot accumulate in the raceway or fittings. This requires that the raceway shall be installed without "pockets," that long runs shall not be truly horizontal but shall always be pitched, and that fittings at low points be provided with drainage openings.

In order to be raintight, all conduit fittings must be made up wrench-tight. Couplings and connectors used with electrical metallic tubing shall be of the raintight type. See Sec. 348-8.

225-24. Outdoor Lampholders. This section applies particularly to lampholders used in festoons. Where "pigtail" lampholders are used, the splices should be staggered (made a distance apart) in order to avoid the possibility of short circuits, in case the taping for any reason should become ineffective.

According to the UL Standard for Edison-Base Lampholders, "pin-type" terminals shall be employed only in lampholders for temporary lighting or decorations, signs, or specifically approved applications.

225-25. Location of Outdoor Lamps. In some types of outdoor lighting it would be difficult to keep all electrical equipment above the lamps, and hence a disconnecting means may be required. A disconnecting means should be provided for the equipment on each individual pole, tower, or other structure if the conditions are such that lamp replacements may be necessary while the lighting system is in use. It may be assumed that grounded metal conduit or tubing extending below the lamps would not constitute a condition requiring that a disconnecting means must be provided.

225-26. Live Vegetation. Coming to grips with a long-standing controversy, outdoor conductors and equipment may not be supported from or mounted on trees. Trees or any other "live vegetation" must not be used "for support of overhead conductor spans." Wording of this rule removed the words "or other electric equipment." The effect is to permit outdoor lighting fixtures to be mounted on trees and to be supplied by an approved wiring method—conductors in raceway or Type UF cable—attached to the surface of the tree. The **Code** Panel defeated several proposals to have a new exception added to this section to specifically recognize use of lighting fixtures and their supply wiring directly on trees (Fig. 225-7).

The one exception to this rule recognizes that temporary wiring may be run on trees in accordance with Article 305.

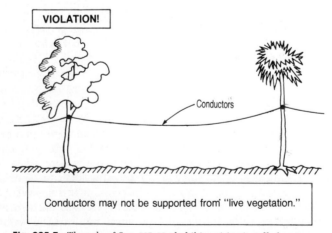

VIOLATION!

Conductors

Conductors may not be supported from "live vegetation."

Fig. 225-7. The rule of Sec. 225-26 phohibits wiring installed on trees.

ARTICLE 230. SERVICES

230·2. Number of Services. For any building, the service consists of the conductors and equipment used to deliver electric energy from the utility supply
lines to the interior distribution system. Service may be made to a building
either overhead or underground, from a utility pole line or from an underground transformer vault.

The first sentence of this rule requires that a building or structure be supplied
by "only one service." Because "service" is defined in Art. 100 as "The *conductors* and equipment for delivering energy from the electricity supply system
to the wiring system of the premises supplied," use of one "service" corresponds to use of one "service drop" or one "service lateral." Thus, the basic
rule of this section requires that a building or other structure be fed by only
one service drop (overhead service) or by only one set of service lateral conductors (underground service). As shown in Fig. 230-1, a building with only one

Fig. 230·1. One set of service-drop conductors supply building from utility line (coming
from upper left) and two sets of SE conductors are tapped through separate metering CTs.
(Sec. 230-2.)

service drop to it satisfies the basic rule even when more than one set of service-entrance conductors are tapped from the single drop (or from a single lateral circuit).

The seven Exceptions to that basic rule cover cases where two or more service drops or laterals may supply a single building or structure.

The second paragraph of this section introduces a requirement that applies
to any installation where more than one service is permitted by the **Code** to
supply one building. It requires a "permanent plaque or directory" to be
mounted or placed "at each service drop or lateral or at each service-equip-

ment location" to advise personnel that there are other services to the premises and to tell where such other services are and what building parts they supply.

Exceptions No. 1 and No. 2 permit a separate drop or lateral for supply to a fire pump and/or to emergency electrical systems, such as emergency lighting or exit lights.

Exception No. 2 to the basic rule that a building "shall be supplied by only one service" recognizes use of an additional power supply to a building from any "parallel power production systems." This would permit a building to be fed by a solar photovoltaic, wind, or other electric power source—in addition to a utility service—just as an emergency or standby power source is also permitted (Fig. 230-2).

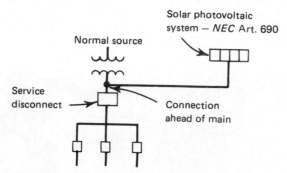

Fig. 230-2. Electric power generated by a solar voltaic assembly or by a wind-driven generator may be used as a source of power in "parallel" with the normal service. (Sec. 230-2.)

Exception No. 3 recognizes another situation in which more than one service (i.e., more than one service drop or lateral) may be used. By "special permission" of the inspection authority, more than one service may be used for a multitenant building when there is no single space that would make service equipment available to all tenants.

Two or more services to one building are permitted when the total demand load of all the feeders is more than 2,000 A, up to 600 V, where a single-phase service needs more than one drop, or by special permission (Fig. 230-3). Exception No. 4 relates capacity to permitted services. Where requirements exceed 2,000 A, two or more sets of service conductors may be installed. Below this value, special permission is required to install more than one set. The term "capacity requirements" appears to apply to the total calculated load for sizing service-entrance conductors and service equipment for a given installation.

Cases of separate light and power services to a single building and separate services to water heaters for purposes of different rate schedules are also exceptions to the general rule of single service. And if a single building is so large that one service cannot handle the load, special permission can be given for additional services.

Exception No. 5 requires special permission to install more than one service to buildings of large area. Examples of large-area buildings are high-rise build-

Ex. No. 4

**1. . . .when the total de-
mand load of all feeders
is greater than 2000 amps
(up to 600 volts), or**

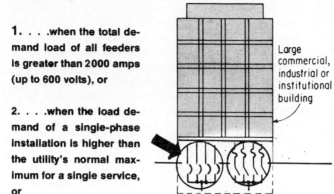

Large
commercial,
industrial or
institutional
building

**2. . . .when the load de-
mand of a single-phase
installation is higher than
the utility's normal max-
imum for a single service,
or**

**3. . . .when special permission is obtained from the inspection
authority.**

NOTE: "Two or more services" means two or more service drops
or service laterals—not sets of service-entrance conductors
tapped from one drop or lateral.

Ex. No. 6

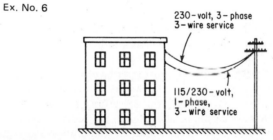

230-volt, 3-phase
3-wire service

115/230-volt,
1-phase,
3-wire service

Fig. 230-3. Exceptions to Sec. 230-2 permit two or more services under
certain conditions. (Sec. 230-2.)

ings, shopping centers, and major industrial plants. In granting special permission the authority having jurisdiction must examine the availability of utility
supplies for a given building, load concentrations within the building, and the
ability of the utility to supply more than one service. Any of the special-per-
mission clauses in the Exceptions in Sec. 230-2 require close cooperation and
consultation between the authority having jurisdiction and the serving utility.

Exception No. 6 is illustrated at the bottom of Fig. 230-3.

Exception No. 7 to the basic rule requiring that any "building or other structure" be supplied by "only one service" adds an important qualification of that
rule as it applies only to Sec. 230-40, Exception No. 2, covering service-entrance

layouts where two to six service disconnects are to be fed from one drop or lateral and are installed in separate individual enclosures at one location, with each disconnect supplying a separate load. As described in Sec. 230-40, Exception No. 2, such a service equipment layout may have a separate set of service-entrance conductors run to "*each or several*" of the two to six enclosures. Exception No. 7 notes that where a separate set of underground conductors of size 1/0 or larger is run to each or several of the two to six service disconnects, the several sets of underground conductors are considered to be one service (that is, one service lateral) even though they are run as separate circuits, that is, connected together at their supply end (at the transformer on the pole or in the pad-mount enclosure or vault) *but not* connected together at their load ends. The several sets of conductors are taken to be "one service" in the meaning of Sec. 230-2, although they actually function as separate circuits (Fig. 230-4).

Although Sec. 230-40, Exception No. 2, applies to "service-entrance conductors" and service equipment layouts fed by *either* a "service drop" (overhead service) or a "service lateral" (underground service), Exception No. 7 is addressed specifically and only to service "lateral" conductors (as indicated by the word "underground") because of the need for clarification based on the **Code** definitions of "service drop," "service lateral," "service-entrance conductors, overhead system," and "service-entrance conductors, underground system." (Refer to these definitions in the **Code** book to clearly understand the intent of Exception No. 7 and its relation to Sec. 230-40, Exception No. 2.)

The matter involves these separate but related considerations:

1. Because a "service lateral" may (and usually does) run directly from a transformer on a pole or in a pad-mount enclosure to gutter taps where short tap conductors feed the terminals of the service disconnects, most layouts of that type literally do not have any "service-entrance conductors" that would be subject to the application permitted by Sec. 230-40, Exception No. 2—other than the short lengths of tap conductors in the gutter or box where splices are made to the lateral conductors.

2. Because Sec. 230-40, Exception No. 2, refers only to sets of "service-entrance conductors" as being acceptable for individual supply circuits tapped from *one* drop or lateral to feed the separate service disconnects, that rule clearly does not apply to "service lateral" conductors which by definition are not "service-entrance conductors." So there is no permission in Sec. 230-40, Exception No 2, to split up "service lateral" capacity. And the basic rule of Sec. 230-2 has the clear, direct requirement that a building or structure be supplied through only *one* lateral for any underground service. That is, either a service lateral must be a single circuit of one set of conductors, or if circuit capacity requires multiple conductors per phase leg, the lateral must be made up of sets of conductors in parallel—connected together at *both* the supply and load ends—in order to constitute a single circuit (that is, one lateral).

3. Exception No. 7 permits "laterals" to be subdivided into separate, non-parallel sets of conductors in the way that Sec. 230-40, Exception No. 2, permits such use for "service-entrance conductors"—*but only* for conduc-

The 1975 *NE Code* **had this limitation on service laterals** (and this is still acceptable)—

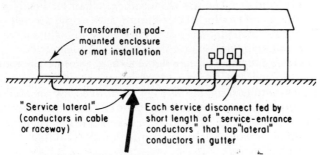

"Service lateral" conductors are not "service entrance" conductors and were, therefore, not applicable to the subdivision permission of Section 230-40, Exception No. 2. The requirement of Section 230-2 for one set of service lateral conductors demanded one circuit of single-conductor or parallel-conductor makeup.

Now, Exception No. 7 considers this type of hookup to be one set of service lateral conductors —

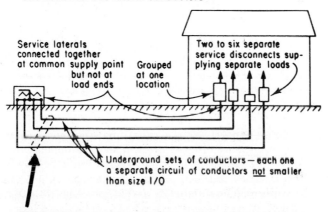

This is **one** service lateral, in the meaning of the basic rule of Section 230-2.

Fig. 230-4. "One" service lateral may be made up of several circuits. (Sec. 230-2.)

tors of 1/0 and larger and *only* where each separate set of lateral conductors (each separate lateral circuit) supplies *one* or *several* of the two to six service disconnects.

Exception No. 7 recognizes the importance of subdividing the total service capacity among a number of sets of smaller conductors rather than a single parallel circuit (that is, a number of sets of conductors connected together at *both* their *supply and load* ends). The single parallel circuit would have much lower impedance and would, therefore, require a higher short-circuit interrupting rating in the service equipment. The higher impedance of each separate set of lateral conductors (not connected together at their load ends) would limit short-circuit current and reduce short-circuit duty at the service equipment, permitting lower IC (interrupting capacity)-rated equipment and reducing the destructive capability of any faults at the service equipment.

230-3. One Building or Other Structure Not to Be Supplied Through Another.   The service conductors supplying each building or structure shall not *pass through the inside* of another building, unless they are in raceway encased by 2 in. of concrete or masonry (Fig. 230-5). Section 230-6 points out that conductors in a raceway enclosed within 2 in. of concrete or masonry are considered to be "outside" the building even when they are run within the building.

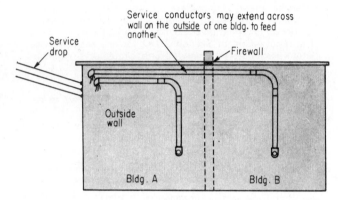

Fig. 230-5.   This is not a violation of the basic rule of Sec. 230-3. (Sec. 230-3.)

A building as defined in Art. 100 is a "structure which stands alone or which is cut off from adjoining structures by fire walls with all openings therein protected by approved fire doors." A building divided into four units by such fire walls may be supplied by four separate service drops, but a similar building without the fire walls may be supplied by only one service drop, except as permitted in Sec. 230-2.

A commercial building may be a single building but may be occupied by two or more tenants whose quarters are separate, in which case it might be undesirable to supply the building through one service drop. Under these conditions special permission may be given to install more than one service drop.

230-6. Conductors Considered Outside of Building.   Conductors in conduit or duct enclosed by concrete or brick not less than 2 in. thick are considered to be outside the building, even though they are actually run within the building. Figure 230-6 shows how a service conduit was encased within a building so that the conductors are considered as entering the building right at the service protection and disconnect where the conductors emerge from the concrete, to satisfy the rule of Sec. 230-70(a), which requires the service disconnect to be as close as possible to the point where the SE conductors enter the building. Fig-

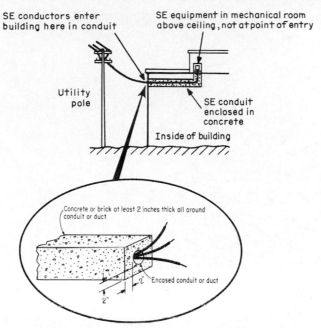

SE conductors enter
building here in conduit

SE equipment in mechanical room
above ceiling, not at point of entry

Utility
pole

SE conduit
enclosed in
concrete

Inside of building

Concrete or brick at least 2 inches thick all around
conduit or duct

2" Encased conduit or duct

2"

Encasement of service raceway can serve to satisfy Sec. 230-70(a).

Fig. 230-6. "Service raceways" in concrete are considered "outside"
a building. [Sec. 230-6].

ure 230-7 shows an actual case of this application, where forms were hung
around the service conduit and then filled with concrete to form the required
case.

230-7. Other Conductors in Raceway or Cable. Although the basic rule permits only service-entrance conductors to be used in a service raceway or service cable exceptions do recognize the use of grounding conductors in service
raceway or cable and also permit conductors for a time switch if overcurrent
protection is provided for the conductors, as shown in Fig. 230-8.

230-8. Raceway Seal. Figure 230-9 indicates that Sec. 300-5(g) may apply to
underground service conduits. Where service raceways are required to be
sealed—as where they enter a building from underground—the sealing compound used must be marked on its container or elsewhere as suitable for safe
and effective use with the particular cable insulation, with the type of shielding
used, and with any other components it contacts. Some sealants attack certain
insulations, semiconducting shielding layers, etc.

230-9. Clearance from Building Openings. Any service drop conductors—open
wiring or multiplex drop cable—must have the 3-ft clearance from windows,
doors, porches, etc., to prevent mechanical damage to and accidental contact
with service conductors (Figs. 230-10 and 230-11). The clearances required in
Secs. 230-24, 230-26, and 230-29 are based on safety-to-life considerations in
that wires are required to be kept a reasonable distance from people who stand,

Fig. 230·7. Top photo shows service conduit carried above suspended ceiling, without the SE disconnect located at the point of entry. When conduit was concrete-encased, the service conductors then "enter" the building at the SE disconnect—where they emerge from the concrete. Service conduit enters building at lower left and turns up into SE disconnect (right) in roof electrical room.

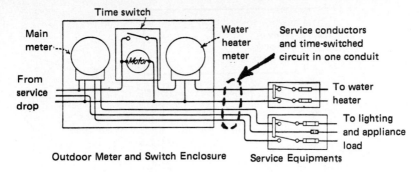

Outdoor Meter and Switch Enclosure   Service Equipments

NOTE: Time-switch conductors may be hooked up so they are in same conduit
as service conductors but the time-switch conductors must be supplied with
over current protection.

Fig. 230-8. A time switch with its control circuit connected on the supply side of the service equipment. (Sec. 230-7.)

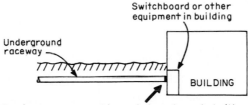

Service raceways must be sealed or plugged at either or both
ends if moisture could contact live parts

Fig. 230-9. Service raceways may have to be sealed. (Sec. 230-8.)

reach, walk, or drive under service-drop conductors. As the Exception notes, conductors run above the top level of a window do not have to be 3 ft away from the window.

The third paragraph of this section says that service-drop or service-entrance conductors must not be mounted on or secured to a building wall directly beneath an elevated opening through which supplies or materials are moved into and out of the building. Such installations of conductors—say, beneath a high door to a barn loft—would obstruct access to the opening and present a hazard to personnel (Fig. 230-12).

230-22. Insulation or Covering. The use of "covered"—not "insulated"—wire, such as TBWP (triple-braid weatherproof wire), has resulted in 14 accidents. Because of nine electrocutions and four hospitalizations, the use of *only* insulated wire for ungrounded conductors is required by this rule.

The only overhead service conductor that is permitted to be bare is a grounded conductor of a multiconductor cable. The grounded neutral of open wiring must be insulated to the same voltage level as the ungrounded conductors.

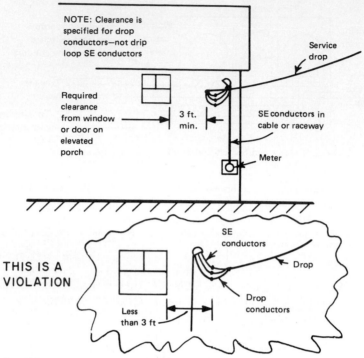

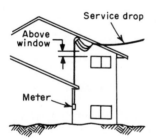

Fig. 230-10. Drop conductors must have clearance from building openings. (Sec. 230-9.)

Fig. 230-11. Drop conductors above top level of a window or door do not require 3-ft horizontal clearance. (Sec. 230-9, Exception.)

230-24. Clearances.   There are three exceptions to the basic rule of part **(a)** that service-drop conductors must have at least an 8-ft vertical clearance from the highest point of roofs over which they pass.

Exception No. 1 to the basic rule calling for 8-ft clearance of service-drop conductors above a roof requires that clearance above a flat roof subject to pedestrian traffic or used for auto and/or truck traffic must observe the heights for clearance of drop conductors from the ground as given in part **(b)** of Sec. 230-24.

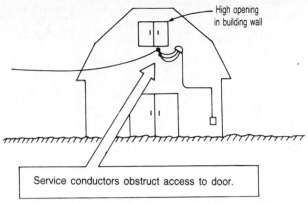

Fig. 230-12. This violates the rule of the last paragraph of Sec. 230-9.

The intent of Exception No. 2 is that where the roof has a slope greater than 4 in. in 12 in., it is considered difficult to walk upon, and the height of conductors could then be less than 8 ft from the highest point over which they pass but in no case less than 3 ft except as permitted in Exception No. 3. Figure 230-13 shows the rule. Figure 230-14 shows the conditions permitted by Exception No. 3.

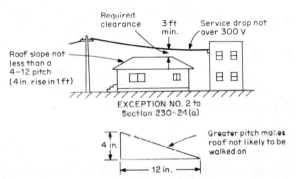

Fig. 230-13. Service-drop conductors may have less than 8-ft roof clearance. (Sec. 230-24.)

Part **(b)** covers service-drop clearance to ground, as shown in Fig. 230-15. The four dimensions of clearance from ground—10, 12, 15, and 18 ft—are qualified by voltage levels and, for the 10-ft mounting height, by the phrase "only for service-drop cables." These **NE Code** rules are in agreement with the *National Electrical Safety Code.* Where mast-type service risers are provided, the clearances in Sec. 230-24(b) will have to be considered by the installer.

230-28. Service Masts as Supports.   Figure 230-16 illustrates this rule.

230-30. Insulation.   The Exceptions to Secs. 230-30 and 230-41(a) clarify the use of aluminum, copper-clad aluminum, and bare copper conductors used as

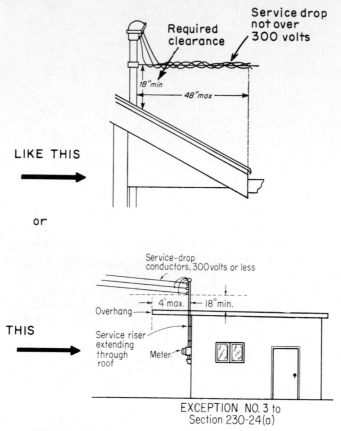

Service drop
not over
300 volts

Required
clearance

Service drop
not over
300 volts

18"min

48"max

LIKE THIS

or

Service-drop
conductors, 300 volts or less

4' max.   18" min.

Overhang

THIS

Service riser
extending
through   Meter
roof

EXCEPTION NO. 3 to
Section 230-24(a)

Fig. 230·14. Reduced clearance for service drop. (Sec. 230-24.)

grounded conductors in service laterals and service-entrance conductors (Fig. 230-17).

For service lateral conductors (underground service), an individual grounded conductor (such as a grounded neutral) of **aluminum** or **copper-clad aluminum** without insulation or covering may *not* be used in raceway underground. A bare **copper** neutral may be used—in raceway, in a cable assembly, or even directly buried in soil where local experience establishes that soil conditions do not attack copper.

The way this rule was worded in the 1975 **NE Code**, an individual *bare* aluminum neutral (along with individual insulated aluminum phase legs) of an underground service lateral appeared to be permitted if the circuit was installed in conduit or other raceway, and that interpretation was common. The wording of part **(d)** of the Exception permits an aluminum grounded conductor of an underground service lateral to be without individual insulation or covering "when part of a cable assembly identified for underground use" where the cable is directly buried or run in a raceway. Of course, a lateral made up

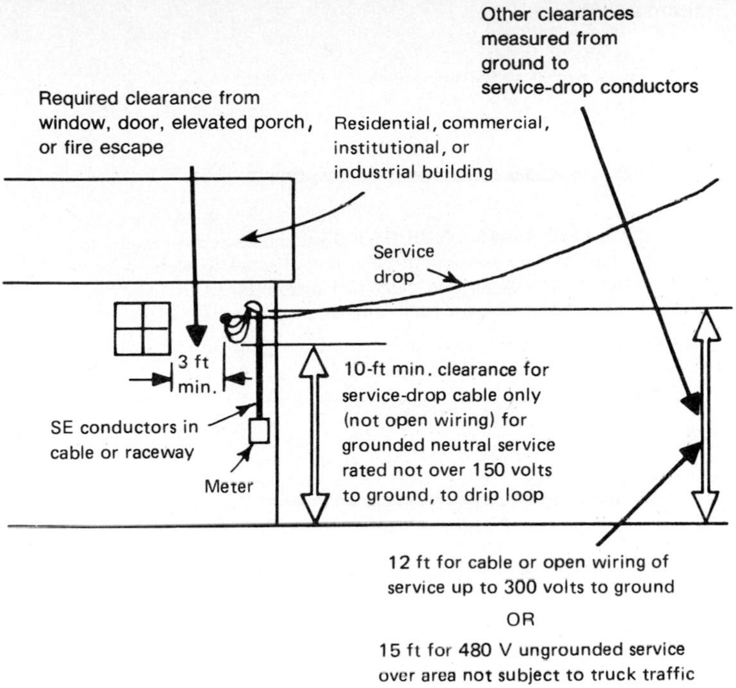

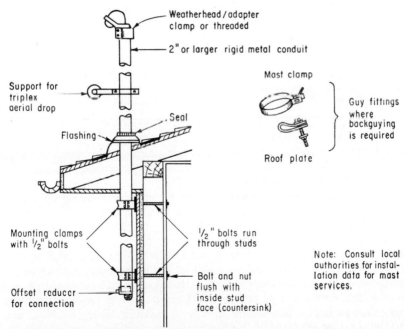

Required clearance from window, door, elevated porch, or fire escape

Other clearances measured from ground to service-drop conductors

Residential, commercial, institutional, or industrial building

Service drop

3 ft min.

SE conductors in cable or raceway

Meter

10-ft min. clearance for service-drop cable only (not open wiring) for grounded neutral service rated not over 150 volts to ground, to drip loop

12 ft for cable or open wiring of service up to 300 volts to ground

OR

15 ft for 480 V ungrounded service over area not subject to truck traffic

Fig. 230-15. Service-drop clearance to ground. (Sec. 230-24.)

Weatherhead / adapter clamp or threaded

2" or larger rigid metal conduit

Support for triplex aerial drop

Seal

Flashing

Mast clamp

Guy fittings where backguying is required

Roof plate

Mounting clamps with 1/2" bolts

1/2" bolts run through studs

Note: Consult local authorities for installation data for mast services.

Bolt and nut flush with inside stud face (countersink)

Offset reducer for connection

Fig. 230-16. Service mast must provide adequate support for connecting drop conductors. (Sec. 230-28.)

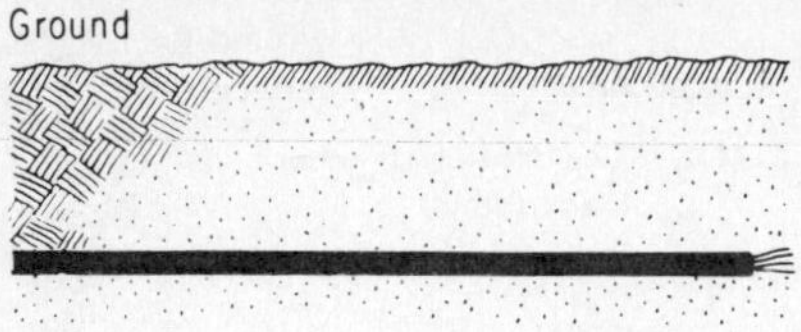

Ground

INSULATED PHASE CONDUCTORS and a bare copper neutral for an underground service lateral in buried raceway. Note: A bare aluminum or copper-clad aluminum neutral could be used here when part of a moisture- and fungus-resistant cable.

Ground

BARE COPPER NEUTRAL in a direct-buried cable assembly with moisture- and fungus-resistant outer covering. Note: A bare aluminum or copper-clad aluminum could be used like this, but it must be within the same type of cable assembly.

Ground

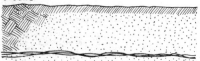

TYPE USE PHASE CONDUCTORS and a bare copper neutral directly buried where soil conditions are suitable for the bare copper.

Fig. 230-17. Sections 230-30 and 230-41 permit bare neutrals for service conductors. (Secs. 230-30 and 230-41.)

of individual insulated phase legs and an *insulated* neutral is acceptable in underground conduit or raceway (Fig. 230-18).

230-32 Protection Against Damage.   Underground service lateral conductors—whether directly buried cables, conductors in metal conduit, conductors in nonmetallic conduit, or conductors in EMT—must comply with Sec. 300-5 for protection against physical damage (Fig. 230-19).

230-40. Number of Service-Entrance Conductor Sets.   As a logical follow-up to the basic rule of Sec. 230-2, which requires that a single building or structure must be supplied "by only one service" (that is, only one service drop or lateral), this rule calls for only one set of SE conductors to be supplied by each service drop or lateral that is permitted for a building. Exception No. 1 covers a multiple-occupancy building (a two-family or multifamily building, a multi-tenant office building, or a store building, etc.). In such cases, a set of SE con-

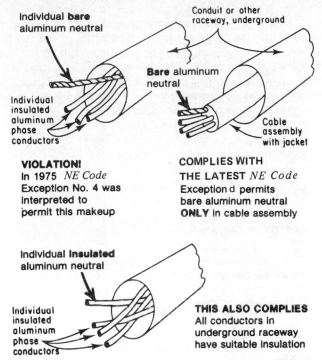

Fig. 230-18. Underground bare aluminum grounded leg must always be in a cable assembly. (Sec. 230-30.)

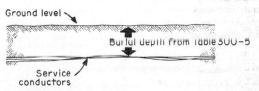

Fig. 230-19. Protecting underground service conductors. (Sec. 230-32.)

ductors for each occupancy or for groups of occupancies is permitted to be tapped from a single drop or lateral (Fig. 230-20).

When a multiple-occupancy building has a separate set of SE conductors run to each occupancy, in order to comply with Sec. 230-70(a), the conductors should either be run on the outside of the building to each occupancy or, if run inside the building, be encased in 2 in. of concrete or masonry in accordance with Sec. 230-6. In either case the service equipment should be located "nearest to the entrance of the conductors inside the building," and each occupant would have "access to his disconnecting means."

Any desired number of sets of service-entrance conductors may be tapped from the service drop or lateral, or two or more subsets of service-entrance

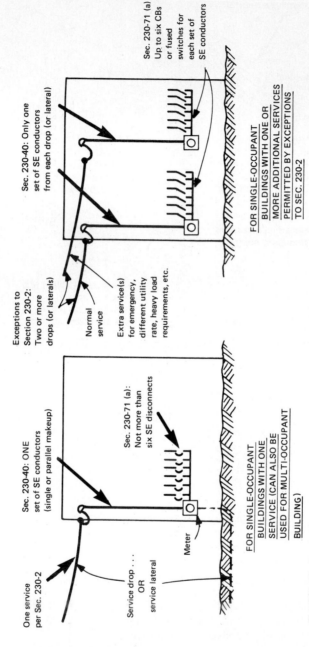

Sec. 230-71 (a)
Up to six CBs
or fused
switches for
each set of
SE conductors

Sec. 230-40: Only one
set of SE conductors
from each drop (or lateral)

Exceptions to
Section 230-2:
Two or more
drops (or laterals)

Normal
service

Extra service(s)
for emergency,
different utility
rate, heavy load
requirements, etc.

FOR SINGLE-OCCUPANT
BUILDINGS WITH ONE OR
MORE ADDITIONAL SERVICES
PERMITTED BY EXCEPTIONS
TO SEC. 230-2

Sec. 230-40: ONE
set of SE conductors
(single or parallel makeup)

Sec. 230-71 (a):
Not more than
six SE disconnects

Meter

One service
per Sec. 230-2

Service drop . . . .
OR
service lateral

FOR SINGLE-OCCUPANT
BUILDINGS WITH ONE
SERVICE (CAN ALSO BE
USED FOR MULTI-OCCUPANT
BUILDING)

Fig. 230-20. Service layouts must simultaneously satify Secs. 230-2, 230-40, 230-71, and all other NEC rules that are applicable. (Sec. 230-40.)

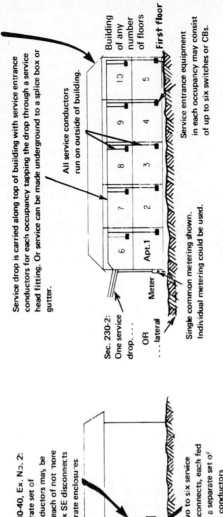

Sec. 230-40, Ex. No. 1: Separate sets of SE conductors tapped from one drop (or lateral) to feed each of any number of occupancy units

Service drop is carried along top of building with service entrance conductors for each occupancy tapping the drop through a service head fitting. Or service can be made underground to a splice box or gutter.

All service conductors run on outside of building.

Building of any number of floors

First floor

Service entrance equipment in each occupancy may consist of up to six switches or CBs.

Sec. 230-2: One service drop.....

OR

...lateral

Meter

Single common metering shown. Individual metering could be used.

FOR MULTIPLE-OCCUPANCY BUILDING (SEPARATE TENANTS IN APARTMENTS, OFFICES, STORES, ETC.)

Sec. 230-40, Ex. No. 2: A separate set of SE conductors may be run to each of not more than six SE disconnects in separate enclosures

Sec. 230-2: One service

Utility pole

Metering from point of drop connection

Meter

Two to six service disconnects, each fed by a separate set of SE conductors

FOR SINGLE OCCUPANCY BUILDINGS SUCH AS FACTORIES, SCHOOLS AND STORES OR FOR MULTIPLE-OCCUPANCY BUILDINGS

Fig. 230-20. (Continued)

conductors may be tapped from a single set of main service conductors, as shown for the multiple-occupancy building in Fig. 230-20.

Exception No. 2 permits two to six disconnecting means to be supplied from a single service drop or lateral where each disconnect supplies a separate load (Fig. 230-21). Exception No 2, recognizes the use of, say, six 400-A sets of service-entrance conductors to a single-occupancy or multiple-occupancy building in lieu of a single main 2,500-A service. It recognizes the use of up to six subdivided loads extending from a single drop or lateral in a *single-occupancy* as well as multiple-occupancy building. Where single metering is required, doughnut-type CTs could be installed at the service drop.

The real importance of this rule is to eliminate the need for "paralleling" conductors of large-capacity services, as widely required by inspection authorities to satisfy previous editions of the NEC (Fig. 230-21). This same approach could be used in subdividing services into smaller load blocks to avoid the use of the equipment ground-fault circuit protection required by Sec. 230-95.

This rule can also facilitate expansion of an existing service. Where less than six sets of service-entrance conductors were used initially, one or more additional sets can be installed subsequently without completely replacing the original service. Of course, metering considerations will affect the layout.

But, the two to six disconnects (circuit breakers or fused switches) must be installed close together at one location and not spread out in a building.

230-41. Insulation of Service-Entrance Conductors.   Except for use of a bare neutral, as permitted, all service-entrance conductors must be insulated and may not simply be "covered"—as discussed under Sec. 230-22. The same wording is used in part **(d)** of the Exception in Sec. 230-41 as described above for Sec. 230-30. In this section, the reference is to "service-entrance conductors" instead of "service lateral conductors." But, again, a **bare individual** aluminum or copper-clad aluminum grounded conductor (grounded neutral or grounded phase leg) may **not** be used in raceway or for direct burial.

Aluminum SE cable with a bare neutral may be used aboveground as SE conductors. *But,* an aluminum SE cable with a bare neutral may be used underground *only* if it is "identified" for underground use in a raceway or directly buried. Conventional-style SE-U aluminum SE cable with a bare neutral is not "identified" for use underground but may be used, as the first sentence of Sec. 230-40 describes, as "service-entrance conductors entering or on the exterior of buildings or other structures." In "SE-U," the "U" stands for "unarmored" not "underground."

230-42. Size and Rating.   Sizing of service-entrance conductors involves the same type of step-by-step procedure as set forth for sizing feeders covered in Art. 220. A set of service-entrance conductors is sized just as if it were a feeder. In general, the service-entrance conductors must have a minimum ampacity—current-carrying capacity—selected in accordance with the ampacity tables and rules of Sec. 310-15, sufficient to handle the total lighting and power load as calculated in accordance with Article 220. Where the **Code** gives demand factors to use or allows the use of acceptable demand factors based on sound engineering determination of less than 100 percent demand requirement, the lighting and power loads may be modified.

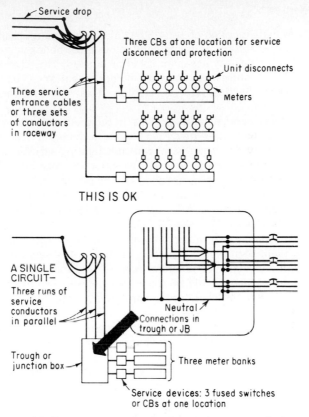

Service drop

Three CBs at one location for service
disconnect and protection

Unit disconnects

Three service
entrance cables
or three sets
of conductors
in raceway

Meters

THIS IS OK

A SINGLE
CIRCUIT—
Three runs of
service
conductors
in parallel

Neutral
Connections in
trough or JB

Trough or
junction box

Three meter banks

Service devices: 3 fused switches
or CBs at one location

THIS WAS COMMONLY REQUIRED TO SATISFY PREVIOUS
NE CODE BUT IS NOT NOW NECESSARY

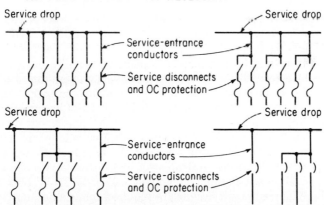

Service drop

Service-entrance
conductors

Service disconnects
and OC protection

Service drop

Service drop

Service-entrance
conductors

Service-disconnects
and OC protection

Service drop

From two to six separate sets of service-entrance conductors
may be supplied by a single service drop for either single- or multiple-occupancy buildings. Disconnects can be of same or different ratings, and each set of service-entrance conductors can be
installed using any approved wiring method.

Fig. 230-21. Tapping sets of service-entrance conductors from one drop
(or lateral). (Sec. 230-40.)

229

According to the Exception of Sec. 230-42(a), the maximum usable ampacity of busways used as service entrance conductors must be taken to be the amp value for which the busway has been listed or labeled. This is an exception to the basic rule that requires the ampacity of service-entrance conductors to be "determined from Section 310-15"—which does not give ampacities of busways.

From the analysis and calculations given in the feeder circuit section, a total power and lighting load can be developed to use in sizing service-entrance conductors. Of course, where separate power and lighting services are used, the sizing procedure should be divided into two separate procedures.

When a total load has been established for the service-entrance conductors, the required current-carrying capacity is easily determined by dividing the total load in kilovoltamperes (or kilowatts with proper correction for power factor or the load) by the voltage of the service.

From the required current rating of conductors, the required size of conductors is determined. Sizing of the service neutral is the same as for feeders. Although suitably insulated conductors must be used for the phase conductors of service-entrance feeders, the **NE Code** does permit use of bare grounded conductors (such as neutrals) under the conditions covered in Secs. 230-30 and 230-41.

An extremely important element of service design is that of fault consideration. Service busway and other service conductor arrangements must be sized and designed to assure safe application with the service disconnect and protection. That is, service conductors must be capable of withstanding the let-through thermal and magnetic stresses on a fault.

After calculating the required circuits for all the loads in the electrical system, the next step is to determine the minimum required size of service-entrance conductors to supply the entire connected load. The **NE Code** procedure for sizing SE conductors is the same as for sizing feeder conductors for the entire load—as set forth in Sec. 220-10. Basically, the service "feeder" capacity must be not less than the sum of the loads on the branch circuits for the different applications.

The *general lighting load* is subject to demand factors from Table 220-11, which takes into account the fact that simultaneous operation of all branch-circuit loads, or even a large part of them, is highly unlikely. Thus, feeder capacity does not have to equal the connected load. The other provisions of Art. 220 are then factored in.

Part **(b)** of Sec. 230-42 makes a 100-A service conductor ampacity a mandatory minimum if the system supplied is a one-family dwelling with more than five 2-wire branch circuits (or the equivalent of that for multiwire circuits) or if a one-family dwelling has an initial computed load of 10,000 W. Now that three 20-A small appliance branch circuits are required in a single-family dwelling, the average new home will need a 100-A, 3-wire service, because even without *electric* cooking, heating, drying, or water heating appliances, more than five 2-wire branch circuits will be installed.

230·43. Wiring Methods for 600 Volts, Nominal, or Less.   The list of acceptable wiring methods for running service-entrance conductors does include flexible metal conduit (Greenfield) and liquidtight flexible *nonmetallic* conduit, which, although not subject to a maximum length of 6 ft and not stated as requiring an equipment grounding conductor run with it, should be used with those limitations. Although such raceways were prohibited under previous **NEC** editions, effectively bonded flexible metal conduit in a length not over 6 ft may be used as a raceway for service-entrance conductors (Fig. 230-22). A length of flex not

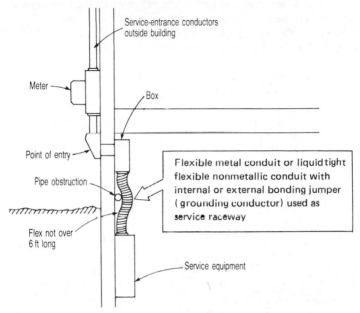

Fig. 230-22. These two flexible conduits may be used for service raceway. [See. 230-43.]

longer than 6 ft may be used as a service raceway provided an equipment grounding conductor sized from Table 250-94 (and with a cross-section area at least 12½ percent of the csa of the largest service phase conductor for conductors larger than 1100 MCM copper or 1,750 MCM aluminum) is used. This rule recognizes that the flexibility of such raceway is often needed or desirable in routing service-entrance conductors around obstructions in the path of connections between metering equipment and service-entrance switchboards, panelboards, or similar enclosures. The required equipment grounding conductor may be installed either inside or outside the flex, using acceptable fittings and termination techniques for the grounding conductor.

It should be noted that *liquidtight* flexible metal conduit is not listed as an acceptable service raceway. But, liquidtight flexible *nonmetallic* conduit may be used as service raceway containing service-entrance conductors. Use of liquidtight flexible nonmetallic conduit for service raceway must satisfy all of the rules of Sec. 351-22 to Sec. 351-27. Such flex may not be used in lengths over 6 ft long and an equipment grounding conductor will normally be required.

230·46. Unspliced Conductors.   For Exception No. 3, an underground service conduit usually terminates at the inside of the building wall unless the building has no basement. A metal conduit or a service cable may terminate at this point or may be run directly to the service equipment. From the terminal box, the conductors are run to the service equipment in rigid metal conduit or electrical metallic tubing or in an auxiliary gutter and may terminate at any suitable point behind the switchboard.

Figure 230-23 shows the conditions of Exception No. 3 and Exception No. 4. The sketch on the right shows a form of construction sometimes employed

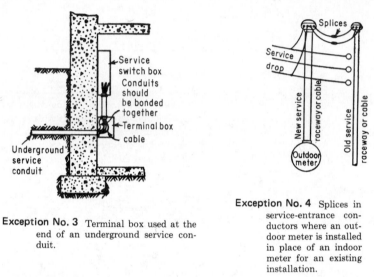

Exception No. 3 Terminal box used at the end of an underground service conduit.

Exception No. 4 Splices in service-entrance conductors where an outdoor meter is installed in place of an indoor meter for an existing installation.

Fig. 230·23. Permitted splices in service-entrance conductors. (Sec. 230-46.)

where the inside meter of an existing installation is removed and an outdoor meter is installed. New service-entrance conductors are connected to the service drop and are carried down to a meter fitting in raceway or cable. From the meter, the outside service conductors return in the raceway or cable and are spliced to the old service-entrance conductors. These splices are permitted by Exception No. 4.

Exception No. 5 recognizes that, where busway is used for service-entrance conductors, the sections must be connected together, and such connections are exempted from the rule that SE conductors must not be spliced.

230·50. Protection of Open Conductors and Cables Against Damage—Above-ground.   In part **(a)**, exposed service-entrance cable that is attached to a building "near sidewalks (and) walkways" must be protected against physical damage by sleeving with rigid metal conduit, IMC, rigid PVC conduit, EMT, or some similar protection—just as it would be if adjacent to a "driveway." This is an important protection rule that has a great number of applications (Fig. 230-24).

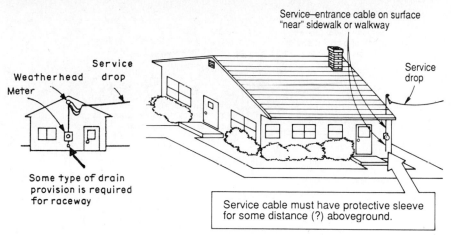

Fig. 230-24. Outdoor service raceway must be raintight *and* drained and SE cable must be protected. (Secs. 230-50 and 230-53.)

Part **(b)** Exception allows use of types MI and MC cables for service entrance or service lateral applications, without need for mounting at least 10 ft above grade—provided they are not exposed to damage or are protected.

230-51. Mounting Supports.   Service-entrance cable must be clamped to building surface by straps at intervals not over 30 in. The spacing of 30 in. replaces the old maximum interval of 4½ ft. Closer spacing of the cable clamps will make a more secure, neater installation. And the cable must still be clamped within 12 in. of the service weather head and within 12 in. of cable connection to a raceway or enclosure.

230-53. Raceways to Drain.   Service-entrance conductors in EMT or rigid conduit must be made raintight, using raintight raceway fittings, and must be equipped with a drain hole in the service ell at the bottom of the run or must be otherwise provided with a means of draining off condensation [Fig. 230-24].

230-54. Connections at Service Head.   When rigid metal conduit, IMC, or EMT is used for a service, the raceway must be provided with a service head (or weather head). Figure 230-25 shows details of service-head installation.

Part **(c)** of this section requires that service heads be located above the service-drop attachment. Although this arrangement alone will not always prevent water from entering service raceways and equipment, such an arrangement will solve most of the water-entrance problems. An exception to this rule permits a service head to be located not more than 24 in. from the service-drop termination where it is found that it is impractical for the service head to be located above the service-drop termination. In such cases a *mechanical connector* is required at the lowest point in the drip loop to prevent siphoning. This Exception will permit the **Code**-enforcing authority to handle hardship cases that may occur.

The intent of part **(g)** is to require use of connections or conductor arrangements, both at the pole and at the service, so that water will not enter connections and siphon under head pressure into service raceways or equipment.

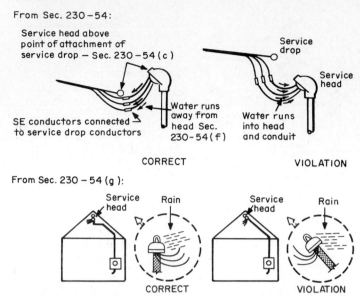

From Sec. 230–54:

Service head above point of attachment of service drop — Sec. 230–54 (c)

Service drop

Service head

SE conductors connected to service drop conductors

Water runs away from head Sec. 230-54(f)

Water runs into head and conduit

CORRECT

VIOLATION

From Sec. 230 – 54 (g):

Service head   Rain

Service head   Rain

CORRECT

VIOLATION

Fig. 230-25. Location of service head minimizes entrance of rain. (Sec. 230-54.)

Where no service head is used at the upper end of a service cable, the cable should be bent over so that the individual conductors leaving the cable will extend in a downward direction, and the end of the cable should be carefully taped and painted to exclude moisture.

230.56. Service-Entrance Conductor with the Higher Voltage-to-Ground. This Code rule repeats the requirement of Sec. 215-8 that the "high" leg (the 208-V-to-ground leg) of a 240/120-V 3-phase, 4-wire delta system must be identified by marking to distinguish it from the other hot legs, which are only 120 V to ground. See Sec. 215-8.

230-70. General. Part (a) covers the place of installation of a service disconnect. The disconnecting means required for every set of service-entrance conductors must be located at a readily accessible point nearest to the point at which the service conductors enter the building, on either the inside or the outside of the building (Fig. 230-26). The service disconnect switch (or circuit breaker) is generally placed on the inside of the building as near as possible to the point at which the conductors come in. And part (b) requires lettering or a sign on the disconnect(s) to identify it (them) as "Service Disconnect."

Although the Code does not set any maximum distance from the point of conductor entry to the service disconnect, various inspection agencies set maximum limits on this distance. For instance, service cable may not run within the building more than 18 in. from its point of entry to the point at which it enters the disconnect. Or service conductors in conduit must enter the disconnect within 10 ft of the point of entry. Or, as one agency requires, the disconnect must be within 10 ft of the point of entry, but overcurrent protection must be provided for the conductors right at the point at which they emerge from the

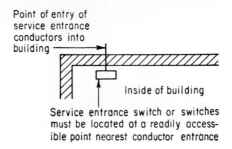

Point of entry of
service entrance
conductors into
building

Inside of building

Service entrance switch or switches
must be located at a readily accessible point nearest conductor entrance

GENERAL CONCEPT

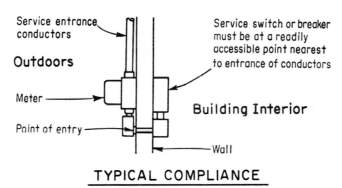

Service entrance
conductors

Outdoors

Service switch or breaker
must be at a readily
accessible point nearest
to entrance of conductors

Meter

Building Interior

Point of entry

Wall

TYPICAL COMPLIANCE

Fig. 230-26. Service disconnect must open current for any conductors within building. (Sec. 230-70.)

wall into the building. The concern is to minimize the very real and proven potential hazard of having unprotected service conductors within the building. Faults in such unprotected service conductors must burn themselves clear and such application has caused fires and fatalities.

Switches or circuit breakers used for service-entrance disconnecting means must be approved for use as service equipment. This rule is meant to require that the switch be listed and labeled by the UL as suitable for service entrance. Check manufacturers' catalogs on this.

230-71. Maximum Number of Disconnects.   Service-entrance conductors must be equipped with a readily accessible means of disconnecting the conductors from their source of supply. As stated in part **(a)**, the disconnect means for each set of SE conductors permitted by Sec. 230-2 and 230-40 may consist of not more than six switches or six circuit breakers, in a common enclosure or grouped individual enclosures, located either inside or outside the building wall as close as possible to the point at which the conductors enter the building. Figure 230-27 shows the basic application of that rule to a single set of SE conductors.

The Exception to part **(a)** says that when control power for a ground-fault protection system is tapped from the line side of the service disconnect means,

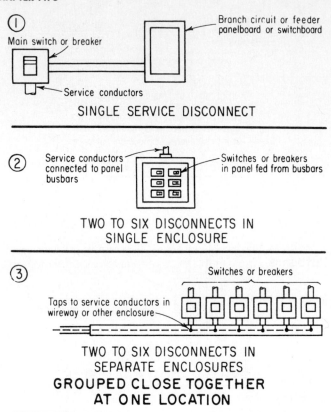

Main switch or breaker

Branch circuit or feeder
panelboard or switchboard

Service conductors

SINGLE SERVICE DISCONNECT

Service conductors
connected to panel
busbars

Switches or breakers
in panel fed from busbars

TWO TO SIX DISCONNECTS IN
SINGLE ENCLOSURE

Switches or breakers

Taps to service conductors in
wireway or other enclosure

TWO TO SIX DISCONNECTS IN
SEPARATE ENCLOSURES
GROUPED CLOSE TOGETHER
AT ONE LOCATION

Fig. 230-27. The three basic ways to provide service disconnect means.
(Sec. 230-71.)

the disconnect for the control power circuit is not counted as one of the six permitted disconnects for a service. A ground-fault-protected switch or circuit breaker supplying power to the building electrical system **counts** as one of the six permitted disconnects. But a disconnect supplying only the control-circuit power for a ground-fault protection system, installed as part of the listed equipment, does not count as one of the six service disconnects.

The rule of this section correlates "number of disconnects" with Secs. 230-2 and 230-40, which permit a separate set of SE conductors to be run to each occupancy (or group of occupancies) in a multiple-occupancy building, as follows:

Section 230-2 permits more than one "service" to a building—that is, more than one service drop or lateral—under the conditions set forth in the Exceptions. As set forth in the first sentence of Sec. 230-40 each such "service" must supply **only** one set of SE conductors in a building that is a single-occupancy (one-tenant) building, and each set of SE conductors may supply up to six SE disconnects grouped together at one location—in the same panel or switchboard or in grouped individual enclosures. If the grouped disconnects for one set of SE conductors are not at the same location as the grouped disconnects for one or more other sets of SE conductors, for those situations described and permitted in the Exceptions to Sec. 230-2, then a "plaque or directory" must be placed at each service-disconnect grouping to tell where the other group (or groups) of disconnects are located and what loads each group of disconnects serves.

Exception No. 1 to Sec. 230-40 says that a single service drop or lateral may supply *more than one set* of SE conductors for a multiple-occupancy building. Then at the load end of each of the sets of SE conductors, in an individual occupancy or adjacent to a group of occupancy units (apartments, office, stores), up to six SE disconnects may be supplied by each set of SE conductors.

The first sentence of part **(a)** to Sec. 230-71 ties directly into Sec. 230-40, Exception No. 1. It is the intent of this basic rule that, where a multiple-occupancy building is provided with more than one set of SE conductors tapped from a drop or lateral, each set of those SE conductors may have up to six switches or circuit breakers to serve as the service disconnect means for that set of SE conductors. The rule does recognize that six disconnects for each set of SE conductors at a multiple-occupancy building with, say, 10 sets of SE conductors tapped from a drop or lateral does result in a total of 6 × 10, or 60, disconnect devices for completely isolating the building's electrical system from the utility supply. Sec. 230-72(b) also recognizes use of up to six disconnects for each of the "separate" services for fire pumps, emergency lighting, etc., which are recognized in Sec. 230-2 as being separate services for specific purposes.

Although the basic rule of Sec. 230-40 specifies that only one set of SE conductors may be tapped from a single drop for a building with single occupancy, Exception No. 2 to Sec. 230-40 recognizes that a separate set of SE conductors may be run from a single service drop or lateral to each of up to six service disconnects mounted in separate enclosures at one location, constituting the disconnect means for a single service to a single-occupancy building.

For any type of occupancy, a power panel (not a lighting and appliance panel, as described in Sec. 384-14) containing up to six switches or circuit breakers may be used as service disconnect. A lighting and appliance panel used as service equipment for renovation of an existing service in an individual residential occupancy (but not for new installations) may have up to six main breakers or fused switches. However, a lighting and appliance panel used as service equipment for new buildings of any type must have not more than two main devices—with the sum of their ratings not greater than the panel bus rating. See Sec. 384-16(a).

The first sentence of Sec. 230-71(a) and that of Sec. 230-72(a) note that from one to six switches (or circuit breakers) may serve as the service disconnecting means for each class of service for a building. For example, if a *single-occupancy* building has a 3-phase service and a separate single-phase service, each such service may have up to six disconnects (Fig. 230-28). Where the two sets of service equipment are not located adjacent to each other, a plaque or directory must be installed at each service-equipment location indicating where the

AS PERMITTED BY EXCEPTIONS TO SEC. 230-2

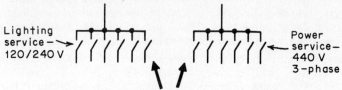

Lighting
service—
120/240 V

Power
service—
440 V
3-phase

Each class of service may consist of 1 to 6
fused switches or CBs in a common enclosure,
or a group of separate enclosures, grouped
together at a common location

Fig. 230·28. Each separate service may have up to six disconnect devices.
(Sec. 230-71.)

other service equipment is—as required by the second paragraph of Sec.
230-2.

Part **(b)** notes that single-pole switches or circuit breakers equipped with handle ties may be used in groups as single disconnects for multiwire circuits,
simultaneously providing overcurrent protection for the service (Fig. 230-29).

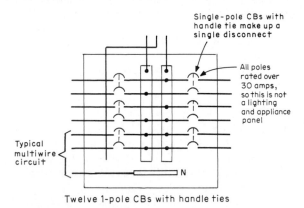

Single-pole CBs with
handle tie make up a
single disconnect

All poles
rated over
30 amps,
so this is not
a lighting
and appliance
panel

Typical
multiwire
circuit

N

Twelve 1-pole CBs with handle ties

Fig. 230·29. This arrangement constitutes six disconnects.
(Sec. 230-71.)

Multipole switches and circuit breakers may also be used as single disconnects.
The requirements of the **Code** are satisfied if all the service-entrance conductors can be disconnected with no more than six operations of the hand—regardless of whether each hand motion operates a single-pole unit, a multipole unit,
or a group of single-pole units with "handle ties" or a "master handle" controlled by a single hand motion. Of course, a single main device for service
disconnect and overcurrent protection—such as a main CB or fused switch—
gives better protection to the service conductors.

The footnote to this section refers to Sec. 384-16(a), which requires a higher degree of overcurrent protection for *lighting and appliance* branch-circuit panelboards. Each such panelboard must be individually protected on the supply side by not more than two main circuit breakers or two sets of fuses having a combined rating not greater than that of the panelboard. Exception No. 2 to Sec. 384-16(a) eliminates the need for individual protection for a lighting and appliance branch-circuit panelboard where such panelboards are used as service-entrance equipment for renovation of an existing installation (but *not* for new jobs) in an *individual residential occupancy*. Examples of these provisions are shown in illustrations in Sec. 384-16. It should be noted that these rules concern only a lighting and appliance branch-circuit panelboard, which is defined in Sec. 384-14 as a panelboard having more than 10 percent of its overcurrent devices rated 30 A or less, for which neutral connections are provided. Panelboards other than that type which are used as service equipment can still follow the basic six-switch rule.

230-72. Grouping of Disconnects. The basic rule of part **(a)** requires that for a service disconnect arrangement of more than one disconnect—such as where two to six disconnect switches or CBs are used, as permitted by Sec. 230-71(a)—all the disconnects making up the service equipment "for each service" must be grouped and not spread out at different locations. The basic idea is that anyone operating the two to six disconnects must be able to do it while standing at one location. Service conductors must be able to be readily disconnected from all loads at one place. And each of the individual disconnects must have lettering or a sign to tell what load it supplies (Fig. 230-30).

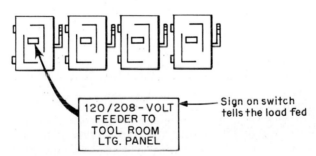

Fig. 230-30. Two to six disconnect switches or CBs must be grouped and *identified.* (Sec. 230-72.)

This rule makes clear that the two to six service disconnects that are permitted by Sec. 230-71(a) for *each* "service" or for "*each* set of SE conductors" at a multiple-occupancy building must be grouped. But, where permitted by the Exceptions to Sec. 230-2, the individual groups of two to six breakers or switches do not have to be together, and if they are not together, a sign at each location must tell where the other service disconnects are. (See Sec. 230-2.) Each grouping of two to six disconnects may be within a unit occupancy—such as an apartment—of the building.

The special or emergency-service equipments permitted by Sec. 230-2 do not have to be grouped with the regular service equipment. It should also be noted that Sec. 700-12(d) and (e) requires emergency services to be widely separated from the other services, to prevent failure of both due to a single fault.

The Exception to part **(a)** *permits* (*Note:* it permits, it does *not require*) one of the two to six service disconnects to be located remote from the other disconnecting means that are grouped in accordance with the basic rule—PROVIDED THAT *the remote disconnect is used only to supply a water pump that is also intended to provide fire protection.* In a residence or other building that gets its water supply from a well, a spring, or a lake, the use of a remote disconnect for the water pump will afford improved reliability of the water supply for fire suppression in the event that fire or other faults disable the normal service equipment. And it will distinguish the water-pump disconnect from the other normal service disconnects, minimizing the chance that firefighters will unknowingly open the pump circuit when they routinely open service disconnects during a fire. This Exception ties into the rule of Sec. 230-72(b), which *requires* (not simply permits) remote installation of a fire-pump disconnect switch that is permitted to be tapped ahead of the one to six switches or CBs that constitute the normal service disconnecting means (see Sec. 230-82, Exception No. 5). The Exception provides remote installation of a *normal service disconnect* when it is used for the same purpose (water pump used for fire fighting) as the *emergency service disconnect* (fire pump) covered in Sec. 230-72(b). In both cases, remote installation of the pump disconnect isolates the critically important pump circuit from interruption or shutdown due to fire, arcing-fault burndown, or any other fault that might knock out the main (normal) service disconnects.

A wide variety of layouts can be made to satisfy the **Code** *permission* for remote installation of a disconnect switch or CB service as a *normal* service disconnect (one of a maximum of six) supplying a water pump. Figure 230-31 shows three typical arrangements that would basically provide the isolated fire-pump disconnect.

Part **(b)**, as noted above, makes it mandatory to install emergency disconnect devices where they would not be disabled or affected by any fault or violent electrical failure in the normal service equipment (Fig. 230-32). Figure 230-33 shows a service disconnect for emergency and exit lighting installed very close to the normal service switchboard. An equipment burndown or fire near the main switchboard might knock out the emergency circuit. And the tap for the switch, which is made in the switchboard ahead of the service main, is particularly susceptible to being opened by *an arcing failure in the board.* The switch should be 10 or 15 ft away from the board. And because the switchboard is fed from an outdoor transformer-mat layout directly outside the building, the tap to the safety switch would have greater reliability if it was made from the transformer secondary terminals rather than from the switchboard service terminals. Although the rule sets no specific distance of separation, remote locating of emergency disconnects is a mandatory **Code** rule.

In part **(b)**, the phrase "permitted by Section 230-2" makes clear that each separate service permitted for fire pumps or for emergency service may be

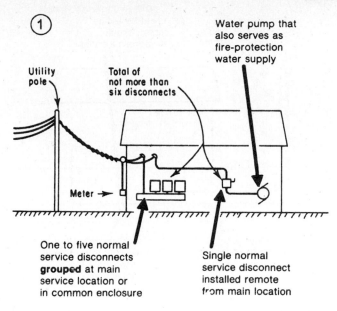

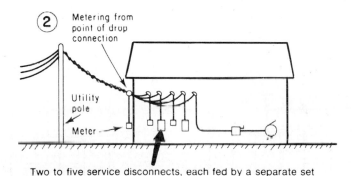

Fig. 230-31. Rule *permits* remote installation of one of two-to-six service disconnects to protect fire-pump circuits (typical layouts). (Sec. 230-72.)

equipped with up to six disconnects in the same way as the normal service—or any service—may have up to six SE disconnects. And the disconnect or disconnects for a fire-pump or emergency service must be remote from the normal service disconnects, as shown in Fig. 230-32.

Part **(c)** applies to applications of service disconnect for multiple-occupancy buildings—such as apartment houses, condominiums, town houses, office buildings, and shopping centers. Part **(c)** requires that the disconnect means for each occupant in a multiple-occupancy building be accessible to each occu-

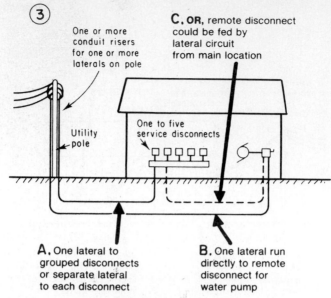

③

One or more
conduit risers
for one or more
laterals on pole

C. OR, remote disconnect
could be fed by
lateral circuit
from main location

Utility
pole

One to five
service disconnects

A. One lateral to
grouped disconnects
or separate lateral
to each disconnect

B. One lateral run
directly to remote
disconnect for
water pump

Fig. 230.31. (Continued)

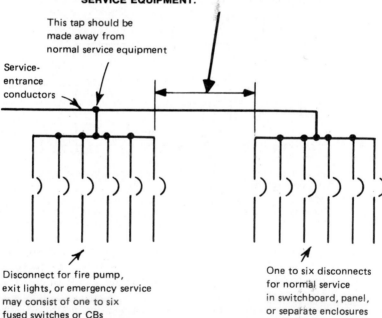

**THIS DISTANCE SHOULD ISOLATE EMERGENCY
DISCONNECT(S) FROM FAULTS IN NORMAL
SERVICE EQUIPMENT.**

This tap should be
made away from
normal service equipment

Service-
entrance
conductors

Disconnect for fire pump,
exit lights, or emergency service
may consist of one to six
fused switches or CBs

One to six disconnects
for normal service
in switchboard, panel,
or separate enclosures

Fig. 230-32. Emergency service disconnects must be isolated from faults in normal SE equipment. (Sec. 230-72.)

Fig. 230-33. Emergency disconnect close to service switchboard and fed by tap from it could readily be disabled by fault in board. (Sec. 230-72.)

pant. For instance, for the occupant of an apartment in an apartment house, the disconnect means for de-energizing the circuits in the apartment must be in the apartment (such as a panel), in an accessible place in the hall, or in a place in the basement or outdoors where it can be reached.

As covered by the Exception to part **(c)**, the access for each occupant as required by paragraph **(c)** would be modified where the building was under the management of a building superintendent or the equivalent and where electrical service and maintenance were furnished. In such a case, the disconnect means for more than one occupancy may be accessible only to authorized personnel.

Multiple-occupancy buildings having individual occupancy above the second floor were required by past **NEC** editions to have service equipment grouped in a common accessible place, with the disconnect means consisting of not more than six switches (or six CBs), as in Fig. 230-34. Although specific provisions requiring that application are no longer in the **NE Code**, it was required under previous **Code** editions. Exception No. 1 to Sec. 230-40 permits a separate set of SE conductors to be run to each tenant unit (e.g., apartment) in any multiple-occupancy building, with the service disconnect for each unit located within the unit—and no limitation is placed on the height or number of floors in the building.

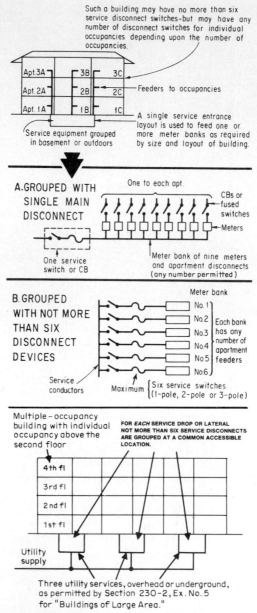

Such a building may have no more than six service disconnect switches-but may have any number of disconnect switches for individual occupancies depending upon the number of occupancies.

Feeders to occupancies

A single service entrance layout is used to feed one or more meter banks as required by size and layout of building.

Service equipment grouped in basement or outdoors

A. GROUPED WITH SINGLE MAIN DISCONNECT

One to each apt.

CBs or fused switches

Meters

One service switch or CB

Meter bank of nine meters and apartment disconnects (any number permitted)

B. GROUPED WITH NOT MORE THAN SIX DISCONNECT DEVICES

Meter bank

No.1
No.2
No.3
No.4
No.5
No.6

Each bank has any number of apartment feeders

Service conductors

Maximum { Six service switches (1-pole, 2-pole or 3-pole)

Multiple-occupancy building with individual occupancy above the second floor

FOR *EACH* SERVICE DROP OR LATERAL NOT MORE THAN SIX SERVICE DISCONNECTS ARE GROUPED AT A COMMON ACCESSIBLE LOCATION.

4th fl
3rd fl
2nd fl
1st fl

Utility supply

Three utility services, overhead or underground, as permitted by Section 230-2, Ex. No. 5 for "Buildings of Large Area."

Fig. 230·34. These rules on grouping of service disconnects are no longer in the **NEC** but represent good and acceptable practice that has been followed widely. (Sec. 230-72.)

230-75. Disconnection of Grounded Conductor.   In this section the other means for disconnecting the grounded conductor from the interior wiring may be a screw or bolted lug on the neutral terminal block. The grounded conductor must not be run straight through the service equipment enclosure with no means of disconnection.

230-76. Manually or Power Operable.   Any switch or CB used for service disconnect must be manually operable. In addition to manual operation, the switch may have provision for electrical operation—such as for remote control of the switch, provided it can be manually operated to the open or OFF position.

Code wording clearly indicates that an electrically operated breaker with a mechanical trip button which will open the breaker even if the supply power is dead is suitable for use as a service disconnect. The manually operated trip button assures that the breaker "can be opened by hand." To provide manual closing of electrically operated circuit breakers, manufacturers provide emergency manual handles as standard accessories. Thus such breaker mechanisms can be both closed and opened manually if operating power is not available.

Local requirements on the use of electrically operated service disconnects should be considered in selecting such devices.

230-78. Externally Operable.   If a switch can be opened and closed without exposing the operator to contact with live parts, it is an externally operable switch, even though access to the switch handle requires opening the door of a cabinet. The Exception pertains to electrically operated switches and circuit breakers, and it explains that such switches or CBs are required to be externally operable only to the *open* position, and not necessarily to the *closed* position (Fig. 230-35).

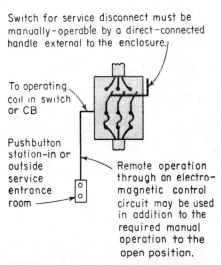

Switch for service disconnect must be manually-operable by a direct-connected handle external to the enclosure.

To operating coil in switch or CB

Pushbutton station-in or outside service entrance room

Remote operation through an electro-magnetic control circuit may be used in addition to the required manual operation to the open position.

Note: Some local codes require both manual and electrical means of operation.

Fig. 230-35. Manual operation of any service switch is required. (Sec. 230-78.)

230·79. Rating of Disconnect.   Aside from the limited conditions covered in parts **(a)** and **(b)**, this section requires that service equipment (in general) shall have a rating not less than 60 A, applicable to both fusible and CB equipment. Part **(c)** requires 100-A minimum rating of a single switch or CB used in the service disconnect for any "one-family dwelling" with an *initial* load of 10 kVA or more or where the *initial* installation contains more than *five 2-wire* branch circuits. It should be noted that the rule applies to one-family houses only, because of the definition of "one-family dwelling" as given in Art. 100. It does not apply to apartments or similar dwelling units that are in two-family or multifamily dwellings.

If the demand on a total connected load, as calculated from Sec. 220-10 through Sec. 220-21, is 10 kVA or more, a 100-A service disconnect, as well as 100-A rated service-entrance conductors [Sec. 230-42(b) (2)], must be used. Any one-family house with an electric range rated 8¾ kW must always have a 100-A rated disconnect (or service equipment) because such a range is a demand load of 8 kW and the two required 20-A kitchen appliance circuits come to a demand load of 3,000 W [Sec. 220-16(a)] at 100 percent from Table 220-11—and the 8 kW plus 3 kW exceeds the 10-kW (or 10 kVA) level at which a minimum 100-A rated service is required.

If a 100-A service is used, the demand load may be as high as 23 kVA. By using the optional service calculations of Table 220-30, a 23-kVA demand load is obtained from a connected load of 42.5 kVA. This shows the effect of diversity on large-capacity installations.

230·80. Combined Rating of Disconnects.   Figure 230-36 shows an application of this rule, based on determining what rating of a single disconnect would be required *if* a single disconnect were used instead of multiple ones. It should be

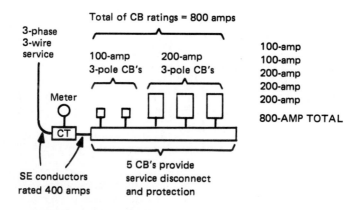

From Art. 220 (Secs. 220-10 through 220-21), calculation of demand load indicated that a single disconnect for this service must be rated at least 400 amps. The rating of multiple disconnects must total at least that value.

Fig. 230-36. Multiple disconnects must have their sum of ratings at least equal to the minimum rating of a single disconnect. (Sec. 230-80.)

noted that the sum of ratings above 400 A does comply with the rule of this section and with Exception No. 3 of Sec. 230-90(a) even though the 400-A service-entrance conductors could be heavily overloaded. Exception No. 3 exempts this type of layout from the need to protect the conductors at their rated ampacity, as required in the basic rule of Sec. 230-90. The **Code** assumes that the 400-A rating of the service-entrance conductors was carefully calculated from Art. 220 to be adequate for the maximum sum of the demand loads fed by the five disconnects shown in the layout.

230-82. Equipment Connected to the Supply Side of Service Disconnect. Cable limiters, fuses or CBs away from the building, high-impedance shunt circuits (such as potential coils of meters, etc.), supply conductors for time switches, surge-protective capacitors, instrument transformers, lightning arresters and circuits for emergency systems, fire-pump equipment, and fire and sprinkler alarms may be connected on the supply side of the disconnecting means. Emergency-lighting circuits, surge-protective capacitors, and fire alarm and other protective signaling circuits, when placed ahead of the regular service disconnecting means, must have separate disconnects and overcurrent protection.

Exception No. 1 to the rule prohibiting equipment connections on the line side of the service disconnect permits "cable limiters or other current-limiting devices" to be so connected.

Cable limiters are used to provide protection for individual conductors that are used in parallel (in multiple) to make up one phase leg of a high-capacity circuit, such as service conductors. A cable limiter is a cable connection device that contains a fusible element rated to protect the conductor to which it is connected.

Meters can be connected on the supply side of the service disconnecting means and overcurrent protective devices if the meters are connected to service not in excess of 600 V where the grounded conductor bonds the meter cases and enclosures to the grounding electrode.

As permitted by Exception No. 6, an electric power production source that is auxiliary or supplemental to the normal utility service to a premises may be connected to the supply (incoming) side of the normal service disconnecting means. This Exception to the basic rule that, "Equipment shall not be connected to the supply side of the service disconnecting means," permits connection of a solar photovoltaic system into the electrical supply for a building or other premises, to operate as a parallel power supply.

Exception No. 8 recognizes that control power for a ground-fault protection system may be tapped from the supply side of the service disconnect means. Where a control circuit for a ground-fault system is tapped ahead of the service main and "installed as part of listed equipment," suitable overcurrent protection and a disconnect must be provided for the control-power circuit.

230-83. Transfer Equipment. The rule on transfer switch disconnection from one source before connection to another source has an exception to apply to "parallel power production systems," as permitted by Exception No. 2 of Sec. 230-2. Exception No. 1 permits two or more sources to be connected in parallel through transfer switches. Either manual or automatic transfer means may be provided (Fig. 230-37).

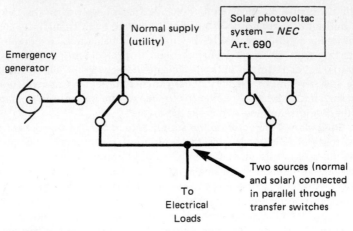

Fig. 230·37. This is an exception to the basic rule that two sources cannot be connected simultaneously to loads. (Sec. 230-83.)

230·84. More than One Building or Other Structure. For a group of buildings under single management, disconnect means must be provided for each building, as in Fig. 230-38. This rule requires that the conductors supplying each building in the group be provided with a means for disconnecting all ungrounded conductors from the supply. Because this is covered under Art.

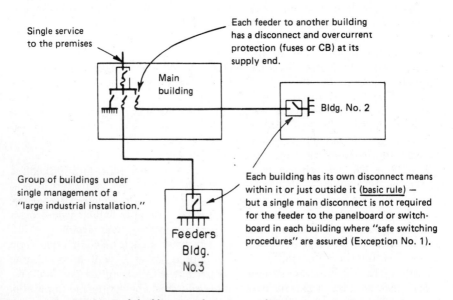

Fig. 230·38. Each building must have its own disconnect means. (Sec. 230-84.)

230, it is usually interpreted to permit the disconnect for each building or structure to be the same kind as permitted for a service disconnect—that is, up to six switches or CBs, as covered in Sec. 230-71.

For large-capacity, multibuilding industrial premises with a single owner, Exception No. 1 permits use of the feeder switch in the main building as the only disconnect for each feeder to an outlying building, provided the switches in the main building are accessible to the occupants of the outlying building.

Where a disconnect is to be used at each outbuilding, the effect of the second sentence of Sec. 230-84(a) (requiring location of the disconnect in accordance with Sec. 230-70) is to clearly require that the disconnect for any outbuilding be located within or just outside each building "nearest the point of entrance of the service-entrance conductors." However, many inspection and engineering authorities prefer a readily accessible feeder disconnect *within* each outlying building, regardless of the distance from the main building.

For any "integrated electrical system" as defined and regulated by Art. 685, Exception No. 2 suspends the basic rule calling for a feeder disconnect at each building.

Part **(b)** requires that the disconnect for each building of a multibuilding layout be recognized for service use—usually that means that the disconnect means for each building must be listed by UL, or another national test lab, as suitable for service equipment. The Exception waives that requirement for wiring device switches (snap switches) used for ON-OFF control of lighting or other loads under the conditions noted.

230-90. (Overload Protection) Where Required.   The intent in paragraph **(a)** is to assure that the overcurrent protection required in the service-entrance equipment protects the service-entrance conductors from "overload." It is obvious that these overcurrent devices cannot provide "fault" protection for the service-entrance conductors if the fault occurs in the service-entrance conductors, but can protect them from overload where so selected as to have proper rating. Conductors on the load side of the service equipment are considered as feeders or branch circuits and are required by the **Code** to be protected as described in Arts. 210, 215, and 240.

Each ungrounded service-entrance conductor must be protected by an overcurrent device in series with the conductor (Fig. 230-39). The overcurrent device must have a rating or setting not higher than the allowable current capacity of the conductor, with the Exceptions noted.

Exception No. 1.   If the service supplies one motor in addition to other load (such as lighting and heating), the overcurrent device may be rated or set in accordance with the required protection for a branch circuit supplying the one motor (Sec. 430-52) plus the other load, as shown in Fig. 230-40. Use of 175-A fuses where the calculation calls for 170-A conforms to Exception No. 2 of Sec. 230-90—next higher standard rating of fuse (Sec. 240-6). For motor branch circuits and feeders, Arts. 220 and 430 permit the use of overcurrent devices having ratings or settings higher than the capacities of the conductors. Article 230 makes similar provisions for services where the service supplies a motor load or a combination load of both motors and other loads.

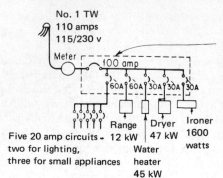

No. 1 TW
110 amps
115/230 v

Meter

100 amp

60A 60A 30A 30A 30A

Five 20 amp circuits –
two for lighting,
three for small appliances

Range
12 kW

Dryer
47 kW

Water
heater
45 kW

Ironer
1600
watts

Service equipment with one overall
100-amp main disconnect and fuse.
Current through service conductors
limited to 100 amperes. Without a
main disconnect and overcurrent
device, current is not limited and
current over 110 amps could flow.
Sum of protective devices is 210 amps
per hot leg.

NOTE: Service-entrance conductors must be selected with adequate
ampacity for the calculated service demand load, from Secs. 220-10
through 220-21.

Fig. 230·39. Single main service protection must not exceed conductor ampacity (or may
be next higher rated device above conductor ampacity). (Sec. 230-90.)

If the service supplies two or more motors as well as other load, then the
overcurrent protection must be rated in accordance with the required protection for a feeder supplying several motors plus the other load (Sec. 430-63). Or
if the service supplies only a multimotor load (with no other load fed), then Sec.
430-62 sets the maximum permitted rating of overcurrent protection.

Exception No. 3.   Not more than six CBs or six sets of fuses may serve as
overcurrent protection for the service-entrance conductors even though the
sum of the ratings of the overcurrent devices is in excess of the ampacity of
the service conductors supplying the devices—as illustrated in Fig. 230-41. The
grouping of single-pole CBs as multipole devices, as permitted for disconnect
means, may also apply to overcurrent protection. And a set of fuses is all the
fuses required to protect the ungrounded service-entrance conductors.

This Exception ties into Sec. 230-80. Service conductors are sized for the *total*
maximum demand load—applying permitted demand factors from Table 220-
11. Then each of the two to six feeders fed by the SE conductors is also sized
from Art. 220 based on the load fed by each feeder. When those feeders are
given overcurrent protection in accordance with their ampacities, it is frequently found that the sum of those overcurrent devices is greater than the
ampacity of the SE conductors which were sized by applying the applicable
demand factors to the total connected load of all the feeders. Exception No. 3
recognizes that possibility as acceptable even though it departs from the rule in
the first sentence of Sec. 230-90(a). The assumption is that if calculation of
demand load for the SE conductors is correctly made, there will be no overloading of those conductors because the diversity of feeder loads (some loads
"on," some "off") will be adequate to limit load on the SE conductors.

Assume that the load of a building computed in accordance with Art. 220 is
255 A. Under Sec. 240-3, Exception No. 4, 300-A fuses or a 300-A CB may be

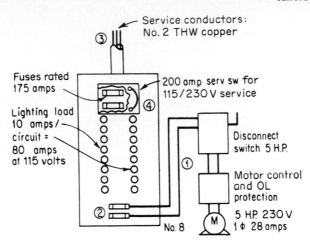

1. Size of motor branch circuit conductors: 125% x 28 amps equals 35 amps. This requires No. 8's.

2. Size of motor branch circuit fuses: 300% x 28 amps equals 84 amps. This requires maximum fuse size of 90 amps. Smaller fuses, such as time-delay type, may be used.

3. Size of service entrance conductors must be adequate for a load of 125% x 28 amps plus 80 amps (lighting load) or 115 amps.

4. Size of main fuses: 90 amps (from 2 above) plus 80 amps equals 170 amps. This requires maximum fuse size of 175 amps. Again, smaller fuses may and should be used where possible to improve the overload protection on the circuit conductors.

Fig. 230-40. Service protection for lighting plus motor load. (Sec. 230-90.)

considered as the proper-size overcurrent protection for service conductors rated between 255 and 300 A if a single service disconnect is used.

If the load is separated in such a manner that six 70-A CBs could be used instead of a single service disconnect means, total rating of the CBs would be greater than the ampacity of the service-entrance conductors. And that would be acceptable.

Exception No. 4 is shown in Fig. 230-42 and is intended to prevent opening of the fire-pump circuit on any overload up to and including stalling or even seizing of the pump motor. Because the conductors are "outside the building," operating overload is no hazard; and, under fire conditions, the pump must have no prohibition on its operation. It is better to lose the motor than attempt to protect it against overload when it is needed.

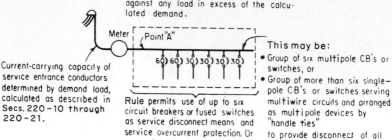

For a demand load of 125 amps, SE conductors could be No. 1 THW copper (130 amps).

In this case, service conductors could be overloaded (up to 240 amps, if CBs here are 2-pole). If main overcurrent protection, rated at 125 amps, were installed at point "A", service conductors would be protected against any load in excess of the calculated demand.

Current-carrying capacity of service entrance conductors determined by demand load, calculated as described in Secs. 220-10 through 220-21.

Rule permits use of up to six circuit breakers or fused switches as service disconnect means and service overcurrent protection. Or one unfused main switch at point "A" and six sets of fuses (for multiwire circuits) may also satisfy code requirements on disconnect and protection.

This may be:
- Group of six multipole CB's or switches, or
- Group of more than six single-pole CB's or switches serving multiwire circuits and arranged as multipole devices by "handle ties" to provide disconnect of all ungrounded conductors with no more than six operations of the hand.

Fig. 230·41. With six subdivisions of protection, conductors could be overloaded. (Sec. 230-90.)

If the service conductors to the fire-pump room enter the fire-pump service equipment directly from the outside or if they are encased in 2-in.-thick concrete . . .

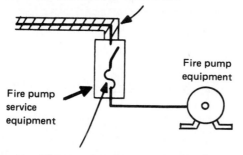

. . . they are judged to be "outside of the building," and . . .

Fire pump equipment

Fire pump service equipment

. . . the overcurrent protective device (fuses or CB) must be rated or set to carry the motor locked-rotor current indefinitely.

Fig. 230·42. (Sec. 230-90.)

230·95. Ground·Fault Protection of Equipment. Fuses and CBs, applied as described in the previous section on "Overcurrent Protection," are sized to protect conductors in accordance with their current-carrying capacities. The function of a fuse or CB is to open the circuit if current exceeds the rating of the protective device. This excessive current might be caused by operating overload, by a ground fault, or by a short circuit. Thus, a 1,000-A fuse will blow if current in excess of that value flows over the circuit. It will blow early on heavy overcurrent and later on low overcurrents. But it will blow, and the circuit and equipment will be protected against the damage of the overcurrent. But, there is another type of fault condition which is very common in grounded systems and will not be cleared by conventional overcurrent devices. That is the phase-to-ground fault (usually arcing) which has a current value less than the rating of the overcurrent device.

On any high-capacity feeder, a line-to-ground fault (i.e., a fault from a phase conductor to a conduit, to a junction box, or to some other metallic equipment enclosure) can, and frequently does, draw current of a value less than the rating or setting of the circuit protective device. For instance, a 500-A ground fault on a 2,000-A protective device which has only a 1,200-A load will not be cleared by the device. If such a fault is a "bolted" line-to-ground fault, a highly unlikely fault, there will be a certain amount of heat generated by the I^2R effect of the current; but this will usually not be dangerous, and such fault current will merely register as additional operating load, with wasted energy (wattage) in the system. But, bolted phase-to-ground faults are very rare. The usual phase-to-ground fault exists as an intermittent or arcing fault, and an arcing fault of the same current rating as the essentially harmless bolted fault can be fantastically destructive because of the intense heat of the arc.

Of course, any ground-fault current (bolted or arcing) above the rating or setting of the circuit protective device will normally be cleared by the device. In such cases, bolted-fault currents will be eliminated. But, even where the protective device eventually operates, in the case of a heavy ground-fault current which adds to the normal circuit load current to produce a total current in excess of the rating of the normal circuit protective device (fuse or CB), the time delay of the device may be minutes or even hours—more than enough time for the arcing-fault current to burn out conduit and enclosures, acting just like a torch, and even propagating flame to create a fire hazard.

In spite of the growth of effective and skilled application of conventional overcurrent protective devices, the problem of ground faults continues to persist and even grows with expanding electrical usage. In the interests of safety, definitive engineering design must account for protection against such faults. Phase overcurrent protective devices are normally limited in their effectiveness because (1) they must have a time delay and a setting somewhat higher than full load to ride through normal inrushes, and (2) they are unable to distinguish between normal currents and low-magnitude fault currents which may be less than full-load currents.

Dangerous temperatures and magnetic forces are proportional to current for overloads and short circuits; therefore, overcurrent protective devices usually are adequate to protect against such faults. However, the temperatures of arcing faults are, generally, independent of current magnitude; and arcs of great and extensive destructive capability can be sustained by currents not exceeding the overcurrent device settings. Other means of protection are therefore necessary. A ground-detection device which "sees" only ground-fault current can be coupled to an automatic switching device to open all three phases when a line-to-ground fault exists on the circuit.

Section 230-95 requires ground-fault protection equipment to be provided for each service *disconnecting means* rated 1,000 A or more in a solidly grounded-wye electrical service that operates with its ungrounded legs at more than 150 V to ground. Note that this applies to the rating of the disconnect, not to the rating of the overcurrent devices or to the capacity of the service-entrance conductors.

The wording of the first sentence of this section makes clear that service GFP (ground-fault protection) is required under specific conditions: only for grounded-wye systems that have voltage over 150 V to ground and less than 600 V phase-to-phase. In effect, that means the rule applies only to 480/277-V grounded-wye and *not* to 120/208-V systems or any other commonly used systems (Fig. 230-43). And GFP is *not* required on any systems operating over 600 V phase-to-phase.

In a typical GFP hookup as shown in Fig. 230-44, part **(a)** of the section specifies that a ground-fault current of 1,200 A or more must cause the disconnect to open all ungrounded conductors. Thus the maximum GF pick-up setting permitted is 1,200 A, although it may be set lower.

With a GFP system, at the service entrance a ground fault anywhere in the system is immediately sensed in the ground-relay system, but its action to open the circuit usually is delayed to allow some normal overcurrent device near the point of fault to open if it can. As a practical procedure, such time delay is designed to be only a few cycles or seconds, depending on the voltage of the circuit, the time-current characteristics of the overcurrent devices in the system, and the location of the ground-fault relay in the distribution system. Should any of the conventional short-circuit overcurrent protective devices fail to operate in the time predetermined to clear the circuit, and if the fault continues, the ground-fault protective relays will open the circuit. This provides added overcurrent protection not available by any other means.

The rule requiring GFP for any service disconnect rated 1,000 A or more (on 480/277-V services) specifies a maximum *time delay of 1 sec for ground-fault currents of 3,000 A or more* (Fig. 230-45).

The maximum permitted setting of a service GFP hookup is 1,200 A, but the time-current trip characteristic of the relay must assure opening of the disconnect in not more than 1 sec for any ground-fault current of 3,000 A or more. This change in the **Code** was made to establish a specific level of protection in GFP equipment by setting a maximum limit on i^2t of fault energy.

The reasoning behind this change was explained as follows:

The amount of damage done by an arcing fault is directly proportional to the time it is allowed to burn. Commercially available GFP systems can easily meet the 1-sec limit. Some users are requesting time delays up to 60 sec so all downstream overcurrent devices can have plenty of time to trip thermally before the GFP on the main disconnect trips. However, an arcing fault lasting 60 sec can virtually destroy a service equipment installation. Coordination with downstream overcurrent devices can and should be achieved by adding GFP on feeder circuits where needed. The **Code** should require a reasonable time limit for GFP. Now, 3,000 A is 250 percent of 1,200 A, and 250 percent of setting is a calibrating point specified in ANSI 37.17. Specifying a maximum time delay starting at this current value will allow either flat or inverse time-delay char-

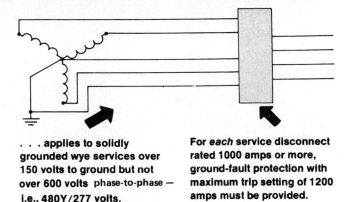

. . . applies to solidly grounded wye services over 150 volts to ground but not over 600 volts phase-to-phase **— i.e., 480Y/277 volts.**

For *each* **service disconnect rated 1000 amps or more, ground-fault protection with maximum trip setting of 1200 amps must be provided.**

GFP IS NOT MANDATORY FOR

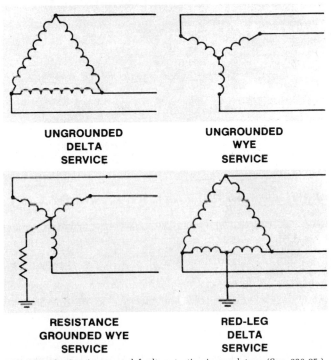

UNGROUNDED
DELTA
SERVICE

UNGROUNDED
WYE
SERVICE

RESISTANCE
GROUNDED WYE
SERVICE

RED-LEG
DELTA
SERVICE

Fig. 230-43. Service ground-fault protection is mandatory. (Sec. 230-95.)

acteristics for ground-fault relays with approximately the same level of protection.

Selective coordination between GFP and conventional protective devices (fuses and CBs) on service and feeder circuits is now a very clear and specific

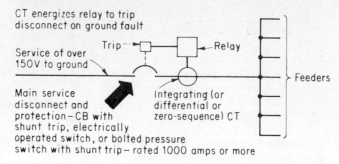

CT energizes relay to trip
disconnect on ground fault

Trip — Relay

Service of over
150V to ground

Main service
disconnect and
protection – CB with
shunt trip, electrically
operated switch, or bolted pressure
switch with shunt trip– rated 1000 amps or more

Integrating (or
differential or
zero-sequence) CT

Feeders

100 hp, 460 V fire-pump motor
has full-load current of
124 A and locked-rotor current
of 906 A . . .

Fire–pump
service

. . . and requires a 1000 A service
CB or disconnect switch to
accommodate the 1000 A fuses
required by Section 230-90, Ex. No. 5

**GROUND-FAULT PROTECTION
MUST NOT BE USED!**

Fig. 230-44. GFP is required for each disconnect rated 1,000 A or more,
but not for a fire-pump disconnect. (Sec. 230-95.)

task as a result of rewording of Sec. 230-95(a) that calls for a maximum time
delay of 1 sec at any ground-fault current value of 3,000 A or more.

For applying the rule of Sec. 230-95, the rating of any service disconnect
means shall be determined as shown in Fig. 230-46.

Because the rule on required service GFP applies to the rating of each service
disconnect, there are many instances where GFP would be required if a single
service main disconnect is used but not if the service subdivision option of Sec.
230-71(a) is taken, as shown in Fig. 230-47.

By Exception No. 1 to part **(a)**, continuous industrial process operations are
exempted from the GFP rules of Sec. 230-95(a) where the electrical system is
under the supervision of qualified persons who will effect orderly shutdown of
the system and thereby avoid hazards, greater than ground fault itself, that
would result from the nonorderly, automatic interruption that GFP would produce in the supply to such critical continuous operations. Exception No. 1
excludes GFP requirements where a nonorderly shutdown will introduce addi-

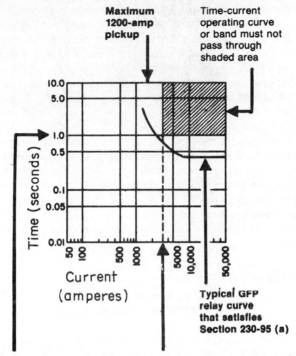

Fig. 230·45. The rule specifies maximum energy let-through for GFP operation. [Sec. 230-95(a).]

tional or increased hazards. The idea behind that is to provide maximum protection against service outage for such industrial processes. With highly trained personnel at such locations, design and maintenance of the electrical system can often accomplish safety objectives more readily without GFP on the service. Electrical design can account for any danger to personnel resulting from loss of process power versus damage to electrical equipment.

Exception No. 2 excludes fire-pump service disconnects from the basic rule that requires ground-fault protection on any service disconnect rated 1,000 A or more on a grounded-wye 480/277-V system.

Because fire pumps are required by Sec. 230-90, Exception No. 4, to have overcurrent protection devices large enough to permit locked-rotor current of the pump motor to flow without interruption, larger fire pumps (100 hp and more) would have disconnects rated 1,000 A or more. Without the Exception, those fire-pump disconnects would be subject to the basic rule and would have to be equipped with ground-fault protection. But GFP on any fire pump is objectionable on the same basis that Sec. 230-90, Exception No. 4, wants nothing less than protection rated for locked rotor. The intent is to give the pump

FUSED SWITCH (bolted pressure switch, service protector, etc.)

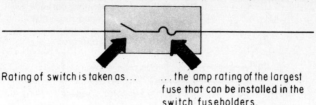

Rating of switch is taken as...   ...the amp rating of the largest
fuse that can be installed in the
switch fuseholders.

EXAMPLE

If 900-amp fuses are used in this service switch, ground-fault protection would be required, because the switch can take fuses rated 1200 amps—which is above the 1000-amp level at which GFP becomes mandatory.

CIRCUIT BREAKER

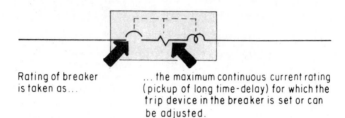

Rating of breaker   ...the maximum continuous current rating
is taken as...   (pickup of long time-delay) for which the
trip device in the breaker is set or can
be adjusted.

Example: GFP would be required for a service CB with, say, an 800-amp trip setting if the CB had a trip device that can be adjusted to 1000 amps or more.

Fig. 230-46. Determining rating of service disconnect for GFP rule. (Sec. 230-95.)

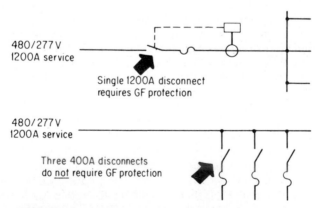

480/277V
1200A service

Single 1200A disconnect
requires GF protection

480/277V
1200A service

Three 400A disconnects
do not require GF protection

Fig. 230-47. Subdivision option on disconnects affects GFP rule. (Sec. 230-95.)

motor every chance to operate when it functions during a fire, to prevent opening of the motor circuit or any overload up to and including stalling or seizing
of the shaft or bearings. For the same reason, Sec. 430-31 exempts fire pumps
from the need for overload protection, and Sec. 430-72, Exception No. 4,
requires overcurrent protection to be omitted from the control circuit of a
starter for a fire pump.

And it should be noted that Exception No. 2 in Sec. 230-95 says that ground-
fault protection "*shall not apply*" to fire-pump motors—appearing to make
omission of GFP mandatory.

Important considerations are given in fine-print notes in this section. Obviously, the selection of ground-fault equipment for a given installation merits a
detailed study. The option of subdividing services discussed under *six service
entrances from one drop* (Sec. 230-2, Exception No. 7) should be evaluated. A
4,000-A service, for example, could be divided using five 800-A disconnecting
means, and in such cases GFP would not be required.

One very important note in Sec. 230-95(b) warns about potential desensitizing
of ground-fault sensing hookups when an emergency generator and transfer
switch are provided in conjunction with the normal service to a building. The
note applies to those cases where a solid neutral connection from the normal
service is made to the neutral of the generator through a 3-pole transfer switch.
With the neutral grounded at the normal service and the neutral bonded to the
generator frame, ground-fault current on the load side of the transfer switch
can return over two paths, one of which will escape detection by the GFP sensor, as shown in Fig. 230-48. Such a hookup can also cause nuisance tripping of
the GFP due to normal neutral current. Under normal (nonfaulted) conditions,
neutral current due to normal load unbalance on the phase legs can divide at
common neutral connection in transfer switch, with some current flowing
toward the generator and returning to the service main on the conduit—indicating falsely that a ground fault exists and causing nuisance tripping of GFP.
The note points out that "means or devices" (such as a 4-pole, neutral-switched
transfer switch) "may be needed" to assure proper, effective operation of the
GFP hookup (Fig. 230-49).
VERY IMPORTANT!

Because of so many reports of improper and/or unsafe operation (or failure
to operate) of ground-fault protective hookups, part **(c)** of Sec. 230-95 *requires*
(a mandatory rule) that *every* GFP hookup be "performance tested when first
installed." And the testing MUST *be done on the job site!* Factory testing of a
GFP system does not satisfy this **Code** rule. This rule requires that such testing
be done according to "approved instructions . . . provided with the equipment."
A written record must be made of the test and must be available to the inspection authority.

Figure 230-50 shows two basic types of GFP hookup used at service
entrances.

230-200. General (Services Exceeding 600 Volts, Nominal).   A definition at the
end of this section is intended to clarify the basic rule on high-voltage services
that the provisions of Art. 230 apply only to equipment on the load side of the
"service-point." Because there has been so much controversy over identifying

3. This GF current coming back on neutral goes through GFP sensor and is **not** sensed as fault current.

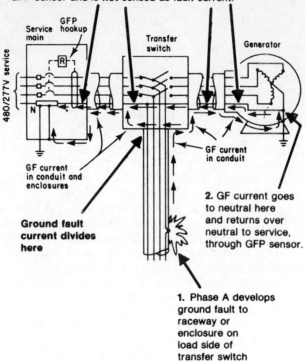

Fig. 230-48. Improper operation of GFP equipment can result from emergency system transfer switch. (Sec. 230-95.)

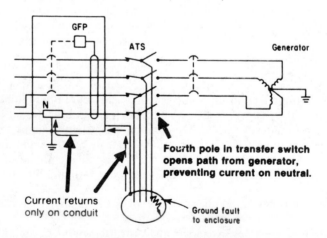

Refer to Fig. 230-48

Fig. 230-49. Four-pole transfer switch is one way to avoid desensitizing GFP. (Sec. 230-95.)

GROUND–STRAP SENSING

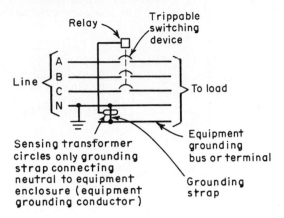

ZERO–SEQUENCE SENSING

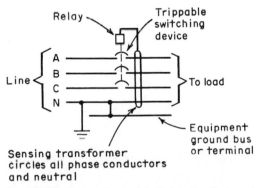

Fig. 230-50. Types of ground-fault detection that may be selected for use at services. (Sec. 230-95.)

what is and what is not "service" equipment in the many complicated layouts of outdoor high-voltage circuits and transformers, the definition provides clarification. In any particular installation, identification of that point can be made by the utility company and design personnel. The definition clarifies that the property line is not the determinant as to where **NE Code** rules must begin to be applied. This is particularly important in cases of multibuilding industrial complexes where the utility has distribution circuits on the property (Fig. 230-51). See Secs. 230-201 and 230-205.

"Service-point" is the "point of connection between the facilities of the serving utility and the premises' wiring." All equipment on the load side of that point is subject to **NE Code** rules. Any equipment on the line side is the concern of the power company and is not regulated by the **Code**. This definition of "service-point" must be construed as establishing that "service conductors" origi-

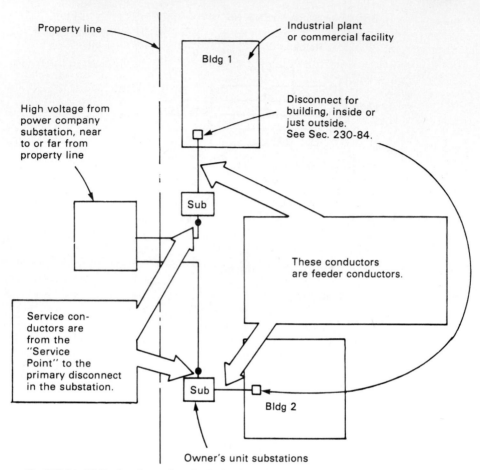

Fig. 230-51. NE Code rules apply on load side of "SERVICE POINT"—not from property line. (Sec. 230-200.)

nate at that point. The whole matter of identifying the "service conductors" is covered by Sec. 230-201.

The definition of "service-point" does tell where the **NE Code** becomes applicable, and does pinpoint the origin of service conductors. And that is a critical task, because a corollary of that determination is identification of that equipment which is, technically, "service equipment" subject to all applicable **NE Code** rules on such equipment. Any conductors between the "service-point" of a particular installation and the service disconnect are identified as service conductors and subject to **NE Code** rules on service conductors.

230-201. Service Conductors.   After noting in Sec. 230-200 that "service conductors and equipment used on circuits exceeding 600 volts" must comply with *all* the rules in Art. 230 (including any "applicable provisions" that cover services up to 600 V), the **NE Code** then proceeds to say that for services over 600

V, the "service conductors" are those conductors—whether on the primary or secondary of a step-down transformer or transformers—that carry current from the "service point" (where the utility connects to the customer's wiring) to the service disconnecting means for a building or structure (Fig. 230-51). All conductors between the defined points—"service point" and "service disconnecting means"—must comply with all requirements for service conductors, whether above or below 600 V.

Section 230-205 says the service disconnect means must be located in accordance with Sec. 230-70 or with Sec. 230-208(b) for circuits over 600 V. Section 230-205 and Sec. 230-208(b) call for the "service disconnecting means" to be either inside or outside the building or structure as close as possible to where the service conductors enter. Those rules identify the service disconnect means and apply to the conductors entering a building or structure. All conductors between the "service point" and the "service disconnecting means" must be treated as "service conductors," regardless of voltage. Conductors operating at over 600 V must satisfy the rules of part **H** of Art. 230 in addition to satisfying all rules of Art. 230 up to part **H**.

Design and layout of any "service" are critically related to safety, adequacy, economics, and effective use of the whole system. It is absolutely essential that we know clearly and surely what circuits and equipment of any electrical system constitute the "service" and what parts of the system are not involved in the "service." For instance, in a system with utility feed at 13.2 kV and step-down to 480/277 V, the mandatory application of Sec. 230-95 requiring GFP hinges on establishing whether the "service" is on the primary or secondary side of the transformers. If the secondary is the service, where the step-down transformer belongs to the utility and the "service point" is on its secondary, we have a mandatory need for GFP and none of the **Code** rules on service would apply to any of the 13.2-kV circuits—regardless of their length or location. If the transformer belongs to the customer and the "service point" is on the primary side, the primary is the service, Sec. 230-95 does not require GFP on services over 600 V phase-to-phase, all the primary circuit and equipment must comply with all of Art. 230, and the secondary circuits are feeders and do not have to comply with any of the service regulations.

The whole problem involved here is complex and requires careful, individual study to see clearly the many interrelated considerations. Let us look at a few important things to note about **Code** definitions as given in Art. 100:

1. "Service conductors" run to the *service equipment* of the *premises* supplied. Note that they run to "premises" and are not required to run to a "building." The **Code** does not define the word *premises,* but a typical dictionary definition is "a tract of land, including its buildings." But for many years, the **Code** rule of Sec. 230-201 did refer to "service conductors to the building." Although that phrase no longer is used in the rule, the wording does clearly aim at establishing the service conductors to the "building or other structure served (Fig. 230-52)."

2. "Service equipment" *usually* consists of "a circuit breaker or switch and fuses, and their accessories, located near the point of entrance of *supply* conductors to a building or other structure, or an otherwise defined area."

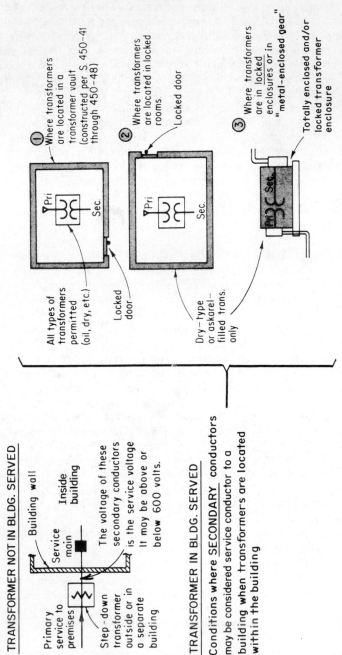

Fig. 230-52. Where the transformer belongs to the utilty, the "service point" is on its secondary and the secondary conductors are the service conductors to the building or structure. (Sec. 230-201.)

Note that the service equipment is the means of cutoff of the supply, and the service conductors may enter "a building" or "other structure" or a "defined area." But, again, a service does not necessarily have to be to "a building." It could be to such a "structure" as an outdoor switchgear or unit substation enclosure.

The wording of Sec. 230-201 bases identification of "service conductors" as being on the primary or secondary side of a "step-down transformer." Because of the definition of "service point," it is essential to determine whether the transformers belong to the power company or the property owner.

If a utility owned transformer that handles the electrical load for a building is in a locked room or locked enclosure (accessible only to qualified persons) in the building and is fed, say, by an underground high-voltage (over 600 V) utility line from outdoors, the secondary conductors from the transformer would be the "service conductors" to the building. And the switching and control devices (up to six CBs on fused switches) on the secondary would constitute the "service equipment" for the building. Under such a condition, if any of the secondary section "service disconnects" were rated 1,000 A or more, at 480/277-V grounded wye, they would have to comply with Sec. 230-95, requiring GFP for the service disconnects.

However, if the utility made primary feed to a transformer or unit substation belonging to the owner, then the primary conductors would be the service conductors and the primary switch or CB would be the "service disconnect." In that case, no GFP would be needed on the "service disconnect" because Sec. 230-95 applies only up to 600 V, and there is no requirement for GFP on high-voltage services (Fig. 230-53). Also, in that case, there would be no need for GFP on the secondary section disconnects, because they would not be "service disconnects"—and those are the same disconnects that might be subject to Sec. 230-95 if the transformer belonged to the utility. However, Secs. 215-10 or 240-13 may require such protection for these secondary section disconnects. See also Fig. 230-54.

230-202. Service-Entrance Conductors.   This section specifies the wiring methods that are acceptable for use as service-entrance conductors where it has been established that primary conductors (over 600 V) are the service conductors or where the secondary conductors are the service conductors and operate at more than 600 V. The basic conduits that may be used are rigid metal conduit, intermediate metal conduit, and rigid nonmetallic conduit. And the NEC no longer requires concrete encasement of the nonmetallic conduit.

Paragraph **(b)** points out that cable tray systems are also acceptable for high-voltage services, provided that the cables used in the tray are "identified as service-entrance conductors." Section 318-3(a) recognizes "multiconductor service-entrance cable" for use in tray, for cables rated up to 600 V. High-voltage (over 600 V) service-entrance cables may be used if the cables are "identified"—which, in today's strict usage, virtually means that such cable must be listed by a nationally recognized test lab (UL, etc.) as suitable for the purpose. Article 338 on "Service-Entrance Cable" does not refer to any high-voltage cable for service-entrance use. Details of this section are shown in Fig. 230-55.

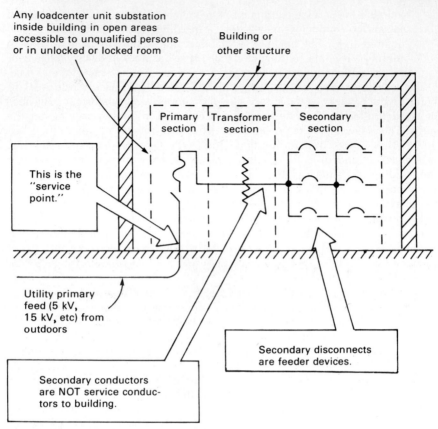

Any loadcenter unit substation inside building in open areas accessible to unqualified persons or in unlocked or locked room

Building or other structure

Primary section | Transformer section | Secondary section

This is the "service point."

Utility primary feed (5 kV, 15 kV, etc) from outdoors

Secondary conductors are NOT service conductors to building.

Secondary disconnects are feeder devices.

Fig. 230-53. The primary is the "service" for any indoor transformer belonging to the owner and fed by utility line. (Sec. 230-201.)

230-203. Warning Signs. Any warning sign for use where unauthorized persons might contact live parts must always include the phrase **"KEEP OUT"** immediately after the phrase **"DANGER HIGH VOLTAGE."** Court cases involving electrical accidents have established the importance of a sign giving a command "KEEP OUT" after advising of the potential hazard "DANGER HIGH VOLTAGE." This is an important factor in making such a sign act as an effective deterrent. And such wording should always be used on signs of this type, whether the sign is required by **Code** rule [see also Sec. 110-17(c) and Sec. 110-34(c)] or not required.

230-204. Isolating Switches. An air-break isolating switch must be used between an oil switch or an air, oil, vacuum, or sulfur hexachloride CB and the supply conductors, unless removable truck panels or metal-enclosed units are used providing disconnect of all live parts in the removed position. This line-side disconnect assures safety to personnel in maintenance [Fig. 230-56]. Part **(d)** requires a grounding connection for an isolating switch, as in Fig. 230-57.

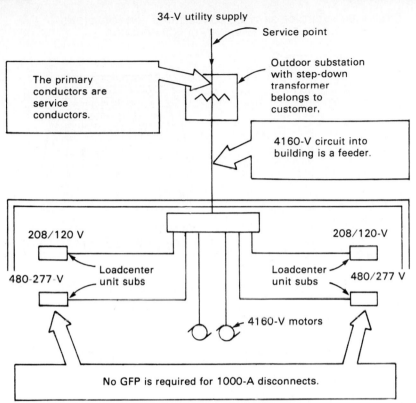

34-V utility supply

Service point

The primary conductors are service conductors.

Outdoor substation with step-down transformer belongs to customer,

4160-V circuit into building is a feeder.

208/120 V

208/120-V

480-277 V

Loadcenter unit subs

Loadcenter unit subs

480/277 V

4160-V motors

No GFP is required for 1000-A disconnects.

Fig. 230-54. The primary circuit must be taken as the "service conductors" where the "service point" is on the primary side of an outdoor transformer.

230-205. Disconnecting Means. In part **(a)**, the basic rule requires a high-voltage service disconnect means to be located "nearest the point of entrance of the service conductors" into the building or structure being supplied—as for 600-V equipment in Sec. 230-70 or as described in Sec. 230-208(b). The Exception permits a feeder to an outlying building on a multibuilding property under single management to have its disconnect in another building on the property. But such a remote disconnect must be capable of being electrically opened by a control device in the building supplied.

Part **(b)**, covering the electrical fault characteristics, requires that the service disconnect be *capable of closing,* safely and effectively, on a fault equal to or greater than the maximum short-circuit current that is available at the line terminals of the disconnect. The last sentence notes that where fuses are used within the disconnect or in conjunction with it, the fuse characteristics may contribute to fault-closing rating of the disconnect. The idea behind this rule is to assure that the disconnect switch may be safely closed on a level of fault that can be safely interrupted by the fuse.

(a) HIGH—VOLTAGE SERVICE CONDUCTORS FOR LOCATIONS ACCESSIBLE TO OTHER THAN QUALIFIED PERSONS

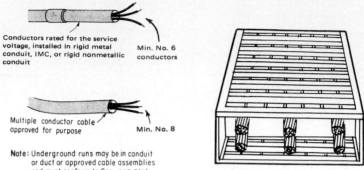

Conductors rated for the service voltage, installed in rigid metal conduit, IMC, or rigid nonmetallic conduit

Min. No. 6 conductors

Multiple conductor cable approved for purpose

Min. No. 8

Note: Underground runs may be in conduit or duct or approved cable assemblies and must conform to Sec. 710-3(b)

In cablebus–5 kV to 35 kV [Article 365]

(h) SERVICE CONDUCTORS OPERATING AT MORE THAN 15 kV

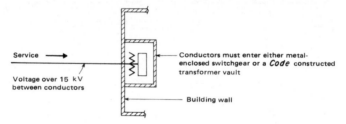

Service →

Voltage over 15 kV between conductors

Conductors must enter either metal-enclosed switchgear or a *Code* constructed transformer vault

Building wall

(f) POTHEAD ON SERVICE CONDUCTORS

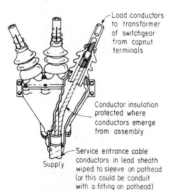

Load conductors to transformer of switchgear from capnut terminals

Conductor insulation protected where conductors emerge from assembly

Supply

Service entrance cable conductors in lead sheath wiped to sleeve on pothead (or this could be conduit with a fitting on pothead)

(i) REMEMBER, SEC. 230-6 ALSO APPLIES TO HIGH-VOLTAGE CONDUCTORS (OVER 600 V NOMINAL) AS GIVEN IN SEC. 230-200, THEREFORE CONDUCTORS ENCLOSED IN MASONRY ARE CONSIDERED AS INSTALLED OUTSIDE THE BUILDING

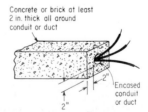

Concrete or brick at least 2 in. thick all around conduit or duct

2"

2"

Encased conduit or duct

Fig. 230-55. Provisions for service conductors rated over 600 V (refer to subpart letter identification of rules). (Sec. 230-202.)

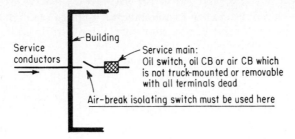

Service
conductors

Building

Service main:
Oil switch, oil CB or air CB which
is not truck-mounted or removable
with all terminals dead

Air-break isolating switch must be used here

EXAMPLE:

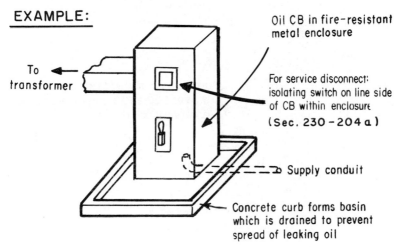

To
transformer

Oil CB in fire-resistant
metal enclosure

For service disconnect:
isolating switch on line side
of CB within enclosure
(Sec. 230-204 a)

Supply conduit

Concrete curb forms basin
which is drained to prevent
spread of leaking oil

Fig. 230-56. Isolating switch may be needed to kill line terminals of service disconnect. (Sec. 230-204.)

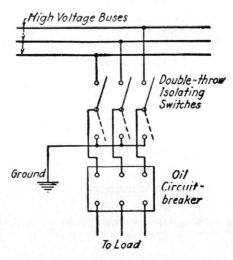

High Voltage Buses

Double-throw
Isolating
Switches

Ground

Oil
Circuit-
breaker

To Load

Fig. 230-57. One method for grounding the load side of an open isolating switch. (Sec. 230-204.)

230-208. Overcurrent Protection Requirements.   Service conductors operating at voltages over 600 V must have a short-circuit (not overload) device in each ungrounded conductor, installed either (1) on load side of service disconnect, or (2) as an integral part of the service disconnect.

FUSED LOAD INTERRUPTER SWITCH

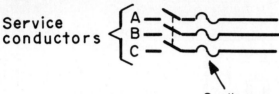

Continuous current rating of each fuse **not over** 300% (3 times) the ampacity of the **service** conductors

AIR, OIL, OR VACUUM CB

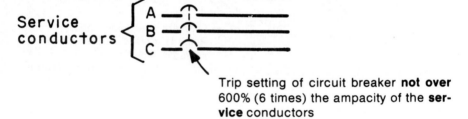

Trip setting of circuit breaker **not over** 600% (6 times) the ampacity of the **service** conductors

TYPES OF DEVICES PERMITTED

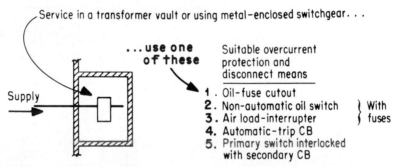

Fig. 230-58. Maximum permitted rating or setting of high-voltage overcurrent protection for service. (Sec. 230-208.)

All devices must be able to detect and interrupt all values of current in excess of their rating or trip setting, which must be as shown in Fig. 230-58.

The difference between 300 percent for fuses and 600 percent for CBs is explained as follows:

The American National Standards Institute (ANSI) publishes standards for power fuses. The continuous-current ratings of power fuses are given with the letter "E" following the number of continuous amps—for instance, 65E or 200E or 400E. The letter "E" indicates that the fuse has a melting time-current characteristic in accordance with the standard for E-rated fuses:

The melting time-current characteristics of fuse units, refill units, and links for power fuses shall be as follows:

(1) The current-responsive element with ratings 100 amperes or below shall melt in 300 seconds at an rms current within the range of 200 or 240 percent of the continuous current rating of the fuse unit, refill unit, or fuse link.

(2) The current-responsive element with ratings above 100 amperes shall melt in 600 seconds at an rms current within the range of 220 to 264 percent of the continuous current rating of the fuse unit, refill unit, or fuse link.

(3) The melting time-current characteristic of a power fuse at any current higher than the 200 to 240 or 264 percent specified in (1) or (2) above shall be shown by each manufacturer's published time current curves, since the current-responsive element is a distinctive feature of each manufacturer.

(4) For any given melting time, the maximum steady-state rms current shall not exceed the minimum by more than 20 percent.

The fact that E-rated fuses are given melting times at 200 percent or more of their continuous-current rating explains why **NE Code** Secs. 230-208 and 240-100 set 300 percent of conductor ampacity as the maximum fuse rating but permit CBs up to 600 percent. In effect, the 300 percent for fuses times 2 (200 percent) becomes 600 percent—the same as for CBs.

Part **(e)** of this section permits overcurrent protection for services over 600 V to be loaded up to 100 percent of its rating even on continuous loads (operating for periods of 3 hr or more).

ARTICLE 240. OVERCURRENT PROTECTION

240-1. Scope.   For any electrical system, required current-carrying capacities are determined for the various circuits—feeders, subfeeders, and branch circuits. Then these required capacities are converted into standard circuit conductors which have sufficient current-carrying capacities based on the size of the conductors, the type of insulation on the conductors, the ambient temperature at the place of installation, the number of conductors in each conduit, the type and continuity of load, and judicious determination of spare capacity to meet future load growth. Or if busway, armored cable, or other cable assemblies are to be used, similar considerations go into selection of conductors with required current-carrying capacities. In any case, then, the next step is to provide overcurrent protection for each and every circuit:

The overcurrent device for conductors or equipment must automatically open the circuit it protects if the current flowing in that circuit reaches a value which will cause an excessive or dangerous temperature in the conductor or conductor installation.

Overcurrent protection for conductors must also be rated for safe operation at the level of fault current obtainable at the point of their application. Every fuse and circuit breaker for short-circuit protection must be applied in such a way that the fault current produced by a bolted short circuit on its load terminals will not damage or destroy the device. Specifically this requires that a short-circuit overcurrent device have a proven interrupting capacity at least equal to the current which the electrical system can deliver into a short on its line terminals.

But safe application of a protective device does not stop with adequate interrupting capacity for its own use at the point of installation in the system. The speed of operation of the device must then be analyzed in relation to the thermal and magnetic energy which the device permits to flow in the faulted circuit. A very important consideration is the provision of conductor size to meet the potential heating load of short-circuit currents in cables. With expanded use of circuit-breaker overcurrent protection, coordination of protection from loads back to the source has introduced time delays in operation of overcurrent devices. Cables in such systems must be able to withstand any impressed short-circuit currents for the durations of overcurrent delay. For example, a motor circuit to a 100-hp motor might be required to carry as much as 15,000 A for a number of seconds. To limit damage to the cable due to heating effect, a much larger size conductor than necessary for the load current alone may be required.

A device may be able to break a given short-circuit current without damaging itself in the operation; but in the time it takes to open the faulted circuit, enough energy may get through to damage or destroy other equipment in series with the fault. This other equipment might be cable or busway or a switch or motor controller—any circuit component which simply cannot withstand the few cycles of short-circuit current which flows in the period of time between initiation of the fault and interruption of the current flow.

A strict interpretation of **NE Code** Sec. 240-2 often raises questions about the approved use of conductors and overcurrent protection to withstand faults.

example Assume a panelboard with 20-A breakers rated 10,000 A IC (interrupting capacity) and No. 12 copper branch-circuit wiring. Available fault current at the point of breaker application is 8,000 A. The short-circuit withstand capability of a No. 12 copper conductor with plastic or polyethylene insulation rated 60°C would be approximately 3,000 A of fault or short-circuit current for one cycle.

Question: Assuming that the CB (circuit breaker) will take at least one cycle to operate, would use of the conductor where exposed to 8,000 A violate Sec. 240-2? This section states that overcurrent protection for conductors and equipment is provided for the purpose of opening the electrical circuit if the current reaches a value which will cause an excessive or dangerous temperature in the conductor or conductor insulation. The 8,000-A available fault current would seem to call for use of conductors with that rating of short-circuit withstand.

This could mean that branch-circuit wiring from all 20-A CBs in this panel-board must be *No. 6 copper* (the next larger size suitable for an 8,000-A fault current).

Answer: As noted in UL Standard 489, a CB is required to operate safely in a circuit where the available fault current is up to the short-circuit current value for which the breaker is rated. The CB must clear the fault without damage to the insulation of conductors of proper size for the rating of the CB. A UL-listed, 20-A breaker is, therefore, tested and rated to be used with 20-A rated wire (say, No. 12 THW) and will protect the wire in accordance with Sec. 240-2 when applied at a point in a circuit where the short-circuit current available does not exceed the value for which the breaker is rated. This is also true of a 15-A breaker on No. 14 (15-A) wire, for a 30-A breaker on No. 10 (30-A) wire, and all wire sizes.

UL 489 states:

A circuit breaker shall perform successfully when operated under conditons as described in paragraphs 21.2 and 21.3. There shall be no electrical or mechanical breakdown of the device, and the fuse that is indicated in paragraph 12.16 shall not have cleared. Cotton indicators as described in paragraphs 21.4 and 21.6 shall not be ignited. There shall be no damage to the insulation on conductors used to wire the device. After the final operation, the circuit breaker shall have continuity in the closed position at rated voltage.

240-3. Protection of Conductors—Other than Flexible Cords and Fixture Wires. Aside from general-purpose lighting and appliance branch circuits [which are clearly and rigidly regulated on overcurrent protection as described in Secs. 210-3, 210-19(a), 210-20, 210-22(c), and 220-3(a)], conductors for all other circuits must conform to the rules and exceptions of Sec. 240-3.

Clearly, the rule wants overcurrent devices to prevent conductors from being subjected to currents in excess of the ampacity values for which the conductors are rated by Tables 310-16 through 310-19 **with all notes.**

That last phrase in the first sentence of this section (about "all applicable notes to these tables") is important because it points out that when conductors have their ampacities derated because of conduit fill (Note 8 to the tables) or because of elevated ambient temperature, the conductors must be protected at the *derated* ampacities and *not* at the values given in the tables.

Specifically, the general rule is that the device must be rated to protect conductors in accordance with their safe allowable current-carrying capacities. Of course, there will be cases where standard ampere ratings and settings of overcurrent devices will not correspond with conductor capacities. In such cases, Exception No. 4 permits the next larger standard size of overcurrent device to be used where the rating of the protective device is 800 A or less. Therefore, a basic guide to effective selection of the amp rating of overcurrent devices for any feeder or service application is given in the exceptions.

For example, if a circuit conductor of, say, 500 kcmil THW copper (not more than three in a conduit at not over 86°F ambient) satisfies design requirements and NE Code rules for a particular load current not in excess of the conductor's table ampacity of 380 A, then the conductor *may* be protected by a 400-A rated fuse or CB.

Section 240-6, which gives the "Standard Ampere Ratings" of protective devices to correspond to the word "standard" in Exception No. 4, shows devices rated at 350 and 400 A, but none at 380 A. In such a case, the NE Code accepts a 400-A rated device as "the next higher standard device rating" above the conductor ampacity of 380 A.

But, such a 400-A device would permit load increase above the 380 A that is the safe maximum limit for the conductor. It would be more effective practice to use 350-A rated protection and prevent such overload.

For application of fuses and CBs, Exception No. 4 has this effect:

1. If the ampacity of a conductor does not correspond to the rating of a standard-size fuse, the next *larger* rating of fuse may be used only where that rating is 800 A or less. Over 800 A, the next *smaller* fuse must be used. However, as the last paragraph of Exception No. 4 says, for circuits over 800 A, a listed fuse or circuit breaker with rating other than a standard value (from Sec. 240-6) may be used.

   For any circuit over 800A, Exception No. 4 prohibits the use of "the next higher standard" rating of protective device (fuse or CB) when the ampacity of the circuit conductors does not correspond with a standard ampere rating of fuse or CB. The rating of the protection may not exceed the conductor ampacity. Although it would be acceptable to use a protective device of the next lower standard rating (from Sec. 240-6) below the conductor ampacity, there are many times when greater use of the conductor ampacity may be made by using a fuse or CB of rating lower than the conductor ampacity but not as low as the next lower standard rating. Listed fuses and CBs are made with ratings between the standard values shown in Sec. 240-6.

   For example, if the ampacity of conductors for a feeder circuit is calculated to be 1,540 A, Exception No. 4 does not permit protecting such a conductor by using the next higher standard rating above 1,540—1,600 A. The next lower standard rating of fuse or CB shown in Sec. 240-6 is 1,200 A. Such protection could be used, but that would sacrifice 340 A (1,540 minus 1,200) of conductor ampacity. Because listed 1,500-A protective devices are available and would provide for effective use of almost all the conductor's 1,540-A capacity, this rule specifically recognizes such an application as safe and sound practice. Such application is specifically recognized by the fine print Note at the end of Sec. 240-6.

   In general, Sec. 240-6 is not intended to require that all fuses or CBs be of the standard ratings shown. Intermediate values of protective device ratings may be used, provided all Code rules on protection—especially the basic first sentence of Sec. 240-3, which requires conductors to be protected at their ampacities—are satisfied (Fig. 240-1).

2. A nonadjustable-trip breaker (one without overload trip adjustment above its rating—although it may have adjustable short-circuit trip) must be rated in accordance with the current-carrying capacity of the conductors it protects—except that the next higher standard rating of CB may be used if the ampacity of the conductor does not correspond to a standard unit rating. In such a case, the next higher standard setting may be used only where

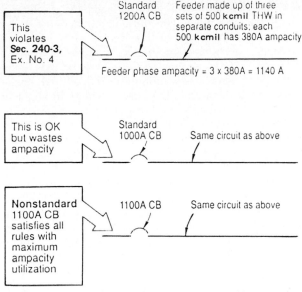

Fig. 240·1. Protection in accordance with Exception No. 4 may use standard or nonstandard rated fuses or circuit breakers. (Secs. 240-3 and 240-6.)

the rating is 800 A or less. An example of such application is shown in Fig. 240-1, where a nonadjustable CB with a rating of 1,200 A is used to protect the conductors of a feeder circuit which are rated at 1,140 A. As shown there, use of that size CB to protect a circuit rated at 1,140 A (3 × 380 A = 1,140 A) clearly violates Exception No. 4 because the CB is the next higher rating above the ampacity of the conductors—on a circuit rated over 800 A. With a feeder circuit as shown (three 500 kcmil THW, each rated at 380 A), the CB must not be rated over 1,140 A. A standard 1,000-A CB would satisfy the **Code** rule—being the *next lower* rated protective device from Sec. 240-6. Or a 1,100-A fuse could be used. Of course, if 500 kcmil THHN or XHHW conductors are used instead of THW conductors, then each 500 is rated at 430 A, three per phase would give the circuit an ampacity of 1,290 A (3 × 430), and the 1,200-A CB would satisfy the basic rule in the first sentence of Sec. 240-3 and Exception No. 4 would not be involved.

The last clause in the first paragraph of Exception No. 4, however, requires that the rating of overcurrent protection must *never* exceed the ampacity of circuit conductors supplying one or more receptacle outlets on a branch circuit with more than one outlet. This final wording in the first paragraph of Exception No. 4 coordinates with the rules described under Sec. 210-19(a) on conductor ampacity. The effect of that last clause in Exception No. 4 is to require that the rating of the overcurrent protection must not exceed the **Code**-table ampacity (**NEC** Table 310-16) or the derated ampacity dictated by Note 8 to the tables for any conductor of a multioutlet branch circuit supplying any receptacles for cord- and plug-connected portable loads. If a standard rating of fuse or CB does not match the ampacity (or derated ampacity) of such a circuit, the next lower standard rating of protective device must be used. *But*, where branch-circuit conductors of an individual circuit to a single load or a multioutlet circuit supply *only* fixed connected (hard-wired) loads—such as lighting outlets or permanently connected appliances—the next larger standard rating of protective device *may* be used in those cases where the ampacity (or derated ampacity) of the conductor does not correspond to a standard rating of protective device—but, again, that is permitted only up to 800 A, above which the next lower rating of fuse or CB must be used, as described under Sec. 210-19(a).

Exception No. 6 refers the matter of protecting motor-control circuits to Art. 430 on motors.

Exception No. 1 applies to the protection of the remote-control circuit that energizes the operating coil of a magnetic contactor, as distinguished from a magnetic motor starter (Fig. 240-2). Although it is true that a magnetic starter is a magnetic contactor with the addition of running overload relays, Exception No. 1 refers only to the coil circuit of any magnetic contactor but not to protection of the coil circuit of a magnetic starter.

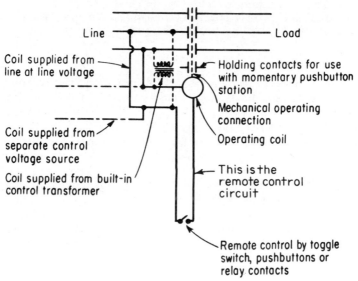

Fig. 240-2. Coil-circuit wires of magnetic contactor must be protected as required by Sec. 725-12. (Sec. 240-3.)

Section 725-12 covers control wires for magnetic contactors used for control of lighting or heating loads, but not motor loads. Section 430-72 covers that requirement for motor-control circuits. In Fig. 240-3, the remote-control conductors may be considered properly protected by the branch-circuit overcurrent devices (A) if these devices are rated or set at not more than 300 percent of (3 times) the current rating of the control conductors. If the branch-circuit

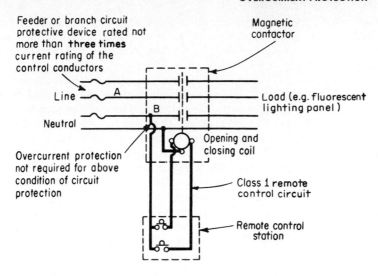

Feeder or branch circuit protective device rated not more than **three times** current rating of the control conductors

Magnetic contactor

Line — A

Load (e.g. fluorescent lighting panel)

B

Neutral

Overcurrent protection not required for above condition of circuit protection

Opening and closing coil

Class 1 remote control circuit

Remote control station

For instance, 30-amp fuses at A would be adequate protection if No. 14 wire, rated at 15 amps, is used for the remote-control circuit because 30 amps is less than 3 × 15 amps. If fuses at A were over 45 amps, then 15-amp protection would be required at B for No. 14 wire.

Fig. 240-3. Protecting a remote-control circuit in accordance with Sec. 725-12. (Sec. 240-3.)

overcurrent devices were rated or set at more than 300 percent of the rating of the control conductors, the control conductors would have to be protected by a separate protective device located at the point (B) where the conductor to be protected receives its supply. (See Sec. 725-12, Exception No. 3.)

Exception No. 2 permits the secondary circuit from a transformer to be protected by means of fuses or a CB in the primary circuit to the transformer—if the transformer has no more than a 2-wire primary circuit and a 2-wire secondary. As shown in Fig. 240-4, by using the 2-to-1 primary-to-secondary turns ratio of the transformer, 20-A primary protection will protect against any secondary current in excess of 40 A—thereby protecting, say, secondary No. 8 TW wires rated at 40 A. As the wording of the Exception states, the protection on the primary (20 A) must not exceed the value of the secondary conductor

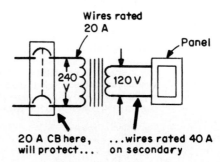

Wires rated 20 A

Panel

240

120 V

Fig. 240-4. Primary fuses or CB may protect secondary circuit for 2-wire to 2-wire transformer. (Sec. 240-3.)

20 A CB here, will protect...

...wires rated 40 A on secondary

ampacity (40 A) multiplied by the secondary-to-primary transformer voltage ratio (120 ÷ 240 = 0.5). Thus, 40 A × 0.5 = 20 A. But it should be carefully noted that the rating of the primary protection must comply with the rules of Sec. 450-3(a) or (b) (1).

A sentence at the end of Exception No. 2 clearly and emphatically states that the secondary conductors from a transformer may *not* be protected by over-current protection on the primary side of the transformer—**except** for a trans-former with a *2-wire* secondary. That has long been the intent of the **Code**, but much discussion and controversy have regularly concentrated on this matter because the **Code** has not previously had the simple prohibition against sec-ondary protection by a primary CB or set of fuses. The whole issue of trans-formers and overcurrent protection is now firmly established as follows.

The basic way to provide overcurrent protection for a dry-type transformer rated 600 V or less (with a rated primary current of more than 9 A) is to use fuses or CBs rated at not more than 125 percent of the transformer primary full-load current (TPFLC) to protect *both* the transformer and the circuit conductors that supply the transformer primary. [This is presented in Sec. 450-3(b).] These circuit conductors must have an ampacity of not less than the rating of the over-current protection or must have an ampacity such that the overcurrent protec-tive device is "the next higher standard device rating" above the conductor ampacity, as described in Exception No. 4 of Sec. 240-3. *But the primary circuit protection is not acceptable as suitable protection for the secondary conductors of a transformer with more than 2 wires on its secondary—even if the second-ary conductors have an ampacity equal to the ampacity of the primary conduc-tors times the primary-to-secondary voltage ratio. Figure 240-5 covers these points.

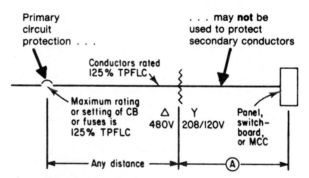

Primary circuit protection . . .

. . . may **not** be used to protect secondary conductors

Conductors rated 125% TPFLC

Maximum rating or setting of CB or fuses is 125% TPFLC

Δ 480V | Y 208/120V

Panel, switch-board, or MCC

⟵ Any distance ⟶ ⟵ (A) ⟶

Distance "A" from transformer to first protection on the secondary side is limited to 10 or 25 ft, subject to the requirements of Exceptions 2, 3 and 8 of Section 240-21. If overcurrent protection is placed at the transformer second-ary connection to protect secondary conductors, the circuit can run any distance to the panel.

Fig. 240·5. Exception No. 2 *clearly* resolves long-standing contro-versy. (Sec. 240-3.)

When primary devices are used for protection of 3- and 4-wire transformer secondaries, it is possible that an unbalanced load may greatly exceed the secondary conductor ampacity, which was selected assuming balanced conditions. As shown in Fig. 240-6, if the primary CB is set at 20 A, it will protect the primary No. 12 wires, which are rated for 20 A. Under conditions of full load of 20 A in the primary and a balanced secondary loading (left), the secondary current is 40 A, and the primary CB will protect the secondary No. 8 TW wires at their 40-A rating. But unbalance (right) can permit overloading of the secondary conductors without an increase in the primary current. Thus, the primary CB will not clear a 100 percent overload on the secondary wires.

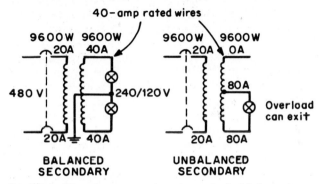

Fig. 240-6. Why primary protection may not do the job for 3-wire or 4-wire secondary 40-A rated wires. (Sec. 240-3.)

However, Exception No. 2 recognizes such primary protection of the secondary conductors of single-phase, 2-wire to 2-wire transformers if the primary OC protection complies with Sec. 450-3 (e.g., not over 125 percent of rated primary current) and does not exceed the value determined by multiplying the secondary conductor ampacity by the secondary-to-primary transformer voltage ratio. In such applications, the lengths of the primary or secondary conductors are not limited.

Exception No. 3 to the basic rule represents a basic concept in **Code** application. When conductors supply a load to which loss of power would create a hazard, this Exception states it is not necessary to provide "overload protection" for such conductors, **but** "short-circuit protection" *must* be provided. By "overload protection," this Exception means "protection at the conductors' ampacity"—i.e., protection that would *prevent* overload (Fig. 240-7).

Several points should be noted about this Exception.

1. Use of this Exception is reserved only to applications where circuit opening on "overload" would be more objectionable than the overload itself, "such as in a material handling magnet circuit." In that example mentioned in the Exception, loss of power to such a magnet while it is lifting a heavy load of steel would cause the steel to fall and would certainly be a serious hazard to personnel working below or near the lifting magnet.

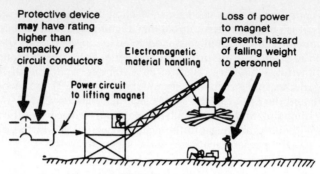

Fig. 240-7. If "overload protection" creates a hazard, it *may* be eliminated. (Sec. 240-3.)

To minimize the hazard created by such power loss, the circuit to it *need not* be protected at the conductor ampacity. A higher value of protection may be used—letting the circuit sustain an overload rather than opening on it and dropping the steel. Because such lifting operations are usually short-time, intermittent tasks, occasional overload is far less a safety concern than the dropping of the magnet's load.

2. The permission to eliminate *only* "overload protection" is not limited to a lifting magnet circuit, which is mentioned simply as an example. Other electrical applications that present a similar concern for "hazard" would be equally open to use of this Exception.

3. Although the Exception *permits* elimination of overload protection and requires short-circuit protection, it gives no guidance on selecting the actual rating of protection that must be used. For such circuits, fuses or a CB rated, say, 200 to 400 percent of the full-load operating current would give freedom from overload opening. Of course, the protective device ought to be selected with as low a rating as would be compatible with the operating characteristics of the electrical load. And it must have sufficient interrupting capacity for the circuit's available short-circuit current.

4. Finally, this Exception is *not* a mandatory rule but a *permissible* application. It says " . . . overload protection *shall not be required* . . ."; it does *not* say that overload protection "shall *not* be used." Overload protection *may be used*, or it *may be eliminated*. Obviously, careful study should always go into use of this Exception.

240-4. Protection of Fixture Wires and Cords.   The basic rules of the first paragraph are that

1. *All flexible cords and extension cords* must be protected at the ampacity given for each size and type of cord or cable in **NEC** Tables 400-5(A) and 400-5(B). "Flexible cords" includes "tinsel cord"—No. 27 AWG wires in a cord that is attached directly or by a special plug to a portable appliance rated not over 50 W.

2. *All fixture wires* must be protected in accordance with their ampacities, as given in Table 402-5.

3. The required protection may be provided by use of supplementary over-current protective devices (usually fuses), instead of having branch-circuit protection rated at the low values involved.

Then the basic rules are modified by an Exception applying to each of the above rules:

Exception No. 1 applies only to a flexible cord or a tinsel cord (not an "extension cord") that is "approved for and used with a specific *listed* (by UL or other recognized test lab) appliance or portable lamp." Such a cord, under the conditions stated, is not required to be protected at its ampacity from NEC Table 400-5 where it is

- Tinsel cord or No. 18 cord or larger, connected to a branch circuit rated not over 20 A.
- No. 16 cord or larger, connected to a branch circuit rated not over 30 A.
- Cord with 20 A or greater ampacity, connected on a circuit rated up to 50 A.

Note that "extension cords" are *not* covered by Exception No. 1 because they are *not* "approved for and used with a specific listed appliance." As a result, No. 16 and No. 18 extension cords *must* be fused at their ampacity values (7, 10, 13 amps, etc., from Table 400-5). *But,* Exception No. 3 of this section says that a "listed" extension cord set that contains No. 16 wire does not require protection at its amp rating and is considered to be protected by a 20-A branch-circuit fuse or CB. Extension cords with larger wire may also be used in any length on a 20-A branch circuit.

Exception No. 2 gives the conditions under which fixture wire does not have to be protected at the ampacity value given in Table 402-5 for its particular size *if* the fixture wire is any one of the following

- No. 18 wire, not over 50 ft long, connected to a branch circuit rated not over 20 A.
- No. 16 wire, not over 100 ft long, connected to a branch circuit rated not over 20 A.
- No. 14 or larger wire, of any length, connected to a branch circuit rated not over 30 A.
- No. 12 or larger wire, of any length, connected to a branch circuit rated not over 50 A.

From those rules, No. 16 or No. 18 fixture wire may be connected on any 20-A branch circuit provided the "run length" (the length of any one of the wires used in the raceway) is not more than 50 ft—such as for 4- to 6-ft fixture whips [Sec. 410-67(c)]. But, for remote-control circuits run in raceway from a magnetic motor starter or contactor to a remote pushbutton station or other pilot-control device, Secs. 430-72(b) and 725-12 require that a No. 18 wire be protected at not over 7 A and a No. 16 wire at not over 10 A—where fixture wires are used for remote-control circuit wiring, as permitted by Sec. 725-16(a) and (b).

The top sketch in Fig. 240-8 shows use of No. 18 or No. 16 fixture wire without need for separate protection when tapped from a 20-A branch circuit supplying recessed fixtures where higher temperature wire is required by Sec. 410-67(c), where, for instance, a fixture calls for 150°C wire to its hot terminal box. Of course, use of fixture wire must also satisfy all other Code rules that apply—as in Art. 400 on cords, Art. 402 on fixture wires, and Sec. 725-16 on fixture wires for control circuits.

In Exception No. 1, the tabulation shows minimum sizes of flexible cords that may be used on circuits rated at 20, 30, 40, and 50 A. A similar tabulation in Exception No. 2 for fixture wire eliminates cross-referencing Sec. 240-4 to amp ratings of tap conductors given in Exception No. 1 of Sec. 210-19(c).

According to Exception No. 3, any listed extension cord set using No. 16 gage wire is considered protected by 20-A branch-circuit protection (bottom of Fig. 240-8). The basic rule of this section requires that "extension cords" be protected against overcurrent in accordance with their ampacities as specified in Table 400-5. Based on that rule, manufactured extension cord sets with No. 18 wire must incorporate overcurrent protection in the plug cap of the set, with a rating of not over 10 A for the No. 18 wire, from Column B of Table 400-5. When such an extension cord is plugged into a receptacle, if an overload (above 10 A) is placed on the cord, the protection will open the circuit.

Although this section in the 1984 **NEC** required a similar protection (rated at 13 A) for No. 16 extension cord sets over 25 ft long, a revision of Exception No. 3 permits a No. 16 extension cord set of any length to be used without any special protection for the cord set—provided it is plugged into a receptacle or a branch circuit rated not over 20 A.

240-6. Standard Ampere Ratings.   This is a listing of the "standard ampere ratings" of fuses and CBs for purposes of **Code** application. However, an important qualification is made by the fine-print note (FPN) at the end of this section. Although this **NEC** section designates "STANDARD ampere ratings" for fuses and circuit breakers, UL-listed fuses and circuit breakers of other intermediate ratings are available and may be used if their ratings satisfy **Code** rules on protection. For instance, Sec. 240-6 shows standard rated fuses at 1200 A, then 1600 A. But if a circuit was found to have an ampacity of, say, 1530 A and, because Exception No. 4 of Sec. 240-3 says such a circuit may not be protected by 1600-A fuses, it is not necessary to drop down to 1200-A fuses (the next lower standard size). This FPN fully intends to recognize use of 1500-A fuses—which would satisfy the basic rule of Sec. 240-3 and the disallowal of Exception No. 4 for protection rated over 800 A. (Fig. 240-1.)

The Exception to the first paragraph of Sec. 240-6 designates specific "additional standard ratings" of fuses at 1, 3, 6, 10, and 601 A. These values apply *only* to fuses and *not* to CBs. The 601-A rating gives **Code** recognition to use of Class L fuses rated less than 700 A. The reasoning of the **Code** panel was:

An examination of fuse manufacturers' catalogs will show that 601 amperes is a commonly listed current rating for the Class L nontime-delay fuse. Section 430-52 (Exception No. 2d) also lists this current rating as a break point in application rules.

Without a 601 ampere rating, the smallest standard fuse which can be used in Class L fuse clips is rated 700 amperes. Since the intent of Table 430-152 and Section 430-52 is to encourage closer short-circuit protection, it seems prudent to encourage availability and use of 601-ampere fuses in combination motor controllers having Class L fuse clips.

Because ratings of inverse time circuit breakers are not related to fuse clip size, a distinction between 600 and 601 amperes in circuit breakers would serve no useful

Exception No. 2 —

Typical use of fixture wire:
4-to-6-ft length of flex for
fixture whip in ceiling, containing
two No. 18 Type AF wires (for 6-A
fixture load, see Section 402-5)
or two No. 16 Type AF wires (for
8-A fixture load). Section 240-4
permits No. 16 and No. 18 fixture
wire to be protected at 20 A.

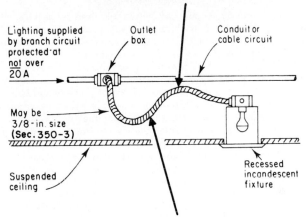

Lighting supplied
by branch circuit
protected at
not over
20 A

Outlet
box

Conduit or
cable circuit

May be
3/8-in. size
(Sec. 350-3)

Suspended
ceiling

Recessed
incandescent
fixture

**IMPORTANT!! Flex is equipment grounding
conductor** because AF wires in flex are tapped
from circuit protected at not over 20-A as permitted
in Section 250-91(b), Exception No. 1.

Exception No. 3 —

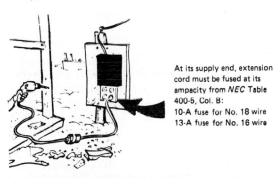

At its supply end, extension
cord must be fused at its
ampacity from *NEC* Table
400-5, Col. B:
10-A fuse for No. 18 wire
13-A fuse for No. 16 wire

NOTE: Exception No. 3 permits a "listed extension
cord set that contains No. 16 wire to be
connected to a receptacle on a branch
circuit protected at 15 or 20 A — without need
for separate protection for the cord set.

Fig. 240-8. Separate rules cover fixture wires and extension cords.
[Sec. 240-4.]

purpose. Hence, inverse-time circuit breaker ratings are listed separately. Such separation also facilitates recognition of other fuse ratings as standard.

The smaller sizes of fuses (1, 3, 6, and 10 A) listed as "standard ratings" provide more effective short-circuit and ground-fault protection for motor circuits—in accordance with Sec. 430-52, Sec. 430-40, and UL requirements for protecting the overload relays in controllers for very small motors. The Code panel reasoning was as follows:

> Fuses rated less than 15 amperes are often required to provide short circuit and ground-fault protection for motor branch circuits in accordance with Section 430-52.
>
> Tests indicate that fuses rated 1, 3, 6 and 10 amperes can provide the intended protection in motor branch circuits for motors having full load currents less than 3.75 amperes (3.75 × 400% = 15). These ratings are also those most commonly shown on control manufacturers' overload relay tables. Overload relay elements for very small full load motor currents have such a high resistance that a bolted fault at the controller load terminals produces a short-circuit current of less than 15 amperes, regardless of the available current at the line terminals. An overcurrent protective device rated or set for 15 amperes is unable to offer the short circuit or ground fault protection required by Section 110-10 in such circuits.
>
> An examination of fuse manufacturers' catalogs will show that fuses with these ratings are commercially available. Having these ampere ratings established as standard should improve product availability at the user level and result in better overcurrent protection.
>
> Since inverse time circuit breakers are not readily available in the sizes added, it seems appropriate to list them separately.

Listing of those smaller fuse ratings has a significant effect on use of several small motors (fractional and small-integral-horsepower sizes) on a single branch circuit as described under Sec. 430-53(b).

Important Last Paragraph: If a circuit breaker has external means for changing its continuous-current rating (the value of current above which the inverse-time overload—or long-time delay— trip mechanism would be activated), the breaker must be considered to be a protective device of the maximum continuous current (or overload trip rating) for which it might be set. This type of CB adjustment is available on molded-case, insulated-case, and air power circuit breakers. As a result of that rule and Sec. 240-3, the circuit conductors connected to the load terminals of such a circuit breaker must be of sufficient ampacity as to be properly protected by the maximum current value to which the adjustable trip might be set. That means that the CB rating must not exceed the ampacity of the circuit conductors, except that where the ampacity of the conductor does not correspond to a standard rating of CB, the next higher standard rating of CB may be used, up to 800 A (Fig. 240-9).

Prior to the 1987 edition, the NEC did not require that a circuit breaker with adjustable or changeable trip rating must have load-circuit conductors of an ampacity at least equal to the highest trip rating at which the breaker might be used. Conductors of an ampacity less than the highest possible trip rating could be used provided that the actual trip setting being used did protect the conductor in accordance with its ampacity, as required in NEC Sec. 240-3. Now, such application may be made only in accordance with the Exception to this rule, which says that an adjustable-trip circuit breaker may be used as a protective

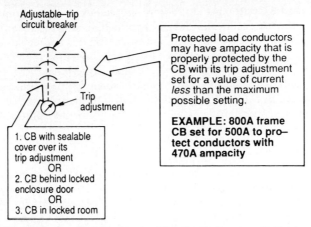

Adjustable–trip circuit breaker

Trip adjustment

Protected load conductors may have ampacity that is properly protected by the CB with its trip adjustment set for a value of current *less* than the maximum possible setting.

EXAMPLE: 800A frame CB set for 500A to pro—tect conductors with 470A ampacity

1. CB with sealable cover over its trip adjustment
OR
2. CB behind locked enclosure door
OR
3. CB in locked room

Fig. 240·9. An adjustable-trip circuit breaker that has access to its trip-adjustment limited only to qualified persons may be taken to have a rating less than the maximum value to which the continuous rating (the long-time or over-load adjustment) might be set. (Sec. 240-6.)

device of a rating lower than its maximum setting and used to protect conductors of a corresponding ampacity in accordance with Sec. 240-3 (and its Exception No. 4) *if* the trip-adjustment is

1. Located behind a removable and sealable cover, or
2. Part of a circuit breaker which is itself located behind bolted equipment enclosure doors accessible only to qualified persons or part of a circuit breaker that is locked behind doors (such as in a room) accessible only to qualified persons

Although this rule and its Exception permit use of conductors with ampacity lower than the maximum possible trip setting of a CB under the conditions given, this does not apply to fusible switches and it is never necessary for a fusible switch to have its connected load-circuit conductors of ampacity equal to the maximum rating of a fuse that might be installed in the switch—provided that the actual rating of the fuse used in the switch does protect the conductor at its ampacity.

240·8. Fuses or Circuit Breakers in Parallel. The basic rule *prohibits* the use of parallel fuses, which at one time was acceptable when fused switches had ratings above 600 A. However, fused switches and *single fuses* (such as Class L) are now readily available in sizes up to 6,000 A. Moreover, this rule prohibits the use of CBs in parallel unless they are tested and approved as a single unit. At one time, this **Code** rule did not mention CBs. However, it is acceptable to factory-assemble CBs or fuses in parallel and have them tested and approved as a unit.

240·10. Supplementary Overcurrent Protection. Supplementary overcurrent protection is commonly used in lighting fixtures, heating circuits, appliances, or other utilization equipment to provide individual protection for specific components within the equipment itself. Such protection is not branch-circuit protection and *the* **NE Code** *does not require supplemental overcurrent protective devices to be readily accessible.* Typical applications of supplemental overcurrent protection are fuses installed in fluorescent fixtures and cooking or heating equipment where the devices are sized to provide lower overcurrent protection than that of the branch circuit supplying such equipment. This is discussed under Sec. 424-19 and Sec. 424-22 on electric space heating equipment.

In application, Sec. 240-10 is frequently tied into the rule of Sec. 240-24. An example of this relationship is explained in the following comments of a consulting engineer:

"It has, for several years, been a common design practice in our office to specify the installation of fusible disconnect switches at motors located above suspended ceilings. As permitted by **NEC** Sec. 424, fuses and/or circuit breakers may be installed above suspended ceilings for the protection of fixed electric space heating equipment. But we specify fusible disconnects for air-handling equipment, with and without integral electric strip heaters and for electric duct heaters.

Possibly the most frequently occurring condition is that of small fan and cooling units that have fractional horsepower (½ to ¼ hp), 120-V, single-phase motors. We have routinely specified the installation of switch-and-plug fuse-combination units as the disconnecting means for the motor. We also routinely specify fusible disconnects for larger 3-phase fan-and-coil units mounted above suspended ceilings."

Question: Is such practice considered to be in compliance with **Code** requirements based upon Secs. 240-10 and 240-24(a), Exception No. 2, and Sec. 380-8, Exception No. 2?

Answer: Section 240-24(a) is a simple, basic rule that requires overcurrent devices (fuses and CBs) to be "readily accessible"—that is, they may not be installed where a portable ladder would be needed to get to them, such as above a suspended ceiling. Exception No. 2 of that rule, however, permits "supplementary overcurrent protection" to be installed where it is not "readily accessible" provided the rules of Sec. 240-10 are observed.

Section 240-10 says that "supplementary overcurrent devices" do not have to be "readily accessible." But such devices must be truly "supplementary"—that is, they must be protective devices that are used in addition to branch-circuit protective devices required by the **Code**. Such devices must not be used as "a substitute" for required branch-circuit protection and must not be used "in place of" such required protection.

In the installations described above, the fuses in the high-mounted disconnect switches are not permitted to serve as the required motor branch-circuit protection. In each circuit to a fan motor, required motor branch-circuit protection must be placed where it is readily accessible—which means down near floor level and not up in the ceiling space. In such a case, it would be permitted for "additional" fuses to be installed in the switch up in the ceiling space because those fuses would be "supplementary" fuses and not *required* fuses. But such application would simply be duplicate protection and would pose the disadvantage that blowing of the high-mounted fuses would require use of a ladder to replace them, which is inconvenient and time wasting and is considered to be the unsafe practice that is the basis for the rule of Sec. 240-24 requiring ready accessibility.

If the fuses in a high-mounted disconnect switch are required by UL marking on the motor controller stating that the controller must be protected by fuses of a specified maximum rating, they would be considered to be supplementary protection "for internal circuits and components of equipment"—as described in Sec. 240-10. But because **NEC** Sec. 110-3(b) makes it a mandatory **Code** rule to follow all "instructions included in the listing" of any product—such as the UL rule that specifies maximum fuse protection for a controller—such fuses are *not* optional or "in addition" to **Code**-required protection. But if such fuses do not constitute required branch-circuit protection they would satisfy Sec. 240-10 as supplementary devices and would be acceptable. Section 424-22 clearly spells out use of "supplementary" protection for subdivided heater circuits and makes clear that "supplementary protection" can be required by the **NEC**. Section 430-53(c) requires supplementary overcurrent protection for "group installation" of two or more motors connected to a *single* branch circuit, and that is commonly encountered in motor devices for air-conditioning equipment.

Fusible switches or CBs mounted so they are not readily accessible are not permitted by the **Code** for other than supplementary protection. Some local codes require *all* overcurrent protective devices to be readily accessible—not more than 6½ ft above the floor or platform from which they may be reached. It is a safety matter to be able to reach protective devices readily for replacement or resetting, and the argument can be made that it is not a hardship in any way to make all protective devices—service, feeder, branch-circuit, and supplementary devices—readily accessible.

240·12. Electrical System Coordination. This rule applies to any electrical installation where hazard to personnel would result from disorderly shutdown of electrical equipment under fault conditions. The purpose of this rule is to permit elimination of "overload" protection—i.e., protection of conductors at their ampacities—and to eliminate unknown or random relation between operating time of overcurrent devices connected in series.

[As worded in previous **NEC** editions, this rule permitted elimination of overload protection for circuit conductors only for "industrial locations." Now, it may be applied in any electrical system (industrial, commercial, institutional, or residential).]

The section recognizes two requirements, both of which must be fulfilled to perform the task of "orderly shutdown."

One is selective coordination of the time-current characteristics of the short-circuit protective devices in series from the service to any load—so that, automatically, any fault will actuate only the short-circuit protective device closest to the fault on the line side of the fault, thereby minimizing the extent of electrical outage due to a fault.

The other technique that must also be included if *overload* protection is eliminated is "overload indication based on monitoring systems or devices." A note to this section gives brief descriptions of both requirements and establishes only a generalized understanding of "overload indication." Effective application of this rule depends upon careful design and coordination with inspection authorities.

It should be noted, however, that it says that the technique of eliminating overload protection to afford orderly shutdown "shall be permitted"—but does *not require* such application. Although it could be argued that the wording implies a mandatory rule, consultation with electrical inspection authorities on this matter is advisable because of the safety implications in nonorderly shutdown due to overload.

240-13. Ground-Fault Protection of Equipment. Equipment ground-fault protection—of the type required for 480Y/227-V service disconnects—is now required for each disconnect rated 1,000 A or more that serves as a main disconnect for a building or structure. Like Sec. 215-10, this section expands the application of protection against destructive arcing burndowns of electrical equipment. The intent is to equip a main building disconnect with GFP whether the disconnect is technically a service disconnect or a building disconnect on the load side of service equipment located elsewhere. This was specifically devised to cover those cases where a building or structure is supplied by a 480Y/277-V feeder from another building or from outdoor service equipment. Because the main disconnect (or disconnects) for such a building serves essentially the same function as a service disconnect, this requirement makes such disconnects subject to all of the rules of Sec. 230-95, covering GFP for services (Fig. 240-10).

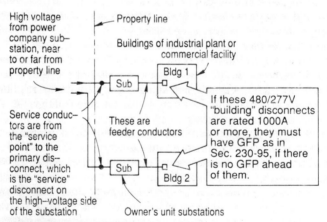

Fig. 240-10. Ground-fault protection is required for the feeder disconnect for each building—either at the building or at the substation secondary. (Sec. 240-13.)

The first exception here excludes the need for such GFP from disconnects for critical processes where automatic shutdown would introduce additional or different hazards. And as with service GFP, the requirement does not apply to fire-pump disconnects.

Exception No. 3 also suspends the need for GFP on a building or structure disconnect *if* such protection is provided on the upstream (line) side of the building disconnect. The rule also stipulates that there must not be any desensitizing of the ground-fault protection because of neutral and/or grounding electrode connections that return current to the neutral on the load side of the service ground-fault sensing hookup.

240-20. Ungrounded Conductors. A fuse or circuit breaker must be connected in series with each ungrounded circuit conductor—usually at the supply end of the conductor. A current transformer and relay that actuates contacts of a CB is considered to be an overcurrent trip unit, like a fuse or a direct-acting CB (Fig. 240-11).

Although part **(b)** basically requires a CB to open all ungrounded conductors of a circuit simultaneously, the Exception covers acceptable uses of a number of single-pole CBs instead of multipole CBs.

The basic rule on use of single-pole versus multipole CBs is covered in this section.

Circuit breakers must open simultaneously all ungrounded conductors of circuits they protect; i.e., they must be multipole CB units, except that individual single-pole CBs may be used for protection of each ungrounded conductor of certain types of circuits, including 3-wire single-phase circuits, or lighting or appliance branch circuits connected to 4-wire, 3-phase systems provided that such lighting or appliance circuits are supplied from a grounded-neutral system and the loads are connected line-to-neutral. Figure 240-12 covers the rules.

Note: Two single-pole circuit breakers may not be used on "ungrounded 2-wire circuits"—such as 208-, 240-, or 480-V single-phase, 2-wire circuits. A 2-pole CB must be used if protection is provided by CBs. Use of single-pole CBs with handle ties but not common-trip is not allowed. This rule is intended to assure that a ground fault will trip open both conductors of an ungrounded 2-wire circuit derived from a grounded system. However, use of fuses for protection of such a circuit is permitted even though it will present the same chance of a fault condition as shown in Fig. 240-12.

Although 1-pole CBs may be used, as noted, it is better practice to use multipole CBs for circuits to individual load devices which are supplied by two or more ungrounded conductors. It is never wrong to use a multipole CB; but, based on the rules given here and in Sec. 210-4, it may be a violation to use single-pole CB units. A 3-pole CB must always be used for a 3-phase, 3-wire circuit supplying phase-to-phase loads fed from an ungrounded delta system, such as 480-V outdoor lighting for a parking lot, as permitted by Sec. 210-6(b).

Refer also to Sec. 210-4 for limitation on use of single-pole protective devices with line-to-neutral loads. And Sec. 110-3(b) requires that use of single-pole CBs be related to UL rules as described in Fig. 240-13.

Part **(c)** of this section excludes "closed-loop power distribution systems" from the need for fuse or circuit-breaker protection. In such systems (covered by **NEC** Art. 780), "listed devices" that provide equivalent protection may be used instead.

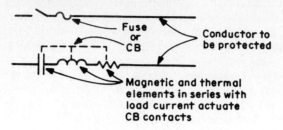

PROTECTIVE DEVICE IN SERIES

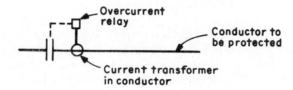

CT—RELAY RESPONDS TO LOAD CURRENT

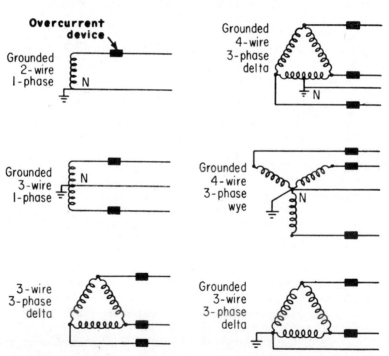

Fig. 240-11. A fuse or overcurrent trip unit must be connected in series with each ungrounded conductor. (Sec. 240-20.)

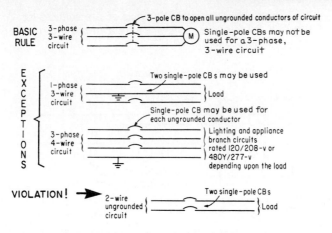

VIOLATION!

THIS IS THE POSSIBLE HAZARDOUS CONDITION —

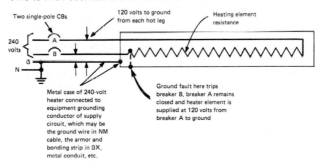

NOTE: A similar faulty condition could develop if the above hookup consisted of two single-pole breakers supplying 480 volts to the primary of a single-phase 480-240/120-volt transformer.

SINGLE-POLE BREAKERS MAY NOT BE USED LIKE THIS —

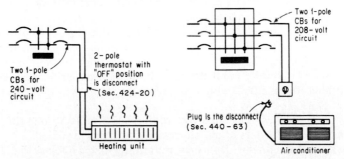

Fig. 240·12. Single-pole vs. multipole breakers. (Sec. 240-20.)

1. "Single-pole CBs rated 120 volts ac are suitable for use in a single-phase multiwire circuit where the neutral is connected to the load."

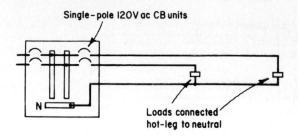

Single-pole 120V ac CB units

N

Loads connected
hot-leg to neutral

2. "Single-pole circuit breakers rated 120/240 volts ac are suitable for use in a single-phase multiwire circuit *with or without* the neutral connected to the load."

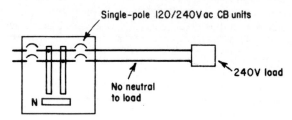

Single-pole 120/240V ac CB units

240V load

No neutral
to load

N

Fig. 240·13. NE Code rules must be correlated with the above UL requirements. (Sec. 240-20.)

240·21. Location in Circuit. The basic rule of this section and Exception No. 1 is shown in Fig. 240-14.

Although basic **Code** requirements dictate the use of an overcurrent device at the point at which a conductor receives its supply, exceptions to this rule are made in the case of taps to feeders. That is, to meet the practical demands of field application, certain lengths of unprotected conductors may be used to tap energy from protected feeder conductors.

Exceptions to the rule for protecting conductors at their points of supply are made in the case of 10-, 25-, and 100-ft taps from a feeder, as described in Sec. 240-21, Exceptions No. 2, No. 3, and No. 10. Application of the tap exceptions should be made carefully to effectively minimize any sacrifice in safety. The tap exceptions are permitted without overcurrent protective devices at the point of supply.

Exception No. 2 says that unprotected taps not over 10 ft long (Fig. 240-15) may be made from feeders or transformer secondaries provided:

1. The smaller conductors have a current rating that is not less than the com-

BASIC RULE

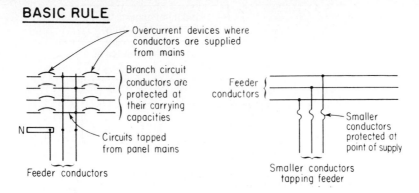

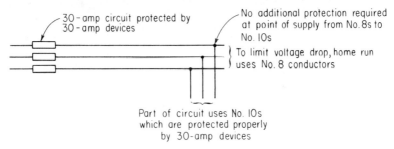

EXCEPTION No. 1

PROTECTING TWO SIZES OF CONDUCTORS

Fig. 240-14. Conductors must be protected at their supply ends. (Sec. 240-21.)

bined computed loads of the circuits supplied by the tap conductors and must have ampacity of—

Not less than the rating of the "device" supplied by the tap conductors, or

Not less than the rating of the overcurrent device (fuses or CB) that might be installed at the termination of the tap conductors.

Important Limitation: For any 10-ft unprotected feeder tap installed in the field, the rule limits its connection to a feeder that has protection rated *not more* than 1,000 percent of (10 times) the ampacity of the tap conductor. Under the rule, unprotected No. 14 tap conductors are not permitted to tap a feeder any larger than 1,000 percent of the 20-A ampacity of No. 14 copper conductors—which would limit such a tap for use with a maximum feeder protective device of not over 10 × 20 A, or 200 A.

2. The tap does not extend beyond the switchboard, panelboard, or control device which it supplies.

3. The tap conductors are enclosed in conduit, EMT, metal gutter, or other approved raceway when not a part of the switchboard or panelboard.

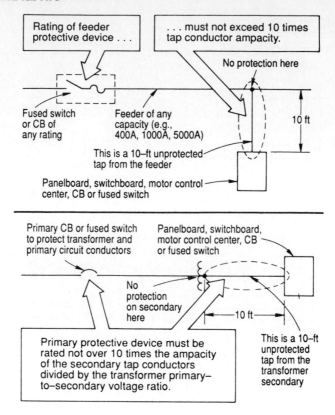

Rating of feeder protective device . . .

. . . must not exceed 10 times tap conductor ampacity.

No protection here

Fused switch or CB of any rating

Feeder of any capacity (e.g., 400A, 1000A, 5000A)

10 ft

This is a 10–ft unprotected tap from the feeder

Panelboard, switchboard, motor control center, CB or fused switch

Primary CB or fused switch to protect transformer and primary circuit conductors

Panelboard, switchboard, motor control center, CB or fused switch

No protection on secondary here

10 ft

Primary protective device must be rated not over 10 times the ampacity of the secondary tap conductors divided by the transformer primary–to–secondary voltage ratio.

This is a 10–ft unprotected tap from the transformer secondary

EXAMPLE: If the above transformer is stepping 480V single phase down to 240/120V single phase, and the 10–ft tap conductors on the transformer secondary have an ampacity of 100A, the primary feeder CB must be rated not more than 10 times 100A divided by two (480/240), or 500A.

Fig. 240·15. Ten-ft taps may be made from a feeder or a transformer secondary. (Sec. 240-21.)

Exception No. 2 specifically recognizes that a 10-ft tap may be made from a transformer secondary in the same way it has always been permitted from a feeder. In either case, the tap conductors must not be over 10 ft long and must have ampacity not less than the amp rating of the switchboard, panelboard, or control device—or the tap conductors may be terminated in an overcurrent protective device rated not more than the ampacity of the tap conductors. In the case of an unprotected tap from a transformer secondary, the ampacity of the 10-ft tap conductors would have to be related through the transformer voltage ratio to the size of the transformer primary protective device—which in such a case would be "the overcurrent device on the line side of the tap conductors."

Taps not over 25 ft long (Fig. 240-16) may be made from feeders, as noted in Exception No. 3, provided:

1. The smaller conductors have a current rating at least one-third that of the feeder overcurrent device rating or of the conductors from which they are tapped.

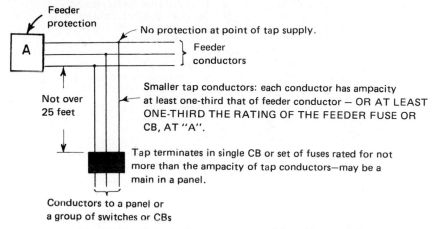

Fig. 240·16. Sizing feeder taps not over 25 ft long. (Sec. 240-21.)

2. The tap conductors are suitably protected from mechanical damage. In previous **Code** editions, the 25-ft feeder tap without overcurrent protection at its supply end simply had to be "suitably protected from physical damage"—which could accept use of cable for such a tap. Now, the rule requires such tap conductors to be "enclosed in a raceway"—just as has always been required for 10-ft tap conductors.

3. The tap is terminated in a single CB or set of fuses which will limit the load on the tap to the ampacity of the tap conductors.

Examples of Taps

Figure 240-17 shows use of a 10-ft feeder tap to supply a single motor branch circuit. The conduit feeder may be a horizontal run or a vertical run, such as a riser. If the tap conductors are of such size that they have a current rating at least one-third that of the feeder conductors (or protection rating) from which they are tapped, they could be run a distance of 25 ft without protection at the point of tap-off from the feeder because they would comply with the rules of Exception No. 3 which permit a 25-ft tap if the conductors terminate in a single protective device rated not more than the conductor ampacity. Because Sec. 364-12 requires that any busway used as a feeder must have overcurrent protection on the busway for any subfeeder or branch circuit tapped from the busway, the use of a cable-tap box on busway without overcurrent protection (as

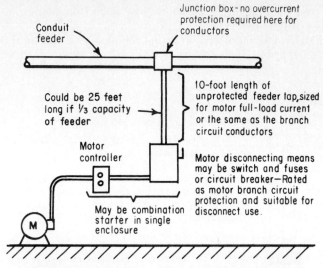

Fig. 240·17. A 10-ft tap for a single motor circuit. (Sec. 240-21.)

shown in the conduit installation of Fig. 240-17) would be a violation. Refer to Secs. 240-24 and 364-12.

A common application of the 10-ft tap exception is the supply of panelboards from conduit feeders or busways, as shown in Fig. 240-18. The case shows an interesting requirement that arises from Sec. 384-16, which requires that lighting and appliance panelboards be protected on their supply side by overcurrent

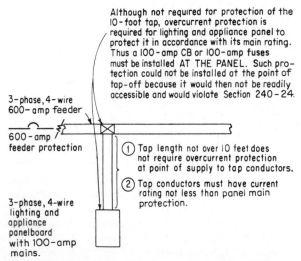

Fig. 240·18. A 10-ft tap to lighting panel with unprotected conductors. (Sec. 240-21.)

protection rated not more than the rating of the panelboard busbars. If the feeder is busway, the protection must be placed (a requirement of Sec. 364-12) at the point of tap on the busway. In that case a 100-A CB or fused switch on the busway would provide the required protection of the panel, and the panel would not require a main in it. But, if the feeder circuit is in conduit, the 100-A panel protection would have to be in the panel or just ahead of it. It could not be at the junction box on the conduit because that would make it not readily accessible and therefore a violation of Sec. 240-24. With a conduit feeder, a fused-switch or CB main in the panelboard could be rated up to the 100-A main rating.

For transformer applications, typical 10- and 25-ft tap considerations are shown in Fig. 240-19.

Figure 240-20 shows application of Exception No. 8 of Sec. 240-21 in conjunction with the rule of Sec. 450-3(b) (2), covering transformer protection. As shown in Example 1, the 100-A main protection in the panel is sufficient protection for the transformer and the primary and secondary conductors when these conditions are met:

1. Tap conductors have ampacity at least one-third that of the 125-A feeder conductors.
2. Secondary conductors are rated at least one-third the ampacity of the 125-A feeder conductors, based on the primary-to-secondary transformer ratio.
3. Total tap is not over 25 ft, primary plus secondary.
4. All conductors are in conduit.
5. Secondary conductors terminate in the 100-A main protection that limits secondary load to the ampacity of the secondary conductor and simultaneously provides the protection required by the lighting panel and is not rated over 125 percent of transformer secondary current.
6. Primary feeder protection is not over 250 percent of transformer rated primary current, as recognized by Sec. 450-3(b) (2), and the 100-A main breaker in the panel satisfies as the required "overcurrent device on the secondary side rated or set at not more than 125 percent of the rated secondary current of the transformer."

In Example 2, each set of tap conductors from the primary feeder to each transformer may be same size as primary feeder conductors **or** may be smaller than primary conductors if sized in accordance with Sec. 240-21, Exception No. 8—which permits a 25-ft tap from a primary feeder to be made up of both primary and secondary tap conductors. The 25-ft tap may have any part of its length on the primary or secondary but must not be longer than 25 ft and must terminate in a single CB or set of fuses.

Figure 240-21 shows another example of Exception No. 8 and Sec. 450-3(b) (2). Because the primary wires tapped to each transformer from the main 100-A feeder are also rated 100 A and are therefore protected by the 100-A feeder protection, all the primary circuit to each transformer is excluded from the allowable 25 ft of tap to the secondary main protective device. The 100-A protection in each panel is not over 125 percent of the rated transformer secondary current. It, therefore, provides the transformer protection required by Sec. 450-

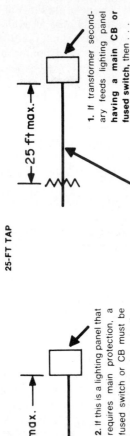

25-FT TAP

1. If transformer secondary feeds lighting panel having a **main CB or fused switch,** then . . .

2. . . . secondary tap conductors from transformer may be 25 ft long, as permitted by Section 240-21, Exception No. 3, but *only* where the tap terminates in a single CB or set of fuses.

3. Or, a 25-ft tap may be made from a transformer to a CB or fused switch in an individual enclosure or serving as a main in a switchboard or MCC.

10-FT TAP

1. A 10-ft tap may be made from transformer secondary to a panel, switchboard, MCC, etc.

2. If this is a lighting panel that requires main protection, a fused switch or CB must be installed as a main protective device in the panel or just ahead of it, at the end of the 10-ft tap.

3. If the panel is *not* a lighting panel (such as a panel with 240-volt or 480-volt heating circuits or other makeup that does not make it a lighting panel as specified in Section 384-14), then main protection is not required at all, and the 10-ft tap conductors terminate in main lugs of the panel switchboard, or other equipment.

NOTE: From a single transformer secondary of adequate capacity, more than one set of 10-ft tap conductors may be run to more than one panel or other distribution equipment.

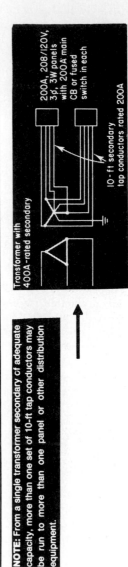

Transformer with 400A-rated secondary

200A, 208/120V, 3ϕ, 3W panels with 200A main CB or fused switch in each

10-ft secondary tap conductors rated 200A

Fig. 240-19. Taps from transformer secondaries. (Sec. 240-21.)

EXAMPLE 1:

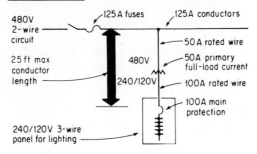

480V
2-wire
circuit

125 A fuses

125A conductors

50 A rated wire

50A primary
full-load current

100A rated wire

100A main
protection

25 ft max
conductor
length

480V

240/120V

240/120V 3-wire
panel for lighting

EXAMPLE 2:

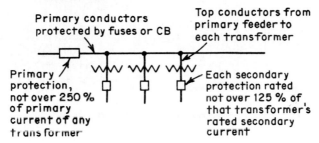

Primary conductors
protected by fuses or CB

Top conductors from
primary feeder to
each transformer

Primary
protection,
not over 250%
of primary
current of any
transformer

Each secondary
protection rated
not over 125% of
that transformer's
rated secondary
current

Fig. 240-20. Feeder tap of primary-plus-secondary not over 25 ft
long. (Sec. 240-21.)

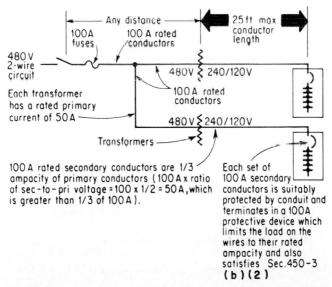

Any distance

25 ft max
conductor
length

100A
fuses

100 A rated
conductors

480 V
2-wire
circuit

480V 240/120V

100 A rated
conductors

Each transformer
has a rated primary
current of 50A

480V 240/120V

Transformers

100 A rated secondary conductors are 1/3
ampacity of primary conductors (100 A x ratio
of sec-to-pri voltage =100 x 1/2 = 50 A, which
is greater than 1/3 of 100 A).

Each set of
100 A secondary
conductors is suitably
protected by conduit and
terminates in a 100A
protective device which
limits the load on the
wires to their rated
ampacity and also
satisfies Sec.450-3
(b)(2)

Fig. 240-21. Sizing a 25-ft tap and transformer protection. (Sec. 240-21.)

3(b) (2). The same device also protects each panel at its main busbar rating of 100 A.

Figure 240-22 compares the two different 25-ft tap techniques covered by Exception No. 3 and Exception No. 8.

As shown in Fig. 240-23, Exception No. 9 gives permission for unprotected

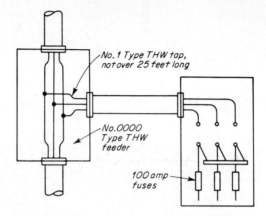

No. 1 Type THW tap, not over 25 feet long

No. 0000 Type THW feeder

100 amp fuses

25-ft tap — EXCEPTION No. 3

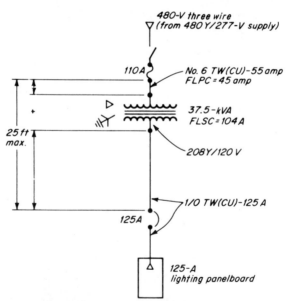

480-V three wire (from 480 Y/277-V supply)

110 A

No. 6 TW(CU)–55 amp FLPC = 45 amp

37.5-kVA FLSC = 104 A

25 ft max.

208Y/120 V

1/0 TW(CU)–125 A

125 A

125-A lighting panelboard

Taps protected from physical damage.
Secondary-to-primary voltage ratio = 208:480 = 1:2.3

25-ft tap — EXCEPTION No. 8

Fig. 240-22. Examples show difference between the two types of 25-ft taps. (Sec. 240-21.)

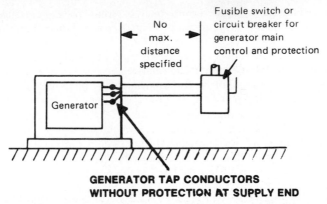

GENERATOR TAP CONDUCTORS
WITHOUT PROTECTION AT SUPPLY END

Fig. 240-23. Unprotected tap may be made from a generator's output
terminals to the first overcurrent device. (Sec. 240-21, Exception No. 9.)

taps to be made from generator terminals to the first overcurrent device it supplies—such as in the fusible switch or circuit breakers used for control and
protection of the circuit that the generator supplies. As the exception is worded,
no maximum length is specified for the generator tap conductors. But because
the tap conductors terminate in a single circuit breaker or set of fuses rated or
set for the tap-conductor ampacity, tap conductors up to 25 ft long would comply with the basic concept given in Exception No. 3 for 25-ft taps. And Sec. 445-
5, which is referenced, requires the tap conductors to have an ampacity of at
least 115 percent of the generator nameplate current rating.

Exception No. 10 is another departure from the rule that conductors must be
provided with overcurrent protection at their supply ends, where they receive
current from other larger conductors or from a transformer. Exception No. 10
permits a longer length than the 10-ft unprotected tap of Exception No. 2 and
the 25-ft tap of Exceptions No. 3 and No. 8. Under specified conditions that are
similar to the requirements of the 25-ft-tap exception, an unprotected tap up to
100 ft in length may be used in "high-bay manufacturing buildings" that are
over 35 ft high at the walls—but only "where conditions of maintenance and
supervision assure that only qualified persons will service the system." Obviously, that last phrase can lead to some very subjective and individualistic
determinations by the authorities enforcing the Code. And the phrase "35 ft
high at the walls" means that this Exception cannot be applied where the height
is over 35 ft at the peak of a triangular or curved roof section but less than 35
ft at the walls.

The 100-ft-tap exception must meet specific conditions:

1. From the point at which the tap is made to a larger feeder, the tap run
   must not have more than 25 ft of its length run horizontally, and the sum
   of horizontal run and vertical run must not exceed 100 ft. Figure 240-24
   shows some of the almost limitless configurations of tap layout that would
   fall within the dimension limitations.
2. The tap conductors must have an ampacity equal to at least one-third of
   the rating of the overcurrent device protecting the larger feeder conductors from which the tap is made.

3. The tap conductors must terminate in a circuit breaker or fused switch, where the rating of overcurrent protection is not greater than the tap-conductor ampacity.

4. The tap conductors must be protected from physical damage and must be installed in metal or nonmetallic raceway.

5. There must be no splices in the total length of each of the conductors of the tap.

6. The tap conductors must not be smaller than No. 6 copper or No. 4 aluminum.

7. The tap conductors must not pass through walls, floors, or ceilings.

8. The point at which the tap conductors connect to the feeder conductors must be at least 30 ft above the floor of the building.

As shown in Fig. 240-24, the tap conductors from a feeder protected at 1,200 A are rated at not less than one-third the protection rating, or 400 A. Although 500 kcmil THW copper is rated at 380 A, that value does not satisfy the minimum requirement for 400 A. But if 500 kcmil THHN or XHHW copper, with an ampacity of 430 A, were used for the tap conductors, the rule would be satisfied. However, in such a case, those conductors would have to be used as if their ampacity were 380 A for the purpose of load calculation because of the

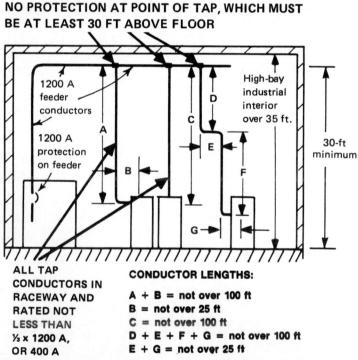

Fig. 240·24. Unprotected taps up to 100 ft long may be used in "high-bay manufacturing buildings."

general UL rule of 75°C conductor terminations for connecting to equipment rated over 100 A—such as the panelboard, switch, motor-control center or other equipment fed by the taps. And the conductors for the main feeder being tapped could be rated less than the 1,200 A shown in the sketch if the 1,200-A protection on the feeder was selected in accordance with Sec. 430-62 or Sec. 430-63 for supplying a motor load or motor and lighting load. In such cases, the overcurrent protection may be rated considerably higher than the feeder conductor ampacity. But the tap conductors must have ampacity at least equal to one-third *the feeder protection rating.*

Exception No. 11 applies exclusively to industrial electrical systems. Conductors up to 25 ft long may be tapped from a transformer secondary without overcurrent protection at their supply end and without need for a single circuit breaker or set of fuses at their load end. Normally, a transformer secondary tap over 10 ft long and up to 25 ft long must comply with the rules of Exceptions No. 3 and No. 8 of Sec. 240-21—which call for such a transformer secondary tap to be made with conductors that require no overcurrent protection at their supply end but are required to terminate at their load end in a single CB or single set of fuses with a setting or rating not over the conductor ampacity. However, Exception No. 11 permits a 10- to 25-ft tap from a transformer secondary without termination in a single main overcurrent device—but it limits the application to "Industrial Installations." The tap conductor ampacity must be at least equal to the transformer's secondary current rating and must be at least equal to the sum of the ratings of overcurrent devices supplied by the tap conductors. The conductors could come into main-lugs-only of a power panel if the conductor ampacity is at least equal to the sum of the ratings of the protective devices supplied by the busbars in the panel. Or the tap could be made to an auxiliary gutter from which a number of individually enclosed circuit breakers or fused switches are fed from the tap—provided that the ampacity of the tap conductors is at least equal to the sum of the ratings of protective devices supplied.

An example of the application of Exception No. 11 is shown at the top of Fig. 240-25. If that panel contains eight 100-A circuit breakers (or eight switches fused at 100 A), then the 25-ft tap conductors must have an ampacity of at least 8 × 100 A, or 800 A. In addition, the tap conductor ampacity must be not less than the secondary current rating of the transformer. The layout of a similar application at an auxiliary gutter is shown at the bottom of Fig. 240-25.

240-22. Grounded Conductors.   The basic rule prohibits use of a fuse or CB in any conductor that is intentionally grounded—such as a grounded neutral or a grounded phase leg of a delta system. Figure 240-26 shows the two exceptions to that rule and a clear violation of the basic rule.

240-23. Change in Size of Grounded Conductor.   In effect, this recognizes the fact that if the neutral is the same size as the ungrounded conductor, it will be protected wherever the ungrounded conductor is protected. One of the most obvious places where this is encountered is in a distribution center where a small grounded conductor may be connected directly to a large grounded feeder conductor.

240-24. Location in or on Premises.   According to part **(a)**, overcurrent devices

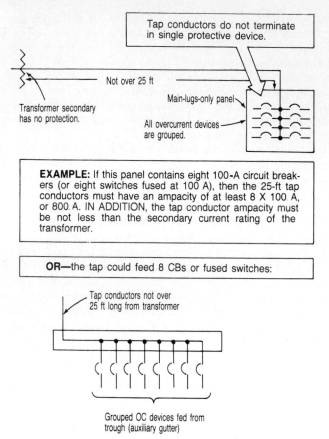

Tap conductors do not terminate in single protective device.

Not over 25 ft

Transformer secondary has no protection.

Main-lugs-only panel

All overcurrent devices are grouped.

EXAMPLE: If this panel contains eight 100-A circuit breakers (or eight switches fused at 100 A), then the 25-ft tap conductors must have an ampacity of at least 8 X 100 A, or 800 A. IN ADDITION, the tap conductor ampacity must be not less than the secondary current rating of the transformer.

OR—the tap could feed 8 CBs or fused switches:

Tap conductors not over 25 ft long from transformer

Grouped OC devices fed from trough (auxiliary gutter)

Fig. 240-25. These tap applications are permitted for transformer secondaries only in "industrial" electrical systems.

must be readily accessible. And in accordance with the definition of "readily accessible" in Art. 100, they must be "capable of being reached quickly for operation, renewal, or inspections, without requiring those to whom ready access is requisite to climb over or remove obstacles or to resort to portable ladders, chairs, etc." (Fig. 240-27).

Although the **Code** gives no maximum heights at which overcurrent protective devices are considered readily accessible, some guidance can be obtained from Sec. 380-8, which provides detailed requirements for location of switches and CBs. This section states that switches and CBs shall be so installed that the center of the grip of the operating handle, when in its highest position, will not be more than 6½ ft above the floor or working platform.

Exception No. 1 covers any case where an overcurrent device is used in a busway plug-in unit to tap a branch circuit from the busway. Section 364-12 requires that such devices consist of an externally operable CB or an externally operable fusible switch. These devices must be capable of being operated from

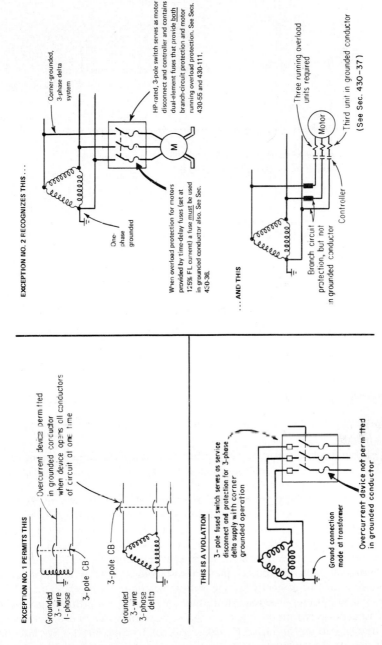

Fig. 240-26. Overcurrent protection in grounded conductor. (Sec. 240-22.)

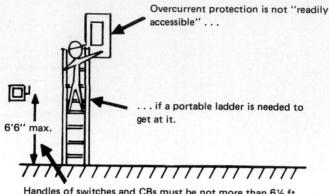

Overcurrent protection is not "readily accessible" . . .

. . . if a portable ladder is needed to get at it.

6'6" max.

Handles of switches and CBs must be not more than 6½ ft above floor or platform (Sec. 380-8).

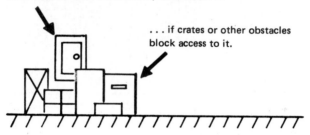

Overcurrent device in a panel, switch, CB, switchboard, MCC is not readily accessible . . .

. . . if crates or other obstacles block access to it.

Fig. 240-27. Overcurrent devices must be "readily accessible." (Sec. 240-24.)

the floor by means of ropes, chains, or sticks. Exception No. 2 refers to Sec. 240-10, which states that where supplementary overcurrent protection is used, such as for lighting fixtures, appliances, or internal circuits or components of equipment, this supplementary protection is not required to be readily accessible. An example of this would be an overcurrent device mounted in the cord plug of a fixed or semifixed luminaire supplied from trolley busway or mounted on a luminaire that is plugged directly into a busway. Exception No. 3 acknowledges that Sec. 230-92 permits service overcurrent protection to be sealed, locked, or otherwise made not readily accessible. Figure 240-28 shows these details.

Section 240-24 clarifies the use of plug-in overcurrent protective devices on busway for protection of circuits tapped from busway. After making the general rule that overcurrent protective devices must be readily accessible (capable of being reached without stepping on a chair or table or resorting to a portable ladder), Exception No. 1 notes that it is not only *permissible* to use busway protective devices up on the busway—it is *required* by Sec. 364-12. Such devices on high-mounted busway are not "readily accessible" (not within reach of a

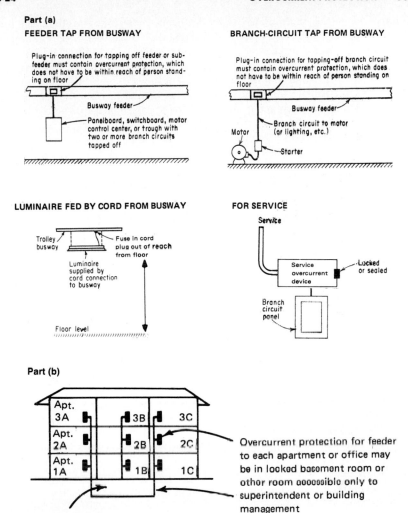

Part (a)

FEEDER TAP FROM BUSWAY

Plug-in connection for tapping off feeder or sub-feeder must contain overcurrent protection, which does not have to be within reach of person standing on floor

Busway feeder

Panelboard, switchboard, motor control center, or trough with two or more branch circuits tapped off

BRANCH-CIRCUIT TAP FROM BUSWAY

Plug-in connection for tapping-off branch circuit must contain overcurrent protection, which does not have to be within reach of person standing on floor

Busway feeder

Branch circuit to motor (or lighting, etc.)

Motor

Starter

LUMINAIRE FED BY CORD FROM BUSWAY

Trolley busway

Fuse in cord plug out of reach from floor

Luminaire supplied by cord connection to busway

Floor level

FOR SERVICE

Service

Service overcurrent device

Locked or sealed

Branch circuit panel

Part (b)

Apt. 3A	3B	3C
Apt. 2A	2B	2C
Apt. 1A	1B	1C

Overcurrent protection for feeder to each apartment or office may be in locked basement room or other room accessible only to superintendent or building management

Service equipment grouped in basement

Fig. 240·28. Fuses or CBs that are permitted to be *not* readily accessible. (Sec. 240-24.)

person standing on the floor). The wording of Sec. 364-12 makes clear that this requirement for overcurrent protection in the device on the busway applies to subfeeders tapped from the busway as well as branch circuits tapped from the busway. The rules of **NE Code** Secs. 240-24, 364-12, and 380-8 must be correlated with each other to assure effective Code compliance.

Part **(b)** applies to apartment houses and other multiple-occupancy buildings, as described in Fig. 240-28.

In addition, it is important to note that parts **(c)** and **(d)** of Sec. 240-24 require that overcurrent devices be located where they will not be exposed to physical damage or in the vicinity of easily ignitible material. Panelboards, fused switches, and circuit breakers may *not* be installed in *clothes closets* in any type of occupancy—residential, commercial, institutional, or industrial. But they may be installed in other closets that do not have easily ignitible materials within them—provided that the working clearances of Sec. 110-16 (30-in.-wide work space in front of the equipment, 6¼-ft headroom, illumination, etc.) are observed and the work space is "not used for storage," as required by Sec. 110-16(b).

240-33. Vertical Position.   Figure 240-29 shows the basic requirements of Secs. 240-30, 240-32, and 240-33.

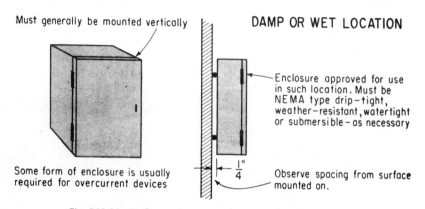

Fig. 240-29.   Enclosures for overcurrent protection. (Sec. 240-30.)

240-40. Disconnecting Means for Fuses and Thermal Cutouts.   The basic rules are shown in Fig. 240-30. Exception No. 2 is illustrated in Fig. 240-31.

240-50. General (Plug Fuses).   Plug fuses must not be used in circuits of more than 125 V between conductors, but they may be used in grounded-neutral systems where the circuits have more than 125 V between ungrounded conductors but not more than 150 V between any ungrounded conductor and ground (Fig. 240-32). And the screw-shell of plug fuseholders must be connected to the load side of the circuit.

240-51. Edison-Base Fuses.

240-52. Edison-Base Fuseholders.

240-53. Type S Fuses.

240-54. Type S Fuses, Adapters, and Fuseholders.   Rated up to 30 A, plug fuses are Edison-base or Type S. Section 240-51(b) limits the use of Edison-base fuses to replacements of existing fuses of this type. Type S plug fuses are required by Sec. 240-53 for all new plug-fuse installations. Type S plug fuses must be used in Type S fuseholders or in Edison-base fuseholders with a Type S adapter inserted, so that a Type S fuse of one ampere classification cannot be replaced with a higher-amp rated fuse (Fig. 240-33). Type S fuses, fuseholders, and adapters are rated for three classifications based on amp rating and are noninterchangeable from one classification to another. The classifications are 0–15, 16–20, and 21–30 A. The 0- to 15-A fuseholders or adapters must not be able to take

THIS IS THE RULE...

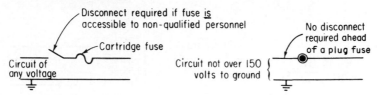

...BUT THIS IS PERMISSIBLE

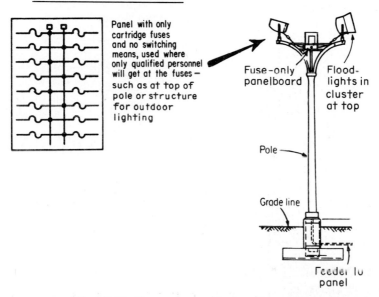

Panel with only cartridge fuses and no switching means, used where only qualified personnel will get at the fuses — such as at top of pole or structure for outdoor lighting

Fuse-only panelboard

Flood-lights in cluster at top

Pole

Grade line

Feeder to panel

Fig. 240·30. Disconnect means for fuses. (Sec. 240-40.)

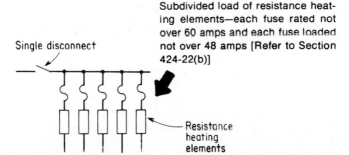

Subdivided load of resistance heating elements—each fuse rated not over 60 amps and each fuse loaded not over 48 amps [Refer to Section 424-22(b)]

Single disconnect

Resistance heating elements

Fig. 240·31. Single disconnect for one set of fuses is permitted for electric space heating with subdivided resistance-type heating elements. (Sec. 240-40.)

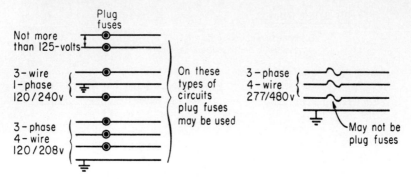

Fig. 240·32. Using plug fuses. (Sec. 240-50.)

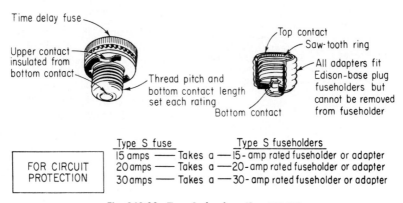

Fig. 240·33. Type S plug fuse. (Sec. 240-53.)

any fuse rated over 20 A. The purpose of this rule is to prevent overfusing of 15- and 20-A circuits.

240·60. General (Cartridge Fuses). The last sentence of part **(b)** must always be carefully observed. It is concerned with an extremely important matter:

The installation of current-limiting fuses demands extreme care in the selection of the fuse clips to be used. Because current-limiting fuses have an additional protective feature (that of current limitation, i.e., extremely fast operation to prevent the flow of the extremely high currents which many modern circuits can produce into a ground fault or short circuit) as compared to noncurrent-limiting fuses, some condition of the mounting arrangement for current-limiting fuses must prevent replacement of the current-limiting fuses by noncurrent-limiting. This is necessary to maintain safety in applications where, for example, the busbars of a switchboard or motor control center are braced in accordance with the maximum let-through current of current-limiting fuses which protect the busbars, but would be exposed to a much higher potential value of fault let-through current if noncurrent-limiting fuses were used to replace the current-limiting fuses. The possibility of higher current flow than that for which the busbars are braced is created by the lack of current limitation in the noncurrent-limiting fuses.

Section 240-60(b) takes the above matter into consideration when it rules that "fuseholders for current-limiting fuses shall not permit insertion of fuses that are not current limiting." To afford compliance with the **Code** and to obtain the necessary safety of installation, fuse manufacturers provide current-limiting fuses with special ferrules or knife blades for insertion only in special fuse clips. Such special ferrules and blades do permit the insertion of current-limiting fuses into standard **NEC** fuse clips, to cover those cases where current-limiting fuses (with their higher type of protection) might be used to replace noncurrent-limiting fuses. But the special rejection-type fuseholders will not accept noncurrent-limiting fuses—thereby assuring replacement only with current-limiting fuses.

The very real problem of **Code** compliance and safety is created by the fact that many fuses with standard ferrules and knife-blade terminals are current-limiting type and are made in the same construction and dimensions as corresponding sizes of noncurrent-limiting fuses, for use in standard fuseholders. Such current-limiting fuses are not marked "current limiting" but may be used to obtain limitation of energy let-through. Replacement of them by standard nonlimiting fuses could be hazardous.

Class J and L fuses   Both the Class J (0–600 A, 600 V AC) and Class L (601–6,000 A, 600 V AC) fuses are current-limiting, high-interrupting-capacity types. The interrupting ratings are 100,000 or 200,000 rms symmetrical amperes, and the designated rating is marked on the label of each Class J or L fuse. Class J and L fuses are also marked "current limiting," as required in part **(c)** of Sec. 240-60.

Class J fuse dimensions are different from those for standard Class H cartridge fuses of the same voltage rating and ampere classification. As such, they will require special fuseholders that will not accept noncurrent-limiting fuses. This arrangement complies with the last sentence of **NEC** Sec. 240-60(b).

Class K fuses   These are subdivided into Classes K-1, K-5, and K-9. Class K fuses have the same dimensions as Class H (standard **NE Code**) fuses and are interchangeable with them. Classes K-1, K-5, and K-9 fuses have different degrees of current limitation but are not permitted to be labeled "current limiting" because physical characteristics permit these fuses to be interchanged with noncurrent-limiting types. Use of these fuses, for instance, to protect equipment busbars that are braced to withstand 40,000 A of fault current at a point where, say, 60,000 A of current would be available if noncurrent-limiting fuses were used is a clear violation of the last sentence of part **(b)**. As shown in Fig. 240-34, because such fuses can be replaced with nonlimiting fuses, the equipment bus structure would be exposed to dangerous failure. Classes R and T have been developed to provide current limitation and prevent interchangeability with noncurrent-limiting types.

Class R fuses   These fuses are made in two designations: RK1 and RK5. UL data are as follows:

Fuses marked "Class RK1" or "Class RK5" are high-interrupting-capacity types and are marked "current limiting." Although these fuses will fit into standard fuseholders that take Class H and Class K fuses, special rejection-type fuseholders designed for Class RK1 and RK5 fuses will not accept Class H and Class K fuses. In that way, circuits and equipment protected in accordance with

Fuseholders in main switch of motor
control center require Class K-1 fuses
for current limitation to protect busbars.
Fuseholders furnished permit replacement of K-1
fuses with non-current-limiting type.

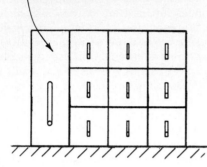

Fig. 240·34. Current-limiting fuseholders must be rejection type. (Sec. 240-60.)

the characteristics of RK1 or RK5 fuses cannot have that protection reduced by the insertion of other fuses of a lower protective level.

Other UL application data that affect selection of various types of fuses are as follows:

Fuses designated as Class CC (0–20 A, 600 V AC) are high-interrupting-capacity types and are marked "current limiting." They are not interchangeable with fuses of higher voltage or interrupting rating or lower current rating.

Class G fuses (0–60 A, 300 V AC) are high-interrupting-capacity types and are marked "current limiting." They are not interchangeable with other fuses mentioned above and below.

Fuses designated as Class T (0–600 A, 250 and 600 V AC) are high-interrupting-capacity types and are marked "current limiting." They are not interchangeable with other fuses mentioned above.

Part **(c)** requires use of fuses to conform to the marking on them. Fuses that are intended to be used for current limitation must be marked "current limiting."

Class K-1, K-5, and K-9 fuses are marked, in addition to their regular voltage and current ratings, with an interrupting rating of 200,000, 100,000, or 50,000 A (rms symmetrical). See Fig. 240-35.

Class CC, RK1, RK5, J, L, and T fuses are marked, in addition to their regular voltage and current ratings, with an interrupting rating of 200,000 A (rms symmetrical).

Although it is not required by the **Code**, manufacturers are in a position to provide fuses that are advertised and marked indicating they have "time-delay" characteristics. In the case of Class CC, Class G, Class H, Class K, and Class RK fuses, time-delay characteristics of fuses (minimum blowing time) have been investigated. Class G or CC fuses, which can carry 200 percent of rated current for 12 sec or more, and Class H, Class K, or Class RK fuses, which can carry 500 percent of rated current for 10 sec or more, may be marked with "D," "time delay," or some equivalent designation. Class L fuses are permitted to be marked "time delay" but have not been evaluated for such performance. Class J and T fuses are not permitted to be marked "time delay."

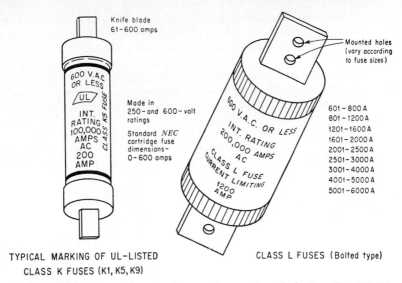

TYPICAL MARKING OF UL–LISTED
CLASS K FUSES (K1, K5, K9)

CLASS L FUSES (Bolted type)

Fig. 240-35. Fuses must be applied in accordance with marked ratings. (Sec. 240-60.)

240-61. Classification.   This section notes that any fuse may be used at its voltage rating or at any voltage below its voltage rating.

240-80. Method of Operation (Circuit Breakers).   This rule requiring trip-free manual operation of circuit breakers ties in with that in Sec. 230-76, although this rule requires manual operation to *both* the closed and the open positions of the CB. According to the Exception, a power-operated circuit breaker used as a service disconnect means must be capable of being opened by hand but does not have to be capable of being closed by hand. The general rule of Sec. 240-80 requires circuit breakers to be "capable of being *closed and opened* by manual operation." That rule also says that if a CB is electrically or pneumatically operated, it must also provide for manual operation. This Exception recognizes that Sec. 230-76(2) only requires a power-operated CB to be capable of being *opened* by hand (Fig. 240-36).

240-81. Indicating.   This rule requires the up position to be the ON position for any CB. *All* circuit breakers—not just those "on switchboards or in panelboards"—must be ON in the up position and OFF in the down position if their

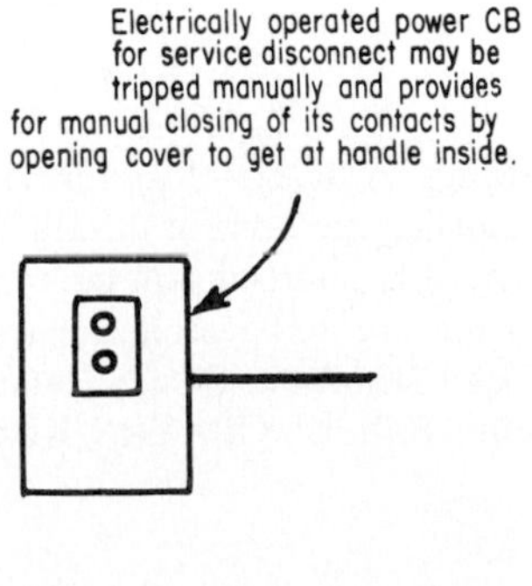

Electrically operated power CB
for service disconnect may be
tripped manually and provides
for manual closing of its contacts by
opening cover to get at handle inside.

Fig. 240-36. Every CB must be manually operable. (Sec. 240-80.)

handles operate vertically rather than rotationally or horizontally. This is an expansion of the rule that previously applied only to circuit breakers on switchboards or in panelboards. This brings the rule into agreement with that of the second paragraph of Sec. 380-7—which makes the identical requirement for *all* circuit breakers *and* switches in individual enclosures. Switches and circuit breakers in individual enclosures must be marked to clearly show ON and OFF positions and vertically operated switches and CBs must be ON when in the up position (Fig. 240-37).

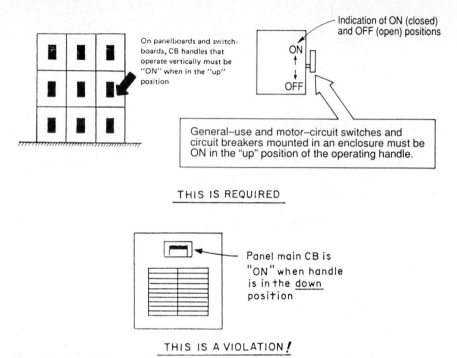

On panelboards and switchboards, CB handles that operate vertically must be "ON" when in the "up" position

Indication of ON (closed) and OFF (open) positions

ON
↑
↓
OFF

General–use and motor–circuit switches and circuit breakers mounted in an enclosure must be ON in the "up" position of the operating handle.

THIS IS REQUIRED

Panel main CB is "ON" when handle is in the down position

THIS IS A VIOLATION!

Fig. 240-37. Handle position of CB in any kind of enclosure must be "ON" in the up position. (Sec. 240-81.)

240-83. Marking.   Part **(a)** requires that the marking of a CB's ampere rating must be durable and visible after installation. That marking is permitted to be made visible by removing the trim or cover of the CB.

The last paragraph of part **(c)** says that enclosures containing series-rated protective devices must be marked with the "additional series combination interrupting rating" of the enclosed devices (Fig. 240-38).

An enclosure containing circuit breakers used at a point in a system with higher available short-circuit current than the breakers' IC rating, as part of a UL-listed series rated system, with an upstream CB of adequate IC must have marking like "Caution: Series Rated System—Additional Series Combination Interrupting Rating: XX,XXXX RMS Symmetrical Amperes." This rule is in

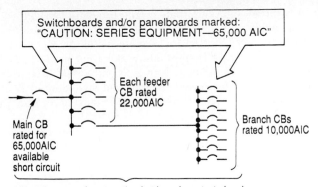

Fig. 240-38. An "additional series combination interrupting rating" must be "marked" on equipment. [Sec. 240-83(c).]

recognition of the safety and effectiveness of tested and UL-listed applications of circuit breakers in series to achieve more economical use of breakers with lower than normal interrupting rating. The requirement calls for marking of "end-use equipment, such as switchboards and panelboards" to advise maintenance and operating personnel of the elevated interrupting rating of the enclosed protective devices that are used as a part of a UL-listed series rated system. By marking end-use equipment, maintenance and operating personnel are alerted that the IC rating of the enclosed devices is greater than that which is marked on the devices because they are used as part of a listed series rated system. This rule in Sec. 240-83(c) corresponds to a similar concern addressed by the wording of Sec. 110-22 of the 1990 NEC.

Part **(d)** of this section requires that any CB used to switch 120- or 277-V fluorescent lighting be approved for the purpose and be marked "SWD" (Fig. 240-39).

In commercial and industrial electrical systems, ON-OFF control of lighting is commonly done by the breakers in the lighting panel, eliminating any local

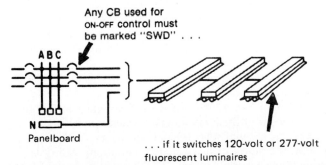

Fig. 240-39. Circuit breakers used for switching lights must be "SWD" type. [Sec. 240-83(d).]

wiring-device switches. UL states that "circuit breakers marked SWD are suitable for switching 120- or 277-V fluorescent lighting on a regular basis." Such listing indicates that any CB used for regular switching of 120- or 277-V fluorescents must be marked SWD and that breakers *not* so marked are *not* suitable for panel switching of lighting. Both 277- and 120-V CBs are required to be designated as suitable for regular or frequent switching of lighting of any kind. Such CBs are available with the "SWD" marking and are suitable for switching duty because they are ruggedly constructed.

Under this rule, only those breakers bearing the designation "SWD" (switching duty) may be used as snap switches for lighting control. Type "SWD" breakers have been tested and found suitable for the greater frequency of ON-OFF operations required for switching duty than for strictly overcurrent protection, in which the breaker is used only for generally infrequent disconnect for circuit repair or maintenance.

The rule of part **(e)** requires specific voltage markings on circuit breakers. A fine print note explains circuit-breaker voltage markings in terms of the device's suitability for grounded and ungrounded systems. Designation of only a phase-to-phase rating—such as "480 V"—indicates suitability for grounded or ungrounded systems. But voltage designations showing a phase-to-neutral voltage by "slash" markings—like 480Y/277 V or 120/240 V—indicate that such circuit breakers are limited exclusively to use in grounded neutral electrical systems.

240·100. Feeders (Over 600 Volts, Nominal).   This section presents rules on overcurrent protection for high-voltage (over 600 V) feeder conductors. It requires short-circuit protection of adequate interrupting capacity for its point of use. Although the rule calls for "short-circuit" protection, it does *not* require that conductors be protected in accordance with their rated ampacities. Refer to Sec. 230-208, which is referenced in this section (Fig. 240-40).

A high-voltage feeder:

1. *Must* have a "short-circuit protective device in *each* ungrounded conductor." OR—

2. It may be protected by a CB equipped with overcurrent relays and current transformers in *only two phases* and arranged as described in Sec. 230-208(d) (2) or (d) (3), which covers overcurrent protection of high-voltage service conductors.

The requirement on maximum value of high-voltage overcurrent protection is as follows:

A FUSE must be rated in continuous amps at *not* more than THREE TIMES the ampacity of the circuit conductor.

A CIRCUIT BREAKER must have a long-time trip element rated *not* more than SIX TIMES the ampacity of the feeder conductor.

As explained under Sec. 230-208, E-rated fuses used for circuits over 600 V can carry 200 percent of their rated current continuously. Therefore, THREE TIMES the current rating of such a fuse is the *same value* of protection as SIX TIMES the current rating of a CB of the same amp rating as the fuse. For instance, three times the 100-A rating of an E-rated fuse is actually three times 200 A, or 600 A—which is the same as six times the 100-A rating of a CB.

TYPE OF DEVICE

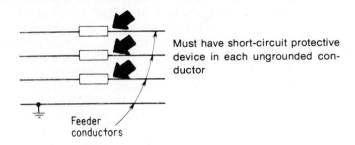

Must have short-circuit protective device in each ungrounded conductor

Feeder conductors

REQUIRED MINIMUM RATING

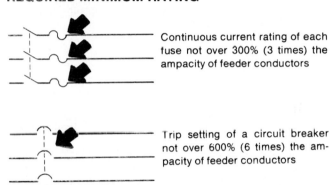

Continuous current rating of each fuse not over 300% (3 times) the ampacity of feeder conductors

Trip setting of a circuit breaker not over 600% (6 times) the ampacity of feeder conductors

Fig. 240·40. Overcurrent protection of high-voltage (over 600 V) feeder conductors. (Sec. 240-100.)

240·101. Branch Circuits. This applies to high-voltage branch circuits, which are invariably branch circuits for high-voltage motors and as such must also satisfy Sec. 430-125 covering overload and fault-current protection for high-voltage motor circuits. A high-voltage branch circuit must be protected by a short-circuit protective device in *each* ungrounded conductor **or** it may be protected by a CB with relays in *only two* phase legs, as described in Sec. 230-208(d) (2) or (d) (3).

ARTICLE 250. GROUNDING

250·1. Scope. One of the most important, but least understood, considerations in design of electrical systems is that of grounding. The word "grounding" comes from the fact that the technique itself involves making a low-resistance connection to the earth or to ground. For any given piece of equipment or circuit, this connection may be a direct wire connection to the grounding electrode which is buried in the earth; or it may be a connection to some other conductive metallic element (such as conduit or switchboard enclosure) which is connected to a grounding electrode.

The purpose of grounding is to provide protection of personnel, equipment, and circuits by eliminating the possibility of dangerous or excessive voltages.

There are two distinct considerations in grounding for electrical systems: grounding of one of the conductors of the wiring system, and grounding of all metal enclosures which contain electrical wires or equipment when an insulation failure in such enclosures might place a potential on the enclosures and constitute a shock or fire hazard. The types of grounding are:

1. *Wiring system ground.* This consists of grounding one of the wires of the electrical system, such as the neutral, to limit the voltage upon the circuit which might otherwise occur through exposure to lightning or other voltages higher than that for which the circuit is designed. Another purpose in grounding one of the wires of the system is to limit the maximum voltage to ground under normal operating conditions. Also, a system which operates with one of its conductors intentionally grounded will provide for automatic opening of the circuit if an accidental or fault ground occurs on one of its ungrounded conductors (Fig. 250-1).

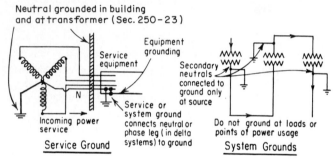

Fig. 250·1. Operating a system with one circuit conductor grounded. (Sec. 250-1.)

2. *Equipment ground.* This is a permanent and continuous bonding together (i.e., connecting together) of all noncurrent-carrying metal parts of equipment enclosures—conduit, boxes, cabinets, housings, frames of motors, and lighting fixtures—and connection of this interconnected system of enclosures to the system grounding electrode (Fig. 250-2). The interconnection of all metal enclosures must be made to provide a low-impedance path for fault-current flow along the enclosures to assure operation of overcurrent devices which will open a circuit in the event of a fault. By opening a faulted circuit, the system prevents dangerous voltages from being present on equipment enclosures which could be touched by personnel, with consequent electric shock to such personnel.

Simply stated, grounding of all metal enclosures of electric wires and equipment prevents any potential-above-ground on the enclosures. Such bonding together and grounding of all metal enclosures are required for both grounded electrical systems (those systems in which one of the circuit conductors is intentionally grounded) and ungrounded electrical systems (systems with none of the circuit wires intentionally grounded).

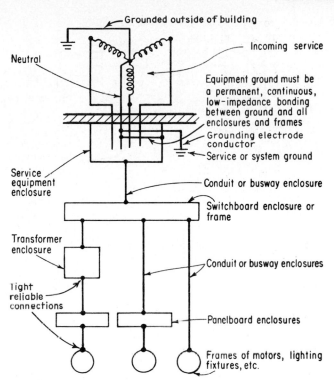

Fig. 250·2. Equipment grounding is interconnection of metal enclosures of equipment and their connection to ground. (Sec. 250-1.)

But effective equipment grounding is extremely important for grounded electrical systems to provide the automatic fault clearing which is one of the important advantages of grounded electrical systems. A low-impedance path for fault current is necessary to permit enough current to flow to operate the fuses or CB protecting the circuit.

In a grounded electrical system with a high-impedance equipment ground-return path, if one of the phase conductors of the system (i.e., one of the ungrounded conductors of the wiring system) should accidentally come in contact with one of the metal enclosures in which the wires are run, it might produce a condition where not enough fault current would flow to operate the overcurrent devices. In such a case, the faulted circuit would not automatically open, and a dangerous voltage would be present on the conduit and other metal enclosures. This voltage presents a shock hazard and a fire hazard due to possible arcing or sparking from the energized conduit to some grounded pipe or other piece of grounded metal.

250·5. Alternating-Current Circuits and Systems to Be Grounded. Part **(a)** does recognize use of ungrounded circuits or systems when operating at less than 50 V. But grounding of circuits under 50 V is required, as shown in Fig. 250-3.

According to part **(b)(1)** of this rule, all alternating-current wiring systems

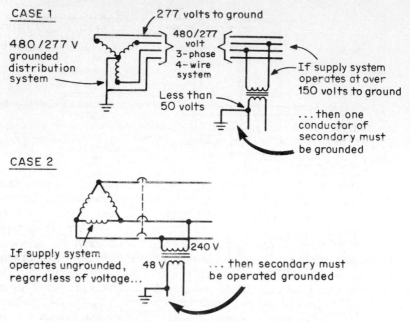

CASE 1

480/277 V grounded distribution system

277 volts to ground

480/277 volt 3-phase 4-wire system

Less than 50 volts

If supply system operates at over 150 volts to ground

...then one conductor of secondary must be grounded

CASE 2

If supply system operates ungrounded, regardless of voltage...

240 V

48 V

...then secondary must be operated grounded

Fig. 250-3. Circuits under 50 V may have to be grounded. (Sec. 250-5.)

from 50 to 1,000 V must be grounded if they can be so grounded that the maximum voltage to ground does not exceed 150 V. This rule makes it *mandatory* that the following systems or circuits operate with one conductor grounded:

1. 120-V, 2-wire systems or circuits must have one of their wires grounded.
2. 240/120-V, 3-wire, single-phase systems or circuits must have their neutral conductor grounded.
3. 208/120-V, 3-phase, 4-wire, wye-connected systems or circuits must be operated with the neutral conductor grounded.

In all the foregoing systems or circuits, the neutrals must be grounded because **the maximum voltage to ground does not exceed 150 V** from any other conductor of the system when the neutral conductor is grounded.

In Parts **(2)** and **(3)** of this section, all systems of any voltage up to 1,000 V must operate with the neutral conductor solidly grounded whenever any loads are connected phase-to-neutral, so that the neutral carries load current. *All* 3-phase, 4-wire wye-connected systems and all 3-phase, 4-wire delta systems (the so-called "red-leg" systems) must operate with the neutral conductor solidly grounded if they are used as a circuit conductor. That means that the neutral conductor of a 240/120-V, 3-phase, 4-wire system (with the neutral taken from the midpoint of one phase) must be grounded. It is also mandatory that 480Y/277-V, 3-phase, 4-wire interior wiring systems have the neutral grounded if the neutral is to be used as a circuit conductor—such as for 277-V lighting. And if 480-V autotransformer-type fluorescent or mercury-vapor ballasts are to be supplied from 480/277-V systems, then the neutral conductor will have to be grounded at the voltage source to conform to Sec. 410-78, even though the neutral is not used as a circuit conductor. Of course, it should be noted that 480/277-V systems are usually operated with the neutral grounded to obtain automatic fault-clearing of a grounded system (Fig. 250-4).

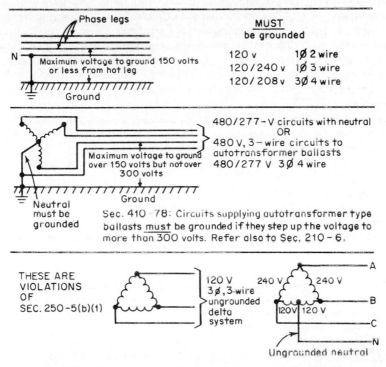

Fig. 250-4. Some systems or circuits must be grounded. (Sec. 250-5.)

Although the NE Code does not require grounding of electrical systems in which the voltage to ground would exceed 150 V, it does recommend that ground-fault detectors be used with ungrounded systems which operate at more than 150 and less than 1,000 V. Such detectors indicate when an accidental ground fault develops on one of the phase legs of ungrounded systems. Then the indicated ground fault can be removed during downtime of the industrial operation—i.e., when the production machinery is not running.

Many industrial plants prefer to use an ungrounded system with ground-fault detectors instead of a grounded system. With a grounded system, the occurrence of a ground fault is supposed to draw enough current to operate the overcurrent device protecting the circuit. But such fault-clearing opens the circuit which may be a branch circuit supplying a motor or other power load or may be a feeder which supplies a number of power loads; and many industrial plants object to the loss of production caused by downtime. They would rather use the ungrounded system and have the system kept operative with a single ground fault and clear the fault when the production machinery is not in use. In some plants, the cost of downtime of production machines can run to thousands of dollars per minute. In other plants, interruption of critical process is extremely costly.

The difference between a grounded and an ungrounded system is that a single ground fault will automatically cause opening of the circuit in a grounded system, but will not interrupt operations in an ungrounded system. However, the presence of a single ground fault on an ungrounded system exposes the system to the very destructive possibilities of a phase-to-phase short if another ground fault should simultaneously develop on a different phase leg of the system (Fig. 250-5).

UNGROUNDED SYSTEMS

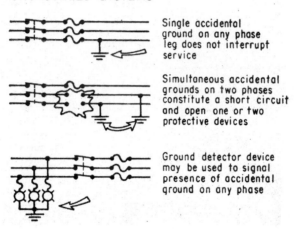

Single accidental ground on any phase leg does not interrupt service

Simultaneous accidental grounds on two phases constitute a short circuit and open one or two protective devices

Ground detector device may be used to signal presence of accidental ground on any phase

Fig. 250-5. Characteristics of ungrounded systems. (Sec. 250-5.)

Grounded neutral systems are generally recommended for high-voltage (over 600 V) distribution. Although ungrounded systems do not undergo a power outage with only one-phase ground faults, the time and money spent in tracing faults indicated by ground detectors and other disadvantages of ungrounded systems have favored use of grounded neutral systems. Grounded systems are more economical in operation and maintenance. In such a system, if a fault occurs, it is isolated immediately and automatically.

Grounded neutral systems have many other advantages. The elimination of multiple faults caused by undetected restriking grounds greatly increases service reliability. The lower voltage to ground which results from grounding the neutral offers greater safety for personnel and requires lower equipment voltage ratings. And on high-voltage (above 600 V) systems, residual relays can be used to detect ground faults before they become phase-to-phase faults which have substantial destructive ability.

Exception No. 3 to the basic rule requiring grounding of one conductor of AC electrical systems recognizes use of *ungrounded* control circuits derived from transformers. According to the rules of part **(b)** of this section, any 120-V, 2-wire circuit *must* normally have one of its conductors grounded; the neutral conductor of any 240/120-V, 3-wire, single-phase circuit *must* be grounded; and the neutral of a 208/120-V, 3-phase, 4-wire circuit *must* be grounded. Those requirements have often caused difficulty when applied to control circuits derived from the secondary of a control transformer that supplies power to the operating coils of motor starters, contactors, and relays. For instance, there are cases where a ground fault on the hot leg of a grounded control circuit can cause a hazard to personnel by actuating the control circuit fuse or CB and shutting down an industrial process in a sudden, unexpected, nonorderly way. A metal-casting facility is an example of an installation where sudden shutdown due to a ground fault in the hot leg of a grounded control circuit could be objectionable. Because designers often wish to operate such 120-V control circuits ungrounded, Exception No. 3 of Sec. 250-5(b) permits ungrounded control circuits under certain specified conditions.

A 120-V control circuit may be operated ungrounded when all the following exist:

1. The circuit is derived from a transformer that has a primary rating less than 1,000 V.
2. Whether in a commercial, institutional, or industrial facility, supervision will assure that only persons qualified in electrical work will maintain and service the control circuits.
3. There is a need for preventing circuit opening on a ground fault—i.e., continuity of power is required for safety or for operating reliability.
4. Some type of ground detector is used on the ungrounded system to alert personnel to the presence of any ground fault, enabling them to clear the ground fault in normal downtime of the system (Fig. 250-6).

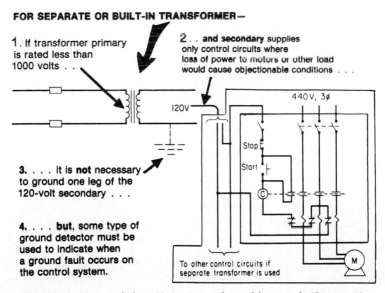

Fig. 250-6. Ungrounded 120-V circuits may be used for controls. (Sec. 250-5.)

Although no mention is made of secondary voltage in this Code rule, this Exception permitting ungrounded control circuits is primarily significant only for 120-V control circuits. The NE Code has long permitted 240- and 480-V control circuits to be operated ungrounded. Application of this Exception can be made for any 120-V control circuit derived from a control transformer in an individual motor starter or for a separate control transformer that supplies control power for a number of motor starters or magnetic contactors. Of course, the Exception could also be used to permit ungrounded 277-V control circuits under the same conditions.

Exception No. 4 excludes from the need for grounded operation the circuits in flammable anesthetizing locations, as covered by Sec. 517-160(a)(1).

A very important permission is given in Exception No. 5: Three-phase AC systems rated 480 to 1000 V may be operated with a high-impedance connection to ground. As an alternative to solidly grounded or ungrounded operation of 3-phase AC systems rated 480 V (or up to 1,000 V), such systems may be high-impedance grounded. Such operation may be used *only* where qualified persons will service the installation, where continuity of power is required, where ground detectors are installed on the system, and where there are no line-neutral (277-V) loads being supplied. Exception No. 5 represents the first NEC recognition of impedance grounding as an alternative to solid grounding or non-grounding of electrical systems. Other sections of Art. 250 coordinate full recognition of high-impedance grounding of electrical systems.

As described in the title of this Exception, the high impedance used to ground the neutral point of the system is usually a resistor, which limits the ground-fault current to a low value. Such application is readily made to a 480/277-V, 3-phase, 3-wire system, with the neutral point connected to ground through the grounding resistor (Fig. 250-7).

As covered by the rule of part **(c),** any AC system of 1,000 V or more must be grounded if it supplies portable equipment. Otherwise, such systems do not have to be grounded, although they *may* be grounded.

Part **(d)** of Sec. 250-5 has special meaning on grounding requirements for emergency generators used in electrical systems. It is best studied in steps:

1. The wording here presents the basic rule that covers grounding of "separately derived systems"—which has always been understood to refer to generator output circuits and transformer secondary circuits because such systems are "derived" separately from other wiring systems and have no conductor connected to the other systems.

2. For a separately derived system, if the voltage and hookup require grounding as specified in Sec. 250-5(b), then such systems have to be grounded and bonded as described in Sec. 250-26.

3. With respect to 2-winding transformers (i.e., single-phase or polyphase transformers that are *not* autotransformers and have *only* magnetic coupling from the primary to the secondary), there is no question that the secondary circuits are "separately derived," and grounding must always be done as required by Secs. 250-5(b) and 250-26.

4. But, when the rule of Sec. 250-5(d), is applied to 208/120- or 480/277-V generators used for emergency power in the event of an outage of the nor-

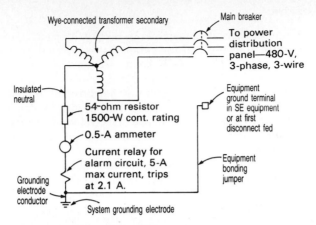

1—Diagram of resistance-grounded system shows how neutral of main transformer(s) is grounded through a resistor, ammeter and current relay. Ground fault on any phase causes current to flow from fault through ground at transformer, through current relay, ammeter and resistor back to transformer neutral. Resistor limits fault current; current relay, which trips at any current level above 2.1 amps, initiates alarm.

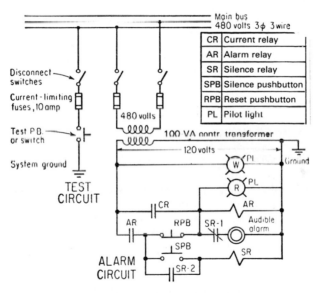

2—Test circuit (on left of diagram) allows application of temporary ground to system to test alarm function. In alarm circuit, contacts CR close when current relay, which is connected in neutral-conductor ground-circuit at main transformer, senses a ground fault (see Fig. 1). Operation of contacts CR initiates audible and visual alarm.

Fig. 250-7. This is a typical application of resistance-grounded system operation. [Sec. 250-5(b), Exception No. 5.]

mal electric utility service, care must be taken with such a generator that is tied into the automatic transfer switch that is also fed from the normal service equipment. With a solidly connected neutral conductor running from the service equipment, through the transfer switch, to the generator neutral terminal, and with the neutral bonded and grounded at both the normal service and the generator, objectionable currents can flow. Section 250-21 prohibits grounding connections that produce objectionable flow of current over grounding conductors or grounding paths. The two grounding connections—at the service and at the generator—can produce objectionable current flow under both normal and fault conditions:

Under normal conditions, neutral current of the connected load in the building has two paths of current flow from the common neutral point in the transfer switch back to the service neutral terminal. One path, of course, is over the neutral conductor from the transfer switch to the service equipment. The other path is over the neutral conductor from the transfer switch to the generator, at which point the current can flow back to the service equipment over the grounding conductor (the conduit and enclosure interconnections) that runs between the service equipment and the generator.

Under ground-fault conditions, a similar double path for current flow can cause desensitizing of ground-fault protective equipment—as discussed and shown under Sec. 230-95, when a 3-pole transfer switch is used.

5. Elimination of the desensitizing of service GF protection can be accomplished by the use of a 4-pole transfer switch that prevents a solid neutral connection from the service equipment to the generator.
6. In the present **NE Code**, the grounding requirements of Sec. 250-5(d) apply to a generator *only* where the generator "has no direct electrical connection, including a solidly grounded circuit conductor" to the normal service. The rule would apply to a generator that fed its load without any tie-in through a transfer switch to *any* other system. The rule would not apply if a generator *does have* a solidly connected neutral from it to the service through a 3-pole, solid-neutral transfer switch (Fig. 250-8).

The first FPN (fine-print note) after Sec. 250-5(d) specifically identifies an on-site generator (emergency or standby) as "not a separately derived system" if the neutral conductor from the generator is connected solidly through a terminal lug in a transfer switch to the neutral conductor from the normal (usually, the power company) service to the premises. Therefore, the generator neutral point does not have to be bonded to the frame and connected to a grounding electrode.

The second FPN cautions that the neutral conductor from a generator to a transfer switch must be sized at least equal to 12½ percent of the cross-section area of the largest associated phase conductor (Sec. 445-5) to assure adequate conductivity (low impedance) for fault current that might return over that neutral when the generator is supplying the premises load, the neutral of both the generator and the normal service are connected solidly through the transfer switch (making the generator *not* a separately derived system), and the generator neutral is not bonded to the generator case and grounded at the generator.

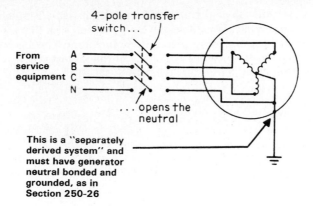

4-pole transfer switch...

From service equipment

A
B
C
N

... opens the neutral

This is a "separately derived system" and must have generator neutral bonded and grounded, as in Section 250-26

Generator neutral *must* be bonded when neutral is opened.

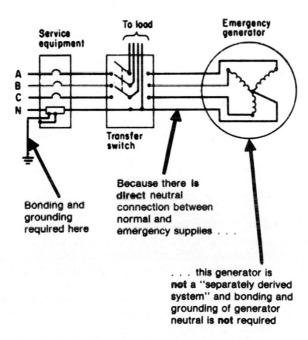

Service equipment

To load

Emergency generator

A
B
C
N

Transfer switch

Bonding and grounding required here

Because there is direct neutral connection between normal and emergency supplies . . .

. . . this generator is **not** a "separately derived system" and bonding and grounding of generator neutral is **not** required

With 3-pole transfer, generator neutral need not be bonded.

Fig. 250·8. These are the choices on bonding and grounding of generator neutral. [Sec. 250-5(d).]

Under such a set of conditions, fault current from a ground fault in the premises wiring system would have to return to the point at the normal service equipment where the equipment grounding conductor (service equipment enclosure, metal conduits, etc.) is bonded to the service neutral. Only from that point can the fault current return over the neutral conductors, through the transfer switch to the neutral point of the generator winding. Section 445-5 requires that such a generator neutral must satisfy Sec. 250-23(b)—which says that a neutral that might function as an equipment grounding conductor must have a cross-section area at least equal to 12½ percent of the csa of the largest phase conductor of the generator circuit to the transfer switch (Fig. 250-9).

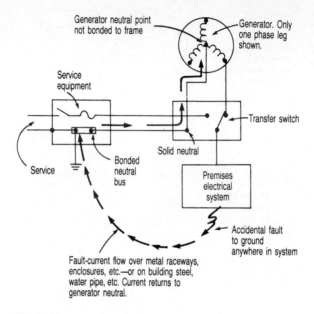

Fig. 250·9. Neutral conductor from service equipment to generator neutral point must be sized at least equal to 12½ percent of the cross-section area of the generator phase leg. [Sec. 250-5(d).]

The effect of the rule of Sec. 250-5(d) on transfer switches is as follows:

3·pole transfer switch   If a solid neutral connection is made from the service neutral, through the transfer switch, to the generator neutral, then bonding and grounding of the neutral at the generator are *not* required because the neutral is already bonded and grounded at the service equipment. And if bonding and grounding were done at the generator, it could be considered a violation of Sec. 250-21(a) and would have to be corrected by Sec. 250-21(b) (Fig. 250-8).

4·pole transfer switch   Because there is no direct electrical connection of either the hot legs or the neutral between the service and the generator, the generator in such a hookup is a "separately derived system" and must be grounded and bonded to the generator case at the generator (Fig. 250-8).

It should be noted that the 4-pole transfer switch and other neutral-switching techniques came into use to eliminate problems of GFP desensitizing that were caused by use of a 3-pole transfer switch **when the neutral of the generator was bonded to the generator housing.** By eliminating that bonding requirement for emergency generators in Sec. 250-5(d) it was the **Code** intent to make possible use of 3-pole transfer switches without disruption of service GFP. But that has not resulted and the neutral-switching concept has prevailed.

Although the rule in Sec. 250-5(d) permits use of an ungrounded and non-bonded generator neutral in conjunction with a 3-pole transfer switch, such application has been found to produce other conditions of undesirable current flow, resulting in other forms of desensitizing of service GFP—such as desensitizing a zero-sequence sensor used for GFP on the generator output. In such a hookup, with the system being supplied by the generator and the normal service open, ground-fault current returning over metal raceway to the metal case of the transfer switch will flow to the bond point between the neutral and equipment ground at the normal service equipment and then return to the generator over the solid neutral, through the zero-sequence sensor. As a result, the use of a 4-pole transfer switch or some other technique that opens the neutral is the only effective way to avoid GFP desensitizing. Ground-fault protection is not compatible with a solid neutral tie between the service and an emergency generator—with or without its neutral bonded.

Refer to the discussion under Sec. 250-23(a) on the relationship between GFP desensitizing and the point of connection of the grounding electrode conductor.

250-6. Portable and Vehicle-Mounted Generators.   Part **(a)** rules that the frame of a portable generator does not have to be grounded if the generator supplies only equipment mounted on the generator and/or plug-connected equipment through receptacles mounted on the generator, provided that the noncurrent-carrying metal parts of equipment and the equipment grounding conductor terminals are bonded to the generator frame. See Fig. 250-10.

A clarification in part **(a)** points out that, where a portable generator is used with its frame *not* grounded, the frame is permitted to act as the grounding electrode for any cord-connected tools or appliances plugged into the generator's receptacles (Fig. 250-10). This assures that tools and appliances that are required by Sec. 250-45 to be grounded do satisfy the **Code** when plugged into a receptacle on the ungrounded frame of a portable generator. It should also be noted that part **(c)** of this section requires the neutral conductor of the generator output to be bonded to the frame of the generator when it is not used as an emergency source connected to a transfer switch.

Part **(b)** notes that the frame of a vehicle-mounted generator may be bonded to the vehicle frame, which then serves as the grounding electrode—but only when the generator supplies only equipment mounted on the vehicle and/or cord- and plug-connected equipment through receptacles on the vehicle or generator. When the frame of a vehicle is used as the grounding electrode for a generator mounted on the vehicle, grounding terminals of receptacles on the generator must be bonded to the generator frame, which must be bonded to the vehicle frame.

If either a portable or vehicle-mounted generator supplies a fixed wiring system external to the generator assembly, it must then be grounded as required for any separately derived system (as, for instance, a transformer secondary), as covered in Sec. 250-26.

The wording of part **(c)** brings application of portable and vehicle-mounted generators into compliance with the concept described above in Sec.

1. . . . the generator supplies equipment mounted on generator and/or cord-and-plug-connected equipment through receptacles on the generator, and

2. metal parts of equipment and equipment grounding terminals of receptacles are bonded to generator frame.

Grounding of portable generator frame is not required if these conditions exist. (Sec. 250-6.)

When frame of portable
generator is left ungrounded
as permitted in Section 250-6 . . .

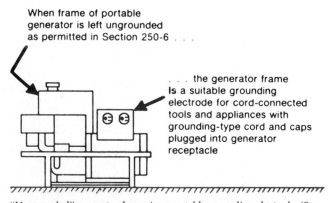

. . . the generator frame
is a suitable grounding
electrode for cord-connected
tools and appliances with
grounding-type cord and caps
plugged into generator
receptacle

"Ungrounded" generator frame is acceptable grounding electrode. (Sec. 250-6).

Fig. 250-10. Grounding details for a portable generator.

250-5(d) on grounding and bonding of the generator neutral conductor. A generator neutral *must be* bonded to the generator frame when the generator is a truly separately derived source, such as the sole source of power to the loads it feeds, and is *not* tied into a transfer switch as part of a **normal emergency** hookup for feeding the load normally from the utility service and from the generator on an emergency or standby basis (Fig. 250-11). A note to this section refers to Sec. 250-5(d) and makes that rule applicable to grounding and bonding of portable generators that supply a fixed wiring system on a premises. In such a case, bonding of the neutral to the generator frame is not required if there is a solid neutral connection from the utility service, through a transfer switch to the generator, as shown in the bottom sketch of Fig. 250-11.

250-21. Objectionable Current over Grounding Conductors.   Although parts **(a)** and **(b)** of this section permit "arrangement" and "alterations" of electrical systems to prevent and/or eliminate objectionable flow of currents over "grounding conductors or grounding paths," part **(d)** specifically prohibits any exemptions from **NEC** rules on grounding for "electronic equipment" and states that "currents that introduce noise or data errors" in electronic data-processing and computer equipment are not "objectionable" currents that allow modification of grounding rules. This paragraph emphasizes the **Code's** intent that electronic data-processing equipment must have its input and output circuits in full compliance with all **NEC** rules on neutral grounding, equipment grounding, and bonding and grounding of neutral and ground terminal buses. Sec. 250-21(b) does offer alternative methods for correcting "objectionable current over grounding conductors" but part **(d)** specifically states that such modifications or alternative methods are not applicable to the on-site wiring for electronic or data-processing equipment if the only purpose is to eliminate "noise or data errors" in the electronic equipment. This paragraph amplifies the revised wording of "Premises Wiring" as given in Article 100.

250-22. Point of Connection for Direct-Current Systems.   On a 2-wire or a 3-wire DC distribution system, a neutral that is required to be grounded must be grounded at the supply station only.

As noted in the Exception, an on-site supply for a DC system must have a required grounding connection made at either the source of the DC supply or at the first disconnect or overcurrent device supplied. Because the basic rule says a DC source (from outside a premises) must have a required grounding connection made at "one or more supply stations" and *not* at "any point on premises wiring," an on-site DC source would be prohibited from having a grounding connection that might be required. This Exception resolves that basic problem by referring to a "DC system source . . . located on the premises."

250-23. Grounding Service-Supplied Alternating-Current Systems.   As noted in part **(a)**, when an electrical system is to be operated with one conductor grounded—either because it is required by the **Code** (e.g., 240/120-V, single phase) or because it is desired by the system designer (e.g., 240-V, 3-phase, corner grounded)—a connection to the grounding electrode must be made at the service entrance (Fig. 250-12). That is, the neutral conductor or other conductor to be grounded must be connected at the service equipment to a conductor

Portable or vehicle generator as sole source or separately derived

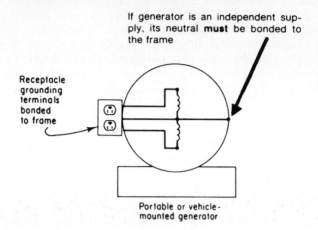

Portable generator supplying premises wiring

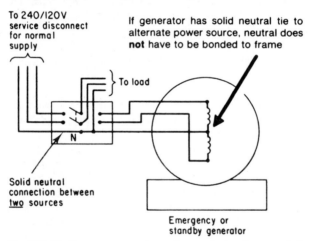

Fig. 250·11. Generator neutral may be required to be grounded. (Sec. 250-6.)

which runs to a grounding electrode. The conductor that runs to the grounding electrode is called the "grounding electrode conductor"—an official definition in the **NE Code**.

The **Code** rule of the second sentence of Sec. 250-23(a) says that the connection of the grounding electrode conductor to the system conductor which is to be grounded must be made "at any accessible point from the *load end* of the

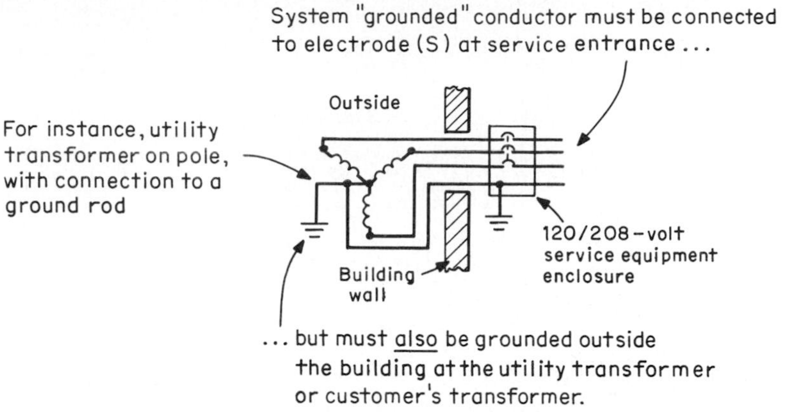

System "grounded" conductor must be connected
to electrode (S) at service entrance ...

Outside

For instance, utility
transformer on pole,
with connection to a
ground rod

120/208-volt
service equipment
enclosure

Building
wall

... but must <u>also</u> be grounded outside
the building at the utility transformer
or customer's transformer.

Fig. 250·12. Grounded interior systems must have *two* grounding points (Sec. 250-23.)

service drop or service lateral" to the service disconnecting means. This means
that the grounding electrode conductor (which runs to building steel and/or
water pipe or driven ground rod) must be connected to the system neutral or
other system wire to be grounded either in the enclosure for the service disconnect or in some enclosure on the supply side of the service disconnect. Such
connection may be made, for instance, in the main service switch or CB or in
a service panelboard or switchboard. Or, the grounding electrode conductor
may be connected to the system grounded conductor in a gutter, CT cabinet, or
meter housing on the supply side of the service disconnect (Fig. 250-13). The
utility company should be checked on grounding connections in meter sockets
or other metering equipment.

In addition to the grounding connection for the grounded system conductor
at the point of service entrance to the premises, it is further required that
another grounding connection be made to the same grounded conductor at the
transformer which supplies the system. This means, for example, that a
grounded service to a building must have the grounded neutral connected to a
grounding electrode at the utility transformer on the pole, away from the building, as well as having the neutral grounded to a water pipe and/or other suitable electrode at the building, as shown in Fig. 250-12. And in the case of a
building served from an outdoor transformer pad or mat installation, the conductor which is grounded in the building must also be grounded at the transformer pad or mat, per Sec. 250-23(a).

This section is concerned with the grounding of a utility-fed AC electric supply circuit that has one of its conductors operated intentionally grounded—such
as any 240/120-V single-phase system; 208/120-V, 3-phase, 4-wire system; or
480/277-V, 3-phase, 4-wire system—as required to have its neutral conductor
grounded by Sec. 250-5(b) or (c). The basic concept being conveyed is as
follows:

1. For such grounding connection, a grounding electrode conductor must be
   connected to the grounded conductor (the neutral conductor) anywhere

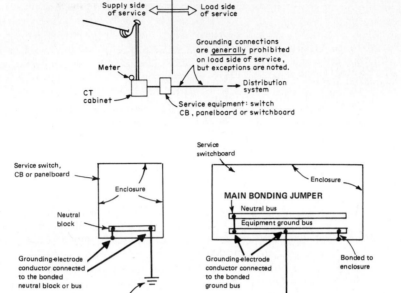

Fig. 250·13. Grounding connection must be made in SE equipment or on its line side. (Sec. 250-23.)

from the "load end of the service drop or lateral" to the *neutral block* or bus within the enclosure for the service disconnect—which includes a meter socket, a CT cabinet, or an auxiliary gutter or other enclosure ahead of the service disconnect, panelboard, or switchboard.

2. The grounding electrode conductor that is connected to the grounded neutral (or grounded phase leg) must be run to a "grounding electrode system," as specified in Secs. 250-81 and/or 250-83.

3. Exception No. 1 notes that the required grounding electrode connection for a local step-down transformer or a generator is treated somewhat differently from that for a utility-fed service.

4. Exception No. 5 permits the grounding electrode conductor to be connected to the equipment grounding bus in the service-disconnect enclosure—instead of to the neutral block or bus—for instance, where such connection is considered necessary to prevent desensitizing of a service GFP hookup that senses fault current by a CT-type sensor on the ground strap between the neutral bus and the ground bus. See Fig. 250-13. However, in any particular installation, the choice between connecting to the neutral bus or to the ground bus will depend on the number and types of grounding electrodes, the presence or absence of grounded building struc-

tural steel, bonding between electrical raceways and other metal piping on the load side of the service equipment, and the number and locations of bonding connections. The grounding-electrode-conductor may be connected to either the neutral bus or terminal lug or the ground bus or block in any system that has a conductor or a busbar bonding the neutral bus or terminal to the equipment grounding block or bus. Where the neutral is bonded to the enclosure simply by a bonding screw, the grounding electrode conductor *must* be connected to the neutral in all cases, because screw-bonding is not suited to passing high lightning currents to earth.

One of the most important and widely discussed regulations of the entire **Code** revolves around this matter of making a grounding connection to the system grounded neutral or grounded phase wire. The **Code** says, "Grounding connections shall not be made on the load side of the service disconnecting means." Once a neutral or other circuit conductor is connected to a grounding electrode at the service equipment, the general rule is that the neutral or other grounded leg must be insulated from all equipment enclosures or any other grounded parts on the load side of the service. That is, bonding of subpanels (or any other connection between the neutral or other grounded conductor and equipment enclosures) is prohibited by the **NE Code**.

There are some exceptions to that rule, but they are few and are very specific:

1. In a system, even though it is on the load side of the service, when voltage is stepped down by a transformer, a grounding connection *must* be made to the secondary neutral to satisfy Sec. 250-5(b) and Sec. 250-26.

2. When a circuit is run from one building to another, it may be necessary or simply permissible to connect the system "grounded" conductor to a grounding electrode at the other building—as covered by Sec. 250-24.

3. Section 250-61 permits frames of ranges, wall ovens, counter-top cook units, and clothes dryers to be "grounded" by connection to the grounded neutral of their supply circuit (Sec. 250-60).

The **Code** makes it a violation to bond the neutral block in a panelboard to the panel enclosure in other than a service panel. In a panelboard used as service equipment, the neutral block (terminal block) is bonded to the panel cabinet by the bonding screw provided. And such bonding is required to tie the grounded conductor to the interconnected system of metal enclosures for the system (i.e., service-equipment enclosures, conduits, busway, boxes, panel cabinets, etc.). It is this connection which provides for flow of fault current and operation of the overcurrent device (fuse or breaker) when a ground fault occurs. But, there must not be any connection between the grounded system conductor and the grounded metal enclosure system at any point on the load side of the service equipment, because such connection would constitute connection of the grounded system conductor to a grounding electrode (through the enclosure and raceway system to the water pipe or driven ground rod). Such connections, like bonding of subpanels, can be dangerous, as shown in Fig. 250-14.

This rule on not connecting the grounded system wire to a grounding electrode on the load side of the service disconnect must not be confused with the rule of Sec. 250-60 which permits the grounded system conductor to be used

1. THIS CONDITION WILL EXIST....AND...

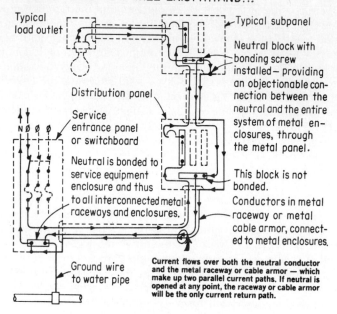

Typical load outlet

Typical subpanel

Neutral block with bonding screw installed— providing an objectionable connection between the neutral and the entire system of metal enclosures, through the metal panel.

Distribution panel

Service entrance panel or switchboard

N Ø Ø Ø

Neutral is bonded to service equipment enclosure and thus to all interconnected metal raceways and enclosures.

This block is not bonded.

Conductors in metal raceway or metal cable armor, connected to metal enclosures.

Ground wire to water pipe

Current flows over both the neutral conductor and the metal raceway or cable armor — which make up two parallel current paths. If neutral is opened at any point, the raceway or cable armor will be the only current return path.

2. THIS HAZARD COULD DEVELOP

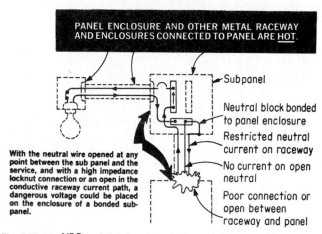

PANEL ENCLOSURE AND OTHER METAL RACEWAY AND ENCLOSURES CONNECTED TO PANEL ARE <u>HOT</u>.

Subpanel

Neutral block bonded to panel enclosure

Restricted neutral current on raceway

No current on open neutral

Poor connection or open between raceway and panel

With the neutral wire opened at any point between the sub panel and the service, and with a high impedance locknut connection or an open in the conductive raceway current path, a dangerous voltage could be placed on the enclosure of a bonded subpanel.

Fig. 250-14. NEC prohibits bonding of subpanels because of these reasons. (Sec. 250-23.)

for grounding the frames of electric ranges, wall ovens, counter-mounted cooking units, and electric clothes dryers. The connection referred to in Sec. 250-60 is that of an ungrounded metal enclosure to the grounded conductor for the purpose of grounding the enclosure.

A very important qualification in the second sentence of Sec. 250-23(a) on grounding connections for AC systems eliminates confusion and controversy about connection of the grounding electrode conductor when a building is fed by service conductors from a meter on a yard pole.

The basic rule of this section says that the grounding electrode conductor required for grounding both the grounded service conductor (usually a grounded neutral) and the metal enclosure of the service equipment *must be* connected to the grounded service conductor *within* or on the *supply side* of the service disconnect. But the rule further requires that the connection of the grounding electrode conductor **must be connected between the load end of the service drop or lateral and the service equipment.**

As a result of that requirement, if a service is fed to a building from a meter enclosure on a pole or other structure some distance away, as commonly done on farm properties, and an overhead or underground run of service conductors is made to the service disconnect in the building, the grounding electrode conductor will not satisfy the **Code** if it is connected to the neutral in the meter enclosure but must be connected at the *load end* of the underground or overhead service conductors. And, the connection should preferably be made *within* the service-disconnect enclosure.

This rule on grounding connection is shown in Fig. 250-15. If, instead of an underground lateral, an overhead run were made to the building from the pole, the overhead line would be a "service drop." The rule of Sec. 250-23(a) would likewise require the grounding connection at the load end of the service drop.

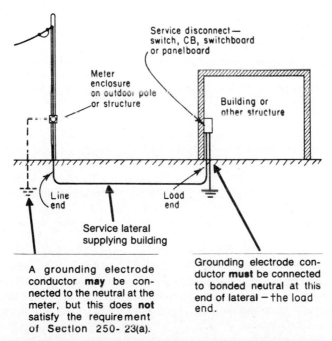

A grounding electrode conductor **may** be connected to the neutral at the meter, but this does **not** satisfy the requirement of Section 250- 23(a).

Grounding electrode conductor **must** be connected to bonded neutral at this end of lateral — the load end.

Fig. 250-15. Connection to grounded conductor at load end of lateral or drop. (Sec. 250-23.)

If a fused switch or CB is installed as service disconnect and protection at the load side of the meter on the pole, then that would establish the service at that point, and the grounding electrode connection to the bonded neutral terminal would be required at that point. The circuit from that point to the building would be a feeder and not service conductors. But, electrical safety and effective operation would require that an equipment grounding conductor be run with the feeder circuit conductors for grounding the interconnected system of conduits and metal equipment enclosures along with metal piping systems and building steel within the building. Or, if an equipment grounding conductor is not in the circuit from the pole to the building, the neutral could be bonded to the main disconnect enclosure in the building and a grounding electrode connection made at that point also. Either technique complies with the concepts of Sec. 250-24(a) and its Exception No. 2.

There is an important Exception to the rule that each and every service for a grounded AC system have a grounding electrode conductor connected to the grounded system conductor anywhere on the supply side of the service disconnecting means (preferably within the service-equipment enclosure) and that the grounding electrode conductor be run to a grounding electrode at the service. Because controversy has arisen in the past about how many grounding electrode conductors have to be run for a dual-feed (double-ended) service with a secondary tie, Exception No. 4 recognizes the use of a single grounding electrode conductor connection for such dual services. It says that the single grounding electrode connection may be made to the "tie point of the grounded circuit conductors from each power source." The explanation on this **Code** permission was made by NEMA, the sponsor of the rule, as follows:

> Unless center neutral point grounding and the omission of all other secondary grounding is permitted, the selective ground-fault protection schemes now available for dual power source systems with secondary ties will not work. Dual power source systems are utilized for maximum service continuity. Without selectivity, both sources would be shut down by any ground fault. This proposal permits selectivity so that one source can remain operative for half the load, after a ground fault on the other half of the system.

Figure 250-16 shows two cases involving the concept of single grounding point on a dual-fed service:

In Case 1, if the double-ended unit substation is in a locked room in a building it serves or consists of metal-enclosed gear or a locked enclosure for each transformer, the secondary circuit from each transformer is a "service" to the building. The question then arises, "Does there have to be a separate grounding electrode conductor run from each secondary service to a grounding electrode?"

In Case 2, if each of the two transformers is located outdoors, in a separate building from the one they serve, in a transformer vault in the building they serve, or in a locked room or enclosure and accessible to qualified persons only or in metal-enclosed gear—then the secondary circuit from each transformer constitutes a service to the building. Again, is a separate grounding connection required for each service?

In both cases, a single grounding electrode connection may serve both services, as shown at the bottom of Fig. 250-16.

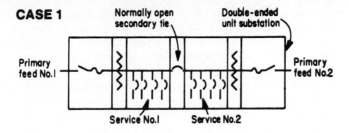

CASE 1

Normally open secondary tie

Double-ended unit substation

Primary feed No.1

Primary feed No.2

Service No.1

Service No.2

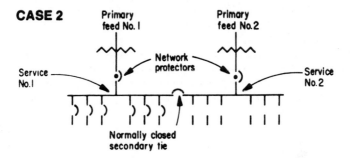

CASE 2

Primary feed No. 1

Primary feed No. 2

Network protectors

Service No.1

Service No. 2

Normally closed secondary tie

FOR BOTH CASES, THIS MAY BE DONE:

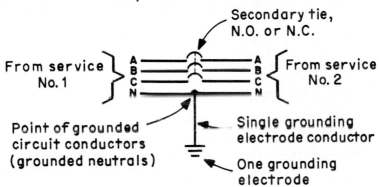

Secondary tie, N.O. or N.C.

From service No. 1

From service No. 2

Point of grounded circuit conductors (grounded neutrals)

Single grounding electrode conductor

One grounding electrode

Fig. 250-16. *One grounding connection permitted for a double-end service.* (Sec. 250-23.)

The **Code** rule in Exception No. 4 refers to "services that are dual fed (double ended) in a *common enclosure or grouped together.*" The phrase "common enclosure" can readily cover use of a double-ended loadcenter unit substation in a single, common enclosure. But the phrase "grouped together" can lend itself to many interpretations and has caused difficulties. For instance, if each of two separate services was a single-ended unit substation, do both the unit substations have to be in the same room or within the same fenced area outdoors? How far apart may they be and still be considered "grouped together"?

As shown in Case 2 of Fig. 250-16, if separate transformers and switchboards are used instead of unit subsubstations, may one of the transformers and its switchboard be installed at the opposite end of the building from the other one? The **Code** does not answer those questions, but it seems clear that the wording does suggest that both of the services must be physically close and at least in the same room or vault or fenced area. That understanding has always been applied to other **Code** rules calling for "grouping"—such as for switches and CBs in Sec. 380-8 and for service disconnects in Sec. 230-72(a).

Part **(b)** requires that whenever a service is derived from a grounded neutral system, the grounded neutral conductor must be brought into the service-entrance equipment, even if the grounded conductor is not needed for the load supplied by the service. A service of less than 1,000 V that is grounded outdoors at the service transformer (pad mount, mat, or unit substation) must have the grounded conductor run to "each service disconnecting means" and bonded to the separate enclosure for "each" service disconnect. If two to six normal service disconnects [as permitted by Sec. 230-71(a)] are installed in separate enclosures (or even additional disconnect switches or circuit breakers for emergency, fire pump, etc.), the grounded circuit conductor must be run to a bonded neutral terminal in *each* of the separate disconnect enclosures fed from the service conductors. Exception No. 3 to this rule clarifies that if multiple service disconnect switches or circuit breakers are installed within "an assembly listed for use as service equipment"—such as in a service panelboard, switchboard, or multimeter distribution assembly—only a single grounded (neutral) conductor has to be run to the single, common assembly enclosure and bonded to it.

Running the grounded conductor to each individual service disconnect enclosure is required to provide a low-impedance ground-fault current return path to the neutral to assure operation of the overcurrent device, for safety to personnel and property. See Fig. 250-17. In such cases, the neutral functions strictly as an equipment grounding conductor, to provide a closed circuit back to the transformer for automatic circuit opening in the event of a phase-to-ground fault anywhere on the load side of the service equipment. Only one phase leg is shown in these diagrams to simplify the concept. The other two phase legs have the same relation to the neutral.

The same requirements apply to installation of separate power and light services derived from a common 3-phase, 4-wire, grounded "red-leg" delta system. The neutral from the center-tapped transformer winding must be brought into the 3-phase power service equipment as well as into the lighting service, even though the neutral will not be used for power loads. This is shown in Fig. 250-18 and is also required by Sec. 250-23(b), which states that such an unused neutral must be at least equal to the required minimum size of grounding electrode conductor specified in Table 250-94 for the size of phase conductors. In addition, if the phase legs associated with that neutral are larger than 1,100 kcmil, the grounded neutral must not be smaller than 12½ percent of the area of the largest phase conductor, which means 12½ percent of the total csa of conductors per phase when parallel conductors are used.

In any system where the neutral *is* required on the load side of the service—such as where 208Y/120-V or 480Y/277-V, 3-phase, 4-wire distribution is to be

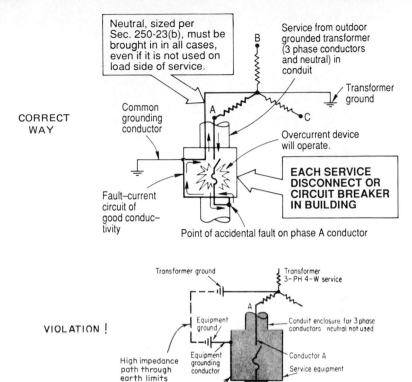

Fig. 250-17. Clearing of ground faults on the load side of any service disconnect depends upon fault-current return over a grounded circuit conductor (usually a neutral) brought into each and every enclosure for service disconnect switch or CB (Sec. 250-23.)

made on the premises—the neutral from the supply transformer to the service equipment is needed to provide for neutral current flow under conditions of load unbalance on the phase legs of the premises distribution system. But, even in a premises where all distribution on the load side of the service is to be solely 3-phase, 3-wire (such as 480-V, 3-phase, 3-wire distribution) and the neutral conductor is not required in the premises system, this **Code** rule says that the neutral must still run from the supply transformer to the service equipment.

The final part of the rule covers cases where the service phase conductors are paralleled, with two or more conductors in parallel per phase leg and neutral, and requires that the size of the grounded neutral must be calculated on the equivalent area for parallel conductors. If a calculated size of neutral (at least 12½ percent of the phase-leg cross section) is to be divided among two or more conduits, and if dividing the calculated size by the number of conduits being used calls for a neutral conductor smaller than 1/0 in each conduit, the FPN calls attention to Sec. 310-4, which gives No. 1/0 as the minimum size of conductor that may be used in parallel in multiple conduits. For that reason,

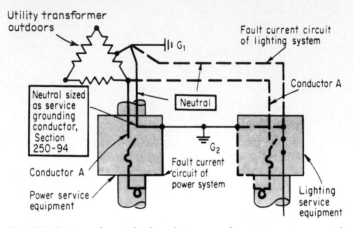

Fig. 250·18. Neutral must be brought in to each service equipment and bonded to enclosure. (Sec. 250-23.)

each neutral would have to be at least a No. 1/0, even though the calculated size might be, say, No. 1 or No. 2 or some other size smaller than No. 1/0. But, the **Code** rule does permit subdividing the required minimum 12½ percent grounded (neutral) conductor size by the total number of conduits used in a parallel run, thereby permitting a multiple makeup using a smaller neutral in each pipe.

As shown in Figure 250-19, the minimum required size for the grounded neutral conductor run from the supply transformer to the service is based on the

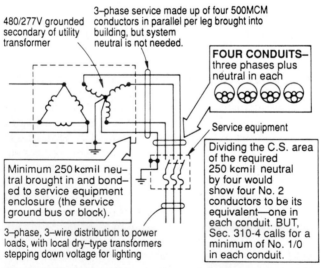

Fig. 250·19. Grounded service conductor must *always* be brought in. (Sec. 250-23.)

size of the service phase conductors. In this case, the overall size of the service phase conductors is 4 × 500 kcmil per phase leg, or 2,000 kcmil. Because that is larger than 1,100 kcmil, it is not permitted to simply use Table 250-94 in sizing the neutral. Instead, 2,000 kcmil must be multiplied by 12½ percent. Then 2,000 kcmil × 0.125 equals 250 kcmil— the minimum permitted size of the neutral conductor run from the transformer to the service equipment. It is **Code** intent to permit the required 250-kcmil-sized neutral to be divided by the number of conduits. From **NEC** Table 8 in Chapter 9, it can be seen that four No. 2 conductors, each with a cross-section area of 66,360 circular mils, would approximate the area of one 250 kcmil (250,000 circular mils divided by 4 = 62,500 circular mils). But, because No. 1/0 is the smallest conductor that is permitted by Sec. 310-4 to be used in parallel for a circuit of this type, it would be necessary to use a No. 1/0 copper conductor in each of the four conduits, along with the phase legs.

250-24. Two or More Buildings or Structures Supplied from a Common Service.   In Sec. 250-23(a), bonding of a panel neutral block (or the neutral bus or terminal in a switchboard, switch, or circuit breaker) to the enclosure is required in service equipment. Exception No. 2 of that section permits bonding of the neutral conductor on the load side of the service equipment in those cases where a panelboard (or switchboard, switch, etc.) is used to supply circuits in a building and the panel is fed from another building. This is covered in Sec. 250-24 which says that, where two or more buildings are supplied from a common service to a main building, a grounding electrode at each other building shall be connected to the AC system grounded conductor on the supply side of the building disconnecting means of a grounded system as shown in Fig. 250-20 or connected to the metal enclosure of the building disconnecting means of an ungrounded system. Those are the basic rules covered in parts **(a)** and **(b)** of this section. But Exception No. 1 to part **(a)** and Exception No. 1 to part **(b)** note that a grounding electrode at a separate building supplied by a feeder or branch circuit is not required where only one branch circuit is supplied and there is no noncurrent-carrying equipment in the building that requires grounding. An example would be a small residential garage with a single lighting outlet or switch with no *metal* boxes, faceplates, or lighting fixtures within 8 ft vertically or 5 ft horizontally from a grounded condition.

Exception No. 2 to part **(a)** states that the grounded circuit conductor of a feeder to a separate building does not have to be bonded and grounded to a grounding electrode if an equipment grounding conductor is run with the circuit conductors for grounding any noncurrent-carrying equipment, water piping, or building metal frames in the separate building. See Fig. 250-21. And, as shown at the bottom of that illustration, the need for a grounding electrode at the outbuilding is eliminated because the words "equipment grounding conductor" as used in Exception No. 2 of Sec. 250-24(a) are understood to include metal "conduit" as indicated by Sec. 250-91(b), which recognizes an "equipment grounding conductor . . . enclosing the circuit conductors." If the separate building has an approved grounding electrode and/or interior metallic piping system, the equipment grounding conductor shall be bonded to the electrode and/or piping system. However, if the separate building does *not* have a

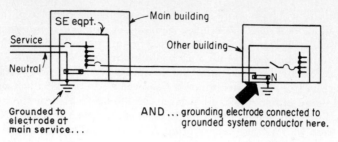

Grounded to
electrode at
main service...

AND ... grounding electrode connected to
grounded system conductor here.

EXAMPLE: ➡

The bonding of the neutral
in the sub-panel and the connection to the ground rod are
required by Sec. 250-24.

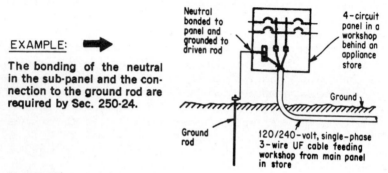

Fig. 250·20. Grounded conductor (e.g., a neutral) must be grounded at each building.
(Sec. 250-24.)

grounding electrode—that is, does not have 10 ft or more of underground metal water pipe, does not have grounded structural steel, and does not have any of the other electrodes recognized by Sec. 250-81—then at least one grounding electrode must be installed. That would most likely be a *made* electrode—such as a driven ground rod—and it must be bonded to the equipment ground terminal or equipment grounding bus in the enclosure of the panel, switchboard, circuit breaker, or switch in which the feeder terminates (Fig. 250-21).

When a grounding electrode connection is made to a grounded system conductor (usually a neutral) at a building that is fed from another building, the necessity for bonding the neutral block in such a subpanel is based on Sec. 250-24 and Sec. 250-54. The latter section says, "Where an AC system is connected to a grounding electrode in or at a building as specified in Sections 250-23 and 250-24, the same electrode shall be used to ground conductor enclosures and equipment in or on that building." Although the **Code** permits and even requires bonding at both ends, if the feeder circuit is in conduit, neutral current flows on the conduit because it is electrically in parallel with the neutral conductor, being bonded to it at both ends.

At one time, the rule of Exception No. 2 of part **(a)** of this section required bonding and grounding of the neutral conductor at any outbuilding in which livestock was housed. That bonding and grounding was required even if an equipment grounding conductor was run from the main building to the live-

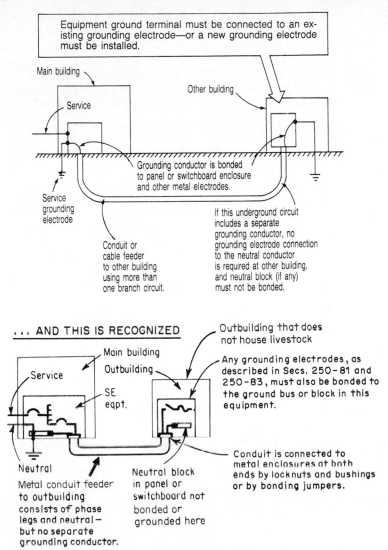

Equipment ground terminal must be connected to an existing grounding electrode—or a new grounding electrode must be installed.

Main building

Other building

Service

Grounding conductor is bonded
to panel or switchboard enclosure
and other metal electrodes.

Service
grounding
electrode

If this underground circuit
includes a separate
grounding conductor, no
grounding electrode connection
to the neutral conductor
is required at other building,
and neutral block (if any)
must not be bonded.

Conduit or
cable feeder
to other building
using more than
one branch circuit.

... AND THIS IS RECOGNIZED

Outbuilding that does
not house livestock

Main building

Any grounding electrodes, as
described in Secs. 250-81 and
250-83, must also be bonded to
the ground bus or block in this
equipment.

Service

Outbuilding

SE
eqpt.

Conduit is connected to
metal enclosures at both
ends by locknuts and bushings
or by bonding jumpers.

Neutral

Metal conduit feeder
to outbuilding
consists of phase
legs and neutral —
but no separate
grounding conductor.

Neutral block
in panel or
switchboard not
bonded or
grounded here

Fig. 250-21. Grounding connection at outbuildings may be eliminated. (Sec. 250-24.)

stock building. That rigid rule has been removed from the **Code,** and it is no longer mandatory that the neutral must always be bonded and connected to a grounding electrode at an outbuilding housing livestock.

As required in the 1981 and previous **NEC** editions, the neutral had to be connected to a grounding electrode and bonded to the disconnect enclosure (and, as a result, bonded to the entire equipment grounding system of interconnected metal raceways and housings in the livestock building being fed). When a neutral is bonded in that way, without connection to a grounding electrode at the livestock building, any flow of normal unbalanced load current on the neutral produces a voltage drop on the neutral from the main disconnect in the livestock building back to the ground reference of the grounding electrode at the service of the main building. That voltage drop then appears as a potential to ground from equipment housings in the livestock building and can have an adverse effect on livestock. The reasoning behind elimination of the mandatory rule on neutral bonding in a livestock building was given as follows:

> When livestock are housed in Building No. 2, and when a separate equipment grounding conductor is run from Building No. 1 to Building No. 2 for the purpose of grounding all metal equipment and parts, it shall be permissible to isolate the grounding conductor from the neutral in Building No. 2 if neutral-to-earth voltages cause distress to the confined livestock.
>
> *Substantiation:* Neutral-to-earth voltages (stray voltages) are caused by many factors. One of the primary causes is voltage drop on secondary circuits due to circuit imbalance and long circuits. Second, voltage drops are imposed on neutral busbars in a building service entrance, which are in turn transmitted to metal grounding conductors, conduit, or panel grounding to a metallic water system. Livestock, particularly dairy animals and swine, are very sensitive to AC voltages that can occur when part of their body makes contact with the described metal equipment and part of their body is in contact with true earth. AC voltages over 1 V are known to cause dairy animals to go out of milk production and to inhibit the growth rate of swine.
>
> (Note attached paper on stray voltage problems, page 11, item 7.) You will note that an alternate solution to resolving stray voltage problems is to isolate the neutral from the grounding conductors in the barn panel and run a separate fourth wire either back to the transformer or metering location (main farm service entrance).
>
> By adding the proposed exception to **NEC** Sec. 250-24, it would make it legal or permissible to run the fourth wire and isolate the neutral and grounding wires at the panel serving building No. 2, which is assumed to be a grounded system having a grounding electrode connected to the neutral.

The last sentence of Exception No. 2 to part **(a)** does require that the equipment grounding conductor that is run with the feeder to the disconnect enclosure in a livestock building be an "insulated or covered copper" conductor and may not simply consist of metal conduit enclosing the feeder conductors. For such a feeder, the equipment grounding conductor must be insulated or covered copper *only* for an underground circuit or for any part of the circuit that is run underground. The purpose of that rule is to assure a more reliable equipment grounding path for such buildings to prevent potentials on equipment that would threaten livestock because of their great sensitivity to even very low voltages—as described earlier. An equipment grounding conductor run underground—directly buried or in a raceway—must be insulated or covered copper to prevent corrosion. *But* an overhead feeder to a barn building may be aluminum or copper multiplex cable with a bare messenger wire used as the equipment grounding conductor. Figure 250-22 shows the considerations in the Exception: (3) applies to any outbuilding; (1) and (2) apply only to a separate building housing livestock.

Figure 250-23 shows another condition in which a grounding electrode connection must be made at the *other* building, as specified in the basic rule of Sec. 250-24(b). For an ungrounded system, when, as shown in the sketch, an equipment grounding conductor is *not* run to the outbuilding, then a grounding

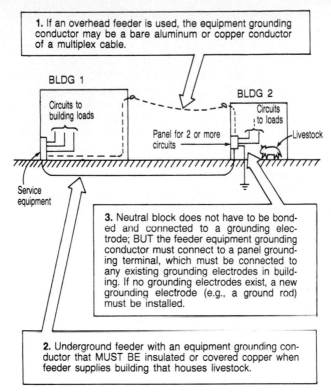

1. If an overhead feeder is used, the equipment grounding conductor may be a bare aluminum or copper conductor of a multiplex cable.

BLDG 1

Circuits to building loads

Service equipment

BLDG 2

Circuits to loads

Livestock

Panel for 2 or more circuits

3. Neutral block does not have to be bonded and connected to a grounding electrode; BUT the feeder equipment grounding conductor must connect to a panel grounding terminal, which must be connected to any existing grounding electrodes in building. If no grounding electrodes exist, a new grounding electrode (e.g., a ground rod) must be installed.

2. Underground feeder with an equipment grounding conductor that MUST BE insulated or covered copper when feeder supplies building that houses livestock.

Fig. 250·22. Building for livestock must be carefully grounded. [Sec. 250-24(a), Exception No. 2.]

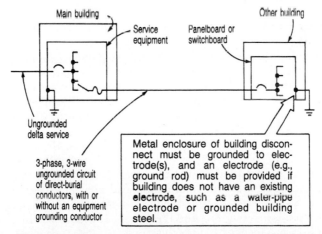

Main building

Service equipment

Panelboard or switchboard

Other building

Ungrounded delta service

3-phase, 3-wire ungrounded circuit of direct-burial conductors, with or without an equipment grounding conductor

Metal enclosure of building disconnect must be grounded to electrode(s), and an electrode (e.g., ground rod) must be provided if building does not have an existing electrode, such as a water-pipe electrode or grounded building steel.

Fig. 250·23. Grounding connection for an ungrounded supply to outbuilding. (Sec. 250-24.)

electrode conductor must be run from the ground bus or terminal in the outbuilding disconnect to a suitable grounding electrode which *must be* provided.

According to Sec. 250-24(b), Exception No. 2, a circuit of an ungrounded system *does not* require a grounding electrode connection to the equipment ground terminal at an outbuilding disconnect *only* where the outbuilding uses not more than one branch circuit, where an equipment grounding conductor is run with the circuit conductors to the outbuilding, and where there are no existing electrodes at the outbuilding. If the ungrounded circuit to the outbuilding is a feeder supplying more than one branch circuit, then connection must be made from the equipment grounding terminal in the outbuilding disconnect to either an existing ground electrode at the building (water pipe, building steel, etc.) or to a new ground electrode installed for the purpose. And such a connection to a ground electrode must be made even if an equipment grounding conductor is run with the feeder conductors to the outbuilding. If the building houses livestock, that portion of the equipment grounding conductor that is run underground to the outbuilding must be insulated or covered copper.

In Fig. 250-23, if the 3-phase, 3-wire, ungrounded feeder circuit to the outbuilding had been run with a separate equipment grounding conductor which effectively connected the metal enclosure of the disconnect in the outbuilding to the grounding electrode conductor in the SE equipment of the main building, a connection to a grounding electrode would not be required provided that conditions a., b., c., and d. of Exception No. 2 are satisfied. But if all those conditions are not satisfied and a grounding electrode connection would be required at the outbuilding, then the equipment grounding conductor run to the outbuilding would have to be bonded to any grounding electrodes that were "existing" at that building—such as an underground metal water service pipe and/ or a grounded metal frame of the building. All grounding electrodes that *exist* at the outbuilding must be bonded to the ground bus or terminal in the disconnect at the outbuilding, whether or not an equipment grounding conductor is run with the circuit conductors from the main building.

Part **(c)** covers design of the grounding arrangement for a feeder from one building to another building when the main disconnect for the feeder is at a remote location from the building being supplied—such as in the other building where the feeder originates. The rule prohibits grounding and bonding of a feeder to a building from another building *if* the disconnect for the building being fed is located in the building where the feeder originates. Part **(c)** correlates the grounding concepts of Sec. 250-24 with the disconnect requirements of Sec. 230-84(a), Exceptions No. 1 and No. 2. This is most easily understood by considering the following sequence of **Code** rules involved:

1. First, in Sec. 250-23(a), bonding of a panel neutral block (or the neutral bus or terminal in a switchboard, switch, or circuit breaker) to the enclosure is required in service equipment. Exception No. 2 of that section permits bonding of the neutral conductor on the load side of the service equipment in those cases where a panelboard (or switchboard, switch, etc.) is used to supply circuits in a building and the panel or switchboard in that building is supplied by a feeder from another building. This is covered in Sec. 250-24(a), which says that where two or more buildings are supplied from a

common service to a main building, a grounding electrode at each other building shall be connected to the AC system grounded conductor on the supply side of the building disconnect means of a grounded system and the neutral must be bonded to the metal enclosure of the disconnect (the enclosure of the panelboard or switchboard or switch or circuit breaker) in the building being supplied. The basic rule calls for grounding and bonding within the building disconnect for the building being fed. That is, the feeder to the second building is treated like a service to the building.

2. But, Exception No. 2 of Sec. 250-24(a) gives the *option* of treating the feeder to a building from another building exactly like a feeder that did not leave the main building—that is, running an equipment grounding conductor and *not* grounding and bonding the feeder neutral in the building disconnect. Exception No. 2 to part **(a)** of Sec. 250-24 states that the grounded circuit conductor of a feeder to a separate building does not have to be bonded and grounded to a grounding electrode if an equipment grounding conductor is run with the circuit conductors for grounding any noncurrent-carrying equipment, water piping, or building metal frames in the separate building. If the separate building has an approved grounding electrode and/or interior metallic piping system, the equipment grounding conductor shall be bonded to the electrode and/or piping system. However, if the separate building does *not* have a grounding electrode—that is, does not have 10 ft or more of underground metal water pipe, does not have grounded structural steel, and does not have any other electrodes recognized by Sec. 250-81—then at least one grounding electrode must be installed. That would most likely be a *made* electrode—such as a driven ground rod—and it must be bonded to the equipment ground terminal or equipment grounding bus in the enclosure of the panelboard, switchboard, circuit breaker, or switch in which the feeder terminates.

3. Although the use of an equipment grounding conductor and elimination of the need for a bonded connection to a grounding electrode, as described in (2) above, is given as an optional alternative to (1) above, part **(c)** of Sec. 250-24 makes elimination of a bonded connection to an electrode a *mandatory* method when the disconnect for the feeder is in the other building where the feeder originates, as covered by Sec. 230-84 (Fig. 250-24).

4. The basic rule of Sec. 230-84(a) says that for a group of buildings under single management, disconnect means must be provided for each building. This rule requires that the conductors supplying each building in the group be provided with a means for disconnecting all ungrounded conductors from the supply. Because this is covered under Article 230, it is usually interpreted to permit the disconnect for each building or structure to be the same kind as permitted for a service disconnect—that is, up to six switches or CBs, as covered in Sec. 230-71.

For large-capacity multibuilding industrial premises with a single owner, Exception No. 1 of Sec. 230-84 permits use of the feeder switch in the main building as the only disconnect for a feeder to an outlying building, provided the disconnect in the main building is accessible to the occupants of the outlying building. Now, when that option of Exception No. 1 of Sec. 230-84(a) is

This is the basic rule of Sec. 250-24(a).

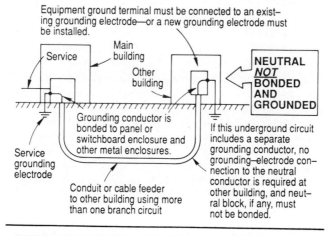

Service

SE eqpt

Main building

Other building

Neutral

N

N

NEUTRAL BONDED AND GROUNDED

Neutral grounded to electrode at main service

Grounding electrode connected to grounded system conductor here

---

This *optional* alternative becomes *mandatory* . . .

Equipment ground terminal must be connected to an exist-ing grounding electrode—or a new grounding electrode must be installed.

Service

Main building

Other building

NEUTRAL *NOT* BONDED AND GROUNDED

Service grounding electrode

Grounding conductor is bonded to panel or switchboard enclosure and other metal enclosures.

Conduit or cable feeder to other building using more than one branch circuit

If this underground circuit includes a separate grounding conductor, no grounding–electrode con-nection to the neutral conductor is required at other building, and neut-ral block, if any, must not be bonded.

. . . if Exception No. 1 of Sec. 230-84(a) is uti-lized to eliminate outbuilding disconnects.

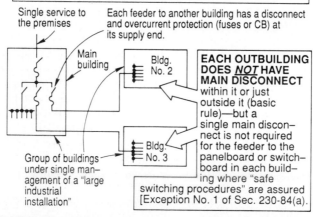

Single service to the premises

Each feeder to another building has a disconnect and overcurrent protection (fuses or CB) at its supply end.

Main building

Bldg. No. 2

Bldg. No. 3

EACH OUTBUILDING DOES *NOT* HAVE MAIN DISCONNECT within it or just outside it (basic rule)—but a single main discon-nect is not required for the feeder to the panelboard or switch-board in each build-ing where "safe switching procedures" are assured [Exception No. 1 of Sec. 230-84(a).

Group of buildings under single man-agement of a "large industrial installation"

Fig. 250-24. Part (c) correlates grounding for multiple buildings under a sin-gle management with rule of Sec. 230-84(a) on location of feeder disconnect for an outbuilding. [Sec. 250-24(c).]

selected, eliminating a main disconnect for the feeder within the outbuilding being supplied, part **(c)** of Sec. 250-24 requires the following conditions to be met:

a. The grounded (neutral) conductor of the feeder *must not* be connected to a grounding electrode at the outbuilding and the grounded conductors must *not* be bonded to the panelboard or switchboard enclosure in the outbuilding.

b. An equipment grounding conductor *must* be run with the feeder circuit conductors to the outbuilding to ground metal equipment enclosures, metal conduit, and other noncurrent-carrying metal parts of electrical equipment in the outbuilding. Any interior metal piping and building and structural metal frames in the outbuilding *must* be bonded to the equipment grounding conductor. In addition, any grounding electrodes at the outbuilding must be bonded to the feeder equipment grounding conductor. And if the outbuilding contains no grounding electrodes as covered in Sec. 250-81, a made electrode (a ground rod, etc.) must be installed and bonded to the equipment grounding conductor of the feeder.

c. The *bond* between the feeder equipment grounding conductor and any grounding electrodes at the outbuilding *must* be made in a junction box "located immediately inside or outside the second building or structure."

As follow-up to part **(c)**, the rule of part **(d)** says the conductor used to bond the feeder equipment grounding conductor to the one or more existing or new grounding electrodes at an outbuilding must be sized from Table 250-95, based on the rating of the overcurrent device protecting the ungrounded conductors of the feeder. This is a rule to clarify the sizing of the bonding conductor to building electrodes as required by Exception No. 2 of Sec. 250-24(a) and part **(2)** of Sec. 250-24(c). In effect, the wording of this rule in part **(d)** calls for the bonding conductor to be the same size as the equipment grounding conductor of the feeder, based on Table 250-95. And the same size of conductor would be used to connect to the interior metal piping systems and structural metal frame of the outbuilding.

Exception No. 1 notes that the grounding conductor would never have to be larger than the circuit ungrounded conductors. And Exception No. 2 says the grounding conductor would not have to be larger than No. 6 copper or No. 4 aluminum where it connects to a driven ground rod or other made electrode.

250-25. Conductor to Be Grounded—Alternating-Current Systems. Selection of the wiring system conductor to be grounded depends upon the type of system. In 3-wire, single-phase systems, the midpoint of the transformer winding—the point from which the system neutral is derived—is grounded. For grounded 3-phase wiring systems, the neutral point of the wye-connected transformer(s) or generator is the point connected to ground. In delta-connected transformer hookups, grounding of the system can be effected by grounding one of the three phase legs, by grounding a center-tap point on one of the transformer windings (as in the 3-phase, 4-wire "red-leg" delta system), or by using a special grounding transformer which establishes a neutral point of a wye connection which is grounded.

250-26. Grounding Separately Derived Alternating-Current Systems. A separately derived AC wiring system is a source derived from an on-site generator (emergency or standby), a battery-inverter, or the secondary supply of a transformer. Any such AC supplies required to be grounded by Sec. 250-5 must comply with Sec. 250-26:

1. Any system which operates at over 50 V but not more than 150 V to ground must be grounded [Sec. 250-5(b)].

2. This requires the grounding of generator windings and secondaries of transformers serving 208/120-V, 3-phase or 240/120-V, single-phase circuits for lighting and appliance outlets and receptacles, at loadcenters throughout a building, as shown for the very common application of dry-type transformers in Fig. 250-25.

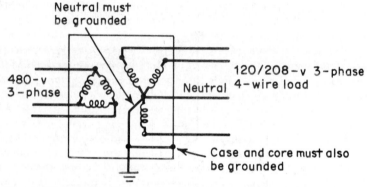

Fig. 250-25. Grounding is required for "separately derived" systems. (Sec. 250-26.)

3. All **Code** rules applying to both system and equipment grounding must be satisfied in such installations.

Referring to Fig. 250-26, the steps involved in satisfying the **Code** rules are as follows:

Step 1—Sec. 250-26(a)

A bonding jumper must be installed between the transformer secondary neutral terminal and the metal case of the transformer. The size of this bonding conductor is based on Sec. 250-79(c) and is selected from Table 250-94 of the **Code**—based on the size of the transformer secondary phase conductors and selected to be the same size as a required grounding electrode conductor. For cases where the transformer secondary circuit is larger than 1,100 kcmil copper or 1,750 kcmil aluminum per phase leg, the bonding jumper must be not less than 12½ percent of the cross-section area of the secondary phase leg.

example Assume this is a 75-kVA transformer with a 120/208-V, 3-phase, 4-wire secondary. Such a unit would have a full-load secondary current of

$$75,000 \div (208 \times 1.732) \text{ or } 209 \text{ A}$$

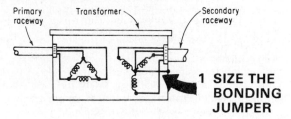

STEP 1 – BONDING JUMPER

1 SIZE THE BONDING JUMPER

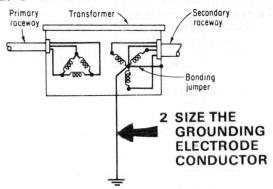

STEP 2 – GROUNDING ELECTRODE CONDUCTOR

2 SIZE THE GROUNDING ELECTRODE CONDUCTOR

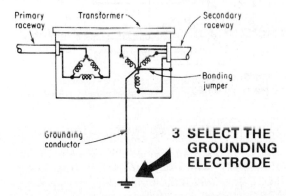

STEP 3 – GROUNDING ELECTRODE

3 SELECT THE GROUNDING ELECTRODE

Fig. 250-26. Grounding a transformer secondary. (Sec. 250-26.)

If we use No. 4/0 THW copper conductors for the secondary phase legs (with a 230-A rating), we would then select the size of the required bonding jumper from Table 250-94 as if we had 4/0 service conductors. The table shows that 4/0 copper service conductors require a minimum of No. 2 copper or No. 1/0 aluminum for a grounding electrode conductor. And the bonding jumper would have to be either of those two sizes.

If the transformer was a 500-kVA unit with a 120/208-V secondary, its rated secondary current would be

$$\frac{500 \times 1,000}{1.732 \times 208} = 1,388 \text{ A}$$

Using, say, THW aluminum conductors, the size of each secondary phase leg would be four 700 kcmil aluminum conductors in parallel (each 700 kcmil THW aluminum is rated at 375 A, four are 4 × 375 or 1,500 A, which suits the 1,388-A load).

Then, because 4 × 700 kcmil equals 2,800 kcmil per phase leg and is in excess of 1,750 kcmil, Sec. 250-79(c) requires the bonding jumper from the case to the neutral terminal to be at least equal to 12½ percent × 2,800 kcmil (0.125 × 2,800) or 350 kcmil aluminum.

Step 2—Sec. 250-26(b)

A grounding electrode conductor must be installed from the transformer secondary neutral terminal to a suitable grounding electrode. This grounding conductor is sized the same as the required bonding jumper in Step 1. That is, this grounding electrode conductor is sized from Table 250-94 as if it is a grounding electrode conductor for a service with service-entrance conductors equal in size to the phase conductors used on the transformer secondary side. But, this grounding electrode conductor does *not* have to be larger than 3/0 copper or 250 kcmil aluminum when the transformer secondary circuit is over 1,100 kcmil copper or 1,750 kcmil aluminum.

example   For the 75-kVA transformer in Step 1, the grounding electrode conductor must be not smaller than the required minimum size shown in Table 250-94 for 4/0 phase legs, which makes it the same size as the bonding jumper—i.e., No. 2 copper or No. 1/0 aluminum. But, for the 500-kVA transformer, the grounding electrode conductor is sized directly from Table 250-94—which requires a 3/0 copper or 250 kcmil aluminum where the phase legs are over 1,100 kcmil copper or 1,750 kcmil aluminum.

The last sentence of Sec. 250-26(a) and (b) permits the bonding and grounding connections to be made either right at the transformer or generator or at the first disconnect or overcurrent device fed from the transformer or generator, as in Fig. 250-27.

The last sentence of Sec. 250-26(a) and (b), however, does say that the bonding and grounding "shall be made at the *source*"—which appears to indicate right at the transformer or generator, and *not* any other point—where the transformer supplies a system that "has no disconnecting means or overcurrent device." A local transformer that "has no disconnect or overcurrent devices" on its secondary is one that supplies only a single circuit and has overcurrent protection on its primary, such as a control transformer to supply motor starter coils. But in such applications, the transformer does not supply a separately derived "system" in the usual sense that a "system" consists of more than one circuit. It is true, however, that for a transformer supplying only one circuit, any required bonding and grounding of a secondary grounded conductor—such as the grounded leg of a two-wire 120-V control circuit—would normally have to be done right at the transformer.

Another interpretation that might be put on that last phrase is that it refers to a hookup in which the transformer secondary feeds *main lugs only* in a panel-

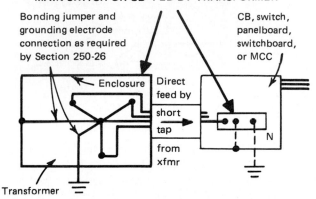

**BONDING AND GROUNDING CONNECTIONS
MAY BE MADE AT TRANSFORMER OR AT
MAIN SWITCH OR CB FED BY TRANSFORMER**

Bonding jumper and
grounding electrode
connection as required
by Section 250-26

CB, switch,
panelboard,
switchboard,
or MCC

Enclosure   Direct
feed by

short

tap

from

xfmr

N

Transformer

Fig. 250·27. Transformer secondary bonding and grounding must be "at the source" or at a secondary disconnect or protective device. (Sec. 250-26.)

board, switchboard, or motor control center. In such cases, the absence of a main CB or fused switch would mean that there is no disconnect means or overcurrent device for the overall "system" fed by the transformer, even though there are disconnects and overcurrent protection for the individual "circuits" that make up the "system." That interpretation would require bonding and grounding of the secondary right *at the source* (the transformer itself).

In both part **(a)** and part **(b)** of this section, Exception No. 2 exempts high-impedance grounded transformer secondaries or generator outputs from the need to provide direct (solid) bonding and grounding-electrode connections of the neutral. This simply states an Exception to each part that is necessary to operate a high-impedance grounded system.

Step 3—Sec. 250·26(c)

The grounding electrode conductor, installed and sized as in Step 2, must be properly connected to a grounding electrode which must be "as near as practicable to and preferably in the same area as the grounding conduction connection to the system." That is, the grounding electrode must be as near as possible to the transformer itself. In order of preference, the grounding electrode must be:

1. The nearest available structural steel of the building, provided it is established that such building steel is effectively grounded.
2. The nearest available metal water pipe, provided it is effectively grounded. Section 250-112 clarifies the term "effectively grounded" by noting that the grounding connection to a grounding electrode must "assure a permanent and effective ground" (Fig. 250-28). Thus, when a nearby cold water pipe is used as a grounding electrode, it would appear

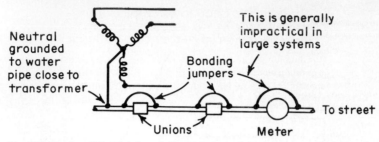

Fig. 250-28. Sec. 250-112 defines "effectively grounded" water-pipe electrode. (Sec. 250-26.)

to be necessary to always bond around any unions or valves that might be opened and thereby break the piping connection to outside earth. And Sec. 250-81(a) requires a bonding jumper to be used around all indoor water meters to assure continuity to earth or through the interior water piping system. The size of such bonding jumpers must be at least the same size as the grounding conductor from the transformer to the water pipe and other electrodes. Of course, the water piping system must satisfy Sec. 250-80. There must be at least 10 ft of the metal water piping buried in earth outside the building for the water-pipe system to qualify as a grounding electrode. There must always be a connection between an interior metal water piping system and the service-entrance grounded conductor (the neutral of the system which feeds the primary of any transformers in the building). That grounding connection for the neutral or other system grounded conductor must be made at the service. And where a metallic water piping system in a building is fed from a nonmetallic underground water system or has less than 10 ft of metal pipe underground, the service neutral or other service grounded conductor must have a connection to a ground rod or other electrode in addition to the connection to the interior metal water piping system. Refer to Secs. 250-80 and 250-81. Where building steel or a metal water pipe is not available for grounding of local dry-type units, other electrodes may be used, based on Secs. 250-81 or 250-83.

Figure 250-29 shows techniques of transformer grounding that have been used in the past but are no longer acceptable along with an example of "case grounding" that *is* specifically recognized by the Exceptions to Sec. 250-26(a) and (b).

Exception No. 1 to Sec. 250-26(b) exempts small transformers for control, signal, or power-limited circuits from the basic requirement for a grounding electrode conductor run from the bonded secondary grounded conductor (such as a neutral) to a grounding electrode (nearby building steel or a water pipe). Exception No. 1 to both parts **(a)** and **(b)** in this section apply to transformers used to derive control circuits, signal circuits, or power-limited circuits, such as circuits to damper motors in air-conditioning systems. A Class 1 remote-control or signaling transformer that is rated not over 1,000 VA simply has to have a grounded secondary conductor bonded to the metal case of the transformer, and no grounding electrode conductor is needed, *provided that* the metal trans-

NOT PERMITTED FOR POWER TRANSFORMERS

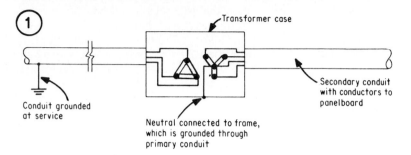

① Transformer case

Conduit grounded
at service

Neutral connected to frame,
which is grounded through
primary conduit

Secondary conduit
with conductors to
panelboard

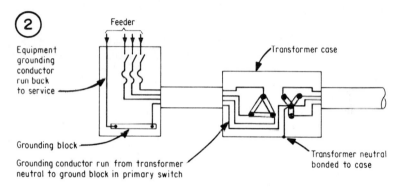

② Feeder

Equipment
grounding
conductor
run back
to service

Transformer case

Grounding block

Grounding conductor run from transformer
neutral to ground block in primary switch

Transformer neutral
bonded to case

THIS IS PERMITTED

**TRANSFORMER NOT OVER 1000 VA — FOR CONTROL,
SIGNAL OR POWER-LIMITED CIRCUIT**

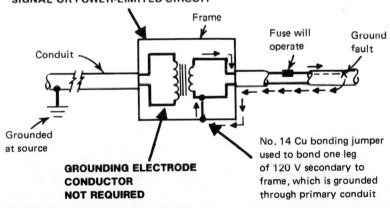

Frame

Conduit

Fuse will
operate

Ground
fault

Grounded
at source

**GROUNDING ELECTRODE
CONDUCTOR
NOT REQUIRED**

No. 14 Cu bonding jumper
used to bond one leg
of 120 V secondary to
frame, which is grounded
through primary conduit

Fig. 250-29. Code rules regulate specific hookups for grounding transformer secondaries. (Sec. 250-26.)

former case itself is properly grounded by grounded metal raceway which supplies its primary or by means of a suitable (Sec. 250-57) equipment grounding conductor that ties the case back to the grounding electrode for the primary system, as indicated at the bottom of Fig. 250-29. Exception No. 1 to Sec. 250-26(a) permits use of a No. 14 copper conductor to bond the grounded leg of the transformer secondary to the transformer frame, leaving the supply conduit to the transformer to provide the path to ground back to the main service ground, but depending on the connection between neutral and frame to provide effective return for clearing faults, as shown. Grounding of transformer housings must be made by connection to grounded cable armor or metal raceway or by use of a grounding conductor run with circuit conductor (either a bare conductor or a conductor with green-colored covering).

Because the rule on bonding jumpers for the secondary neutral point of a transformer refers to Sec. 250-79(c) and therefore ties into Table 250-94, the smallest size that may be used is No. 8 copper, as shown in that table. But for small transformers—such as those used for Class 1 remote-control or signaling circuits—that large a bonding jumper is not necessary and is not suited to termination provisions. For that reason, Exception No. 1 to Sec. 250-26(a) and (b) permits the bonding jumper for such transformers rated not over 1,000 VA to be smaller than No. 8. The jumper simply has to be at least the same size as the secondary phase legs of the transformer and in no case smaller than No. 14 copper or No. 12 aluminum.

250-27. High-Impedance Grounded Neutral System Connections.   This complete section covers grounding connections for a high-impedance grounded neutral system. When high-impedance grounding is used for a 480- to 1,000-V system in accordance with the conditions of Exception No. 5 of Sec. 250-5(b), the grounding connections must be made in compliance with the rules of this section, as follows:

1. The grounding impedance (usually a resistor) must be connected between the system neutral point and the grounding electrode conductor. The neutral point may be that of a wye transformer connection, or a neutral point may be derived from a 480-V delta system by using a zigzag grounding autotransformer.

2. The neutral conductor from the neutral point to the grounding impedance must be fully insulated because it is operating at a substantial voltage above ground.

3. The system neutral must not be connected to ground except through the impedance unit.

4. The neutral conductor from the neutral point to the grounding impedance may be installed in a separate raceway.

5. The equipment bonding jumper (the connection between the system equipment grounding conductors and the grounded end of the grounding impedance) must be an unspliced conductor run from the first disconnect or overcurrent device of the system to the ground end of the impedance device.

6. The grounding electrode conductor must be connected anywhere from the ground end of the impedance to the equipment ground bus or terminal in the service equipment or the first disconnect means.

250-33. Other Conductor Enclosures.   Exception No. 1 permits the installation of short runs as extensions from existing open wiring, knob-and-tube work, or nonmetallic-sheathed cable without grounding where there is little likelihood of an accidental connection to ground or of a person touching both the conduit, raceway, or armor and any grounded metal or other grounded surface at the same time.

250-42. Equipment Fastened in Place or Connected by Permanent Wiring Methods (Fixed).   The word "fixed" as applied to equipment requiring grounding now applies to "equipment fastened in place or connected by permanent wiring," as shown in Fig. 250-30. And that usage is consistently followed in other

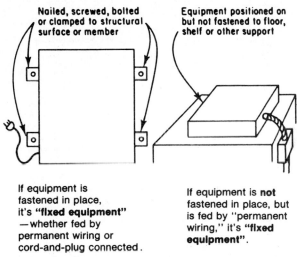

Nailed, screwed, bolted or clamped to structural surface or member

Equipment positioned on but not fastened to floor, shelf or other support

If equipment is fastened in place, it's **"fixed equipment"** —whether fed by permanent wiring or cord-and-plug connected.

If equipment is **not** fastened in place, but is fed by "permanent wiring," it's **"fixed equipment"**.

Fig. 250-30. "Fixed" equipment is now clearly and readily identified for grounding rules. (Sec. 250-42.)

Code sections. As noted in Exception No. 4, enclosures for listed data processing equipment and listed office equiment operating at over 150 V to ground do not have to be grounded if protected by a system of double insulation or its equivalent.

250-43. Fastened in Place or Connected by Permanent Wiring Methods (Fixed)— Specific.   Part (g) requires that all electric signs and associated equipment must have exposed, noncurrent-carrying metal parts grounded. An Exception was removed here that exempted signs that were insulated from ground and from other conductive objects and were accessible only to qualified persons. The Exception was deleted because of two deaths from shock to personnel working on signs that were in compliance with the Exception.

As required by part (k), motor-operated water pumps, including the submersible type, must have their metal frames grounded. This Code rule clarifies an issue that was a subject of controversy. It means that a circuit down to a submersible pump in a well or cistern must include a conductor to ground the pump's metal frame even though the frame is not accessible or exposed to contact by persons.

250-45. Equipment Connected by Cord and Plug. Figure 250-31 shows cord-connected loads that must either be operated grounded or be double-insulated. Except when supplied through an isolating transformer as permitted in paragraph **(d)** of this section, the frames of portable tools should be grounded by means of an equipment grounding conductor in the cord or cable through

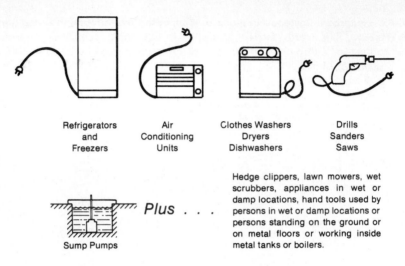

| Refrigerators and Freezers | Air Conditioning Units | Clothes Washers Dryers Dishwashers | Drills Sanders Saws |

Sump Pumps   *Plus . . .*   Hedge clippers, lawn mowers, wet scrubbers, appliances in wet or damp locations, hand tools used by persons in wet or damp locations or persons standing on the ground or on metal floors or working inside metal tanks or boilers.

NOTE: USE OF DOUBLE INSULATION ON TOOLS OR APPLIANCES ELIMINATES NEED FOR GROUNDING.

Fig. 250-31. Grounding cord and plug cap are required for shock protection. (Sec. 250-45.)

which the motor is supplied. Portable hand lamps used inside boilers or metal tanks should preferably be supplied through isolating transformers having a secondary voltage of 50 V or less, with the secondary ungrounded. **Code**-recognized double-insulated tools and appliances may be used in all types of occupancies other than hazardous locations, in lieu of required grounding.

OSHA regulations have made **NE Code** Sec. 250-45 retroactive, requiring grounded operation of cord- and plug-connected appliances in all existing as well as new installations. Check on local ruling on that matter.

250-46. Spacing from Lightning Rods. Lightning discharges with their steep wave fronts build up tremendous voltages to metal near the lightning rods, so the 6-ft separation or bonding is required to prevent flashover with its attendant hazard.

250-50. Equipment Grounding Conductor Connections. Part **(a)** requires that the equipment grounding conductor at a service—such as the ground bus or terminal in the service-equipment enclosure, or the enclosure itself—must be connected to the system *grounded* conductor (the neutral or grounded phase leg). The equipment ground and the neutral or other grounded leg must be bonded together and it must be done on the supply side of the service disconnecting means—which means either *within* or *ahead of* the enclosure for the service equipment (Fig. 250-32).

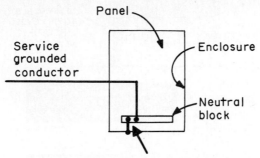

Bonding is the insertion of a bonding screw into the panel neutral block to connect the block to the panel enclosure, or it is use of a bonding jumper from the neutral block to an equipment grounding block that is connected to the enclosure.

NOTE: **Bonding**—the connection of the neutral terminal to the enclosure or to the ground terminal that is, itself, connected to the enclosure—might also be done in an individual switch or CB enclosure.

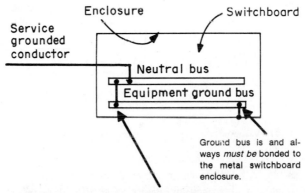

Ground bus is and always *must be* bonded to the metal switchboard enclosure.

Bonding of the neutral is the connection between the neutral bus and the equipment grounding bus or between the neutral bus and the metal enclosure itself.

Fig. 250-32. Equipment ground must be "bonded" to grounded conductor at the service equipment. (Sec. 250-50.)

Part **(b)** requires the ground bus or the enclosure to be simply bonded to the grounding electrode conductor within or ahead of the service disconnect for an ungrounded system.

As shown at the top of Fig. 250-33, some switchboard sections or interiors include neutral busbars factory-bonded to the switchboard enclosure and are marked "suitable for use only as service equipment." They may not be used as subdistribution switchboards—i.e., they may not be used on the load side of the service except where used, with the inspector's permission, as the first discon-

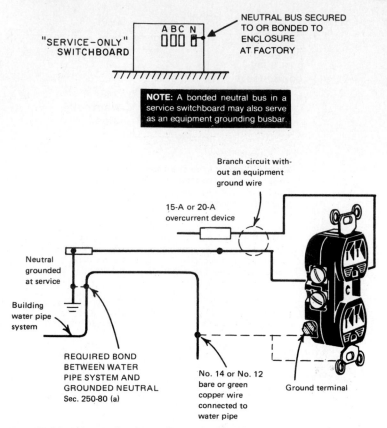

Fig. 250-33. These are bonding and grounding details covered by Sec. 250-50. [Sec. 250-50.]

necting means fed by a transformer secondary or a generator and where the bonded neutral satisfies Sec. 250-26(a) for a separately derived system.

As illustrated at the bottom of Fig. 250-33, the Exception for parts **(a)** and **(b)** describes an accepted technique for using grounding-type receptacles for replacement of existing nongrounding devices or for circuit extensions—on wiring systems that do not include an equipment grounding conductor. The Exception used to say that a grounding-type receptacle could be installed *only* on an *extension* from an existing electrical system that did not have an equipment gounding means in its wiring system—such as nonmetallic-sheathed cable without a ground wire or knob-and-tube wiring. *And*, where a grounding-type receptacle is so installed in a box that is fed as an extension of an existing system, the green hex-head grounding screw of the receptacle has to be grounded by a wire that is connected to a nearby grounded cold-water pipe. In the present code, the rule of this section still recognizes that type of application; but, in addition, the rule now permits the same technique of grounding to a nearby water pipe to be used where a nongrounding-type receptacle is replaced by a grounding-type receptacle in a box that is *part of*, not an *extension of*, an existing wiring system that does not include an equipment grounding conductor.

It should be noted that this addition to the Exception of Sec. 250-50 is actually also an addition to the Exception of Sec. 210-7(d)—which requires that only a nongrounding-type receptacle or a GFCI receptacle must be used when replacing a nongrounding-type receptacle on an existing wiring system without an equipment grounding wire in it.

250-51. Effective Grounding Path.   This section sets forth basic rules on the effectiveness of grounding. In effect, this rule defines the phrase "effective grounding path" and establishes *mandatory* requirements on the quality and quantity of conditions in any and every grounding circuit. The three parts of the section "shall" be satisfied.

Because each of the three required characteristics of grounding paths set forth in **(1)**, **(2)**, and **(3)** is a real and important factor of safety, it is logical and desirable that compliance with the **Code** hinges on carefully establishing each separate condition:

(1).   That every ground path is "permanent and continuous" can be established by the installer by proper mounting, coupling, and terminating of the conductor or raceway intended to serve as the grounding conductor [as permitted by Sec. 250-91(a) and (b)]. And the condition can be visually checked by the electrical inspector, the design engineer and/or any other authority concerned. There is nothing in the wording of that part **(1)** or in other **Code** rules to demand that any kind of actual test be made to verify the condition. However, an inspector could insist that the word "continuous" refers to a path of current and that only a continuity test with a meter or light or bell could positively assure that the path is "continuous."

(2).   That every grounding conductor has "capacity to conduct safely any fault current likely to be imposed on it" can be established by falling back on those other **Code** rules [Secs. 250-93, 250-94, 250-95, 250-23(b), 250-26, 250-79, 680-25(a)(d)(e), etc.] that specifically establish a minimum required size of grounding conductor. Certainly, it is reasonable to conclude that adequate sizing of grounding conductors in accordance with those rules provides adequate "capacity to conduct safely . . . etc."

(3).   But when we come to this part of Sec. 250-51, questions arise as to the intent of the rule; and much logic supports the argument that testing is essential to **Code** compliance. Certainly, on a grounded system, when a phase-to-ground fault occurs, the impedance of the fault-current path over the raceways or equipment grounding conductors must be low enough to cause enough current to flow to operate the fuse or CB nearest the fault on its line side (Fig. 250-34). To *know* for sure that impedance of any and every grounding conductor is "sufficiently low to limit . . . etc." requires that the actual value of impedance be measured; and such measurement not only involves use of testing equipment but also demands a broad and deep knowledge of the often sophisticated technology of testing in circuits operating on alternating current where inductance and capacitance are operative factors. In short, what is "sufficiently low imped-

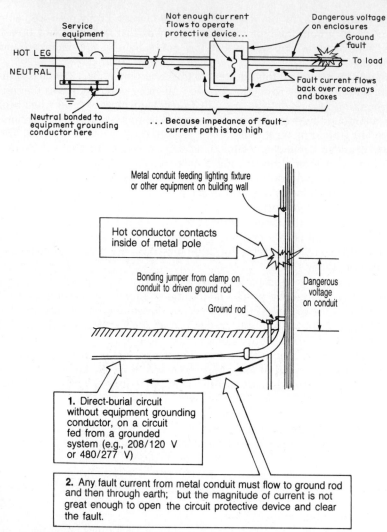

Fig. 250-34. These are violations of the basic concept of effective grounding. (Sec. 250-51.)

ance" and what does "facilitate the operation of the circuit protective devices" mean? And if testing *is* done, is it necessary to test "every" equipment grounding conductor? Are all these possible interpretations of the intent of the **Code** rule unrealistic? Is all of this beyond the capability of personnel and out of the economic reach of customers who have to pay for it? It all comes down to the hard question: *Just how much is safety worth?*

After all these questions and speculations, we are still left with the fact that Sec. 250-51(c) is a mandatory rule that can be fully satisfied only by testing. It is unreasonable to assume that the **Code**-making panel never intended this rule to be enforced. And the concept behind the rule as well as the logic of testing being essential to compliance are theoretical ideals with which every electrical person would agree.

The last sentence in this section prohibits the use of current flow through the earth as the sole equipment grounding conductor because earth impedance is too high and restricts fault-current flow, as shown at the bottom of Fig. 250-34. This rule is also in Sec. 250-91(c). Inspectors as well as computer CATV installers have often overlooked this very important **Code** rule, and the requirement needs to be more obviously emphasized.

250-53. Grounding Path to Grounding Electrode at Services.   Section 250-53(a) requires all the bonded components—the service-equipment enclosure, the grounded neutral or grounded phase leg, and any equipment grounding conductors that come into the service enclosure—to be connected to a *common* grounding electrode (Sec. 250-54) by the single grounding electrode conductor. A common grounding electrode conductor shall be run from the common point so obtained to the grounding electrode as required by **Code** Secs. 250-53 and 250-54 (Fig. 250-35). Connection of the system neutral to the switchboard frame or ground bus within the switchboard provides the lowest impedance for the equipment ground return to the neutral. The main bonding jumper that bonds the service enclosure and equipment grounding conductors [which may be either conductors or conduit, EMT, etc., as permitted by Sec. 250-91(b)] to the grounded conductor of the system is required by part **(b)** of this section to be installed within the service equipment or within a service conductor enclosure on the line side of the service. This is the bonding connection required by Sec. 250-50(a) (Fig. 250-36). And it should be noted that in a service panel, equipment grounding conductors for load-side circuits may be connected to the neutral block, and there is no need for an equipment grounding terminal bar or block.

If a grounding conductor were used to ground the neutral to the water pipe or other grounding electrode and a separate grounding conductor were used to ground the switchboard frame and housing to the water pipe or other electrode, without the neutral and the frame being connected in the switchboard, the length and impedance of the ground path would be increased. The proven hazard is that the impedance of the fault-current path can limit fault current to a level too low to operate the overcurrent devices "protecting" the faulted circuit.

Note that a number of grounding electrodes that are bonded together, as required by Sec. 250-81, are considered to be *one* grounding electrode.

250-54. Common Grounding Electrode.   The same electrode(s) that is used to ground the neutral or other grounded conductor of an AC system must also be used for grounding the entire system of interconnected raceways, boxes, and enclosures. The single, common grounding electrode conductor required by Sec. 250-53 connects to the single grounding electrode and thereby grounds the bonded point of the system and equipment grounds.

In any building housing livestock, all piping systems, metal stanchions, drink-

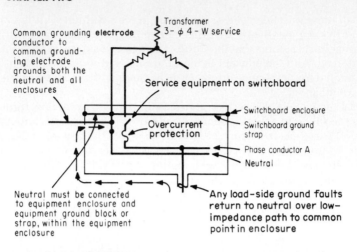

Common grounding **electrode** conductor to common grounding electrode grounds both the neutral and all enclosures

Transformer
3- φ 4 - W service

Service equipment on switchboard

Overcurrent protection

Switchboard enclosure

Switchboard ground strap

Phase conductor A

Neutral

Neutral must be connected to equipment enclosure and equipment ground block or strap, within the equipment enclosure

Any load-side ground faults return to neutral over low-impedance path to common point in enclosure

PROPER CONNECTIONS:

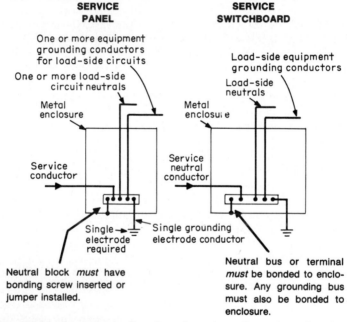

SERVICE PANEL

One or more equipment grounding conductors for load-side circuits

One or more load-side circuit neutrals

Metal enclosure

Service conductor

Single electrode required

Single grounding electrode conductor

Neutral block *must* have bonding screw inserted or jumper installed.

SERVICE SWITCHBOARD

Load-side equipment grounding conductors

Load-side neutrals

Metal enclosure

Service neutral conductor

Neutral bus or terminal *must* be bonded to enclosure. Any grounding bus must also be bonded to enclosure.

Fig. 250·35. Common grounding electrode conductor for service and equipment ground. (Sec. 250-53.)

ing troughs, and other metalwork with which animals might come in contact should be bonded together and to the grounding electrode used to ground the wiring system in the building. See Sec. 250-81.

250·57. Equipment Fastened in Place or Connected by Permanent Wiring Methods (Fixed)—Grounding. This section requires that metal equipment enclo-

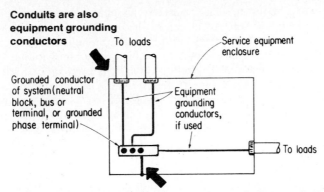

Conduits are also equipment grounding conductors

Main bonding jumper (wire, bus, screw or similar conductor) must be *within* service equipment or service conductor enclosure

Fig. 250-36. Main bonding jumper must be within SE enclosure. (Sec. 250-53.)

sures, boxes, and cabinets to be grounded must be grounded by metal cable armor or by the metal raceway that supplies such enclosures (rigid metal conduit, intermediate metal conduit, EMT, flex or liquidtight flex as permitted by Sec. 350-5 or 351-9), or by an equipment grounding conductor, such as where the equipment is fed by rigid nonmetallic conduit. Refer to Sec. 250-91(b). *But* in Sec. 250-57(b), the rule explicitly requires that *when* a separate equipment grounding conductor (i.e., other than the metal raceway or metal cable armor) is used for alternating-current circuits, it *must* be contained *within* the same raceway, cable, or cord or otherwise run with the circuit conductors (Fig. 250-37). External grounding of equipment enclosures or frames or housings is a violation for AC equipment. It is not acceptable, for instance, to feed an AC motor with a nonmetallic conduit or cable, without a grounding conductor in the conduit or cable, and then provide grounding of the metal frame by a grounding conductor connected to the metal frame and run to building steel or to a grounding-grid conductor. An equipment grounding conductor *must always* be run with the circuit conductors.

If equipment grounding conductor (other than raceway) is used to ground motor, it must be run in raceway with circuit wires

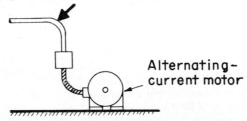

Fig. 250-37. Equipment grounding conductor must be in raceway or cable with circuit conductors for AC equipment. (Sec. 250-57.)

The rule in Sec. 250-57(b) which insists on keeping an equipment grounding conductor physically close to AC circuit supply conductors is a logical follow-up to the rules of Sec. 250-51 which call for minimum impedance in grounding current paths to provide most effective clearing of ground faults. When an equipment grounding conductor is kept physically close to any circuit conductor that would be supplying the fault current (that is, the grounding conductor is in the "same raceway, cable, or cord or otherwise run with the circuit conductors"), the impedance of the fault circuit has minimum inductive reactance and minimum AC resistance because of mutual cancellation of the magnetic fields around the conductors and the reduced skin effect. Under such condition of "sufficiently low impedance," the meaning of Sec. 250-51(c) is best fulfilled—voltage to ground is limited to the greatest extent, the fault current is higher because of minimized impedance, the circuit overcurrent device will operate at a faster point in its time-current characteristic to assure maximum fault-clearing speed, and the entire effect will be to "facilitate the operation of the circuit protective devices in the circuit."

Exception No. 2 of Sec. 250-57(b) *excludes* DC circuits from the need to keep the grounding conductor close to the circuit conductors. Because there are no alternating magnetic fields around DC conductors, there is no inductive reactance or skin effect in DC circuits. The only impedance to current flow in a DC circuit is resistance—which will be the same for a DC ground-fault path whether or not the equipment grounding conductor is placed physically close to the circuit conductors which would supply the fault current in the event of a ground fault. External equipment grounding—by connection to grounded building steel or to an external ground grid—is, therefore, OK for DC equipment, provided the external grounding path is effectively tied back to the grounded conductor of the DC system.

The arrangement shown in Fig. 250-38 violates the basic rule of Sec. 250-57(b) because the lighting fixture, which must be grounded to satisfy Sec. 250-42, is not grounded in accordance with Secs. 250-57 and 250-91(b) or by an equipment grounding conductor contained within the cord, as noted in Sec. 250-57(b).

Note that Sec. 250-91(b) refers very clearly to an "equipment grounding con-

EXTERNAL EQUIPMENT GROUNDING IS A VIOLATION!

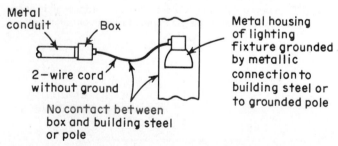

Fig. 250-38. Supply to AC equipment must include equipment grounding conductor. (Sec. 250-57.)

ductor run with or enclosing the circuit conductors." Except for DC circuits [Sec. 250-57(b), Exception No. 2] and for isolated, ungrounded power sources [Sec. 517-19(f) and (g)], an equipment grounding conductor of any type must not be run separately from the circuit conductors. The engineering reason for keeping the ground return path and the phase legs in close proximity (that is, in the same raceway) is to minimize the impedance of the fault circuit by placing conductors so their magnetic fields mutually cancel each other, keeping inductive reactance down, and allowing sufficient current to flow to "facilitate the operation of the circuit protective devices," as required by Sec. 250-51.

The hookup in Fig. 250-38 also violates the rule of the last sentence in Sec. 250-58(a), which prohibits use of building steel as the equipment grounding conductor for AC equipment. And the rules of Sec. 250-58 often have to be considered in relation to the rules of Sec. 250-57.

Note: CARE MUST BE TAKEN TO DISTINGUISH BETWEEN AN "EQUIPMENT *GROUNDING CONDUCTOR*" AS COVERED BY SEC. 250-57 AND AN "EQUIPMENT *BONDING JUMPER*" AS COVERED BY SEC. 250-79(e). A "*BONDING JUMPER*" MAY BE USED EXTERNAL TO EQUIPMENT BUT IT MUST NOT BE OVER 6 FT LONG.

Exception No. 1 recognizes conductors of colors other than green for use as equipment grounding conductors if the conductor is stripped for its exposed length within an enclosure, so it appears bare, or if green coloring, green tape, or green label is used on the conductor at the termination. As shown in Fig. 250-39, the phase legs may or may not be required to be "identified by phase and system" [see Sec. 210-4(d)]. If color coding is used, the phase legs may be any color other than white, gray, or green. The neutral may be white or gray or any other color than green if it is larger than No. 6 and if white tape, marking,

EXAMPLE

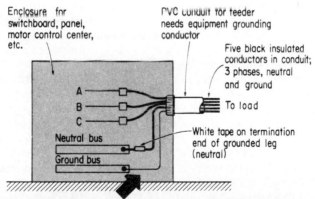

Black insulated conductor used as equipment grounding
conductor has all insulation stripped from entire length exposed
in enclosure

Fig. 250-39. Equipment grounding conductor larger than No. 6 may be a stripped conductor of any color covering. (Sec. 250-57.)

or paint is applied to the neutral near its terminations. The grounding conductor may be green or may be any insulated conductor if all insulation is stripped off for the exposed length. Alternatives to stripping the black insulated conductor used for equipment ground include (1) coloring the exposed insulation green or (2) marking the exposed insulation with green tape or green adhesive labels.

Exception No. 3 permits specific on-the-job identification of an insulated conductor used as an equipment grounding conductor in a multiconductor cable. Such a conductor, regardless of size, may be identified in the same manner permitted by Exception No. 1 of that section for conductors larger than No. 6 used in raceway. The conductor may be stripped bare or colored green to indicate that it is a grounding conductor. But such usage is recognized only for commercial-, institutional- and industrial-type systems under the conditions given in the first two lines of the Exception.

250-58. Equipment Considered Effectively Grounded. This rule clarifies the way in which structural metal may be used as an equipment grounding conductor, consistent with the rule of Sec. 250-57(b) requiring a grounding conductor to be kept physically close to the conductors of any AC circuit for which the grounding conductor provides the fault return path.

Part **(a)** notes that if a piece of electrical equipment is attached and electrically conductive to a metal rack or structure supporting the equipment, the metal enclosure of the equipment is considered suitably grounded by connection to the metal rack PROVIDED THAT the metal rack itself is effectively grounded by metal raceway enclosing the circuit conductors supplying the equipment or by an equipment grounding conductor run with the circuit supplying the equipment. An example of such application is shown in Fig. 250-40. Although this example shows grounding of lighting fixtures to a rack, the Code rule recognizes any "electric equipment" when this basic grounding concept is observed. It is important to note that if a ground fault developed in equipment so grounded (as at point A), the fault current would take the path indicated by the small arrows. In such case, although the fault-current path through the steel rack is not close to the hot conductor in the flexible cord that is feeding the fault—as normally required by Sec. 250-57(b)—the distance of the external ground path is not great, from the fixture to the panel enclosure or box. Because such a short external ground path produces only a relatively slight increase in ground-path impedance, Sec. 250-58(a) permits it. The permission for external bonding of flexible metal conduit and liquidtight flex in Sec. 250-79(e) is based on the same acceptance of only slight increase of overall impedance of the ground path.

The second sentence of Sec. 250-58(a) clearly prohibits using structural building steel as an equipment grounding conductor for equipment mounted on or fastened to the building steel—IF THE SUPPLY CIRCUIT TO THE EQUIPMENT OPERATES ON ALTERNATING CURRENT. BUT, structural building steel that is effectively grounded and bonded to the grounded circuit conductor of a DC supply system may be used as the equipment grounding conductor for the metal enclosure of DC-operated equipment that is conductively attached to the building steel.

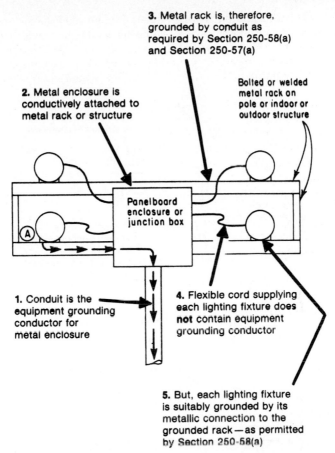

3. Metal rack is, therefore, grounded by conduit as required by Section 250-58(a) and Section 250-57(a)

2. Metal enclosure is conductively attached to metal rack or structure

Bolted or welded metal rack on pole or indoor or outdoor structure

Panelboard enclosure or junction box

Ⓐ

1. Conduit is the equipment grounding conductor for metal enclosure

4. Flexible cord supplying each lighting fixture does **not** contain equipment grounding conductor

5. But, each lighting fixture is suitably grounded by its metallic connection to the grounded rack — as permitted by Section 250-58(a)

Fig. 250·40. This use of metal rack as equipment ground is permitted. (Sec. 250-58.)

It is important to understand the basis for the **Code** rules of Sec. 250-57(b) and Sec. 250-91(b) and their relation to the concept of Sec. 250-58(a):

Note that Sec. 250-91(b) refers very clearly to an "equipment grounding conductor run with or enclosing the circuit conductors." Except for DC circuits [Sec. 250-57(b), Exception No. 2] and for isolated, ungrounded power sources [(Sec. 517-19(f) and (g)], an equipment grounding conductor of any type must not be run separately from the circuit conductors. Keeping the ground return path and the phase legs in close proximity (that is, in the same raceway) minimizes the impedance of the fault circuit by placing conductors so their magnetic fields mutually cancel each other, keeping inductive reactance down and allowing sufficient current to flow to "facilitate the operation of the circuit protective devices," as required by Sec. 250-51.

The second sentence of Sec. 250-58(a) applies the above concept of ground-fault impedance to the metal frame of a building and prohibits its use as an equipment grounding conductor for AC equipment enclosures. As shown in Fig. 250-41, use of building steel as a grounding conductor provides a long fault return path of very high impedance because the path is separated from the feeder circuit hot legs—thereby violating Sec. 250-51(c). Ground-fault current returning over building steel to the point where the building steel is bonded to

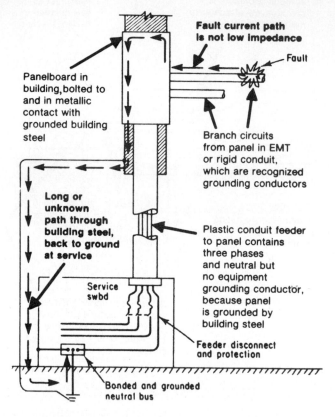

Fault current path is not low impedance

Fault

Panelboard in building, bolted to and in metallic contact with grounded building steel

Branch circuits from panel in EMT or rigid conduit, which are recognized grounding conductors

Long or unknown path through building steel, back to ground at service

Plastic conduit feeder to panel contains three phases and neutral but no equipment grounding conductor, because panel is grounded by building steel

Service swbd

Feeder disconnect and protection

Bonded and grounded neutral bus

THIS LAYOUT IS A VIOLATION

Fig. 250-41. Building metal frame is not an acceptable grounding conductor for AC equipment. (Sec. 250-58.)

the AC system neutral (or other grounded) conductor is separated from the circuit conductor that is providing the fault current. Impedance is, therefore, elevated and the optimum conditions required by Sec. 250-51 are not present, so that the grounding cannot be counted on to "facilitate the operation" of the fuse or CB protecting the faulted circuit. The current may not be high enough to provide fast and certain clearing of the fault.

The first sentence of Sec. 250-58(a) accepts a limited variation from the basic concept of keeping circuit hot legs and equipment grounding conductors physically close to each other. When equipment is grounded by connection to a "metal rack or structure" that is specifically provided to support the equipment and *is* grounded, the separation between the circuit hot legs and the rack, which serves as the equipment grounding conductor, exists only for a very short length that will not significantly raise the overall impedance of the ground-fault path. Figure 250-42 shows another application of that type, similar to the one shown in Fig. 250-40. Although this shows a 2-wire cord as being acceptable, use of a 3-wire cord (two circuit wires and an equipment grounding wire) is better practice, at very slight cost increase.

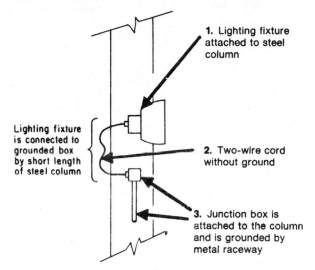

1. Lighting fixture attached to steel column

Lighting fixture is connected to grounded box by short length of steel column

2. Two-wire cord without ground

3. Junction box is attached to the column and is grounded by metal raceway

Fig. 250-42. This satisfies basic rule of Sec. 250-58(a). [Sec. 250-58(a).]

Aside from the limited applications shown in Figs. 250-40 and 250-42, *required* equipment grounding must always keep the equipment grounding conductor alongside the circuit conductor for grounded AC systems. Of course, as long as required grounding techniques are observed, there is no objection to additional connection of equipment frames and housings to building steel or to grounding grids to provide potentials to ground. But the external grounding path is not suitable for clearing AC equipment ground faults.

250-59. Cord- and Plug-Connected Equipment. The proper method of grounding portable equipment is through an extra conductor in the supply cord. Then if the attachment plug and receptacle comply with the requirements of Sec. 250-59, the grounding connection will be completed when the plug is inserted in the receptacle.

A grounding-type receptacle and an attachment plug should be used where it is desired to provide for grounding the frames of small portable appliances. The receptacle will receive standard two-pole attachment plugs, so grounding is optional with the user. The grounding contacts in the receptacle are electrically connected to the supporting yoke so that when the box is surface-mounted the connection to ground is provided by a direct metal-to-metal contact between the device yoke and the box. For a recessed box a grounding jumper must be used on the receptacle or a self-grounding receptacle must be used. See Secs. 250-74 and 250-114.

Figure 250-43 shows a grounding-type attachment plug with a movable, self-restoring grounding member—as covered in the Exceptions of this section.

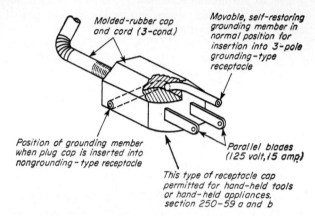

Molded-rubber cap and cord (3-cond.)

Movable, self-restoring grounding member in normal position for insertion into 3-pole grounding-type receptacle

Position of grounding member when plug cap is inserted into nongrounding - type receptacle

Parallel blades (125 volt,15 amp.)

This type of receptacle cap permitted for hand-held tools or hand-held appliances. section 250-59 a and b

Fig. 250·43. This type of plug cap is permitted on cords for tools and appliances. (Sec. 250-59.)

250·60. Frames of Ranges and Clothes Dryers. Under the conditions stated, the frame of an electric range, wall-mounted oven, or counter-mounted cooking unit may be grounded by direct connection to the grounded circuit conductor (the grounded neutral) and thus may be supplied by a 3-wire cord set and range receptacle irrespective of whether or not the conductor to the receptacle contains a separate grounding conductor.

The reason for permitting these appliances to be grounded by connecting them to the circuit neutral is that the circuit is usually short and the grounded neutral conductor is large enough to provide against its being broken. On such equipment if the neutral were broken, the equipment would usually become inoperative and it would be necessary to have repairs made before operation could be resumed.

Parts **(a)** and **(b)** clarify the use of a No. 10 or larger grounded neutral conductor of a *120/208*-V circuit for grounding the frames of electric ranges, wall-mounted ovens, counter-mounted units, or clothes dryers. This method is acceptable whether the 3-wire supply is 120/208 or 120/240 V. However, a provision, applicable to both 3-wire supply voltages, does require that when using service-entrance cable having an uninsulated neutral conductor the branch circuit must originate at the service-entrance equipment. The purpose of this provision is to prevent the uninsulated neutral from coming in contact with a panelboard supplied by a feeder and a separate grounding conductor (in the case of nonmetallic-sheathed cable). This would place the neutral in parallel with the grounding conductor, or with feeder *metal* raceways or cables if they are used. Insulated neutrals in such situations will prevent this (Fig. 250-44).

Wording of the rule that permits frames of ranges and clothes dryers to be grounded by connection to the grounded neutral conductor of their supply cir-

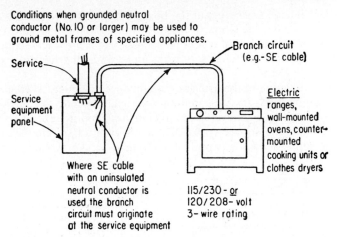

Conditions when grounded neutral
conductor (No.10 or larger) may be used to
ground metal frames of specified appliances.

Service

Service
equipment
panel

Branch circuit
(e.g.-SE cable)

Electric
ranges,
wall-mounted
ovens, counter-
mounted
cooking units or
clothes dryers

Where SE cable
with an uninsulated
neutral conductor is
used the branch
circuit must originate
at the service equipment

115/230 - or
120/208- volt
3- wire rating

Fig. 250-44. Ranges and dryers may be grounded to the circuit neutral.
(Sec. 250-60.)

cuits also permits the same method of grounding of "outlet or junction boxes"
serving such appliances. The rule permits grounding of an outlet or junction
box, as well as cooking unit or dryer, by the circuit grounded neutral (Fig. 250-
45). That practice has been common for many years but has raised questions
about the suitability of the neutral for such grounding. Now, the revised rule

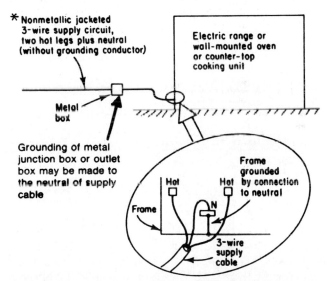

* Nonmetallic jacketed
3-wire supply circuit,
two hot legs plus neutral
(without grounding conductor)

Electric range or
wall-mounted oven
or counter-top
cooking unit

Metal
box

Grounding of metal
junction box or outlet
box may be made to
the neutral of supply
cable

Frame
grounded
by connection
to neutral

Hot   Hot

Frame

N

3-wire
supply
cable

* **Service cable or NM or NMC cable. But NM
or NMC cable must have an insulated
neutral.**

Fig. 250-45. Neutral may be used to ground boxes as well as appliances.
(Sec. 250-60.)

makes clear that such grounding of the box is acceptable. Figure 250-46 shows other details of such application. Without this permission to ground the metal box to the grounded neutral, it would be necessary to run a 4-wire supply cable to the box, with one of the wires serving as an equipment grounding conductor sized from Table 250-95.

Important: As shown in the asterisk note under Fig. 250-45, if a nonmetallic-sheathed cable is used, say, to supply a wall oven or cook-top, such cable is required by part **(c)** of Sec. 250-60 to have an *insulated* neutral. It would be a violation, for instance, to use a 10/2 NM cable with a bare No. 10 grounding conductor to supply a cooking appliance—connecting the two insulated No. 10

FIXED CONNECTION

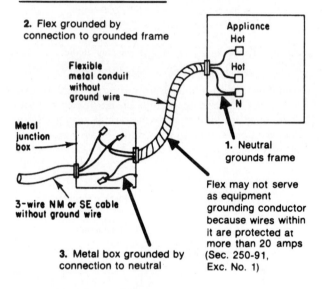

CORD CONNECTION

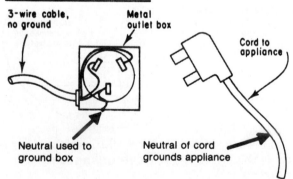

Fig. 250-46. These techniques may be used to ground boxes in circuit. (Sec. 250-60.)

wires to the hot terminals and using the bare No. 10 as a neutral conductor to ground the appliance. An uninsulated grounded neutral may be used only when part of a service-entrance cable.

250·61. Use of Grounded Circuit Conductor for Grounding Equipment. Part **(a)** permits connection between a grounded neutral (or grounded phase leg) and equipment enclosures, for the purpose of grounding the enclosures to the grounded circuit conductor. The grounded conductor (usually the neutral) of a circuit may be used to ground metal equipment enclosures and raceways on the supply side of the service disconnect or the supply side of the first disconnect fed from a separately derived transformer secondary or generator output or on the supply side of a main disconnect for a separate building. The wording here includes the supply side of a separately derived system as a place where metal equipment parts or enclosures may be grounded by connection to the grounded circuit conductor (usually a neutral). It is important to note that, in the meaning of the code [as covered in Sec. 250-26(a) and in Sec. 250-23(a)], the phrase "on the supply side of the disconnecting means" includes connection within the enclosure of the disconnecting means.

Figure 250-47 shows such applications. At A, the grounded service neutral is

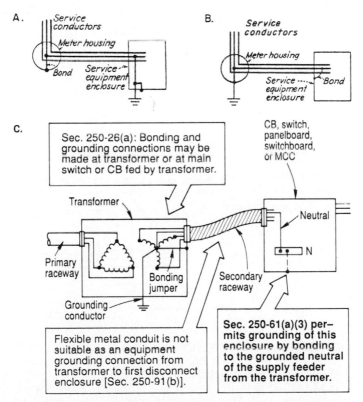

Fig. 250·47. Using grounded circuit conductor to ground equipment housings on line side of service or separately derived system. (Sec. 250-61.)

bonded to the meter housing by means of the bonded neutral terminal lug in the socket—and the housing is thereby grounded by this connection to the grounded neutral, which itself is grounded at the service equipment as well as at the utility transformer secondary supplying the service. At B, the service equipment enclosure is grounded by connection (bonding) to the grounded neutral—which itself is grounded at the meter socket and at the supply transformer. These same types of grounding connections may be made for CT cabinets, auxiliary gutters, and other enclosures on the line side of the service-entrance disconnect means, including the enclosure for the service disconnect. In some areas, the utilities and inspection departments will not permit the arrangement shown in Fig. 250-47 because the connecting lug in the meter housing is not always accessible for inspection and testing purposes. At C, equipment is grounded to the neutral on the line (supply) side of the first disconnect fed from a step-down transformer (a separately derived system).

Aside from the permission given in the five exceptions to the rule of part **(b)** of this section, the wording of part **(b)** prohibits connection between a grounded neutral and equipment enclosures on the load side of the service. The wording supports the prohibition in Sec. 250-23 of grounding connections. So aside from the few specific exceptions mentioned, bonding between any system grounded conductor, neutral or phase leg, and equipment enclosures is prohibited on the load side of the service (Fig. 250-48). The use of a neutral to ground panelboard or other equipment (other than specified in the Exceptions) on the load side of service equipment would be extremely hazardous if the neutral became loosened or disconnected. In such cases any line-to-neutral load would energize all metal components connected to the neutral, creating a dangerous potential

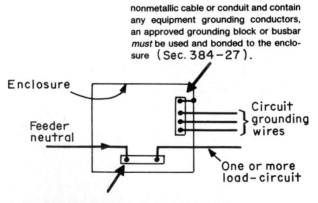

If feeder and/or branch circuits are in nonmetallic cable or conduit and contain any equipment grounding conductors, an approved grounding block or busbar *must* be used and bonded to the enclosure (Sec. 384–27).

Enclosure

Circuit grounding wires

Feeder neutral

One or more load-circuit

NEUTRAL BLOCK OR BUSBAR MUST NOT BE BONDED TO ENCLOSURE TO PROVIDE GROUNDING OF THE ENCLOSURE

Fig. 250-48. Panel, switchboard, CB, and switch on load side of service within a single building. (Sec. 250-61.)

above ground. Hence, the prohibition of such a practice. This is fully described in Fig. 250-15.

Although this rule of the **Code** prohibits neutral bonding on the load side of the service, Secs. 250-50(a) and 250-53(b) clearly require such bonding at the service entrance. And the exceptions to prohibiting load-side neutral bonding to enclosures are few and very specific:

- In a system, even though it is on the load side of the service, when voltage is stepped down by a transformer, a grounding connection *must* be made to the secondary neutral to satisfy Sec. 250-5(b) and Sec. 250-26.
- When a circuit is run from one building to another, it may be necessary, simply permissible, or expressly prohibited to connect the system "grounded" conductor to a grounding electrode at the other building—as covered by Sec. 250-24 and Exception No. 2 of Sec. 250-61(b).
- Exception No. 1 of Sec. 250-61(b) permits frames of ranges, wall ovens, counter-top cook units, and clothes dryers to be "grounded" by connection to the grounded neutral of their supply circuit (Sec. 250-60).
- Exception No. 3 to Sec. 250-61(b) permits grounding of meter enclosures to the grounded circuit conductor (generally, the grounded neutral) on the *load side* of the service disconnect if the meter enclosures are located near the service disconnect and the service is not equipped with ground-fault protection. There is no definition for the word "near," but it can be taken to mean in the same room or general area. This rule applies, of course, to multioccupancy buildings (apartments, office buildings, etc.) with individual tenant metering (Fig. 250-49).

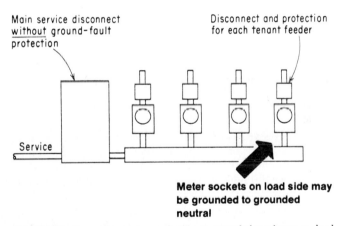

Fig. 250-49. Grounding meter enclosures to grounded conductor on *load side* of service disconnect. (Sec. 250-61.)

If a meter bank is on the upper floor of a building, as in a high-rise apartment house, or otherwise away from service disconnect, such meter enclosures would not meet the rule that they must be "near" the service disconnect. In such cases, the enclosures must not be grounded to the neutral. And if the service has ground-fault protection, meter enclosures on the load side must not be connected to the neutral, even if they are "near" the service disconnect.

Exception No. 4 of this section refers to Secs. 710-72 and 710-74, covering use of neutral conductor and grounding of electrode-type boilers.

250-70. General (Bonding). One of the most interesting and controversial phases of electrical work involves the grounding and bonding of secondary-voltage service-entrance equipment. Modern practice in such work varies according to local interpretations of **Code** requirements and specifications of design engineers. In all cases, however, the basic intent is to provide an installation which is essentially in compliance with **National Electrical Code** rules on the subject, using practical methods for achieving objectives.

In order to ensure electrical continuity of the grounding circuit, bonding (special precautions to ensure a permanent, low-resistance connection) is required at all conduit connections in the service equipment and where any nonconductive coating exists which might impair such continuity. This includes bonding at connections between service raceways, service cable armor, all service-equipment enclosures containing service-entrance conductors, including meter fittings, boxes, and the like.

The need for effective grounding and bonding of service equipment arises from the electrical characteristics of utility-supply circuits. In the common arrangement, service conductors are run to a building and the service overcurrent protection is placed near the point of entry of the conductors into the building, at the load end of the conductors. With such a layout, the service conductors are not properly protected against ground faults or shorts occurring on the supply side of the service overcurrent protection. Generally, the only protection for the service conductors is on the primary side of the utility's distribution transformer. By providing "bonded" connections (connecting with special care to reliable conductivity), any short circuit in the service-drop or service-entrance conductors is given the greatest chance of burning itself clear—because there is not effective overcurrent protection ahead of those conductors to provide opening of the circuit on such heavy fault currents. And for any contact between an energized service conductor and grounded service raceway, fittings, or enclosures, bonding provides discharge of the fault current to the system grounding electrode—and again burning the fault clear. This condition of services is shown in Fig. 250-50.

250-71. (Bonding) Service Equipment. Because of the requirement set forth in Sec. 250-70, all enclosures for service conductors must be grounded to prevent a potential aboveground on the enclosures as a result of fault—which would be a very definite hazard—and to facilitate operation of overcurrent devices anywhere on the supply side of the service conductors. However, because of the distant location of the protection and the normal impedance of supply cables, it is important that any fault to an enclosure of a hot service conductor of a grounded electrical system find a firm, continuous, low-impedance path to ground to assure sufficient current flow to operate the primary protective device or to burn the fault clear quickly. This means that all enclosures containing the service conductors—service raceway, cable armor, boxes, fittings, cabinets—must be effectively bonded together; that is, they must have low impedance through themselves and must be securely connected to each other to assure a continuous path of sufficient conductivity to the conductor which makes the connection to ground (Fig. 250-51).

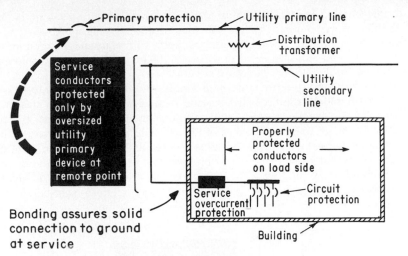

Fig. 250-50. Service bonding must assure burn-clear on shorts and grounds in service conductors. (Sec. 250-70.)

The spirit of the **Code** and good engineering practice have long recognized that the conductivity of any equipment ground path should be at least equivalent to 25 percent of the conductivity of any phase conductor with which the ground path will act as a circuit conductor on a ground fault. Or, to put it another way, making the relationship without reference to insulation or temperature rise, the impedance of the ground path must not be greater than four times the impedance of any phase conductor with which it is associated.

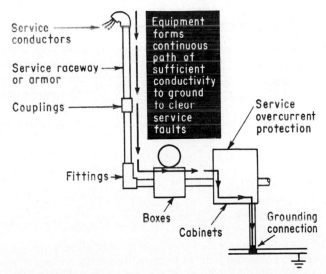

Fig. 250-51. Bonding assures low-impedance path through all service conductor enclosures. (Sec. 250-71.)

In ungrounded electrical systems, the same careful attention should be paid to the matter of bonding together the noncurrent-carrying metal parts of all enclosures containing service conductors. Such a low-impedance ground path will quickly and surely ground any hot conductor which might accidentally become common with the enclosure system.

Specific **NE Code** requirements on grounding and bonding are as follows:

1. Section 230-63 requires that service raceways, metal sheath of service cables, metering enclosures, and cabinets for service disconnect and protection be grounded. An exception to this rule is made in the case of certain lead-sheathed cable services as covered in Sec. 250-55. And, the **Code** requires that flexible metal conduit used in a run of service raceway must be bonded around (Fig. 250-52). Section 230-43 states that rule on flex and lists the *only* types of raceway that may enclose service-entrance conductors.

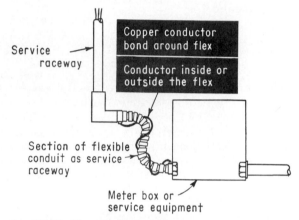

Fig. 250·52. Flex may be used as a service raceway, with a jumper. (Sec. 250-71.)

2. Section 250-32 also requires that service raceways and service cable sheaths or armoring—when of metal—be grounded.

3. Section 250-71 sets forth the service equipment which must be bonded—that is, the equipment for which the continuity of the grounding path must be specifically assured by using specific connecting devices or techniques. As indicated in Fig. 250-53, this equipment includes (1) service raceway, cable trays, cable sheath, and cable armor; (2) all service-equipment enclosures containing service-entrance conductors, including meter fittings, boxes, etc., interposed in the service raceway or armor; and (3) any conduit or armor that encloses a grounding electrode conductor that runs to and is connected to the grounding electrode or "system" of electrodes, as described under Sec. 250-81.

Part **(3)** of the rule on "bonded connections" for all interconnected service equipment makes *clear* that bonded terminations must be used at ends of conduit (rigid metal conduit, IMC or EMT) or cable armor that encloses a ground-

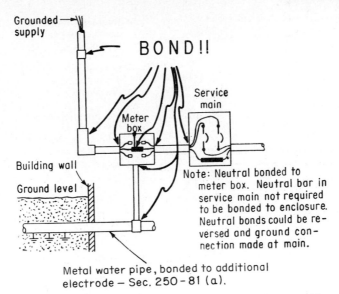

Grounded supply

BOND!!

Service main

Meter box

Building wall

Ground level

Note: Neutral bonded to meter box. Neutral bar in service main not required to be bonded to enclosure. Neutral bonds could be reversed and ground connection made at main.

Metal water pipe, bonded to additional electrode — Sec. 250-81 (a).

Fig. 250-53. "Bonding" consists of using prescribed fittings and/or methods for connecting components enclosing SE conductors. (Sec. 250-71.)

ing electrode conductor. That means that connection of conduit or cable armor must be made using a bonding locknut or bonding bushing (with a bonding jumper around unpunched concentric or eccentric rings left in any sheet metal knockout) or must be connected to a threaded hub or boss. Such connections must comply with the techniques covered in Sec. 250-72.

Section 250-92(b), in the first sentence bears on the same matter and requires a metal enclosure for a grounding electrode conductor to be electrically in parallel with the grounding electrode conductor. As a result, a metal conduit or EMT enclosing a grounding electrode conductor—whether or not such conduit or EMT is mechanical protection required by Sec. 250-92(a)—forms part of the grounding electrode conductor. In fact, such conduit or EMT has a much lower impedance than its enclosed grounding electrode conductor (due to the relation of magnetic fields) and is, therefore, even more important than the enclosed conductor in providing an effective path for current to the grounding electrode.

Assuring the continuity of raceway or armor for a grounding conductor does reduce the impedance of the ground path compared with what the impedance would be if the raceway or armor had poor connections or even opens. Effective bonding of the raceway or armor minimizes the DC resistance of the ground path and reduces the overall impedance which includes the choke action due to presence of magnetic material (steel conduit or armor), the increased inductive reactance of the circuit. Because of that, Sec. 250-71(a)(3) requires "bonding" connection of such raceway to any service enclosure, as shown in Fig. 250-54. Refer to Sec. 250-92(b).

Section 250-71(b) calls for a ready, effective "intersystem" bonding and

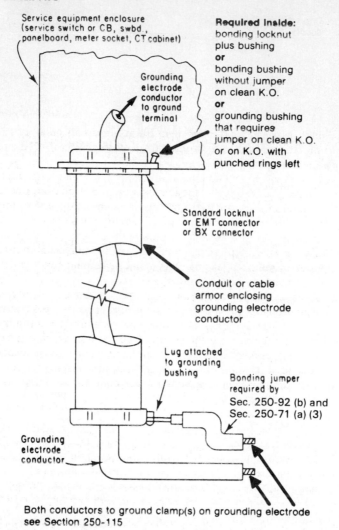

Service equipment enclosure
(service switch or CB, swbd.,
panelboard, meter socket, CT cabinet)

Grounding
electrode
conductor
to ground
terminal

Required inside:
bonding locknut
plus bushing
or
bonding bushing
without jumper
on clean K.O.
or
grounding bushing
that requires
jumper on clean K.O.
or on K.O. with
punched rings left

Standard locknut
or EMT connector
or BX connector

Conduit or cable
armor enclosing
grounding electrode
conductor

Lug attached
to grounding
bushing

Bonding jumper
required by
Sec. 250-92 (b) and
Sec. 250-71 (a) (3)

Grounding
electrode
conductor

Both conductors to ground clamp(s) on grounding electrode
see Section 250-115

Fig. 250-54. Grounding-conductor enclosure must be "bonded" at both ends. (Sec. 250-71.)

grounding of different systems, such as communications (telephone), lightning rod systems, and CATV systems at the service equipment for *all* buildings, not just dwellings. The rule requires that there be an "accessible means external to enclosures" for bonding metal enclosures of, say, telephone equipment to metal enclosures of electrical system components to reduce voltage differences between such metal enclosures as a result of lightning or power contacts. This rule was placed in the **NE Code** because Sec. 800-40(d) requires bonding interconnection between a building's power grounding electrode system and the "protector ground" (grounding electrode conductor) of telephone and other communications systems, and because making that bonded interconnection has become more difficult. Sections 810-21(j) and 820-40(d) also require such grounding interconnections.

The proposal for this **Code** addition included the following commentary:

> In the past, the bond between communications and power systems was usually achieved by connecting the communications protector grounds to an interior water pipe. Where the power was grounded to a ground rod, the bond was connected to the power grounding-electrode conductor or to metallic service conduit, which were usually accessible. With growing use of plastic water pipe, the tendency for service equipment to be installed in finished areas where the grounding electrode conductor is often concealed, and the use of plastic entrance conduit, communications installers no longer have an easily identifiable point for connecting bonds or grounds.
>
> Where lightning or external power fault currents flow in protective grounding systems, there can be dangerous potential differences between the equipment of those systems. Even with the required common or bonded electrodes, lightning currents flowing in noncommon portions of the grounding system result in significant potential differences as a result of inductive voltage drop in the noncommon conductor. If a current flows through a noncommon grounding conductor 10 ft long, there can be an inductive voltage drop as high as 4000 volts. If that noncommon conductor is either the power grounding-electrode conductor or the communications-protector grounding conductor, the voltage will appear between communication-equipment and power-equipment enclosures. The best technical solution to minimizing that voltage is with a short bond between the service equipment and the communications-protector ground terminal. The conductor to the grounding electrode is then common, and the voltage drop in it does not result in a potential difference between systems.
>
> An externally accessible point for intersystem bonding should be provided at the electrical service if accessible metallic service-entrance conduit is not present or if the grounding-electrode conductor is not accessible. This point could be in the form of a connector, tapped hole, external stud, a combination connector-SE cable clamp, or some other approved means located at the meter base or service equipment enclosure.

The first FPN at the end of this section describes a No. 6 copper "pigtail" that can be made available.

A definite shock hazard can arise if a *common* grounding electrode conductor is *not* used to ground *both* the bonded service neutral *and* the communications protector. The problem can be solved by simply bonding the ground terminal of the protector to a grounded enclosure of the service equipment (the service panelboard enclosure or the meter socket) and not using the separate telephone grounding electrode conductor.

250-72. Method of Bonding Service Equipment. Section 250-71 is very specific in listing the many types of equipment that require bonding connections but the actual "how to" is often hazy. For virtually every individual situation where a bonding connection must be made, there is available a variety of products on the market which present the installer with a choice of different methods.

This section sets forth the specific means which may be used to connect service-conductor enclosures together to satisfy the bonding requirements of Sec. 250-71. These means include:

1. Bonding equipment to the grounded service conductor by means of suitable lugs, pressure connectors, clamps, or other approved means—except

that soldered connections must not be used. Section 250-61 permits grounding of meter housings and service equipment to the grounded service conductor on the supply side of the service disconnecting means.

2. Threaded couplings in rigid metal conduit or IMC (intermediate metal conduit) runs and threaded bosses on enclosures to which rigid metal conduit or IMC connects.

3. Threadless couplings and connectors made up tight for rigid metal conduit, IMC, or electrical metallic tubing.

4. Bonding jumpers to securely connected metallic parts. Bonding jumpers must be used around concentric or eccentric knockouts which are punched or otherwise formed in such a manner that would impair the electrical current flow through the reduced cross section of metal that bridges between the enclosure wall and punched ring of the KO (knockout). And the bonding jumpers must be sized from Sec. 250-79(c).

5. Other devices (not standard locknuts and bushings) approved for the purpose.

Based on those briefly worded **Code** requirements, modern practice follows more or less standard methods.

Where rigid conduit is the service raceway, threaded or threadless couplings are used to couple sections of conduit together. Conduit connection to a meter socket may be made by connecting a threaded conduit end to a threaded hub or boss on the socket housing, where the housing is so constructed; by a locknut and bonding bushing; by a locknut outside with a bonding wedge or bonding locknut and a standard metal or completely insulating bushing inside; or sometimes by a locknut and standard bushing where the socket enclosure is bonded to the grounded service conductor. Conduit connections to KOs in sheet metal enclosures can be made with a bonding locknut (Fig. 250-55), a bonding wedge, or a bonding bushing where no KO rings remain around the opening through which the conduit enters. Where a KO ring does remain around the conduit entry hole, a bonding bushing or wedge with a jumper wire must be used to assure a path of continuity from the conduit to the enclosure. Figure 250-56 summarizes the various acceptable techniques. It should be noted that the use of the common locknut and bushing type of connection is not allowed. Neither is the use of double locknuts—one inside, one outside—and a bushing, although that is permitted on the load side of the service equipment. The special methods set forth in Sec. 250-72 are designed to prevent poor connections or loosening of connections due to vibration. This minimizes the possibility of arcing and consequent damage which might result when a service conductor faults to the grounded equipment.

Similar provisions are used to assure continuity of the ground path when EMT is the service raceway or when armored cable is used. EMT is coupled or connected by threadless devices—compression-type, indenter-type, or set-screw type, using raintight type outdoors. Although a threadless box connector is suitable to provide bonded connection of the connector to the metal raceway (rigid metal, IMC, EMT), it is also necessary to provide a "bonded" connection between the connector and the metal enclosure. A threadless box connector on the end of EMT used as service raceway provides satisfactory bonding of the

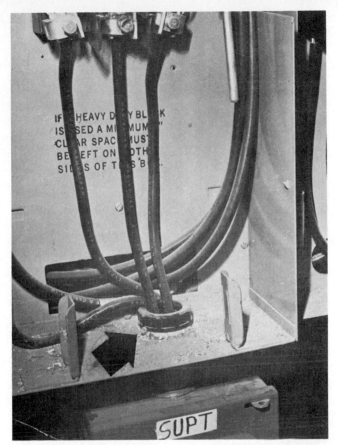

Fig. 250-55. Bonding locknut is a recognized method for bonding a service conduit nipple to a meter socket, when the KO is clean (no rings left in enclosure wall) or is cut on the job. With plastic bushing permitted, this is the most economical of the several methods for making a bonded conduit termination. (Sec. 250-72.)

EMT to the connector, but the last sentence of this rule says that a standard locknut or a standard bushing connected to the threaded end of the connector does not provide the required bonding of the connector to the metal service equipment to which the connector is connected. On the end of the connector, a bonding locknut or bonding bushings with or without jumpers must be used if the knockout is clean (all rings punched out or clean knockout punched on the job). If concentric or eccentric rings are left, a grounding locknut with jumper, a grounding bushing with jumper, or a grounding wedge with jumper must be used to provide bonded connection around the perforated knockout. And fittings used with service cable armor must assure the same degree of continuity of ground path.

The use of bonding bushings, bonding wedges, and bonding locknuts is rec-

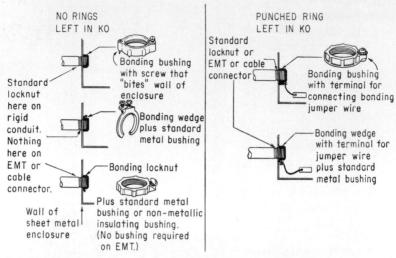

NO RINGS
LEFT IN KO

PUNCHED RING
LEFT IN KO

Standard
locknut or
EMT or cable
connector

Bonding bushing
with screw that
"bites" wall of
enclosure

Bonding bushing
with terminal for
connecting bonding
jumper wire

Standard
locknut
here on
rigid
conduit.
Nothing
here on
EMT or
cable
connector.

Bonding wedge
plus standard
metal bushing

Bonding wedge
with terminal for
jumper wire
plus standard
metal bushing

Bonding locknut

Wall of
sheet metal
enclosure

Plus standard metal
bushing or non-metallic
insulating bushing.
(No bushing required
on EMT.)

Fig. 250-56. Methods for "bonding" wiring methods to sheet metal enclosures. (Sec. 250-72.)

ognized without reference to types of raceways or types of connectors used with the raceways or cable armor. As a result, common sense and experience have molded modern field practice in making raceway and armored service cable connection to service cabinets. The top of Fig. 250-57 shows how a bonding wedge is used on existing connections at services or for raceway connections on the load side of the service—such as required by Sec. 501-16(b) for Class I hazardous locations. A bonding bushing, with provision for connecting a bonding jumper, is the common method for new service installations where some of the concentric or eccentric "doughnuts" (knockout rings) are left in the wall of the enclosure, therefore requiring a bonding jumper. Great care must be taken to assure that each and every type of bushing, locknut, or other fitting is used in the way for which it is intended to best perform the bonding function.

Figure 250-58 shows detailed application of the above rules to typical meter-socket installations. Meter-enclosure bonding techniques are shown in Fig. 250-59. Bonding details for current-transformer installations are shown in Fig. 250-60. Those illustrations are intended to portray typical field practice aimed at satisfying the various **Code** rules.

250-74. Connecting Receptacle Grounding Terminal to Box. The first paragraph requires that a jumper be used when the outlet box is installed in the wall (Fig. 250-61). Because boxes installed in walls are very seldom found to be perfectly flush with the wall, direct contact between device screws and yokes and boxes is seldom achieved. Screws and yokes currently in use were designed solely for the support of devices rather than as part of the grounding circuit.

Although the general rule states that a flush-type box, installed in a wall for a receptacle outlet, does require a bonding jumper from a grounded box to the

FOR EXISTING INSTALLATION

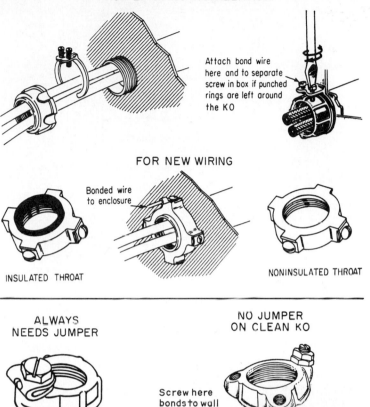

Attach bond wire
here and to separate
screw in box if punched
rings are left around
the KO

FOR NEW WIRING

Bonded wire
to enclosure

INSULATED THROAT   NONINSULATED THROAT

ALWAYS
NEEDS JUMPER

NO JUMPER
ON CLEAN KO

Screw here
bonds to wall
on clean KO

Bonding bushing with lug
for jumper wire – may be
used with jumper for clean
KO or with rings left in
wall of enclosure

Bonding bushing with screw
that "bites" into enclosure
wall may be used without a
jumper on a clean KO or
with a jumper when KO
rings are left in wall

Fig. 250-57. Bonding bushings and similar fittings must be used in their intended manners. (Sec. 250-72.)

receptacle grounding terminal, Exception No. 1 pertains to surface-mounted boxes and eliminates the need for a separate bonding jumper between a surface-mounted box and the receptacle grounding terminal under the conditions described. Although the Exception generally exempts surface-mounted boxes from the need for a bonding jumper from the box to the ground terminal of a receptacle installed in the box—because there is solid contact between the receptacles grounded mounting yoke and the ears on the box when installed—that is not applicable to a receptacle mounted in a raised box cover. A recep-

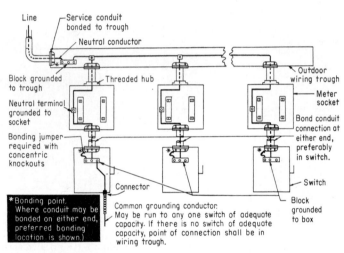

Fig. 250·58. Typical meter socket applications. (Sec. 250-72.)

tacle mounted in a raised box cover is connected to the cover by only a single screw, and that has been judged inadequate for grounding. A bonding jumper must be used on such a receptacle. See Fig. 250-62.

Figure 250-63 illustrates a grounding device which is intended to provide the electrical grounding continuity between the receptacle yoke and the box on which it is mounted and serves the dual purpose of both a mounting screw and a means of providing electrical grounding continuity in lieu of the required bonding jumper. As shown in the sketch, special wire springs and four-lobed machine screws are part of a receptacle design for use without a bonding jumper to box. This complies with Sec. 250-74, Exception No. 2.

Exception No. 3 permits nonself-grounding receptacles without an equipment grounding jumper to be used in floor boxes which are designed for and listed as providing proper continuity between the box and the receptacle mounting yoke.

TROUGH INSTALLATION – MORE THAN 6 METERS

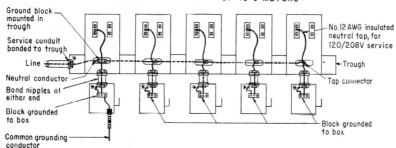

TROUGH INSTALLATION – UP TO 6 METERS

METER ENCLOSURES NIPPLED TOGETHER

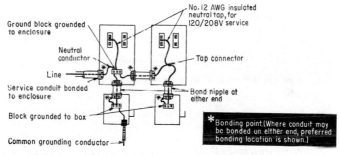

Fig. 250-59. Typical meter-enclosure installations (120/208- or 120/240-V services). (Sec. 250-72.)

Exception No. 4 allows the use of a receptacle with an isolated grounding terminal (no connection between the receptacle grounding terminal and the yoke). Sensitive electronic equipment that is grounded normally through the building ground is often adversely affected by pickup of transient signals which cause an imbalance in the delicate circuits. This is particularly true with highly intricate medical and communications equipment, which often pick up unwanted currents, even of very low magnitude.

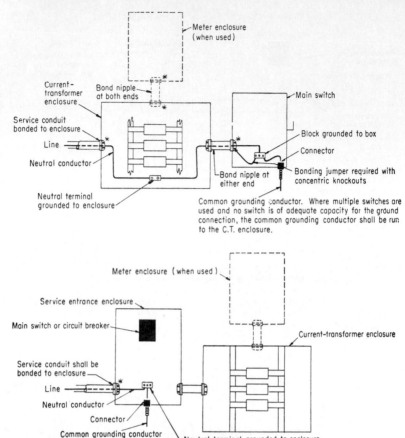

Fig. 250·60. Bonding at CT cabinets. (Sec. 250-72.)

The use of an isolated grounding receptacle allows a "pure" path to be established back to the system grounding terminal, in the service disconnecting means, without terminating in any other intervening panelboard. In Fig. 250-64, a cutaway of an isolated grounding receptacle shows the insulation between the grounding screw and the yoke (top), and the hookup of the insulated grounding conductor to the common neutral-equipment-ground point of the electrical system (bottom).

The last sentence of Exception No. 4 permits an equipment grounding conductor from the insulated (quiet) ground terminal of a receptacle to be run, unbroken, all the way back to the ground terminal bus that is bonded to the neutral at the service equipment or at the secondary of a step-down trans-

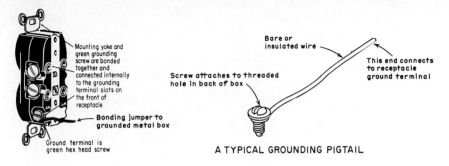

Mounting yoke and green grounding screw are bonded together and connected internally to the grounding terminal slots on the front of receptacle

Bonding jumper to grounded metal box

Ground terminal is green hex head screw

Bare or insulated wire

This end connects to receptacle ground terminal

Screw attaches to threaded hole in back of box

A TYPICAL GROUNDING PIGTAIL

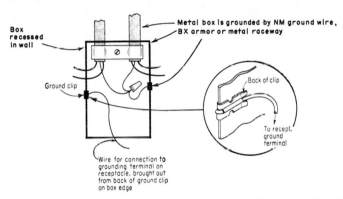

Box recessed in wall

Metal box is grounded by NM ground wire, BX armor or metal raceway

Ground clip

Back of clip

To recept. ground terminal

Wire for connection to grounding terminal on receptacle, brought out from back of ground clip on box edge

Fig. 250·61. Bonding jumper connects receptacle ground to grounded box. (Sec. 250-74.)

former. Or the equipment grounding conductor may be connected to any ground bus in an intermediate panelboard fed from the service or transformer. But, the important point is to be sure the insulated ground terminal of the receptacle does tie into the equipment ground system that is bonded to the neutral.

This Exception must be observed very carefully to avoid violations that have been commonly encountered in the application of branch circuits to computer equipment—where manufacturers of computers and so-called computer power centers specified connection of "Quiet" receptacle ground terminals to a grounding electrode that is independent of (not bonded to) the neutral and bonded equipment ground bus of the electrical system. This practice developed to eliminate computer operating problems that were attributed to "electrical noise." Such isolation of the receptacle ground terminal does not provide an effective return path for fault-current flow and, therefore, constitutes a hazard.

Any receptacle grounding terminal (the green hex-head screw)—whether it is the common type with the mounting yoke or the type insulated from the yoke—must be connected back to the point at which the system neutral is bonded to the equipment grounding terminal and to the grounding electrode.

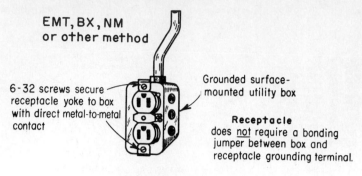

EMT, BX, NM
or other method

6-32 screws secure
receptacle yoke to box
with direct metal-to-metal
contact

Grounded surface-
mounted utility box

Receptacle
does not require a bonding
jumper between box and
receptacle grounding terminal.

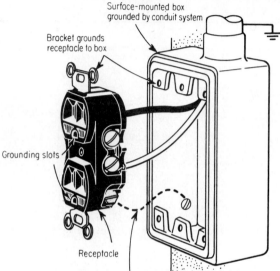

Surface-mounted box
grounded by conduit system

Bracket grounds
receptacle to box

Grounding slots

Receptacle

A jumper wire to connect the grounding-screw terminal to the grounded box
is not required with a surface-mounted box, but is required when receptacle
is used in a recessed box

JUMPER FROM RECEPTACLE
GROUND SCREW TO BOX

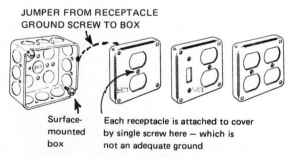

Surface-
mounted
box

Each receptacle is attached to cover
by single screw here — which is
not an adequate ground

RECEPTACLE IN RAISED COVER REQUIRES BONDING JUMPER (cast covers for FS
and FD boxes and other covers may contain a receptacle without a bonding jumper if they
are "listed" as suitable for grounding.)

Fig. 250-62. Typical applications where a surface box does and does not need a receptacle bonding jumper. (Sec. 250-74.)

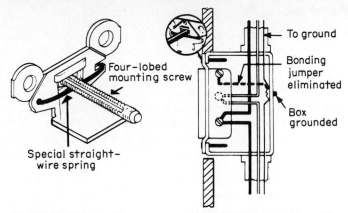

Four-lobed
mounting screw

Special straight-
wire spring

To ground

Bonding
jumper
eliminated

Box
grounded

Fig. 250·63. Self-grounding screws ground receptacle in recessed box without bonding jumper. (Sec. 250-74.)

Insulation separates
ground terminal from
metal mounting strap
for "quiet" grounding

SECTION 250-74, EXCEPTION NO. 4. A
QUIET GROUND MUST MEET THESE
CONDITIONS.

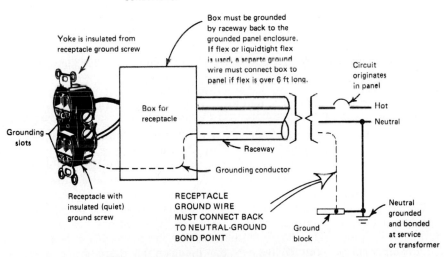

Yoke is insulated from
receptacle ground screw

Box must be grounded
by raceway back to the
grounded panel enclosure.
If flex or liquidtight flex
is used, a separte ground
wire must connect box to
panel if flex is over 6 ft long.

Circuit
originates
in panel

Box for
receptacle

Hot

Neutral

Grounding
slots

Raceway

Grounding conductor

Receptacle with
insulated (quiet)
ground screw

RECEPTACLE
GROUND WIRE
MUST CONNECT BACK
TO NEUTRAL-GROUND
BOND POINT

Ground
block

Neutral
grounded
and bonded
at service
or transformer

A "QUIET" GROUND CONNECTION MUST BE BONDED
BACK TO THE SERVICE OR TRANSFORMER GROUNDING-
ELECTRODE BOND POINT.

Fig. 250·64. Receptacles with isolated ground terminal are used with "clean" or "quiet" ground. (Sec. 250-74.)

That common (bonded) point may be at the service equipment (where there is no voltage step-down from the service to the receptacle), or the common neutral-equipment-ground point may be at a panelboard fed from a step-down transformer (as used in computer power centers).

When an isolated ground connection is made for the receptacle ground terminal, the box containing the receptacle must be grounded by the raceway supplying it and/or by another equipment grounding conductor run with the circuit wires. And those grounding conductors must tie into the same neutral-equipment-ground point to which the receptacle isolated ground terminal is connected.

See comments that follow Sec. 384-27, Exception.

250·75. Bonding Other Enclosures.   Metal raceways, cable sheaths, equipment frames and enclosures, and all other metal noncurrent-carrying parts must be carefully interconnected with Code-recognized fittings and methods to assure a low-impedance equipment grounding path for fault current—whether or not an equipment grounding conductor (a ground wire) is run within the raceway and connected enclosures. The interconnected system of metal raceways and enclosures must itself form a Code-conforming equipment grounding path—even if a "supplementary equipment grounding conductor" is used within the metal-enclosure grounding system (Fig. 250-65).

The Exception to this basic rule recognized that to reduce electromagnetic noise or interference on a grounding circuit, an insulating "spacer or fitting" may be used to interrupt the electrical continuity of a metallic raceway system at the point of connection to a metal enclosure.

This exception permits interrupting the current path between a metal equipment enclosure and the metal conduit that supplies the enclosure—*but only if* the metal conduit is grounded at its supply end *and* an equipment grounding conductor is run through the conduit into the metal enclosure and is connected to an equipment grounding terminal of the enclosure, to provide safety grounding of the metal enclosure. Provisions for an equipment ground reference separate from the metallic raceway system is covered by Sec. 250-74, Exception No. 4 for electronic equipment that is cord-and-plug connected. This Exception covers a separate equipment ground reference for hard-wired sensitive electronic equipment.

250·76. Bonding for Over 250 Volts.   Single locknut-and-bushing terminations are permitted for 120/240-V systems and 120/208-V systems. Any 480/277-V grounded system, 480-V ungrounded system, or higher must use double locknut-and-bushing terminals on clean knockouts of sheet metal enclosures (no concentric rings in wall) for rigid metal conduit and IMC (Fig. 250-66).

Where good electrical continuity is desired on installations of rigid metal conduit or IMC, two locknuts should always be provided on clean knockouts (no rings left) of sheet metal enclosures so that the metal of the box can be solidly clamped between the locknuts, one being on the outside and one on the inside. The reason for not relying on the bushing in place of the inside locknut is that both conduit and box may be secured in place and if the conduit is placed so that it extends into the box to a greater distance than the thickness of the bushing, the bushing will not make contact with the inside surface of the

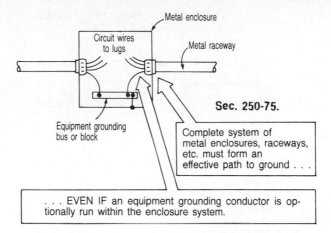

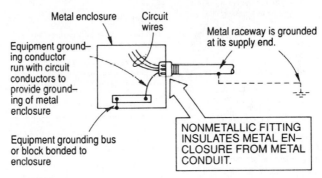

Fig. 250-65. Interconnected metal enclosures (boxes, raceways, cabinets, housings, etc.) must form a continuous equipment grounding path, even if a separate equipment grounding wire is run within the metal enclosure system, except as shown in bottom part of above, to eliminate "noise" on the grounding circuit. [Sec. 250-75.]

box. But that possible weakness in the single-locknut termination does not exclude it from use on systems up to 250 V to ground.

The Exception to the main rule here has the effect of requiring that a bonding jumper must be used around any "oversized, concentric, or eccentric knockouts" in enclosures for circuits over 250 V to ground that are run in metal raceway or cable. For such circuits, a bonding jumper must be used at any conduit or cable termination in other than a clean, unimpaired opening in an enclosure (Fig. 250-66). In any case where all the punched rings (the "doughnuts") are not removed, or, where all the rings are removed but a reducing washer is used to accept a smaller size of conduit, a bonding jumper must be installed from a suitable ground terminal in the enclosure to a lug on the bushing or locknut of the termination of any conduit or cable containing conductors operating at over 250 V to ground. Such circuits include 480/277-V circuits (grounded or ungrounded); 480-, 550-, and 600-V circuits; and higher-voltage circuits. A

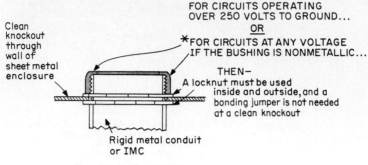

FOR CIRCUITS OPERATING
OVER 250 VOLTS TO GROUND...

OR

*FOR CIRCUITS AT ANY VOLTAGE
IF THE BUSHING IS NONMETALLIC...

Clean
knockout
through
wall of
sheet metal
enclosure

THEN—
A locknut must be used
inside and outside, and a
bonding jumper is not needed
at a clean knockout

Rigid metal conduit
or IMC

* Refer to Sec. 373-5(c).

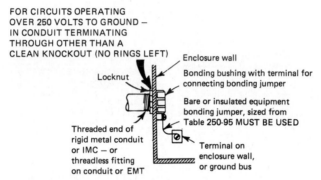

FOR CIRCUITS OPERATING
OVER 250 VOLTS TO GROUND —
IN CONDUIT TERMINATING
THROUGH OTHER THAN A
CLEAN KNOCKOUT (NO RINGS LEFT)

Enclosure wall

Locknut

Bonding bushing with terminal for
connecting bonding jumper

Bare or insulated equipment
bonding jumper, sized from
Table 250-95 MUST BE USED

Threaded end of
rigid metal conduit
or IMC — or
threadless fitting
on conduit or EMT

Terminal on
enclosure wall,
or ground bus

Fig. 250·66. For circuits over 250 volts to ground, a bonding jumper may be needed at conduit termination. [Sec. 250-76.]

bonding jumper is not needed for terminations of conduit that carry such circuits through KOs that are punched on the job to accept the corresponding size of conduit. *But,* double locknuts (one inside, and one outside the enclosure) must be used on threaded conduit ends, or suitable threadless connectors or other fittings must be used on rigid or flexible conduit, EMT, or cable.

250·77. Bonding Loosely Jointed Metal Raceways.   Provision must be made for possible expansion and contraction in concrete slabs due to temperature changes by installing expansion joints in long runs of raceways run through slabs. See Sec. 300-7(b). Because such expansion joints are loosely jointed to permit back-and-forth movement to handle changes in gap between butting slabs, bonding jumpers must be used for equipment grounding continuity (Fig. 250-67). Expansion fittings may be selected as vibration dampers and deflection mediums as well as to provide for movement between building sections or for expansion and contraction due to temperature changes in long conduit runs. The fitting diagrammed in Fig. 250-67 provides for movement from the normal in all directions plus 30° deflection, is available up to 4-in. diameter, and may be installed in concrete.

250·78. Bonding in Hazardous (Classified) Locations.   All raceway terminations in hazardous locations must be made by one of the techniques shown in Fig.

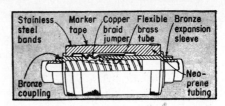

Fig. 250-67. Conduit expansion fitting includes bonding jumper for ground continuity. (Sec. 250-77.)

250-56 for service raceways. And as required by Sec. 501-16(a) such bonding techniques must be used in "all intervening raceways, fittings, boxes, enclosures, etc., between hazardous areas and the point of grounding for service equipment." Refer to Secs. 501-16(a), 502-16(a), and 503-16 (Fig. 250-68).

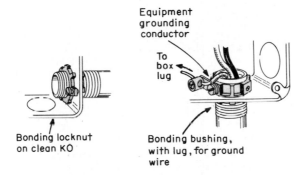

NOTE: Connection of threaded rigid metal conduit or IMC to a threaded boss or hub is considered to be a bonded conduit termination.

Fig. 250-68. Bonded raceway terminations must be used at sheet metal KOs in hazardous areas. (Sec. 250-78.)

250-79. Main and Equipment Bonding Jumpers. Part **(a)** calls for use of copper or other "corrosion-resistant" conductor material—which does include aluminum and copper-clad aluminum. Part **(c)** demands use of connectors, lugs, and other fittings that have been designed, tested, and listed for the particular application.

Part **(d)** covers sizing of any bonding jumper within the service equipment enclosure or on the line or supply side of that enclosure. Refer to the definition of "Bonding Jumper, Main" in Art. 100.

Figure 250-69 shows examples of sizing bonding jumpers in accordance with the first sentence of part **(d)** of this section.

At A, the bonding bushing and jumper are used to comply with part **(d)** of Sec. 250-72. Referring to Table 250-94, with 500 kcmil copper as the "largest service-entrance conductor," the minimum permitted size of grounding electrode conductor is No. 1/0 copper (or No. 3/0 aluminum). That therefore is the minimum permitted size of the required bonding jumper.

At B, with each service phase leg made up of two 500 kcmil copper conduc-

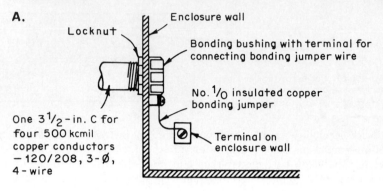

A.

Locknut

Enclosure wall

Bonding bushing with terminal for connecting bonding jumper wire

No. $1/0$ insulated copper bonding jumper

One $3\frac{1}{2}$-in. C for four 500 kcmil copper conductors $-120/208$, 3-∅, 4-wire

Terminal on enclosure wall

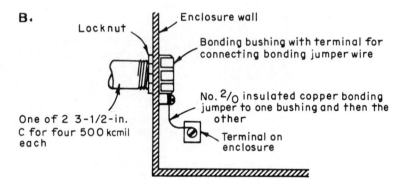

B.

Locknut

Enclosure wall

Bonding bushing with terminal for connecting bonding jumper wire

No. $2/0$ insulated copper bonding jumper to one bushing and then the other

One of 2 3-1/2-in. C for four 500 kcmil each

Terminal on enclosure

NOTE: Bushing with jumper is acceptable bonding for a clean KO or one with punched rings still in place.

Fig. 250-69. Examples of the basic sizing of service bonding jumpers. (Sec. 250-79.)

tors in parallel, the left-hand column heading in Table 250-94 refers to the "equivalent for parallel conductors." As a result, the phase leg is taken at 2 × 500 or 1,000 kcmil, which is the physical equivalent of the makeup. Then Table 250-94 requires a minimum bonding jumper of No. 2/0 copper (or No. 4/0 aluminum).

Figure 250-70 shows an example of sizing a service bonding jumper in accordance with the second sentence of part **(d)** of this section. In this sketch, the jumper between the neutral bus and the equipment ground bus is defined by the **NE Code** as a "main bonding jumper" and the minimum required size of this jumper for this installation is determined by calculating the size of one service phase leg. With three 500 kcmil per phase, that works out to 1,500 kcmil copper per phase. Because that value is in excess of 1,100 kcmil copper, as noted in the **Code** rule, the minimum size of the main bonding jumper must

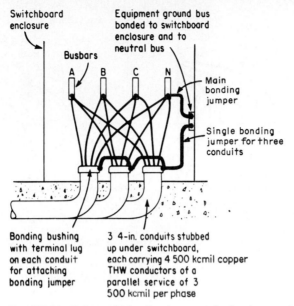

Switchboard
enclosure

Equipment ground bus
bonded to switchboard
enclosure and to
neutral bus

Busbars

A B C N

Main
bonding
jumper

Single bonding
jumper for three
conduits

Bonding bushing
with terminal lug
on each conduit
for attaching
bonding jumper

3 4-in. conduits stubbed
up under switchboard,
each carrying 4 500 kcmil copper
THW conductors of a
parallel service of 3
500 kcmil per phase

Fig. 250·70. Sizing main bonding jumper and other jumpers at service equipment. (Sec. 250-79.)

equal at least 12½ percent of the phase leg cross-section area. Then—

$$12\tfrac{1}{2}\% \times 1{,}500 \text{ kcmil} =$$
$$0.125 \times 1{,}500 = 187.5 \text{ kcmil}$$

Referring to Table 8 in Chap. 9 in the back of the **Code** book, the smallest conductor with at least that cross-section area (csa) is No. 4/0 with a csa of 211,600 CM or 211.6 kcmil. Note that a No. 3/0 has a csa of only 167.8 kcmil. Thus No. 4/0 copper with any type of insulation would satisfy the **Code**.

The jumper shown in Fig. 250-70 running from one conduit bushing to the other and then to the equipment ground bus is defined by the **NE Code** as an "equipment bonding jumper." It is sized the same as a main bonding jumper (above). In this case, therefore, the equipment bonding jumper would have to be not smaller than No. 4/0 copper. And with the calculation that uses the 12½ percent value, if the jumper conductor is to be aluminum instead of copper, a calculation must be made as described below.

In the sketch of Fig. 250-70, if each of the three 4-in. conduits has a separate bonding jumper connecting each one individually to the equipment ground bus, the next to last sentence of part **(d)** may be applied to an individual bonding jumper for each separate conduit (Fig. 250-71). The size of a separate bonding jumper for each conduit in a parallel service must be not less than the size of the grounding electrode conductor for a service of the size of the phase conductor used in each conduit. Referring to Table 250-94, a 500 kcmil copper ser-

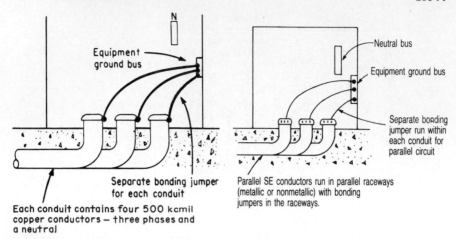

Equipment ground bus

Separate bonding jumper for each conduit

Each conduit contains four 500 kcmil copper conductors — three phases and a neutral

Neutral bus

Equipment ground bus

Separate bonding jumper run within each conduit for parallel circuit

Parallel SE conductors run in parallel raceways (metallic or nonmetallic) with bonding jumpers in the raceways.

Fig. 250·71. An individual bonding jumper may be used for each conduit (left) and *must* be used as shown at right. [Sec. 250-79(d).]

vice calls for at least a No. 1/0 grounding electrode conductor. Therefore, the bonding jumper run from the bushing lug on each conduit to the ground bus must be at least a No. 1/0 copper (or 3/0 aluminum).

The third sentence of part **(d)** requires separate bonding jumpers when the service is made up of multiple conduits and the equipment bonding jumper is run within each raceway (such as plastic pipe) for grounding service enclosures. According to the third sentence of part **(d)**, when service-entrance conductors are paralleled in two or more raceways, an equipment bonding jumper that is routed within the raceways must also be run in parallel, one in each raceway, as at the right in Fig. 250-71. This clarifies application of nonmetallic service raceway where parallel conduits are used for parallel service-entrance conductors. As worded, the rule applies to both nonmetallic and metallic conduits where the bonding jumper is run within the raceways rather than from lugs on bonding bushings on the conduit ends. But for metallic conduits stubbed-up under service equipment, if the conduit ends are to be bonded to the service equipment enclosure by jumpers from lugs on the conduit bushings, either a single large common bonding jumper may be used—from one lug, to another lug, to another, etc., and then to the ground bus—or an individual bonding jumper (of smaller size from Table 250-94, based on the size of conductors in each conduit) may be run from each bushing lug to the ground bus.

The second sentence of part **(d)** sets minimum sizes of copper *and* aluminum service-entrance conductors above which a service bonding jumper must have a cross-section area "not less than 12½ percent of the area of the largest phase conductor." And the rule states that if the service conductors and the bonding jumper are of different material (i.e., service conductors are copper, say, and the jumper is aluminum), the minimum size of the jumper shall be based on the assumed use of phase conductors of the same material as the jumper and with an ampacity equivalent to that of the installed phase conductors (Fig. 250-72).

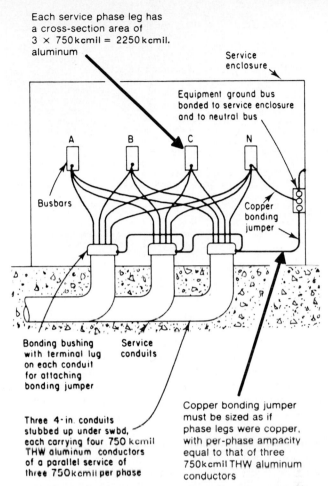

Each service phase leg has
a cross-section area of
3 × 750 kcmil = 2250 kcmil.
aluminum

Service
enclosure

Equipment ground bus
bonded to service enclosure
and to neutral bus

A   B   C   N

Busbars

Copper
bonding
jumper

Bonding bushing   Service
with terminal lug   conduits
on each conduit
for attaching
bonding jumper

Three 4-in. conduits
stubbed up under swbd,
each carrying four 750 kcmil
THW aluminum conductors
of a parallel service of
three 750 kcmil per phase

Copper bonding jumper
must be sized as if
phase legs were copper,
with per-phase ampacity
equal to that of three
750 kcmil THW aluminum
conductors

Fig. 250-72. Sizing a copper bonding jumper for aluminum service
conductors. [Sec. 250-79(c).]

The last sentence in part **(d)** covers the sizing of a bonding jumper that is used
to bond raceway that contains a grounding electrode conductor. Such a raceway is required to provide mechanical protection for a grounding electrode
conductor smaller than No. 6, as noted in Sec. 250-92(a). And protection is frequently provided for larger grounding electrode conductors.

At service equipment, a bonding jumper for a raceway containing a grounding electrode conductor only has to be at least the same size as the required
grounding electrode conductor, as shown in Fig. 250-73. The last sentence
makes clear that the bonding jumper for a grounding electrode conductor conduit does *not* have to be sized at 12½ percent of the cross-section area of the
largest phase conductor of the service—as required by the foregoing text of Sec.
250-79(d), when the largest service phase conductor is larger than 1100-kcmil

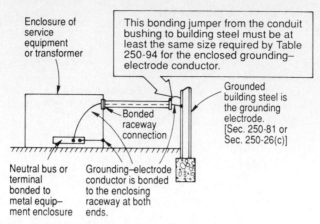

Fig. 250-73. A typical example of the rule on bonding jumpers for raceways enclosing grounding electrode conductors. [Sec. 250-79(d).]

(MCM) copper or 1,750-kcmil aluminum. That requirement for 12½ percent of the service phase size applies only to bonding jumpers that are used with conduits containing ungrounded service phase conductors, but not with raceway sleeves for grounding electrode conductors.

Part **(b)** of Sec. 250-92 covers details on the use of "metal enclosures" (such as conduit or EMT sleeves) for grounding electrode conductors. The grounding conductor must be connected to its protective conduit at both ends so that any current that might flow over the conductor will also have the conduit as a parallel path. The regulation presented is actually a performance description of the rule of Sec. 250-71(a)(3), which specifically and simply requires that any conduit or armor enclosing a grounding electrode conductor be electrically parallel with the conductor. Bonded connections at both ends of an enclosing raceway must be used for any grounding electrode arrangement at a service and for grounding of a separately derived system, such as a generator or transformer secondary. Any bonding jumper for that application simply has to be at least the same size as required for the grounding electrode conductor run inside the conduit.

Part **(e)** requires a bonding jumper on the load side of the service to be sized as if it were an equipment grounding conductor for the largest circuit with which it is used. And sizing would have to be done from Table 250-95, as follows.

Figure 250-74 shows a floor trench in the switchboard room of a large hotel. The conductors are feeder conductors carried from circuit breakers in the main switchboard (just visible in upper right corner of photo) to feeder conduits going out at left, through the concrete wall of the trench, and under the slab floor to the various distribution panels throughout the building. Because the conduits themselves are not metallically connected to the metal switchboard enclosure, bonding must be provided from the conduits to the switchboard ground bus to

Fig. 250-74. Conduits in trench carry feeder conductors from switchboard at right (arrow) out to various panels and control centers. A single, common bonding jumper— run continuously from bushing to bushing—may be used to bond all conduits to the switchboard ground bus. (Sec. 250-79(e).)

assure electrical continuity and conductivity as required by **NE Code** Secs. 250-33, 250-42(e), 250-51, and 250-57.

1. The single, common, continuous bonding conductor that bonds all the conduits to the switchboard must be sized in accordance with **NE Code** Table 250-95, based on the highest rating of CB or fuses protecting any one of the total number of circuits run in all the conduits.

2. Sizing of the single, common bonding jumper would be based on the highest rating of overcurrent protection for any one of the circuits run in the group of conduits. For instance, some of the circuits could be 400-A circuits made up of 500 kcmils in individual 3-in. conduits, and others could be parallel-circuit makeups in multiple conduits—such as 800-A circuits, with two conduits per circuit, and 1200-A circuits, with three conduits. If, for instance, the highest rated feeder in the group was protected by a 2000-A circuit breaker, then the single, common bonding jumper for all the conduits would have to be 250 kcmil copper or 400 kcmil aluminum—determined readily from Table 250-95, by simply going down the left column to the value of "2000" and then reading across. The single conductor is run through a lug on each of the conduit bushings and then to the switchboard ground bus.

In the case shown in Fig. 250-74, however, because the bonding jumper from the conduit ends to the switchboard is much longer than a jumper would be if the conduits stubbed-up under the switchboard, better engineering design might dictate that a separate equipment grounding *conductor* (rather than a "jumper") be used for each individual circuit in the group. If one of the conduits is a 3-in. conduit carrying three 500 kcmil conductors from a 400-A CB in the switchboard, the minimum acceptable size of bonding jumper (or equipment grounding conductor) from a grounding bushing on the conduit end to the switchboard ground bus would be No. 3 copper or No. 1 aluminum or copper-clad aluminum, as shown opposite the value of 400 A in the left column of Table 250-95. If another two of the 3-in. conduits are used for a feeder consisting of two parallel sets of three 500 kcmil conductors (each set of three 500 kcmils in a separate conduit) for a circuit protected at 800 A, a single bonding jumper could be used, run from one grounding bushing to the other grounding bushing and then to the switchboard ground bus. This single bonding jumper would have to be a minimum No. 1/0 copper, from **NE Code** Table 250-95 on the basis of the 800-A rating of the feeder overcurrent protective device.

With such a long run for a jumper, as shown in Fig. 250-74, **Code** rules could be interpreted to require that the bonding jumper be subject to the rules of Sec. 250-95; that is, use of a bonding jumper must conform to the requirements for equipment grounding conductors. As a result, bonding of conduits for a parallel circuit makeup would have to comply with the second sentence in Sec. 250-95, which requires equipment grounding conductors to be run in parallel "where conductors are run in parallel in multiple raceways. . . ." That would then be taken to require that bonding jumpers *also* must be run in parallel for multiple-conduit circuits. And that concept is supported by the next-to-last sentence of part **(d)** of Sec. 250-79. In the case of the 800-A circuit above, instead of a single No. 1/0 copper jumper from one bushing lug to the other bushing lug and then to the ground bus, it would be necessary to use a separate No. 1/0 copper from each bushing to the ground bus, so the jumpers are run in parallel—as required for equipment grounding conductors. Figure 250-75 shows the two possible arrangements. The wording of Secs. 250-79(e) and 250-95 can be used to support either method. Bonding jumpers on the load side of service equipment are sized and routed the same as equipment grounding conductors because such bonding jumpers and equipment grounding conductors serve identical functions. And note that Sec. 250-95 requires the equipment grounding conductor for each of the conduits for a parallel circuit to be the full size determined from the circuit rating. In the case here, a No. 1/0 copper for each conduit is required, based on the 800-A rating of the feeder protective device.

An Exception notes that an equipment bonding jumper never has to be larger than the circuit conductors within a conduit being bonded.

Part **(f)** of Sec. 250-79 follows the thinking that was described in Sec. 250-58(a) for external grounding of equipment attached to a properly grounded metal rack or structure. A short length of flexible metal conduit, liquidtight flex, or any other raceway may, if the raceway itself is not acceptable as a grounding conductor, be provided with grounding by a "bonding jumper" (note: *not* an "equipment grounding conductor") run *either* inside or *outside* the raceway or enclosure PROVIDED THAT the *length* of the *equipment bonding jumper* is *not more* than 6 ft and the jumper is routed with the raceway or enclosure.

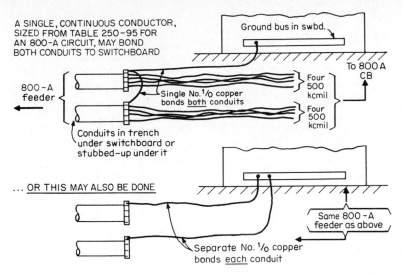

A SINGLE, CONTINUOUS CONDUCTOR, SIZED FROM TABLE 250-95 FOR AN 800-A CIRCUIT, MAY BOND BOTH CONDUITS TO SWITCHBOARD

Ground bus in swbd.

To 800 A CB

800-A feeder

Single No.¹/₀ copper bonds <u>both</u> conduits

Four 500 kcmil

Four 500 kcmil

Conduits in trench under switchboard or stubbed-up under it

... OR THIS MAY ALSO BE DONE

Same 800-A feeder as above

Separate No. ¹/₀ copper bonds <u>each</u> conduit

Fig. 250-75. One jumper may be used to bond two or more conduits on the load side of the service. [Sec. 250-79(e).]

Where an equipment bonding conductor is installed within a raceway, it must comply with all the **Code** rules on identification of equipment grounding conductors. A bonding jumper installed in flexible metal conduit or liquidtight flex serves essentially the same function as an equipment grounding conductor. For that reason, a bonding jumper should comply with the identification rules of Sec. 310-12(b)—on the use of bare, green-insulated or green-taped conductors for equipment grounding.

Note that this application has limited use for the conditions specified and is a special variation from the concept of Sec. 250-57(b), which requires grounding conductors run inside raceways. Its big application is for external bonding of short lengths of liquidtight or standard flex, under those conditions where the particular type of flex itself is not suitable for providing the grounding continuity required by Secs. 350-5 and 351-9. Refer also to Sec. 250-91(b), Exceptions Nos. 1 and 2.

The top of Fig. 250-76 shows how an external bonding jumper may be used with standard flexible metallic conduit (so-called Greenfield). If the length of the flex is not over 6 ft, but the conductors run within the flex are protected at more than 20 A, a bonding jumper *must* be used either inside or outside the flex. An outside jumper must comply as shown. For a length of flex not over 6 ft, containing conductors that are protected at not more than 20 A and used with conduit termination fittings that are approved for grounding, a bonding jumper is *not* required—as covered in Sec. 250-91(b), Exception No. 1.

The bottom of Fig. 250-76 shows use of an external bonding jumper with liquidtight flexible metallic conduit. If liquidtight flex is not over 6 ft long *but* is larger than 1¼-in. trade size, a bonding jumper must be used, installed *either*

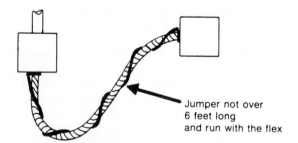

Jumper sized
from Table 250-95

Straight, stretched-out
length of bonding jumper
must not exceed 6 feet

Fittings must have
lugs and be approved
for this use

Box, enclosure or
fitting each end of flex

Jumper must be wrapped
around or attached to flex
so it is "routed with it" as
required in Section 250-79(e)

6- ft bonding
jumper

THIS IS A VIOLATION!
Bonding jumper not
routed with flex and
external bonding
jumper is not permitted
for any length of flex
over 6 ft

Flex over
6 ft long

Bonding jumper required for flex may be outside the flex.

Jumper not over
6 feet long
and run with the flex

Liquidtight flex larger than 1¼ in. size must have bonding
jumper — inside or outside — in any length up to 6 ft.

Fig. 250·76. Bonding jumper rules for standard flex and liquidtight flex. [Sec. 250-79(f).]

inside or outside the liquidtight. An outside jumper must comply as shown. If a length of liquidtight flex larger than 1¼ in. is short enough to permit an external bonding jumper that is not more than 6 ft long between external grounding-type connectors at the ends of the flex, an external bonding jumper may be used. BUT WATCH OUT! The rule says the *jumper,* not the flex, must not exceed 6 ft in length *AND* the jumper "shall be routed with the raceway"— that is, run along the flex surface and not separated from the flex.

250-80. Bonding of Piping Systems. This section on bonding of piping systems in buildings is divided into two parts—metal *water* piping and *other* metal piping. This section is a rather elaborate sequence of phrases that may be understood in several ways. Of course, the basic concept is to ground any metal pipes that would present a hazard if energized by an electrical circuit.

Part **(a)** requires any "interior metal water piping system" to be bonded to the service-equipment enclosure, the grounded conductor (usually, a neutral) at the service, the grounding electrode conductor, **or** the one or more grounding electrodes used. All points of attachment of bonding jumpers for metal water-piping systems must be accessible. Only the connections (and not the entire length) of water-pipe bonding jumpers are required to be accessible for inspection. This rule applies where the metal water piping system does not have 10 ft of metal pipe buried in the earth and is, therefore, not a grounding electrode. In such cases, though, this rule makes clear that the water piping system must be bonded to the service grounding arrangement. And the bonding jumper used to connect the interior water piping to, say, the grounded neutral bus or terminal (or to the ground bus or terminal) must be sized from Table 250-94 based on the size of the service conductors. The jumper is sized from that table because that is the table that would have been used *if* the water piping had 10 ft buried under the ground, making it suitable as a grounding electrode. Note that the "bonding jumper" is sized from Table 250-94 [and not from Sec. 250-79(c)], which means it never has to be larger than No. 3/0 copper or 250 kcmil aluminum. Refer to the illustrations for Sec. 250-81, which also cover bonding of water piping.

The Exception to part **(a)** permits "isolated" metal water piping to be bonded to the main electrical enclosure (panelboard or switchboard) in each unit of a multitenant building—such as in each apartment of an apartment house, each store of a shopping center, or each office unit of a multitenant office building. See the top of Fig. 250-77. This Exception is intended to provide a realistic and effective way to bond interior metal water piping to the electrical grounding system in multitenant buildings where the metal water piping in each tenant's unit is fed from a main water distribution system of nonmetallic piping and is isolated from the metal water piping in other units. In apartment houses, multistore buildings, etc., it would be difficult, costly, and ineffective to use long bonding jumpers to tie the isolated piping in all the units back to the equipment grounding point of the building's service equipment—as required by the basic rule of Sec. 250-80(a). The objective of the basic rule is better achieved in such cases by simply bonding the isolated water piping in each occupancy to the equipment ground bus of the panelboard or switchboard serving the occu-

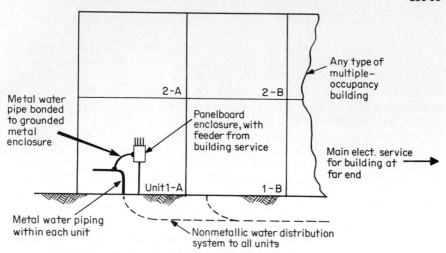

Any type of multiple-occupancy building

Metal water pipe bonded to grounded metal enclosure

2-A   2-B

Panelboard enclosure, with feeder from building service

Main elect. service for building at far end

Unit 1-A   1-B

Metal water piping within each unit

Nonmetallic water distribution system to all units

**THIS WATER-PIPE BONDING IS OK
IN EACH UNIT OF MULTITENANT BUILDING**

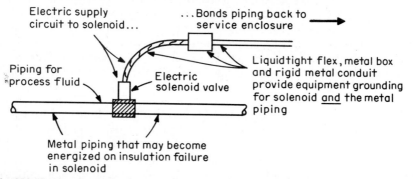

Electric supply circuit to solenoid...

...Bonds piping back to service enclosure

Piping for process fluid

Electric solenoid valve

Liquidtight flex, metal box and rigid metal conduit provide equipment grounding for solenoid <u>and</u> the metal piping

Metal piping that may become energized on insulation failure in solenoid

Fig. 250-77. Certain techniques are permitted as alternatives to the basic rules on grounding of metal piping systems. [Sec. 250-80.]

pancy. The bonding jumper must be sized from Table 250-95 (*not* 250-94)—based on the largest rating of protective device for any circuit within the occupancy.

Part **(b)** requires a bonding connection from "other" (than water) metal piping systems—such as process liquids or fluids—that "may become energized" to the grounded neutral, the service ground terminal, the grounding electrode conductor, or the grounding electrodes. *But, for these* other *piping systems the bonding jumper is sized from Table 250-95,* using the rating of the overcurrent device of the circuit that *may* energize the piping.

Understanding and application of part **(b)** of Sec. 250-80 hinge on the reference to metal piping "which may become energized." What does that phrase mean? Is it not true that any metal piping "may" become energized? Or does the rule mean to apply only to metal piping that conductively connects to metal enclosures of electrical equipment—such as pump motors, solenoid valves, pressure switches, etc.—in which electrical insulation failure would put a potential on the metal piping system? It does seem that the latter case is what the **Code** rule means. And that concept is supported by the second paragraph of part **(b)**, which notes that where a particular circuit poses the threat of energization to a piping system, the equipment grounding conductor for that circuit (which could be the conduit or other raceway enclosing the circuit) may be used as the means of bonding the piping back to the service ground point. That has the effect of saying, for instance, that the equipment grounding conductor for a circuit to a solenoid valve in a pipe may also ground the piping (see bottom of Fig. 250-77).

250·81. Grounding Electrode System. The rules in this section cover the grounding electrode arrangement required at the service entrance of a premise or in a building or other structure fed from a service in another building or other structure, as covered in Sec. 250-24. But, the rules do not apply to grounding of a separately derived system, such as a local step-down transformer, which is covered by part **(c)** of Sec. 250-26 (Fig. 250-78).

Section 250-81 calls for a "grounding electrode system" instead of simply a "grounding electrode" as required by previous **NE Code** editions. Up to the 1978 **NEC**, the "water-pipe" electrode was the premier electrode for service grounding, and "other electrodes" or "made electrodes" were acceptable *only* "where a water system (electrode) . . . is not available." If a metal water pipe to a building had at least 10 ft of its length buried in the ground, that *had* to be used as the grounding electrode and no other electrode was required. The underground water pipe was the preferred electrode, the *best* electrode.

In the present **NEC**, of all the electrodes previously and still recognized by the **NEC**, the water pipe is the least acceptable electrode and is the only one that may never be used by itself as the *sole* electrode. It must always be supplemented by at least one "additional" grounding electrode (Fig. 250-79). Any one of the other grounding electrodes recognized by the **NEC** is acceptable as the *sole* grounding electrode, by itself.

Take a typical water supply of 12-in.-diameter metal pipe running, say, 400 ft underground to a building with a 4,000-A service. From Sec. 250-81(a), that water pipe, connected by a 3/0 copper conductor to the bonded service-equipment neutral, *must* be used as a grounding electrode but may *not* serve as the only grounding electrode. It must be supplemented by one of the other electrodes from Sec. 250-81 or 250-83. So the installation can be made acceptable by, say, running a No. 6 copper grounding electrode conductor from the bonded service neutral to an 8-ft, ½-in.-diameter ground rod. Although that seems like using a mouse to help an elephant pull a load, it is the literal requirement of Sec. 250-81. And if the same building did not have 10 ft of metal water pipe in the ground, the 8-ft ground rod would be entirely acceptable as the *only* electrode.

Although the next-to-last sentence of Sec. 250-81 calls for the grounding electrode conductor to be "unspliced," the Exception in the basic rule says that in

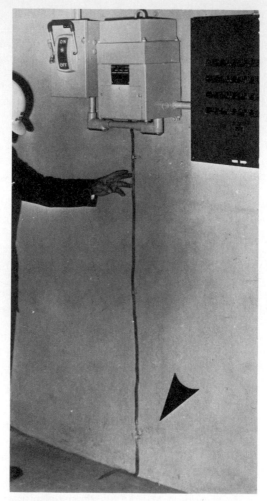

Fig. 250-78. Grounding electrode conductor from the bonded secondary neutral of this local transformer was connected to grounded building steel before concrete floor was poured. This installation is not covered by the rules of Sec. 250-81, but is covered by Sec. 250-26 and complies with those rules. (Sec. 250-81.)

industrial and commercial premises, the rule requiring "unspliced" grounding electrode conductor is relaxed to permit exothermic welded connections to "extend" the grounding electrode conductor. This exception provides for the very common need for adding to the length of grounding electrode conductors because of unforeseen changes or accidental damage to such conductors on larger commercial and industrial jobs.

Fig. 250-79. Connection to an underground metal water-supply pipe is never adequate grounding for electric service equipment. (Sec. 250-81.)

The basic rule of Sec. 250-81 requires that all or any of the electrodes specified in **(a)**, **(b)**, **(c)**, and **(d)**, if they are available on the premises, must be bonded together to form a "grounding electrode system."

(a) If there is at least a 10-ft length of underground metal water pipe, connection of a grounding electrode conductor must be made to the water pipe.

(b) If, in addition, the building has a metal frame that is "effectively grounded," the frame must be bonded to the water pipe—or vice versa, because the rules do not spell out where actual connections are to be made for grounding electrode conductors and bonding jumpers. In the fine-print note, a definition is given for the phrase "effectively grounded" as applied to the metal frame of a building. To be "effectively grounded," the metal frame must be connected to earth by a low-impedance ground connection that will prevent "buildup of voltages" that could present a hazard to equipment or persons. Structural building steel that is bolted into a concrete footing or foundation in the earth would satisfy that definition.

(c) Then, if there is at least a total of 20 ft of one or more ½-in.-diameter steel reinforcing bars or rods embedded in the concrete footing or foundation, a bonding connection must be made from one of the other electrodes to one of the rebars—and obviously that has to be done before concrete is poured for the footing or foundation.

When two or more grounding electrodes of the types described in Sec. 250-81 are to be combined into a "grounding electrode system," the size of the bonding jumper between pairs of electrodes must not be smaller than the size of grounding electrode conductor indicated in Table 250-94 for the particular size of the largest phase leg of the service feeder.

The "unspliced" grounding electrode conductor at the service may be connected to whichever one of the interbonded electrodes that provides the most convenient and effective point of connection.

The last sentence of this paragraph in Sec. 250-81 says that the grounding electrode conductor must be sized as if it were the grounding electrode conductor for whichever one of the interbonded electrodes that requires the largest grounding electrode conductor. If, for instance, a grounding electrode system consists of a metal underground water-pipe electrode supplemented by a driven ground rod, the grounding electrode conductor to the water pipe would have to be sized from Table 250-94; and on, say, a 2,000-A service, it would have to be a No. 3/0 copper or 250 kcmil aluminum, connected to the water-pipe electrode, which would require that size of grounding electrode conductor. A bonding jumper from the bonded grounding terminal or bus in the SE equipment to the driven ground rod would not have to be larger than a No. 6 copper or No. 4 aluminum grounding electrode conductor, just as it would be if the ground rod is used by itself as a grounding electrode. A bonding jumper between the water-pipe electrode and the ground rod would also have to be that size. There is negligible benefit in running larger than a No. 6 copper or No. 4 aluminum to a "made electrode," such as a ground rod, because the rod itself is the limiting resistance to earth.

In parts **(c)** and **(d)** of Sec. 250-81, the "20 feet of bare copper conductor" referred to is going to be "available" at a building only if either 20-ft arrangement has been specified by the electrical designer, because they are clearly and only grounding electrodes; whereas the other electrodes in parts **(a)**, **(b)**, and the rebars in **(c)** are specified by other than the electrical designer and may be "available."

If a building has all or some of the electrodes described, the above applications are mandatory. If it has none, then any one of the electrodes described in Sec. 250-83 may be used for service grounding.

In the last sentence of Sec. 250-81(a), an electrode (such as a driven ground rod) that supplements an underground water-pipe electrode may be "bonded" to any one of several points in the service arrangement. It may be "bonded" to (1) the grounding electrode conductor; or (2) the grounded service conductor (grounded neutral), such as by connection to the neutral block or bus in the service panel or switchboard or in a CT cabinet, meter socket, or other enclosure on the supply side of the service disconnect; or (3) grounded metal service raceway; or (4) any grounded metal enclosure that is part of the service; or (5) interior metal water piping at any convenient point. Part **(a)** calls for a bonding jumper around any water meter within a building and any place where piping on both sides of the meter is required to be grounded.

The second paragraph makes very clear that a ground rod or other "made" electrode that is used to supplement a water-pipe electrode does not require any larger than a No. 6 copper (or No. 4 aluminum) conductor for a bonding jumper that is the only connection from the ground rod to the grounding-electrode conductor, to the bonded neutral block or bus in the service equipment, to any grounded service enclosure or raceway, or to interior metal water piping.

The several requirements set by this section and the conditions established for application of the rules can be best understood by considering a step-by-step approach in making the necessary provisions for typical installations. To restate the above general description of Sec. 250-81:

First, take the case of a building fed by an underground water piping system with at least a 10-ft length of *metal* water pipe buried in the earth ahead of the point at which the metal pipe enters the building (Fig. 250-80). Such buried pipe *is* a grounding electrode, and connection must be made to the underground pipe by a grounding electrode conductor sized from Table 250-94 and run from

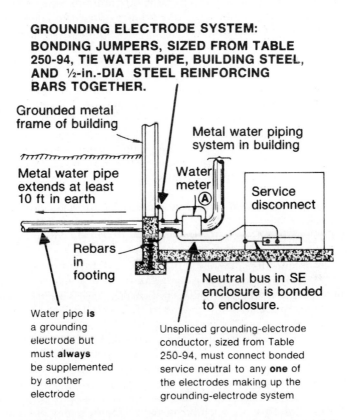

**GROUNDING ELECTRODE SYSTEM:
BONDING JUMPERS, SIZED FROM TABLE 250-94, TIE WATER PIPE, BUILDING STEEL, AND ½-in.-DIA STEEL REINFORCING BARS TOGETHER.**

Grounded metal frame of building

Metal water piping system in building

Metal water pipe extends at least 10 ft in earth

Water meter (A)

Service disconnect

Rebars in footing

Neutral bus in SE enclosure is bonded to enclosure.

Water pipe **is** a grounding electrode but must **always** be supplemented by another electrode

Unspliced grounding-electrode conductor, sized from Table 250-94, must connect bonded service neutral to any **one** of the electrodes making up the grounding-electrode system

NOTE: At point "A", a bonding jumper **must** be used around the water meter and must be not smaller than the grounding-electrode conductor.

Fig. 250-80. Metal building frame and reinforcing bars *must* be used as an electrode if present. (Sec. 250-81.)

the grounding point in the service equipment. But now, a number of other factors must be accounted for, as follows:

1. EVEN THOUGH THE WATER PIPE *IS* A SUITABLE GROUNDING ELECTRODE, SEC. 250-81(a) REQUIRES THAT AT LEAST ONE MORE GROUNDING ELECTRODE MUST BE PROVIDED AND MUST BE BONDED TO THE WATER-PIPE ELECTRODE. A water pipe, by itself, is not an adequate grounding electrode and must be supplemented by at least one other electrode to provide a "grounding electrode system."

2. The additional electrode may be:

▪ The metal frame of the building provided the frame is effectively grounded (embedded in earth and/or in buried concrete). Figure 250-80 shows an example of the metal frame electrode supplementing the water pipe.

▪ OR, a concrete-encased electrode within and near the bottom of a concrete foundation or footing in direct contact with earth. The electrode must consist of at least 20 ft of one or more steel reinforcing bars or rods of not less than ½-in. diameter, or it must consist of at least 20 ft of bare solid copper conductor not smaller than No. 4 AWG. If the building footing or foundation shown in Fig. 250-80 did contain such steel reinforcing, connection of a bonding conductor would have to be made to the steel and the conductor would have to be brought out for connection to the water pipe, the building steel, or the bonded service neutral.

▪ OR, a "ground ring encircling the building or structure," buried directly in the earth at least 2½ ft down. The ground ring must be "at least 20 feet" of bare No. 2 or larger copper conductor. (In most cases, the conductor will have to be considerably longer than 20 ft in order to "encircle" the building or structure.)

▪ OR, underground bare metal gas piping or other metal underground piping or tanks.

▪ OR, a buried 8-ft ground rod or pipe or a plate electrode. An example of bonding of a supplemental grounding electrode is shown in Fig. 250-81. And an interesting point about the bonding of the ground rod to the neutral bus in the SE enclosure is the question of the size of the bonding jumper. Because the first paragraph of Sec. 250-81 requires that all the electrodes that make up a grounding electrode system be "bonded together" by a jumper sized from Table 250-94, and because the last sentence of Sec. 250-81(a) requires the supplemental electrode to be "bonded" to the service neutral or other specified point, it might appear that the conductor shown connecting the ground rod to the neutral bus in the sketch is a "bonding jumper" and must be the same size as the grounding electrode conductor (from Table 250-94). But, the second paragraph of Sec. 250-81(a) describes that conductor as a "bonding jumper," and it is *not* described as a "grounding electrode conductor." Therefore, a No. 6 copper or a No. 4 aluminum is the maximum size required for that connection—as stated in the second paragraph.

In Sec. 250-81(c), the encased grounding electrode may be 20 ft of bare No. 4 stranded copper conductor.

Grounding electrode conductor sized from Table
250-94 must connect bonded service neutral to
clamp on water-pipe electrode, on either side
of water meter, with same size bonding
jumper around water meter.

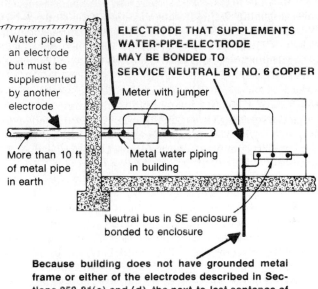

Water pipe **is**
an electrode
but must be
supplemented
by another
electrode

**ELECTRODE THAT SUPPLEMENTS
WATER-PIPE-ELECTRODE
MAY BE BONDED TO
SERVICE NEUTRAL BY NO. 6 COPPER**

Meter with jumper

More than 10 ft
of metal pipe
in earth

Metal water piping
in building

Neutral bus in SE enclosure
bonded to enclosure

**Because building does not have grounded metal
frame or either of the electrodes described in Sections 250-81(c) and (d), the next-to-last sentence of
Section 250-81(a) requires that one of the electrodes of Section 250-83 be used to supplement the
water-pipe electrode—such as a driven ground
rod.**

Fig. 250-81. Supplementing water-pipe electrode in building without
metal frame. (Sec. 250-81.)

Sections 250-81 and 250-83 list the acceptable electrodes and describe
installation requirements.

3. As worded in Sec. 250-81, any of the four types of grounding electrodes
mentioned there [(a), (b), (c), and (d)] must be bonded together IF THEY
ARE PRESENT. Note that the rule does not state that any of those electrodes must be provided. But if any or all of them are present, they must
be bonded together to form a "grounding electrode system," sizing such
bonding jumpers from Sec. 250-79(c). And where a water-pipe electrode,
as described, is present, any one of the three electrodes in Sec. 250-81 may
be used as the required "additional electrode."

In the case of a building fed by a nonmetallic underground piping system or
one where there is *not* 10 ft of metal pipe underground, the water piping system
is *not* a grounding electrode—HOWEVER, THE INTERIOR METAL WATER
PIPING SYSTEM MUST BE BONDED TO THE SERVICE GROUNDING, as

described above under Sec. 250-80(a). But when the water pipe is not a ground-ing electrode, another type of electrode must be provided to accomplish the service grounding. Any *one* of the other three electrodes of Sec. 250-81 [**(b)**, **(c)**, or **(d)**] may be used as the required grounding electrode. For instance, if the metal frame of the building is effectively grounded, a grounding electrode con-ductor, sized from Table 250-94 and run from the bonded service neutral or ground terminal to the building frame, may satisfy the **Code**, as shown in Fig. 250-82. Where none of the four electrodes described in Sec. 250-81 is present, *one* of the electrodes from Sec. 250-83 MUST BE USED, such as a ground rod as shown in Fig. 250-83. Note that any type of electrode other than a water-pipe electrode MAY BE USED BY ITSELF AS THE SOLE ELECTRODE.

As shown in Fig. 250-83, the literal wording of Sec. 250-94, Exception No. 1, would permit use of a No. 6 copper or No. 4 aluminum grounding electrode conductor. It is consistent with long-time **Code** practice, based on tests, that the ground rod shown in Fig. 250-81 be connected to the neutral terminal or to the water pipe by a conductor that is not required to be larger than No. 6 copper or No. 4 aluminum.

The four illustrations shown for this section are only typical examples of the many specific ways in which the new rules on grounding electrodes may be applied.

A very important sentence of Sec. 250-81(a) says that "continuity of the grounding path or the bonding connection to interior piping shall not rely on water meters." The intent of that rule is that a bonding jumper always MUST BE USED around a water meter. This has been added because of the chance of loss of grounding if the water meter is removed or replaced with a nonme-tallic water meter. The bonding jumper around a meter must be sized in accor-dance with Table 250-94. Although the **Code** rule does not specify that the bonding jumper around a meter be sized from that table, the reference to "bonding jumper . . . in accordance with Sec. 250-94," as stated in the first para-graph of Sec. 250-81, would logically apply to the water-meter bond.

The concrete-encased electrode that is described in part **(c)** of Sec. 250-81, known as the "Ufer system," has particular merit in new construction where the bare copper conductor or steel reinforcing bar or rod can be readily installed in a foundation or footing form before concrete is poured. Installations of this type using a bare copper conductor have been installed as far back as 1940, and tests have proved this system to be highly effective.

The intent of "bottom of a concrete foundation" is to completely encase the electrode within the concrete, in the footing near the bottom. The footing shall be in direct contact with the earth, which means that dry gravel or polyethylene sheets between the footing and the earth are not permitted (Fig. 250-84).

It may be advisable to provide additional corrosion protection in the form of plastic tubing or sheath at the point where the grounding electrode leaves the concrete foundation.

For concrete-encased steel reinforcing bar or rod systems used as a ground-ing electrode in underground footings or foundations, welded-type connections (metal-fusing methods) may be used for connections that are encased in con-crete. Compression or other type mechanical connectors may also be used.

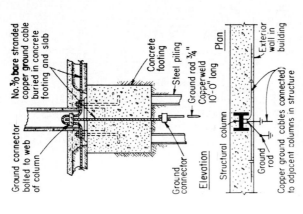

No.%o bare stranded copper ground cable buried in concrete footing and slab

Ground connector bolted to web of column

Concrete footing

Steel piling

Ground rod ¾" Copperweld 10'-0" long

Ground connector

Elevation

Structural column

Exterior wall in building

Plan

Ground rod

Copper ground cables connected to adjacent columns in structure

ONE METHOD of grounding building structural members to ground cable system.

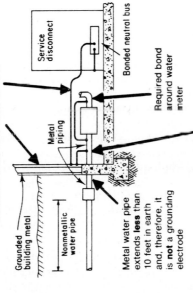

Section 250-81(b) recognizes the grounded metal building frame as a suitable grounding electrode by itself, connected to bonded service neutral by conductor sized from Table 250-94.

Service disconnect

Bonded neutral bus

Required bond around water meter

Metal piping

Metal water pipe extends **less** than 10 feet in earth and, therefore, it is **not** a grounding electrode

Grounded building metal

Nonmetallic water pipe

Section 250-80(a) requires interior metal water piping to be bonded to service grounding, such as by bonding to the grounding electrode (the building frame in this case), with jumper sized from Table 250-94.

NOTE: Rebars in foundation could also serve as the only electrode if building did not have metal frame.

Fig. 250-82. Building metal frame may be sole grounding electrode. (Sec. 250-81.)

Section 250-80(a) requires interior metal water piping to be bonded to service grounding, such as by bonding to grounded neutral bus, using bonding jumper sized from Table 250-94.

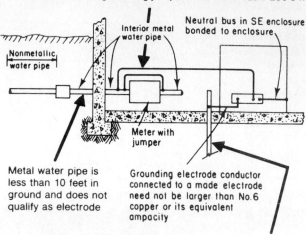

Because building does not have a grounded metal frame or either of the electrodes described in Section 250-81(c) and (d), Section 250-83 requires that at least one of the electrodes described in that Section be used — such as a ground rod.

Fig. 250·83. Ground rod may be only electrode in building without any of the electrodes in Sec. 250-81. (Sec. 250-81.)

250·83. Made and Other Electrodes.   This section covers grounding electrodes that may be used if none of the electrodes of Sec. 250-81 is available. Or one of the electrodes of Sec. 250-83 may be used as the "additional electrode" required by Sec. 250-81(a) to supplement a water-pipe electrode.

Part **(a)** warns that a metal underground gas piping system must never be used as a grounding electrode. A metal underground gas piping system has been flatly disallowed as an acceptable grounding electrode because gas utility companies reject such practice and such use is in conflict with other industry standards.

As a general rule, if a water piping system or other approved electrode is not available, a driven rod or pipe is used as the electrode (Fig. 250-85). A rod or pipe driven into the ground does not always provide as low a ground resistance as is desirable, particularly where the soil becomes very dry. In some cases where several buildings are supplied, grounding at each building reduces the ground resistance. (See Sec. 250-24.) Part **(e)** of Sec. 250-83 prohibits use of an aluminum grounding electrode.

Where it is necessary to bury more than one pipe or rod in order to lower the resistance to ground, they should be placed at least 6 ft apart. If they were placed closer together, there would be little improvement.

Where two driven or buried electrodes are used for grounding two different systems that should be kept entirely separate from one another, such as a

BARE COPPER CONDUCTOR ... OR

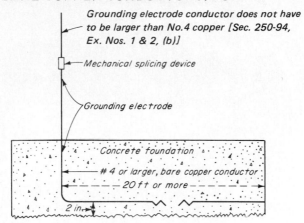

Grounding electrode conductor does not have to be larger than No.4 copper [Sec. 250-94, Ex. Nos. 1 & 2, (b)]

Mechanical splicing device

Grounding electrode

Concrete foundation

 # 4 or larger, bare copper conductor

20 ft or more

2 in.

... 1/2 IN. DIAMETER REBARS OR RODS

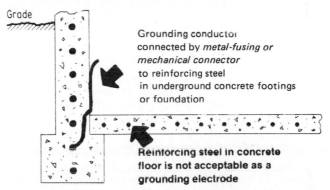

Grade

Grounding conductor connected by *metal-fusing or mechanical connector* to reinforcing steel in underground concrete footings or foundation

Reinforcing steel in concrete floor is not acceptable as a grounding electrode

Fig. 250-84. The "Ufer" grounding electrode is concrete-encased, and the grounding electrode conductor does not have to be larger than No. 4 copper in either case. (Sec. 250-81.)

grounding electrode of a wiring system for light and power and a grounding electrode for a lightning rod, care must be taken to guard against the conditions of low resistance between the two electrodes and high resistance from each electrode to ground. If two driven rods or pipes are located 6 ft apart, the resistance between the two is sufficiently high and cannot be greatly increased by increasing the spacing. The rule of this section requires at least 6 ft of spacing between electrodes serving different systems.

The basic rule of Sec. 250-83(c)(3) calls for a ground rod to be driven straight down into the earth, with at least 8 ft of its length in the ground (in contact with soil). If rock bottom is hit before the rod is 8 ft into the earth, it is permissible to drive it into the ground at an angle—not over 45° from the vertical—to have

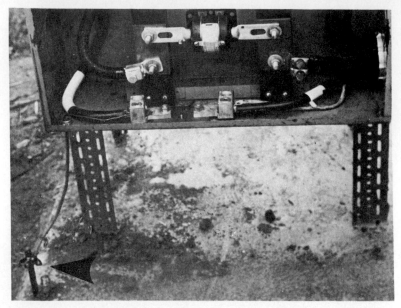

Fig. 250·85. A driven ground rod must have at least 8 ft of its length buried in the ground, and if the end of the rod is aboveground (arrow), both the rod and its grounding-electrode-conductor attachment must be protected against physical damage.

at least 8 ft of its length in the ground. However, if rock bottom is so shallow that it is not possible to get 8 ft of the rod in the earth at a 45° angle, then it is necessary to dig a 2½-ft-deep trench and lay the rod horizontally in the trench. Figure 250-86 shows these rules.

A second requirement calls for the upper end of the rod to be flush with or below ground level—unless the aboveground end and the conductor clamp are protected either by locating it in a place where damage is unlikely or by using some kind of metal, wood, or plastic box or enclosure over the end (Sec. 250-117).

This two-part rule was added to the **Code** because it had become common practice to use an 8-ft ground rod driven, say, 6½ ft into the ground with the grounding electrode conductor clamped to the top of the rod and run over to the building. Not only is the connection subject to damage or disconnection by lawnmowers or vehicles, but also the length of unprotected, unsupported conductor from the rod to the building is a tripping hazard. The rule says—bury everything or protect it!

Of course, the buried conductor-clamp assembly that is flush with or below grade must be resistant to rusting or corrosion that might affect its integrity, as required by Sec. 250-115.

In addition to ground rods, plate electrodes are another form of "made" (manufactured) electrodes. Such electrodes are listed in the UL *Electrical Construction Materials Directory* under the heading "Grounding and Bonding Equipment"—which also covers bonding devices, ground clamps, grounding

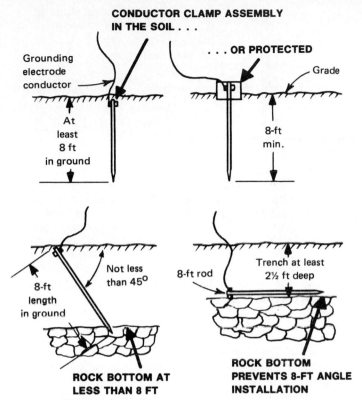

CONDUCTOR CLAMP ASSEMBLY
IN THE SOIL . . .

. . . OR PROTECTED

Grounding
electrode
conductor

Grade

At
least
8 ft
in ground

8-ft
min.

Not less
than 45°

8-ft rod

Trench at least
2½ ft deep

8-ft
length
in ground

ROCK BOTTOM AT
LESS THAN 8 FT

ROCK BOTTOM
PREVENTS 8-FT ANGLE
INSTALLATION

Fig. 250-86. In all cases, a ground rod must have at least 8 ft of its length in contact with the soil.

and bonding bushings, ground rods, armored grounding wire, protector grounding wire, grounding wedges, ground clips for securing the ground wire to an
outlet box, water-meter shunts, and similar equipment. Only listed devices are
acceptable for use. And listed equipment is suitable only for use with copper,
unless it is marked "AL" and "CU."

250-84. Resistance of Made Electrodes.   This section on the resistance to earth
of made electrodes clarifies Code intent and eliminates a cause of frequent
controversy. The rule says that if a single made electrode (rod, pipe, or plate)
shows a resistance to ground of over 25 ohms, one additional made electrode
must be used in parallel, but there is then no need to make any measurement
or add more electrodes or be further concerned about the resistance to ground.
In previous Code editions, wording of this rule implied that additional electrodes had to be used in parallel with the first one until a resistance of 25 ohms
or less was obtained. Now, as soon as the second electrode is added, it does not
matter what the resistance to ground reads, and there is no need for more electrodes (Fig. 250-87).

The last sentence of Sec. 250-84 requires at least a 6-ft spacing between any

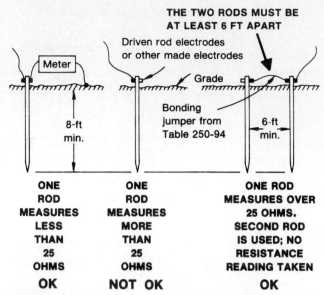

THE TWO RODS MUST BE
AT LEAST 6 FT APART

Driven rod electrodes
or other made electrodes

Meter

Grade

8-ft
min.

Bonding
jumper from
Table 250-94

6-ft
min.

ONE ROD MEASURES LESS THAN 25 OHMS	ONE ROD MEASURES MORE THAN 25 OHMS	ONE ROD MEASURES OVER 25 OHMS. SECOND ROD IS USED; NO RESISTANCE READING TAKEN
OK	**NOT OK**	**OK**

Fig. 250·87. Earth resistance of ground rod must be considered. (Sec. 250-84.)

pair of made electrodes (ground rods, pipes, and/or plates), where more than one ground rod, pipe, or plate is connected to a single grounding electrode conductor, in any case where the resistance of a single grounding electrode is over 25 ohms to ground. And a note points out that even greater spacing is better for rods longer than 8 ft. Separation of rods reduces the combined resistance to ground.

Insofar as made electrodes are concerned, there is a wide variation of resistance to be expected, and the present requirements of the **National Electrical Code** concerning the use of such electrodes do not provide for a system that is in any way comparable to that which can be expected where a good underground metallic piping can be utilized.

It is recognized that some types of soil may create a high rate of corrosion and will result in a need for periodic replacement of grounding electrodes. It should also be noted that the intimate contact of two dissimilar metals, such as iron and copper, when subjected to wet conditions can result in electrolytic corrosion.

Under abnormal conditions, when a cross occurs between a high-tension conductor and one of the conductors of the low-tension secondaries, the electrode may be called upon to conduct a heavy current into the earth. The voltage drop in the ground connection, including the conductor leading to the electrode and the earth immediately around the electrode, will be equal to the current multiplied by the resistance. This results in a difference of potential between the grounded conductor of the wiring system and the ground. It is therefore important that the resistance be as low as practicable.

Where made electrodes are used for grounding interior wiring systems, resistance tests should be conducted on a sufficient number of electrodes to determine the conditions prevailing in each locality. The tests should be repeated several times a year to determine whether the conditions have changed because of corrosion of the electrodes or drying out of the soil.

Figure 250-88 shows a ground tester being used for measuring the ground resistance of a driven electrode. Two auxiliary rod or pipe electrodes are driven to a depth of 1 or 2 ft, the distances A and B in the figure being 50 ft or more. Connections are made as shown between the tester and the electrodes; then the crank is turned to generate the necessary current, and the pointer on the instrument indicates the resistance to earth of the electrode being tested. In place of the two driven electrodes, a water piping system, if available, may be used as the reference ground, in which case terminals P and C are to be connected to the water pipe.

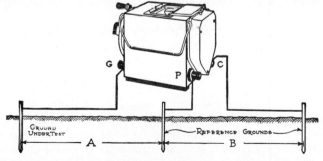

Fig. 250-88. Ground-resistance testing must be done with the proper instrument and in strict accordance with the manufacturer's instructions. (Sec. 250-84.)

But, as noted above, where two made electrodes are used, it is not necessary to take a resistance reading, which is required in the case of fulfilling the requirement of 25 ohms to ground for one made electrode.

250-86. Use of Lightning Rods.   This rule requires an individual "grounding electrode system" for grounding of the grounded circuit conductor (e.g., the neutral) and the equipment enclosures of electrical systems, and it prohibits use of the lightning ground electrode system for grounding the electrical system. Although the rule does *not* generally prohibit or require bonding between different grounding electrode systems (such as for lightning and for electric systems), it does note that such bonding is sometimes required by rules in the sections listed. And the note calls attention to the advantage of such bonding. There have been cases where fires and shocks have been caused by a potential difference between separate ground electrodes and the neutral of AC electrical circuits.

250-91. Material (Grounding Conductors).   Figure 250-89 shows the typical use of copper, aluminum, or copper-clad aluminum conductor to connect the

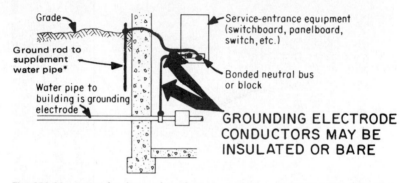

Fig. 250-89.   An insulated grounding electrode conductor may be any color other than white, natural gray, or green. (Sec. 250-91.)

bonded neutral and equipment ground terminal of service equipment to each of the one or more grounding electrodes used at a service. Controversy has been common on the permitted color of an insulated (or covered) grounding electrode conductor. Section 200-7 prohibits use of white or natural gray color for any conductor other than a "grounded conductor"—such as the grounded neutral or phase leg, as described in the definition of "grounded conductor." Green color is reserved for equipment grounding conductors, although there is no **Code** rule clearly prohibiting a green grounding electrode conductor. Refer to Sec. 310-12(b).

Exception No. 2 of Sec. 250-91(a) covers the installation of the grounding electrode conductor for a service layout consisting of two to six service disconnects in separate enclosures with a separate set of service-entrance conductors run down to each disconnect. Such an arrangement is covered in Sec. 230-40, Exception No. 2. Previous **Code** editions required (and it still satisfies the **Code** to use) either a separate grounding electrode conductor run from each enclosure to the grounding electrode or a single, unspliced conductor looped from enclosure to enclosure. And a single grounding electrode conductor used to ground all the service disconnects has to be without splice [the last line in Sec. 250-91(a)]—run from one enclosure to the other and then to the water pipe or other grounding electrode. The specific rule of Exception No. 2 says that when a service disconnect consists of two to six switches or CBs in separate enclosures, a tap from each enclosure may be made to a single, grounding electrode conductor that *must* be without splice or joint. For such an arrangement (shown at the bottom left in Fig. 250-90), the last sentence of Exception No. 2 clarifies that there must be no break in the single, common grounding electrode conductor used to connect the taps to ground two or more service disconnects in individual enclosures.

The wording of Exception No. 2 is clear on the sizing of the main, common grounding electrode conductor. Wording of the exception requires the main grounding electrode conductor to be sized from Table 250-94, which has a footnote that covers multiple sets of SE conductors. The main grounding electrode conductor must be sized for the sum of the cross-section areas of the total number of conductors connected to one hot leg of the service drop. All considerations of function, adequacy, and safety would be satisfied by running the single, common, unspliced grounding electrode conductor from the disconnect for the largest of the several sets of service-entrance conductors directly to the grounding electrode. That single, common conductor could be sized directly from Table 250-94, based on the size of SE conductors as determined from the note under Table 250-94. Each other service-entrance disconnect would then have a tap conductor that taps to the unspliced common grounding electrode conductor.

The wording of the rule makes clear that the size of the grounding electrode tap to each separate enclosure may be determined from Table 250-94 on the basis of the largest service hot leg serving each enclosure, as shown in Fig. 250-91. Although that illustration shows an overhead service to the layout, the two to six service disconnects could be fed by individual sets of underground conductors, making up a "single" service lateral as permitted by Exception No. 7 to Sec. 230-2.

Part **(b)** describes the various types of conductors and metallic cables or raceways that are considered suitable for use as equipment grounding conductors. And the **Code** recognizes cable tray as an equipment grounding conductor as permitted by Art. 318.

Exception No. 1 recognizes flexible metal conduit or flexible metallic tubing (see Art. 349) with termination fittings UL-listed for use as a grounding means (without a separate equipment grounding wire) if the length of the flex is not over 6 ft and the contained circuit conductors are protected by overcurrent devices rated at 20 A or less.

Standard flexible metal conduit (also known as "Greenfield") is not listed by UL as suitable for grounding in itself. However, Sec. 350-5 of the **NE Code** as well as Exception No. 1 in part **(b)** permits flex to be used without any supplemental grounding conductor when any length of flex in a ground return path is not over 6 ft and the conductors contained in the flex are protected by over-

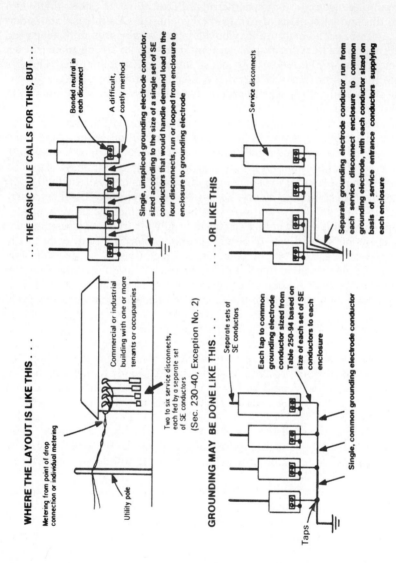

Fig. 250-90. Grounding electrode conductor may be tapped for multiple service disconnects. (Sec. 250-91.)

WHERE THE LAYOUT IS LIKE THIS . . .

Metering from point of drop connection or individual metering

Utility pole

Commercial or industrial building with one or more tenants or occupancies

Two to six service disconnects, each fed by a separate set of SE conductors

(Sec. 230-40, Exception No. 2)

. . . THE BASIC RULE CALLS FOR THIS, BUT . . .

Bonded neutral in each disconnect

A difficult, costly method

Single, unspliced grounding electrode conductor, sized according to the size of a single set of SE conductors that would handle demand load on the four disconnects, run or looped from enclosure to enclosure to grounding electrode

. . . OR LIKE THIS

Service disconnects

Separate grounding electrode conductor run from each service disconnect enclosure to common grounding electrode, with each conductor sized on basis of service entrance conductors supplying each enclosure

GROUNDING MAY BE DONE LIKE THIS . . .

Separate sets of SE conductors

Each tap to common grounding electrode conductor sized from Table 250-94 based on size of each set of SE conductors to each enclosure

Single, common grounding electrode conductor

Taps

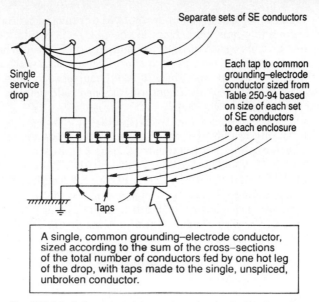

Fig. 250-91. Rule covers sizing main and taps of grounding electrode conductor at multiple-disconnect services. A single common grounding electrode conductor must be "without splice or joint," with taps made to the grounding electrode conductor. (Sec. 250-91.)

current devices rated not over 20 A (Fig. 250-92). Use of standard flex with the permission given in Sec. 250-79(e) for either internal or external bonding must be as follows:

1. When conductors within a length of flex up to 6 ft are protected at more than 20 A, equipment grounding may not be provided by the flex, but a separate conductor must be used for grounding. If a length of flex is short

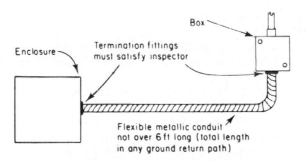

Flex not over 6 ft long is suitable as a grounding means (without a separate ground wire) if the conductors in it are protected by OC devices rated not more than 20 amps.

Fig. 250-92. Standard flex is limited in use without an equipment ground wire. (Sec. 250-91.)

enough to permit a bonding jumper not over 6 ft long to be run between external grounding-type connectors at the flex ends, while keeping the jumper *along* the flex, such an external jumper may be used where equipment grounding is required—as for a short length of flex with circuit conductors in it protected at more than 20 A. Of course, such short lengths of flex may also be "bonded" by a bonding jumper inside the flex, instead of external. Refer to Sec. 250-79(e).

2. Any length of standard flex that would require a bonding jumper longer than 6 ft may not use an external jumper. In the **Code** sense, when the length of such a grounding conductor exceeds 6 ft, it is *not* a BONDING JUMPER BUT *IS* AN EQUIPMENT GROUNDING CONDUCTOR AND MUST BE RUN ONLY *INSIDE* THE FLEX, AS REQUIRED BY SEC. 250-57(b). Combining UL data with the rule of Sec. 250-79(e) and Exception No. 1 to Sec. 350-5, *every length of flex that is over 6 ft must contain an equipment grounding conductor run *only* inside the flex* (Fig. 250-93).

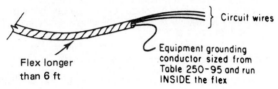

Fig. 250·93. Internal equipment grounding is required for any flex over 6 ft long. (Sec. 250-91.)

In part **a** of Exception No. 1 it should be noted that exemption from the need for an equipment grounding conductor applies only to flex where there is not over 6 ft of "total length in any ground return path." That means that from any branch-circuit load device—lighting fixture, motor, etc.—all the way back to the service ground, the total permitted length of flex without a ground wire is 6 ft. In the total circuit run from the service to any outlet, there could be one 6-ft length of flex, or two 3-ft lengths, or three 2-ft lengths, or a 4-ft and a 2-ft length—where the flex lengths are in series as equipment ground return paths. In any circuit run—feeder to subfeeder to branch circuit—any length of flex that would make the total series length over 6 ft would have to use an internal or external bonding jumper, regardless of any other factors.

In all cases, sizing of bonding jumpers for all flex applications is made according to Sec. 250-79(d), which requires the same minimum size for bonding jumpers as is required for equipment grounding conductors. In either case, the size of the conductor is selected from Table 250-95, based on the maximum rating of the overcurrent devices protecting the circuit conductors that are within the flex.

In part **c** of Exception No. 1, the term "listed for grounding" as applied to termination fittings, will require the authority having jurisdiction to verify the grounding capabilities of fittings by requiring only "listed" fittings to be used with these short conduit lengths. See also Secs. 350-5 and 351-9.

Exception No. 2 presents conditions under which *liquidtight* flexible metal conduit may be used without need for a separate equipment grounding conductor:

1. Both Exception No. 2 and the UL's *Electrical Construction Materials Directory* (the Green Book) note that any listed liquidtight flex in 1¼-in. and smaller trade size, in a length not over 6 ft, may be satisfactory as a grounding means through the metal core of the flex, without need of a bonding jumper (or equipment grounding conductor) either internal or external (Fig. 250-94). Liquidtight flex in 1¼-in. and smaller trade size may

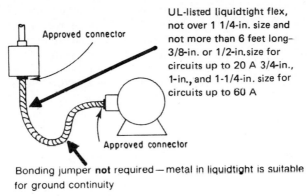

Approved connector

UL-listed liquidtight flex, not over 1 1/4-in. size and not more than 6 feet long– 3/8-in. or 1/2-in.size for circuits up to 20 A 3/4-in., 1-in., and 1-1/4-in. size for circuits up to 60 A

Approved connector

Bonding jumper **not** required — metal in liquidtight is suitable for ground continuity

Fig. 250-94. Liquidtight flex may be used with a separate ground wire. (Sec. 250-91.)

be used without a bonding jumper inside or outside provided that the "total length" of that flex "in any ground return path" is not over 6 ft. Thus, two or more separate 6-ft lengths installed in a raceway run would not be acceptable with the bonding jumper omitted from all of them. In such cases, one 6-ft length or more than one length that does not total over 6 ft may be used with a bonding jumper, but any additional lengths 6 ft or less in the same raceway run must have an internal or external bonding jumper sized from Table 250-95.

The required conditions for use of liquidtight flex without need of a separate equipment bonding jumper (or equipment grounding conductor) are as follows:

Where terminated in fittings investigated for grounding and where installed with not more than 6 ft (total length) in any ground return path, liquidtight flexible metal conduit in the ⅜- and ½-in. trade sizes is suitable for grounding where used on circuits rated 20 A or less, and the ¾-, 1-, and 1¼-in. trade sizes are suitable for grounding where used on circuits rated 60 A or less. See the category "Conduit Fittings" (DWTT) with respect to fittings suitable as a grounding means.

The following are not considered to be suitable as a grounding means:

a. The 1½-in. and larger trade sizes.

b. The ⅜- and ½-in. trade sizes where used on circuits rated higher than 20 A, or where the total length in the ground return path is greater than 6 ft.

c. The ¾-, 1-, and 1¼-in. trade sizes where used on circuits rated higher than 60 A, or where the total length in the ground return path is greater than 6 ft.

Although UL gives the same grounding recognition to their "listed" liquidtight flex, this **Code** rule covers liquidtight that the UL does not list, such as high-temperature type.

2. For liquidtight flex over 1¼ in., UL does not list any as suitable for equipment grounding, thereby requiring use of a separate equipment grounding conductor installed in *any* length of the flex, as required by **Code**. If a length of liquidtight flex larger than 1¼ in. is short enough to permit an external bonding jumper not more than 6 ft long between external grounding-type connectors at the ends of the flex, an external bonding jumper may be used. BUT WATCH OUT! The rule says the *jumper*, not the flex, must not exceed 6 ft in length AND the jumper "shall be routed with the raceway"—that is, run along the flex surface and not separated from the flex.

3. If any length of flex is *over 6 ft*, then the flex is not a suitable grounding conductor, regardless of the trade size of the flex, whether it is larger or smaller than 1¼ in. In such cases, an *equipment grounding conductor* (not a "bonding jumper"—the phrase reserved for short lengths) must be used to provide grounding continuity and IT MUST BE RUN *INSIDE* THE FLEX, NOT EXTERNAL TO IT, IN ACCORDANCE WITH SEC. 250-57(b).

Exception No. 3 of this section covers the same point described under Sec. 250-57 for DC circuits; that is, an equipment grounding conductor for DC equipment may be run separately from the circuit conductors. For all AC equipment, the equipment grounding conductor must be run with the circuit conductors in the same raceway or cable.

Part **(c)** of Sec. 250-91 is an extremely important rule that has particular impact on the use of electrical equipment outdoors. The first part of the rule accepts the use of "supplementary grounding electrodes"—such as a ground rod—to "augment" the equipment grounding conductor; BUT an equipment grounding conductor must always be used where needed and the connection of outdoor metal electrical enclosures to a ground rod is never a satisfactory alternative to the use of an equipment grounding conductor because use of just ground-rod grounding would have the earth as "the sole equipment grounding conductor" and that is expressly prohibited by the last clause of part **(c)**.

This whole matter of earth ground usually comes up as follows:

Question: When direct-burial or nonmetallic-conduit circuits are run underground to supply lighting fixtures or other equipment mounted on metal standards or poles or fed by metal conduit run up a pole or building wall, is it necessary to run an equipment grounding conductor to ground the metal standard or pole or conduit if a ground rod has been driven for the same purpose?

Answer: Yes. An equipment grounding conductor is necessary to provide low impedance for ground-fault current return to assure fast, effective operation of the circuit protective device when the circuit is derived from a grounded electrical system (such as 240/120 V, single-phase or 208Y/120 or 480Y/277 V, 3-phase). Low impedance of a grounding path "to facilitate the operation of the circuit protective devices in the circuit" is clearly and specifically required by **NE Code** Sec. 250-51. When a ground rod is used to ground an outdoor metal standard or pole or outdoor metal conduit and no other grounding connection is used, ground-fault current must attempt to return to the grounded system neutral by flowing through the earth. Such an earth return path has impedance that is too high, limiting the current to such a low value that the circuit protective device does not operate. In that case, a conductor that has faulted (made conductive contact) to a metal standard, pole, or conduit will put a dangerous voltage on the metal—exposing persons to shock or electrocution hazard as long as the fault exists. The basic concept of this problem—and **Code** violation—is revealed in Fig. 250-95.

The same undesirable condition would exist where a direct-burial or non-metallic-conduit circuit feeds up through a metal conduit outdoors. As shown in Fig. 250-96, fault current would have to return through the high impedance of the earth.

The hazard of arrangements using only a ground rod as shown arises from the chance that a person might make contact with the energized metal standard or conduit and have a high enough voltage across the person to produce a dangerous current flow through the person's body. The actual current flow through the body will depend upon the contact resistances and the body resistance in conjunction with the voltage gradient (potential difference) imposed across the body. As shown in Fig. 250-97, a person contacting an energized metal pole can complete a circuit to earth or to some other pipe or metal that is grounded back to the system neutral.

It is important to note that part **(c)** of Sec. 250-91 applies to these situations where outside metal standards or conduits are grounded by means of a ground rod at the standard or conduit. The installations shown in Figs. 250-95, 250-96, and 250-97 are in violation of the last clause of Sec. 250-91(c) as well as Sec. 250-51(c). Figure 250-98 is another example of a violation of the rule.

Compliance with the letter and spirit of those **Code** sections—and other sections on equipment grounding—will result from use of an equipment grounding conductor run with the circuit conductors—either closely placed in the same trench with direct-burial conductors (Type UF or Type USE) or pulled into nonmetallic conduit with the circuit conductors. Such arrangement is also dictated by Sec. 250-57(b), which requires that an equipment grounding conductor *must* be within the same raceway, cable, or cord or otherwise run with the circuit conductors.

Effective grounding methods that are in accordance with **NE Code** rules are shown in Figs. 250-99 and 250-100.

[Although **NE Code** Art. 338 on "Service-Entrance Cable" does not say that Type USE cable may be used as a feeder or branch circuit (on the load side of

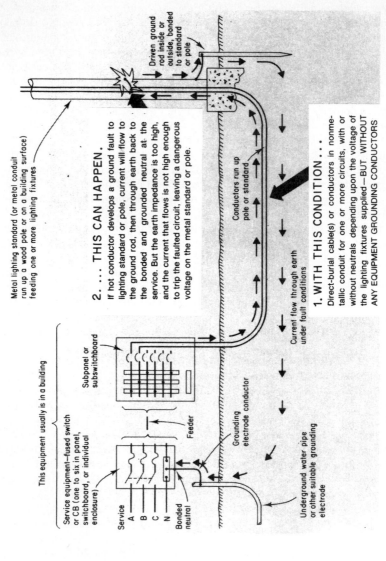

Fig. 250·95. This Code violation produces a dangerous condition at a metal standard. (Sec. 250·91.)

This equipment usually is in a building

Service equipment—fused switch or CB (one to six in panel, switchboard, or individual enclosure)

Service

A
B
C
N

Bonded neutral

Underground water pipe or other suitable grounding electrode

Grounding electrode conductor

Feeder

Subpanel or subswitchboard

Metal lighting standard (or metal conduit run up a wood pole or on a building surface) feeding one or more lighting fixtures

2. ... THIS CAN HAPPEN.

If hot conductor develops a ground fault to lighting standard or pole, current will flow to the ground rod, then through earth back to the bonded and grounded neutral at the service. But the earth impedance is too high, and the current that flows is not high enough to trip the faulted circuit, leaving a dangerous voltage on the metal standard or pole.

Driven ground rod inside or outside, bonded to standard or pole

Conductors run up pole or standard

Current flow through earth under fault conditions

1. WITH THIS CONDITION ...

Direct-burial cable(s) or conductors in nonmetallic conduit for one or more circuits, with or without neutrals depending upon the voltage of the lighting fixtures supplied—BUT WITHOUT ANY EQUIPMENT GROUNDING CONDUCTORS

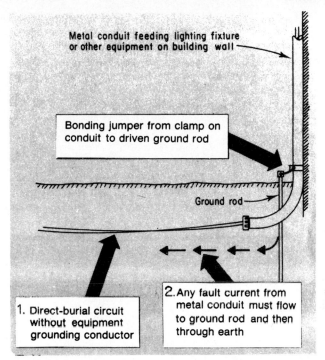

Fig. 250-96. This is also a dangerous condition for conduit up a pole or building. (Sec. 250-91.)

service equipment), the UL listing on Type USE cable says it "is suitable for all of the underground uses for which Type UF cable is permitted by the National Electrical Code."|

If an underground circuit to a metal standard or pole is run in metal conduit, a separate equipment grounding conductor is not needed in the conduit if the conduit end within the standard is bonded to the standard by a bonding jumper (Fig. 250-101). Section 250-91(b) recognizes metal conduits as suitable equipment grounding conductors in themselves.

250-92. Installation. Part (a), in its first paragraph, covers physical protection for a grounding electrode conductor, as shown in Fig. 250-102.

A common technique for protecting bare or insulated grounding conductors (one which grounds the wiring system and equipment cases) makes use of a metal conduit sleeve, run open or installed in concrete. In all such cases, part (b) of this section covers details on the use of "metal enclosures" for grounding electrode conductors. The grounding conductor must be connected to its protective conduit at both ends so that any current which might flow over the conductor will also have the conduit as a parallel path. The regulation presented is actually a performance description of the rule of Sec. 250-71(a)(3) which specifically and simply requires that any conduit or armor enclosing a grounding

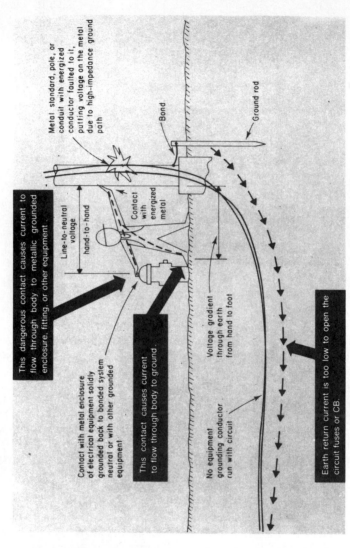

Metal standard, pole, or conduit with energized conductor faulted to it, putting voltage on the metal due to high-impedance ground path

Bond

Ground rod

This dangerous contact causes current to flow through body to metallic grounded enclosure, fitting, or other equipment.

Line-to-neutral voltage

hand-to-hand

Contact with energized metal

Contact with metal enclosure of electrical equipment solidly grounded back to bonded system neutral or with other grounded equipment

This contact causes current to flow through body to ground.

Voltage gradient through earth from hand to foot

No equipment grounding conductor run with circuit

Earth return current is too low to open the circuit fuses or CB

Fig. 250-97. Ineffective grounding creates shock hazards. (Sec. 250-91.)

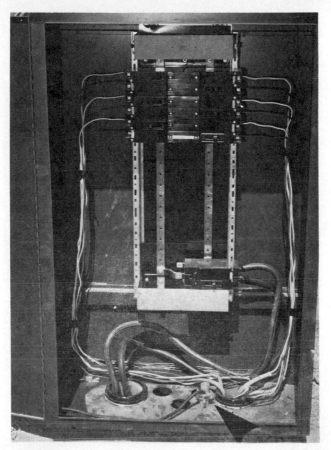

Fig. 250-98. Driven ground rod (arrow) has conductor run to it from a large lug at the left rear of the enclosure. All of the equipment grounding conductors from UF 480-V circuits to pole lights are connected to that lug. But the ground rod and earth path are the sole return path for fault currents. The two larger conductors make up a 480-V underground USE circuit, without the neutral or an equipment grounding conductor brought to the panel. [Sec. 250-91(c).]

electrode conductor be bonded to a service enclosure at one end and to the grounding electrode at the other end. The concept involved is to assure that any metal raceway (or other enclosure) containing a grounding electrode conductor is electrically in parallel with the conductor, as shown in Fig. 250-103. Bonded connection at both ends of an enclosing raceway must be used for any grounding electrode arrangement at a service and for grounding of a separately derived system, such as a generator or transformer secondary, as shown in Fig. 250-104. And in that illustration, where the transformer secondary phase leg is larger than 1,100 kcmil copper or 1,750 kcmil aluminum, the bonding jumper

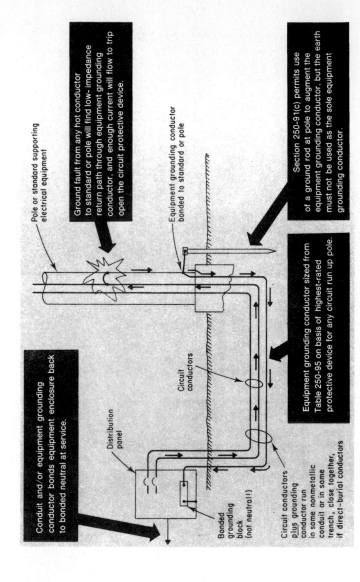

Pole or standard supporting electrical equipment

Ground fault from any hot conductor to standard or pole will find low-impedance return path through equipment grounding conductor, and enough current will flow to trip open the circuit protective device.

Equipment grounding conductor bonded to standard or pole

Section 250-91(c) permits use of a ground rod at pole to augment the equipment grounding conductor, but the earth must not be used as the sole equipment grounding conductor.

Conduit and/or equipment grounding conductor bonds equipment enclosure back to bonded neutral at service.

Circuit conductors

Equipment grounding conductor sized from Table 250-95 on basis of highest-rated protective device for any circuit run up pole.

Distribution panel

Bonded grounding block (not neutral!)

Circuit conductors plus grounding conductor run in some nonmetallic conduit or in some trench, close together, if direct-burial conductors

Fig. 250-99. Equipment grounding conductor assures effective fault-clearing. (Sec. 250-91.)

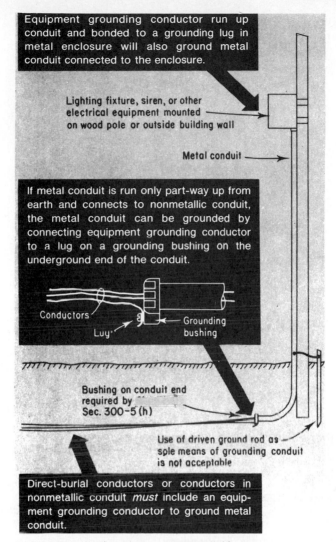

Equipment grounding conductor run up conduit and bonded to a grounding lug in metal enclosure will also ground metal conduit connected to the enclosure.

Lighting fixture, siren, or other electrical equipment mounted on wood pole or outside building wall

Metal conduit

If metal conduit is run only part-way up from earth and connects to nonmetallic conduit, the metal conduit can be grounded by connecting equipment grounding conductor to a lug on a grounding bushing on the underground end of the conduit.

Conductors

Lug

Grounding bushing

Bushing on conduit end required by Sec. 300-5(h)

Use of driven ground rod as sole means of grounding conduit is not acceptable

Direct-burial conductors or conductors in nonmetallic conduit *must* include an equipment grounding conductor to ground metal conduit.

Fig. 250-100. Watch out for grounding details like these! (Sec. 250-91.)

from the conduit bushing to the case will, invariably, have to be larger than the grounding electrode conductor. Table 250-94 shows that a grounding electrode conductor never has to be larger than No. 3/0 copper or 250 kcmil whereas Sec. 250-79(c) requires a bonding jumper to have a cross-section area of at least 12½ percent of the cross-section area of the largest one of the transformer secondary phase legs (or service-entrance phase legs). (Usually, all the phase legs are the same size, so the rule can be read as "12½ percent of *one* of the phase legs.") Refer to Sec. 250-79(c).

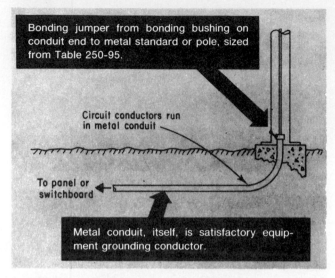

Fig. 250·101. Underground metal conduit to metal standard provides Code-acceptable ground-fault return path. (Sec. 250-91.)

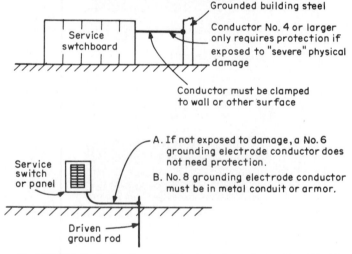

Fig. 250·102. Protection for grounding electrode conductor. (Sec. 250-92.)

The necessity for making a grounding electrode conductor electrically in parallel with its protective conduit applies to all applications of such conductors. If the protective conduit in any such case was arranged so that the conductor and conduit were not acting as parallel conductors—such as the conduit would be in Fig. 250-104 if there were no bonding jumper from the conduit bushing

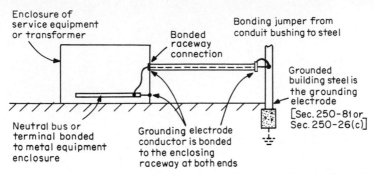

Fig. 250-103. Grounding electrode conductor must be electrically in parallel with enclosing raceway and other enclosures. (Sec. 250-92.)

to the conductor lug—the presence of magnetic metal conduit (steel) would serve to greatly increase the inductive reactance of the grounding conductor to limit any flow of current to ground. The steel conduit would act as the core of a "choke" to restrict current flow. Figure 250-105 shows the "skin effect" of current flow over a conduit in parallel with a conductor run through it, resulting in a condition which makes it critically necessary to keep the conduit connected electrically in parallel with an enclosed grounding electrode conductor. The condition is as follows.

The presence of the steel conduit acts as an iron core to greatly increase the inductive reactance of the conductor. This choke action raises the impedance of the conductor to such a level that only 3 A flows through the conductor and the balance of 97 A flows through the conduit. This division of current between the conduit and the conductor points up the importance of assuring tight couplings and connectors throughout every conduit system and for every metal raceway system and metal cable jacketing. In particular, this stresses the need for bonding both ends of any raceway used to protect a grounding conductor run to a water pipe or other grounding electrode. Such conduit protection must be securely connected to the ground electrode and to the equipment enclosure in which the grounding conductor originates. If such conduit is left open, lightning and other electric discharges to earth through the grounding conductor will find a high-impedance path. The importance of high conductivity in the conduit system is also important for effective equipment grounding, even when a specific equipment grounding conductor is used in the conduit.

Figure 250-105 clearly shows the conduit itself to be a more important conductor than the actual conductor. Figure 250-106 is a clear example of a violation of this rule. Figure 250-107 shows two other examples of violations. Of course, nonmagnetic conduit—such as aluminum—would have a different effect, but it should also be in parallel because it would not be a low-reluctance core for the magnetic field around the enclosed conductor. The inductive reactance of the conductor would not be elevated and the magnetic choking would be minimized. However, the **Code** rules on bonding [Sec. 250-71] and parallel connection of conduit containing a grounding electrode conductor apply to *all*

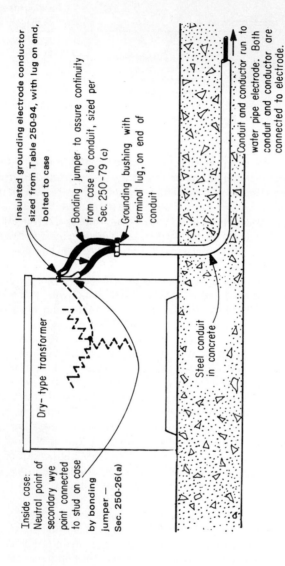

Insulated grounding electrode conductor sized from Table 250-94, with lug on end, bolted to case

Bonding jumper to assure continuity from case to conduit, sized per Sec. 250-79 (c)

Grounding bushing with terminal lug, on end of conduit

Dry-type transformer

Steel conduit in concrete

Conduit and conductor run to water pipe electrode. Both conduit and conductor are connected to electrode.

Inside case: Neutral point of secondary wye point connected to stud on case by bonding jumper — Sec. 250-26(a)

Fig. 250-104. Protective metal conduit on grounding conductor must always be electrically in parallel with conductor. (Sec. 250-92.)

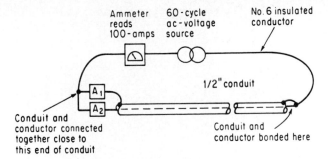

Ammeter reads 100-amps   60-cycle ac-voltage source   No. 6 insulated conductor

1/2" conduit

A_1

A_2

Conduit and conductor connected together close to this end of conduit

Conduit and conductor bonded here

Ammeter A₁ (indicates amount of current in conduit) = 97 amps

Ammeter A₂ (indicates amount of current in conductor) = 3 amps

Fig. 250·105. Enclosing conduit is more important than the enclosed grounding electrode conductor. (Sec. 250-92.)

metal raceways. Aluminum conduit must, therefore, be connected the same as steel conduit or EMT.

PVC conduit may be used to protect No. 4 or smaller grounding electrode conductors used in accordance with this section. Use of nonmetallic raceways for enclosing grounding electrode conductors will reduce the impedance below

Fig. 250·106. Grounding electrode conductors are run in conduit from their connections to an equipment grounding bus in an electrical room to the point where they connect to the grounding electrodes. Without a bonding jumper from each conduit to the ground bus, this is a clear VIOLATION of the second paragraph rule of Sec. 250-92(b). (Sec. 250-92.)

Fig. 250·107. Two examples of very clear violations of the rule that requires enclosing metal raceways (rigid metal conduit at top and flex at right) to be bonded at both ends to a grounding electrode conductor within the raceway. [Secs. 250-71 and 250-92(b).]

that of the same conductor in a steel raceway. The grounding electrode conductor will perform its function whether enclosed or not, the principal function of the enclosure being to protect the conductor from physical damage. Rigid nonmetallic conduit will satisfy this function.

The second paragraph of Sec. 250-92(a) requires special care for aluminum grounding electrode conductors. If such a conductor is to be run, say, along a concrete wall, it would have to be clamped to a wooden "running board" that is nailed to the wall—to keep it from "direct contact with masonry." And outdoors, such a conductor must be kept at least 18 in. above the ground. But, there has been controversy about these rules. Although the wording of this paragraph literally requires those installation methods for *all* aluminum and copper-clad aluminum grounding electrode conductors—whether bare or insulated, installed within or without raceway—some inspectors have taken the rules as applying only to *bare* conductors (Fig. 250-108). Because Sec. 230-30 and the

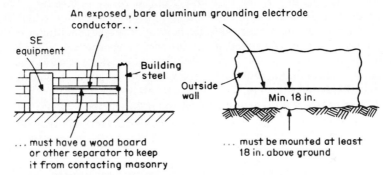

NOTE: An insulated aluminum conductor or a bare conductor installed in conduit may not be subject to these limitations, depending upon the inspector's interpretation.

Fig. 250·108. Does this controversial rule apply only to *bare* aluminum conductors? (Sec. 250-92.)

NEC, in general, recognize insulated aluminum conductors in conduit underground and directly buried in soil, it is argued that *insulated* aluminum conductor may be run in direct contact with masonry and within 18 in. of earth—even directly buried in the soil if it is Type UF or USE, or within conduit or other raceway underground (Fig. 250-109). Of course, all such application must

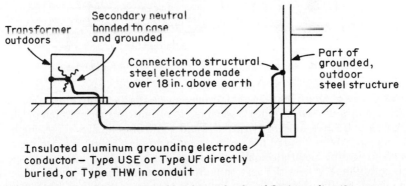

Fig. 250·109. This has been accepted but does violate literal **Code** wording. (Sec. 250-92.)

not have exposed (bare) aluminum, even short lengths, such as at terminations, that would violate the above rules. That means that terminations must be made at least 18 in. aboveground.

Part **(c)** of Sec. 250-92 covers installation of "equipment grounding conductors" as distinguished from "grounding electrode conductors." (Refer to "Definitions," Art. 100.) Where the equipment grounding conductor is a bare or insulated conductor (a cable) that is run by itself, instead of a metal raceway or armor, all the rules of part **(a)**, as described above, must be satisfied. A separately run equipment ground wire is a basic exception to the normal **Code** practice of keeping the ground wire and circuit wires close together. When so run, it must follow the rules for a grounding electrode conductor, which is normally run by itself, either exposed or in raceway. If a steel conduit or tubing is used for mechanical protection of the grounding conductor, it needs to be bonded to the grounding conductor where it enters and where it leaves the protecting steel conduit in order to keep the impedance of the grounding circuit at an acceptable level, as described in part **(a)** above.

250·93. Size of Direct·Current System Grounding Conductor. Figure 250-110 is a diagram of a balancer set used with a 2-wire 230-V generator to supply a 3-wire system as referred to in part **(a)** of this section.

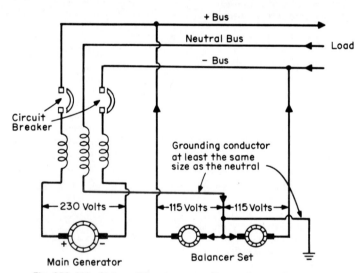

Fig. 250·110. Sizing a DC system grounding conductor. (Sec. 250-93.)

250·94. Size of Alternating·Current Grounding Electrode Conductor. For copper wire, a minimum size of No. 8 is specified in order to provide sufficient carrying capacity to ensure an effective ground and sufficient mechanical strength to be permanent. Where one of the service conductors is a grounded conductor, the same grounding electrode conductor is used for grounding both the system and the equipment. Where the service is from an ungrounded 3-phase power system, a grounding electrode conductor of the size given in Table 250-94 is required at the service.

If the sizes of service-entrance conductors for an AC system are known, the minimum acceptable size of grounding electrode conductor can be determined from **NE Code** Table 250-94. Where the service consists of only one conductor for each hot leg or phase, selection of the minimum permitted size of grounding electrode conductor is a relatively simple, straightforward task. If the largest phase leg is, say, a 500 kcmil copper THW, Table 250-94 shows No. 1/0 copper or No. 3/0 aluminum (reading across from "Over 350 kcmil thru 600 kcmil") as the minimum size of a grounding electrode conductor.

But, use of the table for services with multiple conductors per phase leg (e.g., four 500 kcmil for each of three phase legs of a service) is more involved.

The heading over the left-hand columns of this table is "Size of Largest Service-Entrance Conductor or Equivalent for Parallel Conductors." To make proper use of this table, the meaning of the word "equivalent" must be clearly understood. "Equivalent" means that parallel conductors per phase are to be converted to a single conductor per phase that has a cross-section area of its conductor material at least equal to the sum of the cross-section areas of the conductor materials of the two or more parallel conductors per phase. (The cross-section area of the insulation must be excluded.)

For instance, two parallel 500 kcmil copper RHH conductors in separate conduits would be equivalent to a single conductor with a cross-section area of 500 + 500, or 1,000 kcmil. From Table 250-94, the minimum size of grounding electrode conductor required is shown to be No. 2/0 copper or No. 4/0 aluminum opposite the left column entry, "Over 600 kcmil thru 1100 kcmil." Note that use of this table is based solely on the size of the conductor material itself, regardless of the type of insulation. No reference is made at all to the kind of insulation.

Figure 250-111 shows a typical case where a grounding electrode conductor must be sized for a multiple-conductor service. A 208/120-V, 3-phase, 4-wire service is made up of two sets of parallel copper conductors of the sizes shown in the sketch. The minimum size of grounding electrode conductor which may be used with these service-entrance conductors is determined by first adding

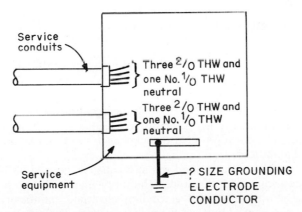

Fig. 250-111. Typical task of sizing the conductor to the grounding electrode. (Sec. 250-94.)

together the physical size of the two No. 2/0 conductors which make up each phase leg of the service:

1. From **NE Code** Table 8 in Chap. 9 in the back of the **Code** book, which gives physical dimensions of the conductor material itself (excluding insulation cross-section area), each of the phase conductors has a cross-section area (csa) of 133,100 kcmil. Two such conductors per phase have a total csa of 266,200 kcmil.

2. The same table shows that the single conductor which has a csa at least equal to the total csa of the two conductors per phase is a 300 kcmil size of conductor. That conductor size is then located in the left-hand column of Table 250-94 to determine the minimum size of grounding electrode conductor, which turns out to be No. 2 copper or No. 1/0 aluminum or copper-clad aluminum.

Figure 250-112 shows another example of conductor sizing, as follows:

1. The grounding electrode conductor A connects to the street side of the water meter of a metallic water supply to a building. The metallic pipe extends 30 ft underground outside the building.

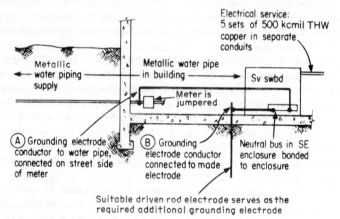

Fig. 250·112. Two different sizes of grounding electrode conductors are required for installations like this. (Sec. 250-94.)

2. Because the underground metallic water piping is at least 10 ft long, the underground piping system is a grounding electrode and must be used as such.

3. Based on the size of the service-entrance conductors (5 × 500 kcmil = 2,500 kcmil per phase leg), the minimum size of grounding electrode conductor to the water pipe is No. 3/0 copper or 250 kcmil aluminum or copper-clad aluminum.

4. The connection to the ground rod at B satisfies the rule of Sec. 250-81(a) requiring a water-pipe electrode to be supplemented by another electrode.

5. But, the minimum size of grounding electrode conductor B required between the neutral bus and the made electrode is No. 6 copper or No. 4

aluminum, as covered by part **(a)** of Exception No. 1 and part **(a)** of Exception No. 2, in this section. Although the **Code** does not require the conductor to a made electrode to be larger than No. 6, regardless of the ampacity of the service phases, a larger size of conductor is commonly used for mechanical strength, to protect it against breaking or damage. As discussed under Sec. 250-81(a) and shown in Fig. 250-81, the conductor at B in Fig. 250-112 can be considered to be a bonding jumper, as covered by the last paragraph of Sec. 250-81(a), which also says that the conductor to the ground rod need not be larger than No. 6 copper or No. 4 aluminum.

Parts **(b)** and **(c)** of Exception Nos. 1 and 2 make clear that a grounding electrode conductor does not have to be larger than a conductor-type electrode to which it connects. Section 250-81(c) recognizes a "concrete-encased" electrode—which must be at least 20 ft of one or more ½-in.-diameter steel reinforcing bars or rods in the concrete or at least 20 ft of bare No. 4 copper conductor (or a larger conductor), concrete-encased in the footing or foundation of a building or structure. Section 250-81(d) recognizes a "ground-ring" electrode made up of at least 20 ft of No. 2 bare copper conductor (or larger), buried directly in the earth at a depth of at least 2½ ft. Because each of those electrodes is described under Sec. 250-81, they are *not* "made electrodes," which are described under Sec. 250-83. As electrodes from Sec. 250-81, such electrodes would normally be subject to the basic rule of Sec. 250-94, which calls for connection to any such electrode by a grounding electrode conductor sized from Table 250-94—requiring up to No. 3/0 copper for use on high-capacity services. *But*, that is not required, as explained in these paragraphs of the two Exceptions.

Parts **(b)** and **(c)** recognize that there is no reason to use a grounding electrode conductor that is larger than a conductor-electrode to which it connects. The grounding electrode conductor need not be larger than No. 4 copper for a No. 4 concrete-encased electrode and need not be larger than No. 2 copper if it connects to a ground-ring electrode—as in parts **(c)** of the Exceptions. Where Table 250-94 would permit a grounding electrode conductor smaller than No. 4 or No. 2 (based on size of service conductors), the smaller conductor may be used—but the electrode itself must not be smaller than No. 4 or No. 2. See Fig. 250-84.

The first note under Table 250-94 correlates to Sec. 230-40, Exception No. 2, and Sec. 250-91(a), Exception No. 2, as follows:

When two to six service disconnects in separate enclosures are used at a service, with a separate set of SE conductors run to each disconnect, the size of a single common grounding electrode conductor must be based on the largest sum of the cross sections of the same phase leg of each of the several sets of SE conductors. When using multiple service disconnects in separate enclosures, with a set of SE conductors run to each from the drop or lateral (Sec. 230-40, Exception No. 2) and using a single, common grounding electrode conductor, either run continuous and unspliced from one disconnect to another and then to the grounding electrode, or with taps from each disconnect to a common grounding electrode conductor run to the electrode—as in Sec. 250-91(a), Exception No. 2, this note is used to determine the size of the grounding electrode conductor from Table 250-94. The "equivalent area" of the size of SE conductors is the largest sum of the cross-section areas of one ungrounded leg of each of the several sets of SE conductors.

250-95. Size of Equipment Grounding Conductors. When an individual equipment grounding conductor is used in a raceway—either in a nonmetallic raceway, as required by Sec. 347-4, or in a metal raceway where such a conductor is used for grounding reliability even though Sec. 250-91(b) accepts metal raceways as a suitable grounding conductor—the grounding conductor must have a minimum size as shown in Table 250-95. The minimum acceptable size of an equipment grounding conductor is based on the rating of the overcurrent device (fuse or CB) protecting the circuit, run in the same raceway, for which the equipment grounding conductor is intended to provide a path of ground-fault current return (Fig. 250-113). Each size of grounding conductor in the table

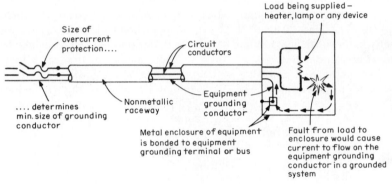

Fig. 250-113. Size of grounding conductor must carry enough current to operate circuit overcurrent device. (Sec. 250-95.)

is adequate to carry enough current to blow the fuse or trip the CB of the rating indicated beside it in the left-hand column. In Fig. 250-113, if the fuses are rated at 60 A, Table 250-95 shows that the grounding electrode conductor used with that circuit must be at least a No. 10 copper or a No. 8 aluminum or copper-clad aluminum.

Whenever an equipment grounding conductor is used for a circuit that consists of only one conductor for each hot leg (or phase leg), the grounding conductor is sized simply and directly from Table 250-95, as described. When a circuit is made up of parallel conductors per phase, say an 800-A circuit with two conductors per phase, an equipment grounding conductor is also sized in the same way and would, in that case, have to be at least a No. 1/0 copper or No. 3/0 aluminum. *But,* if such a circuit is made up using two conduits—that is, three phase legs and a neutral in each conduit—Sec. 250-95 requires that an individual grounding conductor be run in each of the conduits *and* each of the two grounding conductors must be at least No. 1/0 copper or No. 3/0 aluminum (Fig. 250-114). Another example is shown in Fig. 250-115, where a 1,200-A protective device on a parallel circuit calls for No. 3/0 copper or 250 kcmil aluminum grounding conductor.

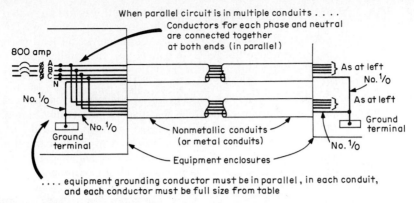

Fig. 250·114. Grounding conductor must be used in each conduit for parallel conductor circuits. (Sec. 250-95.)

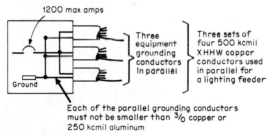

Fig. 250·115. Using equipment grounding conductors in parallel. (Sec. 250-95.)

[Note in that example that each 500 kcmil XHHW circuit conductor has an ampacity of 430 A (Table 310-16), and three per phase gives a circuit ampacity of 3 × 430 = 1,290 A. Use of a 1,200-A protective device satisfies the basic rule of Sec. 240-3, protecting each phase leg within its ampacity. Because the load on the circuit is continuous (over 3 hr), the circuit is loaded to not over 960 A—satisfying Sec. 220-10(b), which requires a continuous load to be limited to no more than 80 percent of the circuit protection rating. Each circuit conductor is actually made up of three 500 kcmil XHHW, with a total-per-phase ampacity of 3 × 430 = 1,290 A. But load is limited to 0.8 × 1,200 = 960 A per phase. Each 500 kcmil is then carrying 960 ÷ 3 = 320 A. Because that value is less than 380 A, which is the ampacity of a 500 kcmil THW copper, the use of XHHW conductors *does* comply with the UL requirement that size 1/0 and larger conductors connected to the equipment be rated at not over 75°C (such as THW) or, if 90°C conductors are used (such as XHHW), they must be used at no more than the ampacity of 75°C conductors of the same size. However, some authorities object to that usage on the grounds that the use of 1,200-A protection would not be acceptable to Sec. 240-3, Exception No. 1, if 75°C (THW) conductors were used, with an ampacity of only 3 × 380 A, or 1,140 A, per phase, because the rating is over the 800-A level and it is not permitted to go to the next larger size of protective device. Therefore, they note, the XHHW conductors are not actually being used as 75°C conductors; the load current could later be increased above the 75°C ampacity; and the application might be taken to violate the letter and intent of the UL rule, thereby violating Sec. 110-3(b) of the NEC.]

The fifth paragraph of Sec. 250-95 covers a similar concern for unnecessarily oversizing equipment grounding conductors. Because the minimum acceptable size of an equipment grounding conductor is based on the rating of the over-current protective device (fuse or CB) protecting the circuit for which the equipment grounding conductor is intended to provide a path of ground-fault return, a problem arises when a motor circuit is protected by a magnetic-only (a so-called "instantaneous") circuit breaker. Because Sec. 430-52 and Table 430-152 permit an instantaneous-trip CB with a setting of 700 percent of (7 times) the motor full-load running current—and even up to 1,300 percent for an instantaneous CB or MSCP (motor short-circuit protector), if needed to handle motor inrush current—use of those high values of current rating permitted in Table 430-152 would result in excessively large equipment grounding conductors. Because such large sizing is unreasonable and not necessary, the rule says when sizing an equipment grounding conductor from Table 250-95 for a circuit protected by an instantaneous-only circuit breaker or by an MSCP, the rating of the motor running overload device must be used in the left-hand column of Table 250-95. [Fig. 250-116.]

Exception No. 2 states that the equipment grounding conductor *need not* be larger than the circuit conductors. The main application for this Exception is for motor circuits where short-circuit protective devices are usually considerably larger than the motor branch-circuit conductor ampacity, as permitted in Sec. 430-52 (up to 1300 percent) to permit starting of a motor without opening on inrush current. In such cases, literal use of Table 250-95 could result in grounding conductors larger than the circuit conductors.

Exception No. 3 points out that metal raceways and cable armor are recognized as equipment grounding conductors and Table 250-95 does not apply to them.

Figure 250-116 shows details of a controversy that often arises about Sec. 250-95 and Sec. 250-57(a). When two or more circuits are used in the same conduit, it is logical to conclude that a single equipment grounding conductor within the conduit may serve as the required grounding conductor for each circuit if it satisfies Table 250-95 for the circuit with the highest rated overcurrent protection. The common contention is that if a single metal conduit is adequate as the equipment grounding conductor for all the contained circuits, a single grounding conductor can serve the same purpose when installed in a nonmetallic conduit that connects two metal enclosures (such as a panel and a home-run junction box) where both circuits are within both enclosures. As shown, a No. 12 copper conductor satisfies Table 250-95 as an equipment grounding conductor for the circuit protected at 20 A. The same No. 12 also may serve for the circuit protected at 15 A, for which a grounding conductor must not be smaller than No. 14 copper. Such application is specifically permitted by the fourth para-

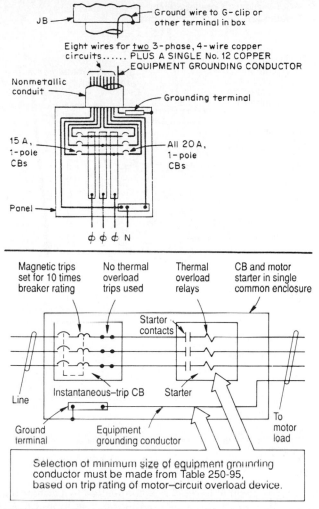

Eight wires for two 3-phase, 4-wire copper
circuits...... PLUS A SINGLE No. 12 COPPER
EQUIPMENT GROUNDING CONDUCTOR

Fig. 250-116. These applications are covered by the fourth and fifth paragraphs of Sec. 250-95. (Sec. 250-95.)

graph of Sec. 250-95, just before the Exceptions. Although this will have primary application with PVC conduit where an equipment grounding conductor is required, it may also apply to circuits in EMT, IMC, or rigid metal conduit when an equipment grounding conductor is run with the circuit conductors to supplement the metal raceway as an equipment grounding return path.

250-112. To Grounding Electrode.   The rule requires that the connection of a grounding electrode conductor to the grounding electrode "shall be accessible" (Fig. 250-117). [Section 250-80(a) also requires that any clamp for a bonding jumper to interior metal water piping must be accessible.] Inspectors want to

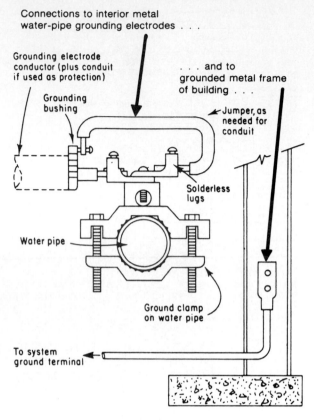

Connections to interior metal
water-pipe grounding electrodes . . .

Grounding electrode
conductor (plus conduit
if used as protection)

Grounding
bushing

. . . and to
grounded metal frame
of building . . .

Jumper, as
needed for
conduit

Solderless
lugs

Water pipe

Ground clamp
on water pipe

To system
ground terminal

. . . must be accessible ! ! !

Fig. 250·117. Whenever possible, connections to grounding electrodes must be "accessible." (Sec. 250-112.)

be able to see and/or be able to get at any connection to a grounding electrode.
But because there are electrodes permitted in Sec. 250-81 and Sec. 250-83 that
would require underground or concrete-encased connections, an Exception
was added to the basic rule to permit inaccessible connections in such cases
(Fig. 250-118). Electrode connections that are *not* encased or buried—such as
where they are made to exposed parts of electrodes that are encased, driven,
or buried—*must* be accessible. This section now places the burden on the
installer to make such connections accessible wherever possible.

The second sentence of this section requires assured connection to a metal
piping system electrode, as shown in Fig. 250-119. In a typical case of grounding
for a local transformer within a building, Sec. 250-26(b) notes that grounding of
the secondary neutral may be made to the nearest water pipe anywhere in the
building; but Sec. 250-112 actually requires that bonding jumpers be used to
assure continuity of the ground path back to the underground pipe, wherever

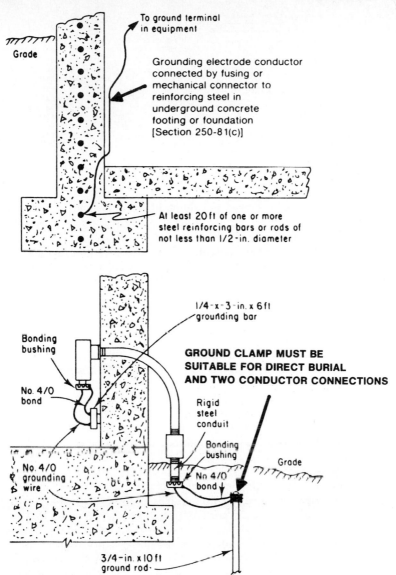

To ground terminal
in equipment

Grounding electrode conductor
connected by fusing or
mechanical connector to
reinforcing steel in
underground concrete
footing or foundation
[Section 250-81(c)]

Grade

At least 20 ft of one or more
steel reinforcing bars or rods of
not less than 1/2-in. diameter

1/4-x-3-in. x 6 ft
grounding bar

GROUND CLAMP MUST BE
SUITABLE FOR DIRECT BURIAL
AND TWO CONDUCTOR CONNECTIONS

Bonding
bushing

No. 4/0
bond

Rigid
steel
conduit

Bonding
bushing

No. 4/0
grounding
wire

No 4/0
bond

Grade

3/4-in. x 10 ft
ground rod·

Fig. 250-118. Encased and buried electrode connections are permitted by Exception to basic rule. (Sec. 250-112.)

the piping may contain insulating sections or is liable to become disconnected. Bonding jumpers around unions, valves, water meters, and other points where a water-piping-system electrode might be opened must have enough slack to permit removal of the part. Hazard is created when bonding jumpers are so short that they have to be removed to remove the equipment they jumper. Dan-

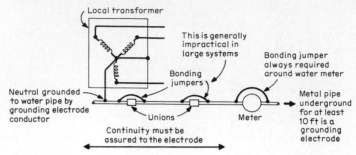

Fig. 250·119. Although required, bonding of metal piping can pose problems. (Sec. 250-112.)

gerous conditions have been reported about this matter. Bonding jumpers must be long enough to assure grounding integrity along piping systems under any conditions of maintenance or repair.

250·113. To Conductors and Equipment.   There are many grounding and bonding fittings on the market which can be used to properly attach the grounding conductors. The one selected should satisfy the following principles:

1. It must be UL listed.
2. It should be rugged, strong, and well plated so that it will fasten and stay tight.
3. It must fasten mechanically.
4. It must have capacity for a large enough ground wire.
5. It must be compatible with the metals used in the system. For example: Aluminum conductors should not be connected with copper connectors. Compatible aluminum connectors are available for such requirements.

In addition to clamps, exothermic welding is recognized as a suitable method for connecting grounding conductors and bonding jumpers to conductors, equipment and grounding electrodes, along with listed clamps, etc. This clarifies long-standing controversy and assures the acceptability of exothermic welding of connections.

250·114. Continuity and Attachment of Branch·Circuit Equipment Grounding Conductors to Boxes.   The basic rule requires all ground wires in boxes to be solidly connected together. Then part **(a)** states that where a grounding conductor enters a metal outlet box it must be connected to the box by means of a grounding screw (used for no other purpose) or by an approved grounding device (such as the popular spring-steel grounding clip). Where several grounding conductors enter the same box they must be properly joined together and a final connection made to the grounding screw or grounding clip. In part **(b)**, covering nonmetallic boxes, grounding conductors must be attached to any metal fitting or wiring device required to be grounded.

From this rule, grounding conductors in any metal box must be connected to each other and to the box itself. Figure 250-120 shows a method of connecting ground wires in a box to satisfy the letter of Sec. 250-114. Note that the two ground wires are solidly connected to each other by means of a crimped-on

Fig. 250·120. Both ground wires are solidly bonded together in the crimped barrel of the spade lug, which is screwed to back of metal box. (Sec. 250-114.)

spade tongue terminal, with one of the ground wires (arrow) cut long enough so that it is bent back out of the crimp lug to provide connection to the green hex-head screw on a receptacle outlet (if required by Sec. 250-74). The spade lug is secured firmly under a screw head, bonding the lug to the box. Of course, the specific connections could be made in other ways. For instance, the ground wires could be connected to each other by twist-on splicing devices; and connection of the ground wires to the box could be made by simply wrapping a single wire under the screw head or by connecting a wire from the splice connector to an approved grounding clip on the edge of the box (Fig. 250-121).

In all the sketches here, connection to the box is made either by use of a screw in a threaded hole in the side or back of the box or by an approved ground clip device which tightly wedges a ground wire to the edge of the box wall, as shown in Fig. 250-122. Preassembled pigtail wires with attached screws are available for connecting either a receptacle or the system ground wire to the box.

Figure 250-123 shows connection of two cable ground wires by means of two grounding clips on the box edges (arrow). In the past, such use has been disallowed by some inspection authorities because the ground wires are not actually connected to each other but are connected only through the box. The clear wording of the **Code** rule here ("all conductors . . . joined within or *to* the box"), however, permits such practice.

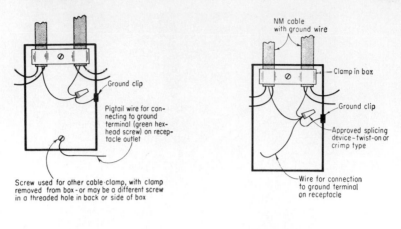

Approved grounding clip
will satisfy bonding
connections specified in
S. 250-74 and S. 250-114

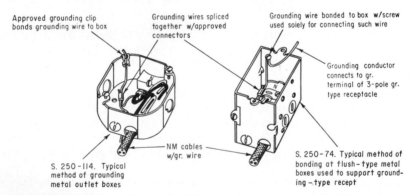

Fig. 250·121. All these techniques bond the ground wires together and to the box. (Sec. 250-114.)

Figure 250-124 shows another method that has been objected to as clear violation of **NE Code** Sec. 250-114(a) which requires that a screw used for connection of grounding conductors to a box "shall be used for no other purpose." Use of this screw, simultaneously, to hold the clamp is for "other purpose" than grounding. Objection is not generally made to use of the clamp screw for ground connection when, in cases where the clamp is not in use, the clamp is removed and the screw serves only the one purpose—to ground the grounding wires.

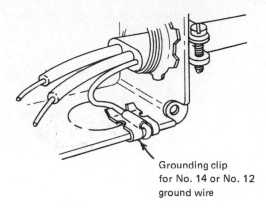

Grounding clip
for No. 14 or No. 12
ground wire

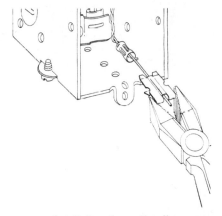

Installation of grounding clip.

Fig. 250-122. Ground clip is "an approved grounding device" of Sec. 250-114(a). (Sec. 250-114.)

250-115. Connection to Electrodes.   Because Sec. 250-83(c)(3) requires *buried* or protected connections of grounding electrode conductors to ground rods, the third sentence of this section requires that a buried ground clamp be of such material and construction that it has been designed, tested, and marked for use directly in the earth. And any clamp that is used with two or more conductors must be designed, tested, and marked for the number and types of conductors that may be used with it. This is shown in the bottom sketch of Fig. 250-118.

250-152. Solidly Grounded Neutral Systems.   Figure 250-125 shows the details of this set of rules. This section does permit a neutral conductor of a solidly grounded "Y" system to have insulation rated at only 600 V, instead of requiring insulation rated for the high voltage (over 1,000 V). It also points out that a bare copper neutral may be used in such systems for service-entrance conductors or for direct buried feeders, and bare copper or copper-clad aluminum may be used for overhead sections of outdoor circuits.

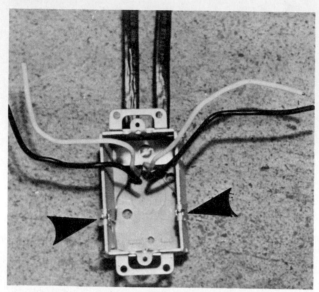

Fig. 250·123. Each ground wire is connected to the metal box by a ground clip (one on each side at arrows). The first sentence of Sec. 250-114 permits ground wires to be "spliced or joined . . . to the box" by use of ground clips or ground screw terminals in the box. (Sec. 250-114.)

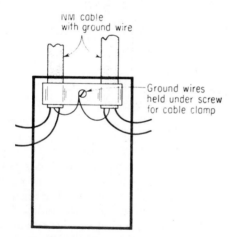

NM cable
with ground wire

Ground wires
held under screw
for cable clamp

Fig. 250·124. This clearly violates Sec. 250-114(a). (Sec. 250-114.)

ARTICLE 280. SURGE ARRESTERS

280·1. Scope. This article is no longer entitled "Lightning Arresters," as it was up to the 1978 NE Code. It is now entitled "Surge Arresters," and a complete editorial rewrite has been done on the content of the article. Article 280 is the result of the work of a subcommittee of the Code-making panel and is

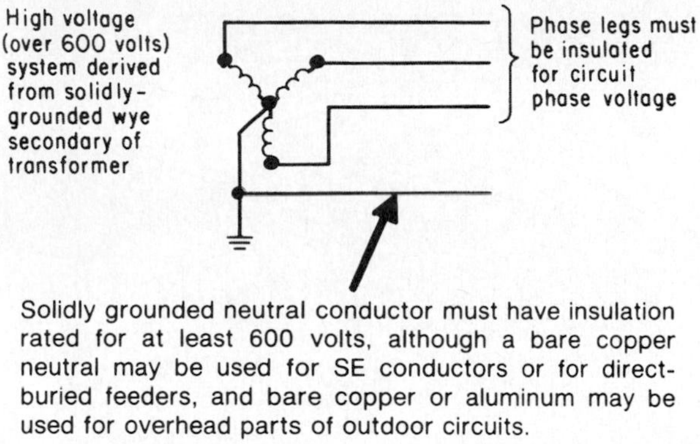

High voltage
(over 600 volts)
system derived
from solidly-
grounded wye
secondary of
transformer

Phase legs must
be insulated
for circuit
phase voltage

Solidly grounded neutral conductor must have insulation
rated for at least 600 volts, although a bare copper
neutral may be used for SE conductors or for direct-
buried feeders, and bare copper or aluminum may be
used for overhead parts of outdoor circuits.

Fig. 250-125. Neutral of high-voltage system generally must be
insulated for 600 V. (Sec. 250-152.)

aimed at updating the scope and details of **Code** rules. Installation, connection,
and grounding requirements are covered for surge arresters installed on premises wiring systems, with completely new renumbering of the various sections.

In previous editions of the **Code**, use of lightning arresters was required for
"industrial stations" where thunderstorms are frequent and lightning protection is needed. Article 280 no longer makes that requirement and is designed
to be applied to any installations where surge arresters might be installed.

This basic requirement used to say that surge arresters are mandatory only
"where thunderstorms are frequent"—but they are *not* needed if some other
type of lightning protection is provided. And the mandatory need used to apply
only to "industrial stations"—such as a generating station or substation serving
principally a single industrial plant or factory, as distinguished from a station
serving several customers of a public utility power company (Fig. 280-1). This
Article no longer makes use of surge arresters mandatory, as previously
required by Sec. 280-10, which has been deleted from the **Code**. Figure 280-2
shows a lightning arrester used on one of several high-voltage circuits serving
the heavy electrical needs of a modern sports stadium.

280-3. Number Required.   A double-throw switch which disconnects the outside circuits from the station generator and connects these circuits to ground
would satisfy the condition for a single set of arresters for a station bus, as covered in the second sentence of this section.

280-4. Surge Arrester Selection.   Figure 280-3 shows the position of a choke
coil where it is used as a lightning-protection accessory to an arrester.

In Sec. 280-4(b), ratings of surge arresters are covered by the basic rule that
applies to silicon-carbide-type surge arresters with a fine-print note pointing
up the difference in voltage rating of MOV (metal-oxide varistor) type arresters.
This addresses the high-technology operating nature of the metal-oxide surge
arrester (MOSA) as applied to premises wiring systems. The concern is to make
an effective distinction between gapped silicon-carbide arresters, widely used
in the past, and the newer metal-oxide block arresters. Manufacturers' application data on rating and other characteristics and the minimum duty-cycle

Fig. 280·1. Surge (lightning) arresters in an electric substation serving an industrial plant are commonly used in areas where lightning is a problem. (Sec. 280-1.)

Fig. 280·2. Lightning arrester (arrow) is a typical "surge arrester" and, where used, one arrester must be connected to each ungrounded circuit conductor–such as shown here for a 2400-V grounded circuit supplying a transformer for stepping voltage down to supply lighting at this athletic stadium. (Sec. 280-3.)

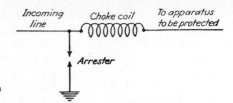

Incoming line — Choke coil — To apparatus to be protected

Arrester

Fig. 280-3. Using a choke coil as an accessory to an arrester. (Sec. 280-4.)

voltage rating of an arrester for a particular method of system grounding must be observed carefully.

280-12. Routing of Surge Arrester Connections.   This rule is particularly important because bends and turns enormously increase the impedance to lightning discharges and therefore tend to nullify the effectiveness of a grounding conductor.

280-24. Circuits of 1 kV and Over.   These rules are aimed at assuring more effective lightning protection of transformers. Lightning protection of a transformer cannot be provided by a primary arrester that is connected only to a separate electrode. Common grounding of gaps or other devices must be used to limit voltage stresses between windings and from windings to case.

280-25. Grounding.   This section refers to Secs. 250-131 and 250-132, which cover connection of lightning arresters. The second sentence covers the need to keep grounding conductors electrically in parallel with their enclosing metal raceway—as discussed under Secs. 250-71(a)(3) and 250-92(b). For instance, assume that a lightning arrester is installed at the service head on a conduit

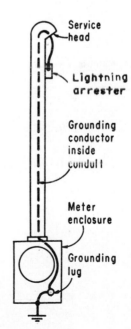

Service head

Lightning arrester

Grounding conductor inside conduit

Meter enclosure

Grounding lug

Fig. 280-4. Arrester grounding conductor must be bonded to both ends of enclosing metal raceway (or other enclosure). (Sec. 280-25.)

service riser, with the grounding conductor run inside the service conduit, bonded to the meter socket at the grounding lug, then run through a hole in the meter socket to the grounding electrode without a metal enclosure from the drilled hole to the electrode. In such a hookup, this rule requires the grounding conductor to be bonded to the conduit at the service head (Fig. 280-4). Ordinarily the meter enclosure has a threaded hub, which would mean the conduit would be in good electrical contact with the meter enclosure and would be bonded at the meter socket end. However, Sec. 280-25 requires that the grounding conductor, if in a metallic enclosure, be bonded at both ends. Therefore, bonding at the service head is necessary.

The reason given for putting that rule in the **NEC** was explained as follows:

When conducting lightning currents, the impedance of a lightning arrester grounding conductor is materially increased if run through a metallic enclosure, especially if of magnetic material. The voltage drop in this impedance may be sufficient to cause arcing to the enclosure, and in any event it reduces the effectiveness of the lightning arrester. Bonding of the conductor to both ends of the enclosure is necessary to eliminate this detrimental effect where metallic enclosures are used.

Chapter Three

ARTICLE 300. WIRING METHODS

300·1. Scope. The Exceptions in part **(a)** of this section indicate clearly that not all the general requirements in Art. 300 apply to remote-control circuits, to signal circuits, to low-energy circuits, to fire protective signaling circuits, and to communications systems. Only those sections of Art. 300 that are referenced in Art. 504, Art. 725, Art. 760, Art. 770, Art. 800, and Art. 810 apply to the types of circuits covered by those articles. In effect, not all the regulations on wiring for general-purpose power and light circuits apply to the specialized circuits covered by Arts. 504, 725, 760, 770, 800, and 810.

300·3. Conductors. Part **(a)** requires that single conductors described in Table 310-13 must be used *only* as part of one of the wiring methods covered in Chapter 3.

Part **(b)** requires that all conductors of the same circuit—including the neutral and any equipment grounding conductors—must be run in the same raceway, cable tray, trench, cable, or cord. An Exception to that rule notes those sections of the **NEC** where an equipment grounding conductor may be run separately from the other conductors of the circuit or where other departures from the basic rule are recognized—such as isolated phase conductors in plastic conduit.

In part **(c) (1)**, the words "cable or raceway" after the words "wiring enclosure" clearly indicate that it is the intent of the **Code** that circuits of different voltage up to 600 V may occupy the same wiring enclosure (cabinet, box, housing), cable, or raceway provided all the conductors are insulated for the maximum voltage of any circuit in the enclosure, cable, or raceway. It is the intent of the **Code** panel to indicate clearly that, for instance, motor power conductors and motor control conductors be permitted in the same conduit. In the past, there has been a long-standing controversy about the use of control-circuit conductors in the same conduit with power leads to motors.

For a long time it was argued that Sec. 300-3(e) in the 1975 **Code** required a separate raceway for each motor when the control conductors were run in the raceway with the power conductors (Fig. 300-1). This was supported by Sec. 725-15, which also indicates that Class 1 control conductors were permitted to be run *only in the raceway* for the power conductors which the control conductors actually control.

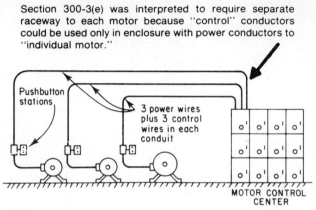

Section 300-3(e) was interpreted to require separate raceway to each motor because "control" conductors could be used only in enclosure with power conductors to "individual motor."

Fig. 300-1. The 1975 **NE Code** limited mixing of control and power wires in raceways. (Sec. 300-3.)

The wording of Sec. 300-3(c) (1) recognizes the use of power and control wires in a single raceway to supply more than one motor, but such usage must be made to conform to the last sentence of Sec. 725-15. The two **NE Code** rules of Sec. 300-3(c) (1) and Sec. 725-15 must be put together carefully.

A common raceway, as shown in Fig. 300-2, may be used *only* where the two or more motors are required to be operated together in order to serve their load function. Many industrial and commercial installations have machines, manufacturing operations, or processes which are based on use of a number of motors driving various parts or stages of the task. In such cases, either all motors operate or none do. Use of all control wires and power wires in the same raceway does not produce a situation where a fault in one motor circuit could disable another circuit to a motor that might otherwise be kept operating.

But when a common raceway is used for power and control wires to separate, independent motors, a fault in one circuit could knock out all the others that do not have to shut down when one goes out. With motor circuits so closely associated with vital, important functions like elevators, fans, pumps, etc., in modern buildings, it is a safety matter to separate such circuits and minimize outage due to any fault in a single circuit. For safety's sake, the **Code**, in effect, says, "Do not put all your eggs in one basket." But the objectionable loss of more than one motor on a single fault does not apply where all motors must be shut down when any one is stopped—as in multimotor machines and processes.

For those cases where each motor is serving a separate, independent load— with no interconnection of their control circuits and no mechanical interlocking

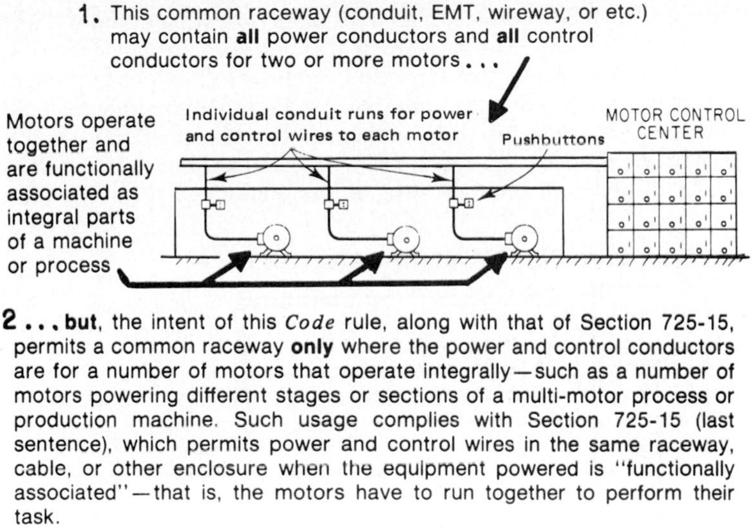

1. This common raceway (conduit, EMT, wireway, or etc.) may contain **all** power conductors and **all** control conductors for two or more motors . . .

Motors operate together and are functionally associated as integral parts of a machine or process

Individual conduit runs for power and control wires to each motor

Pushbuttons

MOTOR CONTROL CENTER

2 . . . **but**, the intent of this *Code* rule, along with that of Section 725-15, permits a common raceway **only** where the power and control conductors are for a number of motors that operate integrally—such as a number of motors powering different stages or sections of a multi-motor process or production machine. Such usage complies with Section 725-15 (last sentence), which permits power and control wires in the same raceway, cable, or other enclosure when the equipment powered is "functionally associated"—that is, the motors have to run together to perform their task.

Fig. 300-2. Mixing of power and control wires in common raceway is still limited. (Sec. 300-3.)

of their driven loads—the use of a separate raceway for each motor is required by the last sentence of Sec. 725-15, **but only** when control wires are carried in the raceways (Fig. 300-3). For the three motors shown, it would be acceptable to run the power conductors for all the motors in a single raceway and all the control circuit wires in another raceway. Such a hookup would not violate Sec. 725-15, although deratings would have to be made and there is the definite chance of loss of more than one motor on a fault in only one of the circuits in either the power raceway or the control raceway.

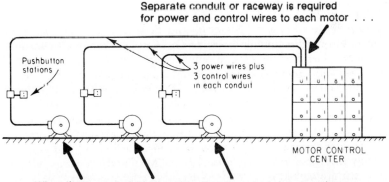

Separate conduit or raceway is required for power and control wires to each motor . . .

Pushbutton stations

3 power wires plus 3 control wires in each conduit

MOTOR CONTROL CENTER

. . . When these are individual motors that do not operate together as parts of a machine or process—that is, each motor has a separate, independent load that may operate by itself.

Fig. 300-3. Section 725-15 prohibits intermixing of power and starter coil-circuit wires when motors are not "functionally associated." (Sec. 300-3.)

Part **(c) (2)** of Sec. 300-3 states that conductors operating at more than 600 V *must not* occupy the same equipment wiring enclosure, cable, or raceway with conductors of 600 V or less. But, the rule lists three exceptions to paragraph **(c) (2)** [not to paragraph **(c) (1)**]. Exception No. 3 is intended to apply to enclosures, not raceways, such as used for high-voltage motor starters, permitting the high-voltage conductors operating at over 600 V to occupy the same controller housing as the control conductors operating at less than 600 V (Fig. 300-4). In addi-

SECTION 300-3(c) (2) PROHIBITS THIS—

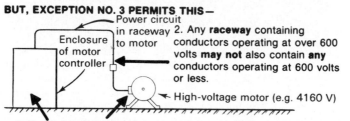

Same conduit carries 5-kV power conductors and control wires under 600 volts

High-voltage motor (e.g. 4160 V)

BUT, EXCEPTION NO. 3 PERMITS THIS—

Power circuit in raceway to motor

Enclosure of motor controller

2. Any **raceway** containing conductors operating at over 600 volts **may not** also contain **any** conductors operating at 600 volts or less.

High-voltage motor (e.g. 4160 V)

1. For any **individual** motor or starter—excitation, control, relay and/or ammeter conductors operating at 600 volts or less **may** occupy the same **starter or motor enclosure** as the conductors operating at over 600 volts.

Fig. 300-4. Control wires for high-voltage starters may be used in the starter enclosure, but not in *raceway* with power conductors. (Sec. 300-3.)

tion, Exception No. 1 of Sec. 300-32 specifically recognizes use of high-voltage and low-voltage conductors in the same enclosure of "motors, switchgear and control assemblies, and similar equipment."

300-4. Protection Against Physical Damage.   Part **(a)** gives the rules on protection required for cables and raceways run through wood framing members, as shown in Fig. 300-5. Where the edge of a hole in a wood member is less than 1¼ in. from the nearest edge of the member, a ¹⁄₁₆-in.-thick steel plate must be used to protect any cable or flexible conduit against driven nails or screws. The same protection is required for any cable or flexible conduit laid in a notch in the wood. *But*, rigid metal conduit, EMT, IMC, and PVC conduits do not require such protection.

Clearance must be provided from the edge of a hole in a wood member to the edge of the wood member. Where the **NE Code** used to require a minimum of 1½ in. from the edge of a cable hole in a stud to the edge of the stud, the present **NE Code** requires only 1¼ in. This permits realistic compliance when drilling holes in studs that are 3½ in. deep. It also was taken into consideration

If BX, NM cable, or raceway wiring
(rigid conduit, EMT, etc.) is used
through holes bored in joists, rafters or
similar wood members. . .

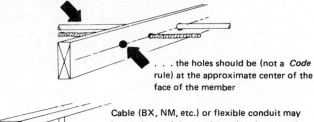

. . . the holes should be (not a *Code*
rule) at the approximate center of the
face of the member

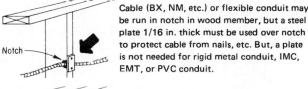

Cable (BX, NM, etc.) or flexible conduit may
be run in notch in wood member, but a steel
plate 1/16 in. thick must be used over notch
to protect cable from nails, etc. But, a plate
is not needed for rigid metal conduit, IMC,
EMT, or PVC conduit.

Notch

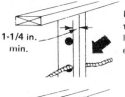

1-1/4 in.
min.

For any raceway or cable wiring (BX, NM, etc.)
through holes bored in studs, edge of bored
hole must be not less than 1-1/4 in. from nearest
edge of stud

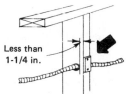

. . . OR . . .

Less than
1-1/4 in.

If hole is less than 1/4 in. from nearest edge,
a steel plate 1/16 in. thick must be used to
protect flexible conduit or cable against driven
nails or screws . . .But a plate is not needed for
rigid metal conduit, IMC, EMT, or PVC conduit.

Any cable and all raceways
except IMC, rigid metal,
rigid nonmetallic and EMT . . .

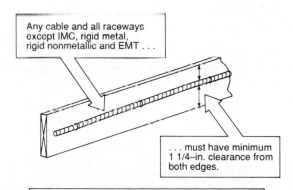

. . . must have minimum
1 1/4–in. clearance from
both edges.

NOTE: If clearance is less than 1 1/4 in., a 1/16 in.
thick steel plate or sleeve must be used to protect
cable or raceway.

Wiring on structural members must have clearance for protection against nails.

Fig. 300-5. Holes in wood framing must not weaken structure or expose cable to nail
puncture. (Sec. 300-4.)

that the nails commonly used to attach wall surfaces to studs were of such length that the 1¼-in. clearance to the edge of the cable hole afforded entirely adequate protection against possible penetration of the cable by the nail.

Figure 300-6 shows typical application of cable through drilled studs, with holes at centers and adequate clearance to edge of stud. Figure 300-7 shows an objectionable example of a drilled hole, violating the rule of part (2) of this section, which warns against "weakening the building structure." Figure 300-8 shows an acceptable way of protecting cables run through holes in wood members.

In part **(b)**, the rules on installations through metal framing members apply to nonmetallic-sheathed cable and to ENT (electrical nonmetallic tubing). Part **(1)** of Sec. 300-4(b) applies to NM cable run through slots or holes in metal framing members and requires that such holes must *always* be provided with bushings or grommets installed in the openings *before* the cable is pulled. But that requirement on protection by bushings or grommets in the holes does *not* apply to ENT run through holes.

Part **(2)** applies to both NM cable and ENT and requires that the cable or tubing be protected by a steel sleeve, a steel plate, or a clip when run through metal framing members in any case where nails or screws might be driven into the cable or tubing.

Part **(c)** requires cables and raceways above lift-out ceiling panels to be supported as they are required to be when installed in the open. They may not be treated as if they were being run through closed-in building spaces or fished through hollow spaces of masonry block.

Part **(d)** requires cables and raceways run along (parallel with) framing members (studs, joists, rafters) to have at least a 1¼-in. clearance from the nearest edge of the member; otherwise the cable or raceway must be protected against nail or screw penetrations by a steel plate or sleeve at least ¹⁄₁₆ in. thick.

Part **(d)** was added because of many persistent reports of nail and screw penetrations of both metallic and nonmetallic cables and raceway. The rule applies to both exposed and concealed locations. Exception No. 1 excludes intermediate metal conduit (IMC), rigid metal conduit, rigid nonmetallic conduit, and electrical metallic tubing (EMT) from the rule. The rule will apply to Romex (Type NM), BX (Type AC), flexible metal conduit, ENT (electrical nonmetallic tubing), Type MC cable and all other cables and raceways, except those excluded (Fig. 300-5, bottom).

Exception No. 2 excludes from this rule concealed work in finished buildings and finished panels in prefab buildings—where cables may be fished. Exception No. 3 excludes mobile homes and recreational vehicles.

300·5. Underground Installations.   This section is a comprehensive set of rules on installation of underground circuits for circuits up to 600 V. (Higher-voltage circuits must satisfy Sec. 710-3.) Table 300-5 in the **Code** book establishes *minimum* burial depths for specific conditions of use. Fig. 300-9 shows burial requirements for rigid metal conduit and IMC. Figure 300-10 shows the basic depth requirements for the various wiring methods.

Because Table 300-5 does not specifically mention EMT, it could be taken to indicate that the **NEC** does not recognize EMT for underground use. But Sec.

Drilled holes at the center of the face of a joist do not reduce the structural strength of the joist.

Signal and alarm wiring is run through the same stud holes as the NM cables. The NEC does not prohibit use of more than one cable through a single hole.

Fig. 300-6. Holes or notches in joists and studs must not weaken the structure of a building. [Sec. 300-4.]

Fig. 300-7. Excessive drilling of structural wood members can result in dangerous notching (arrow) that weakens the structure, violating Sec. 300-4(a) (2). (Sec. 300-4.)

348-1 (in condition No. 3) does recognize EMT for direct earth burial, and so does UL, with this stipulation: "In general, electrical metallic tubing in contact with soil requires supplementary corrosion protection." Note that such protection is not always mandatory. The UL note means to indicate that EMT may be buried without a protective coating (like asphalt paint) where local experience verifies that soil conditions do not attack and corrode the EMT.

Figure 300-11 shows modifications of basic burial depths. If a 2-in.-thick or thicker concrete pad is used in the trench over an underground circuit other than rigid metal conduit or IMC, the basic burial depth in Table 300-5 may be reduced by 6 in. But note that the concrete pad must be "in the trench," right over the cable or raceway. The wording must be taken to mean that it may not be a walk or other concrete at grade level. And the burial depth may not be reduced by more than 6 in. no matter how thick the concrete pad is. This rule is at odds with Exception No. 2 to Table 710-3(b) where burial depth for high-voltage circuits may be reduced "6 inches for each 2 inches of concrete" or equivalent protection in the trench over the wiring method (other than rigid metal or IMC).

Fig. 300-8. Steel plates are attached to wood structure member to protect cable from penetration by nail or screw driven into finished wall, where the edge of the cable hole is less than 1¼ in. from the edge of the wooden member. (Sec. 300-4.)

Note that, in Table 300-5, rigid metal conduit or IMC that is buried in the ground must have at least a 6-in.-thick cover of earth or earth-plus-concrete—even if it has a 2-in.-thick concrete pad over it. But rigid metal conduit, IMC, or other raceways may be installed directly under a 4-in-or-thicker exterior slab that is not subject to vehicle traffic—without any need for earth cover. Given the fact that rigid metal conduit or IMC may be laid directly on the ground (which supports it for its entire length) and would not necessarily require any concrete cover, there is no reason why it cannot be laid on the ground or flush with the ground and covered with at least 4 in. of concrete. See Fig. 300-9.

Section 300-5 only applies to "Underground Installations" and is not applicable if the conduit is laid directly on the ground. No **Code** rule prohibits conduit laid on the ground, provided the conduit is "securely fastened in place" (Sec. 346-12) and is not exposed to physical damage—such as vehicular traffic—and many such installations have been made for years. But, when conduit is installed in the ground, there is serious concern about damage due to digging in the ground, which Sec. 300-5 addresses.

As shown in Fig. 300-12, Table 300-5 recognizes that raceways run under concrete slabs at least 4 in. thick or under buildings have sufficient protection against digging and are not required to be subject to the burial-depth requirements given in the top line of Table 300-5. Where raceways are so installed, the rule requires that the slab extend at least 6 in. beyond the underground raceway.

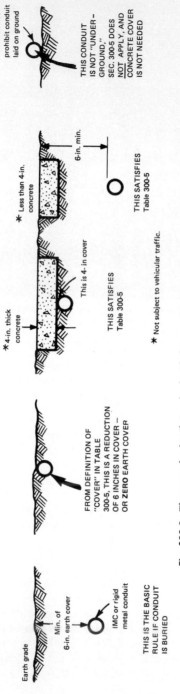

Fig. 300-9.   These are the details involved with the use of rigid metal conduit and IMC underground.

DIRECT-BURIED CABLES

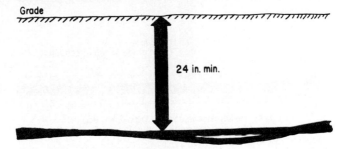

Grade

24 in. min.

RIGID METAL CONDUIT

6 in. min.

INTERMEDIATE METAL CONDUIT

6 in. min.

ELECTRICAL METALLIC TUBING (EMT)

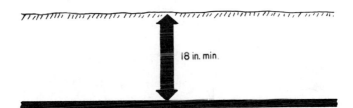

18 in. min.

RIGID NONMETALLIC CONDUIT

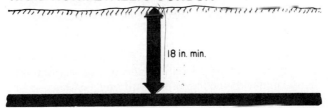

18 in. min.

Conduit approved for burial
without concrete encasement

Fig. 300·10. These are the *basic* burial depths, **but** variations are recognized in Table 300-5 for certain conditions. (Sec. 300-5.)

RIGID NONMETALLIC CONDUIT (ENCASED)

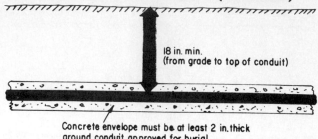

18 in. min.
(from grade to top of conduit)

Concrete envelope must be at least 2 in. thick
around conduit approved for burial
only when encased

Fig. 300-10. (Continued.)

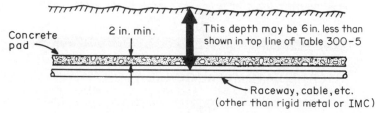

Concrete
pad

2 in. min.

This depth may be 6 in. less than
shown in top line of Table 300-5

Raceway, cable, etc.
(other than rigid metal or IMC)

Fig. 300-11. Concrete pad "in trench" permits only a 6-in. reduction of burial
depth for circuits up to 600 V. (Sec. 300-5.)

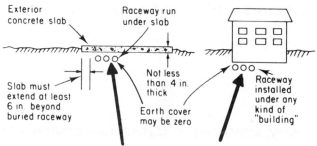

Exterior
concrete slab

Raceway run
under slab

Slab must
extend at least
6 in. beyond
buried raceway

Not less
than 4 in.
thick

Earth cover
may be zero

Raceway
installed
under any
kind of
"building"

Burial-depth requirements of Table 300-5 do not apply
to raceways installed like this.

Fig. 300-12. Table 300-5 eliminates burial-depth requirements for direct
buried "raceways" under specified conditions. (Sec. 300-5.)

1. Any direct burial cable run under a building must be installed in raceway, as required by Sec. 300-5(c), and the raceway may be installed in the earth, immediately under the bottom of the building—without any earth cover.
2. Any direct buried cable under a slab at least 4 in. thick (and not subject to vehicles) is subject to the 18-in. minimum burial-depth requirement of Table 300-5.

Figure 300-13 shows the mandatory 24-in. burial depth given in Table 300-5 for any wiring methods buried under public or private roads, alleys, driveways,

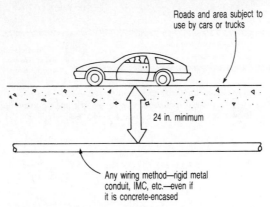

Fig. 300-13. All wiring methods must be at least 2 ft under vehicular traffic. (Sec. 300-5.)

parking lots, or other areas subject to car and truck traffic. A minimum earth cover of 24 in. is required for any underground cable or raceway wiring that is installed under vehicle traffic, regardless of concrete encasement or any other protective measure. This requires the minimum 2-ft earth cover for wiring under the designated areas—including driveways and parking areas of private residences. The minimum earth cover for cables and raceways under driveways and parking areas for one- and two-family dwellings is only 18 in.

Table 300-5 (second vertical column from right) gives limited use of lesser burial depth for the residential circuits described, as shown in Fig. 300-14. Any GFCI-protected residential *"branch circuit"* not over 120 V and protected at 20 A or less may be buried only 12 in. below grade, instead of, say, 24 in. as required for Type UF cable for any nonresidential use or for a residential "feeder."

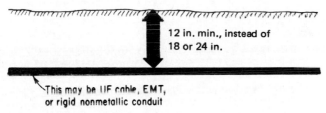

Fig. 300-14. This is OK only for a residential branch circuit rated not over 20 A and protected by a GFCI circuit breaker. (Sec. 300-5.)

Figure 300-15 shows three other special conditions for burial depth.

Table 300-5 (vertical column at right) recognizes reduced burial depth for low-voltage landscape lighting circuits and supply circuits to lawn sprinkler and irrigation valves, as shown in Fig. 300-16. This recognizes the reduced hazards and safety considerations for circuits operating at not more than 30 V.

Part **(b)** of Sec. 300-5 requires **NEC** grounding and bonding for all underground circuits and equipment. For instance, metal conduit and metal sheath

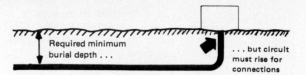

Required minimum burial depth . . .

. . . but circuit must rise for connections

Of course, lesser depths than shown in Table 300-5 are permitted where cable or conductors in raceway come up to terminations or splices in boxes or equipment. NOTE 3.

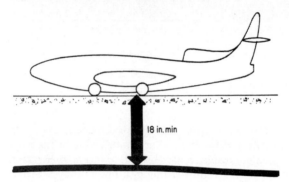

18 in. min

Any cables or raceways may be buried not less than 18 in. deep under airport runways and adjacent defined areas where trespass is prohibited.

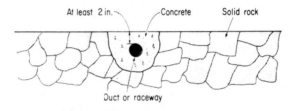

At least 2 in.   Concrete   Solid rock

Duct or raceway

Duct and raceway installed in solid rock may be buried if concrete at least 2 in. thick covers the raceway and extends down to the rock surface.

Fig. 300·15. These applications are also covered in the table burial depths. (Sec. 300-5.)

or electrostatic shielding must be effectively grounded at all terminations by connection to grounded metal enclosure, by bonding jumper, etc., to limit voltage to ground and facilitate operation of overcurrent protective devices, as shown in Fig. 300-17.

Figure 300-18 shows the rule of part **(c)**.

As shown at the top of Fig. 300-19, direct buried conductors or cables coming up a pole or on a building from underground installation must be protected from the minimum required burial distance below grade (from Table 300-5 but never required to be more than 18 in. into the ground) to at least 8 ft above

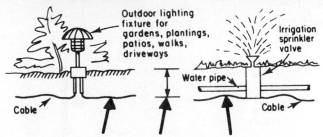

Landscape Lighting   **Irrigation Control**

Outdoor lighting fixture for gardens, plantings, patios, walks, driveways

Irrigation sprinkler valve

Water pipe

Cable

Cable

Minimum burial depth of 6 inches if cable is Type UF and circuit operates at not more than 30 volts

Fig. 300-16. Reduced burial depth for low-voltage landscape lighting and lawn-sprinkler controls. (Sec. 300-5.)

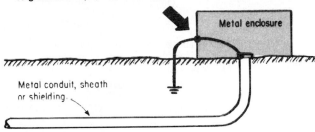

Bonding jumper or other connection to grounded equipment enclosure

Metal enclosure

Metal conduit, sheath or shielding.

Fig. 300-17. Metal of wiring system must be grounded at *all* terminations. (Sec. 300-5.)

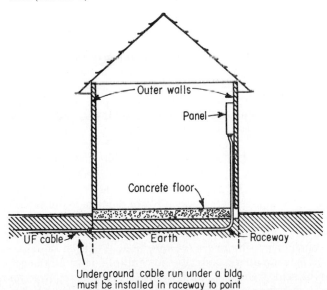

Outer walls

Panel

Concrete floor

UF cable   Earth   Raceway

Underground cable run under a bldg. must be installed in raceway to point beyond outer walls of building.

Fig. 300-18. Burial of cable in earth is not permitted under a building. (Sec. 300-5.)

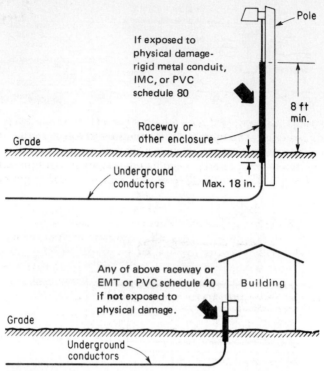

If exposed to
physical damage-
rigid metal conduit,
IMC, or PVC
schedule 80

Pole

8 ft
min.

Raceway or
other enclosure

Grade

Underground
conductors   Max. 18 in.

Any of above raceway or
EMT or PVC schedule 40   Building
if **not** exposed to
physical damage.

Grade

Underground
conductors

Fig. 300-19. Conductors from underground must be protected. (Sec. 300-5.)

grade, as required by part **(d)** of this section. Where exposed to physical damage, raceways on buildings and raceways on poles must be rigid conduit, IMC, PVC Schedule 80, or equivalent, and the raceway or other enclosure for underground conductors must extend from below the ground line up to 8 ft above finished grade. If a raceway on a building or on a pole is not subject to physical damage, EMT or Schedule 40 PVC may be used instead of other raceways.

Figures 300-20 and 300-21 show other rules of Sec. 300-5. Note that part **(f)** specifically requires that backfilled trenches must contain any necessary protection for raceways or cables buried in the trench. It specifies that sand or suitable running boards of wood or concrete or other protection must be afforded in those cases where backfill consists of heavy stones or sharp objects that otherwise would present the possibility of damage to the cable or raceway.

Part **(i)** of this section requires that an underground circuit made up of single-conductor cables for direct burial must have all conductors of the circuit run in the same trench. That rule raises the question: When an underground direct burial circuit is made up of conductors in multiple, must all the conductors be installed in the same trench? And if they are, is derating required for more than three current-carrying conductors in a trench, just as it would be for more than three conductors in a single raceway? The answer to both questions is "yes."

Part (e)

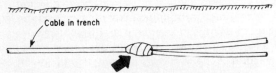

Splices or taps are permitted in trench without a box—but only if approved methods and materials are used.

Part (f)

Backfill of heavy rocks or sharp or corrosive materials must not be used if it may cause damage or prevent adaquate compaction of ground.

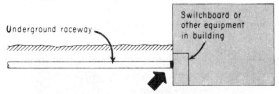

Part (g)

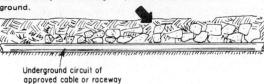

Conduits or other raceways must be sealed or plugged at either or both ends if moisture could contact live parts

Part (h)

Bushing must be used on any conduit end where direct-burial cables leave conduit. Or, a seal that gives the same protection may be used instead of a bushing.

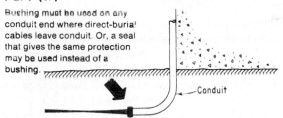

Fig. 300-20. Underground wiring must satisfy these requirements. (Sec. 300-5.)

The wording of the rule in part **(i)** clearly indicates that *all* the conductors making up a direct burial circuit of single conductors in parallel must be run in the same trench and *must* be "in close proximity." The wording of Sec. 300-5(i) also requires that all conductors of a circuit be run in the same raceway if raceway is used (with building wire suitable for wet locations, such as THW).

Fig. 300-21. For direct burial underground conductors, a box must be used at splice points, with conductors brought up in sweep ells and the box properly grounded—*unless approved* materials are used to make directly buried splices in the conductors. (Sec. 300-5.)

But, Exception No. 1 permits parallel conductor makeup in multiple raceways—with each raceway containing all hot, grounded, and (if used) grounding conductors of the circuit.

When multiple-conductor makeup of a circuit is installed with all the parallel-circuit conductors in the same trench, it is necessary to observe the rule of the second paragraph of Note 8 to Tables 310-16 to 310-19 of the **NE Code**. It says:

> Where single conductors . . . are stacked or bundled longer than 24 in. without maintaining spacing and are not installed in raceways, the ampacity of each conductor *shall* be reduced as shown in the above table.

That means that the same deratings must be made as when more than three conductors are used in a single conduit—as explained in Note 8. Certainly, direct burial single conductors are covered by that requirement because Table 310-16 specifically covers direct burial conductors.

Those **Code** rules often make for tricky and troublesome applications. For instance, as shown in Fig. 300-22, an underground circuit of Type USE insulated aluminum conductors might be used for a 3-wire, single-phase service to a multifamily dwelling. Because that is a residential service, Note 3 to Tables 310-16 to 310-19 may be observed to gain a higher-than-normal ampacity for the conductors.

Assuming that a 400-A conductor ampacity is indicated by the calculated demand load from Art. 220, each phase leg of the service feeder must have an ampacity of 400 A. Refer to Note 3 of the ampacity tables: a No. 4/0 THW aluminum has an ampacity of 200 A. Two such conductors per hot leg and two for the neutral would give the required 400-A capacity for the service.

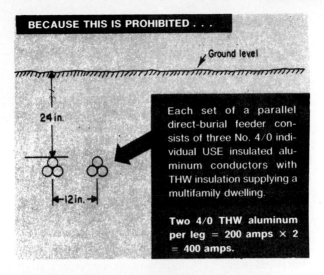

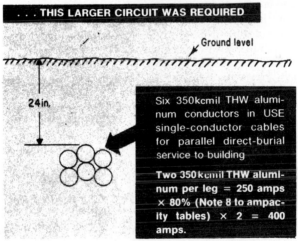

Fig. 300-22. Literal application of Code rules often imposes stiff requirements. (Sec. 300-5.)

But how should the parallel circuit be run?

All the circuit conductors *must* be run in close proximity in the same trench, as required by Sec. 300-5(i). That means all six USE conductors are in the same trench; and because the neutrals do not count as current-carrying conductors, the derating of these "bundled" conductors must be to 80 percent of the 200-A ampacity—as required for four conductors in the table of Note 8. With each 4/0 THW aluminum now derated to 160 A (0.8 × 200), the ampacity of each hot leg is only 320 A (2 × 160).

The rule requiring all conductors to be in the same trench makes the circuit of two 4/0 THW aluminum per leg inadequate. In referring to Table 310-16, it now becomes necessary to pick a larger size of THW aluminum—such that, derated to 80 percent, two of them will provide the required 400-A rating. A 350 kcmil THW aluminum has a normal rating of 250 A. Derated to 80 percent (250 × 0.8), it has the needed ampacity of 200 A, so that two of them in parallel per hot leg and neutral will have the ampacity of 400 A.

If the two parallel sets of conductors could have been run in separate trenches, the 4/0 THW aluminum conductors would have met the need.

Exception No. 1 of part **(i)** permits an underground circuit to be made up in parallel in two or more raceways—*without need for derating.* But, in such cases, each raceway must contain one of each of the phase legs, a neutral (if used) and an equipment grounding conductor (if used). With "A-B-C-N" in each raceway of a multiple group, that would be the same type of multiple-conduit-parallel-conductor makeup as required and commonly used for above-ground circuits.

Exception No. 2 permits "isolated-phase" makeup of underground circuits in multiple conduits—all phase "A" conductors in one conduit, all phase "B" conductors in a second conduit, all phase "C" conductors in a third conduit, all neutrals in a fourth conduit—with an equipment grounding conductor (or conductors, if needed) installed in a fifth conduit or installed in each of the three conduits carrying the phase conductors. *But,* that makeup is permitted only where the conduits are nonmetallic and are "in close proximity" to each other. See Sec. 300-20.

300-6. Protection Against Corrosion. These are general regulations that are repeated in more detail in the various articles covering raceways and enclosures. The last sentence in part **(a)** allows organic coatings to be applied to metallic boxes or cabinets to prevent corrosion when used outdoors, in lieu of the standard "4-dip" zinc galvanizing method.

Part **(b)** is a general rule that is best understood when related to the specific recommendations given in the UL Green Book for the various types of raceways. See Arts. 345, 346, and 348 for such data.

Figure 300-23 shows the *right* and *wrong* ways of installing equipment in indoor wet locations—as covered in part **(c)** of this section.

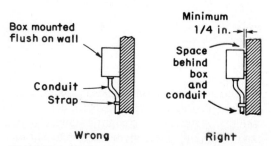

Fig. 300-23. Water or moisture must not be trapped in contact with metal. (Sec. 300-6.)

300-7. Raceways Exposed to Different Temperatures.   Part **(a)** requires protection against moisture accumulation. If air is allowed to circulate from the warmer to the colder section of the raceway, moisture in the warm air will condense in the cold section of the raceway. This can usually be eliminated by sealing the raceway just outside the cold rooms so as to prevent the circulation of air. Sealing may be accomplished by stuffing a suitable compound in the end of the pipe (Fig. 300-24).

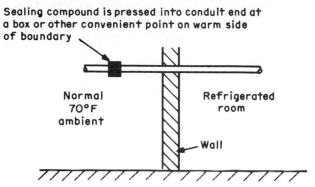

Fig. 300-24. Sealing protects against moisture accumulation in raceway. (Sec. 300-7.)

300-8. Installation of Conductors with Other Systems.   Any raceway or cable tray that contains electric conductors must not contain "any pipe, tube, or equal for steam, water, air, gas, drainage or any service other than electrical."

300-10. Electrical Continuity of Metal Raceways and Enclosures.   This is the basic rule requiring a permanent and continuous bonding together (i.e., connecting together) of all noncurrent-carrying metal parts of equipment enclosures—conduit, boxes, cabinets, enclosures, housings, frame of motors, and lighting fixtures—and connection of this interconnected system of enclosures to the system grounding electrode at the service or transformer (Fig. 300-25). The interconnection of all metal enclosures must be made to connect all metal to the grounding electrode and to provide a low-impedance path for fault-current flow along the enclosures to assure operation of overcurrent devices which will open a circuit in the event of a fault. By opening a faulted circuit, the system prevents dangerous voltages from being present on equipment enclosures which could be touched by personnel, with consequent electric shock to such personnel.

Simply stated, this interconnection of all metal enclosures of electric wires and equipment prevents any potential aboveground on the enclosures. Such bonding together and grounding of all metal enclosures are required for both grounded electrical systems (those systems in which one of the circuit conductors is intentionally grounded) and ungrounded electrical systems (systems with none of the circuit wires intentionally grounded).

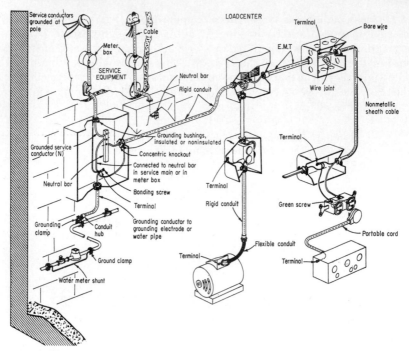

Fig. 300·25. All metal enclosures must be interconnected to form "a continuous electric conductor." (Sec. 300-10.)

But effective equipment interconnection and grounding are extremely important for grounded electrical systems to provide the automatic fault-clearing which is one of the important advantages of grounded electrical systems. A low-impedance path for fault current is necessary to permit enough current to flow to operate the fuses or CB protecting the circuit.

300·11. Securing and Supporting.   Part **(a)** does permit "branch-circuit wiring" to be "supported by the suspended ceiling support wires"—*if* those wires "provide secure support." The wording gives limited acceptance to attaching wiring methods to the ceiling support wires of a hung ceiling. But this method applies only to wiring that supplies or controls "equipment that is supported by or located below a suspended ceiling." Such equipment includes surface and recessed lighting fixtures in the ceiling and wiring for floor-to-ceiling circuit poles, for lighting, receptacles, and communication and data circuits. Other wiring in the ceiling space may not be supported by the ceiling support wires.

In part **(b)**, raceways are prohibited from being used as a means of support for cables or nonelectrical equipment. Telephone or other communication, signal, or control cables must not be fastened to electrical conduits—such as by plastic straps or any other means.

Although raceways must not be used as a means of support for other raceways, cables, or nonelectric equipment, Exception No. 1 permits large conduits

with hanger bars or fittings intended to support smaller raceways. Exception
No. 2 permits such applications as tying Class 2 thermostat cable to a conduit
carrying power-supply conductors for electrically controlled heating and air-
conditioning equipment that is controlled by the Class 2 wires.

300-13. Mechanical and Electrical Continuity—Conductors.   Part **(b)** prohibits
dependency upon device terminals (such as internally connected screw terminals of duplex receptacles) for the splicing of neutral conductors in multiwire
(3-wire or 4-wire) circuits. **Grounded neutral wires** must not depend on device
connection (such as the break-off tab between duplex receptacle screw terminals) for continuity. White wires can be spliced together with a pigtail to neutral
terminal on receptacle. If receptacle is removed, neutral will not be opened
(Fig. 300-26).

This rule is to prevent the establishment of unbalanced voltages should a
neutral conductor be opened *first* when a receptacle or similar device is
replaced on energized circuits. In such cases, the line-to-neutral connections
downstream from this point (farther from the point of supply) could result in a
considerably higher-than-normal voltage on one part of a multiwire circuit and

Do it this way...

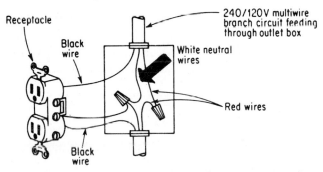

... or this way

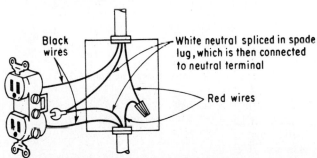

Fig. 300-26. Neutrals of multiwire circuit must *not* be spliced at receptacle terminals. (Sec. 300-13.)

damage equipment, because of the "open" neutral, if the downstream line-to-neutral loads are appreciably unbalanced.

Note that this paragraph does not apply to 2-wire circuits or circuits which do not have a grounded conductor. This rule applies only where multiwire circuits feed receptacles or lampholders. This would most commonly be a 3-wire 240/120-V or a 3- or 4-wire 208/120-V, or even a 480/277-V branch circuit.

The reason for the pigtailing requirement is to prevent the neutral conductor from being broken and creating downstream hazards. The problem lies in the inclination of electricians to work on hot circuits. Assume that a duplex receptacle on a 240/120-V 3-wire circuit becomes defective, and the first thing the electrician does, working hot, is to disconnect the neutral wires from the receptacle. Downstream, 2.4- and 12-A loads have been operating (plugged into additional receptacles on the multiwire circuit), each connected to a different hot leg. When the neutral is broken by the electrician upstream, normal operation of the loads reverts to the condition shown in Fig. 300-27. The two loads are now in series across 240 V. As shown, load A now has 200 V impressed across

An open neutral like this...

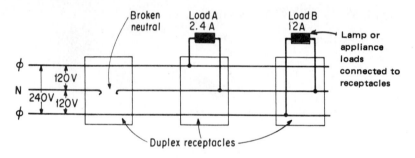

... puts 200 volts across a 120-volt load

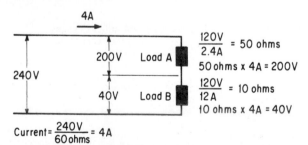

Fig. 300·27. Splicing neutrals on receptacle screws causes "open" in neutral if receptacle is removed. (Sec. 300-13.)

it. It could run extremely hot and burn out. Load B now has only 40 V across it; if it is a motor-operated device, the low voltage could cause the motor to burn up. Both could cause injuries.

Also, in disconnecting the neutral, the electrician could get a 120-V shock if both the disconnected neutral conductor going downstream and the box were touched—not unlikely, since the neutral is usually considered to be dead—that is, at ground potential.

300·14. Length of Free Conductors at Outlets, Junctions, and Switch Points. The rule here applies only to the length of the conductor at its end. The Exception covers wires running through the box. Wires looping through the box and intended for connection to outlets at the box need have only sufficient slack that any connections can be made easily.

300·15. Boxes or Fittings—Where Required. Part **(a)** permits either a "box" or a "fitting" to be used at splice points or connection points in *raceway* systems. The word "fitting" as used here refers to "conduit bodies"—even though the definition of "fitting" in Art. 100 suggests that only locknuts and bushings are fittings. Type T or Type L fittings (conduit bodies) actually become a part of the conduit or tubing and should not contain more conductors than permitted for the raceway. Conduit bodies must not contain splices, taps, or devices unless they comply with the rules of Sec. 370-6(c). For conductors No. 4 or larger see Sec. 370-18(a). Use of boxes and fittings for splicing, for connections to switches or outlet wiring devices, or for pulling must conform to the many detailed rules of Art. 370. Refer to those rules for further discussion.

Exception No. 2 permits splices to be made within lighting fixture wiring compartments where the branch-circuit wires are spliced to fixture or ballast wires.

Part **(b)** accepts *only* a box for splices and connections to devices when the wiring system is *"cable"* instead of raceway (Fig. 300-28).

Exception No. 5 of this section recognizes use of wiring devices that have "integral enclosures." These are the so-called boxless devices made and acceptable for use in nonmetallic-sheathed cable systems (Type NM). Such listed devices do not require a separate box at each outlet because the construction of the device forms an integral box in itself.

Exception No. 6 recognizes the use of manufactured metallic wiring systems—"prefab" or "modular wiring" systems used for distribution of lighting and communications in the space above suspended ceilings. Such UL-listed systems are covered in Art. 604 and are designed with their own components for connections of their cable "whips." Therefore, they are exempted from the usual rule on boxes at splices, junctions, etc.

Exception No. 7 permits use of a "conduit body" at splice, pull, or connection points in cable systems. Of course, where conduit bodies are used in cable runs, they will have to be supported by straps on their hubs or by some other means. When used with rigid metal conduit or IMC, the conduit itself is adequate support for the conduit body if the conduit is clamped within 3 ft on two or more sides of the conduit body.

Exception No. 9 recognizes transition from Type AC cable to raceway without the need for a box, provided that no splice or termination is made in the

This may be a "box"
or "conduit body" per Sec. 370-6 (c)

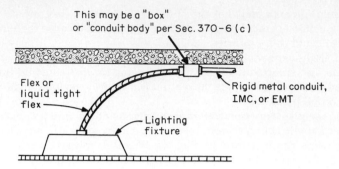

Flex or
liquid tight
flex

Rigid metal conduit,
IMC, or EMT

Lighting
fixture

But with type AC cable (BX) Type NM cable, or any other cable, a "box"
must be used at all splice and outlet points, and even where cable
connects to raceway

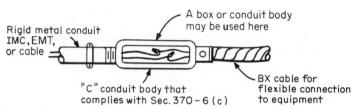

A box or conduit body
may be used here

Rigid metal conduit
IMC, EMT,
or cable

BX cable for
flexible connection
to equipment

"C" conduit body that
complies with Sec. 370 – 6 (c)

Fig. 300·28. Raceways and cables may use boxes or conduit bodies at conductor
splice points. (Sec. 300-15.)

conductors. This permits the common practice of changing from, say, BX to
EMT for a run down a wall, with the armor stripped from a long length of the
BX and the exposed wires run in the EMT. A suitable fitting made for con-
necting BX to EMT must be used (Fig. 300-29).

Part **(c)** of Sec. 300-15 was proposed to address the almost universal misuse
of Type NM (Romex) connectors with other cables and even cords. The wording as it appears in the **Code**, however, requires that *any* fitting or connector
must be "designed and listed" for the wiring method used. Be aware that, while
it will be up to the manufacturers of this equipment to obtain the listing for
these products, it is the designer-installer's responsibility to specify or use ONLY
those fittings and connectors specifically listed for the application.

300·16. Raceway or Cable to Open or Concealed Wiring. Where the wires are
run in conduit, tubing, metal raceway, or armored cable and are brought out
for connection to open wiring or concealed knob-and-tube work, a fitting such
as is shown in Fig. 300-30 may be used.

Where the terminal fitting is an accessible outlet box, the installation may be
made as shown in Fig. 300-30.

Figure 300-31 shows wires pulled into an incomplete raceway system. That
used to be a **Code** violation, but the rule prohibiting it was removed.

300·18. Raceway Installations. This section restores a general **Code** concept
that was in the 1981 and previous **Codes** (it was Sec. 300-18), requiring race-

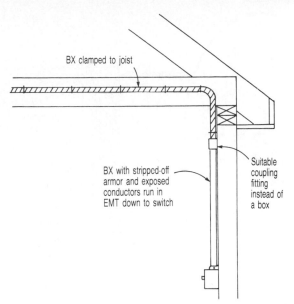

BX clamped to joist

BX with stripped-off
armor and exposed
conductors run in
EMT down to switch

Suitable
coupling
fitting
instead of
a box

Fig. 300-29. This type of no-box connection for cable-to-race-
way change is permitted by Exception No. 9. [Sec. 300-15(b).]

ways to be installed as a complete system, with associated boxes and other
enclosures, before pulling conductors into the raceway and box system. This
rule is reinserted in the **NEC** because of reports of damage to conductors being
pulled into incomplete raceway systems. The exceptions to the rule are
intended to permit wiring of motors and fixture whips after the basic raceway
system has been wired, as well as covering prewired assemblies.

300-19. Supporting Conductors in Vertical Raceways. Long vertical runs of
conductors should not be supported by the terminal to which they are connected. Supports as shown in Fig. 300-32 may be used to comply with Sec.
300-19(a). (See also Figs. 300-33 and 300-34.)

300-20. Induced Currents in Metal Enclosures or Metal Raceways. By keeping
all conductors of an AC circuit close together—in raceway, or a box, or other
enclosure—the magnetic fields around the conductors tend to oppose or cancel
each other, thereby minimizing the inductive reactance of the circuit and also
minimizing the amount of magnetic flux that can cause heat due to hysteresis
loss (magnetic friction) in steel or iron and due to the I^2R losses of currents that
are induced in adjacent metal. The rule of this section calls for always running
a neutral conductor with the phase legs of an AC circuit to minimize such
induction heating. The equipment grounding conductor must also be run close
to the circuit conductors to achieve the reduction in inductive reactance and
minimize the impedance of the fault-current return path when a fault does
occur—thereby assuring the fastest possible operation of the protective device
(fuse or CB) in the circuit (Fig. 300-35).

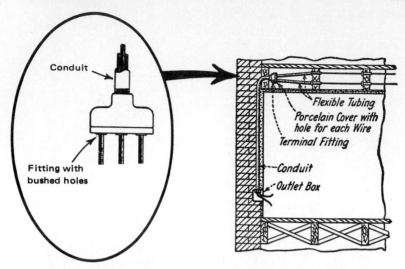

A terminal fitting satisfies the rule on transition from raceway to knob and tube.

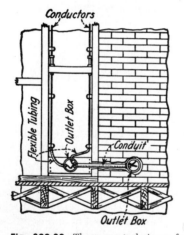

An outlet box may be used where raceway connects to open wiring or concealed knob and tube.

Fig. 300-30. These are techniques for connecting conduit to open wiring. (Sec. 300-16.)

When an AC circuit is arranged in such a way that the individual conductors are not physically close for mutual cancellation of their field flux, it is particularly important to take precautions where a single conductor passes through a hole in any magnetic material—like a steel enclosure surface. The presence of the magnetic material forms a closed (circular) magnetic core that raises the flux density of the magnetic field around the conductor (that is, it greatly strengthens

Fig. 300-31. Conductors shown here have been pulled into the conduit before boxes and continuation of the raceway system were installed to supply underground circuits to outdoor building lighting. Under previous Code editions, this was a violation of Sec. 300-10. That section and its rules were removed after the 1981 NEC.

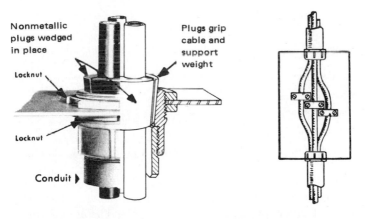

Conductor-support bushing screwed on end of conduit at a cabinet, pull box, or conductor-support box. (*Russell & Stoll.*)

Conductor-support box with single-wire cleats to clamp conductors.

Fig. 300-32. Some type of support must carry the weight of conductors in long risers. (Sec. 300-19.)

Fig. 300-33. Bore-hole cable, with steel wire armor, is permitted by the Exception to be supported only at the top of very high risers because the steel armor supports the length of the cable when the steel wires are properly clamped in the support ring of the type of fitting shown here. (Sec. 300-19.)

the magnetic field). Under such conditions, there can be substantial heating in the enclosure due to hysteresis (friction produced by the alternating reversals of the magnetic domains in the steel) and due to currents induced in the steel by the strong magnetic field. To minimize those effects, the second paragraph of Sec. 300-20 requires special treatment, such as that shown in Fig. 300-36. Or a rigid, nonmetallic board (fiberglass, plastic, etc.) should be used for the enclosure wall that the conductors pass through.

300-21. Spread of Fire or Products of Combustion. Application of this section to all kinds of building constructions is a very broad and expanding controversy in modern electrical work, in particular because of the phrase "substantially increased." The rule here requires that electrical installations shall be made to substantially protect the integrity of rated fire walls, fire-resistant or fire-

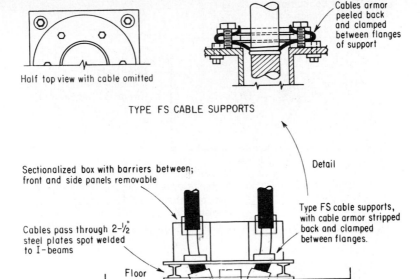

Half top view with cable omitted

Cables armor
peeled back
and clamped
between flanges
of support

TYPE FS CABLE SUPPORTS

Detail

Sectionalized box with barriers between;
front and side panels removable

Type FS cable supports,
with cable armor stripped
back and clamped
between flanges.

Cables pass through 2-½"
steel plates spot welded
to I-beams

Floor

Fiber conduits
and concrete
sheathing stop
at this floor slab

Fig. 300-34. Separate strands of cable armor are snubbed between flanges of support fitting at top of run. Partitioned enclosure protects unarmored sections of cable. (Sec. 300-19.)

In a typical 3-phase circuit

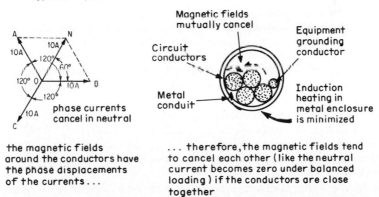

Magnetic fields
mutually cancel

Equipment
grounding
conductor

Circuit
conductors

Metal
conduit

Induction
heating in
metal enclosure
is minimized

phase currents
cancel in neutral

the magnetic fields
around the conductors have
the phase displacements
of the currents...

... therefore, the magnetic fields tend
to cancel each other (like the neutral
current becomes zero under balanced
loading) if the conductors are close
together

Fig. 300-35. Close placement of AC conductors minimizes magnetic fields and induction. (Sec. 300-20.)

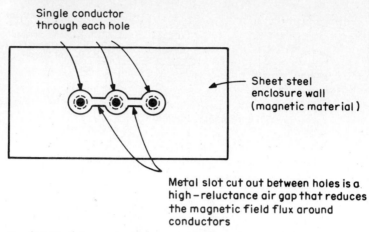

Single conductor
through each hole

Sheet steel
enclosure wall
(magnetic material)

Metal slot cut out between holes is a
high-reluctance air gap that reduces
the magnetic field flux around
conductors

Fig. 300-36. Induction heating is reduced by opening the magnetic core. (Sec. 300-20.)

stopped walls, partitions, ceilings, and floors. Electrical installations must be so made that the possible spread of fire through hollow spaces, vertical shafts, and ventilating or air-handling ducts will be reduced to a minimum. These rules require close cooperation with building officials to avoid destruction of fire ratings when electrical installations extend through such areas.

Floor Penetrations

Certainly, the electrical industry has come to agree that poke-through wiring—that technique in which floor outlets in commercial buildings are wired through holes in concrete slab floors—is an acceptable wiring method if use is made of UL-listed poke-through fittings that have been tested and found to preserve the fire rating of the concrete floor. Throughout the country, the use of poke-through wiring continues to be a popular and very effective method of wiring floor outlets in office areas and other commercial and industrial locations. Holes are cut or drilled in concrete floors at the desired locations of floor outlets, and floor box assemblies are installed and wired from the ceiling space of the floor below. The method permits installation of each and every floor box at the precise location that best serves the layout of desks and other office equipment.

The wiring of each floor outlet at a poke-through location may be done basically in either of two ways—by some job-fabricated assembly of pipe nipples and boxes or by means of a manufactured through-floor assembly (Fig. 300-37) made expressly for the purpose and tested and listed by a nationally recognized testing lab, such as UL.

May either of the methods be used? A clear regulation of the Occupational Safety and Health Administration appears to rule decisively on this question. In the *Occupational Safety and Health Standards*, Subpart S—Electrical, para-

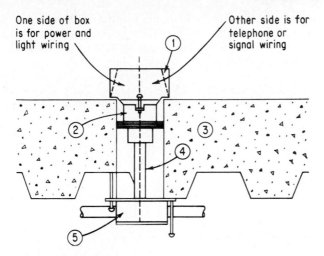

One side of box is for power and light wiring

Other side is for telephone or signal wiring

Numbered components include (1) combination floor service box, (2) fire-rated center coupling, (3) concrete slab, (4) barriered extension, and (5) barriered junction box.

UL-listed assembly is fire-rated for thickest concrete slab.

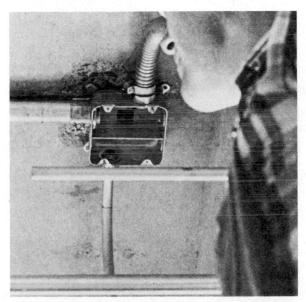

Bottom end of UL-listed poke-through fitting consists of a partitioned box for 120-V circuit and telephone circuit run through vertical channels of fitting into dual-service floor outlet box on top of slab.

Fig. 300·37. Several manufacturers make UL-listed poke-through assemblies. (Sec. 300-21.)

graph 1910.308(d)(2) clearly and flatly *demands* that an installation or equipment determined to be safe by a nationally recognized testing lab must *always* be used in preference to any equipment *not* certified by a testing lab. Thus, if a UL-listed poke-through fitting is available, then the use of any nonlisted, homemade assembly—which has not been determined to be safe—appears to be clearly not acceptable to OSHA and could be construed as a violation of NE Code Sec. 110-2, which calls for all equipment to be "approved."

Section 300-21 also applies to cable and/or conduit penetrations of fire-rated walls, floors, or ceilings without altering the fire rating of the structural surface (Figs. 300-38 and 300-39).

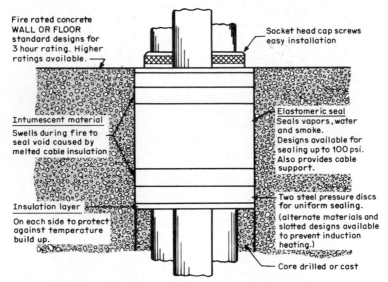

Fig. 300-38. Fire-stop fitting for passing cables or conduit through a fire-rated wall, floor slab, or similar concrete surface, without altering the fire rating of the surface. (Sec. 300-21.)

Ceiling Penetrations

Another similar concern covered by this section is the installation of lay-in lighting fixtures in a fire-rated suspended ceiling. Suspended ceilings are usually evaluated only for their esthetic and acoustic value, but they also serve as fire-protective membranes for the floor above. Although concrete floor structures have various fire-resistance ratings by themselves (depending on the concrete thickness and aggregate used), some assemblies require some type of protective cover. When this is the case, the ceiling is tested in combination with the floor-slab structure for which the rating is desired.

Such a ceiling properly serves its function of fire protection until an installer cuts holes in it, such as for recessed-lighting fixtures or for air diffusers or grilles. Because of that, the acceptability of the overall ceiling system must be carefully determined.

Fig. 300-39. Another type of device to provide for passing cable and/or conduit through fire-rated building surfaces without altering the conditions of fire resistance. (Sec. 300-21.)

First, check the Underwriters Laboratories' *Electrical Construction Materials Directory* (commonly called the UL Green Book), which notes that recessed fixtures that have been shown to provide a degree of fire resistance with the floor, roof, or ceiling assemblies with *which they have been tested* are labeled as follows: "Recessed-type electric fixture classified for fire resistance; fire-resistance classification floor and ceiling Design No. ——."

Next, find the design referred to in the UL *Fire Resistance Index*. This booklet follows the format of the *Electrical Construction Materials Directory*. Refer to a design of the required fire rating and be sure that the fixtures are listed for use with that design.

Designers must specify the particular UL design that suits their requirement, note this in the specifications, and be certain that the lighting fixtures are fire-rated in accordance. But it is advisable for the electrical contractor to investigate the ceiling design for possible fire rating in all cases and to receive from the designer written confirmation of the exact nature and value of the rating, if one exists.

In the UL *Building Materials Directory*, various fire-rated assemblies are listed by "design number" and by "rating time." A companion publication, the *Fire Resistance Index*, contains detailed cross-section drawings of the assemblies, with all critical dimensions shown. Each pertinent element is usually flagged with an identifying number. Keyed to the number are clarifying statements listing additional critical limitations (such as the size and number of penetrations in the ceiling).

The top installation in Fig. 300-40 was tested and given a 1½-hr rating. No protective material was used between the fixture and the floor slab above. A

**Recessed fixture without
protective covering (1½-hr rating)**

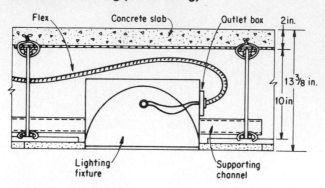

**Recessed fixture with
box board shell (2-hr rating)**

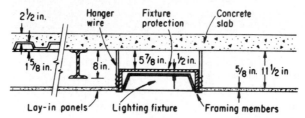

Fig. 300·40. The complete assembly of concrete slab plus fixture and ceiling gets a fire rating. (Sec. 300-21.)

somewhat better rating could have been obtained had protection been provided over the fixture.

At the bottom of Fig. 300-40 is a fixture with protection. When this construction was tested, failure occurred after 2 hr 48 min, and it received a 2-hr time rating. Even with this type of protection, the UL listing will limit the area occupied by fixtures to 25 percent of the total ceiling area. (But a coffered ceiling may contain 100 percent lighted vaulted modules.)

Other Penetrations

Plasterboard (gypsum board) panels used so commonly for interior wall construction in modern buildings are fire-rated. UL and other labs make tests and assign fire ratings (in hours) to wall assemblies or constructions that make use of plasterboard. For instance, a wall made up of wood or metal studs with a single course of ⅝-in. plasterboard on each side of the studs would be assigned a 1-hr fire rating. A wall with two courses of ½-in. or ⅝-in. plasterboard on each side of the studs would be a 2-hr wall (Fig. 300-41). The assigned fire ratings

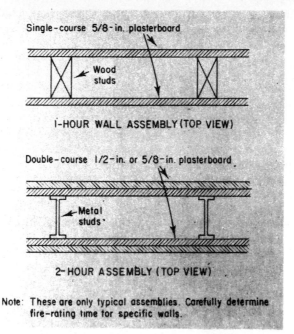

Single-course 5/8-in. plasterboard

Wood studs

I-HOUR WALL ASSEMBLY(TOP VIEW)

Double-course 1/2-in. or 5/8-in. plasterboard

Metal studs

2-HOUR ASSEMBLY (TOP VIEW)

Note: These are only typical assemblies. Carefully determine fire-rating time for specific walls.

Fig. 300-41. Wall assemblies using plasterboard are fire-rated by UL and others. (Sec. 300-21.)

are based on the thickness and number of courses of plasterboard. And the fire rating is for the wall assembly *without any penetrations into the wall.*

Because of the fire rating assigned to the assembly, any wall so constructed is fire-rated. The wall may be between rooms or between a room and a corridor or stairwell. And no distinction is made between an interior wall of an apartment, say, and a wall that separates one apartment from another. All wall assemblies using plasterboard are fire-rated and immediately raise concern over violation of Sec. 300-21 if any electrical equipment is recessed in the wall.

When any electrical equipment is installed as a penetration of a wall, there is the immediate question, Does this substantially increase the possible spread of fire or the spread of products of combustion (smoke and/or heated air)? Building inspectors and electrical inspectors have generally permitted installation of wall switches, thermostats, dimmers, and receptacles in boxes recessed in plasterboard walls. In single-family houses, the entire interior is not considered to be compartmented. It is assumed that individual rooms or areas are not normally closed off from each other and that fire or smoke spread would not be affected at all by those penetrations. The consensus has been that such small openings cut in the plasterboard do not violate the letter or intent of Sec. 300-21, although there is no specific **Code** rule that exempts any wall from the concern of Sec. 300-21.

In apartment houses, office buildings, and other multioccupancy buildings, however, inspectors could logically question use of wiring devices installed in common walls between apartments or between an apartment and a corridor or stairwell. Such walls are assumed to be between interior spaces that are normally closed off from each other by the main doors to the individual apartments. Fire and/or smoke spread, which is normally restricted by the closed doors, might be considered *substantially increased* by any penetrations of those fire-rated walls (Fig. 300-42). Although switch and receptacle boxes are usually accepted, use of a panelboard in a common wall has been rejected.

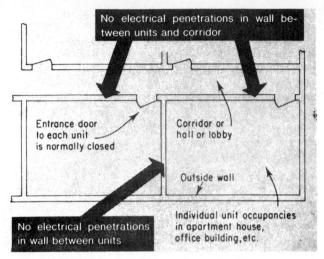

Fig. 300-42. Walls separating closed-off spaces must have maintained fire rating. (Sec. 300-21.)

For larger electrical equipment, such as panelboards, the same general analysis would apply. For interior walls of private houses or individual unit occupancies in apartment houses, hotels, dormitories, office buildings, and the like, a panel installed in a wall between two rooms or spaces that are normally *not* closed off from each other cannot "substantially" contribute to greater fire and/or smoke spread. *But,* panelboards and similar large equipment should normally not be installed in fire-rated walls between spaces that *are* closed off from each other by doors that are normally closed.

When it is necessary to install a panelboard or other large equipment in a wall between areas that are normally closed off from each other, a boxed recess in the wall should be constructed of the fire-rated plasterboard to maintain the fire rating of the wall (Fig. 300-43). This is also common practice for installing recessed enclosures for fire extinguishers in corridor walls and medicine cabinets mounted in walls between apartment units.

Another technique that has been used to maintain fire rating where a panelboard is installed in a wall between individual apartments is to glue pieces of plasterboard to the top, bottom, sides, and back of the recessed panel. In one particular job, this was done as a corrective measure where panelboards had first been installed in such walls without attention to maintaining the fire

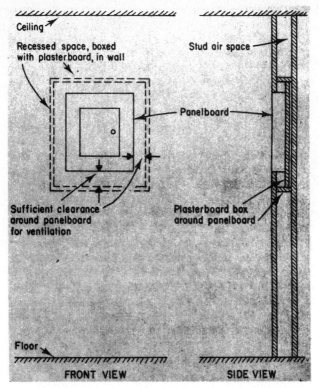

Fig. 300-43. Boxing of large-area penetrations has been required in fire walls. (Sec. 300-21.)

rating of the wall. But the use of plasterboard directly affixed to the panelboard surfaces could be considered an unauthorized modification of the panel that voids UL listing because of improper application.

300-22. Wiring in Ducts, Plenums, and Other Air-Handling Spaces. Part **(a)** of this section applies only to wiring in the types of ducts described.

Part **(b)** covers use of wiring methods and equipment within "ducts or plenums"—which are channels or chambers intended and used only for supply or return of conditioned air. Such "ducts or plenums" are sheet metal or other types of enclosures which are provided expressly for air handling and must be distinguished from "Other Space Used for Environmental Air"—such as the space between a suspended ceiling and the floor slab above it. Space of that type is covered by Part **(c)** of this section. The space between a raised floor (Fig. 300-44) and the slab below the raised floor is also covered by Part **(c)**, unless the air-handling raised floor is within a computer room. Part **(d)** states that an air-handling raised floor used for data processing circuits must comply with Art. 645. NFPA Standard 90A defines a duct system as "a continuous passageway for the transmission of air which, in addition to ducts, may include duct fittings, dampers, plenums, fans, and accessory air handling equipment." The word

Fig. 300-44. Space under a raised floor, which is commonly used for circuits to data processing equipment and provides for passage of conditioned air to the room and to the equipment is covered in part **(d)**. (Sec. 300-22.)

duct is not defined, but a plenum is defined as "an air compartment or chamber to which one or more ducts are connected and which forms part of an air distribution system."

Parts **(b)** and **(c)** of this section clearly limit acceptable wiring methods *ONLY* to the ones described. Part **(c)** permits use of totally enclosed, nonventilated, insulated busway in an air-handling ceiling space *provided* it is a non-plug-in type busway that cannot accommodate plug-in switches or breakers. This one specific busway wiring method was added for hung-ceiling space used for environmental air. Surface metal raceway or wireway with metal covers or solid-bottom metal cable tray with solid metal covers may be used in air-handling ceiling space provided that the raceway is accessible, such as above lift-out panels. The air-handling space under a raised floor in a data-processing location is covered by Art. 645 on electronic computer and data processing equipment.

Figure 300-45 shows wiring methods for use in an air-handling ceiling space.

The **Code** panel has made clear that they generally oppose nonmetallic wiring methods in ducts and plenums and in air-handling ceilings, except for nonmetallic cable assemblies that are specifically listed for such use. It is also the intent of the **Code** that cables with an outer nonmetallic jacket should not be permitted in ducts or plenums. Although the jacket material, usually PVC, would not propagate a fire, it would contribute to the smoke and provide additional flammable material in the air duct. The last paragraph of part **(c)** permits

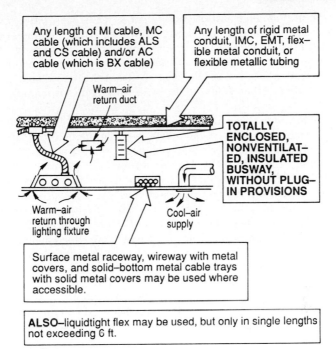

Any length of MI cable, MC cable (which includes ALS and CS cable) and/or AC cable (which is BX cable)

Any length of rigid metal conduit, IMC, EMT, flexible metal conduit, or flexible metallic tubing

Warm–air return duct

TOTALLY ENCLOSED, NONVENTILATED, INSULATED BUSWAY, WITHOUT PLUG–IN PROVISIONS

Warm–air return through lighting fixture

Cool–air supply

Surface metal raceway, wireway with metal covers, and solid–bottom metal cable trays with solid metal covers may be used where accessible.

ALSO–liquidtight flex may be used, but only in single lengths not exceeding 6 ft.

Fig. 300-45. Any wiring method other than these is a violation in air-handling space. (Sec. 300-22.)

use of nonmetallic equipment enclosures and wiring that are specifically UL-listed or classified for use in air-handling ceiling spaces.

In effect, the rules in parts **(b)** and **(c)** exclude from use in all air-handling spaces any wiring that is not metal-jacketed or metal-enclosed, to minimize the creation of toxic fumes due to burning plastic under fire conditions. Section 800-53(a) basically requires telephone, intercom, and other communications circuits to be wired with Type CMP cable or other types installed in compliance with Sec. 300-22 when such circuits are used in ducts or plenums or air-handling ceilings.

Wiring in air-handling space under raised floors in computer centers must use the wiring methods described in Sec. 645-5(d). Ventilation in the raised-floor space must be used only for the data processing area and the data processing equipment.

Although the rules of Sec. 300-22(c) apply only to air-handling spaces above suspended ceilings and beneath raised floors in other than computer rooms, such spaces are also subject to the general rules that apply to non-air-handling spaces. For a thorough understanding of this complex matter refer to these definitions in Art. 100: "accessible," "concealed," "exposed," and "readily accessible."

Because all those words or phrases are used in the **Code** and are critically important to applications of wiring methods and equipment, their definitions must be carefully studied and cross-referenced with each other, as well as related to Code rules using those words or phrases. Many common controversies about Code rules revolve around those words and phrases and interpretation of the definitions. Refer to the discussion on "suspended ceilings" given under the definition for "accessible" in Art. 100 of this handbook. In addition to that information, other rules relate to use above a suspended ceiling as follows:

1. All switches and CBs must be located so they may be operated from a readily accessible place, and the distance from the floor or platform up to the center of the handle in its highest position must not be over 6 ft 6 in. (Sec. 380-8). Exception No. 2 of that rule does permit switches to be installed at high locations that are not readily accessible, even above suspended ceilings, **but only unfused switches**, because use of a fused switch would violate Sec. 240-24 on ready accessibility of overcurrent devices (the fuses in the switch). However, Sec. 430-102 requires a motor disconnect switch to be in sight from the motor controller location. And Sec. 430-107 says one disconnecting means shall be readily accessible. That means *not* above a suspended ceiling, where it would *not* be readily accessible.

2. Section 430-102(b) permits a motor to be out of sight from the location of its controller, and there is no rule requiring that motor controllers be readily accessible. Motor controllers may be installed above suspended ceilings.

3. Section 450-13 requires transformers to be installed so they *are* readily accessible, but certain exceptions are made. Exception No. 1 permits dry-type transformers rated 600 V or less to be located "in the *open* on walls, columns, or structures"—without the need to be readily accessible. And Exception No. 2 permits dry-type transformers up to 600 V, 50 kVA, to be installed in "fire-resistant hollow spaces of buildings not permanently closed in by structure," provided the transformer is designed to have adequate ventilation for such installation. Refer to Sec. 450-13.

Air-Handling Ceilings

All the foregoing rules also apply to wiring and equipment installed above suspended ceilings in space used for air-conditioning purposes. But, in addition to those rules, the broad and detailed rules of Sec. 300-22(c) cover electrical installations in spaces above suspended ceilings when the space is used to handle environmental air. This section makes two basic determinations:

1. It lists all the wiring methods that are permitted in air-handling ceilings (which also may be used in nonair-handling ceiling spaces) and gives conditions and limitations for such use. This is a straightforward materials list which needs little or no interpretation (Fig. 300-45).

2. Section 300-22(c) further comments on other "electric equipment" that is permitted in such spaces. That refers to switches, starters, motors, etc. The basic condition that must be satisfied is that the wiring materials and other construction of the equipment must be suitable for the expected ambient temperature to which they will be subjected.

Application of that **Code** permission on use of "equipment" calls for substantial interpretation. The designer and/or installer must check carefully with equipment manufacturers and with inspection agencies to determine what is acceptable in air-handling space above a suspended ceiling. Practice in the field varies widely on this rule, and **Code** interpretation has proved difficult.

Exception No. 2 of this section recognizes the installation of motors and control equipment in air-handling ducts where such equipment has been specifically approved for the purpose. Equipment of this type is listed by Underwriters Laboratories Inc. and may be found in the *Electrical Appliance and Utilization Equipment List* under the heading "Heating and Ventilating Equipment."

Exception No. 3 is intended to exclude from the requirements those areas which may be occupied by people. Hallways and habitable rooms are being used today as portions of air-return systems, and while they have air of a heating or cooling system passing through them, the prime purpose of these spaces is obviously not air handling.

Exception No. 4 permits modular wiring systems to be used in air-handling spaces *provided* that the wiring system consists of metallic-jacketed cable assemblies and there is *not* a plastic outside sheath over the metal. See Fig. 300-46.

IN CEILING SPACE: COMPLETE SYSTEM OF PREWIRED CABLE LENGTHS WITH SNAP-IN CONNECTORS FOR FIXTURES AND SWITCHES

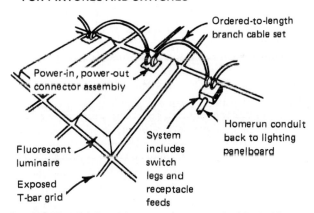

Fig. 300-46. Modular wiring systems, as recognized by Article 604, are permitted to be used in air-handling ceiling spaces.

Exception No. 5 permits Type NM cable to "pass through" a closed-in joist or stud space that is used for cold-air return, as shown in Fig. 300-47. This is allowed because NM cable is suitable to be used under the temperature and moisture conditions in such spaces, as used in "dwelling units," to which the Exception is limited.

Fig. 300·47. A joist space through which Type NM cable passes "perpendicular to the long dimension" of the space may be closed in to form a duct-like space for the cold-air return of a hot-air heating system—but only in a "dwelling unit."

ARTICLE 305. TEMPORARY WIRING

305·1. Scope. Although a temporary electrical system does not have to be made up with the detail and relative permanence that characterizes a so-called *permanent* wiring system, the specific rules of this article cover the only permissible ways in which a temporary wiring system may differ from a permanent system. Aside from the given permissions for variation from rules on permanent wiring, all temporary systems are required to comply in all other respects with **Code** rules covering permanent wiring (Fig. 305-1).

305·3. Time Constraints.   In part **(a)**, the words "maintenance" and "repair" indicate that the less rigorous methods of temporary wiring may be used and that all rules on temporary wiring must be observed wherever maintenance or repair work is in process. This expands the applicability of temporary wiring beyond new construction, remodeling work, or demolition.

Part **(b)** recognizes use of temporary wiring for seasonal or holiday displays and decorations, as shown in Fig. 305-2.

Part **(c)** of this section permits temporary wiring to be used for other than simple construction work. Such wiring, as covered in this article, may also be used during emergency conditions or for testing, experiments, or development activities. As the proposal for this **Code** rule noted:

> Were it not permissible to use temporary wiring methods for testing purposes, it would be impossible to check, before placing in service, many electrical installations. Likewise, emergency conditions would remain without electric power and lighting until permanent installation could be made.

Fig. 305·1. Temporary wiring is not an "anything goes" condition
and must comply with standard **Code** rules to prevent a rat-nest
condition which can pose hazard to life and property. (Sec. 305-1.)

However, part **(d)** of this section is aimed at assuring that the equipment and
circuits installed under this article are really "temporary" and not a back door
to low-quality permanent wiring systems.

305·4. General. Although part **(a)** requires a temporary *service* to satisfy all
the rules of Art. 230, part **(b)** recognizes use of temporary *feeders* that are single-
conductor building wire or single-conductor "cable assemblies" used as open
wiring (Fig. 305-3), multiconductor cable assemblies (Type NM, UF, etc.), or
multiconductor cord or cable of the type covered by Art. 400 for hard usage or
extra-hard usage "Flexible Cords and Cables"—which are not acceptable for
use as feeder or branch-circuit conductors of permanent wiring systems. Section 400-8 specifically prohibits use of such cords and cables "as a substitute for
the fixed wiring of a structure." As shown in Fig. 305-4, prewired portable
cables with plug and socket assemblies are available for power risers in conjunction with GFCI-protected branch-circuit centers, or cable can be run horizontally on a single floor to suit needs. GFCI breakers may be used in temporary panelboards interconnected with cable and feeding standard receptacles
in portable boxes, as shown in Fig. 305-5.

Section 305-4(c) requires temporary branch circuits to consist of single con-

Fig. 305-2. Temporary wiring techniques are permitted for 90 days for such "experimental" work as energy demand analysis. (Sec. 305-3.)

ductors in open wiring, multiconductor cable assemblies (Types NM and UF) or cords or cables covered in Table 400-4, provided that they originate in a panelboard or "an approved power outlet," which is one of the manufactured assemblies made for jobsite temporary wiring. As shown in Fig. 305-6, the temporary branch circuits for receptacle outlets may be part of a manufactured temporary system, which consists of cable harnesses and power centers (or outlets). Several variations of protection may be provided by such portable receptacle boxes, as shown in Fig. 305-6. Box 1 may have GFCI protection for its own receptacles without providing downstream protection. Box 2 may have the same protection as box 1 and in addition have GFCI protection for its 50-A outlet, thus providing protection for box 3. With this arrangement, box 1 will sense the ground fault from the worker at upper left and will trip, allowing boxes 2 and 3 to continue to provide power. Or, all three boxes could receive GFCI protection from a permanently mounted loadcenter feeding the 50-A receptacle outlet at upper left. In this case, the ground fault shown would interrupt the power to all boxes.

Section 305-6 makes it clear that only receptacles used under temporary job conditions require GFCI protection. The implication is that the nonmetallic-sheathed cable runs and pigtail connections traditionally associated with tem-

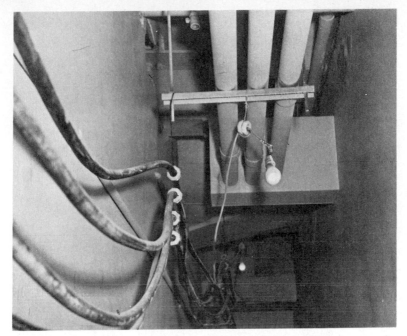

Fig. 305-3. Temporary feeders operating at not over 150 V to ground and where not subject to physical damage may be run as open conductors supported by insulators spaced not over 10 ft apart. (Sec. 305-4.)

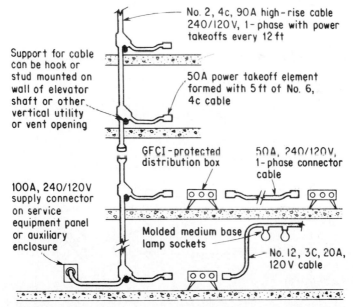

Fig. 305-4. Temporary feeders may be cord assemblies made especially for such use. (Sec. 305-4.)

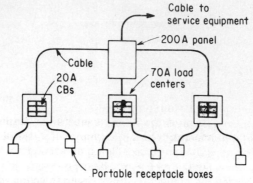

Fig. 305-5. Distribution for temporary power may utilize cable or raceway feeders. (Sec. 305-4.)

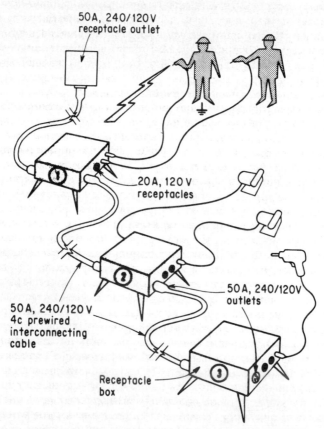

Fig. 305-6. Temporary branch circuits may be part of a manufactured system. (Sec. 305-4.)

porary power on the jobsite would not win awards for neatness and safety, but that once the permanent feeders and panelboards are in place and energized, the shock hazard is considerably reduced.

However, as long as portable tools are being used in damp locations in close proximity with grounded building steel and other conductive surfaces, the possibility of shock exists from faulty equipment whether it is energized from temporary or permanent circuits.

Standard panelboards used for temporary power on the jobsite may be fitted with GFCI circuit breakers for the protection of entire circuits, in accordance with the rules of Sec. 305-6. However, the many varieties of portable power distribution centers and modules have been developed with integral GFCI breakers protecting single-phase, 15- and 20-A, 120-V circuits. Other circuits (higher amperage, higher voltage, and 3-phase) are not required by the **NE Code** to have GFCI protection, and these usually are protected by standard overcurrent devices. A variety of cord sets are also available for use with GFCI-protected plug-in units to supply temporary lighting and receptacle outlets.

While a manufactured system of cable harnesses and power-outlet centers costs more than nonmetallic-sheathed cable runs and pigtail sockets, it is completely recoverable; and its cost can be written off over several jobs. From then on, with the exception of costs for setup and removal, storage, and transportation, much of the temporary power charges included in bids could be profit.

In previous **Code** editions, part **(c)** of this section required temporary wiring circuits to be "fastened at ceiling height every 10 feet." But now, if such circuits operate at not over 150 V to ground and are not subject to physical damage, the fourth sentence in this paragraph permits open-wiring temporary branch circuits to be run at any height "supported on insulators at intervals of not more than 10 feet." Open wiring must not be laid on the floor or ground.

In the interest of greater safety, part **(d)** prohibits use of both receptacles and lighting on the same temporary branch circuit on construction sites. The purpose is to provide complete separation of the lighting so that operation of an overcurrent device or a GFCI due to fault or overload of cord-connected tools will not simultaneously disconnect lighting (Fig. 305-7).

According to part **(e)**, every multiwire branch circuit must have a disconnect means that *simultaneously* opens all ungrounded wires of the temporary circuit. At the power outlet or panelboard supplying any temporary multiwire branch circuit (two hot legs and neutral or three hot legs and neutral), a multipole disconnect means must be used. Either a 2-pole or a 3-pole switch or circuit breaker would satisfy the rule; or single-pole switches of single-pole CBs may be used with "approved" handle ties to permit the single-pole devices to operate together (simultaneously) for each multiwire circuit, as shown for the multiwire lighting circuit in Fig. 305-7.

Part **(f)** requires lamps for general lighting on temporary wiring systems to be "protected from accidental contact or breakage." Protection must be provided by a suitable fixture or lampholder with a guard (Fig. 305-8). OSHA rules also require use of a suitable metal or plastic guard on each lamp. As shown in Fig. 305-9, commercial lighting strings provide illumination where required. Splice enclosure is equipped with integral support means, and a variety of lamp-guard styles provide protection for lamp bulbs.

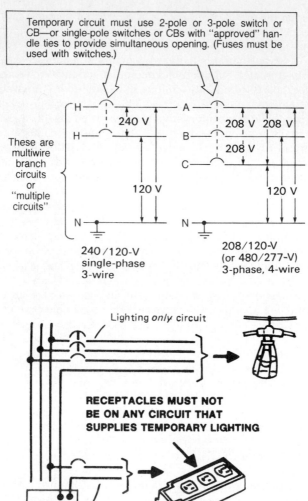

Temporary circuit must use 2-pole or 3-pole switch or CB—or single-pole switches or CBs with "approved" handle ties to provide simultaneous opening. (Fuses must be used with switches.)

These are multiwire branch circuits or "multiple circuits"

240 V

H
H
240 V
120 V

N

240/120-V
single-phase
3-wire

A
B
C
208 V 208 V
208 V
120 V

N

208/120-V
(or 480/277-V)
3-phase, 4-wire

Lighting *only* circuit

**RECEPTACLES MUST NOT
BE ON ANY CIRCUIT THAT
SUPPLIES TEMPORARY LIGHTING**

N

Receptacles *only* circuit

Fig. 305·7. This rule prevents loss of lighting when a defective, high-leakage, or overloaded Code-connected tool or appliance opens the branch-circuit protection of a circuit supplying one or more receptacles. (Sec. 305-4.)

Part **(f)** requires grounding of metal lamp sockets. The high exposure to shock hazard on construction sites makes use of ungrounded metal-shell sockets extremely hazardous. When they are used, the shell *must* be grounded by a conductor run with the temporary circuit.

In part **(g)**, splices or tap-offs are permitted to be made in temporary wiring circuits of cord or cable without the use of a junction box or other enclosure at

Fig. 305·8. A lampholder with a guard is proper protection for a lamp at any height in a temporary wiring system (above). Unguarded lamps at any height constitute a Code violation (right). (Sec. 305–4.)

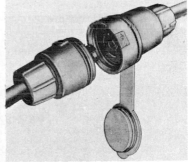

Special watertight plugs and connectors provide insurance against nuisance tripping caused by weather conditions on construction sites.

Fig. 305·9. Temporary lighting strings of cable and sockets are available from manufacturers. (Sec. 305-4.)

the point of splice or tap (Fig. 305-10). But this new permission applies only to nonmetallic cords and cables. A box, conduit body, or terminal fitting must be used when a change is made from a cord or cable circuit to a raceway system or to a metal-clad or metal-sheathed cable.

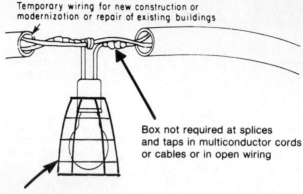

Fig. 305·10. Splices may be used without boxes for cord and cable runs on construction sites. (Sec. 305-4.)

Regulations in part **(h)** require protection of flexible cords and cables from damage due to pinching, abrasion, cutting, or other abuse.

305.6. Ground·Fault Protection for Personnel.   This section covers the rules that concern GFCI protection for all "125-V, single-phase, 15- and 20-A receptacle outlets" on construction sites. (Note that there are no requirements for GFCI protection of 240-V receptacles, 3-phase receptacles, or receptacles rated over 20 A.)

The basic rule of part **(a)** of this section says that ground-fault circuit inter-rupters (either GFCI circuit breakers or GFCI receptacles) must be used to pro-vide personnel protection for all receptacles of the designated rating—that "are not part of the permanent wiring of the building or structure" (Fig. 305-11). That phrase excludes from the need for GFCI protection all receptacle outlets that are intended to serve the occupants of the building after construction is com-pleted and are not simply installed as temporary outlets intended only for use by construction workers during the course of construction activities. Figure 305-12 shows two ways to satisfy the basic rule on GFCI for receptacles on construc-tion sites.

But one phrase in the **Code** rule significantly qualifies the *need* for GFCI protection of the designated receptacle outlets:

GFCI PROTECTION IS REQUIRED *ONLY* FOR THOSE RECEPTACLES THAT "ARE *IN USE* BY EMPLOYEES."

That phrase clearly limits required GFCI protection to receptacles that are actually being used at any particular time. Receptacles *not* in use do not have to be GFCI-protected. This means that *portable* GFCI protectors may be used

BASIC RULE

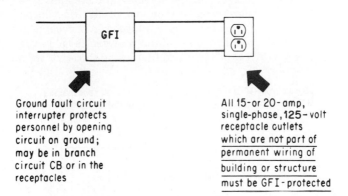

Ground fault circuit
interrupter protects
personnel by opening
circuit on ground;
may be in branch
circuit CB or in the
receptacles

All 15-or 20-amp,
single-phase,125-volt
receptacle outlets
which are not part of
permanent wiring of
building or structure
must be GFI-protected

Fig. 305·11. GFCI protection on construction sites for receptacles in use. (Sec. 305-6.)

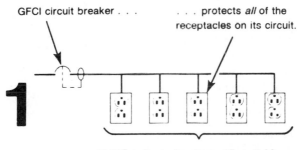

GFCI circuit breaker . . .   . . . protects *all* of the
                                    receptacles on its circuit.

All 125-volt, single-phase, 15- and 20-amp
receptacle outlets connected to
one or more branch circuits
with GFCI-CB protection

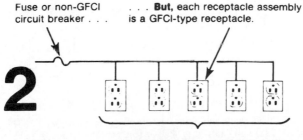

Fuse or non-GFCI   . . . **But,** each receptacle assembly
circuit breaker . . .   is a GFCI-type receptacle.

All receptacles on construction site
are GFCI type.

Fig. 305·12. Two ways to satisfy the basic rule on personnel shock protection at *temporary* receptacles on construction sites. (Sec. 305-6.)

at only those outlets being used (Fig. 305-13). There is no need to use GFCI breakers in the panel to protect "*all*" receptacles or to use all GFCI-type receptacles. This seems to seriously confuse the task of electrical inspection: If all cord-connected tools and appliances are unplugged from receptacles when the inspector comes on the job, then *none* of the receptacles is "in use" and none of them has to have GFCI protection and there is no **Code** violation.

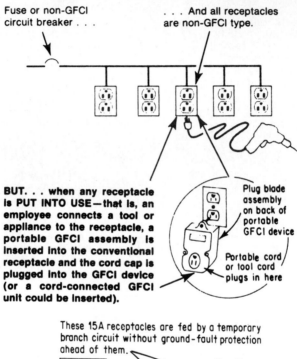

Fuse or non-GFCI circuit breaker . . .

. . . And all receptacles are non-GFCI type.

BUT. . . when any receptacle is PUT INTO USE—that is, an employee connects a tool or appliance to the receptacle, a portable GFCI assembly is inserted into the conventional receptacle and the cord cap is plugged into the GFCI device (or a cord-connected GFCI unit could be inserted).

Plug blade assembly on back of portable GFCI device

Portable cord or tool cord plugs in here

These 15A receptacles are fed by a temporary branch circuit without ground-fault protection ahead of them.

To other receptacles

Temporary panel

Wherever personnel are using cord-connected tools they plug in this portable ground-fault circuit interrupter having protected receptacles on its face for connection of the tools.

Fig. 305·13. Portable GFCI devices may be used to satisfy GFCI rule. (Sec. 305-6.)

Still another option for avoiding use of GFCI protection on construction sites is given in part **(b)** of this section. GFCI protection of receptacles *may be omitted* totally if a "written procedure" is established to assure testing and maintenance of "equipment grounding conductors" for receptacles, cord sets, and cord- and plug-connected tools and appliances used on the construction site (Fig. 305-14). In effect, the **NE Code** accepts such an equipment grounding con-

A written procedure must cover testing of...

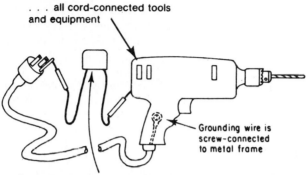

. . . all cord-connected tools and equipment

Grounding wire is screw-connected to metal frame

Continuity tester to assure connection of equipment grounding conductor

. . . and all receptacles, cord sets, and extension cords.

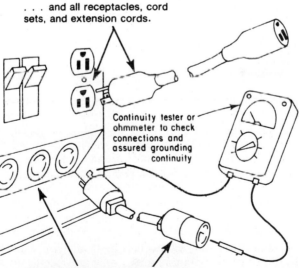

Continuity tester or ohmmeter to check connections and assured grounding continuity

15- and 20-amp locking plugs and receptacles are also covered under the assured grounding program.

Fig. 305-14. Assured grounding program eliminates the need for GFCI. (Sec. 305-6.)

ductor program as a measure that provides safety that is equivalent to the safety afforded by GFCI protection. GFCI protection is not required if all the following conditions are satisfied:

1. The inspection authority having jurisdiction over a construction site must approve a written procedure for an equipment grounding program.
2. The program must be enforced by a single designated person at the construction site.
3. "Electrical continuity" tests must be conducted on all equipment grounding conductors and their connections. The requirements on making such tests are vague, but they do call for:
   a. Testing of fixed receptacles where there is any evidence of damage.
   b. Testing of extension cords before they are first used and again where there is evidence of damage or after repairs have been made on such cords.
   c. Testing of all tools, appliances, and other equipment that connect by cord and plug before they are first used on a construction site, again any time there is any evidence of damage, after any repair, and at least every 3 months.

Obviously, those rules are very general and could be satisfied in either a rigorous, detailed manner or a fast, simple way that barely meets the qualitative criteria. The electrical contractor who has responsibility for the temporary wiring on any job site is the one to develop, write, and supervise the assured equipment grounding program, where that option is chosen as an alternative to use of GFCI protection. This whole **NE Code** approach to use of either GFCI or an "assured equipment grounding program" directly parallels the new OSHA approach to the matter of receptacle protection on construction sites.

ARTICLE 310. CONDUCTORS FOR GENERAL WIRING

310-2. Conductors. Although conductors are generally required by this rule to be insulated for the phase-to-phase voltage between any pair of conductors, bare conductors may be used for equipment grounding conductors, for bonding jumpers, for grounding electrode conductors, and for grounded neutral conductors (Secs. 230-22, 230-30, 230-41, 250-57, 250-60, 250-91, and 338-3).

The application shown in Fig. 310-1 is a commonly encountered violation of Sec. 310-2 because it involves an unauthorized use of a bare conductor. Section 250-60 permits grounding of ranges, cook-tops, and ovens to the neutral conductor *only* where "the grounded conductor (the neutral) is insulated" or is a bare neutral of an SE cable.

Section 310-2 states that "conductors shall be insulated," except when covered or bare conductors (see definition in Art. 100) are specifically approved in this **Code**. As noted above, several sections in Art. 250 state that grounding conductors may be insulated or bare. Article 230 cites several instances when a grounded conductor may be uninsulated or bare.

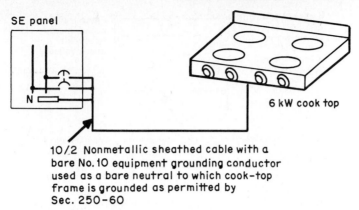

SE panel

N

6 kW cook top

10/2 Nonmetallic sheathed cable with a
bare No. 10 equipment grounding conductor
used as a bare neutral to which cook-top
frame is grounded as permitted by
Sec. 250-60

Fig. 310-1. This is a controversial application that violates Secs. 310-2 and 336-2. (Sec. 310-2.)

Section 338-3(b) permits use of Type SE cable without individual insulation on the grounded circuit conductor to be used as a branch circuit for a range, a wall oven, a cook-top, or a clothes dryer if such a cable originates at the service equipment panel.

Nonmetallic-sheathed cable Types NM and NMC are covered in Art. 336 and do not enjoy the same status as Type SE cable does in Sec. 338-3(b). To the contrary, Sec. 336-25 states: "In addition to the insulated conductors, the [NM or NMC] cable shall be permitted to have an approved size of insulated or bare conductor for equipment grounding purposes *only.*" Use of the bare conductor as a neutral in addition to a grounding conductor would be a violation of Sec. 336-25.

The same evaluation would apply to UF cable, because Sec. 339-3(a) (4) requires UF cable to comply with the provisions of Art. 336 when used for interior wiring as a nonmetallic-sheathed cable. The bare grounding conductor in a Type NM, NMC, or UF cable cannot be used as a neutral conductor.

Although the basic rule of this section requires conductors to be insulated, a note refers to Sec. 250-152 on the use of solidly grounded neutral conductors in high-voltage systems. As an exception to the general rule that conductors must be insulated, Sec. 250-152 does permit a neutral conductor of a solidly grounded "Y" system to have insulation rated at only 600 V (Fig. 310-2). It also points out that a bare copper neutral may be used for service-entrance conductors or for direct buried feeders, and bare copper or copper-clad aluminum may be used for overhead sections of outdoor circuits.

Of course, for such high-voltage systems, the phase legs—the ungrounded conductors—must be insulated for the circuit phase voltage. It is interesting, however, that there is no specific **Code** rule that requires insulation of any circuit to be rated for phase-to-phase voltage. **Code** rules do not distinguish between phase-to-phase voltage and phase-to-neutral voltage on grounded systems, with respect to insulation. Thus, the use of circuit conductors with insu-

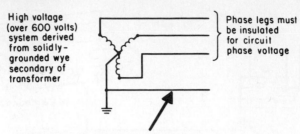

High voltage
(over 600 volts)
system derived
from solidly-
grounded wye
secondary of
transformer

} Phase legs must
be insulated
for circuit
phase voltage

Solidly grounded neutral conductor must have insulation
rated for at least 600 volts, although a bare copper
neutral may be used for SE conductors or for direct-
buried feeders, and bare copper or aluminum may be
used for overhead parts of outdoor circuits.

Fig. 310-2. A note refers to neutral conductors of solidly grounded
high-voltage systems (Sec. 250-152). (Sec. 310-2.)

lation rated only for phase-to-neutral voltage would not constitute a violation
of any specific Code rule, and such practice is used on high-voltage systems.

310-3. Stranded Conductors. No. 8 and larger conductors must be stranded
when they are installed in conduit, EMT, or any other "raceway." The use of
an insulated or stranded No. 8 copper conductor is required for the equipment
bonding conductor required by Sec. 680-20(b)(1). But only a solid No. 8 copper
conductor is required by Sec. 680-22(b) at swimming pools for bonding together
noncurrent-carrying metal parts of pool equipment—metal ladder, diving
board stands, pump motor frame, lighting fixtures in wet niches, etc.

310-4. Conductors in Parallel. The requirements of Sec. 310-4 for conductors
in parallel recognize copper, copper-clad aluminum, and aluminum conductors
in sizes 1/0 and larger. Also, this section makes it clear that the rules for paralleling conductors apply to grounding conductors (except for sizing which is
accomplished in accordance with Sec. 250-95) when they are used with conductors in multiple.

Conductors that are permitted to be used in parallel (in multiple) include
"phase" conductors, "neutral" conductors, and "grounded circuit" conductors.
In the places where this section describes parallel makeup of circuits, a
"grounded circuit conductor" is identified along with "phase" and "neutral"
conductors to extend the same permission for paralleling to grounded legs of
corner-grounded delta systems.

This section recognizes the use of conductors in sizes 1/0 and larger for use
in parallel under the conditions stated, to allow a practical means of installing
large-capacity feeders and services. Paralleling of conductors relies on a number of factors to ensure equal division of current, and thus all these factors must
be satisfied in order to ensure that none of the individual conductors will
become overloaded.

When conductors are used in parallel, *all* the conductors making up *each
phase, neutral, or grounded* circuit conductor must satisfy the five conditions of
the second paragraph in this section. Those characteristics—same length, same

conductor material (copper or aluminum), same size, same insulation, and same terminating device—apply only to the paralleled conductors making up each phase or neutral of a parallel-makeup circuit. All the conductors of any phase or the neutral must satisfy the rule, but phase "A" conductors (all of which must be the same length, same size, etc.) may be different in length, material, size, etc., from the conductors making up phase "B" or phase "C" or the neutral. But, all phase "B" conductors must be the same length, same size, etc.; phase "C" conductors must all be the same; and neutral conductors must all be alike (Fig. 310-3). As the last sentence in the fine-print note explains, it is not the intent of this **Code** rule to require that conductors of one phase be the same as those of another phase or of the neutral. The only concern for safe operation of a par-

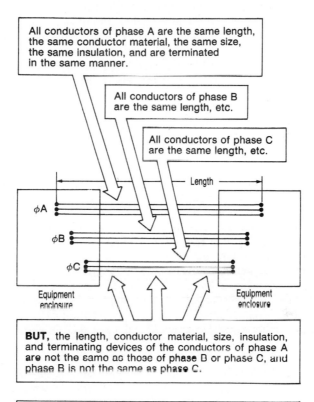

All conductors of phase A are the same length, the same conductor material, the same size, the same insulation, and are terminated in the same manner.

All conductors of phase B are the same length, etc.

All conductors of phase C are the same length, etc.

Length

φA

φB

φC

Equipment enclosure

Equipment enclosure

BUT, the length, conductor material, size, insulation, and terminating devices of the conductors of phase A are not the same as those of phase B or phase C, and phase B is not the same as phase C.

NOTE: This shows three conductors per phase. All nine conductors may be used in a single conduit with their ampacities derated to 70% of the value shown in Table 310-16. Or, three conduits may be used, with a phase A, B and C conductor in each, and no derating would be required.

Fig. 310·3. This is the basic rule on conductors used for parallel circuit makeup. (Sec. 310-4.)

allel-makeup circuit is that all the conductors in parallel per phase leg (neutral, or grounded conductor) will evenly divide the load current and thereby prevent overloading of any one of the conductors. Of course, the realities of material purchase and application and good design practice will dictate that *all* the conductors of all phases and neutral will use the same conductor material, will have the same insulation, will have as nearly the same length as possible to prevent voltage drop from causing objectionable voltage unbalance on the phases, and will be terminated in the same way. The size of conductors may vary from phase to phase or in the neutral, depending upon load currents.

Figure 310-4 shows two examples of parallel-conductor circuit makeup. The photo at bottom shows six conductors used per phase and neutral to obtain 2,000-A capacity per phase, which simply could not be done without parallel conductors per phase leg. Note that a fusible limiter lug is used to terminate each individual conductor. Although limiter lugs are required by the NEC only as used in Sec. 450-6(a) (3), they may be used to protect each conductor of any parallel circuit against current in excess of the ampacity of the particular size of conductor. The CB or fuses on such circuits are rated much higher than the ampacity of each conductor.

Where large currents are involved, it is particularly important that the separate phase conductors be located close together to avoid excessive voltage drop and ensure equal division of current. It is also essential that each phase and the neutral, and grounding wires, if any, be run in each conduit even where the conduit is of nonmetallic material.

The sentence just before the FPN is this section calls for the same type of raceway or enclosure for conductors in parallel in separate raceways or cables. The impedance of the circuit in a nonferrous raceway will be different from the same circuit in a ferrous raceway or enclosure. See Sec. 300-20.

From the Code tables of current-carrying capacities of various sizes of conductors, it can be seen that small conductor sizes carry more current per circular mil of cross section than do large conductors. This results from rating conductor capacity according to temperature rise. The larger a cable, the less is the radiating surface per circular mil of cross section. Loss due to "skin effect" (apparent higher resistance of conductors to alternating current than to direct current) is also higher in the larger conductor sizes. And larger conductors cost more per ampere than smaller conductors.

All the foregoing factors point to the advisability of using a number of smaller conductors in multiple to get a particular carrying capacity, rather than using a single conductor of that capacity. In many cases, multiple conductors for feeders provide distinct operating advantages and are more economical than the equivalent-capacity single-conductor makeup of a feeder. But, it should be noted, the reduced overall cross section of conductor resulting from multiple conductors instead of a single conductor per leg produces higher resistance and greater voltage drop than the same length as a single conductor per leg. Voltage drop may be a limitation.

Figure 310-5 shows a typical application of copper conductors in multiple, with the advantages of such use. Where more than three conductors are installed in a single conduit, the ampacity of each conductor must be derated

Multiple conductors (two in parallel for each phase leg) are used for normal and emergency feeder through this automatic transfer switch.

Six conductors in parallel make up each phase leg and the neutral of this feeder. Fusible limiter lug on each conductor, although not required by Code on other than transformer tie circuits, is sized for the conductor to protect against division of current among the six conductors that would put excessive current on any conductor.

Fig. 310-4. These are examples of circuit makeup using conductors in parallel. (Sec. 310-4.)

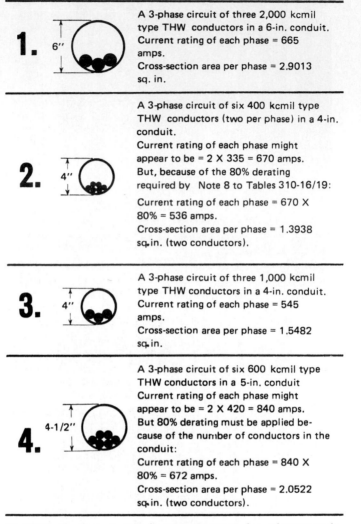

1. 6″

A 3-phase circuit of three 2,000 kcmil type THW conductors in a 6-in. conduit. Current rating of each phase = 665 amps.
Cross-section area per phase = 2.9013 sq. in.

2. 4″

A 3-phase circuit of six 400 kcmil type THW conductors (two per phase) in a 4-in. conduit.
Current rating of each phase might appear to be = 2 X 335 = 670 amps. But, because of the 80% derating required by Note 8 to Tables 310-16/19:

Current rating of each phase = 670 X 80% = 536 amps.
Cross-section area per phase = 1.3938 sq. in. (two conductors).

3. 4″

A 3-phase circuit of three 1,000 kcmil type THW conductors in a 4-in. conduit. Current rating of each phase = 545 amps.
Cross-section area per phase = 1.5482 sq. in.

4. 4-1/2″

A 3-phase circuit of six 600 kcmil type THW conductors in a 5-in. conduit
Current rating of each phase might appear to be = 2 X 420 = 840 amps. But 80% derating must be applied because of the number of conductors in the conduit:
Current rating of each phase = 840 X 80% = 672 amps.
Cross-section area per phase = 2.0522 sq. in. (two conductors).

Fig. 310·5. The above circuit makeups represent typical considerations in the application of multiple-conductor circuits. (Sec. 310-4.)

from the ampacity value shown in **NEC** Table 310-16. The four circuit makeups show:

1. Without ampacity derating because there are more than three conductors in the conduit, circuit 2 would be equivalent to circuit 1.
2. A circuit of six 400 kcmils can be made equivalent in ampacity to a circuit of three 2,000 kcmils by dividing the 400s between two conduits (3 conductors/3-in. conduit). If three different phases are used in each of two 3-

in. conduits for this circuit, the multiple circuit would not require ampacity derating to 80 percent, and its 670-A rating would exceed the 665-A rating of circuit 1.

3. Circuit 2 is almost equivalent to circuit 3 in ampacity.
4. Circuit 4 is equivalent to circuit 1 in ampacity, but uses less conductor copper and a smaller conduit. And the advantages are obtained even with the ampacity derating for conduit fill.

Except where the conductor size is governed by conditions of voltage drop, it is seldom economical to use conductors of sizes larger than 1,000 kcmil, because above this size the increase in ampacity is very small in proportion to the increase in the size of the conductor. Thus, for a 50 percent increase in the conductor size, i.e., from 1,000,000 to 1,500,000 cmil, the ampacity of a Type THW conductor increases only 80 A, or less than 15 percent, and for an increase in size from 1,000,000 to 2,000,000 cmil, a 100 percent increase, the ampacity increases only 120 A, or about 20 percent. In any case where single conductors larger than 500,000 cmil would be required, it is worthwhile to compute the total installation cost using single conductors and the cost using two (or more) conductors in parallel.

The next-to-last paragraph of Sec. 310-4 warns that when multiple conductors are used per circuit phase leg, they may require more space at equipment terminals to bend and install the conductors. Refer to Sec. 373-6.

Figure 310-6 shows an interesting application of parallel conductors. A 1,200-A riser is made up of three conduits, each carrying three phases and a neutral. At the basement switchboard, the 1,200-A circuit of three conductors per phase plus three conductors for the neutral originates in a bolted-pressure switch with a 1,200-A fuse in each of the three phase poles. Because the total of 12 conductors make up a *single* 3-phase, 4-wire circuit, a 400-A, 3-phase, 4-wire tap-off must tap all the conductors in the junction box at top. That is, the three phase A legs (one from each conduit) must be skinned and bugged together and then the phase A tap made from that common point to one of the lugs on the 400-A CB. Phase B and phase C must be treated the same way—as well as the neutral. The method shown in the photo was selected by the installer on the basis that the conductors in the right-hand conduit are tapped on this floor, the center-conduit conductors tapped to a 400-A CB on the floor above, and the left-conduit conductors tapped to a 400-A CB on the floor above that. But such a hookup can produce excessive current on some of the 500 kcmils. Because it does not have the parallel conductors of equal length at points of load-tap, the currents will not divide equally, and this is a violation of the second paragraph of Sec. 310-4, which calls for parallel conductors to "be the same length."

Exception No. 1 of this section clearly indicates long-time **Code** acceptance of paralleling conductors smaller than No. 1/0 for use in traveling cables of elevators, dumbwaiters, and similar equipment.

Exception No. 2 of Sec. 310-4 permits parallel-circuit makeup using conductors smaller than 1/0—but *all the conditions given must be observed.*

This Exception permits use of smaller conductors in parallel for circuit applications where it is necessary to reduce conductor capacitance effect or to

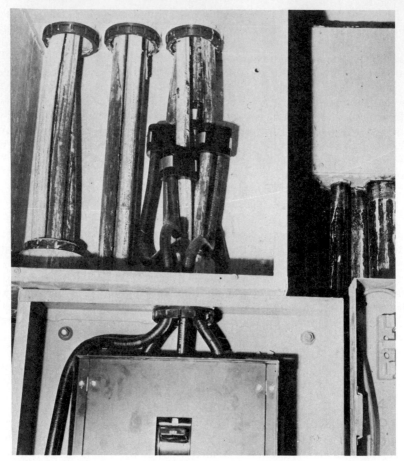

Fig. 310-6. A 1,200-A circuit of three sets of four 500 kcmil conductors (top) is tapped by a single set of 500 kcmils to a 400-A CB (bottom) that feeds an adjacent meter center in an apartment house. This was ruled a violation because the tap must be made from all the conductors of the 1,200-A circuit. (*Note:* The conduits feeding the splice box at top are behind the CB enclosure at bottom.) (Sec. 310-4.)

reduce voltage drop over long circuit runs. As it was argued in the proposal for this Exception—

If a No. 14 conductor, for example, is adequate to carry some load of not more than the 15-amp rating of the wire, there can be no reduction in safety by using two No. 14 wires per circuit leg to reduce voltage drop to acceptable limits—with a 15-amp fuse or CB pole protecting each pair of No. 14s making up each leg of the circuit.

Where conductors are used in parallel in accordance with this Exception, the rule requires that *all* the conductors be installed in the same raceway or cable. And that will dictate application of the last sentence of Sec. 310-4: "Conductors installed in parallel *shall* comply with the provisions of Article 310 Note 8,

Notes to Ampacity Tables of 0 to 2000 Volts.." Thus a single-phase, 2-wire control circuit made up of two No. 14s for each of the two legs of the circuit would have to be considered as four conductors in a conduit, and the "ampacity" of each No. 14 would be reduced to 80 percent of the value shown in Table 310-16. If TW wires are used for the circuit described, the ampacity of each is no longer the value of 20 A, as shown in Table 310-16. With four of them in a conduit, each would have an ampacity of 0.8 × 20, or 16 A. Then using a 15-A fuse or CB pole for each pair of No. 14s would properly protect the conductors and would also comply with the "dagger" footnote of Table 310-16, which says that No. 14 must not have overcurrent protection greater than 15 A. See Fig. 310-7.

Parallel makeup with smaller than 1/0 conductors

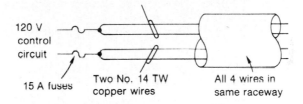

120 V control circuit

15 A fuses   Two No. 14 TW copper wires   All 4 wires in same raceway

From Table 310-16, No. 14 TW copper has ampacity of 20.

"Ampacity reduction" from Note 8 to table:
20 amps × 0.8 = 16 amps.

15-AMP FUSES PROPERLY PROTECT THE NO. 14s AND SATISFY FOOTNOTE TO TABLE 310-16.

Fig. 310-7. Overcurrent protection must be rated not in excess of the ampacity of one conductor when conductors smaller than No. 1/0 are used in parallel. (Sec. 310-4.)

Exception No. 3 permits circuits operating at frequencies of 360 Hz or higher to use conductors smaller than 1/0 in parallel. Exception No. 3 permits parallel use of conductors smaller than 1/0 for circuits operating at 360 Hz or higher frequencies, provided that all the wires are in the same conduit, the ampacity of each wire is adequate to carry the entire current that is divided among the parallel wires, and the rating of the circuit protective device does not exceed the ampacity of any one of the wires. Such use of small conductors in parallel is very effective in reducing inductive reactance and "skin effect" in high-frequency circuits. Interweaving of the multiple wires per phase and neutral produces greater mutual cancellation of the magnetic fields around the wires and thereby lowers inductance and skin effect. Typical application of such usage is made for the 400-Hz circuits that are standard in the aerospace and aircraft industry.

310-6. Shielding.   The effect of this Code rule is to require all conductors operating over 2 kV to be shielded, *unless* the conductor is UL-listed for operation
unshielded at voltages above 2 kV. Because 2,300-V delta (which is over 2 kV)
is the lowest general-purpose, high-voltage circuit in use today, unlisted conductors *must* be shielded for such circuits and any other voltages above that—
such as 4,160/2,300-V, 3-phase, 4-wire wye (grounded or ungrounded neutral).
But note this—UL does list 5-kV unshielded conductors for use in accordance
with Sec. 310-6, Table 310-63, and other Code rules (Fig. 310-8).

Fig. 310-8. A nonshielded conductor (arrow) is permitted for use
on a 2,300-V circuit (phase-to-neutral), as shown here, *only* if the
conductor is listed by UL or another national test lab and approved
for use without electrostatic shielding. (Sec. 310-6.)

UL also lists shielded polyethylene insulated conductors up to 35 kV. And,
in accordance with NE Code Table 310-64, UL has been listing Type RHH insulated conductors (rubber or cross-linked polyethylene insulation) with electrostatic shielding for operation up to 5 kV.

In addition to applicable NE Code, Insulated Power Cable Engineers Association (IPCEA), and UL data on use of cable shielding, manufacturers' data
should be consulted to determine the need for shielding on the various types
and constructions of available cables.

Shielding of high-voltage cables protects the conductor assembly against surface discharge or burning (due to corona discharge in ionized air) which can
be destructive to the insulation and jacketing. It does this by confining and distributing stress in the insulation and eliminating charging current drain to intermittent grounds. It also prevents ionization of any tiny air spaces at the surface
of the insulation by confining electrical stress to the insulation. Shielding,

which is required by this **Code** rule to be effectively grounded, increases safety to human life by eliminating the shock hazard presented by the external surface of unshielded cables. By preventing electrical discharges from cable surfaces to ground, shielding also reduces fire or explosive hazards and minimizes any radio interference high-voltage circuits might cause.

Electrostatic shielding of cables makes use of both nonmetallic and metallic materials. As shown in accompanying sketches of typical cable assemblies, semiconductive tapes or extruded coverings of semiconductive materials are combined with metal shielding to perform the shielding function. Metallic shielding may be done with:

1. A copper shielding tape wrapped over a semiconducting shielding of nonmetallic tape that is applied over the conductor insulation (Fig. 310-9)
2. A concentric wrapping of bare wires over a semiconducting, nonmetallic jacket over the conductor insulation (Fig. 310-10)

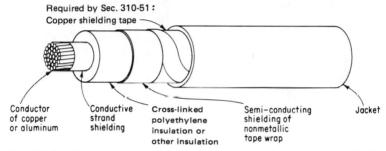

Fig. **310-9.** A flat copper tape spiraled over the insulation is an electrostatic shield. (Sec. 310-6.)

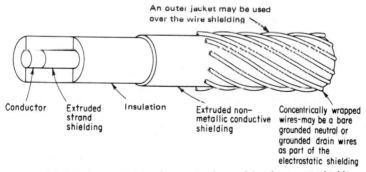

Fig. **310-10.** Wires, instead of metal tape, are also used for electrostatic shielding (URD and UD type). (Sec. 310-6.)

3. Bare wires embedded in the semiconducting, nonmetallic jacket that is applied over the insulation (Fig. 310-11)
4. A metal sheath over the conductor insulation, as with lead-jacketed cable

For many years, high-voltage shielded power cables for indoor distribution circuits rated from 5 to 15 kV were of the type using copper tape shielding and

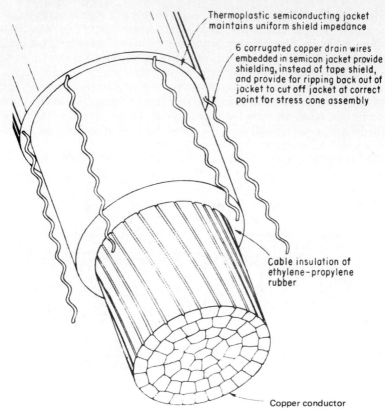

Thermoplastic semiconducting jacket maintains uniform shield impedance

6 corrugated copper drain wires embedded in semicon jacket provide shielding, instead of tape shield, and provide for ripping back out of jacket to cut off jacket at correct point for stress cone assembly

Cable insulation of ethylene-propylene rubber

Copper conductor

Fig. 310·11. Wires embedded in semiconducting jacket form another type of shielding. (Sec. 310-6.)

an outer overall jacket. But in recent years, cables shielded by concentric-wrapped bare wires have also come into widespread use—particularly for underground outdoor systems up to 15 kV. These latter cables are the ones commonly used for underground residential distribution (called "URD"). Such a conductor is shown in Fig. 310-10.

In addition to use for URD (directly buried with the concentric-wire shield serving as the neutral or second conductor of the circuit), concentric-wire-shielded cables are also available for indoor power circuits, such as in conduit, with a nonmetallic outer jacket over the concentric wires. Such cable assemblies are commonly called "drain-wire-shielded" cable rather than "concentric-neutral" cable because the bare wires are used only as part of the electrostatic shielding and not also as a neutral. Smaller-gage wires are used where they serve only for shielding and not as a neutral.

Figure 310-11 shows drain-wire-shielded high-voltage cable with electrostatic shielding by means of drain wires *embedded* in a semiconducting jacket over the conductor insulation. This type of drain-wire-shielded conductor is designed to be used for high-voltage circuits in conduit or duct for commercial and industrial distribution as an alternative to tape-shielded cables. For the same conductor size, this type of embedded drain-wire-shielded cable has a smaller outside diameter and lighter weight than a conventional tape-shielded cable. For the drain-wire cable the assembly difference reduces installation labor, permits reduced bending radius for tight conditions and easier pulling in conduit, and affords faster terminations (with stress cones) and splices. An extremely important result of the smaller overall cross-section area (csa) of the drain-wire-shielded cable is the chance to use smaller conduits—with lower material and labor costs—when conduit is filled to 40 percent of its csa based on the actual cable csa, as covered by Note 4 to the tables in Chap. 9 of the **NE Code**.

Another consideration in conductor assemblies is that of strand shielding. As shown in Fig. 310-12, a semiconducting material is tape-wrapped or extruded

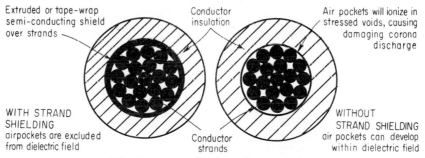

Extruded or tape-wrap semi-conducting shield over strands

Conductor insulation

Air pockets will ionize in stressed voids, causing damaging corona discharge

WITH STRAND SHIELDING airpockets are excluded from dielectric field

Conductor strands

WITHOUT STRAND SHIELDING air pockets can develop within dielectric field

Fig. 310-12. Strand shielding is part of the overall electrostatic shielding system on the conductor. (Sec. 310-6.)

onto the conductor strands and prevents voids between the insulation and the strands, thereby reducing possibilities of corona cutting on the inside of the insulation.

Refer to Sec. 710-6 on terminating and grounding shielded conductors.

310-7. Direct Burial Conductors. The second sentence in this section appears to require shielding only on direct burial cables rated above 2,000 V, although a rule in Sec. 710-3(b) says without reference to voltage that "Nonshielded cables shall be installed" in conduit, which, in effect, prohibits direct burial of any nonshielded cables rated over 600 V (see Fig. 310-13). Correlation between this section and Sec. 710-3 must be carefully made, because the Exception to Sec. 310-7 recognizes "nonshielded multiconductor cables" for direct burial in ratings up to 5 kV provided that the cable has an overall metallic sheath or armor.

This section also requires direct burial high-voltage cables to be "identified for such use," which, in effect, means listed by a test organization or designated by the inspection agency as suitable for direct burial.

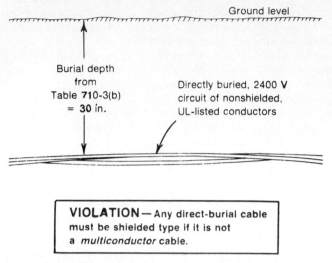

Fig. 310-13. This application is covered by both Sec. 310-7 and Sec. 710-3(b). (Sec. 310-7.)

Code rules on underground use of conductors rated up to 600 V are given in Sec. 310-8.

310-8. Wet Locations.   Any conductor used in a "wet location" (refer to the definition under "location" in Art. 100) *must* be one of the designated types— each of which has the letter "W" in its marking to indicate suitability to **wet** locations. Any conduit run underground is assumed to be subject to water infiltration and is, therefore, a *wet location,* requiring use of only the listed conductor types within the raceway.

Figure 310-14 shows a clear violation of the last sentence of Sec. 310-8. In the photo, conductors marked RHW are run, from the junction box below the magnetic contactor, directly buried in the ground. Although Type RHW is suitable for wet locations, it is not approved for direct burial. If, however, the conductors were of the type that is marked "RHW-USE"—that is, it is listed and recognized as *both* a single-conductor RHW and a single-conductor Type USE (underground service entrance) cable—then such conductors would satisfy this section.

Where Sec. 310-7 refers specifically to "direct burial conductors," requires that they be "identified," and is directed at high-voltage cables, the rule in this section (which applies to conductors rated up to 600 V) simply says "conductors" for direct burial must be "listed"—which means certified by some kind of test lab—and not just "identified"—which means evaluated by other than the manufacturer but not necessarily "listed."

UF cable is acceptable for direct earth burial. Although Sec. 338-1(b) says USE cable is OK for "underground use," it does not say it is OK for direct burial. But the UL *Electrical Construction Materials Directory* (Green Book) notes

Fig. 310-14. Bundle of conductors (arrow) are Type RHW individual building conductors that would be suitable for installation in conduit underground but are not marked "USE"; and their use here, run directly buried to outdoor lighting poles, constitutes a violation of the last sentence of Sec. 310-8. (Sec. 310-8.)

that listed USE cable is recognized for "burial directly in the earth" (Fig. 310-15).

Besides UF and USE, then, what other cables can be directly buried? Section 334-3(5) does recognize MC cable for direct burial "when identified for such use." Sections 330-3(5) and (9) recognize MI cable for direct burial. Note that Sec. 330-3(5) permits MI in "fill" below grade.

For burial-depth requirements on directly buried cables, refer to Sec. 300-5, Table 300-5, and part (i) of that section. Cables approved for direct earth burial must be installed a minimum of 24 in. below grade, as given in Table 300-5, or at least 30 in. below grade for high-voltage cables as covered in Table 710-3(b), with its Exceptions.

Direct burial conductors should be trench-laid without crossovers; slightly "snaked" to allow for possible earth settlement, movement, or heaving due to frost action; and have cushions and covers of sand or screened fill to protect conductors against sharp objects in trenches or backfill. Figure 310-16 shows some recommended details on installing direct burial cables. Moreover, when conductors are routed beneath roadways or railroads, they should be additionally protected by conduits. And, to guard against damage which might occur during future digging, conductors in soft fill should be covered by concrete slabs or treated planks.

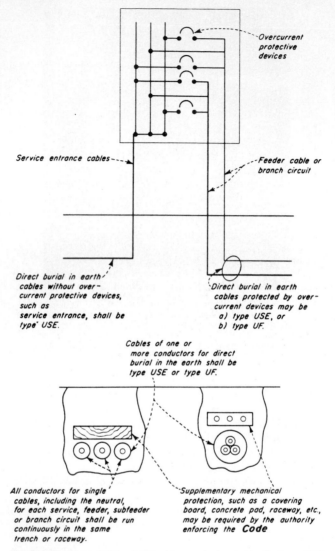

Overcurrent protective devices

Service entrance cables

Feeder cable or branch circuit

Direct burial in earth cables without over-current protective devices, such as service entrance, shall be type USE.

Direct burial in earth cables protected by over-current devices may be
a) type USE, or
b) type UF.

Cables of one or more conductors for direct burial in the earth shall be type USE or type UF.

All conductors for single cables, including the neutral, for each service, feeder, subfeeder or branch circuit shall be run continuously in the same trench or raceway.

Supplementary mechanical protection, such as a covering board, concrete pad, raceway, etc., may be required by the authority enforcing the **Code**

Fig. 310-15. Types USE and UF cables are designated by the letter "U" for underground use. (Sec. 310-8.)

Where prewired cable-in-conduit is being buried, it also should be slightly snaked, although it is unnecessary to provide sand beds or screen the backfill. Inasmuch as these complete conductor-raceway assemblies can be delivered on reels in specified factory-cut lengths, installation is simplified and expedited.

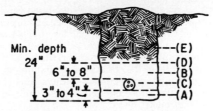

Min. depth
24"
6" to 8"
3" to 4"

---(E)
---(D)
---(B)
---(C)
---(A)

A—Soft bed of sand or screened fill.

B—Blanket of sand or screened fill 6 in. to 8 in. above top of cable.

C—Cable "snaked" slightly in trench for slack when earth settles. Keep single-conductor cables uniformly apart about 6 in. in trench. Avoid cable crossovers. Keep cable below frost line.

D—Add protective slab (creosoted plank, etc.) on sand fill in areas where future digging might occur. Enclose cable in pipe or conduit under highways or rail tracks.

E—Normal backfill.

Fig. 310-16. This satisfies the intent of Sec. 300-5(f). (Sec. 310-8.)

310-9. Corrosive Conditions. Figure 310-17 shows how conductors are marked to indicate that they are gasoline- and oil-resistant, such as Type THHN-THWN, for use in gasoline stations and similar places.

TYPE THHN 600 V OIL AND GASOLINE RESISTANT

Fig. 310-17. Typical marking indicates suitability of conductors for use under unusual environmental conditions. (Sec. 310-9.)

310-10. Temperature Limitation of Conductors. This requirement is extremely important and is the basis of safe operation of insulated conductors. As shown in Table 310-13, conductors have various ratings—60°C, 75°C, 90°C, etc.

Since Tables 310-16 through 310-19 are based on an assumed ambient (surrounding) temperature of 30°C (86°F) (or 40°C), conductor ampacities are based on the ambient temperature plus the heat (I^2R) produced by the conductor (wire) while carrying current. Therefore, the type of insulation used on the conductor determines the maximum permitted conductor ampacity.

example A No. 3/0 THW copper conductor for use in a raceway has an ampacity of 200 according to Table 310-16. In a 30°C ambient the conductor is subjected to this temperature when it carries *no* current. Since a THW-insulated conductor is rated at 75°C, this leaves 45°C (75 minus 30) for increased temperature due to current flow. If the ambient temperature exceeds 30°C, the conductor maximum load-current rating must be reduced proportionally (see "Correction Factors" at the bottom of Table 310-16) so that the total temperature (ambient plus conductor temperature rise due to current flow) will not exceed the temperature rating of the conductor insulation (60°C, 75°C, etc.). For the same reason, conductor maximum load-current ratings must be reduced below the ampacity values where more than three conductors are contained in a raceway or cable (see Note 8 to Tables 310-16 through 310-19).

While it can be shown that smaller conductors, such as Nos. 14 and 12 60°C-insulated conductors, will not reach 60°C at their assigned ampacities (Table 310-16) in a 30°C ambient, ampacities beyond those listed in Tables 310-16 through 310-19 would create excessive voltage drop (*IR* drop) and would not be compatible with most termination devices.

Although conductor ampacities increase with the rating of conductor insulation, it should be noted that most terminations are designed only for 60°C or 75°C maximum temperatures (ambient plus current). Accordingly, the higher-rated ampacities for conductors of 90°C, 110°C, etc., cannot be utilized unless the terminations have comparable ratings or where derating of such higher-amp conductors brings load current down to the allowable ampacities for 60°C or 75°C conductors of the same size.

To find the temperature in degrees Fahrenheit (F) where the temperature is given in degrees Celsius (C), apply the formula

$$\text{Degrees F} = \tfrac{9}{5} \times \text{degrees C} + 32$$

Thus, the maximum operating temperature for Type T insulation is 60°C, $\tfrac{9}{5} \times 60° = 108°$. And $108° + 32° = 140°$, which is the same temperature on the Fahrenheit scale as 60 degrees on the Celsius scale.

Reversing the process, where the temperature is given in degrees F, gives

$$\text{Degrees C} = (\text{degrees F} - 32) \times \tfrac{5}{9}$$

The maximum operating temperature for Type THW insulation is 167°F.

$$167° - 32° = 135°$$

$135° \times \tfrac{5}{9} = 75°$, the corresponding temperature in degrees C.

Watch out when conductors are used in locations with elevated ambient temperatures—in boiler rooms, near furnaces, etc. All load ratings are based on a given ambient—such as 30°C, 86°F for conductors covered by **NE Code** Table 310-16. It is up to the designer and/or installer to make the necessary deratings *required* by the "Correction Factors" given with those tables. Equipment deterioration and ultimate thermal failure are the price of carelessness. Moisture or excessive dampness that may degrade aluminum terminations can also result in high-resistance terminations with resultant heating that damages or destroys equipment and conductors.

310·12. Conductor Identification. For part **(a)**, refer to the discussion given for Secs. 200-6 and 200-7. For part **(b)** refer to Exception Nos. 1 and 3 in Sec. 250-57(b). Section 310-12(a), Exception No. 5, now recognizes the use in multiconductor cables of a *grounded* conductor that is not white throughout its entire length provided that only qualified persons will service the installation. The rule requires that such grounded conductors be identified by white marking at their termination at the time of installation.

Similarly, a *grounding* conductor in a multiconductor cable may be identified at each end and at every point where the conductor is accessible by stripping the insulation from the entire exposed length or by coloring the exposed insulation green or by marking with green tape or green adhesive labels [Sec. 310-12(b), Exception No. 2].

310-13. Conductor Constructions and Applications. Table 310-13 presents application and construction data on the wide range of 600-V insulated, individual conductors recognized by the **NE Code**, with the appropriate letter designation used to identify each type of insulated conductor. Figure 310-18 shows

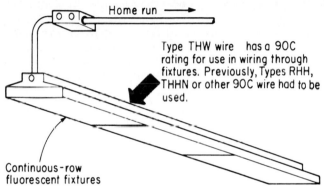

Fig. 310-18. THW wire has the 90°C rating required of conductors within 3 in. of a ballast (Sec. 410-31). (Sec. 310-13.)

a typical detail on application, as covered for Type THW conductor in **NEC** Table 310-13. Type THW wire has a special application provision for electric-discharge lighting, which makes THW the answer for installers needing a 90°C conductor for wiring end-to-end fixtures in compliance with Sec. 410-31.

Important data that should be noted in Table 310-13 are as follows:

1. The designation for "thousand circular mils" is "kcmil," which has been substituted for the long-time designation "MCM" in this table and throughout the **NEC**.

2. Type MI (mineral insulated) cable may have either a copper or an alloy steel sheath.

3. Type RHW-2 is a conductor insulation that is moisture- and heat-resistant rubber with a 90°C rating, for use in dry and wet locations.

4. Type XHHW-2 is a moisture- and heat-resistant cross-linked synthetic polymer with a 90°C rating, for use in dry and wet locations.

5. The suffix "LS" designates a conductor insulation to be "low smoke" producing and flame retardant. For example, Type THHN/LS is a THHN conductor with a limited smoke-producing characteristic.

6. Type THHW is a moisture- and heat-resistant insulation, rated at 75°C for

wet locations and 90°C for dry locations. This is similar to THWN and THHN without the outer nylon covering but with thicker insulation.

7. All insulations using asbestos—A, AA, AI, AIA, AVA, etc—have been deleted from Table 310-13 because they are no longer made.

Conductors for high-voltage circuits (over 2,000 V) must satisfy the specifications of Tables 310-61 through 310-84.

Conductors intended for 600-V (and up to 2,000-V) general wiring under the requirements of the **National Electrical Code** are required to be one of the recognized types listed in **Code** Table 310-13 and not smaller than No. 14 AWG. The **National Electrical Code** does not contain detailed requirements for insulated conductors as these are covered in separate standards such as those of Underwriters Laboratories Inc.

"Dry locations" in this case would mean for "general use" in dry locations.

Table 310-13 permits maximum operating temperatures of 90°C (194°F) in dry and damp (but *not* "wet") locations for Types FEP, FEPB, RHH, XHHW, and THHN wire; but the load-current ratings for Nos. 14, 12, and 10 copper conductors and Nos. 12 and 10 aluminum conductors are limited to those permitted by the maximum overcurrent protection ratings given in the footnote to Table 310-16. One reason is the inability of 15-, 20-, and 30-A CBs to protect these sized conductors against damage under short-circuit conditions. The other reason is that the wiring devices which are commonly connected by these sizes of conductors are not suitable for conditions encountered at higher current loadings.

Terminals of 15- and 20-A receptacles not marked "CO/ALR" are for use with copper and copper-clad aluminum conductors only. Terminals marked "CO/ALR" are for use with aluminum, copper, and copper-clad aluminum conductors. Screwless pressure terminal connectors of the conductor push-in type are for use only with copper and copper-clad aluminum conductors.

Terminals of receptacles rated 30 A and above not marked "AL-CU" are for use with copper conductors only. Terminals of receptacles rated 30 A and above marked "AL-CU" are for use with aluminum, copper, and copper-clad aluminum conductors.

The conductor material known as copper-clad aluminum is made from a metallurgical materials system by using a core of aluminum with a bonded outer skin of copper. There is 10 percent copper by volume (the outer skin) and 26.8 percent by weight. Terminations for copper-clad aluminum conductors should be marked "AL-CU" except where listings by Underwriters Laboratories indicate otherwise.

310-15. Ampacity. Sec. 310-15 states that ampacities of conductors may be determined by *either* of two methods. The first method is described in part **(a)** and is the old, tested, and familiar method of the **NEC**, based on Tables 310-16 through 310-19. The second permitted method is covered in part **(b)** of the **NEC** and is the complex, confusing, incomplete, and defective procedure that was presented in the 1987 **NEC** as the basic method, based on an elaborate formula given in part **(b)**.

The **NEC** ampacity determination procedure using the formula is permitted as an optional alternative "under engineering supervision." All of the ampacity tables based on the formula are in App. B in the back of the **Code** book, where information on the formula method and its related ampacity tables is introduced with the sentence, "This appendix is **not** part of the requirements of this **Code**, but is included for information purposes only." Thus, the 1987 **NEC** ampacity method is given as a nonmandatory, optional alternative to the old standby method.

In part **(a),** a new fine-print note (FPN) points out that "Tables 310-16 through 310-19 are application tables that are for use in determining conductor size on loads calculated in accordance with Article 220." Inasmuch as the **NEC** itself requires that Art. 220 be used at all times in calculating loads, the ampacity-determination method of part **(a)** is completely adequate for all conductor sizing in accordance with all **Code** rules.

The basic ampacity determination procedure of part **(a)** is to use Tables 310-16 through 310-19, with their 11 notes. The most commonly used table will be Table 310-16, which covers all 60°C, 75°C, and 90°C insulated copper, aluminum, and copper-clad aluminum conductors used in *any* raceway or *any* cable, either indoors or outdoors—above ground or underground—and any cable or conductor directly buried in the earth.

Tables 310-16 through 310-19 and accompanying Notes 1 through 11 provide the maximum continuous ampacities for copper, aluminum, and copper-clad aluminum conductors. Table 310-16 covers conductors rated up to 2,000 V where not more than three conductors are installed in raceway or cable or are directly buried in the earth—based on an ambient of 30°C.

Table 310-17 covers both copper conductors and aluminum or cooper-clad aluminum conductors up to 2,000 V where conductors are used as single conductors in free air based on an ambient of 30°C.

Tables 310-18 and 310-19 apply to conductors rated 110°C to 250°C, used either in raceway or cable or as single conductors in free air, based on an ambient of 40°C. Care must be taken in using these tables and in noting references to them throughout the **Code**.

All of these tables and their notes are intended to cover any condition of application that might be encountered. This overall method will indicate the "ampacity" of any of the conductor types for any condition of use. **NEC** Table 310-16, for instance, specifies ampacities for conductors where not more than three current-carrying conductors are contained in a single raceway or cable or directly buried in the earth provided that the ambient temperature is not in excess of 30°C (86°F). For higher ambient temperatures, the ampacity must be derated in accordance with the "Ampacity Correction Factors" at the bottom of each table. For applications of *more* that three current-carrying conductors in a conduit or cable, the ampacity must be derated in accordance with Note 8 to Table 310-16. And where *both* elevated ambient (above 30°C) and more than three conductors in a conduit or cable are present, both deratings must be made—one on top of the other. First, an ampacity must be developed from the appropriate table—correcting for the elevated ambient—then the derating factor given in Note 8 for the number of current-carrying conductors contained within the raceway or cable must be applied to determine conductor ampacity.

Table 310-16 gives ampacities under the two conditions described: that the raceway or cable containing the conductors is operating in an ambient temperature not over 30°C (86°F) and that there are not more than three current-carrying conductors in the raceway or cable. Under those conditions, the ampacity value shown in the table corresponds to the thermal limit of each particular insulation. But in any case, where either or both of the two conditions are exceeded, the ampacity of a conductor is *not* the value shown in the table and must be reduced from that value, using the given derating factors. And then protection must be based upon or provided at the reduced ampacity to ensure that the temperature limit of the insulation is not exceeded.

It should be clearly understood that any reduced ampacity, required because of a higher ambient and/or conductor bundling (Note 8), has the same meaning as the value shown in the table; each represents a current value above which excessive heating would occur under the particular conditions. And if there are two conditions that lead to excessive heating, then a greater reduction in current is required than if only one such condition exists.

Using the Ampacity Tables

An important step in design of circuits is selection of the type of conductor to be used—TW, THW, THWN, RHH, THHN, XHHW, etc. The various types of conductors are covered in Art. 310 of the **NE Code**, and the ampacities of conductors with the different insulations and temperature ratings are given in Tables 310-16 through 310-19 for the varying conditions of use—in raceway, in open air, at normal or higher-than-normal ambient temperatures. Conductors must be used in accordance with all the data in those tables and notes.

In selecting the type and temperature rating of wire for circuits, consideration must be given to a very important UL qualification indicated for the temperature ratings of equipment terminations. Although application data on minimum required temperature ratings of conductors connected to equipment terminals are not given in the **NE Code**, they nevertheless become part of the mandatory regulations of the **Code** because of **Code** Sec. 110-3(b). This section incorporates the instructions in UL and other listing books as part of the **Code** itself. It reads as follows:

Listed or labeled equipment shall be used or installed in accordance with any instructions included in the listing or labeling.

A basic rule in the UL *Electrical Construction Materials Directory* states:

Distribution and Control Equipment Terminations – Most terminals are suitable for use only with copper wire. Where aluminum or copper-clad aluminum wire can or shall be used, (some crimp terminals may be Listed only for aluminum wire) there is marking to indicate this. Such marking is required to be independent of any marking on terminal connectors, such as on a wiring diagram or other visible location. The marking may be in an abbreviated form such as "AL-CU".

Except as noted in the following paragraphs or in the information at the beginning of some product categories, the termination provisions are based on the use of 60C ampacities for wire sizes No. 14-1 AWG, and 75C ampacities for wire sizes Nos. 1/0 AWG and larger, as specified in Table 310-16 of the National Electrical Code.

Some distribution and control equipment is marked to indicate the required temperature rating of each field-installed conductor. If the equipment, normally intended for connection by wire sizes within the range 14-1 AWG, is marked "75C only" or "60/75C", it is intended that 75C insulated wire may be used at full 75C ampacity. Where the connection is made to a circuit breaker or switch within the equipment, such a circuit breaker or switch must also be marked for the temperature rating of the conductor.

A 75C conductor temperature marking on a circuit breaker or switch normally intended for wire sizes 14-1 AWG does not in itself indicate that 75C insulated wire can be used unless (1) the circuit breaker or switch is used by itself, such as in a separate enclosure, or (2) the equipment in which the circuit breaker or switch is installed is also so marked.

"A 75 or 90C conductor temperature marking on a terminal (e.g. AL7, CU7AL, AL7CU or AL9, CU9AL, AL9CU) does not in itself indicate that 75 or 90C insulated wire can be used unless the equipment in which the terminals are installed is marked for 75 or 90C."

Higher temperature rated conductors than specified may be used if the size is based on the above statements.

This temperature limitation on terminals applies to the terminals on all equipment—circuit breakers, switches, motor starters, contactors, etc.—except where some other specific condition is recognized in the general information preceding the product category. Figure 310-19 illustrates this vitally important matter, which has been widely disregarded in general practice. When terminals are tested for suitability at 60°C or 75°C, the use of 90°C conductors operating at their higher current ratings poses definite threat of heat damage to switches, breakers, etc. Many termination failures in equipment suggest overheating even where the load current did not exceed the current rating of the breaker, switch, or other equipment.

When a 60°C-rated terminal is fed by a conductor operating at 90°C, there will be substantial heat conducted from the 90°C conductor metal to the 60°C-rated terminal; and, over a period of time, that can damage the termination— even though the load current does not exceed the equipment current rating and does not exceed the ampacity of the 90°C conductor. Whenever two metallic parts at different operating temperatures are tightly connected together, the higher-temperature part (say 75°C or 90°C wire) will give heat to the lower-temperature part (the 60°C terminal) and thereby raise its temperature over 60°C.

For any given size of conductor, the greater ampacity of a higher-temperature conductor is established by the ability of the conductor insulation to withstand the I^2R heat produced by the higher current flowing through the conductor. But it must not be assumed that the equipment to which that conductor is connected also is capable of withstanding the heat that will be thermally conducted from the metal of the conductor into the metal of the terminal to which the conductor is tightly connected.

Although this limitation on the operating temperature of terminals in equipment does somewhat reduce the advantage that higher-temperature conductors have over lower-temperature conductors, there are still many advantages to using the higher-temperature wires.

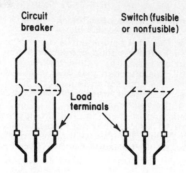

Unless a circuit breaker or switch is marked otherwise, circuit conductors connected to the terminals must not operate at more than a 60C ampacity for conductors in sizes No. 14 to No. 1 AWG and must not operate at more than a 75C ampacity for conductors in sizes No. 1/0 AWG and larger [refer to *NE Code* Tables 310-16 through -19].

IN GENERAL —
FOR CBs, SWITCHES, CONTACTORS, ETC. RATED 125 AMPS OR LESS Use TW wire (or use THW, THHN, RHH, XHHW or other higher-temperature wire at the ampacity of the corresponding size of TW wire).

FOR CBs, SWITCHES, CONTACTORS, ETC. RATED OVER 125 AMPS—Use TW wire at its 60 C ampacities or use THW, THWN or XHHW wire at ampacities permitted up to 75C (or use RHH, THHN or other higher-temperature wire at the ampacity of the corresponding size of 75C wire)

Fig. 310-19. UL specifies maximum temperature rating for conductors connecting to equipment terminals. (Sec. 310-15.)

NEC **Ampacities**

As described in the definition of "ampacity" (in Art. 100), the ampacity of a conductor is the amount of current, in amperes, that the conductor can carry continuously under specified conditions of use without developing a temperature in excess of the value that represents the maximum temperature that the conductor insulation can withstand. For any particular application, one of the many **NEC** ampacity tables must be consulted—depending upon the particular wiring method (wires in raceway, cable, individual insulated wires, etc.) and depending upon the manner of installation (in free air, directly buried in the ground, in raceway underground, as messenger supported wiring, etc.). From the table that corresponds to the specific wiring method and conditions of use, the basic ampacity of any size and insulation of copper or aluminum conductor can be determined. And then any required adjustments can be made to the ampacity value, as needed for ambient temperature and number of conductors in a raceway or cable. NEC Table 310-16, for instance, specifies ampacities for conductors where not more than three conductors are contained in a single raceway or cable in free air provided that the ambient temperature is not in excess of 30°C (86°F). For higher ambient temperatures, the ampacity must be derated in accordance with the "Ampacity Correction Factors" at the bottom of each table. For applications of *more* than three conductors in a conduit or cable, the ampacity of conductors must be derated in accordance with Note 8 to Table 310-16. And where *both* elevated ambient (above 30°C) and more than three conductors in a conduit or cable are present, *both* deratings must be made—one on top of the other.

The NEC approach to setting ampacities of conductors is aimed at designating that level of current that will cause the conductor to reach its thermal limit— the current that the conductor can carry safely *but* above which the temperature rating of the conductor insulation would be exceeded and the conductor exposed to thermal degradation or damage to its insulation. This concept of ampacity is verified in the FPN to Sec. 240-1, where the wording has been virtually unchanged for 30 years and says:

Overcurrent protection for conductors and equipment is provided to open the circuit if the current reaches a value that will cause an excessive or dangerous temperature in conductors or conductor insulation.

For purposes of consistent analysis, the discussions of ampacity here will be based on the first of the ampacity tables, Table 310-16. We will assume that the specific application corresponds to the conditions to which Table 310-16 applies—i.e., not more than three single insulated conductors (0 to 2,000 V) in raceway in free air or Type AC, NM, NMC, or SE cable in free air. The particular considerations given to ampacity value for Table 310-16 can be made for any of the other tables.

NEC Table 310-16 gives ampacities under two conditions: that the raceway or cable containing the conductors is operating in an ambient temperature not over 30°C (86°F) and that there are not more than three current-carrying conductors in the raceway or cable. Under those conditions, the ampacities shown correspond to the thermal limit of each particular insulation. But in any case where either or both of the two conditions are exceeded, the ampacity of the conductors of a circuit must be reduced (and protection must be based upon or provided at the reduced ampacity!) to ensure that the temperature limit of the insulation is not exceeded:

1. If the ambient temperature is above 30°C, the ampacity must be reduced in accordance with the correction factors given with Table 310-16.
2. If more than three current-carrying conductors are used in a single cable or raceway, the conductors tend to be bundled in such a way that their

heat-dissipating capability is reduced, and excessive heating will occur at the ampacities shown in the table. As a result, Note 8 to Tables 310-16 through 310-19 requires the reduction of ampacity, and conductors have to be protected at the reduced ampacity.

It should be clearly understood that any reduced ampacity, required because of a higher ambient and/or conductor bundling, has the same meaning as the value shown in the table: Each represents a current value above which excessive heating would occur under the particular conditions. And if there are two conditions that lead to excessive heating, then a greater reduction in current is required than if only one such condition exists.

In conductor size Nos. 14, 12, and 10, Table 310-16 clearly indicates that 90°C-rated conductors do, in fact, have higher ampacities than those given for the corresponding sizes of 60°C and 75°C conductors. As shown in Fig. 310-20,

1990 Edition
Table 310-16

Size	Temperature Rating of Conductor.			
	60°C (140°F)	75°C (167°F)	85°C (185°F)	90°C (194°F)
AWG kcmil	TYPES †TW, †UF	TYPES †FEPW, †RH, †RHW, †THHW, †THW, †THWN, †XHHW †USE, †ZW	TYPE V	TYPES TA, TBS, SA SIS, †FEP, †FEPB, †RHH, †THHN, †THHW, †XHHW
	COPPER			
18	....	....	....	14
16	....	....	18	18
14	20†	20†	25	25†
12	25†	25†	30	30†
10	30	35†	40	40†
8	40	50	55	55

Fig. 310-20. NE Code table shows higher ampacities for 90°C branch-circuit wires (Nos. 14, 12, and 10). (Sec. 310-15.)

No. 12 TW and No. 12 THW copper conductors are both assigned an ampacity of 25 A under the basic application conditions of the table. *But*, a No. 12 THHN, RHH, or XHHW (dry location) has an ampacity of *30* A. However, the footnote to Table 310-16 (shown in Fig. 310-21) requires that "overcurrent protection"

† Unless otherwise specifically permitted elsewhere in this Code, the overcurrent protection for conductor types marked with an obelisk (†) shall not exceed 15 amperes for 14 AWG, 20 amperes for 12 AWG, and 30 amperes for 10 AWG copper; or 15 amperes for 12 AWG and 25 amperes for 10 AWG aluminum and copper-clad aluminum after any correction factors for ambient temperature and number of conductors have been applied.

Fig. 310-21. Note below Table 310-16 radically alters conductor applications for Nos. 14, 12, and 10. (Sec. 310-15.)

for No. 14, No. 12, and No. 10 copper conductors be taken as 15, 20, and 30 A, respectively, regardless of the type and temperature rating of the insulation on the conductors. And the footnote says that these limitations on overcurrent protection apply after any correction factors for ambient temperature and/or number of conductors have been applied. When applied to selection of branch-circuit wires in cases where conductor ampacity derating is required by Note 8 of Tables 310-16 through 310-19 for conduit fill (over three wires in a raceway), the footnote to Table 310-16 affords advantageous use of the 90°C wires for branch-circuit makeup. The reason is that, as stated in Note 8, the derating of ampacity is based on taking a percentage of the actual ampacity value shown in the table, and the ampacity values for 90°C conductors are higher than those for 60 and 75°C conductors.

Application of Note 8 to Table 310-16 depends upon how many current-carrying conductors are in a raceway. A true neutral conductor (a neutral carrying current only under conditions of unbalanced loading on the phase conductors) is not counted as a current-carrying conductor. If a 208Y/120-V circuit or a 480Y/277-V circuit is made up of three phase legs and a true neutral in a conduit, the circuit is counted as only three conductors in the conduit, and derating for conduit fill, as described in Note 8 of Tables 310-16 through 310-19, is not necessary. But neutrals for circuits with these voltage ratings must be counted as current-carrying conductors if the major portion of the load consists of electric-discharge lighting, data processing equipment, or similar equipment [Note 10(c) of the tables]. Thus, if the circuit supplies fluorescent, mercury, or metal-halide lamps, the neutral is counted as the fourth current-carrying conductor because it carries third harmonic current, which approximates the phase-leg current, under balanced loading. Any such 4-wire circuit must have its load current derated to 80 percent of the ampacity given in Table 310-16, as required by Note 8 to those tables.

As shown in Fig. 310-22, the makeup of a branch circuit consists of selecting the correct size of wire for the particular load current (based on number of wires in raceway, ambient temperature, and ampacity deratings) and then relating the rating of the overcurrent protective device to all the conditions.

In Table 310-16, which applies to conductors in raceways and in cables and covers the vast majority of conductors used in electrical systems for power and light, the ampacities for sizes No. 14, No. 12, and No. 10 are particularly signif-

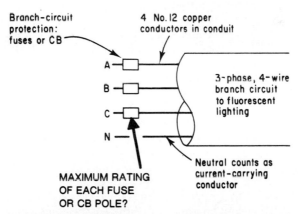

Fig. 310·22. Loading and protection of branch-circuit wires must also account for derating of wire "ampacity." (Sec. 310-15.)

icant because copper conductors of those sizes are involved in the vast majority of branch circuits in modern electrical systems. Number 14 has an ampacity of 20, No. 12 has an ampacity of 25, and No. 10 has an ampacity of 30. The typical impact of that on circuit makeup and loading is as follows:

1. Number 12 TW or THW copper is shown to have an ampacity of 25; and based on the general UL requirement that equipment terminals be limited to use with 60°C conductors in sizes up to No. 1 AWG, No. 12 THHN or XHHW copper conductors must also be treated as having a 25-A continuous rating. *But*, the footnote to Table 310-16 limits all No. 12 copper wires to a maximum load of 20 A by requiring that they be protected at not more than 20 A.

2. The ampacity of 25 A for No. 12 TW and THW copper wires interacts with Note 8 to Tables 310-16 through 310-19 where there are, say, six No. 12 TW current-carrying wires for the phase legs of two 3-phase, 4-wire branch circuits in one conduit supplying, say, receptacle loads. In such a case, the two neutrals of the branch circuits do not count in applying Note 8, and only each of the six phase legs must have its ampacity derated to the "Percent of Values in Tables as Adjusted for Ambient Temperature if Necessary" as stated at the upper right of the table in Note 8. In the case described here, that literally means that each No. 12 phase leg may be used at a derated ampacity of 0.8×25, or 20 A. And the footnote to Table 310-16 would require use of a fuse or CB rated not over 20 A to protect each No. 12 phase leg. Each No. 12 would then be protected at its new ampacity that represents the maximum I^2R heat input that the conductor insulation can withstand. The only other possible qualification is that Sec. 384-16(c) would require the load current on each of the phase legs to be further limited to no more than 80 percent of the 20-A rating of the overcurrent device—that is, 16 A—if the load current is "continuous" (operates steadily for 3 hr or more), a condition not likely for receptacle-fed loads.

3. If two 3-phase, 4-wire branch circuits of No. 12 TW or THW copper conductors are installed in a single conduit or EMT run and supply, say, fluorescent or other electric-discharge lighting, the two neutrals of the branch circuits would carry harmonic current even under balanced conditions and would have to be counted, along with the six phase legs, as current-carrying wires for ampacity derating in accordance with Note 8. In such a case, as the table of Note 8 shows, "7 through 9" conductors must have ampacity derated to 70 percent of the 25-A value shown in Table 310-16 ($0.7 \times 25 = 17.5$ A), which gives each conductor an ampacity of 17.5 A. If 20-A overcurrent protection is used for each No. 12 phase leg and the load is limited to no more than 17.5 or 16 A (0.8×20 A) for a continuous load, the application would satisfy Note 8 to Table 310-16. And Sec. 210-19(a) permits the use of 20-A protection as the next higher standard rating of protective device above the conductor ampacity of 17.5 A, provided that the circuit supplies only hard-wired outlets, such as lighting fixtures, and does not supply any receptacle outlets for "cord- and plug-connected portable loads" that could permit overloading of the conductors above 17.5 A.

Use of 20-A protection on conductors with an ampacity of 17.5 A is recognized only for fixed circuit loading (like lighting fixture outlets) and not for the variable loading that general purpose convenience receptacles permit, because any increase in load current over 17.5 A would produce excessive heat input to the eight bundled No. 12 conductors in that conduit and would damage and ultimately break down the conductor insulation. Of course, the question arises: Over the operating life of the electrical system, how can the addition of excessive current be prevented? The practical, realistic answer is: It can't! It would be better to use 15-A protection on the No. 12 wires or use 90°C rated conductors.

4. No. 12 THHN or XHHW conductors—with their 90°C rating and consequently greater resistance to thermal damage—could be used for the two 3-phase, 4-wire, 20-A circuits to the electric-discharge lighting load, would satisfy all **Code** rules, and would not be subject to insulation damage. With eight current-carrying wires in the conduit, the 70 percent ampacity derating required by Note 8 would be applied to the 30-A value shown in Table 310-16 as the ampacity of No. 12 THHN, RHH, or XHHW (dry locations). Then because $0.7 \times 30 = 21$ A, the maximum of 20-A protection required by the footnote to Table 310-16 would ensure that the conductors were never subjected to excessive current and its damaging heat. And if the original loading on the conductors is set at 16 A [the 80 percent load limiting of Sec. 384-16(c)] for continuous operation of the lighting, any subsequent increase in load even up to the full 20-A capacity would not reach the 21-A maximum ampacity set by Note 8.

Figure 310-23 summarizes the applications described in 3 and 4 above.

Advantage of 90°C Wires

If the four circuit wires in Fig. 310-22 are 90°C-rated conductors—such as THHN, RHH, or XHHW—the loading and protection of the circuit must be related to required ampacity derating as shown in Fig. 310-24. The application is based on these considerations:

1. As described in Figs. 310-20 and 310-21, each No. 12 THHN has an ampacity of 30 A from Table 310-16, but the footnote to that table limits the overcurrent protection on any No. 12 THHN to not more than 20 A.
2. Because the neutral of the 3-phase, 4-wire circuit must be counted as a current-carrying wire, there are four conductors in the conduit—thereby requiring that each conductor have its ampacity derated to 80 percent of its table-value ampacity, as required by Note 8 of Table 310-16. Each No. 12 then has a new (derated) ampacity of 0.8×30, or 24 A.
3. By using a 20-A, single-pole protective device (fuse, single-pole CB, or one pole of a 3-pole CB), which is the maximum protection permitted by the Table 310-16 footnote, each No. 12 THHN easily complies with the Sec. 240-3 requirement that the branch-circuit wire have overcurrent protection in accordance with (usually not greater than) the conductor ampacity (24 A).

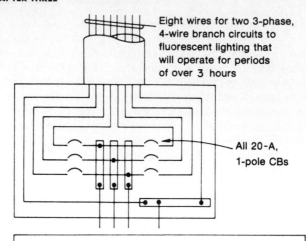

Eight wires for two 3-phase,
4-wire branch circuits to
fluorescent lighting that
will operate for periods
of over 3 hours

All 20-A,
1-pole CBs

CASE 1
With TW or THW No. 12 copper conductors:
No. 12 ampacity = 25 amps, from Table 310-16
From Note 8, derating = 0.7 × 25 = 17.5 amps
From Sec. 384-16(c), max. load = 0.8 × 20 = 16 amps

CASE 2
With THHN, XHHW or RHH No. 12 copper conductors:
No. 12 ampacity = 30 amps, from Table 310-16
From Note 8, derating = 0.7 × 30 = 21 amps
From Sec. 384-16(c), max. load = 0.8 × 20 = 16 amps

**IN CASE 1, CONDUCTORS ARE NOT PROTECTED IN
ACCORDANCE WITH THE 17.5-A AMPACITY, IN CASE
2, THEY <u>ARE</u> PROTECTED AGAINST EXCESSIVE
LOAD CURRENT.**

Fig. 310-23. Conductors with 90°C insulation eliminate the possibility
of conductor damage due to overload.

4. If the lighting load on the circuit is noncontinuous—that is, does *not* operate for any period of 3 hr or more—the circuit may be loaded up to its 20-
A maximum rating.

5. If the load fed is continuous—full-load current flow for 3 hr or more—the
load on the circuit must be limited to 80 percent of rating of each 20-A fuse
or CB pole, as required by Sec. 384-16(c). Then 16 A is the maximum load.
UL rules state that "unless otherwise marked, circuit breakers should not
be loaded to exceed 80% of their current rating, where in normal operation the load will continue for 3 hours or more." CBs under 250 A are not
so marked.

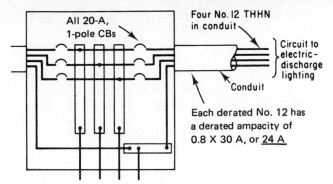

NOTE: TW or THW wires would have to be derated from 20 to 16 A.

Fig. 310-24. Derating of 90°C branch-circuit wires (Nos. 14, 12, and 10) is based on higher ampacities. (Sec. 310-15.)

Figure 310-25 shows the use of two 3-phase, 4-wire circuits of THHN conductors in a single conduit. The 90°C wires offer distinct advantages (substantial economies) over use of either 60°C (TW) or 75°C (THW) wires for the same application, as follows.

Resistive load   If the circuit shown feeds only incandescent lighting or other resistive loads (or electric-discharge lighting does not make up "a major portion of the load"), then Note 10(c) of Tables 310-16 through 310-19 does not require the neutral conductor to be counted as a current-carrying conductor. In such cases, circuit makeup and loading could follow these considerations:

1. With the six phase legs as current-carrying wires in the conduit, Note 8 requires that the ampacity of each No. 12 be derated from its basic table value of 30 A to 80 percent of that value—or 24 A.

2. Then each No. 12 is properly protected by a 20-A CB or fuse—satisfying Sec. 210-20 and the footnote to Table 310-16.

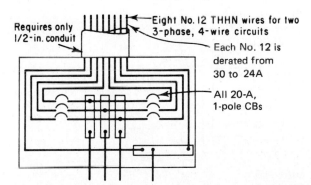

Fig. 310-25. The 90°C conductors can take derating without losing full circuit load-current rating. (Sec. 310-15.)

3. If the circuit load is not continuous, each phase leg may be loaded to 20 A.

4. If the load is continuous, a maximum of 16 A (80 percent) must be observed to satisfy Sec. 384-16(c).

5. If the total load is made up of both continuous and noncontinuous loads, the sum of noncontinuous load *plus* 125 percent of the continuous load must not exceed the rating of the branch circuit, in this case, 20 A [see Sec. 220-3(a)].

Electric-discharge load If the two circuits of Fig. 310-25 supplied electric-discharge lighting (fluorescent, mercury-vapor, metal-halide, high-pressure sodium, or low-pressure sodium), makeup and loading would have to be as shown in Fig. 310-23, Case 2. If that same makeup of circuits supplied noncontinuous loads, the circuit conductors could be loaded right up to 20 A per pole.

In Fig. 310-23, Case 2, the only difference between such circuit makeups using RHH conductors and the ones using THHN is the need for ¾-in. conduit instead of ½-in. conduit because of the larger cross-section area of RHH and XHHW (see Tables 3A and 3B, Chap. 9, **NE Code**).

Feeder Applications

Applying the UL temperature limitation to selection of feeder conductors is generally similar to the procedure described above for selection of branch-circuit conductors.

Refer to Fig. 310-26:

1. Because the load on the feeder is continuous, the 100-A, 3-pole CB must have its load current limited so the 100-A protective-device rating is not less than 125 percent times the continuous current, as required by Sec. 220-10(b). Then, 100 ÷ 1.25 = 80 A. The 76-A load is, therefore, OK. (A CB or fused switch may be loaded continuously to 100 percent of the CB or fuse amp rating only when the assembly is UL-listed for such use.)

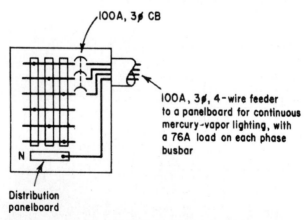

100A, 3∅ CB

100A, 3∅, 4-wire feeder
to a panelboard for continuous
mercury-vapor lighting, with
a 76A load on each phase
busbar

N

Distribution
panelboard

Fig. 310-26. Feeder conductors for up to 100-A equipment must use 60°C ampacity. (Sec. 310-15.)

2. The CB load terminals are recognized by UL for use with 60°C conductors or higher-temperature conductors loaded not over the 60°C ampacity of the given size of conductor.

3. The feeder phase conductors must have an ampacity such that they are protected by the 100-A protective device in accordance with Sec. 240-3. That means they must have an ampacity of 100 A or have a lower value of ampacity for which the 100-A protection rating is the next higher standard rating of protective device above the conductor ampacity, when conductor ampacity does not correspond to a standard rating of protective device. The feeder neutral is not subject to this limitation because the neutral does not connect to the terminal of a switch, CB, starter, etc.—the devices for which heating would be a problem under continuous load. **NEC** Sec. 220-22 is the basic rule that covers sizing of a feeder neutral. Section 220-10(b) covers sizing of feeder phase conductors.

4. If 60°C copper conductors are used for this feeder, reference must be made to the second column of Table 310-16. This feeder supplies electric-discharge lighting; therefore, Note 10(c) of the table requires that the feeder neutral be counted as a current-carrying conductor because of the harmonic currents present in the neutral. Then, because there are four current-carrying conductors in the conduit, the ampacity of each conductor must be derated to 80 percent of its value in column 2 of Table 310-16, as required by Note 8 to Table 310-16. After the conductor is derated to 80 percent, it must have an ampacity such that it is properly protected by the 100 A protection. Because standard ratings of protective devices are 90 A and 100 A (from Sec. 240-6), the derated ampacity of the required conductors must not be less than 91 A—which is the lowest ampacity value that may be protected by a 100-A protective device in accordance with Exception No. 4 of Sec. 240-3, which permits the next higher standard rating of protective device above the conductor ampacity. From Table 310-16, a No. 1/0 TW conductor is rated at 125 A when only three conductors are used in a conduit. With four conductors in a conduit, the 125-A rating is reduced to 80 percent (0.8 × 125 A), or 100 A, which is properly protected by the 100-A CB.

Continuous load on a feeder must be limited to no more than 80 percent of any CB or fused switch that is not UL-listed and marked for continuous loading to 100 percent of its rating—without any relationship to conductor derating. When conductor ampacity is derated because more than three conductors are used in a raceway, the conductors must be protected at the *derated* ampacity. Then—*in addition*—if the CB or fused switch that provides the protection is not UL-listed and marked for 100 percent continuous load, continuous circuit loading must not exceed 80 percent of the rating of the CB or fuses.

The feeder circuit of four No. 1/0 TW conductors, rated at 100 A, would require a minimum of 2-in. conduit. [*Note:* A reduced size of neutral could be used, because the need to upsize hot conductors to be properly protected by the 125 percent protective device required by Sec. 220-10(b) does not apply to the neutral. The neutral could be a No. 2 TW conductor,

which has an ampacity of 76 A after derating of its ampacity from 95 A—
0.8 × 95 A = 76 A, which is adequate for the load current under conditions of maximum unbalance of phase-to-neutral current.]

5. If 75°C conductors are used for this feeder circuit instead of 60°C conductors, the calculations would be different. With THW copper conductors, Table 310-16 shows that No. 1 conductors, rated at 130 A for not more than three current-carrying conductors in a conduit, would have an ampacity of 0.8 × 130 or 104 A when four are used in the conduit and derated. The 104-A conductor ampacity would be properly protected by the 100-A CB that was shown to satisfy Sec. 220-10(b).

Although UL listing and testing of the CB are based on the use of 60°C conductors, the use of No. 1 75°C THW conductors is acceptable because the terminals of the breaker in this case would not be loaded to more than the amp rating of a 60°C conductor of the same size. A No. 1 60°C TW conductor is rated at 110 A when not more than three current-carrying conductors are used in a conduit. When four conductors are in one conduit, the 60°C No. 1 wires are derated to 80 percent of 110 A, or 88 A. Because that value is greater than the load of 76 A on each CB terminal, the CB terminals are not loaded in excess of the 88-A allowable ampacity of 60°C No. 1 conductors, and the UL limitation is satisfied.

Four No. 1 THW conductors, rated at 104 A, would require a minimum of 1½-in. conduit. Or, four No. 1 RHH, THHN, or XHHW conductors could be used in 1½-in. conduit.

6. If 90°C THHN (or XHHW or RHH) conductors are used for this feeder (in a dry location), No. 2 copper conductors could be used. From Table 310-16, No. 2 THHN with a basic ampacity of 130 A would be derated to 0.8 × 130, or 104 A—which would be properly protected within the conductor's ampacity by the 100-A CB. The ampacity of a 60°C No. 2 conductor is 95 A normally and derated to 80 percent is 0.8 × 95 or 76 A—which gives the conductors the same rating as the load. Under such a condition the load current is not in excess of the 76-A allowable ampacity of a 60°C No. 2 conductor, and the UL limitation is satisfied.

Four No. 2 THHN, XHHW, or RHH conductors, rated exactly at 104 A, which is above the required minimum rating of 96 A, would require a minimum of 1¼-in. conduit (in dry locations only).

Note: Of course, voltage drop in the feeder will vary with the different-size conductors and must be accounted for.

Figure 310-27 shows an example where feeder conductors could be used at up to the 75°C ampacity. In this case, because the load on the feeder is not electric-discharge lighting or data processing eqiupment, the neutral does *not* count as a current-carrying conductor. As a result, there are only three current-carrying conductors in the conduit, and derating according to Note 8 is not required. The details are as follows:

1. Because the load on this feeder is continuous, Sec. 220-10(b) limits the load current to not more than 80 percent of the rating of the fuses. Immediately, we know that the feeder load may not exceed 80 percent of the 400-A fuse rating: 0.8 × 400 = 320 A.

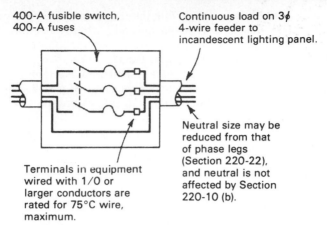

400-A fusible switch,
400-A fuses

Continuous load on 3ϕ
4-wire feeder to
incandescent lighting panel.

Neutral size may be
reduced from that
of phase legs
(Section 220-22),
and neutral is not
affected by Section
220-10 (b).

Terminals in equipment
wired with 1/0 or
larger conductors are
rated for 75°C wire,
maximum.

Fig. 310·27. Equipment wired with conductors No. 1/0 or larger
may use the 75°C ampacity. (Sec. 310-15.)

2. If 75°C conductors are used, because they are permitted by UL test conditions, Table 310-16 shows that 700 kcmil THW aluminum conductors
rated at 375 A could be used and suitably protected by the 400-A fuses in
accordance with Sec. 240-3, Exception No. 1, because 400 A is the next
higher standard fuse rating (from Sec. 240-6) above the 375-A rating of the
conductors. In that case the maximum continuous feeder load of 320 A is
well within the 375-A ampacity of the conductors.

3. If 90°C conductors are used, they must be used at no more than the ampacity of a 75°C conductor of the same size as the 90°C conductor. Table 310-
16 shows that 600 kcmil XHHW aluminum conductors (in a dry location)
have a 385-A rating, and the 400-A fuses constitute acceptable protection
for those conductors in accordance with Sec. 240-3, Exception No. 4. The
load on the feeder phase legs (320 A) is well within the 385-A ampacity of
the 600 kcmil conductors. To check the suitability of the 90°C conductors,
the ampere rating of a 75°C 600 kcmil aluminum conductor is given in
Table 310-16 as 340 A. Because the load of 320 A is not in excess of the
340-A rating of a 75°C conductor, the UL limitation on maximum rating of
conductor termination is satisfied.

4. The smaller conduit size required for the reduced size of higher-temperature conductors is a labor and material advantage.

Notes to Tables 310·16 through 310·19

Note 3   This note has been in the NE Code for a long time and permits use
of certain conductors at ampacity values higher than those shown for the conductors in Table 310-16. For instance, a No. 2/0 THW copper conductor may
be used at an ampacity of 200 A instead of at 175 A, as shown in Table 310-16.
This permission has been given by the NE Code in recognition of the reality
that residential service conductors are supplying loads of great diversity and of

short operating periods or cycles, so that the conductors almost never see full demand load approaching their ampacity and certainly not for continuous operation (3 hr or more).

The higher allowable ampacity ratings for 120/240-V, 3-wire, single-phase dwelling services may also be utilized for feeder conductors, and Type USE is one of the types of conductors given the higher ampacities. The ampere rating of services that are subject to the higher ampacity values has been increased from 200 A to 400 A.

Those higher conductor ampacities permitted by Note 3 are applicable only for service conductors or feeder conductors used in "dwelling units," thereby limiting the application to one-family houses and individual apartments in apartment houses, condominiums, and the like—because only such units conform to the **Code** definition of "dwelling unit," as given in Art. 100. The wording excludes use of Note 3 in relation to service-entrance conductors to a whole building, such as a multifamily dwelling, as shown in Fig. 310-28. And in that sketch, prior to the 1990 **Code**, the wording did prohibit use of the higher ampacities of conductors if each of the SE runs to the individual apartments were a feeder instead of service-entrance conductors, as each run would be if a disconnect and protective device were used at each meter location. But reason dictates that the higher ampacities should be allowed in either case, even though each feeder does not carry "the total current supplied by that service." The phrase "total current supplied by that service" was removed in the 1990 **NEC**, which has the effect of permitting the use of the increased ampacities for feeders to individual "dwelling units" in a multi-family dwelling. And, although they are prohibited by the literal limitation to "dwelling units," it would be reasonable to permit the higher ampacities for service-entrance conductors to the whole building. Refer to Sec. 215-2(b) of the **Code**.

Prior to the 1990 **NEC**, in Note 3, it was clearly indicated that the higher allowable ampacities for residential occupancies using 3-wire, single-phase services also may be applied to 3-wire, single-phase feeders in those cases where the feeder conductors from the service equipment to a subpanel or other distribution point carry the total current supplied by the service conductors. Removal of the phrase "total current supplied by that service" in the 1990 **Code** would recognize use of the increased ampacities given in Note 3 for a feeder as shown in the one-family house sketch of Fig. 310-28, even if, say, swimming pool circuits or other loads are supplied from the service, but are not carried by the feeder. This permission logically permits the feeder conductors to have the same elevated ampacities as are allowed for service conductors.

The last sentence of Note 3 permits the neutral conductor of these 3-wire services and 3-wire feeders to be two sizes smaller than the hot conductors because the neutral carries only the unbalanced current of the hot legs and is not at all involved with 2-wire, 240-V loads. That is how the neutral in SE cable is sized.

Note 5   This note provides that, if an uninsulated conductor is used with insulated conductors in a raceway or cable, its size shall be the size that would be required for a conductor having the same insulation as the insulated conductors and having the required ampacity (Fig. 310-29).

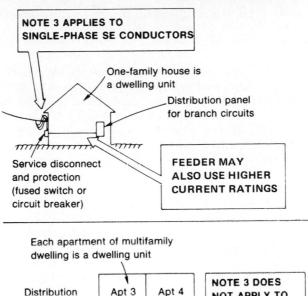

NOTE 3 APPLIES TO
SINGLE-PHASE SE CONDUCTORS

One-family house is
a dwelling unit

Distribution panel
for branch circuits

Service disconnect
and protection
(fused switch or
circuit breaker)

FEEDER MAY
ALSO USE HIGHER
CURRENT RATINGS

Each apartment of multifamily
dwelling is a dwelling unit

Distribution
panel for
branch
circuits
in each apt

Apt 3   Apt 4

Apt 1   Apt 2

NOTE 3 DOES
NOT APPLY TO
SE CONDUCTORS
FEEDING WHOLE
BUILDING

Outdoor group of meters

SE CONDUCTORS TO
EACH APARTMENT
MAY USE HIGHER
AMPACITIES OF NOTE 3

Fig. 310-28. Higher ampacities may be used for service conductors
to "dwelling units."

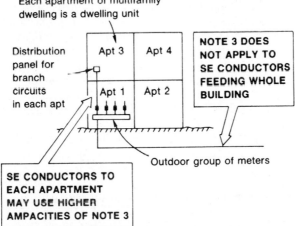

Bare conductor has the capacity of a
conductor of its size that has...

... the same insulation as used
on the insulated conductors
run with the bare conductor.

Fig. 310-29. How to figure ampacity of a bare conductor, where permitted.
(Sec. 310-15.)

example Two No. 6 Type THW conductors and one bare No. 6 conductor in a raceway or cable. The ampacity of the bare conductor would be 65 A.

If the insulated conductor were Type TW, the ampacity of the bare conductor would be 55 A.

Note 8(a) *Where more than three current-carrying conductors* are used in a raceway or cable, their current-carrying capacities must be reduced to compensate for the proximity heating effect and reduced heat dissipation due to reduced ventilation of the individual conductors that are bunched or form an enclosed group of closely placed conductors. Where the number of conductors in a raceway or cable exceeds three, the ampacity of each conductor shall be reduced as indicated in the table of Note 8.

If, for instance, four No. 8 THW copper conductors are used in a conduit, the *ampacity* of each No. 8 is reduced from the 50-A value shown in the table to 80 percent of that value. In such a case, each No. 8 then has a *new* reduced *ampacity* of 0.8 × 50, or 40 A. And, from Sec. 240-3, "Conductors shall be protected in accordance with their *ampacities*." Thus, 40-A-rated fuses or CB poles would be required for overcurrent protection—as the general rule.

The application of those No. 8 conductors and their protection rating is based on the general concept behind the **NE Code** tables of maximum allowable current-carrying capacities (called "ampacities"). The **NE Code** tables of ampacities of insulated conductors installed in raceway or cable have always set the maximum continuous current that a given size of conductor can carry continuously (for 3 hr or longer) without exceeding the temperature limitation of the insulation on the conductor, that is, the current above which the insulation would be damaged.

This concept has always been verified in the FPN to Sec. 240-1, where the wording has been virtually identical for over 30 years and says, "Overcurrent protection for conductors and equipment is provided to open the circuit if the current reaches a value that will cause an excessive or dangerous temperature in conductors or conductor insulation." To correspond with that objective, Sec. 240-3 says, "Conductors, other than flexible cords and fixture wires, shall be protected against overcurrent in accordance with their ampacities as specified in Section 310-15."

Table 310-16, for instance, gives ampacities under the conditions that the raceway or cable containing the conductors is operating in an ambient not over 30°C (86°F) and that there are *not more* than three current-carrying conductors in the raceway or cable. Under those conditions, the ampacities shown correspond to the thermal limit of the particular insulations. But if either of the two conditions is exceeded, ampacities have to be reduced to keep heat from exceeding the temperature limits of the insulation:

1. If ambient is above 30°C, the *ampacity* must be reduced in accordance with the correction factors given at the bottom of Table 310-16.
2. If more than three current-carrying conductors are used in a single cable or raceway, the conductors tend to be bundled in such a way that their heat-dissipating capability is reduced and excessive heating would occur at the ampacities shown in the table. As a result, Note 8 requires *reduc-*

tion of ampacity, and conductors must be protected at the reduced ampacity.

(*Note:* It should be clearly understood that any reduced ampacity—required for higher ambient and/or conductor bundling—has the same meaning as the value shown in a table: Each represents a current value above which excessive heating would occur under the particular conditions. And if there are two conditions that reduce heat dissipation, then more reduction of current is required than for one condition of reduced dissipation.)

Note 8 Requires Derating of "Ampacity"

Note 8 to Table 310-16 says, "Where the number of conductors in a raceway or cable exceeds three, the ampacities shall be reduced as shown in the following table." And that table has a heading on the right to require that any ampacity derating for elevated ambient temperature must be made in addition to the one for number of conductors. If, for instance, four No. 8 THHN current-carrying copper conductors are used in a conduit, the ampacity of each No. 8 is reduced from the 55-A value shown in Table 310-16 to 80 percent of that value. Each No. 8 then has a new (reduced) ampacity of 0.8 × 55, or 44 A. Then, if a derating factor must be applied because the conductors are in a conduit where the ambient temperature is, say, 40°C instead of 30°C, the factor of 0.91 (36–40°C) from the bottom of Table 310-16 must be applied to the 44-A current value to determine the final value of ampacity for the conductors (44 × 0.91 = 40 A). Moreover, Sec. 240-3 of the NEC states, "Conductors, other than flexible cords and fixture wires, shall be protected against overcurrent in accordance with their ampacities as specified in Section 310-15." Thus, fuses or CB poles rated at 40 A would be required. The ampacity of the conductors is changed and the conductors must be protected in accordance with the derated ampacity value and not in accordance with the tabulated value.

Caution on Note 8: The table of Note 8 as it appeared in the NEC up through the 1984 edition was logical, easily understood, and readily applied at all times. As Note 8 now appears in the NEC, however, it is not logical, not even understandable, and defies any possibility of realistic application. The table of Note 8(a) contains two different sets of derating factors for cases where there are more than three current-carrying conductors in a raceway or cable. Column A gives derating factors for 10 or more conductors, with an asterisk notation that "These factors include the effects of a load diversity of 50 percent." Column B gives different derating factors (lower percentages) that are to be applied to 10 or more conductors in a raceway or cable, with the double asterisk notation, "No diversity." This entire concept, as presented, is so confusing as to be fairly described as virtually incomprehensible and practically unusable. In the absence of any solution to the problem, Note 8 should be applied as it appeared in the 1984 NEC, without the asterisked footnote, or to be completely on the safe, legally sound, and most time-efficient side of this issue, always use the derating factors from Column B of the Note 8 table and disregard "diversity factor"— whatever it is.

Because conductor "ampacity" is reduced when more than three conductors are used in a conduit, the overcurrent protection for each phase leg of a parallel makeup in a single conduit would generally have to be rated at not more than the sum of the *derated* ampacities of the number of conductors used per phase leg. That would satisfy Sec. 240-3, which requires conductors to be protected at their ampacities. Because ampacity is reduced in accordance with the percentage factors given in Note 8 for more than three conductors in a single conduit, that derating dictates the use of multiple conduits for parallel-makeup circuits to avoid the penalty of loss of ampacity.

Figure 310-30 shows examples of circuit makeups based on the unsafe concept of load limitation instead of ampacity derating, as applied to overcurrent

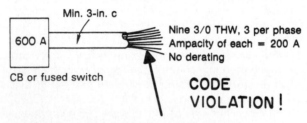

Note 8, max. conductor ampacity per phase
= 0.7 X 600 = 420 A, continuous or noncontinuous

Possible current in excess of conductor thermal limit
= 600 − 420 = 180 A

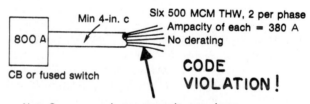

Note 8, max. conductor ampacity per phase
= 0.8 X 760 = 608 A, continuous or noncontinuous

Possible current in excess of conductor thermal limit
= 800 − 608 = 192 A

Fig. 310-30. Parallel-conductor makeup must not be used in single conduits without ampacity reduction, even if load current is limited to the conductor ampacity as shown here.

rating and conductor ampacity—which is a Code violation, because the conductors are *not* protected in accordance with their ampacities.

Figure 310-31 shows a condition of bunched or bundled Type NM cables where they come together at a panelboard location. The paragraph following the table of Note 8 requires conductors in bundled cables to have their load

Fig. 310·31. If a large number of multi-conductor cables are bundled together in a stud space, capacity derating in accordance with Note 8 would be required. If the individual cables are spaced apart and stapled, then the conductors in the cables may be loaded up to their rated ampacity values from Table 310-16. (Sec. 310-15.)

currents reduced from the ampacity values shown in Table 310-16. The ampacity derating is required for conductor stacks or bundles that are longer than 2 ft (24 in.). For shorter bundles, derating is not required. And Exception No. 3 excludes the need for derating groups of (four or more) conductors installed in nipples not over 24 in. long.

Exception No. 4 of Note 8 says that underground conductors that are brought up above ground in a protective raceway [Sec. 300-5(d)] do not require derating if not more than four conductors are used and if the protective conduit has a length not over 10 ft "above grade." The total length of raceway may exceed 10 ft. The phrase "above grade" clearly limits the length of protective conduit that may contain conductors *without* derating in accordance with Note 8(a). The 10-ft length covers the length of 8 ft above grade but not the 1½ ft into the earth given by Sec. 300-5(d) on conductors emerging from underground.

Note 8 does not apply to conductors in wireways and auxiliary gutters, as covered in Secs. 362-5 and 374-5. Wireways or auxiliary gutters may contain up to 30 conductors at any cross section [excluding signal circuits and control conductors used for starting duty only between a motor and its starter in auxiliary gutters (Sec. 374-5)]. The total cross-sectional area of the group of conductors must not be greater than 20 percent of the interior cross-sectional area of the wireway or gutter. And load-limiting factors for more than three conductors do not apply to wireway the way they do to wires in conduit. However, if the derating factors from Note 8 of the NE Code Tables 310-16 through 310-19 are used, there is no limit to the number of wires permitted in a wireway or an auxiliary gutter. But, the sum of the cross-sectional areas of all contained conductors at any cross section of the wireway must not exceed 20 percent of the cross-sectional area of the wireway or auxiliary gutter. More than 30 conductors may be used under those conditions.

Note 10   In the determination of conduit size, neutral conductors must be included in the total number of conductors because they occupy space as well as phase conductors. A completely separate consideration, however, is the relation of neutral conductors to the number of conductors, which determines whether ampacity derating must be applied to conductors in a conduit, as follows.

Neutral conductors which carry only unbalanced current from phase conductors (as in the case of normally balanced 3-wire, single-phase or 4-wire, 3-phase circuits supplying resistive loads) are not counted in determining ampacity derating of conductors on the basis of the number in a conduit, as described. A neutral conductor used with two phase legs of a 4-wire, 3-phase system to make up a 3-wire feeder is not a true neutral in the sense of carrying only current unbalance. Such a neutral carries the same current as the other two conductors under balanced load conditions and must be counted as a phase conductor when more than three conductors in conduit are derated.

Because the neutral of a 3-phase, 4-wire wye branch circuit or feeder to a load of fluorescent, metal-halide, mercury, or sodium lamp lighting or to electronic data processing equipment will carry harmonic current even under balanced loading on the phases (refer to Sec. 220-22), such a neutral is not a true noncurrent-carrying conductor and must be counted as a phase wire when the number of conductors to arrive at an ampacity derating factor is determined for more than three conductors in a conduit. As a result, all the conductors of a 3-phase, 4-wire branch circuit or feeder to a fluorescent load would have an ampacity of only 80 percent of their nominal ampacity from Table 310-16 or other ampacity table. Because the 80 percent is a derating of ampacity, the conductors must be protected at the derated "ampacity" value.

Figure 310-32 shows four basic conditions of neutral loading and the need for counting the neutral conductor in loading a circuit to fluorescent or mercury ballasts, as follows:

CASE 1—With balanced loads of equal power factor, there is no neutral current, and consequently no heating contributed by the neutral conductor. For purposes of heat derating according to the **Code**, this circuit produces the heating effect of only three conductors.

CASE 2—With two phases loaded and the third unloaded, the neutral carries the same as the phases, but there is still the heating effect of only three conductors.

CASE 3—With two phases fully loaded and the third phase partially loaded, the neutral carries the difference in current between the full phase value and the partial phase value, so that again there is the heating effect of only three full-load phases.

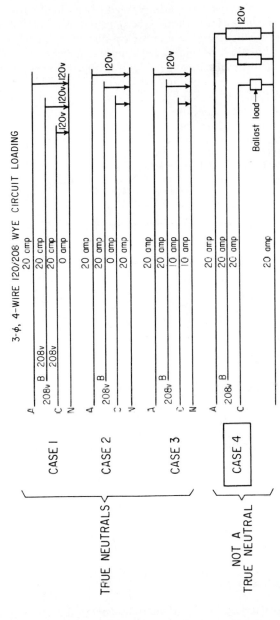

Fig. 310·32. All neutrals count for conduit fill, but only "true neutrals" do not count in determining ampacity derating for number of conductors in a raceway or cable [Note 10(a)]. [Sec. 310-15.]

CASE 4—With a balanced load of fluorescent ballasts, third harmonic current generation causes a neutral current approximating phase current, and there will be the heating effect of four conductors. Such a neutral conductor must be counted with the phase conductors when the load-current limitation due to conduit occupancy is determined, as required in part (**c**) of Note 10.

Although Note 10 exempts only neutral conductors from those conductors which must be counted in determining load-limiting factors for more than three conductors in a raceway or cable (per Note 8), similar exemption should be allowed for one of the "travelers" in a 3-way (or 3-way and 4-way) switch circuit. As shown in Fig. 310-33, only one of the two conductors is a current-carrying conductor at any one time; therefore, the other should not be counted for load-limitation purposes where such switch legs are run in conduit or EMT along with other circuit conductors.

FOR DERATING PURPOSES —

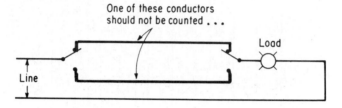

One of these conductors should not be counted . . .

Line

Load

... where these wires are in conduit or EMT with other wires.

Fig. 310-33. The 3-wire run in conduit between 3-way switches contains only two current-carrying conductors. (Sec. 310-15.)

Note 11 This note makes it clear that an equipment grounding conductor or bonding conductor, which under normal conditions is carrying no current, does not have to be counted in determining ampacity derating of conductors when more than three conductors are used in a raceway or cable. As a result, equipment grounding and bonding conductors do not have to be factored into the calculation of required ampacity derating specified in Note 8(a).

Ampacity of conductors over 600 V, nominal Since the 1975 edition, the **NEC** has added a vast amount of information and data for conductors rated over 600 V, up to 35 kV. For instance, Tables 310-69 through 310-84 give maximum continuous ampacities for copper and aluminum solid dielectric insulated conductors rated from 2,001 to 35,000 V.

ARTICLE 318. CABLE TRAYS

318-2. Definitions. Cable trays are open, raceway-like support assemblies made of metal or suitable nonmetallic material and are widely used for supporting and routing circuits in many types of buildings. Troughs of metal mesh construction provide a sturdy, flexible system for supporting feeder cables, particularly where routing of the runs is devious or where provision for change or modification in circuiting is important. Ladder-type cable trays are used for supporting interlocked-armor cable feeders in many installations (Fig. 318-1).

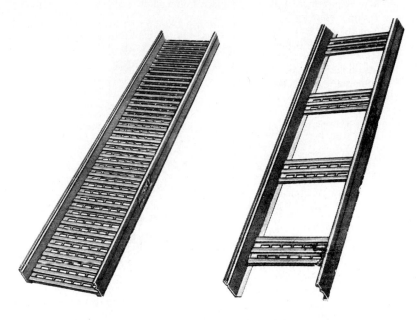

Trough-type (or expanded-   Ladder-type tray
metal-type) tray

Fig. 318-1. Two basic types of cable tray. (Sec. 318-2.)

Where past **Code** editions treated cable tray simply as a support system for cables, in the same category as a clamp or hanger, the **Code** today recognizes cable tray as a conductor support method, somewhat like raceway, under prescribed conditions, and an integral part of a **Code**-approved wiring method. However, cable tray is not listed under the **Code** definition of "raceway" in Art. 100. Any "raceway" must be an "enclosed" channel for conductors. Cable tray is a "support system" and not a "raceway."

318.3. Uses Permitted. The **NEC** recognizes cable tray as a support for wiring methods that may be used without a tray (metal-clad cable, conductors in EMT, IMC, or rigid conduit, etc.), and cable tray may be used in either commercial or industrial buildings or premises (Fig. 318-2). Where cables are available in both single-conductor and multiconductor types—such as SE (service entrance) cable and UF cable—only the multiconductor type may be used in tray. However, Sec. 318-3(b) permits use of single-conductor building wires in tray. Single-conductor cables for use in tray must be 1/0 or larger, listed for use in tray, and "marked on the surface" as suitable for tray applications. In previous **NEC** editions, single-conductor cable in tray had to be 250 kcmil or larger. Sizes 1/0

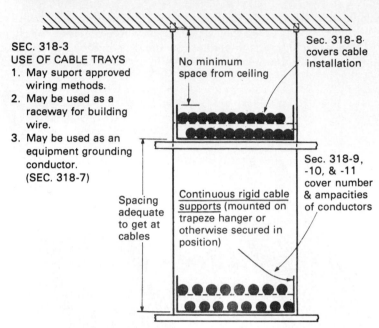

SEC. 318-3
USE OF CABLE TRAYS
1. May suport approved wiring methods.
2. May be used as a raceway for building wire.
3. May be used as an equipment grounding conductor. (SEC. 318-7)

No minimum space from ceiling

Sec. 318-8 covers cable installation

Sec. 318-9, -10, & -11 cover number & ampacities of conductors

Spacing adequate to get at cables

Continuous rigid cable supports (mounted on trapeze hanger or otherwise secured in position)

Fig. 318-2. Cable-tray use is subject to many specific rules in Art. 318. (Sec. 318-3.)

through 4/0 single-conductor cables may now be used but must be used in ladder-type tray with rungs spaced not over 9 in. apart or in ventilated trough cable tray. Sizes 250 kcmil and larger may be used in any kind of tray. This rule states that such use of building wire is permitted in industrial establishments only, where conditions of maintenance and supervision assure that only competent individuals will service the installed cable tray system. This applies to ladder-type tray, ventilated trough, or 4-in. ventilated channel-type cable tray.

Single-conductor cables used in cable tray must be a type specifically "listed for use in cable trays." This is a qualification on the rule that was in previous codes permitting use of single-conductor building wire (RHH, USE, THW, MV) in cable tray. The wording permits any choice of conductor types that may be used, simply requiring that any type must be listed. That adds thin-wall-insulated cables, like THHN or XHHW, to the other types mentioned. Present UL standards make reference to cables designated "for CT (cable tray) use" or "for use in cable trays"—which is marked on the outside of the cable jacket. Such cables are subjected to a "vertical tray flame test," as used for Type TC tray cable and other cables. Only cables so tested and marked "VW-1" would be recognized for use in cable tray.

Part (c) specifically recognizes use of the metal length of cable tray as an equipment grounding conductor for the circuit(s) in the tray—in *both* commercial and industrial premises where qualified maintenance personnel are available to assure the integrity of the grounding path. Section 318-3(d) specifically uses the word "only" when referring to cable types that are permitted to be used in cable trays in hazardous locations. In previous **Code** editions, wording was more open-ended and permitted specific cables without limiting use to only such cables.

As covered in part **(e)**, nonmetallic cable tray may be used in corrosive locations. This permits use of nonmetallic tray—such as fiberglass tray—in industrial or other areas where severe corrosive atmospheres would attack metal tray. Such a tray is also permitted where "voltage isolation" is required.

318-4. Uses Not Permitted. Cable tray may be used in air-handling ceiling space *but* only to support the wiring methods permitted in such space by Sec. 300-22(c). This recognizes cable tray simply as a support for raceways or cables permitted in hung ceilings used for air conditioning. Sec 318-6(h) requires cable trays to be exposed and accessible. Note that the two words "exposed" and "accessible" must be taken "as applied to wiring methods." Cable tray may be used above a suspended, non-air-handling ceiling with any of the wiring methods covered by Sec. 318-3. If used with a wiring method permitted by Sec. 300-22(c), cable tray may be used above an air-handling ceiling.

318-6. Installation. Part **(a)** makes clear that cable tray *must* be used as a complete system—that is, straight sections, angle sections, offsets, saddles, etc.—to form a cable support system that is continuous and grounded as required by Sec. 318-7(a). Cable tray must not be installed with separate, unconnected sections used at spaced positions to support the cable. Manufactured fittings or field-bent sections of tray may be used for changes in direction or elevation.

In the 1971 **NEC**, part **(c)** of Sec. 318-4 on Installation (now Sec. 318-6) read as follows:

(c) Continuous rigid cable supports shall be mechanically connected to any enclosure or raceway into which the cables contained in the continuous rigid cable support extend or terminate.

That wording clearly made a violation of the kind of hookup shown in Fig. 318-3, where the tray does not connect to the transformer enclosures—and is not bonded by jumpers to those enclosures. Although that rule from the 1971 **NEC** has been deleted, it seems clear that the same intent is conveyed by the wording of part **(a)** described above. Whether the tray must come down and connect to the transformer enclosure or whether the continuity may be provided by a bonding jumper from the tray to each enclosure is a matter of local interpretation. Refer also to Sec. 318-7.

Section 318-6(e) notes that any multiconductor cables rated 600 V or less may be used in the same cable tray. Section 318-6(f) points out that although cables rated over 600 V must not be installed in the same cable tray with cables rated 600 V or less, there are two exceptions to that rule. High-voltage cables and low-voltage cables may be used in the same tray if a solid, noncombustible, fixed barrier is installed in the tray to separate high-voltage cables from low-voltage cables. Where the high-voltage (over 600 V) cables are Type MC, it is not necessary to have a barrier in the cable tray, and MC cables operating above 600 V may be used in the same tray with MC cables operating less than 600 V or with nonmetallic-jacketed cables operating at not over 600 V. But for high-voltage cables other than Type MC, a barrier must be used in the tray to separate high-voltage from low-voltage cables (Fig. 318-4).

Figure 318-5 shows the rule of part **(i)**.

Fig. 318-3. This was clearly a violation of Sec. 318-4(c) in the 1971 **NEC** because the tray does not connect to the transformer enclosures. The tray continuity required by Sec. 318-6(a) of the present **NEC** does seem to be violated by lack of connection to the enclosures. (Sec. 318-6.)

Multiconductor cables rated up to 600 volts may be used in the same tray, even when voltage ratings differ.

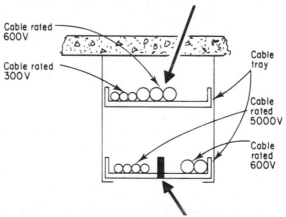

A solid, noncombustible, fixed barrier must be used in tray to separate high-voltage and low-voltage cables with nonmetallic jackets — **but** barrier is not needed in tray if the high-voltage cables are Type MC.

Fig. 318-4. Cables of different voltage ratings may be used in the same tray. (Sec. 318-6.)

No minimum vertical clearance distance from tray
top to ceiling, beam or other obstruction (used to be
6 in.)

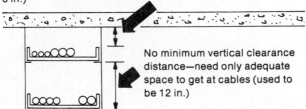

No minimum vertical clearance
distance—need only adequate
space to get at cables (used to
be 12 in.)

Fig. 318-5. Tray spacing must simply be adequate for cable installation and maintenance. (Sec. 318-6.)

318-7. Grounding. Part **(a)** requires cable tray to be grounded, just as conduit or other metal enclosures for conductors must be grounded. That rule combined with part **(a)** of Sec. 318-6—which requires cable tray to be installed as a continuous, interconnected system—makes cable tray comply with the **Code** concept that metal raceways constitute an equipment grounding conductor to carry fault currents back to the bonded neutral at a service, at a transformer secondary, or at a generator. Part **(b)** of Sec. 318-7 combines with the above-described Sec. 318-3(b) (1) to make cable tray a raceway and a wiring method. The **Code** permits steel or aluminum cable tray to serve as an equipment grounding conductor for the circuits in the tray in much the same way as conduit or EMT may serve as the equipment grounding conductor—a return path for fault current—for the circuit conductors they contain, under the conditions specified in part **(b)**.

Note that paragraph **(4)** under part **(b)** requires all tray system components, as well as "connected raceways," to be bonded together—either by the bolting means provided with the tray sections or fittings or by bonding jumpers, as shown in Fig. 318-6.

318-8. Cable Installation. Although splices are generally limited to use in conductor enclosures with covers and are prohibited in the various conduits, part **(a)** permits splicing of conductors in cable tray.

Part **(c)** permits cables or conductors to drop out of tray in conduits or tubing that have protective bushings and are clamped to the tray side rail by cable-tray conduit clamps to provide the bonded connections required by Sec. 318-7(h) (4).

Figure 318-7 shows how single-conductor cables must be grouped to satisfy part **(d)** of this section for a 1,200-A circuit made up of three 500 kcmil copper XHHW conductors per phase and three for the neutral. By distributing the phases and neutral among three groups of four and alternating positions, more effective cancellation of magnetic fluxes results from the more symmetrical placement—thereby tending to balance current by balancing inductive reactance of the overall 1,200-A circuit.

318-9. Number of Multiconductor Cables, Rated 2000 Volts, Nominal, or Less, in Cable Trays. These rules apply to multiconductor cables rated 2,000 V or less. For cables rated 2,001 V or higher, the number permitted in a cable tray is now covered in Sec. 318-12.

Fig. 318-6. Bare equipment bonding jumpers tie all tray runs together, with jumpers carried up to the equipment grounding bus in the switchboard above. (Sec. 318-7.)

Each group of four conductors
is bound in circuit groups of
phases A, B, C and neutral

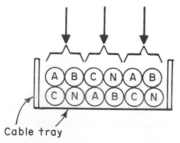

Cable tray

Fig. 318-7. A parallel 1,200-A circuit must have conductors grouped for reduced reactance and effective current balance. (Sec. 318-8.)

Section 318-9 is broken down into parts **(a)**, **(b)**, **(c)**, **(d)**, and **(e)**, each part covering a different condition of use. Section 318-9(a) applies to ladder or ventilated trough cable trays containing multiconductor power or lighting cables or any mixture of multiconductor power, lighting, control, and signal cables.

Section 318-9(a) has three subdivisions:

1. Where all the multiconductor cables are made up of conductors No. 4/0 or larger, the sum of the outside diameters of all the multiconductor cables in the tray must not be greater than the cable tray width, and the cables *must* be placed side by side in the tray in a single layer as shown in Fig. 318-8.

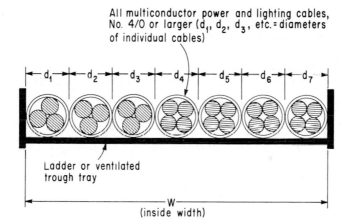

1. Cable-tray width (W) = at least
   $d_1 + d_2 + d_3 + d_4 + d_5 + d_6 + d_7$ in.
2. All cables *must* lie flat, side by side,
   in one layer.

Fig. 318-8. No. 4/0 and larger multiconductor cables must be in a single layer. (Sec. 318-9.)

2. Where all the multiconductor cables in the tray are made up of conductors smaller than No. 4/0, the sum of the cross-sectional areas of all cables *must not exceed* the maximum allowable cable fill area in column 1 of Table 318-9 for the particular width of cable tray being used. The table shows, for instance, that if an 18-in.-wide ladder or ventilated trough cable tray is used with multiconductor cables smaller than No. 4/0, column 1 sets 21 sq in. as the maximum value for the sum of the overall cross-section areas of all the cables permitted in that tray, as in Fig. 318-9.

3. Where a tray contains one or more multiconductor cables No. 4/0 or larger along with one or more multiconductor cables smaller than No. 4/0, there are two steps in determining the maximum fill of the tray.

First, the sum of the outside cross-section areas of all the cables smaller than No. 4/0 must not be greater than the maximum permitted fill area resulting from the computation in column 2 of Table 318-9 for the particular cable tray

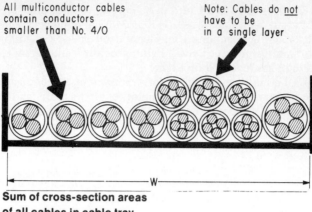

All multiconductor cables contain conductors smaller than No. 4/0

Note: Cables do not have to be in a single layer

Sum of cross-section areas of all cables in cable tray

= not less than cable fill in sq in. given in column 1 of Table 318–9 for the particular cable-tray width involved.

Note: Cross-section area (in sq in.) of each cable can be obtained from cable manufacturers' catalogs or spec sheets. If, in the case shown here, the sum of the cross-section areas of the 10 cables in the tray came to, say, 26 sq in., the smallest permissible width of cable tray would be 24 in., as shown in column 1 of Table 318-9. An 18-in.-wide cable tray would be good only for a sum of cable areas up to 21 sq in.

Fig. 318·9. Smaller than No. 4/0 cables may be stacked in tray. (Sec. 318-9.)

width. Then, the multiconductor cables that are No. 4/0 or larger must be installed in a single layer, and no other cables may be placed on top of them (Fig. 318-10). Note that the available cross-section area of a tray which can properly accommodate cables smaller than No. 4/0 installed in a tray along with No. 4/0 or larger cables is, in effect, equal to the allowable fill area from column 1 for each width of tray minus 1.2 times the sum of the outside diameters of the No. 4/0 or larger cables.

Another way to look at this is to consider that, for any cable tray, the sum of the cross-section areas of cables smaller than No. 4/0, when added to 1.2 times the sum of the diameters of cables No. 4/0 or larger, must not exceed the value given in column 1 of Table 318-9 for a particular cable tray width.

For the installation shown in Fig. 318-10, assume that the sum of the cross-section areas of the seven cables smaller than No. 4/0 is 16 sq in., and assume that the diameters of the four No. 4/0 or larger cables are 3 in., 3.5 in., 4 in., and 4 in. The abbreviation "Sd" in column 2 of Table 318-9 represents "sum of the diameters" of No. 4/0 and larger cables installed in the same tray with cables smaller than No. 4/0. In the example here, then, Sd is equal to 3 + 3.5

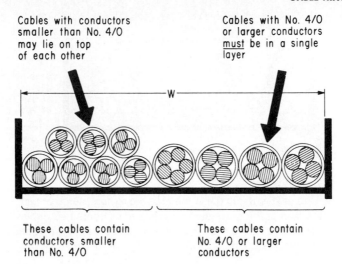

Cables with conductors smaller than No. 4/0 may lie on top of each other

Cables with No. 4/0 or larger conductors <u>must</u> be in a single layer

These cables contain conductors smaller than No. 4/0

These cables contain No. 4/0 or larger conductors

Inside width (W) of tray must not be less than that required by Table 318-9, based on the calculation indicated in column 2 of the table.

Fig. 318-10. Large and small cables have a more complex tray-fill formula. (Sec. 318-9.)

+ 4 + 4 = 14.5, and 1.2 × 14.5 = 17.4. Then we add the 16-sq-in. total of the cables smaller than No. 4/0 to the 17.4 and get 17.4 + 16 = 33.4. Note that this sum is over the limit of 28 sq in., which is the maximum permitted fill given in column 1 for a 24-in.-wide cable tray. And column 1 shows that a 30-in.-wide tray (with 35-sq-in. fill capacity) would be required for the 33.4 sq in. determined from the calculation of column 2, Table 318-9.

Section 318-9(b) covers use of multiconductor control and/or signal cables (not power and/or lighting cables) in ladder or ventilated trough with a usable inside depth of 6 in. or less. For such cables in ladder or ventilated trough cable tray, the sum of the cross section areas of all cables at any cross section of the tray must not exceed 50 percent of the interior cross-section area of the cable tray. And it's important to note that a depth of 6 in. must be used in computing the allowable interior cross-section area of any tray that has a usable inside depth of more than 6 in. (Fig. 318-11).

Section 318-9(c) applies to solid-bottom cable trays with multiconductor power or lighting cables or mixtures of power, lighting, control, and signal cables. The maximum number of cables must be observed, as noted.

318-10. Number of Single Conductor Cables, Rated 2000 Volts or Less, In Cable Trays. This section covers the maximum permitted number of single-conductor cables in cable tray and stipulates that the conductors must be evenly distributed on the cable tray. This section differentiates between (a) ladder or ventilated trough tray and (b) ventilated channel-type cable trays.

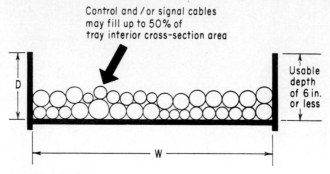

Control and / or signal cables
may fill up to 50% of
tray interior cross-section area

Usable
depth
of 6 in.
or less

Permissible fill:

If the usable depth (D) in the above drawing is 6 in. or less, the sum of the cross-section areas of all contained cables must be not more than $\frac{1}{2} \times D \times W$. If the tray has a depth of more than 6 in., the value of (D) must be taken as 6 in. for computing tray fill.

Fig. 318·11. Tray fill for multiconductor control and/or signal cables is readily determined. (Sec. 318-9.)

In Ladder or Ventilated Trough Tray

1. Where all cables are 1,000 kcmil or larger, the sum of the diameters of all single-conductor cables must not be greater than the cable tray width, as shown in Fig. 318-12. That means the cable tray width must be at least equal to the sum of the diameters of the individual cables.
2. Where all cables are from 250 up to and including 1,000 kcmil, the sum of the cross-section areas of all cables must not be greater than the maximum allowable cable fill areas in square inches, as shown in column 1 of Table 318-10 for the particular cable tray width.

example 1   Assume a number of cables, all smaller than 1,000 kcmil, have a total csa of 11 sq in. Column 1 of Table 318-10 shows that a fill of 11 sq in. is greater than that

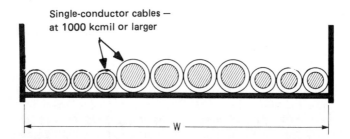

Single-conductor cables —
at 1000 kcmil or larger

Tray must be wide enough to hold all cables side-by-side, as shown.

Fig. 318·12. For large cables, tray width must at least equal sum of cable diameters. (Sec. 318-10.)

allowed for 6-in.-wide tray (6.5 sq in.) but less than the maximum fill of 13 sq in. permitted for 12-in.-wide tray. Thus, 12-in.-wide tray would be acceptable.

example 2   Assume four 4-wire sets of single-conductor, 500 kcmil RHH cables are used as power feeder conductors in cable tray. Table 5 in Chap. 9 of the **NE Code** shows that the overall csa of each 500 kcmil RHH conductor (without outer covering) is 0.8316 sq in. The total area of 16 such conductors would be 16 × 0.8316 or 13.3 sq in. From Table 318-10, column 1, 13.3 sq in. is just over the maximum permissible fill for 12-in.-wide tray, but it is well below the maximum fill of 19.5 sq in. permitted for 18-in.-wide tray. Thus, 18-in.-wide tray is acceptable.

3. Where 1,000 kcmil or larger single-conductor cables are installed in the same tray with single-conductor cables smaller than 1,000 kcmil, the fill must not exceed the maximum fill determined by the calculation indicated in column 2 of Table 318-10—in a manner similar to the calculations indicated above for multiconductor cables.

example   If nine 750 kcmil THW conductors are in a tray with six 1,000 kcmil THW conductors, the required minimum width (W) of the tray would be determined as follows:
1. The sum of the csa of the nine 750 kcmil conductors (those smaller than 1,000 kcmil) is equal to 9 × 1.2252 sq in. (from column 5, Table 5, Chap. 9, **NE Code**) or 11.03 sq in.
2. Each 1,000 kcmil THW conductor has an outside diameter of 1.404 in. The sum of the diameters of the 1,000 kcmil conductors is, then, 6 × 1.404 or 8.424 in.
3. Column 2 of Table 318-10 says, in effect, that to determine the minimum required width of cable tray it is necessary to add 11.03 sq in. (from 1 above) to 1.1 × 8.424 (from 2 above) and use the total to check against column 1 of Table 318-10 to get the tray width:

$$11.03 + (1.1 \times 8.424) = 11.03 + 9.27 = 20.3 \text{ sq in.}$$

From column 1, Table 318-10, the fill of 20.3 sq in. is greater than the 19.5 sq in. permitted for 18-in.-wide tray. But, this fill is within the permitted fill of 26 sq in. for 24-in.-wide tray. The 24-in.-wide tray is, therefore, the minimum size tray that is acceptable.

4. Where any cables in the tray are sizes 1/0 through 4/0, then all cables must be installed in a single layer. And the sum of the single-conductor cable diameters must not exceed the cable tray width as required for "Multiconductor Cables Rated 2000 V, Nominal, or Less" as covered in Sec. 318-9(a)(1).

In 4-in.-Wide Channel-Type Tray

Where single-conductor cables are installed in 4-in.-wide, ventilated channel-type trays, the sum of the diameters of all single conductors must not exceed the inside width of the channel.

318-11.   Ampacity of Cables Rated 2000 Volts or Less in Cable Trays.   Cables in cable tray are not subject to the ampacity derating factors given in Note 8(a) of Tables 310-16 through 310-19.

Multiconductor Cables

When cable assemblies of more than one conductor are installed as required by Sec. 318-9, each conductor in any of the cables will have an ampacity as

given in Table 310-16 or Table 310-18. Those are the standard tables of ampacities for cables with not more than three current-carrying conductors within the
cable (excluding neutral conductors that carry current only during load unbalance on the phases). The ampacity of any conductor in a cable is based on the
size of the conductor and the type of insulation on the conductor, as shown in
Tables 310-16 and 310-18. For cables not installed in cable tray, if a cable contains more than three current-carrying conductors, derating of the conductor
ampacities must be made in accordance with Note 8 to Tables 310-16 through
310-19. But the first sentence of Sec. 318-11 flatly exempts cables in tray from
Note 8.

Exception No. 1 to the above determination of conductor ampacities is made
in the case of any cable tray with more than 6 ft of continuous, solid, unventilated covers. In such cases, the conductors in the cable have an ampacity of not
more than 95 percent of the ampacities given in Table 310-16 or Table 310-18.

Exception No. 2 applies to a single layer of multiconductor cables with maintained spacing between cables, installed in uncovered tray.

Single-Conductor Cables

The ampacity of any single-conductor cable or single conductors twisted
together is determined as follows:

600 kcmil and larger—Where installed in accordance with Sec. 318-10, the
ampacity of any 600 kcmil or larger single-conductor cable in uncovered tray
is *not more* than 75 percent of the ampacity given for the size and insulation of
conductor in Table 310-17 or for the size and insulation of conductor in Tables
310-17 and 310-19. Note that this means 75 percent of the free-air ampacity of
the conductor. And if more than 6 ft of the tray is continuously covered with a
solid, unventilated cover, the ampacities for 600 kcmil and larger conductors
must not exceed 70 percent of the ampacity value in Tables 310-17 and 310-19.

No. 1/0 through 500 kcmil—For any single-conductor cable in this range,
installed in accordance with Sec. 318-10 in uncovered tray, its ampacity is not
more than 65 percent of the ampacity value shown in Table 310-17 or Table
310-19. And if any such cables in this range are used in tray that is continuously
covered for more than 6 ft with a solid, unventilated cover, the ampacities must
not exceed 60 percent of the ampacity values in Tables 310-17 and 310-19.

Where No. 1/0 and larger single-conductor cables are installed in a single
layer in uncovered cable tray with a maintained spacing of not less than one
cable diameter between individual conductors, the ampacities of such conductors are equal to the free-air ampacities given in Tables 310-17 and 310-19, as
shown in Fig. 318-13.

**318-12. Number of Type MV and Type MC Cables (2001 Volts or Over) in Cable
Trays.** This section applies only to high-voltage circuits in tray. Type MV
cable is a high-voltage cable now covered by new Art. 326. Type MC cable is
the metal-clad cable operating above 2,000 V—a cable assembly long known as
interlocked armor cable. [Type MC or other armored cable (e.g., ALS or CS)
operating at voltages up to 2,000 V must conform to Secs. 318-9 and 318-10 on
number and ampacities of cables when used in tray.]

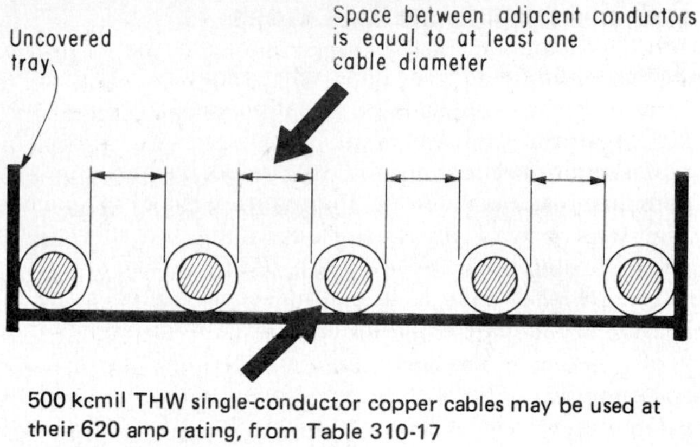

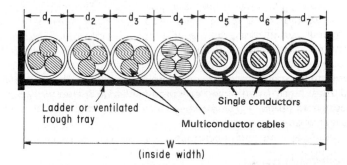

Uncovered tray

Space between adjacent conductors is equal to at least one cable diameter

500 kcmil THW single-conductor copper cables may be used at their 620 amp rating, from Table 310-17

Fig. 318-13. With spacing, cables in tray may operate at free-air ampacity. (Sec. 318-11.)

d_1 d_2 d_3 d_4 d_5 d_6 d_7

Ladder or ventilated trough tray

Single conductors

Multiconductor cables

W
(inside width)

1. Cable-tray width (W) = at least
   $d_1 + d_2 + d_3 + d_4 + d_5 + d_6 + d_7$ in.
2. All cables *must* lie flat, side by side, in one layer.

Fig. 318-14. Tray must be wide enough for all high-voltage cables in a single layer. (Sec. 318-12.)

Type MV and Type MC high-voltage cables must conform to the tray fill shown in Fig. 318-14.

318-13. Ampacity of Type MV and Type MC Cables (2001 Volts or Over) in Cable Trays. This section covers the ampacities of MV and MC cables operating above 2,000 V in cable trays—both single-conductor and multiconductor. Exception No. 2 recognizes the improved heat dissipation afforded by spacing of the cables and allows use of the free-air ampacity tables in loading multiconductor cables. The spacing of "one cable diameter" is also recognized for single conductors in Sec. 318-13(b)(3).

ARTICLE 320. OPEN WIRING ON INSULATORS

320·1. Definition.   Conductors for open wiring may be any of the general-use types listed in Table 310-13 for "dry" locations and "dry and wet" locations such as THW, XHHW, THHN, etc.

The conductors are secured to and supported by insulators, of porcelain, glass, or other composition materials. In modern wiring practice open wiring is used for high-tension work in transformer vaults and substations. It is very commonly used for temporary work and is used for runs of heavy conductors for feeders and power circuits, as in manholes and trenches under or adjacent to switchboards, to facilitate the routing of large numbers of circuits fed into conduits.

320·3. Uses Permitted.   This section limits open wiring on insulators to industrial or agricultural establishments, up to 600 V. Section 320-15 spells out such installations in unfinished attics and roof spaces.

320·6. Conductor Supports.   Methods of dead-ending open cable runs are shown in Fig. 320-1.

Where heavy AC feeders are run as open wiring, the reactance of the circuit is reduced and hence the voltage drop is reduced by using a small spacing between the conductors. Up to a distance of 15 ft between supports the 2½-in. spacing may be used if spacers are clamped to the conductors at intervals not exceeding 4½ ft. A spacer consists of the three porcelain pieces of the same form as used in the support, with a metal clamping ring.

In Exception No. 2, reference to "mill construction" is generally understood to mean the type of building in which the floors are supported on wooden beams spaced about 14 to 16 ft apart. Wires not smaller than No. 8 may safely

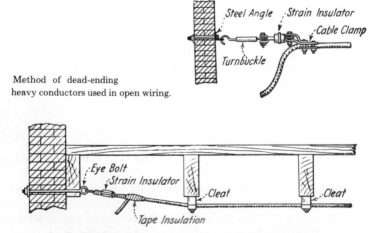

Method of dead-ending
heavy conductors used in open wiring.

Method of dead-ending heavy conductors used in open wiring.

Fig. 320·1. Proven methods must be used for dead-ending open wiring. (Sec. 320-6.)

span such a distance where the ceilings are high and the space is free from obstructions.

320-7. Mounting of Conductor Supports. Figure 320-2 illustrates mounting of knobs and cleats for the support of No. 14, No. 12, and No. 10 conductors. For conductors of larger size, solid knobs with tie wires or single-wire cleats should be used.

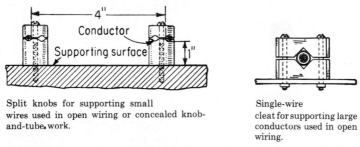

Split knobs for supporting small wires used in open wiring or concealed knob-and-tube work.

Single-wire cleat for supporting large conductors used in open wiring.

Fig. 320-2. Proper wiring support devices must be correctly mounted. (Sec. 320-7.)

320-12. Clearance from Piping, Exposed Conductors, etc. The additional insulation on the wire, referred to in this rule, is to prevent the wire from coming in contact with the adjacent pipe or other metal.

ARTICLE 321. MESSENGER SUPPORTED WIRING

321-1. Definition. This article covers a wiring system that has long been manufactured and widely used in industrial installations. The basic construction of the wiring method has been used for many years as service-drop cable for utility supply to all kinds of commercial and residential properties.

From long-time application, messenger supported wiring is actually an old standard method, even though it has not been covered by the NE Code up until recent years. In Sec. 225-6, the Exception refers to "supported by messenger wire," and that phrase has been in the Code for over 30 years. Figure 321-1 shows an example of triplex service-drop cable used for supplying floodlights at an outdoor athletic field. So coverage of this type of wiring is important—especially for the vast amounts of outdoor use where messenger-cable wiring offers so many advantages over open wiring. But, messenger supported wiring is recognized for both indoor and outdoor branch circuits and/or feeders. Refer to the discussion under Sec. 225-4 for outdoor use of messenger supported wiring.

321-3. Uses Permitted. Messenger support is permitted for a wide range of cables and conductors—for use in commercial and industrial applications. Part **(b)** covers ordinary building wires supported on a messenger and recognizes use

Fig. 321·1. Messenger-supported cable, used here to supply pole-mounted floodlights, may be constructed in a number of different assemblies, such as this service-drop cable with an ACSR messenger cabled with insulated conductors.

of messenger supported wiring in "industrial establishments *only*" with "any of the conductor types given in Table 310-13 or Table 310-62." Tables 310-13 and 310-62 include single-conductor Types MV, RHH, RHW, and THW and also accept all the other single-conductor types, such as THHN, XHHW, TW. All such application is recognized either indoors or outdoors—provided that any conductors exposed to the weather are "listed for use in wet locations" and are "sunlight-resistant" if exposed to direct rays of the sun.

321-5. Ampacity. In any specific application, the ampacity of any conductor "shall be determined by Sec. 310-15"—which covers ampacity tables for all the various conductors in the various wiring methods. The choice of table to be used depends upon the type of cable or conductor assembly being supported by the messenger. Some may opt to use ampacity tables for a "single conductor in free air" (Table 310-17), which is not applicable to, say, triplexed single conductors (bundled together) but is actually applicable only to single conductors that are "isolated" individually in air.

ARTICLE 324. CONCEALED KNOB-AND-TUBE WIRING

324-3. Uses Permitted. Note that this wiring method is restricted to use only for extensions of existing installations and is not **Code**-acceptable as a general-purpose wiring method for new electrical work. Under the conditions specified in **(1)** and **(2)**, concealed knob-and-tube wiring may be used only if special permission is granted by the local inspection authority having jurisdiction as noted in the second sentence of Sec. 90-4.

324-5. Conductors. Conductors for concealed knob-and-tube work may be any of the general-use types listed in Table 310-13 for "dry" locations and "dry and wet" locations such as TW, THW, XHHW, RHH, etc.

324-11. Unfinished Attics and Roof Spaces. Where wires are run on knobs or through tubes in a closed-in and inaccessible attic or roof space, the wiring is concealed knob-and-tube work; but if the attic or roof space is accessible, the wiring must conform to Art. 320 as open wiring on insulators. Both cases are covered by the foregoing rules.

Where the wiring is installed at any time after the building is completed, in a roof space having less than 3 ft headroom at any point, the wires may be run on knobs across the faces of the joists, studs, or rafters or through or on the sides of the joists, studs, or rafters. Such a space would not be used for storage purposes, and the wiring installed may be considered as concealed knob-and-tube work.

An attic or roof space is considered accessible if it can be reached by means of a stairway or a permanent ladder. In any such attic or roof space wires run through the floor joists where there is no floor must be protected by a running board and wires run through the studs or rafters must be protected by a running board if within 7 ft from the floor or floor joists.

ARTICLE 325. INTEGRATED GAS SPACER CABLE TYPE IGS

325-1. Definition.   Type IGS cable is a "factory assembly of one or more conductors, each individually insulated and enclosed in a loose-fit nonmetallic flexible conduit." The cable is for underground use—including direct earth burial—for service conductors, feeders, or branch circuits. The introduction of this cable to the NEC was recommended on the following basis:

Underground cable costs are increasing at a high rate. A need exists for lower material costs and reduced cost for installation. Failures on underground cables are increasing, particularly direct-burial types.

The new cable system overcomes all the above problems. The new cable system has the advantage of low first cost for materials and low installation cost. It eliminates the need for field pulling of cables into conduits and eliminates the cost of assembly of conduit in the field. The new system may be directly buried, plowed in, or bored in for further savings. It is a cable and conduit system.

A tough natural-gas-approved pipe is used as the conduit. When it is pressurized, it will withstand much abuse. The gas pressure keeps out moisture and serves to monitor the cable for damage by insects or mechanical damage that can lead to future failure. The gas pressure can even be attached to an alarm to sound a loss of pressure or to trip a CB for hazardous locations. However, a loss of pressure in the cable will not cause it to fail. Even on dig-ins, the gas serves to warn the digger. The gas prevents combustion and burning on cable failure. The SF_6 gas is nontoxic, odorless, tasteless, and will not support combustion. It acts to put out a fire.

UL has tested a 3/C 250 MCM [kcmil] Type IGS-EC 600-V cable in 2-in. conduit. The UL test at zero gauge pressure shows a breakdown voltage between conductors of 14,000 V after numerous short-circuit, breakdown, and humidity tests. When the cable is single conductor, the breakdown voltage is even higher on loss of pressure, as the polyethylene pipe or conduit provides additional insulating value.

An award-winning installation was made in 1979 at 5 kV. Three installations of 3/C 250 MCM [kcmil] Type IGS-EC cable have been made for residential underground service entrances in Oakland, California. The first was made in May of 1979 and all have been successful.

ARTICLE 326. MEDIUM VOLTAGE CABLE

326-1. Definition.   This is a very limited definition of a relatively new Code designation—Type MV. The description of this cable type is amplified in the *Electrical Construction Materials Directory* of the Underwriters Laboratories, as follows:

Medium voltage cables are rated 2001 to 35,000 volts.

They are single or multi-conductor, aluminum or copper, with solid extruded dielectric insulation and may have an extruded jacket, metallic covering or combination of both over the single conductors or over the assembled conductors in a multi-conductor power cable.

All insulated conductors 8001 volts and higher have electrostatic shielding. Cables rated 2001 to 8000 volts may be shielded or nonshielded.

Nonshielded cables are intended for use where conditions of maintenance and supervision ensure that only competent individuals service and have access to the installation.

Cables marked MV-75, MV-85 or MV-90 are suitable for use in wet or dry locations at 75°C, 85°C or 90°C, respectively.

Cables which are suitable for use in dry locations only are so marked. Cables marked "oil resistant I" or "oil resistant II" are suitable for exposure to mineral oil at 60°C or 75°C, respectively.

Cables marked "sunlight resistant" may be exposed to the direct rays of the sun.

Cables intended for installation in cable trays in accordance with Article 318 of the **National Electrical Code** are marked "for CT Use" or "for use in cable trays."

Cables with aluminum conductors are marked with the word "aluminum" or the letters "AL."

Cables are marked with their conductor size, voltage rating and insulation level (100 percent or 133 percent).

The Listing Mark of Underwriters Laboratories Inc. on the product is the only method provided by UL to identify products manufactured under its Listing and Follow-Up Service.

326-3. Uses Permitted.   Because the **Code** now has an article and cable designation (Type MV) for cables operating above 2,000 V up to 35,000 V, it may be expected that electrical inspection authorities will insist that all cables in that voltage range must be Type MV to satisfy the **NE Code**.

Great care should be exercised in determining the attitude of local inspection authorities toward the meaning of this article. In particular, the relationship of Sec. 110-8 to Art. 326 should be determined. Section 110-8 states that "only wiring methods recognized as suitable are included in this **Code**." The question to be answered is: Will electrical inspection agencies require all high-voltage conductors to be Type MV? Or will inspection agencies accept high-voltage conductors not specifically designated Type MV? In other words, because the **Code** now has an accepted type of high-voltage cable, will it be permissible to use high-voltage cables that are not of this accepted type? For circuits in common use up to 600 V, Sec. 110-8 has consistently been interpreted to require that any conductor or cable must be one of the types specifically designated in the **Code**—Table 310-13 or elsewhere in Arts. 300 to 365. That is, conductors must be Type TW, THW, or one of the other designated types, and cable must be Type AC, NM, MI, MC, or other designated cable. It would be a **Code** violation to use any non-**Code**-designated wire or cable for systems up to 2,000 V. It would, therefore, seem to be similarly contrary to **Code** to use a non-**Code**-designated cable for higher-voltage circuits inasmuch as there is a **Code**-designated type (Type MV) for such applications.

Refer to Table 310-61 on Type MV conductors and to Sec. 310-13(b) for use of Type MV cables in tray.

ARTICLE 328. FLAT CONDUCTOR CABLE
TYPE FCC

328-1. Scope.   This article covers design and installation regulations on a branch-circuit wiring system that supplies floor outlets in office areas and other commercial and institutional interiors. See Fig. 328-1. The method may be used for new buildings or for modernization or expansion in existing interiors. FCC

Fig. 328-1. Flat conductor cable (FCC) supplies terminal base for floor-outlet pedestal at exact location required for desk in office area. FCC cable is taped in position over an insulating bedding tape and then covered with a flat steel tape (not yet installed here) to protect the three conductors (hot leg, neutral, and equipment grounding conductor) in the flat cable. Carpet squares are used to cover the finished cable runs.

wiring may be used on any hard, sound, smooth floor surface—concrete, wood, ceramic, etc. The great flexibility and ease of installation of this surface-mounted flat-cable wiring system meet the need that arises from the fact that the average floor power outlet in an office area is relocated every two years.

Undercarpet wiring to floor outlets eliminates any need for core drilling of concrete floors—avoiding noise, water dripping, falling debris, and disruption of normal activities in an office area. Alterations or additions to Type FCC circuit runs are neat, clean, and simple and may be done during office working hours—not requiring the overtime labor rates incurred by floor drilling, which must be done at night or on weekends. The FCC method eliminates use of conduit or cable, along with the need to fish conductors.

Type FCC wiring offers versatile supply to floor outlets for power and communication—at any locations on the floor. The flat cable is inconspicuous under the carpet squares. Elimination of floor penetrations maintains the fire integrity of the floor, as required by Sec. 300-21.

A typical system might use separate flat-cable circuit layouts for 120-V power to floor-pedestal receptacles, telephone circuits, and data communications lines for CRT displays and computer units. For 120-V power, the flat cable contains three flat, color-coded (black, white, and green) No. 12 copper conductors for 20-A circuits—one hot conductor, one neutral, and one equipment grounding conductor. Telephone circuits use flat, 3-pair, No. 26 gauge conductors. And data connection circuits use flat RG62A/U coaxial cable that is only 0.09 in. high.

328-2. Definitions. The various components of a type FCC system are described here. Figure 328-2 shows typical components of an FCC system.

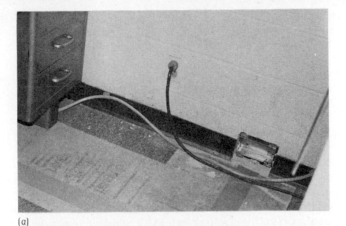

(a)

(b)

(c)

Fig. 328-2. Typical components of a Type FCC system: (a) Bottom shield in place; (b) connecting the conductor; (c) coil of top shield.

328-10. Coverings.   Floor carpet squares used for covering Type FCC wiring must not be larger than 36 by 36 in. This rule eliminates questions that arose about the possibility of using "squares" of broadloom carpet that covered a room floor wall to wall.

In making an undercarpet installation, usual thinking would dictate installation of the cable layout first and then placement of the floor covering of carpet squares over the entire area. But some installers have found it easier and less expensive to first cover the entire floor area with the self-adhesive carpet squares and then plan the circuit layouts to keep the cable runs along the centerlines of carpet squares and away from the edges of the squares. After the layout is determined, it is a simple matter to lift only those carpet squares along the route of each run, install the cable and pedestal bases, and replace the self-stick carpet squares to restore the overall floor covering. That approach has proved effective and keeps carpet cutting to the middle of any square.

328-17. Crossings.   Not more than two FCC cable runs may be crossed over each other at any one point. To prevent lumping under the floor carpets, this rule permits no more than two Type FCC cables to be crossed over each other at a single point. This applies to FCC power cable and FCC communications and data cables.

ARTICLE 330. MINERAL-INSULATED, METAL-SHEATHED CABLE

330-1. Definition.   The data from the UL Green Book expand on the definition (Fig. 330-1) and cover application notes as follows.

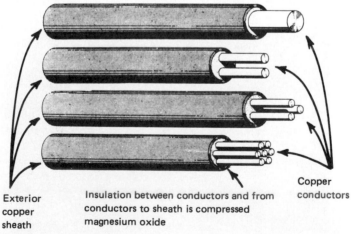

Exterior copper sheath

Insulation between conductors and from conductors to sheath is compressed magnesium oxide

Copper conductors

Fig. 330-1. Type MI is a single- or multiconductor cable that requires special termination. (Sec. 330-1.)

Mineral-insulated metal-sheathed cable is labeled in a single-conductor construction from No. 16 AWG through No. 4/0 AWG, two- and three-conductor from No. 16 AWG through No. 4 AWG, four-conductor from No. 16 AWG through No. 6 AWG, and seven-conductor Nos. 16, 14, 12, and 10 AWG. The exterior sheath may be of copper or alloy steel.

The standard length in which any size is furnished depends on the final diameter of the cable. The smallest cable, 1/C No. 16 AWG, has a diameter of 0.216 in. and can be furnished in lengths of approximately 1,900 ft. Cables of larger diameter have proportionally shorter lengths. The cable is shipped in paper-wrapped coils ranging in diameter from 3 to 5 ft.

The original intent behind development of this cable was to provide a wiring material which would be completely noncombustible, thus eliminating the fire hazards resulting from faults or excessive overloads on electrical circuits. To accomplish this, it is constructed entirely of inorganic materials. The conductors, sheath, and protective armor are of metal. The insulation is highly compressed magnesium oxide, which is extremely stable at high temperatures (fusion temperature of 2,800°C).

330-3. Uses Permitted. This section describes the general use of mineral-insulated metal-sheathed cable, designated Type MI. Briefly, it includes, basically, general use as services, feeders, and branch circuits in exposed and concealed work, in dry and wet locations, for underplaster extensions and embedded in plaster, masonry, concrete, or fill, for underground runs, or where exposed to weather, continuous moisture, oil, or other conditions not having a deteriorating effect on the metallic sheath (Fig. 330-2). The maximum permissible operating temperature for general use is 85°C (determined by present standard terminations). The cable itself, however, is recognized for 250°C in special applications. Permissible current ratings will be those given in Table 310-16 (or Table B-310-3 in App. B in the back of the NEC book). Type MI cable in its many sizes and constructions is suitable for all power and control circuits up to 600 V.

There is no question that MI cable can be used "in underground runs" as indicated in Sec. 330-3(10). But there is a question as to the meaning of "in underground runs." This question arises because of the wording in Sec. 310-7. Section 310-7 and Sec. 310-8(b) state that cable suitable for direct burial in the earth must be of a type specifically approved for the purpose ("identified" and "listed" for such use). That would require that the local inspector be satisfied with direct burial of MI cable and that UL listing recognize such use.

Although the copper sheath of MI cable has good resistance to corrosion, acid soils may be harmful to the copper sheath. Direct earth burial in alkaline and neutral soils would generally be expected to create no problems, but in any direct burial application MI cable with an outer plastic or neoprene jacket would assure effective application and provide compliance with the phrase "protected against physical damage and corrosive conditions" in part **(10)** of Sec. 330-3. Such jacketed MI cables are available, and have been successfully used in direct burial applications.

The fact remains, however, that the Code is not clear on this subject, and local rulings may vary on this subject.

Fig. 330·2. Type MI is recognized for an extremely broad range of applications—for any kind of circuit, indoors or outdoors, wet or dry, and even in hazardous locations, as where MI motor branch circuits supply pumps in areas subject to flammable gases or vapors. (Sec. 330-3.)

330·14. Fittings.   Connections of Type MI cable must be carefully made in accordance with UL and manufacturers' application data to assure effective operation (Fig. 330-3).

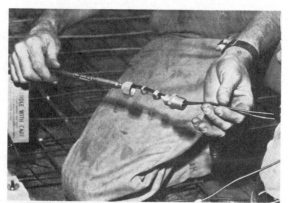

Fig. 330·3. Termination fitting for Type MI cable must be an approved connector, with its component parts assembled in proper sequence. (Sec. 330-14.)

330-15. Terminal Seals. This rule is applied in conjunction with that of Sec. 330-14 to assure *both* sealing of the cable end and means for connecting to enclosures (Fig. 330-4).

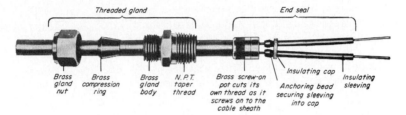

Threaded gland   End seal

Brass   Brass   Brass   N.P.T.   Brass screw-on   Insulating cap   Insulating
gland   compression   gland   taper   pot cuts its   sleeving
nut   ring   body   thread   own thread as it Anchoring bead
                                       screws on to the securing sleeving
                                       cable sheath   into cap

This typical fitting is approved for MI termination in hazardous locations, in accordance with Sec. 501-4.

Fig. 330-4. MI cable termination must provide end sealing and connection means. (Sec. 330-15.)

ARTICLE 331. ELECTRICAL NONMETALLIC TUBING

331-1. Definition. A new type of plastic raceway is defined in a new **Code** article (Fig. 331-1). Commonly referred to as "ENT," electrical nonmetallic tubing is "a pliable corrugated raceway of circular cross section with integral or

Fig. 331-1. ENT is a pliable, bendable plastic raceway for general-purpose use for feeders and branch circuits.

associated couplings, connectors, and fittings listed for the installation of electrical conductors. It is composed of a material that is resistant to moisture [and] chemical atmospheres and is flame retardant." ENT can be bent by hand, when being installed, to establish direction and lengths of runs.

331-3. Uses Permitted.   ENT is permitted to be used as a general-purpose, "flexible"-type conduit in any type of occupancy (Fig. 331-2). Electrical nonmetallic tubing (ENT) is *not limited* to use in buildings up to three stories high. This rule recognizes ENT for use in buildings of any height (Fig. 331-3)—subject to conditions given in Sec. 331-3 and Sec. 331-4. ENT may be used:

   1. Concealed in walls, floors, and ceilings that provide a thermal barrier with

Fig. 331-2. ENT may be used in residential and nonresidential buildings. (Sec. 331-3.)

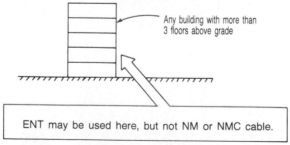

Any building with more than 3 floors above grade

ENT may be used here, but not NM or NMC cable.

Fig. 331-3. ENT (electrical nonmetallic tubing) may be used in any type of building, of any height. (Sec. 331-3.)

at least a 15-min fire rating from listings of fire-rated assemblies. The rule permits ENT above a ½-in. Sheetrock ceiling.

Exception is made to the rule on concealment. ENT may be used *exposed* in a building that is not over three floors above grade. This is limited permission that recognizes ENT for exposed use under the same limitations that Sec. 336-4(a) places on use of Romex in buildings. And the FPN (fine-print note) refers to the revised Sec. 336-4(a), where there is a new definition of the "first floor" that accepts Romex in four-story buildings where the first floor is used totally for vehicle parking, storage, or "similar use," where the space is not used for human occupancy or human habitation. ENT may be used *exposed* in such a four-story building.

2. In severe corrosive locations where suited to resist the particular atmosphere (but not "exposed").
3. In concealed, dry, and damp locations not prohibited by Sec. 331-4.
4. Above suspended ceilings with at least a 15-min fire rating.
5. Embedded in poured concrete with fittings that are listed or otherwise identified for that use.

Note that there is no *general* permission in this section to use ENT *exposed*.

331-4 Uses Not Permitted. ENT may not be used in *exposed* locations, except above suspended ceilings of 15-min fire-rated material and in buildings not

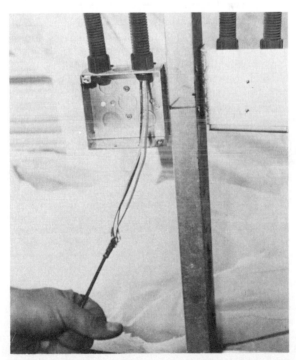

Fig. 331-4. Available in ½-, ¾-, and 1-in. sizes, ENT has a full line of couplings and box connectors. (Sec. 331-5.)

over three floors above grade. This section excludes ENT from hazardous locations, from supporting fixtures or equipment, from use where the ambient temperature exceeds that for which the ENT is rated, from direct burial, and from exposed use, with exceptions as noted.

ENT must not be used in places of assembly, theaters, and similar locations unless the installation satisfies the rules of Arts. 518 and 520. This is intended to warn against improper use of ENT, as reported for installations in these types of locations.

331·5. Size.   ENT is **Code**-recognized in ½, ¾, and 1-in. trade sizes. A full line of plastic couplings, box connectors, and fittings is available, which are attached to the ENT by mechanical method or cement adhesive (Fig. 331-4).

331·10. Bends—Number in One Run.   ENT runs between "pull points"—boxes, enclosures, and conduit bodies—must not contain more than the equivalent of four quarter bends (360°). This rule makes it clear that the practice of making 360° of bends between boxes and "fittings" —such as between "couplings," which comes under the definition for the word "fittings" as given in Art. 100 and previously used in this rule—is prohibited.

ARTICLE 333. ARMORED CABLE

333·1. Definition.   This section identifies Type AC cable, which is the cable assembly long used and known as BX cable. All the regulations on use of Type AC cable are given in the sections of this **Code** article. Type AC armored cable, the commonly used BX cable, is covered by an article of its own and is separated on application and **Code** enforcement from the use of metal-clad cables, which are covered in Art. 334.

Type AC cable (BX) is listed and labeled by UL as "Armored Cable" in the *Electrical Construction Materials Directory*. The assembly contains the conductors within a jacket made of a spiral wrap of steel with interlocking of the edges of the strip (Fig. 333-1).

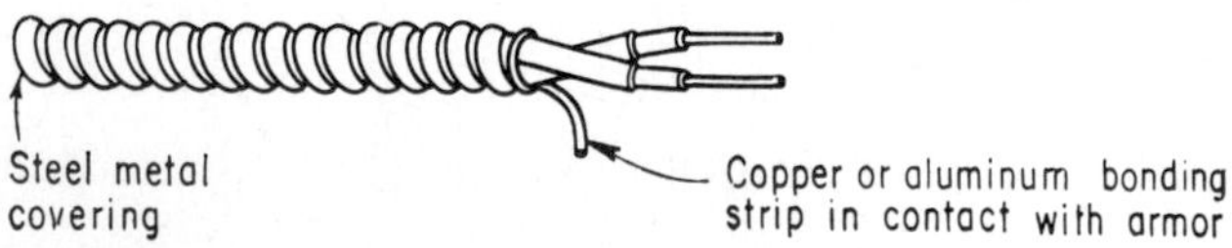

Steel metal covering

Copper or aluminum bonding strip in contact with armor

Fig. 333·1. Type AC cable contains insulated conductors plus bonding conductor under the armor. (Sec. 333-1.)

Armored cable assemblies of 2, 3, 4, or more conductors in sizes No. 14 AWG to No. 1 AWG conform to the standards of the Underwriters Laboratories. These standards cover multiple-conductor armored cables for use in accordance with the **National Electrical Code**, in wiring systems of 600 V or less, at temperatures of 60°C or 75°C depending upon conductor insulation.

Armored cables of other types which do not come under these UL standards are listed by UL as "Metal-Clad Cable, Type MC" and are covered by Art. 334. One type of MC cable is commonly called "interlocked armor cable."

333-4. Construction.   Note that Type AC cable is recognized for branch circuits and feeders, **but not** for service-entrance conductors, which *must* be one of the cables or wiring methods specified in Sec. 230-43. Type MC (metal-clad) cable, such as interlocked armor cable or the other cables covered in Art. 334, is recognized by Sec. 230-43 for use as service-entrance conductors.

Because the armor of Type AC cable is recognized as an equipment grounding conductor by Sec. 250-91(b)(6), its effectiveness must be assured by using an "internal bonding strip," or conductor, under the armor and shorting the turns of the steel jacket. The ohmic resistance of finished armor, including the bonding conductor that is required to be furnished as a part of all except lead-covered armored cable, must be within values specified by UL and checked during manufacturing. The bonding conductor run within the armor of the cable assembly is required by the UL standard.

Because the function of the bonding conductor in Type AC cable is simply to short adjacent turns of the spiral-wrapped armor, there is no need to make any connection of the bonding conductor at cable ends in enclosures or equipment. The conductor may simply be cut off at the armor end.

Construction of armored cable must permit ready insertion of an insulating bushing or equivalent protection between the conductors and the armor at each termination of the armor—such as the so-called "red head."

333-5. Conductors.   UL data on conductors used within Type AC cables refer to the marking on the cable as follows:

ACT—indicates an armored cable employing conductors having thermoplastic (Type T) insulation.

AC—indicates an armored cable employing conductors having rubber insulation of the **Code** grade.

ACH—indicates an armored cable employing conductors having rubber insulation of the heat-resistant (75 C) grade.

ACHH—indicates an armored cable employing conductors having rubber insulation of the heat-resistant (90 C) grade.

ACU—indicates an armored cable employing conductors having rubber insulation of the latex grade.

L—used as a suffix indicates that a lead covering has been applied over the conductor assembly.

As required by the Exception in this section, armored cable (BX) installed within thermal insulation must have 90°C-rated conductors (Types THHN, RHH, XHHW), but the ampacity must be taken as that of 60°C-rated conductors. This requirement recognizes that the heat rise on conductors operating with reduced heat-dissipating ability (such as surrounded by fiberglass or similar thermal insulation) requires that the conductors have a 90°C-rated insulation. That temperature might be reached even with the wires carrying only 60°C ampacities. Although the wires must have 90°C insulation, they must not be loaded over those ampacity values permitted for TW (60°C), as shown in Table 310-16.

333-6. Use. Type AC armored cable is familiarly used in all types of electrical systems for power and light branch circuits and feeders. Figure 333-2 shows use of three runs of 12/2 BX for the supply and two switch legs to a combination light-heat-fan unit in a bathroom. One 12/2 is the supply and the other cables control the appliance as shown in the wiring diagram. But the use of two 12/2 cables for the switch legs violates Sec. 300-20 because the neutral is not kept with all the conductors it serves. As a result, induction heating could be produced.

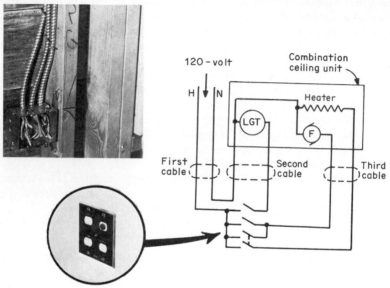

Fig. 333-2. Cable runs of 12/2 BX are used at junction box (above) which was then equipped with switches and pilot light (right) for light-heat-fan unit. Use of two 12/2 cables, with neutral in only one cable, is a violation of the concept covered in Sec. 300-20. A 12/4 cable could serve for all switch legs and satisfy the **Code** rule. (Sec. 333-6.)

As noted in the first sentence of part **(a),** Type AC cable may be used in cable tray *if* "identified for such use." To correlate to Sec. 318-(a)(1)—which recognizes Type AC cable in tray—this rule basically calls for some marking or label attached to the cable to show that it is listed for "CT use" or some other designation that conveys the same idea (to assure that the cable has been tested and found acceptable—such as in accordance with the UL vertical tray flame test).

Type AC is also used for signal and control circuit work. It is particularly effective for running loudspeaker circuits in public address systems and other sound systems where the flexibility of the cable lends itself to ready installation on new construction or rewiring jobs and the armor provides much needed mechanical protection. Armored cable is also especially effective for wiring Class 2 control circuits—such as low-voltage relay switching circuits—where mechanical protection for the conductors and flexibility of installation are required.

For use where Type AC cable is exposed to weather or continuous moisture, for underground runs in raceways and embedded in masonry, concrete, or fill in buildings in course of construction or where exposed to oil, gasoline, or other deteriorating agents, the conductor assembly within the armor must be protected by a lead covering—that is, the cable must be Type ACL. BUT NOTE that the last sentence of part **(b)** in this section PROHIBITS use of *any* Type AC cable, even Type ACL, directly buried in the earth.

Part **(b)(3)** covers use of Type AC cable in hazardous locations, as covered in Secs. 501-4(b) and 504-20. Type AC cable may be used for wiring of intrinsically safe equipment, such as instruments or signals in which the electric circuit is not capable of releasing enough energy under any fault condition to cause ignition of the hazardous atmosphere (Fig. 333-3). This same permission is also given for Type NM cable, Type NMC cable, Type UF cable, rigid nonmetallic conduit, surface raceways, multioutlet assembly, underfloor raceways, cellular metal floor raceways, and wireways in their respective articles.

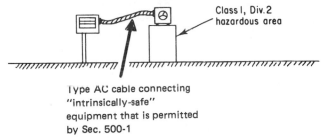

Class I, Div. 2 hazardous area

Type AC cable connecting "intrinsically-safe" equipment that is permitted by Sec. 500-1

Fig. 333-3. Part (b)(3) recognizes BX cable for limited use in hazardous locations. (Sec. 333-6.)

333-7. Supports. Armored cable must be secured by approved staples, straps, or similar fittings, as shown in Fig. 333-4.

In exposed work, both as a precaution against physical damage and to ensure a workmanlike appearance, fastenings should be spaced not more than 24 to 30 in. apart. In concealed work in new buildings, the cable must be supported at intervals of not over 4½ ft for Type AC to keep it out of the way of possible injury by mechanics of other trades. In either exposed work or concealed work, the cable should be securely fastened in place within 1 ft of each outlet box or fitting so that there will be no tendency for the cable to pull away from the box connector.

Exception No. 2 of Sec. 333-7 limits Type AC cable to not over a 2-ft unclamped length for flexibility where such a cable feeds motorized equipment (such as a fan or unit heater) or connects to any enclosure or equipment where the flexibility of the BX length will isolate and suppress vibrations. Section 350-4, Exception No. 2, and Sec. 351-8, Exception No. 2, recognize flexible metal conduit and liquidtight flexible metal conduit for an unsecured length of up to 3 ft at any termination where flexibility is needed. Similarly, Exception No. 3 of this section permits lengths of BX up to 6 ft long to be used without any staples, clamps, or other support where used in a hung ceiling as a lighting fix-

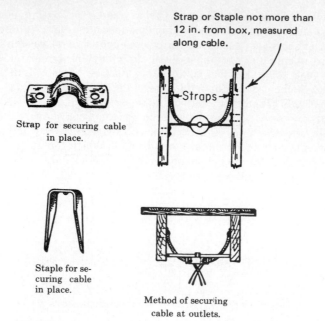

Strap or Staple not more than 12 in. from box, measured along cable.

Straps

Strap for securing cable in place.

Staple for securing cable in place.

Method of securing cable at outlets.

Fig. 333·4. BX must be clamped every 4½ ft and within 12 in. of terminations. (Sec. 333-7.)

ture whip or similar whip to other equipment (Fig. 333-5). This permits use of BX in the same manner as permitted for flexible metal conduit (Greenfield) or liquidtight flexible metal conduit in lengths from 4 to 6 ft as a connection from a circuit outlet box to a recessed lighting fixture [Sec. 410-67(c)]. This use of

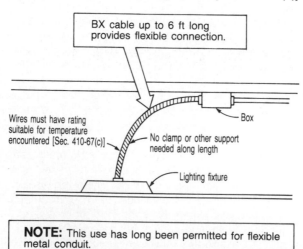

BX cable up to 6 ft long provides flexible connection.

Wires must have rating suitable for temperature encountered [Sec. 410-67(c)]

Box

No clamp or other support needed along length

Lighting fixture

NOTE: This use has long been permitted for flexible metal conduit.

Fig. 333·5. Armored cable (Type AC) may be used for 4- to 6-ft fixture whips, without supports, in an "accessible ceiling." (Sec. 333-7.)

unclamped BX is an exception to the basic rule that it be clamped every 4½ ft and within 22 in. of any outlet box or fitting. Exception No. 3 is an expansion on Exception No. 2 that permits up to a 2-ft length of BX to be used without clamping "at terminals where flexibility is necessary."

Note that the requirements on clamping or securing of BX and flexible metal conduits must be observed for applications in suspended-ceiling spaces, whether for air handling, as covered in Sec. 300-22(c), or nonair handling.

333·9. Boxes and Fittings.   Note that a termination fitting—that is, a box connector—must be used at every end of Type AC cable entering an enclosure or a box (Fig. 333-6) unless the box has an approved built-in clamp to hold the cable armor, provide for the bonding of the armor to the metal box, and protect the wires in the cable from abrasion.

Fig. 333·6. Connectors for BX entering a panelboard cabinet or other enclosure must use approved fittings—some type of single-connector or duplex type (as shown, with two cables terminated at each connector through a single KO). (Sec. 333-9.)

A standard type of box connector for securing the cable to knockouts or other openings in outlet boxes and cabinets is shown in Fig. 333-7. A fiber bushing, as shown, must be inserted between the armor and the conductors. The fiber bushing, which can be seen through slots in the connector after installation, prevents the sharp edges of the armor from cutting into the insulation on the conductors and so grounding the copper wire.

The box shown in Fig. 333-8 is equipped with clamps to secure Type AC cables, making it unnecessary to use separate box connectors. The other box shown is similar but has the cable clamps outside, thus permitting one more conductor in the box. See Sec. 370-6(a)(1).

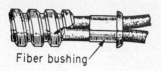

Fiber bushing

Fiber bushing to protect the conductors in Type AC cable from the sharp edges of the armor.

Box connector for Type AC cable.

Fig. 333·7. Every BX termination must be equipped with a protective bushing and a box connector or clamp built into the box. (Sec. 333-9.)

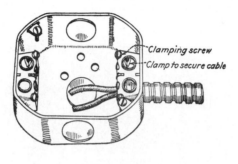

Clamping screw
Clamp to secure cable

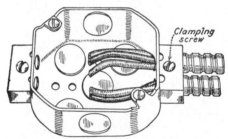

Clamping screw

Fig. 333·8. A box connector fitting is not required if box includes cable clamps for Type AC cable. (Sec. 333-9.)

As covered in the last sentence of Sec. 333-9, "a box, fitting or conduit body"—such as a "C" conduit body—must be used where Type AC cable is connected to another wiring method. Figure 333-9 shows a typical application of this technique, which is also recognized in Exception No. 9 of Sec. 300-15(b).

333·11. Exposed Work.   Exception No. 1 refers to a length not over 24 in. to a lighting fixture, a motor, or a range where some flexibility is necessary, as noted in Sec. 333-7.

Exception No. 3 permits up to a 6-ft length of Type AC cable for a fixture whip as an Exception to the rule requiring AC cable to "closely follow" the building surface. This is related to Sec. 333-7, Exception No. 3, which permits 6-ft fixture whips without clamping of the cable.

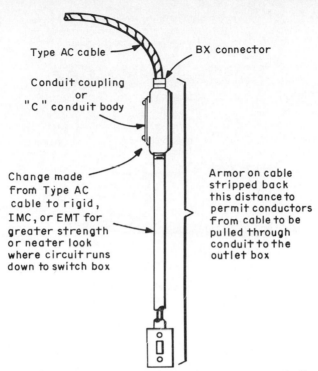

Type AC cable

BX connector

Conduit coupling
or
"C" conduit body

Change made
from Type AC
cable to rigid,
IMC, or EMT for
greater strength
or neater look
where circuit runs
down to switch box

Armor on cable
stripped back
this distance to
permit conductors
from cable to be
pulled through
conduit to the
outlet box

Fig. 333·9. This connection of BX to conduit or EMT is specifically recognized. (Sec. 333-9.)

ARTICLE 334. METAL·CLAD CABLE

334·1. Definition. This article covers "Metal-Clad Cable," as listed by UL under that heading in the *Electrical Construction Materials Directory* (the Green Book). This section defines the type of cable assemblies covered by this article (Fig. 334-1). The definition for metal-clad cable—"a factory assembly of one or more conductors, each individually insulated and enclosed in a metallic sheath of interlocking tape, or a smooth or corrugated tube"—also covers Type ALS and Type CS cables. All metal-clad cables—Type MC, Type ALS, and Type CS—are covered in the single Art. 334.

Aluminum-sheathed (ALS) cable has insulated conductors with color-coded coverings, cable fillers, and overall wrap of Mylar tape—all in an impervious, continuous, closely fitting, seamless tube of aluminum. It may be used for both exposed and concealed work in dry or wet locations, with approved fittings. CS cable is very similar with a copper exterior sheath instead of aluminum.

Because the rules of these three cable types have been compiled into a single article, use of any one of the Type MC cables must be evaluated against the specific rules that now generally apply to all such cables. The **Code** no longer

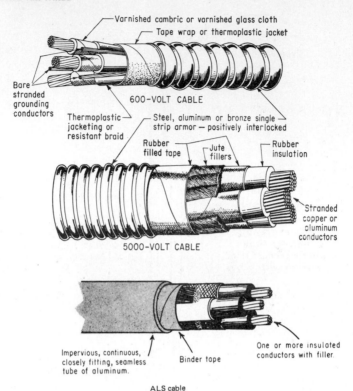

Varnished cambric or varnished glass cloth

Tape wrap or thermoplastic jacket

Bare
stranded
grounding
conductors

600-VOLT CABLE

Thermoplastic
jacketing or
resistant braid

Steel, aluminum or bronze single
strip armor — positively interlocked

Rubber
filled tape

Jute
fillers

Rubber
insulation

Stranded
copper or
aluminum
conductors

5000-VOLT CABLE

Impervious, continuous,
closely fitting, seamless
tube of aluminum.

Binder tape

One or more insulated
conductors with filler.

ALS cable

Fig. 334·1. These are some of the constructions in which Type MC cable
is available. (Sec. 334-1.)

contains the designations Type ALS and Type CS. They are included now along
with interlocked armored cable as Type MC cables.

One type of Type MC cable that has been used for many years under the
name "interlocked-armor cable" is the heavy-duty, industrial feeder type of
armored cable that is similar in appearance to but really different from standard BX armored cable, as covered in Art. 333. MC cable is a different, heavier-
duty assembly than BX (Type AC), and great care must be taken to carefully
distinguish between the design and installation regulations that apply to each
of the cable types. This is particularly important now that the **NE Code** recognizes Type MC cable in the size range from No. 14 and larger. Now, because
both cable assemblies are available in sizes No. 14 up to No. 1, armored cable
must be carefully distinguished as either Type AC or Type MC. As clearly
shown in **NE Code** Art. 334, **Code** rules are different for the two types of cable.
And so are UL regulations as indicated in the Green Book. Always check the
label on the cable.

Type MC is rated by UL for use up to 5,000 V, although cable for use up to
15,000 V has been available and used for many years. Type MC cable is rec-

ognized in three basic armor designs: (1) interlocked metal tape, (2) corrugated tube, and (3) smooth metallic sheath.

334-3. Uses Permitted.   Although this section clearly lists all the permitted applications of any of the various forms of Type MC cable, care must be taken to distinguish between the different constructions, based on the **Code** rules (Fig. 334-2). For a long time, the interlocked-armor Type MC and the corrugated sheath Type MC have been designated by UL as "intended for aboveground use." But part **(5)** of this section recognizes Type MC cable as suitable for direct burial in the earth, when it is identified for such use.

Fig. 334-2. ALS (aluminum-sheathed) Type MC cable was used for extensive power and light wiring in refrigerated rooms and storage areas of a store. The ALS was surface-mounted (exposed) on clamps in this damp location. Because the cable assembly is a tight grouping of conductors within the sheath, there would be no passage of warm air from adjacent nonrefrigerated areas through the cable which crosses the boundaries between the areas. It was therefore not necessary to seal the cables to satisfy Sec. 300-7(a). (Sec. 334-3.)

The Exception to Sec. 334-4, warns against direct burial of Type MC cable. The fine distinction between acceptable and unacceptable use of directly buried Type MC cable will generally require discussion with local inspection authorities to assure clear understanding of the contrasting phrases in Sec. 334-3 and Sec. 334-4.

334-4. Uses Not Permitted.   Type MC cables are permitted by Sec. 334-3 to be used exposed or concealed in dry or wet locations. But such cable must not be subjected to destructive, corrosive conditions—such as direct burial in the earth, in concrete, or exposed to cinder fills, strong chlorides, caustic alkalis, or vapors of chlorine or of hydrochloric acids, unless protected by materials suitable for the condition. But the Exception to this section says that Type MC cable may be used for underground runs where suitably protected against physical damage and corrosive conditions.

334·10. Installation. Figure 334-3 shows the maximum permitted spacing of supports for any Type MC cable. The interlocked-armor Type MC has commonly been used on cable tray, as permitted in part **(b)** of this section (Fig. 334-4).

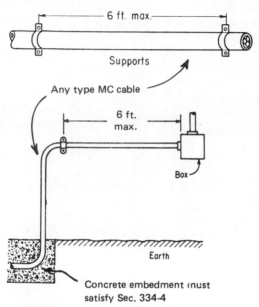

Fig. 334·3. Surface mounting of Type MC cable must be secured. (Sec. 334-10.)

334·11. Bending Radius. Figure 334-5 shows the bending-radius rules for the "smooth sheath" Type MC cables. Cable with interlocked or corrugated armor must have a bending radius not less than 7 times the outside diameter of the cable armor. To conform to IPCEA rules on bending radius for shielded conductors in MC cable, the minimum value must be either 12 times the diameter of one of the conductors within the cable or 7 times the diameter of the MC cable itself, whichever is greater.

334·12. Fittings. Only approved, UL-listed connectors and fittings are permitted to be used with any Type MC cable. Such fittings are listed in the UL Green Book under "Metal-Clad Cable Connectors." Figure 334-6 shows typical approved connectors for interlocked-armor Type MC cable. As shown at left, 600-V terminations for interlocked-armor cable to switchgear or other enclo-

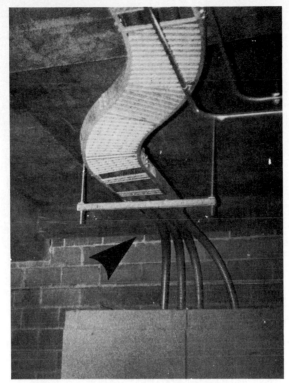

Fig. 334-4. Any Type MC cable is recognized for use in cable tray, and the interlocked-armor version has been widely used in tray, as shown here. But the tray *must* be connected to the enclosure in which the cables terminate. See Secs. 318-5 and 318-6. (Sec. 334-10.)

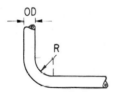

Bends: Radius (R) shall not be less than:
(a) 10 times OD for cables with OD ¾ in. or less.
(b) 12 times OD for cables with OD over ¾ in. but not over 1½ in.
(c) 15 times OD for cables with OD over 1½ in.

Fig. 334-5. Minimum radius values prevent excessively sharp, destructive bending of ALS or CS cable. (Sec. 334-11.)

sures in dry locations can be made with connectors, a locknut, and a bushing in the typical basic assembly shown. In damp locations, compound-filled or other protective terminations may be desired. High-voltage connectors (5 and 15 kV) are generally filled with sealing compound and individual conductors

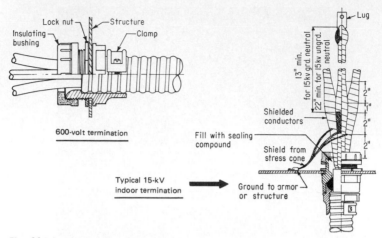

Fig. 334·6. Terminations for interlocked-armor cables must be approved devices, correctly installed. (Sec. 334-12.)

terminated in a suitable manner, depending upon whether the conductors are shielded or not. Or the IA cable may terminate in a pothead for positively sealed and insulated terminations indoors or outdoors.

ARTICLE 336. NONMETALLIC-SHEATHED CABLE

Refer to Sec. 310-2 of this handbook for a discussion on the use of only insulated conductors as circuit conductors and the prohibition on using the bare grounding conductor in NM cable as both a neutral and equipment grounding conductor for a circuit to a cooking appliance (Sec. 250-60).

336·1. Definition.   Nonmetallic-sheathed cable is one of the most widely used cables for branch circuits and feeders in residential and commercial systems (Fig. 336-1). Such cable is commonly and generally called "Romex" by electrical construction people, even though the word *Romex* is a registered trade name of the General Cable Corp. Industry usage has made the trade name a generic title so that nonmetallic-sheathed cable made by any manufacturer might be called Romex. This generic usage of a trade name also applies to the term *BX*, which is commonly used to describe any standard armored cable, made by any manufacturer—even though the term *BX* is a registered trade name of General Electric Co. Type NM cable has an overall covering of fibrous or plastic material which is flame-retardant and moisture-resistant. Type NMC is similar, but the overall covering is also fungus-resistant and corrosion-resistant. The letter "C" indicates that it is corrosion-resistant.

336·3 Uses Permitted.   This type of wiring may be used either for exposed or for concealed wiring (Fig. 336-2) in any kind of building or structure.

    1. NM cable may be used in one-family dwellings.

Type	Construction	Application

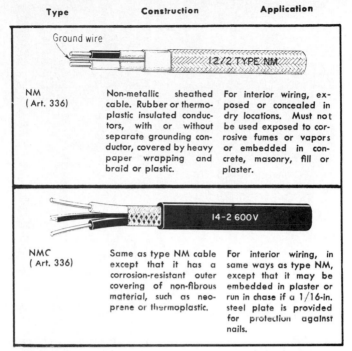

NM (Art. 336)	Non-metallic sheathed cable. Rubber or thermoplastic insulated conductors, with or without separate grounding conductor, covered by heavy paper wrapping and braid or plastic.	For interior wiring, exposed or concealed in dry locations. Must not be used exposed to corrosive fumes or vapors or embedded in concrete, masonry, fill or plaster.
NMC (Art. 336)	Same as type NM cable except that it has a corrosion-resistant outer covering of non-fibrous material, such as neoprene or thermoplastic.	For interior wiring, in same ways as type NM, except that it may be embedded in plaster or run in chase if a 1/16-in. steel plate is provided for protection against nails.

Fig. 336-1. There are two separate types of nonmetallic-sheathed cable. (Sec. 336-1.)

2. NM cable may be used in two-family dwellings.
3. NM cable may be used in multifamily dwellings.
4. NM cable may be used in "other structures.

But in any case, the dwelling or building or structure must not have over three floors above grade. (See definition for building or structure with "three floors above grade" in Sec. 336-4.)

Type NM or NMC cable must be "identified" for use in cable tray. This requirement essentially calls for UL listing and marking on the cable to make it "recognized" as suitable for installation in cable tray.

Although NM cable is limited to use in "normally dry locations," NMC—the corrosion-resistant type—is permitted in "dry, damp, moist, or corrosive locations." Because it has been widely used in barns and other animals' quarters where the atmosphere is damp and corrosive (due to animal vapors), NMC cable is sometimes referred to as "barn wiring."

Part **(b)** says that Type NMC that is run in a shallow chase in masonry, concrete, or adobe and covered over must be protected against nail or screw penetration by a ¹⁄₁₆-in. (minimum) steel plate.

336-4. Uses Not Permitted.   The first sentence of this section limits use of Type NM and Type NMC cables to any building that does not have more than three floors above grade (Fig. 336-3).

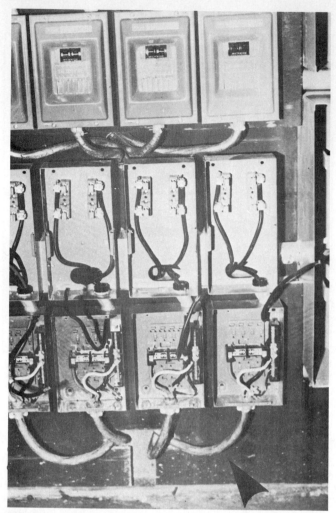

Fig. 336·2. Although NM cable is most widely used for branch circuits, the larger sizes (No. 8 and up) are commonly used for feeders, as run here from apartment disconnects to tenant panelboards. (Sec. 336-3.)

The **Code** rule limiting use of Types NM and NMC cables to buildings not exceeding three floors above grade has produced difficulties in interpretation. The problem arises when buildings are built on hillsides or sloping grades, where the building will have three floors above grade on the uphill side and ·four floors above grade on the downhill side. The question then is: Is this a three-story building or a four-story building, and is use of Type NM cable permitted?

Type NM or type NMC may be used in any building with not more than 3 floors above grade.

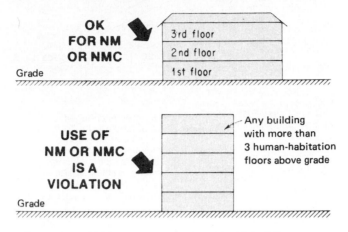

Note: NM or NMC may not be used at all in this building — not even on the first three floors.

Fig. 336-3. Nonmetallic-sheathed cable is limited in application. [Sec. 336-4(a).]

To clarify the issue, the next-to-last sentence of Sec. 336-4(a) defines the first floor of a building and attempts to establish a basis for applying the **Code** rule. Whether or not a particular building will be considered as a three- or four-story building when installed on sloping grade depends upon the definition given for the first floor of a building.

The **Code** spells out that the first floor is that floor that has 50 percent or more of its exterior wall surface area level with or above grade. We must presume that the rule refers to the total wall surface area on all four sides of that floor of the building. And it is not clear how wall "surface area" can be "level with grade." If the bottom floor has over 50 percent of its wall area above adjacent finished grade, then the bottom floor is the first floor. In this rule, the wording is awkward and must be carefully related to building construction and exterior grading in determining whether or not Romex cable may be used in the building. If that bottom floor is the first floor in a building with four floors of dwelling space, then the building is a four-story building and use of Type NM or Type NMC cable is prohibited. But, a bulldozer or backhoe could be used to alter the actual steepness of the grade to create the required conditions that would exclude the bottom floor as the first floor of the building and would thereby permit use of non-metallic-sheathed cable (see Fig. 336-4).

But, the last sentence of this rule says that a three-story building wired in Romex is permitted "one additional level" (four in all) if the first floor level is totally used for auto parking or storage (Fig. 336-5).

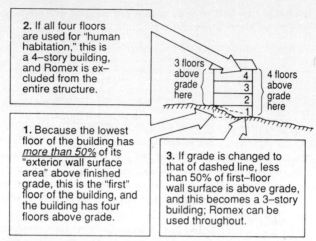

2. If all four floors are used for "human habitation," this is a 4–story building, and Romex is ex–cluded from the entire structure.

3 floors above grade here

4 floors above grade here

1. Because the lowest floor of the building has _more than 50%_ of its "exterior wall surface area" above finished grade, this is the "first" floor of the building, and the building has four floors above grade.

3. If grade is changed to that of dashed line, less than 50% of first–floor wall surface is above grade, and this becomes a 3–story building; Romex can be used throughout.

Fig. 336·4. Definition of "first floor" clarifies use of NM cable in buildings "not exceeding three floors above grade." [Sec. 336-4(a).]

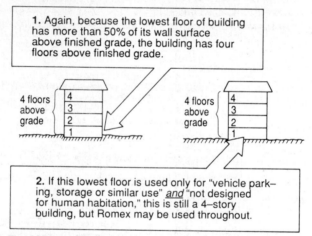

1. Again, because the lowest floor of building has more than 50% of its wall surface above finished grade, the building has four floors above finished grade.

4 floors above grade

4 floors above grade

2. If this lowest floor is used only for "vehicle park–ing, storage or similar use" _and_ "not designed for human habitation," this is still a 4–story building, but Romex may be used throughout.

Fig. 336·5. A first floor that is _totally_ garage or storage area may have three floors above it, and the whole building may be wired with NM or NMC cable. [Sec. 336-4(a).]

The wording of this rule makes clear that NM or NMC may be used only in a building that is not more than three stories high—and may not be used in any mid-rise or high-rise buildings of any type, as described above.

NM cable may not be embedded in masonry as noted in part **(b)(2)**, and the word "adobe" prohibits the use of nonmetallic-sheathed cable embedded in the chases in adobe brick, commonly used in the southwest part of the United States. Adobe is a sun-dried brick material used for building construction. It is brittle and boxes embedded in it tend to become loose. This prohibits the cable from being run in the adobe or in the chases between the adobe bricks.

Although part **(b)** prohibits NM cable embedded in plaster or other construction materials and prohibits it run in chases between bricks, stones, etc., this section does not prohibit use of NMC cable for plaster embedment or in chases, and Sec. 336-3(b)(3) specifically permits it. The 1971 **NEC** had another sentence to the rule shown in part **(b)**, and it allowed use of NMC as follows:

> Where embedded in plaster or run in a shallow chase in masonry walls and covered with plaster within 2 inches of the finished surface, it [NMC cable] shall be protected against damage from nails by a cover of corrosion-resistant coated steel at least 1/16 inch in thickness and 3/4 inch wide in the chase or under the final surface finish.

That sentence permitted use of NMC (but not NM) under plaster, as shown in Fig. 336-6; however it was removed from Sec. 336-3(b) in the 1975 **NEC** and does not appear in the present **NEC**. Omission of that sentence raises the question: Is NMC permitted to be embedded in plaster as covered by the old rule described?

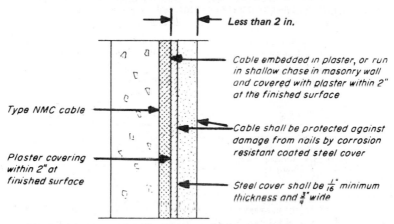

Fig. 336-6. This was permitted by previous editions of the **Code** and may still be acceptable. [Sec. 336-3(b) (3).]

There is no definite answer to that question and the matter must be decided by the local inspector having jurisdiction. No data were made available to explain deletion of the old **Code** rule described. Because the present **NEC** rule prohibits NM embedded in plaster, but does not prohibit NMC in plaster, it can be argued that such use of NMC is **Code**-acceptable. But it would be necessary to protect the cable against the possibility of being damaged by driven nails—such as nails used to hang pictures or add construction elements on the wall. Sufficient protection against nail puncture of the cable is provided by a cover of corrosion-resistant coated steel of at least 1/16 in. thickness and 3/4 in. width. Such metal protection must be run for the entire length of the cable where it is less than 2 in. below the finished surface. The metal strip protection may be run in the chase or under the plaster finish. But, it must be carefully noted that both NM and NMC are prohibited by Sec. 336-4(a)(8) from embedment in cement, concrete, or aggregate—which is distinguished from plaster. Section 336-2 correlates use of NM cable to the rule of the second paragraph of Note 8 to Tables 310-16 to 310-19, which says:

> Where single conductors or multiconductor cables are stacked or bundled longer than 24 inches without maintaining spacing and are not installed in raceways, the ampacity of each conductor shall be reduced as shown in the above table.

Bundled NM or NMC cables will require ampacity derating in accordance with Note 8 to Table 310-16 when the whole bundle is tightly packed, thereby losing the ability of the inside cables to dissipate the heat generated in them. An example of this is shown in Fig. 310-31. This is true of NM cables as well as any other cables. And the derating percentage from the table in Note 8 must be based on the total number of insulated conductors in the group. For instance, fourteen 3-wire cables would have to be ampacity derated to 60 percent of the conductor ampacity (14 × 3 = 42 conductors, at 60 percent, from Note 8).

If the ampacity derating required by Note 8 is not observed, stacking or bundling of groups of NM or NMC cable runs can result in dangerous overheating of conductors and terminations.

336·10. Exposed Work—General. Figure 336-7 shows the details described in parts **(a)** and **(b)** of this section. The rules of this section tie into the rules of Sec. 336-12, covering use in unfinished basements, which are really places of "exposed work."

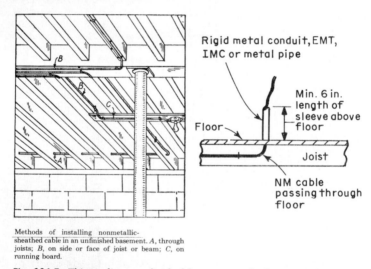

Methods of installing nonmetallic-sheathed cable in an unfinished basement. *A*, through joists; *B*, on side or face of joist or beam; *C*, on running board.

Fig. 336·7. This applies to unfinished basements and other exposed applications. (Sec. 336-10.)

336·12. In Unfinished Basements. Cables containing No. 14, No. 12, or No. 10 conductors must be run through holes drilled through joists. When running parallel to joists, any cable must be stapled to the wide, vertical face of a joist and never to the bottom edge. But, as shown in Fig. 336-8, larger cables may be attached to the bottom of joists when run at an angle to the joists.

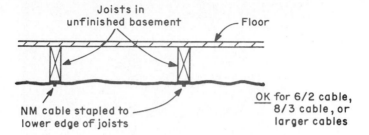

Joists in
unfinished basement

Floor

NM cable stapled to
lower edge of joists

OK for 6/2 cable,
8/3 cable, or
larger cables

Note: Method shown is a VIOLATION for cables
containing Nos. 14, 12, or 10 conductors

Fig. 336-8. Only large cables may be stapled to bottom edge of floor joists. (Sec. 336-12.)

336-15. Supports. Figure 336-9 shows support requirements for NM or NMC cable. Figure 336-10 shows a violation. In concealed work the cable should if possible be so installed that it will be out of reach of nails. Care should be taken to avoid wherever possible the parts of a wall where the trim will be nailed in place, e.g., door and window casings, baseboards, and picture moldings. See Sec. 300-4.

Connectors listed for use with Type NM or NMC cable (nonmetallic-sheathed cable) are also suitable for use with flexible cord or service-entrance cable *if* such additional use is indicated on the device or carton. Connectors listed under the classifications "Armored Cable Connectors" and "Conduit Fittings" may be used with nonmetallic-sheathed cable when that is specifically

Fig. 336-9. NM or NMC cables must be stapled every 4½ ft where attached to the surfaces of studs, joints, and other wood structural members. It is not necessary to use staples or straps on runs that are supported by the drilled holes through which the cable is pulled. But there must be a staple within 12 in. of every box or enclosure in which the cable terminates. (Sec. 336-15.)

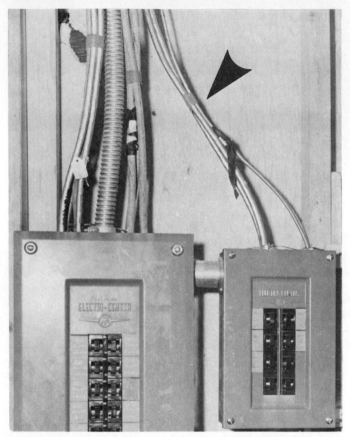

Fig. 336·10. Absence of stapling of the NM cables within 12 in. of entry into the panelboards is a clear violation of Sec. 336-15. (Sec. 336-15.)

indicated on the device or carton. Connectors for NM or NMC cable are also suitable for use on Type UF cable (underground feeder and branch-circuit cable—**NE Code** Art. 339) in dry locations, unless otherwise indicated on the carton. Each connector covered in the listing is recognized for connecting only one cable or cord—unless it is a duplex connector for connecting two cables or if the carton is marked to indicate use with more than one cable or cord.

336·16. Devices of Insulating Material. Note this use of switch and outlet devices without boxes is limited to exposed cable systems and for rewiring in existing buildings. This reference must not be confused with that of Exception No. 2 in Sec. 336-15, which refers to approved wiring devices that incorporate their own wiring boxes, so they are devices "without a *separate* outlet box" and not devices "without boxes."

336·17. Boxes of Insulating Material. By using nonmetallic outlet and switch boxes a completely "nonmetallic" wiring system is provided. Such a system has economic advantage and other advantages in locations where corrosive vapors are present. See Sec. 370-3.

336-26 Conductors. The second paragraph requires that NM and NMC cables always have their conductors applied to the ampacity of Type TW wire—that is, the 60°C ampacity from Table 310-16. However, the insulation on the conductors must be rated at 90°C.

ARTICLE 337. SHIELDED NONMETALLIC-SHEATHED CABLE

337-1. Definition. This article recognizes shielded nonmetallic-sheathed cable as a wiring method, basically intended for use in continuous rigid cable supports, or in raceways, in Class I, Division 2 and Class II, Division 2 hazardous locations. Type SNM cable features an overlapping spiral metal tape and wire shield with an outer nonmetallic jacket. Figure 337-1 shows a cutaway view of a typical Type SNM cable.

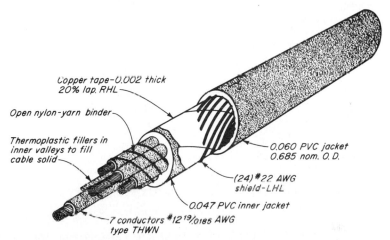

Copper tape—0.002 thick 20% lap. RHL

Open nylon-yarn binder

Thermoplastic fillers in inner valleys to fill cable solid

0.060 PVC jacket 0.685 nom. O.D.

(24) #22 AWG shield—LHL

0.047 PVC inner jacket

7 conductors #12 ¹⁹/₀₁₈₅ AWG type THWN

Fig. 337-1. Type SNM cable is a rugged assembly for industrial-type branch circuits and feeders. (Sec. 337-1.)

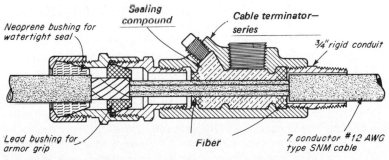

Sealing compound

Cable terminator—series

Neoprene bushing for watertight seal

¾" rigid conduit

Lead bushing for armor grip

Fiber

7 conductor #12 AWG type SNM cable

Fig. 337-2. Design of fitting assures effective application of SNM cable with conduit in hazardous areas. (Sec. 337-6.)

337·6. Fittings. Only fittings approved for use with Type SNM cable may be used. Figure 337-2 shows an approved fitting for use where Type SNM cable enters ¾-in. rigid-metal conduit in Classes I and II, Division 2 hazardous locations.

ARTICLE 338. SERVICE-ENTRANCE CABLE

338·1. Definition. The Code contains no specifications for the construction of this cable; it is left to Underwriters Laboratories Inc. to determine what types of cable should be approved for this purpose. The types listed by the Laboratories at the present time conform to the following data:

> Service Entrance Cable is labeled in sizes No. 12 AWG and larger for copper, and No. 10 AWG and larger for aluminum or copper-clad aluminum, with Types RH, RHW, RHH or XHHW conductors. If the type designation for the conductors is marked on the outside surface of the cable, the temperature rating of the cable corresponds to the rating of the individual conductors. When this marking does not appear, the temperature rating of the cable is 75°C.
> The cables are classified as follows:
> Type SE—Cable for aboveground installation.
> Type USE—Cable for underground installation including burial directly in the earth. Cable in sizes No. 4/0 AWG and smaller and having all conductors insulated is suitable for all of the underground uses for which Type UF cable is permitted by the NEC.

Many single-conductor cables are dual-rated (Type USE or RHW or RHH) and may be used in raceways, for either service conductors or feeders and branch circuits.

> Based upon tests which have been made involving the maximum heating that can be produced, an uninsulated conductor employed in a service cable assembly is considered to have the same current-carrying capacity as the insulated conductors even though it may be smaller in size.

Figure 338-1 shows two basic styles of service-entrance cable for aboveground use. The one without an armor over the conductors is referred to as "Type SE Style U"—the letter "U" standing for "unarmored." That cable is sometimes designated as "Type SEU." The cable assembly with the armor is designated "Type ASE" cable, with the "A" standing for "armored."

Figure 338-2 shows another type of SE cable, known as "Style SER"—the letter "R" standing for "round." In a typical assembly of that cable, three conductors insulated with Type XHHW cross link polyethylene are cabled together with fillers and one bare ground conductor with a tape over them and gray PVC overall jacket. For use aboveground in buildings, it is suitable for operation at 90°C in dry locations or 75°C in wet locations.

The three insulated conductors—a black, a red, and a blue—are used as the phase legs of the service and the bare conductor is used as the neutral.

Figure 338-3 shows Type USE cable for underground (including direct earth burial) applications of service or other circuits. Type USE may consist of one, two, or three conductors, Type RHW insulated wire with neoprene jacket suitable for operation in wet or dry locations at a maximum temperature of 75°C.

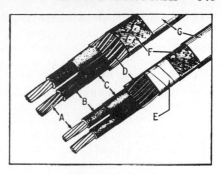

SERVICE ENTRANCE cables may consist of either copper or aluminum phase conductors (A) covered by heat resistant insulation (B) and moisture-resistant braid or tape (C) color coded for circuit identification, while basic assembly is enclosed by concentric neutral (D). Unarmored Type SE Style U is covered by variety of tapes (F) and outer braid (G) such as glass and cotton impregnated with moisture resistant and flame retardant finish labelled with pertinent data. Armored Style A additionally contains flat steel armor (E) as protection against physical abuse.

Fig. 338·1. Two types of aboveground SE cable. (Sec. 338-1.)

Each phase leg is an insulated conductor

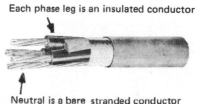

Fig. 338·2. Style SER cable contains individual conductors and no concentric neutral. (Sec. 338-1.)

Neutral is a bare stranded conductor

Fig. 338·3. Type USE cable may be multiconductor or single conductor cable. (Sec. 338-1.)

It is for underground service entrance for direct earth burial, conduit, duct, or aerial applications.

Depending upon whether USE cable is used for service entrance, for a feeder, or for a branch circuit, burial depth must conform to Sec. 300-5 and its many specific rules on direct burial cable.

338-3. Uses Permitted as Branch Circuits or Feeders.   Part **(a)** recognizes use of service-entrance cable fo branch circuits and feeders within buildings or structures provided that all circuit conductors, including the neutral of the circuit, are insulated. Such use must conform to Art. 336 on installation methods—the same as those for Type NM cable. See Sec. 338-4(b).

Part **(b)** covers permitted uses of service-entrance cable that contains a bare conductor for the neutral but limits such application to 120/240-V or 120/208-V systems. When an SE cable has an outer nonmetallic covering over the enclosed bare neutral, this **Code** rule permits the use of SE cable for circuits supplying ranges, wall-mounted ovens, and counter-mounted cooking units (Fig. 338-4). And in such cases, the bare conductor may be used as the neutral of the branch circuit as well as the equipment grounding conductor (see Sec. 250-60). However, price differences between SE cable and NM cable generally determine that SE cable will probably be used only where part of a circuit run is outdoors, or where 75°C supply conductors must be used to connect appliances. SE cables, in sizes 8/3 and smaller, generally cost more than corresponding sizes of NM cables. And even though 6/2, 8/1 SE cable costs slightly less than 6/3 NM cable, additional labor costs usually more than offset the total installation cost in favor of the 6/3 NM cable.

SE cable is also permitted to be used as a feeder from one building to another building, with the bare conductor used as a grounded neutral. Or an SE cable with a bare neutral may be used as a feeder within a building, if the bare neutral is used *only* as the equipment grounding conductor and one of the insulated conductors within the cable is used as the neutral of the feeder. See Fig. 338-5.

Part **(c)** requires that SE cable used to supply appliances not be subject to conductor temperatures in excess of the temperature specified for the insulation involved. The insulated conductors of SE cables are either 60°C or 75°C, and if they are rated at 75°C, such marking will appear on the outer sheath. A cooking unit or oven that requires 75°C supply conductors would be an application for the use of SE cables, rated at 75°C. However, a review of UL listings for cooking units and ovens indicates that the vast majority of such units do not require supply conductor ratings to exceed 60°C. The details in Fig. 338-4 show a method of connecting cooking units where the supply conductors are required to be 75 or 90°C.

338-4. Installation Methods.   Type SE cable used for interior branch circuits or feeders must satisfy all of the general wiring rules of Art. 300. Part **(b)** requires the "installation" of unarmored SE cable (which is the usual type of SE cable) to satisfy Art. 336 on nonmetallic-sheathed cable (Type NM). All the rules of Art. 336 that cover *how* cable is "installed" must be satisfied. But the wording of part **(b)** in this section has caused difficulty.

Because SE cable must be installed in accordance with Art. 336, the relation between Sec. 338-4(b) and Sec. 336-4 raises the question:

Does the **NE Code** permit the use of SER (Service Entrance, Round) cable for feeders in a structure more than three floors above grade?

Inspectors have ruled that Sec. 338-4(b) ("installed in accordance with the provisions of Article 336") would bring SE cable under the provision of Sec.

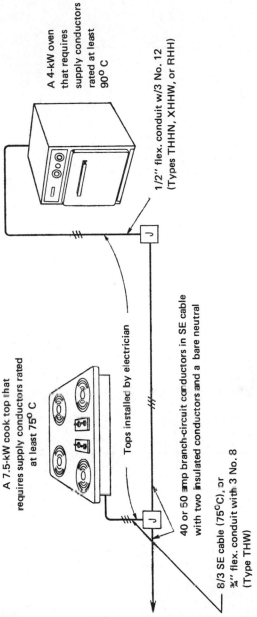

A 4-kW oven that requires supply conductors rated at least 90° C

1/2" flex. conduit w/3 No. 12 (Types THHN, XHHW, or RHH)

A 7.5-kW cook top that requires supply conductors rated at least 75° C

Tops installed by electrician

40 or 50 amp branch-circuit conductors in SE cable with two insulated conductors and a bare neutral

8/3 SE cable (75°C), or ¾" flex. conduit with 3 No. 8 (Type THW)

Fig. 338-4. SE cable with bare neutral may be used for branch circuit to range or other cooking units. (Sec. 338-3.)

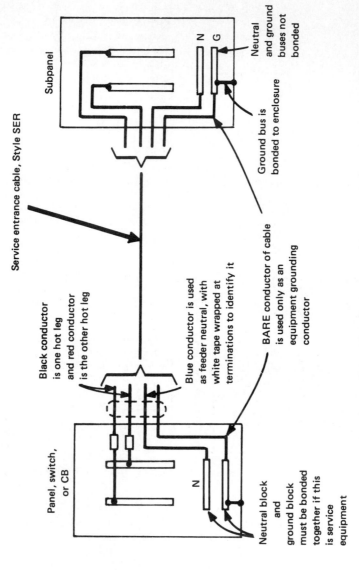

Fig. 338-5. Typical application of SE cable with a bare neutral for use as a feeder within a building. (Sec. 338-4.)

336-4(a) limiting the use of Type SER cable to structures not over three floors above grade.

The chairperson of the **Code** panel says that it is the intent of the **Code** panel that paragraph **(b)** of this rule, in referring to Art. 336, means to limit SE-cable branch circuits or feeders in the same way that Sec. 336-4 limits use of NM or NMC cable. That is, use of NM, NMC, or SE cable is limited to dwellings or other buildings—where the structure is not more than three floors above grade. As a result, the use of SE cable as a feeder, as shown in Fig. 338-5, would be a violation in any building with more than three floors above grade, such as in a high-rise apartment building.

ARTICLE 339. UNDERGROUND FEEDER AND BRANCH-CIRCUIT CABLE

339-1. Description and Marking.   Figure 339-1 shows a violation of the **Code** rule that a bare conductor in a UF cable is for grounding purposes only.

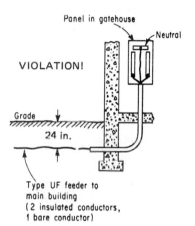

Fig. 339-1. Bare conductor in UF cable may not be used as a neutral. (Sec. 339-1.)

339-2. Other Articles.   Figures 339-2 and 339-3 show details on compliance of UF cable with Sec. 300-5. Where UF comes up out of the ground, it must be protected for 8 ft up on a pole and as described in Sec. 300-5(d).

339-3. Use.   The rules of part **(a)** are shown in Fig. 339-4 and must be correlated to the rules of Sec. 300-5 on direct burial cables. The rule of **(2)** in part **(a)** corresponds to that of Sec. 300-5(i). If multiple conductors are used per phase and neutral to make up a high-current circuit, this rule requires all conductors to be run in the same trench or raceway and therefore subject to the derating factors of Note 8 to Tables 310-16 to 310-31. Refer to the paragraph right after the table in Note 8, in the **NEC**. Also see discussion under Sec. 300-5(i).

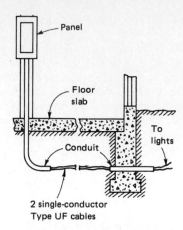

VIOLATION for cable to run under any
building if not totally in raceway
[Sec. 300-5 (c)]

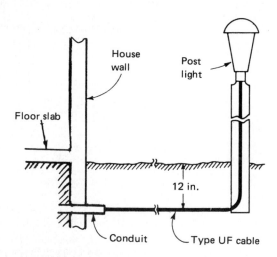

ACCEPTABLE for burial at only 12-in. depth when
used for residential branch-circuit rated not more
than 20 A at 120 V or less where GFCI protection
is also provided [Table 300-5]

Fig. 339·2. UF cable must conform to Sec. 300-5 on
direct-burial cables. (Sec. 339-2.)

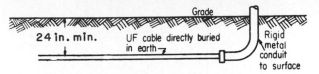

① UF CABLE WITHOUT SUPPLEMENTAL PROTECTION

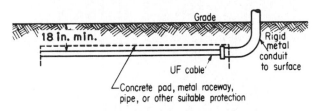

② UF CABLE WITH SUPPLEMENTAL PROTECTIVE COVERINGS

Fig. 339-3. The second qualifier under "Location of Wiring Method or Circuit" in Table 300-5 permits a 6-in. reduction of UF burial depth. (Sec. 339-2.)

UF cable may be used underground, including direct burial in the earth, as feeder or branch-circuit cable when provided with overcurrent protection not in excess of the rated ampacity of the individual conductors. If single-conductor cables are installed, all cables of the feeder circuit, subfeeder, or branch circuit, including the neutral cable, must be run together in close proximity in the same trench or raceway. It may be necessary in some installations to provide additional mechanical protection, such as a covering board, concrete pad, raceway, etc., when required by the authority enforcing the Code. Multiple-conductor Type UF cable (but not single-conductor Type UF cables) may also be used for interior wiring when used in the same way as Type NM cable, complying with the provisions of Art. 336 of the **Code**. And UF may be used in wet locations.

The effect of the wording in part **(a)(4),** where UF cable is used for interior wiring, is to require that its conductors must be rated at 90°C, with loading based on 60°C ampacity. This rule is a follow-up to the requirement that UF for interior wiring must satisfy the rules of Art. 336 on nonmetallic-sheathed cable (see Sec. 336-26, second paragraph).

As noted in part **(b)(8),** single-conductor Type UF cable embedded in poured cement, concrete, or aggregate may be used for nonheating leads of fixed electric space heating cables, as covered in Secs. 424-43 and 426-23.

Application data of the UL are as follows:

Cables suitable for exposure to direct rays of the sun are indicated by tag marking and marking on the surface of the cable with the designation "Sunlight Resistant."

This cable may be terminated by using nonmetallic sheathed cable connectors (see Nonmetallic Sheathed Cable Connectors).

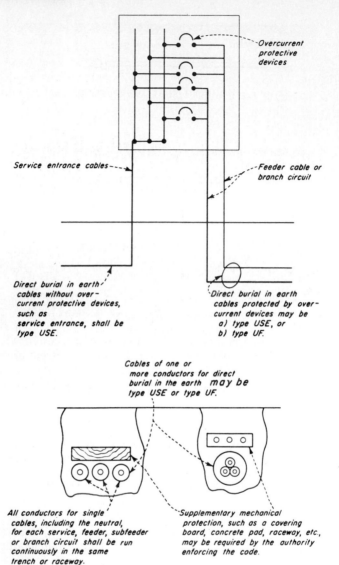

Fig. 339-4. UF cable may be used only as feeders or branch circuits. (Sec. 339-3.)

If single conductor Type UF cable is terminated with a fitting not specifically recognized for use with single conductor cable, special care should be taken to assure it is properly secured and not subject to damage.

Only multiconductor Type UF cable may be used in cable tray, in accordance with Art. 318.

ARTICLE 340. POWER AND CONTROL TRAY
CABLE

340-1. Definition.   This article covers the use of a nonmetallic-sheathed power and control cable, designated Type TC cable (T and C are the initials for "Tray Cable"), which may be used in cable trays, in raceways, or where supported by a messenger wire outdoors (Fig. 340-1).

Fig. 340-1.   This typical 3-conductor tray cable contains bare equipment grounding conductors. (Sec. 340-1.)

340-4. Use Permitted.   Type TC tray cable is limited to use in industrial establishments where maintenance and supervision assure that only competent individuals will work on the cables.

NE Code Sec. 318-2 recognizes the use of Type TC power and control tray cable installed in cable tray. Although specs on the construction and application of Type TC cable are covered in **NE Code** Secs. 340-1 through 340-8, great care must be used in relating those **Code** rules and the rules of **NE Code** Art. 337 to the "Power and Control Tray Cable" in the UL Green Book. Type TC cable is recognized under Sec. 318-3(a)(9).

UL data on "Power and Control Tray Cable" include the following:

Type TC Power and control tray cable is intended for use in accordance with Article 340 of the **National Electrical Code**. The cable consists of two or more insulated conductors twisted together, with or without associated bare or fully insulated grounding conductors, and covered with a nonmetallic jacket. The cables are rated 600 volts.

The cable is Listed in conductor sizes No. 18 AWG to 2,000 MCM [kcmil] copper or No. 12 AWG to 2,000 MCM [kcmil] aluminum or copper-clad aluminum.

Cables with copper-clad aluminum conductors are surfaced printed "AL (CU-CLAD)" or "Cu-clad Al".

Cables with aluminum conductors are surface printed "AL.".

For termination information, see Guide AALZ information.

If the type designation of the conductors is marked on the outside surface of the cable, the temperature rating of the cable corresponds to the rating of the individual conductors. When this marking does not appear, the temperature rating of the cable is 60 C unless otherwise marked on the surface of the cable.

Fittings for use with these cables are Listed by Underwriters Laboratories Inc. under the Outlet Bushings, Nonmetallic-Sheathed Cable Connectors, or Service Entrance Cable Fittings categories. Cables which have been investigated for use where exposed to direct rays of the sun are marked "sunlight resistant."

Cables' surface marked "Oil Resistant I" or "Oil Res I" are suitable for exposure to mineral oil at 60C. Cables suitable for exposure to mineral oil at 75C are surface marked "Oil Resistant II" or "Oil Res II."

Regarding cable seals outlined in Article 501 of the **National Electrical Code**, Type TC Cable has a sheath which is considered to be gas/vapor tight but the cable has not been investigated for transmission of gases or vapors through its core.

The basic standard used to investigate products in this category is UL1277, "Electrical Power and Control Tray Cables With Optional Optical-Fiber Members".

Note that this cable appears to be for cable tray only, but Type TC is recognized by Sec. 340-1 for use in raceway or with messenger support, in addition to use in tray.

340·5. Uses Not Permitted. Although **(4)** of this section has the effect of prohibiting the use of Type TC tray cable directly buried in the earth, the rule is modified by the phrase "unless identified for such use." The result of this wording is to permit Type TC cable directly buried in the earth where the cable is marked or otherwise approved for the purpose by the local electrical inspector. This permission for direct burial was added because the cable assembly was designed to withstand such application and because Type TC cable has been successfully and effectively used directly for years in many installations (Fig. 340-2 with burial conforming to Sec. 300-5). Such cable is listed for direct earth burial by UL, and the performance record has been excellent.

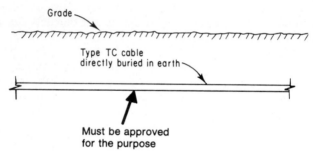

Fig. 340·2. Type TC (power and control tray cable) is recognized for direct earth burial. (Sec. 340-5.)

ARTICLE 342. NONMETALLIC EXTENSIONS

A nonmetallic extension is an assembly of two conductors without a metallic envelope, designed specially for a 15- or 20-A branch circuit as an extension from an existing outlet. Surface extensions are limited to residences and offices. Aerial extensions are limited to industrial purposes where it has been determined that the nature of the occupancy would require such wiring for connecting equipment.

ARTICLE 344. UNDERPLASTER EXTENSIONS

344·1. Use. Such extensions are permitted in order to provide a suitable means of extending from existing outlets to new outlets without excessive expense, where there are no open spaces in walls or floors that will permit fishing from one outlet to another. In installing this work, the plaster is channeled and the conduit, cable, raceway, or tubing is secured to the concrete or tile and then plastered over.

344·2. Materials. Note that Type NM or NMC cable is *not* one of the listed methods for making underplaster extensions. Refer to Sec. 336-3(b), which, prior to the 1975 **NEC**, did permit Type NMC nonmetallic-sheathed cable to be used under plaster, provided it had a continuous protection of sheet steel covering if the cable was less than 2 in. behind the finish surface of the plaster.

344·5. Extension to Another Floor. Such wiring is an expedient permitted for the purpose of avoiding an excessive amount of channeling and drilling of walls and floors. It is an expensive method, and from the standpoint of permanence, safety, and reliability the standard types of wiring are much to be preferred. For these reasons, underplaster extensions are limited to the floor within which they originate. In practice, the use of this method generally is, and should be, limited to short runs feeding not more than two or three additional outlets from one existing outlet.

ARTICLE 345. INTERMEDIATE METAL CONDUIT

This article covers a relatively new type of raceway—a conduit with wall thickness less than rigid metal conduit but greater than that of EMT. Called "IMC," this intermediate metal conduit uses the same threading method and standard fittings for rigid metal conduit and has the same general application rules as rigid metal conduit. Intermediate metal conduit actually is a lightweight rigid steel conduit which requires about 25 percent less steel than heavy-wall rigid conduit. Acceptance into the **Code** was based on a UL fact-finding report which showed through research and comparative tests that IMC performs as well as rigid steel conduit in many cases and surpasses rigid aluminum and EMT in most cases.

IMC may be used in any application for which rigid metal conduit is recognized by the **NEC**, including use in all classes and divisions of hazardous locations as covered in Secs. 501-4, 502-4, and 503-3. Its thinner wall makes it lighter and less expensive than standard rigid metal conduit, but it has physical properties that give it outstanding strength. The lighter weight facilitates handling and installation at lower labor units than rigid metal conduit. Because it has the same outside diameter as rigid metal conduit of the same trade size, it has greater interior cross-section area (Fig. 345-1). Although this extra space is not recognized by the **NEC** to permit the use of more conductors than can be used in the same size of rigid metal conduit, it does make wire-pulling easier.

345·3. Uses Permitted. The data of the UL supplement the requirements of part **(a)** on use of IMC, as follows:

> Listing of Intermediate Ferrous Metal Conduit includes standard 10 ft. lengths of straight conduit, with a coupling, special length either shorter or longer, with or without a coupling for specific applications or uses, elbows, bends, and nipples in trade sizes ½ to 4 in. incl. for installation in accordance with Article 345 of the **National Electrical Code.**

3/4" TRADE SIZES

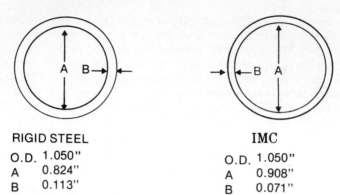

RIGID STEEL
O.D. 1.050"
A   0.824"
B   0.113"

IMC
O.D. 1.050"
A   0.908"
B   0.071"

Fig. 345·1. Typical comparison between rigid and IMC shows interior space difference. (Sec. 345-1.)

Fittings for use with unthreaded intermediate ferrous metal conduit are listed under conduit fittings (Guide DWTT) and are suitable only for the type of conduit indicated by the marking on the carton.

Galvanized intermediate steel conduit installed in concrete does not require supplementary corrosion protection.

Galvanized intermediate steel conduit installed in contact with soil does not generally require supplementary corrosion protection.

In the absence of specific local experience, soils producing severe corrosive effects are generally characterized by low resistivity less than 2000 ohm-centimeters.

Wherever ferrous metal conduit runs directly from concrete encasement to soil burial, severe corrosive effects are likely to occur on the metal in contact with the soil.

Although literature on IMC refers to Type I and Type II IMC because of slight differences in dimensions due to manufacturing methods, the NEC considers IMC to be a single type of product and the rules of Art. 345 apply to all IMC.

Note that the wording in the UL data above includes the word "generally" in stating that IMC does not need additional protective material applied to the conduit when used in soil. That is intended to indicate that local soil conditions (acid versus alkaline) may require protection of the conduit against corrosion. And the UL note about corrosion of conduit running from concrete to soil must be observed. Refer to comments under Sec. 346-1 covering these conditions.

In part **(a)**, wording of the rule is significantly modified by the Exception, which specifically permits use of aluminum fittings and enclosures with steel intermediate metal conduit (Fig. 345-2). This same Exception is also given in Art. 346 on rigid metal conduit and Art. 348 on electrical metallic tubing. Tests have established that aluminum fittings and enclosures create no difficulty when used with steel raceways. The Exception is intended to counteract the implication of that phrase that cautions against use of dissimilar metals in a raceway system to guard against galvanic action. This section prohibits the use of dissimilar metals, "where practicable." This phrase is used frequently in the Code; in effect, it is saying, "You *shall* do it, if you can, or if the inspector thinks

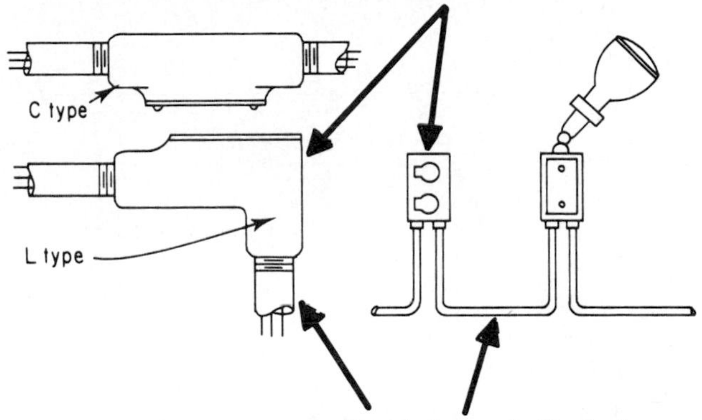

Aluminum fittings, conduit bodies, boxes . . .

C type

L type

. . . are permitted to be used with steel
raceways—rigid steel conduit, IMC and EMT.

Fig. 345·2. NEC warning against use of dissimilar metals does not
apply to this. (Sec. 345-3.)

you can." By using this phrase, the **Code** recognizes that the contractor may not
always be able to comply.

In part **(b)**, wording of the rule intends to make clear that the galvanizing or
zinc coating on the IMC does give it the measure of protection required when
used in concrete or when directly buried in the earth. The last phrase, "judged
suitable for the condition," refers to the need to comply with UL regulations
such as those contained in UL's *Electrical Construction Materials Directory*,
advising how and when steel raceways and other metal raceways may be used
in concrete or directly buried in earth.

The UL data point out that there are soils where some difficulties may be
encountered, and there are other soil conditions that present no problem to the
use of steel or other metal raceways. The phrase "judged suitable for the condition" implies that a correlation was made between the soil conditions or the
concrete conditions at the place of installation and the particular raceway to be
used. This means that it is up to the designers and/or installers to satisfy themselves as to the suitability of any raceway for use in concrete or for use in particular soil conditions at a given geographic location. Of course, all such determinations would have to be cleared with the electrical inspection authority to
be consistent with the meaning of **Code** enforcement.

For use of IMC in or under cinder fill, part **(c)** gives the limiting conditions.
See Sec. 346-3.

345·7. Number of Conductors in Conduit.   The rules on conduit fill are the same
for IMC, rigid metal conduit, EMT, flexible metal conduit, flexible metallic tubing, and liquidtight flexible metallic tubing—for conduits ½ in. size and larger.
Refer to Sec. 346-6.

345·12. Supports.   The basic rule on clamping IMC is simple and straightforward (Fig. 345-3). The two exceptions allowing wider spacing of supports are
the same as those covered in Sec. 346-12 for rigid metal conduit.

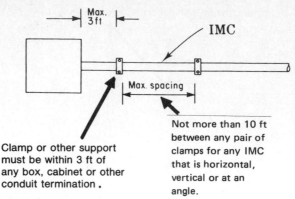

Fig. 345·3. All runs of IMC must be clamped in this way. (Sec. 345-12.)

Spacing between supports for IMC (greater than every 10 ft) is the same as the spacing allowed for rigid metal conduit. The exceptions recognize the essential equality between the strengths of IMC and rigid metal conduit.

ARTICLE 346. RIGID METAL CONDUIT

346·1. Use.   UL data on rigid metal conduit are similar to that on IMC and supplement the rules of this section, as follows:

> Galvanized rigid steel conduit installed in concrete does not require supplementary corrosion protection.
> Galvanized rigid steel conduit installed in contact with soil does not generally require supplementary corrosion protection.
> In the absence of specific local experience, soils producing severe corrosive effects are generally characterized by low resistivity less than 2000 ohm-centimeters.
> Wherever ferrous metal conduit runs directly from concrete encasement to soil burial, severe corrosive effects are likely to occur on the metal in contact with the soil.
> Supplementary nonmetallic coatings presently used have not been investigated for resistance to corrosion.
> Supplementary nonmetallic coatings of greater than 0.010-in. thickness applied over the metallic protective coatings are investigated with respect to flame propagation and detrimental effects to the basic corrosion protection provided by the protective coatings.

For rigid aluminum conduit, the UL application notes state:

> Aluminum conduit used in concrete or in contact with soil requires supplementary corrosion protection.
> Supplementary nonmetallic coatings presently used have not been recognized for resistance to corrosion.

For direct earth burial of rigid conduit and IMC, the UL notes must be carefully studied and observed:

1. Galvanized rigid steel conduit and galvanized intermediate steel conduit directly buried in soil do not *generally* require supplementary corrosion

protection. The use of the word "generally" in the UL instructions indicated that it is still the responsibility of the designer and/or installer to use supplementary protection where certain soils are known to produce corrosion of such conduits. Where corrosion of underground galvanized conduit is known to be a problem, a protective jacketing or a field-applied coating of asphalt paint or equivalent material must be used on the conduit. **But,** UL notes on "Supplementary nonmetallic coatings" must be observed for resistance to corrosion.

2. Aluminum conduit used directly buried in soil requires supplementary corrosion protection. But again, it is completely the task and responsibility of the designer and/or installer to select an effective protection coating for the aluminum conduit, because UL says "supplementary nonmetallic coatings presently used have not been *recognized* for resistance to corrosion." That could also be interpreted as a direct prohibition on the use of aluminum conduit directly buried.

The UL notes must also be observed in all use of metal conduits in concrete, as follows:

1. Galvanized rigid steel conduit and galvanized intermediate steel conduit installed in concrete *do not require* supplementary corrosion protection. See Sec. 348-1 on EMT.

2. Aluminum conduit installed in concrete *definitely requires* supplementary corrosion protection, but the supplementary protective coatings presently used "have not been recognized for resistance to corrosion."

3. *Watch out for this!* UL warns, "Wherever ferrous metal conduit runs directly from concrete encasement to soil burial, severe corrosive effects are likely to occur on the metal in contact with the soil." Supplementary protective coating on conduit at the crossing line can eliminate the conditions shown in Fig. 346-1.

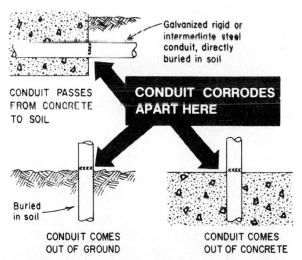

Fig. 346·1. Protective coating on section of conduit can prevent this corrosion problem. (Sec. 346-1.)

346·3. Cinder Fill. Cinders usually contain sulfur, and if there is much moisture sulfuric acid is formed, which attacks steel conduit. A cinder fill outdoors should be considered as "subject to permanent moisture." In such a place conduit runs should be protected as described or buried in the ground at least 18 in. below the fill. This would not apply if cinders were not present.

346·6. Number of Conductors in Conduit. The basic NE Code rule on the maximum number of conductors which may be pulled into rigid metal conduit, rigid nonmetallic conduit, intermediate metal conduit, electrical metallic tubing, flexible metal conduit, and liquidtight flexible metal conduit is contained in the single sentence of this section.

The number of conductors permitted in a particular size of conduit or tubing is covered in Chap. 9 of the Code in Tables 1 and 3 for conductors all of the same size used for either new work or rewiring. Tables 4 to 8 cover combinations of conductors of different sizes when used for new work or rewiring. For nonlead-covered conductors, three or more to a conduit, the sum of the cross-sectional areas of the individual conductors must not exceed 40 percent of the interior cross-section area (csa) of the conduit or tubing for new work or for rewiring existing conduit or tubing (Fig. 346-2). Note 3 preceding all the tables in Chap. 9, in the back of the Code book, permits a 60 percent fill of conduit nipples not over 24 in. long and no derating of ampacities is needed.

When all conductors in a conduit or tubing are the same size, Tables 3A, 3B, and 3C, Chap. 9, give the maximum allowable fill for conductors up to 750 kcmil, for ½- to 6-in. conduit.

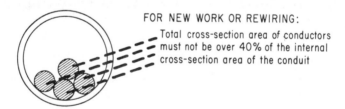

FOR NEW WORK OR REWIRING:
Total cross-section area of conductors must not be over 40% of the internal cross-section area of the conduit

Example:
   From Table 3B, with the 90C conductors used at the ampacity of 75 C 500 kcmil conductors, unless equipment is marked to permit connection of 90C conductors

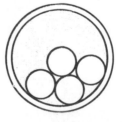

4 No. 500 kcmil THHN or XHHW in 3-in. conduit

Fig. 346·2. For three or more conductors the sum of their areas must not exceed 40 percent of the conduit area. (Sec. 346-6.)

Question: What is the minimum size of conduit required for six No. 10 THHN wires?

Answer: Table 3B, Chap. 9, shows that six No. 10 THHN wires may be pulled into a ½-in. conduit.

Question: What size conduit is the minimum for use with four No. 6 RHH conductors with outer covering?

Answer: Table 3C, Chap. 9, shows that a 1¼-in. minimum conduit size must be used for three to five No. 6 RHH conductors.

Question: What is the minimum size conduit required for four No. 500 kcmil XHHW conductors?

Answer: Table 3B shows that 3-in. conduit may contain four 500 kcmil XHHW (or THHN) conductors.

When all the conductors in a conduit or tubing are not the same size, the minimum required size of conduit or tubing must be calculated. Table 1, Chap. 9, says that conduit containing three or more conductors of any type except lead-covered, for new work or rewiring, may be filled to 40 percent of the conduit csa. Note 2 to this table refers to Tables 4 through 8, Chap. 9, for dimensions of conductors, conduit, and tubing to be used in calculating conduit fill for combinations of conductors of different sizes.

example What size conduit is the minimum required for enclosing six No. 10 THHN, three No. 4 RHH (without outer covering), and two No. 12 TW conductors (Fig. 346-3)?

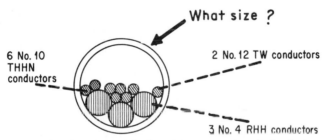

Fig. 346-3. Minimum permitted conduit size must be calculated when conductors are not all the same size. (Sec. 346-6.)

Cross-section areas of conductors:
From Table 5, Chap. 9:
No. 10 THHN . . . . 0.0184 sq in.
No. 4 RHH . . . . 0.1087 sq in.
No. 12 TW . . . . 0.0172 sq in.
Note: RHH without outer covering has same dimensions as THW.

Total area occupied by conductors:
6 No. 10 THHN . . . . 6 × 0.0184 = 0.1104 sq in.
3 No. 4 RHH . . . . 3 × 0.1087 = 0.3261 sq in.
2 No. 12 TW . . . . 2 × 0.0172 = 0.0344 sq in.
Total area occupied by conductors . . . . 0.4709 sq in.

Referring to Table 4, Chap. 9:
The fifth column from the left gives the amount of square inch area that is 40 percent of the csa of the sizes of conduit given in the first column at left. The 40 percent column

shows that 0.34 sq in. is 40 percent fill of a 1-in. conduit, and 0.60 sq in. is 40 percent fill of a 1¼-in. conduit. Therefore, a 1-in. conduit would be too small and—

A 1¼-in. conduit is the smallest that may be used for the 11 conductors.

Example: What is the minimum size of conduit for four No. 4/0 TW and four No. 4/0 XHHW conductors?

From Table 5, a No. 4/0 TW has a csa of 0.3904 sq in. Four of these come to 4 × 0.3904 or 1.5616 sq in.

From column 11 of Table 5 we find that four No. 4/0 XHHW have a csa of 1.3112 sq in.

$$1.5616 + 1.3112 = 2.8728 \text{ sq in.}$$

From Table 4, 40 percent of the csa of 3-in. conduit is 2.9500 sq in. A 2½-in. conduit would be too small.

Therefore—

A 3-in. conduit must be used.

Figure 346-4 shows how a conduit nipple is excluded from the normal 40 percent limitation on conduit fill. In this typical example, the nipple between

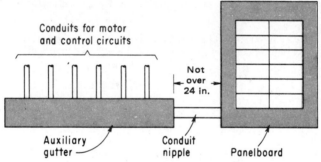

Fig. 346-4. Conduit nipples may be filled to 60 percent of csa and no derating is required. (Sec. 346-6.)

a panelboard and an auxiliary gutter contains 12 No. 10 TW wires, 6 No. 14 THHN wires, 3 No. 8 THW wires, and 2 No. 2 RHH wires (without outer covering). The minimum trade size of nipple that can be used in this case is 1¼ in. [Nipple may be filled to 60 percent of its csa if it is not over 24 in. long. Area of conductors = 12 × 0.0224 sq in. (csa of each No. 10 TW) plus 6 × 0.0087 sq in. (each No. 14 THHN) plus 3 × 0.0526 sq in. (each No. 8 THW) plus 2 × 0.1473, or a total of 0.7734 sq in., which is 60 percent of 1.2890 sq in. **NE Code** Table 4, Chap. 9, shows that a 1¼-in. nipple is the smallest that can be used. Sixty percent of the csa of 1¼-in. nipple = 0.6 × 1.50 or 0.900 sq in.; 60 percent of the csa of 1-in. nipple = 0.6 × 0.86 or 0.516 sq in.] And the conductors do *not* have to be derated in accordance with Note 8 of Tables 310-16 through 310-31. If the nipple had been 25 in. long, calculation at 40 percent fill would have called for a 1½-in. size and all conductors would have had to be derated per Note 8.

THWN and THHN are the smallest-diameter building wires. The greatly reduced insulation wall on Type THWN or THHN gives these thin-insulated conductors greater conduit fill than TW, THW, or RHH for new work and rewiring. Type XHHW wire has the same conduit fills from No. 4 through 500 kcmil. And the nylon jacket on THWN and THHN has an extremely low coefficient of friction. THWN is a 75°C rated wire for general circuit use in dry or wet locations. THHN is a 90°C rated wire for dry locations only.

To fill conduit to the **Code** maximum allowance is frequently difficult or impossible from the mechanical standpoint of pulling the conductors into the conduit, because of twisting and bending of the conductors within the conduit. Bigger-than-minimum conduit should generally be used to provide some measure of spare capacity for load growth; and in many cases, the conduit to be used should be upsized considerably to allow future installation of some larger anticipated size of conductors.

346·8. Bushings. As with IMC, rigid metal conduit always requires a bushing on the conduit end using locknuts and bushing for connection to knockouts in sheet metal enclosures (Fig. 346-5). But simply because a conduit can be

Fig. 346·5. Conduit terminations, other than threaded connections to threaded fittings or enclosure hubs, must be provided with bushings for protection of the conductors. (Sec. 346-8.)

secured to a sheet metal KO with two locknuts [one inside and one outside— as required by Sec. 250-76, Exception (b)], it does not mean the bushing may be eliminated. Of course, no bushing is needed where the conduit threads into a hub or boss on a fitting or an enclosure.

346·9. Couplings and Connectors. Figure 346-6 shows a threadless connection of rigid metal conduit to the hub on a fitting. It is effective both mechanically and electrically if any nonconducting coating is removed from the conduit.

A running thread is considered mechanically weak and has poor electrical conductivity.

Where two lengths of conduit must be coupled together but it is impossible to screw both lengths into an ordinary coupling, the Erickson coupling or a

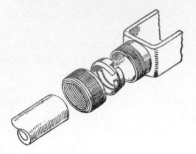

Fig. 346·6. Threadless connectors may be used on unthreaded end of conduit. (Sec. 346-9.)

swivel-coupling may be used (Fig. 346-7). They make a rigid joint which is both mechanically and electrically effective. Also, bolted split couplings are available.

It is not intended that conduit threads be treated with paint or other materials in order to assure watertightness. It is assumed that the conductors are approved for the locations and that the prime purpose of the conduit is for protection from physical damage and easy withdrawal of conductors for replacement. There are available pipe-joint compounds that seal against water without interrupting electrical conductivity.

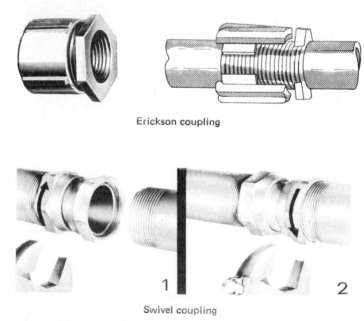

Erickson coupling

Swivel coupling

Fig. 346·7. Fittings provide for coupling conduits where conduits cannot be rotated (turned). (Sec. 346-9.)

346·10. Bends—How Made. *Field bends* means any bend made by workers during the installation of the conduit.

Table 346-10 gives minimum bending radii for field bends in rigid metal conduit, IMC, or EMT using any approved bending equipment and methods. (See Fig. 346-8.) However, the Exception to this rule permits sharper bends (i.e.,

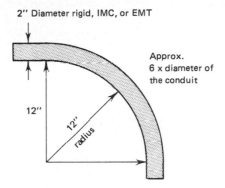

For conduit containing conductors without lead sheath

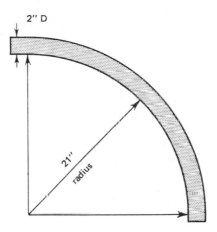

For conduit containing lead-sheathed conductors

NOTE: From Table 346-10 Exception, a bending radius of not less 9½ in. may be used for a one-shot bend on 2-in. rigid, IMC, or EMT if the conductors to be installed do not have a lead sheath.

Fig. 346·8. Minimum bending radii are specified to protect conductors from damage during pull-in. (Sec. 346-10.)

smaller bending radii) if a one-shot bending machine is used in making a bend for which the machine and its accessories are designed. The minimum radii for one-shot bends are given in Table 346-10 Exception. All bending radii apply to any amount of bend—i.e., 45°, 90°, etc.

346·11. Bends—Number in One Run.   There must be not more than the equivalent of four quarter bends (360°) between any two "pull points"—conduit bodies and boxes, as shown in Fig. 346-9. In previous **Codes**, the 360° of bends was

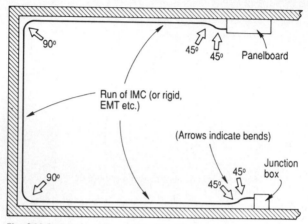

Fig. 346·9. Rigid metal conduit—like all other types of conduits—is limited to not over 360° of bends between "pull points," such as the panelboard and junction box shown here. (Sec. 346-11.)

permitted between boxes and "fittings" and even between "fitting and fitting." Because the word "fitting" is defined in Art. 100 and the term does include conduit couplings, bushings, etc., there could be very many bends in an overall run, totaling far more than 360° if the equivalent of four quarter bends could be made between each pair of conduit couplings. The present wording limits the 360° of bends to conduit runs between "pull points"—such as between switchboards and panelboards, between housings, boxes, and conduit bodies— all of which are "pull points."

The same concept of the number of bends permitted is given in all of the **NEC** Articles on raceways—ENT, EMT, IMC, rigid metal conduit, rigid nonmetallic conduit, etc.

ARTICLE 347. RIGID NONMETALLIC CONDUIT

347·1. Description.   Nonmetallic conduit wiring systems include a wide assortment of products (Fig. 347-1).

All approved rigid nonmetallic conduits are suitable for underground installations. Some types are approved for direct burial in the earth while other types

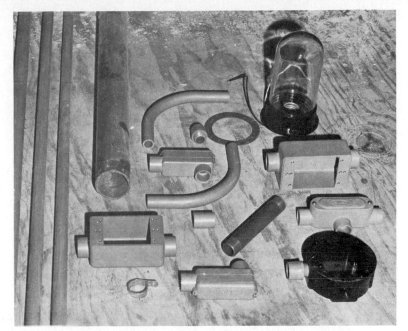

Fig. 347·1. Rigid nonmetallic conduit systems are made up of a wide variety of components—conduit, fittings, elbows, nipples, couplings, boxes, straps. (Sec. 347-1.)

must be encased in concrete for underground applications. The nonmetallic conduits include fiber conduit, asbestos-cement conduit, soapstone, rigid polyvinyl chloride conduit, polyethylene conduit, and styrene conduit. Of these, medium-density polyethylene conduit and styrene conduit are not UL-listed. High-density polyethylene conduit and the others are UL listed. The listed and labeled conduits differ widely in weight, cost, and physical characteristics, but each has certain application advantages.

The only nonmetallic conduit approved for use aboveground at the present time is rigid polyvinyl chloride (PVC Schedule 40, or Schedule 80) (Fig. 347-2). Since not all PVC conduits are suitable for use aboveground, the UL label in each conduit length will indicate if the conduit is suitable for such use. For use of Schedule 80, see Fig. 347-3 and Secs. 300-5(d) and 710-3(b) (1).

UL application data are detailed and divide "Rigid Nonmetallic Conduit" into three categories with specific instructions on each category, as follows:

"Plastic"

This listing covers Rigid Nonmetallic PVC Conduit (Schedule 40 and Schedule 80) intended for installation in accordance with Article 347 of The National Electrical Code. It is suitable for use above ground, underground and for direct burial without encasement in concrete.

Unless marked for higher temperature, rigid nonmetallic conduit is intended for use with wires rated 75C or less including where it is encased in concrete within buildings

Fig. 347·2. PVC conduit is the only rigid nonmetallic conduit that may be used aboveground. And when enclosing conductors run up a pole (shown here feeding a floodlight at top), the PVC conduit must be Schedule 80 PVC conduit if it is exposed to physical damage, such as possible impact by trucks or cars. If the conduit is not so exposed, it may be Schedule 40 PVC conduit. See Sec. 300-5(d). (Sec. 347-1.)

and where ambient temperature is 50C or less. Where encased in concrete in trenches outside of buildings it is suitable for use with wires rated 90C or less.

Schedule 40 conduit is suitable for exposed work where not subject to physical damage.

The marking "Schedule 80 PVC " identifies conduit suitable for use where exposed to physical damage, see Section 347-3(c) of The National Electrical Code.

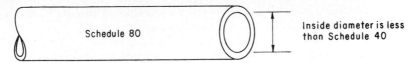

For conductor fill to 40% of the cross-section area, refer to data on wire-fill capacity marked on conduit surface.

Fig. 347·3. Extra-heavy-wall PVC conduit must have conductor fill limited to its reduced csa. (Sec. 347-1.)

Nonmetallic plastic conduit is listed in sizes ½ to 6 in. incl. Listing includes straight conduit, elbows and bends.

For additional Listings of Rigid Nonmetallic Conduit suitable for underground use, see the categories of Conduit, Rigid Non-metallic, Underground, Other Than Plastic, Fiber Type, and Conduit, Rigid Nonmetallic, Underground Plastic.

Schedule 80 rigid PVC conduit has a reduced cross-sectional area available for wiring space. The actual cross-sectional area and the need for reference to National Electrical Code Chapter 9 Table 1 for wire fill capacity are prominently marked on the conduit surface.

Listed PVC conduit is inherently resistant to atmosphere containing common industrial corrosive agents and will also withstand vapors or mist of caustic, pickling acids, plating bath and hydrofluoric and chromic acids.

PVC conduit, elbows and bends (including couplings) which have been investigated for direct exposure to other reagents, may be identified by the designation "Reagent Resistant " printed on the surface of the product. Such special uses are described as follows:

PVC conduit, elbows and bends. Where exposed to the following reagents at 60 C or less: Acetic, Nitric (25 C only) acids in concentrations not exceeding ½ normal; hydrochloric acid in concentrations not exceeding 30 percent; sulfuric acid in concentrations not exceeding 10 normal; sulfuric acid in concentrations not exceeding 80 percent (25 C only); concentrated or dilute ammonium hydroxide; sodium hydroxide solutions in concentrations not exceeding 50 percent; saturated or dilute sodium chloride solution; cottonseed oil, or ASTM No. 3 petroleum oil.

PVC conduit is designed for connection to couplings, fittings and boxes by the use of a suitable solvent-type cement. Instructions supplied by the manufacturer describe the method of assembly and precautions to be followed.

The basic standard used to investigate products in this category is UL651, "Schedule 40 and 80 Rigid PVC Conduit ".

"Other Than Plastic, Underground"

This listing covers impregnated fiber conduit, for use only when installed underground as raceway for the installation of wires and cables in accordance with the **National Electrical Code**. For plastic types of underground conduit, see Plastic Underground.

The conduit is designed for use in underground work under the following conditions:

Fiber conduit and fittings for use in underground work when laid with its entire length in concrete, identified as "Type I."

Fiber conduit and fittings for use in underground work without being encased in concrete, identified as "Type II."

Where conduits emerge from underground installation the wiring method should be of a type recognized by the **National Electrical Code.**

This listing includes straight conduit in lengths up to 10 ft (not for field bends) sizes ½- to 6-in. incl., for use with factory made elbows, couplings, reducers, and other terminal fittings.

"Plastic Underground"

This listing covers plastic types of nonmetallic conduit, for use only when installed underground as raceway for installation of wires and cables in accordance with Article 347 of the National Electrical Code. For other references for underground conduit, see Section 710-3b and Tables 300-5 and 710-3(b). This conduit may be: (1) polyvinyl chloride (PVC) Type A or Type EB; (2) high-density polyethylene (HDPE) Schedule 40; (3) fiberglass reinforced epoxy. The various conduit types differ in their inside and outside diameters. For underground conduit of other than the plastic type, see Conduit, Rigid Nonmetallic, Underground, Other Than Plastic, Fiber Type (EALZ).

The conduit is designed for use in underground work under the following conditions, as indicated on the Listing Mark, (1) when laid with its entire length in concrete (Type A), (2) when laid with its entire length in concrete in outdoor trenches (Type EB) and (3) direct burial with or without being encased in concrete (HDPE Schedule 40 and fiberglass reinforced epoxy). The conduit is intended for use in ambient temperatures of 50 C or less and, unless marked otherwise, Type A and HDPE Schedule 40 conduit are intended for use with wires rated 75 C or less. Type EB conduit, Type A conduit encased in concrete in trenches outside of buildings, may be used with wires rated 90 C or less. HDPE Schedule 40 conduit, when directly buried or encased in concrete may be used with wire rated 90 C or less. Fiberglass reinforced epoxy conduit may be used with wires rated 90 C or less.

Where conduits emerge from underground installation the wiring method shall be of a type Recognized by the National Electrical Code for the purpose.

Plastic underground conduit is Listed in sizes ½ to 6-in. incl. Listing includes straight conduit, elbows and bends unless otherwise noted.

Fiberglass reinforced epoxy conduit, elbows and bends (including fittings) which have been investigated for direct exposure to reagents, are identified by the designation "Reagent Resistant" and are marked to indicate the specific reagents.

PVC conduit is designed for joining with PVC couplings by the use of a solvent-type cement. HDPE conduit is designed for joining by threaded couplings, drive-on couplings, or a butt fusing process. Fiberglass reinforced epoxy conduit is designed for joining by epoxy type cement or drive-on bell and spigot. Instructions supplied by the manufacturer describe the method of assembly and precautions to be followed.

The basic standard used to investigate products in this category is UL651A, "Type EB and A PVC Conduit and HDPE Conduit".

Note: As a result of the wording and intent of **NEC** Sec. 110-3(b), all the above application data constitute mandatory rules of the **NEC** itself—subject to the same enforcement as any other **NEC** rules.

347·2. Uses Permitted. This section applies to use of the conduit for circuits operating at any voltage (up to 600 V and at higher voltages). The rules make rigid nonmetallic conduit a general-purpose raceway for interior and exterior wiring, concealed or exposed in wood or masonry construction—under the conditions stated. Only PVC is acceptable as a rigid nonmetallic conduit for in-building use (aboveground).

Aboveground applications of rigid nonmetallic conduit must be Schedule 40 or Schedule 80 PVC conduit, which is the only nonmetallic conduit listed for use aboveground.

Rigid nonmetallic conduit may be used aboveground to carry high-voltage circuits without need for encasing the conduit in concrete. That permission is also given in Sec. 710-3(a). Aboveground use is permitted indoors and outdoors.

Part **(g)** covers underground applications of all the types of rigid nonmetallic conduit—for circuits up to 600 V, as regulated by Sec. 300-5; and for circuits over 600 V, as covered by Sec. 710-3(b) (Fig. 347-4). Directly buried nonmetallic conduit carrying high-voltage conductors does not have to be concrete-encased if it is a type approved for use without concrete encasement. If concrete encasement is required, it will be indicated on the UL label and in the listing.

Fig. 347-4. All UL-listed rigid nonmetallic conduits are acceptable for use underground. PVC Schedule 40 and Schedule 80 and Type II fiber conduits do not require concrete encasement. Other types must observe UL and NEC rules on concrete encasement. (Sec. 347-2.)

Figure 347-5 shows both underground and aboveground application. Referring to the circled numbers: (1) The burial depth must be at least 18 in. for any circuit up to 600 V. The buried conduit may be Schedule 40 or Schedule 80 (either without concrete encasement) or Type A or Type EB (both require concrete encasement). Refer to Sec. 347-1 and Sec. 300-5. (2) The concrete encasement where the conduit comes up from its 18-in. depth was required at one time by the NEC, but is no longer required. (See Sec. 300-5.) (3) The radius of the bend must comply with Table 346-10 (minimum 18 in.). The conduit aboveground, on a pole or on a building wall, must be Schedule 80 if the conduit is exposed to impact by cars or trucks or to other physical damage. If the conduit is not exposed to damage, it may be Schedule 40.

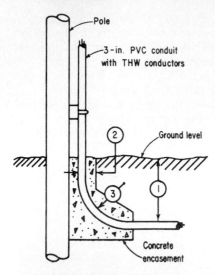

Numbers in circles refer to text.

Fig. 347·5. Schedule 80 PVC conduit may run up pole from earth to above-ground use. (Sec. 347-2.)

In many cases where nonmetallic conduit is used to enclose conductors suitable for direct burial in the earth, inspectors and engineering authorities have accepted use of any type of conduit—PVC, polyethylene, styrene, etc.—without concrete encasement and without considering application of **Code** rules to the conduit. The reasoning is that because the cables are suitable for direct burial in the earth, the conduit itself is not required at all and its use is above and beyond **Code** rules. But temperature considerations are real and related to effective, long-time operation of an installation. Temperature effects must not be disregarded in any conduit-conductor application.

347·3. Uses Not Permitted.   It should be noted that nonmetallic conduit is not permitted in ducts, plenums, and other air handling spaces. See Sec. 300-21 and the comments following Sec. 300-22.

Figure 347-6 shows a difference in application rules between rigid nonmetallic conduit and metal conduit with respect to supporting equipment.

Parts **(d)** and **(e)** require care in use of the conduits so that they are not exposed to damaging temperatures. In using nonmetallic conduits care must be

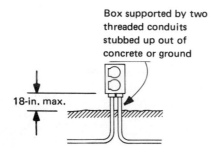

Fig. 347·6. This is O.K. for rigid metal conduit but not for rigid nonmetallic conduit. (Sec. 347-3.)

taken to assure temperature compatibility between the conduit and the conductors used in it. For instance, a conduit that has a 75°C temperature rating at which it might melt and/or deform must not be used with conductors which have a 90°C temperature rating and which will be loaded so they are operating at their top temperature limit. There is available PVC rigid conduit listed by UL and marked to indicate its suitability for use with all 90°C-rated conductors, thereby suiting the conduit to use with 90°C-rated conductors. The UL data described in Sec. 347-1 give the acceptable ambient temperatures and conductor temperature ratings that correlate to these NEC rules. Conductors with 90°C insulation may be used at the higher ampacities of that temperature rating only when the conduit is concrete encased (Fig. 347-7).

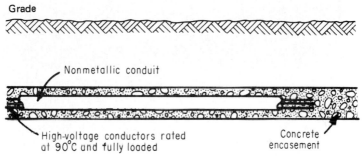

Fig. 347·7. UL data assure that this does not violate Sec. 347-3(e). (Sec. 347-3.)

347·4. Other Articles. When equipment grounding is required for metal enclosures of equipment used with rigid nonmetallic conduit, an equipment grounding conductor must be provided. Such a conductor *must* be installed in the conduit along with the circuit conductors (Fig. 347-8). Refer to Secs. 250-57, 250-58, and 250-45.

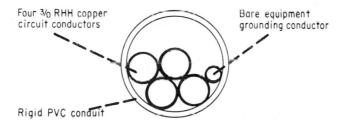

Equipment grounding conductor is sized from Table 250-95, based on the rating of the fuses or CB protecting the circuit conductor in the conduit. With 200-amp protection for the 3/0 conductors here, the equipment grounding conductor must be at least a No. 6 copper or No. 4 aluminum.

Fig. 347·8. Equipment grounding conductor must be used "within" the rigid nonmetallic conduit. (Sec. 347-4.)

Fig. 347·9. PVC conduit is designed for connection to couplings and enclosures by an approved cement, but leaving rough edges in the conduit end is a clear violation of Sec. 347-5. (Sec. 347-5.)

347·5. Trimming.   See Fig. 347-9.

347·8. Supports.   In this section, Table 347-8, giving the maximum distance between supports for rigid nonmetallic conduit, permits greater spacing than previous **NEC** editions. For each size of rigid nonmetallic conduit, a single maximum spacing between supports, in feet, is given for all temperature ratings of conductors used in rigid nonmetallic conduit raceways (Fig. 347-10).

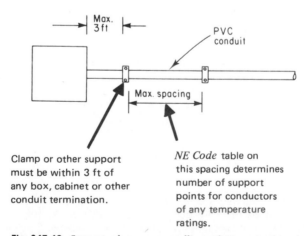

Clamp or other support must be within 3 ft of any box, cabinet or other conduit termination.

NE Code table on this spacing determines number of support points for conductors of any temperature ratings.

Fig. 347·10. Support rules on nonmetallic conduit are simple and direct. (Sec. 347-8.)

347-9. Expansion Joints. Where conduits are subject to constantly changing temperatures and the runs are long, expansion and contraction of PVC conduit must be considered. In such instances an expansion coupling should be installed near the fixed end of the run to take up any expansion or contraction that may occur. Available expansion couplings have a normal expansion range of 6 in. The coefficient of linear expansion of PVC conduit can be obtained from manufacturers' data.

Expansion couplings are normally used where conduits are exposed. In underground or slab applications such couplings are seldom used because expansion and contraction can be controlled by *bowing* the conduit slightly or by immediate burial. After the conduit is buried, expansion and contraction are not a problem. Conduits left exposed for an extended period of time during widely variable temperature conditions should be examined to see if contraction has occurred.

347-11. Number of Conductors. See discussion under Sec. 346-6.

347-13. Bends—How Made. Refer to Sec. 346-10.

347-14. Bends—Number in One Run. Refer to Sec. 346-11.

ARTICLE 348. ELECTRICAL METALLIC TUBING

348-1. Use. EMT is a general-purpose raceway of the same nature as rigid metal conduit and IMC. Although rigid metal conduit and IMC afford maximum protection for conductors under all installation conditions, in many instances it is permissible, feasible, and more economical to use EMT to enclose circuit wiring rated 600 V or less. Because EMT is lighter than conduit, however, and is less rugged in construction and connection details, the NE Code restricts its use (Art. 348) to locations (either exposed or concealed) where it will not be subjected to severe physical damage or (unless suitably protected) to corrosive agents.

EMT distribution systems are constructed by combining wide assortments or related fittings and boxes. Connection is simplified by employing threadless components that include compression, indentation, and set-screw types.

Some questions have been raised about the acceptability of EMT directly buried in soil. The last paragraph of Sec. 348-1 gives EMT exactly the same recognition for direct burial that Sec. 346-1(c) gives to rigid steel conduit. The wording of both paragraphs is identical, and it certainly seems clear that if galvanizing is enough corrosion protection for rigid steel conduit, it must provide equivalent protection for EMT in direct burial. In the UL listing on "Electrical Metallic Tubing," a note says that "galvanized steel electrical metallic tubing in a concrete slab below grade level *may* require supplementary corrosion protection." (That word "may" leaves the decision up to the designer and/or installer.) But note that the rule carefully refers to "*galvanized* steel" EMT and not just to "steel" EMT.

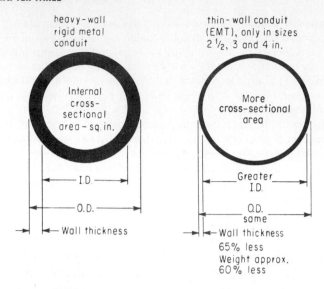

heavy-wall
rigid metal
conduit

Internal
cross-
sectional
area – sq. in.

←——— I.D. ———→

←——— O.D. ———→

→| |← Wall thickness

thin-wall conduit
(EMT), only in sizes
2 ½, 3 and 4 in.

More
cross-sectional
area

←——— Greater ———→
I.D.

←——— O.D. ———→
same

→| |← Wall thickness
65% less
Weight approx.
60% less

Trade size rigid and EMT	Inches outer dia. (O.D.) EMT and rigid	Wall thickness in.		Inside cross-sectional area sq. in.		More C.S.A. % for EMT
		Rigid	EMT	Rigid	EMT	EMT
2½	2.875	0.203	0.072	4.79	5.85	22%
3	3.500	0.216	0.072	7.38	8.84	19%
4	4.500	0.237	0.083	12.72	14.75	16%

Fig. 348·1. Larger sizes of EMT have same outside diameters as rigid and IMC. (Sec. 348-5.)

The next note says, "In general, *steel* electrical metallic tubing in contact with soil requires supplementary corrosion protection." That sentence certainly admits that there are locations where soil conditions are such that supplementary corrosion protection is not required. Since the word "galvanized" is not used ahead of the word "steel" as it was in the preceding paragraph it is at least a possibility that UL left the door open for galvanizing as one possible way of satisfying the requirement for supplementary corrosion protection.

Such an interpretation of UL intent would seem to be consistent with the equal approval that Secs. 345-3(b), 346-1(c), and 348-1 (last paragraph) give to direct burial of galvanized IMC rigid steel conduit and to galvanized electrical metallic tubing. The **Code** makes no distinction, where direct burial is concerned, between rigid conduit and EMT on the basis of their different wall thicknesses and structural strength differences.

It is reasonable to conclude that the phrase "judged suitable for the condition" means that past experience and local soil conditions should be considered in determining the acceptability of direct burial of EMT as well as IMC and rigid conduit, with appropriate attention given to additional protection against corrosion if necessary. Of course, the ruling of the local electrical inspector should be sought and followed.

Where corrosion protection has been provided and deemed suitable for the conditions, EMT burial depths must meet the minimum cover requirements of **NE Code** Sec. 300-5(a). Table 300-5 indicates that EMT would have to be at least 18 in. below grade, except that a 12-in. depth is permissible for residential branch circuits rated 120 V or less, provided with overcurrent protection of not more than 20 A, and provided the circuit also has GFCI protection.

As noted in Sec. 345-3(a), Exception, and Sec. 346-1(b), Exception, permission is given for use of aluminum fittings and enclosures with steel electrical metallic tubing.

348-5. Size.   Up to 2-in. size EMT has the same interior cross-section area as corresponding sizes of rigid metal conduit. EMT sizes of 2½ in. and larger have the *same outside diameter* as rigid metal conduits of corresponding sizes. Accordingly, the interior cross-sectional areas (square inch) are proportionally larger, and this provides more wiring space for greater ease of installation of conductors in these new sizes of EMT. Figure 348-1 illustrates some approximate dimensional comparisons between the larger EMT sizes and those for heavy-wall rigid metal conduit in corresponding sizes. It is significant that the increased internal diameters for respective sizes of EMT provide square inch cross-sectional areas from 16 percent to 22 percent greater. To prevent any misunderstanding, it should be stressed that the greater cross-sectional area of the inside of these EMT sizes, compared with rigid, *does not offer* the chance to fill such EMT runs with more conductors than could be used in corresponding sizes of rigid conduit. Number of conductors permitted in "conduit or tubing" is the same for rigid, IMC, or EMT, from Tables 1 through 8 of **NE Code**, Chap. 9.

348-6. Number of Conductors in Tubing.   Conductor fill for EMT is the same as described under Sec. 346-6 for rigid metal conduit.

348-7. Threads.   Here, the rules clarify **Code** intent. Threading of electrical metallic tubing is prohibited, but integral couplings used on EMT shall be permitted to be factory threaded. Such equipment has been used successfully in the past and has been found satisfactory. The revised **Code** rule recognizes such use. But it should be noted that this applies to EMT using *integral threaded fittings,* that is, fittings which are part of the EMT itself.

348-8. Couplings and Connectors.   Couplings of the raintight type are required wherever electrical metallic tubing is used on the exteriors of buildings. (See Secs. 225-22 and 230-53.)

Sec. 370-7 requires that conductors entering a box, cabinet, or fitting be protected from abrasion. The end of an EMT connector projecting inside a box, cabinet, or fitting must have smooth, well-rounded edges so that the covering of the wire will not be abraded while the wire is being pulled in. Where ungrounded conductors of size No. 4 or larger enter a raceway in a cabinet, the EMT connector must have an insulated throat (insulation set around the edge of the connector opening) to protect the conductors. See Sec. 373-6(c). For conductors smaller than No. 4, an EMT connector does *not* have to be the insulated-throat type. Using THW conductors, a circuit of No. 4 conductors (a 2-wire or 3-wire circuit) requires a 1-in. size EMT (Table 3A, Chap. 9, **NEC**). Therefore, for THW or TW wire, there is no requirement for insulated-throat EMT connectors in ½-in. and ¾-in. sizes. A circuit, say, of three No. 1 THW wires would call for 1¼ EMT, which would require use of insulated-throat connectors—or noninsulated-throat connector with a nonmetallic bushing on the connector end. In the larger sizes, the economics on the makeups can be significantly different. A 4-in. insulated-throat EMT connector might cost $18, whereas a noninsulated-throat connector in that size might cost $10 and $2 for a 4-in. plastic bushing (Figure 348-2).

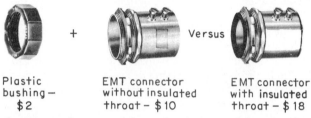

Plastic
bushing —
$2

+

EMT connector
without insulated
throat – $10

Versus

EMT connector
with insulated
throat – $18

Fig. 348·2. Different-cost makeups for 4-in. EMT satisfy **Code** rules on EMT termination. (Sec. 348-8.)

When an EMT connector is used—either with or without an insulated throat to satisfy Sec. 373-6(c)—there is no requirement in Art. 348 that a bushing be used on the connector end. Note, however, that a bushing is required for rigid metal conduit and for IMC as covered in Secs. 346-8 and 345-15.

348·9. Bends—How Made.   Refer to Sec. 346-10.

348·10. Bends—Number in One Run.   Figure 348-3 shows EMT run from a

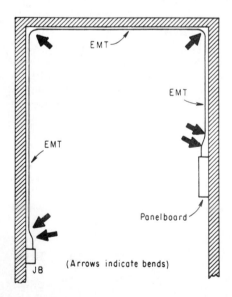

EMT

EMT

EMT

Panelboard

(Arrows indicate bends)

JB

Fig. 348·3. EMT, like other conduit runs, is limited to not over 360° of bends between raceway ends. (Sec. 348-10.)

panelboard to a junction box (JB) along the wall—with exactly a total of 360°
of bend (from the panel: 45°, 45°, 90°, 90°, 45°, 45°).

348·12. Supports. Figure 348-4 shows this rule applied to an EMT layout. If
the word "fitting" is taken to include couplings, then a strap must be used
within 3 ft of each coupling. The definition of "fitting," given in Art. 100,
includes locknuts and bushings, which would logically suggest that the word
also covers conduit bodies ("C," "T," etc.) and couplings.

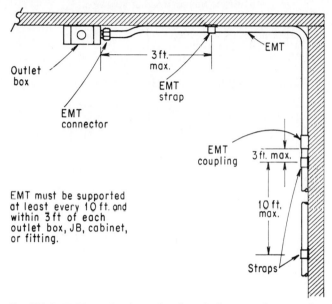

Fig. 348·4. EMT must be clamped within 3 ft of every enclosure or "fitting." (Sec. 348-12.)

As permitted by the Exception, clamps on unbroken lengths of EMT may be
placed up to 5 ft from each termination at an "outlet box or fitting where structural support members do not *readily* permit support within 3 ft." This Exception allows the first clamp to be up to 5 ft from a termination of EMT at an
"outlet box or fitting." It should be noted that the words "junction box" and
"cabinet," which are used in the basic rule of the first paragraph (requiring
clamping within 3 ft) are not used in the Exception permitting a 5-ft distance
from the termination to the first clamp. It must be assumed that those enclosures
are excluded from the Exception permission for the 5-ft distance.

ARTICLE 349. FLEXIBLE METALLIC TUBING

349·1. Scope. The first section of this article defines this NE Code raceway.
The rule indicates that flexible metallic tubing is intended for use where "not
subject to physical damage" and gives use above suspended ceilings as an

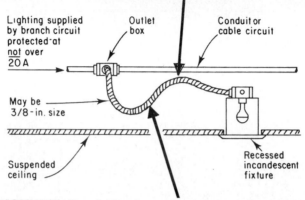

Typical use of flexible metallic
tubing: 4-to-6-ft length for
fixture whip in ceiling, containing
two No. 18 Type AF wires (for 6-amp
fixture load, see Section
402-5, Exceptions)
or two No. 16 Type AF wires (for
8-amp fixture load). Section 240-4
permits No. 16 and No. 18 fixture
wire to be protected at 20 amps.

Lighting supplied
by branch circuit
protected-at
not over
20 A

Outlet
box

Conduit or
cable circuit

May be
3/8-in. size

Suspended
ceiling

Recessed
incandescent
fixture

IMPORTANT!! Flex tubing is equipment grounding conductor

because fittings are listed for grounding, and the AF wires in flex
tubing are tapped from circuit protected at not over 20 amps, as
permitted in Section 250-91(b), Exception No. 1.

Fig. 349-1. New type of raceway seems limited to this application.
(Sec. 349-1.)

example. Although this wording does not limit its use to air-handling ceilings,
it does raise some questions for electrical inspectors with respect to accepting
flexible metallic tubing as a general-purpose raceway.

The meaning of the phrase, "not subject to physical damage," is not clear.
When the proposal was made to add flexible metallic tubing to the **Code** as a
suitable raceway, it was indicated that it had been designed for certain specific
applications and not for general use. It was specifically intended for use as the
fixture whip on recessed fixtures where high-temperature wire is run from the
branch-circuit junction box to the hot wiring compartment in lighting fixtures,
an application long filled by flexible metallic conduit (Fig. 349-1). Although Fig.
349-1 shows Type AF wire, any fixture wire from Table 402-3 may be used provided it has a temperature rating sufficient for the marking in the fixture being
supplied.

349-3. Uses Permitted.   Although flexible metallic tubing is liquidtight without
a nonmetallic jacket, part **(a)** of this section appears to limit its use to dry locations, and part **(d)** appears to limit its use to branch circuits. The problem of
interpretation arises from the wording. The first sentence of Sec. 349-3 indicates where flexible metallic tubing shall be permitted to be used, but it does

not say that other uses would be prohibited. For instance, it is permitted to be used in dry locations, but nowhere in the article is it prohibited from being used in wet locations—except for direct earth burial or embedding in poured concrete or aggregate (Sec. 349-4).

349-4. Uses Not Permitted.   Part **(6)** limits use of flexible metallic tubing to lengths not over 6 ft long. That limitation has the effect of ruling out flexible metallic tubing as a general-purpose raceway and limiting its use to short interconnections so commonly made with flexible metal conduit or liquidtight flexible metal conduit. But it does not appear that flexible metallic tubing, in spite of its resistance to moisture or liquid penetration, is an alternative to the use of liquidtight flexible metal conduit in wet locations.

ARTICLE 350. FLEXIBLE METAL CONDUIT

350-2. Use.   UL data supplement the **Code** data on use of standard flexible metal conduit—known also as "Greenfield" or simply "flex." The UL data note:

> These listings include flexible aluminum and steel conduit in trade sizes $\frac{5}{16}$ to 4 in. incl. and flexible aluminum and steel conduit Type RW (reduced wall), in trade sizes from $\frac{3}{8}$ to 3 in. incl., for installation in accordance with Article 350 of the National Electrical Code.
>
> Flexible metal conduit (steel or aluminum) shall not be used underground (directly buried or in duct which is buried) or embedded in poured concrete or aggregate, or in direct contact with earth or where subjected to corrosive conditions. In addition, flexible aluminum conduit shall not be installed in direct contact with masonry in damp locations.
>
> Flexible metal conduit no longer than six ft and containing circuit conductors protected by overcurrent devices rated at 20 amperes or less is suitable as a grounding means.
>
> Flexible metal conduit longer than six ft has not been judged to be suitable as a grounding means.
>
> See the category Conduit Fittings (DWTT) with respect to fittings suitable as a grounding means.
>
> To prevent possible damage to flexible aluminum conduit, and flexible aluminum and steel conduit Type RW, care must be exercised when installing connectors employing direct bearing set screws.
>
> Flexible aluminum conduit is marked at intervals of not more than one ft with the letters "AL".
>
> Flexible aluminum conduit Type RW is marked at intervals of not more than one ft with the letters "AL" and "RW".
>
> Flexible steel conduit Type RW is marked at intervals of not more than one ft with the letters "RW".

Where Sec. 350-2 prohibits use of flex "in wet locations, unless conductors are of . . . type approved for the specific conditions," interpretation has raised difficulty. Any conductor with a "W" designation—such as THW or XHHW— is recognized by Sec. 310-7 for use in wet locations. From the definition of "wet location" (under "Location" in Art. 100), any indoor place subject to water spray or splashing or outdoors exposed to weather must use "W"-designated wire types—such as outdoor service-entrance conductors tapped from a service drop and run in conduit down the outside of a building. The question then arises: May flex be used in such wet locations if the conductors within it are "W" type (say, THW)? It would seem that the parallel between the two applications would permit use of flex with THW wire in a wet location. However, there would still be concern for water getting inside the flex and running into enclosures or equipment. Because of that, the rule requires that flexible metal conduit used in wet locations (such as exposed to weather outdoors) must be installed to prevent water entering the raceway and thereby entering other raceways or enclosures to which the flex is connected.

Note that the words in this rule require that "installation is such that water is *not likely* to enter other raceways or enclosures. . . ." This is somewhat in conflict with Sec. 225-22, which requires that raceways exposed to outdoor weather "shall be made raintight." That is an absolute requirement, whereas the phrase "not likely" allows some possibility of water entry. Actually, flex exposed to weather outdoors should be of the liquidtight type to satisfy Sec. 225-22.

350-3. Minimum Size.   Exception No. 3 to this rule permits ⅜-in. flexible metal conduit to be used in lengths up to 6 ft for connections to lighting fixtures. This provides correlation with Sec. 410-67(c), which includes 4 to 6 ft of metal raceway for connecting recessed fixtures (generally the nonwired types). Figure 350-1 shows such application, and it is permissible to use No. 16 or No. 18 150°C fixture wire as shown in Fig. 349-1 for flex tubing.

Exception No. 3 also permits ⅜-in. flex if it is "part of a listed assembly," which assumes it is supplied as part of UL-listed equipment.

Exception No. 3 further permits flex in ⅜-in. size to be used "for utilization equipment." This permits 6-ft lengths of ⅜-in. flex to be used for connection of "utilization equipment"—in addition to its use "as part of a *listed* assembly" or for lighting-fixture whips, as in Sec. 410-67(c). Although this rule was intended to cover controls and sensors, use of the phrase "utilization equipment" would lend credence to the concept that ⅜-in. flex may be used with other types of utilization equipment—such as motors, electric heating, etc.

Exception No. 4 permits flex in ⅜-in. size to be used for the cable assemblies of modular wiring systems in hung ceilings [so-called "manufactured wiring systems" covered by Sec. 604-6(a)] in lengths over 6 ft long. This is directed specifically to ceiling modular wiring. And the equipment grounding conductor run in such flex wiring assemblies may be either bare or insulated [see Sec. 604-6(a)(2)] (Fig. 350-1).

350-4. Supports.   Straps or other means of securing the conduit in place should be spaced much closer together (every 4½ ft and within 12 in. of each end) for flexible conduit than is necessary for rigid conduit. Every bend should be rigidly secured so that it will not be deformed when the wires are being pulled in, thus causing the wires to bind.

Figure 350-2 shows use of unclamped lengths of flex, as permitted by Exception No. 2. Figure 350-3 shows another example. Exception No. 3 is illustrated in Fig. 350-1.

350-5. Grounding.   As shown in the UL data under Sec. 350-2, flex in any length over 6 ft is not suitable as an equipment grounding conductor and an equipment grounding conductor must be used within the flex to ground metal enclosures fed by the flex. Exception No. 1 permits flex as an equipment grounding conductor *only* under the given conditions—which would be the same as shown in Fig. 349-1 for flex tubing. Refer to Sec. 250-91(b) and to the discussion of grounding and bonding in Sec. 250-79(e).

The second sentence of this section notes that an equipment bonding jumper used with flexible metal conduit may be installed inside the conduit or outside the conduit when installed in accordance with the limitations of Sec. 250-79. The Exception to this rule makes clear that flexible metal conduit when used

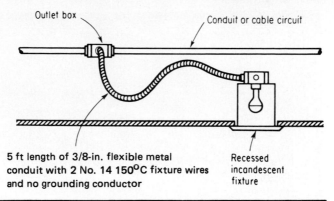

Outlet box

Conduit or cable circuit

5 ft length of 3/8-in. flexible metal
conduit with 2 No. 14 150°C fixture wires
and no grounding conductor

Recessed
incandescent
fixture

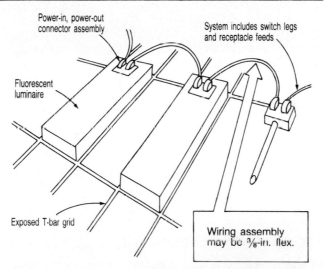

Power-in, power-out
connector assembly

System includes switch legs
and receptacle feeds

Fluorescent
luminaire

Exposed T-bar grid

Wiring assembly
may be ⅜-in. flex.

**complete system in a ceiling space consisting of prewired
cable lengths with snap-in connectors for fixtures and
switches, may use ⅜-in. flexible metal conduit.**

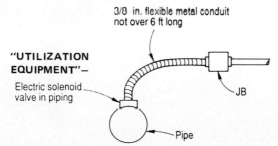

3/8 in. flexible metal conduit
not over 6 ft long

**"UTILIZATION
EQUIPMENT"–**

Electric solenoid
valve in piping

JB

Pipe

Fig. 350-1. Flex of ⅜-in. size may be used for fixture "whip" and for
"utilization equipment." (Sec. 350-3.)

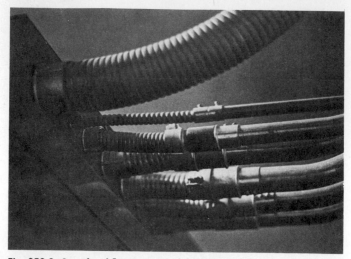

Fig. 350·2. Lengths of flex not over 3 ft long may be used without clamps or straps where the flex is used at terminals to provide flexibility for vibration isolation or for alignment of connections to knockouts. (Sec. 350-4.)

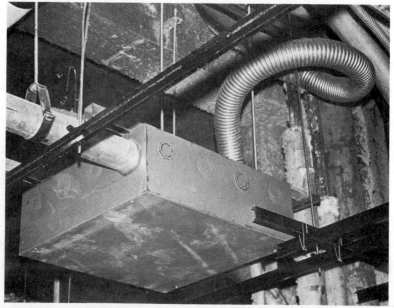

Fig. 350·3. A length of flex not over 3 ft long connects conduit to pull box in modernization job, providing the flexibility to feed from fixed conduit to box. (Sec. 350-4.)

as an equipment grounding conductor in itself is permitted only where a length of not over 6 ft is inserted in any ground return path. The wording indicates that the total length of flex in any ground return path must not exceed 6 ft. That is, it may be a single 6-ft length. Or, it may be two 3-ft lengths, three 2-ft lengths, or any total equivalent of 6 ft. If the total length of flex in any ground return path exceeds 6 ft, the rule appears to require an equipment grounding conductor to be run within or outside any length of flex beyond the permitted 6 ft that is acceptable as a ground return path in itself.

It should be noted that Exception No. 1 of this section is not applicable to the use of flex in a hazardous location. The rules in Sec. 501-16(b) and Sec. 502-16(b) simply require bonding for flex, with only a very narrow Exception given in Sec. 502-16(b) (Fig. 350-4).

Where bonding of standard or liquidtight flex is flatly required, as in Class I, Div. 2 and Class II, Div. 2 locations . . .

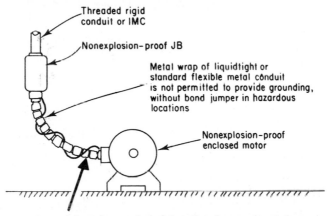

Threaded rigid conduit or IMC

Nonexplosion-proof JB

Metal wrap of liquidtight or standard flexible metal conduit is not permitted to provide grounding, without bond jumper in hazardous locations

Nonexplosion-proof enclosed motor

. . . an internal or external bonding jumper must be used at all times, for any size and any length of the flex and must conform to Section 250-79(e) as noted in Section 501-16(b) and Section 502-16(b).

Fig. 350·4. Flex must always be bonded in Class I and Class II hazardous locations. (Sec. 350-5.)

Exception No. 2 says that an equipment grounding conductor (or jumper) must *always* be installed for a length of metal flex that is used to supply equipment "where flexibility is required," such as equipment that is not fixed in place. Exception No. 2 actually modifies Exception No. 1, which describes the conditions under which a 6-ft or shorter length of metal flex (Greenfield) may be used for grounding through the metal of its own assembly, without need for a bonding wire. Because experience has indicated many instances of loss of ground connection through the flex metal due to repeated movement of a flex whip connected to equipment that vibrates or flex supplying movable equipment, the Exception requires use of an equipment bonding jumper, either inside or outside the flex, in all cases where vibrating or movable equipment is supplied—for assured safety of grounding continuity. The rule applies to those lengths of 3 ft or less that are permitted by Sec. 350-4, Exception No. 2, because "flexibility is necessary."

350-6. Bends.   Figure 350-5 shows the details of this section.

FOR EXPOSED OR CONCEALED WORK . . .

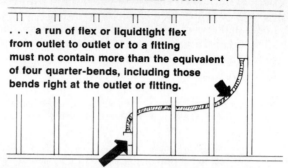

. . . a run of flex or liquidtight flex from outlet to outlet or to a fitting must not contain more than the equivalent of four quarter-bends, including those bends right at the outlet or fitting.

Angle connectors for flex connection to enclosures must not be used for *concealed* flex installations. Straight connectors are OK.

Fig. 350-5. Concealed or exposed flex must not have too many bends that could damage wires on pull-in. (Sec. 350-6.)

In this section and in Sec. 351-10, the limitation to no more than a total of 360° of bends between outlets applies to both exposed and concealed applications of standard metal flex and liquidtight metal flex.

Without restriction on the maximum number of bends in exposed and concealed work, bends could result in damage to conductors in a run with an excessive number of bends or could encourage installation of conductors prior to conduit installation, with conduit then installed as a cable system. A limit on number of bends for exposed and concealed work conforms with the requirements for other raceway systems, such as Secs. 345-11, 346-11, 347-14, and 348-10.

350-7. Number of Conductors.   This section specifies that Table 1 of **NEC** Chap. 9 must be used in determining the maximum permitted number of conductors in ½- through 4-in. flex. Flexible metal conduit is permitted the same conductor fill as other types of conduit and tubing. The number of conductors permitted in ⅜-in. flex is given in Table 350-3.

ARTICLE 351. LIQUIDTIGHT FLEXIBLE METAL CONDUIT AND LIQUIDTIGHT FLEXIBLE NONMETALLIC CONDUIT

351-1. Scope.   This article is divided into two parts. Part **A** covers *metal* liquidtight flex, and part **B** contains seven sections on *nonmetallic* liquidtight flex. Liquidtight metal flex (often called "Sealtite" as a generic term in industry usage, although that word is the registered trade name of the liquidtight flex

Fig. 351-1. Plastic jacket on liquidtight flex suits it to outdoor use exposed to rain or indoor locations where water or other liquids or vapors must be excluded from the raceway and associated enclosures. In lengths under 6 ft, UL-listed metal liquidtight flex does not require a bonding jumper. (Sec. 351-1.)

made by Anaconda Metal Hose Division) is similar in construction to the common type of flexible metal conduit, but is covered with an outer sheath of thermoplastic material (Fig. 351-1).

351-4. Use. UL data on liquidtight metal flex say:

> This listing includes liquid-tight flexible metal conduit in trade sizes ⅜ to 4 in. incl., for installation in accordance with Article 351 of the National Electrical Code.
>
> Flexible liquid-tight conduit is intended for use in wet locations or where exposed to mineral oil, both at a maximum temperature of 60 degrees C and installed in accordance with the National Electrical Code. It is not intended for direct burial or where exposed to gasoline or similar light petroleum solvents unless so marked on the product.

That rule of UL has an effect on the conductors used in the flex. Because UL-listed liquidtight flexible metal conduit is intended for use at a maximum temperature of 60°C, conductors used in liquidtight flex must be 60°C-rated Type TW; or, if higher-temperature-rated conductors are used (THW, RHH, THHN, XHHW), they must be used at the 60°C ampacities of NE Code Table 310-16.

UL also lists the following:

Liquid-tight flexible metal conduit assemblies consist of a length of liquid-tight flexible metal conduit terminated at each end with a permanently attached connector.

Although UL data limit its listed liquidtight flex to use at a maximum of 60°C, there are applications requiring higher-temperature-rated flex for foundries, near boilers, and in other hot places. Even though high-temperature flex is not UL-listed, it is consistent with **NEC** rules [Sec. 110-3(a)(5)] to use the higher-temperature flex when an application would exceed the 60°C rating of UL-listed flex. High-temperature flex is *not* a product listed by any test lab, and its use is, therefore, not contrary to Sec. 110-2. It would violate Secs. 351-4(b)(2) and 110-3(b) to use the listed 60°C flex in any way in which the loading on its contained conductors and the given ambient combined to produce a temperature over 60°C in the plastic jacket of the flex. Refer to temperature correction factors in Table 310-16.

As noted in the UL data quoted above, liquidtight flexible metal conduit is permitted for use directly buried in the earth if it is "so marked on the product." The rule in Sec. 351-4(a) extends **Code** recognition to direct burial of liquidtight flexible metal conduit if it is "listed and marked" for such use. Based on many years of such application, liquidtight metal flex is recognized for direct burial, but any such use is permitted only for liquidtight flex that is "listed" by UL, or some other test lab, and is "marked" to indicate suitability for direct burial, to assure the installer and inspector of **Code** compliance. In the past, successful applications have been made in the earth and in concrete. Standard flexible metal conduit is prohibited from being used "underground or embedded in poured concrete or aggregate" [Sec. 350-2(6)]. But that prohibition is not placed on liquidtight metal flex.

351·5. Size.   Refer to Sec. 350-3. Figure 351-2 satisfies Exception No. 2 of Sec. 350-3 if the No. 12 wires are stranded, as required in Sec. 430-145(b). Table 350-3 accepts four No. 12 THHN in ⅜-in. Greenfield or liquidtight.

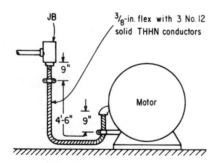

NOTE: The 6 ft length of liquid tight is suitable as an equipment grounding conductor, without bonding.

Fig. 351·2. Both standard flexible metal conduit and liquidtight may be used here. (Sec. 351-5.)

351-6. Number of Conductors.   Refer to Sec. 346-6 for ½-in. to 4-in. sizes, and to Table 350-3 for ⅜-in. size.

351-8. Supports.   As shown in Fig. 351-3, Exception No. 2 permits a length of liquidtight flexible metal conduit not over 3 ft long to be used at terminals where flexibility is required without any need for clamping or strapping. Obviously, the use of flex requires this permission for short lengths without support.

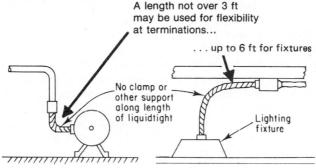

Fig. 351-3. Unsupported length of liquidtight flex is O.K. at terminations. (Sec. 351-8.)

In Exception No. 3, liquidtight metal flex is specifically recognized for a 4- to 6-ft fixture "whip," without clamping of the flex. This covers a practice that has long been common. Either standard or liquidtight metal flex may be used to carry supply conductors to lighting fixtures—such as required by Sec. 410-67(c), where high-temperature wires must be run to a fixture terminal box.

351-9. Grounding.   According to the basic rule, where flexible metal conduit and fittings have not been specifically approved as a grounding means, a separate grounding conductor (insulated or bare) shall be run inside the conduit (or outside, for lengths not over 6 ft) and bonded at each box or similar equipment to which the conduit is connected.

The first sentence of this rule recognizes the metal in liquidtight flex as an equipment grounding conductor, as listed by UL:

> Where terminated in fittings investigated for grounding and where installed with not more than 6 feet (total length) in any ground return path, liquid-tight flexible metal conduit in the ⅜ and ½ in. trade sizes is suitable for grounding where used on circuits rated 20 amperes or less, and the ¾, 1, and 1¼ inch trade sizes are suitable for grounding where used on circuits rated 60 amperes or less. See the category "Conduit Fittings" (DWTT) with respect to fittings suitable as a grounding means.
>
> The following are not considered to be suitable as a grounding means:
>
> 1) The 1½ inch and larger trade sizes,
>
> 2) The ⅜ and ½ inch trade sizes where used on circuits rated higher than 20 amperes, or where the total length in the ground return path is greater than 6 feet,
>
> 3) The ¾, 1, and 1¼ inch trade sizes where used on circuits rated higher than 60 amperes, or where the total length in the ground return path is greater than 6 feet.

When a bonding jumper is required—such as for a length of the flex that is not over 6 ft long but is over 1¼-in. size—the second sentence permits internal or external bonding of liquidtight flex as covered previously for standard flex and spelled out under Sec. 250-79. But for any size of flex run over 6 ft, *only* an internal equipment grounding conductor will satisfy this section and Sec. 250-91(b). The wording of Exception No. 1 focuses on a maximum total length of 6 ft in any equipment "ground return path" where the liquidtight flex itself is used as the equipment grounding conductor. UL applications data in the *Electrical Construction Materials Directory* (the Green Book) make that same limitation to a "total length" of 6 ft.

As required by Exception No. 2, an equipment grounding conductor (or jumper) must *always* be installed for a length of liquidtight metal flex used to supply equipment that is not fixed in one place or location.

Thus Exception No. 2 actually modifies Exception No. 1, which states the conditions under which a 6-ft or shorter length of liquidtight metal flex may be used for grounding through the metal of its own assembly, without need for a bonding wire. [Refer to Sec. 250-91(b), Exception No. 2.] Because experience has indicated many instances of loss of ground connection through the flex metal due to repeated movement of a flex whip supplying movable equipment, Exception No. 2 requires use of an equipment bonding jumper, either inside or outside the flex, in all cases where movable equipment is supplied—for assured safety of grounding continuity. The rule applies to those lengths of 3 ft or less that are permitted to be installed without clamping of the flex—as permitted by Sec. 351-8, Exception No. 2, because "flexibility is necessary."

351·10. Bends. Figure 350-5 shows this rule.

351·22. Definition. Part B of Art. 351 covers liquidtight flexible nonmetallic conduit, which may be used for indoor or outdoor applications in residential, commercial, and industrial applications. It must not be used in any individual length over 6 ft long (unless special approval is given) and is limited to a maximum of 2-in. size. Grounding requires a conductor within or outside the flex.

351·23. Use. Liquidtight flexible nonmetallic conduit may be used exposed or concealed and also may be used for direct burial in earth if "listed and marked for the purpose." This extends similar permission to liquidtight flexible *nonmetallic* conduit that was given for liquidtight flexible *metallic* conduit in the 1987 NEC. And Sec. 351-23(a) recognizes this nonmetallic flex for "concealed" as well as exposed locations.

351·24. Size. Although ½-in. trade size is the smallest recognized size of liquidtight flexible nonmetallic conduit for general use, the Exception notes that ⅜-in. liquidtight flexible metal conduit may be used for motor leads. This was added to coordinate with Sec. 430-145(b) for motors with detached junction boxes.

ARTICLE 352. SURFACE METAL RACEWAYS AND SURFACE NONMETALLIC RACEWAYS

352·1. Use. At one time, this article was titled "Surface *Metal* Raceways." The article now includes both metallic and *nonmetallic* surface raceways (Fig. 352-1).

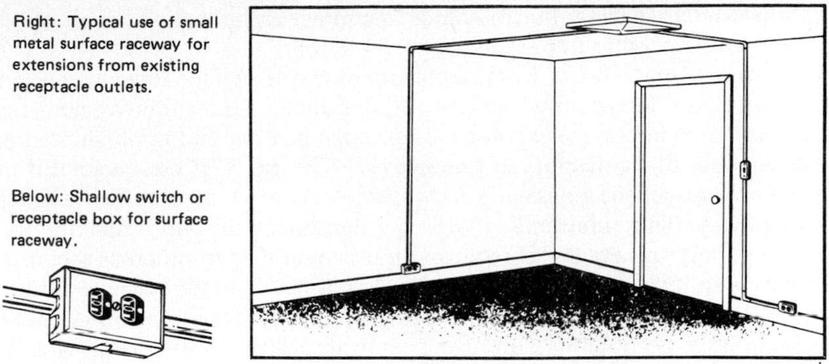

Right: Typical use of small
metal surface raceway for
extensions from existing
receptacle outlets.

Below: Shallow switch or
receptacle box for surface
raceway.

Fig. 352-1. Surface raceway has become popular for new works as well as for modernization.
(Sec. 352-1.)

352-2. Other Articles.   In every type of wiring having a metal enclosure around
the conductors, it is important that the metal be mechanically continuous in
order to provide protection for the conductors and that the metal form a continuous electrical conductor of low impedance from the last outlet on the run
to the cabinet or cutout box. A path to ground is thus provided through the box

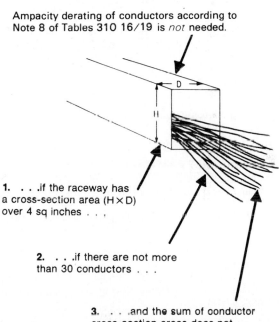

Ampacity derating of conductors according to
Note 8 of Tables 310 16/19 is *not* needed.

D

H

1. . . .if the raceway has
a cross-section area (H × D)
over 4 sq inches . . .

2. . . .if there are not more
than 30 conductors . . .

3. . . .and the sum of conductor
cross-section areas does not
exceed 20% of the interior
cross-section area of the raceway.

Fig. 352-2. NEC rule permits conductor fill of metal surface raceway
without ampacity derating of wires. (Sec. 352-4.)

or cabinet, in case any conductor comes in contact with the metal enclosure, an outlet box, or any other fitting. See Sec. 250-91(b).

352·3. Size of Conductors.   Manufacturers of metal surface raceways provide illustrations and details on wire sizes and conductor fill for their various types of raceway. It is important to refer to their specification and application data.

352·4. Number of Conductors in Raceways.   The rules of conductor fill may now be applied to surface metal raceway in very much the same way as standard wireway. This rule applies wireway conductor fill and ampacity determination to any surface metal raceway that is over 4 sq in. in cross section. As with wireway, if there are not more than 30 conductors in the raceway and they do not fill the cross-section area to more than 20 percent of its value, the conductors may be used without any conductor ampacity derating from Note 8 of Tables 310-16 through 310-19 (Fig. 352-2).

352·6. Combination Raceways.   Metal surface raceways may contain separated systems as shown in Fig. 352-3.

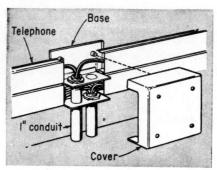

Fig. 352·3. For separating high and low potentials, combination raceway or tiered separate raceways may be used with barriered box assembly. (Sec. 352-6.)

ARTICLE 353. MULTIOUTLET ASSEMBLY

353·1. Other Articles.   UL data are as follows:

This Listing covers metal raceways with factory installed conductors and attachment plug receptacles without provision for field installation of additional conductors except where the product is marked to indicate the number, type, and size of additional conductors which may be field installed. Also covered are nonmetallic raceways with factory installed conductors and attachment plug receptacles either factory installed or separately Listed as Multioutlet Assembly Fittings for field installation.

Multioutlet Assemblies are for installation in accordance with Article 353 of the **National Electrical Code.**

353·2. Use.   These assemblies are intended for surface mounting except that the metal type may be surrounded by the building finish or recessed so long as the front is not covered. The nonmetallic type may be recessed in baseboards. In calculating the load for branch circuits supplying multioutlet assembly, see Sec. 220-3(c), Exception No. 1.

ARTICLE 354. UNDERFLOOR RACEWAYS

354-2. Use.   Underfloor raceway was developed to provide a practical means of bringing conductors for lighting, power, and signaling systems to office desks and tables (Fig. 354-1). It is also used in large retail stores, making it possible to secure connections for display-case lighting at any desired location.

Fig. 354-1. Underfloor raceway system, with spaced grouping of three ducts (one for power, one for telephone, one for signals), is covered with concrete after installation on first slab pour. (Sec. 354-2.)

This wiring method makes it possible to place a desk or table in any location where it will always be over, or very near to, a duct line. The wiring method for lighting and power between cabinets and the raceway junction boxes may be conduit, underfloor raceway, wall elbows, and cabinet connectors.

354-3. Covering.   The intent in paragraphs **(a)** and **(b)** is to provide a sufficient amount of concrete over the ducts to prevent cracks in a cement, tile, or similar floor finish. Figure 354-2 shows a violation. Two 1½- by 4½ in. underfloor raceways with 1-in.-high inserts are spaced ¾ in. apart by adjustable-height supports resting directly on a base floor-slab, as shown. After raceways are aligned, leveled, and secured, concrete fill is poured level with insert tops. But spacing between raceways must be at least 1 in.; otherwise the concrete cover must be 1½ in. deep.

354-6. Splices and Taps.   This section has a second paragraph that recognizes "loop wiring" where "unbroken" wires extend from underfloor raceways to terminals of attached receptacles, and then back into the raceway to other outlets.

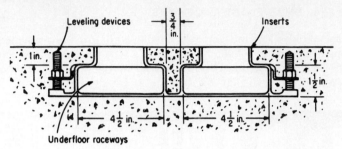

Fig. 354·2. The 1-in. cover is inadequate for raceways less than an inch apart. (Sec. 354-3.)

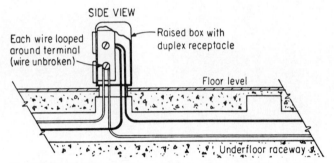

Fig. 354·3. "Loop" method permitted at outlets supplied from under-floor raceways. (Sec. 354-6.)

For purposes of this **Code** rule *only*, the "loop" connection method is not considered a splice or tap (Fig. 354-3).

As noted in the Exception, splices and taps may be made in trench-type flush raceway with an accessible removable cover. The removable cover of the trench duct must be accessible after installation, and the splices and taps must not fill the raceway to more than 75 percent of its cross-section area.

ARTICLE 356. CELLULAR METAL FLOOR RACEWAYS

356·1. Definitions.   This is a type of floor construction designed for use in steel-frame buildings in which the members supporting the floor between the beams consist of sheet steel rolled into shapes which are so combined as to form cells, or closed passageways, extending across the building. The cells are of various shapes and sizes, depending upon the structural strength required.

The cellular members of this type of floor construction form raceways. A cross-sectional view of one type of cellular metal floor is shown in Fig. 356-1.

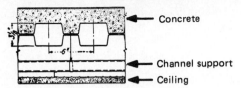

Fig. 356·1. Cross section of one type of cellular method floor construction. (Sec. 356-1.)

356·2. Use. Connections to the ducts are made by means of *headers* extending across the cells. A header connects only to those cells which are to be used as raceways for conductors. Two or three separate headers, connecting to different sets of cells, may be used for different systems, for example, for light and power, signaling systems, and public telephones.

Figure 356-2 shows the cells, or ducts, with header ducts in place. By means of a special elbow fitting the header is extended up to a cabinet or distribution

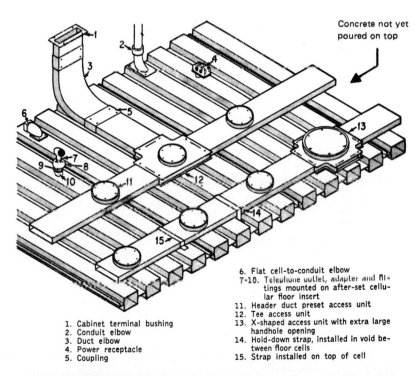

6. Flat cell-to-conduit elbow
7-10. Telephone outlet, adapter and fittings mounted on after-set cellular floor insert
11. Header duct preset access unit
12. Tee access unit
13. X-shaped access unit with extra large handhole opening
14. Hold-down strap, installed in void between floor cells
15. Strap installed on top of cell

1. Cabinet terminal bushing
2. Conduit elbow
3. Duct elbow
4. Power receptacle
5. Coupling

CELLULAR STEEL FLOOR contains unlimited number of channels for enclosing and isolating various electrical services. Wiring is routed from distribution panels to floor outlets through header ducts as shown.

Fig. 356·2. Components for electrical usage in cellular metal floor must be properly applied. (Sec. 356-2.)

center on a wall or column. A junction box or access fitting is provided at each point where the header crosses a cell to which it connects.

356-6. Splices and Taps.   See Sec. 354-6.

356-8. Markers.   The markers used with this system consist of special flat-head brass screws, screwed into the upper side of the cells and with their heads flush with the floor finish.

356-9. Junction Boxes.   The fittings with round covers shown in Fig. 356-2 are termed *access fittings* by the manufacturer but actually serve as junction boxes. Where additional junction boxes are needed, a similar fitting of larger size is provided which may be attached to a cell at any point.

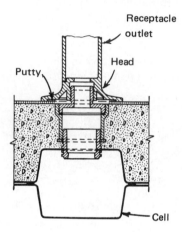

Fig. 356-3. Typical insert for connecting from cell to floor outlet assembly. (Sec. 356-10.)

356-10. Inserts.   The construction of an insert is shown in Fig. 356-3. A 1⅝-in.-diameter hole is cut in the top of the cell with a special tool. The lower end of the insert is provided with coarse threads of such form that the insert can be screwed into the hole in the cell, thus forming a substantial mechanical and electrical connection.

ARTICLE 358.   CELLULAR CONCRETE FLOOR RACEWAYS

358-1. Scope.   The term *precast cellular concrete floor* refers to a type of floor construction designed for use in steel frame, concrete frame, and wall bearing construction, in which the monolithically precast reinforced concrete floor members form the structural floor and are supported by beams or bearing walls. The floor members are precast with hollow voids which form smooth round cells. The cells are of various sizes depending on the size of floor member used.

The cells form raceways which by means of suitable fittings can be adapted for use as underfloor raceways. A precast cellular concrete floor is fire resistant and requires no additional fireproofing.

358-5. Header.   Connections to the cells are made by means of *headers* secured to the precast concrete floor, extending from cabinets and across the cells. A header connects only those cells which are used as raceways for conductors. Two or three separate headers, connected to different sets of cells, may be used for different systems, for example, for light and power, signaling, and telephones.

Figure 358-1 shows three headers installed, each header connecting a cabinet with separate groups of cells. Special elbows extend the header to the cabinet.

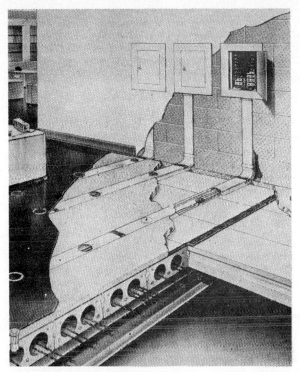

Fig. 358-1. Headers, flush with finished concrete pour, carry wiring to cells. (Sec. 358-5.)

358-7. Junction Boxes. Figure 358-2 shows how a JB must be arranged where a header connects to a cell.

358-8. Markers. Markers used with this system are special flat-head brass screws which are installed level with the finished floor. One type of marker marks the location of an access point between a header and a spare cell reserved for, but not connected to, the header. A junction box can be installed at the point located by the marker if the spare cell is needed in the future. The screw for this type marker is installed in the center of a special knockout provided in the top of the header at the access point. The second type of marker is installed over the center of cells at various points on the floor to locate and identify the cells below. Screws with specially designed heads identify the type of service in the cell.

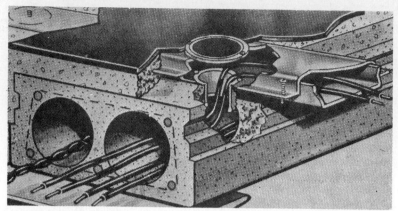

Fig. 358-2. Junction box is used to provide conductor installation from header to cell. (Sec. 358-7.)

358·9. Inserts. A 1⅜-in.-diameter hole is cut through the floor and into the center of a cell with a concrete drill bit. A plug is driven into the hole and a nipple is screwed into the plug. The nipple is designed to receive an outlet with a duplex electrical receptacle or an outlet designed for a telephone or signal system.

ARTICLE 362.   WIREWAYS

362·1. Definition.   Wireways are sheet-metal troughs in which conductors are laid in place after the wireway has been installed as a complete system. Wireway is available in standard lengths of 1, 2, 3, 4, 5, and 10 ft, so that runs of any exact number of feet can be made up without cutting the duct. The cover may be a hinged or removable type. Unlike auxiliary gutters, wireways represent a type of wiring, because they are used to carry conductors between points located considerable distances apart.

The purpose of a wireway is to provide a flexible system of wiring in which the circuits can be changed to meet changing conditions, and one of its principal uses is for exposed work in industrial plants. Wireways are also used to carry control wires from the control board to remotely controlled stage switchboard equipment. A wireway is approved for any voltage not exceeding 600 V between conductors or 600 V to ground. An installation of wireway is shown in Fig. 362-1.

362·2. Use.   Figure 362-1 shows a typical **Code**-approved application of 4- by 4-in. wireway in an exposed location.

362·5. Number of Conductors.   Wireways may contain up to 30 "current-carrying" conductors at any cross section (signal circuits and control conductors used for starting duty only between a motor and its starter are not "current-carrying" conductors). The total cross-sectional area of the group of conductors must not be greater than 20 percent of the interior cross-sectional area of the

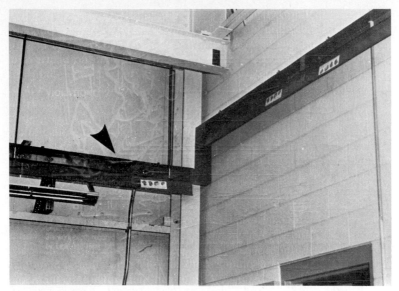

Fig. 362-1. Wireway in industrial plant—installed exposed, as required by Sec. 362-2 provides highly flexible wiring system that provides easy changes in the number, sizes, and routing of circuit conductors for machines and controls. Hinged covers swing down for ready access. Section 326-6 permits splicing and tapping in wireway. Section 362-11 covers use of conduit for taking circuits out of wireway. (Sec. 362-2.)

wireway or gutter. And ampacity derating factors for more than three conductors do not apply to wireway the way they do to wires in conduit. However, if the derating factors from Note 8 of **NE Code** Tables 310-16 through 310-19 are used, there is no limit to the number of current-carrying wires permitted in a wireway or an auxiliary gutter. But, the sum of the cross-section areas of all contained conductors at any cross section of the wireway must not exceed 20 percent of the cross-section area of the wireway or auxiliary gutter. More than 30 conductors may be used under these conditions.

Exception No. 3 says that wireway used for circuit conductors for an elevator or escalator may be filled with any number of wires, occupying up to 50 percent of the interior cross section of the wireway, and no derating has to be made for fill.

The second sentence of the first paragraph has the effect of saying that any number of signal and/or motor control wires (even over 30) may be used in wireway provided the sum of their cross-section areas does not exceed 20 percent of wireway csa. And ampacity derating of those conductors is not required.

Figure 362-2 shows examples of wireway fill calculations. The example at the bottom shows a case where power and lighting wires (which are current-carrying wires) are mixed with signal wires. Because there are not over 30 power and light wires, no derating of conductor ampacities is needed. If, say, 31 power and light wires were in the wireway, then the power and light conductors would be subject to derating. If all 49 conductors were signal and/or control wires, no derating would be required. But, in all cases, wireway fill must not be over 20 percent.

Basic rule

1. Any number of current-carrying conductors up to a maximum of 30, without derating.

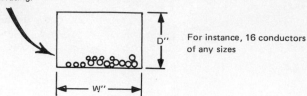

For instance, 16 conductors
of any sizes

2. The sum of the cross-section areas of all the conductors (from table 5 in Chap. 9 of the *NEC*) must not be more than 20% X W″ X D″

Note: Signal and motor control wires are not considered to be current-carrying wires. Any number of such wires are permitted to fill up 20% of wireway cross-section area.

THIS IS OK !

45 conductors in wireway:
29 are current-carrying
power and light wires;
16 are signal-circuit wires

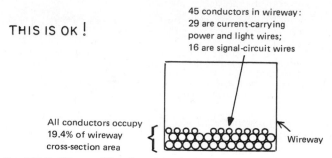

All conductors occupy
19.4% of wireway
cross-section area

Wireway

Fig. 362·2. Wireway fill and need for derating must be carefully evaluated. (Sec. 362-5.)

362·6 Deflected Insulated Conductors.   Deflected conductors in wireway must observe the rules on adequate enclosure space given in Sec. 373-6. This section is based on the following:

Although wireways don't contain terminals or supplement spaces with terminals, pull boxes and conduit bodies don't either. This rule borrows language from both 374-9(d) and 370-18(a)(2), Exception, in an attempt to produce a consistent approach in the **Code.** Although in some cases the deflected conductors travel long distances in the wireway and are therefore easily inserted, in other cases the conductors are deflected again within inches of the first entry. The result is even more stress on the insulation than if they were entering a conduit body.

362·7. Splices and Taps.   The conductors should be reasonably accessible so that any circuit can be replaced with conductors of a different size if necessary and so that taps can readily be made to supply motors or other equipment. Accessibility is ensured by limiting the number of conductors and the space they occupy as provided in Secs. 362-5 and 362-6.

362·8. Supports.   Wireway must be supported every 5 ft. Wireway lengths over 5 ft must be supported at *each end* or *joint,* unless listed for other support. In no case should the distance between supports for wireway exceed 10 ft.

362-11. Extensions from Wireways. Knockouts are provided in wireways so that circuits can be run to motors or other apparatus at any point. Conduits connect to such knockouts, as shown in Fig. 362-1.

Sections of wireways are joined to one another by means of flanges which are bolted together, thus providing rigid mechanical connection and electrical continuity. Fittings with bolted flanges are provided for elbows, tees, and crosses and for connections to cabinets. See Sec. 250-91(b).

ARTICLE 363. FLAT CABLE ASSEMBLIES

363-1. Definition. Type FC cable is a flat assembly with three or four parallel No. 10 special stranded copper conductors. The assembly is installed in an

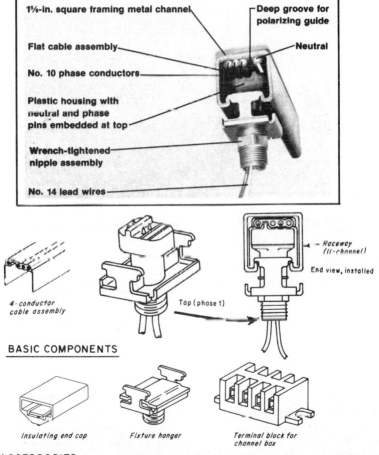

Fig. 363-1. Type FC wiring system uses cable in channel, with tap devices to loads. (Sec. 363-1.)

approved U-channel surface metal raceway with one side open. Then tap devices can be inserted anywhere along the run. Connections from tap devices to the flat cable assembly are made by "pin-type" contacts when the tap devices are fastened in place. The pin-type contacts penetrate the insulation of the cable assembly and contact the multistranded conductors in a matched phase sequence (phase 1 to neutral, phase 2 to neutral, and phase 3 to neutral).

Covers are required when the installation is less than 8 ft from the floor. The maximum branch-circuit rating is 30 A.

Figure 363-1 shows the basic components of this wiring method.

363-3. Uses Permitted.   Figure 363-2 shows a Type FC installation supplying lighting fixtures. As shown in the details, one tap device provides for circuit tap-off to splice to cord wires in the junction box; and the other device is simply a fitting to support the fixture from the lips of the channel.

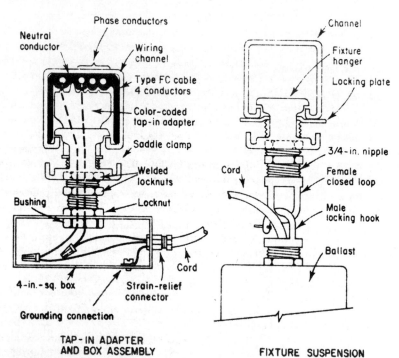

**TAP-IN ADAPTER
AND BOX ASSEMBLY**   **FIXTURE SUSPENSION**

Fig. 363-2. Limited application of Type FC cable system includes use as branch-circuit wiring method to supply luminaires. (Sec. 363-3.)

ARTICLE 364. BUSWAYS

364-2. Definition.   Busways consist of metal enclosures containing insulator-supported busbars. Varieties are so extensive that possibilities for 600-V distribution purposes are practically unlimited. Busways are available for either indoor or outdoor use as point-to-point feeders or as plug-in takeoff routes for power. Progressive improvements in busway designs have enhanced their electrical and mechanical characteristics, reduced their physical size, and simplified the methods used to connect and support them. These developments in turn have reduced installation labor to the extent that busways are most favorably considered when it is required to move large blocks of power to loadcenters (via low-impedance feeder busway), to distribute current to closely spaced power utilization points (via plug-in busway), or to energize rows of lighting fixtures or power tools (via trolley busway).

Busways classed as indoor low-reactance assemblies can be obtained in small incremental steps up to 6,500 A for copper busbars and 5,000 A for aluminum. Enclosed outdoor busways are similarly rated. In the plug-in category, special assemblies are available up to 5,000 A, although normal 600-V AC requirements generally are satisfied by standard busways in the 225-to-1,000-A range. Where power requirements are limited, small compact busways are available with ratings from 250 down to 20 A.

Plug-in and clamp-on devices include fused and nonfusible switches and plug-in CBs rated up to about 800 A. Other plug-in devices include ground detectors, temperature indicators, capacitors, and transformers designed to mount directly on the busway.

364-4. Use. Figure 364-1 shows the most common way in which busway is installed—in the open.

Wiring methods above lift-out ceiling panels are considered to be "exposed"—because the definition of that word includes reference to "behind panels designed to allow access." This section calls for busway to be "located in the open and visible" but does permit busway above lift-out panels of a suspended ceiling, if means of access are provided. It limits such to totally enclosed, nonventilated busway, without plug-in switches or CBs on the busway and only in ceiling space that is not used for air handling. Figure 364-2 shows how other Code rules tie into this section. For instance, fuses and CBs that provide overcurrent protection required by the NE Code must generally be readily accessible—that is, they must be capable of being reached quickly (Sec. 240-24). Fuses and/or CBs are not readily accessible if it is necessary to get a portable ladder or stand on a chair or table to get at them. However, Exception No. 1 in Sec. 240-24 permits overcurrent devices to be used high up on a busway (as *required* by Sec. 364-12) where access to them could require use of a ladder, but Sec. 364-4(a), Exception No. 1, says **not on busway above a suspended ceiling**. But, as noted in Exception No. 2, totally enclosed nonventilated busway with no provisions for plug-in connections may be used in an air-handling space above a suspended ceiling. This Exception correlates to the permission for such busway use in spaces used for environmental air—as stated in Sec. 300-22(c).

Other data limiting application of busway are contained in the UL regulations on listed busway—all of which information becomes mandatory Code rules because of NEC Sec. 110-3(b). Such UL data are as follows:

Busways may carry various markings to indicate the intended use for which the busway was investigated and listed. Busway intended to supply and support

Fig. 364-1. Ventilated-type (with open grills for ventilation) busway may be used only "in the open" and must be "visible." Only the totally enclosed, nonventilating type may be used above a suspended ceiling. (Sec. 364-4.)

industrial and commercial lighting fixtures is marked "Lighting Busway." Busway with sliding or other continuously movable means for tapping-off current to load circuits is marked "Trolley Busway." And, if the same busway is also acceptable for supporting and feeding lighting fixtures, it will *also* be marked "Lighting Busway." If busway is designed to accept plug-in devices at any point along its length and is intended for general use, it is marked "Continuous Plug-in Busway." Busway marked "Lighting Busway" and protected by overcurrent devices rated in excess of 20 A is intended for use only with fixtures having heavy-duty lampholders—unless each fixture is equipped with additional over-current protection to protect the lampholders. This rule correlates with **NE Code** Secs. 210-23(b) and (c), which require only heavy-duty lampholders on branch

When busway is visible –

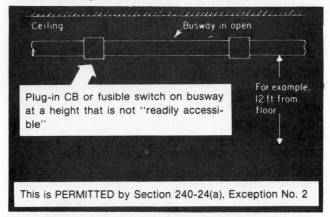

Ceiling   Busway in open

Plug-in CB or fusible switch on busway at a height that is not "readily accessible"

For example, 12 ft from floor

This is PERMITTED by Section 240-24(a), Exception No. 2

When busway is in non–air–handling ceiling space

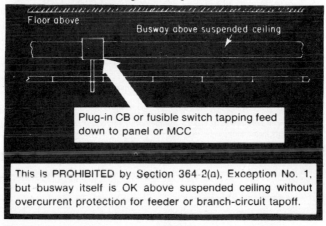

Floor above

Busway above suspended ceiling

Plug-in CB or fusible switch tapping feed down to panel or MCC

This is PROHIBITED by Section 364-2(a), Exception No. 1, but busway itself is OK above suspended ceiling without overcurrent protection for feeder or branch-circuit tapoff.

Fig. 364-2. Use of busway involves NEC rules on accessibility of overcurrent devices. (Sec. 364-4.)

circuits rated 30, 40, or 50 A. A "heavy-duty lampholder" is defined in Sec. 210-21(a) as one having "a rating of not less than 660 watts if of the admedium type and not less than 750 watts if of any other type." Medium-base lampholders— the ordinary 120-V incandescent lampholder—and all fluorescent lampholders are not "heavy-duty" lampholders and are acceptable on lighting busway fed by branch-circuit fuses or breakers rated not over 20 A. But, 50-A lighting busway, for instance, may be used as a branch circuit to supply fixtures with incandescent, mercury-vapor, or other electric-discharge lamps with mogul-base, screw-shell lampholders or other lampholders rated "heavy-duty." In such applications, there is no need for additional overcurrent protection in each fixture. In such a case, the busway is used as a branch circuit in accordance with Sec. 364-12.

However, if fluorescent lighting fixtures are fed by a 50-A lighting busway and each fixture is individually fused at a few amps to protect the nonheavy-duty lampholders with the fuse in each fixture or its cord plug, that is permitted

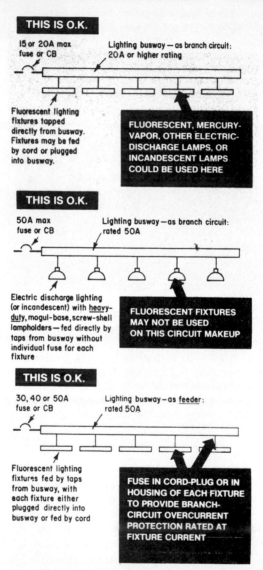

Fig. 364-3. These applications involve UL data and several Code sections. (Sec. 364-4.)

in the UL application information as well as by **NE Code** Sec. 364-12, Exception Nos. 2 or 3. In that case, the lighting busway is a feeder and each fixture tap is a "branch circuit." Note that in such a case the fuse in the plug or in the fixture is not "supplementary overcurrent protection," as described in Sec. 240-10—in spite of the conflict between Secs. 240-10 and 364-12, Exception No. 2. Figure 364-3 shows how those rules are applied. Note that the details involved are related to Sec. 210-21(a)—which prohibits fluorescent lampholders (nonheavy-duty) on circuits rated over 20 A—and Sec. 364-12, Exception No. 2—which identifies the fuse in the cord plug or in the fixture as "branch-circuit overcurrent device."

364·5. Support.   As shown in Fig. 364-4, busway risers may be supported by a variety of spring-loaded hangers, wall brackets, or channel arrangements

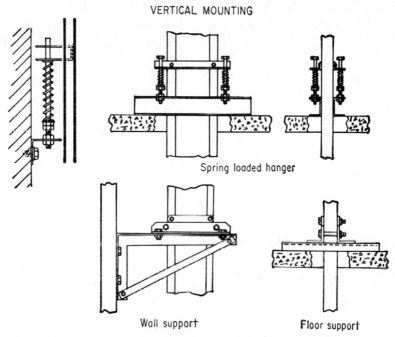

VERTICAL MOUNTING

Spring loaded hanger

Wall support   Floor support

Fig. 364·4. Vertical busway runs should be supported at least every 16 ft. (Sec. 364-5.)

where busways pierce floor slabs or are supported on masonry walls or columns. As shown in Fig. 364-5, spring mounts for vertical busways may be located at successive floor-slab levels or, as indicated, supported by wall brackets located at intermediate elevations. Springs provide floating cradles for absorbing transient vibrations or physical shocks. Fire-resistant material is packed into space between busway and edges of slab-piercing throat.

364·6. Through Walls and Floors.   Figure 364-6 shows a violation of this section, which requires busway to be totally enclosed within the floor slab and for 6 ft above it.

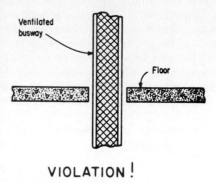

VIOLATION !

Fig. 364-5. Opening for busway riser through slab must be closed off, as required by Sec. 300-21. (Sec. 364-5.)

Fig. 364-6. Ventilated busway may not be used through a floor slab and for 6 ft above the floor. (Sec. 364-6.)

364-8. Branches from Busways. Figure 364-7 shows feeds into and out of busway. The rule here requires that a cord connecting to a plug-in switch or CB on a busway must be supported by a "tension take-up device on the cord."

364-10. Rating of Overcurrent Protection—Feeders and Subfeeders. The rated ampacity of a busway is fixed by the allowable temperature rise of the conductors. The ampacity can be determined in the field only by reference to the nameplate.

364-11. Reduction in Size of Busway. Overcurrent protection—either a fused-switch or CB—is usually required in each busway subfeeder tapping power from a busway feeder of higher ampacity, protected at the higher ampacity. This is necessary to protect the lower current-carrying capacity of the subfeeder and should be placed at the point at which the subfeeder connects into the feeder. However, this section provides that overcurrent protection may be omitted where busways are reduced in size, if the smaller busway does not extend more than 50 ft and has a current rating at least equal to one-third the rating or setting of the overcurrent device protecting the main busway feeder (Figs. 364-8 and 364-9).

Where the smaller busway is kept within the limits specified, the hazards involved are very slight and the additional cost of providing overcurrent protection at the point where the size is changed is not considered as being warranted.

364-12. Subfeeder or Branch Circuits. The rules of this section are interrelated with those of Secs. 240-24 and 380-8. The basic rule of this section makes it clear that branch circuits or subfeeders tapped from busway must have overcurrent protection on the busway at the point of tap. And if they are out of reach from the floor, all fused switches and CBs must be provided with some means for a person to operate the handle of the device from the floor (hookstick, chain operator, rope-pull operator, etc.).

Although no definition is given for "out of reach" from the floor, the wording

Circuits fed from busway may be run in any conventional wiring method—such as EMT or rigid conduit (left) or as "suitable cord," such as "bus-drop" cable down to machines. And cable-tap-boxes may be used (arrow at right) to connect feeder conductors that supply power to busway.

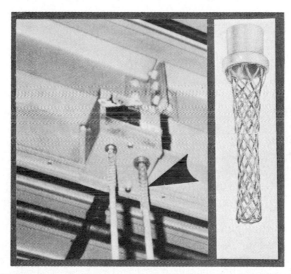

SOME TYPE of tension-relief device must be used on bus-drop cable or other suitable cord where it connects to a plug-in switch or CB on busway. Photo shows strain relief connector with mesh grip (arrow) on cord to bus-tap CB, which is equipped with hookeye lever mechanism to provide operation of the CB by a hookstick from floor level—as required by Sec. 380-8(a), Ex. No. 1 and Sec. 364-12.

Fig. 364-7. Wiring details at busway connections must be carefully observed. [Sec. 364-8.]

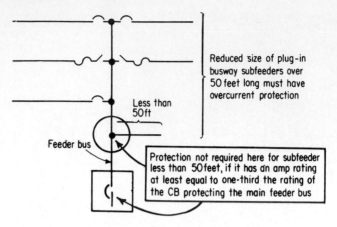

Reduced size of plug-in
busway subfeeders over
50 feet long must have
overcurrent protection

Less than
50 ft

Feeder bus

Protection not required here for subfeeder
less than 50 feet, if it has an amp rating
at least equal to one-third the rating of
the CB protecting the main feeder bus

Example:

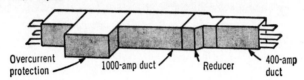

Overcurrent
protection

1000-amp duct

Reducer

400-amp
duct

Fig. 364·8. Busway subfeeder may sometimes be used without protection. (Sec. 364-11.)

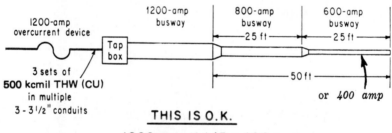

1200-amp
overcurrent device

1200-amp
busway

800-amp
busway
— 25 ft —

600-amp
busway
— 25 ft —

Tap
box

3 sets of
500 kcmil THW (CU)
in multiple
3 - 3½" conduits

— 50 ft —

or *400 amp*

THIS IS O.K.

1200 amp X 1/3 = 400 amps

Fig. 364·9. Total length of reduced busway is not over 50 ft. (Sec. 364-11.)

of Sec. 380-8(a) can logically be taken to indicate that a switch or CB *is* "out of reach" if the center of its operating handle, when in its highest position, is more than 6½ ft above the floor or platform on which the operator would be standing. Thus, busway over 6½ ft above the floor would require some means (hookstick, etc.) to operate handles of any switches or CBs on the busway.

Figure 364-10 relates the rules of Sec. 240-24, Exception No. 2, to Sec. 364-12—with the rule of Sec. 240-24 *permitting* overcurrent devices to be "not readily accessible" when used up on high-mounted busway and Sec. 364-12 *requiring* such protection to be mounted on the busway. To get at overcurrent protection in either case, personnel might have to use a portable ladder or chair

NE Code Section 364-12—Plug-in connection for tapping-off branch circuit shall contain overcurrent protection, which does not have to be within reach of person standing on floor.

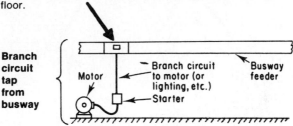

Plug-in connection for tapping-off a feeder or subfeeder shall contain overcurrent protection, which does not have to be within reach of person standing on floor.

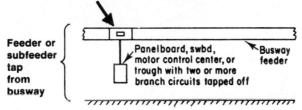

Fig. 364·10. Protection must always be used on busway for these taps—regardless of busway mounting height. (Sec. 364-12.)

or some other climbing technique. Again, 6½ ft could be taken as the height above which the overcurrent protection is not "readily accessible"—or the height above which the **Code** considers that some type of climbing technique (ladder, chair, etc.) may be needed by some persons to reach the protective device.

Then, where the plug-in switch or CB on the busway is "out of reach" from the floor (that is, over 6½ ft above the floor), provision must be made for operating such switches or CBs from the floor, as shown in Fig. 364-11. The plug-in switch or CB unit must be able to be operated by a hookstick or chain or rope operator if the unit is mounted out of reach up on a busway. Section 380-8 says all busway switches and CBs must be operable from the floor. Refer to Sec. 380-8. Figure 364-12 shows a typical application of hookstick-operated disconnects.

Figure 364-13 shows an application that has caused controversy because Sec. 364-12 says that any busway used as a feeder must have overcurrent protection on the busway for any subfeeder or branch circuit tapped from the busway. Therefore, use of a cable-tap box on busway without overcurrent protection could be ruled a **Code** violation. It can be argued that the installation shown— a 10- or 25-ft tap without overcurrent protection on the busway—is covered by Exception No. 1 of that section, which recognizes taps as permitted in Sec. 240-21—including 10- and 25-ft taps. However, wording of Sec. 240-21 refers to "busway taps" in Exception No. 7 which refers the whole matter back to Secs. 364-10 through 364-14—creating a problem in understanding how Exception

Plug-in device must be externally operable circuit breaker or fused switch that provides overcurrent protection for the subfeeder or branch circuit tapped from the busway.

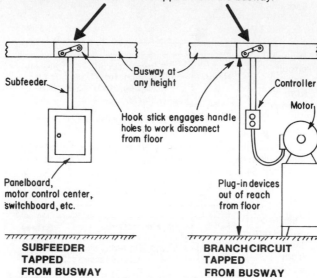

SUBFEEDER TAPPED FROM BUSWAY

BRANCH CIRCUIT TAPPED FROM BUSWAY

Fig. 364-11. Busway plug-in devices must be operable from the floor or platform where operator stands. (Sec. 364-12.)

Fig. 364-12. Disconnects mounted up on busway (top arrow) are out of reach from floor but do have hook-eye lever operators to provide operation by person standing in front of machines. Although the NEC does not literally require ready availability of a hookstick, it is certainly the intent of the Code that one be handy (lower arrow). (Sec. 364-12.)

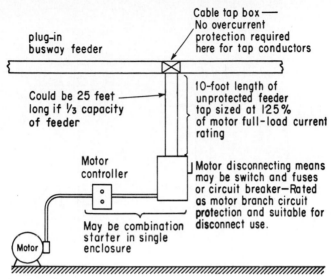

plug-in
busway feeder

Cable tap box ——
No overcurrent
protection required
here for tap conductors

Could be 25 feet
long if ⅓ capacity
of feeder

10-foot length of
unprotected feeder
tap sized at 125%
of motor full-load current
rating

Motor
controller

Motor disconnecting means
may be switch and fuses
or circuit breaker—Rated
as motor branch circuit
protection and suitable for
disconnect use.

May be combination
starter in single
enclosure

Motor

Fig. 364-13. This use of unprotected tap from busway conflicts with Sec. 364-12. (Sec. 364-12.)

No. 1 of Sec. 364-12 is to be understood. Because the phrase "feeder taps" in Sec. 240-21 clearly and certainly means "taps from feeders" and "branch-circuit taps" means "taps from branch circuits," it seems logical to conclude that "busway taps" means "taps from busways." Exception No. 7 of Sec. 240-21, therefore, appears to be applicable to all busway taps and to exclude busway taps from the other provisions of Sec. 240-21. In Fig. 364-13, if the feeder were conduit with conductors instead of busway, the installation shown would be acceptable. [It is also interesting to note that the precise wording of Sec. 240-21, Exception No. 2b, literally calls for the 10-ft tap conductors to have ampacity at least equal to the rating or setting of the fuses or CB (whichever is used) at the load end of the tap. And such protection may be rated up to four times motor full-load current.]

364-13. Rating of Overcurrent Protection—Branch Circuits. Refer to data on busways on lighting branch circuits in Sec. 364-4 and Fig. 364-3.

364-14. Length of Busways Used as Branch Circuits. A busway used as a branch circuit is usually installed for a specific purpose, and the probable maximum load to be supplied by the circuit can be estimated without difficulty.

Figure 364-14 shows details of trolley busway used to supply fluorescent lighting in an industrial plant. Trolley busway runs are fed from four 50-A CBs in lighting panel. The panel is supplied from transformer secondary, powered from a tap to a busway feeder or subfeeder. The lighting fixtures are suspended from the trolley busway, from beams, or from the ceiling. The trolley busway is supported from ceiling, beams, messenger cable, or braces supported from the beams. But because fluorescent fixtures are fed, each fixture cord plug must be equipped with fuse protection at not over 20 A to satisfy Sec. 210-21(a),

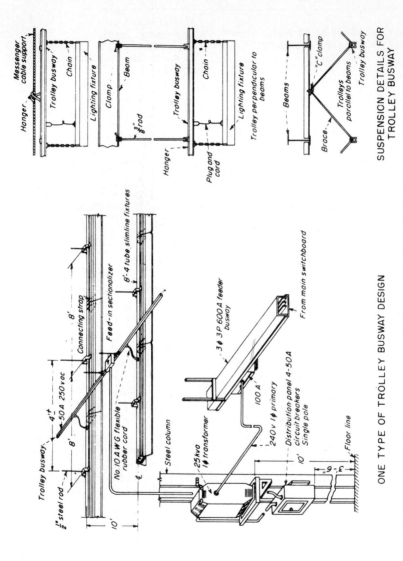

SUSPENSION DETAILS FOR
TROLLEY BUSWAY

ONE TYPE OF TROLLEY BUSWAY DESIGN

Fig. 364-14. Trolley busway may serve as a feeder or as a branch circuit, depending upon circuit protection method.
(Sec. 364-13.)

which permits only heavy-duty lampholders on circuits rated over 20 A. Because Sec. 364-12, Exception No. 2, designates the cord-plug fuse as "the branch-circuit overcurrent device," the 50-A trolley busway is a "feeder" and not a "branch circuit."

ARTICLE 365. CABLEBUS

Cablebus is an approved assembly of insulated conductors mounted in "spaced" relationship in a *ventilated* metal protective supporting structure including fittings and conductor terminations. In general, cablebus is assembled at the point of installation from components furnished by the manufacturer.

Field-assembly details are shown in Fig. 365-1. First, the cablebus framework is installed in a manner similar to continuous rigid cable support systems. Next,

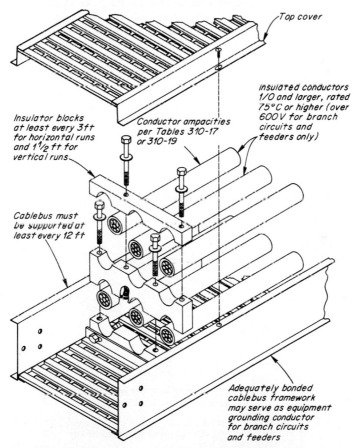

Fig. 365-1. Cablebus systems are field assembled from manufactured components. (Sec. 365-1.)

insulated conductors are pulled into the cablebus framework. Then the conductors are supported on special insulating blocks at specified intervals. And finally, a removable (ventilated) top is attached to the framework.

ARTICLE 370. OUTLET, DEVICE, PULL AND JUNCTION BOXES, CONDUIT BODIES, AND FITTINGS

370·1. Scope. This rule makes clear that Art. 370 regulates use of conduit bodies when they are used for splicing, tapping, or pulling conductors. And this article does refer specifically to conduit bodies, to more effectively distinguish rules covering "boxes," "conduit bodies," and "fittings." The rules of Art. 370 must be evaluated in accordance with the definitions given in Art. 100 for "conduit body" and "fitting." Capped elbows and SE elbows are "fittings" and are not "conduit bodies" and must not contain splices, taps, or devices. The pieces of equipment described in Art. 370 tie into Sec. 300-15, "Boxes or fittings—where required."

370·2. Round Boxes. The purpose of this rule is to require the use of rectangular or octagonal metal boxes having, at each knockout or opening, a flat bearing surface for the locknut or bushing or connector device to seat against a flat surface. But, round outlet boxes may be used with nonmetallic-sheathed cable because the cable is brought into the box through a knockout, without the use of a box connector to secure the cable to the box. However, Sec. 370-7(c) permits only "single gang boxes" to be used without securing the NM or NMC cable to the box itself—as long as it is stapled to the stud or joist within 8 in. of the box. Because "round" boxes are *not* "single gang" boxes, it appears that all such round outlet boxes must be equipped with cable clamps to satisfy the last two sentences of Sec. 370-7(c) (Fig. 370-1). Shallow metal boxes with internal clamps for NM cable are acceptable as round boxes.

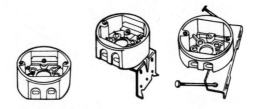

Round nonmetallic outlet boxes
may be used only with NM cable

Fig. 370·1. Round boxes may be used only for connecting cables with internal clamps—such as NM or BX cable. (Sec. 370-2.)

370-3. Nonmetallic Boxes. Growth in the application of nonmetallic boxes over past years is the basis for the two Exceptions to this section, which regulate the conditions under which nonmetallic boxes may be used with metal raceways or metal-sheathed cable. The need and popularity of these boxes developed out of industrial applications where corrosive environments dictated their use to resist the ravages of various punishing atmospheres. In many applications it is desirable to use nonmetallic boxes along with plastic-coated metal conduits for a total corrosion-resistant system. Such application is recognized by the **Code** in the Exceptions of this section, although a limitation is placed requiring "internal" or "integral" bonding means in such boxes (Fig. 370-2).

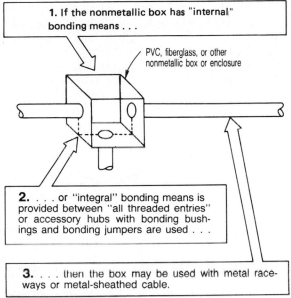

Fig. 370-2. Nonmetallic boxes are recognized for use with metal raceways and metal-sheathed cable. (Sec. 370-3.)

According to the basic rule in the first sentence of this rule, nonmetallic boxes are permitted to be used only with open wiring on insulators, concealed knob-and-tube wiring, nonmetallic sheathed cable, electrical nonmetallic tubing, and rigid nonmetallic conduit (any "nonmetallic raceways"). Exception No. 1 requires internal bonding means in such boxes used with metal cable or raceways. The permission used to apply only to nonmetallic boxes sufficiently large—that is, over 100 cu in. Now, any size of box—PVC boxes, fiberglass boxes, or other nonmetallic boxes or enclosures—may be used with metal raceways or metal-sheathed cable. Exception No. 2 requires that "integral" bonding means between all "threaded" raceway and cable entries must be provided in the box for all metal conduits or metal-jacketed cables. That is, the grounding continuity from each raceway entry to each other raceway entry must be provided by using metal hubs and bonding bushings with lugs for the bonding jumper. And, as further specified in Exception No. 2, there must be a "provision for attaching a grounding jumper inside the box." That requirement assures the safety of effective equipment grounding where metal raceway systems are used with nonmetallic boxes.

As worded, the manufacturer of the nonmetallic box must provide the necessary bonding means for all boxes with "threaded entries" for raceway and/ or cable. The wording of this **Code** rule does recognize the use of accessory hubs with ground lugs to achieve equipment grounding continuity through such boxes. Such application does provide the required grounding continuity and is available for that purpose from the box manufacturers.

370-4. Metal Boxes.   With a metal box in contact with metal walls or ceilings covered with metal, or with metal lath or with conductive thermal insulation, a stray current may flow to ground through an unknown path if a "hot" wire should accidentally become grounded on the box. To prevent this, the box must be effectively grounded by means of a separate grounding conductor.

370-5. Damp, Wet, or Hazardous (Classified) Locations.   "Weatherproof" is defined as meaning "so constructed or protected that exposure to the weather will not interfere with its successful operation." A box or fitting may be considered weatherproof when so made and installed that it will exclude rain and snow. Such a box or fitting need not necessarily be sealed against the entrance of moisture.

The left part of Fig. 370-3 shows a fitting which is considered as weatherproof because the openings for the conductors are so placed that rain or snow cannot enter the fitting. On the right, it shows a fitting made weatherproof by means of a metal cover that slides under flanges on the face of the fitting, and, as required by Sec. 230-53, an opening is provided through which any moisture condensing in the conduit can drain out.

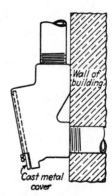

Fitting for use at the outer end of a service conduit.

Type LB conduit fittting used where a service conduit passes through a building wall. See Sec. 370-18.

Fig. 370-3. Fittings must be suited to use in wet locations. (Sec. 370-5.)

See definitions of "wet locations" and "damp locations" in Art. 100.

Weatherproof boxes are for use in "wet locations" as defined by the **NE Code**. In "damp locations," boxes must be "located or equipped" to prevent water from entering or accumulating in the box. Boxes with threaded conduit hubs will normally prevent water from entering except for condensation within the box or connected conduit.

Caution: Extreme care must be exercised in correlating UL and **NE Code** rules on the use of boxes and enclosures in damp or wet locations because of uncertainties about their definitions. UL requires a weatherproof box for wet locations (such as outdoors exposed to rain). Weatherproof, in the **NE Code** definition, means only that it must be constructed or protected so that exposure to weather will not interfere with operation of contained equipment and does *not* mean that entry of water must be excluded. **NE Code** Sec. 370-5 on use of outlet boxes requires that boxes in *either damp or wet* locations must be "placed or equipped" to prevent entry of any moisture; or, if water does enter, the box must be drained so that water will not accumulate within the box. In damp locations (but not in wet locations), UL requires boxes to be "located or equipped" to prevent entry of water into the box.

From the above, it could be argued that a UL weatherproof box, which is intended for wet locations, does not satisfy **NE Code** Sec. 370-5 because that section requires exclusion of moisture from all boxes in wet (and damp) locations, and weatherproof boxes do not necessarily exclude moisture. It also could be contended that UL rules requiring exclusion of water from boxes in damp locations are more strict than the rule on use of weatherproof boxes in wet locations.

However, the last sentence of **NE Code** Sec. 370-5 says that boxes in wet locations "shall be approved for the purpose." Because UL says "weatherproof boxes are intended for use in wet locations," it seems clear that such usage is approved.

370·6. Number of Conductors in Outlet, Device, and Junction Boxes, and Conduit Bodies.   Note that motor terminal housings are excluded from the rules on box conductor fill. And where any box or conduit body contains No. 4 or larger conductors, all the requirements of Sec. 370-18 on pull boxes must be satisfied. Refer to Sec. 370-18 for applications of conduit bodies as pull boxes.

Selection of any outlet or junction box for use in any electrical circuit work must take into consideration the maximum number of wires permitted in the box by Sec. 370-6. Safe electrical practice demands that wires *not* be jammed into boxes because of the possibility of nicks or other damage to insulation—posing the threat of grounds or shorts.

As stated in part **(a)** of this section, Table 370-6(a) shows the maximum number of wires permitted in the *standard* metal boxes listed in that table. But that table applies only where all wires in a given box are all of the same size, i.e., all No. 14 or all No. 12, etc. Table 370-6(b) is provided for sizing a box where all the wires in the box are not the same size, by using so much cubic-inch space for each size of wire.

Table 370-6(a) includes the maximum number of No. 18 and No. 16 conductors that may be used in various sizes of boxes, and Table 370-6(b) gives the required box space for those sizes of conductors. Because of the extensive use of No. 18 and No. 16 wires for fixture wires and for control, signal, and communications circuits, these data are needed to assure safe box fill for modern electrical systems.

Part **(1)** of Sec. 370-6(a) describes the detailed way of counting wires in a box and reducing the permitted number of wires shown in Table 370-6(a) where cable clamps, fittings, or devices like switches or receptacles take up box space.

Important details of the wire-counting procedure of part **(1)** are as follows:

1. From the wording, it is clear that no matter how many ground wires come into a box, whether they are ground wires in NM cable or ground wires run in metal or nonmetallic raceways, a deduction of only one conductor must be made from the number of wires shown in Table 370-6(a) (Fig. 370-4). Or, as will be shown in later examples, one or more ground wires in a box must be counted as a single wire of the size of the largest ground wire

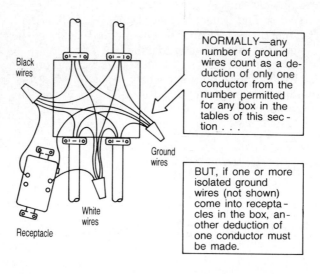

Black wires

NORMALLY—any number of ground wires count as a deduction of only one conductor from the number permitted for any box in the tables of this section . . .

Ground wires

BUT, if one or more isolated ground wires (not shown) come into receptacles in the box, another deduction of one conductor must be made.

White wires

Receptacle

Any wire passing through counts as one, as follows:

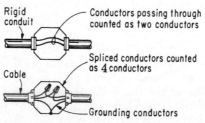

Rigid conduit

Conductors passing through counted as two conductors

Spliced conductors counted as 4 conductors

Cable

Grounding conductors

Fig. 370-4. Count all ground wires as *one* wire (or two wires if isolated-ground wires are also used) of the largest size of ground wire in the box. (Sec. 370-6.)

in the box. Any wire running unbroken through a box counts as one wire. Each wire coming into a splice device (crimp or twist-on type) is counted as one wire. And each wire coming into the box and connecting to a wiring device terminal is one wire.

When a number of "isolated-ground" equipment grounding conductors for receptacles come into a box along with conventional equipment grounding wires, each type of equipment ground wires must be counted as one conductor for purposes of wire count when determining the maximum number of wires permitted in a box. When a number of isolated-ground receptacles are used in a box (as for computer wiring), all the isolated-ground conductors count as a deduction of one from the number of wires given in Table 370-6(a) as permitted for the particular size of box. *And then*, another deduction of one conductor must be made for any other equipment grounding conductors (*not* isolated-ground wires).

2. Regarding the deduction of a wire from the **Code**-given number, Table 370-6(a), for fixture studs, cable clamps, and hickeys, does this apply to the above-mentioned items collectively regardless of number and combination, or does it apply to each item individually, such as clamps—minus one, studs—minus one, etc?

   Answer: It is the intent of the second sentence in this paragraph to clarify that a deduction of one must be made from the number in the table for each *type* of device used in a box. A deduction of one must be made if the box contains cable clamps—whether one clamp or two clamps, a deduction of only one has to be made. A deduction of one must be made if the box contains a fixture stud. A deduction of one must be made if the box contains a hickey. Thus a box containing two clamps but no fixture studs or hickeys would have a deduction of one from the table number of wires for the clamps. If a box contained one clamp and one fixture stud, a deduction of two would be made because there are two *types* of devices in the box. Then, in addition to the deductions for clamps, hickeys, and/or studs, a deduction of two conductors must be made for each mounting strap that supports a receptacle, switch, or combination device. In the 1987 and previous **NEC** editions, a deduction of only one conductor had to be made for each wiring device mounting strap (or yoke) installed in the box.

3. Must unused cable clamps be removed from a box? And if clamps are not used at all in a box, must they be removed to permit removal of the one-wire reduction?

   Answer: Unused cable clamps may be removed to gain space or fill in the box, or they may be left in the box if adequate space is available without the removal of the clamp or clamps. If one clamp is left, the one-wire deduction must be made. If no clamps are used at all in a box, such as where the cable is attached to the box by box connectors, the one-wire deduction is not made.

4. Is the short jumper installed between the grounding screw on a grounding-type receptacle and the box in which the receptacle is contained officially classified as a *bonding jumper*? And is this conductor counted when the box wire count is taken?

Answer: The jumper is classed as a *bonding jumper.* Section 250-74 uses the wording "bonding jumper" in the section pertaining to this subject. This conductor is not counted because it does not leave the box. The next to last sentence of Sec. 370-6(a) (1) covers that point.

The last sentence of Sec. 370-6(a) (1) requires that ganged boxes be treated as a single box of volume equal to the sum of the volumes of the sections that are connected together to form the larger box. An example of wire counting and correct wire fill for ganged boxes is included in the following examples. *Note:* In the examples given here, the same rules apply to wires in boxes for any wiring method—conduit, EMT, BX, NM.

Examples of Box Wire Fill

The top example in Fig. 370-5 shows how deductions must be made from the maximum permitted wires in a box containing cable clamps and a fixture stud. The example at the bottom shows a nonmetallic-sheathed cable with three No. 14 copper conductors supplying a 15-A duplex receptacle (one ungrounded conductor, one grounded conductor, and one "bare" grounding conductor).

After supplying the receptacle, these conductors are extended to other outlets and the conductor count would be as follows:

Circuit conductors	4
Grounding conductors	1
For internal cable clamps	1
For receptacle	2
Total	8

The No. 14 conductor column of Table 376-6(a) indicates that a device box not less than 3 by 2 by 3½ in. is required. Where a square box with plaster ring is used, a minimum of 4- by 1¼-in. size is required.

Table 370-6(a) includes the most popular types of metal "trade-size" boxes used with wires No. 14 to No. 6. Cubic-inch capacities are listed for each box shown in the table. According to paragraph **(b)**, boxes other than those shown in Table 370-6(a) are required to be marked with the cubic-inch content so wire combinations can be readily computed.

Figure 370-6 shows another example with the counting data in the caption. The wire fill in this case violates the limit set by Sec. 370-6(a).

Figure 370-7 shows an example of wire-fill calculation for a number of ganged sections of sectional boxes. The photo shows a four-gang assembly of 3-in. by 2-in. by 3½-in. box sections with six 14/2 NM cables, each with a No. 14 ground wire and one 14/3 NM cable with a No. 14 ground. The feed to the box is 14/3 cable (at right side), with its black wire supplying the receptacle which will be installed in the right-hand section. The red wire serves as feed to three combination devices—one in each of the other sections—each device consisting of two switches on a single strap. When finished, the four-gang box will contain a total of six switches and one duplex receptacle. Each of the 14/2 cables will feed a switched load. All the white neutrals are spliced together and the seven bare No. 14 ground wires are spliced together, with one bare wire brought out to the receptacle ground terminal and one to the ground clip on the

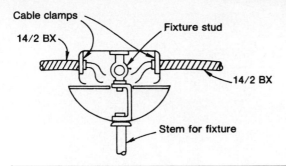

FOR A 4 × 1¼-IN. OCTAGONAL BOX:

From Table 370-6(a) .... 6 No. 14 wires
Minus one for the two cable clamps
and minus one for the fixture stud...... 2 No. 14 wires
_____
MAX. NUMBER PERMITTED .... 4 No. 14 wires

NOTE: If NM cable were used, another deduction of one for the two ground wires would make use of this box a violation.

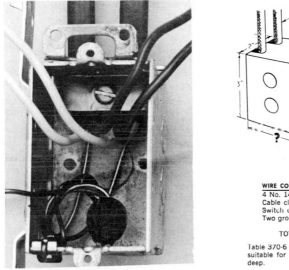

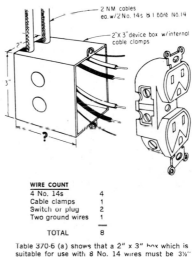

WIRE COUNT	
4 No. 14s	4
Cable clamps	1
Switch or plug	2
Two ground wires	1
TOTAL	8

Table 370-6 (a) shows that a 2″ x 3″ box which is suitable for use with 8 No. 14 wires must be 3½″ deep.

Fig. 370-5. Correct wire count determines proper minimum size of outlet box. (Sec. 370-6.)

bottom of the left-hand section. The four-gang assembly is taken as a box of volume equal to four times the volume of one 3- by 2- by 3½-in. box. From Table 370-6(a), that volume is 18 cu in. for each sectional box. Then for the four-gang assembly, the volume of the resultant box is 4 × 18, or 72, cu in. Then wire fill

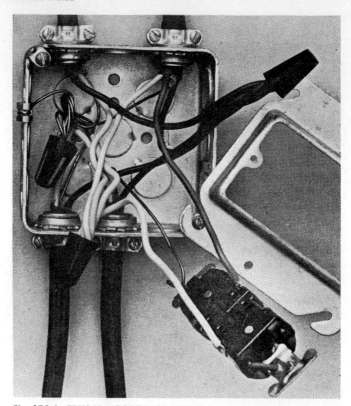

Fig. 370-6. THIS IS A CODE VIOLATION! A 4- × 4- × 1½-in. square metal box, generally referred to as a "1900" box, has four NM cables coming into it. At upper right is a 14/3 cable with No. 14 ground. The other three cables are 14/2 NM, each with a No. 14 ground. The red wire of the 14/3 cable feeds the receptacle to be installed in the one-gang plaster ring. The black wire of the 14/3 feeds the black wires of the three 14/2 cables. All the whites are spliced together, with one brought out to the receptacle, as required by Sec. 300-13(b). All the ground wires are spliced together, with one brought out to the grounding terminal on the receptacle and one brought out to the ground clip on the left side of the box. The wire count is as follows: nine No. 14 insulated wires, plus one for all of the ground wires and two for the receptacle. That is a total of 12 No. 14s. Note that box connectors are used instead of clamps and there is, therefore, no addition of one conductor for clamps. But Table 370-6(a) shows that a 4- × 1½-in. square box may contain only 10 No. 14 wires. (Sec. 370-6.)

for the four-gang assembly may be 4 times that permitted for the basic single gang box used in the assembly. Because a 3- by 2- by 3½-in. box is shown in Table 370-6(a) to have a permitted fill of 9 No. 14 wires, the four-gang assembly may contain 4 × 9, or 36, No. 14 wires—with deductions made as required by Sec. 370-6(a) (1).

Deduct one wire for all the clamps; deduct one No. 14 for all the bare equipment ground wires; and deduct two No. 14s for each "strap containing one or more devices," which calls for a deduction of eight because there are four

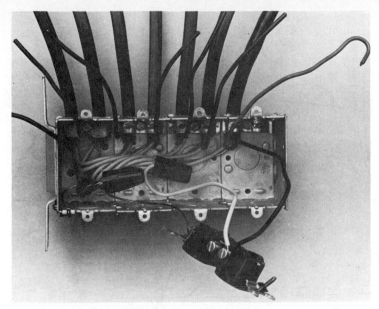

Fig. 370-7. Calculation of the proper minimum box size for the number of conductors used in ganged boxes must follow Sec. 370-6(a) (1), taking the assembly as a single box of the sum of the volumes of the ganged sections and filling it to the sum of the conductor count. (Sec. 370-6.)

device "straps" (one for each of the three combination switches and one for the receptacle). The total deductions come to 1 + 1 + 8, or 10.

Deducting 10 from 36 gives a permitted fill of 26 No. 14 insulated circuit wires. In the arrangement shown, there are 6 cables with 2 insulated wires and 1 with 3 insulated wires, for a total of 15 insulated No. 14 wires. Because that is well within the maximum permitted fill of 26 No. 14 wires, such an arrangement satisfies Sec. 370-6(a)(1).

The alternative method of counting wires and determining proper box size would be as follows:

1. There are 15 No. 14 insulated circuit wires.
2. Add one wire for all the cable clamps.
3. Add one wire for all the No. 14 ground wires.
4. Add two wires for each of the four device straps.

The total of the wire count is: 15 + 1 + 1 + 8, or 25, No. 14 wires.

Then dividing that among the four box sections gives six-plus wires per section—which is taken as seven No. 14 wires per section. Referring to Table 370-6(a), it will be noted that a 3- by 2- by 2½-in. box may contain six No. 14 wires. This calculation, therefore, establishes that the four-gang assembly could not be made up of 3- by 2- by 2½-in. boxes but would require 3- by 2- by 2¾-in. boxes—with a permitted fill of seven No. 14 wires per section, to accommodate the seven No. 14 wires per section.

Although the **Code** wire-counting method in Sec. 370-6(a)(1) does not make reference to the counting method of Sec. 370-6(a)(2)—which applies where all the wires in a box are not the same size—that part **(2)** differs from the calculation made above. As shown in Table 370-6(b), each No. 14 wire in a box must be allowed at least 2 cu in. of free space within the box. In the alternative calculation above, with a total of 25 No. 14 wires determined as the overall count, part **(2)** of Sec. 370-6(a) would require the box to have a minimum volume of 2 × 25, or 50, cu in. Each 3- by 2- by 2½-in. box has a volume of 12.5 [Table 370-6(a)]—for a total of 4 × 12.5, or 50, cu in. volume of the four-gang assembly. That volume satisfies the conductor volume and would permit use of 3- × 2- × 2½-in. boxes. But, the rule of Sec. 370-6(a) would require at least 3- × 2- × 2¾-in. boxes. Use of 3- × 2- × 3½-in. boxes would give more room and provide easier and safer installation.

When different sizes of wires are used in a box, part **(2)** of Sec. 370-6(a) requires that Table 370-6(b) must be used in establishing adequate box size. Using the same method of counting conductors as described in Sec. 370-6(a) (1), the volume of cubic inches shown in Table 370-6(b) must be allowed for each wire depending upon its size. Where two or more ground wires of different sizes come into a box, they must all be counted as a single wire of the largest size used.

When deductions are made from the number of wires permitted in a box [Table 370-6(a)], as when devices, fixture studs, etc., are in the box, the deductions must "be based on the largest conductors entering the box" in any case where the conductors are of different sizes.

Figure 370-8 shows a calculation with different wire sizes in a box. When conduit or EMT is used, there are no internal box clamps and, therefore, no addition for clamps. In this example, the metal raceway is the equipment grounding conductor—so no addition has to be made for one or more ground wires. And the red wire is counted as one wire because it is run through the box without splice or tap. As shown in the wire count under the sketch, the way to account for the space taken up by the wiring devices is to take each one as two wires of the same size as the largest wire coming into the box—i.e., No. 12—as required in the end of the first sentence of part **(a)(2)**. Note that the neutral pigtail required by Sec. 300-13(b) is excluded from the wire count as it would be under Sec. 370-6(a)(1).

From Table 370-6(b) each No. 12 must be provided with 2.25 cu in.—a total of 9 × 2.25, or 20.25, cu in. for the No. 12s. Then each No. 14 is taken at 2 cu in.—a total of 2 × 2, or 4, cu in. for both. Adding the two resultant volumes—20.25 plus 4—gives a minimum required box volume of 24.25 cu in. From Table 370-6(a), a 4- by 4-in. square box 2⅛ in. deep, with 30.3 cu in. interior volume, would satisfy this application.

For the many kinds of tricky control and power wire hookups so commonly encountered today—such as shown in Fig. 370-9—care must be taken to count all sizes of wires and make the proper volume provisions of Table 370-6(b).

FS and FD Boxes—WATCH OUT!

Table 370-6(a) gives the maximum number of wires permitted in FS and FD boxes. But the last sentence of the first paragraph of Sec. 370-6(b) does indicate that FS and FD boxes may contain more wires if their internal volumes are marked and are greater than shown in Table 370-6(a).

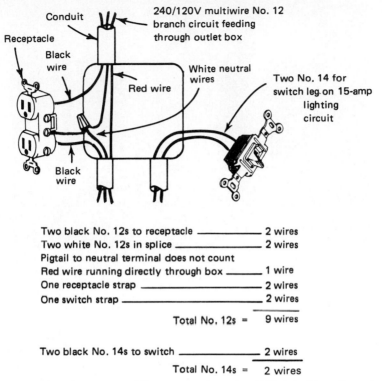

Conduit

Receptacle

Black wire

240/120V multiwire No. 12 branch circuit feeding through outlet box

White neutral wires

Red wire

Two No. 14 for switch leg on 15-amp lighting circuit

Black wire

Two black No. 12s to receptacle	2 wires
Two white No. 12s in splice	2 wires
Pigtail to neutral terminal does not count	
Red wire running directly through box	1 wire
One receptacle strap	2 wires
One switch strap	2 wires
Total No. 12s =	**9 wires**

Two black No. 14s to switch	2 wires
Total No. 14s =	**2 wires**

Fig. 370-8. When wires are different sizes, volumes from Table 370-6(b) must be used. (Sec. 370-6.)

Because the volumes in the table are minimums, most manufacturers continue to mark their products with the actual volume. This in many cases is considerably greater than the volumes shown in the table. The last sentence of Sec. 370-6(b) says that boxes that are marked to show a cubic inch capacity greater than the minimums in the table may have conductor fill calculated in accordance with their actual volume, using the volume per conductor given in Table 370-6(b).

Part **(b)** of Sec. 370-6 covers boxes—metal and nonmetallic—that are not listed in Table 370-6(a) and conduit bodies with provision for more than two conduit entries (cross and T conduit bodies). And the basic way of determining correct wire fill is to count wires in accordance with the intent of Sec. 370-6(a) (1) and then calculate required volume of the box or conduit body by totaling up the volumes for the various wires from Table 370-6(b). The rules of part **(b)** can be broken down into two categories: boxes and conduit bodies.

1. BOXES—Part **(b)** covers wire fill for metal boxes, up to 100 cu in. volume, that are not listed in Table 370-6(a) and for nonmetallic outlet and junction boxes. Although **Code** rules have long regulated the maximum number of conductors permitted in metal wiring boxes [such as given in Table 370-6(a)], there was no regulation on the use of conductors in nonmetallic

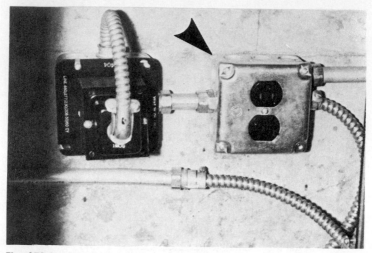

Fig. 370-9. Many boxes contain several sizes of wires—some running through, some spliced, and some connected to wiring devices. Calculation of minimum acceptable box size must be carefully made. The combination switch and receptacle here is on a single mounting strap, which is taken as two wires of the size of wires connected to it. (Sec. 370-6.)

device boxes up to the 1978 **NEC**. Now Sec. 370-6(b) requires that *both* metal boxes not listed in Table 370-6(a) and nonmetallic boxes be durably and legibly marked by their manufacturer with their cubic inch capacities to permit calculation of the maximum number of wires that the **Code** will permit in the box. Calculation of the conductor fill for these boxes will be based on the marked box volume and the method of counting conductors set forth in Sec. 370-6(a). The conductor volume will be taken at the values given in Table 370-6(b), and deductions of space as required for wiring devices or for clamps must be made in accordance with the rules of Sec. 370-6(a). This requirement for marking of both metal and nonmetallic boxes arises from the wording of Sec. 370-6(b), which refers to boxes other than those described in Table 370-6(a) and to nonmetallic boxes.

As shown in Fig. 370-10, a nonmetallic box for a switch has two 14/2 NM cables, each with a No. 14 ground. The wire count is four No. 14 insulated wires, plus two for the switch to be installed, and one for the two ground wires. That is a total of seven No. 14 wires. From Table 370-6(b), at least 2 cu in. of box volume must be allowed for each No. 14. This box must, therefore, be marked to show that it has a capacity of at least 7 × 2, or 14, cu in. (As shown, the ground wires are connected by a twist-on connector, with one end of the wire brought out to connect to a ground screw on the switch mounting yoke. Such a technique is required to provide grounding of a metal switchplate that is used on an outlet within reach of water faucets or other grounded objects. Refer to Secs. 250-42(e) and 410-56(d).

Fig. 370-10. Every nonmetallic box must be "durably and legibly marked by the manufacturer" with its cubic-inch capacity to permit calculation of number of wires permitted in the box—using Table 370-6(b) and the additions of wire space required to satisfy Sec. 370-6(a) (1). (Sec. 370-6.)

2. CONDUIT BODIES—Conduit bodies with provision for more than two conduit entries must be marked with their cubic inch capacity, and conductor fill is determined on the basis of Table 370-6(b). Such conduit bodies may contain splices or taps. An example of such application is shown in Fig. 370-11. Each of the eight No. 12 wires that are "counted" as shown at bottom must be provided with at least 2.25 cu in., from Table 370-6(b). The T conduit body must, therefore, be marked to show a capacity of not less than 8 $\times$ 2.25, or 18, cu in.

For each No. 6 conductor used in the boxes or conduit bodies covered by Sec. 370-6(b), there must be at least 5 cu in. of box volume *and* a minimum space at least 1½ in. wide where any No. 6 is bent in a box or fitting.

Part (c) of Sec. 370-6 contains a number of provisions which must be carefully evaluated. Figure 370-12 shows the first rule. For instance, in that sketch, if a conduit body is connected to ½-in. conduit, the conduit and the conduit body may contain seven No. 12 TW wires—as indicated in Table 3A, Chap. 9—and the conduit body must have a csa at least equal to 2 $\times$ 0.3 sq in. (the csa of ½-in. conduit), or 0.6 sq in. That is really a matter for the fitting manufacturers to observe.

The second paragraph of part (c) covers the details shown in Fig. 370-13. The rule requires that where fittings are used as shown in the sketch, they must be supported in a rigid and secure manner. Because Sec. 370-13 establishes the correct methods for supporting of boxes and fittings, it must be observed, and that section refers to support by "conduits"—which

All such bodies must be durably and legibly marked by manufacturer with their cubic-inch capacities.

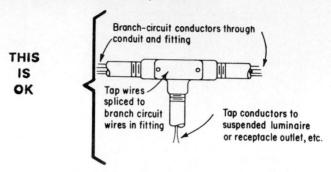

THIS IS OK

Branch-circuit conductors through conduit and fitting

Tap wires spliced to branch circuit wires in fitting

Tap conductors to suspended luminaire or receptacle outlet, etc.

Wire count of fitting:

All No. 12 wires

Two No. 12s straight through	2 wires
Three No. 12s into splice	3 wires
Three No. 12s into splice	3 wires
Total No. 12s =	8 wires

Fig. 370-11. Conduit bodies with more than *two* entries for conduit may contain splices or taps. (Sec. 370-6.)

Cross-section area of conduit body must be . . .

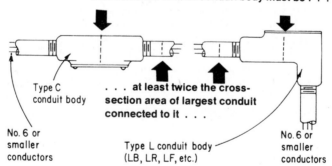

Type C conduit body

. . . **at least twice the cross-section area of largest conduit connected to it . . .**

No. 6 or smaller conductors

Type L conduit body (LB, LR, LF, etc.)

No. 6 or smaller conductors

. . . **and the maximum number of conductors permitted in the conduit body is the number of conductors permitted in the conduit connected to the conduit body, from** *Code* **tables on conduit fill (Chapter 9).**

Fig. 370-12. For No. 6 and smaller conductors, conduit body must have a csa twice that of largest conduit. (Sec. 370-6.)

Although the basic rule still prohibits splicing and
tapping in these fittings . . .

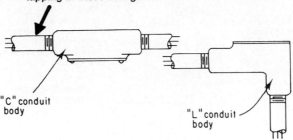

"C" conduit
body

"L" conduit
body

. . . .Permission is **now** given to splice in such fittings, if
Section 370-6(b) is satisfied; that is, if—

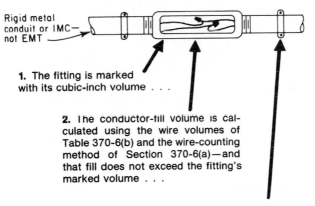

Rigid metal
conduit or IMC—
not EMT

1. The fitting is marked
with its cubic-inch volume . . .

2. The conductor-fill volume is calculated using the wire volumes of
Table 370-6(b) and the wire-counting
method of Section 370-6(a)—and
that fill does not exceed the fitting's
marked volume . . .

3. And the fitting is "supported in a rigid and secure
manner"—such as by the "conduit," if the conduit is
clamped on each side of the fitting as described in the
next-to-last paragraph of Section 370-13.

Fig. 370·13. Splices may be made in "C" and "L" conduit bodies—
if the conditions shown in this illustration are satisfied. (Sec. 370-6.)

seems to exclude such use on EMT because the **NEC** distinguishes between
"conduit" and "tubing" (EMT), as in the headline for Table 1 of Chap. 9
in the back of the **Code** book. Figure 370-14 shows typical applications of
those conduit bodies for splicing.

370·7. Conductors Entering Boxes, Conduit Bodies, or Fittings.   Part **(b)** requires
cable or raceway to be secured to *all metal* outlet boxes, conduit bodies, or
fittings—such as by threaded connection, connector devices, or internal box
clamps.

The first sentence of part **(c)** requires that a nonmetallic box must have a temperature rating at least equal to the lowest-temperature-rated conductor entering the box. This rule assumes that the lowest-temperature-rated conductor in
a box must be suited to the temperature in the box. The box would, therefore,

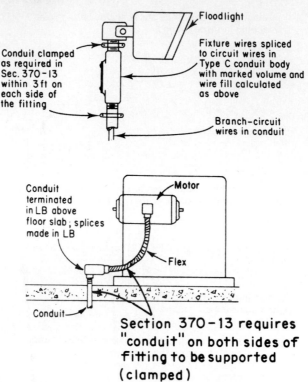

Floodlight

Conduit clamped as required in Sec. 370-13 within 3 ft on each side of the fitting

Fixture wires spliced to circuit wires in Type C conduit body with marked volume and wire fill calculated as above

Branch-circuit wires in conduit

Conduit terminated in LB above floor slab; splices made in LB

Motor

Flex

Conduit

Section 370-13 requires "conduit" on both sides of fitting to be supported (clamped)

Fig. 370-14. Splicing in "C" or "L" conduit bodies is common practice. (Sec. 370-6.)

be properly applied if it has a temperature rating at least equal to that of the lowest-rated conductor.

Part **(c)** also requires that, where nonmetallic-sheathed cable is connected to nonmetallic boxes, the cable must enter through a knockout (KO) opening provided for nonmetallic-sheathed cable, and not through a hole made at any point on the box. At least ¼ in. of the cable sheath must be brought inside the box.

Another very important limitation in this **Code** section applies to the need for clamping nonmetallic-sheathed cable at a KO where the cable enters anything other than a single gang box. The **Code** has always accepted the use of nonmetallic-sheathed cable without box clamps or any type of connector where the cable is stapled within 8 in. of the box. The cable is then brought into the box through an NM cable KO on the box, without any kind of a connector at the KO or any clamps in the box (Fig. 370-15). But the intention of the Exception to part **(c)** is that boxes or enclosures other than single gang boxes must be provided with a clamp or connector to secure nonmetallic-sheathed cable to such boxes (Fig. 370-16). *Only single gang nonmetallic boxes may be used without a cable clamp at the box KOs.* Where the **Code** permits elimination of a cable

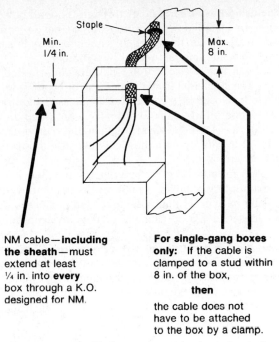

NM cable—**including the sheath**—must extend at least ¼ in. into **every** box through a K.O. designed for NM.

For single-gang boxes only: If the cable is clamped to a stud within 8 in. of the box,

then

the cable does not have to be attached to the box by a clamp.

Fig. 370-15. NM cable does not have to be clamped to single-gang boxes. (Sec. 370-7.)

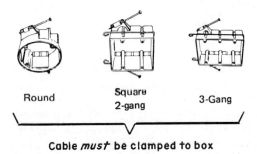

Round   Square 2-gang   3-Gang

Cable *must* be clamped to box

Fig. 370-16. NM cable must be clamped to all nonmetallic boxes that are *not* "single gang boxes." (Sec. 370-7.)

clamp if the cable is clamped to the stud within 8 in. of the box, the rule specifies that the 8-in. length be measured *along the cable* and not simply from the point of the cable strap to the box edge itself.

When used with open wiring on insulators, knob-and-tube work, or nonmetallic-sheathed cable, nonmetallic boxes have the advantage that an accidental contact between a "hot" wire and the box will not create a hazard.

370·9. Boxes Enclosing Flush Devices.   A through-the-wall box is a box which is manufactured to be installed in a partition wall so that a receptacle or switch may be attached to either side; therefore, it is not necessary to use two standard boxes one facing each side and connected by a jumper.

From the literal wording of Sec. 370-9, it could be interpreted to prohibit the use of such boxes. If a single device were used on only one side, then the other side would have to be closed by a cover of a thickness as required in Secs. 370-20(b) and 370-21—generally 14 gage. If a device is installed on both sides and the requirements of Sec. 410-56(d) regarding faceplates are followed, the boxes could be considered to comply with the **Code** because the walls and backs of the boxes would be enclosed.

If the screws used for attaching the receptacles and switches to boxes were used also for the mounting of boxes, a poor mechanical job would result, since the boxes would be insecurely held whenever the devices were not installed and the screws loosened for adjustment of the device position. Hence the prohibition.

370·11. Repairing Plaster and Drywall or Plasterboard.   The purpose of Secs. 370-10 and 370-11 is to prevent openings around the edge of the box through which fire could be readily communicated to combustible material in the wall or ceiling. For this reason inspection authorities do not allow square or hexagonal boxes in ceilings, finished with Sheetrock, without the use of "mud rings."

370·12. Exposed Surface Extensions.   The extension should be made as illustrated in Fig. 370-17. The extension ring is secured to the original box by two screws passing through ears attached to the box.

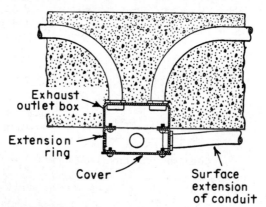

Fig. 370·17. Extension ring must be secured to box for surface extension. (Sec. 370-12.)

As noted in the Exception, a surface extension may be made from the *cover* of a concealed box, *if* the cover mounting design is secure, the extension wiring method is flexible, and grounding does not depend upon connection between the box and the cover. This Exception to the basic rule, which requires use of a box or extension ring over the concealed box, permits a method that provides a high degree of reliability.

370-13. Supports. The Code rule strictly requires all boxes, conduit bodies, and fittings to be fastened in their installed position—and the various paragraphs of this section cover different conditions of box support for commonly encountered enclosure applications. The one widely accepted exception to that rule—although actually not recognized by the Code—is the so-called "throwaway" box or "floating" box, which is a junction box used to connect flexible metal conduit from a recessed fixture to flex or BX branch-circuit wiring, in accordance with Sec. 410-67(c) (Fig. 370-18). In such cases, the connection of the fixture "whip" (the 4 to 6 ft of flex with high-temperature wires, e.g., 150°C Type AF) is made to the branch-circuit junction box which hangs down through the ceiling opening, and then the junction box is pushed back out of the way in the ceiling space and the fixture raised into position. But with suspended ceilings of lift-out panels, there is no need to leave such a loose box in the ceiling space, because connection can be made to a fixed box before the ceiling tiles are laid in place.

Figure 370-19 shows the rule of part **(b)(1)** of this section.

An outlet box built into a concrete ceiling, as shown in Fig. 370-20, seldom needs any special support. At such an outlet, if it is intended for a fixture of great weight to be safely hung on an ordinary ⅜-in. fixture stud, a special fixture support consisting of a threaded pipe or rod is required, such as is shown in Fig. 370-21.

In a tile arch floor (Fig. 370-21) a large opening must be cut through the tile to receive the conduit and outlet box.

The requirement of metal or wood supports for boxes applies to concealed work in walls and floors of wood-frame construction and other types of construction having open spaces in which the wiring is installed. In walls or floors of concrete, brick, or tile where conduit and boxes are solidly built into the wall or floor material, special box supports are not usually necessary.

As covered in part **(c)**, in an existing building, boxes may be flush mounted on plaster or any other ceiling or wall finish. Where no structural members are available for support, boxes may be affixed with approved anchors or clamps. Figure 370-22 illustrates that. For cutting metal boxes into existing walls, "Madison Holdits" are used to clamp the box tightly in position in the opening. Actually, the local inspector can determine acceptable methods of securing "cut-in" device boxes because this provision provides appreciable latitude for such decisions.

And according to part **(c)**, framing members of suspended ceiling systems may be used to support boxes if the framing members are rigidly supported and securely fastened to each other and to the building structure.

Figure 370-23 shows box-support methods that are covered by part **(d)** of Sec. 370-13 for boxes not over 100 cu in. in volume that do not contain devices or support fixtures. The rule there applies to "conduit" [rigid metal conduit and IMC, but not EMT or PVC conduit, Sec. 347-3(b)] used to support boxes—as for overhead conduit runs. A box may be supported by two properly clamped conduit runs (rigid metal conduit or IMC) that are threaded into entries on the box or into field-installed hubs attached to the box. This permission to use separate, field-installed hubs offers a relaxation of the previous demand for direct

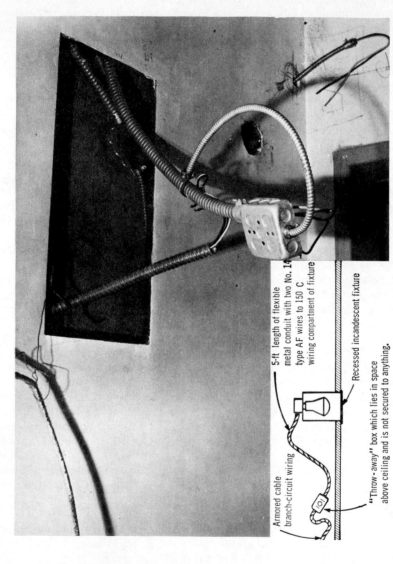

5-ft length of flexible
metal conduit with two No. 14
type AF wires to 150 C
wiring compartment of fixture

Recessed incandescent fixture

"Throw-away" box which lies in space
above ceiling and is not secured to anything.

Armored cable
branch-circuit wiring

Fig. 370-18. Fixture supply flex is tapped out of junction box fed by flex or BX branch-circuit wiring in ceiling space.
Box is later "thrown-away," unattached, into ceiling space. (Sec. 370-13.)

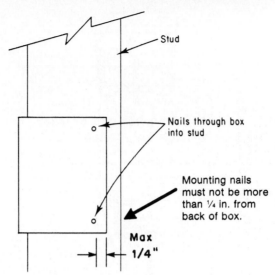

Fig. 370-19. Box-mounting nails must not obstruct box interior space. (Sec. 370-13.)

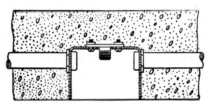

Fig. 370-20. Box in concrete is securely supported. (Sec. 370-13.)

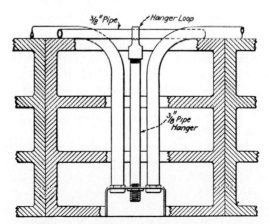

Fig. 370-21. Box in tile arch ceiling requires pipe-hanger support if very heavy lighting fixture is to be attached to the box stud. (Sec. 370-13.)

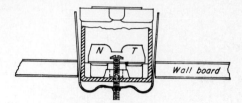

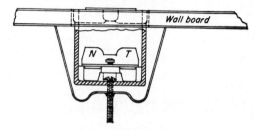

1. Inserting box and bracket through wall board.

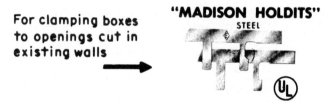

2. Box anchored to wall.

For clamping boxes to openings cut in existing walls ⟶ "MADISON HOLDITS" STEEL

Fig. 370·22. Part **(c)** of Sec. 370-13 refers to these types of clamping devices. (Sec. 370-13.)

threaded connection to the box. Where locknut and bushing connections are used instead of threaded conduit connection to a threaded hub or similar connection, the box must be independently fastened in place. Figure 370-24 shows an installation that is most likely a violation of part **(d)**. However, it may be acceptable because an Exception to part **(d)** permits "conduit or electrical metallic tubing" to support conduit bodies that are not larger than the largest trade size of conduit or EMT used.

The rules of part **(e)** of Sec. 370-13 are shown in Fig. 370-25. The rule recognizes the support of elevated threaded-hub junction boxes (not over 100 cu in.) by conduits emerging from a floor or concrete or the earth, such as those used near swimming pools, patios, or shrubbery. Support by a single conduit is not recognized. Figure 370-26 shows several installations that are in violation of these rules.

The intent of part **(e)** is that a lighting fixture may be supported on a box that is itself supported by two or more rigid metal or intermediate metal conduits

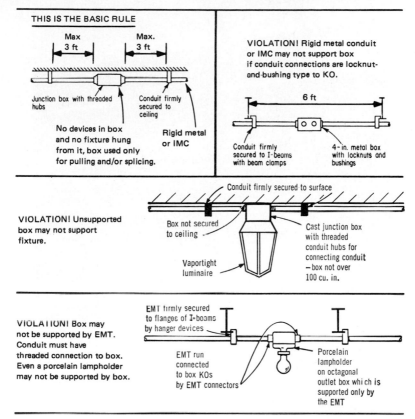

THIS IS THE BASIC RULE

Max
3 ft

Max.
3 ft

Junction box with threaded hubs

Conduit firmly secured to ceiling

No devices in box and no fixture hung from it, box used only for pulling and/or splicing.

Rigid metal or IMC

VIOLATION! Rigid metal conduit or IMC may not support box if conduit connections are locknut-and-bushing type to KO.

6 ft

Conduit firmly secured to I-beams with beam clamps

4-in. metal box with locknuts and bushings

Conduit firmly secured to surface

VIOLATION! Unsupported box may not support fixture.

Box not secured to ceiling

Vaportight luminaire

Cast junction box with threaded conduit hubs for connecting conduit — box not over 100 cu. in.

VIOLATION! Box may not be supported by EMT. Conduit must have threaded connection to box. Even a porcelain lampholder may not be supported by box.

EMT firmly secured to flanges of I-beams by hanger devices

EMT run connected to box KOs by EMT connectors

Porcelain lampholder on octagonal outlet box which is supported only by the EMT

Fig. 370-23. Box may be supported by "conduit" that is clamped, but box must not contain or support anything (Sec. 370-13.)

threaded into the box or into hubs that are field-installed to the box. The wording of this rule permits the two or more conduits to be threaded into either threaded entries in the box itself or into field-installed hubs that are "identified for the purpose" and properly connected to the box. And the wording permits the box to "support fixtures" or contain devices, receptacles, or switches.

Although the wording of part **(e)** does not make it clear, this rule accepts only *metal* conduits as the support. Nonmetallic conduit is prohibited from supporting boxes or any equipment by Sec. 347-3(b).

In the rule of part **(g)**, nonthreaded nonmetallic boxes may be supported by *metal* conduit (rigid or IMC) *but not* by nonmetallic conduit. This requires metal conduit if a nonmetallic box is to be supported by two or more conduits. And the box must be installed "in accordance with instructions contained in the listing or labeling" of the box. The wording of the heading on this rule in the 1987 **NEC** gave virtually literal approval to the support of enclosures by nonmetallic conduit—*but* that was not intended. Such support must comply with the concepts and distances of parts **(d)** and **(e)**.

Fig. 370·24. "T" conduit bodies are supported by the rigid conduit that connects to their threaded hubs, but the conduit body at right does not have the conduit supported on two sides of the conduit body. Note angle iron brace to conduit from I-beam flange. (Sec. 370-13.)

Part **(h)** permits a pendant box (such as one containing a START-STOP button) to be supported from a multiconductor cable, using, say, a strain-relief connector threaded into the hub on the box, or some other satisfactory protection for the conductors.

370·14. Depth of Outlet Boxes.   Sufficient space should be provided inside the box so that the wires do not have to be jammed together or against the box, and the box should provide enough of an enclosure so that in case of trouble, burning insulation cannot readily ignite flammable material outside the box.

370·15. Covers and Canopies.   This rule requires every outlet box to be covered up—by a cover plate, a fixture canopy, or a faceplate, which has the openings for a receptacle, snap switch, or other device installed in a box.

Part **(a)** requires all metal faceplates to be grounded as required by Sec. 250-42. Because metal faceplates are *exposed* conductive parts, they must satisfy Sec. 250-42(a), which, in effect, says that ungrounded metal faceplates shall not be installed within 8 ft vertically or 5 ft horizontally of ground or grounded objects—laundry tubs, bathtubs, shower baths, plumbing fixtures, steam pipes, radiators, or other grounded surfaces—that are subject to contact by persons.

And part **(b)** of Sec. 250-42 requires metal faceplates to be grounded in wet or damp locations (which have been judged to include bathrooms)—unless the faceplates are isolated from contact.

A metal faceplate, if not grounded, may become "alive" by reason of contact of the ungrounded circuit wire with the plate or switch box, and a hazard is thus created if the plate is within reach from any conductive object. The hazard

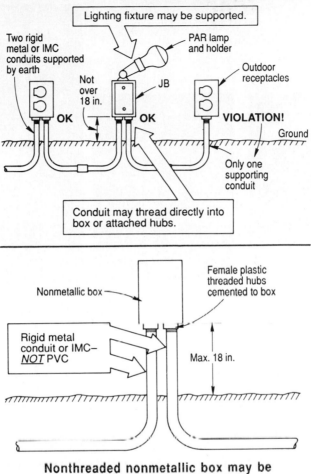

Fig. 370·25. Boxes fed out of the ground or a concrete floor, patio, or walk must observe these rules. (Sec. 370-13.)

still exists, however, if a plate of insulating material is attached by means of metal screws with exposed metal heads. Insulated screws and metal screws with insulated heads are available.

When a metal faceplate is attached to a switch or receptacle in a grounded metal box, it is thereby grounded and complies with Sec. 410-21, which covers grounding of lighting fixtures and faceplates. This is true for a faceplate on a switch or a receptacle because the faceplate attaches to the metal mounting strap of the device and that strap is connected to the ears on the grounded metal box by the mounting screws and, sometimes, additionally by a bonding jumper used for grounding the receptacle ground terminal and strap. In a nonmetallic

Fig. 370·26. A *single* rigid metal conduit may not support a box, even with concrete fill in the ground (left). Box may not be supported on EMT, even with several connections used (center). Method at right is a violation on three counts: EMT, not "conduit," supports the box; only one hub on box is connected; box is more than 18 in. above ground. (Sec. 370-13.)

box fed by NM cable, a receptacle mounting strap is grounded by connection of the cable ground wire to the ground terminal (green hex-head screw)—thereby grounding a metal faceplate attached to the receptacle strap. But in the case of a snap switch in a nonmetallic box, the switch must be equipped with a ground terminal on its strap to permit connection of the NM cable ground wire to the strap—thereby assuring grounding of a metal faceplate attached to the strap of the switch. Figure 370-27 shows such a switch used to ensure effective grounding of metal wall plates when nonmetallic switch boxes are used.

It should be noted that Secs. 370-15(a) and 250-42(a) combine to require grounding of metal faceplates that are "within 8 feet vertically or 5 feet horizontally . . ." etc. But, Sec. 410-56(d), which is referenced after Sec. 370-15(a), flatly requires grounding of *any* metal faceplate if it is attached to a wiring device in a box fed by a wiring system that contains an equipment grounding means—regardless of any distances to grounded objects. In Fig. 370-27, when a metal faceplate is to be used for a switch in a nonmetallic box, Sec. 370-15(a) requires the plate to be grounded if it is "within 8 feet . . ." etc. But, if the faceplate is *not* in a wet or damp location and is *not* "within 8 feet . . ." etc., it does *not* have to be grounded to satisfy Sec. 370-15. *However,* if NM with a ground wire is used, then Sec. 410-18(a) requires use of that type of switch to ground the metal faceplate, no matter where it is used. But, if NM cable without a ground wire is used, Sec. 410-18(b) would make it mandatory to use a faceplate of insulating material—thereby prohibiting the metal faceplate. So to use a

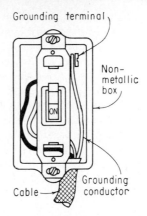

Fig. 370·27. Grounding switch must be used for metal faceplate on any nonmetallic box. (Sec. 370-15.)

metal faceplate on any nonmetallic box, the NM cable must have a ground wire and the type of switch shown must be used.

In part **(b)** of Sec. 370-15, if the ceiling or wall finish is of combustible material, the canopy and box must form a complete enclosure. The chief purpose of this rule is to require that no open space be left between the canopy and the edge of the box where the finish is wood or other combustible material. Where the wall or ceiling finish is plaster the requirement does not apply, since plaster is not classed as a combustible material; however, the plaster must be continuous up to the box, leaving no opening around the box.

370·17. Outlet Boxes.   Part **(b)** requires floor boxes to be completely suitable for the particular way in which they are used. Adjustable floor boxes and associated service receptacles can be installed in every type of floor construction. Metal cap keeps assembly clean during pouring of concrete slabs. After the concrete has cured, this cap can then be removed and discarded and floor plates and service fittings added.

As noted in part **(c)**, a ceiling paddle fan must not be supported from a ceiling outlet box—unless the box is UL listed as suitable as the sole support means for a fan (Fig. 370-28). The vibration of ceiling fans places severe dynamic loads

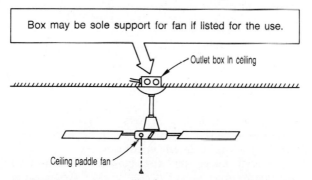

Fig. 370·28. Support for ceiling fans must be suited to the dynamic loading of the vibrating action. [Sec. 370-17(c).]

on the screw attachment points of boxes. But boxes designed and listed for this application pose no safety problems. (See Sec. 422-18.)

370·18. Pull and Junction Boxes.   As noted in Sec. 370-6, conduit bodies must be sized the same as pull boxes when they contain No. 4 or larger conductors.

For raceways of ¾-in. trade size and larger containing conductors of No. 4 or larger size, the **NE Code** specifies certain minimum dimensions for a pull or junction box installed in a raceway run. These rules also apply to pull and junction boxes in cable runs—but instead of using the cable diameter, the minimum trade size raceway required for the number and size of conductors in the cable must be used in the calculations. Basically there are two types of pulls—straight pulls and angle pulls. Figure 370-29 covers straight pulls. Figure 370-30 covers angle pulls. In all the cases shown in those illustrations, the depth of the box

EXAMPLES:

1.

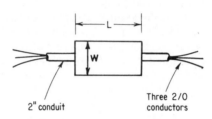

L = 8 × 2 in. = 16 in. minimum
W = Whatever width is necessary to provide proper installation of the conduit locknuts and bushings within the enclosure.

2.

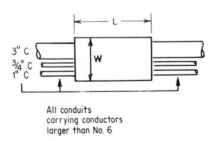

The 3-in. conduit is the largest.
Therefore—
L = 8 × 3 in. = 24 in. minimum
W = Width necessary for conduit locknuts and bushings.

Fig. 370·29. In straight pulls, the length of the box must be not less than eight times the trade diameter of the largest raceway. (Sec. 370-18.)

EXAMPLE:

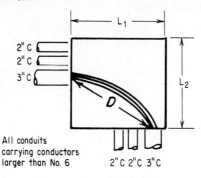

The 3-in. conduit is the largest.
Therefore—
$L_1 = 6 \times 3$ in. $+$ (2 in. $+$ 2 in.) $= 22$ in. min.
$L_2 = 6 \times 3$ in. $+$ (2 in. $+$ 2 in.) $= 22$ in. min.
$D = 6 \times 3$ in. $= 18$ in., minimum distance between raceway entries enclosing the same conductors

Fig. 370-30. Box size must be calculated for angle pulls. For boxes in which the conductors are pulled at an angle or in a "U," the distance between each raceway entry inside the box and the opposite wall of the box must not be less than 6 times the trade diameter of the largest raceway in a row. And the distance must be increased for additional raceway entries by the amount of the maximum sum of the diameters of all other raceway entries in the same row on the same wall of the box. The distance between raceway entries enclosing the same conductors must not be less than 6 times the trade diameter of the larger raceway. (Sec. 370-18.)

only has to be sufficient to permit installation of the locknuts and bushings on the largest conduit. And the spacing between adjacent conduit entries is also determined by the diameters of locknuts and bushings—to provide proper installation. Depth is the dimension not shown in the sketches.

According to the rule of part **(a)(2)** in sizing a pull or junction box for an angle or "U" pull, if a box wall has more than one row of conduits, "each row shall be calculated separately and the single row that provides the maximum distance shall be used." Consider the following:

A pull box has two rows of conduits entering one side (or wall) of the box for a right-angle pull. What is the minimum required inside distance from the wall with the two rows of conduit entries to the opposite wall of the box?
    Row 1: One 2½-in. and one 1-in. conduit.
    Row 2: One ½-in., two 1¼-in., one 1½-in., and two ¾-in. conduits.

Interpretation of 1987 NEC Sec. 370-18(a)(2):

1. $6 \times$ diameter of "largest raceway" entering box wall:

$$6 \times 2½ \text{ in.} = 15 \text{ in.}$$

2. Add "the maximum sum of diameters of all other raceway entries in any one row on the same wall of the box."

Row 2 will give "the maximum sum":

$\frac{1}{2} + (2 \times 1\frac{1}{4}) + 1\frac{1}{2} + (2 \times \frac{3}{4}) = 6$ in.

3. Adding the two results: 15 in. + 6 in. = 21 in.

That is the minimum size box dimension to the wall opposite the wall where the conduits enter.

Calculating with Revised Rule of Present NEC:

Calculating each row "separately" and taking the box dimension from the row that gives the maximum distance.

Row 1: 6 × largest raceway (2½ in.) + other entries (1 in.) = 16 in.

Row 2: 6 × the largest raceway (1½ in.) + other entries [½ in. + (2 × 1¼ in.) + (2 × ¾ in.)] = 9 in. + ½ in. + 4 in. = 13½ in.

Result: The minimum box dimension must be the 16 in. dimension from run No. 1 which "provides the maximum distance" calculated.

Figure 370-31 shows a more complicated conduit and pull box arrangement, which requires more extensive calculation of the minimum permitted size. In this particular layout shown, the upper 3-in. conduits running straight through the box represent a problem separate from the 2-in. conduit angle pulls. In this case the 3-in. conduit establishes the box length in excess of that required for the 2-in. conduit. After computing the 3-in. requirements, the box size was calculated for the angle pull involving the 2-in. conduit.

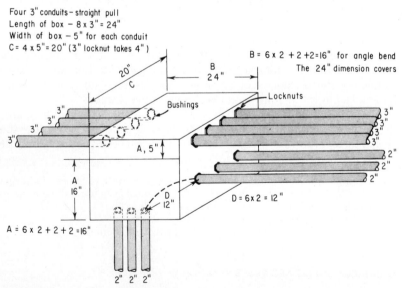

Fig. 370-31. A number of calculations are involved when angle and straight pulls are made in different directions and different planes. (Sec. 370-18.)

Subparagraph **(3)** of Sec. 370-18(a) permits smaller pull or junction boxes where such boxes have been approved for and marked with the maximum number and size of conductors and the conduit fills are *less* than the maximum permitted in Table 1, Chap. 9. This rule provides guidelines for boxes which have been widely used for years, but which have been smaller than the sizes normally required in subparagraphs **(1)** and **(2)**. These smaller pull boxes must be listed by UL under this rule.

There are many instances where an installation is made in which raceways and conductors are not matched so as to utilize maximum conduit fill as permitted by the **Code**. An example would be a 2-in. conduit with six No. 4 THHN conductors. The **Code** would permit up to 16 conductors depending upon the type of insulation. It was felt that in such installations provisions should be made for the use of boxes or fittings which would not necessarily conform to the letter of the law as exemplified by the standards listed in subsections **(1)** and **(2)**, but would compare favorably under test with a box sized as is required for the conductor and conduit.

A pull or junction box used with 2-in. conduit and conductors No. 4 AWG or larger must be 16 in. long if straight pulls are made and must be 12 in. long if angle pulls are to be made. If we have a 2-in. conduit and we are installing eight No. 4 RHH conductors, all pull or junction boxes would have to conform to these measurements. If, however, we are installing five No. 4 RHH conductors, a smaller box would be acceptable, provided it has been tested for and is marked with this number.

Figure 370-32 shows how the rules of Sec. 370-18(a) apply to conduit bodies. **Important:** The Exception given in Sec. 370-18(a) (2) establishes the minimum dimension of L2 for angle runs, but this Exception only applies to conduit bodies which have the removable cover opposite one of the entries, such as a Type LB body. Types LR, LL, and LF do not qualify under that Exception, and for such conduit bodies the dimension L2 would have to be at least equal to the dimension L1 (that is, six times raceway diameter).

Figure 370-33 shows the racking of cable required by part **(b)** of this section.

Figure 370-34 shows another consideration in sizing a pull box for angle conduit layouts. A pull box is to be installed to make a right-angle turn in a group of conduits consisting of two 3-in., two 2½-in., and four 2-in. conduits.

Subparagraph **(2)** of Sec. 370-18(a) gives two methods for computing the box dimensions, and both must be met.

First method:

$$6 \times 3 \text{ in.} = 18 \text{ in.}$$
$$1 \times 3 \text{ in.} = 3$$
$$2 \times 2\tfrac{1}{2} \text{ in.} = 5$$
$$4 \times 2 \text{ in.} = \underline{8}$$
$$\text{Total} = 34 \text{ in.}$$

Second method:

Assuming that the conduits are to leave the box in the same order in which they enter, the arrangement is shown in Fig. 370-34 and the distance A between the ends of the two conduits must be not less than 6 × 2 in. = 12 in. It can be

STRAIGHT RUN

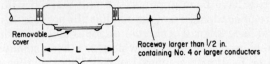

Removable cover

Raceway larger than 1/2 in. containing No. 4 or larger conductors

Type C conduit body must have length L equal to 8 times diameter of the raceway

Examples

If four No. 4 THHN are used in 1-in. conduit, conduit body must be at least 8 in. long.

If four 500 kcmil XHHW are used in 3-in. conduit, conduit body must be at least 24 in. long.

ANGLE RUN

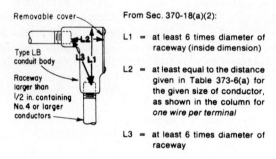

Removable cover

Type LB conduit body

Raceway larger than 1/2 in. containing No. 4 or larger conductors

From Sec. 370-18(a)(2):

L1 = at least 6 times diameter of raceway (inside dimension)

L2 = at least equal to the distance given in Table 373-6(a) for the given size of conductor, as shown in the column for *one wire per terminal*

L3 = at least 6 times diameter of raceway

Examples

If four No. 4 THW conductors are used in 1¼-in. conduit, minimum dimensions would be calculated as follows:

L1 = 6 × 1¼ in. = 7.5 in.
L2 = 2 in., from Table 373-6(a) for one No. 4 conductor per terminal
L3 = 6 × 1¼ in. = 7.5 in.

If four 500 kcmil THW conductors are used in 3½-in. conduit, minimum dimensions would be:

L1 = 6 × 3½ in. = 21 in.
L2 = 6 in., from Table 373-6(a)
L3 = 6 × 3½ in. = 21 in.

Fig. 370·32. Conduit bodies must be sized as pull boxes under these conditions. (Sec. 370-18.)

assumed that this measurement is to be made between the centers of the two conduits. By calculation, or by laying out the corner of the box, it is found that the distance C should be about 8½ in.

The distance B should be not less than 30½ in., approximately, as determined by applying practical data for the spacing between centers of conduits,

$$30\frac{1}{2} \text{ in.} + 8\frac{1}{2} \text{ in.} = 39 \text{ in.}$$

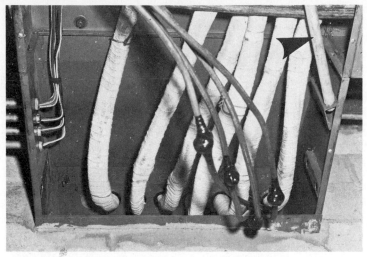

Fig. 370-33. If a pullbox has any dimension over 6 ft, the conductors within it must be supported by suitable racking (arrow) or cabling, as shown here for arc-proofed bundles of feeder conductors, to keep the weight of the many conductors off the sheet metal cover that attaches to the bottom of the box. (Sec. 370-18.)

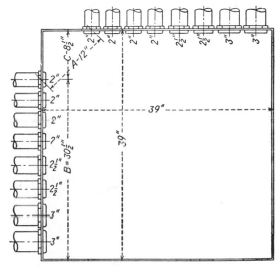

Fig. 370-34. Distance between conduits carrying same cables has great impact on overall box size. (Sec. 370-18.)

In this case the box dimensions are governed by the second method. The largest dimension computed by either of the two methods is of course the one to be used. Of course, if conduit positions for conduits carrying the same cables are transposed—as in Fig. 370-30—then box size can be minimized.

The most practical method of determining the proper size of a pull box is to sketch the box layout with its contained conductors on a paper.

Section 370-18 applies particularly to the pull boxes commonly placed above distribution switchboards and which are often, and with good reason, termed *tangle boxes*. In such boxes, all conductors of each circuit should be cabled together by serving them with twine so as to form a self-supporting assembly that can be formed into shape, or the conductors should be supported in an orderly manner on racks, as required by part **(b)** of Sec. 370-18. The conductors should not rest directly on any metalwork inside the box, and insulating bushings should be provided wherever required by Sec. 373-6(c).

For example, the box illustrated in Fig. 370-34 could be approximately 5 in. deep and accommodate one horizontal row of conduits. By making it twice as deep, two horizontal rows or twice the number of conduits could be installed.

Insulating racks are usually placed between conductor layers, and space must be allowed for them.

370-20. Metal Boxes, Conduit Bodies, and Fittings.   This section through Sec. 370-24 covers construction of boxes. UL data on application of boxes supplement this **Code** data as follows:

1. Cable clamps in outlet boxes are marked to indicate the one or more types of cables that are suitable for use with that clamp.
2. Box clamps have been tested for securing only one cable per clamp, except that multiple-section clamps may secure one cable under each section of the clamp, with each cable entering the box through a separate KO.

Part **(c)** of this section covers the pull boxes regulated by Sec. 370-18. UL data on such boxes are important and must be related to the **Code** rules. Listed pull and junction boxes may be sheet metal, cast metal, or nonmetallic, and all of these have a volume greater than 100 cu in. Because listed boxes of this type are available, the intent of **NE Code** Sec. 110-2 and the clear regulations of OSHA on equipment acceptability demand that only listed pull and junction boxes be used. To use a pullbox or junction box that is not listed is a violation of those regulations. Boxes marked "Raintight" or "Rainproof" are tested under a condition simulating exposure to beating rain. "Raintight" means water will not enter the box. "Rainproof" means that exposure to beating rain will not interfere with proper operation of the apparatus within the enclosure. Use of a box with either designation must satisfy **NE Code** Sec. 370-5, which notes that boxes in wet locations (such as outdoors where exposed to rain or indoors where exposed to water spray) must prevent moisture from entering *or* accumulating within the box. That is, water *may* enter the box if it does not accumulate in the box, where the box is drained. A box that is raintight or rainproof may satisfy that rule. Be sure, though, that any equipment installed in a box labeled "rainproof" is mounted within the location restrictions marked in the box.

In part **(d)** of Sec. 370-20, *connection for grounding conductor is required in metal boxes used with nonmetallic raceway or cable.* This rule is intended to assure a suitable means within a metal box to connect the equipment grounding conductor that is required to be used with such wiring methods to provide equipment grounding. This is required here for metal boxes that are "designed for use" with the nonmetallic systems. Without this rule, use of metal boxes often results in hole drilling in the box to take a nut-and-bolt connection of the grounding conductor. Such unauthorized holes in an enclosure void listing of the box and diminish its concrete-tight or liquidtight integrity.

Note that the "means" for connection of the equipment grounding conductor must be provided "in" each metal box designed for use with a nonmetallic wiring method. Use of a grounding clip (a G-clip) on the edge of the box does not appear to satisfy that wording. Instead, a grounding lug or tapped hole that is part of the box must provide effective grounding connection to the box.

370·51. Size of Pull and Junction Boxes. Figure 370-35 shows the rules on sizing of pull boxes for high-voltage circuits.

370·52. Construction and Installation Requirements. Part **(e)** requires that covers of pull and junction boxes for systems operating at over 600 V must be marked with readily visible lettering at least ½ in. high, warning "DANGER HIGH VOLTAGE KEEP OUT."

STRAIGHT PULLS

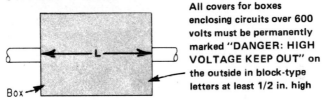

All covers for boxes enclosing circuits over 600 volts must be permanently marked "DANGER: HIGH VOLTAGE KEEP OUT" on the outside in block-type letters at least 1/2 in. high

L - not less than 48 times the outside diameter, over sheath, of the largest shielded or lead-covered *conductor* or *cable* entering the box, *OR* not less than 32 times the outside diameter of the largest nonshielded conductor or cable.

NOTE: The box length must be 48 times the conductor or cable diameter, *not the conduit* diameter.

ANGLE PULLS

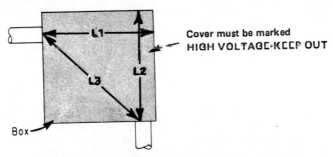

Cover must be marked HIGH VOLTAGE-KEEP OUT

L1, L2, L3—not less than 36 times the outside diameter, over sheath, of the largest *conductor* or *cable*

Fig. 370·35. Minimum dimensions are set for high-voltage pull and junction boxes. [Sec. 370-51(a).]

All required warning signs must be properly worded to include the command "KEEP OUT." While certain sections of the **Code**, such as this one, as well as Secs. 230-203 and 110-34(c), clearly require the inclusion of the command "KEEP OUT," other sections do not (e.g., Sec. 710-43). Be aware that courts have held that warning signs that fail to include some sort of instruction or command with respect to an appropriate action that must be taken are inadequate and constitute negligence on the part of the individual posting the sign. Always include some phrase that will tell the individual what to do about the condition or hazard that exists.

ARTICLE 373. CABINETS AND CUTOUT BOXES

373·1. Scope. Cabinets and cutout boxes, according to the definitions in Art. 100, must have doors and are thus distinguished from large boxes with covers consisting of plates attached with screws or bolts. Article 373 applies to all boxes used to enclose operating apparatus, i.e., apparatus having moving parts or requiring inspection or attention, such as panelboards, cutouts, switches, circuit breakers, control apparatus, and meter socket enclosures.

373·3. Position in Wall. Figure 373-1 shows how the ¼-in. setback relates to cabinets installed in noncombustible walls.

373·5. Conductors Entering Cabinets or Cutout Boxes. Part (c) makes clear that all cables used with cabinets or cutout boxes must be attached to the enclosure. NM cable, for instance, does not have to be connected by clamp or connector device to a single gang nonmetallic outlet box as in Sec. 370-7(c), *but must*

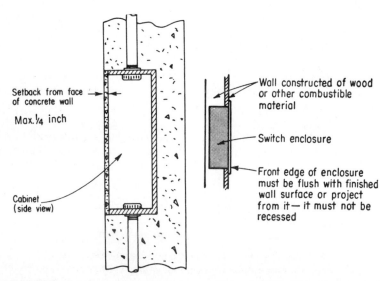

Fig. 373·1. In masonry wall, cabinet does not have to be flush with wall surface—as it does in wood wall. (Sec. 373-3.)

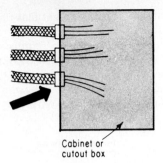

**Any cable (BX, NM, etc.) must
be secured to any cabinet or
cutout box, whether metal or
nonmetallic**

Cabinet or
cutout box

Fig. 373-2. All cables must be secured to all cabinets or cutout boxes. (Sec. 373-5.)

always be connected to KOs in panelboard enclosures and other cabinets (Fig. 373-2).

373-6. Deflection of Conductors. Parts **(a)** and **(b)** cover a basic **Code** rule that is referenced in a number of **Code** articles to assure safety and effective conductor application by providing enough space to bend conductors within enclosures.

A basic concept of evaluating adequate space for bending conductors at terminals of equipment installed in cabinets is presented in this section. The matter of bending space for conductors at terminals is divided into two different configurations, as follows:

1. The conductor does not enter (or leave) the enclosure through the wall opposite its terminals. This would be any case where the conductor passes through a wall of the enclosure at right angles to the wall opposite the terminal lugs to which the conductor is connected or at the opposite end of the enclosure. In all such cases, the bend at the terminals is a single-angle bend (90° bend), and the conductor then passes out of the bending space. It is also called an "L" bend, as shown at the top of Fig. 373-3. For bends of that type, the distance from the terminal lugs to the wall opposite the lugs must conform to Table 373-6(a), which requires lesser distances than those of Table 373-6(b) because single bends are more easily made in conductors.

2. The conductor enters (or leaves) the enclosure through the wall opposite its terminals. This is a more difficult condition because the conductor must make an offset or double bend to go from the terminal and then align with the raceway or cable entrance. This is also called an "S" or a "Z" bend because of its configuration, as shown at the top left of Fig. 373-3. For such bends, Table 373-6(b) specifies a greater distance from the end of the lug to the opposite wall to accommodate the two 45° bends, which are made difficult by the short lateral space between lugs and the stiffness of conductors (especially with the plastic insulations in cold weather).

Table 373-6(b) provides increased bending space to accommodate use of factory-installed connectors that are not of the lay-in or removable type and to allow use of field-installed terminals that are not designated by the manufacturer as part of the equipment marking. Exception No. 1 to part **(b)(1)** is shown in the bottom sketch of Fig. 373-3.

Note: For providing **Code**-required bending space at terminals for enclosed switches or individually enclosed circuit breakers, refer to Sec. 380-18. For conductor bending space at panelboard terminals, refer to Sec. 384-35. In Fig. 373-3, the clearances shown are determined from Table 373-6(a) or Table 373-6(b), under the column for one wire per terminal. For multiple-conductor circuit

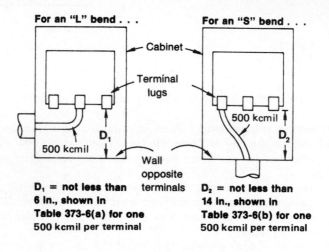

For an "L" bend . . .

Cabinet

Terminal lugs

D_1

500 kcmil

Wall opposite terminals

D_1 = **not less than 6 in., shown in Table 373-6(a) for one 500 kcmil per terminal**

For an "S" bend . . .

500 kcmil

D_2

D_2 = **not less than 14 in., shown in Table 373-6(b) for one 500 kcmil per terminal**

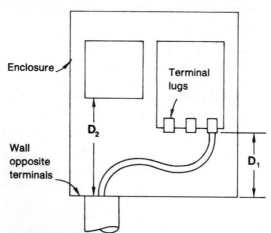

Enclosure

Terminal lugs

D_2

Wall opposite terminals

D_1

EVEN THOUGH CONDUCTOR LEAVES ENCLOSURE THROUGH WALL OPPOSITE LUGS, D₁ MAY BE SIZED FROM TABLE 373-6(a) PROVIDED THAT D₂ CONFORMS TO TABLE 373-6(b)

Fig. 373-3. These clearances are minimums that must be observed. (Sec. 373-6.)

makeups, the clearance at terminals and in side gutters has to be greater, as shown under two, three, four, etc., wires per terminal.

Exception No. 2 of part **(b)(1)** covers application of conductors entering or leaving a meter-socket enclosure, and was based on a study of 100- and 200-A meter sockets.

Paragraph **(c)** applies to all conductors of size No. 4 or larger entering a cabinet or box from rigid metal conduit, flexible metal conduit, electrical metallic tubing, etc. To protect the conductors from cutting or abrasion a smoothly rounded insulating surface is required. While many fittings are provided with insulated sleeves or linings, it is also possible to use a separate insulating lining or sleeve to meet the requirements of the **Code**. Figure 373-4 shows use of a bushing with an insulated edge or a completely nonmetallic bushing to satisfy this rule. Figure 373-5 shows an approved sleeve which may be used to separate the conductors from the raceway fitting, which may be installed after the conductors are already installed and connected.

In the Exception to part **(c)** an insulated throat is not required for conductor protection on enclosure threaded hubs or bosses that have a rounded or flared entry surface. This is recognition of a long-standing reality—that there is no

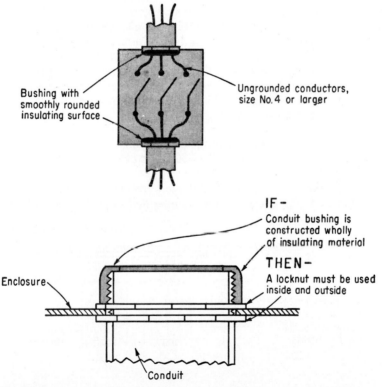

Fig. 373-4. An insulated-throat bushing or other protection must be used at enclosure openings. (Sec. 373-6.)

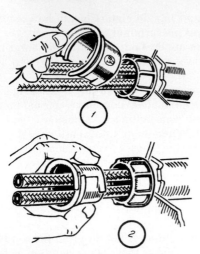

Fig. 373-5. Slip-over nonmetallic sleeve may be used to cover metal bushing throat. (Sec. 373-6.)

need for protective insulating material around the interior opening of integral hubs and bosses on equipment enclosures. Insulated-throat bushings and connectors are needed only for entries through KOs in sheet-metal enclosures.

The last paragraph of part **(c)** prohibits use of a plastic or phenolic bushing ("wholly of insulating material") as a device for securing conduit to an enclosure wall. On a KO, there must be a metal locknut outside and a metal locknut inside to provide tight clamping to the enclosure wall, with the nonmetallic bushing put on after the inside locknut. An EMT or conduit connector must also be secured in position by a metal locknut and not by a nonmetallic bushing.

Part **(c)** also requires that any insulating bushing or insulating material used to protect conductors from abrasion must have a temperature rating at least equal to the temperature rating of the conductors.

373-8. Enclosures for Switches or Overcurrent Devices.   The basic rule here is a follow-up to the rule of Sec. 373-7.

Most enclosures for switches and/or overcurrent devices have been designed to accommodate only those conductors intended to be connected to terminals

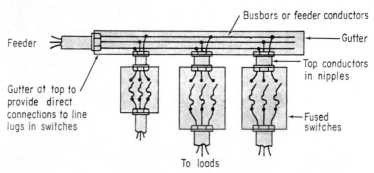

Fig. 373-6. Feeder taps in auxiliary gutter keep feeder cables and tap connectors out of switch enclosures. (Sec. 373-8.)

within such enclosures. And in designing such equipment it would be virtually impossible for manufacturers to anticipate various types of "foreign" circuits, feed-through circuits, or numerous splices or taps.

The rule here states enclosures for switches, CBs, panelboards, or other operating equipment must not be used as junction boxes, troughs, or raceways for conductors feeding through or tapping off, unless designs suitable for the purpose are employed to provide adequate space. This rule affects installations in

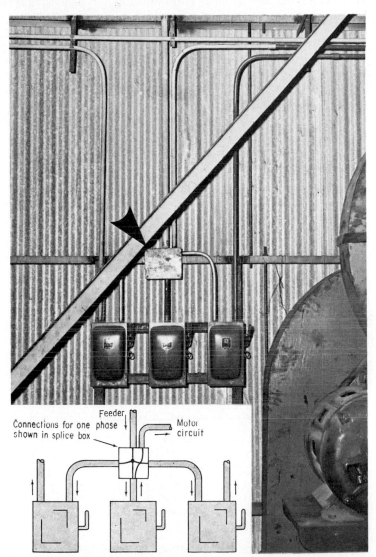

Fig. 373-7. Junction box (arrow) is used for tapping feeder conductors to supply individual motor branch circuits—as shown in inset diagram. (Sec. 373-8.)

which a number of branch circuits or subfeeder circuits are to be tapped from feeder conductors in an auxiliary gutter, using fused switches to provide disconnect and overcurrent protection for the branch or subfeeder circuits. It also applies to feeder taps in panelboard cabinets.

In general, the most satisfactory way to connect various enclosures together is through the use of properly sized auxiliary gutters (Fig. 373-6) or junction boxes. Figure 373-7 shows a hookup of three motor disconnects, using a junction box to make the feeder taps. Following this concept, enclosures for switches and/or overcurrent devices will not be overcrowded.

There are cases where large enclosures for switches and/or overcurrent devices will accommodate additional conductors and this is generally where the 40 percent (conductor space) and 75 percent (splices or taps) at one cross section would apply. An example would be control circuits tapped off or extending through 200-A or larger fusible switches or CB enclosures. The csa within such enclosures is the *free gutter wiring space* intended for conductors.

The Exception to this rule is shown in Fig. 373-8 and applied as follows:

> *Example:* If an enclosure has a gutter space of 3 by 3 in., the csa would be 9 sq in. Thus, the total conductor fill (use Table 5, Chap. 9) at any cross section (including conductors) could not exceed 6.75 sq in. (9 × 0.75).

In the case of large conductors, a splice other than a wire-to-wire "C" or "tube" splice would not be acceptable if the conductors at the cross section are near a 40 percent fill, because this would leave only a 35 percent space for the

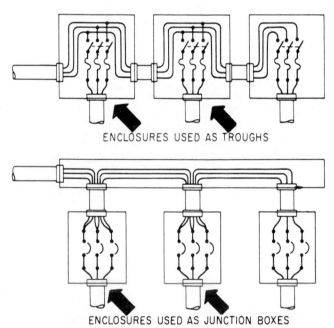

ENCLOSURES USED AS TROUGHS

ENCLOSURES USED AS JUNCTION BOXES

Fig. 373·8. These hookups are permitted where space in enclosure gutters satisfies Exception to basic rule. (Sec. 373-8.)

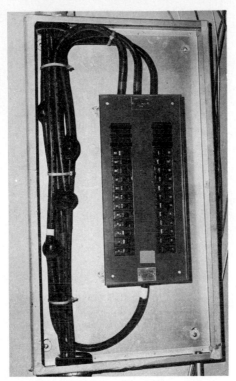

Fig. 373-9. The Exception to Sec. 373-8 permits feeding through and tapping off in cabinets for panelboards on feeder risers, where the side gutter is specially oversized for the application. (Sec. 373-8.)

splice. Most splices for larger conductors with split-bolt connectors or similar types are usually twice the size of the conductors being spliced. Accordingly, where larger conductors are to be spliced within enclosures, the total conductor fill should not exceed *20 percent* to allow for any bulky splice at a cross section.

Figure 373-9 shows an example of feeder taps made in panelboard side gutter where the cabinet is provided with adequate space for the large feeder conductors and for the bulk of the tap devices with their insulating tape wrap.

ARTICLE 374. AUXILIARY GUTTERS

374-1. Use. Auxiliary gutters are sheet-metal troughs in which conductors are laid in place after the gutter has been installed. Auxiliary gutters are used as parts of complete assemblies of apparatus such as switchboards, distribution centers, and control equipment, as shown in Fig. 374-1. But auxiliary gutters

Fig. 374-1. Typical applications of auxiliary gutters provide the necessary space to make taps, splices, and other conductor connections involved where a number of switches or CBs are fed by a feeder (top) or for multiple-circuit routing, as at top of a motor control center (right) shown with a ground bus in gutter (arrow). (Sec. 374-1.)

may not contain equipment even though it looks like surface metal raceway (Art. 352), which may contain devices and equipment (Fig. 374-2).

374-2. Extension Beyond Equipment. Auxiliary gutters are not intended to be a type of general raceway and are not permitted to extend more than 30 ft beyond the equipment which they supplement, except in elevator work. Where an extension beyond 30 ft is necessary, Art. 362 for wireways must be complied with. The label of Underwriters Laboratories Inc. on each length of trough bears the legend "Wireways or Auxiliary Gutters," which indicates that they may be identical troughs but are distinguished one from the other only by their use. See comments following Sec. 362-1 in this handbook.

374-5. Number of Conductors. The rules on permitted conductor fill for auxiliary gutters are basically the same as those for wireways. Refer to Sec. 362-5. Note that Exception No. 3 permits more than 30 general circuit wires; but where over 30 wires are installed, the correction factors specified in Note 8 to Tables 310-16 through 310-19 must be applied.

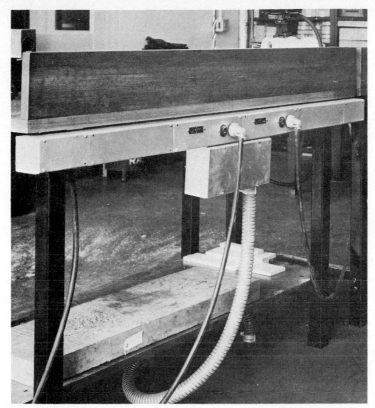

Fig. 374·2. Surface metal raceway may be used with accessory circuit breakers and/or receptacles in cover plates—but auxiliary gutters may not be used like this. (Sec. 374-1.)

No limit is placed on the size of conductors that may be installed in an auxiliary gutter.

The csa of rubber-covered and thermoplastic-covered conductors given in Table 5, Chap. 9, must be used in computing the size of gutters required to contain a given combination of such conductors.

Figure 374-3 shows a typical gutter application where the conductor fill must be calculated to determine the acceptable csa of the gutter. There are several factors involved in sizing auxiliary gutters that often lead to selecting the wrong size. The two main factors are how conductors enter the gutter and the contained conductors at any cross section. The minimum required width of a gutter is determined by the csa occupied by the conductors and splices and the space necessary for bending conductors entering or leaving the gutter. The total csa occupied by the conductors at any cross section of the gutter must not be greater than 20 percent of the gutter interior csa at that point (Sec. 374-5). The total csa occupied by the mass of conductors and splices at any cross section of the gutter must not be greater than 75 percent of the gutter interior csa at that point [Sec. 374-8(a)].

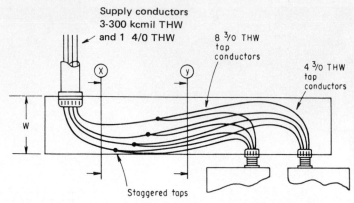

Supply conductors
3-300 kcmil THW
and 1 4/0 THW

8 3/0 THW
top
conductors

4 3/0 THW
top
conductors

W

Staggered taps

Fig. 374-3. Minimum acceptable gutter cross section and depth must be calculated. (Sec. 374-5.)

In the gutter installation shown, assume that the staggering of the splices has been done to minimize the area taken up at any cross section—to keep the mass of splices from all adding up at the same cross section. The greatest conductor concentration is therefore either at section x, where there are three 300 kcmil and one 4/0 THW conductors, or at section y, where there are eight 3/0 THW conductors. To determine at which of these two cross sections the fill is greater, apply the appropriate csa's of THW conductors as given in Table 5, Chap. 9:

1. The total conductor csa at section x is 3 × 0.5581 sq in. plus 1 × 0.3904, or 2.0647 sq in.
2. The total conductor csa at section y is 8 × 0.3288 sq in. or 2.6304 sq in.

Section y is, therefore, the determining consideration. Because that fill of 2.6304 sq in. can at most be 20 percent of the gutter csa, the total gutter area must be at least five times this conductor fill area, or 13.152 sq in.

Assuming the gutter has a square cross section (all sides of equal width) and the sides have an integral number of inches, the nearest square value would be 16 sq in., indicating a 4 by 4-in. gutter, and that would be suitable if the 300 kcmil conductors entered the end of the gutter instead of the top. But because those conductors are deflected entering and leaving the gutter, the first two columns of Table 373-6(a) must also be applied to determine whether the width of 4 in. affords sufficient space for bending the conductors. That consideration is required by Sec. 374-9(d). The worst condition (largest conductors) is where the supply conductors enter; therefore the 300 kcmil cable will determine the required space.

Table 373-6(a) shows that a circuit of one 300 kcmil per phase leg (or wire per terminal) requires a bending space at least 5 in. deep (in the direction of the entry of the 300 kcmil conductors), calling for a standard 6 by 6-in. gutter for this application.

In Fig. 374-3, if the 300 kcmil conductors entered at the left-hand end of the gutter instead of at the top, Sec. 374-9(d) would require Table 373-6(a) to be applied only to the deflection of the No. 3/0 conductors. The table shows, under one wire per terminal, a minimum depth of 4 in. is required. In that case, a 4 by 4 gutter would satisfy.

374-8. Splices and Taps. Part **(a)** is discussed above, under Sec. 374-5.

Part **(b)** covers cases where bare busbar conductors are used in gutters. The insulation might be cut by resting on the sharp edge of the bar or the bar might become hot enough to injure the insulation. When taps are made to bare conductors in a gutter, care should be taken so as to place and form the wires in such a manner that they will remain permanently separated from the bare bars.

Part **(c)** requires that identification be provided wherever it is not clearly evident what apparatus is supplied by the tap. Thus if a single set of tap conductors are carried through a short length of conduit from a gutter to a switch and the conduit is in plain view, the tap is fully identified and needs no special marking; but if two or more sets of taps are carried in a single conduit to two or more different pieces of apparatus, each tap should be identified by some marking such as a small tag secured to each wire.

ARTICLE 380. SWITCHES

380-1. Scope. Note that all the provisions of this article that cover switches *also* apply to circuit breakers, which are operated exactly as a switch whenever they are manually moved to the ON or OFF position.

380-2. Switch Connections. The rule of part **(a)** is shown in Fig. 380-1. Keeping both the supply and return conductors in the same raceway or cable minimizes inductive heating, as described under Sec. 300-20(a).

The rule of part **(b)** is illustrated in Fig. 380-2. The "ACCEPTABLE" three-pole switch satisfies Exception No. 1. Opening only the grounded wire of a 2-wire circuit would leave all devices that are connected to the circuit alive and at a voltage to ground equal to the voltage between wires on the mains. In case of an accidental ground on the grounded wire, the circuit would not be controlled by the single-pole switch.

In Fig. 380-3, the load consists of lamps connected between the neutral and the two outer wires and is not balanced. Opening the neutral while the other wires are connected would cause the voltages to become unbalanced and might burn out all lamps on the more lightly loaded side.

Except for Sec. 514-5, which requires a switch in a grounded neutral for a circuit to a pump at a gas station, the neutral does not need to be switched. But, where a grounded neutral or grounded phase leg is switched, it must never be by a single-pole switch or single-pole CB, even if the CBs are provided with handle ties.

A switch may be arranged to open the grounded conductor if the switch simultaneously opens all the other conductors of the circuit.

380-3. Enclosure. Figure 380-4 shows the basic rule of this section and Sec. 380-4. This rule also requires adequate wire bending space at terminals and in side gutters of switch enclosures. In this section and in other sections applying to wiring space around other types of equipment it is a mandatory **Code**

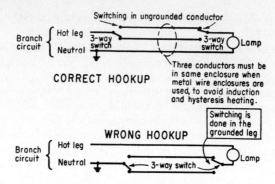

Switching in ungrounded conductor

Branch circuit { Hot leg / Neutral

3-way switch   3-way switch   Lamp

CORRECT HOOKUP

Three conductors must be in same enclosure when metal wire enclosures are used, to avoid induction and hysteresis heating.

Switching is done in the grounded leg

WRONG HOOKUP

Branch circuit { Hot leg / Neutral

3-way switch   Lamp

... AND THE RULE APPLIES FOR ANY LAYOUT OF SWITCH AND OUTLET BOXES

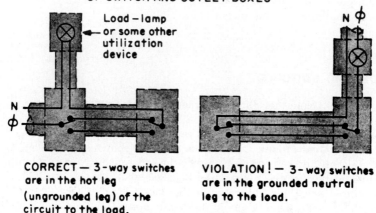

Load — lamp or some other utilization device

N ϕ

N ϕ

CORRECT — 3-way switches are in the hot leg (ungrounded leg) of the circuit to the load.

VIOLATION! — 3-way switches are in the grounded neutral leg to the load.

NOTE: Wiring between switches — in the armor of BX or in metal raceway — must have all three conductors within the single cable or raceway.

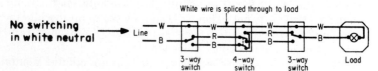

White wire is spliced through to load

No switching in white neutral

Line   W / B   W R B   W R B   W / B   Load

3-way switch   4-way switch   3-way switch

Fig. 380-1. All three-way and four-way switches must be placed in the hot conductor to the load. (Sec. 380-2.)

requirement that wire bending space and side gutter wiring space conform to the requirements of Table 373-6(a) for side gutters and to Table 373-6(b) for wire bending space at the line and load terminals, as described under Sec. 380-18. Those tables establish the minimum distance from wire terminals to enclosure surface or from the sides of equipment to enclosure side based on the size of conductors being used, as shown in Fig. 380-5.

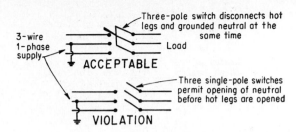

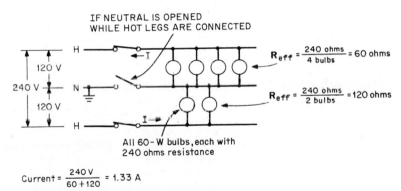

Fig. 380-2. A single-pole switch must not be used in a grounded circuit conductor. (Sec. 380-2.)

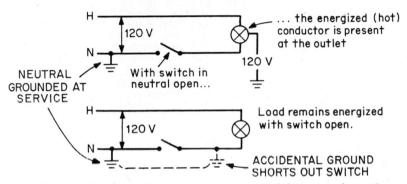

Fig. 380-3. A single-pole switch in neutral can cause damaging load unbalance if opened. (Sec. 380-2.)

This whole concern for adequate wiring space in all kinds of equipment enclosures reflects a repeated theme in many **Code** sections as well as in Art. 110 on general installation methods. One of the most commonly heard complaints from constructors and installers in the field concerns the inadequacy of wiring space at equipment terminals. Section 380-3 is designed to assure suffi-

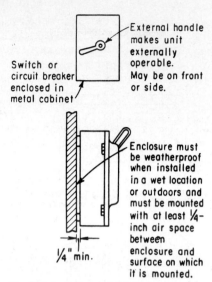

Switch or circuit breaker enclosed in metal cabinet

External handle makes unit externally operable. May be on front or side.

Enclosure must be weatherproof when installed in a wet location or outdoors and must be mounted with at least ¼-inch air space between enclosure and surface on which it is mounted.

¼" min.

Fig. 380·4. Switch and CB enclosures must be suitable. (Sec. 380-3.)

cient space for the necessary conductors run into and through switch enclosures.

380·4. Wet Locations.   Refer to Fig. 380-4 and discussion under Sec. 373-2.

380·5. Time Switches, Flashers, and Similar Devices.   Any automatic switching device should be enclosed in a metal box unless it is a part of a switchboard or control panel which is located as required for live-front switchboards. Such devices must not present exposed energized parts, except under very limited conditions where they are accessible only to qualified persons.

380·6. Position of Knife Switches.   The NE Code requires that knife switches be so mounted that gravity will tend to open them rather than close them (Fig. 380-6). But the Code recognizes use of an upside-down or reverse-mounted knife switch where provision is made on the switch to prevent gravity from actually closing the switch contacts. This permission is given in recognition of the much broader use of underground distribution, with the intent of providing a switch with its line terminals fed from the bottom and its load terminals connected at the top (Fig. 380-7). With such a configuration, an upside-down knife switch provides the necessary locations of such terminals, that is, "line" at bottom and "load" at top. However, use of any knife switch in the reverse or upside-down position is contingent upon the switch being approved for such use, which virtually means UL-listed for that application and also upon the switch being equipped with a locking device that will prevent gravity from closing the switch. The same type of operation is permitted for double-throw knife switches.

As required by part (c), knife-switch blades must be "dead" in the open position, except where a warning sign is used (Fig. 380-8). In a number of electrical system hookups—UPS systems, transformer secondary ties, and emergency generator layouts—electrical backfeed can be set up in such a way as to make

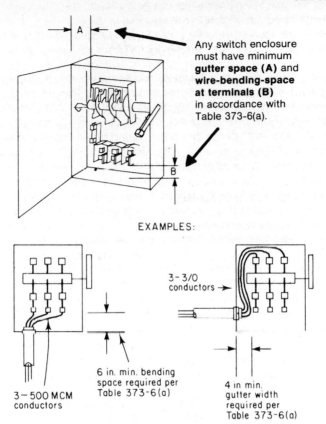

Any switch enclosure
must have minimum
gutter space (A) and
**wire-bending-space
at terminals (B)**
in accordance with
Table 373-6(a).

EXAMPLES:

3-3/0
conductors →

6 in. min. bending
space required per
Table 373-6(a)

3-500 MCM
conductors

4 in min.
gutter width
required per
Table 373-6(a)

Fig. 380·5. Terminating and gutter space in switch enclosures must
be measured. (Sec. 380-3.)

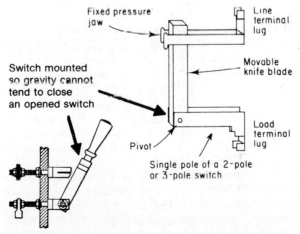

Fixed pressure
jaw

Line
terminal
lug

Switch mounted
so gravity cannot
tend to close
an opened switch

Movable
knife blade

Pivot

Load
terminal
lug

Single pole of a 2-pole
or 3-pole switch

Fig. 380·6. Movable knife blade of a knife switch must be piv-
oted at its bottom. (Sec. 380-6.)

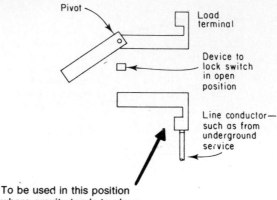

Pivot

Load
terminal

Device to
lock switch
in open
position

Line conductor—
such as from
underground
service

To be used in this position
where gravity tends to close
an open switch, the switch must:
1. Be approved for such use, and
2. Be equipped with a locking
device to hold switch open.

Fig. 380·7. This type of knife-switch operation is permitted.
(Sec. 380-6.)

the load terminals, blades, and fuses of a switch energized when the switch is in the OFF or open position. Where that might happen, the Exception to this section says a permanent sign must be prominently placed at or near the switch to warn of the danger. The sign must read, "Warning—load side of switch may be energized by backfeed."

This potential hazard has long been recognized for high-voltage systems (over 600 V), and Sec. 710-24(o)(2) covers the matter. This Exception to the basic rule that the load side of the switch be de-energized when the switch is open applies the same concept to systems operating up to 600 V.

380·7. Indicating. Switches and circuit breakers in individual enclosures must be marked to clearly show ON and OFF positions, and vertically operated switches and CBs must be ON when in the up position. This is basically a repetition of the rule that has been in Sec. 240-81 for circuit breakers used in switchboards and panelboards.

380·8. Accessibility and Grouping. The rule of part **(a)** of this section, along with the Exceptions, is shown in Fig. 380-9. Exception No. 1 cross-references with Sec. 364-12.

Part **(b)** of this section applies where 277-V switches, mounted in a common box (such as two- or three-ganged), control 277-V loads, with the voltage between exposed line terminals of *adjacent* switches in the common box being 480 V. If the adjacent switches have exposed live terminals, anyone changing one of the switches without disconnecting the circuit at the panel could contact 480 V, as shown in Fig. 380-10. The rule of this section requires permanent barriers between adjacent switches located in the same box where the voltage between such switches exceeds 300 V and terminals are exposed.

If screwless terminal switches (with no exposed live parts) are used, it would *not* be a violation if any number of such switches are ganged in a common box.

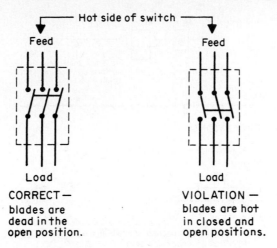

Fig. 380·8. Supply conductors must connect to "LINE" terminals of switch, but backfeed is permitted if carefully marked. (Sec. 380-6.)

Where screwless switches are mounted side by side in a two-gang box, it would seem to satisfy the intent (and literal text) of Sec. 380-8 because the switches would be "arranged" to prevent exposure to 480 V. Of course, the hookup shown would be acceptable if a separate single-gang box and plate are used for each switch, or a common wire from only one phase (A, B, or C) supplies all the three switches in the three-gang box.

380·9. Faceplates for Flush-Mounted Snap Switches. Figure 380-11 shows the basic rule of the first sentence of this section. Note that the recessed metal box is not grounded and that is acceptable because the box is not exposed to contact. Section 250-42 would apply to an exposed box. This rule conforms to the spirit of Sec. 410-18(a), which requires any metal faceplate (metal faceplates come under "exposed conductive parts of . . . equipment") to be grounded when it is

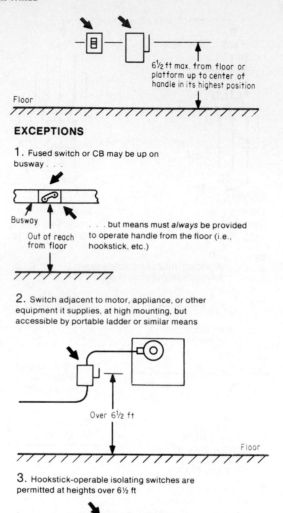

EXCEPTIONS

1. Fused switch or CB may be up on busway . . .

Busway

Out of reach from floor

. . . but means must *always* be provided to operate handle from the floor (i.e., hookstick, etc.)

2. Switch adjacent to motor, appliance, or other equipment it supplies, at high mounting, but accessible by portable ladder or similar means

Over 6½ ft

Floor

3. Hookstick-operable isolating switches are permitted at heights over 6½ ft

Fig. 380·9. All switches and circuit breakers used as switches must be capable of being operated by a person from a readily accessible place. (Sec. 380-8.)

attached to a box fed by a wiring system that contains an equipment grounding conductor. That is discussed also under Sec. 370-15(a).

The wording of this rule of Sec. 380-9 requires the nonmetallic faceplate on an ungrounded metal box only when the faceplate is "within reach of con-

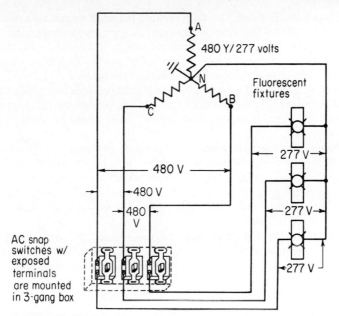

Fig. 380-10. This is a violation if barriers are not used between switches in the box. (Sec. 380-8.)

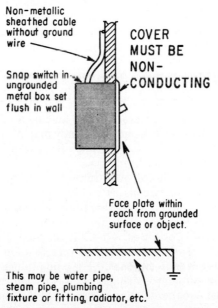

Fig. 380-11. Nonmetallic faceplate eliminates shock hazard. (Sec. 380-9.)

ducting floors," etc. But Sec. 410-18(b) is often taken as requiring a nonmetallic faceplate on every box that does not contain an equipment grounding "means" (metal raceway, metal cable armor, ground wire in NM cable)—whether or *not* it is "within reach of conducting" or grounded parts. Of course, ungrounded metal boxes are not generally encountered in new work.

The last sentence of this section requires that faceplates be installed to cover the wall opening completely to assure that the box behind the faceplate is properly covered and to prevent any openings that could afford penetration to energized parts.

380-10. Mounting of Snap Switches. The purpose of paragraph **(b)** is to prevent "loose switches" where openings around *recessed* boxes provide no means of seating the switch mounting yoke against the box "ears" properly. It also permits the maximum projection of switch handles through the installed switch plate. The cooperation of other crafts, such as dry-wall installers, will be required to satisfy this rule.

380-11. Circuit Breakers as Switches. Molded-case CBs are intended to be mounted on a vertical surface in an upright position or on their side. Use in any other position requires evaluation for such use. ON and OFF legends on CBs and switches are not intended to be mounted upside down.

380-12. Grounding of Enclosures. This section calls for the indicated equipment to be grounded in accordance with Art. 250. Sec. 250-42 requires *all* exposed metal parts (including enclosures) of fixed equipment to be grounded under any of the conditions described. And any switch or CB enclosure that is fed by metal raceway or metal-covered cable must be grounded. Additionally, provisions must be made when nonmetallic enclosures are used with metallic raceways and cables to assure grounding continuity between all interconnected raceways, cables, and any equipment within the enclosure.

380-13. Knife Switches. UL data on ratings and application correspond to the Code data. Specific UL rules are as follows:

1. Nonfusible switches are tested by UL up to 3,600 A, 500 hp, 600 V.
2. UL-listed enclosed switches are rated up to 3,600 A, 500 hp, 600 V.
3. Enclosed switches rated 800 or 1,200 A at more than 250 V are available in two classes. One is for general use and may be used as a disconnect up to its rating; the other is for isolating use only and must be so marked. Any enclosed switch rated over 1,200 A must be marked "For Isolating Use Only—Do Not Open Under Load."
4. Enclosed switches with horsepower ratings in addition to current ratings may be used for motor circuits as well as for general-purpose circuits. Enclosed switches with ampere-only ratings are intended for general use but may also be used for motor circuits (as controllers and/or disconnects) as permitted by **NE Code** Sec. 430-83 (Exception No. 1), Sec. 430-109 (Exceptions No. 2, 3, and 4), and Sec. 430-111. See Fig. 380-12.

380-14. Rating and Use of Snap Switches. For a noninductive load not including any tungsten-filament lamps, a snap switch is merely required to have an ampere rating at least equal to the ampere rating of the load it controls. Electrically heated appliances are about the only common examples of such loads.

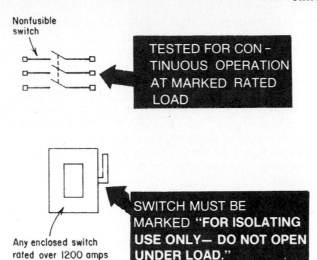

Nonfusible switch

TESTED FOR CON - TINUOUS OPERATION AT MARKED RATED LOAD

Any enclosed switch rated over 1200 amps

SWITCH MUST BE MARKED "FOR ISOLATING USE ONLY— DO NOT OPEN UNDER LOAD."

Fig. 380-12. UL data must be correlated to the Code rules. (Sec. 380-13.)

Fig. 380-13. Top wire-bending space contains off-set ("S") bends and must have dimensions from Table 373-6(b). Bottom wiring space has single ("L") bends—but must conform to Table 373-6(b), not Table 373-6(a). That varies from Section 373-6(b) (1), which permits terminal space from Table 373-6(a) when wires go out the side of the enclosure.

For the control of loads consisting of tungsten lamps alone, or tungsten lamps combined with any other noninductive load, snap switches should be "T" rated, or for alternating current circuits, a general-use AC snap switch should be used.

The term *snap switch* as used here and elsewhere in the **Code** is intended to include, in general, the common types of flush and surface-mounted switches used for the control of lighting equipment and small appliances and the switches used to control branch circuits on lighting panelboards. These switches are now usually of the tumbler or toggle type but can be the rotary-snap or pushbutton type. The term is not applied to CBs or to switches of the type that are commonly known as safety switches or *knife switches*. See definition of "switches" in Art. 100.

380·18. Wire Bending Space. At terminals of individually enclosed switches and circuit breakers, the spacing from lugs to the opposite wall *must* be at least equal to that of Table 373-6(b) for the given size and number of conductors per lug. The larger spacing of that table, rather than the smaller spacing of Table 373-6(a), must be used regardless of how conductors enter or leave the enclosure—on the sides or opposite terminals.

Fig. 380-13 shows the rule on wire bending space in switch or CB enclosures.

ARTICLE 384. SWITCHBOARDS AND PANELBOARDS

384·3. Support and Arrangement of Busbars and Conductors. Part **(a)** notes that only those conductors intended for termination in a vertical section of a switchboard may be run within that section, other than required inner connections and/or control wiring. This rule was intended to prevent repetition of the many cases on record of damage to switchboards having been caused by termination failures in one section being transmitted to other parts of the switchboard. In order to comply with this requirement, it will be necessary in some cases to provide auxiliary gutters. The basic concept behind the rule is that any load conductors originating at the load terminals of switches or breakers in a switchboard must be carried vertically, up or down, so that they leave the switchboard from that vertical section. Such conductors may not be carried horizontally to or through any other vertical section of the switchboard, except as indicated in the sketch at the top of Fig. 384-1. Because of field conditions, in which the installer did not know the location of protective devices in a switchboard at the time of conduit installations, the Exception modifies the requirement that conductors within a vertical section of a switchboard terminate in that section. Conductors may pass horizontally from one vertical section to another *provided* that the conductors are isolated from switchboard busbars by some kind of barrier.

The last sentence of part **(a)** requires that all service switchboards have a barrier installed within the switchboard to isolate the service busbars and the service terminals from the remainder of the switchboard as shown in Fig. 384-1. Because it is commonly impossible to kill the circuit feeding a service switch-

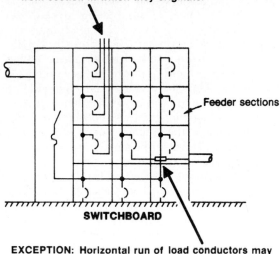

BASIC RULE: Load conductors must vertically exit from section in which they originate.

Feeder sections

SWITCHBOARD

EXCEPTION: Horizontal run of load conductors may be used if isolated from busbars by a barrier

All conductor terminals within a switchboard must be used only for connection to conductors that leave the switchboard vertically from the same switchboard section in which the terminals are located—with the conductors run out the top or out of the bottom of the switchboard.

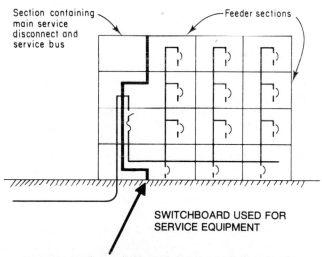

Section containing main service disconnect and service bus

Feeder sections

SWITCHBOARD USED FOR SERVICE EQUIPMENT

In every service switchboard, large or small, a barrier must isolate all feeder sections from the service busbars and terminals.

Fig. 384-1. These are basic rules on switchboard wiring. (Sec. 384-3.)

board, it has become very common practice for mechanics to work on switchboards with the service bus energized. The hazard associated with this has caused concern and is the reason for this addition to the **Code**.

Switchboard manufacturers in many parts of the country have been supplying switchboards with these barriers in place; this **Code** rule aims at making such protection for personnel a standard requirement. With a barrier of this type installed in a service switchboard mechanics working on feeder devices for other sections of the switchboard will not be exposed to accidental or surprise contact with the energized parts of the service equipment itself.

Part **(c)** requires a bonding jumper in a switchboard or panelboard used for service equipment to connect the grounded neutral or grounded phase leg to the equipment grounding conductor (the metal frame or enclosure of the equipment). UL data apply to this rule:

1. Switchboard sections or interiors are optionally intended for use either as a feeder distribution switchboard or as a service switchboard. For service use, a switchboard must be marked "Suitable for use as service equipment."

2. Some switchboard sections or interiors include neutral busbars factory-bonded to the switchboard enclosure. **Such switchboards are marked "Suitable *only* for use as service equipment" and may *not* be used as subdistribution switchboards (Fig. 384-2).** A bonded neutral bus in a service switchboard may also serve as an equipment grounding busbar.

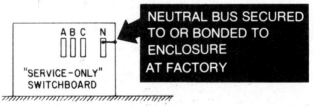

Fig. 384-2. Bonded neutral bus limits switchboard to service applications. (Sec. 384-3.)

3. UL-listed unit substations have the secondary neutral bonded to the enclosure and have provision on the neutral for connection of a grounding conductor, as shown in Fig. 384-3. A terminal is also provided on the enclosure near the line terminals for use with an equipment grounding conductor run from the enclosure of primary equipment feeding the unit sub to the enclosure of the unit sub. Connection of such an equipment grounding conductor provides proper bonding together of equipment enclosures where the primary feed to the unit sub is direct-buried underground or is run in nonmetallic conduit without a metal conduit connection in the primary feed.

4. Unless marked otherwise (with both the size and temperature rating of wire to be used), the termination provisions on switchboards are for 60°C wire from No. 14 to No. 1 and 75°C for No. 1/0 and larger wires.

The rule of part **(e)** is shown in Fig. 384-4 and correlated to the rule of part **(f)**. On a 3-phase, 4-wire delta-connected system (the so-called "red-leg" delta,

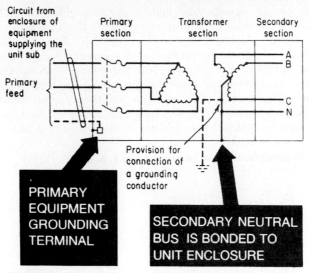

Fig. 384·3. Unit subs have bonded neutral in secondary switchboards. (Sec. 384-3.)

with the midpoint of one phase grounded), the phase busbar or conductor having the higher voltage to ground must be marked, and the higher leg to ground must be phase B, as required by part **(f)**. Without identification of the higher voltage leg, an installer connecting 120-V loads (lamps, motor starter coils,

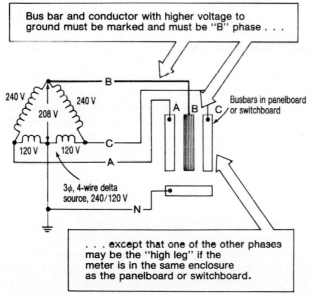

Fig. 384·4. Safety requires "high leg" identification on 4-wire delta systems. (Sec. 384-3.)

appliances) to the panelboard shown in the diagram might accidentally connect the loads from the high leg to neutral, exposing the loads to burnout with 208 V across such loads.

Part **(f)** requires a fixed arrangement (or phase sequence) of busbars in panels or switchboards. The installer must observe this sequence in hooking up such equipment and must therefore know the phase sequence (or rotation) of the feeder or service conductors. This new rule has the effect of requiring basic phase identification at the service entrance and consistent conformity to that identification and sequence throughout the whole system (Fig. 384-5).

Three-phase buses must be arranged as A, B, C . . .

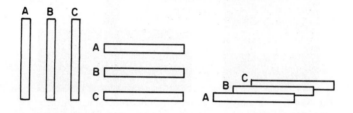

. . . as viewed from the front of the switchboard or panelboard

Fig. 384-5. Phase sequence in panelboards and switchboards must be fixed. (Sec. 384-3.)

Difficulty has been encountered with the rule of part **(f)**, requiring the high leg to be the B phase, because utility company rules may call for the high leg to be the C phase and the right-hand terminal in a meter socket—rather than the middle terminal. As shown in Fig. 384-6, the utility phase rotation can be converted to a **Code** phase rotation by applying the concept that phase rotation is relative, not absolute. If the utility C phase is designated as the NEC B phase, then the other phase legs are identified for NEC purposes as shown. The phase rotation C-A-B is the same as A-B-C, with voltage alternations such that wave B follows wave A by 120 degrees, wave C follows wave B by 120 degrees, wave A follows wave C by 120 degrees, etc. With the phase legs identified as at the bottom of the sketch, each is carried to the appropriately designated phase lug (A-B-C, left to right) at the panelboard shown in Fig. 384-4.

The Exception to part **(f)** will permit the high leg (the one with 208 V to ground) to be other than the "B" phase (such as the "C" phase) where the meter is within the same enclosure as the switchboard or panelboard and the phase configuration of the utility supply system requires other than the "B" phase for the high leg at the meter.

The concept behind this new Exception is to permit the same phase identification (such as "C" phase at 208 V) for the metering equipment and the busbars *within the switchboard or panelboard*. And it is the intent of the **Code** panel that the different service phase identification (such as "C" phase as the high leg) will apply to the entire switchboard or panelboard and that no transposition of phases "B" and "C" is needed within the switchboard or panel-

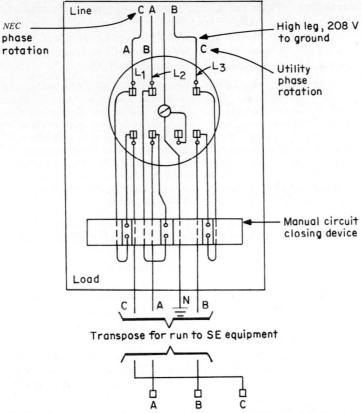

Fig. 384-6. Utility "C" phase becomes NEC "B" phase for high-leg identification. (Sec. 384-3.)

board. However, beyond the service switchboard or panelboard, the basic rule of Sec. 384-3(f) must be observed to have the "B" phase (the middle busbar) as the high (208-V) leg, requiring phase transposition on the load side of the service switchboard or panelboard.

Part **(g)** refers to the need for specific clearances in top and side gutters in both panelboards and switchboards and makes it mandatory that wire bending space at terminals and gutter spaces must afford the room required in Sec. 373-6. This is a repeated requirement throughout the **Code** and is aimed at assuring safe termination of conductors as well as adequate space in the side gutters of panelboards and switchboards for installing the line and load conductors in such equipment. This concern for adequate wire bending space and gutter space is particularly important because of the very large size cables and conductors so commonly used today in panelboards and switchboards. Sharp turns to provide connection to terminal lugs do present possible damage to the conductor and do create strain and twisting force on the terminals themselves. Both of those objections can be eliminated by providing adequate wiring space.

384-4. Installation.   Pipes, ducts, etc., must be kept out of the way of circuits from panelboards and switchboards. This rule is aimed at ensuring clean, unobstructed space for proper installation of switchboards and panelboards, along with the connecting wiring methods used with such equipment.

The argument for this **Code** rule is based on the following:

> Sections 450-47 and 710-9 are the only areas within **NE Code** prohibiting foreign piping (water pipes) in areas containing electrical equipment. With the advent of the large office and apartment-house complexes, it has become more economical to purchase primary voltage power, feed through the switchgear, step down to utilization voltage, and distribute throughout the complex. We have seen hospitals and building complexes wherein chilled-water pipes, steam pipes, cold-water pipes, sanitary cleanouts and other piping pass directly over the building's secondary or primary switchgear. In addition, some architects still utilize the electrical closets as a chase for other than electrical conduit. This rule will aid the inspection authority having jurisdiction in performing its function and assure a safer installation.

The wording of this rule and its four exceptions has created much confusion among electrical people as to its intent and correct application in everyday electrical work.

On first reading, there are certain observations about the rule that can be made clearly and without question:

1. Although the rule is aimed at eliminating the undesirable effects of water or other liquids running down onto electrical equipment and entering and contacting live parts—which should always be avoided both indoors and outdoors—the wording of the first sentence of Sec. 384-2 limits the requirement to equipment within the scope of Art. 384. Section 384-1 makes it clear that only "switchboards, panel-boards and distribution boards . . . for light and power . . . and battery-charging panels . . ." are subject to the rule. Individual switches and CBs, motor-control centers, and all other equipment are not subject to the rule—although the same concern for protection against liquid penetrations ought to be applied to all such other equipment.

2. The designated electrical equipment covered by the rule (switchboards, panelboards, etc.) does *not* have to be installed in "rooms dedicated exclusively to such equipment," although it may be. (See first FPN in this section.) As an alternative to "rooms," the rule of Sec. 384-2 finds it acceptable if the equipment is installed simply in "spaces" that are dedicated exclusively to the equipment.

The second sentence of this rule very clearly defines the "space" for electrical equipment to include any open space *above* the equipment. Dedicated clear working space around switchboards and panelboards must extend to the structural ceiling above the space *but is not* required to extend more than 25 ft from the floor in high-bay locations. This has the effect of permitting water piping, sanitary drain lines, and similar piping for liquids to be located above switchboards or panelboards *if* such piping is at least 25 ft above the floor. The permission for switchboards and panelboards to be installed below liquid piping over 25 ft above the floor must be carefully considered. The object is keep "foreign" piping (chilled-water pipes, steam pipes, cold-water pipes, and other piping) from passing "directly over" electrical equipment and thereby eliminate the problem of destructive arcing and violent burndown that can be caused by water leaking from the piping down onto the equipment (Fig. 384-7). FPN No. 3 clarifies the phrase "structural ceiling:" "For the purpose of this section

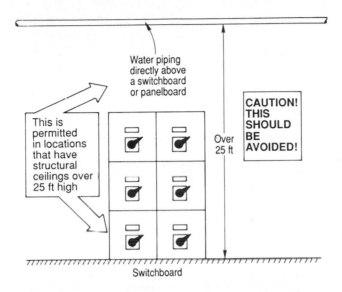

Fig. 384-7. Water pipes and other "foreign" piping must not be located less than 25 ft above switchboard. (Sec. 384-4.)

dropped, suspended, and similar ceilings not intended to add strength to the building structure are not structural ceilings."

Note Carefully: It is *not* a requirement of this rule that "foreign" piping, ducts, etc., must always be excluded from "electrical rooms." Because the rule can be satisfied completely by keeping the "foreign" piping, ducts, etc., out of the "space" dedicated to the equipment, the rule, literally, *permits* such "foreign" piping, ducts, etc., to be installed in electrical rooms, mechanical rooms, electrical closets, and similar enclosed spaces. The second sentence of Sec. 384-2 can be fully satisfied if the "foreign" piping, ducts, etc., are not "installed in" and do not "enter or pass through" the "space" that is "dedicated" to the equipment. It is all right for such piping to be in an electrical room as long as it is not in the "space" dedicated to the equipment—meaning the space taken up by the equipment, the space above the equipment (up to 25 ft) and, of course, the clean and unobstructed working space required around the equipment by NEC Sec. 110-16 (and even Sec. 110-34). (Fig. 384-7.)

From the wording of the argument for this **Code** rule, as quoted above, it seems clear that the object is to keep "foreign" piping (chilled-water pipes, steam pipes, cold-water pipes, and other piping) from passing "directly over" electrical equipment and thereby eliminate the problems caused by water leaking from the piping down onto the equipment.

Sprinkler piping, which is intended to provide fire suppression in the event of electrical ignition or arcing fault, would not be foreign to the electrical equipment and would not be objectionable to the **Code** rule. (See the second FPN at end of section.) Another confirmation of **Code** acceptance of sprinkler protection for electrical equipment (which means sprinkler piping within electrical equipment and even *directly over* electrical equipment) is very specifically verified by Sec. 450-47, which states, "Any pipe or duct system foreign to the electrical installation shall not enter or pass through a transformer vault. Piping or other facilities *provided for vault fire protection* or for transformer cooling shall not be considered foreign to the electrical installation."

It is certainly effective design practice to locate the sprinkler piping in overhead space so it is not directly over electrical equipment, thereby minimizing the chance of water leaking down into the equipment. Layouts of piping can be made to assure effective fire suppression by water from the sprinkler heads when needed, without exposing equipment to shorts and ground faults that can be caused by accidental water leaks from the piping.

Caution: Section 710-9 contains a similar rule on fire-suppression means at high-voltage switching and control assemblies.

The Exceptions to this section identify types of equipment which are not subject to the rules of this section.

384-5. Location of Switchboards. Live-front switchboards, as in Fig. 384-8, must always be applied with cautious regard for the conditions stated in this rule.

384-7. Location Relative to Easily Ignitible Material. A combustible floor under a switchboard must be protected against fire hazard, as noted in Fig. 384-9.

384-8. Clearances. Although it has long been a **Code** rule that a clearance of at least 3 ft be provided from the top of a switchboard to a nonfireproof ceiling

Fig. 384-8. A switchboard with "any" exposed live parts is limited to use in "permanently dry" locations, accessible only to qualified persons. (Sec. 384-5.)

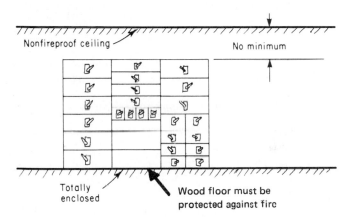

Fig. 384-9. No minimum top clearance is required to nonfireproof ceiling above enclosed switchboard. (Sec. 384-8.)

above, Exception No. 2 of part **(a)** excludes totally enclosed switchboards from this rule. The original rule requiring a 3-ft clearance was based on open-type switchboards and did not envision totally enclosed switchboards. The sheet-metal top of such switchboards provides sufficient protection against heat transfer to nonfireproof ceilings. As a result of this Exception, there now is no minimum clearance required above totally enclosed switchboards, as shown in Fig. 384-9.

As covered in part **(b)**, accessibility and working space are very necessary to avoid possible shock hazards and to provide easy access for maintenance, repair, operation, and housekeeping—as required by Sec. 110-16. It is preferable to increase the minimum space behind a switchboard where space will permit.

384·10. Clearance for Conductors Entering Bus Enclosures. Figure 384-10 shows the rules of this section which is aimed at eliminating high conduit stubups under equipment containing busbars to prevent contact or dangerous proximity between conduit stubups and the busbars. On this matter, UL says that "the acceptability of conduit stubs serving unit sections with respect to wiring space and spacing from live parts can be determined only by the local inspection authorities at the final installation."

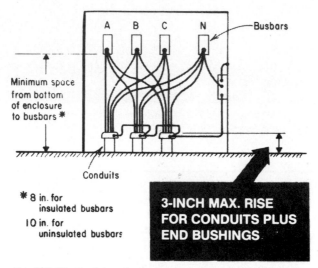

Fig. 384·10. Conduit stubups must have safe clearance from busbars. (Sec. 384-10.)

384·13. General. The first sentence here establishes the minimum acceptable rating of any panelboard.

All panelboards—lighting and power—are required by this section to have a rating (the ampere capacity of the busbars) not less than the **NE Code** minimum feeder conductor capacity for the entire load served by the panel. That is, the panel busbars must have a nameplate ampere rating at least equal to the required ampere capacity of the conductors which feed the panel (Fig. 384-11). A panel may have a busbar current rating greater than the current rating of its feeder but must never have a current rating lower than that required for its feeder. [Although Sec. 220-10(b) notes that a feeder for a continuous load must be rated at least 125 percent of the load current, it is not clear that the panel busbars would have to be rated for more than 100 percent of the load current.]

Although selection of a panelboard is based first on the number of circuits which it must serve, it must be assured that the busbars in a panelboard for any application have at least the **Code**-minimum circuits.

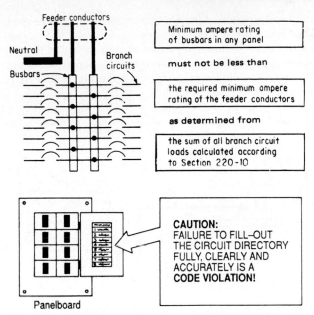

Feeder conductors

Neutral

Branch circuits

Busbars

Minimum ampere rating of busbars in any panel

must not be less than

the required minimum ampere rating of the feeder conductors

as determined from

the sum of all branch circuit loads calculated according to Section 220-10

CAUTION:
FAILURE TO FILL–OUT
THE CIRCUIT DIRECTORY
FULLY, CLEARLY AND
ACCURATELY IS A
CODE VIOLATION!

Panelboard

Fig. 384·11. Rating of panelboard bus must at least match required feeder ampacity and circuits must be identified. (Sec. 384-13.)

With respect to panelboards, marking may appear on the individual terminals, but terminals can often be changed in the field, and wiring space and the means of mounting the terminals may not be suitable. Therefore, panelboards should be marked independently of the marking on the terminals to identify the terminals and switch or CB units which may be used with aluminum wire. If all terminals are suitable for use with aluminum conductors as well as with copper conductors, the panelboard will be marked "use copper or aluminum wire." A panelboard marked "use copper wire only" indicates that wiring space or other factors make the panelboard unsuitable for any aluminum conductors.

The last sentence of this section specifically requires full and legible marking of a panelboard's *circuit directory* to show the loads and functions of each circuit originating in the panel. The FPN also refers to Sec. 110-22, where the general rule requires thorough identification of the loads fed by all circuit breakers and switches (Fig. 384-11).

384·14. Lighting and Appliance Branch·Circuit Panelboard. This definition is intended to describe the types of panelboards to which the requirements in Secs. 384-15 and 384-16(a) are applied.

Even though a panelboard may be used largely for other than lighting purposes, it is to be judged under the requirements for lighting and appliance branch-circuit panelboards if it conforms to the specific conditions stated in the definition.

Watch out for this definition! There are many panel makeups that supply no lighting and appear to be power panels or distribution panels, yet they are technically lighting and appliance panels in accordance with the above definition and must have protection for the busbars. Figure 384-12 shows an example of how it is determined whether a panelboard *is* or *is not* "a lighting and appliance branch-circuit panelboard." The determination is important because it indicates whether or not main protection is required for any particular panel, to satisfy Sec. 384-16.

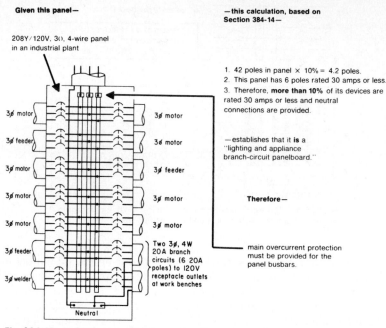

Fig. 384·12. Definition of a "lighting and appliance" panelboard hinges on a specific calculation. (Sec. 384-14.)

Figure 384-13 shows panels that do not need main protection because they are not lighting and appliance panels, which are the only types of panels required by Sec. 384-16 to have main protection. Just as it is strange to identify a panel that supplies no lighting as a lighting panel, as in Fig. 384-12, it is also strange that some panels that supply *only* lighting, as in Fig. 384-13, are technically *not* lighting panels. Because of the definition of Sec. 384-14, if the protective devices in a panel are *all* rated over 30 A **or** if there are *no* neutral connections provided in the panel, then the panel is not a lighting and appliance panel, and it does not require main overcurrent protection.

384·15. Number of Overcurrent Devices on One Panelboard. Figure 384-14 illustrates a panelboard with a 200-A main which provides for the insertion of class CTL overcurrent devices. The top stab receivers are of an F-slot configuration. Each F slot will receive only one breaker pole. The remainder of the slots are of an E configuration which will receive two breaker poles per slot. Thus there is provision for installing not more than 42 overcurrent devices,

Example: No neutral connections provided

Example: OC devices rated over 30 amps

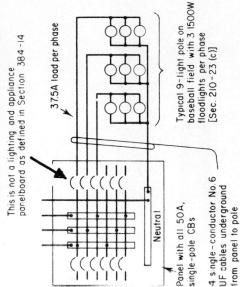

MAIN PROTECTION IS NOT REQUIRED

MAIN PROTECTION IS NOT REQUIRED
This is not a lighting and appliance
panelboard as defined in Section 384-14

37.5A load per phase

Typical 9-light pole on
baseball field with 3 1500W
floodlights per phase
[Sec. 210-23 (c)]

Neutral

Panel with all 50A,
single-pole CBs

4 single-conductor No. 6
UF cables underground
from panel to pole

Supply from ungrounded
480V, 3∅, 3-wire transformer
secondary (no neutral)

All circuits feed lighting:
ungrounded 3-wire circuits
to fluorescent or other
electric discharge lighting
with luminaires connected
phase-to-phase (no neutral
connections)

3-pole CB for each 3-wire circuit per
Section 240-20(b) rated not over 20A
for fluorescent fixtures, up to 50A for other
electric discharge lighting (Sections 210-23
and 210-21 (a)

NOTE: Fusible equipment is also permissible for such
applications.

Fig. 384-13. Some panels that supply only lighting are technically not "lighting and appliance panels." (Sec. 384-14.)

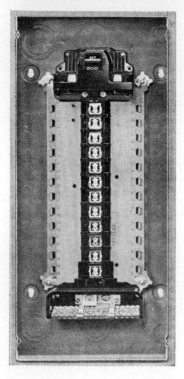

Fig. 384·14. Slots for push-in CB units have different configurations to limit the total number of poles to no more than 42. This is a CTL panelboard (or loadcenter). (Sec. 384-15.)

which does not include the main CB. This panelboard may also be supplied without main overcurrent protection where overcurrent protection is supplied elsewhere, such as at the supply end of the feeder to the panel.

Class CTL is the Underwriters Laboratories Inc. designation for the **Code** requirement for circuit limitation within a lighting and appliance branch-circuit panelboard. It means "circuit-limiting."

384·16. Overcurrent Protection.   Rules in this section of the **NE Code** concern the protection of "lighting and appliance branch-circuit panelboards." In general, lighting and appliance branch-circuit panels must be individually protected on the supply side by not more than two main CBs or two sets of fuses having a combined rating not greater than that of the panelboard, as shown in Fig. 384-15. Individual protection is not required when a lighting and appliance branch-circuit panelboard is connected to a feeder which has overcurrent protection not greater than that of the panelboard (Case 1 in Fig. 384-16), as noted in Exception No. 1.

Because of the wording of the definition in Sec. 384-14, it is vitally important to evaluate a panel carefully to determine if main protection is required.

Where a number of panels are tapped from a single feeder protected at a current rating higher than that of the busbars in any of the panels, the main protection may be installed as a separate device just ahead of the panel or as a device within the panel feeding the busbars (Case 2 and Case 3 in Fig. 384-16).

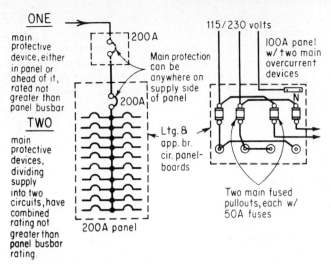

Fig. 384-15. "Main protection" may consist of one or two CBs or sets of fuses. (Sec. 384-16.)

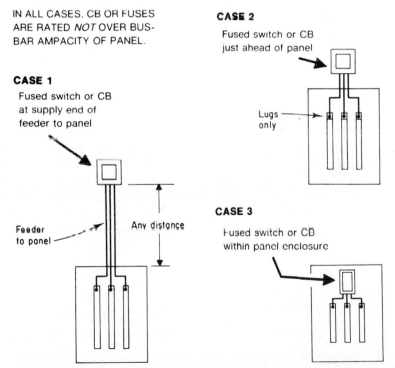

Fig. 384-16. Main panel protection may be located at any one of these locations. (Sec. 384-16.)

The main protection would normally be a CB or fused switch of the number of poles corresponding to the number of busbars in the panel.

Figure 384-17 shows other variations on the same protection requirements. As shown in the sketch with 400-A panels, it is often more economical to order the panels with busbar capacity higher than required for the load on the panels so the panel bus rating matches the feeder protection, thereby eliminating the need for panel main protection.

Although part **(a)** of this section does spell out those general requirements for main protection of lighting and appliance branch-circuit panelboards, Exception No. 2 of that section notes that a panelboard used as residential service equipment for an "existing" installation may have up to six main protective devices [as permitted by Sec. 230-90(a), Exception No. 3]. Such usage is limited to "individual residential occupancy"—such as a private house or an apartment in multifamily dwellings where the panel *is* truly service equipment and not a

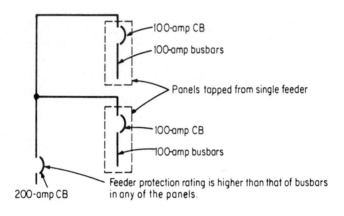

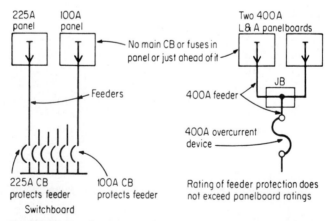

Fig. 384·17. Panel protection may be provided in a variety of ways. (Sec. 384-16.)

subpanel fed from service equipment in the basement or from a meter bank on the load side of a building's service.

But it must be noted that the phrase "for existing installations" makes it a violation to use a service panelboard (loadcenter) with more than two main service disconnect-and-protection devices for a residential occupancy in a new building. See Fig. 384-18. That applies to one-family houses and to "dwelling

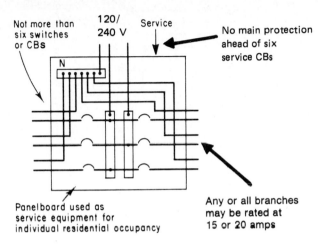

Fig. 384·18. Exception No. 2 eliminates need for main in residential service panel, *but only where* such a panel is installed as a replacement in an existing installation. (Sec. 384-16.)

units" in apartment houses, condominiums, and the like. Use of, say, a split-bus panelboard with four or six main protective devices (such as 2-pole CBs) in the busbar section that is fed by the service-entrance conductors is limited to use only for a service panel in "an individual residential occupancy" in an existing building, such as service modernization. See Fig. 384-19.

Exception No. 2 brings the rule on overcurrent protection for residential service panels into agreement with the basic rule of Sec. 384-16(a) as it applies to all lighting and appliance panelboards in new construction.

The rules of Sec. 384-16(a) have been altered in past editions of the **NE Code** as follows:

1. In the 1975 **NE Code**, Exception No. 2 of Sec. 384-16(a) permitted up to six main protective devices in a residential service panel for *either* new work or additions. But, the rule prohibited use of any 15- or 20-A CBs or fuses without main overcurrent protection ahead of them. Under that rule, a split-bus panel with up to six main CBs or sets of fuses could be used for a residential service, but any 15- or 20-A protective devices had to be

FOR NEW INSTALLATIONS . . .

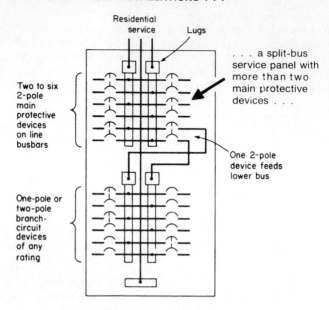

. . . IS A VIOLATION!

Fig. 384-19. Use of a split-bus loadcenter with more than two main overcurrent devices is permitted for residential service equipment *only* in "existing installations." (Sec. 384-16.)

installed in the panel bus section fed by the service-entrance conductors. The rule prohibiting 15- and 20-A protective devices without a main ahead of them ruled out use of small residential panels that had only six single- or 2-pole devices rated 15 or 20 A, with no main ahead. Such panels had been used for a long time for service to one-family houses that required only two small appliance circuits and a few lighting circuits where the dwelling unit had no electric water heating, space heating, or major appliances.

2. In the 1978 **NE Code**, Exception No. 2 was changed to permit use of 15- or 20-A protective devices without need for a main ahead of them, such as in the main busbar section of a split-bus panel or in small six-circuit panels for service in not-all-electric houses or apartments.

3. Now, in the present **NE Code**, for any new job, any panelboard—for service or otherwise, in any type of occupancy—may have no more than two main protective devices if the panel is a lighting and appliance panel (as determined from Sec. 384-14). Residential service panels do qualify as lighting and appliance panelboards.

Panelboards used for service equipment are required by **NE Code** Sec. 230-70 to be marked as "suitable for use as service equipment," and panelboards are so marked.

The rule of part **(b)** of this section is covered in Fig. 384-20. Any panel, a lighting panel or a power panel, which contains snap switches (and CBs are not snap switches) rated 30 A or less must have overcurrent protection and not in excess of 200 A. Panels which are not lighting and appliance panels and do not contain snap switches rated 30 A or less do not have to be equipped with main protection and may be tapped from any size of feeder. Figure 384-21 shows these two examples of overcurrent protection requirements for panelboards.

Fig. 384·20. Any panelboard containing snap switches rated 30 A or less must have main or feeder protection rated not over 200 A. (Sec. 384-16.)

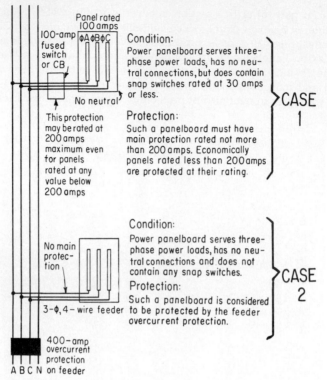

Fig. 384·21. Power panels have very limited requirements for protection. (Sec. 384-16.)

Part **(c)** applies to *any* overcurrent device in a panel and is a similar but stricter rule than those of Sec. 210-22 or Sec. 220-2, as shown in Fig. 384-22. The only exception to the rule is for overcurrent-device assemblies that are "approved" (which means UL listed) for continuous loading at 100 percent of their current rating. Refer to Sec. 220-10(b) on feeder protection.

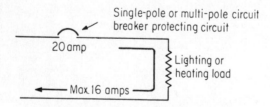

Total load on circuit must not exceed 80% of circuit rating when load is continuous (operates for 3 hours or more) – such as store lighting. CB must not be loaded over 80% of its rating.

Fig. 384·22. This applies for all fuses *and* breakers in a panelboard. (Sec. 384-16.)

Part **(d)** of this section applies to a panelboard fed from a transformer. The rule requires that overcurrent protection for such a panel, as required in **(a)** and **(b)** of the same section, must be located on the secondary side of the transformer. An exception is made for a panel fed by a 2-wire, single-phase transformer secondary. Such a panel may be protected by a primary device. This concept of prohibiting use of panel protection on the primary side of a transformer feeding the panel is consistent with the rules covered under Sec. 240-3 Exception No. 5. Refer to the discussion there.

Part **(e)** is a rule prohibiting the installation of any 3-phase disconnect or 3-phase overcurrent device in a single-phase panelboard. It is now required that any three-pole disconnect or 3-phase protective device supplied by the bus within a panelboard may be used only in a 3-phase panelboard. The effect of this new rule is to outlaw the so-called delta breaker, which was a special three-pole CB with terminal layouts designed to be used in a single-phase panel fed by a 3-phase, 4-wire, 120/240-V delta supply where the loads served by the panel were predominantly single-phase, but where a single 3-phase motor or 3-phase feeder was needed and could readily be supplied from this type of delta breaker. The delta CB plugged into the space of three single-pole breakers, with high leg of delta feeding directly through one pole of the common-trip assembly. Unit was used to protect motor branch circuit or feeder to 3-phase panel, rated up to 100 A.

Use of delta breakers has been found hazardous. When a delta breaker is used in a single-phase panel and the main disconnect for the single-phase panel is opened, there is still the high hot leg supplying the delta breaker. This has caused confusion to personnel who were surprised to find the energized conductor and were exposed to shock hazards.

As noted in part **(e)**, a plug-in circuit breaker that is connected for "backfeed" (with the plug-in stabs being the load-side of the CB) must be mechanically secured in its installed position. This rule requires all plug-in-type protective devices (CB or fusible) and/or main lug assemblies, in panelboards, to have some mechanical means that secure them in position, requiring more than just a pull to remove the devices. This is intended to eliminate the hazard of exposed, energized plug-in stabs of a device that is readily dislodged from its plug-in or connected position (Fig. 384-23).

384·17. Panelboards in Damp or Wet Locations.   UL data supplement the **Code** rules:

Enclosed panelboards marked "Raintight" will not permit entry of water when exposed to a beating rain. Enclosed panelboards marked "Rainproof" will not permit a beating rain to interfere with successful operation of the apparatus within the enclosure but may permit entry of water.

But note this carefully: **NE Code** Secs. 384-17 and 373-2 require that panelboard enclosures in *"damp or wet"* locations must be placed or equipped to *"prevent moisture or water from entering and accumulating within"* the enclosure, and there must be at least a ¼-in. air space between the enclosure and the wall or surface on which the enclosure is mounted. When they are installed exposed outdoors or in other wet locations, the **NE Code** requires that panelboard enclosures must be weatherproof. The **NE Code** definition of "weatherproof" is similar to the **NE Code** and UL definitions of "rainproof." Yet, **NE**

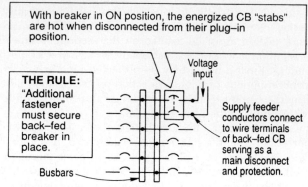

With breaker in ON position, the energized CB "stabs" are hot when disconnected from their plug–in position.

Voltage input

THE RULE:
"Additional fastener" must secure back–fed breaker in place.

Supply feeder conductors connect to wire terminals of back–fed CB serving as a main disconnect and protection.

Busbars

Fig. 384·23. This is an important safety rule for plug-in breakers. (Sec. 384.16.)

Code Sec. 373-2 requires exclusion of water entry—which clearly demands a "raintight" enclosure for outdoor, exposed panelboards (and not "rainproof"). These same considerations apply to other cabinets or enclosures used outdoors.

384·18. Enclosure. UL data cover these considerations:

1. Panelboards labeled as "Enclosed Panelboards" have been established as having adequate wiring space in the enclosure.

2. Unless a panelboard is marked otherwise, the wiring space in the assembly and the current-carrying capacity are based on use of 60°C wire in sizes No. 14 up to No. 1 or the use of 75°C wires for sizes No. 1/0 and larger. This limitation on use is covered in the general data of the UL Green Book. If wires of higher than 60°C or 75°C rating are used, such wires must be used at ampacities not greater than those given in **NE Code** Table 310-16 for wires rated 60°C or 75°C.

384·19. Relative Arrangement of Switches and Fuses. For service equipment, switches are permitted on either the supply side or the load side of the fuses. In all other cases if the panelboards are accessible to other than qualified persons, Sec. 240-40 requires that the switches shall be on the supply side so that when replacing fuses all danger of shock or short circuit can be eliminated by opening the switch.

384·20. Grounding of Panelboards. The effect of this rule is to *require* a panelboard to be equipped with a terminal bar for connecting all equipment grounding conductors run with the circuits connected in the panel. Such a bar must be one made by the manufacturer of the panel and must be installed in the panel in the position and in the manner specified by the panel manufacturer— to assure its compliance with UL rules, as well as the **NEC**. The terminal bar for connecting equipment grounding conductors may be an inherent part of a panelboard, or terminal bar kits may be obtained for simple installation in any panelboard. Home-made or improvised grounding terminal bars are contrary to the intent of this **Code** section.

The terminal bar that is provided for connection of equipment grounding conductors must be bonded to the cabinet *and* frame of a metal panelboard enclosure. If such a panel enclosure is nonmetallic, the equipment grounding

terminal bar must be connected to the equipment grounding conductor of the
feeder supplying the panel.

Equipment grounding conductors must not be connected to terminals of a
neutral bar—unless the neutral bar is identified for that purpose and is in a
panel where Art. 250 requires or permits bonding and grounding of the system
neutral (or grounded) conductor, such as at a service panel or a panel fed from
another building (Sec. 250-24).

Figure 384-24 shows some details of grounding at panelboards. There have
been many field problems relative to terminating grounding conductors in
panelboards where nonmetallic wiring methods have been involved. The rule

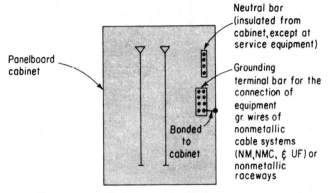

AN "APPROVED" GROUNDING BAR MUST BE USED

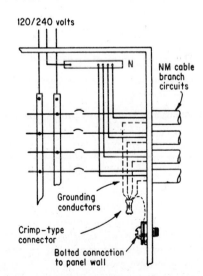

**VIOLATION ! Homemade techniques are not
acceptable.**

Fig. 384-24. Grounding in panelboards must use listed components.
(Sec. 384-20.)

here requires an "equipment grounding terminal bar" in such panels so that these grounding conductors can be properly terminated and bonded to the panel.

In other than service equipment, the grounding conductor terminal bar must not be connected to the neutral bar (that is, the neutral bar must not be bonded to the panel enclosure). Refer to Secs. 250-24, 250-50, 250-53, and 250-61. In a service panel, with the neutral bonded to the enclosure, equipment grounding conductors may, as noted above, be connected to the bonded neutral terminal bar (or block). But the neutral bar must *not* be used for equipment grounding conductors on the load side of the service, except that a bonded neutral block in a subpanel of an outbuilding that is fed from another building is an acceptable grounding terminal bar. Where a panel is used to supply loads in a building, with the panel fed from another building, the equipment ground bus in such a panel must be bonded to the grounded conductor (e.g., the neutral) of the feeder to the building, if the grounded conductor is grounded at the building by a grounding electrode conductor run to a grounding electrode (Fig. 384-25).

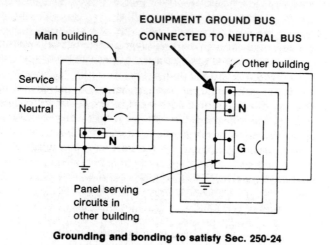

Grounding and bonding to satisfy Sec. 250-24

Fig. 384·25. A grounding terminal bar must be bonded to the neutral conductor in a subpanel, which is not "service equipment," when a grounding electrode is used at an out-building to ground the neutral in the subpanel, as may be required by the rule of Sec. 250-24.

The Exception to this section allows an isolated ground conductor run with the circuit conductors to pass through the panelboard without being connected to the panelboard grounding terminal bar, in order to provide for the reduction of electrical noise (electromagnetic interference) on the grounding circuit as provided for in Sec. 250-74 Exception No. 4.

In order to maintain the isolation of the grounding wire necessary for a low-noise ground, the grounding wire must be connected directly to the grounding terminal bar in the service-entrance equipment. To do this it may be necessary for the grounding wires to pass through one or more panelboards. Of course, such isolated grounding conductors may be spliced together by use of a terminal block installed in the panel but insulated from conductive contact with the metal enclosure of the panel. A "quiet ground" keeps grounding conductors apart from and independent of the metal raceways and enclosures (Fig. 384-26).

Fig. 384-26. "Quiet ground" terminal block for equipment grounding conductors provides for carrying isolated grounding conductors from circuits back to service bonded neutral, with single grounding conductor connecting terminal bar back to service. Terminal block is insulated from metal panel enclosure. Check with manufacturer to assure that isolated bar is approved. (Sec. 384-20.)

Sensitive electronic equipment utilized in hospitals, laboratories, and similar locations may malfunction because of electrical noise (electromagnetic interference) present in the electrical supply. This effect can be reduced by the proper use of an isolated grounding wire which connects directly to the service-entrance panel grounding terminal bar. Such systems are being used in increasing numbers where computers are in use.

384-35. Wire Bending Space in Panelboards. This section of the **Code** correlates wire bending space at terminals in panelboards to the basic concepts of Sec. 373-6(b), as follows:

- The basic rule requires the wire bending space at the top and bottom of a panel to satisfy the distances called for in Table 373-6(b), regardless of position of conduit entries. And the side wiring gutters may have a width in accordance with the lesser distances of Table 373-6(a), based on the largest conductor to be terminated in that space. Exceptions are:
  1. For a "lighting and appliance branch-circuit panelboard rated 225 amps or less," either the top or the bottom bending space may conform to Table 373-6(a)—but the other space at top or bottom (whichever is the terminal-lug space) must comply with Table 373-6(b).
  2. For any panelboard, either the top or bottom bending space may conform to Table 373-6(a), provided that at least one of the side wiring terminal

N = NARROW SPACE, TABLE 373-6(a)
W = WIDE SPACE, TABLE 373-6(b)

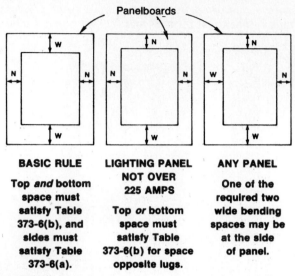

BASIC RULE	LIGHTING PANEL NOT OVER 225 AMPS	ANY PANEL
Top *and* bottom space must satisfy Table 373-6(b), and sides must satisfy Table 373-6(a).	Top *or* bottom space must satisfy Table 373-6(b) for space opposite lugs.	One of the required two wide bending spaces may be at the side of panel.

Fig. 384·27. This summarizes the requirements on wire-bending space at terminals where the feeder conductors supply a panelboard. (Sec. 384-35.)

spaces satisfies Table 373-6(b), based on the largest conductor terminated in that space.

3. Depth of the wire bending space at the top and bottom of a panel enclosure may be as given in Table 373-6(a) rather than Table 373-6(b)—which is a deeper space requirement; but this may be done only where the panel is designed and constructed for a 90° bend (an "L" bend) of the conductors in the panel space and the panelboard wiring diagram is marked to show and describe the acceptable conditions of hookup.

4. This permits minimum space [Table 373-6(a)] where no conductors are terminated, in either the top or bottom of a panelboard.

Figure 384-27 shows the basic rule and Exceptions No. 1 and No. 2. Of course, the rules of Sec. 373-6(b) must be fully satisfied in the choice of location for the wire bending space. And the size of the largest conductor determines the minimum required space for all applications of the tables.

Chapter Four

ARTICLE 400. FLEXIBLE CORDS AND CABLES

400-3. Suitability. This rule requires that any application of flexible cord or cable may require use of "hard usage" cord (such as SJ cord) or "extra hard usage" cord (such as S or SO cord) if the cord is used where it is exposed to abrasion or dragging or repetitive flexing and/or pulling, depending upon severity of use. As noted in Table 400-4, cords for portable heaters must be one of those types when used in damp places. Determination of the need for a particular cable on the basis of use severity is subjective. Table 400-4 also indicates the types of portable cable—that is, for data processing and elevator circuits—and conditions under which each type is suitable, as for hazardous or nonhazardous locations.

Other data on suitability are given in the UL Green Book, as follows:

Flexible cords are constructed as described in, and Listed for use in accordance with Article 400 of the National Electrical Code. All conductors are stranded copper.

Voltage rating:

Types XT and CXT (20-24 AWG) are rated 125 volts.

Types C (14-10 AWG), PD (14-10 AWG), S, SO, SOO, ST, STO and STOO are rated 600 volts.

Types CXT (18 AWG), C (18-16 AWG), PD (18-16 AWG), and all other types are rated 300 volts.

Conductor size:

The conductor size ranges are specified in the National Electrical Code with the following exceptions:

Types XT and CXT, 24-18 AWG; AFS, 18-10 AWG; SVOO and SVTOO, 18-17 AWG; SJOO and SJTOO, 18-10 AWG; SOO and STOO, 18-2 AWG; HSJOO, 18-12 AWG; HSOO, 14-12 AWG.

Temperature rating:

Types XT, CXT, C, PD, SP-1, -2, -3, SRD, E, EO, EN, ET, ETLB, ETP and ETT are rated 60 C.

Type SRDT is rated 60 or 90 C.

Types HPN and HPD are rated 90 C.

Types HS, HSO, HSJ and HSJO have a core temperature rating of 90 C and a jacket temperature rating of 60 C.

The impregnated asbestos insulation on Types AFC, AFPO, AFPD, AFSJ, and AFS has a temperature rating of 150 C. The cotton or rayon overall braid on Types AFPO and AFPD is rated 90 C. The rubber jacket on Types AFSJ and AFS is rated 75 C.

All other cord types are rated 60, 75, 90 or 105 C. Cords having a temperature rating higher than

60 C have the temperature rating printed on the outer surface of the cord; if the cord is rated 60 C, no temperature rating appears.

Additional Markings:

"Water Resistant" indicates the cord is suitable for immersion in water.

"For Mobile Home Use" or "For Recreational Vehicle Use," or "For Mobile Home and Recreational Vehicle Use," followed by current rating in amperes—indicates suitability for use in mobile homes or recreational vehicles.

"Outdoor" or "W-A"—indicates suitability for use outdoors.

"VW-1"—indicates the cord complies with a vertical flame test.

"−50 C"—indicates a cord which complies with a bend test (not a suppleness test) at −50 C.

Cords which have been evaluated for leakage currents between the circuit conductor and the grounding conductor and between the circuit conductor and the outer surface of the jacket may have the values so marked on the cable jacket.

Additional cord types not covered by the National Electrical Code:

Type XT—A twisted or braidless parallel assembly of two conductors intended for use in decorative lighting strings.

Type CXT—A twisted assembly, two conductors intended for use in decorative lighting strings.

Types SVOO (thermoset) and SVTOO (thermoplastic) are vacuum cleaner cords with oil resistant individual conductors as well as oil resistant jackets.

Types SJOO (thermoset) and SJTOO (thermoplastic) are junior hard service cords with oil resistant individual conductors as well as oil resistant jackets.

Types SOO (thermoset) and STOO (thermoplastic) are hard service cords with oil resistant individual conductors as well as oil resistant jackets.

Types HSJOO (hard usage) and HSOO (extra hard usage) are jacketed heater cords with oil resistant individual conductors as well as oil resistant jackets.

Shaver Cord—rated 125 volts, 27 and 20 AWG sizes, no type designation.

A Listing Mark in suitable footage denominations is attached to each coil or spool of flexible cord. The basic standard used to investigate products in this category is UL62, "Flexible Cord and Fixture Wire".

400·5. Ampacity of Flexible Cords and Cables. A three-conductor cord set is permitted by Sec. 250-60(a) to be used with *one* conductor serving as *both* the neutral conductor *and* the equipment grounding conductor, with the frame of the range or dryer grounded by connection to the neutral. The last sentence of this rule points out that the common neutral-grounding conductor does not count as a current-carrying conductor, thereby making the 3-wire cord suitable for use at the higher ampacity shown under column B (fourth from the left) in Table 400-5—which is for cord with not more than two wires.

400·7. Uses Permitted. Figure 400-1 shows accepted uses for flexible cord. Flexible cord may be used for lighting fixtures under **(a) (2).** Refer to Sec. 410-

Fig. 400·1. Permitted uses for flexible cable and cord include pendant pushbutton station for crane and hoist controls (left), and connection of portable lamps. (Sec. 400-7).

14 for limitations on use with electric-discharge lighting fixtures and Sec. 410-30(b) for fixtures that require aiming or adjusting after installation.

Part **(b)** states that *if* flexible cord is used to connect portable lamps or appliances, stationary equipment to facilitate frequent interchange, or fixed or stationary appliances to facilitate removal or disconnection for maintenance or repair, the cord "shall be equipped with an *attachment plug* and shall be energized from an approved *receptacle outlet*."

It should be noted that the cords referred to under this section are the cords attached to the appliance and not extension cords supplementing or extending the regular supply cords. The use of an extension cord would represent a conflict with the requirements of the **Code** in that it would serve as a substitute for a receptacle to be located near the appliance.

Extension cords are intended for temporary use with portable appliances, tools, and similar equipment which are not normally used at one specific location.

But bus-drop cable may be used to feed down to machines in factories. Such cable is UL-listed for that application in accordance with Sec. 400-7 (Fig. 400-2).

Fig. 400-2. Bus-drop power cables are flexible cables listed by UL for feeding power down from plug-in fusible switches on busway to supply machines. Cables here have connector bodies on their ends for machine cord caps to plug into. (Sec. 400-7.)

400-8. Uses Not Permitted.   Although Sec. 400-7 says that flexible cord may be used for "wiring of fixtures," that is a simple, general, broad recognition that may be used by any electrical inspector to accept almost any specific assembly of cord supply to a lighting fixture. It is the kind of rule that actually requires individual inspectors to spell out their own design and installation details. And it ties into the general rule of the second sentence in Sec. 90-4 which makes the inspector the final judge of Code compliance on all questions about NE Code rules.

But Sec. 400-8(1) says that flexible cord must *not* be used "as a substitute for fixed wiring." That rule could be strictly enforced to require all lighting fixtures to be supplied by fixed wiring methods—approved, Code-recognized cables like NM or BX or by a standard raceway method (EMT, rigid, flex, etc.). The rule does create a conflict with Sec. 400-7(a) by raising the question, Is there ever a case where a lighting fixture could *not* be fed by a fixed wiring method? Certainly, any fixture that might be supplied by a cord connection from a junction box to the fixture could just as easily be fed by conductors in flexible metal conduit or in liquidtight flexible metal conduit—both of which conduit-and-wire connections are considered "fixed wiring" methods. If there are no cases where a fixture could not be fed by such a fixed wiring connection, then every use of flexible cord to supply a fixture is "a substitute for fixed wiring." The relationship between Secs. 400-7(a) (2), 400-8(1), 410-14, and 410-30(b) must be carefully evaluated to assure ready compliance with Code rules—particularly since cord connection of lighting fixtures has been used so long and so successfully for both indoor and outdoor applications.

Whether any use of flexible cord is a violation of Sec. 400-8(1) must be related to the rule of Sec. 400-7. If a use of flexible cord does not conform to one of the permitted uses in Sec. 400-7, it becomes a violation of this section.

Figure 400-3 shows one of a number of twin floodlight units that were installed outdoors for lighting of the facade of a building. The use of cord from

Fig. 400-3. This use of flexible cord to supply an outdoor lampholder assembly can readily be described as a "substitute for fixed wiring"—which is a prohibited use of cord. Here, the lampholders could have been attached to one or more threaded openings on an outlet box. (Sec. 400-8).

a junction box to a stab-in-the-ground twin lampholder assembly does not comply with "(2) wiring of fixtures" in Sec. 400-7 because it does not satisfy Sec. 410-14 or Sec. 410-30(e), which regulate use of cord for fixtures, as noted under Sec. 400-7 above. And the application does not comply with the other permitted uses in Sec. 400-7. Because floodlights could have been installed in lampholders that thread into hubs on a weatherproof box, use of the cord is an evasion of a fixed or permanent connection technique that would totally avoid the potential shock hazard of cord pull-out or breakage. Mounting the floodlights on the box would still allow adjustment. This use of cord is a substitute for fixed wiring and is a violation.

Flexible cords and cables may not be installed in raceway, except where the NEC specifically recognizes such uses. Part **(6)** clarifies such use of flexible cords and cables, limiting their use in raceway to applications described or inferred in Sec. 400-7 and other **Code** rules—such as Sec. 550-5(g) for sleeving of a mobile home power-supply cord, Sec. 551-46(a)(2) on the same technique for recreational vehicles, Sec. 645-5(b)(3) for computer-room connecting cables, and Sec. 680-20(b) on the flexible cord run in conduit for a wet-niche lighting fixture, and similar limited applications.

The Exception to this rule permits a flexible cord to have connection to a building surface for a "tension take-up device," as shown in Fig. 400-5. That is an Exception to part **(4)** of Sec. 400-8. Connection of a tension take-up device to support the slack in a run of flexible cord is an exception to the rule prohibiting flexible cord and cable from being "attached to the building surfaces." This is a widely used technique for supporting horizontal lengths of cord that supply equipment that has some movement or travel. Travel from the cord to the tension take-up device is limited to a maximum of 6 ft.

400-10. Pull at Joints and Terminals.   Figure 400-4 shows methods of strain

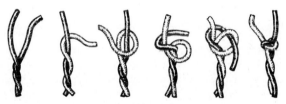

Underwriters' knot

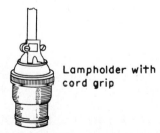

Lampholder with
cord grip

Fig. 400-4. Strain-relief must be provided at cord connections
to devices. (Sec. 400-10.)

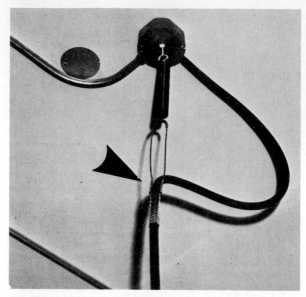

Fig. 400-5. Strain-relief for flexible cord must protect cable jacketing from damage at box connectors and protect wire terminations from pull-out. Spring-loaded come-along support supports cable against weight on bottom end of pendant and also provides up-and-down movement of cable end. (Sec. 400-10.)

relief for cords. The "Underwriters' knot" has been used for many years and is a good method for taking the strain from the socket terminals where lamp cord is used for the pendant, through the hole in the lampholder or switch device. For reinforced cords and junior hard-service cords, sockets with cord grips such as shown in Fig. 400-5 provide an effective means of relieving the terminals of all strain. Figure 400-5 shows a support technique that comes under "other approved means."

400-11. In Show Windows and Show Cases. On account of the flammable material nearly always present in show windows, great care should be taken to ensure that only approved types of cords are used and that they are maintained in good condition.

ARTICLE 402. FIXTURE WIRES

402-5. Ampacity of Fixture Wires. Note that Table 402-5 gives the ampacity for each size of fixture wire **regardless of the type of insulation used on the wire.** For instance, a No. 18 fixture wire is rated for 6 A whether it is Type TFN or PF or any other type.

402-7. Number of Conductors in Conduit. The maximum number of any size and type of fixture wire permitted in a given size of conduit is selected from a different table than the ones used for determining conduit fill for building wire (THW, THHN, etc.). This must be carefully observed, especially when using fixture wires for Class 1 remote-control, signaling, or power-limited circuits, as permitted and regulated by Sec. 725-16 and Sec. 725-17.

402-10. Uses Permitted.   Fixture wires may be used for internal wiring of lighting fixtures and other utilization devices. They may also be used for connecting lighting fixtures to the junction box of the branch circuit—such as by a flex whip to satisfy Sec. 410-67(c) (Fig. 402-1).

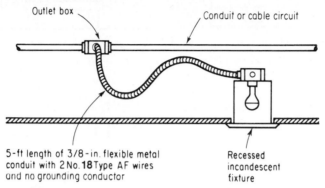

Outlet box

Conduit or cable circuit

5-ft length of 3/8-in. flexible metal conduit with 2 No. 18 Type AF wires and no grounding conductor

Recessed incandescent fixture

Fig. 402-1. Fixture wires may connect fixtures to branch-circuit wires. (Sec. 402-10.)

402-11. Uses Not Permitted.   With the exception of their use for remote-control, signaling, or power-limited circuits, fixture wires are not to be used as general-purpose branch-circuit wires. An example of the use permitted by Sec. 725-16 would be, say, No. 18 fixture wires run as remote-control wires in raceway from a motor starter to a remote push-button station, where the 6-A rating of the wire is adequate for the operating current of the coil in the starter.

402-12. Overcurrent Protection.   This rule refers to Sec. 240-4, which permits No. 18 and No. 16 fixture wire of any type to be protected by a 15- or 20-A fuse or CB. That covers use of No. 18 or No. 16 in fixture "whips" on 15- or 20-A branch circuits and use for remote-control, signaling, or power-limited circuits.

ARTICLE 410.   LIGHTING FIXTURES, LAMPHOLDERS, LAMPS, AND RECEPTACLES

410-4. Fixtures in Specific Locations.   Part (a) covers the kind of installations shown in Fig. 410-1. At left, the lighting fixture on the covered vehicle-loading dock is in a damp location and must be marked "SUITABLE FOR DAMP LOCATIONS" or marked "SUITABLE FOR WET LOCATIONS." At right, the lighting fixtures at a vehicle-washing area are in a wet location and must be marked "SUITABLE FOR WET LOCATIONS"—unless the fixtures are so high

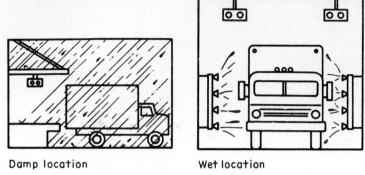

Damp location   Wet location

Fig. 410-1. Fixtures must be marked as suitable for their place of application. (Sec. 410-4.)

mounted or otherwise protected so that there is no chance of water being played on them.

An enclosed and gasketed fixture would fulfill the requirement that water shall be prevented from entering the fixture, though under some conditions water vapor might enter and a small amount of water might accumulate in the bottom of the globe.

Fixtures in the form of post lanterns, fixtures for use on service-station islands, and fixtures which are marked to indicate that they are intended for outdoor use have been investigated for outdoor installation.

An example of fixtures in "damp" locations would be those installed under canopies of stores in shopping centers where they would be protected against exposure to rain but would be subject to outside temperature variation and corresponding high humidity and condensation. Thus the internal parts of the fixture need to be of nonhygroscopic materials which will not absorb moisture and which will function under conditions of high humidity.

The UL listing of "Fixtures and Fittings" notes that—

> These fixtures are incandescent-lamp and electric discharge lamp types (including show-window and showcase type) designed for installation in ordinary locations. Unless marked "Suitable for damp locations" or "Suitable for wet locations," in combination with the Listing Mark, fixtures are only suitable for dry locations.

Part **(c)** recognizes use of lighting fixtures in commercial and industrial ducts and hoods for removing smoke or grease-laden vapors from ranges and other cooking devices. The rule spells out the conditions for using fixtures and their associated wiring in all types of nonresidential cooking hoods. The requirement that such a lighting fixture be "approved for the purpose" may be taken as "listed" by UL for such use.

Part **(d)** covers the use of chandeliers, swag lamps, and pendants over bathtubs, which could pose a potential hazard. Although there is no **Code** prohibition on use of fixtures over tubs and although a bathroom is not technically a damp or wet location, there is considerable concern over exposing persons in water to possible contact with energized parts. Where installed over a tub, a hanging fixture or pendant must be at least 8 ft above "the top of the tub." In addition, hanging fixtures must be excluded from a zone 3 ft horizontally and 8 ft vertically from the top of a bathtub rim. This defines the volume of space from which a chandelier-type lighting fixture is excluded above and around a bathtub. This excludes the entire fixture and its cord or chain suspension. Such application is difficult, if not impossible, in the vast majority of interiors.

410·5. Fixtures Near Combustible Material.   Figure 410-2 shows this rule. Much concern has been expressed by electrical inspectors because of instances where the fixture temperature has done damage to wires in outlet boxes and

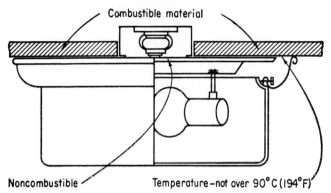

Combustible material

Noncombustible   Temperature –not over 90°C (194°F)

Fig. 410·2. Fixtures must not pose threat of heat to combustible materials. (Sec. 410-5.)

even to nonmetallic boxes themselves. Underwriters Laboratories tests and evaluates fixtures for such heating, with much useful data given in their *Electrical Construction Materials Directory.*

410·6. Fixtures Over Combustible Material.   This refers to pendants and fixed lighting equipment, not to portable lamps. Where the lamp cannot be located out of reach, the requirement can be met by equipping the lamp with a guard.

410·8. Fixtures in Clothes Closets.   The intent is to prevent lamps from coming in contact with cartons or boxes stored on shelves and clothing hung in the closet, which would, of course, constitute a fire hazard.

Use of lighting fixtures in clothes closets is covered by this section, with specific rules based on the given definition of "storage space" in a closet and the isometric drawing that illustrates the locations and dimensions of regulated space within the closet.

This section presents rules that can be divided into three catagories as follows:

1. Part **(a)** is a definition of storage space, and it fully identifies those spaces that must be taken to be storage space for purposes of positioning lighting fixtures, regardless of whether or not any of the space is eventually used for storage of clothes, hats, shoes, etc.
2. Parts **(b)** and **(c)** describe the kind of lighting fixtures that may be used and the kinds that are prohibited from use in closets.

3. Part **(d)** then tells how the various types of lighting fixtures have to be installed in relation to defined storage space.

The **Code** book diagram, Fig. 410-8, clearly shows the closet space from which the various lighting fixtures in **(d)** *must* be spaced. Note that the storage space above the level of the clothes-hanging rod must be as deep as the width of the board used for the shelf if the width of board is greater than 12 in. If the actual width of the shelf is less than 12 in, or even if there is no shelf, the defined space must be taken to be at least 12 in. deep on all sides of the closet and extending vertically from the level of the clothes-hanging rod up to the ceiling.

The 24-in. deep storage space that extends up from the floor must be consid-

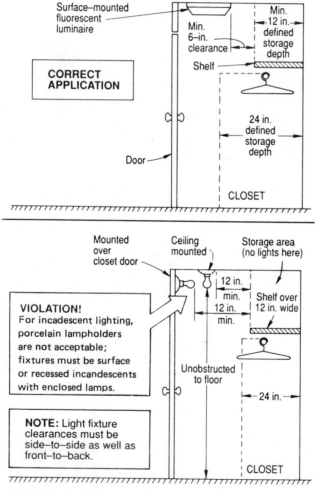

Fig. 410-3. These clearances apply to lighting fixtures in closets. (Sec. 410-8.)

ered to exist up to at least 6 ft above the closet floor or up to the level of the clothes-hanging rod if it is installed at a level over 6 ft above the floor.

Part **(b)** requires that any lighting fixture in a closet must be a UL-listed fixture. The fixture may be surface-mounted or recessed, incandescent or fluorescent. If the fixture is incandescent, the lamp must be "completely enclosed," but if the fixture is fluorescent, the lamp may be exposed or enclosed.

Part **(c)** prohibits use of any incandescent fixture that has a nonenclosed lamp. Pendant fixtures are also prohibited. And it should be especially noted that this rule prohibits use of surface-mounted lampholders—such as the widely used porcelain lampholder.

Part **(d)** notes that a surface-mounted lighting fixture may be mounted on the closet wall space above the closet doorway or on the closet ceiling. For surface-mounted fixtures, an incandescent fixture must have at least 12 in. of clearance from "the nearest point of a storage area" and a fluorescent fixture must have at least a 6-in. clearance from storage space.

Recessed fixtures may be mounted in the closet wall above the door or in the ceiling. Either an incandescent or fluorescent recessed type of fixture must have at least a 6-in. clearance from any storage space. Figure 410-3 shows the clearances for fixtures.

For small clothes closets proper lighting may be achieved by locating fixtures on the outside ceiling in front of the closet door—especially in hallways where such fixtures can serve a dual function. Flush recessed fixtures with a solid lens are considered outside of the closet because the lamp is recessed behind the wall or ceiling line.

410-9. Space for Cove Lighting.   Adequate space also improves ventilation, which is equally important for such equipment.

410-11. Temperature Limit of Conductors in Outlet Boxes.   Fixtures equipped with incandescent lamps may cause the temperature in the outlet boxes to become excessively high. The remedy is to use fixtures of improved design, or in some special cases to use circuit conductors having insulation that will withstand the high temperature.

The first sentence of this rule is related to the rule of Sec. 410-5. Figure 410-

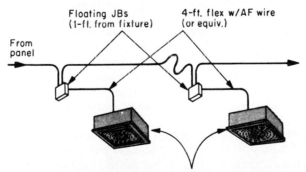

So-called "unwired" recessed incandescent fixtures

Fig. 410-4. Flex "whip" may be used to keep 60°C or 75°C wire away from 150°C terminal space in light fixtures. (Sec. 410-11.)

4 shows how a fixture may be "so installed" that the branch-circuit wires are not subjected to excessive temperature. That hookup relates to Sec. 410-67(c) for recessed fixtures, which requires a 4- to 6-ft length of flex with high-temperature wire (say, Type AF) to connect hot fixture junction point (150°C) to the lower-rated branch-circuit wires.

The second sentence of this section applies to "prewired" recessed incandescent fixtures, which have been designed to permit 60°C supply conductors to be run into an outlet box attached to the fixture. Such fixtures have been listed by UL on the basis of the heat contribution by the supply conductors at *not more* than the *maximum* permitted lamp load of the fixture. Some fixtures have been investigated and listed by UL for "feed-through" circuit wiring. Accordingly, this rule requires careful use of prewired fixtures and, where necesssary, the rule calls for use of fixtures which can be connected at the *start* of the circuit as well as the *end* of a circuit without the need of "throw-away" JBs that are required for "unwired" recessed incandescent fixtures.

For quite some time this problem has created considerable controversy in the field because many inspectors have been enforcing the "feed-through" concept on the basis of an Underwriters Laboratories Inc. ruling which states:

> With the exception of fluorescent-lamp fixtures, recessed fixtures are marked with the required minimum temperature rating of wiring supplying the fixture. Unless marked "Maximum of ____No. ____AWG branch-circuit conductors suitable for at least ____°C (____°F) permitted in junction box," no allowance has been made for any heat contributed by branch-circuit conductors which pass through, or supply and pass through, an outlet box or other splice compartment which is part of the fixture.

The effect of that UL limitation is this: Some prewired fixtures (with attached outlet box) are suitable only for connecting the 60°C branch-circuit wires to the fixture *and* any prewired fixture for feeding the branch circuit through its outlet box must be marked to allow such use—as shown in Figure 410-5. To use a branch circuit to feed a number of prewired fixtures that are listed for only one set of 60°C supply wires, those prewired fixtures must be connected with a flex whip from each to a separate junction box, just as if they were "unwired" fixtures as shown in Fig. 410-4. The top hookup in Fig. 410-5 may be rectified by using two 60°C wires run in a 4-ft flex length to a separate outlet box mounted at least 1 ft away from the fixture.

410-12. Outlet Boxes to Be Covered.   This rule is similar to that of Sec. 370-15. The canopy may serve as the box cover, but if the ceiling or wall finish is of combustible material, the canopy and box must form a complete enclosure. The chief purpose of this is to require that no open space be left between the canopy and the box edge if the finish is wood or fibrous or any similar material.

410-13. Covering of Combustible Material at Outlet Boxes.   See comments under Sec. 370-15.

410-14. Connection of Electric-Discharge Lighting Fixtures.   As Sec. 410-14 is worded, the rules presented apply to *both* indoor and outdoor applications of electric-discharge fixtures. The rules cover general lighting in commercial and industrial interiors as well as all kinds of outdoor floodlighting and area lighting. Part **(a)** of this section covers *only* connection of electric-discharge luminaires "where . . . supported independently of the outlet box." Chain-hung fix-

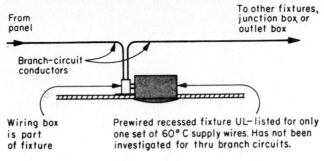

Branch-circuit conductors

From panel

To other fixtures, junction box, or outlet box

Wiring box is part of fixture

Prewired recessed fixture UL–listed for only one set of 60°C supply wires. Has not been investigated for thru branch circuits.

THIS HAS BEEN RULED A VIOLATION

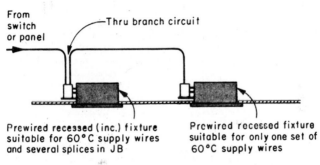

From switch or panel

Thru branch circuit

Prewired recessed (inc.) fixture suitable for 60°C supply wires and several splices in JB

Prewired recessed fixture suitable for only one set of 60°C supply wires

THIS IS O.K.

Fig. 410-5. Care must be exercised in hooking up "prewired" types of fixtures. (Sec. 410-11.)

tures, fixtures mounted on columns, poles, structures, or buildings, and any other fixture that is not "supported" by the outlet box that provides the branch-circuit conductors to feed the fixture are covered by part **(a)**. In the Exception to part **(a)**, cord-fed swag-type lighting fixtures with chain suspension from a ceiling hook independent of the outlet box are recognized.

The basic rule requires a fixed or permanent wiring method to be used for supply to all "electric-discharge lighting fixtures," which includes all fixtures containing mercury-vapor, fluorescent, metal-halide, high-pressure sodium, or low-pressure sodium lamps. BUT *incandescent* luminaires are *not* covered by Sec. 410-14. As a result, incandescent luminaires using cord connection are regulated only by Secs. 400-7(a) (2), 400-8(1), and 410-30(b).

410-15. Supports. Figure 410-6 shows a 7-lb fixture shade that is 17 in. in diameter and supported by the screw-shell of the lamp and holder, on both counts violating the rule of part **(a)**.

In part **(b)**, the rules cover use of metal poles for supporting lighting fixtures. A metal pole supporting a lighting fixture must have a readily accessible hand-hole (minimum 2 in. by 4 in.) to provide access to the wiring within the pole or its base. A grounding terminal for grounding the metal pole must be provided and be accessible through the handhole. Any metal raceway supplying the pole

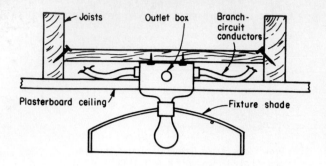

Fig. 410-6. Fixture shade assembly may be supported from a screw-shell lampholder if it is not too heavy or too big in diameter. (Sec. 410-15.)

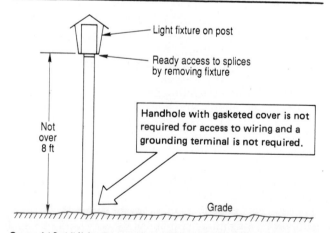

Sec. 410-15(b), **Exception. This type of fixture–on–post does not need an access handhole at base of pole.**

Fig. 410-7. Metal pole must provide access handhole and internal terminal for connecting grounding wire to metal of pole. (Sec. 410-15.)

from underground must be bonded to the pole with an equpiment grounding conductor. And conductors run up within metal poles used as raceway must have vertical supports as required by Sec. 300-19 (Fig. 410-7).

As noted in the Exception to part **(b)(2)**, a metal pole supporting a fixture does not have to have an access handhole at its base if the pole is not over 8 ft in height (such as a common post light) and the enclosed wiring is accessible at the fixture end. This Exception excludes the typical short (not over 8 ft high) post light from the need for a wiring access handhole at its base. That handhole is important for higher poles used on commercial and industrial properties and does add safety. But it is unnecessary for a post light, and this exception allows omission of the handhole where the wiring runs "without splice or pull point" to a fixture mounted on a metal pole not over 8 ft high and where splices of the fixture wires to the branch circuit supply conductors are accessible by removal of the fixture.

410-16. Means of Support.   A lighting fixture may be supported by attachment to an outlet box that is securely mounted in position (see Sec. 370-13), or a fixture may be rigidly and securely attached or fastened to the surface on which it is mounted or it may be supported by embedment in concrete or masonry. As shown in Fig. 410-8, heavy fixtures must have better support than the outlet box.

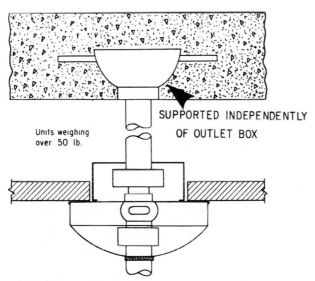

Fig. 410-8. Any fixture over 50 lb must be supported from the structure or some other means than the outlet box. (Sec. 410-16.)

Various techniques are used for mounting luminaires independently of the outlet box, depending somewhat on the total weight of the individual luminaires. In general, pipe or rods are usually used to attach the luminaires to the building structure, and the electrical circuit is made by using flex between the luminaire and the outlet box concealed in the ceiling cavity. If provision is made for lowering the luminaire, by means of winch or otherwise, provision must also be made for disconnecting the electrical circuit.

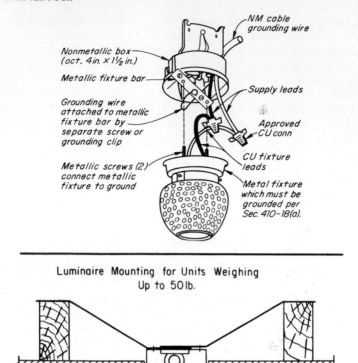

Nonmetallic box
(oct. 4 in. × 1½ in.)

Metallic fixture bar

Grounding wire
attached to metallic
fixture bar by
separate screw or
grounding clip

Metallic screws (2)
connect metallic
fixture to ground

NM cable
grounding wire

Supply leads

Approved
CU conn

CU fixture
leads

Metal fixture
which must be
grounded per
Sec. 410-18(a).

Luminaire Mounting for Units Weighing
Up to 50 lb.

BOX RIGIDLY SUPPORTED

Fig. 410-9. Fixtures must be supported by approved methods. (Sec. 410-16.)

The most common method of supporting fixtures is by means of fixture bars or straps bolted to the outlet boxes, as shown in Fig. 410-9. A fixture weighing over 50 lb can be supported on a hanger such as is shown for boxes under Sec. 370-6 for a tile-arch ceiling. Care should be taken to see that the pipe used in the construction of the hanger is of such size that the threads will have ample strength to support the weight.

Any luminaire may be attached to an outlet box where the box will provide adequate support, but, as noted in Sec. 410-15, units which weigh more than 6 lb, or exceed 16 in. in any dimension, "shall not be supported by the screw-shell of a lampholder."

A normal method of securing an outlet box in place is to use strap iron attached to back of outlet box and fastened to studs, lathing channels, steel beams, etc., nearby. Lightweight units are sometimes attached to outlet box by means of screws through luminaire canopy which thread into outlet box ears, or flanges, tapped for this purpose. For heavier luminaires, fixture studs, hickeys, tripods, or crowfeet are normally used.

Part **(c)** covers the support of fixtures installed in suspended ceilings. The **Code** rule wording was based on the following:

> *SUBSTANTIATION:* The Uniform Building Code requires that suspended ceilings be adequately supported. This is usually in the form of an iron wire support attached to the structural ceiling members and the other end of the wire attached to the suspended ceiling frame members. The lighting fixtures are then laid in the openings and secured only by light metal clips. There have been numerous accidents occur when these metal clips have been dislodged causing fixtures to fall to the floor. There have been several instances, where fixtures are installed in end-to-end rows, when one fixture becomes dislodged from construction vibration causing the entire row to also fall to the floor.
>
> There is also the danger of fixtures being shaken loose by seismic disturbances— Los Angeles, Oroville and Santa Rosa areas, to mention a few locations.
>
> Having these fixtures attached to the framing members also becomes a severe problem to firemen. When the ceiling area becomes involved in a fire or enough heat generated from the fire, the framing members distort and cause the fixtures to fall through the openings.

The last sentence of part **(c)** does clearly recognize support of fixtures by means of "clips" that are listed for use with a particular framing member and type of fixture.

Part **(h)** correlates to Sec. 225-26, which prohibits trees from being used to support conductor spans, by specifically permitting outdoor lighting fixtures and their boxes and support means to be mounted on trees.

410-18. Exposed Fixture Parts.   The wording of this section, in referring to "lighting fixtures and equipment," does not make clear that the rules also apply to faceplates used on snap switches, receptacles, and other devices used in outlet boxes. This section went through extensive revisions and even relocation with Art. 410 since the 1968 **NEC** when, as Sec. 410-95, it referred to "ungrounded metal lighting fixtures, lampholders and face plates." But the intent of the rules was not changed.

Part **(a)** says metal faceplates must be grounded if the box to which they are attached is fed by a wiring system with an equipment grounding means—metal raceway, metal cable armor, or a ground wire in NM cable. That applies to metal and nonmetallic boxes with a metal faceplate attached.

Part **(b)** says if the wiring system to the box does not contain a grounding means, any faceplate must be nonmetallic. That is a stricter rule than the similar rule in the first sentence of Sec. 380-9.

Other discussions on faceplates are given under Secs. 370-15 and 380-9. A note in Sec. 370-15 refers to Sec. 410-18 for faceplates.

Of course, the rules here also apply to lighting fixtures—of the metallic type in part **(a)** and nonmetallic fixtures as required by part **(b)**.

Relating Sec. 250-42(a) to the rule of Sec. 380-9, the effect is to require metal faceplates on switches and receptacles used in such places as kitchens or bathrooms to be grounded if they are within the specified distances of grounded surfaces. This rule requires covers of flush snap switches that are mounted in ungrounded metal boxes and located within reach of conducting floors or other conducting surfaces to be made of nonconducting, noncombustible material. But the way the rule now stands in Sec. 410-18, it simply requires metal faceplates to be grounded if the wiring method permits it.

When a metal faceplate used on a switch mounted in a nonmetallic box has to be grounded, a simple, effective way to do it is to use a switch that has a grounding terminal (a green hex-head screw) attached to the metal mounting yoke. When the grounding conductor in the cable is connected to that screw, the mounting yoke is grounded and so is the metal faceplate that is attached by screw to the mounting yoke.

410-20. Equipment Grounding Conductor Attachment. This rule requires lighting fixtures to have some terminal or other connection for an equipment grounding conductor when such fixtures have exposed metal parts and are supplied by NM cable or nonmetallic raceway, which must carry an equipment grounding conductor for grounding metal parts of the fixture (Fig. 410-10). For

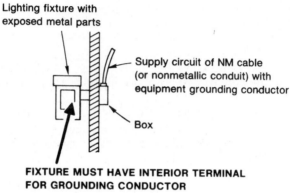

Fig. 410-10. Exposed metal parts of lighting fixtures must incorporate some suitable means for connecting the equipment grounding conductor of a nonmetallic-enclosed supply circuit. (Sec. 410-20.)

fixtures supplied by metal raceway, proper connection of the raceway to the metal of the fixture provides an equipment ground return path through the raceway, in accordance with Sec. 250-91(b).

410-23. Polarization of Fixtures. This method of wiring fixtures is required in order to ensure that the screw shells of sockets will be connected to the grounded circuit wire.

410-28. Protection of Conductors and Insulation. As noted in part **(e),** a lighting fixture fed by a conduit stem suspended from a threaded swivel-type conduit body must be supplied by stranded not solid wires run through the conduit stem—because the swivel fitting permits movement of the conductors.

410-29. Cord-Connected Showcases. Figure 410-11 shows an arrangement of cord-supplied illuminated showcases in a store. The details of this layout are lettered and involve the following rules:

a. The first showcase is supplied by flexible cord plugged into grounding-type receptacle rated 20 A. And that is permitted.

b. Flexible cord feeds second showcase; cord is spliced in JBs in each showcase. That is a clear violation of the requirement that in such connections, separable locking-type (twist-type) cord connectors must be used and spliced cord connections would be a violation.

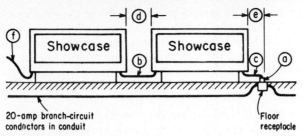

Fig. 410·11. Hookup of lighted showcases must satisfy a number of rules. (Sec. 410-29.)

c. Cord is No. 14 AWG, hard-service type. That is a violation because the cord conductors must be No. 12, the size of the branch-circuit conductors for the 20-A circuit, as required in part **(a)**.

d. Showcases are separated by 2 in. That is OK but is the maximum permitted separation, as noted in part **(c)**.

e. First case is 14 in. from supply receptacle. No good! The maximum permitted distance is 12 in.

f. Second showcase feeds spotlight. Violation! Part **(d)** says no other equipment may be connected to showcases.

410·30. Cord-Connected Lampholders and Fixtures.   Part **(b)** recognizes the use of fixed-cord connection for energy supply to lighting fixtures that require aiming or adjustment after installation (Fig. 410-12). Use of a cord supply to lighting fixtures has been a recurring controversial issue, although Sec. 400-7 has permitted cord supply to lighting fixtures for a long time. Sec. 410-30(c) has required that electric-discharge lighting fixtures, if suitable for supply by cord, must make use of plug-and-receptacle connection of the fixture to the supply

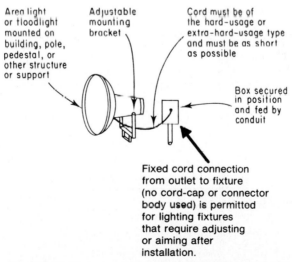

Fig. 410·12. Cord connection—either fixed cord or cord with plug cap—is permitted for adjustable fixtures. (Sec. 410-30.)

circuit. The rule here in part **(b)** permits floodlights—such as those used for outdoor and indoor areas for sporting events, for traffic control, or for area lighting—to have a fixed-cord connection from a bushed-hole cover of the branch-circuit outlet box to the wiring connection compartment in the lighting fixture itself. This rule gives adequate recognition to the type of cord connection that has long been used on floodlights, spotlights, and other fixtures used for area lighting applications.

It should be noted this rule in part **(b)** permits fixed-cord connection but does *not* prohibit use of plug connection to a receptacle or to a connector body. If plug connection is used, however, it might be required that the rules of part **(c)** be satisfied—requiring the receptacle to be mounted directly above the fixture.

In part **(c)** covering electric-discharge fixtures, the rule permits cord-equipped fixtures to be located *directly below* the supply outlet, provided that the cord is continuously visible throughout its entire length outside the fixture (i.e., sight unobstructed by lift-out ceiling panels, etc.) and that it is terminated in a grounding-type cap or busway plug. Except for those fixtures that are UL-listed for cord-and-plug connection as part of listed modular wiring systems for

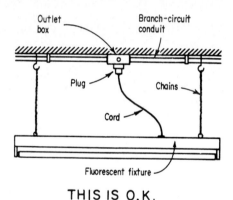

Fig. 410-13. Cord-and-plug fixture supply is O.K. only if cord is "continuously visible." (Sec. 410-30.)

use in suspended ceiling spaces, cord connection may not be used for fixtures installed in lift-out ceilings (Fig. 410-13).

The phrase "directly below the outlet box" has been ruled by inspectors to mean underneath the box and not just at a lower level. The phrase is intended to prevent cases where the fixture is connected by a cord that runs horizontally as well as vertically to an outlet box that is mounted higher than the fixture but off to the side so that the box is not directly above the fixture.

That rule raises a number of questions:

- If an electric-discharge fixture is not mounted "directly below the outlet box," is it a violation to use cord connection from the box to the fixture? The answer seems to be yes.
- Is it a violation any time an electric-discharge fixture is supplied by a flexible cord with fixed cable connectors at both ends of the cord? Yes, except as permitted in Sec. 410-30(b) for fixtures that require aiming or adjustment.
- If outdoor floodlights—mounted on the ground, or on a building, or pole, or crossarms, or standards, or towers—do not comply with the precise conditions of hookup presented in the first and second sentences of Sec. 410-30(c), is it clearly mandatory that a "fixed wiring method" (and not flexible cord) must be used? No, as covered in Sec. 410-30(b).

But, difficulty in interpretation does arise because connection of "electric-discharge lighting fixtures" is strictly regulated and connection of incandescent fixtures is virtually ignored.

The second paragraph of this section permits electric-discharge lighting with mogul-base screw-shell lampholders (such as mercury-vapor or metal-halide

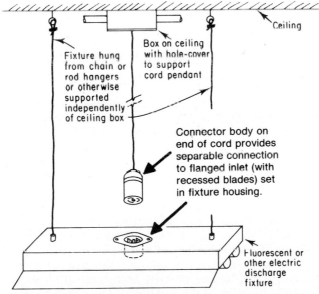

Fig. 410-14. This is the second method recognized for cord supply to lighting fixtures. (Sec. 410-30.)

units) to be supplied by branch circuits up to 50 A with the use of receptacles and caps of lesser ampere rating if such devices are rated not less than 125 percent of the fixture full-load current.

The paragraph at the end of part (c) rule expands coverage of the use of wiring methods suitable for supplying electric-discharge lighting fixtures. Though no longer specified here, such fixtures are permitted to be supplied from busways as described in Sec. 364-12. This paragraph provides for cord connection of a lighting fixture where the cord is equipped with a connector body at its lower end for insertion into a flanged inlet recessed in the lighting fixture housing (Fig. 410-14). This method of cord supply to electric-discharge lighting fixtures presents an alternative to the other method recognized in this section using a cord from the fixture with a plug cap on the other end of the cord for insertion into a receptacle mounted in a box directly above the fixture. The use of a connector body and flanged inlet supply affords greater ease in maintenance of the fixture, since maintenance people can disconnect the fixture at the lower end of the cord to remove it for cleaning or repair.

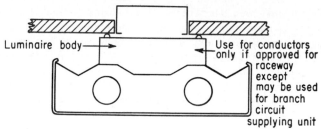

Fig. 410·15. Use of wiring through lighting fixtures is clearly limited. (Sec. 410-31.)

410·31. Fixtures as Raceways. This Code rule has long stated basically that fixtures shall not be used as a raceway for circuit conductors (Fig. 410-15). Exception Nos. 1 and 2 have permitted variations from that rule.

Exception No. 1 permits fixtures to be used for circuit conductors if the fixtures are approved for use as a raceway (i.e., UL-listed and marked for general use as a raceway for conductors other than the circuit supplying the fixture).

Exception No. 2 permits limited use of fixture wiring compartments to carry through the circuit that supplies the fixtures, provided that the fixtures are designed for end-to-end assembly to form a continuous raceway or the fixtures are connected together by recognized wiring methods (such as rigid conduit and EMT). Most self-contained fluorescent luminaire units now available are designed for end-to-end assembly. Each luminaire contains a metal body, or housing, which serves as the structural member of the luminaire and provides a housing for the ballast, wiring, etc., which is of sufficient size to permit running the branch-circuit wiring through the unit. Each luminaire is then tied to the branch circuit by means of a single tap. When a fixture is specifically approved as a raceway, any number of branch-circuit conductors may be installed within the capacity of the raceway. When housings are approved as raceways, luminaires carry an Underwriters Laboratories label which states

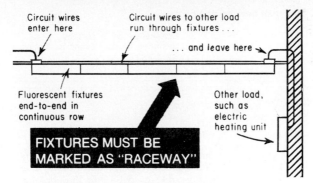

Circuit wires
enter here

Circuit wires to other load
run through fixtures . . .

. . . and leave here ↘

Fluorescent fixtures
end-to-end in
continuous row

Other load,
such as
electric
heating unit

**FIXTURES MUST BE
MARKED AS "RACEWAY"**

Fig. 410·16. Only fixtures approved as "Raceway" may be used for carrying-through circuit wires that supply any load other than the fixtures. (Sec. 410-31.)

"Fixtures Suitable for Use as Raceway." Any type of circuit may be run through the fixture (Fig. 410-16).

It should be noted that in Exception No. 2, the permitted fixture layouts may carry only conductors of either a 2-wire or a multiwire branch circuit where the wires of the branch circuit supply only the lighting fixtures through which the circuit conductors are run. Thus, it is permissible to use a 3-phase, 4-wire branch circuit through fixtures so connected, with the total number of fixtures connected from all the phase legs to the neutral, that is, with the fixture load divided among the three phase legs. But Exception No. 2 limits such use to a single 2-wire or multiwire branch circuit.

Exception No. 3 permits one additional 2-wire branch circuit to be run through such fixtures (connected end-to-end or connected by recognized wiring methods) in addition to the 2-wire or multiwire branch circuit recognized by Exception No. 2, and this additional 2-wire branch circuit may be used only to supply one or more of the connected fixtures throughout the total fixture run supplied by the other branch circuit run through the raceway (Fig. 410-17). This was added to permit separate control of some of the fixtures fed by the additional branch circuit, providing the opportunity to turn off some of the fixtures for energy conservation during the night or other times when they are not needed.

It should be noted that UL rules tie into the above **Code** rules: Fixtures that are suitable for use as raceway—i.e., for carrying circuit wires other than the wires supplying the fixtures—must be so marked and must show the number, size, and type of conductors permitted. **NE Code** Sec. 410-31 correlates with this UL rule.

The last sentence of this section regulates use of wires run through or within fixtures where the wire would be exposed to possible contact with the ballast which has a hot-spot surface temperature of 90°C. Thus, such wires must be rated at least 90°C—which is the temperature at which the wire will operate when carrying its rated current in an ambient not over 30°C (which is 86°F). Note that Type THW wire is permitted for this use in fixtures. Although Type

This may now be done:

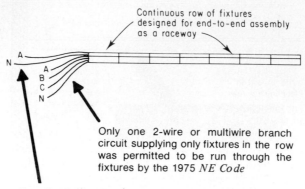

Continuous row of fixtures
designed for end-to-end assembly
as a raceway

Only one 2-wire or multiwire branch
circuit supplying only fixtures in the row
was permitted to be run through the
fixtures by the 1975 *NE Code*

Now the *Code* rule accepts one more circuit—only a **2-wire** circuit—run through the row. But this additional circuit **must** supply one or more of the fixtures in the row, such as night lighting by, say, every fifth fixture, to enable the others to be turned off for energy conservation.

And the same permission applies in this case—

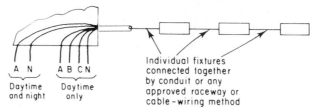

A N   A B C N   Individual fixtures
                         connected together
Daytime   Daytime   by conduit or any
and night only   approved raceway or
                         cable-wiring method

Fig. 410-17. Expanded use of fixtures as raceways provides better control for conservation. (Sec. 410-31.)

THW is listed as a basic 75°C wire in Table 310-13, the table does show it as a 90°C rated wire for use in fixtures in accordance with Sec. 410-31.

The question often arises, May Type AF (150°C) fixture wire be used for circuiting through end-to-end connected continuous-row fluorescent fixtures? Sec. 402-10 permits "fixture wires" to be installed "in lighting fixtures" where they will not be subject to bending or flexing in normal use. That would seem to approve Type AF through the fixtures connected in a row. But, Sec. 402-11 prohibits fixture wires used as branch-circuit conductors. The conductors installed in the fixture "ballast compartment" are referred to as "branch-circuit conductors" in Sec. 410-31, because they feed directly from the branch circuit and are tapped at each fixture to feed each fixture. The branch circuit extends from the point where it is protected by a CB or fuse to the last point where it feeds to the final outlet, device, apparatus, equipment, fixtures, etc. Under these conditions, it seems clear that the wiring must be that approved for

branch circuits. Type AF and any other fixture wires are not approved for
branch-circuit wiring.

To satisfy the last paragraph of Sec. 410-31, conductors such as Type RHH or
Type THHN or Type THW must be installed. Type AF is definitely not permitted to be installed as branch-circuit conductors. But check with the local
inspector if there are any doubts.

410·35. Fixture Rating.   This section specifically requires that any fixture be
suitably marked to indicate the need for supply wires rated higher than 90°C
to withstand the heat generated in the fixture. Such marking must be prominently made on the fixture itself and also on the shipping carton in which the
fixture is enclosed (Fig. 410-18). And UL rules note: Fixtures marked for use in
commercial or industrial occupancies must *not* be used in residential occupancies, because the fixtures have maintenance features beyond the capabilities of
ordinary householders or involve voltages higher than that permitted by the **NE
Code** for residences.

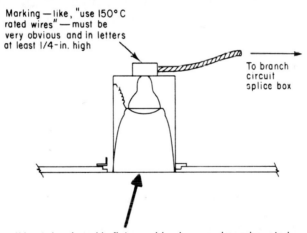

Marking — like, "use 150° C
rated wires" — must be
very obvious and in letters
at least 1/4-in. high

To branch
circuit
splice box

If heat developed in fixture wiring box requires wire rated
over 90C — the required temperature rating of supply
wire must be marked in the fixture and on shipping
carton.

Fig. 410·18. Where high-temperature wire is needed, fixture must
be marked. (Sec. 410-35.)

410·42. Portable Lamps.   Part **(a)** requires portable lamps (table lamps and
floor lamps) to be wired with flexible cord approved for the purpose and to be
equipped with polarized or grounding type attachment plugs. Two-prong non-
polarized attachment plugs are no longer permitted. Polarized type plug caps
permit a single orientation of the plug for insertion in the receptacle outlet.
Such polarizing of the plug will provide for connecting the grounded conductor
of the circuit to the screw shell of the lampholder in the lamp.

In part **(b)**, four specific rules are given on the use of portable handlamps, as
shown in Fig. 410-19. The requirements of part **(a)** calling for polarized or

Portable lamps

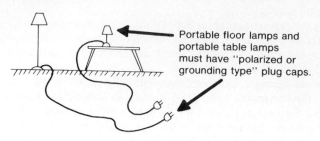

Portable floor lamps and portable table lamps must have "polarized or grounding type" plug caps.

Portable hand lamps

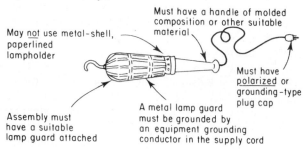

May not use metal-shell, paperlined lampholder

Must have a handle of molded composition or other suitable material

Must have polarized or grounding-type plug cap

Assembly must have a suitable lamp guard attached

A metal lamp guard must be grounded by an equipment grounding conductor in the supply cord

Fig. 410-19. NEC rules aim at greater safety in use of portable lamps and portable handlamps. (Sec. 410-42.)

grounding type attachment plugs also are made applicable to portable handlamps.

410-47. Screw-Shell Type.   This warns against the previously common practice of installing screw-shell lampholders with screw-plug adapters in baseboards and walls for the connecting of cord-connected appliances and lighting equipment and thereby exposing live parts to contact by persons when the adapters were moved from place to place. See Sec. 410-56(a).

410-48. Double-Pole Switched Lampholders.   On a circuit having one wire grounded, the grounded wire must always be connected to the screw shell of the socket, and sockets having a single-pole switching mechanism may be used. (See Sec. 410-52.) On a 2-wire circuit tapped from the outside (ungrounded) wires of a 3-wire or 4-wire system, if sockets having switching mechanisms are used, these must be double-pole so that they will disconnect both of the ungrounded wires.

410-54. Electric-Discharge Lamp Auxiliary Equipment.   Part **(b)** requires that a switch controlling the supply to electric-discharge-lamp auxiliary equipment must simultaneously disconnect both hot conductors of a 2-wire ungrounded circuit. This is required to prevent an energized screw shell where only one circuit wire is disconnected—which would be a hazard during relamping.

410-56. Rating and Type.   Part **(b)** requires that receptacles rated 20 A or less for direct aluminum connections be CO/ALR type. Part **(d)** is intended to prevent short circuits when attachment plugs (caps) are inserted in receptacles mounted with metal faceplates—in which case, the metal of the plate could short (or bridge) the blades of the plug cap if the faceplate is not set back from the receptacle face. The rule requires the "faces" of receptacles to project at least 0.015 in. through the faceplate opening when the faceplate is metallic. And it is necessary to assure a solid backing for receptacles so that attachment plugs can be inserted without difficulty. The requirement for receptacle faces to project at least 0.015 in. from installed metal faceplates will also prevent faults caused by countless existing attachment plugs with exposed bare terminal screws. The design requirements for attachment plugs and connectors in part **(e)** should prevent such faults at metal plates, but the problem of existing attachment plugs in this regard will be around for many years.

With receptacle faces and faceplates installed according to Sec. 410-56**(d)**, attachment plugs can be fully inserted into receptacles and will provide a better contact. The cooperation of other crafts, such as plasterers or dry-wall applicators, will be needed to satisfy the requirements.

As required by part **(e)**, receptacles must be securely mounted in recessed boxes and must assure effective ground continuity. The last two sentences in this section require a receptacle to be tightly screwed to the box in which it is mounted—whether the box is set back from the finished wall surface (not over ¼ in.), is flush with the surface, or projects from the wall surface. This rule is the same as the existing rule in Sec. 380-10(b), which covers snap switches in recessed boxes.

410-57. Receptacles in Damp or Wet Locations.   The definition of "location" in Art. 100 describes places that fall into either the "wet" or "damp" category. Any receptacle used in a damp location—such as an open or screened-in porch with a roof or overhang above it—may not be equipped with a conventional receptacle cover plate. It must be provided with a cover that, although not UL-listed as "weatherproof," will make the receptacle(s) weatherproof when the cover or covers are in place. The type of cover plate that has a thread-on metal cap held captive by a short metal chain would be acceptable for damp locations but not wet locations (Fig. 410-20). And any other plate-and-cover assembly that is not listed as weatherproof and does not satisfy the conditions of part **(b)** of this section may be used in a damp location provided it covers the receptacle when not in use. The type of receptacle cover that has horizontally opening hinged

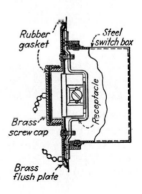

Fig. 410-20. Chain-held screw-cap cover is suitable for damp, but not wet, locations. (Sec. 410-57.)

flaps (doors) to cover the receptacles may be used in a damp but not wet location if the flaps are not self-closing, i.e., if the flaps can stay open (Fig. 410-21). Of course, any cover plate that is listed for weatherproof use may also be used in damp locations.

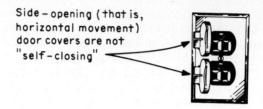

Side – opening (that is, horizontal movement) door covers are not "self-closing"

Note: If door covers were self-closing type, such a cover assembly could be used outdoors to supply a portable tool or equipment that is not left connected.

Fig. 410·21. Cover assembly with stay-open doors may be used in damp but *not* in wet locations. (Sec. 410-57.)

For wet locations, part **(b)** receptacles must be used with either of two types of cover assemblies:

1. For a receptacle outdoors or in any other wet location where a plug-connected load is normally left connected to the receptacle—such as for outdoor landscape lighting or for constant supply to an appliance or other load—only a fully weatherproof, listed cover plate may be used. Such an assembly maintains weatherproof protection of the receptacle at all times—either with the plug out or the plug in. Figure 410-22 shows the way

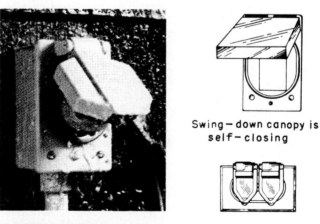

Swing – down canopy is self – closing

Receptacle is kept weatherproof with or without plug inserted.

Duplex cover

Fig. 410·22. UL-listed weatherproof covers protect receptacles at all times. (Sec. 410-57.)

in which a vertically lifting cover shields the receptacle against driving rain (coming at an angle). Such assemblies are made with one cover for a single receptacle or two covers for duplex receptacles. Other cover assemblies use a vertically lifting "canopy" that protects either a single or duplex receptacle.

2. For outdoor receptacles used solely for occasional connection of portable tools or appliances (lawnmowers, hedge-trimmers, etc.), it is permissible, under the Exception, to use a cover that only provides protection against weather when the cover is closed (but not when a plug is inserted.) But such a cover, whether installed for vertical or horizontal movement of the cover, must have spring-loaded *self-closing* covers or gravity-close for vertical-lift covers.

Part **(d)** pertains to flush-mounted boxes in which receptacles are installed in wet locations, and part **(e)** requires an elevation of outdoor receptacles to prevent accumulation of water.

410·58. Grounding·type Receptacles, Adapters, Cord Connectors, and Attachment Plugs.   Paragraph **(3)** of part **(b)** requires a "rigid" terminal for equipment grounding connection in grounding adapters for insertion into nongrounding receptacles (Fig. 410-23). Adapters with pigtail leads are not acceptable to the rule.

Use of grounding adapters to convert a nongrounding receptacle for connection of a three-prong grounding plug cap involves a number of NE Code and UL regulations. When a grounding receptacle connection is required for a cord-

NE Code **AND UL VIOLATION!** The *NE Code* prohibits use of the pigtail grounding adapters that have been available and widely used for many years. Such devices also do not satisfy UL construction standards.

THIS IS UL AND *NE Code* **RECOGNIZED.** Grounding adapter has rigid tab with spade end for connecting grounding terminal of the adapter to metal screw contacting the grounded metal yoke that mounts receptacle to the grounded metal box of the outlet (or to an equipment grounding conductor in NM cable used with a nonmetallic outlet box). Different-width blades on adapter polarize it for insertion in only one way into the polarized blade-openings on the receptacle.

Fig. 410·23. This is the NEC and UL position on grounding adapters. (Sec. 410-58.)

connected appliance or tool, a nongrounding-type receptacle should be replaced with a grounding type, as required by Sec. 210-7(d). And the branch circuit or branch-circuit raceway must include or provide a grounding conductor to which the receptacle ground terminal must be connected.

Plug-in grounding adapters for converting nongrounding (two-slot) receptacles to grounding type are listed by UL under "Attachment Plugs" in the *Electrical Construction Materials Directory* (Green Book). But the **NE Code** makes no reference to the use of such devices. Section 410-58(b) does describe the construction of adapters and thus implies that their use is permitted.

The problem with grounding adapters having a green grounding pigtail is

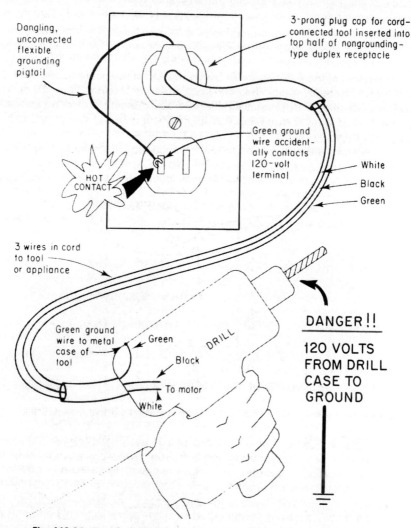

Fig. 410-24. Pigtail adapter can present shock hazard to personnel. (Sec. 410-58.)

that such adapters used on nongrounding receptacles present the inherent risk that they will be used without assuring integrity of the grounding path. It is very easy for anyone to plug such an adapter into a nongrounding receptacle and connect the spade lug in the green pigtail under the screw that secures the faceplate on the receptacle. But experience has shown a number of conditions that might exist and prevent effective grounding of the ground terminal of the adapter. The nongrounding receptacle may be fed by NM cable without a grounding conductor (or even by 2-wire knob-and-tube wiring). If the nongrounding receptacle fed by NM cable is in a nonmetallic box, the screw that secures the faceplate is not grounded, even if the cable includes a grounding conductor.

Another potential hazard of the pigtail adapter is shown in Fig. 410-24. Spade lug on end of the green pigtail wire might accidentally contact a hot terminal through the blade opening of other receptacle on a duplex outlet. Or spade lug could touch the hot blade of a plug cap that is not fully inserted into lower receptacle.

Figure 410-25 shows a very important rule from part **(e)** of Sec. 410-58.

3-PRONG GROUNDING PLUG CAP . . .

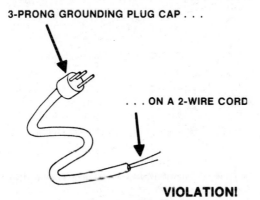

. . . ON A 2-WIRE CORD

VIOLATION!

Fig. 410-25. A 3-wire cord must be used when connecting a grounding-type plug-cap. (Sec. 410-58.)

410-64. General. Underwriters Laboratories rules comment on use of fixtures installed in hung ceilings, as follows:

Fixtures marked "Suitable for Use With Suspended Ceilings" have not been tested for use in ceiling spaces containing other heat sources such as steam pipes, hot-water pipes, or heating ducts.

Air-handling fixtures must be used fully in accordance with the conditions marked on the fixtures. When used in fire-rated ceilings, such fixtures must be related to the "Design Information Section" in the *Fire Resistance Index*, published by UL.

410-65. Temperature. Heat is a major problem in lighting system design, and with the trend to the use of recessed luminaires and equipment, the problem is increased. In the case of luminaires using incandescent lamps, the problem is primarily the prevention of concentrated spots of heat coming into contact with the building structure. In the case of fluorescent luminaires, the major heat problem is related to the ballast, which can build up severely high temperatures when not properly ventilated, or designed for cooler operation through adequate radiation and convection. These are problems which must be solved (1) through proper luminaire design, and (2) through proper installation methods and techniques (Fig. 410-26).

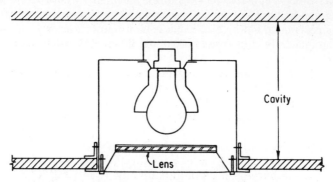

Luminaires shall not subject adjacent combustible material to a temperature in excess of 90°C (194° F).

Fig. 410-26. Recessed fixtures must not threaten combustion of building materials. (Sec. 410-65.)

The rule of part **(c)** requiring thermal protection of recessed incandescent fixtures is intended to prevent fires that have been caused by overlamping or misuse of insulating materials. See Fig. 410-27. As noted in Exception No. 2, a nonthermal-protected recessed incandescent fixture may be used in direct con-

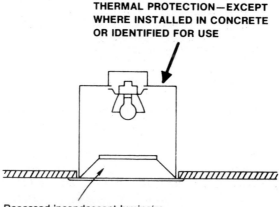

THERMAL PROTECTION—EXCEPT WHERE INSTALLED IN CONCRETE OR IDENTIFIED FOR USE

Recessed incandescent luminaire

Fig. 410-27. Recessed incandescent fixtures that incorporate thermal protection must be "identified as thermally protected," but a fixture without thermal protection may be used if listed and identified for use in contact with insulation. (Sec. 410-65.)

tact with thermal insulation if it is listed as suitable by design for performance equal to thermally protected fixtures and is so identified. There are presently available recessed incandescent fixtures of such design as to prevent overheating even when installled in contact with thermal insulation. Such fixtures cannot be overlamped or mislamped to cause excessive temperature and are listed and marked for such application.

410·66. Clearance and Installation. When recessed fixtures are used with thermal insulation in the recessed space, thermal insulation must have a clearance of at least 3 in. on the side of the fixture and at least 3 in. at the top of fixture and shall be so arranged that heat is not trapped in this space. Free circulation of air must be provided with this 3-in. spacing. If, however, the fixture is approved for installation with thermal insulation on closer spacing, it may be so used (Fig. 410-28). In parts **(a)** and **(b),** the Exception recognizes

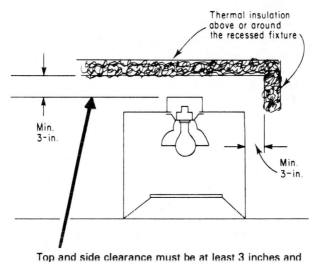

Top and side clearance must be at least 3 inches and insulation must not trap heat.

Fig. 410·28. Clearance of recessed fixture from thermal insulation is required unless fixture is UL-listed for use in direct contact with insulation. (Sec. 410-66.)

recessed incandescent fixtures in contact with thermal insulation or combustible material. Recessed incandescent fixtures must be listed and identified for use in contact with thermal insulation.

In the past, thermal insulation has been installed in direct contact with recessed fixtures not approved for that use and caused overheating in fixtures with resulting failures and fires. Obviously, the installer of thermal insulation will have to be educated on this subject, because electrical installers have little control over how the insulation will be applied.

Figure 410-29 shows an application that involves the ½-in. clearance covered in the first sentence of this section. It shows two 40-W fluorescent strips installed in a residential kitchen ceiling. The ceiling has been furred down on

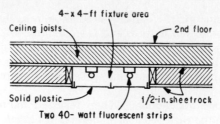

Fig. 410-29. Clearances on custom recessed lighting applications must be evaluated carefully. (Sec. 410-66.)

all sides of the 4- by 4-ft fixture area as shown. The question arises: Is this a "recessed" installation according to the **Code**? How small or large must such an enclosed space be to be considered a recess? The **Code** does not mention "recessed installations" but refers to "recessed fixtures." The installation as shown is basically a field-fabricated recessed fixture. With only two 40-W lamps in this space, it is not likely there will be much of a heat problem. But sufficient information on the total construction of the cavity would be needed for an inspector to make an evaluation. The temperature limitations of Secs. 410-5 and 410-65 must be observed, and wiring must be in accordance with Sec. 410-67.

The next question is: Must a ½-in. clearance be maintained between the fixtures and the Sheetrock? Sheetrock is fire-rated by UL but is not fireproof. It is likely that inspectors would require the ½-in. spacing between the fixtures and the Sheetrock because the paperboard surfaces of the Sheetrock are combustible. The local inspector would have the final say on this concern.

410-67. Wiring. Supply wiring to recessed fixtures may be the branch-circuit wires, if their 60°C or 75°C or 90°C temperature rating at least matches the temperature that will exist in the fixture splice compartment under operating

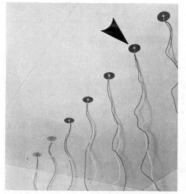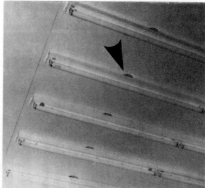

Fig. 410-30. Branch-circuit wires rated at 75°C are brought out of ceiling boxes (left) and then connected to fixture leads within the relatively cool wiring compartment of the fluorescent units. (Sec. 410-67.)

conditions. Typically fluorescent fixtures do not have very high operating temperatures where the branch-circuit wires splice to the fixture wires and branch-circuit conductors may be run right into the fixture. But, incandescent fixtures develop much higher localized heat because all the wattage is concentrated in a much smaller bulb, thereby requiring higher temperature wire where the branch-circuit splices to the fixture leads.

The rules of part **(b)** and part **(c)** of this section are related to the details discussed under Sec. 410-11. Figure 410-30 shows branch-circuit wires rated at 75°C coming out of ceiling boxes (left) and then connected directly to fluorescent strip units mounted over the boxes and attached to the ceiling (right). The 75°C THW branch-circuit wires are rated at 90°C for use within the fluorescent units (Sec. 410-31, last sentence).

Figure 410-31 shows 60°C branch-circuit wiring run directly to integral junction boxes of "prewired" incandescent fixtures. The box protects the branch-circuit wires from the heat generated within the fixtures. Note these fixtures

Fig. 410-31. Prewired recessed incandescent fixtures may have 60°C branch-circuit wiring run directly into their junction boxes. (Sec. 410-67.)

are used for supply and feed-through of the branch-circuit wires and must be UL-listed for that application (refer to Sec. 410-11).

Figure 410-32 shows an application of part **(c)** of this **Code** section, where a fixture wiring compartment operates so hot that the temperature exceeds that of the branch-circuit-rated value and high-temperature fixture wires must be run to the unit. The circuit outlet box supplying the high-wattage incandescent fixture must be mounted not less than 1 ft away from the fixture. The flex whip may be ⅜-in. flex for the number and type of fixture wires as specified in Table 350-3 (Sec. 350-3). If the branch-circuit supplying the fixture is protected at 20 A or 15 A, No. 18 fixture wires may be used for fixture loads up to 6 A or No. 16 fixture wire may be used for loads up to 8 A (Sec. 402-5), and the metal flex may serve as the equipment grounding conductor [Sec. 250-91(b), Exception No. 1]. The flex may not be less than 4 ft long but not more than 6 ft long. The fixture wires could be Type AF for conditions requiring a 150°C rating or could be another type of adequate temperature rating for the fixture's marked temperature, selected from Table 402-3. For flex, refer also to Sec. 350-5.

The 4- to 6-ft fixture "whip" may be Type AC or Type MC cable, with conductors of adequate temperature rating for the temperature of the fixture wiring compartment. This is an alternative to using a 4- to 6-ft length of flexible raceway to enclose the tap conductors of the whip. (Fig. 410-32.)

Recessed fixtures are, in all cases, marked with the required minimum-temperature rating of wiring supplying the fixture. See Sec. 410-35(a), the last sentence. This marking does not allow for any heat contributed by a branch circuit passing through the fixture enclosure or through a splice compartment (outlet box or otherwise) that is part of the fixture construction. An insulation with a temperature rating higher than that indicated on the fixture may be required for such branch-circuit conductors. See Sec. 410-11.

The requirements in part **(c)** are special provisions that apply to recessed fixtures and take precedence over the general requirements. The tap conductors (usually in flexible conduit) connecting an unwired recessed fixture to the outlet box must be in metal or nonmetallic raceway (such as electrical nonmetallic conduit or nonmetallic liquidtight flex) at least 4 ft in length and not over 6 ft. The box is required to be at least 1 ft away from the fixture and the flexible conduit may be looped to use up the excess length (see Sec. 350-4, Exception No. 3). This rule does not apply to "prewired" fixtures designed for connection to 60°C supply wires.

The purpose of this requirement is to allow the heat to dissipate so that heat from the fixture will not cause an excessive temperature in the outlet box and thus overheat the branch-circuit conductors which could be of the general-use type limited to 60°C or 75°C temperatures.

410-73. General. Paragraph **(e)** pertains only to fluorescent lamp ballasts used indoors. The protection called for must be a part of the ballast. Underwriters Laboratories Inc. has made an extensive investigation of various types of protective devices for use within such ballasts, and ballasts found to meet UL requirements for these applications are listed and marked as "Class P." The protective devices are thermal trip devices or thermal fuses, which are responsive to abnormal heat developed within the ballast because of a fault in components such as autotransformers, capacitors, reactors, etc.

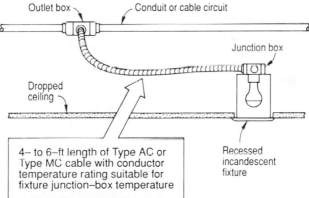

Outlet box — Conduit or cable circuit

Junction box

Dropped ceiling

4– to 6–ft length of Type AC or Type MC cable with conductor temperature rating suitable for fixture junction–box temperature

Recessed incandescent fixture

This is an alternative to tap conductors run in metal flex or liquidtight metal flex.

Fig. 410·32. For fixture with circuit-connection compartment operating very hot, high-temperature wires must be run in flex (other metal raceway or Type AC or MC metal armored cable) between 4 and 6 ft, from an outlet box at least 12 in. away. (Sec. 410-67.)

Simple reactance-type ballasts are used with preheat-type fluorescent lamp circuits for lamps rated less than 30 W. Also, a manual (momentary-contact) or automatic-type starter is used to start the lamp. The simple reactor-type ballast supplies one lamp only, has no autotransformer or capacitor, and is exempted from the protection rule of part **(e).**

The thermal protection required for ballasts of fluorescent fixtures installed indoors must be within the ballast. Previous wording permitted the interpretation that the supplementary protection for the ballast could be in the fixture and not necessarily within the ballast.

Part **(f)** requires that recessed HID fixtures used *either* indoors or outdoors must have thermal protection. The fixture—and not just the ballast—must be thermally protected and so identified. All *indoor, recessed* fixtures using mercury-vapor, metal-halide, or sodium lamps must be thermally protected. If remote ballasts are used with such fixtures, the ballasts must also be thermally protected.

410·75. Open Circuit Voltages Exceeding 300 Volts.   As required by UL, fixtures which are intended for use in other than dwelling occupancies are so marked. This usually indicates that the fixture has maintenance features which are considered to be beyond the capabilities of the ordinary householder, or involves voltages in excess of those permitted by the **National Electrical Code** for dwelling occupancies.

410·76. Fixture Mounting.   Underwriters Laboratories presents data which apply to part **(b)** of this section:

1. Fluorescent fixtures suitable for mounting on combustible low-density cellulose fiberboard ceilings which have been evaluated for use with thermal insulation above the ceiling and which have been investigated for mounting directly on combustible low-density cellulose fiberboard ceilings are marked "Suitable for Surface Mounting on Combustible Low-Density Cellulose Fiberboard" (Fig. 410-33).

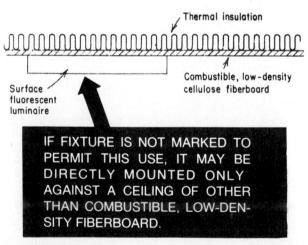

Fig. 410·33. UL lists fluorescent fixtures for surface mounting on low-density cellulose fiberboard ceilings with insulation above. (Sec. 410-76.)

    If a fluorescent fixture is not marked to show it is approved for surface mounting on combustible low-density cellulose fiberboard, it must be mounted with at least a 1½-in. space between it and such a ceiling.

2. Fluorescent fixtures that may not be used directly against any ceiling are marked "For Suspended Mounting Only. Minimum Distance From Ceiling Six Inches."

3. Surface-mounting incandescent and HID fixtures (mercury-vapor, metal-halide, etc.) are suitable for use on any ceiling including low-density fiberboard, without marking—but, except for incandescent fixtures marked "Type I.C.," such fixtures must never be used where there is thermal insulation above the ceiling over the fixture. Type I.C. (insulated ceiling) incandescent fixtures may be mounted on a ceiling with insulation above.

4. If surface-mounted or suspended fixtures require supply circuit wires rated over 60°C, they will be marked to show the required minimum temperature rating of the circuit wires. And where such fixtures are marked to require wires rated over 60°C, the marking does not allow for any heat added by a branch circuit passing through the fixture. In such cases, it is up to the installer to determine the need for using wires of a temperature rating higher than indicated.

The note after this section describes "combustible low-density cellulose fiberboard." Material meeting these requirements is listed in Underwriters Laboratories Inc. *Building Materials Directory* and in addition to other pertinent information includes the following: "This material has been found to comply with the flame spread requirements stipulated in Sec. 410-76 of the **National Electrical Code** as described therein."

410-77. Equipment Not Integral with Fixture.   Part **(c)** covers interconnection of "paired" lighting fixtures, with a ballast supplying a lamp or lamps in both, using up to a 25-ft length of ⅜-in. flexible metal conduit to enclose the circuit conductors. Lighting manufacturers have been making UL-listed pairs of lighting fixtures for use with each other. Because some inspection agencies have questioned use of this equipment, this section describes **Code**-conforming use of such equipment to thereby resolve field controversy.

410-78. Autotransformers.   This rule ties in with the rules of Sec. 210-6 on voltage of branch circuits to lighting fixtures. On neutral-grounded wye systems (such as 120/208 or 277/480) incandescent, fluorescent, mercury-vapor, metal-halide, high-pressure sodium, and low-pressure sodium equipment can be connected from phase to neutral on the circuits. If fluorescent or mercury-vapor fixtures are to be connected phase to phase, some **Code** authorities contend that autotransformer-type ballasts cannot be used when they raise the voltage to more than 300 V, because, they contend, the reference to "a grounded system" in this rule of Sec. 410-78 calls for connection to a circuit made up of a grounded wire and a hot wire (Fig. 410-34). On phase-to-phase connection they would require use of 2-winding (electrically isolating) ballast transformers. The wording of Sec. 410-78 does, however, lend itself to interpretation that it is only necessary for the supply *system* to the ballast to be grounded—thus permitting the two hot legs of a 208-V or 480-V circuit to supply an autotransformer because the hot legs are derived from a neutral-grounded "system." But Sec. 210-9, which calls for a "grounded conductor" to be common to the primary

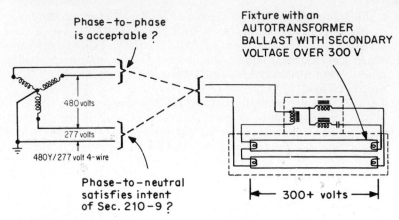

Phase-to-phase is acceptable ?

Fixture with an AUTOTRANSFORMER BALLAST WITH SECONDARY VOLTAGE OVER 300 V

480 volts

277 volts

480Y/277 volt 4-wire

Phase-to-neutral satisfies intent of Sec. 210-9 ?

◄─── 300+ volts ───►

Fig. 410-34. Intent of Sec. 210-9 raises questions about connection of autotransformer ballasts. (Sec. 410-78.)

and secondary of an autotransformer that supplies a branch circuit, can become a complicating factor. Use of a 2-winding (isolating) ballast is clearly acceptable and avoids all confusion.

410-80. General. These sections apply to interior neon-tube lighting, lighting with long fluorescent tubes requiring more than 1,000 V, and cold-cathode fluorescent-lamp installation arranged to operate with several tubes in series. As noted in part **(b)**, electric-discharge lighting equipment with open-circuit voltage exceeding 1,000 V shall not be installed in dwelling occupancies.

410-81. Control. When any part of the equipment is being serviced, the primary circuit should be opened and the servicers should have assurance that the disconnecting means will not be closed without their knowledge.

410-87. Transformer Loading. See comments following Sec. 600-32.

410-88. Wiring Method—Secondary Conductors. This type of cable is not included in the table in Chap. 3 listing various types of insulated conductors, but Underwriters Laboratories Inc. have standards for such cables. The following information is an excerpt from the Underwriters Laboratories Inc. *Electrical Construction Materials Directory:*

> Gas tube sign and ignition cable is classified as Type GTO-5 (5,000 volts), GTO-10 (10,000 volts), or GTO-15 (15,000 volts), and is labeled in sizes Nos. 18-10 AWG copper and Nos. 12-10 AWG aluminum and copper-clad aluminum. This material is intended for use with gas tube signs, oil burners, and inside lighting.
> "L"-used as a suffix in combination with any of the preceding type letter designations indicates that an outer covering of lead has been applied.
> The label of Underwriters' Laboratories, Inc., . . . on the product is the only method provided by Underwriters' Laboratories, Inc., to identify Gas Tube Sign and Ignition Cable which has been produced under the Label Service.

410-100. Definition. This describes the very popular and widely used track lighting made by a number of manufacturers and used so commonly today in residential and commercial interiors (and even exteriors). In Secs. 410-101 through 410-105, extensive rules cover applications of track lighting mounted

Fig. 410·35. Part R of Art. 410 contains rules on installation, application, fastening, and circuit loading for standard and heavy-duty track lighting. (Secs. 410-101 through 410-105.)

on ceilings or walls. Specifically, these rules cover the installation and support of lighting track used to support and supply power to lighting fixtures designed to be attached to the track at any point along the track length (Fig. 410-35).

410·102. Track Load.   In providing minimum required capacity in branch circuits and feeders, a load of 180 VA must be allowed for each 2 ft (or fraction thereof) of lighting track. That amount of load capacity must be provided in branch circuits in both residential and nonresidential installations and would have to be added in addition to the general lighting load in voltamperes per square foot from **NEC** Table 220-3(b), if the track lighting is not used for "general illumination" as described in Sec. 220-3(b). If track lighting *is* used for general illumination in any room or area, its load must be taken as the greater value of either 180 VA per 2-ft length of track or the load determined from the minimum watts per square foot from Table 220-3(b) times the square feet of floor area.

A multicircuit length of lighting track must be taken as a load of 180 VA for each 2 ft or fraction thereof, divided among the number of circuits. For a 2-circuit lighting track, each 2-ft length is a 90-VA load for each circuit. For a 3-circuit track, each 2-ft length is a 60-VA load for each circuit.

ARTICLE 422. APPLIANCES

422·1. Scope.   See definition for "appliance," Art. 100. For purposes of the Code, the definition for an appliance indicates that it is utilization equipment other than industrial and generally means small equipment such as may be used in a dwelling or office (clothes washer, clothes dryer, air conditioner, food mixer, coffee maker, etc.). See also definition for "utilization equipment" in Art. 100.

422·4. Branch·Circuit Sizing.   Part **(a)** states that the amp rating of an individual branch circuit to a single appliance must not be less than the marked ampere rating of the appliance.

422·5. Branch·Circuit Overcurrent Protection.   The second sentence presents a rule based on the fact that some appliances are marked to indicate the maximum permitted rating of protective device (fuse or CB) for the branch circuit supplying that appliance.

422·7 Central Heating Equipment.   This rule requires a dedicated (individual) branch circuit to supply the electrical needs of "Central Heating Equipment" other than fixed electric space heating. This requires a separate circuit for the electrical ignition, control, fan(s), and circulating pump(s) of gas- and oil-fired central heating plants. The Exception notes that auxiliary equipment "such as a pump, valve, humidifier, or electrostatic air cleaner directly associated with the heating equipment" *may* be connected to the same branch circuit (or another branch circuit).

The purpose of this rule is to prevent loss of heating when its circuit is opened due to a fault in a lamp or other appliance that is connected on the same circuit with the heater as was permitted in the 1987 NEC and previous editions. All heating equipment should be supplied by one or more individual branch circuits that supply nothing but the heater and its auxiliary equipment.

422·8. Flexible Cords.   Figure 422-1 shows application of rules on the hookup of kitchen garbage disposers. Hookup of dishwashers and trash compactors is the same, except that the cord must be 3 to 4 ft long, instead of 1½ to 3 ft long.

As required by part **(d)(3)**, a portable high-pressure spray washing machine is required to have a "factory-installed" GFCI. AND this factory-installed device MUST be "an integral part" of the plug cap or in the cord itself no more than 12 in. from the plug cap. An Exception recognizes double-insulated high-pressure spray washers or those rated over 125 V WITHOUT integral GFCI protection provided they are permanently marked that the washer must be connected to a GFCI-protected receptacle.

422·12. Signals for Heated Appliances.   The standard form of signal is a red light so connected that the lamp remains lighted as long as the appliance is connected to the circuit. No signal lamp is required if the appliance is equipped with a thermostatic switch which automatically opens the circuit after the appliance has been heated to a certain temperature.

422·14. Water Heaters.   Part **(b)** ties into Sec. 422-4(a) Exception No. 2 to require 120-gal water heaters or any water heater of lesser capacity to be fed by branch-circuit conductors that have an ampacity and protective device rating not less than 1.25 times the marked ampacity of the water heater (Fig. 422-2). Or, to put it another way, the amp rating of the water heater must not exceed

Receptacle must be accessible and located to avoid
physical damage to the flexible cord

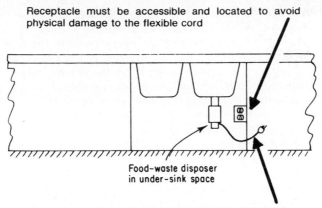

Food-waste disposer
in under-sink space

Cord must be Type S, SO, ST, STO, SJO, SJT. SJTO or
SPT-3—3-conductor, terminated with a grounding-type
plug. Cord must be between 18 and 36 in. long.

NOTE: Double-insulated disposers do not have to be
grounded.

Fig. 422-1. Code rules aim at effective grounding for kitchen garbage
disposers. (Sec. 422-8.)

80 percent of the amp rating of the branch circuit. And that rule must be related
to Sec. 422-28(e). The only case where the water-heater current may load the
circuit to 100 percent is where the circuit protective device is listed for continuous operation at 100 percent of its rating. But there are no standard protective
devices of that type available at the circuit ratings required for water-heater
loads.

Fig. 422-2. Any fixed storage water
heater with capacity of 120 gal or less
must be treated as a "continuous duty
load" that does not load the circuit to
more than 80 percent of its capacity. (Sec.
422-14.)

422·15. Infrared Lamp Industrial Heating Appliances. So-called "infrared" lamps are tungsten-filament incandescent lamps, similar to lamps used for lighting except that they are designed for operation with the filaments at a lower temperature, resulting, for a given wattage, in more heat radiation and less light output, and also in a much longer lamp life. In a typical infrared heating oven for industrial use, the lampholders are mounted on panels which are hinged so that the axis of each lamp is at an angle of about 45° from the surface of the panel, to ensure that all sides of an object passing through the oven will receive a uniform amount of heat radiation.

422·18. Support of Ceiling Fans. A ceiling fan up to 35 lb may be hung from an outlet box identified for such use, and the box must be properly supported. Heavier ceiling fans must be supported independently of the box.

422·21. Disconnection of Permanently Connected Appliances. In part **(a)** lower-rated appliances may use the "branch-circuit overcurrent device" as their disconnect means and such a device could be a plug-fuse or a CB. Part **(b)** for higher-rated appliances does not permit use of a plug-fuse as the disconnect but requires a definite switch-action device—a switch or CB. A permanently connected appliance rated over 300 VA or over ⅛ hp may use its branch circuit switch or CB as the required disconnecting means *if* the switch or CB is within sight from the appliance or it can be locked in the "open" position. Note that this section applies *only* to permanently connected appliances—i.e., those with fixed-wiring connection (so-called "hard wired") and not cord-and-plug connection.

In part **(a)**, the overcurrent device for the circuit to the appliance is not required to be accessible to the user. But the switch or CB in part **(b)** must be "readily accessible" to the user. See definition of "readily accessible" in Art. 100.

Section 422-27 and Sec. 422-25 relate to the rules of this section.

422·22. Disconnection of Cord· and Plug·Connected Appliances. Examples of the application of this section for disconnecting means for appliances are found in the installation of household electric ranges and clothes dryers. The purpose of these requirements is to provide that for every such appliance there will be some means for opening the circuit to the appliance when it is to be serviced or repaired or when it is to be removed.

In part **(b)**, household electric ranges may be supplied by cord-and-plug connection to a range receptacle located at the rear base of the range. The rule permits such a plug and receptacle to serve as the disconnecting means for the range if the connection is accessible from the front by removal of a drawer.

This rule refers to "electric" ranges but the concept also applies to gas ranges. For instance, there have been 115-V receptacle outlets installed behind gas ranges in mobile homes. Such a receptacle is only used as an outlet for the oven light and clock on the range and is not accessible after the range is installed. In order to disconnect the attachment plug or plugs from the receptacle, the range gas supply pipe has to be disconnected, the frame of the range disconnected from its floor fastening, and then the range moved in order to reach the receptacle outlet where the cords are plugged in (Fig. 422-3). Is such an installation in conformity with the intent of the **Code**? The answer seems surely to be no. The inaccessibility of the receptacle would be objectionable.

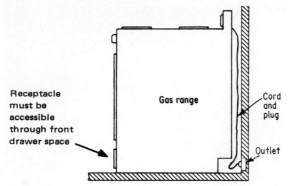

Fig. 422-3. Rule on receptacle behind "electric" ranges could be applied to gas ranges. (Sec. 422-22.)

422-25. Unit Switch(es) as Disconnecting Means.   As shown in Fig. 422-4, the ON-OFF switch on an appliance, such as a cooking unit in a commercial establishment, is permitted by part **(d)** to serve as the required disconnect means if the user of the appliance has ready access to the branch-circuit switch or CB. Note that the wording does not recognize simply "the branch-circuit overcurrent device," and a plug-fuse in the circuit to the appliance would not, therefore, be acceptable as the additional means for disconnection.

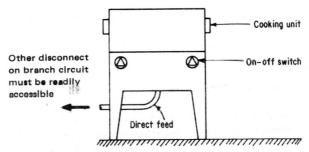

Fig. 422-4. An ON-OFF switch on an appliance must be supplemented by an additional disconnect means. (Sec. 422-25.)

422-27. Disconnecting Means for Motor-Driven Appliances.   The basic rule requires that a switch or CB serving as the disconnecting means for a permanently connected motor-driven appliance of more than ⅛ hp must be within sight from the motor controller, as shown in Fig. 422-5 for the power unit of a built-in vacuum cleaner system. As permitted by Sec. 430-109 Exception No. 2, general-use AC snap switches may be used as the disconnect for motors rated up to 2 hp, not over 300 V, provided that the motor full load is not greater than 80 percent of the ampere rating of the switch.

Under the Exception to this rule, the branch-circuit switch or CB serving as the other disconnect required by Secs. 422-25(a), (b), (c), or (d) is permitted to be out of sight from the motor controller of an appliance that is equipped with

Fig. 422-5. Toggle switch in outlet box on this central vacuum cleaner serves as the disconnecting means within sight from the motor controller installed in the top of the unit. (Sec. 422-27.)

a unit switch that has a marked OFF position and opens all ungrounded supply conductors to the appliance, as shown in Fig. 422-6.

422-28. Overcurrent Protection.   The Exception to part **(a)** requires application of overload protection provisions of Sec. 430-32 and Sec. 430-33 to motors of motor-operated appliances. And overload protection for sealed hermetic compressor motors must satisfy Secs. 440-52 through 440-55. But motors that are not continuous-duty motors—and most appliances are intermittent, short-time, or varying duty types of motor loads—do not require running overload protection. The branch-circuit protective device may perform that function for such motors. See Sec. 430-33.

Part **(e)** sets limits on the maximum permitted branch-circuit protection for an individual branch circuit supplying a single non-motor-operated appliance. This rule is aimed at providing overcurrent protection for appliances that would not be adequately protected if too large a branch-circuit protective device were used ahead of them on their supply branch circuits.

The basic rule says that if a maximum rating or branch-circuit protective device is marked on the appliance, that value must be observed in selecting the

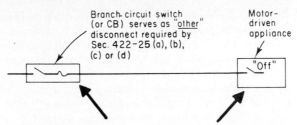

Fig. 422-6. Disconnect for motor-driven appliance may be "out of sight from the motor controller." (Sec. 422-27.)

branch-circuit fuse or CB. If, however, a particular appliance is *not* marked to show a maximum rating of branch-circuit protection, the values specified in this section must be used as follows:

For an appliance drawing more than 13.3 A—the branch-circuit fuse or CB must not be rated more than 150 percent (1½ times) the full-load current rating of the appliance. For an appliance drawing up to 13.3 A—the branch-circuit fuse or CB must not be rated over 20 A.

Those values were chosen to limit the maximum rating of protection to not over 150 percent of the appliance rating to afford greater protection to the appliance, as well as to provide for continuous-load appliances (that operate for 3 hr or more continuously). In the latter case, Sec 210-22(c) requires that a continuous load not exceed 80 percent of the branch-circuit fuse or CB; that is, the protective device is rated not less than 125 percent of the continuous-load current.

An appliance drawing 13.3 A must have protection of not over 150 percent of that value (1.5 × 13.3 = 20 A), which sets 20 A as the maximum protection. And 80 percent of a 20 A rating is 16 A—so that the 13.3-A load does not exceed that value for a continuous load. For appliances drawing more than 13.3 A, the exception says that if 150 percent of the appliance current rating does not correspond to a standard rating of protective device (from Sec. 240-6), the next standard rating of protective device above that value may be used even though it is rated more than 150 percent of the appliance current rating.

Electric water heaters are typical non-motor-operated appliances rated over 13.3 A, and Sec. 422-14(b) says such water heaters of 120-gal capacity or less must have a branch-circuit overcurrent device rated not less than 125 percent of the unit's current rating. And Sec. 422-28(e) says the same branch-circuit device must not be rated more than 150 percent of the unit's current rating.

Part **(f)** of this section covers electric heating appliances using resistance-type heating elements. It requires that, where the elements are rated more than 48 A, the heating elements must be subdivided. Each subdivided load shall not exceed 48 A and shall be protected at not more than 60 A.

The rules of this section are generally similar to the rules contained in Sec. 424-22 for fixed electric space heating using duct heaters as part of heating, ventilating, and air-conditioning systems above suspended ceilings. But Exception No. 2 applies to commercial kitchen and cooking appliances using sheath-type heating elements. This Exception permits such heating elements to be subdivided into circuits not exceeding 120 A and protected at not more than 150 A under the conditions specified.

Exception No. 3 of this same section permits a similar subdivision into 120-A loads protected at not more than 150 A for elements of water heaters and steam boilers employing resistance-type immersion electric heating elements contained in an ASME rated and stamped vessel.

ARTICLE 424. FIXED ELECTRIC SPACE HEATING EQUIPMENT

424-3. Branch Circuits. The basic rule limits fixed electric space heating equipment to use on 15-, 20-, or 30-A circuits, **if the circuit has more than one outlet**. The Exception applies only to fixed infrared equipment on industrial and commercial premises, permitting use of 40-A and 50-A circuits for multioutlet circuits to *fixed* space heaters.

The 125 percent requirement in paragraph **(b)** means that branch circuits for electric space heating equipment cannot be loaded to more than 80 percent of the branch-circuit rating. Even though electric heating is thermostatically controlled and is a cycling load, it must be taken as a continuous load for sizing branch circuits.

The three parts of this rule are as follows:

1. The branch-circuit wires must have an ampacity not less than 1.25 times the total amp load of the equipment (heater current plus motor current).
2. The overcurrent protective device must have an amp rating not less than that calculated for the branch-circuit wires.
3. If necessary, the rating or setting of the branch-circuit overcurrent device may be sized according to Exception No. 4 of Sec. 240-3. That is, if the ampacity of the selected branch-circuit wires does not correspond to a standard rating or setting of protective device (Sec. 240-6), the next higher standard rating or setting of protective device may be used. This accommodates those applications of large unit heaters, where often there is not agreement in ampacity of wires and ratings of standard fuses or CBs.

Figure 424-1 shows an example of branch-circuit sizing for an electric heat unit.

Many line thermostats and contactors are approved for 100 percent load, and derating of such devices is not required.

Section 220-15 covers sizing of feeders for electric space heating loads. The computed load of a feeder supplying such equipment shall be the total connected load on all branch circuits, with an exception left up to the authority enforcing the **Code** which allows permission for feeder conductors to be of a capacity less than 100 percent, provided the conductors are of sufficient capacity for the load serving units operating on duty-cycle, intermittently, or from all

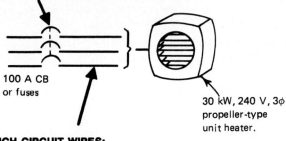

Fuses or CB must be rated not less than 1.25 × 73.7, or 92 amps.

NEXT STANDARD RATING ABOVE 95-AMP RATING OF No. 2 TW OR THW IS 100 amps

100 A CB
or fuses

30 kW, 240 V, 3ϕ
propeller-type
unit heater.

BRANCH-CIRCUIT WIRES:

73.7 × 1.25 = 92 amps.
That calls for No. 2 TW or THW
copper wire, rated at 95 amps.
(60C amp-rating required by UL
for equipment up to 100 amps)

Total load amps
(heater plus motor)
= 73.7 amps.

Fig. 424·1. Branch-circuit conductors and overcurrent protection must be rated not less than 125 percent of heater unit nameplate current. (Sec. 424-3.)

units not operating at one time. The second exception to the rule states that Exception No. 1 does not apply if the optional method in Sec. 220-30 is the method used for calculating the load for a single-family dwelling or individual apartment of a multifamily dwelling.

424·9. General. For instance, heating cable designed for use in ceilings may not be used in concrete floors and vice versa.

This rule ties into that of Sec. 210-52(a). The fine-print note says that UL-listed baseboard heaters must be installed in accordance with their instructions, which *may* prohibit installation below outlets. This applies to all occupancies—residential, commercial, institutional, and industrial.

In buildings warmed by baseboard heaters, the question arises: How can wall receptacles be provided to satisfy the requirement of **NE Code** Sec. 210-52(a) that no point along the floor line be more than 6 ft from an outlet? Should the receptacles be installed in the wall above the heaters? The answer is that receptacles should not be placed above the heaters if they are marked to prohibit that. Fires have been attributed to cords being draped across heaters. Continued exposure to heat causes the cord insulation to become brittle, leading to possible short circuits or ground faults.

Article 210 does not specifically prohibit installation of receptacles over baseboard heaters, and Art. 424 does not specifically prohibit installation of baseboard heaters under receptacles. However, Sec. 110-3(b) says:

Installation and Use. Listed or labeled equipment shall be used or installed in accordance with any instructions included in the listing or labeling.

Underwriters Laboratories now requires in Standard 1042, *Electric Baseboard Heating Equipment,* a warning that a heater is not to be located below an electrical convenience receptacle. A similar statement is included in the UL *Electrical Appliance and Utilization Equipment Directory* (Orange Book):

> To reduce the likelihood of cords contacting the heater, the heater should not be located beneath electrical receptacles.

This instruction and the provisions of Sec. 110-3(b) make it very clear that installation of electric baseboard heaters under receptacles may be a **Code** violation.

Receptacles can be provided in electrically heated (baseboard-type) occupancies as required by Sec. 210-52(a) by making use of the receptacle accessories made available by baseboard heater manufacturers. These units are designed to be mounted at the end of a baseboard section or between two sections.

424·14. Grounding.   The basic rule on grounding applies to all electric space heating equipment. The wiring method supplying any fixed electric space heating equipment must provide a means for grounding all exposed metal parts of such equipment. That must be suitable metal raceway (rigid metal conduit, IMC, EMT) or metal cable armor (BX), or an equipment grounding conductor in NM cable, or nonmetallic conduit.

424·19. Disconnecting Means.   The basic rule requires disconnecting means for the heater, motor controller(s), plus supplementary overcurrent protective devices for all fixed electric space heating equipment.

Part **(a)** of this section applies to heating equipment provided with supplementary overcurrent protection (such as fuses or CBs) to protect the subdivided resistance heaters used in duct heating, as required by Sec. 424-22. The basic rules are shown in Fig. 424-2. The disconnect in that sketch must comply with the following:

1. The disconnect must be "within sight from" the supplementary overcurrent panel. If circuit breakers are used as the supplementary overcurrent protective devices for the subdivided electric heating loads [Sec. 424-22(b)], the circuit breaker may constitute the disconnect required by this section. This rule has to be correlated to the other rules of part **(a)** and **(c)**.
2. The disconnect must also be within sight from the motor controller(s) and the heater, or it must be capable of being locked in the open position.
3. The single disconnect may serve as disconnect for all equipment.

Part **(b)** applies to heating equipment *without* supplementary overcurrent protection.

Care must be taken to evaluate each of the specific requirements in this **Code** section to actual job details involved with electric heating installations.

Figure 424-3 shows two conditions that relate to the rules of part **(b)** of this section. For the two-family house, the service panel is located in a rear areaway and is accessible to both occupants. Circuit breakers in the panel constitute suitable means of disconnect for heaters in both apartments. If the house uses baseboard heaters without motors in them, the breakers would be acceptable as the disconnects in accordance with the rule of **(b) (1)**. For the four-family

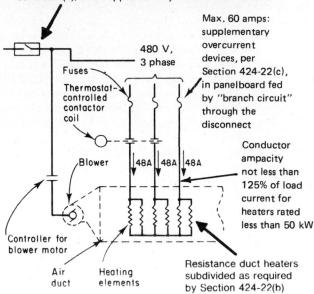

Required disconnect must disconnect heater, motor controller(s), and supplementary overcurrent devices.

480 V, 3 phase

Fuses

Thermostat-controlled contactor coil

Max. 60 amps: supplementary overcurrent devices, per Section 424-22(c), in panelboard fed by "branch circuit" through the disconnect

Blower 48A 48A 48A

Conductor ampacity not less than 125% of load current for heaters rated less than 50 kW

Controller for blower motor

Air duct

Heating elements

Resistance duct heaters subdivided as required by Section 424-22(b)

Fig. 424-2. Rules on disconnects for heating equipment demand careful study for HVAC systems with duct heaters and supplementary overcurrent protective devices. (Sec. 424-19.)

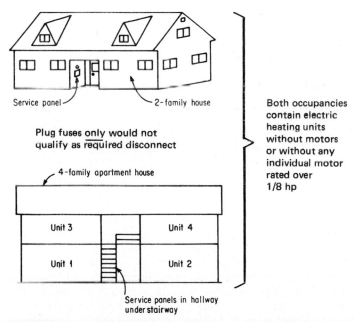

Service panel

2-family house

Plug fuses only would not qualify as required disconnect

4-family apartment house

Unit 3

Unit 4

Unit 1

Unit 2

Service panels in hallway under stairway

Both occupancies contain electric heating units without motors or without any individual motor rated over 1/8 hp

Fig. 424-3. For nonmotored electric heating units, readily accessible branch circuit switch or CB serves as disconnect. (Sec. 424-19.)

house (a "multifamily dwelling"), the service panels accessible to all tenants
are grouped in the hallway under the first-floor stairway in this four-family
occupancy. Switches in the panels may constitute suitable means of disconnect
for heaters in all apartments, under the rule of **(b) (1)**. But note that plug-fuses
(without switches) on branch circuits to the heaters would not satisfy **(b) (1)**.
WATCH OUT! The rules of part **(b)** were revised in the 1978 **NEC**. Previous
Code rules permitted "the branch-circuit overcurrent device"—which could
be a plug-fuse instead of a CB—to serve as the disconnect for electric heaters
up to 300 VA or ⅛ hp. Part **(b) (1)** refers only to "branch-circuit switch or circuit
breaker."

Note that **(b) (2)** requires a disconnect "within sight from" a motor controller
serving a motor-operated space heater with a motor over ⅛ hp, with the limited
Exception referred to part **(a) (2)**c.

Part **(c)** permits the "ON-OFF" switch on the heating unit to be used as the
disconnecting means where "other means for disconnection" are provided,
depending on the occupancy.

424-20. Thermostatically Controlled Switching Devices.   Figure 424-4 shows a
hookup of duct heaters that are controlled by a magnetic contactor that
responds to a thermostatic switch in its coil circuit. The subdivided heater load
of 48 A per leg satisfies the rule of Sec. 424-22(b), *but* the contactor does not

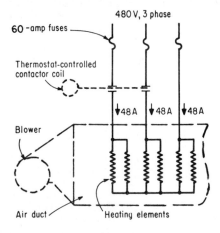

Fig. 424-4. This contactor may not serve
as both controller and disconnect. (Sec.
424-20.)

constitute a combination controller-and-disconnect means because it does not
open all the ungrounded conductors of the circuit. And because the heater contains the 60-A supplementary overcurrent protection, a disconnect ahead of the
fuses would be required by Sec. 424-19(a) even if the contactor did open all
three ungrounded conductors of the circuit.

424-22. Overcurrent Protection.   Heating equipment employing resistance-
type heating elements rated more than 48 A must have the heating elements
subdivided, with each subdivided circuit loaded to not more than 48 A and
protected at not more than 60 A. And each subdivided load must not exceed 80
percent of the rating of the protective device, to satisfy Sec. 424-3(b). Such a

60-A circuit could be classed as an individual branch circuit supplying a "single" outlet that actually consists of all the heater elements interconnected. By considering it as an "individual branch circuit" there is no conflict with Sec. 424-3(a) which sets a maximum rating of 30 A for a multioutlet circuit. The resistance-type heating elements on the market are not single heating elements in the 48-A size. They are made up of smaller wattage units into a single piece of equipment. The **Code** rule states that this single piece of equipment made up of smaller units must not draw more than 48 A and must be protected at not more than 60 A. Thus a heater of this type is limited to 48 A for each subdivided circuit. The subdivision is usually made by the manufacturer in the heater enclosure or housing.

Part **(b)** requires that a resistance load less than 48 A have protection rated not less than 125 percent of heater current. The sentence at the end of this paragraph covers overcurrent protection sizing for subdivided resistance-heating-element loads that are less than 48 A.

Figure 424-5 shows an example of subdivision of heater elements in a heat pump with three 5-kW strip heaters in it. At 230 V, each 5-kW strip is a load of about 22 A. Two of them in parallel would be 44 A and that is not in excess of the 48-A maximum set by part **(b)** of this section. The three heaters would be a load of 66 A in parallel. There are a number of ways the total load might be supplied, but the **Code** rules limit the actual permitted types of hookup:

Section 424-3 states that an individual branch circuit may supply any load, but that permission is qualified by part **(b)** of this section, which requires resist-

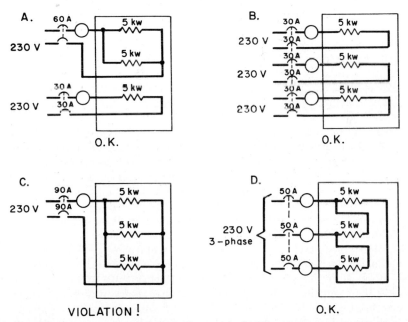

Fig. 424-5. Heater units must be limited to 48-A load with protection not over 60 A. (Sec. 424-22.)

ance heating loads of more than 48 A to be subdivided so that no subdivided heater load will exceed 48 A, protected at not more than 60 A. As shown at A, one possible way to hook up the heaters is to use two strips on one circuit for a connected load of 2 × 22 or 44 A, and the other on one circuit with a connected load of 22 A. The two heaters would require a minimum ampacity for overcurrent protection of 44 × 1.25 or 55 A, calling for a 60-A overcurrent device. For the other circuit, 22 × 1.25 = 27.5 A, requiring a 30-A fuse or breaker. Both circuits would thus be within the limits of a 48-A connected load and 60-A protection. As shown at B, it would also be acceptable to use a 30-A, 2-wire, 230-V circuit to each heater. But use of a single circuit sized at 1.25 × 66 A (82.5 A) and protected by 90-A fuses or breaker would clearly violate the **Code** rule of 60-A maximum protection, as at C.

Another possibility which would give a better balance to the connected load would be to feed the load with a 3-phase, 3-wire, 230-V circuit, if available. For such a circuit, the loading would be:

$$\frac{15,000}{1.732 \times 230} \text{ or } 38 \text{ A}$$

The minimum rating would be 38 × 1.25 or 47.5 A, which calls for 50-A overcurrent protection, as at D.

It should be noted that the rule of part **(b)** in this section applies to *any type* of space heating equipment that utilizes resistance-type heating elements. The rule applies to duct heaters (as in Fig. 424-4), to the strip heaters in Fig. 424-5, and to heating elements in furnaces.

The purpose of paragraph **(c)** of this section is to require the heating manufacturer to furnish the necessary overcurrent protective devices where subdivided loads are required.

Main conductors supplying overcurrent protective devices for subdivided loads are considered as branch circuits to avoid controversies about applying the 125 percent requirement in Sec. 424-3(b) to branch circuits *only*. It is not the intent, however, to deny the use of the *feeder tap* rules in Sec. 240-21 for these *main* conductors.

Paragraph **(e)** requires that the conductors used for the subdivided electric resistance heat circuits specified in Sec. 424-22(c) must have an amp rating not less than 100 percent of the rating or setting of the overcurrent protective device protecting the subdivided circuit(s) (Fig. 424-6). Exception is made for heaters rated 50 kW or more where under the conditions specified it is permissible for the conductors to have an ampacity not less than the load of the respective subdivided circuits, rather than 100 percent of the rating of the protective devices protecting the subdivided circuits.

The wording of part **(e)** clarifies the need for field-wired conductors rated not less than 125 percent of the load-current rating, which must not exceed 48 A. The rating of supplementary overcurrent protection must protect these circuit wires at their ampacity, although the next higher standard rating of protection may be used where the ampacity of the circuit wires does not correspond to a standard protective device rating.

For instance, if the subdivided resistance-heating load is 43 A per phase leg,

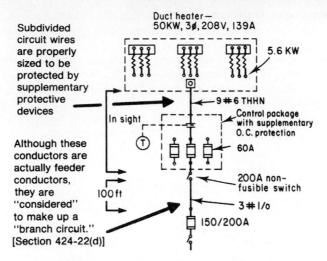

Duct heater—
50KW, 3∅, 208V, 139A

Subdivided circuit wires are properly sized to be protected by supplementary protective devices

5.6 KW

9 # 6 THHN

In sight

Control package with supplementary O.C. protection

60A

Although these conductors are actually feeder conductors, they are "considered" to make up a "branch circuit." [Section 424-22(d)]

100 ft

200A non-fusible switch

3 # 1/o

150/200A

NOTE: There are exceptions for certain equipment.

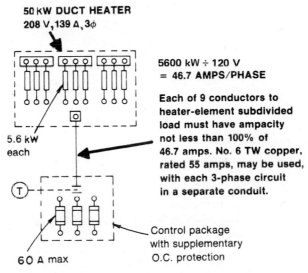

50 KW DUCT HEATER
208 V, 139 A, 3∅

5.6 kW each

5600 kW ÷ 120 V
= 46.7 AMPS/PHASE

Each of 9 conductors to heater-element subdivided load must have ampacity not less than 100% of 46.7 amps. No. 6 TW copper, rated 55 amps, may be used, with each 3-phase circuit in a separate conduit.

Control package with supplementary O.C. protection

60 A max

NOTE: Conditions a, b, and c of the Exception must be satisfied.

Fig. 424-6. Conductors for subdivided heater circuits must fully match overcurrent device rating. (Sec. 424-22.)

the branch-circuit conductors must have an ampacity at least equal to 1.25 × 43, or 53.8 A. That would call for No. 6 TW with an ampacity of 55 A. The next standard rating of protection is 60 A, and that size protection may be used, although 60 A is the maximum size permitted for the subdivided load. The Exception is shown in the bottom part of Fig. 424-6.

424-35. Marking of Heating Cables. Note that there is a color-code for voltage identification of nonheating leads on heating cables to minimize the chance for use on a circuit of excessive voltage.

424-36. Clearances of Wiring in Ceilings. Figure 424-7 shows the details of this rule. The wire at "a." is OK because it is not less than 2 in. above the ceiling, but it must be treated as operating at a 50°C ambient. The same is true of the wire at c, because it is within the insulation. The Correction Factors table below **Code** Table 310-16 shows that TW wire (60°C-rated wire) must be derated to 58 percent (0.58) of its normal table ampacity when operating in an ambient of 41 to 50°C.

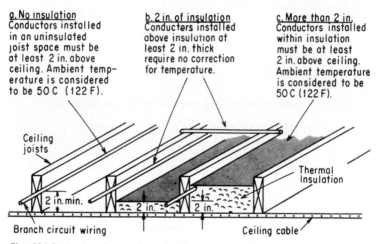

a. No insulation Conductors installed in an uninsulated joist space must be at least 2 in. above ceiling. Ambient temperature is considered to be 50 C (122 F).

b. 2 in. of insulation Conductors installed above insulation at least 2 in. thick require no correction for temperature.

c. More than 2 in. Conductors installed within insulation must be at least 2 in. above ceiling. Ambient temperature is considered to be 50 C (122 F).

Ceiling joists

Thermal Insulation

2 in. min.

2 in.

2 in.

Branch circuit wiring

Ceiling cable

Fig. 424-7. Wiring above a heated ceiling may require derating because of heat accumulation. (Sec. 424-36.)

424-37. Location of Branch-Circuit and Feeder Wiring in Exterior Walls. For branch-circuit wires supplying electric heating cables, this rule no longer requires, as it once did, that branch-circuit wiring "be located outside the thermal insulation." The rule refers to both branch-circuit and feeder wiring in exterior walls and simply references all the wiring rules of Art. 300 and Sec. 310-10, which says in part **(3)** that "Thermal insulation which covers or surrounds conductors will affect the rate of heat dissipation," thereby requiring derating of conductor ampacity.

424-38. Area Restrictions. Figure 424-8 shows installations of heating cables and their relation to **Code** rules.

Heating cable shall not be installed under or over walls or partitions which extend to the ceiling except that "single runs of cable shall be permitted to pass over partitions where they are embedded." The intent here is to avoid repeated crossings of cable over (or under) partitions, since radiation from these sections would be restricted or the cable would be unnecessarily exposed to possible physical damage. While the **Code** specifically speaks of partitions, the same reasoning would apply to arches, exposed ceiling beams, etc.

However, there are times when a small ceiling area (such as over a dressing

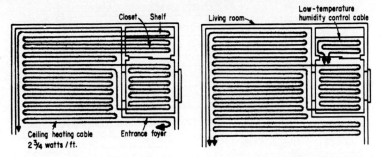

VIOLATION — cable extends beyond room and is installed in the closet. Cable in foyer is O. K.

O. K. — this cable is permitted in closet. Single cable runs that are embedded may cross partition.

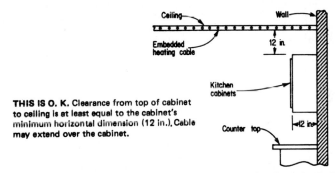

THIS IS O. K. Clearance from top of cabinet to ceiling is at least equal to the cabinet's minimum horizontal dimension (12 in.). Cable may extend over the cabinet.

Fig. 424-8. Layouts of heating cables must generally be confined to individual rooms or areas. (Sec. 424-38.)

room or entryway) is separated from a larger room by such an arch or beam, yet it is impractical to install a separate heating cable and control. The Exception was intended as a solution to this problem. A typical floor plan of such a situation is shown in Fig. 424-9 with two methods of getting the heating cable past the partition or beam. In the upper sketch the cable is brought up into the attic space, through a porcelain tube, and back down through the gypsum board. Plaster is then forced into the tube and puddled over the exposed cable and tube in the attic. This should be the same plaster or joint cement that is used between the two layers of gypsum board.

In the lower sketch a hole is drilled through the top plate of the partition (or beam) and a porcelain tube pressed into the hole. Plaster is packed into the tube after the cable has been passed through. In both cases, the plaster serves to conduct heat away from the cable, avoiding hot spots and possible burnouts.

424-39. Clearance from Other Objects and Openings. Figure 424-10 shows application of the specified clearance distances for different conditions.

424-41. Installation of Heating Cables on Dry Board, in Plaster and on Concrete Ceilings. All heating cables must observe these application methods. Figure 424-11 shows the rules of paragraph (b) and paragraph (f).

Figure 424-12 shows the rule of paragraph (d) and refers to the rule of Sec. 424-43(c) at the outlet box.

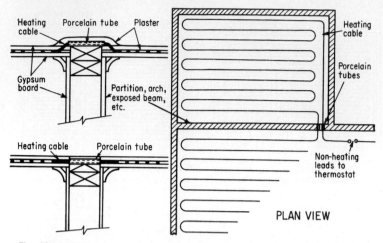

Fig. 424·9. Exception to rule permits single runs across partitions. (Sec. 424-38.)

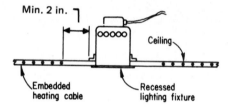

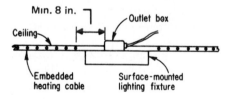

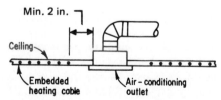

Fig. 424·10. Heating cables and panels must be kept clear of equipment. (Sec. 424-39.)

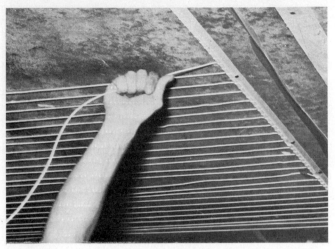

Fig. 424·11. Heating cable not over 2¾ W/ft must have at least 1½-in. spacing between adjacent conductors. (Sec. 424-41.)

Heating cable installed in plaster or between two layers of gypsum board must be kept clear of ceiling fixtures and side walls. In drywall construction, cable must be embedded in mastic or plaster. Without it, dead air space between the cable runs acts as a heat reservoir, increasing the possibility of cable burnouts (Fig. 424-13). Cable movement caused by the expansion and

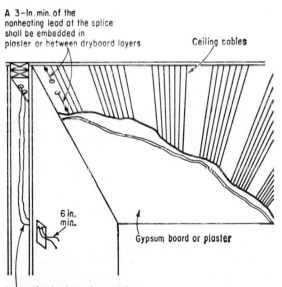

A 3–In. min. of the
nonheating lead at the splice
shall be embedded in
plaster or between dryboard layers

Ceiling cables

6 in.
min.

Gypsum board or plaster

Nonheating leads to thermostat.
Excess leads shall not be cut off,
but shall be embedded in ceiling finish.

Fig. 424·12. Ends of nonheating leads must be embedded in ceiling material. (Sec. 424-41.)

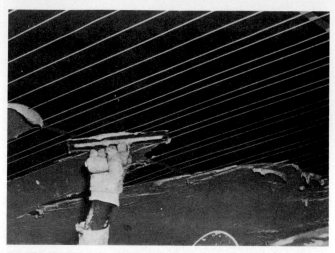

Fig. 424·13. In a drywall ceiling, the heating cable must be covered with a thermally conductive mastic before second course of gypsum board is applied to the ceiling, over the heating cable. (Sec. 424-41.)

contraction accompanying temperature changes is also prevented. Laboratory tests on cable used without mastic have found properly spaced adjacent cable runs actually making contact with each other, producing a hot spot and subsequent burnout. The plaster and sand mixture normally used as a mastic is a good conductor of heat and thus accelerates the dissipation of heat from the entire circumference of the cable. In addition, it improves the conductance from the cable to the gypsum board where the cable does not make direct contact. Even in the most careful installations small irregularities in construction and material prevent perfect contact between the cable and both layers of gypsum board throughout the entire cable length. In no case should an insulating plaster be used. Thickness of the plaster coat should be just sufficient to cover the cable. Installations have been made, unfortunately, with plaster thickness as great as ¾ in. Nails are not capable of supporting the resulting excessive weight, and such ceilings have collapsed. Figure 424-14 shows rules that apply to installation of heating cables in drywall ceilings.

Where the cable is to be embedded between two layers of gypsum board ("drywall" construction), after the cable is stapled to the layer of gypsum lath, it is covered with noninsulating plaster or gypsum cement, and a finishing layer of gypsum board (Sheetrock) is nailed in place covering the cable and plaster. To make sure that nails driven to secure this gypsum board to the ceiling joists do not penetrate the cable, a clear space at least 2½ in. wide must be left between adjacent cable runs immediately beneath each joist. That is, while adjacent cable runs must in general be at least 1½ in. apart, the spacing beneath joists must be increased to at least 2½ in. This means, of course, that the cable must be run parallel to the joists, as in part **(i)**.

Part **(j)** requires that heating cables in ceilings must cross joists only at the ends of the room, except where necessary to satisfy manufacturer's instructions.

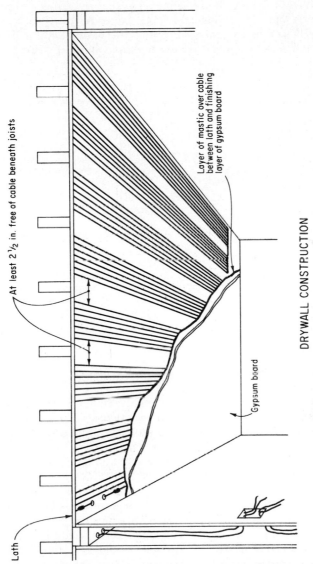

DRYWALL CONSTRUCTION

Fig. 424-14. Additional rules apply only to drywall ceiling construction. (Sec. 424-41.)

If manufacturer's instructions advise the installer to keep the cable away from ceiling penetrations and light fixtures, the Exception here will permit crossing joists at other than the ends of the room.

424-43. Installation of Nonheating Leads of Cables.   Part (c) of this rule prohibits cutting off any of the length of heating leads that are provided by the manufacturers on the ends of heating cable. Any excess length of such leads must be secured to the ceiling and embedded in plaster or other approved material.

424-44. Installation of Cables in Concrete or Poured Masonry Floors.   Details of these rules are shown in Fig. 424-15.

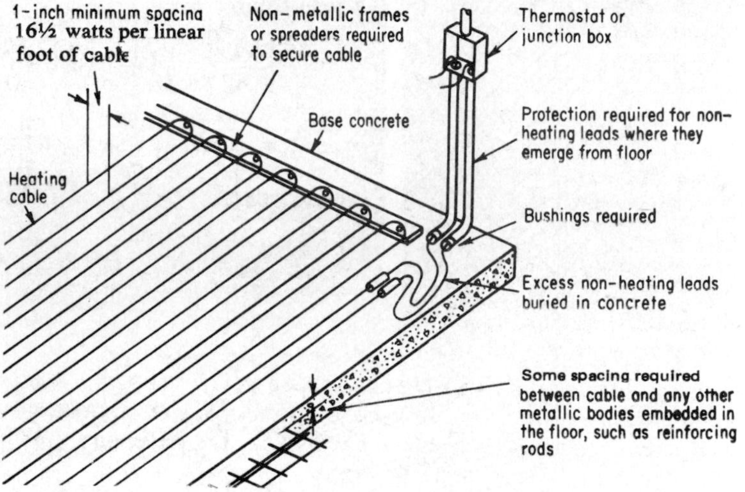

Fig. 424-15. Specific rules apply to heating cable in concrete floors. (Sec. 424-44.)

Paragraph (c) requires cables to be secured in place by nonmetallic frames or spreaders or other approved means. Metallic supports such as those commercially available for use in roadways or sidewalks are not to be used in floor space heating installations. Lumber is often used, although a more common method is to staple the cable directly to the base concrete after it has set about 4 hr. It was not the intention that this **Code** paragraph prohibit the use of metal staples. The object was to reduce the possibility of short circuits because of continuous metallic conducting materials spanning several adjacent cable runs.

Paragraph (d) requires spacing between the heating cable and other metallic bodies embedded in the floor. The intent is to reduce the possibility of contact between the cable and such conducting materials as reinforcing mesh, water pipes, and air ducts (Fig. 424-16).

Paragraph (e) requires leads to be protected where they leave the floor, and paragraph (f) adds that bushings shall be used where the leads emerge in the floor slab. These provisions refer to the nonheating leads which connect the branch circuit home-run to the heating cable. The splices connecting the nonheating leads to the cable are always buried in the concrete. About 6 in. of leads

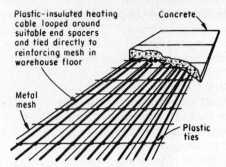

Plastic-insulated heating
cable looped around
suitable end spacers
and tied directly to
reinforcing mesh in
warehouse floor

Concrete

Metal
mesh

Plastic
ties

Fig. 424-16. This would be a violation of paragraph **(d).** (Sec. 424-44.)

is left available in the junction box; any remaining length of nonheating leads is buried in the concrete. The conductors should not be shortened. This applies even though the nonheating leads are Type UF cable. Section 339-3(b) (8) does prohibit the use of UF embedded in poured cement, concrete, or aggregate; however, an Exception to Sec. 339-3(a) is noted for nonheating leads of UF cable because these heating cable assemblies are tested by UL and listed as suitable for such use.

424-57. General. The rules of part **F** of Art. 424 apply to heater units that are mounted in air-duct systems, as shown in Fig. 424-17.

424-70. Scope. In applying **Code** rules, care must be taken to distinguish between "resistance-type" boilers and "electrode-type" boilers (Fig. 424-18).

424-72. Overcurrent Protection. Heating elements of resistance-type electric boilers must be arranged into load groups not exceeding the values specified in paragraph **(a)** or **(b).** Figure 424-19 shows a 360-kW electric boiler used to heat a large school.

Part **(e)** requires that the ampacity of conductors used between the heater and the supplementary overcurrent protective devices for the subdivided heating circuits within such boilers must not be less than 125 percent of the load served.

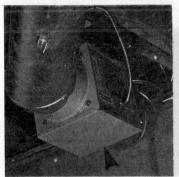

Fig. 424-17. Electric heaters designed and installed to heat air flowing through the ducts of forced-air systems are covered by Secs. 424-57 through 424-66. (Sec. 424-57.)

Fig. 424-18. Electric boilers with resistance-type heating elements are regulated by Secs. 424-70 through 424-75. (Sec. 424-70.)

Fig. 424-19. Electric boiler contains subdivided heating-element circuits, totalling 360 kW. Fuses protect the subdivided circuit loads. (Sec. 424-72.)

Again, however, an Exception is added for heaters rated 50 kW or more under certain given conditions.

424-90. Scope.   The rules of Secs. 424-91 through 424-98 apply to radiant heating panels and heating panel sets. Rules on electric radiant heating panels are separated from the rules on heating cables. The NEC at one time did cover both heating cables and heating panels within the same set of rules. Panels are generically different from cables and require separate specific rules on installation and layout details essential to safety.

424·95. Location of Branch·Circuit and Feeder Wiring in Walls. When electric heating panels are mounted on interior walls of buildings, any wiring within the walls behind the heating panel is considered to be operating in an ambient of 40°C rather than the normal 30°C for which conductors are rated. Because of this, the ampacity of such conductors in wall space behind electric heating panels must be reduced in accordance with the correction factors given as part of Tables 310-16 and 310-18 [Sec. 424-95(b)] (Fig. 424-20).

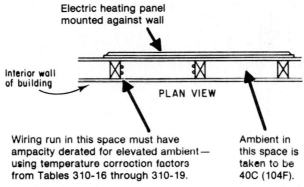

Electric heating panel
mounted against wall

Interior wall
of building

PLAN VIEW

Wiring run in this space must have
ampacity derated for elevated ambient—
using temperature correction factors
from Tables 310-16 through 310-19.

Ambient in
this space is
taken to be
40C (104F).

Fig. 424·20. Wiring in walls behind heating panels must have ampacity corrected for more than 30°C. (Sec. 424-95.)

424·97. Nonheating Leads. Excess length of the nonheating leads of heating panels may be cut to the particular length needed to facilitate connection to the branch-circuit wires (Fig. 424-21).

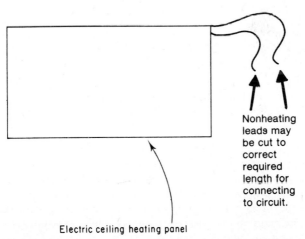

Nonheating
leads may
be cut to
correct
required
length for
connecting
to circuit.

Electric ceiling heating panel

Fig. 424·21. The rule permits cutting of nonheating leads for "panels." (Sec. 424-97.)

ARTICLE 426. FIXED OUTDOOR ELECTRIC DE-ICING AND SNOW-MELTING EQUIPMENT

426-1. Scope. In addition to covering the longtime standard methods and equipment for electric de-icing and snow melting, this article gives detailed coverage of "skin-effect heating"—a system for utilizing the alternating-current phenomenon of skin effect, which derives its name from the tendency of AC current to flow on the outside (the skin) of a conductor. This action is produced by electromagnetic induction, which has an increasing opposition to current flow from the outside to the core of the cross section of a conductor.

In the layout of the article, separate coverage is given to "Resistance Heating," "Impedance Heating," and "Skin-Effect Heating."

426-4. Branch-Circuit Sizing. This basic rule requires that where electric de-icing or snow-melting equipment is connected to a branch circuit, the rating of the branch circuit overcurrent protection and the branch-circuit conductors must be not less than 125 percent of the total load of the heaters (Fig. 426-1).

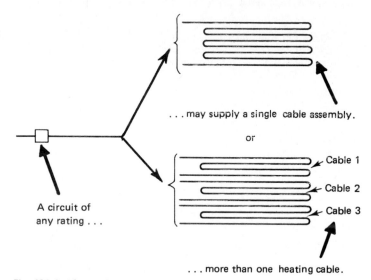

. . . may supply a single cable assembly.

or

Cable 1
Cable 2
Cable 3

A circuit of
any rating . . .

. . . more than one heating cable.

Fig. 426-1. Electric de-icing or snow melting equipment may be fed by a circuit of any rating. (Sec. 426-4.)

Both the circuit conductors and the overcurrent protection must be rated so the load is not over 80 percent of their amp rating. When the branch-circuit conductors are selected to have ampacity of at least 125 percent of the amp value of connected snow-melting and/or de-icing load equipment, it is permissible to go to the next higher amp value of overcurrent protection where the ampacity of the conductors does not correspond to a standard rating of protective device from Sec. 240-6.

426-11. Use. Whether used in concrete, blacktop, or other building material, any de-icing or snow-melting cable, panel, mat, or other assembly must be properly recognized (as by UL) for installation in the particular material.

Application data from the UL's *Electrical Appliance and Utilization Equipment Directory* include the following:

To supplement the general requirements given in the applicable Article of the **National Electrical Code**, the manufacturer is required to provide with the units or mats, specific installation instructions concerning any limitations of the installation and/or use of the equipment. The instructions for mats or cable units intended for burial in concrete will specifically indicate that the slab must be a double pour (poured in two parts) if that is the only acceptable means of installation. If such a limitation is not specifically mentioned, either a single or double pour may be used.

Cable units furnished with nonheating leads of single conductor UF cable, or pre-loomed Type TW wire, have been investigated to determine that the use of additional flexible nonmetallic tubing is not required over the nonheating leads when the cable units are installed. The single conductor UF cable may be identified by the type designation printed at frequent intervals on the cable. Preloomed TW wire consists of Type TW wire with a fabric covering woven over the wire.

Cable units furnished with nonheating leads of Type TW wire or the equivalent shall have the nonheating leads routed through flexible nonmetallic tubing when the cable units are installed.

Radiant heating systems employing cable or other units in installations other than noted above are covered in "listings by report." The description of each system and recommended methods may be obtained upon application to the manufacturer.

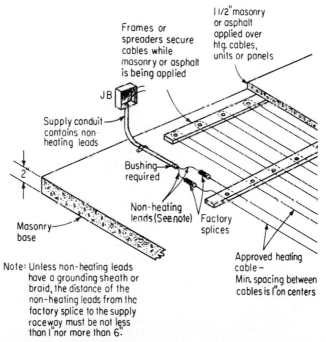

Fig. 426·2. Detailed rules cover installation of heating and nonheating conductors. (Secs. 426-20 and 426-22.)

426·13. Identification.   This rule requires the presence of a de-icing or snow-melting installation to be effectively indicated to assure safety and to prevent disruption.

After a snow-melting installation is made, some type of caution sign or other marking must be posted "where clearly visible" to make it evident to anyone that electric snow-melting equipment is present.

426·23. Installation of Nonheating Leads for Exposed Equipment.   Part **(a)** of this rule permits cutting (shortening) of the nonheating leads provided the required marking on the leads (catalog numbers, volts, watts) is retained. That is not per-

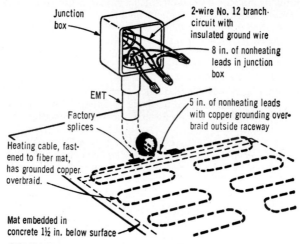

COMPLIES WITH RULES — Nonheating leads with copper grounding braid may have any length embedded in concrete.

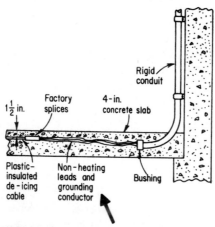

VIOLATION — Excessive length of nonheating leads without a grounding sheath or braid.

Fig. 426·3. Installation of nonheating leads must observe all the rules. (Sec. 426-22.)

mitted for space heating cables, which may not be cut [Sec. 424-43(c)]. The marking on the nonheating leads of snow-melting cable must be within 3 in. of *each* end of the lead. The wording appears to permit cutting the nonheating leads back to the marking closest to the connection to the heating cable—which would mean a length of 3 in. plus that needed for the marking is all that would be required. Or a length could be cut out between the two markings, provided that any splicing that would necessitate is made in boxes, as specified in Sec. 426-24(b).

426-50. Disconnecting Means.   For outdoor de-icing and snow-melting equipment, the CB or fusible switch for the branch circuit to the equipment is adequate disconnecting means as long as it is readily accessible to the user. The cord-plug of plug-connected equipment rated up to 20 A and 150 V may serve as the disconnect device.

ARTICLE 427. FIXED ELECTRIC HEATING EQUIPMENT FOR PIPELINES AND VESSELS

427-22. Equipment Protection.   Electric heating equipment applied to pipelines or vessels must be supplied by a branch circuit with ground fault protection *if* the heating equipment does not have a metal outer covering

Although the title of this section is "Equipment Protection," the major concern is to prevent shock hazard to personnel, which might occur when metal pipe or vessels are energized by a ground fault in electric heating cable or other heating equipment that is not enclosed by a grounded outer metallic enclosure. The "ground-fault protection" referrred to in this rule may be a GFCI.

427-23. Nonmetallic Pipelines.   This rule requires an overall grounded metal jacket on any heating cables intended to be installed on nonmetallic pipelines or vessels. The outer metal covering serves as an equipment ground-return path for fault current in the event of failure of the insulation on the heating conductors. Proper grounding will trip open the faulted circuit and prevent the type of fires that have been reported—as well as providing greater personnel safety.

ARTICLE 430. MOTORS, MOTOR CIRCUITS, AND CONTROLLERS

430-1. Motor Feeder and Branch Circuits.   Two articles in the National Electrical Code are directed specifically to motor applications:

1. Article 430 of the NE Code covers application and installation of motor circuits and motor control hookups—including conductors, short-circuit and ground-fault protection, starters, disconnects, and running overload protection. Article 430 also covers phase converters (3-phase synthesizers) in addition to motors, motor circuits, and controllers. Specific Code rules are given throughout this Article.

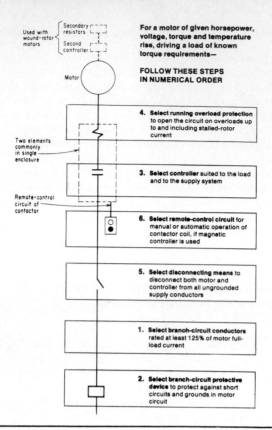

Used with wound-rotor motors
- Secondary resistors
- Second controller

Motor

For a motor of given horsepower, voltage, torque and temperature rise, driving a load of known torque requirements—

FOLLOW THESE STEPS IN NUMERICAL ORDER

Two elements commonly in single enclosure

Remote-control circuit of contactor

4. **Select running overload protection** to open the circuit on overloads up to and including stalled-rotor current

3. **Select controller** suited to the load and to the supply system

6. **Select remote-control circuit** for manual or automatic operation of contactor coil, if magnetic controller is used

5. **Select disconnecting means** to disconnect both motor and controller from all ungrounded supply conductors

1. **Select branch-circuit conductors** rated at least 125% of motor full-load current

2. **Select branch-circuit protective device** to protect against short circuits and grounds in motor circuit

A wide range of new Code rules cover single-to-3-phase converters for motors and other 3-phase loads.

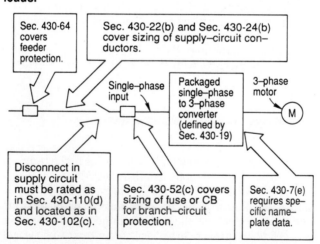

Sec. 430-64 covers feeder protection.

Sec. 430-22(b) and Sec. 430-24(b) cover sizing of supply-circuit conductors.

Single-phase input

Packaged single-phase to 3-phase converter (defined by Sec. 430-19)

3-phase motor

M

Disconnect in supply circuit must be rated as in Sec. 430-110(d) and located as in Sec. 430-102(c).

Sec. 430-52(c) covers sizing of fuse or CB for branch-circuit protection.

Sec. 430-7(e) requires specific name-plate data.

Fig. 430-1. Code rules on motor circuits cover these considerations. (Sec. 430-1.)

2. Article 440, covering "Air-Conditioning and Refrigerating Equipment," contains provisions for such motor-driven equipment and for branch circuits and controllers for the equipment, taking into account the special considerations involved with sealed (hermetic-type) motor compressors, in which the motor operates under the cooling effect of the refrigeration.

Diagram 430-1 in the **NEC** shows how various parts of Art. 430 cover the particular equipment categories that are involved in motor circuits. That **Code** diagram can be restructured, as shown in Fig. 430-1 in this handbook, to present the six basic elements which the **Code** requires the designer to account for in any motor circuit. Although these elements are shown separately here, there are certain cases where the **Code** will permit a single device to serve more than one function. For instance, in some cases, one switch can serve as both disconnecting means and controller.

In other cases, short-circuit protection and overload protection can be combined in a single CB or set of fuses.

Throughout this article, all references to "running overcurrent devices" or simply "overcurrent devices" have been changed to "overload devices." And references to motor "running overcurrent protection" have been changed to "overload protection." This has been done to correlate with the definition of "overload," given in Art. 100, which refers to "Operation of equipment in excess of normal, full-load rating. . . . " A fault, such as a short circuit or ground fault, is not an overload. "Overload" for motors means current due to overload, up to and including locked-rotor current—or failure to start, which is the same level of current.

430-2. Adjustable Speed Drive Systems.   The elements of this rule are shown in Fig. 430-2.

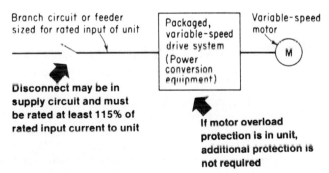

Fig. 430-2. Circuit to packaged drive systems is sized for rating of unit. (Sec. 430-2.)

430-3. Part-Winding Motors.   A part-winding starter is an automatic type of starter for use with squirrel-cage motors which have two separate, parallel windings on the stator. It can be used with the commonly used 220/400-V (dual-voltage) motors when they are used at the lower voltage, with the two windings operating in parallel. Single-voltage motors and 440- and 550-V motors must be ordered as specials if part-winding starting is to be used. The starter contains two magnetic contactors, each of which is rated for half the motor horsepower and is used to supply one winding.

430·6. Ampacity and Motor Rating Determination. For general motor applications (excluding applications of torque motors and sealed hermetic-type refrigeration compressor motors), whenever the current rating of a motor is used to determine the current-carrying capacity of conductors, switches, fuses, or CBs, the values given in Tables 430-147, 430-148, 430-149, and 430-150 must be used instead of the actual motor nameplate current rating. However, selection of separate motor-running overload protection *must* be based on the actual motor nameplate current rating.

As noted in part **(b)**, for any torque motor, the rated nameplate current is the locked-rotor current of the motor, and that value must be used in calculating the motor branch-circuit short-circuit and ground-fault protection in accordance with Sec. 430-52(b). The branch circuit for a torque motor must have its conductors and equipment protected at the motor nameplate rating (locked-rotor current) by selecting a fuse or CB in accordance with Sec. 240-3, Exception No. 4. The rule also requires that conductor ampacity and the setting or rating of the overload protective device be based on this value.

For shaded-pole motors, permanent-split-capacitor motors, and AC adjustable voltage motors, the other rules apply.

430·7. Marking on Motors and Multimotor Equipment. This section covers markings that manufacturers are required to put on the equipment. **Code** Table 430-7(b) can be used to calculate the locked-rotor current of a motor, where that value of current is related to selection of overload protection or short-circuit protection. A typical example would be selection of an instantaneous-trip CB as short-circuit protection of a motor branch circuit. The locked-rotor current of the motor represents the current value above which the breaker (and not the running overload device) must open the circuit. This is described in Sec. 430-52.

430·9. Terminals. As required by part **(b),** unless marked otherwise, copper conductors must be used with motor controllers, and screw-type terminals of control-circuit devices must be torqued. Part **(b)** is intended to assure that only copper wires are used for wiring of motor starters, other controllers, and control-circuit devices because such equipment is designed, tested, and listed for use with copper only. If, however, equipment is tested and listed for aluminum wires, that must be indicated on the equipment, and use of aluminum wires is acceptable.

Part **(c)** requires that a torque screwdriver be used to tighten screw terminals of control-circuit devices used with No. 14 or smaller copper wires. Such terminals must be tightened to a value of 7 lb-in.—unless marked for a different torque value. (See top of Fig. 430-3.)

430·10. Wiring Space in Enclosures. As noted in part **(a)**, standard types of enclosures for motor controllers provide space that is sufficient only for the branch-circuit conductors entering and leaving the enclosure and any control-circuit conductors that may be required. No additional conductors should be brought into the enclosure. Section 430-12 provides a comprehensive set of rules and tables for motor terminal housings to solve the complaint by installers that motor terminal housings are too small to make satisfactory connections.

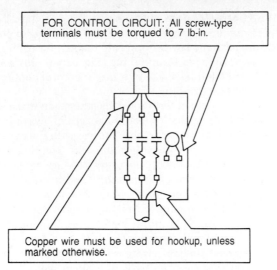

FOR CONTROL CIRCUIT: All screw-type terminals must be torqued to 7 lb-in.

Copper wire must be used for hookup, unless marked otherwise.

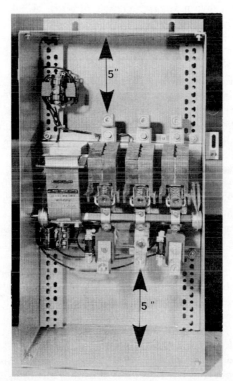

Fig. 430-3. For this size 5 motor starter, use of No. 1/0 THW for the line and load conductors would require a minimum gutter height of 5 in., from Table 430-10(b), to provide **Code**-acceptable wire bending space.

Part **(b)** on "Wire Bending Space in Enclosures" is based on Table 430-10(b), which shows the minimum distance from the end of the lug or connector to the wall of the enclosure or to the barrier opposite the lug, for each size of conductor and for one or two wires per terminal lug (Fig. 430-3). But a provision notes that the minimum wire bending space in a motor control center must conform to the requirements of Sec. 373-6(b).

A further rule applies to use of terminal lugs other than those supplied in the controller by its manufacturer. Such substitute terminal lugs or connectors *must* be of a type identified by the manufacturer for use with the controller, and use of such devices must *not* reduce the minimum wire bending space. That rule would apply, say, where mechanical set-screw lugs are replaced with crimp-on lugs (as for better connection of aluminum conductors). As with switches, CBs, and other equipment, the controller should be marked on its label to indicate acceptability of field changing of the lugs and to specify what type and catalog number of replacement terminal may be used, along with designation of the correct crimping tool and compression die.

430-11. Protection Against Liquids. Excessive moisture, steam, dripping oil, etc., on the exposed current-carrying parts of a motor may cause an insulation breakdown which in turn may be the cause of a fire.

430-12. Motor or Phase Converter Terminal Housings. In part **(e)** the Code rule requires some provision for connecting an equipment grounding conductor at the terminal box where the branch circuit supplies a motor. The grounding connection may be either a "wire-to-wire" connection or a "fixed terminal" connection, and the ground terminal provision may be either inside the junction box—for connection of an equipment grounding conductor run with the circuit wires within the supply raceway—or outside the junction box—for connection of an "equipment bonding jumper" on the outside of a length of flexible metallic conduit or liquidtight flex, either of which is so commonly used. As required by Secs. 350-5 and 351-9, a bonding jumper is required for even short lengths of flex (up to 6 ft) when the wires within the flex are protected at their origin by fuses or CBs rated over 20 A; and liquidtight flex over 1¼-in. size must have a bonding jumper for the typical length (up to 6 ft) used with motor connections. See Sec. 430-145 and Fig. 430-71.

This rule permits either an inside or an outside connection of the bonding jumper to correlate with Sec. 250-79(e), which permits the bonding jumper (up to 6 ft long) to be run either inside or outside the flex.

The Exception to this rule eliminates the need for providing "a separate means for motor grounding" at the junction box where a motor is part of "factory-wired equipment" in which the grounding of the motor is already provided by some other conductive connection that is an element of the overall assembly.

430-13. Bushing. Refer also to Sec. 373-6(c).

430-16. Exposure to Dust Accumulations. The conditions described in this section could make the location a Class II, Division 2 location; the types of motors required are specified in Art. 502.

430-17. Highest Rated or Smallest Rated Motor. Note that the current rating, not the horsepower rating, determines the "highest rated" motor where Code rules refer to such. See Sec. 430-62.

430-22. Single Motor.   The basic rule of part **(a)** says that the conductors supplying a single-speed motor used for continuous duty must have a current-carrying capacity of not less than 125 percent of the motor full-load current rating,
so that under full-load conditions the motor must not load the conductors to
more than 80 percent of their ampacity. For a multispeed motor, selection of
branch-circuit conductors on the supply side of the controller must be based on
the highest full-load current rating shown on the motor nameplate.

Figure 430-4 shows the sizing of branch-circuit conductors to four different
motors fed from a panel. (Sizing is also shown for branch-circuit protection and
running overload protection, as discussed in Secs. 430-34 and 430-52. Refer to
Table 430-150 for motor full-load currents and Table 430-152 for maximum ratings of fuses.) Figure 430-4 is based on the following:

1. Full-load current for each motor is taken from Table 430-150.
2. Running overload protection is sized on the basis that nameplate values
   of motor full-load currents are the same as values from Table 430-150. If
   nameplate and table values are not the same, OL (overload) protection is
   sized according to nameplate.
3. Conductor sizes shown are for copper. Use the amp values given and
   Table 310-16 to select correct size of aluminum conductors.

It is important to note that this rule establishes minimum conductor ratings
based on temperature rise only and does not take into account voltage drop or
power loss in the conductors. Such considerations frequently require increasing the size of branch-circuit conductors.

Exception No. 1 in part **(a)** includes requirements for sizing individual
branch-circuit wires serving motors used for short-time, intermittent, periodic,
or other varying duty. In such cases, frequency of starting and duration of oper-

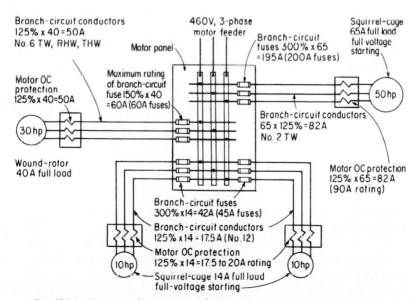

Fig. 430-4. Circuit conductors are sized at 1.25 times motor current. (Sec. 430-22.)

ating cycles impose varying heat loads on conductors. Conductor sizing, therefore, varies with the application. But, it should be noted that the last sentence of Sec. 430-33 says any motor is considered to be for continuous duty unless the nature of the apparatus that it drives is such that the motor cannot operate continuously with load under any condition of use.

When a motor is used for one of the classes of service listed in Table 430-22(a), Exception, the necessary ampacity of the branch-circuit conductors depends upon the class of service and upon the rating of the motor. A motor having a 5-min rating is designed to deliver its rated horsepower during periods of approximately 5 min each, with cooling intervals between the operating periods. The branch-circuit conductors have the advantage of the same cooling intervals and hence can safely be smaller than for a motor of the same horsepower but having a 60-min rating.

In the case of elevator motors, the many considerations involved in determining the smallest permissible size of the branch-circuit conductors make this a complex problem, and it is always the safest plan to be guided by the recommendations of the manufacturer of the equipment. This applies also to feeders supplying two or more elevator motors and to circuits supplying non-continuous-duty motors used for driving some other machines.

Part **(b)** requires that each circuit conductor for the single-phase input to a phase converter have an ampacity at least equal to 2.16 times the full-load current of the 3-phase motors being fed, when input and output voltages are the same. Where input and output voltages are different, the current rating determined as described above must be multiplied by the ratio of output voltage to input voltage. Sec. 430-24(b) covers sizing of feeder conductors to two or more phase converters.

430-23. Wound-Rotor Secondary.   The full-load secondary current of a wound-rotor or slip-ring motor must be obtained from the motor nameplate or from the manufacturer. The starting, or starting and speed-regulating, portion of the controller for a wound-rotor motor usually consists of two parts—a dial-type or drum controller and a resistor bank. These two parts must, in many cases, be assembled and connected by the installer, as in Fig. 430-5.

The conductors from the slip rings on the motor to the controller are in circuit continuously while the motor is running and hence, for a continuous-duty motor, must be large enough to carry the secondary current of the motor continuously.

If the controller is used for starting only and is not used for regulating the speed of the motor, the conductors between the dial or drum and the resistors are in use only during the starting period and are cut out of the circuit as soon as the motor has come up to full speed. These conductors may therefore be of a smaller size than would be needed for continuous duty.

If the controller is to be used for speed regulation of the motor, some part of the resistance may be left in circuit continuously and the conductors between the dial or drum and the resistors must be large enough to carry the continuous load without overheating. In Table 430-23(c) the term *continuous duty* applies to this condition.

Conductors connecting the secondary of a wound-rotor induction motor to

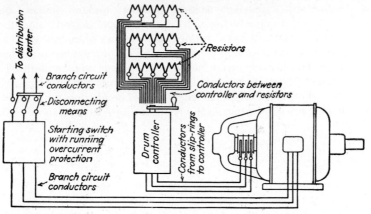

Fig. 430-5. Wound-rotor motor may be used with rotary drum switch for speed control. (Sec. 430-23.)

the controller must have a carrying capacity at least equal to 125 percent of the motor's full-load secondary current if the motor is used for continuous duty. If the motor is used for less than continuous duty, the conductors must have capacity not less than the percentage of full-load secondary nameplate current given in Table 430-22(a) Exception. Conductors from the controller of a wound-rotor induction motor to its starting resistors must have an ampacity in accordance with Table 430-23(c), as shown in Fig. 430-6 for a magnetic starter used for reduced inrush on starting but not for speed control.

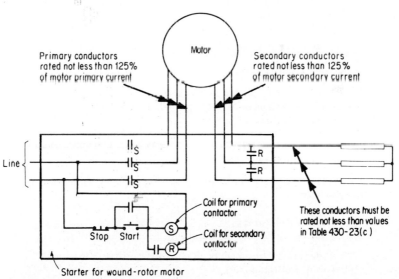

Fig. 430-6. Rules cover conductor sizing for wound-rotor motors without speed control. (Sec. 430-23.)

430·24. Conductors Supplying Several Motors and/or Phase Convert·ers.   Conductors supplying two or more motors (such as feeder conductors to a motor control center, to a panel supplying a number of motors, or to a gutter with several branch circuits tapped off) must have a current rating not less than 125 percent of the full-load current rating of the largest motor supplied plus the sum of the full-load current ratings of the other motors supplied.

Figure 430-7 shows an example of sizing feeder conductors for a load of four motors, selecting the conductors on the basis of ampacities given in Table 310-

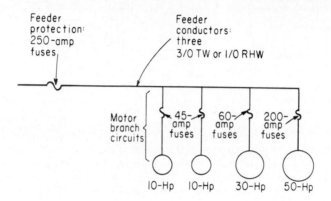

The four motors supplied by the 3-phase, 440-volt, 60-cycle feeder, which are not marked with a code letter (see Table 430-152), are as follows:

    1 50-hp squirrel-cage induction motor (full-voltage starting)
    1 30-hp wound-rotor induction motor
    2 10-hp squirrel-cage induction motors (full-voltage starting).

Step 1. Branch-circuit loads

From Table 430-150, the motors have full-load current ratings as follows:

    50-hp motor—65 amps
    30-hp motor—40 amps
    10-hp motor—14 amps

Step 2. Conductors

The feeder conductors must have a carrying capacity as follows (see Section 430-24):

    $1.25 \times 65 = 81\ amps$
    $81 + 40 + (2 \times 14) = 149\ amps$

The feeder conductors must be at least No. 3/0 TW, 1/0 THW or 1/0 RHH or THHN (copper).

Fig. 430·7. Feeder conductors are sized for the total motor load. (Sec. 430-24.)

16 and using conductors with a 60°C or 75°C insulating rating—or using 90°C-rated conductors at the ampacities of 75°C. UL rules generally prohibit use of 90°C conductors at the 90°C ampacities shown in **Code** Table 310-16. (Refer to Sec. 310-15.)

For the overcurrent protection of feeder conductors of the minimum size permitted by this section, the highest permissible rating or setting of the protective device is specified in Sec. 430-62. Where a feeder protective device of higher rating or setting is used because two or more motors must be started simultaneously, the size of the feeder conductors shall be increased correspondingly.

These requirements and those of Sec. 430-62 for the overcurrent protection of power feeders are based upon the principle that a power feeder should be of such size that it will have an ampacity equal to that required for the starting current of the largest motor supplied by the feeder, plus the full-load running currents of all other motors supplied by the feeder. Except under the unusual condition where two or more motors may be started simultaneously, the heaviest load that a power feeder will ever be required to carry is the load under the condition where the largest motor is started at a time when all the other motors supplied by the feeder are running and delivering their full-rated horsepower.

430-25. Conductors Supplying Motors and Other Loads.

1. The current-carrying capacity of feeder conductors supplying a single motor plus other loads must include capacity at least equal to 125 percent of the full-load current of the motor.
2. The current-carrying capacity of feeder conductors supplying a motor load and a lighting and/or appliance load must be sufficient to handle the lighting and/or appliance load as determined from the procedure for calculating size of lighting feeders, plus the motor load as determined from the previous paragraphs.

The **Code** permits inspectors to authorize use of demand factors for motor feeders—based on reduced heating of conductors supplying motors operating

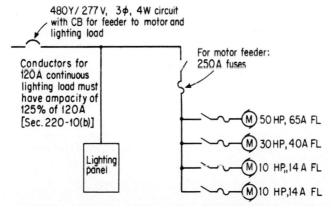

Fig. 430-8. Other load must be properly combined with motor load. (Sec. 430-25.)

intermittently or on duty-cycle or motors not operating together. Where necessary this should be checked to make sure that the authority enforcing the **Code** deems the conditions and operating characteristics suitable for reduced-capacity feeders, as noted in Sec. 430-26.

For computing the minimum allowable conductor size for a combination lighting and power feeder, the required ampacity for the lighting load is to be determined according to the rules for feeders carrying lighting (or lighting and appliance) loads only. Where the motor load consists of one motor only, the required ampacity for this load is the capacity for the motor branch circuit, or 125 percent of the full-load motor current, as specified in Sec. 430-22. Where the motor load consists of two or more motors, the required ampacity for the motor load is the capacity computed according to Sec. 430-24.

Figure 430-8 shows a typical installation for which calculation of required feeder ampacity is as follows:

Step 1. Total Load

Section 430-25(a) says that conductors supplying a lighting load and a motor load must have capacity for both loads, as follows:

$$\text{Motor load} = 65 \text{ A} + 40 \text{ A} + 14 \text{ A} + 14 \text{ A}$$
$$+ (0.25 \times 65 \text{ A}) = 149 \text{ A per phase}$$
$$\text{Lighting load} = 120 \text{ A per phase} \times 1.25 = 150 \text{ A}$$
$$\text{Total load} = 149 + 150 = 299 \text{ A per phase leg}$$

Step 2. Conductors

Table 310-16 shows that a load of 299 A can be served by the following copper conductors:

500 kcmil TW
350 kcmil THW, RHH, XHHW, or THHN

Table 310-16 shows that this same load can be served by the following aluminum or copper-clad aluminum conductors:

700 kcmil TW
500 kcmil THW, RHH, XHHW, or THHN

430-26. Feeder Demand Factor. A demand factor of less than 100 percent may be applied in the case of some industrial plants where the nature of the work is such that there is never a time when all the motors are operating at one time. But the inspector must be satisfied with any application of a demand factor.

Sizing of motor feeders (and mains supplying combination power and lighting loads) may be done on the basis of maximum demand current, calculated as follows:

$$\text{Running current} = (1.25 \times I_f) + (DF \times I_t)$$

where I_f = full-load current of largest motor
DF = demand factor as permitted by Sec. 430-26
I_t = sum of full-load currents of all motors except largest

But modern design dictates use of the maximum-demand starting current in sizing conductors for improved voltage stability on the feeder. This current is calculated as follows:

$$\text{Starting current} = I_s + (DF \times I_t)$$

where I_s = average starting current of largest motor (Use the percent of motor full-load current given for fuses in Table 430-152.)

430-28. Feeder Taps.   This **Code** rule is an adaptation of Exceptions No. 2 and No. 3 of Sec. 240-21, covering use of 10- and 25-ft feeder taps with no overcurrent protection at the point where the smaller conductors connect to the higher-ampacity feeder conductors. The adaptation establishes that the tap conductors must have an ampacity as required by Secs. 430-22, 430-24, or 430-25.

In applying condition (1), the conductor may have an ampacity less than one-third that of the feeder conductors but must be limited to not more than 10 ft in length and be enclosed within a controller or raceway.

If conductors equal in size to the conductors of a feeder are connected to the feeder, as in condition (3), no fuses or other overcurrent protection are needed at the point where the tap is made, since the tap conductors will be protected by the fuses or CB protecting the feeder.

The more important circuit arrangement permitted by the above rule is shown in Fig. 430-9. Instead of placing the fuses or other branch-circuit protec-

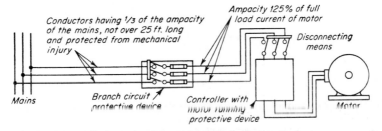

Note: Branch-circuit fuses (or CB) may be rated
higher than ampacity of the tap conductors.

Fig. 430-9. Feeder tap may be sized as provided by Exception No. 3 of Sec. 240-21. (Sec. 430-28.)

tive device at the point where the connections are made to the feeder, conductors having at least one-third the ampacity of the feeder are tapped solidly to the feeder and may be run a distance not exceeding 25 ft to the branch-circuit protective device. From this point on to the motor-running protective device and thence to the motor, conductors are run having the standard ampacity, i.e., 125 percent of the full-load motor current, as specified in Sec. 430-22. If the tap conductors shown did not have an ampacity at least equal to one-third of that of the feeder conductors, then the tap conductors must not be over 10 ft long.

Note that this rule actually modifies the requirements of Sec. 240-21 for taps to motor loads. Section 240-21 Exception No. 2b literally calls for 10-ft tap conductors to have ampacity at least equal to the rating or setting of the fuses or CB (whichever is used) at the load end of the tap. And such protection may be rated up to four times motor full-load current. But condition (1) of this **Code** section does not require such sizing of the tap conductors and simply requires that 10-ft tap conductors be the same size as the branch-circuit wires. And condition (2) does *not* require a 25-ft tap to terminate in a protective device rated to protect the conductors at their ampacity (Fig. 430-10).

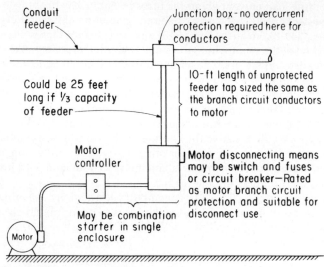

Fig. 430·10. Tap conductors may terminate in protective device rated above their ampacity. (Sec. 430-28.)

example: A 15-hp 230-V 3-phase motor with autotransformer starter is to be supplied by a tap made to a 250 kcmil feeder. All conductors are to be Type THW.

The feeder has an ampacity of 255 A; one-third of 255 A equals 85 A. Therefore the tap cannot be smaller than No. 4, which has an ampacity of 85 A for 75°C ratings.

The full-load current of the motor is 40 A and, according to part **D** of Art. 430, assuming that the motor is not marked with a **Code** letter, the branch-circuit fuses should be rated at not more than 300 percent of 40 A, or 120 A, which calls for 125-A fuses (Sec. 430-52) or less. With the motor-running protection set at 50 A (125 percent × 40 A), the tap conductors are well protected from overload.

The conductors tapped solidly to the feeder must never be smaller than the size of branch-circuit conductors required by Sec. 430-22.

The Exception in this rule notes that a branch-circuit or subfeeder tap up to 100 ft long may be made from a feeder to supply motor loads. The specific conditions are given for making a tap that is over 25 ft long and up to 100 ft long—where no protection is provided at the point of tap from the feeder conductors. This is a motor-circuit adaptation of the 100-ft tap permission, which is fully described under Sec. 240-21, Exception No. 10.

430·29. Constant·Voltage DC Motors—Power Resistors. These rules cover sizing of conductors from a DC motor controller to separate resistors for power accelerating and dynamic braking. This section, with its table of conductor ampacity percentages, assures proper application of DC constant-potential motor controls and power resistors.

430-31. General. Detailed requirements for the installation of fire pumps are not included in the **National Electrical Code**, but this is covered in NFPA Pamphlet No. 20.

As intended by Sec. 430-52, the motor branch-circuit protective device provides short-circuit protection for the circuit conductors. In order to carry the starting current of the motor, this device must commonly have a rating or setting so high that it cannot protect the motor against overload.

For a squirrel-cage induction motor, overload protection must be of the inverse time type with a setting of not over 20 sec at 600 percent of the motor full-load current. It is the intent that the fire-pump motor be permitted to run under any condition of loading and not be automatically disconnected by an overcurrent protection device.

Pamphlet No. 20 requires a CB instead of a fuse as the short-circuit protection for the branch circuit and also requires an unfused isolating switch ahead of the CB.

Except where time-delay fuses provide both running overload protection and short-circuit protection as described in Sec. 430-55, in practically all cases where motor-running overload protection is provided the motor controller consists of two parts: (1) a switch or contactor to control the circuit to the motor and (2) the motor-running protective device. Most of the protective devices make use of a heater coil, usually consisting of a few turns of high-resistance metal, though the heater may be of other form.

430-32. Continuous-Duty Motors. The **Code** makes specific requirements on motor running overload protection intended to protect the elements of the branch circuit—the motor itself, the motor control apparatus, and the branch-circuit conductors—against excessive heating due to motor overloads. Overload protection may be provided by fuses, CBs, or specific overload devices like OL relays.

Overload is considered to be operating overload up to and including stalled-rotor current. When overload persists for a sufficient length of time, it will cause damage or dangerous overheating of the apparatus. Overload does not include fault current due to shorts or grounds.

Typical overload devices include:

1. Heaters in series with line conductors acting upon thermal bimetallic overload relays.
2. Overload devices using resistance or induction heaters and operating on the solder-ratchet principle (Fig. 430-11).
3. Magnetic relays with adjustable instantaneous setting or adjustable time-delay setting.

Of course, the provisions for overload protection are integrated in the enclosure of the controller.

Overload protective devices of the straight thermal type are available with varying tripping and time-delay characteristics. In such devices, the heater coils are made in many sizes and are interchangeable to permit use of the required heater sizes to provide running protection for different motor full-load

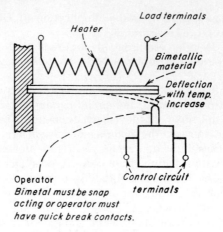

BIMETALLIC TYPE

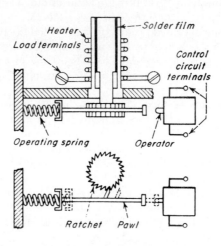

SOLDER-RATCHET TYPE

NOTE: For a manual starter, the contacts
shown are the main load-current contacts of
the switch—connected in series with the
heater coil.

Fig. 430·11. Overload relay devices are made
in various operating types. (Sec. 430-32.)

current ratings. In some units, the heater coil can be adjusted to exact current
values. Individual covers are used on the heating elements in some starters to
isolate the relay from possible effect on its operation because of the temperature of surrounding air.

In general, it is required that every motor shall be provided with a running protective device that will open the circuit on any current exceeding prescribed percentages of the full-load motor current, the percentage depending upon the type of motor. The running protective device is intended primarily to protect the windings of the motor; but by providing that the circuit conductors shall have an ampacity not less than 125 percent of the full-load motor current, it is obvious that these conductors are reasonably protected by the running protective device against any overcurrent caused by an overload on the motor.

Part **(a)** covers application for motors of more than 1 hp. If such a motor is used for continuous duty, running overload protection must be provided. This may be an external overcurrent device actuated by the motor running current and set to open at not more than 125 percent of the motor full-load current for motors marked with a service factor of not less than 1.15 and for motors with a temperature rise not over 40°C. See examples in Fig. 430-4. Sealed (hermetic-type) refrigeration compressor motors must be protected against overload and failure to start, as specified in Sec. 440-52. The overload device must be rated or set to trip at not more than 115 percent of the motor full-load current for all other motors, such as motors with a 1.0 service factor or a 55°C rise (Fig. 430-12).

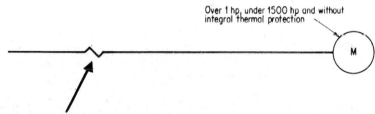

Over 1 hp, under 1500 hp and without integral thermal protection

M

Separate overcurrent device, responsive to motor current, rated or selected to trip at no more than the following percentage of the motor full-load current rating:

Motors with marked service factor not less than 1.15	125%
Motors with marked temperature rise not over 40C	125%
Sealed (hermetic type) motor compressors	
Using overload relays	140%
Using other devices	125%
All other motors	115%

Each winding of a multispeed motor must be considered separately. This value may be modified as permitted by Section 430-34.

Fig. 430-12. Specific rules apply to continuous-duty motors rated over 1 hp. (Sec. 430-32.)

The term *rating* or *setting* as here used means the current at which the device will open the circuit if this current continues for a considerable length of time.

Note: Refer to Sec. 460-9, which discusses the need to correct the sizing of running overload protection when power-factor capacitors are installed on the load side of the controller.

A motor having a temperature rise of 40°C when operated continuously at full load can carry a 25 percent overload for some time without injury to the

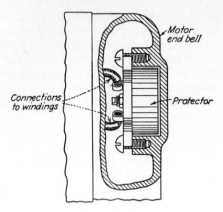

Fig. 430-13. Running overload protection may be built into the motor. (Sec. 430-32.)

motor. Other types of motors, such as enclosed types, do not have so high an overload capacity and the running protective device should therefore open the circuit on a prolonged overload which causes the motor to draw 115 percent of its rated full-load current.

Basic **Code** requirements are concerned with the rating or setting of overcurrent devices separate from motors. However, the **Code** permits the use of integral protection. Paragraph **(2)** of part **(a)** covers use of running overload protective devices within the motor assembly rather than in the motor starter. A protective device integral with the motor as used for the protection of motors is shown in Fig. 430-13. This device is placed inside the motor frame and is connected in series with the motor winding. It contains a bimetallic disk carrying two contacts, through which the circuit is normally closed. If the motor is overloaded and its temperature is raised to a certain limiting value, the disk snaps to the "open" position and opens the circuit. The device also includes a heating coil in series with the motor windings which causes the disk to become heated more rapidly in case of a sudden heavy overload.

Where the circuit-interrupting device is separate from the motor and is actuated by a device integral with the motor, the two devices must be so designed and connected that any accidental opening of the control circuit will stop the motor, otherwise the motor would be left operating without any overcurrent protection.

There is special need for running protection on an automatically started motor because, if the motor is stalled when the starter operates, the motor will probably burn out if it has no running protection.

Part **(b)** of this section applies to smaller motors. Motors of 1 hp or less which are not permanently installed and are manually started are considered protected against overload by the branch-circuit protection if the motor is within sight from the starter (Fig. 430-14). Running overload devices are not required in such cases. A distance of over 50 ft is considered out of sight.

It should be noted that any motor of 1 hp or less which is not portable, is not manually started, and/or is not within sight from its starter location must have

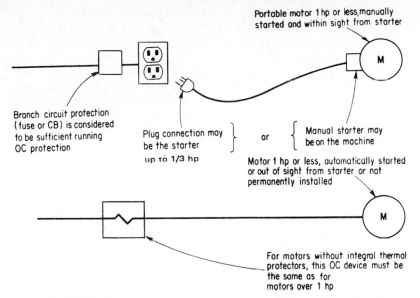

Fig. 430-14. The rules for automatic-start motors are different. (Sec. 430-32.)

specific running overload protection. Automatically started motors of 1 hp or less must be protected against running overload in the same way as motors rated over 1 hp—as noted in part **(c)**. That is, a separate or integral overload device must be used.

There are alternatives to the specific overload protection rules of parts **(a)** and **(c)**. Under certain conditions, no specific running overload protection need be used: The motor is considered to be properly protected if it is part of an approved assembly which does not normally subject the motor to overloads and which has controls to protect against stalled rotor. Or if the impedance of the motor windings is sufficient to prevent overheating due to failure to start, the branch-circuit protection is considered adequate.

430-33. Intermittent and Similar Duty.   A motor used for a condition of service which is inherently short-time, intermittent, periodic, or varying duty does not require protection by overload relays, fuses, or other devices required by Sec. 430-32, but, instead, is considered as protected against overcurrent by the branch-circuit overcurrent device (CB or fuses rated in accordance with Sec. 430-52). Motors are considered to be for continuous duty unless the motor is completely incapable of operating continuously with load under any condition of use.

430-34. Selection of Overload Relay.   This rule sets the absolute maximum permitted rating of an overload relay where values are higher than the 125 or 115 percent trip ratings of Secs. 430-32(a) (1) and (c). Motors with a marked service factor not less than 1.15 and 40°C-rise motors may, if necessary to enable the motor to start or carry its load, be protected by overload relays with trip settings up to 140 percent of motor full-load current. Motors with a 1.0 service factor and motors with a temperature rise over 40°C (such as 55°C-rise motors) must have their relay trip setting at not over 130 percent of motor full-load current.

BUT WATCH OUT! The maximum settings of 140 percent or 130 percent apply only to OL relays, such as used in motor starters.

Fuses or CBs may be used for running overload protection but may not be rated or set up to the 140 or 130 percent values. Fuses and breakers must have a maximum rating as shown in Secs. 430-32(a) and (c). If the value determined as indicated there does not correspond to a standard rating of fuse or CB, the next smaller size must be used. A rating of 125 percent of full-load current is the absolute maximum for fuses or breakers.

430-35. Shunting During Starting Period. As covered in part **(a)** for motors that are *not* automatically started, where fuses are used as the motor-running protection, they may be cut out of the circuit during the starting period. This leaves the motor protected only by the branch-circuit fuses, but the rating of these fuses will always be well within the 400 percent limit specified in the rule. If the branch-circuit fuses are omitted, as allowed by the rule in Sec. 430-53(d), it is not permitted to use a starter that cuts out the motor fuses during the starting period unless the protection of the feeder is within the limits set by this rule. As shown in Fig. 430-15, a double-throw switch is arranged for across-the-line starting. The switch is thrown to the right to start the motor, thus cutting the running fuses out of the circuit. The switch must be so made that it cannot be left in the starting position.

In the Exception to part **(b)**, conditions are given for shunting out overload protection of a motor that is automatically started. In previous **Code** editions, any motor that was automatically started was not permitted to have its overload protection shunted or cut out during the starting period. This Exception now accommodates those motor-and-load applications that have a long accelerating time and would otherwise require an overload device with such a long trip time that the motor would not be protected if it stalled while running.

430-36. Fuses—In Which Conductor. This rule is listed in Sec. 240-22 as Exception No. 2 to the rule that prohibits use of an overcurrent device in an intentionally grounded conductor. When fuses are used for protection of service, feeder, or branch-circuit conductors, a fuse must never be used in a grounded conductor, such as the grounded leg of a 3-phase, 3-wire corner-grounded delta system. But, if fuses are used for OL protection for a 3-phase motor connected on such a system, a fuse must be used in all three phase legs—

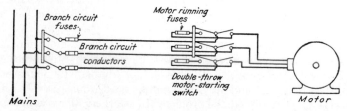

Fig. 430-15. Motor OL fuses may be shunted out for starting. (Sec. 430-35.)

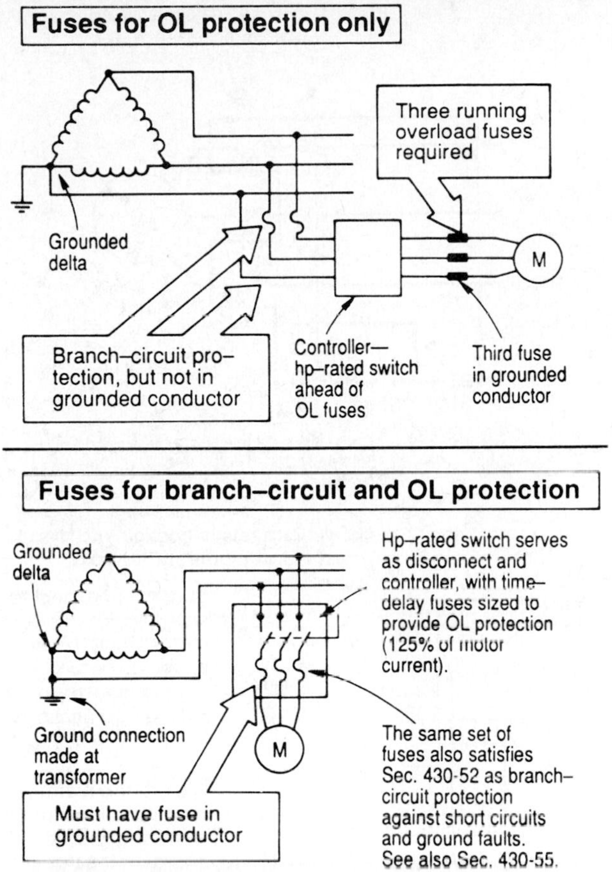

Fuses for OL protection only

Three running
overload fuses
required

Grounded
delta

M

Branch–circuit pro-
tection, but not in
grounded conductor

Controller—
hp–rated switch
ahead of
OL fuses

Third fuse
in grounded
conductor

Fuses for branch–circuit and OL protection

Grounded
delta

Hp–rated switch serves
as disconnect and
controller, with time–
delay fuses sized to
provide OL protection
(125% of motor
current).

Ground connection
made at
transformer

M

Must have fuse in
grounded conductor

The same set of
fuses also satisfies
Sec. 430-52 as branch–
circuit protection
against short circuits
and ground faults.
See also Sec. 430-55.

Fig. 430-16. A fuse for OL protection must be used in each phase leg of
circuit. (Sec. 430-36.)

EVEN THE GROUNDED LEG. Figure 430-16 shows two conditions of such
fuse application for OL protection for a motor.

430-37. Devices Other than Fuses—In Which Conductor.   Complete data on the
number and location of overcurrent devices are given in **Code** Table 430-37.

Table 430-37 requires three running overload devices (trip coils, relays, thermal cutouts, etc.) for all 3-phase motors unless protected by other approved
means, such as specifically designed embedded detectors with or without supplementary external protective devices.

Figure 430-17 points up this requirement.

If fuses are used as the running protective device, Sec. 430-36 requires a fuse
in each ungrounded conductor. If the protective device consists of an automatically operated contactor or CB, the device must open a sufficient number of
conductors to stop the current flow to the motor and must be equipped with the
number of overcurrent units specified in Table 430-37.

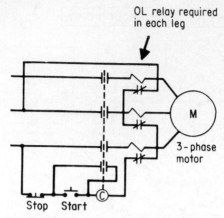

OL relay required
in each leg

Fig. 430·17. Three OL units are required for 3-phase motors. (Sec. 430-37.)

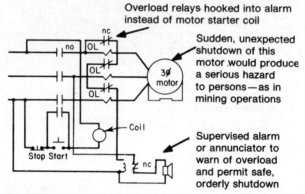

Overload relays hooked into alarm
instead of motor starter coil

Sudden, unexpected
shutdown of this
motor would produce
a serious hazard
to persons—as in
mining operations

Supervised alarm
or annunciator to
warn of overload
and permit safe,
orderly shutdown

Fig. 430·18. This type of hookup may be used to warn of, but not open, an overload. (Sec. 430-44.)

430·42. Motors on General-Purpose Branch Circuits.   Refer to Fig. 430-19, Type 3.

Branch circuits supplying lamps are usually 115-V single-phase circuits, and on such circuits the effect of subparagraphs **(a)** and **(b)** is that any motor larger than 6 A must be provided with a starter that is approved for group operation.

It is provided in Sec. 210-24 that receptacles on a 20-A branch circuit may have a rating of 20 A, and in such case subparagraph **(c)** requires that any motor or motor-driven appliance connected through a plug and receptacle must have running overcurrent protection. If the motor rating exceeds 1 hp or 6 A, the protective device must be permanently attached to the motor and subparagraph **(b)** must be complied with.

The requirements of Sec. 430-32 for the running overcurrent protection of

Type 1

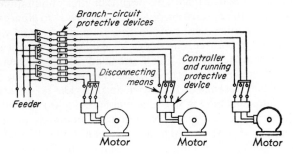

Type 2

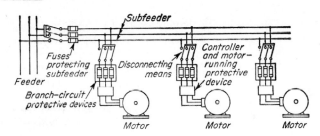

Type 3

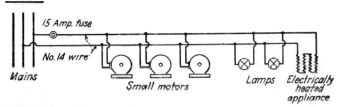

Fig. 430-19. Motor branch-circuit protection is used in various types of layouts. (Sec. 430-51.)

motors must be complied with in all cases, regardless of the type of branch circuit by which the motor is supplied and regardless of the number of motors connected to the circuit.

430-43. Automatic Restarting. As noted in the comments to Sec. 430-32, an integral motor-running protective device may be of the type which will automatically restart, or it may be so constructed that after tripping out it must be closed by means of a reset button.

430-44. Orderly Shutdown. Although the NE Code has all those requirements on use of running overload protection of motors, this section recognizes that there are cases when automatic opening of a motor circuit due to overload may be objectionable from a safety standpoint. In recognition of the needs of many industrial applications the rule here permits alternatives to automatic opening of a circuit in the event of overload. This permission for elimination of overload protection is similar to the permission given in Sec. 240-12 to eliminate overload protection when automatic opening of the circuit on an overload would constitute a more serious hazard than the overload itself. However, it is necessary that the circuit be provided with a motor overload sensing device conforming to the **Code** requirement on overload protection to indicate by means of a supervised alarm the presence of the overload (Fig. 430-18). Overload indication instead of automatic opening will alert personnel to the objectionable condition and will permit corrective action, either immediately or at some more convenient time, for an orderly shutdown to resolve the difficulty. But, as is required in Sec. 240-12, short-circuit protection on the motor branch circuit must be provided to take care of those high-level ground faults and short circuits that would be more serious in their hazardous implications than simple overload.

Note: Section 445-4 also has an Exception that permits this same use of an alarm instead of overcurrent protection where it is better to have a generator fail than stop operating.

430-51. General.   This section indicates the coverage of part **D**, which requires "Motor Branch-Circuit Short-Circuit and Ground-Fault Protection." Although the phrase "ground-fault protection" is used in several of the sections of part **D**, it should be noted that it refers to the protection against ground fault that is provided by the fuses or CB that are used to provide short-circuit protection. The single CB or set of fuses is referred to as a "short-circuit and ground-fault protective device." The rule is *not* intended to require the type of ground-fault protective hookup required by Sec. 230-95 on service disconnects (such as a zero-sequence transformer and relay hookup).

Motor branch circuits are commonly laid out in a number of ways. With respect to branch-circuit protection location and type, the layouts shown in Fig. 430-19 are as follows:

Type 1

An individual branch circuit leads to each motor from a distribution center. This type of layout can be used under any conditions and is the one most commonly used.

Type 2

A feeder or subfeeder with branch circuits tapped on at convenient points. This is the same as Type 1 except that the branch-circuit overcurrent protective devices are mounted individually at the points where taps are made to the subfeeder, instead of being assembled at one location in the form of a branch-circuit distribution center. Under certain conditions, the branch-circuit protective devices may be located at any point not more than 25 ft distant from the point where the branch circuit is tapped to the feeder.

Type 3

Small motors, lamps, and appliances may be supplied by a 15- or 20-A circuit as described in Art. 210. Motors connected to these circuits must be provided with running overcurrent protective devices in most cases. See Sec. 430-42.

Figure 430-20 shows the typical elements of a motor branch circuit in their relation to branch-circuit protection, so that the protection is effective for the circuit conductors, the control and disconnect means, and the motor. Motor controllers provide protection for the motors they control against all ordinary overloads but are not intended to open short circuits. Fuses, CBs, or motor short-circuit protectors used as the branch-circuit protective device will open short circuits and therefore provide short-circuit protection for both the motor and the running protective device. Where a motor is supplied by an individual branch circuit, having branch-circuit protection, the circuit protective devices may be either fuses or a CB and the rating or setting of these devices must not exceed the values specified in Sec. 430-52. In Fig. 430-20, the fuses or CB at the panelboard must carry the starting current of the motor, and in order to carry

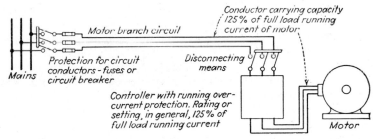

Fig. 430-20. Branch-circuit protection is on the line side of other components. (Sec. 430-51.)

this current the fuse rating or CB setting may be rated up to 300 or 400 percent of the running current of the motor, depending on the size and type of motor. It is evident that to install motor circuit conductors having an ampacity up to that percent of the motor full-load current would be unnecessary.

There are three possible causes of excess current in the conductors between the panelboard and the motor controller, viz., a short circuit between two of these conductors, a ground on one conductor that forms a short circuit, and an overload on the motor. A short circuit would draw so heavy a current that the fuses or breaker at the panelboard would immediately open the circuit, even though the rating or setting is in excess of the conductor ampacity. Any excess current due to an overload on the motor must pass through the protective device at the motor controller, causing this device to open the circuit. Therefore with circuit conductors having an ampacity equal to 125 percent of the motor-running current and with the motor-protective device set to operate at near the same current, the conductors are reasonably protected.

430-52. Rating or Setting for Individual Motor Circuit. The **Code** requires that branch-circuit protection for motor circuits must protect the circuit conductors, the control apparatus, and the motor itself against overcurrent due to short circuits or ground (Secs. 430-51 through 430-58).

The first, and obviously necessary, rule is that the branch-circuit protective device for an individual branch circuit to a motor must be capable of carrying the starting current of the motor without opening the circuit. Then the **Code** proceeds to place maximum values on the ratings or settings of such overcurrent devices. It says that such devices must not be rated in excess of the values given in Table 430-152.

In case the values for branch-circuit protective devices determined by Table 430-152 do not correspond to the standard sizes or ratings of fuses, nonadjustable CBs, or thermal devices, or possible settings of adjustable CBs adequate to carry the load, the next higher size, rating, or setting may be used.

Under exceptionally severe starting conditions where the nature of the load is such that an unusually long time is required for the motor to accelerate to full speed, the fuse or CB rating or setting recommended in Table 430-152 may not be high enough to allow the motor to start. It is desirable to keep the branch-circuit protection at as low a rating as possible, but in unusual cases, it is permissible to use a higher rating or setting. Where absolutely necessary in order to permit motor starting, the device may be rated at other maximum values, as follows:

1. The rating of a fuse that is *not* a dual-element time-delay fuse and is rated not over 600 A may be increased above the **Code** table value but must never exceed 400 percent of the full-load current.

2. The rating of a time-delay (dual-element) fuse may be increased but must never exceed 225 percent of full-load current.

3. The setting of an instantaneous trip CB that is part of a *listed* combination starter (which contains a magnetic short-circuit trip element, without time delay, and separate overload device) may be increased but never over 1,300 percent of the motor full-load current.

4. The rating of an inverse time CB (a typical thermal-magnetic CB with a time-delay and instantaneous trip characteristic) may be increased but must not exceed 400 percent for full-load currents of 100 A or less and must not exceed 300 percent for currents over 100 A.

5. A fuse rated 601 to 6,000 A may be increased but must not exceed 300 percent of full-load current.

6. Torque motors must be protected at the motor nameplate current rating, and if a standard overcurrent device is not made in that rating, the next higher standard rating of protective device may be used.

The rules of this section establish maximum values for branch-circuit protection, setting the limit of safe applications. However, use of smaller sizes of branch-circuit protective devices is obviously permitted by the **Code** and does offer opportunities for substantial economies in selection of CBs, fuses and the switches used with them, panelboards, etc. In any application, it is only necessary that the branch-circuit device which is smaller than the maximum permitted rating must have sufficient time delay in its operation to permit the motor starting current to flow without opening the circuit.

But a CB for branch-circuit protection must have a continuous current rating of not less than 115 percent of the motor full-load current, as required by Sec. 430-58.

Where maximum ratings for the branch-circuit protection are shown in the manufacturer's heater table for use with a marked controller or are otherwise marked with the equipment, they must not be exceeded even though higher values are indicated in **Code** Table 430-152 and in the other rules of this section. That requirement is in the last sentence of this **Code** rule and is also specified in UL regulations which regulate the exposure of motor controllers to short-circuit currents to protect internal components, such as overload relays and contacts, from damage or destruction. Those rules state:

Motor controllers incorporating thermal cutouts, thermal overload relays, or other devices for motor-running overcurrent protection are considered to be suitably protected against overcurrent due to short circuits or grounds by motor branch circuit, short circuit and ground-fault protective devices selected in accordance with the **National Electrical Code** and any additional information marked on the product. Motor controllers may specify that protection is to be provided by fuses or by an inverse time circuit breaker. If there is no marking of protective device type, controllers are considered suitably protected by either type of device. Motor controllers may specify a maximum rating of protective device. If not marked with a rating, the controllers are considered suitably protected by a protective device of the maximum rating permitted by the **National Electrical Code.**

Unless otherwise marked, motor controllers incorporating thermal cutouts or overload relays are considered suitable for use on circuits having available fault currents not greater than [refer to Fig. 430-21]:

Horsepower rating	RMS symmetrical amperes
1 or less	1,000
1½ to 50	5,000
51 to 200	10,000
201 to 400	18,000
401 to 600	30,000
601 to 900	42,000
901 to 1600	85,000

Typical application of the basic rule of Sec. 430-52 on short-circuit protection for motor circuits is shown in Fig. 430-4. Overcurrent (branch-circuit) protection (from Table 430-152 and Sec. 430-52) using nontime-delay fuses is calculated as follows:

1. The 50-hp squirrel-cage motor must be protected at not more than 200 A (65 A × 300 percent).
2. The 30-hp wound-rotor motor must be protected at not more than 60 A (40 A × 150 percent).
3. Each 10-hp motor must be protected at not more than 45 A (14 × 300 percent).

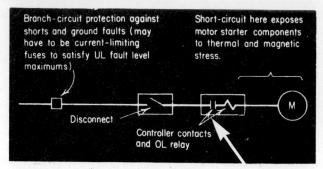

Branch-circuit protection against shorts and ground faults (may have to be current-limiting fuses to satisfy UL fault level maximums)

Short-circuit here exposes motor starter components to thermal and magnetic stress.

Disconnect

Controller contacts and OL relay

M

AVAILABLE SHORT-CIRCUIT CURRENT HERE MUST NOT EXCEED VALUES GIVEN BY UL OR MUST BE LIMITED TO THOSE VALUES

Fig. 430-21. UL specifies maximum short-circuit withstand ratings for controllers. (Sec. 430-52.)

As shown in **Code** Table 430-152, if thermal-magnetic CBs were used, instead of the fuses, for branch-circuit protection, the maximum ratings that are permitted by the basic rule are:

1. For the 50-hp motor—65 A × 250 percent or 162.5 A, with the next higher standard CB rating of 175 A permitted.
2. For the 30-hp wound-rotor motor—40 A × 150 percent or 60 A, calling for a 60-A CB.
3. For each 10-hp motor—14 A × 250 percent or 35 A, calling for a 35-A CB.

Instantaneous Trip CBs

The **NE Code** recognizes the use of an instantaneous trip CB (without time delay) for short-circuit protection of motor circuits. Such breakers—also called "magnetic-only" breakers—may be used only if they are adjustable and if combined with motor starters in combination assemblies. An instantaneous-trip CB or a motor short-circuit protector (MSCP) may be used *only* as part of a "listed" (such as by UL) combination motor controller. A combination motor starter using an instantaneous trip breaker must have running overload protection in each conductor (Fig. 430-22). Such a combination starter offers use of a smaller CB than would be possible if a standard thermal-magnetic CB were used. And the smaller CB offers faster operation for greater protection against grounds and short circuits—in addition to offering greater economy.

A combination motor starter, as shown in Fig. 430-22, is based on the characteristics of the instantaneous trip CB, which is covered by the third percent column from the left in **Code** Table 430-152. Molded-case CBs with only magnetic instantaneous trip elements in them are available in almost all sizes. Use of such a device requires careful accounting for the absence of overload protection in the CB, up to the short-circuit trip setting. Such a CB is designed for use as shown in Fig. 430-22. The circuit conductors are sized for at least 125

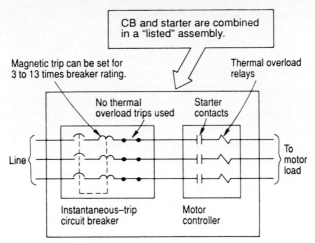

Fig. 430-22. Section 430-52 accepts use of a magnetic-only circuit breaker if it is part of a "listed" assembly of a combination starter. (Sec. 430-22.)

percent of motor current. The thermal overload relays in the starter protect the entire circuit and all equipment against operating overloads up to and including stalled rotor current. They are commonly set at 125 percent of motor current. In such a circuit, a CB with an adjustable magnetic trip element can be set to take over the interrupting task at currents above stalled rotor and up to the short-circuit duty of the supply system at that point of installation. The magnetic trip in a typical unit might be adjustable from 3 to 13 times the breaker current rating; i.e., a 100-A trip can be adjusted to trip anywhere between 300 and 1,300 A. Thus the CB serves as motor circuit disconnect and short-circuit protection.

Selection of such a listed assembly with an instantaneous-only CB is based on choosing a nominal CB size with a current rating at least equal to 115 percent of the motor full-load current to carry the motor current and to qualify under Secs. 430-58 and 430-110(a) as a disconnect means. Then the adjustable magnetic trip is set to provide the short-circuit protection—the value of current at which instantaneous circuit opening takes place, which should be just above the starting current of the motor involved—using a multiplier of something like 1.5 on locked-rotor current to account for asymmetry in starting current. Asymmetry can occur when the circuit to the motor is closed at that point on the alternating voltage wave where the inrush starting current is going through the negative maximum value of its alternating wave. That is the same concept as asymmetry in the initiation of a short-circuit current.

Listed equipment using an instantaneous CB type is available with very simple instructions by the manufacturer to make proper selection and adjustment of the instantaneous-trip CB combination starter a quick, easy matter. The following describes the concept behind the application of combination starters with instantaneous-only CBs.

Given: A 30-hp, 230-V, 3-phase, squirrel-cage motor marked with the code letter M, indicating that the motor has a locked-rotor current of 10 to 11.19 kVA per horsepower, from **Code** Table 430-7(b). A full-voltage controller is combined with the CB, with running overload protection in the controller to protect the motor within its heating damage curve on overload.

Required: Select a CB which will provide short-circuit protection and will qualify as the motor circuit disconnect means.

Solution: The motor has a full-load current of 80 A (**Code** Table 430-150). A CB suitable for use as disconnect must have a current rating at least 115 percent of 80 A. **Code** Table 430-152 will permit the use of an inverse time (the usual thermal-magnetic) CB rated not more than 250 percent of motor full-load current (although a CB could be rated as high as 400 percent of full-load current if such size were necessary to pass motor starting current without opening). Based on 2.5 × 80 or 200 A, a 225-A frame size with 200-A trip setting could be selected. The large size of this CB will generally take the starting current of the motor without tripping either the thermal element or the magnetic element in the CB. The starting current of the motor will initially be about 882 A (30 hp × 11.19 kVA per hp ÷ 220 V × 1.73). The instantaneous trip setting of the 200-A CB will be about 200 × 10 or 2,000 A. Such a CB will provide protection for grounds and shorts without interfering with motor-running overload protection.

But consider use of a 100-A CB with thermal and adjustable magnetic trips. The instantaneous trip setting at 10 times current rating would be 1,000 A, which is above the 882-A locked-rotor current. But starting current would probably trip the thermal element and open the CB. This problem can be solved by using a CB without a thermal element, leaving only the magnetic element in the CB. Then the conditions of operating overload can be cleared by the running overload devices in the motor starter, right up to stalled rotor, with the magnetic trip adjusted to open the circuit instantaneously on currents above, say, 1,300 A (882 × 1.5). But because the value of 1,300 A is greater than 1,300 percent of the motor full-load current (80 × 13 = 1,040 A), Sec. 430-52 Exception (c) would prohibit setting the CB at 1,300 A. The maximum setting would be 1,000 A.

Because the use of a magnetic-only CB does not protect against low-level grounds and shorts in the circuit conductors on the line side of the starter running overload relays, the **NE Code** rule permits such application only where the CB and starter are part of a *listed* combination starter in a single enclosure.

MSCPs

A motor short-circuit protector, as referred to in the second paragraph of Sec. 430-52, is a fuselike device designed for use only in its own type of fusible-switch combination motor starter. The combination offers short-circuit protection, running overload protection, disconnect means, and motor control—all with assured coordination between the short-circuit interrupter (the motor short-circuit protector) and the running OL devices. It involves the simplest method of selection of the correct MSCP for a given motor circuit. This packaged assembly is a third type of combination motor starter—added to the conventional fusible-switch and CB types.

The NE Code recognizes motor short-circuit protectors in Secs. 430-40 and 430-52 provided the combination is a "listed" assembly. This means a combination starter equipped with motor short-circuit protectors and listed by Underwriters Laboratories Inc., or another nationally recognized testing lab, as a package called an MSCP starter.

Part **(c)** requires that branch-circuit conductors for a phase converter must be protected in accordance with their ampacity, determined from new Sec. 430-22(b). The short-circuit protection for the branch-circuit conductors and the equipment must be sized as required by Sec. 240-3, Exception No. 4, based on conductor ampacity.

430-53. Several Motors or Loads on One Branch Circuit.   A single branch circuit may be used to supply two or more motors as follows:

Part **(a):** Two or more motors, each rated not more than 1 hp and each drawing not over 6 A full-load current, may be used on a branch circuit protected at not more than 20 A at 125 V or less, or 15 A at 600 V or less. And the rating of the branch-circuit protective device marked on any of the controllers must not be exceeded. That is also a UL requirement.

Individual running overload protection is necessary in such circuits, unless: the motor is not permanently installed, is manually started, and is within sight from the controller location; or the motor has sufficient winding impedance to prevent overheating due to stalled rotor current; or the motor is part of an approved assembly that does not subject the motor to overloads and that incorporates protection for the motor against stalled rotor; or the motor cannot operate continuously under load.

Part **(b):** Two or more motors of any rating, each having individual running overload protection, may be connected to a branch circuit which is protected by a short-circuit protective device selected in accordance with the maximum rating or setting of a device which could protect an individual circuit to the motor of the smallest rating. This may be done only where it can be determined that the branch-circuit device so selected will not open under the most severe normal conditions of service which might be encountered.

This permission of part **(b)** offers wide application of more than one motor on a single circuit, particularly in the use of small integral-horsepower motors installed on 440-V, 3-phase systems. This application primarily concerns use of small integral-horsepower 3-phase motors as used in 208-V, 220-V, and 440-V industrial and commercial systems. Only such 3-phase motors have full-load operating currents low enough to permit more than one motor on circuits fed from 15-A protective devices.

There are a number of ways of connecting several motors on a single branch circuit, as follows:

In Case I, Fig. 430-23, using a three-pole CB for branch-circuit protective device, application is made in accordance with part **(b)** as follows:

1. The full-load current for each motor is taken from NE Code Table 430-150 [as required by Sec. 430-6(a)].
2. Choosing to use a CB instead of fuses for branch-circuit protection, the rating of the branch-circuit protective device, 15-A, does not exceed the maximum value of short-circuit protection required by Sec. 430-52 and

CASE I—USING A CIRCUIT BREAKER FOR PROTECTION

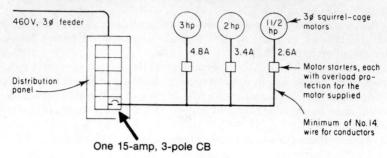

One 15-amp, 3-pole CB

HERE IS THE KEY: A 15-amp, 3-pole CB is used, based on Section 430-52 and Table 430-152. This is the "next higher size" of standard protective device above 250% × 2.6 amps (the required rating for the smallest motor of the group). The 15-amp CB makes this application possible, because the 15-amp CB is the smallest standard rating of CB and is suitable as the branch-circuit protective device for the 1½-hp motor.

Fig. 430-23. Three integral-horsepower motors may be supplied by this circuit makeup. (Sec. 430-53.)

Table 430-152 for the smallest motor of the group—which is the 1½-hp motor. Although 15 A is greater than the maximum value of 250 percent times motor full-load current (2.5 × 2.6 A = 6.5 A) set by Table 430-152 (under the column "Inverse Time Breaker" opposite "polyphase squirrel-cage" motors), the 15-A breaker is the "next higher size, rating, or setting" for a standard CB—as permitted in Sec. 430-52. A 15-A CB is the smallest standard rating recognized by Sec. 240-6.

3. The total load of motor currents is:

$$4.8 \text{ A} + 3.4 \text{ A} + 2.6 \text{ A} = 10.8 \text{ A}$$

This is well within the 15-A CB rating, which has sufficient time delay in its operation to permit starting of any one of these motors with the other two already operating. Torque characteristics of the loads on starting are not high. It was therefore determined that the CB will not open under the most severe normal service.

4. Each motor has individual running overload protection in its starter.
5. The branch-circuit conductors are sized in accordance with Sec. 430-24:

$$4.8 \text{ A} + 3.4 \text{ A} + 2.6 \text{ A} + (25 \text{ percent of } 4.8 \text{ A}) = 12 \text{ A}$$

Conductors must have an ampacity at least equal to 12 A. No. 14 THW, TW, RHW, RHH, THHN, or XHHW conductors will fully satisfy this application.

In Case II, Fig. 430-24, a similar hookup is used to supply three motors—also with a CB for branch-circuit protection.

1. Section 430-53(b) requires branch-circuit protection to be not higher than the maximum amps set by Sec. 430-52 for the lowest rated of the motors.

CASE II—USING A CIRCUIT BREAKER FOR PROTECTION

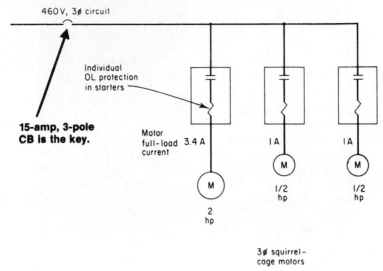

Fig. 430-24. Fractional-horsepower and integral-horsepower motors may be supplied by the same circuit. (Sec. 430-53.)

2. From Sec. 430-52 and Table 430-152, that maximum protection rating for a CB is 250 percent $\times$ 1 A (the lowest rated motor) or 2.5 A. But, 2.5 A is not a "standard rating" of CB from Sec. 240-6; and the third paragraph of Sec. 430-52 permits use of the "next higher size, rating, or setting" of standard protective device.
3. Because 15 A is the lowest standard rating of CB, it is the "next higher" device rating above 2.5 A and satisfies **Code** rules on the rating of the branch-circuit protection.

The applications shown in Case I and Case II permit use of several motors up to circuit capacity, based on Secs. 430-24 and 430-53(b) and on starting torque characteristics, operating duty cycles of the motors and their loads, and the time delay of the CB. Such applications greatly reduce the number of CB poles, number of panels, and the amount of wire used in the total system. One limitation, however is placed on this practice in the last sentence of Sec. 430-52, as noted previously. Where more than one fractional- or small-integral-horsepower motor is used on a single branch circuit of 15-A rating in accordance with **NE Code** Sec. 430-53(a) or (b), care must be taken to observe all markings on controllers that indicate a maximum rating of short-circuit protection ahead of the controller (Fig. 430-25).

In Case III, Fig. 430-26, the same three motors shown in Case II would be subject to different hookup to comply with the rules of Sec. 430-53(b) when fuses, instead of a CB, are used for branch-circuit protection, as follows:

1. To comply with Sec. 430-53(b), fuses used as branch-circuit protection

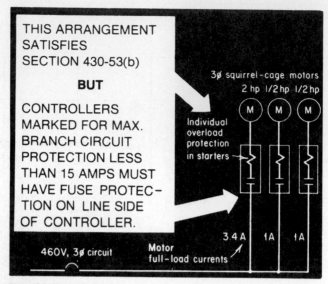

Fig. 430-25. Branch-circuit protection must not exceed marked maximum value. (Sec. 430-53.)

BUT, WATCH OUT!!!

CASE III—USING FUSES FOR CIRCUIT PROTECTION

Interpretation of *NE Code* rules of Section 430-53(b) in conjunction with the "standard" ratings of fuses in Section 240-6 may require different circuit makeup when fuses are used to protect the branch circuit to several motors.

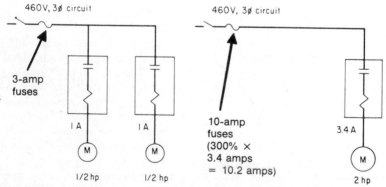

Fig. 430-26. Fuse protection may require different circuiting for several motors. (Sec. 430-53.)

must have a rating not in excess of the value permitted by Sec. 430-52 and Table 430-152 for the smallest motor of the group—one of the ½-hp motors.

2. Table 430-152 shows that the maximum permitted rating of nontime-delay type fuses is 300 percent of full-load current for 3-phase squirrel-cage motors. Applying that to one of the ½-hp motors gives a maximum fuse rating of:

$$300 \text{ percent} \times 1 \text{ A} = 3 \text{ A}$$

3. BUT, there is no permission for the fuses to be rated higher than 3 A— BECAUSE 3 A IS A "STANDARD" RATING OF FUSE (but not a standard rating of CB). Section 240-6 considers fuses rated at 1, 3, 6, and 10 A to be "standard" ratings.

4. The maximum branch-circuit fuse permitted by Sec. 430-53(b) for a ½-hp motor is 3 A.

5. The two ½-hp motors may be fed from a single branch circuit with three 3-A fuses in a three-pole switch.

6. Following the same **Code** rules, the 2-hp motor would require fuse protection rated not over 10 A (300 percent × 3.4 A = 10.2 A).

Note: Because the standard fuse ratings below 15 A place fuses in a different relationship to the applicable **Code** rules, it will require interpretation of the **Code** rules to resolve the question of acceptable application in Case II versus Case III. Interpretation will be necessary to determine if CBs are excluded as circuit protection in these cases where use of fuses, in accordance with the precise wording of the **Code**, provides lower rated protection than CBs—when applying the rule of the third paragraph of Sec. 430-52. And if the motors of Case I are fed from a circuit protected by fuses, the literal effect of the **Code** rules would require different circuiting for those motors.

Figure 430-27 shows one way of combining Case II and Case III to satisfy Sec. 430-53(b), Sec. 430-52, and Sec. 240-6; but the 15-A CB would then technically be feeder protection, because the fuses would be serving as the "branch-circuit protective devices" as required by Sec. 430-53(b). Those fuses might be acceptable in each starter, without a disconnect switch, in accordance with Sec. 240-40—which allows use of cartridge fuses at any voltage without an individual disconnect for each set of fuses, provided only qualified persons have access to the fuses. But, Sec. 430-112 would have to be satisfied to use the single CB as a disconnect for the group of motors. And part (b) of that Exception recognizes one common disconnect in accordance with Sec. 430-53(a) but not 430-53(b). Certainly, the use of a fusible-switch type combination starter for each motor would fully satisfy all rules.

Figure 430-28 shows another hookup that might be required to supply the three motors of Fig. 430-23.

Figure 430-29 shows another hookup of several motors on one branch circuit—an actual job installation which was based on application of Sec. 430-53(b). The installation was studied as follows:

Problem: A factory has 100 1½-hp, 3-phase motors, with individual motor starters incorporating overcurrent protection, rated for 460 V. Provide circuits.

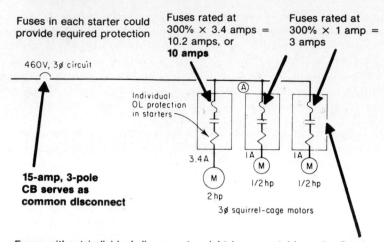

Fuses in each starter could provide required protection

Fuses rated at 300% × 3.4 amps = 10.2 amps, or **10 amps**

Fuses rated at 300% × 1 amp = 3 amps

460V, 3∅ circuit

Individual OL protection in starters

Ⓐ

15-amp, 3-pole CB serves as common disconnect

3.4 A

1 A
(M)
1/2 hp

1 A
(M)
1/2 hp

(M)
2 hp

3∅ squirrel-cage motors

Fuses without individual disconnects might be acceptable under Section 240-40; or a single disconnect switch, fused at 3 amps, could be installed at point "A," eliminating the need for fuses in the two starters for the ½-hp motors.

Fig. 430-27. Multimotor circuit may be acceptable with fused starters. (Sec. 430-53.)

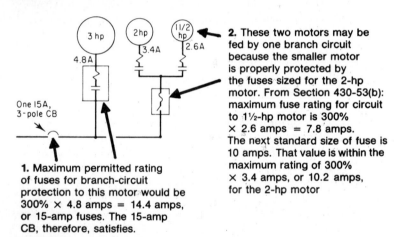

3 hp
4.8A

2hp
3.4A

1 1/2 hp
2.6A

One 15A, 3-pole CB

2. These two motors may be fed by one branch circuit because the smaller motor is properly protected by the fuses sized for the 2-hp motor. From Section 430-53(b): maximum fuse rating for circuit to 1½-hp motor is 300% × 2.6 amps = 7.8 amps. The next standard size of fuse is 10 amps. That value is within the maximum rating of 300% × 3.4 amps, or 10.2 amps, for the 2-hp motor

1. Maximum permitted rating of fuses for branch-circuit protection to this motor would be 300% × 4.8 amps = 14.4 amps, or 15-amp fuses. The 15-amp CB, therefore, satisfies.

Fig. 430-28. This hookup might be required to satisfy literal Code wording. (Sec. 430-53.)

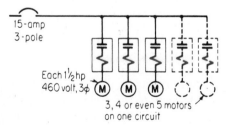

15-amp 3-pole

Each 1 1/2 hp 460 volt, 3∅ (M) (M) (M)

3, 4 or even 5 motors on one circuit

Fig. 430-29. Multimotor circuits offer economical supply to small integral-horsepower motors. (Sec. 430-53.)

Solution: Prior to 1965, the **NE Code** would not permit several integral-horse-power motors on one branch circuit fed from a three-pole CB in a panel. Each of the 100 motors would have had to have its own individual 3-phase circuit fed from a 15-A, three-pole CB in a panel. As a result, a total of 300 CB poles would have been required calling for seven panels of 42 circuits each plus a smaller panel (or special panels of greater numbers than 42 poles per panel).

Under the present **Code**, depending upon the starting torque characteristics and operating duty of the motors and their loads, with each motor rated for 2.6 A, three or four motors could be connected on each 3-phase, 15-A circuit— greatly reducing the number of panelboards, overcurrent devices, and the amount of wire involved, in the total system. Time delay of CB influences number of motors on each circuit.

BUT, an extremely important point that must be strictly observed is the requirement that the rating of branch-circuit protection must not exceed any maximum value that might be marked on the starters used with the motors.

Part **(c)**: In selecting the wording for part **(c)**, it was the intent of the **Code**-making panel to clarify the intent that several motors should not be connected to one branch circuit unless careful engineering is exercised by qualified persons to determine that all components of the branch circuit are selected and specified to meet the present requirements and to function together. The intent is to allow:

a. Completely factory-assembled equipment, or
b. A factory-assembled unit with a separate branch-circuit short-circuit and ground-fault protective device of a type and rating specified, or
c. Separately mounted components which are listed for use together and are specified for such use together by manufacturer's instructions and/or nameplate markings.
It is not the intent to change requirements for supplemental overcurrent protection such as in Sec. 422-28(f) or 424-22(c).
The change will inform the user that no interchange of components should be made without negating the manufacturer's warranty and listing by an approved laboratory.

Two or more motors of any rating may be connected to one branch circuit if each motor has running overload protection, if the overload devices and controllers are approved for group installation, and if the branch-circuit fuse or time-delay CB rating is in accordance with Sec. 430-52 for the largest motor plus the sum of the full-load current ratings of the other motors (Fig. 430-30). The branch-circuit fuses or CB must not be larger than the rating or setting of short-circuit protection permitted by Sec. 430-52 for the smallest motor of the group, unless the thermal device is approved for group installation with a given maximum size of fuse or time-delay CB for short-circuit protective device. (See Sec. 430-40.) Underwriters Laboratories notes that motor controllers for group installation are marked with a maximum rating of fuse required to suitably protect the controller. Section 430-53(c)(2), however, calls for a group installation controller to be marked for the rating of fuse or CB ahead of it.

Part **(d)**: For installations of groups of motors as covered in part **(c)** above, tap conductors run from the branch-circuit conductors to supply individual motors must be sized properly. Such tap conductors would, of course, be acceptable where they are the same size as the branch-circuit conductors themselves.

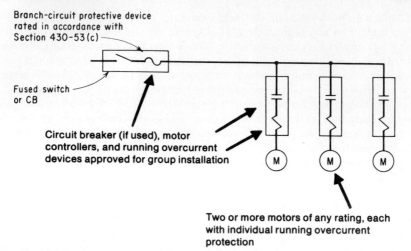

Branch-circuit protective device
rated in accordance with
Section 430-53(c)

Fused switch
or CB

Circuit breaker (if used), motor
controllers, and running overcurrent
devices approved for group installation

Two or more motors of any rating, each
with individual running overcurrent
protection

Fig. 430-30. Motors of any horsepower rating require circuit equipment for group installation. (Sec. 430-53.)

However, tap conductors to a single motor may be smaller than the main
branch-circuit conductors provided that: they have an ampacity at least ⅓ that
of the branch-circuit conductors, their ampacity is not less than 125 percent of
the motor full-load current, they are not over 25 ft long, and they are in raceway
or are otherwise protected from physical damage (Fig. 430-31).

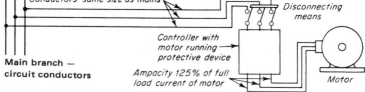

Condition 1

Conductors same size as mains

Disconnecting
means

Controller with
motor running
protective device

Main branch —
circuit conductors

Ampacity 125% of full
load current of motor

Motor

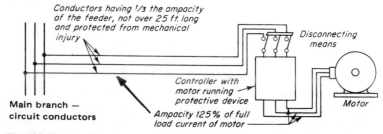

Condition 2

Conductors having ⅓ the ampacity
of the feeder, not over 25 ft. long
and protected from mechanical
injury

Disconnecting
means

Controller with
motor running
protective device

Main branch —
circuit conductors

Ampacity 125% of full
load current of motor

Motor

Fig. 430-31. Overcurrent protection not required for taps to single motors of a group.
(Sec. 430-53.)

The principle applied here is that, since the conductors are short and protected from physical damage, it is unlikely that trouble will occur in the run between the mains and the motor protection which will cause the conductors to be overloaded, except some accident resulting in an actual short circuit. A short circuit will blow the fuses or trip the CB protecting the mains. An overload on the conductors caused by overloading the motor or trouble in the motor itself will cause the motor protective device to operate and so protect the conductors.

430-55. Combined Overcurrent Protection.   A CB or set of fuses may provide both short-circuit protection and running overload protection for a motor circuit. For instance, a CB or dual-element time-delay fuse sized at not over 125 percent of motor full-load current (Sec. 430-32) for a 40°C-rise continuous-duty motor would be acceptable protection for the branch circuit and the motor against shorts, ground faults, and operating overloads on the motor. See bottom of Fig. 430-16 for a typical fuse application.

Figure 430-32 shows a CB used to fulfill four **Code** requirements simultaneously. For the continuous-duty, 40°C-rise motor shown, the CB may provide

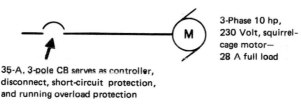

35-A, 3-pole CB serves as controller,
disconnect, short-circuit protection,
and running overload protection

3-Phase 10 hp,
230 Volt, squirrel-
cage motor—
28 A full load

Fig. 430-32. Overcurrent functions may be combined in a single CB or set of fuses. (Sec. 430-55.)

running overload protection if it is rated not over 125 percent of the motor's full-load running current. Therefore, 28 A × 1.25 = 35 A, which satisfies Sec. 430-32(a). Because the rating of the thermal-magnetic CB is not over 250 percent times the full-load current (from Table 430-152), the 35-A CB satisfies Secs. 430-52 and 430-58 as short-circuit and ground-fault protection. The CB may serve both those functions, as noted in Sec. 430-55. The CB may serve as the motor controller, as permitted by Sec. 430-83 Exception No. 2. The CB also satisfies as the required disconnect means in accordance with Sec. 430-111 and has the rating "of at least 115 percent of the full-load current rating of the motor," as required by Sec. 430-110(a). And because it satisfies Sec. 430-110(a) on disconnect minimum rating, it therefore satisfies Sec. 430-58, which sets the same minimum rating for a CB used as branch-circuit protection.

430-56. Branch-Circuit Protective Devices—In Which Conductor.   Motor branch circuits are to be protected in the same way as other circuits with regard to the number of fuses and the number of poles and overcurrent units of CBs. If fuses are used, a fuse is required in each ungrounded conductor. If a CB is used, there must be an overcurrent unit in each ungrounded conductor.

430-57. Size of Fuseholder.   The basic rule of this section covers sizing of fuseholders for standard nontime-delay fuses used as motor branch-circuit protection. The Exception recognizes that time-delay fuses permit use of smaller switches and lower-rated fuseholders.

A fusible switch can take either standard **NE Code** fuses or time-delay fuses—up to the rating of the switch. Because a given size of time-delay fuse can hold on the starting current of a motor larger than that which could be used with a standard fuse of the same rating, fusible switches are given two horsepower ratings—one for use with standard fuses, the other for use with time-delay fuses. For example, a three-pole, 30-A, 240-V fused switch has a rating of 3 hp for a 3-phase motor if standard fuses without time-delay characteristics are used. If time-delay fuses are used, the rating is raised to 7½ hp.

Consider a 7½-hp, 230-V, 3-phase motor (full-voltage starting, without code letters, or with code letters F to V), with a full-load current of 22 A. **NE Code** Table 430-152 shows that such a motor may be protected by nontime-delay fuses with a maximum rating equal to 300 percent of the full-load current (66 A), or time-delay fuses with a maximum rating equal to 175 percent of the full-load current (38.5 A).

If standard, nontime-delay fuses were used, the maximum size permitted would be 70 A (the next standard size larger than 66 A). From the table, this would require a 100-A, 15-hp switch, which would have fuseholders that could accommodate the fuses, as required by the basic rule. Or, a 60-A, 7½-hp switch might be used with standard fuses rated 60 A max. But such a switch would be required by the basic rule to have fuseholders that could accommodate 70-A fuses. Because such a fuse has knife-blade terminals instead of end ferrules and is larger than a 60-A fuse, fuseholders in the 60-A switch could be held in conflict with the **Code** rule even though the level of protection would be better with 60-A fuses in the 60-A switch. Wording of the rule is not clear. But cost, labor, and space savings would be realized using a 30-A, 7½-hp switch with 30-A time-delay fuses, with no worry about nuisance blowing of the fuses on motor starting current, and that would be acceptable under the Exception.

430-58. Rating of Circuit Breaker.   This rule sets a maximum and minimum rating for a CB as branch-circuit protection. Refer to Sec. 430-55.

In the case of a CB having an adjustable trip point, this rule refers to the capacity of the CB to carry current without overheating and has nothing to do with the setting of the breaker. The breaker most commonly used as a motor branch-circuit protective device is the nonadjustable CB (see Sec. 240-6), and any breaker of this type having a rating in conformity with the requirements of Sec. 430-52 will have an ampacity considerably in excess of 115 percent of the full-load motor current.

430-62. Rating or Setting—Motor Load.   Overcurrent protection for a feeder to several motors must have a rating or setting not greater than the largest rating or setting of the branch-circuit protective device for any motor of the group plus the sum of the full-load currents of the other motors supplied by the feeder.

The second paragraph notes that there are cases where two or more motors fed by a feeder will have the same rating of branch-circuit device. And that can happen where the motors are of the same or different horsepower ratings. It is possible for motors of different horsepower ratings to have the same rating of branch-circuit protective device, depending upon the type of motor and the type of protective device. If two or more motors in the group are of different horsepower rating but the rating or setting of the branch-circuit protective device is the same for both motors, then one of the protective devices should be considered as the largest for the calculation of feeder overcurrent protection.

And because Table 430-152 recognizes many different ratings of branch-circuit protective devices (based on use of fuses or CBs and depending upon the particular type of motor), it is possible for two motors of equal horsepower rating to have widely different ratings of branch-circuit protection. If, for instance, a 25-hp motor was protected by nontime-delay fuses, Table 430-152 gives 300 percent of full-load motor current as the maximum rating or setting of the branch-circuit device. Thus, 250-A fuses would be used for a motor that had a 78-A full-load rating. But another motor of the same horsepower and even of the same type, if protected by time-delay fuses, must use fuses rated at only 175 percent of 78 A, which would be 150-A fuses, as shown in Fig. 430-33. If the two 25-hp motors were of different types, one being a wound-rotor motor, it would still be necessary to base selection of the feeder protection on the largest rating or setting of a branch-circuit protective device, regardless of the horsepower rating of the motor.

Figure 430-34 shows a typical motor feeder calculation, as follows:

The four motors supplied by the 3-phase, 440-V, 60-cycle feeder, which are not marked with a code letter (see Table 430-152), are as follows:

- 1 50-hp squirrel-cage induction motor (full-voltage starting)
- 1 30-hp wound-rotor induction motor
- 2 10-hp squirrel-cage induction motors (full-voltage starting)

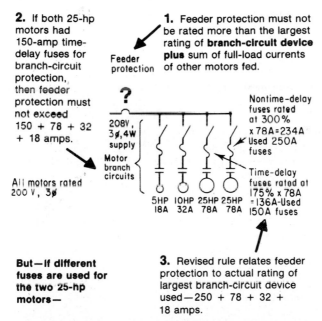

Fig. 430-33. Feeder protection is based on largest branch-circuit protection, not on motor horsepower ratings. (Sec. 430-62.)

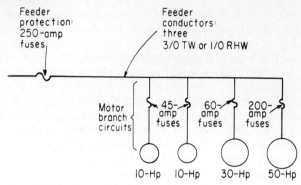

Fig. 430·34. Rating of feeder protection is based on branch protection and motor currents. (Sec. 430-62.)

Step 1. Branch·Circuit Loads

From Table 430-150, the motors have full-load current ratings as follows:

50-hp motor—65 A
30-hp motor—40 A
10-hp motor—14 A

Step 2. Conductors

The feeder conductors must have a carrying capacity as follows (see Sec. 430-24):

$$1.25 \times 65 = 81 \text{ A}$$
$$81 + 40 + (2 \times 14) = 149 \text{ A}$$

The feeder conductors must be at least No. 3/0 TW, 1/0 THW, or 1/0 RHH or THHN (copper).

Step 3. Branch·Circuit Protection

Overcurrent (branch-circuit) protection (from Table 430-152 and Sec. 430-52) using nontime-delay fuses:
1. The 50-hp motor must be protected at not more than 200 A (65 A × 300 percent).
2. The 30-hp motor must be protected at not more than 60 A (40 A × 150 percent).
3. Each 10-hp motor must be protected at not more than 45 A (14 × 300 percent).

Step 4. Feeder Protection

As covered in Sec. 430-62, the maximum rating or setting for the overcurrent device protecting such a feeder must not be greater than the largest rating or setting of branch-circuit protective device for one of the motors of the group plus the sum of the full-load currents of the other motors. From the above, then, the maximum allowable size of feeder fuses is 200 + 40 + 14 + 14 = 268 A.

This calls for a maximum standard rating of 250 A for the motor feeder fuses, which is the nearest standard fuse rating that does not exceed the maximum permitted value of 268 A.

Note: There is no provision in Sec. 430-62 which permits the use of "the next higher size, rating, or setting" of the protective device for a motor feeder when the calculated maximum rating does not correspond to a standard size of device.

According to part **(b)** of this section, in large-capacity installations where extra feeder capacity is provided for load growth or future changes, the feeder overcurrent protection may be calculated on the basis of the rated current-carrying capacity of the feeder conductors. In some cases, such as where two or more motors on a feeder may be started simultaneously, feeder conductors may have to be larger than usually required for feeders to several motors.

In selecting the size of a feeder overcurrent protective device, the NE Code calculation is concerned with establishing a maximum value for the fuse or CB. If a lower value of protection is suitable, it may be used.

430·63. Rating or Setting—Power and Light Loads.　Protection for a feeder to both motor loads and a lighting and/or appliance load must be rated on the basis of both of these loads. The rating or setting of the overcurrent device must be sufficient to carry the lighting and/or appliance load plus the rating or setting of the motor branch-circuit protective device if only one motor is supplied, or plus the highest rating or setting of branch-circuit protective device for any one motor plus the sum of the full-load currents of the other motors, if more than one motor is supplied.

Figure 430-35 presents basic NE Code calculations for arriving at minimum requirements on wire sizes and overcurrent protection for a combination power and lighting load as follows:

Step 1. Total Load

Section 430-25(a) says that conductors supplying a lighting load and a motor must have capacity for both loads, as follows:

$$\text{Motor load} = 65\ A + 40\ A + 14\ A + 14\ A$$
$$+ (0.25 \times 65\ A) = 149\ A \text{ per phase}$$
$$\text{Lighting load} = 120\ A \text{ per phase} \times 1.25 = 150\ A$$
$$\text{Total load} = 149 + 150 = 299\ A \text{ per phase leg}$$

Step 2. Conductors

Table 310-16 shows that a load of 299 A can be served by the following copper conductors:

500 kcmil TW
350 kcmil THW

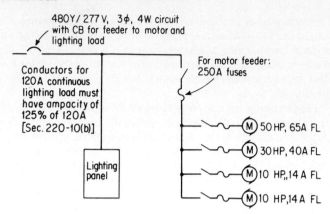

Fig. 430·35. Feeder protection for combination load must properly add both loads. (Sec. 430-63.)

Table 310-16 shows that this same load can be served by the following aluminum or copper-clad aluminum conductors:

700 kcmil TW
500 kcmil THW, RHH, or THHN

Step 3. Protective Devices

Section 430-63 says, in effect, that the protective device for a feeder supplying a combined motor load and lighting load may have a rating not greater than the sum of the maximum rating of the motor feeder protective device and the lighting load, as follows:

1. Motor feeder protective device = rating or setting of the largest branch-circuit device for any motor of the group being served plus the sum of the full-load currents of the other motors:

$$200 \text{ A (50-hp motor)} + 40 + 14 + 14 = 268 \text{ A max}$$

   This calls for a maximum standard rating of 250 A for the motor feeder fuses, which is the nearest standard fuse rating that does not exceed the maximum permitted value of 268 A.

2. Lighting load = 120 A × 1.25 = 150 A

$$\text{Rating of CB for combined load} = 268 + 150 = 418 \text{ A max}$$

   This calls for a 400-A CB, the nearest standard rating that does not exceed the 418-A maximum.

Again: There is no provision in Sec. 430-63 which permits the use of "the next higher size, rating, or setting" of the protective device for a motor feeder when the calculated maximum rating does not correspond to a standard size of device.

Such considerations as voltage drop, I^2R loss, spare capacity, lamp dimming on motor starting, etc., would have to be made to arrive at actual sizes to use for the job. But, the circuiting as shown would be safe—although maybe not efficient or effective for the particular job requirements.

430·71. General.   Figure 430-36 shows the "motor control circuit" part of a motor branch circuit, as defined in part **(a)** of this section. A control circuit, as discussed here, is any circuit which has as its load device the operating coil of a magnetic motor starter, a magnetic contactor, or a relay. Strictly speaking, it

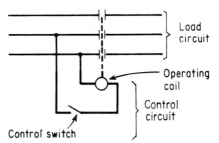

Fig. 430-36. A control circuit governs the operating coil that switches the load circuit. (Sec. 430-71.)

is a circuit which exercises control over one or more other circuits. And these other circuits controlled by the control circuit may themselves be control circuits or they may be "load" circuits—carrying utilization current to a lighting, heating, power, or signal device.

The elements of a control circuit include all the equipment and devices concerned with the function of the circuit: conductors, raceway, contactor operating coil, source of energy supply to the circuit, overcurrent protective devices, and all switching devices which govern energization of the operating coil.

The **NE Code** covers application of control circuits in Art. 725 and in Secs. 240-3 and 430-71 through 430-74. Design and installation of control circuits are basically divided into three classes (in Art. 725) according to the energy available in the circuit. Class 2 and 3 control circuits have low energy-handling capabilities; and any circuit, to qualify as a Class 2 or 3 control circuit, must have its open-circuit voltage and overcurrent protection limited to conditions given in Sec. 725-31.

The vast majority of control circuits for magnetic starters and contactors could not qualify as Class 2 or Class 3 circuits because of the relatively high energy required for operating coils. And any control circuit rated over 150 V (such as 220- or 440-V coil circuits) can never qualify, regardless of energy.

Class 1 control circuits include all operating coil circuits for magnetic starters which do not meet the requirements for Class 2 or Class 3 circuits. Class 1 circuits must be wired in accordance with Secs. 725-11 to 725-20.

430·72. Overcurrent Protection.   Part **(a)** tells the basic idea behind protection of the operating coil circuit of a magnetic motor starter, as distinguished from a manual (mechanically operated) starter:

1. Section 430-72 covers motor control circuits that are derived within a motor starter from the power circuit which connects to the line terminals of the starter. The rule here refers to such a control circuit as one "tapped from the load side" of the fuses or circuit breaker that provides branch-

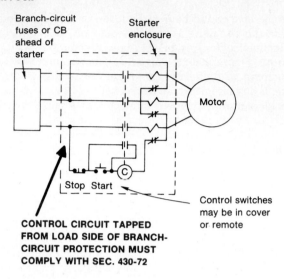

Branch-circuit fuses or CB ahead of starter

Starter enclosure

Motor

Stop Start

CONTROL CIRCUIT TAPPED FROM LOAD SIDE OF BRANCH-CIRCUIT PROTECTION MUST COMPLY WITH SEC. 430-72

Control switches may be in cover or remote

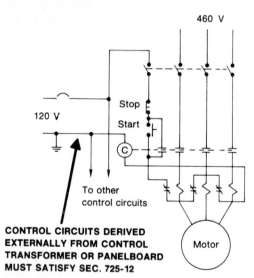

460 V

120 V

Stop

Start

To other control circuits

Motor

CONTROL CIRCUITS DERIVED EXTERNALLY FROM CONTROL TRANSFORMER OR PANELBOARD MUST SATISFY SEC. 725-12

Fig. 430-37. Source of power supply to the control circuit determines which **Code** section applies to the coil circuit. (Sec. 430-72.)

circuit protection for the conductors which supply the starter. See the top of Fig. 430-37.

2. The control circuit that is tapped from the line terminals within a starter is *not* a branch circuit itself.

3. Depending on other conditions set in Sec. 430-72, the conductors of the control circuit will be considered as protected by *either* the branch-circuit

protective device ahead of the starter *or* supplementary protection (usually fuses) installed in the starter enclosure.

4. Any motor control circuit that is not tapped from the line terminals within a starter must be protected against overcurrent in accordance with Sec. 725-12 or Sec. 725-35. Such control circuits would be those that are derived from a panelboard or a control transformer—as where, say, 120-V circuits are derived external to the starters and are typically run to provide lower-voltage control for 230-, 460-, or 575-V motors. See the bottom sketch of Fig. 430-37.

Part **(b)** applies to overcurrent protection of conductors used to make up the control circuits of magnetic motor starters. Such overcurrent protection must be sized in accordance with the amp values shown in Table 430-72(b). And where that table makes reference to amp values specified in Tables 310-16 through 310-19, as applicable, it does *not* specify that Note 8 of those tables must be observed by derating conductor ampacity where more than three current-carrying conductors are used in a conduit. Previously, the rule in part **(b)** of this section specifically recognized the use of control-circuit wires in raceway "without derating factors." Section 725-17, however, does require Class 1 remote-control wires to have their ampacity derated in accordance with Note 8, based on the number of conductors, when the conductors "carry continuous loads" in excess of 10 percent of each conductor's ampacity. The application shown in Fig. 430-38 is, therefore, open to controversy.

The basic rule of part **(b)** requires coil-circuit conductors to have overcurrent protection rated in accordance with the maximum values given in column A of Table 430-72(b). That table shows 7 A as the maximum rating of protection for

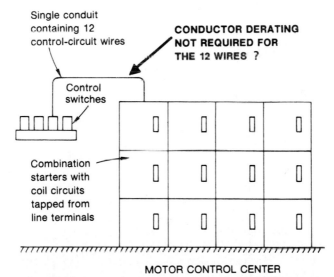

MOTOR CONTROL CENTER

Fig. 430-38. Derating of control-wire ampacity is not specifically required when more than three conductors are run within the same raceway. (Sec. 430-72.)

No. 18 copper wire and 10 A for No. 16 wire and refers to Table 310-16 for larger wires—15 A for no. 14 copper, 20 A for No. 12, etc. The Exceptions to the basic rule cover conditions under which other ratings of protection may be used, as follows:

Exception No. 1 covers protection of control wires for magnetic starters that have their START-STOP buttons in the cover of the starter enclosure.

In Exception No. 1, the value of branch-circuit protection must be compared to the ampacity of the control-circuit wires that are factory-installed in the starter and connected to the START-STOP buttons in the cover. If the rating of the branch-circuit fuse or CB does not exceed the value of the current shown in column B of Table 43-72(b) for the particular size of either copper or aluminum wire used to wire the coil circuit within the starter, then other protection is not required to be installed within the starter (Fig. 430-39). If the rating of branch-circuit protection *does* exceed the value shown in column B for the size of coil-circuit wire, then separate protection must be provided within the starter, and it must be rated not greater than the value shown for that size of wire in column A of Table 430-72(b). For instance, if the internal coil circuit of a starter is wired with No. 16 copper wire and the branch-circuit device supplying the starter is rated over the 40-A value shown for No. 16 copper wire in column B of Table 430-72(b), then protection must be provided in the starter for the No. 16 wire and the protective device(s) must be rated not over the 10-A value shown for No. 16 copper wire in column A of Table 430-72(b).

Because the vast majority of starters are the smaller ones using No. 18 and No. 16 wires for their coil circuits, Exception No. 1 and its reference to column B are particularly applicable to those wire sizes. For No. 16 control wires, branch-circuit protection rated up to 40 A would eliminate any need for a sep-

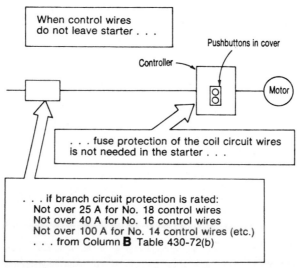

Fig. 430-39. This is the rule of Exception No. 1 to part **(b)** of Sec. 430-72.

arate control-circuit fuse in the starter. And for No. 18 control wires, separate coil-circuit protection is not needed for a starter with branch-circuit protection rated not over 25 A. For No. 14, No. 12, and No. 10 copper control wires, maximum protective-device ratings are given in column B as 100, 120, and 160 A, respectively. For conductors larger than No. 10, the protection may be rated up to 400 percent of (or 4 times) the free-air ampacity of the size of conductor from Table 310-17.

Exception No. 2 covers protection of control wires that run from a starter to a remote-control device (pushbutton station, float switch, limit switch, etc.). Such control wires may be protected by the branch-circuit protective device—without need for separate protection within the starter—if the branch-circuit device has a rating not over the value shown for the particular size of copper or aluminum control wire in column C of Table 430-72(b) (Fig. 430-40). Note that the maximum ratings of 7 A for No. 18 and 10 A for No. 16 require that *fuse* protection at those ratings must always be used to protect those sizes of control-circuit wires connected to motor starters supplied by CB branch-circuit

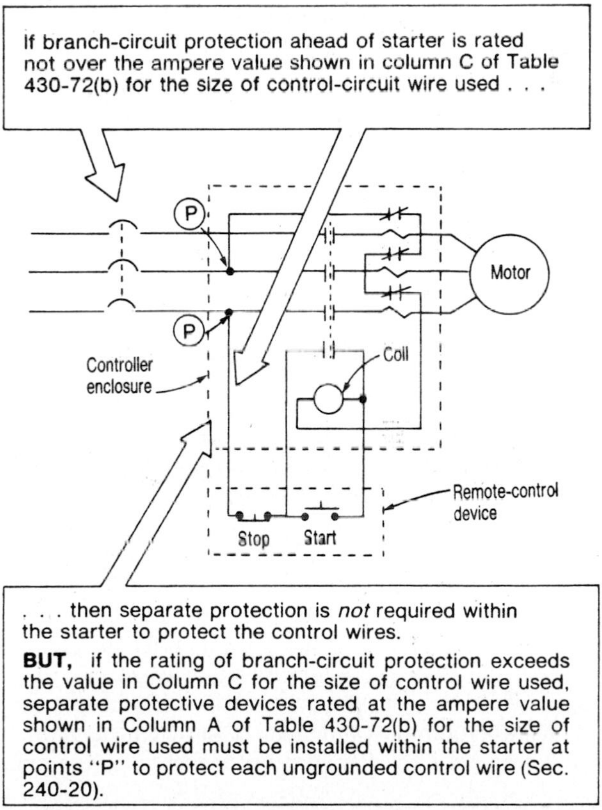

If branch-circuit protection ahead of starter is rated not over the ampere value shown in column C of Table 430-72(b) for the size of control-circuit wire used . . .

. . . then separate protection is *not* required within the starter to protect the control wires.

BUT, if the rating of branch-circuit protection exceeds the value in Column C for the size of control wire used, separate protective devices rated at the ampere value shown in Column A of Table 430-72(b) for the size of control wire used must be installed within the starter at points "P" to protect each ungrounded control wire (Sec. 240-20).

Fig. 430-40. This is covered by Exception No. 2 to part **(b)** of Sec. 430-72.

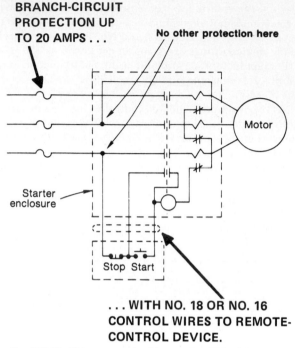

BRANCH-CIRCUIT PROTECTION UP TO 20 AMPS . . .

No other protection here

Motor

Starter enclosure

Stop Start

. . . WITH NO. 18 OR NO. 16 CONTROL WIRES TO REMOTE-CONTROL DEVICE.

Fig. 430·41. This was permitted by previous NEC editions but is now a violation of Exception No. 2 of part **(b)**. (Sec. 430-72.)

protection, because 15 A is the lowest available standard rating of CB. But branch-circuit fuses of 7- or 10-A rating could eliminate the need for protection in the starter where No. 18 or No. 16 control wires are used. Figure 430-41 shows an application that was permitted for many years under previous wording of the **Code** rule but is now contrary to the letter and intent of the rule.

For any size of control wire, if the branch-circuit protection ahead of the starter has a rating greater than the value shown in column C of Table 430-72(b), then the control wire must be protected by a device(s) rated not over the amp value shown for that size of wire in column A of Table 430-72(b). For instance, if No. 14 copper wire is used for the control circuit from a starter to a remote pushbutton station and the branch-circuit protection ahead of the starter is rated at 40 A, then the branch-circuit device is not over the value of 45 A shown in column C, and separate control protection is not required within the starter. But if the branch-circuit protection were, say, 100 A, then No. 14 control wire would have to be protected at 15 A because column A shows that No. 14 must have maximum protection rating from Note 1—which refers to Table 310-16 where No. 14 wire in conduit is shown, by the footnote, to require protection at 15 A.

It should be noted that column A gives the values to be used for overcurrent protection placed within the starter to protect control-circuit wires in any case

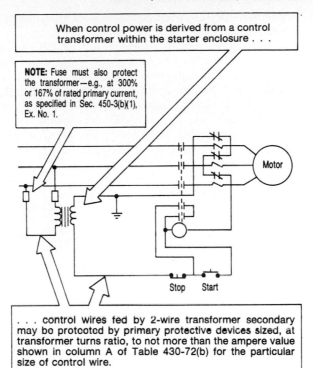

When control power is derived from a control transformer within the starter enclosure . . .

NOTE: Fuse must also protect the transformer—e.g., at 300% or 167% of rated primary current, as specified in Sec. 450-3(b)(1), Ex. No. 1.

Motor

Stop   Start

. . . control wires fed by 2-wire transformer secondary may be protected by primary protective devices sized, at transformer turns ratio, to not more than the ampere value shown in column A of Table 430-72(b) for the particular size of control wire.

EXAMPLE: For No. 16 control wire fed by a 480-120-V transformer, fuses must not be rated over 10 A × (120/480), or 2.5 A.

Fig. 430-42. Exception No. 3 to part **(b)** of Sec. 430-72 permits the secondary wires of the coil circuit to be protected by primary-side overcurrent protection.

where the rating of branch-circuit protection exceeds the value shown in either column B (for starters with no external control wires) or column C (for control wires run from a starter to a remote pilot control device).

Exception No. 3 permits protection on the primary side of a control transformer to protect the transformer in accordance with Sec. 450-3 and the secondary conductors in accordance with the amp value shown in Table 430-72(b) for the particular size of the control wires fed by the secondary. This use is limited to transformers with 2-wire secondaries (Fig. 430-42). Because Sec. 430-72(a) notes that the rules of Sec. 430-72 apply to control circuits tapped from the motor branch circuit, the rule of Exception No. 3 must be taken as applying to a control transformer installed within the starter enclosure—although the general application may be used for any transformer because it conforms to Sec. 240-3, Exception No. 5, and to Sec. 450-3.

Exception No. 4 eliminates any need for control-circuit protection where opening of the circuit would be objectionable, as for a fire-pump motor or other essential or safety-related operation.

Part **(c)** covers the use of control transformers and requires protection on the primary side. And, again, it must be taken to apply specifically to such transformers used in motor control equipment enclosures. The basic rule calls for each control transformer to be protected in accordance with Sec. 450-3 (usually by a primary-side protective device rated not over 125 or 167 percent of primary current), as shown in Fig. 430-42. But, exceptions are given.

Exception No. 1 eliminates any need for protection of any control transformer rated less than 50 VA, provided it is part of the starter and within its enclosure.

Exception No. 2 permits a control transformer with a rated primary current of *less* than 2 A to be protected at up to 500 percent of rated primary current by a protective device in each ungrounded conductor of the supply circuit to the transformer primary, as shown in Fig. 430-43.

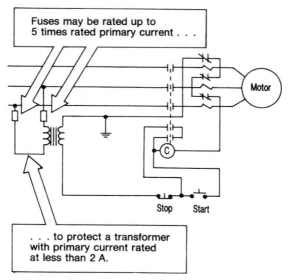

Fig. 430·43. A control circuit fed by a transformer within the starter enclosure may have overcurrent protection in the primary rated up to 500 percent of the rated primary current of a small transformer. (Sec. 430-72.)

In the majority of magnetic motor controllers and contactors, the voltage of the operating coil is the voltage provided between two of the conductors supplying the load, or one conductor and the neutral. Conventional starters are factory wired with coils of the same voltage rating as the phase voltage to the motor. However, there are many cases in which it is desirable or necessary to use control circuits and devices of lower voltage rating than the motor. Such could be the case with high-voltage (over 600 V) controllers, for instance, in which it is necessary to provide a source of low voltage for practical operation of magnetic coils. And even in many cases of motor controllers and contactors for use under 600 V, safety requirements dictate the use of control circuits of lower voltage than the load circuit.

Although contactor coils and pilot devices are available and effectively used for motor controllers with up to 600-V control circuits, such practice has been prohibited in applications where atmospheric and other working conditions make it dangerous for operating personnel to use control circuits of such voltage. And certain OSHA regulations require 120-V or 240-V coil circuits for the 460-V motors. In such cases, control transformers are used to step the voltage down to permit the use of lower-voltage coil circuits.

430·73. Mechanical Protection of Conductor. The condition under which physical protection of the control circuit conductor becomes necessary is where damage to the conductors would constitute either a fire or an accident hazard. Damage to the control circuit conductors resulting in short-circuiting two or more of the conductors or breaking one of the conductors would result either in causing the device to operate or in rendering it inoperative, and in some cases either condition would constitute a hazard either to persons or to property; hence, in such cases the conductors should be installed in rigid or other metal conduit. On the other hand, damage to the conductors of the low-voltage control circuit of a domestic oil burner or automatic stoker does not constitute a hazard, because the boiler or furnace is equipped with an automatic safety control.

The second paragraph of this section focuses on the hazard of accidental starting of a motor. Figure 430-44 shows an example of a control circuit installation that should be carefully designed and is required by the second sentence of Sec. 430-73 to be observed for any control circuit which has one leg grounded. Whenever the coil is fed from a circuit made up of a hot conductor

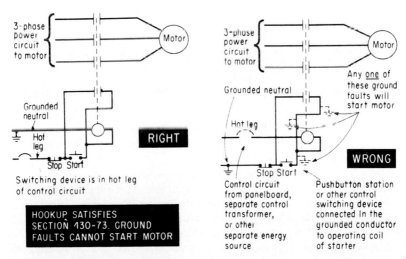

Note : OL relays are not shown in diagrams.

Fig. 430·44. Control hookup must prevent accidental starting. (Sec. 430-73.)

and a grounded conductor (as when the coil is fed from a panelboard or separate control transformer, instead of from the supply conductors to the motor), care must be taken to place the push-button station or other switching control device in the hot leg to the coil and not in the grounded leg to the coil. By switching in the hot leg, the starting of the motor by accidental ground fault can be effectively eliminated.

Combinations of ground faults can develop to short the pilot starting device—push-button, limit switch, pressure switch, etc.—accidentally starting the motor even though the pilot device is in the OFF position. And because many remote-control circuits are long, possible faults have many points at which they might occur. Insulation breakdowns, contact shorts due to accumulation of foreign matter or moisture, and grounds to conduit are common fault conditions responsible for accidental operation of motor controllers.

Although not specifically covered by **Code** rules, there are many types of ground-fault conditions that affect motor starting and should be avoided.

As shown in Fig. 430-45, any magnetic motor controller used on a 3-phase, 3-wire ungrounded system always presents the possibility of accidental starting of the motor. If, for instance, an undetected ground fault exists on one phase of

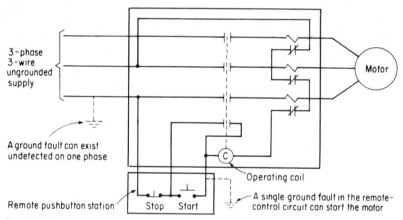

Fig. 430-45.   Accidental motor starting can be hazardous and contrary to **Code** rule. (Sec. 430-73.)

the 3-phase system—even if this system ground fault is a long distance from the controller—a second ground fault in the remote-control circuit for the operating coil of the starter can start the motor.

Figure 430-46 shows the use of a control transformer to isolate the control circuit from responding to the combination of ground faults shown in Fig. 430-45. This transformer may be a one-to-one isolating transformer, with the same primary and secondary voltage, or the transformer can step the motor circuit voltage down to a lower level for the control circuit.

In the hookup shown in Fig. 430-47, a two-pole START button is used in conjunction with two sets of holding contacts in the motor starter. This hookup protects against accidental starting of the motor under the fault conditions shown in Fig. 430-45. The hookup also protects against accidental starting due to two ground faults in the control circuit simply shorting out the START button and energizing the operating coil. This could happen in the circuit of Fig. 430-45 or the circuit of Fig. 430-46.

Another type of motor control circuit fault can produce a current path through the coil of a closed contactor to hold it closed regardless of operation of the pilot device for opening the coil circuit. Again this can be done by a combination of ground faults which short the STOP device. Failure to open can do serious damage to motors in some applications and can be a hazard to per-

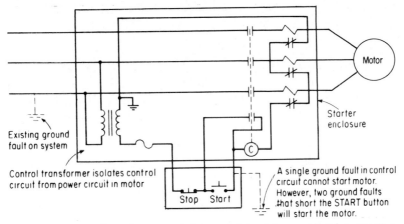

Fig. 430-46. Control transformer can isolate control circuit from accidental starting. (Sec. 430-73.)

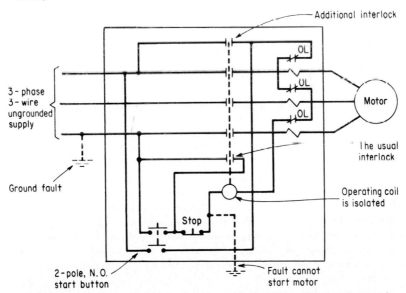

Fig. 430-47. Use of 2-pole start button can prevent accidental starting. (Sec. 430-73.)

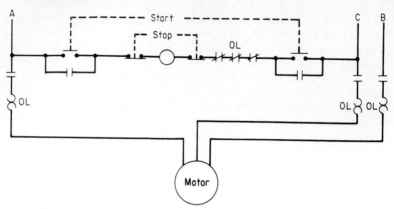

Fig. 430·48. This circuit prevents accidental starting and assures stopping. (Sec. 430-73.)

sonnel. The operating characteristics of contactor coils contribute to the possible failure of a controller to respond to the opening of the STOP contacts. It takes about 85 percent of rated coil voltage to operate the armature associated with the coil; but it takes only about 50 percent of the rated value to enable the coil to hold the contactor closed once it is closed. Under such conditions, even partial grounds and shorts on control contact assemblies can produce paths for sufficient current flow to cause shorting of the stop position of pilot devices. And faults can short-out running overload relays, eliminating overcurrent protection of the motor, its associated control equipment, and conductors.

Figure 430-48 is a modification of the circuit of Fig. 430-47, using a two-pole START button and a two-pole STOP button—protecting against both accidental starting and accidental failure to stop when the STOP button is pressed. Both effects of ground faults are eliminated.

430·74. Disconnection. The control circuit of a remote-control motor controller shall always be so connected that it will be cut off when the disconnecting means is opened, unless a separate disconnecting means is provided for the control circuit.

When the control circuit of a motor starter is tapped from the line terminals of the starter—in which case it is fed at line-to-line voltage of the circuit to the motor itself—opening of the required disconnect means ahead of the starter deenergizes the control circuit from its source of supply, as shown in Fig. 430-49. But, where voltage supply to the coil circuit is derived from outside the starter enclosure (as from a panelboard or from a separate control transformer), provision must be made to assure that the control circuit is capable of being deenergized to permit safe maintenance of the starter. In such cases, the required power-circuit disconnect ahead of the starter can open the power circuit to the starter's line terminals; but, unless some provision is made to open the externally derived control circuit voltage supply, a maintenance worker could be exposed to the unexpected shock hazard of the energized control circuit within the starter.

The disconnect for control voltage supply could be an extra pole or auxiliary

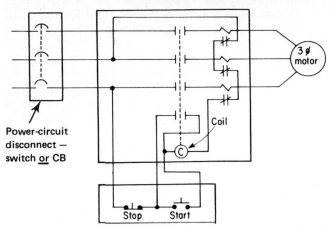

Power-circuit disconnect — switch or CB

Fig. 430-49. Disconnect ahead of starter opens supply to line-voltage coil circuit. (Sec. 430-74.)

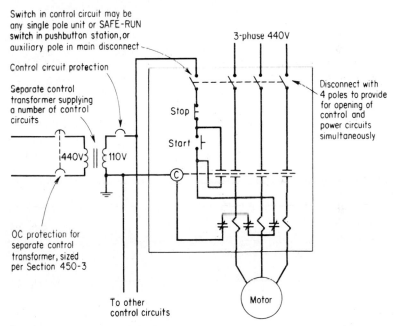

Switch in control circuit may be any single pole unit or SAFE-RUN switch in pushbutton station, or auxiliary pole in main disconnect

Control circuit protection

Separate control transformer supplying a number of control circuits

OC protection for separate control transformer, sized per Section 450-3

To other control circuits

3-phase 440V

Disconnect with 4 poles to provide for opening of control and power circuits simultaneously

Fig. 430-50. Control disconnect means must supplement power-circuit disconnect. (Sec. 430-74.)

contact in the switch or CB used as the main power disconnect ahead of the starter, as shown in Fig. 430-50. Or the control disconnect could be a separate switch (like a toggle switch), provided this separate switch is installed "immediately adjacent" to the power disconnect—so it is clear to maintenance people that *both* disconnects must be opened to kill *all* energized circuits within the starter. Control circuits operating contactor coils, etc., within controllers present a shock hazard if they are allowed to remain energized when the disconnect is in the OFF position. Therefore, the control circuit either must be designed in such a way that it is disconnected from the source of supply by the controller disconnecting means or must be equipped with a separate disconnect immediately adjacent to the controller disconnect for opening of both disconnects. [For grounding of the control transformer secondary in Fig. 430-50, refer to Sec. 250-5(b), Exception No. 3.]

Exception No. 1 of part **(a)** is aimed at industrial-type motor control hookups which involve extensive interlocking of control circuits for multimotor process operations or machine sequences. In recognition of the unusual and complex control conditions that exist in many industrial applications—particularly process industries and manufacturing facilities—Exception No. 1 alters the basic rule that disconnecting means for control circuits must be located "immediately adjacent one to each other" (Fig. 430-51). When a piece of motor control equip-

Fig. 430·51. Industrial control layouts with more than 12 control circuit conductors for interlocking of controllers and operating stations (arrow) do not require control disconnects to be "immediately adjacent" to power disconnects. (Sec. 430-74.)

ment has more than 12 motor control conductors associated with it, remote locating of the disconnect means is permitted under the conditions given in Exception No. 1. As shown in Fig. 430-52, this permission is applicable only where qualified persons have access to the live parts and sufficient warning signs are used on the equipment to locate and identify the various disconnects associated with the control circuit conductors.

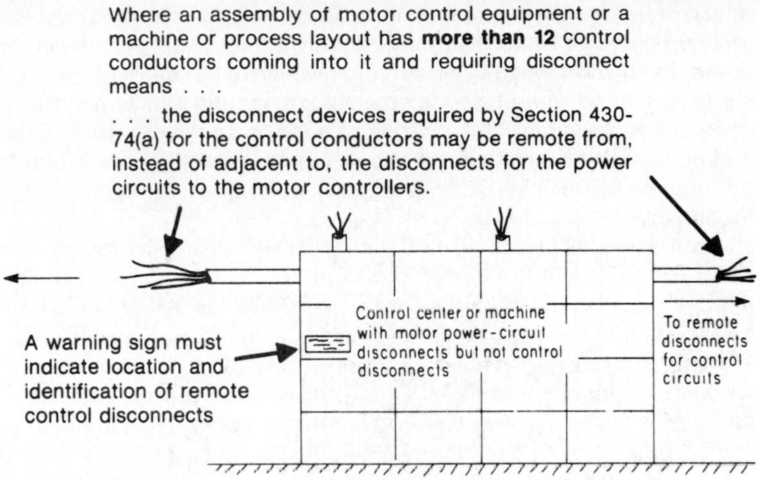

Where an assembly of motor control equipment or a machine or process layout has **more than 12** control conductors coming into it and requiring disconnect means . . .

. . . the disconnect devices required by Section 430-74(a) for the control conductors may be remote from, instead of adjacent to, the disconnects for the power circuits to the motor controllers.

A warning sign must indicate location and identification of remote control disconnects

Control center or machine with motor power-circuit disconnects but not control disconnects

To remote disconnects for control circuits

Fig. 430-52. For extensively interlocked control circuits, control disconnects do not have to be adjacent to power disconnects. (Sec. 430-74.)

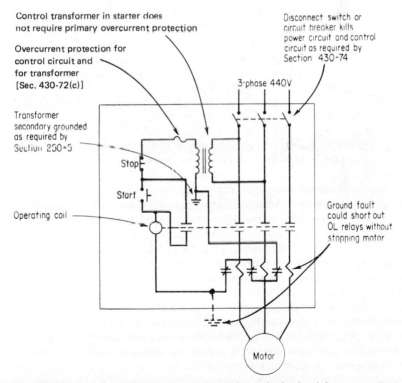

Control transformer in starter does not require primary overcurrent protection

Disconnect switch or circuit breaker kills power circuit and control circuit as required by Section 430-74

Overcurrent protection for control circuit and for transformer [Sec. 430-72(c)]

3-phase 440V

Transformer secondary grounded as required by Section 250-5

Stop

Start

Operating coil

Ground fault could short out OL relays without stopping motor

Motor

Fig. 430-53. Control transformer in starter must be on load side of disconnect. (Sec. 430-74.)

Exception No. 2 presents another instance in which control circuit disconnects may be mounted other than immediately adjacent to each other. It notes that where the opening of one or more motor control circuit disconnects might result in hazard to personnel or property, remote mounting may be used where the conditions specified in Exception No. 1 exist, i. e., that access is limited to qualified persons and that a warning sign is located on the outside of the equipment to indicate the location and the identification of each remote control circuit disconnect.

The requirement of part **(b)** of this section is shown in Fig. 430-53. When a control transformer is in the starter enclosure, the power disconnect means is on the line side and can de-energize the transformer control circuit. Grounding of the control circuit is not always necessary, as noted in Exception No. 3 of Sec. 250-5(b). Overcurrent protection must be provided for the control circuit when a control circuit transformer is used, as covered in Sec. 430-72(b). Such protection may be on the primary or secondary side of the transformer, as described. In Sec. 450-1, Exception No. 2 notes that the rules of Art. 450 do not apply to "dry-type transformers that constitute a component part of other apparatus. . . ." A control transformer supplied as a factory-installed component in a starter would therefore be exempt from the rules of Sec. 450-3(b), covering overcurrent protection for transformers, but would have to comply with Sec. 430-72(c).

430·81. General. As used in Art. 430, the term "controller" includes any switch or device normally used to start and stop a motor, in addition to motor starters and controllers as such. As noted, the branch-circuit fuse or CBs are considered an acceptable control device for stationary motors not over ⅛ hp where the motor has sufficient winding impedance to prevent damage to the motor with its rotor continuously at standstill. And a plug and receptacle connection may serve as the controller for portable motors up to ⅓ hp.

As described in the definition here, a "controller" is a device that starts and stops a motor by "making and breaking the motor circuit current"—that is, the power current flow to the motor windings. A pushbutton station, a limit switch, a float switch, or any other pilot control device that "carries the electric signals directing the performance of the controller" (see the definition of "Motor Control Circuit" in Sec. 430-71) is not the controller where such a device is used to carry only the current to the operating coil of a magnetic motor controller. For purposes of **Code** application, the contactor mechanism is the motor "controller."

430·82. Controller Design. Every controller must be capable of starting and stopping the motor which it controls, must be able to interrupt the stalled-rotor current of the motor, and must have a horsepower rating not lower than the rating of the motor, except as permitted by Sec. 430-83.

430·83. Rating. Figure 430-54 shows the basic requirements on rating of a controller. Although the basic rule calls for a horsepower-rated switch or a horsepower-rated motor starter, there are exceptions as noted in Sec. 430-81 and as follows:

- A general-use switch rated at not less than twice the full-load motor current may be used as the controller for stationary motors up to 2 hp, rated 300 V

THIS IS THE BASIC RULE

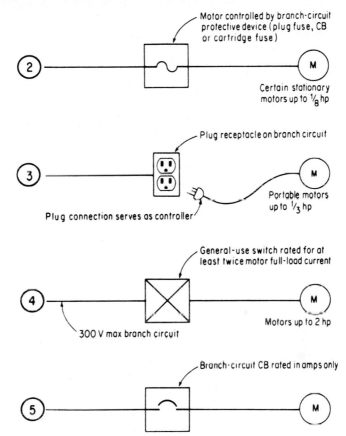

THESE ARE EXCEPTIONS TO THE BASIC RULE

Fig. 430-54. Controller must be a hp-rated switch or CB—but other devices may satisfy. (Sec. 430-83.)

or less. On AC circuits, a general-use snap switch suitable only for use on AC may be used to control a motor having a full-load current rating not over 80 percent of the ampere rating of the switch.

- A branch-circuit CB, rated in amperes only, may be used as a controller. If the same CB is used as controller and to provide overload protection for the motor circuit, it must be rated in accordance with Sec. 430-32.

In the UL's *Electrical Construction Materials Directory*, data are presented on use of switches in motor circuits, as follows:

1. Enclosed switches with horsepower ratings in addition to current ratings may be used for motor circuits as well as for general-purpose circuits. Enclosed switches with ampere-only ratings are intended for general use but may also be used for motor circuits (as controllers and/or disconnects) as permitted by **NE Code** Sec. 430-83 (Exception No. 1), Sec. 430-109 (Exceptions No. 2, 3, and 4), and Sec. 430-111.

2. A switch that is marked "MOTOR CIRCUIT SWITCH" is intended for use *only* in motor circuits.

3. For switches with dual-horsepower ratings, the higher horsepower rating is based on the use of time-delay fuses in the switch fuseholders to hold-in on the inrush current of the higher-horsepower-rated motor.

4. Although Sec. 430-83 permits use of horsepower-rated switches as controllers and UL lists horsepower-rated switches up to 500 hp, UL does state in its Green Book that "enclosed switches rated higher than 100 hp are restricted to use as motor disconnect means and are not for use as motor controllers." But a horsepower-rated switch up to 100 hp may be used as both a controller and disconnect if it breaks all ungrounded legs to the motor, as covered in Sec. 430-111.

Figure 430-55 covers two of those points.

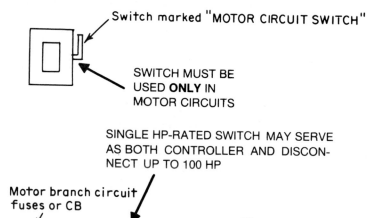

Fig. 430·55. UL rules limit Code applications. (Sec. 430-83.)

For selection of a controller for a sealed (hermetic-type) refrigeration compressor motor, refer to Sec. 440-41.

430·84. Need Not Open All Conductors. It is interesting to note that the **NE Code** says that a controller need not open all conductors to a motor, except when the controller serves also as the required disconnecting means. For instance, a two-pole starter of correct horsepower rating could be used for a 3-

phase motor if running overload protection is provided in all three circuit legs by devices separate from the starter, such as by dual-element, time-delay fuses which are sized to provide running overload protection as well as short-circuit protection for the motor branch circuit. The controller must interrupt only enough conductors to be able to start and stop the motor.

However, when the controller is a manual (nonmagnetic) starter or is a manually operated switch or CB (as permitted by the **Code**), the controller itself also may serve as the disconnect means if it opens all ungrounded conductors to the motor, as covered in Sec. 430-111. This eliminates the need for another switch or CB to serve as the disconnecting means. But, it should be noted that only a manually operated switch or CB may serve such a dual function. A magnetic starter cannot also serve as the disconnecting means even if it does open all ungrounded conductors to the motor.

Figure 430-56 shows typical applications in which the controller does not have to open all conductors but separate disconnect switch or CB is required ahead of the controller. In the sketch, the word "ungrounded" refers to the condition that none of the circuit conductors is grounded. These may be the ungrounded conductors of grounded systems.

Generally, one conductor of a 115-V circuit is grounded, and on such a circuit a single-pole controller may be used connected in the ungrounded conductor, or a two-pole controller is permitted if both poles are opened together. In a 230-V circuit there is usually no grounded conductor, but if one conductor is grounded, Sec. 430-85 permits a two-pole controller.

430-85. In Grounded Conductors.   This rule permits a three-pole switch, CB, or motor starter to be used in a 3-phase motor circuit derived from a 3-phase, 3-wire, corner-grounded delta system—with the grounded phase leg switched along with the hot legs, as in Sec. 430-36.

430-86. Phase Converter Power Interruption.   Automatic control is required to disconnect equipment fed by a *rotary* phase converter in case of power loss at the input of the converter.

430-87. Number of Motors Served by Each Controller.   Generally, an individual motor controller is required for each motor. However, for motors rated not over 600 V, a single controller rated at not less than the sum of the horsepower ratings of all the motors of the group may be used with a group of motors if any one of the conditions specified is met. Where a single controller is used for more than one motor connected on a single branch circuit as permitted under condition *b*, it should be noted that the reference is to part **(a)** of Sec. 430-53. That use of single controller applies only to cases involving motors of 1 hp or less and does not apply for several motors used on a single branch circuit in accordance with parts **(b)** and **(c)** of Sec. 430-53—unless the several motors satisfy conditions *a* or *c* of this section.

See Sec. 430-112, where the same conditions are set for a single disconnect means to serve a group of motors.

430-88. Adjustable-Speed Motors.   Field weakening is quite commonly used as a method of controlling the speed of DC motors. If such a motor were started under a weakened field, the starting current would be excessive unless the motor is specially designed for starting in this manner.

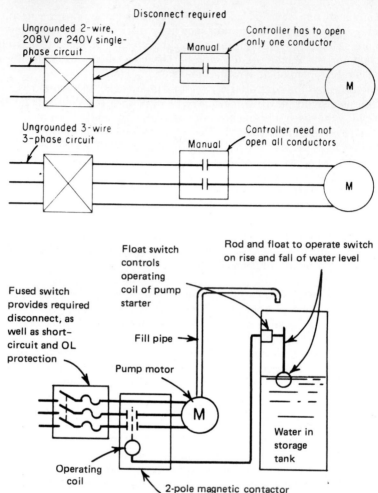

Fig. 430-56. "Controller" does not have to break *all* legs of motor supply circuit. (Sec. 430-84.)

430-89. Speed Limitation. A common example of a separately excited DC motor is found in a typical speed control system that is widely used for electric elevators, hoists, and other applications where smooth control of speed from standstill to full speed is necessary. In Fig. 430-57, G_1 and G_2 are two generators having their armatures mounted on a shaft which is driven by a motor, not shown in the diagram. M is a motor driving the elevator drum or other machine. The fields of generator G_1 and motor M are excited by G_1. By adjusting the rheostat R, the voltage generated by G_2 is varied, and this in turn varies the speed of motor M. It is evident that if the field circuit of motor M should be accidentally opened while the motor is lightly loaded, the motor would reach

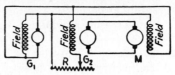

an excessive speed. In many applications of this system the motor is always loaded and no speed-limiting device is required.

The speed of a series motor depends upon its load and will become excessive at no load or very light loads. Traction motors are commonly series motors, but such a motor is geared to the drive wheels of the car or locomotive and hence is always loaded.

Where a motor generator, consisting of a motor driving a compound-wound DC generator, is operated in parallel with a similar machine or is used to charge a storage battery, if the motor circuit is accidentally opened while the generator is still connected to the DC buses or battery, the generator will be driven as a motor and its speed may become dangerously high. A synchronous converter operating under similar conditions may also reach an excessive speed if the AC supply is accidentally cut off.

A safeguard against overspeed is provided by a centrifugal device on the shaft of the machine, arranged to close (or open) a contact at a predetermined speed, thus tripping a CB which cuts the machine off from the current supply.

430·90. Combination Fuseholder and Switch as Controller. The use of a fusible switch as a motor controller with fuses as motor-running protective devices is practicable when time-delay types of fuses are used. The rating of the fuses must not exceed 125 percent, or in some cases 115 percent, of the full-load motor current, and nontime-delay fuses of this rating would, in most cases, be blown by the starting current drawn by the motor, particularly where the motor turns on and off frequently. (See Sec. 430-35.)

It may be found that a switch having the required horsepower rating is not provided with fuse terminals of the size required to accommodate the branch-circuit fuses. For example, assume a 7½-hp 230-V 3-phase motor started at full-line voltage. A switch used as the disconnecting means for this motor must be rated at not less than 7½ hp, but this would probably be a 60-A switch and therefore, if fusible, would be equipped with terminals to receive 35- to 60-A fuses. Section 430-90 provides that fuse terminals must be installed that will receive fuses of 70-A rating. In such case a switch of the next higher rating must be provided, unless time-delay fuses are used.

430·91. Motor Controller Enclosure Types. This section and table cover selection criteria—but no mandatory rule—on types of motor controller enclosures. This section gives selection data, with characteristics tabulated, for application of the various NEMA types of motor controller enclosures for use in specific nonhazardous locations. It can be argued that the data in this section are made mandatory by the general rules of Secs. 110-3 and 110-11—both of which require equipment to be suitable for its environment.

UL and NEMA have developed a new Type 5 motorcontroller that is shown in **NEC** Table 430-91. This is an enclosure for indoor use only and protects against settling airborne dust, falling dirt, and dripping noncorrosive liquids. This type of enclosure is suited to use for motor control centers in industrial environments.

430·102. Location.   Along with Sec. 430-101, this section specifically requires that a disconnecting means—basically, a motor-circuit switch rated in horsepower, or a CB—be provided in each motor circuit. Figure 430-58 shows the basic rule on "in-sight" location of the disconnect means. This applies always for all motor circuits rated up to 600 V—even if an "out-of-sight" disconnect can be locked in the open position.

Because the basic rule here requires a disconnecting means to be within sight from the "controller location," the question arises, Is the magnetic contactor the controller or is the pushbutton station the controller? The **NEC** makes clear that the contactor of a magnetic motor starter *is* the controller for the motor, *not* the pushbuttons that actuate the coil of the contactor. The **NEC** establishes that identification by the definition of "controller" in Art. 100 and by the definition of a "motor control circuit" in Sec. 430-71, as follows:

> *Controller:* A device or group of devices that serves to govern, in some predetermined manner, the electric power delivered to the apparatus to which it is connected.

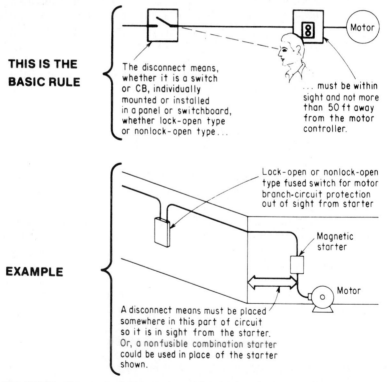

Fig. 430·58. The required disconnect must be visible from the controller. (Sec. 430-102.)

Motor control circuit: The circuit of a control apparatus or system that carries the electric signals directing the performance of the controller, but does not carry the main power current.

In a magnetic motor starter hookup, it is the contactor that actually governs the electric power delivered to the motor to which it is connected. The motor connects to the contactor and *not* to the pushbuttons, which are in the control circuit that carries the electric signals directing the performance of *the controller* (that is, the contactor). The pushbuttons do *not* carry "the main power current," which is "delivered" to the motor by the contactor and which is, therefore, "the controller." It is well established that the intent of the **Code** rule, as well as the letter of the rule, is to designate *the contactor* and *not* the pushbutton station as the "controller," and the disconnect must be within sight from it and not from a pushbutton station or some other remotely located pilot control device that connects into the contactor.

There are two exceptions to this basic **Code** rule requiring a disconnect switch or CB to be located in sight from the controller:

Exception No. 1 permits the disconnect for a high-voltage (over 600 V) motor to be out of sight from the controller location, as shown in Fig. 430-59. But, such use of a lock-open type switch as an out-of-sight disconnect for a motor circuit rated 600 V or less is a clear **Code** violation.

Exception No. 2 is aimed at permitting practical, realistic disconnect means for industrial applications of large and complex machinery utilizing a number of motors to power the various interrelated parts of the machine. The Exception recognizes that a single common disconnect for a number of controllers (as permitted by part *a* of the Exception of Sec. 430-112) is often impossible to be installed "within sight" of all the controllers even though the controllers are

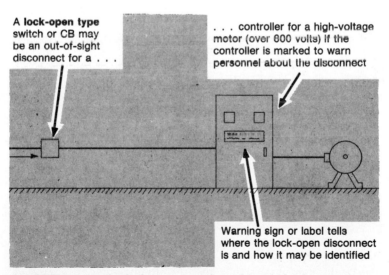

A lock-open type switch or CB may be an out-of-sight disconnect for a . . .

. . . controller for a high-voltage motor (over 600 volts) if the controller is marked to warn personnel about the disconnect

Warning sign or label tells where the lock-open disconnect is and how it may be identified

Fig. 430-59. An out-of-sight disconnect may be used for a high-voltage motor. (Sec. 430-102.)

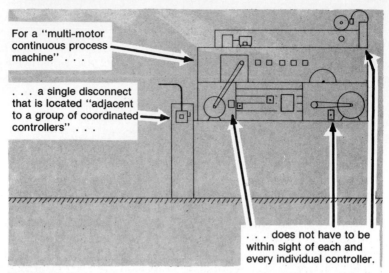

For a "multi-motor continuous process machine" . . .

. . . a single disconnect that is located "adjacent to a group of coordinated controllers" . . .

. . . does not have to be within sight of each and every individual controller.

Fig. 430-60. For multimotor machines, the disconnect may be "adjacent" to controller. (Sec. 430-102.)

"adjacent one to each other." On much industrial process equipment, the components of the overall structure obstruct the view of many controllers. Exception No. 2 permits the single disconnect to be technically out of sight from some or even all the controllers if the disconnect is simply "adjacent" to them—i.e., nearby on the equipment structure, as shown in Fig. 430-60.

Part **(b)** basically requires a disconnect means (switch or CB) to be within sight and not more than 50 ft away from "the motor location and the driven machinery location." But the Exception to that basic requirement says that a disconnect does not have to be within sight from the motor and its load *if* the required disconnect ahead of the motor controller is capable of being locked in the open position.

According to the basic rule of part **(b)**, a manually operable switch, which will provide disconnection of the motor from its power supply conductors, must be placed within sight from the motor location. And this switch *may not* be a switch in the control circuit of a magnetic starter. (The **NE Code** at one time permitted a switch in the coil circuit of the starter installed within sight of the motor. Such a condition is NOT acceptable to the present **Code**.)

These requirements are shown in Fig. 430-61. Specific layouts of the two conditions are shown in Fig. 430-62. (*Note:* **Code** provisions shown in these sketches are minimum safety requirements. Additional use of disconnects, with and without lock-open means, may be made necessary or desirable by job conditions.)

The intent of the Exception to part **(b)** is to permit maintenance workers to lock the disconnecting means ahead of the controller in the open position and keep the key in their possession so that the circuit cannot be energized while they are working on it. Over the years, many questions and controversies have

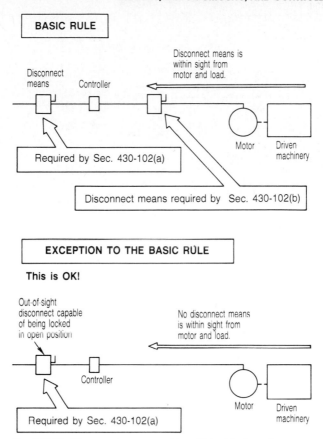

Fig. 430-61. Disconnect means must be within sight from the motor and its driven load, unless out-of-sight disconnect can be locked open. [Sec. 430-102(b).]

arisen over the concept of a lock-open-type disconnect that satisfies the intent of this Exception. The various considerations may be addressed as follows:

Question: Does the rule specify "how" or "by what means" a disconnect must be "locked in the open position"?

Answer: The rule says nothing at all about that and does not actually require "locking" in the open position. It simply stipulates a condition that must be "capable" of being achieved—that is, some provision must assure that the disconnect is simply "capable of being locked in the open position."

Question: Does the **NEC** make it permissible to use the lock on a panelboard door or other enclosure door as the means of making the disconnect capable of being locked in the open position?

Answer: The very clear and straightforward wording of the **Code** rule cannot be construed to prohibit use of such a lock to render the disconnect capable of being locked open. Panelboards made by all of the many manufacturers are

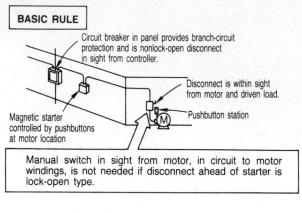

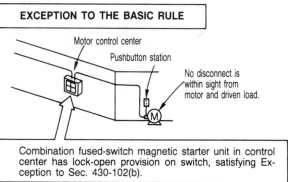

Fig. 430·62. Here's an exmple of the rules, showing physical layout.
[Sec. 430-102(b).]

provided with key-operated locks on their doors and are UL-certified with such locking provision. There is no **Code** rule that prohibits locking of enclosure doors. In fact, in the Exception of Sec. 620-71 covering elevators and moving walks, the **NEC** specifically recognizes use of "cabinets with doors or removable panels capable of being locked in the closed position." And where a number of motors must all operate together, as in "Integrated Electrical Systems" (**NEC** Art. 685), it is more realistic and convenient—and therefore more contributive to effective safety—to be able to use a single lock to lock out *all* the disconnects that must be kept open when *any one* is open. It can be dangerous to lock out a single motor disconnect of a group of integrated motors and leave the others exposed to being turned on during maintenance operations.

Although the literal wording of the Exception of part **(b)** can be fully satisfied either by a lock on the door of a panel containing motor disconnects or by a locking hasp at the handle for each individual disconnect, there are differences between the two methods. The use of individual locking hasps provides greater ease, speed, and convenience of maintenance by limiting lockout to only the disconnect hasps on which locks are placed, keeping other disconencts available. However, the use of a lock on the panel door is really much more conducive to personnel safety than the use of lock hasps for the individual disconnects (switches or breakers) in a panel, for the following reasons:

1. Provision of lock hasps for each circuit disconnect affords no assurance that the disconnect is "capable" of being locked out—that is, that a person who might want to lock open a circuit carries a padlock to accomplish the actual locking. It is totally unrealistic to believe that a significant percentage of maintenance and operating personnel in commercial and industrial buildings carry padlocks in their pockets. Even in the rare case where a worker owns a padlock, he commonly does not have it with him, has misplaced or lost it, or finds it uncomfortable to have the heavy weight in his pocket. Safety cannot be based on fantasy or fiction. And especially in a panel containing two or more disconnects that must *all* be locked in the open position to assure safe maintenance—as for a conveyor system or other multimotor, integrated machine operations—it is totally ridiculous to expect that each person who may have to work on the motors will carry padlocks to use on all the individual disconnects.

2. Where lock-open provision is made by means of a lock installed in the panel door instead of the use of individual lock hasps, it is certain that the lock is always available to be used. Although the use of individual hasps, as described above, does not in itself make the disconnect "capable of being locked in the open position," the use of a panel with a built-in lock more closely follows the **Code** rule because the presence of a "lock" is guaranteed. The lock exists and cannot be removed, and the opportunity for real, effective safety is afforded simply by giving a key to the lock to everyone who needs to lock open the disconnects. People will more readily carry a key than a padlock.

The push-button station in Fig. 430-62, Exception, operates only the holding coil in the magnetic starter. The magnetic starter "controls" the current to the motor; for example, the control wires to a push-button station could become shorted after the motor is in operation and pushing the STOP button would not release the holding coil in the magnetic starter and the motor would continue to run. This is the reason that a disconnecting means is required to be installed within sight from the motor and its load or a lock-open switch installed ahead of the controller. In this case, operating the disconnecting means will open the supply to the controller and shut off the motor.

430.103. Operation.   This rule actually defines the meaning of the term *disconnecting means.*

In order that necessary periodic inspection and servicing of motors and their controllers may be done with safety, the **Code** requires that a switch, CB, or other device shall be provided for this purpose. Because the disconnecting means must disconnect the controller as well as the motor, it must be a separate device and cannot be a part of the controller, though it could be mounted on the same panel or enclosed in the same box with the controller. The disconnect must be installed ahead of the controller. And note that the disconnect must open only the "ungrounded" conductors of a motor circuit.

In case the motor controller fails to open the circuit if the motor is stalled, or under other conditions of heavy overload, the disconnecting means can be used to open the circuit. It is therefore required that a switch used as the disconnecting means shall be capable of interrupting very heavy current.

430·105. Grounded Conductors. Although Sec. 430-103 requires a disconnect means only for the ungrounded conductors of a motor circuit, if a motor circuit includes a grounded conductor, one pole of the disconnect *may* switch the grounded conductor provided all poles of the disconnect operate together—as in a multipole switch or CB. For instance, a 120-V, 2-wire circuit with one of its conductors grounded only requires a single-pole disconnect switch, but a two-pole switch *could* be used, with one pole switching the grounded leg.

430·107. Readily Accessible. Although a motor circuit may be provided with more than one disconnect means in series ahead of the controller—such as one at the panel where the motor circuit originates and one at the controller location—*only one* of the disconnects is required to be "readily accessible," as follows:

The definition of readily accessible is:

Readily accessible: Capable of being reached quickly for operation, renewal, or inspection, without requiring those to whom ready access is requisite to climb over or remove obstacles or to resort to portable ladders, chairs, etc. (See "Accessible.")

The disconnecting means must be reached without climbing over anything, without removing crates or equipment or other obstacles, and without requiring the use of portable ladders.

Note carefully: A disconnect that has to be "readily accessible" must be so only for "those to whom ready access is requisite"—which clearly and intentionally allows for making equipment *not* readily accessible to other than authorized persons, such as by providing a lock on the door, with the key possessed by or available to those who require ready access.

Because the definition of "readily accessible" contains a last phrase that says "See 'Accessible'," logic dictates that the installation must also satisfy the definition of "Accessible." And the wording of the definition clearly establishes that there is no **Code** violation in putting the disconnect means in a room or area under lock and key to make it accessible only to authorized persons.

The definition reads:

Accessible: (As applied to Equipment.) Admitting close approach because not guarded by locked doors, elevation, or other effective means. (See "Readily Accessible.")

Again note carefully: That definition does not say that a door to an electrical room is prohibited from being locked. In fact, the wording of the definition, by referring to "locked doors," actually presumes the existence and, therefore, the acceptability of "locked doors" in electrical systems. The only requirement implied by the wording is that locked doors, where used, must not "guard" against access—that is, disposition of the key to the lock must be such that those requiring access to the room are not positively excluded. The rule is satisfied if the key is available to provide access to authorized persons.

In reference to the definition of "Accessible," the critical word is "guarded."

The definition is *not* intended to mean that equipment *cannot* be "behind" locked doors or that equipment *cannot* be mounted up high where it *can* be reached with a portable ladder. To make equipment "not accessible," a door lock or high mounting must be such that it positively "guards" against access. Equipment behind a locked door for which a key is not possessed by or available to persons who require access to the equipment is *not* "accessible." A common example of that latter condition occurs in multitenant buildings where a disconnect for the tenant of one occupancy unit is located behind the locked door of another tenant's occupancy unit from which the first tenant is effectively and legally excluded. And even that application *is* **Code**-acceptable if the disconnect is *not required* by the **NEC** to be "readily accessible."

Equipment may be fully "accessible" even though installed behind a locked door or at an elevated height. Equipment that is high-mounted but can be reached with a ladder that is fixed in place or a portable ladder *is* "accessible" (although the equipment would not be "readily accessible" if a portable ladder had to be used to reach it). Similarly, equipment behind a locked door *is* "accessible" to anyone who possesses a key to the lock or to a person who is authorized to obtain and use the key to open the locked door. In such cases, conditions do *not* "guard" against access.

Refer to the definitions of "Accessible" and "Readily Accessible" in Art. 100 of this book.

430-109. Type. In a motor branch circuit, every switch or CB in the circuit, from where the circuit is tapped from the feeder to the motor itself, must satisfy the requirements on type and rating of disconnect means. A CB switching device with no automatic trip operation, a so-called molded-case switch, may be used as a motor disconnect instead of a conventional CB or a horsepower-rated switch. Such a device either must be rated for the horsepower of the motor it is used with or must have an amp rating at least equal to 115 percent of that of the motor with which it is used. Figure 430-63 covers the basic rules on types of disconnect means.

For a motor larger than 2 hp, not larger than 100 hp, and not portable, a motor-circuit switch or a CB must be used as the disconnecting means (Fig. 430-64).

A motor-circuit switch is a horsepower-rated switch. If in addition to the disconnecting means there is any other switch in the motor circuit and it is at all likely that this switch might be opened in case of trouble, this switch must have the interrupting capacity required for a switch intended for use as the disconnecting means.

Exception No. 4 to Sec. 430-109 sets the maximum horsepower rating required for motor-circuit switches at 100 hp. Higher-rated switches are now available and will provide additional safety. The first sentence of this section makes a basic requirement that the disconnecting means for a motor and its controller be a motor-circuit switch rated in horsepower. For motors rated up to 500 hp, this is readily complied with, inasmuch as the UL lists motor-circuit switches up to 500 hp and the manufacturers mark switches to conform. But for motors rated over 100 hp, the **Code** does not require that the disconnect have a horsepower rating. It makes an exception to the basic rule and permits the

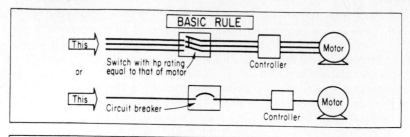

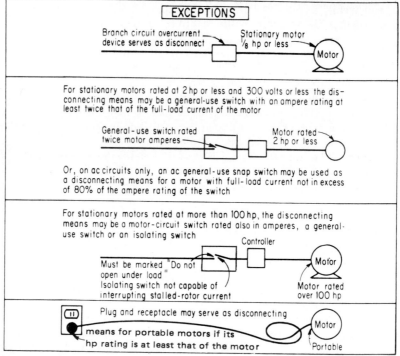

Fig. 430-63. One of these disconnects must be used for a motor branch circuit. (Sec. 430-109.)

use of an ampere-rated switch or isolation switch, provided the switch has a carrying capacity of at least 115 percent of the nameplate current rating of the motor [Sec. 430-110(a)]. And UL notes that horsepower-rated switches over 100 hp *must not* be used as motor controllers. And Exception No. 4 notes that isolation switches for motors over 100 hp must be plainly marked "Do not operate under load," if the switch is not rated for safely interrupting the locked-rotor current of the motor. Figure 430-65 shows an example of disconnect switch application for a motor rated over 100 hp.

example Provide a disconnect for a 125-hp, 3-phase, 460-V motor. Use a nonfusible switch, inasmuch as short-circuit protection is provided at the supply end of the branch circuit.

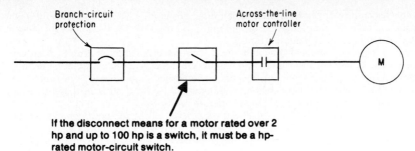

If the disconnect means for a motor rated over 2 hp and up to 100 hp is a switch, it must be a hp-rated motor-circuit switch.

Fig. 430·64. From 2 to 100 hp, a disconnect *switch* must be horsepower-rated. (Sec. 430-109.)

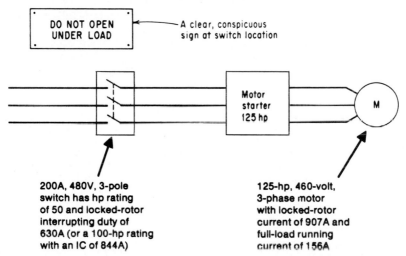

Fig. 430·65. Above 100 hp, a switch does not have to be horsepower-rated. (Sec. 430-109.)

The full-load running current of the motor is 156 A, from **NEC** Table 430-150. A suitable disconnect must have a continuous carrying capacity of 156 × 1.15 or 179 A, as required by Sec. 430-110(a).

This calls for a 200-A, three-pole switch rated for 480 V. The switch may be a general-use switch, a current-and-horsepower marked motor-circuit switch, or an isolation switch. A 200-A, three-pole, 480-V motor-circuit switch would be marked with a rating of 50 hp, but the horsepower rating is of no concern in this application because the switch does not have to be horsepower-rated for motors larger than 100 hp.

If the 50-hp switch were of the heavy-duty type, it would have an interrupting rating of 10 × 65 A (the full-load current of a 460-V, 50-hp motor) or 650 A. But the locked-rotor current of the 125-hp motor might run over 900 A. In such a case, the switch is required by Exception No. 4 to be marked "Do not operate under load."

If a fusible switch had to be provided for the above motor to provide both disconnect and short-circuit protection, the size of the switch would be determined by the size and type of fuses used. Using a fuse rating of 250 percent of motor current (which does not exceed the 300 percent maximum in Table 430-152) for standard fuses, the application would call for 400-A fuses in a 400-A switch. This switch would certainly qualify as the motor disconnect. However, if time-delay fuses are used, a 200-A switch would be large enough to take the time-delay fuses and could be used as the disconnect (because it is rated at 115 percent of motor current).

In the foregoing, the 400-A switch might have an interrupting rating high enough to handle the locked-rotor current of the motor. Or the 200-A switch might be of the CB-mechanism type or some other heavy current construction that has an interrupting rating up to 12 times the rated load current of the switch itself. In either of these cases, there would be no need for marking "Do not operate under load."

Up to 100 hp, a switch which satisfies the **Code** on rating for use as a motor controller may also provide the required disconnect means—the two functions being performed by the one switch—provided it opens all ungrounded conductors to the motor, is protected by an overcurrent device (which may be the branch-circuit protection or may be fuses in the switch itself), and is a manually operated air-break switch or an oil switch not rated over 600 V or 100 A—as permitted by Sec. 430-111.

430-110. Ampere Rating and Interrupting Capacity.   An ampere-rated switch or a CB must be rated at least equal to 115 percent of a motor's full-load current if the switch or CB is the disconnect means for the motor.

SINGLE DEVICE FOR CONTROL AND DISCONNECT

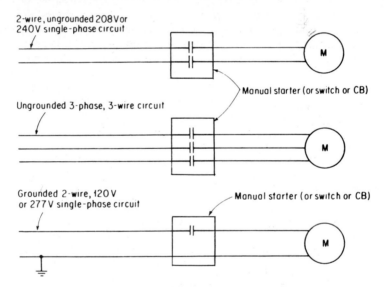

BUT, MAGNETIC STARTER REQUIRES SEPARATE DISCONNECT

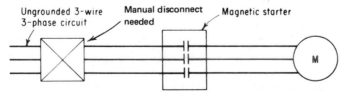

Fig. 430-66.   A manual switch or CB may serve as both controller and disconnect means. (Sec. 430-111.)

When two or more motors are served by a single disconnect means, as permitted by Sec. 430-112, or where one or more motors plus a nonmotor load (such as electric heater load) make use of a single common disconnect, part **(c)** must be used in sizing the disconnect.

430-111. Switch or Circuit Breaker as Both Controller and Disconnecting Means.   As described under Sec. 430-84, a manual switch—capable of starting and stopping a given motor, capable of interrupting the stalled-rotor current of the motor, and having the same horsepower rating as the motor—may serve the functions of controller and disconnecting means in many motor circuits, if the switch opens all ungrounded conductors to the motor. That is also true of a manual motor starter. A single manually operated CB may also serve as controller and disconnect (Figs. 430-66 and 430-67). However, in the case of an autotransformer type of controller, the controller itself, even if manual, may not also serve as the disconnecting means. Such controllers must be provided with a separate means for disconnecting controller and motor.

Although this **Code** section permits a single horsepower-rated switch to be used as both the controller and the disconnect means of a motor circuit, UL rules note that "enclosed switches rated higher than 100 hp are restricted to use as motor disconnecting means and are not for use as motor controllers."

The acceptability of a single switch for both the controller and the disconnecting means is based on the single switch satisfying the **Code** requirements for a controller and for a disconnect. It finds application where general-use switches or horsepower-rated switches are used, as permitted by the **Code**, in conjunction with time-delay fuses which are rated low enough to provide both running overload protection and branch-circuit (short-circuit) protection. In such cases, a single fused switch may serve a total of four functions: (1) con-

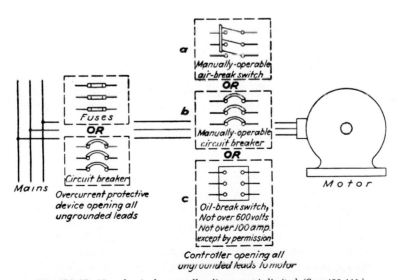

Fig. 430-67. Use of a single controller disconnect is limited. (Sec. 430-111.)

troller, (2) disconnect, (3) branch-circuit protection, and (4) running overload protection. And it is possible for a single CB to also serve these four functions.

For sealed refrigeration compressors, Sec. 440-12 gives the procedure for determining the disconnect rating, based on nameplate rated-load current or branch-circuit selection current, whichever is greater, and locked-rotor current of the motor-compressor.

430·112. Motors Served by Single Disconnecting Means. In general, each individual motor must be provided with a separate disconnecting means. However, a single disconnect sometimes may serve a group of motors under the conditions specified, which are the same as in Sec. 430-87. Such a disconnect must have a rating sufficient to handle a single load equal to the sum of the horsepower ratings or current ratings.

Exception *a*

In Sec. 610-31 it is required that the main collector wires of a traveling crane shall be controlled by a switch located within sight of the wires and readily operable from the floor or ground. This switch would serve as the disconnecting means for the motors on the crane. When repair or maintenance work is to be done on the electrical equipment of the crane, it is safer to cut off the current from all this equipment by opening one switch, rather than to use a separate switch for each motor. Also, in the case of a machine tool driven by two or more motors, a single disconnecting means for the group of motors is more serviceable than an individual switch for each motor, because repair and maintenance work can be done with greater safety when the entire electrical equipment is "dead."

Exception *b*

Such groups may consist of motors having full-load currents not exceeding 6 A each, with circuit fuses not exceeding 20 A at 125 V or less, or 15 A at 600 V or less. Because the expense of providing an individual disconnecting means for each motor is not always warranted for motors of such small size, and also because the entire group of small motors could probably be shut down for servicing without causing inconvenience, a single disconnecting means for the entire group is permitted.

Exception *c*

"Within sight" should be interpreted as meaning so located that there will always be an unobstructed view of the disconnecting switch from the motor, and Sec. 430-102 limits the distance in this case between the disconnecting means and any motor to a maximum of 50 ft.

These conditions are the same as those under which the use of a single controller is permitted for a group of motors. (See Sec. 430-87.) The use of a single disconnecting means for two or more motors is quite common, but in the majority of cases the most practicable arrangement is to provide an individual controller for each motor.

If a switch is used as the disconnecting means, it must be of the type and rating required by Sec. 430-109 for a single motor having a horsepower rating equal to the sum of the horsepower ratings of all the motors it controls. Thus, for six 5-hp motors the disconnecting means should be a motor-circuit switch rated at not less than 30 hp. If the total of the horsepower ratings is over 2 hp, a horsepower-rated switch must be used.

430-113. Energy from More than One Source.   The basic rule of this section, which is similar to that of Sec. 430-74, requires a disconnecting means to be provided from each source of electrical energy input to equipment with more than one circuit supplying power to it, such as the hookup shown in Fig. 430-68, where two switches or a single five-pole switch could be used. And each source is permitted to have a separate disconnecting means. This **Code** rule is aimed at the need for adequate disconnects for safety in complex industrial layouts. But an exception to the **Code** rule states that where a motor receives electrical energy from more than one source (such as a synchronous motor receiving both alternating current and direct current energy input), the disconnecting means for the main power supply to the motor shall *not* be required to be immediately adjacent to the motor—provided that the controller disconnecting means, which is the disconnect ahead of the motor starter in the main power circuit, is capable of being locked in the open position. If, for instance, the motor control disconnect can be locked in the open position, it may be remote; but the disconnect for the other energy input circuit would have to be adjacent to the machine itself, as indicated in Fig. 430-69.

430-124. Size of Conductors.   For motors rated over 600 V, the circuit conductors to the motor are selected to have a current rating equal to or greater than the trip setting of the running overload protective device for the motor.

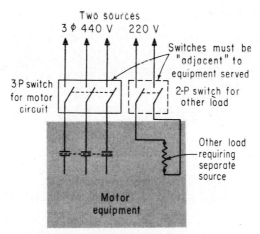

Fig. 430-68. A disconnect must be used for each power input to motorized equipment. (Sec. 430-113.)

If the disconnect for the main power supply to a motor can be locked open, it may be installed remote from the motor . . .

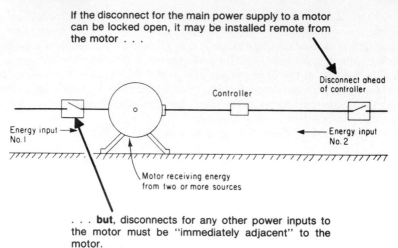

Controller

Disconnect ahead of controller

Energy input No. 1

Energy input No. 2

Motor receiving energy from two or more sources

. . . **but**, disconnects for any other power inputs to the motor must be "immediately adjacent" to the motor.

Fig. 430·69. An exception is made for disconnects for multiple power sources. (Sec. 430-113.)

Fig. 430·70. Liquidtight flex provides flexible connection from rigid conduit supply to motor terminals but does require a separate equipment grounding conductor run within the flex with the circuit conductors or a separate external bonding jumper from the rigid metal conduit to the metal terminal box for each of the two runs. (Sec. 430-145.)

430-125. Motor Circuit Overcurrent Protection.   Overload protection must protect the motor and other circuit components against overload currents up to and including locked-rotor current of the motor. A CB or fuses must be used for protection against ground faults or short circuits in the motor circuit.

430-142. Stationary Motors.   Usually stationary motors are supplied by wiring in metal raceway or metal-clad cable. The motor frames of such motors must be grounded, the raceway or cable armor being attached to the frame and serving as the grounding conductor. [See Sec. 250-91(b).]

Any motor in a wet location constitutes a serious hazard to persons and should be grounded unless it is so located or guarded that it is out of reach. *All* water pump motors, including those in the submersible-type pump, must be grounded, regardless of location, to comply with Sec. 250-43(k).

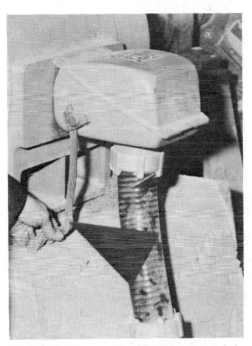

Fig. 430-71. Motor terminal housings must include some lug or terminal for connecting an equipment grounding conductor that may be run inside the raceway with the circuit wires or may be run as a bonding jumper around a length of flex or liquidtight flex, as commonly used for vibration-free motor connections. The terminal box here must have internal provision for connecting the equipment grounding conductor, required for this short length of liquidtight flex, that is larger than 1¼-in. in size. The static grounding connection shown here (arrow) on the box does not satisfy Secs. 351-9 and 250-79(e) as a bonding jumper for the flex, and it does not satisfy Sec. 250-57(b) as an equipment ground for an AC motor. (Sec. 430-145.)

430·145. Method of Grounding. Good practice requires in nearly all cases that the wiring to motors which are not portable shall, at the motor, be installed in rigid or flexible metal conduit, electrical metallic tubing, or metal-clad cable and that such motors should be equipped with terminal housings. The method of connecting the conduit to the motor where some flexibility is necessary is shown in Fig. 430-70. The motor circuit is installed in rigid conduit and a short length of liquidtight flexible metal conduit is provided between the end of the rigid conduit and the terminal housing on the motor. But because the size of flex is over 1¼-in., a separate equipment grounding conductor (or bonding jumper) must be used within or outside the flex as noted in Sec. 351-9 and 250-91(b), Exception No. 2. Refer to Sec. 430-12(e), which requires provision of a suitable termination for an equipment grounding conductor at every motor terminal housing, as shown in Fig. 430-71.

This section permits the use of fixed motors without terminal housings. If a motor has no terminal housing, the branch-circuit conductors must be brought to a junction box not over 6 ft from the motor. Between the junction box and the motor, the specified provisions apply.

According to Sec. 300-16, the conduit, tubing, or metal-clad cable must terminate close to the motor in a fitting having a separable bushed hole for each wire. The method of making the connection to the motor is not specified; presumably, it is the intention that the wire brought out from the terminal fitting shall be connected to binding posts on the motor or spliced to the motor leads. The conduit, tubing, or cable must be rigidly secured to the frame of the motor.

ARTICLE 440. AIR·CONDITIONING AND REFRIGERATING EQUIPMENT

440·3. Other Articles. Article 440 is patterned after Art. 430, and many of its rules, such as on disconnecting means, controllers, conductor sizes, and group installations, are identical or quite similar to those in Art. 430. This article contains provisions for such motor-driven equipment and for branch circuits and controllers for the equipment, taking into account the special considerations involved with sealed (hermetic-type) motor-compressors, in which the motor operates under the cooling effect of the refrigeration.

It must be noted that the rules of Art. 440 are *in addition to* or are *amendments* to the rules given in Art. 430 for motors in general. The basic rules of Art. 430 also apply to A/C (air-conditioning) and refrigerating equipment unless exceptions are indicated in Art. 440.

Article 440 further clarifies the application of **NE Code** rules to air-conditioning equipment and refrigeration equipment as follows:

1. A/C and refrigerating equipment which does not incorporate a sealed (hermetic-type) motor-compressor must satisfy the rules of Art. 422 (Appliances), Art. 424 (Space Heating Equipment), or Art. 430 (Conventional Motors)—whichever apply. For instance, where refrigeration compressors are driven by conventional motors, the motors and controls are subject to

Art. 430, not Art. 440. Furnaces with air-conditioning evaporator coils installed must satisfy Art. 424. Other equipment in which the motor is not a sealed compressor and which must be covered by Arts. 422, 424, or 430 includes fan-coil units, remote forced air-cooled condensers, remote commercial refrigerators, and similar equipment.

2. Room air conditioners are covered in part **G** of Art. 440 (Secs. 440-60 through 440-64), but must also comply with the rules of Art. 422.

3. Household refrigerators and freezers, drinking-water coolers, and beverage dispensers are considered by the **Code** to be appliances, and their application must comply with Art. 422 and must also satisfy Art. 440, because such devices contain sealed motor-compressors.

Air-conditioning equipment (other than small room units and large custom installations) is manufactured in the form of packaged units having all necessary components mounted in one or more enclosures designed for floor mounting, for recessing into walls, for mounting in attics or ceiling plenums, for locating outdoors, etc. Figure 440-1 shows the difference between room A/C units (such as window units) and the larger so-called "packaged units" or central air conditioners. Room units consist of a complete refrigeration system in a unit enclosure intended for mounting in windows or in the wall of the building, with ratings up to 250 V, single phase. Unitary assemblies may be console type for individual room use rated up to 250 V single phase or central cooling units rated up to 600 V for commercial or domestic applications. This type may consist of

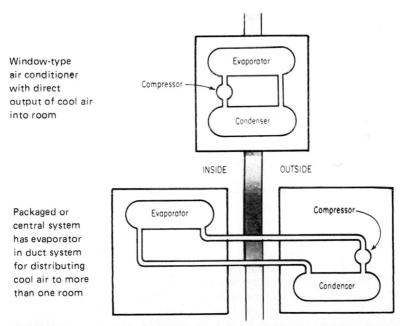

Fig. 440·1. Code rules differentiate between unit room conditioners and central systems. (Sec. 440-3.)

one or more factory-made sections. If it is made up of two or more sections, each section is designed for field interconnection with one or more matched sections to make the complete assembly. Dual-section systems consist of separate packaged sections installed remote from each other and interconnected by refrigerant tubing, either with the compressor within the outdoor section or within the indoor section.

Electrical wiring in and to units varies with the manufacturer, and the extent to which the electrical contractor need be concerned with fuse and CB calculations depends upon the manner in which the units' motors are fed and the type of distribution system to which they are to be connected. A packaged unit is treated as a group of motors. This is different from the approach used with a plug-in room air conditioner, which is treated as an individual single-motor load of amp rating as marked on the nameplate.

440·4. Marking on Hermetic Refrigerant Motor·Compressors and Equipment. Important in the application of hermetic refrigerant motor-compressors are the terms "rated-load current" and "branch-circuit selection current." Definitions of these terms are in notes following Secs. 440-4(a) and (c). When the equipment is marked with the branch-circuit selection current, this greatly simplifies the sizing of motor branch-circuit conductors, disconnecting means, controllers, and overcurrent devices for circuit conductors and motors.

As noted in the last sentence of the FPN in (c), the value of branch-circuit selection current will always be *equal to* or greater than the marked rated-load current. This advises installers that for some A/C equipment that is not required to have a "branch-circuit selection current," the value of rated-load current will appear on the equipment nameplate; and that same value of current will also appear in the nameplate space reserved for branch-circuit selection current. In such cases, the branch-circuit selection current appears to be equal to the rated-load current.

440·5. Marking on Controllers. Note that a controller may be marked with "full-load and locked-rotor current (or horsepower) rating." That possibility of two methods of marking requires careful application of the rules in Sec. 440-41 on selecting the correct rating of controller for motor-compressors.

440·6. Ampacity and Rating. Selection of the rating of branch-circuit conductors, controller, disconnect means, short-circuit (and ground-fault) protection, and running overload protection is *not* made the same for hermetic motor-compressors as for general-purpose motors. In sizing those components, the "rated-load current" marked on the equipment and/or the compressor must be used in the calculations covered in other rules of this article. That value of current must always be used, instead of full-load currents from **Code** Tables 430-148 to 430-150, which are used for sizing circuit elements for nonhermetic motors. And if a "branch-circuit selection current" is marked on equipment, that value must be used instead of rated-load current.

440·12. Rating and Interrupting Capacity. Note that the rules here are qualifications that apply to the rules of Secs. 430-109 and 430-110 on disconnects for general-purpose motors.

A disconnecting means for a hermetic motor, as covered in part **(a)(2)**, must be a motor-circuit switch rated in horsepower or a CB—as required by Sec. 430-109.

If a CB is used, it must have an amp rating not less than 115 percent of the nameplate "rated-load current" or the "branch-circuit selection current"— whichever is greater.

But, if a horsepower-rated switch is to be selected, the process is slightly involved for hermetic motors marked with locked-rotor current and rated-load current or rated-load current plus branch-circuit selection current—but *not* marked with horsepower. In such a case, determination of the equivalent horsepower rating of the hermetic motor must be made using the locked-rotor current and either the rated-load current or the branch-circuit selection current—whichever is greater—based on **Code** Tables 430-148, 149, or 150 for rated-load current or branch-circuit selection current and Table 430-151 for locked-rotor current, as follows:

For example, a 3-phase, 460-V hermetic motor rated at 11-A branch-circuit selection and 60-A locked-rotor is to be supplied with a disconnect switch rated in horsepower. The first step in determining the equivalent horsepower rating of that motor is to refer to **Code** Table 430-150. This table lists 7½ hp as the required size for a 460-V, 11-A motor. To ensure adequate interrupting capacity, **Code** Table 430-151 is used. For a 60-A locked-rotor current, this table also shows 7½ hp as the equivalent horsepower rating for any locked-rotor current over 45 A to 66 A for a 400-V motor. Use of both tables in this manner thus establishes a 7½ hp disconnect as adequate for the given motor in both respects. Had the two ratings as obtained from the two tables been different, the higher rating would have been chosen.

Figure 440-2 shows an example of disconnect sizing for a horsepower-rated

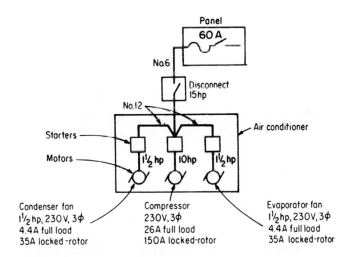

Branch circuit conductors : (125% x 26)+4 4 +4 4 =41.3 amps (No.6)
Compressor conductors : (125% x 26) = 32.8 amps (No.8)
Fan conductors : (125% x 4.4) = 5.5 amps but : 1/3 x 55 = 18.3 amps (No.12)
Fuses : (175% x 26) + 4.4 + 4.4 = 54.3 amps (60-amp fuses) but subject to group fusing restrictions of starters

Fig. 440-2. Disconnect for multiple motors is sized from rated-load or branch-circuit selection currents and locked-rotor currents. (Sec. 440-12.)

switch when a hermetic motor is used, in accordance with Sec. 430-53(c), along with fan motors on a single circuit, as covered in part **(b)** and in Sec. 440-33. Fan motors are usually wired to start slightly ahead of the compressor-motor through use of interlock contacts or a time-delay relay. In some units, however, all motors start simultaneously and that is covered by part **(b)** of this section in sizing the horsepower-rated disconnect switch. Where this is the case, the starting load will be treated like a single motor to the disconnect switch, and the sum of the locked-rotor currents of all motors should be used with **Code** Table 430-151 to determine the horsepower rating of the disconnect. The disconnect normally must handle the sum of the rated-load or branch-circuit selection currents; hence the rating as checked against **Code** Table 430-150 will be on the basis of the sum of the higher of those currents for all the motors. **Code** Table 430-150, using the full-load total of 34.8 A (4.4 A + 26 A + 4.4 A) in this example, indicates a 15-hp disconnect. **Code** Table 430-151, assuming simultaneous starting of all three motors and using the total locked-rotor current of 220 A (35 A + 150 A + 35 A), also shows 15 hp as the required size.

If motors do not start simultaneously, the compressor locked-rotor current (150 A) used with **Code** Table 430-151 gives a 10-hp rating. However, the higher of the two horsepower ratings must be used; hence the running currents impose the more severe requirements and dictate use of a 15-hp switch. See data under Sec. 440-22.

As required by part **(d)** of this section, all disconnects in a branch circuit to a refrigerant motor-compressor must have the required amp or horsepower rating and interrupting rating. This provides for motor-compressor circuits the same conditions that Sec. 430-108 requires for other motor branch circuits.

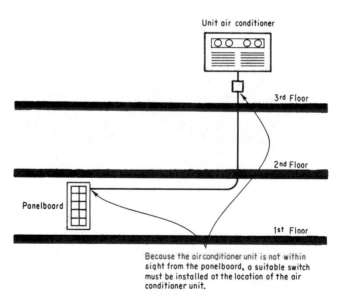

Fig. 440·3. For any fixed-wired A/C equipment, disconnect must be "within sight." (Sec. 440-14.)

440-14. Location. Section 440-13 recognizes use of a cord-plug and receptacle as the disconnect for such cord-connected equipment as a room or window air conditioner. But this section (440-14) applies to fixed-wired equipment—such as central systems or units with fixed circuit connection. For conditioners with fixed wiring connection to their supply circuits, the rule poses a problem. If the branch-circuit breaker or switch which is to provide disconnect means is located in a panel that is out of sight (or more than 50 ft away) from the unit conditioner, another breaker or switch must be provided at the equipment. If the panel breaker or switch does not satisfy the rule here, a separate disconnect means would have to be added in sight from the conditioner as shown in Fig. 440-3. This is also true if the service switch is installed as shown in Fig. 440-4.

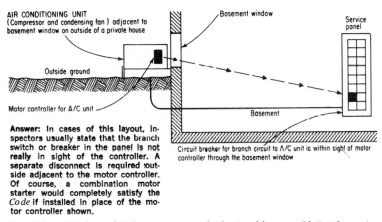

AIR CONDITIONING UNIT
(Compressor and condensing fan) adjacent to basement window on outside of a private house

Basement window

Service panel

Outside ground

Motor controller for A/C unit

Basement

Answer: In cases of this layout, inspectors usually state that the branch switch or breaker in the panel is not really in sight of the controller. A separate disconnect is required outside adjacent to the motor controller. Of course, a combination motor starter would completely satisfy the *Code* **if installed in place of the motor controller shown.**

Circuit breaker for branch circuit to A/C unit is within sight of motor controller through the basement window

Fig. 440-4. "Within sight" disconnect must also be "readily accessible" at the equipment. (Sec. 440-14.)

As stated in the second sentence, the required disconnect means for air-conditioning or refrigeration equipment may be installed on or within the equipment enclosure. That is recognized as an equivalent of the basic rule that the disconnect must be readily accessible and within sight (visible and not over 50 ft away) from the A/C or refrigeration equipment. Such equipment is being manufactured now with the disconnect incorporated as part of the assembly.

440-21. General. Part C of this article covers details of branch-circuit makeup for A/C and refrigeration equipment; Sec. 440-3(a) says that the provisions of Art. 430 apply to A/C and refrigeration equipment for any considerations that are not covered in Art. 440. Thus, because Art. 440 does *not* cover feeder sizing and feeder overcurrent protection for A/C and refrigeration equipment, it is necessary to use applicable sections from Art. 430. Section 430-24 covers sizing of feeder conductors for standard motor loads and for A/C and refrigeration loads. Sections 430-62 and 430-63 cover rating of overcurrent protection for feeders to both standard motors and A/C and refrigeration equipment. That fact is noted by a new phrase added to the end of Sec. 430-62(a).

440-22. Application and Selection. Part **(a)** of this section is illustrated in Fig. 440-5, where a separate circuit is run to the compressor and to each fan motor

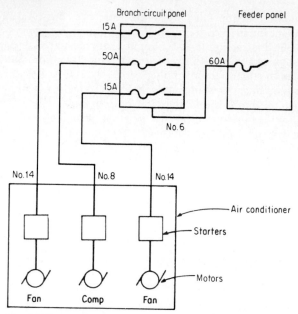

Fig. 440-5. A separate circuit may be run to each motor of A/C assembly. (Sec. 440-22.)

of a packaged assembly, containing a compressor with 26-A rated-load current and fan motors rated at 4.4 A full-load each. The compressor protection is sized at 1.75 × 26 A (175 percent of rated-load current), or 45.5 A—calling for 45-A or 50-A fuses.

Although the two maximum values of 175 and 225 percent are placed on the rating of the branch-circuit fuse or CB, the last sentence of part **(a)** specifies that the branch-circuit protection is *not* required to be rated less than 15 A.

Sizing of branch-circuit protection for a single branch circuit to the same three motors is permitted by Sec. 430-53(c) as well as by Sec. 440-22(b) and is shown in Fig. 440-12. That layout is a specific example of the general rules covered in Sec. 440-22(b) (1), which ties the rules of Sec. 430-53(c) and (d) into the rules of Sec. 440-22(b), as shown in Fig. 440-6. Such application is based on certain factors, as covered in the UL *Electrical Appliance and Utilization Directory*, listed under "Air Conditioners, Central Cooling," as follows:

> The proper method of electrical installation (number of branch circuits, disconnects, etc.) is shown on the wiring diagram and/or marking required to be attached to the air conditioner.
>
> In air conditioners employing two or more motors or a motor(s) and other loads operating from a single supply circuit, the motor running overcurrent protective devices (including thermal protectors for motors) and other factory-installed motor circuit components and wiring are investigated on the basis of compliance with the motor-branch-circuit short circuit and ground fault protection requirements of Sec. 430-53(c) of the 1984 Edition of the **National Electrical Code**. Such multimotor and combination load equipment is to be connected only to a circuit protected by fuses or a circuit breaker

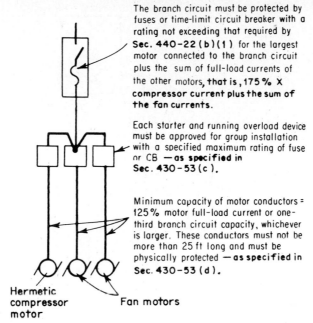

The branch circuit must be protected by fuses or time-limit circuit breaker with a rating not exceeding that required by **Sec. 440-22 (b)(1)** for the largest motor connected to the branch circuit plus the sum of full-load currents of the other motors, **that is , 175 % X compressor current plus the sum of the fan currents.**

Each starter and running overload device must be approved for group installation with a specified maximum rating of fuse or CB **— as specified in Sec. 430-53 (c).**

Minimum capacity of motor conductors = 125% motor full-load current or one-third branch circuit capacity, whichever is larger. These conductors must not be more than 25 ft long and must be physically protected **— as specified in Sec. 430-53 (d).**

Hermetic
compressor   Fan motors
motor

Fig. 440-6. Single multimotor branch circuit must conform to several rules. (Sec. 440-22.)

with a rating which does not exceed the value marked on the data plate. This marked protective device rating is the maximum for which the equipment has been investigated and found acceptable. Where the marking specifies fuses, or "HACR Type" circuit breakers, the circuit is intended to be protected by the type of protective device specified.

The electrical contractor and inspector charged with wiring and approving such an installation can be sure that Code requirements have been met—provided that the branch-circuit protection as specified on the unit is not exceeded and the wiring and equipment is as indicated on the wiring diagram. Provision is made in such a unit for direct connection to the branch-circuit conductors; motors are wired internally by the manufacturer.

Units are sometimes encountered in which the manufacturer has wired separate fuse cutouts for the fan motors inside the enclosure to avoid meeting the requirements of Sec. 430-53(c) for group fusing as shown in Fig. 440-7. The cutouts are normally fed from the line terminals of the compressor starter.

Starter and disconnect sizes are the same as in Fig. 440-2, but starters and their overcurrent protection no longer need be approved for group fusing, and wiring inside the unit need not conform to Sec. 430-53(c). Fan motors may now be wired with No. 14 wire and protected with 15-A fuses. The supply circuit, feeding the same motors, will again be No. 6.

Since the fan motors are not subject to group fusing requirements, they will not restrict the maximum value of the main fuses. However, these fuses provide

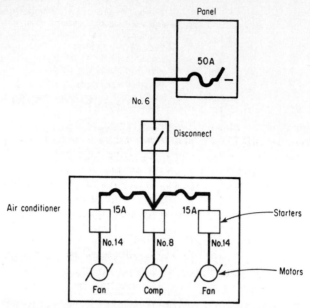

Main fuses: (175 % X 26) = 45.5 amps (50-amp fuses)
Fan fuses: (300% X 4.4) =13.2 amps (15-amp fuses)
Fan conductors: (125% X 4.4) = 5.5 amps (No.14)

Fig. 440·7. Fan circuits are sometimes fused in multimotor assemblies. (Sec. 440-22.)

the only short-circuit protection for the compressor starter and conductors. Unless the compressor starter is approved for group fusing at a higher fuse rating, the fuses must not exceed 175 percent of the compressor full-load rating, or 45.5 A, calling for 50-A fuses. If needed to permit effective starting of all the motors, the fuses at the panel could be increased to 225 percent or 60-A fuses.

Figure 440-8 shows still another hookup for supplying a multimotor assembly. Units are wired with fuse blocks for all motors, as shown. The compressor motor would be fused at 50 A, with remaining fuses and conductors as above.

Main fuses no longer are subject to restriction by motor starters and are sized as feeder protection per Sec. 440-33 as shown by the diagram. This results in 60-A fuses, the differential between the two being too small. The need for time-delay fuses is indicated, using perhaps 30-A fuses for the compressor and 50-A fuses for the main.

The foregoing examples refer exclusively to fused disconnects and fused switches to maintain the continuity of calculations. However, Sec. 430-109 also recognizes the CB as a disconnecting means.

Figure 440-9 shows an arrangement which includes, in addition to the branch-circuit panel, a feeder panel for distribution to other units. The breakers in the branch-circuit panel serve as branch-circuit protection as well as the disconnecting means, and their ratings are computed from Secs. 430-52 and

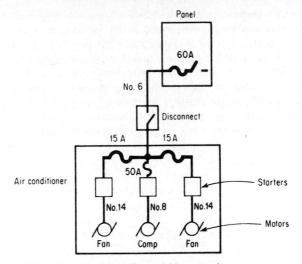

Main fuses : (175 % X 26) + 4.4 + 4.4 = 54.3 amps (60-amp fuses)

Compressor fuses: 175% X 26 = 45.5 amps (45-amp or 50-amp fuses)

Fig. 440-8. Each motor may have individual short-circuit protection. (Sec. 440-22.)

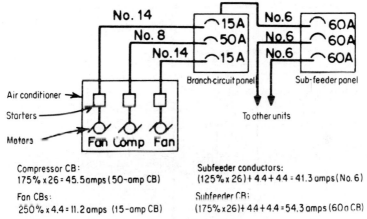

Compressor CB:
175% x 26 = 45.5 amps (50-amp CB)

Fan CBs:
250% x 4.4 = 11.2 amps (15-amp CB)

Subfeeder conductors:
(125% x 26)+ 4.4 + 4.4 = 41.3 amps (No. 6)

Subfeeder CB:
(175% x26)+ 4.4 + 4.4 = 54.3 amps (60 a CB)

Fig. 440-9. Circuit breakers may be used for multimotor A/C assemblies. (Sec. 440-22.)

440-22. Code Tables 430-150 and 430-151 would not be involved, since breakers are not rated in horsepower. Ratings of CBs in the branch-circuit panel are computed at 175 percent of motor current for the hermetic motor and at 250 percent of full-load current for the fan motors, to satisfy Table 430-152. Breakers in subfeeder panel are rated using Secs. 430-62 and 440-33.

Part **(c)** points out that data on a manufacturer's heater table take precedence over the maximum ratings set by Sec. 440-22(a) or (b).

440·32. Single Motor·Compressor. Branch-circuit conductors supplying a motor in a packaged unit are not sized in the same manner as other motor loads (Sec. 430-22). Instead of using the full-load current from **Code** Tables 430-148 to 430-150, the *marked* rated-load current or the *marked* branch-circuit selection current must be used in determining minimum required conductor ampacity. Note that branch-circuit selection current must be used where it is given.

Examples are shown in the typical circuits shown in Figs. 440-2 and 440-6.

440·33. Motor·Compressor(s) With or Without Additional Motor Loads. Where more than one motor is connected to the same feeder or branch circuit, calculation of conductor sizes must provide ampere capacity at least equal to the sum of the nameplate rated-load currents or branch-circuit selection currents (using the higher of those values in all cases) plus 25 percent of the current (either rated-load or branch-circuit selection current for a hermetic motor or **NEC** table current for standard motor) of the largest motor of the group. Examples are shown in Figs. 440-2 and 440-6.

In Fig. 440-6, the question arises as to whether the No. 6 conductors feeding the unit may be decreased to No. 8 inside the unit to feed the compressor motor in the absence of fuses for this motor at the point of reduction. The status of the main feed to the unit—whether it should be considered a feeder or a branch circuit—is in doubt, since it is a branch circuit as far as the compressor motor is concerned and a feeder in that it also supplied the two fused fan circuits.

Considered solely as a branch circuit to the compressor, these conductors normally would be No. 8 to handle the 26-A compressor motor full-load current, protected at not more than 175 percent or 50-A fuses. Therefore, since 50-A fuses (or less) will actually be used for the main feed, they constitute proper protection for No. 8 conductors and their use should be permitted. The existence of No. 6 conductors over part of the circuit adds to its capacity and safety rather than detracting from it.

It is particularly important to keep in mind when selecting conductor sizes that the nameplate current ratings of air-conditioning motors are not constant maximum values during operation. Ratings are established and tested under standard conditions of temperature and humidity. Operation under weather conditions more severe than those at which the ratings are established will result in a greater running current, which can approach the maximum value permitted by the overcurrent device. Operating voltage less than the limits specified on the motor nameplate also contributes to higher full-load current values, even under standard conditions. Conductor capacity should be sufficient to handle these higher currents. Motor feeders are sized according to Sec. 440-33. Since overload protection may permit motors to run continuously overloaded (up to 140 percent full load), feeders must be sized to handle such overload. By basing calculations on the largest motor of the group, the extra capacity thus provided will normally be enough to handle any unforeseen overload on the smaller motors involved with enough diversity existing in any normal group of motors to make consistent overloads on all motors at one time unlikely. However, a group of air-conditioning compressor motors all of the same size on a single feeder have a common function—reducing the ambient temperature. Except for slight possible variations, weather conditions affect each conditioner to the same degree and at the same time. Therefore, if one unit is operating at an overload, it is likely that the rest are also.

440-35. Multimotor and Combination-Load Equipment. This rule ties into the data required by UL to be marked on such equipment. Refer to the UL data quoted in Sec. 440-22.

440-41. Rating. The basic rule calls for a compressor controller to have a full-load current rating and a locked-rotor current rating not less than the compressor nameplate rated-load current or branch-circuit selection current (whichever is greater) and locked-rotor current. But, as noted for the disconnect under Sec. 440-12, for sealed (hermetic-type) refrigeration compressor motors, selection of the size of controller is slightly more involved than it is for standard applications. Because of their low-temperature operating conditions, hermetic motors can handle heavier loads than general-purpose motors of equivalent size and rotor-stator construction. And because the capabilities of such motors cannot be accurately defined in terms of horsepower, they are rated in terms of full-load current and locked-rotor current for polyphase motors and larger single-phase motors. Accordingly, selection of controller size is different than in the case of a general-purpose motor where horsepower ratings must be matched, because controllers marked in horsepower only must be carefully related to hermetic motors that are *not* marked in horsepower.

For controllers rated in horsepower, selection of the size required for a particular hermetic motor can be made after the nameplate rated-load current, or branch-circuit selection current, whichever is greater, and locked-rotor current of the motor have been converted to an equivalent horsepower rating. To get this equivalent horsepower rating, which is the required size of controller, the tables in Art. 430 must be used. First, the nameplate full-load current at the operating voltage of the motor is located in **Code** Tables 430-148, 149, or 150 and the horsepower rating which corresponds to it is noted. Then the nameplate locked-rotor current of the motor is found in **Code** Table 430-151, and again the corresponding horsepower is noted. In all tables, if the exact value of current is not listed, the next higher value should be used to obtain an equivalent horsepower, by reading horizontally to the horsepower column at the left side of those tables. If the two horsepower ratings obtained in this way are not the same, the larger value is taken as the required size of controller.

A typical example follows:

Given: A 230-V, 3-phase, squirrel-cage induction motor in a compressor has a nameplate rated-load current of 25.8 A and a nameplate locked-rotor current of 90 A.

Procedure: From **Code** Table 430-150, 28 A is the next higher current to the nameplate current of 25.8 under the column for 230-V motors and the corresponding horsepower rating for such a motor is 10 hp.

From **Code** Table 430-151, Art. 430, a locked-rotor current rating of 90 A for a 230-V, 3-phase motor requires a controller rated at 5 hp. The two values of horsepower obtained are not the same, so the higher rating is selected as the acceptable unit for the conditions. A 10-hp motor controller must be used.

Some controllers may be rated not in horsepower but in full-load current and locked-rotor current. For use with a hermetic motor, such a controller must simply have current ratings equal to or greater than the nameplate rated-load current and locked-rotor current of the motor.

440·52. Application and Selection.   The basic rule of part **(a)** calls for a running overload relay set to trip at not more than 140 percent of the rated-load current of a motor-compressor. If a fuse or time-delay CB is used to provide overload protection, it must be rated not over 125 percent of the compressor rated-load current. Note that those are absolute maximum values of overload protection and no permission is given to go to "the next higher standard rating"of protection where 1.4 or 1.25 times motor current does not yield an amp value that exactly corresponds to a standard rating of a relay or of a fuse or CB.

Running overload protective devices for a motor are necessary to protect the motor, its associated controls, and the branch-circuit conductors against heat damage due to excessive motor currents. High currents may be caused by the motor being overloaded for a considerable period of time, by consistently low or unbalanced line voltage, by single-phasing of a polyphase motor, or by the motor stalling or failing to start.

Damage may occur more quickly to a hermetic motor which stalls or fails to start than to a conventional open-type motor. Due to the presence of the cool refrigerant atmosphere under normal conditions, a hermetic motor is permitted to operate at a rated current which is closer to the locked-rotor current than is the same rated current of an open-type motor of the same nominal horsepower rating. The curves of Fig. 440-10 show the typical relation between locked-rotor and full-loaded currents of small open-type and hermetic motors. Because a hermetic motor operates within the refrigerant atmosphere, it is constantly cooled by that atmosphere. As a result, a given size of motor may be operated at a higher current than it could be if it were used as an open, general-purpose motor without the refrigerant cycle to remove heat from the windings. In effect, a hermetic motor is operated overloaded because the cooling cycle prevents overheating. For instance, a 5-hp open motor can be loaded as if it were a 7½-hp motor when it is cooled by the refrigerant. The full-load operating current of such a motor is higher than the normal current drawn by a 5-hp load and is, therefore, closer to the value of locked-rotor current, which is the same no matter how the motor is used.

When the rotor of a hermetic motor is slowed down because of overload or is at a standstill, there is not sufficient circulation of the refrigerant to carry away the heat; and heat builds up in the windings. Special quick-acting thermal and hydraulic-magnetic devices have been developed to reduce the time required to disconnect the hermetic motor from the line before damage occurs when an overload condition develops.

Room air conditioners and packaged unit compressors are normally required to incorporate running overload protection which will restrict the heat rise to definite maximum safe temperatures in case of locked-rotor conditions. Room conditioners normally use inherent protectors built into the compressor housing which respond to the temperature of the housing. Larger units also often use inherent protection in addition to quick-acting overload heaters installed in the motor starter, which respond only to current. These protective methods are covered in paragraphs **(2)** and **(4)** of Sec. 440-52(a).

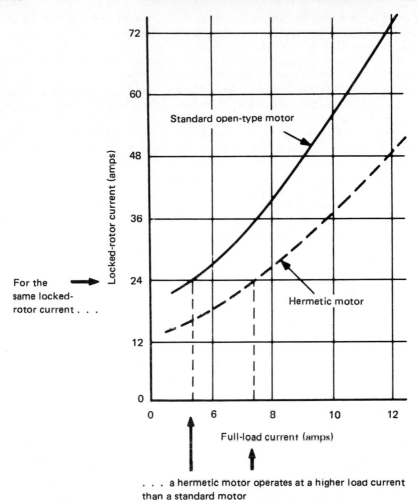

Fig. 440-10. Hermetic motors operate at full-load currents closer to locked-rotor currents. (Sec. 440-52.)

The electrical installer will normally be concerned with the running over-current protection of a hermetic motor only when it becomes necessary to replace the existing devices supplied with the equipment. For this purpose, compressor manufacturers' warranties explicitly specify catalog numbers of replacements which are to be used to ensure proper operation of the equipment.

440-60. General.   These rules on room air-conditioning units recognize that such units are basically appliances, are low-capacity electrical loads, and may be supplied either by an individual branch circuit to a unit conditioner or by connection to a branch circuit that also supplies lighting and/or other appliances. For all **Code** discussion purposes, an air-conditioning unit of the window, console, or through-the-wall type is classified as a "fixed appliance"—which is described in Art. 100 as "fastened or otherwise secured at a specific location." Such an appliance may be cord-connected or it may be fixed-wired (so-called "permanently connected").

Section 210-23 of Art. 210 on "Branch Circuits" must also be applied in cases where a unit room air conditioner is connected to a branch circuit supplying lighting or other appliance load.

When a unit air conditioner is connected to a circuit supplying lighting and/or one or more appliances that are not motor loads, the rules of Art. 210 must be observed:

1. Section 210-22(a) says that "where a circuit supplies only air-conditioning and/or refrigerating equipment, Article 440 shall apply."

2. For plug connection of the A/C unit, Sec. 210-7(a) says that receptacles installed on 15- and 20-A branch circuits must be of the grounding type and must have their grounding terminal effectively connected to a grounding conductor or grounded raceway or metal cable armor.

3. On 15- and 20-A branch circuits, the total rating of a unit air conditioner ("utilization equipment fastened in place") must not exceed 50 percent of the branch-circuit rating when lighting units or portable appliances are also supplied [Sec. 210-23(a)]. It was on the basis of that rule that the 7½-A air conditioner was developed. Being 50 percent of a 15-A branch circuit, such units are acceptable for connection to a receptacle on a 15-A or 20-A circuit that supplies lighting and receptacle outlets.

4. A branch circuit larger than 20 A may *not* be used to supply a unit conditioner plus a lighting load. Circuits rated 25, 30, 40, or 50 A may be used to supply fixed lighting or appliances—but not both types of loads.

440·61. Grounding.   Air-conditioner units that are connected by permanent wiring must be grounded in accordance with the basic rules of Sec. 250-42 covering equipment that is "fastened in place or connected by permanent wiring." Section 250-45 covers grounding of cord- and plug-connected air conditioners by means of an equipment grounding conductor run within the supply cord for each such unit.

The nameplate marking of a room air conditioner shall be used in determining the branch-circuit requirements, and each unit shall be considered as a single motor unless the nameplate is otherwise marked. If the nameplate is marked to indicate two or more motors, Secs. 430-53 and 440-22(b) (1) must be satisfied, covering the use of several motors on one branch circuit.

440·62. Branch·Circuit Requirements.   Even though a room air conditioner contains more than one motor (usually the hermetic compressor motor and the fan motor), this rule notes that for a cord- and plug-connected air conditioner the entire unit assembly may be treated as a single-motor load under the conditions given.

Examples of the rule of part **(b)** are shown in Fig. 440-11. The total marked rating of any cord- and plug-connected air-conditioning unit must *not* exceed 80 percent of the rating of a branch circuit which does not supply lighting units or other appliances, for units rated up to 40 A, 250 V, single phase.

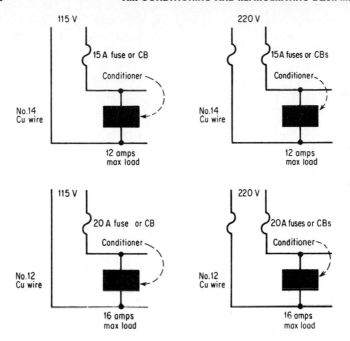

NOTE: 30-A circuits with No. 10 wire may supply units rated 17 to 24 A ; 40- A circuits with No. 8 wire may supply units rated 25 to 32 A ; and 50- A circuits with No. 6 wire may supply units rated 33 to 40 A.

Fig. 440-11. Room air conditioners must not load an individual branch circuit over 80 percent of rating. (Sec. 440-62.)

As noted under Sec. 440-60, Sec. 210-22(a) seems to say that only Art. 440 and not Art. 210 applies when the circuit supplies only a motor-operated load. But, since Arts. 430 and 440 do not "rate" branch circuits—either on the basis of the size of the short-circuit protective device or the size of the conductors—a question arises about the meaning of the phrase "80 percent of the rating of a branch circuit." Does that mean 80 percent of the rating of the fuse or CB? The answer is: It means 80 percent of the rating of the protective device, which rating is not more than the amp rating of the circuit wire. The circuit as described here is taken to be a circuit with "rating" as given in Art. 210 and covered by part **(4)** of Sec. 440-62(a).

As part **(c)** of this section notes, the total marked rating of air-conditioning equipment must *not* exceed 50 percent of the rating of a branch circuit which *also* supplies lighting or other appliances. And Sec. 210-22(a) and Sec. 210-23 must be observed. From the rule, we can see that the Code permits air-conditioning units to be plugged into existing circuits which supply lighting loads or other appliances. By the provisions of this section, such a conditioner must not draw more than 7½ A full load (nameplate rating) when connected to a 15-A circuit; not more than 10 A when connected to a 20-A circuit. In addition, Sec.

210-22(a) requires that the branch-circuit capacity must not be less than 125 percent of the air-conditioner load plus the sum of the other loads. The existing load on the circuit (lights or other appliances) must be low enough so that the total load on the circuit after the addition of 125 percent of the ampere load of the air conditioner is not greater than 15 A in the case of the 15-A circuit, nor greater than 20 A on a 20-A circuit. This is in accordance with Sec. 210-22(a) which restricts the total loading on such a circuit.

Assuming that a 7½-A conditioner is connected to such a 15-A existing circuit, it would mean that the circuit before the addition of the air-conditioner load of 7.5 × 1.25, or 10 A, could have been loaded to no more than 5 A, as shown in Fig. 440-12.

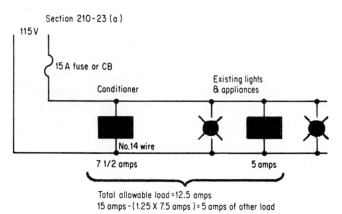

Fig. 440·12. Room air conditioner must not exceed 50 percent of circuit rating if other loads are supplied. (Sec. 440-62.)

A problem exists in connecting two or more conditioners to the same circuit. Compressor and fan motors and their controls, when installed in the same enclosure and fed by one circuit, are approved by UL for group installation when tested as a unit appliance. However, an air conditioner's component parts carry no general group-fusing approval which would permit the several separate conditioners to operate on the same circuit in accordance with Sec. 430-53(c). To connect more than one conditioner to the same branch circuit, the provisions of either Secs. 430-53(a) or 430-53(b) must be fulfilled, treating each cord-connected conditioner as a single-motor load.

According to Sec. 430-53(a), which applies only to motors rated not over 6 A, two 115-V, 6-A conditioners could be used on a 15-A circuit; three 5-A conditioners could be used on a 20-A circuit which supplies no other load; and two 220-V, 6-A units could be operated on a 15-A circuit as shown in Fig. 440-13. But it could be argued that the maximum load in any such application may be calculated at 125 percent times current of largest air conditioner plus the sum of load currents of the additional air conditioners, with that total current being permitted right up to the rating of the circuit.

However, most conditioners sold today exceed 6-A full-load current. As a

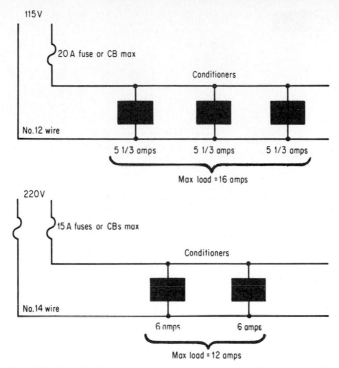

Fig. 440·13. Rules limit use of two or more room conditioners on single circuit. (Sec. 440-62.)

result, the application of two or more units as permitted by Sec. 430-53(a) is limited. But Sec. 430-53(b) does offer considerable opportunity for using more than one air conditioner on a single circuit. Figure 440-14 shows two examples of such application, which can be used if the branch-circuit protective device will not open under the most severe normal conditions which might be encountered. Although that usage is a complex connection among several **Code** rules and requires clearance with inspection authorities, it can provide very substantial economies.

Many local codes avoid the complications of connecting conditioners to existing circuits and connecting more than one conditioner to the same circuit by requiring a separate branch circuit for each conditioner. Multiple installations involving many room conditioners such as are frequently encountered in hotels, offices, etc., require careful planning to meet **Code** requirements and yet minimize expensive branch-circuit lengths.

WATCH OUT! The **NE Code** refers to motor-operated appliances and/or to room air conditioners in Arts. 210, 422, and 440. Great care must be exercised in correlating the various **Code** rules in these different articles to assure effective compliance with the letter and spirit of **Code** meaning. There is much crossover in terminology and references making it difficult to tell whether a room air conditioner should be treated as an appliance circuit load or a motor

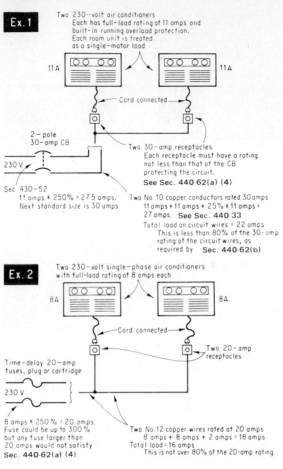

Ex. 1

Two 230-volt air conditioners
Each has full-load rating of 11 amps and
built-in running overload protection.
Each room unit is treated
as a single-motor load

11 A   11 A

← Cord connected →

2-pole
30-amp CB

230 V

Sec. 430-52
11 amps × 250% = 27.5 amps.
Next standard size is 30 amps

Two 30-amp receptacles
Each receptacle must have a rating
not less than that of the CB
protecting the circuit.
See Sec. 440-62(a) (4)

Two No. 10 copper conductors rated 30 amps
11 amps + 11 amps + 25% × 11 amps =
27 amps. **See Sec. 440-33**
Total load on circuit wires = 22 amps
This is less than 80% of the 30-amp
rating of the circuit wires, as
required by **Sec. 440-62(b)**

Ex. 2

Two 230-volt single-phase air conditioners
with full-load rating of 8 amps each

8A   8A

← Cord connected →

Two 20-amp
receptacles

Time-delay 20-amp
fuses, plug or cartridge

230 V

8 amps × 250% = 20 amps.
Fuse could be up to 300%
but any fuse larger than
20 amps would not satisfy
Sec. 440-62(a) (4)

Two No. 12 copper wires rated at 20 amps
8 amps + 8 amps + 2 amps = 18 amps
Total load = 16 amps
This is not over 80% of the 20-amp rating

NOTE: Fuse or CB sizing may be required to conform to Sec.
440-22 (b), with a maximum rating of 175% times load current
of one conditioner plus the current of the other conditioner.
Or the 175% value itself may be held as the maximum rating
of branch-current protection.

Fig. 440-14. These hookups have been accepted as conforming
to rules of Arts. 440 and 430. (Sec. 440-62.)

load. However, a step-by-step approach to the problem which keeps in mind
the intent of these provisions can resolve confusing points. Since the manufacturer is required to supply the motor-running overcurrent protection, no problems should arise concerning these devices. For larger units connected permanently to the distribution system, these can be treated directly as hermetic
motor loads, using the provisions of Art. 440.

It may be assumed that a window or through-the-wall unit will operate satisfactorily on a standard fuse of the same rating as its attachment plug cap if
there is no marking to the contrary on the unit. In any event, a time-delay fuse

of the same or smaller rating could be substituted. If CBs are used for branch-circuit protection, a 15-A breaker will normally hold the starting current if a standard 15-A fuse will, since such breakers have inherent time delay. If the unit is marked to require a 15-A time-delay fuse and a 15-A breaker will not hold the starting current, few inspectors will object to the use of a 20-A breaker, since Art. 430 permits such a procedure for motor loads.

Normally, starting problems are not severe with these units, since the low inertia of present-day motor-compressor combinations permits them to reach full speed within a few cycles. Such a rapid drop in starting current is usually well within the time permitted by the trip or rupture characteristics of the breaker or fuse.

Similarly, the question of wire size may be resolved by application of either Arts. 210, 422, or 440. Rarely do room conditioners even as large as 2 tons take more than 13-A running current; hence No. 12 copper or No. 10 aluminum conductors are more than sufficient. In addition, many local codes prohibit use of conductors smaller than No. 12. In localities where No. 14 wire may be used, provisions of Sec. 440-62(b), restricting the loading to 80 percent of the circuit rating, must determine the wire size, where "rating" is interpreted as referring to the conductor carrying capacity. If Art. 440 is used to determine the wire size, the 125 percent requirement of Sec. 440-32 gives the same result.

Figure 440-15 shows one feeder of an installation involving many room con-

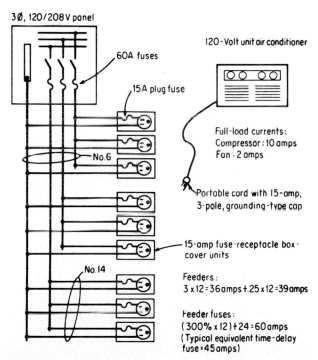

Fig. 440-15. This type of circuiting was used for air conditioners in a hotel modernization project. (Sec. 440-62.)

ditioners which practically eliminates branch-circuit wiring and will serve to illustrate the complications of circuit calculations for a multiple-unit installation. Total running current of each unit is 12 A as shown; hence No. 14 copper wire could be used for branch-circuit conductors, protected by a 15-A fuse—either standard or time-delay. However, if the appropriate conductors of a 4-wire, 3-phase feeder were routed to the location of each conditioner and a combination fuseholder and receptacle installed as shown, the only existing branch-circuit conductors would be the jumpers between the feeder, the fuseholder, and the receptacles. These jumpers, then, could be No. 14 wire. Assuming that the fuse-receptacle unit is mounted directly on or in close proximity with the junction box in which the tap to the feeder is made, the No. 14 wire is justified from the fuse to the feeder since it is not over 10 ft long and is sufficient for the load supplied (Sec. 240-21, Exception No. 2). Since both motors usually start simultaneously, the total unit current is used to compute feeder conductor size and protection. 125 percent times 12 plus 24 is 39 A, permitting No. 8 conductors. However, this is practically the limit of the circuit's capacity; there is no provision for overload, and voltage drop is very likely to be a factor at the end of the feeder. Therefore No. 6 conductors should be used.

Feeder protection is calculated on the basis of 300 percent times 12 plus 24 or 60-A fuses. Substitution of time-delay fuses for this 39-A feeder load would likely permit 45-A fuses.

Important: The rules of Sec. 440-62 apply only to cord- and plug-connected room air conditioners. A unit room air conditioner that has a *fixed* (not cord and plug) connection to its supply must be treated as a group of several individual motors and protected in accordance with Secs. 430-53 and 440-22(b), covering several motors on one branch.

440-63. Disconnecting Means.   A disconnect is required for every unit air conditioner. An attachment plug and receptacle or a separable connector may serve as the disconnecting means (Fig. 440-16).

If a fixed connection is made to an A/C unit from the branch-circuit wiring system (i.e., not a plug-in connection to a receptacle), consideration must be

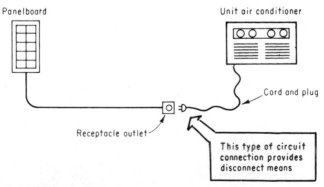

Fig. 440-16. Plug-and-receptacle serves as required disconnect means. (Sec. 440-63.)

given to a means of disconnect, as required in Secs. 422-21 and 422-25 for appliances:

■ For unit air conditioners in any type of occupancy, the branch-circuit switch or CB may, where readily accessible to the user of the appliance, serve as the disconnecting means. Figure 440-17 shows this, but the switch or CB is permitted to be out of sight by the Exception to Sec. 422-27 when the A/C unit has an internal OFF switch—which all units do have. And Sec. 422-27 requires the disconnect means for a motor-driven appliance to be within sight from the air-conditioner unit.

Because air conditioners have unit switches within them, the disconnect provisions of Sec. 422-25 may be applied. The internal unit switch with a marked OFF position that opens all ungrounded conductors may serve as the

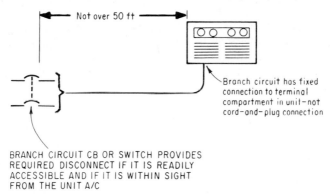

Fig. 440·17. Branch circuit CB or switch may serve as disconnect. (Sec. 440-63.)

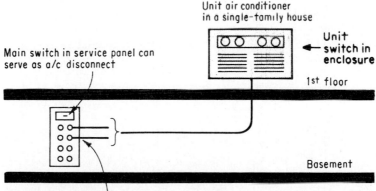

Fig. 440·18. Service disconnect may be the "other disconnect" for A/C unit in private house. (Sec. 440-63.)

disconnect and is considered within sight as required by Sec. 422-26 in any case where there is another disconnect means as follows:

- In multifamily (more than two) dwellings, the other disconnect means must be within the apartment where the conditioner is installed or on the same floor as the apartment.
- In two-family dwellings, the other disconnect may be outside the apartment in which the appliance is installed. It may be the service disconnect.
- In single-family dwellings, the service disconnect may serve as the other disconnect means—whether the branch circuit to the conditioner is fed from plug fuses or from a breaker or switch (Fig. 440-18).

ARTICLE 445. GENERATORS

445-4. Overcurrent Protection. Alternating-current generators can be so designed that on excessive overload the voltage falls off sufficiently to limit the current and power output to values that will not damage the generator during a short period of time. Whether or not automatic overcurrent protection of a generator should be omitted in any particular case is a question that can best be answered by the manufacturer of the generator. It is common practice to operate an exciter without overcurrent protection, rather than risk the shutdown of the main generator due to accidental opening of the exciter fuse or CB.

Figure 445-1 shows the connections of a 2-wire DC generator with a single-pole protective device. If the machine is operated in multiple with one or more other generators, and so has an equalizer lead connected to the positive terminal, the current may divide at the positive terminal, part passing through the series field and positive lead and part passing through the equalizer lead. The entire current generated passes through the negative lead; therefore the fuse or CB, or at least the operating coil of a CB, must be placed in the negative lead. The protective device should not open the shunt-field circuit, because if this circuit were opened with the field at full strength, a very high voltage would be induced which might break down the insulation of the field winding.

Paragraph **(c)** is intended to apply particularly to generators used in electro-

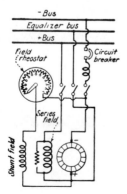

Fig. 445-1. With this connection, a single-pole CB can protect a 2-wire DC generator. (Sec. 445-4.)

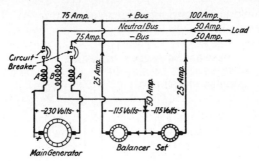

Fig. 445-2. A balancer set supplies the unbalanced neutral current of a 3-wire system, with each generator carrying 25 of the 50-A unbalance. (Sec. 445-4.)

lytic work. Where such a generator forms part of a motor-generator set, no fuse or CB is necessary in the generator leads if the motor-running protective device will open when the generator delivers 150 percent of its rated full-load current.

In paragraph **(d)**, use of a balancer set to obtain a 3-wire system from a 2-wire main generator is covered, as shown in Fig. 445-2. Each of the two generators used as a balancer set carries approximately one-half the unbalanced load; hence these two machines are always much smaller than the main generator. In case of an excessive unbalance of the load, the balancer set might be overloaded while there is no overload on the main generator. This condition may be guarded against by installing a double-pole CB with one pole connected in each lead of the main generator and with the operating coil properly designed to be connected in the neutral of the 3-wire system. In Fig. 445-2, the CB is arranged so as to be operated by either one of the coils A in the leads from the main generator or by coil B in the neutral lead from the balancer set.

445-5. Ampacity of Conductors.   Two sentences at the end of this section clarify sizing of circuit conductors connecting a generator to the control and protective device(s) it serves:

1. The neutral of the generator feeder may have its size reduced from the minimum capacity required for the phase legs. As with any feeder or service circuit, the neutral has to have only enough ampacity for the unbalanced load it will handle   as covered by Sec. 220-22.

2. When a generator neutral is not grounded at its terminals, as is permitted by Sec. 250-5(d), the neutral conductor from the generator must be sized not only for its unbalanced load, as required in Sec. 220-22, but also for carrying ground-fault current. For a generator feeder neutral to be adequately sized as an equipment grounding conductor, to effectively carry enough current to operate overcurrent devices in a grounded system, Sec. 250-23(b) requires that the neutral be not smaller than 12½ percent of the cross-sectional area of the largest phase leg of the generator feeder. See Fig. 445-3.

445-6. Protection of Live Parts.   As a general rule, no generator should be "accessible to unqualified persons." If necessary to place a generator operating at over 50 V to ground in a location where it is so exposed, the commutator or

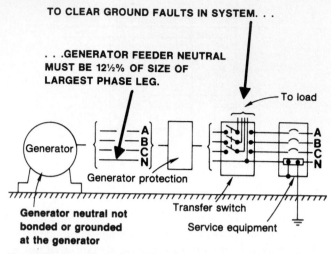

TO CLEAR GROUND FAULTS IN SYSTEM. . .

. . .GENERATOR FEEDER NEUTRAL
MUST BE 12½% OF SIZE OF
LARGEST PHASE LEG.

To load

Generator

Generator protection

Generator neutral not
bonded or grounded
at the generator

Transfer switch

Service equipment

Fig. 445-3. Neutral must have adequate capacity for generator that is not a "separately derived" system source (that is, does not have its neutral bonded and grounded). (Sec. 445-5.)

collector rings, brushes, and any exposed terminals should be provided with guards which will prevent any accidental contact with these live parts.

ARTICLE 450. TRANSFORMERS AND TRANSFORMER VAULTS

450-1. Scope.   The Exceptions indicate those transformer applications that are not subject to the rules of Art. 450. The Exceptions shown in Fig. 450-1 are as follows:

Exception No. 2 excludes any dry-type transformer that is a component part of manufactured equipment, provided that the transformer complies with the requirements for such equipment. Those requirements include UL standards on the construction of the particular equipment. This exclusion applies, for instance, to control transformers within a motor starter or within a motor control center. However, although such transformers do not have to be protected in accordance with Sec. 450-3(b), such control transformer circuits must have their control conductors protected as described under Sec. 430-72(b). But a separate control transformer—one that is external to other equipment and is not an integral part of any other piece of equipment—must conform to the protection rules of Sec. 450-3 and other rules in Art. 450.

Exception No. 6 points out that ballasts for electric-discharge lighting (although they *are* transformers—either autotransformers or separate-winding, magnetically coupled types) are treated as lighting accessories rather than transformers.

Exception No. 8 notes that liquid-filled or dry-type transformers used for

Exception No. 2

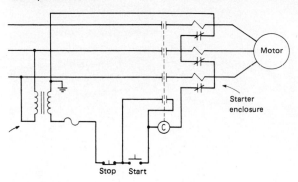

Motor

Starter
enclosure

Stop   Start

Exception No. 6

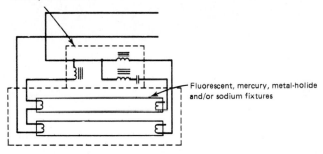

Fluorescent, mercury, metal-holide
and/or sodium fixtures

Exception No. 8

If a transformer is used for
research, development or testing . . .

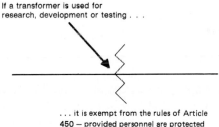

. . . it is exempt from the rules of Article
450 — provided personnel are protected
from energized parts.

Fig. 450-1. These transformer applications are exempt from the rules of
Art. 450. (Sec. 450-1.)

research, development, or testing are exempt from the requirements of Art. 450
provided that effective arrangements are made to safeguard any persons from
contacting energized terminals or conductors. Again, in the interest of the
unusual conditions that frequently prevail in industrial occupancy, this rule
recognizes that transformers used for research, development, or testing are
commonly under the sole control of entirely competent individuals and
exempts such special applications from the normal rules that apply to general-

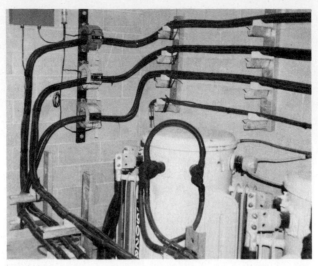

Fig. 450-2. Transformers that are set up in a laboratory to derive power for purposes of testing other equipment or powering an experiment are exempt from the rules of Art. 450 provided care is taken to protect personnel from any hazards due to exposed energized parts. (Sec. 450-1.)

purpose transformers used for distribution within buildings and for energy supply to utilization equipment, controls, signals, communications, and the like. See Fig. 450-2.

UL listing   The *Electrical Construction Materials Directory* of the UL lists "Transformers—Power." To satisfy **NE Code** and OSHA regulations, as well as local code rules on acceptability of equipment, any transformers of the types and sizes covered by UL listing must be so listed. Use of an unlisted transformer of a type and size covered by UL listing would certainly be considered a violation of the spirit of **NE Code** Sec. 110-2.

UL listing covers "air-cooled" types rated up to 500 kVA for single-phase transformers and up to 1,500 kVA for 3-phase units (all up to 600-V rating).

450-2. Definitions.   A "transformer" is an individual transformer, single or polyphase, identified by a single nameplate, unless otherwise indicated in this article. Three single-phase transformers connected for a 3-phase transformation must be taken as three transformers, not one. This definition helps to clarify the contents of some of the rules of Art. 450.

450-3. Overcurrent Protection.   This section covers overcurrent protection in great detail, and other **Code** rules (Secs. 240-21, 240-40, and 384-16 in particular) usually get involved in transformer applications. Although there is no rule on disconnects, use of required overcurrent protection results in the presence of a fused switch or CB that may serve as disconnecting means.

It should be understood that the overcurrent protection required by this section is for transformers *only*. Such overcurrent protection will not necessarily protect the primary or secondary conductors or equipment connected on the secondary side of the transformer. Using overcurrent protection to the maximum values permitted by these rules would require much larger conductors than the full-load current rating of the transformer (other than permitted in the 25-ft tap rule in Sec. 240-21, Exception No. 8). Accordingly, to avoid using oversized conductors, overcurrent devices should be selected at about 110 to 125 percent of the transformer full-load current rating. And when using such smaller overcurrent protection, devices should be of the time-delay type (on the primary side) to compensate for inrush currents which reach 8 to 10 times the full-load primary current of the transformer for about $\frac{1}{10}$ sec when energized initially.

In approaching a transformer installation it is best to use a one-line diagram, such as shown in the accompanying sketches. Then by applying the tap rules in Sec. 240-21 proper protection of the conductors and equipment, which are part of the system, will be achieved. See comments following Sec. 240-21.

Section 230-207 and Sec. 240-3, Exception No. 2, are the only **Code** rules that consider properly sized primary overcurrent devices to protect the secondary conductors without secondary protection and no limit to the length of secondary conductors. The strict requirements in Sec. 230-207 apply where the transformers are in a *vault*, the primary load-interrupter switch is manually operable from outside the vault, and large secondary conductors are provided to achieve reflected protection through the transformer to the primary overcurrent protection. *It is important to note that in all other cases primary circuit protection for transformer protection is not acceptable as suitable protection for the secondary circuit conductors*—even if the secondary conductors have an ampacity equal to the ampacity of the primary conductors times the primary/secondary voltage ratio. See Sec. 240-3, Exception No. 2.

On 3- and 4-wire transformer secondaries, it is possible that an unbalanced load may greatly exceed the secondary conductor ampacity, which was selected assuming balanced conditions. Because of this, the **NE Code** does not permit the protection of secondary conductors by overcurrent devices operating through a transformer from the primary of a transformer having a 3-wire or 4-wire secondary. For other than 2-wire to 2-wire transformers, protection of secondary conductors has to be provided completely separately from any primary-side protection. Section 384-16(d) states that required main protection for a lighting panel on the secondary side of a transformer must be located on the secondary side. However, Sec. 240-3, Exception No. 2, recognizes such primary protection of the secondary of single-phase, 2-wire to 2-wire transformers if the primary OC protection complies with Sec. 450-3 and does not exceed the value determined by multiplying the secondary conductor ampacity by the secondary-to-primary transformer voltage ratio. The lengths of the primary or secondary conductors are not limited by this Exception.

In designing transformer circuits, the rules of Sec. 450-3 can be coordinated with Sec. 240-21, Exception No. 8, which provides special rules for tap conductors used with transformers. This Exception would be used mainly where the primary OC devices are rated according to Sec. 450-3(b) (2), or where the combined primary and secondary feeder lengths from the primary OC device to the secondary tap exceed 10 ft.

Where secondary feeder taps do *not* exceed 10 ft in length, the requirements of Sec. 240-21, Exception No. 2, could apply as in the case of any other feeder tap. In applying the tap rules in Exception Nos. 2 and 8, the requirements of Sec. 450-3 on transformer overcurrent protection must always be satisfied.

Part **(a)** of this section sets rules for overcurrent protection of any transformer (dry-type or liquid-filled) rated over 600 V. Protection may be provided either by a protective device of specified rating on the transformer primary or by a combination of protective devices of specified ratings on both the primary and secondary. Figure 450-3 shows the basic rules of such overcurrent protection. The fact that E-rated fuses used for high-voltage circuits are given melting times at 200 percent of their continuous-current rating explains why this **Code** rule used to set 150 percent of primary current as the maximum fuse rating but permits CBs up to 300 percent. In effect, the 150 percent for fuses times 2 (200 percent) becomes 300 percent—the maximum value allowed for a CB. Now such fuses may be rated up to 250 percent (instead of 150 percent).

- Part **(a)** **(1)** says that *any* high-voltage transformer must have *both* primary and secondary protection based on Table 450-3(a) (1) for maximum ratings of the primary and secondary fuses or circuit breakers.
- Part **(a)** **(2)** gives two alternative ways of protecting high-voltage transformers where "conditions of maintenance and supervision assure that only qualified persons will monitor and service the transformer." The two alternatives are as follows:
  1. Primary-protection-only may be used, with fuses set at not over 250 percent of the primary current or circuit breakers set at not over 300 percent of primary current. And if that calculation results in a fuse or CB rating that does not correspond to a standard rating or setting, the next higher standard rating or setting may be used.
  2. Primary and secondary protection based on Table 450-3(a) (2)b is the alternative.

These rules resulted from concerted industry action to provide better transformer protection. As stated in the "substantiation" for Sec. 450-3(a), "It is felt that this approach will aid in reducing the number of transformer failures due to overload, as well as maintaining the flexibility of design and operation by industry and the more-complex commercial establishments."

Part **(b)** of this section covers all transformers—oil-filled, high-fire-point liquid-insulated, and dry-type—rated up to 600 V. The step-by-step approach to such protection is as follows:

1. For any transformer rated 600 V or less (i.e., the rating of neither the primary nor the secondary winding is over 600 V), the basic overcurrent protection may be provided just on the primary side [Sec. 450-3(b) (1)] or may be a combination of protection on *both* the primary and secondary sides [Sec. 450-3(b) (2)].

   If a transformer is to be protected by means of a CB or set of fuses only on the primary side of the transformer, the basic arrangement is as shown in Fig. 450-4.

   In that layout, a CB or a set of fuses rated not over 125 percent of the transformer rated primary full-load current provides all the overcurrent

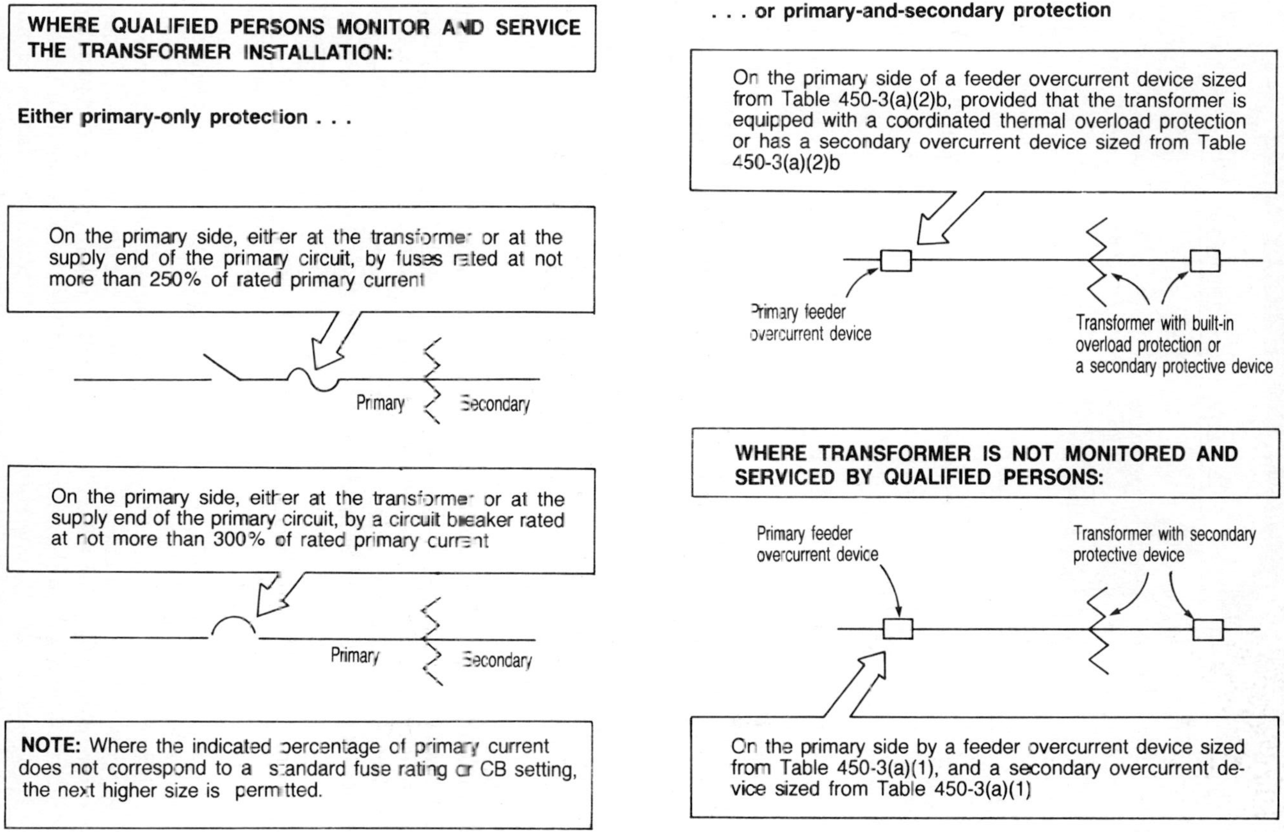

... or primary-and-secondary protection

On the primary side of a feeder overcurrent device sized from Table 450-3(a)(2)b, provided that the transformer is equipped with a coordinated thermal overload protection or has a secondary overcurrent device sized from Table 450-3(a)(2)b

Transformer with built-in overload protection or a secondary protective device

Primary feeder overcurrent device

WHERE TRANSFORMER IS NOT MONITORED AND SERVICED BY QUALIFIED PERSONS:

Transformer with secondary protective device

Primary feeder overcurrent device

On the primary side by a feeder overcurrent device sized from Table 450-3(a)(1), and a secondary overcurrent device sized from Table 450-3(a)(1)

WHERE QUALIFIED PERSONS MONITOR AND SERVICE THE TRANSFORMER INSTALLATION:

Either primary-only protection . . . .

On the primary side, either at the transformer or at the supply end of the primary circuit, by fuses rated at not more than 250% of rated primary current

Primary   Secondary

On the primary side, either at the transformer or at the supply end of the primary circuit, by a circuit breaker rated at not more than 300% of rated primary current

Primary   Secondary

NOTE: Where the indicated percentage of primary current does not correspond to a standard fuse rating or CB setting, the next higher size is permitted.

Fig. 450-3. High-voltage transformers (rated over 600 V, dry or oil- or askarel-filled) must be protected in one of these ways. (Sec. 450-3.)

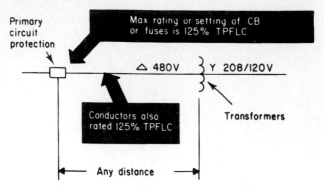

Primary circuit protection

Max rating or setting of CB or fuses is 125% TPFLC

△ 480V ⅜ Y 208/120V

Conductors also rated 125% TPFLC

Transformers

◄── Any distance ──►

TPFLC = transformer primary full-load current (nameplate rating)

Fig. 450-4. This is the basic rule on primary-side transformer protection. (Sec. 450-3.)

protection required by the **NE Code** for the transformer. This overcurrent protection is in the feeder circuit to the transformer and is logically placed at the supply end of the feeder so the same overcurrent device may also provide the overcurrent protection required for the primary feeder conductors. There is no limit on the distance between primary protection and the transformer. When the correct maximum rating for transformer protection is selected and installed at any point on the supply side of the transformer (either near or far from the transformer), then feeder circuit conductors must be sized so that the CB or fuses selected will provide the proper protection as required for the conductors. The ampacity of the feeder conductors must be at least equal to the amp rating of the CB or fuses unless Sec. 240-3, Exception No. 4, is satisfied. That is, when the rating of the overcurrent protection selected is not more than 125 percent of rated primary current, the primary feeder conductor may have an ampacity such that the overcurrent device is the next higher standard rating.

The rules set down for protection of a 600-V transformer by a CB or set of fuses in its primary circuit are given in Fig. 450-5 for transformers with rated primary current of 9 A or more. Note that "the next higher standard" rating of protection may be used, if needed. Figure 450-6 shows the *absolute* maximum values of protection for smaller transformers. When using the 1.67 or 3 times factor, if the resultant current value is not exactly equal to a standard rating of fuse or CB, then the next *lower* standard rated fuse or CB must be used.

When the rules of Sec. 450-3(b) (1) are observed, the transformer itself is properly protected and the primary feeder conductors, if sized to correspond, may be provided with the protection required by Sec. 240-3. But all considerations on the secondary side of the transformer then have to be separately and independently evaluated. When a transformer is provided with primary-side overcurrent protection, a whole range of design

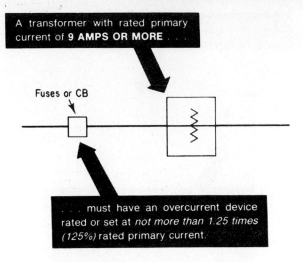

A transformer with rated primary current of **9 AMPS OR MORE** . . . .

Fuses or CB

. . . . must have an overcurrent device rated or set at *not more than 1.25 times (125%)* rated primary current.

NOTE: Where 1.25 times primary current does not correspond to a standard rating of protective device. the next higher standard rating from Section 240-6 is permitted.

Fig. 450-5. Protection sizing for larger transformers is 125 percent of primary current. (Sec. 450-3.)

and installation possibilities are available for secondary arrangement that satisfies the **Code**. The basic approach is to provide required overcurrent protection for the secondary circuit conductors right at the transformer— such as by a fused switch or CB attached to the transformer enclosure, as shown in Fig. 450-7. Or 10-ft or 25-ft taps may be made, as covered in Sec. 240-21.

2. Another acceptable way to protect a 600-V transformer is described in Sec. 450-3(b) (2). In this method, the transformer primary may be fed from a circuit which has overcurrent protection (and circuit conductors) rated up to 250 percent (instead of 125 percent, as above) of rated primary current— but, in such cases, there must be a protective device on the secondary side of the transformer, and that device must be rated or set at not more than 125 percent of the transformer's rated secondary current (Fig. 450-8). This secondary protective device must be located right at the transformer secondary terminals or not more than the length of a 10-ft or 25-ft tap away from the transformer, and the rules of Sec. 240-21 on tap conductors must be fully satisfied.

The secondary protective device covered by Sec. 450-3(b) (2) may readily be incorporated as part of other required provisions on the secondary side of the transformer, such as protection for a secondary feeder from the transformer to a panel or switchboard or motor control center fed from the switchboard. And

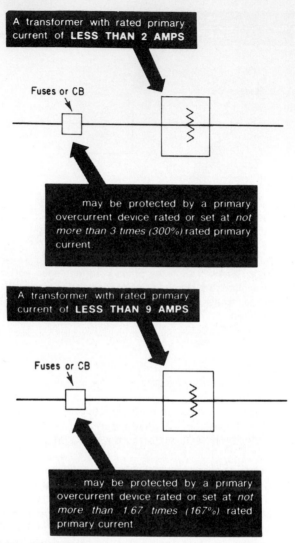

Fig. 450·6. Higher-percent protection is permitted for smaller transformers. (Sec. 450-3.)

a single secondary protective device rated not over 125 percent of secondary current may serve as a required panelboard main as well as the required transformer secondary protection as shown at the bottom of Fig. 450-9.

The use of a transformer circuit with primary protection rated up to 250 percent of rated primary current offers an opportunity to avoid situations where a particular set of primary fuses or CB rated at only 125 percent would cause nuisance tripping or opening of the circuit on transformer inrush current. But the use of a 250 percent rated primary protection has a more common and

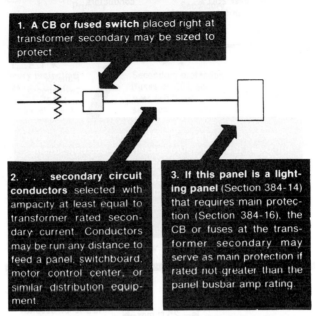

CB OR FUSED SWITCH AT SECONDARY

1. A CB or fused switch placed right at transformer secondary may be sized to protect . . .

2. . . . secondary circuit conductors selected with ampacity at least equal to transformer rated secondary current. Conductors may be run any distance to feed a panel, switchboard, motor control center, or similar distribution equipment.

3. If this panel is a lighting panel (Section 384-14) that requires main protection (Section 384-16), the CB or fuses at the transformer secondary may serve as main protection if rated not greater than the panel busbar amp rating.

Fig. 450·7. Protection of secondary circuit must be independent of primary-side transformer protection. (Sec. 450-3.)

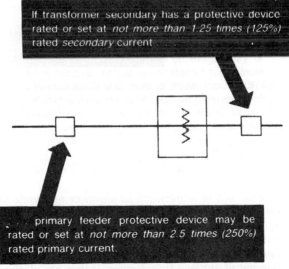

If transformer secondary has a protective device rated or set at *not more than 1.25 times (125%)* rated *secondary* current . . .

. . . primary feeder protective device may be rated or set at *not more than 2.5 times (250%)* rated primary current.

Fig. 450·8. Secondary protection permits higher-rated primary protective device. (Sec. 450-3.)

But a 100-A main would satisfy the 96-A secondary load. *(Note: The overcurrent protective device required at E could be the main protective device required for a lighting and appliance panel fed from the transformer.)*

WATCH OUT FOR THIS TRAP!!

Although the foregoing calculation shows how unprotected taps may be made from feeder conductors by satisfying the rules of Sec. 240-21, Exception No. 8, the rules of Sec. 240-21 are all concerned with PROTECTION OF CONDUCTORS ONLY. Consideration must now be made of *transformer* protection, as follows:

1. Note that Sec. 240-21 makes no reference to *transformer* protection. But Sec. 450-3 calls for protection of transformers, and there is no exception made for the conditions of Exception No. 8 to Sec. 240-21.

2. It is clear from Sec. 450-3(b) (1) that the transformer shown in Fig. 450-11 is *not* protected by a primary-side overcurrent device rated not more than 125 percent of primary current (54 A), because 1.25 $\times$ 54 A = 68 A, maximum.

3. But Sec. 450-3(b) (2) does offer a way to provide required protection. The 110-A protection at E *is* secondary protection *rated not over* 125 percent of rated secondary current (1.25 $\times$ 125 A secondary current = 156 A). With that secondary protection, a primary feeder overcurrent device rated not more than 250 percent of rated primary current will satisfy Sec. 450-3(b) (2). That would call for fuses in the feeder switch (or a CB) (at B in the diagram) rated not over

$$250 \text{ percent} \times 54 \text{ A primary current} = 135 \text{ A}$$

But, the fuses in the feeder switch are rated at 125 A—which are not in excess of 250 percent of transformer primary current and, therefore, satisfy Sec. 450-3(b) (2).

In addition to the two basic methods described above for protecting transformers, Sec. 450-3(b) (2) also provides for protection with a built-in thermal overload protection, as shown in Fig. 450-12.

450-4. Autotransformers 600 Volts, Nominal, or Less.   The rules of this section cover connections and overcurrent protection for autotransformers. The rule calling for overcurrent protection rated at not more than 125 percent of the rated input current for any autotransformer with a rated current of 9 A or more and not more than 167 percent of the rated current for smaller autotransformers is the same as that in Sec. 450-3(b) for 2-winding transformers.

450-5. Grounding Autotransformers.   An existing, ungrounded, 480-V system derived from a delta transformer hookup can be converted to grounded operation in two basic ways:

First, one of the three phase legs of the 480-V delta can be intentionally connected to a grounding electrode conductor that is then run to a suitable grounding electrode. Such grounding would give the two ungrounded phases (A and B) a voltage of 480 V to ground. The system would then operate as a grounded system, so that a ground fault (phase-to-conduit or other enclosure) on the secondary can cause fault-current flow that opens a circuit protective device to clear the faulted circuit.

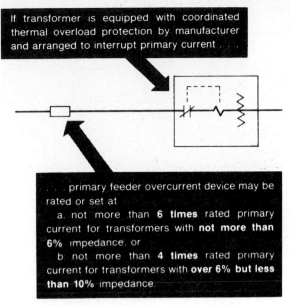

Fig. 450-12. Built-in protection is another technique for transformers. (Sec. 450-3.)

But corner grounding of a delta system does not give the lowest possible phase-to-ground voltage. In fact, the voltage to ground of a corner-grounded delta system is the same as it is for an ungrounded delta system because voltage to ground for ungrounded circuits is defined as the greatest voltage between the given conductor and any other conductor of the circuit. Thus, the voltage to ground for an ungrounded delta system is the maximum voltage between any two conductors, on the assumption that an accidental ground on any one phase puts the other two phases at full line-to-line voltage aboveground.

In recognition of increasing emphasis on the safety of grounded systems over ungrounded systems, Sec. 450-5 covers the use of zig-zag grounding autotransformers to convert 3-phase, 3-wire, ungrounded delta systems to grounded wye systems. Such grounding of a 480-V delta system, therefore, lowers the voltage to ground from 480 V (when ungrounded) to 277 V (the phase-to-grounded-neutral voltage) when converted to a wye system (Fig. 450-13).

A zig-zag grounding autotransformer gets its name from the angular phase differences among the six windings that are divided among the three legs of the transformer's laminated magnetic core assembly. The actual hookup of the six windings is an interconnection of two wye configurations, with specific polarities and locations for each winding. Just as a wye or delta transformer hookup has a graphic representation that looks like the letter "Y" or the Greek letter "delta," so a zig-zag grounding autotransformer is represented as two wye hookups with pairs of windings in series but phase-displaced, as in Fig. 450-14.

With no ground fault on any leg of the 3-phase system, current flow in the transformer windings is balanced, because equal impedances are connected

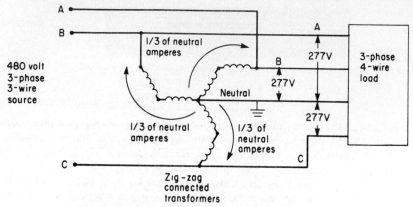

Fig. 450-13. Zig-zag transformer changes voltage to ground from 480 to 277 V. (Sec. 450-5.)

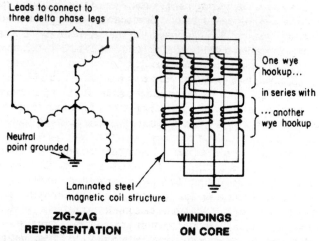

Fig. 450-14. Windings of zig-zag transformer provide for flow of fault or neutral current. (Sec. 450-5.)

across each pair of phase legs. The net impedance of the transformer under balanced conditions is very high, so that only a low level of magnetizing current flows through the windings. But when a ground fault develops on one leg of the 3-phase system, the transformer windings become a very low impedance in the fault path, permitting a large value of fault current to flow and operate the circuit protective device—just as it would on a conventional grounded-neutral wye system, as shown in Fig. 450-15.

Because the kilovoltampere rating of a grounding autotransformer is based on short-time fault current, selection of such transformers is much different from sizing a conventional 2-winding transformer for supplying a load. Careful consultation with a manufacturer's sales engineer should precede any decisions about the use of these transformers.

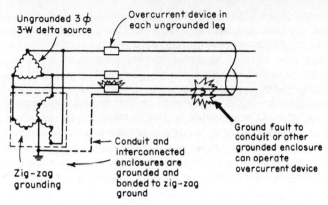

Fig. 450-15. Zig-zag transformer converts ungrounded system to grounded operation. (Sec. 450-5.)

Section 450-5 of the **NE Code** points out that a grounding autotransformer may be used to provide a neutral reference for grounding purposes or for the purpose of converting a 3-phase, 3-wire delta system into a 3-phase, 4-wire grounded wye system. In the latter case, a neutral conductor can be taken from the transformer to supply loads connected phase-to-neutral—such as 277-V loads on a 480-V delta system that is converted to a 480Y/277-V system.

Section 450-5 requires such transformers to have a continuous rating and a continuous neutral current rating. The phase current in a grounding autotransformer is one-third the neutral current, as shown in Fig. 450-13.

Part **(a) (2)** of this section requires use of a 3-pole CB, rated at 125 percent of the transformer phase current. The requirement for "common-trip" in the overcurrent device excludes conventional use of fuses in a switch as the required overcurrent protection. A three-pole CB prevents single-phase opening of the circuit.

450-6. Secondary Ties.   In industrial plants having very heavy power loads it is usually economical to install a number of large transformers at various locations within each building, the transformers being supplied by primary feeders operating at voltages up to 13,800 V. One of the secondary systems that may be used in such cases is the network system.

The term *network system* as commonly used is applied to any secondary distribution system in which the secondaries of two or more transformers at different locations are connected together by secondary ties. Two network layouts of unit subs are shown in Fig. 450-16. In the spot network, two or three transformers in one location or "spot" are connected to a common secondary bus and divide the load. Upon primary or transformer fault, the secondary is isolated from the faulted section by automatic operation of the network protector, providing a high order of supply continuity in the event of faults. The general form of the network system is similar except that widely separated individual substations are used with associated network protectors and tie circuits run between the secondary bus sections. The system provides for interchange of power to accommodate unequal loading on the transformers. Limiters protect

the ties. The purpose of the system is to equalize the loading of the transformers, to reduce voltage drop, and to ensure continuity of service. The use of this
system introduces certain complications, and, to ensure successful operation,
the system must be designed by an experienced electrical engineer.

The provisions of Sec. 450-3 govern the protection in the primary. Refer to
Fig. 450-16. The network protector consists of a CB and a reverse-power relay.
The protector is necessary because without this device, if a fault develops in
the transformer, or, in some cases, in the primary feeder, power will be fed
back to the fault from the other transformers through the secondary ties. The
relay is set to trip the breaker on a reverse-power current not greater than the
rated secondary current of the transformer. This breaker is not arranged to be
tripped by an overload on the secondary of the transformer.

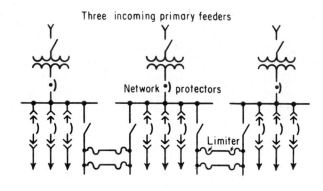

GENERAL NETWORK

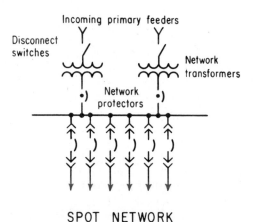

SPOT NETWORK

Fig. 450-16. These are the two basic types of "network" systems.
(Sec. 450-6.)

Section 450-6(a) (3) provides that:

1. Where two or more conductors are installed in parallel, an individual protective device is provided at each end of each conductor.
2. The protective device (fusible link or CB) does not provide overload protection, but provides short-circuit protection only.

In case of a short circuit, the protective device must open the circuit before the conductor reaches a temperature that would injure its insulation. The principles involved are that the entire system is so designed that the tie conductors will never be continuously overloaded in normal operation—hence protection against overloads of less severity than short circuits is not necessary—and that the protective devices should not open the circuit and thus cause an interruption of service on load peaks of such short duration that the conductors do not become overheated.

A limiter is a special type of fuse having a very high interrupting capacity. Figure 450-17 is a cross-sectional view of one type of limiter. The cable lug, the fusible section, and the extension for connection to the bus are all made in one piece from a length of copper tubing, and the enclosing case is also copper. A typical device of this type is rated to interrupt a current of 50,000 A without perceptible noise and without the escape of flame or gases from the case.

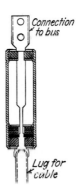

Fig. 450-17. A "limiter" is a cable connection device containing a fusible element. (Sec. 450-6.)

Figure 450-18 is a single-line diagram of a simple 3-phase industrial-plant network system. The primary feeders may operate at any standard voltage up to 13,800 V, and the secondary voltage would commonly be 480 V. The rating of the transformers used in such a system would usually be within the range of 300 to 1,000 kVA. The diagram shows two primary feeders, both of which are carried to each transformer so that by means of a double-throw switch each transformer can be connected to either feeder. Each feeder would be large enough to carry the entire load. It is assumed that the feeders are protected in accordance with Sec. 450-3(a)(2) so that no primary overcurrent devices are required at the transformers. The secondary ties consist of two conductors in multiple per phase and it will be noted that these conductors form a closed loop. Switches are provided so that any section of the loop, including the limiters protecting that section, can be isolated in case repairs or replacements should be necessary.

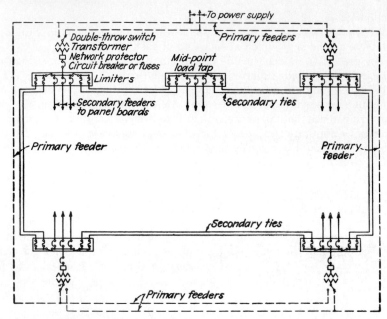

Fig. 450·18. A typical industrial plant network distribution system. (Sec. 450-6.)

1. Transformers must be protected against physical damage.

2. Exposed live parts must be protected against accidental contact by putting the transformer in a room or place accessible only to qualified personnel **or** by keeping live parts above the floor in accordance with Table 110-34(e).

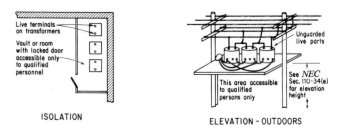

3. Signs or other visible markings must be used on equipment or structure to indicate the operating voltage of exposed live parts

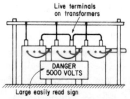

Fig. 450·19. Transformer installations must be effectively guarded. (Sec. 450-8.)

450-7. Parallel Operation. To operate satisfactorily in parallel, transformers should have the same percentage impedance and the same ratio of reactance to resistance. Information on these characteristics should be obtained from the manufacturer of the transformers.

450-8. Guarding. Figure 450-19 summarizes these rules. Refer to Sec. 110-17 on guarding of live parts. Safety to personnel is always important, particularly where a transformer is to operate with live parts. To protect against accidental contact with such components, isolate the unit or units in a room or place accessible only to qualified personnel and guard live parts, such as with a railing. When elevation is used for safeguarding live parts, consult Secs. 110-34(e) and 110-17.

As noted in part **(c),** switches and other equipment operating at up to 600 V and serving only circuits within a transformer enclosure may be installed within the enclosure *if* accessible to qualified persons only. This is intended to be part of the requirement that exposed, energized parts must be properly guarded.

450-9. Ventilation. As noted in the last paragraph, ventilation grills or slots in the sides or back of transformer enclosures must have adequate clearance from walls and objects to ensure free and substantial air flow through the case. Because of the tight quarters in today's electrical rooms and the tendency to give as little space as possible to electrical equipment, this is a critically important installation requirement to ensure safety and trouble-free operation of enclosed transformers. The substantiation for this proposal stated the following:

> Today's widespread use of dry type power transformers indoors has resulted in the common practice of their being installed directly up against walls completely blocking the rear vents. As inspectors, we frequently wind up trying to find out if the transformer installation instructions are anywhere around so we can see what clearances the manufacturer has specified.
>
> Clearly, this is not the best system. Furnaces, for example, commonly have required clearances marked on the nameplate. This proposal will let people know that clearances are required. Secondly, it will let us know what these clearances are.

See Fig. 450-20, top.

450-13. Location. Accessibility is an important location feature of transformer installation. The **NE Code** generally requires a transformer (whether liquid-filled or dry-type) to be readily accessible to qualified personnel for inspection and maintenance (Fig. 450-20). That is, it must be capable of being reached quickly for operation, repair, or inspection without requiring use of a portable ladder to get at it, and it must not be necessary to climb over or remove obstacles to reach it. A transformer may be mounted on a platform or balcony, but there must be fixed stairs or a fixed ladder for access to the transformer (Fig. 450-21). But Exceptions are made:

Exception No. 1 permits dry-type transformers rated 600 V or less to be located "in the open on walls, columns, or structures"—without the need to be readily accessible. A transformer suspended from the ceiling or hung on a wall—in which cases a ladder would be required to reach them because they are over 6½ ft above the floor (see Sec. 380-8)—would be O.K., as shown in Fig. 450-22. And Exception No. 2 permits dry-type transformers up to 600 V, 50 kVA, to be installed in fire-resistant hollow spaces of buildings not permanently

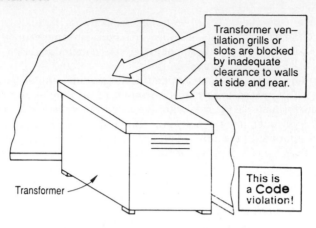

Transformer ven-
tilation grills or
slots are blocked
by inadequate
clearance to walls
at side and rear.

Transformer

This is
a **Code**
violation!

Fig. 450-20. Basic rule calls for every transformer to have adequate ventilation and ready, easy, direct access for inspection or maintenance. (Secs.
450-9 and 450-13.)

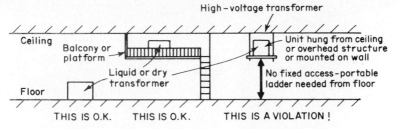

High-voltage transformer

Ceiling

Balcony or platform

Liquid or dry transformer

Floor

Unit hung from ceiling or overhead structure or mounted on wall

No fixed access-portable ladder needed from floor

THIS IS O.K.   THIS IS O.K.   THIS IS A VIOLATION !

NOTE: Installation at far right is O.K. for dry-type transformer rated up to 600 V.

Fig. 450-21. Transformers must be "readily accessible" without need for portable ladder to reach them. (Sec. 450-13.)

Fig. 450-22. Transformer mounted on wall (or suspended from ceiling) would be considered *not* readily accessible because a ladder would be needed to reach it. But, because it is "in the open," such use conforms to Exception No. 1. (Sec. 450-13.)

closed in by structure, provided the transformer is designed to have adequate ventilation for such installation. See Fig. 450-23.

Note in Exception No. 1 that a transformer *may* be *not* readily accessible only if it is located in the *open*. The words "in the open" do not readily and surely relate to such words as "concealed" or "exposed." But it is reasonable to

Fig. 450-23. Recessed mounting of dry-type transformers is permitted within "fire-resistant hollow spaces," as in hospitals, schools, and other commercial or institutional buildings. (Sec. 450-13.)

conclude that "in the *open*" would be difficult to equate with "above a suspended ceiling." The latter location is in a generally smaller, confined space in which the transformers must be readily accessible; Exception No. 1 must be taken as a condition in which a transformer *does* not have to be readily accessible—i.e., that it may be mounted up high where a portable ladder would be needed to get at it. But the words "in the open" could logically be taken to prohibit use of the transformer above a suspended ceiling (Fig. 450-24).

It should be noted that the Exception No. 1 to this rule, which permits high mounting that makes transformers *not* "readily accessible" applies to "dry-type transformers" only. As a result, high mounting of oil-filled transformers—as shown in Fig. 450-25—is not covered by that Exception and could be considered a violation of the *basic* rule of this section. However, Sec. 450-27 on oil-filled transformers installed outdoors actually contains an Exception to the rule of Sec. 450-13. The FPN following Sec. 450-27 points out that additional information can be found in the *National Electrical Safety Code* (*not* the **NE Code**). That code covers use of such transformers as shown in Fig. 450-25.

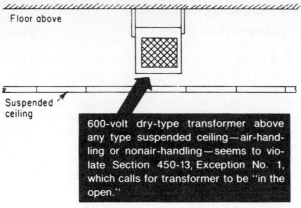

Floor above

Suspended
ceiling

600-volt dry-type transformer above
any type suspended ceiling—air-handling or nonair-handling—seems to violate Section 450-13, Exception No. 1,
which calls for transformer to be "in the
open."

Fig. 450-24. Watch out for transformers above suspended ceilings.
(Sec. 450-13.)

Fig. 450-25. High mounting of oil-filled transformers would require
use of a portable ladder for access to the units. But Sec. 450-27 covers
such units installed on poles or structures. (Sec. 450-13.)

450-21. Dry-type Transformers Installed Indoors. This rule differentiates between dry-type transformers based on kVA rating. All dry-type transformers rated at 112½ kVA or less, at up to 35 kV, must be installed so that a minimum clearance of 12 in. is provided between the transformer and any combustible material.

Exception No. 1 recognizes the use of fire-resistant heat-insulating barriers instead of space separation for transformers rated not over 112½ kVA. But be aware that clearances required to ensure proper ventilation of the transformer must be provided to satisfy Sec. 450-9.

Exception No. 2 permits those transformers rated 600 V or less to be installed closer than the 12-in. minimum, but, consideration must also be given to the requirements of Sec. 450-9. For units rated over 112½ kVA, the rule basically calls for such transformers to be installed in vaults, with two Exceptions provided. Figure 450-26 shows the rules of this section. Related application recommendations are as follows:

- Select a place that has the driest and cleanest air possible for installation of open-ventilated units. Avoid exposure to dripping or splashing water or other wet conditions. Outdoor application requires a suitable housing. Try to find locations where transformers will not be damaged by floodwater in case of a storm, a plugged drain, or a backed-up sewer.
- Temperature in the installation area must be normal, or the transformer may have to be derated. Modern standard, ventilated, dry-type transformers are designed to provide rated kilovoltampere output at rated voltage when the maximum ambient temperature of the cooling air is 40°C and the average ambient temperature of the cooling air over any 24-hr period does not exceed 30°C. At higher or lower ambients, transformer loading can be adjusted by the following relationships.
  1. For each degree Celsius that average ambient temperature exceeds 30°C, the maximum load on the transformer must be reduced by 1 percent of rated kilovoltamperes.
  2. For each degree Celsius that average ambient temperature is less than 30°C, the maximum load on the transformer may be increased by 0.67 percent of rated kilovoltamperes.

Depending on the type of insulation used, transformer insulation life will be cut approximately in half for every 10°C that the ambient temperature exceeds the normal rated value—or doubled for every 10°C below rated levels. Estimates assume continuous operation at full load. With modern insulations this rule is actually conservative for ambient temperature below normal operating temperatures and optimistic above it.

For proper cooling, dry-type transformers depend upon circulation of clean air—free from dust, dirt, or corrosive elements. Filtered air is preferable and may be mandatory in some cases of extreme air pollution. In any case, it can reduce maintenance.

In restricted spaces—small basement mechanical rooms, etc.—ventilation must be carefully checked to assure proper transformer operating temperature. The usual requirement is for 100 cfm of air movement for each kilowatt of transformer loss. Areas of inlet and outlet vent openings should be at least 1 net sq ft per 100 kVA of rated transformer capacity.

TRANSFORMERS RATED 112½ KVA OR LESS

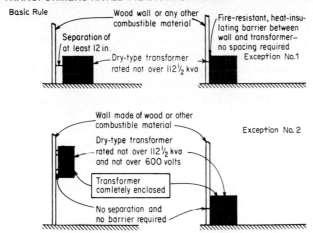

Basic Rule — Wood wall or any other combustible material — Separation of at least 12 in. — Dry-type transformer rated not over 112½ kva

Fire-resistant, heat-insulating barrier between wall and transformer— no spacing required Exception No.1

Wall made of wood or other combustible material — Dry-type transformer rated not over 112½ kva and not over 600 volts — Transformer comletely enclosed — No separation and no barrier required

Exception No. 2

TRANSFORMERS RATED OVER 112½ KVA

Completely enclosed and ventilated unit with 80°C rise or higher insulation...

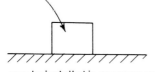

... may be installed in any room or area (need not be fire-resistant)

Clearances from combustible materials in any room or area (not fire-resistant)

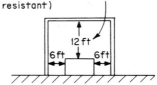

12 ft
6ft   6ft

Dry-type transformer with 80°C rise or higher insulation but not enclosed and ventilated

Room of fire-resistant construction to house transformer

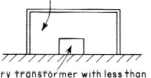

Dry transformer with less than 80°C rise insulation

Dry transformer rated over 35 KV...

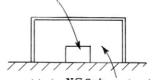

...must be in *NE Code* constructed transformer vault (Part C, Art.450)

Fig. 450·26. Construction of dry-type transformer affects indoor installation rules. (Sec. 450-21.)

Height of vault, location of openings, and transformer loading affect ventilation. One manufacturer calls for the areas of the inlet and outlet openings to be not less than 60 sq ft per 1,000 kVA when the transformer is operating under full load and is located in a restricted space. And a distance of 1 ft should be provided on all sides of dry-type transformers as well as between adjacent units.

Freestanding, floor-mounted units with metal grilles at the bottom must be set up off the floor a sufficient distance to provide the intended ventilation draft up through their housings.

The installation location must not expose the transformer housing to damage by normal movement of persons, trucks, or equipment. Ventilation openings should not be exposed to vandalism or accidental or mischievous poking of rubbish, sticks, or rods into the windings. Adequate protection must be provided against possible entry of small birds or animals.

450-22. Dry-type Transformers Installed Outdoors.   A transformer that sustains an internal fault which causes arcing and/or fire presents the same hazard to adjacent combustible material whether it is installed indoors or outdoors. For that reason, a clearance of at least 12 in. is required between any dry-type transformer rated over 112½ kVA and combustible materials of buildings.

In the Exception, the clearance of 12 in. from combustible building materials is *not* required for outdoor dry-type transformers that have an 80°C rise (or higher) rating and are completely enclosed except for ventilation openings. The same consideration given for an 80°C rise transformer is made outdoors as it is indoors, in Exception No. 2 of Sec. 450-21(b).

450-23. Less-Flammable Liquid-Insulated Transformers.   Section 450-23 covers the liquid-filled transformers designed to replace askarel-insulated transformers. Because oil-filled transformers used indoors require a transformer vault, the "less flammable" (also called "high fire point") insulated transformer offers an alternative to the oil-filled transformers, without the need for a vault. This **Code** section permits installation of these "high fire point liquid-insulated" transformers indoors or outdoors. Over 35 kV, such a transformer must be in a vault.

The rules of this section recognize that these various high fire point liquid-insulated dielectrics are less flammable than the mineral oil used in oil-filled transformers but not as fire-resistant as askarel. Because these askarel substitutes will burn to some degree, **Code** rules are aimed at minimizing any fire hazards:

1. Less-flammable liquid dielectrics used in transformers must, first of all, be listed—that is, tested and certified by a testing laboratory or organization and shown in a published listing as suitable for application. "Less-flammable" liquids for transformer insulation are defined as having "a fire point of not less than 300°C."

2. Transformers containing the high fire point dielectrics may be used *without a vault* but only within noncombustible buildings (brick, concrete, etc.) and then only in rooms or areas that do not contain combustible materials. A "Type I" or "Type II" building is a building of noncombustible construction, as defined in the fine-print note, and there must be no combustible materials stored in the area where the transformer is installed.

3. The entire installation must satisfy all conditions of use, as described in the "listing" of the liquid.

4. A liquid-confinement area must be provided around such transformers that are not in a vault, because tests indicate these liquids are not completely nonpropagating—that is, if they are ignited, the flame will be propagated along the liquid. A propagating liquid must be confined to a given

area to confine the flame of its burning (Fig. 450-27). The liquid-confinement area (a curb or dike around the transformer) must be of sufficient dimensions to contain the entire volume of liquid in the transformer.

A less-flammable liquid-insulated transformer installed in such a way that all of conditions 2 and 3 above are not satisfied must be *either*

1. Provided with an automatic fire extinguishing system and a liquid-confinement area, *or*
2. Installed in a **Code**-specified transformer vault (part **C** of Art. 450), without need for a liquid-confinement area.

Less-flammable liquid-insulated transformers rated over 35 kV and installed indoors must be enclosed in a **Code**-constructed transformer vault. All less-flammable liquid-insulated transformers installed outdoors may be attached to or adjacent to or on the roof of Type I or Type II buildings. Such installation at other than Type I or Type II buildings, where adjacent to combustible material, fire escapes, or door or window openings, must be guarded by fire barriers, space separation, and compliance with instructions for using the particular liquid.

Because these rules are general in nature and lend themselves to a variety of interpretations, application of these requirements may depend heavily on consultation with inspection authorities.

Although askarel-filled transformers up to 35 kV were used for many years

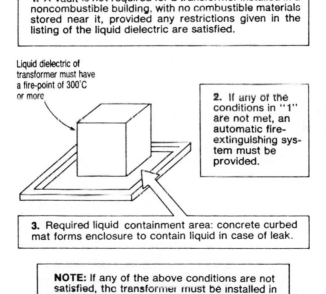

1. A vault is not required for a transformer installed in a noncombustible building, with no combustible materials stored near it, provided any restrictions given in the listing of the liquid dielectric are satisfied.

Liquid dielectric of transformer must have a fire-point of 300°C or more

2. If any of the conditions in "1" are not met, an automatic fire-extinguishing system must be provided.

3. Required liquid containment area: concrete curbed mat forms enclosure to contain liquid in case of leak.

NOTE: If any of the above conditions are not satisfied, the transformer must be installed in a *Code*-constructed transformer vault.

Fig. 450-27. Transformers containing askarel-substitute liquids must satisfy specific installation requirements. (Sec. 450-23.)

for indoor applications because they do not require a transformer vault, there has been a sharp, abrupt discontinuance of their use over recent years. Growth in the ratings, characteristics, and availability of dry-type high-voltage transformers has accounted for a major part in the reduction of askarel units. But another factor that led to rejection of askarel transformers in recent years is the environmental objections to the askarel liquid itself.

A major component of any askarel fluid is polychlorinated biphenyl (PCB), a chemical compound designated as a harmful environmental pollutant because it is nonbiodegradable and cannot be readily disposed of. Thus, although the askarels are excellent coolants where freedom from flammability is important, environmental objections to the sale, use, and disposal of PCBs have eliminated new applications of askarel transformers and stimulated a search for a nontoxic, environmentally acceptable substitute.

Proper handling and disposal of askarel is important for units still in use. A regulation of the EPA (Environmental Protection Agency), No. 311, required that all PCB spills of 1 lb or more must be reported. Failure to report a spill is a criminal offense punishable by a $10,000 fine and/or one-year imprisonment. Both the EPA and OSHA have objected to use of askarels. A manufacturer of askarel has established a program for disposal of spent or contaminated PCB fluid using an incinerator that completely destroys the fluid by burning it at over 2,000°F.

Non-PCB dielectric coolant fluids for use in small- and medium-sized power transformers as a safe alternate to askarels are available and transformers using these new high fire point dielectric coolants have been widely used.

Extensive data from tests on available askarel substitutes show that they provide a high degree of safety. Such fluids do have **NE Code** and OSHA recognition. Responsibility for proper clearances with insurance underwriters, government regulating agencies, and local code authorities rests with the user or purchaser of the fluid in new or refilled transformers. Underwriters Laboratories does not test or list liquid-filled equipment. Both UL and Factory Mutual Research Laboratory have been involved in providing a classification service of flammability. The EPA has commented favorably on such high fire point fluids.

Few physical changes to transformers are necessary when using the new fluid dielectrics. However, load ratings on existing units may be reduced about 10 percent because of the difference in fluid viscosity and heat conductivity compared with askarel. The high fire point fluids cost about twice as much as askarel. Purchase price of a new transformer filled with the fluid (such as a typical 1,000-kVA loadcenter unit) is about 10 to 15 percent more than an askarel-filled unit. But the economics vary for different fluids and must be carefully evaluated.

High fire point liquid-insulated transformers require no special maintenance procedures. The liquids exhibit good dielectric properties over a wide range of temperatures and voltage stress levels, and they have acceptable arc-quenching capabilities. They have a high degree of thermal stability and a high resistance to thermal oxidation that enables them to maintain their insulating and other functional properties for extended periods of time at high temperatures.

Since silicone liquids will ignite at 750°F (350°C), they are not classed as fire-resistant. However, if the heat source is removed or fluid temperature drops below 750°F, burning will stop. The silicone fluids are thus self-extinguishing.

450-24. Nonflammable Fluid-Insulated Transformers. This section permits indoor and outdoor use of transformers that utilize a noncombustible fluid dielectric, which is one that does not have a flash point or fire point and is not flammable in air (Fig. 450-28). As an alternative to askarel-insulated transformers, these transformers offer high BIL ratings and other features of operation similar to high-fire-point dielectric-insulated transformers—without concern for flammability. Such transformers do not, therefore, have the restrictions that are set down in Sec. 450-23 for the high-fire-point-liquid transformers.

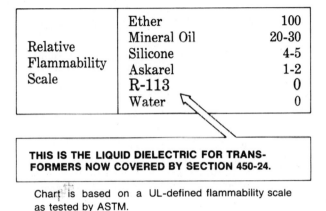

Relative Flammability Scale	Ether	100
	Mineral Oil	20-30
	Silicone	4-5
	Askarel	1-2
	R-113	0
	Water	0

THIS IS THE LIQUID DIELECTRIC FOR TRANSFORMERS NOW COVERED BY SECTION 450-24.

Chart is based on a UL-defined flammability scale as tested by ASTM.

Fig. 450-28. Comparison of the relative flammabilities of liquid dielectrics compared with ether. (Sec. 450-24.)

Nonflammable fluid-insulated transformers installed indoors must have a liquid-confinement area and a pressure-relief vent. In addition, such transformers must be equipped to absorb gases generated by arcing inside the tank, or the pressure-relief vent must be connected to a flue or duct to carry the gases to "an environmentally safe area." Units rated over 35 kV must be installed in a vault when used indoors.

450-25. Askarel-Insulated Transformers Installed Indoors. Although askarel transformers are being phased out, the Code rule says such transformers installed indoors must conform to the following:

1. Units rated over 25 kVA must be equipped with a pressure-relief vent.
2. Where installed in a poorly ventilated place, they must be furnished with a means for absorbing any gases generated by arcing inside the case, or the pressure-relief vent must be connected to a chimney or flue which will carry such gases outside the building (Fig. 450-29).
3. Units rated over 35,000 V must be installed in a vault.

450-26. Oil-Insulated Transformers Installed Indoors. The basic rule is illustrated in Fig. 450-30. Oil-insulated transformers installed indoors must be

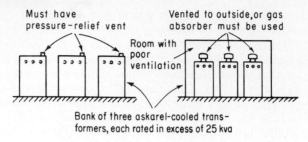

Must have
pressure-relief vent

Vented to outside, or gas
absorber must be used

Room with
poor
ventilation

Bank of three askarel-cooled transformers, each rated in excess of 25 kva

UNITS RATED OVER 35,000 VOLTS MUST BE USED IN A VAULT

Fig. 450-29. Code rules still cover askarel transformers. (Sec. 450-25.)

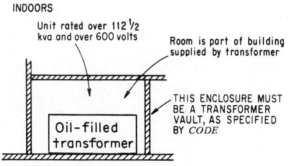

INDOORS

Unit rated over 112 ½
kva and over 600 volts

Room is part of building
supplied by transformer

Oil-filled
transformer

THIS ENCLOSURE MUST
BE A TRANSFORMER
VAULT, AS SPECIFIED
BY *CODE*

Fig. 450-30. Oil-filled transformers generally require installation in a "vault." (Sec. 450-26.)

installed in a vault constructed according to **Code** specs, but the Exceptions note general and specific conditions under which a vault is not necessary. The most commonly applied Exceptions are as follows:

1. A hookup of one or more units rated not over 112½ kVA may be used in a vault constructed of reinforced concrete not less than 4 in. thick.
2. Units installed in detached buildings used only for providing electric service do not require a **Code**-constructed vault if no fire hazard is created and the interior is accessible only to qualified persons.

450-27. Oil-Insulated Transformers Installed Outdoors. Figure 450-31 shows how physical locations of building openings must be evaluated with respect to potential fire hazard from leaking transformer oil.

450-28. Modification of Transformers. Askarel transformers that are drained and refilled with another liquid dielectric must be identified as such and must satisfy all rules of its retrofilled status. This rule is intended to maintain safety in all cases where askarel transformers are modified to eliminate PCB hazards. Marking must show the new condition of the unit and must not create code violations. For instance, an indoor askarel transformer that is drained and refilled with oil may require construction of a vault, which is required for oil-filled transformers as specified in Sec. 450-26.

OUTDOORS

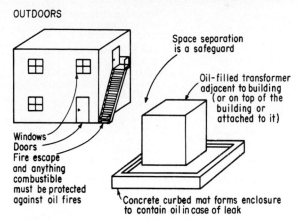

Space separation
is a safeguard

Oil-filled transformer
adjacent to building
(or on top of the
building or
attached to it)

Windows
Doors
Fire escape
and anything
combustible
must be protected
against oil fires

Concrete curbed mat forms enclosure
to contain oil in case of leak

Fig. 450-31. Precautions must be taken for outdoor oil transformers. (Sec. 450-27.)

450-41. Location. Ideally, a transformer vault should have direct ventilating
openings (grills or louvers through the walls) to outdoor space. Use of ducts or
flues for ventilating is not necessarily a **Code** violation, but they should be
avoided wherever possible.

450-42. Walls, Roof and Floor. Basic mandatory construction details are established for an **NEC**-type transformer vault, as required for oil-filled transformers
and for all transformers operating at over 35,000 V. The purpose of a transformer vault is to isolate the transformers and other apparatus and to confine
any fire that might be caused by the failure of any of the apparatus. It is important that the door as well as the remainder of the enclosure be of proper construction and that a substantial lock be provided. Details required for any vault
are shown in Fig. 450-32 and include the following details:

1. Walls and roofs of vaults shall be constructed of reinforced concrete,
   brick, load-bearing tile, concrete block, or other fire-resistive constructions with adequate strength and a fire resistance of 3 hr according to
   ASTM Standard E119-75. "Stud and wall board construction" may not be
   used for walls, roof, or other surfaces of a transformer vault. Although the
   rule here does *not* flatly mandate "concrete" or "masonry" construction,
   that is essentially the objective of the wording. The substantiation for this
   rule said the following:

   The only guidance provided in Sec. 450-42 as to the type of material to be used in
   vault construction is in a fine print note which states that "six-inch (152mm) thick reinforced concrete is a typical 3-hour construction." This, of course, is only advisory.
   Sheet rock can be so installed as to have a 3-hour fire rating, however, it should not
   be considered as being suitable for this type of installation. It would not have adequate
   structural strength in case of oil fire. It is not too difficult to break through such a wall,
   either intentionally or unintentionally.
   Your attention is also called to Sec. 230-6(3), which states that conductors installed
   in a transformer vault shall be considered outside of a building. The major thrust of
   Sec. 230-6 has been that the conductors are to be masonry-encased.

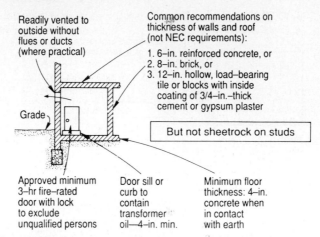

Readily vented to
outside without
flues or ducts
(where practical)

Common recommendations on
thickness of walls and roof
(not NEC requirements):

1. 6–in. reinforced concrete, or
2. 8–in. brick, or
3. 12–in. hollow, load–bearing
   tile or blocks with inside
   coating of 3/4–in.–thick
   cement or gypsum plaster

Grade

But not sheetrock on studs

Approved minimum
3–hr fire–rated
door with lock
to exclude
unqualified persons

Door sill or
curb to
contain
transformer
oil—4–in. min.

Minimum floor
thickness: 4–in.
concrete when
in contact
with earth

Fig. 450-32. Transformer vault must assure containment of possible fire.
(Sec. 450-42.)

2. A vault must have a concrete floor not less than 4 in. thick when in contact
   with the earth. When the vault is constructed with space below it, the floor
   must have adequate structural strength and a minimum fire resistance of
   3 hr. Six-in.-thick reinforced concrete is a typical 3-hr-rated construction.
3. Building walls and floors that meet the above requirements may serve for
   the floor, roof, and/or walls of the vault.

An exception to the basic regulations establishing the construction standards
for transformer fireproof vaults notes that the transformer-vault fire rating may
be reduced where the transformers are protected with automatic sprinkler,
water spray, or carbon dioxide. The usual construction standards for transformer vaults (such as 6-in.-thick reinforced concrete) provide a minimum fire-
resistance rating of 3 hr. Where automatic sprinkler, water spray, or carbon
dioxide is used, a construction rating of only 1 hr will be permitted.

450-43. Doorways.   Each doorway must be of 3-hr fire rating as defined in the
Standard for the Installation of Fire Doors and Windows (NFPA No. 80-1983).
The **Code**-enforcing authority may also require such a door for doorways leading from the vault to the outdoors, in addition to any doorways into adjoining
space in the building.

As required in part **(c)**, vault doors must swing *out* and must be equipped with
"panic bars" or other opening means that requires only "simple pressure." This
is intended to provide the greater safety of a push-open- rather than a rotating-
knob-type of door release. As noted in the substantiation:

Conventional rotating door knob hardware is used on transformer vault doors due
to lack of specific wording in the paragraph as presently written. The *National Electrical Safety Code* is believed to be very specific, or has been formally interpreted to
be, requiring "panic type" door hardware. In an electrical flash or arc an electrical
worker may lose the use of hands for twisting a conventional door knob.

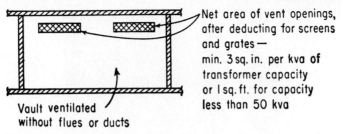

Fig. 450·33. Vault vent opening(s) may be in or near the roof—or near floor level also, if one is at or near roof level. (Sec. 450-45.)

450·45. Ventilation Openings. This rule sets the size and arrangement of vent openings in a vault where such ventilation is required by ANSI C57.12.00-1987—"General Requirements for Liquid-Immersed Distribution, Power, and Regulating Transformers," as noted in Sec. 450-9. Figure 450-33 shows the openings as regulated by part **(c)** of this section. One or more openings may be used, but if a single vent opening is used, it must be in or near the roof of the vault—and not near the floor.

ARTICLE 460. CAPACITORS

460·1. Scope. The sections in this article apply chiefly to capacitors used for the power-factor correction of electric-power installations in industrial plants and for correcting the power factors of individual motors (Fig. 460-1). These provisions apply only to capacitors used for surge protection where such capacitors are not component parts of other apparatus.

In an industrial plant using induction motors, the power factor may be considerably less than 100 percent, particularly when all or part of the motors operate most of the time at much less than their full load. The lagging current can be counteracted and the power factor improved by installing capacitors across the line. By raising the power factor, for the same actual power delivered the current is decreased in the generator, transformers, and lines, up to the point where the capacitor is connected.

Figure 460-2 shows a capacitor assembly connection to the main power circuit of a small industrial plant, consisting of capacitors connected in a 3-phase hookup and rated at 90 kVA for a 460-V system. An externally operable switch mounted on the wall is used as the disconnecting means and the discharge device required by Sec. 460-6 consists of two high-impedance coils inside the switch enclosure which consume only a small amount of power, but, having a comparatively low DC resistance, permit the charge to drain off rapidly after the capacitor assembly has been disconnected from the line.

460·6. Discharge of Stored Energy. If no means were provided for draining off the charge stored in a capacitor after it is disconnected from the line, a severe

Fig. 460·1. A typical power-factor correction capacitor bank is this 300-kvar bank of twelve 25-kvar, 480-V capacitor units installed in a steel enclosure in an outdoor industrial substation. (Sec. 460-1.)

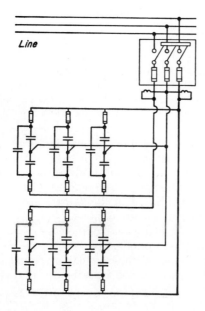

Fig. 460·2. Six internally delta-connected capacitors form a 3-phase capacitor bank. (Sec. 460-1.)

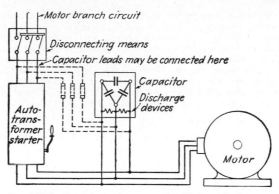

Fig. 460-3. Capacitor voltage must be discharged when circuit is opened. (Sec. 460-6.)

shock might be received by a person servicing the equipment or the equipment might be damaged by a short circuit. If a capacitor is permanently connected to the windings of a motor, as in Fig. 460-3, the stored charge will drain off rapidly through the windings when the circuit is opened. Reactors or resistors used as discharge devices must either be permanently connected across the terminals of the capacitor (such as within the capacitor housing) or a device must be provided that will automatically connect the discharge devices when the capacitor is disconnected from the source of supply. Most available types of capacitors have discharge resistors built into their cases. When capacitors are not equipped with discharge resistors, a discharge circuit must be provided.

Figure 460-3 shows a capacitor used to correct the power factor of a single motor. The capacitor may be connected to the motor circuit between the starter and the motor or may be connected between the disconnecting means and the starter, as indicated by the dotted lines in the diagram. If connected as shown by the dotted lines, an overcurrent device must be provided in these leads, as required by Sec. 460-8(b). The capacitor is shown as having discharge devices consisting of resistors.

In previous NEC editions, Sec. 460-7 covered selection of the size of power-factor capacitors. That section is no longer in the NEC.

Power capacitors, in most applications, are installed to raise system power factor, which results in increased circuit or system current-carrying capacity, reduced power losses, and lower reactive power charges (most utility companies include a power-factor penalty clause in their industrial billing). Also, additional benefits derived as a result of a power capacitor installation are reduced voltage drop and increased voltage stability. Figure 460-4 presents basic data on calculating size of capacitors for power-factor correction. However, manufacturers provide tables and graphs to help select the capacitor for a given motor load.

The former rule of Sec. 460-7 limited power-factor correction to unity (100 percent or 1.0) when there is no load on the motor. That will result in a power factor of 95 percent or better when the motor is fully loaded. The old rule rec-

Power-factor capacitors can be connected across electric lines to neutralize the effect of lagging power-factor loads, thereby reducing the current drawn for a given kilowatt load. In a distribution system, small capacitor units may be connected at the individual loads or the total capacitor kilovolt-amperes may be grouped at one point and connected to the main. Although the total kvar of capacitors is the same, the use of small capacitors at the individual loads reduces current all the way from the loads back to the source and thereby has greater PF corrective effect than the one big unit on the main, which reduces current only from its point of installation back to the source.

Calculating Size of Capacitor:

Assume it is desired to improve the power factor a given amount by the addition of capacitors to the circuit.

Then $\text{kvar}_R = \text{kw} \times (\tan \theta_1 - \tan \theta_2)$

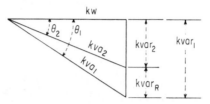

where kvar_R = rating of required capacitor
       kvar_1 = reactive kilovolt-amperes at original PF
       kvar_2 = reactive kilovolt-amperes at improved PF
       θ_1 = original phase angle
       θ_2 = phase angle at improved PF
       kw = load at which original PF was determined.

NOTE: The phase angles θ_1 and θ_2 can be determined from a table of trigonometric functions using the following relationships:
    θ_1 = The angle which has its cosine equal to the decimal value of the original power factor (e.g., 0.70 for 70% PF; 0.65 for 65%; etc.)
    θ_2 = The angle which has its cosine equal to the decimal value of the improved power factor.

Fig. 460-4. Capacitors reduce circuit current by supplying the magnetizing current to motors.

ognized the use of capacitors sized *either* for the value that will produce 100 percent power factor of the circuit when the motor is running at no load *or* for a value equal to 50 percent of the kilovoltampere rating of the motor input for motors up to 50 hp, 600 V (Fig. 460-5).

A number of comments made in the discussions that led to that rule are informative and important:

  1. Setting the capacitor rating at 50 percent of the kilovoltampere rating of the motor input does not afford, in most cases, an appreciable gain in power factor over that achieved by setting the capacitor rating to limit the motor no-load power factor to unity. In two examples, 7.5-hp, 1,200-rpm and 10-hp, 900-rpm ratings, the motor no-load kvar is more than 50 percent of the kilovoltampere rating of the motor input. In these cases, which are typical of ones having inherently low motor power factor and where power-factor improvement would be most beneficial, the italicized "Exception" affords no potential for additional gain in power-factor

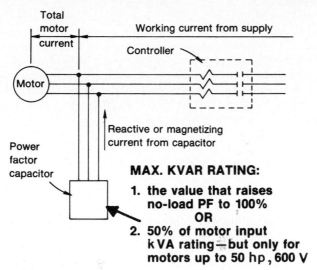

Fig. 460-5. Maximum rating of capacitor kvar may be determined by either of two approaches.

improvement. In other examples, 40-hp, 1,200-rpm and 200-hp, 1,800-rpm ratings, the corrective kvar value to raise the motor no-load power factor to unity yields better power-factor improvement up through 75 percent load than attained by corrective kvar equal 50 percent of the kilovoltampere rating of the motor input. For loads above 75 percent, the converse is true; but there is no notable overall difference in power-factor improvement between the two approaches.

2. Most motor-associated capacitors are related to low-voltage, 5- to 50-hp, 1,800- and 1,200-rpm, across-the-line-start motors. In this range, the no-load rule for determination of maximum capacitor kvar restricts capacitors to less than 50 percent of horsepower.

Noticeable economies can be made by applying larger capacitors to such motors. This has been done for years, with excellent results and no field trouble, as has been attested by several engineers whose views have been made known to the **Code** panel.

The larger motors should certainly have capacitor kvars limited by stringent rules, but this should not interfere with the field-proved use of augmented capacitor sizing of the integral-horsepower motors most commonly used in industrial, commerical, and institutional plants.

The no-load power factor of a motor is a design constant of the motor and may be obtained from the manufacturer of the motor—or it may be measured or calculated. In Fig. 460-4, using the known no-load PF (power factor) of a motor, the kilowatts can be calculated from $kW = PF \times kVA_1$. Then $kvar_1$ (the required rating of PF capacity to raise the no-load value of PF to 100 percent) equals the square root of $(kVA_1)^2 - (kW)^2$, where kVA_1 is calculated from circuit voltage and current measured with a clamp-on ammeter.

A handy rule-of-thumb method for determining the kilovar rating of a capacitor required to provide optimum power-factor correction for a given motor is

1. With no load on the motor, measure the no-load kilovoltampere. That can be determined by using a clamp-on ammeter to measure the amount of current drawn by the motor under no-load condition and then using a voltmeter to get the phase-to-phase voltage of the motor circuit. Then, for a 3-phase motor, the kilovoltampere input to the motor is derived from the formula:

Input kVA = [Phase-to-phase voltage × line current × 1.732] ÷ 1,000

2. Because the power factor of an unloaded motor is very low—say, about 10 percent—the kilovoltampere vector for the original PF condition as shown in Fig. 460-4 is lagging the kilowatt vector by an angle that is approaching 90°. That results from the working current being small (only the resistance of the windings) while the reactive (magnetizing) current is at its normal and very much larger value. In that condition, the reactive current causes the kilovar vector to be almost the same length as the kilovoltampere vector—so close in fact that it is generally safe to take the kilovoltampere input value as the required kilovar rating of capacitor needed to correct to 100 percent PF at no-load, which will result in a 95 to 98 percent PF at full load.

3. Then select a capacitor assembly that has a kilovar rating as close as possible to—but *not* in excess of—the calculated value of input kilovoltampere of the motor. This method may be used on rewound motors or on other motors where it is not possible to make a better determination of needed capacitor kilovar.

Capacitors of the type used for PF correction of motors are commonly rated in kilovoltamperes, or the rating may be in "kilovars," meaning "reactive kilovoltamperes," abbreviated kvar. The capacitors are usually designed for connection to a 3-phase system and constructed as a unit with three leads brought out.

Corrective measures for improving power factor may be designed into motor branch circuits. Generally, the most effective location for installation of individual power-factor-correction capacitors is as close to the inductive load as possible. This provides maximum correction from the capacitor back to the source of power. At individual motor locations, power-factor-correcting capacitors offer improved voltage regulation. As shown in Fig. 460-6, power-factor capacitors installed at terminals of motors provide maximum relief from reactive currents, reducing the required current-carrying capacities of conductors from their point of application all the way back to the supply system. Figure 460-7 shows a typical example. Such application also eliminates extra switching devices, since each capacitor can be switched with the motor it serves.

Capacitors also may be installed as a group or bank at some central point, such as a switchboard, loadcenter, busway, or outdoor substation. Usually this method serves only to reduce the utility company penalty charges; however, in many instances, installation costs also will be lower.

When motors are small, numerous, and operated intermittently, it is often

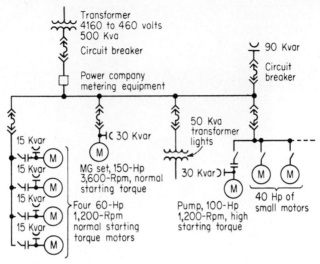

Fig. 460·6. PF capacitors at individual motors offer maximum corrective advantages.

economically more desirable to install required capacitor kvar at the motor control center.

Capacitor installations may consist of an individual unit connected as close as possible to the inductive load (at the terminals of a motor, etc.) or of a bank of many units connected in multiple across a main feeder. Units are available in specific kvar and voltage ratings. Standard low-voltage capacitor units are rated from about 0.5 kvar to 25 kvar at voltages from 216 to 600 V. For high-voltage applications, standard ratings are 15, 25, 50, and 100 kvar. Available in single-, 2-, or 3-phase configurations, power capacitors may be supplied either unfused or equipped with current-limiting or high-capacity fuses (single-phase units are furnished with one fuse; 3-phase capacitors usually have two fuses). On low-voltage units, fuses may be mounted on the capacitor bushings inside the terminal compartment.

Use of capacitor power-factor application is generally not acceptable for *any* motor application involving repetitive switching of the motor load, as in plugging, jogging, rapid reversals, reclosings, etc., because of the severe overvoltages and overtorques that are generated in such motor applications when capacitors of the permitted rating are connected on the load side of the motor starter. The objectionable effects can lead to premature failure of motor insulation.

460·8. Conductors.   Part **(a)** of this section covers sizing of circuit conductors. The current corresponding to the kilovoltampere rating of a capacitor is computed in the same manner as for a motor or other load having the same rating in kilovoltamperes. If a capacitor assembly used at 460 V has a rating of 90 kVA, the current rating is $90,000/(460 \times 1.73) = 113$ A. The minimum required ampacity of the conductors would be 1.35×113 A, or 153 A.

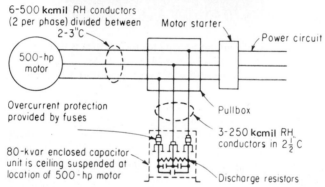

6-500 kcmil RH conductors
(2 per phase) divided between   Motor starter
2-3"C

500-hp
motor   Power circuit

Overcurrent protection
provided by fuses   Pullbox

                                           3-250 kcmil RH
                                           conductors in 2½ C
80-kvar enclosed capacitor
unit is ceiling suspended at
location of 500-hp motor   Discharge resistors

Fig. 460·7. Typical capacitor installation connected on load side of
motor starter for a 500-hp motor consists of ceiling-suspended enclosed
capacitors (arrow) that are rated at 80 kvar, connected through the pull
box to the circuit conductors for the motor. Diagram shows how conductors were added to the equipment shown in the photo.

The manufacturing standards for capacitors for power-factor correction call
for a rating tolerance of "−0, +15 percent," meaning that the actual rating in
kilovoltamperes is never below the nominal rating and may be as much as 15
percent higher. Thus, a capacitor having a nameplate rating of 100 kVA might
actually draw a current corresponding to 115 kVA. The current drawn by a
capacitor varies directly with the line voltage, so that, if the line voltage is
higher than the rated voltage, the current will be correspondingly increased.
Also, any variation of the line voltage from a pure sine wave form will cause a

capacitor to draw an increased current. It is for these reasons that the conductors leading to a capacitor are required to have an ampacity not less than 135 percent of the rated current of the capacitor.

example Given the kvar rating of capacitors to be installed for a motor, determining the correct capacitor conductor size is relatively simple. The rule here requires that the ampacity of the capacitor conductors be not less than ⅓ the ampacity of the motor circuit conductors and not less than 135 percent of the capacitor rated current. The capacitor nameplate will give rated kvar, voltage, and current. It is then a simple matter of multiplying rated current by 1.35 to obtain the ampacity value of the conductor to be installed and selecting the size of conductor required to carry that value of current, from Table 310-16. Then check that the ampacity is not less than ⅓ the ampacity of the motor circuit conductors.

For a motor rated 100 hp, 460 V, 121 A full-load current, a 25-kvar capacitor would correct power factor to between 0.95 and 0.98 at full load. The nameplate on the capacitor indicates that the capacitor is rated 460 V, 31 A. Then 31 × 1.35 = 42 A. From **Code** Table 310-16, a No. 6 TW or THW conductor rated to carry 55 A would do the job. (No. 8 THW rated at 45 A would most likely be considered not acceptable because UL generally calls for use of 60°C wires in circuits up to 100 A.) The motor circuit conductors are found to be 2/0 THW, with an ampacity of 175 A. Since ⅓ × 175 = 58 A, the No. 6 THW, with an ampacity of 65 A, should be used.

If these conductors are connected to the load terminals of the motor controller, the overload protection heaters may have to be changed (or if the OL is adjustable, its setting may have to be reduced), because the capacitor will cause a reduction in line current and adjustment of relay setting is required by Sec. 460-9.

Although part **(b)** of the rule requires overcurrent protection (fuses or a CB) in each ungrounded conductor connecting a capacitor assembly to a circuit, the Exception considers the motor-running overload relay in a starter to be adequate protection for the conductors when they are connected to the motor circuit on the load side of the starter. Where separate overcurrent protection is provided, as required for line-side connection, the device must simply be rated "as low as practicable." When a capacitor is thrown on the line, it may momentarily draw an excess current. A rating or setting of 250 percent of the capacitor current rating will provide short-circuit protection. Being a fixed load, a capacitor does not need overload protection such as is necessary for a motor.

Most power capacitors are factory equipped with fuses which provide protection in case of an internal short circuit. These fuses are usually rated from 165 percent to 250 percent of the rated kilovar current to allow for maximum operating conditions and momentary current surges. When installed on the load side of a motor starter, as noted above, capacitors do not require additional fusing. However, for bank installations, separate fuses are required.

Part **(c)** of the rule requires a disconnecting means for all the ungrounded conductors connecting a capacitor assembly to the circuit—but a disconnect is not needed when the capacitor is connected on the load side of a starter with overload protection. The disconnect must be rated at least equal to 1.35 times the rated current of the capacitor.

Note that part **(c)(2)** requires a multipole switching device for the disconnect. This is a direct reversal from the former statement that "The disconnecting means shall *not* be required to open all ungrounded conductors simultaneously." This change was made because of the inherent danger of single-pole switching of low-voltage capacitors. Normal switching or closing on faults may cause arcs or splattering of molten metal.

Two accepted methods of wiring capacitors are illustrated in Fig. 460-8. Diagram A shows method of connection at a central location, such as at a power center or on busway feeder. In such an installation, the **Code** rule requires an overcurrent device in each ungrounded conductor, a separate disconnecting means, and discharge resistor (usually furnished with capacitors). Current rating of both the capacitor disconnect switch and the conductors supplying the capacitor must be not less than 135 percent of the rated current of the capacitor. In B, the capacitor is connected directly to motor terminals. Installation on load side of motor starter eliminates need for separate overcurrent protection and separate disconnecting means. However, motor-running overcurrent protection must take into account lower running current of motor, as required by Sec. 460-9.

460·9. Rating or Setting of Motor Overload Device.   When a power-factor capacitor is connected to a motor circuit at the motor—i.e., on the load or motor side of the motor controller—the reactive current drawn by the motor is provided by the capacitor and, as a result, the total current flowing in the motor circuit up to the capacitor is reduced to a value below the normal full-load current of the motor. With that hookup, the total motor full-load current flows only over the conductors from the capacitor connection to the motor and the entire

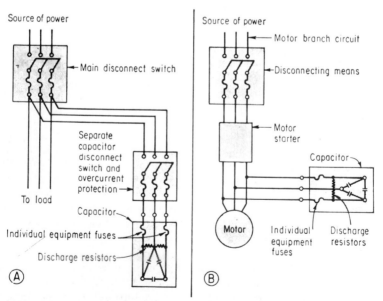

Fig. 460·8. PF capacitor assembly may be connected on the line or load side of a starter. (Sec. 460-8.)

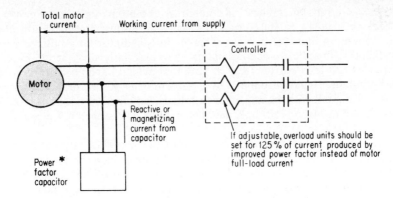

TOTAL MOTOR CURRENT = VECTOR SUM OF REACTIVE AND WORKING CURRENTS

EXAMPLE: Motor with 70% power factor has full-load current of 143 amps. Capacitor corrects to 100% PF.

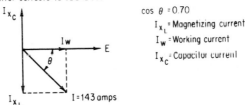

$\cos \theta = 0.70$

I_{x_L} = Magnetizing current

I_w = Working current

I_{x_C} = Capacitor current

I_{x_C} cancels I_{x_L} leaving only working current to be supplied from circuit. Working current = $143 \times \cos \theta$ = $143 \times 0.70 = 100$

OVERLOAD RELAYS SHOULD BE SET FOR 125% OF 100 AMPS

* The rating of such capacitors should not exceed the value required to raise the no-load power factor of the motor to unity. Capacitors of these maximum ratings usually result in a full-load power factor of 95 to 98 percent.

Fig. 460-9. Motor overload protection must be sized for the current at improved PF. (Sec. 460-9.)

motor circuit up to that connection carries only the so-called "working current" or "resistive current." That is shown in the top part of Fig. 460-9.

Under the condition shown, it is obvious that setting the overload relay in the starter for 125 percent of the motor nameplate full-load current (as required by Sec. 430-32) would actually be an excessive setting for real protection of the motor, because considerably less than full-load current is flowing through the starter. The rule of this section clearly requires that the rating of a motor overload protective device connected on the line side of a power-factor correction capacitor must be based on 125 percent (or other percentage from Sec. 430-32) times the circuit current produced by the improved power-factor—rather than the motor full-load current (see Fig. 460-9).

The 25-kvar capacitor used on the 100-hp, 460-V motor in the example in Sec.

460-8 will reduce the motor line current by about 9 percent. Section 430-32(a) (also Secs. 430-34 and 460-9) requires that the running overload protection be sized not more than 125 percent of motor full-load current produced with the capacitor. If the OL protection heaters were originally sized at 125 percent of the motor full-load current (1.25 × 121), they would have been sized at 151 A. With the motor current reduced by 9 percent (0.09 × 121, or 11 A), the motor full-load current with the capacitor installed would be 121 − 11 or 110 A. Since 125 percent of 110 A is 137.5 A, the heaters must be changed to a size not larger than 137.5 A.

If the capacitor conductors could be connected on the line side of the heaters, the heaters would not have to be reduced in size, since the reduction of line current occurs only from the source back to the point of the capacitor connection. Conductor connections at this location are extremely difficult to make because of the lack of space and the large size of the connecting lugs. Controller load terminals are furnished with connectors that will accept an additional conductor, or they can be easily modified to permit a dependable connection.

460·10. Grounding.   The metal case of a capacitor is suitably grounded by locknut and bushing connections of grounded metal nipples or raceways carrying the conductors connecting the capacitor into a motor circuit or feeder.

ARTICLE 470. RESISTORS AND REACTORS

470·1. Scope.   Except when installed in connection with switchboards or control panels that are so located that they are suitably guarded from physical damage and accidental contact with live parts, resistors should always be completely enclosed in properly ventilated metal boxes.

Large reactors are commonly connected in series with the main leads of large generators or the supply conductors from high-capacity network systems to assist in limiting the current delivered on short circuit. Small reactors are used with lightning arresters, the object here being to offer a high impedance to the passage of a high-frequency lightning discharge and so to aid in directing the discharge to ground. Another type of reactor, having an iron core and closely resembling a transformer, is used as a remote-control dimmer for stage lighting. Reactors as well as resistors are sources of heat and should therefore be mounted in the same manner as resistors.

ARTICLE 480. STORAGE BATTERIES

480·1. Scope.   Storage cells are of two general types: the so-called lead-acid type, in which the positive plates consist of lead grids having openings filled with a semisolid component, commonly lead peroxide, and the negative plates are covered with sponge lead, the plates being immersed in dilute sulfuric acid; and the alkali type, in which the active materials are nickel peroxide for the

Fig. 480-1. Article 480 applies only to "stationary installations of storage batteries"—whether they are used for supply to lighting, generator cranking, switchgear control, or in UPS (Uninterruptible Power Supply) systems. (Sec. 480-1.)

positive plate and iron oxide for the negative plate, and the electrolyte is chiefly potassium hydroxide (Fig. 480-1).

480-2. Definitions. "Stationary installations of storage batteries" provide an independent source of power for emergency lighting, switchgear control, engine-generator set starting, signal and communications systems, laboratory power, and similar applications. They are an essential component of UPS systems. This Code article does not cover batteries used to supply the motive power for electric vehicles.

The most commonly used battery is the lead-acid type—either lead-antimony or lead-calcium. Nickel-cadmium batteries offer a variety of special features that, in many instances, offset their higher initial cost. Other types include silver-zinc, silver-cadmium, and mercury batteries.

The *lead-antimony battery* is readily available at a moderate price, has a high efficiency (85 percent to 90 percent), is comparatively small, and has a relatively long life if operated and maintained properly under normal conditions. Voltage output is about 2 V per cell; ratings range to about 1,000 amp-hr (based on an 8-hr discharge rate).

Lead-calcium batteries offer features similar to the lead-antimony type, and they require less maintenance. They do not require an "equalizing" charge (application of an overvoltage for a period of time to assure that all cells in a battery bank will produce the same voltage). For this reason, they are often selected for use in UPS systems.

This type of cell can usually be operated for a year or more without needing water, depending on the frequency and degree of discharge. Sealed or maintenance-free batteries of this type never need water. Voltage output is 2 V per cell, with ratings up to about 200 amp-hr (8-hr rate).

Nickel-cadmium batteries are particularly useful for application in temperature extremes. They are reputed to have been successfully operated at temperatures from −40°F to +163°F. They have a very high short-time current capability and are well suited to such applications as engine starting and UPS operation. Initial cost is higher than lead-acid types; however, they offer long life (25 to 30 years), reliability, and small size per unit. Voltage is about 1.2 V per cell.

480-3. Wiring and Equipment Supplied from Batteries.   As indicated in Fig. 480-2, whatever kinds of circuits and loads a battery bank serves, all rules of the NE Code covering operation at that voltage must be applied to the wiring and equipment.

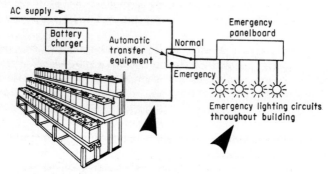

Fig. 480-2. Applicable Code rules must be observed for load circuits fed by batteries. (Sec. 480-3.)

480-6. Insulation of Batteries of Over 250 Volts.   Racks of adjacent batteries must be so placed as to have a minimum of 2 in. of air space between any pair of exposed, live battery terminals of opposite polarity.

480-8. Battery Locations.   Although specific "battery rooms" or enclosures are no longer required for installation of any batteries (not since the 1971 NE Code), part **(a)** does require ventilation at battery locations. A specific "battery room" was previously required for open-tank or open-jar batteries, but such units are no longer made or in use.

The overcharging of a battery can result in the breaking down of the electrolyte into gases that, if permitted to accumulate in the room, may result in an explosive mixture. Overcharging indicates problems with the charging equipment requiring correction. Proper ventilation will resolve this explosive mixture, assuring that the location is not a hazardous location subject to Art. 501.

Because the fumes given off by a storage battery are very corrosive, the type of wiring must be such that it will withstand the corrosive action, and special precautions are necessary as to the type of insulation used, as well as protection of all metalwork. It is stated by the respective manufacturers that conduit made of aluminum or Everdur (silicon-bronze) is well suited to withstand the corrosive effects of the fumes in battery rooms. If steel conduit is used, it is recommended that the conduit be zinc-coated and that it be kept well painted with asphaltum paint.

Batteries of the lead-acid type sometimes throw off a fine spray of the dilute acid which fills the air around the cells; hence steel conduit or tubing should not be brought close to any cell.

There are no special requirements on the type of fixtures or other electrical equipment used in the battery room. Proper ventilation of the room will prevent explosions. See Secs. 300-6 and 410-4(b).

Chapter Five

ARTICLE 500. HAZARDOUS (CLASSIFIED) LOCATIONS

500-1. Scope—Articles 500 Through 504. In the heading of this article, the word "classified" makes clear that hazardous locations are those which have been "classified" as hazardous by the inspection authority. Hazardous locations in plants and other industrial complexes are involved with a wide variety of flammable gases and vapors and ignitible dusts—all of which have widely different flash points, ignition temperatures, and flammable limits. And these explosive or flammable substances are processed and handled under a wide range of operating conditions. In such places, fire or explosion could result in loss of lives, facilities, and/or production.

500-2. Location and General Requirements. Classification of hazardous areas must be approached very carefully, based on experience and a detailed understanding of electrical usage in the various kinds of locations. After study and analysis—and consultation with inspection authorities or other experts in such work—hazardous areas may be identified and delineated diagrammatically by defining the limits and degree of the hazards involved. In all cases, classification must be carefully based on the type of gas involved, whether the vapors are heavier or lighter than air, and similar factors peculiar to the particular hazardous substance.

Locations used for pyrophoric gases, which ignite spontaneously on contact with air, are exempted from designation as Class I hazardous locations. Electrical equipment approved for classified locations is not needed for places where pryophoric gases are handled.

Classification takes into account that all sources of hazards—gas, vapor, dust, fibers—have different ignition temperatures and produce different pressures when exploding. Electrical equipment must, therefore, be constructed and

995

installed in such a way as to be safe when used in the presence of particular explosive mixtures. The source of hazard must be evaluated in terms of those characteristics that are involved with explosion or fire, as follows:

Diesel Oil and Heating Oil

Questions often arise about the need for hazardous location wiring for electrical equipment installed in areas containing diesel fuel oil or heating oil. National Fire Codes (NFC), Vol. 3, classifies diesel fuel oil as a Class II liquid having a flash point at or above 100°F (37.8°C) and below 140°F (60°C). Chapter 6 of the same NFC Vol. 3 on bulk plants, paragraph 6-5-.1, states in part that in areas where Class II or Class III liquids are stored or handled, the electrical equipment *may be* installed in accordance with the provisions of the **NEC** for ordinary (i.e., nonhazardous) locations. Diesel fuel oil is classified as a Class II liquid and does not come under requirements for hazardous (classified) locations. With this type of liquid, explosionproof wiring methods *are not* required and tl ₂ wiring methods listed in Chaps. 1-4 of the **NEC** may be used. The NFC does, however, caution that, if any Class II flammable liquid is heated, it may be necessary that Class I Group D wiring methods be used. In some geographic areas with hot climates, local regulations do require diesel fuel areas to be treated as hazardous areas because of high ambient temperatures. Temperatures in the Southwest often exceed 115°F, especially in closed, nonventilated areas.

Flash point of a liquid is the minimum temperature at which the liquid will give off sufficient vapor to form an ignitible mixture with air near the surface of the liquid or within the vessel used. (This characteristic is not applicable to gases.)

Ignition temperature of a substance is the lowest temperature which will initiate explosion or cause self-sustained combustion of the substance.

Explosive limits: When flammable gases or vapors mix with air or oxygen, there is a minimum concentration of the gas or vapor below which propagation of flame does not occur upon contact with a source of ignition. There is also a maximum concentration above which propagation does not occur. These boundary-line mixtures are known as the lower and upper explosive (or flammable) limits and usually are expressed in terms of the percentage of gas or vapor in air, by volume. (See NFPA Bulletin No. 325M.)

Vapor density is the weight of a volume of pure vapor or gas (with no air present) compared to the weight of an equal volume of dry air at the same temperature and pressure.

Section 500-2 recognizes use of "intrinsically safe" equipment in hazardous locations and exempts such equipment from the rules of Arts. 500 through 517. Intrinsic safety is obtained by restricting the energy available in an electrical system to much less than that required for the ignition of flammable atmospheres such as gases and vapors that exist in processing industries. Intrinsically safe systems operate at low voltage (e.g., 24 V) and are designed safe, regardless of short circuits, grounding, overvoltage, equipment damage, or component failure. But such equipment must be "approved," which requires careful attention to UL listing and application data from the *Hazardous Location Equipment Directory* of UL.

Any applications of "intrinsically safe apparatus" in Class I, II, or III locations must satisfy the rules of Art. 504 covering such apparatus. In this Section the reference to new Art. 504 notes that the "provisions of Article 501 through 503 and 510 through 516 shall not be considered applicable" to intrinsically safe apparatus and wiring "except as required by Article 504."

Intrinsically safe circuits and equipment for use in Division 1 locations must be carefully applied. It is up to the designer and/or the installer to be sure that the energy level available in such equipment is below the level that could ignite the particular hazardous atmosphere. That must be assured for both normal and abnormal conditions of the equipment. Testing of an intrinsically safe system by UL is based on a maximum distance of 5,000 ft between the equipment installed in the nonhazardous or Division 2 location and the equipment installed in the Division 1 location.

Wiring of intrinsically safe circuits must be run in separate raceways or otherwise separated from circuits for all other equipment to prevent imposing excessive current or voltage on the intrinsically safe circuits because of fault contact with the other circuits.

A note in this section: Maximum effort should be made to keep as much electrical equipment as possible out of the hazardous areas—particularly minimizing installation of arcing, sparking, and high-temperature devices in hazardous locations. It is generally economically and operationally better to keep certain electrical equipment out of hazardous areas. Figure 500-1 shows an example.

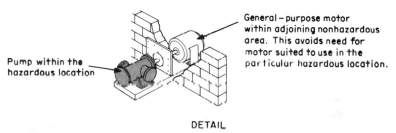

Pump within the
hazardous location

General – purpose motor
within adjoining nonhazardous
area. This avoids need for
motor suited to use in the
particular hazardous location.

DETAIL

Fig. 500-1. Keeping electrical equipment in nonhazardous area eliminates costly hazardous types. (Sec. 500-2.)

There the drive shaft of the motor is extended through a packing gland in one of the enclosing walls. To prevent the accumulation of flammable vapors or gas within the motor room, it should be ventilated effectively by clean air or kept under a slight positive air pressure. A gas detector giving a visual and/or audible alarm would be an additional desirable safety feature.

Positive-pressure ventilation is also cited as a means of reducing the level of hazard in areas where explosive or flammable substances are or might be present. Air-pressurized building interiors can provide safe operation without explosionproof equipment. When explosionproof equipment is not justified financially, pressurized building interiors can alter the need. For example, if a motor control center is to be located in a building in a Class I hazardous location, the entire room may be pressurized. But construction must comply with certain specific requirements:

1. The building area or room must be kept as airtight as possible.
2. The interior space must be kept under slight overpressure by adequate positive-pressure ventilation from a source of clean air.
3. The pressurizing fans should be connected to an emergency supply circuit.
4. Ventilating louvers must be located near ground level to achieve effective air flow within the pressurized room.
5. Safeguards against ventilation failure must be provided.

Purging of electrical raceways and enclosures is another means of reducing the degree of hazard (Fig. 500-2). But that requires both the manufacturer and the user of purged equipment to ensure the integrity of the system. Prepackaged purge controls for both Division 1 and Division 2 locations are on the market.

Fig. 500-2. A seal fitting (upper arrow) is used for equipment enclosure. But nitrogen purging of the conduit system was also applied at this installation at a space-rocket launch-pad. Equipment was specified to be listed for Class I, Division 1, Group B where exposed to hydrogen and for Group D where the equipment was in a rocket-fuel atmosphere. Where motors, panelboards, enclosures, etc., were not available in the proper Group rating, nitrogen purging and pressurization were used in addition to sealing, to add another measure of safety. The valve (lower arrow) was used in the cover of each conduit body to provide continuous bleedoff of the nitrogen to maintain a pressure (2-in. of water) within the conduit, enabling the steady flow of nitrogen to keep the conduit free of any explosive mixture. (Sec. 500-2.)

The purging medium—such as inert gas, like nitrogen, or clean air—must be essentially free from dust and liquids. The normal ambient air of an industrial interior is usually not satisfactory. And because the purge supply can contain only trace amounts of flammable vapors or gases, the compressor intake must be in a nonhazardous area. The compressor intake line should not pass through a hazardous atmosphere. If it does, it must be made of a noncombustible material, be protected from damage and corrosion, and must prevent hazardous vapors from being drawn into the compressor.

500-3. Special Precaution.　Because of the inherently higher level of danger, design and installation of electrical circuits and systems in hazardous locations must be done in particularly strict compliance with the instructions given in product standards. Although **NE Code** Sec. 110-3(b) requires all product applications to conform to the conditions and limitations specified in the directories issued by third-party testing labs (UL, Factory Mutual, ETL, etc.), the correlation of hazardous location electrical equipment is much more thoroughly dictated than that in nonhazardous areas.

1. Section 500-3 requires that construction and installation of equipment in all hazardous areas "will ensure safe performance under conditions of proper use and maintenance." A note urges designers, installers, inspectors, and maintenance personnel to "exercise more than ordinary care" for hazardous location work. The fine-print notes designate the various groups of hazardous locations. Explanatory material describes the nature of various hazardous atmospheres.

2. Paragraph **(a)** of this section requires that all equipment in hazardous locations be approved not only for the class of location (such as Class I, Class II, or Class III) but also for the particular type of hazardous atmosphere (such as Group A, B, C, or D for locations involving gases or vapors, or Group E, F, or G if the atmosphere involves combustible or flammable dusts). The **Code** section describes the specific atmospheres that correspond to those letter designations.

   An important regulation is given in the third paragraph of Sec. 500-3(a), which permits use of "general-purpose equipment" or "equipment in general-purpose enclosures" in Division 2 conditions of Class I, Class II, or Class III locations. That rule permits equipment that is *not* listed for hazardous locations but is listed for general use—BUT such use is acceptable only where a **Code** rule specifically mentions such application. For instance, Sec. 501-4(b) does say that boxes and fittings in Class I, Division 2 locations do *not* have to be explosionproof type; i.e., sheetmetal boxes could be used. But controversy arises over that third paragraph of Sec. 500-3(a) because general-use enclosures are permitted only where the equipment does not pose a threat of ignition "under *normal* operating conditions." Division 2 locations, however, *are* those where the hazardous atmosphere is not present under normal operating conditions. So the last phrase of the **Code** rule seems to be superfluous, unless the phrase "normal operating conditions" is meant to apply to the equipment itself instead of the surrounding atmosphere. Equipment that is operating normally might not pose a threat of ignition, but a ground fault or short in the equipment—which is *not* a "normal operating condition"—could ignite a combustible atmosphere that might exist at a Division 2 location. The **Code** rule here is obscure.

3. In addition to being "approved" for the class and group of the hazardous area where it is installed, equipment is required by paragraph **(b)** of Sec. 500-3 to be "marked" with that data, along with its operating temperature

when used in an ambient not over 40°C. Table 500-3(b) gives identification numbers that are used on equipment nameplates to show the operating temperature for which the equipment is approved.

Position of OSHA

With respect to equipment approval, great care must be taken to understand clearly the rules on hazardous locations equipment as covered in the electrical standards of the Occupational Safety and Health Administration (OSHA) of the U.S. Department of Labor. Those rules constitute federal law on this matter.

In the present OSHA standard, Sec. 1910.307 Hazardous (Classified) Locations is listed as one of the totally retroactive sections that apply to all electrical systems—both new ones and old ones, no matter when they were installed. On the matter of acceptability or approval of equipment used in hazardous locations, Sec. 1910.307(b) says:

> Equipment, wiring methods, and installations of equipment in classified locations shall be intrinsically safe, approved for the hazardous (classified) location, or safe for the hazardous (classified) location. Requirements for each of these options are as follows:
>
> **(1) Intrinsically safe.** Equipment and associated wiring approved as intrinsically safe shall be permitted in any hazardous (classified) location for which it is approved.
>
> **(2) Approved for the hazardous (classified) location.** [i]Equipment shall be approved not only for the class of location but also for the ignitible or combustible properties of the specific gas, vapor, dust, or fiber that will be present.
>
> **Note**—NFPA 70, the **National Electrical Code** lists or defines hazardous gases, vapors, and dusts by "Groups" characterized by their ignitible or combustible properties.
>
> [ii] Equipment shall be marked to show the class, group, and operating temperature or temperature range, based on operation in a 40°C ambient, for which it is approved. The temperature marking shall not exceed the ignition temperature of the specific gas or vapor to be encountered. However, the following provisions modify this marking requirement for specific equipment:
>
> (a) Equipment of the non-heat-producing type, such as junction boxes, conduit, and fittings, and equipment of the heat-producing type having a maximum temperature not more than 100°C (212°F), need not have a marked operating temperature or temperature range.
>
> (b) Fixed lighting fixtures marked for use in Class I, Div. 2 locations only, need not be marked to indicate the group.
>
> (c) Fixed general-purpose equipment in Class I locations, other than lighting fixtures, which is acceptable for use in Class I, Div. 2 locations need not be marked with the class, group, division, or operating temperatures.
>
> (d) Fixed dust-tight equipment, other than lighting fixtures, which is acceptable for use in Class II, Div. 2 and Class III locations need not be marked with the class, group, division, or operating temperature.
>
> **(3) Safe for the hazardous (classified) location.** Equipment which is safe for the location shall be of a type and design which the employer demonstrates will provide protection from the hazards arising from the combustibility and flammability of vapors, liquids, gases, dusts, or fibers.

Those regulations apply to *all* electrical installations in hazardous locations— both new and existing systems. Note that there are actually *three* alternative ways for equipment to be acceptable for use in hazardous locations. A piece of equipment is acceptable if it is "Intrinsically safe" or "Approved for the hazardous (classified) location" or "Safe for the hazardous (classified) location." A piece of equipment would only have to satisfy one of the three conditions described in the rule.

The three alternative conditions can be verified as follows:

"*Intrinsically safe*" equipment must be "approved" as such by UL, Factory Mutual Corporation, or some nationally recognized testing laboratory. In the UL *Hazardous Location Equipment Directory,* listings of various product categories indicate which equipment is intrinsically safe and the class and group of hazardous locations for which they are approved. Such equipment is evaluated and listed in accordance with Standard UL913, Intrinsically Safe Apparatus and Associated Apparatus for Use in Class I, II and III, Division 1, Hazardous Locations. Another source of information on the subject is Installation of Intrinsically Safe Instrument Systems in Class I Hazardous Locations (ANSI/ISA RP12.6-1976).

"*Approved for the hazardous (classified) location*" equipment is basically "listed" and "labeled" equipment certified by a nationally recognized testing laboratory—such as equipment covered in the UL *Hazardous Location Equipment Directory.*

"*Safe for the hazardous (classified) location*" equipment is a category that becomes much more difficult to identify by firm, specific criteria. Just how does an "employer demonstrate" that equipment is safe for a hazardous location application? Although the OSHA rules themselves do not address that question anywhere, the introductory comments to the new OSHA standard as published in the *Federal Register* do state that "guidelines" for making such a judgment "are contained in Chap. 5 of the current **National Electrical Code** (NFPA 70). However, these guidelines are not the only means of complying with the standard. Any equipment or installation shown by the employer to provide protection from the hazards involved will be acceptable. This performance-oriented approach will allow the employer maximum flexibility in providing safety for his employees. Obviously, that is a very general and vague explanation that ultimately leaves determination of acceptability completely up to the OSHA compliance officer.

A clear effect of OSHA regulations is to require "listed," "labeled," "accepted," and/or "certified" equipment to be used whenever available. If any electrical system component is "of a kind" that any nationally recognized testing lab "accepts, certifies, lists, labels or determines to be safe," then that component must be so designated in order to be acceptable for use under OSHA regulations. Every electrical designer and installer must exercise great care in evaluating any and all equipment and products used in hazardous electrical work to assure compliance with OSHA rules requiring certification by a nationally recognized testing lab.

In UL's *Hazardous Location Equipment Directory* (Red Book), limitations and application conditions are first set down for all equipment in general, as follows:

1. When equipment is listed and marked to show that it has been tested and is recognized for use in one or more of the **Code**-designated groups of

hazardous locations, such marking indicates that such equipment is suitable for use in *either* Division 1 or Division 2 location of the particular class of hazardous location, even though no reference is made to the "division." Such equipment is, of course, also acceptable if used in a nonhazardous location. Figure 500-3 shows a typical nameplate used on such equipment, as required by parts **(a)** and **(b)** of Sec. 500-3, showing suitability as "explosion-proof" (Class I) and "dust-tight" (Class II).

Fig. 500-3. Typical UL part of equipment nameplate describes "Approval for Class and Properties." (Sec. 500-3.)

2. BUT, equipment that is marked "Division 2" or "Div. 2" is suitable for use in only such a division and may *not* be used in a Division 1 location. However, a piece of equipment may have other marking to indicate its acceptability for other specific uses. Figure 500-4 shows a nameplate that is an

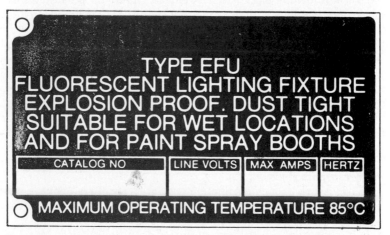

Fig. 500-4. Additional data on a nameplate may show other acceptability—as for "wet locations." (Sec. 500-3.)

addition to the nameplate in Fig. 500-3, noting that the same fixture is
"Suitable for Wet Locations." Section 410-4 of the NE Code requires such
marking on "all fixtures installed in wet locations. . . ." Care must be taken
to distinguish between different parts of nameplates to precisely determine what is third-party certification.

3. Equipment that is listed and marked for "Class I" locations (explosionproof) may be used for "Class II" locations if it is dusttight to exclude combustible dusts and if its external operating temperature is not at or above
the ignition level of the particular dust that might accumulate on it. Obviously, these characteristics must be carefully established before Class I
equipment is used in a Class II location.

4. Equipment listed for Class II, Group G (for flour, starch, or grain dust)—
as used in a grain elevator—is also generally suitable for use in Class III
locations, where combustible lint or flyings are present. The Exception
noted is for fan-cooled type motors which might have their air passages
choked or clogged by large amounts of the lint or flyings.

5. Because hazardous location equipment is critically dependent upon
proper operating temperature, a UL note warns that the ampere or wattage
marking on power-consuming equipment is based on the equipment being
supplied with voltage exactly equal to the rated voltage value. Voltage
higher or lower than the rated value will produce other than rated amps
or watts, with the possibility that heating effect of the current within the
equipment will be greater than normal. Higher than normal current will
be produced by overvoltage to resistive loads and by undervoltage to
induction motors. Because of this, actual circuit voltage, rather than the
nameplate value, must be used when calculating the required ampacity of
branch-circuit conductors, rating or setting of overcurrent protection, rating of disconnect, etc.—all to assure adequate sizing and avoid
overheating.

6. Hazardous location equipment is tested and listed for use at normal atmospheric pressure in an ambient temperature not over 40°C (104°F), unless
indicated otherwise. Use of equipment under higher-than-normal pressure, in oxygen-enriched atmospheres, or at higher ambient temperatures
can be dangerous. Such abnormal conditions may increase the chance of
igniting the hazardous atmosphere and may increase the pressure of
explosion within equipment.

7. Openings or modifications must not be made in explosionproof or dust-
ignition-proof equipment, because any such field alterations would void
the integrity and tested safety of the equipment. Field alteration of listed
products for nonhazardous application is also generally prohibited.

8. All bolts as well as all threaded parts of enclosures must be tightly made
up.

9. Indoor hazardous location equipment that is exposed to severe corrosive
conditions must be listed as suitable for those conditions as well as for the
hazardous conditions.

The requirements of Sec. 500-3 and Code Table 500-3(b) provide the means
of properly identifying and classifying equipment for use in hazardous loca-

tions. The identification numbers in **Code** Table 500-3(b) pertain to tempera-
ture-range classifications as used by Underwriters Laboratories Inc., in UL
Hazardous Location Standards.

While the **Code** rules for Class I locations do not differ for different kinds of
gas or vapor contained in the atmosphere, it is to be noted that it is necessary
to select equipment designed for use in the particular atmospheric group to be
encountered. This is necessary for the reason that explosive mixtures of the
different groups have different flash points and explosion pressures. It is also
necessary because the ignition temperatures vary with the groups of explosive
mixtures.

Underwriters Laboratories Inc. lists fittings and equipment as suitable for use
in all groups of Class I, although the listings for Groups A and B are not as
complete as those for Groups C and D.

In Class II locations the **Code**, in a few cases, differentiates between the different kinds of dust, particularly dusts which are electrically conductive and
those which are not conductive. Here again, as in Class I locations, care must
be used to determine that the equipment selected is suitable for use where a
particular kind of dust is present.

In addition to the use of more than ordinary care in selecting equipment for
use in hazardous locations, special attention should be given to installation and
maintenance details in order that the installations will be permanently free
from electrical hazards. In making subsequent additions or changes, the high
standards that were applied during the original installation must always be
maintained.

For a more thorough knowledge of specific hazardous areas and equipment
selection and location it is essential to obtain copies of the various NFPA and
ANSI standards referenced in Arts. 500 through 517.

500-5. Class I Locations.   In each of the three classes of hazardous locations
discussed in Secs. 500-5, 500-6, and 500-7, the **Code** recognizes varying degrees
of hazard; hence under each class two divisions are defined. In the installation
rules that follow, the requirements for Division 1 of each class are more rigid
than the requirements for Division 2.

Briefly, the hazards in the three classes of locations are due to the following
causes:

Class I, highly flammable gases or vapors
Class II, combustible dust
Class III, combustible fibers or flyings

The classifications are easily understood, and, if a given location is to be
classed as hazardous, it should not be difficult to determine in which of the
three classes it belongs. However, it is obviously impossible to make rules that
will in every case determine positively whether the location is or is not hazardous. Considerable common sense and good judgment must be exercised in
determining whether the location under consideration should be considered as
hazardous or likely to become hazardous because of a change in the processes
carried on, and if so, what portion of the premises should be classed as coming
under Division I and what part may safely be considered as being in Division 2.

ARTICLE 501. CLASS I LOCATIONS

501·1. General. The more common Class I locations are those where some process is carried on involving the use of a highly volatile and flammable liquid, such as gasoline, petroleum naphtha, benzene, diethyl ether, or acetone, or flammable gases.

In any Class I location, an explosive mixture of air and flammable gas or vapor may be present which can be caused to explode by an arc or spark. To avoid the danger of explosions all electrical apparatus which may create arcs or sparks should if possible be kept out of the rooms where the hazardous atmosphere exists, or, if this is not possible, such apparatus must be "of types approved for use in explosive atmospheres."

All equipment such as switches, CBs, or motors must have some movable operating part projecting through the enclosing case, and any such part, for example the operating lever of a switch or the shaft of a motor, must have sufficient clearance so that it will work freely; hence the equipment cannot be hermetically sealed. Also, the necessity for subsequent opening of the enclosures for servicing makes hermetic sealing impracticable. Furthermore, the enclosure of the equipment must be entered by a run of conduit, and it is practically impossible to make conduit joints absolutely air- and gastight. Due to slight changes in temperature, the conduit system and the apparatus enclosures "breathe"; that is, any flammable gas in the room may gradually find its way inside the conduit and enclosures and form an explosive mixture with air. Under this condition, when an arc occurs inside the enclosure an explosion may take place.

When the gas and air mixture explodes inside the enclosing case, the burning mixture must be confined entirely within the enclosure, so as to prevent the ignition of flammable gases in the room. In the first place it is necessary that the enclosing case be so constructed that it will have sufficient strength to withstand the high pressure generated by an internal explosion. The pressure in pounds per square inch produced by the explosion of a given gas-and-air mixture has been quite definitely determined, and the enclosure can be designed accordingly.

Since the enclosures for apparatus cannot be made absolutely tight, when an internal explosion occurs some of the burning gas will be forced out through any openings that exist. It has been found that the flame will not be carried out through an opening that is quite long in proportion to its width. This principle is applied in the design of so-called explosionproof enclosures for apparatus by providing a wide flange at the joint between the body and the cover of the enclosure and grinding these flanges to a definitely determined fit. In this case the flanges are so ground that when the cover is in place the clearance between the two surfaces will at no point exceed 0.0015 in. Thus, if an explosion occurs within the enclosure, in order to escape from the enclosure the burning gas must travel a considerable distance through an opening not more than 0.0015 in. wide.

The basic construction characteristics of equipment for Class I hazardous locations are detailed in various sections of this article and in standards of testing laboratories. Application of the products hinges on understanding those details:

An explosionproof enclosure for Class I locations is capable of withstanding an explosion of a specified gas or vapor which may occur within it and of preventing the ignition of the specified gas or vapor surrounding the enclosure by sparks, flashes, or explosions of the gas or vapor within. Explosionproof equipment must provide three things: (1) strength, (2) joints which will not permit flame or hot gases to escape, and (3) cool operation, to prevent ignition of surrounding atmosphere.

UL requires that explosionproof enclosures must withstand a hydrostatic test of four times the maximum explosion pressure developed inside the enclosure. Explosionproof enclosures are not vapor- or gastight and it is simply assumed that any hazardous gases in the ambient atmosphere will enter them either through normal breathing or when maintenance is performed on the enclosed equipment.

When an explosion occurs inside a rectangular explosionproof enclosure, the resulting force exerts pressure in all directions. The enclosure must be designed with sufficient strength to withstand these forces and avoid rupture (Fig. 501-1).

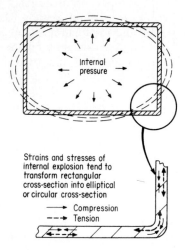

Fig. 501·1. An explosion creates strains and stresses in cross section of enclosure walls. (Sec. 501-1.)

The energy generated by an explosion within an enclosure must be permitted to dissipate through the joints of the enclosure under controlled conditions. There are two generally recognized joint designs intended to provide this control—threaded and flat:

1. Threaded construction of covers and other removable parts that have five full threads engaged produces a safe, flame-arresting, pressure-relieving joint. When an explosion occurs within a threaded enclosure, the flame and hot gases create an internal pressure against the cover, thus locking the threads and forcing the gases out through the path between the threaded surfaces. When the gases reach the outside hazardous atmosphere, they have been cooled by the heat-sink effect of the mass of metal,

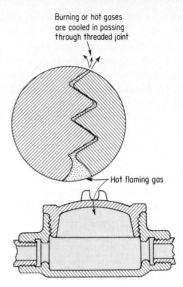

Fig. 501-2. Threaded joints cool the heated gas as it escapes from enclosure under pressure. (Sec. 501-1.)

down to a point below the ignition temperature of the outside atmosphere, as shown in Fig. 501-2.

2. A flat joint is constructed by accurate grinding or machining of the mating surfaces of the cover and the body. This flat joint works in a manner similar to the threaded joint. The two surfaces are bolted closely together, and as flame and hot gases are forced through the narrow opening, they are cooled by the mass of the metal enclosure, so that only cool gas enters the hazardous atmosphere. Figure 501-3 shows the flat joint and a variation on it called a "rabbet" joint. Care must be taken to assure that all cover

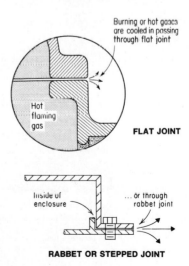

Fig. 501-3. Ground surfaces of flat or rabbet joint provide release and cooling of internal gases. (Sec. 501-1.)

screws are tight and that no particles of dirt or other foreign matter get in between the cover and the body. Even a small particle could prevent tight closing and might allow the joint to pass flame.

UL standards on explosionproof enclosures contain rules on "Grease for Joint Surfaces": "Paint or a sealing material shall not be applied to the contacting surfaces of a joint. A suitable corrosion inhibitor (grease) such as petrolatum, soap-thickened mineral oils, or nondrying slushing compound may be applied to the metal joint surfaces before assembly. The grease shall be of a type that does not harden because of aging, does not contain an evaporating solvent, and does not cause corrosion of the joint surfaces."

501·4. Wiring Methods. Threaded steel intermediate metal conduit has been added to the wiring methods suitable for use in Class I, Division 1 locations. This permission, plus recognition by other sections of the **Code**, gives IMC full recognition as a general-purpose raceway equivalent in application to rigid metal conduit. Type MI cable is the only cable assembly that is permitted in Class I, Division 1 locations (Fig. 501-4).

The term "approved for the location" in paragraph **(a)** means that approval is to be based on the performance of a fitting or equipment when subjected to a specific atmosphere. As applied to rigid metal conduit, to be explosionproof,

Fig. 501·4. Type MI cable is recognized for use in Class I, Division 1 locations, provided that the termination fittings (arrow) are listed as suitable for hazardous location use. (Sec. 501-4.)

threaded joints must be used at couplings, and for connection to fittings the threads must be cleanly cut, five full threads must be engaged, and each joint must be made up tight. Conduit elbows and short-radius capped elbows provide for 90° bends in conduit but only where wires may be guided when being pulled into the conduit, to prevent damaging the conductors by pulling them around the sharp turn in the elbow. Figure 501-5 shows two types of fittings

90°
CONDUIT
ELBOW

CAPPED
ELBOW

ELBOW
CONDUIT BODY

Fig. 501-5. Conduit elbows and similar fittings may be used where wires may be guided into conduit. (Sec. 501-4.)

used in hazardous locations to facilitate pull-in of conductors that have stiff or heavy-wall insulation. The capped elbow is especially suited to use in tight quarters.

All fittings, such as outlet boxes, junction boxes, and switch boxes, also all enclosures for apparatus, should have threaded hubs to receive the conduit and must be explosionproof. Explosionproof junction boxes are available in a wide variety of types (Fig. 501-6). Box covers may have threaded connections with the boxes, or the cover may be attached with machine screws, in which case a carefully ground flanged joint is required.

Fig. 501-6. A wide assortment of boxes, conduit bodies, fittings, and other enclosures are made in explosionproof designs listed for use in Class I locations. (Sec. 501-4.)

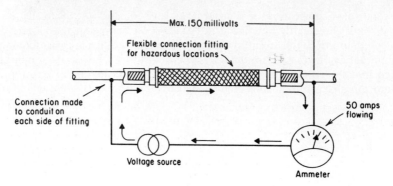

Voltage drop across fitting must not exceed 150 millivolts, measured between points on conduit ¹⁄₁₆ in. from each end of the fitting.

Fig. 501-7. Conductivity of flexible fitting is evaluated by voltage-drop test. (Sec. 501-4.)

A flexible, explosionproof fitting, suitable for use in Class I hazardous locations, is shown in Fig. 501-7. The flexible portion consists of a tube of bronze having deeply corrugated walls and reinforced by a braid of fine bronze wires. A heavy threaded fitting is securely joined to each end of the flexible tube, and a fibrous tubular lining, similar to "circular loom," is provided in order to prevent abrasion of the enclosed conductors that might result from long-continued vibration. The complete assembly is obtainable in various lengths up to a maximum of 3 ft.

Flexible connection fittings that are recognized by **NE Code** Sec. 501-4(a) for use in Class I, Division 1 locations are intended by UL and the **NE Code** to be used where it is necessary to provide flexible connections in threaded rigid conduit systems—as at motor terminals. Use of such flexible fittings must observe the minimum inside radius of bend for which the fitting has been tested. Those data are provided with the fitting.

Note: The UL warns that acceptability of the use of flexible connection fittings must be cleared with local inspection authorities. In general, use of such flexible fittings should be avoided wherever possible and should be limited to situations where use of threaded rigid conduit is completely ruled out by the needs or conditions of the application.

Where flexible connection fittings *are* used, the corrugated metal inner wall and the metal braid construction of the fitting provide equipment grounding continuity between the end connectors and the fitting. The UL test for conductivity through a flexible fitting is shown in Fig. 501-7. Although Sec. 501-16(b) requires either an internal or external bonding jumper to be used with standard flexible metal conduit in Class I, Division 2 locations, that rule does not apply to listed flexible fittings.

At the end of part **(a)**, the exception to the normal wiring methods required in Class I, Division 1 locations indicates that Sec. 501-11 permits flexible cord in Class I, Division 1 locations for portable lighting equipment and portable utilization equipment. This Exception eliminates a long-time conflict between the clear and direct rules of Sec. 501-4(a) on wiring methods and the limited use of portable cord as an alternative to the wiring methods used for fixed wiring. For this, refer to Sec. 516-3 covering places where flammable materials are used for spraying, dipping, and coating—in which applications flexible cord might be used.

In Class I, Division 2 locations explosionproof outlet boxes are not required at lighting outlets nor at junction boxes containing no arcing device. However, where conduit is used, it should enter the box through threaded openings as shown in Fig. 501-6, or if locknut-bushing attachment is used, a bonding jumper and/or fittings must be provided between the box and conduits, as required in Sec. 501-16(b).

As noted in part **(b)** of this section, flexible connections permitted in Class I, Division 2 locations may consist of flexible conduit (Greenfield) with approved fittings, and such fittings are not required to be specifically approved for Class I locations. It should be noted that a separate grounding conductor is necessary to bond across such flexible connections, as required in Sec. 501-16(b).

Ordinary knockout-type boxes may be installed in such locations, but Sec. 501-16(b) rules out the use of locknuts and bushings for bonding purposes, and the requirement specifies either bonding jumpers or other approved means (such as bonding locknuts on knockouts without any concentric or eccentric rings left in the wall of the enclosure) to assure adequate grounding from the hazardous area to the point of grounding at the services.

Cord connectors for connecting extra-hard-service type of flexible cord to devices in hazardous locations must be carefully applied. Section 501-4(b) permits extra-hard-usage flexible cord in Division 2 locations. But Sec. 502-4 permits its use in Division 1 and Division 2 areas of Class II locations. Section 503-3(a) (2) permits cords in Class III, Division 1 and Division 2 locations. Listed cord connectors are recognized for use in Class I, Groups A, B, C, and D or Class II, Group G locations—using Types S, SO, ST, or STO multiconductor, extra-hard-usage cord *with* a grounding conductor.

IMPORTANT! Section 501-4(b) adds power-limited tray cable (Type PLTC) to the list of wiring methods permitted in Class I, Division 2 locations, in accordance with the provisions of Art. 725 covering remote-control, signaling, and low-energy circuits. And, the last paragraph of Sec. 501-4(b) makes clear that high-voltage circuits (i.e., circuits over 600 V) may employ the wiring methods covered in the first part of Sec. 501-4(b) and, where protected from physical damage, may be made up using metallic-shielded, high-voltage cable in cable trays when installed in accordance with Art. 318. And Art. 326 dictates that such cable must be Type MV cable.

Armored cable (Type AC) and liquidtight flexible nonmetallic conduit have been added as acceptable wiring methods in Class I, Division 2 locations. Armored cable has a construction that is considered to be similar to flexible metal conduit, which is already permitted in these locations. It seems clear that the reference to "armored cable" is to Type AC (so-called "BX"), which is the **NEC** designation for "armored cable." Type MC (so-called "metalclad cable" within the **NEC**) has long been acceptable.

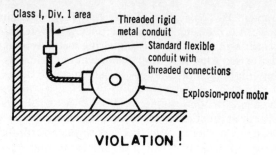

VIOLATION!

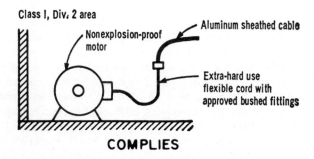

COMPLIES

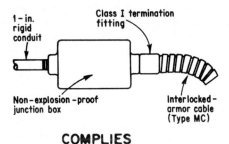

COMPLIES

Fig. 501·8. Wiring methods in Class I locations are clearly regulated. (Sec. 501-4.)

Figure 501-8 shows some applications of wiring methods that are covered by the rules of Sec. 501-4. At top, use of standard flex (Greenfield) in a Division 1 area violates part **(a)** of this section. At center, use of aluminum-sheathed cable (Type ALS) is OK in a Division 2 area. Even though Type ALS is no longer mentioned in part **(b)**, that type of cable is now covered by Art. 334 and is considered as one form of Type MC cable, which is mentioned in part **(b)** as acceptable in Division 2 areas. At bottom, use of Type MC is OK in a Division 2 location.

501·5. Sealing and Drainage.   The proper sealing of conduits in Class I locations is an important matter. In Class I, Division 2 locations, each piece of apparatus that produces arcs or sparks, such as a motor controller, switch, or receptacle, should be isolated from all other apparatus by sealing within the conduit so that an explosion in one enclosure cannot be communicated through the conduit to any other enclosure. Whether used in an enclosure or in conduit, seals are necessary to prevent gases, vapors, or flames from being propagated into an enclosure or conduit run and to confine an explosion that might occur within an enclosure.

The note after the first paragraph points out that seal fittings properly installed are not normally capable of preventing the passage of liquids, gases, or vapors if there is a continuous pressure differential across the seal. However, as indicated, seals may be specifically designed and tested for preventing such passage. This explanation, along with the wording in such rules as Sec. 501-5(a)(4), makes clear that seals will only "minimize," not "prevent," passage of gases or vapors through the seal.

When an explosion takes place within an enclosure because of arc ignition of gas or vapor that has entered the enclosure, flames and hot gases could travel rapidly through unsealed conduits, and the resultant buildup of pressure could exceed the strength of conduit, wireways, or enclosures, causing explosive rupture. *Pressure piling* is the name given to the action that takes place when an explosion occurs inside an enclosure because of flammable gas within the enclosure being ignited by a spark or overheated wiring. When this happens, and there are no seals in the conduits connecting to the enclosure, exploding gas will compress the entire atmosphere within the conduit system and flames or heat will ignite compressed gas some distance down the conduit and cause another, more-powerful explosion. The pressure and succeeding explosions are repeated through the system of raceways and enclosures, with each succeeding explosion increasing in intensity. To prevent such occurrences, it is mandatory that seal-off fittings be used in certain enclosures or conduit runs to block and confine potentially hazardous vapors.

The necessary sealing may be accomplished by inserting in the conduit runs special sealing fittings, as shown in Fig. 501-9, or provision may be made for sealing in the enclosure for the apparatus. An explosionproof motor is made with the leads sealed where they pass from the terminal housing to the interior of the motor, and no other seal is needed where a conduit terminates at the

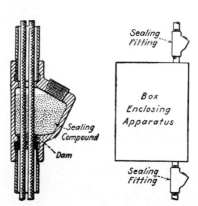

Fig. 501-9. Seal fitting is filled with compound to prevent passage of flame or vapor through the conduit. (Sec. 501-5.)

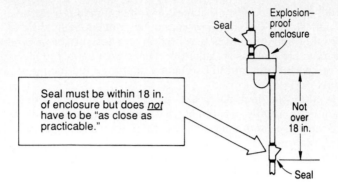

Seal must be within 18 in. of enclosure but does _not_ have to be "as close as practicable."

Seal
Explosion–proof enclosure

Not over 18 in.

Seal

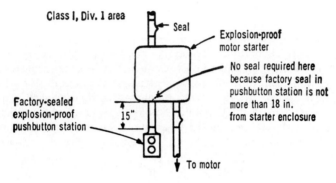

Class I, Div. 1 area

Seal

Explosion-proof motor starter

No seal required here because factory seal in pushbutton station is not more than 18 in. from starter enclosure

Factory-sealed explosion-proof pushbutton station

15"

To motor

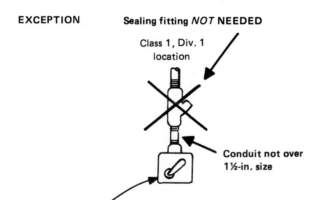

EXCEPTION   **Sealing fitting _NOT_ NEEDED**

Class 1, Div. 1 location

Conduit not over 1½-in. size

Explosion-proof enclosure for tumbler switch with mercury-tube contacts.

Fig. 501·10. Seal should be in each conduit within 18 in. of the sealed enclosure, center, but may not be needed at all, bottom. (Sec. 501-5.)

motor, except that if the conduit is 2 in. or larger in size, a seal must be provided not more than 18 in. from the motor terminal housing.

Class I, Division 1

Part **(a)** of this section covers mandatory use of seals in Class I, Division 1 locations:

1. A seal is required in each and every conduit (regardless of the size of the conduit) entering (or leaving) an enclosure that contains one or more switches, CBs, fuses, relays, resistors, or any other device that is capable of producing an arc or spark that could cause ignition of gas or vapor within the enclosure or any device that might operate hot enough to cause ignition. In each such conduit, a seal fitting must be placed never more than 18 in. from such enclosure. The **Code** rule has eliminated the phrase that said seals had to be installed "as close as practicable" to the enclosure—leaving the remainder of the requirement, that the seal must not be more than 18 in. from the enclosure, intact. As shown in Fig. 501-10, a conduit seal fitting is installed in the top conduit and one of the bottom conduits—close to the enclosure of the arcing device. But a seal is not used in the conduit to the pushbutton because that is a factory-sealed device and that seal is not over 18 in. from the starter. That complies with the intent of the **Code** rule, as well as the rule of Sec. 501-5(c) which recognizes "approved integral means for sealing"—as in the pushbutton. Figure 501-11 shows a seal fitting as close as possible to a box housing a receptacle.

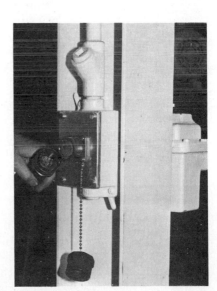

Fig. 501-11. Seal fitting is as close as possible to enclosure, providing maximum effectiveness. (Sec. 501-5.)

The Exception to part **(a)(1)** notes that a seal is not required in a conduit entering an enclosure for a switching device in which the arcing or sparking contacts are internally sealed against the entrance of ignitible gases or vapors. Such conduit is applied to a condition similar to a conduit connection to an explosionproof junction box—that is, any gas that enters the enclosure will contact only wiring terminals and is not exposed to arcs. But because a conduit seal is always required for any conduit of 2-in. size or larger that enters a junction box or terminal housing, this Exception permits elimination of the conduit seal *only* for conduits of 1½-in. size or smaller that enter an enclosure for switching devices with sealed or inaccessible contacts—such as mercury-tube switches, as shown at the bottom of Fig. 501-10. Any switch, CB, or contactor with its contacts in a hermetically sealed chamber or immersed in oil might be applied under this Exception.

Recognition of sealed-contact devices without a separate conduit seal is similar to recognition of "an approved integral means for sealing'" [Sec, 501-5(c)(1)], which is a seal provision that is manufactured directly into some enclosures for Class I equipment.

But questions have always risen about the acceptability of boxes or fittings between the sealing fittings and the enclosure being sealed. This section identifies the devices that may be used between the seal and the enclosure. Explosionproof unions, couplings, reducers, elbows, capped elbows, and conduit bodies similar to L, T, and cross type shall be the only enclosures or fittings permitted between the sealing fittings and the enclosure. A reducing bushing (a "reducer") may be connected at a conduit entry to an explosionproof enclosure so that the bushing is connected between the seal and the enclosure. Because a reducer is commonly used to provide a conduit bushing in the wall of an enclosure and does not pose a threat to the integrity of the seal function, "reducers" have been added to the list of devices permitted to be used between a seal and the enclosure it supplies. The rule goes on to note that any conduit body used in that position must be of a size not larger than the trade size of the conduit with which it is used. This clearly rules out the use of a box or any similar large-volume enclosure between the seal fitting and the enclosure being sealed, as shown in Fig. 501-12.

The fittings listed as acceptable for use between the seal and the enclosure were selected on the basis that their internal volume was sufficiently small as to prevent the accumulation of any dangerous volume of gas or vapor. Acceptability was based on limiting the volume of gas or vapor that may accumulate between the seal and the enclosure being sealed. It was on this basis also that conduit bodies are prohibited from being of a larger size than the conduit with which they are used. If they were permitted, they would present the opportunity for accumulation of a larger volume of gas or vapor, which is considered objectionable.

Figure 501-13 shows an interesting variation on the above concern for use of a box between a seal and an enclosure. *No splices are permitted within seal-off fittings*, according to the UL *Hazardous Location Equipment*

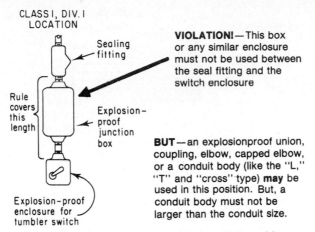

CLASS I, DIV. I
LOCATION

Sealing fitting

Rule covers this length

Explosion-proof junction box

Explosion-proof enclosure for tumbler switch

VIOLATION!—This box or any similar enclosure must not be used between the seal fitting and the switch enclosure

BUT—an explosionproof union, coupling, elbow, capped elbow, or a conduit body (like the "L," "T" and "cross" type) **may** be used in this position. But, a conduit body must not be larger than the conduit size.

Fig. 501-12. Any type of junction "box" may not be used between seal and enclosure. (Sec. 501-5.)

Directory. The illustration shows a round-box type of seal fitting that is used for pulling power and control wires. Such a fitting takes a large, round, threaded cover equipped with a pouring spout. The cover, shown removed, is readily unscrewed to provide maximum unobstructed access to the fitting interior, which facilitates damming either one or both conduit hubs. When the cover is replaced, it can be rotated so the spout points up to permit compound fill. This fitting can be used to seal conduit regardless of its direction or run.

Fig. 501-13. Seal fitting of the round box type is used to seal conduit run into bottom of explosionproof starter enclosure, with flexible fitting connection to the Class I, Division 1, Group D motor below and a watertight Class I cord connector control cable. (Sec. 501-5.)

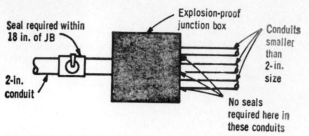

Fig. 501-14. Seals for conduits to junction boxes or fittings are required only for conduits of 2-in. size and larger. (Sec. 501-5.)

2. A seal is required in any conduit run of 2-in. size or larger, where such a conduit enters an "enclosure or fitting" that is required to be explosion-proof and houses terminals, splices, or taps, as shown in Fig. 501-14. Note in such cases, however, the rule does not call for the seal to be "as close as practicable" to the enclosure or fitting, as required for a housing of an arcing or sparking device. Here, it simply requires that the seal be not over 18 in. away from the enclosure.

Another example of seal application in accordance with parts (1) and (2) of Sec. 501-5(a) is shown in Fig. 501-15.

Fig. 501-15. Seal fittings are very close to points where conduits enter the motor starter enclosures. Seals are not required for the conduits entering the junction box (arrow) because they are not 2-in. or larger size—although seals may be used there. (Sec. 501-5.)

The third part of Sec. 501-5(a) covers use of a single seal to provide the required seal for a conduit connecting two enclosures. Where two such pieces of apparatus are connected by a run of conduit not over 3 ft long, a single seal in this run is considered satisfactory if located at the center of the run. Figure 501-16 shows this rule. Although the wording is not detailed, the reference to

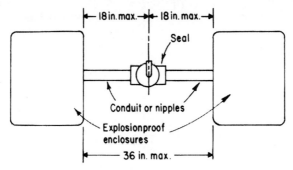

Fig. 501-16. A single seal serves two conduit entries into separate enclosures. (Sec. 501-5.)

"not more than 18 inches from either enclosure" must be understood to be 10 in. measured along the conduit, to avoid the misapplication of the rule shown in Fig. 501-17. The single seal at A is not over 18 in. from the CB enclosure and is literally not over 18 in. from the starter (it is 10 in. from the starter). But that

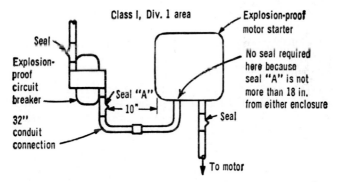

Fig. 501-17. Although this complies with the rule literally, it is a violation of the intent. (Sec. 501-5.)

use of a single seal for the two enclosures violates the **Code** intent that the 18 in. in each case *must* be measured along the conduit.

Part **(4)** requires a seal in each and every conduit that leaves the Class I, Division 1 location—whether it passes into a Division 2 location or into a nonhaz-

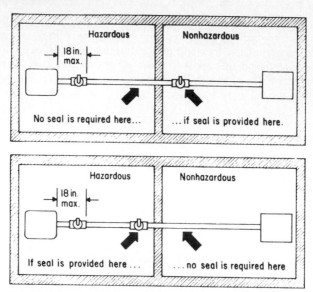

Fig. 501-18. Conduit must be provided with seal fitting where it crosses boundary. (Sec. 501-5.)

ardous location. This required seal may be installed on either side of the boundary (Fig. 501-18). There must be no union, coupling, box, or fitting between the sealing fitting and the point where the conduit leaves the hazardous location. The rule does not specify a maximum distance that must be observed between the sealing fitting and the boundary. The purpose of this sealing is twofold: (1) The conduit usually terminates in some enclosure in the Division 2 or nonhazardous area containing an arc-producing device, such as a switch or fuse. If not sealed, the conduit and apparatus enclosure are likely to become filled with an explosive mixture and the ignition of this mixture may cause local damage in the Division 2 or nonhazardous location. (2) An explosion or ignition of the mixture in the conduit in the nonhazardous area would probably travel back through the conduit to the hazardous area and might cause an explosion there if because of some defective fitting or poor workmanship the installation is not completely explosionproof. If the conduit is unbroken (no union, coupling, etc.) between an enclosure seal and the point where the conduit leaves the hazardous area, an additional seal is not required at the boundary. Figure 501-19 shows two violations where conduit leaves the hazardous area.

The Exception to Sec. 501-5(a) (4) covers the case where a metal conduit system passes from a nonhazardous area, runs through a Class I, Division 1 hazardous area, and then returns to a nonhazardous area. Such a run is permitted to pass through the hazardous area without the need for a seal fitting at either of the boundaries where it enters and leaves the hazardous area. But, the wording of this Exception requires that such conduits, in order to be acceptable, must

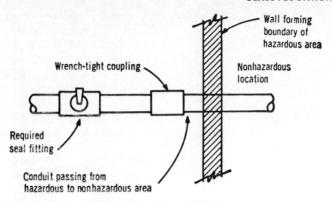

VIOLATION ! — Coupling not permitted between seal and the boundary

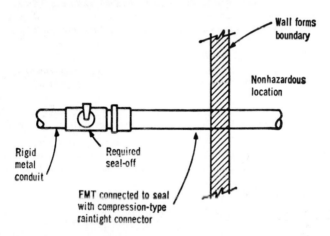

VIOLATION ! — EMT not permitted in Class I location

Fig. 501-19. These violate rules on seal fittings where conduit crosses boundary. (Sec. 501-5.)

contain no union, coupling, box, or fitting in any part of the conduit run extending 12 in. into each of the nonhazardous areas involved (Fig. 501-20).

In the 1975 **NE Code**, the Exception merely referred to "unbroken rigid-metal conduits" that pass through the hazardous area. The effect of the present wording is to clarify the meaning of the word "unbroken."

An identical Exception is made to Sec. 501-5(b) (2) covering the use of a metal conduit passing through a Class I, Division 2 location. It has the same statement prohibiting unions, couplings, boxes, or fittings that are spelled out in the Exception after Sec. 501-5(a) (4).

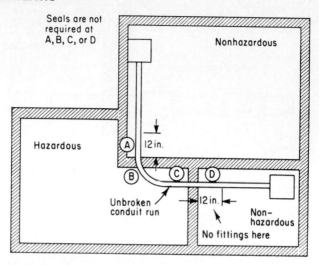

Seals are not
required at
A, B, C, or D

Nonhazardous

Hazardous

Ⓐ 12 in.

Ⓑ   Ⓒ   Ⓓ

Unbroken
conduit run

12 in.

Non-
hazardous

No fittings here

Conduit length in hazardous area must not contain any
union, coupling, box, or other fitting within the hazardous
area and for 12 in. beyond each boundary.

Fig. 501-20. Seals may be eliminated for conduit passing "completely through" hazardous area. (Sec. 501-5.)

For some installations of conduits crossing boundaries, straightforward application of **NE Code** rules on conduit sealing is difficult. Most of these cases involve determination as to what constitutes the boundaries of a hazardous area; the **Code** provides no definition. The inspection authority should be consulted in cases not specifically covered by the **Code**. Because there are no provisions in the **Code** that *prohibit* the use of seals, *"if in doubt, seal"* would be a safe practice to follow.

At the top of Fig. 501-21, the conduit run is sealed within 18 in. of an explosionproof enclosure, as shown below, and extends into a concrete floor slab, emerging in a nonhazardous area. It is not clear what constitutes the boundary of the Class I, Division 1 area. Must a seal be placed at A or might it instead be placed at B in the nonhazardous area? An **NE Code** Official Intepretation, pertaining to a hospital operating room, ruled that the entire concrete slab through which the conduit traveled constituted the boundary of the hazardous area, and that the seal could be placed either at A, where the conduit leaves the hazardous area, or at B, where it enters the nonhazardous area. But some authorities may require seals at A and B. With a seal at A and not at B, a heavier-than-air gas or liquid (like gasoline) might penetrate a crack in the floor, enter the conduit through a coupling, and pass into the enclosure in the nonhazardous area. Or, a seal at B but not at A might not prevent vapor in the conduit from entering the nonhazardous area through a coupling in the concrete and then through a crack in that floor. That kind of gas passage has occurred.

At the bottom of Fig. 501-21, the conduit run is not in the floor slab, but in the ground below the slab. Now what constitutes the boundary? Can the seal still

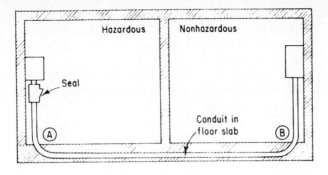

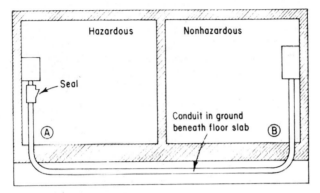

Fig. 501·21. Conduit in floor-slab boundary may require seals at both "A" and "B." (Sec. 501-5.)

be placed either at point A or at point B? **Code** rules applying to gasoline stations and aircraft hangars may be used as a guide. The real question is whether the ground beneath the slab is a hazardous or nonhazardous location. Section 514-8 defines dispensing and service-station wiring and equipment, any portion of which is below the surface of a hazardous area, as a Class I, Division 1 location. Also, Sec. 513-3 requires that the sealing rules of Sec. 501-5(a) (4) and 501-5(b) (2) be applied to horizontal as well as vertical boundaries of defined hazardous areas in aircraft hangars. And the last sentence of Sec. 513-7 says that raceways in or beneath a floor slab are considered as being in the hazardous location above the floor. This is also stated in Sec. 511-3.

A safe conclusion is that, unless specifically defined to the contrary, the ground beneath a hazardous area is an extension of that hazardous area. Or like the concrete floor in the example, the concrete *and* the ground beneath the hazardous area through which the conduit passes can be considered to be the "boundary" when there is any question of boundary. And the boundary itself is considered part of the hazardous location. That means that the conduit does not leave the hazardous area until it emerges at B. The seal should be placed there and an argument can be made that use of two seals—at A and B—would be better practice in both sketches in Fig. 501-21.

It should also be noted that Sec. 514-8 states that the underground Class I, Division 1 location beneath a pump island of a gas station extend at least to the point where underground conduit emerges from the ground. That concept can be logically applied to the sketches in Fig. 501-21.

Figure 501-22 is a wiring layout for a Class I, Division 1 location. The wiring is all rigid metal conduit with threaded joints. All fittings and equipment are

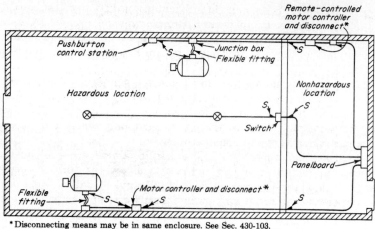

*Disconnecting means may be in same enclosure. See Sec. 430-103.

Fig. 501-22. Required seals are shown in points marked "S." (Sec. 501-5.)

explosionproof; this includes the motors, the motor controller for motor No. 1 (lower part of drawing), the pushbutton control station for motor No. 2 (upper part of drawing), and all outlet and junction boxes. The panelboard and controller for motor No. 2 are placed outside the hazardous area and hence need not be explosionproof.

Each of the three runs of conduit from the panelboard is sealed just outside the hazardous area. A sealing fitting is provided in the conduit on each side of the controller for motor No. 1 (lower part of drawing). The leads are sealed where they pass through the frame of the motor into the terminal housing, and no other seal is needed at this point provided that the conduit and flexible fitting enclosing the leads to the motor are smaller than 2 in. The pushbutton control station for motor No. 2 (upper part of drawing) is considered an arc-producing device, even though the contacts may be oil-immersed, and hence the conduit is sealed where it terminates at this device.

A seal is provided on each side of the switch controlling the lighting fixture. One of these seals is in the nonhazardous room and that single seal serves as both the seal for the arcing device and the seal for conduit crossing the boundary. The lighting fixtures are hung on rigid conduit stems threaded to the covers of explosionproof boxes on the ceiling.

About seal fittings In using seal fittings in conduits in hazardous locations, application data of the UL must be observed, as follows:

- Conduit seal-off fittings to comply with **NE Code** Sec. 501-5 or 502-5 must be used *only* with the sealing compound that is supplied with the fitting and specified by the fitting manufacturer in the instructions furnished with the fitting.
- Seal-off fittings are listed for sealing listed conductors in conduit, where the conductors are thermoplastic insulated, rubber-covered, or lead-covered.
- Any instructions supplied with a seal-off fitting must be carefully observed with respect to limitation on the mounting position (e.g., vertical only) or location (e.g., elbow seal). Figure 501-23 shows a variety of available seal

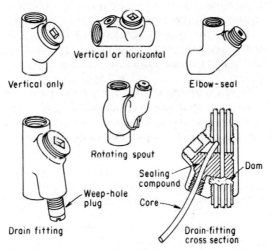

Fig. 501-23. A variety of seal fittings are suited to different applications. (Sec. 501-5.)

fittings. Sealing fittings are designed for vertical orientation only, for optional vertical or horizontal positioning, or as combination elbow seals. Others are compatible with conduits installed at any angle, since covers can be rotated until sealing spouts point upward.

Because conduits are installed vertically, horizontally, and at angles and require ells, tees, and offsets, the fittings used for sealing differ in construction features, orientation, and method of sealing.

Sealing fittings intended solely for vertical orientation have threaded, upward-slanting ports slightly larger than conduit hub openings to permit asbestos-fiber dams to be tamped into fitting bases. The dam prevents the fluid-sealing compound from running down into the conduit before the seal has solidified.

A second type of fitting is designed either for vertical or horizontal positioning. These units are identified by two seal-chamber plugs that can be removed to facilitate tamping dam fibers into both conduit hubs when the device is aligned horizontally. The compound is poured into the chamber through the larger of the two ports. The ports are then replugged, and the plugs tightened flush with their collars. When these fittings are oriented vertically, however, only lower conduit hubs need be dammed.

A third type of seal which can be oriented in any position is shown in the center of Fig. 501-23 and is described in Fig. 501-13. That same fitting may be used as a drain-type seal when its spout is turned down.

Elbow seals (as at upper right of Fig. 501-23) are double-duty devices that are practical either when horizontal conduits must elbow-down to connect with an enclosure's top (as indicated), or when vertical conduits must turn to enter explosionproof enclosures horizontally. In either case, sealant application openings must slant upward.

Another fitting, designed for drainage purposes, is installed only in vertical runs of conduits. Where conduit is run overhead and is brought down vertically to an enclosure for apparatus, any condensation of moisture in the vertical run would be trapped by the seal above the apparatus enclosure. The lower part of Fig. 501-23 shows a sealing fitting designed to provide drainage for a vertical conduit run. Any water coming down from above runs over the surface of the sealing compound and down to an explosionproof drain, through which the water is automatically drained off. These fittings permit passage of condensation while also blocking the passage of explosive pressures or flames. They are equipped with plugs containing minute weep-holes that can either be opened and closed periodically as need develops or allow continuous drainage.

Drain-type seal fittings must be oriented so that compound-application ports remain above the lower downward-slanting drainage plugs. To install seal and drain, both ports are unplugged and the lower conduit hub is dammed. The drainage plug-hole is then closed temporarily by a washer through which a rubber core is inserted. This core protrudes up into the upper part of the sealing chamber, although it must be guided so as not to remain in contact with any of the conductors. Sealing compound then is poured into the chamber through the upper access port, which is replugged and screwed tight.

After the compound has initially set (but has not yet had time to permanently harden), the washer is removed and the rubber core pulled down and out. This creates a clear drainage canal which extends from above the seal down into the drainage weep-hole. A drainage plug is then screwed into the threaded hole, with not less than five full threads engaged to fulfill the requirement for an explosionproof joint.

Class I, Division 2

Because Division 2 locations are of a lower degree of hazard than Division 1, the requirements for sealing are somewhat less demanding, as follows:

1. Where the rules of other sections in Art. 501 require an explosionproof enclosure for equipment in a Division 2 location, all conduits connecting to any such enclosure must be sealed exactly the same as if it were in a Division 1 enclosure. And the conduit, nipple, or any fitting between the seal and the enclosure being sealed must be approved for use in Class I, Division 1 locations—as specified in Sec. 501-4(a).

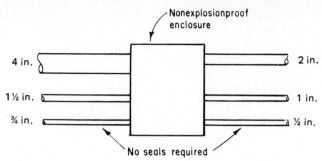

Fig. 501·24. Seals are not required for conduits connected to nonexplosionproof enclosures that are permitted in Division 2 locations. (Sec. 501-5.)

As shown in Fig. 501-24, where a nonexplosionproof enclosure is permitted by other sections to be used in a Division 2 location, a seal is *not* required in any size of conduit. Note that in Division 2 locations, there is *not* always the need to seal conduits 2 in. and larger, as required in Division 1 locations, by Sec. 501-5(a) (2).

2. Any and every conduit run passing from a Class I, Division 2 area into a nonhazardous area must be sealed in the same manner as described above for conduit passing from a Division 1 area into a Division 2 or nonhazardous area (Fig. 501-25). Rigid metal conduit or IMC must be used between the seal and the point where the conduit passes through the boundary.

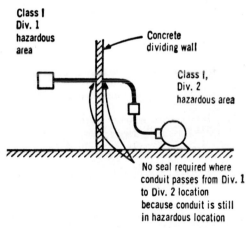

Fig. 501·25. This is a violation; a seal is required. (Sec. 501-5.)

The Exception to part **(b)(2)** is worded the same as the Exception in part **(a)(4)** for Class I, Division 1 locations. The Exception covers the case where a metal conduit system passes from a nonhazardous area, runs through a Class I, Division 2 hazardous area, and then returns to a nonhazardous area. Such a run is permitted to pass through the hazardous area without the need for a seal fitting at either of the boundaries where it enters and leaves the hazardous area, provided that the conduit in the hazardous area does not contain unions, couplings, boxes, or fittings. In a Class I, Division 2 location, the same prohibition against unions, couplings, etc., is applicable, and the method in Fig. 501-26 is not

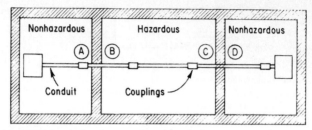

Fig. 501-26. Couplings in conduit through Division 2 location would require seals at the boundaries. (Sec. 501-5.)

acceptable if seals are omitted at the boundary crossings. A seal would not be needed at A, B, C, or D, if the conduit passes through the Class I, Division 2 location without any coupling or other fittings in the conduit.

Part **(c)** of Sec. 501-5 sets regulations about the kind of seals that must be used where seals are required by foregoing rules. Part **(1)** calls for an integral seal within the enclosure itself or use of a separate seal fitting in each conduit connecting to the enclosure, as described above. The use of factory-sealed devices eliminates the need for field sealing and generally is less expensive to install. In fittings of this type, the arcing device is enclosed in a chamber, with the leads or connections brought out to a splicing chamber. No external sealing fitting is required (Fig. 501-27).

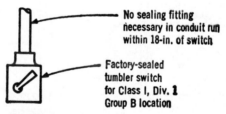

Fig. 501-27. Seal in conduit is not needed where enclosure has built-in seal. (Sec. 501-5.)

Where a seal fitting is used in the conduit, it must be *explosionproof*. The sealing compound must develop enough mechanical strength as it hardens to withstand the forces of explosions. Seals used only to prevent condensation accumulation do not have to be explosionproof; a vaportight seal is sufficient for that purpose.

A seal must be *vaportight* to stop gases and vapors. To do that, the sealing compound must adhere to the fitting and to the conductors. It must expand as it hardens to close all voids without producing objectionable mechanical stresses in the fitting.

Liquid or condensed vapor may present a problem in Class I locations. Where such is the case, joints and conduit systems must be arranged to minimize entrance of liquid. Periodic draining may be necessary, which necessitates the inclusion of means for draining in the original design of the motor (Sec. 501-5).

Installation instructions furnished by the manufacturer must be carefully followed. The seal fitting must be carefully packed with fibrous damming material, which packs more tightly and effectively around conductors when it is dampened, and then filled with the compound supplied with the fitting to a depth at least equal to the inside diameter of the conduit and never less than ⅝ in. deep, as required in part **(3)** and in the UL standard on seal fittings.

Part **(2)** of Sec. 501-5(c) covers the compound used in seals (Fig. 501-28). The sealing compound used must be one which has a melting point of not less than

Fig. 501-28. Conduit seal fitting must be carefully packed with fibrous damming material, which packs more tightly and effectively around conductors when it is dampened and then filled with the compound supplied with the fitting to a depth at least equal to the inside diameter of the conduit and never less than ⅝ in. deep (UL standard). This type of seal is for vertical mounting only. (Sec. 501-5.)

200°F and is not affected by the liquid or gas which causes the location to be hazardous. Most of the insulating compounds commonly used in cable splices and potheads are soluble in gasoline and lacquer solvents and hence are unsuitable for sealing conduits in locations where these liquids are used. A mixture of litharge and glycerin is insoluble in nearly all liquids and gases found in Class I locations and meets all other requirements, though this mixture is open to the objection that it becomes very hard and is difficult to remove if the wires must be pulled out. No sealing compounds are listed by Underwriters Laboratories Inc. as suitable for this use except in connection with the explosionproof fittings of specific manufacturers.

Part **(4)** prohibits splices or taps in seal fittings.

Part **(5)** recognizes use of listed Class I assemblies that have a built-in seal between a compartment housing devices that may cause arcs or sparks and a separate compartment for splicing or taps. Conduit connection to the splice or tap compartment requires a seal fitting only in conduit of 2-in. size or larger, as specified for junction boxes in Sec. 501-5(a) (2).

Part **(d)** covers seals for cables in conduit and for Type MI cable—the only cable permitted by Sec. 501-4(a) to be used in Class I, Division 1 locations. Part **(e)** covers sealing of any of the cables permitted by Sec. 501-4(b).

In part **(f)(3)**, a secondary seal fitting must be installed to prevent flammable or combustible fluids from entering the conduit system after a failure of the primary "single compression seal, diaphragm, or tube." In this section a "compression-type seal" is recognized as a method of sealing between the process fluid and the electrical enclosure. Previous wording of this rule required both draining (or venting) to detect primary seal failure and installation of a second "approved seal" in the conduit system *only* when the primary seal against process fluid entry into electrical conduit was either a single diaphragm or tube. But the same secondary draining and sealing is now also required where a *compression seal* is used.

501·6. Switches, Circuit Breakers, Motor Controllers, and Fuses. Part **(a)** requires explosionproof enclosures (listed for Class I locations, which means suitable for use in Division 1 areas), although purged enclosures are not ruled out. Explosionproof equipment is required in Class I areas only. In addition, the equipment must operate at a temperature low enough that it will not ignite the atmosphere around it.

Division 1   Electrical equipment described must be explosionproof and specifically designed for the specific class and group.

Division 2   Equipment selected must be explosionproof only in certain cases. Purged and pressurized enclosures are recognized as an alternative to explosionproof types, as noted in Sec. 501-3(a). General-purpose enclosures may be used only if all arcing parts are immersed under oil or enclosed within a chamber that is hermetically sealed against the entrance of gases or vapors. In addition, the surface temperature of the apparatus in the general-purpose enclosure should not exceed 80 percent of the ignition temperature of the hazardous substances involved. If those conditions are not satisfied, the enclosure must be explosionproof.

Important: UL standards on explosionproof enclosures contain rules on "Grease for Joint Surfaces": "Paint or a sealing material shall not be applied to the contacting surfaces of a joint. A suitable corrosion inhibitor (grease) such as petrolatum, soap-thickened mineral oils, or nondrying slushing compound may be applied to the metal joint surfaces before assembly. The grease shall be of a type that does not harden because of aging, does not contain an evaporating solvent, and does not cause corrosion of the joint surfaces."

Figure 501-29 shows two explosionproof panelboards. Each panelboard consists of an assembly of branch-circuit CBs, each pair of CBs being enclosed in a cast-metal explosionproof housing. Access to the CBs and to the wiring compartment is through handholes with threaded covers, and threaded hubs are provided for the conduits. Individual CBs and motor starters are also shown. "Panelboards" for light and power are limited in the UL Red Book. Listed panelboards for Class I and Class II hazardous locations are for "lighting and *low-capacity* power distribution." *High-capacity* panelboards (like 1,200-A floor-standing panels) and switchboards must be kept out of hazardous locations wherever possible. Enclosure requirements and details are generally the same as those described under "General rules" and for CBs and boxes. Typical hazardous-location panelboards are shown at the right in Fig. 501-30.

Fig. 501-29. Explosionproof panelboards (arrows) are assemblies made up of circuit-breaker housings coupled to wiring enclosures. Large explosionproof CB enclosure at center feeds the panelboards. Explosionproof motor controllers are at lower left. (Sec. 501-6.)

Fig. 501-30. Explosionproof panelboards (at right) are combined with separate enclosures for motor starters on a rack, to make up a "modular assembly" which is listed by UL under "Industrial control equipment"—which may be assembled either at the factory or in the field. (Sec. 501-6.)

"Industrial control equipment" is a broad category in the UL Red Book, covering "control panels and assemblies" and "motor controllers." Control panels and assemblies include both enclosures and the components within them—such as motor controllers, pushbuttons, pilot lights, receptacles (Fig. 501-31).

Fig. 501·31. Combination motor starter is typical explosionproof control unit for Class I locations. Note the drain-type seal fittings that provide for draining the conduits of any accumulated condensation or other water. (Sec. 501-6.)

Either a single enclosure or a group of interconnected enclosures may be used for mounting the components. Where a number of interconnected enclosures are included in an assembly, it is called a "modular assembly" and may be assembled either at the factory or in the field. An example of that is shown in Fig. 501-30.

Components are provided with the enclosures, to be installed either at the factory or in the plant. Wiring between components of modular assemblies is to be field installed. Conduit seal-off fittings must be used in accordance with Sec. 501-5.

As noted at the end of part **(b)(1)**, in a Class I, Division 2 location, a general-purpose enclosure may be used for a circuit breaker, a motor controller, or switch *if* "interruption of current occurs within a factory sealed explosionproof chamber." This is a condition under which a general-purpose enclosure may

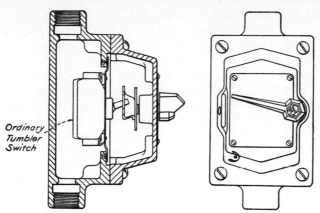

Fig. 501·32. Explosionproof enclosure suits snap switch to use in hazardous location. (Sec. 501-6.)

be used for a current-interrupting device—instead of requiring a Class I, Division 1 enclosure.

A snap switch in an explosionproof enclosure is shown in Fig. 501-32. If a snap switch has an internal factory seal between the switch contacts and its supply wiring connection in its enclosure, it will be so identified by a marking on it. Such switches do not require a seal fitting in a conduit entering the enclosure. The integral seal satisfies Secs. 501-5(a)(1) and 501-5(c)(1).

As noted in part **(b)(2)**, isolating switches in Class I, Division 2 locations may be used in general-purpose enclosures either with or without fuses in the enclosure. In previous **Code** editions, this rule recognized a general-purpose enclosure only for an isolating switch that did *not* contain fuses. But because the fuse in such a switch is for short-circuit protection and neither the switch nor the fuse operates as a "normal" interrupting device, fuses are permitted in isolating switches in general-purpose enclosures.

With reference to subparagraph **(b)(4)**, it is assumed that fuses will very seldom blow, or CBs will very seldom open, when used to protect feeders or branch circuits that supply only lamps in fixed positions. In Division 2 locations the conditions are not normally hazardous but may sometimes become so. There is very little probability that one of the overcurrent devices will operate at the same time that the hazardous conditions exist; hence it is not considered necessary to require that these overcurrent devices be in explosionproof enclosures.

Part **(b)(5)** requires that fuses in lighting fixtures must *not* discharge flame on operation. This rule covers the type of fuse that may be used for internal protection of individual lighting fixtures in Class I, Division 2 locations.

UL Red Book Data

As described under general regulations in the UL's *Electrical Construction Materials Directory* (Green Book) and repeated in the Red Book of UL for individual types of switching and control devices, the wiring space and current-carrying capacity of CBs and other equipment used in hazardous locations are based on the use of 60°C wire connected to the breaker terminals for circuits wired with No. 14 to No. 1 conductors, and on the use of 75°C wire connected to the terminals for circuits wired with conductors of No. 1/0 or larger.

Although the reference clearly bases listing on wires of those maximum-temperature ratings, wires of higher-temperature ratings may be used to take advantage of the smaller conduit sizes needed for thin-wall-insulated wires (such as 90°C THHN and XHHW), along with the greater ampacities of higher-temperature wires, which offer an advantage when conductors are derated. *But,* the load on any such wire must not exceed the ampacity of the same size of 60°C- or 75°C-rated wire. The same rules also apply to switches used in hazardous locations.

Terminal lugs on switches, CBs, etc., are suitable for use with copper conductors, as noted in the UL Red Book. Lugs on equipment are commonly marked "AL-CU" or "CU-AL," indicating that the terminal is suitable for use with either copper or aluminum conductors. But, such marking on the lug itself is not sufficient evidence of suitability for use with aluminum conductors. UL requires that equipment found to be suitable for use with either copper or aluminum conductors must be marked to indicate such use on the label or wiring diagram of the equipment—completely independent of a marking, like "AL-CU," on the lugs themselves. A typical CB, for instance, would have lugs marked "AL-CU" but also must have a notation on the label or nameplate to specify "Lugs suitable for copper or aluminum conductors"—if aluminum conductors are to be used with the breaker.

A hazardous-location *enclosure* for equipment that is to be fed by aluminum conductors must have a marking on it to indicate that it is permissible to use aluminum conductors with the switch or CB that is to be mounted within the enclosure. All enclosures for CBs are marked to indicate what labeled CBs are acceptable for use within the enclosures. Only the breakers specified may be used in an enclosure.

501·7. Control Transformers and Resistors.   The term *control transformer* is commonly applied to a small dry-type transformer used to supply the control circuits of one or more motors, stepping down the voltage of a 480-V power circuit to 120 V.

Part **(a)** requires either explosionproof or purged and pressurized enclosures for Division 1 locations—the same as required for meters and instruments in Sec. 501-3(a).

501·8. Motors and Generators.   Four different types of motor applications are recognized for use in a Class I, Division 1 location. The first is a motor approved for Class I, Division 1 locations—such as an explosionproof motor. The totally enclosed, fan-cooled motor (referred to as a "TEFC" motor) is recognized and listed by UL for use in explosive atmospheres. A motor of a type approved for use in explosive atmospheres of the totally enclosed, fan-cooled type is shown in Fig. 501-33. The main frame and end housings are made with sufficient strength to withstand internal pressures due to ignition of a combustible mixture inside the motor. Wide metal-to-metal joints are provided between the

Fig. 501-33. A motor approved for use in the explosive atmosphere of a Class I, Division 1 location is the basic one of the four types recognized for such locations. (Sec. 501-8.)

frame and housings. Circulation of the air is maintained inside the inner enclosure by fan blades on each end of the rotor. At the left side of the sectional view a fan is shown in the space between the inner and outer housings. This fan draws in air through a screen and drives it across the surface of the stator punchings and out through openings at the drive end of the motor. The motors described in **(2)** and **(3)** of part **(a)** of this section are the only ones available for Class I, Groups A and B locations and for medium-voltage, high-horsepower applications. Cost of ducts and ventilating systems limits their application in other areas.

The UL Red Book lists motors for Class I, Groups C and D locations. To date, UL lists no motors for Groups A and B; therefore, where such conditions are encountered, motors must be located outside the hazardous area or must conform to the alternate arrangements and conditions of Sec. 501-8(a). Air or inert-gas purging are recognized as alternate methods. Motors suitable for Groups C and D, Class I locations are designated as explosionproof.

In part **(b)**, the rule relaxes the requirements for Division 2 areas somewhat. In Class I, Division 2 locations open or nonexplosionproof enclosed motors may be used if they have no brushes, switching mechanisms, or integral resistance devices. However, motors with any sparking or high-temperature devices must be approved for Class I, Division 1 areas—as described above.

"Motors and Generators, Rebuilt" May Be Listed

A procedure has been established to provide third-party certification of rewound or rebuilt motors in hazardous locations. Refer to the UL Red Book on hazardous-location equipment for motor-repair centers authorized to provide certified repairs.

501·9. Lighting Fixtures.   In these locations, part **(a)** requires that each fixture be *approved* for the Class I, Division 1 location and marked to show the maximum wattage permitted for the lamps in the fixture (Fig. 501-34). Reference to

Fig. 501·34. Fluorescent luminaire, fed by Type MI cable, is listed and marked as an explosionproof unit for use in a Class I, Division 1 location. (Sec. 501-9.)

the listings in the UL Red Book shows many manufacturers listed for Class I fixtures for use in various Groups of atmospheres. Listings range from "Class I, Group C" to "Class I, Groups A, B, C, and D." For application of a lighting fixture in a particular Group, it is simply a matter of assuring that a manufacturer's fixture is listed for Class I and the Group. The designation "Class I" indicates the fixture is suitable for Division 1, except where the listing contains the phrase "Division 2 only" following the "Class I" reference or following the "Class I" plus Group references.

But in a Class I, Division 1 location, all fixtures must be listed and marked for such use by UL or other national product testing lab. That is necessary to satisfy OSHA's definition of the word "approved" as it appears in Sec. 501-9(a) (1). And electrical inspectors invariably give the same meaning to the word "approved"—if a test-lab-listed product of the same generic type is a violation of Sec. 110-2.

Part **(a)(3)** permits support of a suspended fixture on rigid metal conduit, IMC, or an explosionproof flexible connection fitting.

Lighting Fixtures Require Careful Application

The UL data on hazardous-location lighting fixtures are given under the heading "Fixtures and Fittings" in the Red Book of UL. A lighting fixture recognized for use in Division 1 hazardous locations will be marked "Electric Lighting Fixture for Hazardous Locations" and will show the one or more Groups of hazardous atmospheres for which it is suited. If a fixture is not recognized for Division 1 locations but is limited to Division 2 installations, it will be marked "Electric Lighting Fixture for Division 2 Hazardous Locations." Other UL data are as follows:

- Class I, Division 1 fixtures with *external* surface temperatures over 100°C will have the operating temperature marked on the fixture.
- Fixtures for Class I, Division 1 and Division 2 locations are designed to operate without igniting the atmosphere of the one or more Groups for which the fixture is listed. A Class I, Division 1 fixture (explosionproof) has its lamp chamber sealed-off from the terminal compartment for the supply conductors. All modern explosionproof lighting fixtures are designed by the manufacturer to be factory-sealed, eliminating the need for seal fittings immediately adjacent to the fixtures.
- Any fixture subject to breakage must be equipped with a guard.
- A fixture with one or more germicidal lamps must have a warning to assure that its method of installation does not present a chance of injurious radiation to any person.
- Fixtures for wet locations and those suitable for use where residue of combustible paint will accumulate on them are marked to indicate such recognition.

Class I, Division 2 locations   In these locations, the selection of a suitable fixture becomes a little more involved and has caused problems in the field. Correlation between the requirements of Sec. 501-9 and the application data and listings of the UL must be carefully established.

Watch Out! Controversy!

Section 501-9(b) (2) does *not* say that a fixture in a Division 2 location must "be approved for the Class I, Division 2 location"—unlike Sec. 501-9(a) (1), which requires a fixture "approved" for the specific location. Instead, Sec. 501-9(b) (2) gives a description of the type of fixture that would be acceptable, citing a number of requirements:

1. The fixture must be protected from physical damage by suitable guards or "by location"—which can be taken to mean that mounting it high or otherwise out of the way of any object that might strike or hit it eliminates the need for a guard.
2. If falling sparks or hot metal from the fixture could possibly ignite local accumulation of the hazardous atmosphere, then an enclosure or other protective means must be used to eliminate that hazard.
3. Where lamps used with the fixture may, under normal conditions, reach surface temperature above 80 percent of the atmosphere's ignition temperature, then either of two conditions must be satisfied—(a) A fixture approved for Class I, Division 1 location must be used, or (b) the fixture must be of a type that "has been tested and found incapable of igniting the gas or vapor if the ignition temperature is not exceeded."

Figure 501-35 shows a Class I, Division 1 fixture that could be used in a Division 2 location. But it is not necessary to use a Division 1 fixture and then questions develop.

Fig. 501·35. In a Class I, Division 2 location, a lighting fixture listed for Class I, Division 1 would satisfy—such as this factory-sealed mercury-vapor luminaire in a Class I, Group D location. Otherwise, a fixture listed for Class I, Division 2 must be used. (Sec. 501-9.)

For many years, in Class I, Division 2 locations simply an enclosed- and gasketed-type fixture was the usual choice. The fixture does not need to be explosionproof but must have a gasketed globe. The primary requirement is that any surface, including the lamp, must operate at less than 80 percent of the ignition temperature of the gas or vapor that may be present. The effect of Sec. 501-9(b) (2) is to recognize the use of general-purpose lighting fixtures if the conditions of fixture-operating temperature and atmosphere-ignition temperature are correlated as required or if the fixture has been "tested" to verify its safety. At best, the described task of determining the suitability of a general-purpose fixture for use in the hazardous location by relating its lamp-operating temperature to

80 percent of the atmosphere-ignition temperature could be difficult for any electrical designer and/or installer. It also seems highly unlikely that any of them would have the facilities or the experience to perform the testing described in the last part of the **Code** rule and make a sound judgment on the suitability, even though the manufacturer provides the necessary temperature data on the fixture. It was the intention of the authors of that last part of the **Code** rule that the testing mentioned be done by a "qualified testing agency" (such as UL, Factory Mutual, ETL). And as a result of such testing, fixtures for Class I, Division 2 locations would be approved and listed on the same basis that fixtures are certified for Class I, Division 1 locations.

Class I, Division 2 fixtures are listed in two ways in the Red Book. Some are listed as "Class I, Division 2 only," without reference to Group or Groups. Others are listed with an indication of the Groups for which they are listed—for instance, "Class I, Groups A, B, C, and D, Division 2 only." Great care must be used in evaluating the detail of these listing designations. If such a fixture is not marked otherwise, the temperature of the fixture is lower than the ignition temperature of any of the atmospheres for which it is listed. Where a Class I Group designation is not mentioned, the fixture must not be used where its marked operating temperature is above the ignition temperature of the hazardous atmosphere. Class I, Division 2 fixtures with *internal* parts operating over 100°C will be marked to show the actual operating temperature of internal parts.

Based on the foregoing, precise enforcement of the **NE Code** and OSHA insistence on the maximum use of third-party certified products would seem to suggest the following approach:

1. In Class I, Division 1 locations, only fixtures listed by a nationally recognized test lab may be used.
2. And because fixtures are listed for Class I, Division 2 locations (in the UL Red Book), any fixture in a Class I, Division 2 location *must be listed* for that application (or, of course, a Class I, Division 1 fixture could be used). Consistent with OSHA's rationale on the matter of listing, if a third-party certified product is available (that is, Class I, Division 2 fixtures), then use of a nonlisted fixture in a Class I, Division 2 location would be a clear violation. Based on that analysis, it seems that the **Code**-rule certification of a general-purpose fixture with lamp-temperature-not-over-80-percent-of-ignition-temperature would be abrogated.

Recessed Fixtures

Recessed fixtures of both incandescent and electric-discharge lamp types are listed in the UL Red Book and are suitable only for dry locations—unless marked "SUITABLE FOR DAMP LOCATIONS" or "SUITABLE FOR WET LOCATIONS." Other rules are:

- Each fixture is marked to show the minimum temperature rating of conductors used to supply the fixture. Care must be taken to observe all such markings on these fixtures with respect to the number, size, and temperature rating of wires permitted in junction boxes or splice compartments that are part of such fixtures. Generally, no allowance is made in such boxes or compartments for heat produced by current to other loads that may be fed by taps or splices in the fixture supply wires within the JB or splice compartment. Allowance is made only for the I^2R heat input of the current to the fixture itself. If the fixture is recognized for carrying through other conductors to other loads, the fixture will be marked to cover the permitted conditions of wiring.

- Fixtures are listed to assure safe application in both Class I, Division 1 and Class I, Division 2 locations.
- In every Class I, Division 1 fixture, the wiring compartment for supply circuit connections is internally sealed from the lamp chambers.
- Fixtures that may be used as raceways for carrying through circuit conductors other than those supplying the fixtures are marked "Suitable for Use as Raceway" and show the number, size, and type of wires permitted.
- Fixtures are marked to show suitability for installation in concrete and some may be used *only* in concrete.
- Fixtures are marked when they may be used *only* with fire-resistive building construction.
- Some fixtures are marked to show acceptable use *only* in Class I, Division 2 locations.

Portable Lighting

Although the basic rule of part **(b)(1)** is that portable lighting in a Class I, Division 2 location must be listed for Class I, Division 1 locations, portable lighting equipment in Class I, Division 2 locations does not have to be approved for Class I, Division 1 use if it is mounted on a movable stand and is cord-connected. This is a relaxation of the rule in the first sentence of part **(b)(1)**. The rule recognizes the common need for temporary lighting for maintenance work in Class I, Division 2 locations, where handlamps would not be adequate.

501·10. Utilization Equipment.   This section covers devices that utilize electrical energy—other than lighting fixtures and motors or motor-operated equipment. Electric heaters in Class I, Division 1 locations must be listed for such application. The UL Red Book lists convection-type heaters under "Heaters," for Groups C and D. Industrial and laboratory heaters are also listed—heat tracing systems, hot plates, paint heaters, and steam-heated ovens.

According to Sec. 501-10(b)(1)a., Exception No. 2, in a Class I, Division 2 location, an electrically heated utilization equipment may be used *if* some current-limiting means is provided to prevent heater temperature from exceeding 80 percent of the ignition temperature of the gas or vapor. Such current limitation may be part of the control equipment for the heater to ensure safe operation by preventing dangerously high temperatures.

501·11. Flexible Cords, Class I, Divisions 1 and 2.   Although Sec. 501-4(a) does not mention flexible cord as an approved method of wiring in Division 1 locations, this rule does permit such cord for connection of portable equipment. The Exception, however, refers back to Sec. 501-3(b)(6), which permits cord and plug connection of process control instruments in Division 2 locations—to facilitate replacement of such units, which are not portable equipment. And Sec. 501-4(b) covers use of cord in Division 2 locations.

An explosionproof handlamp, listed for use in Class I locations, is an example of portable equipment covered by this rule, which requires that a 3-conductor cord be used and that the device be provided with a terminal for the third, or grounding conductor, which serves to ground the exposed metal parts. Such handlamps are listed under "Portable Lighting Units" in the UL Red Book, which notes that flexible cords should be used only where absolutely necessary as an alternative to threaded rigid conduit hookups. Cords, plugs, and receptacles must be protected from moisture, dirt, and foreign materials. Frequent inspection and maintenance are critically important. Consultation with inspection authorities is always recommended where plug and receptacle applications are considered.

As noted in the last sentence of this section, flexible cord may supply submersible pumps in Class I locations. This **Code** section recognizes use of flexible cord with such pumps because they are designated as "portable utilization equipment." Commentary in favor of this **Code** rule stated:

> Many authorities in the wastewater field (sewage, stormwater, etc.) in recognizing especially the contribution to maintenance of submersible pumps, have stipulated that in any wet-well installation they be easily removed without the need for personnel to enter or dewater the wet-well. This is provided by all member companies in the industry by means of guide-rail remote guidance system and a simple automatic discharge connection system which allows indexing and a tight connection (or removal) to be automatically accomplished between the pump discharge flange and the effluent piping flange.
>
> In order to maintain the workability of the system and the intent of the specifying Authorities, it is imperative that flexible cord or cable be used between the place where the service enters the wet-well from the pump control (gas-tight conduit seal or—in the case of Class I, Division 1 locations—explosion-proof junction or splice box hard wired to the pump cable with a suitable compression cable-entry) and the pump cable-entry assembly.
>
> This will allow the pump to the lifted from the wet-well through the opened cover in the access frame in the ground-level slab by its chain or wire-rope without personnel entering or dewatering the wet-well
>
> In the case of Class I, Division 1 locations, the pump is either explosion-proof and suitable for the installation (there are none Approved at the present time) or redundant low-level shut-off sensing is provided which guarantees the uppermost portion of a standard submersible pump is always submerged. These approaches are specified and accepted by the Administrative Code for the State of Wisconsin and the Department of Industrial Safety for the State of California for some time.
>
> Extra hard-usage cord and cable of the S, SO, ST, STO, W, G, PCG, etc., classes have been used for many years in submersible wastewater handling with a perfect safety record in classified locations.

501-12. Receptacles and Attachment Plugs, Class I, Divisions 1 and 2. The basic rule calls for receptacles and plug caps to be approved for Class I locations, which suits them to use in either Division 1 or Division 2 locations. The Exception notes that cord connection of process control instruments in Class I, Division 2 locations does not require devices approved for Class I locations. General-purpose receptacles may be used as outlined in Sec. 501-3(b) (6).

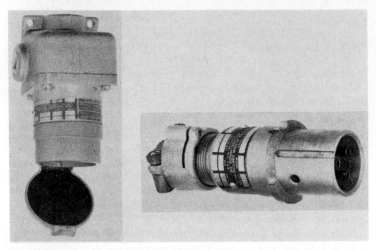

Fig. 501·36. Receptacle and plug must generally be explosionproof type for Divisions 1 and 2. (Sec. 501-12.)

Figure 501-36 shows a three-pole 30-A receptacle and the attachment plug which is so designed as to seal the arc when the circuit is broken, and therefore is suitable for use without a switch. The circuit conductors are brought into the base or body through rigid conduit screwed into a tapped opening and are spliced to pigtail leads from the receptacle. The receptacle housing is then attached to the base, the joint being made at wide flanges ground to a suitable fit. All necessary sealing is provided in the device itself, and no additional sealing is required when it is installed. The plug is designed to receive a three-conductor cord for a 2-wire circuit or a four-conductor cord for a 3-wire, 3-phase circuit, and is provided with a clamping device to relieve the terminals from any strain. The extra conductor is used to ground the equipment supplied.

UL data are as follows:

- Class I receptacles for Division 1 or Division 2 locations are equipped with boxes for threaded metal conduit connection, and a factory seal is provided between the receptacle and its box.
- Receptacles for Class I, Division 2 only may be used with general-purpose enclosures for supply connections, with factory sealing of conductors in the receptacle. The plugs for such receptacles are suitable for Class I, Division 1 locations.
- Frequent inspection is recommended for flexible cords, receptacles, and plugs, with replacement whenever necessary.
- For Class I, interlocked CBs and plugs are made for receptacles so that the plug cannot be removed from the receptacle when the CB is closed and the CB cannot be closed when the plug is not in the receptacle (Fig. 501-37).

Mechanical-interlock construction requires that the plug be fully inserted into the receptacle and rotated to operate an enclosed switch or CB that ener-

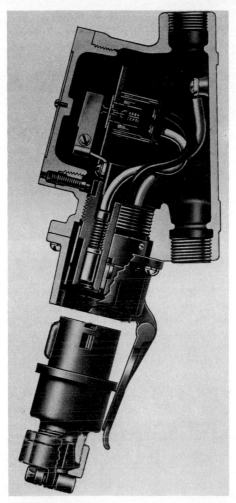

Fig. 501-37. A receptacle with a plug interlocked
with a circuit breaker is an explosionproof assembly
with operating safety features. (Sec. 501-12.)

gizes the receptacle. The plug cannot be withdrawn until the switch or breaker
has first de-energized the circuit.

The delayed-action type of plug and receptacle has a mechanism within the
receptacle that prevents complete withdrawal of the plug until after electrical
connection has been broken, permitting any arcs or sparks to be quenched
inside the arcing chamber. And insertion of the plug seals the arcing chamber
before electrical connection is made. Threaded conduit connection to the CB
compartment is provided. The plug is for Type S flexible cord with an equipment grounding conductor.

501-13. Conductor Insulation, Class I, Divisions 1 and 2.   Because of economics and greater ease in handling, nylon-jacketed Type THHN-THWN wire, suitable for use where exposed to gasoline, has in most cases replaced lead-covered conductors.

An excerpt from Underwriters Laboratories Inc. *Electrical Construction Materials Directory* states as follows:

> Wires, Thermoplastic.
> Gasoline Resistant TW—Indicates a TW conductor with a jacket of extruded nylon suitable for use in wet locations, and for exposure to mineral oil, and to liquid gasoline and gasoline vapors at ordinary ambient temperature. It is identified by tag marking and by printing on the insulation or nylon jacket with the designation "Type TW Gasoline and Oil Resistant I."

Also listed for the above use is "Gasoline Resistant THWN" with the designation "Type THWN Gasoline and Oil Resistant II."

It should be noted that other thermoplastic wires may be suitable for exposure to mineral oil; but with the exception of those marked "Gasoline and Oil Resistant," reference to mineral oil does not include gasoline or similar light-petroleum solvents.

The conductor itself must bear the marking legend designating its use as suitable for gasoline exposure; such designation on the tag alone is not sufficient.

501-14. Signaling, Alarm, Remote-Control, and Communication Systems. Nearly all signaling, remote-control, and communication equipment involves make-or-break contacts; hence in Division 1 locations all devices must be

Fig. 501-38. Explosionproof telephones are made and listed for Class I, Groups B, C, and D, and must be connected with the necessary seal fittings required in conduits to enclosures housing arcing or sparking devices. [Sec. 501-14(b) (4).]

explosionproof, and the wiring must comply with the requirements for light and power wiring in such locations, including seals.

Figure 501-38 shows a telephone having the operating mechanism mounted in an explosionproof housing. Similar equipment may be obtained for operating horns or sirens. Figure 501-39 shows fire-alarm hookups at a distillery. Alcohol

Fig. 501-39. Fire-alarm and control equipment at outdoor tank car delivery and pumping station of a distillery is housed and connected to comply with conduit and seal rules for a Class I, Division 1, Group D location. (Sec. 501-14.)

is generally categorized as creating a Class I, Group G location by Code Table 500-2. A vapor-laden atmosphere with an alcoholic content ranging from 3.5 to 19 percent could become flammable or explode at an ignition temperature of approximately 80°F under certain conditions of air pressure and humidity.

Referring to subparagraph **(1)**, covering Division 2 locations, it would usually be the more simple method to use explosionproof devices, rather than devices having contacts immersed in oil or devices in hermetically sealed enclosures, though mercury switches, which are hermetically sealed, may be used for some purposes. Of course, reference to Sec. 501-3(a) recognizes the use of purged enclosures as an alternative method.

The UL Red Book lists "Telephones" as follows:

■ Telephones, sound-powered telephones, and communications equipment and systems are listed for Class I and Class II use in Division 1 locations and are explosionproof equipment. Such equipment complies with Secs. 501-14(a) and (b).

■ Intrinsically safe sound-powered telephones are also listed for Class I, Division 1, Group D and may be used in both Divisions 1 and 2 locations in accordance with Secs. 501-14(a) and (b).

The Red Book also lists "Thermostats," "Signal Appliances" (which include fire alarms, fire detectors), "Solenoids," and "Sound Recording and Reproducing Equipment."

501·16. Grounding, Class I, Divisions 1 and 2. Special care in the grounding of all equipment is necessary in order to prevent the possibility of arcs or sparks when any grounded metal comes in contact with the frame or case of the equipment. All connections of conduit to boxes, cabinets, enclosures for apparatus, and motor frames must be so made as to secure permanent and effective electrical connections. To be effective, this form of construction is not only necessary in the spaces that are classed as hazardous, but should also be carried out back to the point where the connection for grounding the conduit is made to the grounding electrode system serving the premises. Outside the space where the hazardous conditions exist, threaded connections should be used for conduit, unless bonding techniques are used for connections to knockouts in sheetmetal enclosures. Any conduit emerging from a Division 1 or Division 2 location must have a bonded path of equipment grounding from the hazardous location back to the bonded service equipment or to the bonded secondary of a transformer that supplies the circuit into the hazardous location.

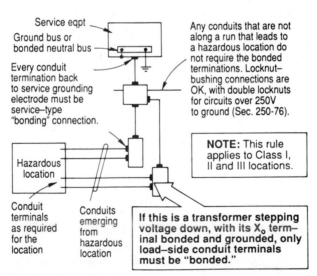

Fig. 501·40. Bonding of raceways and equipment must be made back to service ground. (Sec. 501-16.)

If the circuits to a hazardous location are supplied from a separately derived system (as from a transformer or from a generator on the load-side of the service), "bonded" conduit connections are required *only* back to the transformer or generator and *not* back to the service ground. It is only necessary to bond back to the point where the neutral and equipment grounding conductor of the supply system are bonded together. In that case, the low-impedance ground-fault current return path to the transformer or generator neutral will ensure quick fault-clearing action of the circuit protective devices.

The net effect of the wording in part **(a)** of this section is to require use of "service bonding" techniques (Sec. 250-72) throughout the length of a continuous path from raceway and equipment in a hazardous location all the way back to the *first* point at which the system neutral is bonded to the system equipment grounding terminal or bus and both are connected to a grounding electrode—either at the transformer in the system or at a generator or at the service equipment if there is no voltage change in the system (Fig. 501-40). That means that every raceway termination in the ground return path to the service or

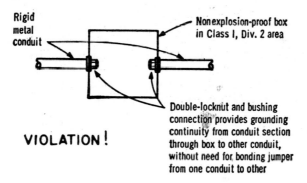

Rigid metal conduit

Nonexplosion-proof box in Class I, Div. 2 area

Double-locknut and bushing connection provides grounding continuity from conduit section through box to other conduit, without need for bonding jumper from one conduit to other

VIOLATION!

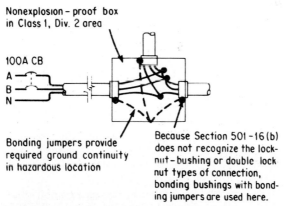

Nonexplosion-proof box in Class 1, Div. 2 area

100A CB
A
B
N

Bonding jumpers provide required ground continuity in hazardous location

Because Section 501-16(b) does not recognize the lock-nut-bushing or double lock nut types of connection, bonding bushings with bonding jumpers are used here.

Fig. 501-41. Bonding bushings with jumpers comply with grounding rule. (Sec. 501-16.)

transformer secondary must be a threaded metal conduit connection to a threaded hub or boss on a fitting or enclosure or any connection to a sheet-metal KO must use one of the following methods:

1. A locknut outside with a bonding locknut inside where connection is made to a clean KO—that is, a KO cut on the job or a KO from which all concentric or eccentric rings (so-called "Donuts") have been removed.
2. A bonding bushing with a bonding jumper to a grounding terminal within the enclosure, on a KO that is clean or has rings left in the enclosure wall.
3. A bonding bushing that does not require a jumper when used on a clean KO (as at bottom right of Fig. 250-57). The various techniques that must be used instead of locknut and bushing or double-locknut-and-bushing are described in Figs. 250-56 and 250-57.

At top, Fig. 501-41 shows a violation of part **(a)**. Although Sec. 501-4(b) permits a sheet-metal junction box (nonexplosionproof) in a Division 2 location, bonding through that enclosure (and all the way back to the service) may not be done simply by locknuts and bushings—not even the double-locknut type. At the bottom, the bonding jumpers satisfy the rule here. From Table 250-95, a No. 8 copper bonding jumper is the minimum acceptable size to be used with a 100-A-rated protective device, for connecting each bushing to the box.

According to the Exception for part **(b)** for Class I, Division 2 areas, liquidtight flexible metal conduit, in lengths not over 6 ft, may be used *without* a bonding "jumper" (an internal or external equipment grounding conductor) to enclose conductors protected at not more than 10 A. This permission is given only for circuits to a load that is "not a power utilization load." The same use of liquidtight flex is permitted for Class II and Class III locations—in Secs. 502-16(b) and 503-16(b).

ARTICLE 502. CLASS II LOCATIONS

502·1. General. Referring to Sec. 500-5, the hazards in Class II locations are due to the presence of combustible dust. These locations are subdivided into three groups, as follows:

- Group E, atmospheres containing metal dust
- Group F, atmospheres containing carbon black, coal dust, or coke dust
- Group G, atmospheres containing grain dust, such as in grain elevators

It is important to note that some equipment that is suitable for Class II, Group G, is not suitable for Class II, Groups E and F.

Any one of four hazards, or a combination of two or more, may exist in a Class II location: (1) an explosive mixture of air and dust, (2) the collection of conductive dust on and around live parts, (3) overheating of equipment because deposits of dust interfere with the normal radiation of heat, and (4) the possible ignition of deposits of dust by arcs or sparks.

A large number of processes which may produce combustible dusts are listed in Sec. 500-6. Most of the equipment listed as suitable for Class I locations is also dusttight, but it should not be taken for granted that all explosionproof equipment is suitable for use in Class II locations. Some explosionproof equipment may reach too high a temperature if blanketed by a heavy deposit of dust. Grain dust will ignite at a temperature below that of many of the flammable vapors.

Location of service equipment, switchboards, and panelboards in a separate room away from the dusty atmosphere is always preferable.

In Class II locations, with the presence of combustible dust, UL standards call for a type of construction designed to preclude dust and to operate at specified limited temperatures. Dust-ignition-proof equipment is generally more economical to use in Class II areas; however, explosionproof devices are often used if such devices are approved for Class II areas and for the particular Group involved.

Dust-ignition-proof equipment is enclosed in a manner so as to exclude ignitible amounts of dusts or amounts which might affect equipment performance or rating and which will not permit arcs, sparks, or heat inside the enclosure to cause ignition of exterior accumulations or atmospheric suspensions of a specified dust on or in the vicinity of the enclosure. Any assemblies that generate heat, such as lighting fixtures and motors, are tested with a dust blanket to simulate the operation of the device in a Class II location.

502·2. Transformers and Capacitors. Part **(a)** requires use of a **Code**-constructed transformer vault for a transformer or capacitor that contains oil or other liquid dielectric that will burn—when used in a Class II, Division 1 location.

The UL Red Book does not list transformers or capacitors for hazardous locations. So far as can be learned, no liquid-insulated or dry-type transformers can be obtained which are dusttight. Capacitors of the type used for the correction of the power factor of individual motors are of sealed construction, but must be provided with dusttight terminal enclosures if installed in these locations.

Dry-type transformers must either be approved as a complete assembly for Class II, Division 1 use (none are UL-listed) or they must be used in a vault. But transformers can be kept out of the hazardous areas, and part **(a)(3)** prohibits any use of a transformer or capacitor in a Class II, Division 1, Group E (metal dust) location.

Part **(b)** requires a vault for any oil-filled or high fire point liquid-insulated transformer or capacitor in a Division 2 area. A dry-type unit in a Division 2 area may be used either in a vault or without a vault if the unit is enclosed within a tight metal housing without any openings and only if it operates at 600 V or less. There are no special requirements for capacitors in Division 2 locations, except that they must not contain oil or any other "liquid that will burn" if they are not within a vault.

502·4. Wiring Methods. Part **(a)** covers Division 1 locations. The wiring methods are essentially the same for Class II, Division 1 as they are for Class I, Division 1. Conduit connections to fittings and boxes must be made to threaded bosses. For fittings and boxes, only those used for taps, splices, or terminals in locations of electrically conductive dusts (metal, carbon, etc.) must be approved for Class II locations (i.e., listed by UL).

As covered in part **(a)(2)**, where a flexible connection is necessary, it would usually be preferable to use a dusttight flexible fitting. Standard flexible conduit may not be used but liquidtight flexible metal conduit or liquidtight flexible nonmetallic conduit may be used, with a bonding jumper as required by Sec. 502-16(b). The use of a hard-service cord having one conductor serving as a grounding conductor is permitted.

In Division 2 locations, in order to provide adequate bonding, threaded fittings should be used with IMC or rigid metal conduit, but EMT may also be used (Fig. 502-1). The requirement for close-fitting covers could best be taken

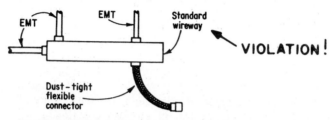

Fig. 502·1. EMT is O.K., but wireway must be dusttight. (Sec. 502-4.)

care of by using dusttight equipment. The standard type of pressed steel box cannot be used in any case where the box contains taps or splices. Where no taps, splices, or terminals are used in a box, a sheet metal box may be used, but all conduit connections to boxes that do not have threaded hubs or bosses must be of the bonded type, as required by Sec. 502-16(b) and described with illustrations under Sec. 501-16(b).

Flexible connections in Division 2 locations must observe the rules given above in part **(a)(2)**.

In part **(b),** for wiring in Class II, Division 2 locations, Type MC cable is acceptable cable for use in ventilated channel-type cable tray. Type MC cable may be used *either* secured to building surfaces or in tray.

502-5. Sealing, Class II, Divisions 1 and 2.   Note that sealing or other isolation is required only for conduits entering a dust-ignition-proof enclosure that connects to an enclosure that is not dust-ignition-proof. Seals are not generally required in Class II areas; however, where raceway connects an enclosure *required to be* dust-ignition-proof and one that is not, means must be provided to prevent dust from entering the dust-ignition-proof enclosure through the raceway. A seal in the conduit is one acceptable way of doing this, with the seal any distance from the enclosure (Fig. 502-2). However, if the connecting raceway is horizontal and at least 10 ft long, or if it is vertical, extending down from the dust-ignition-proof enclosure and at least 5 ft long, no sealing is necessary anywhere in the conduit. The distance between and orientation of the enclosures are considered adequate protection against dust passage. And that applies in Division 1 and Division 2 locations wherever the "dust-ignition-proof" is specifically required to be used by one of the sections of this article.

The next-to-last sentence of this section permits use of conduit *without* a seal

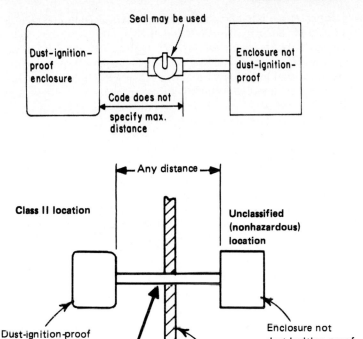

Seal may be used

Dust-ignition-proof enclosure

Enclosure not dust-ignition-proof

Code does not specify max. distance

←— Any distance —→

Class II location

Unclassified (nonhazardous) location

Dust-ignition-proof enclosure

Enclosure not dust-ignition-proof

Boundary

SEAL IS NOT REQUIRED IN CONDUIT RUN

Fig. 502-2. A seal fitting must be used in short (less than 10-ft) connections, as shown at top, but is not required, as shown at bottom.

between a dust-ignition-proof enclosure that is required in a Class II location and an enclosure in an unclassified location (Fig. 502-2, bottom). This added permission is made because, unlike gases or vapors, dust does not travel within conduit.

502-6. Switches, Circuit Breakers, Motor Controllers, and Fuses.   Note that part **(a)(1)** calls for "dust-ignition-proof" enclosures—which might involve the sealing called for in Sec. 502-5.

Most of the enclosed switches and circuit breakers approved for Class I, Division 1 locations are also approved for use in Class II locations.

Switches conforming with the definition of the term *isolating switch* would seldom be used in any hazardous location. Such switches are permitted for use as the disconnecting means for motors larger than 100 hp.

502-8. Motors and Generators.   In Class II, Division 1 locations, motors must be dust-ignition-proof (approved for Class II, Division 1) or totally enclosed with positive-pressure ventilation. The same motors may be used also in Class II, Division 2 areas; however, if dust accumulation is very slight, either a standard, open-type motor (without arcing or sparking parts), a self-cleaning textile motor, or a squirrel-cage motor may be used.

Part **(a)(2)** refers to a totally enclosed pipe-ventilated motor. A motor of this type is cooled by clean air forced through a pipe by a fan or blower. Such a motor has an intake opening, where air is delivered to the motor through the pipe from the blower. The exhaust opening is on the opposite side, and this should be connected to a pipe terminating outside the building, so that dust will not collect inside the motor while it is not running.

For Class II, Division 2 locations, part **(b)** permits use of totally enclosed, non-ventilated motors and totally enclosed, fan-cooled (TEFC) motors in addition to totally enclosed, pipe-ventilated and dust-ignition-proof motors. This rule eliminates any interpretation that only a labeled motor (dust-ignition-proof) is acceptable for Class II, Division 2 locations. Experience has shown the other motors to be entirely safe and effective for use in such locations.

Motors of the common totally enclosed type without special provision for cooling may be used in Division 2 locations, but to deliver the same horsepower, a plain totally enclosed motor must be considerably larger and heavier than a motor of the open type or an enclosed fan-cooled or pipe-ventilated motor.

The UL Red Book lists motors for Class II, Divisions 1 and 2, Groups E, F, and G locations.

502-9. Ventilating Piping. In locations where dust or flying material will collect on or in motors to such an extent as to interfere with their ventilation or cooling, enclosed motors which will not overheat under the prevailing conditions must be used. It may be necessary to require the use of an enclosed pipe-ventilated motor or to locate the motor in a separate dusttight room, properly ventilated with clean air (Sec. 430-16).

The reference to ventilation is clarified in this section. Vent pipes for rotating electrical machinery must be of metal not lighter than No. 24 MSG gauge, or equally substantial. They must lead to a source of clean air outside of buildings, be screened to prevent entry of small animals or birds, and be protected against damage and corrosion.

In Class II, Division 1 locations, vent pipes must be dusttight. In Division 2 locations, they must be tight to prevent entrance of appreciable quantities of dust and to prevent escape of sparks, flame, or burning material.

Typical conditions where these requirements may apply include processing machinery or enclosed conveyors where dust may escape only under abnormal conditions, or storage areas where handling of bags or sacks may result in small quantities of dust in the air.

502-10. Utilization Equipment. As noted in part **(b)(1)**, Exception, dusttight metal-enclosed radiant heating panels may be used in Class II, Division 2 locations even though they are *not* approved for Class II locations. The Exception to this section will permit such electric-heat panels *provided* that surface temperature limitations of Sec. 500-3(d) are satisfied. Heaters of that type are available with low surface temperature.

502-11. Lighting Fixtures. Fixtures used in Class II, Division 1 areas must prevent the entry of the hazardous dust and should prevent the accumulation of dust on the fixture body. In Division 1 locations, all fixtures must be approved for that location. Where metal dusts are present, lighting fixtures must be specifically approved for use in Group E atmospheres. Fixtures are listed by Underwriters Laboratories Inc. as suitable for use in all three of the locations classed as Groups E, F, and G, for Divisions 1 and 2.

The purpose of the latter part of subparagraph **(a)(3)** is to specify the type of cord to be used for wiring a chain-suspended fixture. It is not the intention to permit a fixture to be suspended by means of a cord pendant or drop cord.

The only special requirements for lighting fixtures in Class II, Division 2 locations are that the lamp must be enclosed in a suitable glass globe and that a guard must be provided unless the fixture is so located that it will not be exposed to physical damage. The enclosing globe should be tight enough so that it will practically exclude dust, though dusttight construction is not called for. For Class II, Group G, Division 2 areas, fixtures normally are the enclosed and gasketed type. However, in addition, such fixtures must not have an exposed surface temperature exceeding 165°C.

There are portable handlamps approved for use in any Class II, Group G location, i.e., where the hazards are due to grain dust.

The UL Red Book notes that a Class II fixture for Divisions 1 and 2 is tested for dust tightness and safe operation in the dust atmosphere for which it is listed. A note points out the importance of effective maintenance—regular cleaning—to prevent buildup of combustible dust on such equipment.

502-12. Flexible Cords, Class II, Divisions 1 and 2. Figure 502-3 shows flexible cord used in a Division 2 area of a grain elevator (Class II, Group G).

Fig. 502-3. Flexible cords and listed connectors are used in a grain elevator that handles combustible grain dust. (Sec. 502-12.)

Section 502-4 permits its use in Division 1 and Division 2 areas of Class II locations. Listed cord connectors are recognized for use in Class II, Group G locations—using Types S, SO, ST, or STO multiconductor, extra-hard-usage cord *with* a grounding conductor. Cord connectors for connecting extra-hard-service type of flexible cord to devices in hazardous locations must be carefully applied.

The UL Red Book notes, under "Receptacles with Plugs," that Type S flexible cord should be frequently inspected and replaced when necessary.

502·13. Receptacles and Attachment Plugs. Class II receptacles listed as approved for Division 1 locations are equipped with boxes for threaded metal conduit connection, and a factory seal is provided between the receptacle and its box. Only receptacles and plugs listed for Class II locations are permitted in Division 1 areas.

Receptacles for Class II, Division 2 locations do not have to be approved for Class II but must satisfy the connection method described.

Frequent inspection is recommended for flexible cords, receptacles, and plugs, with replacement whenever necessary.

As shown in Sec. 501-12 for Class I locations, for Class II locations, interlocked CBs and plugs are made for receptacles so that the plug cannot be removed from the receptacle when the CB is closed and the CB cannot be closed when the plug is not in the receptacle.

502·16. Grounding, Class II, Divisions 1 and 2. The requirements of this section are the same as those of Sec. 501-16. Refer to the discussion and illustrations in that section.

502·17. Surge Protection, Class II, Divisions 1 and 2. A common application of this surge protection is found in grain-handling facilities (grain elevators) in localities where severe lightning storms are prevalent. Assuming a building supplied through a bank of transformers located a short distance from the building the recommendations are, in general, as shown in the single-line diagram in Fig. 502-4. The surge-protective equipment consists of primary lightning arresters at the transformers and surge-protective capacitors connected to

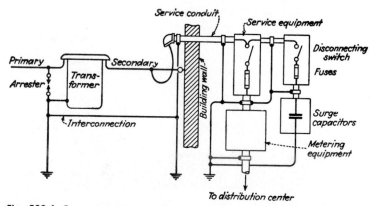

Fig. 502·4. Surge protection is often used to protect Class II systems against lightning.

the supply side of the service equipment. The lightning arrester ground and the secondary system ground should be solidly connected together. All grounds should be bonded together and to the service conduit and to all boxes enclosing the service equipment, metering equipment, and capacitors.

Complete information on methods of providing surge protection may be obtained from the Mill Mutual Fire Prevention Bureau, 2 North Riverside Plaza, Chicago, IL 60606.

ARTICLE 503. CLASS III LOCATIONS

503-1. General. The small fibers of cotton that are carried everywhere by air currents in some parts of cotton mills and the wood shavings and sawdust that collect around planers in woodworking plants are common examples of the combustible flyings or fibers that cause the hazards in Class III, Division 1 locations. A cotton warehouse is a common example of a Class III, Division 2 location.

503-3. Wiring Methods. Rigid nonmetallic conduit, EMT, and Type MC (metal-clad cable) are permitted for Class I and Class II, Division 1 locations—in addition to rigid metal conduit, IMC, Type MI cable, Type SNM cable, and dusttight wireways. Type MC (Art. 334) includes interlocked armor cable, corrugated metal armor, smooth aluminum-sheathed cable (Type ALS), and smooth copper-sheathed cable (Type CS).

Fittings and boxes must be dusttight, whether or not they contain taps, joints, or terminal connections. As part **(a)(2)** notes about flexible connections, it is necessary to use dusttight flexible connectors, liquidtight flexible metal conduit, or extra-hard-usage flexible cord. This clear, simple rule calls for an equipment ground wire in flexible cord, unless some other **NEC**-approved grounding method is used.

Part **(b)** requires the same wiring methods for Division 2 as for Division 1. As indicated in Fig. 503-1, there are no seal requirements in Class III locations.

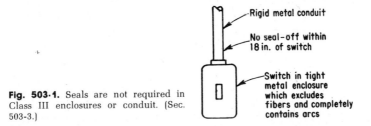

Fig. 503-1. Seals are not required in Class III enclosures or conduit. (Sec. 503-3.)

- Rigid metal conduit
- No seal-off within 18 in. of switch
- Switch in tight metal enclosure which excludes fibers and completely contains arcs

503-4. Switches, Circuit Breakers, Motor Controllers, and Fuses, Class III, Divisions 1 and 2. Equipment suitable for Class III locations must function at full rating without developing surface temperatures high enough to cause excessive dehydration or gradual carbonization of accumulated fibers or flyings. These devices have the same surface temperature limitations as Class II equipment, and construction is similar.

Enclosures for equipment in a Class III location must be dusttight—that is, provided with telescoping or close-fitting covers or other effective means which prevent the escape of sparks or burning material and have no openings through which sparks or burning material might escape, or through which adjacent combustible material might be ignited.

503-6. Motors and Generators, Class III, Divisions 1 and 2. UL lists no Class III motors as such; however, totally enclosed nonventilated motors and the so-called lint-free or self-cleaning textile squirrel-cage motors are commonly used. The latter may be acceptable to the local inspection authority if only moderate amounts of flyings are likely to accumulate on or near the motor, which must be readily accessible for routine cleaning and maintenance. Or the motor may be a squirrel-cage motor, or a standard open-type machine having any arcing or heating devices enclosed within a tight metal housing without ventilating or other openings.

503-9. Lighting Fixtures, Class III, Divisions 1 and 2. In Class III, Divisions 1 and 2 areas, lighting fixtures must minimize the entrance of fibers and flyings and prevent the escape of sparks or hot metal. And again, the surface temperature of the unit must be limited to 165°C. Available fixtures are third-party certified (by a national test lab) for Class III locations, Divisions 1 and 2. In the past, enclosed and gasketed types of fixtures, of the type that was used in Class I, Division 2 areas, have been acceptable as suitable for use in this application. But because there are listed Class III fixtures available, inspection agencies and OSHA might insist on use of only listed fixtures in such applications—to be consistent with the trend to third-party certification.

503-13. Electric Cranes, Hoists, and Similar Equipment, Class III, Divisions 1 and 2. A crane operating in a Class III location and having rolling or sliding collectors making contact with bare conductors introduces two hazards:

1. Any arcing between a collector and a conductor rail or wire may ignite flyings of combustible fibers that have collected on or near to the bare conductor. This danger may be guarded against by proper alignment of the bare conductor and by using a collector of such form that contact is always maintained, and by the use of guards or barriers which will confine the hot particles of metal that may be thrown off when an arc is formed.

2. Dust and flyings collecting on the insulating supports of the bare conductors may form a conducting path between the conductors or from one conductor to ground and permit enough current to flow to ignite the fibers. This condition is much more likely to exist if moisture is present. Operation on a system having no grounded conductor makes it somewhat less likely that a fire will be started by a current flowing to ground. A recording ground detector will show when the insulation resistance is being lowered by an accumulation of dust and flyings on the insulators, and a relay actuated by excessively low insulation resistance and arranged to trip a CB provides automatic disconnection of the bare conductors when the conditions become dangerous.

ARTICLE 504. INTRINSICALLY SAFE SYSTEMS

504-1. Scope This NEC Article covers design, layout, and installation of electrical equipment and systems that are not capable of releasing sufficient electrical or thermal energy to ignite flammable or combustible atmospheres. All equipment and apparatus that is "intrinsically safe" must be "approved"—which can be understood to mean evaluated by a testing laboratory such as UL. Reference to the NEC definition of "approved" and Sec. 110-2 and its fine-print note (FPN) dictate the most rigorous and objective determination that such equipment is "approved."

The substantiation for adoption of this Code Article noted the following:

SUBSTANTIATION: Installation personnel need specific requirements for the installation of intrinsically safe equipment that are clear and concise. The authority having jurisdiction needs requirements that are enforceable.

Currently, NEC Sec. 500-2 exempts intrinsically safe equipment and associated wiring from the requirements of Arts. 500 through 517. The requirements of Art. 500 are applicable to all hazardous (classified) location equipment and intrinsic safety installation should not be expected from them.

The applications of intrinsically safe apparatus and associated apparatus used to be limited to a few specific applications of process control equipment. The need for optimizing process control for quality, economy, and environmental regulations has resulted in a great expansion of the process control industry. In recent years, the use of computerized process control equipment, process logic controllers (PLCs), and similar equipment has grown dramatically. Pneumatic controls are no longer as acceptable as they were years ago and discrete instruments that used to switch 110 V to control processes have also become unsatisfactory.

With the current technology of microelectronics, there is now a vast array of sensors, process transmitters, actuators, etc., that were not possible a decade ago. These devices work with low power levels in the 24-V, 20-mA range and are ideally suited to the application of intrinsic safety techniques. Installation is more cost-effective than other techniques such as purging or use of explosionproof enclosures and conduits. More and more instrument manufacturers are obtaining intrinsic safety approval of their products from UL and FM. One approval agency has indicated an average growth rate of almost 30 percent per year over the last 10 years.

When new requirements are placed in the NEC, they get tremendous coverage by the trade journals, seminars, etc. People in the trade become educated and are able to apply the new requirements in practice. Placing installation requirements for intrinsically safe installations in the NEC will further the practice more than any other single action. Installers and inspectors will have a common basis for proper installation, and final acceptance of installations will be achieved with much less difficulty.

ARTICLE 511. COMMERCIAL GARAGES, REPAIR AND STORAGE

511-2. Locations. At one time (1971 NEC), this section considered parking garages as hazardous locations. Now, the rule no longer requires that this article apply to locations in which more than three cars, trucks, or other gas vehicles are or may be stored. Specifically, parking garages used simply for parking or storage of gasoline-powered vehicles are not classified as hazardous areas, no matter how many vehicles are present. But, such parking areas in enclosed buildings must be adequately ventilated.

Below-grade areas occupied for repairing, or communicating areas located below a repair garage, shall be continuously ventilated by a mechanical ventilating system having positive means for exhausting indoor air at a rate of not less than 0.75 cfm/sq ft of floor area. An approved means shall be provided for introducing an equal amount of outdoor air.

Operations involving open flame or electric arcs, including fusion, gas, and electric welding, shall be restricted to areas specifically provided for such purposes.

All enclosed, basement, and underground parking structures shall be continuously ventilated by a mechanical system capable of providing a minimum of six air changes per hour.

Heating equipment may be installed in motor vehicle repair or parking areas where there is no dispensing or transferring of Class I or II flammable liquids (as defined in the Flammable and Combustible Liquids Code, NFPA No. 30-1984) or liquefied petroleum gas, provided the bottom of the combustion chamber is not less than 18 in. above the floor, the heating equipment is protected from physical damage by vehicles, and continuous mechanical ventilation is provided at the rate of 0 .75 cfm/sq ft of floor area. The heating system and the ventilation system shall be suitably interlocked to ensure operation of the ventilation system when the heating system is in operation.

Approved suspended unit heaters may be used provided they are located not less than 8 ft above the floor and are installed in accordance with the conditions of their approval.

The question often arises, Does diesel fuel come within the classification of volatile flammable liquids, thereby requiring application of Art. 511 to places used exclusively for repair of diesel-powered vehicles? The third paragraph under Sec. 514-1 reads: "Where the authority having jurisdiction can satisfactorily determine that flammable liquids having a flash point below 100°F, such as gasoline, will not be handled, he may classify such a location as nonhazardous."

The NFPA Inspection Manual, under identification of flammable liquids, says, "Minimum flash points for fuel oils of various grades are: No. 1 and No. 2, 100°F; No. 4, 110; No. 5, over 130; No. 6, 150 or higher. Actual flash points are commonly higher and are required to be higher by some state laws. No. 1 fuel is often sold as kerosene, range oil or coal oil."

Diesel fuel is a Class 3 flammable liquid, having flash points above 70°F. One listing of flash points of flammable liquids showed no diesel fuel below 120°F. Therefore, a diesel-fuel installation may be classified as a nonhazardous area and wired as such, unless it can be firmly established that the particular fuel has a flash point under 100°F. But, of course, the authority enforcing the Code is the one responsible for classifying such areas as nonhazardous.

511·3. Class I Locations.   In part **(a)**, the wording (which was significantly revised from the 1971 to the 1975 **NEC**) considers any floor area to be a Class I, Division 2 hazardous location up to 18 in. above the floor. It should be noted

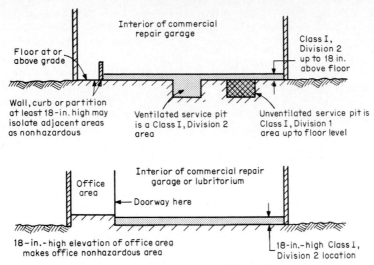

Fig. 511-1. Hazardous areas must be carefully established. (Sec. 511-3.)

that the rule no longer says that "each floor at or above grade" in a commercial garage is considered to be a Class I, Division 2 location up to 18 in. above floor level. The rule no longer refers to "grade" and may be taken to simply apply to any floor whether it is *above* or below grade level. Any wiring within this space must be suitable for Class I, Division 2 locations.

Figure 511-1 shows the basic rule of part **(a)** and part **(b)**. Note that part **(b)** no longer refers to "floor below *grade*," but simply covers "pit or depression below *floor* level." Previous wording of these two parts resulted in the classification as Class I, Division 2 of the total shaded areas in Fig. 511-2, where vehicular servicing is done on the below-grade floor, the first floor, and the second floor. For each floor at or above grade, part **(a)** used to define the entire area up to a level of 18 in. above the floor as a Class I, Division 2 location. And part **(b)** stated that below-grade areas up to a level of 18 in. above the bottom of outside doors

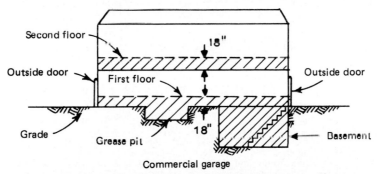

Commercial garage

Fig. 511-2. Previous wording of Code rule identified shaded areas as Class I, Division 2 locations. (Sec. 511-3.)

or other openings that are at or above grade level must be considered Class I, Division 2 locations, which is the lower shaded area in Fig. 511-2. Now part **(b)** simply requires any pit or depression below floor level to be considered as Class I, Division 2 area.

Under the new wording, for floors below grade, such as the basement in the sketch, the enforcing authority may judge that the hazardous location extends up to a level of only 18 in. above the floor. And that means that any wiring and equipment installed in any of these defined hazardous areas must be approved for Class I, Division 2 locations. Above these hazardous areas, Sec. 511-6 applies.

Part **(d)** allows the authority having jurisdiction to classify areas adjacent to hazardous locations as nonhazardous if proper ventilation, air pressure differentials, or physical separation are provided in a specific garage installation.

Equipment located in a suitable room or enclosure provided for the purpose or in a showroom separated from the garage proper by a partition which is reasonably tight up to 18 in. above the floor need not conform to the requirements of this section.

In all garages within the scope of this chapter, because of the possible presence of gasoline vapor near the floor, any equipment which in its normal operation may cause arcs or sparks, if less than 18 in. above the floor, is considered as in a hazardous location. It is seldom necessary to make use of devices having exposed live parts, but where this is unavoidable, even though the device is 18 in. above the floor, any such device should be well guarded.

511·6. Wiring in Spaces Above Class I Locations.   The rules here apply to the lubritorium areas in service stations and *any* other space above the defined hazardous locations.

511·7. Equipment Above Class I Locations.   Part **(a)** notes that equipment that may produce arcs or sparks and is within 12 ft of the floor above hazardous areas must be enclosed or provided with guards to prevent hot particles from

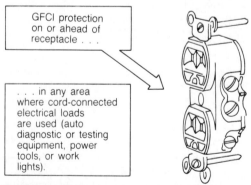

GFCI protection on or ahead of receptacle . . .

. . . in any area where cord-connected electrical loads are used (auto diagnostic or testing equipment, power tools, or work lights).

Fig. 511-3. GFCI protection is required for all 125-V, single-phase, 15- and 20-A receptacles where electrical auto-testing equipment, electrical hand tools, and portable lighting are used. (Sec. 511-10.)

falling into the hazardous area, but lamps, lampholders, and receptacles are excluded. Standard receptacles are O.K. Lighting fixtures that are within 12 ft of the floor over hazardous areas, over traffic lanes, or otherwise exposed to physical damage, must be totally enclosed, as required in part **(b)**.

511-9. Electric Vehicle Charging.   The requirements for battery-charging cables and connectors are similar to the requirements for outlets for the connection of portable appliances, except that when hanging free the battery-charging cables and connectors may hang within 6 in. from the floor. The common form is a plug which is inserted into a receptacle on the vehicle, and, since the prongs are "alive," they must be covered by a protecting hood.

511-10. Ground-Fault Circuit-Interrupter Protection for Personnel.   This rule is shown in Fig. 511-3.

ARTICLE 513. AIRCRAFT HANGARS

513-2. Classification of Locations.   Figure 513-1 shows the details of hangar classifications. The entire floor area up to 18 in. above the floor, and adjacent areas not suitably cut off from the hazardous area or not elevated at least 18 in. above it, are classified as Class I, Division 2 locations. Pits below the hangar

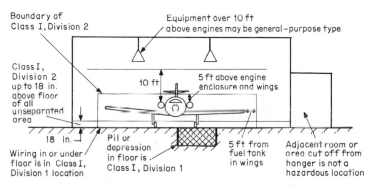

Fig. 513-1. Boundaries of hazardous areas are clearly defined. (Sec. 513-2.)

floor are classified as Class I, Division 1. Within 5 ft horizontally from aircraft power plants, fuel tanks, or structures containing fuel, the Class I, Division 2 location extends to a level that is 5 ft above the upper surface of wings and engine enclosures.

513-5. Equipment Not Within Class I Locations.   Fixtures and other equipment that produce arcs or sparks may not be general-use types but are required to be totally enclosed or constructed to prevent escape of sparks or hot metal particles if less than 10 ft above aircraft wings and engine enclosures, as indicated in Fig. 513-1.

ARTICLE 514. GASOLINE DISPENSING AND
SERVICE STATIONS

514-1. Definition.   As noted under Sec. 511-1, there is a question about application of the rules of Arts. 511 and 514 to areas used for service of vehicles using
diesel fuel and to dispensing pumps and areas for diesel fuel. Fuel with a flash
point above 100°F may be ruled to be *not* "a volatile flammable liquid" to
which the regulations of Arts. 511 and 514 are addressed.

Note that vehicle repair rooms or areas and lubritoriums at gas stations must
comply with Art. 511.

514-2. Class I Locations.   As noted, Table 514-2 delineates and classifies the
various areas at dispensing pumps and service stations. This table brings the
Code rules into agreement with data given in NFPA 30 S/C, General Storage
and Handling of Flammable and Combustible Liquids.

Fig. 1 in the **NEC** book, in Art. 514, gives a visual representation of the dimensions of Class I locations—both Division 1 and Division 2—as described in the
text of Table 514-2. In the wording of Table 514-2, the space within the dis-
pensing-pump enclosure is a Class I, Division 1 location as described in ANSI/
UL 87, "Power Operated Devices for Petroleum Products." This **Code** rule has
become less specific because the previous specific dimensions—"within a dispenser enclosure up to 4 ft vertically above the base except that space defined
as Division 2"—has been removed.

Around the outside of a dispenser pump housing, the Division 2 location
extends 18 in. horizontally in all directions, from grade up to the height of the
pump enclosure or up to the height of "that portion of the dispenser enclosure
containing liquid-handling components" (Fig. 514-1).

In the table, there is no direct statement that the ground under the Division
1 and Division 2 locations at a dispenser island is a Division 1 location. However, that seems to be the intent of the rule given for "Pits" under "Dispensing
Units," where it refers to "space below grade level," where "any part [of that
grade level] . . . is within the Division 1 or 2 location." But the phrase "which
shall extend at least to the point of emergence above ground" is no longer part
of the rule in the table, but is made mandatory at the end of the first paragraph
of Sec. 514-8.

Outdoor areas within 20 ft of a pump are considered a Class I, Division 2
location and must be wired accordingly. Such a hazardous area extends 18 in.
above grade. If a building with a below-grade basement is within this hazardous area, gasoline fumes could enter the building if there were any windows
within the 18-in.-high classified space, thereby making the basement a Class I,
Division 2 area. This condition could be eliminated by "suitably cutting off the
building from the hazardous area" by installing an 18-in.-high concrete curb
between the service station and the residential property or enclosing the window openings up to that height.

Table 514-2 sets a 20-ft-diameter, 18-in.-high, Division 2 area around each
fill-pipe for the underground gasoline tanks at a gas station—as shown in Fig.
514-2.

As noted above, any wiring or equipment that is installed beneath any part

Location   ◼ Class I Div. 1   ▨ Class I Div. 2

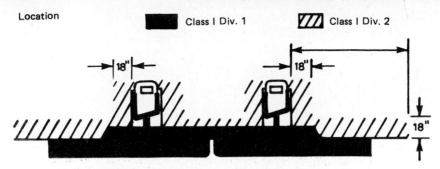

Division 1 space is *within* the dispenser, within any pit or box *below* the dispenser, and within the ground below the Class I, Division 2 location.

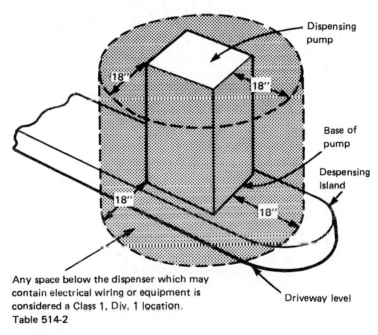

Dispensing pump

Base of pump

Despensing Island

Any space below the dispenser which may contain electrical wiring or equipment is considered a Class 1, Div. 1 location. Table 514-2

Driveway level

Fig. 514-1. The shaded space around the *outside* of the pump enclosure is a Class I, Division 2 hazardous location. (Sec. 514-2.)

of a Class I, Division 1 or Division 2 location is classified as being within a Class I, Division 1 location to the point where the wiring method is brought up out of the ground. That means the Division 1 area may extend far beyond the limits of the 20-ft-radius perimeter around the dispensing pumps. The Division 1 area extends to the point where the conduit comes up to the supply panelboard or runs up to a lighting standard or a sign, as shown under Sec. 514-6.

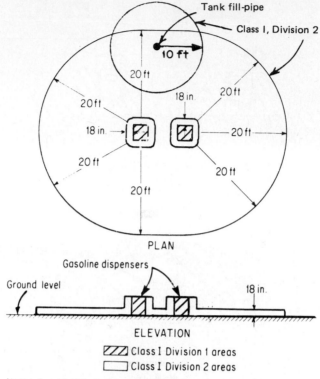

PLAN

ELEVATION

⊿⊿⊿ Class I Division 1 areas

☐ Class I Division 2 areas

Note : Any electrical wiring below the hazardous areas shown is
considered to be in a Class I Division 1 area.

Fig. 514·2. Class I, Division 2 area extends around pumps and tank fill-
pipes. (Sec. 514-2.)

As covered in Table 514-2, under "Dispensing Device, Overhead Type,"
where the dispensing unit and/or its hose and nozzle are suspended from overhead, the space within the dispenser enclosure and "all electrical equipment
integral with the dispensing hoze or nozzle" are classified as Class I, Division
1 areas. The space extending 18 in. horizontally in all directions from the enclosure and extending down to grade level is classified as a Class I, Division 2 area.
The horizontal area, for 18 in. above grade and extending 20 ft measured from
those points vertically below the outer edges of an overhead dispenser enclosure, is also classified as a Class I, Division 2 area. All equipment integral with
an overhead dispensing hose or nozzle must be suitable for a Class I, Division
1 hazardous area.

Table 514-2 notes the hazardous space around any vent pipe for an underground tank at a gas station is simply a 3-ft-radius sphere (a ball-like volume;
Class I, Division 1) and a 5-ft-radius sphere (Class I, Division 2) around the top
opening of a pipe that discharges upward, but the hazardous space around a
pipe opening that does not discharge up includes the sphere described *plus* a

cylinder of space from that sphere down to the ground. The space beyond the 5-ft radius from tank vents that discharge upward and spaces beyond unpierced walls and areas below grade that lie beneath tank vents are not classified as hazardous.

Table 514-2 designates a pit or depression below grade in a lubritorium as a Class I, Division 1 location if it is within an unventilated space, but does allow for the possibility of classification as Division 2, as permitted in Sec. 511-3(b) for a pit in a repair garage where ventilation exists. Refer to Fig. 511-1 on classification of repair area.

514·5. Circuit Disconnects. When the electrical equipment of a pump is being serviced or repaired, it is very important that there be no "hot" wire or wires inside the pump. Since it is always possible that the polarity of the circuit wires may have been accidentally reversed at the panelboard, control switches or CBs must open all conductors, including the neutral.

To satisfy this **Code** rule, a special panel application is commonly used in gas stations. Figure 514-3 shows how the hookup is accomplished using a gas-

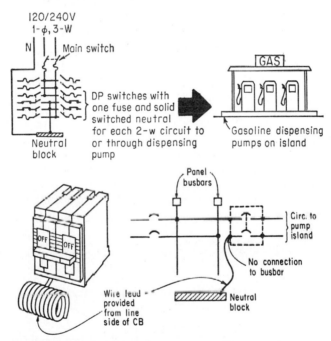

Fig. 514·3. "Gas-station" switches or CBs provide neutral disconnect. (Sec. 514-5.)

station-type panelboard, which has its bussing arranged to permit hookup of standard solid-neutral circuits in addition to the switch-neutral circuits required. Another way of supplying such switched-neutral circuits is with CB-type panelboards for which there are standard accessory breaker units, which have a trip element in the ungrounded conductor and only a switching mech-

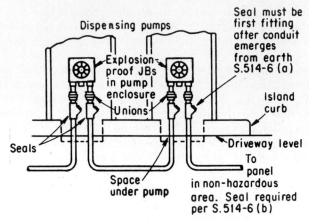

Dispensing pumps

Seal must be
first fitting
after conduit
emerges
from earth
S.514-6 (a)

Explosion-
proof JBs
in pump
enclosure

Unions

Island
curb

Seals

Driveway level

To
panel
in non-hazardous
area. Seal required
per S.514-6 (b)

Space
under pump

Seal required in each conduit entering
or leaving dispensing pump. S.514-6(a)

Fig. 514-4. Seal fitting must be used for every conduit at dispenser.
(Sec. 514-6.)

anism in the other pole of the common-trip breaker, as shown. Either 2- or 3-pole units may be used for 2-wire or 3-wire circuits, rated 15, 20, or 30 A. Use of single-pole circuit breakers with handle ties would be a **Code** violation. No electrical connection is made to the panel busbar by the plug-in grip on the neutral breaker unit. A wire lead connects line side of neutral breaker to neutral block in panel, or two clamp terminals are used for neutral.

514-6. Sealing.   Every conduit connecting to a dispenser pump must have a seal in it, as shown in Fig. 514-4. Conduits connecting to gas pumps are commonly connected through an explosionproof junction box that is set in the pump island, as shown in Fig. 514-5. This box is approved as raintight and provided with integral sealing wells. All the conduits connecting to the box are sealed without need for separate individual sealing fittings. Additional individ-

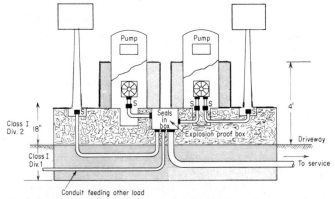

Pump   Pump

Class I
Div. 2   18"

Seals
in
box

Explosion proof box

Driveway

4'

Class I
Div.1

To service

Conduit feeding other load

Fig. 514-5. Seals are required in conduits to pumps and to lighting fixtures or signs at points marked "S." (Sec. 514-6.)

ual seals are required where the conduits enter the pump cavity as shown. And, of course, a seal must be used in each conduit that leaves the hazardous area—such as in the conduit that feeds each lighting standard, with no fitting or coupling between the seal in the base of each standard and the boundary at the 18-in. height where the circuit crosses into nonhazardous areas. And the conduit at bottom right, which extends back to the panelboard, must also be sealed where it comes up out of the earth at the panelboard location.

The lighting fixtures in Fig. 514-5 must satisfy Sec. 511-7(b), which refers to "fixed lighting" that may be exposed to physical damage—such as impact by a vehicle. If the fixtures are not at least 12 ft above the ground, they must be totally enclosed or constructed to prevent escape of sparks or hot metal. Section 514-4 specifies that.

In Fig. 514-6, four seals are shown. Normally panelboards are located in a nonhazardous location so that a seal is shown where the conduit is emerging

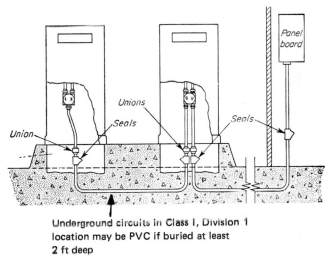

Underground circuits in Class I, Division 1
location may be PVC if buried at least
2 ft deep

Fig. 514-6. Conduit from pump island must be sealed at panelboard location. (Sec. 514-6.)

from underground, which Sec. 514-8 identifies as the point where the conduit is leaving the hazardous location.

514-7. Grounding.   Because of the danger at gas stations, grounding is very important and the rule here calls for thorough grounding.

514-8. Underground Wiring.   Note that Exception No. 2 of this rule permits rigid nonmetallic conduit for circuits buried at least 2 ft deep in the earth, even though the conduit in the earth may be in a Class I, Division 1 area under a Division 1 or Division 2 area, as noted in the second sentence of this rule. Section 347-3(a) normally excludes rigid nonmetallic conduit from hazardous locations but specifically cites Sec. 514-8 as an exception, as shown at the bottom of Fig. 514-6.

Where rigid nonmetallic conduit is buried at least 2 ft in the ground, as permitted for underground wiring at a gas station, a length of *threaded* rigid metal conduit or *threaded* IMC—at least 2 ft long—must be used at the end of the nonmetallic conduit where it turns up from the 2-ft burial depth. This clarifies that the entire length of the nonmetallic conduit must be down at least 2 ft (Fig. 514-7).

The phrase in this rule also requires the 2-ft length of metal conduit to be used on the end of the nonmetallic conduit where the conduit run does *not* turn

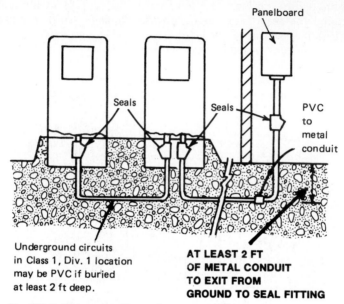

Fig. 514·7. The nonmetallic conduit permitted in the underground Class I, Division 2 location must never come above the required 2-ft burial depth. (Sec. 514-8.)

up, but passes horizontally into the nonhazardous area of a basement. In that case or where the conduit turns up, a length of metal conduit is needed to provide for installation of a seal-off fitting because the conduit is, in effect, emerging from the Class I, Division 1 location below ground; and a seal is required at the crossing of the boundary between the classified location and the nonhazardous location in, say, the office or other general area of a gas station.

ARTICLE 515. BULK STORAGE PLANTS

515·1. Definition. A flammable liquid is said to become volatile when the ambient temperature is equal to, or greater than, its flash point. Typical flash points are gasoline, −45°F; kerosene, 100°F; diesel oil, 100°F. Thus, the status of gasoline is definitely established as a volatile flammable liquid regardless of geographical location of the storage facility. Other liquids may change from one state to another depending upon the relation of the ambient temperature to their respective flash points. (See Fire Hazard Properties of Flammable Liquids, Gases and Volatile Solids, NFPA No. 325M.)

515·2. Class I Locations. This section sets its rules in a table indicating the extent of Division 1 and Division 2 locations at various equipment locations. As with the table in Sec. 514-2, this table brings the **Code** rules into agreement with NFPA No. 30 S/C, General Storage and Handling of Flammable and Combustible Liquids. Figure 515-1 shows rules from Table 515-2, covered

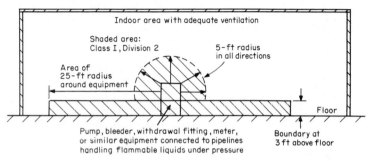

Fig. 515·1. Space around indoor equipment is a Class I, Division 2 location if adequately ventilated; or a Class I, Division 1 location, if not. (Sec. 515-2.)

under "Pumps, Bleeders, Withdrawal Fittings, Meters and Similar Devices, Indoors."

For outdoor use of the same kinds of equipment the 5-ft radius is reduced to 3 ft, the 25-ft radius is reduced to 10 ft, and the 3-ft-high level is reduced to 18 in. And where *transfer* of gasoline or similar liquid is done outdoors or in a ventilated indoor place, the space around the vent or fill opening becomes a Class I, Division 1 location for 3 ft in all directions from the opening and a Division 2 location out to 5 ft from the opening.

The hazardous area around a volatile flammable liquid outdoor storage tank ("Tank-Aboveground" in Table 515-2) extends 10 ft horizontally beyond the periphery of the tank (Fig. 515-2). **Code** designation is Class I, Division 2, and wiring installations within this range must conform to **Code** rules for this category. Space around the vent is a Division 1 location.

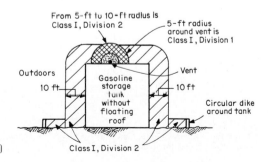

Fig. 515·2. (Sec. 515-2.)

515·5. Underground Wiring.   This rule is somewhat similar to that of Sec. 514-8. However, in this article no underground space is designated as a Class I, Division 1 location—as it is in Table 514-2. Therefore, use of nonmetallic conduit or approved cable buried at least 2 ft underground is *not* made in a hazardous location as it is under Sec. 514-2. But the reference that is made to Sec. 515-5 in Sec. 347-3(a) implies that underground wiring at a bulk-storage plant may be in a hazardous location.

ARTICLE 516.   SPRAY APPLICATION, DIPPING, AND COATING PROCESSES

516·1. Scope.   Note that this article applies to "locations" used for finishing processes—which means open spraying areas as well as enclosed or semi-enclosed "booths."

The safety of life and property from fire or explosion in the spray application of flammable paints and finishes and combustible powders depends upon the extent, arrangement, maintenance, and operation of the process.

An analysis of actual experience in industry demonstrates that the largest fire losses and greatest fire frequency have occurred where good practice standards were not observed.

516·2. Classification of Locations.   Two different types of hazardous conditions are present in a paint-spraying operation: the spray and its vapor which create explosive mixtures in the air; and combustible mists, dusts, or deposits. And each must be treated separately.

In part **(a)**, the interior of every spray booth **(1)** and some area spraying **(3)** are Class I or Class II, Division 1 locations depending on whether the atmosphere contains vapors or dusts. When spray operations are not contained within a booth, there is greatly reduced control of flammable atmosphere, and the area of hazard is increased considerably. This is shown in Fig. 516-1, which is a

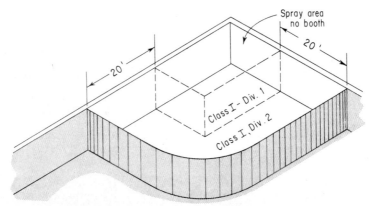

Fig. 516·1. Open spraying involves Division 1 and Division 2 locations, for Class I or Class II conditions. (Sec. 516-2.)

typical specific application of the concept shown in **Code** Fig. 1 of Sec. 516-2(b) (1). A Class I or Class II, Division 1 area exists at the actual spraying operation plus a Division 2 area extending 20 ft horizontally in any direction from the actual spraying area and for 10 ft up. Although only one corner of the room is used for spraying, the entire room area inside the 20-ft line around the spraying is classified as Class I or Class II, Division 2 and must be wired accordingly. And the Division 2 area extends 10 ft above the spray operation.

The NFPA "Standard for Spray Finishing" (No. 33) notes that the inspection department having jurisdiction may, for any specific installation, determine the extent of the hazardous "spraying area."

The interior of any enclosed coating or dipping process must be considered a Class I or Class II Division 1 location. A Division 2 location exists within 3 ft in all directions from any opening in such an enclosure.

516-3. Wiring and Equipment in Class I Locations. In part **(a)**, spray operations that constitute a hazardous location solely on the basis of the presence of flammable vapors (and no paint or finish residues) contain wiring and equipment for Class I locations, as specified in Art. 501.

Part **(b)** places tighter restrictions on spray booths or areas where readily ignitible deposits are present in addition to flammable vapors. In general, electrical equipment is not permitted inside any spray booth, in the exhaust duct from a spray booth, in the entrained air of an exhaust system from a spraying operation, or in the direct path of spray, unless such equipment is specifically approved for both readily ignitible deposits and flammable vapor.

Only rigid metal conduit, IMC, and Type MI cable and threaded boxes or fittings containing no taps, splices, or terminal connections may be installed in such locations.

However, for that part of the hazardous area where the fixtures or equipment may not be subject to readily ignitible deposits or residues, fixtures and equipment approved for Class I, Division 1 locations may be installed. The authority having jurisdiction may decide that because of adequate positive-pressure ventilation the possibility of the hazard referred to in paragraph **(b)** has been eliminated.

Sufficient lighting for operations, booth cleaning, and repair should be provided at the time of equipment installation in order to avoid the unjustified use of "temporary" or "emergency" electric lamps connected to ordinary extension cords. A satisfactory and practical method of lighting is the use of ¼-in.-thick wired or tempered glass panel in the top or sides of spray booths with electrical light fixtures outside the booth, not in the direct path of the spray. Part **(c)** covers lighting fixtures that illuminate the spray operation through "windows" in the top or walls of a spray booth. Any such fixture used on the outside of the booth must be approved for a Class I, Division 2 location when used in any part of the top or sides of a booth that is within the Division 2 locations as shown in Figs. 2 and 3 in Sec. 516-2 of the **Code**.

Automobile undercoating spray operations in garages, conducted in areas having adequate natural or mechanical ventilation, may be exempt from the requirements pertaining to spray-finishing operations, when using undercoating materials not more hazardous than kerosene (as listed by Underwriters-

Laboratories in respect to fire hazard rating 30–40) or undercoating materials using only solvents listed as having a flash point in excess of 100°F. There should be no open flames or other sources of ignition within 20 ft while such operations are conducted.

ARTICLE 517. HEALTH CARE FACILITIES

517-1. Scope.   This article covers the *design and installation* of electric circuits and equipment in hospitals, nursing homes, residential custodial care facilities, mobile health care units, and doctors' and dentists' offices. *But,* this article does not cover "performance, maintenance, and testing" of electrical equipment in such facilities. Such considerations are covered in other industry standards—such as NFPA 56A, 76A, and 76B.

Any specific type of health care location—such as a doctor's office or a dental office—must comply with **Code** rules whether the location is a sole occupancy itself or is part of a larger facility (like a hospital containing other types of health care locations) or is within a school, office building, etc.

Veterinary facilities are not subject to the requirements of Art. 517.

517-2. Definitions.

Patient Vicinity

This term provides a definite value for limiting the area—horizontally and vertically—in which special grounding requirements are to be observed in patient care areas.

Psychiatric Hospital

This is a facility used around the clock to provide only psychiatric care for not less than four resident patients.

Selected Receptacles

This phrase designates specific receptacles that will provide power to appliances used for patient care emergencies. A dissenting vote in the panel acceptance of this definition noted that the wording would allow task receptacles of any kind to be supplied by the emergency system, even receptacles as unimportant as those for floor cleaners—which is contrary to the basic concept that the emergency system is intended to supply only extremely limited loads.

517-10. Applicability.   All the **Code** rules on "wiring design and protection" apply to the entire wiring system in hospitals and to "patient-care areas" of clinics, medical and dental offices, outpatient facilities and doctor examining rooms or treatment rooms in nursing homes and residential care facilities. The rules of Part **B** do not apply to "patient sleeping areas" of nursing homes and residential care facilities or to such buildings that satisfy *a., b.* and *c.* of Exception No. 3.

517·13. Grounding of Receptacles and Fixed Electrical Equipment.   In patient-care areas of *all* health-care facilities, nonmetallic wiring methods are excluded. Electrical nonmetallic tubing, rigid nonmetallic conduit, and non-metallic sheathed cable (Romex) may not be used in any part of a hospital or in patient-care areas of clinics, medical and dental offices, outpatient facilities, nursing homes, or residential custodial-care facilities. (See Exceptions No. 2 and 3 of Sec. 517-10.)

Part **(a)** requires the use of a separate, insulated equipment grounding conductor run with the branch-circuit conductors in metal raceway or metal-clad cable from a panelboard to any receptacle or metal surface of fixed electrical equipment operating over 100 V in all health care facilities. But a separate grounding conductor is not required in a feeder conduit to such a panel. For feeders, the metal conduit is a satisfactory grounding conductor, as recognized generally in Sec. 250-91(b). But for all branch circuits to "receptacles and all . . ." in "areas used for patient care," neither metal conduit, jumpers with box clips (G-clips), nor a receptacle with self-grounding screw terminals (Sec. 250-74, Exception No. 2) may be used alone without the grounding wire run with the branch-circuit wires (Fig. 517-1), which must be in metal raceway or in Type

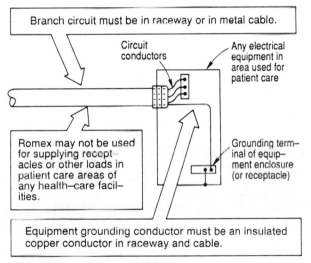

Fig. 517·1. Grounding conductor run with branch circuit in metal raceway or cable must ground receptacles and equipment. (Sec. 517-13.)

MC, Type MI, or Type AC cable (so-called BX). But, those metal-clad cables must have an "outer metal jacket" that "is an approved grounding means of a listed cable assembly." Type AC cable, Type MI cable and Type MC cable with a smooth or corrugated continuous metal sheath—all satisfy that grounding requirement. Type MC with a spiral-wrap metal sheath does not.

It should be noted that the phrase requiring an insulated equipment grounding conductor within these type cables (which appeared in Exception No. 1 to

Sec. 517-11 in the 1987 **NEC**) has been deleted. But it is the intent of the **Code** Making Panel to require an insulated copper equipment grounding conductor, sized in accordance with Sec. 250-95, to be run in any such cable assembly in a patient care area in every health care facility.

The ground terminal of receptacles must be grounded to an equipment grounding conductor run in *metal raceway or metal-covered cables.* Either metal raceway or metal cable must be used for circuits in patient care areas of hospitals, clinics, medical and dental offices, outpatient facilities, nursing homes, and residential custodial care facilities—*always* with an insulated *copper* equipment grounding conductor included in the raceway or cable.

This rule applies to "areas used for patient care"—which, in hospitals, covers patient bedrooms and any other rooms, corridors, or areas where patients are treated, like therapy areas or EKG areas. But, for other than hospitals, Exception No. 1 of Sec. 517-10 excludes waiting rooms, admitting rooms, solariums, recreation areas, as well as business offices and other places used solely by medical personnel or where a patient might be present but would not be treated.

Exception No. 2 to this rule clarifies the use of metal faceplates on wall switches or receptacles without actually connecting an "insulated copper conductor" to each faceplate. They are acceptable as grounded simply by screw connection to a grounded box or grounded mounting strap of a grounded wiring device.

Romex (nonmetallic sheathed cable) is no longer permitted for supplying receptacles or fixed equipment in patient-care areas of clinics, medical and dental offices, outpatient facilities, nursing homes, and residential custodial care facilities. Although Romex was permitted for those areas under Exception No. 3 to Sec. 517-11 of the 1987 **NEC**, it has been excluded for such use because it does not provide "redundant" grounding (i.e., two paths for fault current flow).

Part **(b)** of this section emphasizes that a redundant metallic grounding path is required in patient care areas. Part **(b)** requires that *all* branch circuits supplying patient care areas must be run in a metal-enclosed wiring method—rigid metal conduit, IMC, EMT, or MI, MC, or AC cable—to provide a redundant metallic grounding path in parallel with the insulated copper ground wire in the wiring method. This rule emphasizes high reliability of the ground-fault current return path as major protection against electrical shock.

517·14. Panelboard Bonding. Normal and essential electrical system panelboards serving either the same general care or critical care patient location must have their equipment grounding terminal bars bonded together with an insulated, continuous copper bonding jumper not smaller than No. 10 AWG.

517·15. Maximum Potential Difference. As background to this rule, initial studies of the problem, which has come to be categorized as "microshock," indicated that current values as low as 20 microamperes applied directly to the interior surfaces of the heart produce ventricular fibrillation. These studies utilized dogs as their subjects, and by comparison with human data it was determined that 10 microamperes should be the maximum allowable current leakage in critical care areas. More recent studies actually utilizing human subjects now indicate that there is a wider margin between dogs and humans than was initially anticipated. The new values for permissible potential differences within patient care areas now reflect studies which have been performed both in the United States and abroad on this subject.

In most cases, it will be found that the limits for potential differences permitted in general care areas and critical care areas can be maintained using only the grounding requirements which are set forth in this article. In the 1975 **NE Code**, uncontrolled critical care areas had to have a maximum of 100 mV potential difference maintained under conditions of line-to-ground fault as well as normal operations, and the use of an isolated power system or some equivalent means was necessary to limit the rise of potential difference under fault conditions. Because there is no longer reference to "conditions of line-to-ground fault," there is no need to use an isolated power supply in critical care areas, because under normal operation the rule can readily be satisfied without an isolated power supply. That intent is supported by the elimination of the Exception for permanently installed x-ray equipment—which Exception was in the 1975 **NEC** because the high power needs of such x-ray could not be handled by isolated power supplies.

But this section of the present **Code** requires that critical care grounding limit the potential differences to 40 mV. The maximum permitted potential difference between conductive surfaces exposed to patients has been reduced from 100 to 40 mV for grounding effectiveness in critical care areas. The change was made because of the adverse effect of higher potential difference on physiologic monitoring systems—which creates a hazard in itself—and because the level of 40 mV is readily achieved in even very old systems where only conduit grounds are used.

517·16. Receptacles with Insulated Grounding Terminals. Insulated-ground receptacles must be clearly and externally identified. This rule applies to those receptacles that have their grounding terminals insulated from the metal of the box and conduit.

517·17. Ground·Fault Protection. At least one additional level of ground-fault protection is required for health care facilities where ground-fault protection is used on service equipment (see Sec. 230-95). Where the installation of ground-fault protection is made on the normal service disconnecting means, then each feeder must be provided with similar protective means. This requirement is intended to prevent a catastrophic outage. By applying appropriate selectivity at each level, the ground fault can be limited to a single feeder, and thereby service may be maintained to the balance of the health care facility.

As shown in Fig. 517-2, with a GFP (ground-fault protection) hookup on the service, a GFP hookup must be put on each feeder derived from the service. And part **(b)** requires that selection of the tripping time of the main GFP be such that each feeder GFP will operate to open a ground fault on the feeder, without opening the service GFP. And a time interval of not less than 0.1 sec (i.e., the time of 6 cycles) must be provided between the feeder GFP trip and the service GFP trip. As shown, if the feeder GFP relays are set for instantaneous opera-

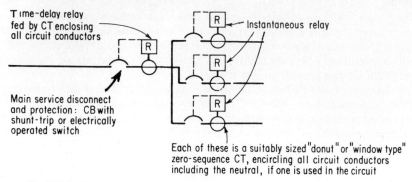

Fig. 517-2. GFP on the service requires GFP on main feeders also. (Sec. 517-17.)

tion, the relay on the service GFP must have at least a 0.1-sec time delay. A zone-selective GFP system with a feedback lock-out signal to an instantaneous relay on the service could satisfy the rule for selectivity.

517-18. General Care Areas. Two circuits must supply each bed used for "inpatient care." But two branch circuits are not required for each patient bed in nursing homes, outpatient facilities, clinics, medical offices, and the like. "Psychiatric, substance abuse, and rehabilitation hospitals" are also exempted from the branch-circuit and receptacle requirements for general care patient bed locations.

As noted in part (b), receptacles at patient bed locations in "General Care Areas" must be "listed hospital grade" and "so identified." The minimum of four required receptacles at each such bed location may be single or duplex types, or a combination of the two. (Two duplex receptacles provides a total of four receptacles.) **ALL** receptacles at **ALL** patient bed locations—general care and critical care—ust be "listed hospital grade" devices.

As noted in part **(c)**, only tamper-resistant receptacles are permitted in pediatric and psychiatric locations. This rule requires that all 15- or 20-A, 125-V receptacles in pediatric and psychiatric locations be "tamper resistant." Although the **Code** does not contain a definition for that word and the UL *Electrical Construction Materials Directory* does not refer to "tamper-resistant" receptacles, the last phrase of part **(c)** gives an indication of its meaning. It seems clear that a tamper-resistant receptacle is one that would make it extremely difficult, if not impossible, to insert a pin, paper clip, or similar small metal object into a slot on the receptacle and make contact with an energized part. Obviously, the concern here is to protect infants, children, and incompetent adults from shock hazard as a result of playful or inadvertent tampering with the receptacle.

Note that protection against tampering must be provided by design of the receptacle and not by attachment of an accessory device, such as a plastic plug, which must be removed to use the receptacle. Receptacles are available with rotating slot covers or internal contact mechanisms, both of which make it necessary to use a cord plug cap to gain access to energized parts.

517-19. Critical Care Areas. Patient bed locations in general care areas (Sec. 517-18) must be supplied by four single or two duplex receptacles,whereas critical care area patient beds must be provided with at least six receptacles (single or duplex devices totaling six points for connecting a cord plug cap). The two or more branch circuits to each critical care area patient bed location must include one or more from the emergency system and one or more from the normal system (Fig. 517-3). In both cases, at least two branch circuits must supply these receptacles. In the case of general care areas, additional receptacles serving other patient locations may be served by these branch circuits, but in the case of critical care areas at least one of these branch circuits is required to be an individual branch having no other receptacles on it except those of a single bed location.

As covered in part **(b)**, "hospital grade" receptacles must be used at patient bed locations in "Critical Care Areas." Six single or three duplex receptacles (or any combination totaling six receptacles) that are UL-listed as "Hospital Grade" devices must be used at each patient bed location and must be so identified at each patient bed location in "Critical Care" patient areas. The best point to call a reference grounding point is the grounding bus in the distribution panel, which is the transition connection point between the branch-circuit grounding wires and the feeder grounding system.

The meaning of part **(c)** is that a "patient equipment grounding point" (defined as a "point for redundant grounding of electric appliances") is *not* mandatory. Such a grounding point may be used, if desired, and connected as described in the rule. In its original application, years ago, the "patient equipment grounding point" was a special jack used to make a grounding connection to the metal enclosures of electrical medical equipment because, at the time, many power cords did not contain a grounding conductor. In addition, this was a carryover from procedures for operating rooms, where all metal surfaces had to be grounded to minimize static charge buildup. With today's universal use of good 3-wire (grounding type) power cords and plugs or double-insulated equipment, there is no real justification for requiring this patient equipment grounding jack. Each three-contact receptacle, in effect, becomes a patient equipment grounding point.

When a patient equipment grounding point is used in a patient vicinity, it must be grounded to the ground terminal of *ALL* grounding type receptacles in the patient vicinity by means of a minimum No. 10 copper conductor looped to all of the receptacles or by individual No. 10 conductors run from the patient grounding point to each receptacle.

Regardless of what additional methods are employed, in order to keep potential differences within the required limits, equipotential grounding is essential to the electrical safety of critical care areas. Some of the earliest equipotential grounding installations consisted of copper busbars run around the walls of patient rooms to which furniture and equipment were attached by means of grounding jumpers. Based on experience obtained through these early installations as well as the refinements produced by the NFPA Committee on Hospitals, the **National Electrical Code** now contains the requirements which cor-

As required by part **(d)** of this section, a bonding-type connection is required for *feeder* metal conduit or metal cable (Type MC or MI) terminations—using a bonding bushing plus a *copper* bonding jumper from a lug on the bushing to the ground bus in the panelboard fed by the conduit (see illustrations in Sec. 250-72). Bonding locknuts or bonding bushings may be used on clean knockouts (all punched, concentric, or eccentric rings removed), and bonding may be provided by threaded connection to hubs or bosses on panel- or switchboard enclosures. This is required for feeder conduits but not branch-circuit conduits. And it seems clear that bonded terminals are required at both ends of each and every feeder to a panelboard that serves the critical care area. (Fig. 517-5.)

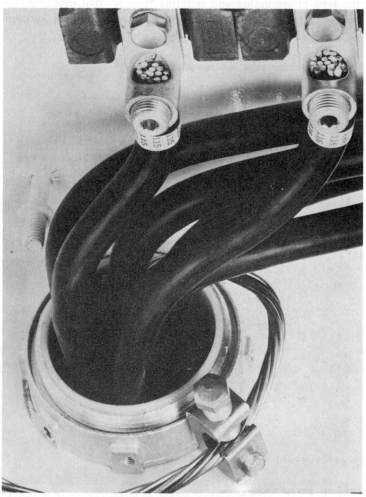

Fig. 517-5. Feeders to branch-circuit panelboards for critical care areas must be bonded. Figure 517-4 covers rules on grounding and bonding for the patient vicinity of a critical care area, with feeder conduit bonding as in photo above. [Sec. 517-19(d).]

Part (e) makes use of an isolated power system for critical care areas a completely optional technique, simply noting that such systems are "permitted" to be used if the design engineer or the hospital-client wants it. That approach ties in with the deletion of the maximum potential difference of 100 mV "under conditions of line-to-ground fault" in a critical care area—which in past Codes made the isolated power system mandatory.

517·20. Wet Locations. As covered by this section, locations intended for ground-fault protection are limited to patient care areas. So, even though the governing body of the hospital may wish to extend this form of protection to such areas as laundries, boiler rooms, and kitchens, the fact that these are not considered patient care areas does not make GFCI (ground-fault circuit interrupter) protection mandatory in such locations. The designer and/or hospital authorities must designate such "wet locations." Locations which are intended for protection would include hydrotherapy, dialysis facilities, selected wet laboratories, and special-purpose rooms where wet conditions prevail.

All receptacles (of any rating) *and fixed electrical equipment* at a wet location must have GFCI protection, where power interruption "can be tolerated." Otherwise, they must be fed from an isolated power supply.

517·25. Scope. Essential electrical systems are covered for hospitals, clinics, medical and dental offices, outpatient facilities, nursing homes, residential custodial care facilities, and other health care facilities for patient care.

517·30. Essential Electrical Systems for Hospitals. This section makes clear that essential electrical systems which are to be installed in hospitals must observe the rules of Part (c). Essential electrical systems in hospitals are subdivided into the emergency system (consisting of the life safety and critical branches) and the equipment system, whereas essential electrical systems for nursing homes and the like are the branches shown in Code diagrams 517-41(1) and (2) for the emergency system. It should be noted that the critical branch in hospitals comprises different equipment and connections than does the critical system in nursing homes.

In Sec. 517-30(c)(3), although wiring of the emergency system is required to be installed in "metal raceway," Exception No. 3 permits Schedule 80 rigid nonmetallic conduit for such circuits. Only the Schedule 80 version of rigid PVC conduit may be used (not Schedule 40 PVC conduit). *BUT* note that although such raceway may be used for emergency circuits, it is *NOT PERMITTED* for such circuits that are "branch circuits serving patient care areas." In addition, Exception No. 3 given for this section in the 1987 NEC has been deleted, which has the effect of disallowing use of cables for emergency circuits "above hazardous anesthetizing locations" and "other-than-hazardous anesthetizing locations."

517·31. Emergency System. Code diagrams 517-30(1), (2), and (3) in the Code book clarify interconnections and transfer switches required. Handbook Table 517-1 summarizes the loads supplied by the hospital emergency system, which must restore electrical supply to the loads within 10 sec of loss of normal supply.

517·41. Essential Electrical Systems. In part (b), a single transfer switch may be used for the entire essential electrical system instead of using a separate transfer switch for each branch, as shown in Code diagram 517-41(3). One

Table 517.1 A Hospital Emergency System Must Serve These Loads (Sec. 517.31)

Life Safety Branch	Critical Branch

Lighting and receptacles for:
—Means of egress illumination
—Exit and directional signs
—Alarm systems
  •Manual fire stations
  •Sprinklers
  •Fire & smoke detection
—Alarms for nonflammable medical gas
—Communications for emergency use
—Generator—set location
	—Isolating transformers in anesthetizing locations
	—Task illumination and selected receptacles in:
	  •Nurseries
	  •Medication preparation
	  •Pharmacy
	  •Acute nursing
	  •Psychiatric beds (no receptacles)
	  •Nurses stations
	  •Ward treatment rooms
	  •Surgery and obstetrics
	  •Angiographic labs
	  •Cardiac catheter labs
	  •Coronary care
	  •Delivery
	  •Dialysis
	  •Emergency
	  •Human physiology labs
	  •Intensive care
	  •Operating rooms
	  •Post-operative
	  •Recovery rooms

transfer switch may supply one or more branches of the essential electrical system in a nursing home or residential custodial care facility where the essential electrical system has a maximum demand of 150 kVA. Separate transfer switches are required only if dictated by load considerations. For small facilities, the essential electrical system generally consists of the life safety branch and the critical branch. For larger systems the critical branch is divided into three separate branches for patients, heating, and sump pumps and alarms. Code diagrams 517-41(1) and 517-41(2) illustrate typical installations.

517-42. Automatic Connection to Life Safety Branch. Part **(a)** describes the switching arrangements for night transfer of corridor lighting. The rule is intended to assure that some lighting will always be provided in the corridor regardless of the mode of operation.

517-43. Connection to Critical Branch. This section details the loads requiring transfer from normal source to the alternate power source. In part **(b)(2)**, elevator operation must not trap passengers between floors. This rule, which was only a recommendation in the 1978 Code, is now mandatory.

517-60. Anesthetizing Location Classifications. Figure 517-6 shows the classified hazardous locations of part **(a)**.

Note that part **(b)** requires designation by the hospital administration that a particular location (operating room, anesthesia room, etc.) is nonhazardous. Section 5-2 of NFPA 56A requires signs *prohibiting* the use of flammable anesthetics.

Hazardous locations rules are separated from those for other-than-hazardous locations. A third category is also designated—"above-hazardous locations."

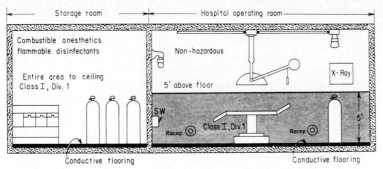

Fig. 517·6. Two types of hazardous locations must be identified. (Sec. 517-60.)

The **Code** covers wiring and equipment in three relations to anesthetizing locations: Sec. 517-61(a) (within-hazardous), Sec. 517-61(b) (above-hazardous), and Sec. 517-61(c) (other-than-hazardous).

517·61. Wiring and Equipment.   Part **(a)** calls for explosionproof wiring methods, in general, for such locations.

Part **(a)(4)** notes an extension of the hazardous boundary. Section 517-60(a)(1) defines the area of a flammable anesthetizing location as a Class I, Division 1 location from the floor to a point 5 ft above the floor. The question then arises, Is the seal required in the upper conduit entering the switch box on the wall of a hospital operating room as shown in Fig. 517-7? The box is partly below and partly above the 5-ft level.

Part **(a)(4)** states that, if a box or fitting is partially, but not entirely, beneath the 5-ft level, the boundary of the Class I, Division 1 area is considered to extend to the *top* of the box or fitting. Therefore, the box or fitting is entirely

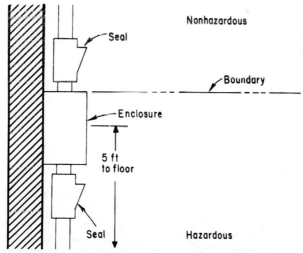

Fig. 517·7. Boundary of Class I, Division 1 location may be extended. (Sec. 517-61.)

within the hazardous area, and a seal is required in conduit entering the enclosure from either above or below, as shown in Fig. 517-7.

If the box or fitting is entirely *above* the 5-ft level, a seal would not be required at the box or fitting, but conduit running to the box from the hazardous area would have to be sealed at the boundary, on the hazardous-location side of the box. If the box shown were recessed in the wall instead of surface-mounted, some means would have to be provided to make the seals accessible [Sec. 501-5(c) (1)], such as removable blank covers at the locations of the seals.

Part **(a)(5)** calls for explosionproof receptacles and plugs within hazardous locations described in Sec. 517-60(a).

In part **(b)(1)** of this section, rigid metal conduit, electrical metallic tubing (EMT), and intermediate metal conduit (IMC) or Type MI or MC cable that has a continuous sheath are permitted in "above-hazardous anesthetizing locations." In "other-than-hazardous anesthetizing locations" [Sec. 517-61(c)(1)], wiring may be in rigid metal conduit, EMT, or IMC—or may be Type MC, Type AC, or MI cable. But rigid nonmetallic conduit may not be used for wiring in anesthetizing locations that use nonflammable anesthetics. And it may not be used in or above a hazardous anesthetizing location. Many of the requirements for safety in the above-hazardous anesthetizing locations are not included for other-than-hazardous locations.

Hospital·Grade Receptacles

The **NE Code** does not contain a "general" requirement that "hospital-grade" receptacles (the UL-listed "Green-dot" wiring devices) must be used in health care facilities. However, it should be noted that Secs. 517-61(b)(5) and 517-61(c)(2) do require use of "receptacles and attachment plugs" that are "listed for hospital use" *above* "hazardous" anesthetizing locations and *in* "other-than-hazardous" anesthetizing locations. As described, those rules require that all 2-pole, 3-wire grounding-type receptacles and plugs for single-phase 120-, 208-, or 240-V AC service must be marked "Hospital Only" or "Hospital Grade," with a green dot on the face of each receptacle (Fig. 517-8). The relation between the phrase "listed for hospital use" and the phrase "Hospital Grade" is explained in the UL *Electrical Construction Materials Directory* (the UL Green Book), under the heading "Attachment Plug Receptacles and Plugs." It says:

> Receptacles listed for hospital use in other than hazardous locations in accordance with Article 517 of the **National Electrical Code** are identified (1) by the marking "Hospital Only" or (2) by the marking "Hospital Grade" and a green dot on the receptacle. The green dot is on the face of the receptacle where visible after installation.

It should be noted that the *requirement* for hospital-grade wiring devices applies only with respect to anesthetizing locations. It does not apply to nursing homes, clinics, or medical offices (Fig. 517-9).

Of course, in the defined hazardous areas of flammable anesthetizing locations [Sec. 517-60 and Sec. 517-61(a)(5)], receptacles must be explosionproof type, listed for Class I, Division 1 areas.

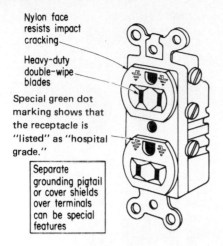

Nylon face resists impact cracking

Heavy-duty double-wipe blades

Special green dot marking shows that the receptacle is "listed" as "hospital grade."

Separate grounding pigtail or cover shields over terminals can be special features

Hospital-grade plugs and receptacles are required *only* for anesthetizing locations. (Sec. 517-61.)

Sec. 517-18(c). Receptacles in pediatric and psychiatric locations must have "construction" that prevents improper contact

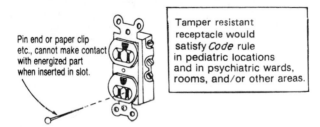

Pin end or paper clip etc., cannot make contact with energized part when inserted in slot.

Tamper resistant receptacle would satisfy *Code* rule in pediatric locations and in psychiatric wards, rooms, and/or other areas.

Fig. 517-8. Hospital-grade plugs and receptacles are required *only* for anesthetizing locations. (Sec. 517-61.)

Underwriters Laboratories Inc. devised a special series of tests for wiring devices intended for hospital use. These tests are substantially more abusive than those performed on general-purpose devices and are designed to ensure the reliability of the grounding connection in particular, when used in the hospital environment. Hospital-grade receptacles have stability and construction in excess of standard specifications and can stand up to abuse and hard usage. Devices which pass this test are listed as "Hospital Grade" and are identified with these words and a green dot, both of which are visible after installation. UL listings include 15- and 20-A 125-V grounding, nonlocking-type plugs, receptacles, and connectors. This class of device is acceptable for use in any nonhazardous anesthetizing location. As noted in the Exception to Sec. 517-61(b)(2), receptacles above a hazardous location do not have to be totally enclosed and may be standard, available hospital-grade receptacles of the type that would be used to satisfy the rule of Sec. 517-61(b)(5).

Fig. 517·9. Although the **NE Code** requires use of hospital-grade receptacles at patient bed locations and in "anesthetizing" locations, the ruggedness and high degree of connection reliability strongly recommend their use for such critical applications as plug-connection of respiratory or life-sustaining equipment.

As covered in part **(c)**(1), in anesthetizing locations that are not hazardous (no flammable agents used), Type AC cable is recognized along with Types MI and MC cable and rigid metal conduit, IMC, and EMT—but any such cable or raceway must contain an insulated-copper equipment grounding conductor and its outer jacket must be an approved grounding conductor. Type AC cable has an excellent record in such an application. Note that although the rule here does not specify a "copper" conductor, because an anesthetizing location is a patient care area, the copper wire is required by Sec. 517-13.

517·63. Grounded Power Systems in Anesthetizing Locations.   Part **(a)** calls for a general purpose lighting circuit, fed from the normal grounded service, to be installed in each operating room. And the Exception recognizes feed from an emergency generator or other emergency service that is separate from the source of the hospital's "Emergency System," as defined in Sec. 517-2. Figure 517-10 shows a layout where such an emergency supply (at lower right) may be the source of supply to the general purpose lighting circuit in the operating room because it is a separate supply from that to the Emergency System (at left).

In part **(f)**, an isolated power system (ungrounded operation with a line isolation monitor) is required only in an anesthetizing location with flammable anesthetics. As the rule has appeared in recent editions of the **NEC**, isolated power systems have been required for locations with both flammable and non-

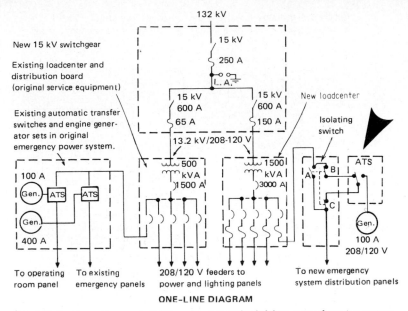

Fig. 517-10. General-purpose lighting circuit must be fed from normal service or separate alternate source. (Sec. 517-63.)

flammable anesthetics. But in 1984, a revision was made in Sec. 517-104(a)(1) to change the phrase an "anesthetizing" to a "flammable anesthetizing" in this section. As a result, an anesthetizing location that does not use flammable anesthetics will not require use of an isolated power system. Section 517-63(f) now makes the requirement for an isolated power system applicable only for anesthetizing locations where "flammable" anesthetics are used. For those cases where the anesthetizing location is used solely for nonflammable anesthetizing materials, an isolated power system is not mandatory in the **NEC** (although NFPS 99 would require it for wet anesthetizing locations).

Figure 517-11 shows the application of a completely packaged transformer loadcenter to provide power for the ungrounded, isolated circuits in hospital operating suites.

517-64. Low-Voltage Equipment and Instruments.   Specific details are given for use of low-voltage equipment in an anesthetizing location. Figure 517-12 shows some of the rules. Section 517-160(a)(2) limits isolating transformers to operation with primary at not over 600 V.

517-160. Isolated Power Systems.   Each isolated power circuit must be controlled by a switch that has a disconnecting pole in each isolated circuit conductor to simultaneously disconnect all power. That is in part **(a)(1)**.

As covered in part **(a)(2)**, any transformer used to obtain the ungrounded circuits must have its primary rated for not more than 600 V between conductors and must have proper overcurrent protection. This **Code** rule used to limit the transformer primary to 300 V between conductors, which often required two

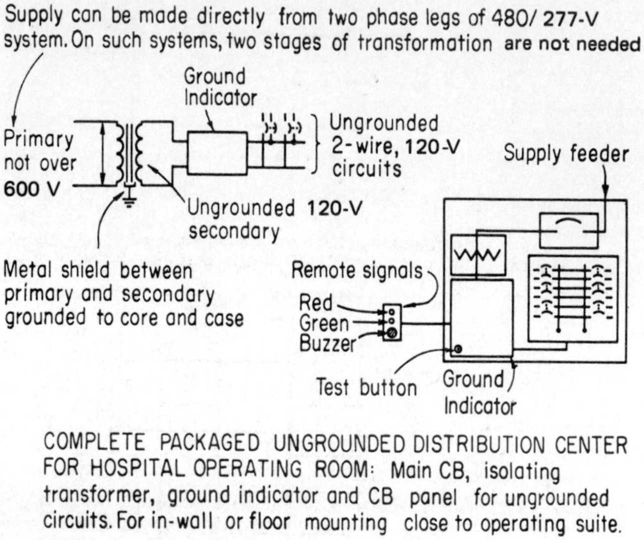

Supply can be made directly from two phase legs of 480/277-V
system. On such systems, two stages of transformation are not needed

Ground
Indicator

Primary
not over
600 V

Ungrounded
2-wire, 120-V
circuits

Supply feeder

Ungrounded 120-V
secondary

Metal shield between
primary and secondary
grounded to core and case

Remote signals
Red
Green
Buzzer

Test button   Ground
Indicator

COMPLETE PACKAGED UNGROUNDED DISTRIBUTION CENTER
FOR HOSPITAL OPERATING ROOM: Main CB, isolating
transformer, ground indicator and CB panel for ungrounded
circuits. For in-wall or floor mounting close to operating suite.

Fig. 517·11. Isolated power supply is required for circuits only in flammable anesthetizing locations. (Sec. 517-63.)

stages of voltage transformation to comply with the rule, as shown in Fig. 517-
13. That diagram shows the circuit makeup used in a hospital to derive the 120-
V ungrounded circuits, with transformation down from 480 to 240 V and then
to 120 V. The ungrounded secondary system must be equipped with an
approved ground contact indicator—to give a visual and audible warning if a
ground fault develops in the ungrounded system.

Isolating transformers must be installed out of the hazardous area [part **(a)(3)**].
The ground indicator and its signals must also be installed out of the hazardous
area [part **(c)(5)**]. In an anesthetizing location, the hazardous area extends to a
height of 5 ft above the floor.

Fixed lighting fixtures above the hazardous area in an anesthetizing location,
other than the surgical luminaire, and certain x-ray equipment may be supplied
by conventional grounded branch circuits [Sec. 517-63(b) and Sec. 517-63(c)].

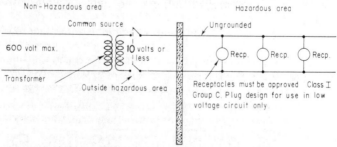

Fig. 517·12. Low-voltage circuits in anesthetizing locations must operate at 10
V or less or be otherwise approved. (Sec. 517-64.)

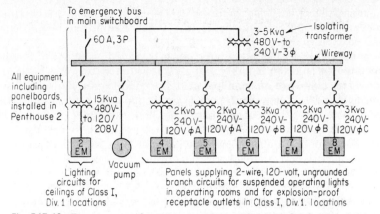

Fig. 517·13. Two-stage transformation was often needed for isolated circuits but is no longer necessary. (Sec. 517-160.)

Part **(a)(5)** requires isolated circuit conductors to be identified by brown and orange colors.

Part **(b)(1)** details a line isolation monitor and clarifies line isolation monitor alarm values, specifying 5.0 mA as the lower limit of alarm for total hazard current. Figure 517-14 shows the basic concept behind detection and signal of a ground fault. The diagram shows major circuit components of a typical ground detector/alarm system. Partial ground energizes current-relay A, opening contact A2 (energizing red light and warning buzzer). Pressing the momen-

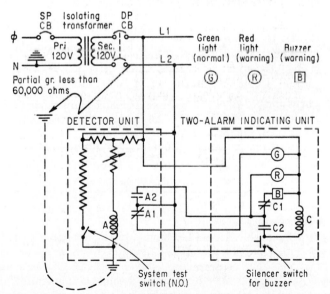

Fig. 517·14. Detection and alarm on ground fault is required for isolated power systems. (Sec. 517-160.)

tary-contact silencer switch energizes coil C, opening contact C1 (disconnecting buzzer), and closing holding contact C2. When ground is cleared, contacts resume position shown in drawing.

The purpose of such a ground indicator is to provide warning of the danger of shock hazard and the possibility of a fault in the system due to accidental grounding of more than one conductor. If one conductor of an isolated system becomes grounded at one point, normal protective devices (fuses or CBs) will not operate because there is no return path and, therefore, no flow of short-circuit fault current. However, if an accidental ground subsequently develops on the other conductor, a short circuit will occur with possible disastrous consequences, such as ignition of ether vapors by arc or a lethal shock to personnel.

ARTICLE 518. PLACES OF ASSEMBLY

518-1. Scope.   This article covers places of assembly which used to be covered along with theaters in Art. 520. This article does not apply to theaters. It covers any single indoor space (a whole building or part of a building) designed or intended for use by 100 or more persons for assembly purposes. That includes dining rooms, meeting rooms, entertainment areas (other than with a stage or platform or projection booth), lecture halls, bowling alleys, places of worship, dance halls, exhibition halls, museums, gymnasiums, armories, group rooms, funeral parlor chapels, skating rinks, pool rooms, transportation terminals, court rooms, sports arenas, and stadiums. A school classroom for less than 100 persons is not subject to this article. See Sec. 518-2.

The clear differentiation given in this section points out that any such building or structure or part of a building that contains a projection booth or stage platform or even just an area that may, on occasion, be used for presenting theatrical or musical productions—whether the stage or platform is fixed or portable—must comply with the rules of Art. 520, as if it were a theater, and not Art. 518. A restaurant, say, that has a piano player for entertainment on Saturday night, could readily be classed as a theater and subject to Art. 520.

The question often arises, Does Art. 518 apply to supermarkets and department-store types of occupancies because such places are regularly crowded with far more than 100 persons? Although occupancies of those types have capacity to hold more than 100 persons at any given time, Art. 518 is not generally applicable.

Article 518 directs attention "to a building or portion of a building" that would be used for the purposes outlined; therefore, you would have to determine how the occupancy is used.

A supermarket generally would not have a public assembly area. However, a department store could incorporate a community room for shows and similar audience functions. This room would be subject to Art. 518. The main areas of supermarkets and department stores, unlike theaters and assembly halls, have many aisles and exits that could be used in case of emergency evacuation of the building. It is these characteristics that permit conventional wiring methods to be accepted.

A proposal was once made to include supermarkets and department stores as "places of assembly," but it was rejected.

Note that places of assembly covered by this article must be for 100 or more people. No rules are given for determining the number of people, but a note refers questions of population to local building codes or to the NFPA Life Safety Code. Of course, number of seats is an index of capacity, and other reasonable indications must be observed.

The following information is found in NFPA No. 101, Life Safety Code, for determining occupant load in places of assembly.

Occupant Load. The occupant load permitted in any assembly building, structure, or portion thereof shall be determined by dividing the net floor area or space assigned to that use by the square feet per occupant as follows:

(a) An assembly area of concentrated use without fixed seats such as an auditorium, church, chapel, dance floor, and lodge room—7 square feet per person.

(b) An assembly area of less concentrated use such as a conference room, dining room, drinking establishment, exhibit room, gymnasium, or lounge—15 square feet per person.

(c) Standing room or waiting room—3 square feet per person.

The occupant load of an area having fixed seats shall be determined by the number of fixed seats installed. Required aisle space serving the fixed seats shall not be used to increase the occupant load.

The occupant load permitted in a building or portion thereof may be increased above that specified in "Occupant Load" if the necessary aisles and exits are provided subject to the approval of the authority having jurisdiction. An approved aisle, exit and/or seating diagram may be required by the authority having jurisdiction to substantiate an increase in occupant load.

518-4. Wiring Methods.   The basic rule says that fixed wiring must be in metal raceway, nonmetallic raceways encased in *not less than 2 in. of concrete,* Type ALS cable, Type MI cable, or Type MC cable. The first Exception says that nonmetallic-sheathed cable, BX (Type AC cable), electrical nonmetallic tubing (ENT), and rigid nonmetallic conduit may be used in building areas that are *not* required by the local building code to be of fire-rated construction. Note that use of those methods no longer relates to the number of persons that the place holds, which was once in this rule. Another Exception permits the use of other wiring methods for sound systems, communication circuits, Class 2 and 3 remote-control and signal circuits, and fire-alarm circuits.

ARTICLE 520. THEATERS AND SIMILAR
LOCATIONS

520-1. Scope.   Where only a part of a building is used as a theater or similar location, these special requirements apply only to that part and do not necessarily apply to the entire building. A common example is a school building in which there is an auditorium used for dramatic or other performances. All special requirements of this chapter would apply to the auditorium, stage, dressing rooms, and main corridors leading to the auditorium but not to other parts of the building that do not pertain to the use of the auditorium for performances or entertainment.

520·4. Wiring Methods.   Building laws usually require theaters and motion picture houses to be of fireproof construction; hence practical considerations limit the types of concealed wiring for light and power chiefly to raceway. Only Type MI or Type MC cables may be used. Cables were long ago found unsuitable for circuits in theaters because they do not readily offer increase in the size of conductors for load growth. Many instances of overfusing dictated the value of raceways, which do permit replacement of larger conductors for safely handling load growth.

Much of the stage lighting in a modern theater is provided by floodlights and projectors mounted in the ceiling or on the balcony front. In order that the projectors may be adjustable in position, they may be connected by plugs and short cords to suitable receptacles or "pockets."

520·23. Control and Overcurrent Protection of Receptacle Circuits.   The term *gallery receptacles* should be understood as including all receptacles, wherever they may be located, that are intended for the connection of stage lighting equipment. Circuits to such receptacles must of necessity be controlled at the same location as other stage lighting circuits.

520·24. Metal Hood.   Because of the large amount of flammable material always present on a stage, and because of the crowded space, a stage switchboard must have no live parts on the front, and the back must be so guarded as to keep unauthorized persons away from the space in back of the board and the wall, with a door at one end of the enclosure.

The more important stage switchboards are commonly of the remote-control type. Pilot switches mounted on the stage board control the operation of contactors installed in any convenient location where space is available, usually below the stage. The contactors in turn control the lighting circuits.

The stage switchboard is usually built into a recess in the proscenium wall, as shown in the plan view, Fig. 520-1. After passing through the switches and dimmers, many of the main circuits must be subdivided into branch circuits so that no branch circuit will be loaded to more than 20 A. Where the board is of the remote-control type, the branch-circuit fuses are often mounted on the same panels as the contactors. Where a direct-control type of board is used, and sometimes where the board is remotely controlled, the branch-circuit fuses are mounted on special panelboards known as *magazine panels*, which are installed in the space back of the switchboard, usually in the location of the junction box shown in Fig. 520-2.

520·25. Dimmers.   Figure 520-2 shows typical connections of two branch circuits arranged for control by one switch and one dimmer plate or section. The single-pole switch on the stage switchboard is connected to one of the outside buses, and from this switch a wire runs to a short bus on the magazine panel. The magazine panel is similar to an ordinary panelboard, except that it contains no switches and the circuits are divided into many sections, each section having its own separate buses. One terminal of the dimmer plate, or variable resistor, is connected to the neutral bus at the switchboard, and from the other terminal of the dimmer a wire runs to the neutral bus on the magazine panel. This neu-

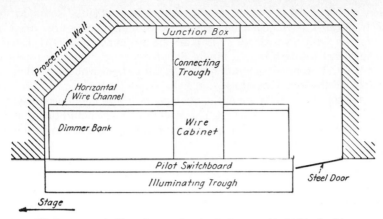

Fig. 520-1. Stage switchboards must be circuited to provide highly flexible usage. (Sec. 520-24.)

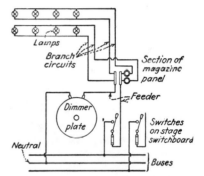

Fig. 520-2. Branch circuits of lighting may be controlled by single dimmer in grounded or ungrounded conductor. (Sec. 520-25.)

tral bus must be well insulated from ground and must be separate from other neutral buses on the panel; otherwise the dimmer would be shunted and would fail to control the brightness of the lamps.

While the dimmer is permanently connected to the neutral of the wiring system, this neutral is presumed to be thoroughly grounded and hence the dimmer is dead. A dimmer in the grounded neutral does not require overcurrent protection, as noted in part **(a)**.

Figure 520-3 shows an autotransformer used as a dimmer. By changing the

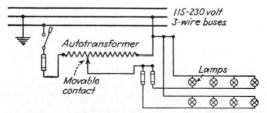

Fig. 520-3. Autotransformer dimmer must have grounded leg common to primary and secondary. (Sec. 520-25.)

position of the movable contact, any desired voltage may be supplied to the lamps, from full-line voltage to a voltage so low that the lamps are "black out." As compared with a resistance-type dimmer, a dimmer of this type has the advantages that it operates at a much higher efficiency, generates very little heat, and, within its maximum rating, the dimming effect is not dependent upon the wattage of the load it controls.

520-43. Footlights. A footlight of the disappearing type might produce so high a temperature as to be a serious fire hazard if the lamps should be left burning after the footlight is closed. Part **(c)** calls for automatic disconnect when the lights disappear.

There is no restriction on the number of lamps that may be supplied by one branch circuit. The lamp wattage supplied by one circuit should be such that the current will be slightly less than 20 A.

Individual outlets as described in part **(b)** are seldom used for footlights, as such construction would be much more expensive than the standard trough type.

A modern type of footlight is shown in Fig. 520-4. The wiring is carried in a sheet-iron wire channel in the face of which lamp receptacles are mounted.

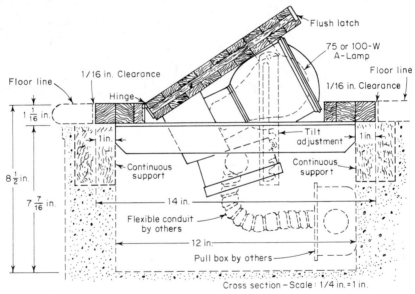

Fig. 520-4. Footlights must be automatically de-energized when the flush latch is closed down. (Sec. 520-43.)

Each lamp is provided with an individual reflector and glass color screen or "roundel." The circuit wires are usually brought to the wire channel in rigid conduit. In the other type of footlight, still used to some extent, the lamps are placed vertically or nearly so, and an extension of one side of the wire channel is shaped so as to form a reflector to direct the light toward the stage.

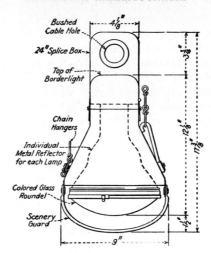

Bushed
Cable Hole

24" Splice Box

Top of
Borderlight

Chain
Hangers

Individual
Metal Reflector
for each Lamp

Colored Glass
Roundel

Scenery
Guard

Fig. 520-5. Border lights must comply with **NEC** construction rules. (Sec. 520-44.)

520-44. Borders and Proscenium Sidelights. Figure 520-5 is a cross section showing the construction of a border light over the stage. This particular type is intended for the use of 200-W lamps. An individual reflector is provided for each lamp so as to secure the highest possible efficiency of light utilization. A glass roundel is fitted to each reflector; these may be obtained in any desired color, commonly white, red, and blue for three-color equipment and white, red, blue, and amber for four-color equipment. A splice box is provided on top of the housing for enclosing the connections between the border-light cable and the wiring of the border. From this splice box, the wires are carried to the lamp sockets in a trough extending the entire length of the border.

Border lights are usually hung on steel cables so that their height may be adjusted and so that they may be lowered to the stage for cleaning and replacing lamps and color screens; hence the circuit conductors supplying the lamps must be carried to the border through a flexible cable. The individual conductors of the cable may be of No. 14, though No. 12 is more commonly used.

520-45. Receptacles. Receptacle load must not exceed 80 percent of its rating if the load is continuous. This is a rule updated to application of modern equipment and not just limited to receptacles for arc lamps and incandescent lamps. Any receptacle for *equipment or fixtures on stage* must have an amp rating of at least 125 percent of the operating current of a continuous load supplied. That presumes that the load to be supplied by a receptacle is clearly known at the time the rating of the receptacle is selected. For a noncontinuous load, the receptacle may be loaded up to 100 percent of its rating.

520-49. Flue Damper Control. A normally-closed-circuit device has the inherent safety feature that in case the control circuit is accidentally opened by the blowing of a fuse, or in any other way, the device immediately operates to open the flue dampers.

520-53. Construction and Feeders. In part **(f)**, specs cover conductors within portable stage dimmer switchboards. A broad detailed rule covers the temperature ratings of conductors permitted in dimmer boards, based on the type of dimmer used. The rule recognizes the difference in temperature of dimmers and permits lower-rated conductors for solid-state dimmers.

520·65. Festoons.   "Lanterns or similar devices" are very likely to be made of paper or other flammable material, and the lamps should be prevented from coming in contact with such material.

520·72. Lamp Guards.   Lamps in dressing rooms should be provided with guards that cannot easily be removed to prevent them from coming in contact with flammable material.

ARTICLE 530. MOTION PICTURE AND TELEVISION STUDIOS AND SIMILAR LOCATIONS

530·1. Scope.   Article 520 covers theaters used for TV, motion picture, or live presentations where the building or part of a building includes an assembly area for the audience. Article 530, however, applies to TV or motion picture studios where film or TV cameras are used to record programs and to the other areas of similar application—but where the facility does not include an audience area.

The term *motion picture studio* is commonly used as meaning a large space, sometimes 100 acres or more in extent, enclosed by walls or fences within which are several "stages," a number of spaces for outdoor setups, warehouses, storage sheds, separate buildings used as dressing rooms, a large substation, a restaurant, and other necessary buildings. The so-called "stages" are large buildings containing numerous temporary and semipermanent setups for both indoor and outdoor views.

The **Code** rules for motion picture studios are intended to apply only to those locations where special hazards exist. Such special hazards are confined to the buildings in which films are handled or stored, the stages, and the outdoor spaces where flammable temporary structures and equipment are used. Some of these special hazards are due to the presence of a considerable quantity of highly flammable film; otherwise, the conditions are much the same as on a theater stage and, in general, the same rules should be observed as in the case of theater stages.

530·11. Permanent Wiring.   The 1975 NEC used the word "metal"—between "approved" and "raceways," in the first sentence. Because the word "metal" no longer appears in the rule, rigid nonmetallic conduit is, therefore, acceptable for use in motion picture and TV studios.

In the Exception, Class 2 and Class 3 remote control or signaling circuits and power-limited fire-protective signaling circuits are exempted from the basic rule requiring permanent wiring to be in raceways or Type MC or MI cable. Those circuits along with communications and sound recording and reproducing circuits are exempt from the basic rule.

ARTICLE 540. MOTION PICTURE PROJECTORS

540·1. Scope. According to the definition of hazardous locations in Art. 500, a motion picture booth is not classed as a hazardous location, even though the film is highly flammable. The film is not volatile at ordinary temperatures and hence no flammable gases are present, and the wiring installation need not be explosionproof but should be made with special care to guard against fire hazards.

540·2. Professional Projector. Figure 540-1 shows a professional movie projector, which is subject to lengthier and stricter requirements than those of nonprofessional projectors.

540·10. Motion Picture Projection Room Required. Professional projectors must be installed in a projector booth, which does not have to be treated like a hazardous (classified) location.

Figure 540-2 shows the arrangement of the apparatus and wiring in the projection room of a large modern motion picture theater. This room, or booth,

Fig. 540·1. Professional projector. But note that Art. 540 applies to *both* professional and nonprofessional movie projectors. The article is divided into part **C** on professional equipment and part **D** on nonprofessional units. (Sec. 540-2.)

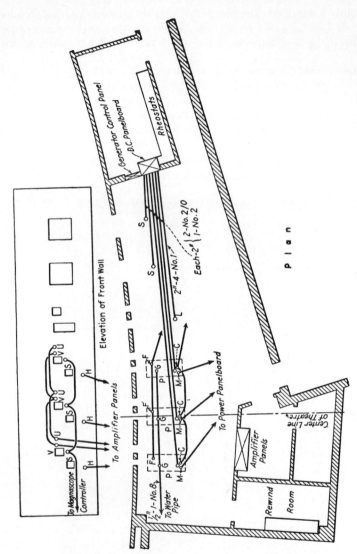

Fig. 540-2. Code rules cover many electrical details in a motion-picture projection room (or "booth"). (Sec. 540-10.)

contains three motion picture projectors P, one stereopticon or "effect machine" L, and two spot machines S.

The light source in each of the six machines is an arc lamp operated on DC. The DC supply is obtained from two motor-generator sets which are installed in the basement in order to avoid any possible interference with the sound-reproducing apparatus. The two motor generators are remotely controlled from the generator panel in the projection room. From each generator a feeder consisting of two 500 kcmil cables is carried to the DC panelboard in the projection room.

From the DC panelboard to each picture machine and to each of the two spot machines a branch circuit is provided consisting of two No. 2/0 cables. One of these conductors leads directly to the machine; the other side of the circuit is led through the auxiliary gutter to the bank of resistors in the rheostat room and from its rheostat to the machine. The resistors are provided with short-circuiting switches so that the total resistance in series with each arc may be preadjusted to any desired value.

Two circuits consisting of No. 1 conductors are carried to the stereopticon or "effect machine," since this machine contains two arc lamps.

The conduit leading to each machine is brought up through the floor.

It is provided in Sec. 540-13 that the wires to the projector outlet shall not be smaller than No. 8, but in every case the maximum current drawn by the lamp should be ascertained and conductors should be installed of sufficient size to carry this current. In this case, when suitably adjusted for the large pictures, the arc in each projector takes a current of nearly 150 A.

In addition to the main outlet for supplying the arc, four other outlets are installed at each projector machine location for auxiliary circuits.

Outlets F are for foot switches which control the shutters in front of the lenses for changeover from one projector to another.

Outlets G are for a No. 8 grounding conductor which is connected to the frame of each projector and to the water-piping system.

From outlets C a circuit is brought up to each machine for a small incandescent lamp inside the lamp house and a lamp to illuminate the turntable. Outlets M are for power circuits to the motors used to operate the projector machines.

Ventilation is provided by two exhaust fans and two duct systems, one exhausting from the ceiling of the projection room and one connected to the arc-lamp housing of each machine. See Fig. 540-1.

A separate room is provided for rewinding films, but as this room opens only into the projection room, it may be considered that the rewinding is performed in the projection room.

540·11. Location of Associated Electrical Equipment. All necessary equipment may be located in a projector booth, but equipment which is not necessary in the normal operation of the motion picture projectors, stage-lighting projectors, and control of the auditorium lighting and stage curtain must be located elsewhere. Equipment such as service equipment and panelboards for the control and projection of circuits for signs, outside lighting, and lighting in the lobby and box office must not be located in the booth.

ARTICLE 547. AGRICULTURAL BUILDINGS

547-1. Scope.   Any agricultural building without the environments covered in **(a)** and **(b)** must be wired in accordance with all other **Code** rules that apply to general building interiors. Article 547 covers *only* agricultural buildings with the dust, water, and/or corrosive conditions described in **(a)** and **(b)**.

547-4. Wiring Methods.   The wording leaves much of the determination of acceptability up to the inspection authority. But Type NMC cable (nonmetallic, corrosion-resistant—so-called "barn wiring cable") is specifically recognized for these buildings. PVC conduit and other nonmetallic or protected products would be suitable for the wet and corrosive conditions that prevail. The rule accepts wiring for Class II hazardous locations, as well as open wiring on insulators (Art. 320).

Note that boxes and fittings must be both dusttight and watertight. Flexible connections must use dusttight flex, liquidtight flex or cord. Also note that NON-METALLIC boxes, fittings, etc. are exempt from the provisions of Sec. 300-6(c). If such components and cables are made from a *metallic* material, then the ¼-in. clearance called for in Sec. 300-6(c) would apply.

547-5. Switches, Circuit Breakers, Controllers, and Fuses.   In this part, the description of the type of enclosure required corresponds to the following NEMA designations on enclosures:

Type 4. Watertight and dust-tight.   For use indoors and outdoors. Protect against splashing water, seepage of water, falling or hose-directed water, and severe external condensation. Are sleet-resistant but not sleet-(ice) proof.

Type 4X. Watertight, dust-tight and corrosion-resistant.   Have same provisions as Type 4 enclosures, but in addition are corrosion-resistant.

The rule of this section seems to clearly call for NEMA 4X enclosures (Fig. 547-1).

NEMA Type 4X

Fig. 547-1. The **Code** rule seems to make use of this type of enclosure mandatory in agricultural buildings. (Sec. 547-4.)

Stainless steel NEMA Type 4X enclosures are used in areas which may be regularly hosed down or are otherwise very wet, and where serious corrosion problems exist. Typical enclosures are made from 14-gauge stainless steel, with an oil-resistant neoprene door gasket.

Epoxy powdered resin coated NEMA Type 4X enclosures are designed to house electrical controls, terminals, and instruments in areas which may be regularly hosed down or are otherwise very wet. These enclosures are also designed for use in areas where serious corrosion problems exist. They are suitable for use outdoors, or in dairies, packing plants, and similar installations. These enclosures are made from 14-gauge steel. All seams are continuously welded with no holes or knockouts. A rolled lip is provided around all sides of the enclosure opening. This lip increases strength and keeps dirt and liquids from dropping into the enclosure while the door is open.

547·8. Grounding, Bonding, and Equipotential Plane. As noted in Exception No. 1 to part **(a)**, panelboard bonding and grounding is not required for a building that houses livestock if an equipment grounding conductor is run as part of a feeder to the panel. This rule is essentially the same as that given in Sec. 250-24(a), Exception No. 2, and permits the main panelboard in the livestock building to be fed and connected as if it were a subpanel in the building where the feeder originates, without the neutral block being bonded to the ground block and panel enclosure. The objective is to separate the neutral conductor and the equipment grounding conductor so that any voltage drop on the neutral as a result of neutral current flow will not be transferred to metal equipment enclosures that might be contacted by cows, hogs, or other livestock—which are very sensitive to even low voltage-to-ground potentials.

The equipment grounding conductor run to the panel must be the same size as the hot legs of the feeder, must be connected to the equipment ground bus in the panel, and must be covered or insulated copper from Sec. 250-24(a), Exception No. 2, if it is run underground. In addition, a grounding electrode must be connected to the ground bus in the panelboard (Fig. 547-2).

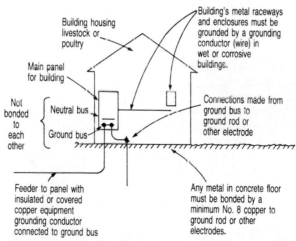

Fig. 547·2. Specific rules cover use of a panelboard in a building housing livestock or poultry. (Sec. 547·8.)

As permitted by Exception No. 2 of part **(a)**, a "listed" *impedance device* may be used to ground interior metal piping in livestock buildings to prevent exposure of animals and humans to neutral-to-earth voltage. This specifically permits a technique that will overcome grounding problems that have caused loss of milk output from dairy cows and other objectionable conditions.

As required by parts **(b)** and **(c)**, reinforcing metal in a concrete floor of an animal confinement area must be bonded to the building's grounding electrode system by a No. 8 copper wire; and in wet or corrosive locations, metal enclosures in the building must be grounded by a copper equipment grounding conductor connected back to the ground bus in the building panel. The concern here is to minimize the possibility of shock hazard and unwanted voltages by assuring the integrity of the entire grounding system. The last sentence of part **(c)** calls for any underground equipment grounding wires to be insulated or covered.

Part **(d)** requires that the uninsulated metal frame of a water-pump motor *must* be grounded. A submersible pump must have any metal well casing bonded to the equipment grounding conductor of the pump or to the ground bus in the panel supplying the pump.

ARTICLE 550. MOBILE HOMES AND MOBILE HOME PARKS

550-1. Scope.   The provisions of this article cover the electric conductors and equipment installed within or on mobile homes, and also the conductors that connect mobile homes to a supply of electricity. But the service equipment which is located "adjacent" to the mobile home is not covered in Art. 550, and all applicable **Code** rules on such service equipment—as in Art. 230 and 250— must be observed.

550-2. Definitions.   A "double-wide mobile home" is manufactured in two sections, each being approximately 12 by 60 ft. Each section is mounted on a chassis, with one side in each section open. The sections are moved to location and joined together to make a 24- by 60-ft complete unit. Because the double-wide will most likely be placed on a foundation, the enforcing authority will usually classify it as a prefabricated structure, because it does not meet the definition of "mobile home." Article 545 would apply.

550-4. General Requirements.   Many so-called mobile homes do not have their main service-entrance equipment located *adjacent* to the mobile home, as required by Sec. 550-5. In some, the service equipment is mounted on the outside of the mobile home, and in others it is mounted inside. That is commonly the case with mobile homes that have had the wheels removed and are on permanent foundations. Some such mobile homes are used as living units, some as business offices, coin-operated laundries, and for many other purposes.

When a mobile home is altered by removing its wheels and installing a permanent foundation, it is no longer mobile and does not satisfy the definition of "mobile home" given in Sec. 550-2. Many inspection authorities treat such installation as a prefabricated building or structure and apply the rules of Art. 545 instead of Art. 550. The requirement for a prefabricated structure is that such buildings must satisfy **Code** requirements the same as a building being built on the site. As with any constructed-on-site building, a prefabricated building can have the service equipment inside or outside.

550-5. Power Supply.   Part **(a)** requires that the mobile home service equipment be located adjacent to the mobile home and not mounted in or on the mobile home. It further specifies that the power supply to the mobile home

Fig. 550-1. Service equipment for a mobile home lot consists of disconnect, overcurrent protection, and receptacle for connecting one 50-A (or 40-A) power supply cord from a mobile home parked adjacent to the service equipment. (Sec. 550-5.)

shall be a feeder circuit consisting of not more than one 50-A rated approved mobile home supply cord, or that feeder circuit could be a permanently installed circuit of fixed wiring. (Fig. 550-1.)

Part **(b)** covers use of a cord instead of permanent wiring. The power-supply cord to a mobile home is actually a feeder, and must be treated as such in applying **Code** rules. The service equipment must be located adjacent to the mobile home and could be either a fused or breaker type in an appropriate enclosure or enclosures, with not over 50-A overcurrent protection for the supply cord (or 40 A, as in the Exception). The equipment must be approved service-entrance equipment with an appropriate receptacle for the supply cord, installed to meet **Code** rules the same as any installation of service equipment. The panel or panels in the home are feeder panels and are never to be used as service-entrance equipment according to Secs. 550-5 and 550-6(a). This means that the neutral is isolated from the enclosure and the equipment grounding goes to a separate bus for the purpose only. As a result, there must be an equipment grounding conductor run from the service-entrance equipment to the panel or panels in the home. This is true whether there is cord connection or permanent wiring.

In the 1975 **NEC**, part **(j)** required special permission to permit two or three 50-A power-supply cords to a mobile home. Most mobile homes parks were not equipped to handle more than one such power-supply cord for each mobile home lot. But in this **Code** edition, Sec. 550-5(a) does *not* permit mobile home parks to be wired with more than one 50-A receptacle at each mobile home lot.

In some areas mobile homes are permanently connected as permitted in paragraph **(i)**. Accordingly, local requirements must be checked in regard to the approved method of installing feeder assemblies where a mobile home has a calculated load over 50 A. In many such cases, a raceway is stubbed to the underside of a mobile home from the distribution panelboard. It is optional as to whether the feeder conductors are installed in the raceway by the mobile home manufacturer or by field installers. When installed, four continuous, insulated, color-coded conductors, as indicated, are required. The feeder conductors may be spliced in a suitable junction box, but in no case within the raceway proper.

550-6. Disconnecting Means and Branch-Circuit Protective Equipment. As shown in Fig. 550-2, the required disconnect for a mobile home may be the

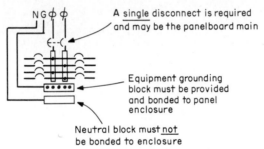

Fig. 550-2. A "distribution panelboard," not "service panelboard" may be used *in* mobile home. (Sec. 550-6.)

main in the panelboard supplying the branch circuits for the unit. Details of this section must be observed by the mobile home builder.

550-7. Branch Circuits.   The manufacturer of the mobile home must assure this minimum circuiting.

550-10. Wiring Methods and Materials.   In the Exception to part **(j)**, the smaller-dimensional box mentioned would usually be a box designed for a special switch or receptacle, or a combination box and wiring device. Such combinations can be properly evaluated and tested with a limited number of conductors and connections and a specific lay of conductors to ensure adequate wiring space in the spirit of the first paragraph in Sec. 370-6.

550-11. Grounding.   The white (neutral) conductor is required to be run from the "insulated busbar" in the mobile home panel to the service-entrance equipment, where it is connected to the terminal at the point of connection to the grounding electrode conductor.

The green-colored conductor is required to be run from the "panel grounding bus" in the mobile home to the service-entrance equipment, where it is connected to the neutral conductor at the point of connection to the grounding electrode conductor.

The requirements provide that the grounded (white) conductor and the grounding (green) conductor be kept separate within the mobile home structure in order to secure the maximum protection against electric-shock hazard if the supply neutral conductor should become open.

A common point of discussion among electrical authorities and electricians is whether or not the green-colored grounding conductor in the supply cord should be connected to the grounded circuit conductor (neutral) outside the mobile home, say at the location of the service equipment. The grounding conductor in the supply cord or the grounding conductor in the power supply to a mobile home is always required to be connected to the grounded circuit conductor (neutral) outside the mobile home on the supply side of the service disconnecting means, but *not* in a junction box under the mobile home or at any other point on the *load side* of the service equipment (pedestal).

550·21. Distribution System.   The mobile home park supply is limited to nominal 120/240-V, single-phase, 3-wire to accommodate appliances rated at nominal 240 V or a combination nominal voltage of 120/240 V. Accordingly, a 3-wire 120/208-V supply, derived from a 4-wire 208Y/120-V supply, would not be acceptable.

While the demand factor for a single mobile home lot is computed at 16,000 VA, it should be noted that Sec. 550-23(b) requires the feeder circuit conductors extending to each mobile home lot to be not less than 100 A.

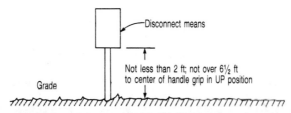

Fig. 550·3. Mobile home service disconnect must comply with new minimum mounting height rule. (Sec. 550-23.)

550·23. Mobile Home Service Equipment.   The service equipment disconnect means for a mobile home must be mounted with the bottom of its enclosure at least 2 ft above the ground, because some very low mounted disconnects are subject to flooding and are difficult to operate. But the disconnect must not be higher than 6½ ft above the ground or platform (Fig. 550-3).

ARTICLE 551. RECREATIONAL VEHICLES AND RECREATIONAL VEHICLE PARKS

551·1. Scope.   Some states have laws that require factory inspection of recreational vehicles by state inspectors. Such laws closely follow NFPA No. 501C, Standard for Recreational Vehicles. This standard contains electrical requirements in accordance with part **A** of Art. 551. It also contains requirements for plumbing and heating systems.

551·10 Low·Voltage Systems. This section concerns 12-V systems for running and signal lights similar to those in conventional automobile systems. Also, many recreational vehicles use 12-V systems for interior lighting or other small loads. The 12-V system is derived from an on-board battery or through a transfer switch from a 120/12-V transformer often equipped with a full-wave rectifier.

551·20. Combination Electrical Systems. As explained in the last Exception of part **(b)**, "momentary" operated electric appliances do not affect converter sizing. This Exception excludes from calculation of the required converter rating any appliance that operates only momentarily (by a momentary contact switch) and cannot have its switch left in the closed position. Such appliances draw current for only momentary periods and do not have to be counted as "load" in sizing the converter rating.

551·42. Branch Circuits Required. This rule coordinates the rules on branch circuits to those of Sec. 551-45 on distribution panelboard.

ARTICLE 553.   FLOATING BUILDINGS

553·1. Scope. This article covers the electrical system in a building—either residential (dwelling unit) or nonresidential—that floats on water, is moored in a permanent location, and has its electrical system supplied from a supply system on land. The rules apply to any floating building and are not limited only to floating "dwelling units."

553·4. Location of Service Equipment. The service-disconnect means and protection for a floating building must not be mounted on the unit. This assures the ability to disconnect the supply conductors to the floating building in an emergency, such as in a storm, in the event that it is necessary to move the unit quickly (Fig. 553-1).

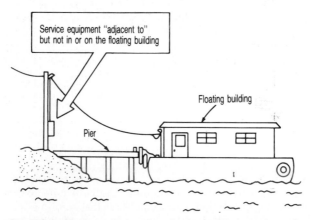

Service equipment "adjacent to" but not in or on the floating building

Floating building

Pier

Fig. 553·1. Service equipment for a floating building must be on the dock, pier, or wharf.

553-8. General Requirements. A green-colored, insulated equipment grounding conductor must be used in a feeder to the main panel of a floating building. This positive equipment grounding conductor must be run to the panel from an equipment grounding terminal (or bonded neutral bus) in the building's service equipment on land.

ARTICLE 555. MARINAS AND BOATYARDS

555-1. Scope. This article covers both fixed and floating piers, wharfs, and docks—as in boat basins or marinas. In Fig. 555-1, branch circuits and feeder cables run from panelboards in the electrical shed at the left, down, and underground into a fabricated cable space running the length of the pier shown at the right, supplying shore-power receptacle pedestals (arrows) along both sides of the pier.

Fig. 555-1. This is one part of a 406-boat marina where shore power is supplied to moored boats from receptacle power pedestals (arrows) supplied by cables run under the pier from a panelboard in the shed at the left (Sec. 555-1.)

555-3. Receptacles. Figure 555-2 shows typical configurations of locking- and grounding-type receptacles and attachment plugs used in marinas and boatyards. A complete chart of these devices can be obtained from the National Electrical Manufacturers Association or wiring-device manufacturers. Locking-type receptacles and caps are required to provide proper contact and assur-

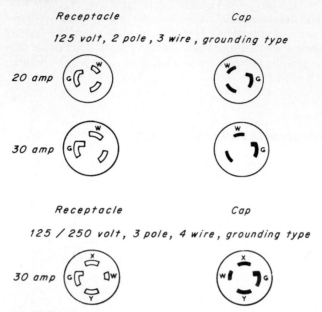

Fig. 555-2. These types of connections provide shore power for boats.
(Sec. 555-3.)

ance that attachment plugs will not fall out easily and disconnect on-board
equipment such as bilge pumps or refrigerators. Shore-power receptacles for
boats up to 20 ft long must be rated at least 20 A, and for boats longer than 20
ft must be rated at least 30 A.

555-4. Branch Circuits.   Each single receptacle must be installed on an individual or multiwire branch circuit, with only the one receptacle on the circuit.
As shown in Fig. 555-3, a receptacle pedestal unit (two mounted back to back
at each location) contains receptacles providing plug-in-power to boats at their
berths along the pier, with CB protection and control in each housing. As
required by **NEC** Sec. 553-3, each receptacle must be rated not less than 20 A
and must be a single locking- and grounding-type receptacle. There is no
requirement for ground-fault circuit interruption on these receptacles. (However, at a marina, any 15- or 20-A 120-V receptacles that are *not* used for shore
power to boats must be provided with GFCI protection.)

Also, as required by **NEC** Sec. 555-4, each individual receptacle in the pedestal unit is supplied by a separate branch circuit of the voltage and current
rating that corresponds to the receptacle rating. At each pedestal location a separate bare, stranded No. 6 copper conductor (arrow) is available as a static
grounding conductor bonded to all pedestals and lighting fixtures. The inset in
Fig. 555-3 shows one receptacle wiring arrangement. Hookup details at pedestal units vary with voltage ratings, current ratings, and phase configuration of
power required by different sizes of boats—from small motorboats up to 100-ft
yachts.

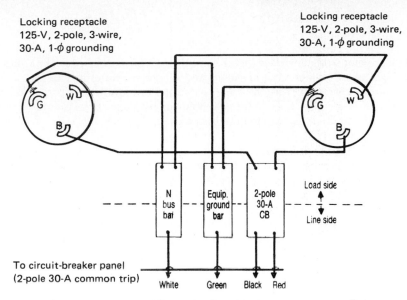

Fig. 555-3. Receptacle providing shore power to each boat is contained in a "power pedestal" (called a "power outlet" in Sec. 555-4) and is a locking and grounding type. (Sec. 555-4.)

555-6. Wiring Methods. The rules here present various options that are available for the circuiting to the loads at marinas and boatyards. This section recognizes any wiring method "identified" for use in wet locations. Examples of wiring methods that are recognized by the **NEC** for use in wet locations are

1. Rigid nonmetallic conduit.
2. Type MI cable.
3. Type UF cable.
4. Corrosion-resistant rigid metal conduit—which is taken to mean either rigid aluminum conduit or *galvanized* rigid steel conduit. The use of the words "corrosion-resistant" is not intended to require a plastic jacket on galvanized rigid steel conduit, although such a jacket does provide significantly better resistance to natural corrosion, like rusting.
5. Galvanized IMC.
6. Type MC (metal-clad) cable.

In the design and construction of a marina it is usually necessary to compare the material and labor costs involved in each of those methods. Emphasis is generally placed on long, reliable life of the wiring system—with high resistance to corrosion as well as high mechanical strength to withstand impact and to accommodate some flexing in the circuit runs. The need for great flexibility in running the circuits under the pier and coming up to receptacle pedestals and lighting poles is often extremely important in routing the circuits over, around, and below the many obstructions commonly built into pier construction. And that concern for flexibility in routing can weigh heavily as a labor cost if a rigid conduit system is used.

Fig. 555-4. PVC-jacketed armored cable—with a continuous, corrugated aluminum armor that is completely impervious to any moisture and water and resistant to corrosive agents—is used for branch circuits and feeders under this marina pier. (Sec. 555-6.)

Any of the recognized types of cable offer the material-labor advantage of a preassembled, highly flexible "raceway and conductor" makeup that is pretested and especially suited to the bends, offsets, and saddles in the circuit routing at piers, as shown in Fig. 555-4. Cable with a metal armor can offer a completely sealed sheath over the conductors, impervious to fluids and water. For added protection for the metal jacket against oils and other corrosive agents, the cable assembly can have an overall PVC jacket.

555-7. Grounding.   The purpose is to require an insulated equipment grounding wire that will ensure a grounding circuit of high integrity. Because of the corrosive influences around marinas and boatyards, metal raceways and boxes are not permitted to serve as equipment grounding conductors.

555-8. Wiring Over and Under Navigable Water.   There are some federal and local agencies that have specific control over navigable waterways. Accordingly, any proposed installations over or under such waterways should be cleared with the appropriate authorities.

555-9. Gasoline-Dispensing Stations—Hazardous (Classified) Locations.   Figure 555-5 shows the rules that define the need for hazardous location wiring at

Fig. 555-5. Gasoline pumping areas at a marina must utilize Class I wiring and equipment within the specific classified boundaries. (Sec. 555-9.)

a marina. A fuel dispensing area at the end of the pier consists of gasoline and diesel fuel pumps at the pier edge, with a shack for service personnel at the right (arrow). A panel installed in the shack supplies lighting and receptacles in the shack, as well as the outdoor sign and pumps in the fuel dispensers. Electrical connections from the dispenser pumps tie into the panel. The inset shows the limits and classifications of hazardous locations around each gasoline-dispensing pump. As indicated, some of the space is classified as Class I, Division 1, and other space as Class I, Division 2—both Group D, gasoline.

Type MC cable is suited for use in the Division 2 spaces, but only threaded metal conduit or Type MI cable is suited for the Division 1 spaces.

Chapter Six

ARTICLE 600. ELECTRIC SIGNS AND OUTLINE LIGHTING

600-1. Scope. In the case of signs that are constructed at a shop or factory and sent out complete and ready for erection, the inspection department must require listing and installation in conformance with the listing. In the case of outline lighting and signs that are constructed at the location where they are installed, the inspection department must make a detailed inspection to make sure that all requirements of this article are complied with. In some cities, inspection departments inspect signs in local shops.

600-2. Disconnect Required. Figure 600-1 depicts the disconnecting means that shall be within sight of the sign, outline lighting, or remote controller. The term "within sight" is clearly defined in Article 100, and it is well understood that it means the same thing as the term "in sight from," which specifies that it shall be visible and not more than 50 ft distant from the other.

Figure 600-2 illustrates the conditions recognized by the Exception—which allows the disconnecting means to be located within sight of the controller where the signs are operated by electronic or electromechanical controllers located external to the sign.

With respect to part **(b)**, any switching device controlling the primary of a transformer that supplies a luminous gas tube operates under unusually severe conditions. In order to avoid rapid deterioration of the switch or flasher due to arcing at the contacts, the device must be a general-use AC snap switch or have a current rating of at least twice the current rating of the transformer it controls.

600-6. Branch Circuits. In part **(a)**, no limit is placed on the number of outlets that may be connected on one circuit for a sign or for outline lighting, except that the total load shall not exceed 20A where "lamps, ballasts, and transformers, or combinations" of these loads are supplied. A 30-A maximum is estab-

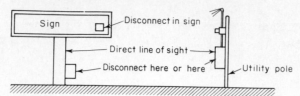

Fig. 600-1. An "in-sight" disconnect may be *in* the sign or visible from the sign. (Sec. 600-2.)

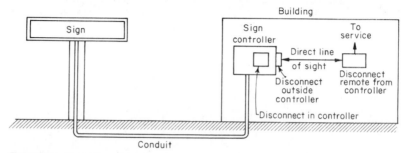

Fig. 600-2. Controller disconnect location may vary but disconnect must be lock-open type. (Sec. 600-2.)

lished for circuits supplying *only* transformers for electric discharge lighting. Where in normal operation the load will continue for 3 hr or more, the load shall not exceed 80 percent of the branch-circuit rating. See Sec. 210-22(c).

Part **(b)** requires a sign circuit. The 20-A branch circuit for sign and/or outline lighting for commercial occupancies with ground-floor pedestrian entry may supply one or more outlets for the purpose but not any other loads. The intent is that one dedicated 20-A circuit supply one or more outlets.

As noted in part **(c)**, a 1,200-VA load must be allowed for the required sign circuit. Part **(b)** of this section requires that a sign outlet be installed for every ground-level store—even if an outdoor electric sign is not actually installed or planned. That also applies to a whole commercial building with ground floor accessible to pedestrians. Part **(c)** follows up on that and requires that this outlet(s) and its required 20-A branch circuit be taken as a minimum load of 1,200 VA (Fig. 600-3).

600-11. Outdoor Portable Signs. This rule applies to outdoor portable or mobile signs that are plug-connected. The rule calls for GFCI protection "on or within the sign" or as part of the plug cap at the end of the supply cord from the sign to protect personnel from potential shock hazards. Documentation for the need for this new rule cited six accidents—three deaths and three shocks—due to ground faults in such outdoor signs that were plug-connected but in which there was no grounding connection or a failed grounding connection.

600-21. Installation of Conductors. In part **(a)**, metal poles are recognized as suitable for running the wires that supply signs, as an alternative to conductors run in one of the raceway or cable methods described.

Part **(b)** permits conductors smaller than No. 14 for portable signs. Portable signs are nearly always small and may be considered as in the same class as

> Every store with ground-floor access to customers must have at least one sign outlet fed by a separate 20-A circuit—but may have two or more outlets on the circuit, which must not supply loads other than sign outlets.

STORE

Show window

Fig. 600-3. Commercial buildings must have outdoor sign outlet. (Sec. 600-6.)

portable lighting equipment, and hence No. 16 or 18 wire may be used inside the sign enclosure, provided that the size used shall always have sufficient ampacity for the load.

In the Exception to part **(c)**, a variety of raceways are recognized and may be used for sign circuits when the raceway is made raintight and arranged to drain. This recognizes such raceways as suitable for weather-exposed locations.

600-32. Transformers. The transformers used to supply luminous gas tubes are, in general, constant-current devices and, up to a certain limit, the voltage delivered by the transformer increases as the impedance of the load increases. The impedance of the tube increases as the length increases and is higher for a tube of small diameter than for one of larger diameter. Hence a transformer should be selected which is designed to deliver the proper current and voltage for the tube. If the tube is too long or of too small a diameter, the voltage of the transformer may rise to too high a value.

600-34. Terminals and Electrode Receptacles for Electric-Discharge Tubing. The component parts of a gas-tube sign or lighting system are:

1. A transformer having a 115- or 230-V primary and a high-voltage secondary. Most primaries are 115 V.
2. High-voltage leads from the transformer to the tube.
3. The tube terminals, by means of which the leads are connected to the electrodes at the ends of the tube.
4. The tube itself.

Aside from the high-voltage leads and the tube terminals, the tube of a gas-tube system involves little accident hazard except that with high voltages a discharge may take place from the tube to conductive objects. The tube should be kept away from flammable material since such material might be slightly conductive, and the tube should not be located where it is likely to be broken.

In outdoor signs the tube terminals usually project within the sign enclosure. They may, however, be contained in separate enclosures of sheet metal or insulating material or may be without any enclosure if kept away from combustible material and inaccessible to unauthorized persons.

For exposed signs in show windows, the tube terminals must be enclosed in sleeves of insulating material and the high-voltage leads may consist of conductors insulated for the operating voltage and hanging free in air, if kept away from combustible or conductive material and not subject to physical damage.

ARTICLE 604. MANUFACTURED WIRING SYSTEMS

604·1. Scope.   This article covers modular prefab wiring systems for ceiling spaces.

Prior to the 1981 **NE Code**, so-called modular wiring systems—those highly engineered, ultra-flexible, plug-in branch-circuit systems for supplying and controlling lighting fixtures in suspended ceilings—encountered opposition in the field. Although these systems have been UL-listed and made of UL-listed raceway, cable, and connector components, inspection agencies adopted a negative attitude toward such systems on the basis that they could not be squared with the **NE Code**. It was a serious contradiction when UL and the **NE Code**, both sturdy cornerstones of electrical safety, were viewed to be in conflict.

But now the **NE Code** has Article 604 to recognize the various types of modular wiring systems that provide plug-in connections to lighting fixtures, switches, and receptacles in all kinds of commercial and institutional interiors that use suspended ceilings made of lift-out ceiling tiles.

These manufactured wiring systems were logically dictated by a variety of needs in electrical systems for commercial-institutional occupancies. In the interest of giving the public a better way at a better price, a number of manufacturers developed basic wiring systems to provide plug-and-receptacle interconnection of branch-circuit wires to lighting fixtures in suspended-ceiling spaces. Such systems afford ready connection between the hard-wired circuit homerun and cables and/or ducts that form a grid- or treelike layout of circuiting to supply incandescent, fluorescent, or HID luminaires in the ceiling.

Acknowledged advantages of modular wiring systems are numerous and significant:

- Factory-prewired raceways and cables provide highly flexible and accessible plug-in connection to multicircuit runs of 120- and/or 227-V conductors.
- Drastic reductions can be made in conventional pipe-and-wire hookups of individual circuits, which are costly and inflexible.
- Plug receptacles afford a multiplicity of connection points for fixtures to satisfy needs for specific types and locations of lighting units to serve any initial layout of desks or other work stations while still offering unlimited, easy, and extremely economical changes or additions of fixtures for any future rearrangements of office landscaping or activities.

- Systems may also supply switches and/or convenience receptacles in walls or partitions, with readily altered switching provisions to provide energy conservation through effective ON-OFF control of any revised lighting layout.
- Work on the systems has been covered by agreement between the IBEW and associated trades.
- Such systems have potential for tax advantage of accelerated depreciation as office equipment rather than real estate.

604-4. Uses Permitted.   Modular systems may be used in air-handling ceilings. Equipment may be used in the specific applications and environments for which it is listed by UL.

604-6. Construction.   Prewired plug-in connections may be BX or MC cable or metal flex. A minimum of No. 12 copper equipment grounding conductor (insulated or bare) is always required in each cable or flex length—even though flex itself is otherwise permitted to be used by the **NE Code** without an equipment

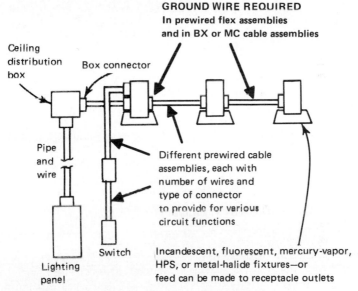

Fig. 604-1. Modular wiring systems are now fully recognized by the **Code**. (Sec. 604-6.)

grounding conductor in lengths not over 6 ft, provided the wires within it are protected at not over 20 A, and BX cable in other uses is recognized by the **Code** and by UL for equipment grounding through its armor and enclosed aluminum bonding wire (Fig. 604-1).

ARTICLE 605.   OFFICE FURNISHINGS

605-1. Scope.   This **Code** article covers electrical equipment that is part of manufactured partitions used for subdividing office space, as shown in Fig. 605-1.

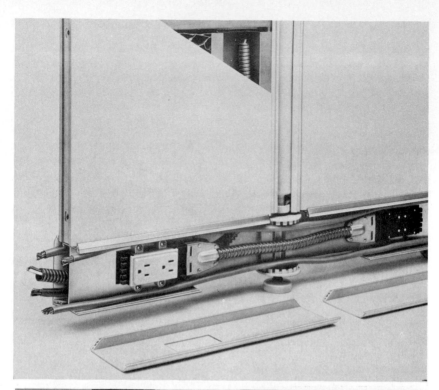

Fig. 605-1. This Article covers electrical wiring and electrical components within or attached to manufactured partitions, desks, cabinets, and other equipment that constitute "Office Furnishings." Photo at top shows interior wiring in base of partitions, to supply lighting fixtures and receptacle outlets—as shown at arrows in bottom photo of a typical electrified office work station.

The substantiation given by the office furniture association that submitted this **Code** article stated:

> This proposal concerns itself with wiring systems as provided by members of our industry, with office furniture systems that are now being used extensively in offices throughout the United States. Although not exclusively office furniture systems are primarily used in areas referred to as "open plan" or "landscape" office layouts.
>
> Within our industry, office systems furniture has grown in popularity to a great extent over the past several years. Today the sales of this type of furniture are well over $800 million dollars annually and growing. Due to energy conservation requirements users have demanded the inclusion of task and ambient lighting with this type of furniture. Current industry estimates show that approximately 80% of all office furniture systems sold contain electrical power. When such power is provided by manufacturers within our association, safety is foremost in their consideration, and all wiring systems have been or are in the process of being submitted to and listed by Underwriters Laboratories Inc.
>
> Our industry is very proud of its concern for product safety and performance and the good record that is currently enjoyed. Our purpose in submitting the enclosed proposal to the National Fire Protection Association is to establish a category within the **National Electrical Code** that deals specifically with products made within our industry that contain wiring systems and to provide in writing the standard of quality that must be adhered to by those making such systems.

605-4. Partition Interconnections.   Wired partitions may be interconnected by a cord and plug. The basic rule calls for interconnection of partitions by a "flexible assembly identified for use with wired partitions."

605-8. Free-Standing-Type Partitions, Cord- and Plug Connected.   A partition or group of connected partitions that is supplied by cord- and plug-connection to the building electrical system must not be wired with multiwire circuits (all wiring must be 2-wire circuits) and not more than thirteen 15-A 125-V receptacles may be used.

ARTICLE 610. CRANES AND HOISTS

610-11. Wiring Method.   In general, the wiring on a crane or a hoist should be rigid-conduit work or electrical metallic tubing. Short lengths of flexible conduit or metal-clad cable may be used for connections to motors, brake magnets, or other devices where a rigid connection is impracticable because the devices are subject to some movement with respect to the bases to which they are attached. In outdoor or wet locations liquidtight flexible metal conduit should be used for flexible connections.

610-21. Installation of Contact Conductors.   Part **(f)** permits use of the track as one of the circuit conductors. In some cases, particularly where a monorail crane or conveyor is used for handling light loads, for the sake of convenience and simplicity it may be desirable to use the track as one conductor of a 3-phase system. Where this arrangement is used the power must be supplied through a transformer or bank of transformers so that there will be no electrical connection between the primary power supply and the crane circuit, as in Fig. 610-1. The secondary voltage would usually be 220 V, and the primary of the transformer would usually be connected to the power-distribution system of the

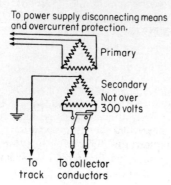

To power supply disconnecting means and overcurrent protection.

Primary

Secondary
Not over
300 volts

To track

To collector conductors

Fig. 610-1. Isolating transformer is used to power track of crane or conveyor. (Sec. 610-21.)

building or plant. The leg connected to the track must be grounded at the transformer only, except as permitted in Sec. 610-21(f) (4).

610-32. Disconnecting Means for Cranes and Monorail Hoists. This disconnect is an emergency device provided for use in case trouble develops in any of the electrical equipment on the crane or monorail hoist, or to permit maintenance work to be done safely.

610-33. Rating of Disconnecting Means. It is possible that all the motors on a crane might be in operation at one time, but this condition would continue for only a very short while. A switch or CB having a current rating not less than 50 percent of the sum of full-load current rating of all the motors will have ample capacity.

ARTICLE 620. ELEVATORS, DUMBWAITERS, ESCALATORS, MOVING WALKS, WHEELCHAIR LIFTS, AND STAIRWAY CHAIR LIFTS

620-1. Scope. These provisions may also be considered as applying to console lifts, equipment for raising and lowering or rotating portions of theater stages, and all similar equipment.

620-11. Insulation of Conductors. A distinction is made here between the conductors carrying the power current and the smaller wires of operating circuits, such as wires connected to the magnet coils of contactors. The operating current passing through the magnet coils may be quite small, and a small current leaking through damp slow-burning insulation where two insulated wires are in contact might be sufficient to operate a contactor.

620-12. Minimum Size of Conductors. Code Tables 310-16 to 310-19 do not include the ampacity for No. 20 AWG copper conductors. However, it is generally considered that No. 20 conductors up to two conductors in cable or cord may safely carry 3 A.

Because of wider use of advanced semiconductor computer equipment, use of wire smaller than No. 20 is permitted for other than traveling cables by part **(b)**, with No. 24 the new minimum.

The development of elevator control equipment, which has been taking place for many years, has resulted in the design and use of equipment including electronic unit contactors requiring very much smaller currents (milliamperes) for their operation.

620-36. Different Systems in One Raceway or Traveling Cable. It would be difficult, if not practically impossible, to keep the wires of each system completely isolated from the wires of every other system in the case of elevator control and signal circuits. Hence such wires may be run in the same conduits and cables if all wires are insulated for the highest voltage used and if all live parts of apparatus are insulated from ground for the highest voltage, provided that the signal system is an integral part of the elevator wiring system.

ARTICLE 630. ELECTRIC WELDERS

630-1. Scope. There are two general types of electric welding: arc welding and resistance welding. In arc welding, an arc is drawn between the metal parts to be joined together and a metal electrode (a wire or rod), and metal from the electrode is deposited on the joint. In resistance welding, the metal parts to be joined are pressed tightly together between the two electrodes, and a heavy current is passed through the electrodes and the plates or other parts to be welded. The electrodes make contact on a small area—thus the current passes through a small cross section of metal having a high resistance—and sufficient heat is generated to raise the parts to be welded to a welding temperature.

In arc welding with AC, an individual transformer is used for each operator; i.e., a transformer supplies current for one arc only. When DC is used, there is usually an individual generator for each operator, though there are also "multioperator" arc-welding generators.

630-11. Ampacity of Supply Conductors. The term *transformer arc welder* is commonly used in the trade and hence is used in the **Code**, though the equipment might more properly be described as an *arc-welding transformer*. Reference should be made here to the FPN following Sec. 630-31 where the term *duty cycle* is explained.

It is evident that the load on each transformer is intermittent. Where several transformers are supplied by one feeder, the intermittent loading will cause much less heating of the feeder conductors than would result from a continuous load equal to the sum of the full-load current ratings of all the transformers. The ampacity of the feeder conductors may therefore be reduced if the feeder supplies three or more transformers.

630-12. Overcurrent Protection. Arc-welding transformers are so designed that as the secondary current increases, the secondary voltage decreases. This characteristic of the transformer greatly reduces the fluctuation of the load on the transformer as the length of the arc, and consequently the secondary current, is varied by the operator.

The rating or setting of the overcurrent devices specified in this section provides short-circuit protection. It has been stated that with the electrode "frozen" to the work the primary current will in most cases rise to about 170 percent of the current rating of the transformer. This condition represents the heaviest overload that can occur, and of course this condition would never be allowed to continue for more than a very short time.

630-31. Ampacity of Supply Conductors.   Subparagraph **(a)(1)** applies where a resistance welder is intended for a variety of different operations, such as for welding plates of different thicknesses or for welding different metals. In this case the branch-circuit conductors must have an ampacity sufficient for the heaviest demand that may be made upon them. Because the loading is intermittent, the ampacity need not be as high as the rated primary current. A value of 70 percent is specified for any type of welding machine which is fed automatically. For a manually operated welder, the duty cycle will always be lower and a conductor ampacity of 50 percent of the rated primary current is considered sufficient.

example 1   A spot welder supplied by a 60-Hz system makes 400 welds per hour, and in making each weld, current flows during 15 cycles.

The number of cycles per hour is $60 \times 60 \times 60 = 216,000$ cycles.

During 1 hr, the time during which the welder is loaded, measured in cycles, is $400 \times 15 = 6,000$ cycles.

The duty cycle is therefore $(6,000/216,000) \times 100 = 2.8$ percent.

example 2   A seam welder operates 2 cycles "on" and 2 cycles "off," or in every 4 cycles the welder is loaded during 2 cycles.

The duty cycle is therefore $\frac{2}{4} \times 100 = 50$ percent.

Transformers for resistance welders are commonly provided with taps by means of which the secondary voltage, and consequently the secondary current, can be adjusted. The rated primary current is the current in the primary when the taps are adjusted for maximum secondary current.

When a resistance welder is set up for a specific operation, the transformer taps are adjusted to provide the exact heat desired for the weld; then in order to apply subparagraph **(a)(2)** the actual primary current must be measured. A special type of ammeter is required for this measurement because the current impulses are of very short duration, often a small fraction of a second. The duty cycle is controlled by the adjustment of the controller for the welder.

The procedure in determining conductor sizes for an installation consisting of a feeder and two or more branch circuits to supply resistance welders is first to compute the required ampacity for each branch circuit. Then the required feeder ampacity is 100 percent of the highest ampacity required for any one of the branch circuits, plus 60 percent of the sum of the ampacities of all the other branch circuits.

Some resistance welders are rated as high as 1,000 kVA and may momentarily draw loads of 2,000 kVA or even more. Voltage drop must be held within rather close limits to ensure satisfactory operation.

630·32. Overcurrent Protection. In this case, as in the case of the overcurrent protection of arc-welding transformers (Sec. 630-12), the conductors are protected against short circuits. The conductors of motor branch circuits are protected against short circuits by the branch-circuit overcurrent devices and depend upon the motor-running protective devices for overload protection. Although the resistance welder is not equipped with any device similar to the motor-running protective device, satisfactory operation of the welder is a safeguard against overloading of the conductors. Overheating of the circuit could result only from so operating the welder that either the welds would be imperfect, or parts of the control equipment would be damaged, or both.

ARTICLE 640. SOUND-RECORDING AND SIMILAR EQUIPMENT

640·1. Scope. Centralized distribution systems consist of one or more disc or tape recorders and/or radio receivers, the audio-frequency output of which is distributed to a number of reproducers or loudspeakers.

A public-address system includes one or more microphones, an amplifier, and any desired number of reproducers or speakers. A common use of such a system is to render the voice of a speaker clearly audible in all parts of a large assembly room.

640·2. Application of Other Articles. In general, the power-supply wiring from the building light or power service to the special equipment named in Sec. 640-1, and between any parts of this equipment, should be installed as required for light and power systems of the same voltage. Certain variations from the standard requirements are permitted by the following sections. For radio and television receiving equipment, the requirements of Art. 810 apply except as otherwise permitted here.

Part **(b)** covers wiring to loudspeakers and microphones and signal wires between equipment components—tape recorder or record player to amplifier, etc. As shown in Fig. 640-1, amplifier output wiring to loudspeakers handles energy limited by the power (wattage) of the amplifier and must conform to the rules of Art. 725. As shown in **Code** Table 725-31(a), the voltage and current rating of a signal circuit will establish it as either Class 2 or Class 3 signal circuit. Amplifier output circuits rated not over 70 V, with open-circuit voltage not

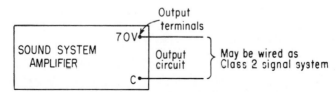

Fig. 640·1. Sound-system speaker wiring may be either Class 2 or Class 3 signal system. (Sec. 640-2.)

over 100 V, may use Class 3 wiring as set forth in **Code** Table 725-31(a) of Art. 725.

Article 725 of the **Code** covers, among other things, signal circuits. A signal circuit is defined as any electrical circuit which supplies energy to a device— like a loudspeaker or an amplifier—that gives a recognizable signal.

640-4. Wireways and Auxiliary Gutters.   Wireways and auxiliary gutters may be used with conductor occupancy up to 75 percent of cross-section area (instead of 20 percent as for power and light wires) and may be used in concealed places where run in straight lines between wiring boxes (Fig. 640-2).

Wireway for sound system

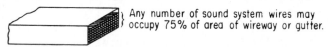

Any number of sound system wires may occupy 75% of area of wireway or gutter.

Fig. 640-2. Signal-circuit wires may fill wireway more fully than power wires. (Sec. 640-4.)

640-6. Grouping of Conductors.   In this class of work, the wires of different systems are in many cases closely associated in the apparatus itself; therefore little could be gained by separating them elsewhere.

The input leads to a motor-generator set or to a rotary converter would commonly be 115- or 230-V power circuits. These wires are not a part of the sound-recording or reproducing system and should be kept entirely separate from all wires of the sound system.

640-10. Circuit Overcurrent Protection.   Although use of solid-state electronic equipment has been steadily replacing vacuum-tube constructions, these rules apply to tube-type components. The overcurrent protection described here is actually involved with the internal circuiting of electronic-tube equipment. Other protection for external signal circuits must comply with Secs. 725-35 and 725-36 on protection of Class 2 and Class 3 circuits.

As mentioned in part **(a)**, a 20 amp-hr battery is capable of delivering a heavy enough current to heat a No. 14 or smaller wire to a dangerously high temperature, and overcurrent protection is therefore quite necessary. A storage B battery might be capable of delivering enough current to overheat some part of the equipment. Several different positive connections may be made to the battery in order to obtain different voltages, and each such lead must be provided with overcurrent protection.

ARTICLE 645. ELECTRONIC COMPUTER/DATA PROCESSING EQUIPMENT

645-1. Scope.   This Article applies only to "an electronic computer/data processing *room*." Because this Article covers all of the designated "equipment," " wiring," and "grounding" that is contained "in an electronic computer/data processing *room*," there is no question about the mandatory application of these rules to such "rooms." But the specific nature of that word *room* in the Sec. 645-1 statement of "Scope" leaves doubt and uncertainty about electronic computer/data processing equipment and systems that are *not* installed in a dedicated room. For such applications, the safest conclusion would be to simply follow Art. 645 rules as closely as possible, especially because all of the rest of the **Code** applies.

The original proposal for Art. 645 (1968) also contained other material that gives insight into the meaning of the concepts, as follows:

Definitions.   In addition to those included in Article 100, the following definitions are applicable to this Article.

(a)   Console.   Unit containing main operative controls of the system.

(b)   Data Processing System.   Any electronic digital or analog computer, along with all peripheral, support, memory, programming or other directly associated equipment, records, storage and activities. The most common types of electronic computer systems are of the digital computer type and are usually classed as Electronic Data Processing Machines (EDPM), Automatic Data Processing Machines (ADPM), and/or Integrated Data Processing Systems.

(c)   Interconnecting Cables.   Signal and power cables for operation and control of the system.

(d)   Raised Floor.   Platform on which machines are installed for housing interconnecting cables, and at times as a means of supplying conditioned air to various units.

(a)   Wiring Under Raised Floors.   Data processing equipment, if connected to the power supply system by means of an approved computer cable or flexible cord and attachment plug cap, or cord set assembly located under a raised floor construction, shall be acceptable provided that:

(1)   Existing combustible, structural floors shall be covered with an insulating noncombustible material before the raised floor is installed.

(2)   The supporting members for the raised floor shall be of concrete, steel, aluminum or other noncombustible material.

(3)   The decking for the raised floor shall be one of the following: (a) Concrete, steel, aluminum or other noncombustible material; (b) Pressure impregnated, fire retardant treated lumber having a flame spread rating of 25 or less. (See NFPA Method of Test Surface Burning Characteristics of Building Materials, No. 255); (c) Wood or similar core material which is encased on the top and bottom with sheet, cast or extruded metal with all openings or cut edges covered with metal or plastic clips or grommets so that none of the core is exposed, and has an assembly flame spread rating of 25 or less. (See NFPA Method of Test of Surface Burning Characteristics of Building Materials, No. 255).

(4)   Access sections or panels shall be provided in the raised floor so that all space beneath is accessible (by the use of simple hand tools, available on the site, if necessary) so that any area or space beneath the floor can be exposed in not over one and one-half minutes.

(5)   The underfloor area, if ventilated, shall be used for air handling associated with the data processing equipment only.

(6)   The power supply computer cable or flexible cord assembly shall be not longer than 15 feet.

Grounding

(a)   All external noncurrent-carrying metallic parts of a data processing system liable to become energized or liable to have a potential above ground, shall be bonded and grounded in accordance with one of the methods outlined in Sections 250-51 to 250-59, and Sections 250-71 to 250-79 inclusive.

(b) One or more individual grounding conductors shall be used to bond the separate units of a data processing system, and the conduit and other metallic raceways associated with the system, and to connect those parts to a common ground point, which, in turn, is connected to the grounded building structure or other recognized system ground.

(c) The grounding conductor required by Section 645-6(b) shall be copper or other corrosion resistant material, stranded or solid, insulated or bare with an ampacity at least as great as the supply wiring connecting that unit or component to the source of supply, and installed so that it will not be subjected to physical damage.

NOTE: The method of grounding is critical to the operation of a data processing system. The design of the system shall determine the grounding method to be used.

Most data processing systems are designed to have a single point for the grounding of the frames and exposed metallic parts of each unit. This point provides both safety ground and logic or DC ground.

Metal conduit, metal clad cable or other metallic raceway systems in most cases do not provide a sufficient ground for the data processing system. If they are used in the supply wiring installation to a system, it may be necessary to connect those portions of the metallic wiring system separately to the common ground point, and isolate them from the frame of the equipment being served so that equipment ground is obtained solely by the separate conductor required by 645-7(b,c).

645·2. Special Requirements for Electronic Computer/Data Processing Equip· ment Room. Six conditions are described under which the rules of Art. 645 may be applied to electronic computer/data processing equipment.

1. One or two "grouped and identified" disconnects must be provided to open the supply to *all* electronic equipment and *all* HVAC equipment in the computer room, with this disconnect (or these disconnects) controlled at the "principal exit doors" of the room.
2. A dedicated HVAC system must be used for the room, or strictly limited use may be made of an HVAC system that "serves other occupancies."
3. Only "listed" (such as by UL) electronic equipment may be installed.
4. The computer "room" must be "occupied only by those personnel needed for" operating and maintaining the computer/data processing equipment.
5. The "room" must have *complete* fire-rated separation from "other occupancies."
6. All applicable building codes are satisfied.

It is very clear from the wording that if any of those conditions are *not* met, the entire computer/data processing installation is *not* subject to the rules of Art. 645. But such an installation would be subject to *all other* applicable rules of the NEC and could even be made subject to Art. 645 on an optional basis.

645·5. Supply Circuits and Interconnecting Cables. Part **(a)** limits every branch circuit supplying data processing units to a maximum load of not over 80 percent of the conductor ampacity (which is an ampacity of 1.25 times the total connected load).

Part **(b)** covers use of computer or data processing cables and flexible cords. As shown in Fig. 645-1 (under a raised floor), part **(c)** permits data processing units to be "interconnected" by flexible connections that are "approved as a part" of the system.

Fig. 645-1. Connection of data-processing units to their supply circuits and interconnection between units (power supply, memory storage, etc.) may be made only with cables or cord-sets specifically approved as parts of the data processing system. (Sec. 645-5.)

Part **(d)** permits a variety of wiring methods under a raised floor serving a data processing system: metal surface raceway with metal cover, metal wireway (as shown in Fig. 645-2), liquidtight flexible conduit, rigid metal conduit, EMT, flexible metal conduit, IMC, Type MI cable, Type AC cable (commonly known as "BX") and Type MC cable (Fig. 645-2).

Although Sec. 352-1 prohibits use of metal surface raceway where it would be concealed, Exception No. 2 of that rule recognizes its use under raised floor-

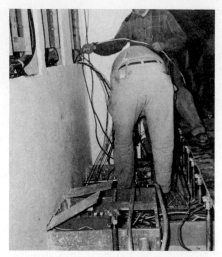

Fig. 645·2. Branch circuits from a panelboard to data processing receptacle outlets must be in a metal-clad raceway system or use Type MI, Type AC, or Type MC cable. (Sec. 645-5.)

ing for data processing by referencing Art. 645. It should be noted that, in addition to surface metal raceway, metal wireway may be used under a raised floor. Section 645-5(d)(2) does recognize use of "wireway" under raised floors. Section 362-2 accepts wireway "only for exposed work," but it may be used under raised floors and above suspended ceilings of lift-out tiles because of the definition of "exposed." In addition, Sec. 300-22(c) does recognize metal wireway above a suspended ceiling space used for air-handling purposes.

Part **(d)(4)** requires openings in raised floors to provide abrasion protection for cables passing up through the floor and requires that openings be only as large as needed and made in such a way as to "minimize the entrance of debris beneath the floor."

Part **(e)** adds important information by stating clearly that any cable, boxes, connectors, receptacles, or other components that are "listed as part of, or for, electronic computer/data processing equipment" are *not* required to be secured in place, *but*, any cable or equipment that is *not* "listed as part of" the computer equipment *must* be secured in accordance with all **Code** rules covering them.

645·10. Disconnecting Means.   As shown in Fig. 645-3, a master means of disconnect (which could be one or more switches or breakers) must provide disconnect for all computer equipment, ventilation, and air-conditioning (A/C) in the data processing (DP) room.

The disconnects called for in this rule are required to shut down the DP system and its dedicated HVAC and to close all required fire/smoke dampers under emergency conditions, such as fire in the equipment or in the room. For that reason, the rule further requires that the disconnect for the electronic equipment and "a similar" disconnect for A/C (which could be the same con-

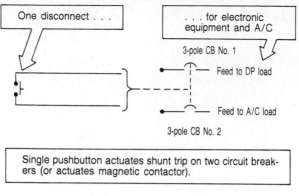

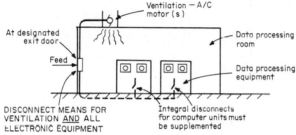

Fig. 645·3. Data processing room must have arrangements like those shown above. (Sec. 645-10.)

trol switch or a separate one) must be grouped and identified and must be "controlled" from locations that are readily accessible to the computer operator(s) or DP manager. And then the rule specifies that these one or more emergency disconnects must be installed at all "principal" exit doors—any doors that occupants of the room might use when leaving the DP room under emergency conditions. The concept is that operators would find it easy to operate the one or more control switches as they exited the room through the doorway. Figure 645-4 shows two control switches—one in the control circuit of the A/C system and the other a shunt-trip pushbutton in the CB of the feeder to the DP branch circuits—with a collar guard to prevent unintentional operation.

Although the present wording of this rule readily accepts the use of a single disconnect device (pushbutton) that will actuate one or more magnetic contactors that switch the feeder or feeders supplying the branch circuits for the computer equipment and the circuits to the A/C equipment, the wording also recognizes the use of separate disconnect control switches for electronic equipment and A/C. Control of the branch circuits to electronic equipment may be provided by a contactor in the feeder to the transformer primary of a computer power center, as shown in Fig. 645-5.

A single means used to control the disconnecting means for both the electronic equipment and the air-conditioning system offers maximum safety. In the event of a fire emergency, having two separate disconnecting means (or their remote operators) at the principal exit doors will require the operator to

Fig. 645·4. Adjacent to the door of a DP room, a break-glass station (at top) provides emergency cutoff of the A/C system in the DP room; and a mushroom-head pushbutton—with an extended collar guard that requires definite, intentional pushing action—energizes a shunt-trip coil in the feeder circuit breaker supplying branch circuits for the electronic DP equipment. (Sec. 645-10.)

Fig. 645·5. Rapidly accelerating application of DP equipment in special DP rooms with wiring under a raised floor of structural tiles places great emphasis on Art. 645. "Computer power centers" (arrow) are complete assemblies for the supply of branch circuits to DP equipment, with control, monitoring, and alarm functions. (Sec. 645-10.)

act twice and thus increase the hazard that only the electronic equipment or the air-conditioning system will be shut down. If only the electronic equipment is disconnected, a smoldering fire will become intensified by the air-conditioning system force-ventilating the origin of combustion. Similarly, if only the air-conditioning system is disconnected, either a fire within the electronic equipment will become intensified (since the electric energy source is still present), or the electronic equipment could become dangerously overheated due to the lack of air conditioning in this area.

Wording of this rule requires means to disconnect the "dedicated"A/C "system serving the room." If the DP room has A/C from the ceiling for personnel comfort and A/C through the raised floor space for cooling of the DP equipment, both A/C systems would have to be disconnected. There have been rulings that only the A/C serving the raised floor space must be shut down to minimize fire spread within the DP equipment and that the general room A/C, which is tied into the whole building A/C system, does not have to be interrupted. In other cases, it has been ruled that the general room A/C must be shut down, while the floor space A/C may be left operating to facilitate the dispersion of fire-suppressant and extinguishing materials within the enclosures of DP equipment that is on fire. Because of the possibility of various specific interpretations of very general rules, this whole matter has become extremely controversial.

The Exception to this rule waives the need for disconnect means in any "Integrated Electrical Systems" (Art. 685), where orderly shutdown is necessary to ensure safety to personnel and property. In such cases, the entire matter of type of disconnects, their layout, and their operation is left to the designer of the specific installation.

645·11. Uninterruptible Power Supplies (UPS). This rule requires disconnects for "supply and output circuits" of any UPS "within" the computer room. The UPS disconnecting means must satisfy Sec. 645-10, and it must "disconnect the battery from its load." The wording of this rule leaves questions about a disconnecting means for a UPS installed *outside* the computer room (Fig. 645-6).

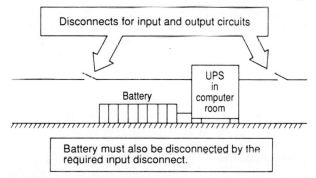

Fig. 645·6. Considerable interpretation latitude is inherent in the rule that requires "grouped and identified" switches or circuit breakers "at principal exit doors" to control an uninterruptible power supply. (Sec. 645-11.)

645·15. Grounding. Electronic computer/data processing equipment must *either* be grounded in full compliance with Art. 250 or it *must* be "double insulated." But contradiction is expressed in two specific rules:

1. Any power system "derived within listed" computer equipment that supplies the computer systems through "receptacles or cable assemblies supplied as part of this equipment" must *not* be considered to be a separately derived system [Sec. 250-5(d)] and may *not* be grounded in accordance with Sec. 250-26 covering such systems.
2. *All* exposed noncurrent-carrying metal parts of an electronic computer/data processing system "*shall* be grounded."

The rule in this section—exempting computer power equipment from the requirements for a separately derived system—is in conflict with the substantiation given of the revision of the definition of premises wiring in Art. 100 of the 1990 **NEC**. It also appears to conflict with part **(d)** of Sec. 250-21. Members of the **Code** Making Panel for Art. 645 made strong objections to the wording and ideas covered here. It seems certain that controversy and confusion will continue.

ARTICLE 650. PIPE ORGANS

650·4. Grounding. Organ control systems are usually supplied from a motor-generator set consisting of a 115- or 230-V motor driving a generator that operates at about 10 V. Neither the generator windings nor the control wires are necessarily insulated for the motor voltage. Assume that the frames of the two machines are electrically connected together by being mounted on the same base and that the frames are not grounded. If a wire of the motor winding becomes grounded to the frame of the motor, the frames of both machines may be raised to a potential of 115 or 230 V above ground, and this voltage may break down the insulation of the generator winding or of the circuit wiring. If the generator is insulated from the motor, or if both frames are well grounded, this trouble cannot occur.

650·5. Conductors. In part **(d)**, the wires of the cable are normally all of the same polarity and hence need not be heavily insulated from one another. The full voltage of the control system exists between the wires in the cable and the common return wire; therefore the common wire must be reasonably well insulated from the cable wires.

650·6. Installation of Conductors. A 30-V system involves very little fire hazard, and the cable may be run in any manner desired; but for protection against injury and convenience in making repairs, the cable should preferably be installed in a metal raceway.

650·7. Overcurrent Protection. The "main supply conductors" extend from the generator to a convenient point at which one conductor is connected through 6-A fuses to as many circuits as may be necessary, while the other main conductor is connected to the common return.

ARTICLE 660. X·RAY EQUIPMENT

660·1. Scope.   An X-ray tube of the hot-cathode type, as now commonly used, is a two-element vacuum tube in which a tungsten filament serves as the cathode. Current is supplied to the filament at low voltage. In most cases unidirectional pulsating voltage is applied between the cathode and the anode. The applied voltage is measured or described in terms of the peak voltage, which may be anywhere within the range of 10,000 to 1,000,000 V, or even more. The current flowing in the high-voltage circuit may be as low as 5 mA or may be as much as 1 A, depending upon the desired intensity of radiation. The high voltage is obtained by means of a transformer, usually operating at 230-V primary, and usually is made unidirectional by means of two-element rectifying vacuum tubes, though in some cases an alternating current is applied to the X-ray tube. The X-rays are radiations of an extremely high frequency (or short wavelength) which are the strongest in a plane at right angles to the electron stream passing between the cathode and the anode in the tube.

As used by physicians and dentists, X-rays have three applications: *fluoroscopy,* where a picture or shadow is thrown upon a screen of specially prepared glass by rays passing through some part of the patient's body; *radiography,* which is similar to fluoroscopy except that the picture is thrown upon a photographic film instead of a screen; and *therapy,* in which use is made of the effects of the rays upon the tissues of the human body.

660·24. Independent Control.   In radiography it is important that the exposure be accurately timed, and for this purpose a switch is used which can be set to open the circuit automatically in any desired time after the circuit has been closed.

660·35. General.   A power transformer supplying electrical systems is usually supplied at a high primary voltage; hence in case of a breakdown of the insulation on the primary winding, a large amount of energy can be delivered to the transformer. An askarel-filled X-ray transformer involves much less fire hazard because the primary voltage is low, and it is therefore not required that such transformers be placed in vaults of fire-resistant construction.

660·47. General.   This section definitely requires that all new X-ray equipment shall be so constructed that all high-voltage parts, except leads to the X-ray tube, are in grounded metal enclosures, unless the equipment is in a separate room or enclosure and the circuit to the primary of the transformer is automatically opened by unlocking the door to the enclosure. Conductors leading to the X-ray tube are heavily insulated.

ARTICLE 665. INDUCTION AND DIELECTRIC
HEATING EQUIPMENT

665·1. Scope.   Induction and dielectric heating are systems wherein a workpiece is heated by means of a rapidly alternating magnetic or electric field.

665-2. Definitions

Induction Heating

Induction heating is used to heat materials that are good electrical conductors, for such purposes as soldering, brazing, hardening, and annealing. Induction heating, in general, involves frequencies ranging from 3 to about 500 kHz, and power outputs from a few hundred watts to several thousand kilowatts. In general, motor-generator sets are used for frequencies up to about 30 kHz; spark-gap converters, from 20 to 400 kHz; and vacuum-tube generators, from 100 to 500 kHz. Isolated special jobs may use frequencies as high as 60 to 80 MHz. Motor-generator sets normally supply power for heating large masses for melting, forging, deep hardening, and the joining of heavy pieces, whereas spark-gap and vacuum-tube generators find their best applications in the joining of smaller pieces and shallow case hardening, with vacuum-tube generators also being used where special high heat concentrations are required.

To heat a workpiece by induction heating, it is placed in a work coil consisting of one or more turns, which is the output circuit of the generator (Fig. 665-1). The high-frequency current which flows through this coil sets up a rapidly

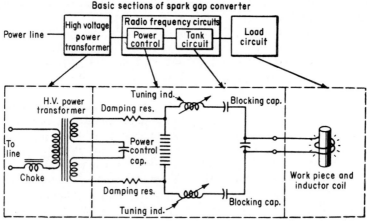

Fig. 665-1. A "generator" circuit supplies the "work coil" of an induction heater. (Sec. 665-2.)

alternating magnetic field within it. By inducing a voltage in the workpiece, this field causes a current flow in the piece to be heated. As the current flows through the resistance of the workpiece, it generates heat (I^2R loss) in the piece itself. It is this heat that is utilized in induction heating.

Dielectric Heating

In contrast, dielectric heating is used to heat materials that are nonconductors, such as wood, plastic, textiles, rubber, etc., for such purposes as drying, gluing, curing, and baking. It uses frequencies from 1 to 200 MHz, especially those from 1 to 50 MHz. Vacuum-tube generators are used exclusively to supply dielectric heating power, with outputs ranging from a few hundred watts to several hundred kilowatts.

Whereas induction heating uses a varying magnetic field, dielectric heating employs a varying electric field. This is done by placing the material to be heated between a pair of metal plates, called electrodes, in the output circuit of the generator. When high-frequency voltage is applied to the electrodes, a rapidly alternating electric field is set up between them, passing through the material to be heated. Because of the electrical charges within the molecules of this material, the field causes the molecules to vibrate in proportion to its frequency. This internal molecular action generates the heat used for dielectric heating.

Generators

In general, both spark-gap and vacuum-tube generators consist of a power-supply circuit, a voltage and/or frequency conversion circuit, a control circuit, and an output circuit. In the spark-gap converter (Fig. 665-1), tank capacitors are alternately charged and discharged, to produce high-frequency oscillations in the output circuit. In vacuum-tube generators, these oscillations are produced by a vacuum-tube oscillator, which is fed by DC power from a high-voltage power supply. The induction heating generator and the dielectric heating generator differ chiefly in their output circuits.

Actual workloads are disconnected from the output circuit, emphasizing the fact that external auxiliary equipment is often needed to ensure the most efficient transfer of power from generator to load.

Except in the case of motor-generator sets, low-power generators will probably contain enough control and cooling apparatus for normal operation. However, on installations of over 50 kW, external switchgear and cooling systems are usually required. Such equipment should comply with the appropriate articles of the **Code.**

665-22. Access to Internal Equipment.   This section allows the manufacturer the option of using interlocked doors or detachable panels. Where panels are used and are not intended as normal access points, they shall be fastened with bolts or screws of sufficient number to discourage removal. They should not be held in place with any type of speed fastener.

665-25. Work Applicator Shielding.   See discussion under Sec. 665-44. This section is intended primarily to apply to dielectric heating installations where it is absolutely essential that the electrodes and associated tuning or matching devices are properly shielded.

665-26. Grounding and Bonding.

Bonding

At radio frequencies, and especially at dielectric-heating frequencies (1 to 200 MHz), it is very possible for differences in radio-frequency potential to exist between the equipment proper and other surrounding metal objects or other units of the complete installation. These potentials exist because of stray currents flowing between units of the equipment or to ground. Bonding is therefore essential, and such bonding must take the form of very wide copper or aluminum straps between units and to other surrounding metal objects such as conveyors, presses, etc. The most satisfactory bond is provided by placing all units of the equipment on a flooring or base consisting of copper or aluminum sheet, thoroughly joined where necessary by soldering, welding, or adequate bolting. Such bonding reduces the radio-frequency resistance and reactance between units to a minimum, and any stray circulating currents flowing through this bonding will not cause sufficient voltage drop to become dangerous.

Shielding

Shielding at dielectric-heating frequencies is a necessity to provide operator protection from the high radio-frequency potentials involved, and also to prevent possible interference with radio communication systems. Shielding is accomplished by totally enclosing all work circuit components with copper sheet, copper screening, or aluminum sheet.

665·44. Output Circuit.

RF Lines

When it is necessary to transmit the high-frequency output of a generator any distance to the work applicator, a radio-frequency line is generally used. This usually consists of a conductor totally enclosed in a grounded metal housing. This central conductor is commonly supported by insulators, mounted in the grounded housing and periodically spaced along its length. Such a line, rectangular in cross section, may even be used to connect two induction generators to the load.

While contact with high-voltage radio frequencies may cause severe burns, contact with high-voltage DC could be fatal. Therefore, it is imperative that generator output (directly, capacitively, or inductively coupled) be effectively grounded with respect to DC so that, should generator failure place high-voltage DC in the tank oscillating circuit, there will still be no danger to the operator. This grounding is generally internal in vacuum-tube generators. In all types of induction generators, one side of the work coil should usually be externally grounded.

In general, all high-voltage connections to the primary of a current transformer should be enclosed. The primary concern is the operator's safety. Examples would be interlocked cages around small dielectric electrodes and interlocking safety doors.

On induction heating jobs, it is not always practical to completely house the work coil and obtain efficient production operation. In these cases, precautions should be taken to minimize the chance of operator contact with the coil.

665·61. Ampacity of Supply Conductors. Quite often where several equipments are operated in a single plant it is possible to conserve on power-line requirements by taking into account the load or use factor of each equipment. The time cycles of operation on various machines may be staggered to allow a minimum of current to be taken from the line. In such cases the **Code** requires sufficient capacity to carry all full-load currents from those machines which will operate simultaneously, plus the stand-by requirements of all other units.

665-67. Keying.   Radio-frequency generators are often turned on and off by applying a blocking bias to the grid circuit of the oscillator tube, for the purpose of obtaining fast, accurate control of power. If this keying circuit does not completely block the tube oscillations, high-frequency power will appear at the work applicator, even though the operator thinks it has been turned off. However, if this residual output voltage is limited to a value of 100-V peak, the operator will be protected from any serious burns.

665-68. Remote Control.   In part **(a)**, if interlocking were not provided, there would be a definite danger to an operator at the remote-control station. It might then be possible, if the operator had turned off the power and was doing some work in contact with a work coil, for someone else to apply power from another point, seriously injuring the operator.

ARTICLE 668. ELECTROLYTIC CELLS

668-1. Scope.   This was a new article in the 1978 **NE Code** and provides effective coverage of basic electrical safety in electrolytic cell rooms.

The presentation of these requirements in the "Proposed Amendments for the 1978 **National Electrical Code**" was accompanied by a commentary from the technical subcommittee that developed them. Significant background information from that commentary is as follows:

In the operation and maintenance of electrolytic cell lines, however, workmen may be involved in situations requiring safeguards not provided by existing articles of the **NEC**. For example, it is sometimes found that in the matter of exposed conductors or surfaces it is the man or his workplace which has to be insulated rather than the conductor. Work practices and rules such as are included in IEEE Trial Use Standard 463-1974 pertinent to such specific situations have been developed which offer the same degree of safety provided by the traditional philosophy of the **NEC**.

As a corollary to this concept, overheating of conductors, overloading of motors, leakage currents and the like may be required in cell lines to maintain process safety and continuity.

Proposed Article 668 introduces such concepts as these as have been proven in practice for electrolytic cell operation.

668-2. Definitions.   The subcommittee noted:

An electrolytic cell line and its DC process power supply circuit, both within a cell line working zone, comprise a single functional unit and as such can be treated in an analogous fashion to any other individual machine supplied from a single source. Although such an installation may cover acres of floor space, may have a load current in excess of 400,000 amperes DC or a circuit voltage in excess of 1,000 volts DC, it is operated as a single unit. At this point, the traditional **NEC** concepts of branch circuits, feeders, services, overload, grounding, disconnecting means are meaningless, even as such terms lose their identity on the load side of a large motor terminal fitting or on the load side of the terminals of a commercial refrigerator.

It is important to understand that the cell line process current passes through each cell in a series connection and that the load current in each cell is not capable of being subdivided in the same fashion as is required, for example, in the heating circuit of a resistance-type electric furnace by Section 424-72(a).

668-3. Other Articles. Electrical equipment and applications that are not within the space envelope of the "cell line working zone," as dimensioned in Sec. 668-10, must comply with all the other regulations of the **NEC** covering such work.

668-13. Disconnecting Means. As shown in Fig. 668-1, each DC power supply to a single cell line must be capable of being disconnected. And the disconnecting means may be a removable link in the busbars of the cell line.

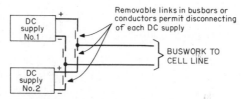

Fig. 668-1. Removal of busbar sections may provide disconnect of each supply. (Sec. 668-13.)

668-20. Portable Electrical Equipment. This section and the rules of Secs. 668-21, 668-30, 668-31, and 668-32 cover installation and operating requirements for cells with exposed live conductors or surfaces. These rules are necessary for the conditions as noted by the subcommittee:

In some electrolytic cell systems, the terminal voltage of the cell line process power supply can be appreciable. The voltage to ground of exposed live parts from one end of a cell line to the other is variable between the limits of the terminal voltage. Hence, operating and maintenance personnel and their tools are required to be insulated from ground.

ARTICLE 670. INDUSTRIAL MACHINERY

670-2. Definition of Industrial Machinery. It should be noted that these provisions do not apply to woodworking machines or to any other type of motor-driven machine which is not included in this definition of machine tools. The provisions do not apply to any machine or tool which is not normally used in a fixed location and can be carried from place to place by hand.

670-4. Supply Conductors. For the disconnect required by part **(b)**, NFPA No. 79 states: "The center of the grip of the operating handle of the disconnecting means when in its highest position, shall not be more than 6½ feet above the floor. The operating handle shall be so arranged that it may be locked in the 'Off' position."

ARTICLE 680. SWIMMING POOLS, FOUNTAINS, AND SIMILAR INSTALLATIONS

680-1. Scope. Electrification of swimming, wading, therapeutic, and decorative pools, along with fountains, hot tubs, spas, and hydromassage bathtubs, has been the subject of extensive design and **Code** development over recent years. Details on circuit design and equipment layout are covered in **NE Code** Art. 680. Careful reference to this article should be made in connection with any design work on pools, fountains, etc.

Because "therapeutic" pools are covered by the **Code**, hot tubs and spas have been added to coverage. A note tells what is meant when any **Code** rule refers to "pool" and what is meant to be covered under the term *fountain*. This is critically important to correct application of the rules of Art. 680.

Research work conducted by Underwriters Laboratories Inc. and others indicated that an electric shock could be received in two different ways. One of these involved the existence in the water of an electrical potential with respect to ground, and the other involved the existence of a potential gradient in the water itself.

A person standing in the pool and touching the energized enclosure of faulty equipment located at poolside would be subject to a severe electrical shock because of the good ground which his body would establish through the water and pool to earth. Accordingly, the provisions of this article specify construction and installation that can minimize hazards in and adjacent to pools and fountains.

Very Important: Therapeutic pools in a health care facility are not exempt from this article. Therapeutic pools in hospitals are subject to all applicable rules in Art. 680.

680-4. Definitions. These definitions are important to correct, effective application of **Code** rules of Art. 680. Figure 680-1 shows a typical dry-niche swimming pool lighting fixture. Figure 680-2 shows a forming shell for a wet-niche lighting fixture.

The definition of "cord-and-plug-connected lighting assembly" covers a lighting fixture of all-plastic construction for use in the wall of a spa, hot tub,

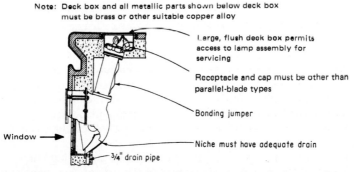

Fig. 680-1. Dry-niche fixture lights underwater area through glass "window." (Sec. 680-4.)

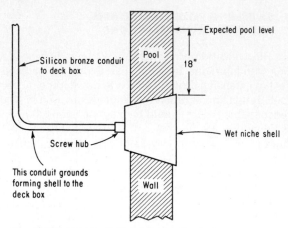

Fig. 680-2. Forming shell is a support for the lamp assembly of a wet-niche fixture. (Sec. 680-4.)

or storable pool. This type of fixture operates from a cord-and-plug connected transformer, and it does not require a metal niche around the fixture.

A "hydromassage bathtub" is a "whirlpool" bath for an individual bather—which is smaller than a hydromassage pool (spa or hot tub)—but is covered by Secs. 680-70 and 680-71.

The definition of "no-niche lighting fixture" covers a fixture for installation above or below the water without any niche. This definition correlates to Sec. 680-20(d), which describes the installation of such fixtures.

Because there are differences in the requirements for "permanently installed" pools and "storable" pools, there has been some confusion in the past as to just what a "storable" pool is. A "storable swimming or wading pool" must be

> . . . so constructed that it may be readily disassembled for storage and reassembled to its original integrity.

The definition of "storable swimming or wading pool" defines such a pool by dimensions—one with wall height not over 3½ ft and no dimension over 18 ft. The introduction of the limiting dimensions now serves to differentiate storable pools from permanently installed pools.

Figure 680-3 shows a "wet-niche lighting fixture."

680-5. Transformers and Ground-Fault Circuit-Interrupters. A swimming pool transformer must be in a weatherproof enclosure to suit it to outdoor use, and a grounded metallic shielding between the primary and secondary winding prevents a primary to secondary short that would connect primary voltage (120 V) to the 12-V secondary circuit—thereby creating a hazardous condition (Fig. 680-4).

Part **(b)** describes general rules on ground-fault circuit-interrupters (GFCI) that are required to be used by other rules of this article. Additional protection may be accomplished, even where not required, by the use of a GFCI. Since

Fig. 680-3. Wet-niche lighting fixture consists of forming shell set in pool wall with cord-connected lamp-and-lens assembly that attaches to the forming shell, with cord coiled within the shell housing. (Sec. 680-4.)

Fig. 680-4. Transformers for low-voltage swimming pool lighting are listed by UL under "Swimming Pool Transformers" and such listing is used by inspectors as evidence that the unit is "approved for the purpose." (Sec. 680-5.)

the ground-fault interrupter operates on the principle of line-to-ground leaks
or breakdowns, it senses, at low levels of magnitude and duration, any fault
currents to ground caused by accidental contact with energized parts of electrical equipment. Because the ground-fault interrupter operates at a fraction of
the current required to trip 15-A CB, its presence is mandatory under following
Code rules and is generally very desirable.

Part **(c)** calls for keeping wires on the load side of a ground-fault interrupter
independent of other wiring. Figure 680-5 shows a hookup that might be considered a violation because of the presence of "other conductors"—the wires

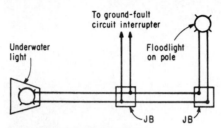

Note: Grounding conductors not shown.

Fig. 680-5. GFCI conductors are in junction box
with other than conductors for underwater light.
(Sec. 680-5.)

in the JB that taps to the floodlight JB. But Exception No. 1 qualifies that rule,
to permit GFCI-protected conductors to be used in a panelboard enclosure with
conductors not protected by GFCI. In the past when a GFCI was used in a
panelboard to supply swimming pool circuits, it was necessary to use supplementary insulation (such as nonmetallic sleeving or tubing) on the GFCI conductors in the panelboard gutter to protect these conductors against excessive
leakage because of capacitive coupling to the other conductors in the gutter.
Excessive leakage was considered a problem because it could cause unwanted
circuit opening due to the sensitivity of GFCI, especially when used in the
highly conductive conditions that exist at wet locations, in such applications as
swimming pools.

Exception No. 1 no longer specifies a need for insulating sleeving on the
GFCI circuit conductors in panelboard gutters. It was concluded that such insulation did not offer sufficient protection against the problem of leakage (Fig.
680-6).

Although conductors on the load side of a GFCI are prohibited from running
in raceways or other enclosures containing "other" conductors, Exception No.
3 permits GFCI load conductors to run in an enclosure that contains other GFCI
load-side conductors. Conductors having equal protection may be used in the
same raceway or enclosure.

**680-6. Receptacles, Lighting Fixtures, Lighting Outlets and Switching De-
vices.** The basic rule here prohibits receptacles within 10 ft from the pool
edge, and part **(a)(3)** calls for GFCIs to protect all 120-V receptacles located
between 10 and 20 ft of the inside walls of indoor and outdoor pools. But the

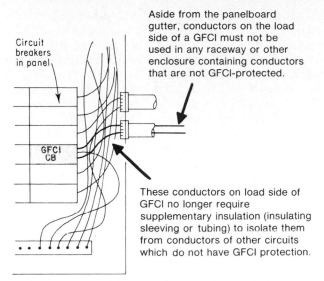

Circuit breakers in panel

Aside from the panelboard gutter, conductors on the load side of a GFCI must not be used in any raceway or other enclosure containing conductors that are not GFCI-protected.

GFCI CB

These conductors on load side of GFCI no longer require supplementary insulation (insulating sleeving or tubing) to isolate them from conductors of other circuits which do not have GFCI protection.

Fig. 680·6. GFCI conductors must be protected against leakage from capacitive coupling to other conductors. (Sec. 680-5.)

Exception to part **(a)(1)** permits the installation of a receptacle for a swimming pool recirculating pump less than 10 ft but not closer than 5 ft from the inside wall of the pool. Normally, receptacles are prohibited from installation anywhere within the 10-ft boundary around the edge of the pool. However, because swimming pool pump motors are commonly cord-connected to permit their removal during cold weather in areas where freezing may damage them, this Exception applies to a receptacle for the pump motor. Such a receptacle must be a single receptacle of the locking and grounding type and must have GFCI protection for any receptacle fed at 120 or 240 V for supply to the cord- and plug-connected pump. A 240-V receptacle for a 240-V pump motor, as well as a 120-V pump, does require GFCI protection. Of course, on a residential property, all outdoor receptacles beyond the 20-ft band around the pool must also have GFCI protection, as required by Sec. 210-8(a) (3). But for any property that does not conform to the definition of "dwelling unit" (Art. 100), GFCI protection is not required for outdoor receptacles more than 20 ft away from the pool's edge.

Part **(a)(2)** requires at least one 120-V receptacle to be "located" within the 10- to 20-ft band around the pool for any permanent pool at a dwelling unit (e.g., a one-family house). The word "located" was put in to replace the word "installed," because there is no need to install such a receptacle if there is already one located within that area around the pool. The rule at one time required this receptacle only where a pool is installed at an "existing dwelling"—which could mean that a receptacle did not have to be installed in the 10- to 20-ft band if the pool was being installed at the same time as the house; that is, the house was not "existing." The rule requires a minimum of one 120-

V receptacle at every pool installed at a dwelling unit. This rule ensures that a receptacle will be available at the pool location to provide for the use of cord-connected equipment. It was found that the absence of such a requirement resulted in excessive use of long extension cords to make power available for appliances and devices used at pool areas.

Part **(a)(3)** requires that all receptacles within 20 ft (it used to be 15 ft) of the inside wall of the pool must be protected by a GFCI. Of course, if the pool is on the property of a private home, *all* outdoor receptacles with direct grade-level access must have GFCI protection—at any distance from the pool.

Figure 680-7 summarizes the rules with respect to receptacles. Note that the **Code** wording does not distinguish between "indoor" or "outdoor" receptacles. The present wording appears to apply to all pools and refers simply to "receptacles on the *property*. . . ."

The fine-print note after part **(a)(3)** says measurement of the prescribed distances of a receptacle from a pool is made over an unobstructed route from the receptacle to the pool, with hinged or sliding doors, windows and walls, floors, and ceilings considered to be "effective permanent barriers." If a receptacle is physically only, say, 3 ft from the edge of the pool but a hinged or sliding door is between the pool edge and the receptacle, then the distance from the receptacle to the pool is considered to be infinite, and the receptacle is thus more than 20 ft from the inside wall of the pool and does not require GFCI protection (Fig. 680-7, bottom).

Figure 680-8 summarizes graphically the rules set forth in part **(b)** of this section.

The reference to "existing lighting fixtures" in Exception No. 1 to part **(b)(1)** must be understood to refer to lighting fixtures that are already in place on a building or structure or pole at the time construction of the pool begins. Where a pool is installed close to, say, a home or country club building, lighting fixtures attached to the already existing structure may fall within the shaded area for a band of space 5 ft wide, extending from 5 ft above the water level to 12 ft above water level all around the perimeter of the pool. The requirement for a lighting outlet so located to be provided with GFCI protection has been removed from this section on the basis that such protection is a negligible safety factor. However, new lighting fixtures may not be installed in that space band around the pool.

Under the conditions given in Exception No. 2, lighting fixtures may be installed less than 12 ft above the water of indoor pools. Lighting fixtures that are totally enclosed and supplied by a circuit with GFCI protection may be installed where there is at least 7½ ft of clearance between the maximum water level and the lowest part of the fixture. Note that this Exception covers *only* indoor pools.

Figure 680-9 applies the foregoing rules to lighting at an enclosed pool.

Part **(c)** requires that switching devices must be at least 5 ft from the pool's edge or be guarded [Fig. 680-8(c)]. To eliminate possible shock hazard to persons in the water of a pool, all switching devices—toggle switches, CBs, safety switches, time switches, contactors, relays, etc.—must be at least 5 ft back from the edge of the pool, or they must be behind a wall or barrier that will prevent a person in the pool from contacting them.

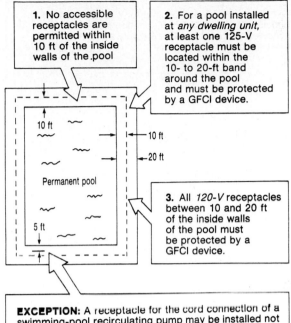

1. No accessible receptacles are permitted within 10 ft of the inside walls of the pool

2. For a pool installed at *any dwelling unit*, at least one 125-V receptacle must be located within the 10- to 20-ft band around the pool and must be protected by a GFCI device.

10 ft

10 ft

20 ft

Permanent pool

5 ft

3. All *120-V* receptacles between 10 and 20 ft of the inside walls of the pool must be protected by a GFCI device.

EXCEPTION: A receptacle for the cord connection of a swimming-pool recirculating pump may be installed not less than 5 ft from the inside wall of the pool; but it must be a single locking- and grounding-type receptacle and must have GFCI protection for a 120-V or 240-V filter pump.

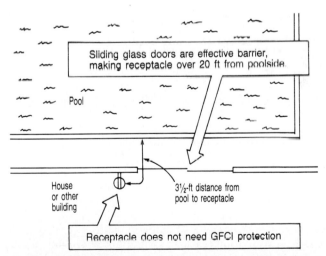

Sliding glass doors are effective barrier, making receptacle over 20 ft from poolside.

Pool

House or other building

3½-ft distance from pool to receptacle

Receptacle does not need GFCI protection

Sec. 680-6(a)(3), Fine Print Note. Doors or windows block a receptacle from connection of appliances that might be hazardous at poolside.

Fig. 680-7. Rules cover all receptacles within 20 ft of the pool's edge. (Sec. 680-6.)

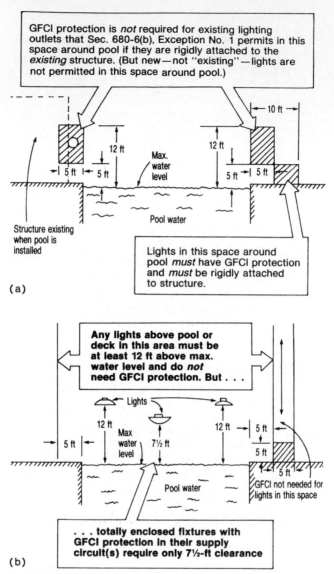

GFCI protection is *not* required for existing lighting outlets that Sec. 680-6(b), Exception No. 1 permits in this space around pool if they are rigidly attached to the *existing* structure. (But new—not "existing"—lights are not permitted in this space around pool.)

10 ft

12 ft

12 ft

Max. water level

5 ft   5 ft

5 ft   5 ft

Pool water

Structure existing when pool is installed

Lights in this space around pool *must* have GFCI protection and *must* be rigidly attached to structure.

(a)

Any lights above pool or deck in this area must be at least 12 ft above max. water level and do *not* need GFCI protection. But . . .

Lights

12 ft

Max water level

7½ ft

12 ft   5 ft

5 ft

5 ft

5 ft

5 ft

Pool water

GFCI not needed for lights in this space

. . . totally enclosed fixtures with GFCI protection in their supply circuit(s) require only 7½-ft clearance

(b)

Fig. 680-8. For lighting fixtures and switching devices, installed locations are governed by space bands around pool perimeter. (Sec. 680-6.)

680-7. Cord- and Plug-Connected Equipment. The 3-ft cord limitation mentioned in this rule would not apply to swimming pool filter pumps used with storable pools under part **C** of Art. 680, because these pumps are considered as portable instead of *fixed or stationary*. See comments following Sec. 680-30.

680-8. Overhead Conductor Clearances. The general rule states that service drops and open overhead wiring must not be installed above a swimming pool

If at all possible, wiring not associated with pool equipment must be kept out of the ground under a pool and under a 5-ft band around the pool. Sec. 680-10

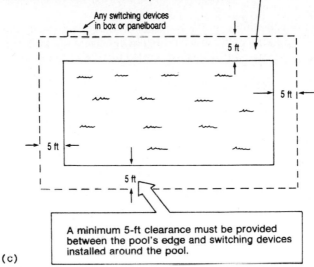

(c)

Fig. 680-8. (Continued)

Fig. 680-9. The lighting fixtures over the pool and for 5 ft back from the edge must be at least 12 ft above the maximum water level if their supply circuit is without GFCI protection. If CFCI protection is provided by a GFCI-type circuit breaker in the supply circuit(s) to these totally enclosed fixtures, their mounting height may be reduced to a minimum of only 7½ ft clearance above water level for an indoor (but not an outdoor) pool. The fixtures at right side do not require GFCI protection because they are over 5 ft back from pool edge and are over 5 ft above the water level. Refer to Fig. 680-8. (Sec. 680-6.)

or surrounding area extending 10 ft horizontally from the pool edge, or diving structure, observation stands, towers, or platforms. But, the Exceptions exempt only utility company lines from the rule, provided the designated clearances are satisfied.

Item C to the table of Exception No. 1 and the diagram clarify the horizontal dimensions around the pool to which the clearances of the table apply for utility lines over a pool area (Fig. 680-10, top). The dimension C, measured hori-

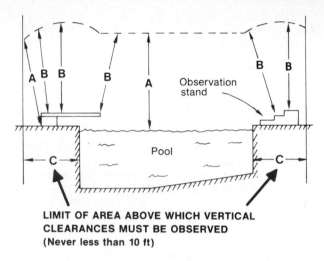

LIMIT OF AREA ABOVE WHICH VERTICAL CLEARANCES MUST BE OBSERVED
(Never less than 10 ft)

PART "C" OF TABLE RAISES QUESTION:

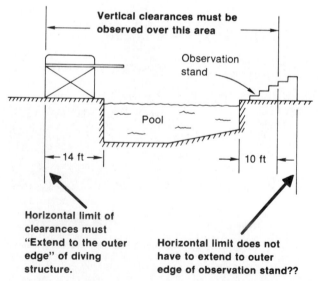

Fig. 680-10. Clearances from Table of Exception No. 1 apply as indicated in these diagrams. (Sec. 680-8.)

zontally around a pool and its diving structure, establishes the area above which utility lines (and *only utility* lines) are permitted, provided the clearance dimensions of A or B in the table are observed. The dimensions A and B do *not* extend to the ground as radii, and the dimension C is the sole ruling factor on the "horizontal limit" of the area above which the clearances of A and B apply.

As the basic rule and Exception No. 1 are worded—and the table and diagram specify—the clearances of A and B must be observed for utility lines above the water and above that area at least 10 ft back from the edge of the pool, all around the pool. But the horizontal distance would have to be greater if any part of the diving structure extended back farther than 10 ft from the pool's edge. If, say, the diving structure extended back 14 ft from the edge, then the overhead line clearances of A and B would be required above the area that extends 14 ft back from the pool edge, not just 10 ft back (Fig. 680-10, bottom).

Part C of the table says that the horizontal limit of the area over which the required vertical clearances apply extends to the "outer edge of the structures listed in (1) and (2) above." That wording clearly excludes item 3 of the basic rule (observation stands) from the need to extend the horizontal limit over 10 ft, as shown at the bottom of Fig. 680-10.

Exception No. 2 in this section provides guidance on use of telephone-company overhead lines and community antenna system cables above swimming pools. Although the first sentence of Sec. 680-8 generally prohibits "service-drop or other open overhead wiring" above pools, it was never the intent that the rules of this section apply to telephone lines. The general concept of this Exception is to specifically permit such lines above pools *provided that* such conductors and their supporting messengers have a clearance of *not less* than 10 ft above the pool and above diving structures and observation stands, towers, or platforms.

680-9. Electric Pool Water Heaters.   A swimming pool heater requires branch-circuit conductor ampacity and rating of the CB or fuses at least equal to 125 percent of the nameplate load current. An electrically powered swimming pool heater is considered to be a continuous load and is therefore made subject to the same requirements given in Sec. 424-3(b) for fixed electric space heating equipment.

680-10. Underground Wiring Location.   This section is aimed at eliminating the hazard that underground wiring can present under fault conditions that create high potential fields in the earth and in the deck adjacent to a pool. Aside from the electric circuits associated with pool equipment, underground wiring must not be run within the ground closer than 5 ft from the sides of a pool. When inadequate space requires that extraneous underground circuits be run within the ground under the 5-ft horizontal band around the pool, such wiring is permitted provided that (1) any such circuits are in rigid metal conduit, IMC, or rigid nonmetallic conduit; (2) the raceways are galvanized steel or otherwise provided with corrosion resistance; (3) the raceways are suitable for the location (by complying with underground application data from the UL's *Electrical Construction Materials Directory*); and (4) the burial depths of the raceways conform to the table of burial depths, given in this section.

680-20. Underwater Lighting Fixtures.   In part **(a)** of this section, the wording must be followed carefully to avoid confusion on the intent.

Part **(1)** starts by requiring that any underwater lighting fixture must be of such design as to assure freedom from electric shock hazard when it is in use and must provide that protection without a GFCI. *But*, a GFCI *is* required for all line-voltage fixtures (any operating over 15 V, such as a 120-V fixture) to provide protection against shock hazard during relamping. A GFCI is not required for low-voltage swimming pool lights (12-V units).

In the 1971 **NE Code**, the rule recognized the use of line-voltage, self-grounding fixtures (listed for use in pools) to prevent shock hazard—without need for a GFCI. But, although such fixtures satisfy the **Code** as safe in operation, the rule now calls for safety during relamping and requires that a GFCI must be installed in the circuit to any fixture operating at more than 15 V to prevent shock hazard during relamping.

The UL presents certain essential data on use of GFCI devices, which must be factored into application of such devices—as follows:

> A ground-fault circuit-interrupter is a device whose function is to interrupt the electric circuit to the load when a fault current to ground exceeds some pre-determined value that is less than that required to operate the overcurrent protective device of the circuit.
>
> A ground-fault circuit-interrupter is intended to be used only in a circuit that has a solidly grounded conductor.
>
> A Class A ground-fault circuit-interrupter trips when the current to ground has a value in the range of 4 through 6 milliamperes. A Class A ground-fault circuit-interrupter is suitable for use in branch and feeder circuits, including swimming pool circuits. However, swimming pool circuits installed before local adoption of ANSI C1-1965 **National Electrical Code** may include sufficient leakage current to cause a Class A ground-fault circuit-interrupter to trip.
>
> A Class B ground-fault circuit-interrupter trips when the current to ground exceeds 20 milliamperes. This product is suitable for use with underwater swimming pool lighting fixtures only.
>
> A ground-fault circuit-interrupter of the enclosed type that has not been found suitable for use where it will be exposed to rain, is so marked.

The last sentence of part **(a)(1)** requires that *only* an "approved" lighting fixture be used—which means only a fixture listed by UL or other test lab. UL data on listed fixtures must be carefully observed:

> These fixtures are for installation in or on the walls of swimming pools not less than 18 in. below the normal water level as measured to the top of the lens opening.
>
> "Wet-Niche" fixtures are intended for installation in a metallic fixture housing (forming shell) mounted in or on the side of a swimming pool wall where the fixture will be completely surrounded by pool water. Such fixtures are provided with a factory-installed, permanently-attached flexible cord that extends at least 12 ft outside the fixture enclosure to permit the fixture to be removed from the forming shell and lifted to the pool deck for servicing without lowering the pool water level or disconnecting the fixture from the branch circuit wiring. Fixtures with longer cords are available for installations in which the junction box or splice enclosure is so located that a 12-foot-long cord will not permit its removal from the forming shell and placement on the pool deck for servicing. To avoid possible cord damage, cord length in excess of that necessary for servicing should be trimmed rather than stored in the forming shell. The trimming must be at the supply end. Each fixture is marked to indicate the proper housing or housings with which it is to be used, and the fixture housing is marked to indicate the fixture or fixtures with which it is to be used.

"Dry-Niche" fixtures are intended for permanent installation in the wall of the pool, having provisions for threaded conduit entries, being designed for servicing from the rear in a passageway or tunnel behind the pool wall, or from the deck surrounding the pool.

Fixtures which are suitable for use only in fresh water pools are marked "Fresh Water Only." Fixtures which are suitable for use in either fresh or salt water pools are marked "Salt Water" or "Salt or Fresh Water."

Fixtures which have been investigated for operation only in contact with water are marked "Submerse Before Lighting," or the equivalent, and such marking is visible after installation of the fixtures.

Part **(2)** sets 150 V as the maximum permitted for a pool lighting fixture— which means that the usual 120-V listed fixtures are acceptable.

Part **(3)** repeats the UL limitation on mounting distance of a fixture below water level. When installed, the top edge of the fixture must be at least 18 in. below the *normal* level of the pool water (Fig. 680-11). This 18-in. rule was

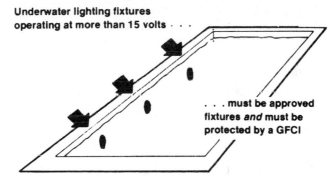

Underwater lighting fixtures operating at more than 15 volts · · ·

· · · must be approved fixtures *and* must be protected by a GFCI

NOTE: 12-volt fixtures do not require a GFCI.

4 in. min. above deck and at least 8 in. above water

Fig. 680-11. Mounting of lighting fixture and circuit components must observe all Code rules and their specific dimensions. (Sec. 680-20.)

adopted to keep the fixture away from a person's "chest area," because this is the vital area of the body concerning electric shocks in swimming pools. Keeping the top of the fixture 18 in. below the normal water level avoids a swimmer's chest area when he is hanging on to the edge of the pool while in the water. *But,* as the Exception notes: An underwater lighting fixture may be used at less than 18 in. below the water surface if it is a unit that is identified for use at a depth of not less than 4 in.

Part **(4)** presents an interesting requirement on the use of wet-niche lighting fixtures. The rule here requires that some type of cutoff or other inherent means be provided to protect against overheating of wet-niche fixtures that are not submerged but are types that depend on submersion in water for their safe operation. Note that UL rules quoted above require some fixtures to be marked "Submerse Before Lighting." Manufacturers of such fixtures should incorporate this protection—such as in the form of a bi-metal switch similar to those used in motor end-bells for motor overload protection.

Part **(b)** details the use of wet-niche fixtures. A wet-niche underwater lighting assembly consists of two parts—a forming shell, which is a metal structure designed to support a wet-niche fixture in the pool wall, and a lighting fixture, which usually consists of a lamp within a housing furnished with a waterproof flexible cord and a sealed lens that is removable for relamping.

Part **(b)(1)** requires that the conduit between the forming shell and junction box or transformer enclosure must be: (1) rigid metal conduit or IMC and made of brass or other approved corrosion-resistant metal, or (2) rigid nonmetallic conduit with a No. 8 *insulated* copper conductor installed in the conduit and connected to the junction box or transformer enclosure and to the forming shell enclosures. The No. 8 insulated copper wire must be stranded. Each enclosure—the forming shell as well as the box—must contain approved grounding terminals.

Figure 680-12 shows a typical connection from a forming shell to a transformer enclosure supplying the 12-V lamp in the fixture. If a 120-V fixture is used, the conduit from the shell terminates in a junction box, as shown in Fig. 680-11. In the sketch of Fig. 680-12, from the forming shell, a length of 1-in. PVC conduit extends directly to a 120/12-V transformer mounted on the back wall of a planter adjoining the pool [observing the 4-ft back and 8-in.-high provisions of Sec. 680-21(b) (4)]. Where the nonmetallic conduit stubs up out of the planter soil, a metallic LB connects the conduit to the transformer. The required No. 8 conductor in the PVC conduit is terminated at the grounding bar in the transformer enclosure and on the *inside* terminal of an inside/outside grounding/bonding terminal on the forming shell. The external bonding lug provides for connecting the forming shell to the common bonding grid, as required by Sec. 680-22(a) and (b). The No. 8 in the PVC conduit bonds the forming shell up to the transformer enclosure. Note that this No. 8 conductor is not needed if metal conduit connects the shell to the transformer enclosure. One of the No. 12 conductors in the supply circuit is an equipment grounding conductor that runs back to the panelboard grounding block and thereby grounds the No. 8 and the metal fittings and transformer enclosure.

Part **(b)(1)** also requires that the inside forming shell termination of the No. 8 be covered with, or encapsulated in, a UL-listed potting compound. Experience

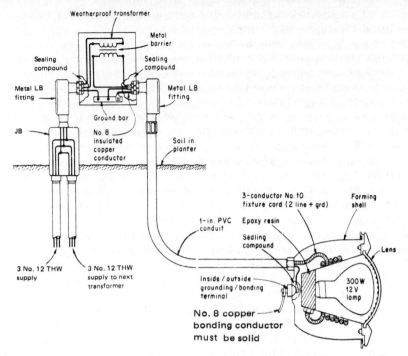

Fig. 680-12. Grounding and bonding is required in a typical hookup of low-voltage wet-niche fixture with PVC conduit. (Sec. 680-20.)

has shown that corrosion occurs when connections are exposed to pool water. Epoxies are available to achieve this protection; however, some inspection agencies do accept a waterproof, permanently pliable silicone caulk compound.

Note that the illustrated assembly includes three noncurrent-carrying conductors: (1) a No. 8 *bonding* conductor connecting the forming shell to the bonding grid; (2) a No. 8 insulated conductor in PVC conduit between the forming shell and the transformer enclosure; and (3) a *grounding* conductor in the fixture flexible supply cord.

Part **(b)(2)** requires sealing of the fixture cord end and terminals within the wet-niche to prevent water from entering the fixture. And grounding terminations must also be protected by potting compounds.

Part **(b)(3)** states that an underwater lighting fixture must be secured and grounded to the forming shell by a positive locking device which will assure a low-resistance contact and which will require a tool to remove the fixture from the forming shell. This provides added assurance that fixtures will remain grounded because, in the case of wet-niche fixtures, the metal forming shell provides a bond between the raceway (or No. 8 conductor in PVC) connected to the forming shell and the noncurrent-carrying metal parts of the fixture.

Part **(c)** permits use of an approved dry-niche lighting fixture that may be installed outside the walls of the pool in closed recesses which are adequately drained and accessible for maintenance. For a dry-niche fixture, a "deck box"—set in the concrete deck around the pool—may be used and fed by metal (rigid or IMC) or nonmetallic conduit from the service equipment or from a panelboard. Where the circuit conductors to the fixture are run on or within a building, the Exception to the rule permits the conductors to be enclosed in EMT—but rigid metal or IMC or rigid nonmetallic conduit must be used outdoors when not on a building. And such a deck box does not have to be 4 in. up and 4 ft back from the pool edge, as required for a junction box for a wet-niche fixture. See Fig. 680-1.

Some approved dry-niche fixtures are provided with an integral flush deck box used to change lamps. Such fixtures have a drain connection at the bottom of the fixture to prevent accumulation of water or moisture.

680-21. Junction Boxes and Enclosures for Transformers or Ground-Fault Circuit-Interrupters. Part **(a)** covers junction boxes that *connect to a conduit that extends directly to a pool-lighting forming shell,* such as shown in Fig. 680-11. The junction box must be of corrosion-resistant material provided with threaded hubs for the connections of conduit.

For line-voltage (120 V) pool fixtures the so-called "deck box" (set in the concrete deck around the pool) is no longer permissible (except where approved dry-niche fixtures include flush boxes as part of an approved assembly), because the deck box, which was installed flush in the concrete adjacent to the pool, was the major source of failure of branch-circuit, grounding, and fixture conductors due to water accumulation within them. The rule of part **(4)** states that these junction boxes must be located not less than 4 in. above the ground level or above the pool deck, and not less than 8 in. above the maximum pool water level (whichever provides the greatest elevation), and not less than 4 ft back from the pool perimeter.

The wording of part **(4)** does make clear that the elevated junction box could be less than 4 ft from the pool's edge if a fence or wall is constructed around the pool, with the box on the side of the wall away from the pool, isolating the box from contact by a person in the pool. Or the box could be within 4 ft of the edge if the box is in a permanent nonconductive barrier.

Important: The Exception to part **(a)** permits flush deck boxes where underwater lighting systems are 15 V or less if approved potting compound is used in the deck boxes and the deck boxes are located 4 ft from the edge of the pool. In Fig. 680-13, a deck box for a 12-V fixture could be used in the deck but the use of the box less than 4 ft from the pool's edge might be considered a violation of *b* of the Exception, which does not recognize the fence along the pool in the same way as in part **(a)(4)**. That is, the fence is not mentioned in the Exception as sufficient isolation of the box from the pool—although the installation certainly does comply with the basic concept in part **(a)(4)**.

Part **(b)** covers installation of enclosures for 12-V lighting transformers and for GFCIs that are required for line-voltage fixtures. Such enclosures may be installed indoors or at the pool location. If a ground-fault interrupter is utilized at a pool, its enclosure must be located not less than 4 ft from the perimeter of the pool, unless separated by a permanent means and must be elevated not less than 8 in., measured from the inside bottom of the box down to the pool deck or maximum water level, whichever provides higher mounting. These rules cover installation of transformer or GFCI enclosures that connect to a conduit that "extends directly" to a forming shell.

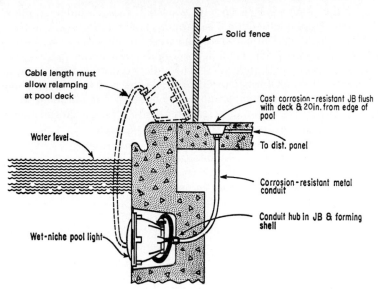

Fig. 680-13. The fence here permits the box to be closer than 4 ft from pool's edge. (Sec. 680-21.)

Part **(b)(1)** requires any such enclosure connected to a conduit that extends directly to an underwater pool-light forming shell to have threaded hubs or bosses. An enclosure of cast construction with raised, threaded hubs or with threaded openings in the enclosure wall would satisfy that rule. But because approved swimming pool transformers are available *only* in sheet metal enclosures with knockouts, some type of threaded hub fitting must be provided in the field and connected to the knockout. The intent of this rule on threaded raceway connections is to provide a high degree of bonding and grounding of the underwater fixture.

Connection to a transformer enclosure has been accepted by inspectors when made up with locknuts. The intent of the section, however, would not be considered satisfied even though the transformer enclosure can be well grounded and bonded by connections at the grounding bar within the enclosure. In most instances, the grounding bar must be added by the contractor.

Part **(b)** also requires that transformer or GFCI enclosures must be provided with an approved seal (such as duct seal) at conduit connections to prevent circulation of air between the conduit and the enclosure; must have electrical continuity between every connected metal conduit and the grounding terminals by means of copper, brass, or other approved corrosion-resistant metal that is integral with the enclosures; must be located not less than 4 ft from the inside walls of the pool (unless separated by a solid fence, wall, or other permanent barrier); and must be located not less than 8 in. from the ground level, pool deck, or maximum pool water level, whichever provides the greatest elevation. This distance is measured from the inside bottom of the enclosure. See Fig. 680-12.

Note that part **(b)(3)** intends to assure a grounding path *from the enclosure and its grounding terminals* to any metal conduit. The section specifically states "metal conduit." Where PVC conduit is used, the provision is not applicable, and the No. 8 ground wire in the PVC bonds to the forming shell. However, the section requires electrical continuity between an enclosure and "every connected metal conduit." The conduit feeding the transformer primary does not seem to be involved with that rule because the concern is with the grounding path between the transformer or GFCI enclosure and the forming shell and because the No. 12 equipment grounding conductor in the primary supply will carry any current from a fault originating within the transformer enclosure. Local **Code** authorities should be consulted on the point.

The phrase "integral with the enclosures" is meant to cover a situation where the enclosure is nonmetallic. In this case, electrical continuity between the metal conduits and the grounding terminals must be provided by one of the metals specified, and this "jumper" must be permanently attached to the nonmetallic box so that it is "integral."

In Fig. 680-12, the transformer enclosure is being used as a junction box to an underwater light, with the equipment grounding conductors terminated at the grounding bar and carried through. However, the primary purpose of this enclosure is to house the transformer. Thus parts **(b)**, **(c)**, and **(d)** of Sec. 680-21 would apply. Section 680-21(a) would apply to boxes connected directly to underwater lights and is intended to cover situations where splices, terminations, or pulling of conductors might be required.

Figure 680-12 also involves Sec. 680-21(b) (1), which requires that the enclosure be equipped with provisions for threaded conduit entries; and Sec. 680-21(b) (3), which requires that the enclosure be provided with electrical continuity between every connected metal conduit and the grounding terminals by means of copper, brass, or other approved corrosion-resistant metal that is integral with the enclosures. The intent of those rules is to assure maximum safety with a high degree of bonding and grounding. An enclosure housing a transformer with conduit connection directly to an underwater light could be equipped with raised hubs for conduit connections, be watertight, and if nonmetallic, be provided with a permanently attached bonding jumper between all metal conduits to provide the required electrical continuity.

Part **(c)** of this section warns against creating a tripping hazard or exposing enclosures to damage where they are elevated as required. It is also important to remember that these junction boxes must be afforded additional protection against damage if located on the walkway around the pool. For protection against impact, they may be installed under a diving board or adjacent to a permanent structure such as a lamp post or service pole.

Part **(d)** must be carefully satisfied and part **(e)** calls for strain relief to be added to the flexible cord of a wet-niche lighting fixture at the termination of the cord within a junction box, transformer enclosure, or a GFCI. If this device is not supplied with the fixture, the contractor must provide it.

680-22. Bonding.   At the beginning of this section, the fine-print note clarifies that the No. 8 pool bonding wire does not have to be taken back to the panelboard. When all the required bonding connections are made at a pool, the entire interconnected hookup will be grounded by the "equipment grounding conductor" that is required to be run to the filter pump and to the lighting junction boxes and is connected to the No. 8 bonding conductor at the pump and in the boxes. In a pool without underwater lighting, the equipment grounding conductor run with a pump-motor circuit will be the sole grounding connection for the bonded parts—and that is all that is required.

The No. 8 bonding conductor does not have to be run to a panelboard, service equipment ground block, or grounding electrode.

Part **(a)** spells out in detail the pool components that must be bonded together. In general, all metal parts that are within 5 ft of the inside walls of the pool and are not separated by a permanent barrier and all metal parts of electrical equipment associated with the pool water circulating system must be bonded together. That usually includes forming shells of underwater lights, ladders, rails, fill spouts, drains, reinforcing bars, transformer enclosures supplying underwater lights, and equipment in the pump room (Fig. 680-14). The bonding

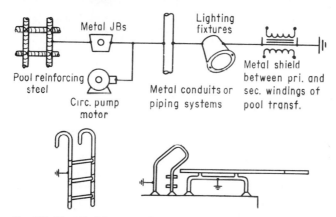

Fig. 680·14. All of these metallic, non-current-carrying parts of a pool installation must be "bonded together." (Sec. 680-22.)

grid must always include metal parts of a pool cover mechanism, including the housing of a drive motor for a power-operated pool cover. The objective of "bonding" all metal together and then "grounding" the interconnected metal components is to bring everything within touch to the same electrical potential—earth potential. This eliminates shock hazard from any stray currents that may be induced in or conducted to the metal from outside the pool environment or from faults in any of the pool electrical equipment that, for one reason or another, are not cleared by the circuit protective devices.

In addition to specifying that underwater lighting fixtures and lighting fixture housings shall be grounded, the rule also requires that all metallic conduit and piping, reinforcing steel and other noncurrent-carrying metal components, located within 5 ft of a pool, must likewise be bonded together and grounded (Fig. 680-15). Part **(a)(6)** states that bonding of metal parts with No. 8 solid copper wire is required within 5 ft horizontally of the inside wall of a pool, *but* bonding is *not* required for parts over 12 ft above the pool area. Any metal piping, raceways, structural parts, or any other metal that is more than 12 ft above the max-

Fig. 680·15. No. 8 insulated bonding conductor connects to clamps on both sides of coupling in brass conduit from forming shell to transformer housing. Section 680-22(a) (5) requires bonding of all "metal conduit" within 5 ft of pool edge. This bonding connection, although literally required, is not always required by inspection authorities because the conduit connects to bonded enclosures at both ends. (Sec. 680-22.)

imum pool water level or above observation stands, towers, platforms, or diving structures does not require connection to the No. 8 solid bonding grid or conductor.

These references are all-inclusive. For example, conduit and piping may relate to power circuitry, intercom or telephone wiring, supply and return water, or to gas lines serving nonelectric heaters. Reinforcing steel refers to that which is installed in deckslabs and walkways, as well as to pool structures which are poured in place, cast in forms, or "gunnited." Other noncurrent-carrying components include metal parts of ladders, diving boards, platforms and supports, scuppers, strainers, filters, pump and transformer housings, etc. All these items must be bonded together with an insulated or bare solid copper conductor not smaller than No. 8 and connected to a common electrode.

Exception No. 1 recognizes that the usual steel tie wires provide suitable bonding for the individual bars of the reinforcing steel and no special type of clamps or welding is required. The structural reinforcing steel may be used as a common bonding grid [part **(b)** of this section] where connections of the No. 8 bonding conductors are made to the steel rods by suitable clamps. Such connections must be used to bond metal parts to the reinforcing steel grid. Usually, the center-line rebars are bonded together and bonded to the No. 8 bonding conductor at several points.

The **Code** does not require each individual reinforcing bar to be bonded. It recognizes that the steel tie wires used to secure the rebars together where they cross each other provide the required bonding of the individual rods. Tests conducted over a period of several years by the **NE Code** Technical Subcommittee on Swimming Pools have shown the resistance of the path from one end to the other through the structural steel to remain at less than 0.001 ohm. The **Code** thus states in Exception No. 1 that clamping or welding these rods at their intersection will not be required.

If the pool is of metal construction and suitably welded or bolted together, only one bonding connection need be made to the pool.

The rule does not require individual sections of such pools to be bonded. However, the overlapping ends of each section to be bolted must not be painted. If they are, the paint must be removed completely to restore conductivity. In addition, resistance tests should be made across each bolted section after assembly to assure low resistance. These sections normally are fastened together by corrosion-resistant bolts at least ⅜ in. in diameter, and such an installation satisfies the bonding objectives (Fig. 680-16). But, electrical parts of such a pool must be tied into that common bonding grid by No. 8 bonding conductors.

Figure 680-17 shows how a metal junction box is bonded into the required bonding grid by No. 8 conductor run in conduit to reinforcing steel. This bonding of metal enclosures within 5 ft of pool edge is required by part **(a)(6)**. When the conduit to the forming shell is PVC, the No. 8 bonding wire required in the PVC by Sec. 680-20(b) (1) bonds the junction box to the forming shell, which is bonded to the rebars. In such cases, some inspectors would not require the No. 8 shown at the bottom of the box.

Important: Exception No. 3 should be carefully noted. It excludes relatively small parts—like bolts, clamps braces, etc.—from the need to be bonded.

Part **(b)** of Sec. 680-22 describes how the bonding must be achieved. Part **(b)** requires all the parts specified in part **(a)** to be connected by means of a No. 8 solid copper conductor (insulated, covered or bare) to a *common bonding grid.* Brass, copper, or copper-alloy connectors or clamps must be used in the common bonding grid, because field reports noted failures of other connectors due to corrosion. This grid could be pool structural reinforcing steel, a metal pool wall, or a solid copper conductor not smaller than No. 8. The idea of connecting all parts to a common grid accomplishes more reliably the objective of equipotential interconnection. Loosening of a connection at one of the parts would not disconnect the bonded parts into two unconnected groups. But it should be noted that the rule does *not* require the common bonding grid to be *continuous,* although the word "grid" does convey the idea of a loop, as in Fig. 680-18.

Figure 680-19 shows how the reinforcing steel of a concrete pool is used as a common grid for connecting all parts together. In that sketch, the steel reinforcing rods, tied together with steel tie wires at intersections, are used as a common bonding grid to bond together pool equipment. Equipment shown here is required to be bonded. In addition, any metal parts (lighting standards, pipes, etc.) within 5 ft of the inside walls of the pool and not separated from the pool by a permanent barrier must be bonded. All connections made must be in accordance with Sec. 250-113, that is, with proper connectors, lugs, etc.

As shown in Fig. 680-10, when all the required bonding connections are made, the entire interconnected hookup will be grounded by the "equipment grounding conductor" that is required to be run to the filter pump and to the lighting junction boxes and is connected to the No. 8 bonding conductor at the pump and in the boxes. In a pool without underwater lighting, the equipment

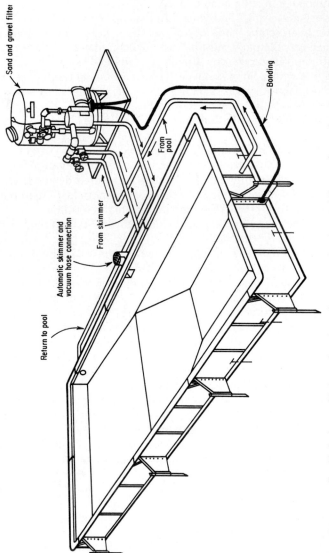

Sand and gravel filter

Bonding

From pool

Automatic skimmer and
vacuum hose connection

From skimmer

Return to pool

Fig. 680-16. Walls of bolted or welded metal pool may be common bonding grid for *nonelectrical parts only.* (Sec. 680-22.)

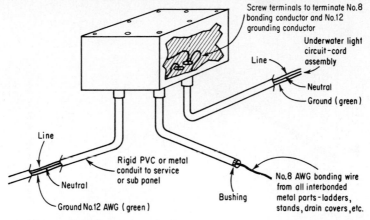

Screw terminals to terminate No.8 bonding conductor and No.12 grounding conductor

Underwater light circuit-cord assembly

Line

Neutral

Ground (green)

Line

Rigid PVC or metal conduit to service or sub panel

Neutral

Ground No.12 AWG (green)

Bushing

No.8 AWG bonding wire from all interbonded metal parts-ladders, stands, drain covers, etc.

Fig. 680-17. Elevated metal junction box within 5 ft of pool edge must be bonded. (Sec. 680-22.)

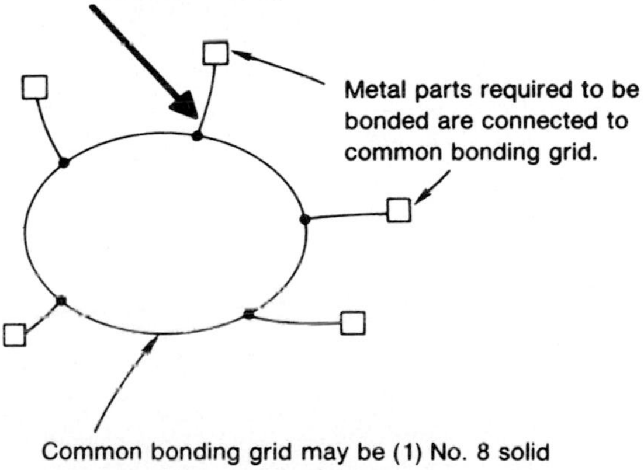

Bonding connections *must* be made with brass, copper, or copper alloy connectors or clamps.

Metal parts required to be bonded are connected to common bonding grid.

Common bonding grid may be (1) No. 8 solid copper conductor, (2) pool reinforcing steel, or (3) metal pool wall.

Fig. 680-18. All designated parts must be connected to a "common bonding grid." (Sec. 680-22.)

grounding conductor run with the pump-motor circuit will be the sole grounding connection for the bonded parts—and that is all that is required.

NOTE: THE NO. 8 BONDING CONDUCTOR DOES *NOT* HAVE TO BE RUN TO A PANELBOARD OR SERVICE EQUIPMENT GROUND BLOCK. Because water-circulating equipment is always used and such equipment is required to be both bonded and grounded, the enclosure of the motor terminal connections provides for bringing the bonding and grounding conductors together. The **Code** does not contain a specific provision requiring the bonding

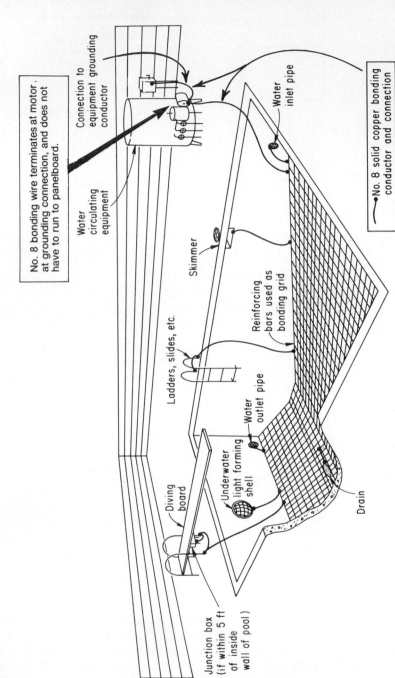

No. 8 bonding wire terminates at motor, at grounding connection, and does not have to run to panelboard.

Connection to equipment grounding conductor

Water circulating equipment

Water inlet pipe

No. 8 solid copper bonding conductor and connection

Skimmer

Reinforcing bars used as bonding grid

Ladders, slides, etc.

Water outlet pipe

Underwater light forming shell

Diving board

Drain

Junction box (if within 5 ft of inside wall of pool)

Fig. 680-19. A No. 8 bonding jumper ties each of the indicated parts to the rebar grid, completing the bonding. (Sec. 680-22.)

network to be grounded. Where wet-niche underwater fixtures are used, the metal conduit between the *bonded* forming shell and the *grounded and bonded* junction box accomplishes another connection between the No. 8 bonded hookup and the equipment grounding conductor. Or the No. 8 wire with the PVC conduit to the forming shell will make the connection.

In part **(b)**, the rule requires that the bonding conductor be of *solid copper* not smaller than No. 8 AWG. It is not required to be insulated. If it is insulated, inspectors might require green color coding at any permanently exposed termination, if a rigid interpretation is put on Sec. 250-57(b), Exception No. 1 and if the "bonding" conductor is considered to be an "equipment grounding" conductor. Section 250-79 on "bonding jumpers" does not specify color of insulation or covering. Because the **Code** rules do not cover the matter of color of bonding jumpers, inspectors commonly do not require green color, permitting black or other colors. The bonding conductor is usually installed underground and under the pool deck, except where it extends into the pump room. At all visible termination points, the conductor can be wrapped with green tape for identification, similar to the permission in *c* of Exception No. 1 of Sec. 250-57(b) which applies to equipment grounding conductors larger than No. 6 (Fig. 680-20).

Fig. 680-20. Water-fill pipe and metal housings associated with the water-circulation system are "bonded" with an insulated No. 8 solid copper conductor, as required. (Sec. 680-22.)

Conflict has arisen in the past over use of this No. 8 bonding conductor because Sec. 310-3 requires No. 8 and larger conductors to be *stranded* where installed in raceways. That rule had the effect of limiting use of *solid* No. 8 conductors, and their manufacture seemed to be curtailed. Section 310-3 has Exception No. 2 which references Sec. 680-22(b) and exempts the swimming pool No. 8 bonding conductor from the need to be stranded. If solid No. 8 copper cannot be obtained, the local inspection agency must be consulted.

To comply with the requirement that all the bonded parts "shall" be connected to "a common bonding grid", it is common practice to connect metal parts of diving boards, slides, and ladders as well as the drain cover, skimmers, and water-circulating equipment to steel reinforcing in the concrete bottom or walls of the pool. These connections are made and inspected prior to the pouring of concrete, of course. The No. 8 copper bonding conductor may, in some instances, have to be connected to aluminum ladders, rails, or junction boxes (Fig. 680-21). Care must be taken to use a connector suitable for copper to aluminum connections. On some jobs, the ladders, spouts, and forming shells are

Fig. 680-21. Fittings for pool ladders have bonding strips attached to them for connection of the No. 8 bonding conductor. When the supports are set in the concrete deck, the bonding connections tie them all together. The No. 8 bonding connections are shown (arrow) and a protective coating is painted on the connectors to protect against corrosion. (Sec. 680-22.)

made of stainless steel, and drains are cast bronze. High-quality, red brass compression connectors can be used, and connections at the iron rebars made with silicon bronze ground clamps.

Part **(c)** points out that water heaters rated over 50 A must have parts of the unit bonded to the other bonded metal parts by a No. 8 conductor and other parts grounded by connection to the equipment grounding conductor of the circuit supplying the heater. And the parts to be grounded or bonded will be designated by instructions with the heater.

680-23. Underwater Audio Equipment.   This section treats connection of loudspeakers for underwater audio output in the same way as a wet-niche pool lighting fixture. Wording and rules are almost identical to that in Sec. 680-20(b). Connection from the speaker forming shell is made to a junction box installed as set forth in Sec. 680-21(a) for a lighting fixture.

680-24. Grounding.   This section lists equipment that must be grounded: wet-niche and dry-niche underwater lighting fixtures, all electric equipment within 5 ft of inside walls of the pool, all electric equipment associated with the recirculating system of the pool, junction boxes and transformer enclosures, GFCIs, and panelboards supplying any electric equipment associated with the pool.

After metal parts have been properly "bonded" to comply with the rules of Sec. 680-22, then "grounding" must be provided to satisfy the many specific rules of Sec. 680-25.

The prime objective of grounding is to provide both connection to the grounding electrode at the service and also to assure a low-impedance path for fault currents to flow back to the grounded neutral to permit proper operation of overcurrent devices. Grounding brings all metallic parts to ground potential, reducing shock hazard.

680-25. Methods of Grounding.   The basic difference between *bonding* and *grounding* becomes evident when the provisions of this section are considered. Essentially, this section calls for grounding with an equipment grounding conductor run in conduit along with the supply conductors. The bonding conductor required by Sec. 680-22 does not have to be in conduit. Also, all equipment grounding conductors must terminate at an *equipment grounding terminal*. Bonding conductors may be connected directly to enclosures.

This section provides rules on methods of grounding metal junction boxes and transformer enclosures, panelboards, underwater lighting fixtures, cord-connected equipment, and other equipment. In general, metal raceways are not depended upon to provide the grounding path for swimming pool electrical systems. This is to make sure that the grounding path is maintained even though the conduit metallic current path might open because of corrosion. This can be a problem in pump houses, for example, where the conduit may be exposed to chlorine or acids. For the same reason, the equipment grounding conductor is required to be insulated.

Section 680-25(b) covers grounding of wet-niche lighting fixtures and grounding required for junction boxes, transformer enclosures, and any other enclosures in the supply circuit to a wet-niche fixture and the field-wiring chamber of a dry-niche lighting fixture. Grounding of all those pieces of equipment must be made by an equipment grounding conductor run with the circuit conductors back to the equipment grounding terminal block of the panel supplying the equipment.

Paragraph **(b)(1)** describes sizing of an equipment grounding conductor that runs from an elevated junction box back to the branch-circuit panel to provide grounding of a wet-niche lighting fixture that is fed from the box. Such an equipment grounding conductor must be sized from Table 250-95, based on the rating of the overcurrent device that protects the circuit supplying the lighting fixture, and may never be smaller than No. 12 insulated copper wire (Fig. 680-22).

Although the basic rule of **(b)(1)** calls for the lighting circuit and its equipment grounding conductor to be installed in rigid metal conduit, IMC, or rigid non-metallic conduit where it is run outdoors, overhead or underground, any part of such a circuit that is installed on or within a building *may* be run in EMT

THIS EQUIPMENT GROUNDING CONDUCTOR must be without joint or splice [Sec. 680-25(b)(2)] and must be installed in IMC or rigid metal or rigid nonmetallic conduit with circuit conductors. It must be sized per Table 250-95 but not smaller than No. 12 AWG. It must be an insulated, copper conductor [Sec. 680-25 (b) (1)]

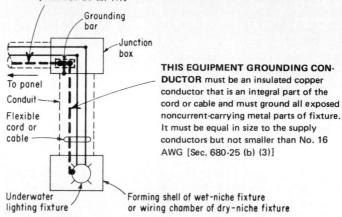

Grounding bar

Junction box

To panel

Conduit

Flexible cord or cable

THIS EQUIPMENT GROUNDING CONDUCTOR must be an insulated copper conductor that is an integral part of the cord or cable and must ground all exposed noncurrent-carrying metal parts of fixture. It must be equal in size to the supply conductors but not smaller than No. 16 AWG [Sec. 680-25 (b) (3)]

Underwater lighting fixture

Forming shell of wet-niche fixture or wiring chamber of dry-niche fixture

Fig. 680-22. Wet-niche fixture must be grounded back to its supply panelboard. (Sec. 680-25.)

instead of the other raceways, as noted in Exception No. 1, because it is a better-protected condition.

Exception No. 2 requires careful sizing of an equipment grounding conductor from the secondary side of a low-voltage transformer for 12-V pool lights to the junction box. That conductor *must* be sized from **Code** Table 250-95 on the basis of the overcurrent-device-rating of the circuit supplying the primary of the transformer. It is not necessary to use a larger grounding conductor on the secondary even though the secondary circuit conductors are larger than the primary conductors because of the 10-to-1 current step-up (120 ÷ 12 V) (Fig. 680-23). A 300-W, 12-V fixture would require No. 10 copper secondary supply conductors (300 W ÷ 12 V = 25 A), but needs only a No. 12 copper grounding conductor (Fig. 680-23).

The rule of part **(b)(2)** on grounding of the junction box for the lighting fixture is also described at the top left of Fig. 680-22. Note that the size of this equipment grounding conductor must be based on the rating of the overcurrent protection for the circuit to the lighting fixture—using Table 250-95, but not smaller

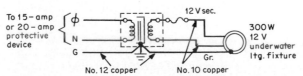

To 15-amp or 20-amp protective device

12 V sec.

300 W 12 V underwater ltg. fixture

No. 12 copper   No. 10 copper

Fig. 680-23 Equipment grounding conductor does not have to be larger on transformer secondary side. (Sec. 680-25.)

than No. 12 [as specified in part **(b)(1)** of this section]. No. 12 would be required for a 15- or 20-A branch circuit.

Exception No. 1 of part **(b)(2)** is shown in Fig. 680-24, where connection of the equipment grounding conductor to the terminal blocks is an *acceptable* joint in the conductor as an Exception to the last sentence of part **(b)(2)**, which calls for the conductor to be "without joint or splice."

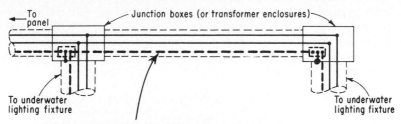

THIS EQUIPMENT GROUNDING CONDUCTOR must be terminated on approved grounding terminals in both enclosures. It must be copper, insulated, sized per Table 250-95, but not smaller than No. 12 AWG. It must be installed with the circuit conductors in IMC or rigid metal or rigid nonmetallic conduit

Fig. 680-24. Grounding conductor between JBs may have terminal "joints" where same circuit supplies more than one pool light. (Sec. 680-25.)

Exception No. 2 is illustrated in Fig. 680-25, showing that the grounding conductor requires joints when a circuit from a panelboard to the lighting fixture(s) feeds through an enclosure for a low-voltage transformer, a GFCI, a time switch, or a manual snap switch.

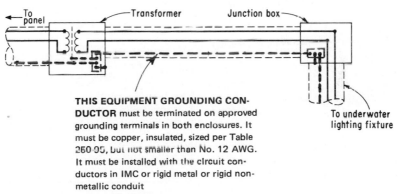

THIS EQUIPMENT GROUNDING CONDUCTOR must be terminated on approved grounding terminals in both enclosures. It must be copper, insulated, sized per Table 250-95, but not smaller than No. 12 AWG. It must be installed with the circuit conductors in IMC or rigid metal or rigid nonmetallic conduit

Fig. 680-25. Proper terminals must be used where grounding conductor runs through enclosures. (Sec. 680-25.)

Part **(b)(3)** requires that the cord supplying a wet-niche lighting fixture must be provided with an equipment grounding conductor in the cord from the forming shell to the junction box, as described in the right-hand text in Fig. 680-22.

In part **(c)**, the rule specifically requires an equipment grounding conductor for "pool-associated motors." This is actually a specific requirement that is a follow-up to the general rule, in part **(a)** of this section, that grounding must be provided for "motors" at pools. The rule here requires that a circuit to a pool filter pump—or any other "pool-associated motor"—*must* be run in rigid metal conduit (steel or aluminum), in intermediate metal conduit (so-called IMC), in rigid nonmetallic conduit (such as Schedule 40 or Schedule 80 PVC conduit), or in Type MC cable that is "listed" for the application. And, for all such circuits to pool motors, a separate equipment grounding conductor of the proper size must be run in the raceway or cable with the branch-circuit conductors. The equipment grounding conductor must be sized from **NEC** Table 250-95, based on the rating of the overcurrent protective device (the fuse or CB) protecting the branch-circuit wires. It must *never* be smaller than No. 12 and must *always* be *copper* and *insulated,* colored green for its entire length in sizes up to No. 6.

Note: THIS RULE CLEARLY ELIMINATES PAST CONFUSION AND DISPUTED **Code** PRACTICE. IT REQUIRES ONE OF THE THREE RACEWAYS OR TYPE MC CABLE TO FEED A FILTER PUMP AND DOES *NOT* PERMIT USE OF TYPE UF OR TYPE USE CABLE FOR THE PUMP CIRCUIT, as shown in Fig. 680-26.

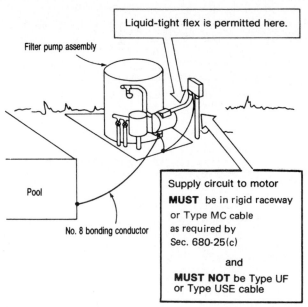

Liquid-tight flex is permitted here.

Filter pump assembly

Pool

No. 8 bonding conductor

Supply circuit to motor
MUST be in rigid raceway
or Type MC cable
as required by
Sec. 680-25(c)

and

MUST NOT be Type UF
or Type USE cable

Fig. 680·26. A very clear rule is now applied to wiring method required for pump. (Sec. 680-25.)

The first two Exceptions to part **(c)** offer only limited use of EMT or liquidtight flexible conduit as part of the circuit to a pool motor. EMT may be used as part of the circuit where the raceway is within or on a building—but may *not* be used overhead or underground outdoors. Any part of the circuit outdoors (not on a building) *must* be one of the three rigid conduits described in the basic rule. Exception No. 2 recognizes the use of liquidtight flexible conduit as the supply raceway for a pool motor where flexibility is needed. Such flex would have to be a metallic type, unless it is nonmetallic flex UL listed for outdoor use, as permitted by Sec. 351-23(a)(3). *But in all cases* where EMT or liquidtight flex is used as permitted by the Exceptions, a separate equipment grounding conductor must be used, as described above, within the raceway.

As permitted by Exception No. 3, wiring to a pool-associated motor may be NM cable or any of the **NEC** wiring methods for that part of the circuit that is run in the interior of a one-family dwelling unit. *But,* it should be noted that Exception No. 3 specifies that interior wiring of a one-family dwelling may be part of the circuit to a filter pump *only* if the interior circuit has at least a No. 12 ground wire. That would recognize Romex with a No. 12 ground wire, but BX (Type AC) with its No. 16 aluminum bonding strip would have to contain an additional insulated grounding conductor that is at least a No. 12. This Exception recognizes that wiring within a building is under better protection for the reliability of the equipment grounding conductor.

Exception No. 4 of this section permits use of flexible cord for cord-and-plug connected equipment, as covered in Sec. 680-7.

Part **(d)** requires an equipment grounding conductor between the service equipment and a panelboard that supplies circuits to pool electrical equipment, as shown in Fig. 680-27. The basic intent is to require an insulated equipment

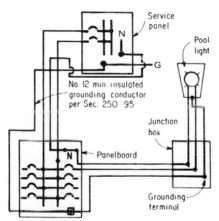

Fig. 680-27. Grounding conductor must connect subpanel ground block to equipment grounding terminal of service equipment. (Sec. 680-25.)

grounding conductor, sized in accordance with Table 250-95, but not smaller than No. 12 AWG, and run back to the equipment grounding terminal in service equipment. Note that this conductor does not have to be copper and may be aluminum.

The equipment grounding conductor required by part **(d)** of this section must be sized from **Code** Table 250-95 in accordance with the rating of the protective device for the circuit that is involved—but No. 12 is the minimum size. From **Code** Table 250-95, a 20-A fuse or CB protecting a branch circuit to pool lighting, as in part **(b)(1)**, would require a No. 12 copper grounding wire with the circuit. But if 40-A fuses or a 40-A CB protected a feeder from the service equipment to a subpanel serving the pool, then **Code** Table 250-95 would require a No. 10 size of copper conductor for the grounding.

The equipment grounding conductor must be installed along with the feeder conductors to the panel in rigid metal conduit, intermediate metal conduit, or rigid nonmetallic conduit. AND ALL OF THESE GROUNDING CONDUCTORS *MUST* BE GREEN IN COLOR FOR THEIR ENTIRE LENGTHS IF THEY ARE UP TO NO. 6 IN SIZE. LARGER THAN NO. 6 MAY BE OF OTHER COLOR IF MARKED GREEN AT TERMINALS [see Sec. 250-57(b)].

Exception No. 1 to part **(d)** is shown in Fig. 680-28. When a nonmetallic cable assembly is used between panels A and B in Fig. 680-29, a No. 12 or larger

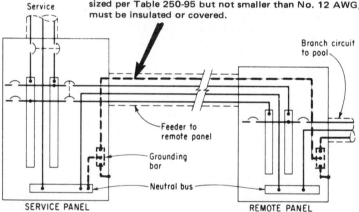

THIS EQUIPMENT GROUNDING CONDUCTOR must be sized per Table 250-95 [Sec. 680-25(d)]. It must be insulated, not smaller than No. 12 AWG, and installed with circuit conductors in IMC or rigid metal or rigid nonmetallic conduit

EXCEPTION: If pool equipment is fed from an *existing* remote panel, the feeder to the remote panel may be in flexible metal conduit or a cable. The equipment grounding conductor must be sized per Table 250-95 but not smaller than No. 12 AWG, and must be insulated or covered.

Fig. 680-28. Equipment grounding conductor may be in cable between panelboards. (Sec. 680-25.)

insulated conductor must be available. Circuit between panel B and deck boxes for lights must be in conduit. In the sketch, a nonmetallic 4-wire cable may be used between the two panelboards. Two conductors can be used for the hot-leg conductors, the third used for the neutral, and the last insulated conductor used for the grounding of pool equipment. The grounding conductor in the cable assembly may be either "insulated or covered." If it is covered or insulated, it must be finished in green color or green with a yellow stripe [Sec. 250-57(b)].

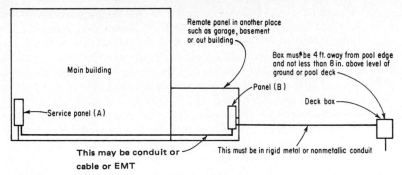

Fig. 680-29. Subpanel is commonly used to supply circuits for pool electrical equipment. (Sec. 680-25.)

Note: Exception No. 1 is applicable only where the subpanel, as shown in Fig. 680-28, is an "existing" panel. With that wording, if a new subpanel were installed in the garage or at the pool location, it would have to be fed from the service equipment by a feeder in rigid metal conduit, IMC, or rigid nonmetallic conduit—with a separate grounding conductor in whatever type of conduit is used. In Exception No. 1, a "remote panel" is one which is "not part of the service equipment."

The integrity of this ground-return path is all the more important now that ground-fault circuit protection is required for outdoor residential outlets, and for circuits supplying electrical equipment used with storable pools. Special attention should be paid to avoiding any connection between grounding terminals and the neutral (except at the service entrance). The grounding terminal block must be connected to the neutral bus in the *service panel* but not in any *remote panel* unless the provisions of Sec. 250-24 are carefully considered and GFCI breakers are not used in the service panel to feed any remote panel. Bonding the neutral to ground in a subpanel can make ground-fault protection in the service panel inoperative.

Exception No. 2 permits use of EMT for the circuits covered by Sec. 680-25(d) where such circuits are under the better-protected conditions when installed on or inside buildings (Fig. 680-29).

Part **(f)** of this section applies to electrical equipment other than the underwater lighting fixture (and its related equipment—the junction box, transformer enclosure or other enclosure in the supply circuit to a wet-niche lighting fixture, and the field-wiring chamber of a dry-niche fixture) and other than motors [covered by part **(c)**] and other than panelboards [covered by part **(d)**]. It simply recognizes that grounding of all such "other" equipment may be done by any of the **Code**-recognized equipment grounding means covered in Sec. 250-57 or 250-59. That means the metal frame of any electrical equipment *other than* the types specifically covered in parts **(b)** through **(e)** of Sec. 680-25 may be grounded by an equipment grounding conductor in raceway or in a recognized cable assembly. Type UF or Type USE cable, with an equipment grounding conductor, is therefore an alternative to the use of raceway for "other" equipment. And if metal raceway is used for such a circuit, the raceway itself—rigid, IMC, or even EMT—would satisfy Secs. 250-57, 250-59, and 250-91(b), and a separate equipment grounding conductor would not have to be run in the raceway. The requirement for an insulated, copper equipment grounding conductor installed in rigid metal conduit, IMC, or rigid nonmetallic conduit—as specified in parts **(b)(1)** and **(c)**—applies only for equipment used in circuits to pool lighting fixtures and pool-associated motors.

680-27. Deck Area Heating.   These rules cover safe application of unit heaters and radiant heaters. Such units must be securely installed, must be kept at least 5 ft back from the edge of the pool, and must not be installed over a pool. Radiant heating cables are prohibited from use embedded in the concrete deck.

680-30. Pumps.   There are portable filter pumps listed by Underwriters Laboratories Inc., and they comply with Sec. 680-30.

680-31. Ground-Fault Circuit-Interrupters Required.   Ground-fault circuit-interrupters must be installed so that all wiring used with storable pools will be protected. For GFCIs see comments following Sec. 210-8.

680-41. Indoor Installations.   Part **(a)** requires that at least one 15- or 20-A, 125-V convenience receptacle must be installed at a spa or hot tub—not closer than 5 ft from the inside wall of the unit and not more than 10 ft away from it. This is intended to prevent the hazards of extension cords that might otherwise be used to operate radios, TVs, etc. (Fig. 680-30).

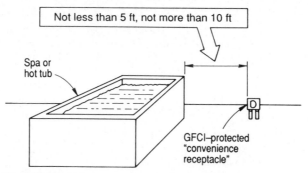

Fig. 680-30. At least one 15- or 20-A general-purpose receptacle must be installed at a spa or hot tub. [Sec. 680-41(a).]

As required by part **(2)** of this section, this receptacle and any others within 10 ft of the spa or tub must be GFCI protected.

Exception No. 2 of part **(b)** permits lighting fixtures of the designated types to be used above a spa or hot tub at any mounting height (less than 7 ft 6 in). Recessed and surface lighting fixtures recognized for use over a spa or hot tub now only have to be suitable for "damp" locations, not for "wet" locations.

680-70. Protection.   Any hydromassage bathtub and its associated electrical equipment must be supplied from a circuit protected by a GFCI.

680-71. Other Electric Equipment.   Hydromassage bathtubs are not subject to the requirements for spas and hot tubs—as they were in the 1984 **NEC**. Receptacles do not have to be at least 5 ft from the tub's inside wall, and lighting fixtures do not have to be mounted at least 7½ ft above the tub's water level.

ARTICLE 690. SOLAR PHOTOVOLTAIC SYSTEMS

690-1. Scope. This complete, detailed article covers this developing technology for direct conversion of the sun's light into electric power.

In 1983, work was completed on the world's largest facility converting sunlight directly to electricity. ARCO Solar, Inc., and Southern California Edison Company are building the facility on Edison property near the community of Hesperia in San Bernardino County. Edison will meter and purchase electricity generated by the facility, which will be designed, built, owned, and operated by ARCO Solar, an Atlantic Richfield subsidiary.

The ARCO Solar photovoltaic system, rated at 6 MW at peak power, will be installed on 20 acres adjacent to an existing Edison station.

The rated capacity of the facility will be at least three times greater than any existing photovoltaic system in the world. The system will provide enough power to serve the electrical needs of more than 2500 typical homes. The electricity will be delivered by Edison to its customers through existing distribution facilities.

Mounting the photovoltaic panels on approximately 100 double-axis trackers will orient the panels toward the sun throughout the day, taking into account seasonal changes of the sun's position. These computer-controlled trackers, developed by ARCO Power Systems, increase the average daily power output of the panels, thus lowering the average cost of electricity.

This is an operating and not a research project. Technology will be used that has not previously been demonstrated commercially on this scale. These technical advances include the combination of double-axis trackers with mass-produced photovoltaic modules, use of large-scale inverters to convert the DC electricity generated by the panels into AC current, and the introduction of a module that achieves the highest efficiency in converting sunlight to electricity of any mass-produced photovoltaic module.

Federal and state tax credits, applicable to photovoltaic installations, enable the project to be built. Improved technology and further cost reductions over the next several years will make such large systems economic in many foreign countries where electricity is more expensive than in the United States. ARCO Solar also believes that photovoltaic technology eventually will be applied economically in large-scale systems in the United States without solar tax credits.

Chapter Seven

ARTICLE 700. EMERGENCY SYSTEMS

700-1. Scope. Note that all the regulations of this article apply to the designated "circuits, systems, and equipment"—ONLY WHEN THE SYSTEMS OR CIRCUITS ARE *REQUIRED BY LAW* AND CLASSIFIED AS EMERGENCY PROVISIONS BY FEDERAL, STATE, MUNICIPAL, OR OTHER CODE OR BY A GOVERNMENTAL AUTHORITY. THE **NE CODE**, ITSELF, DOES *NOT* REQUIRE EMERGENCY LIGHT, POWER, OR EXIT SIGNS.

The effect of the first paragraph of this section is to exclude from all these rules any emergency circuits, systems, or equipment that are installed on a premises but are not legally mandated for the premises. Of course, any emergency provisions that are provided at the option of the designer (or the client) must necessarily conform to all other **NE Code** regulations that apply to the work.

The placement or location of exit lights is not a function of the **National Electrical Code** but is covered in the Life Safety Code, NFPA No. 101 (formerly Building Exits Code). But, where exit lights are required by law, the **NEC** considers them to be parts of the emergency system. The **NEC** indicates how the installation will be made, not where the emergency lighting is required, except as specified in part **C** of Art. 517 for essential electrical systems in health care facilities.

OSHA regulations on exit signs are presented in Subpart E of the *Occupational Safety and Health Standards* (Part 1910). These requirements on location and lighting of exit signs apply to all places of employment in all new buildings and also in all existing buildings.

Prior to OSHA, there was no universal requirement that all buildings or all places of employment have exit signs. The **National Electrical Code** does not require them. And although the NFPA Life Safety Code does cover rules on emergency lighting and exit signs, that code was enforced where state or local government bodies required it—that is, in some areas and for specific types of occupancies. As a result, there are existing occupancies which do not have the exit signs now required by federal law.

Section 1910.35 of OSHA makes clear that every building must have a means of egress—a continuous, unobstructed way for occupants to get out of a building in case of fire or other emergency, consisting of horizontal and vertical ways, as required. Egress from all parts of a building or structure must be provided at all times the building is occupied. The law says:

> Every exit shall be clearly visible or the route to reach it shall be conspicuously indicated in such a manner that every occupant of every building or structure who is physically and mentally capable will readily know the direction of escape from any point, and each path of escape, in its entirety, shall be so arranged or marked that the way to a place of safety outside is unmistakable.

Then it says:

> *Exit marking.* (1) Exits shall be marked by a readily visible sign. Access to exits shall be marked by readily visible signs in all cases where the exit or way to reach it is not immediately visible to the occupants.
> (2) Any door, passage, or stairway which is neither an exit nor a way of exit access, and which is so located or arranged as to be likely to be mistaken for an exit, shall be identified by a sign reading "Not An Exit" or similar designation, or shall be identified by a sign indicating its actual character, such as "To Basement," "Storeroom," "Linen Closet," or the like.
> (3) Every required sign designating an exit or way of exit access shall be so located and of such size, color, and design as to be readily visible.

Note that marking must be supplied for the way to the exit as well as for the exit itself. Further,

> (5) A sign reading "Exit," or similar designation, with an arrow indicating the direction, shall be placed in every location where the direction of travel to reach the nearest exit is not immediately apparent.
> (6) Every exit sign shall be suitably illuminated by a reliable light source giving a value of not less than 5 footcandles on the illuminated surface.

A lot of discussion has been generated by that last rule. Note that an exit sign does not have to be internally illuminated, although it may be. And this lighting is required on "every exit sign" which means signs over exit doors and exit signs indicating direction of travel.

The phrase "reliable light source" raises questions as to its meaning. Just what is reliable? Does this mean that the light source must operate if the utility supply to a building fails? And is there a difference in required application in new buildings versus existing buildings?

Because the OSHA regulations on exit signs do not require emergency power for lighting of such signs, the light units that illuminate exit signs may be supplied from regular (nonemergency) circuits. OSHA does not make it mandatory to supply such circuits from a tap ahead of the service main or from batteries or an emergency generator. And this applies to new buildings as well as existing buildings. As far as OSHA is concerned, Art. 700 of the **NE Code** on emer-

Fig. 700-1. Exit lights and wall-hanging battery-pack emergency lighting units are covered by Art. 700 whenever such equipment or provisions for emergency application are legally required by governmental authorities. (Sec. 700-1).

gency systems does not apply to circuits for exit sign lighting. Of course, OSHA does not object to the extra reliability such arrangements give. But the NEC does classify exit lights as emergency equipment (Fig. 700-1).

An emergency lighting system in a theater or other place of public assemblage includes exit signs, the chief purpose of which is to indicate the location of the exits, and lighting equipment commonly called "emergency lights," the purpose of which is to provide sufficient illumination in the auditorium, corridors, lobbies, passageways, stairways, and fire escapes to enable persons to leave the building safely.

These details, as well as the various classes of buildings in which emergency lighting is required, are left to be determined by state or municipal codes, and where such codes are in effect, the following provisions apply.

700-3. Equipment Approval. This rule has the effect of requiring use of only emergency equipment that is listed for such application by UL or another testing laboratory.

Under the heading of "Emergency Lighting and Power Equipment," the UL's *Electrical Construction Materials Directory* states:

> This listing covers battery-powered emergency lighting and power equipment, for use in ordinary indoor locations in accordance with Article 700 of the **National Electrical Code**. The lighting circuit ratings do not exceed 250 volts for tungsten lamps or 227 volts ac for electric discharge lamps. Other ratings may be included (motor loads, inductive loads, resistance loads, etc.) to 600 volts. This listing covers unit equipment, automatic battery charging and control equipment, inverters, central station battery systems, distribution panels, exit lights, and remote lamp assemblies, but not lighting fixtures. The investigation of emergency equipment includes the determination of their suitability of transferring operation from normal supply circuit to an immediately available emergency supply circuit.

700-4. Tests and Maintenance.   Emergency systems must be tested "during maximum anticipated load conditions." Testing under less than full-load conditions can be misleading and is not a true test.

700-5. Capacity.   It is extremely important that the supply source be of adequate capacity. There are two main reasons for adequate capacity:

1. It is important that power be available for the necessary supply to exit lights, emergency and egress lighting, as well as to operate such equipment as required for elevators and other equipment connected to the emergency system.

2. In such occupancies as hospitals, there may be a need for an emergency supply for lighting in hospital operating rooms, and also for such equipment as inhalators, iron lungs, incubators, and the like.

It is also essential to safety and effective, long-time successful operation of emergency system equipment that it be rated to sustain the maximum available short circuit that the supply circuit could deliver at the terminals of the equipment.

Part **(b)** of this section permits one generator to be used as a single power source to supply emergency loads, essential (legally required) standby loads, and optional standby loads when control arrangements for *selective* load pickup and load shedding are provided to ensure that adequate power is available first for emergency loads, then legally required standby loads, and finally optional standby loads. See Fig. 700-2 (top) and Arts. 701 and 702.

An on-site generator may be used for peak load shaving—in addition to its use for supplying emergency, legally required standby, and optional standby loads. The title of part **(b)** refers to "Peak Load Shaving," which is recognized as a function of the generator in the last sentence of the paragraph. For peak shaving use, however, the generator must be equipped with the selective load-control equipment described in the paragraph to assure the order of priority for various purposes. An FPN essentially calls for the peak load shaving operation to be included in testing and maintenance requirements of Sec. 700-4.

Another important requirement of this section specifies that a portable or temporary generator, or other alternate source of power, must be provided for any time that the emergency generator is out of service for major maintenance or repair.

700-6. Transfer Equipment.   Any switch or other control device that transfers emergency loads from the normal power source of a system to the emergency power supply *must* operate automatically on loss of the normal supply. Transfer equipment must also be automatic for legally required standby systems, as covered in Sec. 701-7, but a manual transfer switch may be used for switching loads from the normal to an optional standby power source, as in Sec. 702-6.

As described in the last paragraph, a bypass switch is recognized on an automatic transfer switch (ATS) to provide for repair or maintenance of the ATS (Fig. 700-2, bottom). Because hospitals and many industrial systems contain transfer switches that cannot be shut down, some means is required to isolate a transfer switch for routine maintenance or for some specific task like contact replacement. When a bypass switch is used, inadvertent parallel operation must not be possible.

Pickup and shedding controller to match generator capacity to load demands—with priority of selection

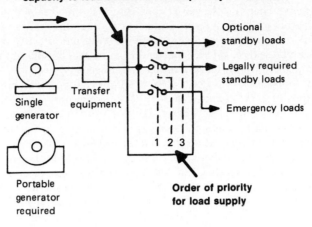

2-WAY BYPASS ISOLATION SYSTEM

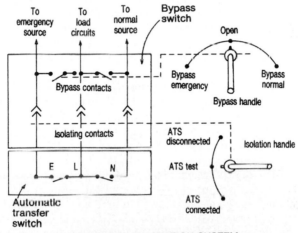

> **NOTE:** Diagram shows only the power (load current) paths through bypass switch and transfer switch.

Fig. 700-2. Special load-control must be used where a single generator supplies emergency and standby loads (top). And a bypass switch may be used to isolate an automatic transfer switch. (Secs. 700-5 and 700-6.)

700-7. Signals. In order to be effective, the signal devices should be located in some room where an attendant is on duty. Lamps may readily be used as signals to indicate the position of an automatic switching device. An audible signal in any place of public assemblage should not be so located or of such a character that it will cause a general alarm.

The standard signal equipment furnished by a typical battery manufacturer with their 60-cell battery for emergency lighting includes an indicating lamp which is lighted when the charger is operating at the high rate, and a voltmeter marked in three colored sections indicates (1) that the battery is not being charged, or is discharging into the emergency system, (2) that the battery is being trickle charged, or (3) that the battery is being charged at the high rate. This last indication duplicates the indication given by the lamp.

Part **(d)** of this section requires the use of a hookup for ground-fault indication on the output of a grounded-wye 480/277-V generator. The rule, however, makes the ground-fault indication signal mandatory only "where practicable." Section 700-26 states that emergency systems do not require ground-fault protection of equipment. Yet, when the load is served by the emergency source, the possibility of a ground-fault is no less than when the load is served by the utility source. Should a ground-fault occur within the emergency system during a power failure, it is debatable whether essential loads should be immediately disconnected from the emergency power supply. However, for reasons of safety and to minimize the possibility of fire and equipment damage, at least an alarm should indicate if a hazardous ground-fault condition exists so appropriate corrective steps will be initiated. When ground-fault indication is used on the generator output, the fault sensor must be located within or on the line side of the generator main disconnect. And the rule also makes it mandatory to have specific instructions for dealing with ground-fault conditions. Refer to Sec. 700-26 and Fig. 700-16.

700.8. Signs.   A sign at the service entrance is required to designate the type and location of emergency power source(s).

700-9. Wiring, Emergency System.   Part **(a)** requires that all boxes and enclosures for emergency circuits must be readily identified as parts of the emergency system. Labels, signs, or some other *permanent* marking must be used on all enclosures containing emergency circuits to "readily" identify them as components of an emergency system. The "boxes and enclosures" that must be marked include enclosures for transfer switches, generators, and power panels. *All* boxes and enclosures for emergency circuits must be painted red, marked with red labels saying "EMERGENCY CIRCUITS," or marked in some other manner clearly identifiable to electricians or maintenance personnel (Fig. 700-3, top).

The bottom of Figure 700-3 shows a clear violation of the rule of part **(b)** because the wiring to the emergency light (or to an exit light, which is classed as an emergency light) is run in the same raceway and boxes as the wiring to the decorative floodlight.

This section requires that the wiring for emergency systems be kept entirely independent of the regular wiring used for lighting and that it thus needs to be in separate raceways, cables, and boxes. This requirement is to ensure that where faults may occur on the regular wiring, they will not affect the emergency system wiring, as it will be in a separate enclosure.

Exception No. 1 for transfer switches is intended to permit normal supply conductors to be brought into the transfer-switch enclosure and that these conductors would be the only ones within the transfer-switch enclosure which

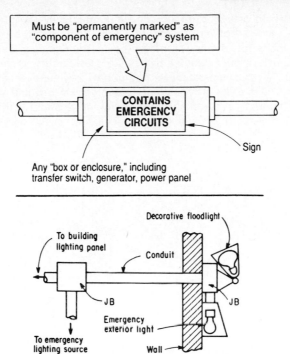

Fig. 700-3. Emergency wiring may not be run in enclosures with wiring for nonemergency circuits, and emergency enclosures must be marked. (Sec. 700-9.)

were not part of the emergency system. Exception Nos. 2 and 3 permit two sources supplying emergency or exit lighting to enter the fixture and its common junction box.

700-12. General Requirements.   This section then lists and describes the types of emergency supply systems that are acceptable—with one or more of such systems required where emergency supply is mandated by law. It specifies that the normal-to-emergency transfer must not exceed 10 sec. This is a change from previous wording that required emergency supply to be "immediately available" on loss of normal supply.

Part **(a)** recognizes storage batteries for emergency source. A storage battery for emergency power must maintain *voltage to the load* at not less than 87½ percent of the normal rated value. This was changed from "87½ percent of system voltage" (that is, battery voltage) because the concern is to keep the voltage to the lamps at 87½ percent. The "electronics" between the battery and the lamps maintains the required "load voltage," and the battery voltage is not in itself the major concern.

Part **(b)** covers use of engine-generator sets for emergency supply as an alternate to utility supply. Engine-driven generators (diesel, gasoline, or gas) are commonly used to provide an alternate source of emergency or standby power when normal utility power fails. Gas-turbine generators also are used.

The first step in selecting an on-site generator is to consider applicable requirements of the **National Electrical Code**, which differ depending on whether the generating set is to function as an emergency system, a standby power system, or as a power source in a health care facility, such as a hospital.

For example, an *internal-combustion* type engine-generator set selected for use under Art. 700 must be provided with *automatic starting and automatic load transfer*, with enough on-site fuel to power the full demand load for at least 2 hr (Fig. 700-4). If a standby power system selected under the regulations of Art.

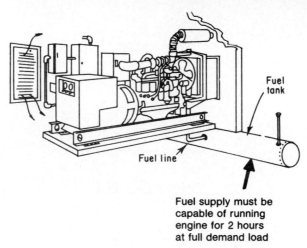

Fig. 700-4. Generator must have automatic start and adequate fuel supply. (Sec. 700-12.)

701 is *legally* required, it must be provided with enough on-site fuel to power the full demand operation of the load for *not less than 2 hr.*

In part **(b)(3)**, the engine driving an emergency generator must not be dependent on a public water supply for its cooling. That means a roof tank or other on-site water supply must be used and its pumps connected to the emergency source (Fig. 700-5).

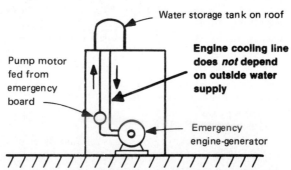

Fig. 700-5. Engine cooling for an emergency generator set must be assured for continuous operation of the generator. (Sec. 700-12.)

An Exception in **(b)(3)** permits use of a utility gas supply to the engine of an emergency generator—at the discretion of the local inspector—where simultaneous outage of both electric power and gas supply is highly unlikely.

As required by **(b)(4)** a battery used with a generator set must have adequate capacity whether it cranks the generator for starting or is simply used for control and signal power for another means (such as compressed air) for starting the generator.

Part **(b)(5)** of this section requires another power supply to pick up emergency load in not over 10 sec where the main generator cannot come up to power output in 10 sec.

As recognized by part **(d)**, two separate services brought to different locations in the building are always preferable, and these services should at least receive their supply from separate transformers where this is practicable. In some localities, municipal ordinances require either two services from independent sources of supply, or auxiliary supply for emergency lighting from a storage battery, or a generator driven by a steam turbine, internal-combustion engine, or other prime mover. Figure 700-6 shows two different forms of the separate-service type of emergency supply. The method at bottom makes use of two sources of emergency input.

Separate Emergency Service

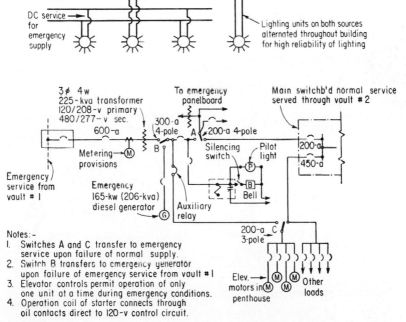

Fig. 700-6. Dual-service emergency provisions can take many different forms. (Sec. 700-12.)

Part **(e)** covers the method shown in Fig. 700-7. In that diagram, the tap ahead of the main could supply the emergency panel directly, without need for the transfer switch.

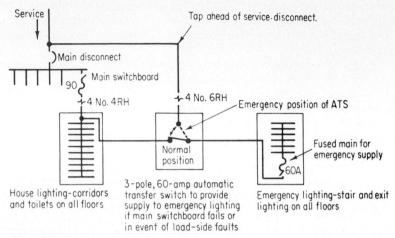

Fig. 700·7 A tap ahead of the service main protects only against internal failures. (Sec. 700-12.)

Part **(f)** covers typical wall-hanging battery-pack emergency lighting units, as shown in Fig. 700-8. The 1971 **NEC** accepted only connection of emergency light units by means of fixed wiring. Part **(f)** now recognizes permanent wiring connection or cord-and-plug connection to a receptacle.

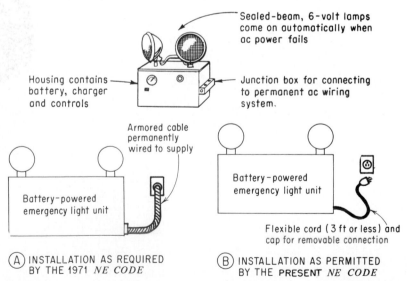

Fig. 700·8. Unit emergency lights may serve as required source of emergency supply. (Sec. 700-12.)

Even though the unit equipment is allowed to be hooked up with flexible cord-and-plug connections, it is still necessary that the unit equipment be permanently fixed in place.

Individual unit equipment provides emergency illumination only for the area in which it is installed; therefore, it is not necessary to carry a circuit back to the service equipment to feed the unit. This section clearly indicates that the branch circuit feeding the normal lighting in the area to be served is the same circuit that should supply the unit equipment.

In part **(f)** the intent of the 87½ percent value is to assure proper *lighting output* from lamps supplied by unit equipment. It is generally considered acceptable to design equipment that will produce acceptable lighting levels for the required 1½ hours, even though the 87½ percent rating of the battery would not be maintained during this period. The objective is adequate light output to permit safe egress from buildings in emergencies. Hence, the unit equipment shall supply and maintain not less than 60 percent of the initial emergency illumination for a period of at least 1½ hours.

As shown at the top of Fig. 700-9, a battery-pack emergency unit must not be connected on the load side of a local wall switch that controls the supply to the unit or the receptacle into which the emergency unit is plugged. Such an arrangement exposes the emergency unit to accidental energization of the

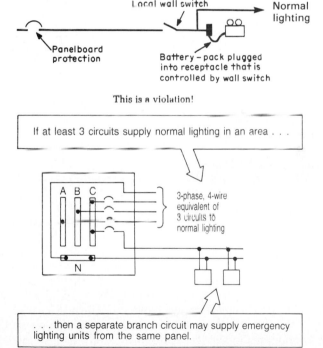

Fig. 700-9. Circuiting of battery-pack emergency lighting may be on normal lighting circuit or separate circuit. (Sec. 700-12(f).)

lamps and draining of the battery supply. But, as permitted by the Exception, if a panelboard supplies at least three normal lighting circuits for a given area, emergency battery-pack lighting units for that area may be connected to a separate branch circuit from the panel, with lock-on provision for that circuit. This is an Exception to the rule of the previous paragraph, which says that unit equipment must be connected on a branch circuit supplying normal lighting in the area. By allowing unit equipment on a separate branch circuit from the same panel, the unit equipment will sense loss of power to the panel and activate. The advantage of such application from a design standpoint is that there is no need to observe the rule that the unit equipment must be "connected ahead of any local switches," which applies when unit equipment is connected on normal lighting circuits.

700·15. Loads on Emergency Branch Circuits.   Figure 700-10 shows a clear violation of this rule, because appliances are excluded from emergency circuits.

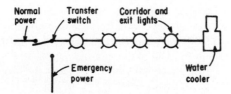

Fig. 700·10. The water cooler may not be on an emergency circuit. (Sec. 700-15.)

700·16. Emergency Illumination.   Note that all exit lights are designated as part of the emergency lighting, and, as such, their circuiting must conform to Sec. 700-17.

Where HID lighting is the *sole* source of *normal* illumination, the emergency light system must continue to operate for a sufficient time after return of normal power to enable the HID lighting to come up to brightness. This rule in the third paragraph is intended to prevent the condition that return of normal power and the disconnect of the emergency lighting leave the building in darkness because of the inherent, normal time delay in the light output upon energizing HID lamps. The Exception after that rule permits "alternative means" to keep emergency lighting on.

700·17. Circuits for Emergency Lighting.   Figure 700-11 shows the basic rule on transfer of emergency lighting from the normal source to the emergency source. If a single emergency system is installed, a transfer switch shall be provided which, in case of failure of the source of supply on which the system is operating, will automatically transfer the emergency system to the other source. Where the two sources of supply are two services, the single emergency system may normally operate on either source, as in Fig. 700-12. Where the two sources of supply are one service and a storage battery, or one service and a generator set, as in Fig. 700-11, the single emergency system would, as a general rule, be operated normally on the service, using the battery or generator only as a reserve in case of failure of the service. Figure 700-13 shows an emergency hookup that has two separate supplies tied into the emergency lighting system.

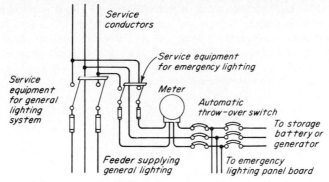

Fig. 700·11. Emergency lighting is automatically switched from normal service to the battery or generator. (Sec. 700-17.)

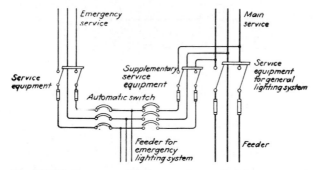

Fig. 700·12. Emergency lighting may be supplied from an emergency service. (Sec. 700-17.)

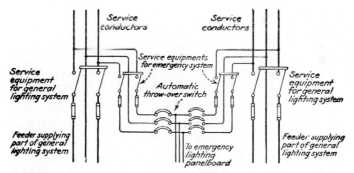

Fig. 700·13. A single emergency lighting system may be fed from two services. (Sec. 700-17.)

Part **(2)** of this section provides for use of two or more "separate and complete" emergency systems. If two emergency lighting systems are installed, each system shall operate on a separate source of supply, as where each emergency disconnect in Fig. 700-12 feeds a separate, independent emergency lighting system. Either both systems shall be kept in operation, or switches shall be provided which will automatically place either system in operation upon failure of the other system.

700-20. Switch Requirements. Figure 700-14 shows a violation of the last sentence of this rule, where use of three- and four-way switches is prohibited.

These switches are a code violation in this circuit...

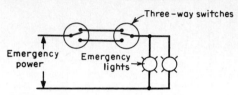

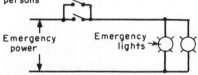

Fig. 700-14. Watch out for switches in emergency lighting circuits. (Sec. 700-20.)

700-21. Switch Location. The sole switch for emergency lighting control in a theater may not be placed in a projection booth (Fig. 700-15). The rule prohibits use of an emergency control switch in the motion-picture projection booth or on stage. In the 1981 **NEC**, the rule that used to be in Sec. 700-19(b)—which prohibited use of an emergency control switch in the motion-picture projection booth or on stage—was deleted. The comment that accompanied the proposal to remove this rule stated:

> Since the place in a theater where there is most likely to be someone present at all times is the projection booth, the emergency lighting switch should be in the projection booth. There was general agreement that this was proper and is conventionally being done. It should be pointed out that the typical motion-picture theater has no one present on the stage to operate the emergency lighting.

In the present **NE Code**, the old rule prohibiting the sole control switch in the projection booth or on the stage is reinstated. The comment that accompanied the proposal to again prohibit installation of an emergency lighting switch in a projection booth or on a stage made the following points:

> The primary control of the life safety emergency system must be restored to those responsible for the management of the building and not rest with those primarily concerned with the performance. These systems are the exit lighting, aisle lighting, and alarm systems that are "first on-last off" during the operation of these occupancies.
>
> Overzealous and unfamiliar production staff persons have been known to disconnect the life safety systems when given the cue to darken the auditorium. Many traveling companies bring their own equipment and do not bother to familiarize themselves with fixed controls nor do they wish to assume responsibility. Motion-picture projectionists in booths are concerned with their equipment, film, and presenting the

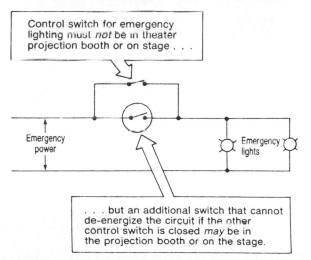

Control switch for emergency lighting must *not* be in theater projection booth or on stage . . .

Emergency power

Emergency lights

. . . but an additional switch that cannot de-energize the circuit if the other control switch is closed *may* be in the projection booth or on the stage.

Fig. 700-15. The sole switch that controls emergency lighting in a theater may *not* be installed in a projection booth or on the stage, with the Exception shown. (Sec. 700-21.)

show. Their function is further compounded by the multi-auditorium theaters of today and the hazards of dealing with xenon lamps in modern projection equipment, leaving little time to monitor the auditorium and render decision regarding the emergency system.

Figure 700-15 has a sketch that shows the Exception to the prohibition against an emergency lighting control switch in a projection booth or on stage. An emergency lighting switch may be used in a projection booth or on a stage if it can energize such lighting but cannot deenergize the lighting if another switch located elsewhere is in the closed (ON) position.

700-26. Ground-Fault Protection of Equipment.   Emergency generator disconnect does not require ground-fault protection. This rule clarifies the relationship between Sec. 230-95, calling for GFP on service disconnects, and the disconnect means for emergency generators. To afford the highest reliability and continuity for an emergency power supply, GFP is not *required* on any 1,000-A or larger disconnect for an emergency generator, although it is permissible to use it if desired (Fig. 700-16).

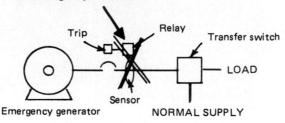

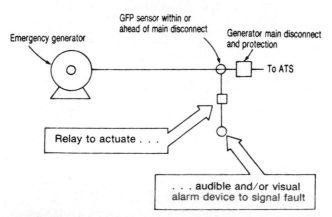

Fig. 700-16. Ground-fault protection is optional for any 480/277-V grounded-wye generator disconnect rated 1000 A or more, but ground-fault "indication" is required. (Sec. 700-26.)

ARTICLE 701. LEGALLY REQUIRED STANDBY SYSTEMS

701-1. Scope. This article covers *standby* power systems that are required by law. Legally required standby power systems are those systems required and so classed as legally required standby by municipal, state, federal, or other codes or by any government agency having jurisdiction. These systems are intended to supply power automatically to selected loads (other than those classed as emergency systems) in the event of failure of the normal source.

Legally required standby power systems are typically installed to serve such loads as heating and refrigeration systems, communication systems, ventilation and smoke-removal systems, sewerage disposal, lighting, and industrial processes that, when stopped during any power outage, could create hazards or hamper rescue or firefighting operations.

This article covers the circuits and equipment for such systems that are permanently installed in their entirety, including power source.

ARTICLE 702. OPTIONAL STANDBY SYSTEMS

702-1. Scope. Life safety is not the purpose of optional standby systems. Optional standby systems are intended to protect private business or property where life safety does not depend on the performance of the system. Optional standby systems (other than those classed as emergency or legally required standby systems) are intended to supply on-site generated power to selected loads, either automatically or manually.

Optional standby systems are typically installed to provide an alternate source of electric power for such facilities as industrial and commercial buildings, farms, and residences to serve such loads as heating and refrigeration systems, data processing and communications systems, and industrial processes that, when stopped during any power outage, could cause discomfort, serious interruption of the process, or damage to the product or process.

Because of the constant expansion in electrical applications in all kinds of buildings, the use of standby power sources is growing at a constantly accelerating rate. Continuity of service has become increasingly important with the widespread development of computers and intricate, automatic production processes. More thought is being given to and more money is being spent on the provision of on-site power sources to back up or supplement purchased utility power to ensure the needed continuity as well as provide for public safety in the event of utility failure.

The intent of Arts. 701 and 702 is to recognize and regulate use of any permanently installed standby system that is not considered to be an "Emergency System" as covered in Art. 517 or 700 of the **National Electrical Code**, or "Essential Electrical Systems for Health Care Facilities" as covered in NFPA Pamphlet No. 76A.

The most fundamental application of standby power is the portable alternator used for residential standby power where electric utility supply is not sufficiently reliable or is subject to frequent outages (Fig. 702-1).

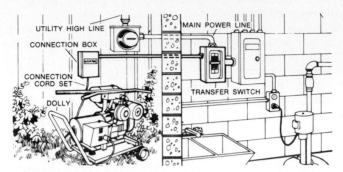

Fig. 702·1. Standby generator with manual transfer is common residential application. (Sec. 702-1.)

Note that an optional "standby" power load may be manually or automatically transferred from the normal supply to the "standby" generator. Any generator used as an "emergency" source or legally required standby system must always have provision for automatic transfer of the load from "normal" supply to the emergency generator. But automatic transfer must be used if a standby power system is required by law to be installed.

702·5. Capacity.   Any standby power source and system must be capable of fully serving its demand load. This can generally be satisfied relatively easily for generator loads. But the task can be complex for UPS systems. The uninterruptible power supply (UPS) is an all-solid-state power conversion system designed to protect computers and other critical loads from blackouts, brownouts, and transients. It is usually connected in the feeder supplying the load, with bypass provisions to permit the load to be fed directly. Figure 702-2 shows a typical basic layout for a UPS system. Such a system utilizes a variety of power sources to assure continuous power. Circuits are shown for normal power operation. If normal power fails, the static switch transfers the load to the inverter within ¼ cycle. The battery is the power source while the engine-generator is being started. When the generator is running properly, it is brought onto the line through its transfer switch, and the static switch transfers the load to the generator supply. Dashed line indicates synchronizing signal, which maintains phase and frequency of inverter output.

Calculation of the required capacity of a UPS system must be carefully made. Data processing installations normally require medium-to-large 3-phase UPS systems ranging from 37.5 to over 2,000 kVA. Some of the typical ratings available from UPS manufacturers are 37.5 kVA/30 kW, 75 kVA/67.5 kW, 125 kVA/112.5 kW, 200 kVA/180 kW, 300 kVA/270 kW, 400 kVA/360 kW, and 500 kVA/450 kW. Larger systems are configured by paralleling two or more of these standard size single modules.

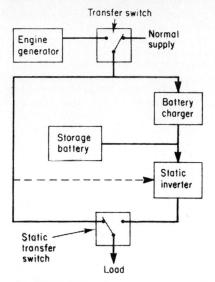

Fig. 702·2. UPS system is a common standby power system. (Sec. 702-5.)

The necessary rating is chosen based on the size of the critical load. If a power profile itemizing the power requirements is not available from the computer manufacturer, the load may be measured using a kilowattmeter and a power-factor meter. Since UPS modules are both kVA- (apparent power) and kW- (real power) limited, a system should be specified with both a kVA and kW rating. The required kVA rating is obtained by dividing the actual load kW by the actual load power factor. For example, an actual 170-kW load with an actual 0.85 power factor would require a 200-kVA-rated UPS. The system should be specified as 200 kVA/170 kW, and the standard 200 kVA/180 kW UPS module should be selected for the application.

ARTICLE 705. INTERCONNECTED ELECTRIC POWER PRODUCTION SOURCES

705·1. Scope. This **NEC** article covers interconnection of electric power sources, including utility supply, emergency systems, standby systems, on-site generator supply, and solar photovoltaic systems.

The substantiation for addition of this **Code** article stated the following:

There is a need for an article within the **NEC** that deals with on-site power production that is interconnected as well as operating in parallel with an electric utility source. This is not the same as emergency generators, which by definition are for an emergency condition when the normal power is not available, nor is it the same as either legally required or optional standby generators not intended to be continuously operated nor interconnected to the utility grid.

The on-site power-production aspect needs to be viewed as possibly ranging from a singular low-wattage, backyard wind machine up to an industrial application that can possibly have a dozen machines all interconnected.

The similar yet even more obvious need exists for multiple power-production sources that are interconnected within the same site or structure: there must be the ability to separate the sources without jeopardizing either the equipment, personnel, or other sources that are allowed to continue operating.

ARTICLE 710.   OVER 600 VOLTS, NOMINAL

710·1. Scope.   An important consideration in selection and application of conductors for systems operating over 600 V is careful correlation of NE Code regulations and the data made available by third-party testing laboratories. Underwriters Laboratories and Electrical Testing Labs have been deeply involved in listing cables for use in high-voltage systems. The expanded testing and listing of high-voltage conductors and cable assemblies have increased the need for the electrical designer and installer to be particularly thorough and careful in establishing full and effective compliance with all applicable codes and standards.

The term *high voltage* is commonly used to refer to any circuit operating at voltage above 600 V, phase to phase. It should be noted, however, that circuits from 601 V up to 35 kV are frequently called "medium-voltage" circuits and the term "high voltage" also is used for circuits operating above 15 kV.

The NE Code contains very extensive rules on all aspects of high-voltage work. These rules must be evaluated and studied carefully. Check all questions about interpretations of Code rules with the authority having jurisdiction for Code enforcement.

710·2. Other Articles.   Article 710 covers general requirements on all circuits operating at more than 600 V between conductors. Specific requirements on high-voltage application are covered within other Code articles on services, motors and controllers, transformers, capacitors, outside wiring, and other specific categories of equipment.

710·3. Wiring Methods.   High-voltage circuits used for commercial and industrial feeders, both outdoors and indoors, most commonly operate at voltages up to 15,000 V (15 kV). But there is a trend to even higher voltages (26 kV, 35 kV) for extremely large installations. Typical circuits today operate at 4,160/2,400 V and 13,200/7,600 V—both 3-phase, 4-wire wye hookups.

Modern high-voltage circuits for buildings include: overhead bare or covered conductors, installed with space between the conductors which are supported by insulators at the top of wood poles or metal tower structures; overhead aerial cable assemblies of insulated conductors entwined together, supported on building walls or on poles or metal structures; insulated conductors installed in metal or nonmetallic conduits or ducts run underground, either directly buried in the earth or encased in a concrete envelope under the ground; insulated conductors in conduit run within buildings; multiple-conductor cable assemblies (such as nonmetallic jacketed cables, lead-sheathed cable, or interlocked armor cable), installed in conduit or on cable racks or trays or other types of supports. Another wiring method gaining wide acceptance consists of plastic conduit containing factory-installed conductors, affording a readily used direct-earth-burial cable assembly for underground circuits but still permitting removal of the cable for repair or replacement.

(a). Conductors aboveground must be in rigid metal conduit, in intermediate metal conduit (IMC), in rigid nonmetallic conduit, in cable trays, in cablebus, in other suitable raceways (check inspector for suitability of EMT), or as open runs of metal-armored cable suitable for the use and purpose. The **NE Code** now equates IMC to rigid metal conduit for indoor and outdoor (including underground) applications for high-voltage circuits.

The phrase "other identified raceway," as used in part **(a)**, seems to mean raceways listed by a testing laboratory and installed in accordance with any instructions given with the listing. If it is meant to accept all raceways covered under the **NE Code** definition for "raceway," then it includes EMT, flexible metal conduit, wireways, and rigid nonmetallic conduit (Fig. 710-1). But that should be checked with the local inspector having jurisdiction.

Rigid nonmetallic conduit has been added to the list of raceways acceptable for running high-voltage circuits aboveground—and the PVC conduit does not have to be encased in concrete. The previous requirement in Sec. 347-2(b), which required concrete encasement of rigid PVC conduit aboveground if it carried circuits operating at over 600 V, is no longer in the **Code**.

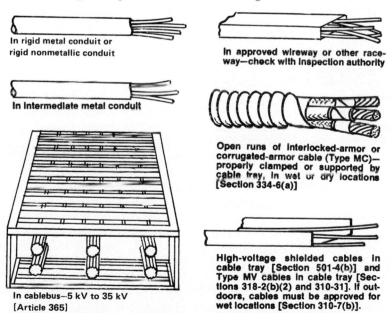

In rigid metal conduit or rigid nonmetallic conduit

In intermediate metal conduit

In cablebus—5 kV to 35 kV [Article 365]

In approved wireway or other race-way—check with inspection authority

Open runs of interlocked-armor or corrugated-armor cable (Type MC)—properly clamped or supported by cable tray, in wet or dry locations [Section 334-6(a)]

High-voltage shielded cables in cable tray [Section 501-4(b)] and Type MV cables in cable tray [Sections 318-2(b)(2) and 310-31]. If out-doors, cables must be approved for wet locations [Section 310-7(b)].

Fig. 710-1. A variety of wiring methods may be used for aboveground high-voltage circuits. (Sec. 710-3.)

Directly buried nonmetallic conduit carrying high-voltage conductors does not have to be concrete-encased if it is a type approved for use without concrete encasement. If concrete encasement is required, it will be indicated on the UL label and in the listing. Sections 347-2(c) and 710-3(b) permit direct burial rigid nonmetallic conduit (without concrete encasement) for high-voltage circuits.

In locations accessible to qualified persons only, open runs of Type MV cable, bare conductors, and busbars may be used (Secs. 710-32 and 710-33). In locations accessible to qualified persons only there are no restrictions on the types of wiring that may be used. The types more commonly employed are open wiring on insulators with conductors either bare or insulated, and rigid metal conduit or nonmetallic rigid conduit containing lead-covered cable.

(b).   Underground conductors may be installed in "raceways identified for the use" or in approved direct burial cable assemblies.

Table 710-3(b) makes clear that underground circuits may be installed in rigid metal conduit, in intermediate metal conduit, or in rigid nonmetallic conduit. Rigid metal conduit or IMC does not have to be concrete-encased, but it may be, of course. Direct burial nonmetallic conduit must be an approved (UL listed and labeled) type, specifically recognized for use without concrete encasement. If rigid nonmetallic conduit is approved for use only with concrete encasement, at least 2 in. of concrete must enclose the conduit. All applications of the various types of nonmetallic conduit must conform to the data made available by UL in the *Electrical Construction Materials Directory*.

In Table 710-3(b), Exceptions No. 2 and No. 3 are modifications to the burial-depth table for high-voltage circuits and provide more specific guidance. Exception No. 2 permits the table burial depth for direct-buried cable or rigid nonmetallic conduit to be reduced by 6 in. for each 2 in. of concrete "placed in the trench over the underground installation." Note that the reduction in burial depth is not allowed for concrete that is above the raceway or cable, up at grade level, such as a roadway, walkway, or patio. The phrase "placed in the trench" indicates that such concrete must be specifically placed in the trench to provide the protection. And both rigid metal conduit and intermediate metal conduit are excluded from this reduction in burial depth because their 6 in. burial depth would become zero. That is consistent with Table 300-5 for underground wiring methods up to 600 V.

Exception No. 3 eliminates the need for any burial-depth in earth for "conduits or other raceways" that are run under a building or exterior concrete slab not less than 4 in. thick and extending at least 6 in. "beyond the underground installation"—that is, overlapping the raceway by 6 in. on each side. Note that in this Exception the 4-in.-thick concrete *may* be up at grade level in the form of a slab or patio or similar concrete area not subject to vehicular traffic.

The last sentence in Exception No. 3 requires a "warning ribbon or other effective means" such as a flag or stake indicating the presence of high-voltage circuits.

Fig. 710-2 covers burial of underground high-voltage circuits and Exceptions 2 and 3.

Part **(b)** notes that unshielded cable (i.e., cable without electrostatic shielding on the insulation) must be installed in rigid metal conduit, in IMC, or in rigid nonmetallic conduit encased in not less than 3 in. of concrete. The effect of this

DIRECT-BURIED CABLES

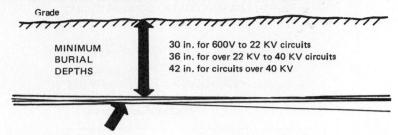

Grade

MINIMUM
BURIAL
DEPTHS

30 in. for 600V to 22 KV circuits
36 in. for over 22 KV to 40 KV circuits
42 in. for circuits over 40 KV

Direct-buried cables must be
concentric-neutral or drain-wire
shielded type or with a conducting
sheath of equivalent ampacity

NOTE: Unshielded cables are not
acceptable directly buried!

IN RIGID METAL CONDUIT
OR INTERMEDIATE METAL CONDUIT (IMC)

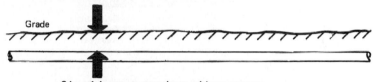

Grade

6 in. minimum at any voltage, without concrete
encasement. See Note 2 below.

IN RIGID NONMETALLIC CONDUIT

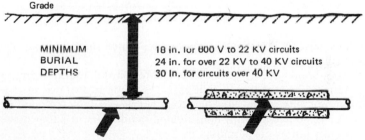

Grade

MINIMUM
BURIAL
DEPTHS

18 in. for 600 V to 22 KV circuits
24 in. for over 22 KV to 40 KV circuits
30 In. for circuits over 40 KV

Rigid nonmetallic conduit approved
for direct burial—i.e., listed by
UL or other nationally recognized
testing agency

Rigid nonmetallic conduit requiring
concrete encasement must have
at least 2 in. of concrete (or equivalent)
above conduit, and the conduit itself
must be at the depths shown.

Fig. 710-2. Direct burial high-voltage cables must be of correct type, at specified depth.
(Sec. 710-3.)

rule is that unshielded, or nonshielded, cables may not be used directly buried
in the earth.

By reference to Sec. 310-7, nonshielded cables may be directly buried up to
2,000-V rating, except that metal-encased, nonshielded conductors (as in Type
MC or lead-jacketed cables) may be used in ratings up to 5,000 V. But *all direct*

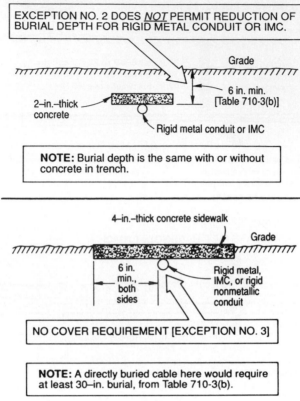

EXCEPTION NO. 2 DOES _NOT_ PERMIT REDUCTION OF BURIAL DEPTH FOR RIGID METAL CONDUIT OR IMC.

Grade

6 in. min.
[Table 710-3(b)]

2–in.–thick concrete

Rigid metal conduit or IMC

NOTE: Burial depth is the same with or without concrete in trench.

4–in.–thick concrete sidewalk

Grade

6 in. min., both sides

Rigid metal, IMC, or rigid nonmetallic conduit

NO COVER REQUIREMENT [EXCEPTION NO. 3]

NOTE: A directly buried cable here would require at least 30–in. burial, from Table 710-3(b).

Fig. 710-2. *(Continued)*

burial cables must be "identified" for such use, which really means listed by a qualified testing agency.

For underground use, all nonshielded cables were required by previous **Code** editions to be installed in rigid metal conduit, in IMC, or in rigid nonmetallic conduit with a 3-in.-thick concrete encasement. Now Type MC cable and lead-sheathed cable—with nonshielded conductors in either assembly—may be directly buried, as permitted by Sec. 334-3(5).

As indicated above, when nonshielded cable (of the nonmetallic-jacket type) is used *underground* in rigid nonmetallic conduit, the conduit must have a 3-in.-thick concrete encasement. But if the same nonshielded cable is used in rigid nonmetallic conduit *aboveground*, concrete encasement is *not* required.

Figure 710-2 demonstrates uses of direct burial high-voltage cables in relation to the **Code** rules. Figure 710-3 covers underground high-voltage circuits in raceways.

Figure 710-4 covers the basic rules of Table 710-3(b), subject to the considerations noted in the rules and Exceptions, as follows:

1. Burial depths shown in diagrams may be reduced 6 in. for each 2 in. of concrete or equivalent above the conductors.

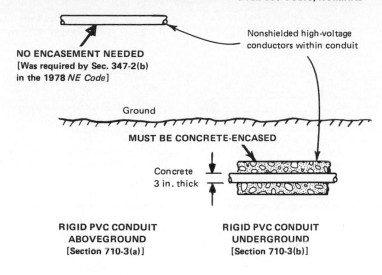

NO ENCASEMENT NEEDED
[Was required by Sec. 347-2(b)
in the 1978 *NE Code*]

Nonshielded high-voltage
conductors within conduit

Ground

MUST BE CONCRETE-ENCASED

Concrete
3 in. thick

**RIGID PVC CONDUIT
ABOVEGROUND**
[Section 710-3(a)]

**RIGID PVC CONDUIT
UNDERGROUND**
[Section 710-3(b)]

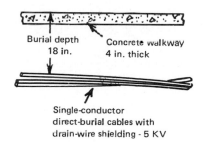

Burial depth
18 in.

Concrete walkway
4 in. thick

Single-conductor
direct-burial cables with
drain-wire shielding - 5 KV

O.K.—From Table 710-3(b), depth
of 30 in. reduced by 6 in. for each 2 in.
of concrete above cables.

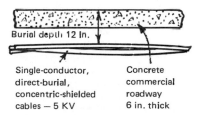

Burial depth 12 in.

Single-conductor,
direct-burial,
concentric-shielded
cables — 5 KV

Concrete
commercial
roadway
6 in. thick

VIOLATION—Under areas subject to heavy vehicular traffic, minimum burial depth must be 24 in. for
any kind of circuit. Exception No. 1 of
Table 710-3(b) does not apply.

Fig. 710-3. Underground raceway circuits may vary widely in acceptable conditions of
use. (Sec. 710-3.)

2. Areas of heavy traffic (public roads, commercial parking areas, etc.) must
have minimum burial depth of 24 in. for any wiring method.
3. Lesser depths are permitted where wiring rises for termination.
4. Airport runways may have cables buried not less than 18 in. deep, without
raceway or concrete encasement.
5. Conduits installed in solid rock may be buried at lesser depths than shown
in diagrams when covered by at least 2 in. of concrete that extends to the
rock surface.

As noted in part **(b)(2)** splices or taps are permitted in trench without a box—
but only if approved methods and materials are used. Taps and splices must be
watertight and protected from mechanical injury. For shielded cables, the
shielding must be continuous across the splice or tap.

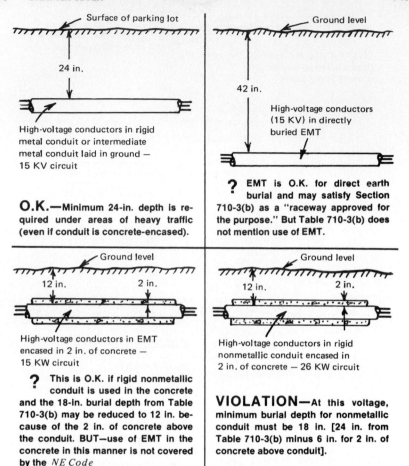

Surface of parking lot

24 in.

High-voltage conductors in rigid
metal conduit or intermediate
metal conduit laid in ground —
15 KV circuit

O.K.—Minimum 24-in. depth is required under areas of heavy traffic
(even if conduit is concrete-encased).

Ground level

42 in.

High-voltage conductors
(15 KV) in directly
buried EMT

? EMT is O.K. for direct earth
burial and may satisfy Section
710-3(b) as a "raceway approved for
the purpose." But Table 710-3(b) does
not mention use of EMT.

Ground level

12 in.   2 in.

High-voltage conductors in EMT
encased in 2 in. of concrete —
15 KW circuit

? This is O.K. if rigid nonmetallic
conduit is used in the concrete
and the 18-in. burial depth from Table
710-3(b) may be reduced to 12 in. because of the 2 in. of concrete above
the conduit. BUT—use of EMT in the
concrete in this manner is not covered
by the *NE Code*

Ground level

12 in.   2 in.

High-voltage conductors in rigid
nonmetallic conduit encased in
2 in. of concrete — 26 KW circuit

VIOLATION—At this voltage,
minimum burial depth for nonmetallic
conduit must be 18 in. [24 in. from
Table 710-3(b) minus 6 in. for 2 in. of
concrete above conduit].

High-voltage conductors in
rigid metal conduit laid on grade
and covered with 2 in. of concrete

Concrete walkway in
shopping center mall
2 in. thick

VIOLATION — Table 710-3(b) calls for a minimum 6-in. burial depth for rigid metal conduit. The depth reductions permitted by Exception No. 2 DO NOT apply to either rigid or
intermediate metal conduit.

Fig. 710-4. Underground high-voltage circuits must observe burial depths. (Sec. 710-3.)

Figure 710-5 shows a permanent straight splice for joining one end of cable
off a reel to the start of cable off another reel, or for repairing cable that is cut
through accidentally by a back-hoe or other tool digging into the ground. "T"
and "Y" splices are made with similar techniques. Disconnectable splice

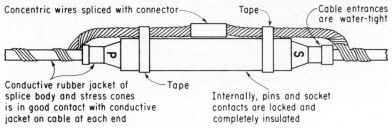

Concentric wires spliced with connector — Tape — Cable entrances are water-tight

Conductive rubber jacket of splice body and stress cones is in good contact with conductive jacket on cable at each end — Tape

Internally, pins and socket contacts are locked and completely insulated

Fig. 710-5. Splice may be made in direct-burial cable if suitable materials are used. (Sec. 710-3.)

devices provide watertight plug-and-receptacle assembly for all types of shielded cables and are fully submersible.

Figure 710-6 covers the rules of parts **(b)(3)** and **(b)(4)**. Figure 710-7 covers part **(b)(1)**.

**BACKFILL MUST NOT DAMAGE
DUCTS, CABLES OR RACEWAYS**

Backfill of heavy rocks or sharp or corrosive materials must not be used if it may cause damage or prevent adequate compaction of ground.

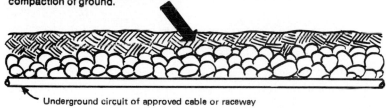

Underground circuit of approved cable or raceway

Protection shall be provided to prevent physical damage to the raceway or cable in the form of granular or selected material or suitable sleeves.

RACEWAYS MUST BE SEALED

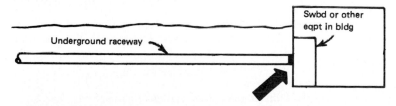

Swbd or other eqpt in bldg

Underground raceway

Where raceway enters from an underground system, the end in the building must be sealed with suitable compound to prevent entry of moisture or gases; or it must be arranged to prevent moisture from contacting live parts.

Fig. 710-6. Circuits must be protected and sealed where they enter equipment. (Sec. 710-3.)

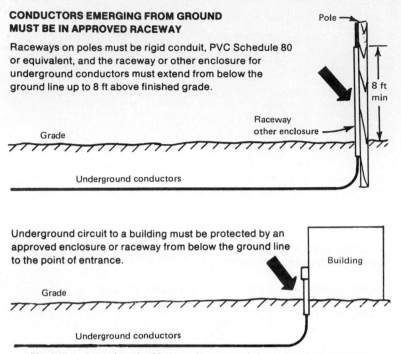

CONDUCTORS EMERGING FROM GROUND MUST BE IN APPROVED RACEWAY

Raceways on poles must be rigid conduit, PVC Schedule 80 or equivalent, and the raceway or other enclosure for underground conductors must extend from below the ground line up to 8 ft above finished grade.

Pole

8 ft min

Raceway other enclosure

Grade

Underground conductors

Underground circuit to a building must be protected by an approved enclosure or raceway from below the ground line to the point of entrance.

Building

Grade

Underground conductors

Fig. 710-7. Direct burial cables must be protected aboveground. (Sec. 710-3.)

710-6. Insulation Shielding. One of the basic decisions to make in selecting high-voltage conductors is whether or not electrostatic insulation shielding is required on the cable. In the 1971 **NE Code** (and previous editions), Table 710-5 set forth an elaborate variety of conditions under which solid dielectric insulated conductors had to be shielded or were permitted to be unshielded. That table set the same basic shielding requirements as recommended by the IPCEA. BUT, the **NE Code** *no longer contains* that table and now takes a different approach to mandatory shielding. The basic requirements on electrostatic shielding of high-voltage conductors are presented in Sec. 310-6 and are explained there.

This section sets forth very general rules on terminating shielded high-voltage conductors. The metallic shielding or any other conducting or semiconducting static shielding components on shielded cable must be stripped back to a safe distance according to the circuit voltage—at all terminations of the shielding. At such points, stress reduction must be provided by such methods as the use of potheads, terminators, stress cones, or similar devices.

The wording of this regulation makes clear that the need for shield termination using stress cones or similar terminating devices applies to semiconducting insulation shielding as well as to metallic-wire insulation shielding systems.

A stress cone is a field-installed device or a field-assembled buildup of insulating tape and shielding braid which must be made at a terminal of high-voltage shielded cable, whether a pothead is used or not. A stress-relief cone is required to relieve the electrical stress concentration in cable insulation directly under the end of cable shielding. Some cable constructions contain stress-control components that afford the cable sufficient stress relief without the need for stress-relief cones. If a cable contains inherent stress-relief components in its construction, that would satisfy Sec. 710-6 as doing the work of a stress cone. As a result, separate stress cones would not have to be installed at the ends of such cable. Or, heat-shrinkable-tubing terminations may be used with stress-control material that provides the needed relief of electrostatic stress.

At a cable terminal, the shielding must be cut back some distance from the end of the conductor to prevent any arcing-over from the hot conductor to the grounded shield. When the shield is cut back, a stress is produced in the insulation. By providing a flare out of the shield, i.e., by extending the shield a short distance in the shape of a cone, the stress is relieved, as shown in Fig. 710-8.

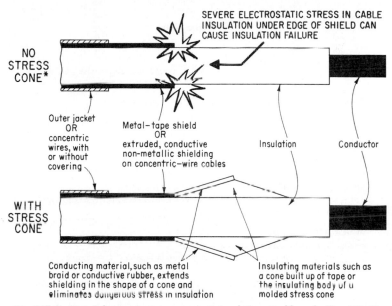

Fig. 710-8. Here is how a stress cone protects insulation at cable ends. (Sec. 710-6.)

Stress cones provide that protection against insulation failure at the terminals of shielded high-voltage cables. Manufacturers provide special preformed stress cones (Fig. 710-9) and kits for preparing cable terminals with stress cones for cables operating at specified levels of high voltage (Fig. 710-10). A wide assortment of stress-relief terminators are made for all the high-voltage cable assemblies used today.

Metallic shielding tape must be grounded, as required by Sec. 710-6 and 300-5(b), which refers to "metallic shielding"—as in Fig. 710-11. The shield on

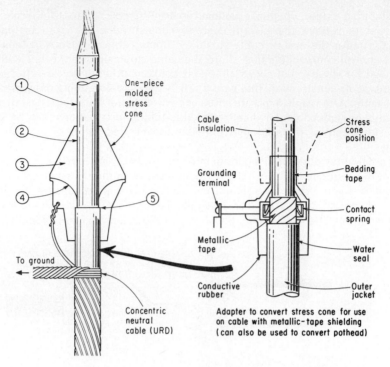

APPLICATION:
Cable shield is cut back about 12 in. Then, using silicone lubricant, the cable insulation surface and the inner bore of the stress cone are lubricated. The stress cone is simply pushed down over the cable end until it bottoms on the cable shield. After cable is prepared, termination takes about 30 seconds.

REFER TO DIAGRAM:
1. Cable insulation with shielding cut back
2. Tight fit between insulation and bore of stress cone
3. Insulating rubber
4. Stress relief provided by conductive rubber flaring away from insulation along bond between insulating rubber and conductive rubber
5. Conductive rubber of cone tightly fit to conductive cable shield

Fig. 710-9. Typical preformed stress cone is readily applied on cables up to 35-kV indoors. (Sec. 710-6.)

shielded cables must be grounded at one end at least. It is better to ground the shield at two or more points. Grounding of the shield at all terminals and splices will keep the entire length of the shield at about ground potential for the safest, most effective operation of the cable. Cable with improperly or ineffectively grounded shielding can present more hazards than unshielded cable.

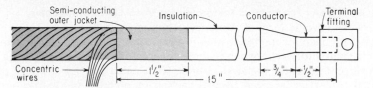

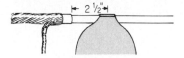 

THIS IS CABLE PREPARED FOR PENNANT STRESS CONE

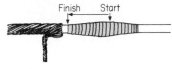 

STEP 1 — Wrap the cone build-up around the insulation at a given place

STEP 2 — Cone assembly with preshaped wrap finished

STEP 3 — Semi-conducting tape contacts semi-conducting cable jacket and extends up to peak of cone

STEP 4 — Entire stress-cone assembly is then wrapped with insulating tape

STEP 5 — Insulate terminal fitting area at end of cable and (for outdoor use) cover entire assembly with silicone tape or use potheads.

Fig. 710-10. "Pennant" method is one of a variety of job-site termination buildups. (Sec. 710-6.)

Metal conduit and metal sheath or electrostatic shielding must be effectively grounded at terminations by connection to grounded metal enclosure, by bonding jumper, etc., to limit voltage to ground and facilitate operation of overcurrent protective devices.

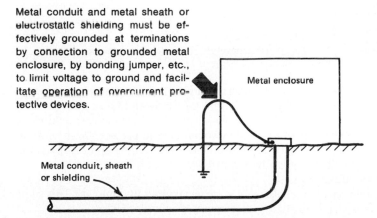

Fig. 710-11. Metallic shielding must be grounded for all high-voltage conductors—under- or aboveground. (Sec. 710-6.)

710-8. Moisture or Mechanical Protection for Metal-Sheathed Cables. A "pothead" is one specific form of stress-reduction means referred to in Sec. 710-6 and has long been a common means of protecting insulation against moisture or mechanical injury where conductors emerge from a metal sheath (Fig. 710-12). Such protection for metal-sheathed cables (such as lead-covered, paper-insulated cables) is required by this section. A pothead is a cable terminal

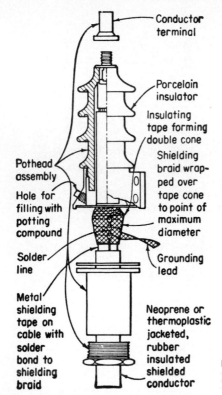

Fig. 710-12. Typical single-conductor pothead protects metallic- or nonmetallic-jacketed cable. (Sec. 710-8.)

which provides sealing to the sheath of the cable for making a moisture-proof connection between the wires within the cable and those outside.

When metal-jacketed high-voltage cables are terminated outdoors exposed to the weather, a pothead is commonly used to protect the insulation of conductors against moisture or mechanical injury where conductors emerge from a metal sheath, as shown in Fig. 710-13.

On use of potheads:

1. Paper-insulated cables must be terminated in potheads. This requirement also extends to such cables operated at under 600 V.
2. Varnished-cambric-insulated cables should be terminated in potheads but may be terminated with taped connections in dry locations.

Fig. 710-13. A pothead is used on the end of each paper-insulated, lead-covered cable to protect against entry of moisture, with a wiped lead joint at the terminal. (Sec. 710-8.)

3. Rubber-insulated cables are commonly terminated in potheads in locations where moisture protection is critical but may be terminated without potheads in accordance with manufacturer's instructions.
4. Although many modern high-voltage cables can be terminated without potheads, many engineers consider potheads the best terminations for high-voltage cable.
5. The use of potheads offers a number of advantages:
   a. Seals cable ends against moisture that would damage the insulation.
   b. Provides a compartment for surrounding the termination with insulating compound to increase strength of electrical insulation.
   c. Seals cable ends against loss of insulating oils.
   d. Provides engineered support of connections.

710-9. Protection of Service Equipment, Metal-Equipment, Metal-Enclosed Power Switchgear, and Industrial Control Assemblies.   The basic rule of the first sentence in this section excludes "pipes or ducts foreign to the electrical installation" from the "vicinity of the service equipment, metal-enclosed power switchgear, or industrial control assemblies." Then, addressing the case where foreign piping is unavoidably close to the designated electrical equipment, the next sentence calls for "protection" (such as a hood or shield above such equipment) to prevent damage to the equipment by "leaks or breaks in such foreign systems."

Piping for supplying a fire protection medium for the electrical equipment is not considered to be "foreign" and may be installed at the high-voltage gear.

The reason given for that sentence was to prevent the first sentence from being "interpreted to mean that no sprinklers should be installed." Fire suppression at such locations may use water sprinklers or protection systems of dry chemicals and/or gases specifically designed to extinguish fires in the equipment without jeopardizing the equipment. Water is sometimes found to be objectionable; leaks in piping or malfunction of a sprinkler head could reduce the switchgear integrity by exposing it to a flashover and thereby initiate a fire.

710-20. Overcurrent Protection.   Figure 710-14 shows the basic rule for high-voltage circuit protection. Refer to Sec. 230-208 for high-voltage service conductors, to Sec. 240-100 on feeders, and Sec. 240-101 on branch circuits. The

OVERCURRENT DEVICE FOR EACH UNGROUNDED CONDUCTOR . . .

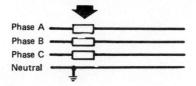

. . . must be either . . .

a **CIRCUIT BREAKER** with three overcurrent relays operated from three current transformers [see Exceptions in Section 710-20(a)]

OR

a FUSE connected in series with each ungrounded conductor.

Fig. 710-14. Basic rule calls for overcurrent protection. (Sec. 710-20.)

specified ratings of protection for high-voltage conductors are presented in those sections.

710-21. Circuit-Interrupting Devices.   High-voltage power CBs provide load switching, short-circuit protection, electrical operation, adjustable time delays of trip characteristics for selectively coordinated protection schemes, quick reclosing after tripping, and various protective hookups such as differential relay protection of transformers. There are oil-type, oil-less (or air-magnetic), and vacuum-break CBs. The air-magnetic CB is the common type for indoor applications in systems up to 15 kV and higher. Oil CBs are sometimes used for indoor and outdoor high-voltage service equipment where they provide economical disconnect and protection on the primary of a transformer.

Modern high-voltage CB equipment meets all the needs of control and protection for electrical systems from the simplest to the most complex and sophisticated. In particular, its use for selectively coordinated protection of services, feeders, and branch circuits is unique. In current ratings up to 3,000 A, CB gear has the very high interrupting ratings required for today's high-capacity systems. Available in "metal-clad" assemblies, all live parts are completely enclosed within grounded metal enclosures for maximum safety. For applications exposed to lightning strikes or other transient overcurrents, CB equipment offers quick reclosing after operation. Drawout construction of the CB units provides ease of maintenance and ready testing of breakers. CB gear offers unlimited arrangements of source and load circuits and is suited to a variety of AC or DC control power sources. Accessory devices are available for special functions.

Figure 710-15 covers the basic rules of this section on use of CBs. Figure 710-16 shows an oil CB, with the line-side isolating switch required by Sec. 230-204(a).

A. Indoor installations of circuit breakers must consist of metal-enclosed units or fire-resistant, cell-mounted units, except that open-mounted CBs may be used in places accessible to qualified persons only.

B. All CBs must be rated for short-circuit duty at point of application.

C. Circuit breakers controlling oil-filled transformers *must* either be located outside the transformer vault *or* be capable of being operated from outside the vault.

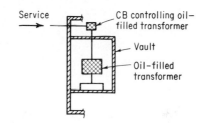

D. Oil CBs must be arranged or located so that adjacent readily combustible structures or materials are safeguarded in an approved manner. Adequate space separation, fire-resistant barriers or enclosures, trenches containing sufficient coarse crushed stone, and properly drained oil enclosures such as dikes or basins are recognized as suitable safeguards.

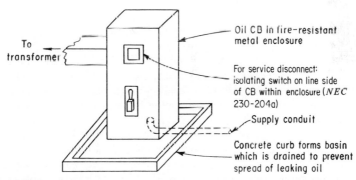

Fig. 710-15. Detailed rules regulate use of high-voltage circuit breakers. (Sec. 710-21.)

Part **(b)** covers power fuses, which are available in current-limiting and non-current-limiting types. (See Fig. 710-17 for an example of the uses to which power fuses may be put.) The current-limiting types offer reduction of thermal and magnetic stresses on fault by reducing the energy let-through. They are constructed with a silver-sand internal element, similar to 600-V current-lim-

Fig. 710-16. Oil circuit breaker for high-voltage application has a disconnecting switch on its supply side to isolate the line terminals of the breaker. (Sec. 710-21.)

iting fuses. Such fuses generally have higher interrupting ratings at some voltages, but their continuous current-carrying ratings are limited.

Noncurrent-limiting types of power fuses are made in two types of operating characteristics: expulsion type and nonexpulsion type. The expulsion fuse gets its name from the fact that it expels hot gases when it operates. Such fuses should not be used indoors without a "snuffer" or other protector to contain the exhaust, because there is a hazard presented by the expelled gases. At the end of part **(b)(1)**, the rule says that vented expulsion-type power fuses used indoors, underground, or in metal enclosures must be "identified for the use." Vented power fuses are not safe for operation in confined space—unless specifically tested and "identified" for such use. Part **(b)(5)** of this section requires that fuses expelling flame in operation must be designed or arranged to prevent hazard to persons or property. The boric-acid fuse with a condenser or other protection against arcing and gas expulsion is a typical nonexpulsion, noncurrent-limiting fuse (Fig. 710-18).

Parts **(b)(6)** and **(b)(7)** cover very important safeguards for the use of fuses and fuseholders:

In coordinating power fuses, care must be taken to account for ambient temperature adjustment factors, because time-current curves are based on an

Fig. 710-17. Typical power fuses are used in load-interrupter switchgear, which is an alternative to circuit-breaker gear for control and protection in indoor high-voltage systems. (Sec. 710-21.)

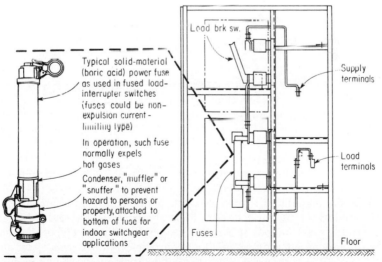

Fig. 710-18. Boric-acid fuse uses a device to protect against flame expulsion. (Sec. 710-21.)

ambient of 25°C. Adjustment also must be made for preheating of fuses due to load current to assure effective coordination of fuses with each other and/or with CBs. Manufacturer's curves of adjustment factors for ambient temperature and fuse preloading are available.

Figure 710-19 shows the time-current characteristic for an R-rated, current-limiting (silver-sand) fuse designed for 2,400-V and 4,800-V motor applications.

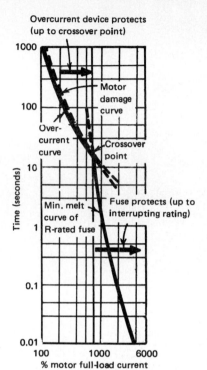

Fig. 710-19. "R-rated" fuses are used in motor starters for 2400- and 4800-V motors. (Sec. 710-21.)

Such fuses must be selected to coordinate with the motor controller overload protection, with the controller clearing overloads up to 10 times motor current and the fuse taking over for faster opening of higher currents up to the interrupting rating of the fuse. The amp rating of R-rated fuses is given in values such as 2R or 12R or 24R. If the number preceding the "R" is multiplied by 100, the value obtained is the ampere level at which the fuse will blow in 20 sec. Thus, the rating designation is *not* continuous current but is based on the operating characteristics of the R-rated fuse. Continuous current rating of such fuses is given by the manufacturer at some value of ambient temperature.

Fused cutouts for high-voltage circuits, as shown in Fig. 710-20, are available for both indoor and outdoor application, as regulated by part **(c)** of this section. Pull-type fuse cutouts are used outdoors on pole-line crossarms or indoors in electric rooms where accessible only to qualified persons, as shown in Fig. 710-21. Such fused cutouts are acceptable for use as an isolating switch, as permitted by Sec. 710-22.

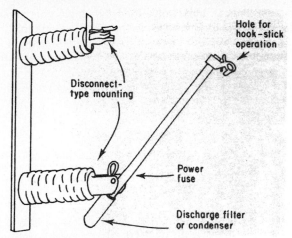

Fig. 710-20. Expanded rules cover use of distribution cutouts. (Sec. 710-21.)

Fig. 710-21. Distribution cutouts are single-pole, fused, protective, and disconnect devices that are hook-stick-operable. Note voltage and current rating on case of each cutout (arrow), as required by part **(c)(5)** of Sec. 710-21. (Sec. 710-21.)

Part **(d)** of this section covers oil-filled cutouts. In addition to air CBs, oil CBs, and fused load-interrupter switches, another device frequently used for control of high-voltage circuits is the oil-filled cutout. Compared to breakers and fused switchgear, oil-filled cutouts are inexpensive devices that provide economical switching and, where desired, overload and short-circuit protection for primary voltage circuits.

The oil-filled cutout is a completely enclosed, single-pole assembly with a fusible or nonfusible element immersed in the oil-filled tank that makes up the major part of the unit, and with two terminals on the outside of the housing. Figure 710-22 shows the basic construction of a typical cutout with a listing of

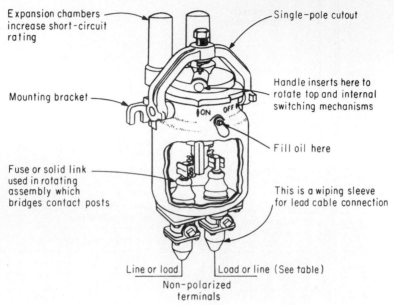

Fig. 710-22. Oil-filled cutout is a fused or unfused, single-pole disconnect device. (Sec. 710-21.)

available entrance fittings for the terminals to suit them to various cable and job requirements. The circuit is broken or closed safely and rapidly by the internal switching mechanism. The switch mechanism is made up of a rotating element that, in the closed position, bridges two internal contacts—each contact connecting to one of the outside terminals. The rotating element is completely insulated from the external case and from the external handle that operates the element. The rotating element may be simply a shorting blade when the cutout is used as an unfused switch. When the cutout is to be used as a fused switching unit, the rotating bridging element is fitted with a fuse. Operation of an oil-filled cutout is controlled at the top end of the shaft extending out through the top of the housing.

As a single-pole switching device, the oil-filled cutout is not polarized—i.e., either terminal may be a line or load terminal. This is a result of the symmetrical construction of the switching element and suits the device to use in circuit sectionalizing or as a tie device in layouts involving two or more primary supply circuits. Note that these **Code** rules on oil-filled cutouts are different from those in part **(c)** on distribution cutouts.

With an oil-filled cutout, the switching of load current or the breaking of fault current is confined within a sturdy metal housing. Operation is made safe and quiet by confining arcs and current rupture forces within the enclosure. This operating characteristic of the cutouts especially suits them to use where there are explosive gases or flammable dusts, where complete submersion is possible, where severe atmospheric conditions exist, or where exposure of live electrical parts might be hazardous.

Oil-filled (sometimes called "oil-fuse") cutouts are made in three sizes based on continuous current—100, 200, and 300 A, up to 15 kV. In one line there are three basic types. *Pole-type cutouts* are equipped with rubber-covered leads from the terminals for use in open wiring. Pothead-type cutouts have a cable lead from one terminal for open wiring and a sleeve on the other for connecting a lead or rubber-covered cable from an underground circuit. *Subway-type cutouts* are for underground vaults and manholes, particularly where submersion might occur, and are equipped with a sleeve on each terminal for rubber- or lead-sheathed cable. Figure 710-23 lists the various types of terminal connections that are available on oil-filled cutouts.

Application	Cable cover	No. of conduits	Entrance type	Method of sealing
Indoor	Rubber or neoprene	Single	Porcelain	Tape Always tape this connection!
		Multiple	Stud bushing	
Indoor or outdoor	Rubber, lead or neoprene	Single	Stuffing box	Compression fittings
	Polyethylene	Single		Compression fittings and tube seal
	Lead	Single	Wiping sleeve	Solder wipe

Fig. 710-23. Terminals on oil-filled cutouts must be matched to application and cable type. (Sec. 710-21.)

For multiphase circuits, two or three single-phase cutout units can be group-mounted with a gang-operating mechanism for simultaneous operation. Figure 710-24 shows 3-gang assemblies. For pole mounting, linkage and long handle are available for operating cutouts from the ground. Or cutouts can be flange-mounted on a terminal box, as shown in Fig. 710-25, where the 3-gang assembly was added to a high-voltage switchgear on a modernization job.

Because oil-filled cutouts provide load-break capability and overcurrent protection, they may be used for industrial and commercial service equipment, for switching outdoor lighting of sports fields and shopping centers, for transformer load centers, for primary-voltage motor circuits, or for use in vaults and manholes of underground systems.

In 100- and 200-A ratings, oil-filled cutouts are available in combination with current-limiting power fuses in double-compartment indoor or outdoor enclosures. These fused oil interrupter switches provide moderate load-break and high fault-current interrupting capability in an economical package.

Single-phase cutouts (top view)

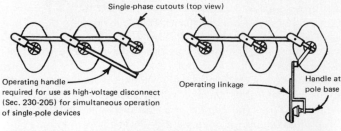

Operating handle
required for use as high-voltage disconnect
(Sec. 230-205) for simultaneous operation
of single-pole devices

Operating linkage

Handle at
pole base

Fig. 710-24. Oil-filled cutouts can be assembled as a 3-pole device for 3-phase circuits. (Sec. 710-21.)

Part **(e)** of this section recognizes the use of so-called load-interrupter switches used in high-voltage systems. In parts **(1)** to **(6)**, a wealth of specific data provides guidance to design engineers, electrical installers, and electrical inspectors on the proper installation, operation, and maintenance of high-voltage interruper switches—with particular emphasis on safety to operators and maintenance personnel.

Switching for modern high-voltage electrical systems can be provided by a number of different equipment installations. For any particular case, the best arrangement depends on several factors: the point of application—either for outside or inside distribution or as service equipment; the voltage; the type of distribution system—radial, loop, selective, network; conditions—accessibility, type of actual layout of the equipment; job atmosphere; use; future system expansion; and economic considerations.

Types of switches used in high-voltage applications include:
1. Enclosed air-break load-interrupter switchgear with or without power fuses
2. Oil-filled cutouts (fused or unfused)
3. Oil-immersed-type disconnect switches

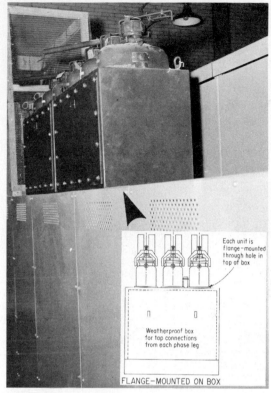

Fig. 710-25. Gang-operated 3-pole assembly of oil-filled cut-outs provided addition of a new high-voltage circuit on a modernization project, but location of the units was questioned because part **(d)(7)** imposes a 5-ft maximum mounting height. (Sec. 710-21.)

Modern load-interrupter switchgear in metal safety enclosures finds wide application in high-voltage distribution systems, in combination with modern power fuses (Fig. 710-26). Section 230-208 of the **NE Code** covers use of air load-interrupter switches, with fuses, for disconnect and overcurrent protection of high-voltage service-entrance conductors. Part **(e)** of Sec. 710-21 covers use of fused air load-interrupter switches for high-voltage feeder in distribution systems.

Metal-enclosed fused load interrupters offer a fully effective alternative to use of power CBs, with substantial economies, in 5- and 15-kV distribution systems for commercial, institutional, and industrial buildings. Typical applications for such switchgear parallel those of power CBs and include the following:

1. *In switching centers*—Switchgear is set up for control and protection of individual primary feeders to transformer loadcenters.
2. *In substation primaries*—Load-interrupter switchgear is used for transformer switching and protection in the primary sides of substations.

Fig. 710-26. Load-interrupter switchgear is generally used with fuses to provide protection as well as load-break switching for high-voltage circuits. The fuses must be rated to provide complete protection for the load interrupter on closing, carrying, or interrupting current—up to the assigned maximum short-circuit rating. (Sec. 710-21.)

3. *In substation secondaries*—Here the switchgear is used as a switching center closely coupled to a high-voltage transformer secondary.

4. *In service entrances*—This is a single-unit application of a switchgear bay for service-entrance disconnect and protection in a primary supply line.

Fused load-interrupter switchgear, typically rated up to 1,200 A, can match the ratings and required performance capabilities of power CBs for a large percentage of applications in which either might be used.

Fuse-interrupter switches for high-voltage circuits are available with manual or power operation—including types with spring-powered, over-center mechanisms for manual operation or motor-driven, stored-energy operators. Available in indoor and outdoor housings, assemblies can be equipped with a variety of accessory devices, including key-interlocks for coordinating switch operation with remote devices such as transformer secondary breakers.

Vacuum switchgear, with their contacts operating in a vacuum "bottle" that is enclosed in a compact cylindrical assembly, has gained wide acceptance as load interrupters for high-voltage switching and sectionalizing. Available in 200-A and 600-A ratings for use at 15.5, 27, and 38 kV, this switching equipment is suited to full-load interruption and is rated for 15,000-A or 20,000-A short-circuit current under momentary and make and latch operations. BIL ratings are 95, 125, or 150 kV.

Vacuum switch assemblies, with a variety of accessories, including stored-energy operators and electric motor operator for remote control, are suited to all indoor and outdoor switching operations—including submersible operation for underground systems. The units offer fireproof and explosionproof operation, with virtually maintenance-free life for its rated 5,000 load interruptions. Units are available in standard 2-way, 3-way, and 4-way configurations, along with automatic transfer options. Accessory CTs and relays can be used with stored-energy operators to apply vacuum switches for fault-interrupting duty.

710-22. Isolating Means.   Air-break or oil-immersed switches of any type may be used to provide the isolating functions described in this section. Distribution cutouts or oil-filled cutouts are also used as isolating switches.

Oil-immersed disconnect switches are used for load control and for sectionalizing of primary-voltage underground-distribution systems for large commercial and industrial layouts (Fig. 710-27). Designed for high-power handling—such as 400 A up to 34 kV—this type of switch can be located at transformer

Fig. 710-27. Oil switches are commonly used for isolating equipment and circuits for sectionalizing and for transfer from preferred to emergency supply. (Sec. 710-22.)

loadcenter primaries or at other strategic points in high-voltage circuits to provide a wide variety of sectionalizing arrangements to provide alternate feeds for essential load circuits.

Oil-immersed disconnect switches are available for as many as five switch positions and ground positions to ground the feeder or test-ground positions for grounding or testing. Ground positions are used in such switches to connect circuits to ground while they are being worked on to assure safety to personnel.

Oil switches for load-break applications up to 15 kV are available for either manual or electrically powered switching for all types of circuits. When electrical operation is used, the switch functions as a high-voltage magnetic contactor.

Switches intended only for isolating duty must be interlocked with other devices to prevent opening of the isolating switch under load, or the isolating switch must be provided with an obvious sign warning against opening the switch under load.

710-24. Metal-Enclosed Power Switchgear and Industrial Control Assemblies. Where the previous sections presented regulations on the individual switching and protective devices, this section covers enclosure and interconnection of such unit devices into overall assemblies. Basically, the rules of this section are aimed at the manufacturers and assemblers of such equipment.

Use of all high-voltage switching and control equipment must be carefully checked against information given with certification of the equipment by a test laboratory—such as data given by UL in their Green Book. Typical data are as follows:

Unit substations listed by UL have the secondary neutral bonded to the enclosure and have provision on the neutral for connection of a grounding conductor. A terminal is also provided on the enclosure near the line terminals for use with an equipment grounding conductor run from the enclosure of primary equipment feeding the unit sub to the enclosure of the unit sub. Connection of such an equipment grounding conductor provides proper bonding together of

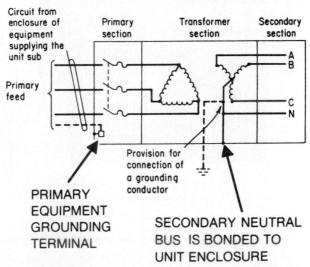

Fig. 710-28. NEC rules on equipment construction are supported by UL data. (Sec. 710-24.)

equipment enclosures where the primary feed to the unit sub is direct-buried underground or is run in nonmetallic conduit without a metal conduit connection in the primary feed (Fig. 710-28).

The rule of part **(o)** is particularly aimed at the designers and installers of equipment, rather than at the manufacturer. Part **(o)(2)** emphasizes that careful layout and application of switching components of all types is important. Figure 710-29 shows the kind of condition that can be extremely hazardous in high-voltage layouts where there is the chance of a secondary to primary feedback—such as the intentional one shown to provide emergency power to essential circuits in Building 2. Under emergency conditions, the main fused interrupter is

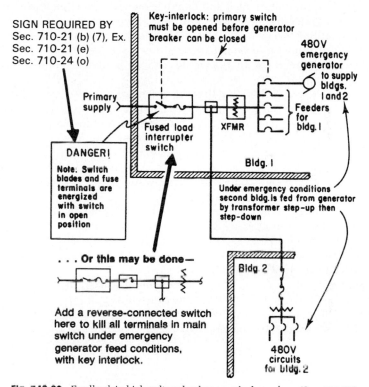

Fig. 710-29. Feedback in high-voltage hookups can be hazardous. (Sec. 710-24.)

opened and the secondary CB for the generator is closed, feeding power to the 480-V switchboard in Building 1 and then feeding through two transformers to supply power to the 480-V circuits in Building 2. This hookup makes the load side of the main interrupter switch alive, presenting the hazard of electrocution to any personnel who might go into the switch thinking that it is dead because it is open. A second switch can eliminate this difficulty, if applied with interlocks.

ARTICLE 720. CIRCUITS AND EQUIPMENT OPERATING AT LESS THAN 50 VOLTS

720-1. Scope. This article covers low-voltage applications that are not power-limited circuits as defined in Sec. 725-3 and are not remote-control or signal circuits. Determination that Art. 720 applies to any circuit or equipment must be carefully made on the basis of the particular load being supplied and circuit conditions. This article covers circuits operating at more than 30 V but not over 50 V—such as 32-V circuiting.

720-4. Conductors. The minimum No. 12 conductor size, rather than No. 14 as permitted for standard power and light wiring, is aimed at the higher current required for a given wattage load at low voltage. For instance, at 32 V, the current corresponding to a given wattage is 3.6 times the current for the same wattage at 115 V. It should also be noted that for a given load in watts and a given size of wire and circuit length, the voltage drop in percentage is about 13 times as great at 32 V as at 115 V.

720-5. Lampholders. Where medium-base sockets are used, there is no good reason for using any but those having a 660-W rating. The ampere ratings of candelabra and intermediate base sockets would permit the use of 25-W lamps at 32 V, but it is not considered safe to allow the installation of these low-wattage sockets on circuits operating at 50 V or less.

Fixtures, regardless of supply voltage, would need to meet the requirements given in Art. 410. If for outdoor use, they would need to comply with Sec. 410-4.

720-10. Grounding. If any circuit connected to the system is carried overhead from one building to another, a system ground must be installed. The grounding conductor should be connected to one of the buses at the switchboard or generator and battery control panel. The requirements of Art. 250 should be followed in general. If water piping connected to a fairly extensive system of street mains is not available, a local water-piping system may be used as the grounding electrode; but unless the piping system is carried for some distance at a depth where it will always be in moist earth, supplementary driven rod or pipe electrodes should also be employed. Refer to Sec. 250-81.

ARTICLE 725. CLASS 1, CLASS 2, AND CLASS 3 REMOTE-CONTROL, SIGNALING, AND POWER-LIMITED CIRCUITS

725-1. Scope. Article 725 of the Code covers power-limited circuits and remote-control and signal circuits. A signal circuit is defined as any electrical circuit which supplies energy to an appliance or device that gives a visual and/or audible signal. Such circuits include those for doorbells, buzzers, code-calling systems, signal lights, annunciators, fire or smoke detection, fire or burglar alarm, and other detection indication or alarm devices.

A "remote-control" circuit is any circuit which has as its load device the operating coil of a magnetic motor starter, a magnetic contactor, or a relay. Strictly speaking, it is a circuit which exercises control over one or more other circuits. And these other circuits controlled by the control circuit may themselves be control circuits or they may be "load" circuits—carrying utilization current to a lighting, heating, power, or signal device. Figure 725-1 clarifies the distinction between control circuits and load circuits.

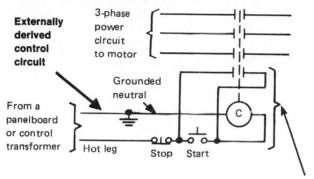

ARTICLE 725 APPLIES

Fig. 725-1. A control circuit governs the operating coil or some other element, to switch the load circuit. (Sec. 725-1.)

The elements of a control circuit include all the equipment and devices concerned with the function of the circuit: conductors, raceway, contactor operating coil, source of energy supply to the circuit, overcurrent protective devices, and all switching devices which govern energization of the operating coil. Typical control circuits include the operating-coil circuit of magnetic motor starters (NEC Secs. 430-71 and 430-72), magnetic contactors (as used for switching lighting, heating, and power loads), and relays. Control circuits include wiring between solid-state control devices as well as between magnetically actuated components. Low-voltage relay switching of lighting and power loads is also classified as remote-control wiring (Fig. 725-2).

Power-limited circuits are circuits used for functions other than signaling or remote-control—but in which the source of the energy supply is limited in its power (volts times amps) to specified maximum levels. Low-voltage lighting, using 12-V lamps in fixtures fed from 120/12-V transformers, is a typical "power-limited circuit" application.

725-2. Locations and Other Articles.   All the applications under this article must observe the specified sections that also rule on use of general power and light wiring.

Part **(a)** prohibits any installation of remote-control, signaling, or power-limited wiring in such a way that there is an appreciable reduction in the fire rating of floors, walls, or ceilings.

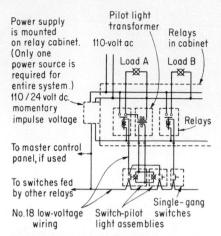

Power supply is mounted on relay cabinet. (Only one power source is required for entire system.) 110/24 volt dc. momentary impulse voltage

Pilot light transformer
110-volt ac
Relays in cabinet

Load A   Load B

Relays

To master control panel, if used

To switches fed by other relays

No.18 low-voltage wiring   Switch-pilot light assemblies   Single-gang switches

Fig. 725-2. Low-voltage switching involves typical "remote-control circuits." (Sec. 725-1.)

Part **(b)** requires that circuits covered by this article must be run in metal raceway or metal cable assembly when used in an air handling ceiling—as required by Sec. 300-22. The Exception permits Class 2 and/or Class 3 circuits (as defined in Sec. 725-3) to be used without metal raceway or metal cable cover in ducts, plenums, or ceiling spaces used for environmental air *provided that the conductors are "listed" as Type CL2P or CL3P, as required in Sec. 725-53(a).* Because of the definition of the word "listed" (see Art. 100, "Definitions"), this rule would require that any such nonmetallic assembly of conductors for those circuits must be specifically listed in the UL's *Electrical Construction Materials Directory* (or with similar third-party certification) as having the specified characteristics for use without metal raceway or covering in ducts, plenums, and air handling ceilings.

Note: For any such application, check that the conductors of the circuit are definitely listed by UL or others.

Part **(e)** notes that Art. 725 does not apply to control circuits tapped from line terminals in motor starters. As described under Sec. 430-72, the control circuit for the operating coil in a magnetic motor starter where the coil voltage supply is tapped from the line terminals of the starter is regulated by the rules of Sec. 430-72 and not by the remote-control rules of Art. 725. Where a control circuit for the operating coil of one or more magnetic motor starters is derived from a separate control transformer, one that is not fed from a motor branch circuit, the control circuit(s) and all components are covered by the rules of Art. 725. In the same way, a control circuit that is taken from a panelboard for power supply to the operating coil of one or more motor starters is also covered by Art. 725 and not by the rules of Sec. 430-72. See Fig. 725-1.

725-3. Classifications. The provisions of this section divide all signaling and remote-control systems into three classes.

Class 1 includes all signaling and remote-control systems which do not have the special current limitations of Class 2 and Class 3 systems.

Class 2 and Class 3 systems are those systems in which the current is limited to certain specified low values by fuses or CBs, and by supply through transformers which will deliver only very small currents on short circuit, or by other means which are considered satisfactory. The current values depend upon the voltage at which the system operates and range from 5 mA up, as shown in Table 725-31(a) and (b). All Class 2 and Class 3 circuits must have a power source with the power-limiting characteristics assigned in the tables in addition to the overcurrent device.

725-4. Safety-Control Equipment.   The application of this rule is illustrated by Fig. 725-3, which is a simplified diagram of a common type of automatic control

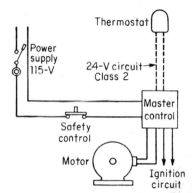

Fig. 725-3. Remote-control circuit must be Class 1 if failure would create a hazard. (Sec. 725-4.)

for a domestic oil burner. Assuming a steam boiler, the safety control is a switch that opens automatically when the steam pressure reaches a predetermined value and, preferably, also opens if the water level is allowed to fall too low. The master control includes a transformer of the current-limiting type which supplies the thermostat circuit at a voltage of 24 V. When the thermostat contacts close, a relay closes the circuits to the motor and to the ignition transformer.

Failure of the safety control or ignition to operate would introduce a direct hazard; hence, the circuits to this equipment are Class 1. The thermostat circuit fulfills all requirements of a Class 2 circuit and can be short-circuited or broken without introducing any hazard. The wiring of this circuit can therefore be done with any type of wire or cable that is sufficiently protected from physical damage to ensure serviceability.

725-11. Power Limitations for Class 1 Circuits.   Class 1 systems may operate at any voltage not exceeding 600 V. They are, in many cases, merely extensions of light and power systems, and, with a few exceptions, are subject to all the installation rules for light and power systems.

Part **(a)** requires that Class 1 power-limited circuits must have energy limitation on the power source that supplies them. And such circuits may be supplied from either a transformer or another type of power supply—such as a generator, batteries, or manufactured power supply. Note that a Class 1 power-limited circuit must be supplied at NOT OVER 30 V, 1,000 VA.

Part **(b)**, however, permits Class 1 remote-control or signaling circuits to operate at up to 600 V, and no limitation is placed on the power rating of the source to such circuits (Fig. 725-4).

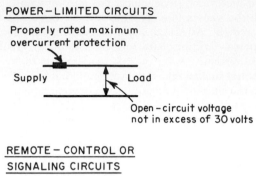

POWER—LIMITED CIRCUITS

Properly rated maximum
overcurrent protection

Supply　　　　　　　Load

Open – circuit voltage
not in excess of 30 volts

REMOTE – CONTROL OR
SIGNALING CIRCUITS

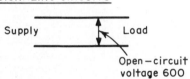

Supply　　　　　　Load

Open – circuit
voltage 600

Fig. 725-4. Class 1 circuits are divided into two maximum voltages. (Sec. 725-11.)

The most common example of a Class 1 remote-control system is the circuit wiring and devices used for the operation of a magnetically operated motor controller. The term *remote-control switch* is used in various **Code** references to designate a switch or contactor used for the remote control of a feeder or branch circuit, with the operating-coil circuit as a Class 1 remote-control circuit.

The signaling systems which are included in Class 1 operate at 115 V with 20-A overcurrent protection, though they are not necessarily limited to this voltage and current. Some of the signaling systems which may be so operated include electric clocks, bank alarm systems, and factory call systems. An example of a lower voltage Class 1 signaling system is a nurses' call system, as used in hospitals. Such systems commonly operate at not over 25 V.

The vast majority of control circuits for magnetic starters and contactors could not qualify as Class 2 or Class 3 circuits because of the relatively high energy required for operating coils. And any control circuit rated over 150 V (such as 220- or 440-V coil circuits) can never qualify, regardless of energy.

Class 1 control circuits include all operating-coil circuits for magnetic starters or contactors which do not meet the requirements for Class 2 or Class 3 circuits. Class 1 circuits must be wired in accordance with Secs. 725-11 to 725-20.

725-12. Overcurrent Protection. In general, conductors for any Class 1 remote-control, signaling, or power-limited circuit must be protected against overcurrent. No. 14 and larger wires must generally be protected at their ampacities from Table 310-16. In the second sentence of this rule, an important statement indicates that it is *not* necessary to take any ampere derating—for either elevated ambient temperature or for more than three wires in a conduit or cable. The wires may simply be used and protected at the ampacity values given in the table.

Important. The statement "Derating factors *shall not* be applied" is a strange prohibition, which can be disregarded without violating this or any **Code** rule. And there seems to be a conflict between that statement and the requirement in Sec. 725-17 that Class I conductors must be derated under some conditions.

It is important to note that No. 18 and No. 16 control or signal-circuit conductors must always be protected at 7 or 10 A, respectively. Those smaller sizes of wire may be used for control and signal circuits supplying coils, relays, or signal devices that are current loads up to 10 A, as recognized by the first sentence of Sec. 725-16(a).

The rule of Exception No. 2 is the same as that of Sec. 240-3, Exception No. 2, but applies to the case where the 2-wire transformer secondary supplies a control circuit to one or more operating coils in motor starters or magnetic contactors. A properly sized circuit breaker or fuses may be used at the supply end of the circuit that feeds the transformer primary and may provide overcurrent protection for the primary conductors, for the transformer itself, and for conductors of the control circuit which is run from the transformer secondary to supply power to motor starters or other control equipment, as follows:

1. The primary-side protection must not be rated greater than that required by Sec. 450-3(b)(1) for transformers rated up to 600 V. For a transformer rated 9 A or more, the rating of the primary CB or fuses must not be greater than 125 percent of (1.25 times) the rated transformer primary current. And if 1.25 times rated primary current does not yield a value exactly the same as a standard rating of fuse or CB, the next-higher-rated standard protective device may be used. Where the transformer rated primary current is less than 9 A—as it would be for all the usual control transformers rated 5,000 VA and stepping 480 V down to 120 V—the maximum permitted rating of primary protection must not exceed 167 percent of (1.67 times) the rated primary current. For a transformer with a primary rated less than 2 A, the primary protection must never exceed 300 percent of (3 times) the rated primary current. With the vast majority of control transformers—with primary ratings well below 10 A—fuse protection will be required on the primary because the smallest standard CB rating is 15 A, and that will generally exceed the maximum values of primary protection permitted by Sec. 450-3(b)(1) (Fig. 725-5).

2. Primary protection must not exceed the amp rating of the primary circuit conductors. And when protection is sized for the transformer, as described above, No. 14 copper primary conductors will be protected well within their 15-A rating.

3. Secondary conductors for the control circuit can then be selected to have an ampacity at least equal to the rating of primary protection times the primary-to-secondary transformer voltage ratio. Of course, larger conductors may be used if needed to keep voltage drop within limits.

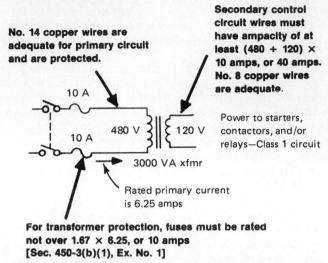

No. 14 copper wires are
adequate for primary circuit
and are protected.

Secondary control
circuit wires must
have ampacity of at
least (480 + 120) ×
10 amps, or 40 amps.
No. 8 copper wires
are adequate.

10 A

480 V   120 V

10 A

3000 VA xfmr

Power to starters,
contactors, and/or
relays—Class 1 circuit

Rated primary current
is 6.25 amps

For transformer protection, fuses must be rated
not over 1.67 × 6.25, or 10 amps
[Sec. 450-3(b)(1), Ex. No. 1]

Fig. 725·5. A separate control transformer supplying a number of coil
circuits for motor starters or magnetic contactors must have primary protection that protects the secondary control conductors as well as the
transformer. (Sec. 725-12.)

In Fig. 725-6, covering use of a magnetic contactor, No. 14 and larger remote-
control conductors may be properly protected by the feeder or branch-circuit
overcurrent devices if the devices are rated or set at not more than 300 percent
of (3 times) the ampacity of the control conductors. If the branch-circuit overcurrent devices were rated or set at more than 300 percent of the rating of the
control conductors, the control conductors would have to be protected by separate protective devices located within the contactor enclosure at the point
where the conductor to be protected receives its supply.

This is covered by Exception No. 3 of this section, which applies to the
remote-control circuit that energizes the operating coil of a magnetic contactor,
as distinguished from a magnetic motor starter. Although it is true that a magnetic starter is a magnetic contactor with the addition of running overload
relays, Exception No. 3 covers only the coil circuit of a magnetic contactor. That
applies to control wires for magnetic contactors used for control of lighting or
heating loads, but not motor loads. Section 430-72 covers that requirement for
motor-control circuits.

In Fig. 725-6, for instance, 45-A fuses at A in the feeder or branch circuit
ahead of the contactor would be adequate protection if No. 14 wire, with its
ampacity of 15 A (reduced from 20 A in Table 310-16 by the footnote to that
table), were used for the remote-control circuit, because 45 A is not more than
300 percent of (3 times) the 15-A ampacity. Larger fuses ahead of the contactor
would require overcurrent protection in the hot leg of the control circuit, at B,
rated not over 15 A. (See footnote to Table 310-16.)

It should be noted that the overcurrent protection is required for the control
conductors and not for the operating coil. Because of this, the size of control

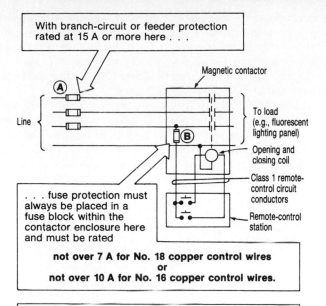

With branch-circuit or feeder protection rated at 15 A or more here . . .

Magnetic contactor

Ⓐ

Line

Ⓑ

To load (e.g., fluorescent lighting panel)

Opening and closing coil

Class 1 remote-control circuit conductors

Remote-control station

. . . fuse protection must always be placed in a fuse block within the contactor enclosure here and must be rated

not over 7 A for No. 18 copper control wires
or
not over 10 A for No. 16 copper control wires.

NOTE: If No. 14 or larger control-circuit wires are used, Exception No. 3 of this Section permits omission of separate protection in the control circuit when the rating of the branch-circuit or feeder protection does not exceed three times the ampacity of the particular size of control wire from Table 310-16.

EXAMPLE: 30-A fuses at "A" would be adequate protection if No. 14 wire, rated at 15 A, is used for the remote-control circuit, because 30 A is *less than* 3 × 15 A. If fuses at "A" were rated over 45 A, 15-A protection would be required at "B" for No. 14 wire.

Fig. 725-6. Protection of coil circuit of a magnetic contactor is similar to that of a starter. (Sec. 725-12.)

conductors can be selected to allow application without separate overcurrent protection. When overcurrent protection is added in the enclosure, its rating must be such that it conforms to the first paragraph of this rule.

725-14. Wiring Method. In general, wiring of Class 1 signal systems must be the same as power and light wiring, using any of the cable or raceway wiring methods that are **Code**-recognized for general-purpose wiring. The two Exceptions refer to the details of wiring permitted by Secs. 725-15, 725-16, and 725-17.

725-15. Conductors of Different Circuits in Same Cable, Enclosure, or Raceway. Any number and any type of Class 1 circuit conductors—for remote-control, for signaling, and/or for power-limited circuits—may be installed in the same conduit, raceway, box, or other enclosure—*if* all conductors are insulated for the maximum voltage at which any of the conductors operates.

Class 1 circuit wires (starter coil-circuit wires, signal wires, power-limited circuits) may be run in raceways by themselves in accordance with the first sentence of this section. A given conduit, for instance, may carry one or several sets of Class 1 circuit wires. And Sec. 725-14 says use of Class 1 wires must conform to the same basic rules from **NE Code** Chap. 3 that apply to standard power and light wiring.

But, it should be noted that two specific sections of the **NE Code** cover the use of Class 1 circuit conductors in the same raceway, cable, or enclosure containing circuit wires carrying power to a lighting load, a heating load, or to a motor load (Fig. 725-7). Section 300-3 covers the general use of "conductors of different systems" in raceways as well as in cable assemblies and in equipment wiring enclosures (i.e., cabinets, housings, starter enclosures, junction boxes, etc.).

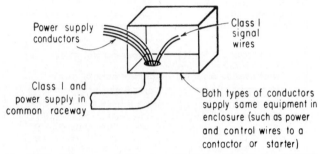

Fig. 725-7. This is permitted by Secs. 300-3(a) and 725-15. (Sec. 725-15.)

But Class 1 circuit wires are also regulated by this section, which strictly limits use of Class 1 wires in the same box and/or raceway with power wires. Figure 725-8 shows a clear violation, if the annunciator has no relationship to the motor load.

Note that this section permits Class 1 circuit wires to be installed in the same raceway or enclosure as "power supply" conductors *only* if the Class 1 wires

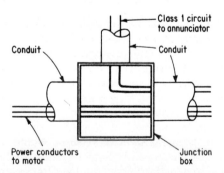

Fig. 725-8. Class 1 wires must *not* be used in raceways with "unrelated" wires. (Sec. 725-15.)

and the power wires are "functionally associated" with each other. That would be the case where the power conductors to a motor are run in the same conduit along with the Class 1 circuit wires of the magnetic motor starter used to control or to start or stop the motor. Refer to the commentary in Sec. 300-3.

The same permission would apply to the hookup of a magnetic contactor controlling a lighting or heating load, as shown in Fig. 725-9. There, the circuit

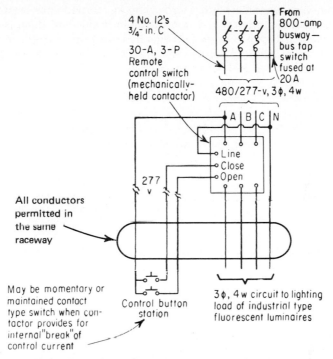

Fig. 725-9. Class 1 wires and power wires may be used in same raceway for "functionally associated" equipment. (Sec. 725-15.)

wires for the Class 1 remote-control run to the pushbutton station may be run in the same conduit carrying the wires supplying the lighting fixtures. A typical application would have the magnetic contactor adjacent to a panelboard, with the control and power wires run in the same raceway to a box at some point where it is convenient to bring the control wires down to the control switch and carry the power wires to the lighting fixtures being controlled. The contactor can be located at the approximate center of its lighting load to keep circuit wiring as short as possible for minimum voltage drop and the control wires are then carried to one or more control points. In such a layout, the control wires and power wires are definitely "functionally associated" because the control wires provide the ON-OFF function for the lighting. BUT, other control or power wires are prohibited from being in the same conduit, boxes, or enclosures with the single set of associated Class 1 and power wires.

Note: Exception No. 1 in this section permits power and control wires for more than one motor in a common raceway. Factory- or field-assembled control centers may group power and Class 1 control conductors that are not "functionally associated." This Exception recognizes the use of listed motor control centers that have power and control wiring in the same wireway or gutter space supplying motors that are *not* "functionally associated." The basic rule generally prohibits that condition when hooking up motor circuits.

Exception No. 2 says that Class 1 circuit conductors and unassociated power-supply conductors are permitted in a manhole if either of them is in metal-enclosed cable or Type UF cable *or* if effective separation is provided between the Class 1 conductors and the power conductors. This new Exception covers the conditions under which Class 1 conductors and unrelated power conductors may be used in the same enclosure (a manhole).

725-16. Conductors.   Figure 725-10 shows this basic rule, which accepts use of building wire to a minimum No. 14 size. BUT, No. 16 or No. 18 fixture wires of the types specified in part **(b)** *may* be used for running starter coil circuits, signal circuits, and any other Class 1 circuits. Of course, use of No. 16 or No. 18

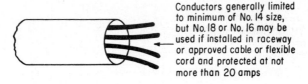

Conductors generally limited
to minimum of No. 14 size,
but No. 18 or No. 16 may be
used if installed in raceway
or approved cable or flexible
cord and protected at not
more than 20 amps

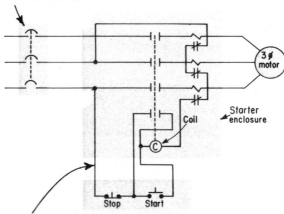

EXAMPLE :

If branch-circuit protection is
rated at 15 A or 20 A . . .

. . . the Class 1 remote-control wires may be
No. 18 or No. 16 fixture wire or No. 14
building wire, depending upon the ampere
load of the starter coil.

Fig. 725-10. No. 16 or No. 18 fixture wire may be used for Class 1 circuits. (Sec. 725-16.)

fixture wire for Class 1 circuits depends upon such conductors having sufficient ampacity for the current drawn by the contactor or relay operating coil or by whatever control device is involved. Wires larger than No. 16 must be building types (TW, THW, THHN, etc.). Class 1 circuits may not use fixture wires larger than No. 16. And ampacity of any Class 1 circuit wires larger than No. 16 must have that value shown in Table 310-16.

Note: Section 402-5 shows that the ampacity of any No. 18 fixture wire is 6 A and the ampacity of any No. 16 fixture wire is 8 A. Any No. 18 or No. 16 fixture wire or No. 14 building wire used for a Class 1 circuit is considered adequately protected by a fuse or CB rated not over 20 A. See Secs. 725-12 and 240-4.

725-17. Number of Conductors in Cable Trays and Raceway, and Derating.   The number of Class 1 remote-control, signal, and/or power-limited circuit conductors in a conduit must be determined from Tables 1 through 5 in Chap. 9 of the NE Code.

When more than three class 1 circuit conductors are used in a raceway, ampacity derating of Note 8, Table 310-16, applies only if the conductors carry continuous loads in excess of 10 percent of the ampacity of each conductor (Fig. 725-11). This rule is aimed at relieving the need to derate conductors that are

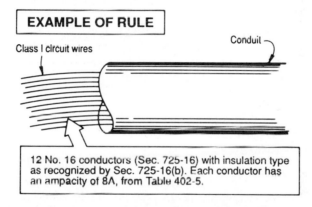

> **EXAMPLE OF RULE**
>
> Class I circuit wires   Conduit
>
> 12 No. 16 conductors (Sec. 725-16) with insulation type as recognized by Sec. 725-16(b). Each conductor has an ampacity of 8A, from Table 402-5.

> **Derating of conductor ampacity (Note 8, Table 310-16) is required (70% of 8A) only if these conductors carry "continuous loads" in excess of 10% of 8A, or 0.8A. If each conductor carries no more than 0.8A, no derating is required.**
>
> With 12 wires at 0.8A, the total heating effect is equivalent to 12 x 0.8, or a total of 9.6A divided among the 12 conductors. If the conductors carry different load currents but their sum does not exceed 9.6A, it would be reasonable to eliminate derating. But even if loading is greater than 9.6A and derating is required, using the 70% factor from Note 8 for 10 to 24 conductors gives each No. 16 wire here an ampacity of 0.7 x 8A or 5.6A—which is the amount of current each conductor is rated to carry continuously.

Fig. 725-11. Determining conductor ampacity for more than three Class I circuit wires in a raceway requires careful evaluation of conditions and the Code rule. (Sec. 725-17.)

usually carrying very low values of current (like up to 2 A for the vast majority of coil circuits of contactors and motor starters). The wording does not spell out whether all the conductors are carrying continuous current or if only some of them are. Actual application of this rule can get involved, depending upon the number of conductors and the type of devices they supply. And it is important to note that there is a direct contradiction of this requirement for derating in the flat statement in Sec. 725-12 that "Derating factors shall not be applied" to Class I circuit wires that are No. 14 or larger.

The same concept of "10 percent of the ampacity of each conductor" has been applied in part **(b)(1)** and **(2)** of Sec. 725-17.

When power conductors and Class 1 circuit conductors are used in a single conduit or EMT run (as permitted by Sec. 725-15), the derating factors of Note 8 must be applied as follows:

1. Note 8 must be applied to all conductors in the conduit when the remote-control conductors carry continuous loads in excess of 10 percent of each conductor's ampacity and the total number of conductors (remote-control and power wires) is more than three. For example, in Fig. 725-12, the conduit size must be selected according to the number and sizes of the wires.

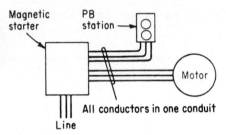

Fig. 725-12. Derating of conductor ampacity is usually not required for this circuit makeup. (Sec. 725-17.)

Because two of the control wires to the pushbutton and the power wires to the motor will carry a continuous load that is usually less than 10 percent of conductor ampacity, a derating factor of 80 percent (from Note 8) does not have to be applied.

2. Note 8 must be applied only to the power wires when the remote-control wires do not carry continuous load and when the number of power wires is more than three. In Fig. 725-13, no derating at all is applied because the control wires do not carry continuous current (only for the instant of switching operation), and there are only three power wires.

Those rules of part **(b)** have created controversy. It usually starts with the question, If a conduit from a starter carries the three power wires of a motor circuit and also contains three control wires run from the starter to a pushbutton station, is it necessary to derate any of the conductor ampacities?

Answer: Section 725-17(b) covers this. (Read that rule several times.) If the starter is the usual magnetically held type of contactor, the two control wires to the STOP button at the pushbutton station will carry the holding current to the coil as long as the starter is closed. Section 725-17(b)(1) says that all conductors

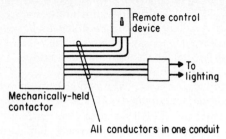

Fig. 725-13. Derating is not required here if Class 1 conductors do not carry continuous load. (Sec. 725-17.)

in the raceway must be derated in ampacity if the total number of conductors (power wires plus control wires) is more than three—*but only if the Class 1 circuit conductors carry continuous loads* of more than 10 percent of conductor ampacities.

The **Code** definition for *continuous load* is: "A load where the maximum current is expected to continue for three hours or more." On that basis, derating of all the conductors (power and control wires) would be required if the starter is left closed for 3 hr or more. It may be argued, however, that because the holding current of the coil is so low (only an amp or less in most cases), the load on the control wires (for instance, No. 14) is nowhere near the ampacity of those wires and does not constitute a "maximum current" in the meaning of the definition for continuous load; therefore, derating is not required for any of the conductors—as noted in Sec. 725-17(b)(2). But it may also be argued that because the three power wires in the conduit are rated at 125 percent of motor current and protected at that value by the OL relays, such conductors could be continuously subjected to maximum operating temperature by motor overload. Under such a condition, any additional current—even 1 A in the control wires—could produce heat that would push the temperature over the limit for the particular insulation.

Because motors are not generally even fully loaded and because continuous operation of motors at 25 percent overload is extremely unlikely, it would seem unreasonable to require derating of conductors for the usual conduit with three power wires and three control wires from a magnetic starter.

Conflict: All this consideration is further confused by a conflict between part **(b)(1)** of Sec. 725-17 and Exception No. 1 to Note 8 of Table 310-16/19, which states that derating factors apply *only* to the number of "power and lighting conductors." Part **(b)(1)** says derating applies to "all conductors"—Class 1 wires as well as the power and light wires.

The certain answer to the puzzle is this: Evaluate each installation on its own conditions and circumstances. Table 310-16 gives maximum continuous current ratings with not more than three conductors in a conduit. If for any control circuit layout, there is indication that the condition of maximum temperature is likely for the power wires, then all the wires must be derated if control wires in the same conduit would be adding any heat at all—even the I^2R of very low coil current.

And because Sec. 725-17, requiring derating under some conditions, is in Part **B Class I Circuits** of Art. 725, it should be noted that the second sentence of Sec. 725-12 (also in Part **B.**) flatly says "Derating factors shall not be applied"— and the words "shall not" makes it strangely mandatory.

We should always keep in mind:

The Code is a guide to safe electrical practice; it is not a design specification. Its rules must be analyzed and applied with knowledge, care, and precision.

725-18. Physical Protection.   This rule aims at providing high reliability and protection for those remote-control circuits where damage to the circuit might cause interruption or malfunction and thereby produce some type of hazard resulting from the controlled load.

725-31. Power Limitations of Class 2 and Class 3 Circuits.   Tables 725-31(a) and (b) set the current and voltage values that define Class 2 and Class 3 remote-control, signaling, or power-limited circuits. Class 2 and Class 3 signaling, remote-control, and power-limited systems are used where the current and voltage requirements are such that it is not necessary to comply with the general requirements for light and power systems.

Current supply from primary batteries is considered as providing satisfactory current limitation as indicated by Note 2 to Table 725-31(a). Where batteries are employed to supply small bell, buzzer, or annunciator systems, it is the usual practice to use several No. 6 dry cells in series. One of these cells will deliver 25 to 30 A on short circuit but the current falls off very rapidly. It would be possible to provide a dry-cell battery that would deliver a fairly heavy current for several hours; however, such batteries are not needed for these systems, and it is therefore safe to assume that they will not be installed and that, in any practical case, supply of the system from a primary battery will provide sufficient current limitation.

Wherever AC service is available, current limitation can be provided by using so-called "current-limiting" transformers. These are transformers having so high a secondary impedance that, even on short circuit, they cannot deliver a current higher than a certain maximum. A doorbell type of transformer will provide the required current limitation for a Class 2 system. In the NEMA Specialty Transformer Standards it is stated that the open-circuit secondary voltage for a doorbell transformer shall not exceed 25 V and that the maximum input with the secondary short-circuited shall be 50 W.

The NEMA Standards include the following data applying to the type known as signaling transformers.

Output ratings: 50 and 100 VA.

Secondary open-circuit voltages for either rating: 4.4, 8.8, 13.2, 17.6, 22.0, and 26.4 volts.

Secondary short-circuit current at maximum voltage: 50-VA rating, 2.1 amp, 100-VA rating, 4.2 amp. The secondary short-circuit current at any lower voltage is proportional to the voltage.

The great majority of small bell, buzzer, and annunciator systems come under Class 2 classification, 0 to 20 V, 5 A. This will also include small intercommunicating telephone systems in which the talking circuit is supplied by a primary battery and the ringing circuit by a transformer.

The Class 2 circuit category is considered to be safe from both a fire and shock standpoint. And, generally speaking, currents of 5 mA or less represent a negligible shock hazard. The maximum power of this 150-V circuit would be approximately 0.75 W.

When the **NE Code** divided low-power control, signal, and power-limited circuits into Class 2 and Class 3, the "Preprint of the Proposed Amendments for the 1974 **National Electrical Code**" presented valuable commentary on the reasons behind the revision. The comments also assist in application of the rules. Excerpts are as follows:

> 725-31 defines the power limitations and overcurrent protection for Class 2 and Class 3 circuits in table form. The separation of existing Class 2 circuits reflect what is now a practical reality since UL does not, in general, list Class 2 power supplies above 30 volts ac because of shock hazard even though the **NEC** permits them. This change together with the installation requirements will allow approved Class 3 systems at voltages above 30 volts ac. The new classifications recognize the acceptability of Class 2 circuits from both a shock and fire standpoint as evidenced by experience and recognizes that Class 3 circuits control fire hazard only and thus require additional safeguards. Also it is recognized that dc is less hazardous than ac from both let-go and fibrillation effects and the classifications reflect this to include the highly desirable 48-volt dc system under Class 2.
>
> Note 5 reflects that the historical acceptance of 30 volts was never intended for use in wet locations or where direct current was interrupted at a low frequency rate. Research work ... supports the need for the lesser voltage limits established where wet contact is likely to occur.
>
> The limitations permit the full 100 VA rating for power supplies irrespective of voltage as opposed to the present unnecessary restriction which permits maximum power only at the upper end of each voltage band. The maximum currents and VA outputs for ac circuits reflect the currently acceptable UL limits on presently listed Class 2 power supplies. The other limits for nontransformer supplies are considered reasonable to limit power to the same degree. It will be noted that the power limits are less restrictive where fuses are used. It will also be noted that the previous permission to derive a Class 2 circuit only from a fuse has been deleted. It was felt that a Class 2 system supplied from a source of unlimited energy and limited only by a fuse (as presently permitted, but probably rarely done in practice) should not be permitted, thus the V_{max}, I_{max} and $(VA)_{max}$ restrictions in Table 725-31.
>
> With regard to overcurrent protection, where adjustable or settable it can be based on 100 VA/V rated but not to exceed 5 amperes (last column). It is not the intent to create a new line of noninterchangeable fuses: the industry standard ratings should still be used.

Important: As Table 725-31 (a) indicates, any remote-control, signaling, or power-limited circuit operating at *less* than 30 V may only be a Class 2 circuit. All Class 3 circuits operate between 30 and 150 V.

725-34. Marking.   The UL presents data on its certification of transformer power supply units, as follows:

> These transformers are intended for use in Class 2 remote control and signal circuits in accordance with the **National Electrical Code.**
> The secondary open circuit voltage rating is 30 V or less.
> The transformers are of two types:
> Energy limiting transformer—The design is such that the short circuit current does not exceed 8 amp.
> Nonenergy limiting transformer—The design includes an over-current protective

device complying with the Class 2 system voltage and current limits specified in the **National Electrical Code**. The rating is 100 va or less.

The Listing Mark of Underwriters Laboratories Inc. on the product is the only method provided by UL to identify products manufactured under its Listing and Follow-Up Service. The Listing Mark for these products includes the name and/or symbol of Underwriters Laboratories Inc. (as illustrated in the Introduction of this Directory) together with the word "Listed," a control number, and the following product name: "Class 2 Transformer."

725·37. Wiring Methods on Supply Side.   Conductors and equipment on the line side of devices supplying Class 2 systems must conform to rules for general power and light wiring.

725·38. Wiring Methods and Materials on Load Side.   The present wording of this rule and its Exceptions clarifies many past misunderstandings about the intent of the rule. Previous **Code** editions only mentioned raceways, porcelain tubes, or "loom" as a means of separating Class 2 circuits, such as "bell wiring," from conductors of light and power systems where such systems were closer than 2 in. And on that basis, some inspectors required such bell wiring or similar Class 2 wires to have a 2-in. clearance from any type of cable (NM, UF, AC, etc.) that contained conductors for power or lighting circuits. The old rule was also commonly applied to prohibit bell wires and NM cables in the same bored holes through studs, etc. With the present wording the 2-in. clearance from Class 2 wiring applies only to "open" light, power, and Class 1 circuit conductors. Power and light circuits or Class 1 circuits that are in raceway or cable do not require 2-in separation from Class 2 and/or Class 3 circuits (Fig. 725-14).

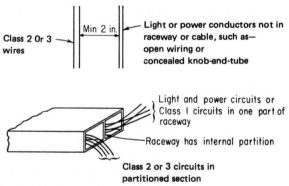

Fig. 725·14. Class 2 or Class 3 wiring must be separated from open-wiring for power and light. (Sec. 725-38.)

Class 2 or Class 3 conductors must be insulated and must be separated at least 2 in. from open power and light conductors, unless the Class 2 or Class 3 conductors are enclosed in a continuous and firmly fixed nonconductor.

Part **(a)(2)** says that Class 2 or Class 3 conductors must not be used in any raceway, compartment, outlet box, or similar fitting with light and power conductors or with Class 1 signal or control conductors, unless the conductors of the different systems are separated by a partition. But this does not apply to wires in outlet boxes or similar fittings or devices, where power-supply conductors have to be brought in to supply power to the signal equipment to which the other conductors in the enclosure are connected.

In hoistways, conductors must be installed in rigid conduit, IMC, or EMT, except as provided for elevators in Art. 620.

In part **(a)(4)**, Class 2 or Class 3 circuit conductors in *shafts* must be separated not less than 2 in. from conductors for light, power, Class 1, or non-power-limited fire-protective signaling circuits in the shaftway.

The rule of part **(b)(3)** requires separation of Class 2 and Class 3 circuits, *unless* the Class 2 wires have insulation that is at least equivalent to that required for Class 3 wires.

725·49. Fire Resistance of Cables Within Buidings.   In Secs. 725-49, 725-50, 725-51, and 725-53, extensive new requirements are presented on fire resistance and other characteristics of UL-listed Class 2 and Class 3 conductors and PLTC (power-limited tray cable). This is very detailed information on the variety of cables commonly used today for signal, remote control, and alarm circuits. These sections cover single- and multiconductor cables of Class 2 and Class 3 circuits installed "within buidlings," in "vertical runs," and in "ducts, plenums, and other airhandling spaces."

Here, distinction must be made between Class 2 and Class 3 wiring. Although any type of insulation is permitted for the conductors of Class 2 systems, in order to ensure continuity of service, a type of insulation should be selected which is suitable for the conditions, such as the voltage to be employed and possible exposure to moisture.

There is a marked distinction between power-limited circuits supplied by limited power sources with overcurrent protection and those without; but within the same source category, little difference exists in the power limitation.

The significant distinction between Class 2 circuits and Class 3 circuits is the character and magnitude of the voltages. The classifications of Class 2 circuits recognize their acceptability from both fire and shock hazard. Class 3 circuits recognize fire hazard only; hence the reason for more restrictive conductor and insulation requirements.

Low-voltage relay switching is a common application of Class 2 remote-control circuits regulated by Art. 725. Low-voltage relay switching is commonly used where remote control or control from a number of spread-out points is required for each of a number of small 120- or 277 V lighting or heating loads. In this type of control, contacts operated by low-voltage relay coils are used to open and close the hot conductor supplying the one or more luminaires or load devices controlled by the relay. The relay is generally a 3-wire, mechanically held, ON-OFF type, energized from a step-down control transformer.

In some cases, all the relays may be mounted in an enclosure near the panelboard supplying the branch circuits which the relays switch, with a single transformer mounted there to supply the low voltage. Where a single panelboard serves a large number of lighting branch circuits over a very large area—such as large office areas in commercial buildings—a number of relays associated with each section of the overall area may be group-mounted in an enclosure in that area.

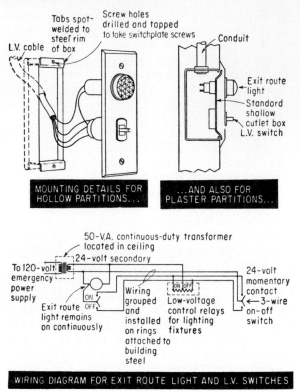

Fig. 725-15. Low-voltage relay switching is a typical application of Class 2 conductors. (Sec. 725-49.)

Figure 725-15 shows 24-V control of 277-V fixtures, with constantly illuminated switchplates alongside doorways to define interior exit routes and practical hollow-partition clip-in switch boxes in interior labs of a medical research center. Control relays are in compact boxes atop luminaires. Relays are connected to switches and to 50-VA continuous-duty 120/24-V transformers by Class 2 remote-control circuits routed through overhead non-air-handling ceiling plenums and supported by insulator rings attached to fixture hangers by spring clips. Wiring of the Class 2 circuits may be done with multiwire low-voltage cable, such as 3-conductor or 4-conductor thermostat cable. Interior-area route-indicating lights and general lighting switches are mounted together in thin boxes set in partitions.

Low-voltage lighting—using recessed and/or surface-mounted fixtures containing 12-V, 20-W incandescent reflector lamps—is another application of Class 2 wiring for the power-limited circuits supplying the lamps from a transformer. In such lighting systems, which have gained popularity for interior decorative and architectural purposes, the supply transformers are available in three ratings—20 VA for one lamp, 60 VA for three lamps, and 180 VA for nine lamps. Note that the 180-VA transformer exceeds the voltampere rating of "5.0

$\times V_{max}$" for a Class 2 circuit up to 20 V. At the specified maximum voltampere rating, the 60-VA transformer (5.0 $\times$ 12 V) is the maximum size that complies with Table 725-31(a).

ARTICLE 760.　FIRE PROTECTIVE SIGNALING SYSTEMS

760-1. Scope. NFPA No. 71, Central Station Signaling Systems, pertains to fire protective signaling alarm services which are transmitted to a privately owned central station building from whence the fire department is notified or other action is taken as deemed appropriate. The types of services provided include manual fire alarm service, guard tour supervisory service, automatic fire detection and alarm service, sprinkler system waterflow alarm, and supervisory signal service.

NFPA No. 72A, Local Protective Signaling Systems, covers provisions for supervised systems providing fire alarm or supervisory signals within the protected premises. These systems are primarily for the protection of life by indicating the necessity for evacuation of the building and secondarily for the protection of the property. The systems may provide for (1) manual fire alarm service; (2) automatic fire alarm service; (3) automatic detection of alarm or abnormal conditions in extinguishing systems, such as sprinkler and carbon dioxide; (4) watchmen's supervisory service; and (5) automatic detection of abnormal conditions in industrial processes which could result in a fire or explosion hazard affecting safety to life.

NFPA No. 72B, Auxiliary Protective Signaling Systems, provides protection to an individual occupancy or building or to a group of buildings of a single occupancy and utilizes the municipal fire alarm facilities to transmit an alarm to the fire department. An auxiliary alarm system deals with equipment and circuits in the protected property and is connected to a municipal fire alarm system to summon the fire department.

There are three types of auxiliary alarm systems, which include (1) local energy type, which provides its own power supply and is electrically isolated from the municipal alarm systems; (2) shunt type, which is electrically connected to and is an integral part of the municipal alarm system; and (3) a direct circuit, in which the alarms are transmitted over a circuit directly connected to the annunciating switchboard at the fire department headquarters.

Proprietary and local systems may be auxiliarized, in which case NFPA No. 72B would apply to the circuitry between the proprietary or local system and the transmitting device.

NFPA No. 72C, Remote Station Protective Signaling Systems, pertains to a system of electrically supervised circuits employing a direct circuit connection between signaling devices at the protected premises and signal receiving equipment at a remote station, such as a municipal fire alarm headquarters, a fire station, or another location acceptable to the authority having jurisdiction. The type of signaling services include (1) automatic fire detection and alarm service; (2) sprinkler system waterflow alarm and supervisory signal service; (3) manual fire alarm service; and (4) automatic smoke alarm service.

NFPA No. 72D, Proprietary Protective Signaling Systems, deals with electrically operated circuits designed to transmit alarms and supervisory and trouble signals for the protection of life and property to a central supervising station at the property to be protected. This system shall be maintained and tested by owner personnel or an organization satisfactory to the authority having jurisdiction.

NFPA No. 73, Public Fire Service Communications, covers the municipal fire alarm system, telephone facilities, and fire department radio facilities, all of which fulfill two principal functions: that of receiving fire alarms or other emergency calls from the public and that of retransmitting these alarms and emergency calls to fire companies and other interested agencies.

Fire alarm systems on private premises from which signals are received directly or indirectly by the communications center are covered by other NFPA standards.

NFPA No. 74, Household Fire Warning Equipment, covers the proper selection, installation, operation, and maintenance of fire warning equipment. The primary intent of this standard is to alert occupants for protection of life. This consists of a system or device which produces an audible alarm indicating the need to evacuate the premises. The types of detection devices used to sense fires are heat detectors and smoke detectors. Heat detectors should never be used by themselves, but must be used in conjunction with smoke detectors.

Many building codes and others (such as NFPA No. 501B, Mobile Homes) require at least one smoke detector located between the sleeping areas and other parts of the residence. Obviously a full-protection system, consisting of heat detectors and/or smoke detectors in each major area of the home, will give the best protection; however, one or more smoke detectors will provide a degree of protection. NFPA No. 74 should be consulted for placement and number of detection devices to be used; in addition, local building codes may require the use of full systems or individual smoke detectors.

760-2. Location and Other Articles.   The Exception to part **(b)** involves use of plastic-jacketed cables in air-handling ceilings. The same considerations are involved here as described under Sec. 725-2.

ARTICLE 770. OPTICAL FIBER CABLES

770-1. Scope.   In the Technical Committee Reports on development of the 1984 NE Code, the following substantiation was given for adding Art. 770 to the Code:

> Fiber optic technology should be included in the Code to permit its orderly development and usage for communications, signaling and control circuits in lieu of metallic conductors. It is reasonable for an optical fiber cable to be installed in electrical raceway and enclosures along with associated electrical conductors. An example of such an application is an optical fiber control circuit for electrically noisy equipment. Since optical fibers are not affected by electrical noise, one could, if permitted by the Code, run the optical fiber cable in the same raceway with the power wiring. A further exam-

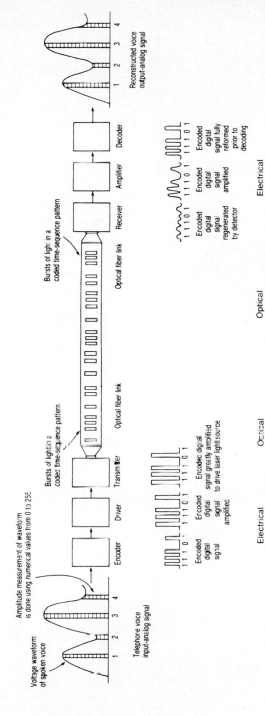

Fig. 770-1. The transmission of a signal (left to right) along an optical fiber link (a cable) at center. At the left, an electrical signal is converted to light pulses that are sent through the fiber cable by a laser diode (a light signal generator), and then, at the right, the light pulses are received and reconstructed into the original electrical signal from the left.

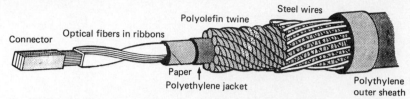

Fig. 770-2. This fiber-optic cable, which is used in a mile-long telephone communication line, is classified as a "conductive" type of optical fiber cable because of the steel wires used to provide an outer mechanical sheath over the fiber assembly.

Fig. 770-3. FO conductors are used as data communication links between five different buildings in which a banking firm has branch locations in a large city. The overall circuiting includes the runs within the buildings (connecting to computers, video equipment, telephones, and telecommunications equipment) and over 5 mi. of underground 30-conductor FO cable with a metal armor sheath—run under the city streets in ducts. A NEMA 3R splice box in the tel-

ple is the use of optical fiber communications cable. One would expect to place this cable in a common raceway along with ordinary metallic conductor telephone cable. However, if the **Code** is not changed to recognize optical fiber technology, a separate conduit system may be demanded by some local authorities.

The proposed article divides optical fiber cables into three types: nonconductive, conductive and hybrid. Obviously the nonconductive types cannot be accidentally energized when placed in raceway so it is proposed that they be permitted in raceway with conductors for electric light, power or Class 1 circuits operating at less than 600 volts only where the functions of optical fiber cables and electrical conductors are associated. Since the conductive optical fiber cables have a potential for inadvertent

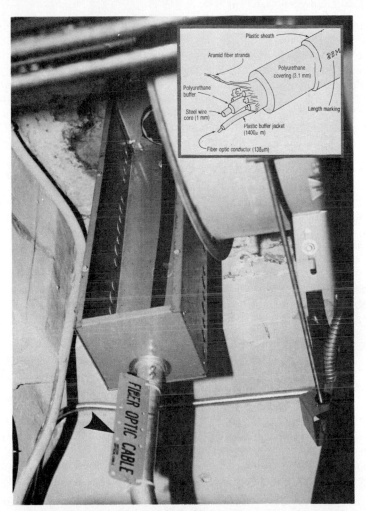

ecommunications room of one of the buildings, with two 10-conductor cables entering at top (arrow) and the individual FO conductors terminated in special connectors (bottom arrow). (Right) A pullbox in a 1½-in. EMT run carrying the 10-conductor cables, with a bright orange tag identifying the FO conduit (inset shows FO cable). (Sec. 770-6.)

energizing of metallic strength members and metallic vapor barriers, it is proposed that
these cables be permitted to share raceway with low voltage wiring systems only, and
the conductive members of these cables must be grounded. Grounding (or isolation) is
also proposed for entrance cables in a manner consistent with the **Code** requirements
for ordinary communications cable.

The proposed article deals with fire properties of optical fiber cables in a manner
identical with other low voltage wiring.

The scope statement, in order to be consistent with the purpose of the **Code**, which
is the "practical safeguarding of persons and property from hazards arising from the
use of electricity," limits the coverage of the proposed article to joint installations of
electrical cable and optical fiber cable.

As part of the high-technology revolution in industrial and commercial building operations, the use of light pulses transmitted along optical fiber cables has
become an alternative method to electrical pulses on metal conductors for control, signals, and communications. The technology of fiber optics has grown
dramatically over recent years as a result of great strides in development of the
fiber cables and associated equipment that converts electrical pulses to light
pulses, and vice versa. For high rates of data transmission involved in data processing and computer control of machines and processes, optical fiber cables
far outperform metallic conductors carrying electrical currents—all at a small
fraction of the cost of metallic-conductor circuiting.

NEC Art. 770, "Optical Fiber Cables," covers the use of such cables in association with conventional metallic-conductor circuits. Nonconductive optical
fiber cables are permitted to be installed in the same raceway and enclosures
as metallic-conductor circuits where the functions of the two different types of
cables are associated with the same equipment, operation, or process.

Figure 770-1 shows operation of a fiber-optic (FO) link in the transmission of
a telephone signal.

770·6. Types.   Figure 770-2 shows an optical fiber cable that is a "conductive"
type, as covered in the descriptions of the three types of cables in this section.
Figure 770-3 shows details of a typical FO cable installation.

ARTICLE 780. CLOSED-LOOP AND
PROGRAMMED POWER
DISTRIBUTION

780·1. Scope.   This NEC article covers electrical distribution systems that are
controlled by signaling between energy-controlling equipment and energy-utilization equipment.

The purpose of this **Code** article is described in the substantiation given with
the proposal to include this in the **NEC:**

Article 780 is included to permit the orderly development and usage of Closed-Loop
Power Distribution systems. This method of power distribution offers advantages in
safety and new features over the present open-loop method.

With closed-loop control, any electrical circuit or appliance is activated only after
proper identification during a power startup sequence, and operation is continued only

so long as an acknowledgement signal is received from the equipment indicating normal operation. The control channel may also be used by the energy-consuming equipment to communicate operational status as well as to call for adjustments in the characteristics of the power being fed to the circuit.

SUBSTANTIATION: Closed-Loop Power Distribution Systems should be permittted because they have the following safety advantages:

a. Power feed to a branch circuit is initiated only when the energy-utilization equipment requests it by a characteristic electrical signal.

b. Power feed to a branch circuit continues only on continuous presence of a nominal operation signal from the energy-utilization equipment.

c. Power consumption is continuously monitored by the energy-control equipment, and power feed to the branch circuit is interrupted at any time that power consumption falls outside the range being requested by the energy-utilization equipment.

d. Low-voltage DC power that does not present a shock hazard is provided to appliances that can utilize it.

Chapter Eight

ARTICLE 800. COMMUNICATIONS CIRCUITS

800-1. Scope.   The sections of this chapter apply basically to those systems which are connected to a central station and operate as parts of a central-station system.

The paragraph titled "**Code** Arrangement" of the "Introduction to the **Code**" (Sec. 90-3) states that Chap. 8, which includes Art. 800, "Communication Systems," is independent of the preceding chapters except as they are specifically referred to.

800-52. Installation of Conductors.   It should be noted that the requirements of Secs. 800-50 and 800-51, covering the listing and marking of the various types of communications wires and cables, are related to the rules of Sec. 800-52 and give authorities enforcing the **Code** the tools whereby they can judge whether the types of cables used in communication circuits substantially contribute to the hazards during fire conditions where fire fighters must of necessity be subjected to these products of combustion. Statistics show that most people die from smoke and products of combustion and not from the heat of fires. Because of this fact it is imperative that electrical materials which contribute products of combustion be held to a minimum. The requirements give electrical inspectors and fire marshals criteria whereby they can judge the hazards which conductors contribute to fire problems.

See discussion of the Exception to Sec. 725-2(b).

ARTICLE 810. RADIO AND TELEVISION EQUIPMENT

810-13. Avoidance of Contacts with Conductors of Other Systems.   For service drops and conductors on the exteriors of buildings, the requirements for insulating covering and methods of installation depend upon the likelihood of crosses occurring between signal conductors and light or power conductors. Where communication wires are run on poles in streets, it is assumed that they are exposed to contact with other wires. But where the overhead wires are run in an alley or from building to building and kept away from streets, lighter insulation is permitted.

Where a communication system is connected to a distribution system that is entirely underground except within the block in which the building is located, and any overhead wires in alleys or attached to buildings are not likely to become crossed with light or power wires, nearly all restrictions as to insulating covering and methods of installation are eliminated.

810-14. Splices.   The antenna may unavoidably be so located that in case of a break in the wire it may come in contact with electric light or power wires. For this reason, the wire should be of sufficient size to have considerable mechanical strength, and the joints should be as reliable as the wire. Joints will have sufficient mechanical strength if properly made with the standard double-tube connectors used in telephone and telegraph work.

810-19. Electric Supply Circuits Used in Lieu of Antenna—Receiving Stations.   The device referred to usually consists of a small fixed capacitor connected between one wire of the lighting circuit and the antenna terminal of the receiving set. As most receiving sets are arranged, a breakdown in this capacitor would result in a short circuit to ground through the antenna coil of the set, and the capacitor should therefore be one that is designed for operation at 300 V or higher in which mica is used as the dielectric so that it will have a high factor of safety.

810-20. Antenna Discharge Units—Receiving Stations.   Where the lead-in is enclosed in a continuous metallic shield, i.e., is run in rigid conduit or electrical metallic tubing, or consists of a lead-covered conductor or pair of conductors, and the metallic enclosure is well grounded, a lightning discharge will usually jump from the lead-in conductor to the metallic shield, because this path to ground offers a much lower impedance than the path through the antenna coil of the receiving set. A lightning arrester is therefore not required where the lead-in is so shielded.

810-21. Grounding Conductors—Receiving Stations.   In order to avoid potential differences between various masses of metal, in or on buildings, and lead-in conductors, the metal portions of antenna masts should never be grounded to soil pipes, soil vent pipes, metal gutters, downspouts, etc. In other words, grounding must be done in accordance with Art. 250, and it is required to use the same grounding electrode for the grounding of masts as for the electrical system in the building.

810-54. Clearance on Building.   The creepage distance is the distance from the conductor to the building measured on the surface of the supporting insulator. The air gap is the distance measured straight across from the conductor to the building.

810-57. Antenna Discharge Units—Transmitting Stations.   A transmitting station should be protected against lightning, either by an arrester or by a switch that connects the lead-in to ground and is kept closed at all times when the station is not in operation.

Chapter Nine

A. TABLES

Tables 1, 3A, 3B, and 3C do not apply where conduit sleeves are used to protect various types of cables from physical damage.

While Note 2 mentions bare (as well as insulated) equipment grounding or bonding conductors, Note 4 to **Code** Table 1 applies to all forms of *bare* conductors (equipment grounding conductors and neutral or grounded conductors). Where any bare conductors are used in conduit or tubing, the dimensions given in Table 8 may be used. Since *all* wires utilize space in raceways, they must be counted in calculating raceway sizes whether the conductors are insulated or bare. The only Exception to this is in the footnote to Table 350-3 for short lengths of ⅜-in. flexible metal conduit.

Note 4 allows compact-strand conductors to be used in conduit or tubing based on use of the actual (reduced) cross-sectional area of such conductors, rather than using the number of conductors permitted by **Code** Table 3A or 3B in Chapter 9.

In regard to Note 4 there are conductors (particularly high-voltage types) that do not have dimensions listed in Chap. 9. Conduit sizes for such conductors may be determined by computing the cross-sectional area of each conductor as follows:

$$D^2 \times 0.7854 = \text{cross-sectional area}$$

where D = outside diameter of conductor, including insulation. Then the proper conduit size can be determined by applying Tables 1 and 4 for the appropriate number of conductors.

example Three single-conductor, 5-kV cables are to be installed in conduit. The outside diameter (D) of each conductor is 0.750 in. Then $0.750^2 \times 0.7854 \times 3 = 1.3253$ sq in. From Tables 1 and 4 (40 percent fill) a 2-in. conduit would be required. **Code** Tables

3A, 3B, and 3C are based on Table 1 allowable percentage fills, and have been provided for the sake of convenience. In any calculation, however, Table 1 is the table to be used where any conflict may occur in Tables 3A, 3B, or 3C.

Table 1 is also used for computing conduit sizes where various sizes of conductors or conductor types are to be used in the same conduit. Tables 1, 3A, 3B, and 3C apply to new work or rewiring, exposed or concealed.

An example of Note 3 would be to determine how many No. 14 Type TW conductors would be permitted in a ½-in. conduit. For three or more such conductors, Table 1 permits a 40 percent fill. From Table 4, 40 percent of the internal cross-sectional area of a ½-in. conduit is 0.12 sq in. From Table 5 (column 5) the cross-sectional area of a No. 14 type TW conductor is 0.0135 sq in. Thus 0.12/0.0135 = 8.8, or 9 such conductors would be permitted in a ½-in. conduit. Where the decimal is less than 0.8 (such as 0.7), the decimal would be dropped and the whole number would be the maximum number of equally sized conductors permitted; e.g., 8.7 would be 8 conductors.

The following is an example for computing a conduit size for various conductor sizes:

Number	Wire Size and Type	Table 5 Cross-sectional Area (ea.)	Subtotal Cross-sectional Area
3	No. 10 TW	0.0224	0.0672
3	No. 12 TW	0.0172	0.0516
3	No. 6 TW	0.0819	0.2457
		Total cross-sectional area	0.3645

Table 1 permits a 40 percent fill for three or more conductors. Following the 40 percent column in Table 4, 1¼-in. conduit or tubing would be required for these nine conductors, which have a combined cross-sectional area of 0.3645 sq in.

Table 5B gives the maximum number of compact conductors permitted in trade sizes of conduit or tubing. Conductors with "compact-strand" construction have the cross-section areas of their strands shaped as trapezoids to provide tight "nesting" of the strands when they are twisted together. Such construction eliminates the air voids that occur when individual strands of circular cross section are twisted together and results in a smaller overall diameter of the total bundle of strands. Thus a 600-kcmil compact-strand assembly has an overall cross-section area of a conventional 500 kcmil with circular strands.

Note 4 of part **A. Tables** in Chap. 9 recognizes the fact that compact-strand conductors have increased conduit fill because of their overall smaller area. To cover such compact-strand conductors, Table 5B is in the **NEC**. The substantiation for the proposal to add this table to the **NEC** stated:

The '87 **NEC** gives maximum number of conductors in conduit or tubing as well as the dimensions for concentric lay conductors (Tables 3A, 3B, 3C, 5, 6, 7). Table 5A gives dimensions and areas for compact aluminum building wire. However, no Table lists maximum number of conductors in conduit or tubing for compact-stranded aluminum conductors. To add this table in Chap. 9 will provide consistency within Chap. 9 as well as providing a reference guide in the field for both installers and inspectors.

Table 10 gives "Expansion Characteristics of PVC Rigid Nonmetallic Conduit." This is an excellent source of important engineering data that ensures proper design, layout, and installation of rigid nonmetallic conduit runs. The substantiation for this proposed **Code** change stated as follows:

> Section 347-9 alerts an inspector to the requirement for expansion joints for rigid nonmetallic conduit. Now, the inspector must rely on manufacturer's literature, which is generally not available at the jobsite, for expansion characteristics. Generally, the expansion coupling will indicate an expansion/contraction range. With this chart included in Chap. 9, the inspector can determine the proper number of expansion couplings for a conduit run in an accurate, timely fashion.

And the same benefit will accrue to design engineers, electrical contractors, and operating personnel.

B. EXAMPLES

In Chap. 9, part **B**, the **NE Code** offers sample calculations using **Code** rules to determine load currents for several types of occupancies. It has been our experience that much confusion and many questions arise in applying the provisions of Arts. 220 and 230 to computing branch-circuit, feeder, and service loads in single-family residences. To clarify the brief calculation data given in the **Code** book, the following presents an expanded discussion of the steps covered in Examples 1(a) and 1(b). This will explore in detail **NE Code** examples of sizing the services and circuits for single-family dwellings (including individual apartments in multifamily dwellings), with and without air-conditioning units.

Two general procedures spelled out at the beginning of part **B**, Chap. 9, involve voltage values to be used and the method of handling fractions of an ampere in the calculations.

To standardize calculations, part **B** of Chap. 9 in previous **NEC** editions had specified that nominal voltages of 230 and 115 V are to be used in computing the ampere load on a conductor. [Dividing these voltages into the watts load will produce higher current values than would 240 and 120 V, thus resulting in larger (safer) conductor sizes.]

Now, however, the paragraph on "voltage" in part **B** has designated voltage values as "120, 240/120, 240, and 208Y/120." Although it says that those values "shall be used in computing the ampere load on the conductor," there would be no **Code** violation in making all ampere calculations with a voltage of 115 or multiples of 115 (or even lower values). Use of the lowest possible voltage value that might be encountered assures the greater adequacy of higher-ampere values when kilowatt or kilovoltampere ratings are divided by voltage to arrive at current values. The higher current values would dictate use of larger conductor sizes, with greater adequacy and safety. The use of values higher than 120 V (or multiples of it) would be a violation and would result in lower ampere values.

Where a particular calculation produces a current value involving a fraction of an ampere, the fraction may be dropped if it is 0.4 or less. Presumably, a value such as 20.7 A should be continued to be used as 20.7. We have chosen here to round off such values as the next higher whole number, in this case 21 A. Again, this is on the safe side. There are occasions, however, when current values must be added together. In such cases, it is on the safe side to retain fractions less than 0.5, since several fractions added together can result in the next whole ampere.

It is assumed that the loads in the following examples are properly balanced on the system. If they are not properly balanced on the system, additional feeder capacity may be required.

Example No. 1(a). One-Family Dwelling.   The basic dwelling we will consider here is assumed to have a total usable floor area of 1,500 sq ft. As indicated in Sec. 220-3(b), when load is determined on a voltamperes/square feet basis, those areas not used as normal living quarters are excluded from the area calculation. Open porches, garages, unfinished basements and attics, and unused areas are not counted as part of the house area. Area calculation is made using the *outside* dimensions of the "building, apartment, or other area involved."

example   A two-story dwelling 30 by 25 ft. First and second floors 30 by 25 ft by 2 = 1,500 sq ft. The "floor" area is computed from the "outside" dimension of the building and multiplied by the number of floors. [Section 220-3(b).]

Cooking will be done using a 12-kW electric range. And the house has a 5.5-kW 240-V electric dryer. The kilowatt ratings are taken as kilovoltampere values.

The steps taken in arriving at the branch-circuit and feeder loads follow.

General Lighting Circuits

Because lighting usage in dwelling occupancies is a random, noncontinuous application—with no control over sizes and types of light bulbs—the **Code** simply requires that a minimum amount of branch-circuit capacity be provided. Based on experience, the minimum required branch-circuit capacity will accommodate a fairly heavy and extensive use of general-purpose lighting fixtures in a home. Of course, if a given dwelling is provided with an unusually heavy amount of built-in indoor and outdoor lighting, then the provision of specific branch circuits for the loads is the best design approach.

Calculation of the **Code** minimum required branch-circuit capacity for general lighting is done also to determine the required capacity in feeders and service-entrance conductors.

In Sec. 220-3(b), the **NE Code** requires a minimum unit load in voltamperes/square feet for general lighting in the various types of occupancies listed in Table 220-3(b). For a dwelling occupancy (other than a hotel), circuit capacity for general lighting must be not less than 3 VA/sq ft times the square-foot area of usable living space. For the dwelling in this example, *minimum capacity for general lighting* would be

$$1{,}500 \text{ sq ft} \times 3 \text{ VA/sq ft or } 4{,}500 \text{ VA}$$

When the total load capacity of branch circuits for general lighting is known, it is a simple matter to determine how many lighting circuits are needed. By dividing the total load by 120 V, the total current capacity of circuits is determined:

$$\frac{4{,}500 \text{ VA}}{120 \text{ V}} = 37.5 \text{ A}$$

Then, using either 15- or 20-A, 2-wire, 120-V circuits (and not dropping the major fraction of an ampere),

$$\frac{3.75 \text{ A}}{15 \text{ A}} = 2.5$$

which means three 15-A circuits.

$$-\text{OR}-$$
$$\frac{37.5 \text{ A}}{20 \text{ A}} = 1.87$$

which means two 20-A circuits.

Small-Appliance Circuits

The next step is to provide for 20-A, 2-wire circuits to supply only receptacle outlets in the kitchen, pantry, breakfast room, dining room, and family room. Section 220-4(b) requires a minimum of *two* such small-appliance circuits.

In addition, Sec. 220-4(c) requires at least one 20-A, 2-wire appliance circuit for the receptacle outlet required by Sec. 210-52(f) at the laundry location.

Range Circuit

A branch circuit for the 12-kW range is selected in accordance with Note 4 of Table 220-19, which says that the branch circuit load for a range may be selected from the table itself. Under the heading "Number of Appliances," read across from 1. The maximum demand to be used in sizing the range circuit for a 12-kW range is shown under the heading "Maximum Demand" to be not less than 8 kW. The minimum rating of the range-circuit ungrounded conductors will thus be

$$\frac{8{,}000 \text{ VA}}{240 \text{ V}} = 33.33 \text{ or } 33 \text{ A}$$

Table 310-16 shows that the minimum size of copper conductors that may be used is No. 8 (TW—40 A, THW—50 A, XHHW or THHN—55 A). A 40-A circuit rating is also designated in Sec. 210-19(b) as the minimum size of conductor for any range rated 8¾ kW or more. And the UL regulation calls for 60°C circuit conductors for sizes No. 14 to No. 1—or use of 75°C or 90°C conductors at the ampacity of the corresponding size of 60°C conductor.

The overload protection for this circuit of No. 8 TW conductors would be 40-A *fuses or a 40-A circuit breaker*. THW or THHN or XHHW conductors must be used as if they are TW (60°C) wires and should not be protected at their higher ampacities.

Although the two hot legs of the 240/120-V, 3-wire circuit must be not smaller than No. 8, Exception No. 1 of Sec. 210-19(b) permits the neutral conductor to be smaller, but it specifies that it must have an ampacity not less than 70 percent of the branch-circuit rating (the rating of the protective device) and may never be smaller than No. 10.

For the range circuit in this example, the neutral may be rated

$$70 \text{ percent} \times 40 \text{ A (the rating of the CB of fuses)} = 28 \text{ A}$$

This calls for a *No. 10 neutral.*

If THHN or XHHW conductors are used for the hot legs, they must be used as 40-A wires, which calls for the No. 10 neutral. The No. 10 neutral would be acceptable for *any* of the conductor insulations (Fig. 1).

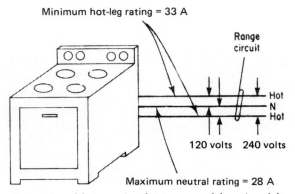

Fig. 1. Neutral for range is only 70 percent of the rating of the circuit protective device. (Chap. 9.)

The branch circuit for the dryer is sized from Sec. 220-18 at 5000 W (VA) or the nameplate rating, whichever is greater. The nameplate value of 5500 VA (5.5 kW) is used here:

$$\frac{5500 \text{ VA}}{240 \text{ V}} = 22.9 \text{ or } 23 \text{ A}$$

That calls for No. 10 wires.

Service Conductors

After calculating the required circuits for all the loads in the dwelling, the next step is to determine the minimum required size of service-entrance conductors to supply the entire connected load.

The **NE Code** procedure is the same as sizing feeder conductors for the entire load—as set forth in Sec. 220-10. Basically, the service "feeder" capacity must be not less than the sum of the loads on the branch circuits for the different applications.

The *general lighting load* is subject to demand factors from Table 220-11, which takes into account the fact that simultaneous operation of all branch-circuit loads, or even a large part of them, is highly unlikely. Thus, feeder capacity does not have to equal the connected load.

Sections 220-16(a) and (b) permit the *small appliance loads* to be added to the general lighting load before applying the demand factor from Table 220-11.

General lighting
[Three 15-A or two 20-A circuits] . . . . 4,500 VA
Kitchen appliance load (two circuits)
[1,500 VA/circuit, Sec. 220-16(a)] . . . . 3,000 VA
Laundry load
[One circuit, Sec. 220-16(b)] . . . . 1,500 VA

Total   9,000 VA

Then the demand factors are applied:
3,000 VA at 100 percent . . . . 3,000 VA
6,000 (9,000 − 3,000) VA at 35 percent . . . . 2,100 VA

Basic feeder load   5,100 VA

The feeder demand load for the 12-kW range must be added to the 5,100 VA. As stated in Sec. 220-19, the range feeder demand load is selected from **Code** Table 220-19. In this case, it is 8 kW (column A, one appliance).

Basic load . . . . 5,100 VA
Range feeder capacity . . . . 8,000 VA
Dryer load . . . . 5,500 VA

Total feeder load   18,600 VA

The minimum required ampacity of the ungrounded service-entrance conductors of a 240/120-V, 3-wire, single-phase service is readily found by dividing the *total feeder load* by 240 V:

$$\frac{18,600 \text{ VA}}{240 \text{ V}} = 77.5 \text{ or } 78 \text{ A}$$

Although a load current of that rating could be readily supplied by No. 3 copper TW, THW, THHN, or XHHW conductors, there is an important provision of Sec. 230-42(b) (2) that comes into play here. Where the initial computed total feeder load is 10 kW or more for a single-family dwelling, the ungrounded conductors of a service feeder must be rated at least 100 A; i.e., **the minimum capacity of the service-entrance hot legs = 100 A** (Fig. 2).

That would call for a minimum of one of the following:
- No. 1 TW copper conductors (110 A)
- No. 1 THW copper conductors (130 A)
- No. 1 THHN copper conductors (150 A)
- No. 1 XHHW copper conductors (150 A)
- No. 1/0 TW, THW, THHN, or XHHW aluminum conductors (100 to 135 A)

IMPORTANT NOTE: It is a basic UL requirement that switches, CBs, and panelboards be listed *only* with 60°C conductors in conductor sizes from No. 14 up to No. 1, unless any such piece of equipment is marked to indicate its use with conductors of higher temperature rating. The terminals on switches and breakers used as service equipment require the use of TW wire, in this case; or if higher temperature wires are used (THW, THHN, XHHW), they must be used at the ampacity of the corresponding size of TW wire. It would violate that

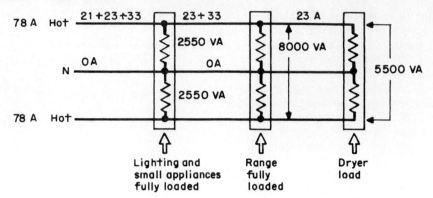

Fig. 2. Service hot legs are based on total demand load. (Chap. 9.)

UL rule to use No. 2 or No. 3 copper THW wire at its 115-A or 110-A rating for the service conductors, because TW wire in those sizes does not have a 100-A rating and would operate too hot with a 100-A load on it. Of course, in the example here, the calculated demand load current is only 78 A, and the 100-A rating of service-entrance conductors is dictated by the **Code** on the basis of experience with load additions over the life of the system. But when and if demand load does come up to 100 A, effective operation of a 100-A service CB or fused switch or panelboard would then require that the thermal condition at terminals not exceed that produced when the 100-A demand load is supplied by No. 1 TW (60°C) conductors, rated 110A. In any situations that pose difficulty in correlating **NE Code** rules and UL limiting conditions, it is in the best interests of real, long-time economy and reliable life of equipment to resolve all choices of conductor selection in favor of larger size and greater adequacy. Certainly, experience indicates that far too many services have to be increased in capacity shortly after installation simply because initial design was skimpy or based on squeezing as much as possible out of "apparent" ratings of equipment.

Service Neutral

Because a neutral conductor of a 3-wire, single-phase service carries only the unbalance (or difference in) current of the two hot legs, the **NE Code** does permit the very realistic reduction of neutral conductor size from the size of the service hot legs.

Section 220-22, which covers sizing of any feeder neutral, also applies to the neutral of a service. The neutral must have an ampacity at least equal to the maximum unbalance of loads connected from the two hot legs to the neutral. This load is taken to be "the maximum connected load between the neutral and any one ungrounded conductor" (hot leg). On a service of the type considered here, it is assumed that all the 120-V loads will be divided between the two hot legs, with one half connected from one hot leg to neutral and the other half connected from the other hot leg to neutral. Section 220-4(d) requires loads to be evenly proportioned among the branch circuits to assure optimum sharing

BALANCED LOAD

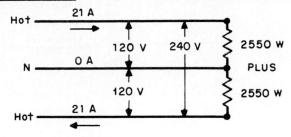

MAXIMUM UNBALANCED LOAD

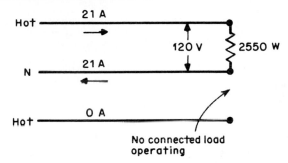

No connected load
operating

Fig. 3. Half of the total 120-V load is considered to be from hot leg
to neutral. (Chap. 9.)

of load by the hot legs of the service (Fig. 3). Thus, in the example here, half of
the 5,100-W basic demand load for the 120-V loads can be considered connected from either hot leg to neutral, and that would require ampacity in the
neutral of

$$\frac{5,100 \text{ W}}{2} \div 120 \text{ V} = 21.25 \text{ A}$$

Then, in addition, the neutral must have capacity for some unbalance in the
3-wire, 240/120-V circuit to the 12-kW range and in the 3-wire circuit to the
dryer. Section 220-22 notes that the feeder neutral load (i.e., the required
ampere capacity in the neutral service-entrance conductor) may be taken to be
"70 percent of the load on the ungrounded conductors." This recognizes that a
circuit to a range or dryer usually has some load connected from each hot leg
to neutral, requiring the neutral to carry *only* the unbalance. From the above
calculation of the current load on the hot legs of the range branch circuit (using
an 8,000-VA demand load for the 8,000-W range), it was found that the load
was 33 (actually 33.33) A. Then, as shown in Fig. 4, the feeder neutral ampacity
for the range load must be not less than

$$70 \text{ percent} \times 33.33 \text{ A} = 23.33 \text{ A}$$

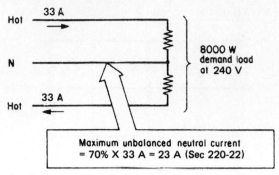

Fig. 4. Range neutral load is taken at 70 percent of hot leg current. (Chap. 9.)

And the feeder neutral ampacity for the dryer load must be at least

$$70 \text{ percent} \times 22.9 \text{ A} = 16.03 \text{ A}$$

Adding the three values of minimum neutral conductor ampacity for the different loads, the total minimum required neutral conductor ampacity is determined:

Neutral load, lights and appliances . . . . 21.25 A
Neutral load, range circuit . . . . 23.33 A
Neutral load, dryer circuit . . . . 16.03 A
      Total neutral load . . . . 60.61 A

Since 0.61 is greater than 0.5, the total neutral load should be rounded off from 60.61 A to 61 A. From the above, it is evident that some judgment must be exercised in dropping fractions. If the contributions to the neutral load had been rounded off to 21, 23, and 16 A, respectively, the total would have been 60 instead of 61. We chose to stay with the larger value since, if it ultimately makes any difference at all, it will be in the safe direction.

Of course, as with so many other calculations, there is more than one way to arrive at the same result. For instance, the total lighting and appliance load can be added to the total range demand load and dryer demand load, with both of the latter modified by a 70 percent neutral demand factor, and the grand total divided by 240 V to get the required amp capacity of the service neutral:

Lighting and small appliance load . . . . 5,100 VA
Range load (8,000 VA × 70 percent) . . . . 5,600 VA
Dryer load (5,500 VA × 70 percent) . . . . 3,850 VA
      Total . . . . 14,550 W

Then, since that is the total load that forms the basis for feeder unbalance to determine the required neutral capacity, there are two ways to determine the neutral load.

1. Under conditions of maximum possible unbalance, half of that total divided by 120 V yields the result:

$$\frac{14,550 \text{ VA}}{2} \div 120 \text{ V} = 60.6 \text{ A or } 61 \text{ A}$$

—OR—

2. Simply take the total load and divide it by 240 V, giving the same result:

$$\frac{14{,}550 \text{ VA}}{240 \text{ V}} = 60.6 \text{ A or } 61 \text{ A}$$

Selection of the neutral conductor can then be made from Table 310-16 as required for either copper or aluminum conductor in raceway or service cable, with 60°C insulation or higher-temperature conductors of the same size as required for a 60°C conductor. The above calculations dictate the following conductor choices for this example:

Copper: Not less than No. 4 (TW, THW, THHN, XHHW)
Aluminum: Not less than No. 3 (TW, THW, THHN, XHHW)

Single-Family Dwelling with Air-Conditioning Units

Example No. 1(b) in Chap. 9 of the **NE Code** deals with the same dwelling as the previous example (1,500 sq ft of living space with a 12-kW range and a 5.5-kW dryer) plus one 6-A 240-V room air-conditioning unit, one 12-A 120-V room air-conditioning unit, one 10-A 120-V dishwasher, and one 8-A 120-V disposal unit. The approach to the calculations is the same as in the preceding example, with simple addition of the extra loads. The amp loadings on the two hot legs and the neutral break down as shown in the following table:

Line A (One Hot Leg), amps	Neutral Leg, amps	Line B (Other Hot Leg), amps	Load
78	61	78	From first example
6	—	6	One 240-V A/C
12	12	10	One 120-V A/C and one 120-V dishwasher
—	8	8	One 120-V disposal
3	3	3	25% largest motor load
99	84	105	Total

Because the unit air conditioners are cord-and-plug-connected units, each may be treated as a single motor load of the A/C unit's nameplate rating. Room air conditioners are considered to be fixed appliances and must be added into required service-entrance conductor capacity as required by Sec. 220-17. As indicated in the listing above, the 6-A 240-V A/C unit places a 6-A load on each service hot leg but has no effect on neutral capacity because it has no neutral supply conductor. The three 120-V loads are divided as shown on the two service hot legs—the 120-V A/C unit connected from line A to neutral and the other two 120-V units connected from line B to neutral. Maximum unbalance of those loads would exist when the 12-A A/C unit on line A is off and the 10- and 8-A loads on line B are running. The current drawn by the neutral under that condition would be 18 A to match the 18 A (10 + 8) drawn by the 10-A dishwasher and the 8-A disposal unit. Thus, 18 A of load capacity must be added to the 61-A neutral load originally calculated.

Section 430-24, on sizing of conductors supplying several motors, requires that such conductors have an ampacity equal to the sum of the full-load current ratings of all the motors plus 25 percent of the highest-rated motor in the group. Because the 12-A-rated 120-V unit has the highest current rating of the motors, a value of 3 A (25 percent × 12 A) is added to line A hot leg and 25 percent × 10, or 2.5 A, is taken as an addition of 3 to line B hot leg. A load of 3 A is also added to the neutral because each 120-V motor load is connected hot-leg-to-neutral, and the neutral is part of the motor circuit and thus is a conductor "supplying several motors."

Note that the calculated demand load here (99 A for line A and 105 A for line B) is above the minimum 100-A required rating of service conductors from Sec. 230-42(b) (2). The service hot-leg conductors may be No. 1 TW copper conductors, with their 110-A ampacity or No. 2/0 TW aluminum conductors, which are rated at 115 A.

The neutral conductor for the service conductors to this house will have to be rated for not less than 61 A + 18 A + 3 A, or 82 A. Such a neutral conductor would be:

No. 3 copper TW, THW, THHN or XHHW; or

No. 1 aluminum TW, THW, THHN, or XHHW.

Index

Boldface numbers refer to article numbers *not* page numbers.

"Accessible" 100
Access to working spaces 110-16, 110-33
Accidents
  motor 430-73
  transformer 430-73, 450-8, 450-28
Adapters 410-58
Adobe, NM cable limitations 336-3
Aerial cables 100, 225-4
Agricultural buildings
  application 547-1
  circuit breakers, type 4/4x 547-4
  fuses, type 4/4x 547-4
  grounding 547-8
  motor controllers, type 4/4x 547-4
  switches, type 4/4x 547-5
  wiring methods 547-4
Air-conditioning equipment
  ampacity 440-6
  application and selection 440-52
  branch-circuit requirements 210-63, 440-22, 440-62
  conductors 440-62
  controller rating 440-41
  disconnects 440-14, 440-63
  feeders 440-62
  grounding 440-61, 450-4
  hermetic motors 440-53
  hotel units 440-62
  motor compressor loads 440-33
  motors 440-3

Air-conditioning equipment (*Cont.*):
  multimotor loads 440-35
  noncoincident loads 220-30
  outlets 210-63
  overload protection devices 440-52
  ratings, 440-6, 440-12
  room units 440-60
  in schools 220-34
  wiring 440-3
  (*See also* Motor-compressors)
Aircraft hangars 513-2, 513-5
Air-handling ceiling, wiring methods 300-22
Alarm systems, hazardous locations 501-14
Aluminum conductors (*see* Conductors, aluminum)
American National Standards Institute (ANSI) 230-208, 500-1
American Wire Gage (AWG)
  mineral-insulated, metal-sheathed cable 330-1
  standards 110-6
  (*See also* Wiring)
Ampacity
  branch circuits 210-19, 440-6
  cable in trays 318-10, 318-12
  conductors 210-19, 300-5, 310-10, 310-15, 310-38, 445-5
    branch circuit 430-52, 430-53
    derating 310-15

1

Ampacity, conductors (*Cont.*):
    electric welders **630-11, 630-31**
    multimotor **430-24**
  cords and cables **400-5**
  definition **100, 310-15**
  fixture wires **402-5**
  heating equipment **665-61**
  messenger-supported wiring **321-5**
  motors **430-6**
  tables **310-15**
Ampacity correction factors 310-15
Ampere ratings, fuses and CBs **240-6,
    430-110**
**Anesthetizing equipment 517-60, 517-
    63**
Antenna, radio/TV equipment **810-20,
    810-57**
Appliances
  branch circuit ratings **210-23**
  branch circuit sizing **422-5, 422-28**
  central heating equipment **422-7**
  circuits **220-3**
  definition **210-4, 422-1**
  disconnect devices **422-21, 422-22, 422-
    25, 422-27**
  electric clothes dryers, feeder capacity
    220-19
  electric cooking, feeder capacity **220-
    19**
  extension cord use **400-7**
  feeder loads, dwelling units **220-16**
  fixed load, dwelling units **200-17**
  flexible cords **400-7, 422-8**
  grounding **250-45, 250-60, 250-70, 422-8**
  infrared lamps, industrial **422-15**
  motor-operated **440-62**
  outdoor **210-52**
  overcurrent protection **230-71, 422-6,
    422-28**
  permanently connected **210-6**
  receptacles **210-50**
  signals for heat **422-12**
  water heaters **422-14**
  wiring methods **220-19**
  (*See also* Motors)
"Approved" 100
"Approved for purpose" (*see* "Identi-
    fied")
**"Approved for the hazardous (classified)
    location" 500-2**
Arcing parts 110-18
Armored cables (*see* Cables, armored)

Askarel, transformer insulation **450-23,
    450-25, 450-28**
Assembly, places of 518
Attachment plugs, hazardous locations
    501-12, 502-13
Attic outlets 210-63
Audio equipment, swimming pools **680-
    23**
Autotransformers
  ballast connections **410-78**
  derived circuits **210-9**
  grounding **450-5**
  600 volts, nominal, or less **450-4**
Auxiliary gutters
  conductors **374-5**
  extensions **374-2**
  splices and taps **374-8**
  use **374-1**

Balancers, generators **445-4**
Ballasts, protection devices **410-73**
Banks, lighting in **220-2**
Barn wiring, NM cable **336-3**
Basements, receptacles **210-52**
Bathrooms
  definition **210-8**
  fixtures in **410-4**
  lighting outlets **210-70**
  receptacles **210-50**
**Bathtubs, hydromassage 680-4, 680-41,
    680-70, 680-71**
Batteries (*see* Storage batteries)
Bends, between outlets **350-5**
Boatyards (*see* Marinas/boatyards)
Boilers, resistance-type **424-70, 424-72**
Bonding
  definition **100, 250-50, 350-70**
  dielectric heating equipment **665-25**
  fittings to conductors, specifications
    250-113
  grounding electrode system **250-81**
  hazardous locations **250-78, 501-16**
  health care facilities **517-14**
  jumpers **100, 250-74, 250-79, 501-16**
  lightning rods **250-46**
  panelboards, health care facilities **517-
    14**
  piping systems **250-80**
  raceways, loosely jointed metal **250-77**
  service equipment **250-71, 250-72, 250-
    92**

Bonding (*Cont.*):
  swimming pool components **680-22,**
    680-25
  swimming pools **680-20**
  techniques **250-75**
  250-V systems **250-76**
  (*See also* Grounding)
Boxes 370-1
  conductors entering **370-7**
  construction **370-20**
  covers **370-15**
  enclosing flush devices **370-9**
  exposed extensions **370-12**
  metal **370-4, 370-20**
  nonmetallic **370-3**
  number of conductors **370-6**
  repair **370-11**
  round **370-2**
  supports **370-13**
  weatherproof **370-5**
  (*See also* Cutout boxes: Junction boxes;
    Outlet boxes; Pull boxes)
Branch circuits 210, 210-1
  air-conditioning equipment **440-22,**
    440-60, 440-62
  aluminum conductors **110-14**
  ampacity and rating **210-19, 440-5**
  appliances **210-23, 422-5, 422-27**
  busways **364-8, 364-12, 364-13, 364-14**
  cables **339-1**
  calculations **220-1, 220-2, 220-3, 220-19**
  CB protection device **430-53**
  CB ratings **430-58**
  classifications **210-3**
  closed-loop and programmed power
    distribution **210-2, 780-1**
  color code **210-5**
  conductor ampacity **430-52, 430-53**
  cord connectors **210-7**
  definition **100**
  de-icing **426-4**
  disconnects, air-conditioning equip-
    ment **440-63**
  double derating **310-15**
  electric signs/outline lighting **600-6**
  emergency systems **700-15**
  feeder protection **430-62**
  fixed electric space-heating equipment
    424-3
  fixture wire use **402-11**
  flat conductor **328-1**
  flexible metal tubing use **349-3**

Branch circuits (*Cont.*):
  fuse protection **430-53**
  grounded **210-5**
  ground fault circuit-interrupter protec-
    tion **210-8, 215-9**
  grounding conductors **210-5, 250-114**
  guest rooms **210-60**
  hot conductors **210-5**
  individual **210-23**
  junction box supports **370-13**
  lighting outlets **210-70**
  loads **210-22, 210-23, 430-25, 430-62**
  luminaire use **410-31**
  marinas/boatyards **555-4**
  maximum loads **210-22**
  maximum voltage **210-6**
  minimum required calculations **220-3**
  mobile homes/parks **550-4, 550-5**
  motor compressor loads **440-33**
  motor protection device **430-62**
  motors **430-22, 430-42, 430-51**
  multiloads and multimotors **430-53**
  multimotor operation **430-53**
  multioutlet **210-23**
  multiwire **210-4**
  nonmetallic extensions **342**
  outlet devices **210-21, 210-50, 210-70**
  outlet receptacles **210-50**
  outside **225**
  overcurrent protection **210-20, 240-101,**
    422-6, 430-72
  protection **430-51**
  protection device ratings **430-52**
  receptacles **210-7, 210-50**
  in recreation vehicles **551-8**
  requirements **210-24, 220-4**
  rooftop outlets **210-63**
  SE cable use **338-3**
  show windows **210-62**
  single motor compressor **440-32**
  sizing for appliances **422-5**
  space heating equipment, overcurrent
    protection **424-22**
  temporary wiring **305-2**
  use **330-3**
  voltage calculations **220, 220-2, 220-3**
  voltage limitations **210-6**
  wall clearances **424-37**
  wiring **220-19, 310-15, 410-67**
  (*See also* Circuit breakers; Circuits)
Brown and Sharp (B & S) gage 110-6
Building 100, 230-3

Building Materials Directory 300-21, 410-76
Bulk storage plants
  definition 515-1
  hazardous location 515-2, 575-5
  underground wiring, hazardous locations 515-5
Burial depth 710-3
Busbars
  bonded, neutral 384-3
  support in switchboards and panelboards 384-3
Bushings (see Conduits, bushings)
Busways
  ampacity rating 364-10
  branch circuits 364-8, 364-12, 364-13, 364-14
  CB accessibility 364-4
  CB radio 100
  definition 364-2
  feeders 364-10, 364-14
  lighting 364-4
  markings 364-4
  overcurrent devices accessibility 100
  overcurrent protection, rating 364-10, 364-13
  plug-in devices 364-12
  size reduction 364-11
  subfeeders 364-10, 364-12
  support 364-5
  through walls and floors 364-6
  trolleys 364-14
  use 364-4
  wiring methods 100, 364-4
BX (see Cables, types, BX)
Bypass isolation switches 100

Cabinets
  definition 100, 373-1
  position in wall 373-3
Cablebus 365
Cable limiters 230-82, 450-6
Cables
  aerial 100, 225-4
  aluminum 338-1
  ampacity, cables in trays 318-10, 318-12
  appliance supply, grounding 250-61
  armored
    boxes 333-9
    construction 333-4

Cables, armored (*Cont.*):
  definition 333-1
  exposed 333-11
  fittings 333-9
  supports 333-7
  use 333-6
  AWG sizes 330-1, 333-1, 338-1
  barn wiring 336-3
  bending radius 334-11
  bore-hole, steel wire armor 300-19
  branch-circuit, description and marking 339-1
  cable tray grounding 318-6
  conductors, types 210-21, 225-4
  copper-clad aluminum 110-14, 338-1
  data processing systems 645-5
  dead-ending 320-6
  electrical nonmetallic tubing (ENT) 331-1, 331-3, 331-5
  FC, number of conductors 363-6
  FC definition 363-1
  FC installation 363-5
  FC use 363-3
  fire-rated structure penetration 300-21
  fittings 330-14
  flat conductor, type FCC 328-1, 328-2, 328-10
  flexible
    ampacity 400-5
    raceways 400-8
    types 400-3
  gang box entry 370-6
  GTO classification 410-88
  hazardous locations 333-6, 501-4, 501-5
  heating
    area restrictions 424-38, 424-39
    in ceilings 424-41, 424-43
    installation 424-41, 426-24
    marking 424-35
  high-voltage shielding 310-61, 710-8
  installation 110-7, 318-7
  installation in concrete floors 424-44
  insulation 310-2
    resistance 110-7
    shielding 710-6, 710-8
  integrated gas spacer (IGS) 325-1
  interconnecting, for data processing systems 645-1
  marking 310-11
  masonry, NM limitations 336-4
  medium-voltage (MV) 318-2, 318-11, 318-12

Cables, medium-voltage (MV) (*Cont.*):
definition **326-1**
uses **326-3**
messenger-supported **225-4, 225-5**
metal-clad (MC)
definition **334-1**
fittings **334-12**
installation **334-10**
mineral-insulated, metal sheathed **330-
1, 331-3**
multiconductor **318-8, 318-10, 330-3**
nonheating leads, cutting **426-11**
nonheating leads installation **424-43,
426-25**
nonmetallic (NM)-sheathed **310-2, 336-
1, 370-7**
conductors **336-26**
exposed work **336-10**
insulation **336-16, 336-17**
supports **336-15**
unfinished basements **336-12**
uses **336-3, 336-4**
number of conductors **725-17**
optical fiber **00-2, 770-1, 770-3**
outlet boxes **370-20**
over 600 V, nominal **710-1, 710-3, 710-
6**
power and control tray, defined **340-1**
power-limited tray (PLTC) **310-10**
PVC jacketed-ALS **334-4**
Romex **336-1**
round boxes connectors **370-2**
secured to cabinet **373-5**
service-drop **225-4, 225-5**
service entrance (SE)
bare neutral conductor **338-3**
branch circuit use **338-3**
definition **338-1**
feeder use **338-3**
with higher voltage-to-ground **230-56**
installation methods **338-4**
use, cooking appliances **338-3**
shielding **310-6**
single-conductor **318-9, 318-10**
SNM fittings **337-6**
SNM sheathed, definition **337-1**
support **300-19**
terminal seals **330-15**
through wood framing **300-4**
types
AC **326-3, 333-1, 333-4, 333-5, 333-6,
333-7, 333-9, 645-5**

Cables, types (*Cont.*):
ACH **333-5**
ACHH **333-5**
ACL **333-5, 333-6**
ACT **333-5**
ACU **333-5**
ALS **334-1, 334-4, 334-11, 334-12**
ASE **338-1**
BX **333-1, 333-6, 333-7, 334-1, 336-1,
370-13, 518-3**
CS **334-1, 334-11**
ENT **331-1, 331-3, 331-5**
FC **363**
FCC **328-1, 328-2, 328-10**
IGS **325-1**
MC **225-4, 318-5, 318-11, 318-12, 326-
3, 333-1, 334-1, 334-3, 334-4, 334-
10, 334-11, 334-12, 518-3, 520-4,
530-11, 645-5**
MI **225-4, 330-1, 330-3, 516-3, 518-3,
520-4, 530-11, 645-5**
NM **225-4, 310-2, 310-15, 326-3, 331-
3, 333-6, 336-1, 336-3, 336-4, 338-
3, 338-4, 339-3, 344-2, 370-6, 370-
7, 370-15, 373-5**
NMC **225-4, 310-2, 333-6, 336-1, 336-
2, 336-4, 338-4, 344-2, 547-3**
SE **310-2, 318-2, 338**
SER **338-1**
SEU **338-1**
SNM **337**
TC **340-4, 340-5**
THW **310-13**
UF **225-4, 310-9, 333-6, 339-2, 339-3,
424-14, 426-10**
UL ratings **334-1, 710-1**
under buildings, limitations **300-5**
under concrete **300-5**
underground **300-5, 330-3**
unfinished basements **336-8**
USE **310-9, 318-2, 338-1**
uses permitted **100, 326-3**
wire connections **300-16**
Cable trays
ampacity **318-11, 318-13**
cable installation **318-8**
channel **318-10**
definition **100, 318-2**
grounding **318-7**
high-voltage cables **318-12**
installation **318-6**
ladder **318-10**

Cable trays (*Cont.*):
multiconductor cables **318-9, 318-11**
number of conductors **725-17**
single conductor cables **318-10, 318-11**
uses **318-3, 318-4**
ventilated trough **318-10**
wiring **230-202**
Canadian Standards Association (CSA)
100
Capacitors
Class II hazardous locations **502-2**
conductor sizing **460-8**
corrective measures **460-6**
fuses **460-8**
grounding **460-10**
installations **460-6**
manufacturing standards **460-8**
overcurrent protection **460-8, 460-9**
power factor correlation, motor circuit
460-6
provisions **460-1**
size calculations **460-6**
stored charge drainage **460-6**
wiring methods **460-8**
x-ray equipment **660-35**
Case grounding 250-45
"CAUTION" signs 110-31
Ceiling fans 422-18
Ceilings
CB installations **300-22**
design and fire-rating requirements
300-21
fire-rated **300-21**
lighting fixtures, lay-in **300-21**
motor controllers, installation **300-22**
penetration **300-21**
suspended **100**
fixtures **410-16**
transformers **450-2**
wiring methods **300-22**
switches installations **300-22**
transformers installations **300-22**
wiring clearances **424-36**
wiring for air-handling space **300-22**
Cellular concrete floor, precast raceway
use **358-1**
Cellular metal floor raceways (See Raceways, cellular metal floor)
Central heating equipment 422-7
Central Station Signaling Systems 760-1
Certification, third-party **100, 110-2, 300-**
21

Cinder fill, conduits **346-3**
Circuit breakers
accessibility **100**
agricultural buildings, type 4/4x **547-4**
ampere ratings **240-6, 463-110**
appliances disconnects **422-21**
as controller **430-83, 430-111**
as disconnects **430-111**
as switches **380-11**
branch circuit protection device **430-53**
branch circuit protection rating **430-58**
ceiling installations **300-22**
Class I hazardous locations **501-6**
Class II, Div. 1 hazardous locations
502-6
Class III, Div. 1/Div. 2 hazarous locations **503-4**
enclosures **373-8**
feeder protection **220-10**
generators **455-4**
ground-fault protection **100, 230-95**
handle position **240-81**
interrupting device over 600 V, nominal **710-21**
locations, overcurrent protection **240-**
24, 240-30
manual operation **240-80**
motors, instantaneous trips **430-52**
panelboards **384-16**
parallel **240-8**
ratings **430-52**
SWD marking **240-83**
swimming pool electric equipment **680-**
5
temperature limitations **110-3**
type 4/4x, agriculture buildings **547-4**
UL Standard 489 **240-1**
(*See also* Disconnects; Fuses; Overcurrent protection; Switches)
Circuit interrupters (*see* Ground-fault circuit interrupters)
Circuits
adjustable speed drive systems **430-2**
alternating-current (AC), grounding
250-3, 250-23, 250-25, 250-26
appliances **220-3**
classifications **210-3**
communications
building clearance **810-54**
conductor installation **800-3**
definition **800-1**
radio/TV equipment **810**

Circuits (*Cont.*):
data processing systems **645-5**
derating **310-15**
design and installation **500-2**
disconnects, gasoline stations **514-5**
emergency systems **700-17**
fixtures for conductors use **410-31**
40-A calculations **220-19**
grounded conductor for grounding
    equipment **250-61**
health care facilities **517-63**
impedance **110-10**
intrinsically safe, wiring **500-1**
large, **210-23**
less than 50 V **720**
motors
    branch-circuit conductor sizing
        430-4
    feeder **430-1**
    noncontinuous **430-22**
    overload protection **430-31, 430-52**
    power capacitors **460-6**
    ratings **430-52**
    switches **430-83**
multiple **210-4**
multiple-conductor **310-4**
multiwire branch **210-4**
over 600 V, nominal **710-2, 710-3**
parallel, underground **300-5**
remote-control **100, 401-14, 725-1**
secondary ties **450-5**
signal **725-1**
single **210-4**
sound equipment **640**
telecommunications **300-22**
theater gallery receptacles, overcurrent
    protection **520-23**
two-wire branch **210-4, 210-10**
type FCC **328-1**
underground raceway wiring **710-3**
ungrounded **200-6, 300-5**
(*See also* Branch circuits; Circuit break-
    ers; Control circuits, Power-limited
    circuits)
Clamping devices 370-13
Clearances, service drop conductors **230-
    9, 230-24**
**Closed-loop and programmed power dis-
    tribution 210-2, 780-1**
Closets, installations prohibited in **240-
    24, 410-8**
Coating (*see* Finishing processes)

Color codes
grounded conductors **200-6, 200-7, 210-
    5, 250-57**
grounding electrodes **250-91**
hot conductors **210-5**
Commercial occupancies
branch circuit maximum voltage excep-
    tions **210-6**
kitchen equipment, branch circuit and
    feeder calculations **220-20**
lighting, SWD circuit breakers **240-83**
(*See also* Show windows/cases)
Communication circuits (*see* Circuits,
    communications)
Communications systems 501-14, 770-1
Compressors (*see* Motor-compressors)
Computers (*see* Data processing systems)
"Concealed" 100
Concrete, poke-through wiring **300-21**
Conductors
AC grounding electrode **250-94**
air-conditioning equipment **440-62**
aluminum **110-3, 110-14, 210-23, 250-
    81, 250-92, 250-95, 430-63**
ampacity **210-19, 300-5, 310-10, 310-15,
    310-38, 445-5**
    derating **310-15**
    electric welders **630-11, 630-31**
    heating equipment **665-61**
approvals **100**
arrester, size and material **280-32**
bare neutral, 3E cable **338-3**
bends in conduits **346-10, 346-11**
bonding, swimming pools **680-22**
branch circuit **250-114, 310-15**
    aluminum **110-14**
    ampacity **430-52, 430-53**
    flat **328-1**
    grounded **210-5**
    motors **430-22**
    splice connector effects **110-14**
building clearance **225-19**
building pass-through service **230-3**
bus enclosures entrance clearance **384-
    10**
cabinet entry **373-5**
cable types **210-21, 225-4**
capacitor sizing **460-8**
color coatings **200-7**
concealed knob-and-tube **324-5**
conduit size **346-6**
conduit sleeve protection **250-92**

Conductors (*Cont*.):

construction **310-13**

contact, installation for cranes/hoists **610-21**

control circuit protection **430-72, 430-73**

controller openings **430-84**

copper **110-114, 250-81, 310-4, 310-10, 310-13, 310-15, 318-7, 430-25, 430-63**

copper-clad aluminum **110-14, 310-13**

copper supply **110-3**

corrosion **310-9**

covering **225-4**

current capacity and heat effects **310-15**

cutout boxes entry **373-5**

DC system grounding, size **250-93**

dead-ending in open wiring **320-6**

defection **373-6**

derating **300-5, 310-15, 725-17**

direct-burial **310-7**

disconnects, grounded motors **430-105**

double derating **310-15**

electrical continuity **300-13**

electric discharge load **310-15**

electric signs/outline lighting **600-21**

EMT **310-15**

enclosures **250-33, 250-72**

equipment, grounding **250-50, 250-95, 310-15, 347-4**

feeder **100, 310-4, 430-24, 430-62**

feeder taps **240-21, 430-28**

field-wired **424-22**

fixtures for circuits use **410-31**

general wiring **310**

ground clearance **225-18**

grounded **100, 200-2, 200-6, 200-7, 210-5, 230-75, 240-22, 240-23, 250-57, 250-61, 310-12, 430-105**

grounded, motors **430-85, 430-105**

grounding

AC system **250-25, 250-26, 250-94**

and bonding fittings **250-113**

electrode **100, 250-112**

enclosures **250-33**

materials **250-91**

objectionable current over **250-21**

receptacles for **210-7**

size of equipment **250-95**

high-voltage, color identification **215-8, 215-9**

hot **210-5**

Conductors (*Cont*.):

identification **310-12**

in parallel **310-4**

installations

with other systems **300-8**

resistance **110-7**

insulaton **230-4, 230-30, 230-40, 501-13**

elevators/escalators **620-11**

requirements **310-2, 310-15**

resistance **110-7**

shielding **710-8**

knob-and-cleaf supports **320-7**

length **300-14**

less than 50 V **720-4**

limited circuits **725-15, 725-16, 725-17, 725-37, 725-38, 725-39, 725-40**

load capacity **430-25**

magnetic flux **300-20**

mechanical continuity **300-13**

mobile homes/parks **550-9**

mounting supports **320-7**

multiloads **430-25**

multimotor service **430-24**

multiple circuits **310-4**

neutral **310-4, 310-15**

nonmetallic extensions **342**

number in conduits **345-7, 346-6**

number in EMT **348-6**

open, spacings **225-14**

organs **650-4, 650-5**

outdoor

clearance from buildings **225-19**

clearance from ground **225-18**

covering **225-4**

lampholders **225-24**

lamps **225-25**

lighting equipment **225-7**

live vegetation **225-26**

minimum size **225-6**

raceways **225-22**

spacings **225-14**

wiring on building **225-10**

outlet box entry **370-6**

over 600 V, nominal **710-1, 710-2, 710-3, 710-9**

overcurrent protection **210-20, 240-3, 430-24**

parallel circuits grouping **318-7**

polyethylene insulation **338-1**

protection **230-50, 310-15**

PVC jacket **338-1**

raceways **210-21, 300-5, 300-18, 310-15**

Conductors (*Cont.*):
  radio/TV equipment **810-13, 810-21**
  remote-control **240-3, 430-72**
  resistive load **310-15**
  secondary **230-201, 230-202, 230-204, 450-6**
  service **100, 220-35, 230-22, 230-201**
  service-drop clearances **230-9, 230-24**
  service-entrance
    bonding jumpers **250-79**
    classification **230-201**
    connections at service head **230-54**
    insulation **230-41**
    mounting supports **230-51**
    number **230-40**
    overcurrent protection **230-90**
    raceways drainage **230-53**
    size and rating **230-42**
    unspliced **230-46**
    wiring methods **230-43, 230-202, 230-205**
  service lateral **230-2, 230-32**
  services, number **230-2**
  shielding **310-6**
  single, construction, AWG **330-1**
  sizes **110-6, 225-6**
    elevators/escalators **620-12**
    motors rated over 600 V **430-124**
    temperature relationship **110-3**
  sound equipment **640-6**
  space-heating equipment ratings **424-22**
  splice points **300-13, 300-15**
  stranded **310-3**
  support in switchboards and panel boards **384-3**
  supports **320-6**
  supports in vertical raceways **300-19**
  surface raceway, metal enclosure **352-2**
  surge arresters **280-12**
  swimming pool **680-5, 680-8**
  tap, branch circuit calculations **220-19**
  tap, overcurrent protection **240-21, 430-53**
  temperature limitations **310-10**
  temperature ratings **110-3**
  types
    AC cables **335-5**
    MCM **318-10, 374-5, 430-25**
    MV **326-3**
    RH **338-1, 370-18**
    RHH **310-15, 310-61, 338-1, 346-6, 351-4, 370-18, 430-25, 430-53, 430-**

Conductors, types, RHH (*Cont.*):
    62, 430-63
    RHW **318-2, 338-1, 430-53**
    THHN **210-21, 310-9, 310-15, 351-4, 370-18, 430-25, 430-53, 430-62, 430-63**
    THW **210-21, 310-4, 310-15, 318-2, 326-3, 348-8, 350-2, 351-4, 374-5, 430-25, 430-53, 430-62, 430-63**
    THWN **310-9, 310-15**
    TW **210-21, 215-2, 310-15, 326-3, 351-4, 430-25, 430-53, 430-62, 430-63**
    XHHW **210-21, 310-15, 318-7, 338-1, 346-6, 350-2, 351-4, 430-25, 430-53**
  UL terminal ratings **310-15**
  underground **310-7**
    protection **300-5**
    service **100**
  ungrounded, overcurrent protection **240-20, 240-21**
  ungrounded, tapped from grounded systems **210-10, 215-7**
  unspliced **230-46**
  wet location **310-8**
  wound-rotor, secondary current **430-23**
  (*See also* Disconnects; Feeders; Services; Wires)
Conduit bodies 100, 370-1
  conductors entering **370-7**
  construction **370-20**
  number of conductors **370-6**
Conduits
  bushings **430-13**
  bushings, cabinets and cutout boxes **373-6**
  conductor derating **310-15**
  EMT bends **348-10**
  feeder terminations, health care facilities **517-17**
  ferrous metals, soil contact corrosive effects **346-1**
  fire-rated structure penetration **300-21**
  flex-temperature relationship **410-11**
  flex wiring **410-67**
  flexible metal
    bends in concealed work **350-6**
    bonding jumper use **250-79**
    grounding **350-5, 430-145**
    liquidtight, separate grounding conductor **230-43, 250-91, 351-21**
    size **350-3**

Conduits, flexible metal (*Cont.*):
  supports **350-4**
  use **350-2**
  (*See also* Liquidtight flexible metal
    conduit)
  galvanized steel **346-1**
  grounding at terminals **300-5**
  intermediate ferrous metal **345-3**
  intermediate metal conduits (IMC)
    aluminum fittings **345-3**
    clamping **345-12**
    steel **345-3**
    use **345-3**
  junction box size **370-18**
  liquidtight metal **90-6**
  motion picture projectors **540-10**
  number of conductors allowed
    345-7
  outlet box supports **370-13**
  over 600 V, nominal **710-3**
  plastic **347-1**
  PVC **250-92, 250-95, 347-1, 347-2,**
    347-3, 347-9, 547-3
  raceway installations **300-5**
  rigid metal
    bends **346-10**
    bushings **346-8**
    cinder fill **346-3**
    conductors **346-6**
    couplings **346-9**
    uses **346-1**
  rigid nonmetallic
    bends **347-13, 347-14**
    conductors number of **347-11**
    description **347-1**
    expansion joints **347-9**
    grounding **347-4**
    supports **347-8**
    trimming **347-5**
    use **347-2, 347-3**
  sealing and drainage, Class I hazardous
    locations **501-5**
  sealings, gasoline pumps **514-6**
  size **310-15**
  stubups **384-10**
  supports **345-13**
  swimming pool **680-20**
  underground installations **300-5**
  underground PVC **347-1**
  wire count **370-6**
  wiring methods, hazardous locations
    501-4

Connections
  cord-and-plug **422-22**
  electrical **110-14**
  end-to-end **410-31**
  fixtures **410-30**
  plug and receptacle **410-30**
Connectors
  armored cable **336-5**
  conduit fittings **336-5**
  cord **210-7**
  round box cable **370-2**
  (*See also* Cords; Fixtures)
Consoles 645-1
Construction sites
  assured grounding program require-
    ments **210-9**
  GFCI protection **305-4**
  shock hazard on **305-2**
Continuous load 100
Control assemblies, industrial, over 600
    V, nominal **710-24**
Control circuits 410-81
  accident hazards **430-73**
  industrial motors **430-74**
  interlocked **430-74**
  motors **430-71**
    disconnects **430-74**
    magnetic **430-71, 430-72**
  overcurrent protection **430-72**
  protection, transformers **430-72,**
    430-73
  (*See also* Branch circuits; Circuit break-
    ers; Circuits)
Controllers
  CB branch circuits **430-83, 430-111**
  design **430-82**
  marking **440-4**
  motor, fusible switch **430-90**
  motor, number served **430-87**
  ratings **430-83, 440-41**
  UL listing **430-52**
Control resistors, Class I hazardous loca-
    tions **501-7**
Control transformers, Class I hazardous
    locations **501-7**
Converters, phase, power interruptions
    430-86
Cooking appliances
  kitchen equipment **220-20**
  ranges, disconnect devices **422-22**
  SE cable use **338-3**
Copper, conductor material **110-14**

Copper-clad aluminum cables 110-14, 338-1

Copper conductors (see Conductors, copper)

Cord-and-plug-connected lighting assembly 680-4

Cord connectors 210-7

Cords
  extension
    protection 240-4
    temporary use 400-7
  fixed, connections 410-30
  flexible
    ampacity 400-5
    appliances, use 400-7, 422-8
    Class I, Div. 1/Div. 2 501-11
    Class II, Div. 1/Div. 2, hazardous locations 502-12
    conflicting rules 400-8
    lighting fixtures 400-7, 400-8
    outdoor lampholder 400-8
    portable lamps wiring 410-42
    protection 240-4
    raceways 400-8
    strain relief 400-10
    uses 400-7, 400-8
  show windows and show cases 400-11
  strain relief 400-10
  swimming pools 680-7
  types 400-3, 502-12

Corrosion 300-6, 310-9

Counter spaces, receptacles 210-25

Couplings and connectors conduit 346-9
  (See also Connectors)

Cove lighting space 410-9

Cranes (see Equipment, cranes)

Crawl space outlets 210-63

CSA (Canadian Standards Association) 100

Current limitation, utilization equipment 501-10

Currents, induced 300-20

Cutout boxes 373-1
  conductors entering 373-5
  deflection of conductors 373-6
  enclosures for switches 373-8
  position 373-3

Data processing systems
  definitions 645-1
  disconnecting means 645-10

Data processing systems (Cont.):
  grounding 250-74, 645-1, 645-15
  interconnecting cables 645-5
  rooms 645-2
  supply circuits 645-5
  uninterruptible power supply 645-11
  wiring under raised floors 300-22, 645-1

Deck area, heating of 680-27

Definitions of terms 100

De-icing and snow-melting equipment
  disconnects 426-50
  fixed outdoor, branch-circuit requirements 426-4
  identification 426-13
  installation 426-23
  use 426-11
  (See also Equipment)

Demand factor 100

Derating circuits 310-15

Deteriorating agents 110-11

Device boxes (see Boxes)

Devices 100

Dielectric heating equipment
  access 665-22
  bonding 665-25
  definition 665-1, 665-2
  generators, vacuum tube, 665-2
  grounding 665–25
  shielding 665-25
  (See also Equipment)

Diesel fuel, commercial garages as hazardous locations 500-1, 511-1

Dimmers, theater 520-25, 520-53

Dining rooms, receptacle outlets in 210-52

Dipping (see Finishing processes)

Direct burial
  cables, underground 300-5, 330-3
  conductors, underground (see Conductors, underground)
  conduits, underground installations 300-5

Direct grade access level 210-8

Disconnecting means
  definition 430-103
  identification 110-22

Disconnects
  air-conditioning equipment 440-14, 440-63
  appliances 422-21, 422-22, 422-25
  branch circuits, AC equipment 440-63

Disconnects (*Cont.*):
  buildings under single management
    230-84
  circuits, gasoline stations **514-5**
  cranes **610-32, 610-33**
  data processing systems **645-10**
  de-icing and snow-melting equipment
    426-50
  electric signs outline lighting **600-2**
  electrolytic cells **668-13**
  energy source **430-113**
  fuses **240-40**
  grounded motor conductors **430-105**
  location, AC equipment **440-14**
  mobile homes/parks **550-4**
  monorail hoists **610-32**
  motor controllers **430-74, 430-102**
  motor-driven appliances **422-27**
  motors, accessibility **430-107**
  motors, rating **440-12**
  multimotor machines, proximity **430-102**
  SE conductors, disconnecting means
    230-205
    equipment connected to supply side
      230-82
    external operation **230-78**
    grouping **230-72**
    manual or power operation **230-76**
    maximum number **230-71**
    ratings **230-79, 230-80**
    switches **230-70, 230-71, 230-72**
  single, for several motors **430-112**
  size, multiple motors **440-12**
  space-heating equipment **424-19**
  switches **422-25, 430-111, 440-63**
  transfer equipment **230-83**
  types **430-109**
  voltage-control **430-74**
  (*See also* Conductors; Feeders; Services; Wires)
Diversity factor, definition **100**
Doors
  garage, receptacles in **210-8**
  transformer vaults **450-43**
  working spaces **110-16**
Dry-niche fixtures (*see* Lighting fixtures; Swimming pools)
Drywall, replacement near outlet boxes
    370-11
Ducts, wiring methods **300-22**
Dumbwaiters (*see* Elevators/escalators)

Dwelling units
  additional loads in existing **220-31**
  appliances, fixed load **200-17**
  branch circuit maximum voltage **210-6**
  definition **100, 210-23**
  electric clothes dryers, feeder calculations **220-18**
  electric cooking appliances, feeder capacity **220-19**
  ground-fault circuit protection **210-8**
  optional feeder sizing calculation **220-33**
  receptacle loads **210-4, 210-21, 210-52**
  service demand load, optional calculation **220-30**
  small appliance and laundry loads **220-16**
  voltage **410-75**
  (*See also* Appliances; Branch circuits; Fixtures)

Electrical Appliance and Utilization Equipment Directory **440-22**
Electrical Appliance and Utilization Equipment Directory (Orange Book) **110-3, 300-22, 424-9, 426-10**
Electrical Baseboard Heating Equipment **424-9**
Electrical connections 110-14
Electrical Construction Materials Directory (Green Book) **110-3, 110-14, 220-10, 300-6, 300-21, 326-1, 333-1, 334-1 340-4, 345-3, 351-8, 400-3, 410-5, 410-58, 410-88, 430-83, 450-1, 501-6, 501-13, 517-18, 700-3, 710-3, 710-24, 725-2**
Electrical equipment
  applications **668-3**
  grounding conductor, swimming pools
    680-25
  portable **668-20**
  swimming pool **680-5, 680-25**
  working space **110-16**
  (*See also* Equipment; Motors)
Electrical loads, residences **310-15**
Electrical nonmetallic tubing (ENT) **331-1, 331-3, 331-4, 331-5, 331-10**
Electrical system coordination 240-12
Electrical Testing Laboratories, Inc. 100, 110-3, 710-1

Electrical vehicle, charging equipment requirements **511-8**
Electric appliances (see Appliances)
Electric cranes (see Equipment, cranes)
Electric discharge
  lighting fixtures **410-14, 410-54**
  load **310-15**
Electric metallic tubing (EMT) 100
  bends **346-10, 348-9, 348-10**
  conductor derating **310-15**
  couplings and connectors **348-8**
  health care facilities **517-13, 517-61**
  junction boxes **370-6**
  number of conductors in conduit **345-7, 348-6**
  sizes **348-5, 348-8**
  supports **348-12**
  threads **348-7**
  underground use **300-5**
  use **348-1**
  wire count **370-6**
Electric signs/outline lighting
  application **600-1**
  branch circuits **600-6**
  conductors **600-21**
  disconnects **600-2**
  electric-discharge tubing receptacles/terminals **600-34**
  emergency systems **700-8**
  grounding **250-43**
  portable **600-11**
  transformers **600-32**
Electric space heating, fixed **220-15**
Electric welders
  application **630-1**
  conductors ampacity **630-11, 630-31**
  overcurrent protection **630-12, 630-32**
Electrodes
  AC grounding conductor **250-94**
  common grounding **250-54**
  grounding conductor connection **250-112**
  grounding path **250-53**
  grounding system **250-23, 250-81**
  manufactured **250-83, 250-84**
  Ufer system **250-81**
Electrolytic cells
  definitions **668-1, 668-2**
  disconnection means **668-13**
Electromagnetic interference, reduction of 250-75

Elevators/escalators
  application **620-1**
  conductor insulation **620-11**
  conductor size **620-12**
  motors **430-22**
  phase protection **620-53**
  wiring system in raceway **620-36**
Emergency conditions 305-1
Emergency systems
  acceptability **700-12**
  applications **700-1**
  batteries **700-12**
  branch circuits **700-15**
  capacity **700-5**
  circuits **700-17**
  definition **700-12**
  dual service **700-12**
  generators **700-12**
  ground-fault protection **700-26**
  health care facilities **517-31**
  Life Safety Code **700-1**
  lighting **700-12, 700-16, 700-17**
  loads **700-15**
  OSHA requirements **700-1**
  signals **700-7**
  signs **700-8**
  switches **700-20, 700-21**
  tests and maintenance **700-4**
  transfer equipment **700-6**
  UL listing **700-3**
  wiring **700-9**
EMT (see Electric metallic tubing)
Enclosures
  circuit breakers **373-8**
  conductors **250-33, 250-72**
  explosionproof, Class I hazardous location **501-6**
  hysteresis heating **300-20**
  junction box use **373-8**
  metal, electrical continuity **300-10**
  metal, induced currents **300-20**
  motor controllers **430-10, 430-91**
  NEMA 4X **547-4**
  operating equipment **373-8**
  panelboards **373-8, 384-18**
  safety of **110-31**
  switches **373-8, 380-3**
  transformers, GFCI, swimming pools **680-21**
  (See also Guarding, transformers, exposed parts; Hazardous locations; Isolation, high-voltage systems)

14 INDEX

Energy source, disconnects **430-113**
Enforcement 90-4
ENT (electrical nonmetallic tubing) 331-
1, 331-3, 331-5
Entranceways (see Doors)
Environmental Protection Agency 450-23
Equipment
  accessibility **100**
  aircraft hangars, hazardous locations
    513-5
  amperage marking **110-3**
  arcing parts **110-18**
  certification, third-party **90-6**
  Class I, explosionproof, hazardous loca-
    tion **501-6**
  commercial garages, hazardous location
    511-6
  concealed **100**
  cranes
    contact conductors installation **610-**
      21
    disconnects **610-32, 610-33**
    electric, Class III hazardous location
      503-13
    wiring methods **610-11**
  disconnect devices **110-22**
  enclosures **373-8**
  examination for installation and use
    110-3
  examination for safety **90-6**
  exposed **100, 426-23**
  finishing processes, hazardous loca-
    tions **516-3**
  ground-fault protection **100, 215-10,**
    240-13
  grounding conductor **100, 250-1, 250-**
    50, 250-95, 310-15, 347-4
  hazardous locations, precautions **500-**
    2
  hoists
    contact conductors installation **610-**
      21
    monorail, disconnects **610-32**
    wiring methods **610-11**
  interrupting rating **110-9**
  intrinsically safe **504-1**
  live parts protection **110-17**
  low-voltage, health care facility **517-64**
  marking **110-21, 430-7**
  motion picture projectors **540-11**
  motors, marking **430-7**
  panelboard penetration and fire ratings
    300-21

Equipment (Cont.):
  plasterboard penetration and fire rat-
    ings **300-21**
  service (see Service equipment)
  transfer **230-83, 700-6**
  use **110-3**
  utilization, Class I hazardous locations
    501-10
  wattage marking **110-3**
  workspace **110-16**
  x-ray, health care facilities **517-2**
  (See also specific items)
Expansion joints (see Conduits, rigid
    nonmetallic)
Explosionproof seal fittings 501-5
Explosive limits, gas or vapor in air **500-1**
"Exposed" 100
Exposed work, NM cables **336-6**
Extension cords (see Cords, extension)

Faceplates (see Outlet boxes, covers and
    canopies)
Factory Mutual Engineering Corp. 100,
    110-3
Factory Mutual Research Laboratory,
    flammability classifications **450-23**
Family rooms, receptacle outlets in 210-
    52
Fans, ceiling 422-18
Faults (see Ground-fault circuit interrupt-
    ers; Ground-fault circuit protec-
    tion)
FC cable 363
FCC type wiring 328-1, 328-2, 328-10
Feedback, high-voltage systems **710-24**
Feeders
  air-conditioning equipment **220-34,**
    440-62
  appliances, dwelling units **220-16**
  application **310-15**
  bonding **250-24**
  branch circuit protection **430-62**
  busways **364-10, 364-14**
  calculations **220-1, 220-2, 220-10, 220-**
    19, 220-30, 220-35
  CB ratings **220-10**
  common neutral **215-4, 215-9**
  conductors **100, 430-24, 430-62**
    ampacity relationship **310-15**
    in parallel **310-4**
    tap **240-21, 430-28**
  conduit terminations, health care facili-
    ties **517-85**

Feeders (*Cont.*):
cooking appliance capacity calculations **220-19**
definition **100, 215-1, 230-205**
demand factor **430-26**
derating **310-15**
electric clothes dryers **220-19**
electric space heating, fixed **220-15**
fuses **220-10**
general lighting calculations **220-11**
ground-fault protection **215-9**
ground-fault protection of equipment **250-10**
grounding **250-24**
high-voltage, overcurrent protection **240-100**
kitchen equipment, commercial **220-20**
load calculations **220-10**
loads **215-2**
minimum rating and size **215-2**
mobile homes/parks **550-3**
motors **220-14, 430-26**
multiple conductors **310-4**
neutral load calculations **220-22**
noncoincident loads **220-21**
outside **225**
overcurrent protection device **430-62**
panelboards **373-8**
protective devices **430-63**
raceways, temporary wiring **305-2**
ratings for power and light loads **215-2, 430-63**
SE cable use **338-3**
show-window lighting **220-12**
small appliance loads **220-16**
subfeeders **215-1**
switches, fuse ratings **450-3**
tap conductors **240-21, 430-28**
transformers **450-3**
underground, description and marking **339-1**
underground use **339-3**
ungrounded conductors **215-7**
(*See also* Conductors; Disconnects; Lighting; Services; Wires)
Festoons 225-6, 520-65
Fiber optic cables 90-2, 770-1, 770-4
Field-wired conductors 424-22
Finishing processes
definition **516-1**
equipment, hazardous location **516-3**
hazardous locations, Class I, Div. 1/Div. 2 **516-2**

Finishing process (*Cont.*):
wiring, hazardous locations **516-3**
Fire doors and windows, installation standards (NFPA) **450-43**
Fire hazards (*see* Hazardous locations)
Fire protection
electrical installations **300-21**
floor penetrations **300-21**
signaling system, definition **760-1, 760-2**
transformers **450-23**
Fire pumps 230-95
Fire-rated outlets 300-21
Fire ratings 300-21
Fire Resistance Index **410-64**
Fire-resistant shells 300-21
Fire wall, definition **100**
Fittings 370-1
conductors entering **370-7**
construction **370-20**
flexible, Class I hazardous locations **501-4**
number of conductors **370-6**
weatherproof **370-5**
Fixtures
bathroom **410-4**
branch circuits **410-31**
circuit conductors use **410-31**
clearances **410-66**
clothes closets **410-8**
conductor temperature limits **410-11**
conductors for movable parts **410-26**
connections **410-30**
cord-connected showcases **410-29**
cord-equipped **410-30**
cove lighting space **410-9**
damp or wet locations **410-4**
electric-discharge connections **410-30**
equipment not integral with **410-77**
exposed parts **410-18**
faceplates exposed **410-18**
fire hazards **410-8**
floodlights **400-8, 410-30**
grounding for **410-20**
HID **410-76**
high-temperature wire, marking **410-30, 410-35**
incandescent connections **410-65**
lampholders **210-3, 225-24, 305-2, 410-47, 410-48, 422-15, 720-4**
lighting, flexible cord use **400-7, 400-8**
mountings **410-30, 410-76**
near combustible material **410-5**

Fixtures (*Cont.*):
  outdoor use **410-4**
  over combustible material **410-6**
  polarization **410-23**
  prewired **410-11**
  raceways **410-31**
  rating **410-35**
  recessed **410-66, 410-67, 501-9**
  supports **410-15, 410-16**
  suspended ceilings **410-16, 410-64**
  tap conductors **410-67**
  thermal insulation **410-66**
  track lighting **410-100, 410-102**
  type I.C. **410-76**
  wires **240-4, 402-10**
  wiring temperatures **410-67**
  (*See also* Connectors; Cords, flexible;
    Lighting fixtures)
Fixture wires
  ampacity **402-5**
  branch circuits **402-11**
  conductors in conduits **402-7**
  overcurrent protection **240-4, 240-6,
    402-12**
  types **402-5**
  uses **402-10, 402-11**
Flashers 380-5
Flash point of liquid 500-1
Flat cable assemblies (FC) 363
Flat conductor cable, type FCC **328-1,
    328-2, 328-10, 328-17**
Flex (*see* Conduits, flexible metal)
Flexible cords (*see* Cords, flexible)
Flexible metal conduits (*see* Conduits,
    flexible metal)
**Flex metal tubing, 349-1, 349-3, 349-
    4**
Floating dwelling units 90-2, 553
Floodlights 400-8, 410-30
Floor penetrations, wiring installations
    300-21
Fluorescent lighting
  commercial and institutional **210-6**
  hazardous locations **501-9**
  limitations **210-23**
Footlights 520-43
"Foreign" piping 384-2
Fountains 680-1
FS and FD boxes, wire count **370-6**
Fuseholders 430-57, 430-90
Fuses
  accessibility **100**
  ampere ratings **240-6**

Fuses (*Cont.*):
  ANSI standards **230-208**
  arrangement in panelboards **384-19**
  branch circuit protection **430-53,
    430-56**
  capacitors **460-8**
  cartridge **240-60**
  CB devices **710-21**
  Class I hazardous locations **501-6**
  Class II, Div. 1 hazardous locations
    502-8
  Class III, Div. 1/Div. 2 hazardous loca-
    tions **503-4**
  classification **240-61**
  compressor motors, short-circuit pro-
    tection **440-22**
  disconnecting means **240-40**
  Edison-base **240-54**
  feeder switch, ratings **450-3**
  feeders **220-10**
  flame protection device **710-21**
  function **230-95**
  holders **240-54, 240-80**
  locations, overcurrent protection **240-
    24, 240-30**
  motors **430-53, 430-56, 430-57**
  overload protection use **430-36**
  panelboards **384-19**
  parallel **240-8**
  plug **240-50, 240-54**
  R-rated **710-21**
  ratings **430-52**
  time-delay **430-57**
  type 4/4x, agricultural buildings **547-4**
  type S, **240-54**
  (*See also* Oil-filled cutouts; Overcur-
    rent protection)

Garage doors
  lighting outlets in **210-70**
  receptacles in **210-8**
Garages
  lighting outlets **210-70**
  receptacles **210-8, 210-50**
Garages, commercial
  electric vehicle charging **511-9**
  equipment in hazardous locations
    511-7
  ground fault protection **511-10**
  hazardous locations **511-2, 511-3**
  wiring in hazardous locations **511-6**

Gasoline dispensing stations (see Gasoline service stations)
Gasoline pumps (see Gasoline service stations)
Gasoline service stations
  circuit disconnects **514-5**
  conduit sealing, gasoline pumps **514-6**
  definition **514-1**
  grounding **514-7**
  hazardous locations **514-2**
  lighting fixtures, sealings **514-6**
  underground wiring **514-8**
Gas pipes, grounding electrodes 250-83
General Cable Corp. 336-1
General Electric Co. 336-1
General Storage and Handling of Flammable and Combustible Liquids
  514-2, 515-2
Generators
  balancers **445-4**
  CB protection **445-4**
  Class I, Div. 1 hazardous location **501-8, 501-16**
  Class I, Div. 1/Div. 2 hazardous locations **502-8**
  Class III hazardous locations **503-6**
  dielectric heating power **665-2**
  emergency systems **700-12**
  grounding requirements **250-5, 250-6, 280-1**
  internal combustion **700-6**
  keying **665-67**
  live-part protection **445-6**
  output circuit, RF lines **665-44**
  overcurrent protection **445-4**
  portable and vehicle-mounted, grounding **250-6**
GFCI (see Ground-fault circuit interrupters)
Greatrooms, receptacle outlets in 210 52
Green Book (see *Electrical Construction Materials Directory*)
Greenfield (see Conduits, flexible metal)
Grounded circuit conductors 310-4
Grounded conductor (see Conductors; Equipment)
Grounded electrical system, voltage-to-ground **100**
Ground-fault circuit interrupters
  branch circuits **100, 210-8**
  Class A **680-20**
  feeders **215-9**

Ground-fault circuit interrupters (*Cont.*):
  swimming pools **680-5, 680-21, 680-25, 680-31**
  temporary wiring **305-6**
  (*See also* Circuit breakers)
Ground-fault circuit protection 215-9, 230-95, 430-51
  construction sites **305-4**
  dwelling units **210-8**
  for emergency systems **700-26**
  feeders **215-9**
  health care facilities **517-17**
  wet locations **517-20**
Ground-fault protection of equipment 100, 215-10, 240-13
Grounding
  AC circuits and systems **250-5, 250-23, 250-25, 250-26**
  AC equipment **250-25, 250-26, 250-94, 440-61, 450-5**
  appliances **250-45, 250-60, 250-70, 422-8**
  bonded jumpers **250-56**
  branch circuit, equipment conductors **210-5, 250-114**
  buildings supplied from single service **250-24**
  cable trays **318-6**
  capacitors **460-10**
  case **250-45**
  circuit conductor for **250-61**
  Class II, Div. 1/Div. 2 hazardous locations **502-16**
  clothes dryers **250-60, 250-70**
  connection point, direct-current systems **250-22**
  critical care areas **517-19**
  data processing systems **250-74, 645-1, 645-15**
  DC systems **250-22**
  definition, types **250-1**
  dielectric-heating equipment **665-25**
  electrodes
    alternative types **250-83**
    bonding **250-81**
    common grounding **250-54**
    grounding path **250-53**
    lightning rods **250-86**
    manufactured **250-83, 250-84**
    system **250-23, 250-81**
  equipment
    AC system **250-25, 250-26, 250-94, 440-61, 450-5**

Grounding, equipment (*Cont.*):
conductor connections **100, 250-1, 250-50**
conductors, size **250-95, 310-15, 347-4**
connected by cord and plug **250-45**
connected by fixed wiring **250-57**
fixed **250-42, 250-43, 250-45**
portable **250-59**
fittings to conductors, specifications **250-113**
fixtures **410-20**
gasoline service stations **514-7**
generators **250-5, 250-6**
health care facility **517-13, 517-19**
high impedance **250-27**
installation **250-92**
less than 50 V **720-4**
lightning rods **250-86**
liquidtight flexible metal conduit **351-9**
marinas/boatyards **555-7**
material **250-91**
mobile homes/parks **550-9**
motor wiring **430-145**
neutral systems **250-152**
organs **650-3**
panelboards **384-20**
path, effective **250-51**
radio/TV equipment **810-21**
ranges and ovens **250-60, 250-70**
services less than 1000 V **250-131**
space-heating equipment **424-14**
structural metal as conductor **250-58**
swimming pools **680-20, 680-22, 680-24, 680-25**
techniques **250-75**
transformers **250-5, 250-45, 450-5**
Ufer system **250-81**
ungrounded system, definition **250-5**
to water pipes **250-50**
water pumps **250-43, 547-8**
x-ray equipment **660-47**
zig-zag, transformers **450-5**
(*See also* Bonding)
Grounding electrode conductor (*see* Conductors)
Ground rods 250-83, 250-84, 250-115
Guarding, transformers, exposed parts **450-8**
(*See also* Enclosures; Isolation, high-voltage systems)
Guest rooms, branch circuits **210-60**
Gutters (*see* Auxiliary gutters)

Habitable rooms 210-70
Handle position, circuit breakers and switches 240-81
Hazardous Location Equipment Directory (Red Book) **110-3, 500-1, 500-2, 501-5, 501-6, 501-8, 501-9, 501-10, 501-11, 501-14, 502-8, 502-11, 502-12**
Hazardous Location Standards **500-3**
Hazardous locations
aircraft hangars, equipment **513-5**
attachment plugs,
Class I, Div. 1/Div. 2 **501-12**
Class II, Div. 1/Div. 2 **502-13**
bonding **250-78**
bulk storage plants **515-2, 575-5**
cables **333-6**
capacitors **502-2**
CB
Class I **501-6**
Class II, Div. 1 **502-6**
Class III, Div. 1/Div. 2 **503-4**
certified motor repair centers **501-8**
circuit design and installation **500-3**
Class I (*see* Hazardous locations, Class I)
Class II (*see* Hazardous locations, Class II)
Class III (*see* Hazardous locations, Class III)
classification and scope **500-1, 500-2**
coating processes, Class I, Div. 1/Div. 2 **516-2**
coating processes, equipment **516-3**
commercial garages **511-1**
construction sites **305-2**
diesel fuel and heating oil **500-2, 511-1**
dipping processes, Class I, Div. 1/Div. 2 **516-2**
dipping processes, equipment **516-3**
electric cranes, Class III, Div. 1/Div. 2 **503-13**
equipment, precautions **500-3**
equipment in commercial garages **511-6**
equipment installation **500-2**
explosionproof enclosures **501-6**
explosions in enclosures **501-1**
explosive limits **500-2**
finishing processes, Class I, Div. 1/Div. 2 **516-2**
finishing processes, equipment **516-3**
fixtures in **410**
flash point of liquid **500-2**

Hazardous locations (*Cont.*):
flexible cords, Class II, Div. 1/Div. 2 **502-12**
flexible fittings, Class I **501-4**
floors in commercial garages, Class I, Div. 2 **511-2**
fluorescent luminaire, Class I, Div. 1 **501-9**
fuses
    Class I **501-6**
    Class II, Div. 1 **502-6**
    Class III, Div. 1/Div. 2 **503-4**
garages **511-1**
gasoline service/dispensing stations, Class I, Div. 1/Div. 2 **514-2**
generators
    Class I, Div. 1 **501-8, 501-16**
    Class II, Div. 1/Div. 2 **502-8**
    Class III **503-6**
grounding, Class I, Div. 1/Div. 2 **501-16**
grounding, Class II, Div. 1/Div. 2 **502-16**
hoists, Class III, Div. 1/Div. 2 **503-13**
ignition temperatures **500-2**
intrinsically safe systems **504-1**
lighting fixtures
    Class I, Div. 1/Div. 2 **501-9**
    Class II, Div. 1/Div. 2 **502-11**
    Class III, Div. 1/Div. 2 **503-9**
motor controllers
    Class I **501-6**
    Class II, Div. 1 **502-6**
    Class III, Div. 1/Div. 2 **503-4**
motors
    Class I, Div. 1 **501-8**
    Class II, Div.1/Div. 2 **502-8**
    Class III **503-6**
OSHA regulations **500-3, 503-9**
panelboards **501-6**
positive-pressure ventilation **500-2**
precautions **500-3**
pressure piling, Class I **501-5**
receptacles, Class I, Div. 1/Div. 2 **501-12**
receptacles, Class II, Div. 1/Div. 2 **502-13**
seal fittings, Class II, Div. 1/Div. 2 **502-5**
sealing and drainage of conduits, Class I **501-5**
spray applications, Class I, Div. 1/Div. 2 **516-2**
spray applications, equipment **516-3**
switchboards and panelboards **384-6**

Hazardous locations (*Cont.*):
switches
    Class I **501-6**
    Class II, Div. 1 **502-6**
    Class III, Div. 1/Div. 2 **503-4**
vapor density **500-2**
ventilating pipes, Class II, Div. 1 **502-9**
wiring and equipment, anesthetizing locations, health care facilities **517-61, 517-63, 517-64**
wiring in commercial garages **511-5**
wiring methods
    Class I **501-4**
    Class II, Div. 1/Div. 2 **502-4**
    Class III **503-3**
Hazardous locations, Class I 500-5, 501-1, 501-5
attachment plugs, Div. 1/Div. 2 **501-12**
CB **501-6**
coating processes, Div. 1/Div. 2 **516-2, 516-3**
dipping processes, Div. 1/Div. 2 **516-2, 516-3**
finishing process, Div. 1/Div. 2 **516-2, 516-3**
flexible fittings **501-4**
floors in commercial garages, Div. 2 **511-2**
fluorescent luminaire, Div. 1 **501-9**
fuses **501-6**
gasoline service stations, Div. 1/Div. 2 **514-2**
generators, Div. 1 **501-8, 501-16**
grounding, Div. 1/Div. 2 **501-16**
junction boxes, seal fittings **505-5**
lighting fixtures, Div. 1/Div. 2 **501-9**
lightning arresters, Div. 1/Div. 2 **501-16**
motor controllers **501-6**
motors, Div. 1 **501-8**
OSHA regulations, Div. 1/Div. 2 **501-9**
panelboard, explosionproof **501-6**
pressure piling **501-5**
receptacles, Div. 1/Div. 2 **501-12**
resistors, control **501-7**
sealing and drainage of conduits **501-5**
signaling systems, Div. 1 **501-14**
spray applications, Div. 1/Div. 2 **516-2, 516-3**
switches **501-6**
wiring methods **501-4**
Hazardous locations, Class II
application **502-1**
attachment plugs, Div. 1/Div. 2 **502-13**

Hazardous locations (*Cont.*):
CB, Div. 1 **502-6**
flexible cords, Class II, Div. 1/Div. 2 **502-12**
fuses, Div. 1 **502-6**
generators, Div.1/Div. 2 **502-8**
grounding Div. 1/Div. 2 **502-16**
lighting fixtures, Div. 1/Div. 2 **502-11**
motor controllers, Div. 1 **502-6**
motors, Div. 1/Div. 2 **502-8**
receptacles, Div. 1/Div. 2 **502-13**
seal fittings, Div. 1/Div. 2 **502-5**
surge protection **502-17**
switches, Div. 1 **502-6**
transformers and capacitors **502-2**
utilization equipment **502-10**
ventilating pipes, Div. 1 **502-9**
wiring methods, Div. 1/Div. 2 **502-4**
Hazardous locations, Class III
applications **503-1**
CB, Div. 1/Div. 2 **503-4**
electric cranes, Div. 1/Div. 2 **503-13**
fuses, Div. 1/Div. 2 **503-4**
generators **503-6**
hoists, Div. 1/Div. 2 **503-13**
lighting fixtures, Div. 1/Div. 2 **503-9**
motor controllers, Div. 1/Div. 2 **503-4**
motors **503-6**
switches, Div. 1/Div. 2 **503-4**
wiring methods **503-3**
Hazardous Locations Classification,
NFPA **500-1**
Health care facilities
anesthetizing locations, **517-60, 517-63**
applicability and scope **517-10, 517-25**
critical branch **517-43**
critical care areas **517-19**
definitions **517-2**
emergency system **517-31**
essential electrical systems **517-30, 517-31, 517-41**
general care areas **517-18**
ground-fault protection **517-17**
grounding **517-13, 517-16**
hospital-grade receptacles **517-61**
insulated-ground receptacles **517-16**
isolated power systems **517-160**
life safety branch **517-42**
low-voltage equipment **517-64**
maximum potential difference **517-15**
panelboard bonding **517-14**
patient areas **517-2**

Health care facilities (*Cont.*):
psychiatric hospitals **517-2**
receptacles in **517-2, 517-13, 517-16, 517-61**
wet locations, ground-fault protection **517-20**
wiring **517-61**
x-ray equipment **660-1, 660-24, 660-35, 660-47**
Heaters, duct-mounted **424-57**
Heating, induced currents **300-20**
Heating equipment
branch circuits **210-63**
central **422-7**
induction **665-1, 665-2, 665-22, 665-44**
noncoincident loads **220-30**
outlets **210-63**
pipelines and vessels **427-22, 427-23**
receptacles **210-50**
remote control **665-68**
RF generators keying **665-67**
swimming pool deck areas **680-27**
(*See also* Dielectric heating equipment)
Heating oil, hazardous locations **500-1**
High-impedance grounding 250-27
High voltage
cable shielding **310-6**
cable trays **318-11**
CB devices **710-21**
feeders **240-100**
guarded areas **110-34**
installations **110-31**
motor disconnect proximity **430-102**
motor starters, wiring enclosures **300-3**
service-point, definition **230-200**
High-voltage systems
definition **710-1, 710-2**
feedback **710-24**
insulation requirements **310-2**
insulation shielding **710-6**
oil-fill cutouts **710-21**
overcurrent protection **710-20**
protection devices **710-8, 710-9**
switching devices **710-21, 710-24**
wiring **710-3**
Hoists (*see* Equipment, hoists)
Hospitals (*see* Health care facilities)
Hotels and motels
air-conditioning equipment **440-62**
ground-fault circuit protection **210-8**
receptacles **210-50, 210-70**
Hot tubs 680-41, 680-70, 680-71

Houseboats 90-2, 555-20
Household Fire Warning Equipment
   760-1
Hydromassage baths 680-4, 680-41, 680-
   70, 680-71

IC (interrupting capacity) rating 110-9
Identification
   electrical connections 110-14
   multiwire branch circuits 210-4
"Identified" 100, 110, 110-14
IEEE trial use standard 463-1974, 668-1
Ignition temperature 500-1
IGS (integrated gas spacer) cable 325-1
Impedance, circuit, IC ratings 110-10
Incandescent lamps 410-65, 422-15
   (See also Hazardous locations, lighting
      fixtures)
Incandescent luminaires 410-14, 410-16
Individual branch circuits 210-23
Induced currents 300-20
Induction heating (see Heating equip-
      ment, induction)
Industrial occupancies
   branch circuit maximum voltage
      exceptions 210-6
   definition 230-72
   electrical system coordination 240-12
   lighting, SWD circuit breakers 240-83
   ungrounded wiring systems 250-5
Industrial station 280-1
Inspection, third-party certification 300-
   21
Inspectors 90-4, 100
Installations
   approvals 110-2
   cable resistance 110-7
   cable trays 318-5
   cables 318-7
   capacitors 460-6
   CB in ceilings 300-22
   circuits, underground raceway wiring
      710-3
   conductors 110-7, 300-8
   definition 90-2
   de-icing 426-23
   equipment examinations and use 110-3
   fire ratings and wall penetrations 300-
      21
   fire spread protection 300-21
   grounding 250-92

Installations (Cont.):
   high-voltage enclosures 110-31
   intrinsically safe 504-1
   mandatory rules 110-1
   motor controllers in ceilings 300-22
   motor location 430-4
   panelboard/plasterboard 300-21, 384-2
   requirements 110
   switchboards 384-2
   switches in ceilings 300-22
   transformers in ceilings 300-22
   underground 330-5
Insulated ground receptacles 517-13
Insulated Power Cable Engineers Associ-
      ation (IPCEA) 310-6, 334-11
Insulation
   cable installations 110-7, 310-2, 710-6,
      710-8
   conductors 110-7, 230-4, 230-30, 230-
      40, 310-2, 310-15, 501-13, 620-11
   integrity 110-7
   motor protection against liquids 430-11
   organs 650-3
   outlet boxes 336-11, 336-12
   over 600 V, nominal 710-6, 710-8
   resistance test 110-7
   service conductors 230-22, 230-30, 230-
      40, 501-13
   switch boxes 336-11, 336-12
   tester 110-7
Insulators, open wiring 320
Integrated gas spacer (IGS) cable 325-1
Intermediate ferrous metal conduit 345-3
Intermediate metal conduit (IMC) (see
      Conduits, intermediate metal
      conduits)
Interpretations, formal 90-5
Interrupting (capacity) rating 100, 110-9
Intrinsically safe systems 500-2, 504-1
IPCEA (Insulated Power Cable Engineers
      Association) 310-6, 334-11
Isolation, high-voltage systems 710-22
(See also Enclosures; Guarding, trans-
      formers, exposed parts; Hazardous
      locations)

Jumpers, bonding 100, 250-74, 250-79,
   501-16
Junction boxes
   branch-circuit supports 370-13
   construction and installation 370-52

Junction boxes (*Cont.*):
  enclosures **373-8**
  metal boxes **370-4**
  nonmetallic **370-3**
  number of conductors **370-6**
  raceways **356-9, 358-5, 370-18**
  seal fittings, Class I hazardous location **505-5**
  size **370-51**
  swimming pools **680-5, 680-21, 680-22**
  weatherproof **370-5**
  wiring methods **370-6**
  (*See also* Outlet boxes; Pull boxes)

Kitchen equipment, commercial, branch circuit calculations **220-20**
Kitchens
  lighting outlets **210-70**
  receptacle outlets **210-52**
Knife switches (*see* Switches, knife)
Knockouts, round boxes **370-2**

"Labeled" 100, 110
Lampholders (*see* Fixtures, lampholders)
Lamps
  infrared **422-15**
  portable **410-42**
Laundry appliance receptacles 210-52, 220-3
Lead-antimony batteries 480-2
Lead-calcium batteries 480-2
Life Safety Code, emergency systems **700-1**
Lighting
  bathroom outlets **210-70**
  branch circuit outlets **210-70**
  busways **364-4**
  dwelling units, outlets **210-70**
  electric-discharge **410-54, 410-80**
  emergency systems **700-12, 700-16, 700-17**
  feeder capacity **220-11**
  feeder neutral sizing **220-30**
  festoon, definition **225-6**
  fixtures **400-7, 400-8**
  garages **210-70**
  low voltages **725-40**
  neon-tube voltage requirements **410-80**
  outdoor lampholders **225-24**

Lighting (*Cont.*):
  outdoor lamp location **225-25**
  outdoor receptacles **210-8, 210-50, 210-52, 410-57**
  overcurrent protection **230-71**
  poles **225-7**
  portable **501-9**
  show windows **220-12**
  track **410-100, 410-102**
  (*See also* Theaters)
Lighting fixtures
  ceiling penetrations **300-21**
  circuits, health care facilities **517-63**
  Class I, Div. 1/Div. 2 hazardous locations **501-9**
  Class II, Div. 1/Div. 2 **502-11**
  Class III, Div. 1/Div. 2 **503-9**
  clothes closets **410-8**
  cord-and-plug-connected **680-4**
  fire resistant installation **300-21**
  no-niche **680-4**
  OSHA regulations
    Class I, Div. 1/Div. 2 **501-9**
    Class III **503-9**
  paired, interconnection of **410-77**
  receptacles **210-50**
  recessed, Class I, Div. 1/Div. 2 **501-9**
  sealings, gasoline pumps **514-6**
  swimming pools **680-4, 680-6, 680-22**
  track **410-100, 410-102**
  trees **410-16**
  UL listing **680-20**
  (*See also* Fixtures; Hazardous locations, lighting fixtures)
Lighting loads, feeder ratings **430-63**
Lightning (surge) arresters 280-1, 280-3, 280-4, 280-12, 280-25, 501-16
Lightning rods
  bonding **250-46**
  grounding electrode system **250-86**
Limited circuits (*see* Power-limited circuits)
Limiters, cable 230-82, 450-6
Liquidtight flexible metal conduit
  bends in concealed work **351-10**
  definition **351-22**
  grounding **351-9**
  grounding conductor, separate **230-43, 250-91**
  number of conductors **351-6**
  scope **351-1**
  size **321-24, 351-5**

Liquidtight flexible metal conduit (*Cont.*):
supports 351-8
use 351-4, 351-23
"Listed" 100, 110
Live vegetation, and outdoor conductors
225-26
Loads
appliances 220-16, 220-17
branch circuits 210-22, 210-23, 430-25,
430-62
calculations, dwelling units 220-31,
220-33, 220-34
computation 220-2
conductors 430-25
continuous, limited circuits 725-17
emergency systems 700-15
feeder neutral 220-22
feeders 215-2
maximum 210-22
noncoincident, in feeder calculations
220-21, 220-30
permissible 210-23
receptacle, nondwelling units 220-13
receptacles 210-4, 210-21, 210-50,
210-52
residence service demand, optional
calculation 220-30
track lighting 410-102
Local Protective Signaling Systems, fire
protection 760-1
Locks, panelboard 430-86
Low voltages 725-40
Low-voltage systems, recreational
vehicles/parks 551-3
Luminaires 410-31, 410-65

Madison Holdits 370-13
Magazine panels 520-24, 520-25
Magnetic contactor, overcurrent
protection 240-3
Manufactured buildings 545-1, 545-13
Manufactured wiring systems 300-14,
300-22, 604
Marinas/boatyards 90-2, 555-1
branch circuits 555-4
gasoline stations 555-9
grounding 555-7
receptacles 555-3
wiring 555-6, 555-8
Masonry, NM cable limitations 336-3

Maximum potential difference, health
care facilities 517-15
Medium-voltage cable [*see* Cables, medium-voltage (MV)]
Meeting places 518-1, 518-3
Messenger supported wiring 225-4, 225-
5, 321-1, 321-3, 321-5
Metal boxes 370-4, 370-20
Metal-clad cable (*see* Cables, metal-clad;
Cables, types, MC)
Metal enclosures, electrical continuity
300-10
Metalworking machine tools, definition
670-2
Microshock 517-15
Mobile homes/parks
branch circuit protective equipment
550-6, 550-7
conductors 550-11
disconnects 550-6
distribution system 550-21
general requirements 550-4
grounding 550-11
power supply 550-5
scope and definition 550-1, 550-2
service equipment 550-23
wiring methods 550-10
(*See also* Recreational vehicles/parks)
Modular wiring systems 300-14, 300-22,
604
Motels (*see* Hotels and motels)
Motion picture projectors
definition 540-1, 540-2
electrical equipment 540-11
projection room 540-10
Motion picture/TV studios 530-1, 530-11
Motor compressors
AC equipment 440-22
branch circuits 440-33
fuses as short-circuit protection 440-22
hermetic refrigerant markings 440-4
motor loads 440-33
single, branch circuit conductors 440-
32
swimming pools, lighting fixtures 680-
20
Motor controllers (*see* Motors,
controllers)
Motors
accident hazards 430-73
AC equipment, loads 440-35
additional rules 440-2

Motors (*Cont.*):

adjustable speed **430-88**

ampacity and rating determination **430-6**

appliances **440-62**

automatic starts **430-32, 430-43**

branch circuit protection device **430-62**

branch circuits, general purpose **430-22, 430-42, 430-51**

bushing **430-13**

CB branch protection **430-52, 430-53, 530-55, 430-56, 430-62**

circuits
  branch-circuit conductor sizing **430-4**
  feeder **430-1**
  noncontinuous **430-22**
  overload protection **430-31, 430-52**
  power capacitors **460-6**
  ratings **430-52**
  switches **430-83**

Class I, Div. 1 hazardous locations **501-8**

Class II, Div. 1/Div. 2 hazardous locations **502-8**

Class III hazardous locations **503-6**

conductors for motors rated over 600 V **430-124**

conductors grounded **430-85**

constant-voltage DC **430-29**

continuous-duty, overloads **430-22**

control circuit disconnects **430-74**

control circuits **430-71, 430-72**

controllers **430-51, 430-52, 430-81**
  agricultural buildings **547-4**
  Class I hazardous locations **501-6**
  Class II, Div. 1 hazardous locations **502-6**
  Class III, Div. 1/Div. 2 hazardous locations **503-4**
  in ceilings **300-22**
  enclosure types **430-10, 430-91**
  speed regulation **430-23**
  thermal overload relays **430-52**
  wiring space in enclosures **430-10**
  wound-rotor **430-23**

current ratings **430-17**

disconnects
  accessibility **430-107**
  controller proximity **430-74, 430-102**
  ratings **440-12**

dust accumulation **430-16**

elevators/escalators **430-22**

equipment markings **430-7**

Motors (*Cont.*):

feeder capacity **220-14**

feeder demand factor **430-26**

fuse branch circuit protection **430-53, 430-56**

fuseholder size **430-57**

fusible switch controller **430-90**

ground-fault protection **430-51**

grounding method **430-145**

hermetic **440-52**

high-voltage, disconnect proximity **430-102**

housings **430-12**

individual circuit ratings **430-52**

instantaneous trip CB **430-52**

intermittent duty **430-33**

manual starts **430-32**

multimotor, branch-circuit connections **430-53**

multiple, disconnects size **440-12**

number served by controller **430-87**

overcurrent protection **430-53, 430-55, 430-62, 430-72, 430-125**

overload protection **430-31, 430-52**

overload protection shut down procedure **430-44**

overload relays **430-34**

part-winding **430-3**

power and control wiring **300-3**

power interruption **430-86**

protection against liquids **430-11**

rating for overcurrent protection **430-62, 430-63**

short-circuit protection **430-52**

shunting **430-35**

single branch circuits for multiload operation **430-53**

single disconnects **430-113**

single-speed **430-22**

speed limitation **430-89**

stationary **430-142**

torque, ratings **430-52**

totally enclosed, fan-cooled (TEFC) **501-8, 502-8**

totally enclosed, nonventilated **502-8**

types of disconnects **430-109**

wound-rotor, secondary current **430-23**

Moving walks (*see* Elevators/escalators)

Multiconductor cables 318-8, 318-10, 330-3

Multioutlet assembly 353-1, 353-2

Multioutlet branch circuits 210-23

Multiple circuits 210-4
Multiple conductor circuits 310-4
    (See also Conductors)
Multiple-occupancy buildings, service
    disconnect applications 230-72
Multiwire branch circuits 210-4
Musical instruments (organs) 650

Nails, penetration by 300-4
National Electric Code, purpose of
    handbook 90-1
National Electrical Manufacturers Associ-
    ation (NEMA) 220-10, 547-4, 555-3
National Fire Protection Association
    (NFPA) 500-1
Network systems, transformers 450-6
Neutral blocks and buses 250-23, 250-24
Neutral conductors 310-4, 310-15
Neutral grounded wires 300-13
NFPA (National Fire Protection
    Association) 500-1
NFPA Fire News, code interpretations
    90-5
Nickel-cadmium batteries 480-2
Noncoincident loads 220-21, 220-30
Nondwelling units, receptacle loads 220-
    13
No-niche lighting fixtures 680-4
Nonmetallic boxes 370-3
Nonmetallic pipelines 427-23
Nonmetallic-sheathed cable (see Cables,
    nonmetallic-sheathed)
Nursing homes 517-30, 517-41

Objectionable current over grounding
    conductors 250-21
Occupational Safety and Health
    Administration (OSHA)
    approvals 110-2
    askarel use 450-23
    disconnects identification 110-22
    electrical equipment, hazardous
        locations 500-3
    emergency systems 700-1
    equipment acceptability, junction boxes
        370-51a
    exit signs, requirements 700-1
    fire-rated outlets 300-21
    inspection approval 100

Occupational Safety and Health Admin-
    istration (OSHA) (Cont.):
    lighting fixtures, Class I, Div. 1/Div. 2
        501-9
    lighting fixtures, Class III hazardous
        locations 503-9
    pull and junction boxes 370-51
    system grounding regulations
        250-1
    temperature wiring 305-2
    testing laboratories listing 100
    third-party certification 90-6
    transformers 430-72, 450-1
    wiring methods standards 300-21
Office buildings, lighting in 220-2
Office furnishings 605-1
    free-standing partitions 605-8
    partition interconnections 605-4
Oil-filled cutouts, high-voltage systems
    710-21
One-family dwellings, definition 210-52
Open wiring (see Wiring, open)
Optical fiber cables 90-2, 770-1, 770-3
Orange Book (Electrical Appliance and
    Utilization Equipment Directory)
    110-3, 300-22, 424-9, 426-10
Organs 650
OSHA (see Occupational Safety and
    Health Administration)
Outdoor appliances 210-52
Outdoor lighting (see Lighting)
Outlet boxes
    cable clamps 370-20
    cable insulation 336-11, 336-12
    clamping devices 370-13
    concrete ceilings, supports 370-13
    conductor entry 370-6
    conductor temperatures for fixtures
        410-11
    construction 370-20
    covers and canopies 370-15, 410-12,
        410-13
    depth 370-14
    EMT supports 370-6
    exposed surface extensions 370-12
    floor boxes 370-17
    flush devices 370-9
    supports 370-13
    through-the-wall 370-9
    weatherproof 370-5
    wire count 370-6
    (See also Junction boxes)

Outlets
  branch circuits **210-21, 210-50, 210-63, 210-70**
  motion picture projectors **540-10**
  receptacle **100, 210-50, 220-3**
  regulations **370-1**
  rooftop **210-63**
  swimming pools **680-6, 680-22**
Overcurrent devices
  accessibility **100**
  busway **100**
  capacitors, motor ratings **460-8, 460-9**
  circuit limiting (CTL) **384-15, 725-12**
  enclosures **373-8**
  grounding conductors **100**
  IC rating **110-9**
  panelboard **384-15**
Overcurrent protection 210-20, 240-1, 650-6
  appliances **230-71, 422-6, 422-28**
  busways **364-10, 364-13**
  capacitors **460-8, 460-9, 712-12**
  circuits, gallery receptacles **520-23**
  conductors **210-20, 240-3, 430-24**
  electric boilers, resistance **424-72**
  electric welders **630-12, 630-32**
  feeders, high-voltage **240-100**
  fixture wires and cords **240-4, 240-6, 402-12**
  fuse and CB locations **240-24**
  generators **445-4**
  health care facilities **517-66**
  lighting **230-71**
  location in circuit **240-21**
  location of devices **240-24**
  motor control circuit **430-72**
  motor rating **430-62, 430-63**
  multibuilding plants **230-201**
  over 600 V, nominal **710-20**
  power-limited circuits **725-12**
  rating, maximum permitted **230-208**
  remote-control circuit conductors **240-3**
  SE conductors **230-90**
  sound equipment **640-10**
  space-heating equipment **424-22**
  supplementary **240-10**
  transformers **240-3, 450-3**
  vertical position **240-33**
  (See also Circuit breakers; Fuses; Overload protection devices)
Overhead service **100**
Overload devices, motor short-circuit protection (MSCP) **430-52**

Overload protection devices 384-16, 430-32, 430-37, 430-53, 430-55, 430-62, 430-125
  AC equipment **440-52**
  feeders **430-62**
  fuses **430-36**
  motor shut-down procedure **430-44**
  ratings **430-32**
  transformers **450-3**

Paired lighting fixtures, interconnection of 410-77
Panelboards
  bonding jumper **384-3**
  branch-circuit, appliances **384-14**
  branch-circuit, lighting **384-14**
  branch-circuit overcurrent protection **384-16**
  bus rating **384-13**
  CB **384-16**
  circuits **310-15**
  clearances needed **110-16, 384-8**
  enclosures **373-8, 384-18**
  explosionproof, Class I hazardous locations **501-6**
  feeders **373-8**
  fuses arrangement **384-19**
  general requirements **384-13**
  grounding **384-20**
  health care facilities **517-14**
  installation **300-21, 384-4**
  location **384-5, 384-7**
  locks on doors **430-86**
  markings **384-13**
  number of overcurrent devices **384-15**
  phase sequence **384-3**
  rainproof/raintight **384-17**
  service equipment **384-16**
  switches arrangement **684-19**
  theaters **520-24**
  UL listing **384-18**
  wet locations **384-17**
  wire bending space in **384-35**
  wiring, temporary **305-2**
    (See also Hazardous locations, wiring methods)
  wiring penetrations and fire ratings **300-21**
Pantries, receptacle outlets in 210-52
Partitions, office space 605-1, 605-4, 605-8
Part-winding motors 430-3

PCB, transformer coolants **450-23, 450-28**

PCEA (Power Cable Engineers Association) 310-6, 334-11

Performance testing, ground-fault protective hookups **230-95**

Phase conductors 310-4

Phase converters 430-86

Phase protection, elevators/escalators **620-53**

Photovoltaic systems, solar **100, 690-1**

Pipelines, heating equipment **427-22, 427-23**

Places of assembly 518

Plants, electrical distribution in **230-201**

Plaster
  NM cable limitations **336-3**
  replacement near outlet boxes **370-11**

Plasterboard
  replacement near outlet boxes **370-11**
  wiring penetration and fire ratings **300-21**

Plastic conduits (see Conduits, PVC)

Plenums
  definition **100**
  wiring **300-22**

Polarization, of fixtures **410-23**

Pools (see Swimming pools)

Portable lighting 501-9

Power Cable Engineers Association (PCEA) 310-6, 334-11

Power capacitors 460-6

Power-limited circuits
  Class 1 systems **725-11**
  Class 2 systems **725-31**
  Class 3 systems **725-31**
  classifications **725-3**
  conductors **725-15, 725-16, 725-17**
  definitions **725-1**
  fire resistance **725-49**
  locations **725-2**
  marking **725-34**
  overcurrent protection **725-12**
  physical protection **725-18**
  safety-control equipment **725-4**
  UL listing **384-15**
  wire size **110-6**
  wiring **725-14, 725-37, 725-38**

Power loads, feeder ratings **430-63**

Power resistors 430-29

Power supply, mobile homes/parks **550-3**

Prefab buildings (see Manufactured buildings)

Prefab wiring systems 300-14, 300-22, 604

Premises wiring (system) 100

Public Fire Service Communications, fire protection **760-1**

Pull boxes 370-18, 370-51, 370-52
  (See also Junction boxes; Outlet boxes)

Pumps
  swimming pool **680-30**
  water, grounding **250-43, 547-8**

Raceways
  bonding, Class I hazardous location **250-77, 501-16**
  boxes, connection points **300-15**
  building exteriors **225-22**
  cellular concrete floor **358-1, 358-3**
    inserts **358-7**
    junction boxes **358-5**
    markers **358-6**
  cellular metal floor
    definition **356-1**
    inserts **356-10**
    junction boxes **356-9, 370-18**
    markers **356-8**
    splices and taps **356-6**
    use **356-2**
  conductor current capacity and heat effects **310-15**
  conductors, insertions **300-18**
  conductors in parallel **210-21, 300-5**
  connections at service head **230-54**
  corrosion protection **300-6**
  definition **100**
  drainage **230-53**
  electrical continuity **300-10**
  electrical nonmetallic tubing (ENT) **331-1, 331-3, 331-5**
  elevators/escalators, wiring systems **620-36**
  feeders, temporary wiring **305-2**
  fittings, connection points **300-15**
  fixtures **410-31**
  flexible cords and cables **400-8**
  flexible metal tubing **349-1**
  installation **300-18**
  junction boxes **356-9, 370-18**
  limited circuits **725-15**
  metal, induced currents **300-20**
  moisture accumulation **300-7**
  number of conductors **725-17**
  seal **230-8**

Raceways (*Cont.*):
secured in place **300-11**
service **230-7, 230-8**
service-entrance (SE) conductors **230-47**
surface
combination **352-6**
metal, auxiliary gutters **374-1**
metal enclosure for conductors **352-2**
number of conductors **352-4**
size of conductors **352-3**
splices and taps **354-6**
use **352-1**
wiring **300-22**
temperature differences **300-7**
underfloor covering **654-3**
underfloor use **354-2**
underground circuits, wiring **710-3**
underground installations, compliance exceptions **300-5**
vertical, conductor supports **300-19**
wire connections **300-16, 300-18**
wire mixing limitations **300-1**
wiring methods **300-22**
Raceway seals 230-8
Radiant heating panels 424-90
nonheating leads **424-97**
wire clearances in walls **424-95**
Radio/TV equipment
antenna discharge units **810-20, 810-57**
conductors **810-13, 810-21**
electric supply circuits **810-19**
grounding conductors **810-21**
splices **810-14**
Raised floors, wiring under **300-22, 645-1**
Ratings, interrupting **100, 110**
"Readily accessible" 100, 430-107
Receptacles
attachment plugs **410-56, 410-58**
bathrooms **210-50**
branch circuits **210-7, 210-50**
Class I, Div. 1/Div. 2 hazardous locations **501-12**
Class II, Div. 1/Div. 2 hazardous locations **502-13**
cord connectors **410-58**
damp and wet locations **410-57**
definition **100, 210-4**
dwelling unit, required **210-50**
family rooms **220-3**
garage doors **210-8**
garages **210-8, 210-50**

Receptacles (*Cont.*):
GFCI protection on construction sites **305-4**
grounding adapters **410-58**
grounding-type **210-7**
guest rooms **210-60**
health care facilities **517-2, 517-13, 517-16, 517-61**
insulated grounds **517-13**
loads **210-4, 210-21, 210-50, 210-52**
loads, nondwelling units **220-13**
marinas/boatyards **555-3**
nondwelling loads, calculations **220-13**
nongrounding-type, exception **210-7**
outdoor **210-8, 210-50, 210-52, 410-57**
outlets **100, 220-3**
ratings and types **410-56**
ratings equal to load **210-21**
rooftop outlets **210-63**
show windows **210-62**
space-heating equipment **424-9**
split-wired, in dwelling units **210-6**
swimming pools **680-6**
theaters **520-45**
weatherproof covers **410-57**
Recessed fixtures 410-66, 410-67, 501-9
Recording equipment 640
Recreational vehicles/parks
branch circuits **551-10**
combination systems **551-6**
definition **551-6**
low-voltage systems **551-5**
(*See also* Mobile homes/parks)
Recreation rooms, receptacle outlets in 210-52
Red Book (*see Hazardous Location Equipment Directory*)
Refrigeration equipment
branch circuits **210-63**
motors **440-3**
outlets **210-63**
Remote-control circuits 100, 240-3, 401-14, 725-1
(*see also* Power-limited circuits)
Remote Station Protective Signaling System, fire protection **760-1**
Resistive load, conductors **310-15**
Resistors, control, Class I hazardous locations **501-7**
Resistors, power 430-29
Rigid metal conduits, (*see* Conduits, rigid metal)

Rigid nonmetallic conduits (see Conduits, rigid nonmetallic)
Rods (see Ground rods; Lightning rods)
Romex cables 336-1
Roof spaces
  concealed knob and tube wiring 324-11
  conductor clearances 225-19
Rooftop outlets 210-63
Round boxes, knockouts 370-2
Round service-entrance cable (SER) (see Cables, service-entrance)

"Safe for the hazardous (classified) location" 500-2
Safety 110-31, 110-34, 230-22, 500-2
Schools 220-34
Screws, penetration by 300-4
SE (service-entrance) cable (see Cables, service-entrance)
Seal fittings
  Class I hazardous locations 501-5
  Class II, Div. 1/Div. 2 hazardous locations 502-5
  drains 501-5
  junction boxes, Class I hazardous locations 505-5
  UL specifications 501-5
  (See also Hazardous locations, seal fittings)
Sealing compounds 501-5
Sealings 501-5, 514-6
Sealtite (see Liquidtight flexible metal conduit)
Secondary ties 450-6
Semiconductors, shielding 310-61
"Series rated" equipment 110-22
Service 100, 230-2
Service conductors 100, 220-35, 225-4, 225-5, 230-6, 230-7, 230-22, 230-201, 230-205
Service drop 100, 230-2
Service-drop clearances 230-9, 230-24
Service-entrance (SE) cable (see Cables, service-entrance)
Service-entrance cable, unarmored (SEU) 338-1
Service-entrance conductors (see Conductors, service-entrance)
Service equipment
  bonding 250-71, 250-72, 250-92
  definition 230-202

Service equipment (Cont.):
  panelboards 384-16
  protection 710-9
Service lateral 100
Service mast supports 230-28
Service points 230-200, 230-205
Service raceways 230-7, 230-8
Shielded nonmetallic sheathed (SNM) cable 337
Shielding
  cables 310-6
  conductors 310-6
  copper tape 310-6
  dielectric heating equipment 665-25
  electrostatic 310-6
  metallic 310-6
  semiconductors 310-6
  strand 310-6
Shock hazard, multipole CB requirements 210-4
Short-circuit protection 110-9, 240-3, 240-12
  (See also Overcurrent protection)
Show windows/cases
  branch circuits 210-62, 220-3
  cord connected 410-29
  lighting 220-12
  receptacles 210-26, 210-62
"Sight" (in sight from) 100
Signal circuits 725-1
  (See also Power-limited circuits)
Signaling systems, Class I, Div. 1 hazardous locations 501-14
Signals, emergency 700-7
Signs (see Electric signs/outline lighting; Warning signs)
Single circuits 210-4
Snap switches
  flush-mounted, faceplates 380-9
  mounting 380-10
  use 380-14
Snow-melting equipment (see De-icing and snow-melting equipment)
Solar photovoltaic systems 100, 690-1
Sound equipment 640-2, 640-4, 640-6, 640-10
Space-heating equipment
  area restrictions 424-38
  conductors 424-22
  disconnect devices 424-19
  fixed electric, branch circuits 424-3
  fixed electric installation 220-15, 424-9

Space-heating equipment (*Cont.*):
 grounding **424-14**
 overcurrent protection, branch circuit **424-22**
 receptacles **424-9**
 thermostatically controlled switches **424-20**
 wiring clearances in ceiling **424-36**
 wiring locations in walls **424-37**
 wiring methods **424-14**
Special permission 100
Split-wire receptacles 210-6
Spray applications (*see* Finishing processes)
Standby power systems 701, 702
Storable swimming pools 680-4
Storage batteries
 definitions **480-2**
 descriptions **480-1**
 emergency systems **700-12**
 lead-antimony **480-2**
 lead-calcium **480-2**
 locations **480-8**
 nickel-cadmium **480-2**
 wiring **480-3**
Stranded conductors 310-3
Surface extensions, boxes, 370-12
Surface raceways (*see* Raceways, surface)
Surge arresters 280-1, 280-3, 280-4, 501-16
 circuits of 1 kV and over **280-24**
 grounding **280-25**
 routing **280-12**
Surge protection, Class II hazardous locations **502-17**
Suspended ceilings (*see* Ceilings, suspended)
Swimming pools
 bonding conductor **680-22**
 bonding of components **680-22, 680-25**
 conductors **680-5, 680-8**
 conduit **680-20**
 cord- and plug-connected equipment **680-7**
 deck area heating **680-27**
 definitions **680-1, 680-4**
 electrical equipment
  CB **680-5**
  grounding conductor **680-25**
 GFCI wiring **680-5, 680-21, 680-25, 680-31**
 grounding **680-20, 680-22, 680-24, 680-25**

Swimming pools (*Cont.*):
 grounding/bonding **680-20, 680-22, 680-24, 680-25**
 junction boxes **680-5, 680-21, 680-22**
 lighting fixtures/outlets **680-6, 680-22**
 mountings, lighting fixtures **680-20**
 overhead conductors **680-8**
 pumps **680-30**
 receptacles **680-6**
 transformers **680-5, 680-21**
 UL listing **680-1**
 underwater audio equipment **680-23**
 underwater lights **680-4, 680-20**
 water heaters **680-9**
 wiring **680-5**
Switchboards
 barriers **384-3**
 bonding jumper **384-3**
 busbars arrangement **384-3**
 busbars support **384-3**
 clearances **110-16, 384-8**
 conductors arrangement **384-3**
 conductors support **384-3**
 installation **384-4**
 location **384-5, 384-7**
 theaters **520-24**
Switch boxes, cable insulation **336-11, 336-12**
Switches
 accessibility **100, 380-8**
 ampere-rated **430-110**
 arrangements in panelboards **384-19**
 as controller **430-111**
 as disconnects **430-111**
 automatic **380-5**
 ceilings installation **300-22**
 circuit breakers **380-11**
 Class I hazardous locations **501-6**
 Class II, Div. 1 hazardous locations **502-6**
 Class III, Div. 1/Div. 2 **503-4**
 clearances needed **110-16**
 connections **380-2**
 controller ratings **430-83, 430-111**
 definition **100**
 disconnect devices **422-25, 422-27**
 disconnects, AC equipment **440-63**
 emergency systems **700-20, 700-21**
 enclosed, horsepower ratings **380-13**
 enclosure grounding **380-12**
 enclosures **373-8, 380-3**
 feeder, fuse ratings **450-3**
 flush-mounted snap, faceplates **380-9**

Switches (*Cont.*):
  fusible, motor controller **430-90**
  ground fault protection **230-95**
  handle positon **240-81**
  health care facilities **517-66**
  high-voltage, marking **110-30**
  high-voltage systems **710-21, 710-24**
  isolating **230-204, 230-205, 280-34**
  knife **380-7, 380-13**
    position **380-6**
  low-voltage **725-1, 725-40**
  oil-immersed **710-22**
  overcurrent protection requirements
    230-208
  panelboards **384-19**
  plug-in **100**
  ratings **380-14**
  remote control **725-11**
  scope **380-1**
  snap, mounting **380-10**
  snap, use **380-14**
  surge arrester **280-3**
  thermostatically controlled **424-20**
  transformers **450-8**
  type 4/4x, agricultural buildings **547-4**
  UL data **380-13**
  wet locations **380-4**
  (*See also* Circuit breakers; Disconnects;
    Hazardous locations, switches)
Systems 250-26, 504-1, 700-12, 701, 702

Tap conductors
  branch circuit calculations **200-19**
  overcurrent protection **240-21, 430-53**
TEFC (totally enclosed, fan-cooled)
    motors 501-8, 502-8
Telecommunications, wiring methods
    300-22
Telephones, explosionproof, Class I
    hazardous locations **501-14**
Temperature 110-3, 310-10, 310-15
**Temporary wiring 225-26, 305-1, 305-3,
    305-4, 305-6**
Terminals 110-3, 110-14, 310-15
  identification of **200-10**
Testing conditions 305-1
Theaters
  application **520-1**
  border lights **520-44**
  dimmers **520-25, 520-53**
  festoons **520-65**
  flue damper control **520-49**

Theaters (*Cont.*):
  footlights **520-43**
  gallery receptacles, circuits, overcurrent
    protection **520-23**
  lamp guards **520-72**
  magazine panels **520-24, 520-25**
  metal hoods, stages **520-24**
  panelboards **520-24**
  proscenium sidelights **520-44**
  receptacles in **520-45**
  switchboards **520-24**
  wiring methods **520-4**
  (*See also* Lighting)
Time delays
  fuses **240-60**
  ground-fault protection **230-95**
Time switches 380-5
**Totally enclosed, fan-cooled (TEFC)
    motors 501-8, 502-8**
**Totally enclosed, nonventilated motors
    502-8**
Townhouses, receptacle outlets in 210-52
Track lighting 410-100, 410-102
Transfer equipment 230-83, 700-6
Transfer switches 100
Transformer arc welder (*see* Electric
    welders)
Transformers
  accessibility **450-2, 450-13**
  accident hazard **430-73, 450-8, 450-28**
  applications **450-1**
  askarel, insulation **450-23, 450-25, 450-
    28**
  ceilings
    installation **300-22**
    suspended **450-2**
  circuits, health care facilities **517-63**
  Class II hazardous locations **502-2**
  conductor protection **430-72**
  control, Class I hazardous locations
    501-7
  control disconnects **430-74**
  cooling, insulation problems **450-21**
  dry-type **450-21, 450-22**
  electric signs/outline lighting **600-32**
  exposed parts, guards **450-7**
  feeders **450-3**
  grounding **250-5, 250-45, 450-5**
  guarding **450-8**
  high-voltage **450-3**
  indoor installation **450-21, 450-23, 450-
    24, 450-25**
  limited circuits, UL markings **725-34**

Transformers (*Cont.*):
  liquid-insulated, high fire point **450-23**
  loading **410-87**
  location **450-2, 450-13**
  modifications **450-28**
  nonflammable fluid-installed **450-24**
  oil-insulated **450-26, 450-27**
  OSHA regulations **430-72, 450-1**
  outdoors **450-22**
  overcurrent protection **240-3, 450-3**
  overcurrent protection device **450-3**
  parallel operation **450-7**
  primary/secondary circuits **450-3**
  secondary, grounding **250-26, 250-45**
  secondary ties **450-6**
  step-down **230-201**
  swimming pools, enclosures **680-5, 680-21**
  taps, overcurrent protection **240-21, 240-24**
  UL listing **725-34**
  ventilation **450-9, 450-21, 450-22**
  x-ray equipment **660-24**
  zig-zag grounding **450-5**
  (*See also* Hazardous locations)
Transformer vaults 450-24, 450-25
  doorways **450-43**
  locations **450-41**
  ventilation openings **450-45**
  walls, roof, and floor **450-42**
Trees
  lighting fixtures on **410-16**
  temporary wiring on **225-26**
Two-family dwellings, definition 210-52

Ufer system 250-81
UL (*see* Underwriters Laboratories)
Underground feeder cable (UF) (*see* Cables, UF)
Underground installations 300-5, 710-3
Underground residential distribution (URD) 100, 310-6
Underground service
  definition **100**
  entrance (USE) cable **310-9**
  (*See also* Cables; Conductors; Raceways; Service)
Underground wiring 514-8, 515-5, 680-10
Underplaster extensions 344-1, 344-2, 344-5
Underwriters Laboratories (UL) 90-6
  ALS cable, listing **334-4**

Underwriters Laboratories, Inc. (UL) (*Cont.*):
  auxiliary gutters, listing **374-1**
  Building Materials Directory **300-21, 410-76**
  cable ratings **334-1**
  cables over 600 V, nominal **710-1**
  CB Standard 489 **240-1**
  circuit limiting (CTL) **384-15**
  Class I hazardous classification **501-1**
  code limitations **430-83**
  controllers short-circuit ratings **430-52**
  Electrical Appliance and Utilization Equipment Directory **440-22**
  Electrical Appliance and Utilization Equipment List (Orange Book) **110-3, 300-22, 424-9, 426-10**
  Electrical Baseboard Heating Equipment **424-9**
  emergency equipment **700-3**
  equipment marking, hazardous locations **500-2**
  feedthrough ruling **410-12**
  Fire Resistance Index **300-21, 410-64**
  fixtures and fittings markings **410-4, 680-20**
  fixtures as raceways **410-31**
  flexible metal conduit listing **350-2, 351-4**
  floor penetration standards **300-21**
  fluorescent fixture mounting **410-76**
  GFCI devices **680-20**
  Hazardous Location Standards **500-3**
  health care facilities, wiring **517-61**
  IMC data **346-1**
  labels **100**
  lighting fixtures **680-20**
  liquid-filled equipment **450-23**
  listing **100, 326-1**
  manufactured building component interconnections **546-13**
  panelboards enclosure **384-18**
  plastic conduits, listing **347-1, 347-2**
  plastic underground conduits, listing **347-1**
  polyethylene conduits, listing **347-1**
  power-control tray cable use **340-4, 340-5**
  protective devices **410-73**
  SE construction specifications **338-1**
  seal fittings, Class I hazardous locations **501-5**
  swimming pools, electric shocks **680-1**

Underwriters Laboratories, Inc. (UL) (Cont.):
  switches **380-13**
  temperature limitations, terminals **110-3**
  terminal lugs, marking **501-6**
  terminal ratings **310-15**
  transformers, limited circuits **725-34**
  underground installations limitations **300-5**
  underwriters knot **400-10**
  weatherproof listing **410-57**
  wire sizes **110-14**
  (See also *Electrical Construction Materials Directory; Hazardous Location Equipment Directory*)
Ungrounded electrical system, voltage-to-ground **100**
Uninterruptible power supply, data processing systems **645-11, 702-5**
United States Testing Co. (UST) 100
USE (underground service-entrance) cable 310-9
UST (United States Testing Co.) 100
Utility companies, circuits and equipment exemptions **90-2**
Utilization equipment, definition **210-4**

Vapor density 500-1
Vaportight seal fittings 501-5
Vegetation, and outside conductors **225-26**
Vehicle doors (see Garage doors)
Ventilating pipes, Class II, Div. 1 hazardous locations **502-9**
Ventilation
  motion picture projectors **540-10**
  transformers **450-9, 450-21, 450-22**
Voltage 110-4
  branch circuits **210-6, 220, 220-2**
  control disconnects **430-74**
  drop in feeders **215-2, 215-6**
  dwellings **410-75**
  maximum, branch circuits **210-6**
  network systems **450-5**
  phase-to-phase **450-3**
Voltage-to-ground 100

Waivers, code rules **90-4**

Walls
  clearance for radiant heating wiring **424-95**
  locations for space-heating wiring **424-37**
  penetrations and fire ratings **300-21**
Warning signs 230-203
Water fountains, definitions **680-1, 680-4**
Water heaters, ampacity rating **422-14**
Water pipes
  grounding to **250-50**
  grounding electrodes **250-81, 250-83**
Water pumps, grounding 250-43, 547-8
"Weatherproof" 370-5
Wet-niche fixtures (see Lighting fixtures; Swimming pools)
Whips, fixture 410-67
Whirlpool baths 680-4, 680-41, 680-70, 680-71
Wire bending space 384-35, 430-10
Wires
  branch circuit **310-15**
  conduit bodies **370-6**
  connections **300-16**
  control conductors **300-3**
  fixtures **240-4, 402-10**
  neutral, grounded **300-13**
  number in outlet boxes **370-6**
  power conductors **310-3**
  types
    AF **410-31, 410-67**
    FEP **310-13**
    FEPB **310-13**
    RHH **310-13, 310-15, 318-2, 346-6, 410-31**
    THHN **310-13, 310-15, 346-6, 410-31, 501-13**
    THW **346-6, 410-31, 410-67**
    THWN **346-6, 501-13**
    TW **336-2, 346-6, 370-6, 424-36, 426-10, 501-13**
    XHHW **310-13, 310-15, 346-6**
  UL listing **110-14**
  (See also Cables; Conductors)
Wireways
  definition **362-1**
  deflected insulated conductors **362-6**
  extensions **362-11**
  hung ceilings **100**
  number of conductors **362-5**
  splices and taps **362-7**
  supports **362-8**
  use **362-2**

Wireways (*Cont.*):
wiring methods **100**
Wiring
AC systems **250-5, 250-23, 250-25**
air-conditioning **440-2**
air-handling ceilings **300-22**
AWG classification **410-88**
barns **336-3**
branch circuit, cooking units **220-19**
branch-circuit ratings **310-15, 410-67**
buildings **225-10**
BX branch circuit **370-13**
cable tray systems **230-202**
ceiling height **305-2**
ceilings, air-handling space **300-22**
commercial garages, hazardous
locations **511-5**
concealed, knob-and-tube **300-16**
data processing equipment, under
raised floors **300-22, 645-1**
ducts **300-22**
emergency system **700-9**
finishing processes, hazardous
locations **516-3**
fixed equipment, grounding **250-42,
250-45**
fixtures, temperature needs **410-67**
floor outlets **328-1**
garages, hazardous locations **511-5**
health care facilities **517-61,**
insulators **320**
messenger supported **225-4, 225-5, 321-
1, 321-3, 321-5**
motion picture/TV studios **530-11**
motors, controllers **430-10**
open
definition **320-1**
supports **320-6**
uses **320-3**
outdoor overhead **225-4**
over/under navigable water **555-8**
panelboard penetrations and fire
ratings **300-21**
plasterboard penetrations and fire
ratings **300-21**
plenums **300-22**
poke-through **300-21**
premises **100**
raceways **300-22**
sound equipment **640-2, 640-4**
space-heating equipment, in walls **424-
37**

Wiring (*Cont.*):
storage batteries **480-3**
suspended ceilings **300-22**
swimming pools, GFCI **680-5**
system ground **250-1**
temporary **305-1, 305-3, 305-4, 305-6**
underground requirements **300-5, 514-8**
under raised floors **300-22, 645-1**
(*See also* Conductors)
Wiring methods and systems
accessible **100**
agricultural buildings **547-3**
air handling ceilings **300-22**
appliances **220-19**
applications **300-1**
busway **100, 364-4**
BX, junction boxes **370-6**
cable trays **100**
capacitors **460-8**
circuit breakers on busways **100**
Class I hazardous locations **501-4**
Class II, Div. 1/Div. 2 hazardous locations **502-4**
Class III hazardous locations **503-3**
concealed knob and tube, uses **324-3**
conductors of different voltage **300-3**
conduit junction boxes **370-6**
conduits, hazardous locations **501-4**
cranes **610-11**
electric cooking appliances **220-19**
electric-discharge lighting fixtures **410-
30**
EMT junction boxes **370-6**
exposed **100**
fixtures polarization **410-32**
floor penetration **300-21**
hoists **610-11**
limited circuits **725-14, 725-37, 725-38**
manufactured **300-14, 300-22, 604**
mobile homes/parks **550-8**
modular **300-14, 300-22, 604**
NM junction boxes **370-6**
OSHA standards **300-21**
over 600 V, nominal **710-3**
places of assembly **518-3**
plenums **300-22**
plug-in switches **100**
prefab **300-14, 300-22, 604**
premises **100**
secondary conductors **410-88**
space-heating equipment **424-14**
suspended ceilings **300-22**

Wiring methods and systems (*Cont.*):
  telecommunications **300-22**
  theaters **520-4**
  underground circuits **710-3**
  wireways **100**
  (*See also* Busways; Wireways)
Wood, cables through framing **300-4**
Work acceptability 110-12
Working space
  accessibility **110-33**
  compliance of rules **110-14**
  electrical equipment areas **110-16**
  high-voltage, guarded areas **110-34**

Working space (*Cont.*):
  lighting requirements **110-16**
Work neatness 110-12

X-ray equipment
  application **660-1**
  capacitors **660-35**
  grounding **660-47**
  grounding, health care facilities **660-47**
  guarding **660-47**
  transformers **660-24**

Zig-zag grounding transformers 450-5

ABOUT THE AUTHORS

Joseph F. McPartland is the Editorial Director Emeritus of *Electrical Construction and Maintenance* magazine. He has authored 28 books on electrical design, electrical construction methods, electrical equipment, and the **National Electrical Code**®. For over 40 years he has been traveling throughout the nation conducting seminars and courses on the many aspects of electrical design, engineering, and construction technology for electrical contractors, consulting engineers, plant electrical people, and electrical inspectors. Mr. McPartland received a Bachelor of Science degree in Electrical Engineering from Thayer School of Engineering, Dartmouth.

Brian J. McPartland, an associate editor of *Electrical Construction and Maintenance* for the past four years, has more than 14 years' experience in electrical technology. After serving in the U.S. Navy Submarine Force, during which time he earned his degree in electrical technology, Brian held positions in both product engineering and sales with various electrical equipment manufacturers. He is coeditor of McGraw-Hill's *Handbook of Practical Electrical Design* and coauthor of *McGraw-Hill's* **National Electrical Code**® *Handbook* and EC&M's *Illustrated Changes in the 1990* **National Electrical Code**®.